The Garland Encyclopedia of World Music

Volume 6

The Middle East

THE GARLAND ENCYCLOPEDIA OF WORLD MUSIC

Volume 1
AFRICA
edited by Ruth M. Stone

Volume 2
SOUTH AMERICA, MEXICO,
CENTRAL AMERICA, AND THE CARIBBEAN
edited by Dale A. Olsen and Daniel E. Sheehy

Volume 3
THE UNITED STATES AND CANADA
edited by Ellen Koskoff

Volume 4
SOUTHEAST ASIA
edited by Terry E. Miller and Sean Williams

Volume 5
SOUTH ASIA: THE INDIAN SUBCONTINENT
edited by Alison Arnold

Volume 6
THE MIDDLE EAST
edited by Virginia Danielson, Scott Marcus, and Dwight Reynolds

Volume 7
EAST ASIA: CHINA, JAPAN, AND KOREA
edited by Robert C. Provine, Yosihiko Tokumaru, and J. Lawrence Witzleben

Volume 8
EUROPE
edited by Timothy Rice, James Porter, and Chris Goertzen

Volume 9
AUSTRALIA AND THE PACIFIC ISLANDS
edited by Adrienne L. Kaeppler and J. Wainwright Love

Volume 10
THE WORLD'S MUSIC: GENERAL PERSPECTIVES AND REFERENCE TOOLS

Advisory Editors
Bruno Nettl and Ruth M. Stone

Founding Editors
James Porter and Timothy Rice

The Garland Encyclopedia of World Music
Volume 6

The Middle East

Virginia Danielson, Scott Marcus, and
Dwight Reynolds
Editors

Alexander J. Fisher
Associate Editor

Stephen Blum, Theodore Levin, Abraham Marcus, and Irene Markoff
Consulting Editors

ROUTLEDGE
New York and London
2002

The initial planning of *The Garland Encyclopedia of World Music* was assisted by a grant from the National Endowment for the Humanities.

Published by
Routledge
29 West 35th Street
New York, NY 10001

Published in Great Britain by
Routledge
11 New Fetter Lane
London EC4P 4EE

Routledge is an imprint of the Taylor & Francis Group.

Project Editor: Susan Gamer
Director of Production: T. J. Mancini
Copyeditor: Usha Sanyal
Indexer: Marilyn Bliss
Music Typesetting: Hyunjung Choi
Maps: Graphic Services at Indiana University, Bloomington
Cover designer: Lawrence Wolfson Design, New York
Publishing Director: Sylvia K. Miller
Vice President: Linda Hollick

Library of Congress Cataloging-in-Publication Data

The Garland encyclopedia of world music / [advisory editors, Bruno Nettl and Ruth M. Stone; founding editors, James Porter and Timothy Rice].
p. cm.
Includes bibliographical references, discographies, and indexes.
Contents: v. 6. The Middle East / Virginia Danielson, Scott Marcus, and Dwight Reynolds, editors.
ISBN 0-8240-6042-3 (alk. paper)
Music—Encyclopedias. 2. Folk music—Encyclopedias. 3. Popular music—Encyclopedias.
I. Nettl Bruno, 1930– II. Stone, Ruth M. III. Porter, James, 1937– IV. Rice, Timothy, 1945–
ML100.G16 2002
780′.9—dc21 97-9671
CIP
MN

10 9 8 7 6 5 4 3 2 1

Cover illustration: © Robert Holmes: Morocco, Tan Tan Moussem.
Photo researcher: Elaine Bernstein

Printed on acid-free, 250-year-life paper
Manufactured in the United States of America

Contents

Part 1

Introduction to the Musics of the Region   1

Part 2

Understanding the Musics of the Middle East: Issues and Processes   29

Audio Examples

The following examples are included in the accompanying audio compact disk packaged with this volume. Track numbers are indicated on the pages listed below in parenthesis for easy reference to text discussions. Complete notes on each example may be found on pages 1139–1144. An abridged version of these notes is provided as liner notes accompanying the compact disk.

1 Eastern Arab Art Music: *taqāsīm* (solo improvisation) in *maqām bayyātī* and *Samā'ī Bayyātī al-'Aryān* (39, 91, 405, 551)

2 Turkish Mevlevi *taksim* (solo improvisation) in *makam beyati* (51, 108, 121, 769)

3 Turkish classical *taksim* (solo improvisation), in *makam beyati* (51, 121)

4 Classical Persian *dastgāh-e shūr* (60, 134, 854, 867)

5 Yemeni drumming from the Ḥaḍramawt: *Īqā' al-Rubūṭ* (97)

6 Yemeni highland drumming: *Ḍarbat Sayyārī* (100, 417)

7 Yemeni drumming from the Ḥaḍramawt: *Īqā' al-Istimā'* (102)

8 Yemeni drumming from the Tihāma: *Raqṣat al-Mansarī* (103)

9 Islamic vocal music: *Inshād* in the public *ḥaḍra* (92, 148)

10 Islamic vocal music: *Ibtihālāt* (167)

11 Jewish cantillation: *Bereshit bara* 'In the beginning' (200, 1016)

12 Eastern Christian chant (214)

13 Berber women's wedding song from the Anti-Atlas (479)

14 Berber wedding song, *aḥwash*, from the Anti-Atlas (480, 488)

15 Berber warrior dance, *taskiwin*, from the High Atlas (489)

16 Palestinian folk song, *dal'onā* (583)

17 Palestinian line dance, *saḥjih* (573, 584)

18 Palestinian shaving song, *zaffih* (578, 589)

19 *Qurba* 'bagpipe' dance at a wedding in Oman (415, 679)

20 Yemeni vocal music with lute accompaniment (407, 686)

21 Yemeni vocal music with copper-plate percussion (403, 687)

22 Saudi women's wedding song, *Bā'ūnī* (692, 698)

23 Kurdish epic song, *Hasu* (747)

24 Kurdish dance songs: *Ax lê Nurê, Henokê gerowwêre, Xwastîme* (748)

25 Turkish Alevī song with *bağlama* accompaniment: *Haydar, Haydar* (84, 759, 797)

26 *Gharībī*, lyric song of Khorasan province, Iran (830)

27 Persian narrative song, *Sayyed Moḥammad Khān* (831)

28 Persian classical music: *Masnavi* in the *dastgāh* of *māhur* (60, 134, 854, 866)

29 Kazakh epic song, *zhyr* (953)

30 Uzbek classical song, *Sarabaxi Ōrōm-i Jōn* 'Peace of the Soul' (903, 907, 909)

31 Uzbek classical instrumental dance piece, *Oynasin Dugah* (903, 907, 909)

Maps

About *The Garland Encyclopedia of World Music*

Scholars have created many kinds of encyclopedias devoted to preserving and transmitting knowledge about the world. The study of music has itself been the subject of numerous encyclopedias in many languages. Yet until now the term *music encyclopedia* has been synonymous with surveys of the history, theory, and performance practice of European-based traditions.

In July 1988, the editors of *The Garland Encyclopedia of World Music* gathered for a meeting to determine the nature and scope of a massive new undertaking. For this, the first encyclopedia devoted to the music of all the world's peoples, the editors decided against the traditional alphabetic approach to compartmentalizing knowledge from A to Z. Instead, they chose a geographic approach, with each volume devoted to a single region and coverage assigned to the world's experts on specific music cultures.

For several decades, ethnomusicologists (following the practice of previous generations of comparative musicologists) have been documenting the music of the world through fieldwork, recording, and analysis. Now, for the first time, they have created an encyclopedia that summarizes in one place the major findings that have resulted from the explosion in such documentation since the 1960s. The volumes in the series comprise contributions from all those specialists who have from the start defined the field of ethnomusicology: anthropologists, linguists, dance ethnologists, cultural historians, and performers. This multidisciplinary approach continues to enrich the field, and future generations of students and scholars will find *The Garland Encyclopedia of World Music* to be an invaluable resource that contributes to knowledge in all its varieties.

Each volume (with the exception of the tenth and final volume) has a similar design and organization: large sections that cover the major topics of a region from broad general issues to specific music practices. Each section consists of articles written by leading researchers, and extensive glossaries and indexes give the reader easy access to terms, names, and places of interest.

Part 1: Introduction to the region, its culture, and its music as well as a survey of previous music scholarship and research.

Part 2: Major issues and processes that link the musics of the region.

Part 3: Detailed accounts of individual music cultures. In Volume 7, East Asia, more than one part serves this function (Part 3, China; Part 4, Japan; Part 5; Korea; and Part 6, Inner Asia).

The editors of each volume have determined how this format is to be constructed and applied, depending on the nature of their regions of interest. The concepts covered in Part 2 will therefore differ from volume to volume; likewise, the articles in Part 3 might be about the music of nations, ethnic groups, islands, or subregions. The picture of music presented in each volume is thus comprehensive yet remains focused on critical ideas and issues.

Complementing the texts of the encyclopedia's articles are numerous illustrations: photographs, drawings, maps, charts, song texts, and musical examples. At the end of each volume is a useful set of study and research tools, including a glossary of terms, lists of audio and visual resources, and an extensive bibliography. An audio compact disk will be found inside the back cover of each volume, with sound examples that are linked (with an icon in the margin) to discussions in the text.

The Garland Encyclopedia of World Music represents the work of hundreds of specialists guided by a team of distinguished editors. With a sense of pride, the publisher offers this series to readers everywhere.

Preface

The intent of this volume is to introduce English-speaking readers to the many and varied musics of the Middle East and Central Asia and to the sociocultural settings in which these musics are learned and performed. Music making is viewed here as a form of human behavior that expresses individual and communal feelings, values, and identities. Social events—indeed, local societies themselves—are, in part, constituted through musical performance.

The geographic area of the Middle East and Central Asia is vast, peopled by many different societies and linguistic groups from Berbers in Morocco to Uygurs in western China. A comprehensive book on music cultures of the region would be impossible. This book, like others in the *Garland Encyclopedia of World Music*, presents essays on selected topics, copious illustrations of music making, and lists of references for further reading. It is not encyclopedic in its organization or in its coverage of its subject. For example, the section entitled "Historical Roots" discusses primarily Arabic sources in order to illustrate one major scholarly history among the many that exist in this region. These literatures—Persian, Turkish, and others—are discussed in individual essays throughout the book. However, the overall effect is a sampling of material that we hope will invite further reading, listening, and exploration, rather than providing all necessary information in a single place.

As a region, the Middle East and Central Asia have been underrepresented in musicological, ethnomusicological, and anthropological research. Although many of the cultures represented here have their own centuries-old scholarly traditions and literature, these are not well-known in the West. This volume is the first English-language reader on Middle Eastern musics. Many of its essays are groundbreaking at the same time that they seek to be introductory.

HOW THE VOLUME IS ORGANIZED

This book follows the pattern of its companion volumes in the Encyclopedia. Part 1 surveys the terrain, presenting a view of musical practices through an initial essay on listening to Middle Eastern and Central Asian musics, followed by one on important narratives and discourses about music in the region.

Part 2, Understanding Musics of the Middle East: Issues and Processes, features essays on major issues relevant to musical theory and practice: systems of modal conceptualization, processes of composition and performance, ways in which local and international "pop" music in the media have manifested themselves in Middle Eastern locales, relationships among musical and devotional practices, and music and the construction of gender, to name a few. We offer samples of musical-religious practices, gendered contexts, popular musics, and processes of performance in hopes of inspiring readers to look further for more information.

Part 3, Music Cultures and Regions, brings the reader into contact with specific local and national musical practices, moving from North Africa through the Mashriq or eastern Arab world, the Arabian Peninsula, Israel, Turkey, Iran, Armenia, Kurdistan, and Central Asia. Many of the subjects of the essays overlap. For instance, one can read about modal practices in the sections on theory, composition, and performance as well as in the sections on the Mashriq, Turkey, and so forth. Similarly, Jewish musical practices are discussed in the sections on North Africa, Israel, the Mashriq, and Central Asia.

The volume includes short articles called "Snapshots." These offer brief descriptions of musical life and musicians that are intended to bring readers closer to the lives of individual musicians and the experience of being present at different kinds of musical performance.

RESEARCH TOOLS

Lists of additional resources—print, audio, and video—appear at the back of the volume. These lists are intended to direct readers to materials that are generally accessible. Most of the resources are in Western languages. More specific lists of references, which sometimes include primary sources and resources in Middle Eastern languages, appear at the ends of relevant articles as a guide to appropriate readings.

The glossary and the index point readers toward information on specific musical instruments, musicians, and concepts about music as these occur throughout the volume.

The volume is accompanied by a compact disk that provides an audio component for many of the articles in the volume and at the same time offers a glimpse of the great variety of musics found in the region. Emphasis is given to musics that are not readily available on commercial recordings. The recorded examples are linked with notes and icons to related discussions throughout the volume. The notes for a single recorded example may direct readers' attention to several essays in the volume and, in some instances, to notated transcriptions of the music printed in the volume. The audio examples were initially recorded in a variety of circumstances over a period of four decades; thus, the sound quality varies. Most are field recordings; a few are commercial releases; and four were made specifically for this volume.

Readers are encouraged to seek out additional recordings, which appear with increasing frequency, whether of famous musicians such as Monajat Yultchieva, Muḥammad ʿAbd al-Wahhāb, or Bracha Zefira, for example, or examples of regional, folk, or other musics. Those interested in a particular artist or tradition would do well to search library or commercial catalogs, where these recordings are often represented.

ACKNOWLEDGMENTS

To call this volume a collective effort is to indulge in incredible understatement. It includes contributions by seventy-three scholars who come from seventeen countries and worked in nearly as many different languages. The project was launched more than ten years ago by Josef Pacholczyk, Lorraine Sakata, and Philip D. Schuyler, who recruited a large number of authors whose works appear in the present volume. When the volume passed to the present editors, authors were added as new writers and fields of information emerged, and to update information. The current editors have worked under three consecutive owners of the publishing company, and no fewer than five production teams have contributed expertise to the project. We thank Josef, Lorraine, and Phil for their initial work; Leo Balk, formerly vice president of Garland Publishing, for his efforts to advance its publication and for his help to us; Soo-Mee Kwon, formerly of Garland-Routledge; and Sylvia Miller, Richard Steins, and Susan Gamer of Routledge's encyclopedia division, who saw the production through to its conclusion.

Our most heartfelt thanks go to the contributing authors. Their fine contributions speak for themselves. More than that, their forbearance, patience, courtesy, and kindness throughout a protracted publication process that concluded with a perhaps inevitable "rush to the cadence" has overwhelmed us, and we are grateful. We mourn those who are no longer with us and will not see the result of their labor: Simon Jargy, JaFran Jones, and Habib Hassan Touma, valued colleagues and friends whom we miss.

The principal editors of the volume owe an indescribable debt of gratitude to Stephen Blum, Theodore Levin, and Irene Markoff, who contributed more to it than they ever intended. From the minutiae of spellings and transliterations to the articulation of major themes in the book to individual contacts with authors in remote locations, their service went well beyond the call of duty and doubtless intruded on other aspects of their professional and personal lives. Abe Marcus has served as an insightful reader of the volume and has assisted in the resolution of countless last-minute problems.

Ali Jihad Racy, Salwa El-Shawan Castelo-Branco, and Kay Kaufman Shelemay have served as valuable advisers to the volume from the time that the present editors took on the project to its final completion. Our gifted and multitalented associate editor, Alex Fisher, contributed his excellent scholarly skills, his fine organizational skills, and his remarkably even temperament and outstanding work ethic to the volume. In especially trying moments, Alex kept us on track. Ruth Ochs assisted Virginia Danielson in the early stages of work. We are grateful to the staff of the Loeb Music Library at Harvard, especially Sarah Adams, who graciously made room for the project. After so many years of collaborative effort with so many contributors, it simply is not possible to thank every individual who has played a role in assembling this volume. We hope, however, that all the participants in this project will find the volume a worthy product of their labors.

—Virginia Danielson, Scott Marcus, and Dwight Reynolds

Guide to Transliteration and Pronunciation

This volume covers cultures whose people speak Middle Eastern and Central Asian languages from three of the world's major language families: Afroasiatic, Indo-European, and Altaic. The primary branches of the Afroasiatic language family include Semitic (Arabic, Aramaic, Hebrew, Syriac), Berber, and Ancient Egyptian (of which Coptic is a later stage). The Indo-European family is represented here by the Iranian language group (Persian, Tajik, Dari, Kurdish, Baluchi) and Armenian. The Altaic language family includes the Turkic languages of Central and western Asia (Azeri, Kazakh, Kyrgyz, Turkish, Turkmen, Uygur, and Uzbek), as well as eastern Turkic languages such as Tuvan.

Many of these languages were at some point, or continue to be, written in the Arabic script, a fact that reflects the spread of Islam throughout this region (and with it the use of the Arabic language as a religious and scientific lingua franca) nearly 1,300 years ago. Although the Arabic script was adopted over a broad geographic expanse, the pronunciation of certain letters varies from one language to another. One result is that a vast array of cognate words are found throughout the Middle East and Central Asia, much as words deriving from Latin can be found scattered throughout the European languages. Some of these terms have retained a similar pronunciation and a single meaning, but many words have, over time, acquired different meanings, different pronunciations, or both. Cognate terms of both types are very much in evidence in the music cultures of these regions. For example, the terms *maqām* (Arabic), *makam* (modern Turkish), *muğam* (Azeri), and *muqam* (Uygur) all refer to similar, though not identical, concepts of melodic mode. In addition, several of these languages have numerous spoken colloquial dialects that use variant pronunciations of the same word: *darbūka*, *dirbaki*, and *darabukka* are all Arabic dialectal variants of one name for the common vase-shaped single-headed drum. In many cases, the spelling of musical terms has been standardized in this volume for the convenience of the reader; in other cases, however, particularly where a specific tradition is stressed, cross-linguistic and dialectal variations have been retained. The glossary at the end of this volume will serve as a basic guide to these variations.

When required by the conventions of English syntax, plural forms of nouns throughout this volume generally follow the norms of each language. Because the syntactic conventions of some languages (such as Persian and Turkish) do not use the plural nearly as often as English uses it, this policy has produced sentences that may seem awkward to readers familiar with these languages.

ARABIC, PERSIAN, AND OTTOMAN TURKISH

The *International Journal of Middle East Studies* (*IJMES*) transliteration system has in general been used for Standard Written Arabic, Persian, and Ottoman Turkish. A guide to the pronunciation of these sounds is found below. Additional vowels have been added to accommodate those of the many Arabic spoken dialects referred to in this volume, some of which differ dramatically from the written literary language

("Standard Arabic"). When lyrics or spoken dialects are quoted, the transliteration follows the speaker's pronunciation as closely as possible.

Arabic vowels and diphthongs

Each Arabic vowel has a long and short form. Short vowels appear unmarked; long vowels are marked with a macron: *ā*. In addition, Arabic vowels are all "darkened" when they occur next to an emphatic or velarized consonant (see below). This difference is most noticeable in the "light" and "dark" pronunciations of the long form of the vowel *a*.

Romanization	Pronunciation
a ā	short as in *tack*; long as in *can*; long in conjunction with a velarized consonant, as in *father*
e ē	short as in *bet*; long as in *mate*
i ī	short as in *bit*; long as in *seek*
o ō	short as in *oak*; long as in *open*
u ū	short as in *put*; long as in *ruler*
aw	*ow* in *how*
ay	*y* in *my*

Arabic consonants

Unless otherwise noted, consonants are pronounced approximately like their English equivalents. Sounds that are pronounced differently from, or do not exist in, English include the emphatic or velarized consonants (most of which are marked with underdots) that have a "dark" pronunciation made with the tongue further back and arched higher in the mouth than in English:

ḍ ṣ ṭ q ẓ (pronounced as a "dark" *z* or *dh*—see below)

Plus the following:

th	*th* in *thin* (never as in *this*)
dh	*th* in *this*
j	*j* in *joke* in the Arabian Peninsula and the Gulf; *s* in *measure* in the Eastern Mediterranean and parts of North Africa
kh	*ch* in Scottish *loch* or German *Bach*
ʿ	uvular fricative, pronounced like a short growling sound deep in the throat
ʾ	glottal stop, like the short silence in *uh-oh*, but occuring at the beginning, middle, or end of a word in Arabic
ḥ	"heavy" *h* pronounced deep in the throat (like the sound made by blowing on a pair of eyeglasses to clean them)
gh	fricated *r*, as in the French pronunciation of *Paris* but stronger

Persian vowels and diphthongs

There are three main dialects of Persian: Farsi (spoken in Iran), Tajik (spoken in Tajikistan and northern Afghanistan), and Dari (spoken in western Afghanistan). Persian is written in the Arabic alphabet but has four additional letters, transliterated here as *p*, *ch*, *zh*, and *g*. (When Persian musical terms were adopted into Arabic, these consonants were changed: for example, *chahārgāh* became *jahārkāh*; *āhang* became *hank*; and *pīsh row* became Turkish *peşrev* and then Arabic *bashraf*.) Four Persian consonants are pronounced differently from the Arabic consonants written with the same letters:

Arabic *th* (as in *mathnavī*) becomes *s* (*masnavī*).
Arabic *dh* (as in *dhikr*) becomes *ẕ* (*ẕekr*).

Arabic *ḍ* (as in *ḍarb*) becomes *ż* (*meżrāb*).
Arabic *w* (as in *wird*) becomes *v* (*verd*).

In everyday speech, Persian vowels are differentiated more consistently by timbre than by length. Speakers and singers of classical poetry, however, take great care to distinguish the three long vowels—*ā*, *ī*, and *ū*—from the three short vowels we have written (in a departure from the *IJMES* system) as *a*, *e* and *o*. The six Persian vowels can also be classified as three front vowels (*a*, *e*, and *ī*) and three back vowels (*ā*, *o*, and *ū*). In many publications *i* and *u* are understood as potentially long vowels without carrying a macron, but we have placed macrons over all three long vowels in order to make the transliteration of proper names and musical terms reasonably consistent in Arabic and Persian. The two Persian diphthongs are written here as *ow* and *ey* or *ei*.

Ottoman Turkish

Because Ottoman Turkish was written in the Arabic script, it is transcribed here using the same system as Persian and Arabic. This has the advantage of giving a precise rendering of the written form of words and also highlights the many Persian and Arabic borrowings. In Ottoman Turkish, most of the letters of the Arabic alphabet were pronounced as in Persian; however, Ottoman Turkish no longer exists as a spoken language; rather, it exists for modern Turks as a literary heritage similar to Latin, Middle English, and Old Provençal for modern Europeans.

Modern Turkish

In 1924, Mustafa Kemal Atatürk launched a reform of the Turkish language as part of his effort to westernize Turkey. This included discarding the Arabic script used over seven centuries of Ottoman culture and adopting the Roman alphabet. Some letters that had been part of Ottoman orthography but were not pronounced by Turkish-speakers (such as the Arabic letter *ʿayn*) were dropped, and a number of distinctions made in Ottoman Turkish (such as vowel length, particularly in words borrowed from Persian and Arabic) were also abandoned. Diacritic marks such as the umlaut, cedilla, hacek, and circumflex on romanized letters allowed the expression of all the sounds of Turkish in the new alphabet. In this volume, names and terms from the Ottoman period have been transliterated from Arabic script according to the system described above; those from after 1924 have been cited in their modern Turkish (romanized) spellings. The spelling of many terms and names has been regularized, but in articles that deal with sources from both the Ottoman period and the modern period, the reader will encounter variant spellings that reflect these two distinct linguistic periods of Turkish culture. Modern Turkish consonants are pronounced as in English, except for the following:

c	*j* in *joke*
ç	*ch* in *church*
ğ	between two vowels as a slight *s* sound, otherwise silent
ş	*sh* in *ship*

Modern Turkish vowels are pronounced as follows:

a	short *u* in *sun*
e	short *e* in *bed*
i	*i* in *bit*
ı	similar to the second vowel sound in *station*, *wanted*
o	*o* in *falsetto*
ö	French *eu*, *feu*
u	*u* in *pull*
ü	German *ü* in *über*

The vowels *a*, *i*, and *u* are occasionally written with a circumflex accent (*â*, *î*, *û*) before the letters *g*, *k*, and *l* to indicate that a slight *y* sound is inserted before the vowel: thus *kâtib* is pronounced *kyatib*. In some words of Arabic or Persian origin, the circumflex is also used to indicate a lengthening of the vowel sound.

Note that the consonant transliterated as *j* from Arabic, Persian, and Ottoman Turkish is written *c* in modern Turkish; thus Arabic *ḥijāz* becomes Turkish *hicaz*. Also, the Persian consonant transliterated as *ch* is written *ç* in modern Turkish. Turkish terms adapted into Arabic have sometimes retained this consonant as they passed into Arabic—for example, Arabic *al-chalghī al-baghdādī*, the basic instrumental ensemble of the Iraqi *maqām*, adapted from Turkish *çalgi* 'musical instrument'.

CENTRAL ASIAN TURKIC LANGUAGES

Many of the Central Asian Turkic languages were at one time or another written in Arabic script. During the Soviet period, however, nearly all of these closely related languages—Azeri, Kazakh, Kyrgyz, Uygur, and Uzbek—came to be written in various forms of the Russian Cyrillic alphabet. This is also true of Tajik, an eastern dialect of Persian. In modern Central Asia one can find examples of the same language written in romanized, Cyrillic, and Arabic scripts.

Azeri

Azerbaijani is now written in an alphabet modeled on that of modern Turkish, with one additional vowel, ə, formerly written *ä*; and two additional consonants, *x* and *q*. *X* stands for the same consonant transliterated as *kh* in the *IJMES* system for Arabic, Persian, and Ottoman Turkish. *Q* does not have exactly the same values in Azerbaijani as in Arabic; musical terms borrowed by Azerbaijani from Arabic are often spelled (and pronounced) differently—for instance, Arabic *maqām* becomes *muğam* in Azerbaijani.

Kazakh, Kyrgyz, Turkmen, Uygur, Uzbek

The romanized spellings in this volume represent a simplified and, for native English-speakers, more intuitive version of transliteration schemes now used in the nations of Central Asia themselves. For sounds that cannot be intuitively or unambiguously transliterated into English orthography, we use the following conventions:

Romanization	Pronunciation
kh	*ch* as in *loch*
gh	similar to *ch* in *loch*, but voiced to sound like *logh*
q	*c* as in *cot* (hard *c*, formed in the back of the throat)
j	*j* as in *joke*
ç (Turkmen)	*ch* as in *choke*
ş (Turkmen)	*sh* as in *shake*
zh	*g* as in *loge*
ā (Uzbek and Tajik)	*a* as in *father*
ä (Kazakh, Turkmen, and Uygur)	*a* as in *cattle*
ö	*e* as in *alert*
ü	*ü* as in German *über*
y	*i* as in *bit*
ÿ (Turkmen)	*y* as in *yellow*

INDIVIDUAL LANGUAGES:

Aramaic and Syriac

Aramaic and Syriac represent two closely related languages of the Semitic branch of the Afroasiatic family. In this volume they are referred to primarily as the liturgical languages of several Eastern Christian communities and thus the language of hymnody and religious cantillation. The transliteration system is that used for Arabic above.

Armenian

Armenian has its own unique alphabet and is transliterated here according to the Library of Congress system.

Berber

Although Berber is often referred to as a single language, this is a misconception. The various languages that form the Berber language family are distinct and often unintelligible to speakers of other Berber languages. The three Berber languages that appear most prominently in this volume are Kabyle, Tashlhiyt (also Tashelhit), and Tamazight. Speakers of Kabyle live primarily in eastern Algeria; speakers of Tashelhiyt live in parts of the High Atlas, the Anti-Atlas, and the Souss plain; speakers of Tamazight (singular, Amazigh; plural, Imazighen) are found in the High and Middle Atlas. (The names of these languages and the peoples who speak them occur in a variety of spellings in the scholarly literature.) Until recent times, these languages were rarely written, but when they were, it was in the Arabic script. Romanized writing systems were created during the French colonial period and have now gained some currency. In recent decades, some people have begun to discard the term *Berber* in favor of *Imazighen* (singular, *Amazigh*), which has been recoined to refer to a pan-Berber identity.

Coptic

Coptic is the final evolutionary stage of the language of ancient Egypt. Over a period of 5,000 years, a number of different writing systems evolved, including the hieroglyphic, heiratic, and demotic systems. Coptic is written in the Greek alphabet, with the addition of seven letters for sounds not found in Greek, and is the language of Christian Egypt. It exists now almost entirely as the language of the hymns and liturgy of the Coptic Church.

Hebrew

Hebrew has been transliterated according to the Library of Congress system.

Kurdish

Two forms of Kurdish are now written in standardized alphabets: Sorani in a modified Arabic alphabet, and Kurmanji in a Latin alphabet modeled on that of modern Turkey with the addition of the consonants *x* and *q* (as in Azerbaijani) as well as a few others that have not been used in this book, which otherwise uses the alphabet devised for Kurmanji. The five long vowels are written *a*, *ê*, *î*, *ô*, *û*; short vowels used in Kurdish words cited here include *e*, *i*, *o*, *ö*, *u*, and *ü*. For further information on the phonemes and orthography of Kurdish, see Amir Hassanpour. 1992. *Language and Nationalism in Kurdistan, 1918–1985*. San Francisco: Mellen.

Contributing Authors

Najwa Adra
New York Foundation for the Arts
New York, United States

Charlotte F. Albright
Seattle, Washington, United States

Walter Armbrust
St. Antony's College
Oxford University
Oxford, England

Stephen Blum
CUNY Graduate Center
New York, United States

Kay Hardy Campbell
Hingham, Massachusetts, United States

Salwa El-Shawan Castelo-Branco
Universidad Nova de Lisboa
Lisbon, Portugal

Margaret Caton
Institute of Persian Performing Arts
Los Angeles, California, United States

Dieter Christensen
Columbia University
New York, United States

Anna Czekanowska
Warsaw University
Warsaw, Poland

Virginia Danielson
Harvard University
Cambridge, Massachusetts, United States

Ruth Davis
Corpus Christi College
University of Cambridge
Cambridge, England

Tamila Djani-Zade
Glinkas State Museum of Music Culture
Russian Academy of Music
Moscow, Russia

Alexander Djumaev
Union of Composers
Tashkent, Uzbekistan

Jean During
Centre National de la Recherche Scientifique
Paris, France

Jürgen Elsner
Insitut für Musikwissenschaft
Humboldt Universität
Berlin, Germany

Yîldîray Erdener
University of Texas
Austin, Texas, United States

Walter Feldman
Bar-Ilan University
Ramat-Gan, Israel

Alexander J. Fisher
Harvard University
Cambridge, Massachusetts, United States

Gila Flam
Jewish National and University Library
Hebrew University
Jerusalem, Israel

Michael Frishkopf
University of Alberta
Edmonton, Alberta, Canada

Jane Goodman
Indiana University
Bloomington, Indiana, United States

Mahmoud Guettat
Institut Supérieur de Musique
Ministry of Cultural Affairs
Tunis, Tunisia

Louis Hage
Université Saint-Esprit
Kaslik, Lebanon

Scheherazade Qassim Hassan
Université de Paris X
Nanterre, France

Jehoash Hirshberg
Hebrew University
Jerusalem, Israel

Amy Horowitz
University of Pennsylvania
Philadelphia, Pennsylvania, United States

Ani Hovsepian
Brandeis University
Waltham, Massachusetts, United States

L. JaFran Jones
(Deceased)

Simon Jargy
(Deceased)

Deborah Kapchan
University of Texas
Austin, Texas, United States

Nedim Karakayali
University of Toronto
Toronto, Ontario, Canada

Alma Kunanbaeva
University of California
Berkeley, California, United States

Jean Lambert
Musée de l'Homme
Paris, France

Theodore Levin
Dartmouth College
Hanover, New Hampshire, United States

Manuk Manukian
Komitas State Conservatory of Music
Yerevan, Armenia

Abraham Marcus
Center for Middle Eastern Studies
University of Texas at Austin, United States

Scott Marcus
University of California
Santa Barbara, California, United States

Irene Markoff
York University
Toronto, Ontario, Canada

Bezza Mazouzi
Paris, France

Kristina Nelson Davies
Arab Arts Project
Cairo, Egypt

Karin van Nieuwkerk
International Institute for the study of Islam in the Modern World (Leiden)
Insitute for Languages and Cultures of the Middle East
Nijmegen University
Nijmegen, Netherlands

Eckhard Neubauer
Institute for the History of Arabic-Islamic Science
Frankfurt, Germany

John Morgan O'Connell
University of Limerick
Limerick, Ireland

Anne Marie Oliver
Harvard University
Cambridge, Massachusetts, United States

Arzu Öztürkmen
Bogazici University
Istanbul, Turkey

Christian Poché
Paris, France

Ali Jihad Racy
University of California
Los Angeles, California, United States

Anne K. Rasmussen
College of William and Mary
Williamsburg, Virginia, United States

Ursula Reinhard
Berlin, Germany

Dwight F. Reynolds
University of California
Santa Barbara, California, United States

Miriam Rovsing Olsen
Université de Paris X
Nanterre, France

Martha Roy
Cairo, Egypt

Magda Saleh
New York, United States

George Sawa
Toronto, Ontario, Canada

Suzanne Meyers Sawa
University of Toronto
Toronto, Ontario, Canada

Ḍirghām Ḥ. Sbait
Portland State University
Portland, Oregon, United States

Philip D. Schuyler
University of Washington
Seattle, Washington, United States

Edwin Seroussi
Bar-Ilan University
Ramat-Gan, Israel

Uri Sharvit
Bar-Ilan University
Ramat-Gan, Israel

Anthony Shay
Avaz International Dance Theatre
Los Angeles, California, United States

Amnon Shiloah
Hebrew University
Jerusalem, Israel

Karl Signell
Silver Spring, Maryland, United States

Paul Steinberg
Harvard University
Cambridge, Massachusetts, United States

Martin Stokes
University of Chicago
Chicago, Illinois, United States

Ruth M. Stone
Indiana University
Bloomington, Indiana, United States

Razia Sultanova
Goldsmiths College
University of London
London, United Kingdom

Ted Swedenburg
University of Arkansas
Fayetteville, Arkansas, United States

Dariush Talai
University of Tehran
Tehran, Iran

Habib Hassan Touma
(Deceased)

Sabine Trebinjac
Université de Paris X
Nanterre, France

Nadia Yaqub
University of North Carolina
Chapel Hill, North Carolina, United States

Ameneh Youssefzadeh
Paris, France

Sławomira Żerańska-Kominek
Warsaw University
Warsaw, Poland

The Garland Encyclopedia of World Music
Volume 6

The Middle East

Part 1
Introduction to the Musics of the Region

The large and diverse geographic area that we call the Middle East and Central Asia supports widely shared, important musical practices. The singing of fine poetry, sophisticated melodic improvisation, and musical composition using a great variety of long, complex rhythmic patterns are the basis for essential aesthetic values. Large, often open-ended forms that offer the potential for spontaneous alteration at the request of an audience are integral to the construction of social time—of entertainment—in this region. Musical performances often grow out of life-cycle events such as weddings. Musicians now work comfortably in the media as well; indeed, "mediated" performances may be a part even of weddings and similar occasions, and during the twentieth century the mass media became patrons of music and musicians.

Within these broad characteristics, countless local musical identities have emerged. For listeners, the many dialects, melodic and rhythmic patterns, musical instruments, and genres produce the rich musical world of the Middle East and Central Asia.

Traditional Moroccan musicians in Marrakech, c. 1990s. Photo © Lawrence Manning, Corbis.

Hearing the Music of the Middle East

Stephen Blum

Improvisation and the Centrality of the Voice
Distinctive Features and Structural Dimensions
Sequences and Compound Forms
Cultural Diversity and Social Distance

For musicians and listeners of the twenty-first century, the Middle East is a region with far-reaching connections that extend across large portions of three continents—Africa, Europe, and Asia—and can be discerned, as well, in large diasporic communities of Australia and the Americas. The contributors to this volume have been more concerned with fundamental principles of the musics of the Middle East, and with ways in which shared resources and values have been adapted to local requirements, than with drawing sharp contrasts between Middle Eastern musical practices and those of neighboring regions.

An especially impressive continuity in Middle Eastern music is the ingenuity with which musicians, in response to changing demands, have systematized resources drawn from many regional practices while devising countless ways for groups and individuals to articulate their differences. Musicians pursuing local interests and those attempting some kind of supralocal synthesis run up against different pressures for change. The desire to construct comprehensive musical systems derives, in part, from the cultural prestige and the intellectual frameworks of the world religions born in the Middle East, which include Zoroastrianism, Judaism, Christianity, and Islam. In no other part of the world have the cantillation of sacred texts and the organization of liturgies occupied a greater share of musicians' energies. Classifications of rhythmic and tonal patterns according to their character and function have served both sacred and secular ends (which have often been closely intertwined).

Musical instruments originating in the Middle East and Central Asia were carried, together with ideas about music, in all directions—to sub-Saharan Africa, South and East Asia, and Europe (Blench 1984; Lawergren 1995–1996, 1997). A striking example is a type of ensemble that served as an emblem of power in countless Asian, African, and European courts from Sumatra and Malaysia to northern Cameroon and northern Nigeria (Dauer 1985:57–65; Farmer 2000). The core instruments of this ensemble, in its various manifestations, are oboes, long trumpets, and kettledrums, though others (cylindrical drums, shorter trumpets, and various metallophones) have often been added and the long trumpets are not always present. The towers called *naubat-khānā* in South Asia and *naqqāra-khāne* or *ṭabl-khāna* in the Middle East were designed for this paradigmatic "outdoor" ensemble, which contrasts in almost every respect with the ensembles that have cultivated more refined sounds, suitable to garden

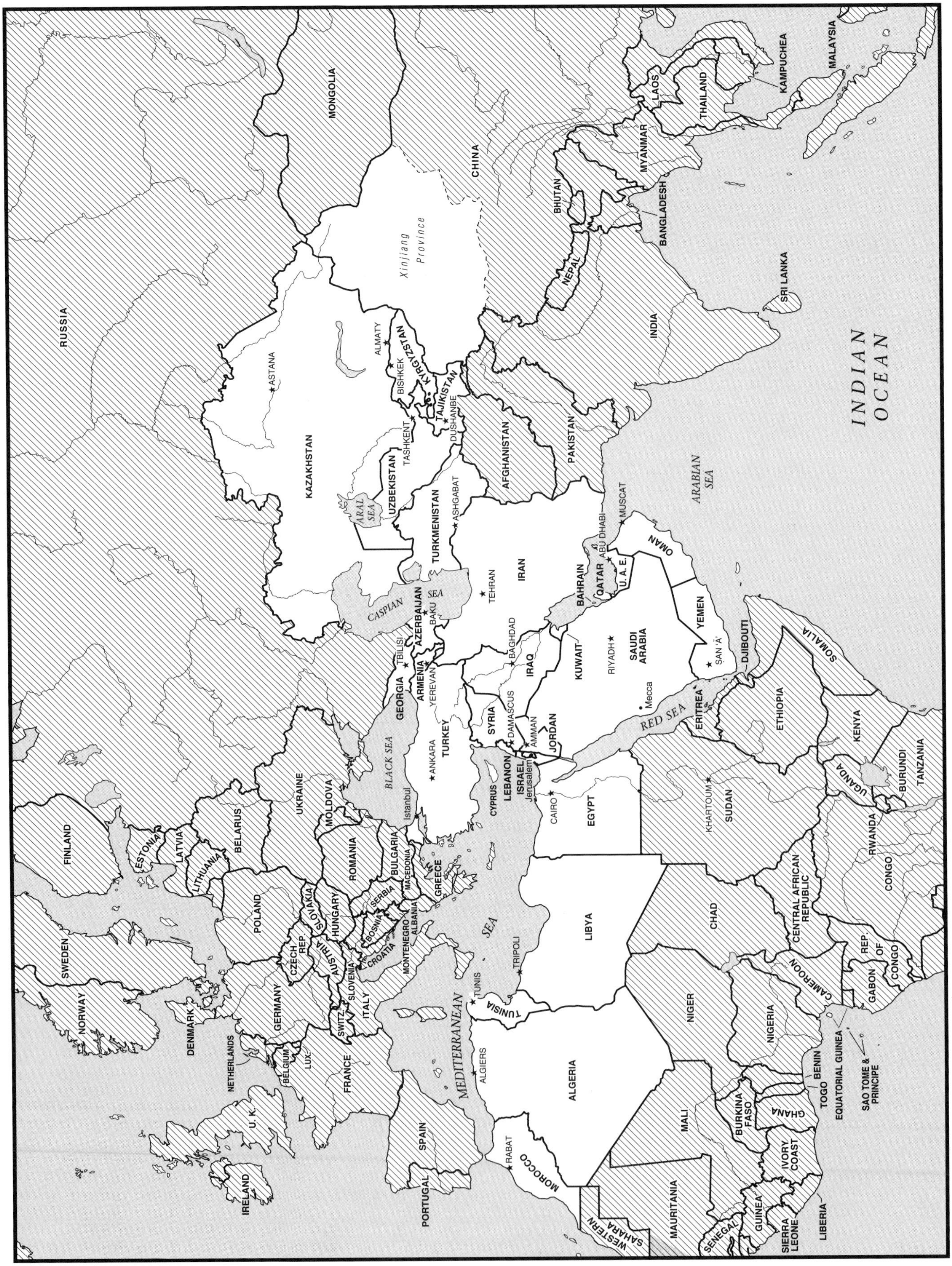

The Middle East.

pavilions or "indoor" settings. Different attitudes and postures were associated with each type of ensemble, as was also the case with the Chinese distinction between "military" and "civic" instrumentation and the medieval European classification of instruments as either *haut* 'loud' or *bas* 'soft'.

The manner in which music solicits (or demands) the attention of potential (or involuntary) listeners is one of the main respects in which genres of performance and roles of performers are distinguished. The need for such distinctions stems from the importance of music as a medium through which people interact and through which they can represent different styles of interaction.

This article introduces a few of the major issues that are explored in greater depth throughout the volume: improvisation and the centrality of the voice, distinctive features of sounds, compound musical forms, and models of cultural diversity. (For basic information on the peoples, languages, religions, geography, and history of the Middle East, see Bates and Rassam 1983; Eickelman 1998; Goldschmidt 1999; Hourani 1991; Lapidus 1988, Mostyn and Hourani 1983; and Rahman 1979.)

IMPROVISATION AND THE CENTRALITY OF THE VOICE

The forms of music making most highly valued in many Middle Eastern societies, as well as in some adjacent regions, require performers to improvise—that is, to adjust patterns and sequences they have mastered in ways they find appropriate for each occasion. Performers may learn such patterns and sequences as a fund of resources assembled for use in composing unique performances, or by way of a repertoire of relatively fixed compositions which they may modify during performance. These terse formulations describe two extremes, neither of which can be wholly absent from a competent musician's learning process. The relationship between resources organized for use in composition and repertoires of more or less finished compositions has varied significantly at different times and places, with the result that important musical terms have acquired multiple meanings.

Some forms of musical interaction depend on face-to-face contact among a restricted number of participants, and some may occur in public as well as in more private spaces. Amateur musicians often create their own relatively private space as they perform for one another in a venue, such as a teahouse or public park, where other activities are also taking place (figure 1). When a group of men or women will sing short responses to a leader's phrases, the leader, in turn, must respond to his or her perceptions of changes in the group's emotional state, noting as well the variable reactions of its individual members. Soloists must be similarly attentive to the responses of listeners who do not sing but utter conventional expressions of pleasure during the performance or even remain silent until they applaud or offer compliments once the performer has finished. Professionals or semiprofessionals who provide music on demand—notably for weddings and other celebrations—must quickly learn the necessary improvisational skills. Members of a circle of amateur musicians who perform for themselves alone are likely to cultivate an acute sensitivity to the ways in which different facets of a musical personality may manifest themselves from one session to the next. A star whose performances give listeners a sense of the links joining a national idiom of their own to a greater world must also make every performance a unique event.

Lila Abu-Lughod (1986:172–175) describes an occasion when two bedouin women sewing tents sang verses about patience and love to each other. Each woman's spontaneous choice of verses that offered an appropriate response to those her friend had just sung resulted in a sequence that other women, hearing Abu-Lughod's recording of the improvised exchange, have found deeply moving. Listening to the sequence aroused strong emotions in women who knew both singers and were well aware of the hardships suffered by one of them in particular. Repertoires of verses,

FIGURE 1 Two friends entertain themselves outside a teahouse, playing a three-stringed dūtār and a goblet drum. Photo by Stephen Blum, Herāt, Afghanistan, 1969.

along with techniques for presenting them musically, take shape as groups of singers find that they can voice their desires and frustrations by drawing on these repertoires and techniques. Quite often a singer or an instrumentalist hears an immediate response from another musician, as when two bedouin women or two Kurdish men exchange verses.

The voice has remained central to the musics of the Middle East because it is the primary instrument of human communication. Voices can be effectively supported, extended, contradicted, or transcended by the other musical instruments. We use our voices much more for dialogue and conversation than for monologues, to the point that speaking or singing to oneself is best understood as internalized dialogue through which a speaker or singer responds to remembered voices of others. Knowledge of a repertoire of poetic and musical resources enables a performer to rearrange familiar sequences and activate the listeners' memories. Listening to music of the Middle East becomes hearing as we expand our capacity for remembering rhythmic and melodic patterns, and for associating these patterns with human actions and emotions.

With his incomparable ability to depict the elaborate networks in which humans move and act, Leo Tolstoy specified each moment in a series of memories experienced by a Muslim warrior as he overhears one of his disciples singing familiar verses about a *ghazavāt*, a military campaign for a religious end. The protagonist of Tolstoy's story *Haji Murad* is about to fight his last battle against the Russian forces of occupation in the Caucasus as he listens to a song in which a dying *jigit* 'warrior' tells birds to carry news of his own and his companions' deaths to their female relatives (who, by implication, will create narrative songs praising their heroic deeds). Haji Murad hears other events in the soundscape—nightingales cooing, knives being sharpened, a cheerful voice responding to the song with *Lā illāhi illā 'l-lāh!* 'No divinity apart from God!'—and he is reminded of a narrative song addressed to his father by his mother, who composed it after the father stabbed her during a quarrel. She concluded her song with the line "I did not fear death, neither will my boy *jigit*." Haji Murad's memory of his mother singing the song as he lay beside her under a fur coat and saw the scar on her side conjures up a long string of further memories of his childhood and of his own wife and son. Tolstoy's finely wrought prose brings out the almost limitless power of song to evoke formative relationships among parents and children, husbands and wives, masters and disciples.

The song that Tolstoy imagined Haji Murad's mother to have composed, like the verses that Abu-Lughod heard bedouin women singing, might have seemed almost meaningless to listeners who did not understand the words, knew nothing of the circumstances to which the singers referred, and lacked the memories of earlier musical experiences that enable a hearer to notice significant differences in a new composition or performance. Several ways of overcoming such limitations are available to singers and instrumentalists who address themselves to a broader public.

When a performer draws attention to one musical segment by repeating it with slight (or extensive) changes, the listeners' short-term memory may retain a provisional "background" against which they can perceive potentially meaningful changes from one repetition to the next. Which of the potentially meaningful differences prove to be decisive in any listener's response to the performance will depend on habits this listener formed during earlier performances as well as on his or her immediate desires.

Structurally, a musical performance in the Middle East normally consists of several sections of varying length. A shift from one section to the next may be quite abrupt, or it may be so gradual that listeners do not immediately realize that the music is taking on a new character. Listening for the most striking contrasts between sections with respect to pitch register, timbre, rhythm, and mode is probably the best way for new listeners to approach Middle Eastern music. With further experience, very subtle contrasts within each section start to register on the ear.

DISTINCTIVE FEATURES AND STRUCTURAL DIMENSIONS

While music always involves coordination of more than one sequence of movements and sounds, musical practices differ with respect to which distinctive features and structural dimensions are most pertinent. Musicians and listeners in the Middle East often enjoy the interplay among accents that are grouped in at least two different ways.

Another type of interplay is that between sounds whose duration is sustained and sounds that fade away more quickly. Two syllables used by speakers of several languages to represent this fundamental contrast are *dum*, for the resonant sounds produced by striking the center of a drumhead; and *tek*, for the drier, brighter sounds produced by rapping on or near the rim of a drum. The oppositions between the initial consonants, central vowels, and final consonants of the two syllables are iconic, with distinctive features of the two classes of drum sounds; moreover, they exemplify principles of rhythmic theory that were richly developed in Arabic writings on music (Neubauer 1995–1996; Sawa 1989:35–71).

An opposition between two types of sound is often replicated by two or more instruments that have complementary timbres. Double-headed cylindrical drums and paired kettledrums are invariably constructed and played so that the sounds produced on one skin will contrast with those obtained from the other. Combining two or more such instruments yields a compact system of differentiated timbres, as in the typical drum ensemble of the Tihāma plateau in Yemen, consisting of a large deep kettledrum (*mirfa'*), a small deep kettledrum (*dumduma* or *tungura*), a double-headed cylindrical drum (*ṭabl marad*), and a single-skinned cylindrical drum (*ṭabl mu'astā*). Each instrument plays rhythmic figures appropriate to its pitch level and flexibility: faster movement and improvised variation are associated with higher-pitched sounds, slower movement and greater predictability with deeper sounds. [See Rhythmic Structure and Drum Improvisation in Yemen.]

The makeup of numerous small ensembles exploits the opposition between the sounds of bowed stringed instruments and those produced by strings that are plucked (with a fingernail or plectrum) or struck (with light hammers). The contrast provides an effective accompaniment to sung poetry, as the string attacks can reinforce the initial consonants of sung syllables and the fiddle can proceed to imitate subtle inflections of vowels. In this respect the most important rival or partner of bowed instruments is the rim-blown flute most often called *nāy* or *nei*.

The Egyptian *takht*, which was replaced in the 1930s by the larger *firqa*, included up to five instruments as well as a solo vocalist and a small group of supporting singers: *'ūd* (a short-necked lute), *qānūn* (a plucked dulcimer), *nāy*, *kamanja* (a spike fiddle) or Western violin, and *riqq* (a small frame drum). A similar Persian ensemble of the late nineteenth century would have *tār* (a long-necked lute) and *santūr* (a hammered dulcimer) rather than *'ūd* and *qānūn*, and a goblet drum (*żarb*) alongside or in place of the frame drum (called *dāīre* and usually larger than the *riqq*). The frame drum was banished from elite Persian ensembles through most of the twentieth century, but it began to return after the Iranian revolution of 1979. It remained essential to the Azerbaijani genre known as *muğam*, which is performed by a trio consisting of Azerbaijani *tar* (distinct from the Persian variety), *kəmançe* (spike fiddle), and a singer who also plays the frame drum (*dəf*) during instrumental interludes. A somewhat similar genre known as *al-maqām al-'irāqī* 'Iraqi *maqam*' requires a minimum of three performers in addition to the vocalist, in one of two standard ensembles. The *chalghī al-baghdādī* consists of *santūr*, *joze* (spike fiddle), *daff* (frame drum), *dumbak* (goblet drum) and perhaps *naqqāra* (paired kettledrums); in the *takht al-sharqī* the *santūr* and *joze* are replaced by *'ūd*, *qānūn*, and *nāy*.

A pair of sounds may be understood as an opposition of two locations—center or rim, upper string (*bam*) or lower string (*zīr*) on a long-necked or short-necked lute. A different but equally important concept of the two options is to locate them with reference to a center: a membrane or a string may be tightened or loosened if it is not left alone; a pitch may be raised or lowered if it is not repeated unchanged; a beat of moderate speed may be halved or doubled (see Neubauer 1995–96:297 on the rhythmic theory associated with Iṣḥāq al-Mawṣilī). The same tripartite structure is apparent in the ancient Greek classification of musical compositions according to ethos and in the Arabic adaptation of this classification that appears in writings of the philosopher al-Kindī (d. c. 866). The Greek hesychastic became *al-mu'tadil* 'the temperate', diastaltic became *al-basṭī* 'the expansive', and systaltic became *al-qabḍī* 'the constrained' (Lachmann and al-Ḥifnī 1931:xx, 30; Strunk 1950:45). More complex classifications by ethos generally include similar distinctions between assertion and withdrawal. Such schemes have proved useful both in classifying repertoires and in spelling out musical itineraries that start with one ethos and end with another. The distinction made by Mauritanian musicians between "blackness" (connoting youth, strength, war, tension) and "whiteness" (connoting maturity, nostalgia, love, loosening) operates on every level of temporal organization; most broadly, every performance moves from the strength of youth to the nostalgia of old age (Guignard 1975). Other modal systems have been designed to allow for a variety of plots.

A relatively "coarse" distinction, such as that between a "taut" and a "loose" string, can gradually be transformed into a set of "fine" distinctions (Picken and Nickson 2000:129). Before or early in the second millennium B.C.E., Sumerian or Babylonian musicians developed systematic procedures for generating seven different orderings (or "octave species") of a set of seven pitches, by tightening or loosening the strings on a lyre or harp to produce different sequences of descending fifths and ascending fourths. The Old Babylonian tablet known as the "tuning text" identifies the string that must be retuned in order to transform the tritone formed between the first and last notes in each such sequence into a perfect fifth (West 1994:162–168). Assigning a name to each string made it possible to name each interval formed by a pair of strings as well as the tuning based on each string; an inventory of Akkadian love songs classified by tuning also survives. In Babylonian musical notation, the interval names are followed by numeral signs that have been variously interpreted (West 1994:171–178).

Assigning names to strings, intervals, tunings, and eventually positions on strings has remained central to many Middle Eastern musical practices, as have the classification of repertoires by tuning or mode and a preference for modes containing seven pitch classes. But in the Middle East musical notation did not attain the same degree of importance that it acquired in East Asia and Europe. Master musicians have tended to regard face-to-face communication over an extended time as the only adequate channel for the transmission of musical knowledge, although this has not prevented students from trying to learn what they could from a variety of sources. [See The Iraqi Maqam and Its Transmission.]

A major reason why most Middle Eastern practices never came to rely on musical notation is the complexity of the rhythms to which verse and prose are appropriately sung or recited. Many musical genres require flexible rhythms that do not depend on a regular, predictable grouping of accents. One could scarcely overemphasize the significance, for musicians of the Middle East and neighboring regions, of poetry composed in quantitative meters, which furnish one rhythmic dimension (a regular distribution of long and short syllables) that musicians are free to coordinate with other patterns involving duration and various types of accent. The enduring cultural prestige of the pre-Islamic *qaṣā'id* 'odes' (singular, *qaṣīda*) in classical Arabic must have motivated, to varying degrees, many of the poets who created quantitative poetry in Persian, Hebrew, Chaghatai Turkish, Ottoman Turkish, Urdu, Swahili, and Hausa—to name only seven of the major languages for which a stock of quantitative meters was developed at some point during the past twelve centuries.

An eloquent and influential argument that "a tune is independent of the [poetic] meter, or of the lesser or greater number of syllables" was advanced by the great Jewish poet and philosopher Yehuda Ha-Levy (d. 1141) in the same section of his *Book of the Kuzari* in which he extolled the advantages of face-to-face conversation over writing (Shiloah 1992:55–56, 96–98). Ha-Levy's argument did not rule out all forms of notation: he remarked that certain features of oral communication—such as changes of pace, pauses that separate subjects, and differences between commands and requests—are effectively communicated by the *te'amîm* accents that were devised for biblical cantillation.

Whether, as al Faruqi (1979, 1985b) argues, secular performance genres came to be more highly esteemed the more closely they resembled the cantillation of religious texts is a controversial issue. But there can be no doubt that the rhythmic sensibilities of countless musicians benefited from hearing and participating in sophisticated practices of cantillation, as well as from exploiting the possibilities made available by quantitative poetry.

SEQUENCES AND COMPOUND FORMS

Listeners who are new to the music of the Middle East can quickly learn to appreciate the diverse ways in which instrumentalists interact with singers (some of whom are also instrumentalists, as in the Azerbaijani trio). No function is more important than supplying instrumental interludes, which in many performance genres offer a much-needed respite after the most intense passages of sung poetry. One large set of variables concerns the rhythmic and tonal relationships of the interludes to the music that precedes and follows them. Great composers, such as Riyāḍ al-Sunbāṭī (1906–1981), have designed impressive sequences in which one interlude is performed between a few sections, then replaced by a new interlude for the next few sections, and so on. Outstanding improvisers may be recognized by their ability to create effective transitions between the emotional coloring of one passage and the frame of mind that suits the poetry of the following passage.

Listeners who are new to the music of the Middle East can quickly learn to appreciate the diverse ways in which instrumentalists interact with singers.

The density of events must vary if a performance is to hold the attention of listeners. Exchanges between singers and instrumentalists often involve overlapping entries which in a conversation would sound like interruptions but in music can show support while at the same time articulating a complementary perspective. Listeners whose musical habits were largely formed by the polyphonic music of Europe and the Americas have sometimes described Middle Eastern music as "monophonic," in other words "single-voiced." This term can be misleading to the extent that it directs attention away from the interactions through which performers create sonorous textures whose components cannot be enumerated as easily as the individual lines in, say, a four-voice fugue by J. S. Bach. Sometimes a singer is "shadowed" by one or more instrumentalists who follow every twist and turn in the singer's line almost (but not quite) as closely as possible. The precise points where instrumental figures begin and end are often left to the performer's discretion; as a result, the number of sounds that can be heard at any given moment and the harmonic relationships among them will fluctuate.

Many instruments and small ensembles are designed to allow for the continuous sounding of a drone—generally a complex sound in which certain partials of a fundamental pitch stand out. Three important classes of such instruments are long-necked plucked lutes with sympathetic strings, drone strings, or both (for instance, the *saz* of Turkey and Azerbaijan); double duct-flutes (such as the *donelī* of Baluchistan); and single-reed double pipes with either a conical or a cylindrical bore (such as the *mijwiz* of the Levant and the *duzele* of Kurdistan). The one- or two-stringed fiddles used to accompany some epic singing (such as the bedouin *rabābah*) for the most part play patterns that function as drones. Double-reed pipes with a conical or cylindrical bore (such as the *zurna* and *mei* or *balaban* of Turkey and Transcaucasia) are often played in pairs, with one player concentrating on the melody and a second player responsible for the drone. Similarly, in ensembles that include two or more stringed instruments, the open strings of one (such as the *setar* or *tanburag* of Baluchistan) may be strummed in a repeating rhythmic pattern. A unique genre in which a group of men responds to a vocal soloist by producing a compound vocal drone is the *nahma* ritual cycle of pearl divers along the Arabian Gulf.

Drones are established in order to be interrupted, then renewed. The same can be said of rhythmic patterns that are repeated a number of times (with or without melodic changes), then replaced by different patterns or by music that avoids repetition of fixed rhythms. The desire for interruptions or departures followed by returns has led to the development of suites or compound musical forms, which have a long history in the Middle East and the rest of Eurasia.

One reason to create a compound form is in order to tell a story without using words. Robert Lachmann (1929) drew a parallel between a flute piece about a fight with a lion that he had recorded from a Tunisian shepherd and the ancient Greek *nomos* describing Apollo's victory over the python. Two recorded versions of a Turkish instrumental narrative, *Kara koyun* 'Black Sheep', use different instruments—the rim-blown flute *kaval* and the duct-flute *düdük*—and different sequences of musical figures to tell what is essentially the same story about a shepherd who wins his bride by meeting her father's challenge to play music that can prevent sheep from slaking their thirst (Brăiloiu 1984:disk 2, side A, track 1; Simon and Wegner 2000:CD 2, track 1). Other stories associated with instrumental pieces also account for the creation of the piece itself, or at least of its culminating section. In one type of plot, a ruler is informed of the death of his son or his favorite horse by an instrumental narrative newly composed for that purpose, in response to the ruler's threat to punish any bearer of bad tidings.

The creation of suites or compound forms must have made it easier for musicians to remember a large repertoire. One model of cyclic organization used by composers from the eighth through the early sixteenth centuries is a sequence of seven songs, such as the cycle about seven fortresses composed by Ma'bad (d. 743; Neubauer 1997:317–18, 352 n. 234). The most richly elaborated compound forms are cycles consisting of pieces and improvisations in a more or less prescribed sequence of genres—such as the *nūba* of North Africa, the *waṣla* of Egypt and the Levant, the Turkish *fasıl*, and the five great *fuṣūl* of the Iraqi *maqām*. Different types of sequence, some more formalized than others, have been worked out to meet the diverse needs of courts, Sufi lodges, circles of amateurs, the *naqqāra-khāne*, and in the twentieth century the concert hall (al Faruqi 1985a; Feldman 1996:177–192; Racy 1983).

A compound form conceived as a sequence of genres may or may not progress through a prescribed sequence of musical *maqāmāt* 'modes' (singular, *maqām*); in some cases each "movement" or major section of the compound form begins and ends in the same mode. Compositions or improvisations that move systematically through every available mode have constituted a genre of their own at certain times and places, sometimes to provide a synopsis of the modal system, at other times to challenge composers or performers to display their command of the entire system. Two Byzantine *stichera*, short monostrophic hymns, which move systematically through all eight modes of the *oktōēchos*, seem to have been composed as a synopsis (Strunk 1942:202–204; Husmann 1970:306, 314–315). As described by the great Timurid musician and theorist 'Abd al-Qāder Ibn Gheibī al-Marāghī (d. 1435), the vocal genre *koll ol-żorūb va 'l-nagham* 'compendium of rhythms and melodies' called not only for modulation through twelve primary modes (*maqāmāt*), six secondary modes (*āvāzāt*), and twenty-four branches (*sho'ab*) but also for systematic use of the available rhythmic cycles (Marāghī 1987 [1415]:249). A musician's ability to make a harmonious arrangement of the full range of modes was also tested by such Ottoman Turkish genres as the precomposed instrumental *küllî külliyat peşrev* 'compendium prelude' and the improvised *taksîm külli* (Feldman 1996:294–299). One Persian *dastgāh* 'system' in current use, *rāst panjgāh*, is sometimes said to have been assembled in large part from portions of other *dastgāh-hā*.

The idea of modulating through several—if not all—parts of a modal system is easily combined with the idea of a compound form made up of several genres. Different ways of joining the two concepts are evident in the Iraqi *fuṣūl* 'cycles', the Persian *radīf* 'row', and the Tajik-Uzbek *shashmaqom*, among others.

The long-standing interest in compound forms stimulated efforts to classify tonal and rhythmic patterns according to their potential functions—such as introducing, continuing or moving away, reaching a culmination, and returning or closing. Terms for music that fulfils these functions occur in all major languages of the Middle East—for example Arabic *qafla* 'lock' (a cadential pattern), Persian *forūd* 'descent' (an extended melodic descent toward a cadence), Azerbaijani *ayaq* 'foot', and Kurdish *paş-bend* 'after the verse'.

CULTURAL DIVERSITY AND SOCIAL DISTANCE

The development of compound forms provided much-needed opportunities for bringing together verses, rhythms, and melodies from highly diverse sources. A ceremony of the Qāderi dervishes in Iranian Kurdistan might include texts in Arabic, Persian, and Sorani Kurdish (During 1994). The Iraqi *maqām* is a particularly impressive achievement, incorporating both rural and urban genres, performed in both religious and secular settings, and with texts and vocables taken from dialectal Arabic, Persian, Kurdish, Turkish, and Hebrew as well as from literary Arabic; before the emigration of Iraqi Jews to Israel in 1949, Jewish instrumentalists and Muslim vocalists collaborated in performance of the *maqām* (Shiloah 1992:200–202). For most of its existence, the Tajik-Uzbek *shashmaqom* accomodated sung poetry in both Tajik (Persian) and Uzbek, but in the twentieth century nationalist pressures led to the artificial construction of separate Tajik and Uzbek "traditions" (Djumaev 1993).

Historians of European music have traced continuities in the traditions associated with a single language and nation, giving us excellent histories of, for example, "Italian music" and "Russian music." However, the model of national music histories is more misleading than helpful when applied to the Middle East, where the norm has been cultural interaction among speakers of two or more languages and among practitioners of several religions. Middle Eastern writers have often described such interactions by attributing a group of innovations to one outstanding individual.

In his remarks on the early history of Andalusian music, Aḥmad ibn Yūsuf al-Tīfāshī (d. 1253) reports that Ibn Bajja (d. 1139) "secluded himself for several years with skilled singing girls, whereupon he improved the *istihlāl* [a vocal prelude] and the *'amal* [another vocal genre] and combined the songs of the Christians with those of the East, thereby inventing a style (*ṭarīqa*) found only in Andalus, toward which the temperament of its people inclined, so that they rejected all others" (Monroe 1986–1987:256–257). Several points are noteworthy in al-Tīfāshī's account: the collaboration of a male innovator with "skilled singing girls"; the identification of vocal practices according to both religion (Christianity) and region (the Mashriq); acceptance of the new style because of its perceived compatibility with the Andalusian temperament (*ṭab'*); and the resulting obsolescence of older styles. In an earlier passage, al-Tīfāshī likewise claims that the adoption of stylistic innovations introduced to al-Andalus by Ziryāb (d. c. 850) caused all other styles to be abandoned. The topics and formats of these statements turn up continually in spoken as well as in written discourse.

A somewhat similar story, as told in the *Kitāb al-aghānī* 'Book of Songs' of al-Iṣfahānī (d. 967), is that of the singer Ibn Misjaḥ, who was active in Mecca during the reigns of the first six Umayyad caliphs (661–715). He is said to have traveled widely in order to assimilate the best aspects of several musical repertoires—Byzantine melodies, the Syrian *oktōēchos* (*al-alḥān al-ustūkhūsīya* or *al-luḥun al-thamāniya* in Arabic), songs from the Persian province of Fars, and the repertoire of the Persian short-necked lute *barbat* (Neubauer 1994:374–375). Two key verbs in al-Iṣfahānī's narrative form a complementary pair: *wa-akhadha* 'he assimilated' and *wa-alqā* 'he discarded'. Selecting the features one wishes to adopt from a foreign musical practice entails identifying and rejecting its undesirable features, in this case certain *nabarāt* 'vocalises' (singular, *nabra*) and melodies (*nagham*) that Ibn Misjaḥ deemed incompatible with Arabic vocal art. A more sociological account of the Arab assimilation of Persian and Byzantine vocal idioms was offered by Ibn Khaldūn (d. 1406), who famously described "the craft of singing" as "the last of the crafts attained in civilization" and noted that the military successes of the Arabs in the first century of Islam led singers to abandon the courts of the Persians and Byzantines in order to seek their fortune in the Hijaz, where "Ma'bad and his class of singers . . . learned from them" (Ibn Khaldūn 1967:ii, 404). If they ever performed at the same gatherings, Ma'bad and some of the singers whose vocalises he had rejected may have found occasion to dramatize their artistic differences.

How perceptions of cultural difference or social distance can be enacted in performance has remained a major concern of Middle Eastern musicians. A musician may avoid any reference to specific dance rhythms or to the whole area of dance. An entire category of performers, such as the *nashshādīn* of Yemen (Schuyler 1990), may be distinguished by its avoidance of all musical instruments. A listener who hears the options that performers have chosen is often in a position to recognize the options they have rejected.

REFERENCES

Abu-Lughod, Lila. 1986. *Veiled Sentiments: Honor and Poetry in a Bedouin Society*. Berkeley and Los Angeles: University of California Press.

Bates, Daniel G., and Amal Rassam. 1983. *Peoples and Cultures of the Middle East*. Englewood Cliffs, N.J.: Prentice-Hall.

Blench, Roger. 1984. "The Morphology and Distribution of Sub-Saharan Musical Instruments of North African, Middle Eastern, and Asian, Origin." *Musica Asiatica* 4:155–191.

Brăiloiu, Constantin, comp. 1984 [1951–1958]. *Collection universelle de musique populaire enregistrée*. Geneva: Musée d'Ethnographie, Archives Internationales de Musique Populaire. (Booklet with six LP records; first issued as forty 78-rpm records.)

Dauer, Alfons. 1985. *Tradition afrikanischer Blasorchester und Entstehung des Jazz*. Beiträge zur Jazzforschung, 7. Graz: Akademische Druck- und Verlagsanstalt.

Djumaev, Alexander. 1993. "Power Structures, Culture Policy, and Traditional Music in Soviet Central Asia." *Yearbook for Traditional Music* 25:43–50.

During, Jean. 1994. *Kurdistan: Zikr et chants. Les derviches qâderi de Sanandaj (Iran)*. Paris: OCORA. (Two compact disks, C 560071-72.)

Eickelman, Dale F. 1998 [1981]. *The Middle East and Central Asia: An Anthropological Approach*, 3rd ed. Upper Saddle River, N.J.: Prentice-Hall.

Elsner, Jürgen. 1997. "Listening to Arabic Music." *World of Music* 39(2):111–126.

Farmer, Henry George. 2000. "Tabl-Khāna." *Encyclopedia of Islam*, 2nd ed., Vol. 10:34–38. Leiden: Brill.

Faruqi, Lois Ibsen al. 1979. "The Status of Music in Muslim Nations: Evidence from the Arab World." *Asian Music* 12(1):56–85.

———. 1985a. "The Suite in Islamic History and Culture." *World of Music* 27(3):46–64.

———. 1985b. "Music, Musicians, and Muslim Law." *Asian Music* 17(1):3–36

Feldman, Walter. 1996. *Music of the Ottoman Court: Makam Composition and the Early Ottoman Instrumental Repertoire*. Berlin: VWB—Verlag für Wissenschaft und Bildung.

Goldschmidt, Arthur. 1999 [1979]. *A Concise History of the Middle East*, 6th ed. Boulder, Colo.: Westview.

Guignard, Michel. 1975. *Musique, honneur et plaisir au Sahara*. Paris: Paul Geuthner. (Includes 45-rpm record.)

Hourani, Albert H. 1991. *A History of the Arab Peoples*. Cambridge, Mass.: Harvard University Press.

Husmann, Heinrich. 1970. "Die oktomodale Stichera und die Entwicklung des byzantinischen Oktoëchos." *Archiv für Musikwissenchaft* 27:304–325.

Ibn Khaldūn. 1967. *The Muqaddimah: An Introduction to History, Translated from the Arabic by Franz Rosenthal*, 2nd ed., 3 vols. Princeton. N.J.: Princeton University Press.

Lachmann, Robert. 1929. "Die Weise vom Löwen und der pythische Nomos." In *Musikwissenschaftliche Beiträge: Festschrift für Johannes Wolf*, 97–106. Berlin: M. Breslauer.

Lachmann, Robert, and Mahmud al-Hifnī, eds. and trans. 1931. *Ja'qūb Ibn Isḥāq al-Kindī: Risāla fī ḥubr ta'līf al-alḥān*. Leipzig: Breitkopf und Härtel.

Lapidus, Ira M. 1988. *A History of Islamic Societies*. Cambridge: Cambridge University Press.

Lawergren, Bo. 1995–1996. "The Spread of Harps between the Near and Far East during the First Millennium A.D.: Evidence of Buddhist Musical Cultures on the Silk Road." *Silk Road Art and Archaeology* 4:233–275.

———. 1997. "To Tune a String: Dichotomies and Diffusions between the Near and Far East." In *Ultra Terminum Vagari: Scritti in onore di Carl Nylander*, ed. B. Magnusson et al., 175–192. Rome: Quasar.

Marāghī, 'Abd al-Qāder Ibn Gheibī al-. 1987 [1415]. *Jāmi' al-alḥān*, ed. Teqī Bīnesh. Tehran: Mo'asese-ye Moṭāle'āt va Tehqīqāt-e Farhangī. (Holograph manuscript dated 1415.)

Monroe, James T. 1986–1987. "A Sounding Brass and Tinkling Cymbal: al-Xalāl in Andalus (Two Notes on the Muwaššah)." *Corónica* 15(2):252–258.

Mostyn, Trevor, and Albert H. Hourani, eds. 1983. *The Cambridge History of the Middle East and North Africa*. Cambridge: Cambridge University Press.

Neubauer, Eckhard. 1994. "Die acht 'Wege' der arabischen Musiklehre und der Oktoechos." *Zeitschrift für die Geschichte der Arabisch-Islamischen Wissenschaften* 9:373–414.

———. 1995–1996. "Al-Halāl ibn Ahmad und die Frühgeschichte der arabischen Lehre von den 'Tönen' und den musikalischen Metren." *Zeitschrift für die Geschichte der Arabisch-Islamischen Wissenschaften* 10:255–323.

———. 1997. "Zur Bedeutung der Begriffe Komponist und Komposition in der Musikgeschichte der islamischen Welt." *Zeitschrift für die Geschichte der Arabisch-Islamischen Wissenschaften* 11:307–363.

Picken, Laurence E. R., and Noël J. Nickson. 2000. *Music from the Tang Court*, Vol. 7, *Some Ancient Connections Explored*. Cambridge: Cambridge University Press.

Racy, Ali Jihad. 1983. "The Waslah: A Compound Form Principle in Egyptian Music." *Arab Studies Quarterly* 5:396–404.

Rahman, Fazlur. 1979 [1966]. *Islam*, 2nd ed. Chicago: University of Chicago Press.

Sawa, George Dimitri. 1989. *Music Performance Practice in the Early 'Abbāsid Era 132–320 A.H. / A.D. 750–932*. Toronto: Pontifical Institute of Mediaeval Studies.

Schuyler, Philip D. 1990. "Hearts and Minds: Three Attitudes toward Performance Practice and Music Theory in the Yemen Arab Republic." *Ethnomusicology* 34:1–18.

Shiloah, Amnon. 1992. *Jewish Musical Traditions*. Detroit: Wayne State University Press.

Simon, Artur, and Ulrich Wegner, comps. 2000. *Music! 100 Recordings, 100 Years of the Berlin Phonogramm-Archiv 1900–2000*. Mainz: Wergo. (Booklet and four compact disks, LC 06357.)

Strunk, Oliver. 1942. "The Tonal System of Byzantine Music." *Musical Quarterly* 28:190–204.

———. 1950. *Source Readings in Music History*. New York: Norton.

West, M. L. 1994. "The Babylonian Musical Notation and the Hurrian Melodic Texts." *Music and Letters* 75:161–179.

History of Scholarship: Narratives of Middle Eastern Music History

Virginia Danielson
Alexander J. Fisher

Theorizing about Musical Sound
Assessing Spiritual Value: Is Music Good or Bad?
Stories, Song Collections, and Biographies: Capturing Performance
Travelers' Tales, Printed Scholarship, and the Oriental Gaze
Ways of Thinking about Music in the Twentieth Century

Over centuries of written history, the peoples of the Middle East have used varied means of analyzing, describing, and recording music and musical life. Some of their narratives are hundreds of years old; others are relatively new and changeable, dependent on more transitory media than the written word. As Touma observes, "the history of researching Arabian music is as old as Arabian cultural history" (1996:168).

The essays in this volume offer discussions and details of major issues and themes in scholarship and the relevant literature. This overview article will outline some broad, widely shared narratives of musical life. Because of the wealth and richness of the resources—many of which have not been thoroughly explored by scholars—the following discussion will rely on only a few examples rather than attempt to encompass the entire breadth of knowledge and information concerning Arabic, Persian, Hebrew, Turkish, and Central Asian music histories.

Unsurprisingly, the narrative strains described here overlap and do not represent discrete forms of knowledge. Moreover, as Feldman argues persuasively with regard to Turkish music history (1996:25), the distinction between "emic" and "etic" discourse is blurred by the commingling of contributions by local writers alongside those by European residents and travelers, "modernized" Middle Easterners and their more locally rooted counterparts, and clerics and practitioners of half a dozen or more religions, all of whom tend to address more than a single aspect of musical practice.

In a book on musical thought in rabbinical Judaism, Heidy Zimmerman (2000) mentions the difficulty of working with written sources in order to understand musical thought that is only partially written down. Much musical thought, not only in Judaism but throughout the Middle Eastern world, has depended on oral transmission and, of course, on shared knowledge of practice. The study of written documents is a necessary step, but only one step, toward understanding the historical musical world; readers must always allow for a broader world than any text may depict.

THEORIZING ABOUT MUSICAL SOUND

Nearly every Middle Eastern music has a centuries-old history of theoretical works. Writers sought to understand music in terms known to them from ancient Greek theories of the harmony of the spheres, consonance and dissonance, and the relationship of music to nature and human moods. They sought to measure and explain

The study of written documents is a necessary step, but only a step, toward understanding the historical musical world.

melodic intervals, modes, and musical instruments. They asked questions about the proper role of music in society and in spiritual life.

Music theory—part of the Greek *quadrivium* that also included arithmetic, geometry, and astronomy—first entered learned discourse through Arabic translations of Greek encyclopedic and scientific works. [See ARABIC SOURCES ON MUSIC: EIGHTH TO NINETEENTH CENTURIES.] Middle Eastern scholars became familiar with Euclid, Pythagoras, Ptolemy, Nicomachus of Gerasa, Plato, Aristotle, and Aristoxenus, the authors of the Greek explanations of tetrachords (Greek *genus*; plural, *genera*—known to this day in Arabic by the cognate *jins*; plural, *ajnās*). The Arabic translations of some of these works served to preserve and perpetuate them; some became known to European scholars of later centuries through these translations.

Subsequent theories of music attempted to name the notes, fundamental melodic structures such as tetrachords, metrical patterns, and modes of local musics. At first, these theories remained close to the Greek models; one example is the writings of Ḥunayn bin Isḥāq (d. 873), which found an enthusiastic reception in Arab and Jewish intellectual circles (Shiloah 1995:45–48). Saadya Gaon's writing on music closely followed al-Kindī (Farmer 1943).

Beginning with al-Fārābī, however, theorists turned away from theoretical models that did not seem to accommodate local practice. Their ideas were, in turn, transmitted in Arabic, Turkish, Persian, and Hebrew works, modified to suit local scholarly and musical practices. Many Middle Eastern societies, despite their different languages and social histories, claim the same theorists as their own. Middle Eastern musics seem to share a "core" of theorists whose works underpin different classical-historic repertoires. Eric Werner provides a good illustration of the results of transmission of the ancient works: "The Greeks were the music teachers of both the Arabs and the Jews . . . but it is also evident that our Judeo-Arabic authors were not content with simply paraphrasing their Hellenic sources. In almost every case, they elaborated upon the Greek ideas. In these elaborations, Arabs and Jews usually parted company" (1965:75). Thus scholars working at different times and in different places created basically similar branches of locally informed theory.

Al-Fārābī (tenth century), who systematized music with a keen ear to actual practice, is certainly the best-known of these "core" writers. Like other theorists, he chose the *ʿūd* as his own instrument; not coincidentally, this is an important instrument of practical performance. Al-Fārābī described instances when the theoretical solutions of the Greeks did not account for the actual sound of music in performance (Sawa 1989). He analyzed characteristic microtones and rhythmic patterns, systematized information about notes and modes, and considered the processes of composition and performance. As a scholar, he was equally interested in Aristotle's *Poetics* and in Aristoxenus's *genera*; this broad view, bringing theory and practice together, was typical of his life's work.

Al-Fārābī's legacy was carried on and augmented by others over the centuries. Ṣafī al-Dīn al-Urmawī (d. 1294) was a well-known theorist, and his *Kitāb al-adwār*, giving a recognizably modern system of modes and meters, relies heavily on al-Fārābī's example. Al-Urmawī's legacy became that of an international systematist, and many treatises, mostly of Persian origin, followed this highly rigorous and analytical trend at least into the sixteenth century. For example, al-Urmawī's student Quṭb al-Dīn al-Shirāzī (d. 1311) transmitted his teacher's work in a Persian encyclopedia (*Durrat al-tāj*) but modified it to "reflect the musical practice of his time much more objectively" (During, Mirabdolbaghi, and Safvat 1991:40) and included a list of melodic modes currently in use. An important treatise from Bukhara or Khiva, Darvīsh-Alī Changī's *Risāle-i Musīqī* (1572), discusses music in terms of a system of twelve *maqāmāt*, twenty-four *shu'be*, and six *āvāz* akin to al-Urmawī's (Levin 1984:10). Angelika Jung (1989), in outlining the sources of Central Asian music theory, found relationships among the early systematist theories and later Central Asian works. Other systematist writers, including al-Marāghī, al-Shirwānī, and al-Lādhiqī, adhered closely to al-Urmawī, but their writings also tend to reflect Eastern styles and traditions; we know comparatively less about medieval musical traditions of the Western Arab regions. In the Ottoman period, theorists tended to reject the systematist approach, favoring poetry and prose that demonstrated the cosmological and affective characteristics of melodic modes. The anonymous *Shajara dhāt al-akmām* of the seventeenth century, for example, connects specific modes to the zodiac, the bodily humors, and physical elements, but its treatment of rhythmic cycles continues to rely on al-Urmawī's legacy.

Early Arab theories of rhythm and meter were closely tied to contemporary systems of poetic meter. As early as the eighth century al-Khalīl ibn Aḥmad systematized meter according to sixteen poetic meters [see THEORIES OF RHYTHM AND METER IN THE MEDIEVAL MIDDLE EAST], and his successors, for instance al-Fārābī (in *Kitāb al-īqā'āt* 'Book of Rhythms') also linked the meters of music and poetry. As in many other areas, al-Fārābī set lasting precedents in his treatment of rhythm, developing a letter notation for rhythmic description and classifying attacks, rhythmic modes, and ornamental techniques.

Modern scholars have brought archaeology to bear on instruments and instrumental music in the ancient Middle East. Beginning with the early-twentieth-century excavations by Sir Arthur Wooley in Sumer (modern Iraq), much research has indicated the prominence of the lyre in this ancient region [see MUSIC IN ANCIENT ARABIA: ARCHAEOLOGICAL AND WRITTEN SOURCES]. Moreover, numerous discussions of musical instruments by early Arab writers have been preserved. These writings differ according to philological, historical, and theoretical approaches: whereas writers like al-Mufaḍḍal ibn Salāma (d. 903) preferred a taxonomic approach (Robson and Farmer 1938), theorists like al-Kindī and al-Fārābī exploited instruments (notably the *'ūd*) as a medium for technical discussion of modal concepts. Al-Fārābī is typical in that (like the Greeks) he gives pride of place to the human voice; in his concept, instruments fall into a hierarchical continuum with the voice at the top, followed by melodic instruments and percussion instruments, with military instruments at the bottom. After the voice, the prominence of plucked chordophones—especially the *'ūd* and *qānūn*—can be seen in the writings of Ibn Sīnā (Avicenna), who classified instruments according to the presence of strings. However, as al-Fārābī had stated in *Kitāb al-mūsīqī al-kabīr* 'Grand Book on Music', imitation of the voice remained an ideal.

Fascination with musical instruments persisted as scholars endeavored to describe, measure, and compare similar instruments. Some attempted to link the histories of peoples by identifying shared instruments or to trace histories by using archaeological sources—for instance, depictions of instruments on tomb walls or in statuary. Writers such as Hans Hickmann (1949) explored the characteristics of musical instruments, ancient and modern, using contemporary performances, museum collections, and iconographic resources. Bathyah Bayer (1963) conducted important archaeological studies of ancient Palestine. Scheherazade Qassim Hassan's work on musical instruments (1980) expands our understanding from the Mediterranean region into Iraq, the Arabian Peninsula, and eastward.

Indeed, a number of instruments are widely shared in the Middle East and Central Asia. End-blown reed flutes, frame drums, hourglass drums, lutes, zithers, and spike fiddles are found nearly everywhere. Scholars have raised questions about comparative tunings and uses. For instance, Veronica Doubleday (1999) probes the gender implications of what she sees as a common use of frame drums by women across times and places.

The potential for musical notation has interested theorists variously. They made occasional attempts to notate music, beginning with al-Kindī's alphabetical notation (Shiloah 1995:50). Little notated music exists before the twentieth century, although there are important exceptions in Ottoman classical music. Two Europeans resident at the Ottoman court made large collections of notated pieces. Ali Ufkî Bey (born Wojciech Bobowski), a slave-musician and then an interpreter in the Ottoman palace service, compiled 300 pages of notated music (*Mecmû'a-i Saz ü Söz* 'Collection of Instrumental and Vocal Works', c. 1650) representing a wide variety of classical genres (Feldman 1996:29). A half-century later, Demetrius Cantemir, a royal hostage in the Ottoman palace, made his own collection of notations, similarly documenting the classical traditions (Wright 1992, 2000). In the nineteenth century, an Armenian cleric, Baba Hamparsum, devised his own system of notation and applied it to religious court melodies.

In the nineteenth century and well into the twentieth, naming and measuring notes and modes remained fundamental to music theory (Marcus 1989). "Science," a principal aspect of Middle Eastern modernism, was brought to bear on rational divisions of the octave. Theorists attempted to measure intervals precisely with a variety of mechanical tools, finding, however (as al-Fārābī had found centuries earlier), that their measurements did not match performance practices. One famous instance occurred at the Cairo Conference on Music (1932), sponsored by the Egyptian government at the behest of Rodolphe d'Erlanger [see BARON RODOLPHE D'ERLANGER]. Trying to rationalize the *maqām* system using an equal (and mathematically measured) division of the octave, Arab musicians and scholars nevertheless found differences in the tunings of the same tone from one *maqām* to another (*Kitāb mu'tamar al-mūsīq 'l-'arabiyya* 1933:331–340; *La musique arabe* 1992:237–241).

As a "scientific" device, notation was widely adopted in the twentieth century; theorists and teachers used it to preserve repertoires, develop modern pedagogical techniques, and facilitate the work of people in new occupations (such as studio musicians). Subjects ranging from musical exercises for beginners (for example, 'Arafa and 'Alī's method book for learning the *'ūd*, now in its seventh printing) to compendiums of the entire *radīf* of a major Persian musician (for example, Barkechli 1963; Massoudieh 1997) found their way into print, even though there were only a few music printing firms in the Middle East, and these were only in major cities. Nevertheless, reading music has not replaced oral-aural means of learning musical style and practice.

Maḥmūd al-Ḥifnī's *Turāthunā* 'Our Heritage', published in four volumes by the Egyptian ministry of culture, was intended to preserve and teach important "pieces." In some places musicians and scholars have reconstituted or recovered traditions using oral and printed sources and have made new printed sources of their own. Yunus Rajabi (1897–1976) in Uzbekistan produced a version of Tajik-Uzbek *shashmaqam* regarded as authoritative and used to teach the tradition (Levin 1993:303). Commercially published transcriptions of notations and song texts throughout the Middle East extend to the lyrics and music of the latest pop artists.

ASSESSING SPIRITUAL VALUE: IS MUSIC GOOD OR BAD?

The value of listening to music has been pondered by Christian, Jewish, and Muslim religious authorities for centuries. All three religions incorporate music in chanting, and devotion sometimes involves physical activity akin to dancing. [See, for example, MUSIC IN PERFORMANCE: WHO ARE THE WHIRLING DERVISHES?] Philosophers such as al-Ghazālī (d. 1111) advanced the view that music brought the devotee closer to God; but other clerics have viewed musical performance, especially for entertainment, as drawing attention away from the desired spiritual life, as wasting time, and as the work of the devil. These opposed views were argued by Ibn Abī 'l-Dunyā (823–894) and Majd al-Dīn al-Ghazālī (d. 1126) in two early treatises (Robson 1938).

Greek philosophy, represented primarily by the Plato's and Aristotle's writings on ethics, informed the attitudes toward music of a number of important Muslim and Jewish philosophers, such as al-Kindī, the Ikhwān al-Ṣafā, Salomon Ibn Gabirol (1021–1069), Judah ha-Levi (c. 1066–1145), and Maimonides (1135–1204); interestingly, Gabirol and ha-Levi were also singers. These writers probed the uses of music in a balanced and ethical life. Their works manifest the variety of themes—music-theoretical, philosophical, spiritual, and, in some cases, practical—that were often present in a single treatise.

Jewish, Christian, and Muslim authorities in the Middle East have attempted (sometimes successfully) to restrict the role of women in musical forms of devotion. While many Muslim women know how to recite the Qur'ān, they rarely do so in public, and few if any women perform Muslim hymns (*inshād dīnī*) publicly. [See ISLAMIC HYMNODY IN EGYPT: *AL-INSHĀD AL-DĪNĪ*.] Similarly, the public role of women in sung or chanted portions of the Jewish and Christian liturgies has often been circumscribed.

Yet music is nearly essential to Sufi practice, in which the sounds of frame drums, end-blown flutes, and many varieties of chanting and singing literally entrance practitioners. And there are many sources of musical inspiration in contemporary Jewish worship. Christian liturgies depend on chant, which may be composed, improvised, or constructed through centonization, and is often embellished with melismas and ornamentation. The accompanying instruments tend to be limited to cymbals and other metallic idiophones.

Thus music is often said to have a powerful effect on the soul, and philosophical and religious works form an important part of the discourses on music. Kristina Nelson (1985) and Roy Choudhury (1957) present histories of what is called in Arabic the *samāʿ* polemic, *samāʿ* referring to the intent listening that engages the mind and soul. Beginning with the Qur'ān and with the *ḥadīth* 'sayings' of the Prophet Muhammad, and continuing through legal and philosophical discourse, they summarize the various positions taken by Muslim thinkers, presenting views of the value of music that clearly change in different times and places. During (1992) has examined musical life in the Islamic Republic of Iran between 1980 and 1990, finding an array of often mutable policies and practices. In her ethnography of an Iranian village during the rule of Ruhollah Khomeini, Erika Friedl (1991, chap. 10) describes acceptance of or resistance to limits on forms of wedding music, and the resulting compromises.

In the twentieth century scholars have increasingly turned to questions of origins and interrelationships in early Christian and Jewish religious song and liturgical chant. Since no notated sources from before the ninth century survive, scholarly investigations have focused largely on liturgy and ritual. Eric Werner's influential work on early Jewish and Christian traditions, culminating in *The Sacred Bridge* (1959–1984), posited close connections between the liturgies of the early Jewish synagogue and the Christian church. The supposition of Jewish influences on early Christian practices has been common in the literature, but more recent work (Smith 1994, for example) has modified this view, suggesting that the destruction of the temple in Jerusalem in

70 C.E. prevented the development of a unified Jewish synagogal tradition and thus precluded any specific, identifiable influence on Christian practice.

The character and history of Christian chant and liturgies stemming from the historical patriarchates of the Mediterranean Christian world—Rome, Jerusalem, Alexandria, Constantinople, and Antioch—have formed an important line of inquiry in scholarship similar to research on European liturgics and chant. Such researchers tend to notate and preserve rites, decipher early forms of notation, codify melodic modes and genres, and look for chronological relationships among the liturgies. Significant contributions have been made toward an understanding of some of these traditions, including those of the Maronite church (see especially Louis Hage, 1972–1991) and the Coptic church (Newlandsmith 1931, followed by the more recent work of Ilona Borsai, Ragheb Moftah, Marian Robertson-Wilson, Martha Roy, and others). Peter Jeffery's work on tenth-century Georgian chant (1994), shedding light on previously unknown antecedents from Jerusalem, is representative of the increasing engagement of Western musicologists with ethnomusicological approaches and the religious traditions of the ancient and medieval Mediterranean.

STORIES, SONG COLLECTIONS, AND BIOGRAPHIES: CAPTURING PERFORMANCE

Writing down song texts and stories about musicians and performances forms the oldest narrative of music in the Middle East. By far the most famous collection is the twenty-three volumes of al-Iṣbahānī's *Kitāb al-aghānī* 'Book of Songs', with its wealth of descriptions of performances and musicians (Neubauer 1965; Sawa 1989). This enormously rich source for musical life in the Abbasid courts has yet to be fully exploited by scholars. Al-Iṣbahānī draws our attention to the roles women played in professional performance; his and other descriptions of female performers yield a history of accomplished and often learned women—poets, singers, instrumentalists, and composers—who for centuries served as artists and teachers in the Islamic empire.

The *Kitāb al-aghānī* is one of a long series of accounts of musical life (and other forms of social life) told anecdotally. Poetry and literary works, such as the essays of al-Jāḥiz (d. c. 868), include descriptions and evaluations of music. A poem by Ibn al-Khaṭīb al-Salmānī of Granada (fl. 1294) describes the classification and attributes of a system of twenty-four Andalusian modes (Farmer 1933). Historical chronicles by such figures as al-Maqrīzī (1364–1442), al-Maqqarī (1591–1632), and al-Jabartī (1754–1822) contain information about music. Ibn Khaldūn, a famous philosopher and chronicler, described musical practices he observed in his travels and advanced one of the first Arab theories of music in society—that singing signifies abundance in society, for it is "in demand only by those who are free of all other worries" (1967, 2:401). Many of these sources have not been mined extensively by music scholars. At the turn of the twenty-first century, a multicultural and interdisciplinary community of scholars remained attracted to archives and libraries from Morocco to Tashkent containing manuscript treatises of musical discourse of the past (Adler 1975; Levin 1993:303; Massoudieh 1996; Shiloah 1979).

Biography was and is an important device for conveying musical knowledge, beginning with al-Jāḥiẓ's discourse on singing girls (1980). Biographies not only tell life stories but also describe musical value and often extrapolate moral and aesthetic principles. Autobiography became popular as a genre in the 1920s, and many famous entertainers published some sort of life story or memoir. Inexpensive biographies of musicians are commonly marketed on street corners. In addition, biographical information appears in both scholarly and general works on music.

Collecting songs has persisted as a means of gathering and preserving texts and also instructions about performance. Muḥammad ibn al-Ḥusayn al-Ḥā'ik collected the Maghribi *nūbāt* in the early eighteenth century (al-Ḥā'ik 1999; Shiloah 1995:84).

Shihāb al-Dīn's instructions (c. 1840) indicate that nineteenth-century suites (*waṣlāt*) consisted primarily of *muwashshaḥāt* unified by melodic mode.

TRAVELERS' TALES, PRINTED SCHOLARSHIP, AND THE ORIENTALIST GAZE

Social histories by scholars like Abu Lughod (1989), Goitein (1967–1993), and Petry (1991) depict Middle Eastern societies as internationally mobile and cosmopolitan, and as center of travel and trade. They suggest that, historically, engagement with the world outside the Middle East has been greater than Orientalist depictions of exotic Middle Eastern "others" may convey.

One of the first travelers to give an account of cultural life in foreign lands was Ibn Baṭṭūṭa (1304–1377), whose journeys and chronicles take readers from the empires of western Africa to China. Later, Evliya Çelebi's travels yielded descriptions of equally diverse places. Both writers included accounts of musical practice. Middle- and upper-class people traveled in the Middle East for reasons of health, business, politics, and adventure, leaving accounts—sympathetic and unsympathetic—of music they usually could not understand. Van Nieuwkerk (1995:21 and chap. 2) characterizes European travelers' view of the Middle East as "imperfect and inferior." Their accounts are interesting nonetheless for their observations, if not for their value judgments.

Perspectives vary greatly, from adventurers such as Charles Doughty and St. John Philby in Arabia to literati, including Lady Mary Wortley Montague, and members of the elite such as the Englishwoman Lady Lucy Duff Gordon, who lived for years in Egypt in search of a more healthful climate. Among the most engaged visitors was Edward Lane (1978), who spent two years in Cairo in the 1830s, learned Arabic, went about in local garb, and later produced a rich and detailed memoir that included much musical information. Turning the tables, Cachia (1973) gives an entertaining account of a nineteenth-century Lebanese traveler's assessment of European music.

One of the great adventurers of the twentieth century was, of course, T. E. Lawrence (1888–1935), known as Lawrence of Arabia, whose exploits have been recounted in books, on stage, and on film. Asking what these writers and producers actually knew about Lawrence or the Middle East, Steven Caton (1999) published a useful study of prevailing attitudes and their effect on public culture.

Elite Middle Easterners became ambassadors to foreign lands, and, of course, elite outsiders became ambassadors to the Middle East. Embassies and the observations of resident officials provided varied documents, such as the early wax cylinder recordings of speech and song made by diplomats (and students of the great Orientalist Snouck Hurgronje) in the Dutch embassy in Jidda, Arabia, at the turn of the twentieth century (Gavin 1985).

European engagement with the arts of the Middle East grew during the seventeenth and eighteenth centuries with exposure to Turkish janissary bands (*yeniçeri*), military symbols of what was then the most powerful empire in the region. European military ensembles adopted techniques, instruments, and accoutrements of the *yeniçeri*. Ottoman officials sent entire bands to foreign courts. In 1805, Vauxhall Gardens featured what must have been one of the first foreign "Middle East ensembles"—a group of men and women playing "Turkish" instruments as part of an evening's entertainment (Farmer 1957). The sense of "Turkish music" extended beyond these into a multitude of "Turkish" opera plots, among which one of the most famous was Mozart's *Entführung aus dem Serail* 'The Abduction from the Seraglio' (1782).

The Napoleonic invasion of Egypt in 1798 is often cited as turning point in the regional balance of power. The subsequent "scientific" expedition launched by the French resulted in the publication of *Description de l'Égypte* (1809–1822), a monumental documentation of contemporary Egyptian culture and society. Edward Said (1978) links its intellectual content with an earlier work, *Voyage en Égypte et en Syrie*, by a French traveler, the comte de Volney (1787), as part of the discourse of "scientific"

There is considerable evidence that local histories are in fact much richer than simple narratives suggest.

inquiry. According to Said, these documents, although perceptive and intelligently composed, had the effect of supplanting local histories with European narratives purporting to be world histories. Said's view forms part of *Napoleon's Egypt*, an interesting juxtaposition of a history written by the Egyptian intellectual 'Abd al-Raḥmān al-Jabartī with memoirs of Louis Antoine Fauvelet de Bourrienne, Napoleon's private secretary (al-Jabartī 1993:167–180).

Other nineteenth-century music historians were less directly engaged and more chauvinistic in their view of non-European musics. Major writers, including Charles Burney, Johann Forkel, and August Wilhelm Ambros, considered Middle Eastern (and often other non-European musics) primitive, unsophisticated, and even ugly. Raphael Kiesewetter, on the other hand, sympathetically applied his experience with source scholarship to Arab music. His *Musik der Araber nach Originalquellen dargestellt* (1842) exhibits a lively interest in Middle Eastern musics (see also Bohlman 1987). Works by others followed, including Salvador-Daniel (1879), Christianowitch (1863), Ribera (1970, 1975), Robert Lachmann (whose *Musik des Orients* of 1929 remains a worthwhile summary volume), and the prolific Henry George Farmer (1929, 1939, 1997). These writers' experiences of Middle Eastern cultures and languages varied considerably, but they all sought to grasp Middle Eastern musics and to explain them, usually in European terms.

Burney, Forkel, and others advanced interest in research on musical antiquity, especially the practices of the ancient Jewish temple. There followed much speculation about the origin of liturgical practices and melodies, and continued interest in the practice of scriptural chanting. Out of European scholarship came systematic study of the music of Jewish communities, at first from printed sources and later, following the work of A. Z. Idelsohn, from oral resources.

As many scholars have noted, much less attention was paid to local voices and local histories. Racy (1983), Massoudieh (1973), and Touma (1973) outline problems in obtaining and using source materials to recapture local music histories before the age of sound recordings. Many manuscript resources in Middle Eastern and European libraries remain unconsulted. Known sources of cultural history are often unindexed and difficult to use. Received wisdom often relays a narrative of decline and downfall that parallels the decline of the Ottoman Empire; this descent then reverses itself with "westernization" or engagement with the "science" of the European Enlightenment. Racy, Touma, Shiloah, and others provide evidence that local histories are in fact much richer than simple narratives suggest.

WAYS OF THINKING ABOUT MUSIC IN THE TWENTIETH CENTURY

A blurring of boundaries and a progressive elaboration of viewpoints persisted throughout the twentieth century, with scholars and musicians traveling internationally in all directions to "discover" and research musical practices for various purposes. European and American ethnographic research sent "foreigners" into the Arab world to collect, ask questions, describe, and analyze, and "Middle Easterners" into the West to learn, teach, perform, and conduct research. New forms of discourse emerged.

Ethnography became a new way of collecting and writing information about musical life. What Levin (1993:300) observed in Central Asia might apply to the entire Middle East: the expanse of the territory and the diversity of its peoples, languages, and practices have yielded ethnographic and folkloric studies focused on single ethnic or national groups rather than on common cultural features over larger areas. Local preferences, both communal and national, for indigenous arts reinforce the scholar's inclination to focus on single communities, however defined. The balance of intellectual power shifted within the Middle East itself as "peripheral" communities challenged hegemonic centers. Many of the essays in *La musique arabe: Le congrès du Caire de 1932*—the proceedings of a conference organized by Scheherazade Qassim Hassan in 1992 that assessed the content of the congress of 1932—address the difficulties experienced by musicians and scholars from Iraq, Algeria, and other places outside the "mainstream" cultural world of Egypt, Palestine, and Greater Syria in trying to affect understandings of what constitutes Arab music. This issue persists today.

Early European work focused on the collection, transcription, and analysis of musics believed to be "traditional." Local scholarship often followed suit, as populations feel compelled to preserve cultural artifacts and productions which they believe are being lost. A striking example is the Nubian and Sudanese populations whose villages were flooded in the 1960s when the High Dam was built. Today in Saudi Arabia, scholars struggle to find practitioners of the diverse musics of remote populations, in the belief that knowledge of these art forms is dying out. Each year the government sponsors arts festivals in the hope of sustaining and capturing manifestations of these forms (Campbell 1999).

European institutes and museums supported ethnographic research in music throughout the twentieth century. The Berlin Phonogrammarchiv, which was followed by a counterpart in Vienna, sponsored some of the first collecting expeditions and supported the notable work of A. Z. Idelsohn, Erich von Hornbostel, and Robert Lachmann. The Musée de l'Homme in Paris has assisted the work of ethnographers such as Bernard Lortat-Jacob, Jean During, Jean Lambert, and Miriam Rovsing Olsen. At present, the Maison des Cultures du Monde and the Institut du Monde Arabe in Paris bring Middle Eastern artists to Europe, where their performances are recorded, scholarly notes on the repertoires are made, and the results are marketed as "world music" and as documents of musical heritage.

Commercial recording has become a medium of scholarly discourse since the mid-twentieth century. The recordings made by the Musée de l'Homme and UNESCO in the Bärenreiter Musicaphon series, with their copious notes and illustrations, initiated an enterprise that has been continued by scholars such as Jean During, Theodore Levin, Jean Lambert, and Dieter Christensen. These products have become effective sources of sound and information often not available elsewhere.

The kinds of ethnographic projects launched by foreigners have been affected and sometimes limited by governmental policies and sensibilities. Arranging research trips, especially to remote locations, can involve lengthy bureaucratic processes. Fieldwork in some places has been discouraged, and the necessary visas and official permissions have been hard to obtain. In other cases, certain kinds of work have been actively encouraged by political authorities—for example, the collection of materials for archives.

Among the fieldwork that has been conducted, some exemplifies pioneering studies on the characteristics and movement of music and musicians in performance: Nettl's work on the Persian *radīf* (1992); During's on the *radīf*, on Sufi music, and on the Azeribaijani *mugam* (1984, 1988a, 1988b); Margaret Caton's on Persian vocal forms (1983); and Blum's on intersecting "folk" repertoires in Meshed, Iran (1972). Later ethnographic work has tended to probe further into relationships between music and social life (Danielson 1997; Schuyler 1990, 1997) and has taken up themes current in ethnomusicological scholarship internationally: ethnography of performance (Reynolds 1995), gender and the roles of women (van Nieuwkerk 1995), music and healing (Lambert 1997), popular music and popular culture (Armbrust 1996; Stokes 1992), and globalization (Zirbel 1999). Increasingly, interdisciplinary studies take up musical performance (S. Caton 1990).

Scholarly frameworks have brought Middle Easterners to Europe and the Americas to contribute to scholarly discourse and, very often, to perform. Ali Jihad Racy, a sensitive and informed scholar and a prominent performer, composer, and teacher, brings all of these sensibilities to bear on his narratives of music history and performance practice (for example, 1991). Hormoz Farhat (1965), working at the time as a Western-trained composer and theorist in an American university, offered as his dissertation a perceptive account of the Persian *radīf.* Raouf Yekta Bey, working in Turkey, became a towering figure in international musical life as the author of the widely read "La Musique Turque" in Lavignac's encyclopedia (Yekta 1922), as a participant in conferences, and as a sponsor of countless local Turkish initiatives in musical research, collecting, publication, and performance.

Journalism became an important form of discourse in the Middle East. During the nineteenth century, newspapers were launched in many major cities. Writers came from the ranks of intellectuals and literati. For example, in Egypt Luṭfī al-Sayyid, an intellectual who later became the head of the Egyptian University, spent part of his career editing a newspaper. Newspapers sometimes printed poetry. In casual social circles, such as coffeehouses and groceries, people read newspapers aloud; thus those who could not read still had access to the papers. The twentieth century witnessed a burgeoning of magazines, from intellectual journals to radio broadcast schedules to theatrical gossip sheets (Armbrust 1996; Danielson 1997:5). These media proved to be tools for serious communication among Middle Eastern thinkers as well as light entertainment. Scholars have found them a rich source of discourse about musical life.

The extent to which European music might be indebted to Arab arts was a persistent question throughout the twentieth century. Julian Ribera (1912, 1970) launched a debate on the influence of musical-poetic forms (including the *muwashshaḥ*) on European poetry and was countered by Higinio Angles (1943–1964). In a famous debate, Henry George Farmer (1925, 1978) insisted that Arab music had exerted an enormous influence on Europe and was countered with equal vehemence by Kathryn Schlesinger (1925). The debate raged in literary circles, centering on the poetry of medieval courtly love in southern France and Spain and its relationship to Arab precedents (Monroe 1970). These questions have significantly affected historically informed performance, as well-known performers of early music such as Thomas Binkley and Joel Cohen have presented interpretations of medieval European music informed by the presumption of Arab, Turkish, or so-called "Mediterranean" influence.

REFERENCES

Abu Lughod, Janet. 1989. *Before European Hegemony: The World System* A.D. *1250–1350.* Oxford: Oxford University Press.

Adler, Israel. 1975. *Hebrew Writings Concerning Music, in Manusripts and Printed Books, from Geonic Times up to 1800.* Munich: G. Henle.

Angles, Higinio. 1943–1964. *La musica de las Cantigas de Santa Maria del rey Alfonso el Sabio.* Barcelona: Disputación Provincial de Barcelona, Biblioteca Central.

ʻArafa, ʻAbd al-Munʻim, and Ṣafar ʻAlī. 1942. *Kitāb dirāsat al-ʻūd.* Cairo: n. p.

Armbrust, Walter. 1996. *Mass Culture and Modernism in Egypt.* Cambridge: Cambridge University Press.

Barkechli, Mehdi. 1963. *La musique traditionnelle de l'Iran*. Tehran: Secretariat d'État aux Beaux-Arts.

Bayer, Bathyah. 1963. *The Material Relics of Music in Ancient Palestine and Its Environs: An Archaeological Inventory*. Tel Aviv: Israel Music Institute.

Blum, Stephen. 1972. "Musics in Contact: The Cultivations of Oral Repertoires in Meshed, Iran." Ph.D. dissertation, University of Illinois.

Bohlman, Philip. 1987. "The European Discovery of Music in the Islamic World and the 'Non-Western' in Nineteenth-Century Music History." *Journal of Musicology* 5(2):147–164.

Cachia, Pierre. 1973. "A Nineteenth-Century Arab's Observations on European Music." *Ethnomusicology* 17:41–51.

Campbell, Kay Hardy. 1999. "Days of Song and Dance." *Aramco World* 50(1):78–87.

Caton, Margaret. 1983. "The Classical Tasnif: A Genre of Persian Vocal Music." Ph.D. dissertation, University of California, Los Angeles.

Caton, Steven C. 1990. *"Peaks of Yemen I Summon": Poetry as Cultural Practice in a North Yemeni Tribe*. Berkeley: University of California Press.

———. 1999. *Lawrence of Arabia: A Film's Anthropology*. Berkeley: University of California Press.

Christianowitsch, Alexandre. 1863. *Esquisse historique de la musique arabe aux temps anciens, avec dessins d'instruments et quarante mélodies notées et harmonisées*. Cologne: M. Dumont-Schaubert.

Danielson, Virginia. 1997. *'The Voice of Egypt': Umm Kulthum, Arabic Song, and Egyptian Society in the Twentieth Century*. Chicago: University of Chicago Press.

D'Erlanger, Rodolphe. 1930–1959. *La musique arabe*. Paris: Geuthner.

Description de l'Égypte. 1809–1822. Paris: Imprimerie Impériale.

Doubleday, Veronica. 1999. "The Frame Drum in the Middle East: Women, Musical Instruments, and Power." *Ethnomusicology* 43(1):101–134.

During, Jean. 1984. *La musique iranienne: Tradition et évolution*. Paris: Recherche sur les Civilisations.

———. 1988a. *Musique et extase: L'audition spirituelle dans la tradition Soufie*. Paris: Albin Michel.

———. 1988b. *La musique traditionnelle de l'Azerbayjan et la science des muqams*. Baden-Baden: V. Koerner.

———. 1992. "L'oreille islamique. Dix années capitales de la vie musicale en Iran: 1980–1990." *Asian Music* 23(2):135–164.

During, Jean, Zia Mirabdolbaghi, and Dariush Safvat. 1991. *The Art of Persian Music*. Washington D.C.: Mage.

Farhat, Hormoz. 1965. "The *Dastgah* Concept in Persian Music." Ph.D. dissertation, University of California Los Angeles.

Farmer, Henry George. 1925. *The Arabian Influence on Musical Theory*. London: Reeves.

———. 1929. *History of Arabian Music to the Thirteenth Century*. London: Luzac.

———. 1933. *An Old Moorish Lute Tutor, Being Four Arabic Texts from Unique Manuscripts in the Biblioteca Nacional, Madrid (no. 334) and the Staatsbibliothek, Berlin (Lbg. 516)*. Glasgow: Civic Press.

———. [1939?] *The Structure of the Arabian and Persian Lute in the Middle Ages*. London: s. n.

———. 1943. *Sa'adyah Gaon on the Influence of Music*. London: Probsthain.

———. 1957. "Janitscharemusik." In *Die Musik in Geschichte und Gegenwart*. Kassel: Bärenreiter.

———. 1978. *Historical Facts for the Arabian Musical Influence*. New York: Arno.

———. 1997. *Studies in Oriental Music*. Frankfurt am Main: Institute for the History of Arabic-Islamic Science at Johann Wolfgang Goethe University.

Feldman, Walter. 1996. *Music of the Ottoman Court: Makam, Composition, and the Early Ottoman Instrumental Repertoire*. Berlin: VWB-Verlag für Wissenschaft und Bildung.

Friedl, Erika. 1991. *Women of Deh Koh: Lives in an Iranian Village*. New York: Penguin.

Gavin, Carney. 1985. "The Earliest Arabian Recordings: Discoveries and Work Ahead." *Phonographic Bulletin* 43:38-45.

Goitein, S. D. 1967–1993. *A Mediterranean Society: The Jewish Communities of the Arab World as Portrayed in the Documents of the Cairo Geniza*. Berkeley: University of California Press.

Hage, Louis. 1972–1991. *Musique maronite*. 4 vols. Kaslik, Lebanon: Bibliothèque de l'Université de Saint-Esprit.

Al-Ḥā'ik, Muḥammad ibn al-Ḥusayn. 1999. *Kunnāsh al-Ḥā'ik*. Rabat: Akadimiyat al-Mamlaka 'l-Maghribiyya.

Hassan, Scheherazade Qassim. 1980. *Les instruments de musique en Irak et leur rôle dans la société traditionnelle*. Paris: Mouton.

Hickmann, Hans. 1949. *Instruments de musique*. Cairo: Impr. de l'Institut Français d'Archéologie Orientale.

Al-Ḥifnī, Maḥmūd Aḥmad, ed. 1969. *Turāthunā 'l-mūsīqī min al-adwār wa'l-muwashshaḥāt*. Cairo: al-Lajna 'l-mūsīqiyya 'l-'ulyā.

Ibn Khaldūn. 1967. *The Muqaddimah: An Introduction to History, Translated from the Arabic by Franz Rosenthal*, 2nd ed. London: Routledge and Kegan Paul.

al-Jabarti, Abd al-Rahman. 1993. *Napoleon in Egypt: Al-Jabarti's Chronicle of the French Occupation, 1798*, trans. Shmuel Moreh. Princeton, N.J.: Markus Wiener.

Al-Jāḥiẓ. 1980. *The Epistle on Singing-Girls of Jahiz*, ed. and trans. with commentary A. F. L.

Beeston. Warminster, Wiltshire, England: Aris and Phillips.

Jeffery, Peter, 1994. "The Earliest Christian Chant Repertory Recovered: The Georgian Witnesses to Jerusalem Chant." *Journal of the American Musicological Society* 47:1–38.

Jung, Angelika. 1989. *Quellen der traditionellen Kunstmusik der Usbeken und Tadshiken Mittelasiens: Untersuchungen zur Entstehung und Entwicklung des Šašmaqam*. Hamburg: Karl Dieter Wagner.

Kiesewetter, Raphael Georg. 1842. *Die Musik der Araber, nach Originalquellen dargestellt*. Leipzig: Breitkopf and Härtel.

Kitāb mu'tamar al-musīqā' l-'arabiyya (Book of the Conference of Arab Music). 1933. Cairo: al-Maṭbā'a al-amiriyya.

Lachmann, Robert. 1929. *Musik des Orients*. Breslau: F. Hirt.

Lambert, Jean. 1997. *La médecine de l'âme: Le chant de Sanaa dans la société yémenite*. Nanterre: Société d'Ethnologie.

Lane, Edward William. 1978 (1836). *An Account of the Manners and Customs of the Modern Egyptians*. The Hague: East-West. (Reprint.)

Levin, Theodore. 1984. "The Music and Tradition of the Bukharan Shashmaqam in Soviet Uzbekistan." Ph.D. dissertation, Princeton University.

———. 1993. "Western Central Asia and the Caucasus." In *Ethnomusicology: Historical and Regional Studies*, ed. Helen Myers, 300–305. New York: Norton.

Marcus, Scott. 1989. "Arab Music Theory in the Modern Period." Ph.D. dissertation, University of California Los Angeles.

Massoudieh, Muhammad. 1973. "Tradition und Wandel in der persischen Musik des 19. Jahrhunderts." In *Musikkulturen Asiens, Afrikas, und Ozeaniens im 19. Jahrhundert*, ed. Robert Günther, 73–96. Regensburg: Gustav Bosse.

———. 1997. *Radif-i avazi-i musiqi-i sunnati-i Iran*. Tehran: Anjuman musiqi Iran.

———. 1996. *Manuscrits persans concernant la musique*. Munich: G. Henle.

Monroe, James T. 1970. *Islam and the Arabs in Spanish Scholarship (Sixteenth Century to the Present)*. Leiden: Brill.

La musique arabe: Le congrès du Caire de 1932. 1992. Cairo: CEDEJ.

Nelson, Kristina. 1985. *The Art of Reciting the Qur'ān*. Austin: University of Texas Press.

Nettl, Bruno. 1992. *The Radīf of Persian Music*. Champaign, Ill.: Elephant and Cat.

Neubauer, Eckhard. 1965. "Musiker am Hof der frühen Abbasiden." Inaug.-Dissertation, Frankfurt am Main, J. W. Goethe-Universität.

Newlandsmith, Ernest, 1931. *The Ancient Music of the Coptic Church*. London, 1931.

Petry, Carl F. 1991. *The Civilian Elite of Cairo in the Later Middle Ages*. Princeton, N.J.: Princeton University Press.

Racy, Ali Jihad. 1983. "Music in Nineteenth-Century Egypt: An Historical Sketch." *Selected Reports in Ethnomusicology* 4:157–179.

———. 1991. "Creativity and Ambience: An Ecstatic Feedback Model from Arab Music" *World of Music* 33(3):7–28.

Ribera, Julian. 1912. *Discursos leidos ante la Real Academia Española*. Madrid: Iberica.

———. 1970. *Historia de la musica arabe medieval y su influencia en la Espanola*. New York: AMS.

———. 1975. *Music in Ancient Arabia and Spain: Being La musica de las Cantigas*. New York: Da Capo.

Robson, James. 1938. *Treatise on Listening to Music*. London: Royal Asiatic Society.

Robson, James, and Henry George Farmer, eds. 1938. *Ancient Arabian Musical Instruments, as Described by al-Muffaddal ibn Salama (Ninth Century) in the Unique Istanbul Manuscript of the* Kitab al-malahi *in the Handwriting of Yaqut al-Mustasimi (d. 1298)*. Glasgow: Civic Press.

Roy Choudhury, M. 1957. "Music in Islam." *Journal of the Asiatic Society, Letters* 23(2):43–102.

Said, Edward. 1978. *Orientalism*. New York: Pantheon.

Salvador-Daniel, Francisco. 1879. *La musique arabe: Ses rapports avec la musique grecque et le chant grégorien*. Algiers: A. Jourdan.

Sawa, George. 1989. *Music Performance Practice in the Early Abbasid Era 132–320 A.H. / A.D. 750–932*. Toronto: Pontifical Institute for Mediaeval Studies.

Schlesinger, Kathryn. 1925. *Is European Musical Theory Indebted to the Arabs? Reply to "The Arabian Influence on Musical Theory" by H. G. Farmer*. London: Reeves.

Schuyler, Philip. 1990. "Hearts and Minds: Three Attitudes toward Performance Practice and Music Theory in the Yemen Arab Republic." *Ethnomusicology* 34(1):1–18.

———. 1997. "*Qat*, Conversation, and Song: A Musical View of Yemeni Social Life." *Yearbook for Traditional Music* 29:57–73.

Shihāb al-Dīn Muḥammad ibn Ismā'īl. c. 1840. *Safīnat al-mulk wa-nafīsat al-fulk*. Cairo: Maṭba'at al-jami'a.

Shiloah, Amnon. 1979. *The Theory of Music in Arabic Writings (c. 900-1900): A Descriptive Catalogue of Manuscripts in Libraries of Europe and the U.S.A.* Munich: G. Henle.

———. 1995. *Music in the World of Islam: A Sociocultural Study*. Aldershot, Hampshire, England: Scolar.

Smith, J. A. 1994. "First-Century Christian Singing and Its Relationship to Contemporary Jewish Religious Song." *Music and Letters* 75:1–15.

Touma, Habib Hassan. 1973. "Die Musik der Araber im 19. Jahrhundert." In *Musikkulturen Asiens, Afrikas, und Ozeaniens im 19. Jahrhundert*, ed. Robert Günther, 49–72. Regensburg: Gustav Bosse.

———. 1996. *The Music of the Arabs*, trans. Laurie Schwartz. Portland, Ore.: Amadeus.

Van Nieuwkerk, Karin. 1995. *A Trade Like Any Other: Female Singers and Dancers in Egypt*. Austin: University of Texas Press.

Volney, Constantin-François, comte de. 1787. *Voyage en Syrie et en Égypte*. Paris: Desenne.

Werner, Eric. 1959–1984. *The Sacred Bridge: The Interdependence of Liturgy and Music in Synagogue and Church during the First Millennium*. 2 vols. London: Dobson; New York: Columbia University Press.

———. 1965. "Greek Ideas on Music in Judeo-Arabic Literature." In *The Commonwealth of Music*, ed. Gustave Reese and Rose Brandel. New York: Free Press.

Wright, Owen. 1992. *Words without Songs: A Musicological Study of an Early Ottoman Anthology and Its Precursors*. London: School of Oriental and African Studies, University of London.

———. 1992–2000. *Demetrius Cantemir: The Collection of Notations*. London: School of Oriental and African Studies, University of London.

Yekta, Raouf. 1922. "La musique turque." In *Encyclopédie de la musique et dictionnaire du Conservatoire*, ed. A. Lavignac. Paris: Delagrave.

Zimmerman, Heidy. 2000. *Tora und Shira: Untersuchungen zur Musikauffassung des rabbinischen Judentums*. Bern: Peter Lang.

Zirbel, Katherine. 1999. "Musical Discursions: Spectacle, Experience, and Political Economy among Egyptian Performers in Globalizing Markets." Ph.D. dissertation, University of Michigan.

Part 2
Understanding the Musics of the Middle East: Issues and Processes

Musical performance helps form the fabric of social life. Musicians sustain and advance certain values: technical virtuosity, aesthetic feeling, spiritual devotion, and social identity. They also create pleasure and fun in a society.

The essays on the following pages explore ways in which the people of the Middle East make "good" music. They approach questions such as who gets to perform music and when, and what sounds are included under the rubric of music—for instance, what constitutes devotional sound. They show how the technology of the mass media has entered the lives of musicians and listeners and how people use and adapt this technology. The essays also show how musical expression relates to social and political identities.

The last group of essays in Part 2 will give an idea of the deep historical roots that characterize most musics of the Middle East and Central Asia. The examples presented here come mostly from the Arab world; later in this volume, other essays will present more historical detail from other parts of the region.

Traditional Tunisian musicians on a beach in the Kerkennah islands. Photo © Ric Ergenbright, Corbis.

Section 1
Theory, Composition, and Performance

One feature uniting many musics of the Middle East and Central Asia is the systems of melodic modes that guide practice and are a central focus for theoretical studies. In order to highlight similarities and differences among individual cultural approaches, three of the following articles focus on similar melodic modes: the eastern Arab *maqām bayyātī*, the Turkish *makam beyati*, and the Persian *dastgāh-e shūr*. Each article seeks to present the concepts, understandings, and practices of one culture, providing the reader with a basis for comparing and contrasting the three modal systems. In each culture, distinct traditions of theory and practice exist in a dynamic relationship, with significant changes occurring over time. A fourth article, on the unique modal system of Turkish folk music, serves, in part, to emphasize the existence of other diverse modal systems in the region (Andalusian, Iraqi, Central Asian, and so on).

The concept of modes is also applied to rhythm in a variety of ways, as seen here in studies focusing on Turkey, the eastern Arab world, and Yemen. The essay on Yemen, presenting findings from the author's ethnographic research, serves as a reminder that many rhythmic practices of the region have received almost no scholarly attention and remain virtually undocumented.

Studies of performers, genres, and formal structures reveal many instances of historical change and transformation. Separate male and female genres have flourished and declined. Suite forms have been developed, reshaped, and then, in some cases, discarded. Government patronage has played a marked role in preserving, transforming, or suppressing musical traditions. Periods of support have alternated with official censure, affording a glimpse of the often unstable locales in which music traditions exist. The composer has gained importance in many traditions, often with a resulting decline in improvisation. Intercultural contact, with the West and among Middle Eastern cultures, has created points of similarity yet has generally not hindered the efflorescence of unique cultural traditions throughout the region.

Saudi musicians in performance. The musician on the right is playing a handheld *ṭabla*; the musician on the left plays a traditional violin. Photo © Byron Augustin, 1989.

The Eastern Arab System of Melodic Modes in Theory and Practice: A Case Study of *Maqām Bayyātī*

Scott Marcus

In broad terms, the entire area of the *mashriq*—the Arab countries of the eastern Mediterranean—shares a melodic modal system that is distinct from the modal traditions of North Africa, Iraq, and the Arabian Peninsula. While moments of polyphony occur on rare occasions, the melodic aspect of eastern Arab music is overwhelmingly monophonic (that is, only one melodic line occurs at a time) or heterophonic (that is, different instruments simultaneously present slightly different renditions of the same melodic line). This is true whether a performance is by one person, a small group of three to five or more musicians (called a *takht*), or an orchestra of more than twenty members (called a *firqa*). The melodies of eastern Arab music are governed by a system of melodic modes, individually called *maqām* (plural, *maqāmāt*) or *naghma* (alternatively spelled *naghama*; plural, *anghām*, *naghmāt*, or *naghamāt*). Although musicians have commonly used the terms *maqām* and *naghma* interchangeably, the word *maqām* is now favored by both younger musicians in Cairo and writers in the Arab world and the West.

LEARNING ABOUT THE MODES

For musicians, the individual modes are generally understood by the way they occur in practice, that is, in existing compositions and improvisations, new and old. The oldest songs and instrumental pieces in the present repertoire date from the nineteenth century and possibly earlier. Recordings preserve music from as early as 1904 (Racy 1976, 1977), and many recordings from the 1940s onward are extremely well known pieces of oral culture. While some pieces—a simple folk song, for example—might exhibit few characteristics of a given mode (perhaps a few typical phrases using only a small part of the mode's larger scale), more sophisticated pieces highlight a number of the mode's unique features (such as characteristic ways of beginning, characteristic accidentals, or common and less common modulations to other modes). Thus by learning pieces of music, one learns the nature of the various *maqāmāt*. Musicians commonly praise a more sophisticated piece by saying that it is full of "work" (*shughl*), perhaps best understood to mean a combination of aesthetic artistry and modal craftsmanship. Enthusiasm for a highly sophisticated piece is often expressed by calling it a "school" (*madrasa*); this indicates that the piece is full of modal knowledge and that there is much one can learn from it.

In broad terms, the entire area of the *mashriq* shares a distinct melodic modal system.

Similarly, students also learn the unique characteristics of each *maqām* by hearing solo improvisations—instrumental *taqāsīm* (also spelled *taqsīm*) or vocal *layālī* and *mawwāl*—either from recordings or by listening to and watching fellow musicians in performance. After listening to such a session, young musicians might come away with one or two new ideas that they will incorporate into their own improvisations. Thus musicians learn the intricacies of the various *maqāmāt* by an ongoing process of osmosis, beginning in early childhood. To the extent that students take music lessons (a rather rare phenomenon until the advent of conservatory training in the twentieth century), they learn to play specific pieces of music during these lessons. There is no direct, explicit teaching of the characteristics of the individual modes beyond, perhaps, their most basic scales.

Theorists, on the other hand, have developed their own traditions for understanding and explaining the *maqāmāt*. These traditions have changed considerably over the last two hundred years, falling into three rather distinct periods (Marcus 1989b). Of the three, contemporary theory is the simplest in that the definition of a *maqām* is confined, for the most part, to a presentation of scales and an analysis in terms of tonic pitch (*qarār* or *asās*), melodic intervals, and tetrachordal structure. This body of knowledge is taught to all who pursue conservatory- or institute-based training and is found in all recently published theory books.

MODERN ARAB MUSIC THEORY: AN INTRODUCTION

The notes of modern Arab music

FIGURE 1

The Arab tonal system is based on a two-octave fundamental scale (a carryover from ancient Greek and medieval Arab music theory), from GG to g (figure 1), usually conceived as containing a primary central octave from C to c. The notes of the fundamental scale are identified in accordance with a system of Persian and Arabic names whose roots go back to the medieval period. The central octave notes are named *rāst*, *dūkā*, *sīkā*, *jahārkā*, *nawā*, *ḥusaynī*, *awj*, and *kirdān* (figure 2). Six of these notes correspond to the notes C D F G A and c of the Western scale. The third and seventh notes, however, fall between the Western flat and the corresponding natural note. Thus *sīkā* falls between E and E-flat; *awj* falls between B-flat and B. In the twentieth century, with the adoption of Western staff notation, Western solfège (do, re, mi, fa, sol, la, and si), and the Western understanding of E-natural and E-flat, the note *sīka* came to be called "mi half-flat" *(mī nisf bīmūl*, pronounced *mī nuṣṣ bīmōl* in Egyptian dialect). This new term for the third note of the Arab fundamental scale is based on the assumption that the Western E-natural is, in fact, the "natural" note, at least in name. While the

FIGURE 2

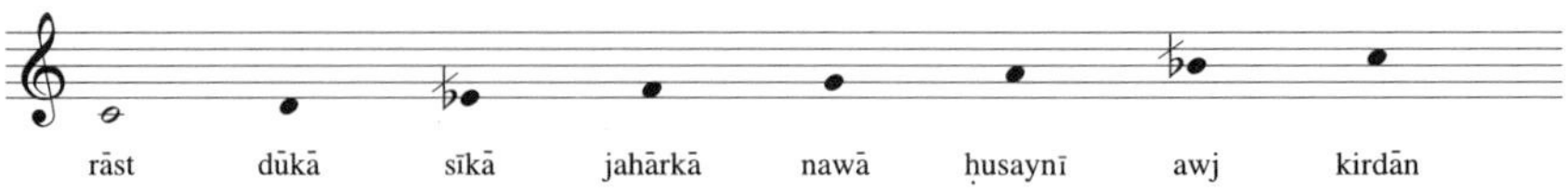

FIGURE 3

C D E♭ E𝄳 E♮

I I
< < < < < < <

I I
< < <

G A B♭ B𝄳 B♮

I I
< < < < < < < <

I I
< < <

note E-flat alters the note E-natural by making it "completely" flat, the Arabic note requires flattening the E only "halfway"; thus, "mi half-flat." Similarly, the note *awj* is now commonly referred to as *sī nisf bīmūl*, or "si half-flat." The symbol for the half-flat in staff notation is most commonly a flat sign with a slash across its stem: 𝄳 (figure 3).

The term *half-flat* (*nisf bīmūl*) and its notation symbol date from the twentieth century, but an important development remarked on in the 1770s (Laborde 1780) had already paved the way for this understanding of the *sīkā* and *awj* notes. This new development was a reconceptualization of the long-standing Arab musical scale in terms of quarterstep intervals. Thus C to D (*rāst* to *dūkā*) came to be understood as a 4-quarterstep interval, *dūkā* to *sīkā* came to be considered a 3-quarterstep interval, and so forth, so that the Arab fundamental scale came to be reconceptualized as containing twenty-four quartersteps per octave (figure 4). The main theoretical conceptualization of the scale prior to this quartertone system was the scale of Ṣāfī al-Dīn in the thirteenth century; it had seventeen steps per octave (see ARABIC SOURCES FOR MUSIC THEORY). The intervals in this earlier scale were conceptualized in terms of limma and comma intervals (Farmer 1936:752–753; Shiloah 1981; Wright 1978).

FIGURE 4

C D E𝄳 F G A B𝄳 c

4/4 3/4 3/4 4/4 4/4 3/4 3/4 = 24/4

C I I I D I I E𝄳 I I F I I I G I I I A I I B𝄳 I I c

Theoretically, the newly developed scale was an equal-tempered quartertone scale, expressible in terms of 50-cent quarterstep intervals (although the cent system is not used by Arab musicians or theorists; figure 5).

FIGURE 5

C I I I D I I E𝄳 I I F I I I G I I I A I I B𝄳 I I c

0 50 100 150 200 250 300 350 400 450 500 550 600 650 700 750 800 850 900 950 1000 1050 1100 1150 1200

Given this tempered scale, the twentieth-century term *half-flat* can be seen as an accurate description of the note's theoretical position: that is, it does occur exactly halfway between a natural note and its corresponding flat. In addition to the half-flats, the notes falling between a note and its corresponding sharp came to be called "half-sharp" (*nisf dīyaz*) in the twentieth century, notated by the symbol ‡ (figure 6).

FIGURE 6

C𝄲 C♯ D𝄲 D♯ E E𝄲 F𝄲 F♯ G𝄲 G♯ A𝄲 A♯ B B𝄲

C I I I D I I E𝄳 I I F I I I G I I I A I I B𝄳 I I c

D♭ D𝄳 E♭ F♭ F𝄳 G♭ G𝄳 A♭ A𝄳 B♭ B c𝄳

Indeed, today there are a few instruments (some keyboards and accordions, for example) that strive for this very tempered system of tuning. Performers using other instruments commonly tune their notes in ways that differ from equal temperament: for example, since the strings of the *'ūd* and the violin are tuned to perfect fourths and fifths, many notes on these instruments tend to be rendered in Pythagorean intonation. In addition, musicians with instruments that allow for self-determination of exact pitch (the violin, the fretless *'ūd*, the human voice, and so on) often speak of special tunings for individual notes in a given *maqām*; for example, the flat third in *maqām nahāwand*, E-flat, is said to be especially low—lower than the E-flat in *maqām ḥijāz*. Similarly, the E-half-flat in *maqām rāst* is commonly understood to be higher than the E-half-flat in *maqām bayyātī* (see Marcus 1993b). In present-day Cairo, such understandings are being lost, as the two main schools of higher learning for music teach only the equal tempered system.

The intervals of modern Arab music

The modes of modern-day Arab music use four melodic intervals, the whole step containing 4 quartersteps, the 3-quarterstep, the half or 2-quarterstep, and the augmented second or 6-quarterstep. In one method used in theory books, intervallic analysis is notated with an ascending arch to indicate 4-quarterstep intervals, a descending arch for 3-quarterstep intervals, a "v" for 2 quartersteps, and three sides of a rectangle to indicate 6-quarterstep intervals (figure 7).

FIGURE 7

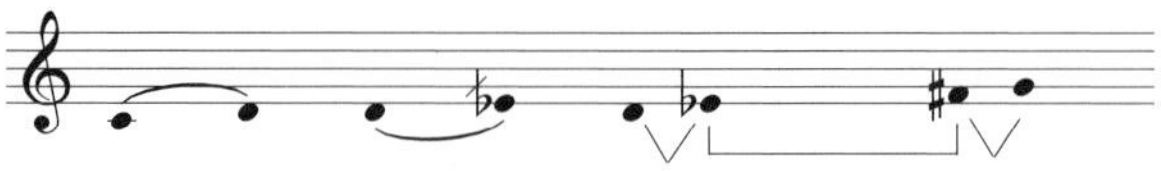

There are also extremely rare instances of a 5-quarterstep interval, found, for example, between the notes C and D-half-sharp and between E-half-flat and F-sharp. Most musicians and theorists agree that Arab music does not contain intervals of a single quarterstep. There is, perhaps, one exception: in modes with a half-flat tonic, such as E𝄳, it is somewhat common to notate the leading tone to the tonic as D-sharp, thus creating a 1-quarterstep interval between D-sharp and E𝄳. Theorists, however, point out that the leading tone should correctly be notated as D-half-sharp. This removes the only instance of a 1-quarterstep interval in Arab music, since the interval between D𝄲 and E𝄳 is 2 quartersteps.

The tetrachords of modern Arab music

Present-day Arab music theory commonly recognizes nine or eleven tetrachords, all using 2-, 3-, 4-, and 6-quarterstep intervals. Here, the term *tetrachord* (*jins*, the Arabic spelling of the Greek *genus*) is used loosely to include three- and five-note groups in addition to the standard four-note groups. Lists that include rarely used tetrachords might name an additional four to six tetrachords (see Marcus 1989a:304). Each of the tetrachords has a specific root position and occurs in a number of common transpositions. For example, the *rāst* tetrachord, consisting of four notes with the intervals of 4, 3, and 3 quartersteps, has its root position on C; it also occurs commonly on GG, G, and c, and less commonly on D and a few other positions. The nine principal Arab tetrachords (in root position) appear in figure 8. The nine principal tetrachords are increased to eleven when the single *sīkā* trichord (E𝄳 F G) is reconceptualized as three distinct tetrachords (figure 9).

FIGURE 8

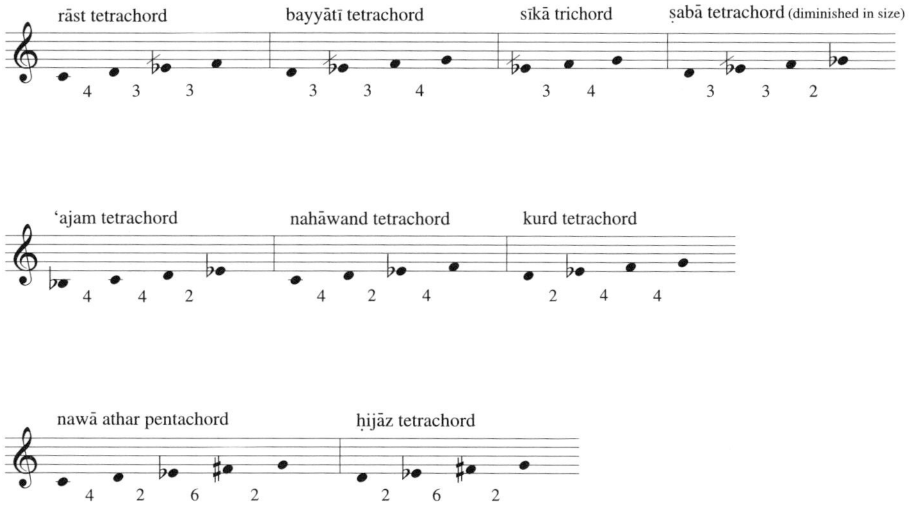

FIGURE 9

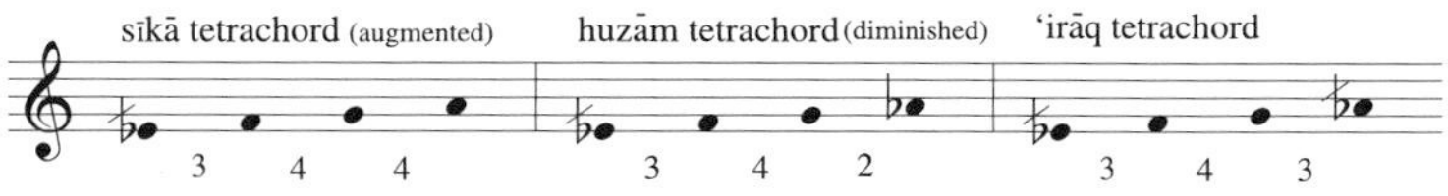

Creating modal scales

Theoretically, modal scales are created by joining together two or more tetrachords. Present-day Arab music theory recognizes three types of tetrachordal joining (*jam'*): disjunct (*munfaṣil*), when the second tetrachord starts after the first without sharing any notes; conjunct (*muttaṣil*), when the second tetrachord begins with the last note of the first tetrachord; and overlapping (*mutadākhil*), when the second tetrachord starts before the last note of the first tetrachord. *Maqām rāst*, for example, contains disjunct tetrachords; *maqām bayyātī* contains conjunct tetrachords; *maqām ṣabā* contains overlapping tetrachords (figure 10).

Note that the scale of *maqām rāst* corresponds with the central octave (C to c) of the two-octave Arab fundamental scale (introduced above). For this reason, *maqām rāst* is considered the preeminent mode of Arab music.

In addition to *maqām rāst*, other commonly used modes include *bayyātī*, *ḥijāz*, *ṣabā*, *huzām*, and *nahāwand*. *Rāst* and *nahāwand* are based on C tonic (and are commonly transposed to G); *bayyātī*, *ḥijāz*, and *ṣabā* are based on D (commonly transposed to G and AA); *huzām* is based on the Arab note E-half-flat (and commonly transposed to BB𝄳) (figure 11).

FIGURE 10

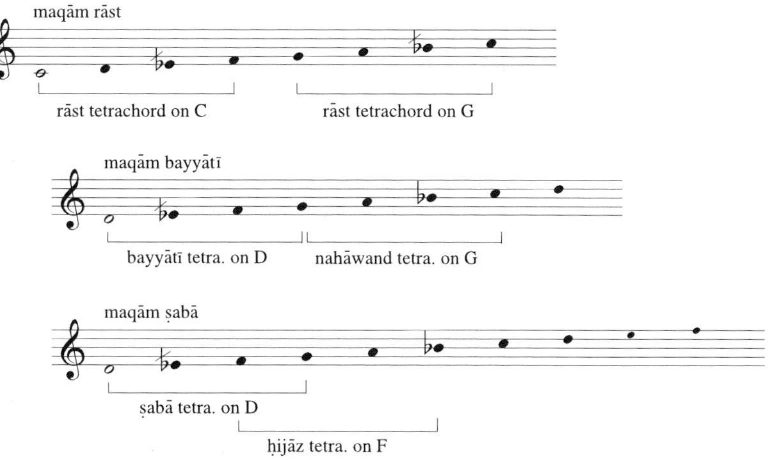

FIGURE II

The above is a presentation of modern-day Arab music theory, which was developed in the first half of the twentieth century and became predominant during the 1930s through the 1970s. According to this theory, the various modal scales are presented in terms of scales with a recognized tonic pitch, and are analyzed in terms of intervals and tetrachords. This is how the modes are presented in most contemporary Arab theory books and in classes in modern institutes and conservatories throughout the eastern Arab world. (See, for example, al-Farjānī 1986; Muḥammad 1984).

THE MODES IN PRACTICE: THE CASE OF *MAQĀM BAYYĀTĪ*

In practice, however, a more complex and dynamic definition of the individual modes emerges, involving such considerations as the notes not duplicating at the octave, specific nontempered intonation for some notes, a common progression or path for moving through the various regions of a mode's scale, additional tetrachords beyond those indicated in the simple scalar presentation of the mode, characteristic accidentals, and a set of standard modulations to other modes. The presence and persistence of this considerably denser definition of the modes in practice speak both to the existence of distinct traditions of music theory and music practice and to another important aspect of traditional Middle Eastern music culture: that performers and composers absorb a "common practice" understanding of the various melodic modes and then seek to work within the existing modal tradition, while improvising or creating fixed compositions. This is in marked contrast to expectations in Western art music, where the composer is supposed to step beyond the tradition, to be on the cutting edge, creating a new grammar. A few Arab composers have actively tried to expand the *maqām* system, for example, by adding moments of Western harmony or by including rare modulations; but even eminent musicians, such as the Egyptian composer Muḥammad ʿAbd al-Wahhāb, who are praised for their innovations, are generally best understood as composing within the long-standing common practice of the *maqām* system.

In order to convey some of the complexity of the "common practice" understandings of the Arab *maqāmāt*, I have chosen to focus on a single *maqām*, *maqām bayyātī*, one of the most common of all the Arab modes. As indicated above, modern-day
TRACK 1 theory defines *maqām bayyātī* as a D-based mode consisting of a *bayyātī* tetrachord on D and a *nahāwand* tetrachord on G (figure 12). Beyond this simple definition, one of the first points students of performance might come across is that, while *maqām bayyātī* uses B-flat above the D tonic, it uses the note BB-half-flat (𝄳) below the tonic. Thus, as with many modes of Arab music, the notes of *maqām bayyātī* do not duplicate at the octave (figure 13).

A second aspect of performers' knowledge is a widely held understanding that the second degree of the *bayyātī* scale, the E𝄳, is tuned slightly lower than a tempered E𝄳. While no studies have sought to quantify the exact pitch (or range of pitch) for this note, I would suggest a lowering from the 150 cents of the tempered half-flat of between 5 and 15 cents. It must be added here that this lowering is not universally recognized, since a number of "fixed pitch" instruments such as the *qānūn* (zither) and the retuned accordion commonly have only a single E𝄳 to be used in all the modes which call for an E𝄳. (A *qānūn* player can retune the strings to give a slightly lowered E𝄳, but this is not generally done in practice.) Similarly, many hold that the B𝄳 of *bayyātī* also differs from its equal-tempered position by being raised slightly above that position. Other examples of specific tuning concern the notes F and B-flat, both of which are generally played lower than their equal-tempered positions of 300 cents and 800 cents, respectively, above the tonic. It is possible, in each case, that the position is best represented by the Pythagorean interval, the Pythagorean minor third being of 294.135 cents and the Pythagorean minor sixth being of 792.18 cents. (Note that the open strings of the *ʿūd* are tuned in a series of perfect fourths and thus create Pythagorean intonation for many of the pitches; see Marcus 1989a:201ff and 1993b.)

A third aspect of the "common practice" understanding for *maqām bayyātī* concerns a common path or progression for movement through the mode's various regions. Compositions and improvisations in *bayyātī* tend to start in the middle of the mode's central octave, possibly somewhere in the region from F to B-flat, and then proceed down to the tonic D. (According to a treatise of 1840 by Mīkha'īl Mashāqa, if one started at or below the tonic rather than in the middle of the mode's central scale, this would be a characteristic feature of a different mode and should not be

FIGURE 12

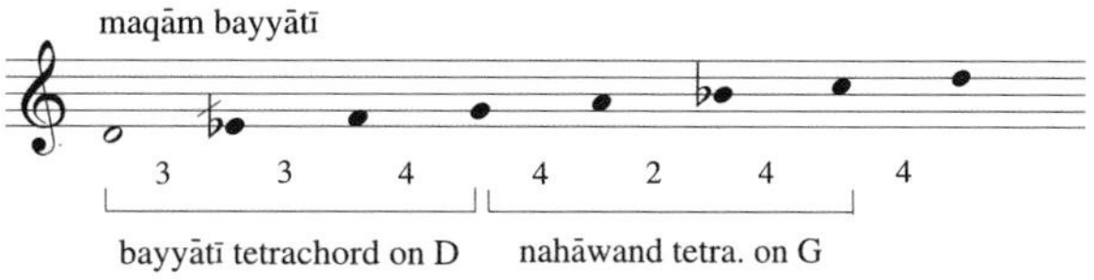

FIGURE 13

considered *bayyātī*, although he admits that "most knowledgeable Syrians" would still have considered it to be *bayyātī* [1899:883].) After the initial moments in the middle of the scale, the melody would commonly descend to settle on the tonic note, often using one or two or more notes below the tonic, the lowest possible note generally being the G one-fifth below the tonic (GG). Note that the BB below the tonic is 𝄳. Then, there will commonly be an ascent up the scale, initially further exploring the mode's central octave and next commonly ascending into the higher octave. In the central octave, the G is often an important resting note, in part because of its function as the base note of the second tetrachord. The note B-flat is also regularly featured, often in conjunction with a phrase that descends to F, leading a few theorists to indicate the presence of a *jahārkā* or *'ajam* tetrachord based on F (F G A B-flat). In one of the mode's most characteristic movements, a sequence often occurs in which a descent from B-flat to F is followed by similar descents from A to E𝄳, and then from G to D (see, for example, the composition *samā'ī bayyātī*, by Ibrāhīm al-'Aryān). Another common movement consists of a held A followed by a fall to A from c using B𝄳: for example, A, c B𝄳 c A. (This movement was once considered a characteristic feature of a distinct mode called *ḥusaynī*. In the present day, however, *ḥusaynī* has virtually disappeared as a distinct mode in performance, and this movement is now generally subsumed within *maqām bayyātī*.)

After presenting the central octave, improvisations and compositions might commonly rise to the octave region. In order to effect this shift in focus, the note B-flat is generally replaced by B𝄳. This might be best understood as a full octave shift of the overall scale of *bayyātī*, wherein the BB below the tonic is half-flat. Now that the focus is being shifted to the octave region, the tonic itself might also be seen as temporarily moving up one octave. Along with it, the BB half-flat below the tonic is also moved up an octave. Tetrachordally speaking, we now have a *rāst* tetrachord on G (G A B𝄳 c) rather than the earlier *nahāwand* tetrachord on G (G A B-flat c). The improviser or composer may explore the octave region at any length, possibly including one or more cadences on the octave note itself (d), and will then eventually descend back into the region of the central octave. This is commonly achieved by first reasserting the note B-flat in place of the B𝄳, with the resulting reappearance of the *nahāwand* tetrachord.

As the descent to the original tonic and the final cadence proceeds, there is often one further dramatic development: a *ḥijāz* tetrachord on G (G A-flat B c) may be introduced temporarily. Jihad Racy (professor of ethnomusicology at the University of California, Los Angeles) has referred to this in his classes as a "precadential" movement. Finally, the improvisation or composition would end by resolving on the tonic D, commonly after replacing the *ḥijāz* tetrachord on G with a *rāst* (or *nahāwand*) tetrachord and often after descending below the tonic at least to the extent of presenting the subtonic note C.

This progression serves to highlight an important aspect of the structure of most of the Arab *maqāmāt*: each has a single root or lower tetrachord, which gives the defining character to the mode. The region above this first tetrachord, however, is not restricted to just one tetrachord; rather, a number of tetrachords, often three, appear in characteristic ways at specific times in the overall progression, with each tetrachord fulfilling specific functions. In our *bayyātī* example, the *nahāwand* tetrachord on G (with its B-flat) can be seen as helping to present the central octave; the *rāst* tetrachord on G (with its B𝄳) can be seen as helping to propel the melodic motion upward to the octave note and above; the *nahāwand* tetrachord is reasserted in order to bring the melodic movement back down into the central octave; the *ḥijāz* tetrachord acts as a momentary coloring before the final cadence, serving to heighten the effect of the cadence; and finally a *rāst* or *nahāwand* tetrachord is brought back to reassert the

FIGURE 14

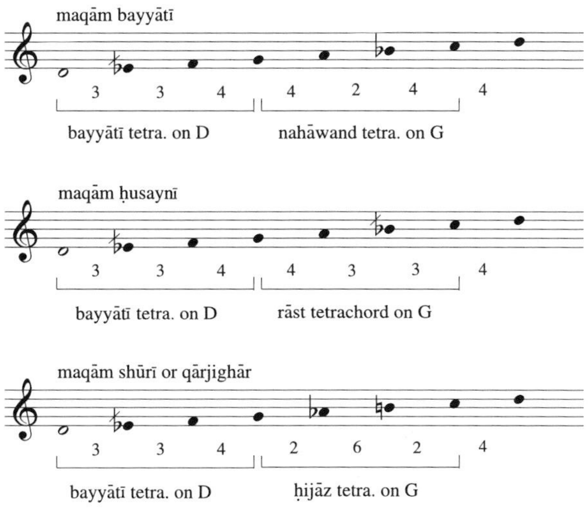

original character of the mode. Thus, like the idea of "functional harmony" within the "common practice" harmony of eighteenth- and nineteenth-century Europe, Arab modal practice can be seen as following a clear "functional" melodic practice.

Interestingly, this progression is not explicitly stated in the present day: it is not taught at institutes that train music teachers or at conservatories whose goal is, in part, to develop professional musicians. Yet it is a body of knowledge that all experienced musicians come upon, unconsciously absorb, and manifest in their performance practice. Theorists do recognize the occurrence of *nahāwand*, *rāst*, and *ḥijāz* tetrachords on G above a *bayyātī* tetrachord on D, but they consider the three upper tetrachords as creating three distinct *maqāmāt*—*bayyātī*, *ḥusaynī*, and *shūrī*, respectively. Performers commonly recognize all three as being part of *maqām bayyātī* (figure 14).

A fourth aspect of a performer's knowledge is an understanding of characteristic accidentals for each mode. While a number of modes, such as *nahāwand* and *kurd*, feature accidental notes prominently, *maqām bayyātī* uses such notes only rarely. There are generally no accidentals that appear in the root *bayyātī* tetrachord on D. The *nahāwand* tetrachord on G might rarely have a momentary B-natural, functioning as a replacement for the B-flat and serving as a discontinuous lowering neighboring tone to the note c, as in the phrase G A B-flat c, c B c, B c d c B-flat A G. Also, when the movement descends from the octave region and the B-flat is reinserted in place of the B𝄳, it is possible to have an e-flat in the octave rather than an e-half-flat. Along with the B-flat, this e-flat serves to propel the melodic line toward a descent from the higher octave (see Marcus 1989a:599–629).

A fifth aspect of a performer's knowledge is a set of common modulations to other modes, for modulation forms a prominent feature of Arab music performance practice. Modulations might be sudden and very conspicuous or subtle and virtually seamless. Either way, they are a highly valued aspect of performance practice. Modulations are common to modes that share the same tonic, in this case, to *ṣabā* on D or to *ḥijāz* on D. It is also standard to modulate to modes based on the root note of the second tetrachord, here commonly to *maqām rāst* or *maqām nahāwand* on G. In these instances, the modulation would differ from simply playing the normal upper tetrachords of *bayyātī*: notes beyond those of the tetrachord will be changed to conform to the notes of the new *maqām*. *Maqām rāst* on G, for example, will have the notes E-natural and F-half-sharp. When these notes are added below the note G within a presentation of the *rāst* tetrachord on G, then the mode is understood to be *maqām rāst* and not *maqām bayyātī*. Similarly, *maqām nahāwand* on G would have E-natural

FIGURE 15

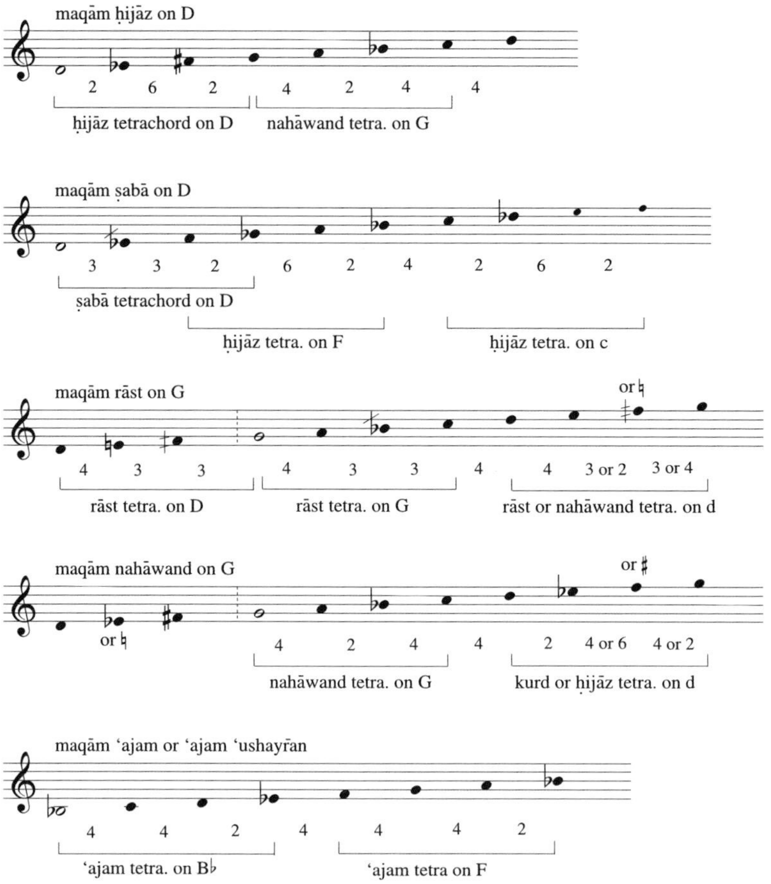

and F-sharp (or E-flat and F-sharp) below the tonic G and thus differs significantly from *maqām bayyātī* on D. Further, within *maqām bayyātī*, a modulation to *maqām ʿajam* with a descent from B-flat to BB-flat is also common (figure 15; see Marcus 1992).

Thus a performer's knowledge of *maqām bayyātī* includes comprehensive knowledge of a large number of other modes that will appear in improvisations and precomposed pieces based in *maqām bayyātī*. The improviser or composer must know all the aspects discussed above for each of these additional modes (aspects of nonduplication at the octave, specifics of intonation, accidentals, and the like) and must also master the many common and rare ways of effecting modulations both to the new *maqāmāt* and back to the original *maqām*. Modulatory excursions might include only a single new *maqām* or a number of new *maqāmāt* in succession before the obligatory return to the original *maqām*.

The central position of modulation in Arab music results in a situation where the *maqāmāt* exist in constant interaction with one another. This stands in contrast to the situation in North and South Indian classical musics, where modulation is not prominent, and where each melodic mode (raga) is commonlly understood to stand on its own, separate from the others. Thus, while a single item of Indian music will generally include only a single raga, an item of Arab music performance might include many related *maqāmāt*.

THE NUMBER OF *MAQĀMĀT* IN MODERN ARAB MUSIC

As mentioned above, theorists recognize three distinct *maqāmāt* (*bayyātī*, *ḥusaynī*, and *shūrī*), whereas performers often recognize all three as aspects of a single mode:

maqām bayyātī. This discrepancy has an impact on discussions seeking to ascertain the exact number of *maqāmāt* in present-day Arab music. On a basic level, one might take a musician's perspective, saying that there are nine main *maqāmāt*, corresponding to the nine tetrachords of modern Arab music listed above. According to this understanding, these nine *maqāmāt* would each have a number of different upper tetrachords, occurring in characteristic fashion and fulfilling specific functions in the melodic development of the mode. Further, each of these modes would occur in one or more transpositions (for example, *maqām bayyātī* might occur on G, AA, or GG) but would still be considered *maqām bayyātī* in each position. Theorists, on the other hand, would give a new name to each unique scale; thus each change in a mode's upper tetrachord would result in a separate *maqām*. Also, transpositions of a given mode are often given their own unique names, so that theorists might recognize fifty, sixty, seventy, or more *maqāmāt*. Theorists generally group their dozens of *maqāmāt* into nine "families" (*faṣīla*; plural, *faṣā'il*) based on the modes' lower tetrachord, providing a significant commonality between performers' and theorists' conceptualizations.

CHANGES IN *MAQĀM* CONCEPTUALIZATION OVER TIME

The second half of the twentieth century saw a rise in institutionalized music education throughout much of the Arab Middle East. As discussed above, in the music theory taught at these institutions each *maqām* is presented as a specific scale, which is then analyzed in terms of tonic pitch and intervallic and tetrachordal structure. Students are not explicitly taught about nontempered tunings, accidentals, or specific paths for the melodic unfolding of each *maqām*. The most talented students will come to learn these aspects of the traditional *maqām* system over time (by prolonged and intimate contact with respected repertoire through transcriptions, recordings, and live performances). Other students, however, seem to accept contemporary theory as if it were comprehensive; they grow up believing that there is only the tempered scale of twenty-four notes per octave, and thus *bayyātī* does not have a slightly lowered E𝄳 and a slightly raised B𝄳. Similarly, they do not understand that a *maqām* might have a specific path for its melodic unfolding; compositions in *maqām bayyātī* are therefore free to follow any path whatsoever. This suggests that melodic modal practice might well change over time.

Such change has, of course, occurred in the past. For example, Mīkha'īl Mashāqa's treatise of 1840 presents dozens of *maqāmāt* from that period which simply no longer exist today. Similarly, from the end of the nineteenth century to roughly 1930, a scholarly or academic Arab *maqām* practice flourished, featuring a number of *maqāmāt* that have since largely faded from common practice. For example, *maqām bayyātī* was considered separate and distinct from two modes of similar scalar structure: *maqām muḥayyar* (in which movement was said to begin in the octave and then descend) and *maqām ḥusaynī* (which emphasized the note A, emphasized the note B𝄳 over B-flat, and had a number of distinct melodic characteristics). Today, however, these latter two modes are largely lost, though they remain as distinct modes by virtue of respected compositions such as *samā'ī Ḥusaynī Ṭātyos* and *samā'ī Muḥayyar Jamīl Bey*. To the extent that they still occur, they are subsumed under an all-encompassing *maqām bayyātī*.

In conclusion, the Arab system of melodic modes exists in parallel dynamic realms of theory and practice. Each realm has experienced significant changes over the last 100 to 150 years. Contemporary theory is a somewhat recent product, largely designed for institutionalized settings. The "common practice" definitions of the present-day *maqāmāt* predate this theory, representing a performance practice from the nineteenth and early twentieth centuries and possibly earlier. However, there have been significant changes in this practice, especially the loss of a large number of modes that once existed. We can expect changes in both theory and practice to continue in the future.

REFERENCES

al-Farjānī, Miftāḥ Suwaysī. 1986. *Maqāmāt al-mūsīqā al-ʿarabiyya: dirāsa taḥlīliyya*. Tripoli: al-Dār al-Jamāhīriyya.

Farmer, Henry George. 1936. "Musiki." In *Encyclopedia of Islam*, 749–755. Leiden: Brill.

Laborde, Jean Benjamin de. 1780. *Essai sur la musique ancienne et moderne*. Vol. 1. Paris: Imprimerie de Ph.-D. Pierres.

Marcus, Scott. 1989a. "Arab Music Theory in the Modern Period." Ph.D. dissertation, University of California Los Angeles.

———. 1989b "The Periodization of Modern Arab Music Theory: Continuity and Change in the Definition of the *Maqāmāt*." *Pacific Review of Ethnomusicology* 5:35–49.

———. 1992. "Modulation in Arab Music: Documenting Oral Concepts, Performance Rules, and Strategies." *Ethnomusicology* 36(2):171–195.

———. 1993a. "Solo Instrumental Improvisation (Taqāsīm) in Arab Music." *Middle East Studies Association Bulletin* 27:108–111.

———. 1993b. "The Interface between Theory and Practice: The Case of Intonation in Arab Music." *Asian Music* 24(2):39–58.

Mashāqa, Mikh'īl. c.1840. "al-Risāla al-shihābiyya fī āl-ṣināʿa al-mūsīqiyya." Unpublished manuscript.

———. 1899. "al-Risāla al-shihābiyya fī āl-ṣināʿa al-mūsīqiyya lī'l-duktūr Mīkh'īl Mashāqa." *Al-Mashriq*. Beirut: Imprimerie Catholique.

Muḥammad, Suhayr ʿAbd al-ʿAzīz. 1984. *Ajandat al-mūsīqā al-ʿarabiyya*. Cairo: Dār al-Kutub al-Qawmiyya.

Racy, Ali Jihad. 1976. "Record Industry and Egyptian Traditional Music: 1904–1932." *Ethnomusicology* 20(1):23–48.

———. 1977. "Musical Change and Commercial Recording in Egypt, 1904–1932." Ph.D. dissertation, University of Illinois, Champaign-Urbana.

Shiloah, Amnon. 1981. "The Arab Concept of Mode." *Journal of the American Musicological Society* 34(1):19–42.

Wright, Owen. 1978. *The Modal System of Arab and Persian Music, A.D. 1250–1300*. London Oriental Series. Vol. 28. Oxford: Oxford University Press.

Music in Performance: *'Ūd* Lessons with George Michel

Scott Marcus

Transmission
Improvisation: *Taqasim*
The Last of the *'Ūd* Players

George Michel was one of Cairo's most respected *'ūd* players from the 1960s until his death in the mid-1990s. He was the lead *'ūd* player in the government's Firqat al-Musīqā 'l-'Arabiyya 'Arab Music Ensemble', and as such often appeared on Egyptian national television and radio and in government-sponsored international tours. He was also a teacher at the two main institutes of higher music education in Cairo: al-Ma'had al-'Ālī li 'l-Musīqā al-'Arabiyya 'Higher Institute for Arab Music' and Kulliyat al-Tarbiyya al-Musīqīyya 'Faculty of Music Education'. In addition, he was a composer; a number of his compositions have entered the standard repertoire of art music ensembles throughout the eastern Arab world.

In the early 1980s, I took *'ūd* lessons twice weekly with George Michel. Always a gentleman, George (as his friends called him) would arrive at my apartment in Cairo for each lesson immaculately dressed, with gracious words of greeting and a big smile. After initial small talk and tea, we would begin our lesson proper, often first addressing a series of questions I had prepared. Eventually, he would check the tuning of my *'ūd* and ask me to play what I had been working on. A very particular man, he would not allow mistakes. A simple missed note might cause him to shake a finger or raise his chin and click his tongue, or both. With some regularity, however, he would perceive a mistake as more grievous and would scream out in disapproval, "What is this?" Was he really angry? Since such outbursts were often followed by a smile, they were, perhaps, better understood as a method of teaching.

Transmission

For his part, George focused the lessons largely on what might be called "monuments" of modern Arab instrumental music: renowned pieces—a few of which were his own compositions—in the genres *samā'ī*, *longa*, *taḥmīla*, and *qiṭ'a*. For many of these pieces, we had commercially produced transcriptions in Western staff notation that used non-Western symbols to indicate the half-flat and half-sharp notes of Arab music. These transcriptions are included in books published from the 1940s on for students and teachers of then newly formed music institutes—for example, 'Abd al-Mun'im 'Arafa's *Dirāsat al-'ūd* and his *Kitāb ustādh al-musīqā 'l-'arabiyya*. However, if there was even a single mistake in a given transcription, George would grab a pen and quickly produce a new transcription, from memory, only occasionally picking up my *'ūd* to check a passage. He would then review what he had written by reading the transcription aloud using the solfège syllables: do, re, mi, fa, sol, la, si. Conservatory-trained, George was an absolute master of solfège and Western notation.

Improvisation: Taqāsīm

For my part, I spent many lessons with George trying to learn the art of *taqāsīm* 'improvisation' on the *'ūd*, an art of which he was an acknowledged master. This was a somewhat frustrating endeavor for George, since he did not feel that this art could be taught. "Play from your heart," he would instruct me. He decided that I should, as a first step, imitate one of his improvisations, which he proceeded to record for me. After many weeks, when he finally decided that I could reproduce his *taqāsīm* to his satisfaction, he declared that I must now come up with my own creation. When I played a phrase that he considered to be from his *taqāsīm*, he stopped me, stating in a loud, forceful voice, "No, that's mine! Play something of your own. Your own creation!" But he was not able to teach how to build individual phrases or how to structure a given *taqāsīm*. My attempts to receive instruction in the improvisatory exploration of individual modes were meeting with little success. Finally, I suggested that we turn our attention to the modulations that occur in *taqāsīm*. "Ah," George exclaimed, "now this I can help you with. Yes, this is my business." In subsequent lessons, with him and others, I learned that the musicians of Cairo conceptualize with great specificity about modulations among the *maqāmāt* 'modes', though much less so about movement within a single *maqām*.

The last of the 'ūd *players*

George was a proud man, declaring, for example, that he had never played in a night club. But he enjoyed joking, and he also had a humble side. He frequently referred to himself as "the last of the *'ūd* players." While I comprehended the self-depreciating nature of this statement, I came to understand that it also had a second meaning. Cairo had recently lost its two superstar *'ūd* players. The favorite of the masses, Farīd al-Aṭrash, known as the "king of the *'ūd*," had died in 1974; and Riyāḍ al-Sinbāṭī, a consummate musicians' musician, had died only a year or so before my lessons with George began. The position of "first *'ūd* player" in Egypt had then, uncontested, passed on to George Michel. Indeed, in large part because of his occasional solos on television and radio, George was widely known and respected in Cairo, though he never approached the fame of either Farīd or Riyāḍ al-Sinbāṭī. He was "the last" in part because he had outlived these other two.

REFERENCES

'Abd al-Mun'im 'Arafa and Ṣafar 'Alī. 1984. *Dirasat al-'ūd* (The Study of the *'Ūd*), 6th ed. Cairo: n. p. (First published in 1942.)

'Abd al-Mun'im 'Arafa. 1976. *Kitāb ustādh al-musīqā 'l-'arabiyya* (The Book of the Arab Music Teacher), 3d ed. Cairo: Maṭba'at al-Sa'āda. (First published in 1944.)

Contemporary Turkish *Makam* Practice

Karl Signell

The Abstract Level: *Makam* Theory
The Empirical Level: Alernative Explanations
Individuality
Related Musics
Extramusical Meaning

To the outsider, the Turkish *makam* is a mystery: is it a scale, a mode, or a melody? But the Turkish theorist defines it, the Turkish performer hears it with the inner ear, and the Turkish music lover often takes it for granted.

A musician playing classical Turkish music at the beginning of the twenty-first century usually reads from a score. At the top of its first page, there is almost invariably the name of a *makam* (figure 1). Names distinguish one *makam*, or classical Turkish melody classification, from another. We should not compare modal systems indiscriminately; but solely with regard to its use of names for types of melodies, the Turkish *makam* (plural, *makamlar*) system resembles European medieval modes (Aeolian, Phrygian), Indian *raga* (*Bhairavi*, *Todi*), and Javanese *patet* (*Nem*, *Sanga*). Historical records list hundreds of *makamlar*, some known only by their names, since no compositions in these modes survive. The best modern performers can improvise in about fifty *makamlar*, and even more if a performer has had a chance to study compositions in an unfamiliar *makam*.

The precisely defined characteristics of the Turkish *makam* hold true for classical compositions and improvisations performed by elite groups of instrumentalists and singers, such as those in government and conservatory ensembles and at radio stations in Istanbul, Ankara, and Izmir. Turks call this genre Turkish classical music (*klasik Türk müziği*, or *klasik Türk musikisi*) or sometimes art music or learned music *(sanat musikisi*).

The Turkish *makam* can be understood on two levels: an abstract level that provides theoretical knowledge, and an empirical level that provides knowledge based on performance. The astute student will learn abstract theory but will approach it with a healthy skepticism until practice bears it out.

FIGURE 1 *Makam* name—*beyati*—at the top of a score. (For the complete score, see figure 16.)

THE ABSTRACT LEVEL: *MAKAM* THEORY

According to the early twentieth-century Turkish theorist Rauf Yekta and his colleague H. Saadettin Arel, a *makam* has six elements: (1) tetrachord and pentachord (scale types), (2) ambitus, (3) beginning, (4) dominant, (5) tonic (finalis), and (6) movement (*seyir*).

One might reformulate twentieth-century Turkish theory and modify it from a performer's point of view by defining *makam* in terms of five elements, not very different from Yekta's (Signell 1986):

1. Scale
2. Melodic unfolding
3. Modulation
4. Stereotyped motives
5. Tessitura

Any one of these elements might indicate the difference between two *makamlar*, but most of them are needed to identify a *makam* clearly, even at the abstract level.

Scale

Intervals

Western music commonly uses seven notes (do, re, mi, and so on) with five auxiliary notes (sharps and flats), so that twelve notes per octave are available: these are the white keys and black keys in an octave on the piano. Theoretically, any two successive notes are separated by the same interval, 100 cents. A cent is one-hundredth of a Western tempered semitone; a perfect octave contains 1,200 cents. Every musical interval, in all musics, can be represented in cents.

FIGURE 2 Turkish and Western notes between whole tones.

Classical Turkish music, which is monophonic, has developed subtleties of intonation; thus one finds three named pitches between whole tones where Western music has only one (figure 2). In their classical music, Turks recognize and name at least twenty-four notes per octave (Signell 1986:28–29). Often, a pitch has the same name as a *makam* in which it plays an important role (for instance, the pitch *segah* is important in *makam segah*). Turkish theorists use the Pythagorean comma (*koma*), equal to 23.46 cents, as the unit of measure for intervals. However, different methods are used to calculate some intervals, and figures may be rounded to whole numbers; as a result, there can be discrepancies in totals.

Turkish theory recognizes five intervals (figure 3), and classical Turkish music notation, for the most part, uses three flats and three sharps (figure 4). Figure 5 compares commas and cents in a widely used *makam*, *beyati*. As figure 6 shows, the same notation represents different intervals, depending on Turkish and Western conventions.

Scale: Examples

Note that for all the scales discussed here, the tones are represented hierarchically: the finalis as a whole note, secondary tonal centers such as the dominant and the upper tonic as half notes, and the other tones of the scale as stemless black heads. Note also

FIGURE 3 The five intervals recognized in Turkish theory.

Turkish name	English translation	Comma value	Cents value
bakiye	small half-tone	4	90
küçük mücennep	large half-tone	5	114
büyük mücennep	small whole-tone	8	180
tanini	whole-tone	9	204
artık ikili	augmented second	12	271

FIGURE 4 The three flats and three sharps of classical Turkish music notation.

Accidental	Turkish notation	Western tempered notation	Example
𝄳	lowers 23 cents (1 comma)	—	Figure 5, 9: A–B𝄳 = 180 cents (small whole tone)
♭̸	lowers 90 cents (4 commas)	—	Figures 8, 9: A–B♭̸ = 114 (large half-tone)
♭	lowers 114 cents (5 commas)	lowers 100 cents	Figures 6, 7: A–B♭ = 90 (small half-tone)
𝄲	raises 23 cents (1 comma)	—	Figure 8: E–F𝄲 = 114 (large half-tone)
♯	raises 90 cents (4 commas	raises 100 cents	Figure 11: E–F♯ = 180 (small whole tone)
♯̸	raises 114 cents (5 commas)	—	

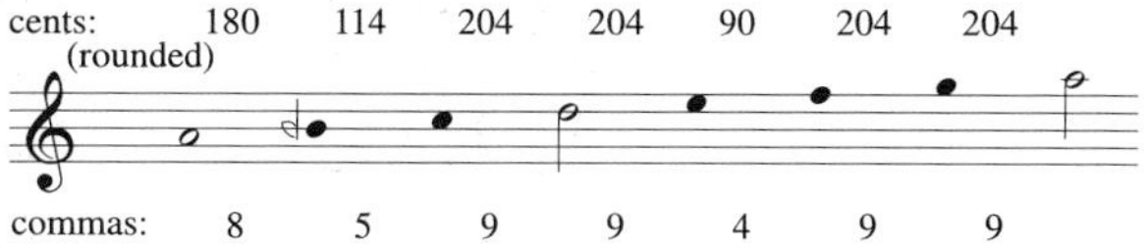

FIGURE 5 Intervals in *makam beyati* in commas and cents.

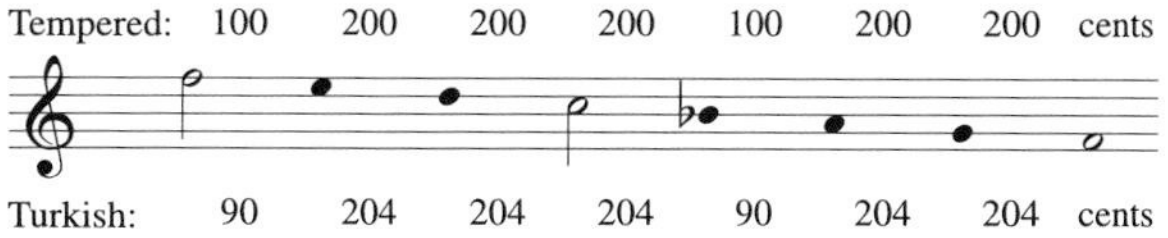

FIGURE 6 *Acemaşiran*: Western tempered intervals versus Turkish intervals.

that Turkish notation is a fifth higher than Arab notation; for instance, the Turkish *makam acemaşiran* ends on f whereas the Arab *ʿajam ʿushayrān* ends on B-flat.

Common practice in Western classical music relies on two scales, major and minor. The scale of the Turkish *makam acemaşiran* is close to the Western major scale (again, see figure 6). *Makam acemaşiran* is a "descending" scale, cadencing an octave below the starting point; Turkish theory represents it as descending from left to right. The scale of *makam nihavent* is close to the Western minor scale (figure 7).

The augmented-second intervals of *makam şehnaz* (figure 8) resemble scales familiar to Western listeners from pseudo-Near Eastern music such as the "Bacchanale" from Saint-Saëns's *Samson and Delilah*; the augmented-second interval is found in various positions in other *makamlar*. To non-Turkish ears, *makam saba* (figure 9) is one of the more exotic scales, with its diminished-fourth interval from its finalis to its fourth scalar degree.

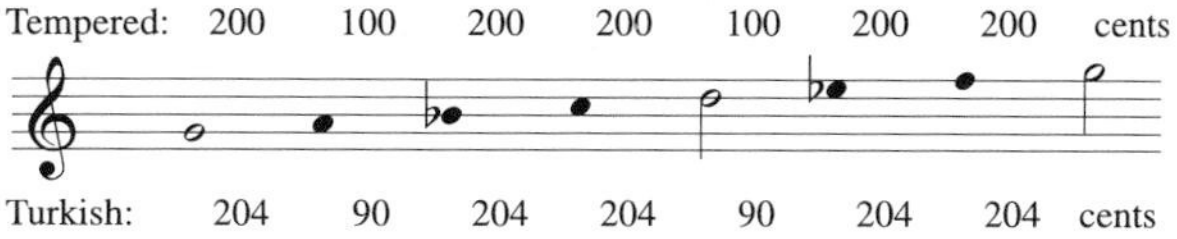

FIGURE 7 *Nihavent*: Western tempered intervals versus Turkish intervals.

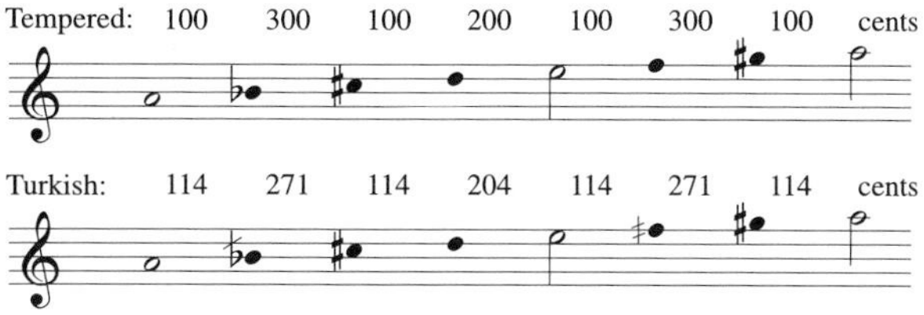

FIGURE 8 *Şehnaz*: Western tempered intervals versus Turkish intervals.

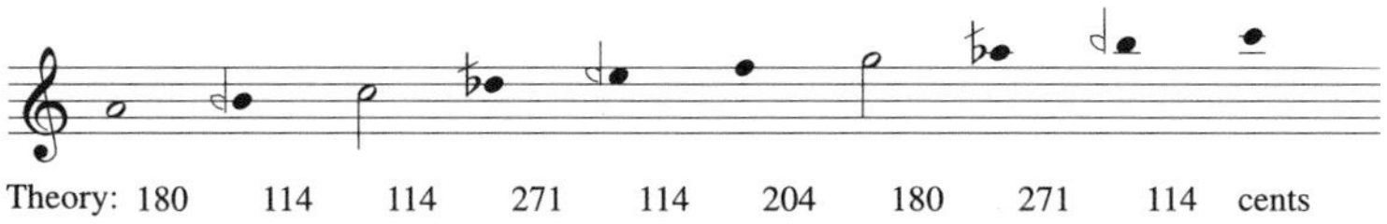

FIGURE 9 *Saba*: intervals

The scale of *makam rast* differs more perceptibly than *makam acemaşiran* from the Western major scale because the third degree of *rast* is clearly flatter than the comparable Western interval. In major scales, the first two intervals add up to 400 (200 + 200) cents; in *acemaşiran*, they add up to 408 (204 + 204); in *rast*, they add up to only 384 (204 + 180; figure 10). The scale of *makam beyati* overlaps that of *makam rast*, beginning on the second degree of *rast*, except for a consistent f-natural in *beyati* (figure 11). To the Western ear, *beyati* sounds similar to the descending melodic minor scale except for the slightly lower pitch *segah*, its second degree.

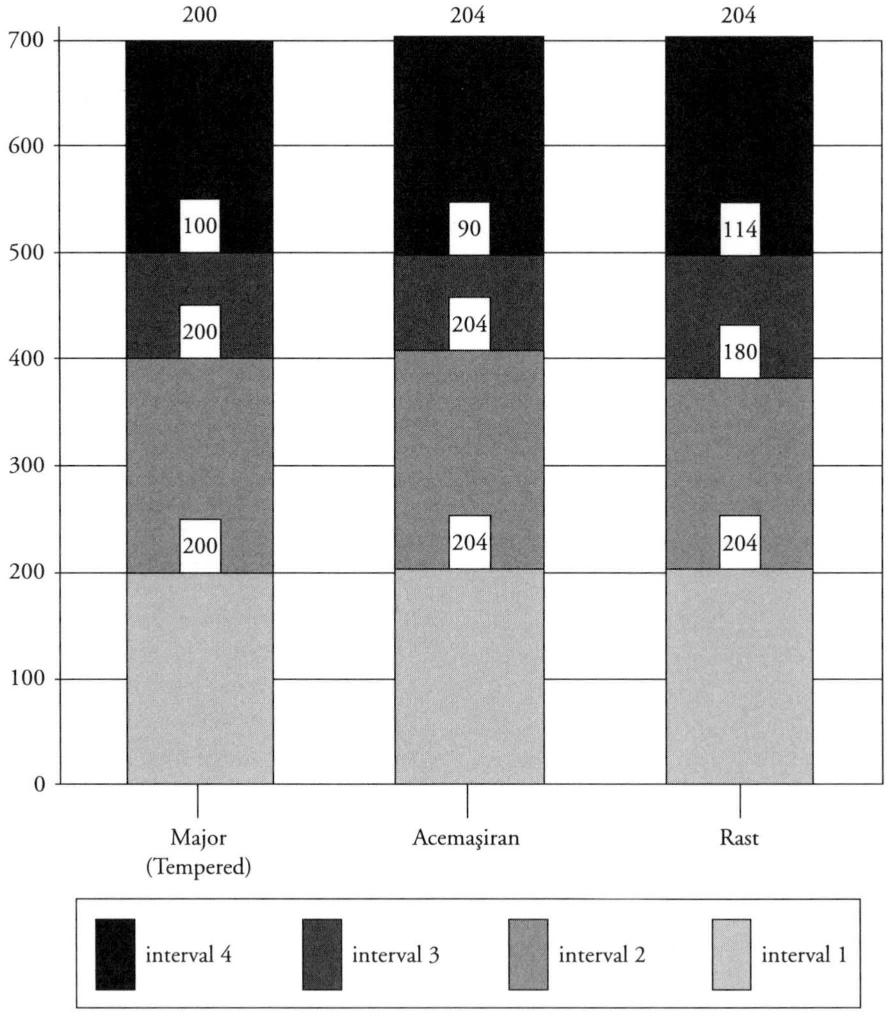

FIGURE 10 Comparison of major, *acemaşiran*, and *rast* pentachords.

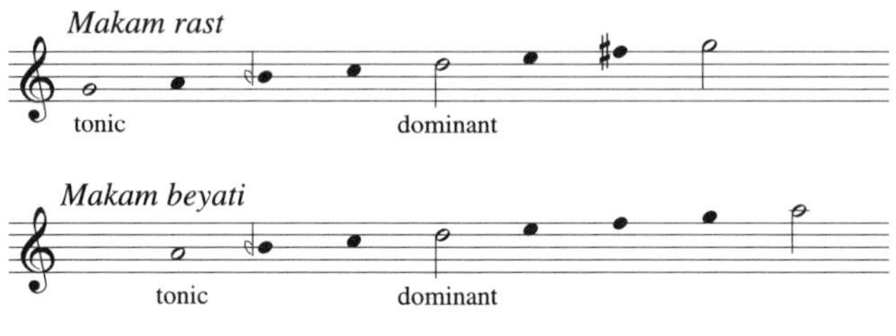

FIGURE 11 Overlap between *rast* and *beyati*.

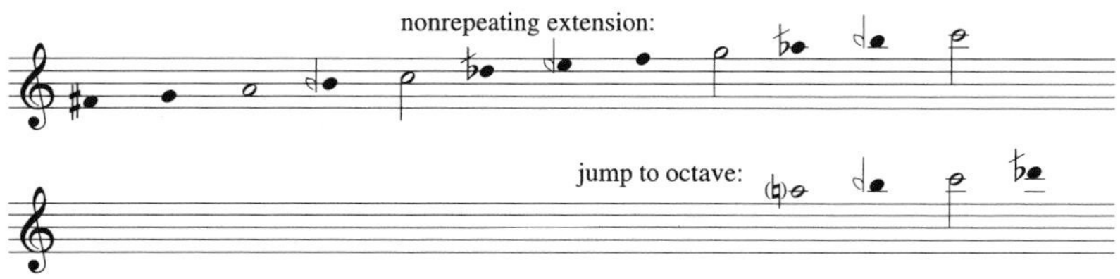

FIGURE 12 Extended *saba* scale and jump to octave.

Western tempered scale intervals repeat exactly in every octave. By contrast, a Turkish *makam* often has different intervals in different octaves. *Rast* repeats the same intervals starting an octave above the finalis, but *makam saba*, for example, does not, except when a performer deliberately jumps up an octave after establishing the *makam* to present it in a higher range (figure 12). *Beyati* commonly uses B-flat (a note called *sünbüle*) in the upper octave instead of B-comma-flat (called *tiz segah*; see figure 16 below, m. 17).

Melodic unfolding

Tonal centers

A scale is an abstract set of pitches that becomes music only when the musician brings it to life. For example: A melody might begin by repeating, holding, or circling around d (*neva*), showing the importance of this note as a backbone or tonal center of the *makam*. As the melody descends and begins to emphasize a (*dügah*), the scale, melodic motives, and tonal centers gradually suggest that *makam beyati* might be taking shape. Returning to d for a cadence makes it clear that d is the secondary tonal center, or the dominant (*güçlü*). A final cadence on a reveals that a is the primary tonal center, or tonic-finalis (*karar*), and confirms that the *makam* is *beyati* (figure 13). Other important tones in *beyati* include f (*acem*) and c (*çargah*).

TRACK 2 In Western music, the dominant is always a fifth higher than the tonic, but the Turkish dominant can be found on the third, fourth, or fifth degree above the tonic. In *makam rast*, the dominant is a fifth above the tonic, but the third degree strongly shapes its melodies. *Makam beyati* uses basically the same scale as *rast* and has the
TRACK 3 same dominant, but in *beyati* the tonic is the note that was the second degree in *rast* (refer back to figure 11).

Direction

If we travel in one direction on a street and then in the opposite direction, we almost seem to be moving along two different streets. *Makam hüseyni* begins in the middle of the octave, like *beyati*, but around e (*hüseyni*), a fifth above the tonic (rather than at d, as in *beyati*). A *hüseyni* melody will next descend to establish the tonic, then explore the upper range to the octave and above. *Makam muhayyer* uses the same scale

FIGURE 13 *Beyati seyir* (Yekta 1920–1931:3003). Yekta's notation, unlike modern notation, assumes B-comma-flat (that is, one-comma flat) without use of an accidental.

as *hüseyni* but begins an octave above the finalis and works its way gradually down to the tonic. These different melodic journeys give the listener an impression of different *makamlar*. Musicians and theorists recognize this difference by giving these *makamlar* different names.

Seyir

Western music theory simplifies sonata-allegro form for students. In Turkish music theory, *seyir* (plural, *seyirler*) is a melody that attempts to capture the essentials of a *makam* for students. Besides the scale and melodic direction, a *seyir* might reveal typical melodic patterns, ranges to be exploited, and notes to be emphasized. The repertoire of all compositions in a *makam* shows the full range of possibilities, but the *seyir* should give the essential features in brief.

Yekta provides a *seyir* for *beyati* (figure 13) and twenty-nine other *makamlar*. The *seyirler* by Yekta and M. N. Beken (figure 14) show a melodic progression basically the same as the exposition (up to *meyan*) of a *beyati* composition (see below, figure 16). Since classical Turkish music typically requires modulation within the exposition of the *makam*, a realistic *seyir* would include modulation. Beken's *seyir* includes a modulation typical of *beyati*, to *hicaz* on d.

Modulation

Definition

In Western music, modulation establishes a new tonal center, as in the first movement of *Eine kleine Nachtmusik*, in which Mozart establishes his first theme in G major, then modulates to the dominant (D major) to introduce his second theme. Turks use the word *geçki* 'modulation' for a shift to another *makam*, which could mean a shift of scale, tonal center or centers, and *seyir*. A modulation can be short and transitory—a *cins* 'taste' of another *makam*—or longer and even permanent (Signell 1986). Except for the simplest improvisation or composition, Turkish music requires modulation.

Obligatory modulation

Although we expect Mozart to modulate to another key for his second theme, we also expect him to return to the home key by the end of the first movement. We can say that his first movement is in G major although it modulates to other keys; indeed, modulations strengthen the sense of G major by providing a contrast. For most *makamlar*, the *seyir* would include an expected temporary modulation to another *makam*. *Makam acemaşiran* often modulates temporarily to *saba*, using a tonal center common to both, c (*çargah*; figure 15).

Among other possibilities, *makam beyati* often includes short modulations to *hicaz* on d and a taste of other *makamlar*, and sometimes a more substantial modulation to *saba* before returning to and cadencing in *beyati* (figure 16).

FIGURE 14 *Beyati seyir* by Yekta and M. N. Beken.

FIGURE 15 Temporary modulation to *makam saba* within *makam acemaşiran*.

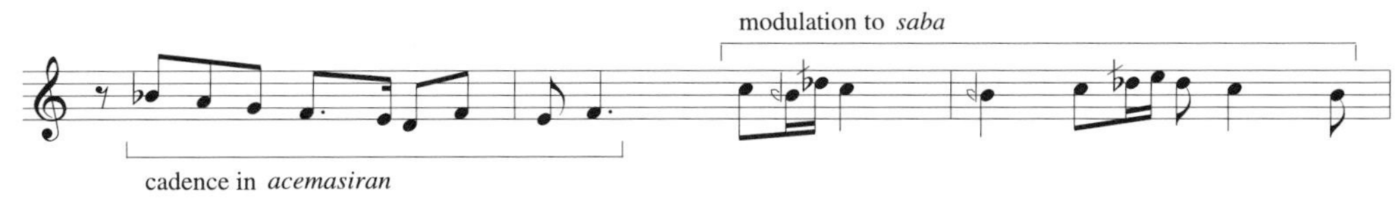

FIGURE 16 Modulations in a *beyati* composition. (This is the same composition as in figure 1.)

Compound makamlar

When a horticulturist grafts a cutting of a domesticated rose onto a wild stock, the two parts form a new, complex whole. Turkish composers, instead of inventing new *makamlar*, sometimes graft together two *makamlar* by starting a composition in one *makam*, modulating to another, and staying in the second until the end of the piece, creating a new tonal structure and a new ethos. *Makam beyati-araban* ends with *beyati*

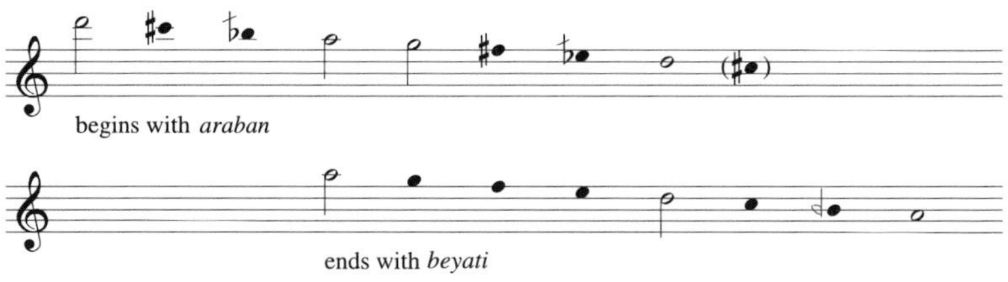

FIGURE 17 The two components of *makam beyati-araban*.

but begins with a different tessitura and different tonal materials (figure 17). Whereas *beyati* establishes its first tonal center a fourth above the finalis on d (*neva*), *beyati-araban* establishes its first tonal center an octave above the finalis on a (the pitch *muhayyer*). The *araban* tonal materials in the upper range are related to the augmented-second family of *hicaz* and *şehnaz* (refer back to figure 8).

Stereotyped motives

We often infer a person's nationality from his or her accent; people have many other, more complex characteristics, but an accent is something we can quickly hear and recognize. Similarly, one immediately recognizes some *makamlar* from a single motive that captures important structural notes. Stereotyped motives appear at the beginning or end of a composition or an improvisation. Some are universal; others are associated with a particular composer or performer (Signell 1986:125ff). When such motives appear, they are a kind of musical shorthand that quickly suggests the *makam* (figures 18 and 19). However, one should not expect to find a stereotyped motive in every composition or improvisation, and one should not jump to a conclusion about the intended *makam* before the performer sounds the finalis.

Tessitura

Tessitura can refer to the range of a *makam*. To bring order to a vast accumulation of *makamlar*, twentieth-century Turkish theorists organized some *makamlar* by scales that seemed to be the same, grouping them under the rubric of *şed* 'transposed' *makamlar*. Theorists considered *makamlar acemaşiran* and *mahur* as *makam çargah* transposed up a fourth and fifth, respectively. *Hicazkar* and *evcara* were considered *zirgüleli hicaz* transposed down a second and a minor third, respectively. In modern theory these transposed modes differ only in name, but performers recognize subtle differences. *Suzidil* and *şedaraban* are both described as descending *zirgüleli hicaz* transposed to different pitches, but each has its own *seyir*.

Tessitura could also refer to the ambitus of a *makam*. For example, *beyati* and *uşşak* have the same basic scale, but *beyati* quickly rises to the fourth degree and rarely descends below the finalis. *Uşşak* begins—unlike *beyati*—by dwelling in the area of the finalis and often descends one or two degrees below the finalis. Violating this rule runs the danger of violating the boundary between *beyati* and *uşşak*.

A listener familiar with these five criteria—scale, melodic unfolding, modulation, stereotyped motives, and tessitura—should be able to identify a *makam* with the reason-

FIGURE 18 Personal *beyati* motive by Neyzen Niyazi Sayın.

FIGURE 19 General stereotyped motives in *makamlar segah*, *şehnaz*, and *karcığar*.

able certainty that most Turkish musicians and theorists would agree. These rules hold within the narrow circle of elite performers in major centers of music in Turkey.

THE EMPIRICAL LEVEL: ALTERNATIVE EXPLANATIONS

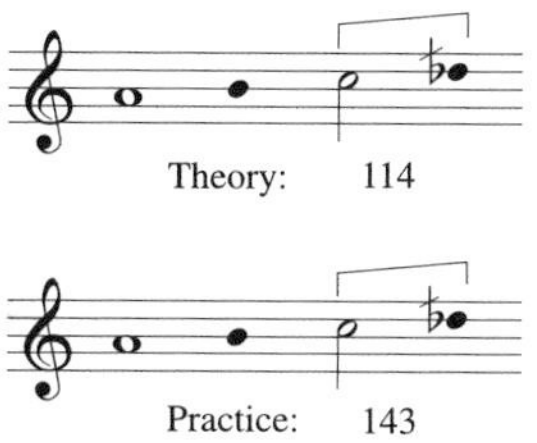

FIGURE 20 *Saba* interval: theory versus practice (Signell 1977:158).

Performers often find traditional theory puzzling. The *makamlar* they play and hear show more flexibility than traditional theory would imply. It is common knowledge among performers that pitches in performance vary from the theoretical pitches. Precise measurements confirm that performed intervals vary from one musical context to another and sometimes depart consistently and substantially from theoretical intervals (Signell 1986: app. A). In *makam saba*, for example, the fourth degree consistently measures an average of 29 cents higher in practice than in theory (figure 20).

Performers and many listeners also know that certain pitches are variable (*oynak*), depending on melodic context. In *makamlar beyati* and *uşşak*, for example, the performer will lower the b-one-comma-flat (the pitch *segah*) in a descending melodic line. When descending toward a final cadence, the performer will lower it even more, usually sliding toward the tonic (figure 21). Performers call this "warming" the pitch. One leading performer, Tanburi Necdet Yaşar, proposed names for three more pitches—making five in all—known to performers but not recognized in theory (Signell 1986:41). Further measurements are likely to show other differences between theory and practice. For example, the concept of a "transposed" *makam* simplifies subtle changes of tessitura, pitch, *seyir*, tonal color, and instrumental idiosyncracies when one finds a scale rendered at another pitch (Signell 1986: ch. 8).

A different paradigm: For larger questions of scale and *seyir*, an empirical methodology might help us understand the dynamic nature of the *makam*. Ignoring traditional theory, one could analyze data from performances, using the array of notes in each phrase as a building block of melodic development. A sequence of such arrays would make up the *seyir* of one performance. One could then observe the extent to which the artist uses tonal materials of the theoretical scale, and the extent to which the melodic line behaves in accordance with ideas presented in theory books.

Comparing performances, one will find some similar arrays, some different arrays, and some arrays that, although similar, appear at different places in the sequence. Such a comparison offers a transparent basis for determining which elements are required to establish a nominal *makam*, which are misleading or playful, and which are conclusive in nailing down the identity of the *makam*. This methodology allows researchers to test one another's conclusions. Anyone can gather and analyze data from other performances in the same *makam*, or from other *makamlar*. This type of analysis may offer a more persuasive explanation of Turkish *makam* than a rigid theory, by showing the relationship between personal choices of individual performers within commonly accepted boundaries (Beken and Signell, in press). A more complete understanding of the word *makam* and its context in Turkish music requires a deeper and fuller explanation of the relationship between the dynamic variability of each *makam* realization and the relatively static limits accepted by most musicians over time.

INDIVIDUALITY

No two speakers of English use the language in exactly the same way. Aside from gross differences between British, American, Indian, and other varieties of English, every

FIGURE 21 Lowered second degree in *makam beyati* in descending melody.

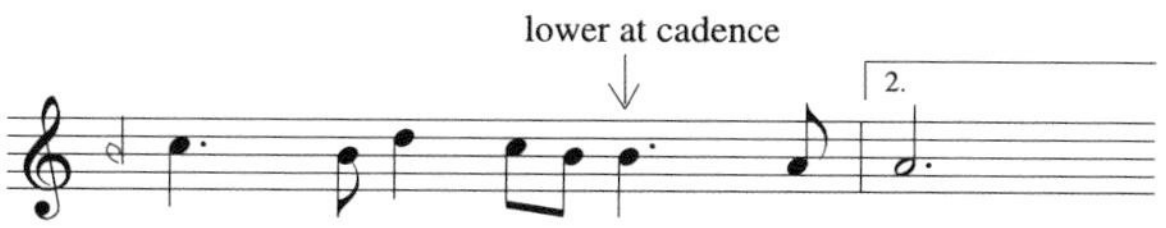

Each improvisation by a master musician shows his knowledge and understanding of the *makam* and its repertoire, his mood at the moment of creation, his personality, his virtuosity, and his musical intelligence.

speaker has a different understanding of words and syntax, based on personal history. Even for one individual, linguistic "performance" varies depending on the day, the year, the context, and the person's mood. No two performers of Turkish classical music understand *makam* in exactly the same way; nor does a single performer realize *makam* the same way from one day to the next or from one context to another. *Makam* exists only in its realization by individual composers and performers at specific times and in specific places.

In jazz, the personality and style of the interpreter are all-important. In Turkish music also, peers and listeners judge how well a performer brings the *makam* to life, touching the right bases while putting a personal stamp on it. This tension between the shared and the personal contributes greatly to the vitality of Turkish music.

A competent but unimaginative musician will observe all the rules of a *makam*, with correct intonation, expected modulations, and stereotyped motives at the right places. This musician does the job required, like a bureaucrat. A master musician might create a personal riff for a given *makam*, a motive that identifies the *makam* and the player (Signell 1986:125ff). More subtly, each improvisation by a master musician shows his knowledge and understanding of the *makam* and its repertoire, his mood at the moment of creation, his personality, his virtuosity, and his musical intelligence. No one can copy this type of performance; like jazz, it is personal and therefore all the more precious.

RELATED MUSICS

The nature of *makam* in contemporary elite Turkish musical circles becomes clearer in comparison with closely related musics. One cannot easily draw a line defining the limits of Turkish classical music. To varying degrees, performers of other kinds of music also participate in the classical tradition. Their interpretation of *makam* varies from that of the elite in ways that give us a fuller understanding of the contemporary realization of Turkish *makam*.

Historic repertoire

If we examine the classical repertoire in history, we find (as mentioned at the beginning of the article) that some *makamlar* have survived in name only, with no compositions to tell us what music these names represent. When contemporary performers approach the compositions that have survived from the sixteenth and seventeenth centuries (the early, anonymous Mevlevi compositions and pieces from the Cantemir and Ufkî collections), they can grasp the *makam* structures intellectually, but the melodic movement may be awkward for someone accustomed to the eighteenth-, nineteenth-, and twentieth-century repertoire. When they are called on to improvise in a *makam* found only in early compositions, musicians feel that they are on shaky ground. A performer can neither draw on a large and familiar repertoire in the *makam* nor create a *taksim* 'improvisation' by analogy to known *makamlar*. This is like asking a modern actor to improvise in the style of seventeenth-century *commedia dell'arte*.

Gypsy music

Gypsies and Gypsy style dominate Turkish nightclub (*gazino*, or *fasıl*) music—a context in which light compositions from the classical repertoire are often played in a lively style with plenty of improvisation and Gypsy intonation.

Gypsy intonation often differs from classical intonation. With the augmented-second interval between the second and the third degrees in *makam hicaz*, for example, Gypsies typically place the second degree a little higher and the third degree a little lower, making the augmented interval smaller than the classical one (figure 22). In any *makam*, for example *beyati*, a Gypsy will usually place the pitch *segah* lower than a classical musician would, approximately one comma flatter, more like the corresponding Arab pitch *sīkā*.

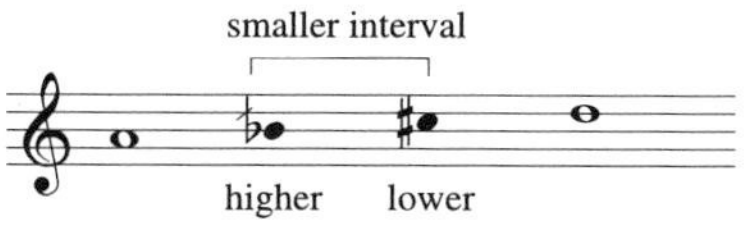

FIGURE 22 Smaller augmented second interval in *makam hicaz* in Gypsy intonation.

Turkish folk music

Mustafa Kemal Atatürk, founder of the modern republic in the 1920s, exalted Turkish folk music as purely Turkish, even Central Asian. He suppressed Turkish classical music as alien—as Middle Eastern. This policy led twentieth-century Turkish theorists to seek ways to make Turkish classical music seem more Turkish by drawing parallels to folk music. They looked for *makam* in folk music, matching classical scales with similar scales in folk song. However, they ignored the specifics of microtonal intonation, modulations, *seyir*, and even tonal centers so minutely prescribed by classical rules. This exercise reminds us that the borders of *makam* are permeable and that defining terms remains a crucial aspect of making comparisons.

EXTRAMUSICAL MEANING

Do not look for extramusical meanings of Turkish *makamlar* in the secular classical tradition in modern times. Vestiges linger in *makam* names such as *saba* (a light zephyr from the east) and *hicaz* (the Ḥijāz, formerly a kingdom, now a region of Saudi Arabia), but one would be hard-pressed to find a Turkish musician or theorist who would say that these *makamlar* still have any meaning associated with breezes or with Arabs. Twentieth-century treatises on *makam* mention no extramusical meanings. In 1972, an informal survey of musicians regarding extramusical meanings for *makamlar* received no consistent responses. Nor did secular classical performance practice in the last decades of the twentieth century prescribe any *makam* for times of the day, days of the week, or special occasions. However, the mosque and Turkish Jews represent an exception with regard to extramusical meaning.

Mosque

Turkish mosque music has preserved extramusical meanings that have disappeared from classical music. According to the noted liturgical singer Kâni Karaca, the first call to prayer (*ezan*, Arabic *adhān*) of the day should be sung in *makam saba*, and the other four *ezan* throughout the day should each be sung in specific *makamlar* (Signell 1970–1972: interview). This statement may apply only to an elite group, however, since no general agreement with it has been found. Professionally trained reciters seem to conform to published descriptions of specific *makamlar* for specific chapters of the *Mevlit* 'Nativity Poem' and *Miraciye* 'Ascension Poem' (Signell 1986:120–121).

Turkish Jews

In addition to the evidence from mosque music, there is indirect historical evidence from other ethnic groups in Turkey suggesting that there were stronger extramusical associations with *makam* in the past. Jewish cantors (*hazanim*) in urban centers such as Istanbul, Izmir, and Edirne were intimately familiar with Turkish classical music for centuries: they include İsak Fresko Romano ("Tanburi İsak"), a noted composer of the eighteenth and nineteenth century; İsak Algazi, one of the greatest singers of early twentieth-century Turkish classical music; and Jewish emigrants from Turkey to the United States in the late twentieth century. Like their coreligionists in many other parts of the world, Turkish Jews adopted local music practice for their liturgy.

The Jewish liturgy in Istanbul prescribed specific *makamlar* for specific times of day, for specific days, and for specific texts. Tradition prescribed a different *makam* for each of the Ten Commandments. A cantor who had been trained in Izmir and had studied with Algazi said, "As a matter of course, Sephardic Jewry recited all the passages of the Sabbath prayer in the specific *maqam* adapted to each particular Sabbath" (Seroussi 1989b). This small subset of contemporary Turkish *makam* practice preserved extramusical meanings that possibly link the history of Turkish music to that of Indian and Iranian classical music.

Makam is a word, like *music*, *Turkish*, *love*, or *God*. The meaning of words is elusive, ever-changing with time, place, context, and personal interpretation. To define such a word is to deny the very nature of words as representations—dynamic, rich markers of complex phenomena. When we talk of "Turkish music," then, we must say whether we mean music of the Ottoman Empire (which century?) or the Turkish Republic (which decade?), and what kind of music we mean—classical (in which circles?), folk, religious, Gypsy, military, arabesk, Turkish pop, Euro-pop, and so on. We can discuss *makam* in terms of well-documented theory and well-known practices that apply to a small cadre of elite musicians, but we must take into account a wide array of related musics, some as far apart as medieval Europe and contemporary India.

REFERENCES

Arel, H. Saadettin. 1968. *Türk Musikisi Nazariyatı Dersleri* (Lessons in Turkish Music Theory). Istanbul: Hüsnütabiat Matbaası.

Beken, Münir Nurettin, and Karl Signell. In press. "Confirming, Delaying, and Deceptive Elements in Turkish Improvisations." In *The Maqām Traditions of the Turkic Peoples. ICTM Study Group "Maqām," Proceedings of the Fourth Meeting, Istanbul, 18–24 October 1998*, ed. Jürgen Elsner and Yalçın Tura. Istanbul: Istanbul Technical University. (Complete transcriptions and audio recordings can be accessed at <http://research.umbc.edu/eol/makam>.)

Cemil Bey, Tanburi. c. 1910–1914. *Tanburi Cemil Bey*. Crossroads/Rounder TCRO426. (Compact disk. Early twentieth century: *makamlar saba* and *nihavent*.)

Ezgi, Subhi. 1933–1953. *Nazarî ve Amelî Türk Mûsikîsi* (Theory and Practice of Turkish Music). 5 vols. Istanbul: Hüsnütabiat.

Feldman, Walter. 1990. "Jewish Liturgical Music in Turkey." *Turkish Music Quarterly* 3(1):10–13.

Masters of Turkish Music. 1990. Rounder Records 1051. (Compact disk. Early twentieth century: *makamlar rast*, *beyati*, *hicaz*, *saba*, and *beyati-araban*.)

Masters of Turkish Music, Vol. 2. 1996. Rounder Records 1111. (Compact disk. Early twentieth century: *makamlar rast*, *hicaz*, *nihavent*, *saba*, *şehnaz*, *beyati*, *segah*.)

Münir Nurettin Beken: The Art of the Turkish Ud. 1997. Rounder Records 1135. (Compact disk. *Makamlar rast* and *hüseyni*.)

Necdet Yaşar Ensemble. 1989. *Music of the World* CDT-128. (*Makamlar nihavent*, *acemaşiran*, *segah*, and *saba*.)

Özkan, İsmail Hakkı. 1987. *Türk Mûsikîsi Nazariyatı ve Ussûlleri/Kudüm Velveleleri* (Turkish Music Theory and Rhythmic Cycles/Drum Ornamentations). Istanbul: Ötüken Neşriyat.

Seroussi, Edwin. 1989a. *Mizimrat Qedem: The Life and Music of R. Isaac Algazi from Turkey*. Jerusalem: Renanot-Institute for Jewish Music.

———. 1989b. "The Turkish *Makam* in the Musical Culture of the Ottoman Jews: Sources and Examples." *Israeli Studies in Musicology* 5:55–68.

———. 1991. "The *Peşrev* as a Vocal Genre in Ottoman Hebrew Sources." *Turkish Music Quarterly* 4(3):1–9.

Shiloah, Amnon. 1992. *Jewish Musical Traditions*. Detroit, Mich.: Wayne State University Press.

Signell, Karl. 1970–1972. Turkish tape recordings. Signell collection, Archive of Folk Culture, Library of Congress, Washington, D.C. (Recordings include concerts, interviews, mosque and Sufi musics, and many examples of *taksim*, *seyir*, and other genres. Index and copies available to qualified scholars.)

———. 1973. "Turkish Makam System in Contemporary Theory and Practice." Ph.D. dissertation, University of Washington. Ann Arbor, Mich.: UMI Research Press.

———. 1977. *Makam: Modal Practice in Turkish Art Music*. Seattle, Wash.: Asian Music Publications.

———. 1986. *Makam: Modal Practice in Turkish Art Music*. New York: Da Capo.

Yekta Bey, Raouf. 1920–1931. "La musique turque." In *Encyclopédie de la musique*, ed. Albert Lavignac, Part 1, 5:2945–3064. Paris: C. Delagrave.

The Concept of Mode in Iranian Music: *Shūr*

Margaret Caton

Poetry and Mode
Māye
Forūd
Motaghayyer
Pitch Hierarchy
Gūshe
Dastgāh
Radīf
Ethos
Historical Note

The concept of mode in Iranian music can be hard to grasp, and though it has long been studied by musicologists, it still remains somewhat ambiguous. In particular, Iranian musical practices are difficult to fit into a Western concept of mode as defined by scale and tonal centers. To some extent, this lack of clarity reflects the mysterious and ineffable nature of Iranian classical music.

In former eras, mode was referred to as *maqām* (plural, *maqāmāt*), a term still used in Arab and Turkish music. In current practice the term *māye* 'essence' conveys the sense of mode. *Māye* refers to the foundation or basis of something; *māye* is the essential ingredient without which a product or enterprise cannot come into being or develop. For example, you need *māye* 'ferment', 'leaven' to start and make yogurt, bread, or cheese, and you need *māye* 'capital' to start a business. In music, *māye* refers to the distinctive or defining features of a mode, such as scale and melodic tendencies.

Mode in Iranian music is conveyed by a loosely unified set of melodic patterns that may be varied in different ways. These melodies are the basis for the expression and communication of feeling through inspired improvisation. In Iranian classical music there may be hundreds of melodic patterns and progressions, and though many of them exist in common practice, each master musician retains and develops his own *radīf* 'repertoire' (plural, *radīf-hā*) with his own style or version of these progressions.

In Iranian music, the simple mode *shūr* is considered the most fundamental and perhaps the most characteristic. The modal complex—the *dastgāh* (plural, *dastgāh-hā*)—of *shūr* has been referred to by Iranians as the mother *dastgāh* (Sadeghi 1971:36), perhaps because it has the most extensive repertoire and has been the source for the development of four subsidiary modal complexes, as well as being related or similar to many other modal complexes in the *radīf* of Iranian music. Many Iranian folk melodies are based on this modal configuration or its derivatives. In addition, *shūr* is usually the first *dastgāh* in the organization of the *radīf*, and its tuning (for example, *shūr* on g) is often a reference point for finding other modes and their starting notes (During and Mirabdolbaghi 1991:72; Farhat 1990:27; Sadeghi 1971:36–37; Zonis 1973:67).

The *radīf* itself is not performed as such but serves as the basis for performance. Traditionally an *ostād* 'master teacher' transmits the *radīf* to students by aural instruction, beginning with the *dastgāh* of *shūr*. Within a single *dastgāh*, the *radīf* consists of a progression of melodies and melodic formulas often presented in an unfolding developmental order that outlines an arch. Each individual melody is usually referred to as a *gūshe* (plural, *gūshe-hā*), though there are some differences as to what actually constitutes a *gūshe* and which melodies in the current versions of the *radīf* conform to this conceptualization.

POETRY AND MODE

Traditional Iranian music is essentially melodic, exploring and ornamenting different tones of emphasis that progress in a primarily stepwise manner, which is suitable for supporting and interacting with poetry. The form, rhythm, and feeling of the classical repertoire (the *radīf*) is closely aligned with Iranian poetry. A lyric poetic form, *ghazal*, is used as the basis for the vocal form of the *radīf*, the *āvāz*. Other poetic forms, such as *dobeytī* and *masnavī*, also appear consistently.

The *ghazal* is a lyric poem of five to seventeen lines, with each line or distich divided into two hemistiches. Each melodic section, or *gūshe*, is sung to a different line or two of poetry, typically from the same *ghazal* throughout a vocal performance of a *dastgāh*. The sequence of a vocal *gūshe* would be, for example, a vocalized introductory phrase, one or two lines of poetry with pauses between hemitiches, and vocalized ornamentation at the end of each line and the end of the *gūshe*.

According to Tsuge, the rhythm and phrasing of the *gūshe-hā* are related to the rhythm of the poetry (1974:168, 175–176). The treatise *Bohūr al-Alḥān* suggests that certain poetic meters are compatible with certain modes (During and Mirabdolbaghi 1991:155–156). Persian musical theory, such as that found in *Bohūr al-Alḥān*, associates a different ethos with each mode. The musician may choose a poem that contains a suitable sentiment for the mode, or perhaps choose a suitable mode for the sentiment of the poetry.

It may be suggested that the melodic phrasing is based at least in part on the requirements of the vocal-poetic form, and that this melodic form also finds its way into the purely instrumental rendition of the *āvāz*. According to Morteza Varzi (an *ostād* of the *kamānche*, a type of bowed lute), "the *dastgāh* exists not in and of itself but only as an aid to poetry, to impart a kind of feeling that brings out the meaning of the poetry" (personal communication 1 May 2000).

MĀYE

Shūr is the most prevalent mode if the criterion is the scalar configuration g–a-*koron* 'half-flat' (roughly)–b-flat–c, which is the focus of the mode, or *māye* (During and Mirabdolbaghi 1991:46, 60; Farhat 1990:23), as found in the introductory section—the *darāmad* 'entrance'—of the *dastgāh* of *shūr*, that is, *dastgāh-e shūr*. This tetrachord appears in many different patterns in the classical Iranian modal system. In addition to being the characteristic tetrachord in the *darāmad* of *shūr*, it appears throughout the *dastgāh* of *shūr* on different pitch levels and also in the final cadence (*forūd*) of many individual melodic formulas in the *dastgāh*, as well as in the concluding cadence. (A pitch level is roughly analogous to a tonal area and pitch emphasis.) It also occurs in the subsidiary *dastgāh-hā* of *shūr* (*abū 'aṭā*, *dashtī*, *afshārī*, and *bayāt-e tork*) as well as in other *dastgāh-hā* such as *navā* and *māhūr*. The same scale degrees in one melody, however, may have a different pattern and pitch emphasis in another and possibly a different emotional connotation, ethos, and effect.

Shūr is the name for a simple mode, or *māye* (as found, for example, in the *darāmad*), which uses the tetrachord g–a-*koron*–b-flat–c, and also for melodic extensions beyond the tetrachord as found in the rest of the *dastgāh* of *shūr*. In one sense, the *dastgāh* of *shūr* may be considered an expansion and development of the initial theme, or *māye*, of *shūr*. Another way of looking at the development of the modal structure in the *dastgāh* can be derived from the term itself. A *dastgāh* 'framework', 'structure' can be likened to the posts and beams of a room. The *darāmad* 'entrance' implies a doorway to that room, and the *gūshe-hā* 'corners' are the four corners and walls. *Dastgāh* also means a loom, and weaving a tapestry of musical motifs is an apt metaphor for music in Iran, a country known for its ornamental carpet designs.

As noted above, a *dastgāh* may be considered a modal complex, consisting of an evolving progression of melodies. In *shūr*, as in other *dastgāh-hā*, this overall progression has the contour of an arch. That is, the *dastgāh* progresses from a low pitch level to the highest point (*owj*) and then, at the conclusion, returns to the original tonal level. These changes occur by extending the melodic range through shifting tonal emphases.

An *ostād* would teach his students the *darāmad* and *gūshe-hā* within the *dastgāh* of *shūr*, each piece taught in order, according to its place in this systematic progression of gradual ascent and return. This particular organization may serve a number of purposes. First, it is a way of increasing and then resolving emotional tension. Second, it corresponds with Iranian mystical philosophy as found in Sufism and expressed in the poetry used in the vocal performance of the *dastgāh*. In this philosophy, the material world is contrasted with the spiritual world through the heightened progression of pitch levels. Third, the arrangement of *gūshe-hā* in this systematic order becomes a mnemonic device in a culture where the traditional musical repertoire was transmitted orally. It can be noted that despite the traditional order of the *gūshe-hā* in the *radīf*, in actual performance the musician is free to choose which *gūshe-hā* to play and, to a certain extent, in what order.

The musical basis and origin of the *gūshe*, and of the *dastgāh*, can be found in some historical treatises on Persian and Arab music, which emphasize different forms of the tetrachords and pentachords forming the octave. This focus on four- and five-note patterns is found today in many of the *gūshe-hā* that form the *dastgāh*. The melodic *ambitus* is extended by auxiliary tones both above and below the central tones, and by shifts in the tonal centers.

Persian music has been conceptualized theoretically within the framework of a tetrachord system (Barkeshli 1976:65; Zonis 1973:30). A seven-tone octave scale can be derived, however, from the overlay of melodies that make up the particular mode. The initial *māye* (mode) of *shūr* in the *darāmad* section may be focused on the tetrachord g–a-*koron*–b-flat–c but in fact makes use of an extended range as found in a number of *radīf-hā* (Farhat 1990:27; Karimi 1978:14; Sadeghi 1971:58). See figure 1.

Transposition and modulation do occur within *dastgāh-hā*; thus the actual tones and intervallic relations would shift as the tonalities shift. Modulation to the *gūshe* of *shahnāz*, for example, involves both a shift in the extended melodic range of the *darāmad* and a change of tuning, and also functions as a transposition of the original *shūr* tetrachord to a higher level (figure 2). A return to *shūr* would involve a reference to d-natural.

Persian music uses whole tones, semitones, and neutral tones. In the *shūr* tetrachord, the neutral tones, for example, occur between g and a-*koron* and between a-*koron* and b-flat. This particular neutral tone is roughly equivalent to a three-quarter tone (between a semitone and a whole tone). There are also five-quarter tones that

FIGURE 1

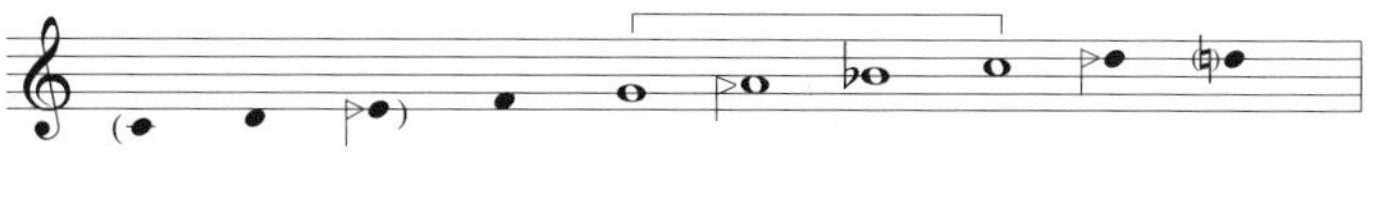

FIGURE 2

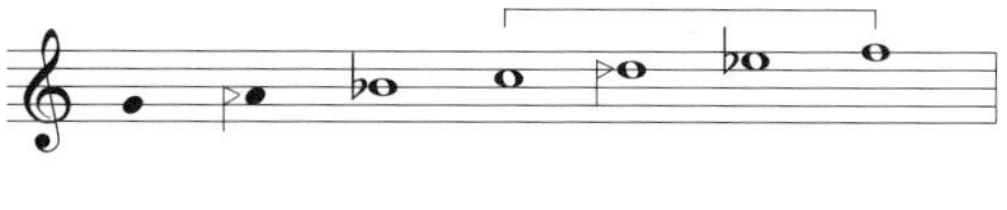

occur in other *dastgāh-hā*. This neutral tone does not imply exact measurement, and some modes may use a neutral tone that is higher or lower in pitch than others. Farhat (1990:15–16) discusses the concept of a flexible neutral tone; he identified two basic types: a small neutral tone (135 cents) and a large neutral tone (160 cents). There has been much study and discussion of the origin, position, and number of these tonal possibilities, in theoretical treatises from at least as early as the ninth century C.E. (Barkeshli 1976:i–ii; Farhat 1990:4–5; Wright 1978:6–8). Regardless of theoretical and scientific measurements, however, the actual tuning of these neutral intervals may vary.

According to Varzi (personal communication), each performer has his own "*koron*," which is not precise but variable—different at different times. Each geographical area may have its own "*koron*" as well. These styles and preferences fall within a limited range of flexibility in the choice of the intonation of the *koron*. Varzi feels that the sadder the mode, the flatter (or smaller) the *koron*; thus, for instance, *shūr* would tend to have a smaller neutral tone and *chahārgāh* a larger one. In addition, it appears that the use of the tetrachord g–a-*koron*–b-flat–c involves a flatter a-*koron* than the tetrachord g–a-*koron*–b-natural–c (*chahārgāh*, *eṣfahān*, and *homāyūn*), so that the size of the initial three-quarter or neutral tone may be influenced by its relationship to the third tone (that is, whether it is the minor or major third). Therefore, the larger the third, the sharper the second.

FORŪD

In the *dastgāh*, cadential patterns are referred to as *forūd*. They may be an auxiliary tone above or below the final tone, they may be a phrase, or they may be listed as a separate *gūshe*. They appear throughout the *dastgāh*, serving as conclusions to phrases and *gūshe-hā*, as links within *gūshe-hā* (for example, resolution to the original *māye* after a melodic extension), as connections between *gūshe-hā*, and as resolutions of developmental modulations in the return to the original mode at the end of the *dastgāh* of *shūr*.

In simple *shūr*, the cadential pattern may include the auxiliary tone below or above; the two tones below (with a raised sixth: e-*koron*); or the fourth above, c (Farhat 1990:27–28). The *forūd* phrase that involves a return to *shūr* from a modulation to an upper tetrachord may also include the fifth scale degree in a raised position, d-natural. To a certain extent, this may have an effect similar to the tendency in some Western classical music to shift to a major tonality at the end of a piece in a minor key. Figures 3 and 4 show two versions of this type of *forūd*. In Ṣabā's *santūr radīf* (figure 5), a *forūd* pattern in the *darāmad* is used with d-natural in the tetrachord below the *shūr* tetrachord.

MOTAGHAYYER

The fifth step of the scale of *shūr* (d) may be raised or lowered in specific contexts (d-*koron*, d-natural). This changing tone—a phenomenon that is present in other

FIGURE 3 Excerpt from *Chahārmeżrāb* (Ma'rūfī 1973:10, no. 12).

dastgāh-hā as well—is referred to as *moteghayyer*. When the melodic *ambitus* is extended in the *darāmad* of *shūr* and related *gūshe-hā*, the upper fifth degree may be in the lower position (d-*koron*); see figure 6. Thus, in the *darāmad* section of Ma'rūfī's *shūr radīf*, d-*koron* appears to be used as an upper auxiliary to c.

FIGURE 4 Excerpt from *Naghme* (Ma'rūfī 1973:11, no. 13).

FIGURE 5 Excerpt from *Darāmad* (Ṣabā 1965:25).

FIGURE 6 Excerpt from *Darāmad-e Sevvom* 'Third *Darāmad*' (Ma'rūfī, 1973:2).

FIGURE 7 Excerpt from *Kereshme* (Maʿrūfī 1973:4, no. 8)

FIGURE 8 Excerpt from *Kereshme* (Maʿrūfī 1973:6–7, no. 10).

In the second *Kereshme* (number 8; see figure 7), d-natural is used in a melodic passage with an ascent to f. However, the third *Kereshme* (number 10; see figure 8) uses d-*koron* in conjunction with a phrase using f. The (subtle) difference is that in the phrase with d-natural, the passage appears to be ascending from c to f, whereas in the phrase with d-*koron* it is descending from f to c.

This upper tetrachord (c–f) is also associated with a modulation to *Shahnaz*, for example, where d-*koron* is fixed and not a *motaghayyer*. Extensions into this upper tetrachord, in addition to using d-*koron* as an auxiliary to c, can eventually result in a shift of tonal centers with the upper c rather than g becoming the cadence tone.

Iranian instruments may shift octaves for the sake of melodic variety or because of the limitations of a particular instrument (such as the *santūr*, a hammered dulcimer, which is often tuned in the upper two octaves to d-*koron* and the lower octave to d-natural). Consequently, octave shifts may involve different forms of d (d-*koron*, d-natural) that may not necessarily be a function of its role as a *moteghayyer*.

FIGURE 9 Excerpt from *Zirkesh-e Salmak* (Maʿrūfī 1973: 12, no. 15).

With *Zirkesh-e Salmak* and *Salmak*, the d comes to have what is perhaps the intended connotation of a changing tone, in that the alternation of d-*koron* and d-natural is an essential part of the melodic and modal characteristics of these *gūshe-hā*. In *gūshe-hā* numbers 15 through 19, d-natural is again associated with phrases that use upper f and also g as an important structural element of the melody, and d-*koron* appears to function as an auxiliary reference to c (figure 9). Note that in Iranian musical notation, an accidental is retained until it is canceled.

Subsequent *gūshe-hā*, numbers 20 through 23—*Mollānāzī*, *Moghadame-ye Golrīz*, and *Moḥammed Ṣādeq Khāni*—also use the *motaghayyer*. It is possible that these *gūshe-hā* act as connections between *shūr* and *gūshe-hā* in the higher tetrachord with the *finalis* (see below) on c, and that part of their character may be a sense of shifting tonality.

The fifth step in *shūr* is a *motaghayyer*, but when a modulation takes place to the next higher tetrachord with a cadence on the fourth (c in *rāst kūk*), this same fifth step commonly remains lowered, as in *Shahnāz*. This tone would be raised (d-natural) only in a cadence back to the mode *shūr*. For instance, in *Golrīz* (number 24; see figure 10), d is no longer used as a *motaghayyer*, because c has become the new *finalis*.

It may be noted that at this point the upper tetrachord duplicates the intervallic relations of the *shūr* tetrachord, with d functioning as the second degree of this new tetrachord rather than as the fifth degree as it does in *shūr* proper.

PITCH HIERARCHY

Besides the use of a particular set of tones that progressively shifts and unfolds, Iranian modes are characterized by melodic tendencies, with certain tones having specific roles, such as the *motaghayyer*. The tone that usually starts a *gūshe* is called *āghāz* 'beginning'. Melodic activity revolves around a pitch called the *shāhed* 'witness tone'. Intermediate cadences may resolve to an *ist* 'stopping pitch' that may or may not be the same as the final pitch of the *gūshe*, which has been referred to as the *forūd-e kāmel* (Caron and Safvate 1966:42) or *finalis* (Farhat 1990:4; Sadeghi 1971:58). In the *darāmad* of *shūr* on g, the *shāhed* (melodic tonal center), *īst*, and *finalis* are the same, g (based on the generic tuning for the male vocal range, or *rāst kūk*). Farhat (1990:27) lists the *āghāz* as the f below the g, but in fact some *gūshe-hā* in *shūr* also begin on g. A melodic contour is shaped from this pitch hierarchy, and in the case of *shūr* the emphasis is on the descending line, although the overall melodic line is an arch.

Studies may find that *shūr* uses a seven-tone scale, such as g–a-*koron*–b-flat–c–d–e-flat–f–g (Caron and Safvate 1966:59). However, for each individual melodic section of a performance, the focus is usually on a more limited portion of the tonal

FIGURE 10 *Golrīz* (Maʿrūfī 1973:19, no. 24).

FIGURE 11 *Darāmad, chap kūk*, on d, vocalized on "ah" (Karīmī 1978:1, no. 1).

possibilities. As has been mentioned, it is common for four or five tones to be the basis for melodic development. For example, in the transcription of the vocal *radīf* of Maḥmūd Karīmī (in *chap kūk*, or *shūr* on d), the opening *darāmad* first establishes the tonal center as d, with c as a lower auxiliary tone. The second phrase increases the melodic range to f, and the subsequent phrase increases it to g. The third returns the top pitch to f, and the final phrase is cadential (figure 11).

GŪSHE

What is sometimes considered unique about Iranian modes is the method of presentation in melodic formulas that convey scale, *ambitus*, range, progression, and melodic shape. The concept of *gūshe* itself is not necessarily the same as mode, which (as noted above) may be better conveyed by the term *māye*. Two *gūshe-hā* with recognizably different melodies may be constructed on what is essentially the same mode. However, it is more likely that these *gūshe-hā* will also differ in pitch emphasis and range and thus constitute at least a modal variation, if not a different mode. Some scholars consider each named melody in the *radīf* a *gūshe* (Nettl 1987:21–24). Farhat (1990:22) considered the *darāmad* distinct from the *gūshe-hā* that follow and considered a smaller melodic pattern in the repertoire a *tekke* 'piece'. In this article, I have called each melody in the *radīf-hā* of Ma'rufi and Karīmī a *gūshe* for purposes of identification and discussion.

A number of scholars have identified a hierarchy of *gūshe-hā* ranging in type from those that constitute the basic elements of the *dastgāh* structure to those that connect or vary the main *gūshe-hā*. Nettl, in his study of the *radīf* (1987:26–27), described twelve types of *gūshe-hā* in order of significance. Sadeghi (1971:56–63) described a three-level hierarchy: *shāh-gūshe-hā* 'kings', secondary *gūshe-hā*, and fixed *gūshe-hā*. An important *gūshe*, such as *shahnāz*, may be called a *shāh-gūshe* (Caron and Safvate 1966:112; Sadeghi 1971:56–57). The more important *gūshe-hā* are those that appear to be more distinct structurally as well as melodically, whereas the secondary and perhaps tertiary *gūshe-hā* are often more melodically distinct than structurally distinct and may even have fairly fixed melodies. The first type—the central *gūshe-hā*—is the basis for improvisation which is more extensive than that in the more melodically defined *gūshe-hā*.

Some pieces, called rhythmic *tekke-hā* by Farhat, are characterized by specific rhythms. The *kereshme*, for example, uses a hemiola pattern and may be found in different *dastgāh-hā*. The instrumental form *chahārmeżrāb* (which is not a *tekke*) uses a short repeating rhythmic pattern as an underlying basis for improvisation or composition in a *gūshe* (Farhat 1990:109–120; Sadeghi 1971:69–73; Zonis 1973:131–137). While a *chahārmeżrāb* may be included in some *radīf-hā*, it may not be distinguished modally from the *gūshe* within which it occurs.

Although in current practice each *gūshe* does not necessarily constitute a different mode, it is hard to state this with certainty, owing to differences of opinion as to what constitutes a mode. This would depend on whether pitch placement, order, melodic-rhythmic characteristics, and subtleties of melodic contour and pitch emphasis actually constitute a different mode, or whether they are simply realizations, extensions, or variations of the same mode.

Iranian performers, in particular, use the term *māye* (During and Mirabdolbaghi 1991:62, 77–79; Farhat 1990:23), which is a more condensed, abbreviated version of a *gūshe* and has a closer resemblance to the concept of mode as the essential formula or outline for improvisation. You may ask a performer to play the *māye* of *shūr*, for example, and he may play a bit of the *darāmad*; or he may improvise briefly, indicating the basic pitches and melodic direction.

Some observers may consider each *gūshe* as constituting a different mode, on the basis of subtle differentiations in contour or melodic formula. However, in the case of a more important or developed *gūshe*, there may be more than one piece that would fit within essentially the same modal parameters in terms of *ambitus*, scale, and pitch hierarchy, though the actual melodies may differ. Additional *gūshe-hā* using that same tonal material might then be considered different realizations of the modal possibilities presented by the main *gūshe*. Often, however, these additional *gūshe-hā* or versions may extend the pitch range or explore a slightly different part of the scale. In his compiled *radīf*, for example, Ma'rufi (1973:1–6) presents more than one *darāmad* for *shūr*, some of which extend the melodic range to the neutral fifth and flat sixth (d-*koron* and e-flat). Other *gūshe-hā* found in the first part of the *dastgāh* of *shūr* may explore a different part of the *shūr* scale from that found in the *darāmad*. For example, the *gūshe-hā* of *zīrkesh-e salmak* and *salmak* extend the range of *shūr*, exploring the upper tetrachord (c–d-*koron*/d-natural–e-flat–f), then returning to the original cadence tone of *shūr* on g (Ma'rufi 1973:12–15).

The number of *gūshe-hā* in the *radīf-hā* of different master musicians varies. To what extent the *gūshe-hā* in *shūr* proper represent different modes would depend on how finely one distinguishes *ambitus*, contour, and melodic as well as rhythmic characteristics. For example, Karīmī's *radīf* lists fifteen different melodies, while Maʿrūfī's *radīf*, which may be a compilation of some different *radīf-hā*, lists seventy. Some of these melodies are tertiary or fixed or are forms such as *chahārmeżrāb* or *kereshme* that may appear in other *dastgāh-hā* and may not be considered distinct *gūshe-hā*.

Babiracki and Nettl studied eighteen *radīf-hā* of *shūr* and identifed fifty distinct *gūshe-hā* distributed among them. Only three *gūshe-hā* (*darāmad*, *salmak*, and *qarache*) appeared in all eighteen *radīf-hā*; Babiracki and Nettl suggested that this may have been due to historical change and sampling. Eight *gūshe-hā* (*darāmad*, *żirkesh-e salmak*, *salmak*, *bozorg*, *dobeytī*, *shahnāz*, *qarache*, and *rażavī*) were common to most of the eighteen *radīf-hā*. The order of the *gūshe-hā* varied somewhat (Nettl 1987:86–87).

DASTGĀH

Maʿrūfī's and Karīmī's *radīf-hā* use a range of about two octaves for the *dastgāh* of *shūr* (figure 12). These octaves may be divided roughly into four tetrachords or pentachords, with three ascending tetrachords with similar intervallic relations based on the tonic, fourth, and octave, though the highest tetrachord often uses a flat second (the tuning for the *santur* in Ṣabā 1965:4). The fourth tetrachord, below the tonic, is used in some cadences, and in the *darāmad-e khārā* of *shūr* (figure 13). Because of differences in the pitch hierarchy, location in the *dastgāh*, and melodic-rhythmic characteristics, the melodies in these different tetrachord ranges are considered distinct

FIGURE 12

FIGURE 13 *Darāmad-e Khārā*, *chap kūk*, on d (Karīmī 1978:2, no. 3).

gūshe-hā and are thus distinguished from the basic *māye* of *shūr* as found in the *darāmad*.

The *dastgāh* has been equated with the concept of modal complex (Powers 1980:426–427). The question remains whether the concept of *shūr* as a mode can be applied to each of the *gūshe-hā* that make up the *dastgāh* and to the *dastgāh* as a whole, or whether it applies solely to the mode of the *darāmad* and subsequent cadential returns to that mode. There are a number of *gūshe-hā* that extend the range of the initial *shūr* tetrachord, shifting the tonal emphases and creating segues between this tetrachord and, say, the next higher tetrachord (as found in the *gūshe* of *shahnāz*, where the cadence pitch is raised a fourth, c as opposed to g). Does the return to the initial *shūr* cadence in these intermediate *gūshe-hā* mean that they are an extension or variation of *shūr* proper, or are they already in another mode? In some ways this is a matter of semantics. Certainly these *gūshe-hā* are distinguished from the *darāmad*, while at the same time being grouped in the same basic tetrachord as the *darāmad*, using the same cadence tone. It is the shift to the next higher tetrachord with a change in cadence tone that indicates a real departure from the simple mode *shūr*, even though this new section uses a transposed version of the initial *shūr* tetrachord: c–d-*koron*–e-flat–f.

The order of *gūshe-hā* differs in different *radīf-hā*. The development and unfolding of the melodic and modal progression are somewhat flexible, following an overall upward progression with periodic references or returns to the original mode *shūr*. The logic of the *dastgāh* performance, or of the modal progression, would be to explore and realize the possibilities in a particular modal region; then to extend its range incrementally; and finally, after exploring this extension, return to the cadence pitch. In *shūr*, the range of melodic expression is gradually extended until the melodic focus shifts to a higher tetrachord, at which point a new cadence pitch is introduced. Thus the melodic focus of the first section of *shūr* progresses to higher and higher pitch levels until the tonic is shifted to c. Periodically, however, at certain points in the *dastgāh* of *shūr* after the tonic c has been introduced, references are made to the original *shūr* tetrachord by using a final cadence to g. Modir (1986:63–84) presents interesting comparative diagrams of several *shūr radīf-hā* that show melodic focus and periodic cadential returns to *shūr*.

In reviewing Ma'rūfī's *radīf*, as an example, the *darāmad* section begins in the *shūr* tetrachord g–c, using lower f as a cadential auxiliary tone. The fourth *gūshe*, which is the third *darāmad*, introduces d-*koron* as an upper auxiliary to c and then adds e-flat. *Gūshe* number 8, *Kereshme*, adds the upper f and also introduces d-natural. Throughout the initial ten *gūshe-hā*, the cadence returns to g, with the melodic focus on the *shūr* tetrachord.

In *gūshe* number 11, *Āvāz*, the cadence is on c for the first time. The melodic focus of the *chahārmeżrāb*, which follows (number 12), is on c but uses the g cadence as *īst* and *finalis*. This is the first time the modulatory *forūd* to *shūr* on g is used at the end of the *gūshe*. *Naghme* (number 13) continues the melodic focus on c, using the g *forūd* as *īst* and the modulatory g *forūd* at the end.

Gūshe-hā numbers 15 through 21 (*Zīrkesh-e Salmak*, *Salmak*, and *Mollānāzī*) focus more on the upper f than previous *gūshe-hā* do, with perhaps more emphasis on the upper tetrachord, using the *motaghayyer*, though these *gūshe-hā* continue to use the g cadence. *Gūshe* number 16, which is another version of *Zīrkesh-e Salmak*, introduces the upper g.

Gūshe number 24, *Golrīz*, introduces an upper a-flat and cadence on c, which an earlier short *gūshe*—number 1, *Āvāz*—introduced. The next two *gūshe-hā*, *Ṣafā* and *Chahārmeżrāb*, use an upper a-*koron* and a cadence on the upper g. With *Bozorg* (number 30), melodic emphasis is on the upper g with the cadence on c. *Ḥazīn* (number 35) uses a final (lower) g cadence, as do numbers 36 and 37. *'Ozzāl* (number 38) extends the range to the c an octave above, with the cadence on the upper g.

In Ma'rūfī's *radīf*, at number 40 a section of *shūr bālā* 'upper, higher *shūr*' is introduced, with a *shūr darāmad* on the upper octave that uses an ascending cadential phrase e-*koron*–f–g. *Āvāz* (number 44) extends the pitch level to high d-*koron*, e-flat, f, and g, two octaves above the original g.

With *Rażavī* (number 46), the tonic is returned to c (upper). *Qajar* (number 47) adds an octave higher a-flat, with the melodic focus on the upper pentachord c–g, *īst* on upper c, and a modulatory final *forūd* to upper g (still "upper" *shūr*). *Shahnāz*, with its melodic focus and *īst* on c, also uses a modulatory *forūd* to *shūr* on g for the final cadence. *Qarache* (numbers 49 through 51) emphasizes e-flat, with *īst* on c and *finalis* on g. It should be noted that in *shūr* proper both *īst*, or intermediate cadences, and *finalis*, or final cadence, are on g. While these two important *gūshe-hā*, *Shahnāz* and *Qarache*, use a final g cadence, this may possibly be a reference or connector to *shūr* rather than an integral or identifiable part of the *gūshe-hā* themselves.

The next *gūshe-hā*, numbers 52 and 53—as well as 54, which is called *Forūd*—gradually return the focus to the g–c tetrachord, though still in the second octave, with a final return to the g in the lowest, or original, octave at the end of the *forūd*. The form *Maṣnavī* (number 55) is often found at or near the end of a *dastgāh*. In the vocal *radīf*, it represents a different poetic form from the bulk of the *gūshe-hā*, which usually use the *ghazal* form.

Starting with number 56, a section in *Bayāt-e Kord* is introduced. Though included as part of the *radīf* of *shūr*, this is considered by some a subsidiary *dastgāh*, such as *Dashtī* and *Bayāt-e Tork*, which developed originally as extensive sections of *shūr* and then gradually were performed on their own (During 1984:114; During and Mirabdolbaghi 1991:72; Farhat 1990:33).

After the return to *shūr* in number 64 (*Forūd be Shūr*), more melodically formed or composed pieces (numbers 65–70) are introduced in metric rhythm, which was traditional for the conclusion of a *dastgāh* performance.

Karīmī's vocal *radīf* of *shūr* is in *chap kūk* (*shūr* on d) and contains fifteen *gūshe-hā*. Using Massoudieh's comparative scales, one can study the modal progression of this *radīf* in terms of extension of range and increase in pitch, particularly in the shifts of prominent tones, melodic *ambitus*, and cadence tones (figure 14). One can observe how the melodic focus gradually shifts, extending the range, changing the cadential tones, and then returning to the original mode. It may be noted that the *gūshe* of *Ḥoseynī* (number 12) traditionally begins in the highest tetrachord position rather than beginning again in the first tetrachord as found in this *radīf*.

Although the *gūshe-hā* in a *radīf* are arranged in a particular order, usually by ascending pitch, the musician may not necessarily follow this order while playing. A performer is somewhat free to choose spontaneously from the repertoire. Though it is usual for a performer to follow the general outline of the *dastgāh* as presented in the *radīf*, he may, for example, choose to perform only one *gūshe*, such as a *shāh-gūshe* like *shahnāz*.

Gūshe-hā form the basis for improvisation. Caron and Safvate note two types of improvisation, "grande" and "petite." Petite improvisation consists of variation in rhythm, melody, and ornaments; grande is a more "spontaneous creation" (1966: 129; see also Nettl 1987:12). The *shāh-gūshe-hā* are more flexible in their presentation and offer more possibilities for improvisation, based on such techniques as sequence, repetition, ornamentation, and combining melodic-rhythmic motifs from a traditional pool of motivic materials. The secondary and fixed *gūshe-hā* mentioned by Sadeghi (1971:56–57, 61) have more defined melodic features, and the performer would limit improvisation in order to keep the melody recognizable.

FIGURE 14 *Gūshe-hā* in *dastgāh-e shūr*: weighted scales with *motaghayyer*, melodic focus, and starting and ending notes. In these comparative scales, the notes are given values that depend on usage and emphasis. Brackets represent melodic focus. At right, the note preceding the vertical line is the beginning tone and the note following the line is the final tone for each *gūshe*. Notes on the same scale degree, such as a-*koron* and a-natural, usually represent a *motaghayyer*. (From Massoudieh, in Karimi 1978, introduction:14.)

RADĪF

Traditional practice is to a great extent defined and influenced by the repertoire—the *radīf*—which was originally an oral repertoire of *gūshe-hā*. Traditionally, students studied with a master (*ostād*) of the *radīf* and learned his particular repertoire, often in three stages: basic, intermediate, and advanced (Caton 1994:78; Loṭfi 1976:13). Karīmī's vocal *radīf* represents, according to his *ostād* Davāmī, an intermediate version of the *radīf*.

These masters were associated with a particular musical tradition in a certain region or city, such as Eṣfahān or Tehran. The repertoires of musicians from similar

Some performers and theorists have ascribed emotional or mystical associations to *gūshe-ha* and to the *dastgāh* as a whole.

traditions would often overlap. *Gūshe-hā* entered a master's repertoire in various ways: by being learned from his own *ostād*; possibly, by being borrowed or adapted from other repertoires; by variation, improvisation, and composition; and as incoroporated and adapted folk and popular melodies (During and Mirabdolbaghi 1991:65–71; Loṭfi 1976:17–18; Nettl 1987:5–19). Each *gūshe* has a name, such as a location, person, mood, or musical quality or some other cultural symbol, and these names may indicate the sources of some *gūshe-hā* (Nettl 1987:17–19; Zonis 1973:51). In the *dastgāh* of *shūr*, for example, the *gūshe Moḥammed Ṣādeq-Khāni* is named after an important Iranian musician. The name *gūshe Qajar* refers to someone from the Qājār tribe; *Raẓavi* is related to Imām Reżā; and *Ḥoseynī* is related to Imām Ḥoseyn. Other names are descriptive, such as *bozorg* 'large', *ṣafā* 'pure', and *ḥazīn* 'sad'.

Sometimes a *gūshe* or *dastgāh*, such as *dastgāh-e shūr*, developed in such a way that certain *gūshe-hā* expanded and gained a number of variations and extensions, gradually becoming so developed that they could be performed separately. These subsidiary progressions have been called *āvāz* 'song', *naghme* 'tune', and also *dastgāh*. For *shūr*, these are *dashtī*, *bayāt-e tork*, *afshārī*, and *abū 'aṭā*. Another *dastgāh* that shares a scale with *shūr* is *navā*, but it is not usually considered to be related to *shūr* by tradition or even by mode, though scholars such as Vazīrī (Farhat 1990:21; Khāleqi 1973:126–127) considered *navā* as well as the four subsidiaries of *shūr* all part of the *dastgāh* of *shūr* itself.

These modal formulas were traditionally transmitted by ear, in two respects. A person following the *radīf* tradition would study with a master for some years and learn his *radīf* by rote. In addition, this student would hear improvised performances by different musicians and familiarize himself with their improvisational styles. By these two methods, a student would learn the pool of melodic and rhythmic motifs that form the basis for improvisation and would come to understand how to use them in performance without departing from the traditional framework. His performance would be a realization of the modal possibilities inherent in a *gūshe* and in a *dastgāh*. A master musician could improvise more freely and might also modulate from one *dastgāh* to another in the course of a performance (*morakkab khānī* or *morakkab navāzī*).

ETHOS

Some performers and theorists have ascribed emotional or mystical associations to *gūshe-hā* and to the *dastgāh* as a whole. Modes have come to be associated with certain moods or images, though there are different opinions about what a particular mode conveys. Usually, Iranians will say that most Iranian music is sad, sometimes for historical reasons and sometimes for ideological reasons.

It is traditional to perform Iranian classical music with the mystical poetry of Ḥāfeẓ, Sa'adī, Rūmī, and others. An Iranian mystic might describe the overall arching melodic contour of the *dastgāh* as a mystical or perhaps cathartic experience, in which the listener is taken from a mundane or worldly state; then, by listening to *gūshe-hā* at incrementally higher and higher pitch levels, in combination with appropriate poetry, reaches the *owj* 'high point', 'climax'; and finally is returned to his original state, having gone through a cleansing or releasing experience (Caton 1988:21–22). The arching melodic line is compared to the dome of the sky, as well as to the eyebrows of one's beloved.

An additional reason for arranging a modal progression in order of ascending pitch could be related to the association of the *radīf* with vocal performance. That is, the range and ordering of *gūshe-hā* by ascending pitch *ambitus* would follow the increasing tension and volume produced by singing at higher and higher pitch levels while at the same time allowing the singer to gradually warm up his voice.

In general, the nuances of intervallic and pitch relationships as well as motivic and ornamental possibilities and combinations are followed closely by the knowledgeable listener who is accustomed to this music. Each subtle change may be associated with differences in emotional nuances. Some associations are made by custom, but such associations can also be a function of the intervallic and pitch relations themselves. A performer, though he may not articulate a specific ideology, would traditionally choose a mode that he felt fit the mood and nature of the audience (Varzi 1988:7).

Varzi (personal communication) has observed that the ethos of each *dastgāh* is based on a different aspect of love. He views *shūr* as describing defeated love, the aspect that is represented by separation from the beloved (*hejrān).* He believes that the climax of all but two of the *dastgāh-hā* (*Segāh* and *Chahārgāh*, which talk about times of togetherness, *vaṣl*) are actually in the mode *shūr*, as a love story usually has moments that convey anxiety.

I once heard an anecdote about a westerner who told an Iranian musician that Persian music was but a drop compared with the ocean of Western music. The Iranian replied, "Yes, but it is a teardrop." That concept lies at the heart of *shūr*, which is itself a term meaning salty or emotional and seems somehow to convey the essence of Iranian music and feeling. It has been described as deriving from the countryside, as expressing mysticism, and as containing the wisdom that comes from years of experiencing and reflecting on life's vicissitudes (Caron and Safvate 1966:62; Khāleqi 1973:147–149; Zonis 1973:68).

HISTORICAL NOTE

The origin of the *gūshe* may be discovered by examining historical treatises on Persian and Arab music. Wright (1978) describes a common Arab-Persian modal system that existed from around 1250 until 1500 C.E., when the two systems began to evolve separately—in part because of conflicts between the emergent Persian Safavid dynasty and the Ottoman Empire. During the period of commonality, music theorists defined many different modes; the result was a system of modal derivations based on combinations and expansions of the basic modes (see also Safvat 1971:39–48).

Wright presents scales found in practice from the thirteenth- and fourteenth-century theorists Ṣafi-al-Din and Qotb al-Din al-Shirāzi; and he quotes Qotb al-Din concerning the pitch hierarchy present in these scales: "In practice musicians do not pursue the same aim in all modes: in some their aim is to give prominence to the interval limiting the mode; in others to give prominence to a lesser interval; and in others to give prominence by a single note" (1978: 46). In his treatise, Qotb al-Din presented each mode with its scale and prominent intervals and pitches; further, he indicated that the modes known as *sho'be* 'branches' had characteristic melodic features. Since Qotb al-Din was from Shiraz in Persia, his modes may have reflected a regional tradition (Wright 1978:7, 194).

Some names of *gūshe-hā* within the present *dastgāh-e shūr* are mentioned and discussed by Ṣafī-al Dīn and Qotb al-Dīn. They include the scales of *rahāvī*, *ḥusaynī*,

FIGURE 15 From Wright (1978:50, 53, 64).

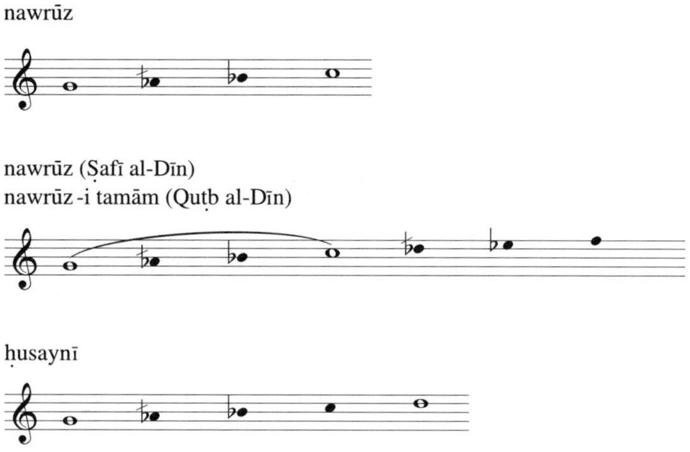

FIGURE 16 The *dāyere* 'circle'. The text reads: "This circle, according to the theoreticians, describes the twelve *maqām*, twenty-four *sho'be*, and forty-eight *gūshe*; and the six *āvāz* and twenty-four *baḥr-e oṣūl*" (Ṣafi al-Din 1967:93).

[دایره]

این دایره از قول حکماء در بیان دوازده مقام و بیست و چهار
شعبه و چهل‌وهشت گوشه [و]شش آوازه وبیست‌وچهار بحراصول است:

۱ ـ C : کردانیه ۲ ـ C : نوروز ۳ـ C : گوشت ۴ ـ C : مایه
۵ ـ C : شهناز ۶ـ C : سلمك ۷ـ C : بزرگ ۸ـ C : کوچك

bozorg, *'ozzāl*, *shahnāz*, and *salmak*, each of which shows some similarity to the scale of the current *gūshe* of the same name. Although *shūr* is not mentioned by name, there are some indications that it may be derived from or related to the mode *nowrūz*, which is the name of the Persian new year. In Wright's discussion of Ṣafī-al-Dīn's classification of modes, *nowrūz* is listed as one of the six *āvāz* (along with *shahnāz* and *salmak*). According to Wright (1978:90; see also During and Mirabdolbaghi 1991:72), the term *āvāz* and the names of five of the six *āvāz* are of Persian origin; in addition, *nowrūz* appeared in earlier lists of Persian modes. The tetrachord scale of *nowrūz* is basically identical to that of *shūr*, with emphasis on the first and fourth degrees. An octave version of *nowrūz* is also presented, with the pitch relations of the lower tetrachord repeated in a conjoint upper tetrachord. *Ḥusaynī* (a *gūshe* in the *dastgāh-e shūr*), with a similar scale, is derived from *nowrūz* (figure 15).

A later Iranian treatise, *Behjat al-Rūh*, thought to have been written in the seventeenth century by 'Abd al-Mo'men Ṣafī al-Dīn, presented a modal system based on the work of earlier theorists but included *gūshe-hā* as part of it. Safvat (1971:40–48), discussing the relationship between the modes in this treatise and earlier treatises, says that the six *āvāz* were formed by combining two of the basic twelve *maqāmāt*, that twenty-four *sho'be* were derived from the twelve *maqāmāt*, and that forty-eight *gūshe-hā* were derived from the *sho'be*, as shown in figure 17 (see also Ṣafī al-Dīn 1967:93, 134–137).

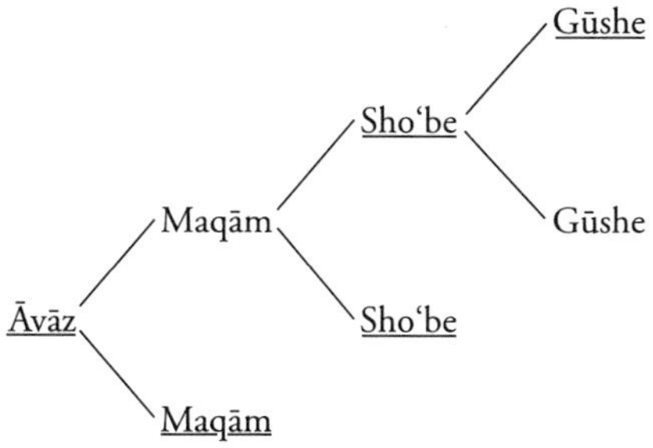

FIGURE 17

Ṣafī al-Dīn (1967) arranges the modes as a series of concentric circles (figure 16) with the six *āvāz* in the center, then the twelve *maqāmāt*, then the twenty-four *sho'be*, then the forty-eight *gūshe-ha*; these are surrounded by twenty-four rhythmic modes, or *bahr-e oṣul* (During and Mirabdolbaghi 1991:84–5; Tsuge 1974:121–129; Zonis 1973:58–61).

Even before the addition of *gūshe-hā* to this system, it was evidently customary in practice to play a combination of modes, specifically starting in one mode, modulating to a related mode, and then returning to the original mode (Wright 1978:180, 192). Some of these progressions may have solidified and developed into what is now the *dastgāh* system. *Dastgāh-hā* such as *shūr* begin in the named mode of the *dastgāh*; progress through a number of modes basically outlined by tradition, with periodic references to the original mode; and then return at the end of the performance to the original *shūr* mode.

REFERENCES

Barkeshlī, Mehdī. 1976. *Modāvemat dar Oṣūl-e Musīqī-ye Irān: Gāmhā va Dastgāh-hā-ye Musīqī-ye Irānī*. Tehran: Ministry of Culture and Art.

Caron, Nelly, and Dariouche Safvate. 1966. *Les traditions musicales: Iran*. Buchet/Chastel: Institut International d'Études Comparatives de la Musique.

Caton, Margaret. 1988. "Melodic Contour in Persian Music, and Its Connection to Poetic Form and Meaning." In *Cultural Parameters of Iranian Musical Expression*, ed. Margaret Caton and Neil Siegel, 18–26. Redondo Beach, Calif.: Institute of Persian Performing Arts.

———. 1994. "Darvīš Khan, Ğolām-Ḥosayn." In *Encyclopaedia Iranica*, ed. Ehsan Yarshater, vol. 7:77–79. Costa Mesa, Calif.: Mazda.

During, Jean. 1984. *La musique iranienne: Tradition et évolution*. Paris: Éditions Recherche sur les Civilisations.

During, Jean, Zia Mirabdolbaghi, and Dariush Safrat. 1991. *The Art of Persian Music*. Washington, D.C.: Mage.

Farhat, Hormoz. 1990. *The Dastgāh Concept in Persian Music*. Cambridge: Cambridge University Press.

Gerson-Kiwi, Edith. 1963. *The Persian Doctrine of Dastga-Composition: A Phenomenological Study in the Musical Modes*. Tel-Aviv: Israel Music Institute.

Hedāyat, Mehdī Qolī. 1938. *Madjma 'al-Advar*. Tehran.

Karīmī, Maḥmūd, comp. 1978. *Radīf-e Āvāzī-ye Musīqī-ye Sonnatī-ye Irān*, transcribed and analyzed by Mohammad Taghi Massoudieh. Tehran: Ministry of Culture and Art.

Khāleqī, Rūhollāh. 1973. *Naẓarī be Musīqī*, vol. 2. Tehran: Ferdowsi.

Khatschi, Khatschi. 1962. *Der Dastgāh: Studien zur neuen persischen Musik*. Regensburg: Gustav Bosse Verlag.

Loṭfī, Moḥammad Reżā. 1976. *Musīqī-ye Āvāzī-ye Irān (Dastgāh-e Shūr): Radīf-e Ostād 'Abd al-llāh Davāmī*. Tehran: Gutenberg.

al-Marāghi, 'Abd al-Qāder b. Gheybī. 1965. *Maqāsed al-Alḥān*. Tehran: Bongāh-e Tarjome va Nashr-e Ketāb.

Ma'rufi, Musá, comp. 1973. *Radif-e Haft Dastgāh-e Musiqi-ye Irāni*. Tehran: Ministry of Culture and Arts.

Massoudieh, Mohammad Taghi. 1968. *Āwāz-e Šur: Zur Melodiebildung in der persischen Kunstmusik*. Regensburg: Gustav Bosse Verlag.

Modir, Hafez. 1986. *Model and Interpretation in Iranian Classical Music: The Performance Practice of Mahmoud Zoufonoun*. Master's thesis, University of California, Los Angeles.

Nettl, Bruno. 1987. *The Radif of Persian Music: Studies of Structure and Cultural Context*. Champaign, Ill.: Elephant and Cat.

Powers, Harold S. 1980. "Mode," in *The New Grove Dictionary of Music and Musicians*, ed. Stanley Sadie, Vol. 12:376–450. London: Macmillan.

Ṣabā, Abolḥasan. 1965. *Dowre Avval-e Santur*. Tehran.

Sadeghi, Manoochehr. 1971. *Improvisation in Nonrhythmic Solo Instrumental Contemporary Persian Art Music*. Master's thesis, California State University, Los Angeles.

Ṣafī al-Dīn, 'Abd al-Mo'men (attributed to). 1967. *Behjat al-Ruḥ*, ed. Rabino de Borgomale. Tehran: Cultural Foundation of Iran. (Modern edition of the original work, c. seventeenth century.)

Ṣafvat, Dāriush. 1971. *Ostādān-e Musiqi-ye Iran va Elḥān-e Musiqi-ye Irāni*. Tehran: Ministry of Culture and Arts.

Shirāzi, Forsat. 1966. *Boḥur al-Alḥān*. Tehran: Forughi.

Tsuge, Gen'ichi. 1974. "Āvāz: A Study of the Rhythmic Aspects in Classical Iranian Music." Ph.D. dissertation, Wesleyan University, Middletown, Conn.

Varzi, Mortezá. 1988. Performance-audience Relationships in the *Bazm*. In *Cultural Parameters of Iranian Musical Expression*, by Margaret Caton and Neil Siegel, 1–9. Redondo Beach, Calif.: Institute of Persian Performing Arts.

Vaziri, 'Ali Naqi. 1913. *Dastur-e Tār*, vol. 1. Berlin.

———. 1934. *Musiqi-ye Naẓari*. Tehran.

Wright, Owen. 1978. *The Modal System of Arab and Persian Music A.D.: 1250–1300*. London: Oxford University Press.

Yar-Shater, Ehsan. "Affinities between Persian Poetry and Music." In *Studies in Art and Literature of the Near East*, ed. Peter Chelkowski, 59–78. Salt Lake City: University of Utah.

Zonis, Ella. 1973. *Classical Persian Music: An Introduction*. Cambridge, Mass.: Harvard University Press.

Aspects of Turkish Folk Music Theory

Irene Markoff

Concepts and Terms: Musical Genres
Folk Poetry
Acoustic Properties of Music
Modal Theory
Modal Classification
Rhythm and Meter

In the 1920s, Mustafa Kemal Atatürk ("Father of the Turks"; figure 1) and his associates launched several ideological campaigns and institutional reforms to bring about social change in their new nation-state, the secular republic of Turkey. Their reforms helped pave the way for the transformation and widespread popularization of Turkish folk music (*Türk halk müziği*), a culture that had formerly been restricted to insular rural communities. This process was facilitated by the institutionalization of the transmission of music, coupled with the urbanization and specialization of talented people who emerged as an elite cadre of performers, educators, scholars, and administrators.

The transformation of Turkish traditional musical culture did not begin immediately. This was because Kemal Atatürk, in his efforts to modernize Turkey, encouraged Western music on state media broadcasts as well as in educational institutions. Exposure to Turkish art music in particular was limited, because it recalled the legacy of the Ottoman Empire, with its Arab- and Persian-influenced high art culture. Folk music, on the other hand, contributed to Atatürk's nationalist vision of an integrated society that would blend Turkish values with aspects of Western civilization. As a major component of unspoiled Turkish folk culture, the designated source for true Turkish values, folk music helped promote a Central Asian Turkic heritage (Berkes 1981). It was also crucial to the creation of a new national Turkish music shaped by a synthesis of Western art music principles with Turkish folk music by a handful of European-trained Turkish composers. For this purpose, full-scale expeditions to collect folk melodies were organized by the Istanbul Municipal Conservatory (Istanbul Belediye Konservatuvarı) in 1926–1929 and the Ankara State Conservatory (Ankara Devlet Konservatuvarı) in 1936–1952 (Ülkütaşır 1973).

FIGURE 1 Mustafa Kemal Atatürk.

Although the state's limited patronage of traditional Turkish music discouraged public familiarity with it, the state did support the teaching of folk arts, including music, by creating and supporting educational institutions called *Halk Evleri* 'People's Houses' throughout Turkey (Karpat 1963). [See also DANCE AND IDENTITY IN TURKEY.] Cultural activities in these institutions, which opened in 1932, included collecting, preserving, teaching, and performing folk music. The *Halk Evleri* were closed in 1950 but were in effect reborn when the ministry of education established the *Halk Eğitim Merkezleri* 'People's Educational Centers' the same year. Many folk music specialists in the major cities of Turkey received their first music lessons at such centers

MAP 1 Turkey

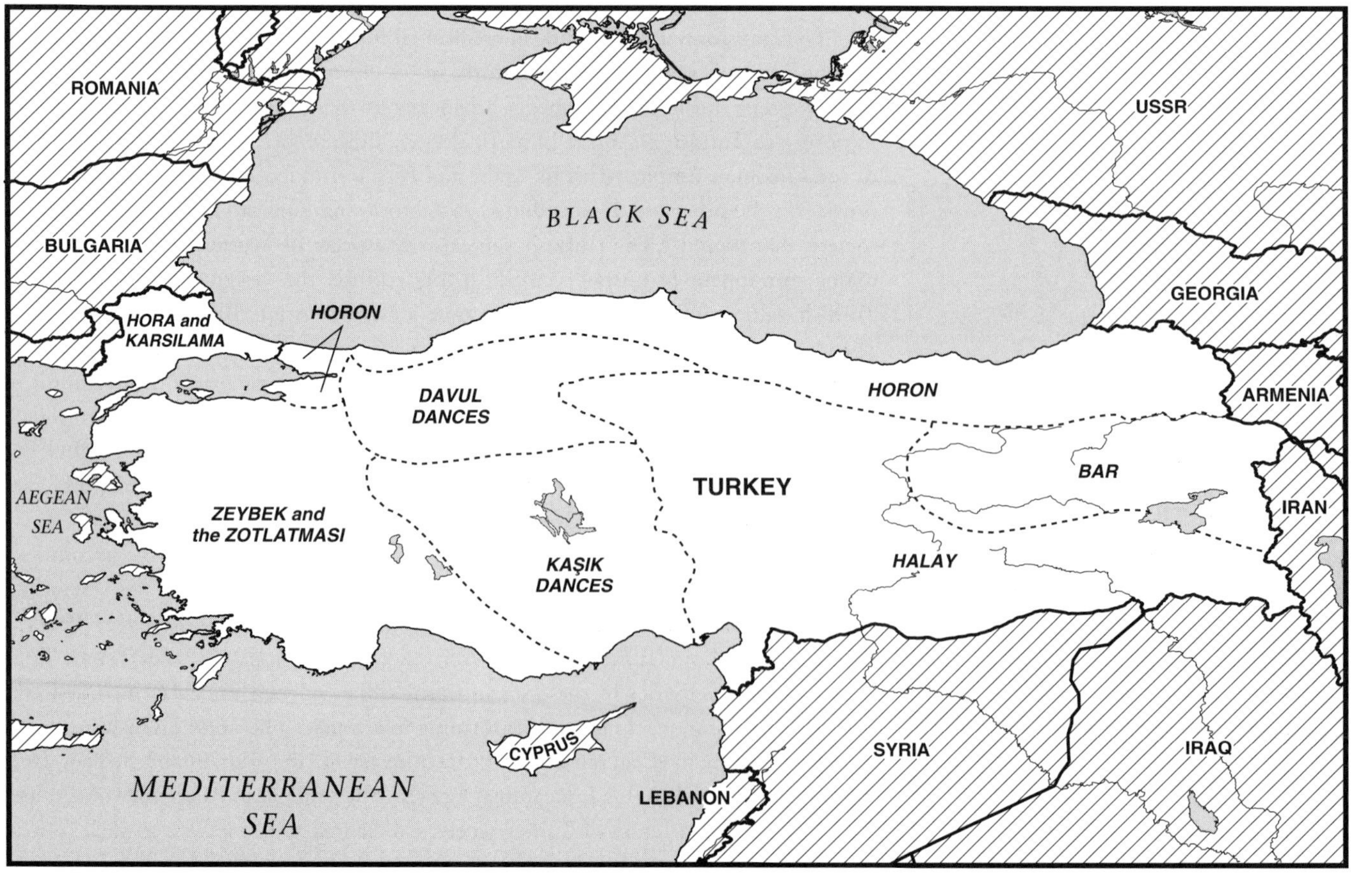

MAP 2 Folk dance regions of Turkey.

FIGURE 2 The vocalist Neriman Altındağ Tüfekçi (wife of Muzaffer Sarısözen and later of Nida Tüfekçi) with members of the first folk music ensemble for the program "Yurttan Sesler" (Voices from the Homeland), Ankara Radio, 1957. Sarısözen is seated to Neriman's right. Photograph from *Türk Halk Müzığı ve Oyunları* 1984. 2(9):338.

and at amateur folklore clubs and societies (*dernek, cemiyet*) established for the preservation and performance of Anatolian folk music and dance.

This marked the beginning of a gradual institutionalization of the learning process, whereby aspiring young performers and educators were instructed at private music schools, at state radio stations, and later at state-supported conservatories in Istanbul, Ankara, and Izmir. For example, the establishment of state radio in Ankara in 1937 allowed for the widespread propagation of folk music traditions. Talented regional performers were recruited for the first live broadcasts and were given a rigorous program: they were drilled daily in solfège, ear training, dictation, sight-reading, and instrumental and vocal techniques as well as regional styles and repertoires. The credit for this accomplishment belongs to Muzaffer Sarısözen, an important person in Turkish folk music history, who handpicked, trained, and conducted performers for these broadcasts (figure 2). He selected the repertoire from the two thousand melodies he had transcribed and helped record for the Ankara State Conservatory of Music's folk music collection as its archivist.

This policy of live broadcasts of rural music was applied at stations in Istanbul, Izmir, Erzurum, Diyarbakir, and Antalya. Although national radio still has a significant role in educating folk musicians, the training it now provides is not as comprehensive as that offered at state conservatories. A case in point is the State Conservatory for Turkish Traditional Music (now affiliated with Istanbul Technical University), founded in 1976. Here students study solfège, musical dictation, Western music theory and history, melodic modes (*makam*), metrical modes (*usûl*), the repertoire of Turkish art music, the theory and practice of folk music, Turkish literary genres, and a major performing medium. State conservatories rely on Western notation and the Western solfège system as teaching aids. This specialized training has stimulated concepts of, and a vocabulary for, materials of music and musical forms that are still being developed and refined, yet are firmly rooted in tradition.

CONCEPTS AND TERMS: MUSICAL GENRES

Türk halk müziği 'Turkish folk music' is classified today according to a tradition established by early scholars such as the French-educated Mahmut Ragip Gazimihâl (1928) and Muzaffer Sarısözen (1962), who divided the folk repertoire into two broad categories according to rhythmic features. These categories are *kırık havalar* 'broken melodies', vocal and instrumental melodies in strict meter; and *uzun havalar* 'long melodies', free-rhythm quasi-improvisational vocal and instrumental melodies.

Kırık havalar include vocal melodies (*sözlü ezgiler*), such as the sung poetry of minstrels, folk songs (*türkü*), and dance songs (*sözlü oyun havalar*); dance melodies (*oyun havalar*) for instruments alone; and solo instrumental repertoire, such as *peşrev* (prelude) and *yanık* 'burned', 'consumed by love' for solo *bağlama*, a long-necked plucked folk lute with frets. *Türkü* is often used as a blanket term for all Turkish folk songs. Dance songs and instrumental dance melodies are more commonly identified by their regional designations, such as *zeybek*, *halay*, *horon*, *bar*, *karşılama*, *teke zo-tlatması* 'goat-leaping dance', and *kaşık oyunları* 'spoon dances'. These regional labels designate not only types of melodies but also dance figures and specific rhythms and meters (figure 3).

Uzun hava 'long melody' is the overall term used primarily for unmeasured vocal melodies, but it can include instrumental melodies as well. Scholars have suggested that this term originated with the word *ozanname*, a corruption of *ozan* 'medieval poet' and *nağme* 'melody', and is thus linked to the melodies of poet-minstrels. The medieval *ozan* recited tales with long recitative-like passages, accompanying himself on the *kopuz* 'folk lute' (Gazimihâl 1954).

Vocal *uzun havalar* are generally identified by ethnic or tribal associations such as Türkmeni (songs of the Türkmen or Oğuz Turks), Afşar (songs of the Afşar Turkic tribes), or Kürdi (in the Kurdish style); by names of poet-minstrels such as Garip (seventeenth century), Kerem (eighteenth century), and Emrah (eighteenth or nineteenth century); by terms borrowed from Ottoman *divan* (high art) literature such as *divan*, *müstezat* 'increased, supplemented', and *semai*; by affiliation with Islamic mystical orders such as the *Kalenderi* (thirteenth-century wandering dervishes); by special regional names such as *maya* 'roots', *hoyrat* 'boorish', *bozlak* 'song of anguish', *Barak* (a Türkmen tribe of the Gaziantep area), *yol havası* 'traveling song', *yayla havası* (songs sung at summer pasture-grazing grounds), and *gurbet havası* (songs of exile); as laments such as *ağıt* and *mersiye*; and finally, as regional musical styles or dialects (*ağız*), such as *Urfa ağzı* (Urfa musical style, southeastern Turkey), *Çamşıhı ağzı* (Erzincan and Sivas style), *Arguvan ağzı* (Malatya style), *Şirvan ağzı* (Elazığ style), *Barak ağzı* (Gaziantep style), and *Summani ağzı* (Erzurum and Kars style). The main concentration of *uzun hava* genres is in eastern Turkey, the greatest variety being in areas such as Erzincan (*maya*, *kürdi*), Maraş, Gaziantep (*barak*, *garip*), Erzurum (*maya*), Elaziğ (*hoyrat*, *maya*, *divan*, *kürdi*, *yol havasi*), Diyarbakir (*kürdi*, *divan*), Urfa (*divan*), and

FIGURE 3 Categories of *kırık havalar*.

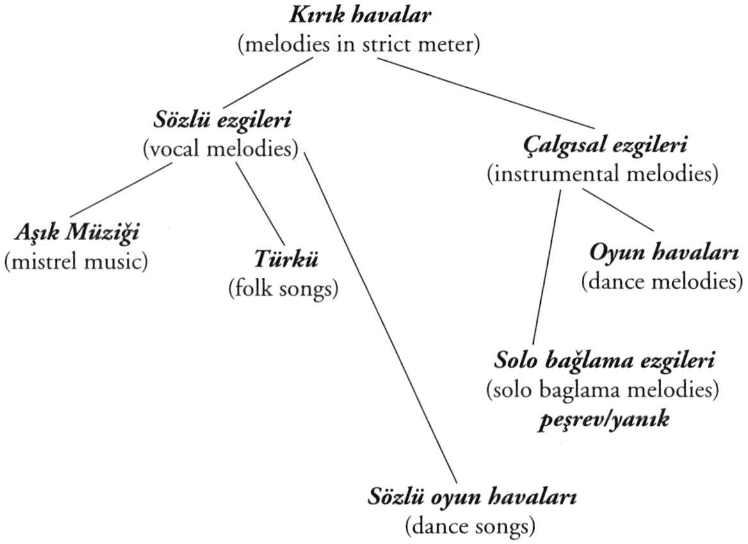

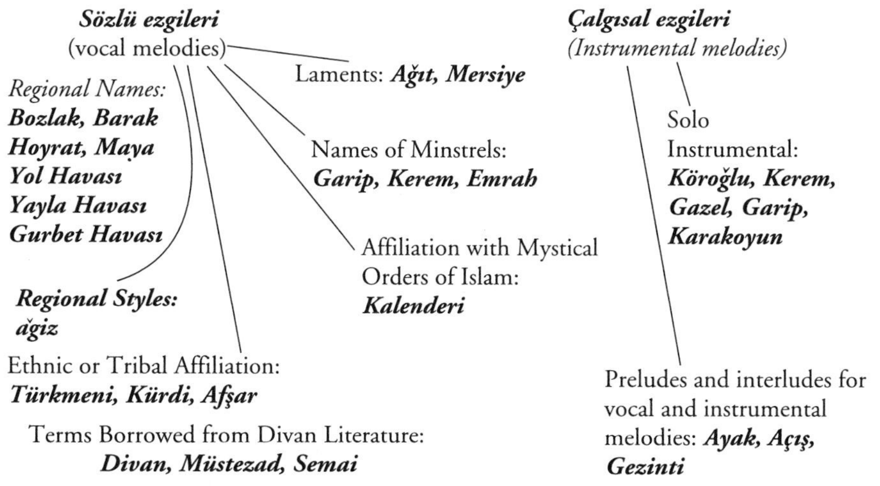

FIGURE 4 Categories and genres of *uzun hava*.

Sivas (*hoyrat*, *maya*, *garip*). The *bozlak* genre is found throughout central Anatolia and the Taurus mountains.

Instrumental forms of *uzun hava* include free-rhythm preludes and interludes that accompany vocal *uzun hava*, such as *açıs* (from the verb *açmak* 'to open' or 'to reveal') or less frequently *ayak* ('base', 'leg', but in this context meaning melody type, or the foundation on which the melody is built). The term *gezinti* (from the verb *gezinmek* 'to run over the notes of a musical instrument') describes instrumental preludes and interludes performed with vocal and instrumental melodies in strict meter. Some free-rhythm instrumental melodies associated primarily with wind instruments such as the *kaval* 'flute' and *mey* 'double-reed aerophone' are performed independently of song. These are known as *köroğlu* 'son of a blind man', from the name of a Central Asian epic; *garip* 'strange', from a romance about the minstrel Garip; *kerem*, from the name of another minstrel; *gazel*, a love poem; and *karakoyun* 'black sheep' (figure 4).

FOLK POETRY

Syllable line (*hece vezni*)

Folk verse forms are characterized by the syllable line. In this type of syllabic prosody (*hece vezne*), the prime focus of rhythmic emphasis is the number of syllables. Three- to four-syllable lines generally combine to form a stanza with specific patterns of rhyme at line ends.

Mani and *koşma* verse forms

The most common forms of folk verse are known as *mani* and *koşma*. The *mani*, which are anonymous, have seven- or eight-syllable lines and are classified according to their function and the context of performance (Boratav 1982:176–178; Dizdaroğlu 1969:67). They are believed to have been the domain of women, who created and sang them spontaneously at social gatherings and while working.

The *koşma* have eleven-syllable or sometimes eight-syllable lines. This form is favored by minstrels, whose pen names (*mahlaslar*) are always cited in the last stanza of their poems. Minstrel poets are representative of two major traditions that are still alive today. One group goes back to the mystical though sometimes outspoken and revolutionary sung works, known as *deyiş* 'poem' (from *demek* 'to speak poetry' and *nefes* 'mystical poem'), of Bektashi dervish-lodge poets (*tekke şairleri*) and poets of the heterodox Alevi sect such as Pir Sultan Abdal (sixteenth century) and Hatai (sixteenth century). The second group recalls medieval bards (*ozan*), singers of epic tales (*destan*) about heroes such as Köroğlu (a warrior bandit renowned throughout Central Asia) and folk narratives (*halk hikayeleri*), combining poetry and prose, of passionate love and the lives of minstrels such as Kerem and Garip. This group is known for the development of on-the-spot composition during song duels (*atışma*). Most minstrels accompany themselves on the *bağlama* (generically called *saz*), a long-necked, fretted, hemipyriform bowl lute whose symbolic value to the identity of the nation-state cannot be overestimated.

ACOUSTIC PROPERTIES OF MUSIC

Melody

The term *ağız* 'dialect' refers to the specific regional (*yoresel, mahalli*) character of folk melodies, and predominantly to regional vocal styles. Urban professional musicians use the term *tavır* 'manner,' 'style', as well as *ağız* to indicate the distinctive regional melodic and rhythmic phrases, ornamentation, intervals, and instrumental techniques that epitomize the main stylistic conventions of different Anatolian melodies. The specific term for mode, *ayak*, is a reasonable facsimile of the concept of *makam* 'melodic mode' in Turkish art music. For rural musicians (*mahalli sanatçılar*), the terms *ayak* and *makam* signify regionally specific types of melodies. Concepts such as the scale and the functions of its individual pitches are foreign to them.

Scale

Urban-trained professional folk musicians in Turkey automatically apply the European solfège syllables to the pitches of melodies they hear or read in Western staff notation. They take the movable-do approach, whereby the syllable do is applied to the tonic (*karar ses*, 'resting tone') of the melody being studied or performed.

The term *diez* is used to indicate raising a pitch a half tone and is represented by the Western sharp symbol; the term *bemol* indicates lowering a pitch a half step and is represented by the Western flat symbol. Microtonal pitches (*koma sesler*) or pitches that fall outside the boundaries of the Western equal-tempered system are identified by the numerals 2, 3, and occasionally 4 placed above flat and sharp signs, indicating two commas flat or sharp, three commas flat or sharp, and so on (figure 5). This convention was borrowed by Sarısözen from the radical musicologist and theorist Kemal Ilerici to account for microtonal piches when he was transcribing his field recordings.

FIGURE 5 Turkish pitch system; microtonal pitches (*koma sesler*) are indicated by numerals above accidental signs.

Intervallic structure

The term *koma sesler* (intervals that are smaller or larger than the Western semitone) is borrowed from Turkish art music, where one comma is equal to roughly 23 cents (after the Pythagorean system), a whole tone is divided into nine commas, and pitches can be raised or lowered by from 1 to 8 commas. In art music, the symbols ɗ, ƀ, and ♭ lower a note one, four, and five commas, respectively, from the natural position. The symbols ‡, ♯, and ǂ raise a note one, four, and five commas, respectively, from the natural position [see CONTEMPORARY TURKISH MAKAM REALIZATION]. In practice, however, the *koma* or *çeyrek* (quarter) tones of the folk music system often differ from those of art music.

In theory, each octave of the classical system is divided into twenty-four unequal pitches as represented by the principal frets of the long-necked classical lute known as *tanbur*. In the folk music system, the character of scaling is inferred from the placement of frets on the folk lutes (*bağlamalar*). In fact, the fundamental folk scales derive from,

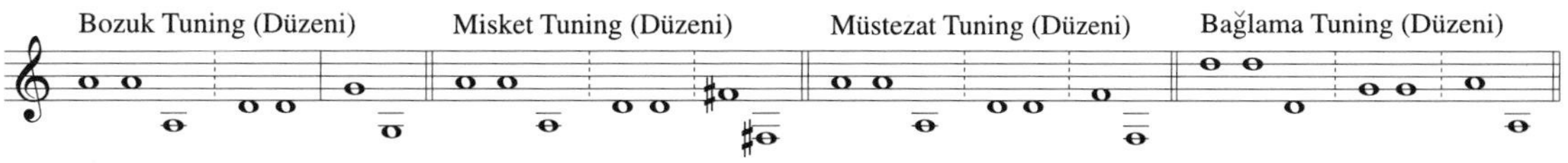

FIGURE 6 Basic *bağlama* tunings.

and are often identified with, actual tunings of the instrument (Markoff 1986a; see figure 6). Contemporary instruments generally have twenty-four frets and can accommodate up to seven microtonal frets on each course of strings with eighteen frets in the first octave. This new feature of high-density microtonal fretting is an obvious adaptation from the modal practice of Turkish art music. However, only a few of these frets are actually used.

The pitches that can be produced on the first course of strings on folk lutes with twenty-four frets can be seen in figure 5. The open strings of this course are generally referred to as *la* (a) in most tunings, regardless of the pitch actually produced. In practice, though, the actual pitches of open strings for various tunings are raised or lowered to accommodate the vocal range of a performer or of a singer being accompanied. *La* is also the tonic used for many scales in the theoretical system.

As mentioned above, microtonal pitches indicate the approximate degree to which a pitch is raised or lowered, as calculated in commas (2, 3, or 4). The microtonal pitches most common in folk music are, in order of frequency of use: $b^{\flat 2}$, $f^{\sharp 2}$, and $b^{\flat 3}$. Although microtonal frets have become standardized in urban musical practice where ensemble work necessitates uniformity of approach, deviations from this norm are common in rural areas. For example, the $b^{\flat 2}$ frets of instruments in Urfa, Aydın, Uşak, Keskin, Maraş, Elbistan, Sivas, and Trabzon are one or two commas lower than the same frets on urban instruments.

MODAL THEORY

Early scholars such as the musicologist and folklorist Mahmut Ragıp Gazimihâl attempted to explain the modal peculiarities of Turkish folk music by comparing its scales to those used in art music. In a major study based on intensive field research, Gazimihâl (1928) observed that the scales used most frequently in folk music resembled the classical modes (*makam*) *hüseyni*, *tahir*, and *uşşak*. However, despite the close resemblance between folk and classical modes, they differ with regard to microtonal pitches, functional tones, melodic progression, and stereotyped phrases. For this reason, in the 1940s folk music educators devised a nomenclature for folk modes based on the jargon of the common "folk" (*halk*). Designations for modes derive from the names of famous minstrels (*garip* and *kerem* are examples), the names of wandering dervishes from Khorosan (*kalenderi*), and the names of *bağlama* tunings and regional melody types such as *misket* and *müstezat*. Certain modes are used almost exclusively with specific tunings of the folk lute, while others commonly have more popular tunings.

Today, enlightened folk musicians use the term *ayak* 'foot', 'base' for the folk mode. *Ayak* was borrowed from folk poetic terminology, where it means a poetic foot or a rhyme or, more specifically, rhyme patterns or words (*uyak*, *kafiye*) established by minstrels particularly in song duels. Thus, the concept of a pattern for the construction of poetic form is echoed in the folk musical term *ayak*, which suggests not only the scale on which a melody is based but also specific features of a type of melody. These include melodic contour, functional tones, stereotyped phrases, and cadential patterns, thus approximating the concept of *seyir* 'progression' in the modal practice of art music.

MODAL CLASSIFICATION

Current practice designates *kerem ayağı* 'the *kerem* mode' as the fundamental mode of the folk theoretical system. The *kerem* mode strongly resembles *makam hüseyni* of the classical system, which Kemal Ilerici (1981) acclaimed as the "mother mode" of Turkish traditional music (figure 7; note that in the transcriptions of *makam* scales, the "white" notes are those most important in the mode, specifically the tonic, dominant, and octave). This view is opposed to that of the respected classical theorists Ezgi and Arel, who consider *çargâh* the principal *makam* of Turkish art music (Signell 1977). *Çargâh* closely resembles the intervals of the Western diatonic C major scale. It was chosen as a "mother" mode because it simplified the creation of scales in the same system by avoiding superfluous accidentals. It also helped Turkish music conform to European conventions. Ilerici's choice of *hüseyni* is based on its widespread use in the Turkish folk and classical repertoire. Some folk music specialists, however, argue that the *kerem* folk mode cannot be accepted as *hüseyni*'s absolute counterpart because certain degrees of the scale are variable. For example, the second degree of the *kerem* mode might be one, two, or three commas flat. When these pitches are used consistently in certain types of melodies, scales deriving from the basic *kerem* alignment are formed. These derivative scales are considered a part of the *kerem* family of scales, headed by *kerem ana dizisi* 'mother scale', the basic *kerem* scale (see figures 8 and 18*a*).

FIGURE 7 *Makam hüseyni.*

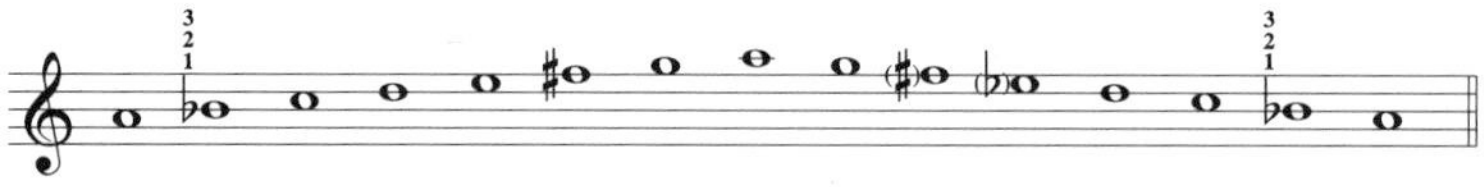
FIGURE 8 Basic *kerem* scale.

This fundamental mode also shares features with *makam muhayyer*, a "brother" *makam* of *hüseyni* that uses the same scale, final, and dominant but is a descending *makam* and, like *kerem*, extends above the upper tonic in range (figure 9). When the folk mode uses f-natural in its tonal row, it resembles the classical modes *uşşak* and *beyati*, which belong to the same family as *hüseyni* and *muhayyer*.

FIGURE 9 *Makam muhayyer.*

When the pitch E-flat is added, the basic *kerem* scale is sometimes called *yanık* 'burned', 'inflamed with love' *kerem ayağı*. The resulting scale can be easily identified with *makam karcığar*, an ascending-descending mode of the classical system that uses a chromatic pentachord built on D, which resembles the lower tetrachord of *makam hicaz* (figure 10).

FIGURE 10 *Yanık* variant of the *kerem* scale *makam karcığar.*

Two other folk modes make use of the augmented second-like interval and seem to belong to the *kerem* family, if only in name. The *yanık kerem* mode (not to be confused with the variant of the "mother" mode) on g resembles the classical *nikriz* mode, although the third degree of its scale is one comma flatter than that of *nikriz* (figure 11). The folk *ayak* known as *tatyan kerem*, on the other hand, is derived from the vocal genre *tatyan* (eastern Turkey) that begins on the relative pitch b and has many similarities with the classical *makam hüzzam* (figure 12). Slight differences in pitch inflection occur on the first and fourth degrees of the two scales.

TRACK 25

FIGURE 11 *Yanık kerem* scale and *makam nikriz.*

FIGURE 12 *Tatyan kerem* scale and *makam hüzzam.*

Two other modes are also widespread, the most popular being *garip ayağı* (named after the minstrel Garip or connoting an exile), which resembles the classical modes *hicaz*, *hümayun*, and *uzzal* (figures 13 and 18*b*). The other mode is known as *kalenderi* (after the wandering dervishes of that name) and is similar to the classical *saba* mode (figure 14).

FIGURE 13 *Garip* scale, *makam hicaz*, *makam hümayun*, and *makam uzzal*.

FIGURE 14 *Kalenderi* scale and *makam saba*.

Misket modes are associated with the *bağlama* tuning of the same name, and the basic scale has close similarities to the classical modes *eviç* and *ferahnâk* (figure 15). The basic *müstezat* folk mode, which also derives its name from a *bağlama* tuning, bears a striking resemblance to the classical modes *acemaşiran* and *mahur* (figure 16).

FIGURE 15 Basic *misket* scale, *makam eviç*, and *makam ferahnâk*.

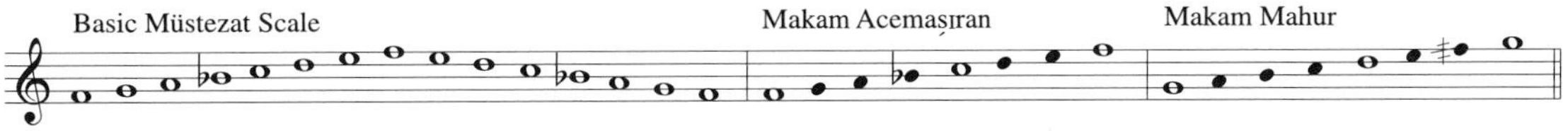

FIGURE 16 Basic *müstezat* scale, *makam acemaşiran*, and *makam mahur*.

Although trained folk music specialists are committed to this folk-derived terminology, many younger conservatory graduates communicate in classical modal terminology.

RHYTHM AND METER

Usûl 'meter' is a generic expression for the concepts of meter and metrical mode in art music practice. Muzaffer Sarısözen appropriated this term in *Türk Halk Musikisi Usulleri* (Meters of Turkish Folk Music; 1962). This study—the product of many years of intensive collection, transcription, and analysis of folk repertoire—is the sole comprehensive treatise on the subject. The term *usûl* is acceptable if construed in the broad sense as meter, since folk music practice uses rhythmic cycles (metric modes) that are commonly transcribed as single-measure units.

Sarısözen grouped meters into three main categories: (1) *ana* 'mother', but here used to mean basic or fundamental meters; (2) *birleşik* 'compound', though a more appropriate translation is 'additive' because of the asymmetric division between rhythmic units in the meters; and (3) *karma* 'mixed' (figure 17).

Ana meters closely resemble the simple and compound meters of Western art music, with their duple, triple, and quadruple features (2/4, 3/4, 6/8, and 4/4).

Birleşik meters are a close facsimile of the classical *aksak* 'limping' or 'lopsided' meters and are considered the most colorful and distinctive folk meters. These additive meters are found in a number of countries in the Balkans (Bulgaria, Macedonia, Romania, and Greece) and in parts of Central Asia, and are characterized by measures in which the relationship between time units is unequal or asymmetrical. Turkish folk meters in the *birleşik* category include 5/8 (23); 7/8 (322; 232; 223); 8/8 (233; 323; 332—rare), and 9/8 (3222; 2322; 2232; 2223).

FIGURE 17 Regional distribution and nomenclature of Turkish folk meters.

Meter	*Nomenclature*	*Location*
Ana (basic)		
2/4 (widespread)	*Uzundere*	Artvin
	Sağma	Tokat
	Delilo	Elaziğ
	Kervan	Eskişehir
	Kaşık oyunlar; sallama	Central Anatolia
	(*Silifke*)	Mediterranean area
	Halay (often fast section)	Central, eastern, and southeastern Turkey
3/4		Eastern Turkey
4/4	*Halay* (slow section)	(see above)
	Misket	Ankara
	Hora	Thrace
6/8 (33)	*Fatmalı*	Elazığ
	Bar	Northeastern Turkey
9/8 (333)	*Sallama*	Northeastern Turkey
	Gelin Ayşe	Southeastern Turkey
12/8	*Halay* (fast section)	Central and eastern Anatolia
Birleşik (additive)		
5/4; 5/8 (23)	*Summani Ağzı; halay; sema*	Eastern Turkey
7/8; 7/16 (322; 223)	*Horon*	Black Sea region
	Hora	Thrace Sea of Marmara
9/4 (3222/2223)	*Zeybek* (ağır)	Aegean/Mediterranean
(2223)	*Ankara zeybeği*	Ankara
9/8 (2223)	*Zeybek* (kıvrak)	Aegean and Mediterranean
	Baş barı	Erzurum
	Halay	Eastern Turkey
	Sarı çiçek	Artvin
		Thrace
(2223; 2323; 3222)	*Karşılama*	Black Sea, Thrace, Bolu
(2223)	*Tamzara*	Elaziğ
(2223; 2322)	*Semah, teke zotlatması*	Aegean, Mediterranean
(3222)	Mengi	
	Bengi	
(2322)	*Uç ayak oyun havası*	Malatya
Karma (mixed)		
10/8 (3223; 2332; 2323; 2233; (3322; 2323 and 3223)	*Çayda Çıra* (2323)-Elazığ	Eastern Turkey
11/8 (7 + 4; 5 + 6)		
12/8 (5 + 7; 7 + 5)		
13/4 (6 + 7; 7 + 6; 8 + 5; 5 + 8)		
14/4 (8 + 6; 6 + 8; 5 = 5 + 4)		
15/4 (7 + 8; 8 + 4)		

FIGURE 18 (a) "Kaşların Karasına," Sivas (*kerem* scale). (b) "Hış Hış Hancer Boynuma," Gaziantep (*garip* scale).

Karma 'mixed' meters are not so widespread. They include 10/8 (3223; 2332; 2233; 3322; 2323); 11/8 (7 + 4 = 22322; 5 + 6 = 32222); 12/8 (5 + 7; 7 + 5); 13/4 (6 + 7; 7 + 6; 8 + 5; 5 + 8); 14/4 (8 + 6, 6 + 8, 5 + 5 + 4); and 15/4 (7 + 8, 8 + 7). Meters of 16 to 20 are rare.

In discussing folk meters, practicing musicians disregard Sarısözen's classification system, preferring to use regional expressions such as the names of regional dance forms (figure 17). For example, the term *zeybek* conjures up a pattern of 9 equal slow pulses with an inner division of 9/4 = 3 + 2 + 2 + 2 and 2 + 2 + 2 + 3 for the so-called *ağır zeybeği* (slow *zeybek*). A pattern of four basic pulses outlines the meter 9/8 with a 2223 division of time units for the *kıvrak zeybeği* (quick *zeybek*). The *karşılama* dance form also has a meter of 9/8, with four basic pulses divided (2323) or (2223); the *horon* dance form is associated with three main pulses that are divided (223)/16 to form a meter of 7/16.

Two musical examples are shown in figure 18.

REFERENCES

And Metin. 1976. *Turkish Dancing*. Ankara: Dost Yayınları.

———. 1987. *Culture, Performance, and Communication in Turkey*. Performance in Culture, no. 4. Tokyo: Institute for the Study of Languages and Cultures of Asia.

Andrews, Walter. 1976. *An Introduction to Ottoman Poetry*. Chicago: Bibliotheca Islamica.

Arseven, Veysel. 1976. "Türk Halk Müzığının Ezgisel Yapısı Üzerine." In *Türk Folklor Araştırmaları Yıllığı*, 83–99. Ankara: Ankara Üniversitesi Basimevi.

Ataman, Sadi Yaver. 1975. *100 Türk Halk Oyunu*. Istanbul: Tifdruk Matbaacılık.

Bartók, Béla. 1976. *Turkish Music from Asia Minor*. Edited by Benjamin Suchoff with an afterward by Kurt Reinhard. Princeton: Princeton University Press.

Başgöz, Ilhan. 1972. "Folklore Studies and Nationalism in Turkey." *Journal of the Folklore Institute* 9:162–176.

Bellah, Robert. 1958. "Religious Aspects of Modernization in Japan and Turkey." *American Journal of Sociology* 64:1–5.

Berkes, Niyazi, ed. 1981. *Turkish Nationalism and Western Civilization: Selected Essays of Ziya Gökalp*. Translated and edited by N. Berkes. Westport, Conn.: Greenwood.

Boratav, Pertev Naili. 1973. "La littérature populaire turque contemporaine." *Turcica* 5:47–67.

———. 1982. *100 Sorunda Türk Halk Edebiyat*. Istanbul: Gerçek Yayınevi.

Demirsipahi, Cemil. 1975. *Türk Halk Oyunları*. Ankara: Türkiye Iş Bankası Kültür Yayınları: 148.

Dizdaroğlu, Hikmet. 1969. *Halk Şiirinde Türler*. Ankara: Ankara Üniversitesi Basımevi.

Finnegan, Ruth. 1979. *Oral Poetry*. Cambridge: Cambridge University Press.

Gazimihâl, Mahmut Ragıp. 1928. *Anadolu Halk Türküleri ve Musiki Istikbalımız*. Istanbul: Marifet Matbaası.

———. 1954. "Uzun Havalar." *Türk Folklor Araştırmaları* 3:883.

Ilerici, Kemal. 1981. *Türk Müzığı ve Armonisi*. Istanbul: Milli Eğitim Basımevi.

Karpat, Kemal. 1963. "The People's Houses in Turkey." *Middle East Journal* 17:55–67.

———. 1976. *The Gecekondu: Rural Migration and Urbanization*. Cambridge: Cambridge University Press.

Kurt, Irfan. 1989. *Bağlamada Düzen ve Pozisyon*. Istanbul: Pan Yayınları.

Lewis, Bernard. 1968. *The Emergence of Modern Turkey*. London: Oxford University Press.

Markoff, Irene Judyth. 1986a. "Musical Theory, Performance, and the Contemporary Bağlama Specialist in Turkey." Ph.D. dissertation, University of Washington, Seattle.

———. 1986b. "The Role of Expressive Culture in the Demystification of a Secret Sect of Islam." *World of Music* 28(3):42–56.

———. 1990–1991. "The Ideology of Musical Practice and the Professional Turkish Folk Musician: Tempering the Creative Impulse." *Asian Music* 22(1):129–145.

Özbek, Mehmet. 1981. *Folklor ve Türkülerimiz*. Istanbul: Otuken.

Öztuna, Mustafa. 1969. *Türk Musikisi Ansiklopedesi*. Istanbul: Milli Eğitim Basımevi.

Picken, Laurence. 1975. *Folk Instruments of Turkey*. London: Oxford University Press.

Reinhardt, Kurt, and Ursula Reinhardt. 1984. *Musik der Türkei. Band 2: Die Volksmusik*. Wilhelmshaven: Heinrichschofen's Verlag.

Sarısözen, Muzaffer. 1962. *Türk Halk Musikisi Usulleri*. Ankara: Resimli Posta Matbaası.

Saygun, A. Adnan. 1976. *Béla Bartók's Folk Musical Research in Turkey*, ed. V. Laszlo. Budapest: Akademia Kiado.

Signell, Karl. 1977. *Makam: Modal Practice in Turkish Art Music*. Seattle: Asian Music.

Stokes, Martin. 1992. *The Arabesk Debate*. Oxford: Clarendon.

Toraganlı, Hasan. 1982. "Türk Halk Musikisinde Ana (*Hüseyni*) Türecinin (*Makam*) Yapısal Özellikleri." In *II Milletlerarası Türk Folklor Kongresi Bildileri (Cilt III. Halk Müziği—Oyun—Eğlence)*, 311–324. Ankara: G. Ü. Basımevi.

Tüfekçi, Nida. 1981. "Türk Halk Musikisi." *Kök* 1(1):14–15.

Ungay, M. Hurşit. 1981. *Türk Mûsikîsinde Usuller ve Küdûm*. Istanbul: Türk Musikisi Devlet Konservatuarı Öğretim Üyesi.

Ülkütaşir, M. Şakir. 1973. *Türkiyede Folklor ve Etnografya Çalışmaları*. Ankara: Başbakanlık Basımevi.

Yekta, Rauf. 1921. "La musique turque." In A. Lavignac, *Encyclopédie de la musique*, Part 1, 5:2945–3064. Paris: C. Delagrave.

Yönetkin, Halil Bedi. 1963. "Türk Halk Musikisinde Oktav Bölümü." In *Türk Folklor Araştırmaları nisan*, 3029–3031.

Rhythmic Modes in Middle Eastern Music

Scott Marcus

Rendering a Rhythmic Mode in Performance
The Great Variety of Rhythmic Modes
Cultural Associations, Cultural Aesthetics

The rhythmic aspect of traditional Arab and Turkish music is governed by a system of rhythmic modes called *īqā‘* (plural, *īqā‘āt*) in Arabic and *usûl* (plural, *usûller*) in Turkish. While there are a great number of Middle Eastern percussion instruments, each capable of producing a variety of sounds, only two sounds are used to define the structure of the individual rhythmic modes. The primary sound is that produced when a drumhead is struck so that the entire head resonates fully and as a single unit; this stroke, called *dumm* (plural, *dumūm*) in Arabic and *düm* (plural, *dümler*) in Turkish, is the deepest or lowest sound a drum can produce. In contrast, the second sound is produced when the drumhead is struck at its edge, at the point where the head meets the rim; this stroke produces a high-pitched sound called *takk* (plural, *tukūk*) in Arabic and *tek* (plural, *tekler*) in Turkish. The structure of each rhythmic mode is defined by a unique skeletal pattern of *dumm* and *takk* strokes. Since this pattern is generally continuous and recurrent in performance, the rhythmic modes are understood to be cyclical.

The following eight-beat pattern of *dumm* strokes (D), *takk* (T) strokes, and rests (*iss* in Arabic, noted here by a hyphen: -) is undoubtedly the most common rhythm used in Arab and Turkish music:

D T - T D - T -

In the eastern Arab world, the rhythm above is called *maqṣūm*, or *düyek* in Turkish. It is completely distinct from the following mode, called *maṣmūdī ṣaghīr* or *baladī* in Arabic:

D D - T D - T -

Although the only difference between these modes is the placement of a *dumm* on the second beat of the rhythm, that itself is considered a major difference in Arab or Turkish music. The presence of two initial *dumm* strokes creates a feel entirely different from that produced by the *maqṣūm* rhythm (and has a different set of cultural associations).

Further, the following is again a completely distinct mode, distinguished from *maṣmūdī ṣaghīr* by an additional *dumm* on the fourth beat. This mode is called *ṣa‘īdī*:

D D - D D - T -

FIGURE 1 Notation of *dumūm* and *tukūk*: (a) *maqṣūm*; (b) *maṣmūdī ṣaghīr*; (c) *ṣa'īdī*.

FIGURE 2 *Ṣa'īdī.*

Because Turkish and Arab music adopted Western staff notation (beginning in the nineteenth century), it is now common to represent these three rhythms as varieties of 4/4 time, where the eight parts of the rhythm are seen as eighth notes. According to one common method of transcribing the rhythms, the *dumm* sound is represented on the staff by notes with an ascending stem, while the *takk* sound is notated with a descending stem (figure 1). Alternatively, *ṣa'īdī* is performed as in figure 2. The two initial sixteenth-note *takk* strokes are orally rendered as "tak" (T) plus "ka" (K). Thus:

TK D - D D - T -

RENDERING A RHYTHMIC MODE IN PERFORMANCE

When performing a given rhythm, a drummer is expected to embellish the skeletal structure by adding *takk* strokes, but not *dumm* strokes, because, generally speaking, the appearance of an additional *dumm* would serve to establish a new rhythmic mode. The following example shows a progression of possible embellishments within the *maqṣūm* rhythm (with the skeletal structure in **bold** type). First, adding a *takk* in the place of the three rests produces:

D **T** T **T** **D** T **T** T

Adding a "turnaround," two sixteenth-note *takk* strokes (tak-ka) that serve as a "pickup" to the downbeat of the next cycle, produces:

D **T** T **T** **D** T **T** TK

Doubling the *takk* strokes (to create tak-ka-s) in the place of the other two original rests produces:

D **T** TK **T** **D** TK **T** TK

Doubling additional *takk* strokes produces:

D **T**K TK **T** **D** TK **T** TK
D **T**K TK **T**K **D** TK **T** TK
D **T**K TK **T**K **D** TK **T**K TK

To preserve the structure and feel of the *maqṣūm* rhythm in these last examples, the primary *takk* sounds (those in bold type) would have to be accented so that they stand out in the context of many successive repetitions of *takk*. Performers speak of a need to maintain the mode's defining weighting (*wazn*) while adding embellishments, although the skeletal weighting can, in fact, be replaced for one or more cycles in the interest of interpreting a given melodic line.

Two additional *takk* strokes might be added to the rhythm above so that there is an unbroken succession of sixteenth notes (DK being a *dumm* followed by a *takk*):

DK **T**K TK **T**K **D**K TK **T**K TK

Any or all of the beats may be further divided. For example, the original three rests may be filled with four thirty-second-note *takk* strokes (represented as tak-ka-tak-ka):

D **T** TKTK **T** **D** TKTK **T** TKTK

Or there may be three sixteenth-note triplets:

D **T** TKT **T** **D** TKT **T** TKT

Further, extended portions of one or more cycles of a given rhythm may be realized by virtuosic drumrolls of continuous *takk* strokes. For example, with the roll represented by the symbol ~~~~~:

D T TK **T D**~~~~~~~~~~~~~~~~~~~~~

When performing any of the rhythms above, the percussion player can substitute a number of different sounds in place of the standard *takk* in the interest of timbral and expressive variety, without creating a change in the named rhythm. One alternative is a muffled sound produced by hitting the area near the center of the drum with an open hand, momentarily leaving the hand in contact with the drumhead. Another alternative, a forceful attack on the head with a slightly cupped hand, produces the loudest sound a drum can make. Another sound is created when one hand presses on the drumhead, restricting the size of the area that is able to vibrate, while the other hand produces a standard *takk*. Two, three, or more successively higher-pitched *takk* sounds can be produced in this manner. On the Middle Eastern tambourine (called *riqq* in Egypt, *daff* in Lebanon and Syria), a number of additional sounds are produced with five sets of metal cymbals fitted into its rim.

Thus a drummer has great freedom when performing a given rhythm. The extent of the embellishment should tastefully reflect the overall context of the rhythm, being restrained when accompanying a slow section of a lyrical song and more lavish when accompanying a rousing dance.

THE GREAT VARIETY OF RHYTHMIC MODES

There are many different rhythmic modes, some with regional origins or associations (see, for example, the rhythms identified as "Tunisian" and "Moroccan" in D'Erlanger 1930–1959, 6:141–152). For the most part, a composer is free to choose the mode or modes to be used in a new composition. There are a few genres, however, where the rhythmic modes are fixed in traditional practice. This is the case with the Turko-Arab instrumental genres *peşrev* (in Turkish) or *bashraf* (in Arabic); *saz semaisi* (Turkish) or *samā'ī* (Arabic); and *longa* (Turkish and Arabic). A *peşrev* is cast in the lengthy Turkish *devr-i kebîr* cycle of 28/4 [see CLASSICAL OTTOMAN TURKISH RHYTHMIC PRACTICES] but is commonly rendered in the present day using a 4/4 cycle. A *samā'ī* usually uses two distinct rhythms: the majority of a given composition is set in the 10/8 *samā'ī* rhythm (whose full name in Arabic is *samā'ī thaqīl*), while the fourth of the four instrumental "verses" (called *khānā* in Arabic and *hane* in Turkish) is commonly in a version of 3/4 or 6/8, such as the 6/8 *sankīn samā'ī* rhythm:

D TK T D T -

Figures 3 and 4 show the skeletal *samā'ī* rhythm and a common ornamented version.

Most Arab music in the second half of the twentieth century used varieties of 4/4 (such as *maqsūm*, *baladī* or *maṣmūdī ṣaghīr*, and *ṣa'īdī*) and 2/4 rhythms, but longer rhythms played a more common role in the past. One defining characteristic of the Arab vocal genre, *muwashshaḥ*, still performed today but much more prevalent in the eighteenth and nineteenth centuries, is the large variety of rhythms, many of greater length. In addition to *samā'ī thaqīl* and versions of 3/4 and 6/8, *muwashshaḥāt* use *dawr hindī* (7/8), *nawakht* (7/4), *maṣmūdī* (8/4), *mudawwar* (12/4), *murabba'* (13/4), *muḥajjar* (14/4), *mukhammas* (16/4), and others.

TRACK -1

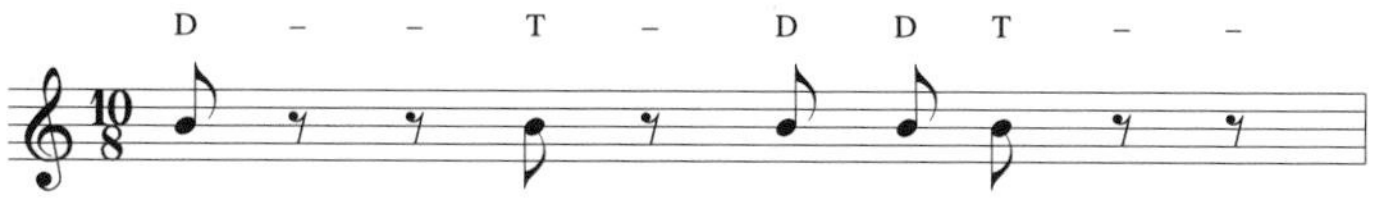

FIGURE 3 The skeletal *samā'ī* rhythm.

FIGURE 4 A common ornamented version of the *samā'ī* rhythm.

When performing a given rhythm, a drummer is expected to embellish the skeletal structure by adding *takk* strokes, but not *dumm* strokes.

CULTURAL ASSOCIATIONS, CULTURAL AESTHETICS

Many of the rhythmic modes have clear cultural and often regional associations. From the last decades of the nineteenth century through the first two-thirds of the twentieth century, new Arab vocal compositions of an artistic and weighty nature were often dominated by the *waḥda* rhythm for the vocal sections, frequently switching to a lighter rhythm such as *maqṣūm* for intermediary instrumental passages.

TRACK 9 Following is the skeletal *waḥda*:

D - - **T** - - **T** -

Below are common ornamented versions of *waḥda*:

D - K **T** - K **T** -
D TK TK **T** - K **T** -
D TK TK **T** TK TK **T** -

The *ṣa'īdī* rhythm mentioned above is named after the region of southern Egypt known as Upper Egypt, the Ṣa'īd, where it is prominent in folk music. Similarly, the *sa'ūdī* rhythm is emblematic of music from Saudi Arabia and many neighboring countries. Along the same lines, *maṣmūdī ṣaghīr* or *baladī* often conveys the feel of folk music (as is implied by the name *baladī*, which means "folk" or "of the folk").

Turkish, Arab, and other Middle Eastern music cultures, while sharing a closely related system of rhythmic modes—created, as we have seen, by consistent placement of structure-defining *dumm* and *takk* strokes—are nevertheless distinguished from each other, in part by distinctive aesthetic senses that govern the realization of the various rhythms in performance. Generally speaking, Turkish drummers are asked to play unobtrusively in the background while the melodic component of the music is dominant. Volume and energetic embellishment are restricted. In contrast, Arab music often gives substantially more prominence to the rhythmic line. The Arab drummer is often encouraged to interpret the melodic line actively and conspicuously, participating in a nearly equal partnership of melody and rhythm.

Although *dumm* and *takk* strokes provide a grammar that defines the modern Arab and Turkish rhythmic systems, they were not, historically, part of the medieval rhythmic system [see THEORIES OF RHYTHM AND METER IN THE MEDIEVAL MIDDLE EAST]. They were, it seems, developed within later Ottoman Turkish music practice and then spread to the Arab world. Neubauer [see ARABIC SOURCES FOR MUSIC THEORY) notes a work of 1672 with "the Turkish düm-tek terminology for which this treatise is one of the earliest witnesses."

REFERENCES

D'Erlanger, Baron Rodolphe. 1930–1959. *La musique arabe*. 6 vols. Paris: Librairie Orientaliste Paul Geuthner.

Donald, Mary Ellen. 1985. *Arabic Tambourine: A Comprehensive Course in Techniques and Performance for the Tambourine, Tar, and Mazhar*. San Francisco: Mary Ellen Books.

al-Ḥilū, Salīm. 1972. *al-Mūsīqā al-naẓariyya*. Beirut: Dār Maktabat al-Ḥayāt.

Kāmil, Maḥmūd. 1978. *Tadhawwuq al-mūsīqā al-'arabiyya*. Cairo: Muḥammad al-Amīn.

Nabīl Sūrah. 1995. *al-Mūsīqā al-'Arabiyya: tarīkh, a'lām, alḥān*. N.p. ISBN 977-5261-51-1.

Rhythmic Structure and Drum Improvisation in Yemen

Jürgen Elsner

The Priority and Diversity of Rhythmic Instruments
Regional Drum Ensembles and Styles
Rhythmic Cycles, Free Rhythm, and Improvisation

Yemen is a beautiful country, and extremely interesting both from a historical perspective and in the present day. Its musical culture is varied and colorful. The rugged topography—mountains, deep wadis, deserts, and semideserts—hinders local communication; as a result, each community, tribe, and so on has an individual culture. If one compares Yemenite music with that of other Arab countries, striking differences are immediately apparent.

In Arab music in general, melody is organized tonally in various ways, is clearly defined, and is accompanied by relatively independent rhythms that are cyclical in structure and improvisational in style. Thus the role of rhythm in Arab music is important, but it pales in comparison with the place of rhythm in Yemenite music, which is shaped primarily by rhythmic rather than melodic elements. Yemenite rhythm is particularly diverse in structure and is worked out in highly differentiated ways: in practice, rhythms based on units of 6, 7, 8, 11, 12, 16, 18, and 24 are all common and are organized in binary, ternary, or mixed forms, such as the 11-beat greater *das'a*, the 7-beat small *das'a*, and the 8-beat *waṣṭā*. Furthermore, rhythm tends to emphasize the more purely sonorous aspect of music. It would be misleading to discount the importance of melody altogether; nevertheless, the number of rhythmic instruments far exceeds the number of melodic instruments. This priority of rhythm is strengthened by the close association between music and dance in Yemen.

THE PRIORITY AND DIVERSITY OF RHYTHMIC INSTRUMENTS

Because detailed research is lacking and musical activity is scattered and diverse, it is difficult to portray Yemenite music accurately. Wherever one goes, one observes deviations from the expected norm. Instruments and ensembles vary from place to place and from region to region. However, there is at least one common element—the predominance of rhythmic instruments. The overview in figure 1 of instruments and ensembles used in particular settlements demonstrates this point.

Figure 1 shows that, apart from the voice, only a few melodic instruments—the *mizmār* (a double clarinet), the *madrūf* and *qaṣaba* (open, end-blown vertical flutes), the *simsimiyya* (a five- or six-stringed lyre), and the larger *ṭambūra*—confront a wide array of drums of many different types. Melodic instruments are solo instruments

FIGURE 1 Ensembles in Yemen: types and local and regional distribution. (Based on research conducted by the author in 1997.)

Melodic instrument	*Drums*	*Region/place*
HADRAMAWT		
Voice	M	Tarīm
Voice/*madrūf*	M Mf	Tarīm, Say'ūn
mizmār	2H	Hadramawt
Voice	H M handcl.	Say'ūn
mizmār	H 2M	Say'ūn
mizmār	H 2M (R)	Say'ūn
Voice/*qaṣaba* or *mizmār*	H 3M or H 2M Mf	Shiḥr, Tarīm, Say'ūn
Voice	H Y D(=R)?	Say'ūn
mizmār	M 3M R (2R)	Say'ūn
Voice	H (2H) 2M 2T, handcl., footst.	Mukallā, Shiḥr, Hadramawt
Voice	H 2M 2T R	Say'ūn
Voice	H T	Shiḥr, Hadramawt
simsimiyya	H T	Shiḥr
simsimiyya (*ṭambūra*)	3T	Tarīm
simsimiyya	2Y (3Y)	Hadramawt (Shiḥr)
HIGH PLATEAU		
—	T	al-Ḍāli'
—	_/	al-Ḍāli', Ibb, al-Ahghūr valley
Voice	_/	al-Turba
mizmār	_/	al-Turba
—	T _/	al-Ḍāli', al-Turba, Ruṣud, Dhamār, Ṣan'ā', al-Ahghūr valley
—	T _/ □	al-Turba
Voice	*ṣaḥn*	al-Ahghūr valley
Voice	□ *ṣaḥn*	al-Ahghūr valley
Voice, *mizmār*	□ *ṣaḥn*	Ṣan'ā', al-Ahghūr valley
—	T 2_/ (4–5_/)	Ibb, Ṣan'ā'
mizmār	T	Ibb, Marzūm (near Ibb)
mizmār	□ *ṣaḥn* T _/	Ḥadda
Voice, *mizmār*	□	Ḥadda
mizmār	D	Ibb
?	_/ 3D	al-Turba
mizmār	□ *ṣaḥn*	al-Turba, Ibb, Dhamār, Ṣan'ā', Ḥadda, al-Ahghūr valley
Voice	2O (-6)	al-Turba, Dhamār, Ibb
TIHĀMA		
Voice	2□	al-Zaydiyya
qaṣaba	u□	al-Mughā
qaṣaba (*mizmār*)	2□ U u	Zabīd
—	2□ U u	Ḥays, Bayt al-Faqīh
mizmār	u -o- □	al-Zaydiyya
—	U u -o- □	northern Tihāma
Voice/*mizmār*	U u -o- □	al-Zaydiyya
mizmār	U 2u 2-o- □	al-Zaydiyya

Legend:

M	*mirwās* (shallow cylindrical drum, the drumheads tensed by cords)
Mf	*mirfa'* (shallow cylindrical drum, the drumheads tensed by cords, somewhat larger than the *mirwās*)
H	*ḥāgir* (cylindrical drum, the drumheads tensed by cords)
T	*ṭasa* (shallow, bowl-shaped kettledrum)
Y	*dumbug* (cup-shaped drum)
_/	*mirfa'* (shallow, pan-shaped kettledrum)
D	*duff* (large frame drum, similar to *ṭār*)
O	*ṭār* (large frame drum with rattles on the inner side of the frame)
□	*ṭabl* (large cylindrical drum, the drumheads tensed by cords)
R	*riqq* (small frame drum with small pairs of cymbals inserted into the frame, also called *duff*)
U	*mirfa'* (large, deep kettledrum)
u	small deep kettledrum (various names)
-o-	*ṣaḥfa* (shallow, open vessel-drum with two antipodal handles)
handcl.	handclapping
footst.	footstamping
ṣaḥn	metal plate or bowl, used as a percussion instrument

FIGURE 2 *Mirfa'* (left) and *mirwās* (right) from Tarīm. Photo by Jürgen Elsner, 13 January 1980.

that appear only occasionally as accompaniment to the voice; percussion instruments appear in groups, as a rule.

Figure 1 also shows regional differences in types of instruments and the makeup of ensembles. In the Ḥaḍramawt, characteristic ensembles consist of *ḥāgir*—cylindrical drums whose drumheads are tuned by cords and gags—and several *marāwīs* (singular, *mirwās*) or two *marāwīs* and a *mirfa'* (plural, *marāfi'*; figure 2), which are played at weddings and other important social events. On the high plain, ancient tribal tradition favors the shallow kettledrums *ṭāsa* and *mirfa'*. In the Tihāma, a low plateau descending to the Red Sea, the instruments that tend to dominate are the *ṭabl*, large cylindrical drums, and deep kettledrums.

The most important deep kettledrum of the Tihāma has the same name—*mirfa'*, closely tied to the drum's function—as certain other drums played in other regions. It is not uncommon for two or more kinds of drums to share a name; in this case, the common name *mirfa'* obscures the differences between three types. In Yemenite usage, *mirfa'* may designate a small, flat, double-skinned cylindrical drum played with one hand; or a single-skinned shallow kettledrum shaped like a pan and played with sticks; or a large clay kettledrum played with large sticks. Conversely, the same drum may have different names.

Of course, figure 1 cannot provide any indication of the highly developed drumming and traditional rhythms associated with these instruments; nor can it hint at the sonic characteristics of the instruments, the drumming techniques, the sonic-rhythmic composition of the ensembles, the rhythmic formulas and sonic-rhythmic contours, their decoration and variation, or the range of possibilities of—or limits on—free rhythmic presentation. However, this table does point to the uniqueness of music making in Yemen. The sonic and rhythmic-functional differentiation and specialization of the drums in Yemenite ensembles vary greatly, depending on geography, tradition, and type of ensemble, and can have quite different effects on the final result.

REGIONAL DRUM ENSEMBLES AND STYLES

In the Ḥaḍramawt, percussion ensembles engaged for weddings (in keeping with the traditional separation of the sexes, these ensembles consist only of men or only of women) usually have four drums. The *ḥāgir*, a large double-skinned cylindrical drum played on both sides with various hand strokes, produces a number of different sounds in a low register. Three *marāwīs* (in Shiḥr; figures 3 and 4), or two *marāwīs* with one

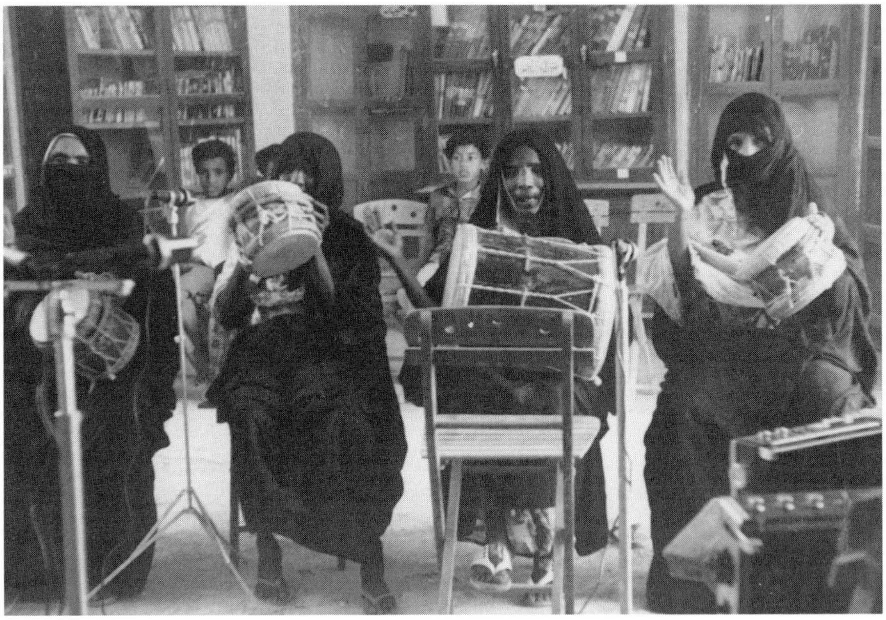

FIGURES 3 AND 4 Nawba Na'īmāt of Shiḥr with *ḥāgir* and *marāwīs*. Photo by Jürgen Elsner, 11 January 1980.

mirfa' (in Sai'ūn)—small shallow cylindrical drums whose proportions are roughly 125 millimeters in height to 170 millimeters in head diameter—are played with only one hand and are tuned differently. The different registers correspond to different functions of these drums in bringing out the basic rhythmic structure, which is like an ostinato and is specific to this region.

In Shiḥr, the small drums have special designations that correspond to their functions in creating the rhythmic fabric; this results in a threefold stratification (figure 5).

FIGURE 5 Classification of small drums in Shiḥr

high/rapid velocity

mirwās (high register) ↑
tarfī' (middle register) |
ṭanna (low register, also understood as *dumm*-stroke) |

low/moderate velocity

FIGURE 6 Musicians of Firqa Ḥadriyya of Sai'ūn with wood blocks; in front (left to right), the drums *ḥāgir*, *mirwās*, *dumbuq*, *mirwās*, and *mirfa'*. Photo by Jürgen Elsner, 15 January 1980.

In Sai'ūn, the low range is occupied by the *mirfa'* and the high range by the two *marāwīs* (figure 6). In both places, however, the small drums contrast with one another in sound, incorporating systematic tuning that is surely one reason why the wedding ensembles of the Ḥaḍramawt are so fascinating. Sonorous—even "harmonious"—rhythmic ostinatos are produced by a combination of individual drumstrokes. These strokes constitute a rhythmic configuration that emerges from the overall texture by means of pitch level, intensity, singularity, and interference effects; together, they create the desired rhythmic configuration.

TRACK 5

For example, in *ṣawt al-rubūṭ*—the first piece in the wedding repertoire of the Nawba Na'īmāt from Shiḥr—the performers drum the sequences shown in figure 7, as an accompaniment for solo and group singing. Note that the varying pitch levels indicated in the music examples refer not to specific frequencies but rather to the approximate center of a "space" determined by pitch and brightness. Also, the durations between strokes indicated by note values are only approximate (as noted earlier, detailed research on the particular characteristics of Yemenite rhythm is still lacking). The rhythmic ostinato that emerges from the combination of stroke sequences has the form shown in figure 8.

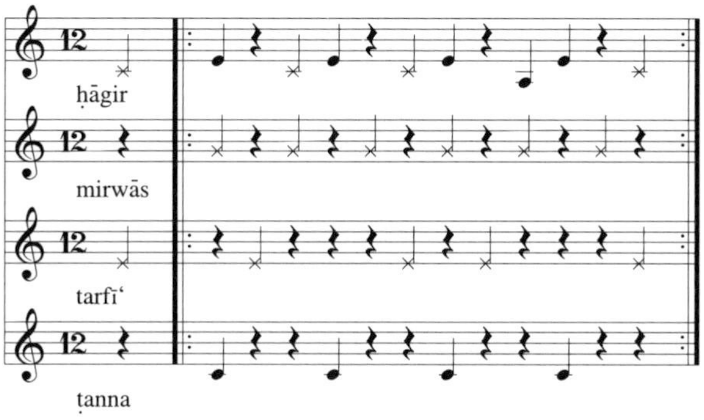

FIGURE 7 Drumming patterns: *ṣawt al-rubūṭ*, Nawba Na'īmāt at Shiḥr, 11 January 1980.

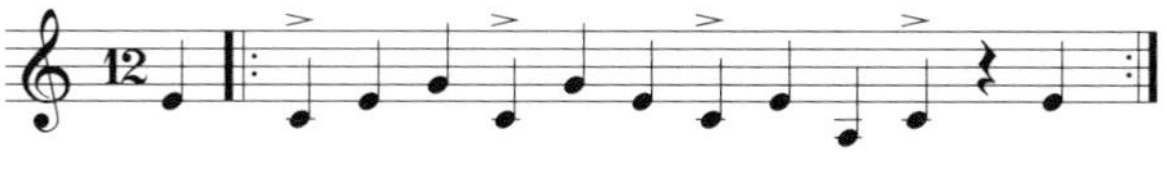

FIGURE 8 Rhythmic ostinato of the *rubūṭ* of Nawba Na'īmāt at Shiḥr.

FIGURE 9 *Mirwās* and *mirfa'* players of Firqa Āl Bā Ṣāliḥ of Sai'ūn. Photo by Jürgen Elsner, 13 January 1980.

FIGURE 10 Relative pitch levels of two drum ensembles from Sai'ūn.

The "harmonic" sound engendered by the drum tuning of the Shiḥr ensemble is rather unusual. Other regional and local traditions of drum tuning in the Ḥaḍramawt differ from it, and from one another. Two examples are the Zirbādī troupe Āl Bā Ṣāliḥ (figure 9) and the women's ensemble Ḥadriyya from Sai'ūn (figure 6). In both of these ensembles, however, the two high-register *marāwīs* are pitched closer together, while the lower *mirfa'* is pitched at a greater distance. The relative pitch levels of these two ensembles are notated in figure 10.

Despite such differences in the Ḥaḍramawt, one common principle underlies the production of the basic rhythmic cycles: the *ḍurūb* (singular, *ḍarb* 'rhythmic cycle'; also *daqqa* 'stroke' and *īqā'*; plural, *īqā'āt*) serve to mesh together the sounds of the differently tuned drums. The individual drums, then, have no independent rhythmic cycles; each drum makes an essential contribution to the overall cycle. The omission of even a single drum would make the rhythmic cycle defective, because the pitch of every drum is necessary to the overall pattern; and one defective cycle would tend to result in another ill-fitting cycle that would soon lead the ensemble astray. (Figure 7 shows this clearly.) The drumming created by this principle can be described as a sonically differentiated combinatory style.

In the Tihāma, drumming and drumming style are entirely different. The drumming of the most important Tihāma ensembles—for example, those that perform at weddings—may be described as a sonically differentiated cumulative style. Here, a *firqa* 'group', 'troupe', or 'ensemble' usually has four drums, divided sonically and functionally into two deep kettledrums and two large cylindrical drums (figure 11). In this hierarchy, the lower-register drums play more slowly than the higher-register drums. With respect to register and mobility, the musicians of Bayt al-Faqīh, Zabīd, and Ḥēs categorize their drums as shown in figure 12. The *mirfa'* is the indispensable foundation of the rhythmic structure unfolded by the small kettledrums (*dumduma* or *ṭungura*) and the low cylindrical drums (*makab*, *ṭabl marad*, and *ṭabl bōga*), which

FIGURE 11 Firqa Sha'biyya of Zabīd with (left to right) *ṭabl mu'asṭā, mizmār, dumduma, mirfa'* and *ṭabl marad*. Photo by Jürgen Elsner, 21 February 1989.

FIGURE 12 Organization of drums in the *firqa* of Bayt al-Faqīh, Zabīd, and Ḥēs.

Bait al-Faqīh	Zabīd	Ḥēs	
			high/rapid velocity ↑
ṭungura	*dumduma* or *ṭungura*	*ṭabl mu'asṭā*	
ṭabl sāgh	*ṭabl mu'asṭā*	*dumduma*	
makab	*ṭabl marad*	*ṭabl bōga*	
large *mirfa'*	*mirfa'*	large *mirfa'*	
			low/moderate velocity

are struck on both sides. Over this rhythmic fabric, a cylindrical drum (*ṭabl sāgh* or *ṭabl mu'asṭā*), played on one head in a distinctive fashion with both hands, provides a brilliant rhythmic improvisation.

The principal difference between this style and the Ḥaḍramawt style is that in the Tihāma, each drummer produces his own independent rhythmic voice, which is constructed from one or more rhythmic figures of varying breadth and freedom. In general, short, quick rhythmic figures are associated with the small kettledrums (*dumduma* or *ṭungura*), whereas the large kettledrums maintain a stable pulse that—depending on the specific dance—may be short and of moderate speed or may unfold at a running pace with shifting patterns of accents and differentiated sequences of sounds. The low cylindrical drum adds broader rhythmic figures that are also repeatedly varied. Over this polyphonic sonic-rhythmic web created by the superimposition of the various drums, the highest cylindrical drum plays a freely organized, virtuosic, solo role. This can be seen in figure 13, a transcription of the dance *al-Ghall* from Zabīd.

In contrast to the complex drumming styles of the Ḥaḍramawt and the Tihāma is the relatively simple style of ensembles in the high plateau. These ensembles accompany the ubiquitous dancing and men's group singing at wedding celebrations, for example. The rhythmic accompaniment is provided by a duo of *ṭāsa-mirfa'*, or by groups with one *ṭāsa* and several *marāfi'* (figures 14 and 15). These two types of drums differ in timbre and register, owing to differences in skin tension, shape, and volume: the *ṭāsa* sounds bright and high while the *mirfa'* sounds dark and low. In general, the *ṭāsa* is the leading instrument and is obligatory; the *mirfa'* is considered supplementary (*murāghi'*). An old *myazzin*—a professional musician—described the

FIGURE 13 *Raqṣat al-Ghall,* Firqa Sha'biyya of Zabīd, 21 February 1989. Transcription by Jürgen Elsner (tapes JAR 11 and 12).

mirfa' as the "echo" of the *ṭāsa*: it may imitate the *ṭāsa* and create periodic relationships and variations over long stretches. *Ḍarbat Sayyārī*, recorded in Ḍāli' in the southeast region of the high plain, is an example (figure 16). However, the *mirfa'* can, on occasion, be dispensed with.

TRACK 6

Because of the functional relationship between the two types of drums, this drumming (in contrast to that of the Ḥaḍramawt or the Tihāma), can be described as a simple supplementary style.

RHYTHMIC CYCLES, FREE RHYTHM, AND IMPROVISATION

The shifting formal structures and relative independence of the individual drums that provide a rhythmic foundation for song and dance cannot be described uniformly. Free interpretation and improvisation are more or less circumscribed in most situations, but a rhythmic voice can still go quite far in this direction. The extent of such freedom depends on norms of traditional musical practice, and these norms are de-

FIGURE 14 *Ṭāsa* (left) and *mirfa'* accompanying the *bar'a* dance, on the Ghabal Saṯḥ at Wadi Żahr northwest of Ṣan'ā'. Photo by Jürgen Elsner, 7 August 1997.

FIGURE 15 *Ṭāsa* and two *marāfi'*, accompanying a dance and procession, on the Ghabal Saṯḥ at Wadi Żahr northwest of Ṣan'ā'. Photo by Jürgen Elsner, 7 August 1997.

termined at the level of systematic thought and articulation as well as at the level of a particular genre. Moreover, the norms vary greatly throughout Yemen. This variety can be attributed to—among other factors—the considerable regional differences in Yemen, which are reflected in the varied instrumental groupings. This differentiation is extensive and suggests that there are numerous relatively independent local systems, each in need of further exploration.

Some norms affecting the degree of rhythmic-formal freedom and improvisation have to do with the position and function assigned to each drum as it spins its rhythmic web. For a particular voice, the conditions of or constraints on its function—that is, the construction of a planned, collectively formed, enjoyable product or effect through rational, practical agreement—can be stricter or freer, depending on the foundation of the rhythmic structure (articulated by the drumming style) and on the rhythmic shape that will emerge. It is important to remember, however, that the determination of what is "free" and what is "obligatory" can vary greatly, according to content. Ideals and criteria for shape and identity, which are understood differently from culture to culture, are decisive. For example, one culture may see the creation of variants as an overall change or even a metamorphosis, whereas another culture may see such variations as representing mobility, animation, topicality, or personality, with little relevance to the formal structure. To all appearances, the latter understanding seems generally to be the case in Yemen.

The same is true of improvisation, in that despite the relatively free rhythmic configurations, (apart from retention of the substratum), there are requirements, standards, and boundaries. In traditional practice, the bounds of individual creativity, parameters, models, sequences, turns of phrase, and the like are predetermined and are realized in practice. Improvisation in this context is neither a free, independent play of ideas nor simple extemporization.

The sonically differentiated combinatory style of the Ḥaḍramawt wedding ensemble makes it clear that the deployment of drums and the drumming sequences are strictly regulated in order to establish the character and rhythmic cycles of the song being accompanied (*ṣawt* 'voice', 'tone', an old traditional vocal genre). Free strokes or rhythmic figures are not called for, as can be seen in the drumming pattern of the *ṣawt al-rubūṭ* (figure 7). In contrast to the strict rhythmic ostinato of the drums, the song of the lead vocalist and the other singers is rhythmically quite free, although it

FIGURE 16 *Ḍarbat Sayyārī*, performed by Aḥmad Muḥammad Gha‘ūf on *ṭāsa* and Ṣāliḥ Muḥammad Ṣāliḥ on *mirfa‘*, Ḍāli‘, 21 December 1979. Transcription by Jürgen Elsner (tape Laḥiğ 4).

follows a fixed, predetermined melodic line, as can be seen by comparing the lead vocalist's lines with the group's answer and the ensuing alternation between them. Variations in detail in the melodic motion enhance the delivery, but the overall form remains unchanged. This is a matter of the arrangement and inner enrichment of the melody, not of variation or ornamentation.

Men's ensembles in the Ḥaḍramawt differ from women's ensembles in repertoire and in their use of a flute (*madrūf*) along with the voice, but they are similar to women's ensembles in their ordering of the individual drums into determined sequences of strokes and in the effect produced by the gliding, rhythmically mobile melodies of the voice and flute. An example is the *īqā‘ al-istimā‘* (figure 17), which accompanies the *zaffa* 'procession' of the groom from his house to the *makhdara*, the "refuge" of the bride. The drums are organized in a fashion similar to the women's ensemble. Superficially, the repeated cyclical figures of the drums seem to diverge; but this impression is due to differences between the instrumental and vocal versions (18

TRACK 8-7

rhythmic units in the introduction and interludes and 12 in the vocal version); actually, the overall rhythmic cycles follow the same principle as the Nawba Naʿīmāt. To the listener, the patterns produced by the individual drums are melded, as with the *rubūṭ*, into unified, pervasive rhythmic ostinatos (figure 18).

In contrast, the sonically differentiated cumulative style of the Tihāma drum ensemble is based on an element of improvisation. However, even this style depends on a relatively fixed rhythmic foundation. The *mirfaʿ* 'kettledrum' and *dumduma* each have a fixed function—an obligation that allows only the *mirfaʿ* some variation in accentuation and in the sequence of sounds. Rhythmic and formal freedom belongs more to the realm of the cylindrical drums, among which the low-pitched drum whose contribution is understood as *hādī* 'leading', 'directing' or as *thaqīl* 'measured', 'slow', 'moderate' typically features short rhythmic figures. The drummer is free to play these figures strictly or to transform or develop them through an exchange of sounds drawn from the two drumheads, diminuition, augmentation, or expansion. These manipulations by an individual drummer can create a highly distinct rhythmic profile that intensifies the music. But these rhythmic voices are also bound by certain conventions related to their respective functions. (In figure 13 the *marad* drummer persists with a certain figure; in figure 19 the same drummer makes a much richer contribution.)

TRACK 8 The high-sounding cylindrical drum that contrasts in movement and shape with the basic drums provides the decisive contribution to the overall rhythmic profile. In

FIGURE 17 Drumming patterns of *īqāʿ al-istimāʿ*, instrumental and vocal sections. Notated from a recording of Firqat al-Zirbādī of Shiḥr, 11 January 1980.

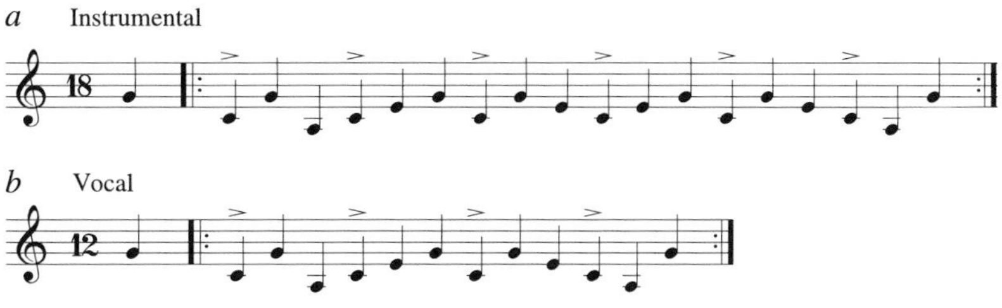

FIGURE 18 Rhythmic ostinato in instrumental and vocal sections of *īqāʿ al-istimāʿ*. Firqat al-Zirbādī of Shiḥr, 11 January 1980.

FIGURE 19 *Raqṣat al-Mansarī*, Firqa Sha'biyya of Zabīd, 21 February 1989. Transcription by Jürgen Elsner.

contrast to the low cylindrical *marad* drum, this drum creates a fast-moving, exciting line (*khafīf* 'light', 'quick'); combinations of strokes by both hands on a single drumhead produce different types of sounds. Sometimes conflicting with the prevailing rhythm and accents, sometimes falling into line with the rhythmic cycle, this drum soars excitedly over the sonic-rhythmic foundation created by the others. (This can be seen clearly in figure 13, *Raqṣat al-Ghall.*) Although it is firmly rooted in the rhythmic play of the dance, and in traditional musical norms, the *ṭabl mu'asṭā*, the leading drum, can improvise freely to stimulate the drumming accompanying dance and heighten its effect.

Also in contrast to the relatively constrained style of the Ḥaḍramawt ensemble is the drumming of the *ṭāsa-mirfa'*-group of the highlands, which displays greater freedom in rhythmic shaping. However, the style of rhythmic improvisation in the highlands does not correspond to the principles applied in the Tihāma. First, the two instruments involved do not have the rich sonic palette of ensembles from the Ḥaḍramawt and the Tihāma. Each drum is restricted to its own range: one high, the other low. Second, the most important elements are the stroke sequences and figures, their inner elaboration, and the accentuation; these have a different significance because of the special functions of the *mirfa'* and the *ṭāsa*. In a duo, the lower-pitched *mirfa'* is assigned the task of securing the underlying beat of the dance—a task the drummer accomplishes by a simple playing of the beat, by the execution of simple rhythmic figures, or both. The *ṭāsa* provides the rhythmic shape, creating a series of rhythmic figures that are repeated, interpreted, varied, and developed in several ways. If necessary, the *mirfa'* can be dispensed with, because the rhythmic figures of the *ṭāsa* always preserve the fundamental beat. In the drum accompaniment to the *bara'* dance in Turba (figure 20), the *mirfa'* provides a simple rhythmic pulse; in the *Ḍarbat Sayyāri* in Ḍāli', further to the east (figure 16), the *mirfa'* is more like the *ṭāsa*, with greater movement and improvisation.

In the tradition of the Ahghūr valley in the northern highlands (northwest of Ṣan'ā'), the *ṭāsa* part is based on the repeated, simple rhythmic "cell" of the *mirfa'*, corresponding closely to the movement of the dance. The spacing and accents of beats, the phrasing and subdivisions, and the runs and countermotions—all of which constitute the rhythmic figures of the *ṭāsa*—have a reciprocal relationship with the foundation of the *mirfa'*. The *ṭāsa* player accompanying the dance executes the rhythmic line with a certain freedom. This imaginativeness is grounded in a rhythmic vocabulary handed down from generation to generation, yet it is made individual through years of practice and is expanded wherever it can be. From this vocabulary the drummer creates and varies the rhythmic figures, usually in two to four rhythmic units and following the development of the dance. Figures that extend over the four units of time are most common (figure 21).

FIGURE 20 *Ḍarb al-Bara'*: Yasīn S. Shamsān (*ṭāsa*) and Sā'id Ṣāliḥ (*mirfa'*). Recorded by the author in Turba, south of Ta'iz, 12 February 1989 (tape JAR 7).

FIGURE 21 One of the most common drumming figures for the *bar'a* dance in the Ahghūr valley (Yammine 1995).

The *ṭāsa* player is expected not only to decorate figures with syncopation and shifts in meter and accent but also to enrich the texture and to display virtuosity through quick strokes, rolls, and mordents. Corresponding with the tempo of their sections, specific dances may be shaped by different figures and allow for different variations and insertions, in which the individuality of the performer can shine through. The ability and talent of a *ṭāsa* player will be prized to the extent that he understands how to vary the structures of his drumming figures and enrich them from within, and how to put together sequences appropriate to the evolution of the dance, all in the context of freedom governed by traditional rules.

In this context, then, the term *improvisation* cannot be understood simply as freedom within the bounds of a historically developed musical system of thought and articulation; still less can it be understood as a transgression or negation of these bounds. More precisely, it refers to a free negotiation with traditional structural elements, based on transmitted forms and genres. In other words, improvisation in this sense is a liberal arrangement and enrichment of musical building blocks, or structural concepts, that are relatively fixed in the repertoire and in practice. The decisive factor in this negotiation is the way in which the performer, while observing the social obligations that are essential for the cohesion of the community, allows individuality and individual achievement to come to the fore and makes possible a creative reinterpretation of the tradition.

TRANSLATED BY ALEXANDER J. FISHER

REFERENCES

Bakewell, Anderson. 1985. "Music." In *Studies on the Tihāmah*, ed. Francine Stone, 104–108. London: Longman.

Elsner, Jürgen. 1990. "Trommeln und Trommelensembles im Jemen." In *Beiträge zur traditionellen Musik*, ed. Andreas Michel and Jürgen Elsner, 18–37. Berlin: Humboldt Universität.

———. 1992. "Trommeln und Trommelspiel im Jemen." In *Von der Vielfalt der musikalischen Kultur: Festschrift für Josef Kuckertz*, ed. Rüdiger Schumacher, 183–205. Anif/Salzburg: Ursula Müller-Speiser.

Ghābir, 'Alī Aḥmad. 1988. "Ḥāḍir wa-mustaqbal al-ghinā' fī 'l-yaman" (Song in Yemen: Today and Tomorrow). In *Dirāsāt al-Yamaniyya* 33 (July/August/September): 109–166. Ṣan'ā': Yemen Center for Studies and Research.

Ghānim, Muḥammad 'Abduh. 1987. *Shi'r al-ghinā' aṣ-ṣan'ānī* (The Poetry of Ṣan'ā' Song). Beirut: Dār al-'Awda.

Halīl Ḥusain 'Ālī. 1988. "Al-'idda Dance in the Yemen." *Al-Ma'thūrāt al-sha'biyya (al-Duḥa/Qatar)* 3(12):6–15.

Lambert, Jean. 1989. "Du 'chanteur' à 'l'artiste' vers un nouveau statut du musicien." *Yemen Sanaa, Peuples Méditerranéens* 46.

———. 1997. *La médecine de l'âme: Musique et musiciens dans la société citadine à Ṣan'ā'*. Nanterre: Société d'Ethnologie.

Serjeant, Robert B. 1951. *Prose and Poetry from Hadramawt*. London: Taylor's Foreign Press.

Yammine, Habib. 1995. "Les hommes des tribus et leur musique (Hauts-plateaux yéménites, vallée d'al-Ahjur)." Ph.D. dissertation, Université de Paris X Nanterre.

Music in Performance: Who Are the Whirling Dervishes?

Walter Feldman

The Mevlevî Order: Historical Background
Musical Actrivity in the Mevlevî Order
The Mevlevî *Ayîn*

In Ottoman times a visit to one of the Mevlevî cloisters (*mevlevîhâne*) of Constantinople was a touristic must comparable to the pyramids of Egypt or the Acropolis in Athens. Travelers' descriptions, such as those of Pietro Della Valle (seventeenth century), Lady Mary Wortley Montagu (early eighteenth century), and Carsten Neibuhr (later eighteenth century), as well as European paintings of the ceremony in the cloisters, furnish some of the earliest documents. In modern times, very few musical institutions of the Middle East have acquired a place in the Western cultural imagination sufficiently important to neccessitate a Western name. Among these is the ceremony of the "whirling dervishes"—virtually a household word even among people who may never have heard of the Mevlevîs. The lyrical poetry of Mevlânâ 'Our Master' Jalāl-uddin Rûmî (d. 1273) is today a best-seller in the United States (mainly in Coleman Barks's translation), although his mystical-didactic *Mesnevî* is virtually unknown. The more expressive aspects of Mevlânâ Rûmî and the Mevlevî tradition have long appealed to the Western imagination, but the deeper structural elements remain obscure.

THE MEVLEVÎ ORDER: HISTORICAL BACKGROUND

The Mevlevî *tarikat* (Sufi order) was organized in Konya by Mevlânâ's son Sultan Veled (d. 1312). It was initially associated with the Saljuk and then the Karaman states of Anatolia; its first permanent establishment (*tekke*) in the new Ottoman capital of Istanbul, the Galata *mevlevîhâne*, was founded in 1494. The second major *tekke*, at Yenikapı, was founded a century later, in 1597. Two others, at Kasımpaş and Beşiktaş, followed in the early seventeenth century, and the Üsküdar *tekke* in the late eighteenth century. There were other major centers Manisa, Karahisar, Bahariyya, Gallipoli, Bursa, and Edirne. Further afield in the Ottoman Empire were the *mevlevîhâne* of Aleppo, Damascus, Hims, Latakia, Tripoli, Beirut, Jerusalem, and Cairo. Still others were built in the Balkan provinces, such as Greece, Bulgaria, and Bosnia.

Until the late seventeenth century, all leaders (*sheikh*) were appointed by the Çelebi, who were descended from Mevlânâ and lived at the central *tekke* (Asitâne) in Konya. Thereafter, families of hereditary sheikhs emerged in Istanbul; these families' views often differed from those of the usually more conservative Çelebi. By the seventeenth century the Mevlevî order in the capital was deeply involved with the Ottoman ruling class and tended to represent the freest and most innovative intellectual currents within that group. As a natural development of the ideas of Mevlânâ—an outstanding poet, thinker, and patron of music—the order saw intellectual and artistic attainments as essential to spiritual advancement. The families of the hereditary sheikhs had members who were outstanding patrons and exemplars of the arts, especially music, poetry, and calligraphy. Because of the continuity created by the hereditary leadership, in recent centuries many of the *mevlevîhâne* also functioned as music conservatories and advanced schools where the Persian language and Persian literature were taught systematically.

By the late eighteenth century, the Ottoman state tended to rely on the Mevlevîs for support as it undertook reforms that were contrary to the interests of the orthodox clergy and the janissary corps. Mevlevîs in Istanbul were also strong supporters of the westernizing reforms of the Tanzimat after 1839. Nevertheless, the Mevlevîye was banned—along with all other *tarikat*—by order of Mustafa Kemal Atatürk in 1925; its central Asitâne in Konya and the Galata *tekke* were turned into museums. After 1925 many leading Mevlevîs became active in secular life; for instance, the last sheikh of the Yenikapı *tekke*, Abdülbaki Dede (d. 1935), became a university teacher of Persian literature, and the dervish musician Rauf Yekta Bey (d. 1935) became the founder of modern Turkish musicology. Still, the demanding training and the elaborate ritual of the Mevlevîye were an obstacle to its continuity after its official dissolution.

MUSICAL ACTIVITY IN THE MEVLEVÎ ORDER

The importance of the Mevlevî order within Ottoman Turkish music must be assessed from several points of view. An organized ritual, known as *âyîn* or *mukabbele*, based on musical compositions emerged in the fifteenth century under the direction of Pîr Adil Çelebi (1421–1460). During this period, Anatolian Turkish art music as a whole developed in original ways, apparently somewhat distinct from the centers of art music in Iran and the Arab countries. For most of the following century (under the sultans Selim I and Süleyman I), however, this originality almost ceased, except for the continuous musical creativity of the Mevlevî dervishes. When an independent Anatolian Turkish art music reemerged in the early seventeenth century, the Mevlevî dervishes interacted with it in several significant ways. By the middle of the century, Mevlevî *neyzen* 'flutists' constituted more than half of the master flutists identified by Evliyâ Çelebi; and by the end of the century they occupied an equally prominent position at the court. Furthermore, their instrument, the *ney* 'reed flute', became the second instrument of the courtly ensemble—a unique development within Islamic art musics. The *ney taksîm* was not only a part of the *âyîn*; it was (and still is) a mature, independent art form.

TRACK 2 The orthodox clergy succeeded in banning the Mevlevî *âyîn* from 1666 to 1684; but even during these years, and immediately afterward, the leading composers of the Ottoman court included several Mevlevî musicians, such as Köçek Mustafa Dede (d. 1683), Buhûrîzâde Mustafa Itrî (d. 1712), and Nayî Osman Dede (d. 1730). In the next century (the eighteenth), their influence increased, and Niebhur (1792) described them as "the best musicians among the Turks." By the beginning of the nineteenth century, the *ney* had displaced other types of flute (notably the panpipe *mıskal*) in the courtly ensemble. The culmination of the Mevlevî musical tradition is represented by Hammamîzâde Ismail Dede (1778–1846), the leading composer of the entire modern era of Ottoman music, who was as crucial in the development of secular music as he was to Mevlevî music.

In the eighteenth century, Greek Orthodox church psalters become serious students of the Mevlevîs, and Petros the Peloponnesian (1730–1777) was known as their musical disciple. During the seventeenth and eighteenth centuries, when it was rare for a provincial musician to enter the court, the principal exceptions seem to have been Mevlevî flutists and kettledrummers.

The Mevlevîs had long assumed a major role in musical pedagogy, and their importance in this regard increased during the economic dislocations of the nineteenth century, when other social groups were unable to perform that function. Consequently, in modern Turkey Mevlevî musicians often stand at the beginning of the line of musical transmission, which frequently involves such central figures as Ismail Dede Efendi, his student Zekâî Dede, his son Zekâîzâde Ahmed Irsoy, Hüseyin Fahreddin Efendi, Azîz Dede, and Emin Dede. For many Turks, this modern link reinforces and even exaggerates the definition of Ottoman art music as "Sufi music," an opinion that has spread to Europe and the Americas because of the whirling dervishes' public tours.

The two earliest indigenous systems of notation developed by the Ottomans were those of Prince Demetrius Cantemir (d. 1723) and the Galata Mevlevî sheikh Osman Dede (d. 1730). Cantemir's notation was perfected by the dervish Mustafa Kevserî (d. 1770); and the sheikh of the Yenikapı *tekke*, Abdülbaki Nâsir Dede (d. 1820), produced both a new system of notation and a major book of theory, *Tetkîk ü Tahkîk* (1795). Modern Turkish musicology is essentially the creation of Rauf Yekta Bey (1871–1935), a student of the Yenikapı *neyzen* Cemal Efendi and Azîz Dede. He founded the Istanbul Conservatory (Dârülelhân) in 1914 and was responsible for numerous major collections of and publications on Ottoman music.

THE MEVLEVÎ *ÂYÎN*

Throughout the Ottoman period, westerners' fascination with the "whirling dervishes" seemed to have little affect on the position of the Mevlevî order within the empire; but in the Republican period the emic and etic perceptions of the order and its ritual have interacted more significantly. Permission was granted to reinstate a form of the traditional annual commemoration of the night of the death of Rûmî (Şeb-i 'Arûs) on December 1953 (although not in the mausoleum in Konya); this quickly met with a positive response in Europe, and later in America. In fact, the commemoration was the one Turkish-Islamic cultural event that began to serve as an international tourist attraction, and soon it was being sponsored by the ministry of tourism of Konya. The initial decision to allow the Şeb-i 'Arûs ceremony seems to have resulted from purely internal pressures, but the many other yearly performances of the general Mevlevî ceremony in Istanbul and in European and North American cities cannot be separated from the demand in the West.

Historically the Mevlevî *âyîn* was conceived of both as a ritual that would benefit the participants and as a spiritual concert, like the medieval Sufi *samâ'*, that would instill belief (*feyz*) in the audience. Unlike the medieval Sufi *samâ'*, the Mevlevî *samâ'* was not restricted: women and non-Muslims were allowed to observe the rituals. Mevlevî *tekke* were constructed with both a musicians' gallery and a clearly demarcated space for nonparticipants.

Collections of lyrics dating from the seventeenth century and later contain texts of compositions for the *âyîn* ceremony, with the names of composers. These texts are generally in Persian and usually taken from the *Divân-i Shams-i Tabrîzî* or from the *Mesnevî* of Rûmî. Such documents attest to the existence of musical compositions corresponding in their formal structure to the *âyîn* of the later tradition. Several *âyîn* are ascribed to well-known musical figures of the eighteenth and seventeenth centuries,

The "whirling dervishes" are virtually a household word even among people who may never have heard of the Mevlevîs.

including Buhurîzâde Itrî (d. 1712) and Osman Dede (d. 1730). The earliest composer known to us by name was Köçek Mustafa Dede (d. 1683), whose work *Beyâtî âyîn* is the best-known *âyîn* today; he is also mentioned in contemporary sources as a composer of secular courtly music. Three *âyîn* earlier than the *Beyatî âyîn* of Köçek Mustafa survive today; they are known collectively as the "ancient compositions" in *makam* 'mode' *pençgâh*, *makam hüseynî*, and *makam dügâh*. (The ancient *dügâh* is the modern *uşşak*.) Of these three only the first is complete, having all four sections (*selâm*). The *dügâh âyîni* has three sections, and the *hüseyni* only one.

Most of the surviving *âyîn* repertoire was composed from the late eighteenth century to the first half of the nineteenth century, when the order received substantial patronage from the Ottoman rulers Selim III (1789–1808) and Mahmud II (1808–1839). In addition to the *âyîn* of Ismail Dede Efendi, compositions continued to be created thoughout the nineteenth century, including major *âyîn* by Mustafa Naki Dede, Haim Bey, Neyzen Salih Dede, Hacî Faik Bey, Zekâî Dede, Hüseyin Fahrettin Dede, and Sermüezzin Rif'at Bey. In the early twentieth century, *âyîn* were created by such musicians as Bolahenk Nûrî Bey (d. 1910), Zekâîzâde Ahmed Irsoy (d. 1943), Ahmed Avnî Konuk (d. 1938), and Kâzim Uz (d. 1938); composers of recent years include Cinuçen Tanrıkorur and Alâettin Yavaşça.

Since the beginning of the nineteenth century the *âyîn* has had the following structure:

1. *Na'at-i şerîf*: a composed rubato form.
2. *Taksîm* on the *ney*.
3. *Peşrev* in *usûl muza'af devr-i kebîr* (56/4).
4. *Selâm-i Evvel* in *usûl devr-i revân* (14/8) or *düyek* (8/4).
5. *Selâm-i Sânî* in *usûl evfer* (9/4).
6. *Selâm-i Sâlis* beginning in *usûl devr-i kebîr* (28/4) and continuing in *usûl semâ'î* (6/8).
7. *Selâm-i Râbi'* in *usûl evfer*.
8. *Taksîm* on the *ney*.
9. *Son peşrev* in *usûl düyek*.
10. *Son yürük semâ'î* (6/8).

The earliest notated Mevlevî *âyîn* dates from 1795—this is the Sûzidilârâ *âyîn* of Sultan Selim III in the "*Tahrîrîye*" of Abdülbakî Nâsir Dede. Since then, and following the fixing of the entire known repertoire in Hamparsum notation in the 1860s, changes in the transmission of the *âyîn* have been relatively minor. Raûf Yektâ's edition of 1923–1939 reperesents an oral tradition predating the Hamparsum manuscript, approaching the style of the 1795 document. Although it is possible to generalize about the form of the repertoire dating from the turn of the nineteenth century, we cannot be certain that various features were not introduced into older compositions at that time. The vocal core and the instrumental introduction and closing of the *âyîn* seem to have been treated differently: the introduction and closing were usually modernized stylistically or replaced with newer items.

In compositional structure, *âyîn* differ substantially from the courtly *fasıl.* For example, AABA structure (known as *zemîn-miyân*) exists only in an altered form in the early *âyîn* and was abandoned by the late eighteenth century; the long *usûl*, with correspondingly retarded tempos and melodic elaboration typical of the courtly *beste* and *kâr*, is found only in a modified form in the opening of the third *selâm*; there are no *terennüm* (nontextual) sections; and the entire *âyîn*, unlike the courtly *fasıl*, is a context of large-scale modulation, so that each *selâm* is often composed in a different *makam*.

REFERENCES

Heper, Sadettin. 1979. *Mevlevî Ayînleri*. Konya: Konya Turizm Derneği.

Montagu, Mary Wortley. 1965–1966. *The Complete Works of Lady Mary Wortley Montagu*, ed. Robert Halshand. Oxford: Clarendon.

Niebuhr, Carsten. 1792. *Travels through Arabia and Other Countries in the East*. Edinburgh: Morison and Son.

Valle, Pietro Della. 1845 (1614). *Viaggi di Pietro Della Valle*. Brighton: G. Gancia.

Yekta, Rauf. 1900 (1318). "Hoca Zekâî Dede Efendi/" In *Esâtîz ül-Elhân*, vol. 1. Istanbul: Mahmûd Bey.

———. 1922 "La musique turque." In *Encyclopedie de la musique et dictionnaire de Conservatoire*, ed. Albert Lavignac, Vol. 5:2945–3064. Paris: Delgrave.

———. 1923–1939 *Mevlevî Ayînleri*. Istanbul: Istanbul Belediye Konservatuarı.

———. 1925. "Dede Efendi" In *Esâtîz ül-Elhân*, vol. 3. Istanbul: Evkaf-i Islâmiyye.

Ottoman Turkish Music: Genre and Form

Walter Feldman

Popular and Elite Forms of *Makam* Music
The Mevlevî *Âyîn*
Cyclical Performance Forms: The Courtly *Fasıl*
The Instrumental *Fasıl* and the *Taksîm*
Aspects of Form in the Classical Repertoire

Anatolia had participated significantly in the *maqām* art music of the Muslim world as early as the thirteenth century. In the fourteenth century, under the Mongols, the southeast part of the country had been particularly active in music, showing close musical relations with the Ilkanid capital in Azerbaijan. During the fifteenth century, under the Ottomans, several musicological treatises were written in Turkish and Arabic, and the musical life of the Mevlevî dervishes continued to develop in the central Anatolian city of Konya. [See Music in Performance: Who Are the Whirling Dervishes?] In secular music, characteristically Ottoman forms begin to appear in the second half of the sixteenth century. By the first half of the seventeenth century, it becomes possible to trace the development of musical form and genre among the Ottomans, through two major notated collections: *Mecmû'a-Ï Saz ü Söz* (c. 1650), by the Ottomanized Pole Wojciech Bobowski (Ali Ufkî Bey); and the collection (c. 1700) of the Moldavian prince Demetrius Cantemir. Other notated collections as well as sporadic notations by travelers and resident foreigners allow us to trace the main lines of development until 1815, when abundant notated documents began to be generated by the local adoption of the Armenian alphabetic notation of Baba Hamparsum.

During the first half of the sixteenth century, the vast expansion of the Ottoman Empire seems to have encouraged the Turkish court to adhere to an international standard for composition, performance practice, and instrumentation which was largely based in Safavid Iran. During this period Iranian musicians had an important place in the music of the court in Istanbul. After the death of Sultan Süleyman "the Magnificent" in 1566, Ottoman court music underwent several changes which appear to have led, by the early seventeenth century, to the establishment of a distinct Ottoman Turkish norm in musical form, performance practice, and instrumentation. These changes include:

1. Arrangement of the concert performance as a cycle (*fasıl*) of composed and improvised items.
2. Dominance of a vocal form known as *beste,* which, among composed genres, used the widest variety of long rhythmic cycles (*usûl*) and the longest melodic lines.
3. Use of the Turkish language for most musical compositions.

4. Establishment of an independent improvised genre (*taksîm*) for both vocal and instrumental music. This new genre was independent of rhythmic cycles and poetic meters, used codified melodic progressions within individual modal entities, and modulated widely among several modes.
5. Establishment of a separate performance cycle for instrumentalists (*fasıl-i sazende*), based largely on the *taksîm*.
6. Development of the instrumental *peşrev* as a major compositional form, structurally independent of any vocal form.
7. Gradual elimination of certain instruments that had been held in common with the broader Islamic culture and their replacement by a new instrumentarium featuring the indigenous long-necked lute *tanbûr* and a newly developed series of reed-flute *ney* with bone mouthpieces.

The dating of these changes in the music of the court is fairly precise, but the development of other musical genres is known only in broad terms. The other major branch of *makam* (*maqâm*) music was represented by the musical-choreographic ritual (*âyîn-şerîf*; *semâ*) of the Mevlevî dervishes, which by the later sixteenth century appears to have assumed something approaching its late-eighteenth-century form. Although they shared one modal system, the music of the Mevlevîs and that of the Ottoman court differed in compositional form, instrumentation, and performance practices. The rhythmic cycles and compositional structures of most of the *âyîn* had been held in common by Ottoman and Persian music in the later sixteenth and early seventeenth century, but the specific approach to composition of most of the extant *âyîn* differs from the courtly repertoire in ways that may reflect the Mevlevîs' development of earlier Persian practices. On the other hand, some parts of the *âyîn* (the third *selâm* and the *peşrev*) seem to reflect the more general Ottoman compositional developments of the eighteenth century. From the seventeenth century to the nineteenth, the influence of the Mevlevîs on the music of the Ottoman court may be seen in the dominance of Mevlevî *ney* players (*neyzen*) at court, in the new position of the *ney* in the courtly ensemble, in the replacement of the Persian *ney* (*ney-i 'Irakîye*) by the local type, and in the eventual displacement of all other wind instruments (such as the panpipe *mıskal*) from the courtly ensemble.

POPULAR AND ELITE FORMS OF *MAKAM* MUSIC

Makam music developed in two large social spheres: on the one hand, the music of the elite, including the court, its grandees, and the upper bureaucracy, as well as the Mevlevî dervishes; and, on the other hand, the urban merchants and artisans. By the seventeenth century, the musical significance of these social categories had become quite permeable, as the music of the court was sometimes performed and composed by musicians coming from the merchant and artisanal classes. Nevertheless, while individuals of these classes entered the sphere of courtly music, as a whole they patronized other musical genres. In addition, the vocal music of the mosque was held in common by the whole urban Muslim population. Beginning in the later sixteenth century, several musical forms that had originated among the largely middle-class Halvetî and Celvetî Sufi orders became accepted in the mosques. The interpenetration of several religious, Sufi, and secular styles was facilitated by the entry of many mosque muezzins into the courtly *fasıl* and into the Sufi *zikr*.

Until their destruction in 1826 the janissaries, the elite military unit, had their own instrumental music (*mehterhâne*), which combined courtly and popular forms. The janissaries also had been major patrons of the urban Sufi music of the Bektaşî dervishes. Their Shiite hymns, called *nefes*, provided a musical bridge between the urban *makam* and the Anatolian hinterland, home of the related Alevî-Shiis. Bektaşî music was performed by professional poet-performers known as *aşık,* and it comprised a liturgical genre for the Bektaşî *âyîn-i cem* as well as paraliturgical or partly secular genres performed in the janissary barracks and coffeehouses. The Bektaşî hymns and *aşık* songs spread far beyond Anatolia, wherever the janissaries were recruited, particularly in Albania, Bulgaria, and Bosnia.

Another link between the musical world of the Ottoman elite and that of the urban population was provided by a number of strophic song forms, accompanied by a variety of long-necked lutes, such as the *bozuk* and *tanbura*. While some popular and rural forms (such as the *deyış* and *ırlayış*) were considered to be outside elite musical taste, certain popular forms, such as the *varsağî*, *türkü*, and *şarkı*, were included in the elite repertoire for solitary entertainment and informal social gatherings. The *varsağî* and the *türkü* were held partly in common by the elite, the urban population, and some rural people; but the *şarkı*, which was apparently of urban origin, was adopted by the elite as early as the middle of the seventeenth century. This development had both musical and poetic aspects. The simple four-line strophes of the *şarkı* were composed by major poets such as Nâ'ilî (d. 1666), Nazîm (d. 1727), and Nedîm (d. 1730), while the music of the *şarkı* was significantly developed in the elite context by Tanbûrî Mustafa Çavuş (d. 1745), a courtier of *ulema* (that is, clerical) origin. The *şarkı* repertoire of Mustafa Çavuş uses a wide range of *makam* and the West Anatolian-Balkan rhythmic cycle in 9/8 called *aksak*, which replaced the Persian rhythms of the seventeenth-century *şarkı*.

Until the nineteenth century several groups and guilds of professional musicians and dancers performed dance music and songs in both outdoor and indoor settings. The principal outdoor ensemble was known as the *mehter-i birûn* 'unofficial *mehter*' and was organized separately from the official *mehter* of the janissaries. Like the latter, it relied on the double-reed shawm *zurna*, but it dispensed with the trumpets (*boru*, *nefîr*) and frequently included panpipes (*mıskal*) and occasionally the *santûr*. With regard to percussion, it differed from the *mehterhâne* by substituting the frame drum (*daire*) and small kettledrums (*cifte-na're*) for the large two-headed drums (*tabl*) and enormous kettledrums (*kös*) of the janissary ensemble. Also, it made no use of the other brass percussion instruments of the military. The dancing that accompanied the *mehter-i birûn* was performed by men, who were usually drawn from the Jewish, Greek, and Armenian minorities; were known as *köçek* and *tavşan* 'rabbit'; and were organized in professional guilds. From the seventeenth to the early nineteenth century, some composers of this dance music were adept in the *makam* system and created elaborate compositions arranged in cyclical form to accompany the movements of the dance. By the nineteenth century *makam karcığar* had become associated with the *köçek* dances, and a famous dance-suite for the *köçek* was composed in that *makam* by the leading Mevlevî musician Ismail Dede Efendi (d. 1846). [See SNAPSHOT: ISMAIL DEDE EFENDI.]

Whereas the male *köçek* generally performed outdoors, a group of female professional dancers appeared indoors. These were the *cengî* dancers, whose name was derived from the harp *çeng*, their principal instrument in early times. They are first documented in the sixteenth century, and they were popular mainly in the homes of the aristocracy. The *çengî* musicians and dancers were female, and—unlike the male *mehter-i bırûn*—the composers of their music seem not to have been adept in the *makam* system. A certain amount of discreet homosexuality seems to have enhanced the appeal of the *çengî* in the harems of the aristocracy. While the choreography of the *köçek* is lost, it appears likely that the modern belly dance originated in the *çengî* repertoire. The *çengî* continued to be extremely popular long after their principal instrument, the *çeng*, had become extinct in the late seventeenth century.

Changes in the structure of Ottoman society from 1826 to 1840 dealt a blow to the organization of public music and dance for entertainment. The destruction of the janissaries in 1826 weakened the entire urban guild organization, in which the

In the eighteenth and nineteenth centuries, the principal settings for public entertainment were the tavern, usually run by Greeks; and the coffeehouse, usually run by Turks.

janissaries had been deeply involved, and this ultimately affected the musicians' guilds as well. In addition, the Ottoman state had become too poor to sponsor the huge public festivities of earlier centuries. The impoverished *köçek* dancers had turned increasingly to prostitution, leading the state to prohibit them, along with the female *çengî*, in 1840. The professional gap was filled by Gypsies who created new, mainly improvisational music and choreography. Gypsy instrumental music sometimes used distinctive intonation and melodic progressions, which became diffused among the lower classes of all religious communities. For example, Turkish and Greek commercial recordings of the 1920s document the adaptation of Gypsy-style vocal improvisation (*taksîm*, *gazel*) in Greek (as the *amane*) and in Judeo-Spanish.

During the eighteenth century and most of the nineteenth century, the principal settings for public entertainment were the tavern (*meyhane*), usually run by Greeks; and the coffeehouse (*kafehane*), usually run by Turks. The *meyhane* featured Greek popular music and dance, while the *kafehane* developed its own repertoire based on urbanized versions of Anatolian songs and urban *şarkı* and *türkü*, in a genre known as *divân*.

The accession of Abdülhamid II in 1876 marked the decline of court patronage of Ottoman art music. At this time a new type of European ("à la franka") entertainment institution, the casino (*gazino*), was introduced in the Greek Pera district of Istanbul, and it quickly eclipsed the musical repertoires of the old *meyhane* and *kafehane*. The music of the *gazino* was usually not European but a modified form of the courtly *fasıl*, featuring a cycle (*takım*) of *şarkı* in contrasting *usûl*, but avoiding the elaborate *beste* and *kâr* compositions. The instrumental *peşrev* and *saz semâ'î* continued to be developed in the new environment, as did the *şarkı* and the improvised *taksîm*. This would create a major problem of self-definition for the Turkish art music of the Turkish republic (1923), because the courtly and nightclub styles and repertoires had interacted closely for two generations. In fact, the interaction of the two styles was so intimate that after World War II the name for the courtly cycle, *fasıl*, was no longer applied to the music of the court but referred only to its nightclub derivative.

Hacı Arif Bey (d. 1885) was the first court composer to concentrate on the *şarkı* rather than on the *fasıl* genres. His student Şevkî Bey (d. 1891), deprived of courtly patronage, spent his life composing *şarkı* for nightclubs; today, these works are considered "classics." There was still important composition of classical *fasıl* by aristocratic amateur musicians and Mevlevî dervishes—for example, Ahmed Avnî Konuk (d. 1938) and Ahmed Irsoy (d. 1943)—but in the early twentieth century new compositions came to be dominated by the *şarkı*. With the beginning of the Turkish republic and a state policy that was hostile to Turkish art music, the *şarkı* began to displace the genres of the classical *fasıl*. Although the classical *fasıl* was still viable among wealthy and middle-class amateurs until the 1960s, urban public performance was dominated by the *şarkı*. Since the 1960s, the conflict between the classical *fasıl* and the nightclub *şarkı* "*fasıl* " has continued, and state and some private cultural institutions have begun to intervene in favor of the former (along with the classical courtly *şarkı*). However, new compositions in the *fasıl* genres are extremely rare, so that, essentially, the dynamics of the classical *fasıl* are being transformed from creation to preservation.

Rauf Yekta Bey (1871–1935), the leading musicologist and music pedagogue of the early twentieth century, attempted to fix the *fasıl* repertoire in notation and to teach this repertoire and *makam* structure in his Dârülelhân Conservatory. He established a mixed chorus at this conservatory and issued many recordings with it. The large mixed chorus emerged for pedagogic purposes and was an innovation with no precedent in the courtly tradition (which had used only soloists and small male choruses). The *tanbûr* and cello virtuoso Mes'ût Cemîl (1902–1963) developed the chorus on radio in Istanbul, while others used choral performance as a means of educating university students in the courtly repertoire. Cemîl's choral performances were further developed by Ruşen Ferîd Kam, the director of radio in Ankara. The chorus became a vehicle for the reestablishment of a canonical repertoire and style, distinguished from the blend of classical and nightclub practice that had been emerging since the end of the nineteenth century. The preservation and reinterpretation of tradition have had a strong impact on the performance of the *fasıl* repertoire. Mes'ût Cemîl removed the improvised vocal *taksîm* ("*gazel* ") from the *fasıl* in his radio chorus, because this genre had been developed in nightclubs for almost two generations and was no longer considered appropriate for the classical *fasıl.* The muezzins who had long been the masters of this genre had participated in this popularization of the *gazel*, and so they were now excluded from the new classical performance. Under the new secular conditions of the Turkish republic, the major solo vocalists born after World War I were never from a clerical (*ulemâ*) educational background. The leading masters of the classical *gazel* in the first half of the twentieth century, such as Munir Nurettin Selçuk (1899–1981) and Rabbi Isak Algazi (1889–1950), were unable to retain the traditional role of the vocal *taksîm* in the *fasıl.*

The concept of the *fasıl* performance as an integration of vocal and metrical compositions with vocal and instrumental improvisations broke down during the 1940s and 1950s under the impact of choral and radio solo performances, which tended to emphasize a single genre. At the death of Mes'ût Cemîl in 1963 the classical chorus of Istanbul radio was taken over by Dr. Nevzat Atlığ (b. 1925), who gradually curtailed any instrumental music, whether composed or improvised, in choral *fasıl* performances. Since the 1970s, this chorus has been subsidized as the Turkish State Classical Music Chorus, and so its artistic policies have become increasingly influential. In this ensemble, the *şarkı* tended to become as prominent as the *fasıl* genres. However, the cyclical *fasıl* was not entirely moribund, and at the same time coherent *fasıl* were still performed on Istanbul radio by a male chorus directed by the noted singer Dr. Allâettin Yavaşça (b. 1927). By the 1980s and 1990s a traditionalist reaction became evident, and some leading soloists such as Meral Uğurlu performed and recorded rather complete classical *fasıl.*

In Ottoman times, the sources of the popular musics of Istanbul were extremely varied and produced different musical forms in different periods and in the same period for different elements of the population. The Turkish, Greek, and Jewish populations all had musical links with an ethnic hinterland: Anatolia for the Turks, mainland and insular Greece for the Greeks, and distant Iberia for the Sephardic Jews. Other minorities, such as Albanians, Bulgarians, and Armenians, also kept up some elements of a separate musical life. In addition, the city always had contact with major cities of the Arab world, such as Cairo, Aleppo, and Damascus, and with the nearby Balkan cities—Salonika, Skoplje (Usküb), Plovdiv (Filibe), and so on. Different genres of popular music at times reflected some of the musical life of these areas. However, the *makam* elements—which were diffused by the musics of the mosques, the dervish lodges (*tekke*), the janissaries, and outdoor entertainment—tended to unify the modal structure (although not the style) of many popular genres. After World War I the loss of the empire and the decline of minorities caused significant changes in the popular music of Turkish cities. Nevertheless, there was considerable continuity with the Ottoman period until the demographic changes of the 1960s.

Today, the popular and classical *şarkı* still retain a dominant role on radio, in nightclub performances, and on recordings, and form much of the repertoire of the older generation of leading popular singers such as Müzeyyen Senar and Zeki Müren. But the "ruralization" of Turkish urban life as a consequence of the mass migration from the countryside since the 1960s has changed the direction of popular music—away from *şarkı* and toward derivatives of the rural *türkü* genre, most recently mixed with elements of Egyptian film music and named *arabesk*. [See ARABESK.] This movement seemed to be becoming dominant in the 1990s, so that the future development of the *şarkı* was in doubt. Now, cyclical performances of the nightclub *şarkı* of the first half of the twentieth century are becoming "classics" that are no longer part of a functioning popular music.

THE MEVLEVÎ *ÂYÎN*

Although the earliest notated Mevlevî *âyîn* dates only from 1795 (in the *Tahrîrîye* of Abdülbaki Nâsir Dede), several *âyîn* are ascribed to well-known musical figures of the seventeenth and eighteenth centuries, such as Köçek Mustafa Dede (d. 1683), Mustafa Itrî (d. 1712), and Osman Dede (d. 1730). Three *âyîn* earlier than the Beyatî *âyîn* of Köçek Mustafa survive today and are known collectively as the *beste-i kadîmler* 'ancient compositions.' The three *beste-i kadîmler* are in *makam pençgâh*, *makam hüseynî*, and *makam dügâh* (modern *uşşak*). Of these, only the first is complete, having all four sections (*selâm*). The *dügâh âyîni* has three sections and the *hüseynî* only one. It is significant that the Mevlevî tradition did not invent composers to go along with the "ancient" *âyîn* composition. While pseudographia was common in the Ottoman secular musical tradition, evidently the Mevlevî dervishes were able to tolerate the existence of works by unknown composers, and even to allow these works to remain fragmentary, without composing appropriate second, third, or fourth sections.

The Mevlevî *âyîn* was conceived of both as a ritual that would benefit the participants and as a spiritual concert, like the medieval Sufi *samâ'*, a "spiritual audition" that would spread spiritual benefit (*feyz*) among the audience as well. Unlike the medieval Sufi *samâ'*, the Mevlevî *semâ'* was not presented to a restricted audience: women and non-Muslims were allowed to observe the rituals in Istanbul. A Mevlevî *tekke* had both a musicians' gallery and a clearly demarcated space for a nonparticipating audience. Thus, while the *semâ' âyîn* was a religious ritual, it was also a concert. In this respect it differed from the religious rituals of Orthodox Sunni Muslims, Orthodox Christians, or Jews, which, while not prohibiting nonbelievers, did not encourage their presence. Likewise, the *fasl-i meclis* at the court, or at a private mansion, was essentially a closed event. In this situation, the only public art music event in Turkey before the nineteenth century was the Mevlevî *âyîn* performance.

A distinctive feature of the Mevlevî *âyîn* is the attribution of each *âyîn* to a single composer. Beginning with Mustafa Dede, every *âyîn* in the repertoire is the work of only one musician. This applied to the vocal *âyîn* proper—the introductory *peşrev* and *semâ'î* were often taken from secular sources. The composition of the four *selâm* of an *âyîn* by one individual meant that the *âyîn* became the longest and most demanding of all Ottoman compositional forms. The bulk of the surviving Mevlevî repertoire was created between the late eighteenth and the late nineteenth century. Composition continued in the twentieth century, most notably by Ahmed Avnî Konuk and Zekâ'îzâde Ahmed Irsoy, even after the banning of the *âyîn* in 1925. After the middle of the century, new composition received some impetus from the renewed public performance of the Mevlevî *âyîn* in Konya beginning in 1958, and the *âyîn* competition that was instituted in 1979.

Eighty-one *âyîn* are known to have been created before the middle of the twentieth century. Of these, sixteen were not notated and are no longer part of the Mevlevî repertoire. Thus the traditional repertoire of the Mevlevî *âyîn* in the twentieth century totaled sixty-five compositions. Between 1934 and 1939, forty-one of these *âyîn* were published by the Istanbul Municipal Conservatory, initially under the direction of Rauf Yekta (d. 1935). Yekta, who was himself a Mevlevî *neyzen*, based his versions on the performed versions that he had learned from Zekâ'î Dede (1825–1897) and Bolahenk Nûrî Bey (1834–1910), two of the last major Mevlevî composers. In 1979 the Mevlevî musicologist Sadettin Heper republished most of these compositions, plus two *âyîn* by the mid-twentieth-century musicians Kemâl Batanay and Kâzim Uz. The twentieth- century musicologist Sadettin Arel also composed a large number of *âyîn*. Heper's source for the older *âyîn* was not the oral tradition but a manuscript in Hamparsum notation dating from the last third of the nineteenth century. This manuscript source is stylistically more modern than the oral versions notated by Rauf Yekta in the 1930s.

The importance of the Mevlevîye for Turkish art music lies in four main areas: the great spiritual significance they attached to music, the beauty and sophistication of their *âyîn* compositions, their high standards and distinct style of performance on the *ney*, and their role in musical transmission and pedagogy. This last point was crucial for the survival of the classical Turkish repertoire into the twentieth century. Throughout the Ottoman period the numerous Mevlevî *tekke* functioned as small conservatories where the principles of Ottoman art music, in addition to the specifically Mevlevî repertoire, were taught to any talented students, including non-Muslims. In several peripheral regions of the empire, there is little or no evidence of art music except for the local Mevlevî *tekke*. During the eighteenth century Mevlevî musicians such as Osman Dede, Mustafa Kevserî, and Abdülbaki Nasir Dede took a keen interest in the possibilities of musical notation, either by inventing their own systems or by preserving the notation of Cantemir. During the later nineteenth century the eclipse of court patronage, the rise of nightclubs, and the decline of other Sufi *tarikat* left the Mevlevî dervishes as the principal bearers and teachers of the courtly repertoire. Most major musicians of the early twentieth century had studied with Mevlevî teachers, if they were not themselves Mevlevîs. By the beginning of the republic in 1923, Mevlevî musicians such as Rauf Yekta and Ahmed Irsoy played a crucial role in preserving the entire classical repertoire and maintaining its distinct performance practice without the pervasive influence of the nightclub. In the middle of the twentieth century Mevlevî *neyzen* such as Halil Can (1902–1953) were among the most respected authorities on Turkish art music, and they were among the first to reinstate the Ottoman repertoire on Turkish radio. The attraction of Western tourists to the revived official *semâ* ceremony in Konya and the smaller *semâ* performances in Istanbul, as well as the high status of everything associated with Jallal ud-Din Rumî in many European intellectual circles, has helped to maintain the prestige of Mevlevî music and musicians in Turkey in recent decades.

CYCLICAL PERFORMANCE FORMS: THE COURTLY *FASIL*

The *fasıl* in the later seventeenth century had the following structure:

1. Instrumental taksîm
2. One or two *peşrev*
3. Vocal *taksîm*
4. *Beste*
5. *Nakş*
6. *Kâr*
7. *Semâ'î*

8. Instrumental *semâ'î*
9. Vocal *taksîm*

During the first half of the seventeenth century several Iranian vocal forms (with Persian or Arabic texts), such as the *'amal,* the *kavl* (*qawl*), and the *savt* (*sawt*), were well known and were probably performed outside of a cyclical format. Later, a few *kavl* items seem to have survived under the misnomer "*kâr*"; however, they are rarely mentioned by the later seventeenth century, and they did not form part of the *fasıl*. The dominant composed forms of the *fasıl* were the *beste* and the *semâ'î*; both used *gazel* and *murabba'* poetry in the Ottoman Turkish language as their texts. The Persian genres, with their Persian texts, remained influential.

In the eighteenth century, Persian texts were the rule for the *kâr* and were not uncommon for the *nakş-semâ'î*, but these forms and their Persian texts constituted a small minority after 1700. The establishment of the *murabba' beste* as the leading form, along with its Turkish-language texts, paralleled the introduction of the cyclical *fasıl* format and the restructuring of the instrumental ensemble, all of which broke the links that had bound Turkey to Iran during the sixteenth century.

By the second half of the eighteenth century, the order and constitution of the *fasıl* had changed, showing an expansion of Turkish compositional forms and a retreat of Iranian forms:

1. Instrumental *taksîm*
2. One *peşrev*
3. [Vocal taksîm?]
4. *Birinci beste* or *kâr*
5. *Iknici beste*
6. *Ağır semâ'î*
7. *Takım* (miniature cycle) of *şarkı*
8. *Yürük semâ'î*
9. Instrumental *semâ'î* (*saz semâ'î*)
10. [Vocal *taksîm*?]

The *semâ'î* had developed into two separate genres, the *ağır semâ'î* in 10/8, 10/4, or 6/4; and the *yürük semâ'î* in 6/8. The *nakş* had begun to merge with other genres and was now called the *nakiş-beste* and the *nakış yürük semâ'î.* These were performed with the genres *beste* and *yürük semâ'î* respectively. The *kâr* seems to have been performed optionally instead of the first *beste*. It became customary to perform one *beste* in a longer *usûl* and slower tempo first (such as *darbayn* or *zincîr*) and then a somewhat quicker *beste* (in *hafîf* or *muhammes*). The *şarkı* was developing classical variants that could be introduced into the *fasıl* following the *yürük semâ'î*, as a minature cycle beginning with the *ağır aksak semâ'î* (10/4) and *ağır aksak* (9/4); continuing with *curcuna* (10/16), *türk aksağı* (5/8), and so on; and usually closing with *aksak* (9/8). The place of the *taksîm* in the *fasıl* is not documented.

THE INSTRUMENTAL *FASIL* AND THE *TAKSÎM*

Cantemir mentioned that there was a separate *fasıl-i sazende* '*fasıl* of the instrumentalist', which had consisted of a *taksîm*, a *peşrev*, and a *semâ'î*. In the *fasıl-i sazende*, the *semâ'î* followed immediately after the *peşrev*. To Fonton, in 1751, the *semâ'î* was like a "fifth part" that succeeded the four parts (*hâne'*) of the *peşrev*, although it was not "the air proper." In the mid-eighteenth century, musicians were able to develop the *taksîm* for "whole hours," so that the *peşrev* and *semâ'î* functioned as a virtual postlude to the *taksîm*. The fact that only one *peşrev* and one *semâ'î* were played, and that no new instrumental genres were invented, indicates that the instrumental *fasıl* had become largely a vehicle for performance of the *taksîm*.

In the seventeenth century, the role of the composer in the *fasıl-i sâzende* appears to have been similar to that in the *fasıl-i hânende* 'vocalist's suite'—the composer created individual items, not entire cycles. By the later eighteenth century, the composer's authority had expanded to the point that it became customary for one individual to create the vocal section of an entire *fasıl*, while instrumentalists composed the *peşrev* and *saz semâ'î* as a unit. There were also situations in which two or more musicians collaborated on a single *fasıl*. In a few cases the same musician (such as Tanbûrî Isak or Vardakosta Ahmed) composed both the vocal and the instrumental sections of the *fasıl*. Thus by the reign of Selim III (1789–1808), the whole *fasıl*, not only the individual item, was coming to be viewed as the unit of composition.

Apparently, no information about the instrumental *fasıl* is available for the nineteenth century; but by the mid-twentieth century its format had changed somewhat, becoming one *peşrev*, *taksîm*, one *saz semâ'î*. The major purpose of this change in format seems to have been to allow the musicians to modulate out of the nominal *makam* during the *taksîm*, and then close the *fasıl* with a *saz semâ'î* in a new *makam*. Until the 1950s musicians seem to have followed the more traditional custom of playing their *taksîm* individually, developing the modulations in succession. In the 1950s the *tanbûr* player and cellist Mes'ût Cemîl developed a new style of *taksîm* in which the musicians played parts of their *taksîm* together (*beraber*), sometimes even over one another. During the 1970s the vurtuosi Necedet Yaşar (*tanbûr*), Niyâzî Sayın (*ney*), and Ihsan Özgen (*kemençe*) developed this style further. Today, it coexists with the more traditional style.

The emergence of the *taksîm* as a genre must be viewed against the broader background of various approaches to temporal organization, composition, and improvisation in the Middle East after the medieval period. However, the various free-rhythm genres of the modern Middle East stand apart from the *taksîm* and its modern vocal counterparts (*layali* in Egypt, *gazel* in Turkey), which are essentially musical features of Turkey and the Ottoman Levant—elsewhere, they are twentieth-century borrowings from Egyptian or Turkish music. Starting in the early seventeenth century Ottoman texts use the term *taksîm* (Arabic *taqsîm* 'division') to refer to an improvised melody in a nonmetrical, "flowing" rhythm, which might be performed either vocally or instrumentally. The *taksîm* as it is known in modern Turkish and Arab music is defined by four major characteristics, which are not present in conjunction in any other nonmetrical genre of the core Muslim world: (1) improvisation ("performance-generation"), which precludes learned, tune-like models; (2) specific rhythmic idioms within an overall flowing rhythm; (3) codified melodic progression (*seyir*); (4) modulation.

In seventeenth-century Turkey the term *taksîm* referred equally to instrumental or vocal music; but in the nineteenth century the alternative term *gazel*, referring to the poetic text, was preferred for the vocal variant of the genre. Sufi vocal *taksîm* are now called *kaside*. In the late nineteenth century the *gazel* was developed in nightclubs, often by professional Qur'anic cantors (*hafiz*). This dual association with the nightclub and religion seems to have doomed the *gazel* in republican Turkey; it was removed by Mes'ut Cemîl from radio and choral performances and was never reinstated. Thus for practical purposes the *taksîm* in contemporary Turkey is almost exclusively an instrumental genre. The alternation of composed and improvised and metrical and nonmetrical music became a basis for the vocal and instrumental *fasıl* and (to a lesser extent) for the Mevlevî *âyîn*.

TRACK-2 The *taksîm* as a genre was known in the twentieth century as essentially a vehicle for the expression of melodic progression (*seyr*) and modulation within the *makam* system. The nearly simultaneous appearance in seventeenth-century Turkish sources of the *taksîm* genre and the terminology for expressing *seyr*, as well as an increasingly
TRACK-3 developed practical application of *seyr* in composition, suggests that the development

of codified melodic progressions had a major effect on the creation of the *taksîm*. In addition to being important as a genre, during the eighteenth century the *taksîm* significantly influenced the development of both transposition and modulation in the composed repertoire. The *taksîm* gave musicians scope to experiment with transpositions and modulations that were not generally current. The combination of flowing rhythm, improvisation, codified melodic progressions, and modulation proved to be highly influential within the Ottoman Empire, where it came to largely define the nature of *makam* music.

ASPECTS OF FORM IN THE CLASSICAL REPERTOIRE

Aside from the performance-generated *taksîm*, the repertoire of Turkish art music consists of compositions. Among compositions, the most fundamental division is between genres that use rhythmic cycles (*usûl*) and those that do not. The latter are a small group of genres all connected with the various Sufi liturgies (the *durak, na'at, temcîd, mersîye, mir'acîye*, and so on). The metrical genres may be divided into vocal and instrumental forms. The vocal forms comprise (1) forms of the secular *fasıl*, (2) the *selâm* of the Mevlevî *ayîn* ceremony, and (3) the *cumhur, tevşîh*, and other Sufi *ilâhî*. The instrumental genres are only the *peşrev* and the *saz semâ'î*, primarily for the *fasıl*, but also the *soñ peşrev* and *soñ semâ'î* of the Mevlevî *âyîn*.

Usûl, tempo, and melodic elaboration

The courtly vocal repertoire was divided into genres that used long *usûl* and those using short *usûl*. The former group consisted only of the *beste* and sometimes the *kâr* (which used either short or long *usûl*). The latter group included various forms of *nakş* and *semâ'î*. In these two genres there was a rather close connection between the rhythmic cycle and the poetic meter of the text. However, no such connection was evident in the *beste* and the *kâr*, which were the dominant genres of the *fasıl*. By the later eighteenth century, the expansion of the *usûl* system had led to a radical break not only between melodic structure and poetic meter (such a break had already developed in the seventeenth century), but also between melodic structure and the *usûl* system.

The Mevlevî *âyîn* reflected a generally more conservative approach to rhythmic and melodic relations. The first, the second, and the end of the third *selâm* retained the short rhythmic cycles that had been essentially unchanged since the seventeenth century (14/8, 9/8, 6/8). Only the opening of the third *selâm* introduced an "expanded" long rhythmic cycle of 28 beats. In earlier times the third *selâm* seems to have used 8/4 (*düyek*).

A process of rhythmic retardation and melodic elaboration apparently began in the last third of the seventeenth century. Cantemir had explained that certain *peşrev* were played at a particularly slow tempo, and that these had what we might call a higher melodic density, necessitating his use of a meter he called the "smallest of the small" (*asğar-i sağîr*) in order to notate what we would call sixteenth notes. As Cantemir stated, this increase in the number of notes implies a decrease in tempo. Notated documents from the middle of the eighteenth century show a 50 percent increase in melodic density over those of Cantemir's time, which suggests a further retardation of tempo. The melodically elaborated slow-tempo *peşrev* of the end of the seventeenth century proved to be the variety of the genre that would evolve into modern forms in the later eighteenth and nineteenth centuries.

Wright (1988:8, 71, 75) found that the number of pitch changes (melodic density) in the seventeenth-century *peşrev* in his corpus, compared with their versions in later nineteenth-century sources, increased by a ratio of 1 to 5. While the *usûl* has increased in length by a ratio of 1 to 2, the melodic density is 1 to 5. The tempo of performance had decreased by a ratio of approximately 5 to 1 ("rhythmic retardation"), thus allowing an increase in melodic density of a reverse proportion ("melodic elaboration"). The gaps in the *usûl* pattern were now filled in by intermediary drum strokes, *velvele.* The tempo of the *velvele* today corresponds almost exactly to the probable tempo of the original seventeenth-century *usûl.* Thus the tempo of Turkish instrumental music has not changed significantly. What has changed is the relationship of a single beat to the larger rhythmic cycle. In terms of quarter notes, the structure of *devr-i kebîr* has been expanded from 14/4 to 28/4 (the quarter note has been expanded to a half note); at the same time, the number of intermediary beats, notated as eighth notes, has created a rhythmic density from four to five times greater than the seventeenth-century structure. The number of drum strokes increased from 13 to 70. Thus the increase in rhythmic density is similar to the increase in melodic density. The fundamental pulse underlying a *peşrev* in the *usûl devr-i kebîr* was much the same in the seventeenth century as it is today, but in a modern piece fourteen beats of this pulse would go through only a quarter to a fifth of one rhythmic cycle. (In the seventeenth century this would have comprehended one entire cycle.)

By the last two decades of the eighteenth century, important changes occurred in the *usûl* system as well. These changes were always in the direction of doubling. For example, *devr-i kebîr* was doubled to 28 beats (from 14), and *muhammes* was doubled to 32 beats (from 16). In the small *usûl,* ağır 'heavy' versions appeared: *ağır aksak* (9/4) alongside *aksak* (9/8) and *ağır aksak semâ'î* (10/4) alongside *aksak semâ'î* (10/8). In the small *usûl,* both the doubled version and the original version continued to be played for different genres. For the larger *usûl,* usually only the new doubled version survived. In some cases, however, the old version continued to be performed as a *nîm* 'half' of the new doubled *usûl*: *nîm hafif* (16 beats—new *hafif* in 32 beats—old *hafif* in 16 beats); *nîm sakîl* (24 beats—new *sakîl* in 48 beats—old *sakîl* in 24 beats).

The two pieces in figure 1 illustrate the difference between melodic usage in the standard and *ağır* versions of the same *usûl,* in this case *aksak semâ'î.* The phrasing of the *usûl* is exactly the same in each, except that the duration of the notes is twice

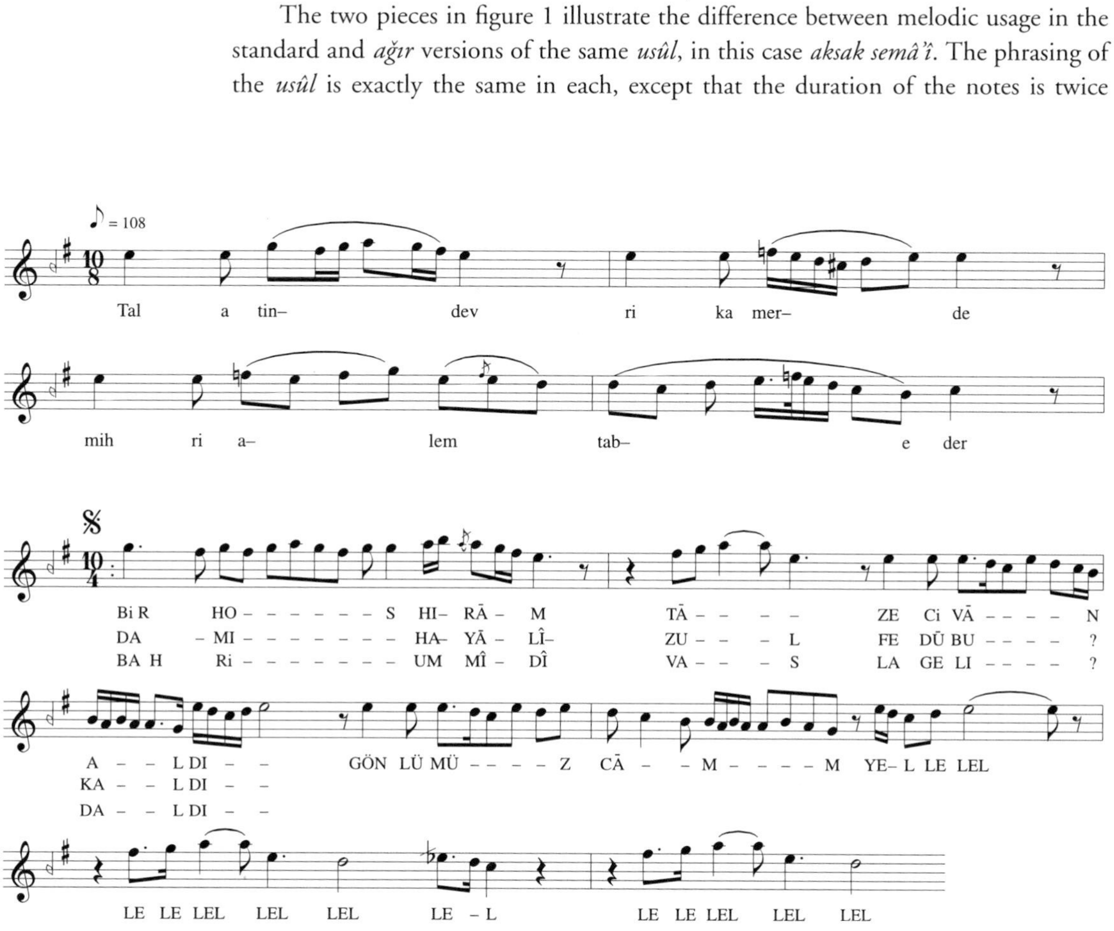

FIGURE 1 (a) *Hüseynî nakış ağır semâ'î, usûl aksak semâ'î*: Zaharya (d. 1740?). (b) *Gülizâr ağır semâ'î, asûl ağır aksak semâ'î*: Isak (d. 1814). The first musical line of each item, comprising four units of the *usûl* pattern, is shown.

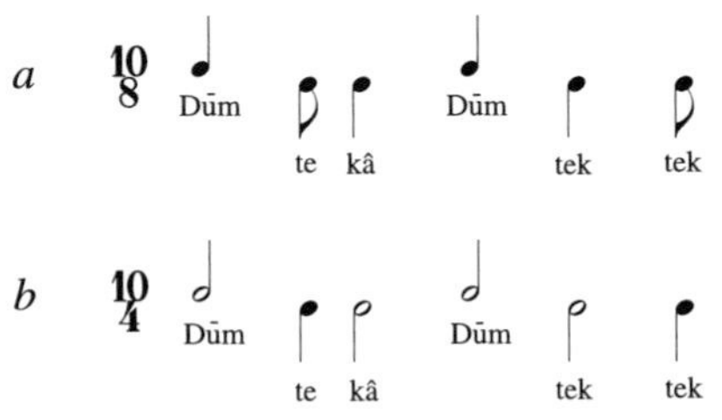

FIGURE 2 (a) *Aksak semâ'î*. (b) *Ağır aksak semâ'î*.

as long in the *ağır* version (figure 2). In Zaharya's piece the number of pitch changes in this four-cycle unit is 28, whereas in Isak's piece the number is 54. This difference corresponds closely to the relationship of the two *usûl*, the first in 10/8 and the second in 10/4. In Zaharya's piece the melodic units correspond to the four constituent units of each *usûl* cycle (3 + 2 + 2 + 3 = 10), and each cycle ends with a rest on an important tonal center of the *makam*. Although the notation occasionally allows us to pick out this pattern in Isak's piece, the frequent pauses and held notes purposely obscure the rhythmic pattern. The melody pauses only after the first and fourth cycles; the melodies of the second, third, and fourth cycles are joined continuously. In performance, the cutting and joining of the melody, quite irrespective of the *usûl*, give this melody almost a sense of rubato. However, this is not reflected in the drum strokes, which continue beating a slower version of the *aksak usûl*.

In short, figure 1 shows rhythmic-melodic variations within two different compositions in a single genre (the *ağır semâ'î*) using standard and "heavy" versions of the same *usûl*. A similar degree of variation in rhythmic-melodic relationships can be seen diachronically where the same item was transmitted orally.

In figure 3, Cantemir's *peşrev* was in the *usûl berefşân* in 16 beats (3 + 3 + 2 + 2 + 2 + 2 + 2), but Fonton used the newer doubled version of the same *usûl* in 32 beats. As expected, the melodic density is doubled in Fonton's version; there are 11 pitch changes in Cantemir and 23 in Fonton. Between the seventeenth and the nineteenth centuries, basic concepts of melody and rhythm had changed, so this long period of transmission resulted in much more drastic alterations of the melody.

In 1800 the relationship of rhythmic pulse to the melodic unit was very different from what it had been in 1650 or even in 1700. In 1650, a given number of pulse beats had formed a discrete rhythmic cycle, the *usûl*. This changed gradually during the 1700s so that at the end the same number of pulse beats were only part of a much longer and slower rhythmic cycle. The melody, however, did not slow down: it continued to move at the same pace. But the core rhythmic unit was five times as large as it had been; hence, the melody was free to expand. By this time the *usûl* cycle was long enough to encompass elaborate melodic movement. The tendency of the music,

FIGURE 3 (a) *Bestenigâr, berefşân*: Cantemir, 1700. (b) *Bestenigâr, berefşân*: Cantemir, according to Fonton, 1750.

however, was to push even beyond the rhythmic cycle and to join the melody outside its boundaries. These tendencies produced the rhythmic-melodic relationships evident in modern Turkish art music since the later eighteenth century, especially within the *beste* and the *peşrev* genres. While the rhythmic idioms of these two genres are somewhat divergent, they have a common relationship to the rhythmic cycle. The divergent concepts of rhythmic cycle and melody of the seventeenth and nineteenth centuries can be observed in the nineteenth-century versions of seventeenth-century *peşrev*.

In figure 4, in the Cantemir version the first half-cycle shows 4 pitch changes; Yekta's verson has 20; the Hamparsum document has 39. Yekta's version, although it was published in the 1930s, seems to reflect mid-nineteenth-century practice, and it shows the fivefold increase in melodic density which was typical of the stylistic change between the seventeenth and the nineteenth centuries (figure 5). The Hamparsum document shows an even more modernized version with almost a tenfold increase in melodic density. In both of the later versions the simple 14-beat *devr-i kebîr* (3 + 2 + 2 + 3 + 2 + 2) has been replaced by the newer doubled version in 28 beats. However, in this example (unlike the previous examples), the melody no longer bears any relationship to the older rhythmic breakup, and its density is at least five times that of the older form.

Within the vocal repertoire, the expansion of the *usûl* system and the processes of tempo retardation and melodic elaboration had the greatest effect on the *beste* and *kâr* genres which used long rhythmic cycles. After the second half of the eighteenth century the *beste* was composed almost exclusively in the new expanded versions of the long *usûl*, such as *çenber* (24/4), *muhammes*, *hafîf* or *berefşân* (32/4), *sakîl* (48/4), *hâvî* (64/4), *zencîr* (120/4), or *darbeyn* in 48/4, 56/4, 60/4, 88/4, 116/4, 118/4, or 120/4.

These changes in the *usûl* system, in tempo and in melodic density and elaboration of the Ottoman metrically composed genres, which occurred gradually from the later seventeenth to the nineteenth century, distinguished it radically from all other

FIGURE 4 *Uşşak peşrev, devr-i kebîr*: (a) Cantemir collection; (b) Rauf Yekta, 1930s; (c) Hamparsum, late nineteenth century. (After Wright 1988.)

FIGURE 5 *Devr-i kebîr*: (a) seventeenth century; (b) nineteenth century.

forms of the *makam* traditions outside the Ottoman Empire. Similar transformations took place in the related art music of Syria but were not apparently carried to the same lengths.

The *terkîb*

The elaboration of the melody over an expanded rhythmic cycle was parallel to other changes in compositional form. These changes are documented primarily in the *peşrev*, which has the longest continuous chain of notations. *Peşrev* of the seventeenth century and the early eighteenth century display several levels of compositional divisions. The largest unit is the *hâne* and the *mülâzime*. In the seventeenth century most *peşrev* were created out of three *hâne* and a *mülâzime* 'ritornello' that was repeated after each *hâne*. The *mülâzime* was the longest unit in the *peşrev* and contained the core of its melodic material. Both *mülâzime* and *hâne* were divided into smaller units called *terkîb*; each *terkîb* consisted of two or more cycles (*devr*) of the *usûl*. A *terkîb* was repeated with alternative endings. The *terkîb* was important in the musical thought of this period because the earliest examples of the *peşrev* (apparently dating from the middle to late sixteenth century) use the *terkîb* in a rather modular fashion, containing much of the melodic development of the *peşrev* within these small units.

As is true of most early (sixteenth-century) *peşrev* in the collections, in the *peşrev* shown in figure 6 the melodic material of the *terkîb* is arranged in antecedent-

FIGURE 6 *Nevâ, devr-i kebîr: serhane, mülâzime, acemi* (from Cantemir).

consequent units; internally, there is a great deal of repetition within these constituent units. In the case of *devr-i kebîr* these melodic units are half-cycles of seven beats. The pattern that emerges from the whole *peşrev* can be charted as shown in figure 7.

The *peşrev* of the seventeenth century maintain the *terkîb* divisions, although they tend to become longer and the melodic relationships between them are more sophisticated. By the middle of the eighteenth century the *terkîb* divisions had apparently been removed from the *peşrev*, allowing for a continuous melodic line throughout the *hâne*. An important document of this change is a *peşrev* recorded by Kevserî and attributed (probably erroneously) to Cantemir. It is likewise in the old form of *devr-i kebîr* (14 beats), but it has a much higher melodic density than the previous piece. Stylistically, this *peşrev* is so modern that it is played in the current repertoire with almost no change, as can be seen from the interlinear score in figure 8.

FIGURE 7

H I: x + x | a + b |

A B C D

M: c + d | c + d | e + d | e + d′ | f + d | f + d′ | c + x | a + b |

H II: A B

e + e′ | e + d′ | e + x | x + b |

H III: A B

c′ + x | c′ + x | e + x | a + b |

FIGURE 8 *Nihavend devr-i kebîr* (*serhâne*): an interlinear score showing the first *hâne* as it appears in Kevserî (K) and in Yekta's Mevlevî *ayinleri* publication (Y).

The abandonment of the *terkîb* marked an important step in the transition from the early modern era of Turkish art music (1580–1780) to the modern era (1780–1920s). This change seems to have been propelled by several factors, principally the rhythmic expansion and melodic elaboration discussed above, along with a more sophisticated use of codified melodic progressions (*seyir*). Whereas compositions of the sixteenth and early seventeenth centuries had often allowed much repetition and imitation which obscured the melodic progression, the more modern style subordinated these compositional techniques to the expression of the *seyir*, spread over a large expanse, comprehending the entire *hâne*. Although modulation increased as well, this was not permitted to hinder the overall melodic progression of the *makam*. Thus the transition from the early modern to the modern era was characterized by an increasingly elaborate and extensive melodic line, spread over an expanding rhythmic cycle, performed at increasingly slow tempi, and expressing an increasingly codified melodic progression within the *makam* while making numerous modulations to other modal entities.

REFERENCES

Feldman, Walter. 1996. *Music of the Ottoman Court: Makam, Composition, and the Early Ottoman Instrumental Repertoire*. Berlin: VWB—Verlag für Wissenschaft und Bildung.

Reinhard, Kurt, and Ursula Reinhard. 1984. *Musik der Türkei*. Wilhelmshaven: Heinrichshofen.

Signell, Karl. 1977. *Makam: Modal Practice in Turkish Art Music*. Seattle, Wash.: Asian Music.

Wright, Owen. 1988. "Aspects of Historical Change in the Turkish Classical Repertoire." *Musica Asiatica* 5:1–108.

———. 1992. *Demetrius Cantemir: The Collection of Notations*. London: School of Oriental and African Studies, University of London.

Yekta, Rauf. 1921. "La musique turque." In *Encyclopédie de la musique et dictionnaire du Conservatoire*, Vol. 5:2945–8064.

Performance Practice in Iran: *Radīf* and Improvisation

Margaret Caton

Classical Persian music is based on a body of traditional melodies arranged according to a musical system known as the *dastgāh* (plural, *dastgāh-hā*). This repertoire, *radīf* (plural, *radīf-hā*), of melodies and melodic ideas forms the basis for improvisation, which ranges from melodic ornamentation and dynamic and rhythmic nuances to development and elaboration of a basic modal structure characterized and unified by motivic suggestions. In the improvisation of the *radīf*, the musician's expertise and inspiration interact with the audience and performance context to create the musical experience.

The *radīf* may be traced to the Sasanian period (third to seventh centuries C.E.), during which the court musician Barbad composed melodies for King Khosros II (r. 590–628). These included seven Khusrovania that some consider the origin of the seven-*dastgāh* system (Zonis 1973:30). Since that time the modes and modal systems that form the basis of the *radīf* have been the subject of research, study, discussion, and debate.

Historically, theoreticians such as Abū Naṣr Fārābī, Abū 'Alī Ebn-e Sīnā, and Ṣafī al-Dīn al-Urmawī incorporated Greek music theory into their analysis of the modal and acoustical properties of Middle-Eastern music. In the fifteenth century, 'Abdalqāder Marāghi incorporated concepts from Turkish music in his theoretical discussions. Contemporary scholars have conducted little research on the music of the period from Marāghi to the middle of the nineteenth century.

Existing historical manuscripts seem to indicate that within the the *maqām* 'mode' tradition, which Iran shared with other Middle Eastern musical cultures, customary modal progressions began to develop. These may have been the origin of the current Iranian classical music system, the *dastgāh*. Much of the scholarship from the late nineteenth century to the present time has continued in the tradition of the medieval theoreticians—the study of tuning systems and modes. Western researchers, for the most part, have focused on musical structure, in particular on the *radīf* itself and more recently on improvised performances based on the *radīf*. More philosophically-minded researchers, both Iranian and Western, have approached the study of performance practice by examining how it expresses the concepts and beliefs of Sufism, or Islamic mysticism. Less studied has been the relationship of music and musical performance to the culture of the Iranian peoples.

APPROACHES TO THE STUDY OF THE *RADĪF*

Scholars have approached the *radīf* from various perspectives, with some degree of polarization in viewpoint. An acoustical approach has emphasized instrumental tuning systems, using the finger positions and frets of the *'ūd*, *tanbūr*, or *tār* (plucked lutes) as standards of measure. Scholars have studied the use of different tuning systems for different *dastgāh-hā* and individual variations found among musicians' performance practice.

One approach has traced the various *radīf-hā* in use today to their historical sources, often emphasizing purity of tradition. The *radīf* compiled by Ma'rufi (published by the ministry of culture and arts) is attributed to the Qajar court musicians Mirzā 'Abdollāh and his brother Āqā Hoseynqoli and before them to their father 'Alī Akbar Farahānī, in the nineteenth century (Sadeghi 1971:17; Tsuge 1974:83–86). Other *radīf-hā*, such as those found outside Tehran in Esfahān and Shirāz, have their own historical roots. A *radīf* was usually passed down from master to disciple with great care, since the *radīf* was learned by ear, without the use of musical notation. It was considered imperative for students to continue the *radīf* of their master teacher (*ostād*) in its purest form. The genealogy of the *radīf* was important in determining not only its authenticity but its quality and status. An essentially unaltered *radīf* traceable to Mīrzā 'Abdollāh was considered more valuable than one attributed to a lesser known or less respected teacher.

Scholars trained in the schools of music of Europe and the United States have taken an analytical approach. These researchers examined different notated and recorded *radīf-hā*, along with realizations in performance. They analyzed and compared the underlying modal structures.

Many Iranian musicians adopted an approach to teaching and performance of their own music that reflected a Western conservatory method. Conservatories and music schools were established, starting with one founded by the French music master Alfred J. B. Lemaire in the mid-nineteenth century (Zonis 1973: 39). In these conservatories, Iranian students were taught both Western and Persian music from scores in Western notation. Exercises, études, and compositions were written for Persian music, often using Western compositional techniques. This composed music, along with notated *radīf-hā*, formed the basis of a systematic teaching method and provided more opportunity for ensemble playing. Beginning in the early twentieth century, concerts were given by different organizations, at the theater of the Grand Hotel in Tehran, and eventually for radio, television, and public concert halls. This tradition of westernized teaching and performance continues to affect the performance practice of the *radīf*, as Iranian musicians tour the West and present their own compositions interspersed with traditional forms.

Another general approach to the study of the *radīf* is philosophical. This has been reflected to some extent in historical treatises which admonished the musician to play for certain audiences and at certain times of day, and which discussed healing properties and astrological signs associated with particular modes.

In addition there was a parallel, often legalistic Islamic tradition of debate over the legitimacy of music. The four legal schools of Islam had different attitudes toward the legality of music, as had different Sufi orders. The issues included the separation of chanting and worship from secular music, whether the Prophet Mohammad had forbidden the performance of music, and whether it was music itself or the listener's spiritual condition that determined the effect.

Promoters of the *radīf* tradition have included advocates of Sufism, who often claim that during the Safavid period, when music was suppressed (Zonis 1973:35–36), Sufi orders preserved and fostered the *radīf*. The *radīf* emerged in the early nineteenth century when the musician 'Alī Akbar moved from Farahān in Iraq to the court of Mohammad Shah in Tehran (During 1975:141–142). It is also held that during the Safavid era, some musicians went to India and Turkey while others sought seclusion in Sufi orders and monasteries (Zonis 1973: 37–38; During 1991: 33).

HISTORICAL BACKGROUND

Iranian music traces its roots to the Sasanian court, where Bārbad (as well as other musicians) entertained the king, singing and accompanying himself on the *barbat*, a precursor of the *'ūd* and the lute. Iranians attribute to Bārbad the tradition of court musicians' conveying ideas and suggestions to kings through music (During and Mirabdolbaghi 1991:154). A story is told of the tenth-century musician Rūdakī, who persuaded the Samanid prince to return to his home in Bukhara by playing a song that would make him homesick (Caton 1984:59).

Some Iranians believe that the seven Khusrovania of Barbad were introduced into Arabic music and helped create the cosmopolitan music culture of the court in Baghdad during the Abbassid period (eighth to tenth centuries). Certainly the musical tradition that developed in the Sasanian court during the pre-Islamic period influenced the development of Middle Eastern musical style, which tended to change and take on new influences, depending on the location of the capital. The capital was an intellectual and cultural center that drew scholars and musicians from various parts of the Islamic empire in the Middle East.

Although there are a number of existing historical manuscripts and a well-defined and respected tradition of theoretical music scholarship, there is little documentation of the lives or performance practices of the musicians themselves, perhaps because the status of the performing musician was lower than that of the scholar. While the theoretical study of music was respected as one of the mathematical sciences, study of performance practice was not. Bārbad, Rūdakī, Ibrāhim al-Mawṣilī, Ishāq al-Mawṣilī, and Ziryāb became part of written history because they were prominent court musicians who influenced the development of music. For example, in the ninth century, Ziryāb was sent from Baghdad to Cordoba in Spain, where he is said to have started a music conservatory associated with the origin of the Andalusian tradition of Middle Eastern music (Schuyler 1984: 14–15).

Some later historical treatises discuss the *gāhs*—different ways of going through a progression of certain *maqāmāt* 'melodic modes'. Some treatises outlined a system of relationships between the *maqām* and the *āvāz* and *sho'be* 'branches' derived from it (Ṣafvat 1971:44–45). This sense of modal relationships continues today in the subsidiary branches of the *dastgāh* of *shur* and *homāyun*.

INFLUENCE OF RELIGION

Issues of Music in Islam

In the Iranian musical tradition, religion has greatly influenced the development of both the form and the performance of the *radīf*. During the time of Muḥammad, music was associated with singing girls and taverns and was linked with paganism and idolatry (Farmer 1973:10–11; Roychoudhury 1957:55). In breaking with existing practices, Muḥammad introduced some reforms, many of which were conveyed not in the Qur'ān itself but in his various *hadith* 'sayings'. Different legal schools of Islam followed different *hadith* and as a result had different attitudes toward music. Eventually, the Shi'ite clergy developed a stricter attitude toward music than the Sunnis, although this attitude fluctuated during different historical periods. During repressive times, many musicians either performed in secret or emigrated to other countries. The Islamic Revolution of 1979, for example, fostered a more repressive attitude toward music, which has continued to affect the development of musical performance. An exodus of Iranian musicians to Western Europe and America in recent times has partially disrupted and in some cases changed the musical tradition. Many artists freed

Religion has greatly influenced the development of both the form and the performance of the *radīf.*

from the constraints of government, religion, and the older musical tradition have introduced innovations in form, rhythm, and performance style.

The clergy traditionally distinguished melodies associated with religious chanting and worship from those associated with music as such. By definition, chanting was an unaccompanied vocal form in a simple melodic style of the Qur'ān, various prayers, and religious texts (Caton 1984:32–33, Farmer 1973:33; Reckord 1987, 1988:29–30). Music per se was associated with musical instruments, a more elaborate ornamentation of melody, and the use of secular or Sufi and Sufi-influenced poetry. According to this definition, music could not be performed on certain Muslim holy days, such as Moḥarram, or in certain religious settings, including mosques. In general, music of the *radīf* was performed in protected locations, such as the court, and in the homes and gardens of the royalty and aristocracy as well as in some Sufi gatherings.

A central issue in the debate concerning music was the belief in the power of music to affect physiology and emotions. Some believed that music had the power to drive people crazy, turn them away from religion, or corrupt their morals. Many Sufis, while agreeing that music was powerful, held that it also could foster the listener's spiritual advancement. Some Sufis held spiritual concerts (*samā'*) that were designed for this purpose. The *ayin*, a spiritual ceremony of the Mevlevi [see MUSIC IN PERFORMANCE: WHO ARE THE WHIRLING DERVISHES?], is a continuing legacy of that tradition. (Although the Mevlevi are based in Turkey, their founder was the Persian poet and mystic Jalāluddīn Rūmī.) Other Sufis, however, felt that music did have the power to corrupt and turn the listener away from God (Caton 1984:50–51). One difference among Sufis concerning this issue was whether the source of corruption was within the music itself or in the listener's lack of spiritual maturity and readiness (Crow 1984:33; Roychoudhury 1957:89–99).

One practice that influenced the development of the *radīf* was Qur'ānic chanting. According to tradition, the angel Gabriel chanted the Qur'ān into Muhammad's ear. Hearing the chanting of the Qur'ān, then, allows the listener to reconnect with the source of the original revelation (Crow 1984:30–31).

Belief in the importance of the sacred word has influenced the form and practice of the *radīf.* In *radīf* performance a soloist sings poetry, primarily the poetry of Ḥāfez, Sa'dī, and Rūmī (thirteenth and fourteenth centuries), accompanied by a melodic instrument that imitates and follows this semi-improvised singing. The instrumental tradition of *radīf* performance follows the vocal tradition in melodic phrasing and tonal contour. Although strictly instrumental forms, such as the *chahārmeżrāb* and *reng*, have been part of the performance tradition, the primary body of the *radīf* is the *gūshe-hā* 'pieces' (singular, *gushe*), which fit the phrasing of poetic forms.

Sufi symbolism

Although not universally applied, Sufi symbolism has been used by some musicians and scholars to describe the meaning of musical structure and the experience of listening to music. A basic concept in Sufism is the arc of descent and ascent. When someone is born, Sufis believe, he is separated from his original unity with God as he descends into the world of matter. For the Sufis, the process of return, or ascent, back to that spiritual union is marked by a number of practices and stages or levels in spiritual progress (Caton 1983:95–96). These levels are called *maqāmāt* (singular, *maqām*), which is also the term for the modes in Arabic and Turkish music, though no longer in Persian music. In Persian music, modes are incorporated into melodic units called *gūshe*, which are arranged in a traditional order within each *dastgāh*. This arrangement follows an arc-shaped tonal contour, beginning with lower-pitched *gūshe-hā* and continuing with progressively higher-pitched *gūshe-hā*, finally resolving on a few *gūshe-hā* that descend to the original pitch. In the Sufi tradition and shamanistic traditions, this arc has been portrayed in various ways—as a rainbow, the rising and setting of the sun, the flight of a bird, a bridge, or a bow (Halifax 1982:22). The arc itself represents the ascent of the soul from an earthly state of being to a more spiritual state and its subsequent return.

Music is thought to transform the listener, through the *ḥāl*, an altered state, to a more spiritual condition and then return him to the everyday world, cleansed and purified. Music acts as a bridge or an archway of change. According to some musicians in the Sufi tradition, the purpose of music is to make the listener better and more spiritual; to cleanse him of impurities such as greed, anger, and lust; and through Sufi poetry, to provide a metaphysical basis for a more balanced, centered life. The *ḥāl* produces a receptive state during which the poetic and musical message may act with full intensity on the listener's cognition and emotions (Varzi 1989, interview).

ART AND MUSIC

Islamic art has generally been characterized by abstraction and stylization, which were considered appropriate for reflecting spiritual concepts. At times, representing animals and human figures was suppressed or banned, partly because this was considered an act of cocreation with God (Martin 1982:70–78). A tradition of abstract geometrical, floral, and calligraphic art developed in rugs and tapestries as well as in architecture, painting, and sculpture. The individual artist creatively combined stylized motifs within traditional forms, much as the musician combined traditional motives within musical structure and style.

Motivic art symbolized the spiritual world, while representational art was felt to embody the physical world. The subtle meanings of geometric and floral motifs included their association with the ambiguous, the elusive, and hence the invisible and infinite world of the spirit. In Persian music, melodic ornamentation, including such individual ornamental tendencies as *eshāre* (a reference or allusion to the next melodic tone), obscures the lines of melodic progression and creates a sense of the indefinite.

Artistic forms were structured so as to convey a sense of symmetry as well as the infinite (al-Faruqi 1978:21; 1985). A Sufi might interpret bilateral symmetry as representing the realms of spirit and matter. For example, one musician related that in playing the *kamānche* (a spiked fiddle), the left hand, representing the world of God, finds the correct notes to play; and the right hand, representing the world of man, actualizes the sound (Varzi 1989, interview).

The interplay of spirit with matter in music and the other arts portrays continuity beyond form. In much artwork the motifs expand outward from a center, cut off only by the border or frame. So also in music, the structure and outline of the *dastgāh* are only the apparent limit of the sound. Any performance of the *radīf* is a sample of the possibilities contained within this repertoire. The music goes beyond the concrete and retreats from the world of the definite. This flight helps the listener transcend his material attachments and brings him closer to the infinite.

MUSICAL STYLE

Musical style is characterized by the primacy of language. Poetic form greatly influences and even determines musical form, with its emphasis on melody and melodic ornamentation. The *dastgāh* structure itself is based on a progression of modes, which contain scale, pitch hierarchy, motives, and mood. Performance practice is based on the concept of a mosaic—choosing musical motives; then expanding them, contracting them, and piecing them together as they follow the progression outlined for a particular *dastgāh*.

Dastgāh

The *dastgāh* structure may have developed as a standardization of some of the more commonly performed modal progressions. The term *dastgāh* means framework, apparatus, system of organization, or arrangement. In music, the *dastgāh* system is a way of organizing the traditional repertoire (the *radīf*) into twelve modal progressions arranged as individual pieces, *gūshe*. The *gūshe-hā*, the basis of the *radīf*, is really a modal nucleus (Powers 1980:426) containing the pitch hierarchies on which improvisation is based. Not all *gūshe-hā* are modal nuclei, however. The primary *gūshe-hā*, each known as a *shāh gūshe*, are the basic modal sections of the *dastgāh* structure and offer the most possibilities for improvisation. Secondary *gūshe-hā* are more developed melodically and may more frequently be omitted from a performance, but they too offer possibilities for improvisation. A third group consists of often fully melodically fixed compositions, with improvisation consisting mainly of variation in ornamentation and rhythmic and dynamic nuance (Sadeghi 1971:56–61).

A *gūshe* may be performed in a musical meter and become, for example, a *żarbī*, *kereshme*, or *chahārmeżrāb*—these are essentially different rhythmic realizations or variations of the basic modal and melodic structure of a *gūshe*. Much has been written on the structure of the *dastgāh* by contemporary researchers (Caron and Safvate 1996; During 1995; Farhat 1990; Nettl 1987; Zonis 1973).

Mode

The *gūshe* has been compared both to *maqām* (Arab Middle East) and to *rāga* (India). Each *gūshe* is located on a particular pitch level within the *dastgāh*, has specific pitches, and contains a characteristic pitch hierarchy as well as melodic motives. In many respects, the *gūshe* is more developed melodically than either the *maqām* or the *rāga*, although, as discussed above, there is considerable variation. The *gūshe-hā* that form the *radīf* originated as rural melodies, religious chants and songs, or other compositions collected by musicians and passed down to their students.

Some *gūshe-hā* have names that indicate their function within the *dastgāh*, such as *darāmad* 'opening', *owj* 'climax', and *forūd* 'closing cadence'. Other *gūshe-hā* are named after people, qualities, or Iranian cities and regions. In one sense, *radīf* refers to this collection of *gūshe-hā*, each master (*ostād*) having his own version. In another sense, the *radīf* is the manner of arranging these *gūshe-hā* in a modal progression within a particular *dastgāh*.

TRACK 4 The *dastgāh* itself is a modal complex, a progression of *gūshe-hā* beginning with the *darāmad*, which is in the mode of the name of the *dastgāh*, such as *shūr* or *segāh*. The performance of the *dastgāh* progresses through a series of pitch levels represented by different *gūshe-hā*. Each *gūshe* has a tonal center, or witness tone (*shāhed*). In addition, there is a ground tone, or *īst* 'stop', at the end of cadences. The *gūshe* is realized within a melodic ambitus, often four to five pitches, with melodic activity centered on the *shāhed*. Thus, a pitch level is established, with a resolution tone as a
TRACK 28 base. Each subsequent *gūshe* raises the pitch of the melodic ambitus or tonal center (or both) slightly above that of the previous *gūshe*. The melodic focus moves progressively higher, still resolving on the stopping tone (*īst*) established in the *shāh gūshe*. This increasing tension between ground and tonal center is resolved when the *dastgāh*

reaches a new *shāh gūshe*, with a higher-pitched resolution tone. Often this may include a slight change in tuning, for example, a shift from d-natural to d-*koron* 'half-flat'. Sometimes particular pitches, known as *motaghayyer* 'changing tones', change according to whether the melodic direction is ascending or descending. These changes in pitch are set by tradition and are located in specific *gūshe-hā* along the structure of the *dastgāh*. Approximately two-thirds of the way through a *dastgāh*, the *owj* 'climax', or highest tonal area, is reached and the *dastgāh* begins resolving downward through a series of *gūshe-hā* until it arrives at the original mode of the *dastgāh* (Farhat 1990:25).

Some *gūshe-hā* are found in more than one *dastgāh*. They retain their pitch hierarchy but may change their tuning and intervallic relations according to the *dastgāh* they are in. Modulation is defined by Iranian musicians as *morākab khānī* or *morākab navāzī*, the practice of moving from one *dastgāh* to another by means of certain passages.

Scale

Traditionally, much attention was given to scale and tuning, whether for the sake of investigating acoustics or mathematical principles, or to discuss the ethical and emotional effects that different pitch relations were believed to have on the listener. In discussions of the *maqām*, the nature of different pitch relations within the tetrachord was explored by medieval Islamic theorists such as Fārābī and Ṣafī al-dīn. Ṣafī al-dīn developed a seventeen-tone scale based on the Pythagorean intervals of limmas and commas. In the twentieth century, 'Alīnaqī Vazīrī developed a standardized tuning system following a Western model, with a theoretical scale of twenty-four quarter tones. Mehdi Barkechli developed a twenty-two-tone scale similar to the seventeen-tone scale of Ṣafī al-dīn (Farhat 1990:7–15).

In performance, intervals such as the neutral second and third and the expanded second may be tuned slightly differently in different *dastgāh-hā*. For example a-*koron* may be somewhat higher in one *dastgāh* and lower in another. Moreover, this note may have different nuances within a *dastgāh* performance, depending on the particular *gūshe* or the position of the pitch within the melody. Further, musicians have individual preferences in intonation. Thus, while the scale degrees are defined in the *radīf*, in actual performance the intonation varies.

Poetry

The primary poetic form used for the *gūshe-hā* of the *radīf* is the *ghazal*, a form of classical poetry that has five to seventeen lines. The poems most often used for the *ghazal* of the *radīf* are by Ḥāfez (1317–1326) and Sa'dī (c. 1213–1292). The *ghazal* itself is arranged in a series of related or associated self-contained lines. Each *gūshe* usually contains one or two lines, or *beyt*, of a *ghazal*, each line consisting of two hemistiches, or *meṣrā'*. Traditionally, these lines are chosen by the singer at the time of the performance. A singer may select one or more of these lines but need not follow the order presented in the *ghazal*.

The form of the *gūshe* itself is based on the presentation of the two *meṣrā'* of the *beyt*. A typical format would be introduction, poetry, and *taḥrir* (Caron and Safvate 1966:111–112). In performing the *gūshe* of *Khārā* (figure 1; Karimi 1978:2), for example, the singer would vocalize an introduction that gives the feeling of the *gūshe*, sing the first *meṣra'* (hemistiche), and then pause while the instrumentalist rephrases either the entire *meṣrā'* or the second half. The vocalist would then sing the second *meṣrā'* and follow this with a more lengthy vocalization, *taḥrīr*. The instrumentalist would then rephrase all or the second part of the second *meṣrā'*, including the *taḥrīr*. Thus, the progression would be:

1. Introduction
2. *Meṣrā'* 1
3. Instrumental recapitulation

FIGURE 1 *Khārā*: a *darāmad* in *dastgāh–e shur*.

4. *Meṣrā'* 2
5. *Taḥrīr*
6. Instrumental recapitulation

Although this is a common way of performing a *gūshe*, there are variations, such as repetition of a *meṣrā'* by the vocalist. Some *gūshe-hā* may have more than one *beyt* or may have no introduction or *taḥrīr* section. Still, a solo instrumentalist would learn and play a version of the *radīf* based on this general format.

The lines from one *ghazal* would be used to perform the main body of the *gūshe* in a particular *dastgāh*. Other *gūshe-hā* placed toward the end of the *radīf* of this *dastgāh* might use different poetic forms, such as the *roba'ī* and the *maṣnavī*. Melodically, these pieces tend to be more fixed.

The lines of the *ghazal* also unify the *dastgāh* performance rhythmically. At one time, Western scholars characterized the *gūshe* as having free rhythm. However, classical Persian poetry uses the *'arūż* system of poetic meters, which is based primarily on syllable length and secondarily on accent (Khanlari 1975:155–157). The poetry is usually sung with rubato but may be sung in a more strictly quantitative rhythm and thus become a *żarbī* 'rhythmic' *gūshe*. Usually the opening phrase of a nonmetric *gūshe* is sung in an iambic pattern according to syllable length (short-long); subsequent phrases tend to lengthen the long syllables (Tsuge 1974:152–153, 164–165).

Metric forms

The rhythm of the *gūshe* is based on classical poetic meters of the *'arūż* system, particularly those of the *ghazal*. The *radīf* originally had few rhythms based on musical meter or rhythmic motives. While the primary focus of the *radīf* has been the nonmetric *gūshe-hā*, metric rhythms did exist that provided variation and a rest from the more elongated rubato of the *gūshe*. These rhythms included motives such as the *kereshme*, a hemiola rhythm that could be played in a variety of different *gūshe-hā* and in different *dastgāh-hā*.

Performance in the twentieth century was influenced by Western musical practices. For example, more emphasis was placed on instrumental ensembles, and thus musical forms were developed or expanded to be played by an instrumental group. In performing a *dastgāh*, the *gūshe-hā* of the *radīf* began to appear under the heading *āvāz*, with metric forms preceding and following the *āvāz*. The *āvāz* could be performed instrumentally or, more commonly, by a singer and an instrumentalist. The term *dastgāh* came to designate not just the *radīf* as a series of *gūshe-hā* but a suite form consisting of *pishdarāmad* 'overture', *āvāz* (*radīf*), *taṣnīf* (a composed metric song; plural, *taṣnīfhā*), and *reng* (a dance form).

The *pīshdarāmad* is the opening instrumental piece, often in 2/4 meter, played by a solo melodic instrument and drum or more often by a small group of instrumentalists. It was invented by Roknaddīn Khān Mokhtārī but was developed and popularized by Darvīsh Khān (Caron and Safvate 1966:146–149; During 1984:156–158). It is sometimes regarded as an adaptation of the Western overture or possibly the Turkish *peshrev*.

The *taṣnīf* is a composed song form, usually in 3/4 or 6/8 meter, performed by a vocal soloist and accompanied by one or more instruments. Some *żarbī* 'rhythmic' *gūshe-hā* within the *radīf* may have originally been *taṣnīf* with melodies composed to classical poetry. The *taṣnīfhā* of 'Alī Akbar Sheydā and 'Āref Qazvīnī in the late Qajar period have come to represent the classical *taṣnif* form, which consists of verse and refrain, with the verse containing either traditional classical poetry or the composer's own poetic lines in the classical style using meters of the *'arūż*. The *taṣnīf* that is now part of a *dastgāh* performance can have a variety of forms.

The *taṣnīf*, as well as the *pīshdarāmad* and *reng*, was based on the *gūshe* of the *radīf*. The traditional *taṣnīf* tended to conform musically to one *gūshe*; the *pīshdarāmad* presented an outline of the major *gūshe-hā* of the *dastgāh*. Later *taṣnīf* composers expanded the melodic form to encompass major *gūshe-hā* of the *dastgāh* (Caton 1983:236–237).

A closing instrumental *reng* would also be performed by a soloist or by an ensemble. The rhythm of the *reng* form is based on a traditional Persian dance rhythm, a particular form of 6/8 time with an emphasis shifting from a division into three accents to a division into two (hemiola). Often this rhythm uses an extended sixth beat with a delayed and shortened first beat. The *taṣnīf* and *reng* bring a lighter and faster finish to the *dastgāh* performance and are believed to be a way of bringing people out of their thoughts into a renewed sense of their surroundings.

The *chahārmeżrāb* may not have originally been part of the *radīf*, but it was gradually introduced as a standard part of the *dastgāh* performance (Borumand 1974–1975, interviews). It is incorporated within the *āvāz* portion as an improvised instrumental solo based on the *radīf* and often precedes or follows an important *gūshe*. The basis of the *chahārmeżrāb* is a rhythmic motive (*pāye*) that incorporates a pedal tone and acts as an ostinato and rhythmic accompaniment to the melody line. A *chahāharmeżrāb* is usually performed in 3/8, 6/8, 6/16, 9/16, or 12/16 meter (Caron and Safvate 1966: 151–155; Sadeghi 1971:69–73; Zonis 1973:131–134).

INSTRUMENTS

The *radīf* has traditionally been performed solo or by a small ensemble, such as a solo vocalist accompanied by one or two melodic instruments and a drum. These instruments include the *setār*, *tār*, *kamānche*, *santūr*, *ney*, *tombak*, and *dāire*.

The *setār*, a four-stringed plucked long-necked lute, developed from a family of instruments indigenous to Iran. The name *setār* actually means three strings, but a fourth was added at the beginning of the twentieth century (Caron and Safvat 1966:166). It has functioned as a teaching instrument for the *radīf*, and as a solo and practice instrument. Its volume has often been considered too low for ensemble performance of the *dastgāh*.

The *tār* is a more recent addition to Iran, believed to have been introduced in the late eighteenth century (Zonis 1973:156). It is a plucked long-necked lute, with six strings plucked with a metal plectrum. It was the preferred performance instrument during the nineteenth century (Caron and Safvate 1966:169), possibly because it was used by the family of ʿAlī Akbar Farahānī and subsequently became prominent in the Qajar court.

The *kamānche* is a vertically held bowed lute, sometimes said to have been the most prominent classical instrument up to the time of ʿAlī Akbar (Caron and Safvate 1966:174; Varzi 1989). Although at one time it was almost replaced by the violin, the *kamānche* is still used by traditional ensembles.

The *ney*, an end-blown flute, is also an indigenous Iranian instrument. Islamic mystics, particularly the Mevlevi order of dervishes founded by Jalāluddīn Rumī (1207–1273), use the *ney* in their spiritual concerts. They believe that it symbolizes the essential condition of man in this world, separated from his spiritual origin. To them, the sound of the ney represents the breath of God or spirit as it flows through man—a hollow reed. This instrument is often included in the classical *dastgāh* ensemble.

The *santūr*, a hammered dulcimer, for the *dastgāh* ensemble usually has seventy-two strings, four strings to a pitch. Partly because of its potentially higher volume, it has sometimes has taken the role of leader of the orchestra. Compared with other classical instruments, it seems to have fewer mystical associations, and it is not as flexible in changing modes or playing certain ornamental nuances. Although its origins in Iran are obscure, it may have either developed from or replaced the *chang* 'harp', an instrument that was once prominent in Iran but disappeared in the seventeenth century (During 1991:101–102; Zonis 1973:165).

The *tombak* is a goblet-shaped drum capable of producing a variety of sounds in addition to its two basic sounds: the lower-pitched *tom* and the higher-pitched *bak*. In addition to playing in the center and on the rim of the *tombak*, the drummer may also play on the wooden frame, using finger rings to produce certain effects. In the past the drummer was often the singer, particularly of the *taṣnīf* (Khāleqī 1974:357–367). At one time, other Iranian musicians did not really consider the *tombak* an instrument. More recently, however, the *tombak* performer Hoseyn Tehrānī raised its status considerably, as he introduced virtuosic playing styles and *tombak* solos.

The *dāire*, a single-headed frame drum, has been less frequently found in the *radīf* orchestra. It is played more often in regional styles of Iranian music.

TEACHING PRACTICES

The *radīf* was traditionally learned by ear, without music notation, and was committed to memory. The *ostād* 'teacher' might instruct students individually or in a group. The teacher would play or sing a phrase, which would then be repeated by each student and corrected by the teacher or a senior student. The well-known musician Darvīsh Khān taught his students the *radīf* at three levels, each of which contained a more complete version of the *radīf* than the previous one. Completion of all three levels took approximately ten years. After the successful completion of each level Darvīsh Khān gave the graduating student the emblem of the Anjoman Okhovat 'Society of Brothers', first in copper, then silver, then gold. No more than twenty people ever received the gold medal from him (Maḥmūdī 1977:12).

The student was expected to work hard, follow the teacher's guidance, and remain loyal to the teacher throughout the training. The student would not perform for an audience until the teacher felt he was ready and gave him permission. The student was often expected to adhere to and reflect a spiritual attitude both in his manner toward his teacher and toward the music itself. This would differentiate him from the *moṭreb*, or entertainer. This distinction between the *radīf* musician and the *moṭreb* is still reflected in Iranians' attitude toward musicians (Caron and Safvate 1966:231–236; During 1991:231–249).

Traditional training was often hard to obtain. Musicians were likely to be secretive about their art and jealously guarded what they knew, both as a way of testing the student's readiness and ability to learn and preserve the *radīf* accurately and as a way of ensuring their own viability in a whimsical and often difficult performance climate.

Over the twentieth century, Iranian musicologists and musicians such as ʻAlīnaqī Vazīrī, Abolḥasan Ṣabā, and Mūsā Maʻrūfī transcribed the *radīf* using Western notation. Eventually teachers began to use these notated versions as instructional aids. Because nearly all the *gūshe-hā* have flexible rhythm, their timing is only approximated by Western music notation with its mathematical rhythmic values. Nor can the slides and other subtle ornaments of this style be precisely notated. Thus the transcribed *radīf* is an approximate version of the original, and a master teacher is still needed to play each *gūshe* for the student.

A number of musicians have objected to the use of notated music and to the concept of standardizing the *radīf*. Since the art of Persian music has been taught aurally and its performance has been based on variation and improvisation, these musicians argue that using notation weakens the memory and the process of internalization necessary to provide the foundation for improvisation. Notation also fosters dependence on written scores and on compositon. Further, presenting a standardized version of the *radīf* limits the traditional process of variation and change and diminishes the richness that comes from a diversity of source material. However, without transcriptions the music is much less accessible to students and its preservation and transmission are more fragile, particularly during periods of change in Iranian society such as those that took place in the twentieth century.

During the 1970s, some musicians and music scholars became concerned that conservatory training was producing a student who could no longer improvise and who tended to rely on notation. They initiated an additional level of training that reintroduced the aural methods of the past. Students studied with older musicians, such as Nūrʻ Alī Borūmand, ʻAlī Akbar Shahnāzī, and ʻAbdollāh Davāmī, hoping to recapture the older tradition before it became inaccessible. In the process they also studied the taped *radīf-hā* and performances of masters that were housed in various archives.

Notated *radīf-hā* and metric compositions and études have created a generation of performers who have facility in Western methods of performance and composition. Their performance of the *dastgāh* reflects this background in Western compositional techniques and greater use of metric orchestral compositions.

LIFE OF THE MUSICIAN

In the nineteenth century the *radīf* musician was often attached to one of the royal offices, such as the retinue of the king or of one of the princes who had jurisdiction over regions of Iran. In the large homes and gardens of the wealthy, individual musicians and small ensembles performed music for gatherings of their patrons. They had little freedom, could not play for others without the permission of their patrons, traveled and moved with their patrons, and were often treated as little better than household servants. Sometimes, because the *hāl*—inspiration—was such an important aspect of the performance, musicians were given alcohol or drugs to enhance or guarantee the effectiveness of their music (Ney-Dāvūd 1996, interview).

The status of the musician was generally low and unstable, partly because of the predominantly antimusical attitudes of orthodox Shiʻa Muslims. Music of the *radīf*, while fostered in the environment of the court, became a closely guarded tradition.

Practiced for centuries by members of the Islamic craft guilds associated with the Sufi brotherhoods, music was treated as a sacred trust; and the passing of the tradition from master to student was done with great care and caution. Musicians played for, and relied on the patronage and protection of, nobles and princes until political and social changes during the late nineteenth century brought music to the general public.

An example of the difficulties experienced by musicians can be found in the biography of Gholām Ḥoseyn Darvīsh, known as Darvīsh Khān, who was one of the innovators of *dastgāh* performance in the early twentieth century. He was originally employed by one of the Qajar princes. After he married and found himself unable to support his family on the income from his patron, he began to perform for other wealthy benefactors. The prince threatened him, but others interceded on his behalf. Later he again began performing for others, and this time, to escape punishment, he took refuge in the British embassy. The ambassador eventually interceded and freed him from his obligation to the prince. In addition to teaching classes, Darvīsh Khān organized his own orchestra at the Society of Brothers, where in 1906 he presented the first public concert, considered the first modern concert (Caton 1994:77–79).

COMPONENTS OF PERFORMANCE

Settings

The secular music of the Qajar period was performed for dinners, evening entertainments (*bazm*), picnics, weddings, and other special occasions. The entertainers might include instrumentalists, singers, dancers, actors, jugglers, fire-eaters, and wrestlers. Accounts of music during the dinner parties commonly mention a musical ensemble, usually consisting of two melodic instruments—*tār* and possibly *kamānche*, and a *tombak*. As mentioned earlier, the drummer was often also the singer. At these entertainments, the entire performance ensemble was male; the dancers dressed up as women.

A notable characteristic of this period was that entertainment ensembles were typically either all-male or all-female. A patron's male musicians usually played for men's parties in the *bīrūne* 'men's quarters'. In the court, women musicians played in the *anderūn* 'women's quarters', or the male musicians were led blindfolded into the *anderūn* and then performed behind a screen. However, there were a few groups of mixed male and female musicians in which the men were blind.

Informal gatherings were held both indoors and outdoors. At one time, a common practice was to play music on rooftops in summer, to cool off from the hot weather, to allow women in the women's quarters to hear the music, and to be out in nature, under the moon and the starlit sky. Another practice—sitting in a room dimly lit by candles—was a way of simulating the effect of being outdoors on a starry night (Varzi 1989, interview).

The playing of music was combined with other activities, such as conversing, dining, and reciting poetry. The *radīf* would often be performed toward the end of the evening, when the gathering had become quieter. In performing the *radīf*, the musician played an improvised version that sometimes lasted for several hours (Zonis 1973:103).

At such an informal gathering, the twentieth-century singer Gholām Ḥoseyn Banān, for example, would open his handwritten book of poetry, leaf through it, stop at a poem, begin to sing a *gūshe* with one of the lines of a *ghazal*, and then continue to sing in the *dastgāh* of this *gūshe*, choosing the lines from the *ghazal* extemporaneously (Varzi 1986, interview). Banān was noted for his ability to convey the feelings and meaning of the poetry and to create an inspired mood (*ḥāl*) in the audience, as well as for his technical ability to sing and to match poetry with musical phrases (Caton 1988:677–678).

Instrumentalists who accompanied the singers at these gatherings followed the singer's phrasing. They knew the *dastgāh* structure and the *gūshe-hā* from which the singer would choose, and they could provide support and interest by approximating the melody, adding or subtracting notes, varying the ornamentation, repeating important tones, delaying and overlapping, or playing in different octaves. They would fill the pauses between poetic hemistiches by reiterating or rephrasing the singer's performance of the phrase.

Improvisation

The music of Banān is a good example of improvisation. He would first choose a poem, basing the choice on his mood and his assessment of the audience's mood and desires. He would also chose the *dastgāh* to go with that poem. In traditional performance, rapport with the audience was an essential part of improvisation (Varzi 1988:6–7). Banān also chose the individual lines of poetry and the *gūshe* that he matched with each line. The rhythmic meter of the poem affected the rhythm of the *gūshe*. The singer interpreted the poetry according to his individual taste, varying the rhythm, length of syllables, and ornamentation within the parameters established for that *gūshe*.

An instrumental rendition would involve similar choices. The musician chose the *dastgāh* as well as the individual *gūshe*. Although the order of *gūshe-hā* in a *radīf* begins with the *darāmad* and progresses according to a traditional arrangement, in actuality a performer might begin in the middle of the *dastgāh* and play only one section. The more experience and expertise a musician had, the more freedom he had in performance. Some musicians would modulate from one *dastgāh* to another.

The degree of freedom in the realization of a *gūshe* varies. *Gūshe-hā* that are more formed, melodically, have less range of variation; improvisation for these *gūshe-hā* consists primarily of ornamentation, rhythmic nuances, and dynamics. The *shāh gūshe-hā*, particularly the *darāmad* (the opening section), are less melodically fixed and have greater possibilities for expansion.

Simple improvisational techniques include ornamentation, repetition, playing in different octaves, dynamic and rhythmic variation, imitation, and sequence. Other improvisatory techniques require more internalization of the *dastgāh* structure and the motivic repertoire and melodic devices of the *radīf*. These include variation, elaboration, compression, and combination (Sadeghi 1971:75–152; Zonis 1973: 98–125).

The art of improvisation was usually not taught separately. Instead, in the process of aural transmission of the *gūshe-hā* the musician internalized a pool of melodic figures as well as the underlying structures that he was intuitively able to draw on during performance. In listening to master musicians, the student was able to comprehend the possibilities and limits of improvisation. In developing a rapport with his audience, he also learned to match his choices to his own mood and the mood of his audience, according to the inspiration of the moment.

The performance of *radīf* music has been changing from *gūshe* improvisation in informal settings to composed orchestral pieces for a concert audience. This trend has reduced the ability and willingness of many performers to improvise in the more difficult improvisational techniques.

Functions of *radīf* music

Music of the *radīf* often served as background and entertainment at wealthy people's parties. For those more intimately acquainted with this music and its philosophical background, listening to it was a means of forgetting troubles and provided emotional catharsis, spiritual cleansing, and enrichment. Musicians themselves distinguished the *radīf* from entertainment music, which was considered a separate genre with a separate purpose, diversion.

As a result of the influence of Western teaching techniques, performance settings, and attitudes, music from the traditional *radīf* was interspersed with additional compositional forms to create a performance of one or more *dastgāh* for the concert stage. The *dastgāh* and the *gūshe-hā* would be chosen in advance. The performance of the *dastgāh* began to lose its philosophical associations, and the audience began to focus on beauty of form and technique. Followers of the older school of intimate music mourn the loss of traditional styles and mystical connotations, while innovative performers and composers continue to create what they feel is a more dynamic music that reflects the reality of their time.

CONTEMPORARY TRENDS

During the Pahlavi dynasty (1925–1979), performance of music was monitored and controlled by the Iranian government. Certain types of music and lyrics were not allowed on public airwaves, and musicians were sometimes imprisoned for performing music that contained political and social criticism or was in some other way threatening to the government. Government offices, such as the ministry of culture and art and the national radio and television, became the new patrons of *radīf* music, sponsoring the teaching of the *radīf* in the conservatory, in universities, and as part of the national broadcast media. Today this patronage has lessened, and although the music of the *radīf* is allowed in Iran where many other musics are discouraged, musical activities have been restricted and many musicians have left Iran to live and perform in the West.

As mentioned above, a common traditional performance context was the informal gathering, indoors or outdoors. In the twentieth century, public concerts were introduced, as well as live and recorded broadcasts of music on radio and television. Conservatory and university instruction became the means of transmitting the *radīf.* These institutions employed traditional musicians, particularly in the revival of traditional *radīf* music in the 1970s. Since the revolution of 1979, music has continued to be taught privately in Iran. Outside Iran, individual musicians and scholars have also studied and performed the *radīf.* Musicians tour Europe and America, bringing a variety of new forms of *dastgāh* performance as well as presenting traditional styles.

The *radīf* has been the subject of much study and analysis in Iran and the West, particularly with regard to mode and organization of the *dastgāh*. Although some historical research has been done on the treatises of various medieval Islamic scholars, the body of theoretical and philosophical manuscripts from the fifteenth to the twentieth century has been little examined. These manuscripts contain clues to the introduction of Turkish elements in the music, philosophical associations of musical modes, and the development of traditional progressions that may have led to the *dastgāh* system.

Often researchers have examined the structure of the music or have presented the mythology associated with its purpose and function. A more integrated approach would involve more study of the relationship of mythology, ideals, and theory to actual conditions and practice. The religious climate and religious attitudes are an interesting area of research for understanding the philosophical foundations of the music itself and the milieu of individual musicians and how their lives and personalities have been shaped. Aspects of Iranian *radīf* music that merit greater investigation include the relationship of the *radīf* to folk music and other forms of music in Iran, the effect of the setting on the performance of the *radīf,* the relationship of the musician's training and attitudes to his performance, the relationship of the sociopolitical and religious climate to the life of the musician and the direction of the music, the function of music within society, the role and status of the musician, and the effects of westernization on attitudes and performance.

REFERENCES

Al-Faruqi, Lois Ibsen. 1978. "Ornamentation in Arabian Improvisational Music: A Study of Interrelatedness in the Arts," *World of Music* 20(1):17–32.

———. 1985. "Structural Segments in the Islamic Arts: The Musical 'Translation' of a Characteristic of the Literary and Visual Arts," *Asian Music* 16(1):59–81.

Arberry, Arthur J. 1962. *Fifty Poems of Hafiz*. London: Cambridge University Press. (See also 1993. Richmond, Surrey: Curzon.)

Borūmand, Nūr Ali. 1974–1975. Interviews. Tehran.

Caron, Nelly, and Dairouche Safvate. 1966. *Les traditions musicales: Iran*. Paris: Buchet/Chastel.

Caton, Margaret. 1983. "The Classical *Tasnif*: A Genre of Persian Vocal Music." Ph.D. dissertation, University of California, Los Angeles.

———. 1984. "Bahá'í Influences on Mírzá 'Abdúlláh, Qájár Court Musician and Master of the *Radíf*." In *From Iran East and West*, ed. Juan Cole and Moojan Monen, 30–64, 187–190. Los Angeles: Kalimát.

———. 1988. "Banān, Ğolām-Ḥosayn." In *Encyclopaedia Iranica*, Vol. 3:669–678. Costa Mesa, Calif.: Mazda.

———. 1994. "Darvīš Khan." In *Encyclopaedia Iranica*, Vol. 7:77–79. Costa Mesa, Calif.: Mazda.

Crow, Douglas Karim. 1984. "Samā': The Art of Listening in Islam." *Maqām: Music of the Islamic World and Its Influences*, ed. Robert H. Browning, 30–33. New York: Alternative Museum.

During, Jean. 1975. "Éléments spirituels dans la musique traditionnelle iranienne contemporaine." *Sophia Perennis: The Bulletin of the Imperial Iranian Academy of Philosophy* 1(2, Autumn):129–154.

During, Jean, and Zia Mirabdolbagahi. 1991. *The Art of Persian Music*. Washington, D.C.: Mage.

Farhat, Hormoz. 1990. *The Dastgāh Concept in Persian Music*. Cambridge: Cambridge University Press.

Farmer, Henry George. 1973. *A History of Arabian Music to the Thirteenth Century*. London: Luzac.

Halifax, Joan. 1982. *Shaman: The Wounded Healer*. London: Thames and Hudson.

Karīmī, Mahmūd, comp. 1978. *Radīf–e Āvāzī-ye Musiqi-ye Sonnati-ye Iran*. Transcribed and analyzed by Mohammad Taghi Massoudieh. Tehran: Ministry of Culture and Art.

Khāleqī, Ruhollāh. 1974. *Sargozasht-e Mūsīqī-ye Irān*, Vol. 1. Tehran: Ebn-e Sina.

Khānlarī, Parvīz Nātel. 1975. *Vazn-e She'r-e Fārsī*. Tehran: Bonyād-e Farhang-e Iran.

Mahmūdī, M. 1977. "'Darvīsh Khān,' Khāleq-e Pishdarāmad," *Rastākhiz* (September):12.

Ma'rūfī, Mūsā, comp. 1963. *Les systèmes de la musique traditionnelle de l'Iran (radif)*. Tehran: Ministry of Culture and Arts.

Martin, Richard. 1982. *Islam: A Cultural Perspective*. Englewood Cliffs, N.J.: Prentice–Hall.

Massoudieh, Mohammad Taghi. 1968. *Awaz-e Sur*. Regensburg: Bosse.

Nettl, Bruno. 1987. *The Radif of Persian Music: Studies of Structure and Cultural Context*. Champaign, Ill.: Elephant and Cat.

Ney Dāvūd, Morteză. 1976, Interview (16 December). Tehran, Iran.

Powers, Harold S. 1980. "Mode." In *New Grove Dictionary of Music and Musicians*, ed. Stanley Sadie, Vol. 12:376–450. London: Macmillan.

Reckord, Thomas. 1987. "Chant in Popular Iranian Shi'ism." Ph.D. dissertation, University of California, Los Angeles.

———. 1988. "The Role of Religious Chant in the Definition of the Iranian Aesthetic," In *Cultural Parameters of Iranian Musical Expression*, ed. Margaret Caton and Neil Siegel. Redondo Beach, Calif.: Institute of Persian Performing Arts.

Roychoudhury, M. L. 1957. "Music in Islam." *Journal of Asiatic Society, Letters* 23(2):43–102.

Sadeghi, Manoochehr. 1971. "Improvisation in Nonrhythmic Solo Instrumental Contemporary Persian Art Music." Master's thesis, California State University, Los Angeles.

Safvat, Dāriush. 1971. *Ostādan-e Mūsīqī-ye Irān va Elhān-e Mūsīqī-ye Irānī*. Tehran: Ministry of Culture and Arts.

Schuyler, Philip D. 1984. "Moroccan Andalusian Music." In *Maqām: Music of the Islamic World and Its Influences*, ed. Robert H. Browning, 14–17. New York: Alternative Museum.

Tsuge, Gen'ichi. 1974. "Āvāz: A Study of the Rhythmic Aspects in Classical Iranian Music." Ph.D. dissertation, Wesleyan University, Middletown, Conn.

Varzi, Morteza. 1986. Interview (25 September). Los Angeles, Calif.

———. 1988. "Performer-Audience Relationships in the *Bazm*." *Cultural Parameters of Iranian Musical Expression*, ed. Margaret Caton and Neil Siegel. Redondo Beach, Calif.: Institute of Persian Performing Arts.

———. 1989. Interviews (February–March). Los Angeles, California.

Zonis, Ella. 1973. *Classical Persian Music*. Cambridge, Mass.: Harvard University Press.

Discography

Anthology of Persian Music, 1930–1990. 1991. Accompanying compact disk to *The Art of Persian Music*. Program notes, 4 pp. Mage: CD 22–1. Performers: Navā'i (*ney*), Musá Ma'rufi (*tār*), 'Ali Khan 'Aref (vocal), Yusof Forutan (*setār*), Yahya Khan Zarrinpanje (*tār*), Sa'id Hormozi (*setār*), Zia Mirabdolbaghi (*zarb*), Asghar Bahari (*kamanche*), Parisa (vocal), Jalil Shahnaz (*tār*), Hoseyn Tehrani (*zarb*) Hatam-e 'Askari-e Farahani (voice), Dariush Safvat (*setār, santur*), Bruno Caillat (*zarb*). Performance of *abū-'aṭā*, *homāyūn*, *māhūr*, *shūr*, *qaṭār*, *bayāt–e eṣfahān*, *segāh*, and *rāst-Panjgāh*.

Classical Music of Iran: Dastgah Systems. 1966. 4 s. Recordings compiled by Ella Zonis. Notes by Ella Zonis (4 pp., illus.). Folkways FW 8831/8832. Contains samples of all twelve *dastgāh-hā*. They include recordings of *setār, tār, kamānche, santūr, tombak*, violin, *ney*, and male and female vocal style.

Iran, Volume 1: Anthologie de la musique traditionnelle. Setâr et Târ par Dariush Talâ'i. 1979. (Musiques traditionnelles vivantes, III: Musiques Savantes). Recorded by Jean During with the help of Mohammad Sadr-e Zade. Notes by Jean During (3 pp., French and English; photos). Ocora 558 540. Performance of *māhūr*, *chahārgāh*, and *eṣfahān*.

Iran, Vol. 2: *Anthologie de la musique traditionnelle. Santur par Majid Kiâni*. (Musique traditonnelles vivantes, III: Musiques Savantes). Ocora 558 550. Performance of *bayāt-e kord*, *reng-e shahr ashūb*, *homāyūn*.

Iran, Vols. 3 and 4: *Anthologie de la musique traditionnelle; Ney par Mohammad Musavi. Chant et ney par Mahmud Karimi et Mohammad Musavi*. 1981. (Musiques traditionnelles vivantes, III. Musiques Savantes). Recorded in Teheran in 1980 by Jean During. Notes by Jean During (10 pp., French and English, illus., photo, texts). Ocora 558 562/563. Performance of *dashtī*, *mokhālef-e segāh*, *homāyūn*, *navā*.

Iran: Dariush Talai et Djamchid Chemirani. Le Son du concert du 11 Mai 1982. 1983. Ocora 4 558 617/618. 2 cassettes. *Setar, tombak*. Performance of *māhūr*, *shūr*, *chahārgāh*.

Iranische Dastgah. 1971. UNESCO Collection: Musical Sources. Notes by Daniélou. Philips 6586 005. Ashgar Bahari (*kamānche*), Omar Sharif (*tār*), Hassan Kassai (*ney*), Hossein Teherani (*zarb*), Hussein Malek (*santūr*). Performance of *afshārī*, *segāh*, *homāyūn*, *eṣfahān*, and *bayāt-e tork*.

Musique Persane. 1971. Notes by Hormoz Farhat (6 pp., French and English, mus. ex., photos). Ocora OCR 57. Faramarz Payvar (*santur*), Jalil Shahnaz (*tār*), Asqar Bahari (*kamānche*), Hasan Nahid (*ney*), Hoseyn Tehrani (*tombak*), Abdolvahhab Shahidi (male vocalist). Performance of *māhūr* and *segāh*.

A Persian Heritage: Classical Music of Iran. 1974. Recorded in Ann Arbor, Mich. Produced by David Lewiston. Notes by Bruno Nettl. Nonesuch H-72060. Faramarz Payvar (*santur*), Khatereh Parvaneh (female vocalist), Houshang Zarif (*tār*), Rahmatollah Badi'i (*kamānche*), Mohammed Esmai'li (*zarb*). Performance of *shūr*, *homāyūn*, *segāh*, *chahārgāh*, *māhūr*, *tombak* solo.

Persische Kunstmusik. 1972. Notes by Eckhard Neubauer (2 pp., German and English). Harmonia Mundi 1C 065–99 632. Performance of *segāh* and *dashtī* by Faramarz Payvar (*santūr*), Khatereh Parvaneh (female vocalist), and Hoseyn Tehrani (*tombak*).

Section 2
Music in Religious Expression

Chanting, singing, playing musical instruments, and even dancing are essential parts of religious expression throughout the Middle East and Central Asia. Over the centuries, devotees have produced some of the world's great chant traditions—for example those of the Syrian, Armenian, and Coptic churches; the several systems of cantillating Jewish holy texts; and the recitation of the Qur'ān. In many practices, singing metrical hymns or improvising devotional songs is an aspect of the religious experience. Sometimes, very good singers have professional careers, and their performances—live and recorded—are commercially marketed. Chant, song, and instrumental music form extended rituals such as the Sufi *ayin* in Turkey, which had a tremendous influence on the shape of more secular Turkish classical music.

Sites throughout the region, including Mecca, Medina, Jerusalem, and Qom, are destinations for pilgrims seeking historic holy places or the tombs of venerated saints. Pilgrimage has given rise to distinct genres of music and song.

Since music is also a form of entertainment and may be heard in places where questionable behaviors such as drinking alcohol and gambling may also take place, the question whether it is actually appropriate in the lives of the devout has been contested in many religions for centuries. Also, the proper use of music in devotional life and daily life has been disputed—as has women's participation in religious devotion, if women particate at all.

The essays that follow detail some important religious practices and show ways in which musical sound has been adapted for devout purpose.

Abraham's Mosque, Hebron, Jordan, c. 1965. Photo © Dean Conger, Corbis.

Snapshot: Shaykh Yāsīn al-Tuhāmī in the Public *Ḥaḍra*: A Typical *Layla* Performance

Michael Frishkopf

Shaykh Yāsīn al-Tuhāmī (figure 1), from Hawātka, Asyūṭ Upper Egypt, is the most famous Sufi religious singer (*munshid*) in Egypt, and widely acclaimed as the greatest. Since 1973, throughout Egypt, he has given thousands of nighttime religious performances called *layālī* (singular, *layla*) for social as well as religious occasions, such as saints' festivals, weddings, and memorials. So great is the demand for his religious singing (*inshād*) that he is completely booked many months in advance. About thirty commercial cassette recordings of his performances are available. His innovations, artistry, fame, and financial success have inspired a large number of imitators, especially in Upper Egypt. Together they form a virtual school, the most influential of its kind. This article examines, in detail, a typical *layla* of Shaykh Yāsīn at a public *ḥaḍra*. *Ḥaḍra* is a Sufi ceremony centered on *dhikr* 'remembrance of God', often accompanied by *inshād* 'Islamic hymnody'. [See Islamic Hymnody in Egypt.]

FIGURE 1 Shaykh Yāsīn al-Tuhāmī performing at a public *ḥaḍra*, the *mūlid* of 'Umar ibn al-Fārid. Photo by Michael Frishkopf, 29 May 1997.

At six in the evening, Shaykh Yāsīn dresses carefully in a fine *jallābiyya* 'robe', a woven *shal* 'shawl', and a *'imma* 'turban' of brilliant white—this distinctive professional attire is now imitated by most *munshidīn* from Upper Egypt—and clasps a rosary in one hand. He and his *firqa* 'musical group' travel to the site of the *layla*, a small village near Tanta in the Nile Delta, where he performs an annual memorial for Shaykh 'Umar Ṭaha, formerly a deputy in the Rifā'ī Sufi order. There Yāsīn is met by members of Shaykh 'Umar's family, who sponsor the *layla*, and by hundreds of local fans who have flocked to see him. He emerges from his car and pushes through the thick crowd, shaking hands and exchanging greetings with his admirers. Slowly he makes his way to the home of one of the sponsors, where a supper is being served for all who come.

The performance space, situated near Shaykh 'Umar's tomb, is clearly marked by color and light. A canvas pavilion, brightly colored with geometric Islamic designs, encloses the space on all sides except one, which is left open to accommodate the overflowing crowd. Against the back flap is a carpeted wooden stage, on which the musicians sit or stand in a semicircle around the *munshid*. In front of the stage is a carpeted strip where *dhikr* 'remembrance of God'—in this case, rhythmic chanting of God's names together with turning or bowing movements—will be conducted. Large loudspeakers are placed on stands around the periphery of the performance

Shaykh Yāsīn is a master of the *layla*, carefully controlling the music and *dhkir.*

space. The pavilion and adjacent buildings are strung with thousands of tiny colored lightbulbs and illuminated with powerful floodlights.

TRACK 3–9 The sponsors have raised money to pay Yāsīn and to rent equipment, but the performance is open to all without charge. In anticipation, people have been gathering all evening; eventually they number several thousand, including many children and hundreds of women who fill overlooking balconies and rooftops. All the main Sufi orders are represented, but a large proportion of those in attendance are not active members of any Sufi order, although most do subscribe informally to a Sufi system of beliefs and practices. They have come out of love and respect for Shaykh 'Umar, wanting to be together, to obtain a blessing, and to acknowledge God through *inshād* and *dhikr*. Others have come, some from a great distance, primarily to see and hear Shaykh Yāsīn. Still others wish merely to join in the celebration.

Around 11 P.M. Shaykh Yāsīn makes his way to the pavilion, ascends the stage, tests the microphone, and supervises the precise placement of the loudspeakers. Yāsīn has established new levels of artistry in his concern for the quality and balance of the sound system; all evening he will continue to make careful adjustments to the mixer. The musicians now take their places. The group consists of *kamanja* (violin), *'ūd* (lute), *ṭabla* (funnel-shaped drum), and two *riqāq* (tambourines; singular, *riqq*). One of Yāsīn's major innovations was his popularization of melodic instruments in the public Sufi *ḥaḍra*. His *firqa* has thus come to resemble the *takht*, the small ensemble of older secular Arab music. Before beginning, Shaykh Yāsīn recites several Qur'ānic verses in the simple *tartīl* style, followed by Rifā'ī prayers. Although the *layla* is open to all Sufi orders, tonight Yāsīn leans toward Rifā'ī texts, in deference to Shaykh 'Umar and his family. These recitations also serve as a benediction for the *layla*, and as a prayer for the inspiration of the performer. Yāsīn finishes after twenty minutes and then takes a break.

Shaykh Yāsīn is a master of the *layla*, carefully controlling the music and *dhikr*. At his signal, the violinist and *'ūd* player connect to the sound system and tune, moving imperceptibly into a nonmetric prelude in which they establish Yāsīn's chosen opening *maqām* 'melodic mode' with a short *taqsīm* 'instrumental improvisation'. Meanwhile a coordinator (*mustaftiḥ*) begins to arrange those who wish to perform *dhikr* into long facing lines, perpendicular to the front edge of the stage. Yāsīn begins the *dhikr* with a slow rhythmic intonation: "Allah . . . Allah." Following Yāsīn's beat, the coordinator sways his body and claps his hands to set a pattern for the others.

At a cue from Yāsīn, the percussionists enter, and the first *waṣla* 'section' is under way. Yāsīn begins with a fixed opening text, *Yā a'ẓam al-mursalīn* 'O greatest of prophets', a *madīḥ* in praise of the Prophet Muhammad. The tempo increases rapidly, building up to a *madad* section, in which Yāsīn asks the family of the Prophet and saints for their blessings; then come three lines of the first *qaṣīda*, closing with a melodic-poetic cadence (*qafla*).

There follows a sequence of three more such "buildups," each in roughly the same form: following a *taqsīm* at slower tempo, Yāsīn sings several lines of poetry, pausing and repeating freely for several minutes, until the *qafla*. An instrumental interlude may follow: either a *taqsīm* or a fixed melody (*mazzīka*), often borrowed from the songs of Umm Kulthūm. Sometimes Yāsīn inserts improvisatory *āhāt*: crying melismas on the syllable "ah." Singing and instrumental interludes may alternate several times. Meanwhile, the tempo increases; the meter intensifies, shifting from *waḥda* to *maqsūm* to *bamb*; and the melodic style changes from nonmetrical to increasingly metrical and short-phrased, until the final *qafla* and culmination of the buildup in *madad*. The buildups themselves increase in length and complexity. (See below, "Notes on Meter and Structure.")

Throughout the performance, vocal melodies are improvised from a set of stock phrases and contours, both metrical and nonmetrical, suitable for the different forms and moods of the poetry. Many of these phrases, originally Yāsīn's, are now widely imitated. The same text can be set to any number of melodies; there are no songs as such. Yāsīn sings in the *maqāmāt* with authority; his intonation is superb, and he modulates skillfully to change the mood. His distinctive style of textual performance features clear, faultless pronunciation and a slow exposition of the text; lines are repeated in many musical guises. By the end of the evening, the attentive listener (even if illiterate) has inevitably memorized large amounts of poetry.

Shaykh Yāsīn draws on many sources of Sufi poetry, most notably the great ʿUmar ibn al-Farīd. Normally Yāsīn's *layla* contains one or two principal *qaṣāʾid*, with shorter excerpts from other poems inserted here and there. From the outset of his career, Yāsīn distinguished himself from his predecessors by singing only classical Arabic poetry and by concentrating on the most exquisite, abstruse poems. Their densely symbolic mystical language of love, longing, and unity challenges the listener's comprehension, despite Yāsīn's clear articulation and his fidelity to the text. Tonight, drawing on an enigmatic poem attributed to Aḥmad al-Rifāʿī, a meditation on mystical union, he sings, *Fa-ṣirtu anā al-dāʿī wa-minnī ʾl-ijābati* . . . 'Then I became the Caller, and from me is the Answer . . .' Each listener understands according to his spiritual station: few grasp the complete meaning intellectually, but everyone feels the words emotionally.

Shaykh Yāsīn points out that he must live a text in order to learn it and sing it; in performance, the words bespeak his own inner state. His richly expressive voice comes from the heart, evoking *shajan* 'wistfulness' in his listeners, who respond with gestures, movements, and vocal cries, particularly at the *qafla*. "What comes from the heart reaches the heart," they say. Using their feedback to guide his poetic and musical choices, Yasīn raises *ṭarab* 'musical emotion' to a peak.

As the pace accelerates, *dhikr* becomes more individualistic, movement more ecstatic. Emotional responses are freely expressed through gesture or vocalization. Mention of saints, with whom many feel a personal relationship, sends waves of enthusiasm through the crowd. Participants may enter a state of mystic rapture, *ḥāl*, whose external manifestations include wild or spasmodic movement, stillness, collapsing, unconsciousness, and *tarjama*—literally 'translation', that is, speaking in tongues.

The majority do not perform *dhikr* but simply watch and listen, swaying to the music, clapping, waving ecstatically after the *qafla*, and shouting, "Allah!" Many hold tape-recorders aloft in front of a loudspeaker in order to make the best possible recording; these tapes will later be copied and distributed to fans around Egypt.

After four buildups, the first *waṣla* is concluded, the *firqa* takes a break, and those wishing to greet Shaykh Yāsīn come onto the stage. Some consider him to possess *baraka* 'blessing', for he is an inspired *munshid* whose father was a *walī* 'saint'. Others shower him with the sort of enthusiastic love usually displayed toward famous popular singers. Part saint, part pop star, he calmly receives them all.

In the second *waṣla*, Shaykh Yāsīn sings nonmetrically, accompanied by melodic instruments only. Everyone sits quietly, concentrating on the singing of poetry. When he finishes a phrase, cries of appreciation rise from his audience. Long *taqāsīm* and *āhāt* provide release from the tension of poetry and lend a meditative cast to this *waṣla*.

The third *waṣla* is a version of the first, but shorter, consisting of two buildups only. The longer final buildup leads to a blessing for the Prophet: *Ṣallā Allāh ʿalayhi wa sallam* . . . ('May God bless him and give him peace'). After the percussion has ceased, Shaykh Yāsīn calls for a recitation of the *Fātiḥa*—the opening chapter of the Qur'ān—and the performance ends.

NOTES ON METER AND STRUCTURE

Waḥda Kabīra	d . . . . . t . . . . . t . . .
Maqsūm	d . t . . . t . d . . . t . . .
Bamb (repeated twice)	dt . td . t . dt . td . t .

Legend: d = *dum,* strong stress, low pitch
t = *tak,* light stress, high pitch
· = *iss,* no stress, rest or filler

FIGURE 2 Principal meters used in musical accompaniment to public *ḥaḍra*.

Figure 2 shows the principal meters in the musical accompaniment to public *ḥaḍra*. Counting *d*'s shows that *maqsūm* is the first harmonic of *waḥda* (twice the frequency) and *bamb* is the first harmonic of *maqsūm*. Metrical shifts from *waḥda* to *maqsūm* to *bamb* (and then back to *waḥda*) create a sense of sudden acceleration (or deceleration), without contradicting the original *waḥda* meter; thus *dhikr* rhythm is never disrupted discontinuously.

In Figure 3 we see a typical structure of a *layla* as performed by Shaykh Yāsīn al-Tuhāmī and his school. Figure 3(a) shows the number of the poetic line being sung as a function of time, thus indicating rate and repetition of poetic material. The nonpoetic sections include interpolated segments of *madad*, *taqsīm*, and *mazzīka*. Figure 3(b) shows tempo and meter as a function of time throughout the performance.

FIGURE 3 Typical structure of a *layla* as performed by Shaykh Yasīn al-Ṭuhāmī and his school. (a) Textual and musical sequencing. (b) Tempo and meter.

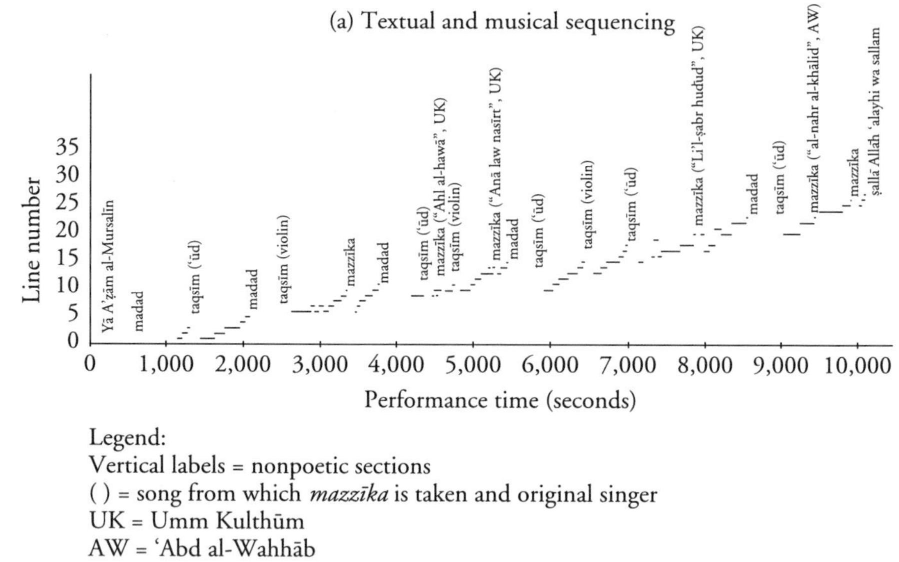

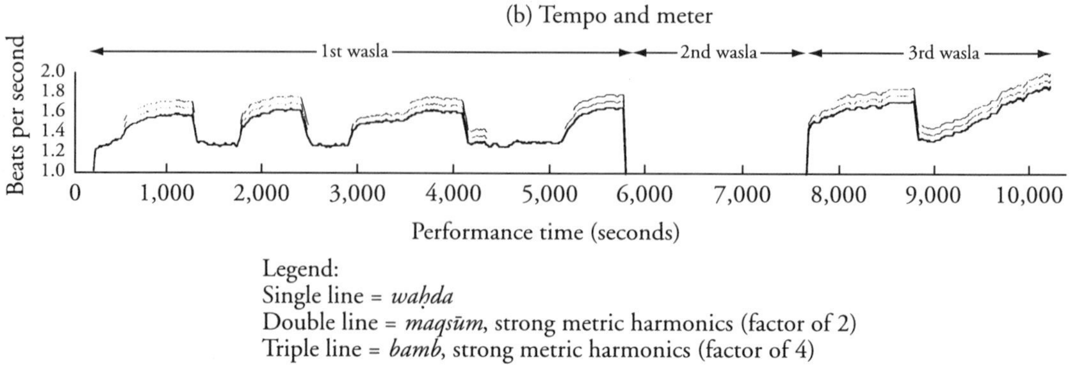

Tempo is defined as four times the strong stress (*dum*) rate of the underlying *waḥda* meter. During the second, nonmetric, *waṣla* no tempo line is plotted. The underlying tempo accelerates continuously within each buildup, while metrical changes provide a sensation of discontinuous tempo doubling.

Although the prevailing strong stress rate may double or quadruple with changes in meter, it is assumed that the fundamental periodicity of the basic *waḥda* meter pulse still maintains perceptual validity, an assumption supported by observations of *dhikr* movements. Faster meters emphasize metrical harmonics at two or four times the basic *waḥda* tempo (analogous to octaves in pitch). Rather than indicate these faster harmonics by doubling or quadrupling the height of the line graph, a quasi-logarithmic notation is used: double or triple lines indicate strong metric harmonics (at factors of two or four, respectively) while the height of the line is still proportional to the basic *waḥda* rate. Thus the two dimensions of tempo (fundamental rate) and meter (harmonic "overtones" of that rate) are decoupled and can be distinguished.

REFERENCES

de Jong, F. 1976–1977. "Cairene Ziyara Days: A Contribution to the Study of Saint Veneration in Islam." *Die Welt des Islams* 17(1–4):26–43.

Hoffman, Valerie. 1995. *Sufism, Mystics, and Saints in Modern Egypt.* Columbia: University of South Carolina Press.

Homerin, Th. Emil. 1994. *From Arab Poet to Muslim Saint: Ibn al-Farid, His Verse, and His Shrine.* Columbia: University of South Carolina Press.

McPherson, J. W. 1941. *The Moulids of Egypt.* Cairo: Nile Mission.

Waugh, Earl H. 1989. *The Munshidin of Egypt: Their World and Their Song.* Columbia: University of South Carolina Press.

The Muslim Call to Prayer

Scott Marcus

Five times a day—before dawn, at high noon, in midafternoon, at sunset, and after sunset—the Muslim faithful are called to perform their prayers. The caller, the *mu'adhdhin* (from which the English term *muezzin* derives), recites the following text, the *adhān*:

Allāhu akbar, Allāhu akbar	God is great, God is great.
Ashhadu an lā ilāha illā llāh	I testify that there is no god but God.
Ashhadu anna Muhammadan rasūl Allāh	I testify that Muhammad is the prophet of God.
Ḥayya 'alā 'l-ṣalāt	Come to prayer.
Ḥayya 'alā 'l-falāḥ	Come to salvation.
al-Ṣalāt khayr min al-nawn	Prayer is better than sleep. [included only in the predawn call]
Allāhu akbar, Allāhu akbar	God is great, God is great.
Lā ilāha illā llāh	There is no god but God.

Every functioning mosque, large or small, has an official *mu'adhdhin* who recites the call to prayer at the appropriate times, five times each day.

On an island in the middle of the Nile river in the heart of Egypt's capital, there is a branch of Helwan University called the College of Music Education that is devoted to teaching music, both Arab and Western. On its small gated campus, the college has a modest one-room mosque. At the appointed times the mosque's mu'adhdhin *stands in front of the doorway and recites the call to prayer. Unamplified, it is heard by students, the faculty, and the staff in the college's small garden and by those in the open-air hallways of the multistoried buildings that line the garden. All but the smallest mosques, however, amplify their* mu'adhdhin*'s call with loudspeakers placed on the mosque's minarets or on the outer walls of the building itself, or hung from neighboring buildings. Thus, within seconds after the college* mu'adhdhin*'s call to prayer has begun, the relative quiet is interrupted by a heavily amplified* adhān *coming from a mosque less than a block away. Unfazed by the competing sounds that render the rest of his call virtually inaudible, the* mu'adhdhin *in the college grounds dutifully completes his task.*

Each caller tends to develop his own unique, often highly complex and artistic, rendition, which he then uses day in and day out.

The times for each prayer are calculated to the minute and are given in daily newspapers and on yearly calendars. Since the times of sunrise and sunset change slightly from day to day, the times for prayers also change accordingly. Calendars in Egypt give distinct times for Cairo and Alexandra, cities that are about 220 kilometers apart.

At a small neighborhood mosque in Cairo, the mu'adhdhin *arrives some ten minutes before the time for the midafternoon call to prayer. He first proceeds to the area of the mosque complex where, prior to prayer, men perform a ritual cleansing that includes washing the hands and face. He then takes off his shoes and enters the mosque itself, going to where a microphone is set on a tall stand. Turning on the sound system, he tests the microphone by breathing into it softly, then looks at his wristwatch. He still has a few more minutes, so he relaxes, in place by the microphone, repeatedly rechecking his watch until it is time for him to begin the call.*

The call to prayer consists of five lines of text that are each performed twice; an additional line ("Prayer is better than sleep"), also performed twice, that is added to the dawn call; and finally a reiteration of the two opening phrases, each now recited just once. Each line is commonly rendered with lengthy unmetered melismas, and a pause of several seconds separates it from the next line. The whole, then, commonly lasts about two to two and a half minutes.

Many Muslim musicians believe that one should not play music during the adhān. *While I was in Cairo researching a folk oboe called the* mizmār, *my teachers would invariably stop my music lessons when we heard the call to prayer. This pause, often treated as a cigarette break, was a time to wait for the call to end. The lesson would resume immediately after the last line of the call.*

In Cairo in the early 1980s, television shows would, at the appropriate times, be interrupted by prerecorded renditions of the call to prayer accompanied by visuals that included the Arabic script for each line of text and a montage of religious images from the holy cities of Mecca and Medina. Arabic-language programs as well as subtitled broadcasts of American programs such as Charlie's Angels *and* CHIPS *were all interrupted. Friends in Cairo told me that this had not always been the case: interpolations of the call to prayer had recently been increased as part of the government's multifaceted response to the Islamic revolution in Iran in 1979 and a subsequent rise of Islamic fundamental sentiments in Egypt.*

The call to prayer is performed by a single male voice without accompaniment. While the text of the call is fixed (an additional line is added in Shi'ite communities), the melodic component is left to the individual caller. Each caller tends to develop his own unique, often highly complex and artistic, rendition, which he then uses day in and day out. At least three normative models have emerged. One version is based on the melodic mode called *maqām rāst* and uses the notes C, D, E-half-flat (E𝄳), F G, and so on; variations of this model prevail in present-day Cairo. Another version is based on *maqām hijāz* (D, E-flat, F-sharp, G, and so on). While renditions in *maqām rāst* or *maqām hijāz* tend to be highly melismatic and virtuosic, a third model, referred to by some as the *adhān sharʿī*, is syllabic and uses only two notes, a whole step apart. The caller simply alternates between these two notes.

Once, while visiting one of Cairo's most famous nāy *makers, I heard the call to prayer come from below. I had become accustomed to artistic, beautiful renditions, but this was the two-note call, rendered by someone with a surprisingly poor voice. The* nāy *maker, perceiving my reaction, offered the explanation that the usual* mu'adhdhin *was not present; he had been called away to his village. The call that day was therefore being given by someone who worked in a neighborhood bakery. "It is a long way from the baker's oven to becoming an artist" (*min al-furn lil-fannān*). Clearly, mosques seek a* mu'adhdhin *with a beautiful, even virtuosic voice; but the* nāy *maker assured me that both fine and poor voices are acceptable before God.*

The Qur'ān Recited

Kristina Nelson Davies

The Oral Nature of the Qur'ān
The Qur'ān and Music
The Recitation Curriculum
Styles of Recitation
The Egyptian *Mujawwad* Tradition
Status of Current Scholarship

The recited Qur'ān is one of the most characteristic sounds of everyday life in the Muslim world. It plays a central role in such expressly religious contexts as collective prayer, the ceremonies accompanying the signing of a marriage contract, funerals, wakes, and memorial services. On many such occasions, the sound is projected by a loudspeaker into the surrounding streets (figure 1). Most radio and television stations open and close their daily broadcasts with recitations from the Qur'ān, and many feature, as part of their regular programming, memorial services and highlights of recitations from their archives. A recitation may also be heard at the start of almost any enterprise for which God's blessing is sought, be it the opening of a shop or an office, a political summit conference, an academic conference, or even a concert of secular music. The sound of the recited Qur'ān may also be heard in a number of informal contexts, as on a bus, in a taxi, in a market, or at a house where friends have gathered to listen to recordings of their favorite reciters. Muslims and non-Muslims alike have testified to the power of this pervasive sound, recounting personal experiences of conversion, repentance, swooning, and ecstasy on hearing it.

FIGURE 1 Shaykh Aḥmad al-Ruzayqī recites the Qur'ān. Photo by Kristina Nelson Davies, Cairo, 1978.

THE ORAL NATURE OF THE QUR'ĀN

For Muslims, the explanation of this power lies in the divine source and significance of the sound. The Qur'ān, the generating source of and ultimate authority within Islam, revealed in Arabic to the Arabs over a twenty-year period in the early decades of the sixth century C.E., is the word of God as it was "laid upon the heart" of the Prophet Muhammad, who subsequently rehearsed it with the angel Gabriel. As such, it represents in some sense the sound of a divine utterance, the sound of God. The Prophet transmitted the revelation to his followers orally, and it was not written down until after his death, at which point the oral text became the primary source for all subsequent written texts. When the written text of the Qur'ān was first disseminated by the caliph 'Uthmān, he sent reciters to accompany it and to teach the unique characteristic sounds of the oral Qur'ān.

Learning correct recitation continues to be the basis of Qur'ānic studies. The prevailing and sanctioned method of instruction is oral and follows the model established by the Prophet when he rehearsed the text with Gabriel: the teacher recites, the student imitates, the teacher corrects. Thus, although the rules for correct recitation

Muslims cite the aesthetic perfection of the Qur'ān as proof of its divine source.

(*tajwīd*) have been set down in many manuals, these rules function primarily as a point of reference for oral instruction. Since the 1960s, when the first recording of the Qur'ān was produced in Egypt for instructional purposes, recordings have proliferated, taking over the role of human teachers among minority Muslim communities where teachers are few. The basic method of instruction still prevails: in a relatively recent multimedia CD-ROM in Urdu, Turkish, Indonesian, Malay, Chinese, and Arabic that includes three English translations of the text and recitations by two Egyptians, as well as a phonetic pronunciation guide, the students are instructed to record, listen, and compare their pronunciation with the reciter's.

THE QUR'ĀN AND MUSIC

Muslims cite the aesthetic perfection of the Qur'ān as proof of its divine source. The exaltation of its language and sound as inimitable has thus introduced aesthetic considerations into the expectations of Muslims listening to it. The contribution of a beautiful voice to an effective recitation has been recognized and documented in Islamic sources since the time of the Prophet Muhammad. All children are encouraged to learn correct recitation as a religious duty, but in Egypt, where the tradition of artistic recitiation has been cultivated most, many professionals recall that they began reciting in public with the support of teachers who singled them out for the beauty of their voices. Scholarly religious consensus recognizes that a reciter's musical artistry is critical in increasing the impact of the Qur'ān because it engages the listeners more fully in the experience. In Egypt, the committee that auditions new reciters for radio and television broadcasts and for the archives may turn down an applicant for aesthetic reasons even though his recitation is correct.

Despite this acknowledgment of aesthetics, debate has continued throughout Islamic history over the propriety of applying musical skills to the recitation of the Qur'ān. The literature on *samā*ʿ 'listening', specifically to music, considers the power of music to sway the emotions a danger as well as an advantage, reflecting a well-established tradition of suspicion toward music because of its secular and even profane associations. Practically speaking, the issue has been resolved by the acceptance by many Muslims of music as an essentially neutral and value-free art. However, while scholarly consensus admits that music may enhance recitation spiritually, melodic practice is not included in the disciplines surrounding Qur'ānic recitation. Instead, this is left to the individual reciter's initiative.

THE RECITATION CURRICULUM

In the context of a body of religious or Qur'ānic studies ranging from grammar and exegesis to biography and literary criticism, a number of disciplines and scholarly debates have served both to provide norms for and to protect the meaning of the Qur'ān as expressed through recitation. The discipline of *qirā'āt* presents and explains the seven (in some schools, ten or fourteen) authoritative variant "readings" representing the traditions of prominent individual transmitters up to the tenth century and now associated with the four different schools of Islamic law and thus, to the degree that these coincide, with different parts of the Muslim world. The disciplines of *adab al-Qur'ān, adab al-tilāwa,* and *adab al-qāri' wa'-mustamī'* (etiquette regarding, respectively, the Qur'ān, recitation, and listener and reciter) explicate recommended behavior and attitudes for reciters and listeners, including the appropriateness of a teacher's or reciter's earning income from the Qur'ān, the merits and risks of different styles of recitation, and the desired effect of the ideal recitation on listeners. The rules of *tajwīd*, codified in the tenth century, seek to preserve the divine sound of the revelation and guard it from distortion. These rules govern the correct pronunciation, timbre, and duration of individual phonemes (hence, rhythm) and link these to meaning by indicating the most appropriate places to break the sound in order to avoid distorting or confusing the meaning of the text. In addition, with regard to duration, tempo, and pauses the rules of *tajwīd* present options that the individual reciter can manipulate for aesthetic effect.

STYLES OF RECITATION

Murattal

The sound and rhythms of *tajwīd* signal the divine origin and nature of the text. A heightened performance mode, distinguished from the pitch patterns of ordinary speech or declamation, marks recitation as an act of worship or devotion. This performance mode encompasses two styles distinguished from each other not only by sound but also by the intent of the reciter. *Murattal* (also called *tartīl* and *tajwīd)* is the unembellished, subdued style heard in the context of prayers, pedagogic classes, and private devotions. It is also a regular part of radio (though not television) programming, and prominent reciters in Egypt have recorded commercially in the *murattal* style. Although emotional intensity and varied personal styles figure in *murattal*, its most prominent feature is its focus on presenting the text simply and clearly. The basic structural unit is the verse, which is performed in a single breath, followed by a pause that is only long enough for the reciter to draw breath. The voice and posture of the reciter are relaxed; the volume is no higher than that of ordinary conversation. Melodic movement is contiguous and kept to a range of a fourth or fifth, although the register may be extended by gradual stepwise motion. The tempo is usually quick. Maximum clarity is ensured by giving each syllable only one pitch or, at most, two pitches for longer syllables; vocal ornamentation is rare. The accessibility of this style to the nonprofessional and its particular suitability for transmitting the text, due to its clarity, make it the standard sound of Qur'ānic recitation in contexts of learning and prayer.

It is the duty of every Muslim to learn correct recitation at least in this standard form, and men, women, and children take advantage of special classes held at mosques and workplaces to learn not only the rules of *tajwīd* but also the variant readings of the text. In addition, memorization and recitation of selected verses are included in the curriculum of government schools in many parts of the Muslim world. Children may also be encouraged to learn and recite the Qur'ān through national and regional competitions.

Murattal is also the public style of women reciters who, with the exception of professionals in Southeast Asia, recite for groups of women only. It is not generally considered suitable for a woman's voice to transmit the Qur'ān to male listeners, the argument being that a woman's voice will distract them from the text. The fact that women reciters use the self-effacing *murattal* style even among themselves reveals the extent to which a woman's voice is considered *'awra,* that is, classed with the parts of the body that should be covered during prayer. In Egypt in the early days of the broadcasting industry, women reciters were heard on radio, and in some parts of Southeast Asia today women reciters perform publicly for mixed audiences, record commercially, and enjoy a public reputation. However, in most of the Muslim world the intentionally "beautiful" or *mujawwad* recitation is reserved for men.

Mujawwad

The *mujawwad* style (also called *tilāwa* and, confusingly, *tartīl* and *tajwīd*) is a more elaborately melodic and intense performance style, identified in modern times with Egypt and widely disseminated throughout the Muslim world by Egyptian reciters and the media. Although both the *mujawwad* style and the *murattal* style should be executed according to the rules of *tajwīd*, with attention to the meaning of the text and with humble and sincere intent (that is, not for personal or commercial gain or glory), a *mujawwad* reciter is expected to engage listeners emotionally in the significance of the text, and the artistry of the individual reciter is, consequently, a prominent feature of this style. Listeners are not necessarily musically literate or able to follow and appreciate the transpositions and modulations of a skilled musician, but they expect the emotional intensity that characterizes an aesthetically satisfying musical perfomance. For this, the reciter as artist, rather than the text, bears responsibility. A performance may last several hours, during which the reciter, like a singer, manipulates text, melodic modulation and transposition, shifts in register, and the emotional connotations of the *maqām*—the melodic mode—to create tension, build suspense, beguile, and enchant his listeners. The slower tempo and longer syllabic durations of this style support melismatic cadences and vocal ornamentation, and the long pauses function both to build and to release tension (figure 2). A *mujawwad* reciter faces the challenge that, unlike a singer, he must use his skills to focus his listeners on the text, not on his own artistry.

FIGURE 2 Shaykh Muḥammad Sallāmā reciting the Qur'ān at a public event. Photo by Kristina Nelson Davies, Cairo, 1978.

While accepting that *mujawwad* recitation has something in common with Arab music and indeed requires musical elements to realize its ideal objective of eliciting an emotional as well as an intellectual and spiritual response from the listener, religious scholarship and public opinion have always been at pains to distinguish it from music. The nature of the text excludes *mujawwad* recitation from the category of "Islamic music" (religious texts set to music) and, of course, from secular music (nonreligious songs and instrumental and dance music). Nor is this classification simply a question of bowing to the popularity of the melodic performance. The melodic recitation of the Qur'ān is subject to unique constraints: rhythm is divinely given, is codified in the rules of *tajwīd*, and must not be changed; melodies must be improvised, inspired by the moment. Setting a text to music is proscribed because it is believed to compromise the text as a divine phenomenon outside the sphere of human endeavor.

This concern for guarding the unique nature of the text carries over into training, practice, and performance. The reciter learns the text and then learns the melodic principles of Arab music composition, applying the one to the other in the context of performance. To ensure melodic spontaneity, reciters warm up the voice with songs and hymns, practice melodic skills with other texts, and use *murattal* to review the text. A performance is a working session: the reciter may repeat a phrase of text in order to polish it musically. In practice, the audience may call for repetitions of the same text in a different register or melodic mode, or for the repetition of an entire section, and reciters on their own initiative or on request may "quote" melodic phrases of other reciters that have entered public memory. Although the availability of recorded performances makes it easier to associate a text with a specific melody, and many reciters do fall into "set texts," the mark of the best reciter continues to be his infinitely creative musicality.

THE EGYPTIAN *MUJAWWAD* TRADITION

Although the recitation of the Qur'ān is significant whoever the reciter may be, the Egyptian *mujawwad* tradition has particular prestige and exerts particular influence.

Egyptian reciters are in demand as teachers, performers, and judges of public recitation competitions in Muslim communities all over the world. Cairo is a host city for reciters who come to learn their art from Egyptian masters. The market for Egyptian recordings is global.

A number of factors contribute to the status of Egyptian reciters. First, most Egyptian reciters train at al-Azhar University in Cairo or at one of its affiliated institutes. Al-Azhar, which was founded more than a thousand years ago, attracts students and scholars from all over the world who seek the authority and prestige of its rigorous and long-established tradition of religious scholarship. Second, Egypt's reputation as a center of musical creativity also extends beyond its borders, thanks to its film, broadcasting, and recording industries. Many Egyptian musicians of the first half of the twentieth century were also reciters, creating a high standard of musicality and aesthetic expectations on the part of the audience. Third, the Egyptian broadcasting and recording industries were quick to exploit the popularity of recitation. Opposition to the broadcasting of recitation was first overcome in Egypt; the first official recordings of recitation were issued in Egypt; and two Egyptians were the first to record and market recitations—Shaykh Muṣṭafā Ismā'īl on phonograph records and Shaykh'Abd al-Bāsiṭ 'Abd al-Samad on cassette tapes. Egyptian reciters continue to expand their audience through broadcasts, cassette tapes, and, increasingly, CDs.

The high demand, in Egypt and elsewhere, for Egyptian reciters encouraged a development unique to that country until the 1980s: the emergence of recitation as a profession. (The Mevlevi Sufis of Turkey, despite their long-established elite tradition of melodic recitiation, do not constitute a profession, because Sufi reciters are not independent of the ritual context.) Increasingly, reciters in other parts of the Muslim world, such as Syria, Saudi Arabia, Tunisia, the Sudan, Pakistan, and Malaysia, establish a professional reputation by recording; but commercial production and distribution are still minimal except in Pakistan, whose recording industry serves Muslim communities in Europe and the United States.

Although the authority and prestige of the Egyptian style of melodic recitation remain undisputed, the largest audience is commanded by the recordings of the great reciters of the period from approximately 1930 to the mid-1980s, such as Shaykh Muḥammad Rif'at, Shaykh Muḥammad Siddīq al-Minshāwī, Shaykh Muṣṭafā Ismā'īl, and Shaykh 'Abd al-Bāsit 'Abd al-Samad. Many listeners lament the passing of what now seems a golden age of Qur'ānic recitation and the lack of sophisticated melodic skills, and especially of improvisation, among the current generation of reciters and musicians. Following the establishment in Egypt in the 1950s of a new style of classical Arab music that turned its back on improvisation, soloists, and the oral transmission of the art in favor of set melodies, choruses, sheet music, and training at Cairo's Higher Institute of Arab Music, musicians of the older generation and aficionados of old-style Egyptian music (*al-mūsīqā al-qadīma*) increasingly looked to reciters as guardians of the authentic musical patrimony [see ARAB MUSIC IN THE TWENTIETH CENTURY]. Since the 1970s, reciters have been increasingly affected by a shift to formal training and a corresponding loss of improvisational skills. Audiences' expectations have also changed: reciters are no longer feted as superstars commanding colossal fees, made the focus of fans and fan clubs, or featured along with singers and film stars in popular magazines and on talk shows; rather, reciters are presented as pious men who put their talent to the service of the Qur'ān. At the same time, melodic recitation, which has always been resisted in more conservative Muslim societies, where it is said to sacrifice the text to the reciter's art and personality, has suffered as this notion has gained currency in Egypt with the growth of religiously based social and political conservatism. Around 1995, for the first time, the monopoly of the Egyptian sound of reciting on the street and in taxis was challenged by Saudi reciters. The Saudi style shares with the Egyptian *murattal* style a quick tempo and a narrow range of three to five pitches

Reciters are no longer feted as superstars commanding colossal fees but rather are presented as pious men who put their talent to the service of the Qur'ān.

but features melisma on the longer durations, or, in the case of one reciter, on the ending syllables. At least one Egyptian reciter, Mohammad Gibril, integrated this style into his own personal style and gained a large popular following.

STATUS OF CURRENT SCHOLARSHIP

Scholarly treatment of recitation has focused on the Qur'ān without regard for the human context. In both Muslim and non-Muslim scholarship, ethnomusicological, sociological, and anthropological approaches to Qur'ānic recitation are notably lacking. Although some Muslim scholarship may describe actual practice, it generally limits itself to listing heretical and unacceptable practices. For most Muslims, the approach inherent in the social sciences has secular connotations inappropriate to the study of the divine. A notable exception is the work of Labīb al-Sa'īd (1967 and 1976), which both acknowledges and contextualizes the orality of the Qur'ān in culture of the Muslim community. Only in the past thirty years have scholars in religion, ethnomusicology, anthropology, and literary and linguistic theory (Graham, Denny, Gade, al-Faruqi, Touma, Hodgson, Sells, and Rasmussen) begun to apply a wider range of disciplines to the study of the Qur'ān and acknowledge the centrality of oral tradition to the Muslim experience in general.

Building on a study by the present author (Nelson 1985), which focuses on the meaning of Qur'ānic recitation in Egyptian society as a cultural performance, the subject would benefit from more research on recitation in the different kinds of communities that make up the Muslim world. For example, the work of Anne Rasmussen and Anna Gade can be counted as a significant contribution to the field: they compare contexts, expectations, and meaning; explore different styles in relation to local music; and consider aesthetic traditions, the influence of the Egyptian model on local traditions of learning and performance, and the strategies by which local communities deal with the authority of the linguistic, aesthetic, improvisational, affective, and musical systems of imported Egyptian styles in the Indonesian context.

A proliferation of recordings bringing the sound of the Qur'ān to non-Arab Muslims also gives non-Muslims easier access to the tradition, and scholars and music producers in Europe and the United States are responding with increased interest in the aesthetic dimensions of Qur'ānic recitation.

REFERENCES

Denny, Frederick. 1980. "The Adab of Qur'an Recitation: Text and Context." In *International Congress for the Study of the Qur'an*, ed. Anthony Johns, 143–160. Canberra: Australian National University

———. 1985. "The Great Indonesian Qur'an Chanting Tournament." *William and Mary: Alumni Gazette Magazine* 54:33–37. (Also published 1986. *The World and I* 6:216–223.)

———. 1988. "Qur'an Recitation Training in Indonesia: A Survey of Contexts and Handbooks." In *Approaches to the History of Interpretation of the Qur'an*, ed. Andrew Rippin, 288–306. Oxford: Clarendon.

———. 1989. "Qur'an Recitation: A Tradition of Oral Performance and Transmission." *Oral Tradition* 4(1–2):5–26.

Eickelman, Dale F. 1978. "The Art of Memory: Islamic Education and Its Social Reproduction." *Comparative Studies in Society and History* 20(4):485–516.

al-Fārūqī, Lois Ibsen/Lamyā'. 1978. "Tartīl al-Qur'ān al-karīm." In *Islamic Perspectives: Studies in Honor of Sayyid Abūl A'lā Mawdūdī*, ed. Khurshid Ahmad and Zafar Ishaq Ansari, 105–119. Leicester, U.K.: Islamic Foundation.

Graham, William A. 1985. "The Qur'an as Spoken Word: An Islamic Contribution to the Understanding of Scripture." In *Approaches to Islam in Religious Studies*, ed. Richard C. Martin, 23–40. Tucson: University of Arizona Press.

Hodgson, M. G. S. 1974. *The Venture of Islam*. Vol. 1. Chicago: University of Chicago Press.

Nelson, Kristina. 1985. *The Art of Reciting the Qur'an*. Austin: University of Texas Press.

al-Qādī, Shukrī. 1999. *'Abāqirat al-tilāwa fī 'l-qarn al 'ishrīn* (Twentieth-Century Genius of Qur'anic Recitation). Cairo: Dār al-Kātib al-'Arabī.

Quershi, Regula. 1969. "Tarannum: The Chanting of Urdu Poetry." *Ethomusicology* 13(3):425–468.

———. 1995. *Sufi Music of India and Pakistan*. Chicago: University of Chicago Press.

Rasmussen, Anne K. 2000. "The Qur'an in Indonesian Daily Life: The Public Project of Musical Oratory." *Ethnomusicology* 45.

al-Sa'īd, Labīb. 1967. *al-Jam' al-ṣawtī al-awwal li 'l-Qur'ān al-karīm aw al-muṣḥaf al-murattal*. Cairo: Dār al-Kātib al-'Arabī.

———. 1970. *al-Taghannī-bi 'l-Qur'ān*. Cairo: al-Maktabah al-Taqāfiyyah.

———. 1976. *al-Maqāri' wa l-qurrā'*. Cairo: Maṭba'at al-Sa'ādah.

Sells, Michael. 1991. "Sound, Spirit, and Gender in *Sûrat al-quadr*." *Journal of the American Oriental Society* 111(2):239–259.

———, trans. and intro. 1999. *Approaching the Qur'an: The Early Revelations*. Ashland, Ore.: White Cloud.

Shalihah, Khadijatus. 1983. *Perkembangan seni baca al-Qur'an dan wiraat tujuj di Indonesia* (The Development of the Art of Reading the Qur'an and the Seven Readings in Indonesia). Jakarta: Pustaka Alhusna.

Touma, Habib Hassan. 1975a. "Die Koranrezitation: Eine Form der religiösen Musik der Araber." *Bessler-Archiv*, Neue Folge, 23:87–133.

———. 1975b. *Die Musik der Araber*. Wilhelmshaven: Heinrichshofen's Verlag.

———. 1976. "Relations between Aesthetics and Improvisation in Arab Music." *World of Music* 18(2):33–36.

Islamic Hymnody in Egypt: *Al-Inshād al-Dīnī*

Michael Frishkopf

Characteristics of *al-Inshād al-Dīnī*
Characteristics of the *Munshid*
Genres and Contexts of *al-Inshād* Outside the Sufi Sphere
***Al-Inshād* in Sufi Contexts**

Al-inshād al-dīnī (often simply *inshād*) is the melodic vocal performance of Arabic poetry as an Islamic practice. The vocalist, called a *munshid* (plural, *munshidīn*), is usually male; he is addressed as *shaykh* to indicate his elevated religious status. By text or context, *al-inshād* is regarded as a form of worship, though it lies outside the core of Islamic ritual. But even when intended as a religious act, *al-inshād* may produce a wide range of emotional experiences, from mystical rapture to aesthetic enjoyment.

Al-inshād thus lies on the border between music and Islam, art and spirituality. Its materials, performance, and emotional impact draw on both. Historically, *al-inshād* is closely associated with the *ṭarab* tradition—musical performance that induces ecstasy—for which it formerly served as an important training ground. On one side, *inshād* borders secular singing (*ghinā'*) in the form of *aghānī dīniyya*, songs combining the urban Arab musical tradition with religious texts but lacking a serious religious context or sincere religious intention. On the other, with regard to performance *inshād* is close to several vocal forms central to Islamic practice, such as the call to prayer (*adhān*) and Qur'ānic recitation (*tajwīd*), which may be melodically elaborate. Yet these are not *inshād*.

The prevailing impression among scholars and laypeople alike is that Islam forbids music in religious ritual and frowns on music in any context; the use of singing in Sufi (mystic) orders is often cited as a rare exception. But in fact melodious use of the voice is seldom absent, even in mainstream Islam.

The prevalence of the melodic voice in Islam stems from the central position of recitation in Islamic practice. Muslims developed melodic versions of recitations in order to beautify and extol them, to draw the listener's attention, to facilitate retention, to clarify meaning, and to develop appropriate emotional responses. In Egypt one hears *tajwīd*, *adhān*, and *ibtihālāt* (supplications to Allah) in ornate melodic style every day.

These recitations are not considered *mūsīqa*, a term that connotes the sounds of instruments, associated with taboo dancing and drinking. *Mūsīqa* is frowned on in religious contexts. Even the term *ghinā'* 'singing' is too laden with secular connotations to be applied to true religious performance. Therefore, intoned recitation of poetry as a religious act is termed *inshād dīnī*; when the recited text is not poetry, special terms

Al-inshād lies on the border between music and Islam, art and spirituality.

such as *tajwīd* or *adhān* are used. Melodically these genres share many features. Differences are determined more by text and context than by musical style.

CHARACTERISTICS OF *AL-INSHĀD AL-DĪNĪ*

Al-inshād and Arab music share many elements: monophony and heterophony; systems of *maqāmāt* and *īqā'āt*; poetic and musical forms; the centrality of poetry and the solo voice; expressive-improvisatory performance of evocative texts; elaborate ornament and melisma; nonmetric improvisation; and ecstatic feedback from the listener. But *inshād* also presents some distinctive features, resulting from three formative factors: (1) the conservative nature of the religious domain, which has preserved features prevalent in Arab music before the 1930s; (2) the tendency of practitioners to parry accusations of heresy by establishing terms and practices distinct from secular music; (3) the functional requirements placed on *inshād* by its special roles and contexts.

The religious import of *inshād* is deeply rooted within particular performance contexts, which condition and socialize meaning while establishing the performer's authority and sincerity and enabling the intensification of emotion through feedback. Although *inshād* has been disseminated and popularized by the media, including phonodisks (from the early 1900s), radio (from the 1920s), television (early 1960s), and cassettes (1970s), these media favored more context-independent commercial entertainment; unlike Arab music, live *inshād* has continued to thrive. Certain *inshād* genres are performed in conjunction with daily and weekly rituals. *Inshād* is performed for annual holidays—especially the Prophet Muhammad's birthday, the holy month of Ramadan, and saints' festivals—and for occasions in the life-cycle, such as weddings, circumcisions, and memorials.

The *munshid* intends to generate powerful emotion. Ideally, performance intensifies his own true feelings; using musical, textual, and expressive techniques, he tries to evoke similar feelings in the listener. While such emotion is normatively religious, in practice and discourse it is ambiguous, interpreted spiritually as *wajd* 'spiritual ecstasy' or aesthetically as *ṭarab* 'musical ecstasy'.

Listeners play an active role in live *inshād*, responding vocally and with gestures after melodic cadences. Performers make use of such feedback to guide their decisions, and thereby optimize the emotional power of the performance. Such optimization requires live performance as well as improvisatory flexibility in the genre. Before 1930, this "cybernetic" process was essential to most Arab music, whereas today it is preserved mainly in *inshād*.

Inshād is fundamentally vocal music, comprising mainly solo and responsorial formats; choral *inshād* exists in Sufi orders. The use of instruments is discouraged by Islamic strictures and is considered by some to be heretical. Pronunciation is precise, facilitating textual communication. The voice is powerful, penetrating, often nasal, and highly expressive; its timbres and long breath-phrases resemble Qur'ānic recitation. Within a wide range, the tenor tessitura is emphasized. Melody features elaborate melisma and subtle ornamentation. The solo *munshid* is ultimately in control of all musical dimensions; traditionally there is no other composer, arranger, or conductor. Much of this control is exercised during the performance, enabling the *munshid* to express inner feeling spontaneously and adapt to context. However, group *inshād* is precomposed. All melody is monophonic or heterophonic in texture.

Most *inshād* uses classical Arabic—the language of the Qur'ān—cast in classical forms such as *qaṣīda* (plural, *qaṣā'id*) and *muwashshaḥ* (plural, *muwashshaḥāt*), which are two genres of metered, rhymed poetry. There are also colloquial styles of *inshād* (especially in the Delta region), using popular forms such as *mawwāl* and *zajal*, but they are criticized by elites as an ignorant degradation. Usually a solo *munshid* selects his own poetry.

Mainstream themes include supplications to Allah (*ibtihālāt*), praise and love of Allah, requests to the Prophet Muhammad for intercession, praise and love of the Prophet (*madīḥ*), religious exhortations, and religious stories (*qiṣaṣ diniyya*), especially stories recounting prophetic miracles. Sufi *inshād* also includes expressions of mystical experiences, intense longing for Allah and the Prophet, and guidance for the Sufi path, often using esoteric or heterodox symbols.

CHARACTERISTICS OF THE *MUNSHID*

Most *munshidīn* are men, because of Islamic conservatism and the public nature of the work. A *munshid* ordinarily receives some formal religious education that provides a general knowledge of Islam and a strong foundation in Arabic language and literature. He memorizes the Qur'ān and learns to recite it. However, there is no formal instruction in *inshād*. The *munshid* memorizes his poetic repertoire from books or aurally. He learns the art of musical performance by listening, imitating, and participating; no musical notation is used. The solo *munshid* is a musical creator; using practical knowledge of the *maqāmāt* and poetics, he sets poetry extemporaneously. He must have an excellent memory, clear diction, a deep feeling for poetry, and the ability to express this feeling vocally.

The *munshid* is distinguished from other singers by his religious identity, which stamps his performance with religious authenticity, even when the text is not overtly religious or when he benefits financially from performance. This identity is supported by his religious education and apparel and certified by the title *shaykh*, attributes that link him to other religious authorities. By excelling in *inshād* and restricting his performance to religious genres, he attains and protects his status as *shaykh*; if he performs secular music or presents himself as *muṭrib*—a singer of urban Arab music—he jeopardizes it.

But there is some ambiguity in this identity. Nearly all *munshidīn* (except within Sufi orders) are professionals, concerned with profit and recognition; some become celebrities. Most consider themselves artists and are well acquainted with the Arab musical tradition; some have performed both religious and secular music, and some have crossed over entirely to the latter.

GENRES AND CONTEXTS OF *AL-INSHĀD* OUTSIDE THE SUFI SPHERE

For the elite religious and media establishments, *al-inshād* comprises two closely related genres sharing performers and themes: *ibtihālāt* and *tawāshīḥ*. By contrast, *qiṣaṣ diniyya* is a "folk" genre.

Ibtihālāt

TRACK 10 *Ibtihālāt* 'supplications' request blessings, mercy, and salvation from Allah, while glorifying him and praising his Prophet. The central poetic genre is the *qaṣīda*, often mixed with prose prayers. The *munshid* is usually a professional, performing *adhān* and often reciting the Qur'ān as well.

Temporally and stylistically, *ibtihālāt* lie close to *adhān* and Qur'ānic recitation (*tajwīd*). Daily before dawn in the larger mosques, following *tajwīd*, a *munshid* performs *ibtihālāt*, closing with the *adhān*. (One such performance is broadcast daily on government radio.) All three entail a vocal soloist, who uses ornamented, unmeasured, improvisatory melody to set a text melismatically; long breath-phrases are separated by silences. In both *tajwīd* and *ibtihālāt*, the performer often repeats text for emphasis, clarification, or emotional effect.

But while Qur'ānic recitation is a resounding of Revelation to mankind, *ibtihālāt* are the reverse: melodic prayer from *munshid* to Allah, and (vicariously) from the listener as well. Whereas Qur'ānic recitation is constrained by rigid rules governing syllable lengths and stopping points, *ibtihālāt* are relatively free, enabling more melisma, more ornamentation, and more personal expressiveness.

Tawāshīḥ dīniyya

Tawāshīḥ dīniyya (also *tawāshīḥ*) is performed by a solo *munshid* together with a small chorus (biṭaāana), standing in a semicircle around him. Alternating precomposed choral segments with improvisatory solo segments, the group performs *qaṣā'id* treating a variety of Islamic themes, especially *madīḥ* and *ibtihālāt*. Other themes are occasional, such as the biographical narratives performed for the Prophet's birthday. *Tawāshīḥ* used to be the prevailing genre of *al-inshād al-dīnī*, a staple for all occasions. Although it is rarely performed today, recordings are broadcast, especially during Islamic holidays.

The heterophonic chorus uses precomposed melodies to perform a line or two, without repetition or pause. Choral melodies are pulsed, but the meter is weak because long melodic phrases transcend metrical units. The soloist then takes up the same text, exploring it in the unmeasured style of *ibtihālāt*, often using a higher tessitura and more melisma. This order may also be reversed, with the soloist leading.

In the excerpt notated in figure 1, the chorus introduces a line of poetry in praise of the Prophet, *Anta al-shāfi'u lanā bī yawmi mi'ādi* 'You are our intercessor on Judgment Day', using *maqām ḥijāz* transposed to G, in a pulsed, quasi-metrical, slightly heterophonic style. Following a brief pause, Shaykh Ṭaha al-Fashnī reviews this textual material in an unmeasured solo. After beginning simply in a narrow range (between the 10- and 15-second marks), he pauses, and then he restates the entire poetic line using an elaborate wide-ranging melody—mainly on the syllable *nā*—while modulating to *bayyātī* on G. This example is transcribed using a modified staff notation, in which the duration of a pitch is approximately proportional to the horizontal length of its extended "notehead"; the scale is given in seconds. (Accidentals are indicated just *below* the notehead and affect only one note.) Below this notation, the choral section is approximately represented in ordinary notation, although meter is ambiguous. True pitch is roughly ten semitones below notated pitch.

Outstanding *munshidīn* of the twentieth century

In the early twentieth century, outstanding specialists in *ibtihālāt*, *qaṣā'id dīniyya*, and *tawāshīḥ dīniyya* included Sayyid Mūsā, Ismā'īl Sukkar (d. 1940), Abū al-'Ila Muḥammad (1878–1927), 'Alī Maḥmūd (1881–1944?), Darwīsh al-Ḥarīrī (1881–1957), Muḥriz Sulaymān, and Ibrāhīm al-Farrān (d. 1940s). Figures in the mid-twentieth century included Ṭaha al-Fashnī (1900–1971), 'Abd al-Samī' Bayyūmī (d. 1970s), Muḥammad al-Fayyūmī (1906–1976), Sayyid al-Naqshabandī (1921–1976), Naṣr al-Dīn Ṭūbār (b. 1921), Muḥammad al-Tūkhī (b. 1925), Kāmil Yūsuf al-Bahtīmī (1920–1969), Muḥammad 'Umrān (1944–1994), and Ibrāhīm al-Iskandarānī. Two contemprary figures are Sa'īd Ḥāfiẓ and Muḥammad al-Hilbāwī. Connoisseurs frequently identify Shaykh Ṭaha al-Fashnī as the greatest of all, although Sayyid al-Naqshabandī became more widely popular through his regular radio appearances during Ramadan. Stars of urban Arab *ṭarab* music, such as Salāma Hijāzī (1852–1917), Sayyid Darwīsh (1892–1923), Zakariyā Aḥmad (1896–1961), Umm Kulthūm (1904?–1975), and Muḥammad 'Abd al-Wahhāb (1910?–1991), along with most other singers and composers born in the nineteenth and early twentieth centuries,

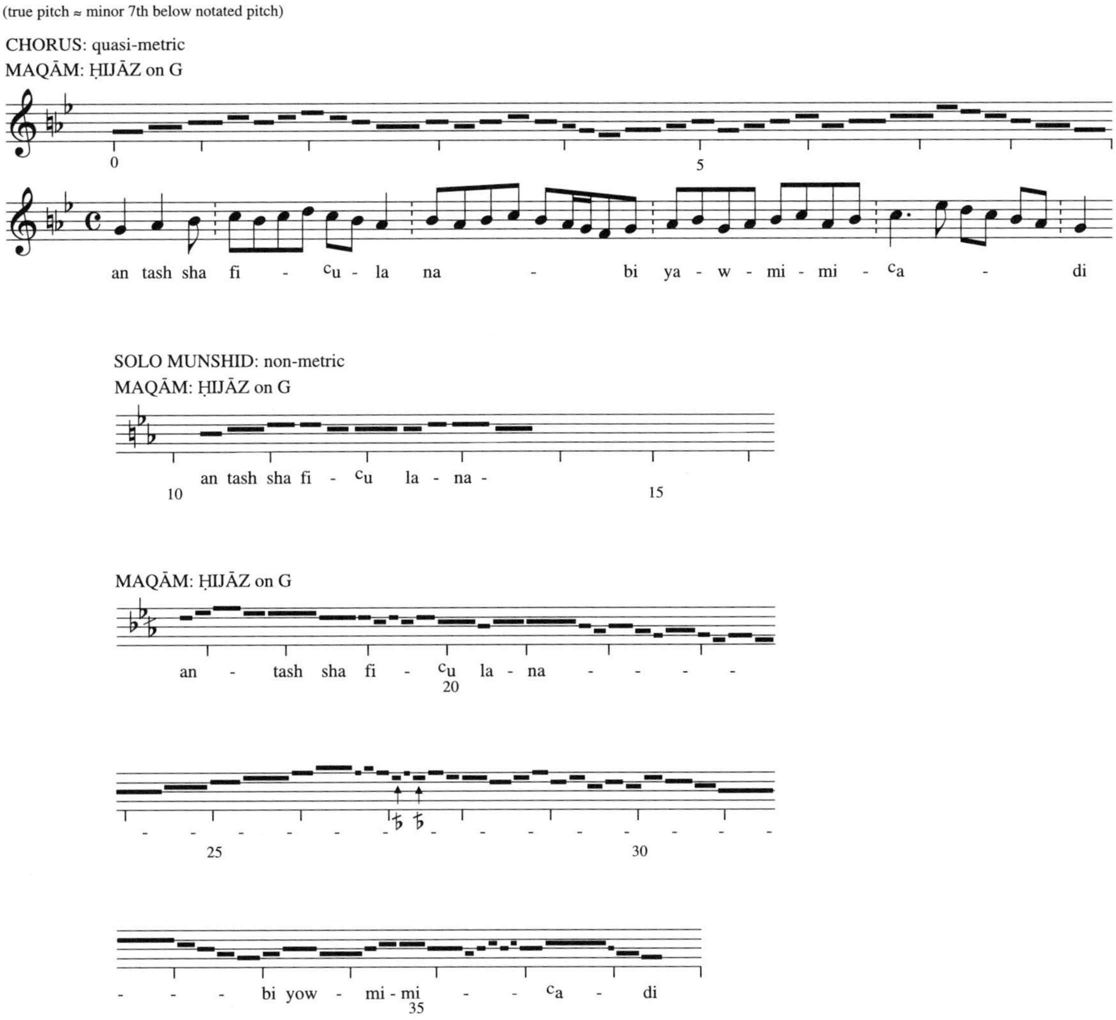
(true pitch ≈ minor 7th below notated pitch)
CHORUS: quasi-metric
MAQĀM: ḤIJĀZ on G
0
5
an tash sha fi - ᶜu - la na - bi ya - w - mi - mi - ᶜa - di
SOLO MUNSHID: non-metric
MAQĀM: ḤIJĀZ on G
an tash sha fi - ᶜu la - na -
10
15
MAQĀM: ḤIJĀZ on G
an - tash sha fi - ᶜu la - na - - - - -
20
25
30
- - - bi yow - mi - mi - - ᶜa - di
35

FIGURE 1 Typical example of *tawāshīḥ dīniyya*, excerpted from a performance by Shaykh Ṭaha al-Fashnī (solo *munshid*) and his chorus (*biṭāna*), for the Prophet Muhammad's birthday celebration (*mawlid al-nabī*). From Sono Cairo 76028/601 *Ṭaha al-Fashnī: Ibtihālāt* and *Tawashīḥ diniyya*, side 1. Transcription by Michael Frishkopf.

acquired their basic vocal and musical training as *munshidīn*, before turning to non-religious forms of Arab music.

Qiṣaṣ dīniyya

Qiṣaṣ dīniyya are religious stories performed by a *munshid*, accompanied by a small ensemble of urban and rural instruments combining the sounds of *ṭarab* and folk music. Each story, related in contrasting literary and musical styles, lasts one or two hours; two stories—separated by an intermission—constitute an evening's entertainment.

In contrast to *ibtihālāt* and *tawāshīḥ*, *qiṣaṣ* draw heavily on folk traditions and *ṭarab* songs. Live performances attract mostly farmers and rural immigrants in cities; the media present *qiṣaṣ* on folklore programs, and the religious establishment looks down on them. *Munshidīn* learn performance through participation, but since texts are usually memorized from books, there is little textual variation between performances of the same story.

Although the atmosphere of the performance is lighter than for other genres of *al-inshād*, *qiṣaṣ* have narrative and exhortative features reminiscent of the Friday sermon. In appearance, the male *munshid* closely resembles a mosque preacher. Yet, of all *al-inshād* genres, only *qiṣaṣ* features a small number of female vocalists. This exception may result from the proximity of *qiṣaṣ* to folk entertainment and from the fact that they are performed outside the mosque; also, propriety is often ensured by the presence of a male family member in the ensemble.

FIGURE 2 Performance of *qiṣaṣ dīniyya* celebrating the saint's festival for the Imām al-Tūnisī, in Cairo, 9 May 1997. The *munshid* (center) is supported by a standard instrumental group comprising (left to right) performers on *tūra* 'large finger cymbals', *kawala* 'reed flute', *'ūd* 'fretless lute', *ṭabla* 'hourglass drum' (partially obscured in this photo), and *mazhar* 'large frame drum with jingles'. The use of amplification equipment by vocalist and melodic instrumentalists is standard. Photo by Michael Frishkopf.

Qiṣaṣ are most commonly performed in the Delta for celebrations of the Prophet's birthday and saints' festivals. Wealthy households may sponsor the *munshid*, or a village may raise funds collectively. Formerly, *qiṣaṣ* also provided entertainment at weddings, though today popular singers are preferred.

Performances generally take place in a brightly lit tent near the home of the sponsor, or near the saint's shrine, starting after the night prayer. The amplified ensemble performs on a stage and usually includes violin, *kawala* 'reed flute', *'ūd* 'fretless lute', frame drums, *ṭabla* 'hourglass drum', and finger cymbals (figure 2).

Often the *munshid* begins with a Qur'ānic recitation or a short *dhikr* (described below). Following a musical overture (a *ṭarab* song, or a series of instrumental improvisations, *taqāsīm*), he sings a religious *mawwāl*—a colloquial poem presented in nonmetrical improvisatory style—without percussion. Then he begins the first story. Stories are of two types: prophet stories (*qiṣaṣ nabawiyya*) from the Islamic canon, and moral fables (*qiṣaṣ khiyāliyya*) drawing on Islamic themes and symbols; the latter are more popular among young people.

The story comprises a series of narrative episodes presented as both colloquial poetry (*zajal*, performed metrically with heterophonic accompaniment) and unaccompanied speech. Following each metric portion, the ensemble plays instrumental excerpts from *ṭarab* songs. Between episodes, the singer inserts a *mawwāl* matching the story's themes, accompanied by melodic instruments and interspersed with *taqāsīm*. In instrumentation and musical style, the ensemble resembles the *takht* of early-twentieth-century Arab music. *Qiṣaṣ* are also shortened and decontextualized through the mass media. Besides television performances, a thriving cassette industry centered in Tanta produces dozens of artists, usually in the studio. Shops in the Delta do a brisk business selling these cassettes, which are frequently played in other shops, taxis, and the homes of connoisseurs.

AL-INSHĀD IN SUFI CONTEXTS

Within *al-inshād al-dīnī* is a subcategory: *al-inshād al-ṣūfī*, that is, *al-inshād al-dīnī* incorporating explicitly Sufi themes or occurring in explicitly Sufi contexts. However, the boundary is never sharp; Sufi concepts, beliefs, and practices permeate Islam, and musically there is interpenetration as well.

Sufism is the mystical aspect of Islam. Motivated by a deep love and longing for Allah and his Prophet, the Sufis seek to rise spiritually through supererogatory devotions. In their view, some people are closer to Allah than others; those who are spiritually advanced provide seekers with spiritual help (*madad*), including blessings, guidance, and intercession. The Prophet Muhammad, being closest to Allah, is the greatest source of *madad*. Next are the saints, pious Muslims whose miraculous deeds indicate their high spiritual level. After death, a saint's blessing radiates from his or her shrine, where a yearly festival may be centered. Among the saints are the founders of the Sufi orders.

The Sufi's spiritual program is formalized in the order (*ṭarīqa*) of his spiritual master (*shaykh*). The *shaykh* guides disciples in the doctrines and practices of the order and monitors their spiritual progress. The central practice is *dhikr* 'remembrance'. Broadly, *dhikr* includes prayers, Qur'ānic recitation, religious study, and *inshād*, all of which are "reminders" of Allah. Specifically, *dhikr* refers to rhythmic group chanting of the Names of Allah, with attendant physical movement. In a group meeting (*ḥaḍra*; plural, *ḥaḍrāt*), held once or more each week, disciples perform various forms of *dhikr*, including the chanted kind, which is commonly accompanied by *inshād*.

Sufism extends far beyond the formal orders. Although each order has distinctive features, the general contours of practice and doctrine are shared. Further, many individuals who are not active in any particular order subscribe to the Sufi worldview. Such commonalities both indicate and support a broader concept that may be termed "informal Sufism"—a larger system of thought, feeling, and action from which the orders emerge as social and ritualistic crystallizations. When a community is permeated by Sufism, all holidays and life-cycle occasions are cause for celebration with informal public *ḥaḍrāt*, in which anyone may participate. The most spectacular public *ḥaḍrāt* take place during saints' festivals.

Al-inshād **within the** ***ḥaḍra*** **of Sufi orders**

Sufis consider poetry the linguistic vehicle most apt for expressing and eliciting mystical feelings and for communicating Sufi teachings. Performed as *inshād*, poems are easier to absorb and retain; singing also heightens the spiritual and emotional atmosphere. Group *inshād* coordinates performance and increases solidarity. But music and emotion are controversial in Islam, so orders must regulate *inshād* and behavior in the *ḥaḍra*.

The order's regular *ḥaḍra* is strictly organized; each participant has a specific role. The *shaykh* presides and maintains ultimate control. The *mustaftiḥ* 'starter' regulates *dhikr* tempo, movement, and chant. *Munshidīn* are usually amateurs: members with good voices and memories, although in several popular orders they are semiprofessionals. A lead *munshid* may select poetry and serve as musical director; occasionally there are accompanying instrumentalists as well.

After night prayer, disciples take seats in formation. Usually there are two or more facing rows. The *ḥaḍra* opens with call-and-response "bidding prayers" (*fawātiḥ*) for the Prophet and saints, followed by a longer group prayer (*hizb*). Next comes *dhikr* chanting, comprising a series of short segments, each characterized by a single chanted phrase and physical movement.

Frequently, *dhikr* is accompanied by *inshād*, which may be performed by a soloist (possibly with a responding chorus), by a chorus, or by antiphonal choirs. Nonmetrical *inshād* may occur in the pauses between segments. The solo *munshid* improvises, delivering poetry in stock melodic motives. Choral *inshād* uses a fixed melody, which ordinarily repeats for each strophe (figure 3). Melodic style often varies with cultural background. Thus, for example, the Burḥaniyya, a Sudanese order, use pentatonic scales in their center in Cairo (where many Sudanese live), whereas their branches in the Egyptian Delta use *maqāmāt*. Instrumental accompaniment is usually limited to frame drums, though occasionally a *kawala* or even an *'ūd* 'fretless lute' appears. No instruments are used in mosques, or by conservative orders.

The example transcribed as figure 3 shows an initial segment of *dhikr* accompanied by choral *inshād*, from the weekly *ḥaḍra* of the Sufi order (al-Ḥāmidiyya al-

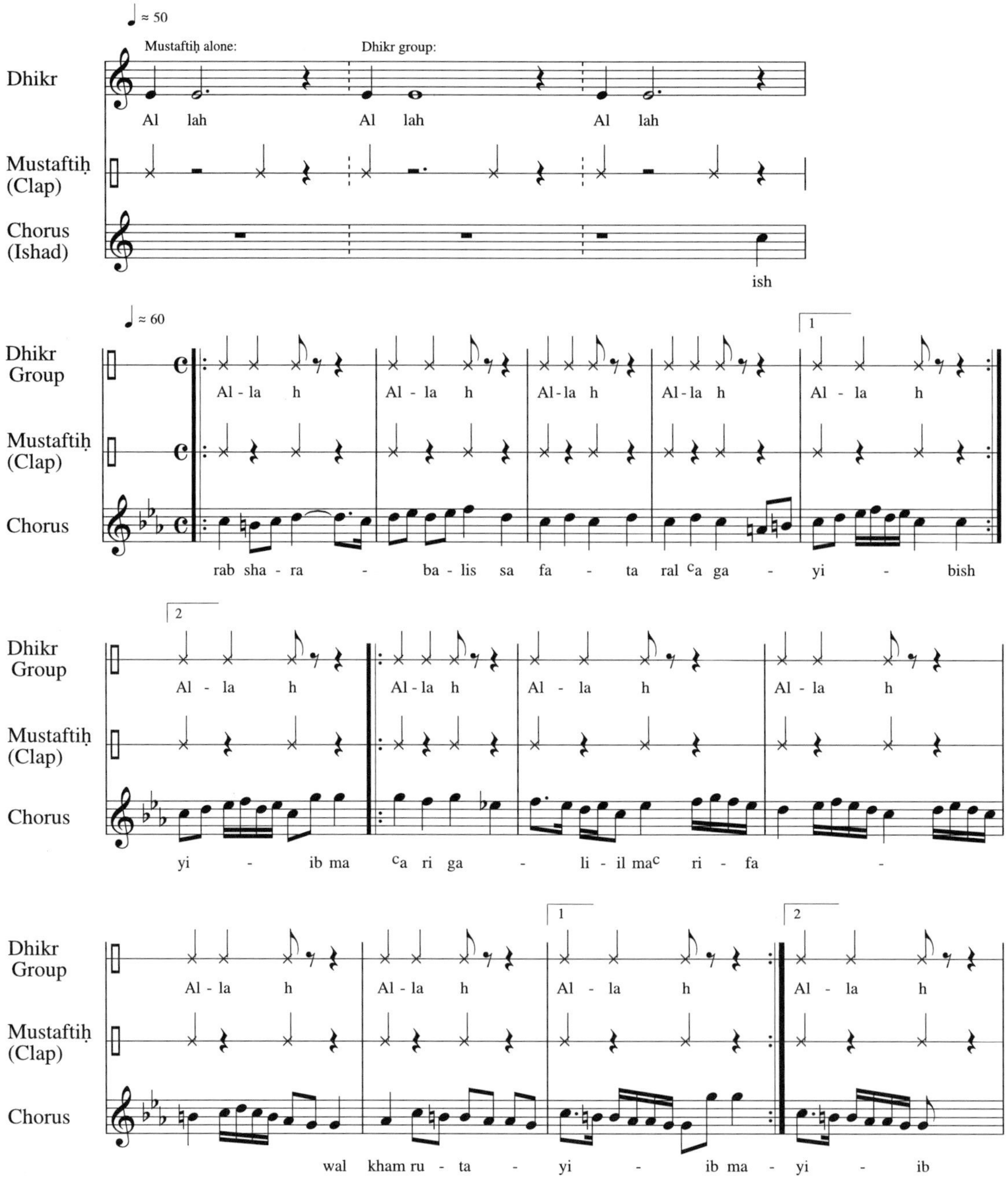

FIGURE 3
Transcription by Michael Frishkopf, from a recording by Shaykh Muḥammad al-Hilbāwī.

Shādhiliyya) in Cairo. While the majority of the brethren bow forward and back, chanting *dhikr* (here, the Name of God, "Allah"), a chorus of *munshidīn* recite poetry. Here they sing the line *Ishrab sharāb āli ṣ-ṣafā tara l-ʿagāyib maʿa rigāli l-maʿrifa wa l-khamru ṭāyib* 'Drink the drink of the people of purity and you'll see wonders with the men of gnosis, for their wine is well-aged'. The *mustaftiḥ*, Shaykh Muḥammad al-Hilbāwī (who is also the lead *munshid*), controls tempo by handclaps. Note that the *dhikr* chant becomes unpitched and metrically regular as soon as the *inshād* begins.

Each *dhikr* segment builds in energy. Its tempo and length are regulated by the *mustaftiḥ*'s handclaps, which gradually accelerate as the *dhikr* movements become more rapid and energetic. There is a gradual rise in tuning; the solo *munshid* may also modulate to raise the tonal center. The volume increases, and the melodic phrases become shorter. After several such segments, the *ḥaḍra* closes with prayers particular to the order and with *fawātiḥ*.

Choral or responsorial *inshād* may also be included as an activity separate from *dhikr*. Figure 4 shows two lead *munshidīn* (first row, at left) with microphones who perform a *qaṣīda*, setting each strophe to a fixed melody. The congregation responds with a recurring refrain, led by a third amplified *munshid* (first row, third from left). All *qaṣā'id* performed as *inshād* are selected from the twelve-volume poetic oeuvre—housed in the open wooden box in front of the lead *munshidīn*—of the order's founder, (Shaykh Ṣaliḥ al-Ja'farī). Such *inshād* is not accompanied by *dhikr* chant or movement, and no instruments are used.

Munshidīn frequently perform poetry composed or selected by a *shaykh* of the order, which may be published as a hymnal. Poetry is also selected from the works of well-known Sufi poets, or from traditional collections. Written poems are usually *qaṣā'id*. In popular orders, colloquial poetry (*zajal* or *mawwāl*) from the oral tradition is also performed. Besides poetry, *munshidīn* perform requests for *madad* 'spiritual help', directed to the Prophet and saints.

Thematically, Sufis divide *al-inshād* into two main types: that which petitions or "remembers" Allah, and that which praises the Prophet (*madīḥ*). *Madīḥ* is most common, for it complements the *dhikr*: while disciples "remember" Allah, *munshidīn* praise the Prophet. Other poems exhort disciples on the Sufi path or express the mystical experience itself. While emotion is important, *al-inshād* of the order is often pedagogical, supporting its spiritual program.

Al-inshād in the public *ḥaḍra*

Sufi *inshād* of the public *ḥaḍra* is more emotionally charged and ambiguous than that of the orders and unfolds outside the jurisdiction of any order. Participants represent a broad spectrum of beliefs and intentions, and strictures are relaxed. Behavior is more ecstatic, and *mūsīqā* is used; the musical group resembles that of *qiṣaṣ dīniyya* but is smaller. Performances begin late and often last until nearly dawn, when the channels between earth and heaven are considered to be most open. Although *munshidīn* who perform in public *ḥaḍrāt* are professionals, many perform free at large saints' festivals, for the saint and for publicity; such performances may draw thousands of participants. In areas where Sufi beliefs and practices are deep-rooted, *ḥaḍrāt* are sponsored by families and communities for a wide variety of holidays and life-cycle occasions; in Upper Egypt, weddings are commonly celebrated with public *ḥaḍrāt*.

FIGURE 4 Performance of strophic responsorial *inshād* during the weekly *ḥaḍra* of the Ja'fariyya Aḥmadiyya Muḥammadiyya order, at their mosque in Cairo, 20 February 1998. Photo by Michael Frishkopf.

Whereas *inshād* is marginal in the orders, it is central in public *ḥaḍrat*. In the orders, performance is unified primarily by commitment to a spiritual master and his practices. But in the public *ḥaḍra*, *inshād* is the central organizing and animating force, forging social and emotional unity through the power of words and music.

Like *qiṣaṣ*, the public *ḥaḍra* takes place in a tent, with *munshid* and ensemble on a stage at one end of the facing lines of *dhikr* performers. Males may perform *dhikr* or join the crowd of onlookers; older women mingle and even perform *dhikr* in the more liberal Delta, though not in Upper Egypt. Attendees include those drawn by the occasion, local residents, and the *munshid*'s fans. Members of different orders mix freely. Motivations vary; participants may seek spectacle, aesthetic pleasure, or spiritual fulfillment.

Socially, participation is more open than in the orders, while performance is more restricted. *Munshid* and ensemble dominate both sonically and visually, owing to the high amplification and their position on the stage. But sonically, the performance is more flexible here than in the orders. According to the exigencies of the context, performers spontaneously adjust content and form to maximize aesthetic and spiritual power.

The performance comprises a sequence of suites, separated by brief intermissions. Each suite (*waṣla*) contains an unbroken series of *dhikr* segments. At the climax of each segment, *dhikr* becomes ecstatic, and the *munshid* switches from poetry to *madad*. Melodic instruments follow the *munshid*'s improvisations heterophonically or play short ostinatos reinforcing meter and tonic. Following the *munshid*'s cadence, musicians fill in with *taqāsīm* or melodies from *ṭarab* songs.

The *munshid* juxtaposes poetic excerpts, gauging listeners' reactions to guide his selections. Especially in the Delta, he may use colloquial poetry to increase comprehension. Responding to context and mood and drawing on a store of melodic fragments, he spontaneously constructs a textual patchwork of authors, themes, and styles. Often he repeats words and lines to emphasize, clarify, or intensify meaning.

The *munshid*'s aim is emotional power, not pedagogy. Texts are often presented more for emotional impact than comprehension. Free of any direct doctrinal or organizational framework, poetry tends toward daring or arcane symbolism. Poetic fragments are further fractured by repetition, allowing the listener to delight in partial meanings and the surfaces of sounds. Vocal technique emphasizes expression: melismas, sighs, and timbral variations that communicate inner feeling. Poetic emotion blends with powerful musical affect generated by strong percussion, improvisation, instruments, popular melodies, and modulation. The *munshid* raises tonality to build emotion or scans to locate the most affective *maqām*, seeking a state of modal concentration called *salṭāna* as a means toward spiritual ecstasy.

Typically the *munshid* belongs to at least one order, which may have provided his first performance opportunities. But after he becomes a professional, his attendance at this order's *ḥaḍrāt* wanes. Often he is traveling. More important, in order to become a *munshid* of the public *ḥaḍra*, he must weaken his allegiance to any particular order. He may even join many orders in order to strengthen his connection with the larger Sufi community.

Skill in selecting and learning poetry is critical to his reputation, for it is on the quality and range of the poetry performed, as much as his musical and expressive skills, that audiences judge him; he is the poet's voice. At first, he imitates the choices of his more successful colleagues. He reads, searching for poetry to express his feeling. He may also employ a poet to compose new poetry by which he may distinguish himself from others; the contemporary Egyptian poet 'Abd al-'Alīm al-Nakhaylī has composed poems for several of the greatest *munshidīn*, including Yāsīn al-Tuhāmī [see SNAPSHOT: SHAYKH YĀSĪN AL-TUHĀMĪ]. Experienced singers have memorized at least one hundred to two hundred poems.

The public *ḥaḍra munshid* has a complex identity. He is a religious figure but also a musician who, like the *muṭrib*, attends to the artistic aspects of his work. Besides his spiritual mission, he aspires to affective power, renown, and wealth. He promotes his career by traveling to the large saints' festivals, producing commercial recordings, and even appearing on folkloric television programs. A successful *munshid* is affluent, and he is booked far in advance. He draws throngs to the *ḥaḍra*, including fans who travel great distances especially to hear him. When the *munshid* is the main object, the meaning of the performance may shift from religious ritual to aesthetic experience, to spectacle, or to celebrity.

REFERENCES

Abdel-Malek, Kamal. 1995. *Muhammad in the Modern Egyptian Popular Ballad*. Leiden: Brill.

Barrayn, Shaykh Ahmad. 1994. *Sufi Songs*. Long Distance 592323. Compact disk. (Sufi *inshād* of the public *ḥaḍra*, representing southern Egypt.)

Danielson, Virginia. 1997. *The Voice of Egypt: Umm Kulthum, Arabic Song, and Egyptian Society in the Twentieth Century*. Chicago: University of Chicago Press.

Frishkopf, Michael. 2001. "Tarab in the Mystic Sufi Chant of Egypt." In *Colors of Enchantment: Visual and Performing Arts of the Middle East*, ed. Sherifa Zuhur. Cairo: American University in Cairo Press. (Forthcoming.)

Nelson, Kristina. 1985. *The Art of Reciting the Qur'ān*. Austin: University of Texas Press.

al-Tuhāmī, Shaykh Yāsīn. 1998. *The Magic of the Sufi Inshād: Sheikh Yasin al-Tuhami*. Long Distance 3039552 ARC 338. Two compact disks, with notes by Michael Frishkopf. (Sufi *inshād* of the public *ḥaḍra* representing middle Egypt.)

Waugh, Earl H. 1989. *The Munshidīn of Egypt: Their World and Their Song*. Columbia: University of South Carolina Press.

The Symbolic Universe of Music in Islamic Societies

Jean During

Heavenly Music: Original Sound
Celestial Beings, Devil, Spirit
Sacred Music: The Patron Saints
People
Symbolic Figures and Numbers
***Samā'*: The Structure and Meaning of Sacred Hearing**
Conditions for Spiritual Hermeneutics

In Islamic cultures of the East, musical practice, both secular and sacred or mystical, has always held a place of remarkable importance. This is probably attributable to the emotional force—even the passion—of the music, which has been codified in an ethical doctrine called *ta'thīr*. Confronted by the mystery and power of music and seeking to create a transcendental aesthetic, scholars, poets, philosophers, and mystics have looked to its origins, invoked myth, invented or resurrected legends, and organized symbolic systems.

Yet an important group of writers and scholars has been utterly unconcerned with the symbolic dimension of music. Al-Fārābī (d. 950), Ibn Sīnā (980–1037), al-Kātib (eleventh century), and Marāghī (d. 1435) eschew myth, legend, and rumor with a circumspection very close to that of the modern scientific method. "We have striven," says Ibn Sīnā, "to propose only what we are certain of, without being concerned by the appeals of tradition" (D'Erlanger 1930–1959, 2:106). On occasion, they explicitly attack a particular superstition, theory, or unverifiable statement, mocking those who, "incapable of arriving at a well-founded result using true science, give themselves over to theories . . . which seem likely, [and] with which they fill their books" (Shiloah 1972:190, 195). For their part, as if to outdo their detractors, the Ismaili gnostics of the tenth century proclaimed that those who denied the music of the spheres were quite simply heretics. Al-Fārābī is among these (D'Erlanger 1930–1959, 1:28).

With a few exceptions, discussions of music are characterized by concern with its origins. Beyond scientific treatises and legal works condemning music (Robson 1938), most texts affirm the divine or heavenly nature of musical science. Its origin, however, varies in different types of writing. Inspirational writings find the origin in God or in Gabriel and other angels; detractors of music associate it with Satan. Less metaphysically, some musical practices are thought to be connected with the prophets.

Like science, music draws its essence from numbers, which also govern other domains of the cosmos, such as the stars and man himself as a microcosm. Music thus establishes a relationship between macrocosm and microcosm on the basis of numbers, and also on the basis of humors; its ritual organization expresses that connection. In all cases, the point is to have an effect on the soul, whether by simple emotion (*ṭarab*) or by communication with higher planes: the spirits, in the case of possession trances (figures 1 to 3); and, for Sufis, the angels, the souls of the founding saints, and the

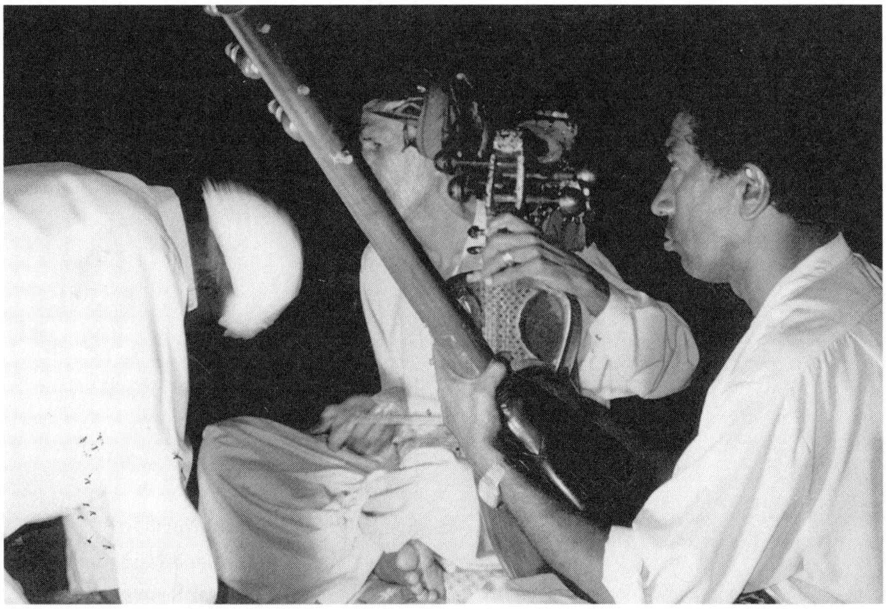

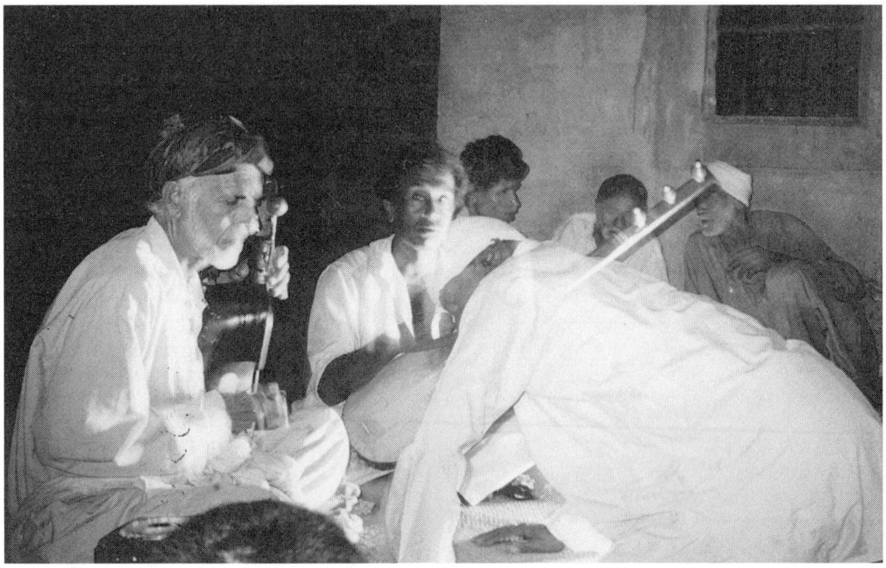

FIGURES 1, 2, AND 3 Baluchi trance session in Damaal in Malir (near Karachi), with a Khalifa in trance. This ritual is performed in gratitude, not to heal illness. Photos by Jean During, 1998.

commemoration of origins. Ultimately, to Sufis, music is a means of reuniting with the deity in a rapturous experience.

HEAVENLY MUSIC: ORIGINAL SOUND

Sufis base their mystical concerts (*samā'* 'hearing') on an event from Muslim sacred history, the primordial covenant (*mīthāq*, referred to in Turkish and Persian texts as *alast*). When Adam was created (whether just his soul or his entire person is not clear), God asked him and all his descendants (for their seed was contained in Adam's loins), "Am I not your Lord?" (*alastu bi-rabbikum*), to which they all responded, "Yes, we witness that you are" (*balī shahidnā*). In the variant of this story in the Qur'ān (7:166–167), everyone is bound by this commitment before birth. This myth does not merely recall that the divine "voice" in all its splendor and with all its indescribable effect is "the supplest melody the inhabitants of Paradise enjoy and the most beautiful song they hear" (Shiloah 1967:193), heard by Moses and by the Prophet when he ascended to heaven. The myth also gives Adam's and his descendants' response, as well as their recognition of their privileged relation to the divine. This transports them into a state of ecstasy that demands expression. Many Sufi hymns phrase their uplifting response as follows: "Yes my Soul, yes my Lord, yes my Beloved" (*balī Jānam, balī miram balī dust*).

Thus the Sufi concert, the *samā'*, is no artificial means of inducing ecstasy, but a ritual that allows people to reactivate a prior state (Molé 1963:134). Or rather, the hearer's manifestation of ecstasy comes from having internalized this myth, as Junayd suggested when he was asked, "What is this ecstasy, that makes a quiet man hear *samā'* and find himself shattered?" "God Most High," he answered, "questioned Adam's future generations after the Pact. . . . Every soul dove into the drunkenness of this word. When they hear *samā'* in this world, they begin to move and to shake" ('Aṭṭār 1959:446).

Thus the myth explains and legitimates *samā'*, which is itself a retelling of the myth. This is also true of another myth that scholars often cite. The Prophet said that *samā'* appeared for the first time on the day when Adam's spirit did not want to enter his body. So that he would not feel anguish, God Most High ordered the angels (or Gabriel, assisted by other angels),

> assembled about His Throne, to go to Adam's side, and to sing there while saying, "Enter the body!" As Adam's spirit did with difficulty enter his body, it also had difficulty getting out when it had to leave him. The echo of the Throne's angels' song rose to the angels of the seven heavens. They all came, and God's praises caused a mystical state to appear within them. . . . All the angels of the seven heavens were thus called to move. They turned so, and no one knew how, on the order of God Most High, the spirit of Adam entered his body." (*Sifat al-jam'īyat*, by Labid ibn Khājegī Tabrīzī, in Molé 1963:215–216)

Some versions add this important coda: "When the voice of the angel had stopped, the soul sought to leave the body, but Adam began to sing through his soul and the soul in ecstasy settled permanently in the body" (Jargy 1971:11). According to this myth, music is the Holy Angel Gabriel's science (*Bihjat al-Rūḥ* 1967:23).

CELESTIAL BEINGS, DEVIL, SPIRIT

The *sīmorgh*

The origin of music is located on quite another plane in the myth of ancient Iran's fabled bird, the *sīmorgh*, whose song is the archetype of all bird song on Earth. According to some traditions, the *sīmorgh* itself originated in China (*Chīn*, Turkestan), and in certain paintings there is a clear family resemblance between the *sīmorgh* and the Chinese phoenix (*feng huang*), which is also believed to be at the source of all music—its name is a synthesis of the cry of the male (*feng*) and the female (*huang*). The *sīmorgh* is sometimes associated with the *qoqnūs* (from the Latin *cygnus* 'swan'), whose beak is pierced with 1,002 holes through which emerge many different melodies ('Aṭṭār 1968: *Manṭiq al-ṭayr*, verse 2295s). Like the phoenix, the *qoqnūs* burns when it grows old, and after forty days a new bird is born from the ashes. Plato is said to have heard its song and to have developed part of his musical science from that song (*Bihjat al-Rūḥ* 1967:26–27). The figure of the *sīmorgh* is found as far back as archaic shamanism and has reappeared several times in new forms in Islam and Sufism.

Diabolus in musica

Arguing against a celestial origin of music, some cite a *ḥadīth* 'narrative' (plural *aḥādīth*) that says, "Satan was the first who lamented and sang." This tradition is reinforced by an Arab myth according to which God taught music to the angels, among them a certain Harit, whose name became Iblis (devil), and then Shayṭān—Satan, the damned. After Satan's disgrace, he and his like "profited from their musical science to tempt people and induce them to sin" (Rouanet 1922:2683). Satan also took the form of a rattlesnake whose tail made a fascinating sound. Adam and Eve were enslaved by it, disobeyed God, and ate of the forbidden fruit (or wheat; Ackerman 1938–1939:2805). However, Gisurdirāz (fifteenth century), a great saint and a passionate lover of *samā'*, turns these arguments around: musical instruments are indeed the devil's invention, but although they have been condemned by jurists, their value can be appreciated by people of heart (Hussaini 1983:113).

Such references to the devil seem to indicate the dangerously seductive power of music, and the hold it can have on the soul. Devils can even intervene during a *samā'* poorly led by Sufis, dancing with the followers and leading them to perdition (Hussaini 1983:112). Some images are very explicit and could stem from a confusion between *samā'* and animist practices, in which possession by some spirits is considered demonic (these are found throughout Islam, particularly in cultures that have had contact with Africa). Often, the term *shayṭān* is to be interpreted as personifying the baser instincts and impulses.

Invisible beings: Ecstasy or possession?

A Sufi cited by Abū Naṣr Sarrāj in the tenth century divided ecstasy (*wajd*) into two categories: ecstasy of possession (*wajd milk*) and ecstasy of meeting (*wajd liqā'in*). A person who does not possess ecstasy must go to meet it. Another Sufi says, "The ecstasy of possession is that which finds you and takes possession of you" (Sarrāj 1914:301). That is true ecstasy. The term *possession* is actually very rare and suggests a greater affinity with pagan practices than one might suppose. In antiquity, Iamblichus (c. 250–c. 330) spoke of possession by gods; in Sufism the being who possesses the subject is not identified; and some religious discredit trance, attributing it to spirits (*ajnān*; singular, *jinn*) and demons.

The participation of "invisible beings" is sometimes felt to be a prima facie condition for the sacred nature of music. Some rituals (*gwātī*, *zār*, *nobān*, *gnāwa*, and others) can even be seen as a kind of offering in sound made to these beings. Thus, as a Kurdish dervish of the Qādirī order explains (personal communication), "each type of *dhikr* has a master (*ṣāḥib*), an attendant (*muwakkil*), that is to say an entity, an angel specifically attached to him. The *dhikr* produces its specific force because of this attendant." When the ritual song leader (*khalīfa*) plays and sings, he must establish a relationship with the divine throne (*'arsh*). Then the angels hear the tambourine (*daf*), and in the invisible world they form a *dhikr* circle (*jam'*), actually in the form of a conical spiral whose vertex points upward. The angels dance and sing along the curves of this spiral, and the musician must harmonize with their music. This is when the effect of the *dhikr* becomes extraordinary and spiritual forces fill the space. It is thus a matter of establishing harmony between earth and heaven and causing the

FIGURE 4 Islamic shamanic session in Khujand: Uzbek women *bakhshis*, devout shamans who chant *dhikr* during healing ceremonies. Photo by Jean During, 1999.

energies between the two to circulate in order to benefit from the graces of the celestial world (During 1989:284).

This concept, although supported by *aḥādīth*, has its roots in shamanic practices still attested to among the Hunza. During sessions of shamanic trance (figure 4), "the fairies [*pari*] . . . bring their own band of musicians to the session. They play much more beautifully than the human musicians." The shaman "should make sure that the two bands play in harmony" (Lièvre and Loude 1990:526).

SACRED MUSIC: THE PATRON SAINTS

In the earthly world, prophets (and sometimes kings) were felt to be the guardians of music, or of one or more of its aspects. In Turkestan, music is said to be the invention of Khidr, the immortal prophet. Scientific authors, on the other hand, attributed musical science to the Greek philosophers and wise men, who transmitted it to scholars, who in turn transmitted it to masters. The invention of human music is commonly attributed to Pythagoras—or Plato, according to some sources—who discovered the twelve *maqāmāt* 'modes' by relating them to the zodiac (Zokā' 1974:192) or listening to the harmony of the spheres (Qoṭb al-Dīn Shīrāzī, cited in Corbin 1964:208, repeating Ikhwān al-Ṣāfā's epistle almost word for word). In any case, the Greek prophets and sages were seen as civilizing heroes who invented musical science to edify the people.

The longing for origins

According to the *aḥādīth*, every prophet had a fine voice, and each apparently sang in his own mode (*maqām*; plural, *maqāmāt*). Primordial hearing (*alast*) and Adam's first *samā'* were accompanied by ecstasy; but in the everyday world, the original ethos of music was more often affliction, sorrow, and separation. The loss of paradise and Adam's awakening to earthly reality were accompanied by tears: in this state of contrition, Adam sang in the *rāst maqām*, the same mode in which his soul had entered his body.

A remarkable thing about the prophets is that each sang in the state of affliction or the exceptional circumstances that marked his particular mission. Originally, there were seven *maqāmāt*—the same number as the seven great prophets (*Bihjat al-Rūḥ* 1967:77). After Adam, Ibrāhīm sang in Nimrod's fire in the *ḥusaynī* and *nowruz-e 'arab maqāmāt*; "Esmā'il in combat, in *rahāvī*, and during immolation, in the *'ushshāq maqām*; Joseph at the bottom of the well and in prison, in the *'irāq*; Moses in the Sinai desert, in the *'ushshāq*; Jonas in the whale's belly, in the *kuchek*; David, repenting at Uriah's tomb, in the *ḥusaynī*" (*Bihjat al-Rūḥ* 1967; for variations, see also Shiloah 1979:288; Zokā' 1974:192).

The human voice was given at the same time as the highest part of the soul, called the "speaking soul" (*nāṭiqa*), which only humans have.

The appearance of certain instruments is also connected with the sadness of music. According to Ibn Khurradādhbih, the lute was invented by Lamek to lament the disappearance of his son. The body of the lute was shaped like his thigh and the neck like his leg, with the foot at the end; the pegs were like toes and the strings like veins. "Then he drew sounds from it and sang a mournful tune" (Rouanet 1922:2683).

Most instruments are attributed to a great man. According to al-Qādirī (1990:17), it was Noah who invented music and made and played the first lute. After the flood, this instrument disappeared and was reinvented by King David. Traditionally, David's instrument was the reed flute, but one legend attributes it to Imam ʿAlī. When the Prophet had given ʿAlī the divine secrets, ʿAlī could not contain them. Leaning over a well, he spoke them to ease his soul. A drop of saliva fell to the bottom, and some time later a reed emerged. A passing shepherd cut the reed and made a flute whose sound filled the soul with spiritual longing.

Maqāmāt: Origin of the modes

A series of myths and legends describe music more concretely. For example, the creation of the twelve canonical *maqāmāt* is associated with a myth about Moses. When Moses parted the waters of the Nile and came to the middle of the river, he saw a stone. Gabriel said to him, "O Moses, take this stone; it will serve you." He took the stone, then went with his people to the desert, where he stayed for forty days. They were beset by thirst. Moses prayed, and Gabriel appeared and told him to strike the stone with his staff. He did so, and a spring burst fort, dividing into twelve streams that each made a different sound. Gabriel said to Moses, "Learn the twelve *maqāmāt*." This is how Moses learned them. After that, the term *musīqī* spread (Zokāʿ 1974:191), playing on the words *mūsī(qī)* and Mūsá (Moses), which are written with the same letters. In a well-known variant (Shiloah 1972:288), Gabriel says, "*Yā Mūsá, isqī*" (O, Moses, give them something to drink), which sounds like *mūsīqī*.

PEOPLE

Being musical is a human quality. The human voice was given at the same time as the highest part of the soul, called the "speaking soul" (*nāṭiqa*), which only humans have. When the soul heard the angels' song, it felt such joy that it lost consciousness. It stood up and entered Adam's body, and immediately Adam sat up and praised God (*al-ḥamdu li-llāh*). Because of this preeminence, the science of music is different from other sciences; and in the eighteen thousand worlds everything is taken up with praising and professing faith in melodies and rhythms (Zokāʿ 1974:191).

People are defined as essentially musical. At least that is what is meant by the following syllogism: Music is the science of Gabriel (*Bihjat al-Rūḥ* 1967:23), who is the Holy Spirit—*rūḥ al-quddūs*, where *rūḥ* 'the breath' is, etymologically, the soul. Therefore, music is the science of the soul, "and those who do not enjoy this science and are not ravished by it (*muḥazaẓ*) are not part of the human species." By analogy, the spirit is defined as the "speaking" soul (*nāṭiq*). Yet this speech is regulated by thought and assumes a listener and a speaker; thus listening (and hearing) define human beings, and hearing is the highest of the five senses.

The effect of music: Stars, numbers, and humors

For several authors the pulse—the audible expression of the vital principle in the blood—is the basis of rhythm (*Bihjat al-Rūḥ*:30). In the ancient world, doctors considered the pulse essential to diagnosis; therefore, they had to understand the science of rhythm. Acccording to *Bihjat al-Rūḥ*, there is a star (or a constellation) called *orqonū* (that is, the *organanon* 'organ') or a "*mūsīqī* planet" that, like blood, flows in the body throughout the lunar month. Each day of the month, it is to be found at a different place in the body. Its position is signaled by the pulse, and a doctor must be careful to treat the organ where it is found, for "the soul takes its sustenance from that organ through that star" (*Bihjat al-Rūḥ*). These curious and rather vague ideas are echoed in an Arabic treatise of the same period: "Doctors claim that a beautiful voice and true melody flow in the body and the veins. Thus they purify the blood, improve the soul, soothe the heart, and cause the senses to vibrate" (al-Qādīrī 1990:10).

There is an intrinsic analogy between temperament and music: "The temperament of every living creature is made of sounds and melodies harmoniously mingled" (Hujvīrī 1976:399). The modes can exert a prodigious influence on the human body, causing, for example, animation, weeping, joy, sadness, courage, and sleep (Farmer 1925–1926). According to the ancients, temperaments are created by the predominance of one humor over another. These vary according to the seasons and the subject's age. In a healthy person, the effect of music will be especially strong, because it conforms to the person's natural temperament. For example, "hot" and "wet" modes will be chosen for a person whose temperament is naturally hot and wet. Conversely, because illness results from an excess of one humor, along with a physiological and psychological imbalance, "cool" and "dry" melodies will be played to heal the patient, to temper the excessive humor, to reinforce the weakened humors, and to reestablish equilibrium (Abu Mrad 1989:120–121).

According to classical physics, only physical bodies, such as organisms, are endowed with qualities like heat, cold, and moisture. A mode, then, could not itself possess these qualities, but it could incite them. How does a mode operate? An Arabic treatise dating from the fourteenth to the sixteenth century explains this as follows: "Modes' influence is not due to their being hot and dry. That is the exclusive property of bodies. Instead it is due to the humor they incite. . . . *Nagham* 'mode' exerts this type of influence because of modes' association with various stars, for the stars hold within them the qualities which govern this influence" (Abu Mrad 1989:127–128).

The author of this treatise says nothing more about how music transmits its influence; for that, we can turn to the Pythagoreans, whose theories were widely known among Muslim authors. The stars modify the states of the human soul and influence human destiny. The influence of music is analogous to the harmonious movements of the stars: both are governed by the laws of numbers. In consequence, the effect of music is due to the effect of the stars.

SYMBOLIC FIGURES AND NUMBERS

In ancient times, music was part of the world system and was based on the cosmic order (the spheres) and numbers (intervals). As early as the Safavids of the sixth century, Bārbad had organized melody according to temporal divisions: 360 days in a year, thirty days in a month, and seven days in a week. During Ṣafī al-Dīn's time (thirteenth century), the modes were arranged in twelve categories, in accordance with the zodiac. Later Persian and Arab authors structured the entire modal repertoire.

Dividing the modes into six *āvāz-hā* and twelve *maqāmāt*, they proceeded to design a system in which each main element corresponded to two other elements from another level. From each of the six *āvāz-hā* came two *maqāmāt*; from the twelve *maqāmāt* came twenty-four *sho'be-hā*; from the twenty-four *sho'be-hā* came forty-eight *gushe-hā*. Some authors went even further, creating a system that started from three fundamental modal types. Rhythmic cycles sometimes corresponded to the twenty-four *sho'be-hā* that completed the pattern. Interrelationships were represented elegantly by what looked like circular mandalas.

Musical performance was also organized into cycles. The *nawba* 'suite' (plural, *nawbāt*), for example, was made up of parts belonging to different genres. Another ancient example is the *āyin*, the Mevlevi Sufis' ritual dance, which symbolizes the movements of the heavens. The word *maqām* also refers to the mystics' spiritual stations and thus to degrees of superior worlds. The structure of the *mandala* 'circle' connected music not only to the numerical order and to the firmament but also to the earthly world, for this world was said to be organized according to the principle of analogy.

Certain symbolic numbers are prominent in inventories and lists. First, there is the number twelve, to which Ṣafī al-Dīn gave a prominent position, In the sixteenth-century Bukhara school, twelve rhythmic cycles and twelve musical forms were used. Today we can still count twelve Persian and Azerbaijani *dastgāh-hā* and twelve Uighur *muqamlar*. This choice of twelve can be explained on theoretical grounds (the twelve notes of the chromatic scale were well known to the ancients), but it is more likely to have proceeded from symbolic reasoning: the twelve signs of the zodiac, the twelve Shi'ite imams, the twelve hours of the day, and so on. Other important numbers have a direct relationship to twelve: the six ancient *āvāz-hā*; the six Tajik-Uzbek *maqāmlar* and their twenty-four derivatives, the *sho'be-hā*. Twenty-four is also the number of rhythmic cycles delineated in certain Persian and Turkish treatises, though in reality there are more or fewer. The twelve *muqāmlar* of the Uighurs also correspond to the twenty-four hours of the day, as do the twenty-four ancient *nawbāt* of Morocco.

Seventeen is also a symbolic number found in many inventories: Ṣafī al-Dīn's seventeen *maqāmāt* and *āvāz-hā* (which are in fact twelve plus six, with two modes reduced to one) and his seventeen degrees of the theoretical scale; the scale of the *tanbur*; and the seventeen rhythmic cycles of seventeeth-century Central Asia. Seventeen, a prime number, is well-known to Muslim esotericists, especially the *ḥurfiyūn*. And seventeen is the number of letters in the Islamic profession of faith, the number of daily ritual prostrations, and the number of Imam 'Alī's companions.

Studying the relationship between the musical modes, sounds, and alternative orders of reality (such as cosmological orders) would lead us too far astray. I will simply note that symbolic relationships have been established between the *maqāmāt* and all levels of the universe, from the stars and constellations in the heavens to the temporal divisions of hours, seasons, and the zodiac; to medicine and physiognomy; and on down to cries in the animal kingdom. Their organizing principle remains to be discovered (for discussion of this point, see Abu Mrad 1989; *Bihjat al-Rūḥ* 1967:78f; Chottin 1939:84; Farmer 1925–1926; Ikhwān al-Ṣafā in Corbin 1964:11, 179–181; Neubauer 1990; Shiloah 1972:288).

SAMĀ': THE STRUCTURE AND MEANING OF SACRED HEARING

A *dhikr* session: The musical *mandala*

The desire to structure the world systematically also affects musical performance, especially in the context of ritual. A circle is the pattern used to organize most rhythmic modes and cycles, and also every level of the *dhikr* ritual and the Sufi *samā'*. This is the *mandala* that represents both the psyche and the cosmos (During 1989:285f; figure 5). In Hinduism and especially in Buddhism, the *mandala* is an image or a sacred space that is always circular, with a center and peripheral ranks. It is at once a "cosmogram" representing divinities grouped around a central deity, and a "psychogram" in which three or four psychic strata are organized around the center (Tucci 1974:31). The center of the *mandala* is the essential place or point—the immobile force that activates all the others. A devotee, by contemplating this center, internalizes a harmonious image of the cosmos and thereby attains an interior state of perfect peace. This process may be seen as a descent to the essence itself. In practice, contemplation of the *mandala* is connected to a mantra—a repetition of an appropriate sacred formula.

Human beings can be seen as structured like a *mandala*, in the sense that the supreme center is the divine part (*ẕarre-ye ẕāt*), enveloped by layers of the "subtle body" or soul (*laṭā'if*) that are themselves surrounded by vital energies delimiting the physical body. Basic spiritual techniques like the *dhikr* consist in penetrating these layers to find their center, the divine part of the person. This work has been described, aptly, as "concentration," because it gradually brings the being toward its own center. The preferred instrument for this kind of asceticism is repetition—musical, verbal, or both—of a single word in a formula, or *dhikr*.

The unfolding of most *dhikr* rituals can be represented by a series of concentric circles starting with the largest and culminating with the smallest, that is, the center. The *dhikr* begins as long, articulated, sung phrases (*wird*), but these are followed by shorter and shorter phrases. The final *dhikr* is no longer articulated and no longer has contrasting differentiated parts. It is reduced to a unity—a breath—as a circle can ultimately be reduced to a point. Thus it is no longer a rhythmic cycle of six, four, or two periods but a simple, pulsating point. Dervishes can be said to have reached the center when they no longer need the material assistance of the *dhikr* but are submerged in an empowering supernatural force. At this stage, they are suffused with the *dhikr*, or rather with its essence. This suffusion (*tajallī*) gives its name to the ritual: *ḥaḍra* 'presence', 'manifestation', or *maḥall-i ẓuhūr* 'epiphanic place'.

Some kinds of Sufi concert have more mandalic qualities than others, but most traditional Middle Eastern musics unfold in this pattern. This is true of *nawbāt*, *faṣā'il*, Mevlevi *'ayinlar*, Uighur *muqāmlar*, and Persian *dastgāh-hā*.

FIGURE 5 Two mullahas, father and son, of Badakhshan (Tajikistan), who specialize in Ismaili religious and mystical repertoire. Photo by Jean During, 1991.

The symbolism of practices and forms

Sages have said that mystical experience is determined, above all, by invention, which gives meaning and value to things by bringing them back to their foundation or origin. This is the hermeneutic meaning of the sacred texts, the *ta'wīl* of symbolic interpretation and ultimately of the imaginal *tawājud*, a condition seen as ecstasy. In this view, everything that takes place in the Sufi's consciousness is invested with meaning; these meanings and interpretations are the flowers of a tree of knowledge which the subject has patiently cultivated through spiritual practice and moral edification. Only at the cost of this patient cultivation can music and its effects truly contribute something.

For example, the *nāy* 'reed flute' is often played in Sufi concerts, notably by Mevlevi dervishes, and is one of the most symbolically charged instruments. For Aḥmad Ṭūsī (1981:10–11) the *nāy* is a metaphor for human essence (*dhāt*), which is supreme divine life (*ḥayāt al-ḥaqq*). The nine holes of the *nāy* symbolize nine levels of the heart: the chest, the heart, fear, the heart's interior, paradise (Eden), lifeblood, the envelope of the heart, and consciousness (the author does not tell us what the ninth level is). The famous Maṣnavī of Mowlānā Jalāl al-Dīn Rūmī describes his thigh, pierced with holes, as reminding him of a mystic's chest that has been ripped open. Indeed, the *nāy* was cut, burned, pierced, carved, and tightened at the joints before becoming a flute. In Mevlevi dervish symbolism, the *nāy* becomes a poetic metaphor for the perfect man, the *shaykh*: devoid of all ego, he is like an instrument in a musician's hands. Only the divine breath that animates him can make him vibrate; he can speak only when touched by the lips of the beloved.

For Aḥmad Ṭūsī (1981:11), the *daf* 'tambourine', because of its circular shape, represents the universe. The skin that covers the frame symbolizes absolute existence. Beating the *daf* is a reference to divine visitation (*vārīdat*), which has been manifested since the mystery of mysteries in absolute existence (*bāṭin-i bāṭin*). The five little cymbals attached to the frame symbolize five degrees: kingship, *valāyat* 'regency' (an allusion to the Shi'ite imams), prophecy, humanity, and spirituality, the degrees through which divine life and divine knowledge become creation.

This is how the ancients interpreted the dervishes' posture and movements during *samā'*. For example, if a dervish jumped or leaped up, it meant (as Ṭūsī said) that he "is pulled from the human degree toward the degree of the One and only." Mowlānā Rūmī said of hand clapping, "Clap your hands and understand how all sounds come from Him/For this sound of two hands cannot be made without separation and union." Taking off one's coat, as dervishes do when seized by ecstasy, conveys the sense of a gift, as Suhrawardī (d. 1191) observes: "It means that we have received news from the other world. So we cast off something of this world" (Corbin 1964:405–406). The coat tossed off cannot be reclaimed but is shared with followers or offered to the musicians.

CONDITIONS FOR SPIRITUAL HERMENEUTICS

In representing the world, ordinary people sharply separate lower realms from higher realms and the sacred from the secular. By contrast, the Sufi and gnostic system is characterized by a hierarchy within the real, in which the levels commingle, opening passageways. We can account for this system by means of two complementary paths to a specific state of that world, which can be approached through the senses: the *ẓāhir/bāṭin* pair and the state of the "imaginal world." This implies a double structure of the world that can be sensed, the imaginal world, and the spiritual senses.

The worldview of Islamic gnosis is structured by the antinomic but inseparable notions of *ẓāhir* and *bāṭin*—exterior and interior, the apparent and the hidden. These ideas, though not clearly defined, refer to various divisions, of which the most typical are the apparent versus the hidden, the letter versus the spirit, and words (*aqwāl*) versus interior states (*aḥwāl*). In such a division, the two levels necessarily coexist:

each needs the other, even when they are in tragic confrontation; and each draws its meaning from the other, even though they are distinct within the hierarchy. As absolutes, then, they are inseparable. God himself is both *ẓāhir* and *bāṭin*.

The *ẓāhir/bāṭin* pair goes beyond a simplified duality like worldliness and otherworldliness, which are both aspects of the world. Because the two levels commingle, the pair is "squared": the *ẓāhir* has a *ẓāhir*, the *bāṭin* has a *ẓāhir*; the *ẓāhir* has a *bāṭin*, and the *bāṭin* has a *bāṭin* (Corbin 1964: for example 46–47). Thus behind each phenomenon there are not one but several meanings and several levels of reality; this is precisely the possibility offered by symbolic thought and hermeneutics. Meaning (*ma'nā*) is also the term used in Islam for the spiritual (*ma'nāwī*). Grasping these meanings changes one's state of awareness radically. Reading a poem or hearing a melody, for instance, can suddenly reveal impassioned meanings (*ma'ānī*) and lead to illumination, ecstasy, and states of grace which the Sufis distinguish from secular emotional states such as *ṭarab*. This is a key to mystical musical practices, especially the *samā'* ritual (Qureshi 1995; During 1988; Hussaini 1983; Molé 1963).

Another road to interpretation is closely connected with the problematic of the beautiful. For the Sufis, the beauty of things bears witness to God and is aesthetic proof of the divine. According to one *ḥadīth*, "God is beautiful and He loves beauty." And the world "is God's mirror. Beauty is never absent from that mirror. . . . The Prophet is a mirror, his heart can be polished like a mirror and reflect the light of the divine" (Bürgel 1988:138–141). Persian metaphysicians used the mirror as an example to illustrate archtypal images; for them, these archetypes were shapes suspended without any support (*mujarrad-i khiyāl*), as images are suspended in a mirror. Iranian metaphysical thought is original because it integrates these independent images, halfway between the world that can be sensed and the world of ideas (Kāshānī, in Corbin 1964: for example 205, 275).

This *'ālam-i mithāl* 'world of analogy' offers itself for imaginal, visionary perception—that is, active, creative imagination, which is a tool and is not to be confused with the conjectural imagination that is merely a kind of representational meandering. A remarkable thing about this world system is that it establishes a direct connection between what can be sensed and what can be reasoned, not by clever mental construction but by basing itself directly on experience and sensation. The imaginal sweetness of which Suhrawardī speaks corresponds to degrees of "more fascinating beauty" and "more overflowing delectation," which are truly felt, not simply imagined or imposed as dogma. This metaphysics is not speculative but experienced or experiential. Cosmology and anthropology are complementary—the hierarchy of states of awareness and forms of knowledge corresponds to the hierarchy of the universe.

Levels of being and levels of reality imply the existence of perceptive organs appropriate to each. Taking this principle to its furthest limit, mystics and sages discover subtle senses that redouble each physical sense. These can be called internal senses or, collectively, a spiritual intellect. Just as the natural intellect dominates the physical senses, this spiritual intellect is, in the hierarchy, the crown of the soul's senses. Thus it is possible to see with another eye and hear with another ear.

However, a problem then arises: how to connect these "supersenses," which perceive the hidden (*bāṭin*) aspect of things, with the ordinary senses that perceive the apparent. In effect, most mystics who use the arts, especially music, are advocating an internal perception. What interests them is not hearing apparent sounds but rather perceiving the other level of reality. As Mowlānā Rūmī says of the *samā'*: "You need the heart's ear, not the body's. . . . We are not aware of the flute and the tambourine." And 'Aṭṭār says of his verses: "One must listen to these words with the heart and soul, not with one's self of water and earth."

When their sublimation ends, mystics have no further need of their apparent senses and sometimes do without any assistance from the world of those senses. When

Suhrawardī read the Qur'ān, he would not even hear a spiritual concert the Sufis were giving in the next room. At the end of his life, Rūzbihān renounced the *samā'* ritual, declaring, "The *samā'* I hear is God himself."

REFERENCES

Abu Mrad, Nidaa. 1989. "Musicothérapie chez les Arabes au Moyen-Age." Thesis, Académie de Paris, Université René Descartes.

Ackerman, Phyllis. 1938–1939. "The Character of Persian Music." In *A Survey of Persian Art*, ed. Arthur Upham Pope, 2805–2817. London: Oxford University Press.

Aflākī, Shams al-Dīn Aḥmad. 1978. *Les saints des derviches tourneurs* (*Manāqib ul-'ārifīn*), trans. Clément Huart. 2 vols. Paris: Sindbad.

'Aṭṭār, Farīd al-Dīn. [1905–1907] 1959. *The Tadhkiratu 'l-awliya* (Memoirs of the Saints), ed. Reynold A. Nicholson. 2 vols. London, Leiden: Luzac.

———. 1968. *Manṭiq al-ṭayr*. Tehran: Kitābfurūshī-i Tihrān.

Bihjat al-Rūḥ (Apocryphe de Safioddin, 1346). 1967. Ed. Rabino de Borgomale. Tehran.

Bürgel, J. Christoph. 1988. *The Feather of Simurgh: The "Licit" Magic of the Arts in Medieval Islam*. New York: New York University Press.

Chottin, Alexis. 1939. *Tableau de la musique marocaine*. Paris: P. Geuthner.

Corbin, Henry. 1964. *Histoire de la philosophie Islamique*. Paris: NRF.

———, ed. 1960. *Terre céleste et corps de résurrection de l'Iran mazdéen à l'Iran shī'ite*. Paris: Buchet/Chastel. (See also 2nd ed.: 1979. *Corps spirituel et Terre céleste: De l'Iran mazdéen à l'Iran shī'ite*.)

During, Jean. 1977. "The 'Imaginal' Dimension and Art of Iran." *World of Music* 19(3, 4):24–34.

———. 1982. "Revelation and Spiritual Audition in Islam." *World of Music* 24(3):68–84.

———. 1987. "Le *samā'* de Ruzbehān Baqli Shirāzi." *Connaissance religieuse* 2(4):191–197.

———. 1988. *Musique et extase: L'audition mystique dans la tradition soufie*. Paris: Albin Michel.

———. 1989. *Musique et mystique dans les traditions de l'Iran*. Paris: Institut Français de Recherche en Iran; Louvain: Éditions Peeters.

———. 1990a. "L'autre oreille: Le pouvoir mystique de la musique au Moyen-Orient." *Cahiers des Musiques Traditionnelles* 3:57–78.

———. 1990b. "Der Mythos der Simorg." *Spektrum Iran* 3(3):3–19.

———. 1992. "What Is Sufi Music?" In *The Legacy of Mediaeval Persian Sufism*, ed. Leonard Lewisohn, 277–287. London: Khaniqahi-Nimatullahi.

———. 2001. *L'âme des sons: La musique d'Ostad Elāhī (1895–1974)*. Paris: Éditions du Relié.

D'Erlanger, Baron Rodolphe. 1930–1959. *La musique arabe*. 6 vols. Paris: P. Geuthner.

Farmer, Henry George. 1925–1926. "The Influence of Music from Arabic Sources." *Proceedings of the Musical Association* 52:89–124.

Ghazzālī, A.-H. 1975. *Kīmiyā-e Sa'ādat*, ed. Khedivjem. Tehran: Arām.

Hujvīrī, 'Alī ibn 'Uṣmān. [1911] 1976. *The 'Kashf al-mahjub': The Oldest Persian Treatise on Sufiism*, trans. Reynold A. Nicholson. Lahore: Islamic Book Foundation.

Hussaini, Syed Shah Khusro. 1983. *Sayyid Muḥammad al Ḥusaynī-i Gīsūdirāz (721/1321–825/1422): On Sufism*. Delhi: Idarah-i Adabiyat-i Delli.

Iamblichus. 1993. *Les mystères d'Égypte*, trans. Édouard des Places. Paris: Les Belles Lettres.

Jargy, Simon. 1971. *La musique arabe*. Paris: Presses Universitaires de France.

Lièvre, Viviane, and Jean-Yves Loude. 1990. *Le chamanisme des Kalash du Pakistan*. Paris: Éditions Recherche sur les Civilisations.

MacDonald, Duncan, ed. 1901–1902. "Emotional Religion in Islam as Affected by Music and Singing: Being a Translation of a Book of the *Ihyā 'Ulūm ad-Dīn* of al-Ghazzālī, with Analysis, Annotations, and Appendices." *Journal of the Royal Asiatic Society* (1901):195–252, 705–748; (1902):1–28, 195–252.

Molé, Marijan. 1963. "La danse extatique en Islam." In *Les danses sacrées*, 145–280. Paris: Éditions du Seuil.

Neubauer, Eckhard. 1990. "Arabische Anleitungen für Musiktherapie." *Zeitschrift für Geschichte der Arabisch-Islamischen Wissenschaften* 6:227–272.

al-Qādirī, 'Askar al-Halabī. 1990. "Rāh al-jām fī Shajarat al-Anghām." In *Traduction et commentaire d'un traité de musique arabe: Mémoire de maîtrise*, ed. and trans. C. Boublil. Strasbourg. (Dissertation typescript.)

Qureshi, Regula Burckhardt. [1986] 1995. *Sufi Music of India and Pakistan: Sound, Context, and Meaning in Qawwali*. Chicago: University of Chicago Press.

Robson, James, ed. 1938. *Tracts on Listening to Music: Being Ḍhamm al-malāhī, by Ibn abī'l-Dunyā; and Bawāriq al-ilmā', by Majd al-Dīn al-Tūsī al-Ghazālī*. London: Royal Asiatic Society.

Rouanet, J. 1922. "La musique arabe." In *Encyclopédie de la musique et dictionnaire du Conservatoire*, ed. A. Lavignac, 1(5):2676–2812. Paris: C. Delagrave.

Sarrāj, Abū Naṣr 'Abd Allāh ibn 'Alī. 1914. *The Kitāb al-luma' fi 'l-Taṣawwuf of Abū Naṣr 'Abdallah b. 'Alī al-Sarrāj al-Ṭūsī*, ed. Reynold Alleyne Nicholson. Leyden: Brill; London: Luzac.

Shiloah, Amnon. 1965, 1967. "L'épître sur la musique des Ikhwān al-Safā." *Revue des Études Islamiques* 33:25–162; 37:159–193.

———, ed. 1972. *La perfection des connaissances musicales (al-Ḥasan ibn Aḥmad ibn 'Alī al-Kātib)*. Paris: P. Geuthner.

Suhrawardī, Yaḥyā ibn Ḥabash. 1976. *L'archange empourpré: Quinze traités et récits mystiques*, trans. and annotator Henry Corbin. Paris: Fayard.

Tucci, Giuseppe. 1974. *Théorie et pratique du mandala*. Paris: Fayard.

Ṭūsī, Aḥmad ibn Muḥammad. 1981. *al-Hadīyah al-sa'dīyah fī ma'ān al-wajdīyah (1360)*, ed. Aḥmad Mujāhid. Tehran: Kitābkhānah-'i Manūchhirī.

Zokā', Yaḥyā. 1974. "Ma'refat-e 'elm-e musīqī" (1353). In *Nāme-ye Minovi*. Tehran.

Manifestations of the Word: Poetry and Song in Turkish Sufism

Walter Feldman

The Bektaşīye
The Sunni *Tarikatlar*
The *Zikr*
Musical Style of the *Zikr*
The *Ilāhī* Hymn
Nonmetrical Composed Genres

During the Ottoman period several dervish orders, *tarikatlar* (singular, *tarika*), created a common liturgical music. Although this *tarikat* music showed a confluence of the court, the mosque, and popular elements, by the seventeenth century it had developed an independent style and repertoire. The repertoire was divided into several musical genres that were performed during the canonical prayer service, during Islamic festivals, and especially during the *zikr* (Arabic, *dhikr*), which evolved into an elaborate musical ritual. In the seventeenth and eighteenth centuries, some of these *tarikat* genres were accepted into the public mosque. The repertoire that survives today was composed between the early seventeenth and the early twentieth century. During the second half of the nineteenth century, there was a decline in both the quantity and the quality of the music created; and after the closing of the dervish lodges, the *tekkeler* (singular, *tekke*), in 1925, new production virtually came to a halt. Over the next three decades, most of this very large repertoire, including several entire genres, was on the way to extinction, although a few *tekkeler* nevertheless preserved much of their Ottoman liturgical practice. In the late 1970s, governmental policies became more permissive toward religious practices, and a somewhat more propitious cultural climate allowed the dervish ceremonies and their music considerably more freedom (especially after the installation of the military government in 1980). Since that time, there have been active efforts to preserve what remains of the dervish music and transmit it to younger generations.

The music of the Ottoman *tarikatlar* can be divided into three groups: that of (1) the Mevlevīye (also Mevlevî, Mevlevī, or Mevlevi); (2) the other Sunni *tarikatlar* (the numerous branches of the Halvetīye order, the Kadirīye, the Rifaīye, and others); and (3) the largely Shiite Bektaşīye order. This article will discuss the Bektaşīye first but will deal primarily with the second group, Sunni *tarikatlar*. [For the Mevlevīye, see Classical Ottoman Turkish Suites.]

Throughout the Ottoman period, the Sunni *tarikatlar* had been important for the music they produced to use within their *tekkeler* and in public mosques, as well as for developing various forms of religious and secular music and, especially, diffusing these forms among the urban population. Thus the music of the *zikr* (plural, *zikrler*) did not exhaust the musical significance of the *tarikatlar*. Observation of the few

Tarikat music showed a confluence of the court, the mosque, and popular elements, but by the seventeenth century it had developed an independent style and repertoire.

tarikatlar still functioning in contemporary Istanbul does not adequately convey their former importance in Turkish musical life.

THE BEKTAŞĪYE

The music of the Bektaşīye, performed in a closed ceremony that was prohibited on several occasions, is less well known than that of most other *tarikatlar*. Nevertheless, it is clear that their ritual was distinct from the others on two major counts. First, the form of their ritual *sema* did not resemble either the Mevlevī *semā* or the various ceremonies of the Sunni *tarikatlar*, but rather shared its basic liturgical features with the *ayīn-i cem* of the rural Alevī order [see ALEVĪ IDENTITY AND EXPRESSIVE CULTURE.] Second, Bektaşī music was partly connected with an old stratum of urban folk music, and it borrowed only selectively from the classical *makam* 'mode' system [see CONTEMPORARY TURKISH *MAKAM* PRACTICE.]

The frequent absence of the *miyan* section where a modulation to a new *makam* occurs indicates the distance between the Bektaşī hymn (*nefes*) and art music. By contrast, many of even the simplest hymns of the Sunni *tarikatlar* have such a section. The Bektaşī hymns commonly use several asymmetrical (*aksak*) rhythms, as well as a very old rhythm called *semāī* 'of the *semā*' in 6/8. None of these rhythms were accepted into the *zikr* of the Sunni *tarikatlar* after the sixteenth century. The *semāī* rhythm had been a mainstay of the music of the Ottoman military or janissary band (*mehter*). It also forms the rhythmic structure of the second part of the third section (*selām-i sālis*) of the Mevlevī *āyīn*. Thus the Mevlevīye and the Bektaşīye—both of which are old, pre-Ottoman Anatolian *tarikatlar*—share this musical feature. The *semāī* rhythm also linked their music with the urban popular music of the sixteenth and seventeenth centuries before the rise of the *şarkı* form caused a transformation of this music. The popular, janissary, and old Anatolian connections of much Bektaşī music are consistent with what is known of the social history of the Bektaşīye. The continuing differentiation of the Bektaşīye from the other *tarikatlar* in Turkey is also illustrated by the fact that at least some Shiite *Bektaşīye* would not sing the hymns of the Sunni *tarikatlar*, considering that doing so would be a sin.

THE SUNNI *TARIKATLAR*

By contrast, most of the Sunni *tarikatlar* developed an essentially homogeneous music. Much (though by no means all) of the music of these *tarikatlar* was performed during the *zikr*. The central position of the *zikr* in their rituals distinguished the Sunni *tarikatlar* from the Mevlevīye and the Bektaşīye, among whom other forms of musical worship eclipsed the *zikr* or made it peripheral. The bases of the various forms of *semā* and *āyīn* among the Mevlevīye, Bektaşīye, and Alevī probably go back at least to the emergence of the Mevlevīye in the later thirteenth century, and possibly go back even further. Since the other *tarikatlar* arrived in Anatolia considerably later, often as late as the fifteenth century, it is the *zikr* that appears as the newcomer in Turkey.

Musically gifted dervishes known as *zākirler* (singular, *zākir*) led the singing during the *zikr* ceremony and produced the bulk of the music sung in the Sunni *tekkeler*. By the seventeenth century it was not uncommon for court musicians who were lay sympathizers (*muhib*) of the orders to compose hymns for their shaykh. Nor was it unusual for a *zākirbaşı*—a lead *zākir*—eventually to become a successor (*halife*, Arabic *khalifa*) of the shaykh of a *tekke*, either the *zākirbaşı*'s own *tekke* or another *tekke* in the same order. Some of the music and much of the poetry of the *tarikatlar* were created by shaykhs of the orders as well. In several of the *tarikatlar* it would appear that musical ability was a requirement not only for the *zākirler* but also for the shaykh. The importance of the office of *zākirbaşı* can be gauged by the fact that, in the Halvetī tradition, the *zākirbaşı* was one of four officers of the *tarikat* who wore the official turban (*tac*) and cloak (*hirka*) during the *zikr* ceremony.

THE *ZIKR*

In the Halvetī, Kadirī, and other Sunni *tarikatlar* the term *zikr* referred to two rather different types of ritual. The one more commonly practiced involved repetition of the litany (*evrad*) of the order, sometimes accompanied by the *ism-i cellāl zikri*, a chanting of the attributes of God. Both the *evrad zikri* and the *ism-i cellāl zikri* were performed kneeling. In many *tekkeler* they were performed daily after the morning prayer and formed part of the morning service. In the Cerrahī *dergāh* they were repeated after the night prayer and on other occasions. This practice was referred to as the *zikr-i şerīf* or *halka-i zikr* 'circle of the *zikr*'. It had only the most rudimentary musical accompaniment.

A more elaborate *zikr* with abundant music and movement was performed once a week, usually between the noon and afternoon prayers or in the evening; on certain days of Ramadan; and on the Prophet Muhammad's birthday. Among some Halvetī groups this was called the *āyīn-i şerīf* or the *mukabbele-i şerīf* 'sacred ritual'; both terms were also used by the Mevlevīye, and it is not clear which group had priority with regard to this terminology. Today the ceremony is simply referred to as the *zikr*.

In the larger *tekkeler* a special structure, called the *tevhīd-hane* 'house of unification', was reserved for the *zikr*. This structure usually adjoined the burial area or the room of the *pīr* (the founder or patron saint of the order) and other resident shaykhs. Its location influenced the performance of the *mukabbele-i şerīf*: much of the directional orientation of the ritual incorporated the physical presence of the cenotaph of the *pīr*.

The three basic types of *zikr* that could be part of the *mukabbele-i şerīf* involved (1) standing in place (*kiyamī zikr*); (2) moving in a circle (*devrān*); and (3) kneeling. The third type had three major branches, the *kelime-i tevhīd zikri* '*zikr* of the word of unification'; the *ism-i cellāl zikri* '*zikr* of the almighty Name'; and the *ku'ūd zikri* 'seated *zikr*'. Most Kadirī groups practiced the *kiyamī zikri*. Some of them, such as the Eşrefīye, practiced the *devrān*. All branches of the Halvetīye apparently practiced the *devrān*. The Halvetīye circled left during the *devrān*; the Eşrefī Kadirīye circled right.

It may be presumed that the various forms of *zikr* were originally produced within, and associated with, different *tarikatlar*. However, by the nineteenth century, just as hymns (the *ilāhīler*) were no longer the sole property of particular *tarikatlar*, their *zikrler*—to which the *ilāhīler* were sung—were often combined in a single *tekke*. That is, several types of *zikr* were performed successively in a single ceremony. In addition, some shaykhs were initiated into more than one *tarikat*, and so they were authorized to perform, and were accustomed to performing, more than one type of *zikr*. Certain *tarikat* branches originated as combinations of branches of larger *tarikatlar*. Some of these heterogeneous *tarikatlar* were venerable, such as the Eşrefīye, a synthesis of Kadirī and Halvetī; and the Gülşenīye, a combination of Halvetī and Mevlevī.

One of the earliest references to the audible *zikr* in Turkey is found in travel writing by the Burgundian ambassador Bertrandon de la Broquiere, who observed a *zikr* ceremony in the region of Adana (Cilicia) in the early years of the fifteenth century: "They sit in a circle and shake their bodies and heads and sing very wildly in their characteristic manner" (Poché 1978:62). While this description could refer to the *ism-i cellāl zikri*, which today involves only the chanting of the names Allah and Hū, the mention of singing suggests something more like the *kelime-i tevhīd zikri*, which is performed on the knees and involves both chanting the formula of the *shahada* (the Islamic credo *La Ilāha illa Lāh* 'There is no God but Allah') and singing *ilāhī* hymns of various musical types.

MUSICAL STYLE OF THE *ZIKR*

The Turkish *zikr* shares several musical features with *zikrler* performed in other parts of the Muslim world. Foremost among these features is a rhythmic chanting of the divine Names, which is coordinated with specific breathing techniques. In terms of musical semantics, the *zikr* may be seen as the opposite of the Qur'ānic *tecvit* (Arabic, *tajwīd*), which represents the word of Allah descending to man. The *tecvit* conveys timelessness, represented by a nonmetrical flowing rhythm; and an emotion that the muezzins characterize as *hüzn* 'sadness', representing Allah's compassion for mankind. The *zikr*, by contrast, is mankind's response to Allah: mankind seeks to imitate the worship of the angels by continually affirming the existence of Allah both through words and through circumambulation of his throne (*'ars*).

In the terrestial *zikr*, time is continually marked by the dervishes' breathing and chanting, which establishes a sense of urgency that is not present in the *tecvit*. While the *tecvit* is a single unique voice addressing mankind, the *zikr* (as noted above) is a collective response by mankind to Allah. Man must listen to the address of Allah through the recitation of the Qur'ān, but his duty in the *zikr* is to affirm the life of Allah by affirming the life that Allah has granted to man. In the *zikr*, the connection between life and time is continually emphasized by changes of tempo, both acceleration and deceleration. The *zikr* must always give the impression of organic life—moving, flowing, and even reversing itself. Although the *ilāhīler* of some parts of the *zikr* may have certain fixed sequences, the ideal is never cyclical (as it is in the *fasıl* or *ayīn*). Rather, the *zākirbaşı* and the shaykh continually alter the order and constitution of the particular hymns in accordance with their perception of the spiritual moment (*ān*).

The Turkish *zikr* represents a fusion of several disparate musical principles. The nonmetrical, performance-generated (improvised) *kaside* chanting by the muezzin, essentially identical to styles used in the mosque, was integrated into a metrical context in which sound was divided into three timbral registers. The uppermost register was the muezzin's high-pitched solo voice. The middle register was occupied by the small group of specialists, the *zākirler*, who sang the metrical hymns (*ilāhīler*). The lowest register was occupied by the mass of dervishes, who chanted and breathed the divine Names. The metrical basis of this chant might be reinforced by percussion, usually large frame drums (*daire*, *bendir*) but also kettledrums (*küdūm*) and cymbals (*halīle*).

In other contexts, the singing of the *kaside* shared much of the purely monophonic aesthetic of the Qur'ānic *tecvit*; but in the *zikr*, elements of polyphony permeated every musical moment. This polyphony, while rudimentary—it was based mainly on octaves—was so pervasive that the music of the *zikr* must be placed in a different category from other genres of Turkish urban music, which insisted on strict monody. For example, the *kelīme-i tevhīd zikri* emphasized successively higher tonal centers within the *makam segāh*, while the chanting of the *shahāda* by the dervishes reinforced each tonal center. The chanting of *Hū* 'It is he' by the dervishes during some of the opening *usūl ilāhīler* also reinforced the shifting tonal centers of the hymns. The *kıyāmi zikri* opens with an improvised *kaside* sung over a low-pitched, growling repitition of the name of Allah without any metrical structure. The closing of the *zikr* always features a three-tiered performance of a blessing on the Prophet in which the dervishes chant the name *Hū* in a low pitch, the *zākirler* sing this blessing to the tune of a metrical *ilāhī* in the *sabā makam* one octave higher, and then the muezzin sings a metrically free version of the prayer two octaves above the continued chanting of *Hū*.

The *zākirler* always perform the *ilāhīler* in a relatively low pitch (often near middle A), never near the pitch used for secular sung genres or even the *cumhur* and *tevşīh ilāhīler*, performed by groups. On the one hand, this pitch allows the muezzins to reach the octave above them comfortably; on the other hand, it connects the *zākir* style with the *nefes* hymns sung by the Alevīye, who prefer a similar pitch. This low pitching of the Alevī hymns contrasts with the singing of rural Sunni *aşıklar*, as well as with the hymns (*kalām*) of the Iranian Kurdish Ahl-e Haqq, whose music and ceremony are otherwise closely related to those of the Alevīye. It would seem that this low pitch of the hymns of the *zikr* reflects a Turkic concept of sacred and shamanistic musical expression. This impression is confirmed by the traditions of certain urban *tekkeler* where the singing of the *kelīme-i tevhīd zikri* is dominated by the *shahāda* singing of the *zākirler*, rather than by the improvised singing of the muezzin. The *zākirler* in these traditions strive to emit a low growling tone that borders on the overtone singing of Turkic Central Asia and Mongolia.

THE *ILĀHĪ* HYMN

The term *ilāhī* 'divine' describes a genre, the hymn, that is both musical and literary—aspects that are not always coterminous. The divine nature of the work sometimes refers to the text and sometimes to the music; this ambiguity has probably encouraged loose usage of the word both in the present day and in the past.

The poetic *ilāhī*

Most *ilāhīler* for the *zikr* ceremony and for the birthday of the Prophet (*mevlīd-i şerīf*) are in the Turkish language. However, the *zikr ilāhī* called *şuğul*, which imitate the dervish hymns of Syrian branches of the Sunni *tarikatlar*, are always in Arabic. They became popular in Turkey only after the second half of the nineteenth century. In addition, the *ilāhīler* sung during Ramadan and in the months of Muharrem and Zilhicce (Dhu al-Ḥijja) are often in Arabic.

Although the poems of Yunus Emre (1240–1322?) and his imitators continued to be used in the *zikr* (as well as in the Bektaşī and Alevī *āyīn-i cem*) throughout the Ottoman period, the *ilāhī* as such is basically a product of this later era. However, a forerunner of the *ilāhī* as we know it from Ottoman times may be found in the early fifteenth century, in the poetry of Hacı Bayram Veli (d. 1429) and his student Eşrefoğlu Rumī (d. 1469); and the *ilāhī* style was essentially formed by the first half of the sixteenth century, as exemplified in the poetry of Ibrahim Gülşenī (d. 1533), his son Gülşenīzade Hayalī (d. 1569), Muslihiddin Merkez (d. 1551), and Muhiddin Uftade (d. 1580), among others (Ergun 1943). This mature *ilāhī* style formed the poetic basis for the *zikr* ceremony among all the Sunni *tarikatlar* until the twentieth century.

After the middle of the sixteenth century, the *ilāhī* appears to have been a remarkably stable poetic quasi genre, in which the principal developments were a progressive limitation of language and literary expression and a corresponding growth of the formulaic. This poetry became increasingly identified with the *tarikat* shaykhs, or "shaykh poets." After the early fifteenth century, there does not seem to have been a single recognized Sufi poet in Turkey who was not affiliated with a *tarikat* organization, and usually the poet was part of its leadership. Although some of the early Ottoman sultans (such as Mehmed the Conqueror) had been hostile toward most Sufi leaders (Martin 1972:280–281), the Ottoman state frequently acted as a patron of the more orthodox *tarikatlar*. From about 1450 until 1620, the principal recipients of imperial favor were the members of the Sufi complex represented by the Halvetīye, Gülşenīye, and Celvetīye. This relationship was especially strong during the reigns of sultans "Sufi" or "Veli" Beyāzid II (1481–1511), Süleymān Kanūnī "The Magnificent" (1525–1566), Mehmed III (1595–1603), and Ahmed I (1603–1617). Throughout this period, and well into the eighteenth century, *ilāhī* poems constituted the principal poetic creations of these *tarikatlar* and formed part of the *zikr* liturgy or the genres *na'at* and *tevşīh*, which were sung at the *mevlīd-i şerīf* 'birthday of the Prophet' and on other occasions. The work of these shaykh poets was often introduced into the musical liturgy during their own lifetime. The poetry of the *divān* of a notable mystic and poet such as Niyāzī-i Misrī (d. 1694) had currency outside the liturgy as well, but the *ilāhī* poems of many shaykh poets lived on principally within the *zikr*. To the Ottomans, the mystical poem became increasingly identified with the Sufi shaykh poem, which might have a primary or secondary liturgical or paraliturgical function.

The musical *ilāhī*

As a musical term, *ilāhī* comprises two broad categories. In the first category are the *ilāhīler* that were sung while the motions of the *zikr* were being performed: *zikr-ilāhīler* (but in Turkish, no special term exists for them). In the second category are the *ilāhīler* sung for all other occasions, including other sections of the *zikr* ceremony. Both of these subgenres had fixed rhythmic cycles (*usūl*). Other dervish musical genres did not use these rhythmic cycles and were not called *ilāhī*, although their texts might be considered *ilāhī*.

Zikr-ilāhīler

Zikr-ilāhīler almost always have a simple binary rhythmic pattern. Only very rarely were pieces in this first category composed in a long rhymthic cycle, such as *hafif* or *muhammes* (in thirty-two beats). More complex *usūller*, such as *çember*, *havi*, *darbeyn*, and *zincir*, common in courtly music, were not used in the *zikr-ilāhīler*, because, unlike *muhmammes* and *hafif*, they were not divided symmetrically. The most common *usūl* for the *zikr-ilāhīler* was the simplest in Ottoman music. In treatises, it is named *sofiyān* 'the Sufis' (figure 1), attesting to an old association with the *zikr* or the medieval *semā*. The other rhythm common in the *zikr* is called *düyek* 'two-one' (a Persian term; figure 2). Unlike *sofiyān*, which was seldom used in courtly music, *düyek* was widely used from the seventeenth to the mid-eighteenth century in the courtly instrumental *peşrev* and in a counterpart, the *peşrev* of the janissary band, the *mehter*.

FIGURE 1 Phrasing of *sofiyān*.

FIGURE 2 Phrasing of *düyek*.

The *zikr-ilāhīler* constitute one of the oldest and most distinctive functioning repertoires in Turkish music. Alongside new or even contemporary compositions, the *zikr* repertoire includes dozens (perhaps hundreds) of *ilāhī* melodies that have been performed continuously in various *tekkeler* since the late seventeenth or early eighteenth century. A still earlier tradition, documented in the mid-seventeenth century in the notated collection of Ali Ufkī Bey, did not survive into the twentieth century. Many current *tarikatlar* in Turkey have initiatory *silsile* that began in the seventeenth or early eighteenth centuries, and many of the *ilāhīler* sung in their *zikrler* evidently represent a continuous tradition dating from that period. Hymns ascribed to dervish composers such as Aziz Mahmūd Hüdāyī (1543–1628), Ali Şīr-u Gani (1635–1714), Hafiz Post (1630–1694), and Cihangirli Ahmed, as well as many anonymous compositions, use *makam* and compositional structure in archaic or idiosyncratic ways. After the latter eighteenth century, *ilāhī* texts were usually set to tunes closely resembling either *türküler* or *şarkılar*, but the *ilāhīler* of the seventeenth and eighteenth centuries cannot be analyzed according to the norms of these later secular genres.

Tevşīh ilāhīsi and *cumhur ilāhīsi*

The second broad category of *ilāhīler* consists of those that are sung apart from the movements of the *zikr*—in other words, those that are not *zikr ilāhīler*. They were referred to by two terms: *tevşīh* and *cumhur*, that is, *tevşīh ilāhīsi* and *cumhur ilāhīsi*. *Tevşīh* designated the panegyrics sung on the *mevlīd-i şerīf* 'ornamentation', which became a musical term apparently as early as the sixteenth century. *Cumhur ilāhīsi* was a more general term that included both the *tevşīh* and hymns for other occasions or hymns with other themes.

Cumhur, from the Arabic word for crowd or mass, was the closest Ottoman equivalent to a chorus, a concept otherwise alien to Ottoman musical practice. In the mosque, *cumhur* referred to a small group of muezzins chanting hymns in unison; in the *tekke*, it denoted the impromptu "chorus" of the entire chain (*halka*) of dervishes in the *zikr*. Whereas the *zikr ilāhīler* were rhythmically and melodically simple, the *cumhur ilāhīler* were as sophisticated as courtly vocal compositions and were generally composed in the complex *evsat usūl* (twenty-six beats) or in the asymmetrical *devr-i hindī* (seven beats). The *cumhur ilāhīler* were still widely sung during the early twentieth century; today, however, they are no longer part of any living tradition but are known mainly by professional musicians who have learned them from notation. Since the early 1980s there has been a movement to popularize these hymns by performing them on television and radio during Ramadan and occasionally at other times of the year, and it is probable that they will regain some of the currency that they lost after 1925.

NONMETRICAL COMPOSED GENRES

During Ramadan, following the *terāvīh* service, one or more muezzins would ascend the minaret and sing a prayer praising and pleading with Allah. The text was called *munacāt* or *temcīd munacati*—the *mināre üzre temcīdāt* of Daī's poem. The *temcīd* was sung solo with the chorus of muezzins entering at certain points. The *na'at* that followed the *temcīd* was always sung as a solo.

What seems to be the only authentic transcription of a *temcīd munacāti* and its *na'at* were made by Abdülkadir Töre (1873–1946). The transcription shows this *temcīd* to be a precomposed piece with no *usūl*. Töre's student Ekrem Karadeniz linked the *temcīd* stylistically with the *durak*, a distinctively *tekke* musical form. Thus, unlike the *tesbīh ilāhīsi*, which appears to have been a feature of the orthodox Ramadan liturgy, the *temcīd munacāti*, the *na'at*, and the unique *mir'acīye* all belong to a separate musical genre that includes, and possibly originated with, the *durak*.

While the *temcīd* and *na'at* have become almost completely extinct, the *durak* still seems to be a step away from oblivion. The sources list more than a hundred *duraklar* in a continuous tradition from the seventeenth until the late nineteenth century, but fewer than a dozen *duraklar* are sung today, and there are few notated sources for the *durak*. The *duraklar* have no *usūl* (rhythmic cycle); nor do they use the rhythmic techniques of Turkish Qur'ānic chant, the secular *gazel*, or the *ezan* (call to prayer)—instead, they favor a leisurely rubato performance style. The *duraklar* are completely precomposed, allowing for virtually no improvisation. Although further analysis is needed, they seem to have an old and close relationship to certain chants of the Greek Orthodox Church. Also, the *durak* also seems to have formed the basis for much of the music of the Sephardic synagogues in Istanbul and other major cities of the Ottoman Empire. Thus a better musicological understanding of the nature of the *durak* form would clarify certain highly significant cultural processes affecting the three major religious groups of Ottoman Turkey: the Mevlevīye, the other Sunni *tarikatlar*, and the Bektaşīye.

The liturgical role of the *durak* is also significant. The chanting of the *durak* after the *kelime-i tevhīd zikri* and before the commencement of the circular standing *zikr* is a period of total silence and meditation—the name *durak* means stopping point. The *durak* invariably uses texts in the Turkish language, generally chosen from the more mystical *gazeller* of Halvetī shaykhs. Purely pious texts were sometimes also used. In the course of the eighteenth century, the *duraklar* became increasingly accepted in mosques outside the *tekkeler*. During the nineteenth century, they were performed by one or more singers before the Friday communal prayer (*cumā namazı*) in mosques that possessed a *vakf* 'pious endowment'.

At least once, the principles of the *durak* were applied to create a continuous work of major dimensions, the *mir'acīye* of Kutb-u Nay Osman Dede (1652–1730). Osman Dede was a significant composer of courtly instrumental music and of four Mevlevī *āyīn* and the inventor of a system of musical notation. Although he was a Mevlevī dede of the Galata Mevlevīhane, his *mir'acīye* was first performed in the *tekke* of the Halvetī shaykh Nasuhī Efendi (d. 1717). It was preserved in various Halvetī and Kadirī *tekkeler* as well as by the Mevlevīhanes. Once again, Abdülkadir Töre produced the most authoritative transcription, in collaboration with Ismail Hakkı Bey (1866–1927). Osman Dede's masterpiece, rather than constituting a new standard that future musicians might seek to imitate or surpass, was regarded as a supernatural feat and therefore inimitable. The very term *mir'acīye* refers only to his composition. Possibly, the *mir'acīye* was part of a tradition of long compositions for narrative texts of a devotional Sufi nature; if so, it is the sole survivor. The earliest work in this lineage was probably the *Mevlūt* (*Mawlid*) of Süleyman Çelebi (d. 1409). This *mesnevi*, which became immensely popular, seems to have been set to music several times over the centuries. In the first half of the twentieth century, a few individuals still knew two sections of an early composition for the *Mevlūt*; today, however, its melody is improvised, or performance-generated, in a style that emphasizes extensive modulation. Subtle differences in the relationship of poetic meter to musical phrase distinguish the *Mevlūt* from the Sufi *kaside*, which—as a close relative of the secular sung *gazel* (vocal *taksīm*)—does not emphasize these poetic and musical relationships to the same degree. In general, the connection between poetic meter and musical line requires basic research within the subject of nonmetrical Sufi musical genres.

Closely connected to the *durak* was the *na'at*, praise of the Prophet Muhammed. Dozens of *na'at* had been composed, mainly by Halvetī musicians, and were sung by dervish musical specialists known as *na'athān*. Today, however, only a single *na'at* is usually performed, the *rast na'at* by Buhurīzade Mustafa Itrī (d. 1712), a court composer connected with the Mevlevīye. This *na'at* is sung at the beginning of the *āyīn* ceremony, regardless of the *makam* in which the *āyīn* is performed. Unlike the *durak*, which generally had a text in Turkish, the *rast na'at* has a Persian text, written by Cellālüddin Rūmī (1207–1273). The *rast na'at* has a more elaborate structure than any surviving *durak*; there are several modulating sections that explore increasingly higher musical ranges. Although the *rast na'at* is apparently composed in the 18/4 *usūl darb-i türkī*, it is sung today in the rubato style of the *durak*.

Of the nonmetrical Sufi genres, only the improvised *kaside* and the improvised style of Mevlūt singing (and to a lesser extent the *mersīye* sung on Muharrem) are widely performed. There are only a handful of competent performers of the composed nonmetrical genres, such as the *durak*, the *na'at*, the *temcīd*, and the composed *mersīye*. The 1990s saw a revival of performances of the *zikr ilāhī* and even of the more elaborate *tevşīh ilāhī*, but it seems unlikely that the composed nonmetrical dervish genres will return to general use. They call for a high level of stylistic specialization, and the *durakçılar* and *na'athanlar* have no professional successors today. Moreover, the extant repetoire is small, few sound recordings have ever been made, and most of the existing transcriptions are unreliable. The more competent transcriptions could possibly be used to reconstruct these genres. However, during the 1960s and 1970s the poor transcriptions of Dr. Subhi Ezgi (1869–1962) occasionally replaced traditional performance practice; thus the combination of a weak performance tradition and transcriptions based on contradictory musical principles threatens to eradicate the musical substance of these genres in the rare instances when some attempt at preservation and transmission has been attempted.

REFERENCES

Birge, John Kingsley. 1937. *The Bektashi Order of Dervishes*. London: Luzac Oriental.

Borrel, Eugene. 1947. "Les poètes Kizil Bach et leur musique." *Revue des Études Islamiques* 15:157–190.

Ergun, Sadettin Nüzhet. 1943. *Türk musikisi, antolojisi*. 2 vols. Istanbul: Rıza Koşkun Matbaası.

Feldman, Walter. 1992. "Musical Genres and *Zikr* of the Sunni Tarikats of Istanbul." In *The Dervish Lodge: Architecture, Art, and Sufism in Ottoman Turkey*, ed. Raymond Lifchez, 187–202. Berkeley: University of California Press.

———. 1993. "Mysticism, Didacticism, and Authority in the Liturgical Poetry of the Halvetī Dervishes of Istanbul." *Edebiyat* NS 4:243–265.

Hickman, William. 1972. "Eşrefoğlu Rumī: Fifteenth-Century Anatolian Mystic Poet." Ph.D. dissertation, Harvard University.

Karadeniz, Ekrem. 1983. *Türk Musikisinin Nazariye ve Esasları*. Ankara.

Martin, B. G. 1972. "A Short History of the Khalwati Order of Dervishes." In *Scholars, Saints, and Sufis*, ed. Nikki R. Keddie, 275–306. Berkeley: University of California Press.

Ömürlü, Yusuf. 1979–1984. *Türk mūsıkīsi klāsikleri: ilāhīler*. Vols. 1–5. Istanbul: Kubbealt, Neşriyat.

Poché, Christian. 1978. "Zikr and Musicology." *World of Music* 20:59–73.

Yekta, Rauf. 1931. *Ilāhīler: Mevlūt Tevşīhleri*. Istanbul.

———. 1933a. *Her Ayinda Okunmağa Mahsus Ilāhīler*. Istanbul.

———. 1933b. *Bektaşī nefesleri*. Istanbul: Feniks Matbaası.

Music in the Religious Experience of Israeli Jews

Edwin Seroussi

The Role of Jewish Religion in the State of Israel
Music and Jewish Religion
Contexts of Performance of Religious Music in Israel
Religious Popular Music
Religious Music Performers in Israel
Music as a Subject of Religious Thought in Israel

When asked about their Jewish identity, Israeli Jews (there are also Israeli Muslims, Christians, and Druze) usually define themselves as "religious" (*dati* 'orthodox'), "traditional" (*masorti*), or nonreligious or "secular" (*ḥiloni*). These labels express different relations to Jewish religious law, *halakhah*, the legal framework that has maintained the social and cultural identity of Jews in the Diaspora within larger non-Jewish societies for the past two thousand years.

Halakhah is based on the Torah (or Pentateuch, the Five Books of Moses in the Old Testament) and on its oral perusals by rabbis, compiled in the Talmud and in countless rulings stretching for almost two millennia. Allegiance to *halakhah* is reflected in every aspect of the individual's existence, specifically in observing the *mitzvot* 'precepts' of Judaism. A "religious" Israeli punctiliously observes all the *mitzvot*, a "traditional" Israeli observes certain precepts or has respect for the precepts without observing them, and a "secular" Israeli ignores the precepts. This rough division, however, is only a working outline; it does not reflect the variety of approaches to the observance of religious precepts found among Israeli Jews.

Among "religious" Jews, one can distinguish between "Zionist religious" or "national religious" (*dati le'umi*) Israelis, who identify with the State of Israel, and "ultraorthodox" Israelis or "zealots" (*ḥaredi*) who oppose or reject the modern state. Because orthodoxy accounts for an absolute majority of Jewish religiosity in Israel, the impact of the modern religious movements—Conservative and Reform—that predominate in the Jewish community of the United States, the largest one outside Israel, is still extremely limited.

Ethnicity also shapes Jewish identity in Israel. There is a division between Ashkenazi (European) Jews and Sephardi Jews (literally, Spanish Jews, though today the term *Sephardi* means non-Ashkenazi, regardless of bonds to Jews in medieval Spain), and this also reflects differences in approaches to religious observance. The idea of a secular, nonobservant Jew developed within European Jewry since the "Emancipation" period, which started in Germany in approximately the second half of the eighteenth century. Thus the critical rift between religious (orthodox) and secular Jews relates primarily to Ashkenazi experience. The alternatives to orthodoxy that developed since the Emancipation, such as the Reform movement and political Zionism (forging a secular nation-state), took shape primarily among European Jews. The division of orthodox Ashkenazi Jews into *ḥasidim* (followers of a mystical movement that developed in Eastern Europe after the mid-eighteenth century) and *misnagdim* 'the opponents' (representing the opposition to Hasidism) is exclusive to Eastern European Jewry. For the most part, Sephardi Jews remained orthodox (though not as extreme as the Ashkenazi *ḥaredim*) or "traditional," their Zionism being of a more spiritual nature.

This diversity of approaches toward religion in Israel has led to an array of religious musical expression. Here, it is impossible to cover the variety of repertoires, performance practices, aesthetic ideas, and conceptualizations of music in all religious settings. What follows, therefore, is a sketch of salient aspects of religious music in modern Israel.

THE ROLE OF JEWISH RELIGION IN THE STATE OF ISRAEL

Nominally secular, the State of Israel defines itself as Jewish (the precise definition of "Jewish" was left open to interpretation by the founders of the state and is still debated) and recognizes *halakhah* as state law in matters concerning the individual. Moreover, Israel's holidays and symbols are those of the Jewish religious tradition.

The state supports an orthodox religious establishment, the Chief Rabbinate, which provides judiciary and other services to its citizens and also runs the synagogues through local religious councils. Since its inception, the Israeli system of public education has reflected the split between religious and secular Jews by segregating the two groups in different schools. The state supports religious public schools that provide musical socialization (in school prayers) and education. It also channels support to other religious institutions, such as rabbinical academies (*yeshivot*) and, in relation to music, schools of synagogue cantors, discussed below.

The social infrastructure for musical creativity and religious performance in Israel is different from that of Jewish communities in the Diaspora. Religious musical activities in Israel are sponsored by the secular state through the religious branches of governmental agencies. This situation engenders new processes, such as the standardization of religious music and its control by a bureaucracy. The contexts of religious musical performance—above all, the synagogues—also function differently from those in the Diaspora. Finally, new technologies allow for the commodification and dissemination of religious music, intensifying the processes of homogenization that result from a public system of religious education and from the intervention of mass media that are partly controlled by the state.

MUSIC AND JEWISH RELIGION

To understand the particular characteristics of religious music among Jews in Israel, one needs to grasp some essential features of music in Judaism. The musical culture of religious Jews is closely connected to practices and rules established by *halakhah*. Religious rituals and festivals determine the contexts for musical performance. These include the Jewish liturgy or "service": the normative order of prayers performed three times a day, usually but not necessarily at a synagogue, by a quorum (*minyan*) of ten adult males. There are more, and more complex, services on the Sabbath and on holidays than on weekdays. Other religious devotions are held in synagogues or in private homes (for example, the ritual recitation of psalms or the reading of the Zohar, a codex of Jewish mysticism); rites of passage (circumcision, bar mitzvah, marriage) are held in synagogues, party halls, or private homes.

TRACK -11

Three phenomena related to music stand out in orthodox Judaism: (1) exclusion of the female voice; (2) exclusion of musical instruments from the synagogue; and (3) a gap between musical ideology and performance practice. The first two are based on rabbinical rulings: a Talmudic passage concerning the "indecency" of the female voice (*Berakhot* 24a) is the basis for excluding women's singing (Schreiber 1984–1985), and the second ruling symbolizes mourning for the destruction of the Temple in Jerusalem (70 C.E.). Because of these two rulings, unaccompanied male singers dominate the "soundscape" of traditional Judaism.

The third phenomenon implies a constant tension between and actual musical practices in Jewish communities and the opinions of the rabbis concerning the uses, powers, and sources of music. For example, rabbis were frequently consulted about the use of "foreign" music in the liturgy, and a literature developed on this issue (Adler 1975; Cohen 1935). This questioning emerged because the music of the Jewish liturgy is an open system. Although the texts of the liturgy were codified in their present form more than a millennium ago, its musical content is theoretically open to change at each performance. *Change*, in this context, means the possibility of singing liturgical texts with new melodies, either original or adopted from non-Jewish coterritorial cultures.

CONTEXTS OF PERFORMANCE OF RELIGIOUS MUSIC IN ISRAEL

The synagogue

The main location in which religiosity is expressed by music is the synagogue. Synagogues in Israel are supported by the state and by public donations (figure 1). To a large extent, the ethnic background of those who attend a synagogue determines the musical style of its services.

In terms of the members of the public who attend them, there are two main types of synagogues: what some anthropologists call an "ethnic" synagogue (Deshen 1969)—one whose congregation is of relatively uniform ethnic origin—and a synagogue with a congregation of diverse ethnic origins. "Ethnic" synagogues are found, for example, in small "development towns" on the periphery where the majority of the population is North African. In these synagogues, Maghribi or Andalusian styles are heard (Sharvit 1986).

The second type of synagogue, which constitutes the majority, is generically divided into Sephardi and Ashkenazi. *Sephardi* refers to synagogues where the predominant musical style is called "Jerusalem-Sephardi." This style, based on the Arab *maqāmāt* of the Middle Eastern tradition, incorporates old Ottoman Sephardi traditions from Turkey, Greece, and Syria (particularly Aleppo) and melodies adopted from modern Egyptian music (such as songs by the Egyptians Muḥammad ʿAbd al-Wahhāb and Farīd al-Aṭrash). Sephardi cantors, many of whom are now trained in schools for

FIGURE 1 Priestly blessing during a morning service at an Israeli synagogue. Photo courtesy of Varda Polak-Sahm, Jerusalem.

cantors, are expected to command the *maqāmāt* and to be acquainted with new Arabic songs. The Jerusalemite style was adopted by most Oriental Jews (for example, Persian, Kurdish, Iraqi, Bucharan, and Yemenite), and by the Sephardi diaspora after World War II by way of wandering cantors and, more recently, cassettes and CDs.

The music of the Ashkenazi Israeli synagogue is loosely based on a style known as "Jerusalem-Lithuanian," an extension of the mainstream style of *ḥazanut* 'cantorial art' of the Eastern European Jews. An alternative approach to this traditional musical style is that of synagogues associated with religious Zionists under the influence of their Bnei Akiva youth movement. This approach advocates the participation of the congregation in the services at the expense of the individualistic cantorial art (Schleifer 1995). These services include metric melodies rather than solo recitations in flexible rhythm. The melodies come from secular Israeli folk songs or from neo-Hasidic tunes, such as those by the "singing rabbi" Shelomo Carlebach.

Besides the liturgy, there are nonliturgical religious gatherings at which the music is extremely rich. Examples are the *baḳashot* of Sephardi Jews and the *tish* of Hasidic courts. *Bakashot* are night vigils held on Saturdays during the winter. These gatherings include study, preaching, and the singing of religious poetry (*piyyutim*). Two traditions of *bakashot* are maintained today: Moroccan and "Jerusalemite." The first is based on the Andalusian music of Morocco (Seroussi 1986). The second, originating in Aleppo (Katz 1968), leans toward the nineteenth-century Middle Eastern Arabic *muwashshaḥ*, Turkish and European military music, melodies of Judeo-Spanish songs, and modern Arab music (usually Egyptian).

The Hasidic *tish* is a continuation of the Eastern European tradition of gathering for a ritual meal on the Sabbath, holidays, and other anniversaries at the court of the community's spiritual leader (*rebbe*). The *ḥasidim* aspire to share the mystical inspiration of their leader by joining him in (sometimes ecstatic) singing and dancing. The repertoire of vocal songs (*nigunim*) for these occasions varies according to the court (Hajdu and Mazor 1971).

The wedding hall

Weddings are a main venue for musical expression in a religious context. In Israel, weddings take place in rented halls and are administered by the Rabbinate. A "secular" weddings opens with the religious ceremony, in which a rabbi or an additional cantor recites the normative blessings. The wedding then proceeds as a dinner party accompanied by a live rock band or by recorded music to which the guests dance. The repertoire includes mainstream national and international pop music. However, some families (usually Sephardi and Oriental) ask performers or disk jockeys to play "ethnic" music. As these requests have increased, rock bands specializing in updated performances of "ethnic" songs (for example, in Moroccan Judeo-Arabic) have emerged.

In "national religious" families, weddings include bands that specialize in neo-Hasidic songs, a style of pop based on the Hasidic *nigun* but influenced by rock or other secular pop styles. Sometimes these weddings feature a traditional klezmer band. Hasidic weddings, on the other hand, feature mostly klezmer bands and vocal *nigunim*. Hasidic weddings also feature a *badḥan* 'jester,' who entertains the audience with improvised rhymes intermingled with songs. At all religious weddings, men and women dance in separate sections of the hall.

It is customary among Sephardi and Oriental Jews to hold a *henna* party a few days before a wedding. The revival of this custom among second- and third-generation Sephardi Jews is a sign of a return to "roots." The need for "authentic" music at henna parties has created a space for the performance of songs specifically related to this event.

Pilgrimages to the tombs of saintly figures

The anniversary of the death of a saintly person is commemorated with a special event that includes prayers, study sessions, a meal, and the singing of sacred poetry. The

FIGURE 2 Ḥasid dancing with child during a hair-cutting ceremony for three-year-olds outside the tomb of Rabbi Simeon bar Yoḥai at his *hilulah* during the festival of Lag ba-'Omer, Meron, Upper Galilee, Israel, 1975. Photo courtesy of Yaakov Mazor, National Sound Archives, Jewish National and University Library, Jerusalem.

Sephardi Jews refer to such celebrations as *hilulot* (singular, *hilulah*). The Hasidic Jews are also fond of *hilulot* because they regard their historical religious leaders (*rebbes*) as saintly (figure 2).

The largest *hilulah* (and the only one shared by Sephardi and Hasidic Jews) is that of Rabbi Simeon bar Yoḥai, to whom folk tradition attributes the codex of Jewish mysticism, the *Zohar*. This *hilulah* takes place on Lag ba-'Omer (the thirty-third day after Passover) at the site of Rabbi Simeon's tomb on Mount Meron in Upper Galilee; it lasts a week and involves setting up a tent city around the tomb, including coffeehouses where live music, religious and secular, is heard (figure 3). On the night of the *hilulah* itself, bonfires are lit around which ecstatic Hasidic vocal music and dances are performed. Later in the evening, klezmer music and Hasidic dances are performed in the courtyard surrounding the tomb. The klezmer repertoire for this occasion is unique; it includes tunes known as *nigunei Meron*, inspired by Arab, Turkish, Greek, and Druze tunes that reflect the interaction between Ashkenazi Jews and non-Jews in Galilee since the nineteenth century.

Another major *hilulah*, developed in Israel in the 1990s, is that of Rabbi Yisrael Abuḥatzira (or Abuhasera), known as Baba Sali. His tomb in the southern city of Netivot became a major site of pilgrimage and musical performances that include songs composed in his honor, some in the form of the Moroccan *qaṣīda* (figure 4).

Other religious festivals

For Moroccan Jews, the arrival of spring, which coincides with Passover, is the focus of a festival called the Mimuna. It starts at the outset of the seventh day of Passover and is celebrated in two settings: receptions for neighbors at people's homes during the evening, and outdoor festivals in public parks on the following day. The Mimuna has become a national holiday in Israel and is a major locus for staged traditional music and dance (figure 5). Other ethnic groups in Israel, such as Kurdish and Persian Jews, have similar festivals at the end of the summer, during Sukkot (Feast of the Tabernacles), in order not to conflict with the Mimuna.

The concert hall

Concert performances of composed religious music outside the synagogue developed in Eastern Europe in the late nineteenth century and continue in Israel today. This music, called *ḥazanut,* is composed by professionals and arranged with instrumental

FIGURE 3 Moroccan Jews celebrating in an improvised coffee shop in a tent outside the tomb of Rabbi Simeon bar Yoḥai at his *hilulah*, 1975. Photo courtesy of National Sound Archives, Jewish National and University Library, Jerusalem.

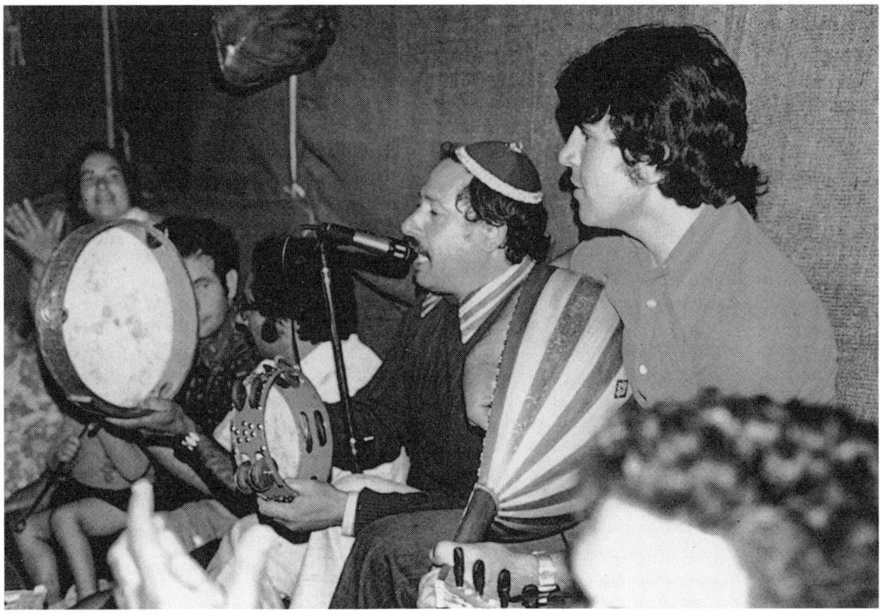

FIGURE 4 *Mizraḥi* women singing next to the tomb of Baba Sali during his *hilulah*, Netivot, Israel. Photo courtesy of Varda Polak-Sahm, Jerusalem.

accompaniment, sometimes by a symphony orchestra. *Ḥazanut* has all the social features of Western art music, such as concert series, advertisements in the mass media, commercial recordings, and radio and television broadcasts. Israeli radio offers programs of *ḥazanut* that include requests from listeners.

Influenced by the Ashkenazi, Sephardi Jews organize their own *ḥazanut* concerts, in which the Jerusalem-Sephardi style predominates. Singers are accompanied by small to medium-sized ensembles that combine Arab instruments (*ʿūd*, *nāy*, violin, *qānūn*, and *darabukka*) with Western European instruments (for example, the flute, double bass, and synthesizer). The Israeli Andalusian Orchestra, founded in 1994, performs Moroccan Jewish religious poetry.

RELIGIOUS POPULAR MUSIC

Apart from the traditional contexts of musical performance discussed here, Israel's local music industry has produced popular music on religious themes. This development was predictable, because the religious segment of Israeli society demanded its own popular music. Mainly connected to the movement of return (*teshuvah*) to traditional Jewish observance in the 1970s and to the influence of the American-born rabbi Shelomo Carlebach (who introduced a folklike style that included acoustic and electric guitars), religious popular music can be traced back to the 1950s, when artists such as the Moroccan-born Joe Amar started to release commercial records including arrangements of religious songs.

A component in the development of religious popular music was the festival of religious songs. The idea of competitive festivals was introduced into Israeli popular music in 1960, when the Israeli Song Festival was first produced by the Israel Broadcasting Authority. The religious song festival modeled after it allowed religious and nonreligious composers to write songs with religious content. Some of the festival songs are performed at synagogue services, weddings, and other religious events.

A style of popular music called *muzika mizraḥit* ("Oriental music"), which has developed since the 1970s (Halper, Seroussi, and Squires-Kidron 1989; Horowitz 1994), includes songs with religious content. Several *mizraḥi* singers returned to religious observance and turned their popular hits (many based on Greek or Turkish songs) into religious songs by replacing the original text with verses from the Bible or other scriptures.

RELIGIOUS MUSIC PERFORMERS IN ISRAEL

Synagogue cantors

FIGURE 5 *Mizraḥi* women singing at the Mimuna, Jerusalem, Israel. Photo courtesy of National Sound Archives, Jewish National and University Library, Jerusalem.

The main musician in the synagogue is the cantor (Slobin 1989). In Israel, the position of cantor is generally voluntary (that is, unpaid), for it is considered an honor to lead the congregation in prayer. However, cantors receive donations from members of their synagogue, particularly during the holiday season, and some do receive a salary.

Until the beginning of the twentieth century, cantors emerged from a traditional social milieu, learning the repertoire through oral tradition. Because it is incumbent on everyone to attend a synagogue regularly, most people learn the liturgical repertoire by heart. Those who advance to the post of cantor need a good voice and a good memory and are required to be knowledgeable in the prayers, "fearful of God" (that is, observant of the religious precepts), and mature (according to tradition, a cantor should be a married man).

The idea of training cantors and synagogue choirs in formal institutions developed in the early twentieth century, under European influence. The Institute Shirat Israel, established in Jerusalem by Zalman Rivlin and Abraham Zvi Idelsohn around 1910, was an early attempt at formal musical education (Bayer 1986). However, Shirat Israel was short-lived, and only since the 1970s have schools of cantors become firmly established, in Tel Aviv for Ashkenazi cantors and in Jerusalem, Tel Aviv, Bat-Yam, and elsewhere for Sephardi cantors. These schools notwithstanding, most cantors are still trained in the traditional way.

Synagogue choirs

Choirs have not made an inroad into Israeli synagogues. Despite efforts by German immigrants who introduced their choral tradition to synagogues in Haifa in the 1930s, and by Sephardi musicians such as Rahamim Amar (in Sephardi synagogues the choir sang in unison), few synagogues employ a trained choir. This lack of choral music can be traced to the fact that the orthodox establishment identified choral music with nonorthodox synagogues, and it has led to a lack of native choral repertoire for the synagogue in Israel (unlike Europe or North America).

Popular religious musicians

Some popular religious artists started their careers as synagogue cantors. Of these, some, such as the Sephardi Uri Shevah and the Ashkenazi Dudu Fischer, remained active in both contexts; others abandoned religious observance and began to sing popular secular music—these included some Yemenite performers of *mizraḥi* popular music. Some singers have taken the opposite route: after being successful as secular musicians, they "returned in repentance" to religious popular music. Among orthodox Ashkenazi Jews, stars of religious popular music, such as Abraham Fried and Mordecai ben David, are not unique to Israel but are part of an international circuit that includes the orthodox communities of North America and Western Europe.

MUSIC AS A SUBJECT OF RELIGIOUS THOUGHT IN ISRAEL

Whenever orthodox Jews have doubts about the uses or the content of music in traditional settings such as a synagogue or a wedding, they refer to their rabbi. In Israel, observant Jews continue to rely on rabbinical opinions (called *responsa* 'answers' to queries from the public) concerning music.

Some relatively recent rabbinical opinions on music have affected Jews in Israel. One example is a ban on instrumental music at Ashkenazi weddings in Jerusalem (although drums accompanying singers are allowed). This ruling should be understood against an Eastern European background in which instrumental music was an essential element of a wedding, stemming from a duty to "rejoice the groom and the bride." The ban, enacted in the second half of the nineteenth century, is attributed to Rabbi Meir Auerbach (1805–1868) of the Old City of Jerusalem, who evidently imposed it in the aftermath of a cholera epidemic that ravaged Jerusalem in 1865 and was interpreted as a punishment for laxity in religious piety. It is also based on a prohibition against instrumental music (noted above) as a symbol of mourning for the destruction of the Temple, and it was enforced by Rabbi Joseph Hayyim Sonnenfeld, a leader of the Ashkenazi community of Jerusalem, at the beginning of the twentieth century. Rabbi Sonnenfeld argued that the destroyed Temple lies before the eyes of the people of Jerusalem, and he threatened the noncompliant with divine punishment. The ban is still observed by ultraorthodox Ashkenazi communities, despite a dissenting opinion that it was intended only for the Old City, the area close to Temple Mount—not for neighborhoods outside the city walls, which constitute the vast majority of the modern city. In practice, the prohibition is circumvented by a style of performance called "mouth music," a vocal imitation of klezmer music; and there is debate as to whether the ban applies to recorded music (Kahn 1986–1989, 10:37–40). The ban is not observed by Sephardi rabbis.

A second influential rabbinical ruling concerning music was that of Rabbi Ovadia Yosef, a spiritual (and political) leader of the Sephardi Jews at the end of the twentieth century and the beginning the twenty-first who is of Iraqi descent and is fond of Arab music. When asked about the use by Sephardi cantors of melodies from popular Arab songs (and about other musical matters), he has decided leniently, following a chain of rulings by his Sephardi predecessors. His opinions, published in his collection of *responsa* called *Yabi'a omer* (Yosef 1954–1955), have affected music in Sephardi synagogues in Israel. He has approved the use of the *maqām* and melodies of mainstream Arabic popular songs, provided that they are set to sacred texts in Hebrew and are performed in religious contexts where men and women are properly separated.

REFERENCES

Adler, Israel. 1975. *Hebrew Writings Concerning Music in Manuscripts and Printed Books from Geonic Times up to 1800*. Munich: G. Henle. RISM B IX[2].

———. 1982. "Problems in the Study of Jewish Music." In *Proceedings of the World Congress on Jewish Music, Jerusalem 1978*, ed. Judith Cohen, 15–26. Tel Aviv: Institute for the Translation of Hebrew Literature.

Bayer, Bathja. 1986. "The Announcement of the Institute of Jewish Music in Jerusalem by A. Z. Idelsohn and S. Z. Rivlin in 1910." *Yuval* 5:24–35.

Ben-Ami, Issachar. 1998. *Saint Veneration among the Jews in Morocco*. Detroit, Mich.: Wayne State University Press.

Ben Rafael, E., and S. Sharot. 1991. *Ethnicity, Religion, and Class in Israeli Society*. Cambridge and New York: Cambridge University Press.

Cohen, Boaz. 1935. "The Responsum of Maimonides Concerning Music." *Jewish Music Journal* 2(2):1–7.

Deshen, Shlomo. 1969. "Beit hakeneset ha'adati: Dfus shinnui dati be-Yisra'el" (The Ethnic Synagogue: A Pattern of Religious Change in Israel). In *Mizug Galuyot: Yemei ciyun bāuniversita hā'ivrit be-yerushalayim* (The Integration of Immigrants from Different Countries of Origin in Israel). Symposium, Hebrew University, 25–26 October 1966. Jerusalem: Magnes Press, Hebrew University.

Deshen, Shlomo, and Moshe Shokeid. 1984. "Cultural Ethnicity in Israel: The Case of Middle Eastern Jews' Religiosity." *AJS Review* 9(2):247–271.

Hajdu, Andre. 1971. "Le nigun Meron." *Yuval: Studies of the Jewish Music Research Center* 2:73–114.

Hajdu, Andre, and Yaacov Mazor. 1971. "Hasidim: The Musical Tradition of the Hasidism." *Encyclopedia Judaica* 7:1421–1432. Jerusalem: Encyclopedia Judaica; New York: Macmillan.

Halper, Jeff, Edwin Seroussi, and Pamela Squires-Kidron. 1989. "Musica Mizrahit: Ethnicity and Class Culture in Israel." *Popular Music* 8:131–142.

Horowitz, Amy. 1994. "Israeli Mediterranean Music: Cultural Boundaries and Disputed Territories." Ph.D. dissertation, University of Pennsylvania.

Kahn, Aharon. 1986–1989. "Music in Halakhic Perspective." *Journal of Jewish Music and Liturgy* 9:55–72, 10:32–49, 11:65–75.

Katz, Ruth. 1968. "The Singing of *Baqqashot* by Aleppo Jews." *Acta Musicologica* 40:65–85.

Kedem, Peri. 1991. "Dimensions of Jewish Religiosity." In *Tradition, Innovation, Conflict: Jewishness and Judaism in Contemporary Israel*, ed. Z. Sobel and B. Beit-Hallahmi, 251–272. Albany: State University of New York Press.

Mazor, Y., ed. 1998. *The Klezmer Tradition in the Land of Israel*. Anthology of Music Traditions in Israel, AMTI CD 9802. Jerusalem: Jewish Music Research Center. Compact disk.

Schleifer, Eliyahu. 1995. "Current Trends of Liturgical Music in the Ashkenazi Liturgy." In *The World of Music*, Vol. 37(1), *Jewish Musical Culture—Past and Present*, ed. Uri Sharvit, 59–72. Basel, Kassel: Bärenreiter.

Schreiber, Baruch David. 1984–1985. "The Woman's Voice in the Synagogue." *Journal of Jewish Music and Liturgy* 7:27–32.

Seroussi, Edwin. 1986. "Politics, Ethnic Identity, and Music in the Singing of *Bakkashot* among Moroccan Jews in Israel." *Asian Music* 17(2):32–45.

Sharvit, Uri. 1986. "Diversity within Unity: Stylistic Change and Ethnic Continuity in Israeli Religious Music." *Asian Music* 17(2):126--146.

Shiloah, Amnon, ed. 1997. "The Performance of Jewish and Arabic Music in Israel." In *Musical Performance*, Vol. 1. Amsterdam: Harwood Academic.

Slobin, Mark. 1989. *Chosen Voices: The Story of the American Cantorate*. Urbana: University of Illinois Press.

Yosef, Ovadia. 1954–1955. *Sefer she'elot u-teshuvot yabi'a omer*, Vol. 1. Jerusalem.

Maronite Music

Louis Hage

The Maronite church is an Eastern Antiochene church that uses the Syriac language. It owes its name to a saint of the fourteenth century C.E. called Maron, who lived in the north of Syria. After his death in about 410, his tomb became an important place of pilgrimage, and his followers immediately started to build the famous Monastery of Saint Maron there. The monastery was a huge building that housed eight hundred monks; in addition, three hundred hermits lived beyond the walls. It was in this monastery that the Maronite church was born and achieved great religious and social importance.

The Council of Ephesus in 431 condemned the Nestorian heresy, that is, the belief that Christ had two distinct natures and persons, one human and one divine. The Council of Chalcedon in 451 condemned the opposite Monophysite teaching that Christ had a single nature, both human and divine. Thus the great Church of Antioch was divided into three groups: the Nestorians, the Monophysites, and the Chalcedonians. The Maronites belong to the last group: the monks of the Monastery of Saint Maron were zealous defenders of the Chalcedonian Council, and as such they attracted many people who gradually came to be called Maronites.

By the seventh century, there was already a strong community surrounding the Monastery of Saint Maron. The monastery existed within a Christian world of four great patriarchates: Alexandria [see THE COPTIC ORTHODOX CHURCH AND ITS MUSIC], Antioch [see SYRIAC RELIGIOUS MUSIC], Byzantium, and Rome. In the seventh century, just after Syria had been conquered by the Arabs, the Patriarchal See of Antioch was left vacant for many decades. During this difficult, troubled period of vacancy, the Monastery of Saint Maron, which had long had jurisdiction over the surrounding population as well as over affiliated convents, became a well-consolidated church with a patriarch and bishops.

Between the seventh and tenth centuries, because of persecutions and religious conflicts in the Middle East, the Maronites fled to the high mountains in northern Lebanon. Here they formed a distinct ethnoreligious community in which secular and clerical power were combined.

Today, the Maronite church embraces more than four million people, the largest number of them in Lebanon, where the church constitutes the oldest ethnoreligious section of the population. There are other Maronite communities overseas, particularly in North and South America and in Australia. The Maronite church, which is in communion with the Roman Catholic church, is presided over by the patriarch and has about thirty bishops. Its main dioceses are in Lebanon, Syria, Cyprus, Egypt, Australia, Canada, Brazil, Argentina, Europe, and the United States.

Until the seventeenth century, the liturgical language of the Maronite church was uniformly Syriac, a language similar to that spoken by Jesus. After the seventeenth century, some of the chants began to be translated into Arabic.

This short account of the origins of the Maronite church is necessary for an understanding of two important characteristics of traditional Maronite music. First, since the Maronite church is a branch of the Syrian church of Antioch, its liturgy and chant are Syro-Antiochene and Semitic. Although it is true that some aspects of the Maronite liturgy—for example, church ornaments and the administration of the sacraments—were influenced at certain times by the Latin liturgy, the traditional Maronite chant bears little resemblance to Gregorian chant or to any Western music. There is no trace of Western art in the composition or performance of Maronite chant earlier than the twentieth century. As for canticles imported from either the East or the West, they are recent additions to the Maronite rite; they form a separate category that has had no influence on the traditional chant; and they are not considered part of the Maronite liturgical repertoire.

Second, the Maronite liturgy has been, since its origin, a monastic liturgy; and this monastic context marked the traditional chant, rendering it simple and austere in character. Even the patriarch and bishops were chosen from among the monks and used to continue to live as monks, and the patriarchal residence was and still is a monastery. The laity, too, used to follow several monastic practices related to fasting and attendance at liturgical offices.

THE SYRO-ANTIOCHENE RITES

The divisions that took place during the fifth century led, little by little, to the development of three independent rites:

1. *Western Syro-Antiochene rite* of the Syro-Orthodox and Syro-Orthodox Malankar Church of India; and of the the Syro-Catholic church (united with the Roman See since the eighteenth century) and Syro-Catholic Malankar church in India.
2. *Western Syro-Antiochene rite* of the Maronite church (Catholic).
3. *Eastern Syro-Antiochene rite* of the Assyrian church, the Chaldean church (united with the Roman See since the seventeenth century), and the Syro-Malabar Church of India.

Nowadays, to understand the musical affinities between the repertoires of the different branches of the Syro-Antiochene church, one must first distinguish the elements that constitute the repertoire of each church. Ignoring these distinctions often leads to error, since the groups within each repertoire are not of the same age, origin, or nature.

SYRIAC POETRY

The Syriac poetry found in liturgical books is for the most part written in strophes, or verses. Strophic poetry in Syriac involves constructing identical, or very similar, strophes, taking into consideration two main complementary elements: a model strophe and a poetic meter.

The model strophe, called *rish qolō* in Syriac, provides the basis for the other strophes and indicates, first, the versification or poetic structure of the strophes and, second, a melody linked to the model. It can be compared to the Byzantine *hirmos* and the Arabic *laḥn*. A compendium of model strophes, called *beth-gazô* 'treasury' by the Syrian Jacobites (Catholics and Orthodox), can be compared to the Byzantine *hirmologion* because it presents the models in relation to a system of eight modes. The Maronites, however, do not seem to have used a *beth-gazô*. In 1700, the Maronite patriarch Stephen Duwayhī wrote a compendium of model strophes, giving detailed versification but not mentioning a system of eight modes, since this system does not exist among the Maronites.

Syriac poetry in the Maronite church is measured. Theorists of meter distinguish between two kinds of measure: by quantity and by number of syllables. Measure by quantity takes note of the long and short character of syllables. Measure by number of syllables is subdivided into two categories: (1) homotony, in which the accented stresses of the syllables of a verse are counted, regardless of the total number of syllables; and (2) isosyllabism, in which all the syllables of a verse are counted, whether they are stressed or atonic. Orientalists who have studied Syriac meter agree about excluding the principle of measure by quantity and keeping the principle of measure by number. But number of what? Some suggest homotony; others favor isosyllabism. Maronite scholars also believe that the number of syllables—not quantity—governs versification; and even if they do not always agree about different kinds of verses and metrical combinations, they provide patterns based on isosyllabism. At all events, the theorists of meter agree that isosyllabism is characteristic of Syriac poetry. This isosyllabism has also influenced the sacred poetry of other Oriental and Occidental liturgies.

MARONITE MUSIC

Musical notation

Before 1939, year when Paul Ashkar's notation of Syro-Maronite melodies was published, musicologists interested in Maronite chant could refer only to Parisot's notation, published in Paris in 1899. And with the exception of Parisot's work, no serious studies of Maronite chant had been undertaken before the 1970s. There were only a few brief discussions based on the assumption that the Maronite chant belonged either to a system of eight modes or to the Arab *maqām* system. Between 1970 and 1990, however, almost all of the Syro-Maronite repertoire was published in new liturgical books (Hage 1972–); and in 1992 another work was published by Fr. Y. El-Khoury.

The repertoire of chants

The repertoire of chants used in the Maronite church is very heterogeneous. A close examination reveals five groups distinct in origin, nature, and significance: Syro-Maronite chant, Syro-Maronite-Arabic chant, improvised melodies, personal or original melodies, and foreign melodies. These groups will be discussed separately later; here, however, is an overview of their distribution in Maronite liturgical books.

Syro-Maronite chant is found in the following liturgical books:

Daily office
Festival Office
Holy Week Office
Funeral Offices
Ritual (Book of Benedictions)
Sacramentary
Pontifical
Syriac Mass

The texts of Syro-Maronite chant are always in Syriac. Most of the melodies are believed to be ancient, dating back to the first centuries of Christianity. They are highly valued and constitute the most genuine and most respected chant of the Maronite tradition. About 150 of these melodies are still in use; in terms of quality, one-third are classified as "great," another third as "medium," and the last third as "common." Musicians and musicologists throughout the world who have come to know these melodies from books, lectures, concerts, and compact disks are intensely interested in them.

Syro-Maronite-Arabic chant is found in the mass and in benedictions and canticles. These texts are in Arabic, but the melodies are Syro-Maronite. Syro-Maronite-Arabic chants composed from the seventeenth century to the mid-twentieth century can be distinguished from those composed later. The earlier ones, which generally have non-classical Arabic texts, number about forty. The others, in classical Arabic, are becoming more and more numerous.

Improvised melodies have been improvised by soloists—priests, deacons, or cantors. The texts may be in Syriac or Arabic.

Personal or original melodies are found especially in the liturgy of the mass and in some benedictions and canticles. These melodies are of recent origin; their texts are in classical Arabic.

Foreign melodies are found in some benedictions and among the canticles. The texts are in classical Arabic.

Methods of composition

Using terminology that has already become classical in the church, we can divide the melodies in Maronite music, according to their methods of composition, into four principal categories: adapted, "centonic," personal, and improvised:

1. *Adapted melodies*. The composer uses an existing traditional melody, modifying it as neccessary for a new text.
2. *"Centonic" melodies* are formed by an eclectic procedure. The composer does not use an existing tradtional melody but rather takes little melodic formulas, arranging, adjusting, or juxtaposing them, according to special rules, in order to make a new melody.
3. *Personal melodies* are formed by free, individual procedures that are the product of a composer's talent and are thereafter associated with him.
4. *Improvised melodies* are made by a special procedure in which traditional guidelines, personal creativity, and (in varying degrees) adaptation or centonization are applied.

Let us now examine the methods of composition in each of the five groups of Maronite music.

SYRO-MARONITE CHANT

Syro-Maronite chant is thought to be a continuation of the chant of the ancient Syro-Antiochene church. This large church probably had a uniform style of music, at least in its western region; only over time, after divisions had occurred within it, did the chant reperoires of different branches of the church diverge.

Composition of Syro-Maronite chant

The Syro-Maronite melodies are composed by two methods: centonization and adaptation. Most of these melodies are centonic—that is, they are created from a number of small fragments, melodic formulas, or patterns. A centonic melody is, therefore, composed in the strict sense of "to compose" (Latin *cumponere*): it results from linking a few small formulas that are already constructed and known. Analysis of these melodies shows clearly that their primary elements are not isolated notes but small formulas, each of which often has its own shape or form. The melodic formulas thus have their own characteristics; detailed study is required to determine these characteristics as well as modifications, relationships with texts, and so on. Centonic Syro-Maronite chant makes no use of personal or original composition—these methods appeared in Maronite music only around the eighteenth century.

FIGURE 1 Three adaptations of a single Maronite melody.

N.B. The note E (mi) is lowered.

The second method of composition frequently used in the Syro-Maronite chant is adaptation of melodic models (figure 1). This procedure sometimes occurs simultaneously with centonization; thus a given melody, A, serves as a model for the composition of another melody, B. The latter reflects two methods of composition—adaptation and centonization—since it too, like its model, is composed of a certain number of small preconstructed melodic formulas.

Like centonization, adaptation obeys rules: it is not haphazard. No description of these rules has come down to us, but since 1964 scholars have been trying to reconstruct the rules by analyzing the melodies. Melodies within the Syro-Maronite repertoire were adapted in either of two ways: by identical reproduction, when an extant melody could be applied to a new text without any significant modification; or by accommodation. Adaptation is easily and frequently applied to Syro-Maronite chant, as to other music, because it requires only metric uniformity between the texts. Accommodation is used when fitting a melody to a new text requires particular temporary modifications: adding or splitting, or joining or omitting, one or several articulated notes.

Characteristics of Syro-Maronite chant

Although it would be impossible to give a detailed analysis of Syro-Maronite chant here, I will describe some general characteristics.

- Syro-Maronite chant forms a sacred repertoire. It is used in the liturgy—never in secular ceremonies.
- It is a living tradition, transmitted orally from generation to generation, that belongs to all Maronites and expresses their sensibility and their musical identity.
- All liturgical texts must be sung or recited, never read as ordinary speech. Although it is permissible to read the text of a prayer or a passage of the holy scriptures, it is never permissible to read a versified text composed for a known melody. In any case, a versified text that was read in this way would lose much of its value.

- The chant is congregational and a cappella; it is considered appropriate for people of all ages and is performed by the whole singing community.
- Certain melodies are devoted to specified rites or liturgical periods; others are not.
- Oral transmission is accomplished within the singing community.
- The chant is strophic. The melody is adapted to a large number of verses whose meter is often uniform. A model strophe (*rīsh qolō*) regulates the meter and the melody of the verses. There is no responsorial chant.
- The chant is syllabic. Except for the final syllable and sometimes the penultimate one, almost no syllable takes more than two notes. Even syllables with two notes are rare; and when such a syllable occurs, the second note is almost always a transient, intermediate step—a movement joining the two notes of an interval of a third.
- The singing is monodic; it has no place for harmony or polyphony.
- The musical scale was originally diatonic but not necessarily tempered. Between C and E, we generally find a third, pitched somewhere between the major and the minor. In practice, the same melody could also be executed according to the tempered system.
- We often have to take into consideration, in the restricted range of Syro-Maronite chant, the mobility of certain degrees or notes, especially the note E. This degree may be lowered slightly relative to the tempered E. This mobility of pitch gave rise to diverging analyses of the Syro-Maronite repertoire and to confusion with Arab music. It is worth pointing out that the lowered E should not be considered a note lowered by a quarter tone.
- The melodic range is relatively small. It is often limited to a fourth or a fifth, sometimes even to a third. Few chants that go beyond this limit show any kind of melodic development. This restricted range often favors the repetition of a melodic formula as well as an unornamented recitative style.
- Melodic formulas are often linked by common notes: the first note of one formula repeats the final note of the preceding formula.
- Many chants are divided into two similar or identical parts.
- Melodies always proceed stepwise. The most frequent intervals are the second and the third. The succession of two diatonic semitones does not occur. The chromatic semitone does not exist. The augmented second is rare.
- A significant characteristic of Syro-Maronite chant is a strong tendency to "correct" thirds; that is, the intermediate note of the third is placed after the second note: for instance, after the interval C–E we find D; after G–E we find F.
- Intervals of a fourth or a fifth are rare and are generally found at the junction of melodic formulas. The larger intervals—the sixth and beyond—are not used. The result is a great simplicity of melody.
- The modal system is of a particular archaic type, not reducible to the Arab musical system or to the system of eight Byzantine or Gregorian modes. Mode is defined by the range of the melody, its scale, its principal notes, its melodic schema, and sometimes its proper melodic formulas. However, in Syro-Maronite chant it is better to speak of a melodic genre than of a mode.
- The repertoire shows a kind of modal evolution, but this has been slow and timid.
- The rhythm is varied. We find syllabic rhythm and patterns of two, three, four, and five beats as well as irregular beats.
- With regard to meter, the melody typically fits the structure and meter of the strophe.
- With regard to textual meaning, the melody bears almost no relationship to

the text, since a melody will find itself set to a large number of different strophes. The three modes or genres used in Syro-Maronite chant have no specific ethos.

- The expression of the chant depends principally on the text, the social and spiritual environment of the singers as well as the hearers.
- Traditional Maronite chant is clearly related to other traditional chants of the Near East, both sacred and secular.
- The chants are generally calm and simple in character, largely as a result of the limited range of the melodies, the repetition of certain preconstructed formulas, and the conjoined movement. In performance, these traditional and communal qualities are sometimes obscured or altered by a poor rendition.
- Instrumental accompaniment of certain chants is limited to four metallic percussion instruments (described later).

SYRO-MARONITE-ARABIC CHANT

The term *Syro-Maronite-Arabic chant* reflects the fact that this chant has an Arabic text and a Syro-Maronite or originally Syro-Maronite melody. Like Syro-Maronite chant, it is almost always strophic. The melody is adapted to a larger or smaller number of strophes, which always have an almost uniform meter. Chants in this group are formed by adapting a Syro-Maronite melody to an Arabic text. This adaptation may take one of three forms: identical reproduction, accommodation, or refashioning.

Around the seventeenth century—the era of the first examples of the Syro-Maronite-Arabic chant—the Maronites seem to have mostly applied a Maronite-Arabic text to a Syro-Maronite melody (figure 2*a* and *b*). This probably involved no great difficulty, because with regard to vocalization and versification the Maronite-Arabic language was very similar to Syriac, the secular language of the Maronites.

Because of the progressive evolution of Maronite-Arabic toward classical, or literary, Arabic, inflections in Maronite-Arabic necessarily increased the number of vocal signs and consequently the number of its syllables. This brought about certain transient or occasional modifications of original Syro-Maronite melodies and necessitated accommodation (figure 2*a* and *c*).

FIGURE 2 Three adaptations of a Maronite melody to suit Arabic texts.

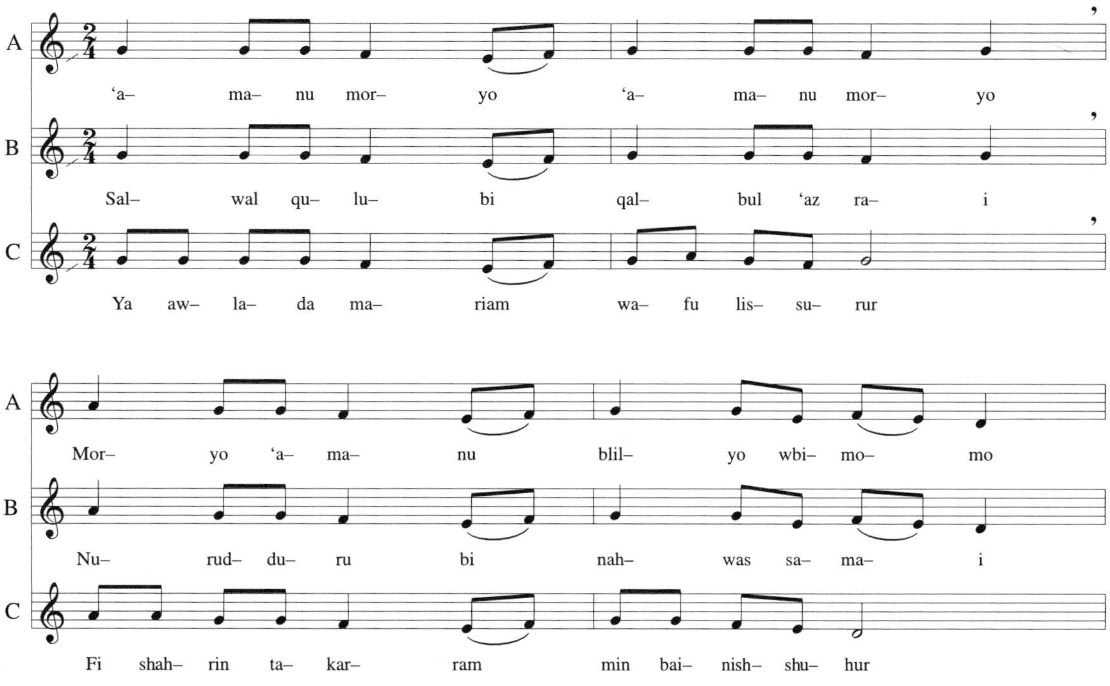

FIGURE 3 Examples of "refashioned" Maronite melodies.

Another consequence of this evolution toward classical Arabic was that added syllables became more numerous; thus accommodation became more difficult and a need arose for refashioning (figure 3). This is a special method of adapting a Syro-Maronite melody to an Arabic text that demands a general and constant modification of the note values of the entire melody. It differs from accommodation in that it affects the entire melody (whereas accommodation affects only certain elements in an irregular manner). However, sometimes accommodation and refashioning can occur simultaneously.

TRACK 12

IMPROVISED MELODIES

Unlike most Western music, that of the Middle East—sacred and secular, vocal and instrumental—reserves an important place for improvisation. Improvisation in Maronite chant is similar to that in Arab and Persian music and the popular music of the Near East. Thus many improvised melodies in the Maronite church stand out very clearly from the rest of the repertoire.

If we wish to group the different kinds of improvisation in the Maronite church according to technique and to the degree of freedom with which the cantor improvises, we can distinguish four principal situations, or categories:

1. The cantor improvises with maximum liberty: he chooses the melodic development he desires; he uses any kind of style, ranging from strict syllabism to

extended melisma; the rhythm is free but generally follows that of the text. Note, however, that despite this complete liberty, there is an unconscious association with some of the musical formulas that the cantor has memorized.

2. The cantor's melodic line can be intuitively sensed by the assembly. In general, this second category has all the features of the first category, but here they are less pronounced. In other words, the cantor's liberty is somewhat limited.
3. The cantor deals with a traditional melody that is already an object of improvisation and instinctively distinguishes between its residual framework (which is more or less fixed) and the subjective element which the melody presents at every new improvisation. The cantor tries to re-create the melody, following its original line or schema.
4. The cantor is dealing with a more fixed melody, which he interprets with individual feeling and technique. In certain places he can sometimes add ornaments or brief developments. Thus in this fourth kind of improvisation we encounter ornamentation, which has a prominent role in the execution and interpretation of Middle Eastern music.

PERSONAL MELODIES

Personal melodies are recent, and their number is growing steadily. They are inspired by many kinds of foreign influences and techniques and thus are manifestly varied and heterogeneous. In general, with regard to technique and inspiration, one may distinguish Western, Arab, combined Western and Arab, and finally Syriac influences. Compositions showing Syriac influences are particularly interesting; to the extent that they meet liturgical, sociological, and artistic needs, they are the most welcome at a time when liturgical and musical reform has already begun.

It is difficult to evaluate the various new compositions. Because they are so new, our judgments could easily be immature and overly subjective; we need time for a more objective appreciation. It is hoped that current research by new scholars will shed more light on these recent chants.

FOREIGN MELODIES

Foreign melodies are found not only in Maronite music but also in other Catholic churches of the Near East. We do not yet know exactly when the Maronites started to apply Arabic texts to foreign melodies taken from the East or the West, although this probably did not happen before the eighteenth century. These foreign melodies are applicable mostly to canticles and paraliturgical poems, and today their use is in decline.

MUSICAL INSTRUMENTS

Traditionally, only four instruments are used in the Maronite church: double cymbals, the large cymbal, the *nāqūs*, and the *marwaḥa* (figure 4). The double cymbals, which have long been in use, can be of different sizes. The large cymbal consists of one suspended disk that is struck with a drumstick.

The *nāqūs* can be single or double. The double *nāqūs* consists of two metallic hemispheres connected to a stem that serves as a handle. It is played with a metallic drumstick. Its tone is reminiscent of the triangle. Probably, this instrument originally had a purely functional role, calling people to prayer and drawing their attention to important moments during prayers—the same function as the bell and the hand bell in the Roman rite.

The *marwaḥa* (plural, *marāwiḥ*) is a metallic disk with some small pieces of metal suspended from the rim. The disk is fixed to a wooden handle, about one meter in length; sometimes a colorful flag is attached to this handle. Performance consists of

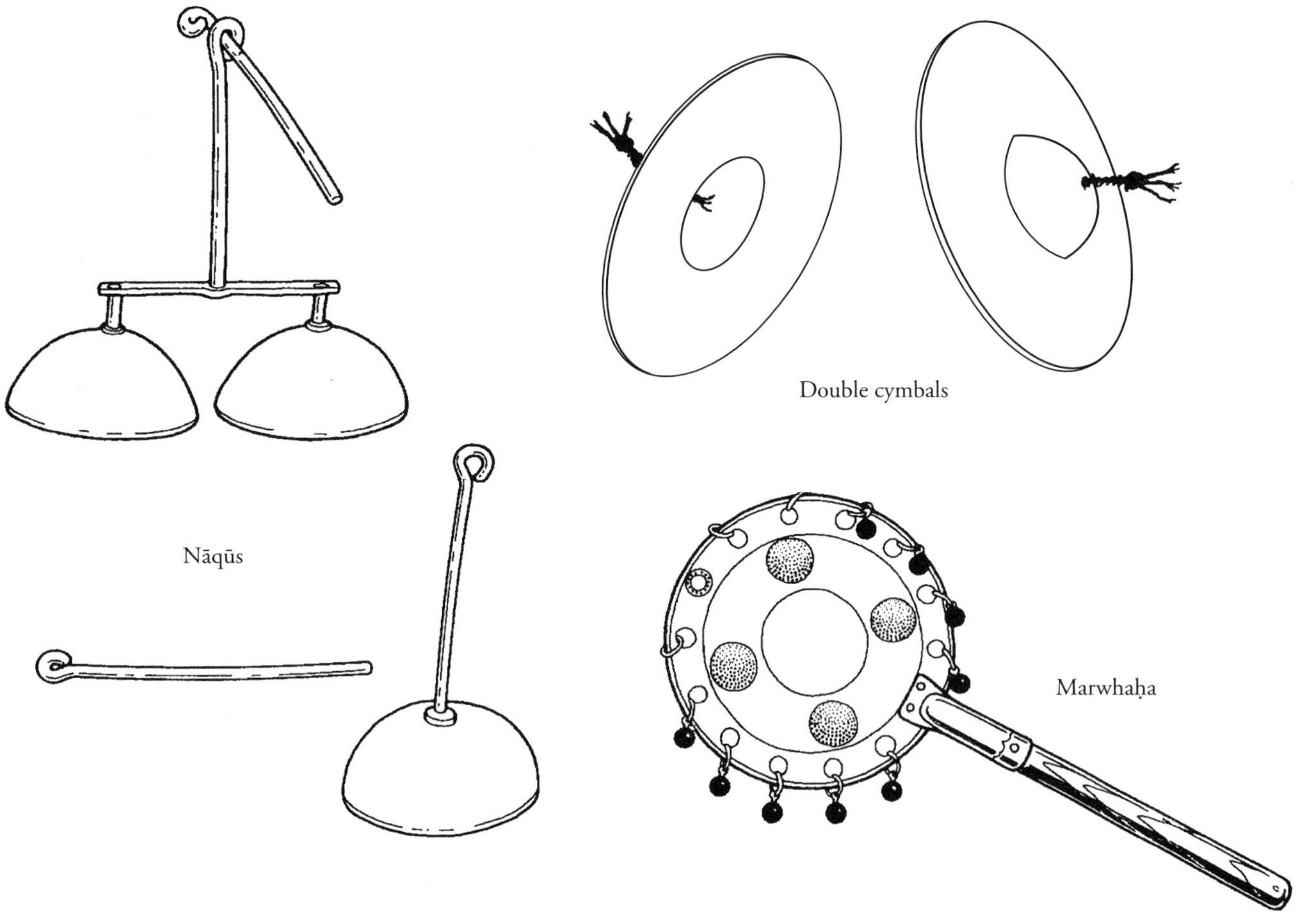

FIGURE 4 Instruments.

gently agitating the handle, slowly raising and lowering it, to produce a light rustling sound.

The playing of these instruments is entrusted to experts who have been trained by their elders, and the instruments are reserved for certain processions and solemn and joyful occasions, such as Christmas and Easter.

The harmonium and the organ, which are to be found in some churches and seminary and college chapels, are of relatively recent usage. Other instruments, such as the violin and the accordion, are more recent still.

REFERENCES

Ashqar, Paul. 1939. *Mélodies liturgiques syro-maronites*. Jounieh, Lebanon.

Gastoué, Amédée. 1931. "La musique byzantine et le chant des églises d'Orient." In *Encyclopédie de la musique et dictionnaire du Conservatoire*, 1:541–556. Paris: Librairie Delagrave.

Hage, Louis. 1963. "Réforme du chant maronite." *Cahiers de philosophie et de théologie* 2: 7–27.

———. 1967. "Les mélodies-types dans le chant maronite." *Melto* 3:325–409.

———. 1969. "Le chant maronite." In *Encyclopédie des musiques sacrées*, 2:218–222. Paris: Éditions Labergerie. (English translations: 1971. "Music of the Maronite Church." *Parole de l'Orient*, 2(1):197–206. Also: 1978. *Maronite Music*. London: Longman for the University of Essex.)

———. 1971–1973. *Traditions musicales du Proche-Orient*. Beirut: Kaslik. (Thirteen 45-rpm disks.)

———. 1972–. *Musique maronite*. Vol. 1: *Le chant syro-maronite* (1972). Vol. 2: *Le chant maronite* (1995). Vols. 3a and 3b: *Monuments du chant maronite* (1990–1991). Vols. 4a and 4b: *Analyse, classement et références* (1990–1991). Kaslik, Lebanon: Bibliothèque de l'Université de Saint-Esprit.

———. 1979a. *Florilège de chants maronites*. Paris: SM. (LP disk.)

———. 1979b. *Chants syriaques de l'Église Maronite*. Paris: SM. (LP disk.)

———. 1980. "Lebanon." In *The New Grove Dictionary of Music and Musicians*, 10:573–576. London: Macmillan.

———. 1982a. *Noëls Maronites*. Paris: SM. (LP disk.)

———. 1982b. *Chants de la Passion et de Pâques*. Paris: SM. (LP disk.)

———. 1983. *Gesänge der maronitischen Kirche*. Christophorus. (LP disk.)

———. 1984a. "Siriaco, canto." In *Dizionario enciclopedico universale della musica e dei musicisti: Il lessico*, 4:308–309. Turin: UTET.

———. 1984b. "Les églises orientales non byzantines." In *Précis de Musicologie*, ed. Jacques Chailley, 114–119. Paris: Presses Universitaires de France.

———. 1986. *Les strophes-types syriaques et leurs mètres poétiques du patriarche maronite Etienne Douayhi*. Kaslin, Lebanon: Bibliothèque de l'Université Saint-Esprit.

———. 1987. *The Syriac Model Strophes and Their Poetic Meters, by the Maronite Patriarch Stephen Douayhi*. Kaslik, Lebanon: University of the Holy Spirit.

———. 1993. *Chants maronites traditionnels*. Paris: SM. (Compact disk.)

———. 1997. *Précis de chant maronite*. Kaslik: Université Saint-Esprit de Kaslik.

———. 2001a. *Musique maronite*. Vol. 5, *Les strophes-types syriaques: Introduction, édition critique, et traduction*. Bibliothèque de l'Université Saint-Esprit de Kaslik.

———. 2001b. *Musique maronite*. Vol. 6, *Les strophes-types syriaques: Étude analytique*. Bibliothèque de l'Université Saint-Esprit de Kaslik.

El-Khoury, Youssef. 1961–1963. "La musique syro-maronite." *As-Sanasbel* (1–6). (In Arabic.)

———. c. 1992. *Tarānimunā: al-alḥān al-suryāniyya li'l-kanisa al-antakiyya al-mā rūniyya* (Syrian Chant of the Antioch Church of the Maronites). Kaslik, Lebanon: Jāmi'at al-Rūḥ al-Qudus.

Nieten, Ulrike. 1998. "Syrische Kirchenmusik." In *Die Musik in Geschichte und Gegenwart*, ed. Ludwig Finscher, 9:185–200. Kassel: Bärenreiter.

Parisot, Dom Jean. 1898. "Essai sur le chant liturgique des églises orientales." *Revue de l'Orient Chrétien* 3:221–231.

———. 1899. *Rapport sur une mission scientifique en Turquie d'Asie*. Paris: E. Leroux.

———. 1901. "Les huit modes du chant syrien." *Tribune de Saint-Gervais* 7:258–262.

Werner, Eric. 1959. *The Sacred Bridge: The Interdependence of Liturgy and Music in Synagogue and Church during the First Millennium*. London: Dobson; New York: Columbia University Press.

The Coptic Orthodox Church and Its Music

Martha Roy

The Coptic Church and Its Language
The Liturgy
The Offices and Hymns
Characteristics of Coptic Music
Transmission of the Tradition

The word *Copt* derives from the Greek *aigyptios* 'Egyptian', which in turn seems to derive from the old Egyptian *ha-ka-ptah* 'house of the spirit of Ptah', an ancient name for the capital city, Memphis (Erian 1986:25). The Greeks called the indigenous community Copts. In the broadest sense, *Copts* may refer to the inhabitants of Pharaonic and Hellenic Egypt and, in later centuries, to the descendants and heirs of this ancient population. Today, the word refers to the Christian Orthodox community of Egypt—the largest of a number of Christian communities in Egypt, which includes Catholics, both Roman and Orthodox, and various Protestant groups.

Copts live throughout the country. Although their communities tend to be in cities—Cairo, Alexandria, al-Minya, and Asyut, for instance—there are also predominantly Coptic villages in the countryside, especially in Upper Egypt. Important monasteries were built in Wadi Natrun, a desert region to the west of the Nile Delta, and in many other places (Meinardus 1989).

Coptic religious practice has produced one of the world's great liturgical traditions. It consists of three important liturgies (St. Basil, St. Kyrollos, and St. Gregory Nazianzes), services for the Offices (Lauds, Terce, Sext, None, Vespers, Compline, the Prayer of the Veil, and Matins), and hundreds of hymns used in a special Office called the Psalmodiyya.

THE COPTIC CHURCH AND ITS LANGUAGE

The Coptic church was founded, according to tradition, by St. Mark in the first century of the Christian era and has continued to be active since then. Its present head is His Holiness Pope Shanuda III, Patriarch of Alexandria and the See of St. Mark, the 117th patriarch in the line of succession.

The Coptic language is a form of ancient Pharaonic and Greek, seldom heard outside the liturgical rites of the church. Historically, the early church is said to have used Greek for its rites, which were translated into Coptic in the third century and into Arabic in the seventh and eighth centuries. Each page in the official prayer book is divided into two columns, one Coptic and the other Arabic, for the benefit of all participating in the service. Today, officiants use both languages interchangeably in performing the rites. Written Coptic consists of the old Greek alphabet, with the addition of seven letters for sounds that are not found in Greek. Much of the

The Divine Liturgy is entirely sung, with the priests, the choir of deacons, and the congregation having assigned roles.

theological terminology derived from early centuries, such as *Kyrie eleison*, is still in Greek. Only a few families have preserved the tradition of speaking Coptic at home; however, an increasing number of young people, interested in their roots, have enrolled in the Coptic language programs of the churches and institutes.

The architecture of the Coptic Orthodox church has its own recognized style and incorporates influences from several civilizations established in Egypt. Often a bell steeple is attached to the basilica; one, two, or three cupolas surmount the sanctuary, which always faces east. There are three entrance doors on the west side: one for men, one for women, and one (in the center) for eminent persons, weddings, and funerals. The nave was formerly divided by a curtain into a men's section and a women's section, but today most churches have discarded this practice. The choir is a platform extending across the church; on it stand the choir of deacons and the readers of the scripture lessons. A high wooden screen separates the choir from the holy sanctuary; on this screen, known as the iconostasis, many saints are represented. Three doors lead from the choir to the sanctuary, which houses the altar where the priest, facing east, offers prayers. All men entering the sanctuary remove their shoes; women do not enter the sanctuary.

THE LITURGY

In the church, the congregation concentrates on the complete liturgy of worship, known as the Divine Liturgy. It is entirely sung—by the priests, the choir of deacons led by the chief singer (the cantor), and the congregation, with each group having assigned roles in the rites, hymns, prayers, readings, and responses. The hymns are sung by the congregants, who depend on the deacons for correct performance.

The liturgical order of the service is (1) preparation for worship; (2) the *synaxis* with the readings and common prayers; and (3) the eucharistic rite. Some of the specific content follows the ecclesiastical calendar, which begins on 11 September: certain prayers, hymns, and scriptural lessons are appointed for each season and each day of the church year, including fasts and feast days to commemorate a figure such as a martyr or a historical event in the life of the church. The choir of deacons needs to have extensive knowledge of the texts and melodies of pieces for each liturgical service.

Coptic music may be heard in the performance of the liturgies. The Liturgy of St. Basil is used on ordinary occasions through the year. The Liturgy of St. Gregory is used for the celebration of the four great feasts: Nativity, Epiphany, Resurrection, and Pentecost. A third liturgy, St. Kyrollos, derived from that of St. Mark, is now seldom heard, and over time most of its melodies have been lost. Historians believe that other liturgies, now unknown or unused, may also have existed in the past. Most of the hymns and prayers of the Divine Liturgy mentioned above resemble the order of the classic rites performed in all Occidental Orthodox churches, but the music is distinctly and uniquely Coptic. The musical patterns have been handed down for centuries from generation to generation, father to son, by rote. This is also the method used to teach the great quantity of melodies to young priests in the Coptic Theological Seminary in Cairo and its branches. There is a firm belief that these melodies originated in the temple rites of Pharaonic Egypt, although no special form or trace of any known decipherable notation or transcription has been found among the papyri and literary tracts of ancient Egypt.

THE OFFICES AND HYMNS

In addition to the services of the Divine Liturgy, there are seven canonical hours or Offices. They are said by laypeople in the city churches and by monks in the monasteries. During each Office, a number of Psalms must be read; the Office also includes two *troparia* (hymns sung between the Psalms) and two *theotokia*, discussed below, to be recited or chanted.

The Psalmodiyya is a choral service sung daily. Its hymns, which differ considerably in style from the liturgical hymns, are called *Psalis* or (in Arabic) *Madayah*; most of them have twenty-four to forty strophes, each of four lines in regular metric patterns. They have various rhyme schemes, and the fourth line often becomes a refrain sung by the congregation. Each strophe may begin with a letter of the alphabet in sequence, thus forming a type of acrostic hymn. Occasionally, the name of the author is included in the acrostic sequence.

The Psalmodiyya includes a wide variety of hymns. The *hos* consist of two Old Testament canticles (Exodus 15:1–18 and Daniel 3:52–58 Apocrypha) and two Psalms (136 and 148–150). All four *hos* have regular meters, bright melodies, and refrains for the congregation. Each *hos* is a hymn of praise to God for his acts of mercy. The *theotokia* are hymns sung in honor of the Virgin Mary as the mother of God. There is a set of *theotokia* for each day of the week, and eighteen for Sunday. They have unrhymed texts but are set to regular rhythmic meters. The *lobsh* is a "crowning hymn" consisting of a nonbiblical text with a biblical theme in four-line unrhymed strophes. The title of each *lobsh* and of most *Psalis* includes the term *Adam* or *Batos*, which may prescribe a form of scale or mode, whose exact meaning is no longer known. The *lobsh* is usually recited rather than sung. The *tarh* is a paraphrase of a biblical text. *Doxologies* are hymns of praise in honor of the Virgin Mary, angels, or saints; they also consist of two unrhymed strophes in Coptic, followed by an Arabic prose text.

In this rich array of choral offerings, a hymn is also sung daily to honor the memory of a martyr or saint or to commemorate a historical occasion. Each hymn has its own melody and its own rhythmic meter. The first word or two indexes the title of each hymn within the assigned order of performance—a significant feat in such a vast heritage of music and tradition.

CHARACTERISTICS OF COPTIC MUSIC

Although historical sources mention the use of the Byzantine system of melodic modes called *octo echos* in Coptic music, the relationship of the *octo echos* to the Coptic repertoire is not completely clear. In the twentieth century, scholars noted a few similarities between the systems of Coptic and Arabic music—predominantly stepwise motion, microtones, melisma, and ornamentation. Nevertheless, the way in which apparently similar structures are used in Coptic music sets it apart from Arab music and gives it a distinctively different sound (Boutros 1976; Erian 1986:275, 296–299). The short version of the Lord's Prayer transcribed here (figure 1) illustrates some of these characteristics.

Coptic music is distinctive in its use of two particular elements of composition: melisma and ornamentation. *Melisma* (plural, *melismata*) refers to a melodic prolongation of a single vowel in a sung text. It may be in free or metrical rhythm, depending on the emphasis of the beats in the melody. Melisma is a common feature in the sacred and secular music of the Middle East. Musical ornamentation is a spontaneous

FIGURE 1 Lord's Prayer, short version sung at funerals and during Lent. Transcription by Martha Roy from a recording made by the choir of the Theological Seminary of the Coptic Orthodox Church, directed by Dr. Ragheb Moftah.

improvisation of pitches around one central tone in a given melody. There are many kinds of ornamentation in the trill, the turn, performed entirely spontaneously by the performer. This is often done within the given melody, and it marks an improvisation of the melody. Both melisma and ornamentation are greatly appreciated by listeners.

Most hymns have only a narrow range of tones, seldom more than five; they follow a stepwise movement. Tonal intervals seldom have more than three or four tones. Brief phrases may be repeated with slight variations and extended by melismatic improvisations. Each piece usually concludes with a recognizable cadential formula.

Only two instruments are used today to accompany the singing of chants. They are played by a deacon, and both are percussive: a pair of small metal hand cymbals (*al-naqūs*), and a metal triangle (*trianto*). Exactly when they began to be used is not known. The Arabic rubrics (see below) added to prayer books in the thirteenth and fourteenth centuries mention that *al-naqūs* accompanied seven hymns; however, in the Arabic dictionary *Lisān al-ʿArab* this term refers to a wooden board beaten rhythmically with a stick—a description that could indicate the *semāntron*. Some early travelers in Egypt make reference to such an instrument (for example, Watson 1904:22). The triangle, which is not mentioned in any of the ecclesiastical prayer books, has a light, pleasing, tinkling sound that offsets the heavier tone of the hand cymbals. The polymetric jingle of the beats of the two instruments in complicated rhythmic patterns is a unique form of accompaniment in Coptic church music.

Several attempts to use a small pump organ in the church have been discouraged. The human voice is considered the most suitable means for offering praise and worship to God.

TRANSMISSION OF THE TRADITION

Although the music of the complete liturgy of the Coptic Orthodox Church has never been written, a number of liturgists have written about it, and musicologists have transcribed particular pieces of the hymns and prayers. In the thirteenth and fourteenth centuries, anonymous writers gave directions in Arabic for the correct performance of the liturgical text. These were known as *rubrics* and were added to the prayer books, where they continue to provide directives for the conduct of services. They were originally written in red (*rubric* means red) but are now written in black ink.

Among the most zealous figures in the preservation of this great treasury of church music is Dr. Ragheb Moftah, head of the Department of Music and Hymns of the Institute of Coptic Studies and of the Coptic Theological Seminary. He has spent a lifetime training students at the seminary in the correct performance of these hymns and chants and has collected from churches and monasteries those sung in southern as well as northern Egypt. He has recorded this valuable material in his studio at the Institute of Coptic Studies and has also encouraged efforts to preserve it by transcribing it into staff notation. He commissioned a transcription from live performances of the hymns and music by the English musicologist Ernest Newlandsmith, from 1926 to 1936. A second project developed under the authority of Dr. Moftah—with the cooperation of Dr. Margit Toth of Hungary, a specialist in the Hungarian school of transcription; and Dr. Martha Roy, the present author, an educator and linguist—produced a full transcription of the Liturgy of St. Basil, the first complete published version (Moftah, Toth, and Roy 1998). The finest details of the music itself are included, and the entire text is given in Coptic, Arabic, and English, preserving this heritagte for posterity.

A number of Egyptians, members of the Coptic Orthodox church, have completed academic dissertations about its music. Also, several groups of young people have served their church through special activities. Some nonclerical groups have performed concerts of liturgical hymns and nonliturgical songs, which they composed for dramatic productions and cassette recordings. These concerts, presented in church halls, are quite popular; the music is distinct in style and demonstrates Western influence with a leaning toward jazz rhythms. The texts are biblical and theologically acceptable—however, the music sometimes is not acceptable; therefore, some community members feel that these forms, attractive as they are, lack the spirituality and dignity of the ancient liturgical tradition. Other youth groups have taken their music on European and American tours, as a way to share their traditions. Their efforts have been received enthusiastically and appreciatively. Young people who do not know Coptic script use texts of the liturgy transliterated into Arabic so that they can participate in chanting the hymns and responses.

Eventually, these developments in Coptic Orthodox music may come into conflict. However, traditional liturgical music and worship have carried the faith of the Coptic Orthodox church through twenty centuries, and loyalty to what they stand for is undiminished. The music continues to be carried across the world through the migrations of the diaspora, and the message and melodies of the church continue to nurture faith and traditional beliefs.

REFERENCES

Borsai, Ilona. 1970–1971. "Charactéristiques générales du chant de la messe copte." *Studia Orientalia Christiana Aegyptica: Collectanea* 14:412–442.

Boutros, Nabīl Kamāl. 1976. "al-Mūsīqā al-qibtiyya fī Miṣr wa'alāqātihā bi'l-mūsīqā al-far'ūniyya" (Coptic Music in Egypt and Its Relationship to Pharaonic Music). M.A. thesis, Helwan University, Cairo.

Daoud, Mary S. 1967. "Mūsīqā al-Kanīsa al-Qibṭiyya" (Music of the Coptic Church). Unpublished study, Cairo.

Erian, Nabila. 1986. "Coptic Music: An Egyptian Tradition." Ph.D. dissertation, University of Maryland.

Khs-Burmeister, O. M. E. 1967. "The Egyptian or Coptic Church: Detailed Description of Her Liturgical Services and the Rites and Ceremonies Observed in the Administration of Her Sacraments." Cairo: Société d'Archaeologie Copte.

Meinardus, Otto Friedrich August. 1989. *Monks and Monasteries of the Egyptian Deserts*. Rev. ed. Cairo: American University in Cairo Press.

Ménard, Réné. 1952. "Notes sur les musiques arabes et coptes." *Les Cahiers Coptes* 2:48–54.

———. 1969. "Tradition copte." In *Encyclopédie des musiques sacrées*, ed. Jacques Porte, 229–233. Paris: Labergerie.

Moftah, Ragheb. 1958. "The Coptic Music." *Bulletin de l'Institut des Études Coptes* 1:42–53.

Moftah, Ragheb, Margit Toth, and Martha Roy. 1998. *The Liturgy of St. Basil of the Coptic Orthodox Church*. Cairo: American University in Cairo Press.

Newlandsmith, E. 1928–1936. "The Music of the Mass as Sung in the Coptic Church and Some Special Hymns in the Coptic Liturgy." Sixteen folio vols. of unpublished transcriptions, given to the Library of Congress in 1996.

Robertson, Marian. 1984–1985. "The Reliability of the Oral Tradition in Preserving Coptic Music: A Comparison of Three Musical Transcriptions of an Extract from the Liturgy of St. Basil." *Bulletin of the Coptic Archaeology Society* 26:84–93; 27:73–85.

———. 1987. "Vocal Music in the Early Coptic Church." *Diakonia* 3:190–198.

El-Shawan, Salwa. 1975. "An Annotated Bibliography on Coptic Music." M.A. thesis, Columbia University, New York.

Watson, Andrew. 1904. *The American Mission in Egypt, 1854 to 1896*. 2d ed. Pittsburgh: United Presbyterian Board of Publication.

Syriac Religious Music
Simon Jargy

The word *Syriac* refers to a Semitic language, derived from Aramaic, that was spoken by the inhabitants of historical Syria, especially in the first centuries of the Christian era (whence its other name, *Christian Aramaic*). Historical Syria encompassed the entire area bounded on the north by the Taurus Mountains, on the east by the Arabian Desert, on the west by the Mediterranean, and on the south by the Sinai Desert. In modern times, *Syria* and *Syrian* refer to a well-defined geopolitical entity, and *Syriacs* refers to a religious minority found mainly outside Syria (figures 1 and 2).

THE MUSIC: A LINK BETWEEN SYNAGOGUE AND CHURCH

This community created an essentially vocal sacred music known as Syrian or Syriac, dating back to earliest Christian antiquity. Historians place the origins of this music

FIGURE 1 Fire ceremony following the celebration of Christmas mass, in Baghdad, by the Syrian Orthodox archbishop. The coals are then taken and burned in the fields of the faithful to enhance fertility. Photo courtesy of Alain Saint-Hilaire.

FIGURE 2 Baptism in a Syrian Orthodox church. After immersing the newborn infant in water and annointing the infant with holy oil, the celebrant offers a benediction with ritual chants. Photo courtesy of Paul-Jacques Callebaut.

at the very beginning of Christianity, or more precisely with the Christian community in the capital of historic Syria, Antioch. Its members were survivors of the first Judeo-Christian community gathered in Jerusalem around James, known as the "Lord's brother," after Jesus' death (30–70 C.E.). These Syrian Jews, who, like Jesus, spoke Aramaic, were the first to welcome the evangelical preaching of the earliest apostles and disciples to leave Jerusalem. They converted as a body to the Christian faith, and the Christianity that even today we call Semitic or Aramaic was born here. The germ of Syriac liturgical song and Christian sacred song generally grew from synagogue chanting.

The most ancient basis of the music that has come down to us is the chanting of biblical scripture, psalmody (Psalms of David; figure 3), and acclamations of God. These sources refer to God indirectly, through vocalizations of consonant and vowel combinations from the words for God: *Yahaweh* and *Elohim*, which is *Alaha* or *Aloho* in Syriac. Such chants, known as *ḥalel*, are a genre unto themselves; they developed into fairly complex melismatic formulas in a later eight-mode framework.

FIGURE 3 Psalm 91, psalmody from the office of Vespers.

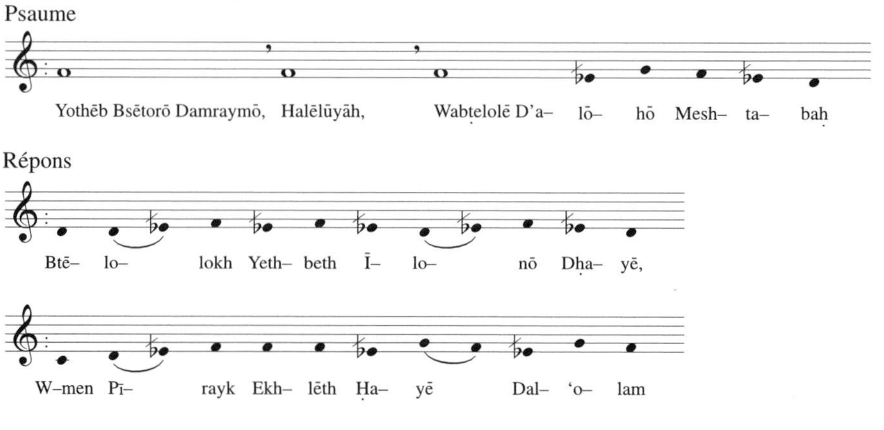
Psaume
Yothēb Bsētorō Damraymō, Halēlūyāh, Wabṭelolē D'a– lō– hō Mesh– ta– baḥ
Répons
Btē– lo– lokh Yeth– beth Ī– lo– nō Dḥa– yē,
W–men Pī– rayk Ekh– lēth Ḥa– yē Dal– 'o– lam

EVOLUTION AND DEVELOPMENT

Antioch, which became the seat of a religious patriarchate (its leader was called the Patriarch), was an eminent city, equal to the other centers of Christian religious power: Rome, Constantinople, and Alexandria.

The process of Hellenization, which made Greek the language of the learned, relegated Syriac to the role of a popular vernacular and indirectly favored the birth of a national movement that adopted Syriac as its rallying point. The movement developed in Mesopotamia, which was one of historical Syria's great provinces but was at the margins of Hellenization. With its cultural capital at Edessa (Urfa in present-day Turkey), Mesopotamia became a center for scriptural and literary study, which, in music, gave birth to a new kind of sung poetry, enriching its original basis in psalmody and recitation. This new genre was hymnody.

HYMNODY: THE IDEAL FORM OF POPULAR RELIGIOUS MUSIC

As early as the second century C.E., a simple poeticomusical genre appeared, a kind of poetry divided into strophes that allow the final verse to be sung as a refrain chanted by the gathering of the faithful, simple in melody and with a clear rhythm. The primary aim of such poetry—based on isosyllables, monophony, and melody structured by several notes over a measured rhythm—is be pleasing in sound, and above all, to be easily memorized.

The earliest hymnographer to revolutionize this religious musical language was a Syriac scholar from Edessa named Bardesanes (154–222 C.E.). Of a noble family, he converted to Christianity while maintaining some relationship with the Manichean gnostics who were found in fairly large numbers in Mesopotamia. Suspected of heresy, he later provoked fierce opposition from the church fathers, notably from the poet and theologian St. Ephraem the Syrian (303–373). For decades, Bardesanes's hymns and especially those of his son Harmonius enjoyed considerable success among ordinary Christians. In fact, they were so popular that St. Ephraem imitated Bardesanes's and Harmonius's poeticomusical model to create hymns that gained widespread currency and had an impact on all kinds of Christian liturgical music. Bardesanes's hymns continue to form the major basis of Syriac liturgical music among both Orthodox and Catholic Syriacs as well as among Maronites and Assyro-Chaldeans.

EVOLUTION AND INDEPENDENCE

While retaining its original basis, enriched by an abundantly varied hymnody, Syriac liturgical music evolved in the context of upsets and divisions that affected the Christian world. The Council of Chalcedon (451) condemned monophysite doctrine (that is, the belief that Christ had a single nature, both human and divine) and brought about another division within the Syrian church, opening the way for the total independence of Mesopotamian Syriac Christians. United around their church hierarchy and their numerous monasteries, monophysite Syriacs created an independent church, which still claimed its authority from Antioch; they were called Jacobite Syrians.

The liturgical music evolved in two directions. One kind developed under the influence of Greek cultural leaders. This "Hellenization" occurred mainly in the sixth century with the adoption of the Byzantine eight-mode system known as *otoechos* (*tekso*). It was the work of the Patriarch Severus of Antioch (c. 465–538).

A parallel development that may be called "Aramaization" took place mostly after the Arab conquest (632). The monophysite Syriac community stood up to western Christianity across Byzantium, enduring violent persecution, and developed a Semito-Aramaic cultural particularism, especially in liturgy and music. This particularism, more than ever before, depended on biblical scripture that the community sought to preserve and spread through a continuous oral tradition. This tradition was based, once again, not on scriptural reading from the original text, which was reserved for a scholarly elite, but on a developing body of paraphrase, commentary, and even para-biblical legends, all drawn from a common oral source. The pedagogical aims of this tradition were initially transmitted by many active monks who had only a rudimentary education.

Developing in this way, the music that has come down to us has been recorded and codified in collections called the *Beth-Gazō* 'thesaurus'. *Beth-Gazō* is not a complete musical manual, properly speaking, as it has no musical notation. It is a collection of extrabiblical liturgical chants in the form of sung hymns and melodies in which only the initial poetic meter is indicated. This is common to an almost constant process of centonization wherein each formula is repeated in the same way in the strophes making up the whole hymn.

The parts of *Beth-Gazō* are ordered as follows.

1. *'Enyonē*: responsa separated by verses from the Psalms. These are also found in Maronite and Assyro-Chaldean liturgical songs.
2. *Madroshē*: hymns based on strophes separated by a refrain. The *Madroshē* Assyro-Chaldean liturgical songs are also in this category.
3. *Qolē*: syllabic song with measured rhythm, which traces its origins to a popular singer known as Shem'ūn Qūqoyō 'Simon the Potter'.
4. *Qonunē Yawnoyē* (Greek canons): the Greek form of the *'Enyonē*, a borrowing that is doubtless due to late Hellenization (eighth century). Based on the Byzantine model, it is also Assyro-Chaldean.
5. *Mawrbē*: variant of the *'Enyonē* genre.
6. *Takhsfothō* (supplications): very decorative songs, difficult to perform, whose meter and rhythm are free. In general, they are reserved for solos by the *shammās* (minor clerics). Like other types of Arab music, they are constructed on a modal system drawing mainly from Eastern *maqām*.

CHARACTERISTICS OF SYRICAC MUSIC

Syriac music, which is essentially vocal and homophonic, is a popular music, and is thus simple in its structures and forms, making it easy to remember and transmit. It is very different from more elaborate Byzantine and Gregorian liturgical music, although it shares with them a choral performance mode of ancient origin, wherein two choirs or the celebrant and the choir alternate.

The poeticomelodic structure consists of short isosyllabic strophes. The poetic meter is based on the number of syllables, not on the progression of quantitative accents. The melody itself develops in short repetitive phrases.

Starting in the fourth and fifth centuries, three syllabic meters were established that were applied uniformly to all later poeticomusical compositions: "Jacob's meter," referring to Jacob of Serug (421–521), the famous fifth-century theologian and Syriac poet, creator of a twelve-syllable meter; "Ephraem's meter," referring to the great St. Ephraem of Edessa, originator of a heptasyllabic meter; and "Balai's meter," referring to the fifth-century Syriac saint and hymnographer, to whom a pentasyllabic meter is attributed.

The rhythm of this music is also folklike. It contains isochronous measures but also undergoes shifts characteristic of other Near Eastern musics. In these rhythms, two- or four-beat cycles predominate, and the ternary remains fairly rare, exemplified by the *bo'ūtō*, which uses Ephraem's meter and paraphrases Psalm 50, "Miserere mei Deus."

Syriac liturgical music, again like other Middle Eastern musics, is essentially modal. The character of each melody is found within the group of notes and their arrangement. It is true that Syriac hymnographers adopted the Greek eight-mode system, but this classification, in the present case, is more or less abstract. In reality, we find in the different types of chants characteristics of the modal system of other Middle Eastern *maqām*-type musics, including Arab, Persian, Turkish, and certainly Kurdish music, with microtonal intervals.

TRANSMISSION AND PRESERVATION

Syriac liturgical music is essentially oral, at least in its specifically musical aspect. Whereas its texts were codified fairly early, according to genre and liturgical use, and were scrupulously preserved, musical notation as such was nonexistent except for a few ekphonetic notations. Thus the music has endured to our day as a result of collective memory, especially in monasteries, seminaries, and religious schools where Syriac and even liturgical songs were part of the curriculum.

But this tradition has very likely undergone alteration over the centuries, and some of it has probably been lost. About a thousand hymns have been notated according to the modern system (Jeannin 1924–1930?; Husman 1969); still, because the religious centers were scattered and far apart, there are melodic variants and even different melodies, especially where sister communities such as the Maronite and Assyro-Chaldean are involved. Moreover, musical notation, despite its utility, cannot replace living oral transmission, a process in which modern recording technology now plays an important role.

The living oral tradition of Syriac liturgical song that remains accessible to its followers has maintained a remarkable link with secular song. Thus in the great majority of popular songs in Syria, in Iraq, and especially in Lebanon, we find Ephraem's heptasyllabic meter or Jacob of Serug's pentasyllabic meter. In Lebanon, the *zajal* and popular songs are often built on models resembling Syriac songs. Here, then, is an example of links between religious and secular musical expression in a part of the Middle East where the spiritual and the temporal are in general intertwined.

More than other Arab oral traditions, Syriac liturgical music faces a challenge resulting from an upheaval in the historical habitat of its communities. The faithful have progressively left the countries of the Middle East for the Western hemisphere: Europe, North and South America, and Australia. Religious leaders have tried to recreate active centers within this diaspora where their musical traditions may be authentically passed down. Although these communities cannot escape the outside influences that have surrounded them over the centuries, the instinct to survive remains strong, and connections to the past have been maintained.

REFERENCES

Dalmais, Irenée Henri. 1957. "L'apport des églises syriennes à l'hymnographie chrétienne." *L'Orient Syrien* 2/3:243–260.

Husman, Heinrich. 1969. *Die Melodien der Jakobitischen Kirche*. Vienna: Bohlau Kommissionsverlag.

Jargy, Simon. 1952. "La musique liturgique syrienne." *Atti del Congresso Internazionale di Musica Sacra*, 166–169. Rome: Desclée et Cie.

———. 1961. "Syrienne (musique)." In *Encyclopédie de la musique*, ed. François Michel, 3:992–993. Paris: Fasquelle.

———. 1978. "The Folk Music of Syria and Lebanon." *World of Music* 1:79–89.

Jeannin, Jules. 1924–1930?. *Mélodies liturgiques syriennes et chaldéennes*. 2 vols. Paris: Leroux.

Levi, Leo. 1958. "Les neumes, les notations bibliques, et le protochrétien." *La Revue musicale* 239/240:147–155. (*Troisième Congrès International de Musique Sacrée de Paris*.)

Nieten, Ulrike. 1998. "Syrische Kirchenmusik." In *Die Musik in Geschichte und Gegenwart*, ed. Ludwig Finscher, 9:185–200. Kassel: Bärenreiter.

Touma, Habib Hassan. 1971. *The Music of the Syrian Orthodox Church*. UNESCO Collection, Musical Sources, Religious Psalmody, 4(2). LP disk.

———. 1996. *Église syriaque orthodoxe d'Antioche. Chants liturgiques du Carême et du Vendredi Saint*. Inédit W 260072. Compact disk.

Wellesz, Egon. 1954a. "Early Christian Music." In *The New Oxford History of Music*, ed. Dom Anselm Hughes, 2:1–13. London: Oxford University Press.

———. 1954b. "Music of the Eastern Churches." In *The New Oxford History of Music*, ed. Dom Anselm Hughes, 2:14–52. London: Oxford University Press.

Wenzel, Jochen, and Christian Poché. 1992. *Syrian Orthodox Church: Antioch Liturgy*. UNESCO/Audivis D 8039. Compact disk.

Werner, Eric. 1952. "The Common Ground in the Chant of Church and Synagogue." In *Atti del Congresso Internazionale di Musica Sacra*, ed. Igino Angles, 134–148. Tournai: Desclée.

Yalcin, Warda, and Esther Lamandier. 1997. *Chants de l'église d'orient en araméen*. Alienor AL 1070. Compact disk.

Section 3
Popular Music and the Media

From Algerian *rai* music to Nubian and Khalījī "Gulfie" pop in the Arabian Peninsula to Uzbeki and Uighur pop, the Middle East and Central Asia offer a rich and varied array of "mediated" musics. While most of these clearly draw on American and European models, many also have strong local roots. Some are not really intended for international consumption but rather appeal to local audiences. Dialects, musical instruments, rhythmic patterns, and melodic styles all serve as ways to infuse local identity into an internationally familiar model.

As a result, there is usually a strong relationship between repertoires that might be called pop and other local repertoires. Sometimes, the designation "popular" disappears altogether in favor of more specific local descriptive terms. Often, these pop repertoires have social and political implications. Repertoires such as *rai* and Turkish *arabesk* bear indications of class and social identity.

Most Middle Eastern communities were quick to adopt the devices of the mass media and found it fairly easy to adapt their own styles of musical performance to the requirements of the media. In cities such as Algiers, Beirut, Cairo and Istanbul, to name only a few examples, the media became important patrons of musicians. Major media such as radio and television have become state-controlled in many places, and the twentieth-century history of the media involved attempts by performers and entrepreneurs to maintain their own control by using such forms as inexpensively produced cassettes, videotapes, and satellite television stations. Although the media have often had a depressing effect on local performance, they have also offered opportunities—locally, nationally, and internationally—for many performers.

Beyazit Tower at the University of Istanbul, topped with communication equipment. Photo © Yann Arthus-Bertrand, Corbis.

The Impact of the Media on Egyptian Music

Walter Armbrust

The Phonograph
Radio
Musical Films
Portability, Piracy, and New Media

In Egypt the only modern mass medium that did not directly involve music at the outset was print, which was first put to use locally in the 1820s by the modernizing ruler Muḥammad ʿAlī (r. 1805–1848). By the late nineteenth century printing had achieved the status of a mass-produced medium with a mass market (Ayalon 1995). Further innovations in media technology followed quickly, including the gramophone (from the turn of the twentieth century), radio broadcasting (from the 1920s on an unregulated basis, and from 1934 as an organized national service), cinema (silent films from the mid-1920s, sound films from 1932), television (from 1960; figure 1), "small" media (audio- and videocassettes from the mid-1970s), and global media (satellite broadcasting from the early 1990s).

In modern Egypt, music figured prominently in the economics and aesthetics of all audio and audiovisual media. Even in the medium of print, the pleasure of reading was often enhanced by news about performers made famous through audiovisual media. From the mid-1920s through the 1950s, many best-selling publications featured extensive news of theatrical and musical performers. For example, in 1947 *al-Ithnayn*, a lavishly illustrated variety magazine that emphasized show business, was estimated by the British Foreign Office to have a weekly circulation of 120,000. According to the available figures compiled by Ayalon (1995:150), this was far more than the circulation of any of the magazine's rivals. Although the popularity of *al-Ithnayn* cannot be attributed solely to its emphasis on music, there is no doubt that Egyptian illustrated magazines from the 1920s to the present have sought to sell themselves through association with musical personalities.

Modernists and political elites have always dreamed of reaching illiterates through audiovisual media. In Egypt music has functioned as a "honey pot," enticing audiences into unfamiliar media terrain. Through the gramophone, music reached mass audiences before other audiovisual content. The radio brought music into homes. Early filmmakers capitalized on preexisting audiences by casting singing stars in their films. At the beginning of the twentieth century music helped create readers; by the end of the twentieth century and on into the twenty-first, satellite television stations were trying to become profitable by drawing in viewers through music videos and rebroadcasts of old musical films. Music in Egypt, therefore, has had a long history of helping

FIGURE 1 The widespread use of the mass media by all strata of Egyptian society is indicated by this drawing of the Colossi of Memnon watching television. (From a notecard sold in Cairo.)

to shape media practices. Of course, the effect of music on the media has its counterpart—the impact of the media on music.

THE PHONOGRAPH

Commercial catalogs of Egyptian music date from 1904, and phonograph records were dominant until the early 1930s, when the introduction of radio and film reduced their importance. Although written information on the character of Egyptian music before recordings is fragmentary, and recordings of noncommercial music are essentially nonexistent (Racy 1977:5–9), there is no doubt that recording technology changed music dramatically. The phonograph removed musical performance from live audiences, and therefore from the "ecstatic feedback" between audience and performer (Racy 1991) on which Arab musical aesthetics were based. Written and oral sources indicate that the live-performance repertoire of recording artists was shaped by the popularity of gramophone recordings (Racy 1977:8).

Initially, because of technical limitations, a record could be no more than two to three minutes long. Consequently, many genres simply could not be represented in the recorded archives other than in truncated form or serialized over several records. The limitations on the length of recorded music became less severe by the mid-1920s, but a general tendency of audiences to have preconceived ideas about a given song based on a recording remained, as did a tendency of performers to gear their live repertoire to recorded performance. By the end of the phonograph era, musicians specialized in popular genres that were tailored to recording and were appreciated by audiences on their own merits (Racy 1977:172). The market for recordings was dominated by three main competitors: the Gramophone Company (based in England), Odeon (in Germany), and Baidaphon (in the Middle East). The buyers consisted initially of the wealthy and public venues such as cafés; later, however, records were increasingly accessible to a broad middle class.

RADIO

Early recorded music gave celebrities much wider fame than could be achieved through live performances. This capacity was further expanded in the 1930s with the introduction of radio and cinema. Radio broadcasting was the most important musical medium from the early 1930s until the 1970s, when more portable means of playing back recorded music were developed. When radio was introduced, some recording stars proved more skillful than others at adapting to it. Through the phonograph, performers such as 'Abd al-Ḥayy Ḥilmī, Shaykh Salāma Ḥijāzī, and Munīra al-Mahdiyya had achieved wide fame among nonspecialist, nonelite audiences. However, two early celebrities of the phonograph era stood out for their ability to extend their fame through new media. One was a man, Muḥammad 'Abd al-Wahhāb (Armbrust 1996:94–115; 'Azzam 1990); the other was a woman, Umm Kulthūm (Danielson 1997). Both were dominant performers whose mastery of the media made them leading figures in twentieth-century Arab music.

Unregulated radio broadcasting in Egypt began in the 1920s. After a tentative beginning, radio was brought under government control and began broadcasting in 1934. Egyptian State Broadcasting (ESB) operated through a contract with the Marconi Company of the United Kingdom and was financed through license fees on receivers, which rapidly became lower in price. In 1947 the contract with Marconi was canceled, probably because of increasing conflict with British policy. After the Free Officers took power in 1952 and definitively ended the direct colonial presence in Egypt, the range of Egyptian radio broadcasting was greatly expanded; its regional broadcasts reached the entire Middle East and beyond to parts of Africa, Europe, Asia, and even North America on a limited basis. By the 1970s Egypt was the sixth largest international broadcaster in terms of weekly program output.

In the 1930s and 1940s the ESB program was not oriented toward politics, and as a consequence a great deal of air time was devoted to music (El-Shawan 1980:111–112). Programming reflected the taste of Muṣṭafā Riḍā, who was the director of the Arabic Music Institute, with the title Arabic Music Consultant at ESB; and of Midḥat 'Āṣim, the director of ESB's Arabic music section. Rida was considered a conservative defender of musical *turāth* 'tradition', in contrast to 'Āṣim, who was trained in both Arabic and Western music. The goals of the ESB have been summarized by Salwa 'Aziz El-Shawan as follows:

> The creation of an instrumental traditional within AMAA [*al-mūsīqā al-'arabiyya*—the Egyptian category of secular urban music] which was comparable to the European tradition; the improvement of the quality of song texts; the encouragement of composers who attempted to incorporate Western musical elements into AMAA; the "improvement" of the audience's musical taste by broadcasting a variety of styles. (1980:112–113)

El-Shawan describes a modernizing agenda closely tied to building a nation-state. Such an agenda commonly emphasizes contestation over canons of taste. Distinctions between "high culture" and "low culture" are never directly transferable from one context to another. Consequently, American or European notions of what distinguishes high culture from low culture do not necessarily make sense in terms of Egyptian music. Therefore, to characterize Muṣṭafā Riḍā as a "conservative" and 'Āṣim as a "modernist" is not at all to say that Rida was a champion of what Americans would call "classical music" (a category that evokes "tradition" but is itself a synthetic and always shifting construct) or that 'Āṣim was an advocate of either fashion-conscious popular music or an elitist avant-garde. Many writers (such as Danielson, Racy, and El-Shawan) caution against imposing Western musical categories on Middle Eastern music. At the same time, one should not underestimate the persistence of a modernist discourse that sought to order expressive culture into opposed categories of artistic value. Nationalists have long seen culture as a means for carrying out an agenda that requires the construction of cultural hierarchies and the association of national identity with the most highly valued range of such hierarchies.

The ESB, with its official imprimatur, was an obvious venue for constructing a national culture. Muḥammad 'Abd al-Wahhāb and Umm Kulthūm, two performers who had already established a reputation through recording and film, solidified their position as dominant figures in the national arena through radio. Both performers had signed contracts with ESB very soon after the service began in 1934 (Danielson 1997:86). Radio offered all performers enormous advantages over recordings. The length of a song was no longer restricted by recording technology. Live concerts could be broadcast, and these broadcasts enabled performers to reconnect with audiences. Umm Kulthūm, for example, thrived on feedback from a live audience; by 1937, radio made this possible in mediated performance (Danielson 1997:86). ʻAbd al-Wahhāb found radio the perfect venue for long, heavily orchestrated compositions, devoid of improvisation, and usually based on texts written in classical Arabic. These "grand songs" of the 1940s (Armbrust 2000) were a perfect vehicle for accomplishing the formal objective of the ESB—to construct a high national culture. Accordingly, Midḥat ʻĀṣim gave ʻAbd al-Wahhāb and Umm Kulthūm pride of place in the ESB programming. From the 1940s until the end of her career (in 1973), Umm Kulthūm's eagerly awaited Thursday evening radio broadcasts became virtually a national ritual (Danielson 1997:86–87).

Between 1934 and the 1970s, music broadcast on radio reached the largest number of listeners of any medium, with the least technical constraints on performance. Radio was, of course, an entirely government-controlled medium, although this is not to say that radio music was either overtly propagandistic or frozen into a state-approved conservatism. Indeed, many recognize the 1930s through the end of the 1960s as a time of exceptional creativity and artistic ferment in music. Of course, radio broadcasts have continued from the end of the 1960s to the present, but after the 1960s the media were significantly reshaped by the introduction of portable devices, specifically the cassette player, which compromised the ability of the state to control performers' access to wide markets.

MUSICAL FILMS

Egypt began producing films in the 1920s (for basic information on Egyptian films, see al-Bindarī et al. 1994). After about a dozen silent films had been made, Muḥammad Karīm directed the first Egyptian talking film, *Sons of Aristocrats* (*Awlād al-dhawāt*, 1932). The first musical, *Song of the Heart* (*Unshūdat al-fu'ād*, 1932), followed immediately. Because *Song of the Heart* was directed by Mario Volpi, an Italian, credit for the first Egyptian musical is often given to Muḥammad Karīm, the director of *The White Rose* (*Al-Warda al-bayḍā'*, 1933), starring Muḥammad ʻAbd al-Wahhāb, who by that time had become a part-owner of Baidaphon (Racy 1977:113), the record company that financed the film. Clearly, musical stars were cast in Egyptian films because they contributed to success at the box office (Shafīk 1998:103–108). These singers were so highly paid that their fees could take half of a film's budget (Armbrust 2000:207; Danielson 1997:87–91).

During the early 1930s most of the technical work in films was contracted to European studios. However, plans were being laid for a more extensive and independent filmmaking infrastructure. These efforts resulted in the expansion of Egypt Studio (Stūdyū Misr), which was part of the financier Muḥammad Ṭalʻat Ḥarb's empire (an empire that included banking, textiles, and large construction projects). Egypt Studio was initially undertaken for the sake of prestige and probably was not very profitable (Davis 1983:206); it is widely regarded as a quasi-national institution (Ibrāhīm and Yūsuf 1996). From the mid-1920s, it documented Ṭalʻat Ḥarb's commercial ventures. Its first full-length fiction film—a public revelation that it could, for the first time, make films entirely on Egyptian soil—was *Widād* (1936), a historical romance starring Umm Kulthūm.

Between the 1930s and the end of the 1960s the musical film occupied a special place among media outlets available to performers. An image on film was intrinsic to the public persona of younger singers such as Laylā Murād, Farīd al-Aṭrāsh, Muḥammad Fawzī, Hudā Sulṭān, and ʿAbd al-Ḥalīm Ḥāfiẓ. During the 1940s and 1950s, popular illustrated magazines such as *al-Ithnayn* and *al-Kawākib* publicized the lives of these young performers as an extension of their film roles, whereas by this time ʿAbd al-Wahhāb and Umm Kulthūm were more likely to be publicized as singers—or, more accurately, as artists—than as film personalities.

Until the 1960s musical films were the private-sector counterpart of the state-owned radio service. The two attracted overlapping audiences and featured many of the same performers. However, cinema never reached as large an audience as radio. From the 1930s to the end of the 1960s, musicals were enormously prestigious, but the songs themselves were not necessarily enjoyed under the best of circumstances. According to el-Mazzawi (1966:200–216), up to the 1960s Egyptian films were often shown not in first-run theaters but in cheaper second-run theaters. Radio undoubtedly helped reconstruct songs that might have been victims of bad prints or worn-out sound systems in theaters. But it was probably not until the advent of television that audiences were regularly able to experience film songs in the context of coherent narratives and under relatively favorable conditions. In terms of how audiences experience films, the musical film—currently an object of nostalgia—is therefore more often a product of television than of theaters.

The theater experience was also strongly gendered. In Egypt, men typically dominate audiences at film theaters. This has probably always been the case, although the actual proportion of men to women in a theater undoubtedly varies historically, by class (more expensive theaters typically accommodate a greater mixing of genders) and perhaps by genre. (For a contemporary description of theatergoing in Cairo, see Armbrust 1998.)

The Egyptian cinema has produced approximately 3,000 feature-length fiction films. The most intense production of musicals took place from the mid-1940s to the early 1960s (Dougherty 1999). By the end of the 1960s, production of musicals virtually ceased, although some directors have attempted to revive the genre in recent years (Shafik 1998:106). The prevalence of musicals in Egypt is often casually exaggerated. In formal discourse, "too much" music is indicative of a general lack of seriousness on the part of filmmakers. Ezzedine (1966:48), for example, said that film producers' prediliction for singing and dancing "almost amounted to an obsession"—a statement that has sometimes been reduced to the stereotype "All Egyptian films are musicals." More accurate assessments suggest that during its heyday, the musical accounted for roughly a third of some 900 feature films produced (Shafik 1998:103; see also al-Sharqāwī 1970:98). However, any attempt to interpret the significance of musicals in Egypt should account for the fact that the decade following World War II was also the most productive period for musicals in Hollywood: for example, as many as 30 percent of the films made by MGM during this time were musicals (Cohan 1993:61, 68, n. 11).

Not surprisingly, given this close quantitative correspondence with Hollywood, Egyptian musicals are often criticized as derivative, both by outsiders and by local commentators (such as Farīd 1986). Indeed, a referendum taken in 1996 on the hundred best Egyptian films of all time included only about ten musicals (Yūsuf, in Bahgat 1996). But such criticism is misleading. For one thing, a referendum among nonspecialists might very well reverse the proportion of musicals to nonmusicals; in other words, it may be that musicals are denigrated only in formal discourse and are highly valued in the more intimate spaces created by national culture.

It is certainly true that many Egyptian films were adaptations of foreign genres, particularly the backstage musical (and also French popular theater, vaudeville, and various forms of diegetic musicals—films in which music is part of the narrative). But if the form of such films was often adapted in this way, the music itself always served to keep cinema locally meaningful. Meaning was not only a function of building on culturally based genres such as the *muwashshaḥ*, *mawwāl*, *qaṣīda*, or *nashīd*, all of

There is every reason to believe that the component of Egyptian musicals which made the most lasting impression was, precisely, the Egyptian music.

which were represented in films. A wide variety of Western music—ranging from contemporary jazz (or, more recently, other forms of contemporary Western popular music) to orchestral classics—was also incorporated into Egyptian films, both as background music and in songs.

Such proliferation of Western music is sometimes viewed with alarm in discourses on authenticity, but there is every reason to believe that the component of Egyptian musicals which made the most lasting impression was, precisely, the Egyptian music. Cinema, together with other media, created a dialectic relationship between styles of music, performers, and audiences. Forms of Arabic music that antedated the modern media would not have been part of this dialectic any more than American popular music would have been part of it, but elements of both could be incorporated in the vigorous hybrid styles facilitated by cinema.

However, it is important to emphasize that the dialectics of musical culture in the media from 1930 to 1970 were shaped by relatively centralized systems of dissemination. Radio and cinema were subject to cultural gatekeepers who applied different logic. In the case of radio, the rationale behind programming was the improvement of pubic taste; for cinema, the rationale was marketability. But these two media drew substantially from the same pools of talent and catered to overlapping audiences. The result was a unique blend of discrimination, responsiveness to audiences' tastes, and incentive for innovation.

In the 1960s the blend of production by private- and public-sector media began to change, as control of the media became more centralized. The print media was nationalized in the early 1960s and the film industry in 1964. Many observers feel that the public-sector production of the middle to late 1960s created the best films in the history of Egyptian cinema, but this evaluation is usually made from the gatekeeper's perspective. Often, the most artistically successful films were commercial failures. In terms of the thoroughly commercialized musical film, the nationalization of cinema undoubtedly hastened the end of the genre. There were a few attempts to make populist musicals during the public-sector period—one example is Ḥusayn Kamāl's *A Bit of Fear* (*Shay' min al-khawf*, 1969)—but these did not resonate with audiences and were largely unsuccessful. ʻAbd al-Ḥalīm Ḥāfiẓ's privately produced *Father Is Up a Tree* (*Abī fawqa al-shajara*, 1969), directed by Ḥusayn Kamāl, was highly successful but proved to be the swan song of the musical. By the beginning of the 1970s the genre was moribund and had ceased to be a significant factor in shaping the public taste in music. The cinema was reprivatized in 1970, at least to the extent that the state no longer directly financed film production (though it maintained ownership of the means of production); but very few musicals were made until the 1990s, when there was a minor revival of the genre (Shafik 1998:105–106).

PORTABILITY, PIRACY, AND NEW MEDIA

Throughout the 1970s, the radio service continued (as it still continues), but the pervasive cross-fertilization between public-sector radio and commercial film music was a thing of the past. Television regularly rebroadcasts musicals, as well as live concerts by approved performers (and more recently, a somewhat less tradition-bound selection of MTV-style music videos). However, starting in the 1970s official approval became increasingly conservative; thus newer singers such as ʿAlī al-Ḥajjār and Sūzān ʿAṭiyya were sometimes perceived as imitating not Western style but the style of the giants of the age of musical film, such as ʿAbd al-Ḥalīm Ḥāfiẓ and Umm Kulthūm (Danielson 1996:305–306).

Affordable audiocassette technology for consumers came in the early 1970s and was highly significant because it provided a new commercial forum for music at a time when the state had gained substantial control over all other mass media. Like radio, audiocassettes projected music into everyday settings that had not been a context for it in the days before modern media. The home, the automobile, public transportation, leisure space, and the workplace all became potential sites for music. With the audiocassette, moreover, the consumer chose the music (or nonmusical content; see Hirschkind 2000 on Islamic audiotapes), whereas music on radio was programmed by someone else. Commercial audiocassettes very nearly eliminate any form of cultural gatekeeping. Cassettes are easier and less expensive to produce and far more portable than records, let alone musical films. The economics of musical production and consumption were further shaken by piracy of cassette tapes. Records cannot be easily pirated, and generally films must be seen in a theater or on television; but by the end of the 1970s almost anyone could have a cassette tape copied very cheaply.

One effect of the new technology was that it became increasingly difficult for singers to dominate the market. When radio and cinema were the primary media outlets for music, from the 1930s through the 1960s, the social capital earned from the culturally discriminating ESB could be converted to financial capital through commercial cinema. Both were relatively centralized forms of media—radio because it was controlled by the state, and cinema because so much funding was required to produce it. Celebrity could be best achieved by those with a foot in both worlds.

By the 1970s, new commercial music began to diverge from state-controlled media. To some extent this was due to economic and political developments beyond the scope of this article (see McDermott 1988; Waterbury 1978). Still, a few landmarks can be mentioned: these include disastrous wars (defeat by Israel in 1967, followed by the destructive though partially redemptive October War of 1973); harsh repression of both leftists and political Islamists; and jarring economic dislocations caused by a transition from state capitalism under Nasser to limited free markets under Sadat. Consequently, national institutions that had been a point of pride in colonial or early postcolonial days were often viewed with skepticism or cynicism by the 1970s. Conditions existed for audiences to tune out radio, and cassette technology offered an alternative.

The range of music available on cassettes is wide compared with what is available on radio. Old favorites by Farīd al-Aṭrāsh, Asmahān, Laylā Murād, and Muḥammad Fawzi occupy shelf space next to music by newer singers who have become known through audiocassettes. They include Ḥamdī Batshān, Shaʿbān ʿAbd al-Raḥīm, ʿAlī Ḥamīda, Muḥammad al-Ḥilū, Muḥammad Munīr, Saḥar Ḥamdī, Iḥab Tawfīq, and Aḥmad ʿAdawiyya. These singers come from diverse backgrounds. The rather cerebral Muḥammad Munīr, for instance, has Nubian roots and associations with European performers that give him a cachet on the world music circuit, as does his acting and singing in films by the celebrated director Yūsuf Shāhīn. The unprepossessing Shaʿbān ʿAbd al-Raḥīm, a *makwagī* 'launderer' who has become a successful, if sometimes controversial, singer, is known for his social and political commentary.

Aḥmad ʿAdawiyya, a popular singer who generally eschews conventional vocal artistry, is perhaps the king of the audiocassette (Armbrust 1996; Danielson 1996). During the 1980s, he probably outsold all his contemporaries, though sales figures are scarce and unreliable. Although there have been diverse musical styles in Egyptian music since 1970, discussion of 'Adawiyya is paradigmatic of the larger discourse on music in the period. His merits (and faults) are framed by a discourse on taste. 'Adawiyya is often derided as a singer for uncouth microbus drivers; as the choice of Gulf Arabs, who are themselves often denigrated in Egypt for their presumed vulgarity; and as the hero of errant young people who have not learned to appreciate "authentic" Arab music. It has often been remarked, though, that disapproval of 'Adawiyya in the context of formal public discourse may mask tacit acceptance in more private contexts (Armbrust 1996:187–188; Danielson 1996:307).

In the larger scheme of things, 'Adawiyya's importance is not that he stands at the head of his generation as a singer. Others, such as Muḥammad Munīr, or more recently the Iraqi singer Kāẓim al-Sāhir, who has become popular in Egypt, have been treated more kindly by the critics; they are largely immune from the scathing comments leveled at 'Adawiyya. Rather, as the most commercially successful singer of the audiocassette age, 'Adawiyya encapsulates a transformation in the media. The audiocassette gives the consumer greater choice because the cultural gatekeeper is absent; therefore, people have greater freedom to listen to whatever they find pleasurable. Such a choice has political implications, even when the music itself has little or no direct political commentary.

However, the audiocassette gives musicians less choice in what they produce. Because anything they sell may be pirated, they have little economic incentive to work for a finely honed performance. If 'Adawiyya has become emblematic of an age in which there are "no more giants" like Umm Kulthūm or 'Abd al-Ḥalīm Ḥāfiẓ, it is also true that even if they wanted to, very few younger musicians have the luxury of creating the highly rehearsed and brilliantly polished performances of earlier generations. Umm Kulthūm's demanding rehearsal standards (Danielson 1997:127–133) are not often applicable today, when a very large proportion of the music available in Egyptian cassette markets features vocalists backed not by live ensembles but by a synthesizer. The liberal use of synthesizers is a sore point for purists; but for most musicians, studio production using synthesizers is simply an economic necessity. The synthesizer can, of course, be adapted for Arabic music (Rasmussen 1996), just as Western instruments were incorporated into the *takht*. Still, the synthesizer is a fault line in discussions of authenticity in Arab music.

Finally, it should be noted that the audiocassette in turn may soon lose its dominance. Compact disks, which are expensive, have had only a limited impact in Egypt. But satellite television is of potentially greater importance. Popular performers such as 'Amr Diyāb and Ḥakīm have begun to produce MTV-style music videos, which are broadcast in Egypt on both terrestrial and satellite television. Music videos are popular and less vulnerable to piracy than audiocassettes. The music can be copied, but there may be continuing demand for the entire package, including the video. Videocassettes of music videos can also be made, but a video player is an unwieldy device compared with a cassette player. Demand for music videos comes from satellite television as well as terrestrial television (now broadcast in Egypt on at least nine channels, each of which needs some unique content), and it is probably the satellite companies that are driving this demand.

Satellite broadcasts to the Arab world began in the early 1990s, and thus far most writing on satellite television has focused on the business itself (see, for example, the on-line journal *Transnational Broadcasting Studies*) or on the political economy of the new medium (Alterman 1998; Sakr 1999). There are now satellite broadcast companies owned by or affiliated with Egypt, Saudi Arabia, Lebanon, Syria, Qatar, and the United Arab Emirates. All are public-sector or quasi-public operations (such as MBC, which is based in London but owned by a brother-in-law of King Fahd of Saudi Arabia). Satellite television is, however, an expensive undertaking; thus even state-run companies have an interest in making this medium pay for itself, though they have not yet been able to accomplish that. Attractive content is, then, a necessity for satellite television, and music videos clearly have the potential to attract paying customers.

From the musicians' point of view, satellite broadcasting offers an opportunity to recapture a more centralized and lucrative media market than was possible during the era of decentralization and the predominance of audiocassettes. Furthermore, the customers for satellite broadcasts will be pan-Arab. The scope of the Egyptian media has always reached beyond Egypt's national borders, but the satellite age promises to be quite different—not an export market but a transnational market. And whereas Egypt had enjoyed a near monopoly of media production in certain fields (particularly cinema), the playing field of satellite television promises to be far more level, or possibly even tilted in favor of Gulf-owned stations.

REFERENCES

Alterman, Jon. 1998. *New Media, New Politics? From Satellite Television to the Internet in the Arab World*. Washington, D.C.: Washington Institute for Near East Policy.

Armbrust, Walter. 1996. *Mass Culture and Modernism in Egypt*. Cambridge: Cambridge University Press.

———. 1998. "When the Lights Go Down in Cairo: Cinema as Secular Ritual." *Visual Anthropology* 10(4): 413–442.

———. 2000. "Farid Shauqi: Tough Guy, Family Man, Cinema Star." In *Imagined Masculinities: Male Identity and Culture in the Modern Middle East*, ed. Mai Ghoussoub and Emma Sinclair-Webb. London: Saqi.

Ayalon, Ami. 1995. *The Press in the Arab Middle East: A History*. Oxford: Oxford University Press.

'Azzam, Nabil Salim. 1990. "Muhammad 'Abd al-Wahhab in Modern Egyptian Music." Ph.D. dissertation, University of California, Los Angeles.

Bahgat, Aḥmad Ri'fat, ed., *Miṣr, mi'at sana sīnimā*. Cairo: Mahrajān al-Qāhira al-Sīnimā'ī al-Duwalī al-'Ishrīn.

al-Bindarī, Mūna, Maḥmūd Qāsim, and Ya'qūb Wahbī eds. 1994. *Mawsū'at al-aflām al-'arabiyya*. Cairo: Bayt al-Ma'rifa.

Cohan, Steven. 1993. "Feminizing the Song-and-Dance Man: Fred Astaire and the Spectacle of Masculinity in the Hollywood Musical." In *Screening the Male: Exploring Masculinities in Hollywood Cinema*, ed. Steven Cohan and Ina Rae Hark, 46–69. New York: Routledge.

Danielson, Virginia. 1996. "New Nightingales of the Nile: Popular Music in Egypt since the 1970s." *Popular Music* 15(3):299–312.

———. 1997. *The Voice of Egypt: Umm Kulthūm, Arabic Song, and Egyptian Society in the Twentieth Century*. Chicago: University of Chicago Press.

Davis, Eric. 1983. *Challenging Colonialism: Bank Misr and Egyptian Industrialization, 1920–1941*. Princeton, N.J.: Princeton University Press.

Dougherty, Roberta. 1999. "The Egyptian Musical Film: Diagesis Derailed?" Presented at the annual meeting of the Middle East Studies Association of North America (MESA), Washington, D.C.

Ezzedine, Salah. 1966. "The Role of Music in Arabic Films." In *The Cinema in the Arab Countries*, ed. Georges Sadoul. Beirut: Interarab Center of Cinema and Television.

Farīd, Samir. 1986. "Sūrat al-insān al-miṣri 'alā al-shasha: bayna al-aflam al-istihlākiyya wa 'l-aflām al-fanniyya." In *Al-Insān al-miṣri 'alā al-shasha*, ed. Hāshim al-Naḥḥās, 205–216. Cairo: GEBO.

Hirschkind, Charles. 2000. "Technologies of Islamic Piety: Cassette-Sermons and the Ethics of Listening." Ph.D. dissertation, Johns Hopkins University.

Ibrāhīm, Munīr Muḥammad, and Aḥmad Yūsuf. 1996. "Studyu Misr: Madrasat al-Sīnimā al-Miṣriyya." In *Miṣr, mi'at sana sīnimā*, ed. Ahmad Ra'fat (Bahgat), 158–166. Cairo: Mahrajān al-Qāhira al-Sīnimā'ī al-Daulī al-'Ishrīn.

Manuel, Peter. 1993. *Cassette Culture: Popular Music and Technology in North India*. Chicago: University of Chicago Press.

Mazzawi, Farīd el-. 1966. "The U.A.R. Cinema and Its Relations with Television." In *The Cinema in the Arab Countries*, ed. Georges Sadoul. Beirut: Interarab Center of Cinema and Television.

McDermott, Anthony. 1988. *Egypt from Nasser to Mubarak: A Flawed Revolution*. New York: Croom Helm.

Racy, Ali Jihad. 1977. "Musical Change and Commercial Recording in Egypt, 1904–1932." Ph.D. dissertation, University of Illinois, Champagne-Urbana.

———. 1991. "Creativity and Ambience: An Ecstatic Feedback Model from Arab Music." *World of Music* 33(3):7–28.

Rasmussen, Anne. 1996. "Theory and Practice at the 'Arabic Org': Digital Technology in Contemporary Arab Music Performance." *Popular Music* 15(3):345–365.

Sakr, Naomi. 1999. "Satellite Television and Development in the Middle East." *Middle East Report* 210 (Spring).

Shafik, Viola. 1998. *Arab Cinema: History and Cultural Continuity*. Cairo: American University in Cairo Press.

Sharqāwī, Galāl al-. 1970. *Risāla fī tārikh al-sīnimā al-'arabīyya*. Cairo: al-Maktaba al-'Arabiyya.

El-Shawan, Salwa 'Aziz. 1980. "Al-Musika al-Arabiyyah: A Category of Urban Music in Cairo, Egypt, 1927–1977." Ph.D. dissertation, Columbia University.

Transnational Broadcasting Studies http://www.tbsjournal.com/ (Website.)

Waterbury, John. 1978. *Egypt: Burdens of the Past, Options for the Future*. Bloomington: Indiana University Press.

Yūsuf, Aḥmad. 1996. "Qirā'a fī istiftā' afḍal mi'at film fī tārīkh al-sīnimā al-miṣrīyya: istiftā' hawla 'ashq al-sīnimā wa 'l-waṭan." In *Miṣr: mi'at sana sīnimā*, ed. Ra'fat Bahgat. Cairo: Mahrajan al-Qahira al-Sīnimā'i.

Music in Performance: Cem Karaca, Live

Martin Stokes

I first saw Cem Karaca (figure 1), rock star and former doyen of the Turkish left, in 1990, in northern Cyprus. We were staying in the same hotel. I eventually plucked up the courage to speak to him but got only as far as "Good morning." "Guten Morgen," he replied, with a nervous smile, and strode past. Two young Kurdish men working in the hotel invited me to his concert in Girne's modest soccer stadium—they had free tickets. The gig started late, but eventually the band (guitars, drums, keyboards) struck up with a crash of fireworks, power chords, and billowing smoke machines as a jeep roared across the stadium with Cem standing on the back, cape swirling. He leaped onto the stage, fist clenched in the air, and snarled a well-known line from the poet Nazım Hikmet: "*Bu memleket bizim*!"—"This country is ours!" The crowd cheered, though apparently more out of relief that the gig had finally started than anything else. One of the Kurds turned to me with a half-smile. He was about to say something when the main fuse blew and the lights went out.

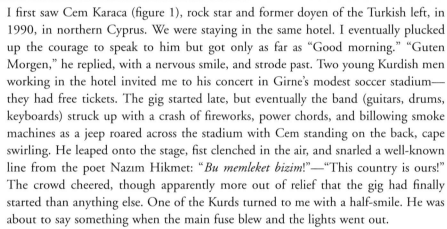

FIGURE 1 The Turkish rock star Cem Karaca, in Beyoğlu, Istanbul. Photo courtesy of Anne Ellingsen.

Six years later, in Istanbul, when power failures at live concerts were less common (although still not unknown), and Cem Karaca's flirtation with liberal-right politics had advanced several discernible degrees, I noticed a small advertisement in *Cumhuriyet*, the main center-left Turkish daily: Cem Karaca was performing in a small club in Beyoğlu. How could this huge, theatrical figure squeeze into a tiny club? I was intrigued, and I telephoned a friend whom I knew to be a fan. Perhaps we could contrive an introduction, and—who knows?—arrange to complete the conversation I had tentatively started in Cyprus.

We meet in a café on Istiklal Caddesi, a street of arty bookshops, smart clothing stores, blaring CD-cassette stalls, art-deco porn cinemas, old consulate buildings, neo-baroque shopfronts, and arcades bearing the names of Greek and Armenian subjects of the Ottoman Empire. It is now a pedestrian mall, with a tram instead of the roaring traffic that I associated with this street in the 1980s. "In the belly of Istanbul," Turks sometimes say, suggesting something both central and secretive. It is midsummer, and the street is seething. Music blares from a thousand speakers, and some of the live acts in the cafés (with windows wide open) are just beginning to make their contribution. The call to prayer sounds distantly from a small mosque halfway down the street; some cassette stalls reverentially turn off their sound systems, but others continue undeterred. The battle between sacred and secular has a taken a new turn in recent

Karaca is among hard-core fans, and the songs hardly need any introduction once the music begins.

years, following the Islamist takeover of the municipality. There is talk of a huge mosque in nearby Taksim Square, facing down the Independence Day monument, the Atatürk cultural center, and Taksim's large Greek Orthodox church. The tense, energetic "soundscape" of the Istiklal Caddesi seems to say it all.

Our café is a meeting place for feminists. Across the way, I am told, is where the Kurdish intelligentsia hang out. I look around and see, through the window, men playing billiards; somebody is picking, inaudibly, at a *bağlama* (a long-necked lute). We leave the feminist café and walk down one of the side streets. The gentrification of Istiklal Caddesi has not yet not gotten this far. Faded photos under rickety neon signs advertise belly dancers; doormen in cheap tuxedos, seeing foreigners, step forward—"Yes please, you want belly dancers?" Our club looks unpromisingly small, and we seem to be early. We establish that there is no cover charge, and we anticipate expensive drinks. By the time the ten or twelve other tables are full, our own table is already a mess of pistachio shells and cigarette ashes. But the others soon catch up. We have left the glamor of Istiklal Caddesi far behind us. People are smartly but cheaply dressed (in contrast to the elegant scruffiness of those in the feminist café); most are smoking Marlboro 100s and drinking the cheaper beer. Two tables away from us, there is a young couple. The man is in jeans and a sharply ironed shirt. The woman wears a glittery top, a long skirt, and a *çarşaf* (head scarf)—the uniform of respectable proletarian Muslims in Turkey at the moment. Both are drinking cola. The father of the family sitting next us, an elderly, rather portly man who has just returned from a twenty-year stint working in an automobile factory in the Netherlands, leans over to introduce himself, curious because we speak Turkish and curious about why we are here.

Cem Karaca has, all along, been sitting at one of the tables, drinking with some friends. There is no band, just keyboards, played by an old colleague, so no tuning up is necessary; they step onto the stage, and the small sound system clicks and hums into life. Karaca embarks on a lengthy, wordy introduction. His humor is spiky and self-conscious, delivered in slightly high-flown language, evoking gentle laughter and nods of approval. He is among hard-core fans, and the songs hardly need any introduction once the music begins. This is clearly a situation Karaca understands and loves. Totally absorbed in his own performance, he sometimes catches the microphone stand with a clumsy blow of a waving hand; sometime he moves to the front of the small, low stage, where he declaims a line with vehement passion to an audience that is no more than six feet away from him. The audience members mouth the words to each song, occasionally catching one another's eye at a particularly meaningful line. For a moment, I think I see tears in the Dutch *Gastarbeiter*'s eyes. Karaca chooses chanson-like songs suitable to a small gathering; the keyboards imitate piano and strings, without electronic rhythm. Some favorites get missed in the process, notably a few directly associated with his more radically politicized period, and he doesn't appear to be taking requests.

After an hour's singing, Karaca announces a break and simply steps off the stage to rejoin his friends. This seems to be our moment; we walk over and introduce ourselves. Karaca's performance appears to be continuing unabated. He is improvising energetically on any subject of conversation that crosses the table, and there is hardly a break in the flow as we are introduced warmly to a group of journalists and assorted literati (many of whom are clearly at the peak of a solid evening's drinking). Karaca, switching with ease from Turkish to English to German, opines on the subjects of Scandinavia and Ireland, Islamists and nightclubs, tolerance and intolerance,. He clinks glasses, greets other well-wishers graciously, and gulps at his *raki*. It is time for the second half. Somehow, we manage to exchange cards and arrange a meeting.

Karaca ends the show after another hour. The penultimate song is one of his most intense and intimate, and the last is an adaptation of a poem by Nazim Hikmet, "*Ben Bir Çeviz Ağaçı*," with a chorus that everybody knows. He repeats it until we are all singing and clapping along, ends the performance, and then returns for two short encores. He steps through a small door I hadn't noticed before, which is evidently the door to the dressing room, and that is the last we see of him.

Most of the audience members look as though they are heading home. My guess is that many have a long journey back to Istanbul's distant, unglamorous suburbs, and their first goal is to establish a place in line at the main *dolmuş* (shared taxicab) terminal in Taksim Square. Istiklal Caddesi, however, seems to be just waking up when we leave the club at about 1:00 A.M. We head back up the hill, toward the noise.

Turkish Rock and Pop Music

Martin Stokes

Pop, Rock, and the Nation
Cem Karaca and Anatolian Rock
Sezen Aksu and Turkish Pop

"At the very heart of [Turkish] pop music lies the urge to melt into a West-leaning universal culture. In Turkey, to succeed in producing music according to Western standards, to attain universal quality, has . . . become the grounds for . . . national pride." With these words, the Turkish critic Tanil Bora (1996:12; translation by the present author) sums up a contradiction at the core of Turkish pop and rock, an issue that continues to haunt the Turkish intelligentsia some seventy years after Mustafa Kemal Atatürk initiated a radical program of Westernizing reforms. What happens when "we" can be truly ourselves only by being like "them"?

Bora, along with other critics on the Turkish left, ties this contradiction to a certain fascistic narcissism that hovers around the fringes of Turkish rock and pop. Bora's comments are made in the context of a discussion of the enthusiastic reception by the Turkish extreme right of the German-Turkish rappers known as Cartel in Istanbul in 1994. Cartel's Islamist iconography and black gang uniforms, together with their lyrics, which many interpret as violent and misogynistic, were of instant appeal to the young, urban, marginal, culturally disenfranchised population on whom the fringe right-wing nationalist parties rely for most of their support. The group's success was undoubtedly connected not only to the cathartic violence and misogyny evident in their act, but also to the simple fact that the group had succeeded in being *onlar gibi* 'like them' while remaining decisively *bizden* 'of us'.

Contrary to Bora's suggestion, Turkish rock and pop musicians have from the outset been deeply concerned with the problem of registering their Turkishness in this assertively international music: Cartel inherited a long tradition. The stated identity politics and artistic ambitions of these musicians have been various, and a significant distinction can be made between Turkish rock and Turkish pop. In general terms, however, Turkish musicians use the words *rock* and *pop* to refer to the genres, dominated by guitar, keyboard, or both, that have emerged since 1960; to vocals using Western techniques and equal temperament; and to an ideal of group musical production organized around harmonic-polyphonic processes. Rock and pop are, in this sense, defined by what they are not: arabesk [see ARABESK] or Turkish commercial folk (*halk*) or art (*sanat*) music, each of which tends to feature a solo voice accompanied by a predominantly monophonic orchestra (often with chordal "backing") organized around the modal principles of Turkish rural and urban musics.

Rock and pop musicians have been courted eagerly by each of the major political parties and have played a part in the politics of identity in Turkey.

The terms *rock* and *pop* are not entirely satisfactory, for at least two reasons. First, the popularity of pop is not easy to define. Even during the pop boom of the mid-1990s, no pop singer could rival the sales of popular arabesk recordings, and it is clear that outside the large cities, listening habits are still firmly rooted in the more indigenous popular genres. The Turkish ministry of culture provided revealing figures for 1995 (Günyeli 1996:8). The highest-selling cassette by far was Mahsun Kĭrmĭzĭgül's arabesk hit "Tam 12d́en . . ." (1,247,000 copies), followed by İbrahim Tatlises's arabesk compilation "Klasikler" (724,000 copies). The highest-selling pop cassette was Kayahan's (661,000 copies); Ercan Saatcĭ's, which was regularly listed on various pop charts as number one throughout the year, sold only 108,000 copies. Second, *pop* and *rock* are not mutually exclusive terms: Kayahan more recently recorded a song by Tatlises, and the large companies have begun to identify a substantial crossover market. However, I will continue to use these terms, since at the most general level they conjure up distinct singers and musical styles in Turkey.

POP, ROCK, AND THE NATION

In 1983 Prime Minister Turgut Özal initiated a process of economic and political liberalization, casting Turkey as a "little American" regional superpower in the Middle East. In many ways, for Turkey's new bourgeoisie, rock and pop have explicitly symbolized this reconciliation of the contradictory demands of being simultaneously Turkish and part of the Western consumer world.

Rock and pop musicians have been courted eagerly by each of the major political parties. Pop and rock have played an important part in the larger-scale politics of identity in Turkey; they have also transformed urban space, and the daily experience of Turkishness, in more subtle and enduring ways. The deregulation of television and radio introduced music video stations (such as Kral TV) and a plethora of specialist pop and rock FM radio stations (such as Açĭk FM). Factory-made guitars from Bulgaria and Indonesia are now as cheap and easy to purchase in Istanbul as the *saz* (the long-necked Turkish plucked lute), and expensive American electric guitars can be found in large shops in upscale neighborhoods in Istanbul. Decreasing prices of foreign-manufactured tapes and CDs (following the entry of PolyGram and Warner Bros. into the Turkish market) mean that foreign popular musical styles can now make a rapid and widespread impact. In 1985, while the indigenous arabesk market was buoyant, the pop and rock icons of America and Europe (in particular Madonna, Michael Jackson, Pink Floyd, and the German heavy metal band The Scorpions) had a small following, imported cassettes were relatively expensive, and although punk rock had a small number of devotees in the suburbs of Istanbul, Turkey's punks were to all intents and purposes invisible. Less than a decade later, the influence of grunge and techno was instantaneous and extensive. Fashions associated with rave (goatees, long hair, tie-dyed T-shirts) and grunge (Doc Martens, dreadlocks) could be seen in profusion in and around Istanbul's universities, challenging the regimented uniformity of youth fashions that had prevailed throughout the 1980s and transforming accepted gender codes for public attire. The streets around Beyoğlu, Kadiköy, and Ortaköy in Istanbul and Yüksel Caddesi in Ankara now teem with flea markets catering to these new fashion subcultures.

Rock bars are perhaps the most significant new phenomenon, attracting young people who want to hear loud live music at cheap club prices. The first of these bars, Kemanci, began as a kind of alternative café under the Galata bridge in 1989, but then, after a fire, moved to its present location in Siraselviler, near Beyoğlu (the main nightclub district). The lone rock journal of the 1980s, *Studyo Imge*, has been replaced by a variety of magazines: some fanzines (*Mega Metal*, *Mondo Trasho*, and *Laneth*) and others scholarly (*Çalĭntĭ* and more recently *Müzük*). Rock and pop, in other words, constitute a sudden, highly visible, provocative presence in urban Turkish life and are a barometer of a rapidly changing experience of Turkishness. For all their sudden visibility, however, Turkish rock and pop draw on a much longer history.

CEM KARACA AND ANATOLIAN ROCK

Cem Karaca's background is in many ways typical of musicians associated today with Anatolian rock. Karaca was born in 1945 and has spent most of his life in Bakĭrköy, a suburb of Istanbul. His parents (his father is from Azerbaijan and his mother is Armenian) ran a theater in Beyoğlu, and his mother was a well-known stage actress. He attended Robert College, a prestigious English-language school, and began to play in amateur rock bands at informal concerts, making use of whatever instruments and amplification were available. In 1967, Karaca's first professional band, Apaşlar, won a "Golden Microphone" competition run by the Turkish daily *Hürriyet* to support emerging acts. The band's winning song, "Emrah," owed much to the French chanson tradition (indeed, Karaca makes much of the influence of Jacques Brel and Gilbert Becaud), but the words were taken from a Turkish folk poet, the Emrah of the title. *Hürriyet* assisted in recording and distributing successful songs from the contest and also arranged national tours, introducing musicians such as Karaca to life in the Anatolian provinces, often for the first time. "Emrah" was arranged and recorded in Germany, reflecting a lack of even the most basic recording facilities in Turkey until the mid-1970s, and beginning a long-standing link between Karaca and the German musical world.

Along with Cem Karaca, a generation of musicians—including Barĭş Manço, Üç Hüreller, Edip Akbayram, Moğollar, Özdemir Erodoğan, Mazhar, Fuat, Özkan (MFÖ), and Erkin Koray—were united by a distinct set of experiences: an upbringing within, or in close proximity to, Istanbul's non-Muslim, suburban petit bourgeoisie; a foreign-language education and European travel; formative encounters with the European counterculture; engagement with a wide range of diasporic musical subcultures in Europe; and success in national competitions, followed by an antagonistic relationship with the official media. Many who entered the eclectic world of commercial music making in the late 1960s were torn between their excitement at the dismantling of the old cultural orthodoxies and their alarm at what they saw as the erosion of a rich Turkish musical heritage. Throughout the 1960s, the popular music market was dominated by a number of singers and bands who specialized in importing and translating currently fashionable foreign popular styles. This has a long history in Turkey. The tango was firmly established in the late 1920s by visiting and local orchestras and was still very much alive in the late 1950s. Orchestras specializing in swing, mambo, calypso, tropical, and cha-cha soon followed. The first Turkish rock 'n' roll orchestra, established at Istanbul's naval college, specialized in school and college dances from 1955 to 1961. In 1961, Erol Büyükburç, later dubbed the Turkish Elvis, made his first recording, "Little Lucy," sung in English. Fecri Ebcioğlu's renditions of European hits in the early 1960s were particularly important for a number of singers and film stars, notably Ajda Pekkan. Between them, Büyükburç and Pekkan cornered the market in importing and translating fashionable European and American pop and rock genres, which became known through the first televised music performances, live tours, musical films, and immensely successful recordings. Anatolian rockers commonly stressed the necessity of using indigenous (that is, Anatolian) culture to challenge the economic and cultural hegemony of the United States and Europe.

In fact, the recording industry in Turkey, dominated in the middle of the twentieth century by Gramophone, Columbia, Odeon, Pathé, and HMV in particular, responded rather slowly to the new presence of Turkish rock and pop. The industry's lists from the early 1960s show the continued strong significance of an older generation of Turkish art singers, notably Münir Nurettin Selçuk and Müzeyyen Sennar, alongside singers of urbanized rural music such as Zekeriya Bozdağ, Ahmet Sezgin, Nuri Sesigüzel, and Abdullah Yüce (a precursor of arabesk). If anything, the multinationals kept the Turkish music market "Turkish" longer than might have been expected. On their lists, rock and pop formed a small subsection, often flagged with explanatory genre terms. Turkish Radio and Television (TRT), for its part, was dominated by the reformist ideals of the 1940s. For Anatolian rockers, TRT was an inward-turning, politically conservative institution, opposed to the kinds of modernization (Western musical instruments and harmonic-polyphonic techniques) that they wanted to see. This antipathy was reciprocated: even today, TRT remains hostile to Anatolian rock.

Cem Karaca often describes his early work as pop and dates the emergence of an oppositional, distinctly Turkish rock to his next band, Kardaşlar, in 1969. From this point on, his career was marked by increasing leftist radicalism, a more emphatic turn to the musical cultures of Anatolia, and restless collaboration with almost every group of musicians associated with Anatolian rock: Kardaşlar (1969–1972), Moğollar (1972–1974), Dervişan (1974–1978), and finally Erdahan (1978–1979). Kardaşlar was the first rock group to experiment with incorporating the *saz* and the *yaylĭ tanbur* (a long-necked Turkish bowed lute). "Lümüne" used folklike lyrics and was written in a 5/8 rhythm, marked out by a *darbuka* 'goblet drum', with the main theme introduced by the *yaylĭ tanbur*. The vocal melody follows the characteristic downward curve of the rural repertoire; the guitar picks out the 5/8 pulse and supplies a harmonic accompaniment that is predominantly I-IV-V.

The most self-conscious musical experimentation was carried out by Moğollar, MFÖ, Erkin Koray, and the more avant-garde Okay Temiz. Moğollar recorded and achieved conspicuous success in France after Karaca left the group in 1974. The titles of the songs of the more experimental groups drew attention to specific Anatolian instruments (Moğollar's "Ikliğ"), modal configurations (MFÖ's "Buselik Makamĭna"), dance genres (Moğollar's "Lorke"), or rhythms (Moğollar's "7/8–9/8") that have an iconic presence in their music. Groups such as Genesis, Deep Purple, Jethro Tull, Led Zeppelin, and Pink Floyd are most frequently cited as sources of inspiration, although precisely what these groups have inspired is often hard to tell. Two distinct musical techniques predominated: a grafting of Turkish texts, techniques, and instruments onto Western rock and pop styles; and "straight" performances of rural melodies on electric keyboards and guitars. Cem Karaca's hallmark, by contrast, has always been lyrics. Karaca specialized in setting to music the texts of the radical leftist poet Nazim Hikmet (then in exile in the Soviet Union), used folk poetry of the *aşĭk* (then identified as a source of indigenous political radicalism), and penned the first Turkish rock opera, *Safinaz*, in 1978. His vocal style is intense, verging on the histrionic. The implicit politicization of the music of the Anatolian rockers of the 1970s thus tended to become explicit when it was connected with Cem Karaca. Kardaşlar was distinguished by outspoken opposition to the military coup of 12 March 1970, beginning an overtly oppositional stance on Karaca's part that led to Dervişan's "1 Mayĭs" (celebrating the international labor movement) and finally to Karaca's self-imposed exile in Germany between 1979 and 1987 to escape constant harassment.

Deteriorating political conditions in the late 1970s, followed by a military coup in 1980, effectively put an end to Anatolian rock. Only a few relatively apolitical musicians associated with the genre—notably Üç Hüreller, MFÖ, and Barĭş Manço—were permitted radio and television time. Arabesk, drawing on a more rural musical aesthetic, had far greater appeal to the large flow of migrants from Anatolia than the experimentalism of Anatolian rock and was tacitly approved by the military government. Local cassette-production firms, which proliferated in the late 1970s, could cater to this new rural-oriented urban audience more rapidly and cheaply than the old record-producing multinationals. Economic austerity and an increasingly authoritarian political culture were not conducive to an underground rock culture: venues were hard to find, hostility to youthful "deviants" increased, and guitars and foreign recordings became difficult to obtain.

In 1985 a genre known as *özgün* 'original' emerged, promoted from within the recording industry (initially as protest arabesk) in response to a more liberal political climate, and to the fact that guitars were gradually becoming available again. Many of the first singers, including Ahmet Kaya and Hasan Hüseyin Demirel (Kaya's producer and a musician in his own right), were Kurds from Tunçeli; the preeminence of the guitar, an intimate bass vocal style reminiscent of the French chanson, and a somewhat self-conscious grafting of the *saz* onto guitar-based harmonic structures meant that their music had much in common with Anatolian rock. The lyrics of *özgün* were complex and often were taken from major leftist poets such as Nazĭm Hikmet. This music enjoyed great popularity between 1986 and 1989 as a "modern" alternative to arabesk; but it was located within the popular cassette industry and was co-opted by the larger labels—and thus, not surprisingly, by the end of this period it was difficult to distinguish from arabesk, except that arabesk had more directly emotional lyrics and a large violin chorus. In the early 1990s, an attempt was made to resurrect the radical potential of arabesk through Kurdish lyrics (involving musicians such as Fĭrat Başkale, and Umut Altĭnçağ), but these could not compete against less politicized Kurdish-language pop (so-called "Kurdobesk"); moreover, Kurdish radicals had become more cautious in the wake of devastating military operations under way in southeastern Turkey during the late 1990s.

SEZEN AKSU AND TURKISH POP

Sezen Aksu (figure 1) began her professional life a decade later than Erol Büyükburç and Ajda Pekkan but had a similar musical background. She trained in Izmir's private music societies and initially made a living singing and recording Turkish art music but gradually introduced Western pop and rock into her performances. Her current prominence followed on her partnership with the producer Onno Tunç (1949–1990). Tunç began as an Armenian church musician in Istanbul; he became fascinated with jazz and American soul in the late 1960s, when the Anatolian rockers were infatuated with European rock counterculture. Throughout the 1980s, he oversaw Turkey's unsuccessful efforts in the Eurovision song contest, but he is best known in Turkey for a series of collaborations with Sezen Aksu from 1984 until his death.

Sezen Aksu has much in common with the Lebanese singer Fayrūz. Both have been supported by influential Western-leaning musicians (in Fayrūz's case, the Raḥbānī brothers) and both have developed an intimate, idiosyncratic vocal style. Also, both have embraced the European pop aesthetic of the 1970s but throughout their careers have retained an ability to evoke and draw upon musical tradition—Turkish and Lebanese, respectively. Each has had the ability to keep herself in the public eye, engaging in fashionable political concerns, and thereby alienating the radical intelligentsia of her country. This comparison gives some sense of Sezen Aksu's enormous cultural significance in Turkey today.

FIGURE 1 The Turkish pop singer Sezen Aksu. Photo courtesy of Necati Sönmez.

The pop boom of the mid-1990s drew heavily on Aksu and Tunç's partnership, whose distinct qualities can be elucidated in relation to Anatolian rock. Both Anatolian rock and Turkish pop have made use of equal temperament, inflected guitar-keyboard functional harmony (increasingly incorporating the peculiarities of Turkish modal configurations), balanced four-measure phrases, and a lyric structure consisting of verse and refrain. Rock musicians have sought to distance themselves from the conventions of the Turkish popular market, presenting themselves as groups rather than as star singers with backing. By contrast, Turkish pop musicians such as Aksu, more firmly rooted in the wider field of Turkish urban popular music, have presented themselves as soloists, and their vocal techniques owe more to earlier urban popular styles. Aksu and Tunç's distinctive sound came from Tunç's compositional style, based on the keyboard and inspired by jazz and soul; and from Aksu's strong, inflected Middle Eastern vocal style and her complex, intimate lyrics. In 1995, breaking away from Tunç's style to work on one album, *Işĭk Doğudan Yükselir*, Aksu set out to integrate "traditional" Anatolian musics into the Turkish popular repertoire. Despite the success of this recording (reported as a lead story on the state's national news program), the Turkish content of her music, in contrast to Anatolian rock, has been implicit rather than explicit; her solo vocal style and the lyrics she writes have made for a distinct continuity with the urban popular aesthetic of the 1930s and 1940s and the arabesk of the 1970s and 1980s. This style has been widely imitated by her "students," Levent Yüksel and Aşkĭn Nur Yengi, and by their imitators in the mid-1990s: Tarkan, Mirkelam, Mustafa Sandal, and Rafet El Roman.

The political intent of Anatolian rock was explicit; by contrast, that of Turkish pop is implicit and has tended toward conservativism. Sezen Aksu has remained in the public eye by espousing progressive approaches to a number of social issues, especially feminism and the plight of the "Saturday Mothers"—a protest movement of women whose sons disappeared after being taken into police custody outside the Galatasaray Lycée in Istanbul. However she rejects the idea that she is a political figure or that she sings political music. When pressed, contemporary pop singers have tended to stress their admiration for leaders of the currently dominant liberal-right parties. The reasons are not hard to find. These musicians are a product of current political and economic conditions. The music industry is increasingly dominated by a few extremely large enterprises (notably Raks-PolyGram) that can channel money into extensive advertising on music video channels and (through copyright organizations such as POPSAV) can intervene effectively against piracy. It is perhaps not surprising that music produced by big business and appealing to bourgeois dreams of self-improvement should have created a generation of politically quiescent musicians, in stark contrast to the radicalism and the anxious identity politics of Anatolian rock. The voice of protest has been superseded by fascination with material goals: the car, the trip to America. Mustafa Sandal's "Onun Arabasĭ Var" ("He's Got a Car") and Rafet El Roman's "Macera Dolu Amerika" ("America, Full of Adventures") were the most conspicuous hits of 1996.

Still, the global spread of rock and pop is not a history of global Westernization. Despite the ambitions of many in the country, the impact of Turkish rock and pop has been largely confined to Turkey and the Turkish diaspora. From the outset, rock and pop musicians in Turkey have taken up the complex, contradictory issues at the heart of contemporary Turkish identity. The energetic and inventive determination with which rock and pop musicians in Turkey have tackled the sterile conundrum that Bora identifies—how to be "ourselves" while imitating others—will doubtless remain an enduring contribution to the experience of those who live in Turkey and those who look on from abroad.

REFERENCES

Akay, Ali, et al. 1995. *Istanbulda Rock Hayati: Sosyoljik Bir Bakiş* (Rock Life in Istanbul). Istanbul: Bağlam.

Berkay, Cahit. 1996. "Cahit Berkay ile Söyleyişi" (Interview with Cahit Berkay). *Dans Müzik Kültür: Folklora Doğru* 62:75–92.

Bora, Tanil. 1996. "Türk Popunda Milliyetçilik Dalgasi" (The Nationalism Craze in Turkish Pop). *Müzük* 1:24–25.

Güneyli, Deniz. 1996. "Yilin Pop Balonari" (Pop Balloons [Successes] of the Year). *Müzük* 1:8.

Hasgül, Necdet. 1996. "Türkiyede Pop Müzik Tarihinde 'Anadolu Pop' Akimin Yeri" (The Place of the Anadolu Pop Movement in Turkish Pop Music History). *Dans Müzik Kültür: Folklora Doğru* 62:51–74.

hira. 1996. "Punkinki Mi Uzun, Hip-hopinki mi?" (Which Has Got the Longest—Punk or Hip-Hop?) *Çalinti* 25(4):57–64.

Kozanoglu, Can. 1994. *Pop Çagi Ateşi* (The Fire of the Pop Age). Istanbul: Iletişim.

Meriç, Murat. 1996. "Türkiyede Pop Müziğin Öyküsü" (The Story of Turkish Pop Music). *Müzük* 1:50–52 (and subsequent issues).

Ok, Akin. 1994. *'68 Çigliklari: Müziğimizde Büyük Atilim Dönemi* (The Cries of '68: A Period of Great Élan in Our Music). Istanbul: Broy.

Özgün, Aras. 1996. "Cartel; Cehennemden Çikma Çikan Faşizm" (Cartel: Mad Fascism from Hell). *Çalinti* 25(4):49–55.

Robins, Kevin, and David Morley. 1996. "Almanci, Yabanci." *Cultural Studies* 10(2):248–254.

Temiz, Okay. 1996. "Okay Temiz ile Söyleyişi" (Interview with Okay Temiz). *Dans Müzik Kültür: Folklora Doğru* 62:93–109.

Arabesk

Nedim Karakayali

The Birth of Arabesk: A Brief History
Musical Organization of Arabesk
Arabesk Lyrics and Films
Arabesk Musicians
The Sociocultural Context of Arabesk

Arabesk is a popular music genre that emerged in Turkey in the late 1960s. The name alludes to elements borrowed from Arab music; it is otherwise unrelated to the term *arabesque* as used in art history. Arabesk composers are mainly inspired by Turkish folk and art music but also experiment with musical material from other cultures (Arab, Western, and so on). Typically, arabesk lyrics are deeply pessimistic, picturing a world filled with loneliness and suffering. Seen from a broader perspective, arabesk extends beyond music, particularly to cinema. Some commentators have even argued that it should be seen as an entire "anticulture." Its sociopolitical repercussions are also important. Despite its huge popularity, arabesk is strongly opposed by the Turkish cultural elite, who see it as a sign of cultural decadence. In fact, the term *arabesk* was originally derogatory. Since the early 1970s, arabesk has remained at the center of heated controversy, which the ethnomusicologist Martin Stokes (1992) has called the "arabesk debate."

THE BIRTH OF ARABESK: A BRIEF HISTORY

In the first decades of the twentieth century, the music media in Turkey were very limited. Few households had record players, and there were no private radio stations. In these circumstances, film music and foreign radio represented an important alternative. Beginning in the early 1930s, Egyptian films and film music began to be very popular in Turkey. Some scholars argued that this popularity was due to a ban imposed temporarily on the broadcasting of Turkish art music, sometimes called Turkish classical music (Tura 1988:41–42). After the establishment of the Turkish Republic in 1923, along with other reforms, the republican elite called for the creation of a new musical culture that would replace Turkish art music, which was associated with the previous political regime, the Ottoman Empire. The ban on broadcasting was a part of this attempt. Whether Egyptian music, which has important similarities to Turkish music, constituted a substitute for the marginalized Turkish art music is hard to ascertain. What is clear, however, is that the popularity of Egyptian music continued even after the ban was ended. Indeed, the state authorities next banned the public performance of Egyptian music with Arabic lyrics. As a result, the entertainment business opted for imitations, and eventually Turkish composers began to write music in "Egyptian" style. It has often been held that arabesk grew out of this practice of

The popularity of arabesk led to strongly negative reactions from modernist intellectuals and proponents of traditional Turkish music, yet it has remained one of the most popular genres.

composing in the Egyptian style—hence the Arab elements in arabesk. However, there has been little research on this topic.

From the 1950s on, several factors—among them the growth of the middle class, the availability of portable record and cassette players, and an increase in the urban population due to migration from rural areas—turned the light-music market into a profitable sector. By the mid-1960s, the number of pop musicians and their fans had increased considerably. In this lively sociocultural context many musicians began to strive for innovation. Some rock bands attempted to merge melodic and rhythmic elements from Turkish music with a rock 'n' roll beat, while others tried to fuse the American country style with Turkish folk music; and some traditional composers began to experiment with new musical ideas and materials.

Orhan Gencebay belonged to this latter group of musicians. Although he composed mainly within the Turkish *makam* system (modal structures in Turkish art music; see CONTEMPORARY TURKISH MAKAM REALIZATION), he often used unconventional elements, some clearly inspired by Arabic music and an elementary polyphony. Gencebay became immensely popular and from the late 1960s on produced many hit songs. He was immediately followed by others, and by the mid-1970s the "arabesk era" was flourishing.

The unprecedented popularity of arabesk led to strongly negative reactions from both modernist intellectuals and proponents of traditional Turkish music, for two main reasons: the abundance of "Arab" elements and the pessimism of the lyrics. Arabesk was also condemned in official circles, and state-controlled radio stations and television channels were forbidden to broadcast arabesk songs. Yet the popularity of arabesk continued, and it has remained one of the most popular music genres. Since the late 1980s, however, both Turkish pop music and arabesk as a genre have seemed to be undergoing a transformation. Turkish pop stars who are not associated with arabesk can now sell their performances just as well as arabesk stars, and several arabesk musicians are trying to modify their music along different lines. Some scholars believe that in the years to come a new synthesis may take place in Turkish pop (Tekelioğlu 1996; see also TURKISH ROCK AND POP MUSIC).

MUSICAL ORGANIZATION OF ARABESK

Most arabesk songs are composed in the *makam* system of traditional Turkish music, but the more sophisticated examples of arabesk deviate from conventional practice—often by using melodic lines that cannot be derived from any known *makam* or by modulating from one *makam* to another in nonstandard ways. Some compositions oscillate skillfully between different *makams*, and at times the exact *makam* of a piece may remain indeterminate, especially when the composer uses polyphonic accompaniment.

The formal and rhythmic organization of arabesk songs usually conforms to the basic principles of Turkish art and folk music (see TURKISH FOLK MUSIC THEORY). One important exception is the extensive use of instrumental introductions and breaks (*taksim*) in arabesk. Such sections are usually unmetered and allow for instrumental or vocal improvisation. However, whereas in art and folk music *taksim* sections are rather brief and modest and have the sole function of establishing the *makam* of a song (or modulating to a new *makam*), in arabesk these sections are often extended and are used to display instrumental or vocal virtuosity. Some musicologists have pointed out that the extension of these unmetered sections may also reinforce the "confusion" and "disorder" expressed by the lyrics (Stokes 1992).

Perhaps the most important differences between arabesk and traditional Turkish music concern the production, dissemination, and instrumental arrangement of arabesk songs. Although arabesk is often often composed on the *bağlama* (the long-necked Turkish lute), arabesk songs are produced in modern recording studios and make full use of the studio's facilities. Arabesk music is mostly disseminated through cassettes recordings, although live concerts are not uncommon.

The size and makeup of arabesk orchestras vary considerably in both studio recordings and live concerts (figure 1). The most vital parts of a prestigious arabesk orchestra are the string section and the percussion section, which usually consists of traditional instruments, although sometimes a drum set may be added. Other frequently used instruments are the *ney* (an end-blown ductless flute) and the *bağlama.* Some arabesk musicians also use an electrically amplifiable version of the *bağlama,* the *elektrobağlama,* which facilitates their display of virtuosity. Although not all arabesk orchestras use it, the *elektrobağlama* is often seen as the trademark of arabesk. Various other traditional instruments of Turkish music such as the *ud* (a short-necked fretless lute) and the *zurna* (a keyless shawm) are occasionally used in solo parts. Arabesk musicians also use Western instruments, either for accompaniment (for example, guitar, bass, accordion, and synthesizers) or for solo sections (for example, flute and trumpet). When such instruments are an accompaniment, their volume is usually very low and their polyphonic capacities are rarely used.

The instrumental arrangement of arabesk songs often presupposes a continuous antiphonal alteration between different blocks of instruments and vocals—a model most probably borrowed from Arabic music. This antiphonal alteration may take place between the lead vocal and the orchestra, or, especially in instrumental introductions and breaks, between the string section and various other solo instruments (figure 2).

ARABESK LYRICS AND FILMS

Perhaps the most characteristic aspect of arabesk songs is their pessimistic lyrics, which describe loneliness, suffering, separated lovers, powerlessness, and hopelessness. There is no place in arabesk for joy, laughter, or humor.

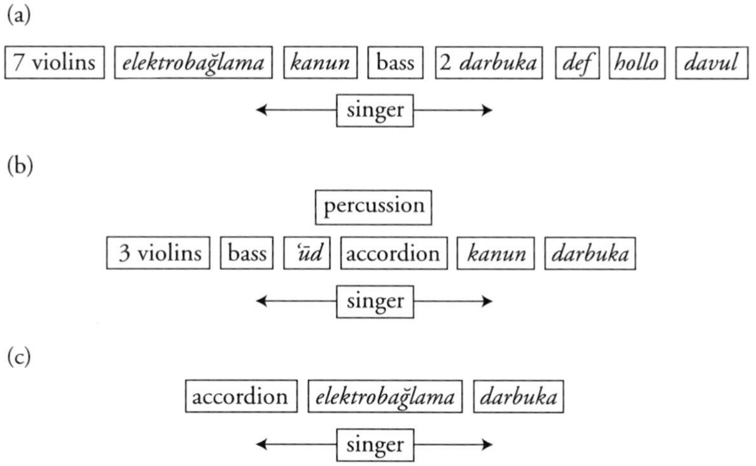

FIGURE 1 Three arabesk orchestras as examples of varying sizes and instruments. (Source: Stokes 1992:171.)

FIGURE 2 Opening section of an arabesk song, "Sarĭşĭnĭm," by M. Kĭrmĭzĭgül and Y. Caner, transposed up a major sixth (voice, up an octave plus a major sixth), from the version recorded by İbrahim Tatlıses. The symbol ^{2} marks a note flattened by two "commas." A comma is a very small interval; two commas "flat" would be less than a half-flat (𝄳) and thus higher in pitch.

The dark picture drawn by arabesk is metaphorical and abstract, seldom if ever referring to any actual event or concrete object. For example, an arabesk song may tell of the intense sufferings of an individual, but without answering questions such as who, where, when, or why. However, it has been pointed out that the abstraction of the lyrics does not make arabesk incomprehensible to listeners, who often interpret the abstract themes in light of their own specific experiences. Furthermore, arabesk lyrics usually allude to stories in the media and in arabesk films. These films often star arabesk musicians in roles as "victims of fate" who suffer in an unjust world.

ARABESK MUSICIANS

The popular myth about arabesk musicians can be summarized as follows: Once they were poor rural migrants trying to survive in the big city. One day, by chance, their musical talent was discovered by a rich producer, and soon they became famous. Despite their fame, however, they did not lose their traditional values. Indeed, it is the memory of their days of suffering that inspires their music.

This is, to a large extent, a constructed story. In reality, there is no typical arabesk musician. Arabesk musicians may have very different backgrounds, regional origins, sexual identities, and lifestyles, and they may belong to any age group. Many arabesk musicians move smoothly among different genres.

Perhaps the best-known arabesk musician is Orhan Gencebay. Paradoxically, he is seen both as the originator of arabesk and as an exception among arabesk musicians. His exceptionality is attributed to his urban background, his high level of education, and his private life, which has been free of scandal. Other important figures in arabesk, among them Ferdi Tayfur and Ibrahim Tatlıses, differ from Gencebay in regional origin, singing style, and lifestyle: these musicians often sing in dialect and use material from their regional folk culture, and the media frequently focus on their eventful private lives.

Many major and minor arabesk stars are known to be transsexuals or transvestites (although it should be noted that two of the most famous Turkish musicians in this group, Zeki Mûren and Bülent Ersoy, made their careers in Turkish art music and performed arabesk only occasionally). Some researchers suggest a link between blurred sexual identity or asexuality and arabesk, reflecting the sense of powerlessness, sexual isolation, and unrealizable desires that animates most arabesk lyrics and films. This argument is supported by the popularity of child arabesk stars, whose identity is asexual. Although there are several arabesk stars who project an unmistakably male or female image, such an image does not always accord with the themes of the music.

THE SOCIOCULTURAL CONTEXT OF ARABESK

Arabesk presents numerous challenges to researchers who want to study its sociocultural aspects—there are perhaps few sociocultural phenomena with so many conflicting attributions and associations. For example, whereas proponents of arabesk characterize it as "people's music," others condemn it as "anticulture" or kitsch.

Some sociologists have tried to place arabesk within a general framework of social movements and identity politics in a rapidly changing society. From this perspective, arabesk appears to be an expression of general discontent with the more pathological aspects of rapid urbanization and modernization. Others argue that arabesk provides an expression for the experience of rural migrants in urban centers who are partly torn from their traditional culture, yet not fully adapted to modern urban life. There is some truth to such arguments, in that arabesk is often popular in migrant communities and marginality is one of its recurring themes. At the same time, however, the popularity of arabesk certainly extends beyond migrant communities. Indeed, one of the most common settings for "arabesk culture" is an expensive nightclub with an upper-class clientele. This has led certain researchers to conclude that arabesk, rather than being a simple expression, gives individuals at all levels of society an idiom for articulating their experiences of marginality or social liminality. Although few, the existing scholarly studies of arabesk provide important insights and frameworks for future research.

REFERENCES

Belge, Murat. 1990. "Toplumsal Değişme ve Arabesk" (Social Change and Arabesk). *Birikim* 17:16–23.

Eğribel, A. 1984. *Nicin Arabesk Değil?* (Why We Are Against Arabesk). Istanbul: Süreç.

Ellingsen, Anne. 1997. "Den Tyrkiske Arabesk-Debatten" (The Turkish Arabesk Debate). *Norsk Antropologisk Tidsskrift* 8(3–4):218–230.

Güngör, N. 1990. *Arabesk: Sosyokültürel Açidan Arabesk Müzik* (Arabesk Music from a Sociocultural Perspective). Ankara: Bilgi Yay.

Karakayalï, Nedim. 1995. "Doğarken ölen: Hafif Müzik Ortaminda Ciddi Bir Proje Olarak Orhan Gencebay" (Stillborn: A Serious Light-Music Project—Orhan Gencebay). *Toplum ve Bilim* 67:135–156.

Özbek, Meral. 1991. *Popüler Kültür ve Orhan Gencebay Arabeski* (Popular Culture and Orhan Gencebay's Arabesk). Istanbul: Iletişim.

Stokes, Martin. 1992. *The Arabesk Debate: Music and Musicians in Modern Turkey*. Oxford: Clarendon.

Tekelioğlu, Orhan. 1996. "The Rise of a Spontaneous Synthesis: The Historical Background of Turkish Popular Music." *Middle Eastern Studies* 32(1):194–215.

Tura, Yaçin. 1988. *Türk Musikisinin Meseleleri* (Problems of Turkish Music). Istanbul: Pan Yayıncılık.

Israeli Mediterranean Music

Amy Horowitz

Musical Style
Historical Background
Technology and Mass Media

Israeli Mediterranean music is a hybrid genre created by Asian- and African-Israeli Jews. The music made its commercial debut in the 1970s on cassettes sold among the stalls of vegetables and household appliances in the marketplace at Tel Aviv's central bus station. Thought to be culturally inferior and "too Arabic," the music was rejected by many *ashkenazi* (that is, European-Jewish) radio editors, record companies, and listeners. Yet African- and Asian-Israeli Jews continued to produce these cassettes, which sold by the hundreds of thousands in their neighborhoods in the 1980s and by the 1990s had infiltrated the national airwaves and mainstream cultural institutions.

MUSICAL STYLE

The voicing of ornamented vibrato (melisma or *silsulim*) in Israeli Mediterranean music evokes the microtonality of Middle Eastern music in general. This ornamented vocal line is the aesthetic heart of the style and is part of its characteristic interaction between Western and Eastern instrumentation, rhythms, and tunes. African- and Asian-Israeli musicians invert European-Israeli compositional practice, in which eastern musical motifs are often sprinkled on a Western musical structure. Instead, they arrange selected Western elements—electric bass, guitar, and synthesizer—around a Middle Eastern vocal center.

The lyrics in Israeli Mediterranean music combine literary Hebrew with Hebrew and Arabic slang and have both sacred and secular themes. Although mainstream *ashkenazi* singers also use a range of linguistic styles, the dialogic combination of archaic Hebrew literary forms and current street language is a distinctive feature of the Israeli Mediterranean genre, readily identifiable by native Israelis.

The performers' repertoire expresses religious, ethnic, national, and generational loyalties. Musicians record sacred prayers with both traditional and modern arrangements to honor the liturgical traditions of the "father's house." Songs in Arabic, Persian, and Kurdish evoke nostalgia, touching on parents', grandparents', and in some cases the composers' own memories of daily life in Yemen, Morocco, Kurdistan, or Iran. Greek, Spanish, and Italian songs refer to the location of Israel—on the Mediterranean—and to its mediation between Eastern and Western musical styles. Rock instrumentation and rhythms attest to the performers' competence in contemporary youth culture.

The ornamented vocal line is the aesthetic heart of the style and is part of its characteristic interaction between Western and Eastern instrumentation, rhythms, and tunes.

Israeli Mediterranean music also utilizes the official repertoire of the Jewish ingathering—*shirei erets Yisrael* 'the songs of the land of Israel'. The incorporation of this genre, with its Eastern European melodies and romantic nationalistic lyrics, signifies the artists' claims of national belonging and competence in the sentimental "soundtrack" of the socialist-Zionist ethos.

As Israeli Mediterranean music took shape, its vocal line, patchwork of genres, and commingling of literary and oral Hebrew dialects threatened the prevailing practice of creating clear national and artistic categories. Indeed, this new panethnic style performed by Asian- and African-Israeli musicians at weddings and other neighborhood events in the 1960s and 1970s exposed the results of the ingathering and blending of diaspora Jewish communities, as overlapping neighborhoods rather than a homogeneous national whole.

HISTORICAL BACKGROUND

The magnitude and pace of the immigration to Israel after 1948 posed a puzzling set of issues for the original Eastern European socialist designers of the new state. They had to translate ideological principles into viable social programs within a now culturally heterogeneous context. Problems of Jewish ethnicity in Israel are rooted in the shortcomings of this absorption program and the unequal treatment and cultural insensitivity experienced by African- and Asian-Jewish immigrants.

The ingathering created conditions for intensified musical interaction between African- and Asian-Jewish musicians through their proximity to each other and their exclusion from the Eurocentric power structures of the new state. Between 1948 and 1953, Israel's Jewish population more than doubled, from 650,000 to 1.5 million. This population explosion led to complex problems not only by its sheer numbers but also in terms of the ethnic and ideological relationships it created. Against the backdrop of recent independence, international censure, economic crisis, and a state of war, Israel absorbed more than 700,000 immigrants divided equally between survivors of the European Holocaust and Jews from predominantly Muslim countries.

By the year 2000, over 50 percent of Israel's 5 million Jewish citizens were of Asian and African ancestry. Many were of multiethnic heritage. Their common socioeconomic marginalization, coupled with cultural affinities, gave rise to a panethnic marker, *mizraḥi* 'easterner'—although this was a loose term and not universally accepted. The concept of *mizraḥi* can be partially understood as a consequence of the encounter between East, Eastern European, and West in the newly formed state.

Asian and African Jews came to Israel with a rich musical history. The arrival of renowned Jewish musicians from Muslim countries in the early 1950s might have provided an opportunity to broaden the local soundscape by fostering a mutually respectful dialogue between easterners and westerners. But these rich and ancient eastern Jewish traditions were reduced to motifs and local texture within a national music industry governed by European tastes.

FIGURE 1 Kurdish *zorna* player from the ensemble Sheva Ahayot 'Seven Sisters'. Folkloric ensembles are acceptable partly because they are seen as preservers of "authenticity" and ethnicity. Photo by Amy Horowitz.

In *mizraḥi* neighborhoods and development towns that grew from the original transit camps, innovations emerged as Western, Mediterranean, African, and Asian urban and rural musics were reshaped through concentrated and intensified interaction. Weddings, births, bar mitzvahs, and religious holidays became occasions for musical transformation as well as community celebrations. Renowned Iraqi *qānūn* and *'ūd* players performed at Iranian, Libyan, Egyptian, and other weddings. Yemenite singers became fluent in Kurdish folk songs. The intermingling of styles was part of the new panethnic *mizraḥi* (Shiloah and Cohen 1983:236).

Alongside these regional musical dialogues, new immigrants encountered the *shirei erets Yisrael*, which had emerged as a popular music genre during the waves of Eastern European immigration from the 1880s through the 1940s. This genre featured a Western musical structure, an Eastern European ethos, and occasional Middle Eastern and Mediterranean textures and tunes. The Israeli ethnomusicologist Natan Shahar notes that this genre developed in a homogeneous, albeit transplanted, European society with a shared sense of national purpose—creating a new Israeli society on reclaimed land. Thus, the songs are often characterized by romantic nationalistic Hebrew lyrics idealize workers, the land, and the communal mission, and they are often set to Eastern European tunes, although at times Yemenite, bedouin, and even local Palestinian melodies were used (Shahar 1989:5–6).

Israel, like many African, Asian, and European countries that gained independence after World War II, established state-controlled media. There was an ideological as well as an economic rationale for this. Nation-building was furthered by broadcasting *shirei erets Yisrael* to the entire population. By controlling access to the airwaves, ethnic variation could be minimized, and new national songs helped shape a national identity.

As Israeli national radio and television and a local recording industry developed, the gap between emerging *mizraḥi* neighborhood traditions and national folk, popular, and art musics intensified. On the radio, Arabic and Mediterranean sounds were relegated to specific time slots; the classical Oriental ensemble was taken to be the official representative of Middle Eastern musics (Shiloah 1992:206), and emergent popular forms were excluded.

Yet the development of radio, television, and the recording industry eventually undermined musical homogeneity. Responding to commercial rather than entirely

FIGURES 2 AND 3 Rubi Chen plays at the City Club accompanied by a young Druze drummer. Photos by Amy Horowitz, 1994.

FIGURE 4 The audience for a concert of Israeli Mediterranean music at a community center in the Yemenite neighborhood of Rosh ha-'Ayin. Photo by Amy Horowitz, 1993.

national incentives, the media began to introduce Greek, French, Spanish, and other Mediterranean popular musics, which came to influence *shirei erets Yisrael* (Shahar 1989:109). In *mizraḥi* neighborhoods, these songs as well as Arab musics were copied from long-playing records and from radio programs (sometimes originating in neighboring countries) onto magnetic tape and distributed widely. By challenging dominant channels of communication and allowing grassroots distribution, these technological and media innovations further destabilized the nationally sanctioned musical genre and made way for the emergence of a commercially viable Israeli Mediterranean music.

By the late 1960s, when Israeli Mediterranean music was emerging, the position of *shirei erets Yisrael* as a style had shifted. These songs were becoming nostalgic devices through which Israeli society preserved memories of its founding. However, for the children of recent *mizraḥi* immigrants growing up during this period, the music was a symbol—for better or worse—of what the Israeli ethnomusicologist Amnon Shiloah defines in sociomusicological terms as *Israelization* (Shiloah and Cohen 1985:202).

While *mizraḥi* musicians were eager to contribute to the formulation of a new Israeli national musical style, their lack of Western training and the fact that they were not skilled in notation were often seen as a justification for excluding them. Moreover, the hybrid genre that was emerging in the *mizraḥi* neighborhoods was perceived as a challenge to the new state's cultural policies of forging a coherent national identity by subsuming ethnic traditions of the diaspora. Thus, Arab and other Middle Eastern sounds were relegated to holiday performances by official folklore ensembles. Only Middle Eastern Israelis whose European training framed their eastern vocal elaborations, such as the Yemenite singer Bracha Zefira (Flam 1982), entered the mainstream music establishment.

It is not surprising that Israeli Mediterranean music became more prominent in the early 1970s, as young people in *mizraḥi* neighborhoods challenged hegemonic cultural policies, which by then were being described as "the mistakes of the 1950s" (Halper, in Horowitz 1985). The *mizraḥi* cultural renaissance and social revolution involved attempts to redefine the artistic as well as political boundaries of Israel during a period of national and international political transformations.

The wars of 1967 and 1973 profoundly altered Israeli society. While the war of 1967 appeared to be a victory for Israel, it actually represented a significant contra-

FIGURE 5 Dress as a marker of Arab aesthetic affinities and Israeli national loyalty: a Moroccan Israeli soldier attending the Mimuna Festival in Jerusalem. Photo by Amy Horowitz, 1994.

diction for a society that had fashioned its political philosophy on a supposedly egalitarian ideal. After the Yom Kippur War (1973), the Ashkenazis' power was shaken by an outcry from the *mizraḥi* underclass against the Labor Party. The alliance of the *mizraḥi* with the right-wing Likud Party might have appeared contradictory, but it voiced decades of frustration with the Labor Party's discriminatory policies. *Mizraḥi* soldiers had been vital in both wars, and *mizraḥi* votes were vital to the victory of the Likud Party; thus the *mizraḥi* expected to be reconfigured as part of the mainstream. Their anger was fed when they continued to experience oppression.

Mizraḥi activism was intensified by the impact of the cultural and political revolution in the United States represented by the black power, antiwar, and students' rights movements. Israeli news broadcasts brought images and sound bites featuring U.S. activists rising in protest against national policies of exclusion and imperialism at a time when *mizraḥi* Israelis had just begun to flex their own political muscle. The name chosen by one *mizraḥi* activist group, *ha-Panterim ha-Sheḥorim* 'Black Panthers', testifies to the impact of these U.S. movements.

Yet, in contrast to some of the separatist political movements emerging in the United States, *mizraḥi* activism was motivated by a desire not to dismantle the system but rather to be accepted as equal parnters in the Israeli mainstream. Thus the struggle did not often take the form of violence or even of demonstrations. Rather, *mizraḥim* sought to contest their exclusion from economic, political, cultural, and social power structures and their marginalization from society itself. Their demand for inclusion was a call for redrawing the contours of society rather than for withdrawing to create their own subculture.

The widely accepted account of how Israeli Mediterrean music was established as a production and distribution network illustrates *mizraḥi* strategies. Their musical subversion combines the sociopolitics that followed the Yom Kippur War and new technology—in the form of a cassette recorder at a Yemenite wedding party. Community musicians had long been thrilling audiences at live performances, and sometimes they recorded their music on reel-to-reel tapes for limited distribution. With the cassette recorder, they saw the possibility of mass reproduction and created their own market.

For Asher Reuveni, who was to become one of the most successful entrepreneurs in Israeli Mediterranean music, the origin myth is a personal story:

> It all started with my wedding. I didn't have a real wedding with a band and dancing and drinking [going on] till morning. My wife's only brother was killed in the [Yom Kippur] war. Our happiness was shattered and we married in a quiet way in the offices of the Rabbinate. My friends promised that when the day comes, three months later, they will make it up to me with a real *ḥafla*. They brought the original *Oud* Band from Kerem Ha-Teymanim, with Daklon [Yossi Levy] and Ben Mosh [Moshe Ben Mosh]. Close to sixty people squeezed into my mother's little living room, three by four meters, and Daklon and Ben Moshe played and sang "songs from our fathers' home." (Reuveni, in Horowitz 1984)

Asher Reuveni and his brothers, Iranian owners of a record and electronics shop in the Yemenite neighborhood of Skhunat Ha-Tiḳvah, recorded the party. Using a new four-way duplicating machine, they made souvenir cassettes for their guests. The sound mix was poor, but the capacity to mass-produce the cassette was revolutionary. The Reuvenis were inundated with requests for the wedding tape. When someone offered them 100 *lirot*, they realized that this music could be a commercial success. Asher's brother Meir said:

> This was 1974, when a *lira* was a *lira*, and don't forget, it was a *partisani* [grassroots] recording, very unsophisticated. So I said, "What's happening here? My friends don't know how to read notes but they play and sing *alakefak* because it

FIGURE 6 Cassette covers suggesting the Yemenite singer Chaim Moshe's desire to attract diverse audiences. *Yemenite Step—Hafla* contains "good feelings" songs about ethinc identity and Arab affinity; *Someone Sings in the Desert*, released in conjunction with his appearance at a mainstream Arab festival, appeals to Ashkenazis.

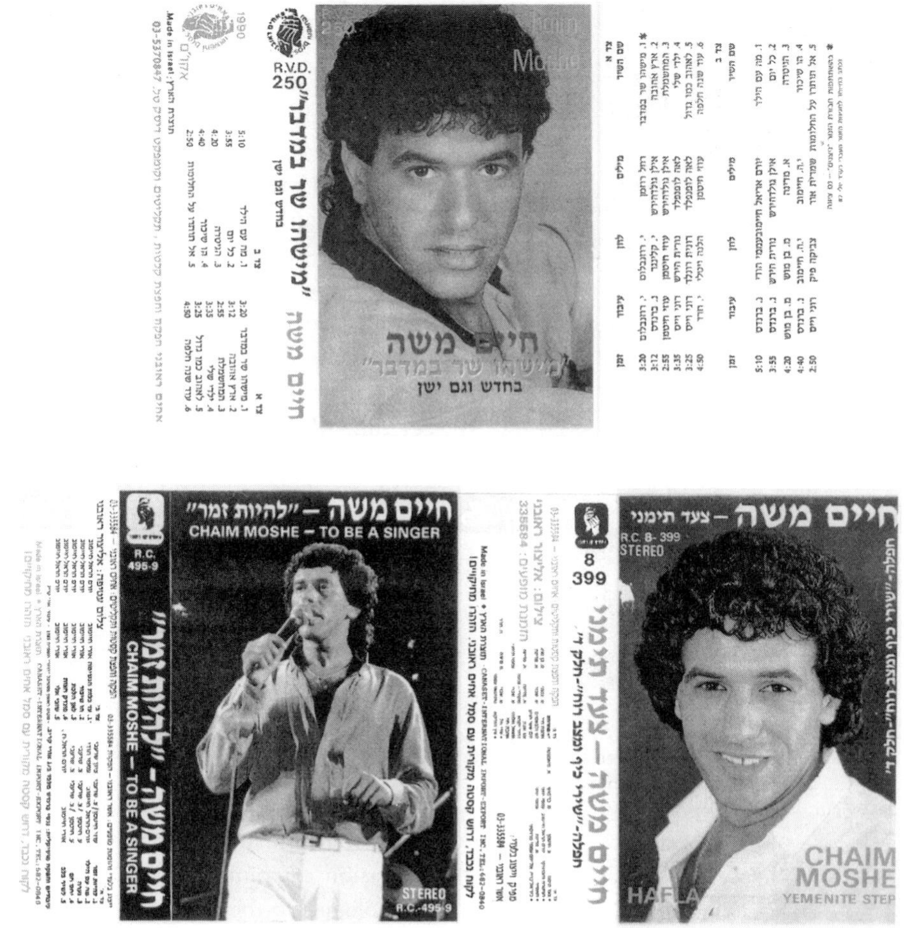

comes straight from the heart. It's good to know that music in this country finally runs according to our tap!" (Reuveni, in Horowitz 1984)

That the setting of this story was a marriage is not surprising; *mizraḥi* neighborhood singers were primarily employed as entertainers at weddings. Although most were Yemenites, they could perform multiethnic vocals, and they provided what was appropriate for each wedding. They rearranged Turkish, Yemenite, and Kurdish songs using rock and roll and Mediterranean popular styles, and they reworked European songs using Middle Eastern elements. For example, in a *mizraḥi* rendition of *Ḥanahleh Hitbalbelah*, a well-known song that joins a Hassidic melody and lyrics of *shirei erets Yisrael*, the Yemenite band Tseliley ha-Kerem moves the piece east of its Eastern European origin by playing guitar and bass lines in Greek popular style. The occasional augmented seconds and bent notes of the guitars are reminiscent of rhythm and blues of the 1960s and also create a sense of the quarter tone. In addition, a live *darbeka* player is juxtaposed with a simple drum machine line—played in halftime—that deepens the Eastern feeling. The music is a counterpoint to the Hebrew lyrics by Natan Alterman, a renowned poet of the *shirei erets Yisrael* period. The poem is a parodic love story of an Ashkenazi boy and a *mizraḥi* girl. Even as the performers navigated Greek, Arabic, rock, Yiddish, and Hebrew elements, their melismatic Middle Eastern vocals were the center of the sound weave.

TECHNOLOGY AND MASS MEDIA

The emergence of Israeli Mediterranean music can be partially explained as a consequence of opportunities created by national and international political movements of the early 1970s. Yet it was an invention by the Philips Corporation that made this musical self-realization possible. The portable cassette recorder allowed *mizraḥi* entrepreneurs to mass-produce and distribute musics that were excluded from the mainstream industry. Using homemade cassettes, *mizraḥi* musicians were able to sidestep the state-controlled media and other mainstream channels that had rejected their combination of Middle Eastern and Mediterranean influences with Western popular music. The affordability and adaptability of the cassette facilitated commercial and musical growth, empowering community-based music and altering local soundscapes forever (Wallis and Malm 1984).

Israeli Mediterranean music, like all hybrid cultural forms, is the result of an intentional process through which *mizraḥi* artists combine memories with their own innovations in a complex scoring of emotional and social life (figure 7). Israeli Mediterranean music is an intricate interconnected practice with national, ethnic, emotional, and social dimensions. It is a tool constructed by and for the music makers themselves in order to fashion a livelihood and a cultural identity. The singer ʿOfer Leṿi, for instance, proclaims himself an "Iraqi, Turkish, Syrian Israeli" (Yermi 1991:48). Leṿi's Israeli nationality, with these contentious ethnic qualifiers, illustrates the complexity of the Middle East—he not only lives in a disputed territory but is made up of the disputants.

Israeli Mediterranean music is a soundscape in which the borders between Arab ethnic and aesthetic affinities and Israeli national loyalty are unclear. In performances that reflect both elements, the sense of being Israeli is reshaped both for Ashkenazi and for *mizraḥi* citizens. Hebrew lyrics combine with Arabic, Persian, Kurdish, and Turkish tunes and texts, attesting to a regionally indigenous Israeli population whose music attracts Egyptian, Jordanian, Lebanese, Syrian, and Palestinian listeners. At the same time, the use of *shirei erets Yisrael* signifies national belonging and nostalgic socialist Zionism.

By the mid-1990s, this homespun genre had been elevated to a new position in the mainstream imagination. The increased acceptability of Israeli Mediterranean music may be part of two national trends: facing up to and embracing the hybrid nature of Israeli society and recognizing its Arab dimension, not only in terms of the presence of Palestinians within Israeli society but as a significant part of Jewish Israeli society

FIGURE 8 The portable cassette player, like cassette recordings, has transformed public soundscapes. Photo by Amy Horowitz.

itself. As Israel's geopolitical relations are reconfigured, this music spans geographic and cultural territories and shows that hybrid musical forms can provide an insight into disputed ground.

REFERENCES

Flam, Gila. 1982. "Pe'ulatah ha-musiḳalit shel Berakhah Tsefirah bishnot ha-sheloshimve-ha-arba'im be-Erets Yisrael" (Bracha Zfira's Attempt at Fusion of Traditions). M.A. thesis, Hebrew University of Jerusalem.

Horowitz, Amy. 1984. Interview with Haim Moshe and Asher Reuveni. Israel Field Tapes, Shkhunat Ha'Tikva, Tel Aviv (5 August).

———. 1985. Interview with Jeff Halper. Israel Field Tapes, Jerusalem (10 August).

———. 1991. Interview with Meir Reuveni. Israel Field Tapes, Tel Aviv (11 January).

———. 1994. "Israeli Mediterranean Music: Cultural Boundaries and Disputed Territories." Ph.D. dissertation, University of Pennsylvania.

———. 1995. "Performance of Disputed Territory: Israeli Mediterranean Music." In *Musical Performance,* ed. Amnon Shiloah, 1(3):43–54. London: Harwood.

———. 1996. "Overcoming Music Ghettos: An Interview with Avihu Medina, *Mizrahi* Musician in Israel." *Cultural Survival Quarterly* 20(4):55–59.

———. 1999. "Israeli Mediterrenean Music: Stradding Disputed Territories." *Journal of American Folklore* 112(summer, 445):450–463.

Regev, Motti. 1986. "The Musical Soundscape as a Contest Area: 'Oriental Music' and Israeli Popular Music." *Media, Culture, and Society* 8(3):345–355.

———. 1996. "Musica *Mizrakhit:* Israeli Rock and National Culture in Israel." *Popular Music* 15(3):275–284.

Shahar, Natan. 1989. "Ha-shir ha-Erets-Yisreeli ṿe-Keren Kayemet le-Yiśra'el" (Eretz-Israeli Song and the Jewish National Fund). Ph.D. dissertation, Hebrew University of Jerusalem.

Shiloah, Amnon. 1992. "Eastern Sources in Israeli Music." *Ariel* 88:4–19.

Shiloah, Amnon, and Erik Cohen. 1983. "The Dynamics of Change in Jewish Oriental Music in Israel." *Ethnomusicology* 27(2):222–251.

Shiloah, Amnon, and Erik Cohen. 1985. "Major Trends of Change in Jewish Oriental Music in Israel." *Popular Music* 5.

Tseliley ha-Kerem. 1986. *Ḥaflah Shel Shirim She-ahavnu* (Party Songs That We Loved). Tel Aviv: Reuveni Brothers RC 161–62. Cassette tape.

Wallis, Roger, and Krister Malm. 1984. *Big Sounds from Small People: The Music Industry in Small Countries.* New York: Pendragon.

Yermi, Amir. 1991. "There Is Almost a Kilo of Gold on Me." *Yedi'ot Aḥaronot* 8 (November):48–50.

Rai

Bezza Mazouzi

Background: *Hadharī, Charqī,* and *'Açrī*
Development of *Rai*: 1950s to 1970s
The Culmination of *Rai*
What *Rai* Means

Rai originated in western Algeria at the turn of the twentieth century, as a folk music of bedouin shepherds, based on bedouin folk forms and Arab love poetry. It began to flourish in the 1920s in the port of Oran. Modern *rai* dates from the 1950s and 1960s, when it was taken up by singers influenced by Western styles. Today, the word *rai* 'opinion' is translated more idiomatically—for example, as "my way," "tell it like it is," and even "oh, yeah!"

BACKGROUND: *HADHARĪ, CHARQĪ,* AND *'AÇRĪ*

In western Algeria, there are several relatively distinct musical genres, though they have greatly influenced each other. In rural areas, bedouin *rai* was popular. Urban genres included the *gharnāti* 'classical suite'; the *hawzī*, an urban popular form; and the *hawfī*, a swing-style song—though these flourished mostly in Tlemcen. In Oran, the urban *hadharī* was common.

Hadharī is closely related to rural *rai* in mode, rhythm, and singing style. Yet it uses different instruments: the *rabāb al-shā'ir/rabāba* (a one-stringed violin), the *gumbrī* (a three-stringed lute like the Moroccan *al-awtār* used by the duo of Ben Amina and Sidi Ahmed), the *tār* (a drum with cymbals attached), and the *darbūka* (an earthenware drum).

In the 1930s and 1940s, *hadharī* was influenced by the popular 78-rpm recordings of Egyptian stars such as Muḥammad 'Abd al-Wahhāb, Umm Kulthūm, and Farid al-Aṭrāsh, and by Egyptian musical films. This early Egyptian influence soon resulted in a change in the makeup of *hadharī* bands: the *'ūd* (a lute with five double strings) replaced the *gumbrī*, and the *kamanja* (a four-stringed violin) replaced the *rabāba*. Even the term *hadharī* was replaced—by *wahrāni* 'from Oran'. This genre was popularized by the singers Belaoui al-Haouari, Ahmed Wahbī, Ahmed Saber, and Chaykha Ouda, among others. In its later phases, the Egyptian influence touched every large Algerian town and city.

In the 1950s, Egypt's popular music, exported as part of Egyptian films, became so influential in Algeria that it gave rise to a new genre, the *charqī* 'Eastern' style. Yet the genre was also influenced by Western music. The trend grew during the 1960s, with many musicians joining it: Cherif Kheddam, Maāmar Missoun, Ahmed Zahār, Moḥammed al-Jamoussi in Tunisia, and later Abd el-Wahab Belkhayāt in Morocco.

In the early 1980s, *rai* entered its triumphant phase: *chāb rai* 'the *rai* of the young'.

It should be noted that during this era, many Algerian musicians had to play in exile, trying to combine local and Egyptian music.

At the same time, starting in the 1950s, another genre developed: *'açrī* 'contemporary'. This genre was strongly influenced by Western styles; drew on rhumba, samba, and waltz rhythms; and used Western instruments exclusively. One of its promoters was 'Abd al-Azīz Mahmoud. It received considerable support from the mass media of the time, but it did not really became popular until the late 1970s and early 1980s, when it caught on especially among groups such as the Djamal 'Allām, Idīr, Izenzaren, and Djurjura.

DEVELOPMENT OF *RAI*: 1950s TO 1970s

Traditional *rai*, which still sung and played today, is exemplified by *shuyūkh* 'masters' like Hamada, Khaldī, Madānī, Būrās, Jilālī, Laïd, and Hadādjī; and by *shaykhāt*, women singers such as Rimiti, Fatima, Kheira, Largam, Dalila, and Rabia. The women sing in a very low voice that usually has a raspy quality. Some of these women began their careers as dancers, like the famous Rimiti, who was followed by Abbassiya, Djaniya, Oudam Zahram Jarba, and others. Women have also been skilled percussionists, playing the *gallāl* and *tār*, but few play the flute, which is reserved for men.

In the early 1950s, signs appeared of what was to become pop *rai*. Belkacem Bouteldja began to use the accordion in place of the *zamr*, a double aulos with horned ends forming a little hollow; the *zamr* has a low sweet sound broken slightly by the breath needed to play it. The advantage of the accordion was that it allowed a *rai* performer to play and sing at the same time. But the accordion could not play quarter tones, so Bouteldja transformed it by changing the length of the strips of metal inside, making it compatible with the traditional Algerian melodic system. His fame is due in part to his introduction and adaptation of the accordion.

In the same era, Messaoud Bellamou, a trumpeter who had been trained at the Aïn Tamouchent conservatory after playing in brass bands in stadiums and Western-style shows, began playing *rai* with Benfissa in cabarets and saxophone with Bouteldja at weddings. Bellamou introduced the saxophone to *rai*. In 1974, inspired by jazz, rock, bossa nova, and reggae, he and Bouteldja named their genre pop *rai*. This name stemmed from the combination of *rai* as sung by Bouteldja and Bellamou's Western-influenced music. Later, other young musicians followed this syncretist path, calling their music *ghinā' rai* 'rai song'.

Thus a way was opened for the introduction of all sorts of Western instruments that had had no aesthetic justification in traditional *rai*. Musicians attempted a kind of compromise between the Western sound of saxophone, accordion, guitar, electric organ, drums and, in the early 1980s, synthesizer and drum machine; and the Algerian sound of *gallāl, tār, darbūka, qarqābū,* and *kamanja*. Of course, all these musicians orchestrated and composed differently, inspired by and borrowing from sources outside their own tradition.

THE CULMINATION OF RAI

With the introduction and spread of the electric organ, synthesizer, and drum machine in the early 1980s, *rai* entered its triumphant phase: *chāb rai* 'the *rai* of the young'. Because the cassette market was flourishing, *rai* could go far beyond its point of origin to reach many young people who were seeking a sharp separation from their elders. In 1985, at the instigation of the mass media, the Algerian ministry of culture organized the first Festival of *Rai*. At this time, *rai* had a short-lived but nonetheless real heyday in the media. There were television and radio programs and reports on *rai*, and many articles about it in the press. The press reported on the production and marketing of *rai* and also debated the ethics of this music—the tone of *rai* and its lyrics were antiestablishment and uninhibited.

The *rai* of the 1980s, represented by *chāb* singers like Khaled, Mami, Moumen, Tati, Messar, Khada, Jallāl, Abelhak, Zahouani, Raïna Raï, Noudjoum el-Raï, and Chaba Zahouanïa, was definitely controversial. One controversy had to do with the "intertextuality" of *rai* as it was cultivated by the younger generation. They incorporated indistinguishable clichés from blues, reggae, and rock into their music, but they also brought in *charqī*, *wahrānī*, *'aytī*, and bedouin music from the high plateaus.

Chāb rai is characterized by an improvisational, impromptu, precarious quality. There are at least two reasons for this. First, this younger generation lacks solid musical training and often knows nothing of the musical universe of older people. Among older generations, musicians have many years of training; in their universe, a disciple takes over only on the death of a master. This type of training severely limits the opportunities available to young musicians, and thus it does nothing to encourage their interest in traditional *rai*.

The second reason is the younger generation's critical attitude toward tradition. Such an attitude is, perhaps, implicit in young people's accrued aesthetics of multiple, converging musical practices from which a new genre—or at least a community of signs—develops at the margins of existing genres. This critical stance is also, of course, implied by the name *rai* itself.

WHAT *RAI* MEANS

As we have seen, *rai* literally means an opinion, and in this sense it is linked to the idea of making a decision. It also means discernment and counsel. Therefore, *rai* refers to freedom of thought and freedom of choice. Popularly, *rai* also has begun to mean individual destiny or fate—a person's future.

Given this breadth, the term *rai* has a technical function and a semantic function. Technically, it is a leitmotiv, a refrain which fills in the gaps when inspiration fails the singer-poet during improvisation. Semantically, it has a psychological effect. Its meaning "destiny" takes on full weight as a symbol or image of daily life. This is how *rai* has become the expressive form of disadvantaged groups in rural society and marginalized city-dwellers, among others. It has also become an accusation, although its identification of the source of a problem is not necessarily realistic.

These, then, are among the reasons why some critics call *rai* revolutionary music. Objectively, *rai* conveys no revolutionary message. But subjectively, it is tempting to say that the young are making a revolution, not in the sense of hoping for it or planning it but rather in the sense of simply accomplishing it by raising ethical and aesthetic questions as members of a social group that has been disadvantaged and shaken by acculturation—by the assimilation of other cultural codes.

On the other hand, today these young musicians are being co-opted by the recordings market, insofar as their art has ceased to be marginal and their creativity has become more conformist. This is a historical fact, though it can be interpreted in many ways. In fact, any interpretation would be in perfect harmony with the meaning of *rai* as opinion. The term *rai* implies that we are free to think what we wish about the phenomenon *rai*.

In western Algeria, music was divided into rural and urban. The sociocultural context favored music, and musicians enjoyed a privileged status, with a stipulated system of compensation. Musicians' long training gave them the necessary bases for performance: for example, knowledge of melodic and rhythmic systems and of specific singing styles. Orchestral training was also well-defined, and performance included dances choreographed for men.

During the 1940s, indications of change emerged. There were greater mutual influences among local genres, and there were strong influences from foreign music, first Eastern and then Western. Gradually, this change became an upheaval on two levels—in performance and socioculturally. The first upheaval was due to a widespread use of Western instruments and motifs that were alien to traditional aesthetics. The younger generation's training in Western conservatories was perhaps one of the most important factors in this development. The second, sociocultural, upheaval was due to new means of recording and marketing: long-playing records, cassettes, and the mass media were important factors in this. Such factors contributed, perhaps inevitably, to the emergence of a new kind of *rai*.

TRANSLATED BY BETH RAPS

REFERENCES

Ben-Naoum, A. 1986. "Le raï, délit d'opinion?" *International de l'Imaginaire* 5:5–16.

Boukella, Djamal. 1985. "Vagues et raï de marais." *Algérie Actualité* (29 August–4 September).

Lazrag, Omar. 1985. "Pop-raï, ordinateur et révolution." *Algérie Actualité* (15–21 November).

Mazouzi, Bezza. 1990. "La musique algérienne et la question raï." *Revue Musicale* 418–420 (June).

Miliani, Hadj. 1986a. "Parcours symbolique de la chanson raï." *International de l'Imaginaire* 5:17–21.

———. 1986b. "Voix de fait et socialité du raï." In *Documents de travail 1 du Groupe de Réflexion sur la chanson oranaise*, 11–25. Oran: Bibliothèque Règionale.

Mouffouk, Ghania. 1985a. "Raï, les chabs, et les cousins." *Algérie Actualité* (22–28 August).

———. 1985b. "Le papillon du raï." *Algérie Actualité* (22–28 August.)

Virolle-Souibes, Marie. 1988a. "Le rây, côté femmes." *Peuples Méditerranéens* 44–45 (July–December):193–220.

———. 1988b. "Ce que chanter erray veut dire." *Cahiers de Littérature Orale* 23:177–208.

Berber Popular Music

Jane Goodman

Music and the Development of Berber Identity
Contemporary Berber Song

Berbers are usually defined as speakers of one of the Berber languages of North Africa. A member of the Afro-Asiatic language family, Berber is related both to Semitic languages, among them Arabic, Hebrew, and Aramaic, and to ancient Egyptian, Coptic, and the Cushitic dialects spoken in Ethiopia. Historical and linguistic evidence suggests that Berbers may have been in North Africa as early as 2500 B.C.E.—long enough to be considered the region's indigenous inhabitants. Many other peoples arrived later, including the Romans (second century B.C.E.), the Arabs (seventh century C.E.), the Turks (sixteenth century), and the French (nineteenth and twentieth centuries). Each group brought with it new forms of political organization, cultural traditions, religions, and languages. The coming of the Arabs was particularly influential, resulting in the adoption of Islam throughout North Africa and the spread of the Arabic language in the region's cities, towns, and plains. As a result, Berber-speaking regions have gradually receded. Today, areas where Berber is the primary language are limited to geographically isolated mountains and desert oases. Of course, Berber-speakers also live in cities, where they often speak Berber in the home and Arabic in shops, schools, and businesses.

Berber-speakers currently make up at least 20 percent of the Algerian population and 40 percent of the Moroccan population, by conservative estimates. Algeria's primary Berber populations include the Kabyles of the Djurdjura mountains, the Shawiya of the Aurès mountains, and the Ibadites of the oases of the Mzab, centered on the Saharan desert city Ghardaïa. In Morocco, Berber-speaking populations inhabit the mountainous regions of the Rif and the Middle Atlas in the north and center, and the High Atlas and Anti-Atlas mountains as well as the Sus valley in the south. A third large group of Berber-speakers consists of the Tuareg populations in the Saharan regions of Niger, Mali, southern Algeria, Burkina Faso, and neighboring countries. Small Berber settlements can also be found further east, from the Siwa oasis in Egypt's western desert to Libya's southeastern border to the Tunisian island of Djerba. Berbers also constitute a sizable percentage of North African immigrant communities in Western Europe, especially France.

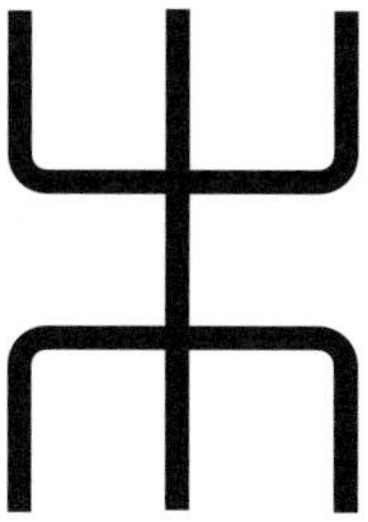

FIGURE 1 This symbol of the Amazigh movement comes from the Tifinagh alphabet, which is native to the Tuareg people.

According to the fourteenth-century historian Ibn Khaldūn, the name *Berber* was bestowed on these populations to describe the "strangeness" of their tongue. Although this anecdote cannot be verified, historians and linguists agree that the name is of external origin, most likely deriving from the Greek word *barbaroi* (Latin *barbari* 'those who speak a foreign tongue'). Increasingly, Berbers prefer to call themselves by the term *Imazighen* 'free men' (singular, *Amazigh*), which is native to the Berber spoken in Morocco's Middle Atlas mountains. It is used today by Berber (*Amazigh*) political activists and their sympathizers in both Algeria and Morocco (figure 1). The conscious selection of an indigenous term reflects the Berbers' growing awareness of their common historical origins as well as their developing transnational (pan-Berber) identity.

MUSIC AND THE DEVELOPMENT OF BERBER IDENTITY

Since the 1970s, music has been crucial to the development of Berber cultural and political identity in both Algeria and Morocco. To understand why, it is necessary to consider the context within which the contemporary Berber movement was born. From the 1930s through the 1950s, Algerians and Moroccans were increasingly involved in anticolonial struggles against France. Revolutionaries from both countries used the Arabic language as one way to rally the population around a vision of a nation united against the colonial power. When independence was achieved by Morocco (in 1956) and Algeria (in 1962), both states proclaimed Arabic the national language and declared it an essential element of their cultural identity. Berber, which the French had favored, was viewed as a threat to national unity. Considered a backward mountain dialect by government authorities, Berber was accorded no place in the new states.

The newly independent nations offered few political contexts in which their vision of national identity could be contested. Neither Algeria's single-party socialist republic nor Morocco's monarchy permitted serious opposition. During the years following independence, many forms of Berber expression, including language courses, academic conferences, and political gatherings, were suppressed by government authorities. The one aspect of Berber culture that was tolerated was its folklore. In fact, the existence of indigenous folk traditions was considered proof that decades of colonial rule had not altered the nation's soul. As a result, Berber cultural and political leaders turned to song to express their divergent views. In postcolonial Algeria, and to a growing extent in Morocco, music has played a vital political role, helping to create and communicate a notion of Berber identity that could not be expressed through other channels.

That music now constitutes an important form of communication among Berber populations is also a function of intersecting historical, sociological, and technological factors. Before the advent of radio, sung poetry had flourished for centuries in Berber regions. Professional poets (called *imeddahen* or *imedyazen*) would travel from village to village to offer sung commentary about recent social and political affairs. These poets helped to chronicle important events, galvanize popular sentiment, and maintain intervillage and intertribal communication. With technological advances, including the creation of national radio stations and the development of recording technologies in the 1940s, Berber music began to be heard by broader audiences. Today, the fact that music is transmitted aurally works to the advantage of a population largely illiterate in the Berber language (still being standardized in writing). In the absence of newspapers or other Berber-language publications, popular music has been until recently the only modern form of mass communication to which various Berber-speaking groups have widespread and simultaneous access.

CONTEMPORARY BERBER SONG

Contemporary Berber music was born in the early 1970s, when the Kabyle song "A Vava Inouva"—composed by a young singer who used the pseudonym Idir 'to live' or 'he lives', in collaboration with the poet Ben Mohamed—caused a sensation throughout North Africa and France. "A Vava Inouva" is built around the refrain of a tale told for centuries by old women throughout Kabylia: a man is banished by his community to a hut outside the village, where his daughter secretly brings him food and water. Each day when she arrives, she shakes her bracelets and sings to her father to let her in, and he sings a reply. One day an ogre imitates the girl's song, the father opens the door, and the ogre devours him. Idir extracted the sung refrain and inserted it into an original song that describes how Berber culture has been passed down from generation to generation through the telling of such tales. Seeking to show that Berber culture was not doomed to disappear but could have a place in the contemporary world, Idir set the familiar refrain in a new musical context: he played it on an acoustic guitar, using arpeggiated chords and harmonies associated primarily with popular Western folk singers of the time, among them Joan Baez and Bob Dylan.

"A Vava Inouva" heralded a new genre, which Berbers refer to in French as *la nouvelle chanson* 'new song'. New song, or new Berber song, is characterized by distinct themes, musical styles, performance practices, and audiences.

Themes

The themes of new song emphasize Berber (*Amazigh*) identity and the history and traditions of the Berber people. A corollary focus is the Tamazight (pan-Berber) language: songs provide commentary about the importance of preserving the language and strengthen a sense of transnational identity by suggesting standard vocabulary and pronunciation (both vocabulary and pronunciation vary considerably from one Berber region to another).

Singers approach the common theme, identity, from various perspectives. Some—Idir, the Kabyle groups Djurdjura (a women's group) and Yugurten (named after a Berber warrior who fought the Romans), the Shawiya singer Dehiya, and the Moroccan group Izenzaren—have focused on reviving traditional texts or melodies within contemporary compositions. Embedding verses from older repertoires into their own songs, these singers have sought to emphasize the value of Berber culture while eliminating aspects felt to be incompatible with contemporary forms of identity. For them, song serves as a forum for the evaluation of Berber cultural practices and a vehicle for their transformation. Others—the Kabyle singers Ferhat Imazighen Imula, Ali Ideflawen, the late Matoub Lounes, and the Shawiyas Amirouche and Les Berbères—have used song as a platform from which to launch incisive critiques of the government's cultural and linguistic policies. Still others—Algeria's Lounes Ait Menguellat and Morocco's Mimoun Lwalid—direct their songs as much at their own population's history, strengths, and shortcomings as at government policies.

To varying degrees, all singers have framed the question of Berber identity in relation to ideas of democracy, social justice, and human rights, particularly the rights of minorities and women. In so doing, they have directly challenged the policies of the state. As a result, most singers have had to contend with a measure of government surveillance, ranging from censorship of the media to confiscation of passports, from cancellations of concerts or recordings to arrests and even torture. For instance, Ferhat Imazighen Imula—whose songs most explicitly confronted the totalitarian policies of the Algerian state—was imprisoned thirteen times between 1976 and 1987. Because of the subversive political role Berber singers have played, they are sometimes referred to as "guerrillas of song."

Musical styles

New song is characterized by contemporary harmonies and instrumental arrangements. In the 1990s, Tak Farinas of Algeria raised this style to unprecedented heights, setting his songs to compelling arrangements and driving rhythms. Although the new musical style epitomized by the guitar-based harmonies of "A Vava Inouva" was adopted by many groups, not all singers play in this style. Matoub Lounes, for example, modified an urban popular style called *sha'bī*; Lounes Ait Menguellat accompanies

As the first Algerian song to resonate outside the North African community, "A Vava Inouva" produced a sense of pride among Algerians.

his searing poetry with a quarter-tone guitar and traditional percussion. However, two musical innovations pioneered by the early new Kabyle singers were subsequently adopted by many North African popular groups. First, the new singers broke with a long tradition of recorded music in which a solo vocalist was accompanied by a large radio orchestra playing in unison. Second, even the most traditional singers began to experiment with new instruments and combinations of instruments, including Western synthesizers and guitars and traditional Berber instruments such as the wooden flute (*ajewwaq*; plural, *tajewwaqt*) and the *bendir* drum.

Performance practices

New song was among the first North African contemporary genres to embrace a new performance modality centered on a shift in the status of the musician and a change in performance venues, audiences, and listening habits. Whereas earlier musicians were socially marginalized, new singers became stars with a local following as intense as fans of the the Beatles or the Rolling Stones. And whereas earlier musicians played primarily for male audiences in intimate venues such as cafés, a central performance setting for new song is a gala concert staged in a large hall or an outdoor stadium. Attendance by women has become more frequent, although in some performance settings women are seated with their families in a separate section.

These changes can be partially attributed to an increasing acceptance of music related to broader changes occurring throughout North African society. In particular, the growing number of public schools and universities founded after independence not only increased educational and professional opportunities but also provided new settings for mixed-gender interaction. Awareness of the Western youth movements of the 1960s, which centered in part on common allegiance to musical stars, may also have helped to transform the ways in which music was appreciated locally. Furthermore, new song does not generally evoke the controversial domain of love or desire, which typically segments North African audiences according to age and sex.

Audiences

When "A Vava Inouva" was broadcast in France in 1975, during a highly symbolic occasion—the first visit of a French head of state to independent Algeria—it became the first Algerian song played on French national radio and the first Kabyle song to enjoy success among European listeners. As the first Algerian song to resonate outside the North African community, "A Vava Inouva" produced a sense of pride among Algerians, and particularly among the Kabyle population. "For the first time in its history," noted the journalist Abdelkrim Djaad, "Algerian song had earned a place in the so-called advanced countries, where third-world cultures had been viewed as subcultures" (1979; translation by the present author). Berber singers have developed strong followings among the growing immigrant audiences in Europe, drawing as many as ten thousand spectators to a single show; some have also played in the United States and Canada.

New Berber song has much in common with the music of other oppressed or minority peoples, for example, the *nueva canción* movement in Latin America, the music of Savuka in South Africa, and the songs of Alan Stivell in Brittany (Stivell recorded one song with Idir). An early form of what we now call world music, contemporary Berber song has played a vital role in creating a sense of pride and cultural identity among North Africa's Berber populations.

REFERENCES

Bourgeot, André. 1989. "Cultures, langues berbères, et folklorisation chez les Touaregs." In *Tradition et modernité dans les sociétés berbères*, ed. Tassadit Yacine, 33–52. Paris: Awal.

Brett, Michael, and Elizabeth Fentress. 1996. *The Berbers*. Oxford: Blackwell.

Chaker, Salem. 1989a. *Berbères aujourd'hui*. Paris: L'Harmattan.

———. 1989b. "Une tradition de résistance et de lutte: La poésie berbère kabyle—Un parcours poétique." *Revue du Monde Musulman et de la Méditerranée* 51(1):11–31.

Djaad, Abdelkrim. 1979. "Idir, entre l'aède et le show." *Algérie Actualité* (2–8 August): 22–23.

Djura. 1990. *Le voile du silence*. Paris: M. Lafon. (Djura. 1992. *The Veil of Silence*, trans. Dorothy Blair. London: Quartet.)

Gross, Joan E., and David A. McMurray. 1993. "Berber Origins and the Politics of Ethnicity in Colonial North African Discourse." *PoLAR: Political and Legal Anthropology Review* 16(2):39–57.

Lacoste-Du Jardin, Camille. 1978. "Chansons berbères, chansons pour vivre." *L'Histoire* 5:104–105.

Lefebure, Claude. 1984. "Ousman: La chanson berbère reverdie." *Annuaire de l'Afrique du Nord* 23:189–208.

Matoub, Lounes. 1995. *Rebelle*. Paris: Stock.

Mehenni, Ferhat. 1983. "La chanson kabyle depuis dix ans." *Tafsut: Série Spéciale "Etudes et Débats"* 1:65–71.

Schuyler, Philip D. 1984. "Berber Professional Musicians in Performance." In *Performance Practice: Ethnomusicological Perspectives*, ed. Gérard Béhague, 91–148. London: Greenwood.

———. 1993. "A Folk Revival in Morocco." In *Everyday Life in the Muslim Middle East*, ed. Donna Lee Bowen and Evelyn A. Early, 287–293. Bloomington: Indiana University Press.

Yacine, Tassadit. 1989. *Ait Menguellat chante . . .* Paris: La Découverte/Awal.

Zoulef, Boudjemaa, and Mohamed Dernouny. 1981. "L'Identité culturelle au Maghreb à travers un corpus de chants contemporains." *Annuaire de l'Afrique du Nord* 20:1021–1051.

The Popular Music of Arab Detroit

Anne K. Rasmussen

Early History: Sana and Amer Khaddaj and Jalil Azzouz
Mainstream Music in Detroit
Iraqi and Yemeni Music
Arab Detroit and Arab America

Detroit, Michigan, and its adjacent city, Dearborn, are in the midwestern United States. Characterized by rich farmland, the natural splendor of the Great Lakes, and major automotive manufacturing plants, this area is part of two quintessentially American economic sectors: agriculture and industry. It is also a kind of living microcosm of the Arab world and a cosmopolitan crossroads of Arab musical activity.

Detroit and Dearborn may not have an equal representation of people from all of the twenty or so nations that make up the Arab world, but there is in fact no place that better approximates an "Arab world mosaic" (see, for example, Coon 1966). Arab immigrants came here throughout the twentieth century, and thousands continue to arrive every year. Early in the twentieth century, immigrants were likely to be Christians from Syria, Lebanon, and Palestine, a region referred to as the Levant and then encompassed by the designation "greater Syria." Arab Detroit today is a mixture including well-established first-wave immigrants, their second- and third-generation American-born children and grandchildren, and immigrants who have arrived more recently from all over the Arab world. There are about 200,000 Americans of Arab heritage in the metropolitan Detroit area, which is said to be the largest Arab community of the diaspora.

EARLY HISTORY: SANA AND AMER KHADDAJ AND JALIL AZZOUZ

While some Arab emigrants came directly to Detroit, others migrated from New York and New England, traveling along peddling routes that had been established at the beginning of the twentieth century. Many more followed in the wake of an economic revolution facilitated by the Ford automobile plant and related industries, which created jobs requiring little skill in the English language and little technical training. The life stories of the musicians Sana and Amer Khaddaj and Jalil Azzouz exemplify the early migration from the Levant to the eastern United States to Detroit.

Amer and Sana Khaddaj first performed together in Lebanon in a musical version of Khalil Gibran's story "The Broken Wings" (its Arabic title is *al-Ajniḥa al-Mutakassira*). Several years later, when they were married, they sang daily, along with a Palestinian-born *'ūd* player, Jalil Azzouz, for Radyū al-Sharq al-Adnā, a station established by the British in Palestine. In 1947, they accepted an invitation to visit the United States, where, they had heard, their performances would be enthusiastically received. A letter (figure 1) from Azmi Nashashibi, controller of Arabic programs in the department of broadcasting of the government of Palestine, helped them obtain the necessary visas. Their trip to America, as it happened, coincided with the outbreak of the Arab-Israeli war, in which both the radio station and their home were destroyed. Amer and Sana Khaddaj, and their colleague Azzouz, stayed in America for the rest of their lives.

Although the Arab community was small compared with some European immigrant groups in the United States, the three musicians found a well-established Arab grassroots music culture that, according to performers of the time, was based on the principles of artistry, philanthropy, and community. Gradually, over a few decades, two contexts for musical performance had become woven into the fabric of immigrant culture: the *ḥafla* (plural, *ḥaflāt*), a formal music party; and the *mahrajān* (plural, *mahrajānāt*), an outdoor weekend festival. Both were usually organized by prominent members of the Arab-American community, by churches, or by social clubs, and they

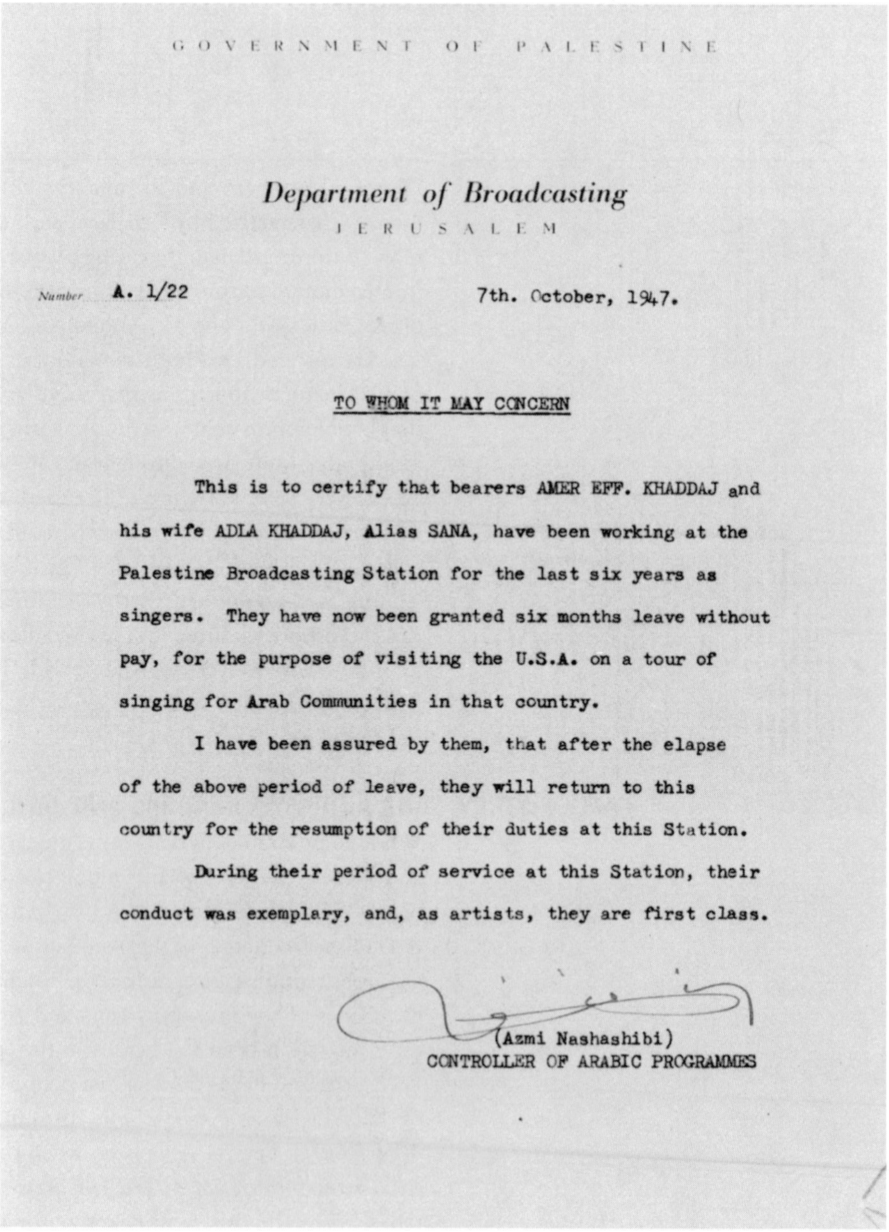

GOVERNMENT OF PALESTINE

Department of Broadcasting

JERUSALEM

Number A. 1/22 7th. October, 1947.

TO WHOM IT MAY CONCERN

This is to certify that bearers AMER EFF. KHADDAJ and his wife ADLA KHADDAJ, Alias SANA, have been working at the Palestine Broadcasting Station for the last six years as singers. They have now been granted six months leave without pay, for the purpose of visiting the U.S.A. on a tour of singing for Arab Communities in that country.

I have been assured by them, that after the elapse of the above period of leave, they will return to this country for the resumption of their duties at this Station.

During their period of service at this Station, their conduct was exemplary, and, as artists, they are first class.

(Azmi Nashashibi)
CONTROLLER OF ARABIC PROGRAMMES

FIGURE 1 The letter of support that helped Sana and Amer Khaddaj obtain a visa for travel to the United States. From the collection of their daughter, Lila Kadaj (who changed the spelling of the family name).

were intended not for profit but to raise money for community causes. These music parties and festivals became a conspicuous feature of Arab-American life, in which the "old country" was evoked or invented during the course of an evening and the goals and accomplishments of Arabs in America were articulated and celebrated. Because music was the centerpiece, these events supported an active group of professional Arab-American musicians. Performing with other community musicians at *ḥaflāt* and *mahrajānāt*, Amer and Sana Khaddaj toured extensively, assisted by the patronage of Aboud Bashir, then bishop of the Orthodox church in America.

The performances of Amer and Sana Khaddaj, along with Jalil Azzouz and several other Arab-American musicians, were captured on thirty-two 78-rpm records made in 1948 in Brooklyn, New York; they were produced by the entrepreneur Farid Alam on his label Alamphon. The community's recording industry complemented its live music events. Several community members became involved in record production, and all the prominent musicians of the 1930s, 1940s, and 1950s made recording of popular hits from home as well as their own compositions and arrangements (Rasmussen 1997a).

After six or seven years in Brooklyn, Sana and Amer Khaddaj moved to Detroit, where, as noted above, a large community of Arab-Americans had formed around the numerous employment opportunities provided by Ford Motor Company. Although a nightclub and restaurant that Amer opened with a partner was short-lived, the couple continued to travel and perform throughout the country (figure 2). Amer was known as a master of lively light songs, and Sana had become famous for her renditions of the serious classical repertoire, but she eventually receded into the shadow of her husband's career and became occupied with raising a family. Jalil Azzouz, who also settled in Detroit, became an artistic leader in the community. Over nearly fifty years, he planned countless programs, prepared written music, coached numerous *'ūd* players and violinists, and continued to teach, practice, and perform long after his retirement. In the absence of formal institutions for Arab music education and performance, such as conservatories, arts centers, or radio and television ensembles, Azzouz's work was crucial to the transmission of a volatile immigrant music culture.

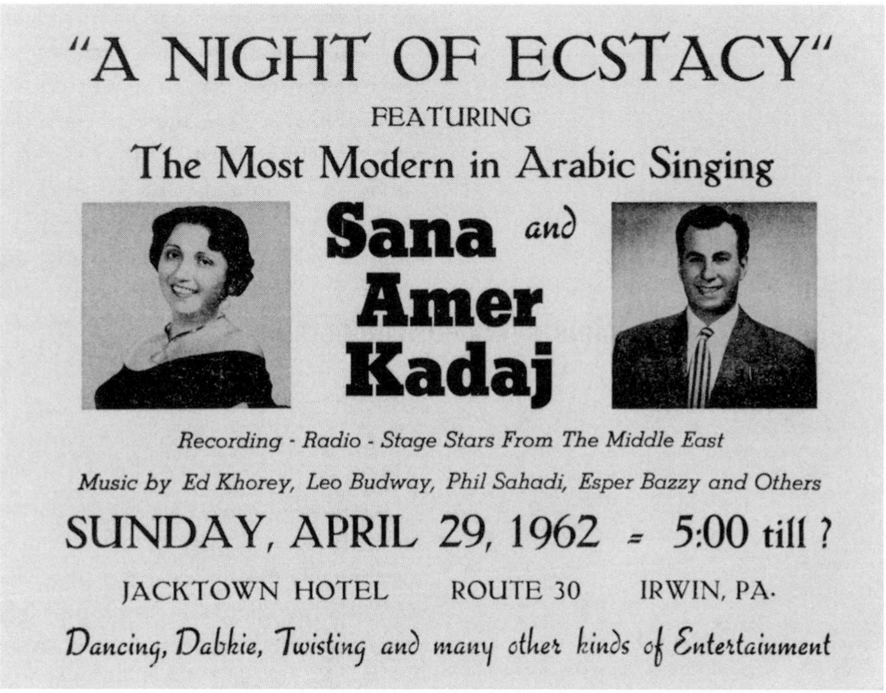
"A NIGHT OF ECSTACY"
FEATURING
The Most Modern in Arabic Singing
Sana and
Amer
Kadaj
Recording - Radio - Stage Stars From The Middle East
Music by Ed Khorey, Leo Budway, Phil Sahadi, Esper Bazzy and Others
SUNDAY, APRIL 29, 1962 - 5:00 till ?
JACKTOWN HOTEL ROUTE 30 IRWIN, PA.
Dancing, Dabkie, Twisting and many other kinds of Entertainment

FIGURE 2 Poster for one of Sana and Amer Khaddaj's engagements in 1962. "Ecstasy" may be a translation of the Arab *ṭarab*, the well-known idea in Arab musical aesthetics that good music, especially singing, leads musicians and their audience to a state of shared ecstasy. From the collection of Lila Kadaj.

The musical mainstream of Arab Detroit resonates with the Levantine and Egyptian style and repertoire.

In the late 1990s, Azzouz was living in a suburb of Detroit where many early immigrants had settled. During the second half of the twentieth century, the first wave of immigrants had been joined by a multicultural mix of newcomers from the Arab world, including many more Muslims and people from peasant families. In an article on popular culture in Arab Detroit in the 1990s, the anthropologist Andrew Shryock (2000:35) drew a demographic profile:

> Highly assimilated middle- and upper-class Christians, whose parents and grandparents came to America from Greater Syria before the fall of the Ottoman Empire, can be found in Detroit's northern and eastern suburbs; Iraqi Chaldeans, a close-knit community of Aramaic-speaking Catholics who own the majority of Detroit's small grocery and liquor stores, live mostly in Detroit, Southfield, and Bloomfield Hills; Palestinian professionals, mostly Christians from the West Bank village of Ramallah, have settled in Livonia; Palestinians from the Jerusalem suburbs of Beit Hanina and Yemenis, both of peasant backgrounds, live together in Dearborn's Southend, a neighborhood which lies in the shadow of the Ford Rouge Plant and boasts its own mosque and business district.

The visible heart of the Arab community is Warren Avenue, in one of the many Lebanese neighborhoods of Dearborn, lined with more than a hundred Arab-owned groceries, restaurants, bakeries, audio-video stores, and businesses.

Like the first Arabs who came at the beginning of the twentieth century, the second wave of Arab immigrants sought educational and economic opportunities in the United States, and some were escaping adverse conditions in their home countries. Their predecessors had in some cases emigrated to escape the political oppression of the Ottoman regime; more recent immigrants have fled conflicts—the Arab-Israeli wars of 1948 and 1967, the civil war in Lebanon that began in 1975, continuing warfare in Beirut and south Lebanon, the Palestinian uprising or *intifāda* that began in 1988, and the war of 1991 in Iraq. Arab immigration to the United States became easier after 1965, when the restrictive quotas first enacted in 1923 were finally lifted.

MAINSTREAM MUSIC IN DETROIT

The musical mainstream of Arab Detroit resonates with the Levantine and Egyptian style and repertoire. Although the Egyptian community here is relatively small, Egyptian music is popular because Egypt is a media hub and a cultural center of the Arab world.

Ensembles consist almost exclusively of men. (In the 1990s, Rama Homaidan, shown in figure 3, may have been the only female singer who performed regularly.) An ensemble usually features a singer backed by two or three percussionists playing *daff* (also *riqq*) and *darabukka* (usually called *ṭabla* or *ṭabli*); two to three musicians playing traditional acoustic instruments such as the *'ūd* (lute), the *qānūn* (zither), the *nāy* (reed flute), and the violin; and a keyboard player at a synthesizer. Performance consists of an astonishingly durable modern repertoire including songs made famous

FIGURE 3 Rana Homaidan, originally from Lebanon, is perhaps the only female singer in Arab Detroit who performed consistently in the late 1990s. She and her husband (a musician and composer, visible in the background) are known for their original pop music. Photo courtesy of Rana Homaidan.

by such Egyptian and Lebanese singers as Umm Kulthūm, Farīd al-Aṭrash, Muḥammad ʿAbd al Wahhāb, ʿAbd al-Ḥalīm Ḥāfiẓ, and Fayrūz. Performances include a good bit of urbanized folk music such as the very popular Levantine genres *ʿaṭābā* and *mijānā* and music for the *dabka* dance. Every year several hits by current pop singers from the Middle East, such as Rāghib ʿAlāmī and ʿAmru Diyāb, make the rounds, and some bands are known for their own original stock of popular music. The occasional concert for traditionalists might include a smattering of classical Arab music (*turāth*) and Syrian songs called *muwashshaḥāt* and *qudūd.* The *nāy* player Nadim Dlaikan, the *ʿūd* player, the violinist Karim Badr, and the *qānūn* player Johnny Sarwat are masters of this repertoire and leaders among Detroit's musicians.

Although some of Detroit's musicians immigrated as conservatory-trained professionals, the great majority of singers and instrumentalists learn on their own. Most young musicians absorb Arab music in America as an oral tradition. They listen to recordings imported from the Middle East and watch televised broadcasts of concerts from the Middle East and local wedding parties on the Arabic cable access channel. They may acquire a musical instrument from a relative returning from the homeland and then pick up techniques here and there, often seeking out experienced musicians for lessons or advice. They see and hear other musicians at numerous weddings and community events. They experiment at home, and they follow along onstage when they are given an opportunity to sit in or perform a few selections with a band. The culture has a certain tolerance for learning by playing as opposed to learning in a rigorous program of formal training and practice. One musician has said, "After just two months with me, my students can play professionally on their own."

Of approximately 150 musicians who can be described as professionals, most are singers, drummers, and keyboard players. A few musicians play traditional acoustic instruments such as the *ʿūd*, the *nāy*, and the *qānūn*; most of them are older and experienced, and their training predated the now widespread digital technology of synthesizers. Those who play synthesizers do so in ways that are distinctively Arab. Keyboard players use microtonal Arab modes (*maqāmāt*), the timbres (tone quality) of Arab instruments, and Arab rhythmic patterns. Thus a keyboard player might imitate the sound of the *mijwiz*, a single-reed double-piped folk clarinet, playing in the mode *bayyātī* (which uses the tone E-half-flat), and accompany himself with a twelve-beat Lebanese rhythm for *dabka* dance sounded using the appropriate percussion samples of *daff* (a tambourine) and *ṭabl baladī* (a double-headed bass drum). It can be argued that although the synthesizer might seem the least "Arab" of all instruments, it has made the greatest contribution to preserving and promoting the distinctive sounds of Arab music in the diaspora—perhaps even inspiring some musicians and audiences to rediscover traditional acoustic instruments (Rasmussen 1996).

IRAQI AND YEMENI MUSIC

The music of the Iraqi Arab community and the Yemeni Arab community complement the prevalent Levantine and Egyptian music of Arab Detroit. In Detroit, numerous refugees from both the Iran-Iraq war and the Gulf war have bolstered the Iraqi population, a group that has been settling here since about 1910. The majority of people of Iraqi heritage are Chaldean: they practice an old form of Catholicism, and their language is neo-Aramaic. (Aramaic is the language thought to have been spoken by Jesus.) The Iraqi community, which preserves its ancient heritage—including its religion and language—nevertheless produces the most modern musical sounds in Detroit. Iraqi bands are extensively electronic, propelled exclusively by keyboards (each band has at least one or two), electric guitar or bass, and drummers who sometimes play digitized drum pads instead of "real" dums. They perform many songs that are specifically Chaldean and are in Aramaic, and dance music with movements and rhythms (such as the pattern *jūrjuna* in 10/8) that are quite different from the Levantine dance music heard throughout the city.

Iraqi music must, of course, be played at a Chaldean wedding, but it has also crept into the "Detroit Arab sound." There are probably several reasons for this mainstreaming of Iraqi music. Every year, Iraqis in Detroit sponsor regular music events and thus hire many musicians, both Iraqi and non-Iraqi. Also, Iraquis are well represented in civic affairs, and they promote their musicians in such venues as the Arab World Festival, an annual downtown festival of Arab music and culture produced by the community. Iraqi young people's bands—for example, Majid Kakka and his Bells Band (figure 4)—have made a splash at this festival, and prominent Iraqi community members are now on its planning committee. While all professional musicians in Arab Detroit cater to a multicultural Arab clientele, mastering some of the distinctive tunes in the Iraqi repertoire has become a prerequisite. As the *ʿūd* and *qānūn* player Victor Ghanam put it, "You don't play Iraqi, you starve!"

In the Yemeni community of south and east Dearborn, around the giant Ford Rouge plant, the musical scene is quieter. This community is relatively new in Arab Detroit; it includes many men who have come to work at the Ford plant and who have had fewer educational opportunities in America than other Arab immigrant groups. Generally, these Yemenis in America are regarded as pious Muslims, and they are not well represented in the civic arena.

In the mid-1990s there was just one regular Yemeni band working to establish a name for itself among its compatriots: Afrāḥ al-Yaman (figure 5). The musicians of *Afrāḥ al-Yaman* report that before the community had its own band, it hired Lebanese musicians. But although they played Arab music, Yemeni people were not familiar with the songs and dances of Lebanon and Egypt, and Lebanese musicians could not play the styles of music familiar to Yemenis, *ṣanaʿānī* and *laḥjī*.

Yemeni music differs significantly in dialect, instrumental style, vocal timbre, and repertoire from the central Arab sound of Egypt and the Levant. Perhaps the most notable difference is in the "groove" of the music: the Yemeni and Levantine-Egyptian rhythmic languages almost seem mutually exclusive. This became clear to the author one evening when an invitation to the home of some Yemeni musicians turned into a sort of jam session. The musicians were eager to learn Lebanese-Egyptian standards, particularly music for *dabka* dancing, but the rhythms were obviously new and challenging to them. On another evening, at a wedding, Lebanese musicians who were

FIGURE 4 The Bells Band, seen from behind. The leader, Majid Kakka, plays three keyboards that can produce hundreds of sampled sounds; the drummer plays a set of pads programmed to reproduce several sampled percussion instruments. Photo by Anne Rasmussen, 1995.

FIGURE 5 Abd al-Nour, the main singer for *Afrāḥ al-Yaman*, performs at a friend's home. Photo by Anne Rasmussen, 1995.

listening to a Yemeni band commented, "They just sound as if they're playing the same rhythm all night long." The Lebanese musicians' impression was far from the truth, though; in fact, if Arab Detroit eventually takes up Yemeni music as it has taken up Iraqi music, the musical mainstream will be infused with another exciting style and repertoire.

At this writing, however, Afrāḥ al-Yaman performs primarily for compatriots from north and south Yemen, two factions of a population that, in recent history, has been split and then reunited. The musicians struggle to get a good time slot at the Arab World Festival and look forward to a future when their community can be more "organized." Meanwhile, they are significant "culture brokers" for the community's celebrations and rituals.

ARAB DETROIT AND ARAB AMERICA

Arab music in the United States is carried on by guardians of traditional ethnic culture, but it also captures the imagination of young people in the community, some of whom have grown up speaking English and listening to alternative rock with their schoolmates. Many young musicians see music not just as a traditional art form but also as a lucrative primary or secondary career.

Detroit's midwestern industrial character distinguishes it from the United States' east and west coasts, which have a rich economy, a culture of international finance, prestigious institutions of education and fine arts, and influential entertainment and mass media cultures. On both coasts, Arab-American communities enjoy the presence of world-class artists such as Ali Jihad Racy and Simon Shaheen, international festivals featuring Arab arts such as the Los Angeles Festival or the annual *Mahrajān al-Fann* in New York, and regular visits by touring pop stars from the Arab world—and this musical activity is reinforced by Arab music studies at a number of universities, notably Harvard and the University of California at Los Angeles and Santa Barbara. In contrast, the University of Michigan, although it is known for its programs in world music, has never paid much attention to Detroit's Arab musical subculture. Shyrock (2000:35) notes that a "broad range of lifestyles and levels of assimilation has made the Detroit Arab community hard to represent, both intellectually and politically. Despite its proximity to the University of Michigan, which houses one of the best

Middle East Studies centers in the country, very few Middle East scholars have worked in Arab Detroit."

The lion's share of institutional support for Arab music and musicians in Detroit comes from the Arab Community Center for Economic and Social Services (ACCESS). Since at least the early 1980s, the cultural arts department at ACCESS has initiated concerts, workshops, festivals, exhibits, research, publications, recordings, films, and conferences about local and worldwide Arab arts; events range from neighborhood street festivals and educational workshops for children to polished performances and prestigious academic conferences. The cultural arts department, particularly under the directorship of Sally Howell, has identified Detroit as a national center of Arab arts. Nevertheless, music making in Detroit remains community-based.

Detroit's blue-collar character suggests that popular music will continue to be made for and by the people rather than by professional musicians from the coasts or stars from overseas. Detroit is not only less affluent but also less assimilated than most of Arab America. Business partnerships, friendships, and especially marriages tend to be endogamous, remaining within national, village, regional, or religious groups. Musicians are cultural specialists for a wide variety of Arab-Americans—Iraqi business owners, Yemeni plant workers, Palestinian professionals, third-generation Syrian-Americans—and are called on to perform the particular songs, dances, and rituals of diverse communities. The celebrations and ceremonies of the many Arab communities of Detroit represent work for musicians. On a summer Saturday, for instance, five weddings may be taking place simultaneously—all with live Arab music. In Detroit, Arab music is an ethnic business. Detroit is a place where young people of Arab heritage are discovering the music of their people and learning how to play it themselves.

Detroit is recognized more for the uncanny resilience of Arab ways in an American context than for any conscientious reworking of Arab traditions in a modernizing world. Yet from another perspective, Detroit—and perhaps other enclaves of the Arab diaspora—might be seen as a landmark on the world map of Arab culture. In a detailed but concise history, the ethnomusicologist Ali Jihad Racy (1984:9) discusses five principal contexts that have shaped Arab music: the cosmopolitan cultural centers of the Umayyad and Abbasid dynasties in the eighth to tenth centuries; the discovery of the classical past in ninth-century Iraq; the Islamic occupation of Spain from 713 to 1492; the 400-year Ottoman period ending in 1917; and contact with the modern West during the eighteenth, nineteenth, and twentieth centuries. In each context, significantly, the evolution of Arab music has been activated by cultural exchange. In the new millennium, histories of Arab music may recognize a sixth context, important and enduring: musical preservation, innovation, and amalgamation in Arab America.

REFERENCES

Abraham, Sameer Y., and Nabeel. 1983. *Arabs in the New World: Studies on Arab-American Communities*. Detroit: Wayne State University Press.

Aswad, Barbara C., ed. 1974. *Arabic-Speaking Communities in American Cities*. New York: Center for Migration Studies of New York.

Coon, Carleton Stevens. 1966. *Caravan: The Story of the Middle East*. Rev. ed. New York: Holt.

Hoogland, Eric, ed. 1987. *Crossing the Waters: Arabic-Speaking Immigrants to the United States before 1940*. Washington, D.C.: Smithsonian Institution.

Howell, Sally. 1998. "Picturing Women, Class, and Community in Arab Detroit: The Strange Case of Eva Habib." *Visual Anthropology* 10(2–4):209–226.

Kayal, Philip M., and Joseph M. Kayal. 1975. *The Syrian-Lebanese in America: A Study in Religion and Assimilation*. Boston: Twayne.

Mandell, Joan. 1998. "Cultural Resilience through Change: Finding the Theme for *Tales from Arab Detroit*." *Visual Anthropology* 10(2–4):189–208.

———. 1995. *Tales from Arab Detroit*. Detroit and Los Angeles: ACCESS and Olive Branch Productions. Videocassette.

McCarus, Ernest. 1984. *The Development of Arab-American Identity*. Ann Arbor: University of Michigan Press.

Naaf, Alexa. 1985. *Becoming American: The Early Arab Immigrant Experience*. Carbondale: Southern Illinois University Press.

Racy, Ali Jihad. 1984. "Arab Music: An Overview." In *Maqam: Music of the Islamic World and Its Influences*, ed. Robert Browning, 9–13. New York: Alternative Museum.

Rasmussen, Anne K. 1996. "Theory and Practice at the Arabic Org: Digital Practice in Contemporary Music Performance." *Popular Music* 15(3):345–365.

———. 1997a. *The Music of Arab Americans: A Retrospective Collection*. Rounder Records CD 1122. Compact disk.

———. 1997b. "The Music of Arab Detroit: A Musical Mecca in the Midwest." In *Musics of Multicultural America: A Study of Twelve Musical Communities*, ed. Kip Lornell and Anne K. Rasmussen, 73–100. New York: Schirmer.

———. 2000. "The Sound of Culture, the Structure of Tradition: Musician's Work in Arab America." In *Arab Detroit: From Margin to Mainstream*, ed. Nabeel Abraham and Andrew Shryock. Detroit: Wayne State University Press.

Reynolds, Dwight F. 1998. "From the Delta to Detroit: Packaging a Folk Epic for a New Folk." *Visual Anthropology* 10(2–4):145–164.

Shryock, Andrew. 2000. "Public Culture in Arab Detroit: Creating Arab-American Identities in a Transnational Domain." In *Mass Mediations: New Approaches to Popular Cultures in the Middle East and Beyond*, ed. Walter Armbrust. Berkeley: University of California Press.

Zogby, James, ed. 1984. *Taking Root, Bearing Fruit: The Arab-American Experience*. Washington, D.C.: American-Arab Anti-Discrimination Committee.

العفو يا سيد الملاح

نغمة نهوند

وضع ماتيلده عبد المسيح

Prix: P.T. 15

الثمن ١٥

EL AFOU YA SID EL MILAH

PAR

Mathilde Abdel Messih

Lith. M. Abdelmessih le Caire

Section 4
Gender and Music

In the Middle East and Central Asia, as in most of the world, music and dance reveal and instantiate gender-related behavior The essays in this section offer a few examples, historical and contemporary, mostly from the Arab world. Other essays, later in the volume, will provide more detail about music and gender elsewhere in the region.

Especially for outsiders, the women of the Middle East tend to attract the most immediate attention in this regard. Common discourse, particularly in North America, might suggest that Middle Eastern women are typically silent, subdued, and even oppressed. But although they may seem to have no voice, there is considerable literature documenting just the opposite. The essays in this volume illustrate the many, often public, voices of female musicians. For centuries, women have been sophisticated and much admired professional singers and composers. Working in a patriarchal society, they have found many paths to creativity—for example, in the domains of courtly singing, dancing for weddings, and contemporary international pop music.

Of course, musical performance also has implications for men regarding gender. One example is which instruments males and females may play (the choice of instruments also has implications for social class and regional identity). Another example is dance: participating in certain forms of dance—such as the male genre *‘arḍa* and female wedding dancing in the Arabian Peninsula—reinforces gender solidarity. Such solidarity may, in turn, contribute to a sense of communal solidarity and local identity.

The relationship between musical performance and gender roles is usually complicated and shifting, and it is not necessarily the same from one part of the region to another. Usually, in any given situation, this relationship is best understood in the context of social, political, and economic relationships.

In the first quarter of the twentieth century, the piano was the favorite musical instrument of middle- and upper-class Egyptian girls who aspired to cosmopolitanism. This is the cover of the sheet music for a piano piece by one such young woman, Mathilde Abdel Messih, a prolific composer of piano music. In this composition, she tries to adapt the piano to the rhythmic patterns and melodic style of local Arab music. The music is undated but was undoubtedly printed in Cairo in the 1910s or 1920s. From the collection of Virginia Danielson.

Snapshot: Sallāma al-Qass

Suzanne Meyers Sawa

Many accomplished poets and musicians of her time admired Sallāma al-Qass 'the pious', one of the most famous slave singing-girls of the early Umayyad era (figure 1). Of mixed blood, she was born in Medina and grew up there. She studied with a number of famous teachers, including Ma'bad (d. 743), Ibn 'Ā'isha (d. c. 743), Jamīla (d. c. 720), and Mālik ibn Abī al-Samḥ (d. 757), and she became highly skilled not only in the vocal arts but in the *'ūd* 'lute', composition, and Qur'ānic recitation. Sallāma was also known for her physical beauty. One poem in the medieval *Kitāb al-aghānī* 'Book of Songs' of Abū al-Faraj al-Iṣbahānī (d. 967) praises her well-rounded figure, slender fingers, white teeth, and pleasant speech (*Kitāb al-aghānī* 17:23; the modern edition is published in Cairo). [See HISTORICAL ISSUES OF GENDER AND MUSIC and SNAPSHOT: PERFORMERS FROM *KITĀB AL-AGHĀNĪ*.]

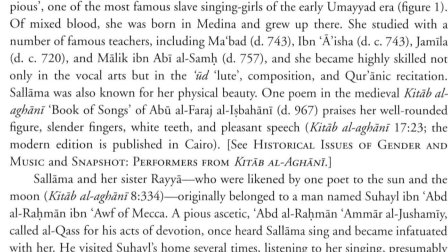

FIGURE 1 Umm Kulthūm in the title role of the Egyptian film *Sallāma*, 1942. Photo courtesy of Dār al-Hilāl.

Sallāma and her sister Rayyā—who were likened by one poet to the sun and the moon (*Kitāb al-aghānī* 8:334)—originally belonged to a man named Suhayl ibn 'Abd al-Raḥmān ibn 'Awf of Mecca. A pious ascetic, 'Abd al-Raḥmān 'Ammār al-Jushamīy, called al-Qass for his acts of devotion, once heard Sallāma sing and became infatuated with her. He visited Suhayl's home several times, listening to her singing, presumably from behind a curtain, though refusing to see her. One day, however, when Suhayl was away, al-Qass did see Sallāma, and they fell in love. Al-Qass resisted his desire and her willingness to consummate their love, quoting a passage in the Qur'ān about the day of resurrection: "Friends on that day will be foes one to another, save those who kept their duty [to Allāh]" (sūra 43:67). The people of Mecca knew of their love and thus also called Sallāma by the name al-Qass. Al-Qass wrote poems about her, including one praising her singing and especially her ability to repeat sections of a poem with new, improvised melodies (*al-tarjī'*). "When she uses the *tarjī'* with her voice, how skillful she is/She prolongs the words of the verse and then repeats them, with a clear ringing in her voice" (*Kitāb al-aghānī* 8:336).

Yazīd ibn 'Abd al-Malik, who was caliph from 720 to 724, bought Sallāma from Suhayl (although according to one account he bought her from the clan of Rummāna, for 10,000 dinars); at the same time, he bought Ḥabāba, another student of the famous teacher Jamīla. Yazīd favored Ḥabāba, who was more beautiful though less talented than Sallāma; and when Habāba died, after choking on a seed, he sickened and himself died of grief shortly thereafter. Sallāma's lament for him "made the eyes weep and hearts burn with pain" (*Kitāb al-aghānī* 8:347); and his son Walīd ibn Yazīd, who ruled from 743 to 744 and whom Sallāma also served—and outlived—could not understand his father's preference for Ḥabāba.

The story of Sallāma enthralled audiences in the Arab world in 1942, when the famous Egyptian singer Umm Kulthūm appeared in the musical film *Sallāma*. The film focused on the unconsummated love of Sallāma and al-Qass and gave Umm Kulthūm a vehicle for her talents in both singing and Qur'ānic recitation.

Historical Issues of Gender and Music

Suzanne Meyers Sawa

The Umayyad Era (661–750 C.E.)
The ʿAbbasid Era (750–1258 C.E.)
The Mamluk Era (1250–1517 C.E.)

Women played a multifaceted role in the music making of the early Arab world, where they contributed to artistic life and helped shape social practices. This survey highlights their musical history from the beginning of Islam in Arabia in 632 C.E. to the end of the Mamluk era in Egypt in 1517, concentrating on the Umayyad era (661–750) and the early ʿAbbasid era (750–932). While Mecca remained the religious capital of the entire Islamic empire, the political capitals shifted, and different dynasties and caliphates coexisted, governing independently though always acknowledging the religious primacy of Mecca. Medina served as the administrative capital for the Prophet Muhammad and also for the first three Orthodox caliphs. Kufa, founded in 638, was the capital city of ʿAli, the fourth and last Orthodox caliph, who was also Muhammad's son-in-law. The power center moved to Damascus under the Umayyads (661–750), then eastward to Baghdad (762–836 and 892–1258) and Samarra (836–892) under the ʿAbbasids. In Spain, the second Umayyad dynasty ruled in Cordova from 756 to 1031; and the Fāṭimids, who originally governed from Qayrawan in Tunisia, moved eastward to establish Cairo as their capital in 969. Cairo maintained its dominant position through several dynasties until the Mamluks were defeated by the Ottoman Turks in 1517. [See ARABIC SOURCES FOR MUSIC THEORY]

FIGURE 1 Enthroned ruler surrounded by courtiers and female musicians, from *Kitāb al-aghānī* (Cairo. Dār al-Kutub Ms. Adab 579/II). Courtesy of Dār al-Kutub.

Numerous sources, of which the most important for information up to the tenth century is the *Kitāb al-aghānī* 'Book of Songs' of al-Iṣbahānī (d. 967), describe women as teachers; repositories of repertoire; transmitters, interpreters, composers, and performers of both vocal and instrumental music; and professional mourners. The *Kitāb al-aghānī* (figure 1), on which later accounts often rely, devotes many chapters to women musicians and poets, although, like many sources, it also contains information about numerous women, named and unnamed, scattered throughout other stories. [See SNAPSHOT: PERFORMERS FROM *KITĀB AL-AGHĀNĪ*.] Primary sources frequently differ in the details of these women's lives; still, the sheer number of accounts presents an overall picture of extraordinary cultural activity not only in the courts and cultivated social circles but occasionally in the lives of the general public.

Appearing continually throughout these accounts is the singing slave girl: in Arabic, *qayna* (plural, *qiyān*) or *jāriya*, the more general term for a slave girl (plural, *jawārī*). These slave girls were of both Arab and mixed origins, Muslim and non-Muslim. The history of Arabic music has been colored by their considerable role in the development and transmission of the repertoire and their prominent places in the social structure relating to musical performance. They were the primary entertainers from pre-Islamic times at least until the eighth century C.E., when evidence of greater activity by male singers and musicians surfaces. Every court, from the Umayyads in Damascus to the ʿAbbasids in Baghdad and Samarra, from the Fāṭimids and Mamluks in Cairo to the second Umayyad dynasty in Andalusia, maintained a retinue of trained female performers who played in all-female orchestras or sang in solo performances for the caliph and his companions, and for the female members of the court. Every slave merchant knew that educating these women increased their value sharply; people of the courtly and upper classes were willing to pay extraordinary prices for women of beauty, charm, and talent who were trained in all the requisites of the "boon companion"—such as knowledge of the Qur'ān, poetry, rhetoric, gaming, and music. Being a slave was not always a permanent condition, nor was it necessarily full of hardship. In addition to the Islamic injunction to treat slaves well, there was a tradition that if a slave bore a child to a master, then both she and her child were freed. Many women, not only singing-girls, entered a court as slaves, bore children, and thereafter spent their lives as free women in the harem, often achieving high status as the mothers of caliphs. The physical setting for performance, at least in ʿAbbasid times, changed after a *qayna* became a mother: she then sang behind a curtain that hid her from the gaze of the caliph's companions.

From the earliest times, there was also another class of singing-girls, those who performed in public taverns. It was probably these performers who were criticized in various *ḥadīth* 'sayings' of the Prophet Muhammad. Though they were often praised by poets for their physical charms, they no doubt did engage in the sex trade, more so than their counterparts who entertained in private settings. After the Islamic state prohibited alcohol, the number of tavern singing-girls probably decreased considerably. Still, the continued association of singing-girls with illicit behavior, listening to music, and drinking wine gave conservative Muslim theologians grounds for criticism.

Some of the most famous musicians were freedwomen, and some were even members of the nobility. The singer and teacher Jamīla was a freedwoman who was also a client (*mawlā*) of a few different tribes around Medina. The composer and performer ʿUlayya bint al-Mahdī (d. 825) was the half sister of both the famous Hārūn al-Rashīd (d. 809) of the *Thousand and One Nights* and the renowned prince and musician Ibrāhīm ibn al-Mahdī (d. 839).

THE UMAYYAD ERA (661–750 C.E.)

The musical centers established in Mecca and Medina before the Orthodox caliphate (632–661) continued to flourish during the Umayyad era (661–750), even though the capital was moved to Damascus. Women musicians and their patrons enjoyed considerable freedom compared with those of the later ʿAbbasid era (750–1258), when more and more restrictions against the public activities of women, particularly women of higher status, would begin to take effect.

One of the most influential performers and teachers of the Umayyed period was Jamīla (d. c. 715), a married freedwoman of Medina who established her own singing school. Her student Maʿbad (d. 743), who was himself one of the most famous teachers and singers of the early eighth century, said of her: "Jamīla is the root of song and we are its branches. Were it not for Jamīla, we would not have become singers" (*Kitāb al-aghānī* 8:186). She claimed to have learned music through listening to her neighbor Sā'ib Khāthir (d. 783), who was famous as a teacher and for bringing the *ʿūd* 'lute' to Medina. Jamīla stated proudly—according to the account of her life in the *Kitāb al-aghānī*—that she took what she had heard from Sā'ib Khāthir to create better songs. Among Jamīla's female students were the Medinese slave singing-girls

Ḥabāba, Sallāma al-Qass 'the pious', and Sallāma al-Zarqā' 'the blue-eyed', who was from Kufa in Iraq. [See SNAPSHOT: SALLĀMA AL-QASS.]

Another famous freedwoman was 'Azza al-Maylā' 'she who walks with a swinging gait' (d. before 710). In addition to her great beauty and refined character, she was known for preserving and performing the songs of earlier slave girls, taught to her by the slave-singer Rā'iqa. One of her students, the Meccan singer Ibn Surayj (d. 746), maintained that 'Azza al-Maylā' was, among both women and men, the most highly skilled in singing and playing the *mizhar* 'skin-bellied lute' and *mi'zafa* 'lyre'. 'Azza was credited with being the first woman of the region to perform measured song and was equally renowned for her skill at the *'ūd* and for composing and singing new Persian styles introduced by the Persian slave Nashīt and her teacher Sā'ib Khāthir. The Medinese singer Ṭuways, notorious for his sarcasm, had only praise for 'Azza and was a frequent visitor to her home. Those attending her public musical gatherings (*majālis*; singular, *majlis*) are said to have sat motionless, in reverence, as if birds were sitting on their heads ready to peck them should they speak or move. Apparently, 'Azza had a daughter, Nā'ila bint al-Maylā', who was also a singer.

The lives of the two Medinese slave singing-girls mentioned above—Ḥabāba (d. 724) and Sallāma al-Qass (d. after 740?)—suggest the power this class of entertainers had over caliphs and society. They were both owned by the caliph Yazīd ibn 'Abd al-Malik (ruled 720–724), who was noted more for his profligacy than for his administrative abilities. Both women were students of Jamīla and Ma'bad, among others. Ḥabāba, a beauty of mixed blood, was first known as al-'Ālīya 'the sublime one' but was renamed by Yazīd after she entered his household. She seems to have performed for Yazīd before he became caliph, accompanying herself on a *duff* that she tossed in the air as she sang. According to some sources, Yazīd purchased Ḥabāba after he came to the throne; according to others, she was acquired by one of Yazīd's wives, who knew of his infatuation with Ḥabāba and gave Ḥabāba to him as a present in order to advance the claim of her own son as heir to the throne. Ḥabāba's influence over Yazīd was so great that, as one account tells, he was willing to hand the control of the government over to her so that he could spend more time drinking wine and listening to music (two activities that were often paired). This disregard for affairs of state was perhaps exaggerated by later 'Abbasid historians eager to discredit an Umayyad ruler, but the story does give a picture of the extramusical roles played by women who were trained to be the boon companions and confidantes of caliphs (*Kitāb al-aghānī* 15:122–146).

At the same time as Yazīd acquired Ḥabāba, he also acquired Sallāma, who was called al-Qass 'the pious' because of an unconsummated love affair with a Meccan ascetic of that name. Of the two women, Sallāma was the better musician and was praised for her ability to recite the Qur'ān, but Ḥabāba was more beautiful and became Yazīd's favorite. Their rivalry for Yazīd's attention, coupled with Ḥabāba's growing arrogance, led Sallāma to chastise Ḥabāba and remind her that the great Jamīla herself had instructed Ḥabāba to defer to Sallāma in all musical matters, and had cautioned her that she would not do well unless Sallāma remained her friend. Ḥabāba subsequently apologized, but she remained the caliph's favorite; indeed, when she died, apparently from choking on a seed, Yazīd died of grief shortly thereafter (*Kitāb al-aghānī* 15:334–351). Sallāma later served under his son Walīd (who ruled 743–744).

There are varying accounts of Sallāma as a singer of laments—a traditional female role. She eulogized Yazīd, Walīd, and the composer and singer Ma'bad, who died while Walīd was caliph. Ma'bad's son Kardam reported that, for his father's funeral, Sallāma sang a lament that Ma'bad had composed on Yazīd's death and had taught to her. Another account suggests that the fame of this lament lasted at least until the death of Hārūn al-Rashīd in 809. The singer Isḥāq al-Mawṣilī (d. 850)—son of the most famous male musician of the 'Abbasid era, Ibrāhīm al-Mawṣilī (d. 804), and

"Jamīla is the root of song and we are its branches. Were it not for Jamīla, we would not have become singers."

himself trained by the renowned singer and mourner ʿĀtika bint al-Shuhda—recounted that he had learned this lament from a Medinese female mourner and had so loved it that he sang it often. When Hārūn died, his wife Umm Jaʿfar (d. 831) commanded Isḥāq to create an appropriate lament. Isḥāq, at a loss for inspiration, finally remembered the Medinese lament and taught it to the *jāriya* of Umm Jaʿfar, Kunayza 'little treasure'. For his services, Isḥāq received 100,000 dirhams and 1,000 robes.

A recognized class of entertainers, based in Medina and Mecca in the early Islamic period and probably in pre-Islamic society, were the *mukhannathūn*, male musicians who dressed as women, dyed their hands with henna, and acted in an effeminate manner. Noted for their wit, they specialized in love songs in the lighter *hazaj* style, usually accompanying themselves on the *duff*. Because of their supposed lack of interest in women, the *mukhannathūn* would be allowed to enter women's quarters and thus could act as marriage brokers. According to several *ḥadīth*, the Prophet Muhammad disapproved of cross-dressing by either sex, and one *ḥadīth* indicates his disapproval and subsequent banishment of a *mukhannath* for making a living from music, presumably because music was associated with wine and and licentiousness.

The first *mukhannath* known by name was Ḥīt, who was evidently banished by Muhammad for describing a woman's body to another man too accurately. The first *mukhannath* to sing *ghināʾ mutqan* (loosely defined as "art music"), as well as the first to sing in the *hazaj* style, was Abū ʿAbd al-Munʿim ʿIsā ibn ʿAbdallāh (632–711), called Ṭuways 'little peacock'. He was famous for his caustic wit and seems to have been the leader of a group of Medinese *mukhannathūn*, some of whom were also known by nicknames: al-Dalāl 'coquetry', Bard al-Fuʾād 'heart's contentment', Nawmat al-Ḍuḥá 'morning nap', Qand 'candy', Raḥma 'compassion', and Hibatallāh 'gift from God'. Musicians from Mecca known by name include al-Gharīd and possibly Ibn Surayj, both of whom played the *ʿūd* rather than the *duff* and whose biographies mention that they sang laments, a genre usually sung by women.

Although there is evidence that *mukhannathūn* were active during the ʿAbbasid era (750–1258), their relatively high status in the musical world of early Islam seems to have been ended sometime in the first two decades of the eighth century by a particularly brutal repression by the government in Medina, during which several *mukhannathūn* were castrated.

THE ʿABBASID ERA (750–1258 C.E.)

When the ʿAbbasid dynasty became the new rulers of the Islamic empire, they moved their capital eastward, to Kufa (750–762), to Baghdad (762–836), to nearby Samarra (836–892), and then back to Baghdad. Kufa and Basra in Iraq continued to rival Mecca and Medina as established musical centers, in part for the fame of their slave singing-girls.

The most renowned female musician of the ʿAbbasid era was ʿArīb (797 or 798–890 or 891), the illegitimate daughter of the Barmakid Jaʿfar ibn Yaḥyā and hence the granddaughter of Hārūn al-Rashīd's favorite vizier, Yaḥyā ibn Khālid (disgraced and assassinated by Hārūn in 803). 'Arīb served ten caliphs and numerous viziers and high-ranking members of the court. More than any other female musician, 'Arīb embodied the ideal of the "boon companion." A woman of great physical beauty and grace, and a prima donna with her own slaves (notably the talented Bid'a and Tuḥfa), she was noted for her knowledge of calligraphy, poetry, chess, and backgammon; for her refined speech and quick wit; and for her skill in singing, playing the *'ūd*, and composition. She was a prolific composer, reporting to the geographer Ibn Khurdadhbih (d. 911) that she had written approximately a thousand songs. No less a personage than the caliph al-Mu'tamid (who ruled from 870 to 892) ordered the belletrist and music theorist 'Alī ibn Yaḥyā (856–912) to make a collection of 'Arīb's songs; and the writer Muhammad ibn Ibrāhīm Qarīḍ made three different collections of them, identifying 1125 unique titles. In contemporary sources, 'Arīb was compared favorably to Jamīla and 'Azza al-Maylā'—legendary Medinese figures of the early Umayyad period—and to Sallāma al-Zarqā', the most famous singer from Kufa (*Kitāb al-aghānī* 21:54–55).

An important example of a woman as a teacher and a preserver and transmitter of the repertoire in the early 'Abbasid era was 'Ātika bint al-Shuhda. Her mother, Shuhda, who had been born in Mecca, was a *jāriya* at the court of the Umayyad caliph Walīd. 'Ātika, who was born in Medina, followed in her mother's footsteps and became a singer and mourner. She was also highly skilled in playing the *'ūd*, and she performed at the court of Hārūn al-Rashīd, where she apparently chastised the singer Ibn Surayj for taking too many liberties in making additions to a song. The musician Isḥāq al-Mawṣilī, mentioned above—who was important in transmitting and preserving the repertoire—is said to have studied with 'Ātika every day for seven years.

'Ātika also seems to have been an independent businesswoman. She acquired a male slave, Mukhāriq (d. c. 845), trained him in the musical arts, and then sold him. He was later acquired by Hārūn al-Rashīd, and he attained both fame and his freedom at Hārūn's brilliant court in Baghdad.

Although the sources usually document the lives of noblewomen and women of professional rank, slave or free, they occasionally offer a glimpse of women's musical role outside the confines of a court or singing school. A story about the Medinese singer Abū Ṣadaqa provides an example. Hārūn al-Rashīd once assembled several singers and asked to hear a certain song. None of the renditions pleased him except the last, by Abū Ṣadaqa (who was known for accompanying himself by tapping the rhythmic mode with a *qadīb* 'wand'). The delighted Rashīd insisted that he repeat the song; when he did, with even more power and passion, the caliph asked him where he had learned it. Abū Ṣadaqa replied that he had first heard it from a black woman, who was singing it as she walked down a street balancing a water jug on her shoulder. The woman agreed to teach it to him for the price of two dirhams; she then set her pot on the ground and—accompanying herself by beating the rhythm on it—sang the song repeatedly until she was certain that he had memorized it. The next day, however, Abū Ṣadaqa had forgotten the song and rushed out to find her. Although he did not know her name or where she lived, he encountered her once more on the street, again with her water jug. She refused to repeat the song until he had paid her another two dirhams, but then she spent more than an hour reteaching it to him (Al-Mas'ūdī 1989:1037–1038).

THE MAMLUK ERA (1250–1517 C.E.)

Despite the political decline of the 'Abbasid state, music—and culture in general—continued to flourish. The musical practices established at royal courts before and during the "golden age" of Islam in Arabia, Syria, and Iraq were reflected at the courts of Mamluk Egypt, and these practices included the vital role of women entertainers.

There were two classes of professional singers (known as *qayna*, *raysa*, or *mughanniyya*): slaves, belonging to the ruling military caste; and popular singers, whose activities were now regulated and taxed by the state under the supervision of a *ḍāmina* (who was both a government tax collector and an independent slave-trader). Women also continued to be professional mourners, accompanying themselves with tambourines; these mourners too were taxed, at about the same rate as singers and prostitutes.

Slave singers, also trained in playing the *'ūd*, were usually gifts to a ruling sultan. As in earlier times, however, rulers might buy a desired performer, paying a high price for the combination of beauty and talent. According to one source, the best singers came from Mecca. These women performed in orchestras of fifteen to fifty players. There is no mention of male orchestra members; presumably, then, the long-established tradition of all-female ensembles had persisted.

How these women were trained is less well known. There is little evidence that women had the freedom to operate the equivalent of a music academy, as the Umayad singer and teacher Jamīla did. One source notes that the sultan al-Nāsir M. B. Qalawūn (ruled 1279–1290) engaged a famous male singer, Kutayla Ibn Qurānghān, to teach singing to his slaves. Another story is that the *ḍāmina* of Cairo bought a black slave, Ittifāq, from the *ḍāmina* of Bilbays, taught her the art of playing the *'ūd*, and then sold her to the ruling caste. Between 1342 and 1347, Ittifāq apparently was married to three different sultans of the Bahrite dynasty; she later married a minister of state and then a North African sultan, 'Abd al-Ḥakīm.

As before, some slave singing-girls had influence outside their role as entertainers and companions. The story of the Syrian singer Dunyā bint al-Uqba'ī (d. 1377) is similar to that of the Umayyad singer Ḥabāba, who manipulated the decisions of the caliph Yazīd. Dunyā, the favorite of the sultan al-Ashraf Sha'bān (ruled 1363–1377), persuaded him to cancel the tax on singers for the year 1377.

Other famous singers of this era include Khadīja al-Rihābīya (d. 1482); Khūbī al-'Awwāda (d. 1340), known as an *'ūd* player; Khadīja bint Nuhayla (d. 1459), the pious singer; and especially 'Azīza bint al-Saṭḥī (d. 1501), who was renowned for her ability to express the poetic beauty of a text.

Despite internal political upheavals, shifting centers of power, and the consequent uncertainties affecting social institutions, women in the Islamic empire helped create, maintain, and transmit a rich musical legacy. As performers, teachers, composers, companions, and businesswomen, as slaves or free women, they, along with their male counterparts, ensured the continuity of musical activities across a vast territory stretching from western Spain to the easternmost border of Iraq.

REFERENCES

al-Iṣbahānī, Abū al-Faraj. 1927–1974. *Kitāb al-aghānī* (Book of Songs). Cairo: Dār al-Kutub.

al-Jāḥiẓ, 'Amr ibn Baḥr. 1980. *Risālat al-qiyān: The Epistle on the Singing Girls of Jāḥiẓ*), ed. and trans. A. F. L. Beeston. Warminster: Aris and Philipps.

Caussin de Perceval, Armand Pierre. 1873. "Notices anecdotiques sur les principaux musiciens arabes des trois premiers siècles de l'islamisme." *Journal asiatique* 7e sér., 2:397–592.

Mas'ūdī. 1989. *Les prairies d'or*, trans. C. Barbier de Meynard and Pavet de Courteille; rev. Charles Pellat. Paris: Société Asiatique.

Meyers Sawa, Suzanne. 1987. "The Role of Women in Musical Life: The Medieval Arabo-Islamic Courts." *Canadian Woman Studies/Les Cahiers de la Femme* 8(2, summer):93–95.

Neubauer, Eckhard. 1995. "Sallāma al-Zarḳā'." In *Encyclopedia of Islam*, 2nd ed., ed. C. E. Boswell et al., Vol. 8, 996. Leiden: Brill.

Pellat, Charles. 1976. "Ḳayna." In *Encyclopedia of Islam*, 2nd ed., ed. C. E. Boswell et al., Vol. 4, 820–824. Leiden: Brill.

Pickthall, Marmaduke, trans. 1982. *Quran.* New Delhi: Kitab Bhava.

Rowson, Everett K. 1991. "The Effeminates of Early Medina." *Journal of the American Oriental Society* 111(4):671–693.

Sawa, George Dimitri. 1989. *Music Performance Practice in the Early 'Abbasid Era 132–320 AH/ 750–932 A.D.* Toronto: Pontifical Institute of Mediaeval Studies.

Stigelbauer, Michael. 1975. *Die Sängerinnen am Abbasidenhof um die Zeit des Kalifen al-Mutawakkil.* Vienna: Verband der Wissenschaftlichen Gesellschaften Österreichs.

Contemporary Issues of Gender and Music

Miriam Rovsing Olsen

When Men and Women Send Messages to Each Other
Musical Metaphors for Social Values
Neutralization of Gender through Music
Urban Environments and Gender Constraints
Transgression of Gender Values
Effects of Modernization in the Rural World

Viewed from the outside, the notion of gender in the Arab-Islamic world is tinged with negative connotations. It calls up visions of sexual segregation, veiled women, and a musical culture in which women's participation seems to be either restricted to the domestic sphere or related to a professional sphere that also includes dance and prostitution. Behind these clichés, however, lies an infinitely more complex reality, which recent research invites us to study in all its subtlety and even to correct.

In effect, the stereotypes stem from observations by city dwellers rather than rural people. The practices they reflect should be seen as extreme manifestations not so much of Islam as of hierarchical social systems strongly marked by moral precepts. The city—or aspiration to an urban money-making way of life—brings about a radical shift in certain principles of behavior. While such principles underlie family, clan, and tribal cohesiveness and are also a basis of much that is of musical importance, they function quite differently in a rural milieu and in a city.

Deference is observed between different age groups and between family members and relatives, imposing varying degrees of reserve among people in different regions. This restraint or modesty—called *amsethi* by the Kabyls, *lhshmat* by the Shilha-speaking Berbers of Morocco, and *hasham* by the Bedouin—functions at both the emotional and the behavioral level, for it encompasses "feelings of shame in the company of the more powerful" as well as "the acts of deference that arise from those feelings" (Abu-Lughod 1986:107–108). The concept is even more decisive in structuring relations between men and women than it is in regulating relations between generations. Among the Bedouin, for example, *hasham* is associated with femininity and dependence, whereas the concept of honor is associated with masculinity and autonomy (Abu-Lughod 1986:118).

Relations between the sexes are fraught with potential consequences for the respective families, including divisiveness and hostility. In Yemen, for instance, the segregation of men and women is explained in terms of *fitna*. Because this term refers to temptation as well as the disorder that can result from it, the concept includes every aspect of relations between males and females (Lambert 1997:160–161). In everyday life, it works to preclude the expression of personal or affective feelings between men and women or adolescent boys and girls. Even newly married couples maintain their distance from each other: they are not seen together in public, and they show no

FIGURE 1 Men and women face-to-face in an *ahidus* (sung dance) at a wedding in Ayt Atta in the central High Atlas Mountains. Photo by Claude Lefébure, winter 1972–1973.

intimacy in either behavior or speech. In societies where marriages are arranged, marriage becomes an alliance between two families rather than just a man and a woman. In fact, once a woman is married and has become a mother, her relationships with her children and elder relatives often provide greater emotional satisfaction than her relationship with her partner. Social life has no place for intimacy between a couple—even at night, when women and children sleep together (Jansen 1987:169–174).

Music and poetry thus serve as a kind of escape valve for emotions that cannot be expressed in the course of daily life. Among the Bedouin, poetry, which is often recited in the midst of a conversation, can express an individual's sense of vulnerability, stemming from painful situations, that would be received with detachment, indifference, or anger if it were expressed in ordinary "discourse" centered on the ideologies of honor and modesty (Abu-Lughod 1986:186–189). Among Atlas Berbers, the notion of *lhshmat* has the effect of prohibiting collective pleasure, but pleasure can be shared during celebrations through music, poetry, and dance (Lortat-Jacob 1980:23; figure 1). The austere behavioral codes that regulate male-female relationships in this part of the world must be understood in order to appreciate the importance of an art form in which words are privileged—a vocal and poetic art that, through its own discourse and mechanisms, permits a dialogue between the sexes.

WHEN MEN AND WOMEN SEND MESSAGES TO EACH OTHER

Dialogue between men and women can unfold in the presence or the absence of the other. It can also become theatrical, as when singers pass on general social messages through ritual, such as rituals celebrating the birth of a son, circumcision, or marriage.

Whatever the circumstances in which the sexes address each other, the mode of address is either derisory or dithyrambic. In Kabylia in the recent past, derision was still a lively tradition. Some couples did not hesitate to display their problems in public in what were known as "mockery songs," performed in a circle (Mahfoufi 1991:284–292). Even in the 1950s, there was real verbal confrontation between the two families being joined by a marriage. The wedding reception was a veritable trial for them: lyrics were improvised for the occasion to emphasize the more or less happy nature of the alliance, and a marriage might actually be broken off if these lyrics were deemed to dishonor either side. Women prepared themselves for these confrontations by seeking information and counsel from female experts in the art of the contest and armed themselves with information about both the bride's and the groom's family history (Mahfoufi 1991:281–284). In the Moroccan Atlas region, derisive stanzas are entirely ritualized in wedding celebrations. One of their functions is to calm the bride's apprehension. They are sung in an intimate all-female setting and, like many ritual songs, they are performed as laments. They make fun of the groom, his mother, and his sisters and thus and help loosen things up and allow the tears to flow (Rovsing Olsen 1984:52–53, 206–211; figure 2).

FIGURE 2 Bride in wedding headgear in Ayt Haddidou in the central High Atlas Mountains. Photo by Claude Lefébure, 1972–1973.

In celebrations in the Moroccan Anti-Atlas mountains, a connection between mockery and praise is made through *ahwash*, collective song and dance accompanied by drums. A celebration includes a series of pieces during which teams of drummers chosen from the audience alternate. The oratorical matches open in a derisive mode but always close in a dithyrambic mode, and the distinction between the two modes is often attenuated by tender refrains sung between derisive stanzas (Rovsing Olsen 1996:92–93).

In some circumstances, emotional expression is solitary and ordinary. Alone or in the presence only of those who do not answer (a baby, for example), isolated from the eyes of others though not necessarily from their hearing, a person may give free rein to his or her feelings and speak to someone who is absent. Women especially express themselves in this way. Daily domestic tasks (grinding grain, washing clothes, preparing meals, and the like) provide numerous opportunities, as does work in the fields, where the vegetation shields a singer from view. Through *maghna* 'song' (also called *maghna 'ātifī* 'sentimental song'), Yemeni peasant women give voice to their disappointments (Yammine 1995:113). Among Shilha-speaking Berbers, the *amarg* 'nostalgia', 'yearning love', 'unrequited love' (Schuyler 1984:146) is sung in similar situations, but often by two women who alternate. Sakata (1983:158) notes that among urban Afghan musicians the majority of songs are about unrequited love and thus are melancholy. Among Kabyls, the *ahiha* 'song that speaks of love' is sung by women (especially while harvesting vetch) when men are absent, and recited by men when women are absent. In both cases, the singer holds a sort of dialogue with the absent one (Mahfoufi 1991:241–244).

Kabyl lullabies allow a female singer to express emotions or complaints that she cannot reveal in any other musical genre. Although she always begins with stanzas concerning the child and sleep, she invariably proceeds to sing stanzas of another kind, which express her personal feelings (Mahfoufi 1991:318–319, 327).

Because it is actually or potentially ambiguous, poetry permits the expression of feelings otherwise condemned. Singers mix up the genders, speaking of women in masculine terms and of men in feminine terms, violating grammatical gender agreement, and the like. The *izran* of the Rifian mountain region, sung first by men and then by women in succession, are formulated as a kind of "insinuation suite," "a kind of 'mini-correspondence' which lovers may exchange in almost complete safety" (Basset 1920:334). The lyrics of *irzan* are sung in such a way that only those concerned understand them; this is important in a region where the separation of the sexes is an inflexible rule. Metaphors expressing the theme of love sometimes permit broader interpretation. In *ghazal* poetry, sung by Yemeni musicians who accompany themselves on the lute, such songs allow not only both feminine and masculine interpretations but also mystical, religious, and earthly interpretations. This is accomplished so effectively that "if certain variations in performance" are made, "one poem can be sung at the same time by libertines and mystics" (Lambert 1997:78–84).

Under these conditions, love is not a simple theme. Simon Jargy emphasizes its importance to poetry in the Arab-Muslim oral tradition, and the shyness and modesty that surround the expression of intimate feelings; he notes a concept called *walif* or *welf* that allows one to keep secret the object of one's love. This term refers simultaneously to "a relative by blood or alliance, a friend, a beloved woman, the clan or the tribe" and thus cannot be translated as "love"—it is much more subtle and complex (1971:110). Feelings distilled into a repertoire sung by men and women (together or separately) also correspond to conventional bodily and verbal expressions.

MUSICAL METAPHORS FOR SOCIAL VALUES

When men and women are exposed to the eye of the community, their attitudes are often conventional. For women, at least, this is in contrast to the easygoing attitudes, laughter, and strong words that they indulge in when they are alone with their children inside the house during a celebration. In public, women's expression is full of modesty and reserve when they are singing or dancing: their eyes are lowered, their body movements are discreet, and their words are difficult to follow and often barely audible (figure 3). In the Moroccan Anti-Atlas, a woman poet will not sing solo (where a man would) but rather will breathe her verses to her female companions in the choir, who will then sing them in unison (Rovsing Olsen 1997:102–103).

No music represents masculine, virile moral values (honor, courage, generosity) as eloquently as the "warrior" genres found throughout the Arab world under various names. These are often accompanied by dancing, flutes, and drums. Men seek to appear virile and warlike through their clothing and accessories (a dagger at the belt, a powderhorn on the shoulder, a rifle) as well as their choreography (which includes sword dances, war exercises, and men on horseback). The dance, directed by a leader, is generally very lively. A dance called *bar'a* 'to surpass oneself', 'excellence', 'bravery' should undoubtedly be considered part of this repertoire: it is a men's collective dance among the tribes in the high plateaus of Yemen (Yammine 1995:160, 173). Sometimes the singing alone suffices to embody warlike tribal values, as in the case of the Yemeni *zamel*, performed by two groups of men in an antiphonal mode on the same occasions as the *bar'a*, sung during wartime "while going to the battlefield to frighten the adversary" (Yammine 1995:122). Even today, this tradition perceives weakness as weakness in both war and the tribe.

In the Rif of Morocco, oratorical matches between men are an important means of expressing honor: each man is defending his territory and his wife. Here the term *honor* derives from *'arḍ*, a word that encompasses the notion of a challenge. A man must show perfect mastery of his message and of poetic speech and must know how

FIGURE 3 Female row of an *ahidus* of blacks-*harratin* in Ayt Atta in the central High Atlas Mountains. Photo by Claude Lefébure, 1972–1973.

to appear modest by praising the enemy (Jamous 1981:65–71). In the Atlas region of Morocco, the prologue of men's and women's sung performances invokes protective saints and expresses the singer's submission to God and to the audience.

In public, mastery of the body through dance is considered all the more admirable because emotions run high in such moments of conviviality. In Yemen, there is unquestionable sensuality in the *la'ba* dance when performed by pairs of men to the sound of the *mizmār*; but the couple must remain indifferent (Yammine 1995:173). In parts of the Atlas region, men and women dance side by side while maintaining a highly controlled posture. Self-mastery is always the aim when all the senses are awakened by flattery or insults in the songs, or by the magnificent presence of so many men and women. In this regard, dance can be seen as a test of social values. This is also true of song. In the Rif region, a man who does not master his words, and does not answer as he should to a challenge in an oratorical match, brings about dishonor (Jamous 1981:70).

NEUTRALIZATION OF GENDER THROUGH MUSIC

A desire for balance between the sexes is often demonstrated in the song repertoires and makeup of musical groups. During celebrations in rural areas, at which hundreds of people might gather, one goes from the narrow family and village group to a much larger one. Although male and female spaces are separated, this separation is blurred by musical similarity. One example from the Moroccan Atlas region is antiphonal song—*naqus*—performed by both groups. Guests take turns dancing to these songs with the help of an idiophone created for the occasion from "found" objects—things in daily use such as a tea tray struck with two skewers. *Tazrrart* responsorial songs are sung at some festivities by male and female guests in two different rooms, who sometimes even respond to each other despite the wall separating them (Rovsing Olsen 1997:51).

Professional musicians respect this apparent desire for symmetry between the sexes. In the Yemeni high plateaus, both male and female groups—males known as *mzayna* (singular, *mzayyin*) and their female equivalent, *mzayyinat* (singular, *mzayyna*)—are hired for major village celebrations (Yammine 1995:175). Symmetry also prevails at weddings, where the *mzayyna* prepares the bride and entertains those surrounding her, while the *mzayyin* does the same for the groom (Yammine 1995:61–62).

Weddings also illustrate a desire for a symmetrical enactment of male and female principles in certain ceremonies. In Iraq, the Islamic wedding ritual includes two simultaneous processions: in one, the bride is brought to her husband's house by women who sing a cappella and ululate; in the other, the groom is brought home from a mosque or a friend's house by men who also sing (Hassan 1980:133). The symmetry of male and female (bride and groom) can also be enacted by women alone. For example, in the High Atlas and Anti-Atlas regions of Morocco symmetry is an important aspect of the wedding ritual: each ceremony at the bride's home has its equivalent at the groom's home (Rovsing Olsen 1989). In the Yemeni high plateaus on the first day of a wedding ceremony, the ritual songs of the *mzayyinat*—the female professional musicians—are sung in both the bride's house and the groom's (Yammine 1995:61; figure 4).

The desire to accord men and women equivalent places in celebrations is also illustrated by the Anti-Atlas Berbers, who divide the night of an *ahwash* into two equal parts: the first part is devoted to men's *ahwash* and the second to women's. At certain high points, members of the audience sing *tazrrart* responsorial songs over the *ahwash* songs. In the first (male) part of the night, women sing the *tazrrart*; in the second (female) part, men sing them.

FIGURE 4 Wedding splendor: young brides in Ayt Haddidou in the central High Atlas Mountains. Photo by Claude Lefébure, 1972–1973.

URBAN ENVIRONMENTS AND GENDER CONSTRAINTS

In a broad sense, then, with regard to gender we can see a dichotomy between ordinary behavior and music. Another important dichotomy related to music is that between rural and urban environments. In an urban milieu, for instance, musicians tend to become professionals and to specialize in string and wind instruments. Natives may be found among these musicians; but usually specialists—paid professional and semi-professional musicians—belong to landless underprivileged or minority groups. In many parts of the Middle East, earning money from music has traditionally been frowned on by the majority population. Thus there have been many musicians among minorities, such as the Romany (or Gypsy) people in Iraq; Jews until the creation of the state of Israel and their emigration there; blacks of slave origin in Iraq, the Gulf countries, and the Maghrib; and a social category, barbers, in Yemen and Afghanistan.

When they leave the land and move to a city, men and women very often abandon their songs. During celebrations, therefore, music is performed by paid specialists who have been hired for the occasion. The only form of active participation for the guests is the dancing, especially by the women—to the point that this has become the main expression of both joy and sadness.

In cities, private "light" entertainment takes on primary importance. During urban celebrations, groups of musicians and female dancers are segregated by sex. But sometimes women participate, especially as dancers, in groups that perform for men. In such cases, the men do not dance. Because the hip movements are different, women's dancing in urban settings has an entirely different character from the dancing one observes in rural environments. Generally, the musicians play short pieces with rapid rhythms, in order, it seems, to give the most people a chance to dance in succession. Laudatory singing in particular is also cultivated, as it confers prestige on those to whom it is addressed.

Whereas in rural areas distress is expressed through sung matches and dancing, urban men and women may express themselves through trance in a religious framework. In Algeria, for instance, for the followers of the Qādiriyya Sufi order the trance would seem to be a therapeutic device and to express an inabilty meet social demands related to gender. For men, such problems may include sexual deviance, inability to marry or to protect a wife or children, and inability to shoulder a man's responsibilities in general. Women's problems may include being widowed or divorced, being a prostitute, being unable to conceive a child, or nearing the end of young womanhood without having found a husband (Jansen 1987:95–97). In Tunisia, young widows or divorcées in the Tijaniya order have their own worship groups that perform "possession" dances, which seem to represent a compensation for being deprived of sexual pleasure (Ferchiou 1972:66).

TRANSGRESSION OF GENDER VALUES

Perhaps the best measure of gender values lies in their transgression. This certainly seems to be true in situations where men and women take on the norms of the other sex.

In the city, traditional gender roles have sometimes known to be violated in a manner which may seem excessive but which is fully explained by the social context. One example is female musicians who perform for men and are generally distinguished (including in name) from female musicians whose audiences are exclusively women. Early in the nineteenth century, discussing the *ghawāzī*, professional women musician-dancers in Egyptian cities, Villoteau noted that the mere fact that they performed with face unveiled in the street was sufficient to give them the reputation of prostitutes (1812:169–182). In the late twentieth century, Sakata found that the same was true of women singers and dancers in the musical orchestra of Herat, in Afghanistan (1983:87–88). Doubleday made a similar observation in Herat at about the same time, regarding other groups of professional female musician-dancers from underprivileged backgrounds, the relatives of barber musicians (1988:158, 161, 167, 195, 211). She suggested that these women's image as "loose" might also have to do with their ability to earn money and negotiate their salaries with men, and that the image might be reinforced by the amorous lyrics of their songs. She also noted that the character traits acquired or sought after among these women—a strong personality, independence, and confidence about performing in public—are the opposite of the "docility, modesty and shyness" normally required of a woman. This imprint of male values may be accepted in an exclusively female context, but elsewhere female musicians are morally condemned. For instance, Algerian women *maddāḥāt* are suspected of working as *shīkhāt* or prostitutes when they are not performing for women (Jansen 1987:195).

While scholars generally agree that *shīkhāt* do combine prostitution with their work as singers and dancers (Jansen 1987:163), studies dealing with professional women musicians in Herat (Doubleday 1988) and Cairo (Danielson 1991, 1997) have found that these professionals may be honorable Muslims, married women, and mothers of families, and that they sometimes perform as a family group such as mother and daughters. Research on the careers of *'awālim* (singular, *'ālima*), professional women musicians in Cairo, from 1850 to 1930 found that although they might come from underprivileged environments, they were not necessarily members of minority groups but were predominantly Egyptian and Muslim (Danielson 1991:301). Today some of these women begin their careers as performers of Qur'ānic cantillation, religious songs, or songs particular to women. Some, very much concerned with their image, have taken advantage of new opportunities, especially public concerts. The most famous example is the phenomenally successful singer Umm Kulthūm.

Gender transgressions often have the same connotations for men as for women. Thus in Ṣan'ā', in Yemen, virility is associated with certain forms of religious chanting and with the traditional qualities of "reason" and "control of oneself, one's words, and one's body," which are incompatible with "musical pleasure." Female musical categories, which include accompanied singing known as *ghinā'* and instrumental music, are believed to cause a loss of reason and bring about state of exultation, *ṭarab* (Lambert 1997:170–171). This feminine connotation is so strong that "whatever his personal virility," a male musician who uses such seductive means with exclusively male audiences is suspected of a "bisexuality unacceptable by the most ordinary male codes" (Lambert 1997:188). Because musicians, by influencing an audience, have the power

Although it may not be acceptable for women to play a wind instrument, they are permitted to hear and see it.

to bring about social disorder, there is a tendency to give them low social value. Throughout the Mediterranean world, therefore, the "desexualization" of musicians is a well-known stratagy for exercising control (Stokes 1994:23).

It is interesting to try to determine the boundaries beyond which one cannot go. An example is the connotation of virility associated with wind instruments in the Arab-Islamic world. Dances in which groups of professional musicians perform in perfect gender symmetry—male musicians among men, female musicians among women—are distinguished only by the absence of wind instruments in the women's groups. Women "replace" such instruments by singing. This is true, for instance, of the *mizmār* in dances in Yemen (Yammine 1995:33, 175) and the *zukra* 'oboe' among religious *ḥaḍra* groups in Sfax (Siala 1994, 1:127–146). A link between music and sex and a notion of sex as created by the devil have been suggested as explanations for this interdiction (Sakata 1983:79; Yammine 1995:33). But although it may not be acceptable for women to play a wind instrument, they are permitted to hear and see it. As a specialist, a male musician is authorized to enter the terrain of women when no other man would. Thus in the oasis of Fezzan in Libya, a male double clarinetist, the *magruna*, performs ritual music for women during wedding celebrations. His presence in this case is "a means of transcending and unifying what is separate to achieve the necessary complementary among all, a presence which unites the male and female principle" (Brandily 1986:55–56). In the Moroccan Rif, male *imdyazn* musicians playing the *zammr* (the counterpart of the Libyan *magruna*) also go among women, a freedom they have because they are not considered men of honor (Jamous 1981:68–69).

EFFECTS OF MODERNIZATION IN THE RURAL WORLD

Influences of urban life are sometimes found in rural environments, though with consequences that differ from one place to another. In the central High Atlas region, for instance, a gradual disappearance of women's special repertoires, and their replacement by young women's dances, suggests a lowering of the status of women resulting from the economic independence of men in a society where men traditionally depended on women's labor (Lortat-Jacob 1980:26). At once time in Egypt, young men and women, responding to the pain of disappointments such as unrequited love, would exchange courtly romantic songs of the Bedouin known as *ghinnāwa* (*'alam* in Cyrenaica in Libya); but today *ghinnāwa* are sung exclusively by young men, who record them on tape (Abu-Lughod 1986:183). That women are no longer able to express themselves through *ghinnāwa* reflects great changes in the economic basis of the tribal system, which have widened the distance between men and women, to women's detriment (Abu-Lughod 1990:38–39).

In rural Yemen, some urban influences have made their way into the male musical world, disturbing the traditional gender balance and symmetry in musical production. Travel between city and countryside is done mainly by men and rarely by women. Thus men introduce changes from the city to the country, and these changes, for the most part, influence men's worlds. For example, the male part of the procession behind a bride and groom is usually performed by both *mzayyin* and *mzayyinat*; as a result of urban influences, this has tended to be replaced by religious hymnody or *nashshād* (Yammine 1995:90). Among the Kabyls, the men's songs that accompanied women's *urar* dances have been supplanted by a professional repertoire—*idebbalen*—played with oboes and double-headed drums (Mahfoufi 1991:135–141).

To understand gender roles better, much more research is needed, especially in rural areas. Many questions remain unanswered, particularly concerning vocal techniques and dance. The unconventional ways in which women express themselves through music demand close consideration and represent many opportunities for research by ethnomusicologists. Some of this research might well focus on those who, in the Middle East, are—even more than men—the true object of women's affection: children.

—Translated by Beth Raps.

REFERENCES

Abu-Lughod, Lila. 1986. *Veiled Sentiments: Honor and Poetry in a Bedouin Society*. Berkeley: University of California Press.

———. 1990. "Shifting Politics in Bedouin Love Poetry." In *Language and the Politics of Emotion*, ed. Catherine A. Lutz and Lila Abu-Lughod, 24–25. Cambridge: Cambridge University Press/ Éditions de la Maison des Sciences de l'Homme.

Basset, Henri. 1920. *Essai sur la littérature des Berbères*. Algiers: Jules Carbonel.

Brandily, Monique. 1986. "Qu'exprime-t'on par et dans la musique traditionnelle? Quelques exemples libyens." *Maghreb Review* 2(2–4):53–57.

Danielson, Virginia. 1991. "Artists and Entrepreneurs: Female Singers in Cairo during the 1920s." In *Women in Middle Eastern History. Shifting Boundaries in Sex and Gender*, ed. Nikki R. Keddie and Beth Baron, 292–309. New Haven, Conn.: Yale University Press.

———. 1997. *The Voice of Egypt: Umm Kulthūm, Arabic Song, and Egyptian Society in the Twentieth Century*. Chicago: University of Chicago Press.

Doubleday, Veronica. 1988. *Three Women of Herat*. London: Cape.

Ferchiou, Sophie. 1972. "Survivances mystiques et culte de possession dans le maraboutisme tunisien." *L'Homme* 12(3):47–69.

Hassan, Schéhérazade Qassim. 1980. *Les instruments de musique en Irak et leur rôle dans la société traditionnelle*. Paris: Mouton (Cahiers de l'Homme).

Jamous, Raymond. 1981. *Honneur et baraka: Les structures sociales traditionnelles dans le Rif*. Paris: Éditions de la Maison des Sciences de l'Homme.

Jansen, Willy. 1987. *Women without Men*. Leiden: Brill.

Jargy, Simon. 1971. *La musique arabe*. Paris: Presses Universitaires de France.

Lambert, Jean. 1997. *La médecine de l'âme*. Hommes et musiques. Nanterre: Société d'Ethnologie. Compact disk included.

Lortat-Jacob, Bernard. 1980. *Musique et fêtes au Haut-Atlas*. Paris: Mouton (Cahiers de l'Homme). Disk included.

———. 1994. *Musiques en fête*. Hommes et musiques. Nanterre: Société d'Ethnologie.

Mahfoufi, Mehenna. 1991. "Le répertoire musical d'un village berbère d'Algérie (Kabylie)." Ph.D. dissertation, Paris X-Nanterre University. 2 vols.

Rovsing Olsen, Miriam. 1984. "Chants de mariage de l'Atlas marocain." Ph.D dissertation, Paris X-Nanterre University. 2 vols.

———. 1989. "Symbolique d'un rituel de mariage berbère: Une approche ethnomusicologique." *Anuario Musical* 44:259–291.

———. 1996. "Modalités d'organisation du chant berbère: Paroles et musique." *Journal of Mediterranean Studies. History, Culture and Society in the Mediterranean World* 6 (1):88–108.

———. 1997. *Chants et danses de l'Atlas (Maroc)*. Preface by Bernard Lortat-Jacob. Musiques du monde. Cité de la Musique/Actes Sud. Compact disk included.

Sakata, Hiromi Lorraine. 1983. *Music in the Mind. The Concepts of Music and Musician in Afghanistan*. Kent, Ohio: Kent State University Press.

———. 1989. "Hazara Women in Afghanistan: Innovators and Preservers of a Musical Tradition." In *Women and Music in Cross-Cultural Perspective*, ed. Ellen Koskoff, 85–95. Urbana: University of Illinois Press. (Originally published 1987. New York: Greenwood.)

Schuyler, Philip D. 1984. "Berber Professional Musicians in Performance." In *Performance Practice. Ethnomusicological Perspectives*, ed. Gerard Béhague, 91–148. Westport, Conn.: Greenwood.

Siala, Mourad. 1994. "La hadra de Sfax: Rite soufi et musique de fête." Ph.D dissertation, Paris X-Nanterre University. 2 vols.

Stokes, Martin, ed. 1994. *Ethnicity, Identity, and Music. The Musical Constuction of Place*. Introduction, 1–27. Oxford: Berg.

Villoteau, Guillaume André. 1812. *De l'état actuel de l'art musical en Egypte, ou relation historique et descriptive des recherches et observations faites sur la musique en ce pays*. Description de l'Egypte ou recueil des observations et des recherches qui ont été faites en Egypte pendant l'expédition de l'armée française, Vol. 14. Paris: Imprimerie de C.L.F. Panckoucke.

Yammine, Habib. 1995. "Les hommes des tribus et leur musique (Haut-plateaux yéménites, vallée d'al-Ahjur)." Ph.D. dissertation, Paris, X-Nanterre University. 2 vols.

70W

Section 5
Learning and Transmission

The ways that music traditions are learned and passed on from generation to generations may be viewed from various sociocultural and musicological perspectives. Centuries-old systems of pedagogy at times continue alongside new approaches, and in some cases the process of transmission has stopped altogether, leading to the rapid demise of once vibrant forms of expressive culture.

Issues surrounding "oral" and "written" transmission have been raised repeatedly as new forms of transcription have been developed and then discarded or widely adopted. Transcriptions of song texts and melodies in a variety of notation systems have raised numerous issues, with each tradition left to shape its own responses over time.

In addition to embracing Western influences in areas as diverse as everyday clothing and city planning, many cultures in the Middle East and Central Asia have adopted elements of Western music pedagogy, including institutionalized training and staff notation. These have led to new pedagogical canons that combine aspects of both Western and indigenous music theory and practice. New vocabulary, concepts, attitudes, instruments, and ensembles have resulted, often leading to efforts aimed at preserving and promoting indigenous music traditions—efforts that, ironically, fundamentally change the very traditions they are supposed to preserve.

The development of printing, records, radio, television, and inexpensive cassettes has changed the face of transmission and pedagogy and has allowed music, as a product, to become more widespread than ever before. It has also allowed unlimited repeated listening and analysis so that students, in many cases, need no longer meet or even know the musicians from whom they learn.

Student-teacher relationships in the region have taken innumerable forms, from intense apprenticeship to modeling one's performance on masters without their knowledge. The following articles highlight many of these issues and offer glimpses of the stages of development from student to master musician.

Open-air store in Cairo, Egypt.
Photo by Scott Marcus, 1983.

The Iraqi *Maqām* and Its Transmission

Scheherazade Qassim Hassan

Classification
Performance and Musical Accompaniment
Performers
Transmission of the Text
Transmission of the Music
Master-Student Relationship
Development of Singers
Institutionalized Teaching

Maqām, as the term is used in the Arab world, is not identical with the Iraqi *maqām*. Except in Iraq, *maqām* has three levels of meaning: a degree of sound, an abstract or theoretical scale, and the modal organization of the Arab-Islamic area—an organization based on predominant tonal centers and specific melodic progressions. In this area, consequently, any piece of urban music depends on a particular modal organization.

In Iraq, however, the general term *maqām*, as well as the more specific term *al-maqām al-ʿirāqī* (plural, *al-maqāmāt al-ʿirāqiyya*), has a fourth meaning: the main urban vocal repertoire. It designates the entire repertoire of *maqāmāt*, or any portion of this repertoire. The appellation *al-ʿirāqī* is believed to have been coined in the nineteenth century, during the Ottoman rule, to distinguish Iraqi tradition from other Islamic repertoires that also are called *maqām*, such as the *mugam* of Azerbaijan and Turkmenistan and the *shashmaqam* of Uzbekistan.

The repertoire of the Iraqi *maqām*, sung in secular and Islamic rituals, consists of some fifty individual *maqāmāt*. Musically, each of these is an independent "composition," more or less complex in structure; but all share the principle of successive, interconnected, variable melodic sections. Between the beginning part, called *taḥrīr* or *badwa*, and an end part called *taslīm*, these melodic sections represent elaborations on the principles mode, new modes and melodic material, and modulations and articulations. The order of transmission of cadences, semicadences, and sections sung in the upper or lower register is scrupulously respected and is different for each *maqām*. The type of poetry—whether it is in colloquial or literary Arabic—and the rhythmic cycles accompanying some *maqāmāt* are fixed by tradition.

The performer must observe the structure of each *maqām*, the order of the constituent melodic sections, the melodic material, and the rhythmic and poetic parameters. However, he is also expected to enhance the traditional framework with personal additions and improvisation.

There are three regional traditions within the Iraqi *maqām*, corresponding to three main cities: Baghdad, Mosul, and Kirkuk. The historical origins of the tradition cannot be dated with certainty, for there are few written records of the repertoire before the nineteenth century. Some contemporary Iraqi specialists have posited that it dates from the ʿAbbasid dynasty (750–1258 C.E.); others think that it is a relatively recent phenomenon dating back only four, five, or six centuries. In any case, until the emergence of modern music in Iraq, the *maqām* was the oldest, and principal, urban repertoire; it is still present in religious rituals and secular traditions; and it inspires modern compositions and provides melodic material for instrumental improvisation.

CLASSIFICATION

The Iraqi *maqām* is based on a complex oral system of classification that describes the parameters of the repertoire, including melodic modes, rhythmic patterns, poetic genres, and the organization of material into set cycles. A primary distinction is drawn between seven "basic" Iraqi *maqāmāt* and the remaining derived ones. The basic *maqāmāt* (*al-maqāmāt al-aṣliyya*) are *bayāt*, *sēgāh*, *rāst*, *ḥijāz*, *'ajam*, *nawā*, and *ṣabā* (Rajab 1983). Each of these *maqāmāt* has the same name as its chief melodic mode; thus the Iraqi *maqām rāst* is in the melodic mode *rāst*. Each of the derived *maqāmāt* (*al-maqāmāt al-far'iyya*) derives from one of these seven basic modes; for example, *maqām humāyūn* is derived from *maqām ḥijāz*. Distinctions are also made between *maqāmāt* whose song texts are in classical Arabic (*al-maqāmāt al-fuṣḥā*) and those whose texts are in colloquial dialects (*al-maqāmāt al-'āmmiyya)*. Rhythmic *maqāmāt* (*al-maqāmāt al-īqā'iyya*) are distinguished from nonrhythmic *maqāmāt* (*al-maqāmāt al-lā īqā'iyya*); and "restricted" *maqāmāt* (*al-maqāmāt al-muqayyada)*, in which the order of melodic pieces must be strictly followed, are distinguished from "free" *maqāmāt* (*al-maqāmāt al-muṭlaqa*), in which the performer is (to some extent) free to change the order of the pieces. A large portion of the individual *maqāmāt* are further organized into *fuṣūl* 'cycles' within which their number and order are dictated by tradition.

PERFORMANCE AND MUSICAL ACCOMPANIMENT

Iraqi *maqām* singing is traditionally referred to as *qirā'at al-maqām* 'reading' or 'reciting' the *maqām*, an expression identical to that used for recitation of the Qur'ān and other religious genres; however, an additional expression, *ghinā' al-maqām* 'singing the *maqām*', came into use around 1930.

In ṣecular contexts, a *maqām* performance is accompanied by the traditional ensemble *al-chalghī al-baghdādī* 'Baghdadi ensemble', consisting of two chordophones, the *sanṭūr* (a box zither struck with two mallets), and the *jōza* (a four-stringed spike fiddle); plus two or three membranophones, the *daff* (a frame drum with snares), the *dumbuk* (a single-headed drum), and optionally the *naqqāra* (a double kettledrum). Since the 1930s, some performers have preferred the Egyptian and Levantine ensemble (*al-takht al-sharqī*), which consists of *'ūd* (short-necked lute), *qānūn* (plucked box zither), and *nāy* (oblique reed flute), as well as the usual membranophones.

In both religious and secular contexts up to the 1940s, Iraqi *maqāmāt* were generally performed in cycles, *fuṣūl*, and were never in fact sung alone, for other independent musical forms are always incorporated into the concert without belonging organically to the *maqām*. The minimal formal elements to be performed with each *maqām* are a *muqaddima* (instrumental introduction) or a *taqsīm* (solo instrumental improvisation) or both, followed by the *maqām* itself, and finally a rhythmic popular song related to the principal mode, a *peste* in secular contexts or a *tawshīḥ* in rituals. Recently, musicians have become more free in altering the order of these forms and even increasing their number.

In theory, no instrumental part stands on its own, either formally or melodically. In practice, however, many singers give the instrumentalists an opportunity to perform important solo improvisations and interludes. With the exception of some compulsory melodic sections that are typical signatures of certain *maqāmāt*, instrumental parts, unlike the vocal part, have no preconceived frame. *Muḥāsaba* (instrumental responses), which have a dialogue with the vocal part, are unique versions created extemporaneously, even when (as is usually the case) they are based on previous group renditions.

PERFORMERS

The Iraqi *maqām* is primarily a vocal repertoire traditionally performed by a male soloist, a *qāri'* 'reciter' or 'reader'. In new settings, and in situations influenced by modern music, the performer is now also called a *mughannī* 'singer' or even a *muṭrib* 'he who provokes musical ecstasy', *ṭarab*.

Maqām singers have traditionally been Muslims, and many are reciters or chanters of the Qur'ān Islamic rituals and ceremonies. They are rarely professionals. Singers are usually from the Arab, Kurdish, and Turkoman ethnic communities and most often belong to the lower urban social classes of merchants and craftsmen. Until 1950, the instrumentalists, *ālātiyya*, were mainly Jewish. Since then, because of the Jewish emigration to Israel, they have been replaced by Muslims. Instrumentalists in earlier times were professionals and specialized only in *maqām* music, but since the 1970s they have tended to diversify their musical practice. Today the popularity of the *maqām* repertoire is increasing, and *maqām* is rapidly becoming an emblem of contemporary Iraqi cultural identity.

TRANSMISSION OF THE TEXT

Two types of poetry are sung in the *maqām*: the colloquial or hybrid *mawwāl,* also known as *zheyrī,* which is composed of seven lines with the rhyme scheme a a a b b b a; and the literary *qaṣīda*, a monorhyme ode based on the rules of classical Arabic prosody. Each individual *maqām* is associated with one of these two poetic forms, although the content is subject to change and may have a wide variety of themes. Poetry of both types can be old or contemporary and may or may not have been created with the specific aim of being set to the *maqām*. The poetry, whether by a literate or an illiterate poet, may be transmitted orally or in writing, because a literate poet can choose to memorize his work and transmit it orally and an illiterate poet can ask someone else to write down his work. Unlike the music, the poetic texts are often compiled in manuscripts and printed collections.

Minor performers usually repeat texts from existing compilations, but a good literate singer often chooses a poem, selects some of its verses, and rearranges them according to his own personal taste. Freedom to change the text of a *maqām* or use the same text for different individual *maqāmāt* allows the singer to perform different versions of the same *maqām* and even of the same text. If a performer's poetic choice is met with approval, it may then be diffused widely among amateurs. A version of a *maqām* that achieves great popularity may come to be more generally associated with the performer than with the author of the text or the composer of the melody, if known.

TRANSMISSION OF THE MUSIC

Oral transmission does not generally occur through a formal, direct master-student relationship. This does not imply, however, that the concept of the master is unknown in the Iraqi tradition. On the contrary, *al-ustādh* 'the master', always a singer, is omnipresent in the life of an apprentice. However, the possible transmission from a professional instrumentalist, known to have conserved the rules and secrets of the vocal part, to a singer of his choice, is not seen as a master-student relationship. Consequently, it does not replace the effective and symbolic role of the vocal master-singer but only complements that role.

Informal learning of the Iraqi *maqām* generally takes place in two stages. The first stage of learning is a self-taught process based on imitation. It involves the acquisition of basic skills through aural, visual, and gestural imitation of a master (or of a number of singers) until the apprentice is able to sing a minimum part of the repertoire. This first period of learning is generally conducted in relative secrecy: the student does not declare his intentions in front of a master he has chosen to imitate. Before 78-rpm records became readily available, the student had to choose a living master, whom he would follow discreetly to concerts, whenever possible, to observe the master's techniques. During this phase, the master would be unaware of being studied or imitated. At this time, also, a passionate student will use any pretext to evoke the particular *maqām* he currently prefers, by indirectly initiating conversation on the subject among knowledgeable people. Throughout this initial period, which might last many years, the student takes an individual path of learning, based on his personal taste and his preference for certain *maqāmāt* and certain masters.

The second period begins when the apprentice performs in front of a specialist audience or in front of a circle of masters and specialists. In this first performance, he reveals the identity of his master and, if the master is living, acknowledges his debt to him. Usually the timing of this passage has not been previously fixed; rather, it depends largely on circumstances. For instance, if illness prevents a master from performing, an aspiring singer (known to the master's friends) may suddenly be thrust onto the stage, taking the place of the accredited performer. Obviously, the student must feel ready to face the *maqām* masters, specialists, and amateurs at any moment, once he has acquired the basic techniques and has learned a number of *maqāmāt*. The future of the new singer depends on the success of this first public encounter. If his performance is appreciated, he will be admitted to the circles of specialists and will attend their informal gatherings and discussions.

MASTER-STUDENT RELATIONSHIP

As far as the master is concerned, the sudden discovery that a new performer has unilaterally designated him as a model for imitation, without his consent, can initially provoke a refusal, and even anger. But when the master receives the new performer's deep respect and gratitude, his attitude usually softens into acceptance, and he agrees to give support and advice. This relationship does not necessarily imply formal teaching. A master could end his life without ever having given a student a single lesson. Rather, his role is based on giving instructions if requested or whenever he deems it necessary. The renowned singer Nāẓim al-Ghazālī (1921–1963), for example, considered al-Gubantchī (1901–1989) his master, although he did not receive lessons from al-Gubantchī.

The essence of the master-student relationship, therefore, is fundamentally moral and, when possible, reciprocal. Although the code of behavior may vary, depending on the individuals concerned, it will evolve around three main precepts: respect for elders; gratitude toward all those who have transmitted any kind of knowledge; and, finally, the expression of solidarity, whether moral or material, on occasions marking important events of life such as marriage and death.

After Nāẓim al-Ghazālī had achieved fame throughout the Arab world, he never missed an occasion to express his respect for al-Gubantchī. Indeed, he was so respectful that at *maqām* evenings he never sang in al-Gubantchī's presence, although it would not have been considered disrespectful for a well-known singer such as himself to do so. The extent to which a student demonstrates solidarity with a master or a master's family in times of difficulty depends on the pupil's personality, his attachment to the master, and the depth of his gratitude. When the great *maqām* singer Aḥmad Zaydān (1829–1912) fell ill, Shaul Gabbay, one of his former students who was by then a professional *maqām* performer, put himself entirely at his master's disposal. When Zaydān died, Gabbay wore black as a sign of mourning and refused to perform himself, or to attend *maqām* performances, for an entire year. A noble and responsible master will return gratitude with gratitude. Al-Gubantchī, who survived many of his students, participated in singing the *mankaba al-nabawiyya* commemorating their death. When al-Ghazālī died at the early age of forty-two, Al-Gubantchī, his master, sang in his memory.

DEVELOPMENT OF SINGERS

The precondition for becoming a *maqām* singer is a natural gift supported by genuine enthusiasm and the determination to follow a long and difficult path. A deep love of this music is essential because of the size of the repertoire (a six-year course in *maqām* given by Sha'ūbī Ibrāhīm, discussed below, did not claim to cover the whole repertoire), its complexity, and the difficulties involved in learning it. In fact, because of the difficulty of the tradition, many singers cannot master the entire repertoire. Most remain specialists in a limited number of *maqāmāt*, and only the greatest performers master all of the repertoire.

A singer is expected to have scrupulous respect for the structure of the Iraqi *maqām*—its parts, sequences, and constitutive pieces. He is judged by the way he shifts between high and low registers, and by his ability to introduce a new modal section and then leave it with equal facility. An acknowledged singer capable of improvisation must also be able to judge the length of time needed to elaborate a particular mode that is not the main mode of the *maqām*, since remaining too long in one modal color can upset the equilibrium and proportion of the entire composition.

In the early and middle twentieth century, lovers of *maqām* considered the beauty of the voice less important than fulfilling the conditions of good singing. But today most lovers and exponents of the *maqām* are more sensitive to good voices than their elders were. Although they admit that a beautiful voice does not in itself create a great *maqām* singer, they criticize the traditional tendency to assign little importance to the voice as such. The fact that the *maqām* is not well known outside Iraq is explained partly by a scarcity of good voices.

INSTITUTIONALIZED TEACHING

Changes in the transmission of the *maqām* appeared with the introduction of institutionalized teaching. The Iraqi *maqām* was first added to the music curriculum at the Ma'had al-Funūn al- Jamīla (Institute of Fine Arts) between 1956 and 1964. At the Ma'had al-Dirāsāt al-Naghamiyya (Institute of Melodic Studies), founded in 1969, it has formed part of the curriculum since 1971. Students at these institutes are usually graduates of intermediate or secondary schools and come from a wide variety of cultural and social backgrounds. Whereas traditional tradition of the Iraqi *maqām* developed new performers, the new teaching methods are aimed at forming generations of learned musicians.

In these institutes, the Iraqi *maqām* is taught as a single element within a general program based on both Middle Eastern and Western music theory, history, and practice. Students acquire some practical and theoretical knowledge of the Iraqi *maqām,* but this alone does not make them *maqām* performers. Any student who plans to become a performer tries to follow the traditional process of learning based on personal research and effort.

From 1971 until his death in 1991, Sha'ūbī Ibrāhīm, who taught at the Institute of Melodic Studies, gave the only classes in *maqām* in Iraq. Sha'ūbī was a well-known *jōza* player in the traditional Baghdadi instrumental ensemble, *al-chalghī al-baghdādī*; originally, he had also been a student of the *'ūd*. He was the only Iraqi *maqām* performer to graduate from the Oriental section of the Institute of Fine Arts.

Sha'ūbī based his teaching on the traditional imitation method. Initially, he would begin by playing recordings of different versions of one *maqām*. Then, he would start to sing the *maqām*, accompanying himself on the *jōza.* To explain each *maqām*, he would use the traditional descriptive terms. In response to specific questions, he would sing several comparable versions, adding commentary to clarify a difficult point. When he only sang a *maqām* and did not play a recording, Sha'ūbī usually rendered a simplified version because he was not, strictly speaking, a *maqām* singer. He would then ask the entire class to repeat it from beginning to end, singing in unison. Sometimes, he would ask one of the pupils to sing alone.

The policy of the Institute of Melodic Studies tended toward written methods of teaching. Accordingly, Sha'ūbī wrote down his lectures. He compiled them into a book, *Dalīl al-anghām li-ṭullāb al-maqām* 'A Guide to Melodies for Students of *Maqām*', which has been published in two editions and is currently used as a textbook. Sha'ūbī's program was designed to cover six years of teaching, and the book is accompanied by six cassettes, one for each year. These cassettes, on which Sha'ūbī himself performs, follow and refer to the text. In the text, Sha'ūbī points to places where modal changes or a particular *qiṭ'a* (melodic piece) occurs.

One way in which Sha'ūbī's teaching differs from that of the traditional masters is his use of a new vocabulary based on the theoretical analysis of modes and tetrachords. As mentioned above, he also used traditional terms, although there is a tendency to replace some local terms with terms from Arabic musical theory. Sha'ūbī's teaching methods have been followed by his students and successors at the Institute of Melodic Studies. This form of class teaching has not completely replaced the traditional oral method of transmission. However, at present we can see that this teaching method has led to fixing one version of each *maqām*, a process that seems to be gaining ground.

REFERENCES

Abou Haidar, Farida. 1977. "The Poetic Content of the Iraqi Maqam." *Journal of Arabic Literature* 19(2, September).

al-'Allāf, 'Abd al-Karīm. 1963. *Al-ṭarab 'inda al-'arab* (Musical Ecstasy among the Arabs). Baghdad: al-Maktaba al-Ahliyya.

al-Ḥanafī, Jalāl (al-Shaykh). 1964. *Al-mughannūn al-baghdadiyyūn wa'l-maqām al-'irāqī* (Baghdadi Singers and the Iraqi *Maqām*). Baghdad: al-Silsila al-Thaqafiyya, Wizārat al-Irshād.

Hassan, Scheherazade. 1987. "Le makam irakien: Structures et realisations." In *L'improvisation dans les musiques de tradition oral*, ed. Bernard Lortat-Jacob. Paris: SELAF.

———. 1989. "Some Islamic Non-Arabic Elements of Influence on the Repertory of al-Makam al-Iraki." In *Maqam, Raga, Zeilenmelodik: Konzeptionen und Prinzipien der Musikproduktion. Materialen der 1. Arbeitstagung der Study Group "Maqām" beim International Council for Traditional Music vom 28 Juni bis 2 Juli 1988 in Berlin*, ed. Jürgen Elsner, 148–155. Berlin: Nationalkomitee DDR des International Council for Traditional Music in Verbindung mit dem Sekretariat Internationale Nichtstaatliche Musikorganisationen.

———. 1992a. "Choix de la musique et de la representation irakienne au Congrès du Caire en 1932: Vers une étude de contexte." In *Musique Arabe: Le Congrès du Caire de 1932*, ed. Philippe Vigreux, 123–146. Cairo: CEDEJ.

———. 1992b. "Survey of Written Sources on the Iraqi *Maqām*." In *Regionale maqam-Traditionen in Geschichte und Gegenwart. Materialien der 2. Arbeitstagung der Study Group "Maqam" des International Council for Traditional Music vom 23 bis 28 März in Gosen bei Berlin*, ed. Jürgen Elsner and Gisa Jähnichen, 252–275. Berlin: Nationalkomitee DDR des International Council for Traditional Music in Verbindung mit dem Sekretariat Internationale Nichtstaatliche Musikorganisationen.

———. 1995. *La maqâm irakien: Tradition de Baghdad—Hommage à Yusuf Omar*. Recordings, text, and photos by Scheherazade Qassim Hassan. Maison des Cultures du Monde, W 260063. (2 compact disks.)

———. 1996a. *Chants de Baghdad*. L'Ensemble al-Tchalghi al Baghdadi, Hussein al A'adhami (vocal). Text by Scheherazade Qassim Hassan. Musicales, Institut de Monde Arabe. IMA CD18 (compact disk.)

———. 1996b. *Irak: Les maqams de Baghdad*. Recordings, text, and photos by Scheherazade Qassim Hassan. OCORA-Radio France.

Ibrāhīm, Sha'ūbī. 1982. *Dalīl al-anghām li-ṭullāb al-maqām* (A Guide to Melodies for Students of *Maqām*). Baghdad: Dā'irat al-Funūn al-Mūsīqiyya, Wizārat al-Thaqāfa wa'l-I'lām.

Qabbanji, Muḥammad. 1994. *Le maqam en Iraq: Congrès du Caire 1932*. Text by A. Hachlef. Club du Disque Arabe AAA 087, AAA 097. France: Les Artistes Arabes Associés, Club du Disque Arabe. (2 compact disks.)

Rajab, Muḥammad Hāshim (al-Ḥājj). 1983. *Al-maqam al-'irāqī* (The Iraqi *Maqām*). Baghdad: Maktabat al-Muthannā.

Music in Performance: A Rehearsal with Firqat al-Musiqa al-'Arabiyya

Scott Marcus

THE ENSEMBLE

Firqat al-Mūsīqā al-'Arabiyya 'Arab Music Ensemble', based in Cairo, is an Egyptian government ensemble founded in 1967 to perform traditional art music (the *turāth*) of the eastern Arab world (the *mashriq*).

The ensemble's unique makeup represents a mix of traditional and modern ideals. The instruments are all "traditional," but their numbers are often found only in this type of government-supported, preservation-oriented ensemble. Thus, while the fifteen or more violinists and two cellos are found in some of the larger commercial orchestras, the multiple performers on the *'ūd* (three), *qānūn* (two or three), *nāy* (two or three), and contrabass (two or three) are extraordinary. Also, the *firqa* uses only a single *riqq* (tambourine) player for percussion, harking back to the aesthetics of the *takht*, a chamber-sized ensemble that was common in the ninteenth century and early twentieth century. The chorus of more than a dozen men and a dozen women singers is also a rather new configuration for Egyptian art music, where choruses of only three or four members were common.

REHEARSALS

During the early 1980s, Firqat al-Mūsīqā al-'Arabiyya met for rehearsals four afternoons a week, in a rundown building near the main Ramsis train station in Cairo. When they arrived for a rehearsal, the instrumentalists, chorus members, directors, and staff would climb a dilapidated staircase to the third floor, where ensemble members would sign in and wait for the rehearsal to begin. The ensemble's conductor, the venerable 'Abd al-Ḥalīm Nuwayra, would arrive and sit in a small office, receiving guests and discussing professional matters with the staff and senior members. While they were waiting, many would order tea or coffee from subordinate staff members who would prepare and then bring over the requested drink, expecting to be paid, and perhaps tipped, before the end of the rehearsal. One could order tea or coffee at any time during the rehearsal by simply summoning the appropriate person.

The ensemble's unique makeup represents a mix of traditional and modern ideals.

While people were sitting and waiting, one staff member would distribute transcriptions of the music to be rehearsed, placing them on each of the instrumentalists' music stands in the rehearsal hall. The transcriptions were kept in a metal filing cabinet and were dutifully collected and returned to the cabinet after each rehearsal. Ensemble members were not allowed to take the transcriptions home, in part because photocopying was not yet common or easily available. Clearly, the ensemble's numerous rehearsals were supposed to be sufficient for all to master the repertoire.

Initially, the chorus would rehearse separately, led by a director who dictated the words and taught the melodic lines by singing and playing the *'ūd*. During the early 1980s, this director was often Kamāl Ḥusnī (who has since died), the son of Cairo's famous Jewish singer and composer Da'ūd Ḥusnī (1871–1937). When Egypt was asked to send performers to the historic Congress of 1932, Da'ūd Ḥusnī was chosen, along with Umm Kulthūm and others. I was told that the Egyptian government had recently recognized Da'ūd Ḥusnī's contribution to Egyptian culture by naming a street in Cairo after him.

Kamāl Ḥusnī had the position of chorus director because of his remarkable command of the *turāth*, a repertoire that he knew and taught by heart. One of the titles for his position recognized this: he was a *muḥāfiẓ* 'keeper', 'guardian' of the repertoire for the ensemble. I found it touching that, well after the present-day territorial conflicts had caused such a profound rift between the region's Muslims and Jews, the chorus of Firqat al-Mūsīqā al-'Arabiyya was still being taught by a Jewish man. The *turāth* was being preserved and passed on by the son of a great Jewish Egyptian singer-composer.

The ensemble's chorus sings monophonically. That is, men and women choristers all learn and sing the same melodic line, although choral arrangements regularly feature alternations among phrases sung by women only, men only, and tutti.

Chorus members do not use written music, though they may have pieces of paper on which they themselves have written song verses by hand. The absence of written music contributes to a situation in which, commonly, the chorus members are not consciously aware of the *maqāmāt* 'melodic modes' of the pieces they rehearse and perform. This came as something of a surprise to me. On a number of occasions when I attended rehearsals, I would ask a chorus member with whom I was sitting what the *maqām* of the song being rehearsed was. Usually, that chorus member would ask another and possibly a third. Finally, someone would lean over toward the instrumentalists and get an answer by asking one of them (George Michel, for example). [See Music in Performance: *'Ūd* Lessons with George Michel.] The instrumentalists, guided by written music and by the observable physicality of their playing, would usually have at least a general sense of the *maqām* being performed.

Nuwayra would finally call for the rehearsal to start and would soon appear from his office and mount a small platform in front of the ensemble. The women's chorus would sit to the left of the instrumentalists, the men's chorus to the right. The first violinist, after first checking with the lead *qānūn* player, would go around and check the tuning of the violinists, cellists, and contrabass players. Then Nuwayra would begin to conduct.

Nuwayra's conducting of a song or instrumental piece was devoid of any flamboyant gestures. There was no attempt to shape the music emotively. Beyond simply keeping the beat and effecting occasional dynamic contrasts, Nuwayra would also cue choral and solo entries, correct mistakes, and direct repeated rehearsing of needy passages.

The rehearsal session was informal in nature, although everyone was expected to pay attention. Many would smoke while rehearsing, holding a cigarette, for example, between the fingers of the bow hand.

Vocal soloists would be called up to stand and rehearse next to the conductor. They would often record the rehearsal on "Walkman" tape recorders so that they could practice at home.

PERFORMANCES

In the 1980s, Firqat al-Mūsīqā al-'Arabiyya's rehearsals led to regular live performances, every Thursday night throughout much of the year, alternating between Cairo one week and Alexandria the next. Videotaped concerts were also broadcast on government television every other Thursday evening. Because of this constant exposure, 'Abd al-Ḥalīm Nuwayra, the *firqa*, and many of its members—especially the instrumentalists and singers who took solos—became very popular figures among the general Egyptian public.

REFERENCES

El-Shawan, Salwa. 1982. "The Role of Mediators in the Transmission of al-Mūsīkā al-Arabiyyah in Twentieth-Century Cairo." *Yearbook for Traditional Music* 21:56–74.

———. 1984. "Traditional Arab Music Ensembles in Egypt since 1967: The Continuity of Tradition within a Contemporary Framework." *Ethnomusicology* 22(2):271–288.

Institutionalization of Learning in Egypt

Salwa El-Shawan Castelo-Branco

Notation
Music Institutions in the Twentieth Century

In contemporary Egypt, informal learning of music coexists with institutional instruction using both oral transmission and written notation. In Islamic hymnody (*al-inshād al-dīnī*) and in musical styles rooted in or evocative of rural life (referred to as *baladī* or *sha'bī*), learning takes place informally through listening and imitation. In recitation of the Qur'ān, training at the Ma'had al-Qir'āt (Qur'ān Recitation Institute) is provided using the rules of *tajwīd*, a system governing proper recitation by regulating phonetics, timbre, rhythm, tempo, beginnings, and pauses. [See The Qur'ān Recited.] However, melodic artistry, an essential ingredient in the *mujawwad* style of recitation, is not included in the curriculum; it is acquired through listening to reputed reciters and secular singers, complemented, in some cases, by formal music instruction. Institutional and private instruction in Western music has been offered since the early nineteenth century. For Arab music, learning was institutionalized and Western notation was gradually adopted in the early twentieth century.

Institutionalized learning of music was introduced in the 1820s and 1830s by the Albanian ruler Muḥammad 'Alī (r. 1805–1848), who founded five schools of Western military music where Italian and French instructors taught young working-class Egyptians band instruments and the rudiments of Western notation and theory. These schools introduced Western notation and inaugurated a tradition of Western-style military music in Egypt, supplying trained musicians to military bands, orchestras, and music institutions.

In the twentieth century, Arab and Western "art" music learning was institutionalized, and Western music was incorporated as a basic component in the training of Arab musicians. In addition, the use of Western notation and solfège for the teaching and performance of Arab music became pervasive.

NOTATION

The earliest example of the use of Western notation in Arab music is Dhākir (1895), quoted in al-Khula'ī (1904:33), who was among the first Arab scholars to use Western solfège syllables to represent the tones of Arab modes (Marcus 1989:123). Since then, Western notation has been used in Arab music theory books, in technical exercises for mastering Arab instruments, in transcriptions of the standard repertoire of Arab music, and in popular music.

In contemporary Egypt, informal learning of music coexists with institutional instruction using both oral transmission and written notation.

The adoption of Western notation for representing Arab music entailed several measures to ensure the articulation of the two systems. Since Arabic is written from right to left, the representation of vocal music posed a problem (Marcus 1989:134). Initially Western notation was written from right to left, a method that was replaced by notation written from left to right with separate syllables of the Arabic text given beneath the notes to which they are sung from left to right. Additional accidentals (half-sharp and half-flat) representing intervals that do not correspond to the tone and half tone were also introduced.

MUSIC INSTITUTIONS IN THE TWENTIETH CENTURY

During the first two decades of the twentieth century, several private institutions in Cairo and other cities offered instruction in Arab music. In 1906, the prominent Arab musicians Manṣūr ʿAwaḍ and Sāmī al-Shawwā founded what has been cited as the first school for Arab and Western music (Kāmil 1975:22). A rival institution, the Egyptian Music Institute (al-Maʿhad al-Mūsīqī al-Maṣrī), was founded by the musician and music journalist Iskandar Shalfūn (1925:4). The most important institution was the Oriental Music Club (Nādī al-Mūsīqā al-Sharqī; figure 1), founded in 1914 by a group of aristocrats and musicians under the leadership of the prominent *qānūn* player and aristocrat Muṣṭafā Riḍā; it provided instruction in Arab music and served as a forum where older musicians debated their concerns about preserving Arab music. In 1929, this influential group secured patronage from King Fu'ād for the founding of the government-supported Arab Music Institute, AMI (Maʿhad al-Mūsīqā al-ʿArabiyya).

The curriculum of AMI emphasizes "bimusical" training in both Arab and Western music. Thus formal training in Arab music requires the acquisition of knowledge and skills in Western music notation, theory, history, and performance. Teachers and professionals acknowledge the limitations of Western notation for the representation of Arab music intervals, ornamentation, and vocal timbre. Solfège syllables are assigned to the notes constituting Arab modes and are sometimes used as "oral notation," often dispensing with the written score. At the same time, the older system of musical instruction relying on attentive listening and imitation and centered on the acquisition of a solid knowledge of modal practice persists within the institutional framework. Furthermore, while instrumentalists use both written and oral-aural transmission, vocalists tend to rely almost exclusively on the latter. Despite its limitations, fluency in Western notation is regarded as an indispensable tool for professional musicians, especially instrumentalists and arrangers who work in Arab music ensembles and in the recording industry, where limited studio time increases reliance on Western notation for the transmission of new compositions.

Music education was introduced in public schools for the first time starting in the academic year 1931–1932, thanks to the efforts of the Egyptian musicologist Maḥmūd Aḥmad al-Ḥifnī (1896–1973), who had been trained in Berlin. Since then, the music curriculum has focused on Western music notation, solfège, and repertoire

FIGURE 1 Nādī al-Mūsīqā al-Sharqī. Photo from Virginia Danielson.

in the major and minor modes. Al-Ḥifnī also organized the Arab Music Conference of 1932, an international meeting in which European and Middle Eastern scholars and musicians documented selected aspects of Arab music performance practice, debated its state, and recommended specific measures for resolving what were then regarded as pressing problems. The Music Education Committee of the conference called for the incorporation of music education at all school grades, as well as the founding of teacher training institutions that could guarantee a supply of qualified teachers (*Kitāb Mu'tamar al-Mūsīqā al-'Arabiyya* 1932:341–373).

The Higher Institute for Music Teachers was founded in 1933. It was integrated into Helwan University and renamed the Faculty of Music Education in 1975. At this institution, training at the undergraduate and graduate levels is provided in both Arab and Western music theory, musicology, performance, and music pedagogy. Graduates work as music teachers, as musicians in Arab music ensembles, and in the popular music industry. A short-lived Higher Institute of Theater Music (Ma'had al-Mūsīqā al-Masraḥiyya, 1944–1950) also offered training in Arab and Western music, producing a generation of musicians conversant in both idioms.

Up to the 1950s, Western "art" music was taught by expatriate musicians in Cairo and Alexandria, either privately or through a few privately owned conservatories. Two generations of Egyptian composers, performers, arrangers, and music teachers received their training within this framework.

Western music was integrated within the official Egyptian system of artistic higher education in 1959 with the founding of the Cairo National Conservatory (CNC). This initiative was one result of a two-pronged cultural policy decreed following the revolution of 1952, a policy that was intended to preserve the cultural heritage of Egypt while promoting "modernity," locally associated with Western cultural products. In the 1980s, CNC expanded its initial offerings to include academic and music curricula from primary through high school as well as specialized programs in music performance, composition, and musicology at the undergraduate and graduate levels. European expatriate musicians and visiting faculty members from the former Soviet Union staffed CNC during its first two decades of existence but were gradually replaced by the best graduates of CNC.

The social organization of CNC is much like that of conservatories in the West. A premium is placed on the individual artistic qualities of teachers, around whom student groups form a patron-client relationship. The CNC has produced highly skilled musicians in Western music. Many completed their training at prestigious institutions in the former Soviet Union and Europe, subsequently filling the ranks of the Cairo Symphony Orchestra and other Western music ensembles.

The CNC does not provide formal training in Arab music. However, many of its students and graduates were socialized in Arab music and acquired basic skills in it as professional studio musicians and arrangers in the popular recording industry.

In sum, in Egypt institutional training has become a requirement for entry into the professional arena in Arab and Western music, and such training is also a source of musical and social prestige. The establishment of Western music as a basic ingredient in the training of Arab musicians and the demand for studio musicians altered the requirements of Arab musicianship and contributed to the development of bimusicality in Arab and Western music by many leading musicians who, informed by new aesthetic ideals and technical skills, introduced radical changes into contemporary Arab music style.

REFERENCES

El-Shawan, Salwa. 1980. "The Sociopolitical Context of al-Mūsīqá al-ʻArabiyyah in Cairo, Egypt: Policies, Patronage, and Musical Change (1927–1977." *Asian Music* 12(1):86–128.

Kāmil, Maḥmūd. 1975. *Tadhawwuq al-mūsīqā al-ʻarabiyya* (The Appreciation of Arab Music). Cairo: Muḥammad Amīn.

al-Khulaʻī, Kamāl. 1904. *Kitāb al-musīqī al-sharqī*. (Book of Oriental Musician). Cairo: Author.

Kitāb mu'tamar al-mūsīqā al-ʻarabiyya (Book of the Arab Music Conference). 1933. Cairo: Al-Maṭbaʻa al-ʻAmīriyya.

Marcus, Scott. 1989. *Arab Music Theory in the Modern Period.* Ph.D. dissertation, University of California at Los Angeles.

Shalfūn, Iskandar. 1925. *Kitāb taʻlīm al-ʻūd* (Book for Learning the 'Ud). Cairo: Author.

The Use of Western Notation in Tunisian Art Music

Ruth Davis

The introduction and use of Western notation in the teaching and performance of Tunisian art music, *al-ma'lūf* 'familiar' or 'customary', was pioneered by the Rashīdiyya Institute, founded in Tunis in 1934 with the aim of preserving and promoting traditional Tunisian music. The Institute was named after the aristocratic patron and amateur of the *ma'lūf*, Muḥammad al-Rashīd Bey (d. 1757). Between 1935 and 1950, the Institute supervised the transcription of the entire repertoire of the *ma'lūf* into Western staff notation, modified slightly to accommodate the neutral intervals of the Arab system of modes, *maqāmāt*, for the use of its ensemble. Rather than crystallizing the traditional melodies into one standard version, these original transcriptions provided an impetus for successive layers of prescriptive notations, each reflecting individual aspects of interpretation by subsequent leaders of the ensemble. After Tunisian independence in 1956, the ministry of cultural affairs published a complete version of the repertoire edited by Ṣāliḥ al-Mahdī, in a series of nine volumes entitled *al-Turāth al-mūsīqī al-tūnisī* 'The Tunisian Musical Heritage'. Distributed to newly created educational and recreational institutions throughout the country, the published notations became the basis for a new national performing tradition inspired by the Rashīdiyya Institute's model.

The Tunisian initiative has parallels in other Middle Eastern repertoires in which, since the nineteenth century, Western notation has been adopted variously as a theoretical tool, a means of documentation, a mnemonic aid to learning, and, exceptionally, as a basis for performance itself. The use of notation is typically associated with other aspects of westernization, including the creation of European-style music academies and ensembles, and it has often been part of a larger mission to revive or preserve traditions perceived to be in decline. The Tunisian example is particularly noteworthy for the relatively early date at which notation was integrated into regular teaching and performance, for the national scope of its use, and for the accompanying radical changes in performance practice generally.

HISTORICAL AND IDEOLOGICAL BACKGROUND

Western notation was first introduced into the *ma'lūf* during the nineteenth century, with the arrival of European music teachers who were invited to form military bands. In 1840, Aḥmad Bey established a school at the Bardo, near Tunis, to train army officers. Alongside the diatonic fanfares imported by the Europeans, the officers' band, and its various civilian offshoots, played melodies from the *ma'lūf* which had been transcribed into Western notation (Rizgui 1967:62; Zghonda n.d.:3ff.).

Outside the specialized sphere of the military bands, *ma'lūf* ensembles generally continued to rely on oral tradition until the founding of the Rashīdiyya Institute nearly a century later. However, both the ideological and the practical foundations for the use of notation in regular performance practice had been laid down during the previous two decades by the European patron and pioneering scholar of Arab music, Baron Rodolphe d'Erlanger [see SNAPSHOT: BARON D'ERLANGER]. From 1921 until his death in 1932, d'Erlanger established himself in a Moorish-style palace in Sidi Bou Said, on the cliffs outside Tunis, and devoted himself to the revival of a tradition he described as moribund (1949, 5:337–338; 340–342).

In his writings (1917:95; 1949, 5:341), d'Erlanger identifed specific European influences (for example, the employment of European music teachers by the local nobility and the widespread use of European instruments of fixed pitch) as factors contributing to the corruption and decline of Arab music in Tunisia. He believed, however, that utlimately the source of decay was inherent in the performing tradition itself, which lacked both notation and a theoretical foundation: "Abandoned to successive generations of musicians increasingly ignorant of the theory of their art and relying solely on oral transmission, the heritage had no means of resisting such a long period of decline" (1949, 5:340).

In 1931, a year before his death, d'Erlanger undertook a comprehensive classification of the melodic and rhythmic genres in current use in Arab music, for presentation at the Cairo Congress of 1932. D'Erlanger was too weak to travel to Cairo (he died in October 1932), and so his collection was presented to the congress by his assistant, Shaykh ʿAlī al-Darwīsh, a Syrian dervish musician from Aleppo who had been provided to him by the Egyptian government. The collection was published posthumously in Arabic in the proceedings of the congress (*Kitāb mu'tamar al-mūsīqā al-ʿarabiyya*, 1933) and in Volumes 5 and 6 of *La musique arabe*, where it was amplified by further musical illustrations and separate sections on the Arab Andalusian traditions of North Africa. D'Erlanger acknowledged his assistant as his source for the "Oriental" Arab traditions (effectively those of Syria); Shaykh ʿAlī al-Darwīsh also transcribed the music examples into Western staff notation (d'Erlanger 1949, 5:xiv, 381).

In hindsight, the significance of d'Erlanger's classification for the future of the *ma'lūf* lay not so much in the resultant publications as in the circumstances of their publication. During Shaykh ʿAlī al-Darwīsh's visit to Tunis in 1931, d'Erlanger arranged for him to give public classes, funded by the government of the French Protectorate, in which he introduced Tunisian musicians to Arab music theory through the use of solmization and Western notation. In effect, this Syrian musician imported to Tunisia the modern teaching methods developed in the music conservatories of Cairo (Racy 1977:37–38; El-Shawan 1980:90, 95–96). Later, at the invitation of his former Tunisian students, Shaykh ʿAlī al-Darwīsh made two further visits to Tunis—in 1938 and 1939, to establish the use of solmization and notation in the recently founded Rashīdiyya ensemble (d'Erlanger 1949, 5:381; al-Mahdi and Marzūqī 1981: 67–68).

INNOVATIONS OF THE RASHĪDIYYA INSTITUTE

Before the founding of the Rashīdiyya Institute in 1934, there were two contrasting types of performance practice for the *ma'lūf*. The first, *ma'lūf khām* 'raw or unrefined *ma'lūf*' was, and to some extent still is, associated with certain Sufi brotherhoods. It was characterized by a male chorus singing in unison accompanied only by hand clapping or by percussion instruments, including the *darbukka* (a vase-shaped drum), *naqqārāt* (a pair of small kettledrums), *ṭār* (a tambourine), and *bandīr* (a frame drum with snares on the underside). Each *firqa* 'musical group' was directed by a shaykh, usually an elderly member chosen for his superior knowledge of the repertoire. He was responsible for selecting and teaching the pieces, controlling the tempo in performance, and leading the transitions from one piece to the next.

The second type of performance practice, restricted to secular contexts, included melody instruments. It was characterized by small, solo instrumental ensembles, traditionally made up of a *rabāb* (a two-stringed fiddle without a separate neck; plural, *rabābāt*), which was replaced by a violin in purely instrumental pieces; an *'ūd 'arbī* (a fretless short-necked Maghreb lute with four pairs of strings; plural, *a'wād*); *naqqārāt* (small kettledrums); and the *ṭār* (al-Mahdī and Marzūqī 1981:49). The instrumentalists doubled as a chorus and sometimes also as solo vocalists. During the twentieth century, Middle Eastern instruments, among them the *'ūd sharqī* (a lute with six courses of strings), *qānūn* (a trapezoidal plucked zither; plural, *qawānīn*), and *nāy* (a reed flute without a mouthpiece) were sometimes added, as were some European instruments of fixed pitch, such as the harmonium, mandolin, and piano (d'Erlanger 1949, 5:341; al-Mahdī and Marzūqī 1981). The shaykh, who normally played either the *'ūd* or the *ṭār*, provided the authoritative renderings for the chorus. Within this framework, however, each soloist interpreted the melodies in his own individual way, embellishing them spontaneously according to the natural articulation of his instrument or voice. The result was a variable, heterophonic texture.

In their efforts to preserve and promote the *ma'lūf*, the founding members of the Rashīdiyya invited the finest shaykhs of Tunis to form an ensemble. The initial response produced six violins, two *rabābāt*, five *a'wād*, three *qawānīn*, *ṭār*, and *naqqārāt*, as well as six male vocalists and one female vocalist (al-Mahdī and Marzūqī 1981:49–50).

Such an ensemble was unprecedented, not only in the size and variety of its instruments but, more critically, in that it combined several instruments of the same type. As the several shaykhs, unaccustomed to performing together, struggled against one another's versions of the melodies, heterophony turned into cacophony. Clearly, in this enlarged format, the musicians would need to conform to a single predetermined rendering, and it was decided that this could best be achieved through the use of notation, in emulation of Western practice. Since none of the shaykhs was competent in this medium, the young violinist Muḥammad Trīkī, versatile in Western, Middle Eastern, and Tunisian music, was invited to supervise the transcription of the entire repertoire, teach the musicians how to read the notation, and lead them in performance. Trīkī had studied the violin with a French priest at a *lycée* in Tunis, and he had practiced conducting in rehearsals of the French symphony orchestra of Tunis. His experience of the *ma'lūf* derived both from the *zawāyā* 'Sufi lodges' and from private lessons with individual shaykhs, and he had studied Middle Eastern song with two visiting Egyptian celebrities—Kāmil al-Khula'ī and Aḥmad Fārūz. Trīkī had also attended the classes in Arab music theory given by d'Erlanger's assistant Shaykh 'Alī Darwīsh during his visit to Tunis in 1931.

Trīkī described to me his very first working session with the shaykhs and the strategy he used to facilitate their acceptance of his direction: he presented himself as their student. Trīkī selected an instrumental piece, the *mṣaddir* of *nūbat aṣbahān* 'suite in the mode *aṣbahān*', and requested each shaykh in turn to play it phrase by phrase. After all of them had performed the first phrase, Trīkī asked them to consult with one another and agree on the best version, which he then transcribed. Trīkī took his "teachers" through the whole piece in this way, notating each phrase as it was chosen. Finally, he played the completed transcription for them. The result, a composite of several different interpretations of the same piece, was unfamiliar to all; nevertheless, each shaykh recognized the portions he had contributed and everyone had to admit that this was the version they had agreed on.

Trīkī emphasized that the primary purpose of the transcriptions was to provide standard versions for performance; they were never intended as a means of preservation in themselves.

Once the shaykhs had accepted Trīkī's project, he relaxed his methods, and most of the subsequent transcriptions were based on performances by one or two musicians only. Chief among these was Shaykh Khamais Tarnān, a master of the *ʿūd ʿarbī* and leader of the Rashīdiyya ensemble. Tarnān is cited as the source for the Tunisian Andalusian traditions represented in Volumes 5 and 6 of *La musique arabe* (d'Erlanger 1949:xv).

Finally, Trīkī's colleague, Ḥabīb al-ʿĀmarī, made fair copies that were kept in the archives of the Rashīdiyya Institute, eventually to become sources for the notations in *al-Turāth al-mūsīqī al-tūnisī* (al-Mahdī n.d.:12). Trīkī emphasized, however, that the primary purpose of the transcriptions was to provide standard versions for performance; they were never intended as a means of preservation in themselves. Trīkī's view was unanimously upheld by the other musicians, who maintained that the transcriptions could never provide independent sources of the melodies: a transcription functioned as an aide-mémoire rather than as a direct tool for learning, and all agreed that it would be impossible to learn new pieces using notated sources alone.

During the first decade of his leadership, Trīkī created a standard format for the ensemble that, he acknowledged, was influenced by the sonorities of both the Western symphony orchestra and contemporary Egyptian ensembles; at the same time, he established conventions for rehearsing and performing that have survived to the present day. Whereas the exact lineup was variable, the basic model included a mixed male and female chorus and an entirely male instrumental section, consisting of several violins, two or three cellos, double bass, *darbukka, ṭār*, and *naqqārāt*, and an arbitrary mélange of traditional urban Arab melody instruments, among them *ʿūd ʿarbī, ʿūd sharqī, qānūn, nāy,* and *rabāb*; instruments of fixed pitch were excluded. According to Trīkī, the chorus and strings were intended to sound in unison "like an army of soldiers," whereas the solo Arab instruments were free to improvise embellishments. In practice, however, any such individual contributions were overwhelmed by the larger, more uniform body of sound produced by the rest of the ensemble.

Patterns of rehearsal and performance were different for the instrumental and vocal sections. Since the nuances of the vocal line were considered too subtle to be taught otherwise than by direct imitation, the singers learned the repertoire from the chorus master, Shaykh Khamais Tarnān, by the traditional method of repetition and memorization. The instrumentalists, in contrast, were coached by Trīkī, aided by parts copied by hand from the original transcriptions. When both sections had mastered a piece, they would reunite to rehearse and perform under Trīkī, the chorus from memory and the instrumentalists still following notation. Trīkī himself either led the ensemble from within, playing the violin, or, more characteristically, directed it from the front with a baton, like the conductor of a symphony orchestra.

Trīkī's early efforts to introduce the techniques of solmization and notation to the resistant shaykhs were unsuccessful. Finally, in 1938 (as noted above), the Rashīdiyya invited their original mentor, Shaykh ʿAlī al-Darwīsh, back from Egypt to take over, with positive results; he paid one further visit in 1939 before judging the Tunisians equipped to manage on their own (al-Mahdī and Marzūqī 1981:67–68). Eventually, the shaykh's original curriculum was expanded into a three-year syllabus including solmization, notation, theory of the *maqāmāt* 'melodic modes' and *īqā'āt* 'rhythmic cycles', Arab music history, and instrumental performance, which was taught independently of the ensemble. By the late 1940s, the ensemble had restricted its new membership to graduates of this curriculum.

ALTERNATIVE TRANSCRIPTIONS

The notations of 'Abd al-Ḥamīd Ben'aljīya and Muḥammad Sa'āda

Over the years, Trīkī's transcriptions were followed by other notated versions of the repertoire prepared by subsequent leaders of the Rashīdiyya and its offshoot, the Radio *ma'lūf* ensemble. It is unclear when these alternative versions began to appear, or indeed whether Trīkī himself ever modified the notations he originally produced. However, the first musician who openly espoused the idea of preparing fresh notations and admitted doing so in practice was 'Abd al-Ḥamīd Ben'aljīya. Formerly a *nāy* player in the Rashīdiyya ensemble under al-Mahdī, Ben'aljīya had learned the *ma'lūf* both in the *zawāya* and in the Rashīdiyya Institute's school and had graduated in piano and flute from the French conservatory in Tunis. Like Trīkī, he had learned how to conduct in rehearsals of the French symphony orchestra. In 1958 he was appointed leader of the new Radio *ma'lūf* ensemble established by the government just two years after independence. It was a special division of the regular Radio ensemble, which was led initially by Egyptians and modeled directly on its contemporary Egyptian counterparts. This larger ensemble, which included Western accordions and harmoniums, specialized in Middle Eastern popular music and Tunisian compositions written in the same style (al-Mahdī and Marzūqī 1981:58). As a professionally contracted body of musicians, the new ensemble, unlike the Rashīdiyya, had a fixed membership: drawing from the elite of the Rashīdiyya's past and present members, it had ten male and ten female singers, ten violins, two cellos, a double bass, *qānūn, 'ūd 'arbī, nāy, darbukka, ṭār*, and *naqqārāt.*

Ben'aljīya wanted to distinguish his elite Radio *ma'lūf* ensemble from the Rashīdiyya by introducing new "professional" standards of performance, which he acknowledged were inspired by Western orchestral models. In contrast to Trīkī, whose notations give a single melodic line undifferentiated between vocal and instrumental renderings, Ben'aljīya prepared separate parts for each type of instrument: in general, the cellos and basses articulate the *īqā',* reinforcing the percussion in a reduced version of the melody. The remaining instruments play the complete melody with characteristic embellishments. Ben'aljīya's scores include contrasts of timbre and register between the various instruments and voices, and between pizzicato and arco strings; they also synchronize bowings and give details of tempo, dynamics, and phrasing.

Ben'aljīya also introduced changes in the melodies themselves, defending the legitimacy of these changes on grounds of authenticity rather than originality: his interpretations, he maintained, were derived from his rich and extensive experience of the *ma'lūf* traditions of the *zawāyā*. Ben'aljīya insisted that there was no such thing as a definitive version of the *ma'lūf*: in oral tradition, he argued, the melodies were being contiuously re-created through recomposition and improvisation; it followed therefore that corresponding changes should be incorporated into the written tradition by continuously revising the notation. Thus, he regarded each transcription he made as provisional, intended for a particular event or season only, to be replaced by fresh transcriptions for subsequent performances. In this way, he believed, his transcriptions would reflect the essentially improvisatory nature of the *ma'lūf* and thus justify the exclusion of improvisation from performance.

Evidently, however, this ideal proved too cumbersome to be realized in practice with any consistency. When Ben'aljīya was appointed leader of the Rashīdiyya ensemble in 1972, he replaced most of its former membership with more disciplined musicians from his Radio ensemble. According to those I interviewed, they continued to use the same scores he had prepared for them a decade earlier.

In 1979, Muḥammad Sa'āda replaced Ben'aljīya as leader of the Rashīdiyya ensemble. Like his predecessor, Sa'āda had learned the *ma'lūf* in the *zawāya* and in the Rashīdiyya school, had played the *nāy* in the Rashīdiyya ensemble under al-Mahdī, and had studied Western music in the conservatory of the French Protectorate. Unlike Ben'aljīya, however, he had continued his music studies in Paris, attending Olivier Messiaen's classes in analysis and taking courses at the Musée de l'Homme. After he returned to Tunis, he had performed in the Radio ensemble and taught at the National Conservatory of Music. Espousing his predecessor's ideologies, Sa'āda too claimed that his personal interpretations were rooted in the traditions of the *zawāya*; he prepared separate parts for each instrument and generally maintained the orchestral conventions established by Ben'aljīya. Occasionally, however, he admitted compromising his ideals and using Ben'aljīya's scores instead of preparing his own.

Ṣāliḥ al-Mahdī and *The Tunisian Musical Heritage*

A radically opposing ideology regarding the status and function of the Rashīdiyya's notations, embodied in the very title *al-Turāth al-mūsīqī al-tūnisī* 'The Tunisian Musical Heritage', was developed by Ṣāliḥ al-Mahdī, who succeeded Trīkī as leader of the ensemble in 1949. Apart from a few brief interruptions, al-Mahdī held the reins until 1972, when he was replaced by 'Abd al-Ḥamīd Ben'aljīya. During this period, although the Rashīdiyya ensemble itself was gradually overshadowed by the achievements of Ben'aljīya's Radio *ma'lūf* ensemble, al-Mahdī rose to become the leading political force in Tunisian music. In 1961 he was appointed both director of music and popular arts in the newly established ministry of cultural affairs and director of the National Conservatory of Music, positions he would hold until 1979.

A cornerstone of the new state-sponsored music education apparatus established after independence in 1956, the National Conservatory of Music replaced both the French conservatory, founded in Tunis in 1896 to teach Western music, and the Rashīdiyya Institute's school. Occupying the colonial buildings of the French conservatory and staffed initially by teachers and graduates of the Institute, the National Conservatory combines studies in Western, Tunisian, and Middle Eastern traditions, using solmization, notation, sight-reading, and dictation in all three. Its curriculum, subsequently adopted by the two younger provincial conservatories of Sousse and Sfax, has provided a blueprint for music education at all levels throughout the country and standardized training for the performers, teachers, and administrators who constitute the new musical establishment (al-Mahdī and Marzūqī 1981:71–74).

In his capacity as director of music and popular arts, al-Mahdī was personally responsible for the government's policies regarding music. These included: (1) the creation of a national network of music clubs in *diyār al-thaqāfa* 'houses of culture', hosting amateur *ma'lūf* ensembles along the lines of the Rashīdiyya; (2) the organization of an annual cycle of competitions and festivals aimed at encouraging the new ensembles and standardizing their performances; and (3) the publication and distribution of the nine volumes of *al-Turāth al-mūsīqī al-tūnisī* containing the Rashīdiyya's transcriptions of the entire *ma'lūf*.

In our conversations, al-Mahdī described the published notations as note-for-note reproductions of Trīkī's original transcriptions, with only slight modifications to simplify certain details of rhythm and phrasing. Trīkī himself maintained that there was no difference between his transcriptions and those al-Mahdī published, although this claim clearly reflected his bitter, long-standing resentment of his younger colleague (in particular, he resented the fact that in certain volumes al-Mahdī's name, rather than his own, appears on the cover), rather than any considered musical judgment. Trīkī's resentment goes back to the period 1949–1951, when he visited Algeria on a personal mission and al-Mahdī replaced him as leader of the Rashīdiyya ensemble. Trīkī had understood this to be a temporary arrangement, and he expected to resume his leadership when he returned. However, by that time al-Mahdī had firmly entrenched himself. Trīkī withdrew from the Rashīdiyya completely and continued his career as an employee of the Radio ensemble, maintaining his reputation as one of Tunisia's best-loved and most respected composers.

In his introduction to the third volume and again in his official history of the Rashīdiyya Institute, al-Mahdī (al-Mahdī and Marzūqī 1981) refers to three national congresses organized by the ministry of cultural affairs in the early 1960s, at which recordings were made of all the *nūbāt* known to shaykhs representing all the regions of Tunisia. These recordings were subsequently transcribed and compared by a committee consisting of al-Mahdī himself, Shaykh Khamais Tarnān, and Muḥammad Trīkī. According to al-Mahdī, the results revealed no fundamental differences (*furūq jawhariyya*) between the interpretations (n.d.:12; al-Mahdī and Marzūqī 1981:81–82). As the title makes explicit, the published notations are presented as the single national tradition of the *ma'lūf*.

For his part, Trīkī denied that the recordings of the shaykhs had been comprehensive, or that any systematic transcriptions or comparisons had ever been made. None of my informants admitted having heard the recordings or having seen the alleged transcriptions, and al-Mahdī himself claimed that they were lost. In general, I found considerable disagreement over the supposed homogeneity of the Tunisian *ma'lūf*. Many people, including past and present representatives of the Rashīdiyya ensemble, the National Conservatory of Music, and the ministry of cultural affairs itself, believed that in fact there were distinct regional variants.

Evidently, the purpose of the three congresses was to establish the authority of the notations published by the ministry of cultural affairs as a pan-Tunisian tradition. Intended for use in the educational and recreational institutions newly established throughout the country, they represented, according to al-Mahdī, the sole "correct" version of the melodies. He admitted that it was legitimate for talented, experienced musicians to improvise embellishments in solo performance (as indeed he himself demonstrated); nevertheless, he insisted that the published notations contained all the essential melodic details.

MUSICAL EVIDENCE OF PERSONAL INTEPRETATION AND REGIONAL VARIATION

The Rashīdiyya and radio ensembles

I have tested various assertions made by Trīkī's successors by comparing five transcriptions of the same piece, the *abyāt* section—the vocal introduction to the *nūba*—of *nūbat al-aṣbahān*, as transcribed and performed by members of the Rashīdiyya and Radio ensembles between 1935 and 1982 (Davis 1992). All my informants, including those whose interpretations are represented here, approved of my choice of repertoire on the grounds that the *abyāt* is a serious, weighty genre, and that the relatively long, slow *baṭāyḥī* rhythm on which it is based offers a rich scope for embellishment and personal interpretation. The sources, in chronological order, are:

- Trīkī (1935): Transcription by Muḥammad Trīkī made in 1935.
- Rashīdiyya (1954): Transcription by the author of a performance by the Rashīdiyya ensemble led by Ṣāliḥ al-Mahdī, recorded by Radio France in Tunis, 1954. This recording was part of the series of twelve of the thirteen Tunisian *nūbāt* (*nūbat al-nawā* was omitted) recorded by Radio France in Tunis in 1954 and reproduced on phonograph records.

- TMH: Transcription in *al-Turāth al-mūsīqī al-tūnisī* 'The Tunisian Musical Heritage', Volume 8 (n.d.:49–63).
- Benʿaljīya (1962): Transcription by ʿAbd al-Ḥamīd Benʿaljīya for a studio performance by the Radio *ma'lūf* ensemble, recorded by Radiodiffusion Télévision Tunisienne on 19 July 1962.
- Saʿāda (1982): Transcription by Muḥammad Saʿāda for a public performance by the Rashīdiyya ensemble at the National Conservatory of Music on 5 November 1982, recorded by the author.

My analysis, although it took into account surface differences of melodic detail, focused primarily on melodic structure as determined by the identity and progression of *ʿuqūd* (singular, *ʿiqd*): tonal units within each mode defined by a characteristic succession of intervals. On this basis, I identified three distinct versions by Trīkī, al-Mahdī, and Benʿaljīya. Saʿāda's interpretation is nearly identical to those of al-Mahdī: despite his ideological convictions, Saʿāda reproduced virtually note for note the version published in *al-Turāth al-mūsīqī al-tūnisī* and recorded by the Rashīdiyya nearly thirty years earlier.

Ironically, the most radical differences occur between Trīkī (1935) and al-Mahdī (1954 and TMH), despite the fact that of Trīkī's three successors only al-Mahdī maintained that he had introduced no significant changes. Despite his claims to the contrary, al-Mahdī's version has not, overall, resulted in simplification of melodic or rhythmic detail.

In general, Benʿaljīya (1962) corresponds closely to al-Mahdī (1954), with one dramatic exception: the second half of each of the three vocal sections, that is, mm. 5–9, 22–26, and 35–39, opens in the uncharacteristic *ʿiqd bayātī* instead of *ʿiqd ḥijāz*, as in all the other sources (see figure 1, which gives mm. 5–8 of both TMH and Benʿaljīya, 1962, indicating the *ʿuqūd* for each source). This radical departure from the regular *ʿuqūd* structure of the *maqām* undoubtedly substantiates Benʿaljīya's claim of a personal interpretation. However, I could find no other musician who would accept this use of *ʿiqd bayātī* in *nūbat al-aṣbahān* as consistent with tradition. Clearly, Trīkī's successors did not always put their theories into practice.

Testūr

Since the late 1960s, the government has held an annual national festival of the *ma'lūf* in the town of Testūr, which is 77 kilometers northwest of Tunis. Testūr, founded by Andalusian refugees in the early seventeenth century, is famous for its indigenous *ma'lūf* tradition.

FIGURE 1 Excerpt from *al-abyāt* of *nūbat al-aṣbahān*, according to versions by ʿAbd al-Ḥamīd Benʿaljīya (1962) and by Ṣāliḥ al-Mahdī in *al-Turāth al-mūsīqī al-tūnisī*. Transcription by Ruth Davis.

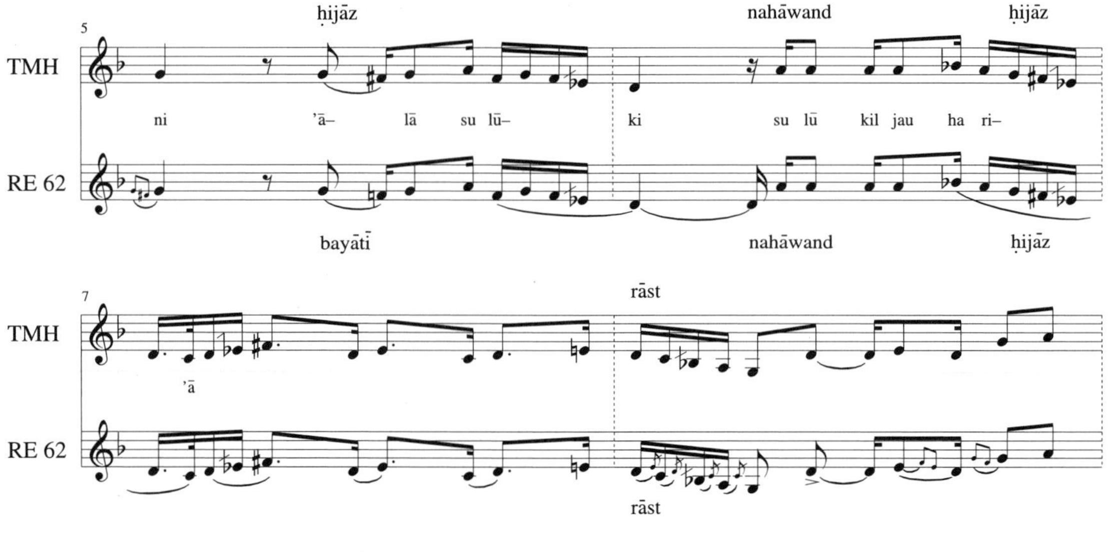

FIGURE 2 *Al-baṭāyḥī "Fī jannati 'l firdawsi,"* according to the traditional version of Testūr (1960; T60) and the version published in *al-Turāth al-mūsīqī al-tūnisī*. Transcription by Ruth Davis.

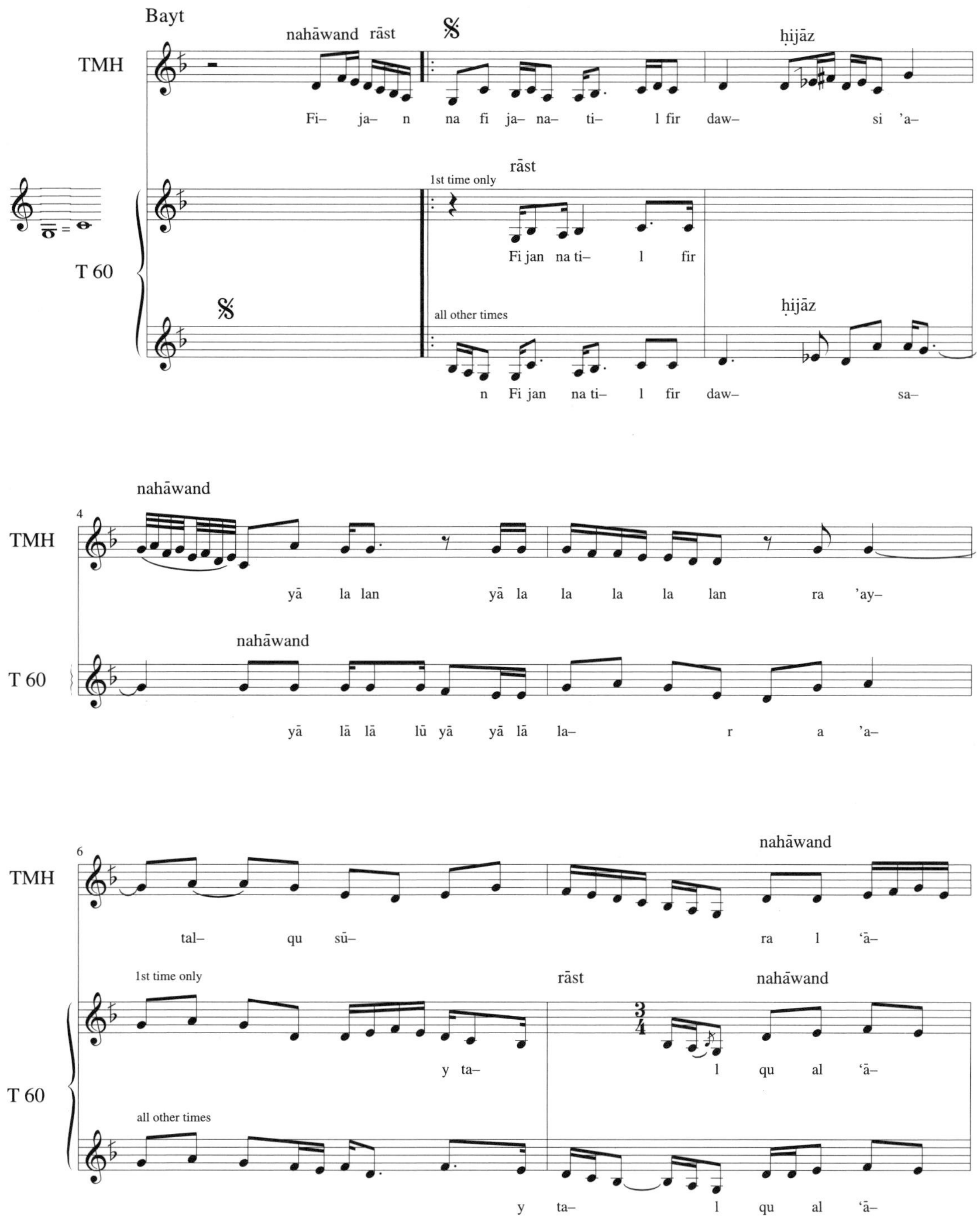

In 1960, before the publication of *al-Turāth al-mūsīqī al-tūnisī*, government representatives visited Testūr to record its musical traditions. The recordings include most of the *nūbāt* of the *ma'lūf* performed by musicians of the ʿĪsāwiyya brotherhood led by Shaykh Muḥammad Ben Ismāʿīl and are kept in the archives of Radiodiffusion Télévision Tunisienne; apparently, no one in Testūr received copies. Ben Ismāʿīl was later to represent Testūr in the three national congresses of the *ma'lūf* organized by the ministry of cultural affairs in the early 1960s.

Figure 2 shows a transcription of the opening piece of *nūbat aṣbahān*, the *baṭāyḥī "Fī jannati 'l-firdawsi"* recorded in Testūr (Testūr 1960) and the version of the same piece in *al-Turāth al-mūsīqī al-tūnisī* (TMH). The musical subsections *bayt, ṭāliʿ*, and

FIGURE 2 (*continued*)

rujū‘ and the progression of *‘uqūd* characterizing each version are indicated above the staff. Figure 3 shows the individual *‘uqūd*: *ḥijāz, nahāwand, nahāwand ong,* and *rāst.*

The *‘uqūd* structure of the *bayt* shown in figure 2 (mm. 1–9) is basically the same in each source. In terms of surface detail, however, TMH is denser and more complex (see, for example, m. 4 and the cadential passage in mm. 7–9).

In figure 2, differences occur in the *‘uqūd* structure of the *ṭāli‘* (mm. 10–14). In Testūr (1960), mm. 11–12, in *‘iqd ḥijāz,* are linked by an ascent into *‘iqd nahāwand*; in the corresponding section of TMH, each segment is instead repeated, thus extending and elaborating the melodic line. In Testūr (1960), mm.12–14 rest within the trichord g–b of *‘iqd nahāwand*; the corresponding section of TMH, in contrast, con-

FIGURE 2 (*continued*)

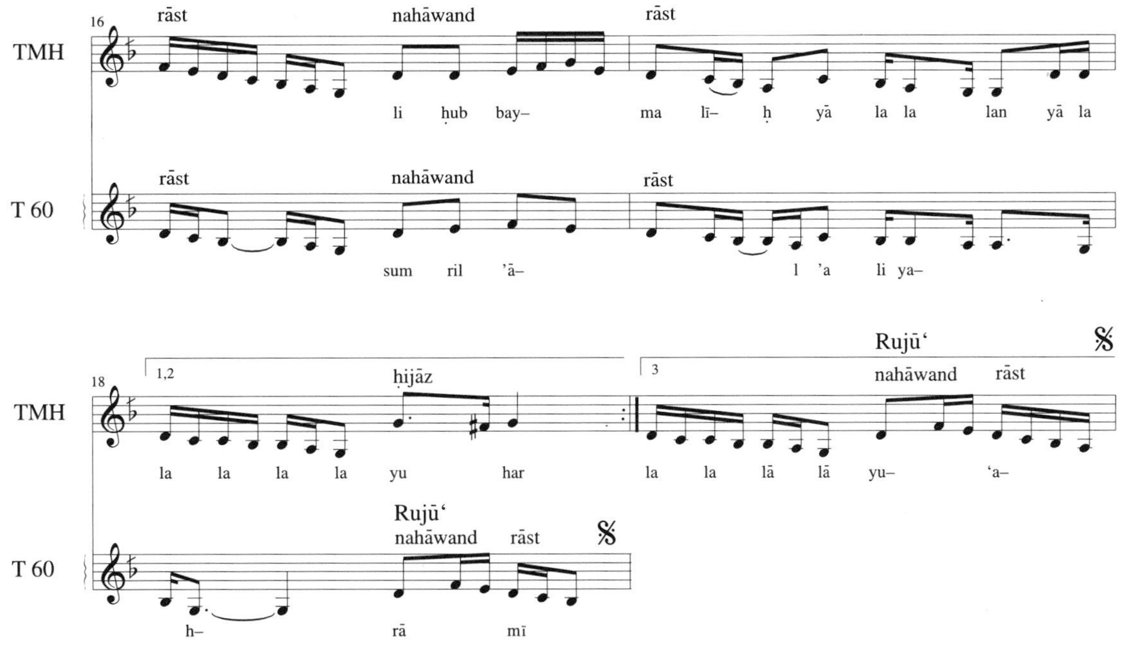

FIGURE 3 The *'uqūd* belonging to two sources: Testūr (1960) and *al-Turāth al-mūsīqī al-tūnisī* of figure 2. Transcription by Ruth Davis.

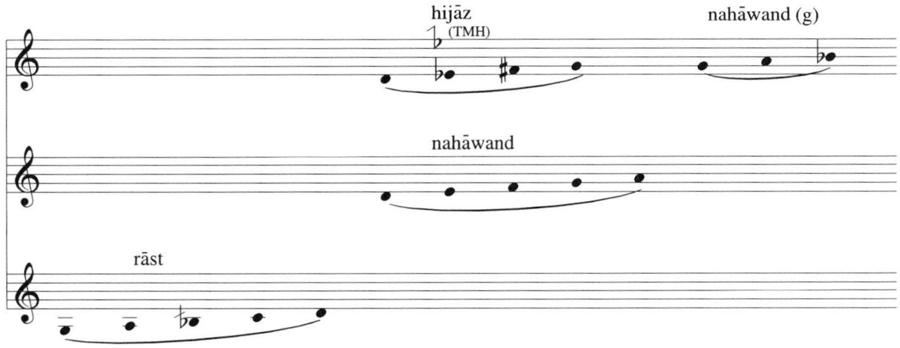

stitutes an elaborate descent from *'iqd nahāwand* through *'iqd ḥijāz* and into *rāst,* followed by an ascent through the same *'uqūd.* In both sources, the second part of the *ṭāli',* mm. 14–18, is identical to the second half of the *bayt* (mm. 5–18), and in each case the *rujū'* is literally a return to the *bayt.*

To summarize, TMH is generally more elaborate than Testūr (1960) in terms of surface melodic detail and is also more dynamic in its contrasting of *'uqūd* and tessitura.

According to al-Mahdī's ideology, promoted by the ministry of cultural affairs, there are no fundamental differences between the two sources: TMH merely represents the "correct" version of Testūr (1960). However, when I visited Testūr in the early 1980s I discovered that the community itself thought otherwise: musicians and non-musicians alike were convinced that there was a distinctive Testūr tradition that was still maintained by former members of the 'Īsāwiyya brotherhood.

At that time there were in Testūr two separate *ma'lūf* ensembles: one of young men and boys, attached to the *dār al-thaqāfa*; and another of older men who had performed under Shaykh Muḥammad Ben Ismā'īl in the 1960s (the shaykh himself had died in 1982). Ousted from the *zāwiya* in the wake of government hostilities shortly after independence, the former Sufi musicians had continued to perform *ma'lūf khām* in cafés and at communal celebrations. [See PATRONAGE AND POLICY IN TUNISIAN ART MUSIC.]

The modern youth ensemble, with its separate choral and instrumental sections, was led by a townsman, Monjī Qarwashī, who had trained in the conservatory of Sfax. Since he was the only person in Testūr who was fluent in notation, Qarwashī taught the ensemble by the traditional method of repetition and memorization, using the published notations as his sources. An imaginative attempt around the mid-1970s to combine the two ensembles—the younger musicians playing instruments supplied by the government, the older ones providing their traditional versions of the melodies—had collapsed after two years, apparently because of conflicts over standards and leadership. Qarwashī had even transcribed some of the traditional melodies for the use of the instrumentalists, but he abandoned this project for want of time and funding.

Evidently, the older musicians had not been influenced by the published notations: a recording I made in 1983 of "*Fī jannati 'l-firdawsi*" is virtually identical to the version of 1960 transcribed in figure 2 (for a comparison, see Davis 1997:16–20). However, by the summer of 1983, the oral tradition of Testūr was clearly on the wane. Deprived of their meeting place, the musicians had neither rehearsed nor performed regularly for more than two decades. The death of Shaykh Muḥammad Ben Ismā'īl the previous summer had been the blow: many traditional melodies were believed to have died with him. According to an old Tunisian proverb, "The death of a single shaykh of art approaches in its effect the burning of a library of manuscripts" (al-Mahdī and Marzūqī 1981:79). Most critically, with declining communal and institutional support, the older musicians were attracting no new recruits: the younger ones gravitated instead to the ensemble attached to the *dār al-thaqāfa*. For the past few summers, the host town has been represented at the annual national festival of the *ma'lūf* by the youth ensemble alone, performing alongside similar ensembles from throughout Tunisia, all using the same notated sources.

Notation—introduced by d'Erlanger in an effort to rescue a dying tradition—was adopted by the Rashīdiyya ensemble to serve an immediate practical need: Trīkī's original transcriptions were intended to create a viable performance practice for a new type of ensemble whose expanded format could no longer follow the procedures developed in oral tradition. Taken from a diversified oral repertoire, the transcriptions provided authoritative but not definitive sources for the ensemble: whether overtly or covertly, at least two subsequent leaders, 'Abd al-Ḥamīd Ben'aljīya and Ṣāliḥ al-Mahdī, modified the original notations to suit their own interpretations.

Al-Mahdī and Ben'aljīya represent opposing ideologies regarding the function of their transcriptions. Ben'aljīya, whose view is shared by his successor, Muḥammad Sa'āda, believes that notation should serve as a vehicle for constant reinterpretation in the authentic manner of oral tradition. In practice, however, considerations of time, effort, and convenience have militated against the realization of this ideal. Al-Mahdī, in contrast, as director of music in the ministry of cultural affairs, has taken a stance that is consistent with the postindependence ideology of a unified national cultural identity. According to this view, the Rashīdiyya's transcriptions served to define and correct an essentially unitary tradition in which superficial deviations were introduced over the years through the inherent fallibility of oral transmission. Published by the ministry of cultural affairs as *The Tunisian Musical Heritage*, al-Mahdī's transcriptions are officially presented as the national tradition of the *ma'lūf*, and as such they have been adopted in teaching and performance by modern, state-sponsored music institutions throughout the country. The published notations have thus served to introduce a new national tradition to regions where the *ma'lūf* was previously unknown, and they have established a new type of performance practice and a uniform version of the melodies in communities that had previously cultivated distinctive local traditions, as in Testūr.

REFERENCES

Davis, Ruth. 1986. "Modern Trends in the Arab-Andalusian Music of Tunisia." *Maghreb Review* 11:58–63.

———. 1992. "The Effects of Notation in the Performance Practice of Tunisian Art Music." *World of Music* 34(1):35–114.

———. 1997. "Cultural Policy and the Tunisian *Ma'lūf*: Redefining a Tradition." *Ethnomusicology* 41(3):1–21.

D'Erlanger, Rodolphe. 1917. "Au sujet de la musique arabe en Tunisie." *Revue Tunisienne* 24:91–95.

———. 1930–1959. *La musique arabe*. 6 vols. Paris: Libraire Orientaliste Paul Geuthner.

———. 1933. *Kitāb mu'tamar al-mūsīqā al-'arabiyya* (Proceedings of the Congress of Arab Music). Cairo: al-Maṭba'a al-Amīriyya.

al-Mahdī, Ṣāliḥ, ed. n.d. *al-Turāth al-mūsīqī al-tūnisī*. 9 vols. Tunis: al-Ma'had al-Waṭanī li'l-Mūsīqā wa'l-Raqṣ.

al-Mahdī, Ṣāliḥ, and Muḥammad Marzūqī. 1981. *al-Ma'had al-Rashīdī*. Tunis: al-Sharika al-Tūnisiyya li-Funūn al-Rasm.

Racy, Ali Jihad. 1977. "Musical Change and Commercial Recording in Egypt." Ph.D. dissertation, University of California, Los Angeles.

Rizgui, Sadok. 1967. *al-Aghānī al-tūnisiyya*. Tunis: al-Dār al-Tūnisiyya li'l-Nashr.

El-Shawan, Salwa. 1980. "The Sociopolitical Context of *al-Mūsika al-'Arabiyya* in Cairo, Egypt: Policies, Patronage, Institutions, and Musical Change (1927–1997)." *Asian Music* 12(1):86–128.

Zghonda, Fatḥī. n.d. *al-Mūsīqā al-nahāsiyya fī tūnis*. Tunis: al-Ma'had al-Waṭanī li'l-Mūsīqā wa'l-Raqṣ.

Note: For sources of music transcriptions, see page 331.

Learning Epic Traditions

Dwight F. Reynolds

Arabic Epic Traditions
Persian Epic Traditions
Turkic Epic Traditions

Although oral epic narrative poems have been documented and studied in Arabic, Persian, and Turkic cultures, only the last have been carefully researched with regard to the processes of learning and transmission, from singer to singer, generation to generation, with or without the mediation of written texts. For the Arabic and Persian traditions we can draw on a mere handful of sources; in a number of traditions there simply are no longer any apprentices or students to observe. Where transmission has been the focus of research, it is the social dimension of that process (as apprenticeship system, "school," or hereditary caste-based occupation) which has most often been documented by scholars. In only a few cases have the more technical dimensions—memorization, improvisation, the role of written texts, the acquisition and use of musical skills, and so forth—been studied. Even with the fragmentary evidence available, however, it is clear that a wide variety of techniques for teaching and transmitting epic traditions have been used in the Middle East, at times side by side within the same region.

ARABIC EPIC TRADITIONS

The versified heroic narratives of the Arabic tradition belong to a genre known as *sīra* (plural, *siyar*) or *sīra sha'biyya* 'folk *sīra*'. In literary contexts the term *sīra* refers to a biography, particularly from the early Islamic period and the Middle Ages; however, that genre was restricted primarily to the biographies of idealized heroic, religious, or political figures. This characteristic probably contributed to the extension of the term *sīra* in the late Middle Ages to include heroic folk epics as well, since they most often treat the exploits of a single extraordinary hero. Nearly a dozen distinct Arabic folk epics have been documented in written and oral traditions, each with its own complex narrative and its own cast of heroes, heroines, and villains. They all share a number of characteristics that clearly link them together into a single genre: they are recounted in a combination of verse, prose, and rhymed prose; the speeches of characters within the story are usually in verse, whereas the third-person narrative segments may be in either verse or prose; the language, whether oral or written, is a form of poetic or artistic colloquial Arabic, rather than classical literary Arabic or the colloquial speech of everyday life. The tales are quite lengthy: a live performance of the epic of the Banī Hilāl, for example, can last over one hundred hours (Reynolds 1995a), and some

Nearly a dozen distinct Arabic folk epics have been documented in written and oral traditions, each with its own narrative and its own cast of heroes, heroines, and villains.

written versions of the epic of the heroine Dhāt al-Himma fill fifty-five volumes (Lane 1895). The stories typically involve not only heroic but also supernatural characters. The distinction between "heroic epic" and "romance" is drawn only with great difficulty in the case of the Arabic folk *siyar*, since they encompass many characteristics of both types of material; individual episodes within a single *sīra*, however, often lean clearly toward one or the other.

The relationship between the written and oral versions of each of these epic traditions is intricate. Although the historical evidence is, unfortunately, only fragmentary, the genre clearly has its roots in oral performances. All the traditions bear at least some marks of "oral composition in performance" as articulated by Milman Parry (1987) and Albert Lord (1960), though we cannot rule out the possibility that material was added to some written versions by literate redactors imitating the style of the oral tradition.

Edward Lane (1895), who lived in Egypt in the 1830s, wrote that in Cairo there were then about fifty professional poets, *shu'arā'* (singular, *shā'ir*), who sang *Sīrat Banī Hilāl*, the epic of the Banī Hilāl bedouin tribe. They performed to the accompaniment of the *rabāb*, a rectangular, one-stringed Egyptian spike fiddle and never used written texts. (A round, two-stringed coconut-shell spike fiddle, at that time known as a *kamanja*, was used in the performance of urban classical music. In the middle to late nineteenth century, the Western violin arrived in Egypt and usurped both the role and the name of the *kamanja*. The coconut-shell spike fiddle came to be considered primarily a folk instrument and was widely adopted by epic singers, who continued to use the term *rabāb*, though the instrument they were using had changed. The rectangular spike fiddle described by Lane is now found in Egypt only among the desert bedouin.)

In contrast, Lane noted that there were about thirty public performers of the *sīra* of al-Ẓāhir Baybars, a thirteenth-century Egyptian ruler. These performers were called *muḥaddithīn* 'reciters' or 'speakers'. They did not sing or use an instrument (in contrast to the *shu'arā'*), nor did they refer to written texts during their performances.

Finally, there were half a dozen performers of the *sīra* of the pre-Islamic hero 'Antar ibn Shaddād and the *sīra* of the heroine Dhāt al-Himma. These reciters always performed from written texts, without music, chanting the verse sections and narrating the prose passages in normal speech. Performances in modern-day coffeehouses of the Persian epic *Shāhnāma* and of traditional Turkic prosimetric romances are reminiscent of their technique (see below).

In the late twentieth century, *Sīrat Banī Hilāl* became the last Arabic epic to remain alive in oral tradition as a sung epic poem and thus is the only example that can be studied in performance. The other epics have survived either as prose folktale cycles or in the form of written redactions from earlier centuries. Although the *Sīrat Banī Hilāl* has recently attracted the attention of a number of scholars, the issues of learning and transmission have not often been addressed.

Susan Slyomovics (1987) reports a mythopoetic version of the way one southern Egyptian epic singer acquired the ability to sing *Sīrat Banī Hilāl*. The account, narrated by the poet ʿAwaḍallah, tells how his grandfather, ʿAlī, received knowledge of the epic in a scene that closely parallels the orthodox version of the way the Prophet Muhammad first received the revelations of the Qur'ān: ʿAlī, who was illiterate, came upon a book in the desert. That night, as he slept in a cave, the voice of a supernatural figure, al-Khiḍr, called to him to read the book, but ʿAlī replied that he did not know how to read. Both the call and ʿAlī's response were repeated a second time. Then, at a third call, ʿAlī rose and was astonished to find that he could read the book. It was the epic of the Banī Hilāl. ʿAlī read it and memorized it; immediately afterward, he lost both his ability to read and the book itself, but he returned home to teach the epic to his son, who then taught ʿAlī's grandson, ʿAwaḍallah. The initiatory dream is also a feature of a number of the Central Asian epic traditions discussed below, some of which also include the figure of al-Khiḍr—in Turkish, Hızır. Slyomovics's account of ʿAwaḍallah's learning of the epic is brief but to the point: when ʿAwaḍallah was seven years old, his father began teaching him, having him repeat each line until he said it correctly and beating him with a stick when he made mistakes. ʿAwaḍallah's apprenticeship lasted until he was fourteen.

During field research in the Nile Delta region of northern Egypt in 1982–1983, 1986–1987, and 1988, I collected fourteen firsthand accounts from hereditary epic singers of *Sīrat Banī Hilāl* (figures 1 and 2) about their apprenticeship and then, for several months, also worked with a master poet, learning small portions of the epic on my own. Unfortunately, the occupation of epic singing was no longer being transmitted from father to son, so I was unable to observe a poet in the process of teaching but had to rely on poets' memories of their own apprenticeship, as much as sixty years earlier.

The process as recalled by each of the poets was very similar. First, a boy heard the stories told and retold by family members in performances. When he reached a certain age, usually between five and seven, family members would begin to quiz him on details of the story. Great emphasis was placed on mastering the complex plots; this process, however, focused only on the narrative elements, not on mastery of the poetry as such. Next, the boy was taught to play drone notes and short melodic phrases as "responses" on the *rabāb* so that, though not yet singing portions of the epic, he could perform alongside his father or an uncle or grandfather. The time spent traveling

FIGURE 1 Poets from the village of al-Bakātūsh, Egypt.

FIGURE 2 Shaykh Ṭāhā Abū Zayd, al-Bakātūsh, Egypt.

between performances was often devoted to more and more detailed questioning about the epic. Since the child had always heard the story in sung verse, it was only a matter of time before he began to respond to questions in verse rather than prose. Quite simply, at some point it would become easier to respond to specific questions in poetry (as heard) rather than recast an idea into prose. I had the same experience during my own struggle to learn portions of the epic: suddenly the answer to the question "What happened next?" or "And what was the name of his sword?" would burst out not as prose but as a fully formed verse of rhymed poetry.

Here is a brief account from an interview with Shaykh ʿAntar ʿAbd al-ʿĀṭī (12 June 1987; Reynolds 1996):

> D.R.: When you were young, how did you memorize the *sīra*?
>
> ʿAntar: I'll tell you. I used to go to the evening gatherings with my father and "support him" [*asniduh*] on the *rabāb*. My hand "supported him," but my ear was toward him [*īdī kānit bitsanniduh wi-widnī luh*]. Afterward, my father would ask me while we were walking or riding the train, "What happened in the story last night?" And I'd tell him.
>
> D.R.: But in ordinary words [*kalām ʿādī*], not in poetry [*shiʿr*]?
>
> ʿAntar: Right, just regular words [*kalām bass*]. The next night he'd sing the same story so I would "drink from it a lot" [*ashrab minhā kitīr*], I'd memorize it [*aḥfaẓhā*]. The next night he'd sing a different story.
>
> D.R.: But how did you get from the level of telling the story in words to singing it? I mean, I can tell many of the stories from hearing them a lot [*min kutrat al-samāʿ*], but I can't sing poetry.
>
> ʿAntar: My father would support me on the *rabāb* when I first started to sing [literally, "to say"]; if I got lost I'd listen to him and repeat what he said [*arudd ʿalēh*].
>
> D.R.: How old were you when you first started to sing the *sīra*?
>
> ʿAntar: Eleven. My father used to present me [*kān biyiqaddimnī*] in the evening gatherings.
>
> D.R.: But, for instance, did you repeat the story to yourself alone, make a review of it [*murājaʿa*]?
>
> ʿAntar: Of course, I'd go over the stories, looking for the right word [*ik-kalima il-munāsiba*] alone [*li-waḥdī*].
>
> D.R.: And you performed at eleven—that's very young!
>
> ʿAntar: I started supporting my mother and [four] sisters, and I married them all off! [When Shaykh ʿAntar was a teenager, his father divorced his mother; ʿAntar became a solo performer, and the breadwinner for a household of six, at that time.]

The epic singers of northern Egypt are quite articulate about one formal feature of their trade: rhyme. For them, the stories of the epic are structured by the monorhyme found at the end of every verse. These singers can discuss, for example, the fact that a given episode starts on a particular rhyme but changes to a new rhyme when a certain character appears on the scene and makes a particular speech. This traditional rhyme scheme helps young poets structure a story as they learn it and also provides a mnemonic device that links specific chunks of verse to specific parts of the narrative and then locks those chunks in place; but the poets never memorize any of the epic in the sense of verbatim repetition. Unlike the South Slavic poets documented by Parry and Lord, the northern Egyptian poets are quite conscious of variation in many aspects of performance: they speak easily of filling out or contracting descriptions and parts of the story according to the audience's willingness to listen; they also speak in detail of stylistic variations from poet to poet. As one poet put it, "The Qurʾān is the

Qur'ān whether you hear it from Shaykh al-Ḥosserī or Shaykh 'Abd al-Bāsiṭ; but not the *sīra*—each poet sings that his own way."

The traditional rhyme scheme described above, moreover, is not rigidly followed by the best of the poets, who are capable of virtuosic improvisation. When I asked Shaykh Ṭāhā Abū Zayd, my teacher, to sing a section of the epic again but on a different rhyme, he was able to do so without hesitation, retaining all the major ideas and even most of the details of the story while simultaneously altering the second half of each and every verse to fit the rhyme that I had selected (Reynolds 1996).

The melodic stock of *Sīrat Banī Hilāl,* in comparison with other Middle Eastern and Central Asian epic traditions, is large and varied. In a single hour of performance, a poet may deploy as many as several dozen different melodies (Reynolds 1995b). The poets of the Nile Delta region, almost to a man, said that learning how to play the *rabāb* was the most difficult aspect of the trade and were continually surprised that my rapid progress on the musical instrument was not matched by an equally rapid mastery of the poetry. During their own learning of the epic tradition, usually in their early teenage years, poets would spend time mentally going over the narratives of the epic, finding the rhyme words necessary to tell the story smoothly, and trying out different melodies; most reported that they never conducted these "rehearsals" out loud. They would then begin performing at least occasionally as soloists, usually before the age of fifteen or sixteen.

According to Parry and Lord, poets, once having mastered the technique of oral composition in performance, should be able to sing in versified form any traditional tale from the stock of the epic. Epic singers of the Banī Hilāl tradition are very specific about which episodes they can and cannot perform, and only a handful of master poets are said to be capable of performing the entire narrative. Many poets can recount in prose tales which, they say, they are unable to sing in poetry. This inability is probably due both to the large amount of narrative detail (names, places, and so on) required to perform a tale "correctly" by local standards and to the requisite mastery of the traditional rhyme scheme, which must be learned from performances rather than invented.

Traditional transmission of *Sīrat Banī Hilāl* thus involves, first, mastery of the narrative and then—gradually, through several years of performing alongside a master poet—acquisition of both the melodic repertoire of the tradition and the underlying rhyme scheme of the epic. These skills are assimilated at the intermediate stages through individual mental reworking of the material and are finally integrated through the experience of performance. Although all the poets in the region quickly named their teachers, they also noted that they had learned additional scenes and entire episodes of the epic from other epic singers whom they encountered in their travels.

This tradition of apprenticeship in northern Egypt seems, however, to have come to an end. The epic is now seen by most people in the region as a provincial and outdated art form; from the early 1970s onward it rapidly lost ground to television and cassette players. During fieldwork in the mid-1980s, I found that not a single young man from a family of epic poets was learning to be an epic singer. Instead, some of these young men were in school, some were training in carpentry and other trades, and some were applying for government jobs. They spoke with pride of the great poets of old, but equally proudly of the fact that they themselves could hardly even hold the *rabāb*, let alone sing the epic.

PERSIAN EPIC TRADITIONS

Almost all the Persian epic traditions are tied to the Iranian national legend, an extensive body of historical narrative that recounts the origins of the Iranian nation before the Islamic conquest. A portion of this tradition was collected and versified by the poet Firdawsī around the year 1000 C.E. in his monumental *Shāhnāma* 'Book of Kings', which consists of some forty thousand couplets. Other written epics emerged later, among them the *Garshāspnāma* and *Borzunāma*, treating characters and story lines connected to this central tradition. Despite its canonical status, Firdawsī's *Shāhnāma* never overwhelmed the popular oral tradition of prose storytelling and poetic recitation known as *naqqāli*; indeed, it seems certain that Firdawsī drew on both written sources and oral performances in assembling his redaction.

One of the few studies dealing with the processes of learning and transmission among Persian-speaking performers of epics is Mary Ellen Page's report of her work with storytellers in Shiraz and Teheran (1977). She demonstrates the close link between written and oral traditions and presents a fascinating case study in which the oral tradition is far more complex and more embellished in narrative structure, details, and interpretive devices than the literary tradition.

The storytellers documented by Page did not come from storytelling families but rather were drawn to the profession by their own personal interests. Typically, a student, having been attracted since an early age by the performances of storytellers, would seek out a master storyteller and work with him for one or two years. The performers in Page's study were completely literate and had not begun their training as professional storytellers until their late twenties.

The training process involved, as a central element of the art, memorizing Firdawsī's *Shāhnāma* from a written text, but also assimilating a vast body of additional narrative material from the oral performance tradition. As part of mastering this additional material, a student would copy his teacher's *ṭūmār* 'scroll', which provides a skeletal summary of the narrative. In actual performance the storyteller recounts most of the epic in prose, drawing on narrative material from Firdawsī for sections that are included in *Shāhnāma*, and from the storytellers' tradition embodied in the *ṭūmār*, while also including sections of poetry quoted from Firdawsī and other sources. Performances in the coffeehouses of Shiraz in the 1970s typically lasted between one and one and a half hours per day; the completion of large segments of the epic might take well over a year of daily performances. Audiences clearly preferred the more heroic and legendary sections of the epic, from the creation to the arrival of Alexander the Great, rather than the more mundane historic portions from Alexander to the Islamic conquest of Iran in the seventh century C.E. (Hanaway 1978; Page 1977).

Page's most interesting contribution is, perhaps, her comparison of oral performances with both the storytellers' texts and Firdawsī's literary version. In some regions performers hold a written text in front of them as a prop, but they rarely refer to it (Blum 1972). The oral performances prove on close examination to be far more complex in detail than either of the written sources; for example, two hundred lines of verse in Firdawsī, covered in one or two pages of summary in a *ṭūmār*, might well constitute several hours of oral performance. Also, the written tradition presents the narrative in a straightforward linear progression, whereas the oral performances are marked by an intricate interweaving of story lines, one tale beginning before another has been concluded, and by extensive historical digressions to provide background material and explanations not found in Firdawsī. Finally, the storytellers include nonhistorical digressions to comment directly on the importance of the story, present the performer's individual interpretation of particular events, and link elements of the story to recent Iranian history. Page's comparisons of performances and *ṭūmār* texts from Shiraz and Teheran show that there is a great deal of cohesiveness in the oral tradition in different parts of Iran. In short, although written forms of the epic—both the canonical literary versions and the summaries found in the *ṭūmār* texts—are central to the oral tradition, the art of oral performance eclipses these sources in both breadth and complexity of structure (Page 1977).

TURKIC EPIC TRADITIONS

Turkic traditions of narrative epic and romance developed in a region stretching from Siberia to modern Turkey and encompass many distinct yet clearly interrelated cultures. Although the generic boundaries between heroic epic and romance are clear in some cases, often they are not; and in discussing learning and transmission, it seems wise to treat the two together. Despite the textual similarities among the various epics and romances of Central Asia, each of the Turkic cultures has its own set of religious, literary, and social associations for both the performers and the performances of these genres. The most prominent of these cultures, along with their terms for epic and romance performers, are: Altay (*qaycı*), Kazakh (*zıraw* or *aqın*), Kirghiz (*manascı* or *semeteycı*), Tatar (*čäčän*), Oghuz (*ozan*), Turkmen (*baxši*), Karakalpak (*baxši*), Uzbek (*šāir*/*baxši*), and Azerbaijani and Turkish (*aşık*; Reichl 1985, 1992). The use of each term varies from region to region; for example, in some places *baxši* refers to singers of heroic epics, and in other places it refers to performers of romances. Most of these traditions include both verse and prose passages and are associated with a musical instrument such as the *qobız* (a horsehair fiddle), the short-necked *dōtār* or *dombira* (lutes), or the Western Asian *sāz* (a long-necked lute). The *Manas* epic of the Kirghiz, however, is sung entirely in verse and with no instrumental accompaniment.

The differing social roles of epic and romance performers strongly influence the means by which the traditions are transmitted; still, despite these differences, several basic patterns are common. One recurring pattern of epic transmission, as reported by singers, involves a sudden and complete acquisition of the ability to perform epics by what is said to be supernatural intervention. Scholars have long noted a connection in Turkic cultures between the singer of epic tales and the figure of the shaman. An important motif linking the two is the initiatory dream, which signals a young person's "calling" to those arts (Başgöz 1952, 1967; Reichl 1992, chap. 3). In the dream, the person being called may see visions of dead heroes or of supernatural figures and may experience some form of physical trial or test. At the conclusion of this test the dreamer may receive some sign of success, such as being handed a musical instrument, and then awakens with the ability to sing heroic epics and to play the musical instrument associated with the tradition. Such initiatory dreams have been recorded and analyzed in places across Central Asia and are still associated, for example, with the modern *aşık* tradition of Turkey and Azerbaijan (Başgöz 1967). The dream as an induction into a tradition clearly associates both the epic and the singer with powerful spiritual forces. Regrettably, the prominence of these dream initiations—although some modern singers are reportedly suspicious of them (Reichl 1992)—has in many cases led to a dearth of scholarly documentation regarding the more practical aspects of learning and transmission.

A second recurring pattern of transmission involves apprenticeships of various sorts, ranging from a formal regimented period of learning in the home of a master singer to a more informal period of contact, often while traveling with one or more performers. One of the most formal traditions is that recorded in the Uzbek "schools" of Bulungur and Nuratin, documented in the nineteenth and early twentieth centuries (Chadwick and Zhirmunsky 1969). It was customary for a young student to live with a master poet, exchanging work around the house for lessons, food, and lodging. The learning process apparently involved first listening to performances by teachers and memorizing essential traditional passages and epic motifs, and then attempting to improvise the remaining narrative within the formulaic language of the genre. After a training period of up to three years, the apprentice would publicly perform a full *dāstān* before an audience of other singers and officially acquire the title of *baxši*.

A third pattern of transmission is hereditary. Both hereditary and nonhereditary lines of teachers are found across Central Asia. In the hereditary lines, singers list not only their immediate teacher or teachers but also a lineage of teachers which may go back several generations. Singers in several regions reported that they were as young as seven when they began their training; this is similar to the testimony of Arab singers of *Sīrat Banī Hilāl* (Reichl 1992).

Finally, a number of performers are documented as having been self-taught. They have learned the tradition only from hearing it performed while they were growing up, without any period of formal training by another poet (Moyle 1990; Reinhard and Pinto, 1989).

These four patterns—dream initiation, formal apprenticeship, hereditary or "genealogical" transmission, and autodidacticism—are not wholly separate but can occur in various combinations. For instance, a singer may have a "calling" dream that then impels him or her to seek out a master singer as a teacher, but later may learn a large part of the repertoire from hearing other performers, or even from written sources.

The degree to which written texts mediate the process of oral transmission in Turkic traditions varies widely from region to region. In general, the traditions of Siberia and eastern Central Asia rely almost entirely on oral transmission, whereas several traditions of western Central Asia have existed in interaction with written versions for a century or several centuries.

REFERENCES

Başgöz, Ilhan. 1952. "Turkish Folk Stories about the Lives of Minstrels." *Journal of American Folklore* 65:331–339.

———. 1967. "Dream Motif in Turkish Folk Stories and Shamanistic Initiation." *Asian Folklore Studies* 26:1–18.

Blum, Stephen. 1972. "The Concept of the *'Asheq* in Northern Khorasan." *Asian Music* 4:27–47.

Chadwick, Nora K., and Victor Zhirmunsky. 1969. *Oral Epics of Central Asia*. Cambridge: Cambridge University Press.

Hanaway, William L. 1971. "Formal Elements in the Persian Popular Romances." In *Iran: Continuity and Variety*, ed. Peter Chelkowski, 139–160. New York: Center for Near Eastern Studies, 1971.

———. 1978. "The Iranian Epics." In *Heroic Epic and Saga: An Introduction to the World's Great Epics*, ed. Felix J. Oinas, 76–98. Bloomington: Indiana University Press.

Lane, Edward. 1895. *An Account of the Manners and Customs of the Modern Egyptians*. London: East-West; Cairo: Livres de France. (Reprinted 1978.)

Lord, Albert B. 1960. *The Singer of Tales*. Cambridge, Mass.: Harvard University Press.

Moyle, Natalie K. 1990. *The Turkish Minstrel Tale Tradition*. New York: Garland. Harvard Dissertations in Folklore and Oral Tradition.

Page, Mary Ellen. 1977. "*Naqqāli* and Ferdowsi: Creativity in the Iranian National Tradition." Ph.D. dissertation, University of Pennsylvania.

Parry, Milman. 1987. *The Making of Homeric Verse*, ed. A. Parry. Oxford: Oxford University Press.

Reichl, Karl. 1985. "Oral Tradition and Performance of the Uzbek and Karakalpak Epic Singers." In *Fragen der mongolischen Heldendichtung*, part 3, Asiatische Forschungen, Vol. 91, ed. Heissig, 613–643. Wiesbaden: Otto Walther Harrassowitz.

———. 1992. *Turkic Oral Epic Poetry: Traditions, Forms, Poetic Structure*. New York: Garland.

Reinhard, Ursula, and Tiago de Oliveira Pinto. 1989. *Sänger und Poeten mit der Laute: Turkische Aşık und Ozan*. Berlin: Dietrich Reimer Verlag.

Reynolds, Dwight F. 1995a. *Heroic Poets, Poetic Heroes: The Ethnography of Performance in an Arabic Oral Epic Tradition*. Ithaca, N.Y.: Cornell University Press.

———. 1995b. "Musical Dimensions of an Arabic Oral Epic Tradition." *Asian Music* 26, 1:51–92.

———. 1996. "Crossing and Re-Crossing the Line." In *The World Observed: Reflections on the Fieldwork Process*, ed. Bruce Jackson and Edward Ives, 110–117. Chicago: University of Illinois Press.

Slyomovics, Susan E. 1987. *The Merchant of Art: An Egyptian Hilali Oral Epic Poet in Performance*. Berkeley: University of California Press.

Section 6
Historical Roots

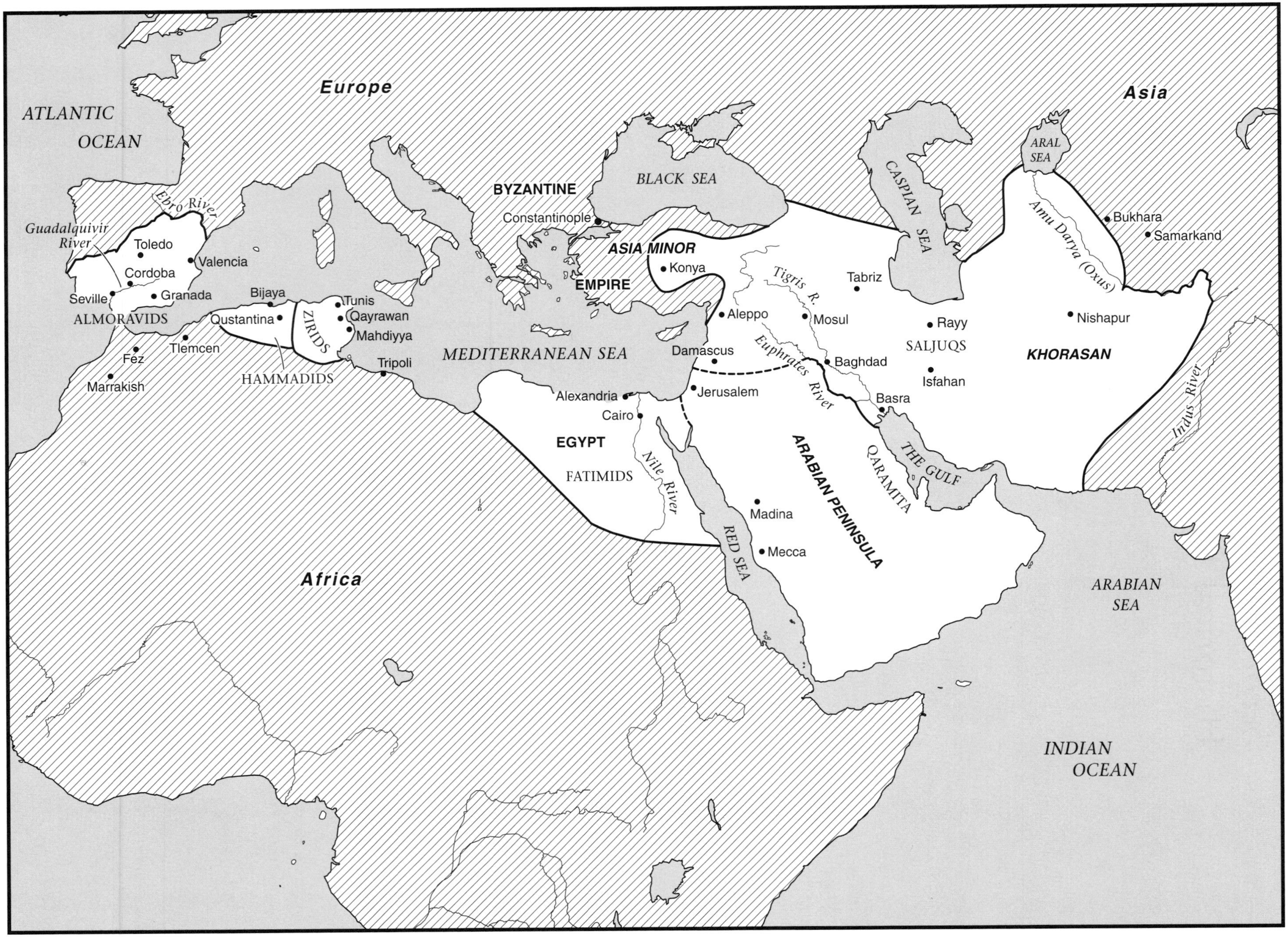

Europe
Asia
Africa
ATLANTIC OCEAN
BYZANTINE
EMPIRE
ASIA MINOR
BLACK SEA
CASPIAN SEA
ARAL SEA
Amu Darya (Oxus)
Bukhara
Samarkand
Nishapur
KHORASAN
Indus River
Tabriz
Rayy
SALJUQS
Isfahan
Tigris R.
Mosul
Baghdad
Basra
Euphrates River
THE GULF
QARAMITA
ARABIAN PENINSULA
Madina
Mecca
RED SEA
ARABIAN SEA
INDIAN OCEAN
Constantinople
Konya
Aleppo
Damascus
Jerusalem
Alexandria
Cairo
Nile River
EGYPT
FATIMIDS
MEDITERRANEAN SEA
Tripoli
Tunis
Qayrawan
Mahdiyya
ZIRIDS
Bijaya
Qustantina
HAMMADIDS
Tlemcen
Fez
Marrakish
ALMORAVIDS
Seville
Cordoba
Granada
Toledo
Valencia
Ebro River
Guadalquivir River

Section 6
Historical Roots

The study of music in the pre-Islamic and medieval periods, relying on a variety of archaeological and literary sources, reveals vibrant worlds of music theory and performance influenced by ongoing intercultural contacts. From rock paintings and etchings to diverse genres of literature—religious texts, histories, lexicographies, studies on medicine, collections of song texts, and narratives about music making—we gain a vivid picture of musical life in these early times.

We learn about the instruments and practices of pre-Islamic societies, in which lyres were featured and often played by groups of women. The adoption of an ancient Greek legacy introduced new concepts, terms, and attitudes that profoundly affected the content and position of music in medieval Middle Eastern culture. The scientific study of music, for example, became an integral part of a learned man's education. The rise and decline of Arabic-, Persian- and Turkish-speaking courts continued these processes of change and development. An unceasing debate about the role of secular music reveals specific attitudes and musical practices in medieval culture.

Rich literary sources, such as the monumental *Kitāb al-aghānī* 'Book of Songs', offer us an intimate sense of music in medieval courts, including descriptions of the contexts in which music was studied and performed, the role and status of musicians, and details of tonal systems, rhythmic concepts and practices, and song texts. Systems of classifying instruments highlight the aesthetic values that shaped the musical culture, and medieval instruments provide the basis for the great variety of instruments that we find in the present day.

The Islamic empire of the golden age, toward the end of the eleventh century.

The *Kitāb al-Aghānī*

George Sawa

Medieval Arabic writings on music can be divided into two main genres: music theory and music literature. Theory deals with sound: acoustics, rhythmic and melodic modes, composition, aesthetics, and performance practice. Musical literature, by contrast, vividly illustrates in narrative format the context of music making. The single most important source of music literature is the monumental *Kitāb al-aghānī* 'Book of Songs' of Abū al-Faraj al-Iṣbahānī (d. 967). The modern edition, published in Cairo, consists of twenty-four volumes, covering ten thousand pages of concise medieval Arabic.

Kitāb al-aghānī reveals much about musical practices in the cities of Mecca, Medina, Damascus, Rayy (present-day Tehran), Isfahan, Basra, and Baghdad from the seventh to the tenth centuries. The narratives are of immense anthropological value because musicians are frequently quoted and thus in effect speak for and about themselves without intermediaries. We learn a great deal about issues related to musical performance, such as musical aesthetics and criteria, the size of programs and the length of concerts, musicians' posture, and the effects of the behavior and interaction of musicians and audiences on the choice and delivery of the music performed. We also learn about compositional techniques, improvisation, processes of musical and textual change, and a very rich vocabulary of music theory as verbalized by practicing musicians. In addition, *Kitāb al-aghānī* is significant in that it depicts music in a sociocultural context. Thus we learn about the uses and functions of songs that were performed not only for entertainment or aesthetic enjoyment but also to depict all aspects of the human life cycle; about the varied educational background and the wide educational role of musicians in court society; about musicians' ethnic origin and socioeconomic status; and about the permissibility of music making—an issue that to this day remains controversial in the Islamic world. Such themes are illustrated in the excerpts that follow.

Early Arab music: Multicultural environment and selective borrowing

Musicians traveled extensively throughout the Islamic Arab empire to learn different musical styles. In the process, they created a dynamic multicultural music environment; and by borrowing selectively from various regions, they developed new musical styles.

> The original name of Ibn Muḥriz (d. c. 715) is Salm, and he was a client of the tribe of Banū Makhzūm. And Isḥāq al-Mawṣilī (d. 850) mentioned that Ibn Muḥriz used to stay in the city of al-Madīna for a while and stay in Makka for a while. When he came to al-Madīna, he stayed three months to learn to play the *'ūd* 'lute' from the songstress 'Azza al-Maylā' (d. ca. 705); then he returned to Makka and stayed three months. Then he journeyed to Persia to study the music of the Persians and learn their songs; then he went to Syria to study the music of the Byzantines and learn their songs. He dropped out what was not likable among the notes and melodies of both people, kept the beautiful ones among them, and blended them together to compose Arabic songs in a new style. (*KA*, 1:378)

Compositional technique

When a singer composed a song orally, he kept time by tapping the rhythmic mode.

> Isḥāq al-Mawṣilī said: Ma'bad (d. 743) was asked: "What technique do you use if you want to compose a song?" He said: "I ride my young camel and tap the *īqā'* 'rhythmic mode' with the wand on my saddle, and I sing the poem till the song becomes straightened up according to the *īqā'*." So it was said to him: "How very apparent is this in the songs which you have composed!" (*KA*, 1:40)

Use of older melodies

In the following anecdote, a sacred melody—the call to prayer—is adapted for a secular text. It is not clear whether or not the melody was changed; in any event, though, a new production was inspired. The fluid nature of the categories "sacred" and "secular" emerges clearly here.

> Isḥāq stayed overnight at the palace of the caliph al-Mu'taṣim (d. 842) when the latter was a prince. Isḥāq heard a melody by 'Abd-al-Wahhāb the muezzin, calling people to prayer at the door of al-Mu'taṣim. He listened to it, liked it, stayed over another night until he learned the melody correctly, and then built on it his melody [with the words]:
>
> Asmā' ridiculed me and said
> O son of al-Mawṣilī, you are old. (*KA*, 5:305)

Transmission and education

The usual method for learning a song orally was to listen to the teacher repeat it as often as needed until the student had mastered it. Another method, according to some accounts, was supernatural: the teacher, in the form of a genie or an animal, would appear to the learner in a dream.

> One day Ibrāhīm al-Mawṣilī (d. 804) longed for a cellar of his. In it there was a pond to which water was fed from a source and from which the water then flowed to a garden. Ibrāhīm said: "I wish to spend my day drinking in this cellar, and sleep in it at night." This he did. And while he was asleep in the middle of the night, two cats, one white and one black, came down the cellar step. One said to the other: "Do you see him asleep?" Then the black one said: "Yes, he is." At this point the black cat burst forth, performing a song in her best voice. Ibrāhīm at this point nearly died of happiness and said: "I wish they would repeat it." So they did repeat it, many times, until he learned it. He then moved in his sleep, and the two cats left. (*KA*, 5:193–194)

The musician's education

To be a court singer required firm knowledge of a repertoire of no fewer than five thousand songs, the ability to play an instrument, and the ability to compose. In addition, musicians had to be thoroughly trained in certain other disciplines—including literature, poetry, prosody, grammar, history, narration of anecdotes, Qur'ānic sciences, astrology, cooking, wine-making, horse-breeding, chess, and backgammon—and in etiquette, so that they would know how to behave properly at court. With this background, they could not only entertain but also educate and befriend rulers. This anecdote shows how long the training process was and illustrates what a would-be court musician's day was like.

> Isḥāq al-Mawṣilī said: "I spent a long period of my life going at daybreak to Hushaym to listen to him; then I would go to al-Kisā'ī (d. 805) or al-Farrā' (d. 822) or Ibn Ghazāla to read a portion of the Qur'ān; then I would go to Manṣūr Zalzal (d. after 842), the lutenist, who would teach me two or three pieces; then to 'Ātika bint Shuhda to learn from her one or two songs; then to al-Aṣma'ī (d. 831) and Abū 'Ubayda (d. 824), from whom I would seek knowledge and discuss belles-lettres, and I would profit from them. Then I would go to my father to tell him what I had accomplished, whom I had met, and from whom I had learned; then I would have lunch with him. At suppertime I would go to the prince of believers, the caliph Hārūn al-Rashīd (d. 809). (*KA*, 5:271–272)

Validating ruling institutions

The roles of a court musician included praising the ruler in song and performing functions that today would be called public relations. This story, related by Isḥāq al-Mawṣilī, is about his father, Ibrāhīm.

> On his accession to the caliphate, the first reward which the caliph Hārūn al-Rashīd (d. 809) gave to a poet was given to Ibrāhīm al-Mawṣilī, when the latter praised him as follows:
>
> Haven't you seen that the sun was ill?
> But when Hārūn ruled, its light shone,
> Enrobing the world with beauty by reason of his countenance.
> Hārūn is its sovereign and Yaḥyā (d. 805) its vizier.
>
> Ibrāhīm sang this, and Hārūn ordered that he be given one hundred thousand dirhams and Yaḥyā ordered that he be given fifty thousand dirhams. (*KA*, 5:242)

Musical excellence

Two prerequisites of musical excellence were skill in the art of composition and skill in the art of performance. Performance involved not only one's own compositions but also those of others; thus the performer needed both skill and versatility, to present many musical styles. The next anecdote illustrates a dichotomy between talent and intellect as a recognized and well-articulated musical concept, in performance or in composition. It is told by Ḥammād, who reports the words of his father, Isḥāq al-Mawṣilī.

> The most skilled among the singers I have seen are four: your grandfather Ibrāhīm al-Mawṣilī, Ḥakam al-Wādī (d. before 809), Fulayḥ ibn abī al-'Awrā', and Siyāṭ (d. 785). So I said: "What did their skills amount to?" He said: "They excelled in what they composed and excelled when they performed the compositions of others." Isḥāq then added: "And my father said to me: None of those singers you see is naturally as musically gifted as Ḥakam al-Wādī and Ibn Jāmi', whereas Fulayḥ ibn abī al-'Awrā' is more aware intellectually of what comes out of his head." (*KA*, 6:280–281)

One musician saved his colleagues from jail by claiming that they were inferior nonprofessionals.

Performance practice, posture, and the effect of music

Posture was recognized as important to full voice production, and competition was seen as a useful means of achieving excellence in performance. The next story illustrates these aspects of music making, as well as the emotional effect of music on the audience.

> We were at the palace of Prince Ibrāhīm ibn al-Mahdī (d. 839) one day, and he had invited every good singer. While Ibrāhīm was leaning on his side and playing chess with one of them, he sang with a soft voice a song of the songstress Farīda. . . . When he had finished, Mukhāriq (d. c. 846) followed him and sang the same song with a soft voice, did well, caused us to be in a state of *ṭarab* 'intense emotion', and exceeded Ibrāhīm's performance. Ibrāhīm repeated the song and added more to his voice in such a way that he effaced Mukhāriq's singing. When Ibrāhīm had finished, Mukhāriq repeated the song and sang it with his full voice and was very careful in his performance, and as a result we almost flew with happiness. At this point Ibrāhīm sat upright—for he had been leaning on his side—and sang it with his full voice and gave the song its full share of notes and ornaments. I saw his shoulders shaking and his whole body moving until he finished the song. In the meantime Mukhāriq was looking fixedly toward him, trembling; his color changed, and his fingers were shaking. It seemed to me, by God, that the chamber was moving and we were moving with it, and when Ibrāhīm finished, Mukhāriq went to him and kissed his hands and said: "May God make me your ransom! ('I'd do anything for you.') How far am I from you!" And Mukhāriq did not enjoy himself for the remainder of the day. (*KA*, 10:107–109)

Musicians and the danger of arrest

Simply because of their profession, musicians were on occasion subject to arrest, and their testimony was sometimes not accepted in a court of law. The next story shows, however, that this handicap might be counterbalanced by extramusical knowledge and a good character, and by humor—one musician saved his colleagues from jail by claiming that they were inferior nonprofessionals.

> When Zabrā' was the governor of the city of al-Madīna . . . he ordered the singers to be brought in and jailed; among them was 'Aṭarrad (d. c. 786). The governor sat down to judge them, and in the meantime a few men from the city of al-Madīna came to intercede on 'Aṭarrad's behalf; they told the governor that he had good qualities, held the ideal of manhood, and was kind and religious. So he summoned 'Aṭarrad and set him free, and asked him if he needed anything. The singer said only: "May God bless you." And as he was leaving he saw the singers being brought in to be judged. So he returned to the governor and said: "May God make the prince prosperous and well. Have you jailed these men because of singing?" The governor replied: "Yes." So he said: "Please do not do

them an injustice, for by God they have not perfected any of that art yet!" At this point the governor laughed and let them go. (*KA*, 3: 307)

> And Isḥāq al-Mawṣilī claimed that ʿAṭarrad had a handsome face, sang well and had a beautiful voice, was good at the craft of composition, and was . . . virtuous, a theologian and a chanter of the Qur'ān. . . . And Ibn Khurdādhbih (d. 911) mentioned that his testimony was accepted at the court in the city of al-Madīna. (*KA*, 3: 303).

The process of change

The inevitability of change sometimes had to be reconciled with the respect and obedience a student owed to his teacher. In the following story, the student Ibrāhīm al-Mawṣilī had to have the permission of his dying master, Siyāṭ (d. 785), to alter Siyāṭ's compositions, and obtained it very artfully. We also learn from this story that the great master had composed sixty songs. This account came from Ibrāhīm's son Isḥāq al-Mawṣilī, who said:

> Siyāṭ was my father's teacher and the teacher of Ibn Jāmiʿ (d. 806) and those who lived in that era. He fell ill, so my father and Ibn Jāmiʿ went to visit him. My father said to him: "O Abū Wahb, your sickness has greatly afflicted me. If there were something I could help you with, I would give anything to do so." He said: "How was I to you both?" We said: "Truly an excellent teacher and master." He said: "I have composed sixty melodies, and I wish you would neither change them nor set these melodies to new texts." So my father said to him: "I shall do that, O Abū Wahb, but which of the following would you dislike: that there be in your songs excellence which I fall short of performing, in which case people would know your superiority over me; or that there be in them a defect which I improve, in which case my improvement would be attributed to you and people would take it away from me and attribute it to you?" So he said: "I absolve you of any wrongdoing." (*KA*, 6:156)

The following passage is a commentary by al-Iṣbahānī on the subject of change in music.

> And despite his knowledge and talent, Prince Ibrāhīm ibn al-Mahdī fell short in his performance of songs of the older repertoire and fell equally short in composing in that style. He used to remove notes from songs that involved much labor and lightened them in accordance with what suited him and with what he was able to accomplish in his performance. If he was reproached for doing so he would say: "I am a king, son of a king. I sing as I wish and in the manner which pleases me." He was the first to spoil songs of the older repertoire, and because of his stature he facilitated and opened the way for others to boldly effect change in this repertoire.
>
> Up to now people are of two types:
>
> (1) Those who followed the belief and practice of Isḥāq and his friends, who disapproved of changing the older repertoire, found such audacity distressing, reproached those who acted in that way, and considered such an act faulty and short of perfection. They sang the older repertoire according to its proper way, or close to it.
>
> (2) And those who followed the belief and practice of Ibrāhīm ibn al-Mahdī or were guided by it, such as Mukhāriq and Shāriya and Rayyiq. And the person who learned from them would sing the older repertoire as they desired it and not the way it was sung by the composer to whom the song was attributed. And the person would find in this endeavor many who cooperated along the same lines, wishing that the learning of such repertoire would become more accessible to them; and the person disliked what was difficult and what had slow cycles,

and he found the time he should spend to learn the good older singing repertoire too long, because of his limited musical knowledge.

And if this continues without interruption, then the composition belongs to whoever is doing the singing at the time and not to the predecessors, because if the new singers change what they have learned as they please, and the one from whom they learned has also, in turn, changed it, and this latter has also learned from others who have changed it—until this process covers a span of five or so generations—then the audience in our era does not receive from the original generation of composers any ancient singing in its original form at all. (*KA*, 10:70)

Improvised song texts

The choice of songs was sometimes dictated by the physical setting of a performance. In the next passage, the setting—an outdoor zoological garden where wine is drunk and race horses are exhibited—is reflected in songs performed by two creative musicians for their patron. When they did not succeed in earning a lavish reward, they improvised a minor textual change in order to settle for less. Their patron was amused and agreed.

The caliph al-Muʿtaṣim was sitting in his zoological garden, and horses were being paraded before him. He was drinking while ʿAllūya (d. 850) and Mukhāriq were singing before him. A reddish-brown horse was led out before him, the like of which had never been seen. ʿAllūya and Mukhāriq signaled to one another, and ʿAllūya sang to the caliph:

If they drink and become intoxicated
They give away every fine race horse.

Al- Muʿtaṣim ignored him. Then Mukhāriq sang to him:

He gives away white-skinned women like gazelles, swift horses
Under their horse-clothes, and white camels too.

Al-Muʿtaṣim laughed and then said: "Shut up, O you two. . . . By God, neither of you will ever own it." Then it was ʿAllūya's turn again, and he sang:

If they drink and become intoxicated
They give away every mule and every donkey.

Al-Muʿtaṣim laughed and said: "As to that, all right," and he ordered a mule for one of them and a donkey for the other. (*KA*, 11:352–353)

Note: Translations from *Kitāb al-aghānī* are by the present author. Dates of death have been included when possible.

REFERENCES

Al-Iṣbāhānī, Abū al-Faraj (d. 967). 1927–1974. *Kitāb al-aghānī* (Book of Songs). 24 vols. Cairo: Dār al-Kutub. (Cited as *KA*.)

Farmer, Henry George. 1929, 1973. *A History of Arabian Music to the Thirteenth Century*. London: Luzac.

Neubauer, Eckhard. 1965. "Musiker am Hof der frühen ʿAbbāsiden." Dissertation. J. W. Goethe-Universität, Frankfurt am Main.

Sawa, George Dimitri. 1981. "The Survival of Some Aspects of Performance Practice of Medieval Arabic Music." *Ethnomusicology* 25(1):73–86.

———. 1984. "Musical Humor in the *Kitāb al-aghānī* (Book of Songs)." In *Logos Islamikos: Studia Islamica in Honorem Georgii Michaelis Wickens*, ed. Roger M. Savory and Dionisius Agius, 35–50. Papers in Medieval Studies 6. Toronto: Pontifical Institute of Medieval Studies.

———. 1985. "The Status and Role of the Secular Musician in *Kitāb al-aghānī*." *Asian Music* 17(1):69–82.

———. 1989a. *Music Performance Practice in the Early ʿAbbāsid Era, A.D. 750–932*. Toronto: Pontifical Institute of Medieval Studies.

———. 1989b. "Oral Transmission in Arabic Music, Past and Present." *Oral Tradition* 4(1–2):254–265.

———. 1997. "Editing and Translating Medieval Arabic Writings on Music." In *Music Discourse from Classical to Early Modern Times: Editing and Translating Texts (Proceedings of the 26th Annual Conference on Editorial Problems, University of Toronto, 19–20 October 1990)*, ed. Maria Rika Maniates, 45–70. Toronto: University of Toronto Press.

Music in Ancient Arabia from Archaeological and Written Sources

Christian Poché

Lyres
Other Instruments
Singers and Dancers

Recent archaeological and epigraphical research has added to our knowledge of the history of musical life in ancient Arabia. Written sources and poetry dating from the sixth century C.E. onward provide additional information. Further, we can compare historical sources with the present-day music of the Arabian Peninsula and consider possible relationships. All these data shed new light on the musical life of this area.

In keeping with tradition, the first Arab historians attempted to establish chronologies dating back to individual ancestors. Thus al-Bayhaqī in the tenth century sought to establish a patronymic for the first man who sang, the first man who sang in Yemen, the first man who sang in Mecca, the man who invented and first played on the *ʿūd* 'lute', the first woman who plucked the *miʿzaf* 'lyre', and so on (1960:367). Archaeological research takes a different approach, not seeking to link the origin of music with named individuals. Similarly, in contemporary field research on the Arabian Peninsula, specific aspects of rural musical life are commonly attributed to a group or tribe rather than to individuals.

LYRES

Perhaps the most ancient evidence of musical instruments in this region is a rock painting showing four lyres, discovered in southern Najran (Saudi Arabia) not far from the border with Yemen, and described by Emmanuel Anati in the 1960s. The lyres appear with other drawings—a warrior, a dagger, camels, ostriches, and small oxen. While it is extremely difficult to assign a precise date to these paintings, Anati (1968:102) concluded that they date back to the "third millennium B.C.E., but they could be considerably later." These lyres are like the Palestinian *megiddo* in shape and are akin to the present-day Ethiopian *begenna*.

Other archaeological evidence of the lyre in southern Arabia (Yemen) probably dates from the second half of the first millennium B.C.E. The best-known example is a funeral stele from Ṣanʿāʾ depicting a seated man who is playing a lyre in the same way as players of present-day lyres—the Yemenite *ṭumbarah*, the Egyptian *ṭanbūrah*, or the Sudanese *rabāba*. The left hand, open, is on the top of the instrument, with the five fingers placed on the strings; the index finger of right hand plays on the bottom. We know from an article by Saint-Saëns describing Egyptian lyre players that the simultaneous playing of two, three, or more notes to produce harmonies is not

FIGURE 1 Funerary stele in two registers from Khawlan (second half of the first millennium B.C.E.).

part of the performance practice of this instrument. The left hand touches the strings to mute them rather than pluck them (1913:538, 539). It is difficult to ascertain exactly how many strings the lyre on the stele has, though today such instruments on the Red Sea coast of the Arabian Peninsula and the Gulf have five or six. But this lyre seems to have fewer strings than the lyres shown in the rock painting at Najran; and its bottom has a shape similar to that of three modern regional versions of the lyre: the Ethiopian *krar*, the Egyptian *simsimiyya*, and the Sudanese *rabāba*.

The San'ā' funeral stele is not the only example of an ancient lyre found in Yemen. Another is shown on the cover of a book, *Al-ghinā' al-yamanī al-qadīm wa mashāhiruhu* 'Ancient Yemeni Music and Its Celebrated Figures' (1983). In this photograph (which is black-and-white and unfortunately has no caption), a seated musician holds a lyre as if it were a psaltery, not like the player shown on the funeral stele: the right hand plays on the top and the left hand plucks on the bottom. Perhaps this musician was left-handed.

Archaeological evidence and written sources confirm that the lyre was found in virtually all the ancient civilizations of western Asia. The oldest and most renowned came from Sumer (Mesopotamia) and were excavated in a royal cemetery at Ur around 1929 by Sir Arthur Woolley; they are now in Iraq, at the National Museum of Baghdad. Archaeologists have also found lyres in Ethiopia (Graziosi 1964:96), ancient Palestine, and Syria (Mari), and more rarely in Egypt (Ziegler 1979:116).

The term for lyre in Semitic languages (and some non-Semitic languages, such as Hittite) is derived from the root *q-n* or *q-n-r*, which is the source of the Hebrew *kinnor*, the ancient Egyptian *kenniniur*, the Ugaritic *knr*, the Babylonian (Mari, in Syria) *kinnāru*, and the Mandaic *kinar*. In early Arabic texts, the word is always in the plural form *kinnārāt* (the singular *kinnāra* was a late contribution by lexicographers and is not supported by tradition; Poché 1984, 2:432). It first appears in its plural form in the collections of *ḥadīth* (sayings of the Prophet), an important source of information about life in the peninsula during the early days of Islam. In the *Musnad* of Ibn Ḥanbal, written in the ninth century and printed for the first time in Cairo in 1895 C.E. (1313 A.H.), the *kinnārāt* are equated with the *qinīn* (1895, 5:267). According to the *Musnad* and the first Arab lexicographers, the *qinīn* was an Ethiopian lyre, analogous to *barābiṭ* (singular, *barbaṭ*—here, a lyre, hence the Greek *bartiton*; 2:165, 3:422). But the term *kinnārāt* soon disappeared from Arabic and became incomprehensible; this is why a copyist misunderstood the word in the *Musnad* and transcribed it as *kiffārāt* 'blasphemers' (1895, 4:66, 5:257). *Kinnārāt* was also misinterpreted by the fourteenth-century jurist Ibn Qayyim al-Jawziyya of Damascus (n.d., 1:263), who wrote it as *kibbārāt*, referring to a drum, the *kabar*, probably of Abyssinian origin (*kabaro*).

Kinnārāt is not the only word in the early written sources that designates a lyre. Two other terms were used at the inception of Islam. The more common was *ma'āzif*, a plural form. The second, less common—indeed rare—was *ṭunbūr*, a singular form. *Ṭunbūr* appeared only in the *Ṣaḥiḥ* of al-Bukhārī, one of the most important books of canonical sayings, in an eschatological chapter: "When the last hour comes and Ibn Maryam [the son of Mary] comes down to you . . . he shall . . . break the idols, the cross, and the *ṭunbūr*" (al-Bukhārī 1981, 3:107). The plural form *ṭanābīr* is found for the first time in the poetry of al-'Asha (d. 628). It is difficult to determine the shape of this instrument. Usually, *ṭunbūr* denotes a long-necked lute, and that is probably what al-'Asha meant by it; but in the *Ṣaḥiḥ* by al-Bukhārī, the word seems to refer to a lyre. The presence of the long-necked lute in the peninsula has never been confirmed; there, the *ṭunbūr* was often defined as a *mi'zaf* (Poché 1984, 3:676).

Four observations can be made from these references. First, the *ma'āzif* were played not individually but in groups—and only female groups, the *qaynāt* or *qiyān* (singular, *qayna*) 'singing-girls' or 'songstresses'. There is no mention of women performing alone, or of male performers.

Second, it was customary, on occasion, for women to play the lyre with the instrument resting on their heads. This is recorded for the first time at the end of the fifth century C.E., in a verse of 'Abīd al-Abraṣ describing a battlefield: "So let the singing women [*qaynāt*] play [*'azf*] on their heads" (Lyall 1913:14, from the Arabic text). Another such description is found in a *ḥadīth* recorded by Ibn Mājah (1953: no. 4020): "It is played on their heads by the singers [*mughanniyyāt*] with the *ma'āzif*." The lyre was not the only instrument played on the head. Ibn Ḥanbal in his *Musnad* recorded a *ḥadīth* in which a black slave (*jāriya*) plays a frame drum (*duff*) on the head of the Prophet (1895, 5:356).

Third, lyres (*ma'āzif*) were also used in battle (Ibn Qutayba 1925, 1:107; Poché 1984, 1:667). It may be assumed that this instrument was associated with death, as this association appears several times in poetry and apocryphal sayings. Until recently, a similar tradition survived in Mauritania: a female griot would play the harp (*ardin*) on horseback, riding behind a warrior to encourage him. In Mauritania the *ardin* is exclusively a woman's instrument and cannot be touched by a man; traditionally it was played in ensembles, not as a solo instrument. All *ardin* players belong to the Hassāniyyah, who are said to have come originally from the Arabian peninsula. In the Darfur area of Sudan, a woman called *hakāmma* would also follow a warrior into battle to incite him with song, but she carried no musical instrument (Carlisle 1973:797).

Fourth, the term *ma'āzif* derives from the root *'azf* 'voice of the jinn'. This aspect of the instrument was frequently noted by different writers (Ibn Manẓūr n.d.: *'Azafa*). Unfortunately, no early reference deals with the relationship between lyre and jinn as it has developed today in the possession cult called *zār*, which is widespread on the Red Sea coast and in the Arabian Gulf area; in this cult, the therapy is for the most part conducted by one man playing the lyre (Poché 1984, 3:183, 519). One *ḥadīth* concerning signs of the end of the world suggests a correspondence between the early lyre and the present-day *zār*: the Prophet Muḥammad says that the singing-girls (*qaynāt*) will be destroyed by a red wind (*rīḥ aḥmar*) for playing on the *ma'āzif* (al-Tirmidhī 1934, 9:58). The expression *rīḥ aḥmar* has not entirely disappeared—it is one of numerous local names for the *zār* in the Sudan (Zenkowsky 1950, 65).

Some general conclusions may be drawn from these archaeological and written sources. The four lyres in the rock painting discovered near Najran seem to have been played together in an ensemble. This may also be deduced from the early written sources in which terms for the lyre first appeared in the plural form, and the inference suggests that there was some continuity in the peninsula from the time of the Najran painting until the writings at the beginning of Islam. In contrast, the funeral stele of San'ā', which shows one male instrumentalist sitting in front of another man who holds a *sistrum* (a handheld rattle) seems to imply a different tradition—a solo male player. That inference is supported by the two singular terms used in early Islam for a lyre, *ṭunbūr* and *qinīn*. *Qinīn*, the Arabic name for the Ethiopian lyre, is probably the first literary designation for this chordophone. This suggests that in Ethiopia at that time, the lyre was already being played by one person (probably a male)—as it still is in the present-day tradition, which regards King David as the ancestor of lyre (*begenna*) players. Thus the funeral stele of Ṣan'ā' seems to correspond with the *ḥadīth*, recorded by al-Bukhārī, predicting that the lyre (singular, *ṭunbūr*) will be destroyed by Ibn Maryam at the end of the world, not only because the instrument is described by a singular term in both contexts but also because in each case there is an association with death.

> Perhaps the most ancient evidence of musical instruments in this region is a rock painting showing four lyres, discovered in southern Najran.

OTHER INSTRUMENTS

Lyres were not the only musical instruments in ancient Arabia, although so far they are the only type of instrument revealed by archaeology. Evidence of additional instruments among Arabs in pre-Islamic times is given by three Greek authors.

The first author, Menander, in the second century B.C.E., briefly mentions the *aulos* of the Arabs (Menandri 1862:4). Here the term should probably be understood as the double-reed wind instrument profusely cited in early writings under the name *mizmār*. The only archaeological evidence of the *mizmār* is found in the writings of the ninth-century Yemenite historian al-Ḥamdānī. In his book *al-Iklīl* (1931, 8:160) he says that he visited a grotto where he saw "two mutilated statues of singing-girls [*qaynatān*], one holding an *'arṭaba*, meaning a *ṭanbūra* [or *ṭunbūra*], the other a *mizmār*, also mutilated." (For a discussion of *'arṭabah*, see Poché 1984, 1:76).

The second author, Pollux, in the first century C.E., attributes the invention of the monochord to the Arabs (1967:60); however, this raises a number of questions that are still unanswered. Nicomachus of Gerasa (modern-day Jarash, in Jordan) wrote of "the monochord, which most people call *phandourai* [three strings] and the Pythagorians *kanones* [a single string]" (Barker 1989:254). Since the single-string monochord is unknown among the Arabs and was never mentioned by them before the classical period, one wonders if the writer does not mean a musical bow. Yet this instrument too seems to be unknown. According to lexicographers, the sound of a finger plucking on a bow is called *'azafa*, a word that has the same root as *ma'āzif*. The appearance of the single-string spike fiddle *rabāba* among the Arabs is of uncertain date; all we can say for sure is that it is a late instrument. The term appeared for the first time as *rabāb* in the ninth century (it was used by al-Jāḥiẓ); but then it seemed to designate a female name: Rabāb is paired with another *qaynah,* Ẓabyah (Pellat 1955:82; Ibn Taḥḥān 1990:25; Pellat has misunderstood this passage, translating it as "What is the relationship between Ẓabyah and the *rabāb*?"). In the Sudan, *rabāba* means a lyre (Poché 1984, 3:183).

The third author, Clement of Alexandria, in the second century C.E., states that cymbals were much liked and were used during wars by the Arabs, as drums were by the Egyptians (1954, 4:4). Among the Arabs, cymbals were called *ṣanj*, although the same term was also used to refer to a harp.

Except for the frame drums (*duff*) of the pre-Islamic period, frequently mentioned in early writings, the only two drums mentioned in the official *ḥadīth* are *ṭabl* and *kūba*. The *ṭabl* is generally considered to be a two-headed cylindrical drum, but that shape was presumably unknown when Islam first began. The *ṭabl*, *ṭbol*, or *ṭobol*, widespread in Sudan, in Mauritania, and among the Tuaregs today, is a single-headed drum. The *kūbā* is assumed to be a single-headed goblet drum, but it was equated with a *ṭabl* in two separate *ḥadīth* recorded by Ibn Ḥanbal (1895, 1:274). A third term, *ghirbāl*, appeared in a *ḥadīth* that had little support and was mentioned only once, in a canonical text by Ibn Mājah (1953: no. 1895). This *ḥadīth*, which deals with marriage, was later made official by al-Ghazālī (Farmer 1929:28; Poché 1984,

2:43), but all other official accounts of it use the term *duff* (a frame drum) instead of *ghirbāl*. Quoting the Andalusian al-Shalaḥī, Sachs (1913:246; 1940:246) claimed that the *ghirbāl* was known in Muḥammad's time. It seems that *ghirbāl* refers to a round frame drum while the Arab *duff* may also be quadrangular (Poché 1984, 1:616).

SINGERS AND DANCERS

Archaeological research in present-day Jordan and northern Saudi Arabia has revealed inscriptions and rock drawings belonging to Thamud culture that date from the first millennium B.C.E. to the fifth century C.E. Epigraphic inscriptions supply a long list of names for a pantheon of gods, among them the *qayn* 'blacksmith' (Arabic, the masculine form of *qayna*). The same word also occurs in Sabean, *qynn* (van den Branden 1966:111), but in the Lihyanit inscriptions from southern Arabia this term designates a slave (Ryckmans 1934:190). The term *qayna* also occurs in the Minean inscriptions from southern Arabia. It is difficult to find a relationship between the designations of a god, songstresses or singing-girls, and a blacksmith; but establishing a relationship between slave and singing-girls is much easier. One should remember that in the Safaitic inscriptions the Arabic term *'arfān* 'seer' refers to a female musician (Ryckmans 1934:171). Blacksmiths and musicians are supposed to have had supernatural powers; it may be hypothesized that as people gradually ceased to believe in these powers, blacksmiths and musicians fell to the bottom of the hierarchy and became slaves. Although this hypothesis cannot be verified at present, we can note that among the Gypsies of west Asia today, men are often blacksmiths and women are musicians.

Besides the Thamud inscriptions, numerous other drawings show naked dancers, female and male, dancing separately and shaking a *sistrum*, a handheld rattle that Arab lexicographers have never included in their impressive lists of sound-producing instruments. It is assumed that these figures are performing a ritual dance (van den Branden 1966:82), and dance is a fundamental issue. Arab writers are very discreet about this art form, discussing it seldom, and then usually to condemn it. Among Arabs, the generic term for dance is *raqṣ*, which has cognates in many Semitic languages. For example, in Syriac *raqd* connotes a dance of lamentation; *teroqṣen* is used today in south Arabic (Shawri and Soqotri); and *raqad* is used in Djibouti in the Afar language.

The first literary references to dance date from the beginning of Islam and concern Ethiopians who danced (*zafina*) in Mecca. The verb *zafina*, equated with the verb *raqaṣa* (Ibn Ḥanbal 1895, 3:153), is still used in the Mehri language (south Yemen) to designate dance (*zefon*; Jahn 1902, 8:238). There is a secondhand reference suggesting that dance is related to the origin of the music among the Arabs; this reference is found in a mythical account of two females, handed down in two versions by the tenth-century historians al-Ṭabarī and al-Mas'ūdī (Poché 1989:11). The women, referred to as *al-Jaradatān* 'two grasshoppers', were able to cause rain or drought by the power of their singing. Of the numerous additional names that later writers gave them, two are significant: Qu'ād 'to limp' and Thumād 'a small quantity of water' (Asad 1960:76). A limping dance, related to fertility, has a long history (Poché 1981); it appears, for example, in the Bible (I Kings 18:25–29), and such a dance exists today in the Sinai Desert. This mythical account links the origin of music among the Arabs to the desert, two females, rainfall, sung poetry, and dance.

Before Islam, the Arabs used only the word *ghinā'* for music, referring to the singing of a poetic text. This term appears as *ghanan* 'to nasalize' in the Safaitic inscriptions from south Arabia (Ryckmans 1934, 1:175)—and that sense survives today, because singing in the peninsula generally has a nasal quality. During his travels in Arabia at the end of the nineteenth century, Doughty remarked that Arab nomads "make to themselves music like David drawing out the voice in the nose to a demesurate length" (1888, 1:41). In pre-Islamic Arabia *ghinā'* was the craft of slave singing-girls, *qaynāt* or *qiyān* (singular, *qayna*). Singing was a collective art, not focused on the individual performer. Numerous classical references (for example, al-Jāḥiẓ and the eleventh-century Egyptian Ibn Ṭaḥḥān) point to a tradition of two women (*qaynatān*) singing together. However, from a *ḥadīth* recorded by al-Bukhārī (1981, 8:181), we know that the camel driver (*ḥādī*) was also included in the category of singer as a male soloist. The first such singer to be recorded in history was called Anjashah; the Arabs trace the tradition of solo male singing to him. The singular term *qayna* was already used around the seventh century.

Histories of Arab music have always emphasized influences from northern countries, especially Mesopotamia, Persia, Byzantium, and Syria. Archaeological and epigraphic findings show that we should also look to southern Arabia, Ethiopia, and eastern Africa as important contributors to the development of music in ancient Arabia. We must remember, for example, that the first muezzin of Islam, Bilāl, was of Ethiopian origin.

REFERENCES

Anati, Emmanuel. 1968. *Rock-Art in Central Arabia*. Louvain: Institut Orientaliste.

Asad, Nāsir al-Dīn. 1960. *Al-qiyān wa 'l-ghina' fī 'l-'aṣr al-jāhilī* (Singing-Girls and Music in Pre-Islamic Arabia). Beirut: Dār Ṣādir.

Barker, Andrew, ed. 1989. *Greek Musical Writings: II*. New York: Cambridge University Press.

al-Bayhaqī, Ibrāhīm Ibn Muḥammad. 1960. *Kitāb al-maḥāsin Wa 'l-māsawī* (Book of the Virtues of Things and Their Contraries). Beirut: Dār Ṣādir.

van den Branden, Albert. 1966. *Histoire de Thamoud*. Beirut: Publications de l'Université Libanaise.

al-Bukhārī. 1981. *Ṣaḥīḥ*. Beirut: Dār al-Fikr.

Carlisle, Roxane Connick. 1973. "Women Singers in Darfur, Sudan Republic." *Anthropos* 68:758–800.

Clement of Alexandria. 1954. "*Paedagogos*" (Christ the Educator). In *Fathers of the Church*, Vol. 23. Washington: Catholic University of America Press.

Doughty, Charles. 1888. *Travels in Arabia Deserta*. Cambridge: Cambridge University Press.

Farmer, Henry George. 1929. *A History of Arabian Music*. London: Luzac.

Graziosi, P. 1964. "New Discoveries of Rock Painting in Ethiopia." *Antiquity* 150:96.

al-Hamdānī. 1931. *al-Iklīl*, ed. Anastās Mārī al-Karmalī. Baghdad: n.p.

Ibn Ḥanbal. 1895. *Musnad*. Cairo: al-Maṭba'a al-Maymaniyya.

Ibn Mājah. 1953. *Sunan*. Beirut: Dār al-Fikr.

Ibn Manẓūr. n.d. *Lisān al-'arab* (Encyclopedia of the Arabic language). Cairo. Reprinted Beirut: Dār Ṣādir.

Ibn Qayyim al-Jawziyya. n.d. *Ighātat al-luhfān min masāyid al-shayṭān* (To Save the Passionate from the Devil's Claws). Cairo. Reprinted Beirut: Dār al-Fikr (n.d.).

Ibn Qutayba. 1925. *'Uyūn al-akhbār* (Choice Histories). Cairo: Dār al-Kutub.

Ibn Taḥḥān. 1990. *Hāwī al-funūn wa salwat al-maḥzūn* (Compendium of a Fatimid Court Musician), ed. Eckhard Neubauer. Frankfurt am Main: Institut für Geschichte der Arabisch-Islamischen Wissenschaften.

Jahn, Alfred. 1902. *Die Mehri-Sprache in Südarabien*. Vienna: A. Hölder.

Lyall, Sir Charles. 1913. *The Diwāns of 'Abīd ibn al-Abraṣ of Asad*. Leiden: Brill.

Menandri. 1862. *Scriptorum Graecorum Bibliotheca Aristophanis, Menandri et Philemoni*. Paris: Firmin Didot.

Nājī, Muḥammad Murshid. 1983. *Al-ghinā' al-yamanī al-qadīm wa mashāhīruhu* (Ancient Yemeni Music and Its Celebrated Figures).

Pellat, Charles. 1955. *Le Kitāb at-Tarbī' wa-t-Tadwīr de Jāḥiz*. Damascus: Institut Français de Damas.

Poché, Christian. 1981. "Rythme impair et danse boiteuse." *Cahiers Musique Culture*: 97–101.

———. 1984. "*'Arṭaba*," "*Duff*," "*Ghirbāl*," "*Kinnārāt*," "*Mi'zaf*," "*Mizmār*," "*Qinīn*," "*Rabāba*," "*Ṭunbūr*." In *The New Grove Dictionary of Musical Instruments*, ed. Stanley Sadie. London: Macmillan.

———. 1989. "Le partage des tâches: La femme dans la musique arabe." *Cahiers de l'Orient* 13:11–21.

Pollux, Julius. 1967. *Pollucis Onomasticon*. In *Lexicographi Graeci*, ed. Ericus Bethe, Vol. 9. Stuttgart: Teubner.

Ryckmans, Gonzague. 1934. *Les noms propres sud-sémitiques*. 3 vols. Louvain: Bureaux du Muséon.

Sachs, Curt. 1913. *Real-Lexikon der Musikinstrumente*. Berlin: J. Bard.

———. 1940. *The History of Musical Instruments*. New York: Norton.

Saint-Saëns, Camille. 1913. "Lyres et cythares." In *Encylopédie de la musique et dictionnaire du Conservatoire*, ed. Albert Lavignac, 1:538–540. Paris: C. Delagrave.

al-Tirmidhī. 1934. *Ṣaḥīḥ*. Cairo: Maṭba'at al-Sāwī.

Zenkowsky, S. 1950. "*Zār* and *Ṭambūra* as Practiced by the Women of Omdurman." *Sudan Notes and Records* 31:65–81.

Ziegler, Christiane. 1979. *Les instruments de musique égyptiens au musée du Louvre*. Paris: Éditions de la Réunion des Musées Nationaux.

Arabic Writings on Music: Eighth to Nineteenth Centuries

Eckhard Neubauer

Schools of Early Arab Music (*Ghinā'*) and Later Modal Styles (*Anghām*)
The Science of Music: *Mūsīqī* in Philosophical Contexts
Song Collections and Biographical Literature
Music as a Legal and Social Problem: *Samā'*
Writings on Musical Instruments
Editions of Arabic Sources

The student concerned with the history of Arab music is faced with the fact that source material in the form of sound recordings and pieces of music in (European) notation are available only from the twentieth century. Authentic Arab musical instruments as assembled in collections date back, with a few exceptions, no earlier than the eighteenth century. For earlier references we are confined to pictorial and literary sources. While a certain number of iconographic depictions of musical scenes have survived from pre-Islamic times, the written documents which represent the main body of sources for the study of Arab music can be traced back to the end of the first century of the Hijra, the seventh century C.E. (Farmer 1965a; this and subsequent citations are to "References" at the end of the article).

The first step toward an Arabic music literature seems to have been the collecting of song texts. This coincided with (and supported) the collecting of traditional poetry, as suggested by the earliest known titles on music and musicians composed in the second/eighth century (dates are given as Muslim era followed by the C.E. equivalent). These earliest books, which are known to us only by their titles (see Ibn al-Nadīm, d. c. 385/995, in "Editions of Arabic Sources" below) or by quotations in later writings, mark the outset of a rapidly increasing literary genre which soon was to cover most aspects of musical theory and practice. Who in the Western world prior to the Romantic era would have thought of developing a typology of musical inspiration? It was the versatile scholar Abū Naṣr al-Fārābī (d. 339/950) to whom we owe this and other methodical attempts at systematizing the phenomena of sound and musical composition. Philosophers such as al-Fārābī shared an interest in music with a great number of philologists and men of letters who had their own approach to the linguistic, historical, and social aspects of music making in international Islamic society.

Indeed, music seems nearly omnipresent in Arabic literature. It appears as musical terminology in lexicographical works (Kurā' al-naml, d. 310/922; Abū Hilāl al-'Askarī, d. after 400/1000; Ibn Sīda, d. 458/1066; al-Maydānī, d. 518/1124), and in metaphorical use in learned literature and letters (al-Washshā', d. c. 325/937; al-Tha'ālibī, d. 429/1038; Ibn al-Sharīf Daftarkhān, fl. ca. 650/1250; Ibn Faḍl Allāh al-'Umarī, d. 749/1348). Music and musicians appear in works on cultural history (Ibn 'Abd Rabbih, d. 328/940; al-Mas'ūdī, d. 345/956; al-Tha'ālibī, d. 429/1038; Bahā' al-Dīn al-Irbilī, d. 692/1293; al-Ibshīhī, d. after 850/1446; Ibn al-Naqīb, d. 1081/

1670), and in writings on social, cultural, and linguistic criticism (al-Jāḥiẓ, d. 255/868-9; Abū Ḥayyān al-Tawḥīdī, d. 414/1023; Ibn Makkī al-Ṣaqallī, d. 501/1107). Biographical data about musicians appear in chronological compendia and biographical reference books (Shiloah 1979) and in monographic compilations such as books on the "first" people (*awā'il*) to have done or invented something (Abū Hilāl al-'Askarī, d. after 400/1000; al-Suyūṭī, d. 911/1505). Musical professions appear in books on arts and crafts (Ibn Su'ūd al-Khuzā'ī, d. 789/1387) and in books on the supervision of trade, *ḥisba* (Ibn al-Ukhuwwa, d. 729/1329; al-Shayzarī, late sixth/twelfth century). Music also appears in medical contexts (Ibn Hindū, d. 420/1029; 'Alā' al-Dīn al-Kaḥḥāl, d. 720/1320; al-Dhahabī, d. 748/1348) and in manuals on how to select talented slaves and slave girls (Ibn Buṭlān, d. 458/1066). The interpretation of dreams has musical aspects (Ibn Sīrīn, d. 110/728; 'Abd al-Ghanī al-Nābulusī, d. 1143/1731), and so does court etiquette (Hilāl al-Ṣābi', d. 448/1056).

Even the orthodox hostility toward secular music would, eventually, stimulate the process of pondering the nature of music, if only to distinguish between "licit" and "illicit" forms. The historical development of Arabic (Persian, and Turkish) literature on music truly reflects the particular tendencies of cultural rise and decline in each of the countries from Transoxania to the Maghreb. Being a literate discipline, it was connected more closely to urban centers than to the rural or bedouin world. Nevertheless, the historian Ibn Khaldūn (d. 808/1406) wrote an essay on music sociology considering all social groups in their historical evolution.

Arabic music theory proper is connected with the short-necked lute (*'ūd*) as a means of experimentation and inspiration in acoustics, in the depiction of the tonal and metrical systems, and in the approach to musical notation (Chabrier 1985; Land 1922; Manik 1969, 1979; Wright 1978). The Arabs' preference for the lute over the Greco-Byzantine lyre or the Iranian harp set the future course—the main character—of art and court music in Islam as well as in the European Renaissance. Medieval Arab writers on music are rightly considered the leading authorities of their time. Although much of their work is lost, an impressive number of titles are known to us from biographical-bibliographical sources or by quotations in later books. What makes it difficult to embark on Arab music history is that only a small number of the extant treatises and books are available in good editions, and that only a few of these have been properly translated or evaluated. The basic sources are therefore still in manuscript form and are scattered in libraries all over the world, constituting a wide field for future research.

The following outline is intended to convey the colorful variety of Arabic music literature. It is divided into several sections representing the main aspects of music theory and practice. Special attention is paid to works available in print or in translation; these are listed chronologically in the survey section "Editions of Arabic Sources." For further details, the reader is referred primarily to the bibliographical reference works of 'A. al-'Alawchī (1964), H. G. Farmer (1965a), and A. Shiloah (1979).

SCHOOLS OF EARLY ARAB MUSIC (*GHINĀ'*) AND LATER MODAL STYLES (*ANGHĀM*)

The theoretical attempts of the early Arabic-Islamic writers on music were laid down in books on *nagham* 'notes', on *īqā'* 'musical metrics', and on *ta'līf* 'composition'.

Books on *nagham* were devoted to describing the basic octave and the then current scales. This emerges from the earliest extant treatise on the subject, which was written by Ibn al-Munajjim (d. 300/912). Here, the notes are identified by letters in their numerical value (for instance, first letter *alif*, "a," numerical value 1 = central note of the system) and named according to their position on the lute (here *muṭlaq al-mathnā*, the open position of the second highest string, called *mathnā*, suggesting an ideal tuning of B-e-a-d′ for the four strings of the lute).

The books on *īqā'* treated the metrical structure of melodies. The methods of describing and defining the *īqā'* meters were, on the one hand, borrowed from the disciplines of Arabic, Greek, and Indian poetical metrics, and, on the other hand, developed from the plucking movements of the lute player. Metrical signs and mnemotechnical syllables were used to depict long and short notes. The writings of al-Fārābī (d. 339/950) on this topic are considered highlights of Arabic music theory.

The beginnings of the literature on composition, *ta'līf,* of which little has survived, seem to have reflected the traditions of individual schools from both the Hijaz and Iraq by using their differing modal terminologies. A Syro-Byzantine wing of Arabic modal theory is mentioned in the writings of al-Kindī (d. c. 252/866), which convey the impression that, at the beginning, several schools existed side by side, some of them in the Syro-Byzantine tradition, others based on Iranian and local Arab models. The widespread early modal names—*muṭlaq, mazmūm, maḥmūl, maḥṣūr*, and so on—which were common in Iraq, in Egypt, and in Muslim Spain, are represented in an early fragment from the Cairo Geniza (Shiloah 1979, no. 287) and in the works of al-Ḥasan ibn Aḥmad al-Kātib (early fifth/eleventh century), Ibn al-Ṭaḥḥān (d. after 449/1057), and al-Tīfāshī (d. 651/1253). The more sophisticated terminology of the Baghdad school of Isḥāq al-Mawṣilī (d. 235/850), which used modal names such as *al-muṭlaq fī majrā al-wusṭā*, (open string via minor third) or . . . *fī majrā al-binṣir* (. . . via major third; Farmer 1965b), thereby differentiating between "female" and "male" scales (as designated by al-Kindī), is immortalized in the "Grand Book of Songs" by Abū 'l-Faraj al-Iṣbahānī (discussed below).

In the course of the fifth/eleventh century a distinctly different nomenclature announces the rise of the "modern" or "Persian" system of twelve modes: *rāst, 'irāq, iṣbahān*, and so forth. This system laid the foundation for the later Near Eastern modal systems described in all subsequent learned writings on music theory based on physical and mathematical principles until the ninth/fifteenth century. It was, to our knowledge, first recorded in the celebrated *Kitāb al-adwār* of Ṣafī al-Dīn al-Urmawī (d. 693/1294). This compendium (discussed below) was to become the most influential of all Arabic books on music theory. It was frequently copied, was translated several times (into Persian), and was commented on in Arabic, Persian, and Turkish. Representatives of al-Urmawī's school were distinguished musicians and scholars, such as Quṭb al-Dīn al-Shīrāzī (d. 710/1311) and 'Abd al-Qādir al-Marāghī (d. 838/1435). One of its last disciples in Ottoman Turkey was Muḥammad ibn 'Abd al-Ḥamīd al-Lādhiqī (d. after 890/1485).

Compared with the "systematic" and more scientific tradition of the Urmawī school, which became the leading doctrine in the centers of courtly and urban music in post-'Abbāsid Iran and Ottoman Turkey, the theoretical literature of the Arab countries developed in a more individual and empirical way. The main currents can be distinguished at first glance by their respective names for "mode" or "modes." While al-Urmawī and his successors speak of *shudūd* (singular, *shadd*) and, from the fourteenth century on, of *maqāmāt* (singular, *maqām*), modes in the Eastern Arab countries are called *anghām* (singular, *naghma*, the term *maqām* being used only in later Ottoman times), and in North Africa *ṭubū'* (singular, *ṭab'*).

Since the written heritage of these local traditions has not yet been duly recognized, a selection of relevant and datable titles is listed here (for some of these, see also "Editions of Arabic Sources," below). Some contain highly unconventional approaches to describing the modes. My dating of several of the authors differs from that given by H. G. Farmer (1965a) and A. Shiloah (1979), to whom the reader is referred for further information.

Titles representing local schools of Iraq, Syria, and Egypt are:

1. *Jawāhir al-niẓām fī ma'rifat al-anghām*, a didactic poem (*urjūza*), written in 729/1329 by **Ibn al-Khaṭīb al-Irbilī,** and commented on in the middle of the twelfth/eighteenth century under the title *Bur' al-asqām, sharḥ al-qaṣīda fī 'l-anghām*. The poem is edited. It is the earliest known text on the Syro-Arab *anghām* tradition, which differed slightly from the system of the *shudūd* described by al-Urmawī.
2. *Ghāyat al-maṭlūb fī 'ilm al-anghām wa 'l-ḍurūb* by Muḥammad ibn 'Īsā ibn Ḥasan al-Baghdādī al-Miṣrī, known as **Ibn Kurr** (d. 759/1358 or 763/1362), Ms. London, Brit. Libr., Or 9247, contains an extensive description of meters and modes in a method of his own. Rather than the seventeen degrees per octave of al-Urmawī's theory, here we find twenty positions over two octaves (a sequence of tetrachords with minor and major thirds) that represent a system related to lute playing. The term *rāst* (here, *rast*), normally understood to refer to the basic note of the mode *rāst* and its scale, occurs in this source as the name of each of the five open strings, the strings being tuned in fourths. So the system elucidates the importance of tetrachord structures and the common practice of transpositions in tetrachordal registers.
3. *Al-Kashshāf fī 'ilm al-anghām* by al-Muẓaffar ibn al-Ḥusayn **al-Ḥaṣkafī** al-Ḥiṣnī, dedicated to the Ayyubid ruler al-Malik al-'Ādil, who ruled over the author's home town Ḥiṣn Kayfa around 780/1378. Al-Ḥaṣkafī describes the modal structures on the basis of a system of eleven degrees in one octave and a fourth, which he calls *buyūt* 'houses' (singular, *bayt*). Mss., see Farmer 1965, no. 332; Shiloah 1979, no. 71.
4. *Muqaddima fī qawānīn al-anghām* by **Jamāl al-Dīn al-Māridīnī** (d. 809/1406), a didactic poem (*urjūza*) with commentary. Mss., see Shiloah 1979, no. 193.
5. *Rawḍat al-mustahām fī 'ilm al-anghām* by Jamāl al-Dīn Ḥasan ibn Aḥmad, known as **al-Jamāl al-Muṭrib** (ninth/fifteenth century), shows certain similarities to the text of al-Ḥaṣkafī (no. 3 above). Ms. Istanbul, see Shiloah 1979, no. 49.
6. An important textbook for singers and composers, written around 900/1500, probably in Syria, by a certain 'Alī ibn 'Ubayd Allāh **al-Saylakūnī** (perhaps Siyalkūtī; Shiloah 1979, no. 281, to be corrected at several points). In a remarkably didactic manner, the modes, meters, musical forms, and repertoire of the time are introduced. Unfortunately, the only extant manuscript is incomplete (hence the title is missing); see Neubauer 2000.
7. *Al-In'ām fī ma'rifat al-anghām* by Shams al-Dīn Muḥammad **al-Ṣaydāwī** al-Dimashqī (d. 911/1506), a didactic poem serving as a commentary on the author's graphic depiction of the modes. This consists of diagrams (unique in the Arab world, yet resembling the staff systems of the ninth-century Greco-Latin *Musica enchiriadis* and those given by Vincenzo Galilei in 1581 and Athanasius Kircher in 1650) showing a number of colored, eight-lined octave schemes into which the melodic development of the modes is entered in numbers, abbreviations, and connecting lines. The text was studied by Berthier and Shiloah, 1985.
8. A didactic poem (*urjūza*) on the modes (*anghām*) by 'Abd al-Qādir ibn Maḥmūd **al-Qādirī** (fl. 1050/1640). Ms. Gotha, see Shiloah 1979, no. 159.
9. *Rāḥ al-jām fī shajarat al-anghām,* written in 1083/1672 by **'Askar al-Ḥalabī** al-Ḥanafī al-Qādirī. It is an interesting document on the survival of Arab tradition in Ottoman times. Modes and meters are depicted in the form of genealogical trees, the meters being represented in the Turkish *düm-tek* ter-

minology for which this treatise is one of the earliest witnesses. Ms. Paris [Ms. Gotha, Germany is missing], see Shiloah 1979, no. 160.

10. *Al-Durr al-naqī fī ʿilm al-mūsīqī*, an Arabic adaptation of a Persian treatise, written c. 1124/1712 by Muḥammad ibn ʿAbd al-Raḥmān al-Qādirī al-Rifāʿī, known as **al-Musallam al-Mawṣilī.** It is available in print.

In the twelfth/eighteenth century the traditional music theory of the Arab east continued to be transmitted in some anonymous treatises before it lost any importance in the first half of the thirteenth/nineteenth century. It was superseded by a "modern" theory recorded by Muḥammad al-ʿAṭṭār and his successors (see below).

The comparatively modest and provincial tradition of the *ṭubūʿ* in North Africa is also documented in a series of datable texts. The following titles may give an idea of the history of Maghribī music theory.

1. A didactic poem on the modes (*ṭubūʿ*) and their relation to the four humors, written by ʿAbd al-Wāḥid ibn Aḥmad **al-Wansharīsī** (d. 955/1548) from Fes (edited and translated).
2. *Kitāb al-Jumūʿ fī ʿilm al-mūsīqā wa ʾl-ṭubūʿ*, another didactic poem, composed by **Abū Zayd** ʿAbd al-Raḥmān ibn ʿAbd al-Qādir **al-Fāsī** al-Fihrī al-Mālikī (d. 1096/1685). It is partly edited and translated into English.
3. *Īqād al-shumūʿ li-ladhdhat al-masmūʿ bi-naghamāt al-ṭubūʿ* by Muḥammad **al-Būʿiṣāmī** (c. 1100/1700). It was recently edited from a manuscript in Rabat. The author reproduces an older, anonymous treatise (*Maʿrifat al-naghamāt al-thamān*), which was edited and translated by H. G. Farmer in *An Old Moorish Lute Tutor* (1933).
4. The introduction to the best-known collection of *nūba* (*nawba*) texts called *Kunnāsh al-Ḥāʾik* (late twelfth/eighteenth century).
5. *Qānūn al-asfiyāʾ fī ʿilm naghamāt al-adhkiyāʾ* by Muḥammad ibn Muḥammad al-Ṣafāqusī al-Qādirī, known as **Siyāla** (d. after 1285/1868). Mss. Baghdad, Tunis.
6. *Aghānī al-sīqā wa maʿānī al-mūsīqā*, or *al-Irtifāʿ ilā ʿulūm al-mūsīqā*, written in 1307/1890 by Ibrāhīm ibn Muḥammad **al-Tādilī** al-Ribāṭī. Mss. Rabat, Casablanca.

It is hoped that the Eastern as well as the Western Arabic texts which are still in manuscript form will find editors and translators to improve our knowledge of the local movements, developments, and periods of stagnation in Arab music history.

THE SCIENCE OF MUSIC: *MŪSĪQĪ* IN PHILOSOPHICAL CONTEXTS

In the Hellenistic period, the four "mathematical" sciences—arithmetic, music theory, geometry, and astronomy—were joined to the traditional canon of Aristotle's philosophical works, in order to complement the curriculum of philosophical studies. Consequently, when an interest in philosophy arose in the young Muslim society, music theory was found among these "foreign" philosophical disciplines, and it was introduced into the growing body of Arabic encyclopedic works and books on the enumeration and classification of the sciences (Reinert 1990; Werner 1965). Some of the latter works were translated, in medieval or modern times, into Western languages. These are the *Iḥṣāʾ al-ʿulūm* of al-Fārābī (d. 339/950), which was intended to work out the structure of the sciences; the celebrated *Rasāʾil* 'Epistles' of the Ikhwān al-Ṣafāʾ 'Brethren of Purity' from the second half of the fourth/tenth century; the scientific dictionary *Mafātīḥ al-ʿulūm* of Muḥammad ibn Aḥmad al-Khwārazmī (late fourth/tenth century); Avicenna's (Ibn Sīnā, d. 428/1037) encyclopedic works *Kitāb al-Shifāʾ* and *Kitāb al-Najāt*, with their extensive chapters on music theory; and the *Irshād al-qāṣid* of Ibn al-Akfānī (d. 749/1348), which gives a concise description of all aspects of the science of music, including bibliographic references supplied by the author. This genre of literature, which continued to exist up to the eleventh/seventeenth century in Ottoman Turkey, provides a great variety of definitions and descriptions of music, and of its branches and terms.

The literary basis of the "foreign" science of music consisted of translations from Greek. An early text that has survived in different redactions is a collection of sayings about music ascribed to Greek and Byzantine philosophers. It was attributed to someone called Būlus (Paulus); translated by Ḥunayn ibn Isḥāq (d. 260/873); propagated in the writings of al-Kindī (d. c. 252/866), the Ikhwān al-Ṣafā', and others (Rosenthal 1966; Shiloah 1979, nos. 28, 78); and relatively recently edited and interpreted (Kazemi 1999). Originating in about the same period was the translation of the *Sectio canonis*, ascribed to Euclid (Mss. Rampur; Teheran; Sezgin 1974:400), which became the *locus classicus* of Arabic mathematical music theory.

However, the first scholar of like leanings to profit from this and other products of classical and later Greek music literature was Abū Naṣr al-Fārābī (d. 339/950). His predecessor al-Kindī had produced a diffuse blend of Oriental, Byzantine, and contemporary Arabic sources, all of which he considered "Greek." The surviving part of his work is a mine of information still to be extracted from the ore and will be of great importance to future research on late antique and early Arab music theory.

The Brethren of Purity, Ikhwān al-Ṣafā' (fourth/tenth century), who relied on sources similar to al-Kindī's, subordinated musical science to a general esoteric concept. Not being especially interested in assimilating contemporary musical research, they favored the idea of the harmony of the spheres and concentrated on proportion, harmony, and topics of a symbolic nature.

In sharp contrast is al-Fārābī's *Kitāb al-mūsīqī al-kabīr* 'Grand Book on Music', which is not only the most extensive but the most important book on this subject written in Arabic. With his broad knowledge, thorough method, and critical respect for his predecessors, al-Fārābī is an exemplary scholar. Trained in the tradition of Greek philosophy and science, he describes the musical reality of his time (tonal system, metrics, composition, and instruments) in order to detect its constructive elements and build up a systematic music theory of general validity. He was the first to define the neutral or middle third, which is the constitutive element of the *rāst* scale, the basic scale of Arab music. A lost part of his book was devoted to, or intended as, a critical history of music theory.

Among the "ancient" writers on music known to the Arabs, the names of Euclid, Pythagoras, Ptolemy, Nicomachos of Gerasa, and Aristoxenos were the most prominent apart from Plato and Aristotle (Farmer 1929–1930). Al-Fārābī quotes Ptolemy, Themistios, and Aristotle while discussing the delicate question of how musical a musicologist ought to be.

Controversial questions were discussed between *aṣḥāb al-mūsīqī* 'advocates of Greek music theory' and *aṣḥāb al-ghinā' al-'arabī* 'advocates of Arab music'—these discussions were analogous to the contests on logical questions held by advocates of Greek philosophy and advocates of Arab grammar. Thābit ibn Qurra (d. 288/901), from the old scholarly center of Ḥarrān in Northern Mesopotamia, who preceded al-Fārābī in systematizing the sciences and in writing an extensive (lost) *Kitāb al-mūsīqī* 'Book on Music', is reported to have collected the results of such discussions as well as the answers to *masā'il* 'musical problems' addressed to himself, in another book (also lost). Only one of these musical problems has come down to us. It is a reply to a question raised by the father of the aforementioned Ibn al-Munajjim regarding the doubling at the octave in singing and instrumental accompaniment. *Organon* techniques using consonant intervals had already been touched on by al-Kindī and were later on treated by Ibn Sīnā.

Ibn Sīnā (d. 428/1037), referred to as Avicenna in the Latin West, discusses basically the same subjects as al-Fārābī in his encyclopedias—*Kitāb al-Shifā'* and *Kitāb al-Najāt*— but he took a different approach and sometimes reached different conclusions, especially in his treatment of musical metrics (*īqā'*), where he favors a theoretical system derived from (Greek and Arabic) poetical metrics. Regarding musical practice, he prefers the basic patterns (*ajnās*) known from Isḥāq al-Mawṣilī to those given by al-Fārābī. Of great interest is his treatment of embellishments in the composition of melodies, a complement to the texts of al-Fārābī and Ibn Sīnā's disciple Ibn Zayla (d. 440/1048), who also left a useful treatise on music theory and practice.

After a longish gap for which we have no information, we suddenly find the results of two centuries of further evolution in two works: *Kitāb al-adwār* and *al-Risāla al-sharafiyya* of Ṣafī al-Dīn al-Urmawī (d. 693/1294). Basing his methodology on al-Fārābī, Ibn Sīnā, and other unnamed predecessors, al-Urmawī treats a "modern" system of twelve modes and the contemporary meters so as to combine *'ilm* 'theoretical knowledge' with *'amal* 'practical experience'. He is celebrated for having first described the octave of seventeen degrees with its "Persian" *rāst* scale (using the Pythagorean diminished fourth of 384 cents in the position of the third, called *wusṭā Zalzal*), in contrast to the "Arab" *rāst* scale of al-Fārābī (with the neutral or middle third of 355 cents in the same position). In defining the characteristic degree of the *rāst* scale, which he had obviously adapted from the (Persian) long-necked lute to the short-necked lute, he unconsciously introduced what we today call a schismatic substitution (of the natural major third of 386 cents by the Pythagorean diminished fourth of 384 cents, the 2 cents in between being called *schisma*, which is the difference between the Pythagorean *comma* of 24 cents and the *comma* of Didymos of 22 cents; Manik 1969:88–92).

Al-Urmawī's teachings survived in the writings of his successors, who wrote their extant works in Persian, as well as in some translations of and commentaries on his own work. The scientific approach to music was revived in the Arabic-speaking world with the formulation of a quarter-tone system (see the treatise by Muḥammad al-'Aṭṭār, 1243/1828, discussed in Shiloah 1979, no. 16; and a more detailed presentation in *al-Risāla al-shihābiyya* by his disciple, Mīkhā'īl Mushāqa, d. 1305/1888, discussed in Marcus 1989). In these attempts the heritage of al-Fārābī was brought into contact with ideas borrowed from modern Europe.

SONG COLLECTIONS AND BIOGRAPHICAL LITERATURE

When Yūnus al-Kātib (d. c. 147/765), a scribe and musician of Persian origin who lived in Medina, put together the first known Arabic *Kitāb fī 'l-aghānī* 'Book of Songs', he succeeded in assembling 825 song texts from compositions of thirty-eight previous and contemporary male and female musicians. The book was a great success and left traces in later song collections. Yūnus al-Kātib also wrote a *Kitāb al-qiyān* on the lives of famous songstresses. Both kinds of anthological compilations, the collecting of songs (*aghānī*) and the collecting of biographies (*akhbār*), developed rapidly from the early third/ninth century on and led to an astonishingly broad literature. We know of many titles of monographic and collective biographical works and of song collections, some of the latter being provided with musical indications as to the melodic mode and meter of the songs and biographical data about the composers. The collection made by the songstress Badhl (fl. 195/810), for example, is said to have contained 12,000 song texts with the names of their composers, though with no indication of their modes. This and all the other early collections and biographical works are lost, with the exception of a book on the historical "stages" or "levels" of the composer-musicians (*Kitāb ṭabaqāt al-mughannīn*) written by the versatile *littérateur* and scholar Ibn Khurradādhbih (d. 300/911).

Many of the lost *aghānī* and *akhbār* books, however, were incorporated later into the *Kitāb al-aghānī al-kabīr* 'Grand Book of Songs', compiled by Abū 'l-Faraj al-Iṣbahānī (d. 356/967). They could even be reconstructed, to a certain extent, from quotations in the *Kitāb al-aghānī*. This outstanding cultural document, consisting of more than twenty printed volumes, is a unique mine of information not only on hundreds of song texts with their modes and meters, but also on the lives of their poets and composers, and on the social context of music making in early Islam and at the courts of the caliphs in Damascus and Baghdad. [See *Kitāb al-Aghānī*.]

A century later, al-Iṣbahānī found a successor in Ibn Nāqiyā (d. 485/1092), who compiled a supplement to the *Kitāb al-aghānī* under the title *Kitāb al-muḥdath fī 'l-aghānī* 'The Renewed Book of Songs'. Though not preserved in full, this book was excerpted by Ibn Faḍl Allāh al-'Umarī (d. 749/1349) in the volume on musicians in his encyclopedic *Masālik al-abṣār fī mamālik al-amṣār*. Ibn Faḍl Allāh's book is our principal source for the music history of the later 'Abbāsid and the Mongol periods in the East, and of Egypt and the Islamic West.

The eastern tradition of songbooks was also introduced into Muslim Spain. Singing girls from twelfth- and thirteenth-century Seville were not sold, as Aḥmad ibn Yūsuf al-Tīfāshī (d. 651/1253) relates, unless they had with them "a book (*daftar*) containing every song they knew" (Ṭanjī 1968:103). A small collection of early "Andalusian" song texts, together with the names of their composers and modes, has survived in al-Tīfāshī's extraordinary work on Arab music in the West, entitled *Mut'at al-asmā' fī 'ilm al-samā'*.

Both the eastern and the western repertoires of medieval Arab music consisted mainly of "compositions" by individual musicians. The songs, whether performed separately or in a *nawba* 'suite' (al Faruqi 1985), were considered their "work" and were transmitted as such in the song collections. This tradition continued after the fall of Baghdad (656/1258) in the cultural centers of Iran and, later on, in Turkey. In Iran it can be traced to the end of the Safavid era (early twelfth/eighteenth century); in Ottoman Turkey the genre of song collections flourished under the name of *sarki mecmuasi* into the nineteenth century, when it changed from handwritten collections to printed books.

On the Arab side, the growing predilection for the *muwashshaḥ* and other popular forms led, from the seventh/thirteenth century on, to new kinds of songbooks. Collections of the verses of *muwashshaḥ* and *zajal* poets like those of Ibn Sanā' al-Mulk (d. 608/1211) or al-Shushtarī (m. 668/1269) were primarily collections of song texts. Some of these collections, such as the *Dīwān* of the poet Abū 'l-Mawāhib al-Tūnisī (d. 882/1477; Farmer 1965, no. 316), contained musical indications. Others consisted of mostly anonymous anthologies of poetry assembled alphabetically, according to their poetical form (*muwashshaḥ*, *zajal*, *mawwāl*, *dūbayt*, and so on) or according to musical forms (such as *dawr*, *shughl*, and *naqsh*). Most of the later comprehensive anthologies are arranged by mode (*maqām*; listed by *nawba* or *waṣla*). From the Syrian and Egyptian repertoire, the following may be mentioned (Neubauer 2000):

1. Two anonymous collections, originating from the tenth/sixteenth and eleventh/seventeenth centuries, preserved in Munich (Shiloah 1979, nos. 292, 293). One contains 492 song texts (with 409 modal and 417 metrical indications) and the other 328 song texts (227 modal and a few metrical indications), arranged for the most part in alphabetical order.
2. The important collection compiled by 'Abd al-Ḥayy ibn Muḥammad al-Ṭāluwī al-Dimashqī al-Ḥanafī, known as **(Ibn) al-Khāl** or **Ibn al-Ṭawīl** (d. 1117/1705), preserved in Berlin (Shiloah 1979, no. 121): 698 song texts (597 modal and 618 metrical indications), arranged alphabetically.

3. The *Safīna* of Ḥusayn ibn Aḥmad **al-Kubaysī** al-Ḥanafī al-Shādhilī from the second half of the twelfth/eighteenth century. Mss. Berlin (Shiloah 1979, no. 158), and Damascus: 740 song texts (complete modal and 668 metrical indications), arranged in suites (*nawba*, singular) of 29 modes, some of them divided into song texts with "Turkish meters" and others with "Arabic meters."
4. An anonymous collection from the end of the twelfth/eighteenth century, preserved in Vienna (Shiloah 1979, no. 295): 334 *muwashshaḥ* song texts (293 modal, 100 metrical indications), arranged in suites of 14 modes (Manuscript is incomplete.)
5. *Safīnat al-mulk wa nafīsat al-fulk* by **Muḥammad Shihāb al-Dīn** (d. 1274/1858), lithographed in 1892: 364 *muwashshaḥ* song texts with complete modal and metrical indications, arranged in 30 suites (here, *waṣla*) and in an unusual sequence of modes (divided into 6 *uṣūl* 'roots' and 6 *furū'* 'branches'.
6. *Sulāfat al-ḥān fī 'l-alḥān*, from an anonymous compiler, 1277/1860. The autograph of about 500 pages is preserved in Damascus: 562 song texts with complete modal and metrical indications, arranged in suites of 24 modes.

In addition to these, the lives and works of twenty-six musicians from Syria in the eleventh/seventeenth and twelfth/eighteenth centuries are the subject of the (printed) book *Bulūgh al-munā fī tarājim ahl al-ghinā'*, written in rhymed prose by **Muḥammad** Efendī **al-Kanjī** (al-Ganjī) in the middle of the twelfth/eighteenth century. Some musicians of Arab origin who lived in the Ottoman capital are included in the (not yet published) Turkish book *Eṭrebü 'l āthār* by the Sheykhü 'l-islām (that is, a high-ranking religious official) and musician (!) Meḥmed **Es'ad Efendi** (d. 1166/1753). It contains the names and dates of nearly one hundred contemporary musicians who worked in the Ottoman Empire.

The nineteenth-century Syro-Egyptian movement of vocal composition is represented in two impressive collections of *qaṣīda* and *dawr* texts together with the names of their composers. Both collections were compiled by 'Abd al-Malik ibn 'Abd al-Wahhāb **al-Fattanī** al-Makkī al-Madanī (d. 1327/1909; mss., Shiloah 1979, nos. 290, 296). It was Muḥammad Kāmil **al-Khula'ī** (d. 1357/1938) who continued to collect the Egyptian repertoire in three books printed in Cairo. By contributing biographies of the composers, al-Khula'ī revitalized the old tradition of *akhbār* and *aghānī* books, and by adding photographs of the musicians and some melodies in European notation he was the first to use these "foreign" means for documenting and preserving the musical heritage.

In North Africa, the traditional "Andalusian" repertoire of *nūba* texts was collected in the *Kunnāsh al-Ḥā'ik* of Tetouan (late twelfth/eighteenth century). This rather important local collection is preserved in different versions and was printed several times. It is complemented by some undated and anonymous collections of *nūba* texts in North African and other libraries.

MUSIC AS A LEGAL AND SOCIAL PROBLEM: *SAMĀ'*

Most Arabic literature on music is devoted to the question whether or not, or to what extent, *samā'* 'listening' to music is licit for a Muslim according to the teachings of the *Qur'ān*, the sayings of the Prophet Muḥammad (*ḥadīth*), and legal practice. Secular song, instrumental music, and dance are the main points of discussion. Orthodox Sunnī Islam, represented by the law schools of the Mālikīs, Shāfi'īs, Ḥanafīs and Ḥanbalīs, as well as Shī'ī authorities share a dislike of any secular music with their Christian and Jewish paragons, and even use the same arguments, such as that music is a pagan custom or that music was invented by the devil.

Theory and practice, however, often diverged. While the pious Ibn Abī 'l-Dunyā (d. 281/894) wrote his rigid *Dhamm al-malāhī* 'Censure of Instruments of Diversion'—the earliest *samā'* text available in English translation—his disciple, the future caliph al-Mu'taḍid (d. 289/902), was composing love songs.

Reduced to the strictest position of Islamic law, only the call to prayer (*adhān*) and the chanting of the Qur'ān (*qirā'a, tajwīd*) are licit. Those with a slightly more liberal attitude tolerate religious hymns and, by interpreting certain sayings of the Prophet, allow some forms of folk music at weddings—but never the sort of music that is connected with *lahw* 'idle pleasure' and hence is capable of detracting body and soul from the proper way (Farmer 1952; al Faruqi 1982a, b; Gribetz 1991; Michot 1988; Pouzet 1983; Robson 1957; Shiloah 1997b). The Ẓāhirī theologian and well-known poet and writer Ibn Ḥazm (d. 456/1064) may have been the only jurist to defend the notion of *ghinā' mulhī* 'entertaining music'.

Ḥanbalī authorities used to be the most consequential opponents of secular and instrumental music, as seen in the extant works of Ibn al-Jawzī (d. 597/1200), Ibn Qudāma al-Maqdisī (d. 620/1223), and Ibn Qayyim al-Jawziyya (d. 751/1350). By his influence on the later Wahhābī movement, the outstanding Ḥanbalī scholar and reformer Ibn Taymiyya (d. 728/1328) initiated the austere attitude toward music that still prevails in Saudi Arabia.

In contrast to the Ḥanbalī position, Shāfi'ī views varied considerably in the course of time, and according to local circumstances. Judgments against "instruments of diversion" were expressed by authorities such as al-Ājurrī (d. 360/970), Ṭāhir ibn 'Abdallāh al-Ṭabarī (d. 450/1058; Shiloah 1979, no. 248), and Taqī al-Dīn al-Ḥiṣnī (d. 829/1426; Shiloah 1979, nos. 75–77). Ibn Ḥajar al-Haytamī (d. 974/1567) condemned the notoriously pleasure-seeking youth of Mecca, albeit with limited success, as a contemporary historian relates. In late 'Abbāsid and early Mamlūk days, however, some Shāfi'īs were rather liberal. As a result, the distinguished Shāfi'ī authority al-Nawawī (d. 677/1278) had to reject the opinion that his school favored secular music (Ms. Dublin, Chester Beatty, arab. 3296, fol. 13r). But again it was a Shāfi'ī scholar, Kamāl al-Dīn al-Adfuwī (Udfuwī, d. 748/1347) who, in his excellent book *Al-Imtā' bi-aḥkām al-samā'* 'The Benefit of Judgments on Music', turned the legal approach into a comprehensive study of all branches of vocal and instrumental music, including such topics as the technique of women's hand clapping (*tasfīq*) and its four common meters, which are rarely touched on in professional treatises on music. Al-Adfuwī draws on a great number of legal, literary, and historical sources. He even reveals to us the earliest Arabic title on music history, *Kitāb ibtidā' al-ghinā' wa 'l-'īdān* 'Book on the Beginnings of Music and Lute Playing', written by the historian Ibn al-Kalbī (d. c. 203/819). The importance of al-Adfuwī's book as a source for both music history and sociology can hardly be overestimated.

In contrast to their Christian counterparts, the leading dogmatists and jurists of Sunnī as well as Shī'ī Islam never attempted to "de-demonize" instrumental music or to integrate it into the services at mosques. The only group to do this were the Ṣūfīs, the Islamic mystics. They introduced instruments and even dancing (*raqṣ*) into their worship. As a result, Ṣūfī writers from North Africa to India argued for their understanding of religious music and were attacked, again and again, by advocates of the orthodox view. Among the many extant Ṣūfī writings on music, those of the following authors are available in editions: Al-Sarrāj (from Iran, d. 378/988), Abū Ṭālib al-Makkī (Iraq, d. 386/996), Abū 'Abd al-Raḥmān al-Sulamī (from Khorasan, d. 412/1021), Abū Manṣūr al-Iṣbahānī (lived in Isfahan, d. 418/1027), al-Qushayrī (Iran and Iraq, d. 465/1072), Ibn al-Qaysarānī (Palestine, Iraq, who traveled widely, d. 507/1113), Shihāb al-Dīn al-Suhrawardī (Iraq, d. 632/1234), Ibn al-'Arabī (Spain, North Africa, Syria, d. 638/1240), Abū 'l-Mawāhib al-Tūnisī (d. 882/1477), Badr al-Dīn al-Mālikī (Egypt, eleventh/seventeenth century), and 'Abd al-Ghanī al-Nābulusī (Syria and abroad, d. 1143/1731), whose book *Īḍāḥ al-dalālāt fī samā' al-ālāt* evoked several rebuttals and defenses.

An essential influence in favor of *samā'* was exerted by the celebrated theologist and philosopher Abū Ḥāmid al-Ghazālī (d. 505/1111), who had shown an inclination toward Ṣūfī ideas in the music chapter of his masterpiece *Iḥyā' 'ulūm al-dīn* 'Revival of the Religious Sciences'. At the same time, his brother, the Ṣūfī Majd al-Dīn al-Ghazālī (d. 520/1126), openly defended religious music in his *Bawāriq al-ilmā'* (both texts can be studied in English translation). The jurist Ibn al-Darrāj al-Sabtī from Ceuta in North Africa (second half of the seventh/thirteenth century) expressed himself definitely in favor of Ṣūfī music in his substantial book *Kitāb al-imtā' wa 'l-intifā' fī mas'alat samā' al-samā'*.

WRITINGS ON MUSICAL INSTRUMENTS

From the *samā'* literature, we learn about aspects of musical life that other sources rarely divulge, such as wedding and funeral customs, dance, and the use of instruments on these and other occasions. Valuable information on musical instruments is given by two of the authors noted above: Ibn al-Darrāj and Kamāl al-Dīn al-Adfuwī. They complement the literature proper, which usually approaches this subject from a philological, a historical, or a descriptive and purely organological viewpoint.

Philology and history prevail in the early *Kitāb al-malāhī wa asmā'ihā* 'Book on the Musical Instruments and Their Names' by al-Mufaḍḍal ibn Salama (d. after 290/903). Writers on music theory such as al-Kindī, al-Fārābī, Ibn Sīnā, Ibn Zayla, Ibn al-Ṭaḥḥān, al-Tīfāshī, and later Persian and Turkish authors describe the tuning or formal aspects of instruments. In one of his extant treatises, al-Kindī deals at length with the construction of the lute (Shiloah 1974). In another text, which seems to be based on a Greek model, he writes about *al-muṣawwitāt al-watariyya* 'chordophones' with one to ten strings, including some of Indian and Byzantine origin, and some instruments mentioned in the Old Testament. Ibn al-Ṭaḥḥān relates in detail how lutes were manufactured in Egypt in the fifth/eleventh century and gives advice on how to avoid imperfections in materials and construction. Unique information on the production of gut and silk strings is given in the anonymous (Persian) *Kanz al-tuḥaf* of the eighth/fourteenth century.

Three Byzantine texts on the construction of organs, ascribed to someone named Mūristus, or Mūristes, though lost in their original form, are preserved in Arabic translation, as are some treatises on the construction of mechanical instruments ascribed to Archimedes (d. 212 B.C.E.), to Heron of Alexandria (fl. 62 C.E.), and to Apollonius (d. c. 190 C.E.). Banū Mūsā ibn Shākir (third/ninth century) developed and described an automatic hydraulic organ, and al-Jazarī (early seventh/thirteenth century) left us descriptions of several devices fitted with musical instruments, such as a giant clock mounted with a military band.

The curious *Kashf al-humūm wa salwat al-maḥzūn* (eighth/fourteenth century; Shiloah 1979, no. 285) is a different kind of book on musical instruments. Its anonymous author follows an esoteric doctrine of music similar to the Ismā'īlī ideas of the Ikhwān al-Ṣafā' (fourth/tenth century). He describes the instruments as manifestations of macrocosmic and microcosmic harmony and numeric symbolism. Despite this orientation, the *Kashf al-humūm* has brought to our knowledge some firsthand information on Egyptian instruments from the Mamlūk period, such as the *jank miṣrī* 'Egyptian harp'.

The history of Arab musical instruments was investigated in particular by the late H. G. Farmer. Some of his numerous studies in both this field and the general realm of the sources of Arab music (Neubauer 1987/1988) are listed in the following bibliography.

EDITIONS OF ARABIC SOURCES

The purpose of this section is to provide a survey of editions and translations of the Arabic titles mentioned above, along with a selection of relevant studies related to them. The list is in chronological order; the symbol // separates works.

- **Abūlūniyūs al-Najjār** (Apollonius "the Carpenter", d. c. 190 C.E.): *Ṣan'at al-āla al-zamriyya*, or *Ṣan'at al-zāmir*, Mss. London, Paris, New York and Damascus (see Shiloah 1979, no. 2). German trans., see Wiedemann 1914. Ed. and English trans., see Shehadeh et al. 1994. Studies, see Hammerstein 1986; Hassan and Hill 1986.
- **Mūrisṭus,** or Mūristes (Mawristes, Mawristos, etc.): l. *Ṣan'at al-urghīn al-būqī* . . . , 2. *Ṣan'at al-urghīn al-zamrī* . . . , 3. *Ṣan'at al-juljul* . . . Ed. Louis Cheikho. 1906. "Thalāth maqālāt 'arabiyya fī 'l-ālāt al-munaghghima," *Majallat al-Mashriq* (Beirut) 9: 18–28. English trans., see Farmer 1931; German trans., see Wiedemann and Hauser 1918. Studies, see Hammerstein 1986; Hassan and Hill 1986.
- **Būlus** (Pavlos, Paulus of Aigina?): *Kitāb 'unṣur al-mūsīqī wa mā faraqat 'alayhi al-falāsifa min tarkībihi wa mā'īyatihī* (Shiloah 1979, no. 28). Ed. and German trans., see Kazemi 1999. Study, see Rosenthal 1966.
- Abū Bakr Muḥammad **Ibn Sīrīn** (d. 110/728): *Muntakhab al-kalām fī tafsīr al-aḥlām* (Interpretation of Dreams), attributed to Ibn Sīrīn, compiled by al-Ḥusayn ibn Ḥasan ibn Ibrāhīm **al-Khalīlī** al-Dārī (early ninth/fifteenth c.), printed in the margin of *Ta'ṭīr al-anām* by 'Abd al-Ghanī al-Nābulusī (d. 1143/ 1731, see below). Chapter 23 on dance and singing, chapter 56 on musical instruments, vol. 2, 103, 270–273.
- Abū Yūsuf Ya'qūb ibn Isḥāq **al-Kindī** (d. c. 252/866): Ed. Zakariyyā Yūsuf. 1962. *Mu'allafāt al-Kindī al-mūsīqiyya*. Baghdad: Maṭba'at Shafīq. Suppl. 1965: *Risālat al-Kindī fī 'l-luḥūn wa 'l-nagham*. Study, see Baffioni 1984. // *Risālat al-Kindī fī Ajzā' khabariyya fī 'l-mūsīqī*. Ed. Maḥmūd Aḥmad al-Ḥifnī. N.d. Cairo: Maṭba'at al-Amīn. Ed. Zakariyyā Yūsuf, see above. English trans., see Farmer 1955–1956. // *Risālat al-Kindī fī Khubr ṣinā'at al-ta'līf*. Ed. Yūsuf Shawqī. 1969. Cairo: Dār al-Kutub. Ed. Zakariyyā Yūsuf, see above. Ed. with German trans., see Lachmann and el-Hefni 1931. Facs. ed. and English trans., see Cowl 1966. // *Mukhtaṣar al-mūsīqī fī ta'līf al-nagham wa-ṣan'at al-'ūd allafahū li-Aḥmad ibn al-Mu'taṣim (Risāla fī 'l-luḥūn wa-'l-nagham)*. Ed. Zakariyyā Yūsuf, see above. French trans., see Shiloah 1974. // *Kitāb al-muṣawwitāt al-watariyya*. Ed Zakariyyā Yūsuf, see above.
- Abū 'Uthmān 'Amr ibn Baḥr al-Baṣrī **al-Jāḥiẓ** (d. 255/868–869): *Kitāb al-Qiyān*. Ed. Joshua Finkel. 1926. In: *Thalāth rasā'il li-Abī 'Uthmān . . . al-Jāḥiẓ*. Cairo: al-Maṭba'a al-Salafiyya. Ed. 'Abd al-Sallām Muḥammad Hārūn. 1965. In: *Rasā'il al-Jāḥiẓ*. Cairo: Maktabat al-Khānjī. Vol. 2. French trans., see Pellat 1963. Ed. and English trans., see Beeston 1980. // *Ṭabaqāt al-mughannīn*, excerpt made by 'Ubayd Allāh ibn Ḥassān, latest ed. 'Abd al-Sallām Muḥammad Hārūn. 1979. In: *Rasā'il al-Jāḥiẓ*. Cairo: Maktabat al-Khānjī. Vol. 3. // *Kitāb mufākharat al-jawārī wa-'l-ghilmān*. Ed. 'Abd al-Sallām Muḥammad Hārūn. 1965. In: *Rasā'il al-Jāḥiẓ*. Cairo: Maktabat al-Khānjī. Vol. 2. // For passages on music in other works written by or attributed to al-Jāḥiẓ, see Shiloah 1979, nos. 40–48 passim.
- Pseudo **al-Jāḥiẓ:** *Kitāb al-tāj fī akhlāq al-mulūk*. Ed. Aḥmad Zakī Bāshā. 1949. Cairo: al-Maṭba'a al-Amīriyya. French trans., see Pellat 1954.
- Abū Bakr 'Abd Allāh ibn Muḥammad ibn 'Ubayd **Ibn Abī 'l-Dunyā** (d. 281/ 894): *Dhamm al-malāhī*. Ed. Hāshim Muḥammad al-Rajab. 1984. In: *Al-Mawrid* (Baghdad) 13, 4: 111–116. Ed. and English trans., see Robson 1938.

- Abū 'l-Ḥasan **Thābit ibn Qurra** al-Ḥarrānī (d. 288/901): *Mas'ala fī 'l-mūsīqī*. Ed. and French trans., see Shiloah 1971a, b.
- Abū Ṭālib **al-Mufaḍḍal ibn Salama** ibn 'Āṣim (d. after 290/903): *Kitāb al-malāhī wa asmā'ihā*. Ed. 'Abbās al-'Azzāwī. 1951. In: *Al-Mūsīqā al-'irāqiyya fī 'ahd al-mughūl wa 'l-turkumān*. Baghdād: Shirkat al-Tijāra wa 'l-Ṭibā'a al-Maḥdūda. Ed. Ṣādiq Maḥmūd al-Jumaylī. 1984. In: *Al-Mawrid* (Baghdad) 4, 3:35–64. Ed. Ghaṭṭās 'Abd al-Malik Khashaba. 1985. Cairo: Al-Hay'a al-Miṣriyya al-'Āmma li-'l-Kitāb. English trans., see Robson and Farmer 1938.
- Abū Aḥmad Yaḥyā ibn 'Alī ibn Yaḥyā **Ibn al-Munajjim** (d. 300/912): *Kitāb al-nagham*. Ed. Muḥammad Bahjat al-Atharī. 1950. In: *Majallat al-majma' al-'ilmī al-'irāqī* (Baghdad) l:113–124. Ed. Zakariyyā Yūsuf. 1964. // *Risālat Yaḥyā ibn al-Munajjim fī 'l-mūsīqī*. Cairo: Dār al-Qalam. Ed. Yūsuf Shawqī. 1976. *Risālat Ibn al-Munajjim fī 'l-mūsīqī wa kashf rumūz kitāb al-aghānī*. Cairo: Al-Hay'a al-Miṣriyya al-'Āmma li-'l-Kitāb. Ed. with Turkish trans. Ruhi Kalender, Necati Avcı. 1981. In: *Ankara Üniversitesi Ilâhiyat Fakültesi dergisi* 25:395–418. Facs. ed., German trans. and study, see Neubauer 1995–1996, 1998. Study, see Wright 1966.
- Abū 'l-Qāsim 'Ubayd Allāh ibn 'Abd Allāh **Ibn Khurradādbih** (d. 300/911): [*Kitāb ṭabaqāt al-mughannīn*:] Ed. Ighnāṭiyūs 'Abduh Khalīfa. 1961. *Mukhtār min kitāb al-lahw wa 'l-malāhī*. Beirut: Al-Maṭba'a al-Kāthūlīkiyya. Cf. al-Mas'ūdī (d. 345/956), below.
- **Banū Mūsā ibn Shākir** (third/ninth century): *al-Āla allatī tuzammir bi-nafsihā:* Ed. Louis Cheikho. 1906. In: *Majallat al-Mashriq* (Beirut) 9:444–458. German trans., see Wiedemann 1910; English trans., see Farmer 1931. Studies, see Hammerstein 1986; Hassan and Hill 1986.
- Abū 'l-Ḥasan 'Alī ibn al-Ḥasan al-Hunā'ī **Kurā' al-Naml** (d. 310/922): *al-Muntakhab min gharīb kalām al-'arab*. Ed. Muḥammad ibn Aḥmad al-'Umarī. 1409/1989. Mecca: Markaz Iḥyā' al-Turāth al-Islāmī. Chapter on musical terms, vol. 1, 243–247.
- Abū 'l-Ṭayyib Muḥammad ibn Isḥāq ibn Yaḥyā **al-Washshā'** (d. c. 325/937): *al-Kitāb al-muwashshā*. Several editions. German trans. of the music chapters, see Bellmann 1984.
- Abū 'Umar Aḥmad ibn Muḥammad **Ibn 'Abd Rabbih** (d. 328/940): *Kitāb al-'iqd (al-farīd)*. Ed. Aḥmad Amīn et al. 7 vols. 1940–1953. Cairo: Lajnat al-Ta'līf wa 'l-tarjama wa 'l-Nashr. Music chapter, vol. 6 (1949), 3–81. English trans., see Farmer 1942.
- Abū Naṣr Muḥammad ibn Muḥammad ibn Ṭarkhān **al-Fārābī** (d. 339/950): *Iḥṣā' al-'ulūm*. Ed. and English trans. of the music section, see Farmer 1934. Studies, see Beichert 1931; Randel 1976. // *Kitāb al-mūsīqī al-kabīr*. Ed. Ghaṭṭās 'Abd al-Malik Khashaba, Maḥmūd Aḥmad al-Ḥifnī. [1967.] Cairo: Dār al-Kātib al-'Arabī. Facs. ed. 1998. Frankfurt: Institute for the History of Arabic-Islamic Science. French trans., see d'Erlanger 1930, 1935. Partial translations, studies, see Chabrier 1985; Dzhanybekov 1974; Haas 1989; Land 1885; Matyakubov 1986; Mokri 1995; Reinert 1979; Sawa 1982, 1989, 1990; Shiloah 1979, sub no. 57; Zemcovskij 1987. // *Kitāb al-īqā'āt*. German trans., see Neubauer 1968–1969. Facs. ed., see Neubauer 1998. // *Kitāb fī iḥṣā' aṣnāf al-īqā'āt*. German trans., see Neubauer, 1994. Facs. ed., see Neubauer, 1998. Studies, see Nazarov 1995; Sawa 1983–1984, 1989.
- Abū 'l-Ḥasan 'Alī ibn al-Ḥusayn **al-Mas'ūdī** (d. 345/956): *Murūj al-dhahab wa ma'ādin al-jawhar*. Several editions. Ed. with French trans. A. C. Barbier de Meynard, Pavet de Courteille. 1861–1877. *Maçoudi. Les prairies d'or*. 7 vols. Paris: Imprimerie Nationale. Revised by Charles Pellat, text Beirut 1966–1974,

trans. Paris 1962–1971. Contains (vol. 8:88–103) two lectures on music history, theory, and dance of which the first was given by Ibn Khurradādhbih (see above) at the Baghdad court of al-Muʿtamid. Separate ed. ʿAbbās al-ʿAzzāwī. 1951. In: *Al-Mūsīqā al-ʿirāqiyya fī ʿahd al-mughūl wa ʾl-turkumān.* Baghdad: Shirkat al-Tijāra wa ʾl-Ṭibāʿa al-Maḥdūda. Studies, see Farmer 1928; Shiloah 1962.

- Abū ʾl-Faraj ʿAlī ibn al-Ḥusayn **al-Iṣbahānī** (d. 356/967): *Kitāb al-aghānī al-kabīr.* Ed. in 24 vols. 1927–1974. Cairo: Dār al-Kutub al-Miṣriyya. Partial trans., paraphr., see Berque 1995; Caussin de Perceval 1873; Christianowitsch 1863; Huart 1884. Studies on musical topics, see Farmer 1953–1954; Kilpatrick 1997, 1998, 1999; Rowson 1991; Sawa 1984, 1985, 1989; Stigelbauer 1975. See Shiloah 1979, no. 156. // *Kitāb al-qiyān.* Compiled from quotations about female singers going back to Abū ʾl-Faraj, by Jalīl al-ʿAṭiyya. 1989. London: Riad El-Rayyes.
- Abū Bakr Muḥammad ibn al-Ḥusayn **al-Ājurrī** (d. 360/970): *Taḥrīm al-nard wa ʾl-shaṭranj wa ʾl-malāhī.* Ed. Muḥammad Saʿīd ʿUmar Idrīs. 1984. [Riyadh:] Dār Iḥyāʾ al-Sunna al-Nabawiyya.
- Abū Naṣr ʿAbd Allāh ibn ʿAlī **al-Sarrāj** (d. 378/988): *Kitāb al-lumaʿ.* Ed. Reynold A. Nicholson. 1915. Leiden: Brill; London: Luzac. Chapter on music (*Kitāb al-samāʿ*), pp. 267–300. Ed. ʿAbd al-Ḥalīm Maḥmūd, Ṭāhā ʿAbd al-Bāqī Surūr. 1960. Cairo. Chapter on music (*Kitāb al-samāʿ*), pp. 338–374. German trans., see Gramlich 1990.
- Abū Bakr Muḥammad ibn Isḥāq ibn Ibrāhīm **al-Kalābādhī** al-Ḥanafī (d. 380/990 or later): *al-Taʿarruf li-madhhab ahl al-taṣawwuf* (Shiloah 1979, no. 161; Mss. and commentaries, see F. Sezgin, *Geschichte des arabischen Schriftitums*, Leiden: Brill 1967, vol. 1:668–670). Several editions, chapter 75 on *samāʿ*. English trans., see Arberry 1935.
- Abū ʾl-Faraj Muḥammad ibn Isḥāq **Ibn al-Nadīm** al-Warrāq al-Baghdādī (d. c. 385/995): *al-Fihrist.* Ed. Gustav Flügel. 1871–72. Leipzig: Vogel. English trans. of the chapter on music literature, see Farmer 1959–61.
- **Abū Ṭālib** Muḥammad ibn ʿAlī al-Ḥārithī **al-Makkī** (d. 386/998): *Qūt al-qulūb.* Printed several times in Egypt (*samāʿ* chapter missing, see Shiloah 1979, no. 189). German trans. of the chapter on *samāʿ* (part 2, chap. 32), see Gramlich 1994.
- **Ikhwān al-Ṣafāʾ** wa Khullān al-Wafāʾ (second half fourth/tenth century): *Rasāʾil.* Ed. Khayr al-Dīn al-Ziriklī. 1928. Cairo (4 vols.). Music chapter, vol. 1:132–180. Reprint 1999. Frankfurt: Institute for the History of Arabic-Islamic Science (Islamic Philosophy, vol. 26). Ed. 1957. Beirut: Dār Ṣādir, Dār Bayrūt (4 vols.). Music chapter, vol. l:183–241. German trans., see Dieterici 1865; French trans., see Shiloah 1964–1966. English trans., see Shiloah 1978a, b. Study, see Żerańska 1972.
- Abū ʿAbd Allāh Muḥammad ibn Aḥmad **al-Khwārazmī** (late fourth/tenth century): *Mafātīḥ al-ʿulūm.* Ed. Gerlof van Vloten. 1895. *Liber mafâtîh al-olûm* . . . Leiden: Brill. Reprint Leiden 1968. Music chapter, pp. 235–246. English trans., see Farmer 1957–58; German trans., see Wiedemann and Müller 1922–1923.
- **Abū ʾl-Muṭahhar** Muḥammad ibn Aḥmad **al-Azdī** (ca. 400/1000?): *Ḥikāyat Abī ʾl-Qāsim al-Baghdādī.* Ed. Adam Mez. 1902. Heidelberg: Carl Winter. Music, passim; on the effect of music, pp. 77–88 (corresponds with Abū Ḥayyān's *Kitāb al-imtāʿ*, see below).
- **Abū Hilāl** al-Ḥasan ibn ʿAbd Allāh ibn Sahl **al-ʿAskarī** (d. after 400/1000): *Kitāb al-talkhīṣ fī maʿrifat asmāʾ al-ashyāʾ.* Ed. ʿIzzat Ḥasan. 1389/1969. Damascus: Majmaʿ al-Lugha al-ʿArabiyya. Chapter 39 on musical instruments, vol. 2, 716–718. // *Kitāb al-awāʾil.* Ed. Muḥammad al-Miṣrī, Walīd Qaṣṣāb.

1975. Damascus: Wizārat al-Thaqāfa wa 'l-Irshād al-Qawmī. 2 vols. On "inventors" of arts, musical activities, passim.

- **al-Ḥasan ibn Aḥmad ibn 'Alī al-Kātib** (early fifth/eleventh century): *Kamāl adab al-ghinā'.* Ed. Zakariyyā Yūsuf. 1973. In: *Al-Mawrid* (Baghdad) 2, 2:101–154. Ed. Ghaṭṭās 'Abd al-Malik Khashaba, Maḥmūd Aḥmad al-Ḥifnī. 1975. Cairo: Al-Hay'a al-Miṣriyya al-'Āmma li 'l-Kitāb. French trans., see Shiloah 1972a.
- **Abū 'Abd al-Raḥmān** Muḥammad ibn al-Ḥusayn ibn Muḥammad **al-Sulamī** al-Nīshābūrī (d. 412/1021): *Kitāb al-samā'.* Ed. Naṣr Allāh Pūrjawādī. 1367sh./1988. In: *Ma'ārif* (Teheran) 5, 3:22–30, 40–72. Study, see Pourjavady 1990.
- **Abū Ḥayyān** 'Alī ibn Muḥammad ibn al-'Abbās al-Tawḥīdī (d. 414/1023): *Kitāb al-imtā' wa 'l-mu'ānasa*. Ed. Aḥmad Amīn, Aḥmad al-Zayn. 1939–1944. Cairo. Beginning of part 3, on the effect of music, vol. 2:165–183 (corresponds with Abū 'l-Muṭahhar al-Azdī's *Ḥikāyat Abī 'l-Qāsim*, see above). // *al-Muqābasāt*. Ed. Muḥammad Tawfīq Ḥusayn. 1970. Baghdad: Maṭba'at al-Irshād. Chapter 19 on natural gift (*ṭabī'a*) and craftsmanship (*ṣinā'a*) in music, pp. 112–115. // *al-Hawāmil wa 'l-shawāmil li-Abī Ḥayyān al-Tawḥīdī wa-Miskawayh*. Ed. Aḥmad Amīn, Aḥmad Ṣaqr. 1370/1951. Cairo: Lajnat al-Ta'līf wa 'l-Tarjama wa 'l-Nashr. Question no. 61 (pp. 162–164): what is superior, singing or the playing of instruments; question no. 155 (pp. 335–337), on the effect of music.
- **Abū Manṣūr** Ma'mar ibn Aḥmad ibn Muḥammad ibn Ziyād al-Iṣbahānī (d. 418/1027): *Kitāb adab al-mulūk*. Chapter on "Listening to Music According to the Sufis" (*bāb samā' al-ṣūfiyya*), ed. Naṣr Allāh Pūrjawādī. 1367sh./1988. In: *Ma'ārif* (Teheran) 5, 3:30–50, 73–78. Study, see Pourjavady 1990.
- Abū 'l-Faraj 'Alī ibn al-Ḥusayn ibn Muḥammad **Ibn Hindū** (d. 420/1029 or 410/1019): *Miftāḥ al-ṭibb*. Chapter 8 on medicine and music, facs. ed. and trans. Shiloah 1972b.
- Abū 'Alī al-Ḥusayn ibn 'Abd Allāh **Ibn Sīnā** (Avicenna) (d. 428/1037): *Kitāb al-shifā'.* Ed. Zakariyyā Yūsuf. 1956. *Al-Shifā'. Al-Riyāḍiyyāt. 3—Jawāmi' 'ilm al-mūsīqī*. Cairo: Al-Maṭba'a al-Amīriyya. Ed. and study, see El-Tawil 1992. French trans., see d'Erlanger 1935. Studies, see Cruz Hernández 1981; Dzhumaev 1980a, b, 1984; Farmer 1937; Gulisaschwili 1967; Nazarov 1995; Nizamov 1980. // *Kitāb al-najāt,* Ed. and German trans. of the music chapter, see Hefny 1931. Ed. and study, see El-Tawil 1992.
- Abū Manṣūr 'Abd al-Malik ibn Muḥammad ibn Ismā'īl **al-Tha'ālibī** (d. 429/1038): *Kitāb laṭā'if al-ẓurafā' min ṭabaqāt al-fuḍalā'.* Facs. ed. Qāsim al-Sāmarrā'ī. 1978. Leiden: Brill. Chapters 8 and 9 on male and female singers. // *al-Tamthīl wa 'l-muḥāḍara*. Ed. 'Abd al-Fattāḥ Muḥammad al-Ḥilw. 1381/1961. Cairo: 'Īsā al-Bābī al-Ḥalabī. Chapter on metaphorical and proverbial sayings about music and musicians, pp. 207–209.
- Abū Manṣūr al-Ḥusayn ibn Muḥammad ibn 'Umar **Ibn Zayla** (d. 440/1048): *al-Kāfī fī 'l-mūsīqī*. Ed. Zakariyyā Yūsuf. 1964 Cairo: Dār al-Qalam.
- Abū 'l-Ḥusayn **Hilāl** ibn al-Muḥassin ibn Ibrāhīm **al-Ṣābi'** (d. 448/1056): *Rusūm dār al-khilāfa*. Ed. Mīkhā'īl 'Awwād. 1383/1964. Baghdad: Maṭba'at al-'Ānī. Chapter 16 on the use of drums at times of prayer, pp. 136–137. English trans., see Salem 1977.
- Abū 'l-Ḥusayn Muḥammad ibn al-Ḥasan **Ibn al-Ṭaḥḥān** al-Mūsīqī (d. after 449/1057): *Ḥāwī al-funūn wa salwat al-maḥzūn*. Facs. ed. 1990. Frankfurt: Institute for the History of Arabic-Islamic Science.
- Abū Muḥammad 'Alī ibn Aḥmad ibn Sa'īd **Ibn Ḥazm** al-Qurṭubī al-Andalusī al-Ẓāhirī (d. 456/1064): *Risāla fī 'l-ghinā' al-mulhī a mubāḥ huwa am maḥ-*

ẓūr. Ed. Iḥsān Rashīd ʿAbbās. [1956.] In: *Rasāʾil Ibn Ḥazm al-Andalusī*. Cairo: Al-Khānjī. Catalan trans., see Terés 1971.

- Abū ʾl-Ḥasan al-Mukhtār ibn al-Ḥasan ibn ʿAbdūn **Ibn Buṭlān** al-Baghdādī al-Mutaṭabbib (d. 458/1066): *Risāla jāmiʿa li-funūn nāfiʿa fī shirā al-raqīq wa-taqlīb al-ʿabīd*. Ed. ʿAbd al-Salām Hārūn. 1370/1951. In: *Nawādir al-makhṭūṭāt*. Cairo: Lajnat al-Taʾlīf wa ʾl-Tarjama wa ʾl-Nashr. Vol.1:352–389, esp. 372ff., 385ff. on the musical qualities and deficiencies of slaves and slave girls. Study, see Müller 1980.
- Abū ʾl-Ḥasan ʿAlī (ibn Aḥmad) ibn Ismāʿīl **Ibn Sīda** (d. 458/1066): *Kitāb al-mukhaṣṣaṣ* (17 parts). Ed. Maḥmūd al-Shanqīṭī et al. 1316/1898–1321/1903. Būlāq. Chapters on musical terms, part 13, pp. 9–16.
- Abū ʾl-Qāsim ʿAbd al-Karīm ibn Hawāzin **al-Qushayrī** (d. 465/1072): *Al-Risāla al-Qushayriyya*. Printed several times. German trans. of the *samāʿ* chapter, see Gramlich 1989. // *Kitāb al-samāʿ*. Ed. Pīr Muḥammad Ḥasan. 1964. In: *Al-Rasāʾil al-Qushayriyya*. Karachi.
- Abū Ḥafṣ ʿUmar ibn Khalaf **Ibn Makkī al-Ṣaqallī** (d. 501/1107): *Tathqīf al-lisān wa talqīḥ al-janān*. Ed. ʿAbd al-ʿAzīz Maṭar. 1386/1966. Cairo: Lajnat Iḥyāʾ al-Turāth al-Islāmī. Chapter 40 on errors in the Arabic language made by musicians, mainly in song texts, pp. 274–281.
- Abū Ḥāmid Muḥammad ibn Muḥammad al-Ṭūsī **al-Ghazālī** (d. 505/1111): *Iḥyāʾ ʿulūm al-dīn*. Printed several times. English trans. of the chapter on *samāʿ*, see Macdonald 1901–1902. Studies, see al Faruqi 1982; Michot 1988.
- Abū ʾl-Faḍl Muḥammad ibn Ṭāhir ibn ʿAlī al-Maqdisī **Ibn al-Qaysarānī** (d. 507/1113): *Kitāb al-samāʿ* (MS Cairo, Azhar). Ed. Abū ʾl-Wafāʾ al-Marāghī. 1970. Cairo: Lajnat Iḥyāʾ al-Turāth al-Islāmī.
- Abū ʾl-Fatḥ **ʿUmar** ibn Ibrāhīm **al-Khayyāmī** (ʿOmar Khayyām, d. 515–516/1122): *al-Qawl ʿalā ajnās alladhī bi-ʾl-arbaʿa* (Ms. Manisa, Turkey, see Shiloah 1971). Ed., Persian trans., and study, Ṣafūrā Hūshyār, Muḥammad Bāqirī. 1376/1997. "Risālah-i Khayyām az dīdʾgāh-i riyāýiyyāt," *Rahʾpūyah-i hunar* 43:43–63. Russian trans., see Rozenfelʾd and Khayretdinova 1974.
- Abū ʾl-Faḍl Aḥmad ibn Muḥammad ibn Aḥmad **al-Maydānī** al-Naysābūrī (d. 518/1124): *al-Sāmī fī ʾl-asāmī* (Arabic-Persian dictionary). Ed. Muḥammad Mūsā Hindāwī. 1967. Chapter on musical terms, pp. 172–174.
- **Majd al-Dīn** Aḥmad ibn Muḥammad al-Ṭūsī **al-Ghazālī** (d. 520/1126): *Bawāriq al-ilmāʿ fī ʾl-radd ʿalā man yuḥarrimu ʾl-samāʿ bi-ʾl-ijmāʿ*. Ed. Hāshim Muḥammad al-Rajab. 1984. In: *Al-Mawrid* (Baghdad) 13, 4:65–78. Ed. and English trans., see Robson 1938.
- Abū Bakr Muḥammad ibn al-Walīd ibn Muḥammad **al-Ṭurṭūshī** (vernacular pronunciation al-Ṭarṭūshī) al-Fihrī al-Mālikī, also known as **Ibn Abī Randaqa** (d. probably 520/1126): *Kitāb taḥrīm al-ghināʾ wa ʾl-samāʿ* (Shiloah 1979, no. 258). Ed. ʿAbd al-Majīd Turkī. 1997. Beirut: Dār al-Gharb al-Islāmī.
- Muḥammad ibn ʿAlī **al-Hindī** (fl. 529/1135). *Jumal al-falsafa*. Facs. ed. Fuat Sezgin. 1985. Frankfurt: Institute for the History of Arabic-Islamic Science. Study on the music chapter, see Neubauer 1987–1988, 1998.
- Jalāl al-Dīn ʿAbd al-Raḥmān ibn Naṣr ibn ʿAbd Allāh **al-Shayzarī** (late sixth/twelfth century): *Nihāyat al-rutba fī ṭalab al-ḥisba*. Ed. Albāz al-ʿUraynī. 1365/1946. Cairo: Lajnat al-Taʾlīf wa ʾl-Tarjama wa ʾl-Nashr. Chapters on music and musical instruments, pp. 108–113.
- ʿAbd al-Raḥmān ibn ʿAlī ibn Muḥammad **Ibn al-Jawzī** (d. 597/1200): *Talbīs iblīs*. Printed several times. English trans., see Margoliouth 1935–1938, 1945–1948.

- Abū 'l-Qāsim Hibat Allāh ibn Ja'far ibn al-Mu'tamid **Ibn Sanā' al-Mulk** (d. 608/1211): *Dār al-ṭirāz fī 'amal al-muwashshaḥāt*. Ed. Jawda al-Rikābī. 1949. Damascus. Partial Spanish trans., see García Gómez 1962.
- Badī' al-Zamān Abū 'l-'Izz Ismā'īl ibn al-Razzāz **al-Jazarī** (early seventh/thirteenth century): *Kitāb fī ma'rifat al-ḥiyal al-handasiyya*. Ed. and English trans., see Hill 1974. Partial German trans., see Wiedemann 1910b; Wiedemann and Hauser 1918.
- Muwaffaq al-Dīn Abū Muḥammad 'Abd Allāh ibn Aḥmad ibn Muḥammad **Ibn Qudāma al-Maqdisī** (d. 620/1223): *Futyā fī dhamm al-shabbāba wa-'l-raqṣ wa 'l-ghinā'*. Ed. Muḥammad ibn 'Umar Ibn 'Aqīl. 1976. Cairo: Maṭba'at al-Jabalāwī.
- **Shihāb al-Dīn** Abū Ḥafṣ 'Umar ibn Muḥammad **al-Suhrawardī** (d. 632/1234): *'Awārif al-ma'ārif*. Printed several times. German trans. of the chapters on *samā'*, see Gramlich 1978.
- Muḥyi 'l-Dīn Muḥammad ibn 'Alī ibn Muḥammad **Ibn al-'Arabī** (d. 638/1240): *al-Futūḥāt al-makkiyya fī asrār al-mālikiyya wa 'l-mulkiyya*. Ed. 'Uthmān Yaḥyā, Ibrāhīm Madkūr. 1392/1972ff. Cairo: al-Hay'a al-Miṣriyya al-'Āmma li 'l-Kitāb. Chapters 182 and 183 on *samā'*, to be expected in vol. 15, the next volume to appear. See Shiloah 1979, nos. 90–93.
- Aḥmad ibn Yūsuf **al-Tīfāshī** (d. 651/1253): *Mut'at al-asmā' fī 'ilm al-samā'*. Description of the Ms., see Qaṭṭāṭ 1987. Partial edition of the chapters on Arabic-Andalusian music, see al-Ṭanjī 1968. Trans. and studies, see Monroe 1989; Poché 1993.
- 'Alī ibn Muḥammad ibn al-Riḍā **Ibn al-Sharīf Daftarkhwān** al-Ḥusaynī al-'Ādilī (wrote his book prior to 654/1256): *Alf jāriya wa jāriya*. Partial edition in transcription with German trans., see Weil 1975–1978.
- Abū 'l-Ḥasan 'Alī ibn 'Abd Allāh al-Numayrī **al-Shushtarī** (d. 668/1269): *Dīwān*. Ed. and Spanish trans., see Corriente 1988.
- **Naṣīr al-Dīn** Muḥammad ibn Muḥammad ibn al-Ḥasan **al-Ṭūsī** (d. 672/1274): A fragment on intervals and pulse (Shiloah 1979, no. 259). Ed. Zakariyyā Yūsuf. 1964. *Risāla fī 'ilm al-mūsīqī*. Cairo: Dār al-Qalam.
- **Bahā' al-Dīn** 'Alī ibn 'Īsā ibn Abī 'l-Fatḥ **al-Munshi' al-Irbilī** (d. 692/1293): *al-Tadhkira al-fakhriyya*. Ed. Nūrī Ḥammūdī al-Qaysī, Ḥātim Ṣāliḥ al-Ḍāmin. 1404/1984. Baghdad: al-Majma' al-'Ilmī al-'Irāqī. Chapters 3 and 4 on wine, music, etc., pp. 72–382 passim.
- **Ṣafī al-Dīn** 'Abd al-Mu'min ibn Yūsuf ibn Fākhir **al-Urmawī** (vernacular spelling al-Armawī or even al-Armāwī) al-Baghdādī (d. 693/1294): *Kitāb al-adwār*. Facs. ed. Ḥusayn 'Alī Maḥfūẓ. 1961. Baghdad: Wizārat al-Irshād. Mudīriyyat al-Funūn wa 'l-Thaqāfa al-Sha'biyya. Ed. Hāshim Muḥammad al-Rajab. 1980. Baghdad: Wizārat al-Thaqāfa wa 'l-I'lām. Facs. ed. 1984. Frankfurt: Institute for the History of Arabic-Islamic Science. Ed. Ghaṭṭās 'Abd al-Malik Khashaba, Maḥmūd Aḥmad al-Ḥifnī. 1986. Cairo: Al-Hay'a al-Miṣriyya al-'Āmma li-'l-Kitāb. French trans., see d'Erlanger 1938. // *Al-Risāla al-sharafiyya fī 'l-nisab al-ta'līfiyya*. Ed. Hāshim Muḥammad al-Rajab. 1982. Baghdad: Wizārat al-Thaqāfa wa 'l-I'lām. French paraphrase, see Carra de Vaux 1891b. French trans., see d'Erlanger 1938. Studies on both works, see Chabrier 1985; Land 1922; Manik 1975, 1979; Reinert 1979; Wright 1978, 1995; further titles, see *The Encyclopaedia of Islam*, Leiden: Brill, vol. 8, 1995, 805–807.
- **Ibn al-Darrāj al-Sabtī** (second half seventh/thirteenth century): *Kitāb al-imtā' wa 'l-intifā' fī mas'alat samā' al-samā'* (wrongly attributed, in secondary literature, to the copyist, Muḥammad ibn Ibrāhīm al-Shalāḥī). Ed. Muḥammad Ibn Shaqrūn. 1982. *Ittijāhāt adabiyya wa ḥaḍāriyya fī 'aṣr Banī Marīn aw Kitāb*

al-imtāʿ. . . Rabat. Partial English trans., see Robson 1947–1953, 1952. Studies, see Farmer 1935; Odeimi 1991; Robson 1958, 1961.

- **ʿAlāʾ al-Dīn** ʿAlī ibn ʿAbd al-Karīm ibn Ṭarkhān al-Ḥamawī **al-Kaḥḥāl** (d. 720/1320): *al-Aḥkām al-nabawiyya fī ʾl-ṣināʿa al-ṭibbiyya*. Ed ʿAbd al-Salām Hāshim Ḥāfiẓ. 1374/1955. Cairo: Muṣṭafā al-Bābī al-Ḥalabī. Chapter on *samāʿ*, vol. 2, 27–32.
- Taqī al-Dīn Aḥmad ibn ʿAbd al-Ḥalīm **Ibn Taymiyya** (d. 728/1328): *Fatāwā*. Comp. and ed. ʿAbd al-Raḥmān ibn Muḥammad ibn Qāsim al-ʿĀṣimī al-Najdī. *Majmūʿ fatāwā shaykh al-islām Aḥmad ibn Taymiyya*. Reprint Riyadh 1398/1978. Legal opinions on *samāʿ* in vol. 11:295–299, 557–669 passim; see Shiloah 1979, nos. 144–147. Study, see Michot 1988. // *al-Istiqāma*. Ed. Muḥammad Rashād Sālim. 1403–04/1983–1984. 2 vols. Riad: Jāmiʿat al-Imām Muḥammad ibn Suʿūd al-Islāmiyya. Chapter on *samāʿ*, vol. 1:216–421.
- **Ibn al-Khaṭīb al-Irbilī** (fl. 729/1329): *Jawāhir al-niẓām fī maʿrifat al-anghām*. Ed. Louis Cheikho. 1913. In: *Majallat al-Mashriq* (Beirut) 16:895–901. Ed. ʿAbbās al-ʿAzzāwī. 1951. In: *Al-Mūsīqā al-ʿirāqiyya fī ʿahd al-mughūl wa ʾl-turkumān*, Baghdad: Shirkat al-Tijāra wa ʾl-Ṭibāʿa al-Maḥdūda.
- Ḍiyāʾ al-Dīn Muḥammad ibn Muḥammad ibn Aḥmad **Ibn al-Ukhuwwa** (Ibn al-Ikhwa?) al-Qurashī (d. 729/1329): *Maʿālim al-qurba fī aḥkām al-ḥisba*. Ed. and English trans. R. Levy. 1938. London: Gibb Memorial Series; ed. Muḥammad Maḥmūd Shaʿbān, Ṣiddīq Aḥmad ʿĪsā al-Muṭīʿī. 1976. Cairo: al-Hayʾa al-Miṣriyya al-ʿĀmma li-ʾl-Kitāb. Chapter on wine and musical instruments, pp. 84–91.
- Shams al-Dīn Muḥammad ibn Aḥmad ibn ʿUthmān **al-Dhahabī** al-Shāfiʿī (d. 748/1348): *al-Ṭibb al-nabawī*. Ed. Aḥmad Rifʿat al-Badrāwī. 1404/1984. Beirut: Dār Iḥyāʾ al-ʿUlūm. Chapter on *samāʿ*, 312–318.
- Kamāl al-Dīn Jaʿfar ibn Thaʿlab ibn Jaʿfar **al-Adfuwī** (vernacular pronunciation al-Udfuwī) al-Shāfiʿī (d. 749/1348 according to Ṣalāḥ al-Dīn al-Ṣafadī, *Aʿyān al-ʿaṣr*, facs. ed. Frankfurt 1990, vol. 1:297–298): *Kitāb al-imtāʿ bi-aḥkām al-samāʿ* (Shiloah 1979, no. 3). The most detailed and comprehensive text on the function of music and musical instruments in Islamic society, not edited, not translated. Study, see Guardiola 1990.
- Raḍī al-Dīn Abū ʿAbd Allāh Muḥammad ibn Ibrāhīm ibn Sāʿid **Ibn al-Akfānī** (d. 749/1348): *Irshād al-qāṣid ilā asnā ʾl-maqāṣid*. Latest ed. ʿAbd al-Laṭīf Muḥammad al-ʿAbd. 1978. Cairo: Maktabat al-Anjelo al-Miṣriyya. Ed. and French trans. of the section on music, see Shiloah 1968. German trans., see Wiedemann and Müller 1922–1923.
- Shihāb al-Dīn Aḥmad ibn Yaḥyā **Ibn Faḍl Allāh al-ʿUmarī** (d. 749/1348): *Masālik al-abṣār fī mamālik al-amṣār*. Vol. 10, on musicians. Facs. ed. 1988. Frankfurt: Institute for the History of Arabic-Islamic Science. // *al-Taʿrīf bi-ʾl-muṣṭalaḥ al-sharīf*. Ed. Muḥammad Masʿūd. 1312/1894. Cairo: Maṭbaʿat al-ʿĀṣima. Chapter on poetic descriptions of musical instruments, p. 215.
- Shams al-Dīn Muḥammad ibn Abī Bakr **Ibn Qayyim al-Jawziyya** (d. 751/1350): *Kashf al-ghiṭāʾ ʿan ḥukm samāʿ al-ghināʾ* [= *al-Kalām ʿalā masʾalat al-samāʿ*, Shiloah 1979, no. 119]. Ed. Rabīʿ ibn Aḥmad Khalaf. 1412/1992. Beirut: Dār al-Jīl.// *al-Muwāzana bayn dhawq al-samāʿ wa dhawq al-ṣalāt wa ʾl-Qurʾān*. Ed. Majdī Fatḥī al-Sayyid. 1410/1990. Ṭanṭā (Egypt): Dār al-Ṣaḥāba.
- Muḥammad ibn Muḥammad ibn Muḥammad **al-Manbijī** (fl. 775/1373): *Kitāb al-samāʿ wa l-raqṣ* [compiled from texts by Ibn Taymiyya]. Printed in Ibn Taymiyya, *Majmūʿat al-rasāʾil al-kubrā*, Cairo 1323/1905, vol. 2:277–314. French trans., see Michot 1991.

- ʿAlī ibn Muḥammad ibn Aḥmad **Ibn Suʿūd al-Khuzāʿī** (d. 789/1387): *Takhrīj al-dalālāt al-samʿiyya ʿalā mā kān fī ʿahd rasūl Allāh min al-ḥiraf wa ʾl-ṣanāʾiʿ wa ʾl-ʿamālāt*. Ed. Iḥsān ʿAbbās. 1405/1985. Beirut: Dār al-Gharb al-Islāmī. Chapter 9 on those who called out the *adhān* (call to prayer) in the Prophet Muḥammad's day, chapter 33 on singers who performed in the presence of the Prophet Muḥammad, pp. 122–128, 756–768.
- Walī al-Dīn ʿAbd al-Raḥmān ibn Muḥammad ibn Muḥammad . . . **Ibn Khaldūn** (d. 808/1406): *Muqaddimat* [*Kitāb al-ʿibar wa dīwān al-mubtadaʾ wa ʾl-khabar fī ayyām al-ʿarab wa ʾl-ʿajam wa ʾl-barbar*]. Several editions. English trans. of the chapter on music, see Rosenthal 1958. Further translations, see Shiloah 1979, no. 122.
- Bahāʾ al-Dīn Muḥammad ibn Aḥmad ibn Manṣūr **al-Ibshīhī** (vernacular spelling al-Abshīhī) (d. after 850/1446): *al-Mustaṭraf fī kull fann mustaẓraf*. Printed several times (see Shiloah 1979, no. 153), chapters 68–70 on music. French trans., see Rat 1899–1902.
- Fatḥ Allāh **al-Shirwānī** (d. c. 857/1453): *Majalla fī ʾl-mūsīqī*. Facs. ed. 1986. Frankfurt: Institute for the History of Arabic-Islamic Science.
- **Abū ʾl-Mawāhib** Muḥammad ibn Aḥmad ibn Muḥammad **al-Tūnisī** al-Shādhilī, alias **Ibn Zughdān** (Ibn Zaghdūn?, d. 882/1477): *Faraḥ al-asmāʿ bi-rukhṣ al-samāʿ*. Ed. Muḥammad al-Sharīf al-Raḥmūnī. 1985. [Tunis:] Dār al-ʿArabiyya li-ʾl-Kitāb.
- Muḥammad ibn ʿAbd al-Ḥamīd **al-Lādhiqī** (d. after 890/1485): *Al-Risāla al-fatḥiyya*. Ed. Hāshim Muḥammad al-Rajab. 1986. Kuwait: Al-Majlis al-Waṭanī li-ʾl-Thaqāfa wa ʾl-Funūn wa ʾl-Ādāb. French trans., see d'Erlanger 1939.
- Jalāl al-Dīn ʿAbd al-Raḥmān ibn Abī Bakr ibn Muḥammad **al-Suyūṭī** al-Shāfiʿī (d. 911/1505): *al-Mustaẓraf min akhbār al-jawārī*. Ed. Ṣalāh al-Dīn al-Munajjid. 1963. Beirut: Dār al-Kitāb al-Jadīd.
- Abū Muḥammad ʿAbd al-Wāḥid ibn Aḥmad ibn Yaḥyā **al-Wansharīsī** (d. 955/1548): Poem on the modes (*ṭubūʿ*) and their relation to the four humors, quoted in and edited together with the *Kunnāsh al-Ḥāʾik* (late twelfth/eighteenth c., see below). Ed. with English trans., see Farmer 1933. Study, see Valderrama 1986.
- Shihāb al-Dīn Abū ʾl-ʿAbbās Aḥmad ibn Muḥammad **Ibn Ḥajar al-Haytamī** (d. 974/1567): *Kaff al-raʿāʿ ʿan muḥarramāt al-lahw wa ʾl-samāʿ*. Printed 1980. Cairo: Dār al-Shaʿb. // *Al-Zawājir ʿan iqtirāf al-kabāʾir*. Printed several times. Last edition 1980. Cairo: Dār al-Shaʿb. Chapter on *samāʿ* pp. 649–660.
- **al-Ṣafadī** (not the well-known Ṣalāḥ al-Dīn Khalīl ibn Aybak al-Ṣafadī, d. 764/1363, but a later Syrian author, difficult to date): *Risāla fī ʿilm al-mūsīqā*. Ed. ʿAbd al-Majīd Dīyāb, Ghaṭṭās ʿAbd al-Malik Khashaba. 1411/1991. Cairo: al-Hayʾa al-Miṣriyya al-ʿĀmma li'l-Kitāb.
- ʿAbd al-Raḥmān ibn Muḥammad **Ibn al-Naqīb** al-Ḥusaynī (d. 1081/1670): *Qaṣīda fī dhikr Banī Umayya wa-Banī ʾl-ʿAbbās wa nudamāʾihim wa-arbāb al-ghināʾ min al-mashāhīr*. Ed. Khalīl Mardam. 1375/1956. "Dīwān Ibn al-Naqīb (1038–1081H)," *Majallat al-majmaʿ al-ʿilmī al-ʿarabī* 31:3–22. Commentary by Muḥammad al-Amīn ibn Faḍl Allāh al-Muḥibbī (d. 1111/1699) in his *Khulāṣat al-athar fī aʿyān al-qarn al-ḥādī ʿashar*, printed Cairo 1284/1867, vol. 2:390–404.
- **Abū Zayd** ʿAbd al-Raḥmān ibn ʿAbd al-Qādir ibn ʿAlī **al-Fāsī** al-Fihrī al-Mālikī (d. 1096/1685): *Kitāb al-jumūʿ fī ʿilm al-mūsīqā wa ʾl-ṭubūʿ*. Partial facs. ed. and English trans., see Farmer 1933.
- **Badr al-Dīn** ibn Sālim ibn Muḥammad **al-Mālikī** (eleventh/seventeenth century): *Qūt al-arwāḥ fī aḥkām al-samāʿ al-mubāḥ*. Ed. and German trans., see Schmidt-Relenberg 1986.

- Anonymous (eleventh/seventeenth or twelfth/eighteenth century): *Kitāb shajarat dhāt al-akmām al-ḥāwiya li-uṣūl al-anghām*. Ed. Ghaṭṭās 'Abd al-Malik Khashaba, Īzīs Fatḥ Allāh. 1983. Cairo: al-Hay'a al-Miṣriyya al-'Āmma li'l-Kitāb.
- Muḥammad **al-Bū'iṣāmī** (c. 1100/1700): *Īqād al-shumū' li-ladhdhat al-masmū' bi-naghamāt al-ṭubū'*. Ed. 'Abd al-'Azīz Bin 'Abd al-Jalīl. 1995. Rabat: Maṭbū'āt Akādīmiyyat al-Mamlaka al-Maghribiyya. Silsilat "al-Turāth". Same text as *Ma'rifat al-naghamāt al-thamān*, ed. and English trans. Farmer 1933.
- Muḥammad ibn Yūsuf al-Ḥalabī **al-Sāqizī** (fl. 1116/1704): *al-Muhannad al-ṣārim al-bāriq fī radd ahl al-bid'a ma'a qiyāsihim al-fāriq* [against *raqṣ* and *samā'* of the dervishes]. Study, see Vajda 1980.
- Muḥammad ibn 'Abd al-Raḥmān al-Qādirī al-Rifā'ī, known as **al-Musallam al-Mawṣilī**, or **Akhī Bābā** (fl. 1124/1712): *Al-Durr al-naqī fī 'ilm al-mūsīqī*. Ed. Jalāl al-Ḥanafī. 1964. Baghdad: Wizārat al-Thaqāfa wa 'l-Irshād.
- **'Abd al-Ghanī** ibn Ismā'īl **al-Nābulusī** al-Ḥanafī al-Qādirī al-Naqshabandī (d. 1143/1731): *Īḍāḥ al-dalālāt fī samā' al-ālāt*. Printed 1302/1885. Damascus: Al-Maṭba'a al-Ḥanafiyya. Ed. Hāshim Muḥammad al-Rajab. 1984. In: *Al-Mawrid* (Baghdad) 13, 4:79–110. // *Ta'ṭīr al-anām fī ta'bīr al-manām* (Interpretation of dreams). Printed 1316/1898. Cairo. Chapter on wine and music, vol. 1:102–103.
- **Muḥammad** Efendī **al-Kanjī** (al-Ganjī) (middle of the twelfth/eighteenth century): *Bulūgh al-munā fī tarājim ahl al-ghinā'*. Ed. 'Abd al-Ḥamīd Murād. 1988. Damascus: Dār al-Ma'rifa.
- Abū 'Abd Allāh Muḥammad ibn al-Ḥusayn al-Tiṭwānī al-Andalusī **al-Ḥā'ik** (late twelfth/eighteenth century): *Kunnāsh*. Ed. and Spanish trans. Fernando Valderrama Martínez. 1954. *El cancionero de al-Ḥā'ik*. Tetouan. Ed. 'Abd al-Laṭīf Muḥammad Bin Manṣūr. 1977. *Majmū' azjāl wa tawāshīḥ wa ash'ār al-mūsīqā al-andalusiyya al-maghribiyya al-ma'rūf bi-'l-Ḥā'ik*. Rabat. Ed. Idrīs Bin Jallūn al-Tuwaymī. [1979.] *Musta'malāt nūbāt al-ṭarab al-andalusī al-maghribī. Shi'r tawshīḥ azjāl barāwil. Dirāsa wa-tansīq wa-taṣḥīḥ Kunnāsh al-Ḥā'ik*. Casablanca: Maṭba'at al-Rāyis. Ed. Mālik Bannūna, 'Abbās al-Jirārī. 1999. *Kunnāsh al-Ḥā'ik*. Rabat: Akādīmiyyat al-Mamlaka al-Maghribiyya. Studies, see Cortés García 1993; Valderrama 1986.
- Muḥammad ibn Ismā'īl ibn 'Umar **Shihāb al-Dīn** (d. 1274/1858): *Safīnat al-mulk wa nafīsat al-fulk*. Lithogr. [1892.] Cairo.
- **Mīkhā'īl** ibn Jirjis ibn Ibrāhīm **Mushāqa** (vernacular pronounciation Mashāqa, Mishāqa, d. 1305/1888): *Al-Risāla al-shihābiyya fī 'l-ṣinā'a al-mūsīqiyya*. Ed. Louis Ronzevalle. 1899. In: *Al-Mashriq* (Beirut) 2:146–151, 218–224, 296–302, 408–415, 561–566, 629–632, 726–731, 883–890, 928–934, 1018–1026, 1073–1082, and separately Beirut: Imprimerie Catholique 1899. Ed. and French trans., see Ronzevalle 1913. English trans., see Smith 1847.
- Muḥammad Kāmil ibn Sulaymān **al-Khula'ī** (d. 1357/1938): *Nayl al-amānī fī ḍurūb al-aghānī*. N. d. [prior to 1904.] Cairo. // *Al-Mūsīqī al-sharqī*. [1904]. Cairo: Maṭba'at al-taqaddum. // *Al-Aghānī al-'aṣriyya*. Ed. Ḥusayn Ḥasanayn. 1921. Cairo: Maṭba'at al-Sa'āda.

REFERENCES

al-'Alawchī, 'Abd al-Ḥamīd. 1964. *Rā'id al-mūsīqā al-'arabiyya*. Baghdad: Wizārat al-Thaqāfa wa 'l-Irshād. Mudīriyyat al-Thaqāfa al-'Āmma.

Arberry, Arthur J., trans. 1935. *The Doctrine of the Ṣūfīs* (Kitāb al-Ta'arruf li-madhhab ahl al-taṣawwuf). Translated from the Arabic of Abū Bakr al-Kalābādhī. Cambridge: Cambridge University Press. Reprint 1977. Chapter 75 on music (*samā'*).

Baffioni, Carmela. 1984. "La scala pitagorica in al-Kindī." In *Studi in onore di Francesco Gabrieli nel suo ottantesimo compleanno*, edited by R. Traini. Rome: Università di Roma "La Sapienza," Dipartimento di Studi Orientali.

Beeston, A. F. L., ed. and trans. 1980. *The Epistle on Singing-Girls of Jāḥiẓ*. With translation and commentary. Warminster: Aris and Phillips.

Beichert, Eugen. 1931. *Die Wissenschaft der Musik bei al-Fârâbî.* Regensburg: Pustet.

Bellmann, Dieter, trans. 1984. *Ibn al-Wassā'. Das Buch des buntbestickten Kleides.* 3 vols. Leipzig, Weimar: Kiepenheuer. Chapters on music, see vol. 2:7–46, 186–190.

Berque, Jacques. 1995. *Musiques sur le fleuve. Les plus belles pages du Kitâb al-Aghânî.* Paris: Michel.

Berthier, Annie, and Amnon Shiloah. 1985. "A propos d'un 'Petit livre arabe de musique.'" Oxford, Bodleian Library, Manuscrits Turcs XLII. Paris, Bibliothèque Nationale, Arabe 2480," *Revue de musicologie* 71:164–177.

Braune, Gabriele. 1990. "Puls und Musik. Die Wirkung der griechischen Antike in arabischen medizinischen und musikalischen Traktaten." *Jahrbuch für musikalische Volks- und Völkerkunde* 14:52–67.

Bürgel, Johann Christoph. 1979. "Musicotherapy in the Islamic Middle Ages as Reflected in Medical and Other Sources." In *History and Philosophy of Science*, ed. Hakim Mohammed Said. Islamabad: Hamdard Foundation Press.

Burnett, Charles. 1993. "European Knowledge of Arabic Texts Referring to Music: Some New Material." *Early Music History* 12:1–17.

Carra de Vaux, Baron. 1891a. "Notice sur deux manuscrits arabes." *Journal Asiatique*, 8th series, 17:295–322.

———. 1891b. "Le traité des rapports musicaux ou l'Épître à Scharaf ed-Dîn, par Safi ed-Dîn 'Abd el-Mumin Albaghdâdî." *Journal Asiatique*, 8th series, 18:279–355.

Caussin de Perceval, A. 1873. "Notices anecdotiques sur les principaux musiciens arabes des trois premiers siècles de l'Islamisme." *Journal asiatique*, 7th series, 2:397–592.

Chabrier, Jean-Claude. 1985. "Éléments d'une approche comparative des échelles théoriques arabo-irano-turques." *Revue de Musicologie* 71:39–78.

———. 1996. "Musical Science." In *Encyclopedia of the History of Arabic Science*, ed. Roshdi Rashed, vol. 2. London: Routledge.

Christianowitsch, Alexandre. 1863. *Esquisse historique de la musique arabe aux temps anciens.* Cologne: Dumont-Schauberg.

Corriente, Federico, ed. and trans. 1988. *Poesía estrófica (cejeles y/o muwasshāt) atribuida al místico granadino As-Sustarī (siglo XIII d.C.). (Preedición, traducción, estudio e índices).* Madrid: Consejo Superior de Investigaciones Científicas. Instituto de Filologia. Departamento de Estudios Arabes.

Cortés García, Manuela. 1988. "Revisión de los manuscritos poético-musicales árabes, andalusíes y magrebíes de la Biblioteca Nacional de Madrid." in *IV Congreso Internacional de civilización andalusí. Universidad de El Cairo.* Cairo, pp. 95–108.

———. 1993. "Vigencia de la transmisión oral en el Kunnās al-Ḥā'ik (Cancionero de al-Ḥā'ik)," *Revista de musicología* 16:1942–1952.

———. 1995. "Nuevos datos para el estudio de la música en al-Andalus de dos autores granadinos: As-Sustarī e Ibn al-Jaṭīb." *Música oral del sur* 1:177–194.

———. 1996. "Sobre la música y sus efectos terapéuticos en la 'Epístola sobre las melodías' de Ibn Bā'a," *Revista de musicología* 19:11–23.

Cowl, Carl, trans. 1966. "The Risāla fīhübr tā'līf al-'alḥān of Ja'qūb ibn Isḥāq al-Kindī (790–874)." *Consort* 23:129–166.

Cruz Hernándes, Miguel. 1981. "La teoría musical de Ibn Sīnā en el Kitāb al-Sifā'." In *Milenario de Avicena*, ed. A. Badawi et al. Madrid: Instituto Hispano-Árabe de Cultura.

Dieterici, Friedrich. 1865. *Die Propaedeutik der Araber im zehnten Jahrhundert.* Berlin: Mittler. Reprint 1969, Hildesheim: Olms. Reprint 1999, Frankfurt: Institute for the History of Arabic-Islamic Science. Trans. of the music chapter of the Ikhwān al-Ṣafā', 100–153, 199–201.

Dzhanybekov, E. 1974. "Muzykal'naja akustika u al-Farabi." *Proceedings of the Thirteenth International Congress of the History of Science, Moscow, August 18–24, 1971*, Section 3, 177–180. Moscow: Izdatel'stvo "Nauka."

Dzhumaev, Aleksandr. 1980a. "Avicenna i muzyka." *Zvezda Vostoka* (Tashkent) 3:145–151.

———. 1980b. "Ibn Sina ob obshchestvennych funkcijach muzyki." *Obshchestvennye nauki v Uzbekistane* (Tashkent). Nos. 8–9.

———. 1984. "Muzykal'no-esteticheskie vzglyady Abu Ali Ibn Siny." *Muzyka Narodov Azii i Afriki* 4:161–178.

Ehrenkreutz, Stefan. 1980. "Medieval Arabic Music Theory and Contemporary Scholarship." *Arab Studies Quarterly* 2:249–265.

d'Erlanger, Rodolphe, trans. 1930. *La musique arabe.* Vol. 1: *Al-Fārābī: Grand traité de la musique. Kitābu l-Mūsīqī al-kabīr. Livres I et II.* Paris: Geuthner.

———, trans. 1935. *La musique arabe.* Vol. 2: *Al-Fārābī (260 H. 872 J.-C.): Livre III du Kitābu' l-mūsīqī al-kabīr et Avicenne (370/980 428/1037): Kitābu' As-Sifā' (Mathématiques, chap. XII).* Paris: Geuthner.

———, trans. 1938. *La musique arabe.* Vol. 3: *Ṣafiyu-d-Dīn al-Urmawī: I. As-Sarafiyyah ou Epître à Sarafu-d-Dīn. II. Kitāb al-Adwār ou Livre des Cycles musicaux.* Paris: Geuthner.

———, trans. 1939. *La musique arabe.* Vol. 4, second part: *Al-Lādhiqī: Traité al-Fatḥīyah (XVIe s.).* Paris: Geuthner.

Farmer, Henry George. 1928. "Ibn Khurdādhbih on Musical Instruments." *Journal of the Royal Asiatic Society*:509–518. Reprint 1997 in H. G. Farmer, *Studies in Oriental Music.*

———. 1929–1930. "Greek Theorists of Music in Arabic Translation." *Isis* 13:325–333. Reprint 1997 in H. G. Farmer, *Studies in Oriental Music.*

———. 1931. *The Organ of the Ancients. From Eastern Sources (Hebrew, Syriac, and Arabic).* London: Reeves. Reprint 1997 in H. G. Farmer, *Studies in Oriental Music.*

———, ed. and trans. 1933. *An Old Moorish Lute Tutor: Being Four Arabic Texts from Unique Manuscripts in the Biblioteca Nacional, Madrid (No. 334) and the Staatsbibliothek, Berlin (Lbg. 516).* Glasgow: Civic Press. Reprint 1997 in H. G. Farmer, *Studies in Oriental Music.*

———, ed. and trans. 1934. *Al-Fārābī's Arabic-Latin Writings on Music in the* Iḥṣā' al-'ulūm *(Escorial Library, Madrid, No. 646),* De scientiis *(British Museum, Cott. MS. Vesp. B.X., and Bibl. Nat., Paris, No. 9335), and* De ortu scientiarum *(Bibl. Nat., Paris, No. 6298, and Bodleian Library, Oxford, No. 3623), etc.* Glasgow: Civic Press. Reprint 1997 in H. G. Farmer, *Studies in Oriental Music.*

———. 1935. "A Maghribī Work on Musical Instruments." *Journal of the Royal Asiatic Society*: 339–353.

———. 1937. "The Lute Scale of Avicenna." *Journal of the Royal Asiatic Society*:117–120. Reprint 1997 in H. G. Farmer, *Studies in Oriental Music.*

———. 1941. "The Jewish Debt to Arabic Writers on Music." *Islamic Culture* 15:59–63. Reprint 1997 in H. G. Farmer, *Studies in Oriental Music.*

———, trans. 1942. *Music: The Priceless Jewel. From the "Kitāb al-'iqd al-farīd" of Ibn 'Abd Rabbihi (d. 940).* Bearsden: Author. Reprint 1997 in H. G. Farmer, *Studies in Oriental Music.*

———. 1945. *The Minstrelsy of "The Arabian Nights": A Study of Music and Musicians in the Arabic "Alf Laila wa Laila."* Bearsden: Author. Reprint 1997 in H. G. Farmer, *Studies in Oriental Music.*

———. 1952. "The Religious Music of Islām." *Journal of the Royal Asiatic Society*: 60–65. Reprint 1997 in H. G. Farmer, *Studies in Oriental Music.*

———. 1953–1954 (publ. 1955). "The Song Captions in the *Kitāb al-aghānī al-kabīr.*" *Transactions of the Glasgow University Oriental Society* 15:1–10. Reprint 1997 in H. G. Farmer, *Studies in Oriental Music.*

———, trans. 1955–1956 (publ. 1957). "Al-Kindī on the 'Ēthos' of Rhythm, Colour, and Perfume." *Transactions of the Glasgow University Oriental Society* 16:29–38. Reprint 1997 in H. G. Farmer, *Studies in Oriental Music.*

———, trans. 1957–1958 (publ. 1959). "The Science of Music in the *Mafātīḥ al-'Ulūm.*" *Transactions of the Glasgow University Oriental Society* 17:1–9. Reprint 1997 in H. G. Farmer, *Studies in Oriental Music.*

———, trans. 1959–1961. "Tenth-Century Arabic Books on Music: As Contained in 'Kitāb al-Fihrist' of Abu 'l-Faraj Muḥammad ibn al-Nadīm." *Annual of Leeds University Oriental Society* 2:37–47. Reprint 1997 in H. G. Farmer, *Studies in Oriental Music.*

———. 1965a. *The Sources of Arabian Music. An Annotated Bibliography of Arabic Manuscripts Which Deal with the Theory, Practice, and History of Arabian Music from the Eighth to the Seventeenth Century.* Leiden: Brill.

———. 1965b. "The Old Arabian Melodic Modes." *Journal of the Royal Asiatic Society*: 99–102. Reprint 1997 in H. G. Farmer, *Studies in Oriental Music.*

———. 1997. *Studies in Oriental Music.* Vol. 1: *History and Theory.* Reprint of writings published in the years 1925–1966. Vol. 2: *Instruments and Military Music.* Reprint of writings published in the years 1925–1969. Frankfurt: Institute for the History of Arabic-Islamic Science. (First published 1986.)

al Faruqi, Lois I. 1982a. "Al Ghazālī on samā'." In *Essays in Islamic and Comparative Studies: Papers presented to the Islamic Studies Group of the American Academy of Religion*, ed. Isma'il Raji al Faruqi and Abdullah Omar Nasseef. Washington, D.C.: International Institute of Islamic Thought.

———. 1982b. "The Shari'ah on Music and Musicians." In *Islamic Thought and Culture*, ed. Ismail R. al Faruqi. Herndon: International Institute of Islamic Thought.

———. 1985. "The Suite in Islamic History and Culture." *The World of Music* 27, 3:46–64.

Fischer, August. 1918. *Das Liederbuch eines marokkanischen Sängers. Nach einer in seinem Besitz befindlichen Handschrift herausgegeben, übersetzt und erläutert*. Leipzig: B. G. Teubner.

Frolova, Olga B. 1981. "Rukopis' biblioteki vostochnogo LGU [Leningrad University Library] 'Mawawil' ('Narodnye pesni')." *Pis'mennye pamjatniki Vostoka. Istoriko-filologicheskie issledovanija, 1974*, 110–136, 341–360. Moscow.

———. 1995. "Egyptian Folk Songs in the Unique Manuscripts of the Saint Petersburg University Library." *Studia Orientalia* (Helsinki) 75:87–93.

García Gómez, Emilio. 1962. "Estudio del Dār al-ṭirāz, preceptiva egipcia de la muwaššaḥa." *Al-Andalus* 27:21–104.

Gramlich, Richard, trans. 1978. *Die Gaben der Erkenntnisse des 'Umar as-Suhrawardī ('Awārif al-ma'ārif)*. Wiesbaden: Steiner. Chapters on *samā'*, pp. 165–192.

———, trans. 1989. *Das Sendschreiben al-Qušayrīs über das Sufitum*. Wiesbaden: Steiner. Chapter on *samā'*, pp. 461–479.

———, trans. 1990. *Schlaglichter über das Sufitum. Abū Naṣr as-Sarrāǧs Kitāb al-luma'*. Stuttgart: Steiner. Chapter on *samā'*, pp. 389–428.

———, trans. 1994. *Die Nahrung der Herzen. Abū Ṭālib al-Makkī's Qūt al-qulūb*. Stuttgart: Steiner. Chapter on *samā'*, pp. 509–524.

Gribetz, Arthur. 1991. "The *Samā'* Controversy: Sufi versus Legalist." *Studia Islamica* 74:43–62.

Guardiola, María Dolores. 1990. "Biografías de músicos en un manuscrito de al-Udfuwī." *Estudios onomástico-biográficos de al-Andalus* 3:335–350.

———. 1991. "La figure de la ḳayna dans les sources musicales." In *Le patrimoine andalou dans la culture arabe et espagnole*. Tunis (Actes du VIIe colloque universitaire Tuniso-Espagnol. Tunis 3–10 février 1989).

———. 1995. "Licitud de la venta de esclavas cantoras." In *Homenaje al Profesor José María Fórneas Besteiro*, 2:938–996. Granada: Universidad de Granada.

Guettat, Mahmoud [Maḥmūd Qaṭṭāṭ]. 1980. *La musique classique du Maghreb*. Paris: Sindbad.

———. 1987. "Min al-makhṭūṭāt al-mūsīqiyya. Taqdīm li-ba'ḍ al-makhṭūṭāt ḥawl al-turāth al-mūsīqī li-'l-Maghrib al-'arabī al-kabīr (wa bi-ṣūra khāṣṣa makhṭūṭ al-Tīfāshī: 'Mut'at al-asmā' fī 'ilm al-samā'." In *Dirāsāt fī 'l-mūsīqā al-'arabiyya*, ed. L. M. Qaṭṭāt. Latakia (Syria): Dār al-Ḥiwār.

Gulisaschwili, Boris A. 1967. "Ibn Sina und die reine Stimmung." *Beiträge zur Musikwissenschaft* 9:272–283.

Haas, Max. 1989. "Antikenrezpetion in der arabischen Musiklehre: Al-Fārābī über musikalische Fantasie." In *Kontinuität und Transformation der Antike im Mittelalter*, ed. Willi Erzgräber, 261–269. Sigmaringen: Jan Thorbecke.

Hammerstein, Reinhold. 1986. *Macht und Klang: Tönende Automaten als Realität und Fiktion in der alten und mittelalterlichen Welt*. Bern: Francke.

Haq, Sirajul. 1944. "Samâ' and Raqṣ of the Darwishes." *Islamic Culture* 18:111–130.

al-Hassan, Ahmad Y., and Donald R. Hill. 1986. *Islamic Technology: An Illustrated History*. Cambridge: Cambridge University Press; Paris: UNESCO.

el Hefny, Mahmoud, ed. and German trans. 1931. *Ibn Sina's Musiklehre hauptsächlich an seinem "Naǧāt" erläutert*. Berlin: Hellwig.

al-Heitty, Abd al-Kareem. 1990. "The Contrasting Spheres of Free Women and Jawārī in the Literary Life of the Early 'Abbāsid Caliphate." *Al-Masāq* (Leeds) 3:31–51.

Hill, Donald R, ed. and English trans. 1974. *Al-Gazarī: Kitāb fī ma'rifat al-ḥiyal al-handasiyya: The Book of Knowledge of Ingenious Mechanical Devices*. Dordrecht: Reidel.

Huart, Clément. 1884. "Étude biographique sur trois musiciennes arabes." *Journal Asiatique*, 8th series, 3:141–187.

Jones, Dalu. 1975. "Notes on a Tatooed Musician: A Drawing of the Fatimid Period." *AARP* [Art and Archaeology Research Papers] 7:1–14.

Kazemi, Elke, ed. and German trans. 1999. *Die bewegte Seele: Das spätantike Buch über das Wesen der Musik (Kitāb 'Unṣur al-mūsīqī) von Paulos/Būlos in arabischer Übersetzung vor dem Hintergrund der griechischen Ethoslehre*. Frankfurt: Institute for the History of Arabic-Islamic Science.

Kennedy, Ph. F. 1998. *The Wine Song in Classical Arabic Poetry: Abū Nuwās and the Literary Tradition*. Oxford: Clarendon.

El-Kholy, Samha A. 1984. *The Function of Music in Islamic Culture in the Period Up to 1100 A.H.* Cairo: General Egyptian Book Organization.

Kiesewetter, Raphael Georg. 1842. *Die Musik der Araber, nach Originalquellen dargestellt*. Leipzig: Breitkopf und Härtel. Several reprints.

Kilpatrick, Hilary. 1997. "Cosmic Correspondences: Songs as a Starting Point for an Encyclopaedic Portrayal of Culture." In *Pre-Modern Encyclopaedic Texts (Proceedings of the Second COMERS Congress, Groningen, 1–4 July 1996)*, ed. P. Binkley. Leiden: Brill.

———. 1998. "The Transmission of Songs in Medieval Arabic Culture." In *Philosophy and Arts in the Islamic World (Proceedings of the Eighteenth Congress of the Union Européenne des Arabisants et Islamisants held at the Katholieke Universiteit Leuven [September 3 September 9, 1996])*, ed. U. Vermeulen and D. de Smet. Leuven: Peeters.

———. 1999. "Princes, musiciens, et musicologues à la cour abbasside." In *Les intellectuels en Orient musulman: Statut et fonction*, ed. F. Sanagustin. Cairo: Institut Français d'Archéologie Orientale.

Kosegarten, Johann Gottfried Ludwig. 1844. "Die moslemischen Schriftsteller über die Theorie der Musik." *Zeitschrift für die Kunde des Morgenlandes* (Bonn) 5:137–163.

Lachmann, Robert, and Mahmud el-Hefni, eds. and trans. 1931. *Ja'qūb Ibn Isḥāq al-Kindī: Risāla fī hubr tā'līf al-alḥān: Über die Komposition der Melodien*. Leipzig: Kistner and Siegel.

Land, Jan Pieter Nicolaas. 1885. "Recherches sur l'histoire de la gamme arabe." In *Actes du Sixième Congrès international des Orientalistes tenu en 1883 à Leide*. Deuxième partie, ṣection 1, Sémitique:37–168. Leiden: Brill.

———. 1892. "Remarks on the Earliest Development of Arabic Music." In *Transactions of the Ninth International Congress of Orientalists. (Held in London, 5th to 12th September 1892)*, 2:155–163. London.

———. 1922. "Tonschriftversuche und Melodieproben aus dem muhammedanischen Mittelalter." *Sammelbände für vergleichende Musikwissenschaft* 1:79–85. Reprint from *Vierteljahrsschrift für Musikwissenschaft*. 1886. 2:347–356).

Macdonald, Duncan Black, trans. 1901–1902. "Emotional Religion in Islām as Affected by Music and Singing: Being a Translation of a Book of the *Iḥyā' 'Ulūm ad-Dīn* of al-Ghazzālī." *Journal of the Royal Asiatic Society* [1901]:195–252, 705–748; [1902]:1–28.

El-Mallah, Issam. 1997. *Arab Music and Musical Notation*. Tutzing: Hans Schneider.

Manik, Liberty. 1969. *Das arabische Tonsystem im Mittelalter*. Leiden: Brill.

———. 1979. "Zwei Fassungen einer von Ṣafī al-Dīn notierten Melodie." *Baessler-Archiv*, Neue Folge 23:145–151.

Marcus, Scott. 1989. "Arab Music Theory in the Modern Period." Ph.D. dissertation, University of California Los Angeles.

Margoliouth, David Samuel, trans. 1935–1938, 1945–1948. "The Devil's Delusion [*Talbīs iblīs*] by Ibn Al-Jauzi." *Islamic Culture* 9–12, 19–22:passim. Chapter on *samā'*, 19 (1945): 171–188, 272–289, 376–383.

Matyakubov, Otanazar. 1986. *Farabi: ob osnovakh muzyki Vostoka*. Tashkent: Fan.

Michot, Jean R. 1988. "L'Islam et le monde: al-Ghazâlî et Ibn Taymiyya à propos de la musique (*samâ'*)." In *Figures de la finitude: Études d'anthropologie philosophique*, ed. G. Florival et al. Louvain-la-Neuve: Éditions de l'Institut Supérieur de Philosophie, Librairie Peeters; Paris: Vrin.

———. 1991. *Musique et danse selon Ibn Taymiyya: Le Livre du Samâ' et de la Danse* (Kitāb al-Samā' wa l-Raqṣ) *compilé par le shaykh*

Muḥammad al-Manbijī. Traduction de l'arabe, présentation, notes, et lexique. Paris: Vrin.

Mokri, Mohammad. 1995. "La mélodie chez al-Fârâbî. Rôle, fondement et définition." In *Persico-Kurdica. Contributions scientifiques aux études iraniennes*, ed. M. Mokri. Paris, Louvain: Peeters.

Monroe, James T. 1989. "Aḥmad al-Tīfāshī on Andalusian Music." *Modern Philology* 125:35–44.

Müller, Hans. 1980. *Die Kunst des Sklavenkaufs nach arabischen, persischen und türkischen Ratgebern vom 10. bis zum 18. Jahrhundert*. Freiburg: Klaus Schwarz (on musical qualities and deficiencies of slaves and slave girls, passim).

Nazarov, Abdumannon. 1995. *Forobiy va Ibn Sino musiḳiy ritmika khususida (mumtoz iyḳo' nazariyasi)*. Tashkent: Uzbekiston Respublikasi Madaniyat Ishlari Vazirligi.

Neubauer, Eckhard. 1968–1969. "Die Theorie vom *īqā'*. I. Übersetzung des *Kitāb al-Īqā'āt* von Abū Naṣr al-Fārābī." *Oriens* 21–22:196–232. Reprint with facs. ed. of the text in Neubauer 1998.

———. 1987–1988. "Das Musikkapitel der *Jumal al-falsafa* von Muḥammad ibn 'Alī al-Hindī (1135 n.Chr.)." *Zeitschrift für Geschichte der arabisch-islamischen Wissenschaften* 4:51–59. Reprint 1998 with facs. ed. of the text in E. Neubauer, *Arabische Musiktheorie*.

———. 1990. "Arabische Anleitungen zur Musiktherapie." *Zeitschrift für Geschichte der arabisch-islamischen Wissenschaften* 6:227–272.

———. 1993. "Der Bau der Laute und ihre Besaitung nach arabischen, persischen und türkischen Quellen des 9. bis 15. Jahrhunderts." *Zeitschrift für Geschichte der arabisch-islamischen Wissenschaften* 8:279–378.

———. 1994. "Die Theorie vom *īqā'*. II. Übersetzung des *Kitāb Iḥṣā' al-īqā'āt* von Abū Naṣr al-Fārābī." *Oriens* 34:103–173. Reprint with facs. ed. of the text in Neubauer 1998.

———. 1995–1996. "Al-ńalīl ibn Aḥmad und die Frühgeschichte der arabischen Lehre von den 'Tönen' und den musikalischen Metren. Mit einer Übersetzung des *Kitāb an-Nağam* von Yaḥyā ibn 'Alī al-Munağğim." *Zeitschrift für Geschichte der arabisch-islamischen Wissenschaften* 10:255–323. Reprint with facs. ed. of text in Neubauer 1998.

———. 1998. *Arabische Musiktheorie von den Anfängen bis zum 6./12. Jahrhundert. Studien, Übersetzungen und Texte in Faksimile*. Frankfurt: Institute for the History of Arabic-Islamic Science.

———. 2000. "Glimpses of Arab Music in Ottoman Times from Syrian and Egyptian Sources." *Zeitschrift für Geschichte der arabisch-islamischen Wissenschaften* 13:317–365.

Neubauer, Eckhard, and Elsbeth Neubauer. 1987–1988. "Henry George Farmer on Oriental Music: An Annotated Bibliography." *Zeitschrift für Geschichte der arabisch-islamischen Wissenschaften* 4:219–266.

Nizamov, Asliddin. 1980. "Ibn Sīnā i ego muzykal'no-teoreticheskie sochinenija." In *Abuali Ibn Sino i ego epoha: K 1000–letiju so dnja ego rozhdenija*, ed. Numan Negmatov, 181–190. Dushanbe: Donish.

Odeimi, Bechir. 1991. "Kitāb al-Imtā' wa-l-intifā': Un manuscrit sur la musique arabe de Ibn al-Darrāğ." *Arabica* 38:40–56.

Pellat, Charles, trans. 1954. *Le livre de la couronne. Kitāb at-Tāğ . . . attribué à Ğāḥiẓ*. Paris: Les Belles Lettres.

———, trans. 1963. "Les esclaves-chanteuses de Jāḥiẓ." *Arabica* 10:121–147.

Poché, Christian. 1993. "Un nouveau regard sur la musique d'al-Andalus: le manuscrit d'al-Tīfāshī." *Revista de musicología* 16, 1:367–379.

Poché, Christian, and Jean Lambert. 2000. *Musiques du monde arabe et musulman. Bibliographie et discographie*. Paris: Geuthner.

Pourjavady, Nasrollah. 1990. "Zwei alte Werke über *samā'*." *Spektrum Iran* (Bonn) 3(2):37–59; 3(3):36–61.

Pouzet, Louis. 1983. "Prises de position autour du *samā'* en Orient musulman au VIIe/XIIIe siècle." *Studia Islamica* 57:119–134.

Randel, Don M. 1976. "Al-Fārābī and the Role of Arabic Music Theory in the Latin Middle Ages." *Journal of the American Musicological Society* 29:173–188.

Rat, Gustave. 1899–1902. *Al-Mostaṭraf. Recueil des morceaux choisis ça et là dans toutes les branches de connaissances réputées attrayantes* par Šihâb-ad-dîn Aḥmad al-Abšîhî. *Ouvrage philologique, anecdotique, littéraire et philosophique traduit pour la première fois*. 2 vols. Paris, Toulon. Chapters on music, vol. 2:372–415.

Reinert, Benedikt. 1979. "Das Problem des pythagoräischen Kommas in der arabischen Musiktheorie." *Asiatische Studien* 33:199–217.

———. 1990. "Die arabische Musiktheorie zwischen autochthoner Tradition und griechischem Erbe." In *Die Blütezeit der arabischen Wissenschaft*, ed. Heinz Balmer and Beat Glaus. Zürich: Verlag der Fachvereine.

Rice, David Storm. 1958. "A drawing of the Fatimid period." *Bulletin of the School of Oriental and African Studies* 21:31–39 (Venus depicted as a musician, see Jones 1975).

Robson, James, ed., trans. 1938. *Tracts on Listening to Music. Being* Dhamm al-malāhī *by Ibn abī 'l-Dunyā and* Bawāriq al-ilmā' *by Majd al-Dīn al-Ṭūsī al-Ghazālī*. London: Royal Asiatic Society.

———. 1952. "A Maghribi Ms. on Listening to Music." *Islamic Culture* 26:113–131.

———. 1957. "Muslim Controversy about the Lawfulness of Music." *Islamic Literature* 9:305–314.

———. 1958. "Some Arab Musical Instruments." *Islamic Culture* 32:171–185.

———. 1961. "Muslim Wedding Feasts." *Transactions of the Glasgow University Oriental Society* 18:1–14.

———, trans. 1947–1953. "The Meaning of Ghinā'." *Journal of the Manchester University Egyptian and Oriental Society* 25:1–8.

Robson, James, and Henry George Farmer, trans. and facs. 1938. *Ancient Arabian Musical Instruments. As described by Al-Mufaḍḍal ibn Salama (ninth century) in the unique Istanbul manuscript of the* Kitāb al-malāhī *in the handwriting of Yāqūt al-Musta'ṣimī (d. 1298)*. Glasgow: Civic.

Ronzevalle, Louis, ed. and trans. 1913. "Un traité de musique arabe moderne." *Mélanges de la Faculté Orientale. Université Saint-Joseph* 6:1–120.

Rosenthal, Franz, trans. 1958. *Ibn Khaldûn: The Muqaddimah—An Introduction to History*. New York: Pantheon. Chapter on music, vol. 3:395–405.

———. 1966. "Two Graeco-Arabic Works on Music." *Proceedings of the American Philosophical Society* 110:261–268. Reprint in F. Rosenthal. 1991. *Science and Medicine in Islam*. Aldershot: Variorum.

Rowson, Everett K. 1991. "The Effeminates of Early Medina." *Journal of the American Oriental Society* 111:671–693.

Rozenfel'd, Boris A., and N. G. Khayretdinova, trans. 1974. "Rech' o rodakh, kotorye obrazuyutsya kvartoy Omar Khayyam." *Istoriko-matematicheskie issledovaniya* 19:279–284.

Salem, Elie A. 1977. *Hilāl al-Ṣābi': Rusūm Dār al-Khilāfah* (The Rules and Regulations of the 'Abbāsid Court). Translated from the Arabic. Beirut: American University of Beirut.

Sawa, George Dimitri. 1982. "Bridging One Millenium: Melodic Movement in al-Fārābī and Kolinski." In *Cross-Cultural Perspectives on Music*, ed. R. Falk and T. Rice. Toronto: University of Toronto Press.

———. 1983–1984. "Al-Fārābī's Theory of Īqā': An Empirically Derived Medieval Model of Rhythmic Analysis." *Progress Reports in Ethnomusicology* l(9):1–32.

———. 1984. "Musical Humour in the *Kitāb al-Aghānī*." In *Logos Islamikos: Studia Islamica in honorem Georgii Michaelis Wickens*, ed. Roger M. Savory and Dionisius A. Agius. Toronto: Pontifical Institute of Mediaeval Studies.

———. 1985. "The Status and Roles of the Secular Musicians in the *Kitāb al-Aghānī* (Book of Songs) of Abū al-Faraj al-Iṣbahānī (d. 356 A.H./ 967 A.D.)." *Asian Music* 17:69–82.

———. 1989. *Music Performance Practice in the Early 'Abbāsid Era 132–320 A.H./750–932 A.D.* Toronto: Pontifical Institute of Mediaeval Studies.

———. 1990. "Paradigms in al-Fārābī's Musical Writings." In *Paradigms in Medieval Thought: Applications in Medieval Disciplines*, ed. Nancy van Deusen and Alvin E. Ford. Lewiston, N.Y.: Edwin Mellen.

Schmidt-Relenberg, Markus, ed. and trans. 1986. "Hören, Tanz, und Ekstase nach Badraddīn ibn Sālim al-Mālikī. Qūt al-arwāḥ fī aḥkām as-samā' al-mubāḥ. Text, Übersetzung und Kommentar." Ph.D. dissertation, University of Kiel.

Sezgin, Fuat. 1974. *Geschichte des arabischen Schrifttums*. Vol. 5: *Mathematik bis ca. 430 H.* Leiden: Brill.

Shehadeh, Kamal, Donald R. Hill, and Richard Lorch, eds. and trans. 1994. "Construction of a Fluting Machine by Apollonius the Carpenter." *Zeitschrift für Geschichte der arabisch-islamischen Wissenschaften* 9:326–356.

Shehadi, Fadlou. 1995. *Philosophies of Music in Medieval Islam*. Leiden: Brill.

Shiloah, Amnon. 1962. "Réflexions sur la dance artistique musulmane au moyen âge." *Cahiers de civilisation médiévale* 5:463–474.

———. 1963. *Caractéristiques de l'art vocal arabe au Moyen-âge*. Tel-Aviv: Israel Music Institute.

———, trans. 1964–1966. "L'épître sur la musique des Ikhwān al-Ṣafā'." *Revue des études islamiques* 32:125–162; 34:159–193.

———, ed. and trans. 1968. "Deux textes arabes inédits sur la musique." *Yuval* l:221–248. Reprint in Shiloah 1993.

———, ed. and trans. 1971a. "Un 'Problème Musical' inconnu de Thābit ibn Qurra." *Orbis Musicae* 1:25–38. Reprint in Shiloah 1993.

———. 1971b. "Les sept traités de musique dans le manuscrit 1705 de Manisa." *Israel Oriental Studies* 1:303–315.

———, trans. 1972a. *Al-Ḥasan ibn Aḥmad ibn 'Alī al-Kātib: La perfection des connaissances musicales*. Paris: Geuthner.

———. 1972b. "Ibn Hindū, le médecin et la musique." *Israel Oriental Studies* 2:447–462. Reprint in Shiloah 1993.

———, trans. 1974. "Un ancien traité sur le *'ūd* d'Abū Yūsuf al-Kindī." *Israel Oriental Studies* 4:179–205.

———, trans. 1978a. *The Epistle on Music of the Ikhwān al-Ṣafā'.* Tel Aviv: Tel Aviv University. Reprint in Shiloah 1993.

———. 1978b. "Reflets de la musique des divers peuples dans les écrits arabes sur la musique." In *Actes du Deuxième congrès international d'études des cultures de la Méditerranée occidentale*, ed. Micheline Galley, vol. 2. Alger: Société Nationale d'Édition et de Diffusion.

———. 1979. *The Theory of Music in Arabic Writings (c. 900–1900). Descriptive Catalogue of Manuscripts in Libraries of Europe and the U.S.A.* Munich: Henle.

———. 1986. "Music in the Pre-Islamic Period as Reflected in Arabic Writings of the First Islamic Centuries." *Jerusalem Studies in Arabic and Islam* 7:109–120. Reprint in Shiloah 1993.

———. 1990. "Techniques of Scholarship in Medieval Arabic Musical Treatises." In *Music Theory and Its Sources: Antiquity and the Middle Ages*, ed. André Barbera. Notre Dame, Ind. Reprint in Shiloah 1993.

———. 1991. "Musical Modes and the Medical Dimension: The Arabic Sources (c. 900–c. 1600)." In *Metaphor: A Musical Dimension*, ed. Jamie Croy Kassler. Sydney. Reprint in Shiloah 1993.

———. 1993. *The Dimension of Music in Islamic and Jewish Culture*. Aldershot: Variorum.

———. 1994. "Notions d'esthétique dans les traités arabes sur la musique." *Cahiers de Musiques Traditionnelles* 7:51–58.

———. 1997a. "L'approche humaniste et métaphorique dans les premiers écrits arabes sur la musique." In *Festschrift Walter Wiora zum 90. Geburtstag*, ed. Christoph-Hellmut Mahling and Ruth Seiberts, 446–456. Tutzing: Hans Schneider.

———. 1997b. "Music and Religion in Islam." *Acta Musicologica* 69:143–155.

Smith, Eli, trans. 1847. "A Treatise on Arab Music, Chiefly from a Work by Mikhâ'il Meshâḳah, of Damascus," *Journal of the American Oriental Society* 1:171–217.

Sobh, Mahmud. 1995. "La poesía árabe, la música, y el canto." *Anaquel de Estudios Árabes* 6:149–184.

Stigelbauer, Michael. 1975. *Die Sängerinnen am Abbasidenhof um die Zeit des Kalifen Al-Mutawakkil. Nach dem Kitāb al-Aġānī des Abu-l-Farağ al-Iṣbahānī und anderen Quellen dargestellt.* Vienna: VWGÖ.

Al-Ṭanjī, Muḥammad ibn Tāwīt. 1968. "Al-Ṭarā'iq wa 'l-alḥān al-mūsīqiyya fī Ifrīqiyya wa 'l-Andalus." *Majallat al-Abḥāth* 21:93–116.

El-Tawil, M. A. 1992. "Ibn Sina and Medieval Music (370–428 A.H. / 980–1038 A.D.): A New Edition of the Musical Section of Kitab al-Shifa and Kitab al-Najat plus a Comprehensive Study of his Life and Works on Music." Ph.D. dissertation, University of Exeter.

Terés, Elías, trans. 1971. "La epístola sobre el canto con música instrumental, de Ibn Ḥazm de Córdoba." *Al-Andalus* 36:203–214.

Vajda, Georges. 1980. "Un libelle contre la danse des soufis." *Studia Islamica* 51:163–177.

Valderrama, Fernando. 1986. "La música arábigo-andaluza." In *Actas del XII Congreso de la U.E.A.I. (Malaga, 1984)*. Madrid: Huertas.

Weil, Jürgen W. 1975–1978. "Epigramme auf Musikerinnen [part 2 and 3: Künstlerinnen] in der Gedichtsammlung *Alf ğāriya wa-ğāriya*." *Rocznik orientalistyczny* 37 (1975):7–12; 39 (1977):137–141; 40 (1978):83–93.

Werner, Eric. 1965. "Greek Ideas on Music in Judeo-Arabic Literature." In *The Commonwealth of Music: In Honor of Curt Sachs*, ed. Gustave Reese and Rose Brandel. New York: Free Press; London: Collier Macmillan.

Werner, Eric, and Isaiah Sonne. 1941–1943. "The Philosophy and Theory of Music in Judaeo-Arabic Literature." *Hebrew Union College Annual* 16 (1941):251–319; 17 (1942–43):511–573.

Wiedemann, Eilhard. 1910a. "Über die Herstellung von Glocken bei den Muslimen." *Mitteilungen zur Geschichte der Medizin und der Naturwissenschaften* 9:475–476. Reprint in Wiedemann, *Gesammelte Schriften zur arabisch-islamischen Wissenschaftsgeschichte*. Frankfurt 1984, vol. 1:475–476.

———. 1910b. "Über Musikautomaten bei den Arabern." In *Centenario della nascita di Michele Amari*, vol. 2. Palermo: Virzì. Reprint in E. Wiedemann. 1984. *Gesammelte Schriften zur arabisch-islamischen Wissenschaftsgeschichte*, vol. 1:451–472. Frankfurt.

———. 1914. "Über Musikautomaten." *Sitzungsberichte der Physikalisch-Medizinischen Societät in Erlangen* 46:17–26, esp. 20–26. Reprint in E. Wiedemann. 1970. *Aufsätze zur arabischen Wissenschaftsgeschichte*, vol. 2:47–56. Hildesheim: Olms.

Wiedemann, Eilhard, and Fritz Hauser. 1918. "Byzantinische und arabische akustische Instrumente." *Archiv für die Geschichte der Naturwissenschaften und der Technik* 8:140–166. Reprint in E. Wiedemann. 1984. *Gesammelte Schriften zur arabisch-islamischen Wissenschaftsgeschichte*, vol. 3:1580–1606. Frankfurt.

Wiedemann, Eilhard, and Wilhelm Müller. 1922–1923. "Zur Geschichte der Musik. l. Abschnitt über die Musik aus den Schlüsseln der Wissenschaft. 2. Angaben von al Akfânî über die Musik." *Sitzungsberichte der Physikalisch-Medizinischen Societät in Erlangen* 54/55:7–22. Reprint in E. Wiedemann. 1970. *Aufsätze zur arabischen Wissenschaftsgeschichte*, vol. 2:580–595. Hildesheim: Olms.

Wright, Owen. 1966. "Ibn al-Munajjim and the Early Arabian Modes." *Galpin Society Journal* 19:27–48.

———. 1978. *The Modal System of Arab and Persian Music A.D. 1250–1300.* Oxford: Oxford University Press.

———. 1983. "Music and Verse." In *Arabic Literature to the End of the Umayyad Period*, ed. A. F. L. Beeston et al. Cambridge: Cambridge University Press.

———. 1995. "A Preliminary Version of the *Kitāb al-Adwār*." *Bulletin of the School of Oriental and African Studies* 58:455–478.

Yammine, Habib. 1999. "L'évolution de la notation rythmique dans la musique arabe du IXe à la fin du XXe siècle." *Cahiers de Musiques Traditionnelles* 12:95–121.

Zemcovskij, Izalij. 1987. "Učenie o forme al'-Farabi i aktual'nye voprosy analiza muzykal'noj formy." *Zbornik Matice Srpske za scenske umetnosti i muziku* 2:7–18.

Żerańska, Sawomira. 1972. "Traktat Braci Czystoçi (Ihwan as-Safa) "O muzyce," mal o znane żródlo do mediewistyki orientalnej." *Muzyka* 17:49–64.

Theories of Rhythm and Meter in the Medieval Middle East

George Sawa

Al-Khalīl ibn Aḥmad, Isḥaq al-Mawṣilī, al-Kindī, and al-Fārābī
Al-Fārābī's Three Types of Attacks
Al-Fārābī's Categories of Rhythmic Modes
Al-Fārābī's Sixteen Ornamental Techniques

AL-KHALĪL IBN AḤMAD, ISḤĀQ AL-MAWṢILĪ, AL-KINDĪ, AND AL-FĀRĀBĪ

The father of the theory of Arabic rhythms and metrics is the prosodist al-Khalīl ibn Aḥmad (718–786 C.E.), who lived in Basra, Iraq. Medieval biographers inform us that he was a lexicographer, grammarian, and belletrist who created the science of Arabic prosody out of his knowledge of the discipline of music. With it, he succeeded in unlocking the metric system that had regulated pre-Islamic and early Islamic poetry. He found that the poetry was built on sixteen meters, each made up of metric feet. The metric feet, eight in number, were in turn made up of short and long syllables. For example, the poetic meter *al-khafīf* was represented as | *fā'ilātun mustaf'ilun fā'ilātun* | *fā'ilātun mustaf'ilun fā'ilātun* |, where *fā'ilātun* and *mustaf'ilun* are poetic feet. The sixteen poetic meters were not only used in their basic form but were also varied by means of many techniques. Al-Khalīl ibn Aḥmad also wrote a treatise entitled *Kitāb al-īqā'* 'Book of Rhythm'. His treatises are no longer extant, but later quotations from and commentaries on his work on prosody had a profound influence on the theory of musical rhythm and meter with respect to technical names, concepts, and variation techniques.

For instance, Isḥāq al-Mawṣilī (d. 850), the earliest writer whose works on the theory of rhythms are still extant, said that the role of rhythm in music is equivalent to the role of prosody in poetry. Isḥāq was a singer, composer, and lutenist as well as a theorist; he devoted one chapter of his treatise *Kitāb fī ta'līf al-nagham* 'Book on the Composition of Melodies' to rhythm. Most of the surviving fragments of his work contain definitions of the various rhythmic modes that were used in his time. Unfortunately, however, because Isḥāq was primarily a practitioner—rather than a logician accustomed to precise discourse—his definitions are vague. Although we can understand that a rhythmic mode is a pattern of durations, their values are not clearly indicated.

After Isḥāq came the philosopher al-Kindī (d. after 870). He had access to Arabic translations of ancient Greek music theory, but because he was not a practitioner of the art he simply copied Greek theories of rhythms uncritically, and some of them did not apply in the Middle East. Also, he defined some rhythmic modes that were not Arabic and left out some important Arab modes.

Al-Fārābī imagines an attack as the striking of a large, solid body by a very thin body. The thinner the striking body, the more appropriate is the term "attack" to describe the contact.

In the tenth century, Al-Fārābī (d. 950), who was both a logician and a performer, made a great contribution to Arab music theory, although of his 160 works only eight dealt with music and only four of those have survived. He treated the subject of rhythm extensively in three of these surviving works:

1. *Kitāb al-mūsīqī al-kabīr* 'Grand Book of Music'
2. *Kitāb al-īqā'āt* 'Book of Rhythms'
3. *Kitāb iḥṣā' al-īqā'āt* 'Book for the Basic Comprehension of Rhythms'

In the Grand Book of Music, al-Fārābī treated the subject of *īqā'* 'rhythm' in two chapters, modeling his theory on ancient Greek musical theory and mathematics, Arabic grammar, phonetics, prosody, and the Qur'ānic sciences. He defined rhythm as "motion through notes within durations well defined as to their length and proportions," and muscial sounds as the product of an "attack" such as the plucking of a string instrument, the beating of a drum, or the impact of air striking a wind instrument or human vocal cords. In itself, an attack has no time value; it occurs in the present and separates past from future. Here, I represent the attack by a downward arrow ↓.

Al-Fārābī imagines an attack as the striking of a large, solid body by a very thin body. The thinner the striking body, the more appropriate is the term "attack" to describe the contact, which is imagined as striking at a point. The concept of the timelessness of the attack comes directly from Euclid's geometrical postulate that inasmuch as a point has no length, a straight line has no surface (width), and surface has no volume (thickness), an attack carries no time in itself. Also, inasmuch as one point is separated from another by a straight line, one straight line is separated from another by a surface, and one surface is separated from another by a volume, one attack is separated from another by a duration. Al-Fārābī then proceeds to define the duration. It must be finite, so that the ear can perceive it; it must not be too long, since then the ear cannot keep count of the pulses; and it must not be too short, as in fast tremolos, for then the ear cannot count the number of attacks in a beat. With regard to fast attacks, he defines the shortest perceptible duration between two attacks as one in which no other attack could be inserted, and he compares an overly fast attack to the sound of thunder. He argues, further, that the ratios of durations should be finite—that is, they should be ratios of integers. Without this finiteness, we would have the free rhythm encountered in the musical genres then known as *nashīd* and *istihlāl*. These are comparable rhythmically to modern-day *taqsīm, mawwāl*, and *layālī*—instrumental and vocal improvisation in free rhythm.

Al-Fārābī borrowed the concept of a shortest perceptible duration from the ancient Greek *chronos protos*. This is a unit of measurement that, when multiplied by 2, 3, 4, and so forth, will create temporal building blocks. When only one building block is used and repeated ad infinitum, the result is a *conjunctive* rhythm (such as | 𝅗𝅥 | 𝅗𝅥 | 𝅗𝅥 | or | ♩ | ♩ | ♩ | . Such a rhythm is artistically uninteresting; it is used only for theoretical purposes, not in practice. However, a bar of a theoretical conjunctive rhythm is used with one or more conjunctive rhythms of a different size to create a *disjunctive* rhythm (such as | ♩ 𝅗𝅥 | or | ♩ 𝅗𝅥 𝅗𝅥. |); the ethnomusicological term is *additive* rhythm. Often, the last duration is longer than any duration in the created "musical bar" or cycle and is called a *separator*.

A disjunctive rhythm, then, is a rhythmic cycle or mode consisting of a pattern of attacks and durations. Each duration is called a rhythmic *part*, which for al-Fārābī is equivalent to a poetic foot. Rhythmic parts combine to create a rhythmic mode in the same way that poetic feet combine to create Arabic poetic meters. In composition or performance, a rhythmic mode or cycle is repeated but is rhythmically varied with a number of alterations (explained below). To some extent, this mirrors poetic practice, since poetic meters are also altered by means of variation techniques. Al-Fārābī borrowed amply from these and applied them to music.

There are two main problems with the chapters on rhythm in the Grand Book of Music: first, they contain contradictory statements regarding the value of the durations; second, the value of the separator is often left unspecified when al-Fārābī discusses particular rhythmic modes. In the Book of Rhythms and Book for the Basic Comprehension of Rhythms, al-Fārābī took a step back from the concept of "rhythmic mode," defining *īqā‘* in its basic form as "the movement of attacks separated from each other by equal durations in consecutive and equal time periods." This is unquestionably a concept of musical bars containing a number of equal beats—that is, musical meters in the modern sense.

The Book of Rhythms and Book for the Basic Comprehension of Rhythms are a welcome revision of the two chapters on rhythm in the Grand Book of Music: the definitions are clearer, and the system of notation is greatly improved. As a result, we are able to determine the precise nature of the early Arab rhythmic modes and transcribe them in Western notation.

AL-FĀRĀBĪ'S THREE TYPES OF ATTACKS

Al-Fārābī distinguishes between three types of attacks on the basis of the durations that separate them. To identify them, he uses letter notations inspired by grammar and prosody.

1. *Light attack* (*naqra khafīfa*), notated as the short syllable *ta*. This is separated from the next attack by the shortest perceptible time, and following convention it is notated here as an eighth rest 𝄾. Thus, ↓ 𝄾 ↓ 𝄾 = ♪ ♪
2. *Medium attack* (*naqra mutawassiṭa*), notated as *tā* (a long syllable) or *tan* (the short syllable *ta* plus an unvoweled consonant *n*). This is separated from the next attack by double the shortest perceptible time: ↓ 𝄾 𝄾 ↓ 𝄾 𝄾 = ♩ ♩
3. *Heavy attack* (*naqra thaqīla*), notated as *tann*. This is separated from the next attack by four times the shortest perceptible time: ↓ 𝄾 𝄾 𝄾 𝄾 ↓ 𝄾 𝄾 𝄾 𝄾 = 𝅗𝅥 𝅗𝅥

Note that these three durations are a geometric progression (1: 2: 4).

AL-FĀRĀBĪ'S CATEGORIES OF RHYTHMIC MODES

Depending on the type of attack used, three categories of *īqā‘āt* in their basic form can result: (1) *light* (*khafīf*), (2) *medium* (*mutawassiṭ*), and (3) *heavy* (*thaqīl*). As in the Grand Book of Music, each cycle is separated from the next by a disjunction (or separator), and its value is double that between the attacks of a cycle. Figure 1 illustrates these categories of *īqā‘āt*. (In the Book for the Basic Comprehension of Rhythms, al-Fārābī notates the first rhythm shown in figure 1, *ramal*, as follows: | tann ○ tann ◯ | tann ○ tann ◯ |. He uses small and large circles to clarify the meaning of the two *tanns*. In this example, the small circle has the value of a half note; the large circle is a separator and has the value of two half notes.)

FIGURE 1 Al-Fārābī's categories of rhythmic modes.

Category 1: Heavy *(thaqīl)*

I.1 *Ramal.* 2 heavy attacks plus disjunction

3/2 | ↓ 𝄾 𝄾 𝄾 𝄾 ↓ 𝄾𝄾𝄾𝄾 𝄾𝄾𝄾𝄾 | ↓ 𝄾 𝄾 𝄾 𝄾 ↓ 𝄾𝄾𝄾𝄾 𝄾𝄾𝄾𝄾 |

time of disjunction =
twice the time between first and second attacks

= 3/2 | 𝅗𝅥 𝅝 | 𝅗𝅥 𝅝 |

first cycle second cycle

I.2 *Al-thaqīl al-awwal. First heavy:* 3 heavy attacks plus disjunction

4/2 | 𝅗𝅥 𝅗𝅥 𝅝 |

I.3 *Al-thaqīl al-thānī. Second heavy:* 4 heavy attacks plus disjunction

5/2 | 𝅗𝅥 𝅗𝅥 𝅗𝅥 𝅝 |

Category 2: Medium *(mutawassiṭ)* **or light-heavy** *(khafīf-thaqīl)*

II.1 *Khafīf al-ramal. Light ramal:* 2 medium attacks plus disjunction

3/4 | ♩ 𝅗𝅥 |

II.2 *Khafīf al-thaqīl al-awwal. First light-heavy:* 3 medium attacks plus disjunction

4/4 | ♩ ♩ 𝅗𝅥 |

II.3 *Khafīf al-thaqīl al-thānī. Second light-heavy:* 4 medium attacks plus disjunction

5/4 | ♩ ♩ ♩ 𝅗𝅥 |

Category 3: Light *(khafīf)*

III.1 *Al-khafīf al-awwal. First light:* 2 light attacks plus disjunction

3/8 | ♪ ♩ |

III.2 *Al-khafīf al-thānī. Second light:* 3 light attacks plus disjunction

4/8 | ♪ ♪ ♩ |

III.3 *Al-khafīf al-thālith. Third light:* 4 light attacks plus disjunction

5/8 | ♪ ♪ ♪ ♩ |

III.4 *Al-khafīf al-rābiʿ. Fourth light* (known as *hazaj*): 5 light attacks plus disjunction

6/8 | ♪ ♪ ♪ ♪ ♩ |

III.5 *Al-khafīf al-khāmis. Fifth light:* 6 light attacks plus disjunction

7/8 | ♪ ♪ ♪ ♪ ♪ ♩ |

III.6 *Al-khafīf al-sādis. Sixth light:* 7 light attacks plus disjunction

8/8 | ♪ ♪ ♪ ♪ ♪ ♪ ♩ |

The formulas in figure 1 would not have been used in practice as presented; they need fillings, changes, variations, and ornaments or embellishments in order to be aesthetically pleasing. Thus fundamental forms of the *īqāʿāt* (in the sense of meter) are merely general formulas from which one can derive particulars such as patterns (rhythmic modes), ornamented patterns, and variations (rhythms).

AL-FĀRĀBĪ'S SIXTEEN ORNAMENTAL TECHNIQUES

By analyzing the rhythm of the musical repertoire of his time, Al-Fārābī codified sixteen ornamental techniques (figure 2). These were not only compositional methods

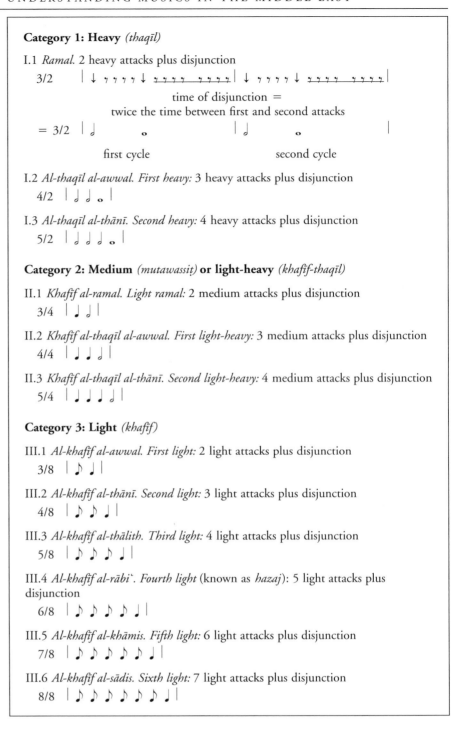

FIGURE 2 Al-Fārābī's sixteen ornamental techniques.

1. *Taḍʿīf: Doubling* of an attack, which consists of inserting a [timeless] attack inside the duration separating two attacks:

3/2 | ↓ 𝄾 𝄾 𝄾 𝄾 ↓ 𝄾 𝄾 𝄾 𝄾 𝄾 𝄾 𝄾 𝄾 | ⇒⇒ | ↓ 𝄾 𝄾 𝄾 𝄾 ↓ 𝄾 𝄾 ↓ 𝄾 𝄾 𝄾 𝄾 𝄾 𝄾 |

or

3/2 | 𝅗𝅥 𝅝 | ⇒⇒ | 𝅗𝅥 ♩ 𝅗𝅥. |

Fundamental *ramal* Popular *ramal*

2. *Ṭayy: Suppression* of an attack but not the duration before it or after it.

6/8 | ♪ ♪ ♪ ♪ ♩ | ⇒⇒ | ♩ ♪ ♪ ♩ | or | ♪ ♩ ♪ ♩ |

Fundamental *hazaj* Popular patterns of *hazaj*

3. *Takrīr: Repetition* of a part (akin to a poetic foot), which results in metric expansion and pattern alteration.

6/8 | ♩ ♪ ♪ ♩ | ⇒⇒ 10/8 | ♩ ♪ ♪ ♩ ♪ ♪ ♩ |

4. *Tarkīb: Assembling* of parts existing in one *īqāʿ* or *assembling* two *īqāʿāt*. This also results in metric expansion, and according to al-Fārābī it is quite common in the light *īqāʿāt.*

7/8 | ♪ ♩ ♩ ♩ | ⇒⇒ 10/8 | ♪ ♩ ♩ ♪ ♩ ♩ |

7/8 | ♪ ♪ ♪ ♪ ♪ ♩ | + 4/8 | ♪ ♪ ♩ | ⇒⇒ 11/8 | ♪ ♪ ♪ ♪ ♪ ♩ ♪ ♪ ♩ |

5. *Majāz: Passage*—one attack (or more) is placed in the time of disjunction in order to facilitate the passage from one cycle to the next, especially when the time of disjunction is long, as in the categories *heavy* and *light-heavy.*

5/4 | ♩ 𝅗𝅥 𝅗𝅥 | ⇒⇒ | ♩ 𝅗𝅥 ♩ ♩ |

6. *Iʿtimād: Support*—one attack (or more) is placed in the time of disjunction of the last bar of a section or piece, to facilitate and mark off the termination of the section or piece. (See example 5.)

7. *Tawṣīl: Joining*—shortening the time of disjunction or making it disappear. This results in metric contraction.

5/4 | ♩ 𝅗𝅥 𝅗𝅥 | ⇒⇒ 4/4 + 1/8 | ♩ 𝅗𝅥 ♩. |

or 3/4 | ♩ 𝅗𝅥 |

8. *Tafṣīl: Disjoining*—elongating the time of disjunction or elongating another part of the *īqāʿ*. Both result in metric expansion.

3/4 | ♩ ♪ ♪ ♩ | ⇒⇒ 3/4 + 1/8 | ♩ ♪ ♪ ♩. | or 4/4 | 𝅗𝅥 ♪ ♪ ♩ |

9. *Taṣdīr: Introduction*—introducing the *īqāʿ* by its last part. This term is borrowed from a poetical device in which the rhyming word has already occurred at the beginning of the line of poetry.

3/4 | ♩ ♪ ♪ ♩ | ⇒⇒ ♪ ♪ ♩ | ♩ ♪ ♪ ♩ |

10. *Tartīl: Slow tempo*—the term *tartīl* is borrowed from Qurʾanic sciences and refers to slow, ornate chanting of the Qurʾān. The *tartīl* in music slows down the tempo of an *īqāʿ* and, when carried to a maximum, transforms the category *light* into *light-heavy* and *light-heavy* into *heavy.*

3/8 | ♪ ♩ | ⇒⇒ 3/4 | ♩ 𝅗𝅥 | ⇒⇒ 3/2 | 𝅗𝅥 𝅝 |

11. *Ḥadr* or *ḥathth: Fast tempo*—the term *ḥadr* is borrowed from Qurʾanic sciences and refers to fast but careful recitation of the Qurʾān. The *ḥadr* in music speeds up the tempo of an *īqāʿ* and, when carried to a maximum, transforms the category *heavy* into *light-heavy* and *light-heavy* into *light.* Reversing the arrows in example 10 will illustrate this technique.

continued

FIGURE 2 *(continued)*

12. Daraj or *idrāj: Gradation—doubling* all attacks including those of *passage.*

3/4 | ♩ 𝅗𝅥 | ⇒⇒ 3/4 | ♩ ♩ ♩ | ⇒⇒ 3/4 | ♪ ♪ ♪ ♪ ♪ ♪ |

fundamental — with *passage* — with *doubling*

Al-Fārābī remarked that this technique leads to complete conjunction and gives a false impression of speed. Comparing *fast tempo* with *gradation,* al-Fārābī says that *fast tempo* shrinks the time of the *īqā*ʿ whereas *gradation,* which adds attacks in the place of silences, gives an impression of motion and hence of speed, but in fact does not alter the time span of the cycle.

13. Tamkhīr: Specific technique that turns the attacks of *light* and *heavy īqāʿāt* into a succession of *medium* attacks: ♩

3/2 | 𝅗𝅥 𝅝 | ⇒⇒ 3/2 | ♩ ♩ ♩ ♩ ♩ ♩ |

2/4 | ♪ ♪ ♩ | ⇒⇒ 2/4 | ♩ ♩ |

14. Timbral and dynamic changes: Here al-Fārābī borrows heavily from Arabic grammar and phonology. An attack may be any of the following.

a. *Qawiyya, tāmma: strong, loud, and complete.* Al-Fārābī refers to this and notates it as *tan* and compares its sound to the sound of the Arabic indefinite accusative ending *an.*

b. *Mutawassiṭa: moderate.* Al-Fārābī refers to this and notates it as *ta* and compares its sound to the sound of the definite accusative ending *a,* less loud and resounding than the one above.

c. *Layyina: soft.* Al-Fārābī compares its sound to that of an unvowelled consanant.

These types of attacks are interchangeable for the purpose of rhythmic variations and ornamentations.

15. Mushākala: homogeneity. Two or more successive cycles having exactly the same pattern are rhythmically homogeneous.

3/4 | ♩ ♪ ♪ ♩ | ♩ ♪ ♪ ♩ |

16. Mukhālafa: heterogeneity. Two successive cycles differing in pattern.

3/4 | ♩ ♪ ♪ ♩ | ♪ ♩ ♩ ♪ |

but also techniques for performance, intended to enhance creativity and produce a unique aesthetic effect—as is amply and eloquently corroborated in the narratives of the *Kitāb al-aghānī* 'Book of Songs' of Abū al-Faraj al-Iṣbahānī. [See SNAPSHOT: PERFORMERS FROM *KITĀB AL-AGHĀNĪ*.] However, not every technique applies to all the *īqāʿāt.*

Al-Fārābī views the *īqā*ʿ as rhythms organized according to modes. He observed that a meter was not frozen—it could be contracted and expanded in a composition. He explained rhythmic variations in terms of prosodic models and held that they consisted of additions or substractions of timeless attacks. Finally, he included tempo and dynamic and timbral changes as an integral part of his theory of rhythm.

After al-Fārābī, Ibn Sīnā (d. 1037), Ibn Zaylā (d. 1048), Ikhwān al-Ṣafā (fl. eleventh century), and Ṣafī al-Dīn al-Urmawī (d. 1294) also wrote about rhythm; their work, though, came nowhere near his theoretical achievements. The durational values of the old rhythmic modes changed, and new modes were created. However, rhythmic notation continued to use al-Fārābī's letter symbols, supplementing them with the paradigms of poetic rhythmic feet and meters as well as the circle notation of the prosodists (figure 3).

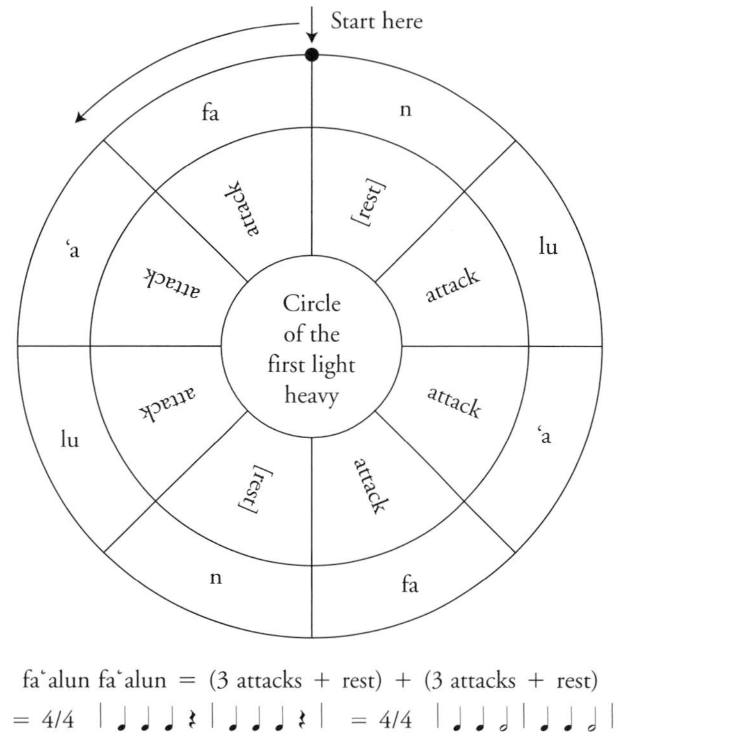

FIGURE 3 Thirteenth-century circle notation, in English transliteration, combining prosodic and musical notation in circular form. From Ṣafī al-Dīn al-Urmawī's *al-Risāla al-sharafiyya*. See II.2 in figure 1, above.

REFERENCES

D'Erlanger, Baron Rodolphe. 1930–1938. *La musique arabe*. Vols. 1–3. Paris: Librairie Orientaliste Paul Geuthner.

Al-Fārābī, Abū Naṣr. 1413 (copied). *Kitāb al-īqāʿāt* (Book of Rhythms). Istanbul: Topkapı Sarayı MS. III, Ahmet 1878, fol. 160b–167a.

———. 1240 (copied). *Kitāb iḥṣāʾ al-īqāʿāt* (Book for the Basic Comprehension of Rhythms). Manisa Public Library MS 1705, fol. 59–90a.

———. 1967. *Kitāb al-mūsīqī al-kabīr* (Grand Book of Music), ed. Ghaṭṭās ʿAbd-al-Malik Khashaba; rev. (with introduction) Maḥmūd Aḥmad al-Ḥifnī. Cairo: Dār al-Kātib al-ʿArabī.

———. 1968–1969. "Die Theorie von Īqāʿ. 1: Übersetzung des Kitāb al-Īqāʿāt von Abū Naṣr al-Fārābī," trans. Eckhard Neubauer. *Oriens* 21–22:196–232.

———. 1994. "Die Theorie von Īqāʿ. 2: Übersetzung des Kitāb iḥṣāʾ al-īqāʿāt von Abū Naṣr al-Fārābī," trans. Eckhard Neubauer. *Oriens* 34:103–173.

Farmer, Henry George. 1943. *Saʿadyah Gaon on the Influence of Music*. London: Arthur Probsthain. (Reprinted in Eckhard Neubaur, ed. 1986. *Studies in Oriental Music*, Vol. I, 573–695. Frankfurt: Institut für Geschichte der Arabisch-Islamischen Wissenschaften an der Johann Wolfgang Goethe-Universität.)

Ibn Zaylā, Abū Manṣūr (d. 440/1048). 1964. *al-Kāfī fī 'l-mūsīqī*, ed. Zakariyyā Yūsuf. Cairo: Dār al-Qalam.

Ikhwān al-Ṣafā (fl. second half of fourth/tenth century). 1928. "Al-Risāla al-khāmisa min al-qism al-riyāḍī fī 'l-mūsīqī." In *Rasāʾil Ikhwān al-Ṣafā*, Vol. I, ed. Khayr al-Dīn al-Ziriklī, 132–180. Cairo: al-Maṭbaʿa al-ʿArabiyya.

———. 1976. *The Epistle on Music of the Ikhwān al-Ṣafā: Risāla fī al-mūsīqī*, trans. Amnon Shiloah. Tel Aviv: Tel Aviv University.

Al-Iṣbahānī, Abū al-Faraj (d. 967). 1927–1974. *Kitāb al-aghānī* (Book of Songs). 24 vols. Cairo: Dār al-Kutub.

Al-Kindī, Abū Yūsuf Yaʿqūb ibn Isḥāq (d. after 256/870). 1962a. "Kitāb al-muṣawwitāt al-watariyya min dhāt al-watar al-wāḥid ilā dhāt al-ʿashara awtār." In *Muʾallafāt al-Kindī al-mūsīqiyya*, ed. Zakariyyā Yūsuf, 67–92. Baghdad: Maṭbaʿa Shafīq.

———. 1962b. "Risāla fī ajzāʾ khabariyya fī 'l-mūsīqī." In *Muʾallafāt al-mindī al-mūsīqiyya*, ed. Zakariyyā Yūsuf, 91–110. Baghdad: Maṭbaʿa Shafīq.

Sawa, George Dimitri. 1983–1984. "Al-Fārābī's Theory of the Īqāʿ: An Empirically Derived Medieval Model of Rhythmic Analysis." *Progress Reports in Ethnomusicology* 1(9):1–32.

———. 1989. *Music Performance Practice in the Early ʿAbbāsid Era, 132 A.H./A.D 750.–320 A.H./A.D. 932*. Toronto: Pontifical Institute for Medieval Studies.

———. 1990. "Paradigms in al-Fārābī's Musical Writings." In *Paradigms in Medieval Thought: Applications in Medieval Disciplines*, ed. Nancy van Deusen and Alvin E. Ford, 81–92. Lewinston, N.Y.: Mellen.

Classification of Musical Instruments in the Medieval Middle East

George Sawa

Medieval Middle Eastern Instruments
Al-Fārābī's Classification
Ibn Sīnā's Classification
Ibn Zayla's Classification
Classification in the *Kanz al-Tuḥaf*
Ibn Ghaybī's Classification

From the seventh century onward, musical instruments are mentioned frequently in the sources on medieval Middle Eastern music. These sources include not only treatises on music and instruments but also anecdotal writings, anthologies, song collections, poems, books on entertainment, books on love and passion, biographies of poets and musicians, geographical writings, and sociocultural histories.

MEDIEVAL MIDDLE EASTERN INSTRUMENTS

The most common instrument was the *ʿūd*, a fretted plucked lute. This was the instrument singers preferred for accompanying themselves while they performed or composed. Other instruments (listed alphabetically here) included: the *ʿanqāʾ* 'zither' or 'dulcimer'; the Chinese *ṣanj* (probably a Chinese gong); the *duff* 'tambourine'; the *chang* 'Persian harp'; the *dūnāy* 'reed flute', with two tubes; the *ghichek* 'Persian spike fiddle'; the *juljul* 'bell'; the *kankala* (a single-string plucked instrument of Indian origin with a gourd-shaped box); the *miʿzafa* 'lyre'; the *mizmār* 'single- or double-reed pipe'; the *mizmār al-jarāb* 'bagpipe'; the *naqqāra* 'kettledrum'; the *nāy* 'flute' or 'pipe', with a single or double reed; the *nozheh* 'Persian dulcimer'; the *pisheh* 'Persian flute'; the *qaḍīb* 'wand'; the *qānūn* 'plucked zither'; the *rabāb* 'spike fiddle'; the *rubāb* 'lute' with two bellies, similar to the modern Persian *tār*; the *saffāqatān* 'castanets'; the *ṣanj* 'cymbals' or 'harp'; the *sulyāq* (probably a lyre); the *surnāy* 'flute'; the *shāhrūd* (perhaps a box zither); the *ṭabl* 'drum'; the *ṭunbūr* 'long-necked lute'; the *urghanīn* 'Byzantine organ'; and the *yarāʿa* 'flute'.

Although these instruments are mentioned in the early sources (and sometimes the construction of a specific instrument is described in copious detail), classification systems do not appear until the tenth century, when Abū Naṣr al-Fārābī (d. 950) laid down a unique system of classification. In the eleventh century, Ibn Sīnā (980–1037), known in the medieval West as Avicenna, developed a system radically different from al-Fārābī's. These two systems were later summarized by Ibn Zayla (d. 1048). Subsequent theorists who wrote in Arabic ignored the topic of instrument classification; but during the late medieval era, in the fourteenth and fifteenth centuries, systems of classification are mentioned in an anonymous Persian treatise called *Kanz al-tuḥaf* 'Treasure of Rarities', and by Ibn Ghaybī (d. 1435). They were inspired to some extent by the systems of al-Fārābī and Ibn Sīnā, respectively.

Considering the voice the most perfect instrument, al-Fārābī classified the other instruments hierarchically on the basis of their imitation of it.

AL-FĀRĀBĪ'S CLASSIFICATION

To understand al-Fārābī's system of classification, it is useful to look briefly at his educational background and scholarly interests. Al-Fārābī was not only a music theorist but also a political philosopher who wanted to develop a system of virtuous government for the purpose of bringing happiness to humanity; a performer on the *'ūd* 'lute', and hence an active participant in his musical culture; and a logician, considered second only to the Greek philosopher Aristotle.

As a music theorist, al-Fārābī was somewhat indebted to the ancient Greeks. His classification of musical instruments was centered on the human voice, which he considered preeminent. In this regard, he reflected both the ancient Greek theorists and the culture of medieval Arab society, which greatly esteemed sung poetry. This cultural value is documented in the narratives of *Kitāb al-aghānī* 'Book of Songs' by al-Iṣbahānī (d. 967): medieval Arab society gave the singer a higher status, and more remuneration, than it gave the instrumentalist.

Al-Fārābī's hierarchical division

Considering the voice the most perfect instrument, al-Fārābī classified the other instruments hierarchically on the basis of their imitation of it: those that imitated it best were higher in his classification; those that imitated it least were lower.

Because of his political philosophy, he placed inhuman sounds—which in his terms were unnatural, frightening, and thus unbearable—at the very bottom of the hierarchy. To him, unnatural instruments were akin to poison to the body. Their function was military: to frighten the enemy by their loudness and unpleasantness. Such instruments included the bells used by ancient Egyptian kings, instruments (which he did not specify) used by Byzantine kings, and the shouters used by Persian kings.

Next up on the scale he placed instruments that created visual rhythm but no sound. The human body, for example, can produce visual but silent rhythm when it performs the *zafn*, a type of dance that consists of moving the shoulders, the eyebrows, the head, and so on. Although such an instrument is near the bottom of al-Fārābī's classification, it is superior to the instruments of war, which produce unnatural, inhuman sounds.

Above the soundless instruments he placed the percussion instruments. These have to do with the arts of clapping, dancing, and playing the tambourines, drums, and cymbals. They are all of a similar class and are superior to the *zafn* by virtue of the fact that they produce sounds. However, they do not produce musical notes (pitches).

Above the percussion instruments were the melody instruments: the *'ūd* 'lute', *ṭunbūr* 'long-necked lute', *mi'zafa* 'lyre', *rabāb* 'spike fiddle', and wind instruments. These produce musical notes and therefore are superior to the percussion instruments.

At the apex, as we have seen, is the human voice, the most perfect instrument because it encompasses the qualities of all the lower instruments with respect to rhythm and pitch, while also using meaningful words that stir the imagination. Furthermore, the human voice can express emotions.

Al-Fārābī subdivided the melody instruments hierarchically according to how closely they imitated the human voice. At the top of this category came the *rabāb* and the wind instruments; below them were the *'ūd* 'plucked lute' and the *ṭunbūr* 'long-necked lute'; below them, in turn, were the plucked open-stringed instruments such as the *mi'zafa* 'lyre' and the *ṣanj* 'harp'. He explained why the bowed *rabāb* and the wind instruments were on the highest level within their class: not only could they imitate the human voice best (presumably because they were capable of sustained sounds), but they were able to some extent to imitate its emotionality. Al-Fārābī provided no clear explanation of why he considred the plucked lutes superior to open-stringed instruments, but one may assume that the actions involved in pressing a lute's strings to the fingerboard would allow performers to imitate some vocal techniques better than they could with open-stringed instruments.

The role of instruments in al-Fārābī's system

Al-Fārābī explained that, in addition to being inferior to the human voice, instruments play a role subservient to the voice. They accompany a vocal line by imitating it as closely as possible; their purpose is to amplify and enrich it, give it brilliance, make it more pleasant, and beautify it by performing idiosyncratic ornamentation. Instruments also play another important role, that of guardian to or support for the singer, giving him or her the proper intonation, correct durations, and a reminder of the melodic line. Instruments also provide a prelude to prepare for the singer's entrance, interludes to give the singer a rest, and a postlude to mark the end of a song.

IBN SĪNĀ'S CLASSIFICATION

Ibn Sīnā was a famous physician whose work on medicine had a profound impact on Europe. He was also a philosopher, logician, metaphysician, and scientist, but he was not a performer. In his classification system, instruments are viewed as physical entities without reference to cultural values or aesthetic considerations. At the core of his system is one main criterion: the presence or absence of strings.

Stringed instruments (chordophones)

Ibn Sīnā divided stringed instruments into three categories. In the first category he placed stringed instruments that are plucked and have frets, such as the *barbaṭ* 'lute' and the *ṭunbūr* 'long necked-lute'. In the second category he placed plucked or hammered stringed instruments that have no frets, by which he meant open-stringed instruments. He further divided his second category into two main subclasses: instruments that have strings stretched over the surface of the instrument, such as the *shāhrūd* 'zither' and the *'anqā'* 'dulcimer' or 'zither'; and instruments that have strings stretched over an empty space between the string holder and the resonator, such as the *ṣanj* 'harp' and the *sulyāq* 'lyre'. In his third category Ibn Sīnā placed bowed instruments that have frets, such as the *rabāb* 'spike fiddle'.

Nonstringed instruments

Ibn Sīnā placed both the aerophones and the idiophones in his group of nonstringed instruments. He divided the aerophones into four classes: (1) those in which the air is blown from one side with the mouthpiece placed inside the mouth, such as the *mizmār* 'single- or double-reed pipe'; (2) those in which the air is blown across a hole, such as the *yarā'a*, also known as the *surnāy* 'flute'; (3) those in which the air is blown by means of a mechanical device, such as the *mizmār al-jarāb* 'bagpipe'; (4) those in which air is blown into pipes, such as the Byzantine *urghanīn* 'organ'. Of the idiophones, he mentioned only the Chinese *ṣanj* (very likely a Chinese gong), which was struck with mallets.

After explaining his classification system, Ibn Sīnā added a prophetic note, saying that one can also invent other instruments.

IBN ZAYLA'S CLASSIFICATION

Ibn Zayla, a student of Ibn Sīnā, was a philosopher and mathematician as well as a music theorist. He summarized the systems of both al-Fārābī and Ibn Sīnā and added useful information regarding the nature of some instruments. We learn from Ibn Zayla, for example, that Ibn Sīnā's plucked or hammered *'anqā'* 'zither' or 'dulcimer' had movable bridges like today's Persian *sanṭūr* 'dulcimer'; and Ibn Sīnā's *mizmār* 'single- or double-reed pipe' is called *nāy*. Ibn Zaylā also added to Ibn Sīnā's idiophones the *qaḍīb* 'wand' and hand clapping. Unlike Ibn Sīnā, he did not overlook the membranophones; he cited the *duff* 'tambourine' and the *ṭabl* 'drum'.

CLASSIFICATION IN THE *KANZ AL-TUḤAF*

The *Kanz al-tuḥaf* 'Treasure of Rarities' is an anonymous fourteenth-century Persian treatise from the city of Iṣfahān. It is most valuable because—unlike many other treatises—it deals with the construction of musical instruments; it also offers a classification system.

In the *Kanz al-tuḥaf*, instruments are divided into two broad categories: perfect and imperfect. The "perfect" instruments include the *'ūd* 'lute', *ghichek* 'Persian spike fiddle', *rubāb* 'lute' of a type with two bellies, *mizmār* 'oboe', and *pisheh* 'flute'.

The category of "imperfect" instruments consists exclusively of open-stringed instruments, which are then subdivided into degrees of imperfection. Imperfect instruments include the *chang* 'harp', which the anonymous author considered the most nearly perfect of the imperfect instruments; the *nozheh* 'dulcimer', considered next after the harp in closeness to perfection; the *qānūn* 'plucked zither'; and the *moghnī*, a plucked instrument in the shape of a lute but with open strings. The author did not explain either the reason for the distinction between perfect and imperfect instruments or the reasoning behind the subcategories of imperfection. Regarding the division of instruments into perfect and imperfect, however, al-Fārābī's system may offer some clarification: the *Kanz al-tuḥaf* may have placed open-stringed instruments below winds and lutes because the author followed al-Fārābī's line of thought—that open-stringed instruments are less able to imitate the voice.

IBN GHAYBĪ'S CLASSIFICATION

Ibn Ghaybī was a court lutenist and singer, a poet, and a painter as well as a music theorist. In his *Jāmi' al-alḥān* 'Compiler of Melodies', he listed more than forty instruments, which he classified into three broad categories: instruments with strings (chordophones); wind instruments (aerophones); and "cups, bowls, and slabs of metal" (idiophones).

The chordophones included open-stringed instruments and the various types of lutes, with or without frets, plucked or bowed; the latter included an instrument resembling the hurdy-gurdy. Wind instruments were divided into those with holes (flute and reed pipe) and those without holes (horn, trumpet, panpipes, and organ). The idiophones, as noted above, included cups filled with water, bowls, and slabs. Ibn Ghaybī did not limit himself to instruments of the Middle East but also included some from Central Asia, East Asia, and Europe. Like both Ibn Sīnā and Ibn Ghaybī, however, he overlooked the membranophones.

In brief, then, medieval writers articulated various systems of classification. The most interesting, perhaps, is al-Fārābī's hierarchical system, since it reflects his educational background and his interests as a researcher and—most important—is culture-specific. The preeminence of the voice in this system derives from two sources: ancient Greek theorists and medieval Middle Eastern cultural and aesthetic values. The instruments are then arranged hierarchically in terms of how well they imitate the human voice and how natural and pleasant they are. Al-Fārābī was concerned not only with the voice, but also with the human body as an instrument that can clap and dance and, in dancing, generate visual but soundless rhythm. Ibn Sīnā's system, ignoring membranophones, classifies instruments on the basis of whether or not they have strings; this system is broadly based on the physical properties of instruments and their method of sound production. Ibn Zayla combines al-Fārābī's and Ibn Sīnā's systems. The *Kanz al-tuḥaf* presents a system based partially on al-Fārābī's hierarchical classification. Finally, Ibn Ghaybī reflects Ibn Sīnā's approach.

REFERENCES

D'Erlanger, Baron Rodolphe. 1930, 1935. *La musique arabe*. Vols. 1 and 2. Paris: Librairie Orientaliste Paul Geuthner.

Al-Fārābī, Abū Naṣr (d. 950). 1967. *Kitāb al-mūsīqī al-kabīr* (Grand Book of Music), ed. Ghaṭṭās 'Abd-al-Malik Khashaba; rev. with introduction Maḥmūd Aḥmad al-Ḥifnī. Cairo: Dār al-Kātib al-'Arabī.

Farmer, Henry George. 1929. *A History of Arabian Music to the Thirteenth Century*. London: Luzac. (Reprinted 1973.)

———. 1965. *The Sources of Arabian Music*. Leiden: Brill.

———. 1966. *Islam: Musikgeschichte in Bildern*, ed. Heinrich Besseler and Max Schneider. Band 3: Musik des Mittelalters und der Renaissance. Lf. 2. Leipzig: VEB Deutscher Verlag für Musik.

———. 1986. *Studies in Oriental Music*, ed. Eckhard Neubauer. 2 vols. Frankfurt: Institut für Geschichte der Arabisch-Islamischen Wissenschaften an der Johann Wolfgang Goethe-Universität.

Ibn Ghaybī, 'Abd al-Qādir (d. 1435). *Jāmi' al-alḥān* (Compiler of Melodies). Oxford: Oxford University, Bodleian Library Marsh 282.

Ibn Zayla, Abū Manṣūr (d. 1048). 1964. *al-Kāfī fī 'l-mūsīqī*, ed. Zakariyyā Yūsuf. Cairo: Dār al-Qalam.

Al-Iṣbahānī, Abū al-Faraj (d. 967). 1927–1974. *Kitāb al-aghānī* (Book of Songs). 24 vols. Cairo: Dār al-Kutub.

Kanz al-tuḥaf (Treasure of Rarities). 14th century (anonymous). Cambridge: Kings College 211. Leiden: Rijksuniversiteit Bibliotheek, Cod. 271(2) Warn. London: BM Or 2361; and India Office, 2067 Ethé 2763. Paris: Bibliothèque Nationale, 913.

Lerner, Ralph, and Muhsin Mahdi, eds. 1972. *Medieval Political Philosophy: A Source Book*. Ithaca, N.Y.: Cornell University Press.

Sawa, George Dimitri. 1982. "Musical Instruments, Middle Eastern." *Dictionary of the Middle Ages*. New York: Scribner.

———. 1989. *Music Performance Practice in the Early 'Abbāsid Era: 132 A.H./A.D. 750 320A.H./A.D. 932.* Toronto: Pontifical Institute for Medieval Studies.

Musical Instruments in the Arab World

Scheherazade Qassim Hassan

Terminology and Classification
Role of Musical Instruments: Concepts and Continuity
Traditional Instruments in Contemporary Performance
Adopted and Adapted Western Instruments

Most of the basic musical instruments used in the contemporary Arab world were already known in the ancient civilizations of Mesopotamia, Egypt, and southern Arabia; in the Islamic period; or in both. Consequently, a certain continuity with the past—in some cases dating back 5,000 years—is evident in the morphology, denomination, or function of the basic instrument types, and even in the role of ensembles.

Perhaps the most persistent similarity has to do with the secondary status of musical instruments relative to the voice. Throughout the history of the region, instruments have generally been at the service of the voice, and this status is still considered the quintessence of contemporary Arabo-Islamic civilization. In the twentieth century, modern trends in music began to change this status and liberate urban instruments from their historical association with the voice; but this trend has not really changed the primacy of the voice. In "classical" music, instruments rarely perform outside the framework of a vocal repertoire; in folk music, some instrumental performances are unrelated to the voice but are always connected with a social occasion of which music is only one aspect. Still, there are numerous musical instruments of all categories in traditional urban and folk music.

TERMINOLOGY AND CLASSIFICATION

In Islamic sources, a number of terms are used to designate musical instruments in general. *Āla mūsīqāriyya* 'tool of the musician', referring to the musician himself; and *ālāt al-lahū* 'instruments of amusement and diversion', linked with "forbidden pleasures" (Farmer 1986:79), appear in the ninth and tenth centuries. *Ālāt al-ṭarab* 'instruments evoking emotion', an old term still in use, suggests the emotional effect of instruments generally in secular contexts. In the twentieth century, the appellation most widespread in the Arab world is *ala mūsīqiyya* 'musical instrument' (plural, *ālāt mūsīqiyya*), often reduced, in a musical milieu, simply to *āla* 'instrument'. In some regions, *'idda* 'ensemble of tools' indicates specific groups of instruments connected with specific musical arts.

Arab authors have various criteria for distinguishing between types of musical instruments. The most ancient sources refer to ethnic preferences in the use of instruments among peoples of the ancient world, including the non-Muslim Indians and Greeks. But the first explicit musical classification in Arabo-Islamic civilization must be attributed to al-Fārābī in the ninth century, who presented more than one system of classification in his *Kitāb al-mūsīqā al-kabīr* 'Grand Book of Music'. The most detailed and complete classification is hierarchical and is based on the capacity of an instrument to maintain a musical sound—that is, to imitate the human voice (D'Erlanger 1930). [See CLASSIFICATION OF MUSICAL INSTRUMENTS IN THE MEDIEVAL MIDDLE EAST.]

The great majority of modern writings (as well as most ancient writings) use an explicit tripartite classification based on the acoustical principles of sound production. Contemporary musicians, musicologists, and amateurs, like most of their predecessors, use three categories. The first category, *al-ālāt al-watariyya* 'instruments with strings', corresponds to the old *ālāt dhāt al-awtār* 'instruments possessing strings'. The second category, *al-ālāt al-hawā'iyya* 'wind instruments', corresponds to *ālāt dhāt al-nafkh* 'instruments possessing breath' (al-Faruqi 1981:9). The third category is *al-ālāt al-īqa'iyya* 'rhythmic instruments', a term that refers to both membranophones and idiophones and is used interchangeably with *ālāt al-naqr* 'percussion instruments' although it does not cover exactly the same instruments. *Ālāt al-naqr* includes idiophones whereas *ālāt al-iqa'iyya* exludes them. Another category—*al-ālāt al-jildiyya* 'membranophones' or *ālāt dhāt al-jild* 'instruments with membranes'—should presumably be covered by the other three; but these terms probably appear when, to avoid confusion, more specificity is needed.

ROLE OF MUSICAL INSTRUMENTS: CONCEPTS AND CONTINUITY

Arab music has always been considered essentially vocal, and before the twentieth century there was no question about the superiority of the voice. Nevertheless, Islamic musicological sources discussed instruments theoretically and regarded them as being outside the realm of the voice. Short and long-necked lutes, the flute, or the plucked zither often served for theoretical discussions of intervals, tetrachords, melodic modes, and tonal systems. The short-necked lute was used to illustrate tablatures indicating finger positions on the strings. Modern musicologists continue to address the same theoretical issues.

In performance, solo instrumental parts, preludes, interludes, and independent instrumental forms either are based on vocal renditions of regional repertoires, serving to reinforce the voice, or are played within a formal framework that is essentially vocal. Some performers of religious and religiously inspired forms sing without instrumental accompaniment. Good performers of urban and classical traditions, who also sing in religious settings, are often able to sing without accompaniment. Some secular singers claim that they can sing without instruments, and indeed that instruments may impede the development of singing, although others maintain that instruments can be helpful to a new singer (Hassan 1980). This idea was expressed in the ninth century by al-Iṣfahānī in *Kitāb al-aghānī* 'Book of Songs': he contrasts solo singing—*irtijāl* 'improvisation'—and singing with instrumental accompaniment, suggesting that instruments thwart the singer's desire for complete freedom (Sawa 1989:105).

The capacity of musical instruments to exceed what they usually do is an old preoccupation. As early as the tenth century, al-Fārābī demonstrated not only how instruments were used but also what they could be capable of in the hands of an expert musician (D'Erlanger 1930:164). In modern times, some musicians have attempted to broaden the techniques and sounds of musical instruments such as the *'ūd,* for reasons other than accompanying singing. In general, however, the results remain either theoretical or, if applied, experimental and limited. The most important experiments were by the Baghdad school of the *'ūd* 'lute', which sought to develop this instrument, create a new repertoire for it, and make it independent of singing; but these efforts were seen as alienating and failed to find a solid audience. To save solo *'ūd* playing, some representatives of this school had to go back to the traditional vocal repertoire and perform it on the *'ūd*. Thus in concerts and records devoted to the *'ūd*, famous instrumentalists sometimes depend on paraphrasing regional vocal traditions; for example, Iraqi solo *'ūd* performers base their content largely on the vocal material of the Iraqi *maqām*.

TRADITIONAL INSTRUMENTS IN CONTEMPORARY PERFORMANCE

Idiophones

The most common contemporary idiophones, found all over the Arab world, are the metallic *ṣunūj* 'cymbals'. They come in three sizes. The smallest are called *ṣunūj al-aṣābi'* 'finger cymbals', or *sagāt* in Egypt, *chumpārāt* in Iraq, *nuiqsāt* (the diminutive of *nāqūs*) in Morocco, and *zel* in Libya. The player uses two pairs, holding one pair in each hand between the thumb and index or middle finger. Small cymbals are used by women dancers, Gypsies, and effeminate men to accompany solo dancing with other string and percussion instruments. Medium-size cymbals (about 10 centimeters in diameter), called *tura* in Egypt, are played by groups that specialize in religious music. In Oman the same cymbal *ring*, *sehal*, or *ṭāsa* (plural, *ṭūs*) is played by men or women to accompany the singing and dancing of professional groups. A pair of *ṭūs* are used in the bedouin dance *'ayāla* of the Gulf region, in which two rows of men sing antiphonally. [See Dance in the Arabian Peninsula.] Large cymbals (15 centimeters in diameter) are often the most popular idiophone in both secular and religious contexts. They are usually played with an ensemble of other instruments that differ according to the country and the occasion.

At many outdoor festivities, time is structured by the metallic sound of *ṣunūj*. In rural Mesopotamia, in the original war dance *al-sās*, the dancers (who carry shields and are sometimes on horseback) are accompanied by cymbals, a shawm, a large circular drum, and a small double kettledrum. Cymbals have an important role in religious ceremonies, accompanying monodic chant and group singing. Large cymbals are used in Oriental Coptic, Chaldean, and Syriac churches; in Shi'a mourning ceremonies in Iraq, Lebanon, and Bahrain; and in the ceremonies of different Sufi orders.

TRACK 21

In the Afro-Arab traditions of North Africa, there are two pairs of medium-size circular cymbals connected by a clasp: the *karākīb* or *karkabūs* in Morocco and Algeria, and the *shikshakāt* in Libya. *Karākīb* are used in ceremonies called *gnāwa* in Morocco, *dīwān* in Algeria, and *stambūlī* in Tunisia; these are rituals in colorful symbolic settings combining dance, music, poetry, and singing. To reconcile the visible and the invisible worlds and communicate with spirits—thanking them and asking them for advice and deliverance—up to four pairs of *karākīb*, accompanied by drums and frequently a *gimbrī* lute (see below) are used. This idiophone is used all over Libya during religious ceremonies and pilgrimages to the shrines of saints, as well as in folk music.

FIGURE 1 Metal dish used in *al-ghinā' al-San'ānī* in Yemen. Photo by Scheherazade Qassim Hassan, San'a, 1997.

The metallic tray, the metallic can, and the terra-cotta jar are important struck idiophones. In Yemen, the flat circular copper tray *ṣaḥn nuḥāsī* is played like a tambourine—alone or with the *ṣan'ānī* lute—to accompany the classical song genre *ṣan'ānī* (figure 1). [See *Al-Ghinā' al-Ṣan'ānī*: Poetry and Music in Ṣan'ā'.] This tray is also played in folk traditions by men and women, and is known as *dish* or *chinchāna* in this context. During the *'Īsāwa* Sufi ritual in Morocco [see The Issawiyya of Tunis], where trance is combined with spectacular practices such as eating glass and piercing the flesh with metal skewers, the *ṭāsa*, a copper bowl struck with sticks, is played along with a variety of drums and frame drums. In middle and south Iraq (Mesopotamia), rural singing is accompanied by striking a tray on which coins, a chapelet, or other objects that will jingle have been placed.

Between Basra in southern Iraq and Oman, all along the Gulf—in Bahrain, Qatar, and the Emirates—the *tanaka* or *pāto*, a large metallic jerrycan for oil or fat, is used by Afro-Arabs in a musical tradition called the *lewa*. In a *lewa* performance, a group of men and women sing and dance, accompanied by an ensemble called *'iddat al-lewa* 'tools of *lewa*' which also includes a large shawm and some drums. The *tanaka* usually has recessed sides and is played with two palm or rubber sticks. This idiophone is very light in weight and can slip while being played. Some performers therefore fill it with stones; but even so, the percussion style is so frenetic that the jerrycan does not usually survive a performance and a new one is required each time. This fragility led one major *leīwa* ensemble in Bahrain to devise a more durable substitute, a copper tray fixed on four legs; this tray is surrounded by jingles and has attached to it three metallic receptacles of different sizes producing three different sounds (figure 2).

The *jaḥla* (pronounced *yiḥla*), a terra-cotta jar originally used for food or water, is an indispensable idiophone for pearl fishers' leisure songs, *fijiri,* along the Gulf shores, particularly between Bahrain and Qatar. The players combine three different strokes: striking the sides of the jar with both hands; striking one side with one hand while the thumb of the other hand holds the rim of the mouth; and striking the mouth with an open palm to cover it entirely. Three or four jars are used to accompany the choral singing of the sailors and pearl fishers, with an equal number of small two-headed drums, *mirwās.* A large horizontal barrel drum, *hājar,* is also used. These different sounds add to the rich polyrhythmic texture.

Mortars and pounders called *mihbash,* made in many sizes, are used by the bedouin to pound coffee beans. The mortar and the act of pounding in a particular rhythm, which is different for every bedouin *shaykh,* symbolize hospitality.

Struck idiophones are also signaling instruments, used to produce specific rhythms known by a population. In Morocco, the Berbers beat a copper or brass tube with a pair of short rods. Nowadays, the tube has been replaced by the circular cast-iron brake drum taken from a car, called *naqūs* 'bell'. This same idiophone is used in the streets of Baghdad to announce that a kerosene dealer is coming. Bells of various types and sizes are signaling instruments for pets and other animals. Large and small handbells are used in Christian churches, and some large empty suspended bells have been observed in Egyptian and Iraqi villages, summoning devotees to Sufi ceremonies.

The *khirkhāsḥa* 'rattle' (plural, *khirkhāshāt*) is intended mainly for children. Some rattles, however, have specific functions. The *beiraq,* a metallic ball rattle fixed on top

FIGURE 2 *Tanaka* used by the Afro-Arab community in Bahrain. Photo by Scheherazade Qassim Hassan, 1997.

of a pole, is shaken during bedouin battles and Shiʿa mourning ceremonies for Ḥusayn. In Libya, *khirkhashāt* made of gourds are played in pairs on festive occasions to accompany dances, as well as during religious ceremonies; they are also used by Sufi orders.

In southern Iraq, the Gulf countries, Oman, Yemen, and Saudi Arabia, the *manjūr* (also pronounced *manyour*), a jingle girdle or skirt made of hooves sewn onto a piece of cloth, is indispensable in *al-nuban* or *fann al-nubān* 'art of *nuban*', also called *zār* or *ṭambūra* (after the lyre; Racy 1988). *Al-nuban* is the major Afro-Arab musical ritual of possession and healing; it combines the singing of poetry with dancing, accompanied by an ensemble called *'iddat al-nubān* 'tools of *nubān*'. This ensemble comprises a *ṭambūra* (lyre) and four kettledrums as well as the *manjūr*. The *manjūr* produces sound when it is activated by the dancer's hip movements. In some cases (though these are exceptional), two *manjūr* are used, one for the basic rhythm and the second for ornamentation. In some countries of the Arabian Peninsula, spirit possession ceremonies are regarded with suspicion and have been marginalized; in fact, they have almost disappeared in Yemen and the Emirates. In Bahrain, the music of *nuban* may be heard in many professional music houses, apart from its original context.

Throughout the region, jingles attached to strings are a type of female jewelry worn during dances. In healing ceremonies in Oman, the sick person is supposed to wear copper jingles; when activated by dance movements, these produce sounds that are said to drive away evil spirits. The *mirwaḥa* is used in Coptic, Syriac, and Armenian Oriental churches [see MARONITE MUSIC; THE COPTIC ORTHODOX CHURCH AND ITS MUSIC; SYRIAC RELIGIOUS MUSIC]. This instrument consists of silver jingles attached to a circular silver disk, fixed to the the top of a wooden stick so that when the stick is turned, the jingles strike the edges of the disk. The *mirwaḥa* symbolizes the murmuring of angels, and so it is turned whenever a holy text refers to angels. Another rhythmic percussion instrument, used in Algeria, in the Gulf area, and elsewhere in the Arab world, consists of jingles or five pairs of metallic disks attached to a tambourine frame without the membrane.

A scraped idiophone, which otherwise is a children's instrument, is used in Latin monasteries of the Middle East during days of fasting, when handbells and large bells are forbidden. It is also used by farmers as a scarecrow.

Chordophones: *Al-ālāt al-watariyya*

For Arabs, strings have always been the most important category of instruments. Four types of stringed instruments have been used in modern times: lutes, fiddles, zithers, and lyres. (Harps completely disappeared from the core area of the Arab world after the sixteenth century, leaving only traces in the southern periphery in contact with Africa.)

Both short- and long-necked lutes are used. Short-necked lutes include the *'ūd*; the *kwitra*; and the *'ūd 'arbī* or *tūnīsī*, specific to North African music. These are all associated with urban music. Long-necked lutes, by contrast, are associated with folk music. The *ṭanbūr*, *sāz*, and *buzuq* in eastern Arab lands and the *lōtār* and *gimbrī* in North Africa are used mainly by non-Arab populations; the *tidinit*, however, is a classical instrument played by the Arab tribes of Mauritania. The *qanbūs* of Yemen associated with urban music must be considered a category between long and short lutes.

Short-necked lutes: The 'ūd

TRACK 1 The *'ūd* or *al-'ūd al-sharqī* (plural, *'īdān*) is by far the most important and most prestigious Arab instrument. It was used in Middle Eastern centers of civilization even before the "golden ages" of the ninth and tenth centuries; but although it was known by all Arabs, many local traditions, whether art or folk, did not use it. Today the *'ūd*

The *'ūd* is the symbol of high Arab musical culture and indeed is called the *sulṭān* or *amīr* 'prince'.

is widespread in the Arab world, even in remote villages; it accompanies folk song. In some places where there is a distinct local version of the short-necked lute, the term *'ūd sharqī* 'eastern lute' is used.

The *'ūd* is the symbol of high Arab musical culture and indeed is called the *sulṭān* or *amīr* 'prince'; it represents both secular musical pleasure and scientific and intellectual thought, and its history is closely connected with the splendors of urban Arab civilization. From Arabic manuscripts written from the ninth and tenth centuries to the present day, no other instrument has been studied so extensively or from so many perspectives—mythological, historical, cosmological, theoretical, acoustical, morphological, technical, ethnological, and sociological.

The modern *'ūd* is an unfretted instrument with five or six courses, played with a plectrum. The sixth string was apparently added in Baghdad in the 1940s. It has been adopted by Arab instrumentalists to give prominence to solo improvisation. In general, it is agreed that the Egyptian and Syrian schools are primarily based on vocal aesthetics, whereas the Baghdad school established an instrumental technique and style independent of the needs of the voice.

In many parts of the Arab world, the second half of the twentieth century saw a remarkable renaissance of the *'ūd* in which its production and use expanded. Evidently, its modest size (which makes it easy to transport) and its technical capabilities (relative to those of regional short-necked lutes) met musicians' need for a practical master reference instrument that could be used anywhere to accompany any singing, including popular song. Thus the *'ūd* supplanted many local lutes in the Arabian Peninsula and North Africa. Today, the *'ūd* still has multiple roles. It accompanies solo singing and is part of the *takht sharqi* 'Oriental ensemble' (*'ūd*, *qanun* 'zither', *nāy* 'flute', violin, and percussion) and modern enlarged orchestras. Its new role as a solo improvisational instrument has been accepted in almost all Arab capitals. In many Arab centers, concertos for *'ūd* and symphony orchestra bring together traditionally trained and Western-trained musicians. In Cairo, Damascus, Aleppo, Mosul, and Baghdad, famous manufacturers produce unique instruments on demand. In the 1970s, when the use of the *'ūd* expanded, large-scale machine manufacturing flourished. Baghdad and Cairo became important exporters of medium-quality instruments to the Gulf countries. Instruments can now be bought in special music shops everywhere and are even offered in the tourist markets of Damascus, Cairo, and Tunis.

The *'ūd 'arbī*—also called *'ūd maghribī* to distinguish it from the *'ūd sharqī*—is used in Algeria, mainly in the city of Constantine; and in Tunisia, where it is also known as *'ūd tūnsī*. This lute closely resembles the Oriental *'ūd* but has a smaller, more elongated sound box; and it is losing ground to the Oriental *'ūd*—which can be played in both the upper and the lower register. In traditional Tunisian ensembles, these registers require two instruments: the *'ūd tūnsī* for the upper octaves and the *rabāb* for lower notes. The *'ūd 'arbī* has a melodic and rhythmic role in urban Arab-Andalusian music; it is also used for improvisational passages and was part of small traditional ensembles. Today, these ensembles have grown to become large orchestras.

The Rashidiyya ensemble of Tunis, for example, has more than thirty musicians and heterogenous instruments, such as numerous violins, cellos, a contrabass, and at least two Oriental *'īdān*, two *qawānīn* (singular, *qānūn*) and two *nāyāt* (singular, *nāy*)—and only one *'ūd 'ārbī*, which in such a configuration is hardly audible. To revive small groups, the High Institute of Music in Tunis created a Tunisian ensemble in which the *'ūd tūnsī* and the Oriental *'ūd* play together, the former providing high tones and the latter providing the low register, thus taking over the traditionally vigorous role of the *rabāb*. The *'ūd tūnsī* is also used to accompany old urban Tunisian songs.

In Algeria, in the contemporary Constantine *nūba* ensembles, the *'ūd 'ārbī* is played with the *kwitra*, the *sniṭra* 'mandoline', the *rabāb* 'spike fiddle', the viola, and the *qānūn*. These instruments are accompanied by a drum (the *darbūka*), a *ṭār* (tambourine), cymbals, and small kettledrums. Other instrumental groups include guitar, *buzūkī*, and a flute (*juwwāk* or *shabāba*), or even piano and banjo. In Morocco, violins join the *rabāb*, the *'ūd 'ārbī*, and the *'ūd sharqī*; they are accompanied by one percussion instrument. These modern Arab-Andalusian orchestras, which always include the lute as a major instrument, are very popular and attract large audiences, although the instruments of the old *nūba* ensemble are hardly heard in these new settings.

Other short-necked lutes

The *kwitra* is another regional short-necked lute, used only in Arab-Andalusian urban ensembles in Morocco and in the Algerian cities Tlemcen (in the Moroccan quarter) and Algiers. This instrument resembles the *'ūd sharqī* but has a more elongated, smaller, less bulging sound box. In the classical *nūba* repertoire, it is played by the master of the ensemble, the *ma'allem* or *bāshā kyatrī*, who is the first lutenist. In Tlemcen, it accompanies *ḥawzī*, a song style that falls between the classical and the popular. The Moroccan equivalent of these two lutes was the *'ūd al-ramal* or *'ūd inqilāb*, which had the same construction, the same number of strings, and the same function but is no longer used in the Arab-Andalusian (*ṣan'a*) repertoire of Morocco.

TRACK 20 The *qanbūs* (also known as the *gabūs*, *'ūd ṣan'ānī*, and *turbī*) is used today to accompany the classical *ṣan'ānī* singing of Yemen. The *qanbus* is a four-string lute made from a single piece of wood; its sound box is covered with a skin membrane. It is probably descended from a tenth-century south Arabian lute. It is believed that in the nineteenth century the *qanbūs* was played in the Hijaz, Aden, Oman, and the Comores. Today in the Arabian Peninsula, it is played only in Yemen. The introduction of the *'ūd sharqī* into Yemen in the 1950s almost led to the disappearance of the *qanbūs*; but young Yemeni performers are now reviving it, and different forms and sizes are made on demand for individual musicians. Like all traditional lutes, the *qanbūs* is at the service of the voice, paraphrasing its melodic lines.

Long-necked lutes

In the Arab world of the Middle East, long-necked lutes such as the *ṭanbūr*, the *sāz*, and the *buzuq*—as well as other varieties, like the *junbush*, that are no longer in use—are primarily instruments of folk music among non-Arab populations. In North Africa, the *ginbri*, the *suisen*, and many less-known varieties are used mainly by Berbers and peoples of African origin. The oldest evidence of long-necked lutes in the region was found in archaeological digs in Iraq. Seals and reliefs attest to the existence of lutes from the Akkadian period (2350–2170 B.C.E.) onward. These artifacts show male musicians, standing or seated, holding the lute horizontally or, later, at an angle. In some depictions, the lute is accompanied by a small harp. In Egypt during the New Kingdom (1580–1090 B.C.E.), a long-necked lute was played by women.

Early Arabic written sources mention the long-necked lute, already named *ṭanbūr*, as the instrument preferred by the people of Lot. In the tenth century the *ṭanbūr baghdādī*, known in the region of Baghdad, was distinguished from the *ṭambūr khurasānī*, known in eastern Persia. The *ṭanbūr baghdādī* disappeared from the region of Baghdad and moved to the north; it still survives there among non-Arabic populations. This type of lute, with its metallic sound and high register, is favored by non-Arab populations, for whom it is equivalent in importance to the short-necked Oriental lute (*ʿūd*) of the Arabs.

The contemporary long-necked lutes, the *ṭanbūr* and *sāz*, are very popular among Kurds, Turkomans, and Yezidis, and the Gypsies in nothern Iraq and Syria. These lutes are made in different sizes and shapes. They have a varying number of frets, generally twelve to seventeen, and two or three courses of strings (Hassan 1980, 1982). The sound box is made of wood, metal, or vegetal materials. The *ṭanbūr* is the most popular instrument among amateurs, specialists, and professionals in these minority groups; it accompanies secular solo singing and the ritual and ceremonial songs of some esoteric Islamic groups. The *ṭanbūr* has flourished in the past few decades. When Baghdad Radio presented Kurdish and Turkoman programs in the 1970s, this instrument was featured and thus was reintroduced, after many centuries, to the musical life of Baghdad, becoming part of various radio ensembles that combined local and regional Arab instruments. In the north, it was introduced into the ensembles of cultural centers and schools.

To meet the needs and aesthetic standards of radio, another long-necked lute, probably of Turkish origin, the *buzuq*—which has enlarged tonal capacities and thus can compete with the *ʿūd*—was introduced into the capitals of the eastern Arab world. The *buzuq* has twenty-four frets, allowing the full range of sound preferred in cities like Baghdad, Damascus, and Beirut. The *buzuq* became an instrument for solo improvisations, *taqāsīm*, and is also played with the *ʿūd* and in modern ensembles.

The *ginbrī*, *gimbrī*, or *jumbrī*, also called a *hajiy*, is a popular long-necked lute used mainly by an originally African population that, through the slave trade, began arriving in Morocco in the eighteenth century. Today the *gimbrī* is also played by the Berbers of Morocco and by the Tuareg of Algeria. It has also been adapted and Arabized in Morocco, Algeria, and Tunisia. There are three types of *gimbrī*, which differ in origin: *sūdānī*, *gnāwī*, and *ʿarabī*. As a popular instrument, the *gimbrī* is made in more than one shape and usually in two sizes: the smaller *gimbrī ṣaghīr*, *souīdsī*, or *hajhūj*, which has nearly disappeared in Morocco; and a larger bass instrument, which is still in use. The sound box, which can be more or less voluminous, is made from wood, tortoiseshell, or a metal jerrycan. A *gimbrī* usually has two or three strings, attached to an ancient type of knob pegs. It is plucked with the fingers rather than a plectrum.

The *gimbrī* has a role in spiritual healing ceremonies called *jeddeba* or *stambūlī* in Tunisia and *līla* in southern Algeria. In these ceremonies, opposed good and evil spirits are each symbolized by a specific melody and color. Through music, dance, poetry, hand and foot clapping, and animal sacrifices to good spirits and saints, the body is said to be freed from bad vibrations, and the proper order of things is reestablished. The *gimbrī* is played by a *maʿallem* 'master' and is accompanied by a pair of concussion idiophones, *karākīb*, and several drums. This rhythmically driving music has a large following among young people and foreigners.

In Morocco, the *lotār*, a circular spike lute, is played by Berbers. Its sound box is covered with skin; it has three or four strings plucked with a plectrum; and the musician often stands while playing. It is accompanied by the *rabāb* and the *nāqūs*.

The Arab tribes of Mauritania and the Tuareg in the Sahara play the *tidīnīt*, a lute for art music. The *tidīnīt* has a long sound box (from 40 to 50 centimeters in length) made from a single piece of wood covered by a membrane; the neck passes beneath the skin. It has four strings, of which only the longer two are played with a plectrum or the fingers; the two shorter strings sound open. On convivial evenings, the *tidīnīt* is played by male specialists—along with the harp *ardin*, which is played by women—to accompany a repertoire of love songs and songs glorifying the Prophet Muhammad.

The bowed fiddle: Rabāb

Rabāb is the generic name for bowed fiddles in the Arab world. These fiddles are of two types: popular spike fiddles and classical polystring fiddles such as the Moroccan two-string *rbeb* and the Iraqi four-string *jōze*.

The oldest and best-known spike fiddle is the bedouin monochord *rabāba*, which has a thin wooden frame, rectangular or waisted, covered with skin stitched on one or more sides. In Yemen, in the Tihama region on the Red Sea, the *rabāba* is circular and has a wooden or metal sound box. At the beginning of the nineteenth century, a rectangular type was used in Egypt (Villoteau 1823), and probably thoughout the Middle East; this form, which has disappeared in urban Egypt, had the same characteristics as the current bedouin *rabāba*.

The neck stick of the bedouin *rabāba*, which holds the single peg, pierces the whole body and is extended on one end by a metal spike. The single horsehair string is rubbed with resin. For intonation, *rabāba* players make movable frets of thread or fine cloth bands tied around the neck. To produce the three to five notes of this instrument, the player touches the string very lightly with the fingers of the left hand; he sits cross-legged on the ground, holding the instrument at an angle with the spike on his thigh—a position that makes it easy to turn the instrument right and left and facilitates bowing. In Saudi Arabia, Kuwait, and the Gulf area, this way of playing is called *yisḥab al-rabāba* 'pulling the *rabāba*', and some of the musical styles are called *masḥūb* 'that which is pulled'.

The rectangular *rabāba* is used by bedouin in the Arabian Peninsula, Jordan, Iraq, Syria, and Lebanon; the waisted *rabāba* is usually found among rural and semisedentary tribes in contact with towns east of the Mediterranean. This instrument is used in two kinds of reperoires. The first repertoire includes the *qaṣīd* and *hujeinī*, sung solo; and the *samrī*, a communal dance of the Arabian Peninsula, Jordan, Syria, and Iraq, accompanied by antiphonal singing. The second repertoire is that of semisedentary tribes. It includes the free solo singing of *'atāba* and the rhythmic dances of the Euphrates, such as the *mijāna* and *dal'ūna* in Iraq and Syria, extending to Lebanon and Palestine.

The *rabāba* is also used by Gypsies in the Middle East. In the desert and semidesert regions, Gypsies are the only professional musicians invited as groups to celebrate festive occasions.

Since bedouin music is based on the word, a *rabāba* player is expected to be primarily a poet, capable of memorizing poetry and of improvising it instantly. He is called *al-shā'ir* 'the poet' (not a musician); he uses the *rabāba* to punctuate his poetic recitation; and his verbal talent (not his musicianship) gives him his authority in the tribe. He is perceived as the main entertainer and the person who communicates social information and commentary; above all, he is feared, for the *shaykh's* reputation is in his hands: his poems praising or criticizing the *shaykh* might be transmitted and repeated for generations.

Because a *rabāba* is fragile, various devices have been used to prevent damage. Gypsies were the first to use gasoline cans and barrels of different sizes as sound boxes. New shapes (triangular and circular) are being experimented with in urban centers in the eastern Arab world. One Palestinian *rabāba* player from Jerusalem, who is often engaged for celebrations, built a large wooden instrument that has a sound board with a circular plastic membrane, which does not need to be adjusted during cold or hot weather. Although musicians prefer the sound of natural membranes, an artificial membrane does not loosen or tighten when the weather changes.

Since bedouin music is based on the word, a *rabāba* player is expected to be primarily a poet, capable of memorizing poetry and of improvising it instantly.

Among the Berber populations of Morocco, the *ribāb* is a monochord spike fiddle with a circular or curvilinear frame body, covered with skin on both sides; it is played with a short bow that has one or two strands of beads whose vibration gives this instrument its characteristic timbre. Because the musican plays standing, the spike of the *ribāb* is attached to his belt with a leather hoop. The *ribāb* accompanies *rwais*, itinerant poets (a function similar to that of the bedouin *rabāba*). A few such instruments may be played together along with the other long lute, the *lotār*.

In the central and southern Sahara of Algeria and the south of Libya, the *imzad*, a circular monochord fiddle played with a short bow or the fingers, is reserved for women. In Algeria, the sound box of the *imzad* is made from a calabash and, as with many African instruments, has an arched neck. In southern Libya, in the region of Ghadames and Ghat, this instrument is called a *rabāba* and can be made from a gourd. The *imzad* accompanies women's singing at festive celebrations and in mourning ceremonies. As with other Saharan instruments, the repertoire of the *imzad* is pentatonic.

With the exception of the Andalusian *rabāb*, all multiple-stringed fiddles in the Arab world are spike fiddles. Both the North African and the Iraqi fiddles are classical instruments.

The only polychord fiddle used for a popular repertoire is the two-stringed Egyptian *rabāb*. In the early nineteenth century this instrument was known in Egypt as *rabāb al-mughannī* '*rabāb* of the singer', as opposed to the bedouin *rabāb al-sha'ir* '*rabāb* of the poet'. The Egyptian *rabāb* and the bedouin *rabāb* were both still used in Egypt at the beginning of the twentieth century, but today only the *rabāb* of the singer survives in nonbedouin populations. According to Villoteau, at the time of Napoleon's expedition to Egypt in 1798 the two-stringed *rabāb* could be found in two sizes: the larger was the *kamanja 'ajūz* 'old *kamanja*', and the smaller was the *kamanja farkh* 'young *kamanja*' or *ṣughayyir* 'the small'. From Villoteau's detailed description, we can conclude that the overall morphology of these traditional two-stringed *rabābs* has remained the same to the present day; only the name has changed, from *kamanja* to *rabāb*. However, what Villoteau called the *rabāb al-sha'ir* corresponds to the trapezoidal single-stringed frame fiddle and now exists only among desert bedouin.

Today, the sound box of a traditional *rabāb* in Egypt is still made from a coconut shell cut open on one side to fix the skin. If the sound emanating from the coconut is judged good or *dhakar* 'male', the box is kept; if the sound is considered female, the box is either thrown away or opened at the back. The strings are horsehair and must be taken from a living animal. Current innovations include a plastic membrane mounted on a metal-rimmed sound box, and the use of one metal string (the other string is still horsehair).

In the Egyptian delta and Upper Egypt, the *rabāb* accompanies epic songs, ballads, popular music, and dance. One particular function of this *rababa* is to accompany the long epic of the Banu Hilal bedouin, *Sīrat Banī Hilāl* [see LEARNING EPIC TRA-

DITIONS]; the musicians are specialists—poet-singers who recite this epic within a narrow melodic range. Two *rababāt* are sometimes played together by seated or standing musicians, accompanied by a percussion instrument. The complete recitation of the lives and deeds of many historical and mythological heroes, as well as their migration from Yemen to Egypt, once took about ninety evenings; it was usually performed in popular coffeehouses and at village festivities, for intensely involved audiences. This tradition still exists, but in a very abbreviated form (Reynolds 1995).

The Andalusian *rebāb, rbāb* or *rbeb andalusī*, which was brought to medieval Europe as the rebec, is used exclusively in the classical music of North Africa and is also known as *rabāb maghribī*. This *rbeb* has an ovoid or boat shape with a small neck angled backward. The Algerian *rbeb* has a long body; the Moroccon *rbeb* is wider but shorter. The sound box has two parts: the upper part is covered with a layer of thin copper in Tunisia and Algeria, or with wood in Morocco; the lower part of the face is covered with skin. There are two thick gut strings, widely separated from each other and from the face. The bow is short, curved, and fairly heavy; the bowing is like that of a contrabass. This instrument, with its low, purring sonorities, once had the major role in traditional *nūba* ensembles in Libya, Tunisia, Algeria, and Morocco; but it is falling into disuse because of its nasal tone and its technical difficulty, even though certain masters developed techniques for playing faster and more brilliantly. Some instrument makers have added a third string; others have changed the construction of the body from a sculptured piece of wood to a lute-like back made of wooden strips. In large modern orchestras the current tendency is to combine one *rbeb* with a dozen violins and violas, a configuration that completely hides its sound.

The Baghdadi spike fiddle—the *jōze* or *kamāna*—has a sound box made of a section or frame cut from a coconut. The sound box is always left open, while its face is covered with skin. There are four strings. This instrument figures only in the *chalghī baghdādī* ensemble (the Baghdadi ensemble), which specializes in accompanying the classical urban tradition *al-maqām al-ʿirāqī* 'Iraqi *maqam*' [see THE IRAQI *MAQĀM*: TRANSMISSION, TEACHING, AND LEARNING].

Board zithers: The **qānūn** *and* **sanṭūr**

The only zithers used in the Arab world are table zithers, the *qānū* and *sanṭūr*. These are instruments of classical and urban music. The *qānūn* is more widespread in urban Arab centers and is taught in its conservatories as a pan-Arab instrument. Although Arab musicians generally know of the *sanṭūr*, its use is now restricted to Iraq.

In the Arab world, the first mention of the *qānū*, a trapezoidal table zither, was in Egypt in the early fourteenth century. The *qānū* has about twenty-six triple strings, played with two plectra attached to rings worn on the first finger of each hand. It is considered an aristocratic instrument and is sometimes referred to as "the sultan." It forms an essential part of the *takht sharqī* ensemble (the small Oriental ensemble) along with the *ʿūd*, the *nāy* 'flute', violin, and percussion and has maintained a prominent place in large modern orchestras. It has also become a solo instrument. By the 1930s, multiple levers, *ʿurab*, were commonly added to each course of strings so that the performer could switch easily from one scale to another. For example, a course of strings tuned to E-flat would become E-half-flat when one lever was raised and would become E-natural when two levers were raised.

The *sanṭūr* (a name of Aramaean origin) is mentioned in the Old Testament as the *sintir*, which was part of the orchestra of the Babylonian king Nebuchadnezzar (604–562 B.C.E.). Very probably, the *sanṭūr* derived from an ancient Babylonian horizontal harp that was struck with two sticks, as the modern instrument still is. The *sanṭūr* was popular in Spain and known in North Africa and Egypt. At the beginning of the nineteenth century, Villoteau mentioned it as a marginal instrument in Egypt—he did not see any examples. Today, it is used only in Iraq. The face of the Iraqi *sanṭūr* is an isosceles trapezoid; there are twenty-three to twenty-five triple strings tuned in unison and stuck with a pair of light sticks. The *santūr* is one of two essential melodic instruments accompanying the classical Iraqi *maqām*. It is part of the local ensemble *chalghī baghdādī*, along with the spike fiddle and two percussion instruments. Nowadays it is also used as a solo instrument.

The lyre: Ṭambūra

The lyre is one of the oldest instruments in the world. It has existed in many shapes and sizes in Mesopotamia since the third millenium B.C.E. Five types of lyres, some circular, are depicted on seals from the second century B.C.E. found in Dilmun (present-day Bahrain). In Yemen, murals dating from the first millenium B.C.E. depict a five-stringed lyre with circular sound box.

In the modern Middle East, the *ṭambūra* (plural, *ṭambūrāt*) is an emblem of *nuban*, the major Afro-Arab ritual of possession. In the Gulf region—from southern Iraq down to Yemen, all along the Gulf shores—and through Kuwait, Bahrain, Qatar, the Emirates, and Oman, the instrument is uniform in shape and size (more than 1 meter high), and the same terms are used for its parts. This *ṭambūra* is a symmetrical triangular lyre with a shallow, circular wooden sound box (or, in more recent instruments, metal bowls) to which a covering of cow membrane is nailed or pegged. Almost everywhere in this region, *ṭambūrāt* have five strings, though some have six. Each string has a name. The *ṭambūra* is placed on the ground to the left of the musician, who leans it against himself and plays it with the right hand. In one technique, a finger strikes the desired strings; in another technique, a large wooden or horn plectrum strikes all the strings and the left hand stops the unwanted strings from sounding.

The *nuban* ceremony of musical therapy, also called *ṭambūra* in some Gulf states, is conducted by a spiritual authority (a man or woman) in a special house called *al-makīd*. It combines sung poetry (in Arabic and Swahili), specific rhythms, and dances and is accompanied by an ensemble, *'iddat al-nubān* 'tools of *nuban*', consisting of several drums and the girdle or skirt, *al-manjūr*, described above. The ceremony is called *al-khiyāṭ* 'the thread' when only the lyre and the girdle are used, with no drums. In Yemen, on the Red Sea, although the large lyre is in use, a small lyre called a *ṭambra* or *ṭumbara* is more popular; its sound box is made of wood or a gourd, and it is played in *zār* ceremonies, the counterpart of *nuban,* to expel evil spirits that cause illness. For all the lyres used in these possession ceremonies, the musical repertoire is pentatonic.

On the African coast of Egypt, the lyre is called a *kisr* (like the Nubian *kisar*) and is played by bedouins along the shore of the Red Sea. In Sudan, where the Arab-Islamic world and black Africa meet, the *ṭambūra,* also known as a *ṭanbūr*, is a unifying symbol amid ethnic and tribal diversity. It is found in both the circular shape (called *kisār* or *kisir* in northern Nubia) and the rectangular shape common in the south (also called *rabāba*). Either kind can be played standing or seated, with a plectrum or the fingers, and with one or two hands, like a harp. Often a singer plays the instrument to accompany other singers and dancers during festive ceremonies, to the rhythm of hand clapping and foot stamping.

Another type of lyre, the *simsimīyya*, is primarily a secular instrument. It has a small circular or rectangular sound box that can be made of various materials. The face is metal or skin, and there are five metal strings. The *simsimīyya* is used on the coast of the Hadramawt, in Aden, in Tihama in Yemen, and in the Hijaz in Saudi Arabia (in these regions, it overlaps with the geographic distribution of the *ṭambūra*), and its use continues northward up the coast of the Red Sea to the Sinai and Egypt, where it can be found particularly in Suez and Port Said. In the latter regions, a larger lyre with seven, eleven, or more strings has developed in recent years. The *simsimīyya* accompanies the songs of fishermen and sailors; popular songs of Egypt and the Peninsula; and songs of the Gulf, Yemen, Aden, and the Hijaz in Saudi Arabia. It also accompanies the *simsimiyya* dances in the Red Sea region up to Aqaba in Jordan. The repertoire of the *simsimiyya* (unlike that of the *ṭambūra*) is diatonic and microtonal.

Another secular lyre, the *qitāra*, can be found in Upper Egypt. It has five strings and a circular metal sound box covered with a thick membrane.

Aerophones: *Al-alāt al-hawa'iyya*

Aerophones include end-blown oblique flutes, single-reed clarinets, double-reed oboes, horns, trumpets, and some other, minor wind instruments. With the exception of the flute (*nāy*), all aerophones are folk instruments played in nonurban settings.

Flutes

End-blown flutes were known in both ancient Egypt and Mesopotamia (where a silver flute from the third millenium B.C.E. has been excavated). The generic name for all varieties of flutes is *nāy* 'reed' (plural, *nāyāt*); this is also the only name for the urban and classical flutes used in cities of the Arab world. The *nāy* is made from Persian reed and is found in at least seven sizes. Whatever the size of the reed, all *nāyāt* have six holes plus one thumbhole, always disposed in the same parts of the reed: eight nodes and nine antinodes. A good *nāy* player, called a *nāyātī*, can produce almost three full octaves.

There have been individual attempts to adapt the *nāy* to modern music, such as adding keys to facilitate chromatic playing and other Western flute techniques. Modern Arab composers in Western idioms have introduced the *nāy* into some of their compositions, including concertos for *nāy* and symphony orchestra.

The *nāy* is the only wind instrument used in art music in the Middle East. It is an essential member of the traditional *takht* ensemble, along with the *'ūd*, the *qānūn*, and percussion instruments. It is also present in most large modern orchestras. The *nāy* also accompanies religious hymns glorifying the Prophet and was used in the original Sufi *mawlawiyya* order, known as the whirling dervishes, which has now mostly disappeared from the Arab world.

The Arab world uses a great variety of popular flutes, in different sizes. They are made of wood or metal, but above all of reed, with three to ten holes (figure 3). These flutes have many regional names: *juwwāk*; *fḥāl* 'male'; *gaṣba* 'reed' (plural, *gaṣbāt*); *shbēb* 'young' or *shabbāba* in North Africa and the eastern countries (where *shabbāba* is also a generic term for flutes); and *'uffāta*, *qawwāla*, *ṣuffāra*, and *salāmiyya* in

FIGURE 3 Metal flute accompanying the bedouin Dān Ghayyathī (singing) during a marriage ceremony in Mukalla, a city in the Hadramawt region of Yemen. Photo by Scheherazade Qassim Hassan, 1997.

Egypt—to mention only a few. In Algeria, a pair of large *gaṣbāt* are played, usually by two itinerant musicians, to accompany bedouin songs. The Egyptian *qawwāla* (*kawwala*), which can have different lengths and sizes and always lacks a thumbhole, is theoretically an instrument for religious music but in practice is multifunctional. It is used by the *mawlawiyya* and other Sufi orders; is played in mosques during *al-mawlid al-nabawī* (the anniversaries of the Prophet's birth and death); and accompanies Sufi poetry and religious *madīḥ* (glorification of the Prophet). This flute is also played in secular contexts—at weddings, in popular settings, and, though now rarely, in coffeehouses—and with secular instruments such as a tambourine with disks and a pair of finger cymbals. The *qawwāla* is considered one of the most authentic sounds of Egypt and has gained popularity in modern compositions.

Most of the popular flutes are oblique flutes played by blowing on the edge of the mouth hole. However, duct flutes are also found in some parts of the Arab world, such as Iraq and Tunisia. Flute performers include amateurs and professionals.

Single-reed instruments: Clarinets

Among the single-reed instruments, idioglotte clarinets, called *bous* in Saudi Arabia and *magrūna* in Tunisia, are solo instruments played by shepherds and amateurs. The double-barrel reed clarinet—two clarinets, side by side, each with its own single reed—is perhaps the most widespread aerophone in the Middle East. Although in the past its generic name, *mizmār*, denoted any aerophone, today *mizmār* designates single- and double-reed instruments. Many local names for the clarinet—such as *mizwij* and *mitbej* in Iraq, *mijwiz* in Lebanon, *jiftī* (from the Persian *joft* 'pair') in the Gulf countries and Oman, and *dozala* among the Kurds in Syria and Iraq—refer to the double form. Other local names include *zummāra* in Yemen, occasionally *al-ānnāna* in Syria, *gurma* or *sittawiyya* in Egypt, and *magrūna* in Tunisia.

In the double-reed instruments (of the clarinet type), two identical pipes, made of reed or an eagle's leg bones (called *fḥāl* 'male' in Tunisia), are attached to each other, and five, six, or seven identical fingerholes are pierced in each reed. The two smaller reeds, with a narrow rectangular tongue cut in each, and inserted into the larger reeds, are held entirely in the performer's closed mouth and are played with a circular breathing technique (Hassan 1980; Racy 1994). The performer generally plays the same melody with both pipes; the sound is especially vibrant because of the beating that results from the two pipes' being slightly out of tune with each other.

North African and some Egyptian identical double clarinets differ from the eastern Arab double clarinet: they have cow horn bells attached to the ends of each pipe, to amplify the sound. These clarinets are called *tormāy* in Egypt, *magrūna* in Tunisia and Libya, and *suggārāt* in Algeria. In general, each pipe has five or six fingerholes, but sometimes only one pipe is melodic and the second functions as a drone tube.

Double-piped clarinets have a purely secular character. In countries east of the Mediterranean, they are used in rural areas and on the edge of the desert and are played by all ethnic groups. North African double clarinets are treated as a national instrument and appear at important festivities, often decorated with beads and colored cloth. When a festivity is limited to women, a man is invited to play the double clarinet. In the Libyan countryside, the performer communicates with animals by playing special melodies.

A third type of double clarinet is the *arghūl*, traditionally made of pipes of unequal lengths. It is almost exclusive to Egypt, though it is found to a lesser extent in Palestine. The short pipe has fingerholes; but to change the pitch of the longer one, which serves as a drone, the pipe is lengthened by adding pieces. The *arghūl* has three sizes: *al-arghūl al-kabīr* 'big *arghūl*', which can be as long as 180 to 250 centimeters; *al-arghūl al-ṣaghīr* 'small *arghūl*', which is about 60 to 85 centimeters long; and the *arghūl ghāb*. It is played by shepherds, boatmen, rural and bedouin in Palestine to accompany folk songs and dances on festive occasions. Today, most Egyptian instruments have melody and drone pipes of the same length.

Single-reed instruments: Bagpipes

Traditional bagpipes in the Arab world are single-reed instruments attached to a skin bag that holds the air. They are used in two areas: in North Africa; and in Southern Iraq, the Gulf states, and the eastern coast of Saudi Arabia. In the Gulf states they are called *jirba*, *qurba*, *gurba*, or *habbān* (these names refer to the skin bag). These instruments have two pipes, each with six holes, and no drone. *Fann al-habbān* 'the art of the bagpipe'—one of the various *funūn* 'arts' of the Gulf region—combines singing and dancing with instrumental music; the bagpipe is played along with several drums. In the multiethnic region between Basra in southern Iraq and the Emirates, this art

TRACK 19

is attributed to the Baluch and Persian communities. In Oman, the Scottish bagpipe, introduced by the British military forces, is used in this musical tradition. The Scottish bagpipe is also found in military bands and in some wedding procession ensembles in Egypt. The North African bagpipe, *al-mizwed*, has a double clarinet with bell horns and a separate mouthpiece attached to the skin bag.

FIGURE 4 *Ṣrnāj*. The oboe played with drums is used only by the Afro-Arab population in southern Iraq and in the Gulf region. Here a woman has the spiritual function of directing the space. Photo by Scheherazade Qassim Hassan, Bahrain, 1997.

Double-reed instruments: Shawms

The shawm is an ancient instrument of this region. It is known as *zurna* east of the Mediterranean; *ṣrnāj* in the Gulf area (figure 4); *mizmār* or *mizmār baladī* and *sibs aba* (*sibs* being a small instrument, *aba* a large one) in Egypt; *al-ghaita* or *al-gaida* in Libya; and *zūkra* in Tripoli, Tunisia, Algeria, and Morocco. (The Turkomans in Iraq have a cylindrical shawm called a *qarnāta*.) The parts of the shawm and their names, described at the beginning of the nineteenth century by Villoteau, are almost the same today. The shawm is a wooden tube that gradually widens into a fairly large conical open end. Shawms in the eastern Arab lands have seven fingerholes and those in the Gulf region have five or six; all have a thumb hole. Sometimes, there are small additional intonational holes on the cone. The upper part of the shawm consists of a double reed attached to a metal staple and a circular disk on which the lips rest. The staple is inserted into a cylindrical fork that enters the body of the instrument.

In most Arab countries, there are shawms of different sizes that correspond to voice registers. In Iraq, there are at least three sizes: the smallest is the Kurdish, in the north; the largest belongs to the black population in the south. In Libya, the mountain shawm is distinguished from the coastal *zukra* (also called a *zenga*), in which the holes are closer together.

In the Arab world, shawms are associated with open spaces and gatherings, military or festive, including weddings. In lands east of the Mediterranean they are entirely secular and are usually played in a duo with a large circular drum, called *ṭabl wa zurna* in Arabic and *dhol wa zurna* in Kurdish, to accompany collective singing and dances. In Egypt the common ensemble, called *mizmār wa ṭābl baladī*, consists of three *mizmār* players and two drummers. In North Africa, the oboe is used on popular festive occasions, at marriages, and in religious and ritual contexts. In Morocco, it is used by the Aissawa Sufi congregation for popular melodies; in the Sufi rituals of Tunisia and Libya, it accompanies the classical *m'alūf* repertoire, together with tambourines.

Trumpets and horns: **Nafīr** *and* **būq**

A trumpet or a horn produces a single fundamental sound that depends on the size of the instrument; and each type of instrument is found in various sizes. These instruments are blown in religious and ritual ceremonies and in outdoor proccessions. Conical metal trumpets, called *ṭuāṭa* in Iraq, are used in Shi'ite religious centers during the mourning ceremony for Husayn. In North Africa, the metallic *nafīr* is blown during Ramadan and also, together with a shawm and a large circular drum, is part of an instrumental ensemble in wedding street proccessions. About ten gourd trumpets

In the Arab world, shawms are associated with open spaces and gatherings, military or festive, including weddings.

of different sizes, under the supervision of a chief blower, constitute an ensemble in Sudanese Berta villages. On festive occasions in the region of the Blue Nile, trumpets are blown together to produce a melody. The *bargham* or *barghum*, the horn of a wild cow, blown vertically through a hole at its pointed end, is used in Oman in two tribal musical traditions. In the Gulf region between Basra and Oman, a marine shell horn, called *lapinka* or *pinka* in the Gulf region and *yim* or *buq* in Oman, is blown from its smaller end by an elderly man to announce Afro-Arab musical ceremonies.

Membranophones: *Al-ālāt al-jildiyya*

The folk music of the Arab world—particularly in the Gulf, the Arabian Peninsula, and the southern parts of North Africa—is characterized by a wealth of membranophones. However, although rhythm is important in the classical and urban repertoires of the Middle East and North Africa, only three types of membranophones are used: the *ṭabla*, a portable drum; tambourines of various sizes; and a pair of kettledrums.

Single-headed portable drums: Ṭabla

Single-headed portable drums with an open shell at their distal end are known in urban music as *ṭabla* (plural, *ṭablāt*) or *darbūkka* (or *dumbuk* in Iraq). Those used in art music have various forms, such as a vase shape in Egypt and regions to the east and a goblet or a jug shape in North Africa. Traditionally, *ṭablāt* of urban and art music were made of clay with the skin either glued on or laced on through holes along its edge, but metal drums with metal pegs are also common.

In folk music, *ṭablāt* vary greatly in shape, the most common being tubular or waisted *ṭablāt*, some with a suspension belt. Most of the popular *ṭablāt* are terra-cotta, but wooden and, more recently, metal drums are also used. In Egypt, children's clay instruments are usually painted and decorated. In North Africa, clay drums have a ceramic glaze with geometrical designs. East of the Mediterranean, *ṭablāt* are more sober. They are produced in all sizes, including children's sizes, and are sold in popular and tourist markets. In Morocco, the *ta'rija*, a small version of the popular ceramic *ṭabla*, is used as a pair, frequently to accompany the urban repertoire of *melḥūn* [see MALHUN]. In Algeria, the *gelāl* is a tubular *ṭabla* that may be as long as 60 centimeters and is played under the arm. In Ghadames in Libya, the *galāl*, played by an ensemble of women, is a small short-necked drum with a large head onto which the skin is simply glued. Popular wooden *ṭablāt* are found in Mesopotamia and in the Arab-African traditions of the Gulf. The slender, wooden Mesopotamian *khashba* is symmetrically waisted and has a very small skin diameter (6 to 11 centimeters); it is played by rural and marsh populations and by Gypsies at weddings and other festive events. Much larger versions are used the region of Basra downward in the Gulf, in connection with the Afro-Arab music. The skin, as in all African-influenced intruments, is quite thick and is secured with wooden pegs. *Ṭablāt* are held under the arm or across one thigh and are played with the fingers of both hands; the musician can sit or stand. In Libya, a paste made from dates is usually put on the center of the skin of wooden and clay *ṭablāt*, to maintain the desired tone.

Truncated and large-footed single-skin drums

Truncated and goblet-footed drums, positioned on the ground, are traditionally made of wood and covered with cow skin secured with wooden pegs. They are used in Afro-Arab musical ceremonies in regions between Iraq and Oman. The truncated form called *msōndō* in Iraq and the Gulf (70 to 110 centimeters high) is attached by a belt around the waist of the performer, who stands and plays with the palms of the hands. A smaller version is called *katāngo* or *shkānga*. The *msōndō* is the principal rhythmic instrument in an ensemble.

A large heavy-footed goblet drum (about 75 centimeters high) called *pīpa* in Iraq, *msōndō* or *msūndū* in Oman. In Yemen the *madif* has a wooden body covered with cowhide. A seated drummer strikes the membrane with two lengths of rubber. This drum is used in several Afro-Arab ceremonies in Yemen and elsewhere; in *zār* spirit ceremonies; and to accompany dances celebrating crops and the harvest.

Kettledrums

The *ṭabl bāz* or *bāz* (whose name is now explained in Iraq as referring to an epithet of Sufi Shaykh ʿAbd al-Qādīr al Gaylānī) was originally a kettledrum used for signaling in hunting with falcons. It is a small truncated copper kettledrum used by the Qadīrī or Qādiriyya Sufi order in Baghdad and by affiliated orders in Egypt and Libya. In Palestine and Egypt, the *bāza* or *bāz* is used during Ramadan. The *bāz* is held in the palm of the left hand while the right hand strikes the skin, often with a leather ribbon. A recent form of the kettledrum with a foot positioned on the ground is used by the Rifāʿiyya Sufi order in Baghdad, either alone or with cymbals.

Other simple kettledrums are folk music instruments. Yemen seems to have the largest variety. The best-known is the *ṭāsa*, a shallow circular clay or metal kettledrum (from 28 to 50 centimeters in diameter), played in the high plateau, the Tihama, and TRACK 6 the Hadramawt. The *ṭāsa* is suspended from the waist of a standing player, who beats it with two bamboo sticks. It is part of ensembles accompanying popular dances, such as the collective tribal *barʿa* dance.

Two other simple types of kettledrums in Yemen—the *mirfaʿ* and *mishkāl*, made of clay; and the metal *ṭanjara* (also called *damdama*, *jawhal*, and *jahif*)—have two membranes: the one on top of the instrument is to play on; the second, on the bottom, is lashed to the top skin and serves in part to attach it. The *mirfaʿ* is widely used in the upper and middle plateau in Yemen, as well as in the Tihama. The clay body is deeper than its diameter (in a medium-size instrument, about 40 centimeters). The *mirfaʿ* is hung around the waist of a standing musician, who plays with two sticks. This instrument is used in *zār* possession ceremonies, and, with the flute, accompanies community dances on festive occasions. In Tunisia, the *gundwa* is used by Sufi groups and the *ṭbayla* is played during Ramadan. The *kuenda* (plural, *kuendāt*) is a clay kettledrum used in Afro-Arab ceremonies in Iraq and the Gulf region, mainly in the *nūbān* possession ritual. Many other varieties of kettledrums are used in different parts of the Arab world.

The *naqqāra*, a simple shallow hemispheric suspended kettledrum, is used in Iraq during Ramadan and in Shiʿa mourning ceremonies. Before the 1950s, this kettledrum was also played by Jewish women called *daggāgāt* at weddings and on other festive occasions. In Tunisia, the *ṭabla tījāniyya* is played by women who are attached to the Tījāniyya Sufi order. In Libya this kettledrum is called a *ṭabl*; it is set on the ground and played by more than one male drummer during festivities. In southern Algeria, the *tagennewt*, a shallow hemispheric bowl, has a skin that is tied to surrounding stones by cords whose tension holds it in place.

Double kettledrums, *naqqāra*, which may or may not be the same size, are part of classical ensembles in North Africa and Iraq. They are also used in large modern urban ensembles, in Sufi orders, in popular music, and in some Afro-Arab traditions.

In Tunisia and Libya, pairs of *naghārāt* or *naghra* are fixed to a wooden table; during Sufi ceremonies, the musician may carry the whole table when he makes his rounds. In classical Tunisian *ma'lūf* ensembles, *naqqārāt* have two vessels of different sizes, described as the "old" and the "young." In the popular music of Tunisia and Morocco, double kettledrums of glazed colored ceramic are frequently used. *Kurktu*, double egg-shaped kettledrums played with two sticks, are used in Afro-Arab musical ceremonies in North Africa.

Single-skin frame drums

Frame drums are generally of two kinds: single-skin or double-skin. Single-skin frame drums can be subdivided, with respect to their additional elements, into at least four types, each of which comes in different sizes: (1) simple, without any additional sonorous elements; (2) with cymbals; (3) with jingles and bells; (4) with one or more strings that create the effect of a snare drum. Their names vary from country to country, and there is some confusion about nomenclature. *Daff* (also pronounced *deff*) would be an appropriate generic name.

All tambourines are held with the thumb and index finger of the left hand, leaving the other fingers free to play on the instrument's edge. The right hand plays low sounds (*dumm*) in the center; high sounds (*takk*) are played on the edge. When an instrument has additional sonorous elements, it is commonly, at times, either shaken or moved up and down. The *daff* is often played only by the chief of an ensemble, to provide the basic rhythmic formulas. A name or names—of God, saints, or the owner of the instrument—or other decorative elements or religious and protective signs are sometimes written on the skin of a tambourine. In many parts of the Arab world, a fairly large number of tambourines (up to twenty) are played together in certain religious and popular secular contexts.

The *daff* with disks—usually five pairs (less frequently three or four pairs) of small cymbals—is called *daff zinjārī* in Iraq; *riqq* (if medium-size) or *mazhar* (if larger and with a deeper frame) in Egypt and Yemen; *ṭār* in Morocco; and *bendīr* in Libya and Tunisia. The largest of these tambourines (up to 50 centimeters in diameter) is a sacred instrument used by the Yezidi sect in northern Iraq and Syria. The smallest *ṭār* (about 15 centimeters in diameter) has a deep frame with two rows of four pairs of cymbals and is part of Moroccan classical ensembles. The middle-size version, which is the most widespread tambourine, is a secular instrument of *takht* ensembles in the Levant and Egypt (where it is occasionally held with the thumb and index finger of both hands), the *chalghī baghdādī* ensemble in Iraq, and *m'alūf* or *nūba* ensembles in North Africa. It is also played by the Aissawiyya ('Issawiyya) Sufi order in Libya, where it is called *al-bendīr al-'Īsāwī*; but this use must be regarded as an exception.

On tambourines about 35 to 40 centimeters in diameter, the jingles are small jingle bells, chains, or coins attached inside the frame. Such instruments are generally called *ṭār* (plural, *tīrān* or *tārāt*) or *mizhar* (plural, *mazāhir*) in Iraq, Syria, and Yemen and *bendīr* in North Africa. They are used in religious and Sufi contexts in many parts of the Arab world, in the leisure song repertoire of pearl fishermen in the Gulf, and by itinerant hymn singers.

Tambourines with one to four removable pieces of string, of any material, attached so as to bisect the interior side of the skin, are called *bendir*. They accompany folk music and dances in Tunisia, Algeria, and Morocco, where they are also an instrument of Sufi orders.

Double-skin frame drums

Circular frame drums with two heads attached directly to each other by braces are used between southern Iraq and Oman along the Gulf shores. A thin frame drum called *ṭabl* or *ṭabl al-'ardha* in Iraq and *kāsir mufalṭaḥ* in Oman varies between 30 and 50 centimeters in diameter. It is used only in the context of tribal traditions of

FIGURE 5 *'Ayyāla* bedouin ensemble of drums and frame drums. Photo by Scheherazade Qassim Hassan, Bahrain, 1997.

the Arabian Peninsula, particularly a communal dance—originally a war dance—called *al-'ardha* in Iraq up to the Emirates and *'ayyāla* in the Emirates and Oman (figure 5). This drum is struck by a stick held in the right hand and by the left hand directly. Various double-skin frame drums—*qanqa* and *dendoun* or *dendoun toaurgī* (the *dendoun* of the Tuareg)—are used in Libya and southern Algeria, where they are played mainly by the Tuareg, by Berber women, and by Arabs to accompany song, along with the fiddle. The Algerian *ṭbel* is played with two rounded sticks as part of the duo *ṭbel-zurna*, which performs at outdoor festivities (its counterpart in eastern Arab countries is the *ṭabl wa zurna* or *mizmār ṭabl baladī*).

A type of double-skin frame drum called *saḥfa* or *mard* is used in Hudaida in Yemen. The name depends on the size; the smaller drum plays the basic rhythm while the larger one adds rhythmic ornamentation. The clay frame of this drum juts out to cover a portion of the back; thus the size of the skin is not exactly the same on both sides. A stick like a spike extends out from both the upper and the lower side of the frame: the lower spike is pushed into the player's belt; the upper spike serves to hold the instrument on his belly. The musician may stand, sit, or (exceptionally) lie down. This frame drum is played on festive occasions.

The square tambourine, a very old instrument, is becoming rare in the Arab world. The *deff* or *deff qabā'ilī* is a square or sometimes rectangular double-skin frame drum. Its frame is very thin on the side farther from the skin but is thicker on the inside immediately under the membrane. Several of these instruments are usually played at the same time, accompanied by circular frame drums. A man or woman holds the drum between the palms of the hands while four fingers strike it on both sides. This instrument, used in communal festivities, is still played by the Berbers in Morocco and Algeria.

A polygonal frame drum called the *dammām,* which exists in many sizes, is played exclusively during Shi'a mourning ceremonies in the religious centers in Iraq. It is held obliquely by the left hand while the right strikes it with a curved stick (Hassan 1980).

Double-headed drums

The great variety of double-headed drums in the Arab world can be reduced to three basic shapes: circular, tubular, and barrel-shaped. The best-known circular double-headed drum is a large wooden drum known from ancient times, generically called *ṭabl* or *al-ṭabl al-kabīr* 'the big drum', though it also has many regional names. The *ṭabl* and a shawm form the famous duo *ṭabl wa zurna*; this drum is also paired with a second drum to accompany three shawms in the *mizmār ṭabl baladī* ensembles of Egypt. Whatever the configuration, the double-headed drum is often obligatory at festivities throughout the Middle East. This *ṭabl* comes in many sizes; the largest is about 65 centimeters in diameter. It has two skins of different thicknesses—one perhaps cow skin, the other perhaps sheepskin—that are played with two sticks: one heavy and the other very light. In general, both membranes are attached indirectly through an outer ring with braced lacing, but many variations, including some inspired by Western drums with metal pegs, are also found.

The smallest tubular drum—and one of the most frequently used—is the *mirwās* (12 to 17 centimeters in diameter). It is found from southern Iraq all along the Gulf and the Arabian Peninsula up to Oman and Yemen. The *mirwās* has two skins attached indirectly through rings. It is held in the palm of the left hand, and the right hand strikes only one head. A *mirwās* is never played alone; at least three or four instruments are used together. In Yemen, the *mirwās* is played with the flute in men's ensembles, and with a large cylindrical drum and a kettledrum in women's ensembles. In the Gulf
TRACK-5 it is used to accompany the classical art of *ṣawt* 'voice' in various different forms, recently with *'ūd* accompaniment. In the leisure song tradition of Gulf pearl fishers, the *mirwās* is played with a terra-cotta jerrycan or with frame drums and cylindrical drums.

The *kāsar*, which is larger than the *mirwās*, is played in Afro-Arab ceremonies in Iraq by both men and women. In Yemen, *al-ṭabl al-ṣaghīr* 'the small drum' is played by women singers on festive occasions. This tubular drum is either held upright, with both hands striking the same skin, or held horizontally and struck on both skins. It is also used to accompany the *'ayyāla*, the official tribal dance in the Emirates. Between two rows of dancers, a large drum—the *ṭabl al-rās* 'head drum'—and a smaller one called *ṭabl al-takhmīr* are moved constantly until the musicians finally stop in the center to play. Both skins are struck; the right hand uses a stick, and the left strikes directly. At the center of the skin, henna is applied in a small circle as a decorative and protective element. In Yemen, the *būga* or *mu'asṭī*, a metallic tubular drum about 50 to 60 centimeters long and 26 to 32 centimeters in diameter is present on all important national, social, and personal occasions. *Ṭabl al-leīwa* is another tubular drum of Yemen, played specifically in possession ceremonies. It is held on the knees of the musician, who strikes it with a stick in his right hand and with his bare left hand. The *hājar* is a cylindrical drum, varying in length between 25 and 60 centimeters, that is the principal instrument of women's ensembles in the Hadramawt. Usually, it is suspended from a shoulder belt and played with both hands. In Oman, a wealth of cylindrical drums, such as *dammām*, *kāsar*, *raḥmānī, dannān*, *dīwī,* and *ṭabl al-zār*, are used in the different musical traditions. Those in the category *raḥmānī* have the widest variety of names, such as *iblīs* 'devil' and *kāfir* 'unfaithful' (Shawqi 1994).

Barrel drums

Barrel drums are usually made of real barrels, which bulge in the middle. In Iraq and the Gulf region, this type of drum is associated with Afro-Arab musical traditions.

ADOPTED AND ADAPTED WESTERN INSTRUMENTS

Certain European musical instruments are used to perform Arab music. These were chosen, in part, on the basis of two apparently contradictory criteria. On the one hand, most stringed instruments were adopted because they sounded like local instruments and could imitate regional vocal intonation and ornamentation. On the other hand, keyboard instruments were chosen for their equal-tempered tuning, which some people saw as a model for the Arab music of the future.

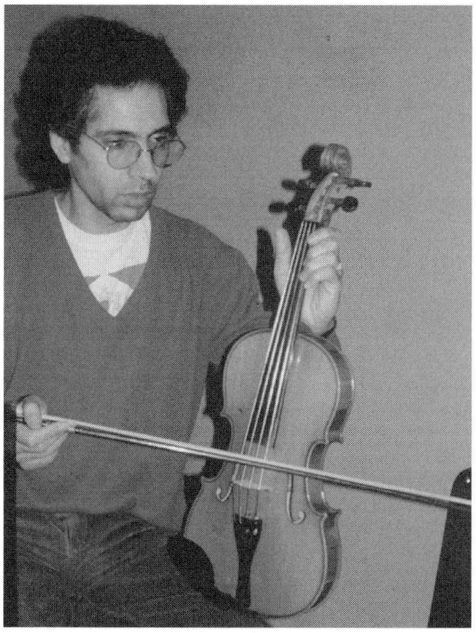

FIGURE 6 Western viola used in Arab-Andalusian ensembles in North Africa, replacing the *rabāb*. Photo by Scheherazade Qassim Hassan, Paris, 1991.

FIGURE 7 Shop selling musical instruments in Tunis, Tunisia. Photo by Scheherazade Qassim Hassan, 1992.

Among the stringed instruments, the violin (called *kamān* or *kamānja*, after indigenous fiddles, and *jrāna* in Tunisia) has been adopted most widely and most successfully; it has found a firm place in the music of North Africa and the eastern Arab world. Because it can perform the subtlest details of local music, both vocal and instrumental, without sacrificing any modal or stylistic qualities, it met with no opposition from traditionalists; and as a nontempered instrument, it was adopted without any structural modification. However, the Western tuning of the open strings was modified to fifth, fourth, and fifth (GDgd). The violin is played as a solo instrument; can be part of any Arab ensemble, small or orchestral; and accompanies folk, urban, and classical repertoires. A number of violinists have achieved renown in Syria, Egypt and Iraq.

The viola, too, has been adopted; but in North Africa its playing position is inverted so that the sound box end rests on the player's knee. This position resembles the manner of holding the local spike fiddle, which the viola supplants (figure 6). The Western cello and contrabass have also been widely adopted in the Middle East (figure 7).

Algeria is the only Arab country to use Western types of lutes. The Western mandolin was introduced to Algeria by colonials in the eighteenth century. Because of its bright, metallic sonorities, it was called *snīṭra*, a diminutive of *sanṭūr*, the Middle Eastern zither, probably recalling a historical North African instrument that no longer exists. The *snīṭra* is part of Arab-Andalusian classical ensembles. In Algerian classical ensembles, all the other lutes are tuned traditionally; only the *snīṭra* has kept its Western tuning in fifths.

The *mandole* is another adopted lute, used in *sha'bī* 'popular' music in Algeria since the 1930s. This instrument is said to have been created by an Italian musician who was inspired to combine the lute and the mandolin. The *mandole*, like the mandoline, has a flat sound box with four single or double strings. There is also a larger version called the *mandonlocel.*

The electric guitar was introduced to North Africa around the 1930s, and later to the eastern Arab world. It fascinated modern musicians because of its similarity to the *'ūd* and *buzuq*; its capacity for solo improvisation, *taqāsīm*; and its appropriateness in accompanying local traditional songs. Two extra frets are occasionally added to the guitar to allow for non-Western notes used in Arab music.

Keyboard instruments had much success in the first half of the twentieth century and became pervasive by its end. In 1922, a piano capable of playing all the quarter tones of Arab music (in equal-tempered tuning) was first created in Cairo. During the 1930s, pianos were in vogue in Arab capitals open to Western influence, and the cosmopolitan Arab aristocracy in Tunisia, Egypt, and Lebanon bought pianos to accompany traditional songs, played by both hands in the octave. Musicians and piano makers experimented with different models capable of playing twenty-four tempered quarter tones. Lebanese and Egyptian pianos were discussed at the conference for Arab music in Cairo in 1932. In the 1950s, 'Abdallah Shāhīn devised an Oriental piano with a pedal to modify scale degrees. A late example of such experiments is a double-board piano called the "kithāra of Damascus" created in 1974 by a Syrian woman, Wajiha 'Abdul-Haqq, to facilitate the playing of Arab music in both harmonic and polyphonic textures: besides the normal diatonic keyboard, it had a second posterior keyboard to produce microtones.

Today, electric organs and synthesizers are popular and are used for a wide variety of music, both traditional and modern, in small and orchestral ensembles. These instruments are capable of playing quarter tones (often in both tempered and non-tempered tunings); with the use of sampling, they can be made to resemble traditional Arab instruments such as the *nāy* 'reed flute' and *qānūn* 'plucked zither' (Rasmussen 1996).

The Western aerophone that has been most widely adopted is the accordion; retuning a few specific reeds makes it capable of playing the non-Western notes of Arab music. The saxophone has also been successfully introduced to Arab music, and a few saxophonists have become famous. Brass instruments, including the trumpet and trombone, are also used. With a saxophone or a trumpet, quarter tones are commonly achieved by lip control. However, the Egyptian musicologist Muḥammad al-Ḥifnī experimented with adding a key to brass instruments to produce quarter tones; and later the Lebanese trumpeter Nasīm Maʿlūf added a fourth key to the trumpet for this purpose. These instruments were intended for use in large Arab orchestras.

Finally, Western drum sets are widely used in modern popular music throughout the Middle East. Drum machines and electronic drum sets are also used extensively in this music.

REFERENCES

Allao, Nabil, and Anne-Marie Bianquis. 1993. "Luth, luthistes, et luthiers." *Autrement: Damas mirroir brisé d'un orient* 65 (January; special issue on Damascus).

Centre des Musiques Arabes et Méditerranéennes, ed. 1992. *Les instruments de musique en Tunisie.* Tunis: Ministère de Culture.

Elsner, Jürgen. 1969. "Remarks on the Big Argul." *Yearbook of the International Folk Music Council* 1:234–239.

Elsner, Jürgen, and Paul Collaer. 1983. *Nordafrika. Musikgeschichte in Bildern*, Band 1: *Musikethnologie*, Lieferung 8. Leipzig: Deutscher Verlag für Musik.

D'Erlanger, Rodolphe (Baron), ed. 1930. "Al Farabi, abu Nasr: *Kitāb al-mūsīqī al-kabīr*, (Grand traité de la musique)." Livre II. In *La musique arabe*, Tome I. Paris: Paul Geuthner.

Farmer, Henry George. 1986. *Studies in Oriental Music*, ed. Eckhard Neubauer. 2 vols. Frankfurt am Main: Institut für Geschichte des Arabisch-Islamischen Wissenschaften an der Johann Wolfgang Goethe-Universität.

al-Faruqi, L. I. 1981. *An Annotated Glossary of Arabic Musical Terms*. Westport, Conn.: Greenwood.

Guettat, Mahmoud. 1980. *La musique classique au Maghreb*. Paris: Sindbad.

Guignard, Michel. 1975. *Musique, honneur et plaisir au Sahara*. Paris: Geuthner.

Hassan, Scheherazade Qassim. 1980. *Les instruments de musique en Irak et leur role dans la société traditionnelle*. Paris: Cahiers de l'Homme.

———. 1981. *Al-mūsīqā al-ʿarabiyya: dirāsāt fī 'l-mūsīqā al-ʿirāqiyya* (Arab Music: Studies in Iraqi Music). Beirut: al-Mu'assasa al-ʿArabiyya li-'l-Dirāsāt wa 'l-Nashr.

———. 1982. "The Long-Necked Lute in Iraq." *Journal of the Society of Asian Music, New York* 23(2):1–18.

Hickmann, Hans. 1954. "Ägyptische Volksinstrumente." *Musica* 8:49–52, 97–100.

al-Ḥifnī, Maḥmūd Aḥmad. 1987. *ʿIlm al-ālāt al-mūsīqiyya* (Science of Musical Instruments). Cairo: al-Hay 'a al-Misriyya al-ʿAmma li-ʿl-Kitab (Egyptian National Council for Books).

Ibrahim, Amal Mohamed. 1986. *Ṣināʿat alāt-al ʿūd fī baghdād munthu inbithāq al-ḥukm al-waṭanī fī al-irāq* (Fabrication of the *ʿAūd* in Baghdad since the Rise of National Rule). Baghdad: Ministry of Culture and Information.

Jenkins, Jean, and Paul Røvsing Olsen. 1976. *Music and Musical Instruments in the World of Islam.* London: Horniman Museum.

Kartomi, Margaret. 1990. "National Identity and Other Themes of Classification in the Arab World." In *On Concepts and Classifications of Musical Instruments*. Chicago: University of Chicago Press.

Lane, E. W. 1981. *Manners and Customs of the Modern Egyptians 1833–1835*. The Hague: East-West; Cairo: Livres de France.

al-Majlis al-waṬanī Lilthakafa wa-l-Funūn wal Adab (National Council for Culture, Arts, and Literature), ed. 1981. *Ma'radh al alat-il mosikiyya* (Exposition of Musical Instruments). Kuwait.

al-Mallah, Issam. 1993. "The Increasing Role of Instrumental Music and Its Influence on Musical Life in Egypt." In *Revista de musicología*. Vol. 16, *Actas del XV Congreso de la SIM*. Madrid: La Sociedad.

Ministry of Information and Culture. n.d. *Al alāt al mosqīiyya al shaʿbīyya* (Instruments of Folk Music). Tripoli.

Plumley, A. Gwendolen. 1976. *El Tanbur: The Sudanese Lyre or the Nubian Kissar.* Cambridge: Town and Gown.

Racy, Ali Jihad. 1988. *Tanbura Music of the Gulf.* Doha: Arab Gulf States Folklore Center.

———. 1994. "A Dialectical Perspective on Musical Instruments: The East Mediterranean Mijwiz." *Ethnomusicology* 38:37–57.

Rashid, Subhi Anwar. 1975. *Al-ālāt al-mūsīqīyya fī al-ʿuṣūr al-islāmīyya* (Musical Instruments in the Islamic World). Baghdad: Dār al-Ḥurrīyah lil-Ṭibāʿah (Ministry of Information).

———. 1984. *Mesopotamien. Musikgeschichte in Bildern*, Band 2: *Musik des Altertums*, Lieferung 2. Leipzig: Deutscher Verlag für Musik.

Rasmussen, Anne. 1996. "Theory and Practice at the 'Arabic Orq': Digital Technology in Contemporary Arab Music Performance." *Popular Music* 15:345–365.

Reynolds, Dwight. 1995. *Heroic Poets, Poetic Heroes: The Ethnography of Performance in an Arabic Oral Epic Tradition*. Ithaca, N.Y.: Cornell University Press.

Rimmer, Joan. 1969. *Ancient Musical Instruments of Western Asia in the British Museum*. London: Trustees of the British Museum.

Sachs, Curt. 1968. *The History of Musical Instruments*. London: Dent.

Sawa, George Dimitri. 1989. *Music Performance Practice in the Early 'Abbasid Era 132–320 A.H. / 750–932 A.D.* Toronto: Pontifical Institute of Medieval Studies.

Shawqi, Yusuf. 1994. *Dictionary of Traditional Music of Oman*, rev. and expanded Dieter Christensen. Intercultural Music Studies 6, International Institute for Traditional Music. Wilhelmshaven: Florian Noetzel Verlag.

Shiloah, Amnon. 1972. "The Simsimiyya: A String Instrument of the Red Sea." *Asian Music* 4:15–26.

al Shu'aibi, Fahad. 1997. "Al alāt al mosīqīyya almustakhdama fi muṣaḥabat al ghīna' al sha'bī bi manṭaqat Tihāma" (Musical Instruments Used to Accompany Folk Singing in Tihama, Yemen). Paper presented at the first scientific colloquim of Yemeni music, San'a.

Taymūr Pacha, Aḥmad. 1963. *Al-mūsīq'a wa-al-ghinā' 'inda al-'Arab* (Arab Music and Singing). Cairo: Lajnat Nashr al-Mu'allafāt al-Taymūrīyah (Committee for the Publication of the Taymouride Works).

Vigreux, Philip. 1985. *La Derbouka: Technique fondamentale et initiation aux rhythmes arabes*. Aix-en-Provence: Edisud.

Villoteau, G. A. 1823. "Description historique, technique, et littéraire des instruments de musique des Orientaux." In *Description de l'Egypte*. Paris: Pancoucke. (Based on research conducted between 1798 and 1801.)

Ziegler, Christine, 1979. *Catalogue des instruments de musique égyptiens. Musée du Louvre. Département des Antiquités Egyptiennes*. Paris: Éditions de la Réunion des Musées Nationaux.

Part 3
Music Cultures and Regions

This part of the book adds color and depth to the issues and processes described in previous essays. Within the framework of broad, widely shared musical practices, an amazing variety of local differences may be found. Beyond national musics, one finds many regional distinctions. For instance, varying "Andulusian" traditions have developed in the cities of Tlemcen, Algiers, and Constantine in Algeria, and these traditions in turn differ from related practices in Tunisia and Morocco. A large repertoire might be rightly called *mashriqī*—belonging to musical practice in Syria, Lebanon, Palestine, Jordan, and Egypt. Yet the tuning and performance style of a Syrian musician may be recognizably different from those of an Egyptian. Political borders established by governments have divided or moved countless ethnic groups such as the Kurds, Armenians, Palestinians, Azerbaijanis, and Uygurs, resulting in different patterns of musical development and—perhaps more important—musical responses to political situations.

Saudi dancers. Photo © by Byron Augustin, 1989.

Section 1
North Africa: The Maghrib

North Africa has long been the cultural contact point between Africa, Europe, and the Middle East. Musical traditions of Berbers, Arabs, Sephardic and Mizrahi Jewish communities, Ottoman Turks, and the remnants of Portuguese, Spanish, and Italian coastal outposts have existed side by side, and occasionally intermixed, for centuries. Despite a variety of historical and local influences, the four countries that form the Arab Maghrib 'where the sun sets'—modern Morocco, Algeria, Tunisia, and Libya—share an art music tradition known as Andalusian music, which has its roots in the courtly traditions of medieval Islamic Spain. The musical traditions of the North African Sufi brotherhoods provide another unifying element. Yet many regions also maintain richly distinctive folk and urban traditions: *malḥūn* from northern Morocco and *gnāwa* music from the south, *sha'bī* music from Algiers, *rai* from the region of Oran, *ḥawzī* from Tlemcen, Jewish liturgical traditions from the island of Djerba, and many others. Today popular musics of North Africa, particularly *rai* and *malḥūn*, are finding a global audience and interacting freely on the world music scene with traditions of Europe and West Africa.

Musicians in Fez, Morocco.
Photo © Craig Aurness, Corbis.

North Africa: Overview

L. JaFran Jones

Islamic Period
Peoples and Influences
Traditional Art Music
Religious Music
Folk Music
Emigrant Communities
Current Trends

Although it supplied the name "Africa" for the entire continent, the southern coast of the Mediterranean, with its desert and mountain hinterlands, is quite distinct from the rest of Africa and constitutes an ethnic and cultural, as well as geographic, unit. This distinctiveness was noted by early Arab writers, who called the region *Jazīrat al-Maghrib* 'island of the west' or, literally, 'place of the sun's setting'; and it is inherent in the perception of modern inhabitants, who feel themselves closer to Europe and the Arab east and regard Africa as "someplace else."

The four independent countries of the Maghreb (North Africa) are Libya, Tunisia, Algeria, and Morocco. They cover approximately 1,830,000 square miles (roughly half the size of the United States) and are home to some 40 million people. The official language throughout the region is Arabic, and the religion of the overwhelming majority is (Sunni) Islam. In the era of European expansion, the region fell variously under the power of France, Spain, and Italy; it regained independence after World War II: Libya in 1951, Tunisia and Morocco in 1956, and Algeria in 1962. Recognition of a common heritage and goals continues to prompt aspirations for a united Maghreb, currently in the form of l'Unité du Maghreb Arabe, a supranational structure somewhat like the European Community.

On the broad scale of history, the entire Maghreb from western Egypt to the Atlantic has shared major trends; but their effect has been uneven, and generalizations should not blind one to important local variations. The "original" inhabitants, according to the earliest written sources, may be considered ancestors of the modern Berbers, a "Mediterranean" people of more or less uniform ethnic stamp with related, though not mutually intelligible, languages. The name is not their own: it derives from an epithet the Greeks used for all peoples whose languages they found unintelligible. Berbers have been an important background presence throughout North African history, often playing a more important role than has been acknowledged in official histories written by outsiders. There are still sizable Berber populations in the Maghreb, particularly in the mountainous regions away from the coastal centers of population and colonization and their spheres of political and cultural influence.

The description "crossroads of civilizations" generally fits the history of North Africa. This has been a theater where foreign powers have acted out their destinies, largely independently of the indigenous Berbers. First to arrive in historic times were

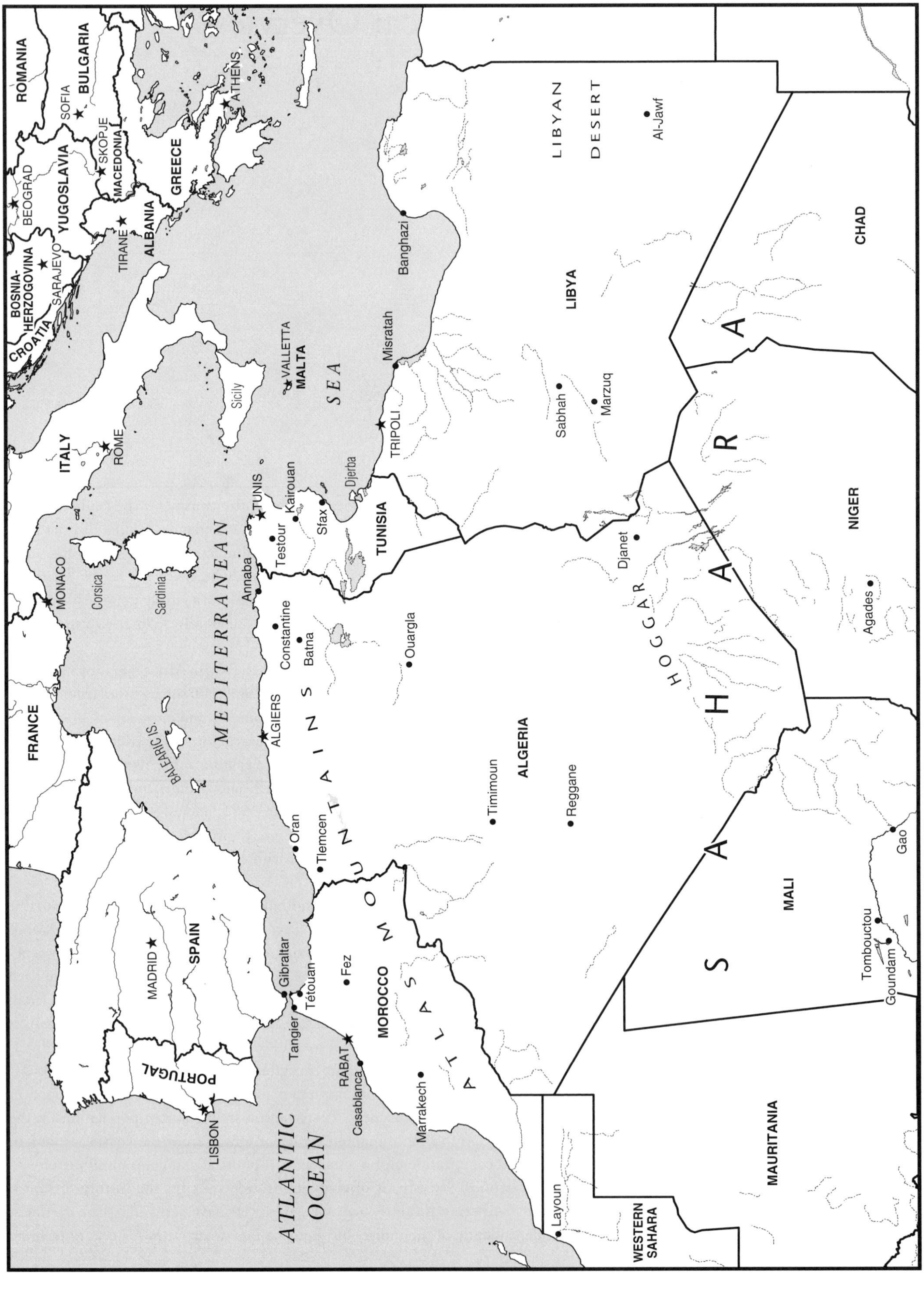

North Africa.

the Phoenicians from c. 800 B.C.E. Their center was Carthage, near Tunis, and they extended their Punic emporiums throughout the Mediterranean.

The Romans called their central province (around Carthage) "Africa," a name of uncertain origin which was subsequently adopted for the entire continent. Whether the music of our own day still has any echoes of Roman music cannot, unfortunately, be determined. During the Roman period, the Jewish diaspora also touched North Africa, although the extent of immigration is unknown. The Jewish community on Jerba, a southeastern Tunisian island which was reputedly Ulysses' "Land of the Lotus Eaters," has a tradition dating back two millennia. Christianity found fertile ground in the region and was well established there by the time it achieved official status in Rome. The region also produced its share of religious dissent, including the Donatists and the curious Circumcelliones, possible prefigurations of the Kharijite rebellion and certain Sufi practices under Islam.

As the Roman empire weakened, North Africa fell under Byzantine influence and into various stages of anarchy, with a brief episode (429–533) of domination by Gothic (Vandal) tribes from Spain. Their importation of the Arian sect of Christianity is seen by some as a preparation for Islam, which became a prominent force in the world only a century after Belisarius of Byzantium retook Carthage.

ISLAMIC PERIOD

Islam reached the Maghreb by the mid-seventh century, and the first permanent Arab encampment, Kairouan (or Qayruwān, in central Tunisia), was established in 670. From there the conquerors continued along the coast to the Atlantic, entering Spain in 711 and extending their apparently irresistible course of victory beyond the Pyrenees as far as Poitiers (732), feats accomplished largely by Berber armies.

Arabization and Islamization proceeded slowly and superficially, however—until the eleventh century, when nomadic Arabs poured into the Maghreb from Egypt, overrunning the country as far as the mountains of Morocco, changing the face of the land, and spreading their language and religion to a degree that would have been unobtainable by a political or military force perched on the coast. These were the redoubtable Banī Hilāl (and other associated Bedouin tribes), who virtually remade the Maghreb and left in their wake, among other things, a great epic cycle—*chanson de geste*—of their feats, an oral tradition of poetry and song that has persisted to our day. At the same time, the great Berber empires emanated from the other extreme of the Maghreb: the Almoravids (*al-murābiṭūn*, 1054–1147) and the Almohads (*al-muwaḥḥidūn*, 1129–1269), encompassing and dominating the entire region (including Muslim Spain) with both their military power and their severe religious orthodoxy, until their decline and other forces from the east and west shifted the balance.

By the time the Almohads had lost their last stronghold, Seville had already fallen to the Christians, and the Mongols had laid waste to Baghdad. The Maghreb lapsed into a period of isolation—though also of relative peace and prosperity—under several independent kingdoms, prefiguring the regional subdivisions that exist in our day. Eventually, the Ottomans became masters of much of North Africa, beginning in the sixteenth century. Only Morocco retained a margin of independence. The era of the Barbary pirates was under way, but behind the glitter of the corsairs and their coastal palaces the brilliance of Maghrebi civilization had faded. The region slid into a long decline that made it easy prey to European ambitions in the nineteenth century once Turkish power had waned.

Meanwhile, events in Spain wrought changes in the complexion of the North African population. Each surge of Christian reconquest—Seville (1248), Granada (1492), and the final expulsion of Spanish Muslims (1609)—sent waves of refugees into the Maghreb, enriching it culturally and musically but creating new problems. When the Jews were expelled in 1492, many of them also found their way to the

Maghreb, either directly or by stages through Europe. They also brought with them an important cultural heritage and came to play a unique role during the era of European colonization. The French took Algeria by force in 1830 and Tunisia by stratagem in 1881. Morocco was officially divided between French and Spanish "protection" in 1912, the same year Libya fell to the Italians. Colonization forced the Maghreb to absorb a deluge of outside influences in a relatively short time. This created tension and resentment, but also certain benefits. It did not, as some had hoped, weaken the religious fabric; rather, it tended to strengthen people's identification with their Arab-Islamic heritage, and it prepared the ground for the era of independence.

PEOPLES AND INFLUENCES

The ethnic tapestry of North Africa is rich and complex, as is its multifaceted music. All the peoples who have lived or passed through the region have no doubt left musical, linguistic, and cultural traces, but those whose contact is more recent are easier to identify. Remnants of pre-Islamic cultures—Punic, Greek, Roman, and Vandal—can sometimes be found in the language and customs of today, as well as in their stone monuments; however, their possible contributions to North African musics are lost to our knowledge, though they still feed our imagination. Other peoples' influences are more discernible.

Berbers

Berbers have remained the unbroken backdrop of the Maghreb since prehistoric times. They have from time to time been politically preponderant, and although they have seldom exerted cultural influence beyond their own sphere, some Berber words have found their way into Spanish, Sicilian, and Maltese. The Berbers are still numerous today, especially in Algeria and Morocco, and their languages and musics are very much alive. We can only guess to what extent today's Berber music resembles that of previous eras. It is transmitted orally, without theoretical elaboration and without traditional links to "classical" Arab or European systems. One may, indeed, question whether there is a general concept of "Berber music." Each group has its own music, with no particular reference to that of the others. In any case, the influence on mainstream North African music is scant.

Arabs

Arab music is the foundation and the point of reference for most music in the Maghreb. This is true not only because the independent Maghreb nations have a strong Arab identity but also as a consequence of sizable Arab emigration to the Maghreb in the wake of the Islamic conquest and the invasion by the Banī Hilāl. It also follows from the fact that the great centers of Arab-Islamic learning in the East and West (Spain) were the major sources of intellectual and artistic culture in the Maghreb before the centuries of decline. The theoretical underpinnings of Maghrebi art music—modes, rhythms, performance techniques—as well as classical instruments, hark back to Arab prototypes. And in rural regions the epic tales of the Banī Hilāl are heard and their influence is felt in other genres of music such as *malḥūn*.

Egypt

Egyptian music constitutes a special case of Arab influence in our time. Egypt has been the prime center from which culture has radiated throughout the Arab world—not only because of its eminent Islamic university al-Azhar, its scholars, and its reformers, but also because of its popular artists and writers. Egypt was prompt to take advantage of the new media: gramophone, film, and, later, television. Early in the twentieth century, Egyptian music ensembles toured the Maghreb, inspiring local artists, implanting new ideas, and shaping popular (urban) taste. There were also music teachers and "artists in residence" in Maghrebi cities. With regard to "classical" music, Cairo was the host city for the pivotal Congress on Arab Music in 1932—largely at the urging of a Tunisian Jewish immigrant, Baron Rodolphe d'Erlanger. [See SNAPSHOT: BARON D'ERLANGER.] But Egypt's forte was popular music. It absorbed influences from West and East and passed them on to other Arab countries. Egyptian operetta (*à la Sayyid Darwīsh*) became the rage in the prewar decades. The Egyptian "diva" Umm Kulthūm was the superstar of Arab music, unsurpassed in the twentieth century. Cairene dialect and Egyptian song conventions have become a lingua franca of pop music throughout the Arab world, and indeed an intimidating force against which Maghrebi composers and performers must struggle if they wish to imbue their own work with a more national flavor. Egyptian-style songs still sell better and more quickly at home, and find a far more ready market abroad, than those that are Maghrebi in character. This is part of a perceived crisis in popular song about which Tunisian music journalists, for example, have been agonizing for decades.

Ottoman Turks

Ottoman Turks controlled much of North Africa from the sixteenth century until European colonization. They remained largely aloof, exploiting but doing little to benefit their subjects. In music, however, they left a worthy legacy. Admired as well as feared, they served as models for imitation in music as well as in military power. This accounts for a good measure of the Turkish influence on music in Morocco, which was not directly under Ottoman rule. In the rest of the Maghreb, the Turkish influence was more direct. Some Ottoman rulers were musically adept and worked at revitalizing and refashioning local repertoires. Muḥammad Rashīd Bey, in the eighteenth century, was a notable example. His compositions still form part of the Tunisian *ma'lūf* repertoire, and the Rashīdī Institute is named after him. Also, Turkish phrases occur as "filler" syllables in some of the repertoire. The Ottomans' military bands and palace ensembles provided employment for Maghrebi musicians and teachers. These performing groups adapted much local art music for their repertoires and gave many concerts that were open to the public, bringing their version of this national heritage to the urban masses, who might not otherwise have been exposed to it. Band clubs sprang up in some cities, calling for teachers and giving urban youth an opportunity to make music outside traditional contexts. Many Ottoman rulers had European wives and permitted them to bring artifacts from their home culture, including musical instruments, into the palaces. Through this avenue several Western instruments (and some elements of the Western repertoire) gained currency in North African music. Some harem women and slaves, from both East and West, were accomplished musicians and dancers. Their influence also filtered into Maghrebi culture on several levels, such as the teaching of children. Music teachers were also brought in from the East and from Europe for this purpose.

Spanish Muslins

Spanish Muslims, or "Andalusians," poured into North African cities in the wake of Christian reconquests and particularly after the expulsion order of 1609. They had a generally higher level of culture and technology than the Maghreb—which was already stagnating—and their innovative contributions were admired, to the extent that even today anyone who claims Andalusian descent is asserting a certain nobility. The music they brought enriched and vitalized cognate genres in the Maghreb, particularly "classical" art music, which subsequently came to be called Andalusian. This should not be taken to mean that the entire genre is an importation. The Andalusian endowment was substantial, in terms of both textual and musical material, but it merged with an existing repertoire and other influences to form a uniquely North African idiom, with important regional variations. The modern Andalusian music of Spain—such as flamenco—is another matter. It emerged long after the refugees had been integrated into Maghrebi society, and its possible influence on the region's music must be sought in more recent contacts.

The ethnic tapestry of North Africa is rich and complex, as is its multifaceted music.

Jews

Jews have lived in North Africa at least since Roman times, but their presence became more prominent when Sephardic refugees arrived from Spain and later immigrants came from Europe (particularly from Leghorn, Italy, since the late eighteenth century). Although these people were a minority with "separate" status, they were nevertheless tolerably well integrated into Maghrebi society and often played important social roles. Compared with their Muslim compatriots, they typically maintained closer ties to Europe. Under the French they had special privileges, which brought some benefit to the colonized people in general but also stirred resentment and began to open a rift in what had been a mutually comfortable relationship. The independence of the Maghrebi states ushered in changes that Jewish communities saw as an unfavorable omen. As the issue of Palestine intensified and Jewish-Arab polarization increased, many Jews departed, leaving only aging vestiges of their community in the Maghrebi homeland. The Jews' private music, in the synagogue and the family, probably had little influence on the Maghreb at large, but their public musical activities had a very significant influence.

Because Jews were not subject to the Islamic sanctions regarding music, their opportunity to perform in public was unrestricted, and by the beginning of the twentieth century they had become a major contingent among professional musicians in the Maghreb. It may be true, as some have claimed, that Jews had a virtual monopoly of popular music during this period, but they drew their material from Muslim sources (traditional and folk repertoire, Egyptian innovations, and some European currents), sang in classical Arabic and local dialects, and were enthusiastically received by both Muslim and Jewish urban audiences. Jewish pop stars used their wealth and influence to benefit the common cause of artistic activity in their homeland and advanced the careers of Muslim as well as Jewish colleagues. They were also significant in the restoration and revitalization of the Andalusian repertoire and may be credited, along with the Sufi brotherhoods, with having preserved it from eclipse. As Muslims became more active in professional public music, the Jews became less prominent, but their influence remained palpable until the Jewish communities themselves dwindled after independence. In fact, many Jews who once had some degree of stardom in their native Maghreb have spread North African popular music abroad—for example, in Paris and New York.

Africans

Some black people from south of the Sahara entered the Maghreb as slaves, others as free persons. The integration of free blacks differed from that of slaves, for free people were not forcibly deprived of their native heritage or their sense of identity. Their influence on the music of the Maghreb has been felt largely in the popular milieu, both urban and rural. They have retained the musical traditions and customs of their homelands, with the result that theirs is a somewhat separate music, though part of the Maghrebi tapestry. Blacks have traditionally had the status of professional musicians, albeit in different contexts from the Jews. For instance, they are engaged for local festivals, where they perform "outdoor music" on drums and wind instruments, in the folk idioms of the region. There are also black brotherhoods, analogous to those of the the Sufis, who merge homeland traditions with local popular religions. The Bū Saʿdiyya of Tunisia, for example, perform at the shrines of certain saints and in private homes; these performances combine dance, trance, and spirit possession, often said to be of therapeutic value. The itinerant Gnāwa are a frequent sight in the streets and squares of Moroccan towns. A trademark of such groups is the *gumbrī*, a plucked chordophone with a rectangular body.

Mediterranean connections

Maltese, Sicilians, and Spaniards have historically lived in close contact with North Africans, often intermarrying, both on their own soil and in the Maghreb. This is true particularly of fishing and seafaring people, but also of laborers and tradespeople. During French domination, many poor people from Sicily and Malta came to live and work in Tunisia and Algeria; their social status was different from that of the French colonists—it was closer to the level of the North Africans themselves. The legacy of this contact, which goes back to the era of Aghlabite hegemony (ninth to eleventh centuries), and perhaps even to Roman times, is easy to see in mutual borrowings in language and customs but less so in music, although it invites speculation. More concretely, one may cite the Maltese who participate in band clubs in North Africa, and apparent similarities between Sicily and Tunisia in *mattanza* 'tuna harvest' songs (which may also include echoes from elsewhere, such as the Balearic Islands).

Europe

European cultural influence intensified with colonization and has not abated despite independence. The Maghreb therefore cannot be described as musically isolated from Europe. From the Ottoman era through the colonial and postcolonial periods, and by way of Egypt, many elements of European music have become commonplace in North Africa. Some Western instruments have all but displaced their Maghrebi counterparts, not only in bands but also in traditional ensembles. Violins and cellos routinely appear in even the most traditional Andalusian ensembles; a type of mandolin and a small guitar are virtually folk instruments in Algeria; electronic and electronically enhanced instruments are no longer a rarity. Music ensembles have grown from a few *shaykhs* clad in the *jibba* or *jallabiyya* to chamber orchestras of musicians in white tie and tails, led by a conductor with baton, and presenting orchestrations that abandon traditional unison or heterophony, counterpointing, if not actually harmonizing, the instruments' differences in dynamics and timbre.

Western musicology has been brought to bear on traditional and folk repertoires, codifying them and committing them to writing. The learning of music has moved from the Sufi *zāwiya* 'shrine' or the feet of a *shaykh* to the conservatory classroom, where lessons in solfège and reading notation have replaced oral transmission. In the music of the popular media, European influence is even more palpable and pervasive—in the fusion of Western and Maghrebi styles, in outright imitation, and in a growing allegiance to foreign imports. At another level, Europeans' interest in savoring and studying the "exotic" components of Maghrebi folk music has drawn North Africans' attention to their own musical heritage and has inspired a folkloric mentality. North Africans now see their music—once simply a part of life of which they were almost unconscious—as something to reprocess and market to tourists, something to be embalmed and encased in a "museum of song," something imbued with nationalistic pride and repackaged as a spectacle of heritage and folklore.

TRADITIONAL ART MUSIC

The so-called Andalusian music of the Maghreb is cultivated and performed in most major cities as a national heritage. The term *Andalusian* refers not to the modern Spanish province of Andalucía but to *al-Andalus*, the Arabic name for Muslim dominions on the Iberian Peninsula in the eighth to fifteenth centuries. In its main regional variants the genre is known as *ma'lūf* 'customary', *gharnāṭī* 'Granadan', *ṣan'a* 'art', and *āla* 'instrument'. It also has a religious component, *jadd* 'serious', traditionally the preserve of Sufi brotherhoods. The repertoire consists in each case of a set of *nūbāt* 'suites' (singular, *nūba*), one for each melodic mode. [See ANDALUSIAN *NŪBA* IN MOROCCO.] After instrumental and free-rhythm solo vocal introductory material, each *nūba* has perhaps five rhythmic sections, based on a succession of rhythmic modes that progress from stately to lively and give an impression of acceleration and increasing tension. These sections are sung in unison (heterophony) by a traditionally all-male vocal ensemble with instrumental accompaniment, using strophic poems in literary and dialectical Arabic. The rhythms seem more distinctively Maghrebi than the modes, which correspond roughly to counterparts in eastern Arab music. Both the rhythmic and the melodic modes, however, vary from region to region and have different names.

That the repertoire is genuinely North African should not be obscured by the designation "Andalusian," as nationalist music scholars point out. The Andalusian import may have been a major part of the fusion that developed into this genre, but it was still only a part. The music survived and evolved on Maghrebi soil for centuries after the Andalusian influx. Manifold contact and exchange between North African and Andalusian cultures took place in the centuries before the waves of refugees, and influence flowed in both directions. Intellectual and artistic contact with the Arab east was also frequent, particularly at the great centers of learning in Tunis and Fez. Much independent musical input must have come through this channel, as historical records suggest. After the demise of al-Andalus, the Maghreb took possession of the music as its own and shaped it, absorbing other influences that never touched Muslim Spain. Nevertheless, noting the Andalusian character of this music is not entirely amiss. The the strophic *muwashshaḥ* and *zajal* song genres, the mainstay of the textual component, are of acknowledged Andalusian invention; and the repertoire has a strong flavor of nostalgia for the golden days of Cordoba, Seville, and Granada—a time of which modern Maghrebis have little knowledge but which is still a sort of "paradise lost" in the collective consciousness. Ironically, the historical record tells us very little about what this music was actually like in *al-Andalus*, but the Maghrebi repertoire that is available to us has a certain historical depth.

Among the various musics competing for an audience today, Andalusian music has an equivocal status. On the one hand, it is a monument to the creative genius of each Maghrebi nation; but on the other hand, it takes a backseat—for composers, performers, and consumers—to many more readily appreciated genres, including European imports. To judge from writers such as d'Erlanger and Chottin, it was on the verge of eclipse at the beginning of the twentieth century. It has subsequently been rescued and restored, put on a pedestal, and clad in the robes of national pride, but not made measurably more palatable to popular taste. Composers find it stifling and prefer more open-ended genres that invite innovation. Few serious attempts have been made to compose new *nūbāt*, and for enrichment these have looked beyond Magrhebi tradition to Eastern models. Audiences lack the concentration and commitment to savor an entire full-scale *nūba*, or even a concert consisting exclusively of selections from the genre. Performing ensembles, even those nominally devoted to cultivating this repertoire, are often forced to organize mixed programs in which brief obligatory traditional selections are followed by more accessible pieces and recent works of popular artists. Standard selections from the repertoire are served up in comfortably small doses on radio and television, and melodic fragments find their way into commercials.

But this never was a music for the masses, and it seems to breathe more contentedly in its own rarefied atmosphere.

RELIGIOUS MUSIC

Terms such as "music" and "song" are inappropriate in discussions of the sacred practices at the heart of Islam. The Qur'ān is "chanted"; the call to prayer is "intoned." These are the apparently musical manifestations of Islam with which Westerners have become familiar through television documentaries. They are also cultivated to a high degree, and with a measure of local flavor, in the Maghreb, but that topic belongs in a different context.

Beyond this, though still near the core of approved devotion, are certain traditional poems sung by men or boys in the mosque or its courtyard during high feasts and on pivotal occasions connected, for example, with the Qur'ānic school or rites of passage. The best-known are the *Burda* and *Hamziyya* and the *Mūlidiyya*, the "cantata" of the Prophet's birth. Although these draw on local Maghrebi tradition, they are part of a broader practice and invite comparative study.

More specifically North African is the music of the many Sufi brotherhoods, most of which are at least roughly beholden to the Shādhiliyya movement. All practice a variety of *dhikr* 'remembrance' in their *zwāyā* 'shrines' (singular, *zāwiya*), usually built around the tomb of a saintly personage. *Dhikr* certainly involves what Western ears hear as musical elements, but the emphasis is on the repetition of divine names and the recitation of sacred texts. The brotherhoods' more frankly musical repertoires bear the general title *madā'iḥ w-adhkār* 'songs' of praise and remembrance. The music they draw on varies from brotherhood to brotherhood and from region to region, as do their customs regarding musical instruments, dance, and trance. Some are within the sphere of Andalusian music. Indeed, certain Sufi brotherhoods have been credited with an important role in preserving this genre over the centuries. Others maintain the music of the deep Sahara. The Tījāniyya, with its major centers in desert regions, has been a chief transmitter of Saharan music into urban milieus. There are also Berber brotherhoods, black brotherhoods, and brotherhoods that are custodians of rural and urban folk music genres.

Other groups resembling the brotherhoods, though perhaps concerned more with music than with devotion, also have repertoires similar to the *madā'iḥ w-adhkār*. They perform professionally, for pay, at festivals, weddings, and other private celebrations. Many women's ensembles—for example, the *zamzamāt* of Libya, the *ḥaḍrāt* of Tunisia, and some varieties of *shaykhāt* in Morocco—fit into this category, since women are typically denied any official status in the brotherhoods. (The female Tījāniyya in Tunisia are an exception.) There are also black troupes. Their practice hovers between Sufi affinity, popular religion, and the frankly secular and may also include trance, spirit possession, and therapeutic functions. Sufi-like repertoires may also be reworked for political aims, as in the case of the "national" *madā'iḥ w-adhkār* performed daily on Tunisian radio during Bourguiba's reign.

FOLK MUSIC

Folk music is possibly the wellspring from which other musics are drawn. It has been claimed that new musical ideas are seldom invented but rather are rediscovered by reaching back and down to the roots of a tradition. In a region as broad and diverse as the Maghreb, folk music is rich, varied, and subtle, almost bafflingly so. This may be the most important type of music to discuss, but it is also the type about which the least is known.

It is relatively easy to compile a list of genres: names with facile one-line descriptions. Such lists can be found in several sources; but none is comprehensive, and all give the impression of eclectic gleanings, selected not for what might be most significant but for what happens to be known. It is also possible to establish presumably useful categories, such as urban versus rural, Arab versus Berber, female versus male, or work versus recreation. These offer a deceptive familiarity with an essentially unwieldy topic. Some more specific labels, such as "Saharan" and "agrarian," may seem more promising, but on closer examination they make about as much sense, and provide about as much help in coping with musical reality and human diversity, as "black" and "white." Even so modestly and narrowly delimited a topic as women's songs for preparing couscous, or lullabies, if extended to cover the entire Maghreb, would defy the capacity of a lifetime's research (and has rarely been undertaken).

Folk music of the Maghreb (and elsewhere) may be the variety most resistant to change. Events and customs long forgotten elsewhere are preserved in this music; and it is in this music that we may seek echoes of melody and rhythm from bygone ages and peoples. But folk music is also frighteningly fragile, vulnerable to disappearing altogether in the wake of a single event. A generation may take its folk songs to the grave if the line of transmission is broken, for as simple a reason as girls going to school or young men emigrating to cities. A pastoral community absorbed into the tourist trade or oil industry will lose its songs for shearing lambs. A community that begins to buy processed flour will lose its songs for preparing grain.

EMIGRANT COMMUNITIES

Millions of North Africans now live outside the Maghreb, largely in France, Spain, Italy, and other European countries, and increasingly in North America. Many young people have scant command of Arabic or Berber and know the homeland only through occasional holiday visits. Their status with respect to Islam is similarly equivocal. Maghrebi governments make efforts to keep national and religious identity alive in these people and alleviate some of the problem of belonging neither here nor there—for the ties with home become thin, and integration into host societies is hindered not only by cultural and ideological clashes but more and more by xenophobia and racism. As a counterbalance, mosques are sponsored, as are programs of religious and Arabic instruction. Host governments cooperate in cultural projects for mutual understanding and in other special programs. Recent examples are the Maghrebi programming of Antenne 2 in France and the Tunisian-Sicilian cultural center at Gibellina.

Emigrant young people are drawn away from their musical heritage by the same international media that attract those at home. In both cases, young people come to know less and less of their own music and more and more of music that has become international currency. Nevertheless, popular artists from the Maghreb frequently tour emigrant centers in Europe and America and are acclaimed by their compatriots. There are also North African artists who live abroad permanently and who cater to the musical needs of their fellow emigrants.

In the wave of "world music" and the atmosphere of multiethnic musical creativity that pervades centers like Paris, some artists from the Maghreb are fusing their musical idiom with that of other cultures and are rising to international stardom. Exponents of Algerian *rai* music [see RAI] are perhaps the most striking example, but there are also others, such as the Tunisian singer Amina, who came close to winning the Eurovision song contest in 1991 (under the French banner), and the *'ūd* virtuoso Anwar Brahim, who improvises a fusion of many musical cultures.

Emigrants returning for visits or repatriation have multiple effects on their home communities. With regard to traditional and folk music, they have the effect of accentuating a "folklore" or "museum" attitude. Returning emigrants are a new class of tourists—nationals, yet spectators rather than participants in the music making of their community. The music must be staged, choreographed, and served up to them as a show rather than being something that fits seamlessly into the fabric of life.

CURRENT TRENDS

It seems clear that changes in Maghrebi society are accelerating, contacts with the outside are multiplying, assimilation of foreign elements—cultural and material—are spreading, and the tenacity of tradition is weakening. Traditional art music remains on its pedestal of national honor; Sufi *zwāyā* continue to perform their function, though in a restrained manner, in popular milieus; and folk music is still enjoyed at celebrations. But there are torn places in the fabric. The media are creating a community of spectators rather than participants. Foreign music is engulfing and diluting indigenous music. The process of embalming and showcasing musical traditions in expanding. For better or worse, the Maghreb is become integrated into a world community and its music is being fused into world music.

REFERENCES

Abassi, Hamadi, et al. 1991. *Tunis chante et danse: 1900–1950*. Éditions de la Méditerranée. Tunis: Alif.

Abun-Nasr, Jamil M. 1975. *A History of the Maghrib*. 2nd ed. Cambridge: Cambridge University Press.

———. 1987. *A History of the Maghreb in the Islamic Period*. Cambridge: Cambridge University Press.

Centre des Musiques Arabes et Méditerranéennes. 1992. *Les instruments de musique en Tunisie*. Tunis: Centre des Musiques Arabes et Méditerranéennes.

Chottin, Alexis. 1938. *Tableau de la musique marocaine*. Paris: P. Geuthner.

Chottin, Alexis, and Prosper Ricard. 1931–1933. *Corpus de musique marocaine*. 2 vols. Paris: Au Ménestrel/Heugel.

Davis, Ruth F. 1986. "Modern Trends in the Ma'luf of Tunisia." Ph.D. dissertation, Princeton University.

D'Erlanger, Rodolphe. 1930–1959. *La musique arabe*. 6 vols. Paris: Geuthner.

Farmer, Henry George. 1929. *A History of Arabian Music to the XIII Century*. London: Luzac.

Guettat, Mahmoud. 1980. *La musique classique du Maghreb*. Paris: Sindbad.

Ḥa'ik, Abū 'Abd Allāh Muḥammad. 1972, 1977, 1981. *Majmū'*. (Various printings of a late-18th-century manuscript.) Casablanca (1972 and 1981); Rabat (1977).

Jones, L. JaFran. 1977. "The 'Isawiya of Tunisia and Their Music." Ph.D. dissertation, University of Washington.

———. 1987. "A Sociohistorical Perspective on Tunisian Women as Professional Musicians." In *Women and Music in Cross-Cultural Perspective*, 2nd ed., ed. Ellen Koskoff, 69–83. Champaign-Urbana: University of Illinois Prss.

———. 1991. "Women in Non-Western Music." In *Women and Music: A History*, ed. Karin Pendle, 314–330. Bloomington: Indiana University Press.

Julien, Charles-André. 1970. *History of North Africa from the Arab Conquest to 1830*. New York: Praeger.

al-Mahdī, Ṣāliḥ, and Muḥammad al-Marzūqī. 1981. *Al-ma'had al-rashīdī li-'l-mūsīqā al-tūnisiyya*. Tunis: Manshūrāt al-Ma'had al-Rashīdī li-'l-Mūsīqā al-Tūnisiyya.

el-Mahdi, Salah. 1972. *La musique arabe*. Paris: Alphonse Leduc.

Qadriduh, 'Abd al-Salām Ibrāhīm. 1974. *Ughniyāt min baladī*. Beirut: Maṭba'at Samāya.

Rizqī, al-Ṣadiq. 1967. *Al-aghānī al-tūnisiyya*. Tunis: Al-Dār al-Tūnisiyya li-'l-Nashr.

Rouanet, Jules. 1913–1922. "La musique arabe" and "La musique arabe dans le Maghreb." In *Encyclopédie de Lavignac* (*Histoire de la musique*), 5:2676–2812, 2813–2942. Paris: Delagrave.

Al-turāth al-mūsīqī al-tūnisī. n.d. Tunis: al-Ma'had al-Waṭanī li-'l-mūsīqā wa'l-raqṣ.

The Andalusian Musical Heritage

Mahmoud Guettat

Historical Background
The Andalusian–North African Musical Edifice
Andalusian Music in the Maghreb Today

Starting from their own indigenous cultures, North Africa and Andalusia arrived at an important artistic tradition by way of Islam and the Arabic language. To understand its uniqueness, we need to consider this tradition within the framework of a much larger Arab-Islamic cultural legacy. Despite its diversity, that legacy remains a distinct entity shaped by two elements: a supranational unity which crystallized over centuries, owing to a common spiritual and linguistic basis; and local traditions determined by specific ethnic, cultural, and social situations. These two components are manifest in the refined and carefully structured classical repertoire of the *nūba*—a highly cultivated fruit of urban Andalusian–North African society, within which it continues to flourish and develop. As we observe the course of this music, we can discern "high" periods of development and intense production; periods of retreat, reflection, and preservation; and today, resurrection, renaissance, and widespread diffusion.

HISTORICAL BACKGROUND

Origins and Development

As early as the seventh century, there was much communication among the urban centers of the Islamic West. Such exchanges continued and increased over time, particularly under the Almoravids and Almohads in the eleventh to thirteenth centuries, when there were cultural borrowings whose influence would still be felt during later reigns. Immigrations, which began in the twelfth century and increased throughout the period of reconquest until the fall of Granada (1492), contributed greatly to this cultural interaction.

One result of this cultural exchange was the formation and development of a distinct, original Andalusian–North African music. Although this began in North Africa, which remained an important site of the music, al-Andalus—Andalusia—was also a decisive factor in its flowering. Indeed, for more than 750 years (the seventh to fifteenth centuries), Arab-Andalusian civilization had a splendor and magnificence rarely surpassed.

Several influences fashioned Andalusian–North African music, including ancient traditions from throughout the Mediterranean world and, later, a gradual synthesis of more heterogeneous eastern, western, northern, and southern elements. In al-Andalus, we can identify three phases of development: first, the period preceding and through the reign of al-Ḥākam I (796–822); second, the reign of ʿAbd al-Raḥmān (822–852); third, the period following the fall of the Umayyad dynasty (1027).

First phase

Until the reign of al-Hakam, two musical trends coexisted peaceably:

- An indigenous tradition that was marked by popular lyricism, Gregorian and Visigothic-Mozarabic liturgical chant, and Byzantine elements before it was altered under the direction of Isidore of Seville (565–636).
- An Afro-Eastern tradition that included musical forms from various North African and Eastern urban centers, notably Medina, Baghdad, and Kairouan (Qayrawān); this tradition was spread by musicians such as ʿAjfā', ʿAllūn, Zarqūn, ʿAbbās Ibn al-Niṣārī, and Manṣūr al-Mughannī.

Second phase

During the reign of ʿAbd al-Raḥmān II (822–852), music was greatly encouraged, and the Eastern tradition, especially that of Arab North Africa, solidified. The Medina school was held in high esteem and had a special pavilion reserved for the famous female singers of Medina, jewels of the Umayyad court. Its influence on both song and ways of life was considerable, at least until the arrival of Ziryāb (789–857), who founded a specifically Andalusian musical school in the great classical tradition of Baghdad. The residence in Cordova of this uncontested arbiter of fashion, taste, and *savoir vivre*, beginning around 822, was a turning point for Andalusian music, completing its "reorientalization." In al-Andalus, the sun of the Umayyads then shone with all its earlier luster—the old Arabic school had triumphed. It was Ziryāb's genius that restored the school's vitality. He was a disciple of the famous Isḥāq al-Mawṣilī (767–850), the undisputed master of the *ʿūd* 'lute' players in Baghdad. Ziryāb had spent about ten years in Kairouan (in northeastern Tunisia); this had opened new horizons to him, including Berber (Imazighen) music.

Gifted with a prodigious memory, Ziryāb knew by heart more than ten thousand songs (*aghānī*) along with their tunes (*alḥān*) and also had a remarkable ability to discuss and teach them. His reforms profoundly marked his era. In music, his innovations included changes in the construction of the *ʿūd*, the quality of the strings, and the plectrum, and the addition of a fifth string. He also developed an original pedagogical process and regulated song in accordance with the *nūba*.

Many other artists, musicians, and poets also made contributions. For example, Ibn al-Firnās (d. 888) is said to have been the first to codify music in Andalusia and to introduce al-Khalīl's science of metrics. Maslama al-Majrītī spread the writings of the Ikhwān al-Ṣafā 'Brothers of Purity' (tenth century), and thereby also spread the thought of al-Kindī (796–874) on music and mysticism.

Third phase

The fall of the Umayyad dynasty in 1027 fragmented the country into small kingdoms or principalities known as the *tawāʾif* (singular, *tāʾifa*). The largest of these were Banū ʿAbbād (1023–1091) in Seville and Banū al-Aḥmar (1235–1492) in Granada. Relations with North Africa became very close under the Almoravids (1056–1147) and especially the Almohads (1130–1269). Artistic and intellectual activity flourished and was enlivened by rivalry among the kingdoms. The "Andalusian community" was now a unique entity, bonded and shaped by more than three centuries of common life. Local imagination replaced the Eastern model, and language, literature, and the arts took on a personal stamp. New music and poetry had a spontaneity, originality, elegance, and color that appealed widely wherever the Andalusian influence was felt.

This metamorphosis of Andalusian society transformed its poetic and musical expression into a collective, popular art. Music now took to the streets, plazas, and public gardens. It developed as a theatrical form, adapted to the taste of the people and combining song, dance, and instrumental accompaniment. Despite its choral nature, it remained an art of solos in which the performers played off one another.

The Moorish principalities nurtured many poets, musicians, and dancers, some of whom had careers in both Andalusia and North Africa. One was the illustrious philosopher and musician Abū Bakr Ibn Bājja, or Avempace (b. Saragossa 1070–d. Fez 1138). A remarkable *'ūd* player whose practical and theoretical knowledge were widely praised, he is considered the most eminent figure after Ziryāb, and many of the most beautiful musical and poetic works constituting the basis of the Andalusian–North African tradition are attributed to him. Like Ziryāb, he instituted a number of reforms, related to the tuning of the *'ūd*, the structure of the *nūba*, and the musical *muwashshaḥ*. His *Risāla fī 'l-mūsīqā* 'Epistle on Music' (now lost) is said to have had an importance in the West comparable to that of the *Kitāb al-mūsqī al-kabīr* of al-Fārābī (d. 950) in the East.

This was the golden age of the *muwashshaḥ* and the *zajal*, forms to which almost all the great poets of the time contributed—including al-Tutaylī (d. 1126), Ibn Bājja (d. 1138), Ibn Baqqī (d. 1145), Ibn Zuhr (Avenzohar, d. 1198), Ibn Rushd (Avveroes, d. 1198), Ibn Ṭufayl (d. 1186), Ibn 'Arabī (d. 1240), and al-Shushtarī (d. 1269). Averroes, in particular, studied the aesthetics and expressive power of music, its influence on morals, and its effect on the human soul; his doctrines evidently had a significant impact on the greatest masters of Spanish music.

Many other important figures deserve mention. Abū al-Ṣalt Umayya Ibn 'Abd al-'Azīz (b. Dania 1068–d. Mahdiyya 1134), who came from al-Andalus, played an important role in music as a composer of songs who developed a new compostional method that survived long after his death, and as the author of an "epistle on music" (which, however, is known to us only in a poor, anonymous Hebrew translation). Al-Mu'taṣim d'Alméria (dethroned in 1090) was a poet and musician as well as a king. Abū 'Abd Allāh (d. 1126) was a legendary figure whose love affair with a Christian woman, Leonor, was immortalized in his songs. Al-Raqūtī (thirteenth century) was a musician, mathematician, and renowned doctor. Lisān al-Dīn Ibn al-Khaṭīb (d. 1374) left a body of work of exceptional quality, especially in music and poetry. Two famous female singers of Granada—Layla and Maryam—were known for their art and for their beauty. Al-Anṣārī of Malaga was a popular figure. Ibn Jot of Valencia is said to have created the popular song *Aragon jota*. Ibn Jūdī and Ibn Ḥimāra were noted by al-Tifāshī (d. 1253) as bearers of the tradition of Ibn Bājja's school. Ibn Ḥāsib of Murcia was said to have no equal in knowledge of musical practice and theory.

An artistic flowering

Exceptional artistic development was fostered by the profound love Andalusians had for music, poetry, and dance. From the ninth century on, these were the preferred forms of worldly entertainment and were performed nearly everywhere: in the humblest homes, in palaces, in the streets, in gardens, and in town squares and plazas.

Here, as in the East, music was beloved despite all attempts to prevent it; even the pious submitted to its charms. One chronicle tells us that "the Qāḍī Muḥammad Ibn Abī 'Īsā could not keep himself, on hearing one female singer, from writing the text of the song in the palm of his hand. He then left for a funeral, taking the precious poem with him in this way." Some Cordovan families, during intimate gatherings, had each young woman sing in turn. Some monarchs had large orchestras at court; Vizir Ibn 'Abbās in Alméria had five hundred female singers in his palace; and each prince or nobleman had his own *sitāra*, or personal orchestra. According to Ibn Mālik, the common people also loved music and music making; and al-Tijībī, in the eleventh century, said that in Malaga no neighborhood, no street, or even any street corner was silent: "I heard strings played incessantly—*ṭunbūr* and zithers."

Exceptional artistic development was fostered by the profound love Andalusians had for music, poetry, and dance.

Many other reports attest to the love of poetry, especially sung poetry, and to abundant creativity and improvisation. Two examples that epitomize the high level of music in thirteenth-century Andalusia and North Africa come to us from al-Tifāshī, who was present at musical sessions that took place in Tunis under the Hafsides (r. 1228–1574): in just one verse of a poem by Abū Tammām (d. 842), *Wa-munfaridun bi-'l-ḥusni*, sung by an Andalusian musician, Tifāshī counted seventy-four shakes (*hazza*); and a female singer's improvisation on one verse of a poem by 'Umar Ibn Abī Rabī'a (644–711), *Tashki 'l-kumaytu*, lasted two hours.

Like music and poetry, dance in Andalusia took various forms. Most female dancers were also singers and musicians; but there were also artists—men and women—who were solely dancers, such as the female dancers of 'Ubayda al-Shaqundī, famous in the twelfth century for the beauty and liveliness of their art. Ibn Khaldūn speaks of dance troupes in which female performers imitated calvary in combat.

Feast days and ceremonies were celebrated sumptuously—and noisily. Surrounded by a large crowd, wedding processions advanced slowly through the city streets, accompanied by the sonorous *būq* 'buccin', *ṭabl* (a drum), and *zamr* (a trumpet or oboe). The bride was received with music and led to her future husband, before whom paraded a line of women in a swarm of flutes, zithers, and oboes. When the wedding party arrived at the bride's home, a ball would begin, with singing and dancing. At a concert, the audience took an active part, clapping to the rhythm of a particular dance or to certain refrains—an artistic effect called *al-muṣāfaḥa*.

In Portugal, an inventory of Don Manuel's wardrobe took up five long pages and included objects related to Arab-Andalusian dance. Tales of the Castilian palace of King Don Sancho IV, son of Alfonso X the Wise, give Arabic names for dancers, lute players, flutes, and trumpets.

Instruments

According to chronicles, Andalusia had industries manufacturing many kinds of musical instruments, and some cities—such as Seville—were famous for the perfection of their instruments. Iconographic documentation of these instruments is very poor, but among the few depictions that have come down to us intact are these:

- Ivory instrument cases, one of which, dedicated to 'Abd-al-Mālik, who was al-Manṣūr's eldest son, dates from 1005.
- Miniatures attributed to Alphonse X the Wise (1221–1284) found in one of the two manuscripts of the *Cantigas* of Santa Maria. This collection, which is of great iconographic value, contains representations of fifty-one thirteenth-century musicians, each playing a different instrument. Among the instruments are the Moorish guitar, the *būq zamrī* (a horn), the *jank* (a harp), and the *'ūd*.
- A miniature of a young Andalusian woman playing the harp, after a thirteenth-century manuscript.

- A reliquary of 1390 from the Cistercian monastery of Our Lady of Piedra, in Aragon.
- A beautiful Arab-Andalusian horn from the tenth to twelfth centuries, now in the Victoria and Albert Museum in London.

Knowledge of instruments also comes to us from literature, including poetry, and from historical works, particularly writings that treat questions of theology or musical aesthetics. Some of these works simply list musical instruments as either licit or illicit according to religious law, without providing any specifics about how they were manufactured or played. Still, we know that instruments were very numerous. To cite just one example, Ziryāb is said to have introduced to Andalusia all the instruments used in the Islamic East, at least forty all together. Tifāshī notes that the most popular instruments were the *'ūd*, *zamr*, *nāy*, *duff*, *shīz*, *rūta*, *rabāb* (Andalusian and Eastern), and *būq*. The *būq* was considered the noblest and most perfect instrument. Here, it is important to emphasize the importance of North Africa and sub-Saharan Africa in the spread of some rhythmic instruments, and thus their importance to Andalusian rhythmic music.

THE ANDALUSIAN–NORTH AFRICAN MUSICAL EDIFICE

The Andalusian–North African musical "edifice" will be considered in terms of several components: its pedagogy, musical language, rhythm and poetics, and mysticism. In addition, we will look briefly at the influence of this edifice on diverse cultures.

Pedagogical procedures

Since the ninth century, interest in musical training has been characteristic of the Andalusian school. Its rules were established by Ziryāb in Cordoba, and the efficacy of its teaching methods made its students part of the glory of al-Andalus. Its pedagogical procedures were designed to give practical training in vocal and instrumental music and took place in stages.

First, a voice test was given: the candidate was asked to sit completely straight on a high stool (*miswara*) and cry out as strongly and loudly as possible, *Yā ḥajjām*! 'O barber!'—or to sustain the sound *ah* for a long time, going from low to high and then the reverse. This allowed the candidate's vocal characteristics to be evaluated. The tester could note whether the candidate spoke without nasality and without obstruction of tongue or breath. If breathing was weak, a turban was wound around the candidate's stomach; this also facilitated the proper placement of sound. Candidates who had a hard time opening the mouth wide and separating the jaws were advised to hold a piece of wood about 7 to 8 centimeters thick between their teeth for several nights. Where the problem was irreparable, the master would advise the candidate to abandon singing and take up some other activity.

For candidates who were accepted, the teaching would proceed from the simplest to the most complicated skills:

- Recitation of a poem with tambourine accompaniment, so as to learn the different rhythmic parts and placement of accents.
- Learning the outlines of the melody, avoiding any embellishment or additions.
- Exploring different possibilities of nuance, ornamentation, and improvisation that would give the work under study the desired expressivity and charm—the criteria by which the quality and creativity of an artist, singer, or instrumentalist was judged.

This pedagogy developed and enriched by more than one genius.

Young women's education included musical training, with practical exercises using the *'ūd*, the *rabāb*, and other instruments. In the thirteenth century, Seville was renowned for the training of slave singing-girls, who were taught by older women "aestheticians." Al-Tifāshī reported that the price of these singing-girls would depend on the number and quality of the songs they knew (in fact, a notebook listing a girl's repetoire would be demanded as part of the sale); that the prospective purchaser would ask the girl to perform a piece of his choosing, accompanying herself on one or more instuments; and that to be considered "perfect" a girl would have to complete her demonstration by performing a corresponding dance. The price of a singing-girl of the highest quality, according to al-Tifāshī, could be more than ten thousand gold dinars.

Musical language: Scale and mode

The edifice of Andalusian–North African music is based on two concepts: *ṭab'* 'mode' (plural, *ṭubū'*), discussed here; and the *nūba* 'musical session' or 'suite' (plural, *nūbāt*), discussed next.

Concerning scale

A controversial argument has been advanced that the troubadours' music is inseparable from their poetry, and that this characteristic is hardly "Arabic"; according to this view, Andalusian music, which is still alive in North Africa, has a solely Oriental aesthetic. This concept seems to involve a musical anachronism: admittedly, North African music by no means represents a simple cultural transmission from Andalusia; but in the tenth century there was actually no great difference between Andalusian–North African music and European music.

In effect, all data confirm that the musical system popular at the time was identical to the system of the old Arab school of the 'ūdists. That is, it was based on the same harmonic principle as the so-called Pythagorean system, which was in reality of much more ancient Semitic origin: a series of consonances of fourths, fifths, and octaves. In practical terms, this system results in dividing the octave into five tones and two proportional half tones between them. This is what is called the diatonic or natural scale. It has middle tones (*tanīn*, *tanīnī* = 9/8) and diatonic half tones or limma (*baqiyya* = 256/243), with the possibility of using another kind of half tone engendered by alterations within these notes—the chromatic or *apotome* half tone (*niṣf tanīnī* = 2187/2048). Thus, with all its chromatic intermediates, the octave has twelve unequal half tones.

The Imazighen (Berber) element not only contributed to the spread of this system but also helped it resist the additions that were grafted onto it later in schools of the Islamic East, especially the specifically Eastern interval of a second or third known as neutral, about three-fourths or one and three-fourths of a tone.

Ṭab'

Essentially modal, this musical system is based on the concept of the *ṭab'*, the *maqām* 'mode' of the Arabic East—a concept that has philosophical and psychological as well as musicological aspects. The term *ṭab'* is generally accepted as meaning innate character, nature, or temperament; characteristic human reactions to and feelings toward other beings and things; and also an impression, stamp, or imprint. Less mystically, *ṭab'* refers to a modal scale, its characteristics, and its potential effect on the listener.

Ṭab' is a coherent set of components that mark a type of musical organization: *darajāt* 'degrees' (singular, *daraja*), which constitute its essence; melodic or melodic-rhythmic motifs, some of which are final cadences *qaflāt* (singular, *qafla*); and *talwīn* 'modulations' or 'changes in color', in which the character of one mode is confirmed by movement toward another *ṭab'*. The *ṭab'* results from melodic structures (and rhythmic structures for some *ṭubū'*) and from the use of the degrees of the scale according to function. This is achieved by combining features such as tension and resolution, attraction, imbalance, dynamics, cadences, and rests that aesthetically—

and specifically—characterize the degrees of each type of *ṭab'* and thus are decisive in distinguishing one *ṭab'* from others.

Two principal factors, space and time, give structure to a work, depending on whether they are organized in a free or fixed manner. All this makes direct contact indispensable: by listening to a true master, we learn to enter the modal universe; and by practice, we come to communicate with the *rūḥ* 'soul' of the *ṭab'* and assimilate its laws. This is why notation abstracted from sound—for example, a note on a scale—is not enough to transcribe this music faithfully, for the function of a sound within the scale depends not on its absolute value but on its value relative to the chosen register and on the interval that separates it from its neighbor. Absolute values become relative to the overarching value of the instrumental chord, which can vary up to a third from one musician to another without modifying the character of the *ṭab'*.

That character depends above all on the nature and order of the intervals of which a *ṭab'* consists. Traditionally, the *ṭab'* is performed in a particular "tonality" which can be transposed to a fourth, a fifth, and sometimes a second. However, a *ṭab'* played in a low register has a particular expression which it does not have if played higher; thus the choice of register is often decisive.

Musical rhythm and poetic metrics: *Nūba* and *muwashshaḥ*

Nūba

The first use of the term *nūba* 'substitution', 'taking turns' dates from the eighth century, during the prosperous reigns of the third 'Abbasid caliph al-Mahdī (775–785) and his son Hārūn al-Rashīd (786–809). Beginning in the ninth century, *nūba* 'suite' was used to refer to the program of a musical session.

Singing according to the *nūba* had a unique history in the Islamic West, notably in Kairouan and Cordoba after Ziryāb's arrival. Ziryāb set down rules for singers of *nūbāt*: a suite would begin with a *nashīd*, a recitative modulated in free rhythm; would continue with a *basīṭ*, a song in a broad, solemn rhythm; and would conclude with *muḥarrakāt* (singular, *muḥarrak*) and *ahzāj* (singular, *hazaj*), songs in light, lively rhythms with a tempo increasing until the end.

The *nūba* had its flowering with Ibn Bājja (d. 1138), who perfected the *istihlāl* (the *nashīd*) and the *'amal* (the *basīṭ*), adding the *muwashshaḥ* and the *zajal* (see below). Other elements added were later attributed to Ibn Jūdi, to Ibn Ḥimāra, and especially to Ibn Ḥāsib al-Mursī.

The significance and the complexity of this repertoire are suggested by Tifāshī's report that among Andalusian musicians, men and women, there were some who knew about five hundred *nūbāt*. The *nūba* continues to develop today, especially within the North African tradition, where it remains a fundamental element of the classical repertoire.

Muwashshaḥ *and* zajal

In the *nūba*, singing emphasized musical rhythm over poetic metrics; this resulted in a succession of innovations in musical and poetic composition that proved to be of great value. Because the poet was spared the obligation of crafting verses from the structure of a preexisting melody, different possibilities could be imagined, and these led to the creation of two new genres: the *muwashshaḥ* 'embellished' and its popular version, the *zajal* 'lyrical'. Their integration into the *nūba* represented a significant advance.

Both the *muwashshaḥ* and the *zajal* can be subdivided into *aqfāl* (singular, *qufl*) or *abyāt* (singular, *bayt*) 'stanzas'. Each stanza is made up of a variable number of hemistiches or short verses: *aghṣān* (singular, *ghuṣn*) for the *aqfāl*, and *asmāṭ* (singular, *simṭ*) for the *abyāt*. This was a true musical and poetic revolution that allowed the rigid form of the ancient *qaṣīda* to be broken by going beyond the structure of classical

Ziryāb's addition of a fifth string, "as red as blood," to the *'ūd* was an expression of mystical aspirations dear to the traditional Arabic school.

metrics and adopting new combinations and varieties for the purposes of both rhythm and rhyme. Without going into technical details, we can note that the creation of the two poetic genres—the *muwashshaḥ* toward the end of the ninth century, about fifty years after Ziryāb's death; and then its popular version, the *zajal*—was a result of poetic, musical, and social evolution. Observers at the time considered this poetic renewal an exclusively Andalusian invention and attributed it to the predominance of rhythm over metrics. (Indeed, the most widespread genre had a meter that resisted any systematic codification.) The popularity of this poetic and musical art spread throughout the Arab-Islamic world and influenced the repertoire of the Catalan and Provençal troubadours in both form and content.

Mysticism in the Andalusian–North African musical edifice

Although the mystical aspect of this music became an object of gratuitous speculation in the Islamic East after al-Kindī (d. 874) and the Ikhwān al-Ṣafā (tenth century), it was considered more seriously in the Islamic West. In fact, the mysterious, magical, mystical, and religious side of the music, as well as its expressive and therapeutic aspects and its effects on the human soul (its ethos), are part of the foundation of the Andalusian–North African musical edifice.

Ziryāb's addition of a fifth string, "as red as blood," to the *'ūd* was an expression of mystical aspirations dear to the traditional Arabic school. Its placement between the second and third original strings was not dictated solely by a need to expand the *ambitus* of the instrument, or by a need to simplify the fingering and thus make it easier to play, or by a desire to increase its intensity or deepen its sonority. The fifth string, with its central position, was also—and more importantly—a way to complete the living body of the *'ūd*. Ziryāb's new string was a synthesis of the four existing elements; it represented the soul and symbolized life. Ziryāb himself recounted that on several occasions he had been inspired by dreams; often, he said, he would awake in the middle of the night to perform these "nocturnal illuminations." His listeners too believed that he was visited by genies who taught him delectable melodies.

Ibn Bājja and his disciples continued this mystical tendency. They found concordances among the strings of the *'ūd*, cosmic elements, and human emotions; postulated close connections between the magical-religious origins of music and cosmology, medicine, mathematics, and ethics; and developed a symbolic tree of humors or modes (*shajarat al-ṭubū'*) and twenty-four imaginary *nūbāt*. Each *nūba*, with its respective *ṭab'* (which gives the *nūba* its name), evokes a feeling, a particular state; and according to a formal rule, each should be performed at a specific time of day.

Influence of Andalusian–North African music

Despite a paucity of information, it seems obvious that this intense activity profoundly marked musical production both in the East and in the West, where it reached not just Christian Spain but all of medieval Europe. In the transmission and continuity of Andalusian music, the role of the Moorish *rāwīs* and *troteras*, Catalan and Provençal troubadours and trouvères, and, later, flamenco singers was considerable. Through

Spanish and Portuguese elements, the influence of Andalusian music exended throughout South America, the Antilles, Central America, and Mexico.

The impact of this contribution persists in several forms of *cancionero*, a song with instrumental sections and dances characteristic of the different traditions. Innummerable forms and rhythmic and melodic techniques attest to the depth and charm of this art, in which singing, dancing, and instrumental accompaniment are inseparable. It is appropriate here to mention flamenco (*cante jondo* and *canto chico*, with their many derivations), *caña*, *seguidilla*, *siguiriya*, *soleares*, *fandango*, Aragonian *jota*, *alala*, popular songs of diverse regions of the Iberian peninsula, the Portuguese *fado*, certain pieces in the religious repertoire (for example the plaints of the Holy Virgin drawn from the Mystery of the Traneito de Nuestra Señora, which came from the city of Elche), and dances such as the *zapateado*, tango, tap dancing, *jaleo*, *bolero*, *sarabande*, *saltarella*, and Portuguese *lenga lenga*.

Thanks to this Andalusian influence, Spanish musicians of the great era of the sixteenth and seventeenth centuries distinguished themselves in many ways from their Italian and Flemish contemporaries. One example among many is Tomás Luis de Victoria (c. 1548–1611) of Avila. Despite his long stay in Rome as the chapel master of the Germanic College, he always remained fundamentally Spanish, and according to one description, "a little Arabic blood" ran in his veins and he had a taste for Moorish guitars. Later, the Andalusian influence was part of the originality of composers of the Spanish national school—Pedrell, Albeniz, Granados, Morera, Vives, and de Falla.

Without listing here all the Andalusian instruments that were popular in the West, it is worthwhile to note that the sixteenth century was the century of the *'ūd*: the lute was the instrument of choice in many contexts. According to the *Crotalan* of Cristobal de Villalon, there were a great many beautiful lutes of various types, some with a golden neck, played by wealthy musicians and noble amateurs, while strolling singers accompanied themselves on less elaborate lutes.

Still, it should be reemphasized that Andalusian music is original and distinct from the rest of the Western tradition, and even from the Spanish tradition, in terms of vocal and instrumental performance methods and in terms of its particular modes, ornaments, poetic melismas, and rhythms.

Nothing, perhaps, helps us understand the soul of Andalusia better than the *zambra*, a term that comes from the Arabic *samra*. A *zambra* is a festival, a complete performance of songs, musical instruments, and dances. This was the nighttime celebration of the Spanish Moors, with dancing, music making, and storytelling. Today, traditional *zambras* and *leilas* are still inseparably associated with the great Andalusian cities—Seville, Granada, Cadiz, and Jerez, among others—where the *zambra* singers and dancers transport audiences into an atmosphere that recalls the fabled world described in Andalusian sources.

ANDALUSIAN MUSIC IN THE MAGHREB TODAY

Andalusian music has continued to be practiced with all its ardor in different centers of North Africa, even after the Islamic West exploded politically. This continuation is due, at least in great part, to the old system of religious corporations and brotherhoods, especially after the sixteenth century. Currently, the repertoire of classical *nūbāt* which emerged from a secular, urban civilization and was continuously enriched by new elements is a unique and prestigious musical monument. It is called *ma'lūf* 'usual', 'traditional' in Libya, Tunisia, and Constantine; *ṣan'a* 'elaborate', 'artistic' in Algiers; *gharnāṭī* in Tlemcen; and *āla* or *ṭarab* 'instrument', 'profane music', 'emotion' in Morocco [see ANDALUSIAN *NŪBA* IN MOROCCO.] Within each of these these different schools, cultural specificity and sociopolitical context have always influenced the *nūba* repertoire and performance styles. But all these names, from Tripoli to Morocco, nevertheless designate a single thing: the traditional North Africa *nūba.*

The major formal characteristics are the same for each *nūba*: the suite is constructed on a principal *ṭab'* from which it gets its name; it encompasses several vocal and instrumental pieces in different rhythmic and dynamic phases succeeding each other in a given order. A traditional *nūba* has two parts: a preparatory part consisting of musical and vocal overtures and preludes; and a main part made up of vocal phases (in general, five), each with its own rhythm and dynamics, and its own internal introduction, transitional passages, and conclusion. In addition to these two basic parts, there may also be "enrichments."

Nūba *in Morocco*

Al-Ḥā'ik wrote at the end of the eighteenth century that it was customary to use eleven *nūbāt* and twenty-six *ṭubū'*, as follows: four *ṭubū'*, each with its own complete *nūba*; and seven *ṭubū'* containing isolated parts (*yatāma* or *itāma* 'orphans') of the fifteen remaining *tubū'* in their *nūbāt*.

The Moroccan *nūba* includes these components:

- *Mishāliya*, an instrumental prelude in free rhythm that takes place over one or several *ṭubū'*.
- *Inshād ṭab' al-naghma*, a vocal prelude.
- This is followed by the *bughya*, an unmeasured instrumental prelude.
- This in turn is followed by the *nūbat tūshiya*, an overture that began as a purely instrumental piece, to which words were later adapted.
- The core of the *nūba* has five rhythmic phases or vocal cycles: (1) *basīṭ*, (2) *qāyim wa-niṣf*, (3) *bṭāyḥī*, (4) *draj*, (5) *quddām*.

The *basīt*, *qāyim wa niṣf*, *btāyhī*, *draj*, and *quddām* are autonomous units, and each unfolds in the following manner:

> *Taṣdīra*, the first song—fairly slow
> *Ṣan'it muwassa'a*, a series of songs—broad rhythm
> *Qanṭara ūla*, the first bridge, or a slightly faster song
> A series of songs of the same tempo
> The *qanṭara* itself, a noticeably faster song (*mahzūz*)
> *Inṣirāfāt*, a series of faster and faster songs
> *Qafl*, the final song—very fast

The framework of the *nūba* is embellished by internal segments: instrumental *tūshiya* (singular, *tawāshī*), and vocal *baytayn* or *muwwāl*, which are mainly performed by the *munshid* 'leading singer'. beyond the *nūbat tūshiyya* described above, there are *mawāzīn tuwāshiya* (before the *qāyim wa-niṣf* and the *quddām*); *tūshiya* performed at the end of certain *ṣanāyi'* of the *quddām*; and *tūshiya* performed within the *ṣan'a bṭāyḥi* and the *qāyim wa niṣf.* The *baytayn* and *inshād* are two verses in classical style, sung over a free rhythm and requiring great virtuosity. In present times, improvisation has given way to a form that is fixed even in its embellishments. However, the *muwwāl* or *mawwāl* is generally a freer and more majestic quatrain that remains fundamentally improvised.

***Nūba* in Alger'**

The Algerian *nūba* repertoire is represented by three schools: Tlemcen, Algiers, and Constantine. Traditionally, there are twelve *nūbāt*. To these, some isolated pieces have been added, as well as seven *nūbāt inqlābāt* (singular, *inqlāb*). These are a kind of abbreviated *nūba* of recent origin.

The Algerian *nūba* includes the *dā'ira*, a short vocal prelude in free rhythm; followed by the *mistakhbar al-ṣan'a* in Algiers or the *mishāliya* in Tlemcen, an instrumental prelude in 4/4 or 2/4 time ending with a fermata. After a *kursī*—a short allegretto instrumental introduction—come an initial series of vocal pieces, the *mṣadrāt* (singular, *mṣaddar*), in 4/4 or 4/8 and a serious, solemn adagio demanding great mastery on the part of the singer. Another *kursī* introduces the second vocal series of *bṭāyhiyya* (singular, *bṭāyḥī*) sung in a less majestic tempo; sometimes, between two *bṭāyhiyya*, a *mistakhbar* related to the *inqlābāt* is sung. A new *kursī* introduces the third vocal series of *adrāj* (singular, *draj*), in a faster tempo. (Some pieces use irregular measures in 5/8 toward the end of their couplets.)

After this first part, made up almost entirely of majestic binary rhythms, the second vocal cycle of thirds, in a livelier tempo, begins. First comes the *tūshiya*, a slightly "limping" instrumental overture in 5/8 of the *aqṣāq* type. This introduces, after a *kursī*, the *inṣirāfāt* (singular, *inṣirāf* or *neṣrāf*), a light, lively vocal series in 5/8, or sometimes in 3/4 or 6/8. After this comes—with no *kursī*—the last vocal piece, the *mukhliṣ* or *khlāṣ*, in 6/8—an alert, dancing tempo, sometimes moderato, which ends in a generous free-rhythm phase that displays the the final signature of the *ṭab'*. Some *nūbāt* closed with an instrumental piece, *tūshiya al-kamāl*, but only one example has survived.

The *nūba inqlāb* has a *shanbar* or *bashraf*—an overture in a fairly lively tempo—and an *istikhbār*, *mistakhbar*, or *ṣayyāh*, an improvised vocal prelude. Then, after a *kursī* or *mīzān*, come the *neqlābāt* (singular, *neqlāb*) or *inqilābāt* (singular, *inqilā*). These are made up of one or more independent vocal pieces of the same poetic form and musical structure as the songs of the grand *nūba*, but with more varied measures and a lighter melody. To modulate to a second *nūba neqlāb*, the musicians go through the subtonic of the *ṭab'*, which is none other than the tonic of the *ṭab'* for the coming *nūba*. The seven *nūba neqlāb* follow this order:

Ramal-māya (la)
Ika (*sīkā*) (si)
Muwwāl (do)
Zīdān (re)
'Irāq (mi)
Jarka and mazmūm (fa)

Nūba *in Tunisia*

Traditionally, the Tunisian repertoire has thirteen *nūba*, to which have been added others that are of more recent composition but still have the traditional rhythmic and formal framework. In some of these, the modal character stems from the *maqāmāt* of the Eastern school.

Currently, the first phase of a Tunisian *nūba* includes the following:

- *Istiftāḥ*, an instrumental prelude in free rhythm.
- *Mṣaddar*, an instrumental overture whose main part is the *tawq* and *silsila*.
- *Dukhūl*, a short instrumental prelude whose rhythm is first a *barwal* (plural, *barāwīl*), sometimes with an *istikhbār* or instrumental improvisation, and then a *bṭāyḥī*.
- *Abyāt*, which was once two verses in a classical style improvised by the *shaykh* or the *munshid* (the main singer). This is a slow, solemn song in the *btāyhī* rhythm with two short intermezzi or *fārigha* between the first repeated verse and the second.
- A second *dukhūl*, in a *barwal* and then a *btāyhī* rhythm, introduces the first vocal part.

- First vocal part, *bṭāyḥiyya* (singular, *bṭāyḥī*), fairly slow, in which a *fārigha* is intercalated.
- The orchestra then performs the *tūshiya* in the *ṭab'* of the next *nūba*. This is an instrumental piece whose rhythm is first a *barwal*, then an *istikhbār* in the same rhythm and the same *ṭāb'*, then a *bṭāyḥī* that closes with a second *istikhbār* on the *'ūd*, in free rhythm in the *tāb'* of the *nūba*.
- This can lead to a performance of either *sawākāt* or *mshāghlāt*, whose tunes are taken from popular songs.
- Sometimes the main singer improvises on several verses before performing the *muwashshaḥ*.
- This first phase of the *nūba*, whose rhythms are exclusively binary, closes with the second vocal part, in which the *barāwīl* are sometimes introduced by a sung *dukhūl*, fast, lively, and joyful.

The second phase unfolds as follows:

- *Fārigha*, introducing the third vocal part.
- Third vocal part, the *adrāj*, in a tempo that accelerates gradually and then, at the end—after a brief silence—returns to the tempo of the beginning.
- *Fārigha*, leading to the fourth vocal part.
- Fourth vocal part, the *khfāyif* (singular, *khafīf*), in a faster tempo that becomes a 6/8 rhythm with the final song and serves to introduce the fifth and final vocal part.
- Fifth (final) vocal part, the *akhtām* (singular, *khatim*)—a lively, even bubbly melody in a tempo that accelerates from a rapid moderato to a very fast rapido. The theme of this final song is often religious.

In addition to the instrumental overtures (*bashraf, bashraf-samā'ī*, and *shanbar*), musicians insert vocal forms—both popular and classical in character—into the thirteen classical *nūba*: the *qaṣīda* (vocal improvisation over classical verses); the *tawshīḥ* or *muwashshaḥ*; the *shughl* or *sjul*, elaborate songs like the *nūba* itself; the *fūndū*, based on a refrain (*radda*) and couplets (*adwār*). In general, these more recent compositions are performed as a *waṣla* 'suite' of two, three, or four pieces.

Nūba *in Libya*

On the whole, the *ṭubū'* of the Libyan *mālūf* are almost identical to those used in Tunisia, although a certain Eastern influence appears in practice. But unlike other North African repertoires, the Libyan *nūba* does not take the name of its basic *ṭab'*; rather, it has the name of the first *dakhla* or *tashtira*—the first phrase or hemistich of the sung poem. We say, for example, *nūba hādiya al-'īs* or *nūba bushra haniyya*. The *nūbāt* so named are subdivided into two rhythmic categories.

First, the *barwal nūba*, the shorter, consists of:

- *Istiftāḥ* (or *istaftūḥ*, according to an ancient manuscript), a vocal prelude performed in a free rhythm (sometimes measured) in a fairly broad tempo, by the *shaykh*, accompanied by the *ghayta*, and repeated after every verse or hemistiche by the group. *Barāwīl*, a series of vocal pieces (two, three, or more) performed in the rhythm of the same name (4/4 or 2/4), rapidly and joyfully. This becomes very accelerated with the final *barwal* or *khatm*.

Second, the *mṣaddar nūba*, longer and more significant, consists of:

- *Istikhbār* (*inshād*) or *baytayn*—two verses. At once time these were improvised during the main *ṭab'* by the *shaykh*, accompanied by the *ghayta*. Currently, this prelude is often composed, and its rhythm is a sometimes open, sometimes measured *mṣaddar*.

FIGURE 1 Traditional ensembles.

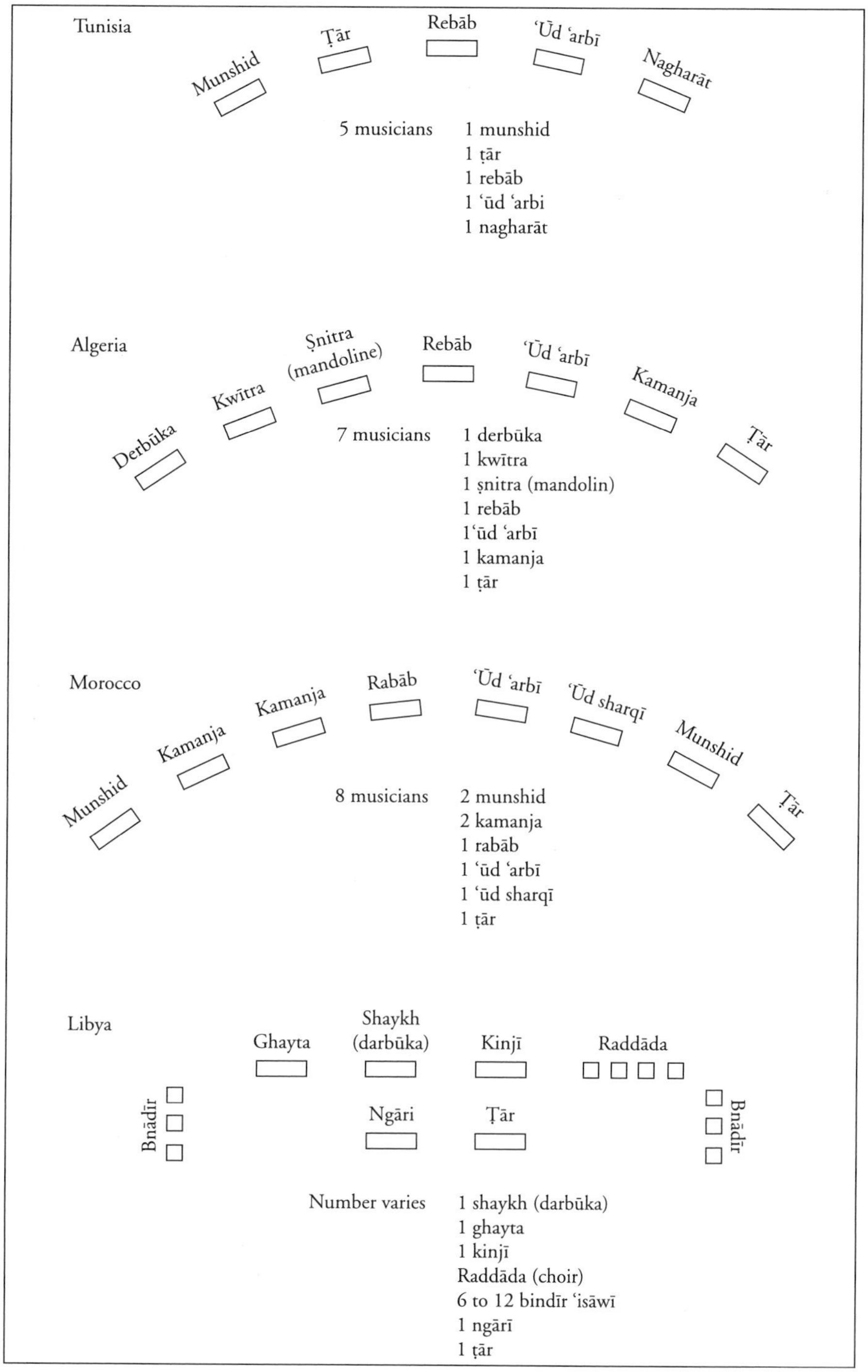

- *Mṣaddar awwal* and *thānī* 'first and second *mṣaddar*'—two songs that unfold in the rhythm of the same name (4/4) at a fairly slow tempo resembling the Tunisian *bṭāyḥī*.
- *Murakkaz awwal and thānī* 'first and second *barwal*'—two more songs performed in the rhythm of the same name. These are actually only another, faster, *mṣaddar* in 4/4 or 2/4. As with the *nūba barwal*, the tempo becomes progressively livelier and more alert toward the *barwal malūf* or *khafīf* until it reaches the near ecstasy or delirium of the finale (*khatm* or *barwal sarī*ʿ).

Melodic structure and instrumentation

The scale generally used in the North African *nūba* repertoire is essentially modal. There are two schools, whose center, and link, is the Constantine region of Algeria.

This region also represents a line of demarcation between the west (Morocco and Algeria) and the east (Tunisia and Libya). In the west, autochtonal components win out, and the continuity of the Andalusian–North African school can be discerned, perpetuating the old lineage of the ʿūdists. This school essentially borrows from a diatonic scale. The school in the east, by contrast, clearly shows an Arab-Ottoman influence and uses intervals of neutral seconds (about three-quarter tones).

The *nūba* songs, whether melismatic, syllabic, or a mixture of both, draw from literary language and dialect and use the classical form of the monorhyme *qaṣida* as well as postclassical strophic forms, especially *muzdawaj*, *musammaṭ*, *muwashshaḥ*, and *zajal*. These are carefully chosen extracts (generally of from two to seven verses) on various subjects: God, love, nature, mystical "drunkeness," and so on. The melodic structure of these songs has several variations.

The traditional orchestra (*firqa* or *jawq*; figure 1) generally consists of a main singer (the *munshid* or *shaykh*) or perhaps two main singers, and numerous instruments: *ṭār* (a drum whose frame has cymbals attached), *rabāb* (a two-stringed instrument), *ʿūd ʿarbī* or *kwītra* (a four-stringed North African lute), *nagharāt* (two small semicircular scoop-shaped timbals, used in Libya and Tunisia), *darbūka* (a goblet-shaped drum used in Algeria), *nāy* or *juwwāq* (an oblique flute), *qānūn* (a tabletop trapezoidal zither), and, more recently, *ʿūd sharqī* (an Eastern lute), plus one or two violins or violas.

Both the voices and the instruments of the modern orchestra have been greatly expanded, often in a way that is incompatible with the nature of the repertoire.

TRANSLATED BY BETH RAPS. ADAPTED FROM THE ORIGINAL BY THE EDITORS.

REFERENCES

Būdhayna, Muḥammad. 1992–. *Al-Turāth al-mūsīqī al-tūnisī* (The Tunisian Musical Heritage). Tunis: Dīwān al-Mālūf.

Chottin, Alexis.1939. *Tableau de la musique marocaine*. Paris: P. Geuthner.

D'Erlanger, Rodolphe. 1937. *Mélodies tunisiennes: Hispano-arabes, arabo-berbères, juive, nègre*. Paris: P. Geuthner.

Guettat, Mahmoud. 1980. *La musique classique du Maghreb*. Paris: Sindbad.

———. 1984. "Al-Turāth al-mūsīqī al-jazā'irī (The Algerian Musical Heritage)." *Al-Ḥayāt al-thaqāfiyya* 32:141–167.

———. 1989. "Dawr Tūnis fī irsā'al-turāth al-mūsīqī al-maghribī al-andalūsī (The Role of Tunisia in the Transmission of Maghribi Andalusian Music)." In *Mūsīqā al-madīna*, ed. Scheherazade Q. Hassan. Beirut: al-Mu'assasat al-ʿArabiyya li 'l-Dirāsāt wa-'l-Nashr.

Al-Ḥā'ik, Muḥammad ibn al-Ḥusayn. 1999. *Kunnāsh al-Ḥā'ik*. Rabat: Akadimiyat al-Mamlaka al-Maghribiyya.

Al-Ḥājjī, ʿAbd al-Raḥmān ʿAlī. 1969. *Tarīkh al-mūsīqā al-andalūsī* (The History of Andalusian Music). Beirut: Dār al-Irshād.

Al-Shāmī, Yūnus. 1984–. *Nawbāt al-āla al-maghribiyya ʿal-mudawwana bi-'l-kitāba 'l-mūsīqiyya*. Casabamce: Mu'assasat Banshara li 'l-Ṭibāʿa wa 'l-Nashr.

Yalas, Jallūl, and al-Ḥifnāwī Amuqrān. 1976–1982. *Al-Turāth al-ghinā'ī al-jazā'irī* (The Algerian Song Heritage). Algiers: SNED.

Andalusian *Nūba* in Morocco

Habib Hassan Touma

Origins of Andalusian Music
Nūba
Mīzān
Ṣan'a
The *Jawq*
Oral Transmission of the *Nūba* Repertoire

Medieval Islamic Spain is referred to in Arabic as *al-Andalus*, a term ultimately derived from the Vandals who ruled the Iberian peninsula and portions of North Africa at the time of the first Arab contact with the region. The musical traditions that originated in Spain during the golden age of Islamic rule are thus known collectively as Andalusian music (not to be confused with the music of Andalucía, a southern province of modern Spain). Andalusian music constitutes an extensive, highly sophisticated musical repertoire of vocal and instrumental pieces—vocal forms predominate—in the Maghrib (Morocco, Algeria, and Tunisia). Transmitted orally for more than twelve centuries, it comprises approximately 1,200 pieces in Morocco, more than 900 in Algeria, and about 350 in Tunisia.

Andalusian music is organized in a distinctive form known as *nūba* 'suite' (plural, *nūbāt*), which has a long history and a characteristic procedure of performance and claims its own audience and connoisseurs. As a musical form, the *nūba* is urban, as is its primary audience. Three regional "schools"—whose centers are Fez, Tetouan, and Rabat in Morocco; Tlemcen in Algeria; and Tunis in Tunisia—determine the stylistic parameters of the *nūba* repertoire. The reperoire is known in Morocco as *āla* 'instrumental', in Algiers as *ṣan'a* 'skill' or 'craft', and in Tunisia as *ma'lūf* 'familiar'. To become an interpreter of the *nūba* repertoire requires years of musical training, a solid knowledge of music theory, an excellent memory, and a beautiful voice.

ORIGINS OF ANDALUSIAN MUSIC

The Andalusians—that is, the medieval Spanish Muslims—first developed this repertoire, preserved it, and then introduced it into North Africa, where it was later augmented by new texts and musical compositions in the Andalusian style. The Andalusians were the transmitters of a culture that had flourished in Islamic Spain during the reign of the Umayyad dynasty (750–1031), the "factional party states" (1031–1089), the Almoravids and Almohads (1089–1231), and Granadan Nasrid dynasty (1231–1492). It would be difficult to discuss the contemporary *nūba* repertoire without referring to these eight centuries of Islamic Spanish history. Indeed, the cultural history of the Iberian Peninsula played a major role in the development of the *nūba* repertoire not only until 1492, when Granada, the last bastion of Muslim rule, surrendered to the Catholic monarchs of Spain, but even until 1609–1614, when the

According to tradition, Ziryāb's personal repertoire included ten thousand memorized songs.

last Moriscos (Muslims living in Christian Spain after the *reconquista*) left the peninsula and emigrated to North Africa.

In 822, the great musician, singer, and courtier of Baghdad, Ziryāb, whose full name was Abū Ḥasan 'Alī Ibn Nāfi', arrived in Cordoba, Spain. He was an authority on the *ṣawt* (an early Arabic song form) repertoire of the old classical music tradition in the eastern half of the Arab world, and he was the highly gifted pupil of the most prominent advocate of this musical form, the master musician Isḥāq al-Mawṣilī (d. 850). The emigration of Ziryāb from Baghdad to al-Andalus was of great significance musically as well as socially. In Cordoba, he is said to have been the creator of the *nūba* form, and he enthusiastically disseminated the elegant manners and accoutrements of the 'Abbasid court of Baghdad. Thus, the year 822 was significant both for the development of the *nūba* and for its eventual maturation in a courtly context in al-Andalus. Ziryāb is said to have organized his performances using musical modes (*ṭubū'*; singular, *ṭab'*) and concepts of pitch that accorded with classical Greco-Arabic medical theory regarding the four temperaments and their corresponding bodily fluids, *sawdā'* 'gall', *balgham* 'phlegm', *dam* 'blood', and *ṣafrā'* 'bile': certain melodic modes were to be performed only at certain times of the day and were thought to evoke certain emotional responses.

It is said that Ziryāb would, in a single night, compose songs ranging from one stanza to much longer; he would preserve them by singing them to his two singing-girls, Ghuzlūn and Hunayda, who would then repeat each melody on the *'ūd* 'short-necked lute' (plural, *a'wād*). It is also said that, night after night, *jinn*—invisible higher beings—inspired his compositions. According to tradition, his personal repertoire included ten thousand memorized songs. Ziryāb's tremendous fame overshadowed the lives and creations of almost all other contemporary singers until the eleventh century. Long after his death, singers continued to follow his practice of beginning a performance with a *nashīd* 'song' to the accompaniment of any *naqr* 'rhythmic pattern'; then proceeding directly to a simple, light section called the *basīṭ*; going on next to a an emotionally moving section, the *muḥarrikāt* or *muḥarrakāt*; and finally singing the *ahāzīj* 'swift songs', which brought the performance to a close.

It was not until the twelfth century, during the rule of the Almoravids (1061–1147) over both Spain and Morocco, that another musician of Ziryāb's caliber emerged. This was the vizier Abū Bakr Ibn Bājja (Avempace), who contributed immensely to the *nūba* repertoire and, in later periods, was renowned as the composer of all the best-known melodies.

NŪBA

The formal structure of a *nūba* comprises five main vocal sections, *mayāzīn* (singular, *mīzān*), usually preceded by two introductory instrumental genres—the nonmeasured *bughya* (or a *mīshāliya*) and the measured *tūshiya* (plural, *tūshyāt*). Each of the main vocal sections, which can take an hour or more to perform, consists of a number of smaller vocal pieces called *ṣan'āt* (singular, *ṣan'a*; see below). In Morocco, the five primary vocal sections of the *nūba* are called *basīṭ*, *qāyim wa-nisf*, *bṭayḥī*, *darj*, and *quddām*. In Algeria, they are called *mṣaddar*, *bṭayḥī*, *darj*, *inṣirāf*, and *khlāṣ*; in Tunisia, *bṭayḥī*, *barwal*, *darj*, *khafīf*, and *khatm*. The name of each section also designates the rhythmic pattern that accompanies it. Thus, the *bṭayḥī* section has the rhythmic pattern *bṭayḥī* as its base, the *darj* has the rhythmic pattern *darj*, and so forth. Originally, the *nūba* repertoire is said to have consisted of twenty-four *nūbāt*, each in a different melodic *ṭab*ʿ 'mode'—literally 'nature' or 'character'. Of these *nūbāt*, however, only eleven have been preserved in Morocco, fifteen in Algeria, thirteen in Tunisia, and nine in Libya.

MĪZĀN

Each of the five sections of a Moroccan *nūba* is called a *mīzān* 'balance' or 'measure'. A sequence of all five sections together constitutes a complete *nūba*. Each *mīzān* is bound to a prescribed elaboration of tempo, which goes through several stages during the performance. The temporal plan includes an introductory segment, three major phases separated by two intermediary stages known as bridges, and a concluding segment. The three main phases are called *muwassa*ʿ 'spacious', *mahzūz* 'shaken', and *inṣirāf* 'departure'. The overall temporal plan thus takes the following course: *taṣdīra* 'introduction', *muwassa*ʿ 'spacious', first *qanṭara* 'bridge', *mahzūz* 'shaken', second *qanṭara*, *inṣirāf* 'departure', and *qufl* 'lock'. The tempo of the *muwassa*ʿ is 1 beat per second. That of the *mahzūz* is 1.8 beats per second up to the first *qanṭara*, which then accelerates to 2.7 beats per second at the beginning of the second *qanṭara* and later, during the course of the second *qanṭara*, reaches 3.5 beats per second. The third temporal phase, the *inṣirāf*, reaches 4.5 beats per second. The tempo, therefore, accelerates fourfold during the performance of a *mīzān*. The acceleration from the first to the third temporal phases changes from, say, quarter note = 60 during the first temporal phase, the *muwassa*ʿ, to quarter note = 270 during the third temporal phase, the *inṣirāf*. However, the time signature of the music, as well as that of the recurring rhythmic pattern maintained by the percussionists, remains constant throughout the *mīzān*.

The time signatures of the five *mayāzīn* are: *basīṭ* 6/4, *qāyim wa-nisf* 8/4, *bṭayḥī* also 8/4, *darj* 4/4, and *quddām* 3/4. The rhythmic pattern of each *mīzān* is executed in performance on the *darabukka* (a vase-shaped drum) and the *ṭār* (a frame drum with jingles). The recurring rhythmic pattern played on the *ṭār* and *darabukka* in each of the five *mayāzīn* must coincide with the time signature of the music being performed.

The term *mīzān* also indicates the period of several *naqarāt* 'beats' (singular, *naqra*) that accompanies the singing in the *nūba*. Such a period of beats is described by Moroccan musicians as an imaginary *dā'ira* 'circle', on whose circumference the sequence of beats is shown. A period of beats in a *mīzān* represents the primary rhythmic type in each of the five *mayāzīn*. The first *mīzān*, in 6/4 time, thus forms a cycle of six beats; the second and third form cycles of eight beats; the fourth forms a cycle of four beats; and the fifth a cycle of three: the sequence of cycles is, then, 6, 8, 8, 4, and 3. The rhythmic pattern of a *mīzān* consists of a characteristic combination of identifiable beats, recurring continuously throughout the course of the performance. A beat is described as muffled, bright, brighter, stressed, accented, unaccented, unoccupied, unchanging, veiled, or variable. The melodic structure within a section is based on the rhythmic pattern of that section and coincides with its structure; this is why a section (*mīzān*) is named after its rhythmic pattern. Thus, *basīṭ* (figure 1) indicates both the name of the first main section of every *nūba* and the name of the six-beat rhythmic pattern. The same is true for the remaining sections and their rhythmic patterns.

FIGURE 1 The rhythmic pattern *basīṭ*.

Moroccan musicians call such a rhythmic pattern a *dawr* 'cycle' (plural, *adwār*), in the sense of a measure or a period; accordingly, a *dawr* in *basīṭ* consists of six beats. Musicians identify the length of a melodic passage by the number of *adwār*, that is, the sum of its measures. A melodic passage in *basīṭ*, for example, is identified as being made up of four, twelve, or even more *adwār* of the *basīṭ* six-beat pattern. In this manner, the *dawr* also serves as a measuring unit to preserve the flawless performance of a specific melodic passage. The number of *adwār* in each *ṣan'a*—a sung stanza of poetry—within a *nūba* is marked at the end of each line of poetry in the songbooks of performers of Andalusian music.

ṢAN'A

A complete *nūba* is the stringing together of the sung *ṣan'āt* 'stanzas of poetry' within the five main vocal sections, the *mayāzīn*. Although the focus is primarily on the progression of the vocal pieces, the *nūba* also includes instrumental passages within the vocal pieces as well as separate instrumental pieces called *tūshyāt* (singular, *tūshiya*). A single *ṣan'a* does not make a *nūba*, nor does a simple series of *ṣan'āt* sung one after the other: a complete *nūba* must contain *ṣan'āt* strung together into the five *mayāzīn*. The *ṣan'at*, then, form the musical backbone of the *nūba*.

Most of the sung poetry in the Andalusian repertoire belongs to either of two genres: *zajal* or *muwashshaḥ* 'adorned' (plural, *muwashshaḥāt*; this term is derived from *wishāḥ*, a woman's scarf decorated with pearls and jewels). However, other forms, such as the *barwala* (a Moroccan form) and the classical *qaṣīda*, are also found. A sung poem in *qaṣīda* form consists of two or four lines of poetry ending with the same rhyme—that is, aa for a two-line *ṣan'a* or aaaa for a four-line *ṣan'a*--whereas the *zajal* and *muwashshaḥ* forms have a wide variety of rhyme schemes.

Form of the *muwashshaḥ*

The poetic form of the *muwashshaḥ* incorporates a number of lines of verse grouped into three categories: *maṭla'* (or *madhhab*), *bayt*, and *qafl*.

The *maṭla'*, that is, the introduction, comprises at least two verse lines, whose end rhymes may be identical (aa) or different (ab). A *muwashshaḥ* is called *kāmil* 'perfect' or *tāmm* 'complete' if it has such an introduction; however, many *muwashshaḥāt* do not have this element and are called *aqra'* 'bald'. The first *muwashshaḥ* in a sequence should always be perfect or complete; later *muwashshaḥāt* can be bald.

The introduction—which is short—is followed by one or more stanzas, each of which consists of two parts; the first part, known as the *bayt*, is the body of the stanza. A *bayt* contains at least three verses, and each section of the *bayt* introduces a new end-rhyme. In a complete *muwashshaḥ*, the *bayt* follows the *maṭla'*; in a bald *muwashshaḥ*, the *bayt* is the beginning of the piece.

The second part of each stanza is the *qafl*, most often comprising two verse lines, which repeats the rhyme of the *maṭla'* and concludes the stanza. The final *qafl* is called the *kharja* 'exit'. In medieval times, the *kharja* was sometimes in colloquial Arabic or in a dialect of Romance.

The rhyme scheme of a *muwashshaḥ* may thus look like this: aa (*maṭla'*) bbb (*bayt*) aa (*qafl*). If the *maṭla'* verses have different rhymes, the rhyme scheme may be: ab ccc ab. The *muwashshaḥ* is composed and sung in classical literary Arabic; a cognate form called *zajal* uses almost exactly the same rhyme format but is composed in colloquial Arabic.

The following *muwashshaḥ* is sung as the first *ṣan'a* in the Moroccan *nūba māya*, that is, in the melodic mode *māya*, and is identified by musicians as a seven-line *ṣan'a* (*ṣan'a subā'iyya*). Note that internal rhyme *-ya* at the end of the first hemistich of each line remains constant throughout the poem:

unẓur ilā rawnaqi l-ʿashiyya//kasat bi-ḥulla ʿalā l-ghurūs (a)
billāhi yā sāqī l-ḥumayya//adir ʿalaynā khamrata l-kuʾūs (a)
daʿūnī naghnam sāʿa haniyya//mā dumtu fī waqti l-ʾaṣīl (b)
zāranī ḥibbī wa-ʿṭaf ʿalayya//mā li-l-raqībi ʿalayya sabīl (b)
saqānī min fīhi al-ḥumayya//mawlā l-dībāji wa-l-ṭarfi l-kaḥīl (b)
sharab wa-ghannā wa-māla ilayya//wa-dhabulat ʿaynāhu l-naʿūs (a)
qabbaltuhu qublatan bilā khafiyya//wa-qultu yā rāḥata l-nufūs (a)

Behold the glow of the evening light!//Like a veil it lays itself over tree and bush.
By God, O cupbearer//Fill our wine glasses one after the other!
Let us seize an hour full of happiness//While the day draws to a close.
My beloved visited me and took pity on me//When no one could spy upon us.
From his mouth I drank wine//As he faced me dressed in silk brocade, his eyelids dark with kohl
He drank, then sang, then leaned toward me//As his sleepy eyes did close.
I gave him a kiss with no shyness//And said, "O soother of souls!"

Structure of the *ṣanʿa*

The poetic and melodic structure of a *ṣanʿa* can be built on a stanza of two (*thunāʾiyya*), five (*khumāsiyya*), or even seven (*subāʿiyya*) lines, each of which has its own traditional melodic plan of performance. This plan determines whether a verse is to be sung in a single melodic phrase or in parts, and whether, when, and how often the instrumentalists are to repeat melodic phrases from the verse. The traditional musical sequence (figure 2) for a five-line *ṣanʿa*, for example, is divided into three parts, as follows—the text is rhymed ab ab ab cb cb:

yā ʿashīya dhakkartanī shawqī (a) // *wa-zamān al-nuḥūl* (b)
rawnaqu al-shamsi ṣāra fī l-ufqi (a) // *māʾilan li-l-khumūl* (b)
ayyuhā l-sāqī jud lanā wa-sqi (a) // *ʿalā ghayẓ al-ʿadhūl* (b)
unẓur al-shamsa kayf badat taṣfar (c) // *janaḥat li-l-ufūl* (b)
jullanār qad ḥaffa bi-l-ʿanbar (c) // *fitnatan li-l-ʿuqūl* (b)

O evening light, you bring to mind my yearning//and a time of pining
The splendor of the sun upon the horizon//inclining toward slumber
O cupbearer, be generous and pour again//despite the jealousy of rivals
Look at the sun, how it turns golden//leaning toward the setting stars
A pomegranate blossom surrounded with amber//enrapturing our minds.

*Entrance (*dukhūl*): aa′ aa′ a*

The first verse is sung to the accompaniment of the instrumentalists (a); it is followed by an instrumental reprise of the melody in slightly altered form (a') known as the *jawāb* 'response'. The second verse is then sung to the same melody as the first (a); it too is followed by the slightly different instrumental response (a'). Finally, the third verse is performed (a) with no response.

*Covering (*taghṭiya*): bb′ b*

The first half of the fourth verse is sung to a new melody (b) with the accompaniment of the instrumentalists; it is followed by the instrumental response in slightly altered form (b'). The second half of the verse is sung to the original form of the melody (b).

*Exit (*khurūj*): a*

The final line of poetry is sung with a return to the opening melody to the accompaniment of the instrumentalists.

FIGURE 2
Transcription of a five-line *ṣan'a*, the sixth *ṣan'a* in the section *mīzān basīṭ*, placed at the beginning of the *mahzūz* temporal phase. Transcription by Habib assan Touma.

THE *JAWQ*

The ensemble in Moroccan Andalusian music is called a *jawq* and usually includes players of the *'ūd* 'short-necked lute', *qānūn* 'box zither', *rabāb* 'bowed fiddle', violin, viola, cello, *ṭār* 'frame drum with jingles', and *darabukka* 'vase-shaped drum'. The members of the ensemble are instrumentalists and also constitute the choir; typically, only the lead vocalist, the *munshid*, sings without also playing an instrument. Customarily, the *rabāb* player is considered the head of the group and leads the performance. The *munshid* sings in unison with the other members of the *jawq* during the *ṣan'āt* but at certain points in the performance is featured in vocal solos.

The vocal pieces, in either classical Arabic or colloquial Moroccan, have themes such as love, happiness, evening twilight, groups of companions drinking wine, longing for al-Andalus and its landscapes, and praise of the Prophet Muhammad. The very

FIGURE 2 *(continued)*

first piece in a *nūba* performance is the instrumental *bughya* or *mīshāliya*, a nonmeasured piece performed by all the instrumentalists except the percussionists. This introductory piece displays and elaborates on the *ṭabʿ* 'musical mode' and its characteristics. A measured instrumental piece, the *tūshiya*, is then performed, with the percussionists now joining in. This is followed by the first *mīzān* of the *nūba*, then the second *mīzān*, the third, the fourth, and finally the fifth. In each *mīzān*, a chosen number of *ṣanʿāt*—perhaps as many as forty—are rendered. Generally, shortly before the performance starts, the leader of the *jawq*, along with his musicians, chooses the order of the *ṣanʿāt* to be sung.

ORAL TRANSMISSION OF THE *NŪBA* REPERTOIRE

Within the framework of traditional oral transmission, the rhythmic patterns have a special function in the teaching of the *nūba* repertoire to the younger generation.

FIGURE 2 (*continued*)

Before students begin to learn to sing a *ṣan'a* in a *nūba*, they must have a command of the rhythmic pattern, the *mīzān*. The ultimate task facing the student is to sing the poem clearly while correctly accentuating the rhythmic pattern. When practicing, the student makes use of a technique called *tawsīd*—beating out the rhythmic pattern with alternating open palm and closed fist to mark the strong and weak accents. Not until this phase of study is completed does the student begin to learn the corresponding melodies. At first the teacher accompanies the student's singing on the *'ūd*; later, the the singer is accompanied by the entire ensemble.

By means of the *tawsīd* technique, the student marks out the rhythmic patterns in each line of the *ṣan'a*, reckoning the number of *adwār* 'measures' for that particular verse. Each line thus comprises a fixed number of measures, which the student notates in the *kunnāsh* 'songbook' at the end of each line of poetry as he or she memorizes

FIGURE 2 (*continued*)

the *ṣanʿa*. Shortening or lengthening the melody of a line of poetry is, therefore, out of the question. Each *ṣanʿa* is identified according to how many lines of poetry it contains and the number of measures in each line; one line of poetry may extend over as many as thirty-seven measures in some songs and as few as six in others.

In addition to this, the student learns to identify each *ṣanʿa* as *mashghūla* 'occupied' or as *khāwiya* 'empty'. A *ṣanʿa* is described as *mashghūla* when it contains *ṭarāṭīn*, nonsense or "filler" syllables such as *yā lā lā*, *ṭīrī ṭān*, and *yā lā lan*, which are worked into the sung poetry. If a *ṣanʿa* contains no such filler syllables, it is called *khāwiya*. The student also learns the proper placement of each *ṣanʿa* within its division of the *mīzān*—that is, in the *muwassaʿ*, *mahzūz*, or *inṣirāf*—for each *ṣanʿa* can be sung only in its appropriate section.

In summary, the student learns first the rhythmic pattern and its relationship to the words of the text both in terms of strong versus weak beats and in terms of the number of measures per line. Next, the student masters the melody, within its specific melodic mode (*ṭabʿ*); this mastery includes the use of filler syllables in certain songs and the interaction between the vocal and instrumental sections. Finally, the student learns the placement of a piece: its proper section within the *mīzān*. This implies the placement of a piece within the larger *nūba* reperoire; for example, a *ṣanʿa* learned as part of the *muwassaʿ* section of *mīzān basīṭ* in *nūba māya* is performed only at that specific point of the repertoire.

REFERENCES

Anthologie al-āla: Musique andaluci-marocaine. 1992. Paris: Maison des Cultures du Monde and Rabat: Ministère de la Culture.

Vol. 1. Haj Abdelkrim al-Raïs and the Orchestre al-Brihi de Fès: *Nūbat gharībat al-ḥusayn*. W 260010. 6 compact disks.

Vol. 2. Haj Mohamed Toud and the Orchestre Moulay Ahmed Loukili de Rabat: *Nūbat 'ushshāq*. W 260014. 6 compact disks.

Vol. 3. Mohammed Larbi-Temsamani and the Orchestre du Conservatoire de Tètouan: *Nūbat iṣbahān*. W 260024. 6 compact disks.

Vol. 4. Ahmed Zaytouni Sahraoui and the Orchestre de Tanger: *Nūbat raṣd*. W 260027. 6 compact disks.

Vol. 5. Haj Abdelkrim al-Raïs and the Orchestre al-Brihi de Fès: *Nūbat istihlāl*. W 260028. 7 compact disks.

Vol. 6. Haj Mohamed Toud and the Orchestre Moulay Ahmed Loukili de Rabat: *Nūbat raṣd al-dhil*. W 260029. 6 compact disks.

Vol. 7. Ahmed Zaytouni Sahraoui and the Orchestre de Tanger: *Nūbat 'irāq 'ajam*. W 260030. 7 compact disks.

Vol. 8. Haj Abdelkrim al-Raïs and the Orchestre al-Brihi de Fès: *Nūbat al-ḥijāz al-kabīr*. W 260031. 7 compact disks.

Vol. 9. Mohammed Larbi-Temsamani and the Orchestre du Conservatoire de Tétouan: *Nūbat ramal al-māya*. W 260032. 8 compact disks.

Vol. 10. Haj Abdelkrim al-Raïs and the Orchestre al-Brihi de Fès: *Nūbat al-ḥijāz al-mashriqī*. W 260033. 5 compact disks.

Vol. 11. Ahmed Zaytouni Sahraoui and the Orchestre de Tanger: *Nūbat al-māya*. W 260034. 7 compact disks.

Vol. 12. Mohammed Briouel and the Ensemble al-Āla du Ministère de la Culture du Maroc: *Mīzān quddām bawākir al-māya* and *Mīzān al-quddām al-jadīd*. W 260035. 2 compact disks.

Chottin, Alexis. 1934. *Corpus de musique marocaine: Fascicule 1—Nouba de Ochchâk (Prélude et Première Phase rhythmique: Bsīṭ) Transcription, traduction, et notes*. Paris: Au Ménestrel Heugel.

———. 1938. *Tableaux de la musique marocaine*. Paris: Librairie Orientaliste Paul Geuthner.

Guettat, Mahmoud. 1980. *La musique classique de Maghreb*. Paris: Bibliothèque Arabe Sindbad.

Larrea Palacin, Arcadio de, and Alfredo Bustani. 1956. *Nawba Iṣbahān*. Instituto General Franco. Tetuan: Editora Marrroqui.

Touma, Habib Hassan. 1998. *Die Nūbah Māyah: Zur Phänomenologie des Melos in der arabisch-andalusi Musik Marokkos*. Hildesheim: George Olms Verlag.

Tuwaymī, Idrīs bin Jallūn. 1980. *al-Turāth al-'arabī al-maghribī fī 'l-mūsīqā*. Casablanca: Maṭba'at al-Ra'īs.

Yafil, Edmond. 1904. *Majmū' al-aghānī wa 'l'alḥān min kalām al-andalus: nūba wa 'inqilābāt*. Algier: Rue Bruce.

Urban Music of Algeria

Jürgen Elsner

History
Music in the Cities: Diversity and Differentiation
The Classical Tradition: "Andalusian" Music
Urban Folk Music: *'Arūbī* and *Ḥawzī*
Women's Music: *Qādriyya* and *Ḥawfī*
Music in Religious Practice
Popular Music: *Sha'bī* and *Rāi*

Algeria, with a total land area of nearly 2.4 million square kilometers, is a vast country; however, more than 85 percent of it is covered by the Sahara Desert, which is bounded in the north by the high Chotts plateau between the Saharan Atlas and the Tell (or Little) Atlas mountains. The desert and steppes are thinly settled and contain only a few centers which in recent years have evolved from small market towns into larger settlements with several thousand inhabitants. Most Algerians live within the relatively narrow, yet fertile and moist, coastal areas on the Mediterranean Sea. In 1989 approximately 95 percent of the population lived in this area; between 1962 (the year of national independence) and 1997, this population increased to 30 million.

Since ancient times, cities along the coast and in the nearby Tell Atlas mountains (which enjoy the climatic influence of the Mediterranean) have developed into military, administrative, and trading centers. These cities were shaped ethnically, socially, and culturally by their relationships with other communities of the Mediterranean, the Near East, and the Middle East. With the changing fortunes of history, some of these centers achieved great importance and experienced swift and lasting development, while others were marginalized, decayed, or were destroyed with the downfall of regional dynasties. In more recent times many of these locales have experienced a rebirth. At the time of the massive French colonization at the end of the nineteenth century, these communities became destinations for rural populations whose land had been expropriated; and during the war of independence in the 1950s and 1960s colonial repression forced nearly half of the farmers—a third of the total population of the country—into the cities. With the population continuing to increase even after the conclusion of the war, urbanization continued unabated. In 1997 roughly 50 percent of all Algerians lived in cities.

The recent urbanization of considerable numbers of uprooted rural dwellers has had lasting effects on urban culture as well. The destruction of inherited economic and social structures has led to a dissolution of traditional modes of behavior and a reordering of cultural frames of reference. Thrown into the cities, with their conveniences of modern civilization and their differentiated and highly developed cultures, these people have been uncertain in assessing the new offerings and have experienced contradictions between material possibilities and spiritual demands. This has been the ground from which new genres and musical styles have arisen and developed.

HISTORY

Algeria has had a long history. Fantastic rock paintings in the central Sahara dating from approximately 10,000 years ago demonstrate the existence of a black population. Some 5,000 years ago Hamitic tribes of Berber extraction invaded the region from the east. After them, Phoenicians, Romans, Vandals, Byzantines, Arabs, their slaves from black Africa, Turks, and Europeans all left their mark. The present ethnic and social structure of the population is complex, and the traditions are many and various, having been nourished by many sources. The influence of the Arabs has been particularly lasting. Beginning in the seventh century they entered Algeria in several waves, subjecting or driving out the Berbers, who persisted in peripheral areas such as the Aurès mountains, Kabylia, the Mzab, and the Hoggar. The steppe areas and the bordering desert regions were taken by the Banī Hilāl and other bedouin populations, whose traditions experienced a fruitful development and remain significant even today. In the Saharan Atlas between Aflou and Bousaada, the ethical-meditative song genre *aiyāi*, which is performed by singer-poets known as *qawwāl* (figure 1)—accompanied in recent times by one or more *qaṣbāt* (singular, *qaṣba*), edge-blown open transverse flutes with six finger-holes—alone encompasses some thirty-five types. This genre has even been taken up by the media, which has popularized it throughout Algeria as part of the national musical heritage.

MUSIC IN THE CITIES: DIVERSITY AND DIFFERENTIATION

Arab culture enjoyed exceptional development and influence in the thickly populated coastal zone with its many cities. Both language and musical life were considerably shaped by this culture, even if the regional dialect and vernacular, musical design, articulation, instruments, and so forth, reveal other sources as well. Owing to the disruptive history experienced in Algeria, the musical culture of the cities is remarkably diverse in structure. It is highly differentiated according to traditions, musical spheres, classes, functions, instruments, genres, forms, and presentation. Moreover, even some of its strictures, grounded as they are in social and regional-historical differences, are

FIGURE 1 The *qawwāl* Boukrab and his group, Aflou. Photo by J. Elsner, 5 May 1985.

in no way homogeneous, despite overlapping characteristics, common functional links, and increasing distribution via modern media. This is the case not only with religious music but also with the dominant courtly-urban art music tradition introduced in the wake of the Arab conquest, a repertoire which in its present development is known as *mūsīqā andalūsiyya* 'music of Andalusia', *mūsīqā ġharnāṭa* 'music of Granada', or increasingly as "classical" music. Neither is this musical culture a closed tradition. The repertoires, performance practices, and instruments of the three main centers of transmission and cultivation—Tlemcen, Algiers, and Constantine (figures 2, 3, and 4)—have much in common, even if, individually, they have distinct features.

The classical music (known in older usage as *ṣan'a* 'art' or 'artistic skill') of Tlemcen, and the surrounding areas under its influence, resembles in some respects the traditions of nearby Moroccan cultural centers, while the *ma'lūf* 'usage', 'custom' of Constantine and its sphere in the east shares not only its name but many features with the Tunisian tradition. Algiers, lying between these two centers, has connections

FIGURE 2 Abdel-Kader plaza in the center of Tlemcen. Photo by J. Elsner, 6 November 1972.

FIGURE 3 The white city of Algiers, view from the harbor to the train station and the shore boulevard. Photo by J. Elsner, 23 March 1973.

FIGURE 4 View of Constantine with the Rhumel canyon. Photo by J. Elsner, 1970.

with both. An interesting example is the wonderful *tūshiya Zīdān*, a classical overture found in all three areas. This instrumental piece, whose melodic profile in all three versions has great similarities, nevertheless demonstrates important differences in melodic progression and formal shape. The Constantine *tūshiya* concisely strings together in sequence five nearly identical extended melodic double lines (figure 5). The Tlemcen version also begins with a succession of melodic pairs of lines. However, this procedure is soon abandoned in favor of a series of individual short lines and segments, or in favor of the kind of melodic sequencing which is particularly preferred in Tlemcen. The piece ends, as in the Constantine *tūshiya*, with a pair of long lines. The version of the *tūshiya Zīdān* in Algiers shares with the version in Tlemcen breadth as well as a multitude of melodic elements and formal sections; with the Constantine tradition, however, the Algiers *tūshiya* shares the unbroken series of long pairs of lines. Its distinctiveness lies in the suggestion of a closed form: at the end of the piece, the pair of lines from the beginning is repeated.

The distinctiveness of these regional traditions is also demonstrated with respect to their rhythmic periods (called *mīzān*), tempo, timbre, and performance practice. For example, a moderate tempo is preferred in Algiers (quarter note = 120), while a broader tempo prevails in Tlemcen and a tendency toward a more volatile tempo can be seen in Constantine. This peculiarity has less to do with surface movement than it does with the underlying tempo—the inner differentiation of basic rhythmic units—and expresses itself in an apparent contradiction: conflicting metronome markings. In Tlemcen, quarter-note values are less frequently divided and tend to move faster than in Algiers, even though the melodic motion is more modest. On the other hand, in Constantine, where the musicians often develop a breathless momentum, the fundamental quarter-note pulses tend to be longer.

In terms of register, or, in other words, the relationship of pitch-space and scale, instruments are normally pitched at a higher level in Constantine than in Algiers or Tlemcen. As the well-known Constantine musician Abdelkader Toumi remarks, "In Constantine the strings are more tightly stretched." The difference between this tuning and that of Algiers and Tlemcen can reach a whole tone or even a minor third. The makeup of the Constantine ensemble indicates a preference for a brilliant, radiant sound; in the production of this sound, the bright, pure-sounding *naqarāt* (a pair of drums, tuned differently from each other) play an important role. By contrast, the Tlemcen ensemble, which uses the *ṭār* (a tambourine) and *darbuka* (a single-headed

FIGURE 5 *Tūshiya Zīdān*, Constantine (parts 1 and 2).

goblet-shaped drum) as percussion instruments, contents itself with a somewhat duller, louder, yet richer sound.

THE CLASSICAL TRADITION: "ANDALUSIAN" MUSIC

The so-called Andalusian music of Algerian cities, which was rooted in the social sphere of feudal lords and required thorough knowledge and training in order to be understood, was originally the domain of relatively few initiates. Despite considerable changes in its social context in the course of history, it lost neither its prestige nor its effectiveness. With the development of early capitalist or mercantile attitudes, the urban bourgeoisie in areas of commerce and manufacturing increasingly appropriated the courtly and aristocratic fine arts, which thus experienced a certain democratization. As the famous Algerian singer Mahieddine Bachetarzi (Muḥyī al-Dīn Bāshṭarzī) reports, this music was heard in public and at family festivals and had great appeal well into the first half of the twentieth century. It embellished the celebration of births, circumcisions, and marriages of the well-to-do and accompanied prominent people to assemblies known as *nazāha* that lasted several days. This music was also heard in urban cafés well into the twentieth century. After Algeria achieved independence, classical music was adopted in many locations by newly founded amateur ensembles and was disseminated nationwide by festivals, radio, records, and television.

The repertoire of Algerian classical music, which has been incompletely transmitted and is only partly understood theoretically, consists primarily of the elaborately structured *nūbāt* (singular, *nūba* or *nawba* 'sequence', 'change') and the lighter *nūbāt al-inqilābāt* (singular, *inqilāb*, a term referring to a folklike, musically simple vocal form). The known Algerian classical compositions number in the thousands and continue to increase. This repertoire, transmitted differently from region to region, is organized into twelve complete *nūbāt*. Of four further cycles only a few pieces are known. The term *nūba* refers to a distinct cycle of various instrumental and vocal pieces featuring gradually increasing tempi. In Tlemcen, the *nūba* opens with an instrumental *mshālya* (known in Algiers as *mustaḥbar al-ṣan'a*) in free rhythm, followed by an instrumental introduction—usually a *tūshiya*, less frequently a *bashraf*. The *bashraf* is customary in Constantine. This is followed by one or more songs in the rhythmically distinct forms *mṣaddar*, *bṭā'iḥī*, *darj*, *inṣirāf*, and *khlāṣ*, which in turn are modeled on the old equal-rhymed *qaṣā'id* (singular, *qaṣīda*), or the *muwashshaḥāt* (singular, *muwashshaḥa*) or *azjāl* (singular, *zajal*), laid out in different strophic forms.

All pieces in a *nūba* are subjected to a common *ṭab'* (plural, *ṭubū'*) 'nature', 'stamp', or 'character'; as a musical term, this refers to the underlying tonal-melodic organization and its associated expressive character, which guarantees the uniformity of the genre. The rhythmic period, *mīzān* (plural, *mawāzīn*), on the other hand, varies according to the type of piece that follows it. In recent times there has been an increasing tendency to simplify the rhythmic accompaniment. For example, the complex *mīzān* known as *qṣīd* (units of 3 + 3 + 2 + 4 + 4) is usually replaced today with the *bashraf*, which despite its syncopated character has a simply executed binary form. However, the "limping" rhythm known as *inṣirāf* (which is difficult to describe), whose pulses involve the proportional relationship 3 : 4 : 4 : 3 : 4 : 4, has endured and has remained very popular.

To some extent, the *nūbāt al-inqilābāt* use different rhythms from the large-scale *nūbāt*; examples include the seven-*mīzān* *ṣūfyān* (units of 3 + 4, known in Constantine as *'āyib* 'limping') and the fast *qubbāḥī* (units of 3 + 3 + 2). Similarly, they open with a *bashraf* or a *shambar* (both instrumental forms of Turkish origin) and an improvised vocal-instrumental *istikhbār*. A series of *inqilābāt* follows. The overall unity of the *ṭab'* is also valid for this folklike *nūba*.

Classical music was performed by small troupes known as *jawq*. These consisted of four to six musicians who performed as vocal soloists, as members of a chorus, and as instrumentalists. They were usually professional musicians—often Jewish—whose social standing was, for religious reasons, low. Two instruments are characteristic of Algerian ensembles into the present time: the four-stringed *kwītra* or *'ūd 'arbī* 'Arabian lute', with its interesting old Arabian tuning (G-e-A-d); and the two-stringed *rabāb* (figure 6), which is boat-shaped, has a bent neck, and is bowed roughly with a short, curved bow. By the end of the nineteenth century, these instruments were joined by the *kamanja kabīra*, the European viola, which is played resting on the knee. In Constantine it has entirely replaced the *rabāb*. Rhythmic instruments include the tambourine known as the *ṭār* and, more recently, the goblet-shaped drum known as the *darbuka*. By the 1930s there was tendency toward larger and larger ensembles, and after Algerian independence ensembles of twenty or more musicians were not uncommon. The introduction of other European instruments further altered the nature of the ensemble.

The performance of a *nūba* can vary greatly in length, depending on the knowledge and ability of the musicians, as well as on the interest and reaction of the audience. According to Abdelkader Toumi (figure 7), the Constantine musician mentioned above, it was customary into the 1960s for traditional marriage celebrations to be accompanied by several *nūbāt*, which were performed before spellbound listeners all night long, until daybreak. The order of the *nūbāt* corresponded to specific times of

FIGURE 6 *Rabāb* player of the Tlemcen SLAM-Orchestra at the Third National Festival of Classical Algerian Music. Photo by J. Elsner, Algiers, 28 October 1972.

FIGURE 7 Abdelkader Toumi (b. 1906), *kamānja*; and Muḥammad Reggānī (b. 1913), *'ūd 'arbī*, at a studio recording of classical music. Photo by J. Elsner, Constantine. 17 May 1985.

day. Thus, the *nūbāt Zīdān* and *Raml* were to be performed in the late afternoon; at nightfall the *Raml al-Māya* and *Mazmūm* were played, although the *Sīka*, *Mjennba*, and *Ḥsīn* were also possible; at midnight, the *Raṣd al-Dhīl* was played; and dawn would be greeted with the *nūba Māya* or *Raṣd*. Since the 1960s, as ways of life in Algeria have changed, such attributions of meaning and forms of organization in classical musical practice have become outmoded or have disappeared. There has been a tendency to perform only excerpts or parts of different *nūbāt* and to shorten the length of performances.

URBAN FOLK MUSIC: *'ARŪBĪ* AND *ḤAWZĪ*

Apart from classical music, other socially or functionally determined musical practices, folk music and folklike music, popular music, religious or cult music, and "Western" music can be found in Algeria's cities and in regions influenced by them. These musics cannot simply be differentiated according to their sources and characteristics; they also differ from one another in how they are rooted in society. In the course of history these types have differed greatly in relative importance. In particular, folklike music and popular music have increasingly moved into the foreground, overshadowing other musical traditions.

In connection with the social dislocations of the nineteenth and twentieth centuries, new folk music practices have emerged in Algerian cities. The petit bourgeois and plebeian classes have contributed the most to this development. These new forms of urban folklike music arising from the lower social classes have drawn on various traditions, such as classical music, music for religious functions, and folk and tribal music. However, the borrowed material has been given a unique stamp, and new stylistic standards have been developed that have their own historical significance. The texts are usually in *malḥūn*, the colloquial language. Originally, the performers were for the most part professional folk musicians, but these repertoires have also been adopted by classical musicians.

'Arūbī

Regional traditions have given rise to vocal genres such as *'arūbī* (or *'arbī*) and *ḥawzī*. Though simpler in design and less rich in repertoire, the *'arūbī* is nevertheless related to, and has grown out of, classical "Andalusian" music. It first developed in the rural area surrounding Algiers, influenced by the *nūba* tradition of that city. The name itself implies an emphasis on "authentic" ethnic roots as opposed to "Andalusian" repertoires. The basis of the *'arūbī* is formed by strophic poetry in various forms, transformed into broad melodic arches that resemble those of classical music but lack its characteristic richness. These pieces are usually performed responsorially by a soloist and a group and sometimes close with an improvised solo in free rhythm.

Ḥawzī

The folk genre known as *ḥawzī* (from *ḥawz* 'boundary') was originally associated with the region around Tlemcen but has also been adopted by the other regional centers of Algiers and Constantine. Appealing to popular taste in language as well as content, the *ḥawzī* embraces serious themes (*klām el-jedd* 'serious words' or 'serious speech') concerned with religion, saints, Muḥammad and his companions, miracles, and the beauty of nature, as well as lighter themes (*klām el-hezl* 'frivolous' or 'idle' words or speech)—wine, women, love, dance, and music. Since the seventeenth century many poets have devoted themselves to this form, and, despite the occasional persecution and exile of poets on moralistic grounds, many of the thousands of examples of their work survive today. The most famous of these poets were Aḥmad Ibn al-Trīkī (who died at the beginning of the eighteenth century); Muḥammad Ibn Msāyib (d. 1766), who left behind more than two thousand poems; and Būmidyān Ibn Sahla (who lived to see the end of Turkish occupation in 1830).

With respect to poetic form, the *ḥawzī* closely resembles the "Andalusian" *zajal*. As a rule it is organized strophically and has a complex rhyme structure, in which internal rhymes play a large role and the ending lines of each stanza have the same rhyme. Like the *'arūbī*, the *ḥawzī* melodies are much plainer than those of the "Andalusian" *nūba*, and the underlying binary and ternary rhythmic periods (*mawāzīn*) are simpler. Very common in the modern tradition are the *qubbāḥī* and the uniquely buoyant *inṣirāf*, an accelerated penultimate *mīzān*.

Along with the *nūbāt*, the *'arūbī* and *ḥawzī* have long since found their way into the private as well as the public sphere. During traditional wedding concerts the musicians would occasionally throw in refreshing lighter songs, often at the request of the audience. In earlier times, in cafés featuring musicians, the colorful assemblage of listeners would often call for lighter, more easily digestible fare.

WOMEN'S MUSIC: *QĀDRIYYA* AND *ḤAWFĪ*

Qādriyya

In the sexually segregated society of Algeria, the *'arūbī* and the *ḥawzī* belong to the realm of men. Women have developed their own striking musical forms for their own circles, forms which have also been adopted by classical musicians and have served especially as refreshing, unaffected additions at the end of the *nūba*. These are the *qādriyyāt* (singular, *qādriyya*), sung in dialect, which belong to the repertoire of traditional women's ensembles (*msama'āt* or *msāma'*). These groups, engaged by rich families for celebrations such as marriages, betrothals, and circumcisions, have fulfilled ceremonial functions and provided entertainment. The *qādriyyāt* are pretty, elegantly formed melodies setting multiple stanzas of love poetry, classified as *qādriyya ṣan'a* (elaborated *qādriyya*) in classical music or as *qādriyya zendānī* in the context of urban folk music. The songs of the first group are generally tied to the *mīzān inṣirāf*, according to local understanding a three-part rhythmic period, while those of the second group are characterized by the rocking meter (6/8 or 12/8) of the *zendānī*—a name derived from a light dance song.

Ḥawfī Folk Music

There are very old and intimate bonds with respect to language, form, rhyme, and content between the *ḥawzī* and the *ḥawfī*, a genre of urban folk music. This genre, which is cultivated in northern Algerian cities from Tlemcen to Algiers and about which little is known, is the exclusive domain of women. The *ḥawfī* features short rhymed texts of few verses, which are improvised in free rhythm on a melodic model of usually four or five lines (figure 8).

A *ḥawfī* song, performed by a soloist, serves as entertainment and can encompass a wide range of themes, from nature poetry to poetry about the joys and sufferings of love to the glorification of Allah and the saints.

Women of lower social standing, who in Muslim society are for the most part ostracized by the public and must provide for their own musical needs, cultivate along with the *ḥawfī* numerous other genres, including incantations; cradle songs; work songs; songs of ritual or entertainment relating to birth, circumcision, marriage, pilgrimage, and veneration of the dead; jocular songs; dance songs; and laments. When rhythmic accompaniment is called for, the women clap their hands or use the *darbuka*, traditionally considered a women's instrument.

Since children belong generally to the sphere of women, their musical expressions should be mentioned in this context. These expressions include songs of mockery, prayer, and play, as well as songs sung during Ramadan, at the great feast (*'īd el-kebīr*), and during the *mulūd* (birthday of the Prophet).

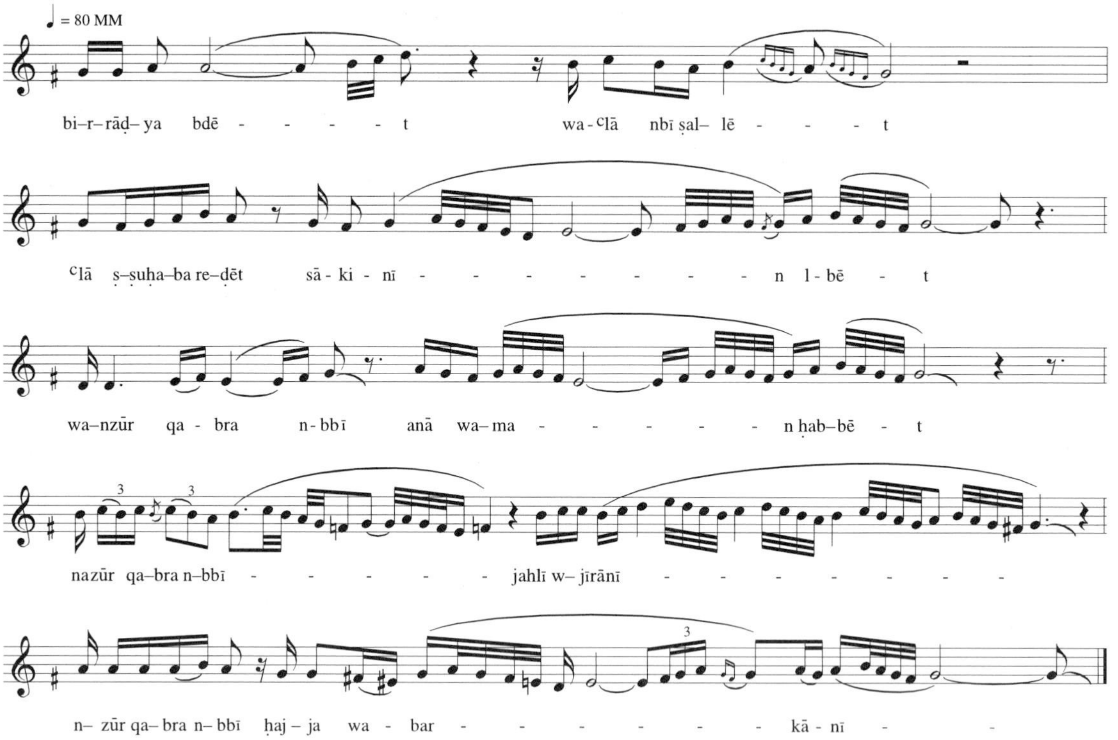

FIGURE 8 *Bi-r-rāḏya bdēt* (*ḥawfī*/Tlemcen).

Like those of women, the folk music traditions of men in Algerian cities are relatively little researched and, with the modernization of urban life, are rapidly disappearing. It is increasingly difficult to hear the traditional songs of various tradesmen, including the weavers, basketmakers, and smiths; the calls of street vendors; or the music of itinerant entertainers and beggars. Music for entertainment as well as for the celebration of important annual events in people's lives, performed by variously constituted troupes of semiprofessional or professional musicians, is retreating more and more in the face of popular music disseminated by the media.

The music of the descendants of black African slaves in the large city centers was reported at the beginning of the twentieth century but has largely disappeared since then. It continues to have a role only in regions with large concentrations of these people, where it is performed at secular as well as sacred celebrations.

MUSIC IN RELIGIOUS PRACTICE

In the Muslim world, religion penetrates all phases and aspects of life. This is reflected in music, which is subtly woven into both liturgical-cultic practice and into everyday acts and articulations of a ritual or ceremonial character. References to religious ideas mark invocations, meditations, formulas for intercession and blessing, procession songs, songs of praise, and so forth. Even dances accompanied by singing and *bendīr* rhythms, such as the *saf* (*ṣaff*) performed by the women of the Sahara Atlas for religious feasts, serve to praise Allāh and the Prophet and thus also fall into the category of religious practice.

In Muslim Algeria, singing and music making within a religious context are considered not music as such but rather as a means of adding urgency to the presentation of sacred texts and of shaping the religious act more effectively. Any obscuring or overshadowing of the text by the music is considered uncalled for and is actively resisted by the orthodox. The greater role allowed to music as a medium for the union with and veneration of Allāh by various religious brotherhoods in their exercises (*samāʿ* 'listening' or *ḥaḍra* 'presence') has only deepened the suspicions of the orthodox with regard to these groups. Significantly, the recitation of the Qur'ān, even when it is not simply spoken but rather is presented with a raised voice and musical pitch, is assigned not to a singer but rather to a reciter (literally, a reader). And the *adhān*, the call to prayer which today can usually be heard melodiously wafting through Algerian cities, projected by loudspeakers, can still be heard occasionally in the open land in a loud and sometimes rough voice.

In the cultic functional context of Algerian life, songs of praise, *amdāḥ* (singular, *madḥ/madīḥ*), performed by soloists or groups and glorifying or expressing love for Allāh, the Prophet, and the saints, have a particularly important role among the different musical renditions of religious texts. The texts of these songs, usually in the popular *malḥūn* dialect, derive their form from the isometric, equal-rhymed old Arabic *qaṣīda* or from the revived strophic *qaṣīda*, which in turn developed under the influence of the *muwashshaḥa* and the *zajal*. In musical terms, songs of praise are closely related to the tradition of classical music, especially in the urban milieu.

POPULAR MUSIC: *SHA'BĪ* AND *RĀI*

Sha'bī

New musical practices and genres associated with the enormous social upheavals and developments of the twentieth century have taken their place beside such forms as *'arūbī*, *ḥawzī*, and *qādrīyya*, themselves considered modern in the nineteenth century. In this creation of new musical forms, the *madḥ*, which has been widely disseminated and is deeply rooted in popular consciousness, has assumed a particularly important and highly interesting role. It represents one source of the music called *sha'bi* 'popular', or relating the common people, which developed in Algeria during the 1930s. Like other types of traditional music, the *sha'bī* used the vernacular (*malḥūn*) and was formally related to the *qaṣīda* in its strophic structure and equal rhymes over several lines and half-lines of verse. On the other hand, it was influenced by classical music as well as by popular genres, although it tended to orient itself toward forms developed in other countries, which were subsequently adopted with great eagerness in Algeria. These included newer Egyptian music (often called *sharqī* 'eastern'), jazz, and European dance music. These genres gradually spread from east to west through concerts of Egyptian, Tunisian, and Algerian music in the 1920s; eventually, they were disseminated throughout the French colonial empire in North Africa, since the French recruitment of Algerian soldiers in the First World War led to greater knowledge of and influence by popular European music. To a certain extent the distribution of phonograph records and radio (since the early 1930s) also contributed to this phenomenon.

The influence of jazz and of European dance music on the *sha'bī* are unmistakable, even if its forms and articulation remain firmly rooted in Algerian musical culture. Particularly striking has been the adoption of fretted stringed instruments like the mandolin, guitar, and banjo and the disappearance of other traditional instruments. This has led to changes in the overall profile of the sound, which has become sharper, more vigorous, more penetrating, and more subjective; at the same time, the reinforcement of higher frequencies gives the overall sound a greater stridency. Structurally, these changes have reinforced a tendency toward simplifying the music and making it more understandable—it demands little in the way of specialized training or knowledge. The newer *sha'bī* are characterized by shorter sections and phrases; the melodies tend to be structured on fifths and thirds, triadic groupings, chromatic passages, and *cante-jondo* turns. Simple rhythmic patterns are preferred, and the vocal style is elastic, light, and swinging, yet rhythmic and impulsive. As a result of this process, participation in the world of professional music making has become democratized.

Mohamed Idir Ait-Ouarab, known and loved under the name Mohamed El-Anka, or al-ʿAnqā (figure 9), is an exemplary figure in the origin and development of the genre of *shaʿbī*. El-Anka was born in the Algerian casbah in 1907. His parents, who came from the Great Kabylia Mountains, were deprived of their lands by the colonialists and were forced to flee. Having spent a number of years in the Qur'ān school and in the native school, El-Anka began elementary school as a ten-year-old. He was irresistibly attracted to music and could always be found wherever it was, listening at marriages and other family celebrations and in cafés. As an eleven-year-old he became acquainted with the troupe of the famous musician Mustapha Nador, who, just for fun, entrusted the aspiring child with a tambourine; however, the banjo was El-Anka's first instrument. His parents were powerless to discourage his under-appreciated, insatiable thirst for music; finally, they allowed him to learn and practice, and he found his way to a number of renowned musicians. At first El-Anka was a musician and singer at "henna evenings," ceremonies accompanied by *madḥ* songs. At age eighteen he was accepted into Mustapha Nador's orchestra, where he learned the mandolin and, above all, the *madḥ* repertoire of his teacher. One year later Nador died, and the musicians of the troupe agreed that El-Anka was his most suitable successor. To overcome his qualms and trepidations at the prospect of becoming a *maddāḥ* ʻ*madḥ* singer' and orchestra leader, El-Anka visited the *ḥaḍrāt* 'presence' or 'assembly' of *madḥ* singers in the mosque of Sidi Abderrahmane Etaʿālibī (ʿAbd al-Raḥmān al-Thaʿālibī), regularly for five years. There, twice a week, ancient hymns and songs of praise were offered by groups accompanied by the *deff* (a small frame drum), *bendīr* (a large frame drum), and *zunūj* (small hand cymbals).

In 1929 El-Anka founded his own orchestra, which consisted of instruments that reflected his desire for a pleasant, rich sound, including viola, flute, banjo, *darbuka*, and tambourine. With this formula, he achieved great success. As his popularity grew, he began to treat the established repertoire with greater freedom, experimenting with new turns of phrase and accents. Many listeners were pleased by his departures from the usual fare. He was invited by the newly constituted, fragile Algerian radio network to introduce the popular *madḥ* over the airwaves. Recordings of his performances were enthusiastically sought. His innovative, refreshing style of popular song, despite its controversial content, was by 1932 known as *shaʿbī* (*chaâbi*) 'the epitome of the popular'. The new genre was laconic, mutable, pleasing, and accessible. Many musicians of El-Anka's generation and especially of later generations, motivated and stimulated by current social and cultural events and trends, dedicated themselves to the

FIGURE 9 Mohamed El-Anka during a concert in Algiers. From Photo Archive, Institut National de Musique Algier.

inherited traditions of popular music, particularly the new genre. Even in the difficult times after World War II and independence, much hope was in the *sha'bī*, which remained accessible to the masses of the dispossessed who had fled into the cities and reflected their ideas and aspirations. The genre remained popular into the 1980s, when it was displaced by *rai*, a new kind of music that gained ground despite official resistance.

Rai

Rai (in classical Arabic, *ra'y*) 'opinion' or 'view' has become known as *musique moderne*, playing on the customary interaction of old and new [see RAI]. Its origins go back to the area around Oran in western Algeria, during the period after World War II. As with *sha'bī*, the beginnings and development of *rai* were indebted to the new social situation, newly available instruments, and new technology. Like the earlier Egyptian music, jazz, and European dance music, contemporary Western dance and pop music influences and fascinates young audiences and musicians. On a foundation of urbanized bedouin and urban folk traditions of the Oran region, young amateur musicians have built a music which reflects the conditions and needs of many of those born after the war, a music which has had great success and has been transmitted internationally via France since the 1980s.

TRANSLATED BY ALEXANDER J. FISHER

REFERENCES

Bachetarzi, Mahieddine. 1968–1986. *Mémoires*. 3 vols. Algiers: Entreprise Nationale du Livre.

Bouzar-Kasbadji, Nadya. 1988. *L'emergence artistique algérienne au XX siècle*. Algiers: Offices des Publications Universitaires.

Collaer, Paul, and Jürgen Elsner. 1983. "Nordafrika." In *Musikgeschichte in Bildern*, 1(8), ed. Werner Bachmann. Leipzig: Deutscher Verlag für Musik.

Daoudi, Bouziane, and Hadj Miliani. 1996. *L'aventure du rai*. S.n.: Éditions du Seuil.

Elsner, Jürgen 1982. "Instrumentalstücke der klassischen algerischen Musik." Algiers: Institut National de Musique. (Typescript.)

———. (1985) 1990. "Der Rhythmus Inṣirāf. Zum Problem quantitativer Rhythmik." In *Schriftenreihe des Mecklenburgischen Folklorezentrums, Abteilung Tanz*, ed. Rosemarie Ehm-Schulz, 59–74. Neubrandenburg: Mecklenburgisches Folklore-Zentrum. Also in *Rhythmik und Metrik in traditionellen Musikkulturen*, ed. Oskár Elschek, 239–249. Bratislava: VEDA, Verlag der Slowakischen Akademie der Wissenschaften.

———. 1991a. "Formation of New Music Traditions in the Arab Countries of North Africa." In *Studies in Ethnomusicology*, Vol. 1, ed. Jürgen Elsner and Gisa Jähnichen, 33–45. Berlin: Humboldt-Universität.

———. 1991b. "The Forms of Classical Algerian Instrumental Music." In *Studies in Ethnomusicology*, Vol. 1, ed. Jürgen Elsner and Gisa Jähnichen, 20–32. Berlin: Humboldt-Universität.

———. (1992) 1993a. "Présentation de la musique algérienne au Congrès du Caire." In *Musique arabe, Le Congrès du Caire de 1932*, ed. Sheherazade Qassim Hassan, 191–208. Cairo: CEDEJ. German version: "Zur Darstellung der algerischen Musik auf der ersten Konferenz für arabische Musik Kairo 1932." In *Studies in Ethnomusicology*, Vol. 3, ed. Jürgen Elsner and Gisa Jähnichen, 111–136. Berlin: Humboldt-Universität.

———. 1993b. "Some Remarks on New Developments in the Music of Algerian Cities." *Revista de Musicología* 16(3):1240–1245.

———. 1997. "Bashraf und Shambar in Algerian Art Music." In *The Structure and Idea of Maqām: Historical Approaches. Proceedings of the Third Meeting of the ICTM Maqām Study Group Tampere—Virrat, 2–5 October 1995*, ed. Jürgen Elsner and Risto Pekka Pennanen, 65–85. Tampere: Department of Folk Tradition, University of Tampere.

Guettat, Mahmoud. 1980. *La musique classique du Maghreb*. Paris: Sindbad.

———. 1986. *La tradition musicale arabe*. S.n.: Ministère de l'Education Nationale.

Plenckers, Leo J. 1989. *De muziek van de algerijnse muwashshaḥ*. Alkmaar: Rapporta B.V.

———. 1993. "Changes in the Algerian *San'a* Tradition and the Role of the Musicologist in the Process." *Revista de Musicología* 16(3):1255–1260.

Poché, Christian. 1995. *La musique arabo-andalouse*. S.n.: Cité de la Musique/Actes Sud.

Rouanet, Jules. 1922. "La musique arabe dans le Maghreb." In *Encyclopédie de la musique et dictionnaire du Conservatoire*, ed. Albert Lavignac, 2813–2944. Paris: C. Delagrave.

Saadallah, Rabah. 1981. *Le chaâbi d'el-hadj M'hamed el-Anka*. Algiers: Dār al-Kutub (La Maison des Livres).

Schade-Poulsen, M. 1994. "Music and Men in Algeria. An Analysis of the Social Significance of Rai." Ph.D. dissertation, University of Copenhagen.

Yafil, Edmond-Nathan. 1904–1924. *Répertoire de musique arabe et maure*. Nos. 1–29. Algiers.

Yelles-Chaouche, Mourad. 1986. *Le ḥaufī: Poésie féminine et tradition orale au Maghreb*. Algiers: Office des Publications Universitaires.

Yillis, Jalūl, and Amuqrān al-Ḥafnāwī. 1975–1982. *Al-Muwashshaḥāt wa 'l-azjāl* (The *Muwashshaḥāt* and *Azjāl*). Parts 1–3. Algiers: 'l-shirka al-Wataniyya li 'l-Nashr wa 'l-Tawzī'.

Music in Performance: A Wedding in the Atlas Mountains

Miriam Rovsing Olsen

After harvesting barley for two months, women are taking pleasure in gathering at the bride's house and relaxing during a wedding celebration that began a few days ago. They are draped in heavy indigo cloth fastened with a silver fibula. On their heads, and falling to their shoulders, they wear a black scarf with red, green, and yellow designs; the scarf is held in place by a thick cord and sometimes covered by a white veil. Two or three of these women, whose veils are pinned on, are the bride's "initiators"; they assist her during the ritual, never leaving her side. Unwedded girls wear great gilt tiaras mounted on a long multicolored band of woven cloth that drops down the back all the way to the feet in two wide halves.

It is late—10 p.m.—and the men of the honor guard (*imsalan*) have arrived on muleback to seek the bride. One bears a bundle decorated with sprigs of basil. They are received by women, some at the doorstep, others further inside the house. One of the women utters three long, strident ululations. Then in a low, calm voice, the women—arranged rather theatrically in two separate antiphonal groups—begin their

TRACK 13 songs (*izwirrign*):

> In the name of the compassionate and merciful God
> He is First in everything
> Prayers to Lord Muhammad.

Then, to a different tune, they begin to sing the following words, which are passed back and forth between the groups and repeated:

> O my daughter's boys of honor, be welcome
> Be welcome; you bring happiness.

Then the tune changes again, this time for two verses:

> Every messenger holds
> white plow beams.
>
> You kings, hold tightly to each other
> to hold hard-wearing plow beams.

One of the initiators (called a *tamzwarut*) then takes up the bundle, puts it on her head, and brings it to the bride. The bride is settled in a room, surrounded by her girlfriends. They have heard the *izwirrign* from a distance. The bride, draped in blue cloth, is sobbing; when she sees the bundle, her sobbing intensifies. Everyone on all sides is crying. A woman opens the bundle and displays its contents: clothing, all white—undergarments, a long shirt, two large veils (one thicker than the other), and a long turban—jewelry, dates, almonds, henna, a very fine red head scarf, another thicker one, and slippers (*babauches*). Immediately, the women hang up one of the white veils as a curtain to isolate the bride from her friends. Two women then care for her, dress her, and prepare her. She reappears, still draped in blue but now with a transparent red veil covering her head and face. She remains unmoving in a corner of the room. When a woman or a friend wants to talk to her, the bride lifts her veil, extending it to cover both of them. The room is intensely hot. One of the initiators prepares the bride's henna. A meal is served. In another room, the men conclude the contractual aspects of the marriage. After midnight, outside the house, the villagers
TRACK 14 are now gathered to sing and dance the *aḥwash* until sunrise [see Berber Musics in Morocco].

A few hours later, in the late morning, a dozen women get ready to clothe the bride for her departure to the village of the groom's family. They are in the central courtyard, which is open to the sky; the sun is burning hot. The women have spread a mat out on the ground. In their hands they hold a large white blanket. One of them utters three piercing ululations; then, dividing into two groups, they sing the first song exactly as they did the night before on the arrival of the men of honor. Sharp laments are heard from two of the women. Now the bride, led by a boy and followed by her friends and other women, enters the courtyard and steps onto the mat. Two initiators stand on each side, and immediately a dozen women raise the large white blanket over her to shield her from the eyes of onlookers. At a distance, an old woman recites a few words from time to time, in an authoritative voice. These are in fact the first words of verses that the women then sing, along with the number of repetitions: "twice," "three times," "four times."

Now the women change tunes. They now sing a tune from the night before—the last of the three songs. The words are addressed directly to the bride:

> Don't cry, bride, you mustn't cry.
> The one marrying you is welcome in your father's and your mother's eyes
> In the eyes of your elder brothers too.
>
> I pin the edges of your garments
> With fibulae like Aisha's, the Prophet's wife.
>
> I dress you as she was dressed,
> Aisha, the Prophet's wife.
>
> Rise, bride, may God support you
> so that you carry yourself as supple as a reed.
>
> My daughter, may God bless you; your father tells you
> to return his keys to him.
>
> Mother, I put the keys
> to my father's room in [my] right hand.

The effect of the singing is immediately apparent: the bride sobs, as do the women around her, over the continued lamentations of the women holding the veil. Ready for her departure, the bride is now entirely hidden under her white veils, and the women guide her toward the door of the house while starting up a new song that enjoins the boys of honor to give a silver coin in exchange for the bride's departure:

> Call one of the boys of honor so that his brothers may bring the bridle.

Then the heavy door opens in front of the procession. A man bears the bride before him on his mule. The lamenting continues, and the women have changed tunes again; they now sing a more markedly rhythmic tune, for walking:

A sawl a illi s-unfrad nnm ad amd imun.	My daughter, call your procession, so they can ready themselves for departure.

In this last song, which is repeated as often as necessary, there is a particular relationship between text and melody: the melody starts with the last four syllables of the verse (that is, the words *ad amd imun*) and goes on with the rest of the verse (*a sawl a illi s-unfrad nnm*). This constant shifting between the beginning and the end of the verse and of the melody implies a circular process, appropriate for walking. Other songs follow, executed in the same manner.

The procession is imposing. Groups of men, who have been invited on this occasion because of their qualities as musicians or singers, join in and add their *tizrrarin* (singular, *tazrrart*) to the processional songs. Using a melodic formula of a single type, a male soloist sings—in a high register—the first verse of a distich whose final syllables are picked up by a group of men. He concludes with the second verse, joined by the group for its second half. The soloists each sing *tizrrarin* in turn. Other men begin to play the drum. A listener would probably be stunned by this multilayered singing, in such strong contrast to the ceremony that has just been observed. The predominant mood now is euphoria. In front of the groom's house, a crowd awaits the procession, which is hailed by *tizrrarin* sung by the men of the village. The procession stops. Some women are sitting on the roof above the entrance. Three ululations pierce the sonorous atmosphere, and then the initial song heard at the bride's home begins again; it is passed between the women seated on the roof and those surrounding the bride. Then they begin a singing contest in which each verse is sung only once. The tune is the one with which, earlier, they invited the men of honor to make a gift:

> I greet you as a believer does when he meets another believer.
> I return your greeting as a believer does when he meets another believer.
>
> Tell me whether my daughter will find adversaries in this house.
> In this house there will be support for her and not adversaries.
>
> We have brought fifty horses with saddles and harnesses.
> Take off their bridles and give them grain in the manger.
>
> We have brought a king's daughter, her arms filled with flowers.
> She is the fiancée of the son of a king who owns fields and water.
>
> My daughter is beautiful, my daughter is of age; give her the keys to your wealth.
> If your daughter pleases me, I will give her the keys to our stores.
>
> If he wants my daughter, he must know she loves to rest on cool terraced roofs.
> If your daughter wants rest, she will have to raise lambs and calves.
>
> My daughter doesn't want to be despised like a kitchen tripod; she wants to be respected like the foyer of the mosque.
> My son wants his honor preserved; spring water will not wash away dishonor.

I have brought white corn; I will be happy if skillful hands take care of it for me.
At the top of the mountain, I see a cloud swollen with water, coming toward me.

As for me, I will not enter until it rains almonds and sweets.
Rise to enter, you young women; almonds and sweets are falling on us from over the door.

At these final words, the women seated above the doorway drop not only almonds and dates but also milk, and a great white veil intended to protect the bride. Things begin happening at a faster pace: children throw themselves on the nuts and dried fruits and toss them at each other. The bride is carried up an outside staircase, to a room where she is settled in a corner opposite the door, on the right. Again, three ululations are heard, and *izwirrign* are now exchanged between one group of women in the room where the bride is and another group at the door of the room. Holding a little boy by one hand and carrying a small bucket of milk in the other, a woman goes to and fro between the bride's room and the groom's, going up and down the staircase several times. The first song is the same as in the other phases. It is followed by another song:

I want to be like you in all that is white
Of whiteness as pure as the young ewe's milk
Ram, call your mother to bring you milk
When she's brought the milk, let her bring you the tool
When she's brought you the tool, let her bring you leaves
When she's brought you leaves, let her bring you the fleece
When she's brought you the fleece, let her bring you some water.

The *izwirrign* songs are followed by a round dance in the bride's room to the beats of a frame drum played by a woman. An initiator brings the bride toward the door, to open and close it three times. The women engage in *tizrrarin* while they drink the spicy coffee they have just been served. The man who brought the bride enters. He sits down before her, and together they begin a ritual meal. Then the bride's room empties out.

On the ground floor, large, beautiful rugs have been spread out in rooms that are normally left bare; the guests, who had been seated in different rooms according to sex and age, now crowd in. Relaxed, the women chat and joke, sitting on the rugs, tightly packed together along the walls of the rectangular room, filling the whole space. They are dressed in their most beautiful clothing and wear much jewelry. The women begin a *tazrrart*, and immediately the men respond from their own room with another one; this dialogue—between men and women separated by a wall which is pierced only by their voices—continues for a long time.

Drums can now be heard in the distance. On the square in front of the house, men have begun poetic contests that will last until about midnight, interrupted only by meals. On this night, the young women are draped in white cloth. In their tiaras are yellow and orange flowers and basil. Only the dawn will put an end to the festivities. In the bride's room, the ritual picks up again. The three ululations, now familiar, sound again, and the first song of a new series. . . .

Note: This description is a general account of several marriages observed by the author in the Atlas Mountains from 1977 to 1990, during the months of July to September.

Berber Musics in Morocco

Miriam Rovsing Olsen

Musical and Agricultural Aesthetics
The Art of Sung Poetry
Ladkar
Aḥidus* and *Aḥwash
Professional Performers

The Berber peoples of Morocco live mainly in the mountains, where they have maintained a vibrant musical culture. While the music of the Rif region to the north is still little known, the music of some tribes in the Atlas region has been researched in depth. The Atlas Mountains, a long ridge descending diagonally from Fez in the northeast to Goulimine in the southwest, are divided into the High Atlas in the center (the largest of the massifs), the Middle Atlas in the north, and the Anti-Atlas in the south. There are two groups of Berbers in the Atlas region, distinguished from each other by their language and way of life: the Imazighen seminomadic herders of the eastern High Atlas and the Middle Atlas, who speak Tamazight; and the sedentary farming Shleuh of the central and western High Atlas, Anti-Atlas, and Souss plain, who speak Tashlḥiyt. Among the Berbers, Qur'ānic recitation and hymns sung in Arabic do not indicate that Arabic is the everyday language.

MUSICAL AND AGRICULTURAL AESTHETICS

The primary explanation for the vitality of musical traditions in the Atlas is probably found in their relationship to the natural environment. Among the Shleuh, not only do musical performances follow the farming calendar, but some forms embody growing cycles. As a result, a single term often refers to both music and agriculture: *iriẓi*, a rhythm drummed while the performers are walking in a procession, also refers (in the Anti-Atlas) to plowing; *tamssust*, a sung dance, also refers to knocking fruit down from trees; and *aqqayn* (in the western High Atlas) means both sung lyrics and seeds or certain nuts, such as walnuts. Musical aesthetics are based on what one might call an agricultural aesthetic, which has developed from daily observation and attention to plants and seasonal cycles (figures 1 and 2).

Music is a result of communal efforts similar to farming. Local people bring their knowledge to this collective vocal, poetic, and gestural art, which varies from one region to another. Each person's way of participating depends on criteria such as sex and age, as well as on the principle of taking turns. In singing, a performance always alternates between two parties—groups or soloists.

Religious songs performed with no instrumental accompaniment mark the end of natural cycles: seasons (frost in winter), barley growing (planting out and winnowing), a woman's unmarried life (weddings), and human beings on earth (death). The

FIGURE 1 Berber men winnowing barley in the Atlas Mountains, Morocco. Photo by Claude Lefébure, 1972.

FIGURE 2 Threshing in the Atlas Mountains, Morocco. Photo by Claude Lefébure, 1972.

word *ladkar* (plural, *ddikr*) 'mention', 'repetition' is used for such songs, whose texts are entirely or partially an invocation of God and the Prophet; *ladkar* encompasses each of these situations among the Shleuh people. Among the Imazighen, the *ahellil* seems to fulfill the same function, though we do not at present have an accurate description of this music. Wedding songs in particular bear specific names that vary from one tribal group to another: *asallaw* (Ida Ouhmahmoud), *urar* (Ayt Mgoun), *asnimmr* (Ayt Bougmez), *urraḥman* (Ayt Haddidou), *izwirrign* (Ida Ouzddout). Some peoples—such as the Ayt Atta in the central High Atlas (Lefébure 1977:112–113)—have no generic names for these songs, but they seem to be the exception.

The more spectacular side of Berber musical life is the great group dances. These are performed mainly at night, with drum accompaniment, and in the Anti-Atlas they depict life or growth cycles. Those performed during the dog days of summer, at the end of the farming period, take place at weddings, at circumcisions, on local saints' days, or at religious festivals.

Such times of conviviality are propitious for music and dance—hence the expression "festival season" (Jouad and Lortat-Jacob 1978). Festivals can give rise to a little music or a great deal of music, depending on the region. Weddings are the most important occasions for performance, because they are so lengthy, because an amazing number of guests are often invited, and because both sides of Berber musical life—religious singing and dance—are present at weddings.

Berber music generally gives pride of place to song: that is, singing and poetry. Berber singing deserves far more detailed study than it has yet received; suffice it to say here that vocal register changes according to whether the songs are performed indoors or outdoors. Generally, high and very high (even falsetto) voices belong outdoors; singing indoors is often in a middle range. Outdoors, only choruses change registers, from low to medium to high; in sung group dances, the rise in register is actually prescribed by the form.

THE ART OF SUNG POETRY

In societies without a written language, such as these, purely instrumental music is rare, but poetry is everywhere. All important language is poetic—words expressing divinity, clairvoyance, wisdom, love, teaching, and social criticism. For the Berbers, poetic language is beautiful, orderly, and a product of reflection. Poetry is shaped by song, even when it is sometimes also repeated in its own rhythm without music, in order to give weight to certain statements (Jouad 1995:227–297).

The ability to sing poetry and translate community feelings and concerns into veiled and conventional language is not given to everyone. Among the Berbers, a poet is *bu lmeana*, someone "who has sense, who is able to reflect," a "guide as much as interpreter of people's opinion" (Lefébure 1987:31). Throughout Berber lands, this gift indicates that poets are divinely inspired and have a special relationship to the saints. And that is true not only of poetic talent but also of musical talent (Schuyler 1979b:20). Numerous witnesses tell us that pilgrimages are made to the tombs of saints so as to obtain their favor, *baraka*. During such a pilgrimage, dreams reveal whether an aspirant's vocation is indeed the one desired. When musical and poetic inspiration result, a relationship is established between the aspirant and the saint: the aspirant becomes the saint's "child" and will henceforth invoke this saint, along with God, in the prologue of every song (Schuyler 1985:122).

LADKAR

Several traits characterize *ladkar*, which is always sung antiphonally. First, there is a close link to a specific occasion. Each occasion (a wedding ritual or threshing, for example) is divided into a series of phases or acts associated with a specific series of songs.

Second, there is no improvisation; singers perform from memory. Although we do not have much historical documentation for these songs, recently published works presenting songs collected at the beginning of the twentieth century (Laoust 1993) include verses from the western High Atlas that can still be heard today. The persistence of archaic Berber terms and Arabic words, which are incomprehensible to many villagers, attests to the fact that improvisation is absent. The aim is to reproduce songs exactly. Even the number of repetitions of some verses is prescribed (two, three, or four); in more strictly religious circumstances—such as the *ladkar* of mature women's gatherings—the prescribed number of repetitions may be as high as a hundred or even a thousand. Among women, tunes and verses are dictated by a female poet—that is, a person whose vocation and link with the divine have been attested to and who can thus impose divine will concerning the order of verses and sometimes even the melody. She is an experienced person, generally older, who, when the time comes, gives the beginning of each verse and the number of repetitions, and sometimes hums the tune.

Third, poems are always sung in dialogue: either the singers play different roles, or they address a mute hearer who cannot or must not speak. Thus a *ladkar* for threshing is sung to the animals who stamp the grain, and many ritual wedding songs are sung to the bride, who must neither sing nor speak.

Fourth, the songs are designed to cause weeping and are accompanied by lamentation: they are sung to a living being who "agonizes" and cannot respond, except perhaps by lamenting—such as a bride (these songs never fail to produce that effect in brides) or one of the animals to whom threshing songs are addressed (the animals respond by braying). The translation "lament" is, therefore, also appropriate for *ladkar*.

AḤIDUS AND *AḤWASH*

Aḥidus (figure 3) and *aḥwash* both refer to a gathering of villagers and the villagers' participation in a group of songs and dances, as well as to the songs and dances themselves. *Aḥidus* is the term used in the Tamazight region; *aḥwash* is used in the Tashlḥiyt region. These gatherings are occasions for poetic creativity, and for all the poetic-musical types that are also performed in other, more intimate circumstances.

The importance of such events, where people of all ages and both sexes gather to interact through song and dance, cannot be overemphasized. What takes place at these festivals is a veritable education in the rules of communal behavior, particularly in values such as unpretentiousness, sexual modesty, moderation, patience, timing, and self-control. Until recent times, young Amazigh men had to prove their virtuosity and elegance not only in war but also in *aḥidus* (Peyron 1991:34). The desired effect of these sung dances—in contrast to the mournful effect produced by the *ladkar*—is joy, even euphoria. The ululations of the women in the audience are the most explicit manifestation of joy.

Aḥidus and *aḥwash* both include sung poetic contests between individual poets or groups and sung group dances. These dances draw dozens of people close together in a circle or line, accompanied by frame drums known as *illuna* (singular, *allun*) or *tilluna* (singular, *tallunt*, the diminutive of *allun*). The frame drum is the basic instrument in the Atlas. For the *aḥidus*, it has snares; in other contexts it may have cymbals. The skin of the drum should be stretched taut for the occasion. During the dance, a fire is lit near the dancers; this allows the musicians to retighten the skin of the drum by warming it from time to time.

FIGURE 3 A line of men facing a line of women during the *aḥidus* of the Ayt Atta of the southern outfall of Jabal Saghro. Photo by Claude Lefébure, 1972.

Aḥidus among the Amazigh

In the *aḥidus* in Timahdite, near Azrou in the Middle Atlas, men and women alternate in a circle, side by side, holding their hands out horizontally and swaying their hips; this arrangement has been described as a great undulating chain. Sometimes there are deep, unexpected bows, and postures in which the hands are held out as in Islamic prayer. Only the men sing. Depending on the length of the strophe, the initial solo song is called *izli*, *aferdi*, or *tamdyazt* (Chottin 1938:18–22).

In Tounfite, a large village in the eastern High Atlas, the *aḥidus* of the Ayt Yahya can take one of two forms, according to whether mature men or youths are performing with the women. When it is *hayfa* or *taghzzaft* 'the long one' (this term refers to the length of the musical phrase), mature men perform in an ancient style: they sing and dance with great reserve in a five-beat rhythm, using two different ways of striking the drum. The initial distich is repeated antiphonally. When the *aḥidus* is *amssad*, it is performed by young men, and the dance style is lively, with music marked by "contrasts in intensity" and tempo (Lortat-Jacob 1994:52–53).

Among the Ayt Brahim of the eastern High Atlas, the dancers form two lines facing each other. The *aḥidus* begins with a song based on a distich *izli* sung by the leader; during this song, the dancers rock back and forth in a movement known as *assergig* 'trembling'. The *izli* is then picked up alternately, in turn, by each line of dancers; the dancers slowly sink while swaying their hips before rising—then, also in turn, the rows do "three bends of the knee" before "rising onto the tips of their toes" and letting themselves "fall down again" (Peyron 1994:2208).

In the northeastern Atlas, the melodic range is reduced to a fifth, and the chromatic character often includes intervals smaller than a half tone. Kárpáti notes a predominant range of a minor third, with occasional extensions up to a fourth, and a syllabic recitative. A single rhythmic cycle predominates, defined as five beats or ten beats divided into two groups of five. Distinct timbre also helps to define this rhythm (Chottin 1938:28, 29; Kárpáti 1961:456–457; Lortat-Jacob 1994:53–53).

Aḥwash among the Shleuh

Drummers from one or several villages of the Shleuh gather into groups known as *l'mat* (or *l'wmt* in the western High Atlas). In these groups, which are formed each year, they learn to play and improvise. They are invited, or come on their own initiative, to play in the *aḥwash* of villages other than their own. The drummers use different playing positions: soloists hold the drum vertically whereas group players hold it horizontally. The large two-headed drum is played with two curved sticks known as *ganga* in the Anti-Atlas or *bengri* in the western and central High Atlas. It is most commonly played in the Anti-Atlas, where it is often combined with *tiqrqqawin*—metal clappers, such as those used by *gnawa* musicians.

Descriptions of the central High Atlas *aḥwash* from different places and periods (Paris 1921; Chottin 1938:15–31; Lortat-Jacob 1980) allow us to identify a few shared characteristics.

In the *aḥwash* of the Ayt Mgoun (Lortat-Jacob 1980), the musicians' processional entrance takes place to a dance tune in a "limping" rhythm known as *tazrrart* in three unequal beats (an eighth note followed by two dotted eighths) lasting a total of one second, repeated over and over (124). Men and women dance and sing together here, but only men improvise poetry and play the drum in public. Dancers in the central High Atlas stand upright, undulating, pushing the body forward and pulling it backward. The soloist's initial melodic phrase, sung over a distich, grows shorter and then is divided into parts performed by the men's group and parts performed by the women's group. The drummed rhythm goes gradually from a cycle of four heavy beats to a cycle of three unequal beats during what the Ayt Mgoun call a "rise," and then stops to make way for *tizzrarin* singing (singular, *tazrrart*, which here can refer to two different types of music) sung solo by the drummers taking turns. The *aḥwash* concludes with a drummed formula.

The *aḥwash* is sometimes preceded by a singing contest (*lmsaq*) among several soloists, in which a verse of twelve syllables is used. The soloists' melodic phrases, whose schema is based on a fifth, are punctuated by two beats of the drum from the group of drummers (*thrrim*). The verses and syllables, "devoid of meaning," belong to the "matrix formula" of this poetic form and are repeated first by the men and then by the women (Jouad 1995:22–38).

In the Anti-Atlas, an *aḥwash* night is divided into two halves—one in which the men perform, and one in which the women perform. As in the central High Atlas, there is a processional entrance of the musicians, to a dance tune, here called *iriẓi*, which is also performed by the women when they enter, clapping their hands to the tune and preceded by two or three women drumming on the *tallunt* (plural, *tilluna*). The three unequal beats are slower here than in the *tazrrart* rhythm of the central High Atlas.

The men perform a sung dance that is called *ddrst* among the Ida Ouzddout and *ahnaqqar* or *taḥwasht* elsewhere. *Ddrst* 'row' or 'chain' refers to the arrangement of the singer-dancers, who are in a long line with the *tallunt* drummers in the middle; it also refers to the verses and melody, which are parallel, the beginning and end of each melodic phrase coinciding with the beginning and end of the lyrics. *Ddrst* tunes number only about a dozen.

Men often have poetic contests in this context. Each poet enters the contest with a quatrain preceded—as in all improvised poetry in the Atlas—by formulaic syllables "devoid of meaning," which conform to the matrix for the true verses (Jouad 1995:15–51). The melodic phrase is interspersed not with drumbeats (as in the central High Atlas) but by long silences. The last verse is a kind of saying, known as *tasrgwlt* 'the lid', and is always repeated at least once by the two alternating groups of men, who thus approve and reinforce it. Another poet-singer then takes the floor with a new quatrain, whose last verse will also be picked up by the two groups; and so forth. When no more poets interrupt the men's groups, the contest is over; but the groups continue to exchange the "lid" verse as the drums gradually move into the middle. The line then closes into a circle and, at the dance leader's instigation, the dance begins.

In the same fashion, there are two parts in the *aḥwash n'timgharin* 'women's
TRACK 14 *aḥwash*'. One part, the *amkhllf*, centers on poetic contests; the other part, *tamssust*, is performed at the end of these contests and consists mainly of dancing. *Amkhllf* and *tamssust*, like other musical terms, encompass a web of meanings that cannot be discussed fully here. However, we can note that *amkhllf* 'the one who is offset' and 'crossing between' refers both to the offsetting of melodies by verses and verses by melodies (whose beginnings and endings do not coincide) and to the crisscrossing dance figures and rhythmic figures on the drum. *Tamssust* 'the one who shakes' refers to the shaking shoulders of the women dancers and to their singing voices as well; it also refers to the shaking up of the circle, from which the dancers often diverge.

The *amkhllf* and *tamssust* unfold as responses to a soloist who joins the women's group before regaining his place in the audience once he has performed his song. His song is unaccompanied and punctuated by long silences. It is called *amarg*, and it can take two forms. One form is critical, even insulting; the women respond to this with a singing contest, the *amkhllf*. The other form is laudatory; the women respond to this with *tamssust* dancing.

In the *tamssust*, the melodic phrase includes a distich. Like the danced part of the central High Atlas *aḥwash*, the *tamssust* accelerates, and this acceleration is also considered a "rise" in rhythm and melodic phrase, which gradually get shorter (going from four beats to three beats). As in the central High Atlas, there is also a phase with *tizrrarin* (responsorial songs), but the singing groups here continue to sing and the *tizrrarin* come instead from the onlookers, whose tunes, rhythm, and words are heard over those of the dancers,. The *aḥwash* ends, as in the central High Atlas, with formulaic drumming.

Finally, in the western High Atlas, the *aḥwash* includes men's warrior dances
TRACK 15 known as *taskiwin* 'powderhorns', performed in a circle. Each man plays an *agwal*, a small goblet-shaped clay drum. The dancers' costume includes an actual powderhorn, *tiskt*, which is richly decorated and has rattles attached to it. The movements and rhythms are performed over tunes played on the *tal'wwatt* (a flute) by two or three musicians, whose performance is related to their work as shepherds, and by three *tallunt* drummers. Every so often, at the end of the night, young women sing and dance. They intervene with a short dance, especially during the "breaks" in the *taskiwin*, during which they shake their shoulders. This is called *astara-n-ighariwn* 'shoulder walk'; it is accompanied by flutists and drummers. The breaks may also be filled by slapstick comedy, which is much appreciated by villagers in this part of the Atlas.

PROFESSIONAL PERFORMERS

Among the Imazighen, a poet-singer *amdyaz* forms a troupe with two *irdaddn* 'respondents' or 'accompanists', who play the *allun* and sometimes the *lkamanja* (alto or violin); and a double-clarinet player (*bu ughanim* 'he of the reed'), who also takes the role of a clown (Lortat-Jacob 1980, 1994). These troupes sometimes include an oblong glazed clay drum called a *tarija*; a two- or three-stringed lute, the *lginbri*; or—in place of the clarinet—a six- or seven-holed flute, the *juak* (Chottin 1938:33; Kárpáti 1961:454–455). The groups have two repertoires: (1) *Tamdyazt*, which is of a moral and political character, is often sung without instrumental accompaniment. It is sometimes given other names, such as *tayffart* in the Middle Atlas. (2) *Izli* (plural, *izlan*) is often accompanied by violin and drum and is sung by the accompanists. *Izli* consists of two or four verses and treats light, amorous themes. It is used in the *aḥidus* (Lortat-Jacob 1994:55).

Kárpáti (1961:455) combines the *tamdyazt* and the *izlan* into a single category characterized by a long series of lyrical "strophes" with an amorous or heroic subject and distinguished from the *tayffart* by the manner in which it is performed. The *tayffart* is sung ("recited") by a soloist with two or three accompanying singers. In addition, there are rhythmic differences—a "parlando-rubato" style in the *tayffart*, and "giusto" for the *izlan-tamdyazt*, which evokes dancing.

Professional Imazighen musicians are called *shikhāt*. In their singing and dancing of the *izlan*, they are accompanied by *shikh* musicians on the violin or alto (*lkamanja*) or on the lute (*loṭar* or *lginbri*; Lortat-Jacob 1994:54). According to Kárpáti (1961:454–455), *imdyazn* groups in the Middle Atlas traditionally perform with *shikhat*. When the songs performed are *izlan-tamdyazt*, they sing antiphonally, whether between men and women or between two groups of women. The basic accompaniment on the frame drum is played by both men and women, but aside from this only men play musical instruments here.

Rways musicians are of great importance in the Tashlḥiyt region. The main poet-singer accompanies himself on a single-stringed viol, *rribab*, and is also accompanied by *loṭar* 'lute' players (who also sing as a group) and by a musician playing the *nāqūs*—a bell, generally made of a piece of cast iron, which the musician strikes with two metal sticks. Chottin (1933:24) also mentions an oblique flute and a frame drum.

The terminology is clearly of village origin, as are some features: the unmeasured instrumental prelude known as the *astara*, *amarg* sung poetry, the increasingly accelerated *tamssust*, shaking the shoulders while dancing, and the interjection of slapstick comedy. Only the use of stringed instruments is different.

Rways musicians incorporate aspects of everything they have heard during their travels, making their music "an amalgam of village styles from every part of the High Atlas and Sus," and this mixture is intensified because the membership of *rways* groups changes all the time (Schuyler 1978:72). To these Berber borrowings must be added Arabic, African, and European borrowings, especially military music (Chottin 1938:51). On the other hand, the rapid style of *rways* music is not really compatible with the Anti-Atlas style.

Since *rways* musicians often travel, they must satisfy diverse listeners. They have traveled since the beginning of the twentieth century, all the way to France, Belgium, and the Netherlands. As performers, they pay close attention to what is around them, and often insert elements of it into their poetry. They comment and sometimes strongly criticize, taking on the role of cultural "mediators." Permanent contact with urban centers—they settle especially in areas that have seen the largest emigrations of Shleuh since the 1970s (Casablanca, Agadir, and Marrakesh)—has apparently had the effect of increasing the influence of Arabic, including in their poetry. Religious themes are prominent because some *rways* are former religious scholars or have received extensive religious training (Schuyler 1978:73, 74; 1985:123). But songs of praise for local figures form the bulk of their material and on many occasions earn them immediate recompense. Urban *rways* groups include *raysat*, female singer-dancers who play *nuiqsat* 'finger cymbals'. They have replaced the young, effeminate-looking male musicians who performed in these groups at the beginning of the twentieth century (Chottin 1938:47). Since at least the 1990s, women have also performed as poets.

Rways music has been able to adapt to different listeners and different places (Schuyler 1979, 1984). For instance, in the *ḥalqa* 'circle', an outdoor performance, verbal entertainment (slapstick comedy) is given priority. At private parties, praise-songs for prestigious guests and hosts, and even dances, predominate (when the *raysat* join the group). Dance also predominates in commercial establishments for non-Shleuh audiences. *Amarg* sung poetry is found mainly in electronic media (records and cassettes). More research remains to be done on the effects of audiovisual recordings on this music, which remains very popular in areas where the Shleuh have immigrated.

TRANSLATED BY BETH RAPS

REFERENCES

Chottin, Alexis. 1938. *Tableau de la musique marocaine*. Paris: Geuthner.

Jouad, Hassan. 1995. *Le calcul inconscient de l'improvisation: Poésie berbère, rythme, nombre, et sens*. Paris: Peeters.

Jouad, Hassan, and Bernard Lortat-Jacob. 1978. *La saison des fêtes dans une vallée du Haut-Atlas*. Paris: Seuil.

Kárpáti, J. 1961. "Mélodie, vers, et structure stophique dans la musique berbère (imazighen) du Maroc Central." *Studia Musicologica* 1(3–4):451–473.

Laoust, Émile. 1993. *Noces berbères: Les cérémonies du mariage au Maroc*. Aix-en-Provence: Edisud.

Lefébure, Claude. 1977. "Tensons des ist—εṬa: La poésie féminine beraber comme mode de participation sociale." *Littérature Orale Arabo-Berbère* 8:109–142.

———. 1987. "Contrat mensonger, un chant d'amdyaz sur l'émigration." *Études et Documents Berbères* 3:28–46.

Lortat-Jacob, Bernard. 1980. *Musique et fêtes au Haut-Atlas*. Paris: Mouton-EHESS.

———. 1994. *Musiques en fêtes*. Nanterre: Société d'Ethnologie.

Paris, André. 1921. "Haouach à Télouet." *Hespéris* 1:209–216.

Peyron, Michaël. 1991. *"Isaffen ghbanin (rivières profondes)": Poésies du Moyen-Atlas marocain traduites et annotées*. Casablanca: Wallada.

———. 1994. "Danse." *Encyclopédie Berbère* 14:2204–2213.

Rovsing Olsen, Miriam. 1997. *Chants et danses de l'Atlas (Maroc)*. Paris: Cité de la Musique/Actes Sud.

Schuyler, Philip. 1978. "*Rwais and Aḥwash*: Opposing Tendencies in Moroccan Berber Music and Society." *World of Music* 21(1):65–80.

———. 1979a. "A Repertory of Ideas: The Music of the Rwais, Berber Professional Musicians from Southwestern Morocco." PhD. dissertation, University of Washington.

———. 1979b. "Music Education in Morocco: Three Models." *World of Music* 22(3):19–31.

———. 1985. "The *Rwais* and the *Zawia*: Professional Musicians and the Rural Elite in Southwestern Morocco." *Asian Music* 18(1):114–131.

Music in Performance: Following the Entranced Ones—*Gnāwa* Performances and Trance in Rabat, Morocco

Deborah Kapchan

U tb'atī nās l-ḥāl
urā nsitī walidīk.

You followed the entranced ones
and forgot your parents.
(From a popular song)

Soumaya is sitting on a low foam mattress, leaning against unevenly stuffed pillows, when suddenly her body jerks and she throws her arms up over her head, flailing in the direction of her neighbors. Arching her back, she sends her legs out toward the center of the floor. Women help her to turn over as she gets on hands and knees and crawls toward the musicians who are seated on sheepskins against the north wall. Smoking incense rises up into the cool air from a clay brazier placed before the musicians. Soumaya bathes her face in the fragrance of burning sandalwood, turning her head from side to side, opening her jaw and waving the smoke into her mouth. Then she is up on her feet, arms extended out to the sides, her head thrown violently back and forth as if her neck were loose. She stamps the ground with the heel and ball of first her left foot, then her right foot; then she jumps up with both feet, her torso quaking from the impact when she lands on the hard ceramic floor tiles.

We are in a courtyard covered over with a tarp; the high walls are lined with green and red velour draperies. We can see, between the top of the walls and the tarp, that the clouds are beginning to catch the first glints of dawn. Inside we are many, sitting huddled together on sinking mattresses or on the floor, shoulder to shoulder; women wrapped against the night in scarves and long silky robes. The lights are turned off, and the *gnāwa* musicians are playing loudly, clacking their heavy *qrāqab* 'cymbals' (singular, *qarqaba*), calling 'Aisha Qandīsha, the *jinniyya* of threshold and danger.

O 'Ā'isha, beautiful 'Ā'isha
'Ā'isha the Gnāwiyya.

In a trance, gyrating, two women dance madly before us. Despite the din, calm reigns. We are all drunk on fatigue and incense and sound.

The dancers collapse on the floor. They are caught by other women, caressed, sprinkled with flower water. Another song begins, and a woman rises, moving her weight heavily from side to side. A friend drapes a black cloth over her shoulders, but she is barely conscious of it. The *gnāwa* master (*m'allem*) nods his head in time with her movements; he speeds up, and her movements keep time; they are in tandem. *Khdem 'lihā* 'Work for it', he tells her.

When the music stops, the possessed woman falls backward into the arms of the *mqadma*, who begins to speak with the possessing *jinn*. "What do you want?" she asks several times. No answer. "Do you want a sacrifice?" Barely perceptibly, the girl's head nods a "yes." "Who are you?" the *mqadma* continues: "Who are you? Are you 'Ā'isha?" Another affirmative nod of the head. The girl's eyes are glazed; her vision is unfixed; her long curly hair is strewn across a forehead running with orange-blossom water, which is used to revive those who are "taken in trance."

To be inhabited—*meskūn*—is to be possessed by a disembodied spirit, a *jinn* (plural, *jnūn*), one with its own character, personality, and whims. One spirit or many may possess a body, which then becomes the material agent for the desires and volition of what are called its owners—*l-mulūk*, the possessing spirits. To say that someone is possessed by Lalla Mīra, for example, is to say that the attributes of this *jinniyya*—her frivolity, humor, and vanity—are mapped onto the possessed. This is more than simply a metaphor. The possessed woman embodies these qualities, becoming an icon of the *jinniyya*, laughing her laughter, demanding her beat, and delighting in it. Resisting a possessing spirit causes illness; but placating the spirit brings health and possibly power. Witnessing the performances of one another's spirits while experiencing their own, women practitioners embody a plurality of personalities. They also condone what many of them refer to as an addiction or an intoxication—*l-blīa*—an inebriation with the music, the incense, in short, the *ḥāl* or state of ecstasy in movement, the pain and bliss of being other.

"You must know how to listen to the *hajhūj*," one "trancer" told me. "You listen, and the spirits pass through the music of the *m'allem* and rise up within you." The resultant trance, or *jadhba*, is thought to be healing and to assuage the afflicting *jinn*.

In Morocco, people "fall" into trance—*kay-tīḥū*. There is a relinquishing, a capitulation to the experience, a submission. Once this happens, however, the spirits "rise up" in the body"—*l-jnūn kay-ṭal'u fīk*. "My body is pins and needles from my head to my toes" (*det-i kat t-shūwak-lī min ar-rās ḥetta ar-rjlīn*), one woman said, describing the experience.

Now Miriam appears wearing a red lace gown pulled over her *qafṭān* and a red knit hat sewn with cowrie shells; she carries two knives in her hands. She is Sidi Hammou, the *jinn* of the slaughterhouse. She dances in front of the *gnāwa*, moving her hips and arms backward, the knives puncturing air and incense. She has removed her cap, and she now hits the blades against her newly bared head, though not too hard. Tonight she is taking it easy. A few songs later, she is in black, holding a bundle of lit candles in each hand. She pushes up her sleeves and, stamping head and feet in time to the music, waves the candles under her forearms. She brushes them under her chin, risking burns, and moves around the periphery of the room. Separating a single candle from its set, she opens her toothless mouth as wide as possible above the flame, then hands the candle to the person before whom she performs, inviting the observer to partake in the blessing of absorption. She continues moving around the room.

"A young woman has to be courageous," offers a wrinkled old woman, turning to me. "If you cry all the time, spirits will strike you. They are everywhere. If you cry all the time and are unhappy, they'll possess you. In the bathroom, in the kitchen; wherever there is water. You have to be courageous."

The woman sitting to my left is a member of the Bushishiyya *ṭarīqa*, a Sufi sect. She is about fifty, with thick bones and regular features. There is a Bushishiyya pilgrimage site (*zāwiya*) here in Rabat, she informs me. Early on in the night, she gets up and "trances" to Jilālī, one of the saints of her lineage. Her movements are awkward, jerky. She tells me later that she began to trance to the Jilāliyya beat soon after her father died. One day when the family was gathered for a ceremony to propitiate the spirit, she went into a trance and remained totally unconscious until she woke up in the middle of the floor. Her trancing made the entire family cry and also trance. She was the catalyst for a heated session.

The woman to my right is much younger, although she already has three children. She was married at thirteen. Now her husband has just returned from the pilgrimage to Mecca. He is forty-eight. "Does he object to your having trancing ceremonies?" I ask. "No. He sees me having a *crise*, and what can he do?" she replies. She first tranced only four years ago. She heard *gnāwa*-style music on television, dropped everything, and started trancing. She has been attending ceremonies ever since and holds a ceremony of her own every year during the week of the *mulud*, the Prophet's birthday. She says that she is possessed (*meskūna*). "With whom?" I ask. She says, "*Bezzāf* 'many'—Lalla 'Ā'isha, Lalla Mālika, Lalla Mīra, others. Every time, a new one shows up." She had a *crise* just yesterday, she tells me, and then she leaves my side in order to trance to the spirits in black.

The man who is the host of this *līla* 'evening gathering' trances all through the night and knows all the songs. He is called by the honorary title *l-Ḥājj* because he has made the pilgrimage to Mecca. When Buhali, the *jinn* of water, is invoked, the host becomes childlike and tries to run away to the beach. Only when several other men in the room restrain him does he really let himself go, screaming bleakly, a desperate empty look in his eyes. He trances and sways, crying out for forgiveness (*Allāh yasmaḥ linā*); he is bathed with water and finally falls down, his small feet and hands yellow, his mouth gaping.

At Lalla Mimouna's song, I get up to trance, but I do not find my rhythm right away. The floor beneath my feet is littered with crumbs, and I can feel the uneven rough cement under the carpet. Closing my eyes, I initially lose my balance and have to slow my movements down to a steadier rhythm in order to keep from falling backward. Finally someone grabs me by the back of my belt (I later learn that it is the woman from the Bushishiyya), and I begin to release my hold and relinquish my control, counterbalancing my movements to her support, swaying my head back and forth. When the music is over, I return to my seat next to her, and she tends to me. Later in the evening, when I can't find a seat, she pulls me down on the floor in front of her, settling my body between her heavy thighs, resting her chin on the top of my head. Her large toenails, painted red, catch my peripheral vision.

After trancing, women wish each other good health: *b-ṣaḥt-ek*.

At seven o'clock in the morning I leave, accompanied by the son of the *m'allem*, who is always sent with me for protection. Those who remain wait for a breakfast of *harira* soup and boiled eggs. The streets of Rabat are empty except for mangy cats and an occasional taxicab. I flag one taxi down and get in. I have a pain in my leg, my skin is sticky with sweat, and the incense of the night is clinging to my pores. The odor of the entranced ones mixes with the diesel of the taxi as I return home, as light as the morning sky over Rabat.

Malḥūn: Colloquial Song in Morocco

Philip D. Schuyler

Poetic Form
Themes, Language, and Imagery
Training
Instrumentation and Ensembles
Performance

"*Malḥūn*," a young Moroccan once told me, "is the true classical music of Morocco." The young man was a university student, I was a fledgling researcher, and we were both attempting to learn to sing *malḥūn* at the conservatory in Fez. His comment surprised me, because the status of *malḥūn* at the conservatory was far below that of *al-'ala al-andalusiyya*, the style of music that had pride of place as the national art music on radio and television, at state fesitivities in the royal palace, and at family celebrations among the bourgeoisie. [See ANDALUSIAN *NŪBA* IN MOROCCO.] Outside the conservatory, many Moroccans thought of *malḥūn* not as music at all, but rather as the incantation of poetry.

The name *malḥūn* itself contributes to this ambiguity. The term stems from the standard Arabic root *laḥana*, which has derivatives that mean speaking ungrammatical Arabic, chanting, and setting something to music. Moroccan scholars themselves differ on which derivation is most appropriate. The late Mohamed el-Fassi, a minister of culture, scholar, and great compiler of *malḥūn* texts, maintained that all *malḥūn* was meant to be sung (1964:37). On the other hand, Abbas Jirari, perhaps the most distinguished literary scholar of a later generation, has pointed out that some of the poetry of *malḥūn* is meant to be recited, not sung. There is a similar debate among scholars in Yemen, where an analogous form of dialectical song poetry (commonly called *homayni*, but also sometimes known as *malḥūn*) bears a remarkable resemblance to the Moroccan form. The debate is unlikely to be resolved, because both sides are, in fact, correct: *malḥūn* often uses nonstandard vocabulary and violates the rules of standard Arabic grammar, for the sake of meter or poetic effect. But it is best appreciated when it is *heard*, whether recited or, particularly, sung.

The exact origins of *malḥūn* are unclear. Arabic dialect poetry, known as *zajal*, first appeared in Muslim Spain in the twefth century C.E. (sixth century A.H.). The first evidence of dialect Arabic poetry in Morocco comes from the fifteenth century C.E. (ninth century A.H.; Jirari 1969:563–65), and the word *malḥūn* itself was first used in a poem about one hundred years later. *Malḥūn* thus appeared long after the Andalusian *zajal*, but it seems to have developed independently. The earliest poets of Moroccan *malḥūn* were from the Tafilalet region, an area on the edge of the desert, far from the cities where Andalusian refugees settled after their departure from Spain in the years leading up to 1492. The Tafilalet was, rather, an area populated both by indigenous Berbers and by Arabs who had migrated west from the Arabian peninsula. The presence of the eastern Arabs, and the poetic form and themes of some of the early poems, has led a number of scholars to conclude that *malḥūn* was based on an Arabian model. At least one observer, however, has also noted similarities between *malḥūn* and Berber poetry (Jouad 1995:315–327).

The Tafilalet was the home of the 'Alawite family, descendants of the Prophet Muhammad who gained control of the rest of the Morocco in the seventeenth century (and who still rule the country today). As the 'Alawites moved north to the great cities of Fez, Marrakech, and especially Meknes, they took *malḥūn* with them. Many members of the 'Alawite dynasty were supporters of *malḥūn* and some—including the founder, Moulay 'Ali Cherif—were poets themselves. The most revered poets, however, seem to have come from more humble origins. The greatest flowering of *malḥūn* took place in the eigtheenth and nineteenth centuries, when the form was refined (some say perfected) by such poets as Jilali Mtired, a greengrocer; Abdel Hadi Bennani, a spice merchant; and al-Hajj Ahmad al-Gharabli, a weaver.

Even today, *malḥūn* continues to appeal to both the elite and the working class. King Hassan II (r. 1961–1999) was a great patron of many varieties of Moroccan music, including *malḥūn*. During his reign, a growing cultural nationalism encouraged the study of traditional Moroccan forms, including not only *malḥūn* but also proverbs and other forms of oral literature in both Arabic and Berber, as a way of asserting Moroccan identity in the face of previous intellectual domination by France, on the one hand, and by Egypt and Lebanon on the other. A new generation of scholars, such as Abbas al-Jirari and Ahmed Suhum, wrote extensively about the form. The playwright Tayyeb Siddiqi incorporated *malḥūn* into his theater pieces, which in turn generated a new genre of folk-revivalist popular music (Schuyler 1993b).

At about the same time, in the old centers of *malḥūn* such as Fez and Marrakech, intellectuals began to stage festivals and conferences, and also to organize societies that met regularly for discussion and performance of the music. The most highly regarded performers of the traditional style, however, continued to come from the artisanal groups. For example, observing one of these societies in Marrakech in the 1990s, Sibylle Vocke noted that the membership included three university professors, three secondary school teachers, three lawyers, a judge, and a tax collector, but also two weavers, two leather workers, a tailor, a brass smith from the royal palace, and (like Jilali Mtired) a greengrocer (1990:30). When I attended the same group in the mid-1970s, the gatherings were held in rotation at certain members' houses, with the middle-class members serving as patrons and hosts and also providing historical information and poetic interpretation. The artisans in the group, for their part, animated the gathering, serving tea and cookies, telling jokes, and above all—following the tradition—singing the songs.

POETIC FORM

A poem in *malḥūn* shares both its name, *qaṣīda*, and its basic organizational device—a bipartite line form—with classical Arabic poetry. Each line of a *qaṣīda* is divided into two hemistichs, or half-lines (Arberry 1965:6). In the classical *qaṣīda,* both rhyme and meter are established in the first verse (*bait* 'house') and maintained throughout the entire poem, which generally includes twenty-five to one hundred lines.

Andalusian poets, in the eleventh century C.E., replaced the classical form with more elaborate patterns, grouping together lines of different lengths, with rhyme schemes such as aa bbb aa or aa bba ccca (Chottin 1939:91). The new rhyme schemes were the basis of a strophic form, known as *muwashshaḥ*, that was probably a result of the ecumenical atmosphere of the Muslim states of medieval Spain, which fostered collaboration between Iberians, North Africans, and Eastern Arabs, and between Christians, Muslims, and Jews. [See THE ANDALUSIAN MUSICAL HERITAGE.]

Like the *muwashshaḥ*, the *qaṣīda* of *malḥūn* is strophic in form. The patterns of the stanzas are often very simple (for instance, four lines with a pattern such as aaab, cccb, or dddb), but they can also be very long and complex, sometimes appearing to approach free verse. A *qaṣīda* may have anywhere from four to a dozen or more stanzas.

THEMES, LANGUAGE, AND IMAGERY

A *qaṣīda* of *malḥūn* can touch on any subject, from pleas to Allah and praise of the Prophet Muhammad to elegies and descriptions of nature to social advice and political commentary. Most common of all are songs of love, which may include explicitly erotic descriptions of the beloved and depictions of intoxication by wine (which is forbidden in Islam). The theme of the poem is developed in successive stanzas, which may describe an imagined voyage, parts of the body, or the efforts of a lover to join his beloved. In the poem *Al-Herraz* 'The Magician', for example, the beloved is held captive by a crafty magician, and in each stanza the lover attempts a different disguise in order to gain access to the magician's house. His efforts are consistently foiled until the last stanza, when he finally defeats his enemy. Similarly, each stanza of *A-Naḥla* 'The Bee' describes, in botanically correct terms, different areas of a nineteenth-century royal garden.

As Jouad points out, the language of *malḥūn* is characterized by "the heterogeneity of its lexical sources" (1995:299), drawing on literary and dialect Arabic from different periods, as well as slang and even other languages, including Berber. There is a profusion of synonyms (including fifteen different names for the Prophet Muhammad in one *qaṣīda* alone), and extensive punning. The vocabulary is often obscure in itself and is often made more so by the intentional distortion of pronunciation for sonic effect. Even when the surface meaning is clear, it may conceal a rich network of metaphors. Some of these images, such as the comparison of the beloved's eyebrows to bows shooting arrows at the lover's heart, are drawn from the repertoire of classical Arabic, while others are unique to Morocco.

Often an entire poem is an extended metaphor. "The Bee," mentioned above, describes not only the passage of a bee through a garden but also political maneuvering in the sultan's court (Hamid Triki, personal communication; see also Vocke 1990:85–103). More commonly, songs describing erotic love or intoxication are, in fact, discussing the love of Allah or the Prophet Muhammad. In one famous instance, the mystic poet Sīdī Qaddūr al-ʿAlamī, in his *qaṣīda Tamu bhiz al-Kheddad* 'Tamu with the Resplendent Cheeks', describes a woman in intimate detail:

> Her legs were a pillow for me at night
> And her saliva was my liquor as I sipped on delicious nourishment.

The text seems so erotically charged that once, when Sīdī Qaddūr attended a wedding toward the end of his life, a singer was too embarassed to sing the song in front of its author, because such a saintly man should not be exposed to such scandalous language. When he heard this, Sīdī Qaddūr (who is said to have remained celibate his entire life) replied, "Tell the singer that, by God, I know neither Tamu nor Fettuma. Let him sing what the [wedding guests] want; each listener will understand it as he wishes" (Buret 1938:88).

TRAINING

Traditionally, professional music education in Morocco resembled craft training. Students were apprenticed to master musicians (who were often relatives by blood or marriage) and worked closely with them for long periods of time. Initially, the child acted as a domestic servant to the master (*mʿallem*), doing small household tasks, running errands, and so on. For these services, the master provided food and clothing and occasionally gave a small tip or a gift. During this period the apprentice stayed with the master the better part of the day, sometimes moving into the master's house. The child was thus exposed to a great deal of musical activity, including planning, rehearsal, instrument repair, and aesthetic debate, as well as actual performance. After a time, the apprentice began to learn songs directly; he was given the words to the songs he had been hearing, and when he had memorized them completely, he was allowed to sing. Eventually, he also began to play an instrument or two. After this period of training, which might last for several years, and during which the apprentice continued his domestic work, he was finally ready for public performance. The master then began to take him along to parties and other performances as an accompanist and, if he showed talent, even as a soloist.

In the case of *malḥūn*, this type of training was both more clear-cut and more ambiguous. That is, the practice of *malḥūn* has never been as thoroughly professionalized as some other styles of music, such as *al-'ala al-andalusiyya* or that of the *ghaita* and *ṭbel* (shawm and side drum) ensembles used for wedding processions and some religious ceremonies. Performers of *malḥūn*, like the poets, generally came from the artisanal classes; many continued to practice a craft in addition to music, and many others performed music more as a hobby than a profession. In other words, apprentices might serve a master—and learn skills—simultaneously in two disciplines: *malḥūn* and a more conventional craft, such as carpentry or leatherwork.

The master-apprentice system allowed for an exchange of goods and services between teacher and student, and as long as the mutual obligations were met, there was a bond between the two. The long and intimate association of teacher and student transmitted a great deal more than song texts and intrumental techniques. Apprentices learned a whole range of behavior and attitudes and at the same time gained an introduction to the professional world. The teachers, for their part, received years of cheap labor and accompaniment in their music.

Over the past forty years, *malḥūn* has been added to the curriculum in conservatories. Unlike Andalusian music, the main subject in the conservatories, *malḥūn* does not have a traditional theoretical system, nor does it lend itself well to notation. And while the instructors of Andalusian music are themselves products of the conservatory, in Morocco or Europe, the instructors of *malḥūn* are typically drawn from the ranks of practicing performers. As a result of all this, conservatory education in *malḥūn* still follows traditional patterns. Students must first memorize an assigned text and then develop their own rendition under the watchful eye and critical ear of the instructor. The most serious students still attach themselves to individual masters, much as in the apprentice system of old.

INSTRUMENTATION AND ENSEMBLES

Malḥūn can be found in a wide variety of contexts, from street performance to religious lodges to the royal palace, accompanied by a wide variety of ensembles. According to some sources, a singer of *malḥūn* originally accompanied himself on the *deff*, a square double-headed frame drum (about 20 to 25 centimeters on a side). Since poetry was the point, no additional accompaniment was necessary. Even today, singers in the marketplace (Schuyler 1993a, 1996) sometimes still use only a *deff* or a *bendīr* (a round frame drum) when presenting a *qaṣīda*.

When *malḥūn* is used in the rituals of Muslim religious associations, such as the 'Aissawa ('Īssāwa), the song is generally accompanied by a variety of drums, including both the *bendīr* and the *naqqāra* (or *ṭbila*, a bound pair of pottery kettledrums). In these sacred performances, the singing alternates with instrumental passages, accompanied by the same set of drums, played by a wind ensemble of double-reed pipes (*ghaita*) and six-foot-long trumpets.

Over the course of the last century, *malḥūn* was increasingly incorporated into the repertoires of urban string ensembles, which usually include several European-style violins or violas (played upright on the knee rather than on the shoulder), at least one *ʿūd* (a pear-shaped fretless lute with eleven strings in six courses), a *suisin* (a small, three-stringed fretless lute with a skin-covered body), a *derbuka* (a single-headed goblet-shaped drum), a *ṭar* (a small tambourine, about 18 centimeters in diameter), and one or more *tʿarija* (small single-headed drums). This is similar to the standard ensemble for many urban popular musics in Morocco, and, with the addition of the *rebāb* (a two-stringed, boat-shaped bowed lute), it is also much like the ensemble used in the performance of *al-ala al-andalusiyya*, the style favored by both the royal court and the bourgeoisie (Schuyler 1984). Indeed, a number of Andalusian orchestras include some *malḥūn* in their performances to lighten the mood during interludes or at the end of an evening.

Despite these (and other) variations in ensemble form, a performance of *malḥūn* is characterized in particular by the presence of the *tʿarija* (plural, *tʿarij*), a small pottery vase drum. According to legend, the *tʿarija* was introduced to the *malḥūn* ensemble by Jilali Mtired from the "other world," where the great poet-singer entertained the spirits at a wedding party (El-Fassi 1964:41). "Bringing back" an instrument from the spirit world—or from a remote region of the real world—is a recurrent theme in Moroccan musical lore. The image may be meant to represent the tangible result of a musician's divine inspiration (a thread that runs throughout the history of Arabic literature and folklore), or it may simply be a justification for adding a new instrument or procedure to a musical style. In any case, the *tʿarija*, at least since the nineteenth century C.E., has become the main instrument in the *malḥūn* ensemble. The lead singer uses it to measure his own singing and to control the rhythm and tempo of the orchestra; and in instrumental interludes or at the end of a song, to add rhythmic energy to the performance, polyrhythmic improvisations are played with a supporting *tʿarija.*

PERFORMANCE

The performance of a *qaṣīda* follows the repetitive structure of the poem, but the rendition is almost always elaborated by the addition of other elements. The result is a kind of suite built of a variety of melodies, meters, and forms, both poetic and musical. A song is generally preceded by a *taqsīm,* an unmeasured solo instrumental improvisation. In some instances, all the featured instruments—violin, *ʿūd*, *suisin*—may each take a solo in turn. When there is only one opening *taqsīm*, the other musicians will get their turn as soloists in other *qaṣīda* later in the event. Less frequently, the lead singer may present a *muwwāl* or *bitein*, a solo vocal improvisation in free rhythm. This improvisatory introduction may be followed by a short introductory song, known as *serraba*, composed by a different, often anonymous, poet. The *serraba* is distinguished from the rest of the performance by its quick tempo, asymmetrical meter (*gobbahi*, 5/8), and call-and-response style.

The presentation of the *qaṣīda* itself usually begins with a statement of the refrain (*harba* 'pike' or 'spear point') by the lead singer. The accompaniment here, and throughout the song, is very restrained; the melodic instruments quietly underline the contours of the tune while the drums provide a spare metric framework in 2/4. The musical focus is entirely on the singer, who is esteemed particularly for the clarity of his enunciation and his ability to navigate rhythmically through the tongue-twisting text.

After the solo presentation of the *harba,* the refrain is taken up by the rest of the orchestra, singing in chorus and then giving an instrumental statement of the tune. The *harba* contains the kernel of the entire piece—the poetic form, the theme of the poem, and the basic melody. Following this introduction, the solo singer performs each of the stanzas, which alternate with the choral refrain and instrumental interludes.

The three initial repetitions of the refrain—as solo, chorus, and instrumental passage—thus present a summary of the overall form of the music, which is repeated throughout the performance.

Although the first stanza establishes the basic form, variations and elaborations may be introduced later in the performance. For example, subsequent stanzas may be preceded by three or four short lines of poetry (*na'ura*), sung in call-and-response style. At several points in the performance, the singer may modulate from one melodic type to another, raising the pitch level and raising tension among the listeners at the same time. Then, toward the end of the last stanza, he begins to acclerate the tempo, and at the very end of the song he modulates the meter to a vigorous 5/8 (*gobbahi*) or, more commonly, 6/8 (*dridka*). The final *harba* is repeated over and over in a joyous chorus while the tempo continues to accelerate and the instrumental accompaniment, particularly the dialogue of the *t'arij*, becomes louder and louder. The song concludes with a brief, unmeasured melisma by the lead singer, bringing the melody back down to the tonic as the ensemble dissolves in laughter and shouts of approval. After a break for some tea and conversation, the musicians will begin again.

In short, *malḥūn* is a bundle of contradictions. The form, according to Moroccan scholars, had its birth on the edge of the desert but reached maturity in the grand imperial cities of Fez and Marrakech. The language is "incorrect" dialect Arabic, but the poetry makes use of richly allusive vocabulary and complex plays on words. Both poets and, especially, practitioners are principally drawn from the artisinal classes, but the genre has long benefited from the patronage and artistic contributions of the aristocracy and, indeed, royalty. Today it is both a popular form and an art form, commercially exploited and esoteric.

The name *malḥūn* itself appears throughout the Arabic-speaking world, from Morocco and Algeria to Yemen, and everywhere the term signifies a similar phenomenon: sung poetry in dialect Arabic, characterized by subtle manipulations of language and a distinctly urban sensibility. And yet Moroccans think of *malḥūn* as a distinctly—indeed, uniquely—Moroccan art of their own invention. Yemenis and others feel equally possessive of the style. And, in fact, they are all right, because it is the nature of the phenomenon, however widespread, to manifest itself locally, in the choice of instruments and melodic styles and, above all, in the skillful manipulation of regional dialect.

REFERENCES

Arberry, A. J. 1965. *Arabic Poetry.* London: Cambridge University Press.

Buret, M. T. 1938. "Sidi Qaddur el-'Alami: Notes biographiques." *Hespéris* (1st trimester): 84-92.

Chottin, Alexis. 1939. *Tableau de la musique marocaine.* Paris: Paul Geuthner.

El-Fassi, Mohamed. 1964. "Al-Adab al-sha'bī al-maghribī al-malḥūn." *Majjalat al-baḥth al-'ilmī* 1(1).

———. 1965. "Lughat al-malḥūn." *Majjalat al-baḥthi al-'ilmi* 2(1):199–203.

Jirari, Abbes ben Abdallah. 1969. *Al-Qasīda: Al-zajal fī al-maghrib.* Rabat: Maktabat al-Ṭālib.

Jouad, Hassan. 1995. *Le calcul inconscient de l'improvisation: Poésie berbère—Rhythme, nombre, et sens.* Paris: Éditions Peeters.

Kapchan, Deborah. 1999. "*Zajal* Poetry: A Preface." *Mediterraneans/Méditerranéennes* 11:45.

Schuyler, Philip D. 1984. "Moroccan Andalusian Music." In *Maqam: Music of the Islamic World and Its Influences,* ed. Robert Browning. New York: Alternative Museum.

———. 1993a. "Entertainment in the Marketplace." In *Everyday Life in the Muslim Middle East,* ed. Donna Lee Bowen and Evelyn Early, 276–280. Bloomington: Indiana University Press.

———. 1993b. "A Folk Revival in Morocco." In *Everyday Life in the Muslim Middle East,* ed. Donna Lee Bowen and Evelyn Early, 287–293. Bloomington: Indiana University Press.

———. 1996. "Jamaa el-Fna." *Natural History* 105(5, May):38-45. (With photographs by Lori Grinker.)

Suhum, Ahmed. 1993. *Al-Malḥūn al-maghribī.* Rabat: Shu'un Jam'iyya.

Vocke, Sibylle. 1990. *Die markkanische Malhunpoesie.* Wiesbaden: Otto Harrassowitz.

Wansbrough, John. 1969. "Theme, Convention, and Prosody in the Vernacular Poetry of North Africa." *Bulletin of the School of Oriental and African Studies* 32:477–495.

Discography

Maroc, Anthologie d'Al-Melhûn: Traditions de Fès, Meknes, Salé, Marrakech. 1990. Royaume du Maroc, Ministère de la Culture and Maison des Cultures du Monde. W60016.

Musique et chants du Maroc: Le Malhun de Meknes. 1994. Institut du Monde Arabe 50305-2.

Baron Rodolphe d'Erlanger

Ruth Davis

Rodolphe Francis d'Erlanger (figure 1) was the third and youngest son of a wealthy banker of German Jewish extraction and an American mother. He was born in Boulogne-sur-Seine on 7 June 1872 and brought up in Paris as a Roman Catholic. Rather than enter the family bank, he studied art at the Académie Julian, and he pursued a lifelong career as a painter, specializing in portraits, landscapes, and local scenes in oil on canvas, inspired by his travels and life in North Africa. In 1911, d'Erlanger settled with his wife Bettina and his son Leo in Tunisia, where he had received substantial lands and property from his father as a wedding gift. His research into the principles of traditional Arab architecture culminated in 1921 in the completion of his magnificent palace, Ennajma Ezzahra (*al-najma al-zahrā'* 'resplendent star'), in Sidi Bou Said, overlooking the Gulf of Tunis. With its plain white exterior, ornate interior, and landscaped gardens descending to the sea, Ennajma Ezzahra is a masterpiece of Tunisian architecture, combining local and other North African styles.

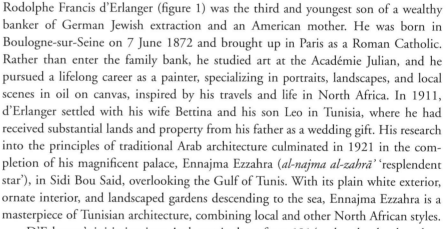

FIGURE 1 Baron Rodolphe d'Erlanger (1872–1932).

D'Erlanger's initiation into Arab music dates from 1914, when he developed an intense and highly productive relationship with the Tunisian musician and literary scholar Shaykh Aḥmad al-Wāfī, who was unrivaled in his mastery of the Tunisian Andalusian repertoire, *al-ma'lūf*, and was equally knowledgeable in Qur'ānic recitation, sacred Tunisian songs, and eastern Arab styles. Al-Wāfī remained d'Erlanger's close friend and mentor until his own death in 1921.

D'Erlanger outlined his musical ideology and goals in an article published in Tunis in 1917, "Au sujet de la musique arabe en Tunisie." Contrasting the rich Arab musical heritage of Tunisia with its current state of decadence and neglect, d'Erlanger blamed the beys (local nobles) for employing European music teachers in their courts: ignorant of the principles of Arab music, these foreigners were promoting "an illegitimate type of music which has neither rational basis nor aesthetic appeal" (d'Erlanger 1917:95). In the fifth volume of his monumental work *La musique arabe* (figure 2), d'Erlanger lamented the widespread use of European instruments of fixed pitch—such as the piano, harmonium, and fretted mandolin—whose tunings were incompatible with the nontempered, variable intervals of the Arab modes (1949:341). Ultimately, however, d'Erlanger believed that the causes of decadence lay within the traditional musical culture, and particularly in the musicians' ignorance of theory and notation. He urged Europeans to support the efforts of native musicians rather than teach them

- Volume 1 (1930): Al-Fārābī's *Kitāb al-mūsīqī al-kabīr* 'Great Book of Music', books 1 and 2.
- Volume 2 (1935): *Kitāb al-mūsīqī al-kabīr*, book 3; a short treatise by Ibn Sīnā, Avicenna (*Mathematics*, ch. 12), extracted from *Kitāb al-shifā'* 'The Book of Healing'.
- Volume 3 (1938): The first complete translation of Ṣāfī al-Dīn's monumental two-part work *Al- risāla al-sharafiyya* 'The Sharafian Treatise'; and *Kitāb al-adwār* 'Book of Cycles'.
- Volume 4 (1939): Anonymous treatise dedicated to Ottoman Sultan Mehmet II (fifteenth century), compiling al-Fārābī, Ibn Sīnā, and Ṣāfī al-Dīn; al-Lādhiqī's *al-Fatḥiyya* 'The Conquest'.
- Volume 5 (1949): On the general scale and melodic modes of modern Arab music.
- Volume 6 (1959): On the rhythmic system and compositional forms of modern Arab music.

FIGURE 2 Summary of contents of d'Erlanger's *La musique arabe*.

directly, and he encouraged European scholars to provide Arab musicians with a theoretical basis for their teaching: "We sincerely hope that one day we shall be given the opportunity of providing the shaykhs of Arab music with the means of explaining to their pupils all the rules of that art" (1917:95).

D'Erlanger dedicated the rest of his life to achieving that goal. Throughout the 1920s, as both patron and apprentice, he gathered in his palace an entourage of outstanding Tunisian musicians, singers, and scholars, including the ensemble that was to represent Tunisia at the Cairo Congress in 1932: Muḥammad Ghānim on *rabāb* (a two-stringed boat-shaped fiddle without a separate neck), Khumais Tarnān on *'ūd 'arbī* (a fretless short-necked Maghrebi lute with four strings), Khumais al-'Āṭī on the *naqqarāt* (a pair of small kettledrums), 'Alī ibn 'Arafa on the *ṭār* (tambourine), and the solo falsetto vocalist (*ṣawt al-tays*) Muḥammad ibn Ḥasan. Far from typifying contemporary performance practice, these musicians represented d'Erlanger's unique attempts to reconstruct an older type of ensemble that excluded both European and eastern Arab instruments. In addition, d'Erlanger commissioned and sponsored numerous research projects, including the translation into French of Arab musical treatises.

It was d'Erlanger's role as both an organizer of and a contributor to the Cairo Congress of 1932 that enabled him to bring his musical projects to completion. His own task was to prepare a comprehensive classification of the melodic and rhythmic genres and compositional forms of modern Arab music, and in 1931 the Egyptian government sent the Syrian musician Shaykh 'Alī al-Darwīsh to Tunisia to serve as his assistant.

During his visit, al-Darwīsh gave public classes in the *medina* (the old city) of Tunis; in these classes, he introduced local musicians to modern Arab music theory using solmization and Western notation. The classes were hosted by the École Supérieure de Lange et de Littérature Arabes and were funded by the government of the French Protectorate. In 1938, al-Darwīsh returned to Tunis at the invitation of his former pupils to establish the teaching curriculum of the Rashīdiyya Institute, which had been founded in 1934 with the aim of preserving and promoting traditional Tunisian music. He paid a final visit to Tunis in 1939, leaving the musicians of the Rashīdiyya equipped to manage their own teaching.

D'Erlanger was too ill to attend the Cairo Congress, and his musicians were escorted to Cairo by al-Darwīsh instead. There, they performed alongside ensembles from other Arab countries in concerts and recording sessions directed by Robert Lachmann, assisted by Béla Bartók. The recordings made at the congress—which were cut directly onto metal disks—not only include the earliest examples of the Tunisian *ma'lūf* but also provide unique documentation of an archaic type of performance practice that was soon to become obsolete, when d'Erlanger's ensemble was dissolved after his death in October 1932. The results of d'Erlanger's classification project were presented to the congress by al-Darwīsh and were published posthumously in its proceedings.

The full fruits of d'Erlanger's scholarship are presented in his six-volume work *La musique arabe* (1930–1959). The five posthumous volumes (1935–1959) were edited, and their publication was supervised, by d'Erlanger's personal secretary, Manoubi Snussi. The first four volumes of *La musique arabe* comprise annotated translations into French of major Arab musical treatises written before the sixteenth century, including works by al-Fārābī, Ibn Sīnā (Avicenna), Ṣāfī al-Dīn, and al-Lādhiqī. The last two volumes are expanded versions of d'Erlanger's reports to the Cairo Congress on the general scale and melodic modes (Volume 5) and the rhythms and compositional forms (Volume 6) of modern Arab music. In his introduction to Volume 5, d'Erlanger acknowledged al-Darwīsh as his source for "Oriental" traditions (effectively those of Syria and the Levant); the Tunisian shaykhs Aḥmad al-Wāfī (d'Erlanger's original mentor) and Khumais Tarnān (the *'ūd* player of his ensemble) had provided the data for the Tunisian Andalusian tradition; al-Darwīsh was responsible for the musical transcriptions (1949:xiv–xv). According to d'Erlanger, Volumes 5 and 6 contain the first codification of the elements of modern Arab music based on the analytical methods of the ancient Arab theorists (1949:viii). D'Erlanger's specific innovation, taken from al-Darwīsh, was to reintroduce into modern Arab music theory the medieval concept of tetrachords (*genres* in French and *ajnās*—singular, *jins*—in Arabic). Thus the individual melodic modes, *maqāmāt,* are presented as ascending and descending scales, each comprising a specific sequence of conjunct, disjunct, or overlapping tetrachords (occasionally trichords or pentachords). D'Erlanger's method of presenting the *maqāmāt* was subsequently adopted by Tunisian and other Middle Eastern music theorists (Marcus 1989:47ff.).

In 1987, in anticipation of a transfer of ownership of Ennajma Ezzahra, d'Erlanger's ashes were removed from the garden of the palace to Montreux, Switzerland. The following year, the palace and its grounds were taken over by the Tunisian government, and on 20 December 1991, Ennajma Ezzahra was designated the Centre des Musiques Arabes et Méditerranéennes. As a state-run institution, it functions variously as a museum dedicated to d'Erlanger's life and work; the national sound archive; a center for research, study, concerts, and conferences; and an instrument workshop. Many of d'Erlanger's paintings are on display there.

In the urban Tunisian society of the 1920s, public music making was generally regarded as shameful, professional musicians were invariably either Jews or members of the lowest social classes, and the typical colonial attitude toward the indigenous culture was a mixture of ignorance and contempt. In such an environment, the sustained interest and patronage of an influential European aristocrat, culminating in the participation of Tunisians in the Cairo Congress of 1932, had a pivotal role in giving Tunisian music a new dignity and new respect. Moreover, through their representation in *La musique arabe,* their presence at the Cairo Congress, and their continuing association with Shaykh 'Alī al-Darwīsh, Tunisian musicians effectively placed their efforts to promote the *ma'lūf* within an international movement to revive Arab music.

REFERENCES

Congrès du Caire 1932, vol. 2: *Musique citadine de Tlemcen/Algérie; Musique savante de Fès/Maroc; Musique citadine de Tunis/Tunisie*. 1988. Édition Bibliothèque Nationale—France/Institut du Monde Arabe, APN 88–10. Compact disk.

Davis, Ruth. 1989. "Links between the Baron Rodolphe d'Erlanger and the Notation of Tunisian Art Music." In *Ethnomusicology and the Historical Dimension*, ed. Margot Lieth Philipp, 47–59. Ludwigsburg: Philipp Verlag.

———. 1993. "Tunisia and the Cairo Congress of Arab Music, 1932." *Maghreb Review* 18:83–102.

D'Erlanger, Rodolphe. 1917. "Au sujet de la musique arabe en tunisie." *Revue Tunisienne* 24:91–95.

———. 1930–1959. *La musique arabe*. 6 vols. Paris: Librairie Orientaliste Paul Geuthner.

———. 1937. *Mélodies tunisiennes: Hispano-Arabes, Arabo-Berbères, Juive, Nègre.* Paris: Librairie Orientaliste Paul Geuthner.

Guettat, Mahmoud. 1992. "La Tunisie dans les documents du Congrès du Caire de 1992." In *Musique Arabe: Le Congres du Caire de 1932*, ed. Philippe Vigreux, 69–86. Cairo: Editions CEDEJ.

Kitāb mu'tamar al-mūsīqā al-'arabiyya (Book of the Congress of Arab Music). 1933. Cairo: al-Maṭba'a al-Amīriyya.

Louati, Ali. 1995. *Le Baron d'Erlanger et son palais Ennajma Ezzahra à Sidi Bou Said.* Tunis: Éditions Simpact.

Marcus, Scott. 1989. "Arab Music Theory in the Modern Period." Ph.D. dissertation, University of California Los Angeles.

Ministère de la Culture. 1995. *Centre des Musiques Arabes et Méditerranéenes.* Tunis: Simpact.

Moussali, Bernard. 1988. "Tunisia, Urban Music of Tunis." In *Congrès du Caire 1932*, 145–151. France: Édition Bibliothèque Nationale avec le concours de l'Institut du Monde Arabe. Insert booklet to APN 88/9–10. Vols. 1 and 2.

Musique tunisienne: Enregistrements du Congrès du Caire. Gramophone HC 40–55 and HC 83–86. 20 compact disks.

Racy, Ali Jihad. 1991. "Historical Worldviews of Early Ethnomusicologists: An East-West Encounter in Cairo, 1932." In *Ethnomusicology and Modern Music History,* ed. Stephen Blum, Philip V. Bohlman, and Daniel M. Neuman, 68–91. Urbana and Chicago: University of Illinois Press.

Patronage and Policy in Tunisian Art Music

Ruth Davis

Musical and Poetic Content
Patronage and Social Contexts before Tunisian Independence
Patronage and Policies since Tunisian Independence

Tunisian art music, *al-ma'lūf* 'familiar' or 'customary', belongs to the North African branch of urban Arab music often called Andalusian. Its early history is shrouded in legend, but according to popular belief, endorsed by certain scholars, the various Arab-Andalusian repertories were originally imported from the Moorish courts of medieval Spain by Muslims and Jews fleeing the Christian reconquest between the twelfth and seventeenth centuries (d'Erlanger 1930–1959:334ff.; al-Mahdī and Marzūqī 1981:9–10). The Tunisian scholar Mahmoud Guettat has proposed a modified version of the legend—that the Arab-Andalusian traditions flourished in parallel in Andalusia and the Maghreb and that the Andalusian refugees merely enriched and reinforced a pre-existing tradition (1980:173–174). In Tunisia, the *ma'lūf* was generally confined to towns and cities of the northern and coastal regions (that is, the principal areas of Andalusian settlement), where it was cultivated by aristocratic and bourgeois amateurs, Jewish and other lower-class professional musicians, and members of certain Sufi brotherhoods. Until the rise of state patronage in the 1960s, the repertoire was virtually unknown among the rural and nomadic populations of the interior and south ('Abd al-Wahhāb 1918:117).

From around the beginning of the twentieth century, the musical life of Tunis became increasingly dominated by eastern Mediterranean and European influences, resulting in neglect of the local *ma'lūf* tradition. A revival was pioneered by a foreign patron and scholar of Arab music, Baron Rodolphe d'Erlanger, who lived in Tunisia from 1911 until his death in 1932. [See Snapshot: Baron d'Erlanger.] The European presence in Tunisia during the French Protectorate (1881–1956) challenged traditional aesthetic values and attitudes regarding the social status of music and the contexts for its performance.

Under the influence of the rising nationalist movement, the *ma'lūf* acquired a new symbolic value, and d'Erlanger's initiative was taken up after his death by the Rashīdiyya Institute, founded in Tunis in 1934 and named after the aristocratic patron and amateur musician Muḥammad al-Rashīd Bey of Tunis (d. 1959). Subsidized by the government and modeled on the European concept of a music conservatory, the Rashīdiyya represented a radically new institutional context for the *ma'lūf*. In its efforts to conserve and promote the tradition, it laid the foundations for the government's musical policies after independence in 1956.

Tunisian independence was accompanied by a hostile reaction to the Sufi movement, which consequently fell into decline. When the ministry of cultural affairs was created in 1961, with the mission of forging a national identity, the *ma'lūf* was designated the national musical heritage, and the government effectively replaced the Sufi brotherhoods as the principal source of patronage. The Rashīdiyya provided the model for a nationwide network of new musical institutions, and the *ma'lūf* became the official repertoire of state-organized music education and amateur performance.

MUSICAL AND POETIC CONTENT

The *ma'lūf* is a melodic tradition, conceived according to the principles of *maqām* 'melodic mode' (plural, *maqāmāt*) and *īqā'* 'rhythmic-metric organization' (plural, *īqā'āt*) characterizing urban Arab music generally. It is primarily a vocal repertoire, although in some regions, notably Tunis, some purely instrumental pieces were added, supposedly by Muḥammad al-Rashīd Bey in the eighteenth century (Guettat 1980:215; al-Mahdī and Marzūqī 1981:35). Although both words and music were transmitted by oral tradition, the poetic texts, belonging to the literary Arabic forms *qaṣīda, muwashshaḥ*, and *zajal,* were also recorded in special handwritten or printed collections called *safā'in* 'vessels' (singular, *safīna*). Tunisians generally concede that the texts must have been recomposed in Tunisia or altered in transmission, since they combine features of literary Arabic and Tunisian dialect. The themes of the texts—mostly romantic descriptions of nature, love, and wine—have traditionally been exploited for their ambiguity, particularly in Sufi contexts. Thus love could be either worldly or divine, and wine could be earthly wine or the elixir of paradise.

Most of the repertoire, including all that is regarded as the authentic Andalusian core, is classified by *maqām* into thirteen *nūbāt* 'suites' (singular, *nūba*). [See ANDALUSIAN *NŪBA* IN MOROCCO.] A *nūba* comprises a common stock of vocal and instrumental genres, each representing a particular *īqā'* or, exceptionally, *īqā'āt*, which are performed in a characteristic sequence (Davis 1992). Since not every genre nor every example of any one genre need be included, two performances of the same *nūba* may in principle consist of totally different pieces; in practice, however, musicians keep to a limited, habitual repertoire, which varies from one ensemble to the next.

PATRONAGE AND SOCIAL CONTEXTS BEFORE TUNISIAN INDEPENDENCE

Rodolphe d'Erlanger provides vivid descriptions of the traditional social contexts for the *ma'lūf.* They included: (1) the Sufi lodges where pupils of all social classes could learn the entire art music tradition under the tutelage of a shaykh; (2) communal celebrations for religious festivals, pilgrimages, and family occasions; (3) private entertainments in the idyllic gardens and luxurious chambers of aristocratic and bourgeois homes; and (4) coffeehouses where professional musicians gathered to rehearse.

Apart from the aristocracy, the principal patrons of the *ma'lūf* before independence were Sufi brotherhoods, popular religious organizations that used special repertories of music and dance as a means of attaining a trance. Certain lodges, notably those of the 'Īsāwiyya and the 'Azūziyya brotherhoods, cultivated the *ma'lūf* alongside their sacred repertoire, both as a recreational activity and, according to some, as an act of duty to preserve the Andalusian heritage. The *ma'lūf* was typically sung after the public ceremonies on Fridays and other holidays: the secular songs were supposed to calm the heightened emotional atmosphere and allow the participants to recover from their physical exertions before returning home. The Sufi concerts also provided opportunities to learn the repertoire, since everyone present would participate in the singing.

Urban Islamic society regarded public musical activity outside the lodges as shameful. Professional musicians were generally either Jews or members of the lowest classes, and amateur musicians of higher social standing were obliged to confine their musical activities to the privacy of their homes. The lodges thus functioned as a musical haven, providing musical instruction and entertainment for professionals and amateurs alike, regardless of their social class. Many people attended the Sufi lodges as an excuse to enjoy the *ma'lūf*. In Tunis, the various lodges chose different days of the week to host special performances in addition to those following the religious ceremonies; thus a devotee might conceivably participate in a *ma'lūf* concert every evening of the week.

The Sufi lodges adoped a performance style called called *ma'lūf khām* 'raw' or 'unrefined' *ma'luf*, characterized by a male chorus singing in unison accompanied only by percussion or hand clapping. In many communities, the lodges were a springboard for performances of *ma'lūf khām* elsewhere: according to d'Erlanger, the musicians who sang in local cafés and in celebrations on religious holidays and at pilgrimages, weddings, and circumcisions were members of the Sufi groups (1917:93). But in larger towns and cities, *ma'lūf khām* was generally confined to the lodges, and the *ma'lūf* was performed in other contexts by small instrumental ensembles that included melody instruments; the players doubled as a chorus, alternating with a solo voice.

Members of the aristocracy maintained instrumental *ma'lūf* ensembles in their palaces. The celebrated patron and amateur Muḥammad al-Rashīd Bey, who is said to have abdicated his throne in order to devote himself to his art, is traditionally credited with the organization of the *nūba* cycle, the composition of its instrumental pieces, and the introduction of new musical genres reflecting Ottoman influences (Guettat 1980:214–15; al-Mahdī and Marzūqī 1981:35). He founded a *ma'lūf* ensemble and music school in his palace that continued to train and promote eminent musicians until the early 1940s.

D'Erlanger himself patronized a private *ma'lūf* ensemble that rehearsed in a special building in the grounds of a magnificent Moorish-style palace he had built according to his own specifications in Sidi Bou Said, a clifftop village on the outskirts of Tunis. His description of a *ma'lūf* concert in a princely home may well be based on his own experience:

> Let us now make our way into the palace of a nobleman, even that of the prince. Courtyard follows upon courtyard, garden upon garden, one could get lost in such a maze: here an orange grove is surrounded by colonnades; there a pool reflects the high walls of this gigantic home, creating the illusion of an enchanted city. . . . The master of the house is looking forward to the night, when he will gather together his close friends and summon his musicians. He too will take part in the concert, perhaps playing the lute or, if he is gifted with a pleasant voice, he will sing. . . . He has chosen the finest room in his palace for his concert hall; his musicians will be wearing the most magnificent costumes, and everyone will be dressed in harmonious colors. No sound will be allowed to distract the listeners; the servants waiting on him will be shod in the softest leather. The low tables will be laden with the most beautiful dishes containing savories and sweetmeats; perfumes will drift through the atmosphere; often in his rapture he will forget the passing hours. (1917:94)

D'Erlanger's descriptions may seem highly romanticized, but musicians in Sidi Bou Said attest that his images of an aristocrat passing the nights in the luxurious atmosphere of a private concert, of Sufis practicing under their shaykh in the lodge, of musicians playing in idyllic gardens, of jasmine-scented rooms in bourgeois villas, and of women crowding to listen from behind the grilles that separated them from the men (d'Erlanger 1917:92–94) were indeed scenes from the traditional *ma'lūf* in Sidi Bou Said—and that the aristocrat was d'Erlanger himself.

The role of Baron Rodolphe d'Erlanger

The seeds of the government's musical policies after independence were first sown by d'Erlanger, who was probably the single most influential patron of the *ma'lūf* in the twentieth century. Ensconced in his palace, d'Erlanger devoted himself to the preservation and promotion of the indigenous culture, especially its music. From the early 1920s (his palace was completed in 1921) until his death in 1932, he dedicated his home to the pursuit of Arab musical scholarship and performance. As both patron and apprentice, d'Erlanger employed local scholars to translate Arab music treatises into French, and he selected five leading musicians of Tunis to form a unique type of ensemble that would reconstruct performance styles of the past.

D'Erlanger maintained that the chief reasons for the vulnerability of the *ma'lūf* in the face of foreign influences were the musicians' total reliance on oral transmission and their lack of theoretical knowledge. For the tradition to survive, therefore, the musicians needed a theoretical foundation comparable to that of Western art music (d'Erlanger 1917:95). His own contribution lay in the completion of his monumental six-volume work *La musique arabe*, which was published posthumously. Volumes 1–4 (1930–1939) contain French translations of treatises written before the sixteenth century by al-Fārābī, Ibn Sīnā (Avicenne), Ṣafī al-Dīn, and al-Lādhiqī; volumes 5 (1949) and 6 (1959) provide comprehensive classifications of the modes, rhythms, and compositional forms that were in use in d'Erlanger's time.

D'Erlanger was a principal organizer of the Cairo Congress of 1932, and the last two volumes of *La musique arabe* are expanded versions of reports he originally prepared for that congress. He was assisted by a Syrian, Shaykh 'Alī al-Darwīsh, who had been sent to Tunis at d'Erlanger's request in 1931. During 'Alī al-Darwīsh's visit, d'Erlanger arranged for him to give public classes, funded by the Tunisian government, in the medina in Tunis; these classes introduced local musicians to contemporary Arab music theory using solmization and notation. The shaykh's direct contact with Tunisian musicians proved definitive in advancing d'Erlanger's cause. In 1938 and 1939, at the invitation of his former students, the shaykh paid two more visits to Tunis to introduce solmization, notation, and Arab music theory to the Rashīdiyya Institute's ensemble, laying a foundation for the curriculum subsequently adopted by the ensemble and the institute (d'Erlanger 1930–1959:381; al-Mahdī and Marzūqī 1981:29–30, 68).

D'Erlanger was too ill to attend the Cairo Congress himself (he died in October of the same year). However, he sent his own *ma'lūf* ensemble, trained and escorted by Shaykh 'Alī al-Darwīsh, thereby establishing a link between Tunisian musicians and modern ideological, educational, and institutional developments in Egyptian art music. On their return, the musicians reported to their colleagues the congress's official recommendation that institutions be established throughout the Arab world to preserve and promote indigenous music traditions. Tunisians today acknowledge this recommendation as a catalyst in the founding of the Rashīdiyya Institute two and a half years later (al-Mahdī and Marzūqī 1981:27–28).

The Rashīdiyya Institute

Founded in November 1934 in Tunis and subsidized by the government of the French Protectorate, the Rashīdiyya Institute represented a new social context for the *ma'lūf*. Taking as its immediate model the French music conservatory founded in Tunis in 1896, it was the first public secular institution to devote itself exclusively to music. Its fundamental goals—to preserve and promote traditional Tunisian music—were a continuation of d'Erlanger's aims, and they foreshadowed those of the government after independence.

The founders' motives were essentially twofold. First, they wanted to protect the *ma'lūf* from an influx of foreign, particularly Egyptian, influences, seen as dominating the musical life of the capital. Second, they wanted to raise the social status of the *ma'lūf* by removing it from its presumbly vulgar secular environments (for example, cafés where people smoked hashish and wedding celebrations where alcohol was served) and provide it with a respectable public secular setting, comparable in status and function to a European music conservatory (Davis 1996). The social status of the new institution was reflected in the roster of its founding members, which included prominent members of the Tunisian bourgeoisie; its president was Muṣṭafā Ṣfār, the mayor of Tunis (al-Mahdī and Marzūqī 1981:30–31).

The activities of the Rashīdiyya Institute centered on an ensemble that rehearsed and gave public concerts at the institute and at a school that trained prospective members of the ensemble. In its efforts to preserve and promote the *ma'lūf,* the institute introduced radical changes in performance practice and transmission. It organized the transcription into Western staff notation of the entire repertoire known to the shaykhs of Tunis from oral tradition, establishing these transcriptions as the basis for teaching and performance. [See WESTERN NOTATION IN TUNISIAN ART MUSIC.] Eventually, it created a new, enlarged ensemble that included new instruments, instrumental doublings, a conductor, and separate male and female choruses and had been inspired both by the Western symphony orchestra and by contemporary Egyptian ensembles.

The ensemble gave regular public performances in the large inner courtyard of the institute, and as the official representative of Tunisian music it gave concerts to honor important political events and figures, such as visiting foreign dignitaries (al-Mahdī and Marzūqī 1981:104–106). When the Tunisian Broadcasting System, or Tunisian Radio, was founded in 1938, its director general was 'Uthmān Ka'ak (who would later, in 1941, succeed Muṣṭafā Ṣfār as president of the Rashīdiyya Institute). Its artistic director, responsible for its musical policies, was Muṣṭafā Bushshūsha, brother-in-law of Muṣṭafā Ṣfār. Tunisian Radio adopted the policy of restricting its broadcasts to Tunisian music, whether traditional or modern. At first, the Rashīdiyya broadcast live programs two evenings a week; eventually, Tunisian Radio devoted each evening of the week to a live performance by a different group. The Rashīdiyya continued to give weekly live broadcasts until after independence; these performances were transmitted from the radio studio until 1949, after which they were transmitted directly from the Rashīdiyya Institute (al-Mahdī and Marzūqī 1981:52–54).

The Rashīdiyya's activities had no obvious effect on the *ma'lūf* traditions of the Sufi brotherhoods, or indeed, until after independence, on *ma'lūf* practices outside the capital. However, in its efforts to raise the social status of the *ma'lūf,* the Rashīdiyya discouraged its members from performing in traditional secular public contexts. It is difficult to gauge the effects of these prohibitions on the traditional *ma'lūf* activities, since other factors, particularly increasing competition from foreign and newer Tunisian repertoires promoted by the media, must inevitably have contributed to their decline. Whatever the primary cause, by the eve of Tunisian independence the *ma'lūf* had virtually disappeared from cafés in the city, its songs were rarely heard at Muslim wedding celebrations, and the Rashīdiyya represented virtually the sole public secular context for the *ma'lūf* in the capital.

PATRONAGE AND POLICIES SINCE TUNISIAN INDEPENDENCE

After Tunisian independence in 1956, the new government adopted certain policies that contributed, either intentionally or inadvertently, to a radical transformation of traditional *ma'lūf* practices. It designated the *ma'lūf* as the national musical heritage and claimed a monopoly over patronage of the *ma'lūf*; it created a mechanism whereby the achievements of the Rashīdiyya would be extended throughout the nation; and it fostered a negative attitude toward the Sufi brotherhoods that critically undermined their musical traditions.

Although the *ma'lūf* was unknown to a large part of Tunisia, in certain respects this art was well qualified for its official designation. It was common at least to several communities, unlike the rural musical traditions, which tended to be more regionally

As an Arab musical and literary tradition, the *ma'lūf* reflected the government's general policy of "arabizing" Tunisian culture.

diversified ('Abd al-Wahhāb 1918:106). As an Arab musical and literary tradition, the *ma'lūf* reflected the government's general policy of "arabizing" Tunisian culture. It had the prestige associated with the Arab-Andalusian heritage, and its legendary origin passed for history in the popular imagination and even among some scholars. But the most valuable asset of the *ma'lūf* was the fact that it had been systematically classified, studied, and documented by the Rashīdiyya Institute. The government had merely to assimilate the Rashīdiyya's aims, methods, and achievements into its own cultural and educational policies. The Rashīdiyya, with its ensemble and school, provided a complete Tunisian musical repertoire in notation, a standard performance style, an institutional model, and a source of music teachers, administrators, and advisers. With these resources and a new national network of cultural and educational institutions, the government extended the Rashīdiyya's work from its center in Tunis to the whole of Tunisia.

The demise of the Sufi traditions

The new government regarded the Sufi brotherhoods as politically corrupt and socially regressive. During the protectorate, certain brotherhoods had cooperated with the French against the Tunisian resistance movement, and the government was suspicious of their loyalty as well as their esoteric spiritual practices. At best, the Sufis were seen as an unworthy distraction from the new national cause; at worst, they were considered a potential source of opposition (Jones 1977:39–40). Moreover, the new leadership regarded many of the Sufis' beliefs and customs, particularly the extreme physical practices performed in trances, as shameful relics of a backward society, counterproductive to the new goals of modernization and progress. The official attitude was summed up, a decade after independence, by the Reverend R. Marston Speight: "Modern activist politicians accuse the Sufi brotherhoods of being largely responsible for the backwardness of the Tunisian nation. The followers of the mystic way are uniformly described as obscurantists, fatalists, and exaggerated pietists" (1966:58).

The government suppressed the Sufis' extreme physical practices, confiscated their lands and other possessions, and officially denigrated the brotherhoods. As their activities were restricted and their social prestige plummeted, the membership of the brotherhoods declined, and lodges throughout the country emptied and ceased to function (Speight 1966:58). In some provincial communities, among them Testūr, Zaghuan, and Sidi Bou Said, where Sufi musicians had traditionally also performed *ma'lūf khām* in secular contexts, the uprooted musicians were to some extent able to maintain their traditions; however, they operated in a social and spiritual limbo, a situation scarcely alleviated by the new alternative social contexts provided by the government.

The new institutions

Shortly after independence, the French music conservatory, founded in Tunis in 1896, was converted into a new National Conservatory of Music. This new institution, the cornerstone of the government's music education apparatus, effectively combined the functions of the former Western conservatory and the Rashīdiyya school. Its syllabus, defined by presidential decree on 23 January 1958, grew to include practical, historical, and theoretical studies in Tunisian, Egyptian, and Western music; and in all three traditions solmization, Western staff notation, and the skills of sight reading and dictation were used (al-Mahdī and Marzūqī 1981:71–74). The course is taught over a period of seven years to children and young people up to the age of twenty; the classes are free, subsidized by the government. The Rashīdiyya school offered the same course to adults until 1972, when a special adult conservatory was created and the Rashīdiyya dropped its independent teaching functions altogether.

In 1961, a ministry of cultural affairs was created to promote and harmonize cultural activities throughout the nation. In particular, the new ministry was to: (1) cultivate the national cultural heritage, (2) provide a basic popular education in all aspects of that heritage, and (3) develop cultural links with foreign countries, especially with international cultural organizations (Kacem 1973:36). To effect its policies, the ministry established a nationwide network of cultural and recreational institutions called *diyār thaqāfa* 'houses of culture' coordinated by a parallel network of national, regional, and local cultural committees. The ministry itself had various specialized departments, including a department of music and popular arts that was directed until 1979 by Ṣāliḥ al-Mahdī, who had been the leader of the Rashīdiyya ensemble since 1949 and was simultaneously appointed director of the new National Conservatory of Music. For the next eighteen years, until he was replaced in both posts by his former student Fatḥī Zghonda, al-Mahdī was personally responsible for the government's musical policies.

During the 1960s and 1970s, the ministry of cultural affairs created a network of amateur ensembles and music schools along the lines of the Rashīdiyya in new *diyār thaqāfa* throughout the country. The ministry supplied these institutions with instruments and sent out graduates of the Rashīdiyya school and the National Conservatory to organize and teach the new ensembles, at first using the Rashīdiyya's transcriptions as sources. Over the same period, the ministry published a version of the Rashīdiyya's transcriptions in a series of nine volumes entitled *al-Turāth al-mūsīqī al-tūnisī* 'The Tunisian Musical Heritage' that were distributed to the new ensembles. Thus the *ma'lūf* was introduced to areas where it had been unknown, and new performance practices, new institutional contexts, and unfamiliar versions of the melodies were introduced to communities where it was traditional. Over the years, some of the *diyār thaqāfa* expanded their musical programs to include systematic teaching along the lines of the National Conservatory, offering the same syllabus and examinations up to a certain level. Some, such as those of Sfax and Sousse, have developed into self-contained regional conservatories, offering the complete syllabus up to the final diploma examination.

In order to encourage and monitor the new state-sponsored ensembles, the department of music and popular arts established a program of intensive residential music courses, held during school vacations, and an annual cycle of competitions and festivals, culminating in a national competition and festival held each summer in Testūr, the traditional center of *ma'lūf*. In 1969, the government instituted a policy requiring professional musicians to hold qualifying cards for their particular types of repertoire. Since then, the regional *ma'lūf* festivals have also served as examination centers for the licensing system. The examiners and adjudicators are selected from the Rashīdiyya and the conservatory; the ministry of cultural affairs gives the ensembles guidelines for their choice of programs and regulates the criteria by which the performances are judged. According to Fatḥī Zghonda, the criteria include choice of program and instruments, intonation, vocal and instrumental technique, and manner of interpreting the melodies. The desirable program includes repertoire from *al-Turāth al-mūsīqī al-*

tūnisī and new compositions in traditional Tunisian styles. The guiding principles for the choice of instruments are correct intonation and the correct balancing of timbres; Western instruments of fixed pitch, which inevitably compromise the subtle intervals of the *maqāmāt*, are particularly to be avoided. Melodic interpretation should be based on the published notations.

Except for a brief period (1972–1979) when the government funded a professional ensemble led by ʿAbd al-Ḥamīd Benʿaljīya, the Rashīdiyya has maintained its amateur status, subsidized by the government. On the whole, its members are recruited from the staff and former students of the National Conservatory. A bastion of the *ma'lūf*, the Rashīdiyya is effectively the national ensemble, providing the model for provincial ensembles.

The media

Since independence, the *ma'lūf* has maintained a relatively low profile on radio, on television, and in the Tunisian mass media generally. In 1958, the government provided funds for a professional radio ensemble modeled on counterparts in Egypt; its repertoire consisted primarily of Egyptian popular songs and Tunisian songs in a similar style. Within this framework, a special reduced ensemble, made up of the elite of the Rashīdiyya's past and present membership, was formed for performances of the *ma'lūf*. Rather than continue the custom of broadcasting regular live performances, however, Tunisian Radio built up a stock of studio recordings by both the radio ensemble and the Rashīdiyya ensemble; it broadcast these recordings repeatedly—at first weekly, but this was decreased to alternate weeks around the mid-1980s. When a television section was added in 1965, it adopted the same policy of transmitting prerecorded studio performances. These token offerings were occasionally supplemented by live radio and televion broadcasts of, for instance, concerts by the Rashīdiyya ensemble or highlights from the international festival of the *ma'lūf* held annually in Testūr.

The relative lack of interest of Radiodiffusion Télévision Tunisienne (R.T.T.) in the *ma'lūf* was mirrored in the catalogs of the Tunisian record and cassette companies. In the mid-1980s, neither of the two privately owned companies, Mallouliphone (Tunis) and Société de la Cassette (Carthage), had issued recordings of the *ma'lūf*; and the state-owned company Ennaghem had released only a handful, all of them from archival recordings made by the R.T.T. In the early 1990s, the ministry of culture collaborated with Maison des Cultures du Monde in Paris to reissue on compact disks the archival recordings of *nūbāt* performed by the radio ensemble. The series included one new recording (1994) of *nūbat al-sīkā* by an ensemble created especially for the purpose.

Rehabilitation of the Sufi musicians

During the 1960s, the government began to relax its earlier prohibitions against the Sufi brotherhoods. While remaining officially disapproving of their religious beliefs and practices, it came to recognize their artistic traditions as a valuable and harmless part of the national folklore that deserved to be fostered. In some communities, lodges were reopened, and there, under the auspices of municipalities, the former Sufi ensembles were allowed to resume their musical activities, divorced from their sacred functions. Alternatively, some surviving Sufi ensembles gravitated toward the new cultural institutions, cooperating to a greater or lesser degree with emissaries of the ministry of cultural affairs. The government subsidizes the upkeep of the lodges and provides for the musicians' costumes and instruments, promotes performances by the Sufi ensembles on national and religious holidays, and holds competitions for the performance of the Sufis' sacred repertoires along the lines of the competitions for the *ma'lūf*. Traditional *ma'lūf* centers not uncommonly support two ensembles: one, descended from a former Sufi ensemble with a nucleus of older musicians, performs *ma'lūf khām* at weddings and other communal celebrations; the second, a modern instrumental ensemble with a membership predominantly of young people, represents the town at competitions and festivals.

In certain respects, the "official" *ma'lūf,* originally promoted by the Rashīdiyya Institute and then taken up by the ministry of cultural affairs, amounts to an invented tradition, in the sense that a repertoire which was once the popular entertainment of certain urban communities confined to a limited geographical area, and in which performance practices were local and even personal, has been transformed into a symbol of national identity. For the music and its performers, this transformation involved changes in social function, contexts, and status; the process also resulted in radical changes in performance practice, affecting the form of the melodies themselves.

By creating a special environment for the *ma'lūf*—an environment that effectively replaced the traditional secular contexts—the founders of the Rashīdiyya succeeded in setting the traditional repertoire apart and protecting it from the competition of new commercial repertoires fostered by the mass media. The *ma'lūf* was thus elevated in both social and musical status. As a national tradition, it acquired a new symbolic value and academic and intellectual prestige comparable to that of Western art music. When the state took control of cultural policy after Tunisian independence, it also took over the musical ideology, values, and methods represented by the Rashīdiyya and promoted them nationwide in new state-funded music clubs and conservatories. With the demise of the Sufi brotherhoods, the last stronghold of traditional patronage, *ma'lūf,* seemed to be moving into the state-controlled secular domain of academic, education, and recreational music.

Yet despite the efforts of the ministry of culture to monopolize the *ma'lūf,* grassroots activities and older performance styles have persisted, both within and outside the official establishment, to the extent that in the 1990s musicians and audiences were speaking of a popular revival (Davis 1996). In historic centers of *ma'lūf* such as Zaghuan, Sidi Bou Said, and Testūr, Sufi-style ensembles continue to sing *ma'lūf khām* at communal celebrations and give concerts sponsored by the municipality on national and religious holidays. In Tunis and other large towns, leading musicians perform in small vocal and instrumental ensembles in formal concerts, at cafés, in hotels, and at weddings. The transcendence of the government's institutional frameworks, with their limitations on performace, is strikingly illustrated by a recording of the popular singer Lotfi Bushnak in the *ma'lūf* series by the ministry of culture and Maison des Cultures du Monde. Along with conventional performances of the *nūbāt,* the series includes four abbreviated *nūbāt* called *waṣlāt,* featuring Bushnak as the solo vocalist, backed by an ensemble of eight top-ranking solo instrumentalists.

REFERENCES

'Abd al-Wahhāb, Ḥassan Ḥusnī. 1918. "Le développement de la musique arabe en Orient, Espagne, et Tunisie." *Revue Tunisienne* 25:106–117.

Davis, Ruth. 1986. "Links between the Baron Rodolphe d'Erlanger and the Notation of Tunisian Art Music." In *Ethnomusicology and the Historical Dimension,* ed. Margot Lieth Philipp, 47–59. Ludwigsburg: Philipp Verlag.

———. 1992. "The Tunisian *Nūba* as Cyclic Genre." In *Regionale maqām-Tradition in Geschichte und Gegenwart,* 1. *Proceedings of the Second Meeting of the ICTM Study Group on Maqām, Berlin 1992,* 83–114.

———. 1996. "The Art/Popular Music Paradigm and the Tunisian *Ma'lūf. Popular Music* 15(3):13–23.

D'Erlanger, Rodolphe. 1917. "Au sujet de la musique arabe en Tunisie." *Revue Tunisienne* 24:91–95.

———. 1930–1959. *La musique arabe.* 6 vols. Paris: Libraire Orientaliste Paul Geuthner.

Guettat, Mahmoud. 1980. *La musique classique du Maghreb.* Paris: Sinbad.

Jones, Lura Jafran. 1977. "The 'Isawiyya of Tunisia and Their Music." Ph.D. dissertation, University of Washington.

Kacem, Abdelaziz. 1973. "La politique culturelle tunisienne." *Annuaire de l'Afrique du Nord* 12:29–44.

al-Mahdī, Ṣāliḥ, ed. n.d. *al-Turāth al-mūsīqī al-tūnisī* (The Tunisian Musical Heritage). 9 vols. Tunis: al-Ma'had al-Waṭanī li'l-Mūsīqā wa'l-Raqṣ.

al-Mahdī, Ṣāliḥ, and Muḥammad Marzūqī. 1981. *al-Ma'had al-Rashīdī* (The Rashīdiyya Institute). Tunis: al-Sharika al-Tūnisiyya li-Funūn al-Rasm.

Speight, R. Marston. 1966. "Tunisia and Sufism." *Muslim World* 26:58–59.

The ʻĪsāwiyya of Tunis

L. JaFran Jones

Sufism
The ʻĪsāwiyya
Traditional ʻĪsāwiyya Practice
The ʻĪsāwiyya in Modern Tunisia

Of the diverse Sufi groups in North Africa, the ʻĪsāwiyya have received particular attention from Western scholars and travelers because of their relative accessibility, their role in the transmission and preservation of traditional art music (*ma'lūf*), and certain unusual devotional practices that arouse curiosity. By the beginning of the twentieth century, ʻĪsāwiyya "ensembles" had "performed" in European cities. Their accommodating response to the European vogue of cultural tourism caused them to be shunted into categories like "folklore" and "music" in Western eyes, obscuring their essentially religious identity. The ʻĪsāwiyya themselves remain Sufis of characteristically Maghrebi and Tunisian cast.

SUFISM

Sufism provides believers with an enhanced, more immediate religious experience through devotional practices such as music, the repetition of sacred formulas, the manipulation of breath and body movement, and trance. There are analogous and not unrelated movements within Christianity and other religions. The generally acknowledged derivation of the term *Sufi* is that it relates to the wool (*ṣūf*) traditionally worn by adepts. Tunisian ʻĪsāwiyya still wear a body shirt of coarse white wool, often over bare skin. Sufis have rarely received the approval of the custodians of orthodoxy, whose attitude has ranged from disdain to aggressive persecution, yielding occasional Sufi martyrs. More recently, reformers, both religious and secular, have made Sufism a scapegoat for the spectrum of ills that put the Muslim world at the mercy of European colonizers.

Full-scale Sufi brotherhoods became prominent in the Maghreb beginning in the eleventh and twelfth centuries and tended to radiate from Morocco to the rest of the Maghreb and Muslim Spain. The most influential of these brotherhoods was the Shādhiliyya order, based on the teachings of Sīdī Abū'l-Ḥasan (Bel-Aḥsan) (1196–1258), who was born in Morocco, became a Sufi in Tunisia, and finished his work in Egypt. The Shādhiliyya movement has maintained unequaled spiritual authority for centuries. With a few exceptions, virtually all Sufi brotherhoods in North Africa, including the ʻĪsāwiyya, are branches of the Shādhiliyya order.

THE ʿĪSĀWIYYA

The founder of the ʿĪsāwiyya, Sīdī Muḥammad ben ʿĪsā of Meknès (c. 1467–1526, north-central Morocco), claimed the standard sherifian descent from the Prophet and a direct spiritual lineage extending back to Sīdī Bel-Aḥsan. Sīdī ben ʿĪsā was a charismatic leader, renowned in his own time for his palpable piety and for his power to work miracles and to protect against foes, both seen and unseen. This power is still believed to emanate not only from his tomb in Meknès but also from the words he taught his followers to repeat in their devotions.

The ʿĪsāwiyya were established in Tunisia at least by the end of the sixteenth century, but their history in Tunisia has yet to be adequately researched. An important aspect of this history is the traditional assertion that the ʿĪsāwiyya figured most prominently among brotherhoods in Tunisia that attracted Muslim refugees from "reconquered" Spain. The Andalusian influx and its impact on Tunisian culture were particularly intense in the early seventeenth century and introduced, among other things, a musical tradition that blended with local repertoires and other influences to create the *maʾlūf* genre. This became an intimate part of ʿĪsāwiyya practice and, in its secular manifestation, an art form in which Tunisians take pride.

Until well into the twentieth century the Sufi brotherhoods were a pervasive element in Tunisian society, and practically everyone was associated with some brotherhood. The *zāwiya* 'shrine' (plural, *zwāyā*) served as an all-purpose center for the social life of young and old, providing recreation, education (including musical training), socialization, and a setting for family celebrations. It also cared for the poor. From their beginnings in Tunisia, the ʿĪsāwiyya were chiefly a brotherhood of the popular urban masses, and their status among brotherhoods reflected this. Their ecstatic practices and unreserved espousal of music also earned the disapproval of the more staid brotherhoods. Nevertheless, the ʿĪsāwiyya, one of the largest brotherhoods, had enough status and included enough important families to confer on music a legitimacy it would not otherwise have enjoyed.

TRADITIONAL ʿĪSĀWIYYA PRACTICE

The rapid and fundamental changes in Tunisia since independence (1956), which have accelerated and expanded in recent years, make it difficult to speak with confidence about tradition. What one reads, even in relatively recent sources, and what one witnessed at first hand only a decade or two ago may no longer be valid today. But although one may be tempted to assume that all old things have been eclipsed, this would be an exaggeration. The ʿĪsāwiyya and their practices have not disappeared from modern Tunisia. Still, they have declined, changed, and lost much of their former raison d'être. The future may see their demise, their revival, or their fossilization into "folklore." One must be cautious about evaluations and predictions in so volatile a context.

In the *zāwiya*: *Dhikr*

A *zāwiya* is a sacred place, typically built around the tomb of a holy man. It is not subject to the same restrictions as a mosque. There are rooms for women's activities and spiritual consultations with the shaykh. Food is normally permitted, as are, at the discretion of the brotherhood, certain types of musical instruments and ecstatic practices. Various noncanonical devotional activities take place, particularly around the tomb itself.

There may be activities in a *zāwiya* every day, but normally (male) members of the *ṭarīqa* 'way'—the Sufi brotherhood—meet once a week for their official devotions. Since this involves mainly "remembering" God by repetition of his name or names, the ceremony is called *dhikr* 'remembrancing'. It does not entail music per se, although to Western ears, melody and rhythm can be perceived in the recitations. The ʿĪsāwiyya of Tunis are more strict in excluding music from these devotions than those elsewhere in Tunisia. Farther south, *ʿaml* (*maʾlūf*-type singing) may be included, even with musical instruments and full-blown ecstatic practices (*takhmīr*).

Dhikr is a ceremony with many parts and a complex structure. Each *ṭarīqa*, and indeed each group within a *ṭarīqa*, has its particular conventions. At the heart of the *dhikr* is the repetition of God's names and of short formulas containing the divine name, such as the *shahāda* 'credo'. There may be hundreds or thousands of iterations, depending on the customs of the *zāwiya* and on the shaykh's discretion. At Sīdī al-Ḥārī in Tunis, for example, *dhikr* of the name *Allāh* begins after several hundred repetitions of the *shahāda*. At first, four iterations are grouped rhythmically in one breath: *Allāhu Allāhu Allāhu Allāh*, often with a lilting "melody." As the tempo increases, syllables drop, so that a sound like *Al-la-wa-la-wa-la-wa-la* and then simply *La-la-la-la* is produced. At the climax all stop abruptly and are briefly silent. A new and different sequence then begins: slow and low-pitched, with one breath for each iteration: *Al-lāh*. Every other man bends forward and pronounces the divine name, then returns to an upright position and is silent while those next to him bend for *dhikr*. With acceleration this changes to *La-ha-la-ha-la-* . . . at a higher pitch. On a cue from the shaykh, the *dhikr* halts and the group breaks into a quasi-melodic litany of blessings on the Prophet.

Other texts, also repeated generously, are important not only for "remembrancing" God but also for their power to bring blessings upon those who keep them ever on the mind and tongue. Chief among these is *al-Fātiḥa*, the opening chapter of the Qur'ān, for which each brotherhood has its own distinctive style of delivery. Besides a number of conventional prayers and invocations, there are special collages of inspired texts assembled and in part written by Sīdī ben ʿĪsā. Each of these pericopes, or lections, is a *ḥizb*. It consists of selections from the Qur'ān, praise of God, eulogies to the prophets and saints, vignettes of (Sufi) doctrine, and supplications. At least one *ḥizb* is recited in a *dhikr* ceremony, with a special candle burning before the shaykh. *Ḥizb* recitation is more melodic than that of the Qur'ān, which also takes place at junctures in the ceremony.

Maʾlūf tradition

An aspect of Sufism that has chronically placed it at odds with orthodox Islam is the affirmation of *samāʿ* 'listening' (to music) as a legitimate means of expressing devotion and drawing near the divine. Since the Prophet lauded the merits of a "beautiful voice," even rigid orthodoxy cannot exclude a modicum of what might be called music: for example, *ʾadhān* (the call to prayer) and *tajwīd* (cantillation of the Qur'ān). But Sufis went well beyond this, admitting the intonation of noncanonical poetry with more elaborate melody and rhythm, instruments, and even music without words. All this is anathema to the orthodox.

Popular brotherhoods such as the ʿĪsāwiyya have taken a further step, using music that is virtually indistinguishable from that enjoyed in the secular sphere (*ṭarab*), including very lively rhythms. Purists of Sufi theory would assert that these brotherhoods have taken unwarranted license with the principle of *samāʿ*: their music goes beyond the spiritual into physical stimulation and pleasure and detracts from the higher goal. The ʿĪsāwiyya take a different view, for they have embraced *maʾlūf*, and it would be difficult to subtract this from the essence of their *ṭarīqa*.

Maʾlūf is traditional Tunisian art music. Very similar repertoires exist elsewhere in the Maghreb, but with different names. The repertoire consists of a set of *nūbāt* 'suites' (singular, *nūba*), each based on one of the traditional melodic modes (*naghma*). Five different rhythmic modes provide the five sections of each suite, and although they do not consistently increase the tempo throughout, they convey a sense of progressive acceleration from a languid beginning to a precipitous conclusion. Individual

From their beginnings in Tunisia, the ʿĪsāwiyya were chiefly a brotherhood of the popular urban masses.

selections are strophic poems sung in unison (or heterophony) to melodies composed in the respective rhythm (*mīzān*) and *naghma*.

The ʿĪsāwiyya make a primary distinction between *maʾlūf al-jadd* 'serious' and *maʾlūf al-hazl* 'frivolous'—that is, between the sacred and profane. Musically the two repertoires differ little, with variations mainly in instrumentation and execution. The chief difference lies in the poetic texts: those of the ʿĪsāwiyya extol God, praise the prophets and saints, and are supplications for blessings or intercession. The two repertoires share poems by notable mystics, ostensibly about love and wine but permitting a symbolic, religious interpretation.

The closeness of sacred and secular *maʾlūf* is easy to understand in view of the role that the ʿĪsāwiyya and other brotherhoods have played in preserving and perpetuating the tradition. At the time of the Andalusian influx in the sixteenth and seventeenth centuries, they provided a crucible for the fusion of indigenous and imported elements and the extraction of the Tunisian *maʾlūf.* Over the centuries they fostered the repertoire and provided the principal opportunity for learning and practicing *maʾlūf.* In musical families, mothers often served as unofficial music teachers, but otherwise the young received their musical as well as their devotional initiation in the *zāwiya*. Boys and men could continue to receive training in the group or from a shaykh until they had mastered the repertoire, and in the *zāwiya* they had a safe haven for exercising their art. When the time came in the twentieth century for transcribing and codifying *maʾlūf,* shaykhs of the ʿĪsāwiyya were an indispensable source.

Today secular *maʾlūf* is quite separable from that of the ʿĪsāwiyya, and the repertoire is more comprehensive. The work of restoration and unification drew from the ʿĪsāwiyya but did little to alter their repertoire, which continued as before as an oral tradition with regional diversity and whatever imperfections, lacunae, or "corruptions" may have accumulated over the centuries. In the *maʾlūf ʿĪsāwī* that survives, we may have a glimpse of what Tunisian *maʾlūf* was like in general before the scholars took it in hand. Yet there are elements one could consider distinctively *ʿĪsāwī*: a preference for certain modes, such as *ḥsīn* and *aṣbaʿīn*; a tendency to modulate into "folk" modes, such as *ṣālḥī* and *ʿarḍāwī*, or to incorporate regional folk material; considerably more attention to rhythm; and a few ʿĪsāwiyya "trademarks," such as *brāwal ʿĪsāwiyya* and *mjarrad*. *Barwal* (plural, *brāwal*)—a lively, syncopated pattern—is one of the five canonical *maʾlūf* rhythms, but the ʿĪsāwiyya have become specialists in it, acknowledged virtuosos. Their *brāwal* are particularly appreciated, not always for purely spiritual reasons. *Mjarrad*, a five-beat rhythm, is virtually synonymous with the ʿĪsāwiyya and is eagerly anticipated toward the end of a ceremony, after *maʾlūf* (with *brāwal*) and preceding trance music (if any).

Music and trance: *ʿAml* and *takhmīr*

ʿĪsāwiyya groups vary considerably in their restrictions on music and trance in the *zāwiya*. In Tunis instruments are excluded, music is normally not used in devotions, and trance, although it occurs spontaneously, is neither acknowledged nor consciously induced. Elsewhere, various combinations of music, instruments, and trance are allowed. Virtually all 'Īsāwiyya groups make music outside the *zāwiya* on appropriate occasions. Throughout Tunisia the brotherhoods now exercise much more restraint with regard to trance practices than formerly. Officially there is little tolerance for the "eccentric" side of 'Īsāwiyya practice, except perhaps when it is choreographed and "faked" in the context of folklore.

When it is part of devotional offices, *ma'lūf* is called *'aml* 'work', 'craft' and has a religious purpose, though it is also lively and stimulating to the senses. The texts, full of devotion and exaltation, some exquisite, are an apt continuation and affirmation of *dhikr*. The music and its rhythm drive toward special consciousness of the divine. *Nūbāt 'Īsāwiyya* are usually shorter than in secular *ma'lūf*, but like *ma'lūf* they begin with verses of classical poetry, improvised solo (*qaṣīda*, *nashīd*) in free rhythm with considerable melisma. Choral selections follow with mounting tension through the *brāwal* to a quick-paced *khitm* 'conclusion', which usually ends with the rapid repetition of the name of God or a brief formula. Then the next *nūba* begins with its sedate and mellifluous *nashīd*. Since the *nūbāt* are relatively short, the alternation between the calm of the *nashīd* and the mounting ebullience of the choral segments is pronounced and has a singular effect. The 'Īsāwiyya are conscious of the distinction between the repertoire of *ma'lūf* and extraneous material from the folk and popular milieus, but they are not purists in practice. Normally they hold more rigidly to *ma'lūf* at the outset and insert more folk material as they progress, sometimes ending with sheer folk music (which remains, nevertheless, devotional: typically a lively panegyric to a local saint).

Instruments are less welcome for *'aml* in the *zāwiya* than on more frankly musical occasions outside, and rhythm instruments are preferred over melodic instruments. The instrument par excellence for many brotherhoods is the *bandīr*, a circular frame drum with snares. The single-headed, vase-shaped *darbūka* is also used, particularly when there are melodic instruments. When there is an emphasis on the *ma'lūf* character of the music, a leading shaykh may play the *ṭār*, a small tambourine, de rigeur in secular *ma'lūf*. Preferred melodic instruments are the *zukra* (a double-reed conical aerophone) and the *mizwid* (a bagpipe). Both of these are folk instruments appropriate for the outdoors, and their exclusion from the *zāwiya* is understandable. The *zukra* has a wide range and prodigious capabilities, and Tunisia has many local virtuosos. When the *zukra* is used with 'Īsāwiyya singing, there are many improvised excursions between verses and selections, drawing on a wide range of musical material, delighting listeners and enhancing the effect of the *'aml*.

In Sufi theory, *wajd* 'ecstasy' is a heightened state of consciousness in which the devotee draws near the divine. The 'Īsāwiyya call their ecstatic states *jadb* 'captivation', 'being carried away' and *takhmīr* 'leavening', 'fermentation'. A mild form of *jadb* occurs spontaneously, even during *dhikr*, among both participants and spectators. A person appears to faint and is eventually revived by the shaykh. There is always characteristic body movement during devotions. In *dhikr* people sit cross-legged and sway back and forth. Those who sense ecstasy approaching will stand up, with more pronounced swaying and knee movements, until they collapse in *jadb*. When *takhmīr* is to be intentionally induced, it begins at a fixed point in the music, typically after the *mjarrad* section. The voluntary participants stand in a row, holding hands, sway forward and backward, and bend the knees. When one falls, the row is closed and the others continue. Those in *jadb* remain essentially immobile until the shaykh revives them. This "standard" *takhmīr* is still not uncommon.

Rarely seen today is the *takhmīr* behavior which has drawn so much curiosity and scholarly interest to the 'Īsāwiyya. It requires men of strength, experience, and a particular disposition. In *takhmīr* they do not faint but appear to acquire exceptional powers. One, called 'Akkāsha, wears a woolen hooded *qashshabiyya* and is fettered with chains, held firmly by several others. He shakes the chains, often breaking them, and makes the other men appear insubstantial. Others take on the stereotypical behavior of certain animals, such as a chicken, camel, or cat, and may perform amazing feats. The chief practice, however, involves those who inflict bodily assaults on themselves with no apparent injury. This is associated with scorpion-eating; older accounts imply that scorpions were routine fare during the *takhmīr 'Isāwī*. A later innovation in Tunisia was chewing and swallowing lightbulbs. There are also those who puncture themselves with long, sharp awl-like instruments or lacerate themselves with swords, and those who roll in a bed of cactus leaves, piercing their bare torsos with spines. All this is done with no apparent pain and, as some medical experts have reported, with no particular aftereffects.

Outside the *zāwiya*: *Kharja* and *ḥaḍra*

On festive occasions—all of which were traditionally religious—the brotherhoods typically served as masters of ceremony, and the activities centered on the *zāwiya*. A high point of a celebration was the *kharja* 'procession'. This practice has abated but not disappeared.

Members of the *ṭarīqa* and their supporters take the flags and emblems from the *zāwiya*, prepare instruments of music and sometimes of *takhmīr*, and parade through the streets. *Dhikr* is performed before leaving and occasionally en route, but most of the activity in *kharja* consists of chanting and playing instruments, sometimes with a modicum of pyrotechnics. Earlier accounts mention feats of *takhmīr*. The 'Īsāwiyya perform the most popular selections of their repertoire. *Zukra* and drums are kept busy, and a crowd follows along. There is a mildly military air about all this. Smaller-scale *kharjāt* are organized for family celebrations, such as weddings and circumcisions.

At its destination, the *kharja* disbands and a *ḥaḍra* 'immanence', 'holy presence' is performed. *Kharja* is not a prerequisite to *ḥaḍra*; indeed, even regular *zāwiya* devotions may be so called. There is, however, a sense of something out of the ordinary: something more solemn or compelling than is usual. Holy personages—saints or prophets—are expected to attend and impart their blessing. The believers desire union with these beings in the higher sphere, just as there is a union of the participants through music and movement. Some seek boons in their personal lives. At family events they hope for blessings and good portents to grace the wedding or circumcision. And of course there is enjoyment, and celebration.

A *ḥaḍra* begins with *dhikr*, including special invocations for the occasion. There may also be recitation of the Qur'ān. An ample session of *'aml* is usual, including traditional songs for the occasion. Some individuals almost always experience "ordinary" *wajd*, and there may also be *takhmīr* lines or "specialist" manifestations.

Traditionally a *ḥaḍra* was imperative for any momentous event, from community festivals and pilgrimages to individual family occasions. It belonged to the category of things which could not be omitted without risking misfortune and whose proper consummation was a guarantee of support from on high. Today many see it as entertainment, and there are more popular, more fashionable forms of that.

Women and the 'Īsāwiyya

In describing the 'Īsāwiyya and other Sufi brotherhoods, there is no need to avoid masculine words that exclude women, for only men (and boys) belong to the brotherhood, participate in the offices, perform the *'aml*, join hands in *takhmīr* rows, and the rest. However, women are almost always present, even if they are relegated to separate "invisible" rooms. Increasingly, they provide a raison d'être for the brotherhood. Their devotion, spiritual experience, therapeutic practices, and *takhmīr* are certainly no further from Sufi ideals than those of the brothers. Likewise, their response to the musical aspects of 'Īsāwiyya practice, to the *dhikr*, and to the music they learn in the *zāwiya* and pass on to their children is essential for the life of the *ṭarīqa*. Nevertheless, the brothers are men and the brotherhood is conceived of in male terms.

THE ʿĪSĀWIYYA IN MODERN TUNISIA

Reform movements throughout the twentieth century sapped the vitality of the brotherhoods. At its inception the independent government was openly hostile to the ʿĪsāwiyya and other brotherhoods, dispossessing them and demolishing or desacralizing many *zwāyā*. Cultural politics tended to regulate and tone down the aspects of their practices that were considered bizarre and relegate these to the status of *arts populaires*. Secular institutions, including conservatories, usurped many of their former functions. The postindependence generation has turned away from tradition, ridiculing rather than venerating the ways of elders. There is a tone of nostalgia, but the current cultural climate in Tunisia emphasizes "renewal" and innovation, not revival. When one asks a young couple planning marriage if they intend to have an ʿĪsāwiyya evening, one may well be answered with a laugh.

Early in the period of colonization the ʿĪsāwiyya appeared to be accommodating tourists from Europe and offering them "performances." In recent decades it appeared that younger people with ʿĪsāwiyya experience were commercializing their knowledge and selling ʿĪsāwiyya traditions in sanitized form to tourists, who could thus experience simulated ʿĪsāwiyya performances in their hotels. Perhaps inevitably, a further development has followed: the internal folklorization of ʿĪsāwiyya and other traditions, with modern Tunisians themselves as tourists, watching a show of their own heritage.

Many people still attend a *zāwiya* for the same reasons as ever; there are still weekly *dhikr* devotions, ʿĪsāwiyya weddings, *kharjāt*, pilgrimages, and even, perhaps, full-scale *takhmīr* exercises. But the future must be left to reveal itself.

REFERENCES

Brown, Kenneth L. 1985. "The Discrediting of a Sufi Movement in Tunisia." In *Islamic Dilemmas: Reformers, Nationalists, and Industrialization*, ed. Ernest Gellner, 146–168. The Southern Shore of the Mediterranean: Religion and Society No. 25. Amsterdam: Mouton.

Brunel, René. 1926. *Essai sue la confrérie religieuse des Aîssâoûa au Maroc*. Paris: Geuthner.

Dermenghem, Émile, and Léo Barbès. 1951. "Essai sur la hadhra des Aïsaouia d'Algérie." *Révue Africaine* 84:289–314.

Johnson, Pamela Ryden. 1979. "A Sufi Shrine in Modern Tunisia". Ph.D. dissertation, University of California, Berkeley.

Jones, L. JaFran. 1977. "The ʿIsawiya of Tunisia and Their Music." Ph.D. dissertation, University of Washington.

———. 1982. "The Role of Sufi Brotherhoods in the Preservation of Tunisian Art Music." In *Essays in Islamic and Comparative Studies*, ed. Ismaʿil Raji al-Faruqi, 109–120. Herndon, Va.: International Institute of Islamic Thought.

Keddie, Nikki R., ed. 1972. *Scholars, Saints, and Sufis: Muslim Religious Institutions since 1500*. Berkeley: University of California Press.

Nayyāl, Muḥammad al-Buhlī. 1965. *al-Ḥaqīqa al-taʾrīkhiyya li'l-taṣawwuf al-islāmī*. Tūnis: Najāḥ.

Rizqī, al-Ṣādiq. 1967. *al-Aghānī al-Tūnisiyya*. Tunis: al-Dār al-Tūnisiyya Li'l-Nashr.

Trimingham, J. Spencer. 1971. *The Sufi Orders in Islam*. Oxford: Clarendon.

Zghonda, Fatḥī. 1991. *Al-Ṭarīqa al-Sulāmiya ashʿāruhā wa-alḥānuhā*. Carthage: Bayt al-ḥikma.

Music of the Jews of Djerba, Tunisia

Ruth Davis

The Jewish Community
Music of Ḥāra Ṣghīra in 1929
Music of Ḥāra Kebīra in 1978
Musical and Social Change
Relationships between Sacred and Secular Songs

Djerba is a small Mediterranean island lying just off the southern edge of Tunisia's eastern coastline, not far from Libya. It is said to be the land of the lotus-eaters in Homer's *Odyssey*, and its mythical image as a paradise has some reflection in reality. It is a fertile island inhabited by a Berber majority belonging to the Kharijite Muslim sect, Arabs, black Africans, and an ancient Jewish community whose legendary origins date back to the Babylonian exile—that is, the exodus following the destruction of the first temple in Jerusalem in 586 B.C.E. Until the radical social and political upheavals of the 1940s and 1950s, these disparate ethnic and religious groups lived together peacefully and relatively prosperously, supporting themselves by fishing, farming, trading, and crafts such as weaving and pottery (among the Muslims) and jewelry (among the Jews).

THE JEWISH COMMUNITY

The Jews are concentrated in two villages: Ḥāra Kebīra 'big Jewish quarter' lies on the outskirts of Houmt Souk, the island's main port and market town, while Ḥāra Ṣghīra 'little Jewish quarter' nestles among olive groves in the open countryside some seven kilometers inland. In local accounts, Ḥāra Kebīra is the younger community, associated particularly with migrations from the Western Maghrib after the expulsion of the Jews from Spain in 1492. It is also the more worldly, and superior in scholarly prestige. Ḥāra Ṣghīra, in contrast, is the holier settlement, linked directly with the original migrations from Jerusalem. Its inhabitants are all Cohenim, that is, descendants of the priestly caste, and on its outskirts stands a miraculous synagogue known as the Ghrība (Arabic, 'lonely one' or 'stranger'; figure 1), whose foundation is believed to contain a stone from King Solomon's temple. Venerated by Muslims as well as Jews, the Ghrība attracts pilgrims from the Tunisian mainland, Libya, and beyond, most notably for the festival of *Lag ba-'omer*, celebrated in early summer with two days of spectacle and processions accompanied by music making. (For a detailed description of the festivities at the Ghrība, see Udovitch and Valensi 1984:125–131.)

FIGURE 1 Rabbis in the Ghrība, Ḥāra Ṣghīra. Photo by Ruth Davis, 1978.

The music of the Jews of Djerba was first documented by Robert Lachmann, who visited the island in the spring of 1929, bringing an Edison phonograph. His twenty-two recordings from Ḥāra Ṣghīra form the basis of his classic study *Jewish Cantillation and Song in the Isle of Djerba*, published posthumously in 1940 in an incomplete English translation (only nine of the twenty-two music transcriptions were included). In 1978, the complete text appeared in the original German, edited by Edith Gerson-Kiwi. Lachmann's own wax cylinder recordings are held in the department of ethnomusicology at the Museum for Ethnomusicology (formerly the Phonogram archive) in Berlin. Wax cylinder copies taken from copper negatives of his originals (a technique for which the Phonogram archive was famous) are held in the National Sound Archive of the Jewish National and University Library in Jerusalem. These copies have recently been transferred onto tape, thus becoming newly accessible to scholars.

In 1960, Wolfgang Laade recorded a circumcision ceremony in Ḥāra Kebīra which appears with a photograph and notes in the second volume of his three-volume anthology of Tunisian music (1962). However, to my knowledge, my own research in Ḥāra Kebīra, in the spring of 1978, represents the only large-scale survey of Jewish music on Djerba since Lachmann. A comparison between Lachmann's findings and my own, nearly fifty years apart, reveals the major social and cultural changes affecting both communities since his visit.

MUSIC OF ḤĀRA ṢGHĪRA IN 1929

Lachmann's original purpose was to discover whether the supposed age of the Jewish community was reflected in its musical traditions: he based his research in Ḥāra Ṣghīra on the assumption that its relatively isolated position would have served as a buffer against external influences. In the event, he concluded that Jewish music on Djerba showed no more ancient characteristics than Jewish music on the mainland (Lachman and Gerson-Kiwi 1978:28). Nevertheless, he justified his detailed study, based on complete musical and textual transcriptions and analyses of all twenty-two recorded examples, on the grounds that it constituted the first investigation into Tunisian Jewish cantillation and song.

Like Near Eastern music generally, that of Ḥāra Ṣghīra was an oral tradition. Exceptionally, it was entirely vocal: while most orthodox Jewish communities forbid the use of musical instruments in synagogues and on religious holidays, the rabbis of Ḥāra Ṣghīra forbade the very presence of musical instruments in the village. This extreme position at first threatened Lachmann's research; the community mistook his Edison phonograph, with its horn, for a musical instrument, and special expiatory prayers had to be offered before the machine was eventually accepted (Lachman and Gerson-Kiwi 1978:28). Lachmann recorded three types of repertoire: liturgical cantillation (exs. 1–9), festival songs (exs. 10–15), and women's songs (exs. 16–22). The first two genres, based on written Hebrew texts, were performed exclusively by men; the last, in the Judeo-Arabic vernacular, was sung only by women. Each genre is distinguished by its musical system, textual characteristics, and social function, and by its relationship to the musical traditions of the Tunisian-Arab environment.

Liturgical music

Liturgical cantillation denotes the chanting of the Jewish liturgy in free rhythm to melodies classified according to the particular prayers or parts of the Bible with which they are associated. While the relationship between melody and text is therefore fixed, the tunes themselves may vary from one community to the next. The nine examples from Ḥāra Ṣghīra are settings of biblical texts taken from the Pentateuch (exs. 1 and 2), Prophets (ex. 3), Esther (exs. 4 and 9), Psalms (ex. 5), Proverbs (exs. 6 and 7), and Job (Ex. 8). Within the bounds of their flexible intonation, characteristic of the genre as a whole, Lachmann describes their melodies as essentially diatonic with occasional chromatic digressions, approximating the *maqāmāt* 'melodic modes' of Tunisian urban music.

Festival music

The festival songs, *piyyutim* (singular, *piyyut* 'poem'), are settings of Hebrew rhymed poetry. Like liturgical cantillation, the *piyyut* is a genre common to all Jewish communities, but it is far more versatile. In the synagogue, *piyyutim* form part of the liturgy and are sung spontaneously at climactic points in the service; they are also sung in domestic prayer and for entertainment in family and communal celebrations. While certain texts are confined to specific regions or communities, others are known to Jews everywhere; but in either case, the melodies generally reflect local traditions. Sung by an entire congregation or domestic gathering, *piyyut* tunes are popular in the most general sense of the word. Lachmann's six examples are associated with particular religious holidays (Rosh Hashana, Pesach, and Purim), weddings, and in one case circumcisions; their melodies, he maintains, belong to the various *maqāmāt*, *īqā'āt* 'rhythmic-metric cycles', and styles of Tunisian urban music. Individually, according to Lachmann, they reflect classical, popular, and Ottoman musical styles; in one case, he hypothesizes that they reflect specifically Jewish styles. However, in associating the melodies with Tunisian urban traditions, Lachmann cautions that "this does not mean that they are taken from the Arab-Tunisian repertoire, but only that they are conceived in a similar style" (Lachman and Gerson-Kiwi 1978:126).

Women's music

Lachmann's women's songs focus on biblical and other themes specifically related to women. Though metrically ambiguous, they are in definite time and are accompanied by hand clapping. Compared with festival and liturgial music, their melodic range is smaller, their pitch fluctuation is more pronounced, and their tonal system is generally less defined. Lachmann notes that their melodies bear no relation to the *maqāmāt* or *īqā'āt* of Tunisian urban traditions but belong, rather, to the sphere of rural music.

Lachmann's study is a classic in comparative musicology. In the introduction to her edition of the original German text, Gerson-Kiwi describes it as "a musical portrait" whose "method of detailed analysis of a single unit, supported by parallels from the musical traditions of various peoples," was pioneering in its time. Apart from relating the Jewish repertoires to those of the immediate Arab environment, Lachmann draws detailed comparisons with a startling array of other Eastern, folk, ancient, and Western (notated) traditions; the result is "a compendium of ideas and methods" with far-reaching general musical significance (1978:15–16, 21). The chapter on liturgical cantillation, for instance, includes, among other topics, penetrating discourses on the nature of musical time, the transcription and analysis of "free rhythm" and its various manifestations and principles, methods of notating pitch and its transposition, the relationship between text and musical structures, the concept of the musical phrase, and criteria for melodic integrity in oral traditions. Issues such as these remain of pressing interest to ethnomusicologists today.

MUSIC OF ḤĀRA KEBĪRA IN 1978

The social and musical conditions I discovered in Ḥāra Kebīra (Davis 1985) were radically different from those Lachmann described. The creation of the state of Israel in 1948 and Tunisian independence in 1956 had provoked waves of mass emigration: in general, the Jews from the north, including Tunis, who had come under French cultural influence during the protectorate, emigrated to France, while those from Djerba and the southern mainland, where French influence was weaker, gravitated toward Israel. In 1929, according to Lachmann, there were 3,500 Jews in Ḥāra Kebīra and 1,500 in Ḥāra Ṣghīra; by the late 1970s the figures had dropped to about 800 and 300 respectively. Continuing emigration since then has further depleted the community. At first, the abandoned Jewish homes remained empty; then, in the late 1960s, Muslim Tunisians from the mainland began to move in. A mosque was erected at the entrance of Ḥāra Kebīra, its minaret towering above all the other buildings in the flat landscape, and a crackling recording of the *adhān*—the call to prayer—could now be heard five times a day. The mutual trust established over the centuries between Djerban

Jews and Muslims tended not to be extended to the newcomers, who constituted an unprecedented intrusion into the *ḥāra*. Economic factors also undoubtedly came into play: in general, it was the wealthier Jews who had remained behind, while the new arrivals were among the poorest inhabitants of the island.

MUSICAL AND SOCIAL CHANGE

FIGURE 2 Rabbi from Ḥāra Kebīra reciting prayers at home. Photo by Ruth Davis, 1978.

In contrast to Lachmann's examples, the songs I recorded in Ḥāra Kebīra extended beyond the bounds of Tunisian tradition to embrace other Arabic and European repertoires and styles. Both men and women sang sacred Hebrew songs, as well as secular songs in Arabic and modern Hebrew: liturgical cantillation was the only genre that remained exclusive to men (figure 2). There was no specific repertoire of women's songs, nor was there any repertoire representing rural traditions. Various musical instruments were used, and on certain occasions mixed bands of Jewish and Muslim male professional musicians were hired to perform in Jewish homes.

Some of these musical differences may have existed at the time of Lachmann's visit. The Jews of Ḥāra Kebīra maintained that their rabbis had never imposed a total ban on musical instruments but had merely prohibited their use in the synagogues and on religious holidays (as is customary in orthodox Jewish communities). Their more exposed position next to the island's main port and capital, their stronger links to trade and scholarship, and their generally more worldly outlook may have made the inhabitants of Ḥāra Kebīra historically more receptive than those of Ḥāra Ṣghīra to new secular musical trends—including foreign Arab music—from the mainland. Since the beginning of the twentieth century, Egyptian songs introduced by visiting artists and promoted in the newly emerging recording market had become fashionable in Tunis, where Jewish musicians had long had a prominent role. [See PATRONAGE AND POLICY IN TUNISIAN ART MUSIC.] Meanwhile, the influx of Jewish refugees from Tripolitania at around the same time had further enriched the musical life of the capital (al-Mahdī and Marzūqī 1981: 23–35). As for Lachmann's "women's songs," not even the older women of Ḥāra Kebīra had any recollection of such a genre: they insisted that they had always sung the same Arabic songs as their Muslim neighbors, which were also sung by Muslim and Jewish men. The only difference, they maintained, was in the accompaniment: the men sang to a variety of instruments (see below) while the women were confined to the *darbūka* and hand clapping.

Despite these intrinsic differences, certain aspects of the musical culture of Ḥāra Kebīra in 1978 may be attributed to specific social changes that had occurred since Lachmann's research: the introduction of modern, secular Hebrew education; the large-scale emigration of the majority of the community, including most of its musicians; the development of tourism and modern transportation; and the introduction of radio, television, and other mass media.

Education

In the 1940s, Zionist emissaries from Palestine established modern, secular Hebrew schools on the island for both girls and boys, to supplement the traditional *yeshivot*, religious Hebrew schools from which girls were excluded. This new initiative had the full support of the Djerban rabbis, who had previously resisted attempts by the Alliance Israélite Universelle—an organization (based in Paris) dedicated to improving the social and educational conditions of the Jews of North Africa and the Levant—to introduce French secular education there. Although girls and boys were educated in separate buildings, the curriculum was the same. In addition to purely academic subjects, the emissaries introduced secular songs, often with Zionist themes, composed by Jews of European origin, and *piyyutim* belonging to Ashkenazi traditions (those relating to German and Eastern European Jews) and Ladino (Judeo-Spanish) traditions. After 1948, the dissemination of such foreign repertoires was facilitated through contacts with relatives abroad, and some of the new *piyyut* melodies entered synagogue and domestic worship, supplementing the traditional Djerban tunes.

In general it was the girls, whose social outlets were otherwise more restricted, who took greater advantage of the new educational opportunities. Free from the conflicting demands of the *yeshivot* and later of earning a living, girls had more time than boys to devote to secular studies; and many girls continued to attend the Hebrew school until they married, often when they were well into their twenties or older. The girls' school also served as a general meeting place or club hosting a range of extracurricular activities, including music making. Since Djerban women were still barred from synagogue worship, a devout group held services in the school instead, a custom introduced in the early 1970s by the daughter of the director of the modern Hebrew school on her return from religious studies abroad. The girls literally read rather than chanted the liturgy—cantillation remained the exclusive domain of men— but on the sabbath and other holidays, the girls' services were interspersed with *piyyutim* sung to melodies they had learned at school. On festive afternoons, while the boys played soccer outside, the girls gathered in the school to celebrate with readings, modern Hebrew songs, and games. They sang in unison, without instruments but sometimes accompanied by hand clapping.

Tourism

Since the late 1960s, a coastal *zone touristique* had been developed, with a string of luxury hotels and discotheques, providing new business outlets for the Jewish jewelers of Ḥāra Kebīra and expanding musical horizons. Catering primarily to a European clientele, the tourist venues promoted almost exclusively Western—especially French—popular music. In 1972, an international airport opened on Djerba, facilitating visits to and from relatives abroad. By 1978, the annual *Lag ba-'omer* celebrations at the Ghrība, traditionally a setting for exchanges of musical repertoires, had become a focal point for family reunions and a touristic bonanza as pilgrims arrived on charter flights via Paris.

Mass media

Probably the most intrusive threat to traditional culture came from the mass media: transistor radios since the 1960s and television soon thereafter were bringing contemporary European lifestyles and values directly into the home; reinforced by commercial records and cassettes, they were also providing continuous exposure to an ever-changing spectrum of popular Tunisian, Middle Eastern, and European music. Many Jewish families had substantial collections of French popular music and modern Hebrew songs on records and cassettes imported from abroad. French songs were conspicuously absent from live performance, but many of the Tunisian and foreign Arabic songs popularized in the media were sung by both men and women at weddings and other domestic celebrations. Particularly popular were songs recorded by famous Tunisian Jewish singers of the 1930s and 1940s such as Shaykh al-Afriāt and Ḥabība Msīka; some used the *franco-arabe* dialect then in vogue—though this dialect is now now generally despised by Tunisian Muslims and obsolete in contemporary song lyrics.

Arab songs were typically performed by bands of male musicians formed and hired for specific occasions. Mass emigration had depleted the Jewish community of instrumentalists, and those who remained mostly played only the *darbūka* and *ṭār:* of the two who played the *'ūd sharqī,* only one, the middle-aged merchant Jacob Bṣīrī, performed in public. As a result, Muslims—invariably Djerbans from outside the village—were hired to make up a band. The standard ensemble for wedding celebrations comprised Jacob Bṣīrī as solo singer and *'ūd* player, with fellow Jews on the *darbūka* and *ṭār* and Muslims playing violins and accordion. The entire band would double as chorus, and it was usually amplified.

Weddings

The typical Jewish wedding in Ḥāra Kebīra was a lavish affair celebrated for two weeks preceding the marriage ceremony itself, which was conducted by a rabbi in the groom's house. Ritual preparations of the bride and groom were punctuated by nights of feasting and music making, at the bride's home during the first week and at the groom's house during the second week. The principal celebrations were held in the large inner courtyard: the male guests sat at tables laden with hot food and drink, while the women and girls huddled against the surrounding walls. The musicians sat at a table supporting microphones and jugs of *bukha* 'fig spirits', on a dais erected at the far end of the courtyard. The voices of the guests rose in competition with the amplified music: guests neither sang nor danced, and they generally seemed to ignore the musicians.

Arab songs accompanied by the *darbūka* and hand clapping were sung by women at all-female gatherings, such as those marking the various ritual preparations of the bride; the most important of these were the blanching of her skin with a paste of flour and water and the dyeing of her skin with henna. Each ritual took place on a separate evening in the bride's home and was followed by celebrations that included music making. On a typical occasion, the bride—attended by her family and close friends—would have her skin blanched in small room opening onto the courtyard; then she would remain recumbent on a sofa while the rest of the guests sat on the floor outside, consuming soft drinks and sweet foods and intermittently raising high-pitched ululations. There were no hired musicians: instead, a group of guests ranging from small children to old women would sing a continuous stream of Arab songs, clapping their hands and beating the *darbūka,* apparently ignored by everyone else. Their songs were part of the general ambience, like the French popular songs which would be simultaneously blasting out from a record player.

Other festivities

On certain occasions, considered holy, such as the last night of a wedding celebration after the religious ceremony or the *Lag ba-ʿomer* rituals at the Ghrība, Arab songs were banned by the rabbis and only *piyyutim* were allowed; these were performed by a reduced band of Jewish musicians led by Jacob Bṣīrī on the *ʿūd*, without amplification (figure 3). The term *piyuṭ* was also applied to a genre of Judeo-Arabic songs about the Ghrība, which were performed at the annual festivities alongside the regular *piyuṭim* to Hebrew texts.

FIGURE 3 Jacob Bṣīrī, musician from Ḥāra Kebīra, singing *piyyutim* with *ʿūd* accompaniment at the *Lag ba-ʿomer* celebrations at the Ghrība. Photo by Ruth Davis, 1978.

The Ghrība celebrations took place in the inner courtyard of a *funduq* 'hostel' adjacent to the synagogue, where pilgrims of modest means set up temporary lodgings. Streamers bearing Tunisian flags, portraits of President Bourguiba posted on the walls, and a conspicuous array of policemen gave the occasion the character of a national holiday. On the two festival afternoons, a golden wagon decked with hundreds of empty candleholders was wheeled out of the synagogue into the courtyard, where it became the focal point of a mock auction to aid the rabbis of the Ghrība. A pilgrim from the crowd tossed a shawl to the auctioneer standing on the wagon, and bids were made. At the highest bid the musicians struck up a *piyyut,* dancing and turning as they played, the crowd cheered, and the shawl was draped over the wagon. The ritual was repeated until by the early evening the wagon was covered in multicolored scarves. On the first day it was wheeled back into the Ghrība, the shawls were removed, and the candleholders were filled with hundreds of burning lights. On the second day, it was wheeled in full array in a procession led by the musicians, the pilgrims joining in the singing and cars hooting alongside, down the hill into Ḥāra Ṣghīra, where the ceremonies closed in the courtyard of a small synagogue, with speeches in honor of the president.

RELATIONSHIPS BETWEEN SACRED AND SECULAR SONGS

In Jewish communities throughout the world, the melodies of well-known songs in the vernacular have been transferred to Hebrew texts, and secular texts have often served as models for Hebrew poems set to the same tunes. Lachmann believed that the six *piyyutim* he recorded in Ḥāra Ṣghīra constituted a unique melodic repertoire, which merely adopted stylistic features associated with various Tunisian Arab urban traditions. In contrast, certain *piyyutim* I recorded in Ḥāra Kebīra were identified, by the singers or by informants from outside the community, with particular songs in the vernacular.

I have found and illustrated (Davis 1986; Davis in press) melodic and in some cases textual relationships between six *piyyutim* from Ḥāra Kebīra and the six secular songs with which they were identified. Five secular songs represent Ukrainian, Ladino, Libyan, and (in two cases) Tunisian-Andalusian traditions; the sixth, "*'Andik baḥrīya, yā rāyis*," an Arabic song popular in the media, was variously described as Egyptian, Lebanese, or Tunisian in origin. Some Muslim musicians attributed this sixth song to the celebrated Egyptian composer and singer Muḥammad 'Abd al-Wahhāb; others associated it with the Lebanese singer Wadī' al-Ṣāfī, whose version was frequently broadcast on Tunisian radio. However, Jacob Bṣīrī, the chief musician of Ḥāra Kebīra, said that it was a genuinely Tunisian song, originally performed in Tunis in the 1930s by the Jewish female singer Habiba Msika.

The Ukrainian and Ladino melodies, set to the liturgical texts "*Lekha dodi likrat khala*" and "*Tsur mishelo akchalnu*," had apparently been imported to Djerba as *piyyutim*. In contrast, the two Tunisian-Andalusian melodies were described as traditional Djerban settings of their respective texts. The melodies themselves belong to the repertoire known as *al-ma'lūf*, which is said to have beeen introduced by Muslims and Jews fleeing Spain after the Christian reconquest. The *piyyutim* identified with "*'Andik baḥrīya, yā rāyis*" and the Libyan song were of more recent origin. According to Jacob Bṣīrī, they had been composed in Tunis in the 1930s, when he was a young man; in each case, the Hebrew version was inspired by both the words and the tune of its Arab counterpart.

The *piyyut* "*go'eli ya*" clearly has textual as well as melodic correspondences with its Libyan model, "*Yā mā yā ghālīya*"—an Arabic song about a woman who vows to remain faithful to her lover even though he has often betrayed her. The *piyyut* prays for the redemption of the Jews of the Diaspora and affirms their trust in God's faithfulness. It has no written text; it is sung voluntarily by the congregation when the *sefer torah* 'scroll of the law' is taken out of the ark and carried in procession around a synagogue. Muslim musicians told me that "*Yā mā yā ghālīya*" was brought to Tunisia by Jewish refugees from the Fazzan region of Tripolitania in the early years of the twentieth century. Apparently it was very popular among Jewish musicians of Tunis in the 1930s; some Jews of Ḥāra Kebīra associated with a Jewish female singer called Dalel. Jacob Bṣīrī, who had sung both the Arabic and the Hebrew version, said that the *piyyut* modeled on "*go'eli ya*" was written by his cousin, Gaston Bṣīrī, at that time.

Figure 4 shows the Arabic and Hebrew versions of this song. The Arab song comprises an indefinite number of six-line stanzas alternating with a six-line refrain; the stanzas and refrain are set to the same melody. The opening refrain, as sung by a Jewish woman with a Muslim friend playing the *darbūka*, follows (the rhyme scheme is noted in parentheses):

Refrain
wā yā mā yā ghālīya (a)
li naḥsibik khawwān yā ghālīya (ba)
li naḥsibik khawwān (b)

FIGURE 4 (a) Opening refrain of Arabic song "*Yā mā yā ghālīya*" as sung by a Jewish woman from Ḥāra Kebīra. (b) First stanza and refrain of its Hebrew counterpart "*go'eli ya*," as sung by Jacob Bṣīrī, a musician from Ḥāra Kebīra. Transcription by Ruth Davis.

wā yā mā yā ghālīya (a)
ya shmātat el-'adwān fīk ū fīya (ba)
li naḥsibik khawwān (b)

O precious one
We'll consider you a traitor, O precious one
We'll consider you a traitor
O precious one
How the enemies will gossip maliciously about you and me
We'll consider you a traitor.

I recorded the same song, performed by Jacob Bṣīrī accompanied by a mixed band of Muslims and Jews, at a Jewish wedding party in Ḥāra Kebīra.

The *piyuṭ* comprises three stanzas, each of which has five lines followed by a single-line refrain. Following are the first verse and refrain as sung by Jacob Bṣīrī, accompanying himself on the *'ūd*, in the courtyard of his home.

Verse
go'eli ya (a)
el melekh ne'eman go'eli ya (ba)
el melekh ne'eman (b)
go'eli ya (a)
ga al ben hagvirah hayefihfiyah (a)

Refrain
melekh ne'eman (b)

The Lord is my redeemer
God is a faithful king—the Lord is my redeemer
God is a faithful king
The Lord is my redeemer
He redeemed the son of the extraordinarily beautiful lady.
(Refrain) The Lord is my redeemer.

A comparison between the two shows how the rhyme scheme of the Arab refrain provides an exact model for the first verse and refrain of the *piyyut*; in the following two stanzas of the *piyyut,* the same pattern is repeated with different rhymes.

In the other five examples from Ḥāra Kebīra, the melodic relationship between the sacred and secular sources is not always as clear-cut; nor are there always comparable textual correspondences. In the Tunisian-Andalusian melodies, individual phrases are rearranged and varied; it is possible that Lachmann intepreted features corresponding to Tunisian musicians' notions of melodic identity as evidence of mere "stylistic similarity." However, the fact that "traditional" settings of *piyyutim* dating from the eighteenth century were identified with specific tunes from the Tunisian-Andalusian repertoire suggests that transferring melodies between sacred and secular texts was a well-established Djerban custom. Moreover, the identification of certain *piyyut* melodies with popular mass-media songs of the 1930s or later indicates that this traditional practice survived well into modern times.

My findings in Ḥāra Kebīra call into question Lachmann's assumption that the *piyyutim* of Ḥāra Ṣghīra constituted a unique melodic repertoire. Lachmann maintained that the singers there "had scarcely any contact with secular urban music" (Lachmann and Gerson-Kiwi 1978:128). However, the proximity of the village to the Ghrība, a famous pilgrimage site attracting Muslims and Jews from the Tunisian mainland and abroad, and particularly the annual *Lag ba-'omer* celebrations, would surely have provided opportunities for exposure to external repertoires: even in 1929, the community may not have been quite as isolated as Lachmann supposed. Further examination of this historic material (as noted above, it has now been transferred onto tape) may yet reveal that the practice of adapting secular tunes to sacred Hebrew texts was also part of the tradition of Ḥāra Ṣghīra, just as it appears to have been in Ḥāra Kebīra, only seven kilometers away.

REFERENCES

Davis, Ruth. 1985. "Songs of the Jews on the Island of Djerba: A Comparison between Two Surveys." *Musica Judaica* 7:23–33.

———. 1986. "Some Relations between Three *Piyuṭim* from Djerba and Three Arab Songs." *Maghreb Review* 11:134–44.

———. In press. "*Piyuṭ* Melodies as Mirrors of Social Change in Djerba, Tunisia." *Musica Judaica* 14.

Laade, Wolfgang. 1962. *Tunisia*. Vol. 2, *Religious Songs and Cantillations from Tunisia*. Folkways FW 8862.

Lachmann, Robert. 1940. *Jewish Cantillation and Song in the Isle of Djerba*. Jerusalem: Azriel Press, Archives of Oriental Music, Hebrew University.

Lachmann, Robert, and Edith Gerson-Kiwi, eds. 1978. *Gesänge der Juden auf der Insel Djerba*. Yuval Monograph Series 7. Jerusalem: Magnus Press, Hebrew University.

al-Mahdī, Ṣāliḥ, and Muḥammad Marzūqī. 1981. *Al-Ma'had al-Rashīdī*. Tunis: Ministry of Cultural Affairs.

Udovitch, Abraham L., and Lucette Valensi. 1984. *The Last Arab Jews: The Communities of Jerba, Tunisia*. London: Harwood Academic.

Section 2
The Eastern Arab World: The Mashriq

In contrast to the Maghrib—'the place where the sun sets'—the Mashriq, from a historic Arab perspective, is where the sun rises: that is, in the lands of Iraq, Syria, Lebanon, Palestine, Jordan and Egypt. The Mashriq—with its cosmopolitan urban centers such as Cairo, Beirut, and Jerusalem; its historic institutions, including the thousand-year-old Azhar University and mosque; and its aggressive development of the mass media in the twentieth century—has become in a sense a cultural heartland for the Arab world. Historically at the forefront of Arab political, economic, and cultural life, the Mashriq is home to centers of education that draw together a wide range of populations ranging from rural to international. Its large mosque and religious establishment train reciters of the Qur'ān and Christian priests. Its modern-day conservatories train symphonic orchestra musicians, members of national folk ensembles, and internationally known stage and session musicians. Historic centers of musical performance such as Aleppo continue to attract student musicians. Until the late twentieth century, most media productions originated in Cairo. Film, television, and recording studios were all located there, drawing performers from other parts of the Arab world who were seeking opportunities. Its relationship with Europe resulted in opera houses and musical theaters, which were sometimes settings of elegance and sophistication but at other times were vilified as institutions of the foreign oppressor. The *mashriqi* amalgam of musical richness draws from the rural and the "folk," the European and the Turkish, and the historically Arab—and from its own versions of the "modern."

Blind musician near Ctesiphon, Iraq.
Photo © Dean Conger, Corbis.

Overview of Music in the Mashriq

Ali Jihad Racy

The music of the Arab world—a vast region extending from western North Africa to the Arabian Peninsula and Mesopotamia—can be studied as one broad domain, particularly if we consider such unifying traits as the prevalence of Islam and Islamic institutions, the predominance of the Arabic language, and the historical, political, and artistic threads that link the various Arab communities. At the same time, however, this music has tremendous internal diversity (figures 1–4).

THE ARAB NEAR EAST

It has been customary for historians and music scholars to distinguish between two major areas: the *Maghrib*, or North Africa; and the *Mashriq*, or the Arab Near East. Although this essay touches on various aspects of Arab music and music history, it will focus on the music of the Mashriq, a large area that incorporates Egypt, the Arabian Peninsula and the Gulf states, Iraq, and the Levant, a subregion comprising Lebanon, Syria, Jordan, and Palestine. Despite their considerable cultural, religious, and musical differences, the inhabitants of the Arab Near East tend to share certain overall historical experiences based on material, cultural, and demographic contacts, and a general identification with intellectual and musical legacies.

FIGURE 1 Drummers at a *zār* ceremony in Doha, Qatar. The diversity of Arab music can be seen in figures 1–4. Photo by Barbara Racy.

HISTORICAL BACKGROUND

The music of the Near Eastern Arab world has historical roots in antiquity, although its overall character owes much to the court traditions and theoretical legacy of medieval Islam. The history of Near Eastern music has been a concern of Arabists, Orientalists, archaeologists, philologists, biographers, historical musicologists, and a few researchers with a leaning toward ethnomusicology and the social sciences. In the early twentieth century, Western scholars—such as A. Z. Idelsohn, Eric Werner, Egon Wellesz, Hans Hickmann, Curt Sachs, and more recently Subḥī Anwar Rashīd—investigated music in Near Eastern antiquity. Their studies covered a wide range of topics, from religious rites, including biblical, Byzantine, and Syrian liturgies, to pharaonic and Sumerian musics and musical instruments. Henry George Farmer, Julian Ribera, Baron Rodolphe d'Erlanger, and later Owen Wright, Amnon Shiloah, George Sawa, and others addressed music in medieval Islamic times. These medievalists discussed topics that included performance practice; biography; music theory and cos-

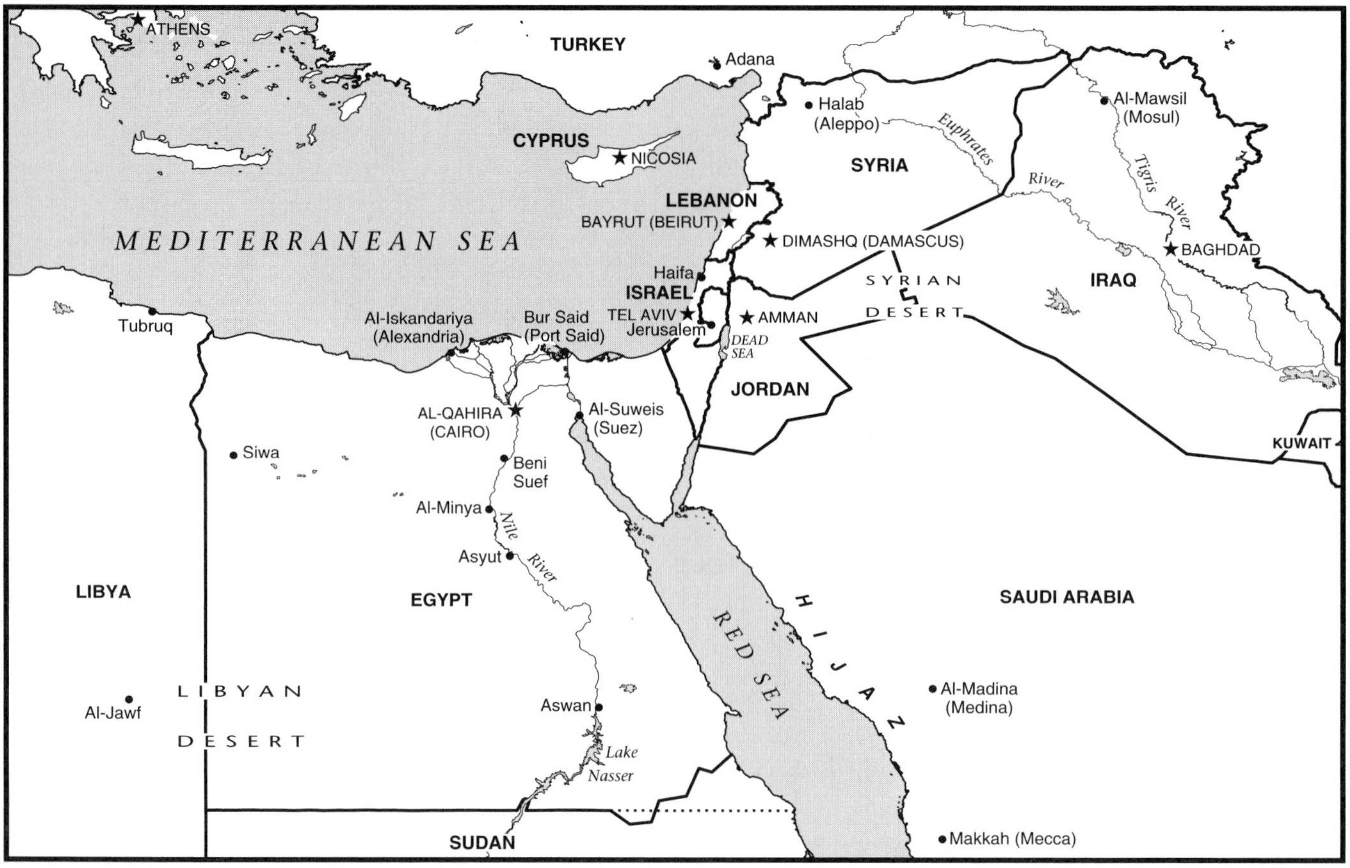

The Mashriq.

mology, with reference to the influence of ancient Greek scholarship; and musical contacts between Europe and the Islamic Near East. Their focus was usually the historical period generally considered as marking the height of Islamic civilization and extending roughly from the early Islamic epoch in Arabia after 632 C.E. to the fall of Baghdad in 1256.

Numerous medieval theoretical treatises have been edited and published in the original Arabic—the language of the Qur'ān and the scientific lingua franca of the medieval Islamic world. The editors included Ghaṭṭās Khashaba, Maḥmūd al-Ḥifnī, Zakariyyā Yūsuf, and Yūsuf Shawqī in Egypt; and Muḥammad Hāshim al-Rajab in Iraq. Some major treatises have been translated and published in Western languages, particularly French, by d'Erlanger, Shiloah, and others.

FIGURE 2 Female ensemble in Doha, Qatar. Photo by Barbara Racy.

Near Eastern music history is usually considerd in terms of well-demarcated epochs, largely on the basis of literary accounts, theoretical (often highly speculative) music treatises, and to a smaller extent pictorial art and other physical artifacts. Musical notation was used in some liturgical traditions and by a few theorists, but it does not constitute a significant source of information. Traditionally, the music has been transmitted orally. Historical constructs, then, reflect the nature and the limitations of sources and seem to be restricted to the more documented, typically formal, or "learned" traditions. Furthermore, such constructs usually imply that musical developments follow social, political, and cultural trends and can be conveniently organized into political periods such as dynasties, and along a linear path of cultural history. Such implications notwithstanding, the various histories testify to the enormous role music has played in secular and religious life in general.

Writings on music in ancient civilization inform us about the cosmological connotations of music and about religious rituals in which music was indispensable. Ac-

FIGURE 3 The Egyptian dancer Fīfī ʿAbduh and her ensemble. Photo by Barbara Racy.

FIGURE 4 The singer Muḥammad ʿAbduh of Saudia Arabia performing with his ensemble. Photo by Barbara Racy.

cordingly, music was also imbued with magical and other supernatural meanings. Also documented are specific music theories and notational devices and various musical instruments, such as harps and lyres in Sumeria and lutes, harps, reed instruments, and trumpets in ancient Egypt. Henry George Farmer's classic *History of Arabian Music to the Thirteenth Century* (1929) indicates that music occupied an important position in pre-Islamic Arabian life as an art and a ritualistic medium. Sung poetry was usually a significant means of social and political expression. Music had supernatural connotations because it was believed to invoke *jinn* 'spirits'. There were folk songs of numerous types, particularly laments and the *ḥidā'*, which was associated with camel-driving. Musical entertainment was typically provided by *qiyān*, female slaves who sang in the homes of wealthy, noble Arab families. Arabs played a variety of instruments, including frame drums and a skin-bellied lute, which eventually seems to have been replaced by a wood-bellied counterpart, the *ʿūd* 'wood'.

With the spread of Islam from Arabia to Syria, Mesopotamia, and Persia and through North Africa and Spain (roughly between 638 and 750), the music of the Near East underwent an extensive process of ethnic blending, acquiring new features and associations. Attitudes toward music also changed. Conservative Islam is known

With the spread of Islam, the music of the Near East underwent an extensive process of ethnic blending, acquiring new features and associations.

to have developed a negative attitude toward music and musicians, deeming the performance of certain genres unlawful. Although the Qur'ān itself neither condones nor prohibits music, the *ḥadīth*—a collection of sayings attributed to the Prophet Muhammad and his companions—contains numerous admonitions against singing, *nawḥ* 'wailing', and certain musical instruments. Although some early religious authorities expressed reservations about music, such strictures applied mostly to music as a secular profession, often referred to as *lahu* (*lahw*) 'entertainment' or 'diversion' and *ghinā'* 'singing'—activities that, to purists, may have evoked morally dubious contexts and conduct, as well as un-Islamic or pagan practices. The vast realm of folk or ritualistic expressions that accompanied such events as weddings, circumcisions, and battles, and those that served a religious purpose and therefore were not considered music proper, were exempted. A prime example is the *adhān*, the call to prayer, traditionally performed five times a day from minarets throughout the Islamic world. Another example is Qur'ānic chanting, the most revered expression of the faith, an established practice founded on *'ilm al-tajwīd* 'art of cantillation', which incorporates rules for the enunciation and delivery of the Qur'ānic text, considered a divine utterance revealed through the Prophet as God's messenger.

Moreover, Muslim rulers increased their patronage of music, particularly when their courts became highly affluent and cosmopolitan. Close contacts with conquered civilizations contributed to a new humanistic milieu marked by artistic tolerance and at times a strong interest in music and musicians on the part of the ruling classes. As sociopolitical establishments, medieval Islamic courts were a primary setting for music and lent prestige to performers. Similarly, the cultures in which these courts existed were becoming increasingly multiethnic, multireligious, multilingual, and—understandably—multimusical. Indeed, the courts of Damascus, Cordova, Seville, and Baghdad patronized musicians, poets, philosophers, and scientists from varied backgrounds. In the time of the Orthodox caliphs in Arabia (632–661), when al-Madina was a political center, the singer Ṭuways (632–710) is said to have been the first male to pursue the art of singing in the Ḥijāz; his career supposedly marks the appearance of male singing in Islam—before that, musical entertainment was provided by the socially less prestigious *qiyān*. Ṭuways himself belonged to a low social class known as *mukhannathūn* 'effeminate men' who affected women's ornaments and mannerisms; but although he was criticized by his society in general, he was highly admired by the nobles. In later Arabic accounts, Ṭuways is credited with being the first to master the "serious" art of music, *al-ghinā' al-mutqan*, and to have introduced the *īqā'*, or metric pattern. Metric modes are thought to have become prevalent in Arab music at this time. Other singers also became well known, particularly Ṣā'ib Khathīr (d. 683), who is sometimes said to have been the first in Madina to accompany himself on the *'ūd* and to introduce certain rhythmic modes into his compositions. The female singer 'Azza al-Maylā' supposedly scandalized conservative Muslims but was supported by notable patrons and is said to have cultivated a type of measured song (*ghinā' mu-*

waqqa'), developed a repertoire with Arabian and Persian components, and performed on some instruments herself.

Further developments occurred during the Umayyad dynasty (661–750), which had its capital at Damascus. This period witnessed a confluence of Syrian, Greek, Persian, and Arabian cultures and artistic expression. Whereas Caliph Mu'āwiya I (r. 661–680) was less open about his appreciation of music, his son Yazīd I (r. 680–683) took great pleasure in it and was described in a later Arab source as the first Muslim ruler to admit singers and instrumentalists to the court. Other caliphs, such as 'Abd al-Malik (r. 685–705) and Yazīd II (r. 720–724), brought a number of musicians into their courts. Music was sometimes practiced by free men, although musicians were still looked on as a separate social class.

One early Umayyad singer was Ibn Misjaḥ (d. c. 715), a black slave from Mekka who was liberated at a young age. His musical talent flowered when, as a boy, he heard Persian music being sung by masons who had been brought from Iraq to Damascus by Caliph Mu'āwiya. Ibn Misjaḥ's rise to fame, we are told, offended some conservatives in Mekka, who accused him of using his profane art to seduce believers—an accusation that had prompted his departure to Damascus in the first place. Ibn Misjaḥ was a pioneer in integrating new and different styles, particularly Persian and Byzantine, into Arabian music. A student of Ibn Misjaḥ, Ibn Muḥriz (d. c. 715), the son of a Persian free man, also assimilated Persian and Byzantine elements. He is credited with a number of musical innovations, including a rhythmic mode and songs in which the melody was longer than one line of poetry; before that, we are told, a melody covered only a single poetic line. Also famous was Ibn Surayj (c. 634–726), the son of a Turkish slave in Mekka. He originally specialized in singing elegies but gave this up in favor of the regular professional *al-ghinā'* and then performed at the court of al-Walīd I (r. 705–715) in Damascus. Another important singer of the Umayyad era was Ma'bad (d. 743), a free individual who was the son of a black man. He was born in Madina, sang at the courts of the Umayyad caliphs, and was known for cultivating his own style. Other outstanding artists of the Umayyad era included Yūnus al-Kātib (d. c. 765) and a number of female singers such as Jamīla (d. c. 720), who was a freed slave and a renowned singing teacher.

The 'Abbāsid era, which Farmer divided into three periods—"golden age" (750–847), "decline" (847–945), and "fall" (945–1258)—is noted by both early and modern historians for its material splendor, its cosmopolitanism, and its intellectual and artistic output. It is also known for enthusiastic patrons of music, such as the caliphs al-Mahdī (r. 775–785), Hārūn al-Rashīd (r. 786–809), al-Amīn (r. 809–813), and al-Wāthiq (r. 842–847), generally recognized as the first 'Abbāsid caliph who was a "real musician" (Farmer 1929:96–97). Centered in Baghdad, the 'Abbāsid civilization witnessed an increase in Persian influence in both the cultural and the political domain. Some 'Abbāsid rulers imitated the courts of Persia and Khurasan, "where music and Islam did not come into conflict" (Farmer 1929:92).

In addition to the *qiyān*—the singing-girls—'Abbāsid artists included vocalists and instrumentalists from distinguished social backgrounds. A notable example is Ibrāhīm al-Mawṣilī (d. 804), who was descended from a noble Persian family but had an Arab upbringing; he traveled to northern Persia, Basra, and later Baghdad to learn Persian and Arab singing. This artist earned "the foremost position among the court musicians" of Hārūn al-Rashīd (Farmer 1929:116). According to medieval historians, Ibrāhīm al-Mawṣilī created hundreds of compositions, devised new modes, and taught a number of famous artists—such as Mukhāriq (d. c. 845), who was originally the slave of a female singer but became a well-paid celebrity; and Manṣūr Zalzal (d. 791), a renowned lute player. Zalzal was Ibrāhīm al-Mawṣilī's brother-in-law and *'ūd* accompanist, and he too is acknowledged for his contributions to musical practice, specifically for introducing the "neutral" third interval named after him and for inventing a new type of *'ūd* that supposedly took the place of the Persian lute.

Prince Ibrāhīm Ibn al-Mahdī (779–839) was Hārūn's half brother, from a different mother. Prince Ibrāhīm's mother was a musician, as was the mother of his stepsister 'Ulayya, also a well-known singer. We are told that Prince Ibrāhīm was well-educated in several disciplines but showed special talent as a singer and instrumentalist, and that Hārūn supported his educational and artistic career despite the predominant view of music as a demeaning activity. Historians also mention that Ibrāhīm Ibn al-Mahdī became a theorist and a proponent of what Farmer calls "the Persian Romantic music movement," which put him at odds with Iṣḥāq al-Mawṣilī (767?–850), an advocate of "the old Arabian traditional school" (1929:120).

Iṣḥāq al-Mawṣilī, the son of Ibrāhīm al-Mawṣilī, was extremely well-educated and was trained by a number of artists including his uncle, Zalzal. He became an eminent court musician, earned lavish sums, and made a deep impression on his patrons. Al-Ma'mūn (r. 813–833) said, "Were Iṣḥāq not so publicly known as a musician, I would have appointed him a judge (*qāḍī*), for he is more deserving of it than any of the judges that we now have, and he surpasses them all in virtuous conduct, piety, and honesty" (Farmer 1929:124). A poet, a man of literature, and a musician with a strong theoretical bent, Iṣḥāq is described by Farmer as "an all-round musician, . . . the greatest that Islam produced" (125).

Another celebrated and multifaceted personage was Zaryab. Having begun his career in Baghdad, he moved westward to North Africa as a result of a rivalry between himself and Iṣḥāq, eventually settling in Moorish Spain. There he joined the court of Sultan al-Hakam I (r. 796–822), where he was cherished and handsomely rewarded. Early historians have described Zaryāb as well-versed in various fields and have attributed to him artistic and pedagogical innovations that included an *'ūd* plectrum made from an eagle's feather and a special system for vocal training: the proper production of sound and the use of textual, rhythmic, melodic, and ornamental elements. He is also credited with devising an order in which metric and nonmetric songs were combined into the *nawba*, a traditional multipart or suite-like format. He is also believed to have brought the *nawba* to Moorish Spain, where he contributed to its further refinement.

Moorish Spain witnessed the introduction of new poetic forms set to music, a legacy that survived as part of Hispano-Arabic or Andalusian music, especially in the urban centers of North Africa. These were two strophic forms: the *zajal*, which used the colloquial idiom of the Iberian Peninsula under the Moors; and the *muwashshaḥ*, which was primarily in classical Arabic and had an elaborate stanzaic form that distinguished it from the classical Arabic *qaṣīda* 'poem' (the latter used continuous parallel lines, each line consisting of two hemistitches, rather than separate strophes).

MUSIC AS A SCIENCE

The emergence of *'ilm al-mūsīqā* 'the science of music' broadened the scope and significance of music in medieval Islamic culture. This new science was derived mainly from ancient Greek writings and was developed during the 'Abbāsid period. Through *Bayt al-Ḥikma* 'the house of wisdom', a scholarly institution founded by Caliph al-Ma'mūn in Baghdad, Greek treatises, many on music, were translated into Arabic. Such translations had far-reaching and long-lasting effects; one result was that *al-mūsiqa* 'music' became a primary concern of philosophers, physicians, and acousticians and was regarded as part of the quadrivium, the four major sciences. *'Ilm al-mūsīqā* was the speculative counterpart of *'ilm al-ghinā'* 'the science of singing'—that is, the practical art of music making. Among the ancient Greek importations were the Pythagorean doctrine of the "harmony of the spheres" and the Platonic teachings about *ethos*, which referred to the emotional and moral influence of music and was presented in Arabic writings under the heading *ta'thīr* 'influence'. These and other doctrines had counterparts in the ancient Semitic civilizations of the Near East and established direct links between music, numerology, therapeutics, and cosmology.

Perhaps the most significant development in music was the adoption of technical terminology and analytical concepts, which either retained their basic Greek linguistic forms or were translated into Arabic. Among the concepts that became important in Arabic writings were tetrachords, pentachords, octave species, the great perfect system (double octave); intervals (diatonic, chromatic, enharmonic), consonance and dissonance, and conjunct (overlapping) and disjunct (consecutive) patterns of tetrachords. Also of basic importance was the Pythagorean system of intonation and the use of mathematical ratios to represent melodic intervals.

Like the Greeks, Muslim music theorists tended to organize their treatises from the simple to the compound. As illusrated in the second volume of *Kitāb al-mūsīqā al-kabīr* 'Grand Treatise on Music', by the renowned philosopher Abū Naṣr al-Fārābī (c. 870–950), such works usually discussed the concept of *sawt* 'sound' and then proceeded to other areas such as intervals, tetrachords, pentachords, octave species, double-octave systems, rhythm, instruments and their tuning, compositional techniques and the application of texts, and the influence of music (*ta'thīr al-alḥān*) on the soul. Although these writers generally imitated ancient models, they also expressed their own concerns, as the following examples demonstrate.

The system of finger modes, thought to be old and deeply rooted in Arabian practice, was expounded by Iṣḥāq al-Mawṣilī and later by Ibn al-Munajjim (d. 912). It featured a set of melodic modes based on a Pythagorean diatonic fretting of the lute neck; this whole- and half-tone fretting produced eight octave scales beginning on different steps or frets within the scale and were identified in reference to (1) the name of the first note of the scale, whether that note was an open string or stopped; and (2) the name of one of the two adjacent chromatic notes that happened to be included on the third degree on each of the four open strings of the *'ūd*—this choice depended on which of the two notes the mode used. The system was known as finger modes because the frets and the notes were conceived of and described in part through the names of the performer's fingers, or *aṣabi'*. There are numerous historical references to the actual use of this system. The famous multivolume work *Kitāb al-aghānī* 'Book of Songs' of Abū al-Faraj al-Iṣfahānī (897–967), which gives extensive information on social, literary, and artistic life in the medieval courts, mentions the use of specific modes in connection with actual song texts. It is generally believed (for example, by Farmer) that the finger modes continued to be used until the eleventh century, when the region began to experience strong musical influences from Persia.

A further contribution was made by the philosopher al-Kindī (d. c. 874), whose musical writings include two treatises. Well versed in Greek philosophy, al-Kindī discussed consonant and dissonant intervals using the lute strings for illustration and proposed the addition of a fifth string on the lute to achieve a wider melodic range, thus reaching the span of a "great perfect system." He also presented a lute fretting in which the Pythagorean whole-step gap between the nut on the neck of the instrument and the first fret was furnished with two different semitonal frets in order to accommodate the two unequal semitones in the chromatic Pythagorean scale. In addition to extending the chromatic possibilities of the lute fretting of the so-called Old Arabian school, al-Kindī wrote about the cosmological, emotional, and therapeutic functions of music, as did his Jewish student Sa'īd Ibn Yūsuf (892–942), also known as Saadia Gaon.

As a music theorist, Abū Naṣr al-Fārābī had a profound impact on later generations. Knowledgeable about the doctrines of Greek philosophers such as Plato and Aristotle, and a philosopher himself, he is also thought to have been an accomplished

As a music theorist, Abū Naṣr al-Fārābī had a profound impact on later generations.

musician. In his *Kitāb al-mūsīqā al-kabīr*, we learn of a peculiar pre-Islamic Arab system of tuning that used very small, approximately quarter-tone intervals represented by the frets of a long-necked lute called *al-ṭanbūr al-baghdādī*. Al-Fārābī also presented an elaborate fretting on the short neck of the *'ūd* of his time, based on a diatonic Pythagorean matrix to which he added two microtonal (or neutral) intervals that were evidently popular. The two new frets were applied to the intervals of the second and the third of each of the five lute strings. One of these was slightly higher than a minor third, at an interval of 303 cents; this non-Pythagorean third was called *wusṭa al-Furs* 'the Persian middle fret', possibly reflecting an emerging ethnic-musical influence. The other new fret was only a bit higher; as a third step, it was almost equidistant between a minor and a major third and measured 355 cents. This intermediary or "neutral" step was attributed to the virtuoso lutenist Manṣūr Zalzal and was called *wusṭa Zalzal*. Al-Fārābī also used this fretting of diatonic and microtonal intervals as a basis for creating different tetrachords, pentachords, and octave species; some of these roughly resembled our minor and major scales, but others differed because they incorporated the neutral *wusṭa Zalzal*.

Al-Fārābī described another tuning system associated with the province of Khorasan, in what is now northeastern Iran. It was presented in the form of a fretting found on the long neck of *al-ṭunbūr al-khurāsānī*. In this fretting, the Pythagorean diatonic whole step, which measured 204 cents (as compared with the modern equal-tempered whole step, which consists of two equal 100-cent semitones), is divided into three parts: one *limma* (or Pythagorean semitone of 90 cents); another *limma*; and a *comma*, or the remainder, 24 cents. The fretting also incorporated Pythagorean semitonal steps of 90 cents each.

Later generations of scholars were also preoccupied with intonation and fretting, as can be seen, for example, in the works of the physician and philosopher Ibn Zayla (d. 948) and a tenth-century group of thinkers called Ikhwān al-Ṣafā' 'Brothers of Purity'. The physician and philosopher Ibn Sīnā, or Avicenna (980–1037), was also interested in tuning; he proposed a scordatura, an unconventional tuning of the lute strings, in order to allow for the reproduction of the *zalzal* third in the upper octave.

A later landmark was the systematic model of Ṣafī al-Dīn al-Urmāwī (d. 1294), the author of *Kitāb al-adwār* 'Book of Modes'. This scholar, who was also a practicing musician, was one of the first to present a system of melodic modes based on a detailed seventeen-interval scale. Referring to twelve modes (presumably common during his time) by their specific names—such as *'ushshaq, nawā, busāik,* and *rāst*—he presented the value of each interval within them in terms of Pythagorean *limma* and *comma* units similar to those used on the *ṭunbūr* of Khurāsān described earlier by al-Fārābī. Through his scale, Ṣafī al-Dīn, who worked out systems of fretting for the *'ūd* and the *ṭanbūr*, was able to accommodate the half steps (90 cents), whole steps (204 cents), and neutral steps (180 cents) of the modes. He influenced many theorists of later periods.

SUFISM

Another development affecting the status and significance of music was the rise and proliferation of Islamic mysticism, also known as Sufism. It began as an ascetic movement during the Middle Ages and became quite prevalent in the thirteenth century. The Sufis belonged to separate *ṭuruq* 'paths' or 'religious orders' (singular, *ṭarīqa*), each of which usually gave allegiance to a founding saint, as implied in the names of some of the main orders: the Qādiriyya, the Shādhiliyya, the Rifā'iyya, and the Mawlawiyya, or Mevlevis. Although the Sufis adhered to the teachings and duties of Islam, they had an all-encompassing spiritual worldview. Basic to their mystical quest are the doctrines of divine oneness—the unity of the universe, including God and humankind—and divine love, the human yearning for the divine. The mystics or dervishes (Sufi adepts) sought reunion with God through direct experience, including music and dance; thus they saw the arts as a means toward a desirable mystical state, spiritual ecstasy. Their rituals typically incorporate chanting and dancing and sometimes give an important role to instruments such as the *nāy*, a reed flute. Through the centuries, the Sufis have produced a considerable repertoire of mystical love poetry and devotional songs. Their rituals are also associated with the practice of *dhikr* 'remembrance' or 'reiteration'. *Dhikr* often means the combination of music and dance typical of a specific order, in other words the ritual as a whole. However, it refers specifically to performances in which the dervishes repeat a formula such as *lā ilāha illā l-Lāh* 'there is no god but Allah', thus creating a low-pitched ostinato or a constantly repeated melodic motif, also called *arḍīyyah* 'ground' or 'foundation', that accompanies a solo performance by the leading vocalist, the *munshid*. This practice usually involves rhythmic movements of the head and torso and can be accentuated by clapping or playing percussion instruments or even by breathing rhythmically.

The effects of Islamic mysticism on Near Eastern music in general have been profound and multifaceted. The spiritual connotations of music and dance, epitomized in the mystical religious performance called *samā'* 'listening' or 'auditioning', have shaped the concept and appreciation of music. Furthermore, many Sufi sects—such as the Mevlevis in Turkey and in the city of Aleppo in Syria—have preserved and propagated their musical practices. Numerous dervishes were music theorists and composers and performers of secular and sacred works. Many secular artists, particularly singers, received Sufi religious and musical training, and Sufi poems that spoke of love in a mystical or symbolic sense were used as lyrics by mainstream Arab singers.

POSTMEDIEVAL PRACTICES

During the postmedieval period, roughly from the fourteenth to the nineteenth century, music continued to dominate secular and spiritual life. Many scholars have depicted preceding eras, especially the 'Abbāsid dynasty, as a golden age of Arab music (Farmer 1929) and have associated the succeeding centuries with musical, cultural, and political decline, but there is no reason to assume that postmedieval music had lost its vital social and religious role. Music theories still existed, although as Amnon Shiloah has demonstrated, these theories focused on music and cosmology and borrowed considerably from earlier authorities. As both a popular and an exclusive medium of entertainment, music thrived under the Fāṭimids (909–1171) and the Mamlūks of Egypt (1250–1517) and seems to have been prominent in Sufi, court, and military contexts throughout the Ottoman period, from the early sixteenth century until World War I. In fact, the Ottoman traveler Evliya Efendi Chelebi identified dozens of musically specialized professional guilds whose members had particular patron saints; these guilds were the backbone of musical life throughout the Ottoman world, including Syria, Egypt, and North Africa. The Sufi orders also had a clear influence on music. Aleppo in Syria had numerous Sufi orders, including the Mevlevis, and Cairo and other North African cities became major centers for musically diverse Sufi groups.

The importance of music as social entertainment was noted by a number of Western visitors in the eighteenth and nineteenth centuries. Musicians, who generally belonged to lower social ranks, were nevertheless an essential part of folk and popular festivities. In his two monumental volumes on the city of Aleppo, Alexander Russell, a British physician who visited Syria in the first half of the eighteenth century and published a book in 1794, wrote extensively about Aleppan social life, including detailed descriptions of musical events, instruments, and performance genres, and people's ways of listening and reacting to music. He found that "the Aleppeens, in general, have a correct ear, and are fond of music," and he speaks of their musical sophistication and their well-established theory, which had been developed despite the oral nature of their music. Russell provides information on such phenomena as the Ottoman military band, Sufi flutes, panpipes, and the typical seating of ensembles in a courtyard. He describes the listeners' enthusiasm and the active participation of men, and sometimes women, as they occasionally joined in the chorus. He notes the "natives'" special fondness for the *mawwāl*, an improvisatory vocal genre, and exuberant and extroverted responses to music, particularly among Christians and Jews—although he observed that "the Turks of condition, in mixed company, very seldom lay aside their usual solemnity."

Russell's ethnographic data on making and listening to music are comparable to those presented by later Western observers. Among them were Villoteau, who led a research team as part of Napoleon's scientific mission to Egypt and wrote two detailed volumes on Egypt's music and musical instruments around the turn of the nineteenth century (published in 1823 and 1826). Edward Lane, a British Orientalist, wrote *An Account of the Manners and Customs of the Modern Egyptians* (first published in 1836) that gives a wealth of firsthand observations on Egyptian culture during the first half of the nineteenth century, including music, musical instruments, attitudes toward music, epic singers in coffeehouses, public dancers, and religious festivals. As Lane recounts, although musicians belonged to a very low social rank, music itself was ubiquitous and had a tremendous emotional effect. Such accounts not only give us valuable data on postmedieval musical life but also indirectly presage the musical mosaic that exists in the region today.

LITURGICAL AND FOLK PRACTICES

The Near Eastern Arab world has many liturgical and folk styles that have interacted with secular urban culture but have also maintained their regional and contextual diversity. In Egypt, for example, some liturgical practices of the Coptic church—including the use of centuries-old percussion instruments—are thought to retain elements of pharaonic music. In Lebanon, the Maronites have historical roots that go back to Saint Maron (d. c. 410), and their church repertoire, which uses the Syriac and Arabic languages, goes back at least to the seventh and eighth centuries, when members of this sect first settled in northern Lebanon. Modern Syriac churches use hymns attributed to the fourth-century saint Ephraim; the Greek Orthodox church has chants derived from ancient Byzantine music that are similarly represented in a currently used system of notation. Non-Christian religious expressions are also prevalent, including those of the Druze sect of Lebanon. Throughout the Arab world, Muslims have rites for religious holidays, such as the *aḍḥā* feast at the end of the *ḥajj* pilgrimage and the Prophet's birthday. Sacred expressions also appear in the annual Shiʿite celebration of the ʿĀshūrāʾ (*taʿziya*) in Lebanon, in Iraq, and elsewhere, commemorating the martyrdom of the saints Ḥasan and Ḥusayn in 680.

Folk musical traditions include an array of styles and instruments and have many social and political connotations. Among the bedouin—the nomadic tribal cultures of northern Arabia and the Levant, including Jordan, Palestine, and Syria—the *shāʿir* 'poet-singer' uses a *rabāba*, a single-stringed quadrilateral upright fiddle, to accompany heroic songs, generally known as *qaṣīda* or *shurūqi*, and love songs such as the genre *ʿataba*. The bedouin, for whom serving coffee at the *maḍāfa* 'guest house' of a tribal chief is an important social ritual, may also play the *mihba*, a large wooden mortar and pestle used to grind coffee beans, as a musical instrument—since the person who uses a *mihba* usually produces intricate, aesthetically pleasing rhythmic patterns. The *mihba* is also a status symbol, indicating the host's high rank, his honor, and his hospitality.

In villages of the eastern Mediterranean—for example, in Lebanon—music is part of many social events and rituals. At funerals, particularly in Christian and Druze villages, lament genres are performed by either men or women, following a social tradition known collectively as *nadb*. Folk songs performed at weddings deal with love and social commentary related to village life and society at large. The genre *ʿatābā* consists of verses sung by a soloist, often with a choral refrain called *mijāna*. Other genres, such as the *dalʿūna*, are sung by performers of the *dabka*, a line dance, to the accompaniment of folk instruments: an end-blown reed or metal flute known as *minjayra* in Lebanon and *shabbāba* in Palestine and the *mijwiz*, a double-pipe or double clarinet that has two single reeds and requires the technique of "circular breathing." In Palestinian communities the *yarghūl* may be used; this instrument differs from the *mijwiz* in having one pipe for the melody and another with no holes for a drone. In Lebanon and some parts of Palestine, there is a very popular tradition of sung folk poetry known as *zajāl* in which the *qawwāl* 'poet-singer' usually improvises, particularly during poetic duels among contestants who may represent their villages or communities. The *zajāl* repertoire encompasses genres that have their own meters, their own types of melodies, and in some case their own rhyme schemes.

The folk music of Egypt also has considerable variety, ranging from the distinctly accentuated collective song of the Siwa oases in the west (which has a North African sound) to the more lyrical singing accompanied by the *simsimiyya*, a small lyre, in Port Said and the Red Sea area—or to the pentatonic, rhythmically complex Nubian music of the south, for example the Aswan region (which sounds more African). In the Nile communities, folk music typically uses a wide variety of instruments, such as an end-blown reed flute usually known as the *ṣuffāra* (also called a *salamiyya*), and the *arghūl*, a double pipe with two single reeds (one tube for the melody; and another, without holes but sometimes with extensions, used as a drone). The *rabāba* is also played; this is a two-stringed spike fiddle whose body is made from a coconut shell and has an opening covered with fish skin. The *rabāba* is typically used by the *shāʿir* to accompany his recitation of traditional epics, particularly an epic named after the eleventh-century Arab hero Abū Zayd al-Hilālī.

FIGURE 5 *Ṭār* players at a public festival in Doha, Qatar. Photo by Barbara Racy.

Percussion instruments include the *ṭār*, a large frame drum without cymbals (figure 5); the *mazhar*, a large frame drum with cymbals; and *sajāt*, small brass finger cymbals. *Sajāt* are used by dancers such as the local entertainers known as *ghawāzī*, who are also accompanied by a typical instrumental ensemble, usually three double-reed wind instruments of the type known as *mizmār* and a large double-sided drum known as *ṭabl baladī* (figure 6). In general, the music of the Nile tends toward highly coordinated ensemble playing. Furthermore, the repertoire includes a considerable number of purely instrumental genres as well as vocal genres; it borrows more extensively from urban music: its melodic and rhythmic modes, patterns of intonation, and improvisational techniques are often reminiscent of the urban aesthetic.

The Arab Gulf region is also rich and diverse in instrumentation and styles of performance, in part because throughout its history, it has interacted closely—for instance, by sea trade—with East Africa, Persia, and India. An important category,

FIGURE 6 *Mizmār* and *ṭabl baladī* ensemble from Egypt. Photo by Barbara Racy.

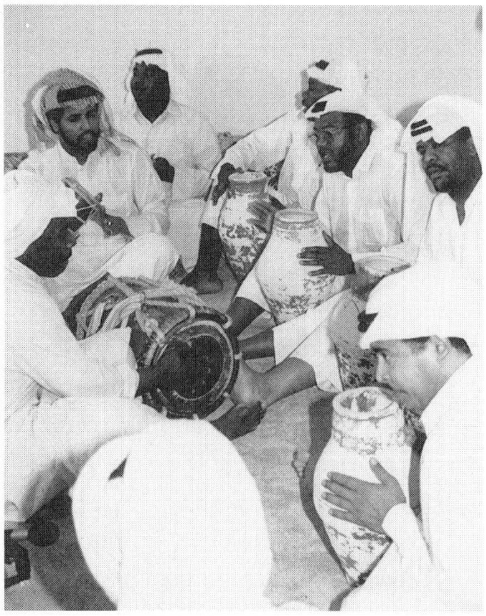

FIGURE 7 A performance of pearl-diving music in Doha, Qatar. Photo by Barbara Racy.

FIGURE 8 *Ṭanbūra* performance in Doha, Qatar. Photo by Barbara Racy.

especially in Kuwait, Bahrain, and Qatar, is an elaborate legacy that was associated with pearl fishing (figure 7). Although pearl fishing is no longer practiced, this repertoire, generally known as *fjirī*, is still performed, especially by older people. It incorporates numerous song genres, each related to a specific aspect of pearl diving, and tends to be rhythmically complex, with long metric patterns, syncopation, and polyrhythm. Hand clapping is typical, as are percussion instruments, including the *jahala* 'clay pot' (a few such pots are beaten together) and the *mirwās*, a small double-sided cylindrical drum. The singing is led by a vocal soloist, the *nahhām*, who usually opens the performance against a low-pitched vocal drone maintained by the rest of the ensemble.

The Gulf region has other art forms, some of which are connected with specific rituals as well as with entertainment, often in combination with dance. These include the *ṭanbūra* tradition (figure 8), practiced largely by people of East African origin in the Basra region of southern Iraq, Kuwait, Bahrain, the United Arab Emirates, and Oman. The word *tanbūra* comes from the name of a large lyre used in the ritual, which is also collectively known as the *nūban*—a reference to its Nubian roots. The performance is directed by a spiritual leader and may be either a weekly social event or a special ritual to treat maladies related to spirit possession. In these performances, rows of either women or men dance to the accompaniment of a lyre, several single-headed cylindrical drums, and a *manjūr*, a rattle belt made of animal hooves. Other genres include the *lēwa*, a performance of dance and music derived from Africa which features large cylindrical single-headed drums and a tin can beaten with a stick that produce a complex polymetric layer accompanying a *ṣurnāy*, a type of oboe. The popular *'arḍa* is a stylized war-procession dance that typically uses a double-sided cylindrical drum, a pair of medium-size brass cymbals, and several large frame drums. The dancers may also brandish swords or muskets. The *'arḍa* and its many variants are prevalent in tribal and national ceremonies throughout Saudi Arabia and the Gulf states.

URBAN MUSIC AND MODERNISM

The nineteenth century was a turning point in Arab music. Napoleon's conquest of Egypt and the subsequent military and cultural contacts inspired a series of musical borrowings from the West. Early in the century, Egypt's rulers, who had considerable autonomy within the Ottoman Empire, made systematic attempts at westernization. Muhammad ʿAli (r. 1804–1848), impressed by Europe's military establishment, brought French experts to train his army and to establish military schools in which the instruments of the European brass band were taught. In Egypt, as in other Ottoman regions, European-style brass bands gradually replaced the traditional Turkish military ensembles, although the new bands often performed works of local composers—marches and adaptations of Near Eastern popular and folk songs. Many local officers were trained in Western theory and notation and then notated local tunes; some of their writings reflected their newly acquired Western perspectives on music theory and pedagogy. This period also saw the rise of published teaching methods for various instruments and the appearance of Arab Protestant hymnals, in which classical Arabic lyrics were set to Western hymn tunes—these hymnals sometimes had introductory sections about teaching Western theory and harmony. Such developments paved the way for the Western-type conservatory, a pedagogical institution that used European notation and became prevalent in Arab cities, particularly after World War I.

The nineteenth century also saw the rise of musical theater and the importation of European opera into Egypt by Khedive Ismāʿīl (r. 1863–1879). Ismāʿīl, a modernist-minded ruler, had commissioned Verdi's opera *Aida* to inaugurate the new Cairo Opera House as part of the festivities for the opening of the Suez Canal in 1869. Because *Aida* was not ready in time, Verdi's *Rigoletto* was used for the inauguration; but in 1871 *Aida*, followed by other romantic operas, was performed at the opera house—a symbol of westernization that stood for more than a century (it was erected by Ismāʿīl in 1869 and destroyed by a fire in 1971). In the late nineteenth century and afterward, particularly during the British occupation of Egypt (1882–1922), many European orchestras and theatrical groups visited Cairo, inspiring local artists and contributing to the cosmopolitanism of urban life.

Late-nineteenth-century Egypt also saw the emergence of talented and tremendously famous artists. This period, sometimes descibed as a golden age of modern Arab music, was also marked by government patronage of some celebrated artists. For instance, Ismāʿīl supported the female singer Almaz (1860–1896) and the male singer ʿAbduh al-Hamūlī (1841–1901), who was also a prolific composer. During this time the innovative composer Muḥammad ʿUthmān (1855–1900) contributed a wealth of works to Egypt's music, particularly in the vocal genre *dawr*. These and other artists were accompanied by the *takht*, a small instrumental ensemble that comprised an *ʿūd*, a *qānūn* (a type of zither), a *nāy*, a violin (a nineteenth-century import that had been preceded by the *kamānja*, a two-stringed spike fiddle), and a *riqq* (a small tambourine), in addition to a chorus of three or four men. Similarly, the *ʿawālim*, female musical entertainers who performed for female audiences, had their own ensemble, which usually included the *ʿūd* and several percussion instruments.

Egypt also had a theater movement, which emerged in the second half of the nineteenth century and continued though the early twentieth century. Dramas, typically inspired by old Arab plots or adapted from classical European tragedies, were staged with a musical component, mostly in the form of sung classical poetry. Among the theater pioneers was the Syrian-born actor Aḥmad Abū Khalīl al-Qabbānī (1841–1902), who also led a theater group at the Columbian Exposition in Chicago in 1893. Another major artist was Shaykh Salāma Ḥijāzī (1852–1917), a Sufi-trained singer who acted and sang classical Arabic *qaṣāʾid* 'poems' (singular, *qaṣīda*) as part of the dramatic repertoire. From about 1916 to the late 1920s, operettas—a popular genre that combined singing, acting, and sometimes dancing and vaudeville—were performed in Egypt; one of the people associated with operetta was the modernist singer and composer Shaykh Sayyid Darwīsh (d. 1923).

FIGURE 9 Umm Kulthūm. Photo courtesy of Dār al-Ṣayyād.

The early twentieth century also brought new musical instruments. The piano became increasingly prevalent in middle-class homes, as did piano sheet music, mostly adaptations of popular Arab songs transcribed in Western notation with simple harmony. Other European instruments, particularly the accordion and some brasses and woodwinds, also became widespread and were usually played in the Arab musical idiom. Local brass bands were formed in Arab cities such as Beirut, Damascus, Alexandria, and Baghdad.

A significant contributor to change was the rise of commercial recording, particularly after 1904. Although cylinder phonograph records, mostly privately made, were available at the turn of the twentieth century, it was the flat 78-rpm disk, in the 1920s, that achieved dramatic popularity and became the primary commercial medium. Phonographic disks—promoted by companies such as Gramaphone, Odeon, Pathé, Columbia, and Bardophone—enabled people throughout the Arab world to hear the voices of celebrities: the Egyptians Shaykh Yūsuf al-Manyalāwī (1850–1911), ʻAbd al-Ḥayy Ḥilmī (1857–1912), Shaykh Abū al-ʻUla Muḥammad (1876–1927), Munīra al-Mahdiyya (d. 1965), and Umm Kulthūm (1896–1975; figure 9), and many others from neighboring Arabic-speaking countries. Although current music was available on phonographic disks, the medium was perhaps most significant with regard to the popularity of genres such as the Egyptian *ṭaqṭūqa*, a short precomposed strophic song, particularly in the 1920s. It also became a major medium for a new type of song, the *munūlūj* 'monologue', that was through-composed, was irregular in structure, and depicted emotions in an aria-like fashion. The *munūlūj* was composed by famous Egyptian artists such as Muḥammad al-Qaṣabjī (1892–1966) and sung by celebrities such as Umm Kulthūm, especially in the early 1930s.

Commercial sound recording was a factor in the transformation of traditional Arab music, because record companies favored precomposed, short, self-contained songs over long, improvised, interactive live performances, which did not fit the limited duration of early phonograph disks. These developments, along with an interest in westernizing the traditional idiom and the rise of a mass pan-Arab public for music, paved the way for the film song in the early 1930s. The first musical film in Cairo, made in 1932, ushered in a flourishing Egyptian film industry, and the musical film became a popular medium featuring artists such as the renowned singer, film actor, and composer Muḥammad ʻAbd al-Wahhāb (c. 1901–1991; figure 10).

MELODIC AND RHYTHMIC MODES

FIGURE 10 Muḥammad ʻAbd al-Wahhāb. Photo courtesy of Dār al-Ṣayyād.

Modern urban music has inherited much from the medieval and postmedieval periods, but it also has contemporary features. Today's Arab musicians have a basic repertoire of melodic modes known as *maqāmāt* (singular, *maqām*). According to theoretical sources, each *maqām* is a melodic framework with a tonic note, or *qarār*, and a scale of one or two octaves—that is, a sequence of intervals consisting of any of the following approximate melodic distances: a half tone, a whole tone, three-quarters of a whole tone, and an augmented second. In some theories, particularly those written in Syria (for example, by the violinist and music educator Tawfīq al-Ṣabbāgh), we encounter Pythagorean divisions that take into account the tendency for such intervals to vary slightly in magnitude, depending on the modal and melodic context. Accordingly, the intervallic variants are accounted for by varying the number of commas (smaller units) within each interval. However, in prevalent thinking—for example, in the system of the nineteenth-century Lebanese-born theorist Mikhā'il Mashshāqa—the octave scale is divided into twenty-four equal quarter tones. This equal-tempered quarter-tone division is appealing, particularly to modernist Egyptians, because it is compatible with the European equal-tempered twelve-semitone scale. In some theories, certain note clusters within each modal scale are bracketed separately in the form of tetrachords, pentachords, and trichords. Some sources also present a *sayr* 'path' as a brief synopsis describing how the mode unfolds, what direction it takes, which notes are momentarily emphasized, and which notes are altered with accidentals, for example, to initiate a descent toward the final note, or tonic. Theory books often list several dozen modes, each with its own name, and typically these modes are grouped by the tonic notes that they share.

In practice, the modes, about a dozen of which are most commonly used, are realized in compositions and improvisations. Improvisation, because it is typically devoid of meter and in some cases also devoid of text, is considered flexible enough to represent the modal design directly and eloquently. In a typical instrumental improvisation, for example, the performer presents modal creations that combine conventional and original elements. In the process, he highlights certain notes, progresses gradually from one pitch center to another, organizes the performance in terms of phrases and pauses, executes certain cadential patterns (*qaflāt*; singular, *qafla*), and may modulate to other modes before returning to the original one. A talented practitioner is able to produce correct intonation beyond the arbitrary system of equal-tempered quarter tones, which if literally applied distorts traditional intonational practice. As an approximate representation, this system has provided the basis for modern notation, which uses conventional European symbols with two additional signs: one for lowering a note by roughly a quarter tone, and another for raising a note by roughly a quarter tone. However, when interpreting notated pieces, traditional artists would execute the intervals more accurately, producing, for example, augmented seconds that are a bit narrower than the bare notational representation would suggest, and adding embellishments and melodic and rhythmic nuances that the notation does not explicitly indicate.

Ultimately, all such stylistic adjustments, in combination with further creative and contextually inspired applications, help to evoke the musical ecstasy inherent in each *maqām*. Ideally, the performer produces such ecstasy and is also inspired by it—a process of feedback that fosters highly affective renditions and compositions. Musicians usually speak of *salṭana*, an ecstatic state which they experience before or during a performance and which is directly linked to the modes. The modal ethos overpowers musicians and also empowers them to excel. They also speak of *ṭarab*, an ecstatic feeling evoked by the music as a whole; this is the musical emotion that a truly inspired modal performance will produce in the listener.

Music theory also presents a collection of rhythmic modes, or meters, known as *īqāʿāt* (singular, *īqāʿ*) or *awzān* (singular, *wazn*). As generally illustrated, each pattern consists of a cycle of beats and rests, represented on a straight horizontal line following a time signature. Two types of beats are recognized. One is the *dumm*, often represented by a note with a downward-pointing stem; this is an emphatic, deep-sounding beat that can be produced by hitting a drumhead close to its center. The second is the *takk*, usually marked by a note with an upward-pointing stem; this is a higher-pitched sound that can be produced closer to the rim of a drum or on a tambourine cymbal. A rest, sometimes referred to as *iss*, is indicated by a regular rest sign. The patterns themselves vary greatly in length, from two or three beats to twenty-eight, thirty-two, or more.

In actual compositions, the rhythmic patterns are reflected in the length and accents of each melodic unit or phrase. They are also interpreted on percussion instruments to reinforce the metric foundation and enhance the temporal coordination of a performance. However, when interpreted by percussionists, such skeletal patterns become highly ornate. Certain beats are subdivided, and rests may be filled with different types of beats, as long as the *īqāʿ* retains its basic beat structure and accents. Indeed, the percussive vocabulary has a wide gamut of timbral and dynamic effects, and artistic percussion evokes its own ecstasy.

In practice, a traditional performer or composer creates *tarab* by combining technical skills with personal traits. A traditional singer, for example, can evoke ecstasy by several means: a "natural" chest voice, ample embellishments, clear enunciation of textual syllables, good intonation, full command of the *qaflāt*, flexible improvisation or interpretation, and—sometimes—calculated departures from or playing around the regular meter or beat. Many of these attributes belong to the realm of practice rather than written, formalized theory.

THE MUSICAL REPERTOIRE

Near Eastern Arab music has a number of basic genres. During the late nineteenth and early twentieth centuries, traditional music emphasized flexibility, spontaneity, and direct participation by the audience, but several standard genres were performed either separately or together in the form of traditional medleys. These include *taqāsīm* (singular, *taqsīm*), instrumental improvisations; *layalī*, improvised vocalization on a few syllables, mostly *ya layl*, usually leading to a *mawwāl* or vocal improvisation on a poetic text in colloquial Arabic; and the *muwashshaḥ* (plural, *muwashshaḥāt*), a strophic song which uses a text in classical Arabic, but often with sporadic colloquialisms and *tarannumāt* (singular, *tarannum*)—added expressions such as *lalli* and *aman*, usually vocalized in a florid melismatic style, that "stretch out" vocal phrases to fit long, complex metric patterns. The *muwashshaḥāt* of Syria and Egypt have medieval literary features but apparently use formal structures and metric patterns typical of Turko-Arab or Ottoman classical music and are influenced by the Mawlawi dervishes of Syrian cities, particularly Aleppo. Nineteenth- and twentieth-century *muwashshaḥāt* are precomposed, accompanied by instruments, and typically sung by a chorus, sometimes with occasional solo vocal parts. Formally, they have a number of patterns. AABA is very prevalent: A represents verses that use the same melody; B represents a momentary shift to the higher register of the melodic mode and often a brief modulation to another mode. In Syria, the *muwashshaḥ*, has been associated with several celebrated names: the composers Aḥmad Abū Khālil al-Qabbānī (1841–1903), ʿUmar al-Baṭsh (1885–1950), and Shaykh ʿAli al-Darwīsh (1872–1952); and the singers Muḥammad Khayrī and Ṣabāh Fakhrī.

Egypt is associated with the *dawr*, a highly sophisticated genre developed largely in the late nineteenth century which became virtually obsolete in Egypt by the early 1930s. Customarily performed by a leading soloist with choral and instrumental accompaniment by a *takht*, it was metric and largely precomposed. However, it had a flexible middle section of improvised vocalizations on the syllable *ah* and elaborate and modally complex passages in which a technique known as the *hank* (probably from the Turko-Persian musical term *ahang*) was used. This section consisted of virtuosic and modally varied alternations between the soloist and the chorus, usually on a few syllables or textual fragments. Other early vocal genres include the *qaṣīda*, which was usually improvised with or without a beat pattern and used a classical Arabic text, often a Sufi-related love poem.

Instrumental genres, although not very numerous, were important in the *takht* repertoire. These include the *dulāb*, a short precomoposed instrumental piece that functioned as a prelude to the performance proper, for example a *qaṣīda*. Another genre, the *taḥmīla*, is a lively instrumental composition incorporating call-and-response or solo-ensemble passages for each melodic instrument. Two genres, the *bashraf* and the *samāʿī*, are of Ottoman origin. The *bashraf* (Turkish *peşrev*) is metric, is precomposed, and has a form similar to a rondo: verse-like passages alternating with a repeated refrain-like component (AxBxCxDx, with x representing the refrain). The *samāʿī* (Turkish *saz semai*) is more prevalent among Arab performers; its form is similar to that of a *bashraf*, but it has a ten-beat pattern for all but the last "verse" section, which comes before the final refrain and uses a shorter pattern, usually three to six beats.

In performance, these genres were strung together in traditional although often loose or flexible formats. As a rule, the pieces of the medley, often referred to as a "suite" or a "compound" form, share a melodic mode, although internally they vary stylistically and rhythmically, some being improvised solos and others precomposed tuttis. The flow of the components tends to build to a climax by increasing the tempo, the metric activity, and the overall stylistic complexity. A prime example is the Egyptian *waṣla* 'stretch' or 'connection' (plural, *waṣlāt*) of the late nineteenth and early twentieth centuries. This compound structure, which was gradually abandoned after the 1920s, was often presented at a *sahra*—an evening festivity, usually held during a wedding. The internal flow of the *waṣla* and the way the individual genres were strung together were perfectly suited for creating a continuous sense of ecstasy in both the listener and the musicians, particularly the leading vocalist. Its internal generic structure seemed to entail an effective accumulation of creative modal ecstasy and to provide an organic progression through which the *muṭrib* undergoes musical warm-ups leading to a climactic phase toward the end of the performance. Although flexible in terms of its generic ingredients, a typical *waṣla* often began with a solo *taqsīm*—an instrumental improvisation on the *'ūd*—followed by an instrumental prelude, usually a *dūlāb* or TRACK 1 *samā'ī*, by the ensemble, at times with *taqāsīm* interpolations by some *takht* instruments, such as the violin or the *nāy*. Then the chorus and the soloist together sang a *muwashshah*, or part of one, in a typical heterophonic style; this gave the soloist a chance to work out his voice and become more attuned to the mode of the *waṣla*. Then the *qānūn*—the preferred accompanying instrument, in part because of its sonorous timbre and because its open strings provided a stable or fixed pitch reference—played a short *taqāsīm* that prepared for the lead soloist's *layālī* and *mawwāl*. These were accompanied heterophonically, with the *qānūn* artfully paraphrasing or echoing the main vocal phrases, as well as filling in with short *taqāsīm* after each vocal phrase. The *waṣla* culminated in the *dawr*, during which the leading vocalist and the rest of ensemble would reach a peak of ecstasy. The early-twentieth-century Egyptian theorist and music reformer Kāmil al-Khula'ī, the author of *Kitāb al-mūsīqā al-sharqī* (from about 1904) tells us that an evening performance customarily incorporated three *waṣlāt*, and that the last *waṣla* would end with an additional piece, typically a *qaṣīda*, as a finale.

Such compound structures are prevalent in the Islamic world, although the content differs considerably from one country to another. For example, the Syrian *fāsil* consists largely of *muwashshaḥāt* in which the meters tend to become progressively shorter and the tempi livelier. As performed today, the typical Syrian medley has a flexible content. An ensemble instrumental prelude, usually a *dūlāb* or a *samā'ī*, leads into the vocal segment, which incorporates a nonmetric improvisatory *qaṣīda* and sometimes an Egyptian *dawr*, as well as a series of *muwashshaḥāt*. As a rule, the medley ends with a chain of *qudūd* (singular, *qadd*)—strophic songs in colloquial Arabic, a genre associated with Aleppo. The *fāṣil* and the *waṣla* differ from other Arab compound forms such as the North African *nūba* or *nawba* and the Iraqi *maqām*. The latter uses a traditional ensemble known as *tshalghī* or *tshalghi Baghdādī* and is associated with numerous celebrated vocalists, *qurrā'* 'readers' or 'reciters' (singular, *qāri'*), such as Muḥammad al-Qubbānjī, whose artistry was captured on documentary 78-rpm disks at the Cairo Congress of Arab Music in 1932, and later Yūsuf 'Umar.

Numerous features distinguish the Iraqi *maqām* from neighboring Arab styles. Its modes are different from and more prestructured than the standard *maqāmāt* used, for instance, in Cairo and Beirut. Also, it has a typical sequence in which an instrumental prelude leads to a long improvisatory vocal segment, the *taḥrīr*, that may call for metric accompaniment; this segment in turn leads to a number of *bastāt* (singular,

Despite the enlarged ensembles and the influence of electronics and the media, the mainstream style of composition and performance remains rather faithful to traditional models.

basta)—traditional strophic songs, often well-known. *Tshalghī* music uses a special combination of instruments: the *santūr*, a type of hammer dulcimer; the *jawzah*, a four-stringed spike fiddle comparable to the Persian *kamānche*; and the *dumbak*, a small single-headed drum, usually metal. In these respects, the Iraqi *maqām* performance can be compared to other compound forms in Iran and Central Asia, such as the Azerbaijani *mogam*. The *ṣawt* 'voice' is also related to the Iraqi *maqām*, although the *sawt* has local rhythms and intonations. It is typical of the Arab Gulf region, where it can be heard especially in Kuwait and Bahrain, and it has been a specialty of well-known artists such as the late 'Awād al-Dukhī.

TRADITION AND MODERNITY

After World War II, westernization continued and the technological mass media expanded. Arab cities, which received an influx of people from rural areas, became larger and more cosmopolitan. European-derived repertoires usually developed along with an outlook that favored Western classical music, especially among Western-minded educators, thinkers, and policy makers.

From the 1950s to the 1970s, urban music encompassed a large stylistic mainstream, usually referred to as *fann* 'art', *mūsīqā* 'music', and *ṭarab* 'ecstasy' or 'enchantment'. This mainstream represented the indigenous urban style, associated with professional music and local music theory and rooted in the *takht* tradition. It is characterized by a thick orchestral texture created by unison and octave relationships, in contrast to the transparent, subtle heterophonic texture of the *takht*. The mainstream sound is usually produced by the larger *firqa* 'ensemble' or *urkestr* 'orchestra', which traditionally accompanied a leading singer or a dancer and somewhat resembles the European classical orchestra. It incorporates the original *takht* instruments but usually adds a large violin section (sometimes ten or more violins) and often cellos, a double bass, and—especially in popular contexts—a *ṭabla*, a vase-shape single-headed drum.

Despite the enlarged ensembles and the influence of electronics and the media, the mainstream style of composition and performance remains rather faithful to traditional models. This is illustrated by Umm Kulthūm's songs of the late 1940s and early 1950s, which were often performed live and, although essentially precomposed, allowed for some flexibility. These songs had texts by well-known lyricists such as Aḥmad Rāmī and music by major composers such as Zakariyya Aḥmad (1896–1961) and Riyāḍ al-Sinbātī (1906–1981), who were among the most prolific twentieth-century Egyptian composers.

However, mainstream music tends to be eclectic, combining—sometimes juxtaposing—traditional and Western-inspired elements, often in a patchwork of contrasting styles. Each patch, commonly referred to as *lawn* 'color', was grafted onto a traditional style, the indigenous urban sound. The multicolored aesthetic has been typical of the songs of 'Abd al-Wahhāb of Egypt, above all the songs that he composed for films in the 1930s. Stylistically, the mainstream songs, *aghānī*, are precomposed and have a strophic, often irregular structure. By and large they adhere to conventional urban designs—intonational, modal, and metric—but they may have other regional and Western-derived components. In some of his songs, ʻAbd al-Wahhāb uses Latin and ballroom dance meters, motifs from European romantic and postromantic composers, and Western-inspired programmatic compositional devices.

This urban mainstream has influenced the urban styles of many countries in the region. It thus serves as a standardized idiom or musical lingua franca throughout the Near East, North Africa, and the Arabian Peninsula.

In large cities, such as Cairo, the mainstream has been linked to a periphery: religious-oriented music that includes Sufi performances and repertoires; an older *takht*-related repertoire, mostly pedagogical works and "classics" that are still performed at conservatories and in intimate gatherings of connoisseurs; urbanized rural folk music; a locally conceived and locally supported classical European idiom, primarily romantic and postromantic symphonic works that often use indigenous folk and traditional elements; and urban music that seems to be directly inspired by European popular music.

RECENT TRENDS

The late twentieth century brought far-reaching musical developments. For one thing, the earlier configuration of a large traditional mainstream with a varied periphery became less well defined as its components were transformed or blended. For instance, many *aghānī* departed from the mainstream. In the late 1960s, Muḥammad ʻAbd al-Wahhāb wrote songs for Umm Kulthūm that moved toward a more "vernacular" or popular style: short meters, popular-sounding melodies, and a highly structured, heavily orchestrated format with little room for flexible interpretations. These and comparable works of the 1960s and 1970s seemed to cater to mass tastes rather than to the diehard *ṭarab* connoisseur, and they often combined elements from folk dance and short electric-guitar motifs intended to evoke American popular music.

Some older genres were modernized. An outgrowth of the *takht* repertoire—an outgrowth inspired by the urban *firqa* and the large European choral ensemble—was the rendering of older precomposed and improvisatory vocal works in preset, or fixed, choral formats; this became a prevalent practice in some Near Eastern Arab cities. A leader of this trend was Firqat al-Mūsīqā al-ʻArabiyyah ʻEnsemble of Arab Music', established by the Egyptian ministry of culture in 1967 as a counterpart of the Cairo Symphony Orchestra. Such ensembles, in Cairo and other Arab cities, generally have some twenty male and female singers and a large orchestra that resembles a large *firqa* and, like a *firqa*, performs in octaves and unison but typically has several *ʻūd* and *qānūn* players. As a rule, solo improvisations are consciously avoided; the chorus performs under a conductor who controls the tempo and adds prominent dynamic effects. The performances usually take place in a formal theater setting.

New art forms have also emerged. One very popular urban genre has been the so-called Lebanese *fulklur* 'folklore', which is a repertoire of music, dance, and drama. It developed in the late 1950s, largely with government sponsorship, and has often been presented as a local national form of expression. It has been performed in various settings, especially at festivals during the tourist season. Among the most prolific and influential composers and lyricists have been the two Raḥbānī brothers, Asi (b. 1923) and Manṣūr (b. 1925), who were associated with Asi's wife, the well-known female singer Fayrūz (b. 1935). In addition to individual songs and instrumental works, Lebanese *fulklur* generally centers on musical plays with plots that have been derived from village life and dialogue, songs, and "folk" dances. These dances are inspired by the Lebanese village *dabka*—traditional line dances—but they are newly created and fitted to new folkloric songs, frequently by local Soviet-inspired choreographers.

The music represented by the Raḥbānīs—for example, the songs of Fayrūz—has the familiar modal and metric vocabulary of Near Eastern urban music but presents novel sonorities and instrumental blends. A typical work highlights certain instruments, notably the accordion, adjusted to play the "neutral" microtonal intervals; the *buzuq*, a long-necked fretted lute with metal strings that can produce drone effects (this instrument is typically used by local Gypsies); and the recorder, a local Near Eastern fipple flute with an agile tone and a brilliant timbre, as compared with the *nāy*, which sounds more reedy and more traditional. Other instruments are the *riqq*, the *ṭabla*, and a lyrical backdrop of strings playing in the well-coordinated, streamlined style of European classical orchestras, often with a piano that provides colorful arpeggiated fillers and outlines the basic melodic structures. Fayrūz's singing has a distinctive falsetto-like effect and a pure, flowing quality that sets her apart from more conventional female vocalists, particularly those who specialize in *ṭarab*. In general, the Raḥbānīs' songs are carefully structured, are nonimprovisatory, and indicate great attention to orchestral detail. The lyrics, in either Lebanese colloquial or classical Arabic, are picturesque and display impressive literary workmanship, often using romantic rural imagery. The vocal material includes numerous adaptations of folk songs, although much of it is newly composed.

Many other Lebanese artists have been connected with the folklore movement. Among them are Walīd Ghulmiyya, a composer of folkloric and symphonic works; Zākī Naṣīf, a composer and singer; Tawfīq al-Bāshā and Boghos Jalalian, who are composers and arrangers; the female singer Ṣabah; and the male singer and composer Wadīʿ al-Ṣāfī (figure 11), who is acclaimed throughout the Arab world for his phenomenal voice and his talent as an improvisor. Somewhat related in style are the modern political songs and instrumental works, often in Western popular and classical-inspired forms, of Marcel Khalifa (b. 1950), a composer, singer, and accomplished *ʿūd* player.

Since the early 1980s, Near Eastern Arab music has departed further fom the modernized traditional models of the 1960s and 1970s. With the gradual decline of earlier mainstream genres and aesthetic criteria, and the death of mainstream celeb-

FIGURE 11 Wadīʿ al-Ṣāfī performing in Lebanon, in an intimate setting. Photo courtesy of Dār al-Ṣayyād.

rities, new forms have been developed, some of which are now predominant and have international appeal. In Lebanon, there is Ziyād Raḥbānī (b. 1956), the son of Asi Rabḥānī and Fayrūz, a young, multifaceted renegade (and a skilled pianist) whose songs, instrumental pieces, and theatrical works have combined traditional mainstream devices with components from the "folklore" repertoire of his own family, Western classical and popular musics, and traditional jazz. Some of the works of Ziyād Raḥbānī recontextualize or juxtapose disparate elements so as to parody or caricature traditional and modernist works, including some by earlier Lebanese folklorists. His music, though rebellious, often uses traditional instruments such as the *buzuq* and the *'ūd*, as well as the piano and accordion; but it also has some very novel timbres and experimental sounds. Ziyād Raḥbānī, like his father and uncle, sometimes features the singer Fayrūz.

The Near Eastern Arab world has also seen the rise of a new artistic movement that is associated with young singers and with recent means of distribution, including satellite broadcasting, and indicates a further blurring of musical boundaries. It has become a prevalent popular genre, particularly since the mid-1980s, when it was represented by Cairo's *aghānī shabābiyya* 'youth songs' or *al-jīl* 'new generation'. This new mainstream is almost exclusively based on songs. A typical song is only a few minutes long and—like earlier mainstream music—features one leading singer and a relatively small accompanying ensemble in which electronic instruments are prominent; this ensemble includes the tonally modified synthesizer, the bass guitar, the Western drum-set, and local percussion instruments such as the *ṭabla* and *riqq*. The sound is highly "synthetic" and studio-based. The emphatic beat, which gives the songs their powerful, danceable rhythmic drive, is often produced on an electronic drum machine.

Despite its electronic ambience and novel stylistic features, the new popular music is in some ways local and folklike. The lyrics are predominantly amorous and use the same stylized concepts and expressions as the earlier urban repertoires. The metric patterns are typically short, mostly two- or four-beat patterns derived from the indigenous, and very accessible, folk dance repertoire. Similarly, the tunes emphasize a few familiar or "popular" melodic modes, such as *bayyātī*, *nahāwand*, *rāst*, *ḥijāz*, and *ṣabā*.

Within this urban repertoire, certain ethnic and stylistic threads stand out. These include Nubian-based popular songs in Cairo, which have introduced Africanism into the new movement by using traditional Nubian pentatonicism and syncopated meters. Some new features tend to cross national and geographical boundaries. For example, meters and melodic structures of the Khalījī, the Arabian Gulf, can be heard in the Arab nightclubs of Cairo, Beirut, London, and Los Angeles. Another common trait is pastiche-like structures, particularly in the recent Egyptian *rāp* songs, which may use digitally sampled bits from Western rap and set them in collages of other musical components, some local.

Lately, Arab music has been disseminated through multimedia channels, a trend epitomized by the Arab music video or "video clip." Music video achieved great pan-Arab popularity during the 1990s. The songs often remained within the bounds of the new popular mainstream and applied visual themes to amorous lyrics and the overall musical content. At times, however, the visuals were related to the content more loosely and (as in some Western counterparts) were even abstract.

At the turn of the twenty-first century, the music of the Arab Near East was highly eclectic and strongly influenced by the media in its conception, content, and distribution. It had modern and postmodern features, and the urban movement seemed increasingly detached from earlier mainstream practices and to some extent from the traditionalist-modernist rhetoric of the preceding decades. However, today's music is by no means a stylistic monolith. Traditional musical practices and aesthetic criteria tend to remain recognizable, although mostly in sacred and secular contexts that may have become specialized or even marginalized. Such practices and criteria also permeate various novel and unconventional musical expressions.

REFERENCES

Danielson, Virginia. 1997. *The Voice of Egypt: Umm Kulthūm, Arabic Song, and Egyptian Society in the Twentieth Century*. Chicago: University of Chicago Press.

D'Erlanger, Baron Rodolphe. 1930–1959. *La musique arabe*, Vols. 5–6. Paris: Paul Geuthner.

El-Shawan Castelo-Branco, Salwa. 1984. "Traditional Arab Music Ensembles in Egypt since 1967: The Continuity of Tradition within a Contemporary Framework." *Ethnomusicology* 28(2):271–288.

Farmer, Henry George. [1929] 1973. *A History of Arabian Music to the Thirteenth Century*. London: Luzac.

Lagrange, Frédéric. 1996. *Musiques d'Egypte*. Paris: Cité de la Musique/Actes Sud.

Lane, Edward W. [1860] 1973. *An Account of the Manners and Customs of the Modern Egyptians*. New York: Dover.

Marcus, Scott Lloyd. 1989. "Arab Music Theory in the Modern Period." Ph.D. dissertation, University of California, Los Angeles.

Nelson, Kristina. 1985. *The Art of Reciting the Qur'ān*. Austin: University of Texas Press.

Racy, Ali Jihad. 1976. "The Record Industry and Egyptian Traditional Music: 1904–1932." *Ethnomusicology* 20(1):23–48.

———. 1983a. "Music in Nineteenth-Century Egypt: An Historical Sketch." *Selected Reports in Ethnomusicology* 4:157–179.

———. 1983b. "The *Waṣlah*: A Compound-Form Principle in Egyptian Music." *Arab Studies Quarterly* 5(4):396–403.

———. 1991. "Creativity and Ambience: An Ecstatic Feedback Model from Arab Music." *World of Music* 33(3):7–28.

———. 1992. "Music." In *The Genius of Arab Civilization: Source of Renaissance*, 3rd ed., ed. John R. Hays, 151–171. New York: New York University Press.

———. 1996. "Heroes, Lovers, and Poet-Singers: The Bedouin Ethos in Music of the Arab Near-East." *Journal of American Folklore* 109(434):404–424.

Sawa, George. 1989. *Music Performance Practice in the Early 'Abbāsid Era, 132–320 A.H./750–932 A.D.* Toronto: Pontifical Institute of Medieval Studies.

Touma, Habib Hassan. 1996. *The Music of the Arabs*. Portland, Ore.: Amadeus.

Performance of Arab Music in Twentieth-Century Egypt: Reconciling Authenticity and Contemporaneity

Salwa El-Shawan Castelo-Branco

Concepts
The Performance of Emotion
The Representation of Tradition

Arab music in Egypt is a dynamic arena in which different performance practices and aesthetics coexist. During much of the twentieth century, performance was a medium for individual creativity, and the sonic and emotional content of music was largely shaped in the course of performance in response to feedback from the audience. This model gradually gave way to an approach whereby musical compositions were treated as essentially fixed texts, while still allowing for some creative input from solo performers. Since the late 1960s, a new model for the representation of Arab music has been established, and performances have become highly formalized and fixed.

What accounted for the diversity of performance of Arab music in twentieth-century Egypt? What are the distinctive features of the various performance models? When, how, and why did changes occur? What is the role of Arab music in Egyptian culture and society? These questions will be addressed from the perspective of Arab music aesthetics and cultural politics, particularly the central concern with the construction of a contemporary Egyptian identity that is at once *aṣīl* 'authentic' and *mu'āṣir* 'contemporary', reconciling *al-turāth wa al-hadātha* 'tradition and modernity'.

CONCEPTS

In Egypt, *al-mūsīqā al-'arabiyya* 'Arab music' refers to a central group of indigenous urban musical domains that share basic characteristics, most importantly melodic and rhythmic modes, the primacy of words, the central role of the voice as an expressive medium, and melodic artistry. *Al-mūsīqā al-'arabiyya* was used as a generic term following the landmark Arab Music Conference (an international scholarly meeting held in Cairo in 1932 to document and debate the state of Arab music at the time); it replaced the term *al-mūsīqā al-sharqiyya* 'Oriental music', which had been widespread until then.

In Egypt, musicians include within the domain of Arab music different styles, repertoires, and performance practices going back to the mid-nineteenth century. The earliest is *maghna* or *ṭarab*, a Turkish-influenced urban repertoire, style, and performance practice that predominated from the mid-nineteenth century until World War I. Its demise in the 1910s and 1920s was an impetus for efforts at revival by conservative musicians who conceptualized *maghna* as a historical repertoire and performance practice, referring to it as *al-qadīm* 'the old'. In the 1930s and 1940s, a new

FIGURE 1 Umm Kulthūm and her *firqa*. Photo from Salwa El-Shawan Castelo-Branco, c. 1940.

Western-influenced repertoire, style, and performance practice was introduced within Arab music and was often promoted by journalists and the music media as *al-jadid* 'the new'. The composer and singer Muḥammad 'Abd Al-Wahhāb was one of its leading proponents.

Arab music also includes a wide range of musical styles and types deriving from early repertoires and practices and drawing some elements from other musical domains, most notably rural music and Western music. These types are intended to reach large audiences, live and through the media; they include songs from musical theater (1870s to 1920s), songs from films (1930s to 1950s), and the *ughniyya*, a popular song that was developed in the 1940s and 1950s and was largely shaped by the singer Umm Kulthum (figure 1) in collaboration with a few composers with whom she worked closely. [See SNAPSHOT: OPENING NIGHT FOR A STAR PERFORMER—UMM KULTHŪM AND *INTÁ 'UMRĪ*.]

In the late 1960s, earlier repertoires of Arab music were revived and new norms were established for their performance. Both the repertoire and its performance practice were designated *al-mūsīqā al-'arabiyya* 'Arab music', here used as a specific term; or *al-turāth* 'heritage' a concept that merges substance, ideology, and emotions and was central in twentieth-century debates concerning the modernization of Egyptian culture (El-Gābirī 1991).

THE PERFORMANCE OF EMOTION

In Arab music, words occupy a central place and the solo voice is the main expressive medium. The creativity of composers and performers lies in their effectiveness in interpreting and transmitting the layers of meaning and emotions contained in texts through melodic invention and—most important—through vocal interpretation. The musical setting of a text usually consists of a skeletal melody in the appropriate mode and rhythmic pattern. But it is through the artistry of the solo vocalist using many expressive tools (articulation, melodic improvisation, ornamentation, sectioning, repetition, variation, tone color, vocal register, cadences, rhythmic changes, silences, and so on), in a dialogue with the audience, that the meanings and emotions embedded in texts and melodies are communicated and the heightened state of emotion or ecstasy known as *ṭarab* is experienced by both performers and audiences. In Egypt, the model of performance practice that predominated from the 1850s up to the 1960s served the expressive ideals of *ṭarab*. It was based on the central role of the solo vocalist, the accompaniment of a small instrumental ensemble with which the soloist worked closely, and a close interaction between musicians and audience. Within this model, a musical composition was open-ended; its final shape depended on the creativity of the solo vocalist and the instrumentalists, and on continous feedback from a musically informed audience (*sammīa*).

While Arab music continued to depend on the central role of the solo vocalist up to the 1960s, the size and makeup of the accompanying ensemble changed considerably. From the mid-nineteenth century until the 1910s, a small accompanying ensemble called a *takht* had predominated. It consisted of two to five instrumentalists and a chorus of four or five vocalists (*sannida* 'supporters'). *Takht* 'stand' or 'platform', a Persian term, originally referred to an elevated structure on which the performers stood or sat. The instrumental section of the *takht* consisted of a *qānūn* (a trapezoidal plucked zither with twenty-six courses of three strings), an *'ūd* (a fretless short-necked lute with five or six pairs of strings), a *nāy* (an end-blown cane flute with seven holes), a violin designated *kamān* or *kamānja*, and a *riq* (a round frame drum, approximately 25 centimeters in diameter, with jingles). The solo vocalist (*muṭrib*, masculine; or *muṭriba*, feminine) was the central figure in a *takht* performance; there was much solo vocal improvisation, both within the framework of musical compositions and as separate items (*layālī* and *taqsīm*). All *takht* instrumentalists rendered an ornamented version of the melody performed by the solo vocalist, a technique known as *tarjama* 'translation'. The *riq* also performed rhythmic ornamentation. Musical leadership in the instrumental *takht* was provided by the *qānūn*. The *riq* player maintained the rhythmic coherence of the performance, adding ornamentation to the basic metric cycle (*īqā*). A famous solo vocalist might have his or her own *takht*; and *qānūn* players would often form a *takht*, usually named after themselves, which would be hired to accompany different solo vocalists.

Several changes in the size and makeup of *takht* ensembles were introduced during the first quarter of the twentieth century. By the 1930s, an ensemble called a *firqa* (plural, *firaq*) was established. The solo vocalist continued to be the central element, but the accompanying ensemble was much larger. *Takht* instruments (except the *riq*) were multiplied, and new instruments were added.

In the 1930s, a *firqa* typically had three or four violins, a number that increased to about fifteen by the 1960s. The *qānūn*, *'ūd*, and *nāy* were doubled, and new instruments were introduced, including the *ṭabla* (a goblet-shaped drum), cello, double bass, accordion, and clarinet. Some of these instruments, including the cello and double bass, became permanent members of the *firqa*, but others were only used occasionally. A male, female, or mixed chorus ranging from just a few singers to fifteen or more was also added to the *firqa*. In some *firaq*, the *qānūn* continued to lead; in others, a Western-style conductor was introduced.

The changes that occurred in *takht* ensembles were initially brought about through musical theater. The original *takht* was considered too small to portray the events and emotions represented onstage, and so larger ensembles including Western musical instruments were used. Other media also encouraged large instrumental groups. The Egyptian state radio formed large instrumental ensembles for which it commissioned Westernized instrumental compositions as part of its policy of modernizing Arab music. Singers starring in musical films, a popular genre from the 1930s to the 1950s, were generally accompanied by a large *firqa*.

In brief, during the 1930s the *firqa* was established, replaced the *takht*, and became the standard ensemble for accompanying the *ughniyya*. In general, solo vocalists and their *firaq* preserved a creative approach to Arab music, maintaining the norms of performance practice of the *takht* and the aesthetic of the *ṭarab*. In these *firaq*, when the solo vocalist improvised, only a small core of instrumentalists provided an accompaniment. At the same time, there was an increasing tendency toward approaching musical compositions as fixed texts and limiting solo vocalists' creative input to occasional ornamentation.

THE REPRESENTATION OF TRADITION

In 1967, the Egyptian ministry of culture founded Firqat al-Mūsīqā al-'Arabiyya 'Arab Music Ensemble' (figure 2) with the purpose of reviving and disseminating earlier Arab repertoires. [See Music in Performance: A Rehearsal with Firqat al-Mūsīqā al-'Arabiyya.] This ensemble constructed a "heritage" for Arab music and instituted a new model for its performance that was tantamount to the invention of a new performance practice and aesthetic.

The founding of an "official" governmental ensemble for Arab music was informed by a two-pronged cultural policy that called for the revival and preservation of Egypt's cultural heritage while at the same time stressing the need for modernizing cultural production (Wahba 1972). The ministry of culture initially invested in the creation of Western-type music institutions, such as a symphony orchestra, a conservatory, and opera and ballet companies (Ukasha 1988, Vol. 1:413–29). Prominent Arab musicians such as Umm Kulthūm and 'Abd Al-Wahhāb called for equal support for Arab and Western musics and were important in bringing about the founding of a governmental ensemble for the revival and dissemination of the Arab music heritage of Egypt. A committee of scholars and musicians was formed to select the repertoire to be revived, determine its temporal boundaries and characteristics, and cast it into an appropriate mold for modern representations.

The development of the repertoire was based on temporal and stylistic criteria. To be selected as part of the "heritage," a composition had to have been composed at least fifty years earlier and had to adhere to the stylistic norms of Arab music, especially those that predominated up to the 1920s. During its first few years of activity, Firqat al-Mūsīqā al-'Arabiyya gave priority to performing vocal and instrumental forms that had fallen out of use by the 1920s, such as the *muwwashaḥ*, *dawr*, *bashraf*, and *samā'ī*. Gradually, however, this ensemble—and others modeled after it—began to be more flexible in selecting a repertoire, gradually incorporating within *turāth* more recent Western-influenced compositions.

The committee also created a radically new format for the performance of *turath*; these changes in the performance of Arab music were intially applied and consolidated by 'Abd Al-Ḥalīm Nuwera, the first conductor of Firqat al-Mūsīqā al-'Arabiyya. A

FIGURE 2 Firqat Al-Mūsīqā Al-'Arabiyya performing at the Cairo Opera House and Cultural Center. Photo from Salwa El-Shawan Castelo-Branco, November 1995.

large chorus of twelve men and twelve women replaced the solo vocalist, who had been the quintessence of Arab music. The conductor was established as the leader and central figure of the ensemble. The large *firqa* was retained, but Western instruments, except for the violin family, were excluded. Compositions were transcribed into Western notation, and the resulting scores were used by instrumentalists and the conductor—though not by the chorus, which relied exclusively on oral transmission. Melodic improvisation and ornamentation were eliminated; only the *riq* and other percussion instruments added rhythmic ornamentation. Musical compositions became crystallized and were replicated almost identically in each performance. The concert hall was established as the performance setting for Arab music, and the norms of performances by Western symphony orchestras were imposed, including printed programs, silence on the part of the audience during a piece, and formalized applause at the end of each composition. The committee members justified the replacing the solo vocalist with a chorus as a means of distinguishing between *turāth* and other domains of Arab music in which the solo vocalist is central, especially those that are widely transmitted through the media. The committee's decision was also inspired by a Turkish music ensemble from Istanbul which visited Cairo in the mid-1960s; that ensemble consisted of a large instrumental section and a chorus. Approximately five years after the founding of Firqat al-Mūsīqā al-ʻArabiyya, some compositions featured vocal soloists, duos, or trios selected from the chorus, but their musical role was identical to that of the chorus.

Thus cultural policies and musicians instituted *turāth* as a "new" domain of Arab music and established a new model for performance practice and aesthetics. Firqat al-Mūsīqā al-ʻArabiyya, the first ensemble to launch *turāth*, attracted a large audience drawn from Cairo's educated elite and stimulated the formation of other, similar ensembles in Egypt and throughout the Arab world.

The increased Western influence on Egyptian culture since the mid-nineteenth century engendered debates among politicians and intellectuals about Egyptian cultural identity and its relationship to the West. Central to these debates was an evaluation of contemporary Egypt's relationship to its past and its vision of a future in the modern world. Issues that have been discussed and debated include biculturalism (*al-izdiwāg al-thaqāfī*), cultural invasion (*al-ghazw al-thaqāfī*), cultural continuity (*al-tawāṣul al-thaqāfī*), intellectual and cultural independence (*al-dhatiyya al-thaqāfiyyah*), and potential conflicts between authenticity and contemporaneity (*al-aṣāla wa al-muāṣara*) and tradition and modernity (*al-turāth wa al-hadātha*). These issues were echoed in musical discourse, concepts, and performance practices, and in Arab music itself. *Turāth* performances symbolically address some of these issues and, for the audience, reconcile authenticity and contemporaneity and create Egyptian modernity through music.

REFERENCES

Danielson, Virginia. 1997. *The Voice of Egypt: Umm Kulthūm, Arabic Song, and Egyptian Society in the Twentieth Century*. Chicago, Ill.: University of Chicago Press.

El-Gābirī, Muhammad ʻĀbid. 1991. *Al-Turāth wa 'l-hadātha: dirāsāt wa munāqashāt* (Heritage and Modernity: Research and Debates). Beirut: Marqaz Dirāsāt al-Wiḥāda al-ʻArabiyah.

Racy, Ali Jihad. 1983 "The Waslah: A Compound Form Principle in Egyptian Music."

Arab Studies Quarterly 5(4):396–403.

———. 1998a. "Improvisation, Ecstasy, and Performance Dynamics in Arab Music." In *In the Course of Performance: Studies in the World of Musical Improvisation*, ed. Bruno Nettl and Melinda Russell. Chicago, Ill.: University of Chicago Press.

———. 1988b. "Sound as Society: The *Takht* Music of Early Twentieth Century Cairo." *Selected Reports in Ethnomusicology* 7:139–170.

El-Shawan, Salwa. 1982. "The Role of Mediators in the Transmission of Al-Musiqa Al-ʻArabiyyah in Twentieth Century Cairo." *Yearbook for Traditional Music* 14:55–74.

———. 1984 "Traditional Arab Music Ensembles in Egypt since 1967: 'The Continuity of Tradition Within a Contemporary Framework.'" *Ethnomusicology* 28(2): 271–288

Ukāsha, Tharwat. 1988. *Mudhākarāti fī 'l-siyāsa wa 'l-thaqāfa* (My Memoires in Politics and Culture). 2 vols. Cairo: Dār al-Hilāl.

Wahba, Magdi. 1972. *Cultural Policy in Egypt*. Paris: UNESCO.

Snapshot: Ṣabāḥ Fakhrī

Ali Jihad Racy

When I spoke with Ṣabāḥ Fakhrī in 1990 about music and performing, the great Syrian singer told me:

> In order to perform best, first I have to be sure that I am physically in good condition and that I am accompanied by good musicians as well as equipped with an appropriate sound system, one that I have tried out and adjusted in advance. Beyond that it is the audience that plays the most significant role in bringing the performance to a higher plateau of creativity. I like the lights in the performance hall to remain on so that I can see the listeners and interact with them. If they respond, I become inspired to give more. Thus we become reflections of one another. I consider the audience to be me and myself to be the audience.

With his phenomenal talent, his legendary voice, and his close connection to his audience, Ṣabāḥ Fakhrī (figure 1) has become a respected and beloved *ṭarab* singer—that is, one who completely engages his audience with the feeling of the music and the lyrics. He moves his listeners through the expressiveness of his melodic renditions and through the spontaneity of music created on stage. He has attracted a large number of followers, particularly learned ones who understand and love the music.

His performances typically combine instrumental improvisations (*taqāsīm*), historic songs (such as *qudūd ḥalabiyya* and *muwashshaḥāt*), and folk songs. A performance has the suite-like format that can be found throughout the Middle East, for instance, the *waṣla* or *fāṣil*. In the Aleppan tradition, the *fāṣil* usually begins with a precomposed instrumental piece (*samāʿī* or *dūlāb*) and continues with a succession of *muwashshaḥāt*, all in the same melodic mode (*maqām*). The *fāṣil* includes instrumental improvisations and a vocal improvisation on a classical text (*qaṣīda*). The performance ends with *qudūd*, strophic songs that are rendered in call-and-response fashion by the chorus and soloist and, especially in performances by Ṣabāḥ Fakhrī, involve a great deal of virtuosity. Fakhrī's artistry is clearly displayed in his interpretations and treatments of these different genres. His enthusiastic listeners often motivate his creative impulses, so that the performance is shaped collectively. "A good listener," Fakhrī told me, "knows the value of the music, as the jeweler can tell diamond from glass. I sense

FIGURE 1 Ṣabāḥ Fakhrī performing in Los Angeles. Photo by Barbara Racy, 1990.

people's reactions from their movements and by observing their inner emotional tribulations and their responses to what I am singing."

In the Middle East, these performances last, uninterrupted, for hours—in at least one case, fourteen hours. Fakhrī transforms the listeners and brings them to ecstasy through active and emotionally charged audience participation. In this respect he carries forward an old and valued Arab art. Literary sources such as *Kitāb al-aghānī*, a ninth-century compilation of stories about musical life in the opulent Abbāsid courts [see THE *KITĀB AL-AĀNĪ*.], recount tales of singers who transfixed audiences with compelling and beautiful songs.

Born in Aleppo in 1933, Fakhrī grew up with the rich musical tradition of that city. He studied with Shaykh ʻAlī al-Darwīsh and Shaykh ʻUmar al-Baṭsh, who had both absorbed the musical legacy of the Mawlawī Sufi order in Syria. Fakhrī also attended the Conservatory of Music in Damascus. Through his diligent research on older musical sources, including vintage recordings by major artists from Cairo and other Arab cities, he learned a tremendous repertoire of Arab song classics. He became known for his superb renditions of Andalusian *muwashshaḥāt*, a repertoire, thought to have originated in Spain, that had long flourished in Aleppo. By now he has become internationally acclaimed as a performer of the *turāth*, the heritage of Arabic song.

Fakhrī has made hundreds of recordings and international tours. His firm grounding in Arab music theory and his expertise in classical Arabic poetry have enabled him to document traditional Arab music in a multipart audio series, *Nagham al-Ams* 'Tunes of the Past', consisting of more than 150 songs in various genres and melodic and rhythmic modes. Yet it is in his live performances that we can most fully grasp his art, as we watch him interacting with and profoundly moving his listeners and experience a musical tradition whose roots go back to the medieval Islamic courts.

Musical Life in Aleppo, Syria

Christian Poché

Written Sources
Modern Musical Forms
Secular and Sacred Traditions

Aleppo is an ancient town in northern Syria, on the old Silk Road. Today it has approximately one million inhabitants. In the past, Aleppo was considered an "open town" in contrast to Damascus, which was regarded as a holy Islamic city and therefore closed to non-Muslims. For this reason, Europeans settled in Aleppo and eventually came to be referred to as "Levantines." Most were Italians, but Maltese, Greeks, British, Dutch, and French lived there as well. As a result of negotiations between François I (r. 1515–1547) and Sultan Süleyman the Magnificent (r. 1520–1566), a French consulate was opened in Aleppo in 1562, following that of the Venetians in 1548. The Aleppans have generally been merchants and traders, and the city has retained a cosmopolitan, polyglot character. Although Arabic is the official language and the population is dominated by Syrian Arabs (Muslim and Christian), the city also contains communities of Armenians and Kurds, as well as Turks and Greeks. Most of the Jewish community that flourished there in the past departed after 1948, leaving only a handful of families. The community historically played a role in supplying good musicians and instrumentalists. Traditionally, Muslims sang and accompanied themselves with frame drums or small kettledrums, whereas Christians and Jews served as instrumentalists (although this was not a hard and fast rule). Aleppo is famous both for its cuisine and for its musical traditions, which are regarded as among the richest in the Arab world.

WRITTEN SOURCES

Little documentary evidence exists from earlier centuries that pertains to musical life specifically in Aleppo. Aleppo was the center of a brilliant court life under the Ḥamdānid dynasty (944–1003). The great music theorist al-Fārābī (d. 950) settled there for a while, and one of the most important Arabic works ever written about music, the *Kitāb al-aghānī* 'Book of Songs', by Abū al-Faraj al-Iṣfahānī (d. 967), was dedicated and presented to the tenth-century Ḥamdānid ruler of Aleppo, Sayf al-Dawla. [See The *Kitāb al-Aghānī*.] A treatise on music, *Rāḥ al-jām fī shajarat al-anghām* 'The Wine of the Goblet Regarding the Tree of Melodies', probably dating from the seventeenth century, was signed by an Aleppan, at least insofar as we can guess from his name, al-Ḥalabī 'the Aleppan' al-Ḥanafī al-Qādirī; but it contains no specific references to musical life in Aleppo. The manuscript gives information on the musical

Aleppo is famous both for its cuisine and for its musical traditions, which are regarded as among the richest in the Arab world.

instruments used in wartime by Arabs, Turks, Europeans, and Kurds. It deals chiefly with the origin of the short-necked lute, the *'ūd* (Shiloah 1979:240). It also contains a drawing showing the musical modes in the form of a tree (that and the circle being the customary diagrams for representing the modal system).

According to Jean Benjamin de Laborde (1780, 1:191), the first statement on Arab music by a European was written in Aleppo in 1670 by the Frenchman Pétis la Croix, who studied Arab music there (Neubauer 1989:132). Unfortunately, that manuscript seems to be lost. From other European sources of the seventeenth century, we find observations on a private concert accompanying a dinner given in Aleppo around 1681 by the French consul, the Chevalier d'Arvieux. The text mentions a chamber orchestra consisting of "oboes, flutes, timbales, violins, psalteries, and manicordions. . . . The Jews thereafter danced" (1735, 5:63). Those instruments were presumably the double-reed oboe (*zurna*), the reed flute (*nāy*), the small kettledrum (*naqqāra*), the plucked box zither (*qānūn*), and the long-necked lute (*ṭanbūr*). This appears to be the oldest account of an Aleppan orchestra, which, with the exception of the *zurna* and the replacement of the *ṭanbūr* with the short-necked *'ūd* in modern times, has remained the structure of the Arab *takht*, or chamber orchestra, in Syria.

Only at the beginning of the eighteenth century do we find, again from European sources, a significant statement about musical life in Aleppo. Two British doctors, Alexander and Patrick Russell, in their *Natural History of Aleppo* (1794), devoted one long chapter to musical life. Two kinds of music were performed: outdoor and indoor. The first kind (outdoor) referred to music of the Ottoman troops stationed in Aleppo, the *nawba-khāna*, called "the Bashaw's band," which performed "twice a day in the court of the Seraglio" (1:151). The band consisted primarily of oboes (*zummār*), with the accompaniment of trumpets (*nafīr*), and a percussion section consisting of cymbals (*ṣanj*), double-headed drums (*ṭabl*), and small kettledrums (*naqqāra*). The performance was divided into three parts, each progressively faster, and the whole concert took about half an hour. The second kind of Aleppan music (indoor) was "chamber music," performed by singers accompanied by a hammered box zither (*sanṭūr*) or a plucked box zither (*qānūn*), a long-necked lute (*ṭanbūr*), kettledrums (*naqqāra*), the reed flute (*nāy*), and the frame drum (*duff* or *dā'ira*). No short-necked lute (*'ūd*) is mentioned. The chamber concert, "consist[ing] of vocal and instrumental music, continues more than an hour, without intermission" (1:147). Unfortunately, only one musical form is mentioned by name—the *mawwāl*, placed between "an air and a recitative" (1:153).

MODERN MUSICAL FORMS

Vocal improvisation: The *mawwāl*

From the British consul Edward B. B. Barker (1876), who spent many years in Aleppo during the early nineteenth century, we learn that the *mawwāl* (plural, *mawāwīl*) was much appreciated at that time. This improvised form seems to have been popular throughout much of the Middle East during the eighteenth century. In Cairo, the Frenchman Claude Etienne Savary informs us that the *mawwāl*, which he described as an "elegy" (1785, 2:149), was the musical genre of sung poetry performed at private Cairene parties by female vocalists known as *'awālim* (singular, *'ālma*), in contrast to Aleppo, where the *mawwāl* was performed by male singers. Nowadays, it is possible to hear Aleppan concerts devoted exclusively to the performance of *mawāwīl*. Some performers became specialists in this form. Muḥammad al-Dāyikh (b. 1938), for example, is currently recognized as the foremost singer of *mawāwīl* as a separate performance genre. This type of specialization is an exception, however, for the *mawwāl* is more commonly integrated into the traditional Aleppan vocal suite known as the *waṣla*, in which it is but one of several sections.

In Aleppo (unlike Egypt), *mawwāl* is sung with a guttural accent reminiscent of the nomadic bedouin of the Syro-Iraqi desert. For example, the word *qalbī* 'my heart' is pronounced *galbī* as in bedouin dialects. The *mawwāl* is built on a structure of four, five, seven, or ten verses, depending on its origin. It also integrates exclamatory syllables, such as *amān* 'safety' and *yā bā* 'O father'. The performance is generally preceded by an instrumental improvisation called a *taqsīm*. In Aleppo, the *mawwāl* can be freely accompanied by a single instrument, or it can be rendered in a rhythmic structure of 8/8 or 4/4, as practiced by the Turks under the name *çiftetelli*. When the *mawwāl* is sung within a *waṣla*, the performer may also insert a vocal improvisation called *layālī*. In short, the *mawwāl* remains a strong part of Aleppo's musical tradition; a local variant of the genre is called *mawwāl ḥalabī* 'Aleppan *mawwāl*.'

Composed song: The *muwashshaḥ*

The second important vocal form of Aleppo is the *muwashshaḥ*. According to the people of Aleppo, this is an old classical form, traditionally sung by a small choir and accompanied only by a frame drum. Today, however, it is often sung by a mixed choir and a full orchestra (*firqa*), a practice found throughout Syria and Egypt. This short, fixed composition is based on verses of strophic poetry. The poetic form itself originated in medieval Islamic Spain (al-Andalus), but there is no evidence of a direct historical link between the Aleppan *muwashshaḥ* repertoire and that of Muslim Spain. No written sources mention any direct transmission, and the association of the two is found primarily in oral tradition. The link between the Aleppan repertoire and al-Andalus is not mentioned in older texts and appears for the first time, as far as can be determined, in a small work published in Beirut, Lebanon, in 1864 by Buṭrus Karāmī entitled *al-Darārī al-sab' ay al-muwashshaḥāt al-andalusiyya* 'The Seven Roads, or The Andalusian *Muwashshaḥāt*'. The booklet contains only the poems themselves. The first scholarly attempt at establishing a historical link is to be found in a book published in 1955 in Aleppo, *Min kunūzinā: al-muwashshaḥāt al-andalusiyya* 'From Our Heritage: The Andalusian *Muwashshaḥāt*' by Fu'ād Rajā'ī and Nadīm 'Alī al-Darwīsh. Yet even this work does not treat the actual origins of the Aleppan *muwashshaḥ* but merely gives an account of the form's history and development in al-Andalus and an extensive collection of the most famous Aleppan *muwashshaḥāt* transcribed in Western notation. No historical evidence is provided to link the diachronic historical study dealing with medieval al-Andalus to the synchronic collection of the modern Aleppan repertoire.

Nevertheless, other sources shed some light on the history of the Aleppan *muwashshaḥ*. In a famous book published in Cairo in 1856, *Safīnat al-mulk wa nafīsat al-fulk* 'The Royal Ship and the Sumptuous Boat', containing a vast compilation of *muwashshaḥāt*, the author, Muḥammad Ismā'īl Shihāb al-Dīn, notes that he heard a particular *muwashshaḥ* from a Syrian singer named Shākir who had visited Egypt in 1820 (42). Some scholars have maintained that Shākir was in fact from Aleppo. In addition, Shihāb al-Dīn groups his collection into suites (*waṣlāt*) that consist entirely of *muwashshaḥāt*, a form that is still known today in Aleppo as *waṣlāt al-muwashshaḥāt*. This Aleppan suite form begins in a slow tempo and gradually progresses to faster tempi. It also usually begins with poems in older classical Arabic and closes with compositions in contemporary Aleppan Arabic. These suites may be sung separately or may be integrated into the larger *waṣla* as a separate section. The current master of the separate *muwashshaḥ* suites is Ṣabrī Mudallal (b. 1918).

Another important source concerning the history of the Aleppan *muwashshaḥ*, which incidentally does not claim any connection to the Andalusian repertoire, is the work of Ṣāliḥ al-Jadhba (1858–1922; Adham al-Jundī 1954, 1:322), a religious shaykh who in 1906 met the French ethnomusicologist D. M. Collangettes (1906). In his manuscript, al-Jadhba cites old Aleppan musicians who mastered the *muwashshaḥ* and the *qudūd* (see below) and refers to the Aleppan sacred dance *samāḥ*, which may be related to the Turkish Alevi *semah* dance. He mentions one of the oldest known Aleppan musicians, al-Bashank (1765–c.1845) who, like many famous singers, was a muezzin (Ṣabrī Mudallal is today the head muezzin of Aleppo). Al-Bashank, who was given the nickname Imām al-fann 'imam of art', was head muezzin of Aleppo in his day. He was a specialist in the *muwashshaḥ*, which formed a part of both the religious and the secular repertoires, for many religious compositions in the genre *madīḥ* 'praise of the Prophet Muhammad' were based on the *muwashshaḥ* form.

From these various references it is possible to conclude that the *muwashshaḥ* form has long played a major role in the musical traditions of Aleppo, but that the local repertoire cannot be shown to have been historically transmitted from al-Andalus. Rather, it seems to be specifically Aleppan, and to have been valued by Muslims and Christians alike.

A brief contrast with modern North African *muwashshaḥ* traditions (presumed to be closer to medieval Andalusian sources because of their geographic proximity) reveals several distinguishing characteristics of the Aleppan tradition. The Aleppan *muwashshaḥ* is based on melodic modes (*maqāmāt*) found throughout the Arab Eastern Mediterranean that include microtones, such as the three-quarter tone, and differ significantly from the diatonic modes found in North Africa. In addition, the Aleppan *muwashshaḥ* often includes nonsense syllables such as *yalalallī*, already attested to in Ottoman manuscripts of the sixteenth and seventeenth centuries, that differ from the Moroccan use of the nonsense syllables *ha-na-na*. The Aleppan *muwashshaḥ* is based on complex rhythmic cycles—3/4, 17/8, 20/4, 24/4, and so forth—possibly inherited from Ottoman music during the same time period, which contrast markedly with the metrical simplicity of the common Moroccan and Algerian *muwashshaḥ* rhythms: 2/4, 4/4, 4/8, and 6/8. In addition, the Aleppan *muwashshaḥ* opens the suite and possesses a distinctively solemn mood that contrasts sharply with other genres in the performance, whereas in North Africa the performance aesthetic of the *muwashshaḥ* is indistinguishable from the other genres within the suite (*barwal*, *shughl*, and *zajal*) (Poché 1995).

A sacred and secular song cycle: *Isqī al-'iṭāsh*

One of the most famous anonymous compositions sung in modern times, very much appreciated by the inhabitants of Aleppo and unique to that city, is the cycle called *Isqī al-'iṭāsh* 'Give Water to the Thirsty'. Aleppan musicologists (al-Ṣabbāgh 1954; al-'Aqīlī 1979) attribute the text and music to various authors. Originally a religious chant (*inshād*), it is sung during periods of drought as a propitiation. Although quite short—only two stanzas—to begin with, it accumulated various *muwashshaḥāt*, *qudūd*, and even the *samāḥ* dance form over time, eventually growing into a lengthy cycle of more than an hour's duration. The text of the introductory poem is found at the end of a fifteenth-century manuscript entitled *Kitāb al-an'ām bi-ma'rifat al-anghām* 'The Book of Well-Being in the Science of Melodies', signed by Shams al-

Dīn al-Ṣaydāwī al-Dimashqī. The poem was published for the first time in 1929 by Aḥmad Ubarī in a collection taken chiefly from a nineteenth-century compilation by Muḥammad al-Warrāq (1828–1910), an Aleppan hymnodist and muezzin, entitled *Sulāfat al-alḥān wa safīnat al-alḥān* 'The Choicest Melodies and the Ship of Songs'. Thus the historical continuity of the Aleppan tradition can be traced through Ubarī and al-Warrāq to al-Ṣaydāwī al-Dimashqī, whose fifteenth-century text currently stands as the oldest known documentation of the musical traditions of Aleppo.

The suite: *Waṣla*

The main form of Aleppan music, both sacred (without musical instruments other than frame drums) and secular (with a *takht* ensemble), is the *waṣla* 'suite'. This suite may be derived from the Ottoman *fasil* described for the first time by the eighteenth-century Romanian theorist Dimitri Cantemir (Popescu-Judetz 1973). The Egyptian Shihāb al-Dīn wrote of the *waṣla* (1856), but only in regard to the *muwashshaḥ*. Not until the late nineteenth century did a published work in Egypt describe the Arab *waṣla* that combines instrumental and vocal sections, as well as improvised, fixed, and measured compositions. The *Risālat rawḍ al-massarāt fī 'ilm al-naghamāt* 'Treatise on the Garden of Joys in the Knowledge of Musical Modes' by 'Uthmān al-Jundī, published in Cairo in 1899, describes the Egyptian *waṣla* as follows: the performers begin with a succession of *muwashshaḥāt*, then the vocalist enters with a *qaṣīda* (a monorhyme poem freely improvised within the rules of the modal *maqām* system), followed by an instrumental improvisation known as *taqsīm*. Then come the *qudūd* and the *taḥmīla* (a short, fixed composition). Finally, the *waṣla* concludes with a succession of *adwār* (singular, *dawr*, a fixed composition that allows for some improvisation). Curiously, Egypt did not preserve the *waṣla*, which, in the contemporary Middle East, survives only in Aleppo.

The modern Aleppan *waṣla* is constructed as follows: a short instrumental introduction of the *samā'ī* genre or a *dūlāb*, then a series of chorally performed *muwashshaḥāt*, followed by an instrumental *taqsīm* improvisation, then a solo vocal improvisation of *layālī* which is connected to the *qaṣīda*. Then come the *dawr* (introduced from Egypt) and the *mawwāl*. The whole concludes with a series of *qudūd* that may be interspersed with *taqsīm* or *layālī* improvisations. A complete *waṣla* may exceed an hour in length and is always performed in a specific mode (*maqām*) which is announced to the listeners, with modulations that demonstrate the soloist's musical erudition and skill (Poché 1985).

An Aleppan genre: The *qudūd*

The *qudūd* (singular, *qadd*; but they are usually referred to in the plural) are short poems in Aleppan dialect that loosely follow the *muwashshaḥ* form but are sung with the addition of a refrain. They are currently found only in the repertoire of Aleppo and are regarded as light urban music. To some degree, the genre can be related to the Egyptian *ṭaqṭūqa* or the Iraqi *pasta* (or *basta*) in the sense of a "simple song." The origin of the *qudūd* cannot be traced with certainty, but according to al-Jabaqjī (1970:6), they are old songs whose original semiclassical texts have been replaced by lyrics in local dialect. In this case, the *qadd* 'mold' or 'model' would refer to the original rhythm.

The *qudūd* are often grouped together, sometimes mixed with other song genres, and performed as the concluding section of a *waṣla*. They are sung in a joyful manner to a tempo that steadily becomes faster and faster. They can also be sung separately, in which case they are at times referred to simply as *ughniyya* 'song'. In the past, many of the lyrics were tied to mysticism, but most of the *qudūd* performed nowadays address themes of love, nature, and the relations between men and women, and are occasionally satirical in tone. Among the most popular *qudūd* is "*al-Qaraṣiyya*" (pronounced *arasiyyé*); the title refers to a small, red, acidic plum that grows in the region of Aleppo and is featured in certain renowned Aleppan dishes. The song begins: *al-qaraṣiyya akl al-afandiyya* 'Sour plums are the food of gentlemen'.

An Aleppan instrument: The *nash'at kār*

A musical instrument quite typical of and specific to Aleppo is the short-necked plucked lute known as the *nash'at kār*. It is shaped like a standard *'ūd* and uses the same tuning but is smaller and an octave higher. Although its pegbox mechanism has been borrowed from the guitar or mandolin, it is otherwise simply a small *'ūd* whose timbre resembles that of the *qānūn* 'plucked box zither'. It was still being used by the town's *takht* chamber ensemble in the 1960s, but it has now become obsolete and has been superseded by the *'ūd*. There are no references to the *nash'at kār* in written sources, and its history is therefore unknown.

SECULAR AND SACRED TRADITIONS

The description of Aleppan musical life apparently cannot be traced further back than the above-mentioned eighteenth- and nineteenth-century sources. These sources demonstrate, however, that secular and sacred musical traditions coexisted, and further, that the creation of new compositions came primarily from the realm of sacred music. In the beginning of the twentieth century, two distinct trends can be discerned. The first emanated from the mosque and private religious institutions, called *takiyyāt*, the second from the public concerts performed in coffeehouses, music halls, and, later, movie houses. The two trends came into contact at weddings and private parties where both religious and secular music is performed.

In modern times, Aleppo has achieved great renown for its musical arts. Between 1900 and 1930, the most famous Egyptian celebrities, among them 'Abduh Ḥamūlī and Salāma Ḥigāzī, performed there, giving concerts in the city's music halls. The Lebanese dancer Badī'a Maṣabnī wrote in her memoirs about the atmosphere of the Luna Park music hall and described the Aleppan public as both knowledgeable and appreciative (Bāsīla c. 1965:148). When the Egyptian singer Ṣāliḥ 'Abd al-Ḥayy appeared there, he announced: "I am today in Aleppo, the city of musical artistry (*ṭarab*)" (Ḥallāq 1982:5).

REFERENCES

al-'Aqīlī, Majdī. 1979. *al-Samā' 'inda 'l arab* (Music among the Arabs). 5 vols. Damascus: Maṭba'at Dimashq.

d'Arvieux, Laurent. 1735. *Mémoires du Chevalier d'Arvieux*. 6 vols. Paris: Charles Jean-Baptiste Delespine.

Barker, John. 1876. *Syria and Egypt under the Last Five Sultans of Turkey*. London: Tinsley.

Bāsīlā, Nazīj. c. 1965. *Mudhakkirāt Badī'a Maṣabnī* (Memoirs of Badī'a Maṣabnī). Beirut: Dār Maktabat al-Ḥayāh.

Chants sacrés et profanes de Syrie. Sabri Moudallal: Premier muezzin d'Alep. 1994. Notes by Christian Poché. Paris: Institut de Monde Arabe, no. 303. Compact disk.

Collangettes, D. M. 1906. "La musique d'Alep." *Revue Musicale* 6:142.

Ḥallāq, 'Abdallah Yurkī. 1982. "al-Ṭarab fī Ḥalab" (Musical Entertainment in Aleppo). *al-Ḍād* 52:3–9.

al-Jabaqjī, 'Abd al-Raḥmān. 1970. *al-Fulklūr al-'arabī wa-l-qudūd al-ḥalabiyya* (Arab Folklore and the Aleppan *Qudūd*). Aleppo: Maṭba'at al-Sharq.

al-Jundī, Adham. 1954–. *A'lām al-adab wa 'l-fann* (Celebrities in Literature and Art). 2 vols. Damascus: Maṭba'at Majallat Ṣawt Sūriya.

al-Jundī, 'Uthmān. 1899. *Risālat rawḍ al-massarāt fī 'ilm al-naghamāt* (Treatise on the Garden of Joys in the Knowledge of Musical Modes). Cairo: Maṭba'at al-'Umūmiyya.

Karāmī, Buṭrus. 1864. *al-Darārī al-sab' ay al-muwashshaḥāt al-andalusiyya* (The Seven Roads, or The Andalusian *Muwashshaḥāt*). Beirut: n. p.

de Laborde, Jean Benjamin. 1780. *Essai sur la musique ancienne et moderne*. 4 vols. Paris: Chez Eugene Onfroy.

L'art sublime du Ghazal. 1994. Poèmes d'amour au Bīmāristān d'Alep. Adīb Dāyikh (chant), Julien Jalaeddin Weiss (*qānūn*). Notes by Bernard Mousali. Nanterre: al Sur, ALCD 143, 144. 2 compact disks.

Mélodies judeo-arabes d'autrefois Maghreb et Moyen Orient. 1997. Notes by Bernard Mousali. Contains two songs by the Jewish Aleppan singer Fayrūz al-Ḥalabiyya. Paris: Blue Silver Mélodie, 50556–2. Compact disk.

Neubauer, Eckhard. 1989. "Musique arabe en France 1630–1830." In *Le monde arabe dans la vie intellectuelle et culturelle en France*. Paris: Institut du Monde Arabe.

Poché, Christian. 1985. "Syrie: Les muezzins d'Alep." Nanterre. Concert program notes.

———. 1995. *La musique arabo-andalouse*. Arles and Paris: Actes Sud et Cité de la Musique.

Popescu-Judetz, Eugenia. 1973. *Dimitri Cantemir: Cartea Ştiinţei Muzicii*. Bucharest: Editura Muzical.

Rajā'ī, Fu'ād, and Nadīm 'Alī al-Darwīsh. 1955. *Min kunūzinā: al-muwashshaḥāt al-andalusiyya* (From Our Heritage: The Andalusian *Muwashshaḥāt*). Aleppo: Maṭba'at al-Sharq.

Russell, Alex[ander], and Pat[rick] Russell. 1794. *Natural History of Aleppo*. 2 vols. London: G. G. and J. Robinson.

al-Ṣabbāgh, Tawfīq. 1954. *al-Anghām al-sharqiyya* (Oriental Modes). Aleppo: Maṭba'at al-Ma'ārif.

Savary, [Claude Etienne]. 1785. *Lettres sur l'Egypte*. 3 vols. Paris: Chez Onfroy.

Shihāb al-Dīn, Muḥammad Ismā'īl. 1856. *Safīnat al-mulk wa nafīsat al-fulk* (The Royal Ship and the Sumptuous Boat). Cairo: al-Maṭba'a al-Ḥajariyya.

Shiloah, Amnon, 1979. *The Theory of Music in Arabic Writings (c. 900–1900)*. Munich: G. Henle Verlag.

Syrie: Adīb Dāyikh et l'ensemble al-Kindī. 1995. Notes by Bernard Mousali. Paris: Institut de Monde Arabe, no. 50314–2. Compact disk.

Ubarī, Aḥmad. 1929. *Faṣl isqī al-'iṭāsh* (The Song Cycle "Give Water to the Thirsty"). Aleppo: Maṭba'at al-'Aṣr al-Jadīd.

The Palestinian Groom's Wedding Eve Celebration

Nadia Yaqub

A Groom's Celebration in Fandaqumiyya
A Groom's Celebration in al-Rayne

In the northern part of Palestine, the major musical and poetic event of a traditional Palestinian wedding is the groom's celebration, *sahrit il-ʿarīs*, held on the evening before the wedding itself. Typically, hundreds of men will gather to participate in the dancing and singing and to listen to oral poetry duels. Although there is a cluster of core traditions associated with this event, individual performances may vary greatly.
TRACK-17 To convey the variety that exists within this tradition, I will describe two wedding eve parties. Although they differ significantly, both are considered traditional. (I should note that weddings in other parts of Palestine may differ signficantly from those described here.)

A GROOM'S CELEBRATION IN FANDAQUMIYYA

It is about nine o'clock on an evening in June 1995. In Fandaqumiyya, a tiny village in the hills between Janin and Nablus, a wedding eve party is taking place in the street in front of the groom's family home. I and the others who have chosen to leave the women's party are crowded on a rooftop overlooking this all-male celebration in honor of the groom and his father. Some women are quietly chatting among themselves or listening to the proceedings below while others are more intent on adding their own voice to the party with *zaghārīd*—one-line tunes sung at a high pitch and characterized by yodeling. Girls move among us, going back and forth between our vantage point on the roof and the women's party that continues indoors.

As I arrive on the rooftop, the men below have finished setting up the broadcasting equipment—microphones for each of the two poets, a mixing board, and loudspeakers. The cameraman has set up a video station from which he will roam around during the evening with a handheld camera. Chairs are arranged along either side of the road where, for most of the evening, about half the guests, especially older men, will stand or sit. The performance space is well lit and decorated with colored lights and streamers.

The *ṣaff*

Mūsā Ḥāfiẓ and his brother Jihād are the poets who have been hired as this evening's entertainment. Mūsā is in his early forties but has already built a reputation for himself as the finest poet in northern Palestine. He performs daily during the wedding season,

FIGURE 1 Mūsā Ḥāfiẓ performs at a wedding eve celebration in the village of Kufr Kanna, Israel. Photo by Nadia Yaqub, July 1995.

May through October (figures 1 and 2), and supports himself entirely from his poetry. Although he has performed with many other poets, he prefers to sing with a regular partner, his brother Jihād. (Most Palestinian oral poets prefer a regular partner.) Mūsā begins tonight's performance by inviting the audience to form a *ṣaff*, a line of men who will act as a chorus. He does so with some verses of *yā ḥalālī yā mālī*, a form in which the poet recites a line and is answered by the audience with that refrain—*Yā ḥalālī yā mālī*. The form has a measured beat and a melody in a minor key that well suit the religious exhortations and solemn praise of this section of the performance. Men of all ages join the *ṣaff*, which will eventually number well over two hundred. As the line lengthens, it loops around the poets, who stand about forty feet apart in the middle of the road.

Within a few minutes, the *ṣaff* is ready, and Mūsā switches to a faster *murabba'* quatrain. Jihād now joins his brother in the performance. The two poets alternate "turns"; a turn consists of two short lines, separated by the *ṣaff*'s refrain. The *ṣaff* now claps enthusiastically in time to the singing. Soon, the enthusiasm of the *ṣaff* encourages the poets to switch to yet another genre. After one verse of *'atābā*, which serves as a transition, they move into the *far'āwī*, during which the ring of men dance while clapping and singing a refrain of the poet's choosing: *Abu 'Ābīd ḥayy al-ḍayf* 'Abu 'Ābīd, greet the guest'. Although the tempo is fixed, the poet can affect the level of excitement by changing the melody or by raising or lowering the register in which he sings. With the commencement of the *far'āwī*, a few young men enter the ring of men and dance facing the *ṣaff*, encouraging and helping them to maintain the rhythm of their clapping. The groom, his brother, and, later on in the performance, his father, are carried around the square on the shoulders of friends and relatives.

As the poets move from form to form, their poetry continues to treat the central themes of greeting and praising the hosts and their guests. A dominant theme at this party, and indeed at many such events, is praise for the chivalrous virtues of the *ṣaff*. The men are described as fierce knights ready to do battle, as fine riders, and as the protectors of their families and villages. The poetic arena is compared to a battlefield. The poets do not address political themes or events directly, but love of country and willingness to protect it are topics of praise. Guests are also praised for their hospitality, piety, and education.

Far'āwī

After some minutes, Mūsā introduces a new refrain, which defines a new meter and melody for the *far'āwī*: "Unfurl it, unfurl it. Unfurl our flag." He again changes the refrain a few minutes later and continues to do this every few minutes until he is ready to switch to another genre, which he marks by singing a drawn-out *ōf*, the signature beginning of the *'atābā*. Before continuing the verse, however, he pauses to admonish some young men who are not ready to stop dancing and listen quietly, as the *'atābā* demands. A woman near me takes advantage of the pause in the performance to sing *zaghārīd* and continues to sing as the poets trade *'atābā* verses.

'Atābā

'Atābā offers poets an opportunity to display their musical and poetic compositional skills. Composed in the *maqām* 'melodic mode' *bayāt*, as are the *murabba'* and the *far'āwī*, each verse is preceded and followed by long-drawn-out vowels that allow the poet to improvise vocally within the *maqām*. The two-line composition, characterized by paronomasia at the end of the first three hemistichs and a final hemistich ending in the syllable *āb*, demands that a poet be well versed in wordplay and composition within a strict formal structure. Although the themes of praise and chivalry that characterize the *far'āwī* and *murabba'* continue in the *'atābā*, the slower tempo makes it particularly suitable for the quotation of proverbs, religious statements, and description. The tempo of the party slows down considerably when poets begin to compose

FIGURE 2 A musician performs on the *yarghūl* during the celebration in Kufr Kanna. Photo by Nadia Yaqub, July 1995.

ʿatābā, for not only are turns separated by the vocal improvisations that begin and end each turn, but poets will often pause between hemistichs, or repeat a hemistich or line. A *murabbaʿ* will typically last less than ten seconds, whereas an *ʿatābā* verse takes thirty to sixty seconds to sing and can last as long as two minutes.

Murabbaʿ and *muthamman*

The *ʿatābā* is not conducive to active participation by the audience but requires instead that the *ṣaff* listen quietly and clap and cheer only at the conclusion of each poet's turn. Tonight, however, the audience is clearly eager to participate, so Mūsā and Jihād limit their *ʿatābā* exchange to a few verses and then move on to the more inclusive *murabbaʿ*. The audience, as before, claps in time to the singing, but now the poets answer each other so quickly that they do not allow the *ṣaff* time to respond with a refrain. The *murabbaʿ* soon becomes the *muthamman*, which is similar in form and meter and melody but consists of eight hemistichs instead of four. Two *ʿatābā* prepare the *ṣaff* to move again to the *farʿāwī* genre.

As the evening progresses, the performance space as defined by the *ṣaff* becomes diffuse. Young boys are shooed away from the arena, and the poets (in verse) encourage the *ṣaff* to line up properly. An older relative of the groom walks into the circle and fires a pistol into the air—a practice that, though forbidden, is usually ignored by the Israeli authorities. Young men weave in and out of the *ṣaff* offering coffee, water, and cigarettes to the guests. Mūsā and Jihād begin to lengthen the time they spend on each poetic form, but the *farʿāwī*, which allows for the fullest participation from the audience, continues to dominate the performance.

Poetic dueling

About one hour into the performance, a local poet takes Jihād's microphone, much to the excitement of the women around me, who begin to ululate and again sing *zaghārīd*. In *murabbaʿ* verse, the local poet challenges Mūsā to "duel" with him in poetry. The *ṣaff*, also greatly excited, begins clapping more complex rhythms. The poets do not debate a topic; rather, the duel consists mainly of boasting by each poet and predictions of his opponent's imminent defeat—a metalinguistic commentary on the performance in process—interspersed with the themes of praise and chivalry that have dominated the evening. This exchange lasts only a few minutes and is ended by the local poet with an *ʿatābā* verse. Jihād then takes over once more to perform a long *'atābā* section with Mūsā, which elicits renewed enthusiasm from the crowd and another round of firing into the air.

Dabke

It is now midnight, and the poets have been singing for nearly three hours when the host takes the microphone to introduce a local *dabke* dance troupe and invite the guests to attend the wedding festivities the next day. Then, the costumed *dabke* troupe begins to perform to the music of a *mijwiz* (a two-piped double reed wind instrument) and a *darbakke* (a handheld drum), and the singing of a local poet. The *dabke* is a line dance performed by men. There are several Palestinian *dabke* song patterns, each consisting of a basic tune that allows for a great deal of vocal or instrumental ornamentation. Once the dance troupe's performance ends, the floor is open to the audience members, about twenty of whom form a circle around the musicians and dance.

Mūsā has been given a chair, and at the conclusion of the *dabke* a smaller ring forms around him and the musicians, who begin to play and sing the henna song. Two women—the mother and a great-aunt of the groom—dance into the circle. Each is wearing a brightly colored long dress and a white scarf. The groom's mother carries a small basket containing flowers and henna. They dance with the groom for some minutes and then seat him on a chair and begin to decorate his hands with henna. As the older women work, several other women—all aunts of the groom—enter the ring and begin to dance. It is nearly two o'clock in the morning when the festivities end.

A GROOM'S CELEBRATION IN AL-RAYNE

Three weeks later I attend a wedding in al-Rayne, a small village just east of Nazareth on the road to Tiberias. The wedding eve party takes place in a small parking lot along the main road. The performance area has been covered with a green canopy and is well lit. Chairs are arranged around the space where the poets, musicians, and *ṣaff* will stand.

As the performance space and the recording equipment are set up, I talk with Mu'īn Khalīl, the musician who has been hired for tonight's performance. Mu'īn is a well-known musician with a regular program on Israeli radio. He opens a small leather case and carefully draws out his *mijwiz*, which he will play at tonight's wedding (figure 3). "I made it myself," he says, "from the wing bones of a hawk." The instrument is small, less than a foot long, and its two pipes, each with six holes, are held together by beeswax and tape. Mu'īn proceeds to tune the instrument by adjusting its bamboo mouthpiece and reeds.

Dabke

As the only woman present, and because I do not want my presence to affect the performance, I try to be inconspicuous, seating myself behind the chairs that ring the *ṣaff*. The party begins with Mu'īn playing *taqāsīm* 'instrumental improvisations'. The music serves as an invitation to the gathering guests to prepare to dance the *dabke*. Mu'īn then launches into one of the many popular *dabke* songs, *Yā ẓarīf al-ṭūl* 'O Tall Handsome One', and he is joined by the poet Abū Mājid. Like most *dabke* songs, this one has a simple melody on which a skilled musician can elaborate at length. Thus the sung verses tend to be short and separated by long instrumental stretches in which Mu'īn plays, accompanied only by the rhythmic stamping of the dancers' feet. Mu'īn is in his sixties and a chain-smoker, but he still has tremendous lung power, and he plays continuously for more than half an hour.

By this time, a crowd of approximately 150 people has gathered at the party. It is time for the two poets—Abū Mājid and Abū Jawhar–to begin their performance. Abū Mājid is a younger brother and Abū Jawhar a nephew of the late Tawfīq al-Raynāwi, a well-known poet who performed from the 1930s to the 1970s. Both are

FIGURE 3 Muʿīn Khalīl plays the *mijwiz* during a wedding eve celebration in al-Rayne, Israel, while guests dance the *dabke* around him. Photo by Nadia Yaqub, 1995.

also relatives of the groom. Indeed, I am told that this is a family wedding and that all the guests are related to the groom.

Saḥje

Abū Mājid and Abū Jawhar begin by singing *ʿatābā* verses and then move on to *murabbaʿ* and *farʿāwī*. Like their counterparts in Fandaqumiyya, they vary the tempo of their performance by moving from form to form. After about half an hour of poetry, however, their place is taken by Muʿīn, who again performs on his *mijwiz*. He plays a simple melody, which he calls *saḥje*, again with continual elaboration. The men in the *ṣaff* dance and clap, as they would for the *farʿāwī*, but there is no singing. Muʿīn's performance lasts about fifteen minutes, after which he relinquishes the floor to the poets. He will play the *saḥje* two more times in the course of the evening, each time for about ten or fifteen minutes. I later asked Muʿīn about his practice of performing during the poetry section. He acknowledged that this is unusual, claiming that he is the only musician in the Galilee who does so.

Poetic dueling

The singing of Abū Mājid and Abū Jawhar tonight is similar to that of Mūsā and Jihād at Fandaqumiyya, but Abū Mājid and Abū Jawhar perform little *farʿāwī*, since Muʿīn's *saḥje* solo generally occurs when the *farʿāwī* would usually be performed. This wedding at al-Rayne also differs from the one at Fandaqumiyya in that it includes *ʿatābā al-nashal*, a type of dueling in *ʿatābā*. In *ʿatābā al-nashal*, the poets sing very quickly, omitting the pauses and vocal ornamentation that characterize the regular *ʿatābā*, and focus on quickly trading verses. The effect can be quite thrilling, especially when poets follow a particular theme or compositional restriction (for example, composing a string of verses that end in the same rhyme letter or morphological root). In this performance, however, the *ʿatābā al-nashal* sections are short and serve mainly as transitions to a spirited *murabbaʿ* exchange.

Although considerably smaller, this wedding is just as lively as the one at Fandaqumiyya. The performance space is not as large, and the poets are more tolerant of the horseplay of young boys, perhaps because the wedding party is a more intimate family gathering.

FIGURE 4 The shaving of the groom at the end of the wedding party at al-Rayne. The groom and the poet Abū Mājid are on the shoulders of the young men. Photo by Nadia Yaqub, 1995.

Shaving the groom

TRACK 8–18 Three hours into the performance, Mu'īn again performs *taqāsīm*, and then *yā ẓarīf al-ṭūl*, inviting the men to another round of *dabke* dancing. After half an hour of dancing, the host takes the microphone to invite those present to participate in *ziyānat al-'arīs*, the shaving of the groom (figure 4). Women from the groom's family join the *ṣaff* as Abū Mājid sings a shaving song to the accompaniment of the *darbakke* and clapping and chanting. The groom and the barber are raised onto the shoulders of some of the young men at the party, as is Abū Mājid, and one of the women takes the second microphone and begins trading lines with Abū Mājid. Much of the singing consists of instructions to the barber: "Shave him, barber, shave him"; "Wait, barber, wait, wait for his cousins to come"; and later, "Wipe him, barber, wipe him." Other family members take their turns at the microphone. Finally, the poets Abū Mājid and Abū Jawhar again take the microphones and sing alternating turns of the henna song—the same one that was sung during the adorning of the groom with henna at the wedding in Fandaqumiyya—although here at al-Rayne the groom's hands are not decorated with henna. The wedding ends shortly after midnight.

REFERENCES

'Arnīṭa, Yusra. 1968. *al-Funun al-sha'biyya fī filasṭīn*. Beirut: Munaẓẓamat al-Taḥrīr al-Filasṭīnī.

Bailey, Clinton. 1974. "Bedouin Weddings in Sinai and the Negev." In *Studies in Marriage Customs*, ed. Issachar Ben-Ami and Dov Noy, 117–132. Jerusalem: Magnes.

Al-Barghūthī, 'Abd al-Laṭīf. 1986. *Dīwān al-'atābā al-filasṭīnī*. Jerusalem: Bir Zeit University.

———. 1990. *Dīwān al-dal'awna al-filasṭīnī*. Al-Bīra: Jam'iyyat In'āsh al-Usra.

Ḥāfiẓ, Mūsā. 1988. *Funūn al-zajal al-sha'bi al-filasṭīnī*. Jerusalem: Manshurāt al-Baydar.

Sbait, Dirgham. 1982. "Improvised Folk-Poetry of the Palestinians." Ph.D. dissertation, University of Washington.

———. 1986. "Poetic and Musical Structure in the Improvised-Sung Colloquial *Qaṣidah* of the Palestinian Poet-Singers." *Al-'Arabiyya* 19:75–108.

———. 1989. "Palestinian Improvised-Sung Poetry: the Genres of *Ḥidā'* and *Qarrādī*—Performance and Transmission." *Oral Tradition* 4:213–235.

———. 1993. "Debate in the Improvised-Sung Poetry of the Palestinians." *Asian Folklore Studies* 52:93–117.

Shiloah, Amnon. 1974. "A Group of Arabic Wedding Songs from the Village of Deyr al-Asad." In *Studies in Marriage and Custom*, ed. Issachar Ben-Ami and Dov Noy, 267–296. Jerusalem: Magnes.

Palestinian Wedding Songs

Ḍirghām Ḥ. Sbait

Historical Background
Social-Cultural Context
Traditional Wedding Songs
Modern Palestinian Weddings and Songs

The oral literary heritage of the Palestinians includes various genres of folk poetry, folk songs, and popular songs, many of which are intended for weddings and, to a lesser degree, for other joyous events. There are five distinct categories of Palestinian wedding songs:

1. *Folk songs* by earlier anonymous Palestinian composers.These are transmitted orally and are still performed by nonprofessional Palestinian folk singers, and also (though less frequently) by professional popular singers.
2. *Women's folk songs*. These usually have precomposed texts, but they are occasionally improvised by the vocalist.
3. *Audience folk songs*. These are sung by an individual or a group in specific wedding contexts.
4. *Improvised sung poems*. These are classified as defined poetic genres. They are improvised in spoken Palestinian Arabic and are sung by professional male poet-singers. Their melodies are almost fixed, are transmitted orally from the older generation of Palestinian poet-singers, and include established precomposed and newly composed refrains, introduced by the poet-singers and then repeated by folk dancers and the audience.
5. *Urban songs popularized on radio and television*. These are composed by literary poets and professional musicians and are sung by professionals to entertain the wedding guests. This category may include traditional folk songs of category 1, renovated and played in a different fashion.

Songs of categories 1, 2, and 3 are mostly precomposed, but new verses are often added by folk improvisers. The melodies are transmitted orally and are mostly fixed, but with several variations. Except for category 5, all these songs are characterzed by "orality." Almost all the songs are composed in spoken (colloquial) Palestinian Arabic, which differs slightly from literary (formal) Arabic in grammar and idiom; the only exception is some songs in category 5, which are originally composed in literary Arabic. The orally composed songs use distinct poetic techniques, despite their similarity to formal literary Arabic poetry. There is a wide spectrum of forms, genres, subjects, melodies, and folk and modern instruments in Palestinian wedding celebrations, but only few representative examples—mostly from categories 1 through 4—will be discussed here.

Modern Palestinians celebrate three types of weddings: mostly traditional weddings, with old folk songs and sung poetry; traditional urban weddings, with a mixture of old folk songs and contemporary songs; and totally urban weddings, with modern Arabic urban music and contemporary popular radio and television songs.

HISTORICAL BACKGROUND

The Palestinian tradition of folk songs and improvised sung poetry in spoken Arabic is probably as old as the Palestinian people. Before the twentieth century, during what has been called an "era of literary stagnation," there was no scholarly interest in this oral discipline, despite its importance as an original art form that gives a true, vivid picture of the life of the Palestinians—their character, aesthetic values, customs, social-ethnic oral history, literature, and music. Early Arab literary scholars disregarded most works not written in literary Arabic. The Palestinian wedding songs, which constitute a serious part of Palestinian folk literature, were also ignored by early scholars, probably because there was little interest in the common man and his position in society, let alone his way of life, traditions, values, literature, and music.

Modern scholars, both Arab and non-Arab, are paying increasing attention to folk traditions and literature; above all, they are interested in studying the original culture depicted by folk texts. This is perhaps especially because modernization presents a threat to traditional artistic expression. For one thing, orally composed folk songs and poems—which are being supplanted by songs of more sophisticated urban composers and musicians popular with the young and promoted by the media and the music industry—are in danger of dying with the older generation. Also, the vast majority of Palestinian wedding songs are associated with villages; and since most villages are gradually becoming modernized, this art form faces an uncertain future. The Palestinian identity and nation face an uncertain future as well. Therefore, a number of scholars have dedicated themselves to collecting, studying, analyzing, and publishing materials that will preserve these unique traditions.

Two pioneer scholars were Dalman, whose *Palästinischer Diwan* (1901) is a broad collection of early Palestinian wedding songs and other folk songs; and Saarisalo, whose *Songs of the Druzes* (1932) is a general collection of improvised Palestinian poetry, more limited in scope. These works by Western Arabists paved the way for a new generation of Palestinian authors who published Arabic works dealing directly with Palestinian folk songs, many of which are performed at weddings. ʿArnīṭah (1968) covers a wide range of Palestinian folk songs, their melodies, and related traditions; Sirḥān (1979) examines wedding songs in their sociocultural context; al-Barghotī (1979) studies folk songs and poetic genres of Palestinians of the West Bank and Jordan. Two dissertations written in English, both based on fieldwork, are al-Barghotī's "Arab Folk Songs from Jordan" (1963) and the present author's "Improvised-Sung Folk Poetry of the Palestinians" (Sbait 1982). Three essays in English by the present author (Sbait 1986, 1989, 1993) take up the most popular genres of improvised sung Palestinian wedding songs. Works such as these, presenting the rich and complex oral folk tradition of the Palestinians, provide Arab readers, Arabists, Western folklorists, ethnomusicologists, social anthropologists, literary critics, and others with a detailed scholarly record of Palestinian wedding songs.

SOCIAL-CULTURAL CONTEXT

For most Palestinians, their wedding is the most important event of their life. Among people of all religions, divorce is a last resort if marital problems arise, particularly when couples have children; therefore, Palestinians take a wedding very seriously and spend much effort and money celebrating it. The couple will meet openly or secretly, or in the family circle. The groom tells his parents of his choice, and they do the groundwork for a meeting in which the groom's family, or a *jāha* (a delegation of respectable people representing the family of the groom), asks the bride's parents for her hand. When a proposal is accepted, Christian families discuss the details of the *khuṭbih* 'engagement' and Muslim families decide the date of the *katb liktāb* (or *'aqd izzawāj*) 'marriage contract'. These two events can be celebrated quietly by the two families, or with festivities to which many guests are invited. On this occasion, Christians invite a priest to bless the engagement, and Muslims invite a *ma'dhūn* or *ma'zūn* (an official authorized by a Muslim judge of the religious courts to perform a marriage) to sign the marriage contract. After the official ceremony, precomposed folk songs are sung, but rarely is a poet-singer or a professional singer invited to this brief celebration.

As the wedding approaches, a date is set, lists of guests are prepared, and invitations are printed and mailed or delivered in person. A best man, who may be a friend or brother of the groom, and a maid of honor, who may be a sister or friend of the bride, are selected. If the bride is from another village, buses must be hired to transport the crowd of guests, and a special taxi or private car must be obtained to take the bride from her village to the groom's home. The bride's car will be specially decorated for the occasion, as in the West. The parents of the bride and the groom prepare all that is required for the festive dinner if the wedding is to take place in the village; but when a wedding is to be held in a city, food is prepared by professional caterers in a rented hall (Sbait 1982:1–58).

TRADITIONAL WEDDING SONGS

For a traditional village wedding, the father of the bride usually invites a professional musical group to entertain his family's guests. However, the groom's father invites a team of two poet-singers and a folk musician to entertain his family's guests. Palestinians who have just moved to a city continue to include traditional wedding songs, in addition to urban songs. Hence, it is not at all strange to have a traditional or semitraditional wedding in a town or city with a Palestinian community.

In the old days, a wedding involved everyone in the village during the week of *ta'ālīl* (singular, *ti'līlih*)—the wedding eve entertainments. The villagers would come to the house of the host (the groom's father) to sip coffee, sing wedding songs, dance, and help with some of the preparations.

During this time two separate *hinna* 'henna' parties took place—one for the bride and one for the groom. *Tarawid* (light songs) of henna were performed by a female lead vocalist who would sing the basic verses, which the women would repeat after her. One example is *Mnayn jibt il-hinna?* 'Where Did You Bring the Henna From?' (Sbait collection, cassette 19):

> Where did you bring the henna from? Tell me, O groom.
> The henna is from our country, and the wedding clothes are from Paris.

In recent times, henna parties have gone out of fashion, and only a few traditional people perform the ceremony. Also, these lengthy evening celebrations are no longer practical because wedding guests are too busy to participate every night in such events—nor can the host afford the cost.

The time then arrives for two separate musical parties, which take place simultaneously, beginning at about eight o'clock in the evening. These are the groom's night and the bride's night.

The groom's night

Āwīhā

On the evening of the groom's celebration, known as *sahrit il-'arīs*, or *it-ti'līlih*, the groom's relatives and close friends arrive first. Guests from outside the village then begin to appear at the host's house. As they reach the door, older female relatives sing *āwīhā* quatrains praising the groom's parents, especially his mother, and expressing their own happiness on this occasion.

Āwīhā is based on four lines of poetry sung by a female soloist and followed by women's *zarāghīt* 'ululation'. Each line has seven to seventeen syllables. The common rhyme schemes are aaaa and aaba. Every quatrain deals with one subject, usually praise or congratulations. Here is an example (Sbait 1982:70, 366–375; collection, cassette 21):

> *Soloist*: Ah, I came to sing, nobody sang like me.
> Ah, amidst a courtyard in which the bird is waiting.
> Ah, I wish you, the groom, to be delighted with your bride-to-be.
> Ah, you married the good (bride) and the other (young men) are still waiting.
> *Women*: Ululation.

As people assemble in the guests' room, sipping coffee and chatting, a short time before the formal evening begins, the poet-singers improvise quatrains called *'atābā* in honor of the groom, his father (the host), or their guests.

'Atābā is mostly improvised. It has four basic lines, sung by one poet-singer at a time; each line has eight to fifteen syllables. A feature of this genre is the *jinās*, or homonym: the last word of all the lines (except the last) must have a *jinās*. The most common rhyme scheme is aaab. The rhyme of the last verse must end with either *nā* or *ab*. *'Atābā* ending with *nā* and sung indoors is normally followed by a refrain; *'atābā* ending with *ab* and sung outdoors is not followed by a refrain. However, either type, if sung indoors, may occasionally be followed by another popular refrain, such as "Welcome, our beloved who have honored us with their visit." The basic subjects are praise of the hosts, the groom, the bride, their families, and their guests; a description of the evening; love; and social and political events. In the following example, "your eyes are our eyes" is a metaphor expressing praise (Sbait 1982:59–146; collection, cassette 34).

> *Poet-singer*: Welcome to the guests who arrived at the host's house.
> My eyes became pleased by greeting the respected people.
> In the past and the future lifetime
> I will not forget the people of generosity, and my friends.
> *Audience's refrain*: All the eyes are mere eyes, but your eyes are our eyes.

Dabkih *songs*

When most of the guests have gathered, a light dinner is offered. Soon, the best man, who acts as an informal master of ceremonies, asks the *shabāb*—the young men—to perform a *dabkih*, a circle dance. At a traditional wedding, a folk musician plays popular folk tunes on a *shubbābih* (a reed or a brass flute), a *mijwiz* (a wind instrument with a double pipe), or an *arghūl* known as *urghul* (a woodwind with two pipes of unequal length). The *rawwīs* 'head' leads the *dabkih shamāliyyih*, a popular folk dance of Palestinian villages in northern Galilee; during it, occasionally, he performs an artistic solo dance in the middle of the circle.

The folk musician plays *taqāsīm* (singular, *taqsīm*), improvised solo passages. Then he approaches one or more well-recognized male or female folk singers while playing a folk tune; the singer or singers will respond by performing a quatrain from an appropriate folk song in category 1. This may last for an hour; meanwhile, the folk singers take turns singing quatrains of popular wedding folk songs such as *dal'onā* and *ẓarīf aṭ-ṭul*. However, at modern weddings professional singers and instrumentalists are the main entertainers.

TRACK 3-16

The dominant form for these songs is the quatrain, except for *jafrā*, which is based on eight short verses. In *dal'onā* songs, the rhyme scheme is aaab or aaba; the last verse of any quatrain must end with the rhyme *nā* ('Awaḍ 1983:30-31; Frayḥa 1973:57). In *ẓarīf aṭ-ṭul* the rhyme scheme is aaab; the preferred rhyme of the last verse in the quatrain is usually *nā* but may vary. In *jafrā* the common rhyme scheme is ab/cb/db/cb; the last verse of this song ends with the rhyme *iyyā*. In *'al-hawa* the rhyme scheme is aaba; the last verse of this quatrain must end with *wā*. In order, the verses have ten, eleven, six, and sixteen syllables. The subjects are love (*ghazal*), implied sex, rebuke of the beloved, and politics. What distinguishes these songs from each other, given the similarilty of their poetic forms, is mainly the melody (Sbait 1982:1–58).

There are hundreds of established quatrains. Four of the most popular are *Dal'onā* 'The Charming, Spoiled Girl', *Ẓarif aṭ-ṭūl* 'The Charming Tall Person', *'al-Hawa* 'Concerning Love' (Sbait collection, cassettes 3 and 5), and *Jafra wya harrabi'* 'She Is Young, O Folks!' (al-Barghotī 1979:26–27).

Occasionally, a popular piece may be sung, such as *Wayn 'a-Ramallah* 'Going to the City of Ramallah', or an old-fashioned song such as *Baddar qamarna* 'Our Moon Is Shining Full in the House' ("our moon" is a metaphor for the beloved).

Ṣaff saḥjih *songs*

As the folk dance progresses, the crowd continues to grow, and the folk poet-singers are ready to begin. The best man invites the leader of the folk dance, the dancers, and the guests to form *ṣaff saḥjih*, a line of about fifty to two hundred people (figure 1). As the dancers line up, they clap and chant *Widaḥaw* 'Spread out'; two or more *saḥjih* organizers (*ḥāshī*) dance in front of the line, helping the others to get arranged and clap in rhythm. At the same time, several hundred guests and neighbors are seated on chairs. The groom and his best man sit with them in the front row, facing the dancers. Between the audience and the dancers, a space is left for the poet-singers and the line organizers to stand.

Then both poet-singers begin their performance. Each holds a microphone in one hand, holds the other hand to his ear, and sings *of* (a sigh of relief) on a high

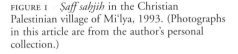

FIGURE 1 *Ṣaff saḥjih* in the Christian Palestinian village of Mi'lya, 1993. (Photographs in this article are from the author's personal collection.)

note several times; this will echo throughout the space and will be answered by an *of* from the dancers. As soon as the crowd calms down, the singing and dancing begin.

Outdoor ʿatābā. The poet-singers first alternate outdoor *ʿatābā* (the celebration having moved outdoors), slightly varied in form and melody from the indoor *ʿatābā* described above; they praise the host, groom, and guests or their communities. The following improvisation is an example; "a Subaytī" refers to the poet himself (Sbait 1982:77; collection, cassette 28):

> O my village, I will never forget my house while absent from you.
> Who else but my heart your love captured?
> Take an oath of love from a Subayti—
> I will never forget you, no matter how long the absence will be.

Ḥidā. Next, the poet-singers switch to improvisation of several types of *ḥidā* (plural, *ḥadādī*), another popular genre, which differs from *ʿatābā* in structure and
TRACK 17 melody. *Ḥidā* is sung in couplets (*ḥidā muzdawjī*), quatrains (*ḥidā mrabbaʿ*), eight-line stanzas, or stanzas of more lines, followed by the dancers' refrains. A line has seven or eight syllables. The rhyme scheme for couplets is ab, ab, cb, db, and so on; the rhyme scheme for quatrains is aaab, cccb, and so on. The most common refrain is *Yā ḥalālī yā mālī* 'Oh, how fortunate I am!' The subjects are mostly praise; descriptions of the occasion; social, educational, and intellectual issues; zeal; political issues; humor; and love. The melody varies from one type of *ḥidā* to another. Usually, the couplets are in a slow tempo and the quatrains in a fast tempo; but couplets sung in the bedouin style (*is-saḥjih il-badāwiyyih*) have the fastest tempo of all types of *ḥidā*. Thus a feature of this genre is the possibility of accelerating the tempo from one type to another (Sbait 1982:147–225; collection, cassettes 1 and 34).

As the poets improvise *ḥidā mrabbaʿ* (quatrains), they may debate in a friendly manner. A debate in *ḥidā*, called *mḥāwarah* in Palestinian Arabic, can involve one subject, such as "the importance of education," or contrasting subjects such as "imprisonment and freedom." One long debate, for instance, was called "He Who Has Taught His Son" (collection, cassette 23). *Mḥāwarah* is the most advanced form of this genre: the poets debate intellectual subjects requiring a great deal of argumentation. Audiences look forward to such a debate and consider it the climax of the groom's night (Ḥaydar 1989:189–212; Sbait 1982:221–224, 1986:75–108, 1993:93–117; Sowayān 1989:151–173).

Farʿāwī. Thereafter, the poet-singers switch to improvisation in a genre called *farʿawi*, and the dancers sing various rhythmic refrains, clap, and dance to the rapid tunes. *Farʿāwī* poems are based on single improvised rhythmic verses, couplets, or quatrains followed by varying refrains. The refrain of any individual improvisation is the first verse or the couplet introduced by the poet-singers. Depending on the opening line, a verse has six, seven, eight, ten, or eleven syllables. Single lines use the rhyme scheme a; couplets and quatrains use ab, ab. The subjects are descriptions of the occasion, love, politics, praise, zeal, religious sentiments, congratulations, and words of welcome (Sbait 1982:226–253; collection, cassette 30).

Dūrah. When they have reached a high point, the poet-singers and dancers together perform *dūrah*, a spontaneous circular rotation of the line of dancers. Some individuals from the audience dance inside this circle; in Christian villages, women, relatives of the groom, or whoever wants to may do this. Some men dance with a sword in the hand, others with a cane; most women hold an embroidered handkerchief or scarf. Other women, outside the circle, sing *āwīhā*, followed by ululation. *Dūrah* is another climactic point of the groom's night.

Qaṣīdih. One of the poet-singers may chose to improvise a *qaṣīdih* (plural, *qaṣāyid*) in which he enhances the occasion by presenting his congratulations to the hosts or by discussing an important social, pedagogical, or political issue. *Qaṣīdih* is also known by the colloquial Arabic name *zajaliyyih* (plural, *zajaliyyāt*); this is derived from the general name *zajal*, commonly used for all improvised sung, precomposed, and improvised Palestinian poems that follow the model of the classical Arabic *qaṣīda*: two hemistiches (or couplets) and a monorhyme at the end of all couplets. Other *qaṣāyid* are based on sections (stanzas), each of which has a concluding line; the last stanza of all includes a *kharjah* (the last verse of the poem), which normally conveys a special message—this structure is like the the Andalusian *muwashshaḥ*, a postclassical stanzaic Arabic poem. Refrains are uncommon in this genre. A *qaṣīdih* verse has eight to thirteen syllables. Monorhyming poems use the scheme ab/db and so on. Five-line stanzas may have the rhyme scheme abacb/abadb and so on. Three common topics are congratulations, love, and politics (Sbait 1982:326–357, 1986:75–108).

Here is an excerpt from an improvised *qaṣīdih* based on a five-line stanza (Sbait collection, cassette 17):

> I came to attend your wedding, O Nazih [the groom]
> And to congratulate your parents and family who invited me.
> I came to stay awake all night.
> I am ready to sing until sunrise
> If the beloved ones like listening to me.

Mḥorabih: *Procession songs*

It is now time to return from the village square to the groom's house. Many local people return to their homes; guests from outside the village who are not planning to return for the next day of the wedding may congratulate the groom and leave. Other guests, who will be attending the next day, may go to the groom's house immediately, or they may join their own hosts, or friends from the groom's village may invite them to stay overnight. The young friends of the groom and his family, and relatives, usually led by the poet-singers, walk back to the host's house at about midnight, while singing *mḥorabih*, wedding procession songs.

Since *mḥorabih* is slow, it is not accompanied by dancing or clapping. A *mḥorabih* is based on improvised single lines or pairs of lines improvised one at a time. The first line or pair is the refrain, to be sung by the listeners as they walk; this refrain will be used until the poet-singer switches to another verse. A single line has twelve syllables; a pair of lines have eight syllables each. Single lines use the steady rhyme scheme a; pairs use the steady rhyme scheme ab. The subjects are mainly praise and congratulations, as in the following excerpt (Sbait 1982:254–265; collection, cassette 4):

> Our groom has superiority over the lion with his esteem;
> All the young men obey his word today.
> We came today to attend his wedding.
> Our groom, all the young men are in his service.

After the groom arrives at his parents' house, it is traditional in some villages, particularly Christian villages, to pay a visit to the bride's family. If the bride is from another village, a small delegation will drive there and greet her family on behalf of the groom's family. If the bride lives in the same village, the groom himself and everybody associated with him can go on this brief visit. The route to and from the bride's house is traveled in a procession while the crowd sings *mḥorabih*.

The bride's night: *Jalwih* songs

The bride's night, *sahrit il-ʿarūs*, is held simultaneously with the groom's, but her musical celebration is rather different. The guests, mostly women, are usually members of the immediate or extended family and friends. The performers are professional male musicians (this is due to a lack of professional female Palestinian singers). They play instruments, mainly the *'ud* (a short-necked plucked lute); *kamanja* (a spike fiddle); *durbakkih*, also known as a *tablih* (a single-headed goblet drum); *qānūn* (a zither); and *daff* (a tambourine). Western electric instruments—such as electric guitar, drums, and, most recently, keyboards—are also used. In most cases a professional male soloist is invited to sing; many of these singers hve formed their own groups. The musicians sit on the stage below the *ṣamdih*, the bride's elevated space, with microphones and loudspeakers in front of them. They first play instrumental dance music, and the maid of honor invites young girls, and others, to dance. Then the musicians sing popular folk songs and popular songs from radio and television, familiar to audiences around the Arab world.

The climax of the bride's night is her bridal song and dance, *il-jalwih*, or *jalwit il-'arūs*. The *jalwih* songs are precomposed couplets or quatrains of poetry, the last of which is followed by a refrain for the audience. The lines vary in length from nine to twelve syllables. Rhyme schemes are (1) abcd and so on; (2) aaba and so on; and (3) aaab. The tempo for rhyme scheme 1 is very slow; rhyme scheme 2 has a tempo that is faster but still suitable for a slow bride's dance; rhyme scheme 3 has an even faster tempo suitable for a fast dance. The first song is not accompanied by instruments, but the last two are. The subject of all these songs is praise of the bride's beauty and uniqueness.

Halfway through the evening, the bride puts on her best dress, or possibly her white wedding gown, and appears with her maid of honor and a sister, a relative, or the village's most recent bride. Each of these women takes the bride by one hand and holds in her other hand a long white lighted candle with a colorful ribbon tied around it (figure 2).

A traditional *jalwih* is usually conducted by an older woman from the village. She faces the bride, and they hold their hands palm to palm. The bride closes her eyes and stands still while the woman sings *Hadhi l-asiliyyih* 'This Bride Is of Noble Origin', an old traditional Palestinian bridal song in a slow, free rhythm:

> This is the girl of noble origin, the daughter of the noble family;
> This is the girl, of whom nothing bad has been said or done.

FIGURE 2 Bridal dance with candles during a Christian wedding in Mi'lya, 1993.

Her young men [brothers, uncles, and so on] have never been condemned in
public;
Nobody has condemned or disgraced her.
Young men, do not get married to a daughters of people of ill repute;
Do not get married to a girl unless she is like her mother
and the full moon is her brother, and the crescent is her cousin.

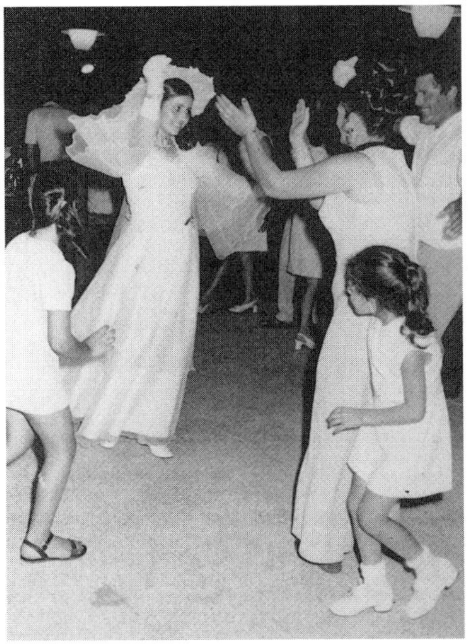

FIGURE 3 Individual bridal dance after a *jalwih*, at a Palestinian Christian city wedding in Haifa, 1972.

Now the bride's two companions put their candles on the floor, and the bride (perhaps to symbolize peace) extinguishes them with her foot. She then takes her companions' hands, and the musicians sing the most popular song, *Witkhaddari* 'Stay Behind Your Curtain' (collection, cassette 5), in a slow rhythm, as the three women dance. (This dance consists of swaying the body and swinging one foot right and left while remaining stationary.)

Stay behind your curtains. May God protect you, O beautiful bride!
O rose in the garden!
O bride! You are like the twig of a carnation
And the jasmine's settled down on us.
Rise and go up, in the name of Allah.
Daughter of the notable people, how amazing you are!
And the blond [or brown] hair is cascading down
And the eyes are hazel.

As this song concludes, the bride is left alone to dance in the circle (figure 3). The musicians play *Yā nūr* 'O You Are the Light' (collection, cassette 19) in a rapid tempo, praising her beauty and describing the dresses she has worn during the evening.

At the end of the *jalwih* songs, the bride is seated and popular music, singing, and dancing resume. As the groom's party arrives, the bride's father, brothers, and uncles go out to welcome the guests. For a few minutes, all sing and dance together, rather chaotically, as the women perform their particular *āwīhā* song and ululation comes from every direction. Afterward, the groom and his delegation returns to his parents' house to resume their celebration.

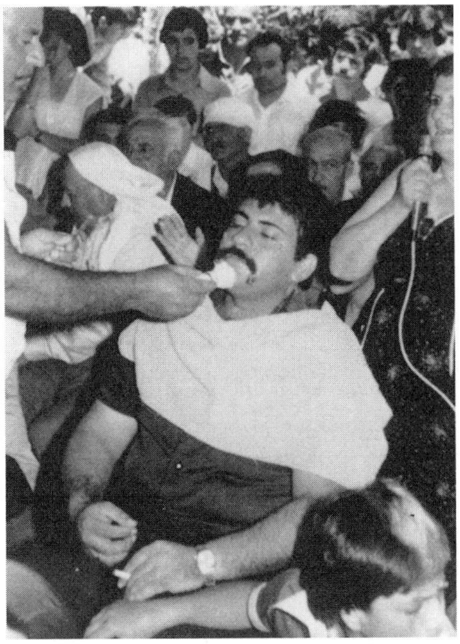

FIGURE 4 *Zaffih* (shaving ceremony) in the Christian Palestinian village of Fassutah, 1980. The barber is at the left, the groom in the middle, and the folk singer at the right; guests can be seen in the background.

At this point, the bride's night ends; but in most communities the groom's closest friends stay with him after midnight for a *sahrit il-'azzābiyyih*, or bachelor party, where they chat, drink, sing, and dance on their own. Christian Palestinians in Galilee often hold an extended party indoors after midnight: the guests dine while poet-singers entertain them with "table songs," mostly indoor *'atābā* and refrains, *qarrādī* (a genre of improvised sung poetry) and refrains (Sbait 1982:293–325), popular songs, and folk songs. This concludes the first major part of the wedding, the groom's and bride's nights.

The groom's shaving party

Preparations for the groom's public shaving party—*ḥlaqit il-'arīs*; also called *zyānit il-'arīs*, *zaffit il-'arīs*, or (in short) *iz-zaffih* (figure 4)—starts early in the morning on the wedding day. Soon after the barber's arrival, a crowd gathers in the home of the groom's father. If the groom has been invited somewhere else for this part of the wedding, the best man invites the whole crowd along.

The *zaffih* is long, and so is the repertoire of songs for it. A *durbakkih* player and a *mijwiz* player begin warming up. The shaving party generally begins with the singing of *dal'onā* and the dancing of the *dabkih*. In Muslim villages, women sing and dance separately in a side room close to the area where the groom's party is going on, but older female relatives of the groom may join the men. In Christian villages men and women celebrate all the wedding festivities together, including the shaving party.

FIGURE 5 Two poet-singers improvising at a traditional Palestinian wedding in Miʿlya, 1980.

M'annā

Soon, the poet-singers (figure 5) take the place of the folk musicians and improvise *mʿannā* poems. *Mʿannā* are based on four, six, or more lines. The last line is the refrain and is sung twice by the audience. Each line has ten to fifteen syllables. Quatrains of *mʿannā* have the rhyme scheme aaab. The words mostly express the poets' feelings—love, praise, congratulations. Musical instruments may accompany the poet-singers (Sbait 1982:266–292). The following excerpt illustrates a basic *mʿannā* quatrain (collection, cassette 8):

> I came to this house when the loved ones were far away;
> I found the roses without blooms in their house.
> I am coming now to congratulate my relatives faithfully;
> I found the roses blooming throughout the house.

Qarrādī

Normally the poet-singers follow this performance by singing *qarrādī* couplets or quatrains in honor of the host and the groom. *Qarrādī* is based on improvised couplets, quatrains, or eight-lines stanzas. It is sung solo or in alternation by professional poet-singers and is followed by the audience's refrains, which may vary. It is usually accompanied by musicians who play folk or modern instruments, and by folk dancing by the crowd. A pair of lines have seven and seven, seven and eight, or seven and four syllables. Couplets usually have the rhyme scheme ab/cb/db and so on; quatrains are usually aaab, or abab/cccb and so on. The subjects include love, praise, and descriptions of the occasion. These songs are mainly rhythmic and are accompanied by folk dances and hand clapping (Sbait 1982:293–325, 1989:213–235). Here is an example of *qarrādī* (collection, cassette 20):

> *Poet-singer, improvising*: In the day of predicament
> The poet saddles his horse.
> The virtuous man
> Feels proud when his friends are rejoicing.
> *Audience's refrain*: The virtuous man
> Feels proud when his friends are rejoicing.

Shaving songs

Soon after a lengthy musical introduction, the mother of a Christian Palestinian groom, followed by many other women, starts the precomposed rhythmic *zaffih* ‘shaving’ songs. If she cannot sing herself, she invites a female soloist who will lead these songs; if no women are available, male singers are acceptable. There are many traditional folk songs for this occasion.

TRACK 18 Shaving songs are mostly based on precomposed verses but also on some improvised verses. The soloist sings one verse or couplet at a time, and the audience repeats it as a refrain. Songs based on one verse have various rhyme schemes, such as abcd and so on; songs based on couplets may have the rhyme scheme ab/cd/ef or ab. A line has eight to twelve syllables. Shaving songs congratulate the groom and his family (uncles and others). These songs are mostly rhythmic and are accompanied by enthusiastic folk dancing and clapping. They are also accompanied by folk instruments such as the *mijwiz* and *durbakkih*, classical instruments such as the *‘ūd*, or Western instruments such as the violin or electric guitar or keyboard.

As the poet-singers and folk singers perform the shaving songs, the barber first gives the groom one actual shave and then gives him six mock shaves (a lucky number) with the blunt edge of the razor, though still with shaving soap. At the climax of this celebration, the young men carry the groom on their shoulders and dance with him, whereupon his mother, sisters, and other female relatives shed tears—as do the groom himself and some of the more emotional guests. The barber is the first to say, *Mabrūk yā ‘arīs* ‘Congratulations, groom’; and women start to sing *āwīhā*.

The repertoire may open with a song urging the barber to start the job, such as *Bmus idh-dhahabiyyih* ‘With Golden Razor’ (collection, cassette 40). Then there will songs in honor of the groom’s mother and the groom himself, such as *Bilhanā* ‘With Bliss’ or ‘Congratulations’ (collection, cassette 5); and songs praising other relatives, such as *Wayn aziffak yā ‘arīs* “Where Shall I Celebrate Your Wedding Shaving Party, O Groom?’ (collection, cassette 21):

> . . . I like to celebrate your shaving party at the house of your paternal uncles . . .
> I like to celebrate your shaving party at your brother’s house
> As the respected men are standing in two lines . . .

Now the shaving ceremony is coming to an end, and the soloist offers thanks to certain participants, as in *Mzayyin il-‘arīs* ‘The Groom’s Barber’ (collection, cassette 21). Immediately afterward, the young men accompany the groom as he goes to take a bath while singing the *mḥorabih* (procession song) *‘Araysaynā yā raytā ḥalqah mbārakih* ‘Our Groom, We Wish You a Blessed Shaving’ (Sbait 1982:1–58).

The groom then puts on his wedding suit. When he enters the guests’ area, an older person from the village sings a precomposed *shūbāsh* praising him and his parents. *Shūbash*, usually sung solo, is based on four verses, followed by the phrase “May God forgive” or “Ah, alas!” sung by the audience, and women’s cries of joy. Each line has six to eight syllables. The common rhyme schemes is abcb. The subjects are usually praise of the groom, good wishes to the groom and his family, and gratitude for those who gave wedding presents (Sbait 1982:358–365; see also “This House Is Not Ours,” collection, cassette 3).

The bride’s party during the shaving festivity

While the shaving festivity is going on, a separate daytime party for the bride is held in her parents’ home. The bride is seated in an elevated armchair inside or outside the house. She is surrounded by her girlfriends and relatives. Since the professional musicians have left by now, an amateur musician from the village may play. If no musician is available, girls will play the drum, dancing and singing songs popular on radio and television. After the bride has put on her white wedding dress, they may (with the

The bride's impending departure for the groom's home is a dramatic and emotional moment.

help of older women) perform another *jalwih*, which may include songs from the bride's night.

Half an hour or so before the arrival of the groom's delegation, the relatives and friends of the bride kiss or embrace her and give her valuable gifts. Because unmarried girls are so secluded and protected, and because a married women can rarely return to her parents' home, the bride's impending departure is a dramatic and emotional moment. As the groom's delegation arrives, the bride is ready to leave. Holding a bouquet of white roses, she walks at the front of a procession back to the groom's house in Muslim and Druze villages, or to the church in Christian villages. She is accompanied by her maid of honor and her father or a brother or uncle. One of the women who walk behind her plays the *durbakkih*, and the rest sing the folk song *Yikhlif ʿalayku w-kaththar Allah khayrkuh* 'Thank You, the Bride's Family; May God Increase Your Wealth' (Sbait 1982:1–58).

The wedding day

In Muslim villages, the groom is taken from his host's house back to his father's house in an impressive procession through the main streets. A line of people dance while the poets improvise *farʿāwī*. Soon after the groom's arrival, the bride arrives with the delegation. The groom is brought to unveil her, amid dances and songs. Shortly after the marriage ceremony, the bride and groom leave on their honeymoon, and the formal wedding is over.

In Christian villages, the parts of the wedding that take place after the shaving celebration are more elaborate. A festive dinner for all the guests is usually offered right after the shaving party, and before the church ceremony. Immediately after that, the guests, with the groom and his best man at their head, march to the church in a procession while the poet-singers improvise *farʿāwī*. The poets hold microphones, and an amplifier and a loudspeaker are carried on a jeep. As the procession approaches the church, the young men ring the church bell to announce the occasion. When the groom arrives, he sits with his best man and the guests, waiting for the bride, while a group of young men perform a brief folk dance to entertain the crowd. The bride is brought to the church with *mḥorabih*.

After the church wedding, the married couple leave the church as the poet-singers and the young men form a dance line. The bride, her maid of honor, the groom, and his best man are at the end of the line, and the women walk behind them. Elderly people and children walk ahead of the line. The two poet-singers hold their microphones, and the line organizers clap rhythmically to start the procession back to the host's house.

The poets sing rhythmic *farʿāwī* verses such as *Mabrūk iklīl il-ʿursān* 'May This Marriage Ceremony of the Newlywed Couple Be Blessed' or *Halfarḥah likbīrih lal-ʿarīs il-ghālī* 'This Great Wedding Is for the Dear Groom' (Sbait 1982:226–253). The dancers repeat the opening verses as refrains, clap, and dance; the poets improvise matching verses; and the line keeps moving.

As the procession passes by a house, the owner and his family may become temporary hosts of the wedding procession. The procession will then stop for a few minutes, while the poets improvise quatrains of *'atābā* praising the host's generosity; some of the women may also improvise *āwīhā* of praise.

When the bride arrives at the home of the groom's parents, before she enters the house, the women sing several *āwīhā* quatrains to welcome her. Then guests congratulate the couple, offer gifts, and start to leave. In some villages it is customary for the guests to give money to someone who will sing a *shūbāsh*—a song of congratulations and gratitude for the guests' generosity, as in this excerpt (Sbait 1982:358–365):

> May God return this gift to you, O the father . . .
> And may God increase your wealth,
> And this is a gift for the groom . . .

The last line of the quatrain may actually specify the gift.

MODERN PALESTINIAN WEDDINGS AND SONGS

Weddings of modern urban Palestinians, particularly Christians who are more open to a Western lifestyle, have taken a different direction. Most families still hold a small evening party and a shaving party for the groom, and an evening party for the bride with a limited number of guests. But the important parts of the wedding are the church ceremony, the formal *iklīl*, to which both families and as many as several hundred guests are invited; and, on the same evening, a festive dinner and a musical celebration in a local club, a hotel, or a *muntazah* (an outdoor restaurant). Recently, this format has also been adopted by secular liberal Palestinian Muslims and Druzes. It is, in fact, a Western-style celebration with the addition of Palestinian traditions, particularly folk traditions.

Urban Palestinian wedding music combines traditional folk songs and modern urban songs. City people prefer *al-ghinā al-mutqan*—modern Arab singing—performed by professional singers and instrumentalists, who offer popular love songs from television and radio. They also perform an almost complete repertoire of innovative *dal'onā* folk songs, accompanied by the Palestinian *dabkih* (folk dance) and modern instruments. This repertoire is becoming a hallmark of village as well as city weddings (collection, cassette 4).

Modern Palestinian musicians use traditional Arab instruments such as the *'ūd*, *durbakkih* (a drum), *daff* or *ṭār* (a tambourine), and *nāy* (a flute). They also use Western instruments, generally the electric guitar, the violin, and the keyboard, even for a *dabkih*.

In some weddings of rural Palestinians who have recently settled in a city, a friend or relative who is a poet-singer will be asked to improvise an *'atābā*, *m'annā*, *qarrādī*, or *qaṣidīh*. At many weddings, a *saḥjih*—the line dance—is performed. Women also sing *āwīhā*.

The following might be the order of a modern Palestinian city wedding: The musical ensemble takes its place on the stage, where the bride, the groom, and the immediate family are also seated. At first, the ensemble plays light music as the guests arrive. When most of the guests have arrived and are seated, the bride leaves the stage and then reappears, from a side room, with her maid of honor, both holding white, decorated, lighted candles. She is preceded by perhaps two dozen girl friends, also holding candles, who form opposite lines. She walks slowly to the dance floor, while the singer performs this popular song, which is also a *jalwih* song:

> *Tmakhtarī smallah yā 'arūsah*
> Walk slowly with pride; may God protect you, O beautiful bride.

Meanwhile the groom joins the bride on the dance floor, and they start to dance; a favorite song at this point is *Wayn il-'aris waynuh*, which begins "Where is the groom, where is he?" (Sbait collection).

Next the bride and groom are seated to dine. The musicians sing popular love songs and occasionally nationalistic Palestinian songs by local compsers, or familiar songs from Arab radio and television. They often sing pieces associated with the popular Lebanese stars W. al-Ṣafī, M. Barakāt, Fayrūz, Ṣabāḥ, and S. Tawfīq; the Egyptians F. al-Aṭrash, 'A. Ḥāfiẓ, Umm Kulthūm, 'U. Dhyāb, and I. Tawfīq; the Syrian S. Fakhrī; or the Iraqi K. al-Sāhir—and many others. Thus a modern urban Palestinian wedding may combine modern songs, popular folk songs, and improvised sung poetry.

In conclusion, Palestinian wedding songs, traditional or contemporary, including improvised sung poetry, women's folk songs, and audiences' refrains, which are composed in spoken Palestinian Arabic, as well as orally transmitted folk songs, constitute a rich, complex literary, musical, and artistic heritage. This heritage provides details of and insight into the social-cultural traditions and the character of the Palestinian people.

REFERENCES

'Arnīṭah, Y. 1968. *al-Funūn al-sha'biyya fī Filasṭīn* (Folk Arts in Palestine). Beirut.

'Awaḍ, 'A. 1983. *Dirāsāt fī 'l-fulklūr al-filasṭīnī.* (Studies in Palestinian Folklore). Damascus.

al-Barghotī, 'A. 1979. *al-Aghānī al-'arabiyya al-sha'biyya fī filasṭīn wa 'l-urdunn* (Arabic Folk Songs in Palestine and Jordan). Jerusalem and al-Quds.

———. 1963. "Arab Folk Songs from Jordan." Ph.D. dissertation, University of London.

al-Bāsh, Ḥ. n.d. *al-Ughniya al-sha'biyya al-filasṭīniyya* (The Palestinian Folk Song). Damascus.

Dalman, G. 1901. *Palästinischer Diwan.* Leipzig: Hinrichs.

al-Fākhūrī, Ḥ. n.d. *Tārīkh al-adab al-'arabī* (History of Arabic Literature). Beirut.

Frayḥa, A. 1973. *Mu'jam al-alfāẓ al-'āmmiyyah* (Dictionary of Colloquial Expressions). Beirut.

Granqvist, H. 1931–1935. *Marriage Conditions in a Palestinian Village.* Helsingfors.

Ḥaddād, M. 1986. *Palestinian Folk Heritage between Obliteration and Revival.* Taybih.

Ḥaddād, Yūsuf. 1987. *al-Mujtama' wa 'l-turāth fī filasṭīn* (Society and Folklore in Palestine: A Case Study of al-Baṣṣah Village). Acre.

Ḥaydar, 'Adnān. 1989. "The Development of Lebanese Zajal: Genre, Meter, and Verbal Duel." *Oral Tradition* 4(1–2):189–212.

Jargy, S. 1970. *La poésie populaire traditionelle chanteé au Proche-Orient arabe.* Paris.

———. 1978. "Kasida." *Encyclopaedia of Islam,* vol. 4:713–714. Leiden.

Libbis-Azzām, Nā'ilah. 1989. *al-Aghānī al-fulklūriyya limunāsabāt al-khiṭba wa 'l-zawāj* (Folk Songs for Engagements and Weddings). al-Quds.

Linder, S. 1952. *Palästinische Volksgesänge.* Upssala: Lundquistska.

Saarisalo, A. 1932. "Songs of the Druzes." *Studia Orientalia* 4(1).

Sbait, Ḍirghām Ḥ. 1982. "The Improvised-Sung Folk Poetry of the Palestinians." Ph.D. dissertation, University of Washington.

———. 1986. "Poetic and Musical Structure in the Improvised-Sung Colloquial Qaṣīdih of the Palestinians." *al-'Arabiyya* 19:75–108.

———. 1989. "Palestinian Improvised-Sung Poetry: The Genres of Ḥidā and Qarrādī—Performance and Transmission." *Oral Tradition* 4(1–2):213–235.

———. 1992. "'Dīwān al-Dal'onā al-Filasṭīnī' by 'A. al-Barghūtī." *Middle East and South Asia Folklore Bulletin* 9(3). (Book review.)

———. 1993. "Debate in the Improvised-Sung Poetry of the Palestinians." *Asian Folklore Studies* 52:93–117.

Sbait collection. 1972–1994. This consists of 120 hours of live improvised sung poetry, approximately 16,000 verses; 20 hours of interviews with sixteen Palestinian poet-singers; 8 videos of Palestinian weddings; 3 Arabic *ṭarab* 'joy of music' concerts including classical, popular, and folk songs from fifteen Arab countries (1988–1991. Ḍ. Sbait, producer. Oregon: Portland State University); and 40 weddings and other social occasions on cassettes, including folk and popular songs.

Sirḥān, Nimr. 1979. *Aghānīnā al-sha'biyya Fī al-ḍaffa al-gharbiyya* (Our Folk Songs in the West Bank). al-Kuwait.

———. 1979–1982. *Mawsū'at al-fulkūr al-filasṭīnī* (Encyclopedia of Palestinian Folklore). 5 vols. Amman.

Sowayān, Saad A. 1989. "'Tonight My Gun Is Loaded': Poetic Dueling in Arabia." *Oral Tradition* 4(1–2):151–173.

Snapshot: Munir Bashir

Christian Poché

On 28 September 1997 the Iraqi *'ūd* player Munir Bashir (b. 1930 in Mosul) died in Budapest. His rich musical career, characterized by a renewal of the *'ūd* as a solo instrument, was celebrated around the world, particularly in the West. A respected artist in the East, he was widely admired for his numerous official activities. He was entrusted, most notably, with the responsibilities of secretary general of the Arab Academy of Music, an organization influenced by his stature for many years, until his retirement in 1995.

Munir Bashir and I were linked in a profound friendship. We met for the first time in Lebanon in 1968. At this time Bashir lived in the village of Falūgha in the heart of the Lebanese Mountains. Then he played the *'ūd* very differently from the manner that he would later develop. Like many musicians of his time, he opted resolutely for modern styles; as he wrote in his memoirs, his father once advised him, "My son, if you want to have a career, you must choose modernism." Soon, however, Bashir curbed or at least moderated his emphasis on modernism, thanks above all to his many European friends who encouraged him not to overlook the value of traditional music, hoping to find in him a spokesman capable of responding to westerners' expectations.

In those years, as the complexities of the Indian *raga* system captivated many listeners, Bashir endeavored to raise knowledge of the Arab musical world to the same level. This is why he became a soloist, renouncing the role of the *'ūd* as a mere accompaniment to the voice. Bashir invented the *'ūd* recital. The *'ūd* had never lost its dignity, but he sought to restore nobility to this instrument. He quickly realized that his objectives could not be achieved without a dedicated repertoire, and so he began, with a real sense of urgency, to create one.

Until then 'ūdists had been content to introduce a vocalist with a brief improvisation, preparing the atmosphere for the music to come. But no matter how talented the interpreter, the instrument could never dominate the performance; the voice always remained in the limelight. The *'ūd* never appeared in any other role than to play *taqsīm*, an improvisation that lasted no more than a few minutes. Munir Bashir felt compelled to bring a new dimension to this form, making it the focal point of the musical experience. To do this he joined several *taqāsīm* together into a suite that immediately assumed a new breadth. This is precisely what he presented during his

Munir Bashir's concerts involved a kind of torment: glued to their seats and holding their breath, the audience members feared to make the slightest sound.

'ūd recitals: four or five improvisations ordered to create a series of small *taqāsīm*, cleverly joined to one another according to the rules of musical grammar. But even this result, which was successful for more than a decade, never seemed to satisfy him.

Munir Bashir realized that he could not insist on concerts consisting solely of improvisation. Pieces in distinct rhythms, based on Arab musical styles, were noticeably absent. Slowly he began to "reinject" rhythmic sections based on well-known tunes, showing that improvisation could be alternately free and measured. At the same time he abandoned the term *taqāsīm* as inappropriate for this style. In the 1980s, Bashir was content to develop the idea of mode in his music, and the pieces that formed the framework of his recitals henceforth carried the name *maqām*.

Between 1993 and 1995, however, Bashir resisted this temptation once more. He did away with the term *maqām* and yielded to the fascination of endowing his improvisations with poetic allusions, which to the end of his life were not abstract but tangible, and suggested a mystical bent that contrasted with the "good life" he cultivated in social circles. Although he was known for his frankness and spicy anecdotes, his music sent a different message, one of contemplation, of reflection.

He always enjoyed repeating, "Arab music is a beautiful music, but one must be able to understand it on its own terms." He balanced his creation of a new, unpublished repertoire with the development of a new sonority for his instrument, one derived from Turkish methods. With the silkiness of Bashir's playing as a foundation, two techniques for playing the *'ūd* that until then had dominated the Arab world were henceforth mingled: the thin, sinewy plucking of the individual note doubtless formed a secular aesthetic, developed through the ages; the other method, developed principally in Egypt, joined the striking of the plectrum with a sonorous approach. With Bashir a third way appeared, already practiced in the Turkish school: that of the beauty of the note itself, its tone, its vibrato. Legions of young interpreters, even if not his own students—he was hardly a teacher himself—adopted it. At the end of the twentieth century, this way of touching the strings of the *'ūd* predominated in the Arab world.

Munir Bashir was the first to insist on a religious silence during his concerts, displeasing audiences who demanded nothing more than simple pleasure and followed traditional modes of listening, seeking to reach the psychological and physiological state known as *ṭarab*. His concerts involved a kind of torment: glued to their seats and holding their breath, the audience members feared to make the slightest sound. Bashir believed that the music he played required a veritable asceticism which manifested itself through suffering. This attitude, so unlike his everyday social relations, dumbfounded his audiences but gradually led them to a more intellectualized listening. This was not always received gladly, though, and his admirers in the East as in the West sometimes became his detractors.

His intent was no less than to raise the *'ūd* to the same aesthetic level as the human voice. In November 1996, I heard him for the last time. He was passing through Cairo on the occasion of the Fifth Festival and Congress of Arab Music. The other concerts took place in the great hall of the Cairo Opera, a large space with 1,800 seats. It was not here, however, that Bashir gave his recital. Instead, he chose an intimate adjoining space. It is said that the intimacy of the *'ūd* will not allow grandiloquence. This is true, but it is also likely that in the collective consciousness, the *'ūd* has not yet reached the point where it may be considered equal to the voice.

My most vivid memory of Munir Bashir is from October 1973. I met him in a thick fog, passing between East and West Berlin, in a surreal atmosphere reminiscent of a film. At that time I had invited him to give a recital in West Berlin, his first in Germany. On the day he was expected to arrive, war broke out in the Middle East. As a precaution, the airports closed all their gates, but Bashir had been able to rush through and onto the last departing plane. At the very moment when I had lost all hope, in the middle of the night, he emerged from the no-man's-land that separated the two Berlins. He has now returned to that fog out of which he once appeared, leaving a legacy that will not soon disappear.

Translated by Alexander J. Fisher

Stardom in Egyptian Music: Four Case Studies

Virginia Danielson

Sayyid Darwīsh
Umm Kulthūm
Muḥammad 'Abd al-Wahhāb
'Abd al-Ḥalīm Ḥāfiẓ

Commercial recordings, radio broadcasts, films, television, and videotapes have created internationally famous stars of Arab music. [See The Impact of the Media on Egyptian Music.] Many listeners came to know a few performers against whom they measured others. A focus on accomplished professional performers is nothing new in the Arab world. Historical records show that Arab societies have supported professional musicians who became well-known in courts and urban areas, arguably "stars," for centuries. At the beginning of the twentieth century in Egypt, well-known performers of all sorts traveled long distances, sometimes by invitation, to sing for celebratory events. Fame, if not stardom, is not exactly new.

Nevertheless, the status attained by a relatively small number of performers in the mid-twenthieth century created new pressures, which were recognized by the musicians themselves. The stars could command more money and better performance settings than their less-known counterparts. They could influence patrons concerning whom else to hire. Umm Kulthūm, for instance, sold thousands of recordings, largely because she had become well-known in the Egyptian delta as a child and young woman. She became the object of a bidding war between Gramophone and Odeon Records in 1926 and obtained a startlingly high sum of money which included a retainer for her services. She used this price to back up her claim that she was the best singer (and also to avoid less desirable performance contexts). In hot pursuit, Muḥammad 'Abd al-Wahhāb used similar tactics; and when Egyptian Radio began broadcasting in 1934, these two artists dominated the airwaves.

Use of the media allowed performers to expand their presence and achieve stardom. Some performers aggressively sought and held on to such exposure, at the expense of less spectacular local performers. Record players, radios, cassette players, and television sets, presenting the music of the "stars," occupied the space in coffeehouses and other public settings that live performers had formerly held.

The technology of the media became centered in major cities. Throughout most of the twentieth century, Cairo and Beirut held sway as the media production capitals of the Arab world. They drew in aspiring stars and, in turn, sent performances, through the media, back out into a world of ever-growing audiences for broadcast and recorded music.

SAYYID DARWĪSH

Sayyid Darwīsh (1892–1923) was one of the first "media" stars. So popular were his songs—marketed on 78-rpm disks—that contemporary listeners all over the Mashriq reported hearing and learning these songs within days of their first release in Cairo.

Sayyid Darwīsh was born in a working-class district in Alexandria. When he was still young, his father died, and so Sayyid was reared primarily by his mother and his uncles. He went to a Qur'ān school and a local primary school. He attended *dhikr* with his uncles. He learned to sing the popular songs of his day and also the religious songs performed on local saints' days and at other celebrations. As a young man, he began to perform in the coffeehouses of Alexandria, where he was considered a good and entertaining singer.

At that time, a Syrian entrepreneur launched a musical theater in Alexandria. Darwīsh worked with him and eventually toured in Syria. The tour was unsuccessful, however, and in about 1917 Darwīsh sought his fortune in the theater district of Cairo.

There he found work with major theatrical troupes that were then flourishing: George Abyaḍ 'Alī al-Kassar, Munīra al-Mahdiyya, the 'Ukkāsha Brothers, and Najīb al-Rīḥānī. He worked with popular Italian pit orchestras and wrote European-style duets and choruses into his plays alongside songs in Arab *maqāmāt* 'modes'. He composed thirty musical plays and dozens of individual songs in many genres: religious songs, virtuosic neoclassical *adwār* (singular, *dawr*), and simple strophic tunes. He often collaborated with the poet Badī' Khayrī to produce songs and comic plays in colloquial language, drawn from the idioms and images of working-class Egypt and often anti-imperialist in sentiment. He is strongly associated with the "Egypt for Egyptians" movement, represented by the revolution of 1919, and he remains a dominant symbol of Egyptian culture and local pride to the present day. The play *al-Ashara al-Ṭayyiba*, a satire against Turkish governance, is one famous example. The song *Zurūnī kull sana marra* 'Visit Me Once a Year' exemplifies his popular, folklike tunes; *Sālma yā Salāma* is one of a number of songs he wrote that were centered on workers, in this case sailors returning to port; and *Anā maṣrī* expresses, typically, his pride in being Egyptian. His song *Bilādī, bilādī* is currently the Egyptian national anthem.

FIGURE 1 Muḥammad 'Abd al-Wahhāb in front of the specter of Sayyid Darwīsh. Photo courtesy of Dār al-Hilāl, c. 1970.

He appears to have lived hard; certainly, he died young. But his very short and tumultous life belies the actual place he holds in Egyptian culture. His recorded songs carried him into the future; their locally rooted style made him an icon of Egyptianness. This narrative was carried forward by sophisticated musicians and ordinary listeners alike. So great was his impact that within a few years of his death, other stars—including such luminaries as Zakariyya Aḥmad and Muḥammad 'Abd al-Wahhāb—were vying with each other in the popular press for the honor of being regarded as his "successor" in the musical world (figure 1). Virtual every "star" composer of the twentieth century in Egypt claimed to have learned his style from the music of Sayyid Darwīsh. At the turn of the twenty-first century, Darwīsh's songs were still well-known and were often sung; many people believe them to be folk songs. He remains venerated as the "father" of Egyptian music.

UMM KULTHŪM

Umm Kulthūm (1904?–1975), in her later years, said that she moved to Cairo from her rural village on the day Sayyid Darwīsh died, thus drawing his image and stature into her own public persona. Yet she became a very different kind of star, and perhaps the most famous singer in the twentieth-century Arab world.

Born in a village in the delta of Egypt, Umm Kulthūm was reared in a poor family, attended Qur'ān school, and in general shared a socioeconomic background with many of her contemporaries. Her father, the village *imām*, made extra money

FIGURE 2 Muḥammad ʿAbd al-Wahhāb with ʿAbd al-Ḥalīm Ḥāfiẓ. Photo courtesy of Dār al-Hilāl, c. 1955.

by singing religious songs at weddings and on other special occasions. While listening to him teach these songs to her brother so that the son might accompany and assist the father, Umm Kulthūm learned the songs too. Her father discovered that her voice was very strong and included her in the lessons and ultimately in the performances, although he dressed her as a boy in an attempt to avoid gossip and the censure he might receive for putting his young daughter on the public stage.

Despite her odd garb, the child became the family star, touring the delta for years until, in about 1923, the family decided to try to break into the lucrative world of commercial music in Cairo. This they did; and by 1928 Umm Kulthūm was established at the top of the ranks of performers in the city. She had a lucrative recording contract with Gramophone Records and gave public and private concerts. In the 1930s and 1940s, her fame and artistic authority continued to develop, and she made six musical films.

Umm Kulthūm was known throughout her life for her powerful voice and her ability to use melody and improvisation to bring out the meaning and mood of the poetry she sang. She cultivated a public persona of great dignity and cast herself as a "real" Egyptian, untainted by anything foreign. She carried the art of singing poetry through the twentieth century with her accomplished renditions of elegant, literary, and musically difficult *qaṣāʾid* in addition the clever colloquial lyrics and modern love songs that she also sang. She improvised on everything and "never sang a line the same way twice." Her performances lasted for hours and became cultural events, attracting the attention of millions throughout the Arab world.

In the 1960s she began to sing the simple love lyrics that had become popular with younger stars such as ʿAbd al-Ḥalīm Ḥāfiẓ. In 1964, she began her famous collaboration with Muḥammad ʿAbd al-Wahhāb. [See SNAPSHOT: OPENING NIGHT FOR A STAR PERFORMER—UMM KULTHŪM AND *INTÁ ʿUMRĪ*.] Following the defeat of Egypt in 1967, she toured the Arab world on behalf of her country, donating the proceeds of her concerts to the Egyptian government. These trips took on the characteristics of state visits. All together, she recorded more than 300 songs, among the most famous of which are *al-Aṭlāl* by Riyāḍ al-Sunbāṭī, *Intá ʿumrī* by Muḥammad ʿAbd al-Wahhāb, *Raqq al-ḥabīb* by Muḥammad al-Qaṣabjī, and many *zajal* by Zakariyya Aḥmad. When she died, at the end of a performing career that had spanned more than fifty years, her funeral was described as being bigger than that of President ʿAbd al-Nāṣir.

MUḤAMMAD ʿABD AL-WAHHĀB

A self-proclaimed disciple of Sayyid Darwīsh, Muḥammad ʿAbd al-Wahhāb became the greatest Arab modernist of the twentieth century. His compositions form the backbone of *mashriqi* Arab music not only in the region of Syria, Lebanon, and Egypt but also in the Arab diaspora, where his music is a staple of Middle Eastern university ensembles and accomplished Arab-American artists such as Simon Shaheen, who frequently pay tribute to his genius (Shaheen 1990).

ʿAbd al-Wahhāb was born to a religious family in working-class Cairo. As an adolescent, he became drawn to the stage and performing—an interest that struck horror into his family. He persisted, however, and, at a very young (if indeterminate) age, found himself singing on the stages of the most important theaters in Cairo. He studied music and became skilled not only at musical theater but in the complicated art of improvising melodies for sophisticated poems, *qaṣāʾid* (singular, *qaṣīda*). The poet laureate of Egypt, Aḥmad Shawqī, was one of ʿAbd al-Wahhāb's patrons and wrote elegant verse for him to sing.

An accomplished musical classicist, ʿAbd al-Wahhāb was at the same time an inveterate innovator. He probed the possibilities of all musics that came his way, borrowing from the nineteenth-century European symphonic literature; Spanish, Latin American, North American, and local Middle Eastern dance rhythms; and instruments from everywhere, including the Hawaiian guitar. An early (and successful) example of his experimentation is the song *Fīʾl-Layl*.

In the 1930s, the handsome ʿAbd al-Wahhāb became a major film star. Like many of his peers, he grew tired of the costs and control of various entertainment agencies. Instead, he founded his own film production company, which remained successful and profitable for the rest of his life. Among his famous films is *al-Ward al-baydāʾ* 'The White Rose'.

After 1950, he turned his attention from performing to composing. He used increasingly large ensembles, which he conducted himself; and he adopted musical notation even for such genres as *taqāsīm*, which historically have been improvised. He wrote songs for many singers and became a mentor to such luminaries as ʿAbd al-Ḥalīm Ḥāfiẓ.

From the perspective of the twenty-first century, ʿAbd al-Wahhāb's legacy is inestimable. His grasp of international musical styles is unparalleled. His songs are a cherished part of people's memories of home and childhood. As Kay Kaufman Shelemay (1998) has poignantly shown us, his melodies constitute hymn tunes for Syrian Jews living in New York who fondly remember them from years gone by.

ʿABD AL-ḤALĪM ḤĀFIẒ

ʿAbd al-Ḥalīm Ḥāfiẓ (1929–1977) was a romantic crooner and a film star. "I heard him," an Arab-American woman of his generation told me, "and I fell in love."

Born in a village in the Egyptian delta, ʿAbd al-Ḥalīm was orphaned at an early age and reared by his uncle. He attended a Qurʾān school as well as a public school and, at the age of eighteen, matriculated at the Institute of Arab Music—an increasingly common path for aspiring professional musicians in his day. He aim was to study voice and *ʿūd*; however he was persuaded to transfer to the Higher Institute for Theater Music, where he studied oboe instead. There he met three men who were to become lifelong colleagues: the composers Kamāl al-Ṭawīl and Muḥammad al-Mūjī and the conductor Aḥmad Fuʾād Ḥasan. After his graduation, he worked as a music teacher in primary schools and played oboe in the Egyptian Radio Orchestra.

However, ʿAbd al-Ḥalīm never lost his ambition to become a professional singer. He began singing pieces by his friends al-Mūjī and al-Ṭawīl and in 1951 successfully auditioned to be a singer on Egyptian Radio. His first successful song was *Liqāʾ* 'Meeting' by al-Ṭawīl. Shortly after recording it, he signed a contract with the superstar Muḥammad ʿAbd al-Wahhāb to sing ʿAbd al-Wahhāb's songs and to appear in films made by his company (figure 2).

In the following years ʿAbd al-Ḥalīm sang many love songs and appeared in romantic films that became extremely popular. He typically appeared as a handsome and virtuous young hero, a good boy who was wronged but triumphed in the end. Among his famous films was *Laḥn al-wafāʾ* 'Song of Good-Bye'. Many of the songs he recorded, including *Ahwāk* 'I Love You' and *Qāriʾat al-finjān* 'The Tea-Leaf Reader', remain popular throughout the Arab world to the present day.

His songs and films were incredibly successful. The plots and lyrics positioned him as a "nice young man." In his public life, he became close to the charismatic populist President Jamāl ʿAbd al-Nāṣir, and this connection augmented the public's sense of ʿAbd al-Ḥalīm as a solidly grounded Egyptian who cared about family, neighbors, and community.

In 1939, ʿAbd al-Ḥalīm was diagnosed with schistosomiasis or bilharzia, a debilitating parasitic disease from which numerous rural Egyptians used to suffer. He suffered increasingly severe attacks beginning in 1955 and died of the disease in 1977.

Throughout his life and after it, his great appeal was as a sympathetic local hero with whom many Egyptians identified. His own recordings were still widely sold in 1995, and at the turn of the twenty-first century young male singers continued to copy his vocal style.

REFERENCES

Armbrust, Walter. 1996. *Mass Culture and Modernism in Egypt*. Cambridge: Cambridge University Press.

Azzam, Nabil. 1990. "Muḥammad ʿAbd al-Wahhāb in Modern Egyptian Music." Ph.D. dissertation, University of California, Los Angeles.

Danielson, Virginia. 1997. *"The Voice of Egypt": Umm Kulthūm, Arabic Song, and Egyptian Society in the Twentieth Century*. Chicago: University of Chicago Press.

al-Ḥifni, Mahmūd. 1974. *Sayyid Darwīsh: Ḥayātuhu wa-āthār ʿabqariyyabhi* (Sayyid Darwīsh: His Life and Genius). Cairo: al-Hayʾa al-Miṣriyya al-ʿĀmma li-'l-Kitāb.

Saḥḥāb, Fiktūr. 1987. *Al-Sabʿa al-kibār fi-'l-mūsīqa 'l-ʿarabiyya al-muʿāṣira*. Beirut: Dār al-ʿIlm li-'l-Malāyīn.

Shaheen, Simon. 1990. *The Music of Mohamed Abdel Wahab*. Axiom Records 422-846 754-2. (Compact disk.)

Shelemay, Kay Kaufman. 1998. *Let Jasmine Rain Down: Song and Remembrance among Syrian Jews*. Chicago: University of Chicago Press.

Snapshot: Opening Night for a Star Performer—Umm Kulthūm and *Intá 'Umrī*

Virginia Danielson

On the evening of 6 February 1964, the Azbakiyya Cinema, one of the largest theaters in Cairo, would be completely full by 9:30. Men and women were finding seats, talking, milling around—just as audiences had been doing for decades on the first Thursday of every month—as they waited for the international star Umm Kulthūm (figure 1) to begin her performance. Tonight, though, was special. Umm Kulthūm had finally agreed to perform a song by the great modernist composer Muḥammad 'Abd al-Wahhāb.

Although Umm Kulthūm and 'Abd al-Wahhāb were both gifted and accomplished musicians, they represented different points on the musical spectrum of their time and were professional rivals. 'Abd al-Wahhab advanced the "modern." He had learned much from Western musical practices: he performed his music exactly the same way from one occasion to another; he used large, meticulously rehearsed instrumental ensembles; he had included accordions, clarinets, and saxophones for the first time in Arab music, and for this new song he would introduce the electric guitar into Umm Kulthūm's repertoire; he asserted the importance of the composer over the performer in musical production; and he had composed numerous instrumental pieces performed independently of singing.

Umm Kulthūm, by contrast, had been trained in the historic vocal arts of the Arab world. She sang poetry, improvising and repeating lines at will, shaping and reshaping the poetry and the composed melody that carried it. She considered herself the principal creator of a musical performance. A composition provided a starting point; the instrumental music supported the singer. She was, in her own view and that of many others, "authentically" Arab and Egyptian.

On the night of February sixth, most of the audience had come to hear Umm Kulthūm, the singing star, the center of the performance. Nevertheless, most were well aware of 'Abd al-Wahhāb's role in the performance. The new song, *Intá 'umrī* 'You Are My Life', had been in preparation for a year. Newspapers had carried stories about its preparation, about how the two stars had agreed to work together, and about the difficulties of reconciling their disparate views of music.

It was said that the president of Egypt, Jamāl 'Abd al-Nāṣir, had been the motivating force. Like many others, he was a fan of Umm Kulthūm and 'Abd al-Wahhāb. According to reports, he wanted their collaboration to be part of his own legacy and,

FIGURE 1 Umm Kulthūm performing. Photo by Fārūq Ibrāhīm, c. 1969.

a year earlier, he had prompted a discussion between the two by inviting them to his supper table at a benefit concert they attended at the army officers' club. The audience that was gathered on February sixth knew this story.

This concert would be broadcast live from Cairo and also transmitted by Radio Damascus. 'Abd al-Nāṣir, a charismatic leader of nonaligned nations, had committed substantial resources to the development of Egyptian Radio, sending his message of Arab unity and socialism throughout the Middle East; and to help his citizenry through the years of political and economic transition, he encouraged entertainment.

While people streamed into the hall, Umm Kulthūm paced behind the curtain, listening to one of her accompanists, the *qānūn* player Muḥammad 'Abduh Ṣāliḥ, improvise in the *maqām*—the melodic mode—of the first song on the program. She watched the audience and tried to absorb the musical character and possibilities of the *maqām*. This first piece was *Kull layl wa-kull yawm* 'Every Night and Day', a love song by Bāligh Ḥamdi that most people already knew. *Intá 'umrī* would be second.

'Abd al-Wahhāb, who was always nervous about his premieres, stayed at home until the first song ended. He came to the theater, with a reporter, in time for *Intá 'umrī*, staying out of sight in the wings, fidgeting tensely, while the new song began. "*Tawakkilna 'alā Allāh*" 'We entrust ourselves to God', he said.

Intá 'umrī had a long, sectionalized instrumental introduction, typical of 'Abd al-Wahhāb's compositions. In older styles of music, such a beginning would occupy perhaps two to ten minutes, but this one was twenty minutes long, with some sections that sounded like *taqāsīm* and others that used Western and Egyptian dance rhythms. The ensemble played the introduction; by its end, people had jumped up and were standing on their chairs, cheering. Umm Kulthūm quieted them for the first line of the song: "Your eyes return me to the days that are gone . . ." The words were set in a nonmetrical declamatory style. Umm Kulthūm sang them carefully, drawing the audience into the nostalgia and sadness of this torch-like song. She sang the line four times. By the time she reached the climax of the verse—the refrain, "You are my life, which begins its mornings in your light"—the audience was roaring its approval. She had spent an hour on the first verse. ʿAbd al-Wahhāb, obviously overjoyed, went home with friends and heard the rest of the performance on the radio.

Umm Kulthūm sang many lines repeatedly. When she sang the line "*Al-laylá 'l-ḥilwa wa-'l-shūq wa-'l-maḥabba min zamān wa-'l–qalb shāyilhum ʿashānak*" 'The sweet night and longing and love from long ago, and the heart carrying them for you', the audience was overcome with pleasure. Her longtime poet, Aḥmad Rāmī, was holding a lit cigarette that he had clearly forgotten about. She repeated this line over and over. One of her listeners in the first row, al-Ḥājj Ḥāfiẓ al-Ṭaḥḥān, personally requested four more repetitions.

The performance of *Intá ʿumrī* lasted more than two hours. Traffic stopped completely in the working-class district of Shubra as one car after another pulled over and parked for the entire two hours while the song was being broadcast. Newspapers called it "the longest, and most beautiful, Arabic song."

Umm Kulthūm began her third song of the evening at 3:20 A.M. Few people could remember, later, what it had been, and the newspapers did not bother to report on it.

Intá ʿumrī remained a mainstay of Umm Kulthūm's repertoire for the rest of her life. By the late twentieth century it had passed into the *turāth*, the heritage of Arab music.

Western Music, Colonialism, Cosmopolitanism, and Modernity in Egypt

Salwa El-Shawan Castelo-Branco

An Egyptian Opera
The Advent of European Military Music
The Establishment of European Music in Cosmopolitan Egypt
The Localization of Western Music in Egypt

AN EGYPTIAN OPERA

Cairo, Opera House and Cultural Center, Sunday, 23 June 1996. Tonight will probably make history. *Anas Al-Wugud*, an opera by the Egyptian composer Aziz El-Shawan (1916–1993), has just had its premiere at the Cairo Opera House (figure 1). Strict security measures were in place because Susan Mubarak, Egypt's first lady, was expected to attend. The state television interviewed specialists and selected audience members and recorded the entire performance. Playbills were distributed as the audience walked through the lobby. At 9:15, Yusif El-Sisy walked energetically to the conductor's podium and acknowledged the polite applause. The curtain opened in silence. The setting was a courtyard outside the vizier's palace during the early Islamic period in Egypt. Following a short overture, a chorus of thirty men and women in bright costumes walked onto the stage,

FIGURE 1 Cairo Opera House and Cultural Center. Photo from Salwa El-Shawan Castelo-Branco.

FIGURE 2 Scene from the opera *Anas al-Wugud* by Aziz El-Shawan at the Cairo Opera House. Photo from Salwa El-Shawan Castelo-Branco, June 1996.

> took up their positions, and sang to celebrate a harvest. This festive atmosphere was enhanced by a brief ballet. The protagonist, Anas Al-Wugud, a soldier in the sultan's army, then sang an aria praising the beauty of the evening, the Nile, and the moon.

The premiere of *Anas Al-Wugud* (figure 2), evoked by this excerpt from the present author's field notes, is a landmark in the music of twentieth-century Egypt. This multitextual work set to an Arabic libretto by the poet Salama Al-Abasy—based in turn on a tale from the *Arabian Nights*—is the story of the love between a soldier and the vizier's daughter, set in Egypt during the early Islamic period. The music is tonal, in Western style, but with occasional allusions to Arabic *maqāmāt* 'modes'. It is sung in Western operatic style, except when Arabic phonetics channel vocal production closer to Arab singing. The sets, designed by the French stage director Michel Giess; and the costumes, designed by Alain Roussel, reflect European images of an exuberant, colorful "Orient." The dances that punctuate this opera recall Orientalist dances in nineteenth-century European operas and ballets.

Like much twentieth-century Egyptian urban music, *Anas Al-Wugud* draws on Arab and Western musics to create a new synthesis. This process has been stimulated by Western musical activities in Egypt for two hundred years. Western music was initially brought by colonial agents (rulers, armies, missionaries, and European settlers) in the nineteenth century; by the early twentieth century, several domains of Western music had been integrated into the musical life of Cairo and Alexandria, where they became localized. This article describes the introduction and appropriation of Western music in Egypt and its repercussions—an overview that is central to the understanding of musical and cultural processes characterizing nineteenth- and twentieth-century Egypt. The overview will be presented within the framework of colonialism, cosmopolitanism, and ideologies of resistance to Western domination, such as nationalism and Islam.

THE ADVENT OF EUROPEAN MILITARY MUSIC

European music first came to Egypt through Napoleon's expedition (1798–1802). A military band accompanied the French army and performed at official celebrations and local festivities. The French pianist, teacher, and composer Henri-Jean Rigel (1772–1852) was a member of the expedition and became the music director of the newly founded French theater in Cairo, for which, in 1799, he composed a comic opera in one act, *Les deux meuniers* (Brook and Viano 1980).

This initial incursion of European music in Egypt did not seem to have an immediate effect on local musical life. However, the brief French sojourn had considerable cultural consequences for both Egypt and Europe. The expedition included a team of 146 scholars who documented Egypt's contemporary life and ancient history in a monumental twenty-two-volume work, *Description de l'Egypte* (1812–1829), that included two volumes on music by Guillame A. Villoteau (1759–1839). Villoteau described the musical instruments and practices depicted in ancient Egyptian monuments as well as contemporary music practice in Egypt and other Middle Eastern countries. Napoleon also founded the Institut de l'Egypte, a research center for the advancement of knowledge in and about Egypt, and set up the first Arabic printing press that issued regular publications. In all, the exposure of Egyptian leaders and intellectuals to French military organization and administration, to the ideas of the French revolution, and to European scholarship provided a model for subsequent modernization plans.

Shortly after the French had departed, Muḥammad ʿAlī (1805–1848), an Albanian officer in the Ottoman army, seized power, founding a dynasty that would rule until the revolution of 1952. He embarked on a wide-ranging modernization program, using European experts and Egyptians whom he sent to Europe for training. European music was first institutionalized in Egypt as part of Muḥammad ʿAlī's modernization program for the army. In the 1820s and 1830s, he founded five schools of military music where French instructors trained Egyptian peasant recruits in band instruments and the rudiments of Western notation and theory. The graduates formed Western military bands attached to Muḥammad ʿAlī's army.

How did Egyptians react to European military music? In 1840, in a survey of life in Egypt during Muḥammad ʿAlī's reign, A. Clot-Bey—a French physician who was the head of the first Egyptian medical school—described Egyptians as indifferent to European military music and expressed his own skepticism about the utility of Western military music in an Egyptian context:

> Our music does not affect Egyptians at all. Even the patriotic hymn "Marseillaise" . . . neither causes their hearts to vibrate, nor opens their chests, nor catches their attention. Requiring that Egyptians use our instruments and sing our hymns does not fulfill the aim of military music. Egyptians who faint with joy when they hear their own singers and instrumentalists are bored and upset when they hear European instruments and songs. (From the translation by Maʿsūd 1982: 83–54)

Instruction in military music weakened during the reign of Muḥammad ʿAlī's immediate successors but was then reinforced by Khedive Ismāʿīl (r. 1863–1879), who made large financial investments in the establishment of European musical institutions. The Italian composer and librettist Ruggiero Leoncavallo (1859–1919) was hired to supervise the military music department of the Egyptian army. With the British invasion in 1882, the training of military musicians was transferred to British hands. By the 1930s, a generation of trained Egyptian military musicians took over military music instruction and performance and created a new repertoire of Egyptian military music. Following the revolution of 1952, considerable financial support was provided for instruction in and performance of Western-style military music; the performance groups included several military bands and a symphony orchestra staffed by highly proficient Egyptian military musicians—some of whom also filled the ranks of Western orchestras and music institutes.

THE ESTABLISHMENT OF EUROPEAN MUSIC IN COSMOPOLITAN EGYPT

During the second half of the nineteenth century, an influential cosmopolitan social and cultural milieu formed in Egyptian cities. There was a large influx of Europeans and Syrians during the reign of Khedive Ismāʿīl and during the subsequent British occupation (1882–1922), adding to the existing mix of Italians, French, Greeks, Armenians, Turks, and Europeanized Egyptians (Jews, Christians, and Muslims).

For cosmopolites in Egypt, European "art" music was an important cultural resource, and a symbol of social ascension and power. Through the sustained patronage of the ruling dynasty and well-to-do sectors of the cosmopolitan community, it occupied an important place in the musical life of Cairo and Alexandria. During the nineteenth century, there was a cleavage between European and local cultures and musics; but by the early twentieth century local urban styles were being influenced by Western models, and Egyptians trained in Western music were creating Western-based musical idioms.

From the mid-nineteenth to the mid-twentieth century, training in the performance and composition of European "art" music was available in Cairo and Alexandria through European private instructors and in private conservatories run by Europeans. Several prominent Egyptian performers and composers received their musical training within this framework. Exposure to and rudimentary instruction in Western music (notation, Christian hymns, band instruments, and piano) was also provided in several hundred private schools run by European and American missions and foreign communities in cities throughout the country. From the mid-nineteenth century until they were nationalized or closed after 1952, these schools, estimated to have absorbed as much as 50 percent of all students, trained generations of Egyptians who later occupied leading positions (Vatikiotis 1985:454).

The piano had an important place among Egyptian cosmopolites. The first pianos were probably brought by the French expedition. By the late nineteenth and the early twentieth century, there was a high demand for pianos, as evidenced between the 1890s and the 1940s by the commercial activities of some twenty music stores in Cairo, where pianos and other musical instruments, gramophones, 78-rpm records, and music scores were sold. Up to the mid-twentieth century, playing the piano and owning a piano were a symbol of high social status and an asset for marriageable women. A repertoire of Arab "salon music" developed and was disseminated through sheet music and commercial recordings. It consisted of arrangements for piano of selected Arab compositions and a new Arab piano repertoire, most of which was created by a few women composers trained in Arab and Western music—notably Matilda and Sophie Abd El-Massih. Some of the pianos sold in Egypt were adapted by adding a pedal that produced a timbre reminiscent of the Middle Eastern plucked zither (*qānūn*); this timbre was considered appropriate for performances on what was then referred to as *al-biānō al-sharqī* 'the Oriental piano'.

During the late nineteenth century, the Western violin was appropriated for the performance of Arab music in Egypt. By the early twentieth century, it had totally supplanted the two-stringed *kamangah* or *kamān* (a spiked fiddle) and had taken its name. This adapted violin is played in the same position as the Western violin, but it has a different tuning (g-d-g-c).

The inauguration of the Cairo opera house on 1 November 1869, as part of Khedive Ismāʿīl's lavish celebrations for the opening of the Suez Canal, reinforced Western music in Egypt as a symbol of power and was an important factor in its localization. Verdi's *Rigoletto* was performed at the opening. *Aida*, commissioned by the khedive, was premiered on 24 December 1871. A product of imperial domination, "it does a great many things for and in European culture, one of which is to confirm the Orient as an essentially exotic, distant, and antique place in which Europeans can mount certain shows of force" (E. Said 1993:112). For the Europeanized Egyptian elite, it symbolized the recognition of Egypt's grandeur and place in world history and provided a model of a European musical representation of Egypt that has inspired certain Egyptian composers. From its inauguration until it was destroyed by a fire in 1971, the Cairo opera house became a bastion of Western music in Egypt, offering seasons of ballet as well as opera and featuring prominent opera companies and soloists.

THE LOCALIZATION OF WESTERN MUSIC IN EGYPT

During the twentieth century Western music was gradually woven into the complex web of urban musical life in Egypt. Western "art" music has been performed regularly in Cairo and Alexandria. During the first half of the century, concert seasons were organized, presenting visiting artists, orchestras, and opera and ballet companies as well as resident European musicians. The nucleus of a symphony orchestra was founded within the Egyptian Broadcast Corporation in 1934 and gave regular performances until 1959, when the Cairo Symphony Orchestra (figure 3) was founded. Starting with the academic year 1931–1932, Western music education was introduced in the Egyptian public school system by the Egyptian musicologist Maḥmūd Aḥmad al-Ḥifnī (1896–1973), who had been trained in Berlin. Instruction in Western music was also integrated into the curricula of the Arab Music Institute (founded in 1929), the Higher Institute for Music Teachers (founded in 1933), and the short-lived Higher Institute for Musical Theater (1944–1950).

The nationalist ideology and modernization program of the revolution of 1952 resonated in its cultural policy, which called for reviving the heritage of Arab music while at the same time supporting the institutionalization of Western "art" music as part of a modernization of Egyptian musical and cultural life. In 1959, a state-supported national conservatory and a symphony orchestra were founded in Cairo; these were followed, a few years later, by opera and ballet companies. From the 1960s on, several generations of Egyptians were sent to study at conservatories in Europe and the former Soviet Union; these students would gradually replace the Russian and Eastern European musicians who staffed government-supported institutions in the 1960s and 1970s. In 1988, a new cultural center including an opera house was built in central Cairo, largely with the financial support of the Japanese government, and

FIGURE 3 The composer Aziz El-Shawan, the pianist Bengt-Ake Lundin, the conductor Mustapha Nagui, and the Cairo Symphony Orchestra. Photo from Salwa El-Shawan Castelo-Branco, 19 March 1993.

Western "art" music stimulated the emergence of a new musical idiom created by Egyptian composers whose work weaves local melodies, rhythms, and modal flavor into Western models from the eighteenth century up to the twentieth.

has since housed nine government-sponsored ensembles of Arab and Western music and dance. Performances of Western and modern Egyptian music are given regularly in this new cultural center; they attract a small audience of educated Egyptians and occupy limited broadcast time on radio and television. Western popular musics have also been disseminated in urban Egypt through radio broadcasts, commercial recordings, and live performances by visiting and local groups.

Western "art" music stimulated the emergence of a new musical idiom created by three generations of Egyptian composers whose work weaves local melodies, rhythms, and modal flavor into Western models from the eighteenth century up to the twentieth. Yusif Greis (1899–1961), Hasan Rashid (1896–1969), and Abū Bakr Khayrat (1910–1963), the first generation of composers, created Egyptian symphonic music in eighteenth- and nineteenth-century styles. Aziz El-Shawan (1916–1993), Gamal Abd Al-Rahim (1924–1988), and Rif'at Garranah (b. 1924) developed distinct nationalist styles. El-Shawan uses lush melodies and a tonal harmonic language that alludes to Egyptian melodic types. Gamal Abd Al-Rahim develops a modal framework with a dissonant vocabulary and a contrapuntal texture. Garranah frequently quotes traditional melodies, setting them to Western tonal harmony. A third generation of composers graduated from the Cairo National Conservatory, completing their studies at the Vienna and Moscow conservatries; they include Gamal Salamah (b. 1945), Rageh Daoud (b. 1954), and Mona Ghoneim (b. 1955). This generation has attempted to develop a new modal style inspired by local *maqāmāt*.

Western music has also influenced indigenous urban musics. Exposure to opera and Western-inspired Arabic theater stimulated the emergence of an Egyptian musical theater that was most productive from the 1870s to the 1930s, with notable contributions by prominent singers of Arab music and composers such as Salāma Ḥigāzī (1852–1917), Sayyid Darwīsh (1892–1923), Kāmil Al-Khula'ī (1880–1928), Daoud Husnī (1871–1937), and Zakariyya Aḥmad (1896–1961).

Western instruments, especially the violin family, were adopted for Arab music, and the size of ensembles increased from the *takht*, consisting of five different instruments, which had been predominant until the 1920s; to the *firqa*, including thirty or more instrumentalists and led by a Western-style conductor, since the 1930s.

Training in Arab and Western music became a requirement for Egyptian musicians after the study of music was institutionalized in the 1930s. As a result, composers and performers acquired skill in both Western and Arab music, and Western notation was established as a medium for the transmission of Arab music. The aesthetic ideals and technical skills that musicians acquired through their bimusical training had far-reaching effects on concepts and styles in Arab music.

Since the 1970s, large segments of Egypt's population have adopted Islamic principles and lifestyles as part of their search for authenticity and identity and their resistance to modernization through westernization. Researchers have observed that cosmopolitanism and internationalism in Egyptian culture are in decline (M. Said 1999:183). Thus far, however, this trend has not had a direct impact on Western and Western-inspired musical domains in Egypt, which continue to receive strong government support and to have a following among a small segment of the educated elite.

REFERENCES

Abdun, Salih, ed. 1971. "Genesi della 'Aida': Con documentazione inedita." *Quaderni dell'Istituto di Studi Verdiani*, vol. 4. Parma: Tipografia "La Nazionale."

———. 1973. *Ṣafaḥāt fi ta'rīkh opera al-Qāhira: Aida wa Mi'at Sham'a* (Pages from the History of the Cairo Opera: Aida and One Hundred Candles). Cairo: Al-Hay'a al-Miṣriyya li'l-Kitāb.

Brook, Barry, and Richard Viano. 1980. "Rigel, Henri Jean." In *The New Grove Dictionary of Music and Musicians*, ed. Stanley Sadie. London: Macmillan.

Clot-Bey, A. 1840. *Aperçu général sur l'Egypte*. Paris: Fortin, Massin et Cie. (Arabic translation: Muḥammad Mas'ūd. 1982. Cairo: Dār al-Mawqif al-Arabī.)

Al-Ḥifnī, Maḥmūd Aḥmad. 1968. *Salāma Ḥijāzī: Rā'id al-masraḥ al-'arabī* (Salamah Higazi: The Pioneer of Arab Theater). Cairo: Dār al-Kātib al-'Arabī.

Al-Kholy, Samhah, and J. Robinson, eds. 1993. *Festschrift for Gamal Abd Al-Rahim*. Cairo: Binational Fulbright Commission in Egypt.

Al-Kholy, Samhah, ed. 1999. *Al-Ta'līf al-miṣrī al-mu'āṣir* (Contemporary Egyptian Compositions). Cairo: Ministry of Culture, Prism Series.

Landau, Jacob M. 1958. *Studies in the Arab Theater and Cinema*. Philadelphia: University of Pennsylvania Press.

Said, Edward. 1993. *Culture and Imperialism*. New York: Vintage.

Said, Mohamed Sayyid. 1999. "Cosmopolitanism and Cultural Autarky in Egypt." In *Cosmopolitanism, Identity, and Authenticity in the Middle East*, ed. Roel Meijer. Surrey, England: Curzon.

El-Shawan, Salwa. 1985. "Western Music and Its Practitioners in Egypt (c. 1825–1985): The Integration of a New Musical Tradition in a Changing Environment." *Asian Music* 27(1):144–153.

Vatikiotis, P. J. 1985. *The History of Egypt from Muhammad Ali to Mubarak*, 3rd ed. Baltimore, Md.: Johns Hopkins University Press.

Villoteau, M. [Guillaume A.]. 1823. "Description historique, technique, et littéraire des instruments de musique des Orientaux." In *Description de l'Egypte*, Vol. 13. Paris: Panckoucke.

———. 1826. "De l'état actuel de l'art musical en Egypte." In *Description de l'Egypte*, Vol. 14. Paris: Panckoucke.

The Performers of Muḥammad ʿAlī Street in Cairo, Egypt

Karin van Nieuwkerk

Contexts of Entertainment in Egypt
Transformations in Entertainment between 1900 and 1970
Developments since 1970
Professionalization and Trade Unions
The Status of the Muḥammad ʿAlī Street Performers

In Cairo, members of the same profession often used to live together in one neighborhood, and to a large extent they still do. Most of the entertainers who work at weddings and saint's day celebrations cluster around Muḥammad ʿAlī Street, a thoroughfare that cuts diagonally across the old city and connects the center, by way of the palace, to the citadel built by Ṣalāḥ al-Dīn on the outskirts of town. Muḥammad ʿAlī Street was completed in the 1870s, and the area between the palace and the center seems to have been favored by entertainers since at least the late nineteenth century. Its official name is now Citadel Street, but most people, and certainly most performers, stick to the old name.

Muḥammad ʿAlī Street retains its reputation as a locus for performers and wedding agencies, if only for the lower classes. Yet the character of the street has changed considerably since the 1970s. For example, only a few music shops have survived; most of the shops that sold instruments have been replaced by furniture firms (figure 1). The offices and signs of the *ʿawālim*—women performers who sang only for female

FIGURE 1 View of Muḥammad ʿAlī Street. Photo by Karin van Nieuwkerk, 1991.

audiences—have disappeared. The male musicians no longer work solely at weddings and saint's day celebrations; they now combine that circuit with the world of nightclubs. During the day, the coffeehouses are still filled with musicians waiting for wedding customers; but in the evening the musicians sitting there wear black suits and white shirts, their working clothes for the nightclubs. Older performers still live in the back streets, and newcomers from the provinces may find refuge with them or stay in a nearby hotel; but many of the younger generation have saved enough money to move out, to a neighborhood around Pyramid Street.

Thursday is the peak day for weddings, so on Thursdays 'Arḍ Sharīf—the place where people gather on Muḥammad 'Alī Street—is very crowded and chaotic. Large Peugeots come and go, carrying performers to weddings all over Cairo and to neighboring villages.

CONTEXTS OF ENTERTAINMENT IN EGYPT

Egyptian entertainment has three main contexts. First is the circuit of weddings and saint's day celebrations, the traditional context for the performers of Muḥammad 'Alī Street. Second is the nightclub circuit, which exists mainly for Arab and European tourists. Third is the performing arts circuit, which centers on concert halls, theaters, radio, and television. We should be wary of equating the Egyptian scene with that of Western music. The clear-cut distinction made in the West between highly esteemed classical music and lower-status popular music does not apply in the Arab world. There are distinctions among the Egyptian contexts, in that the most talented performers tend to work in theaters and to receive more respect than performers at saint's day celebrations or in nightclubs; but the genres of songs and instrumental music may well be the same in all three contexts. The famous songs of Umm Kulthūm or Muḥammad 'Abd al-Wahhāb, for instance, can be heard in concert halls, in nightclubs, at weddings, and on radio.

The male performers of Muḥammad 'Alī Street are typically instrumentalists and singers; women work mainly as singers and dancers. The most important instruments played at weddings and saint's day celebrations are percussion instruments like the *ṭabla* 'hourglass drum' and the *riqq* 'tambourine', as well as the accordion, the saxophone, and the electronic keyboard. In the past, there were many female instrumentalists, who worked at at separate women's parties, but this tradition has disappeared; today there are hardly any women instrumentalists on Muḥammad 'Alī Street. Many female performers used to be *shamla*, that is, they worked as both singers and dancers; at present, however, most are just one or the other. Male dancers are rare at weddings and at saint's day celebrations, although some perform in the *zaffa* 'wedding procession'. Most male dancers are folk dancers who work in theaters. Few women perform as dancers in wedding processions in the street; most work at the party after the *zaffa*, as "belly-dancers" on stage (figure 2).

FIGURE 2 A dancer from Muḥammad 'Alī Street at a wedding in a working-class neighborhood. Photo by Karin van Nieuwkerk, 1989.

Typically, it is the weddings of lower-class and lower-middle-class people that are served by the musicians, singers, and dancers of Muḥammad 'Alī Street. Weddings in lower-class neighborhoods are usually celebrated on the street (figure 3). Red lights are strung between the houses; chairs and tables are set out in the street; and a wooden platform draped with multicolored cloth serves as a stage. The program usually starts after the wedding procession, at around ten or eleven at night. The bride is sometimes inside her apartment, and women lean over the balconies to witness the show downstairs; but sometimes the bride and groom sit apart with some female guests in a separate section of the street. Singers and dancers take turns, and the musicians are asked to play a *tōba*, an improvised solo, which is followed by a dance rhythm, the *tit*.

Every two or three minutes, the entertainers are interrupted by tippers. A tipper comes on stage and yells congratulations to the families of the bride and groom into the ear of the man with the microphone—the *nabatshī*—who relays the message to

FIGURE 3 Performers at a wedding procession. Photo by Karin van Nieuwkerk, 1988.

the audience. Waving ten-pound banknotes, the tipper, by way of the *nabatshī*, then continues to greet friends, neighbors, and colleagues. The ritual is concluded with a *salām*, a musical salutation consisting of a popular song, while the tip, the *nuqṭa*, quickly disappears into the musicians' bag. The *salām*, in turn, is interrupted by the next tipper who wants to give greetings and congratulations. As guests arrive, they have a right to be announced, and to be greeted by a short musical salutation. Accordingly, the party is rather hectic. Now and then, people quarrel if they think their tip has received insufficient respect or too much time has been given to the salutations of others. The entertainers find it virtually impossible to perform until late at night, when the guests have settled down.

Many performers of Muḥammad ʿAlī Street also work at saint's day celebrations (figure 4), such as the *mūlid* of the Prophet Muḥammad—an important celebration in the provincial city of Ṭanṭā—or the *mūlid* of Dessūq. In the evenings during Ramadan, entertainment programs are offered in large theaters and small tents. A saint's day celebration usually lasts for a week. Several productions take place side by

FIGURE 4 A saint's day celebration. Photo by Karin van Nieuwkerk, 1989.

During a saint's day celebration, several performances take place side by side, each trying to attract customers by making more noise than the others.

side, each trying to attract customers by making more noise than the others. A program often consists of a band of musicians, singers, dancers, acrobats, and magicians and lasts for twenty minutes. Then a new group of people will elbow their way to the front, in order to have the best view of the dancers' legs. In the course of a typical evening, the performers give the same program six times. During the *laylā al-kabīra*, the last evening of the *mūlid*—and its climax—they perform the same show more than ten times.

TRANSFORMATIONS IN ENTERTAINMENT BETWEEN 1900 AND 1970

The performers of Muḥammad 'Alī Street have witnessed many changes in the circuit of weddings and saint's day celebrations. Often, such changes have entailed a loss of esteem.

At the beginning of the twentieth century, wedding celebrations were still segregated; as a result, women were prominent in the entertainment market. Female singers, dancers, and instrumentalists were in great demand. They formed groups that regularly worked together under the leadership of an experienced performer, the *usṭá*, who taught the trade to family members and new girls. Female performers often lived in the same house, and most *usṭāwāt* clustered together in an alley, the *ḥārit il-'awālim*, off Muḥammad 'Alī Street. The male performers of Muḥammad 'Alī Street worked under a male leader and performed at men's parties.

At that time, there seems to have been a distinction between female performers for the women's parties and those for the men's parties: a men's party was not attended by *'awālim*, who performed only for women. From the 1940s onward, however, there was no difference between these two types of female performers except in name: the female performers working at women's parties (and the parties themselves) were still called *'awālim*, whereas the female entertainers at a *sahra*, a men's party, were called *artistes*; but in fact most female performers of the 1940s were both *'awālim* and *artistes*, first performing for the women upstairs and afterward singing and dancing until early morning for the men.

In the late 1940s, the *'awālim* had vanished from urban weddings, which had become less extravagant and, more significantly, less segregated. This development was related to social changes in the larger society, where the separation of the sexes in general had become less strict. Separate women's parties lingered on in the countryside, but by the 1960s they had disappeared there as well: either professional entertainment was abolished at the women's party, or female guests were allowed to be present at the men's party. In the latter case, women would usually sit apart with the bride and groom and leave early; after their departure the male party would continue until morning. This is still the pattern at weddings in working-class neighborhoods.

From the 1940s through the 1970s, women of Muḥammad 'Alī Street's families remained active at weddings and saint's day celebrations. At weddings they were mainly important as singers and dancers, but several women also managed to build up a male clientele. Once more they undertook the organization of weddings parties themselves.

Performers no longer worked with one specific *usṭā* but started working with several male and female employers. Yet entertainers still formed a relatively small society of loosely related groups. After the 1970s, however, this too would change.

DEVELOPMENTS SINCE 1970

During Sadat's presidency (1970–1981) Egypt adopted an open-door policy in order to attract foreign investments. With the changes in the economy, a middle class emerged that took advantage of the new situation; this newly wealthy class spent a great deal on recreation, creating demand for entertainers and a climate in which performers flourished. Weddings and other festive occasions were celebrated on a large scale. Wedding processions took on new vigor; and the bride's procession was enlarged and supplemented with dance performances, mostly male folk dancing, although sometimes women performed the *shamʿidān*, a candelabra dance.

This growing demand for entertainers resulted in higher wages. Prices had been on the rise since the 1950s, but under Sadat they increased tenfold. In the 1940s, entertainers earned less than a pound for a performance, including their wages and tips; in the 1960s they earned five pounds; during the 1970s, about fifty pounds. In the 1990s, one hundred pounds a performance was not an especially high offer for a dancer. Not only did wages rise, but so did tips. In the past, only someone like a village headman could afford to show off by tipping a pound—most men gave only a piaster or two, while women could afford only a few millimes. Now a man usually tips ten pounds, and this tip is matched by other men, so that the total can amount to a thousand pounds.

In general, performers who are at the peak of their careers are better off than, say, civil servants, but not as well off as audience members may think. Instrumentalists usually receive no more than twenty or thirty pounds for an evening's work. Female entertainers working in wedding processions may receive fifteen pounds, and they have to be on their feet for a long time in order to earn that. It should be noted that female entertainers must usually stop working at a fairly young age, and dancers and performers of the older generation have no pensions. Moreover, all entertainers face a slack season during the winter. A growing number of musicians work at two jobs in order to make ends meet: some combine work at weddings with work in an orchestra; others work during the day as government employees and in the evening as nightclub or wedding entertainers. Yet despite these reservations, it is clear that performers' income has increased.

The increased earnings have led to changes in the system of payment. At the beginning of the twentieth century, wedding performers received no wage but shared all their earnings (*ḥeṣaṣ*). In the 1950s, performers received an advance payment and half of the tips. Today, they usually agree on a fixed sum (*ḥaqq* 'right') and do not receive a share of the tips. People sometimes reject the ritual of tipping for fear that it will lead to quarrels. If tips are given, they may now disappear into the pocket of the person who has arranged the wedding.

Such changes in the system of payment reflect a growing individualization of performers. Since the 1970s, performing groups have increasingly consisted of individuals working for the highest bidder. This individualization is related to the end of the monopoly once held by the entertainers of Muḥammad ʿAlī Street. Higher profits have attracted many people from outside the profession to work not only as musicians, singers, and dancers but also as impresarios and employers. Now, the latter are called not *usṭāwāt* but *aṣḥāb il-firqa* 'owners of the band'. The Muḥammad ʿAlī Street performers refer to these newcomers as *dukhālā'* or *khashānā* 'intruders' and refer to themselves as *awlād il-kār* 'the people of the trade'. But they acknowledge that their trade is an "inn without a doorkeeper"—anyone can enter it and perform at weddings.

The heritage of the 1970s—the growing individualization of the Muḥammad ʿAlī Street performers and the end of their monopoly—combined with the recent economic recession, has affected the entertainment market in several ways. First, people tend to economize on parties and entertainment, and so they hire professional performers only for weddings. At other festive occasions, live entertainment is replaced by cassette players and radios. Even at weddings, some people have only a long, extensive wedding procession with folk-dancing; there is no program after it. Others entertain a small number of guests at a respectable nightclub. People who do hold a traditional wedding party sometimes give the entertainers a fixed sum and pocket the tips themselves.

Second, Muḥammad ʿAlī Street performers say that professional ethics have been abandoned at weddings since their monopoly was broken. The older generation of Muḥammad ʿAlī Street performers had a shared code of honor. For a long time, they had formed a community of cooperating families, which exercised strict social control. Because of their sense of community, a group's reputation was considered to be tarnished if any of its members misbehaved. For instance, performers considered it a disgrace to accept food, since that might lead people to think that the entertainers were poor and hungry, without a home of their own to eat in. There were also rules for proper relations between female performers and men—male colleagues and customers. The *usṭāwāt*, the leaders, kept a close eye on the women's conduct toward customers. They guarded the women and fined or beat those who behaved improperly. It was not considered respectable for a woman to talk, laugh, or dance with customers. Receiving tips was, of course, acceptable; but this too was bound by rules of honor; thus it was dishonorable for a woman to let men put money in her costume—the money had be placed in her hand. Today performers of the older generation say the women entertainers' success is based principally on wearing scanty costumes and going out with the customers, not on artistry.

Third, at weddings today there are increasing problems of drugs, alcohol, and quarrels, which can cause a party to break up before the entertainers have gathered enough tips to cover their basic costs. Because of such financial hazards, many women have become reluctant to organize weddings. There are also risks for female performers. Hard drugs, which were introduced in the early 1980s when Egypt became a transit country for heroin and cocaine, have caused a rise in criminal behavior. Currently, gangs sometimes assault entertainers after a wedding, to steal their earnings or to kidnap the women performers. Some female entertainers from Muḥammad ʿAlī Street have left the trade altogether, and most have kept their children out of it.

Fourth, the circuit of saint's day celebrations and weddings has lost esteem. As a result of restrictive government policies, secular entertainment at saint's day celebrations is limited, and the large-scale artistic productions have mostly disappeared. "Intruders" have entered this branch of the trade as well, and the performers of Muḥammad ʿAlī Street accuse them of causing performers at saint's day celebrations to be disrespected. Entertainment at a saint's day celebration is currently considered the cheapest form of amusement. Today—in sharp contrast with the past—most Muḥammad ʿAlī Street performers say that they no longer work at these celebrations.

Because weddings celebrated in the streets are now held in low regard, more hosts are choosing to celebrate a wedding in a private venue, such as a club (figure 5). Since the late 1970s, the government has built a growing number of clubs for sports and festive occasions. In part, this represents an attempt by the authorities to restrict uncontrolled street weddings. To a significant extent, the disorderly and unpredictable happenings of the street have been replaced by weddings limited to a number of invited guests, at which no alcohol is served and which end by midnight. At present, weddings in many towns of the Delta, and increasingly in Cairo as well, take place in clubs.

FIGURE 5 Performers from Muḥammad ʿAlī Street taking a rest during a private party. Photo by Karin van Nieuwkerk, 1988.

Finally, the performers have relocated their sphere of activity. In order to perform in an army club or sports club, they must be registered by an agent and obtain official papers. In former times, female performers would remain at one party all evening, alternating as singers and dancers. Some women still do work like this, but others have adopted the *nimar* system prevailing in nightclubs: that is, they drop by at a wedding for only half an hour to do one show, and then leave for another wedding in a club or on the street. Several chose this system after having experienced trouble with drunken customers and criminal gangs. A few female entertainers have chosen to work in nightclubs, as many of the male performers of Muḥammad ʿAlī Street have already been doing for some time.

PROFESSIONALIZATION AND TRADE UNIONS

Since about the 1950s, a third circuit—the performing arts—has developed, to the detriment of weddings and saint's day celebrations. Theater, film, recordings, radio, and television have become the most respectable media for art and entertainment. A growing number of art schools and academies certify and license entertainers, who now monopolize the respected state-controlled cinema, television and radio stations, and theaters. The performing arts have, moreover, become the standard against which nonrecognized forms of art and entertainment are measured. This too has resulted in a loss of status for the circuit of weddings and saint's day celebrations.

At the outset, these new options were open to many. In fact, some of the performers of Muḥammad ʿAlī Street had minor film roles as dancers, and a few worked in radio. But after the 1960s, because of an ongoing professionalization of their trade, star performers who reached the higher echelons of their art would stop working in the less prestigious popular circuit; and many common entertainers were barred from state-controlled radio and television. Today, singers and instrumentalists who are not graduates of the Institute for Arab Music cannot perform on radio or television. One female singer of Muḥammad ʿAlī Street, for instance, sang on radio for a time but then was no longer allowed to do so, because she had no institutional training. In addition, the increasing number of specialized training institutes has fragmented the unity of the performing arts; once, a performer could be an actor, singer, dancer, and acrobat at the same time, but this is no longer true. Professionalization has thus led to a split between those with a certificate, who work in ensembles, in orchestras, on radio, or on television; and those who may have a lifetime of experience but have no formal training, who work at weddings and saint's day celebrations and in nightclubs. This trend has brought greater respect to some performers at the expense of others. In particular, belly dancing, which involves no form of schooling, receives no serious recognition.

These tendencies are reflected in the policies of trade unions. Actors and actresses have a well established trade union. Dancers belong to their union in theory, but in reality only those with training are admitted. Thus most dancers, except for folk and ballet dancers—a relatively small group–are denied membership. Musicians and singers are united in another trade union, from which they receive benefits in case of illness and on retirement. This union's policy is to keep unqualified people and "intruders" out of the trade. The unions plan to establish a vocational training course that will include instruction not only in music but also in reading and writing. Most musicians from Muḥammad 'Alī Street approve of excluding unqualified "intruders," but they would prefer to be examined only on their skill in music.

THE STATUS OF THE MUḤAMMAD 'ALĪ STREET PERFORMERS

Egyptians are fond of music, singing, and dancing, and performers are very important in Egypt. Professional entertainers are a central part of the most important occasions in people's lives, such as births, engagements, and weddings. Despite this, however, performers are generally not honored or accorded much prestige.

Many people are ambivalent about performance as a profession. Strictly religious people, for instance, are likely to condemn entertainers. Many people would not allow their children to work as performers and would object to their child's marrying an entertainer. Lower-class and lower-middle-class people, who are acquainted with financial hardship and a lack of options, generally do not condemn male professional entertainers; but they may still think it improper for a woman to work as a singer or dancer.

Still, even though the entertainment profession is generally not held in high esteem, the performers of Muḥammad 'Alī Street are not a marginal group. Many Egyptians acknowledge the contribution of musicians, singers, and dancers to weddings and say that these performers enliven the party and create a merry atmosphere. Besides, the presence of performers confers prestige on a host—and the more entertainers appear, or the more expensive and famous they are, the more the prestige of the host family is enhanced. Entertainers are viewed as necessary because they make people happy—they encourage people to express their happiness. A celebration without performers is not considered a real celebration.

REFERENCES

Danielson, Virginia. 1991. "Artists and Entrepreneurs: Female Singers in Cairo during the 1920s." In *Women in Middle Eastern History*, ed. Nikki R. Keddie and Beth Baron, 292–310. New Haven, Conn.: Yale University Press.

al-Faruqi, Lois Ibsen. 1979. "The Status of Music in Muslim Nations: Evidence from the Arab World." *Asian Music* 12(1):56–85.

Graham-Brown, Sarah. 1988. *Images of Women*. London: Quartet.

Koskoff, Ellen, ed. 1989. *Women and Music in Cross-Cultural Perspective*. Urbana: University of Illinois Press.

Nieuwkerk, Karin van. 1995. *"A Trade Like Any Other": Female Singers and Dancers in Egypt*. Austin: University of Texas Press.

Racy, Ali Jihad. 1981. "Music in Contemporary Cairo: A Comparative Overview." *Asian Music* 13(1):4–26.

———. 1982. "Musical Aesthetics in Present-Day Cairo." *Ethnomusicology* 26: 391–407.

el-Shawan, Salwa. 1980. "The Sociopolitical Context of *al-Musika al-'Arabiyyah* in Cairo, Egypt: Policies, Patronage, Institutions, and Musical Change (1927–1977)." *Asian Music* 12(1):86–129.

Dance in Egypt

Magda Saleh

The *Bambūtiyya*
Bedouin Dances
Combat Dance of the Ababda Bedouin
Būrmiyya
***Raqs Sharqī* (Oriental Dance)**
Dhikr
Al-Hinna al-Suwaysī
***Raqs Iskandarānī* (Alexandrian Dance)**
***Kaff* (*Kafāfa*)**
***Raqs al-Khayl* (Horse Dancing)**
Nubian Dance
***Rongo* (Sudanese Dance)**
Taḥṭīb
Zār

Egypt has a number of regional and social subcultures, each enriched by its own dance forms—ceremonial, communal, ritual, martial, and entertainment dances. The culture of this ancient land was founded, enduringly, on thirty centuries of pharaonic civilization and through the succeeding eras has absorbed many influences. In modern times, rapid change was spearheaded by the Napoleonic invasion from the West in 1798; today, two centuries later, the nation remains in transition, with increasing erosion of its native local culture. Although serious study has long focused on Egypt's political and cultural history, dance has been neglected, and research on dance is still in its initial stages. This essay introduces and outlines the multifarious dance genres of Egypt.

THE *BAMBŪTIYYA*

The *bambūtiyya* is a dance from the Suez Canal Zone, in particular Port Said, Ismailiyya, and Suez. Its name—a corruption of the English "bumboat"—refers to boat peddlers who sell their wares to sailors and passengers on ships in transit through the canal. Some of the songs accompanying this dance, rendered by a soloist with chorus, originated as far away as the Arabian Gulf region. The lead singer plays the *simsimiyya*, a five-stringed zither peculiar to the area, supported by *riqq* (a tambourine), *darabukka* (a clay hourglass drum), and rhythmic clapping.

The origin of the dance itself is uncertain. It may be an example of recent adoption and adaptation of a foreign dance form to local dance culture—in this case the foreign dance might be the Charleston, a Western social dance that was much in vogue in Egypt after its appearance in the 1920s. The *bambūtiyya* consists of a lively Charleston-like leg action with intermittent pelvic shimmies. The upper body mimes a variety of work-related movements such as rowing, winding ropes, and bargaining.

BEDOUIN DANCES

After the Arab conquest of Egypt (639–642 C.E.), Arab tribes, migrating in waves, settled in the Sinai peninsula, Upper Egypt, and the eastern Delta in Lower Egypt, and along the Mediterranean littoral west of Alexandria. Communities of bedouin still live in these areas.

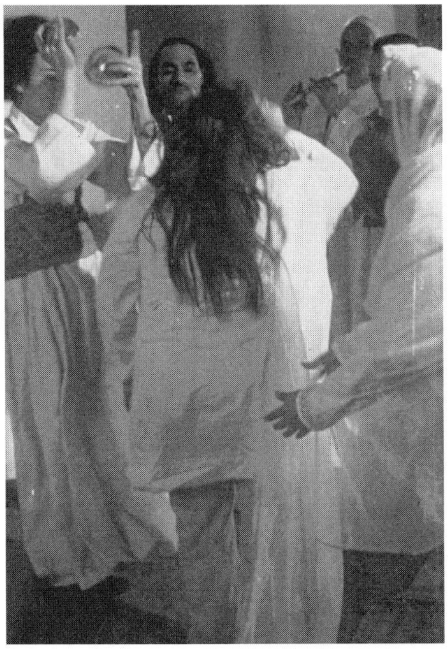

FIGURE 1 Arab *haggāla* near Marsa Matrūh, Western Desert. The *ḥāshiya* spins, revealing the padding around her waist; the men, singing and dancing, lunge toward her. Photo by Magdi Kamel, 1975.

Kaff al-ʿarab is a common bedouin dance. One or more female dancers face a row of male singers who clap their hands in rhythmic accompaniment. The dance song is performed in three distinct parts. The *shittaywa*, which includes the dance proper, is sung by the men. A poet renders the *ghannaywa* in free rhythm which does not lend itself to dance. Action usually stops during the *magrūda*, which is sung by a soloist and chorus. The dancer, *al-ḥāshiya*, advances and retreats, favoring those male singers who are clapping and lunging most fervently. This interplay between the dancer or dancers and the men is central to the action. It is a provocative exchange suggesting dalliance and flirtation, but it is maintained as a playful fiction, preserving the strict decorum that governs behavior between the sexes. The woman's movements consist of pelvic rotations and oscillation, and her hips are sometimes padded or girdled to emphasize the motion. Accessories manipulated during this dance include sticks or staves, rifles, daggers, and swords. In a form of "courage dance," the *ḥāshiya* may wield a sword dangerously, both with the flat and on edge.

The *kaff al-ʿarab* is widespread throughout the Arab world and has numerous variations. In Egypt, there are regional variants known by different names: *haggāla* (figure 1), *dahiyya*, *razʿa*, *samar*, *kaff*, *mashraqiyya*, and *khojar*—with improvisation by female poets.

COMBAT DANCE OF THE ABABDA BEDOUIN

The nomadic Ababda, roaming the eastern desert of Egypt between the Nile Valley and the Red Sea, are a branch of the Hamitic Beja tribes. These wanderers over the African deserts east of the Nile and north of the Atbara river are not always considered "Arab" by other Arab tribes.

A display of martial dancing skills in which warriors are paired in freely improvised mock combats, a form both ancient and widespread, is accompanied by choral singing, clapping, stamping, and strumming on the *tanbūr* (*qithār* 'zither'). With raucous taunts, the adversaries circle each other, brandishing straight swords and round hide shields, jumping high off both feet from an upright stance or a crouch (figure 2). They squat, lunge, thrust, parry, and feint. With the flick of a wrist, a combatant whips his sword arm, causing the long blade to shiver along its entire length—a notable feat.

FIGURE 2 *Abbadi* combat dance with sword and shield, Naj al-Shadhliyya, Eastern Desert, near Aswān. Photo by Magdi Kamel, 1975.

BŪRMIYYA

The Siwa oasis, at the tip of a crescent of oases bisecting Egypt's western desert, close to the border with Libya, is inhabited by tribes related to Berber, Arab bedouin, and African groups. The merry gatherings of the *zaqqalīn* 'club-bearers' (singular, *zaqqal*) are the liveliest and most frequented in Siwa. *Zaqqalīn*—who work in the fields or as night watchmen—spend their leisure hours singing, dancing, and drinking. One of their dances, the *būrmiyya* (from *barama* 'to twist') is simple and quasi-stationary, with minimal ornamentation. It can be enhanced by the artful manipulation of accessories such as a stick, or a scarf wrapped or held around the pelvic area. Its most notable feature is a shuffling, hip-swinging action. The musical instruments accompanying the dance and song include the *ṭabl* 'double-headed drum', the *tishbibt* 'metal flute', and the double-horned *magruna*.

A dance akin in character to some African animal dances was disseminated by descendants of black slaves and adopted locally. An energetic group of *zaqqalīn* form a circle. They dance around, hips swinging rhythmically, with jerks of the body, hops, and forward jumps. The action climaxes in erotic movements punctuated by excited shouts and shrieks as the participants close in for the finale.

RAQS SHARQĪ (ORIENTAL DANCE)

Raqs sharqī, a seductive dance also called *raqs baladī* 'native dance', *raqs maṣrī* 'Egyptian dance', *raqs ʿarabī* 'Arab dance', and (by Westerners) "belly dance," is regarded as preeminently Egyptian, although the current style was shaped, for more than two millennia, by other cultural influences as well. In fact, the term *raqs sharqī* refers only to the most familiar aspect of an ancient dance form that is varied and widespread. Its defining element is a range of articulated pelvic movements. Numerous theories, many associated with fertility and maternity, have been developed to explain its origins and function. Ancient Tanagra-type pottery figurines depict long-vanished dances and rites; in the nineteenth century, special feats requiring exceptional muscular control, skill, strength, and balance—and even a risqué striptease dance—were documented, but these too seem to have all but died out. A popular dance of this type that survives today is the *raqs al-sham'īdān* 'candelabrum dance', in which the dancer executes various specialty tricks while balancing on her head a tall, weighty, ornate candelabrum with lighted candles (figure 3).

FIGURE 3 *Sham'īdān* (candelabrum) dance, performed by Maḥāsin Milāl, Cairo. Photo by Magda Saleh, 2000.

Within this tradition, a distinctive form in a unique style distinguished by a rapid vibration of the hips is practiced by the *ghawāzī* (singular, *ghāziyya*; figures 4 and 5). These dancers' name may refer to their predilection for adorning themselves with cascades of *ghāzī*, an early Ottoman coin, but their origin is uncertain. The patriarch of the Māzin family of Luxor in Upper Egypt claimed to be of the Nawar; this people and the Ḥalab and Ghajar are Gypsy tribes resident in Egypt. They are said to have entered Egypt in the wake of the conquering Ottoman armies in 1517. According to later European travel writings, particularly nineteenth-century sources, these mostly itinerant dancers had become the main attraction at the great religious festivals and other public festivals. They were also hired privately to dance at celebrations of births and circumcisions, at weddings, and at all-male gatherings. Their present-day costume derives from the apparel of the nineteenth-century dancers, who wore padding below the waistline under their skirts. Generally performing in pairs, trios, and quartets, the *ghawāzī* present their varied repertoire in a choreographed or semichoreographed form or in an improvised style. Some dancers also sing. Dancing girls are sometimes referred to as *'awālim* (singular, *'alima*, originally a specific term describing a learned female singer).

Strictures against these dancers were not uncommon. For example, Egypt's ruler Muḥammad 'Alī Pāshā banned all dancing girls from Cairo in 1834, causing a marked increase in the ranks of male dancers performing in a feminine style (*khawal*). These male dancers were already popular; the tradition of dancing youths goes back to ancient times, although the practice is regarded with the opprobrium attaching to a male performer who does not create a masculine presence.

Dance schools existed in the past. Children were reportedly bought or stolen from peasant mothers to swell the numbers of the *ghawāzī*. In Cairo, professional dancers are now drawn from sources other than the families of hereditary dancers. The better-trained and better-paid dancers appear in nightclubs, at private celebrations, and in films. Retired dancers may teach their routines to others.

DHIKR

In the twelfth century, religious fraternities of dervishes, *ṭuruq* (singular, *ṭarīqa*), appeared, advancing an identity of Muslim organization and worship. In Egypt alone, Sufism, a spiritualization of Islam, resulted in the establishment of a considerable number of such *ṭuruq*. Full members wandered as mendicants or lived in monasteries that had evolved from cells clustered around the grave or shrine of a saint. A saint's day (*mūlid*) centers on such a shrine, which is the focus of a saint cult, and these cults are at the core of popular belief and practice in the Middle East. The *ṭuruq* also had a vast number of lay members. The last monastery in Egypt closed in 1967, and the *ṭuruq* survive with a mainly lay membership.

The practice of *dhikr* 'reminding oneself' or 'remembrance' is based on Qur'ānic texts. [See ISLAMIC HYMNODY IN EGYPT: AL-INSHĀD AL-DĪN.] Worshipers seek iden-

FIGURE 4 *Ghawāzī* dancers performing a duet. Photo from *Arabesque* magazine.

tification with the divine, achieved through a difficult technique of spirituality that entails prolonged asceticism. Those who have progressed significantly along the spiritual path practice a solitary *dhikr* of the privileged (*khawāṣ*). Others who are less advanced (*'āmma* 'commonality') gather in collective *dhikr* sessions. Certain Sufi fraternities seek the same goal by purely physical procedures, ecstatic dance, and thaumaturgical practices. The ordinary Muslim thus obtains and renews emotional reinforcement and release through the spiritual and physical exercise of *dhikr* and other ceremonial performances, inducing trance.

During *dhikr*, *munshidīn* 'singers' recite spiritual odes (*qaṣā'id*) and poetry (*muwashshaḥāt*). They are accompanied by the *nāy* 'flute', *mazhar* (a large tambourine), *bāza* (a pair of small kettledrums of different sizes), and *sagat tūra* (large finger cymbals). The beat may also be maintained by clapping or other means.

A complete session of *dhikr* or *majlis* is begun by recitation of the *Fātiḥa*, the opening sura of the Qur'ān; blessings; and invocations. The participants in the ecstatic dance are seated or stand shoulder to shoulder in one row or several rows. Proceeding slowly, they chant *Lā illāha illā-Allāh* 'There is no god but Allah', bowing their heads and bodies twice in unison at each repetition. This may be later shortened to *Allāh ḥayy!* 'God lives!' or even to *ḥayy!* or a guttural explosion of breath as the dance switches to a more rapid tempo. At the climax, the participants drop the whole body, or they bend back and forth, swinging violently and more and more widely as the intensity deepens. They may also twist sideways and turn their heads, or they may jump. Excited calls for spiritual aid (*madad*) burst out, and an excess of fervor may cause a participant to become possessed, falling to the ground in a fit or frenzy. The close of the ceremony contrasts strikingly with the gravity of its earlier sections.

While *dhikr* is at the heart of a *mūlid* celebration, the event, great or humble, combines ceremonial and devotional practices with the secular activities and entertainments of a popular fair. Multitudes of local people and pilgrims accompany dervishes in a joyous procession (*zaffa*) to a saint's shrine through gaily decorated streets. (The most important *mūlid* celebrated in Egypt is that of the Prophet, *Mūlid al-Nabī*.)

The dervishes engage in a variety of thaumaturgical feats, among which are ritual piercing, walking on burning embers, directly exposing themselves to flames, licking red-hot knives, and swallowing fire, live coals, glass, snakes, and scorpions. In a dramatic spectacle called a *dōsa* 'treading', the shaykh of the order, accompanied by his

FIGURE 5 *Ghawāzī* trio entertaining foreign visitors in the nineteenth century. From *Arabesque* magazine.

entourage, once rode in ceremonial procession over prostrate devotees, apparently inflicting no harm. This practice was suppressed but later revived in a different form, in which the shaykh walked over the faithful. Whether it survives today is uncertain.

AL-HINNA AL-SUWAYSĪ

Celebrated in Egypt, *laylat al-ḥinna* 'henna night', one of the festivities preceding a wedding, is dedicated to the ritual dyeing of the bride's and sometimes the groom's hands and feet with henna as a prophylactic against the evil eye. This practice is common in most of the Muslim world, but the city of Suez, at the tip of the Gulf of Suez, has a unique version of *laylat al-ḥinna*: a ritual perambulation. Its provenance is uncertain; over the ages, foreign influences may have shaped this *ḥinna al-suwaysī* 'Suez hinna', or the parade through the streets might hark back to ancient Egypt.

In the bride's home, a large, gaily decorated tray of henna paste is prepared; this tray will be paraded through the quarter from dusk to dawn, with song and merriment. The male relatives of the families that are being united, and their guests, deposit the tray before the homes of the bridegroom and the relatives and friends of the couple in the neighborhood. The men dance energetically, circling the henna tray while miming swimming, rowing, the hoisting of sails, and the drawing of ropes. These gestures are reinforced by movements such as jogging, squatting hops, sidestepping across the body, and kicking. The dancers are led in song by a solo vocalist accompanied on a *darabukka*, and each sequence culminates in the complex syncopated *saqfa suwaysī* 'Suez clapping'.

RAQS ISKANDARĀNĪ (ALEXANDRIAN DANCE)

A link has been suggested between older weapon dances, with swords, knives, and daggers and those still practiced in Alexandria and some towns of lower Egypt. The *ṣuḥba* 'friends' or 'companions', an individual dance with martial features, is intended to reflect the indomitable character of the Alexandrians. In a tradition that is now waning, youths of the popular quarter Rās al-Tīn display their skill, balance, and strength in various feats. The movements include wide side-to-side hopping, undulating sidestepping and cross-stepping, balancing and pivoting on one leg, and crouching and bouncing. The dance incorporates a stylization of the formidable Alexandrian *rūsiyya* (from *rās* 'head'), the use of the head to deal a literally stunning blow, as well as mimetic gestures such as stabbing, slashing, and throat slitting. Upright thumbs and pointed fingers indicate knives, and stabbing rapidly at oneself while bouncing in a crouch actually constitutes a dangerous trick. One gesture, raising the hands alternately to the forehead. is typical of the Alexandrian style. A performer uses accessories such as shawls, scarves, and a chair on which he dances.

Alexandrian acrobat dancers were a popular feature of the secular entertainments associated with *mūlid* celebrations. These dancers were forerunners of the *zaffa*; on the forehead or chin, they balanced a long pole topped by *sistra* 'rattles'. More recent feats have included spinning, dancing, upending a bicycle clamped in the teeth by the handlebars, and balancing a chair on the chin. The display is accompanied by *darabukka*, *mazhar*, and accordion.

KAFF (*KAFĀFA*)

In the *kaff* (figure 6), a social dance of Upper Egypt performed on a variety of festive occasions, one or several veiled women parade, pivot, advance, and retreat before a row of men. Up and down the Nile Valley, there are many versions of the elements, motifs, sequences, and dynamics of the movements in this dance, most of which are performed by men. These movements include stamping, leaping, skipping, hopping, lunging, swaying, swinging, inclining the torso, taking short steps forward and backward, and performing sequences of two-footed jumps, sometimes combined with nod-

FIGURE 6 *Kaff* dance in Baharif village near Aswān, Upper Egypt. The veiled woman's shawl spreads out like the wings of a bird as she sways from side to side, swinging her arms open and across her upper body. Photo by Magdi Kamel, 1975.

ding. A solo singer accompanies the dance; the men also punctuate this vocalist's song sequences by providing choral responses and clapping. The beat of the *tār* (a large tambourine without jingles), the *ṭabl*, or both, leisurely at first, switches to a rapid tempo. The overall pattern, reminiscent of the *kaff al-'arab*, may imply that older dance forms of the Nile valley merged with those of Arab settlers.

RAQS AL-KHAYL (HORSE DANCING)

Arab poets composed some of their most memorable verse in praise of their prized steeds. The horse features prominently in the oral traditions of epic poetry (*sīra*) and narrative ballads (*mawāwīl*). Today, the Arabian horse and his master perpetuate a fabled relationship of prowess and mutual devotion.

The horse learned to dance in many cultures. The Arabian horse, trained in forms of horsemanship, dressage, and dancing peculiar to Arab societies, plays an important role in social celebrations. The horse was introduced to Egypt in the early seventeeth century B.C.E. Later archaeological evidence attests to its participation in enduring seasonal rituals.

FIGURE 7 Dancing horse performing the *taḥiya* 'salute' or 'greeting', Giza. Photo by Magdi Kamel, 1975.

Horse dancing and games enliven many popular events. At the level of serious training and competition, the requirements for appearance and accomplishment in the high art of dressage are stringent. Dance is a prime feature, and the horse performs a variety of exercises to the lilting rhythms of *ṭabl* and *mizmār*. Among these are the *murabba'* 'square', a cadenced on-the-spot prance; the *ta'aqīla* (from *aqala* 'to hobble'), in which the animal propels itself rhythmically off its hind legs, flexing a foreleg to its chest; and the *ijwāz* (from *gāz/jāz* 'couple', 'pair'), a combination of the *murabba'* in front and the *ta'aqīla* at the rear. An equine "Charleston" is sometimes attempted: the horse's forelegs are in the *ta'aqīla* position; the rear legs kick sideways. The horse firmly extends a foreleg in a salute, *taḥiya* (figure 7). It may kneel and lie, and the rider may dance standing on its back.

Equestrian art served a martial purpose, training the horse for battle. Ancient Arab horse entertainments inspired and spread games and dances. In Egypt, a dangerous combat game of presumed bedouin origin, the *tarda* (from *tārada* 'to chase'), involved a large number of horsemen armed with palm-frond spines, *jarīd*. The horsemen split into two groups, taking turns at hotly pursuing each other. The challenger attempted to touch his fleeing opponent with his *jarīd*, or even hurled it after him. Another game, the *birjas* 'tournament', is a form of jousting or mounted stick play (*taḥṭīb*).

NUBIAN DANCE

The rich Nilotic culture of the three main Nubian groups—the southern Fadikka; the Wādī al-ʿArab, Arabic-speaking Nubians; and the northern Kenuz—was forever changed when ancient Nubia disappeared under Lake Nasser behind the High Dam. [See NUBIAN MUSIC IN CAIRO.] There are social and cultural differences among the people who once inhabited a thousand miles of Nile shoreline. No longer a Nilotic people, they had to adjust their pattern of life to a radically different environment as they moved from sparsely populated isolated villages to compact contiguous settlements where they were exposed to Upper Egyptian customs. This adaptation was accomplished through a series of social transformations, as major occasions of ceremonial life were simplified or altered by a new residential situation.

The most significant event in the life of a Nubian man or woman, the marriage ceremony, embodies a network of relationships within the society. The most vital of these is a system of mutual obligation by which the community mobilizes to produce ceremonies and complete tasks. A syncretism of Islamic and animist customs, embodied in intricate pageantry, marks the crucial events of birth, circumcision, marriage, and death. Weddings and circumcisions—the latter replete with symbols of marriage—are sometimes held simultaneously, or a cooperative circumcision ceremony is held for several boys, to minimize costs. At a wedding, the actual marriage ceremony is the culmination and highlight of long days of joyous, exhausting festive activities, arrangements, parties, and announcements. Continuous dancing, singing, and drumming are an essential feature of the celebrations. At last, the groom is danced in procession to his bride, who awaits him in the wedding room.

Nubian dance movements, delicate and supple, are accompanied by vigorous drumming on the *ṭār* complemented by a rich variety of complex rhythmic clapping, or clapping and stamping patterns (figure 8). Singing is punctuated by choral responses—the piercing ululations of the women. While the musicians drum, standing to one side, men and women dance simultaneously but in discrete groups. The singer may position himself between them. Strict decorum is maintained.

The dance tempi vary. In a sedate dance, shuffling a step at a time, the groups advance toward and retreat from one another in orderly rows. The participants clasp hands. In another dance, while the men stand opposite, drumming, clapping, and singing, women—clad in a fine black overdress (*jirjār*) that subdues their own bright clothing—dance in a semicircle. They move half a pace forward, then backward, with

FIGURE 8 Nubian musicians playing the *ṭār*, Tushka, New Nubia. Photo by Magdi Kamel, 1975.

the right foot; then they repeat this with the left foot. Advancing with slight inclinations of the torso, they sway gently from side to side, hands clasped. A solitary woman may move out to dance more rapidly. Yet again, a cluster of young men, displaying nimble footwork, vie with one another in the impetuosity of their dancing and clapping. Occasionally, they move apart to dance an inspired solo, compete in pairs, or dance a duet.

The saint cult is highly developed among the Kenuz. In a colorful ceremonial procession to the saint's shrine, to which visits are made throughout the year, a crowd of people will spread out along the route, singing and dancing. Locking arms, the men move backward. Positioned between them and the women, a singer regulates the pace of the procession. A considerable distance can be covered in several hours. At the shrine, ecstatic *dhikr* is performed, along with prayers, dancing, singing, feasting, and offerings of food. Such visits highlight a variety of occasions.

Arab influence may be inferred from the sword and shield dance, and a version of the *kaff,* which appears to be limited to the Wadī al-'Arab Nubians.

RONGO (SUDANESE DANCE)

There is ample archaeological evidence for the presence of black people in ancient Egypt, and for contacts deep within black Africa. In more recent times, migration, the slave trade, and the induction of Sudanese soldiers following the conquest of the Sudan by Egypt's ruler Muḥammad 'Ālī Pāshā in 1820 led to an influx of blacks into the country. Sudanese fleeing internal strife also settled there in the late nineteenth century.

In the mid-nineteenth century, Nubian and Sudanese performers were featured in bridal processions, offering mock combat dances, acrobatic feats, clowning, and other entertainment. Early in the twentieth century, the Sudanese *rongo* (*ringu, ringa*) gained prominence as a popular feature of *mūlid* entertainment and had a steadily increasing vogue. This dance was established permanently in some places in Cairo.

The *rongo* (figure 9) owes its name to its principal accompanying instrument, the *ringu*. This is a xylophone made of gourds attached to wooden blocks and struck by mallets, akin to similar instruments found as far away as West Africa. Two iron rods produce metallic tones from a short section of railway track, the *kuria*. The *darabukka* can also be featured in the accompaniment, which is complemented by singing.

FIGURE 9 Sudanese *rongo* at Naj al-Sudaniyya near Qena. Photo by Magdi Kamel, 1975.

FIGURE 10 Common steps in *raqṣ al-taḥṭīb*.

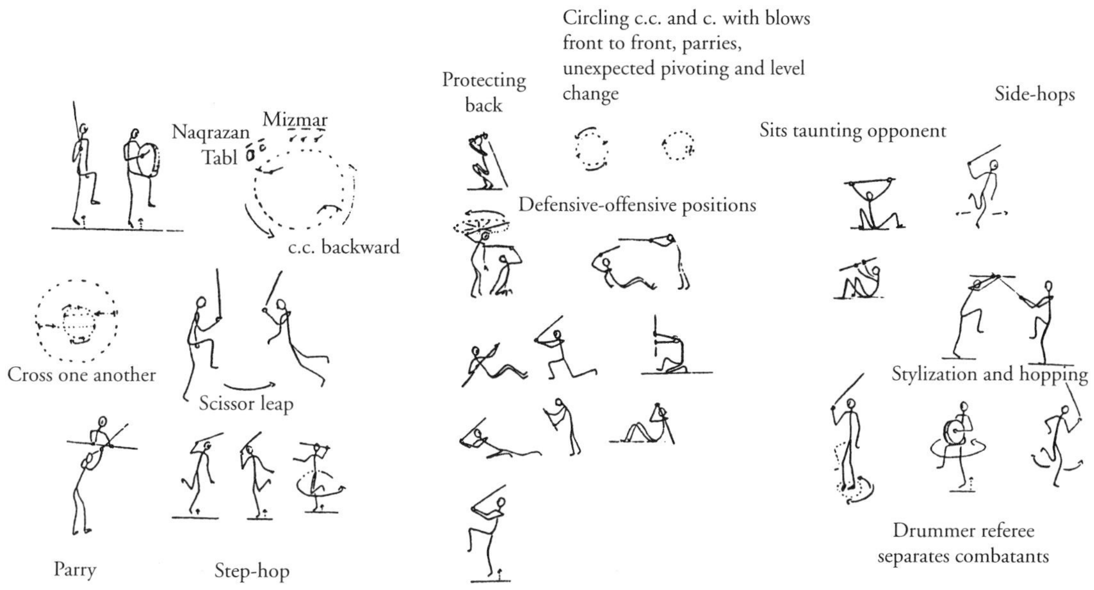

This dance, rendered by performers of both sexes, is graceful and rhythmic. Men and women circle, group, and pair off. They may clasp hands and may dance face to face, back to back, or side to side. Their movement consists essentially of a "treadmill" step, with the thrusting of a buttock to the rear, elbows flapping, arms held close to the body. The males court their female partners, leaping and brandishing one or more rattles (*shakhshāka*) whose use complements the *ringu* and *kuria*. Performance of the *rongo*, if not extinct, appears to be on the wane.

TAḤṬĪB

FIGURE 11 *Raqṣ bi 'l-'asā*, al-Shaykh Shibl, Suhaj, Upper Egypt. Photo by Magdi Kamel, 1975.

Complex and highly structured, the dynamically powerful offensive and defensive techniques of *taḥṭīb* (from *ḥaṭab* 'wood'—that is, firewood), formulated many centuries ago, are the oldest surviving form of Egyptian martial art (figure 10). These stylized techniques involve behavior closely related to the art of dance. In a fight, graceful "stick play" is transformed into a dangerous, even vicious melee. Opponents wield a formidable weapon, a long, thick bamboo or wood stave (*'asā* or *nabbūt*) grasped in one or both fists. (The *nabbūt* is still used in self-defense, particularly in Upper Egypt.) When the game is practiced as a pastime, strict rules and restrictions apply.

Taḥṭīb can be preceded or followed by *raqṣ bil-'asa* 'dance with stick' (figure 11) in procession or in place. This allows a player to demonstrate skill, inventiveness, and musicality in the manipulation of his weapon, alone or in an ensemble. As the men pace through dignified evolutions, step out to the catchy beat of the *waḥda wa-nuṣṣ* (a common rhythmic mode), or mince to a lively staccato, tempi and rhythms vary. In the venerable tradition of musician-dancers, the musicians, playing the large *ṭabl baladī*, the *naqrazān* (a small kettledrum suspended from the neck), and the *mizmār*, sometimes mingle with the dancers, stepping and swaying rhythmically. The drummer often contributes a tour de force, such as drumming while spinning dizzyingly on one leg.

Each combatant in the duel of *taḥṭīb* seeks to penetrate his opponent's guard. With taunts, verbal challenges, or guttural outbursts, he slashes, parries, feints, and tries to elude his adversary. He waits, tense and motionless, for the other to flinch, and sometimes breaks away, stick upheld, to hop with raised leg held at a right angle to the body—a position inherited from ancient Egyptian dance. All the while, he maintains his defense by circular sweeps of the *nabbūt* around the body. The drummer regulates the game, intervening to separate overly aggressive combatants. *Taḥṭīb* is a favorite feature of *mūlid* entertainments and other festive occasions.

ZĀR

The word *zār* is of uncertain etymology. A ritual of pacification and propitiation enacted in cases of possession, the *zār* is found in countries of the Middle East and North Africa, transcending religion and social class. Its practice is particularly widespread in Ethiopia. The presumed introduction of the *zār* into Egypt from Ethiopia may have occurred no earlier than the nineteenth century. The oldest recorded reference to it dates from 1862.

The existence of spirits and spirit possession—a belief ingrained in the traditional lore of many cultures—is the basic premise underlying the *zār*. The *jinn*, beings intermediate between angels and men, are said to have the power to cause evil among humans. They roam the earth, permeating solid matter and the firmament. Possession is caused by a perceived lapse or transgression. Women in particular are seen as susceptible. A variety of ailments, neuroses, psychosomatic complaints, and psychotic conditions may afflict the victim. Spirits entering the human body are known as *asyād* 'masters'; to refer to them as *'afrīt* or *shayṭān* 'spirits' or 'devils' is derogatory. To neutralize the power of a spirit, an individual in a position perceived as vulnerable endeavors to placate it by resorting to the *zār*. During a period of preparation, the patient may attend a weekly public *zār* held by the *kudya*, an instrument and intermediary of the *asyād*, in her home. Thereafter, the patient must continue to attend regularly.

Undertaking all functions endowed with a spiritual mystique, the *kudya* expresses the wishes of the spirits, translating them into demands for material wealth. The complex ritual can last up to seven days, although financial considerations now limit most *zār* to a day or two, culminating with pomp and celebration during the *laylā al-kabīra* 'great night'.

An altar to the spirits, the *kursī al-asyād* 'masters' seat', is erected at sunset, laden with food that will later be distributed. The patient, *'arūsa* 'bride', bedecked in bridal finery, jewels, and amulets, is paraded in procession around the altar (figure 12). Blessings are invoked, incantations are intoned, and the proceedings are interspersed with recitations from the Qur'ānic *Fātiḥa*. Various animals with peculiar coloring or markings may be sacrificed at prescribed times, and the patient smeared with their

FIGURE 12 *Zār* in Cairo. For the *'arūsa*, mounting frenzy as the *kudya* stands by protectively. Photo by Magdi Kamel, 1975.

blood, which she may also drink. Other aspects of the ritual involve the application of henna, purification with incense for all in attendance, and—for the *'arūsa*—stepping over fire.

Singing and drumming, which are believed to ensure the success of the ceremony, heighten the charged though festive atmosphere. Musical instruments include *ṭabl*, *tār*, *ṭanbūr*, *bandīr* (a large tambourine), *suffarā'* (a small flute), *sagāt tūra*, and *oksh* or *mangour* (a belt rattle of goats' hooves). Communing with the spirits, the female singer, *munshida*, renders the repertoire of *zār* songs, while the musicians chant to the refrain. The songs are associated with specific individual spirits, which also have specific accoutrements and other paraphernalia.

At the core of the complex ritual is dance, violent and unrestrained, peaking in crises and subsiding when the dancers become exhausted. The convulsive movements include tripping in a tight circle, running in place, stamping, bending and plunging forward and backward, and jerking and twisting the torso and head from side to side with arms held close to the body or swinging back and forth. Emotion reaches a height as constraints are removed and repressed impulses are released. *Zār*, then, displays universal characteristics of therapy in a "primitive" form, and it often relieves symptoms and improves the patient's funtioning; indeed, its power to heal is often held to be greater than that of many methods based on rational assumptions.

Several genres of *zār* may be identified throughout the country, differing in dialect and local performance practices. *Zār* is called *faraḥ ma'a 'l-asyād* 'wedding with the masters', and parallels have been noted between wedding ceremonies and *zār* ceremonies.

REFERENCES

Alexandru, Tiberiu, and Emile A. Wahba. 1967. *The Folk Music of Egypt*. Cairo: Ministry of Culture.

Berger, Morroe. 1961. "A Curious and Wonderful Gymnastic. . . ." *Dance Perspectives* 10:4–41.

Buonaventura, Wendy. 1989. *Serpent of the Nile: Women and Dance in the Arab World*. London: Saqi.

Fahmy, Farida Melda. 1987. "The Creative Development of Mahmoud Reda, a Contemporary Egyptian Choreographer." M.A. Thesis, University of California, Los Angeles.

Fakhri, Ahmed. 1973. *The Oases of Egypt*, vol. 1. Cairo: American University in Cairo Press.

Fernea, Robert A. 1966. "Initial Adaptations to Resettlement: A New Life for Egyptian Nubians." *Current Anthropology* 7(3):349–354.

———. 1973. *Nubians in Egypt: Peaceful People*. Austin: University of Texas Press.

Kennedy, John G. 1967. "Nubian Zar Ceremonies as Psychotherapy." *Human Organization* 26(4):185–194.

el-Khadem, Saad. 1972. *Al-raqṣ al-sha'bī fī Miṣr* (Folk Dance in Egypt). Cairo: Cultural Library Series, Egyptian General Book Organization.

Lane, Edward W. 1936. *The Modern Egyptians*. London: Dent.

el-Malouk, Qamar. n.d. "The Mystery of the Ghawazi." *Habibi* 3, 4, and 5.

al-Maṣrī, Fāṭima. 1975. *al-Zār: dirāsa nafiyya taḥlīliyya anthrūpūlūjiyya* (The Zar: A Psychological Anthropological Study). Cairo: Egyptian General Book Organization.

McPherson, J. W. 1941. *The Moulids of Egypt*. Cairo: Ptd. N. M. Press.

Murray, G. W. 1935. *Sons of Ishmael*. London: Routledge.

Saleh, Magda. 1979. "A Documentation of the Ethnic Dance Traditions of the Arab Republic of Egypt." Ph.D. Thesis, New York University.

Saleh, Maher. 1965. "Horsemanship and the Horse Dance." *Al Funun al Shaabiya* (Folk Arts) 2:68–81.

St. John, Bayle. 1973. *Village Life in Egypt*. New York: Arno.

Wood, Leona. 1976. "Danse du Ventre: A Fresh Appraisal." *Dance Research Journal* 8(2):18–30.

Zuhur, Sherifa, ed. 1998. *Images of Enchantment: Visual and Performing Arts of the Middle East*. Cairo: American University in Cairo Press.

Popular Music of the *Intifāḍa*

Anne Marie Oliver and Paul Steinberg

Protest and Defiance
Nationalist Songs, Islamist Chants
Myth, Mastery, and Martyrdom

The *intifāḍa*, the Palestinian revolt against Israeli rule that began in 1987 and ended with the signing of the Oslo Accords in the early 1990s, changed the political landscape of the Middle East irrevocably. Of the popular media that helped to create and sustain it, music was perhaps the most powerful. Capable of lending emotional appeal to revolutionary ideas in a way that more staid media like leaflets and official proclamations could not, political music was an intrinsic part of street rallies, mass demonstrations, folk dance or *dabka* festivals, weddings, and celebrations commemorating martyrs. Whether in the form of anthems, popular chants, or mourning songs, the music of the uprising owes its origins to a long tradition of sung protest and defiance in Palestine. Resistance to Ottoman rule, the revolts of 1929 and 1936, and the war of 1948 all produced their own musical expression, the offspring of which could be found throughout the West Bank and the Gaza Strip during the *intifāḍa*.

PROTEST AND DEFIANCE

As, arguably, the most immediately emotive of aesthetic systems, music was the natural ally of *intifāḍa* activists, whose primary goal was to nationalize and mobilize the Palestinian population as quickly as possible. One song of the time stated the major objective as, "Every citizen becomes a revolutionary." The ways and means of revolution were not always clear to the general populace, however, and music, particularly in the early months of the uprising, functioned as a primer of sorts, as in the following verses from the audiocassette "State":

> Close the street at Manara Square
> When a car passes, attack at once
> O children of the stones, O heroes,
> close the streets and bring out the tires.
>
> The leaflet came out, telling the people to gather
> All the street is afire against the occupation
> O children of the stones, O heroes,
> close the streets and bring out the tires.
>
> When the merchant got the news, he ran to close his door
> then the soldier came and broke the lock

O children of the stones, O heroes,
close the streets and bring out the tires.

The upright popular committees
lead the struggle with spirit and morale
O children of the stones, O heroes,
close the streets and bring out the tires.

Peopled with heroes and martyrs, soldiers and saviors, peasants and merchants, heretics and spies, enemies and infidels, the songs of the *intifāḍa* told its story. A singer might recount a clash between soldiers of the Israel Defense Forces (IDF) and the *shabāb*, the young activists of the uprising; or villagers' refusal to pay taxes to the military authorities; or a prisoner's resistance under interrogation—and, depending on factional allegiances, singers would use nationalist, Marxist, or Islamist motifs.

Regardless of its orientation, all popular music of the *intifāḍa* shared certain time-honored traditions. Rhyme was standard; introductions were chanted; greetings were lengthy; the language was colorfully poetic; and the themes focused on lost childhood, martial heroism, victory, anger, injustice, revenge, and martyrdom. The common assumption of all *intifāḍa* song, nationalist and Islamist, was that the heady turmoil and onward rush of the *intifāḍa* would usher in a dawn of freedom, an era of liberation and justice in which past wrongs would be avenged and long-standing goals achieved. While old maximalist objectives like the elimination of the "Zionist entity" disappeared from the official documents of the Palestine Liberation Organization (PLO), they lived on in popular song, uncensored.

The songs of the *intifāḍa* not only reflected life under occupation and revolt in all its forms, real and fantastic, but also called for commitment and action on the part of their audience, as in the commands, "Revolt! Revolt! Revolt!" and "Declare war on them!" and "Those who honor the martyr must follow in his footsteps." Whether emotionalizing issues, narrating identity, commemorating the dead, or instructing the populace on correct revolutionary behavior, music was an important part of the uprising. Its perceived power was such that it was often considered a weapon in its own right, as in the lines, "This is my great people, fighting with bottles and stones/With daggers and Molotovs, with poetry and song."

NATIONALIST SONGS, ISLAMIST CHANTS

The explosion of popular song during the *intifāḍa* created ever-new opportunities for semiotic competition and ideological differentiation between the dominant nationalist groups under the leadership of Fatah and the oppositional Islamist groups led by the Islamic Resistance Movement, Ḥamās (figure 1). There were major and minor differences between the two blocs. While nationalists saw Palestinians as constituting a nation much like other nations of the world, Islamists had reservations about the idea of nationalism, promoting instead a vision of a unified Islamic community, or *umma*. While nationalists relied on a lexicon drawn from Marxism and third-world liberation movements, Islamists used the language of the Qur'ān and *sunna*, the recorded words and acts of the Prophet Muhammad. Nationalists used a variety of instruments in their music, including folk instruments like the *shibāba* (figure 2) and the *yarghūl*, both shepherd's flutes; the *ṭabla*, a type of drum; and modern instruments such as the synthesizer. By contrast, the Islamists banned all musical instruments except the drum from their troupes. The nationalist groups often consisted of men and women who sang and danced together, whereas the Islamists proscribed both dancing and mixed groups. Many nationalist songs were based on old *dabka* dance tunes; the Islamists favored *zajal* (metrical verse sung in colloquial Arabic) and other chantlike forms.

FIGURE 1 Accompanied by gunmen, young people affiliated with the Islamic Resistance Movement, Ḥamās, sing at the *ḥaflat ta'bīn,* or commemorative celebration, of Muḥammad 'Azīz Rushdī, a "general" in the Battalions of the Martyr 'Izz al-Dīn al-Qassam, the underground military wing of Ḥamās. Still from "The Hero-Martyr Muḥammad 'Azīz Rushdī" (videotape).

FIGURE 2 *Shibāba* player in traditional peasant dress, performing in honor of a recent nationalist martyr of the *intifāḍa*. Still from "Commemorative Celebration of the Hero-Martyr 'Amr al-'Ālūl" (Fatah videotape.)

For decades, popular Palestinian political culture, particularly that of young people, had centered on folk music and dance, which reflected the Palestinians' rich agrarian past and were widely viewed as a potent expression of national and ethnic identity. Many adherents of Ḥamās had grown up within this culture, but with the advent of the *intifāḍa* and the founding of an Islamist front it was denounced as suspect. Some even labeled it "un-Islamic," a term that Ḥamās defined in its covenant of 1988, in a section titled "The Role of Art in the Liberation Battle": "Man is an amazing form made from a handful of mud and a puff of spirit, and Islamic art addresses man on this basis, while un-Islamic art speaks only to the body and favors the mud." In the same vein, an Islamist singer on the Islamic Jihad audiocassette "The Call of Jihad" bemoans the nationalist pastime of folklore song and dance, suggesting that this has diverted the attention of the *umma* from its proper goals:

> O our nation, where is honor? Where dignity and freedom?
> Where the fervor for glory? Where the proud souls?
>
> In the Name of Allāh, Allāh Allāh
> In the Name of Allāh, Allāh Allāh
> In the Name of Allāh, Allāh Allāh
> In the Name of Allāh, Allāh Allāh.
>
> They taught us only dancing and they taught us only singing
> They made us learn all kinds of dancing—shaking and folk *dabka.*
>
> In the Name of Allāh, Allāh Allāh
> In the Name of Allāh, Allāh Allāh
> In the Name of Allāh, Allāh Allāh
> In the Name of Allāh, Allāh Allāh.

The Islamists also rejected the nationalist values of land and country, peasant and shepherd in the folkloric tradition. In nationalist music of the *intifāḍa*, land is typically equated with honor, and one who lives off the land, whether a shepherd roaming the hills with flock and flute, or a peasant harvesting fields of wheat, is portrayed as a steward of both land and culture. He is an intensely poetic, nostalgic, romanticized

In nationalist music of the *intifāḍa*, land is typically equated with honor, and a shepherd roaming the hills with flock and lute, or a peasant harvesting fields of wheat, is portrayed as a steward of both land and culture.

figure, as in the following lines from the "Sharaf al-Tibi Band": "O shepherd, O you taking your flock out early in the dewy morning/How beautiful is your flute letting fall the sweetest melodies, the flowers spreading smiles around you." He is often spoken of in sacrificial language reminiscent of that applied to martyrs, as in these lines from the audiocassette "'Ayun Qara": "O laborer, O peasant! O laborer, O peasant! A drop of sweat rises on your forehead/A drop falls, a drop falls, a flower appears, a flower grows."

Islamist music, in contrast, refers to the land in almost exclusively religious terms, and its nostalgia takes the form of longing for a golden age when Islamic heroes vanquished "the enemies of God and man." In the music of Ḥamās and the Islamic Jihad, contemporary armed operations are commonly compared to great Muslim battles of old, as in the following song from an underground videotape of the military wing of Ḥamās, the 'Izz al-Dīn Battalions. The song makes reference to the twelfth-century battle of the Horns of Ḥiṭṭīn, a definitive victory over the Crusaders by Muslims under the command of the Kurdish military leader Ṣalāḥ al-Dīn:

> If the heroes of Ḥiṭṭīn
> could witness the deeds of our Battalions,
> Ṣalāḥ would get down off his horse and proclaim,
> "At your service, Ḥamās, our inheritor."

Another historical event used as a harbinger of a future Palestinian victory is the battle of Khaybar, the last in a series of battles for the control of western Arabia, fought between Muhammad's followers and the Jewish tribes of the region. The Jews were defeated at Khaybar and were subsequently expelled from most of the Arabian peninsula. References to this famous battle abound in Islamist media, as in the popular chant, "In the Name of Allāh, *Allāhu akbar* /In the Name of Allāh, Khaybar has come!" or in the sung line, "Khaybar, Khaybar, O Jews, the Army of Muhammad will return!"

MYTH, MASTERY, AND MARTYRDOM

Despite their differences, the music of the nationalists and the Islamists shared a number of important functions during the *intifāḍa*. It was largely through music that Palestinians transformed current events into the stuff of myth and solidarity. Song dealt not only with internal concerns and problems but also with international issues from the civil wars in Somalia, Lebanon, Afghanistan, and the former Yugoslavia to the immigration of Jews from Ethiopia and the former Soviet Union. The Gulf war was a turning point that received particular attention. In the following song from the tape "Ayun Qara," President Saddam Hussein of Iraq is extolled as a heroic avenger, and the night when he rained Scud missiles on the Israeli city of Tel Aviv becomes a symbol of retribution and revenge:

When we hear the siren, the air-raid siren
we run up to the roof of the house
The ululation of my mother rises with the cry of the siren
The Zionist army and all its dens are destroyed.

When we go up, we see the Hussein missile
We shout praises to you and swear by your name, Saddam Hussein
Greetings from my homeland to all those
rising up against, not bargaining with, the tyranny of the unbelievers.

When we hear the siren, the air-raid siren
we run up to the roof of the house
The ululation of my mother rises with the cry of the siren
The Zionist army and all its dens are destroyed.

When we hear the siren, we see you [the missile] coming
We listen to the radio, to Nachman Shai [IDF's spokesman during the Gulf war]
"Put up plastic sheeting! Make it tight!
Put on your gas mask! Get under your rock, O mouse!"

When we hear the siren, the air-raid siren
we run up to the roof of the house
The ululation of my mother rises with the cry of the siren
The Zionist army and all its dens are destroyed.

Mythicizing history, *intifāḍa* song provided narratives of epic identity. For Palestinian youth, in particular, it helped answer the question, "What am I?" and it did so, paradoxically, through the negation of that "I" in the name of the people and on behalf of the eternity of the land. The refrain of the following song of the "Al-Qala' Band" answers the question "What am I?" with the assertion, "I am a *fidā'ī*," a self-sacrificer:

What am I? What will I be?
What am I? What will I be? And what will be my words?
I am a *fidā'ī*, standing at the border
I am a *fidā'ī*, standing at the border.

I am searching for a loaf of bread, while listening to the millstone turning
Before the sun sets, I will return to see the wheat flashing in the sun.

What am I? I am a *fidā'ī*.

The land, O my comrades, is thirsty; the blood of the martyrs will irrigate it
I listen to the sound of guns, in which the poor seek help
The land, O my comrades, is thirsty; the blood of the martyrs will irrigate it
I listen to the sound of guns, in which the poor seek help.

What am I? I am a *fidā'ī*.

I will fight until the last drop of my blood, for the land is calling me
Then make from my body torches, and from my love bombs for the homeland
I will fight until the last drop of my blood, for the land is calling me
Then make from my body torches, and from my love bombs for the homeland.

What am I? I am a *fidā'ī*.

The other side of such celebrations of sacrificial transformation was the contempt commonly displayed in *intifāḍa* song for those seen as devaluing this kind of transcendence. In "The Call of Jihad," for instance, the singer mocks Arab leaders who make empty promises to the Palestinians as well as Palestinians who put their faith in them. Listed among the false saviors are King Hussein of Jordan; King Fahd ibn ʿAbdul al-ʿAzīz of Saudi Arabia; Qabus bin Said, Sultan of Oman; and Husni Mubarak, president of Egypt:

> Some said, "Hussein," and some said, "Fahd"
> They counted many men
> Some said, "Qabus," and some said, "Mubarak"
> They counted many men.
> I said, "What a pity.
> Mighty Jerusalem, liberated by midgets!"

The liberation of Jerusalem and Palestine, many *intifāḍa* songs asserted, would be catalyzed by "the children of the stones," who, unlike "the sleepers," were ready and willing to risk humiliation, arrest, injury, and death. Indeed, it was largely through media like music that the children and youth of the uprising confronted and mastered their fear of such dangers. In *intifāḍa* song, fear was commonly transformed into defiance, and weakness into a source of inspiration, as in the lines, "My people are not afraid of fire/O enemy, your bullets are but sparks," and "We are afraid neither of desert tents nor of shooting/Neither of transfer nor of the demolition of houses." Some verses recalled with pride how even children successfully confronted enemy soldiers, as in the lines, "Young girls, as beautiful as roses, go down to battle/Defying the thuggery of the soldiers and joining in the attack."

Countless *intifāḍa* songs and chants called for self-sacrifice on the altar of God and country. Commemorating the deaths of young people who had answered the call was yet another function of *intifāḍa* song. Drawing on a long tradition in Palestinian culture of treating the untimely death of the young in terms usually reserved for marriage celebrations, *intifāḍa* song commonly referred to the martyr as a "bridegroom" or "bridegroom-martyr" or even, in an interesting reversal of gender, as female. Martyrs were said to live forevermore in the Gardens of Allāh, attended by perpetually virginal maidens; those who remained behind on earth were to follow in their footsteps. A common vow, chanted or sung, was: "O martyr, rest; we will continue your path."

REFERENCES

Abū-Fāris, Muhammad ʿAbd al-Qādir. 1990. *Shuhadāʾ filisṭīn* (Martyrs of Palestine). Amman: Dār al-Farqūn.

Barghūtī, ʿAbd al-Laṭīf. 1979. *al-Aghāni al-ʿarabiyya al-shaʿbiyya fī Filistīn wa ʾl-Urdunn* (Popular Arab Songs in Palestine and Jordan). Jerusalem: Maṭbaʿat al-Sharq al-ʿArabiyya.

———, ed. 1990. *al-Adab al-shaʿbī fī ẓull al-intifāḍa* (Popular Culture in the Shadow of the *Intifāḍa*). Taibe: Markaz Iḥyā al-Turāth al-ʿArabī.

Schiff, Ze'ev, and Ehud Ya'ari. 1989. *Intifāḍa: The Palestinian Uprising—Israel's Third Front*, ed. and trans. Ina Friedman. New York: Simon and Schuster / Touchstone. (Reprinted 1991. Originally in Hebrew.)

Sulaiman, Khalid A. 1984. *Palestine and Modern Arab Poetry*. London: Zed.

Nubian Music in Cairo

Ted Swedenburg

Two Nubian Musicians
Contexts of Nubian Music
Features of Nubian Music
Music and Nubian Identity

Contemporary Nubian music is largely a by-product of displacement and migration. Although long-distance migration from Old Nubia (south of Aswan, Egypt) to Cairo predated the twentieth century, it was the construction of the first Aswan Dam in 1902 and subsequent raisings of the dam in 1912 and 1933 that began the flooding of agricultural land in Nubia and that set off the contemporary migration of Nubian men to seek work. In 1963–1964, construction of the Aswan High Dam caused a total inundation of Old Nubia. By that time, about half the Nubian population was already living outside Old Nubia; the remaining 56,000 residents were then resettled in New Nubia, in the Kom Ombo region north of Aswan. Although the residents of Nubia shared broadly similar customs, in fact they belonged to three quite distinct groups: the Kenuz (speakers of Matokki, a Nilotic language), the Fadikka (speakers of Fadikka, a related language) and the 'Alayqāt, who spoke Arabic. The Nubians were essentially created as a distinct people—a modern ethnic group—by their common experience of permanent exile from a flooded homeland.

TWO NUBIAN MUSICIANS

Two of the most important and best-known Nubian musicians, Hamza 'Alā' al-Dīn (known abroad as Hamza El Din) and 'Alī Ḥassan Kūbān, are products of migrations that took place before the High Dam was built. Both made substantial innovations in the traditional musical styles of Old Nubia, in which singing was accompanied only by hand clapping, the *ṭār* 'frame drum', and sometimes the *kisr* 'five-stringed lyre.'

Hamza belonged to a group that began composing, playing, and singing Nubian music in the 1950s, but his own chief contribution was performing Nubian music to the Arab *'ūd*. He moved to the United States in the early 1960s and gained international fame performing in folk clubs in Greenwich Village, and at Woodstock in 1969; but his recordings, although readily available in the United States, never appeared in Egypt. Hamza now lives in Tokyo; he occasionally performs in Egypt and is still regarded with great respect by Nubians.

Today, many Nubian musicians play the *'ūd*, but performances or recordings with *'ūd* accompaniment are somewhat rare. Instead, the music that is most sought-after by Cairene Nubians, whether on cassette or for live performances, is that of the

FIGURE 1 Ali Hassan Kūbān's band (with Kūbān on the left) rehearsing at his club. Photo by Ted Swedenburg, summer 1997.

modern *firqa* 'musical ensemble'. 'Alī Kūbān (figure 1) had a major role in its development.

Kūbān moved with his family to Cairo in the 1940s, and in the 1950s, as a Boy Scout, he learned to play the bagpipes and clarinet. In 1956—inspired, he says, by a jazz band from Harlem that he had seen perform in Cairo in the late 1940s—he started his own group, which performed mainly at Nubian weddings. Kūbān's group transformed traditional Nubian music both by adding new instruments, which included the accordion, violin, *'ūd*, and *ṭabla*, and by composing new songs, which it performed along with traditional ones. Over the years, the group became larger and further transformed its instrumentation. By the late 1970s, it had added saxophone, trumpet, electric guitar, electric bass, electronic keyboards, and Western-style drums. In 1979, Kūbān made his first recording for Egypt's burgeoning cassette market; at the same time, wedding performances were becoming more lucrative, in part as a result of migration by Nubians to the oil states of the Arabian Gulf. Nubian musicians proliferated in both enterprises—cassette recordings and performances at weddings—and some of the most prominent belonged to Kūbān's "group," a pool of performers who were hired out for weddings through Kūbān's agency. In the late 1980s, Kūbān made the leap from the wedding circuit in Cairo to the "world music" scene. Today Kūbān, in his seventies, tours Europe and the United States, performing for world music audiences. He records only abroad and rarely performs in Egyt, but the 'Alī Ḥassan Kūbān "group" still dominates the Nubian wedding circuit.

CONTEXTS OF NUBIAN MUSIC

Nubian music is virtually absent from Egyptian radio, televised music videos, and nightclubs and is only rarely performed at concerts. However, it thrives in the cassette market and at weddings. People who buy Nubian music cassettes are mainly Nubians themselves, but a few Nubian musicians have "crossed over" into the wider Egyptian market. Weddings are almost the only occasion for the live performance of Nubian music.

A wedding is a major event in the Nubian community, and weddings are numerous during the summer. Larger wedding parties are typically held outdoors, on the grounds of social clubs, and attract hundreds of guests. Very few people who are not Nubians attend, but many Nubians without a formal invitation do come, particularly young men, who enjoy the music, the dancing, and the chance to meet unmarried Nubian women. The event starts with the *zaffa*, a procession which ushers in the bride and the groom, and which usually features traditional Nubian music by a troupe in traditional garb, singing to the accompaniment of hand clapping and drumming. After the bride and groom take their seats on an elevated stage, the festivities begin: nonstop live music and dancing, which often go on into the early hours of the morning. The size of the band and the number of singers vary from wedding to wedding. A large, expensive wedding may feature a big band and as many as ten or twelve major Nubian singers. At less elaborate weddings, the musical entertainment may consist of a single singer backed up by an electronic keyboard equipped with a drum machine. Men and women often dance together, and dances combine traditional Nubian and contemporary steps. The most notable modern dance, which Nubians call "rap" dancing, is actually the "electric slide," an American funk dance from the early 1980s.

The songs include conventional wedding pieces about love and in praise of the bride and groom, as well as nostalgic laments that contrast the difficulties of life in exile with the lost world of Old Nubia. Usually the band also plays a "nationalist" song that explicitly raises Nubian issues. The most common is "Al-ḥigra al-murra" ("The Bitter Relocation"), composed by the recording artist Khidr al-ʿAṭṭār (figure 2). Although this song was never recorded, its words are known to everyone. When the strains of "Al-ḥigra al-murra" begin, a wedding takes on the character of a rally: the guests dance with great enthusiasm and chant along with the music, especially to the line "They imposed the bitter migration upon us"; some people even break into tears. The song goes on:

They said Kom Ombo is a green paradise
We lived sad nights there
We walked for years in the long exile
My name is there [in Old Nubia]
My homeland is there.

Significantly, this song—which brings Nubians together so emotionally—is in Arabic. Today, Arabic is the lingua franca of Nubians in Cairo, especially the younger gen-

FIGURE 2 The singer Khidr al-ʿAṭṭār at a wedding in Zamalek, Cairo. Photo by Ted Swedenburg, summer 1995.

Contemporary Nubian music is largely a by-product of displacement and migration.

erations, who generally do not speak a Nubian language. Some popular Nubian singers (including Vīkā, 'Abbūd Ṣāliḥ, and Ḥassan 'Abd al-Majīd) sing mainly in Arabic; they are popular among Nubian young people and sometimes achieve success in mainstream music. Many Nubians are critical of a performer who sings only in Arabic; they argue that artists should help keep the Nubian languages alive. In fact, some performers do continue to sing in the Nubian languages: two examples are 'Alī Ḥassan Kūbān (who sings in Matokki) and Khidr (who sings in Fadikka), although both also perform some songs in Arabic.

FEATURES OF NUBIAN MUSIC

The Nubian languages are just one of several striking stylistic features that differentiate Nubian music from other Egyptian popular musics. Even though so many Nubians have lived in Cairo for decades, speak Arabic, and are consumers of Egyptian mass culture, Nubian music has mostly resisted the influence of Egyptian pop. Actually, influence appears to flow the other way: Egyptian pop artists, particularly young *shabābī* artists, tend to borrow from Nubian styles, especially rhythms.

Nubian music is lower-pitched, sounds more "African," and is more polyrhythmic than Egyptian pop. Nubian groups have preserved the rhythms of the *ṭār* but have integrated additional percussion instruments (bongo and *tabla*) and new rhythms (such as salsa, samba, and Afro-Cuban). Each Nubian subgroup also has its own unique rhythms; therefore, rhythm can be used both to distinguish "Nubian" from "Egyptian" and to distinguish among Kenuz, Fadikka, and Arab Nubians. With regard to mode (*maqām*; plural, *maqāmāt*), Nubians use the pentatonic (five-note) *maqām khumāsī*. This, too, sharply distinguishes Nubian music from other Egyptian musics, which use the characteristically Arab microtonal *maqāmāt*. As for instrumentation, Nubian musicians tend to rely more on horn sections and sounds generated by an electronic keyboard than Egyptian pop artists do.

Contemporary Nubian music closely resembles the popular musics of the Sudan, which also use *maqām khumāsī*, have "African" polyrhythms, and rely heavily on brass instruments. This testifies to the fact that Nubia remains a part of the greater Sudanese cultural area, and that there is considerable contact between Nubians and Sudanese in Cairo. Some Nubians specialize in popular Sudanese songs, in Arabic; and some Sudanese singers who live in Cairo perform at Nubian weddings and concerts. Another influence on Nubian music is the music of the Arabian Gulf region. Significant numbers of Nubian workers have migrated to the Gulf since the 1970s, and several songs from the Gulf have been incorporated into the repertoire of Nubian performers. Such borrowing is facilitated by the similarity between Gulf and Nubian rhythms, especially in the use of the *daff* (Nubian, *ṭār*), and by the strong effects of African music in Gulf music. The Sudan, then, has been a major influence on Nubian music, although 'Alī Kūbān and other Nubian artists have been inspired to a lesser extent by musicians of the African diaspora such as James Brown and Bob Marley.

MUSIC AND NUBIAN IDENTITY

The transformations that have developed in Nubian music have not been unanimously welcomed. Some Nubians say that the music popular among young people is merely commercial rather than artistic or ethnic. They accuse some artists of producing vulgar music and senseless lyrics, and of overrelying on electronic keyboards and drum machines, to the detriment of "true" Nubian rhythms that are said to be possible only with the *ṭār*. Other artists, though, are held up as exemplars of true Nubian music, and these include both musicians performing in the traditional style (backed by the *ṭār* and hand clapping) and musicians with bands that use electronic instruments.

Such debates indicate the liveliness and heterogeneity of the Cairene Nubian music scene. Through performances of music and rituals involving music, Nubians articulate their own narrative of Egypt's modernization and progress, a narrative that is counter to the official version. Music provides a means of expressing the bitterness of relocation and cultural loss, of remembering life in Old Nubia, and, on occasion, of pronouncing a desire to "return"—to reestablish the Nubian community on the banks of Lake Nasser. Nubians' music also reflects their hope of receiving governmental and international support to maintain their culture, their heritage, and in particular their languages.

Most important, and most fundamentally, music is a significant part of the articulation and reconfiguration of Nubian identity because it underlines the differences between that identity and the hegemony of Egyptian culture. Rituals such as weddings can serve as a way to sharpen and strengthen ethnic boundaries that have, under the threat of assimilation, become ambiguous. At wedding ceremonies, through complex networks of pleasure, political expression, ritual, celebration, and desire, music may take on its most salient role in the expression of the Nubians' collective "difference."

REFERENCES

Fernea, Elizabeth, and Robert A. Fernea (with Aleya Rouchdy). 1991. *Nubian Ethnographies*. Prospect Heights, Ill.: Waveland.

Fernea, Elizabeth, Robert A. Fernea, et al. 1973. *Nubians in Egypt: Peaceful People*. Austin: University of Texas Press.

Werner, Louis. 1991. "World Musician." *Aramco World* July-August:19.

Section 3
The Arabian Peninsula

For well over a thousand years the singing of fine poetry has been a central art form in the Arabian Peninsula. The region has produced a plethora of song genres—often solo; sometimes improvised; some, such as the *sāmrī*, highly localized; and others, such as the *qaṣīda*, familiar throughout the Arab world. The effect of words and of good singing is at the basis of aesthetic values. The region has produced genres of antiphonal song, many forms of dance, and songs related to work, the most famous of which are undoubtedly the genres associated with pearl diving along the eastern coast of the peninsula.

The interior of the peninsula, although relatively isolated, has for centuries welcomed Muslim pilgrims from all over the world. Coastal populations have had long and extensive contact with other societies, particularly in Africa, Iran, and the Indian subcontinent. Musical performances provide evidence of these relationships in adopted genres and performance practices. Local scholars try to capture and preserve the rich musical heritage of the populations of the interior.

Many important forms of performance are related to gender. In the *ʿarḍa* (or *razḥa* in Oman), for instance, the men of a community are brought together in a demonstration of local and masculine solidarity. Women's wedding music helps to construct lively communities in which women function as professional singers, instrumentalists, entrepreneurs, and patrons of performance, sustaining local styles and practices over the years.

Commercial recording attracted musicians early in its history; recordings of local genres such as *ṣowt* were made beginning in the 1920s. Since the 1960s, when Muḥammad ʿAbduh marketed songs in Saudi dialect internationally, pop musicians from the peninsula have been increasingly prominent in the world music scene.

Al-ʿarḍa: a solo performer with a stick dances between two lines of male compatriots. Photo by Jean Lambert, March 2000.

The Arabian Peninsula: An Overview

Jean Lambert

The Arabian Gulf Region
Saudi Arabia
Yemen
Unity and Diversity of Music in the Arabian Peninsula

There are many obstacles to understanding the music of the Arabian Peninsula. For a long time, most of the region was closed off to research. The available information is scattered and fragmentary and is never approached as a whole. Owing to the prevalance of oral tradition, much of the historical data is unreliable. Moreover, certain European concepts do not accord with the specificity of the peninsula: for example, as scholars have noted, the conventional distinction between "classical" and "popular" is largely irrelevant, since some of the main musical forms lie between what is usually meant by these terms (Jargy 1986:23). Therefore, I have focused here on areas and musics that are little known and have tried to make the best possible use of fieldwork and the available literature.

This article discusses three of four main areas that can be distinguished in the Arabian Peninsula: the Arabian Gulf, Saudi Arabia, and Yemen. A fourth area, Oman, is examined separately [see MUSICAL LIFE IN SOHAR, OMAN]. As in many other parts of the world, modern boundaries have arbitrarily separated natural cultural units. Fishermen's songs exist throughout the peninsula, and bedouin songs are prevalent in the central region. Although other connections could be established, for practical reasons fishermen's music will be discussed in the section on the Gulf, and bedouin music in the section on Saudi Arabia. The section on Yemen will be concerned mostly with sedentary villagers. Urban music is noted in the sections on the Gulf and Saudi Arabia, but Yemeni urban music is taken up elsewhere [see *AL-GHINĀ´ AL-ṢAN`ĀNĪ*: POETRY AND MUSIC IN ṢAN`Ā´, YEMEN]. Purely religious genres (recitations of the Qur'ān, calls to prayer) will not be treated here. They have drawn little attention from scholars, as they have been considered, correctly or not, less specific than other genres (for the Gulf, refer to Maṭar n.d.:133–136; for Yemen, Poché 1976). Finally, the Jewish music of Yemen will be set aside, since a large majority of Jews left for Israel in 1948 (for a bibliography, see Staub 1979).

THE ARABIAN GULF REGION

Two main musical styles are characteristic of the Gulf: pearl divers' songs and traditional urban music (for an overview, see Dōkhī 1984; Ḥanẓal 1987; Maṭar n.d.; Røvsing-Olsen 1980).

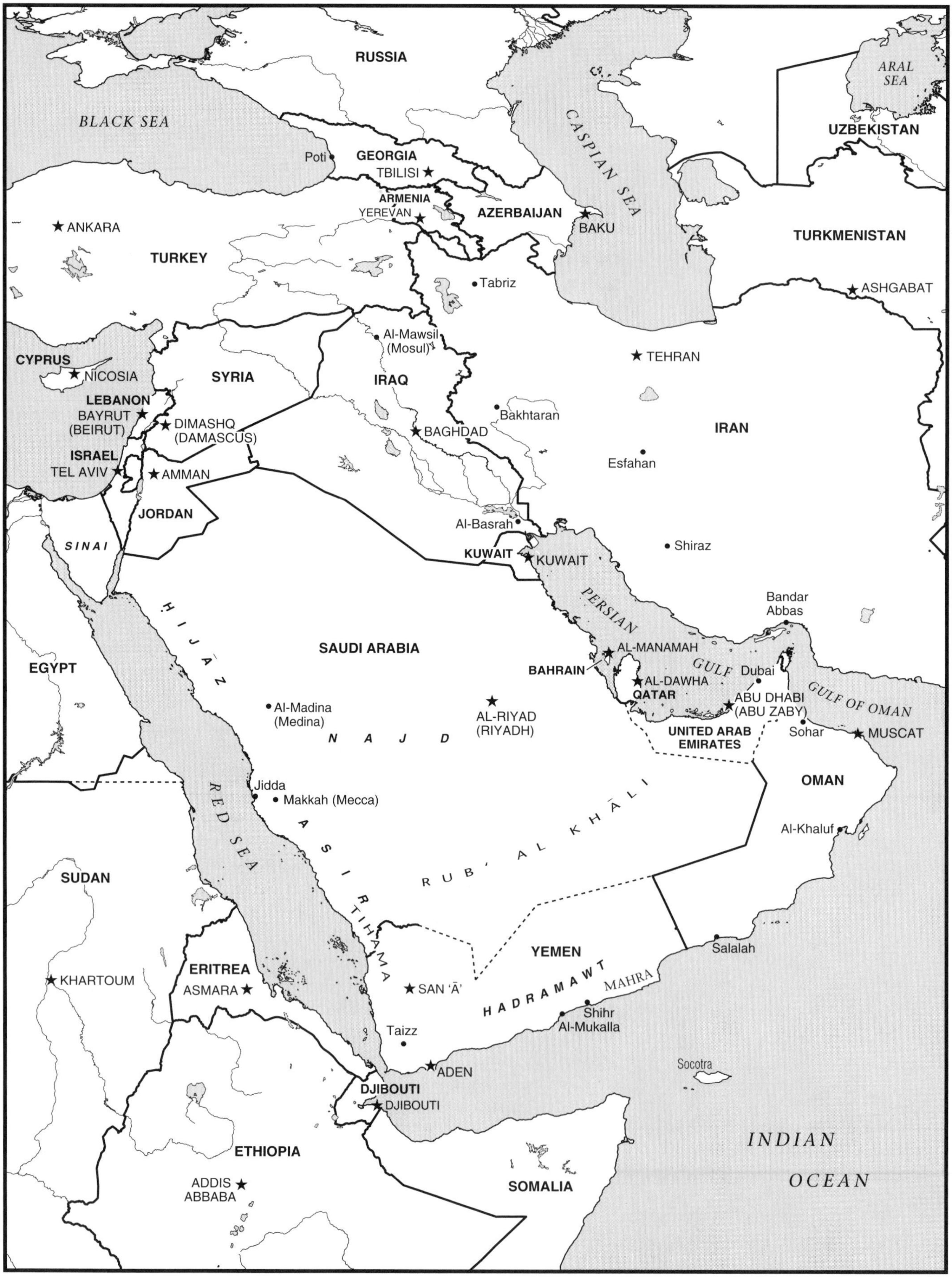

The Arabian Peninsula.

Pearl divers' songs

Pearl divers' songs are known locally as *aghānī al-ghawṣ* 'diving songs' or *nahma* 'animal sound' or 'voice of the whale'. The first transcriptions were published in 1960, and the first commercial recordings were issued in 1968 (by Røvsing-Olsen, whose archives are preserved at the Danish Folklore Institute, Copenhagen). The social context of the *nahma* and the status of the professional singer, the *nahhām*, are documented in Kuwait by al-Harbi (1980) and Maṭar (n.d.), in Qatar by Sulaymān (1992) and Ghānim (n.d.), and in Bahrain by Ḥarbān (n.d.). The *nahma* includes several forms that differ little from country to country.

The repertoire can be divided into two categories. First, there are songs that accompany every aspect of labor on the boats: hoisting the sail, dropping the anchor, opening the oysters, and so on. Except for the *yamāl*, which is unmeasured, these songs have short rhythmic cycles (Maṭar n.d.:80–86). Second, there are entertainment songs known—since some of them, such as the *ḥaddādī*, are sung only at night—by the generic term *fjīrī* 'until dawn' (Røvsing-Olsen 1980:513). These have long rhythmic cycles (16/8 and 32/8). They are prestigious forms, and their origin is the subject of rich legends (Maṭar n.d.:50).

There are two types of lyrics in pearl divers' songs, called *zuhayrī* and *muwaylī* respectively (Dōkhī 1984:302–313; Rifā'ī 1985:91). The *muwaylī* has an old fixed style, while the *zuhayrī* is more lively and may consist of five, six, or seven verses. The themes include pleas for religious protection from the dangers of the sea (in work songs), the transmission of navigational knowledge, love, and moral exhortations.

The accompanying instruments are mainly percussive and include the *ṭār*, a frame drum; the *ṭabl*, a cylindrical drum; and *ṭwaysāt*, small metal cymbals. Some instruments are everyday objects such as water jars (*jaḥla*) and mortars for grain or coffee (*hāwon*). Refined hand clapping involves various techniques called base (*asās*), divergence (*sudūd*), answer (*rudūd*), and intricacy (*sharbaka*), and a binary-ternary polyrhythmic pattern (Kerbage n.d.). There are at least three major vocal techniques: the *naḥba* 'lament'; the *janda*, an introductory improvisation; and the *hamhama*, a bass vocal drone which is the most characteristic feature of *nahma* (Dōkhī 1984:300; Røvsing-Olsen 1978). *Hamhama* seems to be related symbolically to the voice of the whale, and it suggests that more anthropological research is needed to illuminate the deep meaning of *nahma*.

Besides sailors' songs, the *mu'alleyā*, a type of urban popular music, used to be performed in the harbors of Kuwait City, Manama, Bahrain, and Sohar, Oman. The lyrics were satiric poetry, often political, and these songs were performed in coffee shops by professional musicians who were often members of marginal social groups associated with prostitution, homosexuality, and transsexuality (Wikan 1982).

Art music: The *ṣawt*

The *ṣawt* is a traditional urban genre in which the singer is accompanied by the short-necked lute, the *'ūd* or *makbas* 'plucked'. *Ṣawt* is found mainly, and with few differences, in Kuwait and Bahrain. The lyrics include classical Arabic poetry and colloquial poetry, mostly of Yemeni origin (al-'Ammārī 1991–1996). The history of its forms, its melodies, and external influences on it is unknown earlier than its use by the Kuwaiti singer 'Abdallah Faraj (d. 1901), who spent twenty years in India and may also have been a composer ('Abduh Ghānim 1986). The *ṣawt* was recorded for the first time by 'Abd-al-Laṭīf al-Kuwaytī in Baghdad in 1927 and in Cairo in 1929; and by Muḥammad Ben Fāris (for his biography, see al-'Ammārī 1991–1996) and Ḍāḥī Ibn al-Walīd in Baghdad in 1932 for His Master's Voice (Hachlef 1994). More recently, famous performers have included Muḥammad Zwayd (Jargy 1994) and 'Abdallah Bughayth from Kuwait.

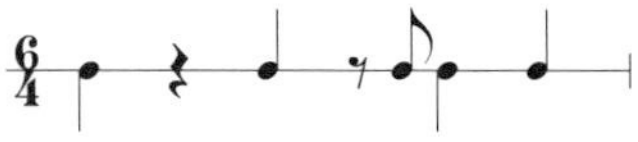

FIGURE 1 *'Arabī*, a ternary rhythmic cycle.

FIGURE 2 *Shāmī*, a binary rhythmic cycle.

There are two main rhythmic cycles: the *'arabī*, which is ternary (figure 1); and the *shāmī*, which is binary (figure 2). These two rhythms underlie a suite which, ideally, unfolds as follows:

- *Istihlāl*: an instrumental prelude.
- *Istimā'* or *taḥrīra*: a short introductory poem sung in a free rhythm.
- The *ṣawt* itself, the main part, either in *shāmī* or in *'arabī*.
- *Tawshīḥa*: a short concluding poem sung to a conventional melody in a mode close to *rast*.

The modes (*maqāmāt*; singular, *maqām*) are related to those of classical Arab music (*bayātī*, *rast*, *sīkā*, and *ḥijāz*). The names of the lute strings (the treble, *sharāra* 'spark'; and the bass, *bām*) are similar to those for the harp; this seems to indicate some historical connection between the two instruments. The voice and lute are supported by hand clapping and the *mirwās*, a small cylindrical double-skinned drum. The dance that goes along with the *ṣawt*, the *zafan*, is characterized by sudden leaps and kneeling (Ḥarbān n.d.).

Although some melodies have been transcribed ('Alī 1980; Dōkhī 1984), the exact nature of *ṣawt* requires more research on polyrhythm, modal practice, and vocal techniques. Because of its oral character and its hand-clapped rhythmic articulation, the *ṣawt* belongs to a popular environment; but its poetry, its use of the lute, and its modal system situate it closer to classical Arab music. These characteristics make it a very original genre that cannot be easily classified.

SAUDI ARABIA

Little if any musicological fieldwork has been carried out in Saudi Arabia. The Najd will be taken as a point of reference here, since for the past two centuries it has influenced the other regions by virtue of its political centrality (due to the Wahhabi movement). Comparisons will be made with similar forms in Arabia's margins such as the Sinai and the Gulf. The Ḥijāz, which is historically important, will also be taken into account. Very little is known about Asir, which has been significantly influenced by the Najd, the Ḥijāz, and Yemen (Bā Ghaffār 1994:286–326).

The Najd

Four main categories of music can be distinguished in the Najd: the *dewīnih*, the *sāmirī*, the *'arḍa*, and the *riddiyya*.

Dewīnih

The *dewīnih*—from *dīwān* 'poetry collection' (Sowayan 1985:139)—is emblematic of the nomads in Arabia (though *dīwān* also refers to the classical songs of the Yemeni Jews). It is interpreted by a solo vocalist who sings a capella or accompanies himself on the *rabāba* or *ribābih*, a single-stringed fiddle. According to legend, this instrument was first made by a woman from the Ṭayy tribe who was lamenting the loss of her child and had her tongue cut ('Obayd Mbārek 1992:105). The colloquial poetry—which is lyric, sapient, and epic—is of the genre *nabaṭī*, whose most famous author is Ibn Li'būn (1790–1831), a Najdi who settled in Kuwait (Rubay'ān 1996).

The melodies are usually limited to a pentachord (Shiloah 1980), and they may show the oldest modal forms in Arab music, precursors to the *maqāmāt bayātī*, *sikā*, and *rast*. In local theory, rhythm is referred to as *ṭarg* and melody as *shālih* (Sowayan 1985:158). There are several variants of *dewīnih*, named after tribes or poetic meters: the *masḥūb* 'pulled' is melismatic (Jargy and al-Ansari 1994, vol. 1), the *marbū'* has a light rhythm, and the *hjēnī* is a cameleers' song ('Obayd Mbārek 1992:105). Many of these forms are practiced in the Gulf as well as in Sinai and northern Arabia (Jenkins and Røvsing-Olsen 1976:1A; Shiloah 1972).

Usually, the poet, *al-shā'ir*, who sings a capella, is an ordinary tribesman, whereas *ribābih* players, who may sing lyrics created by others, are often professionals and belong to pariah groups such as the Ṣulayb (Røvsing-Olsen 1964:141). A famous singer and *ribābih* player who died in the 1970s was called Ibn Ṣāfī (Sowayan 1985:12). Although the Wahhabis fought it, the *ribābih* is said to be found in the tent of every leading *shaykh* (Maṭar n.d.:152).

The sāmirī

The *sāmirī* or *sāmrī* 'of nighttime' is an important popular genre among nomads, sedentary villagers, and urban people (for examples from the Gulf, see Kerbage c. 1984:63). It is sung at festivals and weddings and on Thursday evening (the first night of the weekend). It has several variants including the *sḥīrī*, *khammārī*, and *'ashūrī* and can also have some healing functions ('Abd al-Ḥakīm n.d.:74).

Kneeling in the sand facing each other—and leaving ample space for the dancers—are two lines of ten to twenty people who will have the role of two choirs. The song is accompanied by several frame drums, *ṭārāt* (singular, *ṭār*; the plural form of this word is seldom used); by one or two cylindrical double-skinned drums (*ṭabl*); and by hand clapping (Sowayan 1985:158). Usually the singer and the *ṭār* players sit at one end of the two lines, and the *ṭabl* is closer to the middle. The members of one line hold the *ṭār* and sing while those of the other line answer antiphonally and make dancelike movements with their shoulders; both lines remain kneeling (Maṭar n.d.:129).

The poetry is lyrical and, as in *dewīnih*, it is of the genre *nabaṭī* (Sowayan 1985:140–142). According to 'Aqīlī (n.d.:100), the *sāmirī* has the richest repertoire in Saudi Arabia. There are only two rhythms, however, one binary and one ternary; and many of the melodies are based on less than one octave (Bois 1999; Jargy and al-Ansari 1994; for transcriptions, see Dōkhī 1984:49–76).

In the Gulf, *ṭār* bands performing the *sāmirī* are professional or associative groups; the name of the group is painted on each instrument. These bands also accompany the *furaysa* (Dōkhī 1984:265–269), a dance in which men disguise themselves in women's clothes (Maṭar n.d.:125, 129–130). There are also female orchestras (*ṭaqqāqāt*) that accompany dances in which women display their hair ('Obayd Mbārek 1992:86). There are some famous women soloists (al-Khulayfi 1995). [See WOMEN'S MUSIC OF THE ARABIAN PENINSULA.]

"Sung dances" of the desert

In the center of the Arabian Peninsula are found some forms that combine collective war dance and poetry extolling the honor of the tribe. The melodies are simple and rhythmic (involving hand clapping and eventually drums), and the singing is syllabic.

The *'arḍa* (or *'ardih*) 'demonstration of force' is the most famous of these "sung dances." It gathers all the men of the village or tribe. [See DANCE IN THE ARABIAN PENINSULA and OVERVIEW OF MUSIC IN THE MASHRIQ.] Two ranks of dancers are disposed in a semicircle; they wave swords and serve as a choir. The steps are hieratic, but there are also acrobatic movements that display the dancers' agility and endurance. Between the two ranks, several poets may sing. As a celebration of the manly ideal of bedouin life, the *'arḍa* is central to Saudi identity—the rulers have always danced it publicly. It is explicitly distinguished from the concept of more frivolous dance, *raqṣa* ('Aqīlī n.d.:113). A military procession or fantasia, *sabḥa*, often takes place at the same time (Dōkhī 1984:236; 'Obayd Mbārek 1992:53–65). Every region in the kingdom has its own style. The *'arḍa* also has a *baḥriyya* variant in the Gulf (Dōkhī 1984:235).

The *'arḍa* comprises a suite that uses two or three rhythms, the *taḥmīr* and the *'irqāb* ('Aqīlī n.d.:117; Sowayan 1985). The accompanying instruments are the *ṭabl* and *ṭār*, and also small cymbals (*ṭūs*). A large cylindrical drum, *dammām*, is carried to circulate around the dancers (Maṭar n.d.:102–104). Usually the *'arḍa* is accompanied by an antiphonal syllabic song, the *ḥidwa*, which praises the tribe's honor and the ruler.

In the *'ayyāla* of Oman and the Emirates (Awḥān 1988; Jenkins and Røvsing-Olsen 1976:6B), two lines of dancers armed with swords or sticks face each other, step forward, then withdraw; their heads make a little back-and-forth movement that recalls the head of a walking camel. They are accompanied by polyrhythmic patterns played by the drummers who stand in the middle. Also named *wahhābiyya* in Oman, this dance shows evidence of influences from the Najd.

From the north to the south, there is a continuum of dances whose names are based on the close linguistic roots *rzf*, *rzḥ*, *rdḥ*, and *dḥḥ*; they are all tribal dances accompanied by antiphonial song and hand clapping but no instruments: the *razfa* of the Emirates (Røvsing-Olsen 1980:513), the *razāf* of Qatar (Kerbage n.d.), the *razḥa qaṣafiyya* of Oman, the *radḥa* in Sharja (Jenkins and Røvsing-Olsen 1976:1B4), and the *radīḥī* of Sinai (Shiloah 1972:17). In the Ḥaḍramawt the *razfa* is performed at religious festivals; solo dancers step forward from the ranks to perform acrobatic feats (Saqqāf n.d.:37), which are very similar to the *zafan* of the Gulf. In Yemen the *razfa* is an antiphonal song performed by tribes and the army when marching (Rossi 1939:11). The *radḥa* in Kuwait is a female processional dance. The *daḥḥa* (in Sinai, *daḥḥiyya*) is a collective dance of northern Arabia and northern Syria (Shiloah 1972:17), accompanied by hand clapping and rhythmic respiration. In northern Arabia, the *daḥḥa* is accompanied by improvised poetry (Bā Ghaffār 1994:215).

Poetry contests, sociable rhythms, and tribal calls

When poetry is improvised (a very old tradition in Arabia), music has a lesser role in the performance, although it is not entirely absent. In the *riddiyya* (or *mrādd* or *galṭa*), two poets improvise in turn (*radd* means "answer") and a choir sings the last verse a capella (Sowayan 1985:142–143). A similar structure of performance is found in the *habbūt* of Oman, the *bāla* in Yemen (Caton 1991; Yammine 1995), and the *dān* in the Ḥaḍramawt.

In northern Arabia, social occasions and festivals are necessarily accompanied by coffee, a symbol of hospitality. Coffee grinding—the beans, in a pestle, are ground by being pounded with a mortar—is an occasion for a rhythmic "call" (Shiloah 1978, side A).

Throughout Arabia, tribal calls may take a more or less musical form. In the Gulf, the *nadba* shows a superimposition of several different animal-like shouts (from a high-pitched head voice to the lowest drone), concluding with a rhythmic contrapuntal pattern.

The Ḥijāz

Although Ḥijāz was the historical birthplace of Islam and the cradle of Arab music in the Umayyad period, it remains relatively unknown in the modern world. At first a cosmopolitan center, the Ḥijāz declined under the Wahhabis, who mistrusted its liberal tradition.

The first modern evidence of music in the Ḥijāz was recorded by Snouk Hurgronje, a Dutch Orientalist who had converted to Islam and who described a wedding ceremony and the songs performed there (1931 [1888]:44, 119, 130–140). He transcribed a song for the headdress (of the bride), *ghunā al-kharīṭ*, as well as some religious songs performed by a *meqaṣṣid* along with a choir of *raddādīn*. He also evoked the golden youth of Mecca who used to listen to the *qānūn* and to the South Arabian lute, the *qanbūs*, near the shrine of a holy woman, Sittanā Mēmūna. Hurgronje also gathered the oldest recordings of the Arabian Peninsula, in Jidda between 1904 and 1907 (Gavin 1985), and deposited one *qanbūs* in the Ethnographic Museum of Leiden.

Many popular genres exist in the Ḥijāz (Bā Ghaffār 1994:34–210), but I will deal mainly with the urban *ḥijāzī* tradition. The cylinders of 1904–1907 include a rich sampling of this tradition (as well as several Yemeni pieces). In later recordings by Muḥammad al-Sindī (who died in the 1970s), the solo singer, playing the lute himself, is accompanied by a bass drum and a *mirwās*, a kettledrum struck with the hands. There seems to have been a significant evolution between the recordings from Jidda and those from al-Sindī: as in Yemen, the *qanbūs* has been substituted for the Egyptian lute.

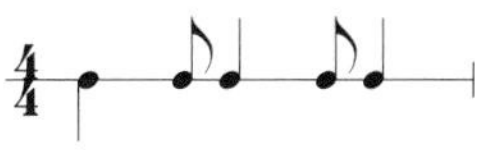

FIGURE 3 Binary rhythmic cycle of the *ḥijāzī* style.

The *ḥijāzī* style has a nonmeasured part, called the *mawwāl* or *majaṣṣ* (from *jaṣṣa* 'to explore'; Bā Ghaffār 1994:52), sung in classical Arabic and often found in the middle of a measured piece. The rhythmic cycles are binary (figure 3); one resembles the Yemeni *wasṭā*, another one the Egyptian *waḥda*. There is also a ternary cycle (figure 4).

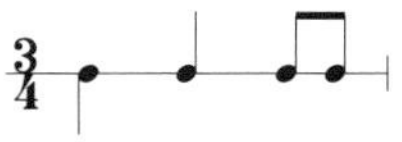

FIGURE 4 Ternary rhythmic cycle of the *ḥijāzī* style.

The most common melodic modes are variants of the *bayātī* and *rast*, but without flat notes. Poetry is often of Yemeni origin (notably of eighteenth-century Yaḥyā 'Umar), reflecting a continuity of culture between the Ḥijāz and Yemen. Nevertheless, the specificity of a *ḥijāzī* style is obvious in the syncopated beats of the drum, whose timbre punctuates the musical phrases.

YEMEN

Unified in 1990, the two Yemens represent a huge variety of regional styles and circumstances of performance, due to their natural and social diversity: there are sedentary farmers, nomads, and fishermen as well as townspeople. Although Yemeni music has a very specific identity rooted in an old culture, it also has some points in common with other musics of the Arabian Peninsula. Roughly, three major regions can be distinguished: the Zaydi Highlands, the Shāfi'ī coastal plains, and the inner Ḥaḍramawt (for details, see Lambert 2000).

Villagers of the Highlands

As the stronghold of the Zaydis, a moderate Shi'ite sect, the Highlands are the historical heart of Yemen. They offer a good exemple of the importance of music in social life: work songs, tribal songs and dances, magical invocations, and festival music.

The *mahjal* is sung during harvests and other collective work. It is usually chanted on two notes in a very simple rhythm and has humorous lyrics. The *ḥādī* is sung by women while they thin out sorghum leaves; it is a love song, unmeasured, with a large ambitus. Other songs accompany more solitary labor; examples are the plower's *maghrad*, the cameleers' *jammālī* (Yammine 1995), the well diggers' *masnā*, and the housewives' *aghānī*.

The *bāla* is a poetry contest, usually performed at weddings. The *zāmil* is a song extolling honor and the warlike virtues of tribesmen. It is composed and performed for local political events, wars, and weddings (Caton 1991). It is a responsorial form whose rhythm is close to a march and whose melodies are usually tetratonic (Yammine 1995). A dance analogous to the *zāmil* is the *bara'*, an occasion for the tribe to represent its political solidarity in choreography. This dance is a suite of three or four sections. The dancers—as many as fifty, arranged in a semicircle—make stylized movements with a *janbiyya* dagger (Adra 1982). The *bara'* is accompanied by two kettledrums (*ṭāsa* and *marfa'*), which show the influence of the Mamluk or Ottoman *ṭubul-khāne*. They are struck with sticks by *mzayyin*, professional musicians who have important social and ritualistic functions in various events and situations of villagers' daily life—religious festivals, weddings, announcements, alarms.

Aside from the Islamic ritual genres, music also has magical functions which are linked to agriculture and cosmology. During a drought, prayers for rain (*ṣalāt al-istisqā'*) are offered, and a specific farmers' song, the *tasgiya*, is sung to call the rain. During eclipses of the moon, specific hymns are sung to plead for the remission of sins.

In the villages, wedding ceremonies are conducted by the *mzayyin*, who play in small bands of three instruments: the *mizmār*, a double-reed clarinet; the *ṭabl*, a double-skinned drum; and one copper plate. While playing their instruments, the drummers also sing in unison with the clarinet. This orchestra accompanies the dance *lu'ba* 'game'. The dancers gather in groups of two or three and wave their daggers. Women dance in the same style, but without daggers and without the *mizmār* (Yammine 1995).

The coastal plains: Tihama, the outer Ḥaḍramawt, and Mahra

The coastal plain regions (as well as some mountains like Ḥugariyya and Yāfi') have certain historical links and cultural similarities. The inhabitants belong to the mainstream of orthodox Islam (the Shāfi'ī legal school), and local Sufism plays an important role in their music. They have more links with the rest of the peninsula than the isolated Highlands. Tihama music is little known, but the practice of the *zār* is definitely similar to that in the Gulf, as well as the use of the harp, *ṭanbūra* (Bakewell 1985a, b; Poché 1976). The Ḥaḍramawt is even less well known, but its fishermen's songs are related to those of the Gulf ('Obayd 1989), especially in the use of hand clapping and the lyre, *samsamiyya* (see Lambert 2000).

A widespread feature is the drum band (Elsner 1990). [See also RHYTHMIC STRUCTURE AND DRUM IMPROVISATION IN YEMEN.] In Tihama, it consists of several cylindrical frame drums and kettledrums of various sizes. They are usually played by people of low status, the *aḥdām* (Bakewell 1985a, b). These popular bands have important social functions. In Tuhayta, drummers conduct pilgrimages to shrines of local saints, compelling every merchant in the *sūq*, by playing and dancing in front of his shop, to give alms to the saint on the day of the festival. In Shihr (Ḥaḍramawt), a similar band, *al-'idda*, leads processions in town. Inhabitants of different quarters confront each others in dance; these confrontations sometimes give rise to actual fights ('Alī 1988). These two kinds of drum bands show a strong African influence. The most widespread musical form is the *sharḥ*, a quick polyrhythmic cycle also called *sawāḥilī* 'coastal'.

In the ancient harbors of Mukalla and Shihr, there is a strong tradition of urban music, the *'awādī* 'the one of the lute', which is associated with the famous singer and *'ūd* player Muḥammed Jum'a Khān (d. 1965). This style is at a crossroads of many influences from India, Africa, and the Gulf. The little orchestras that play the *'awādī* always include at least one violin.

It is not yet possible to discuss the variety of music in Mahra and Socotra. These regions have been linguistically isolated (four different South Arabian languages are still spoken there), and their isolation has favored the preservation of archaic features in a mainly vocal music. Incantations are notably used in an exorcism ceremony, the *rābūt* (Lonnet and Simeone-Senelle 1987). Some of this music was recorded as early as 1902 (Adler 1903).

The inner Ḥaḍramawt

Popular music is very rich in the Ḥaḍramawt valley. It is particularly famous for the Beni Maghrāh songs that accompany the ibex hunt (*al-qanīs*) and the theatrical game that follows it (Saqqāf n.d.:31–32; Serjeant 1951). This section will focus on the music of the old towns of Seyyun, Shibam, and Tarim (see also Lambert 2000).

The *dān* is a poetic contest with improvisation which takes place indoors at nighttime gatherings. It is as much a social ritual as an entertainment. Two or three poets confront one another, each in turn composing a quatrain, in a speaking voice. A specialized singer helps them by repeating a refrain based on rhymed combinations of the nonsense syllables *dān, dān*. To help the singer put the words into a melodic shape, a scribe repeates them for him and writes them out for posterity (Hassan 1998). In a variant called *shabwānī*, the *dān* is performed in the open air, after long preparatory dances accompanied by the *ʿidda* band.

At weddings, the most common genre is the *zerbādī* dance, which is accompanied by a beveled flute, the *madrūf*; an oblong double-skinned drum, the *hājir*, which comes from India; and several *mirwās*. The *zerbādī* shows influences from South Asia, remnants of ancient migrations to Java and Gujarat: a slow tempo, delicate rubato, and varied drum timbres.

FIGURE 5 A musician from Ḥijāz plays double percussion parts simultaneously on a *derbūka* and a *ṭār*, which he holds together in his left hand and forearm. Photo by Jean Lambert, 1 March 2000.

UNITY AND DIVERSITY OF MUSIC IN THE ARABIAN PENINSULA

This brief overview suggests the great variety as well as the undeniable unity of music in the Arabian Peninsula (figures 5–9). There are many common features from the Gulf all the way to Yemen, across the Najd and the Ḥijāz. However, these similarities are often obscured by varying terms—although it is also true that similarities of vocabulary sometimes hide real differences.

Tribal dances related by their form and function include the *ʿardih* of Najd, its variants in the Gulf, and the Yemeni *baraʿ* (a word that also exists in Oman). All along the coasts, African influences can be found: in the Gulf (Røvsing-Olsen 1967), in Yemen (Bakewell 1985a, b), and in the Ḥijāz (Hurgronje 1931:13). Polyrhythmic patterns of a binary rhythm against a ternary rhythm (Røvsing-Olsen 1967:150–151), as well as refined hand clapping, are found in the coastal areas, though they are found less in the interior. It is difficult to determine whether these features are a result of external influences.

History has separated genres that appear to have had a common origin: the *nabāṭī* poet Ibn Liʿbūn, who was born in the Najd and settled in southern Iraq, inspired both the *dewīnih* and the *sāmirī*; in the Najd, *ʿarḍa* tribal dance and *ḥadwa* song are parts of the the same form; in Yemen, the *baraʿ* and *zāmil*, which have similar functions, are performed separately. On the other hand, some styles overflow national or natural borders: through the desert, the *dewīnih* and *sāmirī* have spread to almost every country; in the Gulf, the *sāmirī* and the *ʿarḍa*, which are presumably of bedouin origin, are also performed by fishermen. Sailors' musical forms throughout Arabia are related to each other not only by simple contact but also through distant meeting points including Zanzibar and Singapore. Arabia conceals many unexplored common features: the *muwaylī* poetry of the Gulf is attributed by pearl divers to a figure in Omani legend, Ḥumaydī b. Manṣūr (Dōkhī 1984:303), who is also said to have composed many work songs in the Yemen Highlands (Yammine 1995) that have a similar poetic style.

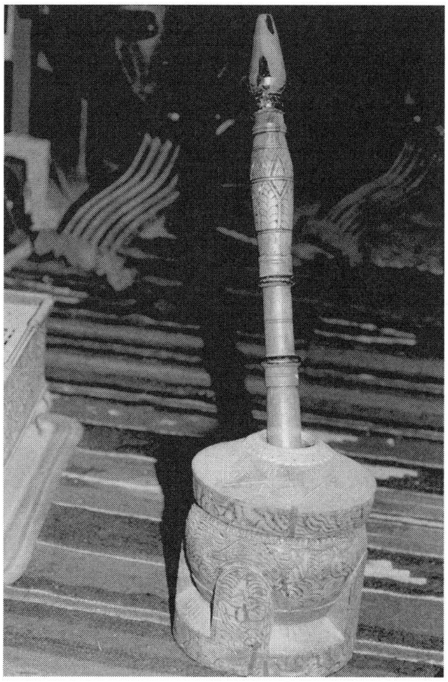

FIGURE 6 Bedouin coffee grinder, *al-mahbash*, from Jidda. In northern Arabia, coffee grinding is an occasion for a rhythmic "call"; and pearl divers' songs of the Gulf region may be accompanied by a coffee mortar used as a musical instrument. Photo copyright © 1989 by Byron Augustin.

Various forms of traditional urban music also have common features characteristic of the Arabian Peninsula. The *ṣawt* of the Gulf, the *ḥijāzī* of Arabia, and the *ʿawādī* of the Ḥaḍramawt or the *ghināʾ ṣanʿānī* have a large number of common texts (ʿAbduh Ghānim 1986; ʿAmmārī 1991–1996), though fewer common melodies. More significantly, they have preserved a classical tradition in which the soloist is both a singer and a lute player—a practice that is fading away elsewhere in the Arab world. The lyrics are composed in a literary style marked by local dialects. Poetry and music are closely linked. This traditional urban art was cultivated in all-male social sessions (*dīwāniyya* in the Gulf, *magyal* in Ṣanʿāʾ, *mabraz* in Aden), although that is changing now.

In the peninsula, theory focuses more on rhythmic variations than on modal variations, which are rare. The dominant scales are based on tones and three-quarter tones, while diatonic modes have a smaller range and seem to have been spread through foreign influences (as in Yemeni fishermen's songs). Although these modal structures are very empirical, there are some particular variations: the *tawshīḥa* of the *ṣawt* is reminiscent of the various forms of *tawshīḥ* in Yemen; the *majaṣṣ* in Tihama and the

FIGURE 7 *Right:* Polyrhythmic clapping by a chorus accompanying pearl-diving songs and *zafan* dancing; in this series of pictures (a, b, and c), the hands are clearly clapping against each other's beat. Photos by Jean Lambert, Bahrain, 2 March 2000.

(a)

(b)

(c)

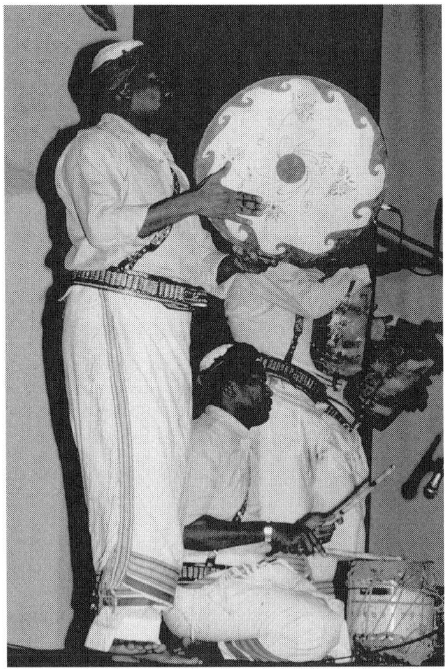

FIGURE 8 *Above:* Saudi Arabian musicians: the man who is standing is playing a *duff*; the seated man is playing a type of *ṭabl*. Photo copyright © by Byron Augustin.

(a)

(b)

FIGURE 9 *'Arḍa baḥriyya*: In this dance, one or two *tabl* drummers (a) face a rank of *ṭār* drummers (b), playing a polyrhythmic dialogue. Photos by Jean Lambert, Bahrain, 2 March 2000.

Ḥijāz seem to be a mixture of melodic material and modal concepts; and the tendency to end a piece on a pitch other than the fundamental of the melody is widespread.

Long before the advent of recording, music traveled throughout the peninsula, and Yemen seems to have had a major role in this circulation: in the past hundred years, there were Yemeni texts and melodies in the Gulf and as far as the Sinai; and Yemeni musicians were to be found in Mecca at the beginning of the twentieth century and are found in the Gulf today. In the Ḥijāz, there were also singers who came from other regions, like Ibrāhīm al-Sammān (d. 1964), a Syrian who became a *muezzin* of the Great Mosque of Medina toward the end of his life (Mahdī 1986:133–134).

Today, these musicians and arts are responding to intense pressure for change and commercialization (Poché 1994) caused by the rise of the cassette industry, petroleum production, and emigrant labor. Henceforth, melodies will still cross the seas and the desert (al-Qāsimī 1987), but at an accelerated pace.

REFERENCES

'Abd al-Ḥakīm, Ṭāriq. n.d. 1980. *Ashhar al-fulklūrāt al-sha'biyya* (The Most Famous Forms of Folklore). Riyadh: al-Jam'iyya al-'Arabiyya al-Sa'diyya li'l-Thaqāfa wa 'l-Funūn.

'Abduh Ghānim, Nizār. 1986. "Al-judhūr al-yamaniyya li-fann al-ṣawt al-khalījī" (The Yemeni Roots of the *Ṣawt* in the Gulf). *Al-Ma'thūrāt al-sha'biyya* 4:9–28.

Adler, Guido. 1903. "Sokotri-Musik." In *Die Mehri- und Soqotri-Sprache. II: Südarabische Expedition der Akademie der Wissenschaften*, ed. David Heinrich Müller, 6:377–382. Vienna: A. Hölder.

Adra, Najwa. 1982. "Qabyala: The Tribal Concept in the Central Highlands Yemen Arab Republic." Ph.D. dissertation, Temple University.

'Ali, Aḥmad. 1980. *Al-mūsīqā wa 'l-ghinā fī'l-Kuwayt* (Music and Singing in Kuwait). Kavet: Sharikat al-Rabī'ān li'l-Tawzī' wa 'l-Nashr.

al-'Ammārī, Mubārik. 1991–1996. *Muḥammad bin Fāris. Ashhar man ghannā al-ṣawt fī 'l-Khalīj* (Muḥammad bin Fāris, the Most Famous *Ṣawt* Singer of the Gulf). 3 vols. Bahrain: Wizārat al-I'lām.

'Alī, Khalīl Ḥusayn. 1988. "Al-'idda Dance in Yemen." *Al Ma'thūrāt al-sha'biyya* 12:8–15.

Anonymous. n.d. *Min turāthinā* (From Our Inheritance). Doha: Wizārat al-I'lām. Cassette tape.

al-'Aqīlī, Majdī. n.d. (c. 1979.) *Al-samā' 'inda al-'arab* (Music among the Arabs). Vol. 5. Damascus: Maṭba'at Dimāshq.

Awḥān, Fārūq. 1988. "Raqṣat al-'ayyāla fī 'l-Imārāt al-'Arabiyya al-Muttaḥida." *al-Ma'thūrāt al-sha'biyya* 9.

Bā Ghaffār, Hind. 1994. *Al-aghānī al-sha'biyya fī'l-Mamlaka al-'Arabiyya al-Sa'ūdiyya* (Folk Songs in the Saudi Arabian Kingdom). Jidda: Dār al-Qādisiyya li 'l-Tawzī' wa 'l-Nashr.

Bakewell, Anderson. 1985a. "Music of the Tihamah." In *Studies on the Tihamah: The Report of the Tihama Expedition* 1982, ed. F. Stone, 104–108. London: Longman.

———. 1985b. *The Afro-Arabian Crossroad: Music of the Tihama on the Red Sea, North Yemen*. Lyricord LLST 7384. LP disk.

Bhattacharya, Deben. n.d. (c. 1970.) *Musique des bédouins*. Paris, Bam, Folklore et Musiques de l'Univers. LD 5783. LP disk.

Bois, Pierre. 1999. *Arabie Saoudite: Musique de 'Unayzah, Ancienne Cité du Najd.* Paris: Maison des Cultures du Monde, Inédit, CD W 260087. Compact disk.

Caton, Steven. 1991. *Peaks of Yemen I Summon: Poetry as Cultural Practice in a North Yemen Tribe*. Berkeley: University of California Press.

Ḍōkhī, Yusuf Farḥān. 1984. *Al-aghānī al-kuwaytiyya* (The Kuwaiti Songs). Doha: Markaz al-Turāth al-Sha'bī li-Duwal al-Khalīj (Arab Gulf States Folklore Center).

al-Duwayk, Muḥammad Ṭālib. 1991. *Al-ughniya al-sha'biyya fī Qaṭar.* 2 vols. Qatar: Wizārat al-I'lām wa 'l-Thaqāfa.

Elsner, Jürgen. 1990. "Trommeln und Trommelensembles im Jemen." In *Beiträge zur traditionellen Musik*, ed. A. Michel and Jürgen Elsner, 18–37. Berlin: Humboldt Universität.

Faraj, 'Abdallah. 1953. *Dīwān*, ed. Khālid al-Faraj. Dimashq: Maṭba't al-Tarqī.

Gavin, Carney E. S. 1985. "The Earliest Arabian Recordings: Discoveries and Work Ahead." *Phonographic Bulletin* (September):38–45.

Ghānim, Kalthūm 'Alī. n.d. (c. 1995.) *Al-Iḥtifālāt al-jamā'iyya wa ba'ḍ al-ashkāl al-thaqāfiyya al-muṣāḥaba li-mujtama' al-ghōṣ* (Ceremonies and Some Related Cultural Forms among Pearl Divers). 2 vols. Doha: Idārat al-Thaqāfa wa 'l-Funūn.

Grandguillaume, G. 1982. "Valorisation et dévalorisation liées aux contacts de cultures en Arabie Saoudite" ("Valorization" and "Devalorization" Related to Cultural Contacts in Saudi Arabia). In *Péninsule arabique aujourd'hui: Études par pays*, ed. P. Bonnenfant, 623–654. Paris: Éditions du CNRS.

Hachlef, Ahmed. 1994. *La musique de Bahreïn: Anthologie de la musique arabe.* Club du Disque Arabe, AAA 104. Compact disk.

Ḥanẓal, Fāliḥ. 1987. *Mu'jam al-qawāfī wa 'l-alḥān fī 'l-Khalīj al-'Arabī* (Dictionary of Rhymes and Melodies in the Arab Gulf). Al-Shārqa: Ittiḥād Kuttāb wa-Udabā' al-Imārāt al-'Arabiyya al-Muttaḥida.

Ḥarbān, Jāsim Muḥammad. n.d. (c. 1998.) *Al-fīrī*. Bahrain: al-Mu'assasa al-'Arabiyya li'l-Ṭibā'a wa 'l-Nashr.

al-Harbi, Salih. 1980. "Hommes et société des pêcheurs de perles au Koweit." (People and Society among the Pearl Fishers of Kuwait." Diplôme, Ecole des Hautes Études, Paris.

Hassan, Schéhérazade. 1998. *Yémen: Chants du Ḥaḍramawt*. Auvidis-UNESCO D 8273. Compact disk.

Hurgronje, Snouck. [1888] 1931. *Mekka in the Latter Part of the Nineteenth Century*, trans. James Henry Monahan. Leiden: Brill.

Jargy, Simon. 1986. "Comments on the Concept and Characteristics of the Folk Music in the Gulf and Arabian Peninsula." *Al-Ma'thūrāt al-sha'biyya* 1 January.

Jargy, Simon, and Ali Zakariyya al-Ansari. 1994. *A Musical Anthology of the Arabian Peninsula.* 1, Sung Poetry of the Bedouins; 2, Music of the Pearl Divers; 3, *Ṣawt*: Music from the City; 4, Women's Songs. Geneva: VDE-Gallo, CD-758-59-60-61. 4 compact disks.

Jenkins, Jean, and Poul Røvsing-Olsen. 1976. *Music in the World of Islam.* 1, The Human Voice; 2, Lutes, Strings; 4, Flutes and Trumpets; 5, Reeds and Bagpipes; 6, Drums and Rhythms. Tangent Records, TGS 131–136. LP disk.

Kerbage, Toufik. n.d. (c. 1984.) *The Rhythms of Pearl Divers' Music in Qatar*. Dōḥā: Ministry of Information.

al-Khulayfi, Samia. 1995. *Le chant des femmes du Koweit* (The Song of Kuwaiti Women). Paris: DEA, Université de la Sorbonne-Paris IV.

Lambert, Jean. 2001. "Yemen." In *The New Grove Dictionary of Music and Musicians*, 2nd ed., ed. Stanley Sadie, 27:652–657. London: Macmillan.

Lonnet, Antoine, and Marie-Claude Simeone-Senelle. 1987. "Rābūt: Trance and Incantations in Mehri Folk Medicine." *Proceedings of the Seminar for Arabian Studies* 17:107–115.

al-Mahdī, Ṣālih. 1986. *Al-mūsīqā al-'arabiyya* (Arab Music). Tunis: Al-Dār al-Tūnisī li'l-Nashr.

al-Mannā'ī, 'Abd al-Raḥmān, and Muḥammad al-Maslamanī. 1987. *Aghānī al-'amal 'alā sufun al-Ghawṣ fī 'l-Khalīj* (The Work Songs of Pearl Divers in the Gulf). Doha: Markaz al-Turāth al-Sha'bī li-Duwal al-Khalīj.

Maṭar, Būlus. n. d. (c. 1982.) *Khalīj al-aghānī* (The Gulf of Songs). Beirut: Dār al-Muthallath.

'Obayd, 'Alī Muḥammad. 1989. "Aghānī ṣayādī al-samak fī qaryat Shuqrā al-yamaniyya" (Fishermen's Songs of Shuqra in Yemen). *Al-Ma'thūrāt al-sha'biyya* 14:51–66.

'Obayd Mbārek, Bandar. 1992. "Dirāsāt taḥlīliyya li-aghānī al-bādiyya fi-l-Kuwayt" (Bedouin Songs of Kuwait). Master's thesis, University of Helwan.

'Obaydalī, Aḥmad. 1982. "Al-mūsīqā wa 'l-ghinā bayna 'l-Khalīj wa 'l-Yaman" (Music and Song between the Gulf and Yemen). *Dirāsāt yamaniyya* 10:159–170.

Poché, Christian. 1976. *Zaidi and Shafi': Islamic Religious Chanting from North Yemen*. UNESCO Collection, Musical Sources, Philips 6586 040. LP disk.

———. 1989. "Scander, scander, scander. Musique." In *Koweiti*. Paris: Institut du Monde Arabe.

———. 1994. "Pays du Golfe: De la frénésie sociale à l'accélération musicale." *Adib*, ed. Y. Gonzales-Quijanio and R. Boustani. Paris: IMA. CD-ROM.

al-Qāsimī, Khalid. 1987. *Al-awāṣir al-mūsīqiyya bayna 'l-Khalīj wa 'l-Yaman* (Musical Links between the Gulf and Yemen). Beirut: Manshūrāt al-ʿUwaydāt.

———. 1993. *Al-ughniya al-yamaniyya al-khalījiyya bayna 'l-turāth wa 'l-muʿāṣira* (Yemeni and Gulf Songs from Past to Present). Sharja: Dār al-thaqāfa al-ʿArabiyya li-n-Nashr wa-t-Tarjama wa-t-Tawzīc; Beirut: al-Falāḥ.

Racy, Ali Jihad. 1988. *Tanbura Music of the Gulf.* Doha: Arab Gulf Satates Folklore Center. Booklet and cassette.

al-Rifaʿi, Hessa. 1985. "Sea Chanteys of Kuwait." *Arabian Studies* 7:88–95.

Rossi, Ettore. 1939. *L'arabo parlato a Sanaa: Grammatica, testi, lessico* (The Arabic Spoken in Sanʿa: Grammar, Texts, and Lexicon). Rome: Istituto per l'Oriente.

Røvsing-Olsen, Poul. 1964. "Enregistrements faits à Kuwait et à Bahrein" (Recordings Made in Kuwait and Bahrain). In *Les colloques de Wegimont, IV, 1958–1960; Ethnomusicologie III*, 137–170. Paris: Les Belles Lettres.

———. 1968. *Pêcheurs de perles et musiciens du Golfe Persique* (Pearl Fishers and Musicians of the Persian Gulf). 1068 Ocora, 42, Paris. LP disk.

———. 1978. "The Vocal Bourdon in the Arab Gulf." *Anthropologiska Studier* 25–26:12–20.

———. 1980. "Arabian Gulf." In *The New Grove Dictionary of Music and Musicians*, ed. Stanley Sadie, 1:513–514. London: Macmillan.

Rubayʿān, Yaḥyā. 1996. *Muḥammad ibn Liʿbūn.* Kuwait: Sharikat al-Rubayʿān.

Saint-Hilaire, Alain, and Karen Saint-Hilaire. 1971. *Les Emirats du Golfe Arabique* (The Emirates of the Arabian Gulf). Alvarès, C 471. LP disk.

al-Saqqāf, Jaʿfar Muḥammad. n.d. (c. 1980.) *Lamaḥāt ʿan al-aghānī wa 'l-raqṣāt al-shaʿbiyya fī muḥāfaẓat Ḥaḍramawt* (Popular Songs and Dances of the Ḥaḍramawt). Aden: Wizārat al-Thaqāfa; Beirut: al-Fārābī.

al-Saud, Noura bint Muḥammad, al-Jawharah Muḥammad al-ʿAnqari, and Madeha Muḥammad al-ʿAtroush, eds. 1989. *Abha, Bilad Asir: Southwestern Region of the Kingdom of Saudi Arabia.* Riyadh: Editors.

Serjeant, Robert B. 1951. *Saudi Arabian Poetry and Prose of Ḥaḍramawt.* London: Taylor's Foreign Press.

Shiloah, Amnon. 1972. "The *Simsimiyah*: A Stringed Instrument of the Red Sea Area." *Asian Music* 4(1):15.

———. 1978. *Bedouin Music of Southern Sinai.* Ethnic Folkways Records EE 4204. LP disk.

———. 1980. "Arab Music: II. Folk Music." In *The New Grove Dictionary of Music and Musicians*, ed. Stanley Sadie, 1:526–539. London: Macmillan.

Sowayan, Saad Abdullah. 1985. *Nabati Poetry: The Oral Poetry of Arabia.* Berkeley and Los Angeles: University of California Press.

Staub, Shalom. 1979. *A Review of the Literature and a Selective Bibliography of Yemenite Jewish Folklore and Ethnology with a Special Emphasis on Dance and Music, 1893–1978.* n.p.

Sulaymān, Ṣādiq. 1992. *Al-nahhām* (The Sea Singer). Doha: Markaz al-Turath al-Shaʿbī li-Duwal al-Khalīj.

Tayash, Fahad. 1988. "Sameri Tradition and Zār Dance in Saudi Arabia." *al-Maʾthūrāt al-Shaʿbiyya* 9:23–36.

Touma, Habib Hassan. 1977. "Le Fidjri, forme de chant caractéristique des pêcheurs de perles de Bahrein" (The Fidjri: Characteristic Song of the Pearl Divers of Bahrain). *World of Music* 19:3–4:128–132.

———. 1979. *Fidjeri Songs of the Bahrain Pearl Divers.* Musical Sources, Vol. 23, UNESCO. Philips, Milan. 064-18371. LP disk.

Wikan, Unni. 1982. *Behind the Veil in Arabia: Women in Oman.* Baltimore, Md.: Johns Hopkins University Press.

Yammine, Habib. 1995. "Les hommes de tribu et leur musique (Hauts plateaux yéménites, vallée d'al-Ahjur)" (Tribal Men and Their Music in the High Yemenite Plateaus, Valley of Ahjur). Ph.D. dissertation, Université de Paris X-Nanterre.

Sung Poetry in the Arabian Peninsula

Simon Jargy

The Primacy of the Spoken Word
The Tradition: Diversity and Synthesis
Orality and Living Masters
Improvisation and Memorization
Sociocultural Functions

THE PRIMACY OF THE SPOKEN WORD

Paradoxically, it is in the Middle East—site of the earliest alphabets and the first tablets containing civil and religious laws—that the spoken rather than the written word has held pride of place throughout the past and today.

A word consists of sound and rhythm, and so it is aimed at the ear—but in fact it touches all one's sensibilities. When an aesthetic intention meets the word, it becomes poetry: *shi'r* 'sensation'. The emotional aspect of poetry thus has priority over its cerebral aspect, giving it greater impact in the mysterious universe of intuition. For the Semitic peoples, among whom Arabs are a major group, this is how the poetic spoken word can be understood, as sound, rhythm, and music. It is sometime said that Semitic peoples are averse to intellectualizing, and indeed that this aversion is the essence of their genius: the image and melody of the spoken word take precedence over the concept, and sensation is expressed in a spontaneous, often fiery way, without apparent logical order. This is why a poem in Arabic is made up of independent, interchangeable verses and couplets, and why hyperbole and emphasis take on such importance. These elements are propitious for the improviser, who is at once a singer, reciter, poet, and creator—and a memorizer. Oral transmission, though it depends on sound, is ultimately made possible by memorization; memory is crucial in the chain of oral transmission through generations of masters and disciples.

THE TRADITION: DIVERSITY AND SYNTHESIS

Even oral traditions do not arise spontaneously. Those in the Arabian peninsula have resulted from a confluence of several civilizations that gave rise to two different heritages. One heritage comes from the desert interior, bedouin civilization; this civilization includes nomadic, seminomadic, and sedentary groups who appear Arab and whose traditions center on cantillated or sung poetry accompanied by a fiddle called the *rabāba*. The second heritage is regional, resulting from interaction with the musical cultures of the surrounding civilizations: African, Iranian, and Indian. Today, the specific synthesis of these legacies is the traditional music of the Arabic peninsula.

Sung poetry should not be considered separately from its geocultural context. In this immense desert region, perhaps even more than elsewhere, humans are an integral part of their environment. For millennia, they have been shaped by their environment

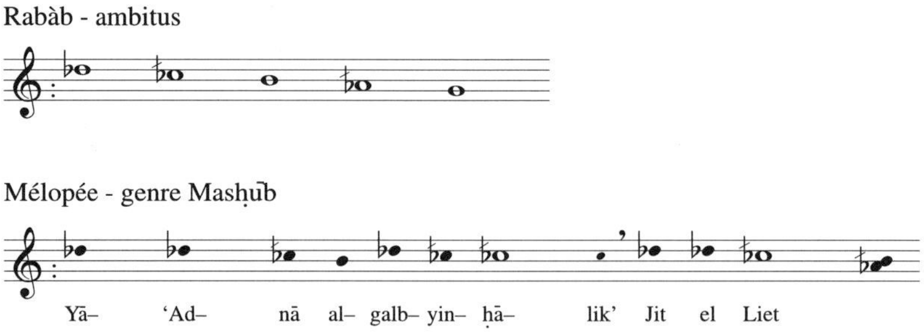

FIGURE 1 (a) Ambitus of the *rabāba*. (b) *Mélopée*: the genre *mashụb*.

as well as by the vicissitudes of history, and their destiny has been linked to the desert and the sea.

In the desert interior, then, we find the nomadic bedouin peoples. The word *bedouin* comes from *badawi* 'desert inhabitant', and these peoples are part of a land where, from time immemorial, human life has been set to the rhythm of desert migrations. Such migrations were determined by the location of water and pastures, by normal seasonal changes, and by capricious weather. The people developed a kind of civilization which we call nomadism and which has endured, in its basic form, to the present day. Nomadic Arabia has retained the ways of its earliest ancestors, who wandered in search of hunting grounds, habitats, and physical conditions friendly to life.

Nomadism is, of course, an unstable existence. No doubt as a counterbalance, the need was felt for a permanent tradition. For the bedouin Arab, this was sung poetry, which early on became the most natural means of expression. It also became the distinct emblem of bedouin genius, and this remains true today. There is a popular saying, "The whole history of the Arabs is told in poetry"; and in the ninth century Al-Jahiz—one of the greatest masters of Arabic, who broke with the exclusivity of the language to create Arabic prose—said of the Arabs, "Their whole genius is found centered on poetry, language and its derivations, and rhetoric" (from *Kitab al-Bayan wa 'l-Tabiyhin* 'Rhetoric and Demonstration', in which Al-Jahiz discusses the particular genius of each civilization of his time).

This poetry has always included a form of music comprising intonation, accent, and long and short syllables. The earliest historical sources indicate that the *sh'ir* bedouin—the creator and guardian of the tradition—was also considered a singer. In ancient classical Arabic, *shi'r* 'poetry' is related to *nashid* 'song' or 'cantillation'; and reciting poetry is synonomous with singing it (*anshada al-shi'r*). The indissoluble link between *shi'r* and *inshad* 'song' or 'recitative' can still be discerned in spoken bedouin Arabic in the peninsula, where *nishida* is synonomous with *gisida* 'poem'.

Sung poetry in ancient Arabia seems to have had a dual function—religious and social. The few surviving examples of ancient rhymed prose (*saj'*) indicate that sung poetry was linked to magical incantations. Etymologically, the *sha'ir* 'creator of songs' was not only a maker of words, rhythms, and rhymes but essentially a visionary in touch with the invisible, a kind of prophet familiar with gods and spirits. More concretely, the *shai'r*'s inspiration, expressed in lyrical language and rhythmic syllables, was both a matter of magical powers—described by the word *tarab* 'rapture'—and also at the service of his social group, his tribe. He incarnated an emblematic power, defending the tribe's honor in the face of its enemies and extolling its virtues. Very early on, the range of cantillated poetry was expanded by another social function: the marking of events in the life cycle and in society, such as birth, circumcision, marriage, work, and warriors' great deeds.

FIGURE 2 Four-year-old girl with drum in the Salt Market in San'a, Yemen. Photo by Marie-Georges Jargy, 1995.

We still see this heritage in the sung poetry of the Arabian Peninsula. It uses spoken bedouin and is most often accompanied by the *rabāba*, a one-stringed bowed instrument that produces a rather nasal sound limited to a range of a diminished fifth (figure 1*a*), within which intervals often shift. For group songs, percussion instruments were later added—the drums *ṭār* and *ṭabl* (figure 2). This cantillated poetry, mainly

FIGURE 3 Al-'Ayn in the Buraymii desert, United Arab Emirates. The *nabaṭi* poet Murbarak al-Misfir chants a *gisid*, a sung love poem. Photo by Marie-Georges Jargy, 1974.

a popular art, is distinct from the learned classical poetry that specialists study: it is referred to as *nabaṭi* (figure 3) to distingush it from the classical form, and many scholars treat it as a poor relation. Despite this, sung poetry of bedouin origin remains a noble art highly esteemed by the Arabs; and it has always escaped the attacks of rigorous Islamic movements that, in certain historical periods, considered music anathema.

Bedouin sung poetry retains its connection to the desert and centers on three main traditional genres:

1. *Al-hjini* of the *hida'* type. This genre began as camel-riders' music, sung to a rhythm that suggested the camel's gait. We are told that this was the earliest form of sung poetry, and thus the earliest music, in Arabia. As it evolved later among the bedouin, it began to resemble a warriors' song, often in triple meter.
2. *Al-'arḍa* 'war song'. This is a more ostentatious form of warrior song, practiced especially by sedentary bedouin (figures 4 and 5).
3. *Al-samri*. Traditionally, these are love songs preserved by sedentary bedouin who live near urban centers. They comprise a more sophisticated cycle of rhythmic songs and dances, intended for public celebrations and feasts.

ORALITY AND LIVING MASTERS

What has allowed this sung poetry to endure, overcoming all obstacles and remaining a living tradition, is oral transmission. Oral transmission can without exaggeration be called miraculous; and it is an especially astounding phenomenon in modern times, when writing and recording have become the main means of dissemination and preservation. In the modern era, writing has been used to compile and set the poetic texts of certain traditional songs, and some examples have been set in Western musical notation; nevertheless, such techniques have not replaced the essential living mastery of the *sha'ir*, and the relationship between master and disciple remains the one way to ensure the survival of this tradition across generations. One has only to speak with popular musicians in Arabia to hear them say that they received their art from an older person—father, mother, uncle, aunt, grandfather, grandmother (figure 6). Some memorizers distinguish themselves as much for their talent as "transmitters" as for their poetry or their singing; they become the keepers of the poetical-musical tradition. A

FIGURE 4 *'Arda* simulating war, accompanied by *ṭār* and *ṭabl*, on the holiday 'Ild al-Fitir in Abu Dhabi, 1974. The two enemy camps stand face to face and advance on each other alternately, while an "arbiter" in the center marks the rhythm. Photo from Ministry of Information, Abu Dhabi.

FIGURE 5 *Ṭabl* players accompanying an *'arḍa*. This ancient war song is now an entertainment and also marks solemn events such as Muslim holidays. Photo from Ministry of Information, Abu Dhabi.

FIGURE 6 The poet Abu 'Adnan and his family, of the Bani Khaalid tribe, in the desert of Palmyra after a session of sung poetry accompanied by the *rabāba*. Photo by Marie-Georges Jargy, 1971.

process of selection takes place in which the best masters are identified by a broad, if tacit, consensus.

Oral transmission does not lend itself to literary or musical notation. No poetic or melodic notation system has been found that can faithfully reproduce it, phonetically and morphologically, or capture the complexity of its microtones. The written Arabic used to compile and set the poetic texts is inadequate. Although it is perfectly suited to the classical language, this alphabet is insufficient for spoken Arabic dialects—and those dialects are used nearly exclusively in traditional music. The problem of musical transcription is even more complex. Since the nineteenth century, Western musical notation has been much used, even more by Arab musicians than by Western ethnomusicologists; but—at least among the westerners—the intention has been to develop a working tool for research and analysis, with no claim whatsoever that this notation is an infallible means of preservation or transmission. In sum, we can quickly see that textual notation and musical notation are incapable of replacing oral transmission.

IMPROVISATION AND MEMORIZATION

One consequence of this oral mastery, so unsuited to being set down in writing, is that it must remain alive and ever-changing if it is to fulfill its social, cultural, and spiritual functions in a civilization which is itself both living and oral. This is a quality that popular music in modern industrialized countries has largely lost. Living oral transmission is linked to another characteristic of the Arab poetic-musical form: improvisation.

Improvisation—which seems to be experiencing a resurgence, even in some Western musical forms—has always been a natural, spontaneous process in a civilization like that of the Arabian Peninsula, where the spoken word is more important than the word "frozen" in writing. For improvisation itself to be received, it must necessarily enter the mind of the listener, whose memory then becomes a link in the chain of transmission and preservation. If we go back to pre-Islamic origins, we can see that the great classical Arabic poetry follows this pattern. Thus we find, alongside the *sha'ir*—the creator of songs—another very important personage, the memorizer: the *rawi* 'bard' or 'rhapsodist'. The *rawi* must have an exceptional memory and a passion for poetic and melodic expression. Most often, the *rawi* is himself a poet. Not only is he capable of memorizing poetry by declaiming and singing it, but his own creativity in effect authorizes him to fill out the poetry he sings, or sometimes to add his own improvisations. In this way, the original work of the *sha'ir*, as transmitted by the *rawi*, or singer, fluctuates and is modified in a kind of continual polishing that is at the same time an adaptation to a changing environment.

This aspect of the music in particular struck one eminent nineteenth-century traveler, Aloys Musil, who tells the following anecdote about the *sha'ir*:

> Often the *sha'ir* argued that a verse had been expressed in this way or that, but his friends, the *ruat*, contradicted him. This caused him to exclaim that all versions were right and original and to end by invoking the omniscience of Allah.

SOCIOCULTURAL FUNCTIONS

One general observation seems appropriate. Over the centuries, the communal spirit of this music can be seen most clearly in a refusal to lionize individual authors, even great geniuses. In fact, this heritage is more collective than personal. Its repository and true guardian is the group. Though some famous names have been remembered in classical poetry, we find mostly an anonymous poetic tradition, a common pool from which all can draw freely—in sharp contrast to the principle of authors' rights so jealously defended in the West. Often, one cites a verse or even an entire poem without knowing who its original author was. There is even a formula for this kind of quotation: "As the poet sang it. . . ." Such citation is even more marked in popular sung poetry, a genre in which the author began to be named only during the contemporary era, doubtless under the modernizing influence of the West.

Today, some economic or simply social activities have disappeared, and the poetic-musical cycles associated with them no longer have a reason to exist. Warrior songs (*'arda*), for example, have had to adapt to peaceful circumstances and are preserved in playful scenes and even religious supplications. It will be the same for other poetic-musical traditions; the main thing is to keep them alive in some form.

Therefore, traditional music and poetry have a new role in maintaining cultural identity threatened by technology. This role has developed as an almost spontaneous transfer that attests to the adaptivity and strength of the popular genius. As they left fishing boats, tents, caravans, battlefields, and empty Qur'ānic schools, these poetic-musical traditions took refuge in the *dar* (plural, *dur*), a traditional "patio" that became a setting for occasional performances of songs and dances; or, even more simply, they were performed in public squares or before governors' palaces on holidays such as Mulid, Ramadan, and 'Id al-Adha. These sociological and economic changes—brought about to a large extent by the technological revolution, in particular the advent of gasoline—entailed two other transformations that contributed to keeping the tradition alive.

The first of these consequent transformations was an increasing number of *joqa* 'troupes' of singer-poets, dancers, and musicians—male and female—who specialized in preserving and performing different kinds of traditional music. Some *joqa* are devoted to a specific genre; thus we find groups dedicated to pearl-fishing songs and others, most often women, devoted to wedding songs such as the *samri*. Still others perform bedouin songs: *'arda*, *hjini*, and *mashūb* 'drawn out' (figure 1*b*). In general, a troupe has a director who is famous for collecting an elder's poetic and musical knowledge, and the group takes this elder's name. As the director's popularity increases, the troupe receives more and more invitations to perform at family parties and ceremonies. In this context, it is important to avoid the term "professional" as understood in Western milieus and by westernized Arabs. Musicians of the Arabian Peninsula do not receive a formal musical education and do not make music their primary profession. They are simply working-class people who have fine voices and have assimilated a part of the traditional repertoire. They hold all sorts of other jobs and perform music in their leisure hours.

Still, it is true that since the advent of radio and—above all—television, there has been a new trend toward professionalization among some individual musicians and even among some *joqa*. This presents the dangerous possibility that an organizational structure will emerge which would compromise the authenticity of the traditions the *joqa* are intended to safeguard.

The second transformation has been the role of the media in encouraging a wider distribution of traditional music, especially on television, where the best groups can perform. Significant funding is placed at the disposition of the best troupes, and some poets and musicians have salaried positions in radio and television. This too has contributed to keeping traditions alive. But here as well, there is a danger of professionalization, which is contrary to the essence of any truly popular music and can gradually erode its spontaneity and its integrity.

From the perspective of ethnomusicology, evolution seems incompatible with traditional music. But it is perhaps important to make the point that the popular music of the Arabian Peninsula, like that of other Arab regions, should not and cannot remain frozen in unchanging forms or structures. In Arabia, unlike many industrialized countries, popular songs are not preserved mainly in archives or museums. The oral tradition on which they are based is itself never static but always changing—if only because of the creativity of poets, singers, and musicians.

Of course, even a cursory exposure to the words, melodies, rhythms, and instruments of this music will reveal clearly that some of these elements are immutable, that they form the backbone or archetype of the tradition, and that they will serve as a model for all future creations. But beyond these basic structures, creativity implies being able to choose, apply, adapt, and enrich according to the needs of the moment. We can observe this in many popular songs of the East, and in liturgical music such as Christian hyms. There are well-known vocal and instrumental ornaments for songs that have never been imposed or codified, tempi that are left to the director's discretion, and hand clapping and scansion by percussion instruments that punctuate weak and strong tempos in a variety of rhythms without ever failing to observe the fundamental rules of a genre. Thus this music appears to us as the oral expression—unwritten and uncodified, using sound, words, rhythm, and gestures—of the collective genius of a people, shaped by layer upon layer of the cultures that have fused into one of humanity's oldest civilizations.

TRANSLATED BY BARBARA RAPS

REFERENCES

Burckhardt, J. L. 1831. *Notes on the Bedouins and the Wahabys*. 2 vols. London: Coburn and Bentley.

Dickson, H. R. P. 1967. *The Arab of the Desert*, 4th ed. London: George Allen and Unwin.

Farmer, H. G. 1967. *A History of Arabian Music to the Thirteenth Century*. London: Luzac. (Originally published 1929.)

Galley, Micheline, issue ed. 1996. "Creativity and Tradition: Mediterranean Folk Poetry in Sung Form." *Journal of Mediterranean Studies* 6(1). (This journal is issued semiannually by Mediterranean Institute, University of Malta, ed. P. Sant Cassia.)

Jargy, Simon. 1988. *La musique arabe*, 3rd ed. Paris: Presses Universitaires de France.

———. 1989. "Sung Poetry in the Oral Tradition of the Gulf Region and the Arabian Peninsula." In *Oral Traditions*. Vol. 4, *Arabic Oral Tradition*, ed. John Miles Poley, guest ed. Issa Boullata, 175–187. Columbus, Ohio.

Sowayan, Saad 'Abdullah. 1982. "The Prosodic Relationship of Nabati Poetry to Classical Arabic Poetry." *Journal of Arabic Linguistics* (Wiesbaden) 8:72–79.

"Sung Poetry of the Beduins." 1994. In *Archives internationales de musique populaire*, 4 vols., ed. Laurent Aubert. Geneva: VDE-Gallo. (Compact disks, with accompanying notes by Simon Jargy.)

Musical Life in Sohar, Oman

Dieter Christensen

Geographic and Historical Setting
The Arts
Performance Groups and Their Arts
Occasions
Musical Life, Social Order, and Cultural Diversity

GEOGRAPHIC AND HISTORICAL SETTING

Sohar's highly diverse population is historically linked to East Africa, the Arabian Gulf, and the Makran coast of Iran and Pakistan, as well as to the interior of the Arabian Peninsula. In 1975, the anthropologist Fredrik Barth identified more than thirty distinct groups in Sohar, the most numerous being sedentary Arabs, descendants of African slaves, bedouin, Baluchis, Fārisī, and Ajam (Persians). All these were cross-cut by their adherence to one or another of various schools of Islam, which include the Sunni, Shi'ite, and Ibadite (Barth 1983). Within this urban diversity and transience, ethnic identity and social balance must be continually negotiated.

Expressive behavior—speech beyond basic communication, and "the arts"—constitutes a medium in which the negotiation of social relationships and identities is symbolically acted out. Orderly relationships between the individual and the local community, among local communities, among groups of people within and across local communities, and between the people of Sohar and the state all require the enactment of "arts" (Arabic *funūn*; singular, *fann*). In that sense, music making—as one of the arts—is an integral part of life in Sohar.

The Sultanate of Oman is the easternmost country on the Arabian Peninsula. It borders on the Arabian Gulf and is part of the coast that faces the Gulf of Oman and the Indian Ocean, an important waystation on the Mesopotamian-Indian-East African sea routes since antiquity. Oman is also part of the great South Arabian desert, the Empty Quarter, with all that this implies about being a "true Arab": a bedouin roaming the sands on camelback, searching for water and pasture, singing the great tales of ancestors.

Geographic conditions, orientation toward the desert or the sea, and migrations within southern Arabia and from beyond the waters have all contributed to the considerable regional diversity of culture within Oman. The few fortified marketplaces along the littoral—from Salala and Mirbat in the south to Sur, Muscat, Muttrah, and Sohar in the north—have attracted people from many lands and have mediated between the desert people and the fishers, traders, and date palm growers of the coast.

Since 1970 the people of Oman have experienced profound and rapid changes in their ways of life. A major maritime power on the Indian Ocean in the eighteenth and nineteenth centuries, Oman governed possessions along the East African coast to

Lines of dancers, all men or boys, move back and forth under the walls of the old citadel of Sohar. There are more than twenty groups, each group representing its own village or tribe and following its own rhythm and melody.

Zanzibar in the south, in the Arabian Gulf, and on the Baluchistan coast (now Pakistan). Oman's fortunes faded with the rise of the British Empire in India, the advent of the steamship, and the suppression of the East African slave trade. After having been at the center of a wide net of trade relations and movements of people—from India to Mesopotamia and Europe, from Africa to the Middle East—Oman slipped into increasing isolation, which became extreme during the rule (from 1932 to 1970) of Sultan Said bin Timur, whose policies included minimizing contacts with the outside world. There were almost no schools in Oman, no hospitals outside Muscat, no roads, no telephones, no radios. All this changed in 1970, when the present ruler, Sultan Qabus bin Said, succeeded his father and steered the country toward a gradual opening to the rest of the world. Since then, electricity, radio, television, rapid transportation, health services, and formal education have become universally available, as have satellite dishes (since 1992) and all manner of electronic communications equipment. Contract workers from other Arab countries (including administrators and teachers from Egypt, the Sudan, and Jordan) and from South Asia (including engineers, physicians, nurses, and unskilled workers from India, Pakistan, and the Philippines) have added to the diversity of a population that for centuries has accommodated substantial African and Baluchi elements within its South Arabian majority, especially in the coastal regions.

Since 1970 Oman has been transformed from a locally oriented subsistence economy, with a way of life that had changed little for centuries, to a nation that participates in global economic and information exchange. Profound transformations are continuing at a rapid pace and are affecting everything from the way babies are born and circumcisions are conducted (now at the hospital) to notions of identity. Sohar is part of these ongoing, all-encompassing changes.

Sohar

The town of Sohar is an important trading center on the northeastern coast of the Arabian Peninsula; it is the administrative seat of its province and was once a capital of the Sultanate of Oman. Medieval travelers described it in glowing colors as a wealthy city, but by the latter half of the twentieth century its physical appearance was unassuming. In 1975, Barth noted that Sohar could be perceived as an "overgrown fishing village" (1983:21). Sohar has benefited from the general economic and technological evolution of the Sultanate since 1970, and from a special development project in the 1980s and 1990s. Blacktop roads and concrete construction are now ubiquitous; the medieval walls that surrounded the market quarter and the citadel have been torn down; a mile-long "corniche" and a tourist hotel (opened in 1993) have been built on the beach. Although as yet there has been no census, the population of the province of Sohar is estimated at 25,000, with no more than 15,000 people living in the town proper.

THE ARTS

The Sohari concept of *fann* 'art' involves the enactment of skills of expressive behavior by an organized group of people in a formal setting on an appropriate occasion. This is in contrast to expressive behavior enacted by people who are not organized formally into a group or are judged locally not to be skilled, or in a setting that is not judged locally as formal or appropriate.

There also are or were other forms of music making, in the Western sense of the term—for instance as part of agricultural work, fishing, and seafaring until these domains were revolutionalized by the economical and technological changes of the 1970s. However, work songs were not considered among the arts. Music as transmitted by television, radio, audiocassettes, and the like is readily accessible to all Omanis but so far is not a significant factor in the social life of Sohar. The *adhān*, the call to prayer [see THE MUSLIM CALL TO PRAYER], broadcast by loudspeakers everywhere, is a pervasive and highly significant marker of social time, but Soharis do not consider it in any sense music or art.

Arts, then, are public rituals, most of which have music as an integral ingredient. These rituals, in turn, are themselves an integral part of social life: without them boys cannot be circumcised, weddings cannot be celebrated, mental illnesses cannot be cured; and relationships between villages, tribes, and the state cannot be negotiated or affirmed—though many such concepts are changing, as are specific practices.

A few images can serve to illustrate aspects of musical life in Sohar.

Feast at the end of the Holy Month of Ramadan, June 1985

Lines of dancers, all men or boys, move back and forth under the walls of the old citadel of Sohar; the sound of drums and lines of sung poetry echo from the governor's new office across the street; noisy pickup trucks bring more groups of men, who form lines and advance, dancing, in a broad front, to join the whirling crowd between the fortress and the new seat of government (figure 1). It is after the fourth prayer, the sun is setting, but there is no breeze to relieve the oppressive heat of June; the dancers' white gowns are drenched with sweat. The *wālī*—the governor of the province of Sohar, who represents the sultan of Oman—appears with his retinue, somber-looking, with a dagger glistening under the *abbāya*, the brown mantle of office worn over the white *dishdasha* that is the official everyday dress of Omani men. The dancing becomes more energetic; there are more than twenty groups, each group representing its own village or tribe and following its own rhythm and melody. This is the second day of the *'īd al-fiṭr* 'small feast' that ends the month of Ramadan, and the *wālī*, on behalf of the sultan, is receiving congratulations and expressions of loyalty from the communities in his province. (Two recordings made in Nizwa, in the interior of Oman—a song of praise, *'āzī*; and a dance with weapons, *qaṣṣafiyya*—very closely resemble what one would hear in Sohar. See Christensen 1993, tracks 2–3.)

FIGURE 1 Dancers moving toward the fortress of Sohar to greet the governor during the feast at the end of Ramadan. Photo by Dieter Christensen, June 1985.

FIGURE 2 *Dān*. Drummer and the lead singer Haluma with a line of dancers in a "standing dance" at a wedding in Sohar. Photo Dieter Christensen, August 1992.

Wedding, August 1990

In Ṣobāra, a section of Sohar close to the citadel, a house is festooned with hundreds of colored lights. The edges of the flat roof, the television antenna on top, the crowns of the walls surrounding the large courtyard, and the sheds that have been erected outside the courtyard are all illuminated with garlands of green, red, yellow, and blue lightbulbs, some blinking. People go busily in and out. A group of women and a few men are huddled under the reed roof of the shed near the gate, outside the courtyard wall. They adjust the microphone and amplifier and fuss over the loudspeakers, metal cones that are to be strung on nearby trees. Then the leader of a women's ensemble or *dān* group—her name is Haluma (figure 2)—puts her water pipe aside, pulls the microphone close to her mouth, and clears her throat. Two drummers "begin the knock," falling into their interlocking beats. The women, sitting in a circle, clap their hands, picking up the rhythm. Small hand cymbals join in. Haluma begins her song, "I repent; I did not mean to do anything bad . . ." The chorus of women answers. It is the first night of a wedding that will end on Thursday around midnight, and the women's singing signals the official beginning of the ritual at the house of the bridegroom's parents, the "owners" or "masters" of the wedding. In the middle of the song, the groom's mother, two of his sisters, and a few other woman relatives emerge from inside the courtyard to the public space in front, drop coins onto a large metal tray in the circle of the singers, then slowly withdraw. Haluma, her dark face glistening with sweat, praises their beauty and their generosity. The presence of the singers has been acknowledged; the "owner" of the wedding has been honored. Now the loudspeakers spread the news throughout the settlement. A wedding has begun.

A few hundred feet down the beach, another house is similarly adorned, though more modestly; in its courtyard are women musicians—another *dān* group. This is the house of the bride, where the wedding will be celebrated separately until the evening of the last day, when the bride is taken by car, in a splendid circuitous procession passing through all the main roads of Sohar and covering dozens of miles, to the groom's house.

FIGURE 3 *Zār* ritual in Sohar. The "father of the *zār*," standing, flagellates the possessed person (at center, crouching under a white veil), who has fallen into a trance. Photo by Salwa El-Shawan Castelo-Branco, August 1992.

Zār, a healing ritual, August 1992

The crisscrossed car tracks through dry wadis, marking the way to the *bayt al-zār* 'house where the *zār* is held', are hard to find in the fading daylight. Nobody actually lives at the *bayt al-zār*; it is a compound in the bush, far from the beach or any settlement, that serves only as a place for healing ceremonies. A dozen pickup trucks are parked near the gate of the high-fenced cluster of houses and sheds. The even beat of the *zār* drums signals that a healing ritual (figure 3) is in progress.

In a house made of palm fronds, some thirty people, men and women, face a slowly rocking figure veiled with green cloth. The walls and ceiling are covered with printed shawls and paper cuttings. A number of cylindrical drums are lined up against one wall. Two large drums are being played in an even, unaccented rhythm. One man, who gestures and waves incense around the veiled figure, is reciting; the women and men will answer in chorus, persistently, for hours. The movements of the veiled figure become more erratic and more violent. He is ill and been brought here for treatment of his *jinn*, the evil spirit that is said to possess him. Some of his relatives are watching while others squat outside in the courtyard, preparing food and drinking tea. The ritual will take the whole night and will be repeated on the following two nights.

Mālid, a votive ritual, January 1990

In a broad open space on the beach, outside the sea gate of a large compound, mats and rugs have been laid out in a long-sided rectangle for a *mālid*, a votive (or "votivic") ritual celebrating the birth and life of the Prophet Muhammad. There are cushions and backrests on two sides; in the middle is a small table, covered with a green cloth, that holds incense burners and flasks of rosewater. After the last prayer, at about eight

FIGURE 4 *Mālid* ritual in Sohar. The line of *hawwīm*, kneeling, dance their adoration of the Prophet Muhammad. Photo Dieter Christensen, July 1992.

o'clock in the evening—it is getting dark quickly—men assemble solemnly, talking softly, and seat themselves on a precious rug in two facing rows. Incense is lit, then carried around and waved at everyone in turn; rosewater is sprayed on all; then a very old man, propping himself up on his cane, begins to read from the Holy Qur'ān. The *ḥalqat al-mālid* '*mālid* circle' has begun a *naḏr* ceremony for the well-being of a baby.

The ceremony lasts until well after midnight, with recitations of prose and poetry, hymns, and rhythmic body movements. Late in the evening, fires are lit on the beach to heat and tune the large frame drums (*ṭārs*) that accompany the final segment, when the baby boy, for whom the "owner of the *naḏr*" has pledged the ceremony, is carried twice around the ceremonial space. Throughout the evening a few neighbors, all men, drift in and out. Tea and coffee are offered. Women pass by, but they do not stay, and they hardly glance at the men. (Figures 4 and 5 show a *mālid* ritual; for an excerpt of a *mālid* performance, see Christensen 1993, track 6.)

PERFORMANCE GROUPS AND THEIR ARTS

All the arts—and there were sixteen that could be distinguished in Sohar in 1993—are enacted by organized groups, called *firāq* 'teams' (singular, *al-firqa*) or *ḥalāq* 'circles' (singular, *al-ḥalqa*). In the province of Sohar, there is usually more than one group for an art, and some arts can be found in each residential or tribal group; also, some groups perform more than one art. Performance groups have an established leadership and hierarchy and a more or less fixed membership, and they are associated with particular localities. The most important kinds of performance groups are *firāq al-razḥa, firāq al-dān, ḥalāq al-mālid, ḥalāq al-lewa, ḥalāq al-pākit*, and *firāq al-qurba*.

Firāq al-razḥa and *al-razīf*

The "arts with the sword"—sometimes called generically *al-razīf*—are performed by groups of men who represent, and are perceived as acting on behalf of, larger communities. These groups do not seek material gain or even spiritual blessings, but individual members do take pride in acting out a communal ethos in local rituals such as weddings and circumcisions and in state rituals—religious and national feasts celebrating the social order of the Sultanate. *Firāq al-razḥa* usually also perform the *'āzī*, a processional recitation of poetry of praise that emphasizes religious invocations.

The arts with the sword share several characteristics. First, they center on Arabic poetry that recalls heroic deeds of the past—usually with tribal associations—or that praises leaders of the present, usually the sultan. Second, the poetry is sung antipho-

FIGURE 5 Reader reciting the praise of the Prophet in a *mālid* ritual in Sohar. Photo by Dieter Christensen, July 1992.

nally and is in strophic form, with each verse repeated numerous times before the next is sung. Third, the enactment of these arts—exclusively by men—requires one or two "poets," who "give" the lines of poetry; two opposing lines of dancers and singers, who carry swords or camel sticks; and sometimes, between these lines, individual dancers, who parade their swords or perform ritual sword duels. Fourth, the groups are always from a residential or tribal community, which they are considered to represent. Distinctions among forms of the *razīf* and the organization of groups arise from those communities.

The sedentary Arabs in the town of Sohar and the villages to the south perform the *qaṣṣafiyya* (figure 6), a fast, even-metered dance that is considered easy; and the complex *lāl al-'ūd* 'great shout', which consists of antiphonal, highly melismatic unmetered calls followed by slow, even-metered singing and dancing. An essential element is a pair of drummers beating interlocking rhythms on the smaller *kāsir* and the larger *raḥmānī*, both double-headed "y-laced" cylindrical drums. The drums symbolize the group; in fact, preparing for a performance is described as "carrying the drums." The *ra'īs* 'leader'—a position that commands respect—accepts invitations to "make a knock" and is responsible for all arrangements, such as notifying and transporting the performers.

In theory, membership in a *firqat al-razḥa* is open: that is, any male may join regardless of residence, social status, ethnicity, or religion. In reality, the drummers are almost always, as a local phrase puts it, "from the servants," and the majority of dancers and singers tend to be from the locality or tribe that the group represents. However, to ensure that there will be enough performers for a given event (the minimum number is twenty), leaders may resort to inviting individual dancers from other groups, in a mutual-aid arrangement; such exchanges of performers are, evidently, necessitated by diminished social support for this art.

Sedentary Arabs north and west of Sohar town prefer the *wahhābiyya* (figure 7), a dance with weapons that shares many traits with the *qaṣṣafiyya*. What distinguishes the *wahhābiyya* is a slower tempo, a triple meter, and the very characteristic nodding head movements made by the dancers when the two drummers, sometimes reinforced by frame drum players, "visit" a line. (For a *wahhābiyya* from Majīs, a village in northern Sohar province, see Christensen 1993, track 4.)

The *razīf* of recently settled bedouin—there are no longer any fully nomadic bedouin in Sohar province—is distinct in that drums are not used.

FIGURE 6 *Razḥa qaṣṣafiyya* in Sohar. The two musicians with the cylindrical drums *raḥmani* (left) and *kāsir* move between two lines of dancers and individual dancers who carry weapons—swords or sticks and shields. Photo by Dieter Christensen, August 1992.

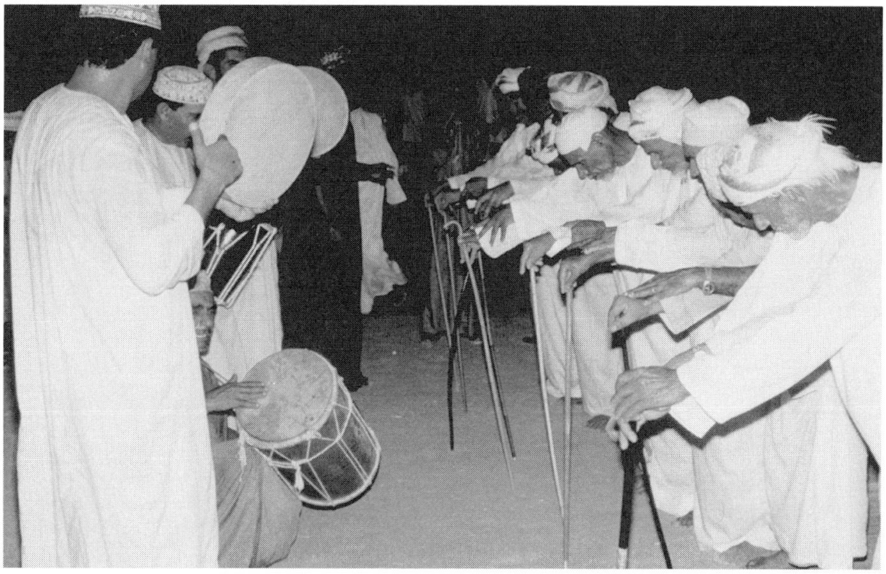

FIGURE 7 *Wahhābiyya* in Sohar. Dancers, bowing and nodding, lean on their camel sticks. The sound of the cylindrical drums (*raḥmani*, left, and *kāsir*) is made "stronger" with frame drums, an innovation of the 1990s. Photo by Dieter Christensen, August 1992.

Firāq al-dān

Ghinā' (*al-nisā'*) 'women's songs' are performed primarily for profit by *dān* groups (figure 8). The performers are contracted for weddings and circumcisions; the "owner" of a local social event issues an invitation to a performance group by undertaking to pay its leader a flat fee and to render certain services, such as transportation, meals, and refreshments. In addition, the group receives ritual cash donations. The proceeds are shared by the group members according to an established schedule.

The *firqa* is always "owned" by an individual, usually the lead singer, who may be a woman or a man. Ownership in the Western sense extends to the equipment—drums, small cymbals, amplifiers, loudspeakers, and often a minivan—and, in a less tangible way, to the services of twelve to twenty-five group members; but it does not include the repertoire: the songs of ritual, love, and praise. The group in turn "belongs" to the locality of the *ra'īs* (masculine) or *ra'īsa* (feminine), though without representing it.

All *firāq al-dān* in Sohar have at least two male drummers for the pair of cylindrical drums (*kāsir* and *raḥmānī*), but some female lead singers may also occasionally play the *raḥmānī* themselves. The chorus (*ḥarīm*) has varying proportions of women and men. All professional woman musicians and all professional drummers in Sohar are descendants of slaves.

The repertoire of a *dān* group is fluid. In addition to ritual songs—such as songs for applying henna to a bride and groom—and formulaic songs of praise, each group develops a repertoire that may draw extensively on the poetry of popular music from the Arabian Gulf and elsewhere disseminated on radio, television, and cassettes. These songs are all strophic, metered, and based on a limited number of named rhythmic patterns. Most groups also dance; that is, they perform "standing songs" which involve antithetical movements of rows of the *ḥarīm*, the drummers, and the lead singer or singers. All *dān* groups use amplification.

Ḥalāq al-mālid

The celebration of the birth (*mawlūd*) and life of the Prophet Muhammad is the subject matter of poetry and prose recited, sung, and danced by formally organized groups of men known as *ḥalāq al-mālid* '*mālid* circles'. The spiritual head, distinguished by his mastery of both the content and the diction of *mālid* poetry, is known as the *khalīfa*. He is assisted by the *shawūsh*, whose responsibilities include organiza-

FIGURE 8 *Dān* group performing "women's songs" at a wedding in Sohar. In this *firqa*, the lead singer and several members of the chorus, *al-ḥarīm* 'the women', are male. Photo by Khalfan al-Barwani, August 1992.

tional and practical matters. A *mālid* group consists of twenty to fifty men functioning either as "readers" or as *huwwīma* 'those who adore', who respond with singing and body movements to "readers'" chanting. At the time of this writing there were six *mālid* circles in Sohar. Membership is open to all males who want to join, regardless of their residence, ethnic group, or social status, if they are willing and able to acquire the considerable skills—memorizing and correctly enunciating prose and poetry in classical Arabic, and moving vigorously in complex patterns.

Mālid circles are invited to perform at weddings, at circumcisions, and in votive rituals enacted to praise the Prophet and to invoke his blessing for themselves and their hosts. On these occasions, a group is not paid or otherwise rewarded, although the "owner" of the event has to provide transportation and certain other services. Some *mālid* circles also perform healing rituals in which the patient is put into a trance to be freed of evil spirits; for these rituals, a group receives a substantial payment.

The repertoire of the *mālid* groups is very limited: texts are drawn from the Qur'ān and from a specific set of prose hagiography and poetry in classical Arabic, and only two forms, the *mālid* proper and the *jalāla*, are practiced.

Mālid begins with a recitation from the Holy Qur'ān, followed by recitation of a prose *riwāya* 'story' from the life of the Prophet and by chanting of *qaṣīda* 'poetry of praise', which is accompanied by highly expressive body movements in the *huwāma* 'adoration' section and leads to the *tawḥīd* 'becoming one' or achieving unity with God—the goal of a *dhikr*. When *mālid* is performed for healing, it is usually the *huwāma* section that leads to the trance. Frame drums are used in the closing part (*tashwīsha*) of the *mālid*, and in the other form practiced by *ḥalāq al-mālid*, the *jalāla*.

The *jalāla* follows the *mālid* proper in weddings, leading any of the wedding processions with rhythmic chanting of poetry of praise accompanied by frame drums (figure 9). *Ḥalāq al-mālid* do not use amplification.

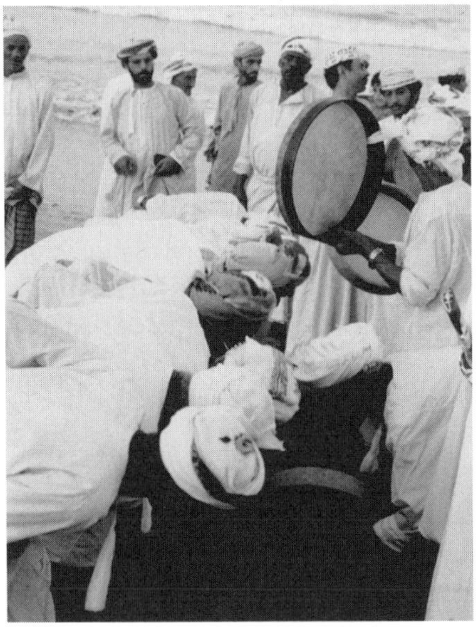

FIGURE 9 *Jalāla* leading a wedding procession in Sohar. The "readers" carry frame drums (*ṭarāt*). Photo by Dieter Christensen, July 1990.

Ḥalāq al-lewa

Lewa groups, consisting of men who are descendants of slaves, perform for profit. They are led by the *abū al-lewa* 'father of the *lewa*', who owns most of the equipment—several drums, including African-type drums called *musundu*; conch trumpets (*jīm*), and metal trays of canisters used to beat the time line. The owner has a claim to the services of the drummers and dancer-singers (all together, twenty to forty people) who make up the group. The central figure is the *zammār*, who plays a double-reed instrument and has to be hired from outside, at a high fee, since there is no longer a resident player of the oboe *mizmār* in Sohar.

The repertory of *ḥalāq al-lewa* is limited to a set of three named dances—*lewa*, *sabāta*, and *bum*—in which the individual dancers and singers revolve while circling around the instrumentalists. The song texts, in poorly understood Swahili and Arabic, abound with references to East Africa and seafaring. *Lewa* carries strong African connotations that are neither Arab nor Muslim; performances frequently lead to a trance. (A *lewa* ritual is shown in figure 10; for an excerpt from a performance see Christensen 1993, track 5.)

FIGURE 10 Players of the double-reed *mizmār* or *zurna* and the *musundu*, a kettledrum of African origin, in a *lewa* ritual in Sohar. Photo by Dieter Christensen, July 1985.

Ḥalāq al-pākit

There is only one group in Sohar that presents a musical theater called *pākit*. This group is clearly identified as *'Ajam* 'Persian', and the song texts and named roles in the plots are in colloquial Persian, which is disappearing rapidly as a spoken language in Sohar. The group, which performs at weddings, on invitation and for a substantial fee, is all-male and consists of lead singers (*khand*), drummers, a chorus that also claps hands and moves expressively while sitting, and several masked actors: the old man, the crow, the horse riders, the leopard, the pregnant woman. The "pregnant woman" gives birth to hand puppets who dance on her belly—a play within the play (figure 11).

Firāq al-qurba

The most recent kind of performance groups in Sohar is the *firāq al-qurba* 'bagpipe teams'. They began in 1988 in the Youth Club of Sohar with a few drummers and a player of the Scottish bagpipes, a native of Sohar, who was on leave from his job as military musician in the United Arab Emirates Forces; by 1994, bagpipe teams were to be found all over northern Oman and enjoyed great popularity, especially among young men. Drawing on *dān*, *lewa*, popular music of the Arabian Gulf, and other arts, the initial experimentation evolved into a new kind of group structure: a Scottish bagpipe as the central, eponymous instrument (figure 12); two or more drummers
TRACK 19 playing cylindrical and African-type *musundu* drums, tambourines, and cymbals; dancers; and a chorus. Although the dancers and chorus are part of the group, anyone may join the single or couples' dancing, for which a large circle is formed by the group members and the spectators. High-volume amplification has become an integral part

FIGURE 11 *Pākit* in Sohar. The dance of the hand puppets borne by the "woman"—on his back in the foreground—and the lead singer of the group to the right. Photo by Dieter Christensen, August 1992.

of the performances. By 1992, *qurba* had become widely recognized as an art—and as an alternative to *lewa* in weddings, since *qurba* is more readily available, its performers demand much lower fees, and its attractiveness to young and older men is unsurpassed.

OCCASIONS

Soharis are very much aware of acting on a public stage wherever they are, unless it is the *ḥaram* sphere of their own house. The public stages of men and women differ dramatically. Those of most older women are primarily their own neighborhood (*balād*), with excursions to the hospital or to a wedding. Men, on the other hand, roam widely and freely; their primary social stages are the market, where one sees and is seen; the mosque; and formal ritual settings that are de facto public: religious and secular feasts, weddings, circumcisions (formerly), and votive—or votivic—rituals. The most important of these occasions are "great feasts" and weddings.

FIGURE 12 Lead musician of a *qurba* in Sohar with his instrument, a Scottish bagpipe. Photo by Dieter Christensen, August 1990.

"Great feasts"

The important Islamic feasts—the end of the month of Ramadan (*'īd al-fiṭr*) and the beginning of the month of pilgrimage (*'īd al-aḍḥa* or *'īd al-kabīr*)—and the secular National Day celebrations on November 16 are all associated with public display, through the arts, of loyalty to the supreme ruler of Oman, the sultan. The norm is that the governor of Sohar sends invitations to the *shaykhs*, who will pass them on to the "responsibles" of the groups they want to perform. Only arts that are performed by men, that display male prowess, and that praise the sultan are deemed suitable; hence, only the *razīf, lāl al-'ūd, qaṣṣafiyya, razḥa, razfa, wahhābiyya, 'ayyāla*, and *'āzī* are performed on these occasions.

On the first day of *'īd al-fiṭr* relationships within the extended family are celebrated through visits and shared meals, without any enacted arts. On the second day, visits of respect are paid to tribal and residential heads—the *shaykhs*—and to socially more remote officials, such as the *wālī*. The afternoon of the second and third day of the *'īd* is the time for the enactment of arts as an expression of respect for and loyalty to the sultan. The proper place in Sohar is in front of the official seat of the *wālī*, who represents the sultan and who should be present during the performances that begin after the third prayer (between 4 and 5 P.M.) and last until the fifth prayer (around 8 P.M.), with an interruption for the fourth prayer. The teams representing tribal and residential entities throughout the province arrive by whatever transportation they have; at one time they came on foot or riding horses or camels, but since the 1970s they have usually traveled by pickup truck. When they arrive, they dance formally into the venue—at least since the 1970s under a national flag—performing their distinctive versions of the *razīf*. The town of Sohar and the coastal villages to the south will "make" *qaṣṣafiyya* and *lāl al-'ūd*, the villages to the north will "make" *wahhābiyya* or *'ayyāla*, and the bedouin of the interior will "make" the *razīf* without drums. Weapons are much in evidence, and ritual sword fights between the rows of dancers attract the milling all-male crowd. Ten to twenty groups may be performing at the same time, competing with each other to display their skill in the din of drums and the dust they all raise. There are memories of olden times when horse races and the reciting of poetry on camelback were part of the celebrations; and pride in one's own group as part of all the groups that make up Sohar is evident.

Since the early 1980s, the national government has instituted procedures for the direct representation of the provinces through the arts on National Day, at religious feasts, and at other major events of national significance if they are celebrated in the presence of the sultan—events that receive extensive coverage on television in Oman.

For Sohar, a *firqat al-funūn al-sha'biyya li'l-Ṣuhār* was created by order of the governor, with officials appointed by him. This group (for which uniforms in the style of folkloric troupes familiar from television were considered at one point) draws its members from the traditional residential and tribal *firāq*. Although it was originally intended to represent the province only at events outside Sohar, the leadership has claimed all provincial events, religious and secular, as well. By recruiting key performers from "local" groups on these occasions and by claiming to represent the entire province, the *firqat al-funūn al-sha'biyya li'l-Ṣuhār* has preempted and precluded local and tribal representation: the governor issued his invitation only to the *firqat al-funūn al-sha'biyya li'l-Ṣuhār*. The consequences of this policy on the local political level, as well as for the functioning and form of the arts, have been far-reaching and have caused considerable controversy among performers, who are involved in an ongoing process of negotiation. A critical point was reached in November 1992, when National Day celebrations in the presence of the sultan were held in Sohar. The venue was not the fort but the sports stadium, to which admission was selective. Instead of the "making" of traditional arts that had dominated all previous National Day celebrations in Sohar, troupes organized and trained ad hoc performed a historical melodrama written by an Egyptian, with music by a Kuwaiti. The drama included dances named after traditional Sohari arts, but these were not recognized by Soharis in the audience as having anything to do with those arts. For instance, a piece called *Al-mālid*—referring to a highly stylized ritual enacted exclusively by men to praise the Prophet Muhammad—was performed by girls to Western-style orchestral music. However, the following day, after the departure of the sultan and his guests, a large number of local *firāq*, which had been excluded from the performances in the stadium, conducted a procession through the town and around the fort.

Weddings

In Sohar, a wedding is understood as a social contract between extended families and is celebrated as publicly as possible to construct the social locus and to affirm the mutual commitment of the partners—that is, the families.

Normally, a wedding extends over four days and ends on a Thursday (or, in the case of traditional Baluchis, on a Friday), but there are also three-day weddings. There are several constraints on when a wedding may be held. The entire month of Ramadan is "respected"—that is, no arts, and and hence no weddings, can be performed. Where there is any sensitivity to Shi'ite beliefs, the first ten days of the month of Muharram are also barred. Summer is preferred, but winter weddings are not uncommon. The groom's family must be "ready"—that is, must have accumulated the agreed-on bride-price, acquired the food and beverages for the celebration (grain, meat, fruits, soft drinks), and engaged the performers. A new constraint is the work obligations of the groom and bride—for example, weddings tend to "stop" toward the end of August, when young women return to school. The death of a close relative on either side precludes the performance of all arts that make *ṭarab* and thus precludes the wedding, for a negotiable period. A wedding has to be postponed when performers of the one art that is considered essential for it—*ghinā'*—cannot be procured, as occasionally happens in peak wedding seasons.

The cultural complexity of Sohar is reflected by ethnic differences in wedding customs. Ongoing and rapid change has necessitated adaptations and negotiations on many levels of the wedding ritual. I describe here the typical structure of weddings among Arabized Baluchis in 1990–1992.

The first song performed by the *dān* group in front of the groom's house—usually on a Monday evening, or, in a three-day wedding, on Tuesday evening—signals the beginning of the event. From then on, a predetermined ritual unrolls: women relatives and friends of the bride assemble at the bride's house, usually entertained by a *firqat al-dān* in the evening. At the groom's house, relatives and friends arrive, and additional, prearranged arts are performed: *razḥa* or *wahhābiyya*, *qurba*, *lewa*, perhaps even *pākit*.

On Monday, Tuesday, and Wednesday, these groups will perform after the fourth prayer and until about midnight, all at the same time and often in close proximity to each other. On Wednesday afternoon, henna exchanges take place by way of processions between the wedding houses. On the last day of the wedding, which culminates—normatively—in the consummation of the marriage, music making begins in the morning with *dān*, followed by a ritual noon meal of *harīs*, a porridge of wheat with beef and butter, to which all are invited. This is an offering to the larger community, and trays with *harīs* are sent from the groom's house to neighbors and relatives. More *ghinā'* follow immediately after the meal and until the third prayer (around 4 P.M.), when preparations are made for the *zaffat al-'arīs*—the procession to wash the groom, the ritual hair cutting usually having taken place the previous afternoon. If there is a *ḥalqat al-mālid*, it will lead the procession, performing *jalāla*. The *dān* is next, and other arts follow, all the way to the place of the ceremonial washing, which must have a clean running water—a *falaj* (pumped irrigation water in a palm grove) or running water in a mosque. The procession winds its way through the village to spread the news of the wedding, with all groups performing simultaneously and the *dān* using a bullhorn; it always returns by a different route.

After the return of the *zaffat al-'arīs*, there are more performances until it is time for the bride's procession, the *zaffat al-'arūs*, to set out; it will return well after the last prayer. Whether the house of the bride is next door or many miles away, the *zaffa*—now always traveling in cars—will take a long route, passing through places to which the groom and bride have connections. While other *firāq* may stay behind and rest or entertain the guests who cannot join the *zaffa*, the *firqat al-dān* will always accompany the *zaffa* and will sing during the procession. On its return, both *firaq al-dān* will join it. The official end of the wedding ritual is marked by the bride's *firqat al-dān* guiding her into the nuptial chamber—the *killa*—at the groom's house and the bright ululation with which the singing breaks off.

A recent trend among many "owners of a wedding" is to hire a *muṭrib*, a singer of popular songs who accompanies himself on an *'ūd* 'lute' and who may bring a *dumbak* player, to perform songs from the Gulf States and Yemen softly into the morning; but this is not thought to be part of the wedding. The social event ends when the bride enters the *killa*. The guests then leave.

MUSICAL LIFE, SOCIAL ORDER, AND CULTURAL DIVERSITY

Musical life in Sohar is an integral part of the processes through which Soharis negotiate their relations with the state, with the various and constantly shifting groupings of people in the province, and with their immediate community. By participating in a *mālid* circle or by arranging for a performance of *mālid*, an individual can convey his devoutness as a Muslim but at the same time proclaim his adherence to a form of Islam other than Ibadhism—the form of Islam, embraced by the ruling dynasty, that rejects the notion of attaining *tawḥīd* 'oneness' through Sufi practices. By participating in the "arts with the sword" at great feasts, Soharis can sustain the political hierarchy. By beating the drum in a *firqat al-razḥa*, a descendent of "free Arabs" can either place himself among descendants of slaves or demonstrate his belief that such social distinctions are obsolete. By singing and dancing with a *firqat al-dān*, a man can publicly proclaim and reaffirm his sexual orientation. By putting together a set of wedding customs from many options, and by inviting performers of certain arts rather than others, the "owner" of a wedding can attempt to construct a public image of his and his family's ethnicity and social status that may not closely correlate with his genealogy, achievements, or means. For instance, a family descended from slaves may invite Baluchi artists to perform at its wedding, to project a Baluchi identity that the family deems superior to its inherited social status.

In this way, patronage generated by diverse social needs supports the diversity of arts in Sohar; the arts provide a medium for the symbolic expression of cultural diversity and social status and contribute to the climate of tolerance that characterizes life in Sohar.

REFERENCES

Barth, Fredrik. 1983. *Sohar: Culture and Society in an Omani Town*. Baltimore: Johns Hopkins University Press.

Christensen, Dieter. 1991. "Traditional Music, Nationalism, and Musicological Research." In *Music in the Dialogue of Cultures*, ed. M. P. Baumann, 215–223. Wilmhelmshaven: Noetzel.

———. 1992. "Worlds of Music, Music of the World: The Case of Oman." In *World Music, Musics of the World*, ed. M. P. Baumann, 107–122. Intercultural Music Studies, 3. Wilhelmshaven: Noetzel.

———. 1993. *Traditional Arts of the Sultanate of Oman*. UNESCO Collection AUVIDIS/D8211. Compact disk.

———, ed. 1994. *Dictionary of Traditional Music in Oman*. Rev. trans. of Yūsuf Shawqī, *Mu'jam mūsīqā 'Umān al-taqlīdiyya*. Intercultural Music Studies, 6. Wilhelmshaven: Noetzel.

Al-ghinā' al-Ṣan'ānī: Poetry and Music in Ṣan'ā', Yemen

Jean Lambert

Ḥomaynī Poetry
The Music of Ṣan'ā': *Al-ghinā' al-Ṣan'ānī*
Poetry and Music

The song of Ṣan'ā, *al-ghinā' al-ṣan'ānī,* is the oldest tradition of urban music known in Yemen and in the Arabian Peninsula. In this classical vocal and instrumental genre, the singer accompanies himself on a short-necked lute, the *'ūd.*

The history of this music is not well known, because of the disdain of many learned historians for oral tradition and because of religious puritanism directed at musicians. However, the music developed along with a poetic tradition, the *ḥomaynī*, and developments in this poetry are better documented, allowing us to follow the genre historically. There is another good reason why we should study the poetry and the music together: in Yemen, one can hardly imagine music without sung words, for they are crucial to its meaning. Consequently, the word *ghinā'* can be translated not only as "song" but also as "music."

Despite its name, *ṣan'ānī* music must not be isolated from the other genres in Yemen. The *ghinā' ṣan'ānī* had an influence on other musical traditions: the lute was added to other vocal music which had not used instruments, or it replaced other instruments, as in the *laḥjī* style of south Yemen (Lambert 1993). The meaning of *ṣan'ānī* itself is open to question. *Ḥomaynī* poetry was not born in the Ṣan'ā' region, and the origin of the melodies is very controversial. Some modern artists, such as al-'Antarī (d. 1965) and Bā-Sharāḥīl (d. 1952), were not from Ṣan'ā'. The exodus of musicians to Aden at the beginning of the twentieth century raised a new question (Lambert 1993): is the *ghinā' ṣan'ānī* specific to Ṣan'ā', or is it the common property of the whole nation?

ḤOMAYNĪ POETRY

Lyrical poetry (*ghazal*) can be written in classical Arabic—that is, *ḥakamī* 'according to the rules'—or in a literary style, *ḥomaynī*, influenced by colloquial Yemeni Arabic. (The etymology of the word *ḥomaynī* is unknown.) The absence of declensions in *ḥomaynī* makes composition and the adaptation of words to music easier. Thus there is a close connection between the literary use of dialect and the development of the musical genre. Yemenis are very proud of this genre because it is representative of a major proportion of Yemeni poetry and stresses national specificity.

The rise of *ḥomaynī* poetry coincided with the emergence of a strong, wealthy state, the Rasūlī dynasty, in Ta'izz and Zabīd in the fourteenth and fifteenth centuries.

Is the *ghinā' ṣan'ānī* specific to Ṣan'a', or is it the common property of the whole nation?

This was a period when art, science, and mysticism flourished. The first writers of *ḥomaynī* were Ibn Fulayta (who died c. 750 A.H./1349 C.E.) and Abū Bakr al-Mazzāh (who died c. 835/1431). When the center of power moved to the highlands, poetry and music followed. Henceforth, the main *ḥomaynī* poets were members of the ruling Zaydī aristocracy: Muḥammad Sharaf al-Dīn (d. 1016/1607), 'Alī al-'Ansī (d. 1139/1726), and Aḥmad al-Ānisī (d. 1241/1825) and his father 'Abd al-Raḥmān al-Ānisī (d. 1250/1834). Only some of the manuscripts from this "golden age" have been published ('Abduh Ghānim 1980; Lambert 1997a, ch. 3).

Ḥomaynī poetry depends on lyricism and elegy and includes strong religious expression. Love is celebrated in the pastoral style of the *muwashshaḥ* and the metaphoric spirit of the ancient Arabs who compared beautiful women to graceful antelopes, to colored birds with enchanting voices (as messengers of love), and to the shining full moon or the thin crescent moon. *Ḥomaynī* forms follow the general evolution of Arabic poetry, from the classical monorhymed *qaṣīda* toward the quatrain, *mubayyit*, and the *muwashshaḥ*, here a threefold stanza.

THE MUSIC OF ṢAN'Ā': *AL-GHINĀ' AL-ṢAN'ĀNĪ*

Although, as noted above, very little is known about the history of music in Yemen, literary history provides indications of some important developments. Like poetry, court music moved from the luxurious palaces of the Rasūlī kings to the more ascetic life of the Zaydī imams. Between the fifteenth and eighteenth centuries, it changed from a public activity, encouraged by the sovereign, to a more intimate art. As *ḥomaynī* was written in small towns such as Shahāreh, Thulā, and Kawkabān that periodically served as the royal capital, music had to respond to the contingencies of unstable power and to the puritanism of the intellectual elite in the highlands. These circumstances may explain the ambiguous status of the traditional performer—the *mughannī* 'singer'—as well as the pragmatism that characterizes music in Yemen and the aesthetic influence of poetry on music. Also, the structure of the lute determines a great deal of musical aesthetics.

TRACK 20

FIGURE 1 Ḥasan al-'Ajamī playing the *qanbūs* or *ṭarab*. Photo courtesy of Jean Lambert, 1997.

The South Arabian lute

Until the beginning of the twentieth century, the most common instrument was a locally built lute, the *ṭarab* (figure 1). It was also played in Aden, where it was called the *qanbūs* (as well as in the Ḥijāz in the nineteenth century; Farmer 1931). This instrument was introduced to Indonesia and East Africa by Yemeni immigrants (Poché 1984). In Yemen, only a few artists are still able to play it today.

The body of the *qanbūs* is carved from one piece of wood from an apricot tree or a local *ṭunub* (*abrus bottae*) and covered with goatskin, which gives it a very organic sound with rich overtones. It has three double courses and a single string, with an ambitus of one and a half octaves. The strings are struck by a plectrum made of an eagle feather. The recent introduction of the Egyptian *'ūd* has brought some technical innovations, although it has not entirely transformed the local performing style. As with the *ʿūd*, the names of the parts of the *ṭarab* or *qanbūs* provide evidence of anthropomorphic symbolism (Lambert 1997a, ch. 4). They also give some indication of its aesthetics. The tuning is from bass to treble (the pitches are relative, not absolute):

C1: *al-jarr, al- yatīm* 'the orphan' (single string)
D1: *al-rakhīm* 'the mild, refined one' (double course)
G2: *al-awsaṭ* 'the middle one' (double course)
C2: *al-ḥāziq* 'the well tensed' (double course)

The tonic of the majority of the melodies is G. This course is known as the instrument's *lisān* 'tongue' (Poché 1984:168).

If no *ṭarab* was available, the singer would accompany himself with a brass plate (*ṣaḥn mīmiyeh*) held horizontally between his two thumbs (figure 2). Nowadays, the South Arabian lute has been superseded by the *ʿūd*, without drastically affecting musical techniques or aesthetics (for musical examples of both, see Lambert 1997a, b).

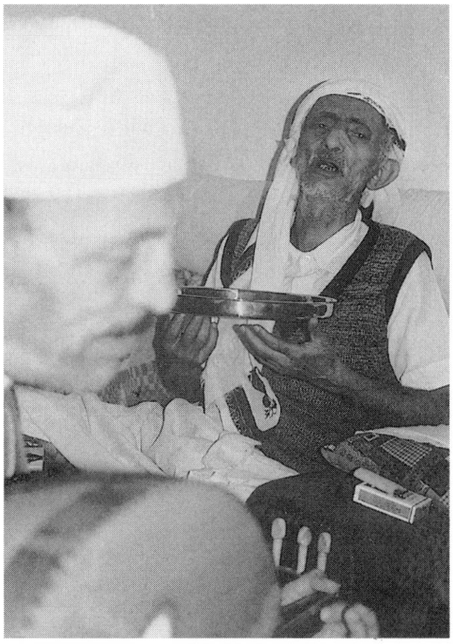

FIGURE 2 Muḥammad al-Khamīsī playing the *ṣaḥn mīmiyeh*. Photo courtesy of Jean Lambert, 1997.

Melody and rhythm

Ṣanʿānī melodies are distantly related to *maqām*, but until recently the modes had no specific names. They are based on a main scale made up of combinations of whole tones and three-quarter tones, and very rarely of half-tones (where E1, B2, or E2 can be flat).

The most common modes are a kind of *rast* on G2 (*awsaṭ* course) and a kind of *ʿushshāq*, sometimes on D2 (*ḥaziq* fingered with the forefinger) and sometimes on A2 (*awsaṭ* with the forefinger). There are also a few melodies of the *sika* type. The melodies rarely have any modulation in pitch or flat leading notes. Many pieces end on a tone that is not the tonic, giving them a characteristic feeling of modal instability.

TRACK 21

Although Yemenis have no mathematical theory for their rhythms, most of the rhythmic cycles have specific names. Two asymmetrical cycles—one with 11 beats (figure 3*a*), the other with 7 beats (figure 3*b*)—are very characteristic of *ghināʾ ṣanʿānī*. These two rhythms have the same name, *dasʿa* 'step', but they are distinct in practice. The *wasṭā* (figure 3*c*) is the most common rhythm in Yemen. It has a slow binary variant, *muṭawwala*, and a development in triplets with a switch of accent, *al-wasṭā al-kawkabāniyya* 'the Kawkabān *wasṭā* (figure 3*e*), which can be written with either 12 beats or 4 beats. The *sāriʿ* (figure 3*d*) follows the same rhythmic pattern as the *wasṭā* but is quicker. The *sajʿ* (figure 3*f*) is similar to a march rhythm; it has a quick tempo but fits melismatic melodies because it is not syncopated. The *fartāsh* 'search' is a development of variations on a short melodic motif according to a simple binary rhythm that tradition suggests is a Turkish military march. It is purely instrumental, and that is rare enough to be noteworthy. The *muṭawwal* 'stretched' is an unmeasured form whose composition is relatively fixed. Often alternating with measured sections in the same piece, and interweaving vocal and instrumental parts, it is the most sophisticated form in Ṣanʿāʾ. Its distinctive character lies in the way the lute accompanies the voice, more closely than in the Oriental *mawwāl*.

Variation and improvisation: The "philosophy of the melody"

In order to "make the lute talk," the artist builds his performance on stable forms from which he develops variations. This is called *falsafat al-laḥn* 'the philosophy of the melody'. Every song has a basic melodic-rhythmic structure called *al-qāʿida* 'basis', 'stand', 'law', 'custom', or 'pattern' that the learner must closely reproduce. In contrast, the *kharsha* 'decoration' is a more or less improvised variation on sections (*maqṭaʿ*) of the basic melody, using either the voice or the instrument. Thus the dialectic relationship between *qāʿida* and *kharashāt* is precisely the relationship between repetition and variation. Every accomplished musician has his own *kharashāt*, which characterize his personal style. *Qāʿida* and *kharashāt* are articulated by a *lāzima*, a very short coda which is played on two courses and which underlines the basic rhythm and the characteristic pitches of the mode.

Given the neutral level of performance represented by the *qā'ida*, variation is produced by three basic techniques of the right hand. The *fard* 'individual' (figure 4*b*) consists in playing the melodic line "one by one," with a regular pulsation. For the *sils* 'chain' (figure 4*c*), the right hand plucks two courses alternately, mainly G2 and C2. While the melodic line is being played on G2, a quick pedal in C2 (free of

FIGURE 3 Rhythmic cycles.

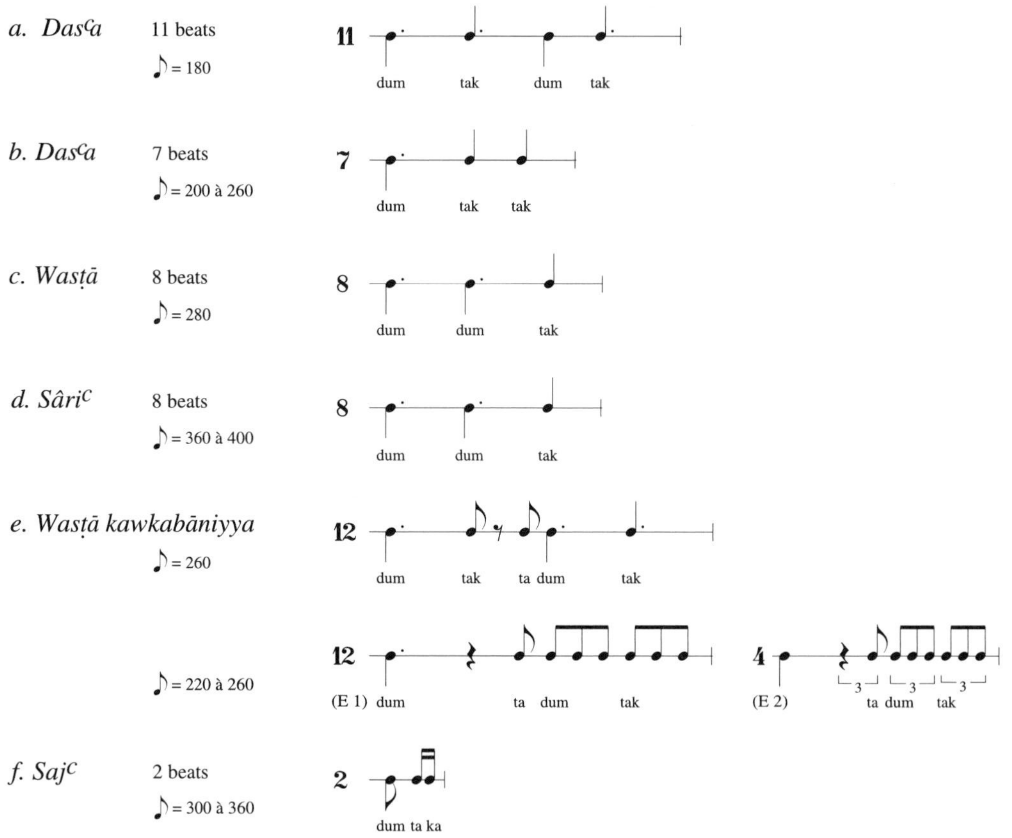

FIGURE 4 Basic melody with *fard*, *sils*, and *ḍafāra* renditions.

fingering) doubles it as an ostinato, giving the impression of a polyphonic dialogue. In the *ḍafāra* 'plaiting' (figure 4*d*), the plectrum simultaneously plucks the *awsaṭ* course (G2), for the main melodic line, and the *rakhīm* (B1); this produces a harmonic echo to the main notes of the melody, generally on a fourth or a fifth. For its part, the left hand ornaments many notes of the *qāʿida* with "answers" on an interval of a second, without any plucking by the right hand, relying on the specific resonance of the *qanbūs*.

Playing involving these contrasts (course alone, courses plucked alternately, courses plucked simultaneously) allows for a range of expressive nuances. The right hand, which is particularly active, secures the rhythmic, the melodic, and the ornamental aspects of the melody at once.

Compound forms

Stock pieces can be executed in two main styles: either with the instrument in a *qawma* 'suite' or in a purely vocal style, the *tawshīḥ*, another kind of compound form.

The qawma

The *qawma* is a suite in the sense of the Andalusian *nawba*: a succession of pieces whose modes, rhythms, and tempi are fixed by traditional practice and are more or less linked to dance. The *qawma* of Ṣanʿāʾ has particular stylistic features.

The *qawma* contains three melodies of different rhythmic cycles and tempi, which must be performed in a fixed order: *dasʿa, wasṭā*, and *sāriʿ*. Usually these correspond to three or more different songs. In addition to this standard definition, which is representative of modern practice, the other forms already mentioned (*muṭawwal, wasṭā muṭawwala, sajʿ*, and the instrumental *fartāsh*) can be included in the suite, instead of or in addition to the *dasʿa*. The variation lies mainly in the choice of cycle at the beginning of the suite; as far as the *wasṭā* and the *sāriʿ* are concerned, they drive the listener toward the feeling of a binary and always quicker rhythm, well suited for dance. Thus the main organizing principle seems to be an acceleration of tempo.

As a concept, the suite is clearly defined by the *nagla* 'passing, transition', which marks the transition between two melodies. Its sophistication is unique to each musician. The main constraint is rhythmic: one must avoid silence between the two melodies. Tradition forbids the musician to stop playing during the suite. The *qawma* must be built as a structure in the architectural sense (Lambert 1995:167). The continuum sustains the acceleration of tempo toward an emotional crescendo which is greatly appreciated. But the *nagla* is also an opportunity to play on sound perception: sometimes the listener still continues to sense the rhythm of the previous section after the performer has switched to the next one.

Verse	*Melodies*	*Rhythmic formulas*
1–2	A	muṭawwal
3–4	B	sāriʿ
5	A	muṭawwal
6	C	sajʿ
7–15	B	sāriʿ
16–17	C	sajʿ
18–23	B	sāriʿ

FIGURE 5 "*Iqbis matā shiʾt nār al-shawq min kabadī*" 'Pick up when you wish the fire of love from my liver'. *Ḥakamī* poem sung by ʿAbdallāh al-Ḥammāmī (Lambert 1997a:124–125 and sound example 12).

The vocal suite: Tawshīḥ *or* tathlīth

The word *tawshīḥ* is rich in meanings in Yemen, but in this case it designates a purely vocal variant of the *ghināʾ ṣanʿānī*. The interpreter of *tawshīḥ* is not a *mughannī* but another type of performer, a *nashshād*, who draws from the same stock pieces, the same modes, and the same rhythmic formulas as in the *qawma*. The most spiritual lyrics, often written in classical Arabic, are chosen.

The *tawshīḥ* (or *tathlīth* 'tripling') is a compound form with three sections. The logic of its concatenation is diametrically opposed to that of the *qawma*: rather than being linear and ending in a crescendo, the *tathlīth* is circular, and its melodies alternate freely. Figure 5 is a model of a distinctive *tathlīth* in which three melodies—A, B, and C—alternate.

The sense of acceleration is disrupted, as a quick rhythm is usually followed by a slower one or by a nonmeasured part. In the absence of an instrument, the melody is interpreted in a psalmodic way (*ṭarīqa inshādiyya*). This results in a blurring of rhythmic perception. Like a reciter of the Qurʾān, the singer pauses at length between verses and introduces a great deal of melisma. Instead of the predominantly musical succession of the poems in a *qawma*, the *tathlīth* presents an interweaving of melodies around one poetic form.

POETRY AND MUSIC

The interaction between poetry and music in *al-ghinā' al-ṣan'ānī* is significant on several levels. The combination of rhythmic formulas and verse makes it easy for the singer to memorize the sections of the melody (*maqṭa'*) as well as different combinations of texts and melodies, which evolve continuously according to the technique of contrafacture. This also helps the poet during composition. Poetic content has an influence on musical interpretation: the tradition of Ṣan'ā' defines the order of lyrical thematic exposition as *'itāb* 'blame, reproach', *firāq* 'separation', and *wasf* 'description'.

Moreover, a performance must provoke a kind of anamnesis of emotion that reflects the real or imagined meaning of the poem. For example, it is said that the poem "*Yā ḥamāmī amāna mā dahāk*" 'O my turtledove, by God what happened to you?' was composed by a father who had killed his daughter and later discovered that she was innocent of the crime of which he had accused her. A good singer must relive the father's emotions—sorrow and guilt—and bring the poem to life for the audience through the genuineness of his interpretation. Such concerns are expressed in many legends in which musicians recount the circumstances of poetic composition.

Given the ideological priority of language in Islam, music is sometimes looked down on and has to be accompanied by poetry (Lambert 1997a, ch. 5). However, musicians often express a preference for music over language, considering music a more direct means of expression, closer to "natural" communication, especially that of birds. Thus the "monodic" unison between voice and instrument is interpreted as a dialogue in which the instrument is a human voice and "says" what the words cannot say (Lambert 1997a, ch. 10). Therefore, for both the musician and the listener, the relationship between poetry and music is suffused by a strong, effective symbolism.

REFERENCES

'Abduh Ghānim, Muḥammad. 1980. *Shi'r al-ghinā' ṣan'ānī* (The Poetry of Ṣan'ā' Song). 2nd ed. Beirut: Dār al-'Awda. (Later editions were published in 1983 and 1985.)

'Alī Aḥmad, Jābir. 1988. "Ḥāḍir wa mustaqbal al-ghinā' fi'l-Yaman" (Present and Future of Singing in Yemen). *Dirāsāt yamaniyya* (Yemeni Studies) 33:109–166.

Farmer, Henry G. 1929. "Meccan Musical Instruments." *Journal of the Royal Asiatic Society* Part 3:489–505. (Reprinted in Henry G. Farmer. *Studies in Oriental Music*, ed. Eckhard Neubauer, Vol. 2, 79–100. Frankfurt am Main: Institute for the History of Arab-Islamic Science at Johann Wolfgang Goethe University.

Johnson, Ragnar. n. d. *Music from Yemen Arabia: Sanaani, Laheji, Adeni.* Lyricord LLST 7283. LP recording.

Lambert, Jean. 1993. "Identité nationale et régionalisme musical." *Revue d'Études du Monde Musulman et Méditerranéen* 67(1):171–186.

———. 1995. "La musique dans la Maison-tour: Harmonies et Dissonances." In *Sanaa, architecture domestique et société*, ed. P. Bonnenfant, 165–173. Paris: CNRS-Éditions.

———. 1997a. *La médecine de l'âme: Le chant de Ṣan'ā' dans la société yéménite*. Hommes et Musiques Series. Nanterre: Societé d'Ethnologie.

———. 1997b. *Mohammed al-Hārithī: Chant et luth de Ṣan'ā'*. Musicales, Institut du Monde Arabe, Media 7 IMA-CD 26. Compact disk.

Murshid Nājī, Muḥammad. 1984. *al-Ghinā' al-yamanī al-qadīm wa mashāhiruhu* (Ancient Yemeni Music and Its Famous Names). Kuwait City: Al-ṭalī'a.

Poché, Christian. 1984. "Qanbūs." In *The New Grove Dictionary of Musical Instruments*, ed. Stanley Sadie, Vol. 3, 168–169. London: Macmillan.

———. 1975. *North Yemen: Traditional Music.* Musical Atlas, Unesco Collection. Recorded by J. Wenzel. EMI Odeon O64 18 352.

Schuyler, Philip. 1990. "Heart and Mind: Three Attitudes toward Performance Practice and Music Theory in the Yemen Arab Republic." *Ethnomusicology* 34:1–18.

al-Shāmī, Aḥmad. 1974. *Min al-adab al-yamanī* (About Yemeni Literature). Beirut: Dār al-Shurūq.

Music in Performance: A Saudi Women's Wedding Party

Kay Hardy Campbell

One by one the conversations around us stopped, as the crowd strained to hear distant drumming, in a majestically slow 4/4 rhythm, that announced the bridal procession. From the same distance came women's cries of joy, *zagharīt*, filling the pauses between drumbeats. The drumming grew louder, and the crowd turned toward the back of the reception room at the Meridien Hotel in Jidda. An Iranian friend and I also turned, to look beyond the hundreds of Saudi women, unveiled and formally dressed, who had gathered there to celebrate the marriage of a young Saudi couple from the prosperous merchant class. All of us had waited several hours for this moment, and we had passed the time in the traditional way by enjoying the sights and sounds of a Saudi women's wedding party, a *ḥaflat al-zaffāf.*

It was 1979, and I was gathering material for a story about Saudi women's music for the *Arab News*, a Saudi English-language daily published in Jidda, where I was then living. Since this music is most frequently played at *ḥaflāt* attended by women only, I had been angling for invitations to parties where Saudi women singers who were famous throughout the kingdom would be performing. So far, the few weddings I had attended featured singers whose popularity was only local; but now my editor had gotten me an invitation to this wedding party, where Sāra 'Uthmān, a rising star from Riyāḍ, was being flown in to sing and play the *'ūd* with her orchestra of women drummers. I had brought my Iranian friend with me, to be a second pair of outsider's eyes.

Our gilded invitation in hand, we had arrived at the hotel an hour later than the official starting time of 9 P.M., but we were still quite early. We made our way into the reception room, which was large enough to hold the eventual crowd of three hundred women easily. As soon as we sat down, a servant came by with fragrant aloewood incense, which (like the instrument) is known as *'ūd*. We waved it over us, as is traditional for women guests who are presented with incense on entering a friend's home or arriving at a party, and again on leaving. The air was filled with its rich fragrance; and it would cling to our gowns for days afterward—an indication of good-quality (and very expensive) *'ūd*. While we waited for the orchestra to arrive, servants brought soft drinks, juice, tea, and Saudi coffee. The rustling of voluminous taffeta and satin gowns could be heard at every turn as the guests streamed in to greet friends and family and then to find good seats close to the stage.

The crowd strained to hear distant drumming, in a majestically slow rhythm, that announced the bridal procession.

About an hour later Sāra ʿUthmān walked on stage. Her entrance elicited no reaction at all from the audience. She wore a full-length white dress that contrasted with her dark skin; her hair was cut in a simple chin-length bob. She sat down and began to tune her *ʿūd* and test the microphones. Then her drummers walked slowly onto the stage, each carrying a few frame drums (*ṭārāt*; singular, *ṭār*). One drummer also had a *darbukka*, and another had brought a *daff*. A brazier of live coals was brought to the stage and set down there; this was to enable the drummers to tune their skin drumheads, which quickly go limp in Jidda's humidity, even in this air-conditioned hotel. The drummers arranged their chairs in a row on either side of Sāra ʿUthmān and began to tap the drum skins, holding them over the coals and raising the pitch of each drum as the skin tightened. Well out of sight of the women, a young man set up equipment to make a casette recording of the evening's performance; this cassette would be on sale in Jidda's marketplace within days.

Sāra ʿUthmān began the performance with a simple *taqāsīm* on her *ʿūd*, exploring the notes of the melody she was about to play. It seemed more like a warm-up than a serious exploration of the song's *maqām* 'mode'. Then she played the metrical melody. The drums came in, one by one, adding rich layers of polyrhythms from high to low. The audience reacted immediately with cheering, clapping, shouting, whistling, and *zagharīt*.

The musicians repeated a single melodic phrase throughout each song. Sāra ʿUthmān sang the refrain and verses, and her chorus repeated the refrains. Each song lasted ten or fifteen minutes. The crowd seemed to urge the orchestra on, and the musicians played songs with progressively livelier rhythms. There were thrilling 6/8 patterns that I was told were Kuwaiti, and 4/4 patterns that I would later learn were called *ʿadanī* [see WOMEN'S MUSIC OF THE ARABIAN PENINSULA]. Although each song remained in just one steady rhythm, the drummers varied their playing with syncopation, fitting multitone drumbeats into every nook of each rhythmic pattern. With the livelier rhythms, one of the drummers would play the *daff* and add the bright jingling of its cymbals to the mix. Others would pound smaller, high-pitched *ṭārāt* to accent the syncopation in the offbeats. I noticed that one of these small *ṭārāt* was bright-green—unlike all the others, whose natural skin tone had been left unpainted. When the music inspired them, women in the
TRACK 22 audience would add another layer of syncopation with rhythmic clapping (*tasfīq*). On top of this rhythmic complexity, audience members occasionally let out boisterous whistles and *zagharīt*.

It was not long before young girls and teenagers approached the stage area and began to dance in pairs. Some of them were wearing party dresses. Others had put on the traditional long dancing dress, the *thōb nashal*, a caftan-like garment worn over an evening gown; such dancing dresses are in bright colors like hot pink, turquoise, blue, red, orange, and purple, as well as in black, and are lavishly embroidered with gold thread and dotted with sparkling sequins. The dancers lifted their skirts an inch or two and began to swing them from side to side. When they twirled and their gowns

FIGURE 1 Cassandra, an American dancer, captures the joyful spirit of Arabian women's dancing. Photo by Zone V Photography; courtesy of Cassandra Shore, artistic director, Jawaahir Dance Company and the Cassandra School.

floated around them, they looked like bright flowers in full bloom. Even the older women in the audience sang and clapped.

That night, the pounding 6/8 rhythms inspired the most dancing. During these songs, the girls would swing their hair back and forth in the traditional bedouin way, winning more encouragement from the audience. There were also 4/4 rhythms, and during one 4/4 piece, two young women did a simple pair dance while both played finger cymbals. My Iranian friend found that some of the 4/4 rhythms were familiar to her, since they are also played in Azerbaijan, a region of Iran that is close to Iraq and Kuwait. Late in the evening, the orchestra played popular pan-Arab pop tunes that inspired one teenager to get up and perform an Egyptian-style solo dance with a scarf tied around her hips.

The audience continued to socialize all through the evening's performance, alternating between watching silently, clapping, letting out *zagharīt*, whistling, dancing, and talking with friends. After the applause for each song, the musicians took a break to tighten their drums, take a glass of tea, and retune the *'ūd*. The audience seemed to expect the musicians to stop between numbers, breaking the musical spell for a few minutes. As soon as the musicians began playing again, the intense excitement returned.

The evening passed in this way until well after midnight. It was at this point, during a break between songs, that we heard the distant drumming in a slow 4/4 rhythm. At last the bride and groom appeared at the back of the room and made their slow, stately procession to the stage. The *zagharīt* and the deep tones of the *tārāt* rang through the room. A dozen women walked with the couple, including the drummers as well as others who carried large, thick candles in tall candlesticks. The audience murmured in admiration and let out occasional *zagharīt*. The bride wore an exquisitely ornate Western-style white wedding gown. Her brilliant diamond necklace and earrings, wedding gifts from her husband, sparkled in the candlelight. Her makeup and hairstyle were as glamorous as a film star's. The groom wore the traditional formal Saudi men's costume—a full-length white silk *thōb*, a headdress (white *ghuṭra* and black *agāl*), and a fine brown cloak (*mishlaḥ*) of lightweight wool. He smiled broadly, probably both from the excitement of the moment and from the pleasure of seeing his female relatives and friends dressed up and unveiled, in honor of himself and his bride.

As the procession entered, cameramen filmed it on video, and some older women among the guests, not wanting to appear in the video, quickly covered their hair and faces. Many Saudi women still prefer not to be photographed; and out of deference to the more conservative guests, someone at the microphone in front of the room said, "No photos, please," to warn off any amateur photographers in the audience. The groom and the video cameramen were very careful not to stare at the dazzling sea of unveiled faces around them.

As the procession reached the stage, the drumming changed to a faster 3/4 rhythm. The bride and groom posed for some still photographs before sitting down in two formal chairs that had waited on stage all night for them. Then the music and dancing began again for another hour or so, in honor of the couple. When the bride and groom paraded offstage to their wedding chamber, the guests were invited to a sumptuous feast. But many of the young women stayed behind, begging the musicians to keep playing.

My friend and I stayed to talk to the musicians. Sāra 'Uthmān was happy with the performance: "I like to experience my audience. I enjoy the fact that they never want the parties to end, as you have just seen here tonight. We are happy when the audience reacts this way." One band member, Jawāhir, added that the most important thing "is the audience members' response. They feel as though the time has gone quickly. After all, the artist is up there for the sake of the audience."

At this time, Sāra 'Uthmān was twenty-eight years old. She had begun to play for her own family at the age of twenty. After playing for a few private parties, she had been asked to perform for prominent clients and eventually had been offered engagements outside Riyāḍ. We spoke to her at the height of the wedding season, the month before Ramadan. She and her group—made up of her friends and relatives—were flying around the country, playing three or four nights a week. She had even traveled to Egypt to give some public concerts, at which she performed several songs composed especially for her. Her group spoke of a possible trip to the United States, for a private engagement.

As we parted, Sāra 'Uthmān gave me the high-pitched green-painted *tār*. I remembered that the drummers had used this instrument to hit distinctive accented beats that seemed to float above the deep pounding of the other drums. Then one of her drummers handed me a *daff* and insisted that I keep it as a memento of the evening. We left the hotel at the same time as the performers did, just as the glow of dawn was spreading across Jidda's skyline.

Women's Music of the Arabian Peninsula

Kay Hardy Campbell

Origins
Women's Music and Women Musicians Today
Performance and Music Traditions
The Role of Women's Patronage
Government Support
World Music and Modern Technology

The women of the Arabian Peninsula, or Arabia—Saudi Arabia, the countries of the Arabian Gulf, and Yemen—participate fully in the folk life of their culture. Whether they are city dwellers, villagers, or bedouin, successive generations of Arabian women inherit and pass on to their sons and daughters many folk traditions and arts, including the hypnotic song and musical forms, believed to date from the time of the Prophet Muhammad, that are still chanted at weddings and other celebrations. These song styles play a crucial role in rites of passage and have survived through the centuries because Arabian women have long been enthusiastic patrons and practitioners of local music.

Today's Arabian women are also part of the world music audience and are bombarded with outside musical influences. Yet the same modern technology that brings world music to this area also offers women an opportunity to take more control of their own music traditions: now they can hear their music more often on cassettes and CDs; and radio and television broadcasts bring their songs to a larger regional and global audience. Also—and most important—the role of music in Arabian rites of passage allows it to resist outside influences and should ensure its survival despite the popularity of other world musics throughout the region.

Scholars consider women's music a separate genre in Arabia because women there lead a distinct social life, with many activities taking place in the company of female family members. Although their lives are not separated from men's within the extended family, for centuries Arabian women have gathered with other women to celebrate religious holidays and family events such as births and weddings. On these occasions, they still sing special songs that have a specific social role and a distinct sound.

ORIGINS

The modern folk music of Arabian women is far removed from the sophisticated ensemble music that developed in the courts of the Arab and Islamic empires [see Historical Issues of Gender and Music]. Folk melodies are relatively simple, and the instrumental parts require little virtuosity or theoretical knowledge to be rendered well. Yet important elements of Arab court music have their origins in the Arabian Peninsula, in musical performance traditions centered on women and in patterns of social life and patronage in which women were prominent at the time of the Prophet.

In 1909, members of the Dutch legation in Jidda made a wax recording of a local women's folk orchestra—the earliest known recording of Arabian women's music.

It can be argued that, in many senses, Arabian women's music is a potent predecessor of this court music. Today, many practices among Arabian women involving music performance and patronage seem little changed from the seventh century C.E., when the origins of classical Arab court music were first chronicled.

At the dawn of Islam, the ancient cities of Medina and Mecca in western Arabia were centers of trade and religious pilgrimage. Public salons for travelers were held by women entertainers (*qiyān*; singular, *qayna*), who recited and sang poetry, promoting the work of contemporary poets as well as the careers of the political leaders whose praises they sang in verse. Early Arab historians chronicled the lives of prominent women singers, noting that these women played a stringed instrument (which is related to the modern-day *'ūd*) and were sometimes accompanied by percussion instruments. Three genres of art song were frequently attributed to them: heavy, highly ornamented songs sung to classical Arabic poetry and known as *sinād*; simple, lighthearted tunes that came under the classification *hazaj*; and laments, known as *nawḥ*.

In addition to the *qiyān*, who performed in the salons and the homes of the wealthy, less well known women musicians sang simple folk tunes within tribal and extended-family settings to celebrate rites of passage. Their singing is mentioned in anecdotes about the life of the Prophet Muhammad, in which he reportedly condoned women's singing on such occasions. Although the acceptability of musical performance is still debated in Arabia today, it is possible that the Prophet's attitude toward such festival singing has helped keep the Arabian women's folk song tradition alive.

A brief sampling of these anecdotes illustrates both the acceptability of women's singing and its important role in weddings in early Islam. On one occasion, "The Prophet said, 'Announce this wedding; play the *ghirbāl* (frame drum) about it'" (Ibn Mājah 1952, 4:611). On another occasion, it is related, "The Prophet was passing through part of the city, and happened upon a group of women who were playing the tambourine and singing. . . . He answered them, 'God knows I am fond of all of you'" (Ibn Mājah 1952, 4:612). On still another occasion, the Prophet is said to have asked his wife 'Ā'isha about a wedding, "Did you send the girl to her husband?" "Yes," 'Ā'isha answered. "And did you send a singer with her?" "No," she replied. The Prophet then said to her, "Didn't you know that the *Anṣār* [supporters of Islam from Medina] are fond of love poetry? You should have sent a singer" (al-Bustānī 1964:75).

No musical notation survives to give us the melodies of these songs. However, examples of the lyrics sung by the *qiyān* and court singers are preserved in several texts such as the *Kitāb al-aghānī* 'Book of Songs' by Abū al-Faraj al-Iṣbahānī (c. 897–967). [See SNAPSHOT: PERFORMERS FROM *KITĀB AL-AGHĀNĪ*.]

In 1909, members of the Dutch legation in Jidda made a wax cylinder recording of a local women's folk orchestra—the earliest known recording of Arabian women's music (Gavin 1985). Today, cassette tapes and CDs of traditional women's music, recorded both in studios and at live performances such as wedding parties, are available in the Arabian Gulf.

WOMEN'S MUSIC AND WOMEN MUSICIANS TODAY

Contexts of performance

Among women in Arabia, there is still a distinction between "art" and "folk" song, with nearly all women musicians performing folk music. A few famous folk singers, including Rabāb of Kuwait and ʿItāb of Saudi Arabia, have crossed the line from traditional folk singing to more sophisticated art singing, like modern-day *qiyān*; they collaborate with famous recording stars and composers, performing in concert halls with full-size Arab orchestras, and their CDs are available worldwide. However, these women musicians are exceptions to the general practice.

In many countries of the Gulf—Kuwait, Bahrain, Qatar, and the United Arab Emirates—one can hear women's folk music on the radio, see it performed on television, and attend live performances during religious and national celebrations, school graduation parties, and family rites of passage. Throughout those countries, folk music groups made up of men and women (figure 1) are in great demand for private parties. These groups, led by men, form a kind of extended family of musicians who perform for men and women (sometimes separately), as requested by the hosts. In Saudi Arabia, by contrast, only women musicians play for women's wedding parties.

Even in the countries where men and women sing together, women have occasion to sing for all-female audiences. Wedding celebrations are a common setting for such performances, since they involve several events held only for women—for example, the *laylat al-ḥinna*, the night when the bride's friends gather to decorate her hands and feet with henna. At a *laylat al-ḥinna*, folk musicians entertain the bride, who must sit still for hours while the henna dries and its designs "set" on her skin.

Outside these formal venues, in all countries of the Arabian Peninsula, women get together to sing, often among themselves, with or without professional musicians, when their extended family or tribe is celebrating. The bedouin, traditional farming and pearling communities, also generate their own songs. In the agricultural communities of Yemen, and among bedouin throughout the peninsula, women sing as they work in the fields or at home. The thriving pearl-diving culture that dominated

FIGURE 1 Mixed-gender folk music group from Kuwait. Photo from Kuwait Office of Information.

the Arabian Gulf until the early twentieth century had a women's song tradition known as *guffāl*; these songs were performed as the crews of pearl-diving ships returned home after the arduous season. In Yemen, songs performed during the milling of grain (*dagg al-ḥabb*) are still played today as a folk genre, although hand milling—the process that gave rise to them—is now practiced only in remote areas of the country.

In many parts of the Gulf it is also acceptable for women singers to perform at renditions of *ṣawt*, a highly stylized song cycle. This music is most often played at private soirées held in the *dīwān* 'salon' of prosperous homes. During such evenings, the audience participates fully in rhythmic clapping (*tasfīq*), singing, and dancing. The women who sing on these occasions are more skilled and have a more diverse repertoire than the women's folk bands. They most closely resemble *qiyān* in that they remain within traditional performance venues and musical genres. Because they wear traditional costumes and follow the formal aesthetics of the region, they have more glamorous clothing, jewelry, and hairstyles than the singers in the women's folk bands, whose appearance is generally more subdued. Occasionally, videos of such performances with women singers are broadcast on television in the Gulf region. But these more intimate evenings, in a traditional *dīwān* decorated with oriental carpets, are best experienced in person. Pillows for audience seating are placed along the walls, with an open space left in the middle of the room for dancing; this arrangement puts the audience members close enough to the performance area that they can clap and sing along with the vocalists and musicians.

Women's folk music ensembles and instrumentation

TRACK 22 A traditional women's musical *firqa* 'group' (figure 2) is led by a singer known as the *muṭriba* 'entertainer'. The *firqa*, made up of her women friends and relatives, is named after her, and often she is the only musician in the group who is known to the audience. Even when a women's folk band is a subset of a larger mixed music ensemble, the women's group is led by a *muṭriba*.

The *muṭriba* is usually the most accomplished musician in her group. She carries the vocals and often also plays the *'ūd*. To accompany her, ensemble members play percussion instruments, including the *ṭār* 'frame drum', the *daff* 'tambourine', and occasionally a *darbukka* 'cylindrical clay drum'. What gives such a band its distinctive sound is its use of at least four *ṭārāt* with varying pitches ranging from low to high. The small *ṭār* adds high decorative accent beats to the syncopated rhythms of the tunes. The players of the *ṭār* and *daff* also double as chorus singers. In cities, the

FIGURE 2 Women musicians playing in the Gulf style. Courtesy of Martha Carr Moussa.

ensemble sometimes also includes violinists or keyboard players, who add modern and electronic sounds to the traditional instrumentation.

PERFORMANCE AND MUSIC TRADITIONS

Music at weddings

Throughout the peninsula, wedding celebrations are the primary settings where one can see and hear traditional Arabian women's music performed. A wedding joins two large extended families and involves days of celebration, music, and dance. Because specific wedding customs vary by tribe and town, each celebration becomes a delightful meld of family and regional traditions—including music.

The grandest night of a wedding celebration, and the one with the most music, is the *laylat al-zffāf*, when the bride and groom come together as husband and wife and their families and friends gather for an all-night party to celebrate their union. In Saudi Arabia, women and men celebrate separately, at elaborate soirées featuring folk bands hired for the occasion. These parties are held in the home, either in the courtyard of a family compound or on the high-walled roof of the family's apartment building. Some upper-class weddings are held in public facilities, for example in hotels and in outdoor party areas known as "wedding gardens." In any of these settings, the outside of the building is often decorated with long strings of white lights.

When the musicians arrive at the party, they slowly set up their instruments and their simple microphones and modifiers on the stage. The hosts provide them with a charcoal brazier full of hot coals that is set beside the drummers' chairs. The drummers hold the faces of their instruments over the coals to tighten the skins, turning each drumhead in their hands and tapping its surface gently to test the pitch and to gauge the tautness. As each drum (*ṭār*) is heated, its skin tightens, raising its pitch and also increasing its volume to a powerful, resonant sound.

The *'ūd* player, who is often also the singer, tunes her instrument slowly, playing short improvised phrases as she moves from string to string. She also tests her microphones—there are two, one for the voice and the second for the *'ūd*—and makes sure that all the percussionists and the other singers are ready to begin; then she opens with a quiet *mawwāl* 'vocal improvisation', while strumming her *'ūd* and adding simple embellishments on it between her sung phrases. When a singer is very popular or accomplished, the audience reacts immediately to her improvisations, clapping and cheering after each phrase. But when the performers are just an average local band, the audience will show little appreciation, or even awareness, until the whole *firqa* begins to play.

Finally, as the *muṭriba* begins the actual melody of the first folk song, the drummers join in tentatively, taking a few measures until the entire complement of drums has begun to play. This process gradually reveals the many layers of rhythmic texture. Starting at the low pitches with the *darbukka*, the frame drums fill in the medium range. One particularly good drummer plays a small *tār* with a higher tone, which she strikes to accent the syncopation. The multilayered quality of the percussion section and the syncopated beats the percussionists play have a hypnotic effect on the listeners. (Figure 3 shows one favorite rhythmic pattern, called *sa'ūdī* or *khalījī*; figure 4 shows another popular rhythm, with layers of syncopated lines added by high-pitched *tārs* and by clapping.) Gradually the tempo of the song picks up. The audience joins in with singing, clapping, and *zaghārīt* 'ululation'. Each song lasts ten or fifteen minutes.

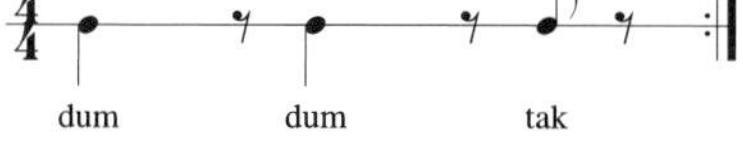

FIGURE 3 *Sa'udī* or *khalījī*.

Women's songs

Women musicians play popular tunes from all over the Arab world as well as traditional Arabian women's songs passed down through the generations. The traditional songs

FIGURE 4 Rhythm with syncopated lines.

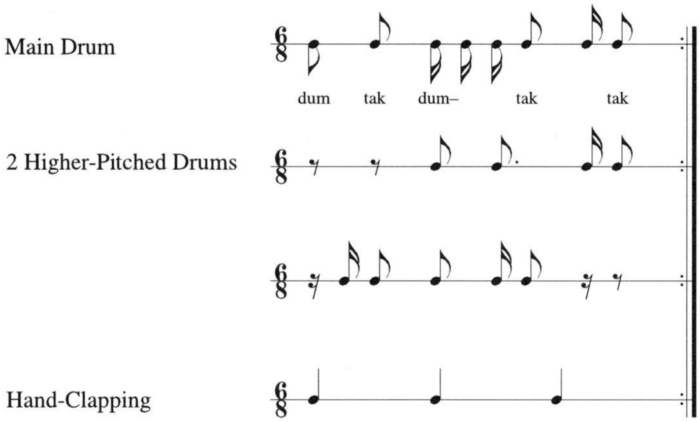

are little known outside the Arabian Peninsula, although there are similar women's folk music traditions in many parts of the Arab world.

The lyrics of traditional songs focus on love in all its details and permutations. In addition, there are many songs about weddings and marriage; one example, often performed in Saudi Arabia, is *Yā layla dāna* 'O Night, O Black Pearl' (figure 5), a song extolling the joys of the wedding night.

Each region has traditional songs for such occasions. In the United Arab Emirates, for example, *al-murāda* is a traditional style of song and dance performed by two lines of women who sing the praises of their tribe's leaders and its beautiful women.

FIGURE 5 *Yā layla dāna*, a traditional women's wedding song of the Gulf. In the refrain, *dāna* is a word for a large Gulf pearl; it is also used—and so is *layla*—as a filler in lines like this. In verse 2, *laylat al-farḥ* 'night of joy' is sometimes sung instead of *laylat al-'urs* 'wedding night'. (Translation by Abla Shocair and Kay Hardy Campbell.)

Refrain:

Yā layla dāna	O night, O black pearl
Yā layla dāna	O night, O black pearl
Yā layla dāna dān	O night, O black pearl
Yā layla dāna	O night, O black pearl!

Verse 1:

Nawwrī 'alaynā	Shine on us,
Nawwrī yā zayna	Shine, O beauty.
Yā shama 'atan bil-bayt	You are the candle in the house.
Intī illī fīnā	You are shining among us.

Refrain.

Verse 2:

Laylat al-'urs, hiyya layla fi-'umr	The wedding night is the night of your life.
Laylat al-'urs fīhā al-hana wa-al surūr	The wedding night is filled with happiness.
Laylat al-'urs, hiyya layla fi-'umr	The wedding night is the night of your life.
Laylat al-'urs fīhā al-hana wa-al surūr	The wedding night is filled with happiness.

Refrain.

Verse 3:

Haggich 'alaynā	Blame us if you are unhappy,
Haggich 'alaynā	Blame us if you are unhappy.
Yā ahlá al-bunayyāt	You, the loveliest and most innocent girl,
Haggich 'alaynā	Blame us if you are unhappy.

Refrain.

In women's songs, the melody line is simple and is repeated throughout a song. The only embellishment to the melody is the *muṭriba*'s subtle vocal ornamentation with tremolos and grace notes. Usually, a song remains within one melodic mode, or *maqām*; its melody is confined to a five-tone subset (*jins*) of the *maqām*, with small intervals between notes. Each song takes the form of several verses and a refrain interspersed with instrumental breaks. The soloist sings the refrain and verses; the chorus echoes the refrain. Although the rhythms do not shift, the drummers experiment with syncopation; this results in a deep rhythmic texture under the simple melody line. During the musical interludes between verses, the *muṭriba* might perform a rhythmic *taqsīm* on the *'ūd* before letting the drummers explore the potential syncopations in the rhythmic structure. It is no wonder that many lively dance forms have evolved to accompany this music [see DANCE IN THE ARABIAN PENINSULA].

Many of the traditional songs heard at performances by women's groups come from bedouin ancestral traditions. As with all folk music of the Arabian Peninsula, echoes of African and Indian music also find their way into these songs, in the use of certain intervals, lyrics, and rhythms which may have originated in the neighboring continents. Yet the combination of these qualities and instrumentation within the Arabian social context makes the sound of an Arabian women's orchestra distinct.

Between songs, the drummers tap their drumskins over the charcoal, and the *'ūd* player retunes her instrument, since it can slip out of tune easily by the end of each song. Sometimes the musicians take time to drink a cup of tea. In this relaxed atmosphere the women partygoers enjoy their reunion with family and friends and sit back in anticipation of the building excitement. Each song seems to be livelier than the preceding one; finally, the music beckons the women to perform their traditional dances and everyone, including the grandmothers, to sing along with favorite tunes. The high point of the evening is reached after midnight, when the bride and groom arrive at the party and are entertained by music and dance. Historically, the women's orchestra accompanied the bridal couple to their bridal chamber and serenaded them just outside the door until the dawn prayer. It is this stage of the evening—the *zaffa*, or *dazza*—that forms the core of the women's wedding music tradition.

THE ROLE OF WOMEN'S PATRONAGE

In the United Arab Emirates, Bahrain, and Kuwait, women's groups are featured on radio and television. Thus their fame and reputation has spread through this modern means as well as through a more open tradition of mixed-gender performance. But in areas where women's music is not broadcast—for example, in Saudi Arabia—patronage by other women is crucial if a singer and her group are to widen their audience. This reliance on women patrons is reminiscent of the early years of Islam, when aristocratic women of the Ḥijāz, such as Sukayna Bint al-Ḥusayn and 'Ā'isha Bint Ṭalḥa, were generous patrons of their favorite singers and poets. The tradition continues today.

Modern Saudi women's ensembles gain fame through referrals and through support from prominent women patrons, who hire them for highly visible performances within the female social realm: for example, at benefits for charities. It is through such endorsements and referrals that Saudi women musicians begin to travel more widely around the country, attract a larger audience, and become famous. The ease of jet travel throughout the region has made it possible for very popular women's groups to cover an entire country on a regular basis.

GOVERNMENT SUPPORT

Governments throughout the Arabian Peninsula support the preservation of folk art, including music. They have established music institutes to foster the study of music and folklore, and many of these institutions welcome women students. Although most of the institutes are less than twenty years old and therefore have little history of training women, they have the potential to raise the level of women's musicianship in the future.

In addition, governments sponsor folk music and dance groups as official representatives at regional and international festivals of folk art. Thus women musicians from Kuwait, Bahrain, Qatar, and the United Arab Emirates can participate in regional performances, gaining exposure to the arts of their counterparts in other countries. In Saudi Arabia, women's music is still sheltered from the public eye, and women do not participate in music institutes or folklore centers, nor are they part of the national folkloric groups that tour internationally. However, the organizers of the annual Saudi folk arts festival *Janādiriyya* do set aside specific days when women may attend. On those days, Saudi women sponsor and organize a full program of cultural events, including the folk arts. Although this practice reinforces the tradition of keeping women's folk arts separate, it also allows women to to be celebrated in a prominent national venue.

WORLD MUSIC AND MODERN TECHNOLOGY

The arrival of electronic music technology in the Gulf region has helped traditional women's music to survive and flourish. Cassette and compact disk recordings of women's music are circulated among women, making it possible for them to listen to their folk tunes whenever they want. Even in Saudi Arabia, some families have women's wedding parties recorded by local studios, which then sell the tapes so that local residents can hear the latest wedding music performed by the most popular bands. Radio and television are bringing women's folklore traditions to a wider audience in most Gulf countries—including Saudi Arabia, where broadcasts from the Gulf region can be received.

As noted above, because of its unique instrumentation and its important social role, Arabian women's folk music is not very susceptible to Western musical trends. Even when women's groups play pan-Arab pop tunes, and when they are joined by violinists and electronic keyboard players, these new influences are filtered through tradition—the drums and the singing style—and thus take on the rich folkloric sound of the Gulf region. Women's music also remains somewhat apart, and resistant to foreign musical influences, because it continues to be performed for live audiences in traditional settings. A wedding requires at least one evening of traditional women's music, with many *ṭārāt* and much singing; even the most modern families are proud of this music and still include it in their weddings, and this helps ensure the survival of women's wedding song as a genre. The distinctive sound of Arabian women's folk bands—simple melodies overlaying rich syncopation—combined with its role in marking rites of passage and the continued support it receives from women patrons will help it survive as a distinct musical form and performance tradition.

REFERENCES

al-Bustānī, Karam. 1964. *Al-nisā' al-'arabiyyāt*. Beirut: Dār Ṣādir.

Campbell, Kay Hardy. 1979. "Arabian Wedding Nights." *Arab News* (1 August).

———. 1985. "Saudi Arabian Women's Music." *Ḥabībī* 9(3).

———. 1977. "The Lives and Literary Patronage of 'Āisha Bint Ṭalḥah Ibn'Ubayd Allāh and Sukayna Bint al-Ḥusayn Ibn 'Alī in *Kitāb al-aghānī*." Undergraduate honors thesis, University of Minnesota.

Gavin, Carney. 1985. "The Earliest Arabian Recordings: Discoveries and Work Ahead." *Phonographic Bulletin* 43:38–45.

Ibn Mājah. 1952. *Sunan Ibn Mājah*. Cairo: 'Īsā al-Bābī al-Ḥalabī.

al-Iṣbahānī, Abū al-Faraj Ibn Ḥusayn. 1927–1974. *Kitāb al-aghānī* (Book of Songs). Cairo: Dār al-Kutub.

Jargy, Simon. 1994. *A Musical Anthology of the Arabian Peninsula*. Vol. 4, *Women's Songs*. Geneva: Archives Internationales de Musique Populaire. (VDE CD-783.)

Dance in the Arabian Peninsula

Najwa Adra

General Characteristics of Dance in the Peninsula
Classification of Dances
Dance as a Social Issue

Because much of the Arabian Peninsula is covered by desert, most people live along the coasts and in the fertile mountains of Yemen, Oman, and the Hijaz in Saudi Arabia. Economically, the population can be divided into coastal fishing communities, farming communities, and nomadic herders. Although folklore polarizes the nomadic and settled populations, historically they have depended on each other economically and culturally. Besides supplying the sedentary populations with livestock products, the nomadic populations traditionally provided military protection as well. Their self-reliance, courage, strength, and generosity were admired by the urban population, and both segments valued what was defined as a tribal code of honor.

The mountains of Yemen, which extend into Asir in southwestern Saudi Arabia, are very fertile and extensively cultivated with small, individually owned terraces. Here, the population is predominantly sedentary, although it defines itself as tribal and shares in the tribal honor code. The combination of rivalry and mutual dependence between urban and rural populations that is traditional in the communities farther north is also found here. Along the eastern coasts that border the Arabian Gulf, the majority of the population was traditionally engaged in pearl diving, fishing, and overseas trade. The development of cultured pearls in the 1930s and the discovery of major oil reserves on the coasts and offshore put an end to these activities.

In the past, immigrants into the region came largely from the east coast of Africa, the Indian subcontinent, and Iran. These immigrant communities date back centuries and have had an important influence on the dance and music traditions of the region.

GENERAL CHARACTERISTICS OF DANCE IN THE PENINSULA

Dancing has long been considered indispensable at Arabian weddings and other social celebrations. Dancing forms part of religious and national holidays, harvest celebrations in agricultural areas, and rituals connected with fishing and, in the past, with pearling. Small social gatherings of friends and family often include some dancing. Each district, and sometimes each village, has its own dances, and there are more than a hundred named dances in the region. These constitute an important folk tradition in which people dance for pleasure. Professional dancers, recruited from low-status social groups, may be hired to perform at weddings and other celebrations.

FIGURES 1 AND 2 Men performining *al-shabwānī* in a wedding procession in Hadramawt, Yemen, 1991. Photo by Daniel Varisco, 1991.

Dancing is most commonly referred to in Arabic as *raqṣ*, a generic term that denotes dancing for entertainment. It is also called *ghinā'* 'song' or *lu'b* 'play'. Particular genres of dance may be named after the genre of poetry that they accompany, their meter, or the major musical instrument used.

Dances may be performed outdoors or indoors, depending on the dance and the occasion. A public square, a threshing floor, or any open area may be considered a suitable space for outdoor dancing. At weddings and other festive events, dancing is most frequently performed in large reception rooms in private houses or in enclosed garden or patio areas. A large room or patio may be filled with guests seated on mattresses or carpets on the floor, with a space kept clear in the middle or at one end for dancing. Dancing may also take place in smaller rooms where family members and close friends congregate in the evenings. At weddings, dancing is also part of the processions (figures 1 and 2). During national holidays, choreographed dances are sometimes performed on a proscenium stage in large public halls. Both folkdancing and choreographed dancing are often shown on local television. With the possible exception of televised productions and staged performances, the audience actively supports the dancers by ululating, sounding out the rhythm, clapping, or expressing loud praise. However, the audience is not expected to concentrate totally on the dancing. Members of the audience may talk among themselves or walk around during any particular dance.

Gender

Although a few genres of dance are specifically identified as "men's" or "women's," most dances in the Arabian Peninsula are performed by men and women. At large festive gatherings, separate spaces are usually reserved for men and women. Women dance together for female audiences while men dance together for male audiences. Even in these gender-segregated contexts, however, female professional dancers may perform for women or men. Whether a dance is segregated or mixed depends on the particular dance, the context of performance, and local attitudes. In general, urban social settings are more likely than rural settings to be gender-segregated. Dances are also likely to be gender-segregated in religiously conservative communities and families. In some contexts women perform unveiled, with their hair loose; in others they are fully veiled. This also may vary with the dance, the community, and individual whim. Many women in the peninsula cover their hair and sometimes parts of the face when they appear in public. The practice of veiling may range from a towel quickly thrown over the head to an elaborate scarf or mask. Veiling is an expression of modesty;

but because it focuses attention on the eyes, it is also considered beautiful and seductive.

Line dances

In the Arabian Peninsula, most dancing involve lines of dancers that define the performance space. Parallel lines are common, but sometimes the dancers are arranged in a square, horseshoe, or circle. Shoulders touching, dancers may sway to the music, step sideways or backward and forward, move toward each other and away from each other, or turn in unison. They may brandish weapons, clap, or play drums or tambourines. The dancers in a line usually perform in a standing position, but in some dances of fishing and pearling communities in the Gulf and on the southern coasts, they perform kneeling or sitting as they might on board a boat or ship. Line dancers are usually judged on their coordination with each other. When a dance event also includes poets or solo or couple dancers, their performance space is delimited by the line dancers, who also support them by singing or maintaining the beat.

Improvisation

As in other parts of the Middle East, this dance tradition is characterized by improvisation. Consequently, there is a wide variety of steps and movements. Elements of dance that are shared in the peninsula region include running steps, step-hops, step-together-step-hops, and step-together-step-steps, with the last step or hop often initiating a turn. Dancers may propel themselves forward and up by pressing down on the ball of one foot (samba-fashion), as is commonly done in other Arab dancing. Shifts of level, such as knee bends, leaps, and straight vertical jumping on flat feet, are common. Variations of the grapevine (a pattern in which one foot steps sideways while the other alternates stepping forward and back) are typical of Yemeni dancing, as is shaping a space with one's steps. In all parts of the peninsula, when line dancers move forward, they may do so with a scooping movement of the arms and torso.

Women commonly swing the head and loose tresses while holding the right hand lightly on the upper chest. This movement is called *na'ash, tanawush, nuwwāsh* (in Yemen), or *rishī* (in parts of southern Yemen) and is similar to the *danse des cheveux*, described by French travelers in North Africa. In Saudi Arabia and the Gulf countries, it is usually performed by young girls, although in the Yemeni highlands it is more often performed by older women to imply suffering. A woman may go into *nuwwāsh* at the end of a dance, moving out of the dance space and into the audience area. As she passes women in the audience, they ululate or verbally express their support and empathy.

The dancing of seafaring communities is characterized by large arm movements that mimic rowing. The line dancers often perform in a kneeling position. With the arm leading, the upper torso is propelled forward to the floor; then it is raised to an upright position, with the back straight; then it moves forward and down again.

Poetry

In most cases, dancing accompanies sung or chanted poetry, and the lyrics are an important element of the performance. Some of these dances involve responsorial poetry, and some, like the Yemeni *bālah* or the Saudi *mzayyan,* include poetic competition. In a competition, one poet improvises a verse to a set rhyme or meter; then, using the same structure, another poet tries to improvise a better verse. Poets who create the best or wittiest verses gain social esteem.

Musical instruments

Musical instruments associated with dancing include the *'ūd* 'lute' in towns and cities and wind instruments—such as the *mizmār* 'single- or double-reed pipe' and the *surnāy* 'flute'—in rural areas. The *ṭanbūra* 'bowl lyre' lends its name to a number of dances performed in the Gulf countries. When such instrumentalists are involved in a dance event, the dancers give them small gifts of money at the conclusion of the performance.

A number of dance genres are accompanied by drumming alone or by drumming and rhythmic hand clapping. Clapping along with drums, in double time or in polyrhythms, produces an effect that has been likened to the sound of castanets. Rhythmic foot stamping marks time in some dances. Frequently, objects that jingle with the movements of the dancers are worn to intensify the percussive effects; examples include ankle bracelets and small metal bells worn on the dancers' belts. In healing dances (*zār*) along the coasts, dancers tie goats' hooves to their belts for this purpose.

Clothing and accessories

Typically, performers wear their best clothing (except in devotional dancing, as noted below). Dancers often hold daggers, swords, or bamboo poles that they wave while dancing.

CLASSIFICATION OF DANCES

Dances of the Arabian Peninsula are classified locally as exhibition dances, dances related to work, dances purely for entertainment, *zār* 'healing dances', and dances performed during mystical (*ṣūfī*) rituals. A few are described in this section. Each of these dances has a number of variations, involving differences in movements and steps, musical and percussive accompaniment, the presence or absence of poetry, and the identity of the performers. Whereas one dance may be performed in mixed groups in a certain community or at a particular time, it may be performed only by men or by women in another context. Sometimes, also, a particular social group may be associated with a dance.

Exhibition dances

Some of the most highly esteemed dances in the Arabian Peninsula are exhibition dances performed by men only. These dances are often associated with warfare. In the past, some were performed in conjunction with raiding, or with agreements establishing peace between warring groups. When poetry is included, its subjects are valor, heroism, and chivalry. These dances are performed on religious and national holidays as well as at weddings and on other festive occasions. In the Hadramaut of southern Yemen, men traditionally celebrated an ibex hunt with dancing.

For both performers and spectators, exhibition dances represent the chivalry, strength, and courage associated with Arab tribes. These dances are a source of pride, whereas many other dances of the region are derided as frivolous. Even heads of state openly participate in exhibition dances with no loss of prestige. What is admired most is the cohesion and interconnectedness of the performers: these dances manifest a sense of social solidarity.

Allowing for regional variations, the exhibition dances of the peninsula can be loosely divided into *al-'arḍa*, performed in Saudi Arabia and the Gulf countries, and the Yemeni *bara'*. The term *al-'arḍa* is derived from a verb meaning to present, exhibit, or expose and also connotes width and expansion, which is metaphorically represented by the long lines of men facing in the same direction as they dance. The term *bara'* connotes skill or excellence.

Al-'arḍa

Al-'arḍa is also known as *razīf* or *galaṭa* in Saudi Arabia; *al-'arḍa al-ḥarbiyya* 'war *'arḍa*' in Kuwait, Bahrain, and Qatar; *al-'ayyāla* in the United Arab Emirates; and *al-razha* in Oman. Most commonly, this dance involves two lines of men, touching shoulders, who chant responsorial poetry while carrying swords, rifles, or thin bamboo canes. The dancers step gracefully and lightly sideways or backward and forward to the beat of the drum while waving their swords or sticks. In Oman, the two lines approach each other slowly and bow low before retreating.

A few dancers at a time leave the line to improvise duets or solos. This improvisation is more expressive than the line dance and often includes shimmying the shoulders and torso. When the dance is well under way, young girls enter the space between the lines, swinging the hair, head, shoulders, and upper torso in *na'ash*. In some cases, a man holding a sword or pole will dance facing a girl, matching his arm movements to her swinging.

The poetry of *al-'arḍa* consists of traditional verses that were once used to goad men into participating in raiding forays. These verses address tribal honor and its ideals and eulogize heroes and courageous women of the tribe. A lead poet dictates a verse or hemistich to one line of dancers, who repeat the verse. He listens to and encourages the recitation, much like a conductor of a chorus, then moves to the other line of dancers. The fervor of this poetry is said to intensify the dancers' emotion.

Al-'arḍa is performed during religious and national holidays. Class and other status distinctions are erased in this dance, for political leaders perform alongside the poorest members of the population. While performing, the dancers leave off their outer cloaks, which indicate their status or relative wealth. Large, public dances are advertised in newspapers; smaller groups perform at weddings and other family celebrations.

FIGURE 3 Men performing *bara'* in al-Maḥjar, al-Ahjur, Yemen. One of the two drummers can be seen on the left. Photo by Daniel Varisco, 1979.

Bara'

Bara' (figures 3 and 4) is the signature dance of the highland Yemeni tribes, and each tribal region is associated with a particular beat, style of dancing, and steps. Like *al-'arḍa*, *bara'* represents chivalry and tribal honor.

Bara' is a lively dance performed to drums and sometimes to the chanting of tribal poetry. It involves anywhere from two to a hundred dancers in a circle. Dancers step-hop or move in grapevine fashion to the right and left; they close in to the middle with a flourish, scooping the space before them, then turn back to their original places. Dancers hold daggers, which they wave above their heads. As in *al-'arḍa*, the steps are not complicated, but coordination with the other performers and with the music takes considerable skill. Also like *al-'arḍa*, this is an egalitarian dance in which dignitaries and heads of state participate.

Work-related dances

Seafaring

A number of dances in the Arabian Peninsula were traditionally related to subsistence activities. Perhaps the most dramatic were the sea dances of pearling and merchant boats and ships, performed nowadays purely as entertainment. Some sea dances have

FIGURE 4 Men learning a new *bara'*. The drummers are seen on the right. Knives are held in the right hand; a shawl is held in the left. Photo by Daniel Varisco, 1979.

Every phase of the pearling process was associated with a genre of poetry, and most phases were also occasions for dancing.

the same names as land dances but differ in movements and poetry; most sea dances are variations on the dancing already described. The songs for these dances are almost always mournful, and the dances are slow and emotive. Most involve a solo dancer and a chorus of men, kneeling on the ground and making large circular movements with their arms in imitation of rowing. These arm movements lead the upper body forward, up, and sideways.

Every phase of the pearling process was associated with a genre of poetry, and most phases were also occasions for dancing. At the beginning of each pearling season, it took three to four days for the boats to be readied for the sea. During these days, a dance called *al-sinkinī* was performed to mournful poetry. This dance was accompanied by hand clapping and the *ṣurnāy*, a reed instrument. On board their boats, pearl divers would dance variations of the *fijīrī* in the evenings. Dancers kneeling in a line strike the floor rhythmically with their hands. Then, with elaborate hand and arm movements, they come up to a sitting position. After some time, they repeat the process, again lowering the upper body and striking the floor with their hands. Meanwhile, a soloist may stand and improvise; sometimes he dances while holding the anchor. Pulling up anchor also occasioned dancing. When the pearling vessels were ready to return to shore, a dance called *al-ʿarḍa al-baḥriyya* 'the sea *ʿarḍa*' was performed. They would meet in a designated area to await the arrival of the prince's vessel, then celebrate for two or three days. Two lines of men chanted poetry while lines of drummers stood behind them and sword carriers stood behind the drummers. Local leaders *(shaykhs)* and sometimes the prince himself would participate in a sea *ʿarḍa*.

Large merchant ships, which had more space and afforded more leisure time, would sometimes take along a professional singer and master of ceremonies *(nahām)* who would organize nightly music and dancing events.

Agriculture

In Bahrain, farm workers thresh wheat using rhythmic work-related movements that are locally classified as agricultural dances. Men, carrying a palm frond in the right hand, circle a large pile of wheat. To a musical rhythm, they take turns beating the wheat until it is all threshed. The process of cracking wheat to make a special dish, *harīsa*, is an occasion for another of these dances in Bahrain and Qatar. The wheat is placed in a long wooden container and crushed by being pounded with a large, heavy stick. Dancers—men and women—take turns rhythmically pounding the wheat while moving their bodies backward and forward. Lightly stepping on sorghum seeds in the process of sowing constitutes a dance in the northern highlands of Yemen. The evenings after harvests also provide an occasion for dancing in parts of the Arabian Peninsula.

Entertainment dances

The vast majority of dances in this region—only a few of which can be described here—are performed purely for entertainment.

The traditional dance of Ṣan'ā', the capital of Yemen, and its surrounding communities is a couple dance called *dasa'*. The two dancers perform three parts, each part characterized by a slightly faster beat than the preceding one. In the first part, the dancers, side by side, outline a square on the floor through a series of weight shifts punctuated by small, quick circles drawn by the left foot, held slightly above floor level. Dancers, remaining side by side, may turn and perform with their backs to the seated audience. (By the 1980s, the more accomplished performers were omitting this first part of the dance, considering it to be too slow.) The second part has a faster beat and more complicated footwork. Again, a square is outlined on the floor, but now this is done with considerably more flourish and with faster turns, and the orientation of the body remains forward. A good dancer barely touches the floor during this second segment. The last part is also fast, but the step is a simple sideways weight shift. When two men perform *dasa'*, they face each other and move around each other instead of dancing side by side. They hold daggers in their right hands and hold each other's left hand. Some men also shimmy the upper body.

This dance is usually performed in gender-segregated contexts but may be performed by a man and a woman in the intimacy of the home. In both women's and men's dancing, partners are chosen from close friends and relatives. The dance accompanies sung poetry and *'ūd* music in towns and cities, and *mizmār* in rural areas. [See Sung Poetry in the Arabian Peninsula and *Al-ghinā' al-ṣan'ānī*: Poetry and Music in Ṣan'ā'].

The dancing performed to *ṣawt*, a genre of music that has become popular in Kuwait, Bahrain, and Qatar, is reminiscent of the *dasa'* of San'ā' in its rhythm, forward focus, and weight shifts.

Sharḥ, a dance from southern Yemen, currently competes with *dasa'* in popularity. Also a couple dance, it is more expansive and more flowing than *dasa'*. The dancers begin at opposite ends of the performance space and appear to glide toward and then past each other, turning 180 degrees when they reach the far end of the space. They step forward with one foot, then press downward on the ball of the other foot (again, as in the samba) to propel themselves up and forward before stamping the forward foot lightly; then they repeat this step starting on the other foot. Their hips and shoulders may sway with the movement. This dance is fast and light. Depending on the context and the community, it may be performed by a man and woman, two men, or two women. In one variation, a man leads a woman by the hand in and around a space formed by a curved line of men. The men in the line take turns dancing with her.

Several dances accompany a genre of poetry known as *al-sāmirī*. In Saudi Arabia, two lines of kneeling men face each other. A poet stands between them and dictates verses, which are then repeated by each line in turn, much in the manner of *al-'arḍa*, although the poetry used is of a different genre. In *al-sāmirī*, poet and drummers remain in their lines. The lines of dancers move their backs in undulating movements. In *sāmir*, also called *masāmir*, two or three veiled women dance between two lines of men. The songs, composed extemporaneously, praise the beauty and artistry of dancers. Dancers may teasingly snatch an article of clothing from the lines of men, to be redeemed with a token gift.

In Saudi Arabia and Yemen, the mother of the bride or the groom dances with a tray on her head. On the tray are lit candles, arranged in a circle around incense, spices, flowers, and eggs. It is considered bad luck if the candles do not remain lit for the duration of the dance.

An appealing traditional dance performed by women in coastal towns along the Gulf is the *farīsa* 'hobbyhorse dance'. The chorus is made up of a circle of women playing tambourines. A dancer wearing a cardboard "horse" performs in the middle of this circle. Sometimes another dancer, dressed as a man, leads the "horse" around.

Al-murādā is performed by women in Qatar and Bahrain. In this dance, no musical or percussive instruments are used; the beat is maintained by fast stamping. Two lines of women stand shoulder to shoulder and hand in hand. The two lines alternate singing, while the women lift a foot to step forward and back. After two or three verses, the first line moves forward to meet the second, then retreats while the second line comes to meet it.

Dances imported to the peninsula by immigrant communities include *al-līwa*, a genre performed on the Red Sea coast as well as in the Gulf countries. This dance, which consists of a slow walk in an open circle, has no leaps or deep knee bends. The dancers step forward with a slight turn, step back, and sometimes execute a complete turn. *Al-līwa* dances, performed by men and women to pentatonic music, are emotive. The songs speak of separation and sorrow, and the musical instruments are the *ṣurnāy* and drums. Some of the lyrics contain Swahili expressions, indicating an East African origin.

Another import is *al-hubbān*, which is performed in Kuwait and the United Arab Emirates by Iranian immigrants. This dance is named after the bagpipe, its signature instrument, and is so popular that professional groups are hired to perform it at weddings and other celebrations. A line of women faces a line of men, with a large number of musicians in the middle. Men begin the dance by singing (the women in this dance do not sing). The *hubbān* follows the singers, playing the melody associated with the song, and then the drumming begins. The movement begins with the line of men retreating two steps while the line of women advances two steps. Then the women retreat while the men advance. This pattern is repeated for the duration of the song. The lines then take two steps sideways. The player of the largest drum begins to dance between the two lines. After this, a woman holding handkerchiefs in her hands goes into the middle and begins to twirl. A man joins her, moving with bent knees, shifting his weight forward and back while pressing on his insteps.

New dances are continually being added to individual repertoires. Those who are exposed to Western dances or Egyptian belly dancing through television or travel often teach these dances to their friends. Thus contemporary urban celebrations may include the latest Western popular dances as well as traditional dances.

Dancing at healing ceremonies, *zār*

Zār is a healing ceremony intended to exorcise *jinn* (spirits) from people who are believed to be possessed. *Zār* dancing frequently ends in a trance. Variations of *zār* are widespread throughout the region. In Saudi Arabia, *zār* dancing is linked with *sāmirī* poetry. On the Gulf, this dancing is named after the *ṭanbūra* or *nūbān* 'bowl lyre' because of the importance of this instrument to it. There are a number of variations, some of which are performed only at healing ceremonies whereas others may also be performed at celebrations. A defining characteristic of *ṭanbūra* is that (as noted above) the dancers wear belts hung with goats' hooves, which rattle when they stamp their feet.

Religious dancing

Devotional dancing, when combined with praise of God and the ritualistic repetition of the names of God, is thought to lead to inner harmony and oneness with God. It is performed during Sufi mystic rituals. On these occasions (in contrast with occasions when dancing is performed for entertainment), the clothing worn is plain and simple. Devotional dances vary according to the Sufi order. Movements may involve a simple swaying back and forth, small sideways steps, or shimmying and leaping. Leaps may be accompanied by sensational feats such as piercing the body with a sword or some other sharp object. If no blood flows or if the wound heals quickly during the ceremony itself, that is taken as a sign of the devotee's deep faith. Religious orthodoxy frowns on Sufi rituals, and they have declined or gone underground in recent years because of increased religious conservatism in this region.

DANCE AS A SOCIAL ISSUE

Traditions related to dancing in the Arabian Peninsula are relatively unknown in the West, for a number of reasons. For one thing, the peninsula—unlike Southeast Asia or Europe—has no established tradition of classical theater that would have interested early historians of dance. Second, belly dancing, which has captured the imagination of people in Europe and the United States, was not traditionally performed in the peninsula. Third, most dancing in the penisula is informal entertainment and takes place in or near the home and at traditional evening celebrations, which foreign visitors are not likely to attend. Fourth, in some parts of the peninsula dancing is important at festivals associated with visits to saints' shrines, and such visits are not widely publicized, because religious leaders tend to disapprove of them. Finally, Arab scholars rarely write about dancing, which is considered secondary to poetry and music and indeed is often regarded as frivolous play unworthy of scholarly attention. When Arabic treatises on science, mathematics, and medicine were translated into European languages, there were no comparable works on dancing.

Prohibitions against dancing are a significant social issue. In the late 1940s, for example, *lu'b* dancing was banned by the ruling imamate of North Yemen, ostensibly for religious reasons but most likely because some of the poetry sung at dance events was critical of the imamate. The ban did not stop dancing: a small *'ūd* was developed that could be carried unseen under loose clothing; people stuffed their windows with cushions to muffle the sound of music or danced in windowless storage rooms that had been transformed into reception rooms; and the ban was not enforceable in rural areas. Ironically, Imam Ahmad, who ruled North Yemen from 1948 to 1967 and maintained the official ban, is rumored to have been an excellent dancer, and fond of *lu'b*. Nevertheless, as a consequence of this ban, a number of musicians left San'ā'to form music schools in the southern Yemeni towns of Hadramaut and Aden.

In the recent past, negative influences on dance have included a spreading religious conservatism that disapproves of dancing, especially mixed-gender dancing. This ties into a larger debate on the legality of dancing in Islam. Some religious scholars argue that dance, like music, can excite the emotions and lead people to improper behavior. Others believe that dancing in itself is permitted. In practice, one finds a range of interpretations, with most families in the region permitting dancing in prescribed contexts.

Political and economic changes have resulted in a decline of some dance traditions. Television has also influenced practices. On the one hand, watching television means that people have less time available for dance: instead of dancing during afternoon and evening visits, people are now likely watch televised serials. On the other hand, choreographed versions of traditional dances are often presented on television as "folk" dances. In some cases, such presentations have expanded dance repertoires by enabling people to learn and perform dances of other communities. In the final analysis, dancing in the Arabian Peninsula remains alive and well.

REFERENCES

Adra, Najwa. 1982. "Qabyala: The Tribal Concept in the Central Highlands of the Yemen Arab Republic." Ph.D. dissertation, Temple University.

———. 1993. "Tribal Dancing and Yemeni Nationalism: Steps to Unity." *Revue du Monde Musulman et de la Méditerranée* 67(l):161–168.

———. 1998. "Dance and Glance: Visualizing Tribal Identity in Highland Yemen." *Visual Anthropology* 11(1–2):55–101.

al-'Ardāwī, 'Ādil. 1978. "*Lamaḥāt fī aghānī wa raqṣāt al-ṣayd fī 'l-Khalīj*" (Observations on Fishing Songs and Dances in the Gulf). *Al-turāth al-sha'bī* 9(7):125–138.

al-Khalīfī, 'Ā'isha. 1986. "*Al-murādā: raqṣat al-nisā' fi'l-Khalīj al-'Arabī*" (*al-murādā*: A Women's Dance in the Arabian Gulf). *Al-Ma'thurāt al-sha'biyya* 1(3):105–129.

Rihani, Amin. 1930. "The Dance." In *Around the Coasts of Arabia*. Boston: Houghton Mifflin.

al-Sāmirī, 'Abd al-Jabbār. 1978. "*Maṣādir wa marāji' fī fūlklūr al-Khalīj al-'Arabī wa 'l-Jazīra: al-raqṣ al-sha'bī*" (Sources and References in the Folklore of the Arabian Gulf and the Peninsula: Folk Dance). *Al-Turath al-sha'bī* 9(7):268–270.

al-Shukrī, Ibrāhīm. 1978. *al-Raqṣāt al-sha'biyya al-kuwaytiyya: dirāsa fanniyya* (Kuwaiti Folk Dances: A Technical Study). Kuwait: I. al-Shukrī.

Music Making among Western Expatriates in the Arabian Peninsula

Ruth M. Stone

Music as Public Counterpoint
Recorded Music
Music Lessons
Holiday Music Making

Americans, Europeans, South and East Asians, Africans, Latin Americans, Australians, and others—people of more than fifty nationalities—have left their own countries to work in the oil fields of the Arabian Peninsula. These "expatriates," as they call themselves, have developed a rich musical life that symbolically transports them home while also opening up new vistas for exploration. The groups actively reconstruct community through the performing arts. They re-create the arts of their home even as they draw inspiration from the people around them for new kinds of performances. The performance practices described here were observed by the author over more than fourteen years, but location and names of individuals have been omitted in deference to local sensitivity.

The American expatriates, with whom I worked mostly closely, created their music, particularly Western music, in concerts in homes, at school events, and during music lessons. They spent long hours practicing together, building community through music. Their music was performed in private settings with restricted access—not in public concert halls, for that was not permitted.

MUSIC AS PUBLIC COUNTERPOINT

During the course of my research, the Muslim call to prayer punctuated the flow of activity five times a day, when the faithful left their work or leisure to turn toward Mecca. As television stations took a "prayer intermission," all sound except for Muslim prayers ceased to be transmitted. These calls, amplified by loudspeakers, became part of the soundscape for the people working in this area.

In this context, surprising sounds subtly but powerfully countered the public sounds of prayer. At breakfast one morning, I heard a sound like a calliope. Stepping into a nearby alley, I discerned the tune "Santa Claus Is Coming to Town." There was a large dump truck, driven by a Filipino expatriate, backing up to a construction site. Whenever it moved in reverse, the truck played one of a variety of Christmas selections, including "We Wish You a Merry Christmas." So, in the middle of June, there was a gentle but insistent counterpoint.

The hearers of these sounds might receive them in very different ways, depending on their background knowledge and sensibilities. Many local residents would not know what was being performed. Others might know and might enjoy the music. Still others

The expatriates have developed a rich musical life that symbolically transports them home while also opening up new vistas for exploration.

might be offended if they were aware of the text. Some expatriates would feel a sense of solidarity with this clever presentation.

Performance in this rather unusual contact zone takes place in a social space where "disparate cultures meet, clash, and grapple with each other" (Pratt 1992:4). The asymmetrical relations derive from a situation in which local residents have money to buy Western expertise. The expatriates value the chance to earn better wages than they can in their home countries, even as they sometimes feel yoked to a kind of economic servitude.

RECORDED MUSIC

Expatriates in a place I'll call "Oilville" recorded, with their ubiquitous video cameras, all kinds of musical events within the community. Furthermore, at certain moments of high drama, such as massive layoffs, they made audio- and videotapes that circulated, underground, to a wide audience. In 1986, when many expatriates were given termination notices as oil prices plummeted, two enterprising men made a cassette on which they layered track on track of instrumental and vocal music. To the tune of "Surfin' USA" they sang:

> Everybody got their notice, it came just today.
> Seems we've all been surplused, we got thirty days.
> So we're packing the kids up, we're going home to stay.
> Everybody's been surplused, surplused USA.

The music circulated within a certain restricted group of people. Containment, defined through a series of symbolic or real walls, enclosed these people and their interactions in Oilville. These walls allowed the expatriates to enjoy freedom and to behave in ways that could not be presented to the public view. For the expatriates in Oilville, week after week, hearing and performing music became a way of achieving *communitas*, of developing a sense of "we." Ironically, this avenue to a sense of oneness was often the very medium that local authorities found objectionable and that they moved to forbid. Thus what was highly valued by the expatriates was restricted by the local authorities. This conflict played out in numerous ways as one group sought a valuable form of aesthetic expression and another attempted to suppress something it considered harmful.

People reported that they spent a great deal of time listening to music on cassette tapes or compact disks. One former resident of Oilville, whom I interviewed in her home in Santa Fe, New Mexico, several years after she had left the Arabian Peninsula, said that she had developed what she now considered a strange kind of spiritual relationship with several singers whose music had special meaning for her and to whom she felt close. She fantasized about her relationship with these singers, constructing a reality that she would not have experienced in Santa Fe.

In the local communities near Oilville, there were a great number of stores that sold tapes and compact disks. During the early 1980s many of the tapes were pirated copies that sold for about US$1.50 each, although by the mid-1990s attempts to curb piracy had limited the number of quickly duplicated tapes. Compact disks were less easily pirated, and most of those were legitimate copies.

Even these recordings—microcosms of home—were perceived as a threat by the local authorities. In the autumn of 1993, signs were posted in local music stores announcing that women were not allowed to enter. One could only surmise that because music was played in these stores, they were perceived as places where people might become sexually aroused, and that a woman, as the bearer and symbol of her family's honor, should not be present in such a setting.

MUSIC LESSONS

Musicians in Oilville fashioned and developed their artistic selves. Children as well as adults formed a relatively large group of aspiring artists. Extensive leisure time represented varied possibilities and new horizons for the invention and reinvention of performers. Budding pianists were among the most numerous of these developing artists. There were many piano teachers in Oilville, organized in the Oilville Piano Teachers' Guild, and they taught a veritable army of novices. As in many American communities, families with aspirations for their children turned to the piano for their initial musical training.

One measure of the willingness and ability of expatriate parents to invest in this musical training was the price charged for lessons. Teachers received between US$20 and $40 per hour; and of the expatriate women in the community, a hardworking piano teacher could earn one of the highest incomes. While a number of these teachers were highly trained, the professional qualifications of others were only meager.

The luster of studying piano extended beyond the immediate American and British communities. Other expatriate families, including Indians, as well as elite local families, sought to have their children receive lessons. One teacher reported teaching a range of children:

> Because my husband's nationality is not American, I became known as the piano teacher who took students other than American, which really was an asset. . . . They would come to me rather than go to somebody else because they felt like they said, that I would be more sympathetic to the problems of international students. But what happened, it was as much an experience for me, because I was able to develop an international teaching style, which was far beyond what an American teacher would have been able to develop just with American students. . . . Even the [West Asians] that I teach . . . their interest is learning Western music. (Stone 1992:211)

Two pupils in this teacher's studio illustrate the different motivations for studying music. The first, a girl of sixteen, came on Fridays for a lesson that would last an hour and a half. She played only Western art music and aspired to continue as a pianist and eventually teach. When she began, the girl had only a small Yamaha keyboard, but she loved it—and she wanted tapes of her teacher's Mozart and Beethoven works.

> After one year of working on this keyboard, her father said, "She won't stop, she keeps after me. She wants a piano. Will you sell me yours?" . . . And I thought, well, I'll get rid of it eventually. So I said, "I'll sell it to you for a certain price. And he said, "Fine." So now she has this piano. They have a three-floor house. She lives on the top floor. They carted that piano up three floors to her bedroom. She locks it up every night because she's got five brothers and sisters. She locks it, and she locks all her music. She has a box and she locks all her music in the box. (Stone 1992:211)

Another of this teacher's students represented a quite different approach to music.

> With [this student's parents] it was, "We have to teach our daughter Western music because we have to appear Western. We have to know those things Western. And it doesn't matter if she's not any good, it doesn't matter. We have the money. She has the time." (Stone 1992:211)

For the first girl, music was a consuming passion, and she did everything necessary to learn to play. For the second girl, music was a badge of westernization and the quality of the music was largely irrelevant.

Many children in the community took lessons in tap dance and modern dance. A recital, entitled "K's Dance Explosion," presented students in elaborate costumes; each dancer had several costumes for each performance. Personal appearance meant everything, and even the teacher—who came on stage to speak—wore an elaborate white sequined outfit. While the dances in the show were well rehearsed, the emphasis was evidently on the costumes.

The tap dance and jazz show, choreographed by a dancer who had been teaching in this area for more than ten years, also emphasized another theme—American patriotism. There were three performances, with about 300 people present at each. The versions were called "Red," "White," and "Blue" respectively and were all staged on a weekend close to the Fourth of July. The color scheme of the costumes and stage decorations followed the theme of red, white, and blue. But none of this precluded the presence of other nationalities, and the event attracted people who valued things Western in general or things American in particular. The audience also applauded a circumscribed display of sexuality: the youngest dancers, three-year-olds making their debut, danced to a song with the words, "I dance with my hands, I dance with my lips, I dance with my hips." In addition, some of the dances gave a nod to local aesthetics: the dancers overtly centered the movements on their hair and on swinging their hair. It was fascinating to watch high steppers in a line like the Rockettes, taking people "home" through patriotic symbols and American popular music, even as they reminded the audience of where they were and of local ideas.

These lessons in music and dance of the West were clearly vehicles to transport learners home. A piano or a dance costume can provided a concrete visual representation of the music of home and help to create it in ways that the expatriates consider authentic. The instruction that I encountered centered on the arts of the West, though some of the lessons focused on arts of expatriates from various other countries. Nowhere did I encounter a single young person being taught the arts of the Arabian peninsula.

The arts constituted a lucrative market in Oilville. People valued and were willing to pay well for instruction in the arts. The company that employed the expatriates had only limited positions available for women, and so music instruction of all sorts became a top-paying alternative form of work. As more and more women entered the scene, competition for positions as teachers sometimes became fierce. Moreover, success did not always depend solely on musical knowledge or experience. Entrepreneurship and community networking were critical aspects of developing a studio.

HOLIDAY MUSIC MAKING

The Christmas season, more than any other, evoked nostalgia for home, and people planned, prepared, and performed elaborately during this time—though against a backdrop of increasingly systematic opposition. Concerts proliferated as many groups scheduled events during the month of December.

For example, in 1992, the Oilville Community Chorale began to work in late summer for the two concerts it would give at Christmastime. The director noted that after the previous year's concert people had asked for more music which was familiar and with which they could sing along. Favorites included such numbers as "Jingle Bell Rock."

On the afternoon of the first concert, the gymnasium in the junior high school was set up with chairs facing the stage, which was lit by spotlights. Tables holding candles dotted the aisles, and two small artificial Christmas trees stood at the sides of the stage, with wrapped boxes piled underneath. While the Community Chorale rehearsed, a woman working for the employees' association supervised a group of Sri Lankan contract laborers, who put up tinsel on the edge of stage, placed lights on the trees, and otherwise prepared the area. When the candles were lit, the architecture of the gym was muted and the space began to take on a festive glow.

The performing groups—the Children's Chorus, the Barbershop Chorus, The Gentlemen (a double quartet of Filipino singers)—gathered and sat in their assigned sections. Most of the performers were dressed in white shirts or blouses and black pants or skirts. The Barbershop Chorus added cummerbunds and red bow ties. The Gentlemen's white shirts were satin and had ruffles down the front; their cummerbunds and bow ties were red and green satin. The Chorale added ascots and sashes of red and green plaid with gold threads. The Children's Chorus wore robes of red, dark green, and blue.

Small details proved strong reminders of home and Christmas: the jingle bells that someone shook to accompany one of the songs by the Chorale; the pure, wispy timbre of the children's choir; "Away in a Manger" sung by the Gentlemen, holding only pen-lights to illuminate themselves.

The Chorale led several sing-along carols, providing a chance for the audience to commune in song. Even this simple act, however, was performed with a consciousness that the conservative local authorities were opposed to the texts. The song sheets had been edited to delete potentially offending words. Other reminders of home came in songs that spoke of snow, which is associated with Christmas in many parts of the Northern Hemisphere: "White Christmas," "The Snow Lay on the Ground," "Let It Snow," and "Sleigh Ride."

The inclusion of The Gentlemen in the concert was thought-provoking for several reasons. The announcer identified them as a Filipino group, although she did not indicate the nationality of any other group. Clearly, they were outsiders allowed to perform by special invitation. Furthermore, the audience seemed fascinated to hear American and European songs interpreted by non-Americans. The Gentlemen were quite competent. They used no printed music; they had sophisticated amplification equipment with reverberation capabilities; they used a synthesizer for accompaniment; they had choreographed hand gestures and foot movements for each of the songs. They showed an impressive mastery of a tradition they had learned through contact with others, and their skill won a great deal of admiration from the audience and from the other singers.

Another feature of the Christmas season was the pantomime, a genre from the British that over time had become part of this season within and outside Oilville. In its British incarnation, it was a musical production that used a children's fairy tale for the basic plotline, to which was added improvised commentary on the local situation. One thread of the story was for children and was a funny retelling of the tale. The other thread, premised on a reversal of sex roles and intended for adults, was based on innuendo and sexual references. In the early 1980s, pantomimes were typically performed at a predominantly British compound, and Americans and others went there to see this genre, with which they were unfamiliar. The Americans in Oilville became so enamored of pantomime that they soon began performing one themselves each season. One year, the residents of Oilville presented *Robinson Crusoe*, supported by a small band with piano, electronic keyboard, and drums. The jokes centered on the inane aspects of life in Oilville. There was a vague allusion to a pirate captain

The pantomime was an act of community building and a chance for humorous exploration of the outrageous.

symbolizing the president of the oil company; and the parrot in the cage was the employee, subject to the whims of his owner. One straitlaced employee from the personnel department, cast amusingly against type, was a very credible Mrs. Crusoe. Two normally shy women whom I knew well played cannibals—blatant caricatures of the "other." One song that the audience was asked to sing along with the cast counterpointed travel themes with images of home:

> I am sailing, I am sailing home again, 'cross the sea.
> I am sailing stormy waters to be near you, to be free.
>
> I am flying, I am flying like a bird 'cross the sky.
> I am flying, passing white clouds, to be near you, to be free.
>
> Can you hear me, can you hear me through the dark night?
> Far away, I am dying, forever trying, to be with you.
> Who can say?

And the central plot of searching for buried treasure had parallels in the Oilville residents' search for financial gain.

The pantomime in Oilville indicates how, in the 1990s, Americans were making an ostensibly British tradition their own. They had watched the British present pantomime in a neighboring compound, had chosen certain elements, and had incorporated these into a quintessential celebration of home. Since this event called for considerable improvisation and audience participation, they also added American elements—local humor and details that would resonate with the largely American audience.

The event was an act of community building and chance for humorous exploration of the outrageous. For example, the role reversal that was featured prominently took on a special accent in this setting where sexuality was so guarded, so noticed, and so commented on. The topical jokes also allowed pent-up anger to be defused through humor.

The residents of Oilville spoke fondly of the Christmases they spent in West Asia. They liked the opportunity to focus on family gatherings, socialize with friends, and attend musical performances of all kinds. Many knew that when they returned home they would not have the same amount of leisure time to devote to creating Christmas, and that home would never be so cozy, so intimate, or so celebrated as it was here, perhaps in part because of the local objections.

As we can see from the events described here, travel is a powerful theme for American and European expatriates in West Asia. They leave the United States or Europe to travel to the Orient, a place portrayed in the media and even in academic literature as exotic. "Likewise, the application of the metaphor of travel to thought conjures up the image of an innovative mind that explores new ways of looking at things or which opens up new horizons" (Abbeele 1992:xiii). Home, another theme, contrasts with travel, bringing to mind ideas and memories of rootedness, containment, and security. Music, as sound and as interaction, often facilitates travel back home or to new horizons.

REFERENCES

Abbeele, Georges Van Den. 1992. *Travel as a Metaphor: From Montaigne to Rousseau.* Minneapolis: University of Minnesota Press.

Pratt, Mary Louise. 1992. *Imperial Eyes: Travel Writing and Transculturation*. London: Routledge.

Stone, Ruth M. 1992. Interview transcripts. (Unpublished.)

Section 4
Armenia

Armenia is both a country located in Transcaucasia and a multinational community with significant representation in many other countries. Its music bears relationships to European and Middle Eastern musical systems and so has a readily distinguishable character. With a history that extends over thousands of years, Armenia's musical heritage includes one of the world's great liturgical traditions, numerous genres of folk music, and contributions to international symphonic and choral repertoires. Armenian scholars and musicians developed written theories of music and their own systems of musical notation. Colloquial song genres such as the *gusan* are demonstrably centuries old. Armenian church music depends on its own system of modes, similar in character to those of Armenian folk music. Together, these repertoires sustain a sense of community and identity in the widespread diaspora that constituted Armenian life for most of the twentieth century.

Armenian folk musician, in Yerevan, 1967. Photo © Dean Conger, Corbis.

Music of Armenia

Manuk Manukian

Historical Overview
Theoretical Overview
Folk Music
Professional Music
Church Music

Traditional Armenian folk, professional, and sacred music has always been an important factor in the Armenian ethos. For millennia, this music has reflected and reinforced the nation's spiritual life, the beauty of its land, and its difficult but heroic history. Ancient roots and never-fading vitality are the essence of contemporary Armenian music.

HISTORICAL OVERVIEW

The Armenian nation, its language, and its music originated in the third millenium B.C.E. as a result of a union of local ethnic groups. The existing material culture was well developed (it included crafts, raising cattle, and agriculture that used irrigation) and was a foundation for the development of immaterial culture: language, folklore, songs, dances, and instrumental music. According to historical and archaeological documents, music in ancient Armenia was a versatile art form, very common in everyday life and also constituting an integral part of secular and religious rites, agriculture, and military operations. Music, like other arts, reflected the aesthetics of the time and the region and can be taken as indicative of the people's collective mind.

The first epic poems about Armenian heroes, real and mythological—Vahagn, Tork-Angegh, Haig and Bel, Ara Geghetsik and Shamiram, Sasuntsi Davit, and others—date from this period. These poems were recited by professional poets and singers called *vipasanner* and *gusanner*, who passed them on from generation to generation; indeed, the epics have survived to the present day.

The development of literature, architecture, the arts, and sacred and secular music was also stimulated by historical events: the adoption of Christianity in Armenia as a state religion in 301 C.E., the invention of the Armenian alphabet in 404, the foundation of the first schools, and the decisive battle of Avarair in 451. Significant works were produced by the first Armenian historiographers, Movses Khorenatsi, Akatangeghos, and Yeghishe; the translators Mesrop Mashtots and Sahag Partev; and the philosophers Davit Kerakan and Davit Anhakht. These were followed by important studies in art and music, including the first theoretical classification of melodies.

In the Middle Ages, many new genres of sacred and secular music developed. Music theory and practice reached a point where the need for notating this musical wealth became urgent, and a system of ecphonetic musical notation, *khazer,* known

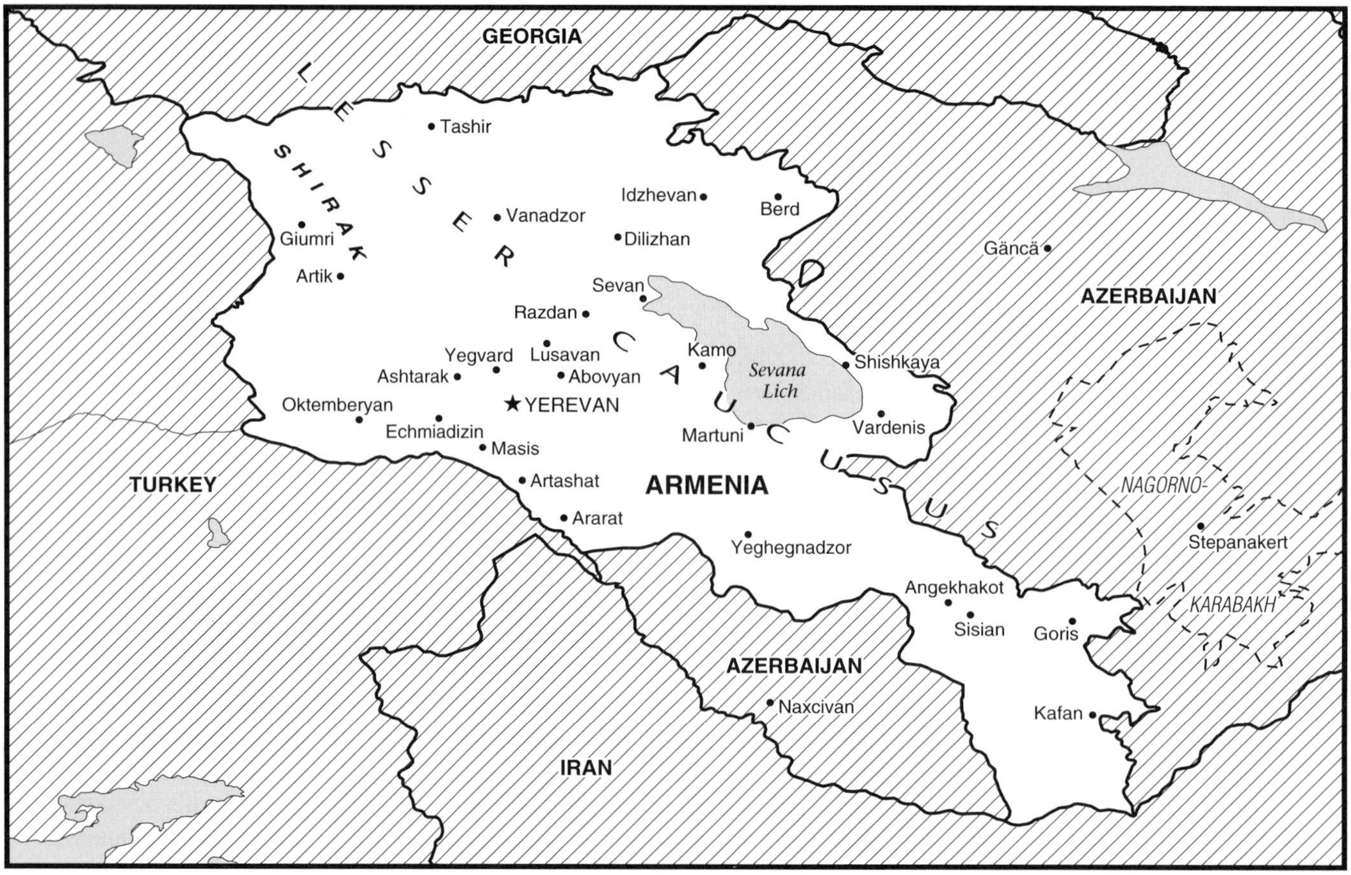

Armenia.

as Armenian neumes, was created. It was soon being widely used by scholars and, as an aspect of music theory, became a main subject in the curriculum of medieval Armenian universities.

In the ninth century, after massive invasions by Turks, Mongols, and Tatars, the Armenian economy and culture appeared on the verge of ruin. The invaders subjugated most of Armenia, enslaving the population, systematically destroying cultivated land areas and irrigation canals, and setting fire to forests and gardens. In 1080, a new Armenian kingdom, Kilikia (Cilicia), was founded on the northeastern shore of the Mediterranean; here, the civilization and culture continued to develop for the next three centuries. Among the cultural highlights of Kilikia was the work of the miniaturist artist Toros Roslin and the musician and poet Nerses Shnorhali.

In 1375, however, this last Armenian kingdom was also devastated. Those who survived and were able to escape founded new settlements in Crimea, Persia, India, and Europe; thus the concept of the *spiourk*, the Armenian diaspora, came into being. As if in compensation for the loss of the homeland, and of so much material culture, music became a citadel of the Armenian national spirit. New genres of folk songs emerged, reflecting the new reality. Along with patriotic songs and songs of social protest, there were the *antouni* and *pandoukhti*—songs expressing the spirit of an exiled people. Numerous manuscripts preserved the texts of sacred music and folk songs; one of the first was the the famous songbook *Tagharan* (1513). From the late Middle Ages (the fifteenth century) to the eighteenth century, there was a new phase of Armenian cultural development. It included, significantly, the foundation of printing houses and educational institutions and the art of the *ashughs* 'minstrels'.

In the nineteenth century, the land and the nation were split, in the sense that whereas many peasants remained under Turkish and Persian rule, large numbers of the bourgeoisie, intellectuals, and aristocrats were part of the diaspora. A powerful process of self-awareness, initiated by Armenian students in Europe, led to new genres of patriotic songs. The early nineteenth century also marked a new era in Armenian professional music. One of its main features, which would become a basis for further developement, was a synthesis of the ancient heritage of Armenian folk, professional, and sacred art with modern European traditions and means of expression.

In 1813, the *khazer* notation system gave way to system devised by a prominent music theorist and composer, Hambardzum Limondjian (1768–1839). Unlike European notation, Limondjian's system (see below) was able to capture the unique Armenian monody without forcing it into a into a well-tempered order. The Limonjian system was of enormous importance in preserveing an extensive portion of the Armenian musical heritage, especially sacred music. This development was followed by new studies in sacred music and the foundation of the first professional music societies. Talented performers and composers such as Karol Mikuli, Stepan Elmas, and Nadezda Papayan began to appear on European stages, and concerts by various instrumental and choral groups began to gain popularity. In 1868 Tigran Chukhadjian (1837–1898) composed the first Armenian opera, *Arshak Erkrord* 'Arshak the Second'. This was followed by the first musical, *Leblebiji*, (1875), earning the composer the name "the Armenian Verdi."

The composer and choir director Khristofor Kara-Murza (1853–1902) played an important role in introducing homophony to Armenian music. In 1885 he organized his first concert of choral music in Tiflis, which was then the Eastern center of Armenian culture. For the next seventeen years he traveled extensively, visiting more than forty towns populated by Armenians to spread Armenian music, organize choirs, and present concerts of patriotic, folk, *gusan*, and sacred songs in his own harmonization. It is due to his efforts that homophony was firmly established, and that traditional music became a foundation for what would be called the "new professional music."

Makar Ekmalyan (1856–1905), a composer, choir conductor, and educator, is primarily known for his harmonization of the Armenian liturgy. In effect, he summarized the ancient traditions of the church music by harmonizing, selecting, and categorizing. Although his version of the liturgy has been a subject of controversy, it is still the one performed most frequently.

The composer and pianist Nikoghayos Tigranyan (1856–1951), whose work drew on instrumental folk traditions, was very important in shaping Armenian professional music. In 1887, Tigranyan published his first piano collection, *Transcaucasian Folk Songs and Dance Music*. Later, he transcribed and arranged for piano the instrumental *mughamms* performed on the traditional *t'ar* by its prominent exponent Melik Aghamalyan. Written in a free, improvisational form, those piano transcriptions represented the first attempts in the Transcaucasus to arrange traditional melodies for a European instrument.

The original language of the new professional Armenian music was due to these creative efforts by Kara-Murza, Ekmalyan, and Tigranyan. However, their use of folklore was based mainly on European harmonies, which often clashed with authentic Armenian music. Komitas (1869–1935; figure 1), the great composer, ethnomusicologist, and choirmaster, found the way out of this incongruity. The new professional music was made possible by his versatile and learned work in folklore—collecting, research, composition, and performance. National features became more vivid, and a new period of development began.

FIGURE 1 Komitas as a young man.

Komitas always remained committed to his assertion that Armenians have their own unique music. To prove it, he transcribed more than 4,000 melodies, which became the subject of his theoretical studies, as well as the main inspiration for his original compositions and transcriptions. He revealed the tetrachordal basis of Armenian music and argued that the fourth and the fifth chord harmonies, later developed by other composers, were close to its nature. Komitas also revealed a contrasting polyphony, according to which each voice of the musical texture is perceived as an independent monody so that the monodic nature of a melody is not lost in the polyphonic texture.

Komitas's own work is an example of the classical style in Armenian professional music and has become a permanent part of the national heritage. Although the major part of it was lost during the genocide of 1915, the works that were found and preserved later (about 1,200 records of folk songs) influenced the subsequent development of Armenian music and demonstrated the value of this music to the world.

In the early twentieth century, several important events and musicians contributed to the further growth of Armenian professional music. The composer Armen Tigranyan (1879–1950) wrote the lyric opera *Anoush*, which was staged by amateur actors in Giumri in 1912. With its subject—an episode from rural life—and its clear, folklike melodic language, *Anoush* became the first national opera and found a permanent place in the repertoire; it is still one of the favorite pieces in this genre.

Spiridon Melik'yan (1880–1993), in partnership with Anoushavan Ter-Ghevondyan (1887–1961), undertook a scientific expedition to Shirak, one of the most musically fertile regions. This trip resulted in the recording of 252 folk melodies that were of great value and have been widely used ever since by Armenian composers and musicologists.

An invaluable contribution to the establishment of a classical style in Armenian music was made by another great composer and conductor, Alexandr Spendiaryan (1871–1928). Along with a great deal of chamber and orchestral music, he wrote an opera, *Almast*, based on a historical subject, in which he used fourteen melodies from the Shirak ethnographic collection.

The founder of the classical style in Armenian romance, Romanos Melik'yan (1883–1935), was a famous composer, a teacher, and a public figure. His numerous solo songs and choruses are based on folk songs as well as on his own melodies. Among his most important pieces are the vocal cycles *Ashnan Togher* (1907–1913), *Z'mrukhti* (1918–1928), and *Z'arvar* (1922–1930). In 1908, Melik'yan participated in the founding of the League of Armenian Music Teachers. In 1921, in Yerevan, the capital of Armenia, he initiated and organized the Music Studio, which in 1923 became the State Conservatory of Music. In 1925, he founded a music school in Stepanakert, the capital and cultural center of the autonomous republic of Nagorno Karabakh, populated by Armenians. He also took part in establishing the Yerevan Theater of Opera and Ballet, becoming its first artistic director.

In the 1920s and 1930s, new folklore expeditions were undertaken, inspiring composers to a broader use of the national melodic and stylistic heritage in various genres. In addition to the State Theater of Opera and Ballet, several musical groups and ensembles were founded under state auspices: the State Symphony, String Quartet, Cappella, Ensemble of Folk Song and Dance, Ensemble of Folk Instruments, and Jazz Orchestra.

A high point of the Armenian professional school of composition is the work of Aram Khachaturian (1903–1978). His compositions, based on folk music and a modal system, convey, simultaneously, the colorful, highly emotional national style; its profound lyricism; and its monumentality. Khachaturian, who wrote many ballets and instrumental works, always tried to use Armenian folk music—a tendency that became typical among his successors, including the avant-garde.

Armenian musicology of the second half of the twentieth century extended the study of folk music by viewing it in the context of, and as an element of, national culture as a whole. Scientific expeditions, studies, edited versions, and publications of *gusan*, *ashugh*, and ancient sacred music have been part of ethnomusicology and the history and theory of Armenian music. The major centers of collective research have been the institutes of arts and sciences, and archaeology and ethnography, of the Armenian Academy of Science; the Komitas State Conservatory of Music; and the Matenadaran Research Institute, one of the world's oldest manuscript depositories.

THEORETICAL OVERVIEW

The most important characteristics of Armenian music are as follows:

- Monody and monodic (monophonic) concepts.
- Rich, expressive melodies featuring melisma and usually accompanied by an instrument. (A tonic pedal point is still common in most genres of sacred and instrumental music.)
- A mainly tetrachordal structure (C–D–E–F; F–G–A–B-flat; B-flat–C–D–E-flat; and so on) of the nontempered scale, in which the third tone of each tetrachord is a little lower than that in the tempered scale. As a result, D–E is considered a "tight" tone, and E–F is a "loose" semitone because E is low. In developing his "New Armenian Notation" (figure 2), Hambardzum Limondjian took this characteristic into consideration.
- A system of different melodic models with specific intonations; specific rhythmic and final cadential formulas; and various modal structures using diatonic; altered, diminished, or augmented major-minor; Locryan; and harmonic scales. These structures are believed to have been shaped in ancient times and are still considered a fundamental feature of the national music.
- The specific function of the tonic antithesis around which a melody begins to unfold. The interval between the antithesis and the tonic can vary from a minor third to a seventh, and it defines both the diapason and the emotional substance of the melody.
- A metric system that includes simple, compound, regular, irregular, and altering measures. The most common meters include 5/8 and 7/8. However, some songs may have no metric accents at all.

Today, after more than a century of contact with European music, all these characteristic features are still preserved in the national music, although to a different extent in different genres.

FOLK MUSIC

Folk genres

Since its inception, Armenian music has developed as two mutually enriching branches: folk music and professional music. Folk music, in turn, has several branches or genres: labor, ritual, epic, lyrical, and other songs. These branches of folk music are interconnected; for example, some typical themes of labor songs can also be found in ritual and lyric songs.

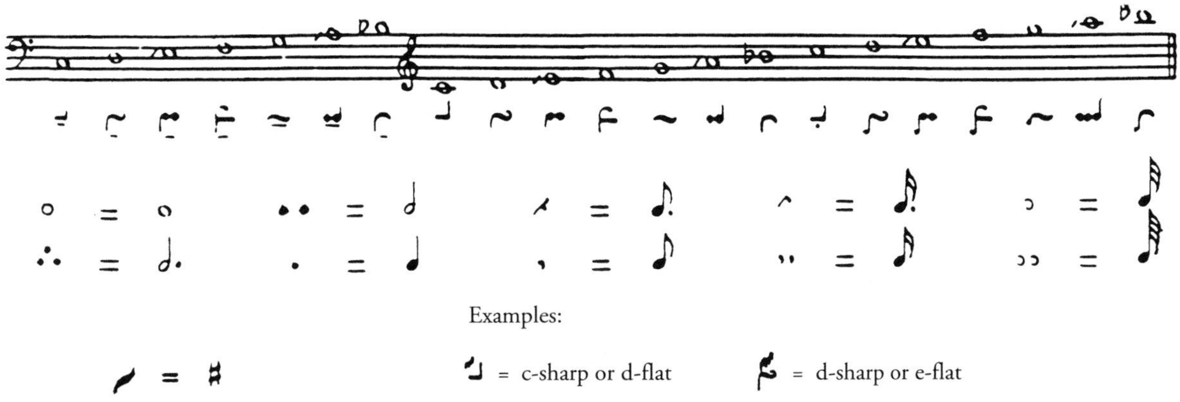

FIGURE 2 Limondjian notation.

Labor songs, because they are a part and thus an immediate reflection of Armenian peasants' work and life, are a particularly rich and interesting group. Today, they still attract the attention of musicologists and composers, as a subject of research and a source of inspiration. These songs are distinguished by their own themes and performers. For instance, there are many *horovels*, or plowing songs (figure 3), threshing songs, and shepherds' pipe melodies (figure 4), usually performed by men. Another group of labor songs are sung by women while milking, churning, grinding wheat, or rocking their babies (figure 5).

Ritual songs (figures 6 and 7), perhaps uniquely, preserve some features of pre-Christian music. They are connected with various Christian or family festivities and are represented by Christmas carols, girls' fortune-telling songs, cycles of wedding songs, and funeral songs.

Epic songs include songs from the tale *Sasuntsi Davit*, which depicts a struggle of the Armenian people against foreign invaders, and the famous epic-historical song *Mokats Mirza*. At the first hearing, these songs may seem grim, but they are full of wisdom and vitality.

FIGURE 3 Fragment of a *horovel* 'plowing song' from the Lori district.

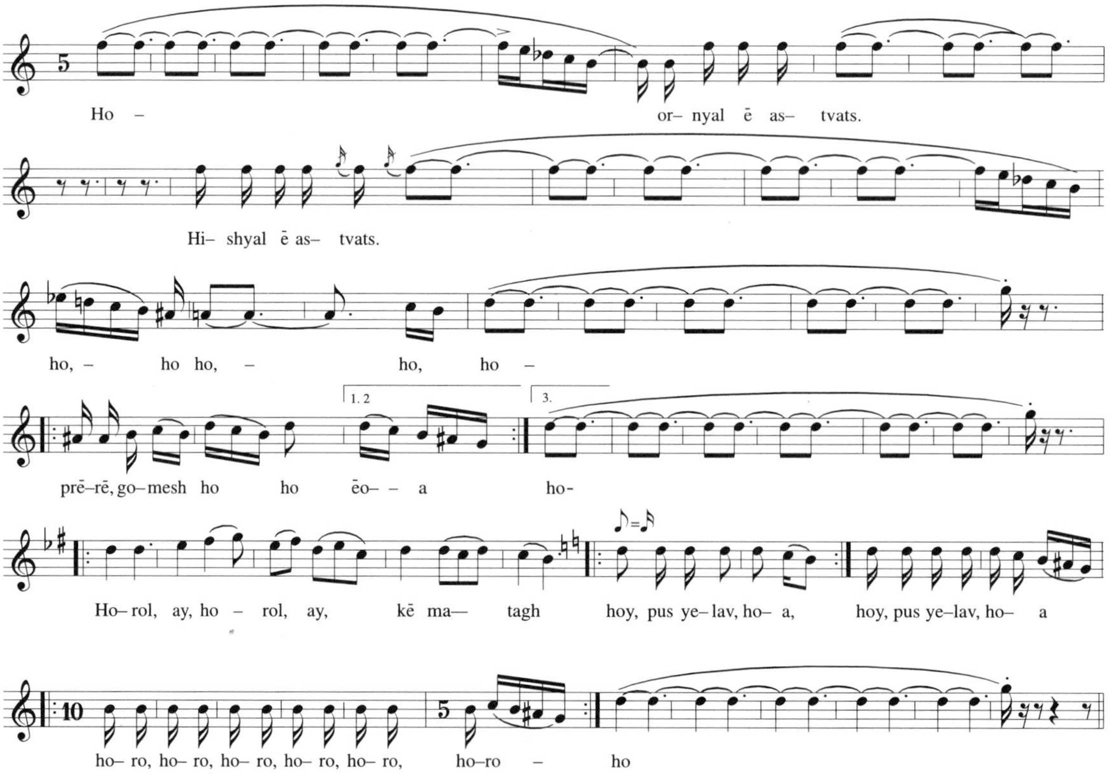

FIGURE 4 Shepherd's pipe melody.

FIGURES 5a AND b Two lullabies.

(a)

(b)

Lyric songs, expressing a wide range of sentiments, such as love and patriotism, are possibly the richest branch of Armenian folk music. Their emotionalism is expressed in an abundance of beautiful tunes, and in modal nuances, verse structures, interchangeable use of cantilena and recitative, and song and dance rhythms.

One of the oldest genres, falling between lyric songs and dance songs (see below), are the *habrbans*. They have been known since the age of matriarchy and are usually presented by girls and boys alternately (figure 8). Their love themes can frequently be traced in dance songs.

Dance songs are usually performed in a ring. The chorus is typically sung by the group, whereas the stanza is sung each time by a different individual, who expresses himself or herself by creating a new text for the stanza and also varying the melody.

"Romance" lyric songs, profoundly psychological and dramatic, are a genre known as *antouni*. Their unique synthesis of personal, social, and national dreams has raised them to the classical level. As a separate branch, they are highly significant and are considered gems of the national culture.

Folk instruments

Folk instruments and instrumental groups are used in all spheres of national music. They may accompany dances or songs, or they may be used for performing difficult instrumental masterpieces. A variety of percussion, wind, and string instruments have been known since ancient times. Armenian historiographers and medieval miniaturists provide evidence of many types of drums, lyres, and flutes, as well as trumpets, hunting horns, and other brass military instruments.

The tradition of instrument-making was highly developed by dynasties of manufacturers. The preferred material for instruments was the wood of an apricot tree, *Prunus armeniaca*; it was valued for its appearance and its acoustical qualities—moreover, the apricot tree was considered a symbol of Armenia, and this symbolism is reflected in a number of songs. These traditions were lost during the massacre of 1915 but were restored many years later.

Nowadays one of the most popular instrumental groups consists of two woodwind reed *z'urnanerner* or *dudukner* accompanied by a two-membrane drum, the *d'hol*. As

FIGURE 6 Christmas carol.

FIGURE 7 Song for the Ascension holiday.

FIGURE 8 *Habrban*, setting by Komitas.

Continued.

a rule, one of the two wind instruments, the *d'amkash*, holds the *d'am*, the tonic drone tone.

In the twentieth century, taking the violin family as a model, Vahagn Bouni (1888–1960) created bass, baritone, tenor, alto, and soprano versions of folk instruments. This enabled him to organize the Eastern Symphonic Orchestra, which has performed in many places since 1928. Currently, instrumental traditions are carried on by the Ensemble of Folk Instruments of Armenian Radio and Television and by the folk or *gusan* song and dance ensembles.

PROFESSIONAL MUSIC

Gusan

The *gusan* art, an important branch of secular professional music, has had great popularity. In structure, *gusan* songs are similar to folk songs. They usually consist of three

FIGURE 8
Continued.

or four stanzas with varied repetitions. These songs have a wide range of themes from simple to profoundly philosophical, and from personal to national. A *gusan* performer is a versatile and gifted individual who is at once the composer, the poet, the singer, and the accompanist (figure 9). *Gusan* songs have developed in several phases, gradually widening their themes, though always maintaining the virtue of reflecting vital current issues.

In the ancient period there were two types of *gusan* songs. One type was primarily joyful or lyrical; these songs and instrumental pieces served as entertainment in various settings, such as the theater and the courts of the local nobility. The second type was created by *vipasans*. Using features of epic songs, they praised legendary or historical events and heroes, thereby compiling an oral history of Armenia. Movses Khorenatsi, known as the "father of Armenian history," quoted fragments of those stories and songs in his works. He observed that they had the character of a recitative and were

FIGURE 8
Continued.

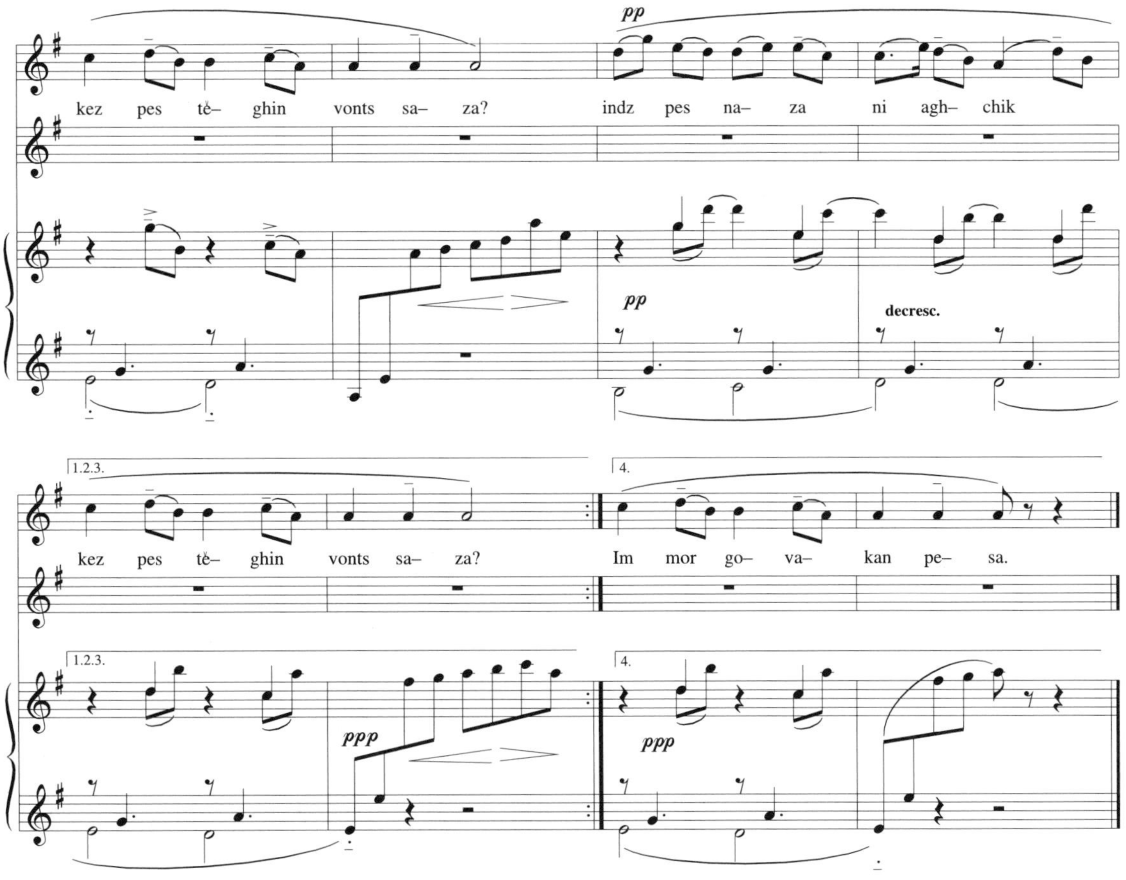

accompanied by a string instrument, the *bambirn*. Traces of the *vipasan* art can be found in the epic *Sasuntsi Davit*, which is still sung today.

Medieval *gusan* art shared pride of place with church music. At the same time, it continued to be an important influence on other branches of Armenian music, which it enriched and was enriched by. Such influence is evident in the folk songs *Antouni* and *Mokats Mirza*. However, the influence of the *gusan* song on professional genres, and especially on secular songs called *tagher* (figure 10), seems to have been more significant. The latter soon captured the attention of the clergy, who composed numerous spiritual *tagher*. But even in *tagher* based on biblical themes (the favorite being about Mary), a secular mentality was still apparent.

In the sixteenth and seventeenth centuries, when Armenia became a battlefield of the perpetual Turkish-Persian wars, its songs reflected and generalized about the devastating political events.

FIGURE 9 *Gusan* Ashot with his *k'amanch'a*, 1970s.

Ashugh

The late Middle Ages marked a new stage in the development of the *gusan* art. The allegorical language gradually came to seem pompous and antiquated, and simpler poetry and more accessible music were sought. Consequently—although the term *gusan* persisted—the *gusanner* and the popular professional performers joined a group of musicians known in the Middle East as *ashughner* (singular, *ashug*; Turkish *ašiq*; Persian *ašik*).

In the community of Middle Eastern *ashughner*, Armenian artists found their own aesthetic and stylistic directions, their own themes, their own vocal and instrumental interpretations, and some new principles of combining cantilena, recitative, and dance rhythms and intonations. They perpetuated national traditions and also played an important role in international culture. Traditionally, after a term of ap-

A– ror'n a– sats tat– rak hav– kun vay, le, le, le,
In– chu ku– las kuts– kuts a– run
3
3
le, le, le, le, vay, lo, lo, lo, lo, lo, lo, lo.

FIGURE 10 Secular *tagh*: *Arorn Asats* 'The Wooden Plow and the Bird'.

FIGURE 11 *Gusan* Shahen with his *k'anon*, 1970s.

prenticeship with a master, a young *ashugh* had to make a pilgrimage to the Sourb Karapet monastery in Moosh. By traveling across the country, the *ashugh* would become acquainted with the life of the people, comprehend issues concerning the nation, and appreciate the charm of the various dialects of Armenian folklore.

Typically, an *ashugh* treated his profession—and his instrument—with deep respect. He would often create songs dedicated to his own role or to the instrument he was using. The instruments, primarily strings, varied; they included the *k'amanch'a*, *k'eman*, *k'anon* (figure 11), *s'az* (figure 12), *t'ar*, and violin. As a rule, the last stanzas of a song would give the author's name or pseudonym. Many Armenian *ashughner* compiled manuscripts of their lyrics, although the melodies were transmitted as an oral tradition. The most prominent representatives of the *tagher* and *ashugh* art of this period are Naghash Hovnat'an (1661–1722) and Paghtasar Dpir (1683–1768); their lyrics have been published, and their melodies are still sung today.

FIGURE 12 *Gusan* Havasi playing a *s'az*, with the author, 1973.

As it developed during the seventeenth and eighteenth centuries, the *ashugh* art took several directions, distinguished by styles and dialects. The main geographic regions were, among others, New-Jugha, Astrakhan, Tiflis, Karabagh, New-Nakhijevan, and Shirak. In the mid-eighteenth century, in one of the largest Armenian cultural centers, Tiflis, we find an especially important *ashugh*: Sayat-Nova (1712–1795), whose legacy reveals his uniquely rich and versatile melodies, rhythms, structures, and modal treatments. It is not surprising that his songs remain popular today, since they are marked by cheerfulness, warmth, tenderness, drama, and knightly dignity. Indeed, Sayat-Nova has become a national symbol for beauty, and his work continues to inspire not only composers but also other artists. Hakhverdyan's research on Sayat-Nova's lyrics was published in 1852, and this research began the serious study of the *ashugh* art.

Miskin Boorji and Shirin were the most famous Armenian *ashughner* of the first half of the nineteenth century, and their development of themes was continued in the second half of the century. Owing to their artistic influence and their ability to express the national consciousness in general terms, *ashugh* songs were both popular and important at this time, helping the people to endure war, exile, and genocide. Songs such as *ashugh* Djivani's "The Unpleasant Days Will Come and Go" (figure 13) have a significance that is more than merely artistic.

The old versification system used by an *ashugh* had about seventy formulas with corresponding melodic modes; these were definite modal, rhythmic, and compositional structures. The rules were sometimes adopted by the new generation of *ashughner*, but these younger artists might also ignore them, creatively using elements and techniques of other genres. For instance, *ashugh* Djivani in his song "I Am an Apricot Tree" used the style of a rustic dance.

FIGURE 13 Ashugh Djivani, *Dzakhord Orer* 'The Unpleasant Days'.

Djivani's rich body of work—more than 1,000 lyrics and about 100 melodies—is now published and well known. His successors were once again called *gusaner*. One of them, *gusan* Sheram (1857–1938), created a new melody for every song—a departure from the old tradition of using the same melody with different lyrics, This increased the importance of the musical element and also strengthened the unity between the melody and the lyrics. After the 1930's, in the works of Havasi (1896–1978), Ashot (1907–1989), Shahen (1909–1991), Razmik (1927), and others, this creative principle became characteristic of contemporary *gusan* art.

Today, many nonprofessional singers and poets in Armenian villages create songs following the *gusan* and *ashugh* style, and some of their works have been spread throughout the nation.

CHURCH MUSIC

Church music is often considered the most important branch of Armenian music, and it is certainly one of the oldest and richest branches. Significantly, at each stage of its development it has been closely connected with secular music. The system of modes that constitutes the basis of the church music was also common in folk songs and *gusan* songs.

Christian music had an earlier foundation, pre-Christian sacred music. The old temples seem to have been centers of musical education, where vocal solo, choral, and instrumental music was performed and taught. The pagan cymbals persisted in Armenian sacred music until the end of the seventeenth century, and the ancient *k'shots*, a silver plate with jingles, is still important in the modern Armenian liturgy.

The adoption of Christianity in the year 301 was not only a religious reform but also a factor in national self-affirmation and thus, of course, in the national culture. Long before the invention of the Armenian alphabet in 404, the Psalms had been

FIGURE 14 Grigor Narekatsi, *tagh* Resurrection.

translated into Armenian and were in wide use in everyday life. After 405, church music became increasingly developed. Along with the Psalms, new genres—*k'tsurt, sharakan*, and *tagh* (figure 14)—and other new forms of sacred music emerged. These new forms called for systematic study and classification, a task that was undertaken over the course of several centuries by a number of prominent individuals in the Armenian church, including Anania Shirakatsi and Barsegh Tchon (seventh century), Stepanos Siunetsi (eighth century), Grigor Narekatsi (940–1003), and Nerses Shnorhali (1101–1173).

The developing sacred music also needed a notation system, and this in turn was the impetus for practical and theoretical musicology. A system of modes and melodic models was created, and the principles and structures of the liturgy were worked out. The unique system of Armenian neumes was also created, allowing thousands of manuscripts to enter the scriptoria of Armenia, Kilikia, and the Armenian diaspora; however, although this system was used for centuries, the key to deciphering it was eventually lost. The national awakening of the nineteenth century made it necessary once again to develop a distinctive system of notation. As mentioned above, Hambardzum Limondjian accomplished this, synthesizing the symbols of the old *khazer* and some principles of European notation; his system was used effectively in both church and secular music. In 1875, thanks to the efforts of the musicologist Nikoghayos T'ashchyan, the largest collection of church music, the *Sharaknots*, was published in Limondjian's notation.

Until the late nineteenth century, Armenian church music preserved its monodic character. Among the first homophonic arrangements of the liturgy, Makar Ekmalyan's was the most successful; it was published in 1896 in European notation and has been used ever since in all Armenian churches. Komitas's polyphonic version of the liturgy was published in 1933 in Paris. The most recent arrangement of the Armenian mass, by Khoren Mekhanadjian, was published in Echmiadzin in 1985. Various instrumental, solo, and choral arrangements of parts of the liturgy appear regularly on concert programs. In fact, the perennially popular Armenian liturgy is considered one of the richest and most remarkable manifestations of Eastern Christian music.

EDITED BY ARI HOUSEPIAN

REFERENCES

Arevshatyan, Anna S. 1991. *"Mashtots" zhoghovatsun orpes hay mijnadaryan erazhshtakan mshakuyt'i hushardzan*. Yerevan: Hayastani GA hratarakch'ut'yun.

Arménie: Chants liturgiques du moyen-âge. Ocora OCR 66. LP disk.

Arménie: Musique de tradition populaire. Ocora OCR 50. LP disk.

Arménie: Musique des Achough. Ocora OCR 59. LP disk.

Arménie: Musique instrumentale. Ocora OCR 67. LP disk.

At'ayan, Robert A. 1955. *Armen Tigranyan: kyank'e, erazhshtakan-hasarakakan gortsuneut'yun e ev steghtsagortsut'yun e*. Yerevan: HSSṘ GA Hratarakch'ut'yun.

———. 1959. *Haykakan khazayin notagrut'yune: Usumnasirut'ian yev verdsanut'yan hartser* (Armenian *khaz* notation: questions of study and transcription). Yerevan: HSSṘ GA Hratarakch'ut'yun.

———. 1962. *Gusan Avasi*. Moscow: Sovetskii Kompozitor.

———. 1965. *Armianskaia norodnaia pesnia* (Armenian Folk songs). Moscow: Izdatel'stvo Muzyka.

———. 1999. *The Armenian Neume System of Notation*, trans. V. N. Nersessian. Richmond, Surrey, England: Curzon.

At'ayan, Robert A., M. G. Arutiunian, and G. E. Budagian, eds. 1960. *Muzyka sovetskoi Armenii: Sbornik statei*. Moscow: Gos. muzykal'noe izd-vo.

Barsamyan, A. A., and M. Harutyunyan. 1968. *Hay erazhshtut'yan patmut'yun* (History of Armenian Music). Yerevan: Luys Hratarakch'ut'yun.

Belyayev, V. M. 1963. "Muzïkal'naya kul'tura Armenii" (The Musical Culture of Armenia). In *Orcherki po Istorii Muzïki Narodov S.S.S.R.* (Outline of the History of the Music of the Peoples of the Soviet Union), ed. G. A. Balter, 2:82–204. Moscow.

Brutyan, Margarit. 1971. *Hay Zhoghovrdakan Erazhshtakan Steghtsagortsut'yun* (Armenian Musical Folklore: Rural Songs). Yerevan: Luys Hratarakch'ut'yun.

———. 1973. "Ladovaya sistema armyanskoy narodnoy (krest'yanskoy) muzïki" (The Modal System of Armenian Folk [Peasant] Music). In *Problemï Muzïkal'nogo Fol'klora Narodov S.S.S.R.*, ed. I. I. Zemtsovsky, 3:226. Moscow.

———, and A. P'ahlevanian. 1995. *Hayrenakan Meds Paterazmë hay Zhoghovrdakan ev Gusanakan Ergerum* (The Great Patriotic War [1941–1945] in Armenian Folk Songs and the Songs of the *Gusanner*). Yerevan.

Chants liturgiques arméniens: Chants liturgiques du Carême et des fêtes de Pâques (Armenian Liturgical Chant: Chant for Lent and Easter). 1989. Auvidis D 8015. Compact disk.

Chants liturgiques du moyen-âge et musique instrumentale. 1988. Ocora C559001. Compact disk.

Daian, L. D., ed. 1960–1976. *Sharakan hayastaneayts ekeghetswoy / Les hymnes de l'église arménienne* (Hymns of the Armenian Church). Vols. 2–8. Venice.

Dowsett, Charles, 1997. *Sayat'-Nova: An Eighteenth-Century Troubadour: A Literary and Biographical Study*. Louvain: Peeters.

Ertlbauer, A. 1985. *Geschichte und Theorie der einstimmigen armenischen Kirchenmusik: eine Kritik der bisherigen Forschung*. Vienna.

Gasparian, Djivan. 1996. *Apricots from Eden*. Traditional Crossroads CD 4276. Compact disk.

———. 1999. *Armenia*. WDR/World Network 32.377. Compact disk.

Geodakian, Georgii S., and M. Rukhkian, eds. 1986. *Traditsii i sovremennost': Voprosy armianskoi muzyki*. Yerevan: Izd-vo AN Armianskoi SSR.

Grigor Narekatsi and Armenian Music, Fifth to Fifteenth Centuries. 1985. Yerevan. (In Armenian; summary in English and Russian.)

Hagopian, Richard. 1993. *Armenian Music through the Ages*. Smithsonian/Folkways SF 40414. Compact disk.

Kazandjian, Sirvart. 1984. *Les origines de la musique arménienne*. Paris: Éditions Astrid.

Kerovpyan, A. 1991. "Les *charakan* (*troparia*) et l'octoéchos arménien selon le *charaknots* (*tropologion* arménien) édité en 1875." In *Aspects de la musique liturgique au Moyen-Age*, ed. Christian Meyer, 93–123. Paris: Creaphis.

———. 1995. "Mündliche und schriftliche Überlieferung in der Musik der Armenier." In *Armenien: Wiederentdeckung einer alten Kulturlandschaft*, ed. K. Platt, 445–449. Bochum.

———. 1996. "Armenian Liturgical Chant: The System and Reflections on the Present Situation." *St. Nersess Theological Review* 1:25–42.

———. 1999. *Manuel de notation musicale arménienne moderne*. Vienna.

Komitas, Vardapet. 1895. *Shar Akna zhoghovrdakan ergeri* (Collection of Akn Folk Songs). Vagharshapat.

———. 1931. *Zhoghovrdakan erger* (Folk Songs). Yerevan.

———. 1950. *Hay zhoghovrdakan erger ev parerger* (Armenian Folk Songs and Dances). Yerevan.

———. 1960–. *Erkeri zhoghovatsu / Komitas* (Komitas: Collection of Compositions), ed. R. A. At'ayani. Yerevan: Haypethrat.

———. 1970. *The Music of Komitas*. KCC 100 Komitas Centennial Committee. 2 LP disks.

———. 1989. *Arménia: Chants et danses populaires d'Arménie*. Empreinte digitale ED 13002. Compact disk.

———. 1995. *The Voice of Komitas Vardapet*. Traditional Crossroads CD 4275. Compact disk.

———. 1998. *Armenian Sacred and Folk Music*, trans. Edward Gulbekian. Richmond, Surrey: Curzon.

Korganov, Vasilii. 1900, 1908. *Kavkazskaya muzïka* (Caucasian Music). Tblisi: M. Martirosianets.

Manukian, Manuk. 1977. *Gousans of Armenia: Soviet Composer*. Moscow.

———. 1995. *Zhoghovrdakan avetisner: Nvirvum ē Hayastanum k'ristoneut'yan orpes hamazgayin petakan kron ĕndunman 1700-amyaki*. Ējmiatsin: Mayr At'oṛ S. Ējmiatsni tparan.

Markarian, Varoujan. [1995.] *Armenian Chant*. Holyland 17. Compact disk.

Mazmanyan, Ruzanna. 1986. *Sovetahay erazhshtakan kyanki taregrutyun (1946–1960)* (Annals of Soviet-Armenian Musical Life, 1946–1960). Yerevan: Haykakan SSH GA Hratarakch'ut'yun.

Melik'ian, S., and G. Gardashian. 1927–1928. *Vana zhoghovrdakan erger* (Folk Songs from Van). Yerevan.

Melik'ian, S., and A. Ter-Ghevondian. 1917. *Shiraki erger* (Songs from Shirak). Tblisi.

Moses of Khoren. 1978. *History of the Armenians*, trans. Robert W. Thomson. Cambridge, Mass.: Harvard University Press.

Muradyan, Mat'evos Hovhannesi. 1989. *Urvagits arevmtahay erazhsht'ut'yan patmut'yan (XIX dar ev XX daraskizb)* (Essay on the History of Western Armenian Music). Yerevan: Haykakan KhSH GA Hratarakch'ut'yun.

Nersessian, Vrej, ed. 1978. *Essays on Armenian Music*. London: Kahn and Averill for Institute of Armenian Music.

P'ahlevanian, A., and A. Sahakian. 1984. *T'alin: Haykakan zhoghovrdakan erger ev nvagner* (T'alin: Armenian Folk Songs and Melodies). Yerevan.

Pashinian, E. 1983. "Superladovaya sistema armianskoy narodnoy muzïki i yeyo proyavleniye v tvorchestve sovremennïkh kompozitorov" (The Supermodal Tonal System of Armenian Folk Music and Its Appearance in the Works of Contemporary Composers). In *Theoretical Problems of Non-European Musical Cultures*, 104–154. Moscow.

Rukhkian, Margarita. 1980. *Armianskaya simfoniya* (The Armenian Symphony). Yerevan: Izd-vo AN Armianskoi SSR.

Sarkisian, S. 1983. *Voprosï Sovremmenoy Armianskoy Muzïki* (Problems in Contemporary Armenian Music). Yerevan.

Shahverdyan, Alek'sandr. 1959a. *Hay erazhshtut'yan patmut'yan aknarkner: XIX–XX d.d. minch 'sovetakan srjan* (Sketches of the History of Nineteenth- and Twentieth-Century Armenian Music). Yerevan: Haypethrat.

———. 1959b. *Ocherki po istorii armianskoi muzyki XIX–XX vekov; dosovetskii period*. Moscow: Gos. Muzykal'noe Izd-vo.

T'adevosyan, Alek'sandr. 1973. *Sovetakan Hayastani erazhshtut'yunĕ: Hodvatsneri zhoghovatsu*. Yerevan: Hayastan Hratarakch'ut'yun.

Talyan, Shara, and Vaghinak Chakmishyan. 1966. *Ergaran: Kazmetsin Shara Talyan ev Vaghinak Chakmishyan*. Yerevan: Hayastan hratarakch'ut'yun.

T'ahmizian, Nikoghos. 1973. *Nerses Shnorhali: Composer and Musician*. Yerevan. (In Armenian; summary in Russian and French.)

———. 1977. *Teoriia Muzyki v Drevnei Armenii* (Theory of Music in Ancient Armenia). Yerevan: Izd-vo AN Armianskoi SSR.

———. 1982. *Muzyka v Drevnei i Srednevekovoi Armenii* (Music in Ancient and Medieval Armenia). Yerevan.

———. 1994. *Komitas ev hay Zhoghovoordi Erazhshtakan Zharangut'yun* (Komitas and the Musical Legacy of Armenian Notation). Pasadena, Calif.

Tashjian, N., ed. 1874, 1878. *Dzyaynagreal Ergetsoghut'iwnk' Srboy Pataragi* (Musical Transcription of the Chants of the Divine Liturgy). Vagharshapat.

Tigranov, Georgii. 1956–1960. *Armianskiy Muzïkal'nïy Teatr* (Armenian Musical Theater). Yerevan: s.n.

Tigranyan, Nikoghayos. 1981. *Hodvatsner, Husher, Namakner*. Yerevan: Haykakan SSH GA Hratarakch'ut'yun.

T'umachan, Mihran. 1972–. *Hayreni erg u Ban: Armianskie Narodye Pesni* (Armenian Folk Songs). Yerevan: Haykakan SSH GA Hratarakch'ut'yun.

Section 5
Kurdistan

Section 5
Kurdistan

With no modern state of their own, Kurds live as a substantial minority in Turkey, Syria, Iran, and Iraq and in communities of the diaspora in Europe and North America. They form the largest nonstate nation in the world. Their communities live in environments that are quite different from each other and that are, in many cases, oppressive. Language, dress, and expressive culture have become powerful means of establishing and maintaining Kurdish social identity, both local and international.

The larger community may draw on widely shared "pan-Kurdish," behaviors to project its identity. Simply listening to songs in Kurdish becomes important where Kurdish minorities see themselves as challenged. Smaller, localized groups of Kurds may use dialects, songs, and clothing to differentiate themselves within the Kurdish whole.

Song genres and dances with particular characteristics have an important role in this world, establishing links between individuals and groups. While sharing broad musical genres—such as sung epic poetry—with neighboring Middle Eastern communities, Kurdish communities carve out their own artistic space with specific styles of vocal delivery, songs, and dances that articulate pan-Kurdish or regional identities.

Kurdish dervish, Hakkari, Turkey.
Photo by Dieter Christensen.

Kurdistan

Dieter Christensen

Kurdistan and the Kurds: Geography, Demography, Political History
Musical Instruments
Pan-Kurdish Musical Forms
Regional Musical Forms
Music in Cities and in the Diaspora

KURDISTAN AND THE KURDS: GEOGRAPHY, DEMOGRAPHY, POLITICAL HISTORY

Perhaps more than any other people, the Kurds depend on music for their sense of belonging. Kurdistan 'the land of the Kurds', is an expanse of mountainous country in West Asia roughly the size of Great Britain, dissected by the modern boundaries of Turkey, Syria, Iraq, Iran, and Armenia. Its backbones are the Taurus mountains in southeastern Turkey and the Zagros mountains in northwestern Iran, but the territory in which Kurds live extends beyond the Taurus over much of eastern Turkey, adjoining northern Syria and the northern part of Mesopotamia in Iraq. Outside of contiguous Kurdistan, numerous Kurds live in Khorasan in eastern Iran, as a result of a relocation in the sixteenth century. As a consequence of political and economic developments in the twentieth century, substantial numbers of Kurds have moved voluntarily or involuntarily from eastern Turkey to western Turkey, especially to the area of Istanbul, and from all over Kurdistan to various European countries.

Kurds—people who consider themselves Kurds and distinct from others, such as Turks, Arabs, and Armenians—are estimated variously to number between 20 million and 30 million. They speak a West Iranian language, of which three dialects are prominent: Sorani in the south and southeast, Kurmanji in central Kurdistan, and Zaza in the northwest. Many Kurds, especially men, are multilingual, speaking the national language of their own state as well as two or three Kurdish dialects. The ethnogenesis of the Kurds is a matter of debate. Whether Xenophon's Karduchoi were the ancestors, or even among the ancestors, of today's Kurds is subject to speculation; it is most likely that today's Kurds are the result of partial assimilation among populations that have been living in western Asia for millennia. Regional differences in physical makeup and ways of life have survived or evolved in these processes.

Throughout known history and into the twentieth century, the relative inaccessibility of their mountainous homeland has protected the Kurds from complete domination by other powers. Islam has spread in Kurdistan since the seventh century but did not become dominant until the fifteenth century and has always remained somewhat superficial. (According to a Turkish proverb, "Compared with a horse, a Kurd is a Muslim.") The Mongol invasion in the thirteenth century touched Kurdistan, and the Ottoman Empire took nominal control in the fifteenth century and established a border with the Persian Empire that cut right through Kurdistan. However, Kurdish

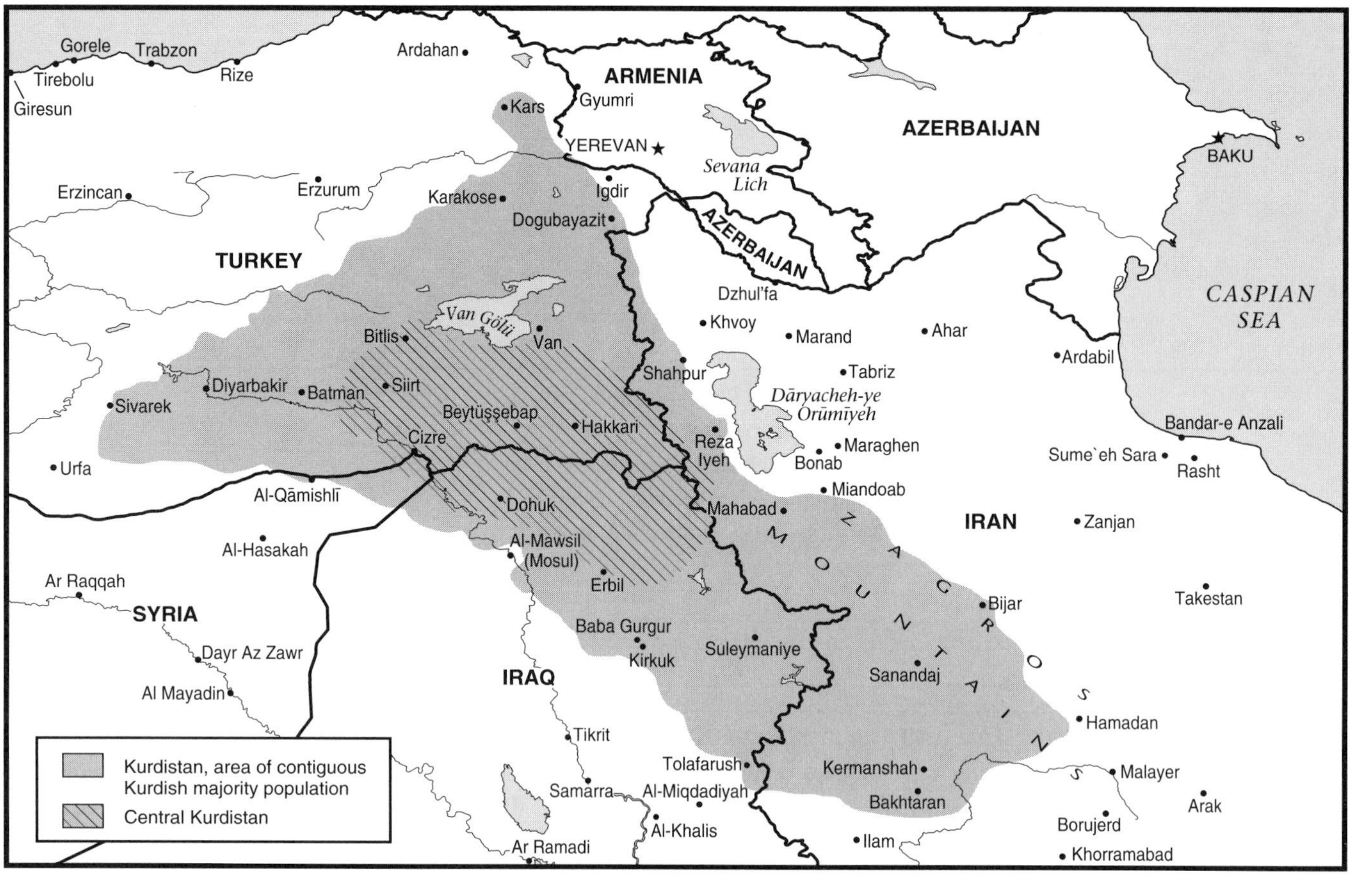

Kurdistan.

principalities, such as those of Badinan and Culamerg-Hakkari, remained de facto independent until the middle of the nineteenth century. Even at the end of the twentieth century, neither the Turkish Republic nor the government of Iraq had been able to extend complete control over the Kurdish mountains.

The Kurds have no state of their own in the modern world. They are a minority in all states in which they live, and they are marginalized in various ways and to different degrees. Turkey's policies of monocultural national integrity have tended to deny the very existence of the Kurds. In Iraq, the Kurds have clashed violently with the centralist Arab hegemony, especially since the Iraqi-Iranian conflicts, during which they were seen as sympathizing with Iran (to whose northwestern provinces many Iraqi Kurds are tied by blood). In Iran, where they occupy a major part of the northwestern Zagros mountains, Kurds have a long history of seeking independence from central governance. They succeeded briefly, under Soviet influence, in the Mahabad Republic of 1945–1946. In Soviet Armenia, Kurds enjoyed cultural recognition and support under the Soviet policy of ethnic diversity, but this is waning in the independent Armenia of the post-Soviet period. Overall, the Kurds, who are not known to have developed a political sense of comprehensive nationhood in recorded history, have lost out in the territorial battles of the evolving nation-states of West Asia. This has heightened the importance of projecting or hiding Kurdishness in modern times, making it in many cases an issue of physical survival.

At the bottom of the current political situation and the historical processes that led to it lie the multilayered notions of identity that unite Kurds, setting them apart from others while at the same time emphasizing differences among Kurdish groups and thus weakening coherence. The motivations for these ideas come from a wide array of cultural domains—concepts of ancestry and social status, loyalty to tribal leaders or territorial rulers, ownership of land, political ideologies, religious beliefs—and they are played out daily in "expressive behavior": acts that are intended to convey messages, in this context messages about distinctiveness or sameness ("I am myself"; "I am a Kurd, not an Arab, not a Turk . . ."; "I am like you; we are together"). Such expressive behavior is manifested in dress, language, music and musical implements, and body movement, including dance—any kind of action that is intended to convey messages. The choice of tribal Kurdish dress rather than, say, European-style clothing as it is commonly worn in western Turkey may convey the message "I am a Kurd, not a Turk"; or, to set Kurdish groups apart, "I am a Herki, not a Goyan." Similarly, musical instruments; certain kinds of songs and dances; Kurdish or a local Kurdish dialect rather than Arabic, Turkish, or Persian—all these can convey meanings intended to evoke in others notions of distinctiveness or inclusiveness and a perception of the performer as an individual of certain social qualities and a certain social identity. By constructing social identities in performance, Kurds in Kurdistan and in the extensive diaspora negotiate their existence as individuals and as members of groups. This essay on musical performance as expressive behavior will survey what is known of Kurds everywhere but will focus on rural central Kurdistan.

MUSICAL INSTRUMENTS

The human voice is doubtless the primary instrument for making music in Kurdistan. Voice quality is carefully controlled in performance to meet aesthetic ideals that apply to all singers, whether men or women, semiprofessional bards, or performers of dance songs. The voice should be "fine" or "thin" but still strong, and the pitch as high as the melody range and the vocal cords allow. Indeed, in competitions, singers of narratives and dance songs try to outperform others not only in repertoire and content but also in voice control and timbre by driving the pitch range to its upper limits.

Musical instruments proper are few among the Kurds, and their use is subject to social restrictions. Frame drums—consisting of a more or less circular wooden frame over which a single membrane of goat- or sheepskin is stretched—are known as *erebane*, *bendêr*, *def* or *defe*, or *daire*. With metal rings attached to the inside of the frame, they are the signifying attribute of dervishes. Without the rattle rings, they are used by men and women in some areas to accompany dance songs.

The other widely used drum, the double-headed cylindrical *dehol*, is the instrument of professional musicians, *mitirp* (from Arabic *muṭrib* 'one who makes *ṭarab*', that is, a musician-singer). These *mitirp* are generally understood to be "Gypsies," a minority that is "different." *Mitirp* usually live in or at the edge of towns and are hired for celebrations in rural areas. While their performance is essential for weddings among Kurdish farmers and pastoralists, the instruments are considered "not Kurdish." The *dehol* (Turkish *davul*, Arabic *ṭabla*) is built from a circular frame, over which are stretched two strong hides held by wooden hoops. These are then laced together to provide the necessary tension. The player carries the drum vertically before him, the right hand striking it with a heavy wooden club, the left hand with a thin stick.

The *dehol* is always played together with one or two oboes called *zorne* or *sez* (Turkish *zurna*, Arabic *mizmār*; figure 1). This is a double-reed instrument usually turned from mulberry wood. It has a conical bore, a flared bell, seven finger holes, and one thumbhole. The metal mouthpiece with the tied-on double reed is inserted into the body of the instrument through a lip disk. The double reed vibrates freely within the player's mouth cavity without being modulated by the lips. Circular breathing is essential to the playing technique.

FIGURE 1 *Mitirp* with *sez* and *dehol*, southern Kurdistan, Iran.

End-blown flutes—*blûr*, *bulûl*, *belwêr*—with six or seven finger holes on top plus one hole for the thumb are generally made of wood. In central Kurdistan, these instruments, 80 centimeters long, are often turned, with a pear-shaped bell. Similar

FIGURE 2 *Mitirp* with the spike fiddle *riçek*, Hakkari, Turkey.

flutes made from iron pipe (*bilûlê asin, şimşal*) are common in western Iran. These flutes are most often used for self-entertainment, for instance by shepherds.

The double clarinet—*dûzele* 'two reeds' (Kurdish), *dödük* (from Turkish *düdük*), or *zimare* (from Arabic *zummāra*)—consists of two reeds or bird bones tied side by side, each with six finger holes, a thumbhole, and a clarinet mouthpiece. Played by Kurdish peasants rather than by *mitirp*, it accompanies dances.

String instruments are known among the Kurds, but they are always associated with or derived from urban settings or a specific national culture. The spike fiddle called *riçek* or *kemençe* (figure 2), played mostly by the professional *mitirp*, is identical to the Persian instrument of the same name. In Turkey, Syria, and Northern Iraq, the long-necked lute *tanbur*, in various sizes, is identical to the Turkish *saz*. The long-necked lute *tembûr*, a sacred instrument of the Ahl-e Haqq sect in western Iran, is derived, with much of its repertoire, from urban Iranian tradition.

PAN-KURDISH MUSICAL FORMS

The historical cultural diversity of the Kurds is evident in their musical practices, which differ considerably from region to region as well as among distinct groups within the same region. There are very few pan-Kurdish musical forms—modes of expression that Kurds consider their own and that have similar characteristics across Kurdistan. The most important forms are sung narratives and dance songs, probably because many performers of narratives travel widely and because dance songs are among the most public manifestations of expressive behavior. Since the inception of Kurdish broadcasts from Soviet Armenia and northern Iraq in the late 1930s and in the 1950s in Iran, narratives and dance songs have been staples of programming.

Sung narratives

For urban and rural Kurds alike, listening to a recounting of historical events tends to be a deeply moving experience, evocative of what it means to be a Kurd among non-Kurds, and perhaps also what it means to be a member of the tribe or lineage to which a narrative relates. The recounting is always a performance for an audience, and it calls for highly developed skills. Most important are a vast memory for names, episodes, and historical contexts; the ability to shape a story into a compelling musical and spoken (prose) rendition; and the ability to sustain a highly controlled vocal style and to underscore the dramatic content with auditory, mimetic, and bodily gestures.

Another essential ability is sensing the mood of an audience and choosing the appropriate subject and performance style for the occasion. The few singers who have these qualities are highly respected and widely recognized, and they were known over large distances even before the advent of radio and recordings. Great singers of the past are remembered for generations, and their recordings—rarely made before the 1950s—are treasured regardless of technical quality.

Narration may take the form of *hekayat* or *çîrok û stran*, in which spoken prose is mingled with sung prose; narratives in rhymed verse are called *beyt*. Purely sung narratives are of three kinds, distinguished by the general character of their content: heroic songs about men, narratives involving the love of a woman, and *beyt* with themes that are often religious or fabulous.

Heroic songs

Heroic songs deal with battles among men and, while recounting more or less historical events, glorify courage, bravery, and honesty in situations that are usually tragic and fatal. These narratives appeal to what Kurds consider specifically male Kurdish values. Such heroic songs—*şer, merxoş*, and so on—can serve to reaffirm and project group identity or can function as mere entertainment; but in rural life, and to a lesser degree also in urban life, they often serve other distinct social functions as well.

TRACK 23 In central Kurdistan, having a well-known singer of heroic songs (*şa'ir* 'poet' or *lawjebij* 'sayer of songs') as a retainer contributes much to the prestige of a tribal or village chief. The poet will sing whenever important guests arrive, praising the valor and might of his tribe by recounting heroic deeds of the past. At weddings, he may represent the chief. In disagreements among tribes that might lead to violent confrontations, a noble competition between the poets of the respective leaders may contribute to a resolution as much as direct negotiation.

Scene 1:

July 1965, in the summer pasture of the Gewdan (figure 3). Black tents are set up in two rows, with space left between them for people and flocks. The grass is already brown, so it is time to take the camp to an even higher pasture, but no one is preparing for the move. There is a palpable tension in the atmosphere. The women—who are usually occupied with their looms, with making butter at tripods from which goatskins filled with creamy yogurt are suspended, or with baking bread or cooking—are all hiding in their tents. The men are milling

FIGURE 3 At the visitors' tent, Hakkari, Turkey.

around two large visitors' tents, set apart from the rest. Armed with all their weapons—pistols, carbines, short daggers—worn conspicuously, they listen to the sounds that come from inside these two tents. In one tent are the elders of the Gewdan and those of the Herki—another seminomadic tribe with pastures further north which they can reach only by driving their flocks over Gewdan land. The pastures are already strained, and the Gewdan are demanding a high price for permission to cross them. The negotiations have gone on for many hours.

In the second tent are the poets of the Gewdan and the Herki, in noble competition, trying to outsing each other, raising their voices to ever higher registers, spinning longer and longer tales, and holding their audience—men from both tribes—spellbound. When it seems that the voice of Ramazan, the *şa'ir* of the Gewdan chief, is about to give out, the elders of the two tribes enter the singer's tent. They have come to an impasse, and now they too listen. When the voice of Ramazan breaks and his opponent continues triumphantly, the two chiefs stand up and embrace. There are shouts of joy; the women emerge from their tents; lines of dancers form; "it is like a wedding." The two singers have settled what the chiefs could not settle.

Narratives of love

Narratives, *hijikirini* (from *hij kirin* 'to make love'), always involve the love of a woman as a central element. They differ from lyrical love songs in that they have an unhappy ending and praise female beauty only marginally. In form and musical structure, they are indistinguishable from heroic songs. Only by those who know or understand the text can they be recognized as "love narratives."

Beyt*: Rhymed verses*

While these two kinds of sung narratives rely on the recitation and melodic-rhythmic rendering of prose, a third kind, *beyt*, is presented in rhymed verses. These narrative poems, often with religious or fabulous rather than historical content, are performed by semiprofessional singers (*beytbij*), by roving dervishes, or by *mitirp*, professional musicians who are not considered Kurds. The content is not historical in the sense of referring to a specific area, tribe, or time in recent Kurdish experience. These stories are the most pan-Kurdish of the Kurdish oral literature.

Lyrical songs, known especially in northern and western Iran as *lawik*, *heyran*, or *qatar*, emphasize melodic models over text. They may also be performed on instruments alone—for instance, on a flute.

Dances: *Govend*

Dance is the other broad category of performance that exists among Kurds everywhere—as among other peoples—and serves to project group identity. Dancing as a social activity always involves sound, "music," but also much more: the patterned and coordinated movement of people; the setting; the occasion; dress; and the explicit content of song texts, or the meanings associated with song melodies performed on instruments. In any performance, the participants make choices that are determined, or steered, by how they want to be perceived as individuals or as a group.

In terms of movements in relation to sound, there are three main types of dance. TRACK 24 In the first type, two groups of two or three men or women alternate in singing a usually short melody that is repeated many times. The dancers position themselves side by side, forming a single line holding each other by the hands or touching shoulders, the feet moving essentially in place. The song texts are in rhymed verses, and each line is repeated once.

There are many named categories of these line dances with antiphonal singing. Rich terminologies refer to various aspects of body movement, such as action of the

FIGURE 4 *Govendê dehol*, Hakkari, Turkey.

shoulders or the lower arms and hands, step patterns, choreographic figures, text content, or presumed origin. In any given enactment, the dancers-singers may run through several individually named dance songs that all belong to the same category. The outsider who cannot follow the lyrics will assume that one and the same dance has been going on for a long time because nothing seems to change: the movements, the rhythm, the tempo, and the expression of the dancers all remain the same. Actually, the dancers have performed six or seven dances that they consider different because the song texts and names differ.

The second type has a lead singer whose calls are answered by a chorus—often all the other dancers—in line similar to that in type 1. This second dance type is particularly popular in Iraqi Kurdistan.

In the third type (figure 4), instrumentalists provide the music for a line of dancers who move in a wide open circle, with the lead dancer often waving a small scarf. The instruments are typically a pair consisting of oboe and drum—*dehol û zorneh, sez û dehol*—or sometimes two drums, and usually played by *mitirp*; but in some areas a double clarinet, *duzele*, may be used instead of the oboe. The tunes played by the melody instrument are usually those of locally known dance songs, though dancers may disagree on which song text the instrument is "saying." The perceived association of instrumental melodies with song texts underscores the essentially vocal basis of Kurdish music making. This third type is common to all ethnic groups in northwestern Asia and is closely associated with nontribal professional musicians.

Like the performance of narratives, dancing has important social functions in rural as in urban and diaspora settings. Foremost is its role in the wedding ritual (figure 5).

Scene 2:

June 1965, high in the mountains above the Zab river in central Kurdistan. The normally calm summer camp of the Mamhoran tribe has been astir with excitement. Guests have come from far away, sheep are being slaughtered, smoke from cooking and roasting rises like a cloud, and the sounds of oboe and drum are heard. With two hired musicians in the middle, a loose, open circle of dancers has snaked around the camp for two days, joined by anyone who wishes—guests and hosts, mostly men, at times a chain of women in between them. The *govendê dehol* 'drum dance' (figure 6) brings them all together to celebrate the wedding of a Mamhoran man and a Gewdan woman. At night, after the meal in the guests' section of the largest tent, one of the musicians will take his spike fiddle,

FIGURE 5 Wedding dance, southern Kurdistan, Iran.

FIGURE 6 *Govendê dehol*, Hakkari, Turkey.

his *riçak*; praise the hosts and the great men of the tribe; and then entertain everyone with stories of love and battle as they are known everywhere in central Kurdistan.

The next morning, the *mitirp* (*mitrib*) will lead the procession to collect the bride, a journey that takes six hours on horseback—for the *mitirp*, on donkeys—and ends with a full-fledged attack on the bride's camp, guns blasting, men shouting. When the dust settles, the families of the bride and groom have already confirmed their agreement. Men from each tribe form lines, holding hands closely, shoulders touching, moving slowly to the alternating voices of their best singers; other lines of dancers are formed by women. The vanquished camp is full of dancing groups, each proudly displaying the skill of the tribe. Only later will the musicians start up again with the drum and oboe to entertain everyone.

Meanwhile, the family and friends of the bride will sing the wedding songs, *narinik*, that mark this stage of the ritual. The next day, the procession will return to the camp of the groom, with the bride on horseback under a green veil as its prize, the musicians at her side. Sung dances, ritual wedding songs "over the head of the groom," then the entertainment by the professional musicians—the wedding ends as it began, a social event which brings people together and in which each stage is marked by music and dance.

REGIONAL MUSICAL FORMS

Some musical forms associated with domestic activities and with women's rituals are regional, in the sense of being known and practiced only within a limited geographic area. Among these are lullabies, work songs, and bridal songs performed as part of the wedding ritual.

Lullabies

In central Kurdistan, lullabies (*narinik*) are hummed or sung in a soft voice by women to comfort babies, always solo and never for an audience other than the child. The same name, *narinik*, also designates certain wedding songs.

Work songs

Communal work, specifically work that requires the coordination of several people to complete a task, occurs among the Kurds primarily in conjunction with harvesting and the preparation of food. The cutting of grain with sickles calls for group singing. In central Kurdistan, women swing and shake sheepskins or barrels filled with yogurt in a tripod to separate butter from buttermilk. This requires at least two women working in conjuction and is often accompanied by their singing. In agricultural communities of northern Iraq, wheat is squashed to produce a staple of much Kurdish cooking. Two or three men using wooden mallets pound the wheat in turn in a mortar while singing special short-phrased songs that regulate and stimulate the heavy work. There are also special songs for making wool into felt for clothing and mats. Other forms of work—plowing, the preparation of potters' clay, and so on—are occasions for individual singing.

Bridal songs

Ritual songs generically called *narinik*—the same term that is used for lullabies—or *şeşbendi* are performed in central Kurdistan as part of the wedding ritual by close relatives of the bride and groom. There are specific categories for the different phases of the wedding ritual; for instance, *serkê zawa* 'over the groom', is to be sung only on the arrival of the bride at the groom's house, when the pair first sit together. In all cases two groups of two or three singers (all women or all men) alternate. The strophes are short, the meter is loose, and the melodies often have a wide range.

MUSIC IN CITIES AND IN THE DIASPORA

Within contiguous Kurdistan, the musical life of towns with a Kurdish majority has always interacted to some extent with that of nearby non-Kurdish towns. The urban elite of Mahabad and Sanandaj in Iran, Suleymaniye and Erbil in Iraq, and Bitlis and Diyarbakir in Turkey adopted and adapted urban practices of the respective country. Kurdish musicians in Mahabad perform in the style of classical Persian music including *avaz-ha* 'songs' with Kurdish texts. In Turkey, urban Kurdish singers accompany themselves on the long-necked lute *saz* or *tanbur* in the manner of Turkish bards.

The disintegration of the Ottoman Empire during World War I and subsequent international treaties (Treaty of Sèvres, 1920) first raised hopes of Kurdish autonomy but then split the contiguous area inhabited by Kurds among four states: Turkey, Syria, Iraq, and Iran (Treaty of Lausanne, 1923). The Kurds, a minority in each state, experienced increasing repression, which led to antiassimilationist sentiments, Pan-Kurdish nationalism, and separatism. Since the 1950s, emigration has created a substantial Kurdish diaspora in Europe (especially Sweden, Austria, Germany, and England), North America, and Australia. Attaining an autonomous Kurdish state is a political project that calls for a pan-Kurdish identity to supersede the various regional, tribal, linguistic, and political identities. Kurdish musicians and writers like Hooshang

Kamkar and Naser Rezazi are elaborating a national music theory and music history in an effort to authenticate the antiquity of Kurdish culture.

Aided by technological advances and global mass communications since the 1950s (radio, recordings, and since the late 1990s websites), the Kurds' dual and sometimes conflicting goals increased cultural homogeneity while making things distinctively Kurdish more familiar and more appealing to the rest of the world. Music has taken a leading place in this effort; in turn, the effort has affected musical content and form. Nationalistic songs have become a pan-Kurdish genre popularized by singers in exile like Şivan Perwer (b. 1955 near Urfa, Turkey) and Naser Rezazi (b. 1955 in Sanandaj, Iran). Instrumental music and lyrical songs with instrumental accompaniment are emphasized over unaccompanied performance of narratives in regional dialects, which would highlight the cultural diversity among Kurds while limiting potential audiences and thus the potential market. To appeal to younger audiences among Kurds, especially in the diaspora, as well as to non-Kurds, singers like Şivan Perwer (the "king of Kurdish music") have adopted the vocal styles and backups of Western pop music while retaining Kurdish lyrics and using elements of Kurdish dress in their advertising. Song texts and the titles of compact disks may draw on widely known rural songs and may be identified as *geliri* 'folk'. Through radio and recordings, urban musical practices in Kurdistan and in the diaspora draw from rural practices and then feed back into all parts of Kurdistan.

REFERENCES

Blum, Stephen, and A. Hassanpour. 1995. "'The Morning of Freedom Rose Up': Kurdish Popular Song and the Exigencies of Cultural Survival." *Popular Music* 15:325–343.

Bruinessen, Martin van. 1992. *Agha, Shaikh, and State: The Social and Political Structures of Kurdistan*. London: Zed.

Christensen, Dieter. 1961. "Kurdische Brautlieder aus dem Vilayet Hakkari. Süd-Ost Türkei." *Journal of the International Folk Music Council* 13:70–72.

———. 1963. "Tanzlieder der Hakkari-Kurden." *Jahrbuch für Musikalische Volks- und Völkerkunde* 1:11–47.

———. 1965. *Kurdish Folk Music from Western Iran*. New York: Ethnic Folkways Library FE 3103. (LP disk.)

———. 1975. "Musical Style and Social Context in Kurdish Songs." *Asian Music* 6:1–6.

Kendal, Nezan. 1979. "Kurdish Music and Dance." *World of Music*: 19–32.

Kurdistan. 1974/1989. UNESCO Collection Audivis D8023. Compact disk.

Perwer, Şivan. 1989. *Chants du Kurdistan*. Audivis B6145. Compact disk.

———. Dotmam CD-28 (1985–1994); Lê Dîlberê CD-32 (1986/1996); Ya star CD-15 (1995). Ses Plak Yapim (Istanbul).

Section 6
Turkey

Section 6
Turkey

Bridging Europe and Asia, the region of present-day Turkey has interacted throughout history with an array of surrounding cultures—Central Asian, Persian, Arab, Balkan, Greek, and Western European—both influencing and being influenced by each. The Anatolian peninsula is home to a celebrated classical music tradition, numerous forms of religious music, a historic tradition of military music, a wealth of unique musical instruments and genres of regional folk music and dance, and many forms of popular music.

Lavish patronage of court and religious musics aided the development of classical traditions of Ottoman court and Mevlevi ritual music, each with elaborate suite forms. While some Middle Eastern Muslim traditions rejected instrumental music, Mevlevi Sufis gave a central position to the *ney* (a reed flute) in their rituals and symbolism; Alevi Sufis gave a central position to the *bağlama saz* (a long-necked lute).

The birth of the Turkish Republic after the fall of the Ottoman Empire led to a profound reevaluation of Turkish culture. Courtly Ottoman culture was looked on with suspicion and either put aside or transformed. The Arabic script of the Ottoman Turkish language and Ottoman forms of dress, like religious and musical traditions, were banned in the new westward-looking nation. Music and dance of the countryside were brought into newly founded conservatories in urban centers as part of an effort to construct a modern national identity—a process that often altered these forms. Shifting ideologies led various Sufi groups to experience periods of efflorescence and decline, periods of suppression, and spirited revivals.

New recording industries, government radio and conservatories, and new concert settings have interacted with new styles and aesthetics, enlarged ensembles, standardized repertoires, and new systems of music pedagogy based on European models. Influences from abroad continue, often contested but frequently enthusiastically embraced.

Dancing Dervish, Instanbul, c. 1985–1995. Photo © Hans Georg Roth, Corbis.

Snapshot: Tanburī Cemīl Bey

John Morgan O'Connell

The life of the acclaimed Turkish instrumentalist Tanburī Cemīl Bey (1871?–1916) is a story of transition, set in the final years of the Ottoman Empire and resonating with the revolutionary ethos and the cosmopolitan character of the time. This was a period in which major social and administrative changes were instituted under the provisions of the *Tanzimat* reforms (1839–1876), and Western aesthetic preferences (*alafranga*) competed with—and in some instances replaced—native urban sensibilities (*alaturka*) in a wide range of cultural practices, including music. In this context of political uncertainty and cultural fragmentation, Tanbūrī Cemīl Bey offered the possibility of a new future. His remarkable artistic innovations and diverse aesthetic interests not only reflected the instability of his own time but also anticipated the major musical and cultural reforms that followed the foundation of the Turkish Republic in 1923.

The life of this great artist mirrored the historical uncertainty of his social world: it was informed by volatile social conditions, changing musical tastes, and unpredictable professional opportunities. Tanburī Cemīl Bey was born into a privileged family with courtly connections, but he had an insecure youth, owing to the early deaths of his father, Mehmed Tevfik Bey (1836–1874), and his uncle, Refik Bey (1839–1888); and the professional commitments of his cousin and protector, Mahmud Bey, a bureaucrat. Ignoring the professional advice of his cousin and adopting instead the artistic interests, modernizing ideals, and cosmopolitan values of his deceased uncle, Tanburī Cemīl Bey did not excel in his appointed career as a civil servant. Instead, after 1908 he opted exclusively for the lifestyle of a musician, which, although it was unsuited to his impoverished circumstances, accorded well with the revolutionary zeal and the westernizing character of the *Tanzimat* period. Although he was able to secure the patronage of Sultan Abdülhamīd II (1842–1918) and could rely on the support of his aristocratic connections, he preferred the solitary existence of an independent musician. Such a life reflected an earlier precedent in Western classical music and imbued his life story with a distinctively mythological flavor. Emulating many of the Epicurean attributes associated with this romantic ideal, he conducted his personal and professional life according to the rigorous demands of his art and the aesthetic demands of contemporary expectations. True to character, he avoided the responsibilities of family life—especially his obligations to his son, Mesʻūd Cemīl Tel (1902–1963)—cultivating instead the melancholic disposition and nervous temperament of a romantic artist.

He was personally isolated and physically debilitated (partly as a result of his consumption of alcohol), but he achieved the ultimate distinction in his chosen role—an undocumented life, an untimely death, and an unmarked grave.

The musical world of Tanburī Cemīl Bey was forged from the multifaceted soundscape of his upbringing. Having received only fragmentary musical training during his formative years, he perfected his own style of instrumental performance, characterized by technical innovations, extended transpositions, melodic variations, and motivic embellishments. He demonstrated his artistry on a wide range of classical and nonclassical instruments, including the classical long-necked lute (*tanbur*), the bowed *tanbur* (*yaylı tanbur*), the pear-shaped bowed lute (*kemençe*), the lute (*lavta*), and the cello (*viyolonsel*). By the time he eventually received a classical education (*meşk*) in the tradition from recognized practitioners such as Tanburī Ali Efendi (836–1890) and theoreticians such as Kemanī Aleksan Ağa (1852–1925?), he had not only consolidated his reputation as an exceptional virtuoso and an up-and-coming composer but had also developed his own nonclassical performance style. This style was shaped by childhood experiences—an interest in folk music, and westernizing influences—and was manifested in the thematic content and the programmatic embellishments of his instrumental improvisations (*taksimler*). While his stylistic innovations were not universally accepted—in particular, they tended to be rejected by traditionalists like Raūf Yektā Bey (1871–1935)—his rapid plectrum technique on the *tanbur*, the remarkable agility of his left hand on all instruments, and his fluid bowing style on the *kemençe*, combined with his faultless musicianship and his skill as an improvisor, secured his position in the canonic line (*silsile*) of Turkish music and made him influential among a new school of Turkish instrumental practitioners. To put it simply, Tanburī Cemīl Bey mediated musically between the traditional and the innovative—a schism indicative of a world in transition.

The professional world of Tanburī Cemīl Bey was profoundly influenced by these musical prerequisites. Shunning the traditional path of courtly patronage, and unable to support his own participation in the amateur musical activities of his rank, he developed a new professional class, that of the soloist. This role was consistent with his romantic desire for artistic independence. By elevating the status of instrumental performance, by composing a classical selection of instrumental pieces to suit such performance, and by ignoring public disapproval of his performances in the nightclub circuit, he was at once able to bestow a classicizing distinction on his stylistic innovations and to reap the financial rewards of doing so. He was helped significantly in this by the record industry. Between 1910 and 1914, as a soloist and accompanist, he recorded more than 180 disks for the Blumenthal, Orfeon, and Regent labels. This gave him an independent income and also an opportunity to reconfigure the aesthetic expectations of his bourgeois audience—an audience that became familiar with the eclectic sound of his improvisations, was eager to applaud his stylistic innovations, and was prepared to buy his exclusive artistic labels. In addition, he was able to maintain his social standing as a professional musician by giving solo recitals in concert settings for the first time, by publishing a number of musicological treatises (such as *Rehber-ī Mūsıkī*) for an academic following, and by nurturing an aristocratic circle of students who were able to transmit his unique style and romantic vision to later generations. In this way, he mapped out a musical future for a changing world.

Tanburī Cemīl Bey's life is, then, a story of anticipation as well as transition. Nurtured in the cosmopolitan *Tanzimat* era and reflecting the westernizing predilections of his upbringing, Tanburī Cemīl Bey was able to anticipate musically the political and social reforms of the twentieth century. By revolutionizing Turkish instrumental practice and by disseminating his improvisations and compositions to an international audience through the record industry, he influenced, both temporally and spatially, an emergent bourgeois elite. Captivated by his new, revolutionary musical worldview, this elite would subsequently translate it into political reality.

Turkey: An Overview

Ursula Reinhard

Folk Music
Military Music
Religious Music
Art Music
Popular Music

The territory of contemporary Turkey links the Orient and the Occident, reflecting the dual heritage of Turkish culture. The Turks who entered Anatolia from Central Asia and founded the Seljuk Empire (eleventh to thirteenth centuries) brought their folk music with them. Folk elements have, to this day, imbued Anatolian music with characteristic tone colors, polyphonic texture created by a drone, and vestiges of pentatonicism. The music absorbed influences from all the groups the Turks came into contact with during their wanderings, and from their neighbors when they settled—particularly the Byzantines, the Persians, and the Arabs, who brought melodic components along with the Islamic faith. Cultural influences, for example in rhythms and forms, also came from the defeated peoples of the Balkans. All these links encouraged the evolution of a distinct music on Anatolian soil.

Turkish music has received little scholarly attention in the West. With regard to historical studies, the reason is probably that all the treatises on music theory, even those by Turks, were written in Persian or Arabic. However, the influence of Turkish music can be seen, for example, in the overlay of Turkish elements on the music of the Balkans, where several musical instruments, or their names, reflect Turkish culture.

TRACK 8–25

In Turkish culture, as in most cultures, music can be divided into folk and art, though the boundaries are sometimes fluid. Close to folk music are military music and some religious music, but other religious music is art music. Folk music continues to flourish and will be discussed before Ottoman art music, which belongs to the past.

FOLK MUSIC

Types of folk nusic

Folk music has traditionally been based on oral transmission and manifests itself anew in each musical realization. The folk song (*türkü*) sung by all segments of the population, and in particular by villagers and nomads, can be classified minimally in terms of two musical styles: *kırık hava* 'broken melody' and *uzun hava* 'long melody' [see ASPECTS OF TURKISH FOLK MUSIC THEORY].

Kırık hava (figure 1), often sung to accompany dance, is simple in its melodic structure, has a relatively limited range and scarcely any melismas, but has a pro-

Turkey.

nounced meter. Meters are often asymmetrical, with rhythms of 5, 7, 10, 11, 16, 20, or 21 beats; and rhythms of 6, 8, 9, 12, 16, or 18 beats that commonly contain uneven groupings. Thus a 6/4 unit can break down to 4 + 2 quarters, an 8/8 rhythm to 3 + 2 + 3 eighths, a 9/8 rhythm to 2 + 2 + 2 + 3 eighths, and so on. This 9/8 *aksak* 'limping', 'staggering', or 'unevenly flowing' rhythm has entered into art music; this term indicates that one of the four metric portions has been extended by half its length, interrupting a homogeneous measure. The origin of asymmetrical meters is uncertain; but presumably they resulted from contact between different groups. Similar asymmetrical rhythms are found in Asian, Turkic, and Balkan musics.

FIGURE 1 *Kırık hava*. (K. Reinhard 1962:21). Translation: "The moon rises over the beanfield. / Sweat beads between the brows. / Two hearts become one. / What can we then do? / (Refrain) Ah, what do you say, bride? / I speak, but you say nothing. / Say nothing, I will go away. / Girl, you make me crazy."

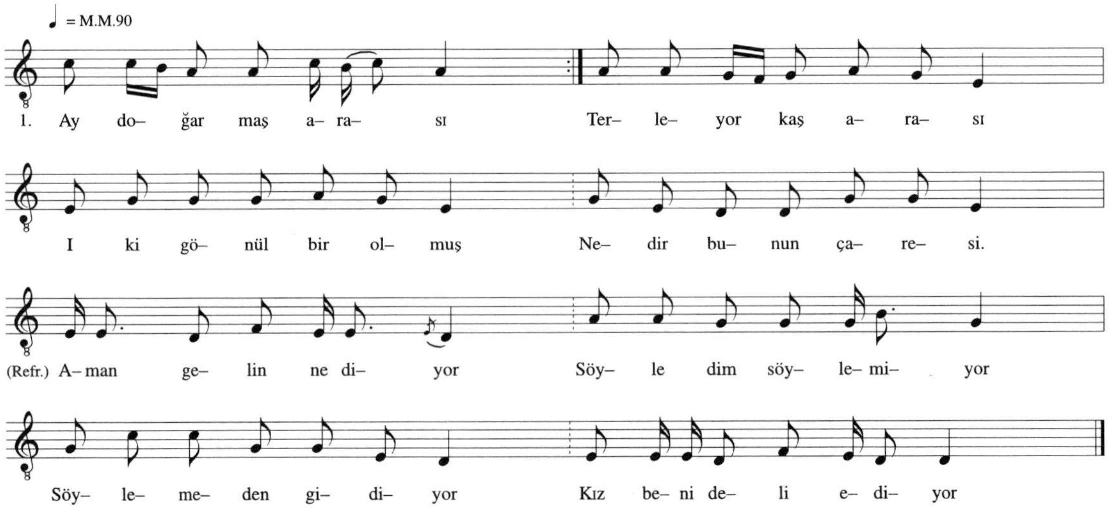

Uzun hava (figure 2), which is ubiquitous in love songs, is characterized by free rhythms. The melodies are expansive, with rich ornamentation and melismas. The melodic contour is generally descending. Similarities between *uzun hava* and some religious chanting, such as the Muslim call to prayer, suggest a mutual influence between Islamic and early Turkish music. *Uzun hava* is highly regarded, and people show little reluctance to sing it, despite the prohibitions against music in orthodox Islam. This type of song has various names in different provinces: for example, *bozlak* in the south and *maya* (or *varsağı* or *hoyrat*) in the northeast.

There are several other categories of songs, among them songs of mourning, particularly a type of death dirge called *ağıt.* Some of these dirges are very close to the free-meter *uzun hava*, with wide-ranging ornamentation; an added feature is a de-

FIGURE 2 *Uzun hava* (Bartók, 1976:124–125). Translation: "I am the son of the lord of the land, but I made a mistake. / I wanted to do good, but began to do bad. / I wanted to kiss her; I bit her red cheek. / Nothing hurts me, but my teeth should be pulled. / Because of you I have left my homeland. / I have wasted everything that I had. / Who made my sweet, pretty love cry? / Your eyelashes are all thick and round from tears."

FIGURE 3 *Ağıt: Nenni Ibrahim nenni.* (Ahrens et al. 1984:32.) Translation: "Ah, my Ibrahim. / Why do you lie so full of defiance? / My lion son, he came here, / ate in a lively way his bread."

scending fourth within the fourth poetic line. A second type of *ağıt* is less ornamented (figure 3). Here, each line is separated from the next by a pause. In *ağıt,* the ranges of the lines are smaller than the overall compass. As in *uzun hava,* the lines often descend gradually toward the end of the song. The most definitive criterion is the shaping of the fourth line of the stanza: the melody begins here at the upper limit of a given range that encompasses a fourth, and proceeds to the final note. If an *ağıt* does have a regular meter, it is often 6/8.

There are also different genres in the songs of Turkish bards, *aşıklar* (singular, *aşık,* or *aşîk*), which are sung by the general population as well. Among the most important is a "melodic-recitative" song, limited to a range of one to two notes, or at the most a fifth. This is sung psalmodically, generally to a text with a religious worldview. Another popular type has two melodic lines of equal or unequal length within one line of poetic text. The singer usually makes a pause or caesura between two melodic lines. An 11-syllable line, for instance, is divided into 6 and 5 syllables for singing, and a pause is used to give the 5-syllable line the value of a 6-syllable line. This tendency to halve the line sometimes results in a division of words that disregards the flow of language. The songs are often bound by meter but lend themselves very much to improvisation. With regard to texts, love songs dominate, followed by dirges, soldiers' songs, descriptions of nature, ballads, and other content.

FIGURE 4 *Kaval player* in Sivas, Hafık, 1963.

Folk songs have various poetic forms, such as *türkü* (as a poetic form), *koşma,* and *mani;* the last two were improvised and have four lines. All these are usually lighthearted or associated with dance, or both. The 8- or 11-syllable ballad form is called *destan.* In northeastern Turkey, there are a number of different forms, such as the 15-syllable *divani,* the *müstezad,* and the *muhammes,* all identified with classical poetry. A stanza generally has four lines but can also have five, six, or seven lines if a refrain has been added. There is always an end rhyme, though the rhyme pattern varies with the poetic form. The *mani,* for example, has the pattern aaba. In the *koşma,* the first stanza is aaab, abab, or abac and aaaa; all subsequent stanzas are aaab. Generally, a textual image at the beginning of a song indicates the content to follow. Thus a first

FIGURE 5 *Right: Saz* player and *aşık* in Malatya, 1970.

FIGURE 6 *Tulum* player in Ardeşen, on the Black Sea, 1963.

FIGURE 7 *Kemençe* player in Rize, on the Black Sea, 1990.

line with the words "Mist on the high mountains" foretells an uncertain or even a hopeless fate. Many symbolic words are used in the texts: the rose and the nightingale, for instance, symbolize two lovers; a thirst for water means longing; a fire means the agony of love.

Folk instruments and ensembles

All folk songs can be accompanied by instruments, and the drum has a special role in dance songs. *Uzun hava,* in which texts with an 11-syllable prosody are popular, is either sung solo or accompanied by a long-necked lute, the *saz.*

Folk music instruments include the single-headed hourglass-shaped drum, *deblek* (or *dümbelek, dümbek, darbuka;* Arabic *darabukka*); the end-blown flute, *kaval* (figure 4); the recorder, *düdük;* and the long-necked lute, *bağlama* or *saz* (figure 5), which has a body shaped like half a pear.

The long-necked lute is made in different sizes, the smallest being the *cura* and the largest the *meydan sazı.* Depending on its size, a lute can have from three to twelve strings. If there are more than three strings, they are arranged in courses (where one or more of the strings are doubled). The *saz* has frets; its open strings are often tuned to three notes, la-re-sol (from high to low), a tuning called *karadüzen.* The *bağlama düzen* or *aşık düzen* is la-re-mi; there are also other tunings. The lute is played with a plectrum, and the lower strings are often played simultaneously to provide drive and rhythmic accompaniment. It is played all over Turkey, and its importance is indicated by the fact that *saz* is a general term for all musical instruments.

In the south and west, dances are often accompanied by two spoons played like castanets (*kaşık*). In the recent past, various bowed instruments were played, such as the *kabak kemane* 'gourd fiddle'; this is a spike fiddle. The *kemane* resembles the Greek lyre. The *tırnak kemençe* 'fiddle played with the fingernails' is used by nomads of the southwest. These instruments have now been replaced by the European violin. To the east of the Black Sea, the bagpipe *tulum* (figure 6) and the box-shaped fiddle *kemençe* (figure 7) are played. The double clarinet *argul* is limited to the midsouth. In the region of Burdur and Fethiye there is a small bamboo or reed clarinet, the *sipsi.* In Fethiye and in the province of Izmir, Gypsy women play a frame drum, the *deblek,* at weddings (figure 8). A tambourine without cymbals, the *mazhar,* accompanies dervish songs. In bear dances and also in women's dances, a tambourine with cymbals, the *def,* is played.

FIGURE 8 *Deblek* players, Günlükbaşı, Fethiye, 1986.

The most widespread instrumental ensemble consists of the *davul*, a large double-headed drum; and the *zurna*, a double-reed oboe (figure 9). These two instruments always appear together, sometimes in two pairs, and are usually played by Gypsies. The main accents are played with a heavy stick on the right head of the drum, while the left head is struck with a light stick to mark rhythmic subdivisions. The *zurna* player uses circular breathing in order to execute long uninterrupted passages.

Davul and *zurna* players appear at important celebrations, especially weddings and circumcisions, where they accompany open-air male dances. Different versions of this ensemble are found all over Turkey and beyond: from the Near East to India and China and to the south across North Africa. In northeastern Anatolia, the shrill *zurna* is replaced as the partner of the *davul* by the deep, warm *mey*, a double-reed recorder. In recent times, the *zurna* has also been replaced by the European clarinet, *klarnet*, particularly in Thrakia, in the south and the west.

Some ensembles in small towns consist of clarinets with small *deblek* drums and a *saz*. In the west, in the southwest, and along the western Black Sea, there are ensembles consisting of a fiddle (*keman*), a banjo-type lute (*cümbüş*), and a *deblek* or

FIGURE 9 *Zurna* and *davul* players, Milas, Dibekdere, 1968.

FIGURE 10 *Deblek* and *düdük* players, Adana, Karataş, 1956.

a *davul*. The small bamboo or reed clarinet *sipsi* is played only in the province of Burdur, in an ensemble with the *deblek*, the *bağlama*, and an idiophone, the *zilli maş* 'fire tongs with bells'. In the south, the *kaval* or *düdük* is often played with the *deblek* (figure 10). Until about 1975, a double clarinet (*çifte*) with a box-shaped body was played in the western Black Sea region to the accompaniment of a *davul* struck only with the hands. This ensemble appeared at weddings, in performances by dancing boys (*köçek*).

Until a few decades ago, instruments in Turkey were played either solo or in small groups. There is now a growing tendency for many instruments to be played together. In large and medium-size cities, there is also an increasing tendency, at the festivals of wealthier groups, to add European and electronic instruments. All over Turkey, folk music groups have incorporated a variety of instruments, both Western and traditional, to create small orchestras; these perform with amateurs and professional singers at festivals.

Folk singers and poets

Professional and semiprofessional poet singers are called *aşıklar* or *ozanlar* (singular, *ozan*). Accompanying themselves on the *bağlama*, they sing both worldly and religious songs, which they have either composed or taken from their contemporaries or earlier *aşıklar*. [See SNAPSHOT: ARIF SAĞ—ALEVI BAĞLAMA TEACHER AND PERFORMER PAR EXCELLENCE.] Such poet-musicians already existed in pre-Islamic times, as wandering minstrels. Even today, they travel around to bring their songs to a broader audience. They have a large and varied repertoire of types of songs in which they compose their poetry. These songs can be close to *kırık* and *uzun hava*, or a mixture that expressses individual creativity. The songs are often polyrhythmic and very complex. The *aşıklar* present their audiences with a variety of content, particularly critical songs addressing religious and current topics. They improvise at song competitions with other *aşıklar*, singing in praise of women, friends, guests, and notable people. Their creations are often transmitted from generation to generation—examples include the songs of Pir Sultan Abdal and Karacaoğlan (in the sixteenth and seventeenth centuries) and, in modern times, Aşık Veysel (d. 1973). The name of the composer of a song appears in the first or last line of the final stanza, as in the tradition of the European troubadours. The *aşıklar*, who are almost always Shi'ite-Alevi, often sing at the religious ceremonies of the Bektashi and Alevi orders.

FIGURE 11 *Gerdaniye Köroğlu Türküsü.* (Nazari 1935, cilt 3: 313.) Translation: "I am Köroğlu. I wander through the mountains, / In the blowing wind, I sense deception and trickery. / With an iron club, I crush heads. / Ah, white horse, let me find my beloved. / I've had a fight with her; reconcile me with my beloved."

Some *aşıklar* are also transmitters of dramatized prose epics that can be traced back to the sixteenth century in Anatolia. Among these is an epic brought by Turkic people from Central Asia, *Köroğlu* 'The Blind Man's Son', which is known from the Near East to China and India; its hero is a noble robber who takes from the rich and gives to the poor (figure 11).

There are also a large number of love epics, such as *Aslı and Kerem* and *Leyla and Mecnun.* The songs of such epics are based on melodic models with various alternating rhythms, often asymmetrical. There are different types of songs, depending on whether the text is heroic, lyric-melancholic, and so on; but whatever type is used, it is transformed in each rendition according to the fancy of the singer.

Apart from these epics, many *aşıklar* invent their own short or long narratives, punctuated by songs that often link the past with the present; or they describe their own lives. These traditions are alive in northeastern Turkey, mostly in the provinces of Erzurum and Kars.

The Adana Plain in the south once had *halk hikayecileri* 'popular storytellers', who performed epics at festivals and weddings to the accompaniment of a long-necked lute (the *cura* or *bağlama*); some of these epics were as much as twenty hours long and took several days to perform. The *halk hikayecileri* told their stories in an impressive, highly dramatic style. Their songs, unlike those of the *aşıklar* in the north, were limited to melodies with minimal variations. These epic singers are now extinct; the last of them, Kır Ismail (whom Béla Bartók met during his travels in Turkey in 1936), died in 1963. All this music was and is sung for men, though women may also listen.

FIGURE 12 *Ağıt* singer of a lament for the dead, *Nenni Ibrahim nenni*, in Adana, Bahçeköy.

Women's folk music

Religious practice requires that women celebrate weddings and other festivals in separate spaces. Their dances are accompanied by the *def* 'tambourine' or the *deblek*; in earlier times, the short-necked lute, the *'ūd*, was also used. Ritual songs are performed on the night when the bride's face, hands, and feet are dyed with henna. Cradle songs are sung only in intimate settings; superstition and habit dictate that they may not be sung in the presence of outsiders. However, certain women are permitted to sing dirges publicly; although no music is permitted at a burial, women compose dirges and sing them before the corpse is taken for burial. These *ağıt* dirges (figure 12) describe the goodness of the dead person and the conditions in which he died; the women also sing stanzas in which the dead person speaks as if still alive. Close relatives, such as the widow or mother, give free vent to their agony by speaking directly to the departed.

Work songs

Until recently, work songs were common in folk music; for example, boys and girls sang improvised *mani* during the hazelnut harvest. Musical fishermen's calls were still heard in the early 1960s, and Bartók was able to record pleas for rain in 1936.

MILITARY MUSIC

Military music represents a link between folk and art music. Since about the 1970s, there has been a revival of the *mehterhane* 'janissary band' (figure 13), which had ceased to exist in 1826, with the destruction of the elite janissary corps. The *mehter* band had its roots in the early Ottoman period. It gradually developed into a large orchestra with nine players for each kind of instrument: oboes (*zurna*), trumpets (*boru*), large drums (*tabıl* or *davul*), pairs of small kettledrums (*nakkare*), cymbals (*zil*), and Turkish crescent cymbals (*çağana*). In addition, there was one player of the large kettledrum (*kös*). This configuration—particularly the central group of *davul* and *zurna*—highlights the relationship between military music and folk music. However, the actual musical forms (such as *peşrev*) and rhythmic modes (*usûl*) indicate the proximity of military music to art music.

The instruments of the *mehter* became known in the West, and were sometimes adopted there, through the Turkish wars. Western military music that used these instruments was sometimes called janissary music; and the instruments were even absorbed into opera orchestras, particularly in the fashionable, exotically colored "Turkish operas" of the eighteenth and nineteenth centuries. It is unclear, though, how many rhythmic or melodic elements were adopted from the *mehter* (for instance, in "alaturka" pieces). This adoption was possible in part because *mehter* music was sometimes played at diplomatic receptions at Turkish embassies; every ambassador had a *mehter* ensemble. A letter of Mozart's indicates that he may have heard such music at a camp near Vienna.

Depending on their rank, officials of the Ottoman court had large or small bands, which played when an official was on his way to the reception hall of the castle, the *divan*. Of the musical instruments in the *mehter* ensemble, the *kös* was reserved exclusively for the sultan. At a court, the day started and ended with music. Early in the

FIGURE 13 *Mehterhane*, Istanbul, 1970. *Zurna, boru, kös, davul, çağana*, and *zil* are shown.

morning, the *mehter* played the *nevbet* 'striking the watch' at the gates of the castle and from its towers. Music was played on many occasions: at all large festivals, at weddings, at the birth of the sultan's children, at circumcision celebrations, on the ascension of a ruler to the throne, at state receptions, and to celebrate victories; music was even played when the sultan was being shaved. According to Evliyâ Çelebi, a seventeenth-century travel writer, one thousand musicians were employed at the court in Istanbul. During military campaigns, musicians were sent on horseback or camel-back close to the enemy lines; their music was said to be so loud that heaven and earth shook and the enemy often fled in panic. In camp, the night was marked by muffled drumbeats interspersed with cries of "Allah is great"—this was intended to prevent the soldiers from going to sleep. Even today, Turks are stirred when, on a national occasion, they see a *mehter* ensemble with its traditional instruments and costumes. *Mehter* bands can also be heard twice a week at the military museum in Istanbul.

RELIGIOUS MUSIC

Religious music has an important role in Turkish culture. Some is linked to folk music, as is the ritual music of the Turkish Alevi, the Bektashi order (whose members were once the preachers of the janissaries), and certain other Sufi orders. Mystical songs of the great thirteenth-century poet Yunus Emre (and other mystical *aşık* through the centuries) remain popular, as do the songs of Pir Sultan Abdal, who was executed for revolutionary religious activities in the sixteenth century. This music includes hymns (*nefes*), songs of praise (*ilahi*), songs of mourning (*mersiye*) for martyrs, songs for Ali (the son-in-law of the Prophet Muhammad, who is a central figure for Sufi religious groups), and songs for the religious dance *sema*. Among the Alevi, all songs (especially the *cem* or religious service) are accompanied by the *bağlama* or *saz*; and *saz* players are often also religious functionaries. With the exception of *sema*, mystical-religious love songs have the same musical conception as worldly love songs, differing only in content—for example, references to saints. Members of the Bektashi order often sing in unison, accompanied by instruments. In the *zikir* (or *zikr* 'recitation of the name of Allah') ceremonies of some Sufi orders such as the Halveti, a trance is reached through musical recitation in different modes and rhythms, and through body movements. Such religious ceremonies also include art music; thus there is no clear boundary between folk and art music in the religious context.

The music of the Sunni Muslims is classical, though only a few decades ago they also had fasting songs accompanied by the *davul*. These were entertaining folk songs of the genre *mani*, seven syllables to a line, sung during the month of fasting by a man or young boys at sunrise and sunset, to mark the beginning and end of each day's fast. The musicians went through the streets, collecting money for their message. (The Sunni are the largest religious community of Turkey, and Sunni Islam was the state religion until Atatürk declared Turkey a secular nation in 1923.)

Orthodox Islam is not sympathetic to music; strict theologians believe that music can intoxicate the senses, leading the faithful away from God. Instruments are the primary target of the ban on music. A large variety of vocal musical forms have developed, but they are regarded as recitation (*tecvit*), not music. These forms are drawn from elements of classical music and follow the rules of *makam*, discussed below. [See also Contemporary Turkish *Makam* Practice.] This category includes the call to prayer, *ezan* (Arabic *adhān*), which is heard five times a day—in Arabic, the liturgical language of Islam—from all minarets in the Islamic world. [See The Muslim Call to Prayer.] Qur'ān recitation, with its melodic contours, ornaments, free meter, and long pauses for concentration, is also in this category. There are also epics in the religious music of the Sunni. Süleyman Çelebi (d. 1429) wrote his epic

Mevlût or *Mevlit* on the life of the Prophet in the *mesnevi* poetic style; the music, composed soon afterward, consists of Qur'ānic recitation followed by hymns. The four parts of this epic are now based on four melodic modes—*dügâh, hüseyni, rast,* and *ırak*—and are recited at births, deaths, and circumcisions. The voyage of the Prophet to heaven (*miraciye*) is also rendered musically. The morning prayer recited during the month of fasting in the mosque is called *tesbîh*; the night prayer is called *temcîd.* The prayer for mercy (*tekbîr*) heard at festivals praises Allah's greatness and the hereafter. It is recited in the *ırak makam* and in the *durak* meter: 1 + 1 + 1 + 2 + 4 + 4 + 4 + 4 = 21 metric units. The same rhythm is applied in *salat,* another prayer for mercy. The dead are remembered in the *mersiye* songs. *Tevşîh, na't,* and *ilahi* are songs of praise.

A very famous *na't* composed by Buhûrîzâde Mustafa Itrî in the seventeenth century is heard every December in Konya to begin the ceremony of the whirling dervishes (Mevlevi). It is composed in the *rast makam* and has the 18-beat *türkî zarp* meter. Other dervish orders in which music has a central role also use the *na't,* which, like the religious dance *semâ,* is believed to bring mankind closer to God. This is achieved by means of long artistic hymns, sustained instrumental music, and rhythmically chanted calls to Allah (*zikir*). The texts for this music are taken from the poetry of the mystics.

In contrast to orthodox Muslims, many Sufi groups embrace music in their rituals. The founder of the Mevlevi order, Celaleddin Rumi (Celâleddin-î Rumî, 1207–1273), freed himself from the ban on music; this is why musical instruments were used at Mevlevi ceremonies. Initially, these instruments consisted of the end-blown flute *ney* (TRACK 8-2) (figure 14), whose sound is similar at times to that of a crying human; and the pair of small drums, the *kudüm.* Other instruments were added later, and today the ensemble consists of several *ney, kudüm,* long-necked lutes (*tanbur*), spike fiddles (*rebab*), and a pair of *halile* cymbals. Each dervish and novice is trained not only in religion but also in playing an instrument and singing. The Mevlevi order thus produced many composers, and even a few sultans belonged to it. Mevlevi music can be seen as the inception of Turkish-Ottoman art music (figure 15).

FIGURE 14 Religious music: *ney* player at a Mevlevi ceremony in Konya.

FIGURE 15 *Dördüncü Selâm* 'Fourth Greeting' from a Mevlevi hymn (*Mevlevi Âyini*) in *makam pençgâh*, by an unknown composer, c. 1450. (*Türk Musikisi Klasiklerinden*. 1934. Band 6, *Mevlevi âyinleri* 1:273.) Translation: "You are my sultan, you are my sultan. / In my heart, in my life, you are my faith. / When you breathe on me, I become brave. / What is the importance of a soul? You are a hundred times more (worthy) than my soul."

ART MUSIC

Art music in Ottoman times: Music at the court

In Turkey, art music is known as *klasik müziği* 'classical music'. During Ottoman times, art music was patronized mainly by the sultan's court. A great deal of our information about life at the sultan's court comes from the book *Serai Enderun* 'The Castle of Enderun', written in Italian in the seventeenth century by a Polish prisoner of war. The author, whose Islamic name was Ali Ufkî (d. 1672), was a music teacher and composer at Enderun. The court had a practice house (*meşkhane*) in which musicians, teachers, and pages worked. A number of musicians lived in the castle, and others came every day from outside. "They were above all virtuous musicians and poets," writes Ali Ufkî. He describes in detail the music and instruments of the *mehter*; and he divides music into "Cammer and Field music"—that is, art (chamber) and military music—placing performers of religious music within the category of art music. If the ruler wanted "Cammer Music," he addressed the *sâzende başi* 'master of music', who would prepare a suitable program and summon the musicians. The sultan was often in his pleasure castle, in a room with a window, through which he granted audiences. The musicians sat in a raised place called the *makam*, with the singers in front and the instrumentalists behind them. If they were positioned in front of the sultan and his wives, they had to play with closed eyes and bowed heads; any transgression of this etiquette would be punished by a blow to the Adam's apple (*happas*). When the sultan chose a wife from his harem for his bedchamber, she was accompanied by female companions who sang and played instruments. Unfortunately, Ufkî does not tell us which music or which instruments were used—as a man, he could not know this. He did know, however, that female musicians were trained in the harem and that at weddings women celebrated in separate quarters by singing and playing instruments.

If the sultan liked a certain piece, the musicians were rewarded with precious gifts from the treasury. They were also paid, more or less according to their abilities. They could be freemen or (like Ali Ufkî) slaves; and slaves could eventually be freed and even raised to high office. No distinction was made on the basis of nationality, ethnic group, skin color, or even religion. Ufkî reports that all were treated equally, although those who "were higher than the others in virtue and wisdom" were held in great esteem. Ufkî describes Turkish music as "pleasant" and harmonious. He says that the musicians "composed their pieces by heart"—that is, they composed and played without written notes, which were then not known in Turkey. "The beat was given by successive drumbeats for the compositions." Ufkî wrote down classical and folk music in European notation. He did not pass on this skill, but his collection of scores, *mecmû'a-i sâz-ü söz,* was found in 1948, in London. A large number of musical pieces from this era have thus been preserved.

Development of art music

There is little information about the earliest Turkish classical music, because it was transmitted only orally and because its composers (unlike composers of Western music) were anonymous or have been forgotten. Data from the fifteenth and sixteenth centuries are sparse—we have only names, and there would be little point in simply listing them here. It is only in the seventeenth century that attempts at notation begin to provide definite information. The most important source is the Romanian prince Kantemiroğlu, or Demetrius Cantemir (1673–1723). In his *Kitâb ilmü'l-mûsıkî alâ vechi'l-hurûfât* 'Knowledge of Music and the Representation of Sounds through Letters', he wrote 350 instrumental pieces in an alphabetical notation, with numbers below to indicate time. This work includes religious, worldly, and *mehter* music.

Music reached its high point in the second half of the seventeenth century, the time of the two great composers Hafız Post (d. 1693) and Buhurîzâde Mustafa Itrî (1640–1711). *Yürük Semai,* composed by Hafız Post in the *rast makam,* is still a favorite song. Itrî is sometimes referred to by westernized Turks as the "Turkish Bach," because of his religiosity. He wrote a great deal of religious and secular music.

A cultural renaissance called the "tulip age" (*lâle devri,* 1718–1730) began a few years after Itrî's death. Common people were permitted to attend festivals in the imperial gardens at the Bosphorus. It was here that court musicians began to show interest in the *aşık* folk poets and in folk music in general, weaving it into their compositions. This synthesis is recognizable in the compositions of Eyyubi Bekir Ağa (c. 1685–1759). One of the greatest composers was Sultan Selim III (1761–1808): he had a unique musical style, and his compositions are still featured in concert programs. Other rulers who were composers were Mahmud I (1696–1754) and Abdülaziz (1830–1876).

Among the masters of the nineteenth and twentieth centuries was Ị smail Dede (1778–1846), whom everyone knows today. Under Western influence, he created seven new melodic modes (*makamlar*) and even composed a waltz (*vals*) which, apart from its meter, was an example of true Turkish classical music (figure 16). Even more famous are the instrumental pieces by Santuri Edhem Efendi (1855–1926), such as the Romanian *longa*. Şevkı Bey (1860–1891) composed more than 500 songs and has therefore been compared to Schubert, although there are no musical similarities between the two.

A turning point came in 1828, with the appointment of Giuseppe Donizetti (1788–1856) as the chief conductor of the court. This brought Turkish music under Western influence. Donizetti founded a Western-style orchestra and introduced Western notation, and a division between Western and Turkish music began to develop in the capital. The old letter notation invented by an Armenian church musician, Hamparsum Limonciyan (1768–1839), in which 360 mostly religious melodies had been recorded, became superfluous, although traditional musicians stayed with the old notation for a while.

Among the last great classical composers are Tanburi Cemil Bey (1871–1916), whose work can be heard in the first recordings by the Istanbul conservatory from the

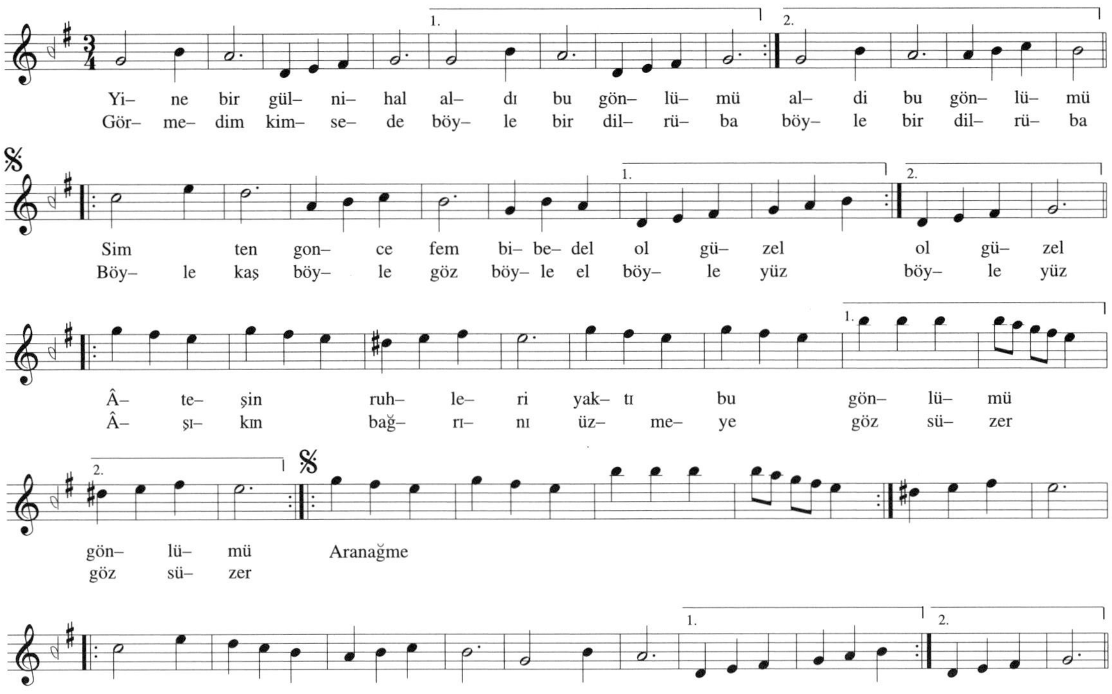

FIGURE 16 *Hamami Zâde* by İsmail Dede, *şarkı* in *makam rast*, *vals* 'waltz'. (Edipoğlu 1962:57.) Translation: "Again my heart was enflamed for a rose branch, / For a beauty with silver-shimmering skin and a rosebud mouth. / Your fire burned my soul, my heart. / You beauty with the silver-shimmering skin and the rosebud mouth."

1930s; and Lem'i Atlı (1869–1945), who is currently in vogue again. Turkish classical music is today patronized by the upper classes; but it has only a "museum existence," although one can hear and see old music on radio and television.

Elements of art music

The formal elements of art music—particularly the melodic system—have been studied in detail in Turkey. Along with Suphî Ezgi (1869–1962), who wrote a six-volume work on Turkish music, the most important modern Turkish music writers and theoreticians were Raûf Yektâ (1878–1935) and Sadettin Arel (1880–1955).

Melodic system and makam

Al-Farabi in the ninth to tenth century had already established a link with the Greek theorists with regard to melody. A twelve-note theoretical scale was expanded by Safi al-Din (1230–1294) to seventeen notes, from which seven were chosen to create different modes. Finally, the system was expanded to include twenty-four notes per octave; some practitioners recognize more (for example, the forty-one tones of Ekrem Karadeniz) while retaining the features of seven-note scales. The intervals are not quarter steps; in the twenty-four-note scale there are three different semitones (60, 90, and 114 cents) and three sizes of whole tones (180, 204, and 228 cents).

The various scales form the basis of the *makam* system. Apart from the scales, each *makam* has a starting note, an ending note, and a dominant note, which, according to Gültekin Oransay, is a rule of composition. The dominant note (*güçlü*) is often the fourth or the fifth. For example, in *makam rast*, which starts with sol, the *güçlü* is the fifth; in *makam uşşak*, which starts with la, the *güçlü* is the fourth, re. There are thirteen basic modes (figure 17), of which six include versions of the one-and-a-half step interval common in Oriental music. Although a few of these scales approximate Western scales, they do not have precisely the same notes, since the intervals have different cent sizes.

Rhythm

Like the notes, the meters or rhythms of Turkish classical music are theoretically fixed, with all compositions built on one or more specific rhythmic modes. These rhythmic patterns (*usûl*) consist of deep-sounding main beats (*düm*) and higher and lighter

FIGURE 17 The thirteen fundamental *makamlar*.

beats (*tek*). Shorter *usûl* have 2 to 6 beats. Longer *usûl* can be viewed as combinations: for example, a 7-beat *usûl* combines 3-beat and 4-beat units; an 8-beat *usûl* combines 2 + 3 + 3; and so on. Even longer *usûl* can be made by combining several shorter meters. For example, one *usûl* no longer in use, the *darb-i fetih* 'rhythmic pattern of conquest', consisted of 88 beats. During a performance, the drummer can vary the *usûl* by subdividing the various beats in any number of ways (*velvele*). While the possibilities for rhythmic improvisation are endless, the tendency today is to use the same standard traditional *velvele*. [See Rhythmic Modes in Middle Eastern Music.]

Melodic formation

Melodic formation is very flexible and strongly ornamented. Descending modes can occasionally be heard, but melodies usually develop in arches or undulating patterns, in which steplike movements dominate but ascending leaps upward are popular. Traditionally, each composition consists of a melody that exists only as an idea and can be easily changed in each rendition to reach its final form.

Forms

The *taksim* is a solo instrumental improvisation. It is performed mostly before songs and instrumental pieces and serves, among other functions, to introduce the essence of a *makam*. In the nineteenth century, there were vocal versions of *taksim* called *gazel*, but these have been sung scarcely at all in the twentieth century. The *taksim* is rhythmically and metrically free and is generally not accompanied by drums, although on occasion an instrumental ostinato can provide an underlying rhythmic pattern. There are no rules for the length of the *taksim*, but it often has a tripartite structure. The most important task of the *taksim* is to introduce the *makam*, its melodic intervals, and its dominant notes.

The most important composed instrumental forms are *peşrev* and *saz semaisi*. Each consists of four parts (*hane*), each part followed by the same refrain (*teslim*). *Hane* and *teslim* are often of equal length with the same underlying *usûl* in various renditions. In longer rhythmic modes, a *hane* or *teslim* may last only two cycles, or even only one cycle. The *makam* for instrumental pieces can be chosen freely. The composer of a *peşrev* need not choose any particular *usûl*; but for a *saz semai*, one of the *semai* meters is traditionally chosen.

There is a large variety of vocal forms (usually in verse), the preferred form being four lines, though a refrain can be added. Complete lines of vocables are also often added. There are instrumental interludes (*saz payı*) consisting of very few notes, as well as longer instrumental introductory and concluding sections. The most important types of song are *şarkı*, *kâr*, *beste*, and *murabba*. The texts of the songs are arranged according to Persian-Arabic conventions of *dīwān* poetry. In this arrangement, the syllables are not counted as in folk poetry: instead, the lines consist of certain groups with regularly ordered open and closed syllables—a principle to which the Turkish language does not readily lend itself. An important principle of composition is that the third line of four-line songs is prominent. This line, which has a name of its own (*meyan*), is set apart by modulation, a changed melody, a higher scale, or the like. It is a peculiarity of Turkish art music that the climax of a piece is in its second half, usually at the link between the second and third lines or the third and fourth lines. In many cases, the highest note of the composition is found here, naturally creating a special effect in this monodic music.

For performances of classical music, selected pieces, all from the same *makam*, are performed consecutively. Such a cycle is called *fasıl*. It commonly begins with a *peşrev* and includes *taksim* and a *saz semai*. Five song genres are often included: *kâr*, *beste*, *ağır semai*, *şarkı*, and *yürük semai*. This suite form has changed over the centuries, and no single structure is generally followed today.

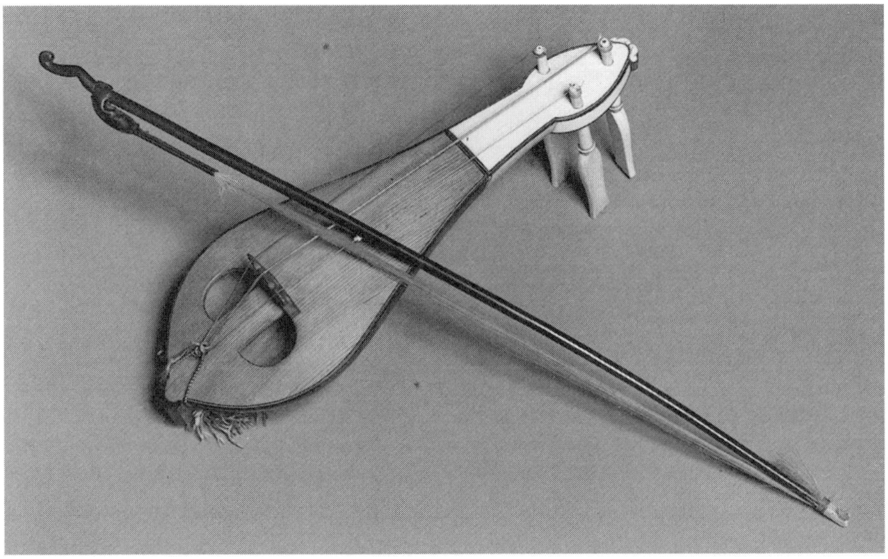

FIGURE 18 *Kemençe rûmî.*

Instruments of art music

The instruments used for religious and secular art music are the small tambourine with cymbals (*def*) and without cymbals (*mazhar*), the drum pair (*kudüm*), cymbals (*zil*), and the end-blown flute (*ney*). The *ney*, made from reed, is related to the rustic *kaval* and is made in different sizes. Stringed instruments include the *rebab*, a spike fiddle found across large areas of the Orient; the small, three-stringed *kemençe rûmî* (the half-pear-shaped bowed fiddle with very short fingerboard shown in figure 18); the fretted long-necked lute (*tanbur*); the fretless short-necked lute (*ud*), adopted with little change by the West; the Persian hammered zither *santur*; and the plucked zither *kanun*. (Several instruments are shown in figure 19; the *kanun* is shown in figure 20.) Some other instruments have been lost over the centuries; examples are the harp (*çeng*) and the pan flute (*mıskal*), lost in the eighteenth century.

The choice of instruments to be used in solo or choral singing is generally left to the performers. There are, however, certain norms, particularly in the religious

FIGURE 19 A court festival, shown in a seventeenth-century miniature. Left to right: one *rebab*, one *tanbur*, two *zilli def*, three *ney*, one *santur*.

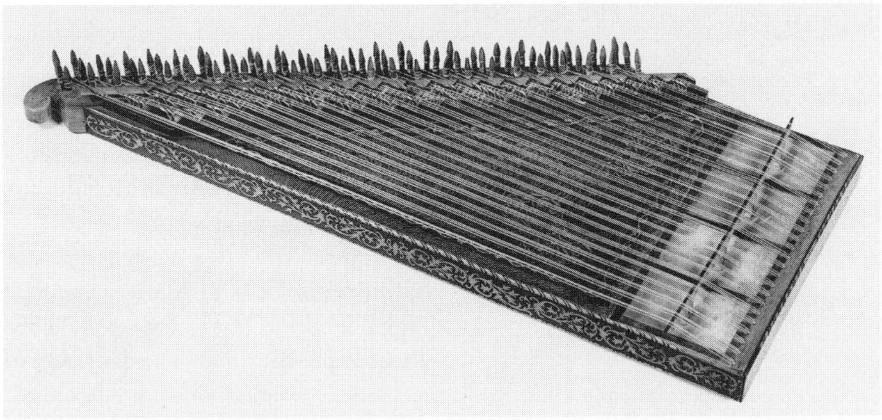

FIGURE 20 *Kanun.*

sphere. The adoption of European instruments has increased the variety of instrumentation.

Modern art music

Europeanization has resulted in a modern Western-style art music. Opera houses in Istanbul and Ankara feature Western operas; conservatories teach Western music. The decisive period in this trend toward Western music was the 1930s, when Paul Hindemith and Eduard Zuckmayer brought students closer to polyphony at the conservatory in Ankara. Hindemith believed that the new generation of composers who were to be sent to Europe for higher studies should work on the basis of their own folk music and link it to European harmony. The composers of that time, the "Turkish five" (*Türk beşleri*)—Adnan Saygun (1907–1990), Ulvi Erkin (1906–1972), Necil Kazım Akses (1908–1996), Cemal Reşit Rey (1904–1985), and Hasan Ferid Alnar (1906–1978)—worked in the Western style and were influenced by the impressionists and Bartók. This is particularly true of the most famous among them, Saygun, whose oratorio *Yunus Emre* is internationally known. Saygun included folk melodies in his work, and the next generation of composers followed him in this regard—Ilhan Baran (b. 1934), Bülent Tarcan (b. 1914), Sabahattin Kalender (b. 1919), Ferit Cenan Akın (b. 1932), and the two best-known, Muammer Sun (b. 1932) and Nevit Kodalli (b. 1924). However, these later composers sought a polyphony based on the primary intervals of folk music, fourths, and Western music, taking Bartók as their model. Other composers stayed within the Western limit of twelve notes; these included Bülent Arel (1919–1990), Ilhan Usmanbaş (b. 1921), and Cengiz Tanç (b. 1933).

It is interesting that despite the orientation toward the West, there are very different approaches. These include classical music with microtones (for example, Alnar) and a predominant leaning toward traditional rhythms (for example, Erkin), or an interweaving of folk music by integrating tetrachordal and pentachordal structures. These were amalgamated with triads and Western harmonies or modal scales (as by Kodalli). The compositions of Muammer Sun are full of contrasts: they have a comprehensive harmonic foundation but also, for instance, Turkish drone effects. Sun—like Ilhan Baran, Cengiz Tanç, Necati Gedikli (b. 1944), and Hayrettin Akdemir—was a student of Kemal Ilerici, who sought to synthesize Turkish classical music with polyphony. Accordingly, he developed a sound aesthetic using layers of fourths and fifths. Younger composers have created avant-garde linear pieces or original folk songs (as well as variations on folk songs) based on free sounds: for example, melodic patterns written for specific instruments might be exchanged with other instruments (as in Akdemir's *Düğün*). Other new practices, such as musical graphics and a chaotic melodic intensification of sound, are alternated with traditional melodies, drones, and rhythms, all with the intention of referring to Turkish culture while keeping up with Western modernism.

POPULAR MUSIC

Popular music has long shown Western influences in different ways. After World War II and until the 1970s, a popular version of vocal art music with Turkish instrumental ensembles was received favorably; this was called the *şarkı* 'art song'. Since then, there have been Western-style hit songs accompanied by European instruments, but with a Turkish coloring. A parallel trend is for pop music to use Turkish folk songs clothed in a pleasing melody.

So-called *arabesk* music [see Arabesk] is viewed with considerable ambivalence. Some people actually consider *arabesk* immoral, and in fact it was, for a time, banned from television and radio; on the other hand, it is also seen as the consummate folk song of present times. The derivation of the term *arabesk* for this genre is unclear, but it signifies inspiration from Arab music. This music evolved in urban slums around the 1970s, in a milieu of ever-increasing rural immigration into the cities. Rural newcomers came with the dream of a better life but often fell deeper into poverty; *arabesk*, with its depressing texts foretelling a dark future, was a safety valve for these people. Osman Gencebay was apparently the first composer of this genre. Some, though not all, *arabesk* is characterized by ornamentation and throaty trills and sobs. The genre also has melodic characteristics of Turkish folk and art music and elements of non-European music. Most of all, however, it shows a proximity to Western music, particularly with regard to its large European ensembles, which also include Turkish instruments. Electronic instruments, effects, and rhythms are integral to this music. The song is always in the foreground and may be accompanied by one or more voices. Many musicians claim that any kind of music can be transformed into *arabesk* and that any kind of ensemble, Turkish or Western, is appropriate for it. Nevertheless, the rhythm instruments are always important because they carry the driving rhythms underlying the singing. *Arabesk* is being disseminated through recordings (such as cassettes), but the oral tradition also continues.

Adapted by the Editors.

REFERENCES

Ahrens, Christian. 1970. *Instrumentale Musikstile an der osttürkische Schwarzmeerküste, eine vergleichende Untersuchung der Spielpraxis davul-zurna, kemençe und tulum*. Munich: Kommissionsverlag K. Renner.

Ahrens, Christian, et al. 1984. "Weine meine Laute . . ." In *Gedenkschrift Kurt Reinhard*. Laaber-Verlag.

Akdemir, Hayrettin. 1992. *Die neue türkische Musik*. Berlin: Hitit-Verlag.

Bartók, Béla. 1976. *Turkish Folk Music from Asia Minor*, ed. Benjamin Suchoff. Princeton, N.J.: Princeton University Press.

Birge, John K. 1937. *The Bektashi Order of Dervishes*. London: Luzac; Hartford, Conn.: Hartford Seminary Press.

Campbell, Richard G. 1968. "Zur Typologie der Schalenlanghalslaute." In *Collection d'études musicologiques/Sammlung musikwissenschaftlicher Abhandlungen*, vol. 47. Strasbourg, Baden-Baden: Heitz.

Christensen, Dieter. 1963. "Tanzlieder der Hakkari-Kurden." *Jahrbuch für Musikalische Volks- und Völkerkunde* 1:11–47.

Eberhard, Wolfram. 1955. *Minstrel Tales from Southeastern Turkey*. Berkeley: University of California Press.

Edipoğlu, Baki Süha. 1962. *Ünlü Türk Bestekârları*. Istanbul.

Elçin, Sükrü. 1976. *Ali Ufkî: Hayatı, eserleri ve Mecmûa-i sâz ü söz*. Istanbul: Millî Eğitim Basımevi.

Farmer, Henry G. 1940. "Turkish Instruments of Music in the Seventeenth Century." *Journal of the Royal Asiatic Society*.

———. 1966. "Islam." In *Musikgeschichte in Bildern*, vol. 3. Leipzig: Deutscher Verlag für Musik.

Fisher, C. G., and A. W. 1987. "Topkapı Sarayı in the Mid-Seventeenth Century: Bobovsk's Description." *Archivium Ottomanicum* 10:5–81.

Gölpınarlı, Abdülbâki. 1963a. "Pir Sultan Abdal: Hayatı, sanatı, eserleri." *Varlık Yayınları, sayı*, 152; *Türk klâsikleri*, 13. Istanbul: Varlık Yayınevi.

———. 1963b. *Alevî-Bektâşî nefesleri*. Istanbul: Remzi Kitabevi.

Hindemith, Paul. 1983. *Türk Küğ Yaşamının Kalkınması için Öneriler* (Recommendations for the Development of Turkish Musical Life), ed. Gültekin Oransay. Izmir.

Kantemiroğlu. c. 1700/1976. *Kitāb-i 'ilmü'l-Mūsikī 'alā vechi'l-Hurūfāt*, ed. Tura Yayınlarī. 4 vols. Istanbul.

Markoff, Irene. 1986. "The Role of Expressive Culture in the Demystification of a Secret Sect in Islam: The Case of the Alevis in Turkey." *World of Music* 28(3):42–45.

Nazari, Suphi. 1935. *Ameli Türk Musikisi*. Istanbul.

Okyay, Erdoğan. 1976. *Melodische Gestaltelemente in den türkischen "Kırık hava."* Ankara.

Oransay, Gültekin. 1957. "Das Tonsystem der türkei-türkischen Kunstmusik." *Musikforschung* 10:250–264.

———. 1964. *Die traditionelle türkische Kunstmusik*. Ankara: Küğ-Veröffentlichung.

———. 1966. *Die melodische Linie und der Begriff Makam der traditionellen türkischen Kunstmusik vom 15. bis 19. Jahrhundert*. Ankara: Küğ-Veröffentlichung.

———. 1973. "Dinî Türk Musikisinde XVII. Yüzyılda Kullanılmiş Makamlar." *Ankara Üniversitesi Ilâhiyat Fakültesi Dergisi* 19:75–82.

Öztuna, Yılmaz. 1969–1976. *Türk Musikisi Ansiklopedisi*. 3 vols. Istanbul: M. E. B. Devlet Kitaplar.

Picken, Laurence. 1975. *Folk Musical Instruments of Turkey*. London: Oxford University Press.

Popescu-Judetz, Eugenia. 1981. *Studies in Oriental Arts: Dimitri Cantemir's Theory of Turkish Art Music*. Pittsburgh, Pa.: Institute of Folk Arts.

Reiche, Jens Peter. 1970. "Stilelemente südtürkischer Davul-Zurna-Stücke." *Jahrbuch für Musikalische Volks- und Völkerkunde* 5:9–54.

Reinhard, Kurt. 1956a. "Zustand und Wandel der bäuerlichen Musik in der türkischen Provinz Adana." *Sociologus* (neue Folge) 6:68–78.

———. 1956b. "Types of Turkmenian Songs in Turkey." *Journal of the International Folk Music Council* 9:49–54.

———. 1960. "Ein türkischer Tanzliedtyp und seine außertürkischen Parallelen." *Baessler-Archiv* (neue Folge) 8:131–169.

———. 1961. "Trommeltänze aus der Süd-Türkei." *Journal of the International Folk Music Council* 13:19–26.

———. 1961. "Zur Variantenbildung im türkischen Volkslied, dargestellt an einer Hirtenweise." In *Festschrift Heinrich Besseler zum 60. Geburtstag*, 21–34. Leipzig: Deutscher Verlag für Musik.

———. 1962. *Türkische Musik*. Berlin: Museum für Völkerkunde.

———. 1966a. "Türkische Musik." In *Die Musik in Geschichte und Gegenwart* 13:954–968. Kassel: Bärenreiter.

———. 1966b. "Musik am Schwarzen Meer: Erste Ergebnisse einer Forschungsreise in die Nordost-Türkei." *Jahrbuch für Musikalische Volks- und Völkerkunde* 2:9–58.

———. 1967a. "Die Gegenwärtige Praxis des Epengesanges in der Türkei." In *Grazer und Münchener Balkanologische Studien: Beiträge zur Kenntnis Südosteuropas und des Nahen Orients*, 83–96. Munich: Trofenik.

———. 1967b. "Die Quellensituation der türkischen Kunstmusik. Gedanken zur Frage mündlicher und schriftlicher Tradition und zum Problem Improvisation-Komposition." In *Festschrift Walter Wiora*, 578–582. Kassel.

———. 1969. "Cultivation and Encouragement of Traditional Music in Turkey: Creating a Wider Interest in Traditional Music." In *International Institute for Comparative Music Studies and Documentation, Berlin, 1969*, 160–169. Berlin.

———. 1970. "Strukturanalyse einer Hymne des türkischen Komponisten Itrî." In *Festschrift Walter Graf*, 158–177. Vienna: H. Böhlau.

———. 1972. "Grundlagen und Ergebnisse der Erforschung türkischer Musik." *Acta Musicologica* 44:266–280.

———. 1973. "Musikalische Gestaltungsprinzipien der âyın, dargestellt an der anonymen Komposition im Makam pençgâh." In *Uluslararası Mevlâna Semineri*, 315–333. Ankara: Türkiye İş Bankası Kültür Yayınları.

———. 1974. "Die türkische Doppelklarinette çifte." *Baessler-Archiv* (neue Folge) 22:139–163.

———. 1975a. "Über die Beziehungen zwischen byzantinischer und türkischer Musik." In *Musica Antiqua*. Vol. 4, *Acta Scientifica*, 623–632. Bydgoszcz.

———. 1975b. "Die Musikpflege türkischer Nomaden." *Zeitschrift für Ethnologie* 100:115–124.

———. 1976. "Über einige Beziehungen zwischen türkischer und griechischer Volksmusik." *Beiträge zue Ethnomusikologie* 4:9–18.

———. 1978. "Albert Bobovsky's Aufzeichnungen türkischer Musik als geschichtliche Quelle." In *Musica Antiqua*. Vol. 5, *Acta Scientifica*, 373–382. Bydgoszcz.

———. 1979. "Spieltechnik und Musik der türkischen Kurzoboe mey." *Studia Instrumentorum Musicae Popularis* 6:111–119.

———. 1980a. "Turkey." In *The New Grove Dictionary of Music and Musicians*, Vol. 19, 165–179. London: Macmillan.

———. 1980b. "Türkei." In *Außereuropäische Musik in Einzeldarstellungen*, 165–179. Munich: Deutscher Taschenbuchverlag; Kassel: Bärenreiter.

———. 1981a. "Mozarts Rezeption türkischer Musik." In *Bericht über den Internationalen Musikwissenschaftlichen Kongress, Berlin 1974*, 518–523. Kassel: Bärenreiter.

———. 1981b. "Turkish Miniatures as Sources of Music History." In *Music in East and West: Essays in Honor of Walter Kaufmann*, 143–166. New York.

———. 1984a. "Gestalten südtürkischer Totenklagen." In *'Weine, meine Laute . . .'. Gedenkschrift für Kurt Reinhard*, ed. Christian Ahrens, Rudolf Maria Brandl, and Felix Hoerburger. Regensburg: Laaber-Verlag.

———. 1984b. "Das Na't des İtrî und seine Versionen." *Jahrbuch für Musikalische Volks- und Völkerkunde* 11:9–13.

Reinhard, Kurt, and Ursula Reinhard. 1968. "Auf der Fiedel mein. . . . Volkslieder von der osttürkischen Schwarzmeerküste." *Veröffentlichungen des Museums für Völkerkunde Berlin* (neue Folge), vol. 14. Berlin: Museum für Völkerkunde.

Reinhard, Kurt, and Ursula Reinhard. 1969. *Turquie: Les traditions musicales*. Paris: Buchet-Chastel.

Reinhard, Kurt, and Ursula Reinhard. 1983. "Volksmusikelemente in der Türkischen Kunstmusik." In *II: Milletlerarası Türk Folklor Kongresi Bildiriler*, vol. 3, 225–239. Ankara: Kültür ve Turizm Bakanlığı.

Reinhard, Kurt, and Ursula Reinhard. 1984. *Musik der Türkei*. 2 vols. Wilhelmshaven: Heinrichshofen.

Reinhard, Ursula. 1965. "Vor seinen Häusern eine Weide. . . . Volksliedtexte aus der Süd-Türkei." *Veröffentlichen des Museums für Völkerkunde Berlin* (neue Folge), vol. 8. Berlin: Museum für Völkerkunde.

———. 1985a. "Konstanz und Wandel im bağlama-Spiel und Gesang türkischer âşık und ihrer Lieder." *Studia Instrumentorum Musicae Popularis* 8:86.

———. 1985b. "Das Musikleben in osmanischer Zeit." In *Türkische Kunst und Kultur aus osmanischer Zeit*, vol. 1, 159–163; 213–222. Recklinghausen: A. Bongers.

———. 1987. "Westliche Einflüsse auf das türkische Musikleben einst und heute." In *Mozaik: Türkische Kultur in Berlin*, 37–44. Berlin: Arenhövel.

———. 1990. "The Veils Are Lifted." In *Music, Gender, and Culture*, ed. Marcia Herndon and Susanne Ziegler. Wilhelmshaven: Florian Noetzel Verlag.

———. In press (a). "Epische Gesänge in der Türkei am Beispiel des Köroğlu-Epos."

———. In press (b). "Musik am türkischen Hof des 17. Jahrhunderts." Lecture, Akademie der Wissenschaften in Göttingen, June 1988.

Reinhard, Ursula, and Tiago De Oliveria Pinto. 1989. *Sänger und Poeten mit der Laute, Türkische Âşık und Ozan*. Veröffentlichungen des Museums für Völkerkunde Berlin, Abteilung Musikethnologie Berlin. Berlin: Museum für Völkerkunde, Dietrich Reimer Verlag. (With 2 cassettes.)

Sarısözen, Muzaffer. 1962. *Türk Halk Musikisi Usulleri*. Ankara: Resimli Posta Matbaasî.

Satıroğlu, Aşık Veysel. 1974. "Doslar beni hatırlasın." In *Türkike İş Bankası Kültür Yayınları*, 96. Ankara: Türkiye İş Bankası Kültür Yayınları.

Say, Ahmet. 1985. *Müzik Ansiklopedisi*. 4 vols. Ankara.

Saygun, Adnan. 1948. *Les divers aspects de la musique turque*. Ankara.

———. 1976. *Béla Bartók's Folk Music Research in Turkey*, ed. László Vikár. Budapest: Akadémiai Kiadó.

Sieglin, Angelika. 1984. *Instrumentalkompositionen der türkischen Kunstmusik in ihrer Beziehung zum Makam*. Hamburg: K. D. Wagner.

Signell, Karl L. 1977. *Makam: Modal Practice in Turkish Art Music*. Seattle: Asian Music Publications.

Wannig, Klaus-Detlev. 1980. "Der Dichter Karaca Oğlan: Studien zur türkischen Liebeslyrik." In *Studien zur Sprache, Kultur, und Geschichte der Türkvölker*, vol. 1. Freiburg: Schwarz.

Yekta Bey, Raouf. 1922. "La musique turque." In *Encyclopédie de la musique*, ed. Albert Lavignac, Vol. 5, 2945–3064. Paris: C. Delagrave.

Zimmermann, Cornelia-Kalyoncu. 1985. *Deutsche Musiker in der Türkei im 20. Jahrhundert*. Frankfurt am Main: P. Lang.

Snapshot: Ismail Dede Efendi

Walter Feldman

Hammâmîzâde Ismail Dede Efendi (1778–1846) had a dominant role in almost every aspect of the current repertoire of Turkish classical music. Although the Ottoman musical culture produced many great masters over its centuries-long history, none of its historical figures can rival the significance of Ismail Dede. In attempting to assess this significance, we may note that his long career represents a bridge between the high classicism of the court of Selim III (r. 1789–1808), which opens the modern era of Ottoman music, and the various developments of the nineteenth century, when the court gradually ceased to be the major patron of this music. His sheer output is staggering—more than 500 items, of which 268 survive today—and thus his own compositions occupy a dominating position within the entire known Ottoman vocal repertoire. His great productivity was matched by his dedication to instruction, so that his numerous students, themselves frequently musicians of the highest caliber, transmitted his compositions into the present day. It is also fortunate that Necib Pasha (1812–1883), whose Ottoman musical education was supplemented by a study of Western music at the court with Donizetti Pasha, included many of Dede Efendi's works, during the composer's lifetime, in his own collection of Turkish music in Western notation.

Ismail Dede had an almost uniquely catholic taste within Ottoman music, and he composed extensively within every vocal genre, including the mystical *âyîn* of the Mevlevî dervishes [see Music in Performance: Who Are the Whirling Dervishes?], the *beste* and *semâ'î* of the courtly *fasıl*, the light-classical *şarkı*, and even the songs of the *köçek* dancing-boys of the taverns of Istanbul. While his style has never been subjected to extensive analysis, it can be said that he developed a form of the crystallized classical style of the court of Selim III, which then became a standard for the remainder of the nineteenth century. His students, drawn from many walks of life, included Mevlevî dervishes such as Zekâ'î Dede (d. 1897); men of the court, such as Dellâlzâde Ismail (d. 1869), Haim Bey (d. 1868), Hacı Faik Bey (d. 1891), and Hacı Arif Bey (d. 1885); and the Armenians Baba Hamparsum (d. 1839) and Nikoaos Ağa (d. 1890?). Moreover, his students were numerous enough to ensure that almost the entire Ottoman vocal repertoire would be transmitted in the form in which he had shaped it. It would not be an exaggeration to say that the preponderance of the style and repertoire of twentieth-century Turkish classical music can be traced back to Ismail Dede through his students.

Although Ismail Dede lived until the mid-nineteenth century—a relatively recent period—and despite the great fame of his music, the sources for his life are few. They consist of a few documents of the court, a few brief notices in the *Defter-i Derviân* of his teacher Ali Nutkî Dede (1762–1804), and some stories in the *Letâif-i Enderûn* of Hızır Ilyas Bey (1859) and in the *Tarîh-i Enderûn* of Atâ Bey (1876). These have been supplemented by anecdotes told by his student Zekâ'î Dede Efendi (d. 1897) to Rauf Yekta Bey (1924), but the historicity of several of them has been questioned by Sadettin Nüzhet Ergun in a monumental study of the music of the dervish orders (1943).

Ismail Dede's father, Süleyman Ağa, was born in Korica, near Manastir. He became the *mühürdar* 'seal bearer' of the infamous Ahmad Jazzar Pasha in Sidon but later resigned from official service and settled in Istanbul, where he purchased a *hammâm* 'bathhouse' in the Ehzâde neighborhood. As a child, Ismail studied for seven years with a local amateur musician, Uncuzade Mehmed Efendi. As an adolescent. he was registered in the *muhasebe kalemi* 'office of accounts', but he began to study music at the nearby Yenikapı Mevlevî *tekke* 'lodge'. At the age of twenty, he decided to leave his office work and enter the three-year retreat of the Mevlevî dervishes. During the second year of his service he composed a *şarkı* song in the *makam* 'mode' *buselik* that was eventually performed for Sultan Selim III by his imperial singer. This led to the sultan's requesting Ismail's service at court. Ismail's superior, Ali Nutkî Dede, shortened his service by one year so that he could begin to attend the imperial *fasıl* twice a week. As a dervish, Ismail received the title *dede* and continued to teach and compose in his cell in the *tekke.* In 1802, he married a woman of the court and left the *tekke* to live with her in the Akbıyık neighborhood. They had one son, who died in 1805.

Ismail Dede withdrew from the court during the troubles resulting from the assassination of Sultan Selim III in 1808; but with the accession, later that year, of Mahmud II (1808–1839) he entered the most productive period of his career. He attained the posts of *musahib-i şehriyârî* 'imperial companian' and chief muezzin. It was in this period that he composed seven Mevlevî *âyîn*: *Saba* and *Neva* in 1823, *Bestenigâr* in 1832, *Saba-Buselik* and *Hüzzam* in 1833, the lost *Isfahan* in 1836, and *Ferahfeza* in 1839. He also completed his *fasıl* in the same *makam* in 1834.

The death of Sultan Mahmud II in 1839 marked the end of this creative period, as the new ruler, Abdülmecid (r. 1839–1861), attempted to install Western music at court. In 1846, Ismail Dede is reported to have remarked that "there is no longer any taste in this game"; he left the court and embarked on a pilgrimage to Mecca, where he composed his last piece, an *ilâhî* hymn in the *şehnaz makam*, and where he died of cholera the same year.

REFERENCES

Aksoy, Bülent. 1994. "Ismail Dede Efendi." In *Istanbul Anseklopedisi*, vol. 4: 211–212. Istanbul.

Dede, Ali Nutkî, *Defter-i Derviân*. Süleymâniye Ktp. Nafiz Paa no. 1194.

Ergun, Sadettin Nüzhet. 1943. *Türk Musikisi Antolojisi,* vol. II. Istanbul.

Hızır Ilyas Efendi. 1859. *Letaif-i Enderûn*. Istanbul.

Inal, Ibnülemin Mahmud Kemal. 1964. *Ho Sada.* Istanbul.

Öztuna, Yılmaz. 1987. *Dede Efendi*. Istanbul.

Yekta Bey, Rauf. 1924. *Esâtîz-i Elhân III: Dede Efendi*. Istanbul.

From Empire to Republic: Vocal Style in Twentieth-Century Turkey

John Morgan O'Connell

Debating Vocal Style
Reforming Vocal Style
Performing Vocal Style
Personalizing Vocal Style

Vocal style in Turkish music was a subject of intense public debate during the twentieth century. After the inception of the Turkish republic and the formulation of a suitable nationalist ideology, Turkish vocalists had to address the ideal of musical purity espoused in the dominant Republican perspective and determine acceptable limits of musical practice in light of a redefined Turkish identity. Responding to contemporary intellectuals' criticism of Ottoman culture, they attempted to classify styles of vocal performance into two categories—Ottoman and Republican—and rejected styles that did not conform to the modernist aspirations and westernizing predilections of the new political elite.

Vocal styles, including transmission, performance, and presentation, were defined according to a wide variety of criteria. Such issues were at the heart of the discourse surrounding admissible artistic practices and acceptable aesthetic values. While this discourse was neatly articulated in a number of academic publications and also widely manipulated by legislators for political purposes, it enabled individual musicians to validate deviant musical practices for strategic advantage and foreign commercial interests to commodify vocal performance in line with the aesthetic demands of an expanding Turkish market. In short, vocal style provided a locus for debating larger social and political issues in Turkey during the early twentieth century.

DEBATING VOCAL STYLE

In fact, the debate over style in Turkish vocal performance has a well-established pedigree connected to the gradual appropriation of Western cultural practices throughout the Eastern Mediterranean during the eighteenth century and intimately associated with the political and social upheavals consequent to the demise of Ottoman political influence. The instability associated with almost a century of intermittent reforms (known as the *Tanzimat* period) was characterized by a transformation—based on European principles—of outmoded Ottoman military, educational, and bureaucratic institutions. These westernizing reforms, in turn, had a profound influence on the administrative structure and the cultural fabric of Ottoman society. In the administrative realm, the widespread adoption of European political and philosophical ideals precipitated two attempts at constitutional reform (in 1876 and 1908) and eventually paved the way for the dramatic events of the 1920s, when Turkey became a republic

European aesthetic preferences (*alafranga*) competed with—and in some instances replaced—native urban sensibilities (*alaturka*).

in 1923 under the leadership of Mustafa Kemal Atatürk (1881–1938). In the cultural realm, European aesthetic preferences (*alafranga*) competed with—and in some instances replaced—native urban sensibilities (*alaturka*) in a wide range of areas that were subsequently classified historically as Ottoman versus Republican and geographically as Eastern versus Western. These areas encompassed sartorial preferences, temporal designations, culinary interests, and particularly musical activity.

The division between *alaturka* and *alafranga* in stylistic discourse had important implications for Turkish musical performance. During the twentieth century, *alaturka* was generally considered unsophisticated in musical conception, outdated in performance technique, degenerate in emotive content, and above all unsuited to Turkish nationalistic purism. *Alafranga*, on the other hand, provided an alternative to Ottoman musical practice and promoted the reform of Turkish music according to European principles. The debate over *alaturka* and *alafranga* reflected, in part, an intense scrutiny by contemporary Republican ideologues, who, inspired by Ziya Gökalp (1876–1924; see Gökalp 1923), sought to standardize cultural practices—dress, language, customs, and music—according to contemporary notions of Turkish respectability. Modifying Gökalp's original ideas, they argued that *alaturka* belonged to the imperial or Ottoman stage of civilization and that it had not progressed to the national or Republican level of artistic development exemplified by *alafranga*. With regard to Turkish music, the debate also reflected a related modernist urge to systematize terminology in published lexicons, standardize repertoires in notated anthologies, codify methods, and control performance as a public (rather than private) expression of normative (rather than singular) practices. The result of the Republican effort was the emergence of a national style (*millî musiki*) that appealed to the Western biases of Republican taste and offered the possibility of a Turkish style expunged of its Eastern elements.

The distinction between *alaturka* and *alafranga* was especially apparent in regard to vocal performance. Turkish art song, in contrast to Western vocal performance and its variants, was relegated to the *alaturka* category. Not only was the monophonic compositional style of this ancient tradition—based on a sophisticated relationship between mode (*makam*), rhythmic cycle (*usûl*), and prosodic structure (*aruz*)—deemed unsuited to the modernist sensibility of contemporary audiences, but the elusive language of its texts, the cosmopolitan character of its musical forms, and the cyclical configuration of its compound structures (*fasıllar*) served to endorse the Eastern provenance and hence the non-Turkish attributes of *alaturka*. The method of its transmission, the manner of its performance, the context of its presentation, and above all the lifestyle of its proponents were all subjected to critical attention.

Turkish vocal style, especially in improvisations (*gazeller*), symbolized these concerns. Turkish vocal technique was denigrated for its chest register, guttural nasality, sobbing character, and amplitude. Turkish vocal performance was criticized for its intense melismas, melancholic character, textual inaccuracy, incorrect pronunciation, and scruffy presentation. In addition, the lifestyle of Turkish vocalists was portrayed as degenerate, combining alcoholic excess, sexual promiscuity and, implicitly, gender ambiguity. This lifestyle was said to be cultivated nocturnally in drinking houses (*meyhaneler*) and was equated with the multicultural provenance—and debauchery—of Ottoman musical performance. Simply put, *alaturka* was seen as a benighted product of Ottoman disorder. It was a vast domain of unspoken meanings that had to be defined, debated, and changed for the sake of Republican order and control.

REFORMING VOCAL STYLE

The transformation of Turkish style according to the etic rules of *alafranga* rather than the emic principles of *alaturka* reflected a more general concern with social and political change in Turkey during the 1920s. In an attempt to erase the culture of the Ottoman past, Mustafa Kemal Atatürk instituted a set of reforms—religious (1924–1925), sartorial (1925), economic (1926), and linguistic (1928)—which served to underscore the modernist and westernizing aspirations of his new state. These reforms, subsequently legitimated (1932) according the ideology of revolutionism (*inkılâpçılık*), nurtured a discourse about change that permeated many aspects of Turkish life. In music, Atatürk's preoccupation with revolutionary change resulted in a reification of Western styles (*alafranga*), to the detriment of Ottoman practice (*alaturka*). Turkish folk music, a category that mediated between *alafranga* and *alaturka*, provided a conceptual space for the construction of a national style (*millî musiki*) and for contestation of its boundaries [see ASPECTS OF TURKISH FOLK MUSIC THEORY]. On the one hand, orthodox opinion was that Turkish folk music should be molded within a Western compositional framework to create a modernized national music, polyphonic in texture but Turkish in essence. On the other hand, proponents of Turkish art music, which had to address orthodox nationalist ideals, proposed a heterodox solution—the reconstitution of *alaturka* according to European musicological principles. In this way, *alaturka* was "alafrangized" (a neologism, *alafrangalaştırmak*).

This modernist synthesis had profound consequences. Turkish music was codified and notated according to European musicological standards. That is, *alaturka* was fossilized within—or, to use another image, put into the straitjacket of—Western notation and published in a series of authoritative editions by the Committee for the Examination and Standardization of Turkish Music (Türk Musıkisi Tedkik ve Tesbit Heyeti). Turkish music theory, following a precedent set by Raûf Yektâ Bey (1871–1935), was standardized by Subhî Ezgi (1869–1962) and Sâdeddin Arel (1880–1955) according to European acoustic principles. Turkish musical performance, too, faced the inexorable thrust of modernism: ensembles were expanded, unison replaced heterophony, and individual invention was curtailed as part of a wholesale adaptation of European orchestral conventions. A new glossary of musical terms was invented under the auspices of the Turkish Language Society (Türk Dil Kurumu) to satisfy the revolutionary provisions of language reform; and this revised vocabulary was published in *Tarama Sözlüğü* 'Research Dictionary' after 1932, institutionalized in conservatories for instructional use, and subsequently collected in authoritative reference sources for research purposes. While these terms reflect the nationalist concern for a purified Turkish lexicon freed from Arabic and Persian influences, they also demonstrate a modernist concern for adopting Western musical terminology in the realm of *alaturka*. Consequently, the vocabulary of vocal style—technique and performance—has the unmistakable stamp of European musical taxonomy, which was seen as modernizing in principle and Republican in spirit.

In this climate of taxonomic rigor, Turkish vocal performance was itself classified as a style, rather than as a distinctive musical system, to distinguish it from a world of possible styles. All aspects of style—technical expertise, rendition, artistic expressiveness, and the manner and presentation of performance—were scrutinized for their national validity and, by extension, for their Western character. Vocal styles were

FIGURE 1 Arab stereotype: a street musician of African descent performing on a three-stringed, long-necked bowl lute in Istanbul. This photograph, taken by the Swedish photographer Guillaume Bergson in 1875, depicts a contemporary Orientalist representation of Arab music making in Turkey. Photo courtesy of the Abdullah Frères Collection at the German Archaeological Institute, Istanbul.

classified generically according to their regional qualities, historic characteristics, and normative functions. They were also distinguished by individual attributes, including context or setting, religious associations, and ensembles' affiliation. Technical terms (describing vocal practice) and timbral definitions (describing vocal quality) were formulated to replace the practical metaphors of the past and to give a critical edge to the polemical discourse concerning authentic modes of Turkish performance. Vocal styles that did not conform to the standards of *alafranga* practice were expunged from the musical canon, subjected to public scrutiny, and ridiculed as deviant. In this process, individual musical practices were bracketed as styles, equated with stereotypes, and inspected for their Turkish pedigree. Nightclub (*gazino*), mystic (*tekke*), and Arab (*arap*) styles were not only linked to a representative range of musical practices but also equated with characteristic contemporary stereotypes—respectively, the drunken Christian, the mad Sufi, and the itinerant Arab (figure 1).

The emergence of Arab style (*arap tarzı*) as a musical category was especially significant. This term, appearing in Turkish musical discourse after 1928, began to replace *alaturka* to designate a class requiring critical attention. That is, the musical practices associated with Ottoman vocal performance were no longer identified with a Turkish provenance (*alaturka*) but rather were equated with the non-Turkish attributes of an alien Arab tradition. By extension, musical practices and musical genres that did not conform to the westernizing goals of Republican orthodoxy were classified as foreign and rejected accordingly. Musical styles associated with Sufi religious houses, Christian drinking establishments, and Gypsy festivities were scrutinized for their non-Turkish attributes, labeled for their discursive interest, and vilified for their heterodox character. While these styles were sometimes identified with different aspects of Ottoman cultural life and assigned to correspondingly distinctive stylistic categories, they were often grouped together and simply subsumed under the pejorative category "Arab style." As part of the same process, the term *goygoy* was applied to an eclectic range of vocal practices: those that included intense glottalization and melismatic embellishment, those that were often associated with non-Muslim performers, and those that were identified as Arab rather than Turkish in origin. Although it is true that a number of contemporary Turkish instrumentalists—most notably Kemânî Hayday Tatlıyay (1890–1963)—consciously emulated Egyptian musical styles for commercial reasons, Turkish commentators manipulated the pejorative designation *goygoy* to denigrate the musical practices of the Ottoman era and to undermine the Turkish pedigree of *alaturka*.

PERFORMING VOCAL STYLE

This climate of revolutionary change had important implications for the transmission of Turkish vocal style. Although the reform of music education can be traced back as far as the formation of the Imperial Band (Mızıkay-ı Hümâyûn) in 1827, and although several Turkish music societies institutionalized these reforms by applying Western didactic methods before 1923, in practice traditional methods of instruction continued to be used. The traditional system fostered by a number of Sufi sects was oral in character and was ideally suited to the training of Turkish vocalists. This system, called *meşk* 'lesson' or 'model', focused on the poetic rather than the melodic attributes of the Turkish vocal repertoire and organized the training process accordingly. Students would sit in a circle on the floor with their teacher (*hoca*) and, in one instructional operation, memorize text (*güfte*), rhythmic cycles (*usûller*), modes (*makamlar*), interpretation, and performance, though the lesson was divided into literary and rhythmic components. This format served to structure the learning experience; to blend all textual, musical, and performance criteria into one palatable whole; and above all to aid memorization.

In contrast, the reforms by the new national government entailed a completely different method of vocal instruction. This method was literate rather than oral, Western rather than Eastern, and melodic rather than poetic. The new approach to music education—modeled on the European conservatory—encouraged not only Western vocal techniques, to replace traditional practices, but also Western aesthetics that were in keeping with the westernizing Republican ethos and the transformation of *alaturka* into a national style.

After 1927, this reformation of *alaturka* vocal performance was profoundly affected by the creation of the new Turkish Music Conservatory. The conservatory did have a precedent—the Darül'elhan (1917–1926)—but now the ministry of education initiated reforms proscribing the teaching of Turkish music in schools (1924), promoting instruction in Western music in teachers' colleges (1924), and bringing existing institutions into the new conservatory under the auspices of the Fine Arts Commission (1926). All this was detrimental to *alaturka*. It was no longer taught or performed in the new academy, whereas *alafranga* was promoted by means of generous funding, active recruitment of staff and students, and a well-advertised series of public performances. In fact, of the eighteen full-time staff members in the *alaturka* section of Darül'elhan in 1924, the new conservatory kept only three—and these three were employed as musicologists (under the direction of Raûf Yektâ Bey) to document and notate the Turkish classical repertoire from oral sources, in a new institutional body called the Society for the Fixing and Classification of Turkish Music (Alaturka Musiki Tasnif ve Tesbit Heyeti). The annual budget published in *Düstur* 'Codex' shows the disproportionate allocation of government funds in the new institution: more than 78 percent went to the *alafranga* section, and only the remainder went to the *alaturka* division. This, of course, reflected a significant withdrawal of support. Thus institutional reform, functioning in the Republican context, confined *alaturka* both temporally and substantively within an edifice of *alafranga*, the Turkish Music Conservatory.

The establishment of the new music academy pushed *alaturka* further out toward the periphery. Turkish vocal performance continued to be taught in some public schools (such as Darüşşafaka, a school for orphans) and in some private institutions that emerged soon after the new conservatory and benefited from its dismissal of so many musicians. However, because Turkish musical performance had been expunged from the music curriculum and Turkish musical instruction had been eliminated from state establishments, vocalists needed to devise new strategies for professional employment and advancement. Some retreated to the drinking houses (*meyhanelar*) and nightclubs (*gazinolar*) in large Turkish cities, thereby confirming the low status of *alaturka* in Republicans' eyes. Others regrouped into professional ensembles—some already established (such as the Darüttа'limi Musiki Cemiyeti) and some (such as the Türk Musiki Heyeti) newly formed in response to the influx of unemployed artists. The most accomplished performers were also offered generous recording contracts with leading foreign companies (including Columbia, Pathé, and Gramophone), technologically advanced competitors in the lucrative Turkish market. In particular, after 1927 the development of electronic recording not only opened up new opportunities in Turkish radio stations but also facilitated the development of a new Turkish style. Modern technology enabled performers to realize in practice the aesthetic aspirations of the Republican ideal—a national style that used Turkish materials within a framework of European musical practices.

PERSONALIZING VOCAL STYLE

The famous vocalist Münîr Nûreddin Selçuk (1899–1981; figure 2) was supremely adept at navigating through this ideological quagmire. Advocating a heterodox solution to the problem of developing a national music, he performed *alaturka* using European

FIGURE 2 Reforming a stereotype: Münîr Nûreddin Selçuk (1899–1981).

vocal methods. To this end, he developed his own performance style, combining Western techniques of diaphragm control and voice production with traditional practices. He also studied in Paris (reportedly at the Paris Conservatoire in 1928) to further his knowledge of Western music, to perfect his technical expertise, and perhaps to acquire the prestige attendant on a foreign education. His westernizing strategies also encompassed musical interpretation. His careful choice, precise enunciation, and delicate programmatic embellishment of ancient Ottoman texts reflect his wide heterodox concern with correct, descriptive performance of a Turkish literary canon. Moreover, his judicious application of dynamics and his restrained use of ornamentation and inessential syllabization bespeak an artistry at once respectable, neoclassic in intent, and acceptable to the reformist sensibility of Republican orthodoxy.

Selçuk's search for Western respectability extended beyond vocal style. In performance, Selçuk was the first vocalist to present Turkish music as a soloist, standing in front of his audience, wearing a tuxedo, adopting the format of a recital or concert rather than a traditional *fasıl*—and thus avoiding the modal specificity and cyclical structure of traditional practice. His professional style—including his choice of concert venues, his impeccable sartorial sense, his aristocratic stage manner, and his insistence on the *alafranga* terms "artist" and "solist" (in contrast to the pejorative *alaturka* terms *hanende* and *gazelhan*)—also suggested his pride in having achieved distinction in the face of contemporary ideological prejudice.

However, although Selçuk's performance style seemed to embody Republican modernism, and although his personal style seemed to confirm the Republican taste for westernization, it would be simplistic to view his stylistic innovations only in terms of ideological discourse. In truth, long before the creation of a Turkish state in 1923, his interest in Western music had been nurtured by his teachers—Bestenigâr Hoca Ziyâ Bey (1877–1923) and [Zekâîzâde] Ahmed Irsoy (1869–1943)—within the eclectic musical circles of Istanbul. His professional style also reflected an antiquated concern with social distinction made possible by his ancient Selçuk lineage. This concern was evident in his exclusive circle of professional contacts, in his courtly manner of personal address, and in his aristocratic lifestyle as a gentleman of Istanbul (*İstanbul efendisi*). In addition, his much publicized concert format, his distinctive sartorial preferences, and even his interest in westernization had precedents in earlier musical—especially instrumental—performance practices. Indeed, it could be argued that his stylistic innovations were tailored to suit the technological innovations (especially electronic recording) and commercial interests of recording companies. A number of recording companies, notably His Master's Voice (Sahibinin Sesi), promoted Selçuk by creating exclusive artistic labels (the FF and FE series), sponsoring his trip to Paris in 1928, backing his international concert series, and patronizing his debut at the Fransız Tiyatrosu 'French Theater' in 1930. By sponsoring a contemporary artist in this way, they used the ideological concerns of Republican orthodoxy for economic gain—perhaps for commercial survival. Simply put, musical discourse had its financial benefits.

When Münîr Nûreddin Selçuk called for a reconstitution of *alaturka* according to the principles of *alafranga*, he was offering a heterodox solution to a contemporary discourse concerning the appropriate character of national music (*millî musiki*). By integrating European techniques with traditional performance practices, he not only addressed the political sensibilities of Republican orthodoxy but also forged his own individual vocal style and his own manner of performance and presentation. These were as politically respectable as they were financially advantageous. Selçuk was thus able to circumvent the political prejudices and the commerical volatility of contemporary Turkish life and, with ideological impunity, create his own type of Turkish vocal performance.

REFERENCES

Aksoy, Bülent. 1989. "Is the Question of the Origin of Turkish Music Not Redundant?" *Turkish Musical Quarterly* 2(4):1–8.

Arel, Hüseyin. 1988. *Türk Musikisi Kimindir?* Ankara: Kültür ve Turizm Bakanlığı.

Behar, Cem. 1987. *Klasik Türk Musikisi Üzerine Denemeler*. Istanbul: Bağlam Yayınları.

Bourdieu, Pierre. 1984. *Distinction: A Social Critique of the Judgment of Taste*, trans. Richard Nice. Cambridge, Mass.: Harvard University Press.

Erguner, Ahmed. 1990. "Alla turca—alla franca: Les enjeux de la musique turque." *Cahiers de Musiques Traditionnelles* 3:45–56.

Ezgi, Subhi. 1933–1955. *Nazari ve Amelî Türk Musikisi*. 5 vols. Istanbul: Millî Eğitim Basımevi.

Feldman, Walter. 1993. "Ottoman Sources on the Development of the Taksîm." *Yearbook for Traditional Music* 25:1–28.

Foucault, Michel. 1969. *L'Archéologie du savoir*. Paris: Gallimard.

Gazimihal, Mahmut. 1924. "Musiki ve Ziya Gökalp." *Millî Mecmua* 24:383–385.

———. 1961. *Musiki Sözlüğü*. Istanbul: Millî Eğitim Basımevi.

Gökalp, Ziya. 1923. *Türkçülüğün Esasları*. Ankara: Matbuat ve İrtibarat Matbaası.

Hall, Leslie. 1989. "The Turkish *Fasıl*: Selected Repertoire." Ph.D. dissertation, University of Toronto.

O'Connell, John M. 1996. "*Alaturka* Revisited: Style as History in Turkish Vocal Performance." Ph.D. dissertation, University of California, Los Angeles.

Oransay, Gültelkin. 1985. *Atatürk ile Kuğ*. 2nd ed. Izmir: Kuğ Yayını.

Öztuna, Yılmaz. 1990. *Büyük Türk Mûsikisi Ansiklopedesi*. 2 vols. Ankara: Kültür Bakanlığı.

Saygun, Adnan. 1965. *Atatürk ve Musiki*. Ankara: Ajans-Türk Matbaacılık.

Shaw, Stanford. 1976–1977. *History of the Ottoman Empire and Modern Turkey*. 2 vols. Cambridge: Cambridge University Press.

Signell, Karl. 1988. "Mozart and the Mehter." *Turkish Music Quarterly* 1(1):34–36.

Stokes, Martin. 1989. *The Arabesk Debate: Music and Musicians in Modern Turkey*. Oxford: Oxford University Press.

Yektâ Bey, Raûf. 1921. "La musique turque." In *Encyclopédie de la musique et dictionnaire du conservatoire*, ed. Albert Lavignac, 1945–3064. Paris: Delagrave.

Snapshot: Arif Sağ—Alevi *Bağlama* Teacher and Performer Par Excellence

Irene Markoff

The *bağlama*—a long-necked folk lute—is a symbol of religious and cultural identity, and the mystical poetry associated with it can be traced back to the thirteenth century. When I arrived at the Turkish State Conservatory of Music in 1981 for my first lesson on this sacred instrument, I was introduced to a tall, casually dressed man in his late thirties with an overhanging mustache and intense dark eyes whose facial features could easily be placed in the steppes of Central Asia. Little did I know, then, that my first instructor and future mentor was one of Turkey's great *bağlama* virtuosos, who not only had mastered a pan-Turkish musical repertoire but also was dedicated to popularizing the sacred and secular minstrel traditions associated with his Alevi sectarian roots. Because of his powerful artistic presence, Arif Sağ (figure 1) was then becoming recognized as a musical guru whose talent and vision would influence and shape generations of young performers schooled in his lyrical, technically innovative style of playing. Arif confirmed this, and with good reason, when he confided to me

FIGURE 1 Arif Sağ in his studio. Photograph by Irene Markoff, Istanbul, 1982.

that if one were to observe 100,000 *bağlama* players, 90,000 would be prone to imitate him.

The early 1980s were a time of deliberate transition for Arif Sağ, who had always been unyielding in his efforts to realize his creative and entrepreneurial ambitions. Born in 1945 in the Alevi village of Dallı (in the Aşkale district of Erzurum Province), Arif had begun playing the *bağlama* at a young age, at first with the technique called *şelpe*, an open-handed fingertips style of Central Asia. At age seventeen, Arif made his way to Istanbul to expand his musical knowledge and to search for new opportunities. Even though he cut his first 45-rpm record there (in 1962), economic hardship forced him to return to Erzurum in 1963. He found employment as an instrumentalist at Erzurum Radio for two years. In 1966, he was hired by Istanbul Radio as a staff soloist and ensemble player (he worked there from 1966 to 1969 and, later, from 1975 to 1982), but he also spent time making commercial recordings of folk and *arabesk* (urban popular) music. During this formative period, Arif studied with Nida Tüfekçi, an established and respected radio and recording artist from Central Anatolia who had performed in folk music ensembles under Muzaffer Sarısözen's direction at the state radio station in Ankara. Nida Bey (*bey* is a term of respect) went on to assume administrative duties and conduct vocal and instrumental ensembles at Istanbul Radio and was appointed director of the folk music division at the newly formed Turkish State Conservatory of Music in 1976. Through Nida Bey, Arif was invited to teach *bağlama* and lecture at the conservatory (1975–1982). This experience prepared him for the opening of his own music school and instrument shop in Aksaray, Istanbul, in 1981. He now has approximately 600 students and expects 1,000 to enroll at a new music school, which is located near the studio of his recording company, ASM (created in 1988).

Arif's strategic planning continued in 1982 with an unprecedented event in the folk music milieu, a two-hour solo recital at the Şan Theater in Istanbul that was recorded live; the recording was released under the title of the show, *Işte Bağlama, Işte Arif Sağ* 'Wherever You Find the *Bağlama*, There You Will Certainly Find Arif Sağ'. I attended this historic event. It began with masterful renditions and arrangements of Alevi *deyişler* (mystical poetry set to music), sung by Arif as he accompanied himself on the *bağlama*, and other selections from the repertoire performed in the *bağlama* tuning. Next came a set of pan-Turkish selections executed in the *bozuk* tuning. It was during this performance that Sağ, who loves innovation, subjected a brief phrase in the Ankara dance tune "Yandım Şeker" to sequential chromatic variations; this unconventional, fantasy-like treatment shocked traditionalists. Sağ's maverick tendencies, however, did not undermine the performance: he continued to create a magical quality with his subtle embellishment of the melodic line, and his augmentation of rhythmic density through unexpected rhythmic variation caused the music to "swing."

In Sağ's recordings, one can observe a growing tendency toward experimentation through bona fide compositions in traditional style whose polyphonic arrangements use mainly parallel fifths and fourths ("Insan Olmaya Geldim," 1983; "Halay," 1988; and "Duygular Dönüştü Söze," 1989). In the 1980s, Sağ began to describe his music as "contemporary folk" that would maintain and evoke the essence of tradition through stylistically correct regional modes of expression. In the 1990s, he began to collaborate with the composer Cengiz Özdemir, who provided subtle arrangements for *bağlama* with the Western symphony orchestra ("Direniş," "Umut," and "Seher Yıldızı"). Sağ's strong commitment to his roots also led him to perpetuate and politicalize Alevi expressive culture through the "Muhabbet" recordings (1984–1987; figure 2), which featured Alevi artists such as Yavuz Top, the minstrel Muhlis Akarsu (d. 1993), and Musa Eroğlu, a Tahtacı performer (the Tahtacı are a sect related to the Alevi). This politicization manifested itself, in part, in Arif's move from a general folk

FIGURE 2 Cover of the cassette *Muhabbet 2*. (Şah Plak ve Kasetçilik, 1984.)

repertoire to songs that actively promoted his image as an Alevi artist. Before a widespread cultural revival that started in the 1980s, Alevis tended to hide their identity; indeed, some still do. Now, Arif and others no longer feared to perform the Alevi repertoire that had been seen as suspect: songs in praise of the twelve imams, with their strong Shi'ite character, and songs associated with Kurdish Alevi poets or leftist poets whose work had sometimes been censored by state radio and television (as was the case with the *aşık* minstrel Nesimi, who died in 1993). [See ALEVI IDENTITY AND EXPRESSIVE CULTURE.] This commitment drew Arif into the world of politics; he was the first musician elected a deputy of the Turkish National Assembly (1987–1991). His continued involvement in Alevi affairs includes the directorship of a foundation associated with the Karaca Ahmet shrine in Istanbul, and participation in annual Alevi festivals.

The release of the Concerto for *Bağlama* in 1998 was another coup for Arif, advancing his collaboration with Özdemir and the young *bağlama* masters Erdal Erzincan and Erol Parlak. This unusual six-part concerto pits two forces against each other: a *bağlama* trio (Sağ, Erzincan, and Parlak playing selections from the traditional folk, Alevi, and composed repertoire primarily with the *şelpe* technique) and the Istanbul State Symphony Orchestra. The orchestral accompaniment is in classical Western style until the last selection, "Yandım Şeker," which features an upbeat jazz-like accompaniment and incorporates another "take" on the memorable chromatic exercise of 1982. Arif's aim in this piece, which he described as an experiment, was to engage in an artistic and cultural debate between East and West, adapting Turkish musical concepts and practices to universal standards. Tolga Sağ, Arif's son, has followed suit in his first solo recording, "Yol" (1998), which includes renditions in Western classical and "pop jazz" styles.

Arif Sağ is clearly a musical giant who is bound to tradition yet driven by a need to explore new avenues that challenge his creativity. He was described as "the Ravi Shankar of Turkey" by Preston Reed, an American acoustic steel guitarist who "jammed impromptu" with Arif during a live satellite broadcast on Turkish national television in 1997; this broadcast reached 100 million viewers and drew a "flood of calls." In an E-mail that he sent to a number of people after his return from Turkey, Reed described the experience as having taken on a "cosmic transformational quality" as he applied his "Western chord voicings, syncopated rhythms, and simple harmonic progressions" to the "snake-like quarter-note trilling and Middle Eastern licks." In Arif's view, Preston's percussive guitar technique has actually been a part of *bağlama* performance practice for centuries.

Arif Sağ's superstardom has not yet been eclipsed. His search for innovative ideas continues, and there are plans for a recording with a sitarist, more world and local concert tours, solo recordings, and recordings with other artists such as the vocalist Belkis Akkale.

Alevi Identity and Expressive Culture

Irene Markoff

The Alevis
Rituals and Religiosity
The Musical Perspective
Master Musicians since the Establishment of the Turkish Republic
Revivalism and the Reconstruction of Alevi Identity

Islamic mysticism has, for centuries, been defined and enhanced through sung poetry, instrumental music, and dancelike movements. In the context of ritual ceremonies, these expressive cultural forms have been embraced as aids to articulating and perpetuating religious doctrines and beliefs and intensifying the emotional expression of faith. In the case of the heterodox Alevis of Turkey (and the related Tahtaçıs and village Bektashis), esoteric ceremonies reveal shamanistic survivals of a Central Asian Turkic past, Shi'ite tendencies whereby the imam 'Ali is almost deified, and affiliation with the Bektashi order of dervishes.

THE ALEVIS

Alevis trace their genesis to Central Asian Turkmen, who encountered Islam in the form of Sufism first in Khurasan (in the eleventh to thirteenth centuries) and later in Asia Minor, where they submitted to the influences of an assortment of Haydari, Kalenderi, Abdal, and finally Bektashi dervishes. The name Alevi 'followers of 'Ali' is a self-identification used by the community since the nineteenth century. It replaces the pejorative appellation Kızılbaş, given in the sixteenth century to their Turkmen ancestors who supported the Safavids. The major concentration of Alevis is in Central Anatolia; but there are pockets throughout the Aegean and Meditteranean coastal areas (where the Alevis are also known as Tahtacıs and Abdals), as well as Kurdish-speaking communities in Malatya, Erzincan, Tünceli Gazaiantep, Maraş, and Sivas.

Despite their connection to Sufism, always tolerated and revered in Turkey, Alevis continue to be viewed with suspicion and mistrust by outsiders because of activities that are considered clandestine, behavior that is considered nonconformist, and tendencies that are considered subversive and revolutionary. Because an element of secrecy and mystery has surrounded Alevi beliefs and social behavior, outsiders conjured up a mythology in which the Alevis were branded as heretics who failed to observe the five pillars of Islam and denied the mosque and as irreligious (*lādinī*) individuals who participated in drinking parties (*cem bezmi*) with music and dance where men and women engaged in communal sex after a candle-extinguishing ceremony, *mum söndü* (Eyuboğlu 1980; Mélikoff 1974). Hostility toward the Alevis was exacerbated by their overt rebellion against Ottoman Sunni authority in the sixteenth century, when they were purged ruthlessly during the reign of Sultan Selim I. The Alevis, then known as

FIGURE 1 Hacı Bektaş Veli; a poster from Hacı Bektaş village.

FIGURE 2 Bektashi Alevi pictorial art with figurative and calligraphic elements illustrating the manifestation of ʿAli in the human face. The caption reads, "I held the mirror up to my face and there I saw Ali" (Eyuboğlu 1980).

Kızılbaş, supported the Safavids of Persia and deified the Safavid leader Shah Ismail. (Kızılbaş 'redheads' referred to a turban with twelve folds worn by Shah Ismail's Turkmen military elite.) The charismatic Ismail, under the pen name Hatâyî, wrote ecstatic religious verses (Inalcik 1973) that reinforced the shamanistic leanings of the Kızılbaş and their allegiance to a heretical sect of Islam founded in the thirteenth century by Safi al-Dīn of Ardabil (not to be confused with the philosopher and music theorist of the same name). The poetry in Shah Ismail's *divan* conveys an intense Shiʿite message combined with heterodox concepts, such as the manifestation of God in human form (*tecelli*) and metempsychosis (*tenasüh*): Ismail believed that he himself was a reincarnation of the imam ʿAli, and a manifestation of God (Roemer 1990).

Misunderstood and persecuted since Ottoman times, Alevis were forced to protect themselves by suppressing their true religious identity through a practice known as *taqiya* 'dissimulation'—a masking of identity by Shiʿite and heterodox sects to ensure their survival in a hostile environment. As a result, they organized themselves into tight-knit rural communities where recruitment into the sect was limited to blood lineages, ritual activities were closed to outside scrutiny, and commitment to the institution of Alevi *communitas* was strengthened by social mechanisms and a system of checks and balances to prevent violations of the moral code. A tripartite formula, in fact, embodies and summarizes Alevi rules for *edep* 'ethical behavior': *Eline, diline, beline, sahip ol* 'Be master of your hands, tongue, and loins', meaning that one should not steal, lie, or commit adultery. Disrespect for the rules and uncooperativeness in resolving problems could lead to exclusion from religious ceremonies and shunning of the *düşkün* 'fallen' individual (Andrews and Markoff 1987; Markoff 1993).

A more informed "insider" discourse about Alevi culture clarifies negative misinterpretations that have persisted to this day. Alevis owe spiritual allegiance to Hacı Bektaş Veli, founder of the Bektashi order in the thirteenth century (figure 1), whom they regard as their patron saint; they venerate Bektashis such as the sixteenth-century saints Balım Sultan, Abdal Musa, Kaygusuz Abdal, Seyyid ʿAli, and Şahkullu Sultan and the fifteenth-century saint Şeykh Bedreddin. Alevi holy men (*dede*, *pir*, *baba*, *murşid*), who supervise rituals and religious instruction, are recruited from privileged lineages (*ocak*, *seyid*), a mystical elite claiming superior ritual status because of its links to the spiritual hierarchy connected from the founding saint of the Bektashis to Imam ʿAli (figure 2), the Prophet Muhammad, and finally, God. Reverance toward the twelve Shiʿite imams, the family of the Prophet (*ehl-i beyt*—Muhammad, Ali, Fatima, Hasan, and Huseyn), is prominent in Alevi lore and rites, as is the martyrdom at Kerbala in 680 C.E. The holy book (*buyruk*) of the *dede* elite contains what is believed to be a collection of the sayings of the sixth of the twelve Shiʿite imams, Imam Cafer Sādik (inTurkish, Sadık), as well as ritual prescriptions, religious anecdotes, and facets of the mystical experience.

The charisma and *baraka* 'blessings' of Imam ʿAli are celebrated and acknowledged through idioms and ritual behavior restricted to closed musical religious services, referred to collectively as *cem* or sometimes *ayin*. ʿAli's courage is crystallized in a phrase exclaimed by the *dede* during *cem* ceremonies: *Lā fetā illā ʿAli lā seyfe illā Zülfikār* 'There is no one more valiant than Ali, no sword like Zülfikār' (Ali's sword, Zülfikār, is a recurring symbol). Alevis believe that Muhammad passed the divine light to ʿAli, and with this gift of esoteric knowledge ʿAli and his descendants were given the ability to interpret the hidden meaning of the Qurʾān.

RITUALS AND RELIGIOSITY

Cem ceremonies can take place during specific Muslim religious festivals such as Kurban Bayramı 'Festival of the Sacrifice'; Nevruz, the Persian new year; Muharrem; and Hıdrellez, a celebration on the fortieth day after the spring equinox in honor of the legendary Hızır, who is equated with St. George. Other *cem* ceremonies are organized when the need arises and can be categorized according to their functions: for example, the celebration of extrafamilial brotherhood between pairs of males of the same age to provide nurturance and interdependence (*musahip tutma*); the symbolic ritual initiation and affirmation of beliefs of sect members who have established ritual kinship (*ikrar verme*); the reviewing of sectarian beliefs, doctrines, and rules for behavior; the settling of disputes within the community in a central ritual known as *görgü cemi, ayin-i cem* 'rite of integration'; the pronouncement of judgment on wrongdoers (*sorgu*); and the introduction of young sect members to rituals and beliefs in a more informal setting (*Abdal Musa cemi*; *muhabbet*). These ceremonies are attended by families bound by kinship who assemble in private prayer houses (*cemevi*) where religious beliefs, doctrines, and spiritual affiliations are reviewed and renewed under the direction of the *dede*, who acts in a judiciary capacity to settle familial and community disputes. The *dede* leads all ceremonies with the aid of twelve assistants, who are named according to their specialized ritual function and the historical-mythological figures they represent. For example, the water carrier (*ibriktar*, *ibrikçi*, Selman) plays the role of Selman Farisi, who supported 'Ali's rightful ascension to the caliphate; and the primary keeper of order, who maintains discipline throughout the ceremony (*gözcü*), plays the role of Karaca Ahmet, the famous mystic of Anatolia (Andrews and Markoff 1987).

Collective ritual during these highly structured, highly disciplined gatherings includes recitations from the Qur'ān; religious formulas; prayers; blessings; legends; spiritual exercises that include elements of *zikr* (without controlled breathing but with some body posturing); and ritual dance (*sema*), accompanied by sung mystical poetry in the vernacular and the sacred ritual instrument known as the *bağlama*, *saz*, or, sometimes, *çöğür*—a long-necked plucked folk lute with movable frets.

Sema is a dignified dance, performed by couples chosen by the *gözcü*, who then monitors dance movements and conduct. The choreography involves circle and line formations; walking steps and restricted arm movements during the first (slow) part of the dance, *ağırlama*; and faster steps with more animated movements in the second part, *yeldirme*, *yelleme* (in which the tempo increases). A third part, *hızlanma*, in which the figures become even more complex and intense, is sometimes performed. In Tokat, for example, the dancers are described as whirling spinning wheels, *çarh gibi dönerler* (Yönetken 1986:80). The dance suite usually ends with a decrease in tempo that allows the dancers to regain their composure and make their way to the *dede* for his blessings and prayers. Of the many regional variants of *sema*, the most widespread and important are *Kırklar Semahı* 'Dance of the Forty Saints' and *Turnalar Semahı* 'Dance of the Cranes', with their symbolic figures of ascent. In the *Turnalar Semahı*, the image of the elegant crane (*turna*) preparing for flight symbolizes both the ascending soul of Imam 'Ali and the metamorphosis of Central Asian miracle-working shamans into birds. In the *Kırklar Semahı*, the nocturnal ascent of the Prophet Muhammad (*miraç*) to heaven leads him to the gathering of the forty saints. There he is said to have beheld the manifestation of divine reality in 'Ali and to have recognized 'Ali's possession of the mystery of saintship, *sırr-ı vilāyet* (Birge 1937:266).

THE MUSICAL PERSPECTIVE

The sacred specialized Alevi musical repertoire also includes *deyiş* or *deme* (songs of mystical love); *nefes* (songs concerning the mystical experience); *düvaz* or *düvazdeh imam* (hymns in honor of the twelve Shi'ite imams); *mersiye* (laments for Imam Huseyn, who was martyred at Kerbala); *miraçlama* (songs about the ascent of Muhammad to heaven); and the *illalah*, a genre that incorporates the *tahlil* formula (*lāilāhe illāllāh*, in a spelling standard among Turkish Sufis) into the poem to create an atmosphere of *zikr*.

Common meters include Western duple meter and the asymmetric (*aksak*) varieties such as 5/8, 7/8, 9/8, and 10/8. The *sema* repertoire of Central and Eastern Anatolia uses 9/4 (2232) in the first movement, moving to 9/8 (2322) or (2223) in the fast movement, sometimes leading to an even faster third movement in triple meter, and finally ending with a brief close in slow duple. The Alevis of the Mediterranean and Aegean areas use the 9/8 (2223) and (2322) meter predominantly.

For the Alevis, the *bağlama* has become a powerful symbol of their group identity and their creed. It is also a material representation of Imam 'Ali and the tenets of his faith: the resonator is said to represent his body, the neck his sword Zülfikār, the twelve strings (and sometimes frets) the twelve Shi'ite imams, and the lower course of strings the Prophet Muhammad (Markoff 1986b:48). When played in the traditional manner of the Alevi Türkmen, the *bağlama* is strummed and plucked in the Central Asian open-handed *şelpe* style (that is, *parmakla* 'with the fingers'). The deeper symbolic association of the term *şelpe* is with a drawing in the form of a hand, known as *pençe-i Āl-i-ābā* 'family of the mantle', in which the names of the Prophet's family members are written. The bond with Shi'ism is emphasized during the first twelve days of the month of Muharrem, when Alevis fast, all festivities are curtailed, and the instruments are tied up in silence and respect to commemorate the martyrdom of Huseyn.

The Alevi-Turkmen la-re-mi (from high to low pitch) tuning known as *bağlama düzeni*, Alevi *düzeni*, and sometimes *Veysel düzeni* (in honor of a contemporary minstrel) is traditional for the Alevi repertoire. This *düzen* 'tuning' facilitates the crossing of strings and the creation of an intricate texture featuring the movement of two instrumental voices in parallel fourths and fifths played on the same instrument, a distinctive feature of nomadic Turkmen lute performance. Another tuning, *bozuk düzeni* (la-re-sol), is used mainly in the Aegean region by Tahtaçı and village Bektashis, and by professional urban musicians as well. [See Aspects of Turkish Folk Music Theory.]

The musicians in *cem* ceremonies are often descendants of *dede* lineages and are highly respected in the community. They are referred to as *zākir*, *güvende*, *sazende*, or *aşık*, depending on regional usage. Many are known as poet-minstrels—*aşık* or *ozan*—who perpetuate the tradition of the poets of the dervish lodges such as Yunus Emre (thirteenth century); Nesimi (fourteenth century); Pir Sultan Abdal, Hata'i, and Genç Abdal (sixteenth century); Kul Himmet and Kul Hüseyn (seventeenth century); Dertli, Seyrani, and Sümmani (nineteenth century); and Nesimi (figure 3), Veysel, Ali Izzet, Davut Suları, and Daimi (twentieth century). The poetry is in Turkish and follows the principles of *hece vezne*, in which the focus is the number of syllables. Religious themes include the mystical experience; spiritual intoxication; the twelve imams; the family of the Prophet; the story of Ali's martyrdom; the role of Imam 'Ali as a guide through the world of divine knowledge; respect for the Qur'ān; and the Old and New Testaments. In more secular poetry, we encounter echoes of nomadic life, with its shamanistic survivals; we also find a didactic tone, and a defiant spirit that reproachfully addresses the fate and rights of the individual in a world without justice or equality (*fani dünya*). This poetry still appeals to many levels of Turkish society, as it expresses the Alevi view of unity, tolerance, understanding, and openness to other beliefs.

MASTER MUSICIANS SINCE THE ESTABLISHMENT OF THE TURKISH REPUBLIC

After the establishment of the Turkish Republic in 1923, it was through the minstrels that some aspects of Alevi expressive culture came to be tolerated and popularized. They gave secular policy of the state strong ideological support through their poetry and music and thus helped bolster national identity and ensure the support of the masses (Başgöz 1972:168). For example, Alevi minstrels and musicians such as *Aşık* Veysel (d. 1973), *Aşık* Ali Izzet, and Hasan Hüseyn were popularized through perfor-

FIGURE 3 *Aşık* Nesimi, Istanbul, 1983. Photo by Irene Markoff.

mances at cultural centers known as *Halk Evleri* 'People's Houses'; through appearances at festivals and concerts and on state radio programs; and through recordings by Columbia, Odeon, and RCA Victor. Alevis, in fact, became fervent supporters of Kemal Atatürk and his vision of a secular state free from religious domination.

The secularizing policies of the state, together with the large migration of Alevis to the cities of Ankara, Istanbul, and Izmir in the 1950s, paved the way for the rise in popularity of a generation of Alevi professional musicians who were trained at private music studios, music clubs, state radio stations, and conservatories. Many of these performers were *bağlama* virtuosos (and vocalists as well) who found it necessary to expand their repertoire. Mastery of pan-Turkish folk music styles was crucial to their careers as members of radio ensembles, conservatory teachers, and instructors in their own private music studios. These activities ran parallel to their careers as recording and concert mega-artists. The most important artists—in terms of innovative style and composition—include Ali Ekber Çiçek (now in his sixties) and Arif Sağ, Musa Eroğlu, and Yavuz Top (now in their mid-fifties). These technically superior and creative artists were active in revitalizing Alevi music traditions by applying refinements and innovations to rurally derived sources.

An important model for such artistic experiments was the brilliant *Haydar* (1965), composed for voice and *bağlama* by the Alevi radio and recording artist Ali Ekber
TRACK-25 Çiçek. *Haydar* was inspired by twentieth-century Bektashi poets (especially *aşık* Sıdkı) and by Alevi melodies from the Malatya area of Eastern Turkey (borrowed from *aşık* Süleyman Elver). In the technically challenging instrumental prelude, Çiçek has created a complex texture in which innovative plectrum techniques, changing meters, and moments of tension created by stacked chord-like configurations are propelled along by rhythmic ostinatosi. *Haydar*, which is both artistic and expressive, exemplifies Çiçek's efforts to elevate Alevi spiritual values through musical exploration of the timbral and harmonic potential of the *bağlama*.

Following in the footsteps of Çiçek is Arif Sağ, one of Turkey's most impressive and subtle *bağlama* virtuosos, whose style is still imitated by young *bağlama* players. [See ARIF SAĞ: ALEVI *BAĞLAMA* TEACHER AND PERFORMER PAR EXCELLENCE.] During a recital at the Şan Theater in Istanbul in 1982), Sağ applied his creative and technical wizardry to a refashioning of the *Kırklar Semahı*, in which the solo instrument, with refined plectrum techniques and left-hand ornamentation, captured the expressive qualities of the sung verse and succeeded in conveying the expected emotional impact.

Today Alevis are still actively searching for a new identity by reinventing their culture.

Arif Sağ's contemporary Yavuz Top has been called a radical innovator and was one of the first Alevi artists to subject the traditional Alevi repertoire to complex orchestration combined with attempts at Western functional harmony. His skillful arrangement of the music for Pir Sultan Abdal's poem *Ötme Bülbül Ötme* 'Don't Sing, Nightingale', as performed by *aşık* Feyzullah Çınar, combines a mixed choir that sings periodically in two parts (imitating the parallel fifths heard in *aşık düzeni* lute peformances) with an instrumental ensemble comprising Turkish traditional and Western instruments. Arif Sağ later met Top's challenge with his recording *Insan Olmaya Geldim*, with a title track inspired by the poetry of Nimri *dede*. Sağ also uses a chorus singing in parallel fifths with the melody line, as well as a *ney* (a dervish reed flute) and a *kabak kemane* (a bowed spike lute); these elements contribute to the contrapuntal texture with countermelodies and phrases that often form parallel-fifth intervals with other instruments. In the late 1990s, Sağ used a full string orchestra plus *bağlamalar* played in *şelpe* and traditional Alevi style (with plectrum) to accompany arranged selections in his recording *Seher Yıldızı*. The university-educated vocalist Hasan Yükselir did the same in *Su Türküler*.

Until the 1960s, most Alevi musicians and minstrels limited the Alevi repertoire they performed in public to the truly mystical *deyiş* and *nefes* that espoused humanistic ideals and love and understanding among men. However, in the 1970s a group of minstrels, including Daimi, Nesimi, Mahsuni, and Muhlis Akarsu, chose to follow in the revolutionary footsteps of the sixteenth-century poet Pir Sultan Abdal, who was hanged for his religious beliefs (he was an antinomian). Their poems of social protest sometimes enraged government authorities: state broadcasts were censored to exclude their work, and their reputation was blackened—they were considered a threat to national security. This was a period in history when many urbanized Alevis, alienated from the state, supported left-of-center political parties. Their alientation was a result of anti-Alevi pogroms in regions inhabited mainly by Kurdish-speaking Alevis: Malatya, Maraş, and Corum (Van Bruinessen 1996). Their musical repertoire was politicized and appropriated by leftist revolutionaries because its themes spoke to contemporary struggles. During this time and until the late 1980s, Alevi performers concealed their sacred repertoire: they replaced the names 'Ali and Huseyn with *dost* 'friend', or they used less threatening texts with the melodies of sacred works such as hymns in praise of the twelve Shi'ite imams.

REVIVALISM AND THE RECONSTRUCTION OF ALEVI IDENTITY

The early 1990s marked the beginning of the visibility of the Alevi sacred repertoire in performance and on recordings. This heralded a sectarian focus on cultural revival and a new interest in religiosity that had begun in European immigrant communities in the 1980s when the state imposed Sunni Islam in Turkey and supported ultraconservative Sunni religious activities in the diaspora (Van Bruinessen 1996). Cassettes of entire *cem* ceremonies appeared in the marketplace, and several recordings presented a regional variety of the *sema* repertoire organized by the Tahtaçı artist Musa Eroğlu.

This was no doubt a result of the relaxation of the government ban on Sufi houses of worship and activities in 1989 after a hiatus of more than sixty years. Thereafter, many new Alevi associations sprang up in Turkey, foundations and trusts were organized, saints' tombs were rebuilt, and *cem* ceremonies were performed publicly. In an attempt to assert their identity, Alevi intellectuals and community leaders set out to resolve and clarify issues relating to Alevi origins, rituals, and doctrines: they published books and articles, and they organized seminars at annual festivals held at saints' shrines such as those of Haci Bektaş (in Kırşehir Province in August) and Abdal Musa (in the village of Tekke, in the Elmalı district of Antalya Province, in June).

Today Alevis are still actively searching for a new identity by reinventing their culture. Their number is now estimated at 20 million, and they have gradually integrated and assimilated into mainstream Turkish society. Despite their strong identification with Kemalist secularism and social justice, they are still divided into factions, each with its own strategies for survival, recognition, and solidarity in a changing, unstable homeland. Secularists in the Turkish political establishment support the Alevi revival, considering the Alevis (discounting the Kurdish element) natural Turkish allies against the rise of political Islam; but several incidents in the 1990s heightened the Alevis' fear of continued violence and persecution at the hands of the extremist right-wing Sunni. The most notorious incident occured in 1993, at a festival in Sivas in honor of Pir Sultan Abdal—Sunni and right-wing activists torched a hotel, and sixty-seven Alevis were killed. The victims included two *aşık* poet-singers: Nesimi Çimen and Muhlis Akarsu. Hasret Gültekin, a young Alevi performer in the modern *özgün müziği* style—free or alternative music with didactic leftist tendencies—was also killed.

At the same time, Islamist fundamentalists have attempted to entice and assimilate Alevis into the Islamic brotherhood by contributing financially to Alevi cultural foundations and committing themselves to the removal of barriers to religious practice. This appeal to an orthodox strain within the community is criticized by secularist Alevis, who bemoan the crossover of former leftists into the comfort zone of the rightist camp.

Despite these conflicting tendencies, it appears that Alevi culture is leaning toward a national identity that values an attachment to Kemalist ideals and to religiosity. This is illustrated by a tendency among many young Alevis in Turkey and the diaspora to re-evaluate their Marxist-Leninist sentiments, acknowledge their roots, and mobilize. Today, young people often wear chains with Alevi symbols (such as 'Ali's two-edged sword Zülfikār), and participate actively in associations where they attend *cem* ceremonies and are taught to perform the ritual *sema* dance and mystical sung poetry.

In this milieu, Alevi music and poetry continue to flourish. Many younger Alevi musicians look to the Anatolian *aşık* poet-minstrels as well as the more enlightened contemporary approach of Arif Sağ, Musa Eroğlu, and Yavuz Top as models for their *bağlama* reworkings of the traditional Alevi repertoire. Some prefer the more traditional approach—pure *bağlama* accompaniment to singing, as exemplified by Tolga Sağ, Ismail Özden, and Erdal Erzincan. Others (such as Güler Duman and the vocalist Sabahat Akkıraz) gravitate toward a folk-infused modern sound that combines guitars, bongos, and other Western instruments with *bağlama*, *ney*, *mey* (a double-reed woodwind), *kaval* (an end-blown flute), *darbuka* (a goblet-shaped drum), and *bendir* (a frame drum). A third Alevi group has embraced *özgün müziği* (genuine or alternative music), a syncretic style that protests against worldly values and espouses mystical love and sometimes political militancy; this group includes Hasret Gültekin and Ferhat Tunç.

Despite the recent emergence of Alevis aspiring to a united front that could revitalize and celebrate their culture, there is some fear that overexposure of rituals and expressive culture as staged mass entertainment will eventually cheapen and weaken traditions. Whatever the future holds for Alevis, it appears that the Alevi network has become stronger through communication and activism generated by a new enlightened leadership. This leadership has in turn gained public support through associations, foundations, federations outside Turkey, publications, Websites, and the continued popularity and impact of Alevi music and poetry on contemporary Turkish culture.

REFERENCES

Akkıraz, Sabahat. n.d. *Insana Muhabbet Duyalı*. Şah Plak. (Cassette.)

Alevilikte Cem 2. 1993. Pınar Müzik Üretim ve Yapımcılık (12271; cassette).

Andrews, Walter, and Irene Markoff. 1987. "Poetry, the Arts, and Group Ethos in the Ideology of the Ottoman Empire." *Edebiyat* 1(1):28–70.

Aygün, Belgin. 1982. *Alevi-Bektaşi Törenler Içinde Semah*. Ankara: Ankara University Department of Theater.

Başgöz, Ilhan. 1972. "Folklore Studies and Nationalism in Turkey." *Journal of the Folklore Institute* 9:162–76.

Bin Yıllık Yürüyüş. Musa Eroğlu ve Semah Grubu 1 and 2 (012, 013). 1999. Istanbul: Koda Plak ve Kasetiçilik.

Birdoğan, Nejat. 1984. "Samahlar." In *Folklor ve Etnografya Araştırmalar* 1:31–51.

Birge, John Kingsley. 1937. *The Bektashi Order of Dervishes*. London: Luzac.

Çiçek, Ali Ekber. n.d. *Turkish Sufi Music: Folk Lute of Anatolia*. Lyrichord Stereo LLST 7392.

Duman, Güler. 1995. *Bu Devran*. Duygu Müzik Merkezi. (Cassette.)

Duygulu, Melih. 1997. *Alevi-Bektaşī Müziğinde Deyişler*. Istanbul: n.p.

Eliade, Mircea. 1974. *Shamanism: Archaic Techniques of Ecstasy*. Princeton, N.J.: Princeton University Press.

Eroğlu, Musa. 1996. *Halil Ibrahim: Kerbela Destanı*. Duygu Müzik Merkezi. (Cassette.)

Eyuboğlu, Ismet Zeki. 1980. *Bütün Yönleriyle Bektaşilik (Alevilik)*. Istanbul: Yeni Ciğır Kitabevi.

Gölpınarlı, Abdülbâki. 1963. *Alevī-Bektaşī Nefesleri*. Istanbul: Remzi Yayınevi.

Gronhaug, Reidar. 1974. *Micro-Macro Relations*. Bergen: University of Bergen.

Gültekin, Hasret. n.d. *Rüzgarın Kanatlarında*. Neba Müzik. (Cassette.)

Inalcik, Halil. 1973. *The Ottoman Empire: The Classical Age, 1300–1600*. New York: Praeger.

Karişik Özgün Müzik, Özgürlik Için. 1990. Güney Plak (260; cassette).

Karpat, Kemal. 1976. *The Gecekondu: Rural Migration and Urbanization*. Cambridge: Cambridge University Press.

Mardin, Serif. 1984. "A Note on the Transformation of Religious Symbols." *Turcica* 16:119–120.

Markoff, Irene. 1986a. "Musical Theory, Performance, and the Contemporary *Bağlama* Specialist in Turkey." Ph.D. dissertation, University of Washington.

———. 1986b. "The Role of Expressive Culture in the Demystification of a Secret Sect of Islam." *World of Music* 28(3):42–56.

———. 1990–1991. "The Ideology of Musical Practice and the Professional Turkish Folk Musician: Tempering the Creative Impulse." *Asian Music* 22(1):129–145.

———. 1993. "Music, Saints, and Ritual: Samā' and the Alevis of Turkey." In *Manifestations of Sainthood in Islam*, ed. Grace Martin Smith and Carl. W. Ernst, 95–110. Istanbul: Isis.

———. 1995. "Introduction to Sufi Music and Ritual in Turkey." *MESA Bulletin* 29(2):157–160.

Mélikoff, Irène. 1974. "Le problème Kızılbaş." *Turcica* 6:49–67.

Muhabbet 1–2 (Arif Sağ, Musa Eroğlu, Muhlis Akarsu). 1984. Istanbul: Şah Plak ve Kasetçilik. *3* (Arif Sağ, Musa Eroğlu, Muhlis Akarsu, Yavuz Top). 1985. Istanbul: Şah Plak ve Kasetçilik. *4* (Arif Sağ, Musa Eroğlu, Yavuz Top). 1986. Istanbul: Zirve Plak, 1002. *5* (Arif Sağ, Musa Eroğlu, Yavuz Top, Muhlis Akarsu). 1987. Istanbul: Zirve Plak, 1008. *6–7* (Musa Eroğlu, Muhlis Akarsu, Yavuz Top). 1995. Istanbul: Kalan Müzik Yapım Ltd, 071 and 072. (Cassettes.)

Roemer, Hans R. 1990. "The Qizilbash Turcomans: Founders and Victims of the Safavid Theocracy." In *Intellectual Studies on Islam: Essays Written in Honor of Martin B. Dickson*, ed. Michel M. Mazzaoui and Vera B. Moreen. 27–39. Salt Lake City: University of Utah Press.

Ruhi Su. Sultan Suyu. 1993. "*Pir Sultan Abdal'dan Deyişler*." Imece Müzik Yapım. (Compact disk.)

Sağ, Arif. 1983. *Insan Olmaya Geldim*. Sembol Plak. (Cassette.)

Sağ, Arif, with Belkis Akkale. 1996. *Seher Yıldızı*. ASM Müzik Üretim. (Cassette.)

Sağ, Tolga, Erdal Erzincan, and Ismail Özden. 1997. *Türküler Sevdamız*. ASM Müzik Üretim. (Cassette.)

Şener, Cemal. 1997. *Şaha Doğru Giden Kervan. Alevilik Nedir*. Cologne: Avrupa Alevi Birlikleri Federasyonu Yayınları.

Şerif, Ashık Mahsuni, Musa Eroğlu, Ashık Bahattin Kader, Ashık Nuri Kılıç, and Ashık Ali. 1999. *Ashiklar, Those Who Are in Love*. Golden Horn Records. (Compact disk.)

Tahtaçılar. Arşiv serisi. 1997. Istanbul: Kalan Müzik Yapim. (Compact disk.)

Top, Yavuz. n.d. *Deyişler-1*. Sembol Plak. (1098, cassette.)

Turkey. An Esoteric Sufi Ceremony. 1994. JVC World Sounds. (VICG-5345, compact disk.)

Ulusoy, A. Celalettin. 1980. *Hünkār Hacı Bektaş Veli ve Alevi-Bektaşī Yolu*. Hacı Bektaş: n.p.

Van Bruinessen, Martin. 1996. "Kurds, Turks, and the Alevi Revival in Turkey." *Middle East Report* 200 (summer):7–10.

Yalman, Nur. 1969. "Islamic Reform and the Mystic Tradition in Eastern Turkey." *European Journal of Sociology* 10(1):41–60.

Yönetken, Halil Bedi. 1986. *Derleme Notları*. Istanbul: Orkestra Yayınları.

Yükselir, Hasan. 1997. *Su Türküler*. Nepa MüzikYapım. (Compact disk.)

Turkish Song Duel

Yîldîray Erdener

In Turkey song dueling is practiced exclusively by semiprofessional minstrels known as *aşîklar* (singular, *aşîk*). The Turkish word for song duel is *karsîlasma* 'to encounter' or 'to meet each other'. The English term *song duel* is actually misleading, because in a Turkish song duel the songs have only a secondary role—the most important aspect of the event is improvised poetry.

In a song duel, an *aşîk* does not compose new songs but rather uses well-known traditional tunes. Such a tune is called a *makam*: among *aşîklar* in northeastern Turkey, the term *makam* refers to a tune rather than to a musical mode. *Aşîk* Seref Taslîova (figure 1), one of my informants in Kars, told me that 157 different *makamlar* are used in song contests. He pointed out that in earlier times an apprentice would initially learn 16 to 32 *makamlar* from his master. When the apprentice had learned between 72 to 112, the master would recognize him as an *aşîk* and give him a *mahlas*—in effect, a pseudonym, pen name, or stage name. An *aşîk* in Turkey uses the *mahlas* as a kind of signature in the last stanza of each improvised poem.

FIGURE 1 *Aşîk* Seref Taslîova (left) and *aşîk* Murat Çobanoglu in a song contest in the coffeehouse of Kars. Photo by Y. Erdener, 1982.

FIGURE 2 *Aşîk* Murat Çobanoglu in a solo performance. Photo by Y. Erdener, 1982.

LOCATIONS OF THE SONG DUEL IN TURKEY

The primary center for song dueling is Kars. In this city, with a population of more than 60,000, there are nearly a hundred coffeehouses. With the exception of Asîklar Kahvesi 'Aşîks' Coffeehouse', these establishments entertain their guests with a radio, a cassette tape player, or a television set. In Asîklar Kahvesi, song duels take place every night except Saturday. This coffeehouse is owned and operated by the nationally known *aşîk* Murat Çobanoglu (figure 2). In 1966, at age twenty-six, Çobanoglu shared the first prize in song dueling with a famous, well-established, elderly *aşîk* at the annual Konya Aşîks' Festival and instantly became a star. In the following year, Çobanoglu won more prizes, bringing renown and honor to Kars, his hometown, which had been virtually forgotten. As a gesture of appreciation, the mayor of Kars offered him an inexpensive plot of land in the business district to build a coffeehouse where *aşîklar* would have a permanent place to keep their tradition alive.

In northeastern Turkey, some song duels also take place in the city of Erzurum. The *aşîklar* in Erzurum, however, do not always have a permanent place to perform, and so their duels are not as accessible to the public as those in Kars.

A third city where song duels take place is Konya, in central Anatolia. Since 1966, Konya has been the home of the Aşîks' Festival, held each year during the last week of October. The organizers invite the best *aşîklar* (numbering from thirty to fifty) to challange one another in various categories, including song dueling. The Konya festival is an important event for an *aşîk* because people will evaluate his talent on the basis of how many prizes he wins there.

BECOMING AN *AŞÎK*

According to tradition, a teenage boy has a dream in which he falls in love with a girl and becomes an *aşîk* 'lover' or 'the one in love'. This dream transports the boy into a new life and gives him a new identity. The experience might take place at a grave, at the tomb of a saint, at a fountain, or at home. In the dream a prophet, a saint, or a dervish (a holy man) introduces a beautiful maiden to the novice, telling him her name or her father's name and the name of town where she lives, and telling him that the girl is his destiny and that he should therefore make every effort to find and marry her. However, it will not easy be to reach her by foot or by horseback, because she is in a faraway place, perhaps in another country, such as Iran, Iraq, Afghanistan, or China. When the novice opens his eyes, he is disappointed because neither the beautiful girl nor the holy man is real, and yet he wants to start searching immediately for the girl.

This same tradition can also can be found in Turkish folk tales. A *hikaye* 'folk story' is told primarily in prose and interspersed with poems sung to the accompaniment of the *saz* (a long-necked plucked lute). The plot of a *hikaye* consists of a several episodes held together by the hero *aşîk*, who travels from one place to another to find the girl of his dream. For example, in the story *Aşîk Garip and Shah Senem* the hero (Garip) awakens from his dream and tells his mother that he has fallen in love with Shah Senem, the daughter of Hoca Sinan of Tbilisi, and he wants to go and look for her.

When an *aşîk*, such as Garip, arrived in a town in search of his beloved, he would hang his *saz* on the wall of a coffeehouse. This would communicate the message that a guest *aşîk* was in town. If there was another guest *aşîk* or a local *aşîk* in the town, a song duel would be arranged almost immediately to test the newcomers's sacred and secular knowledge and his poetic and musical skills. Whenever possible, the newcomer would sing love songs for the girl of his dream and then would continue his search, wandering from one town to another. Thus his platonic love would become a burning passion and a continual source of poetic inspiration.

Another way of receiving the gift of poetry is directly from the dream. Some very well-known *aşîklar* such as Senlik of Kars (1850–1913) and Sümmani of Erzurum (1860–1915) declared that they received knowledge through the dream itself. For example, upon awakening from his dream, *aşîk* Senlik found that he could compose poetry spontaneously. Although he was nonliterate, he said that he now could read Persian and Arabic (the Qur'ān) because he had received divine inspiration in his dream. His contemporary, *aşîk* Sümmani, also learned how to read the Qu'rān in an initiatory dream:

Aldîlar abdesti uyandîm habdan
Aslîmîz yapîlmîs hak-ü türabdan
Okudular üç had yesil yapraktan
Okudum harfini, noktasîn tek tek

They [holy people] performed an ablution, and I woke up [from my ignorance].
We are created out of dust.
They read three times from green pages [from the Qur'ān].
I read the letters and dots one by one (Hînçer 1968:30).

Sometimes, a hero *aşîk* in a *hikaye* also receives the gift of music. Upon awakening, he may play the *saz* masterfully, although he has never before even touched a *saz*; the *hikaye Emrah and Selvi* is one example (1971:15–19). In *Aşîk Garip and Shah Senem*, a woman more than ninety years old plucks the strings of a *saz* to awaken Garip—who has never played this instrument—from his deep sleep; when he wakes up, he says, "Old woman, give me the *saz*. That isn't the way to play it. This is how."

In contemporary Turkey, an *aşîk* falls in love in reality rather than in a dream. However, because of the strict segregation of the sexes in rural areas of Turkey, and because of social and economic differences, the *aşîk* cannot talk to his beloved, or even see her. For instance, in his teenage years *aşîk* Deryami (1926–1989) of Artvin saw a girl who was picking plums in her garden; when her head scarf fell down, he saw her face and instantly fell in love. That was, however, the last time he saw her, because she was the daughter of a rich man and Deryami's family was very poor. He started improvising poetry about her lovely face and learned how to play the *saz* while tending cows in the pasture (interview with the author). *Aşîk* Pünhani (1917–1991) of Kars, another poor boy, fell in love with a girl whose father had many cows and oxen; this love too was unfulfilled, and Pünhani "cried day and night." To express his frustration, he went to lonely places to compose poems about his love. *Aşîk* Mevlüt Ihsani (b. 1928) of Kars told me that he fell in love with the daughter of a landowner in his village. He had been blind since the age of nine, and when he proposed marriage to her, she replied: "You're poor and disabled. Why should I marry you?" This pattern of falling in love hopelessly is very common among *aşîklar* in Turkey. I interviewed about forty *aşîklar* in Kars, most of whom had begun to experiment with improvising poetry in this way—composing poems was the only outlet that was socially accepted and encouraged.

In times past, when an *aşîk* such as Senlik, Sümmani, or the hero of a *hikaye* dreamed of falling in love, he would interpret the dream as a revelation from God and would therefore, of course, take it very seriously. As *aşîk* Garip said: "I shall either find the one I love or die searching." However, because of vast distances, rough roads, and other adversities, he would usually be unable to find the object of his love. Today, an *aşîk* is still usually frustrated, but the primary reason is social or economic differences. Still, an *aşîk*—past or present—never forgets his first love. Fifty years after seeing his beloved, *aşîk* Pünhani said, "She sits in my heart. If I had married ten women I would still be unable to forget her." *Aşîk* Reyhani (b. 1932) of Erzurum told me that he too kept his beloved in his heart: "Although I'm married, I'm still in love with her." For an *aşîk*, at least at the beginning of his career, this love is his poetic inspiration.

Although the beloved is the inspiration, poetic skills are obtained from the holy man who appears in the initiatory dream. This holy personage offers the future *aşîk* something to eat or drink, and drinking or eating from the hands of a such a personage symbolizes the transmission of poetic and musical skills, and in some cases immediate knowledge. It is believed that the drink, called "the wine of truth," comes directly from the "seven layers of Heaven." Upon awakening, an *aşîk* sometimes describes the holy wine as having magical qualities and says that drinking it ignites a fire in the veins, so that the gift of poetry is immediately felt. This, indeed, is considered the ideal way to become an *aşîk*, because the gift comes from God. Only chosen individuals have such a dream; these individuals are called *ilhamli aşîklar* 'God-inspired poets', and only they can spontaneously compose poetry with no difficulty:

> I can sing any song whatever, for God had implanted this gift of song in my heart. He gives the words to my tongue without my having to seek them. (Radloff 1885:xvii)

Contemporary *aşîklar* in Turkey claim that it is not necessary to eat or drink anything from the hands of a holy person, nor need they fall in love with a beautiful maiden. The visual image of the holy man in the dream appears to be sufficient for acquiring the gift of poetry and the inspiration to create it. Coming into contact with a holy man, even in a dream, is believed to make the dreamer himself partly holy. For example, *aşîk* Reyhani (b. 1932) and *aşîk* Ilhami Demir (1932–1988) of Kars were convinced of this.

Aşîk Çobanoglu (1940) of Kars is one of very few contemporary *aşîklar* who say that they have had a dream identical to the dreams of earlier *aşîklar*. While going to a summer pasture, Çobanoglu fell asleep near a fountain. Veysel Karani (a well-known follower of the Prophet Mohammed) appeared to him in a dream, offered him water, and taught him how to read the Qur'ān.

Except for the hero of a *hikaye*, no one begins to improvise poetry overnight, whether in a dream or in real life. Learning how to compose poetry orally is a long process. Just as a child learns a language, a future *aşîk* learns a poetic and musical language by listening, memorizing, and imitating past and present masters. During this period, if the young man is in love there is an established tradition that tells him what to do to become an *aşîk*.

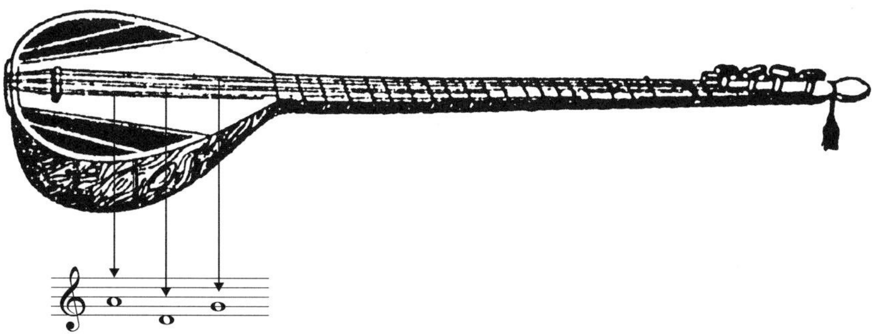

FIGURE 3 *Kara düzen* or *bozuk düzen* on the *saz*.

THE *AŞÎK*'S INSTRUMENT: THE *SAZ*

The *saz*, with its long fretted neck, is an integral part of any song contest. Even someone who cannot play the *saz* well feels obligated to hang one over his shoulder during a duel.

The *saz* family consists of a number of instruments of various sizes, each with its own name. *Aşîklar* use the largest size (about 80 to 90 centimeters long). The pear-shaped body of the *saz* is preferably carved out of a single piece of mulberry wood. The T-shaped tuning pegs are inserted directly into the neck from the front and the sides. Today, the strings are plucked with a plastic plectrum, but the traditional plectrum was made of cherry bark. There are fourteen to twenty-four movable frets, which allow quartertones to be produced. The lower string is the melody string whereas the upper two strings are strummed for a drone effect. Depending on the region, and on individual taste, the three pairs of metal strings can be tuned in a different ways. *Aşîklar* in northeastern Turkey prefer the *kara düzen* 'black tuning' (figure 3), in which the middle strings are tuned a fifth below the melody string and the upper strings a fourth above the middle string. Although the *saz* is a string instrument, one can also produce a percussive effect by striking its top with the ring finger of the strumming hand.

Most *aşîklar* in northeastern Turkey say that the *saz* is a source of inspiration for improvising poetry. If they have trouble constructing a line or finding the most powerful word or the best rhyme, they turn to the *saz*. One *aşîk* in Kars described the importance of his instrument during a song contest by saying, "If I don't know what to say next, I continue playing my *saz*." In addition to gaining time, playing the *saz* helps the *aşîk* adapt the poetic line to the musical line by holding one syllable for two rhythmic beats instead of one syllable for each beat. In general, an *aşîk* prefers to sing one syllable for each note (syllabic style).

SONG DUELS IN KARS

The Asîklar Kahvesi

During a year in Kars, I observed more than 600 song duels in the the coffeehouse of *aşîk* Çobanoglu. This coffeehouse is about 8 by 12 meters in area, and when it is crowded it holds about 100 listeners (all male). Seating, to some degree, is associated with wealth and prestige. Although everyone pays the same cover charge (40 to 50 cents), high-status guests are usually seated at a head table that is close to the stove in winter and away from the dust of the street in summer. Tables are arranged in rows, with enough space between them for two dueling *aşîklar* to walk up and down, each with his *saz* over his shoulder. Because there is no fixed stage, the *aşîklar* can make eye contact with audience members and interact with them. The walls of the coffeehouse are decorated with sacred and secular representations of the past and present, instruments in black linen covers, photographs of well-known *aşîklar*, and—most important—framed certificates won by *aşîklar* at the annual festival in Konya.

The audience

Song duels take place at dusk. During the day, Çobanoglu's coffeehouse, without this attraction, becomes simply one of ninety-five coffeehouses where *aşîklar* and local people socialize, drink tea, play cards or backgammon, and talk business. In the evening, the audience consists of men from three groups: the townspeople (shopowners, their apprentices, laborers, and friends and relatives of the *aşîklar*); villagers (farmers, stock raisers, cattle dealers, and people who have come to town to do errands); and outsiders from neighboring cities (businessmen, truck drivers, and "guest workers" who have come home from Europe to visit relatives). Thus, the evening audience is drawn from different geographical areas, ethnic groups, social statuses, incomes, occupations, and religious sects.

Aşîklar are very responsive to the composition of the audience. Before the performance, they carefully study the audience members and decide what topics and music would please them. For example, if the majority of the audience is from a certain ethnic group (Azerbaijani, Turkoman, Terekeme, Kurd, Yerli), the competing *aşîklar* will choose this group's favorite traditional tunes and issues that are important to it. If many audience members are bearded and are wearing skullcaps, the *aşîklar* know that they would like religious themes. If many audience members are young, the main theme of the evening will be unrequited love.

Performances

Although the performances start at dusk, the most generous tippers usually do not arrive until about eight o'clock or eight-thirty. Therefore, the people who arrive early are usually entertained by apprentices who walk up and down among the tables, singing various songs to the accompaniment of the *saz*. Next, two lesser-known master *aşîklar* will present a song duel. At about eight or nine o'clock the nationally known masters will appear. Either the older *aşîk* or the one with the greater reputation will welcome the audience, in brief speech full of traditional formulas. He will wish the audience and the Turkish state well and will ask the audience to listen carefully. Then he will play a well-known *makam* that may last from one to three minutes. At this point, the audience members stop talking and take care not to make any noise with their tea glasses. Thus the instrumental music serves as a framing device and helps to focus the audience's interest and attention.

As they walk up and down, the *aşîklar* study the audience, greet acquaintances, and make eye contact with others. On the basis of what they see and how they analzye it, they decide what kind of music and poetry will be most appreciated and what ideas, concepts, and images will move the audience emotionally. At the same time, the audience looks for information about the competence of the *aşîklar* and their mood on that night; this lets the audience know what to expect.

FIGURE 4 *Aşîk* Ilhami Demir (right) negotiates with *aşîk* Seref Taslîova about who will sing next. Photo by Y. Erdener.

The length of a song duel depends on the mood of the competing *aşîklar*. It can have from five to seven sections, and traditionally one of the final sections will always include with personal attacks and insults. In each section, the *aşîklar* sing their improvised verse to a different traditional tune.

In the coffeehouse, when the listeners are ready for the song duel, the *aşîklar* will openly negotiate to decide who will sing first (figure 4). Usually, the one who greets the audience will start singing the first stanza of a *divan*, which should be composed in the classical Arabic-Persian metric pattern (*aruz*) and based on an alternation of long and short syllables. However, in a song duel, the *aşîklar* are under the pressure inherent in oral performance, and so it is impossible for them to alternate long and short syllables properly. Therefore, they have changed the classical *aruz* to the syllabic meter, and they use fifteen syllabes per line.

In the first section of a song duel the *aşîklar* do not improvise; rather, they use a poem composed by a well-known *aşîk* of the past. The content of a *divan* generally deals with the transitory nature of life, religious practices, or religious personages from the Qur'ānic heritage. Religious ideas, images, and symbols unifiy the audience at the outset. As soon as the first *aşîk* finishes the first stanza, the opponent will start to play his instrument for one to two minutes. During this time, he will decide whether to continue with the second stanza of the original verse or to reply with a *divan* from another past master. Relative to other songs in a duel, a *divan* is in a slow tempo. It uses the lower tones of the scale and generally has a narrow melodic range (between the perfect fifth and sixth). According to *aşîklar*, starting a song duel with a *divan* is similar to saying "hello" in everyday life—this is a a piece for warming up the audience, and the performer's voice. This first section of the song duel is completed when the competing *aşîklar* take turns and finish singing the whole *divan* of the past master.

The two *aşîklar* strictly respect each other's alternate turns. The second *aşîk* has to follow the exact metric and rhyme patterns of his opponent. For instance, in a stanza each line must have a definite number of syllables (eight, eleven, or fifteen), and there are certain rules for rhyming each stanza. If the second *aşîk* makes any changes, he will be reminded of his mistakes both by his opponent and by the audience members—an embarrassing situation for the *aşîk*.

After the first section (the *divan*), which has fifteen syllables per line, the following sections can have eight or eleven syllables in a line and can deal with any subject matter, such as the beauty of nature or the seasons; love, including unrequited love; social problems; local or national politics; unfair distribution of wealth; the importance of money or of traditional and religious values; geography; local or national history; and teasing and insults.

The poetic content

In a song duel, the content of the poetry is not always a prime issue. Since the folk poet composes without pen and paper, he does not have the luxury of revising. Also, he is not trying to find novel images or fantastic ideas, because there is no time to do so in front of a live audience. Therefore, whenever he is under pressure to construct his next line but cannot find the best rhyme or words, he will draw on a repertoire of formulas and clichés. These traditional elements are also part of the repertoire of the listeners, and so they are a bridge between the performer and the audience. Since a song duel is a social event, other aspects of the experience—such as spontaneity, competition, interaction, and the sharing of traditional knowledge through music and poetry—are sometimes more important than the poetic content or the number of syllables in a line.

BUILDING A REPUTATION

In olden days, a young, unknown *aşîk* would build his reputation through successful song duels with established, even famous, masters. In those days, religous issues and mystical and spiritual concepts were prominent topics of song duels. Therefore, *aşîklar* had to be knowledgeable about the Qur'ān and religious matters; and religious leaders of the village or a neighboring village were usually the jury that decided who had won a duel. The *asşîklar* would propound riddles and ask each other questions about sacred issues, such as how many holy books or prophets there were, what were their names, what was the content or meaning of certain verses in the Qur'ān, how often Muhammad had experienced God's revelations, when God created the world, and what was created first. Usually, at the end of a song duel, the victor would humorously disparage his opponent's knowledge and competence. To show his respect, the loser would hand his *saz* to the victor; the victor would then kiss the loser on the forehead and return the *saz* to him.

Contemporary *aşîklar* build their reputation somewhat differently. For one thing, they seek success at an *aşîk* festival. Winning a prize at a festival increases their chance of performing on national or local radio and television, and this media exposure can spread their reputation rapidly across the country.

Second, today's *aşîklar* and their listeners—unlike those of the past—prefer secular themes. After the separation of church and state in 1926 and the law introducing the Latin alphabet and banning the use of Arabic letters in 1928, religious issues gradually lost prominence in song dueling. Now, issues of daily life are the dominant themes.

Third, in the coffehouse, the song duel has become a commercial activity, and there is no winner or loser as such; thus the major goal of *aşîklar* in the coffeehouse of Kars is to entertain the audience members, who have paid a cover charge. One of the best ways to succeed in this is to become proficient with insults. In the insult section of the duel, the *aşîklar* use their wit and their poetic and musical talent to cast aspersions on each other's physical appearance (long or short arms, neck, or hair; height; face; feet), behavior (ways of walking or talking), intellectual capacity (education, general knowledge), or relatives (father, brother, or grandmother, and—especially—the opponent's mother-in-law). Another common way to entertain the audience is to avoid certain letters in improvising poetry: *b*, *f*, *m*, *p*, and *v*. These five consonants (like *p* and *b* in English) cannot be pronounced without closing the lips. Before the performance begins, each of the competing *aşîklar* places a pin in his mouth so that if he inadvertently uses one of the prohibited letters, the pin will prick him as his lips close—he may even bleed slightly. This feature of a contest is called *dudakdegmez* 'lips don't touch'. Festivals may also include *dudakdegmez*.

ASPECTS OF MODERN SONG DUELING

In conclusion, it is worthwhile to note some significant aspects of the song duel as it exists today. These include the relative importance of poetry and music, the importance of improvision, and the place of song dueling in Turkey.

Poetry and music

As has already been mentioned, poetry is considered more important than music in the song duel. Nevertheless, *aşîklar* still have a *saz* over the shoulder during a performances. They say that playing the instrument poorly does not affect their improvisation, and they note that the famous *aşîklar* Senlik and Sümmani left behind hundreds of beautiful poems, although neither of them could play the *saz* well (nor did either of them have a beautiful voice). Modern *aşîklar* who do play the *saz* well say that it is a source of inspiration and a good way to gain time during a performance. They also find that the *saz* helps them to hide and correct errors while they are constructing the lines of a stanza. In rapid composition, a line may turn out to be a syllable too short or too long. With the help of the *saz*, an *aşîk* can adjust the poetic line to the musical line by holding one syllable for two beats instead of one, or by making a dactyl out of a trochee. Without the *saz*, in fact, most *aşîklar* would be unable to improvise poetry during a song duel.

Combining the rhythm of the music with that of the words creates a state of mind, enabling the performer to formulate ideas and to express them artistically. In the coffeehouse of Kars, the *aşîklar* can use music and poetry to explore with impunity themes that would otherwise be risky. To put this another way, music allows them to make statements that would be forbidden in other contexts. Music gives the *aşîklar* a special kind of of license and freedom—for example, to sing obscene lyrics in public. Such obscenity, expressed in the rhythms of music, somehow does not seem to be a personal attack or affront, as it would be in normal speech (Erdener 1995:122–141).

Improvisation and spontaneity

In Turkey, traditional culture emphasizes improvisation. *Aşîklar* who can improvise easily, as we have seen, are said to be inspired by God, and they are admired and praised. During a song duel talented *aşîklar* can easily incorporate into their poetry an unexpected situation or topic, or the presence of an individual.

To be able to improvise poetry, one must have been born and raised in an environment where the *aşîk* tradition is part of daily life, as it is in northeastern Turkey, especially around Kars. There, learning how to recite poetry is virtually the same as learning one's native tongue. Like a child learning to speak, a young *aşîk* lays a foundation for improvising poetry by hearing thousands of poems created extemporaneously by other *aşîklar*. By hearing, memorizing, and imitating the poems of others, the young *aşîk* absorbs the rhythm of singing and rhyming and internalizes the basic rules of poetic improvisation. With music and improvised poetry, a competent *aşîk* can catch every heart in the audience.

The place of song dueling

Finally, it sould be noted that song dueling is not a prevalent tradition in modern Turkey. Although it can be found in Konya, its primary center—in terms of a natural context—is northeastern Turkey. This is due to the historically close contact between Turkish *aşîklar* and the *aşîklar* of Russian and Iranian Azerbaijan. The province of Kars was geographically part of the Ottoman Empire, but culturally it has always been part of Russian and Iranian Azerbaijan. The people of Kars share many cultural elements with those of Azerbaijan, including the song duel. When the province of Kars became Russian territory (1878–1918), *aşîklar* often traveled to Azerbaijan and exchanged ideas with *aşîklar* there, and well-known *aşîklar* of northeastern Turkey were in close contact with the *aşîklar* of Russian and Iranian Azerbaijan. For example, the legendary *aşîk* Senlik traveled extensively in Russian Azerbaijan (to Tiflis, Baku, Revan, and elswhere). Senlik had a tremendous impact on the *aşîk* tradition, especially on the song duel in northeastern Turkey. During his time, song contests were prevalent among Turkish-speaking peoples in Central Asia and Azerbaijan, and although there is very little literature from that period, we can probably assume that the song duel was introduced to Turkey by him and his contemporaries. The song dueling tradition in northeastern Turkey, with Kars as its center, flourished during the second half of the nineteenth century and the early twentieth century.

REFERENCES

Aslan, Ensar. 1975. *Çîldîrlî Aşîk Senlik*. Ankara: Sevinç Matbaasî.

Bali, Muhan. 1975. "Aşîk Karsîlasmalarî-Atîsmalar (Song Dueling of *Aşîklar*: Satiric Poems)." *Türk Folklor Arastîrmalarî* 314.

Basgöz, Ilhan. 1952. "Turkish Folk Stories about the Lives of Minstrels." *Journal of American Folklore* 65:331–339.

———. 1967. "Dream Motif and Shamanistic Initiation." *Asian Folklore Studies* 1:1–18.

Brands, Horst Wilfrid. 1978. "Aytîs-Deyisme, Formen des Dichterwettstreits bei den Türkvölkern." In *Studies in Turkish Folklore*, ed. Ilhan Basgöz and Mark Glazer. Indiana University Turkish Studies No 1. Bloomington, Ind.: Maccallum.

Eberhard, Wolfram. 1955. *Minstrel Tales from Southeastern Turkey*. Los Angeles: University of California Press.

———. 1971. *Emrah ile Selvi*. Istanbul: Halk Kitapçîlîk.

Emsheimer, E. 1956. "Singing Contests in Central Asia." *International Folk Music Journal* 8:26–29.

Erdener, Yîldîray. 1995. *The Song Contests of Turkish Minstrels: Improvised Poetry Sung to Traditional Music*. New York: Garland.

Hînçer, Ihsan. 1968. "Aşîklîk, Bade içme, Irtical, Atîsma ve Muamma." *Türk Folklore Arastîrmalarî*, 20, *Yîl Özel Sayîsî*.

Özder, Adil. 1965. *Dogu Illerimizde Aşîk Karsîlasmalarî*. Bursa: Emek Basîmevi.

Radloff, V. 1885. *Proben der Volksliteratur der türkischen Stamme*, Vol. 5. Saint Petersburg: Kaiserliche Akademie der Wissenschaft.

Dance and Identity in Turkey

Arzu Öztürkmen

The Ottoman Past
Dance and Nationalism in Turkey
The Modern Folk Dance Movement
The Art of Dance and the Stage Experience

Many people associate Turkish dance either with the whirling dervishes or with belly dancing. Although both these dance forms are rooted in the Ottoman past and still constitute an important part of tourists' experience in Turkey, Turkish dance today is considerably more complicated. Different historical trends helped shape what is currently perceived as "Turkish folk dancing." The Ottoman Empire, which controlled the Mediterranean, the Balkans, and the Middle East between the thirteenth and nineteenth centuries, was at the crossroads of a variety of regional cultures. Today's Turkish dance tradition reflects this diversity, combining within it elements of Caucasian, Balkan, Islamic, and Anatolian culture. Following the collapse of the Ottoman Empire, the Republican regime (which was established in 1923) tried to foster a national culture based on the historical and regional heritage of the Ottomans and on Western culture.

THE OTTOMAN PAST

In the Ottoman period, dance had an important place in religious rituals and at court as well as in village life.

Dancelike religious rituals were not confined to the whirling dervishes of the Mevlevi sect; many other religious groups had similar practices, which to the outsider looked like dance. (It should be noted that today many believers see their rituals as a form of prayer and reject the term "dance.") Historically, these rituals were part of the Sufi practice of Islam. They were performed by religious groups such as the Mevlevis and the Kadiris in the main towns. In smaller towns and villages around Anatolia, there was a more expanded tradition of such religious rituals among the Alevi people. Historians believe that in Ottoman times Sufi practices fused Islamic beliefs with shamanistic elements inherited from Central Asian Turkic ancestors.

The two best-known forms of ritual dancing are the Mevlevi *sema* and the Alevi *semah*—both terms refer to rotation of the body. Although the Ottomans respected most of the religious orders as social institutions, the Alevi sects around Anatolia have historically suffered at the hands of state authorities. The main reason for this was the government's concern that the Alevis might be in league with the Safavid state to the east. Despite this oppression, however, both the Alevi ritual *cem* and its *semah* have survived to the present.

Ottoman social life was also characterized by various genres of entertainment dance, especially at court. The most extravagant court dances took place during imperial festivals held in honor of the sultan's family; such a celebration—for example, a wedding or the circumcision of a prince—lasted at least two weeks, and usually more. Four types of dancers performed at these festivities.

The first two types, the *köçekler* and the *çengiler*, were professional dancers trained for group performances. A *köçek* was a male dancer who wore long hair, jewelry, and women's clothes; a *çengi* was a female dancer in the service of the harem. The *köçekler* and *çengiler* used tightly controlled movements of the upper body—such as elegantly extended arms and very elastic motion around the waist—in skillful belly dancing.

During performances at imperial festivals, the *köçekler* and the *çengiler* would often be accompanied by a third type of dancers—a group of grotesque dancers called *soytarı* or *curcunabaz*. The main function of these grotesque dancers was to ridicule the elegance and skill of the *köçekler* by distorting their movements and exaggerating their figures; they appealed to the audience's sense of humor by calling attention to themselves. In contrast to the *köçekler* and *çengiler*, the grotesque dancers performed very earthbound movements that were often sexually suggestive or even obscene; they would bump into one another and pause with twisted arm and hand gestures.

There was also a fourth type of dancers, the *tasbaz*. These were acrobatic dancers who displayed their skill by rhythmically whirling a plate on a finger.

The main sources for the study of the imperial festivals are the official "festival books." A festival book, called a *surname*, was illustrated with numerous miniatures that show performances in great detail. In addition, useful descriptions of dance performances are found in narratives by travelers, mostly Europeans who witnessed dancing and wrote their observations in letters, diaries, reports, or books.

The status of the court dancers appears to have been mixed. It is possible that, relative to other professions, dancing was undervalued; but the most competent *köçekler* and *çengiler* are known to have had their own fans and to have been supported at least during the peak of their careers.

The lifestyle of the court had an influence on peripheral parts of the empire. During the eighteenth and nineteenth centuries, for example, the prestige of local notables and high-ranking bureaucrats increased; and at their mansions, called *konaklar*, they organized their own festivities, similar to those celebrated at court but smaller in scale. These festivals included dancing by professional *köçekler* and *çengiler*, who usually lived in the *konak* and entertained the family and guests on various occasions, such as circumcisions and weddings.

DANCE AND NATIONALISM IN TURKEY

In the early twentieth century, during the last decades of the Ottoman Empire, Turkish intellectuals—who were shaken by nationalist rebellion and by the loss of their lands—turned to the study of their culture and discovered dance as a symbol of national identity. The pioneers of dance research were two Ottoman intellectuals of the Young Turk movement, Rıza Tevfik and Selim Sırrı Tarcan. In 1900, Rıza Tevfik wrote an article, "Dance and Its Various Forms in the Ottoman Countries," that discussed the importance of dance as representative of its cultural context. He identified different dance genres such as *zeybek* and *horon* and described how they were related to local traditions.

Selim Sırrı Tarcan not only wrote about dance but also collected folk dances for the first time and performed them on stage. Tarcan's interest in folk dance began as early as 1898, in İzmir, where he observed Aegean soldiers performing their local dances. In 1909, the Ottoman government sent him to Sweden to study physical education, and his experiences there heightened his awareness of the growing relationship between dance and national identity. He was deeply impressed by the teachers in Nees, where national and local dances were "disciplined" and given a more "refined form." On his return to Istanbul, he began stylizing the dances he had collected from various sources. In 1916, he choreographed a dance that he named *Tarcan zeybeği*, after himself. As he would write later, he first chose a folk song, then speeded up its rhythm while "preserving the national character of both the song and the dance." He taught his choreographed dance to students at the Teacher's College.

Tarcan's contribution to the history of dance in Turkey also has to do with the fact that he was able to make a smooth transition to the Republican era. By the early years of the republic, Tarcan was actively promoting its ideals of westernization and modernization. Because he was in close contact with high-ranking bureaucrats, he found the opportunity to present his choreography to the president, M. Kemal Atatürk. Atatürk praised Tarcan for having transformed the *zeybek* into a "civilized" form that could be accepted and enjoyed by the entire country as its national and social dance. Interestingly, he also asked Tarcan to perform in a tuxedo and, later, to perform accompanied by a woman.

Tarcan wanted the national dance to be modern while preserving a touch of the traditional, and to be performed as a ballroom dance. He held that national folk dances are "a live expression of people's characteristcs, temperament, and morals" and that this noble tradition should be offered to the people "as a sacred book, once it goes through the artistic filter" (Tarcan 1948).

The *Tarcan zeybeği*, however, remained little more than a fantasy in Turkey's dance history. Although it achieved a certain popularity during the 1930s through the efforts of Tarcan's students, who carried it to various parts of the country as elementary school teachers, it never became Turkey's unique "national dance" as Tarcan and Atatürk had dreamed. Other trends in Turkish folk dance were developing concurrently with Tarcan's attempts to create a national dance. The most influential of these trends were the People's Houses of 1932 to 1951 [see also ASPECTS OF TURKISH FOLK MUSIC THEORY].

People's Houses (*Halk Evleri*) were semiofficial cultural clubs, established in towns and villages to conduct local research and to promote the cultural reforms of the Republican regime. Each People's House focused on different kinds of artistic performance, such as music, drama, and literature, in addition to educational and charitable activities. The anniversary of the founding of the People's Houses was celebrated every year in the capital city, Ankara, as a public festival in which regional groups gathered to present staged performances. By the end of the 1930s, the leading performing artists of each town or village had been identified and invited to these annual celebrations.

These festivals were beneficial for local performers in several ways. First, the dancers gained a reputation, and prestige, in their own localities when reviews of their performances were published in the journals of the People's Houses. (This, however, also had a negative aspect: to retain a monopoly, many of these dancers declined to train younger people.) Second, by representing their local identity to urban audiences and then, when they returned home, by recounting their experience of a national festival, the dancers acted as agents of a nation in formation. Third, for many local dancers the experience of performing at an anniversary festival for the People's Houses constituted a rite of passage. They organized "formal" groups for the first time and decided on the order of the dances to be performed for audiences who were not familiar with their traditions. This was a challenge but also a significant opportunity to make their own local identity part of a national repertoire. Fourth, seeing other dance genres that were now also part of this national repertoire was another new experience, and it made many local dance groups aware that the nation-state took pride in diversity as a sign of a richer culture. As for the audiences, this presentation of what were called national dances helped them understand, in more concrete terms, the nation envisioned by the new regime.

Most regional genres were previously performed as either men's or women's dances, but that changed when the Republican regime promoted women's appearance on stage and encouraged mixed group dancing.

Today, in fact, the main genres of Turkish folk dance are classified by region. Borderlands in northeastern and southern Turkey had rather varied dance traditions, reflecting an Ottoman heritage. The *halay* genre, widespread in central and eastern Anatolia, has a markedly linear structure: the dancers hold hands, and the focus is on movements of the legs and feet while the upper body suggests the unity of the group. The *zeybek* genre belongs to the Aegean tradition and is something more than a group dance: the individual performers, in a circle, dance independently of one another, executing slow movements, holding their arms outstretched, snapping their fingers rhythmically, and from time to time kneeling down. *Horon* is the characteristic genre of the Black Sea coast: it is distinguished by a very fast, energetic rhythm accompanied by trembling shoulders and stamping feet. The *karşılama* genre is seen mostly in Thrace and is in some ways similar to the Balkan *hora*: these Thracian dances are characterized by moving the feet rapidy and rhythmically and pulling the legs up in various ways. Dancers in a *karşılama* group link their little fingers; sometimes they face one another while snapping their fingers. Most of these regional genres were previously performed as either men's or women's dances, but that changed when the Republican regime promoted women's appearance on stage and encouraged mixed-group dancing.

During the festivals for the People's Houses, these dances were performed for the first time before urban audiences; thus many local dances were subject to a process of selection. Dances that had elements of spectacle or drama (such as an enactment of a harvest, women's housework, or jealousy involving two girls and a boy) became fashionable. Similarly, dances with very fast, energetic rhythms, which gave the performers a chance to display their skill and talent, were preferred to slower, more repetitive dances. Depending on the audience's response, many dances were kept short, and repetitions might be eliminated. Individual dances that could be adapted for performance by a group, especially a mixed group, were favored over solo dances. Overall, in these performances, audiences favored "regularity" and "uniformity." Synchronized, harmonious group movement was praised as a sign of civilization and modernity.

The performances commemorating the People's Houses lasted for two decades; during that time, they created in the major cities an audience devoted to staged folk dance. In 1950, with the transition to a multiparty system, the parliament voted to close the People's Houses (which, as quasi-official institutions, had been linked to the former single ruling party, the Republican People's Party). This development was a threat to the new tradition of bringing local dance groups to large cities; but in 1954, a private bank, Yapı ve Kredi Bankası, decided to continue the custom by organizing annual folk dance competitions and festivals in Istanbul. The bank's festivals were not very different from those that had been held to commemorate the founding of the People's Houses: local dance groups, each representing a particular region and genre, were invited to perform. Perhaps the most important achievement of these festivals was to introduce a repertoire of folk dances, later framed as "national Turkish dances."

THE MODERN FOLK DANCE MOVEMENT

By the 1960s a new trend became dominant in folk dance: an increasing number of student groups were interested in performing folk dances in large cities. One of the main reasons behind this interest was that more students of Anatolian origin were coming to İstanbul and Ankara for higher education. Most of them lived in dormitories named after, and usually sponsored by, well-off people in their native towns. Such dormitories provided Anatolian students with a support system in an urban context, and by teaching their local dances to others, the students could build a bridge between their local and new identities. This started a significant process: the university clubs now taught many local dances at the same time, enabling not only members of a particular dance tradition but any young performer to learn the developing repertoire of what was called Turkish folk dance. The process was new in two important ways. First, performers were now exposed to other dance traditions not only visually but also experientially, through their own bodies, as they learned the systems of movement in those traditions. This was quite a different experience from simply being a spectator at the festivals for the People's Houses. Second, the age profile of the dancers changed strikingly. The members of local dance groups had been the most experienced dancers, so they were usually adults and often elderly people; by contrast, many performers of the 1960s were university and high school students—and the age profile would become even younger as university students seized a new business opportunity by teaching the repertoire to elementary school pupils.

This new kind of folk dance practice spread rapidly during the 1970s and 1980s, especially in educational institutions and in small private folk dance associations that offered weekend courses attended mostly by young people. They had a fixed repertoire of six to ten dances from different regions, and two or three teachers who taught the full repertoire. The dances were named after the towns they were associated with, instead of by genre; a typical repertoire included dances from Edirne, Diyarbakır, Antep, Sivas, Artvin, and Kars, and a few from the Black Sea and Aegean regions. The goal for the students would be to perform at a year-end show, in a folk dance competition, or in a folk dance festival abroad.

The folk dance associations also played an important role in offering a setting for the socialization of boys and girls. Conservative Turkish families regarded folk dance as perhaps the most legitimate dance form, and as something they could tolerate. Compared with the settings in which ballet was taught or disco dancing took place, the folk dance associations—which had a paternalistic structure—gave parents a sense of security, reassuring them that their children would be safe and well supervised. Moreover, families took pride in watching their young people perform "national" dances on stage in colorful traditional costumes. For the state authorities, too, folk dancing was an acceptable activity for the young. In the politicized context of the 1970s, folk dance associations, unlike many other youth organizations, presented no threat to the state order. In fact, the state began to promote folk dance and to control it through competitions organized by the ministries of sports and education at all levels, from elementary school through the folk dance associations.

The folk dance movement of the post-1970s was distinguished from that of the 1970s by three changes in stage techniques, involving choreography, musical accompaniment, and costuming. The first of these, floor patterning, was inspired by the Soviet-style "ensemble" and became a predominant concern at year-end shows and folk dance competitions. The folk dance repertoire, which had more or less stabilized since the early 1930s, was now subject to a set of floor patterns such as circles, crosses, diagonal or perpendicular lines, and rows (figures 1 and 2). Floor patterning had an important impact on the urban folk dance tradition. When the same patterns were applied over and over again to the various folk dances in the national repertoire, movements came to be standardized. Putting a regional motif into a choreographic arrangement on stage, sometimes hastily, involved devising movements that were almost new and that looked alike from dance to dance regardless of the original locality of a genre. For example, movements such as kneeling down or pulling one's legs up can be done in different ways, and in fact each of these was once executed in two totally different styles in the *zeybek* and *halay* genres—but when its nuances were eliminated for the sake of efficient floor patterning, the movement began to look the same in both genres. A related effect was that floor patterning tended to speed up the rhythm of all the dances in the repertoire.

The second change in stage technique had to do with music. Since the 1930s, the musical accompaniment to folk dance had been provided by local instruments that varied from genre to genre; now, a new set of instruments were added to these. For example, the *davul* and *zurna*, the Turkish drum and horn, had been the two main instruments of the *halay* genre, but in the post-1970s other instruments, such as the accordion and the *saz*, were added to performances. Because similar additions were made to various dance genres, a certain standardization of musical accompaniment occurred.

A third change was in costuming. To meet the increased demand for costumes, most folk dance associations and school clubs began to buy all kinds of regional costumes from the same urban tailors, rather than taking the time to order each costume from its original town or village. Thus the same array of colors, and similar synthetic fabrics, began to be used for a variety of dances, resulting in a standardized visual impression that was analogous to the standardized sound of the musical instruments.

One consequence of these developments was a unification of local elements—movement, music, and costumes—that had been diverse. Folk dancing as such emerged as a new genre, called *halk oyunu oynamak*. Its popularity was unequaled by other forms of dance such as ballet, modern dance, and disco. Notably, for the performers, the social significance of folk dance was perhaps greater than its nationalistic significance. Folk dance clubs and associations were a milieu that offered dancers unique opportunities for socializing, traveling, and gaining the approval of their families and the state authorities.

FIGURE 1 Floor patterning of the Kırklareli folk dance performed by Boğaziçi University Folklore Club at a college-level folk dance competition in Elazığ, 1986. Photograph courtesy of Laleper Aytek.

FIGURE 2 Floor patterning of the Afyon-Dinar folk dance at the competition in Elazığ, 1986. Photograph coutesty of Laleper Aytek.

THE ART OF DANCE AND THE STAGE EXPERIENCE

The Western performing arts were among the major art forms promoted by the Republican regime in Turkey after the early 1930s. The People's Houses had special art sections offering courses in drama, classical music, and painting. The state openly praised "high art," including opera and ballet. In 1936, the first state conservatory—specializing in the teaching of music, drama, and opera—was opened in Ankara.

Training in ballet came a decade later, in 1948, when a small school was opened in Istanbul under the guidance of Ninette de Valois. This school made a breakthrough in legitimizing ballet in Turkey: the Ottoman world had been familiar with ballet performances since the sixteeth century, but teaching ballet to Turkish performers was a novelty. In 1950, the ballet school became a state conservatory. Today, with branches in the large cities, the state conservatories train young dancers, and two state ensembles sponsored by the ministry of culture regularly perform the classical and modern repertoire. Many private institutions also offer ballet courses in the large cities. However, the number of private ballet companies is small; and although ballet is sponsored and supported by the state's cultural policies, it is not a widely acclaimed dance form in Turkey. Compared with folk dancing or social dancing in night clubs or at weddings and circumcision celebrations, ballet has few performers and a limited audience. This is partly because of a scarcity of ballet schools, partly because there are few employment opportunities outside the state ensembles, and partly because the public tends to think of ballet as an art for elite performers and elite audiences.

Modern dance became part of the curriculum in state conservatories only in the 1990s, although foreign dance troupes had introduced this form in the 1980s. Modern dance found many supporters among students who preferred its free expression to the strict rules of ballet. As with ballet, however, the groups who perform modern dance are very few.

What both ballet and modern dance represent symbolically in Turkey may reveal more than their actual performance does. Debates between tradition and modernity are easily transferred to the discussion of why the state sponsors a Western art rather than traditional arts. In Turkey, ballet and modern dance have failed to produce a genuine synthesis of "modern" forms and the Turkish experience. Domestic ballet and modern dance companies may choose their themes from traditional tales and legends, but they have not developed an original theme emanating from contemporary Turkish life.

REFERENCES

And, Metin. 1976. *A Pictorial History of Turkish Dancing: From Folk Dancing to Whirling Dervishes—Belly Dancing to Ballet*. Ankara: Dost Yayınları.

Ataman, Sadi Yaver. 1975. *100 Türk Halk Oyunu*. Istanbul: Yapı ve Kredi Bankası.

Büfk-Eçy. 1987. "Folklor Derneklerine Bir Bakış" *Folklora Doğru* 56:33–40.

Çeçen, Anıl. 1990. *Halkevleri*. Ankara: Gündoğan Yayınları.

Demirsipahi, Cemil. 1975. *Türk Halk Oyunları*. Ankara: Türkiye İş Bankası Kültür Yayınları.

Evliyaoğlu, Sait, and Şerif Baykurt. 1988. *Türk Halkbilimi*. Ankara: Ofset Reprodüksiyon Matbaacılık.

Karpat, Kemal H. 1963. "The People's Houses in Turkey: Establishment and Growth." *Middle East Journal* 17(1, 2):55–67.

Mélikoff, Irène. 1993. *Uyur İdik Uyardılar: Alevîlik-Bektaşîlik Araştırmaları*, trans. Turan Alptekin. Istanbul: Cem Yayınevi.

Öztürkmen, Arzu. 1993. "Folklore and Nationalism in Turkey." Ph.D. dissertation, University of Pennsylvania.

———. 1994a. "Folk Dance and Nationalism in Turkey." In *Seventeenth Symposium of the Study Group on Ethnochoreology: 1992 Proceedings*, 83–86. Nafplion: Peloponnesian Folklore Foundation.

———. 1994b. "The Role of the People's Houses in the Making of National Culture in Turkey." *New Perspectives on Turkey* 11:159–181.

Sözen, Muzaffer. 1941. Halk Rakslarından Halaylar. *Ülkü* 17:111–119.

———. 1995. "The Alevi *Cem* Ritual and the Nationalization of *Semah* Dances." In *Dance, Ritual and Music: Proceedings from the Eighteenth Symposium of the Study Group on Ethnochoreology, International Council for Traditional Music, August 9–18, 1994, in Skierniewice, Poland*. Warsaw: Polish Society for Ethnochoreology.

Tarcan, Selim Sırrı. 1948. *Halk Dansları re Tarcan Zeybeği*. Istanbul: Ülkü Basımevi.

Section 7
Iran

Section 7
Iran

In no other part of the world has sung poetry been more highly valued than in the territories where Iranian civilization has flourished for millennia. The public and private lives of most Iranians include activities during which verses are sung or recited, either by specialists or by most of those who are present. Some types of singing do not allow for instrumental accompaniment; others require it. Verses of the great classical Persian poets—Sa'dī, Mowlānā Jalāl al-dīn Rūmī, and Hāfez—are performed in a variety of ways and have remained poems that must be heard, remembered, and reproduced orally, not just experienced through silent reading. Each language spoken in Iran has its own genres of sung poetry, some of them oriented toward narrative and philosophical reflection.

Iranian instruments are heard to best effect in small ensembles, where the different ways of producing sounds can register on the listener's ear. Musicians must move in order to play instruments; and more often than not, their listeners are inclined to move in response. In many situations the responses must remain within the bounds of decorum; in other circumstances some participants enjoy a temporary release from the inhibitions of everyday life.

Following the revolution of 1979 and the abolition of an oppressive monarchy, many Iranians questioned their cultural traditions and argued about what cultural practices might best meet their needs. Some groups have attempted to limit the types of performance offered in public spaces. Throughout Iran's long history, men and women who wished to cultivate their artistic and spiritual interests freely have often found themselves in conflict with political and religious authorities. The twentieth century saw vigorous efforts toward creating a civil society in Iran, and this project continues in the first decade of the twenty-first century.

Street violinist playing Iranian folk music in front of a shop at the old bazaar in Tehran. Photo © Earl and Nazima Kowall, Corbis.

Iran: An Introduction

Stephen Blum

Venues and Purposes
Roles of Performers
Musical Knowledge

The territory occupied by the modern nation of Iran, a vast plateau ringed by mountain ranges, has supported a distinctive civilization for several millennia. At various times the sphere of influence of Iranian civilization has extended outward in many directions—toward the Arabian peninsula, Mesopotamia, Anatolia, Transcaucasia, Central Asia, Afghanistan, Kashmir, and South Asia. Persian, the mother tongue of slightly more than half of Iran's population, is at once the national language of Iran and the primary language of Iranian civilization. Classical Persian poetry is deeply imbued with musical imagery, and musical terms adopted from Persian are found in each of the areas named. The term *Īrān bozorg* 'greater Iran' is sometimes applied to those regions of Afghanistan and Transoxiana where Persian is a major language for poetry and music. In recent centuries Sufi religious orders have provided the main channels for the diffusion of Iranian musical practices and ideas about music.

This overview begins with singing in the primary venue of Iranian Sufism, the *khāneqāh*, and continues through other venues, some of them more private than public. The ways in which people learn to interact in each type of venue enable them to assume specific roles in the performance genres that require or allow for the singing of poetry, the playing of instruments, or rhythmically coordinated exercises, marching, or dancing. One's sense of what is appropriate in each situation provides a basis for organizing one's knowledge of music, poetry, and other disciplines. The three main sections of this introduction thus deal with venues, roles of performers, and musical knowledge.

The cultural prestige of Persian notwithstanding, Iran is a multilingual nation. In the cultural politics of the Islamic Republic (established in 1979), the musical practices of groups whose mother tongue is not Persian—Azerbaijani Turks, Kurds, Baluchis, Turkmen, Arabs, etc.—are classified as "regional." The musical cultures of Baluchistan, the Gulf region, Kurdistan, Azerbaijan, and the Turkmen Plain stretch across national boundaries, while other regional practices (such as those of the northern provinces of Gilan and Mazanderan) are unique to Iran. Two government units—the Ministry of Culture and Islamic Guidance, and the Arts Division of the Islamic Propaganda Organization—have organized festivals and issued recordings of regional musics. Iran's *mirās-e farhangī* 'cultural heritage' is now rather widely understood to include the performing arts of the country's *navāḥī-ye mokhtalef* 'diverse regions' as

Iran.

well as the varieties of music that are cultivated, or diffused by means of recordings and broadcasts, throughout the nation. Regional musics are sometimes called *mūsīqī-ye maqāmī* 'music using melodic types', in order to distinguish them both from urban popular music and from the elite music based on a system of seven principal modes—*haft dastgāh* 'seven systems'—and five or more *āvāzāt* 'annexes'. This highly refined music is most strongly identified with the region once known as *'Irāq al-'ajam* 'Persian Iraq', which includes such artistic centers as Qazvīn, Tehrān, Eṣfahān, and Shīrāz; a closely related musical system is cultivated in major cities of the republic of Azerbaijan.

The history of the changing relationships among the diverse musical idioms of "greater Iran" is long and intricate. Much fundamental research remains to be done before music historians can attempt to describe these changes and identify some of the principal causes. Scholars and critics have not always resisted the temptation to represent the past in terms of modern dichotomies, such as regional versus national and folk versus classical. The first extensive inventory of Persian writings on music was published as recently as 1996, and most treatises are not yet available in modern editions. Intensive fieldwork has been carried out in only a few of Iran's many regions. For much of the country, the best available documents are recordings and other publications resulting from the festivals mentioned above.

VENUES AND PURPOSES

Khāneqāh and *zūr-khāne*

A male visitor to Iran, entering the meeting place (*khāneqāh*) of a Sufi order on a Thursday evening as the guest of a man who regularly attends the sessions (*majāles*; singular, *majles*), will be warmly received as he kisses the hand of the leader (*morshed*) and sits in the place he is offered in the circle of devotees. As one man after another sings a *ghazal* of his choice, an attendant serves tea, sweets, and perhaps fruits to the visitor and the other listeners. If the visitor has attended similar sessions in other Iranian cities, he is likely to recognize poetry he has heard before. Perhaps a special place in the sequence of events is reserved for poems composed by the founder or another important figure of this order, poems in which everyone can take part by singing the refrain stanzas. The session culminates with the most important event: performance of *ẕekr* 'remembrance' of God, through unison recitation of a few phrases, each initiated by the *morshed* and repeated many times, beginning with *Lā ellāhe ellā 'llāh!* 'No divinity apart from God!'

Each Sufi order has its own norms of worship, which always include specific ways of performing *ẕekr* and often involve a communal meal early in the evening. Separate sessions for women are sometimes held in a different room from the men's gathering. In certain orders sung poetry is accompanied by frame drums (*def*) or by long-necked lutes (*tanbūr* or *dūtār*); the lutes are also used for instrumental solos among the Naqshbandī in Khorasan and the Ahl-e Ḥaqq of Kurdistan (who are neither Sufis nor, by orthodox standards, Muslims). Singers of the Cheshtī order in Baluchistan accompany themselves on the short-necked double-chested lute *rabāb* as a companion adds a rhythmic drone on the long-necked lute *tanbire* and other dervishes join in singing the refrain lines. Such uses of instruments are among the many reasons given by orthodox religious leaders for their opposition to the Sufi brotherhoods and to the Ahl-e Ḥaqq.

Many of the venues in which Iranian musical practices have been developed over the centuries have a distinctively urban cast. The *khāneqāh* is one such venue; another is the *zūr-khāne*, an athletic club where men gather in the early morning or early evening to perform a sequence of exercises. Here as well the leader is called *morshed*, but his role is unique to the *zūr-khāne*: he plays a large clay goblet-shaped drum (*żarb*) while singing religious verses and short passages from the Persian epic poem *Shāh-nāme* 'Book of Kings', composed in the tenth century by Ferdowsī on the basis of earlier oral and written sources. Each motion of the athletes is tightly coordinated with the rhythms played on the *żarb*. Two metal instruments also have prominent roles: the *morshed* intensifies certain drum strokes by striking a small suspended bell, and in one exercise the athletes lift and shake a heavy rattle (*kabbāde*) that has metal disks attached to the links of a chain. The athletes are scrupulously polite to one another and to any visitors. The room usually has an octagonal pit that can accommodate a limited number of athletes, and it is common for a man within the octagon to offer his place to a latecomer. The *morshed* seldom fails to sing verses in praise (*madḥ*) of Imām 'Alī, the first imām of Shī'a Islam, who is remembered as a brave and adept warrior and whose portrait hangs on the wall of every *zūr-khāne* (and is often seen in a *khāneqāh*). Toward the end of the sequence a difficult exercise is performed individually by those who wish to attempt it: the arms are crossed, then gradually extended outward as the athlete turns in an accelerating circular motion (*charkh*) which is not unlike the (slower) motions of the so-called whirling dervishes of the Mevlevi order in Turkey.

The *khāneqāh* and *zūr-khāne* differ in their prevailing ethos: in the first venue, this is a contemplative love of the divine in all its manifestations; in the second, it is a resolve to train body and soul for service to the Shī'a community. Men who regularly attend either type of session find a warm sociability (*moḥabbatī*) that enhances their everyday lives. Knowledge of music and poetry is highly prized in most Sufi orders, whose leaders may or may not have engaged in formal study of these subjects. The *morshed* of a *zūr-khāne* acquires his art either through an extended apprenticeship of up to twelve years or through various formal and informal means, perhaps including lessons in the classical *dastgāh* system. One *morshed* in the city of Sabzevār who took such lessons at a music school came to realize that his own master had always sung in the *dastgāh* of *shūr* without knowing its name. The heroic aspects of particular *dastgāh-hā* and *gūshe-hā*, which are emphasized in the *zūr-khāne*, might seem out of place in the *khāneqāh*—but some of the very same verses by the classical Persian poets Sa'dī, Mowlānā Jalāl al-dīn Rūmī, and Ḥāfeẓ are sung in both venues.

Ceremonial mourning

A third type of gathering, especially common in villages and among countless thousands of rural migrants to cities, is the *hey'at*, a group of devotees who meet for religious observances in a private home or in a public building known as *Ḥoseiniye*. Banners displaying the name of the *hey'at* are often hung on the outer wall of a home on days when the group has scheduled a session. Several performance genres are cultivated in these gatherings, which are viewed favorably by the official religious hierarchy. Responsorial singing of *nowḥe* 'lamentation' involves two types of rhythmic movement: in *sīne-zanī*, men and boys beat their breasts on every third, fourth, or sixth pulse; in *zanjīr-zanī*, they strike small chains lightly against their shoulders. The purpose is to express anguish over the sufferings of the martyred Shī'a imams. Soloists take turns singing verses that gradually move to a higher vocal register but always lead back to the short group response in the lower register. On the anniversaries of the martyrdom of Imām Ḥosein (the tenth day of the month of Moḥarram), Imām Ḥasan (the twenty-eighth of Ṣafar), Imām Reżа (the twenty-ninth of Ṣafar), or others, many groups (now called *daste*) participate in processions, with loudspeakers carried in trucks to amplify the soloists and sometimes with instruments (cymbals, bass and snare drums, trumpets, and saxophones). Patterns of lifting and lowering each foot are well coordinated with the rhythms of singing, drumming, breast-beating, and striking one or both shoulders with the small chains (figure 1). The solemnity of the occasion does not prevent singers from occasionally imitating the vocal mannerisms of well-known performers of urban popular music.

A powerful experience at many devotional gatherings is provided by a *rowże-khān*, who sings extended narratives about the martyrdom of Imām Ḥosein and others as listeners weep profusely. Separate sessions are often arranged for women and girls, with the male performer seated behind a screen. A *rowże-khān* must know how to manipulate his voice and shape his performance in ways that will elicit highly emotional responses. The manipulative aspects of his art, and the fact that he is usually paid for his services, make the *rowże-khān*'s profession less than honorable in the

FIGURE 1 A group of men in Mashhad perform *nowḥe sīne-zanī* on the anniversary of the martyrdom of Imām Reżā. Photo by Amir Ḥosein Pourjavady, 1995.

eyes of some Iranians. Yet no performing art has deeper roots throughout the nation, and cassettes of the best-known *rowże-khānān* are sold in every city and town.

Enacting the same stories in dramatic form (*ta'zīye* 'mourning', or *shabih* 'likeness') is almost universally viewed as meritorious and is the most ambitious undertaking of a *hey'at*. One experienced member usually looks after the props and scripts and provides advice during rehearsals. A villager who has memorized a specific role (*naqsh*) from his father's teaching may proceed to teach the same role to his son. The performances usually take place on anniversaries of the martyrdom of an imam, in the courtyard of a private home or on an outdoor stage constructed for the purpose, with men and women seated in separate areas. A group that makes a pilgrimage to the shrine (*īmām-zāde*) of one of the imam's numerous descendants may prepare and perform a *ta'zīye* as an offering to the other pilgrims. No instruments are indispensable, but drums and trumpets are often used to evoke the wars waged against the imāms by their opponents. These opponents are deemed incapable of singing and can merely declaim their lines of verse in a raspy voice. The imams, members of their families, and their supporters sing all their lines, praising one another's merits and lamenting their cruel fate. Most spectators weep profusely, just as they do during a *rowże-khān*'s performance.

The power of sung poetry to evoke the deepest meanings of human existence makes singing and recitation an indispensable component of religious observances for most Iranians, especially during the two months of mourning, Moḥarram and Ṣafar. Two fundamental lyric impulses, praising and lamenting, are activated by devotion to the imāms and their families. Many villagers welcome visits by professional *ta'zīye* troupes; the members of these troupes pause during a performance to collect donations from spectators. Itinerant shaykhs, preachers, and *rowże-khānān* also travel to villages to perform various services, which may include storytelling and sung poetry. The least reputable itinerants are wandering dervishes who belong to brotherhoods that do not prohibit begging, notably the Khāksār order. Despite their low status, mendicant dervishes have long played a major role in the transmission of oral repertoires from one region to another.

Public spaces in cities

Before the Iranian revolution of 1979, many kinds of performance were regularly offered in urban teahouses, parks, and other open spaces where the performers might attract listeners. Villagers could experience these genres during visits to the cities. A genre closely associated with begging was *parde-dārī*, recitation of a story while pointing with a stick to some of its key scenes as depicted in a canvas painting (*parde*). Some of the more respectable genres are now treated as "folklore" or "cultural heritage" (figure 2). Prime examples are the Azerbaijani *dāstān* or *ḥikāye*, performed in teahouses by an *'āsheq* (spelled *aşıq* in Azerbaijani), and the similar narratives in spoken prose and sung verse performed by a *bakhshī* (in Turkmen, *bagşy*) among the Turks of northern Khorasan and the Turkmen of eastern Mazanderan. Another major genre that once attracted listeners to teahouses was recitation of Ferdowsī's *Shāh-nāme* by a *naqqāl* 'carrier', 'narrator', who was often a member of a dervish order. Teahouses were especially popular in periods of high unemployment and underemployment, which were frequent under the regime of the late shāh. Most have since been closed, eliminating the primary venue for *naqqālī*. In parts of Azerbaijan and Khorasan, the Turkic *dāstān* has retained its prominent place in the celebration (*toy*) of a wedding, a circumcision, or some other major event. Among the Turkic-speaking Qashqa'i of Fars Province, however, the vocation of *'āsheq* has largely vanished.

Open spaces near bus stations formerly served as a prime venue for performances by troupes of popular entertainers known as *daste-ye moṭreb*. One such troupe active in Mashhad in the late 1960s included two female dancers, two wrestlers, and players

FIGURE 2 A cameraman for national television films the Kurdish *bakhshī* Ṣohrab Moḥammadī playing the *dūtār* in a tomato field behind his home, in the village of Ashkhāne, west of Bojnūrd. A *bakhshī* does not normally perform in a tomato field, except when prevailed on to do so by photographers with an interest in "cultural heritage." Photo by Amir Ḥosein Pourjavady, 1995.

of the *tār* (a double-chested long-necked lute), violin, *sornā* (a conical oboe), *żarb* (a goblet drum), *dohol* (a double-headed cylindrical drum), *dāire* (a frame drum), and *dāire-zangī* (a frame drum with jingles). In addition to wrestling and dancing accompanied by music (some of it taken from current Iranian and Indian films), the troupe performed comic skits with stock characters, one of them in blackface. Such troupes, like the Turkic storytellers, traveled widely to perform at rural weddings. Since the revolution of 1979, performances of comic skits, dancing, and instrumental music are no longer allowed on the streets of Iranian cities. *Moṭreb-hā* who continue to perform at rural or urban weddings are more likely to work as duos or trios than as members of larger groups. They are accorded none of the esteem that is readily bestowed on a gifted *muṭrib* in the Arab world.

In the 1960s, ensembles of urban musicians (many of them Jewish or Armenian) could be hired at agencies to perform at upper-middle-class weddings. The musical idiom was essentially that of radio ensembles consisting of *tār*, violin, *ney* (a rim-blown flute), *santūr* (a dulcimer), and *żarb*. The agencies also served as gathering spots where musicians might socialize and give lessons. While the Islamic Republic has no need for such agencies or for radio ensembles, musicians still gather in shops where they pursue other occupations, in their own homes, and in cultural institutions of various sorts. In northern Khorasan a number of *bakhshī-hā* work as barbers, and their shops serve as centers for informal sessions.

The dominant voices heard in public spaces of the Islamic Republic are those of men. Women are not permitted to sing solos or dance before audiences that include men, a restriction that applies to films and the broadcasting media as well as to live performances. Even instrumental solos that could remind male listeners of a woman's singing were excluded, for a time, from festivals of regional music. Iranian-born women living outside the Islamic Republic are pursuing roles as performers and artists that may include strong criticism of the silencing of women's voices within Iran. *Turbulent*, a work by the artist Shirin Neshat (b. 1957 in Qazvīn, now living in New York City), juxtaposes a film of a man singing to a packed hall and a second film of the composer Sussan Deyhim performing her music in an empty hall; the work was awarded a Golden Lion at the 1999 Venice Biennale.

ROLES OF PERFORMERS

Restrictions on public performance have been a constant factor in Iranian music history; but before the Islamic Republic, efforts to prevent women from performing in public were commonly made by their families rather than by the state. The sensual pleasure that music so readily affords performers and listeners makes it a sensitive subject from the point of view of religious authorities. Performers have necessarily developed rationales that emphasize ways in which their own modes of behavior are superior, or somehow preferable, to certain others. Singers and reciters may insist that the poetry in their repertoires has didactic value, and they may claim that they do not accept, or at least do not solicit, donations from listeners. Musicians who perform at weddings but do not sing or play dance music enjoy a higher status than those who perform at dances. In Mukri Kurdistan (the area around Māhābād), for instance, the former are paid by the bridegroom's family whereas the latter call out lines in praise of individual male dancers, who are expected to reward them in return.

Amateurs and professionals

Although the desirability of a high level of professional expertise is taken for granted in such arts as architecture and miniature painting, music is valued all the more in some circumstances if the performers do not claim to have acquired exceptional skills. Moreover, professionalism is by no means synonymous with the highest levels of artistry. Musicians who consider themselves amateurs may boast that they are not subject to the same demands as professionals but may freely choose when, where, and what to perform—choices they nonetheless make with respect to the social networks in which they are active. Gatherings of amateurs in private homes are a primary venue for performances of elite music.

Many performance roles presuppose considerable breadth and depth of experience, to which performers must continually apply their gifts of analysis and synthesis. Mastery of a large repertoire allows a performer to choose the items and the manner of presentation that will best meet the needs of a particular occasion, whether the venue is a *khāneqāh*, a teahouse, or a private gathering. An Azerbaijani *aşıq*, or a Turkmen or Khorasani *bakhshī*, is likely to have heard more than one version of certain stories, and listeners may want him to reconcile some of the differences. When asked whether the Azerbaijani hero Koroğlu 'son of a blind man' was the same person as the Turkmen hero Görogly 'son of the grave' (that is, the grave in which his mother had been prematurely buried), one Khorasani *bakhshī* replied that perhaps they were two different men, "or perhaps the stories are two ways of remembering one man." Another *bakhshī* described to Ameneh Youssefzadeh his efforts to collect, in different villages, the numerous sections of the story *Bābā Rowshān*. The musical resources available to performers enable them to discover new combinations of ideas as they remember or collect old ones.

This is true even with respect to the simplest vocal genres, some of which are appropriately sung by individuals working or traveling alone. The names of such genres as *beyābānī* (from *beyābān* 'open, uninhabited space' or 'desert') and *faryādī* (from *faryād* 'cry'), both of which are sung in southern Khorasan, refer to the place in which individuals may feel moved to sing, or to the utterance through which a singer may express strong emotion. Singing that is directed toward listeners may still retain powerful connotations of loneliness and isolation. Amateur singers who like to sing when they are alone are sometimes prevailed on to entertain their family, friends, and neighbors at informal social gatherings and at weddings.

Topics and voices

One particularly important genre, *gharībī*, takes its name from the condition of someone who is *gharīb*—a stranger or outsider—and gives voice to a yearning for a home that has been lost or abandoned. Each text stanza can be described either as a distich (*dobeitī*) or, by counting each half-line separately, as a quatrain (*chārbeitī*). Figure 3 is a transcription of one distich (or quatrain) of *gharībī* as sung by a *moṭreb* who emigrated from Zābol to Mashhad. The melodic range is often limited to a perfect

FIGURE 3 One strophe of the genre *gharībī*, as sung by a *moṭreb* in Mashhad. Translation: "Loneliness keeps me in the grip of melancholy;/fate holds a chain around my neck./Fate! Lift the chain from around my neck,/As I am held fast in a strange land."

fourth, as in this case. Similar verses are sung (also within a narrow melodic range) in Afghanistan and Tajikistan, where they are generally called *felak* 'fate', 'destiny' rather than *gharībī*. In these texts, as well, the singer addresses "Fate," asking to be released from his condition of isolation in a strange land.

TRACK 26

In figure 3, each half-line has 11 syllables in a regular sequence of short (S) and long (L) values, and the durations of the sung syllables conform to the poetic meter S L L L / S L L L / S L L. Singers are free to insert additional syllables at the beginning, in the middle, or at the end of the half-line; these are in brackets in the transcription. The added syllables function as interjections and intensify the expressive effect.

The same text is just as easily sung to melodies with a wider range, extending perhaps to an octave. Many of them, like the melody in figure 3, accommodate half of a quatrain (22 syllables) and are repeated with variation in the second half, in which the text usually takes a new direction (as does the request addressed to "Fate" in figure 3). The melody to which the first 11 syllables are sung always lies in a higher register, or emphasizes higher pitches, than the second segment; both segments invariably end by descending to a cadence.

In most regions of Iran, singers use a small number of melody types to present sequences of distichs (or quatrains) on various topics. In addition to complaints about fate, the topics may include complaints about unrequited love or requests for a lover's favors; praise of family members (especially father, mother, and brother); the beauty and destructiveness of nature; complaints of hunger, illness, or lack of work; transgressions of the rules of hospitality; and many others. Verses on religious topics are also common, not least because they are often sung and spread by wandering dervishes. The following quatrain, sung by a worker who repaired the underground canals that bring water to villages around Mashhad, is representative of the texts that singers may learn from dervishes:

Avval nām-e Khodā rā yādu kerdom	First I remembered the name of God.
Dovvom beit o ghazal bonyādu kerdom	Second I made verses and ghazals.
Ey, sar-e man dar fedāyet, yā Moḥammad!	I place myself wholly at your disposal, O Mohammad!
Be chārom khedmat-e ostādu kerdom.	Fourth I served a master [as his apprentice].

Here, as in figure 3, the third line shifts from description to direct address. The various types of semantic change that may occur at this point are options offered by the musical-poetic structure, which singers exploit as they group familiar lines and quatrains to form new sequences. The structure is at once economical and powerful. As they select the verses they will sing on a given occasion, singers also decide on a sequence of voices and attitudes.

The melody types, which can also be played on instruments, offer singers a number of possibilities for coordinating verses (which do not invariably use quantitative meters) with gradually descending melodic contours. Singers may add a refrain after every quatrain or at irregular intervals. The melody types to which quatrains are sung vary from one region to another, as do the names of the pertinent vocal genres (for example, *dastūn* in Gilan, *katūlī* and *kele-ḥāl* in Mazanderan, *chārbeitī* in Khorasan, and *sharve* in Fars and the Gulf region). Names of some genres refer to ethnic groups and localities as well as to topics (such as *gharībī*) and situations (such as *kuche-bāghī*, from *kuche-bāgh*, a lane between two gardens). In addition to its importance for amateur singers, the singing of quatrains (*qoşmələr*) in Azerbaijani forms the basis of the professional *aşıq*'s repertoire. [See THE AŞIQ AND HIS MUSIC IN NORTHWEST IRAN (AZERBAIJAN), text of figure 1.]

It was once common for Iranian singers to assemble new songs from familiar materials and perform them in the presence of those whose actions they praised, or in the presence of their surviving relatives. Songs that recount the exploits of outlaws or rebels generally end with the protagonist's execution or death in battle, followed by the singer's expression of grief and admiration. Few such songs have found a place in the folkloric repertoires presented at festivals and distributed in printed and recorded form.

Socially marginal groups are widely considered to be especially inclined toward music making, practiced alongside such other occupations as ironworking, tooth extraction, and barbering. Itinerants called *qereshmol*, *ghorbatī*, *kūlī*, and so on are a good source of songs for those who wish to expand their repertoires. Figure 4*a* is an excerpt from a narrative song in Persian, sung by an itinerant ironsmith living in a tent outside Mashhad. According to a friend of the singer, "the birds of the desert fell in love with
TRACK 27 his voice." The melody type he chose for the story joins three contrasting registers: after one half-line in the upper register, two more are sung in the middle register, followed by three half-lines set within the lower tetrachord. The poetic meter is the same as in figure 3 but is treated flexibly. Figure 4*b* is another version of these lines, sung by a villager to a much simpler melody type which lies entirely within one tetrachord (like figure 3) and is repeated with little variation for each half-line. In both versions, Golzār Khān tells a messenger about a dream in which he saw his brother fall into a fire, and the messenger confirms that his brother, Seyd Moḥammad Khān, has indeed been killed by their enemy, Mokhtār. Both singers introduce this brief dialogue with one or two lines (omitted from figure 4) describing the messenger's ride from the site of the shooting to Golzār's home, and both conclude with the moral that one who has lost his brother is better off dead than alive. The more elaborate melody type of figure 4*a* allows the singer to dramatize his own presence as he varies the durations and intensities of the sung syllables.

If anguish over the loss of loved ones and other feelings of deprivation have long been central topics of sung poetry in Iran, the expression of desire for union with a human or divine beloved may be considered a further manifestation of the same fundamental motivation for producing music. The romantic narratives that are sung in Persian, Kurdish, Azerbaijani, Turkmen, and the Turkic language of Khorasan portray lovers as impelled to sing, not only when they are kept apart for some reason but also when they are reunited. Instrumental solos may likewise be perceived as generated by an awareness of separation, as in the famous opening line of the *Masnavī* of Mowlānā Jalāl al-dīn Rūmī:

Beshno az ney chū ḥekāyat mīkonad / az jedā'ī-hā shekāyat mīkonad.

Listen to the *ney* as it narrates its tale and complains of separations.

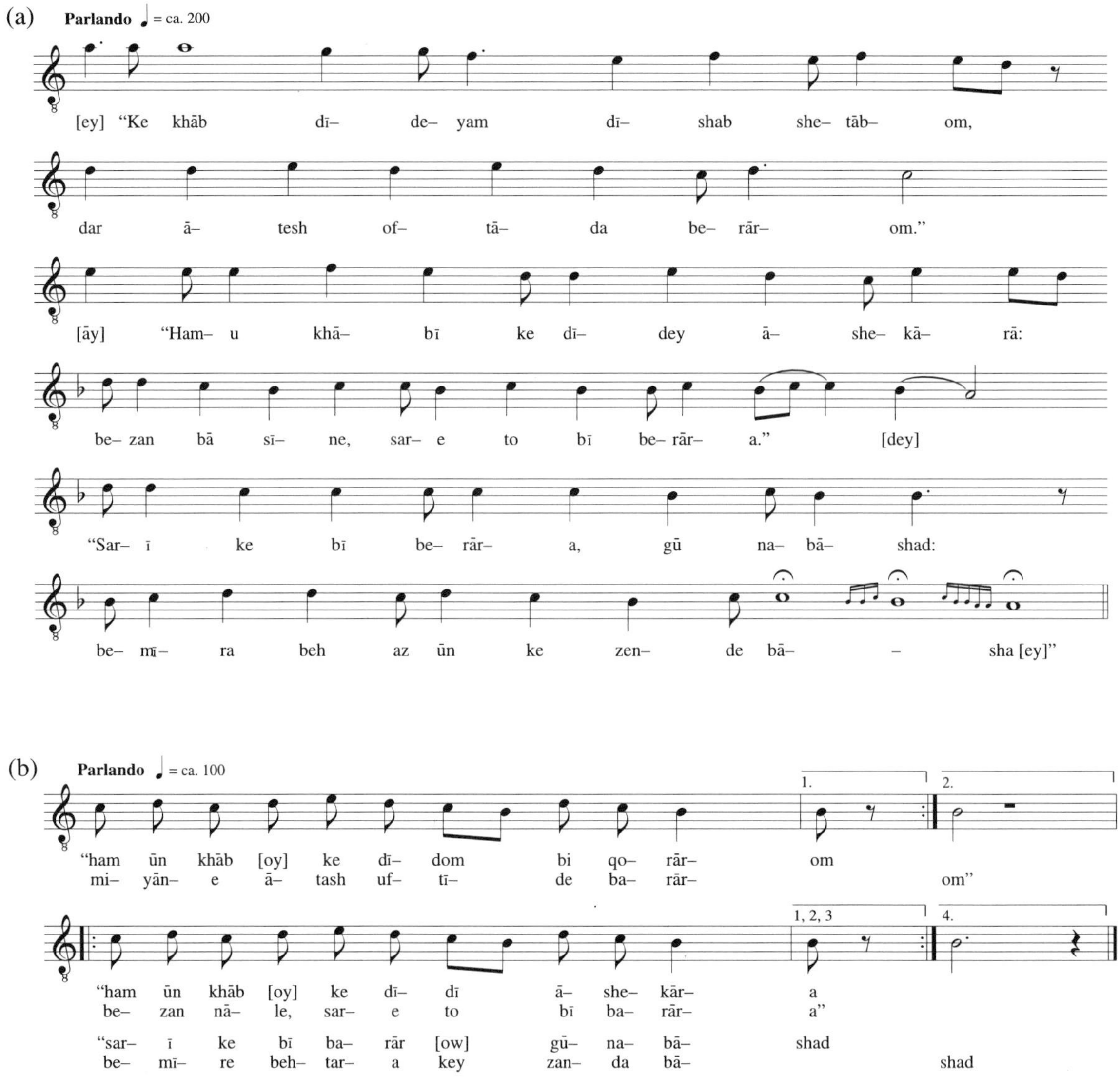

FIGURE 4 Excerpts from two performances of a narrative from southern Khorasan, sung by (a) an itinerant ironworker and (b) a villager. Translation: "Last night, restless, I saw, in a dream,/my brother fallen into a fire./Your dream has come true:/strike your breast; you've become a brotherless man./'A brotherless man'—let that not be said:/better to die than to remain alive."

Rhythms of interaction

Classification of musical genres and idioms by social stratum and relative prestige has sometimes obscured significant continuities in underlying values, techniques, and habits. Performances in most idioms normally juxtapose sequences of equal pulses against other sequences in which sounds are separated by unequal (and relatively unpredictable) intervals of time. By manipulating the transitions between less predictable and more predictable rhythms, performers can control the ways in which their music approaches, or keeps its distance from, listeners. A series of sharp attacks on a string instrument or a drum, whether equally or unequally spaced, may easily surpass the articulatory possibilities of the human voice (though it may just as easily imitate them); hence instrumentalists may choose either to play variations on the meters of sung poetry or to replace them with rhythms of greater density. Iranian musical idioms offer many options for creating dialogue and other types of complementarity among voices and instruments.

Melodies performed by a solo vocalist or instrumentalist may call to mind several kinds of behavior, perhaps including predictably timed motions that others can perceive as invitations or even a command to participate in the performance—for example, by moving in rhythm or singing a refrain line. Such invitations or commands may or may not come at predictable intervals of time. Soloists fulfill roles that individuals commonly enact as members of groups, in nonmusical as well as musical activities. They attract and hold the attention of the group by stimulating, encouraging, and challenging its members, and by repeating rhythmic patterns and melodic progressions while at the same time demonstrating flexibility and sensitivity. Soloists need the reassurance and support that the group is able to provide in various ways; audible and visible signs of acceptance cannot be deferred too long. Depending on the genre and the venue, an appropriate response may involve singing, weeping, shouting, or nodding encouragement to the performer or performers, hand clapping, dancing, and other rhythmic motions (as in the *zūr-khāne* exercises and in *nowḥe sīne-zanī* or *zanjīr-zanī*).

A leader may initiate a responsorial performance of *zekr* or *nowḥe* by singing the refrain line that the group must repeat at regular intervals (figure 5). Sometimes none of the leader's lines exceeds the length of the response, whereas in other cases the solos become progressively longer and more elaborate until a descent to the lower register cues the group to enter with the refrain. The usual practice among groups that meet to perform *nowḥe* is for several men to take turns acting as leader (*rāhber*).

Though it is entirely possible to sing or recite poetry without any instrumental accompaniment, the addition of instrumental sounds creates a richer ambience and enhances the effect of each sung syllable. A single frame drum (*dāire*) is enough to accompany singing or dancing and to hold a listener's attention with contrasting sounds—sharp and dry when the instrument is struck near the rim, more resonant when several fingers strike the center of the skin. When voice and drum are joined by one or more melodic instruments, the performance may evoke human interactions of many kinds.

The most prestigious manner of performing classical poetry is the *āvāz* of a solo vocalist, accompanied by a small instrumental ensemble, which usually includes *tār*, *ney*, *kamānche*, and *żarb*, perhaps with the addition of *santūr* or *'ūd*. The singer may choose a different melodic model (*gūshe*) for each line of the poem (normally a *ghazal*), and one instrumentalist provides a response (*javāb-e āvāz*) to each of the singer's phrases in that *gūshe* (or group of related *gūshe-hā*). A change in the instrument offering responses dramatizes the subsequent modulation to a new *gūshe*.

Group (refrain, as before), etc.

FIGURE 5 Kurdish verses sung in preparation of the "seated" phase of a Qāderī *zekr* ceremony, Sanandaj, 1993. Translation: "'Ali is the friend, 'Ali is my master, 'Ali is the lord of dervishes./One who loves is one who suffers: the zeal of Ghows-e Gīlānī!

Performances of vocal *āvāz* are almost always followed by the singing of one or more *taṣnīf-hā*—composed settings of classical, popular, or contemporary poems. The lyrics of many *taṣnīf-hā* use the quantitative meters of classical versification; the most common musical meters are 2/4, 3/4, 6/8, and 4/4. The sequence *āvāz-taṣnīf* moves from unpredictable to relatively predictable timing of the vocal and instrumental attacks, enacting a shift from introspection to renewed sociability. The relationship is potentially effective on more than one level. Singers may interrupt their *āvāz* to perform a *taṣnīf*, momentarily replacing the rhythmic intricacy of *āvāz* with the more straightforward rhythms of a short *taṣnīf*. Such interruptions are obligatory in a performance of an Azerbaijani *muğam*. Azerbaijani musicians invariably interpolate a short instrumental dance piece (*reng*) after each *ghazal* in a sequence that is otherwise analogous to Persian *āvāz*; Azerbaijani singers are expected to play the frame drum (*def*) during each *reng* and during the *taṣnīf* that concludes their performance. In Persian classical music, the playing of a *reng*—often an extended, multisectional piece in a rapid 6/8—marks the end of a performance.

MUSICAL KNOWLEDGE

Attitudes toward history

The antiquity of their civilization is a topic that Iranians approach in a number of ways. The most important, with respect to musical practice, are an emphasis on singing verses that have withstood the test of time and an interest in identifying legitimate chains of transmission from master to pupil. Iranian art forms are dependent on face-to-face communication, in which stories about the past and its meanings can be transmitted in ways that inhibit listeners from aggressively questioning them on the spot. Questions arise later, as the pupil comes into contact with multiple sources of authority and begins to compare their prescriptions and stories.

Unlike that of China, the music history of Iran has not been marked by periodic efforts to restore ancient standards of tuning and rectify the performance of ceremonies, although a few contemporary musicians believe that, at some unknown time, Arab intervals were rejected in favor of a return to "purely Iranian" intervals [see TRADITION AND HISTORY: THE CASE OF IRAN]. Compared with their counterparts in South Asia, Iranian musicians are far less likely to appeal to the doctrinal authority of treatises.

The need to place a high value on artistic resources inherited from the past is responsible for a remarkable continuity in musical terminology and in the structure of theoretical and pedagogical systems (for example, in the number of modal entities and in the relationships among them). Any musician must ultimately satisfy the desires and demands of patrons with differing tastes, and pedagogical systems have been organized with this need firmly in mind. The archetypal story is that of Bārbad (figure 6), chief minstrel of the Sasanian ruler Khosrow Parvīz (r. 590–628 C.E.), who is said to have organized a collection of seven royal modes (*al-ṭurūq al-mulūkīya*), thirty melody-types (*alḥān*), and 360 melodies (*dastān*). Similar hierarchical arrangements of entities in three orders of magnitude—between roughly 4 to 8, 12 to 30, and 200 to 400—are evident in many subsequent pedagogical systems. Seven has remained the preferred number at the highest level of classification. In identifying the modal entities deemed appropriate to one or another type of patron, Iranian writers on music have emphasized differences in age, occupation, temperament, and ethnicity.

FIGURE 6 The Sasanian court musician Bārbad playing the lute (*barbat*) for Khosrow. Painting attributed to Mīrzā ʿAli. From a *Khamsa* of Neẓāmī, 1539–1543. British Museum Oriental 2265, folio 77v.

Instruments

Like their counterparts in other parts of the Middle East and Central Asia, Iranian musicians have much to say about musical knowledge or musical "science" (Arabic *ʿilm*, also used in Iranian and Turkic languages). It is usually linked to the instrument or instruments a musician has mastered. In describing his *dūtār* (a long-necked lute with two strings) as "an instrument of knowledge," the *bakhshī* ʿAlī Āqā Almājoqi added that "no one will reach the outermost limits of this knowledge." He did not hesitate to evaluate one competitor's competence as "zero." The full extent of a master performer's knowledge can only be hinted at in actual performances. Musicians are evaluated on the basis of their performances and on the basis of what one has heard or been told about them. It is essential to praise one's master, difficult to praise one's rivals.

Knowledge that is articulated with reference to an instrument's construction may include stories about its creation. One Khorasani *bakhshī* described three stages in the invention of the *dūtār*. The inventor (who, in this account, might have been Solomon, Galen, or a minister of the Sasanian ruler Kei Qobād) began with the idea that the *dūtār* needed seven frets (*haft parde*) to match the seven heavenly bodies, *haft kavākeb* (Saturn, the sun, the moon, Mars, Mercury, Jupiter, and Venus, corresponding to the days of our week). When seven frets had been attached to its neck, the *dūtār* still lacked a voice (*sedā*). The inventor noticed the sound produced by the wind blowing against a hollow mulberry tree and realized that, since silkworms eat mulberry leaves, strings of silk and a body of hollow mulberry would have a substance in common, thus "adorning one another" harmoniously. The final step was to use two strands of silk for a looser string named *bam* 'above', 'upper' and one strand of silk for a tighter string named *zīr* 'below', 'lower'. On the *dūtār*, the "lower" string (closest to the ground) is usually tuned a fourth or fifth above the string with a "higher" location (and the contemporary *dūtār* of northern Khorasan has eleven or twelve frets rather than seven, although most melody types have seven pitch-classes).

All three steps point to relationships that turn up in many other stories and theories: correspondences between a given number of entities belonging to different categories, harmonies produced through appropriate junctures, and relationships between upper and lower locations or sources of sound. The two skins of a pair of kettledrums (*naqqāre*) or of a double-headed cylindrical drum (*dohol*), no less than the upper and lower strings or upper and lower courses of a long-necked lute, can be distinguished as *bam* and *zīr*. According to one Turkmen story, the sounds produced as the phoenix (*qoqnos*, perhaps from Greek *kyknos*) flapped its wings inspired Plato to create the *dūtār*; here the image of flapping wings is perhaps a metaphor for the up-and-down movement of the player's right hand as several fingers strike both strings simultaneously. According to another Turkmen story, the instrument lacked a voice until Satan assisted its inventor, in this case the groom of Imām ʿAlī, Qambar, who remains the patron saint of the Turkmen *bagşi*.

Some of the most important Persian writings on music devote considerable space to comparative descriptions of instruments. Among these are the treatises of ʿAbdolqāder Ibn Gheibī Marāghī (d. 1435), which offer information on forty-three instruments; and the anonymous *Kanz al-tuhaf* 'Treasure of Rarities' of the mid-fourteenth century, which has fuller accounts of eight instruments. The first attempt at a comprehensive inventory of Iranian instruments, made in the final decades of the twentieth century by Moḥammad Reżā Darvīshī, awaits publication.

Names

The extent to which names are assigned to positions on instruments and to musical resources associated with these positions varies considerably. In the elite music derived from nineteenth-century court practices, three of the canonical *haft dastgāh* 'seven systems' [see A NEW APPROACH TO THE THEORY OF PERSIAN ART MUSIC: THE *RADIF* AND THE MODAL SYSTEM] bear names that were once assigned to frets, then incorporated within a general scale: *segāh* 'position three', *chahārgāh* 'position four', and *rāst panjgāh* 'the mode *rāst* at position five'. For the various types of *dūtār*, names are given either to specific frets (as on the large *dūtār* of the Torbat-e Jām region in southern Khorasan) or to groups of frets (as on the *dūtār* of northern Khorasan and, most often, the Turkmen *dūtār*). *Dūtār* players in Torbat-e Jām also have names for six different tunings. Turkmen musical terminology classifies tunings and registers alike as low, middle, and high. In northern Khorasan, the name *navā'ī* designates the highest fret and the only modal entity in which that fret is used. *Navā'ī* is also the name of the celebrated fifteenth-century poet-musician with whom the modal entity is associated, and of a modern song derived from that modal entity and composed by a musician of southern Khorasan, O̱sman Moḥammad Parast.

While the provision of names for frets and groups of frets makes the *dūtār* something of an exception among Iranian instruments, it is extremely common for melody types and modal entities to carry their own proper names, so that musicians may treat them as "personalities" with multiple attributes (Caron and Safvate 1966:115), such as greater or lesser importance and varying degrees of flexibility in performance. Many names are those of regions (such as Karabākh, in Azerbaijan), ethnic groups (Jamshīdī), protagonists of stories (Kòroğlu), or poets who intended their verses to be sung (Shāh Khatā'ī, Ja'far Qolī). The latter two categories overlap, since the protagonists of many stories are poet-musicians. Names of birds make effective titles of pieces: *Chakāvak* 'Lark' is a *gūshe* in the *dastgāh* of *homāyūn*, and *Ṭorqe* 'Thrush' is a Khorasani piece for *dūtār* or *qushme* (a double clarinet) which depicts a bird soaring beyond the limits of our vision, then slowly reappearing.

Proper names help performers to learn and remember the available options, the appropriate sequences of units, and the lore associated with each named entity. In other words, a set of names serves as an apparatus (*dastgāh* in its general sense) with which to organize an ever-expanding fund of information and experience pertaining to the selection, combination, and reference of melodic and rhythmic units. This principle is most fully developed in the multiple versions of the Persian *radīf* compiled for singers and instrumentaliṣts. [See PERFORMANCE PRACTICE IN IRAN: *RĀDIF* AND IMPROVISATION.] The availability of names makes it possible to specify combinations that are best avoided as well as those that are prescribed or favored. Most names of *gūshe-hā* in the canonical *radīf* denote places, situations, emotional states, or actions such as *rūh-afzā* 'refreshing the soul' and *majles-afrūz* 'animating the gathering'. The names of the *gūshe-hā* in a short sequence may suggest a miniature drama—for example the sequence *'oshshāq* 'lovers', *nahoft* 'concealed', and *khojaste* 'auspicious' in the *dastgāh* of *navā* as taught by the great singer Maḥmūd Karīmī (see Massoudieh 1978:169–171; 2nd ed., 1997:135–137).

A sequence of names commonly identifies a succession of contrasts in register and rhythmic character. Generic names, such as the Kurdish *paşbend* 'after the verse' and the Persian *darāmad* 'coming out', often refer to the genre's function or position in a temporal sequence. The sequence of *gūshe-hā* that constitutes one *dastgāh* normally begins with one or more *darāmad-hā* and often includes at least one *gūshe* whose name designates a rhythmic pattern. One such pattern, *kereshme* 'wink', 'amorous gesture' (figure 7), may be played in any *dastgāh* and corresponds to one of the primary quantitative meters of classical Persian poetry: S L S L S S L L / S L S L S S L (L). When students of an instrument are taught to play *kereshme* in one or another *dastgāh*, they may also learn a verse or two in this meter.

Na- dā- na- mat be ḥa- qī- qat ke dar ja- hān be che mā- nī

FIGURE 7 Beginning of the *gūshe kereshme* in the *dastgāh* of *shūr*, with a verse in the corresponding poetic meter. Translation: "I don't know, in truth, what in the world you resemble."

Generic names are used for many of the same purposes as proper names. Regional norms may prescribe a relatively fixed sequence of dance types, as in Lorestan, where the sequence usually begins with *sangīn se-pā* 'heavy, three steps' and concludes with *shāne-shakī* 'shaking shoulders'. Musicians in northern Khorasan are less likely to group dance pieces in a predictable sequence; before the Iranian revolution, tunes learned from radio and recordings were often inserted alongside older pieces. How Iranian instrumentalists follow prescribed sequences and create new ones is a topic that merits further study.

Considerations that have governed the use of names in Iranian musical practices become evident as performers discuss their readiness to meet the requests of friends and patrons. The *bakhshī* 'Alī Aqā Almājoqī told Ameneh Youssefzadeh that he chooses tunes which are happy (*shād*), moving (*sūznāk*), martial (*razmī*), or melancholy (*ḥoznāvar*) according to the mood of each audience and the character of each poem. The tune he described as *sūznāk* has the same tonal structure as the lower tetrachord of the Turkish *makam suznak*, and the common Arabic root *ḥzn* shared by the adjective *ḥoznāvar* and the name of the Persian *gūshe ḥazīn* is easily recognizable. Matching a sequence of modal entities to the changing moods of listeners as well as to a sequence of verses has been a major concern of Persian-language writers on music from the eleventh century onward.

Today, as in the past, Iranian discourse on music is informed by an awareness of spiritual and emotional energies brought into play by sung poetry and by sequences of instrumental sounds that support, imitate, or transcend voices. Repeated efforts to control and limit the memories and experiences that music may evoke among Iranians furnish compelling evidence of its range and power. By continually drawing distinctions among performance genres—some more elevated, others more down-to-earth—individuals and groups can, as they wish, confirm past allegiances or create new relationships.

REFERENCES

Bina, Sima. 1997. *Āvā-ye sahrā / Sounds from the Plain*. Canoga Park, Calif.: Caltex. Compact disk.

Blum, Stephen. 1978. "Changing Roles of Performers in Meshhed and Bojnurd, Iran." In *Eight Urban Musical Cultures*, ed. Bruno Nettl, 19–95. Urbana: University of Illinois Press.

———. 1996. "Musical Questions and Answers in Iranian Xorāsān." *EM: Annuario degli Archivi di Etnomusicologia, Accademia Nazionale di Santa Cecilia* 4:145–63.

Caron, Nelly, and Dariouche Safvate. 1966. *Iran. Les traditions musicales*. Paris: Buchet/Chastel.

Chelkowski, Peter J., ed. 1979. *Ta'ziye: Ritual and Drama in Iran*. New York: New York University Press.

———. 1991. "Popular Entertainment, Media, and Social Change in Twentieth-Century Iran." In *The Cambridge History of Iran*, Vol. 7, *From Nadir Shah to the Islamic Republic*, ed. Peter Avery, Gavin Hambly, and Charles Melville, 765–814. Cambridge: Cambridge University Press.

Darvīshī, Moḥammad Rezā. 1994. *Moqademe-ye bar shenākht-e mūsīqī-ye navāḥī-ye Irān, 1: Manāṭeq-e janūb (Hormozgān, Būshehr, Khūzestān)*. Tehran: Sāzmān-e Tablīghāt-e Eslāmī.

Deyhim, Sussan, and Shirin Neshat. 2000. *Turbulent*. New York: Isle X Records. Compact disk.

Digard, Jean-Pierre, comp. 1974. *Iran: Baxtyâri, nomades de la montagne*. SELAF-OROSTOM CETO 747. LP record.

During, Jean. 1989. *Musique et mystique dans les traditions de l'Iran*. Bibliothèque iranienne, Vol. 36. Paris and Tehran: Institut Français de Recherche en Iran.

———. 1992. "L'oreille islamique: Dix années capitales de la vie musicale en Iran: 1980–1990." *Asian Music* 23(2):135–164.

———, comp. 1993. *Asie centrale: Les maîtres du dotâr*. Geneva: Archives Internationales de Musique Populaire, AIMP 26. Compact disk.

———. 1996. "La voix des esprits et la face cachée de la musique: Le parcours du maître Hâtam 'Asgari." In *Le voyage initiatique en terre d'Islam: Ascensions célestes et itinéraires spirituels*, ed. Mohammad Ali Amir-Moezzi, 335–373. Louvain and Paris: Peeters.

Farhat, Hormoz. 1990. *The Dastgāh Concept in Persian Music*. Cambridge Studies in Ethnomusicology. Cambridge: Cambridge University Press.

Fatemi, Sasan. 1997. "La musique et la vie musicale du Mazanderan: Le problème du changement." Thesis, Université de Paris-X.

The Kamkars. 1997. *Nightingale with a Broken Wing*. London: Womad WSCD 009. Compact disk.

Kuckertz, Josef, and Mohammad Taghi Massoudieh. 1976. *Musik in Bušehr (Süd-Iran)*. 2 vols. Ngoma: Studien zur Volksmusik und aussereuropäischen Kunstmusik, 2. Munich and Salzburg: Katzbichler. (Persian version, *Mūsīqī-ye Būshehr*. 1978. Tehran: Rādyū-Televīzyūn-e Mellī-ye Īrān.)

Massoudieh, Mohammad Teqi. 1978. *Radif vocal de la musique traditionelle de l'Iran*. Tehran. (2nd ed., Tehran: Sorūsh, 1997.)

———. 1980. *Mūsīqī-ye Torbat-e Jām*. Tehran: Sorūsh.

———. 1985. *Mūsīqī-ye Balūchestān*. Tehran: Sorūsh. (German version: *Musik in Balūčestān*. 1988. Hamburg: Karl Dieter Wagner.)

———. 1988. *Mūsīqī-ye mazhabī-ye Irān, 1: mūsīqī-ye ta'ziye*. Tehran: Sorūsh.

———. 1992a. "Der Begriff des Maqām in der persischen Volksmusik." In *Von der Vielfalt musikalischer Kultur: Festschrift Josef Kuckertz zum 60. Geburtstag*, ed. Rüdiger Schumacher, 311–334. Anif/Salzburg: U. Müller-Speiser.

———. 1992b. "Die Begriffe Maqām und Dastgāh in der turkmenischen Musik des Iran." In

Regionale maqām-Traditionen in Geschichte und Gegenwart, ed. Jürgen Elsner and Gisa Jähnichen, 377–397. Berlin: Study Group "Maqām" of the International Council for Traditional Music.

Moradi, Shahmirza. 1994. *The Music of Lorestan, Iran: Shahmirza Morādi, Sornā*. Wyastone Leys, Monmouth, England: Nimbus NI 5397. Compact disk.

Mūsīqī-ye navāḥī-ye Irān (Regional Music of Iran). 1998. Tehran: Anjoman-e Mūsīqī-ye Irān. 16 albums, each with 6 cassettes and a booklet.

Nettl, Bruno. 1972. "Persian Popular Music in 1969." *Ethnomusicology* 16:218–239.

———. 1974. "Aspects of Form in the Instrumental Performance of the Persian *Āvāz*." *Ethnomusicology* 18:405–414.

———. 1978. "Persian Classical Music in Tehran: The Processes of Change." In *Eight Urban Musical Cultures*, ed. Bruno Nettl, 146–185. Urbana: University of Illinois Press.

———. 1992 [1987]. *The Radif of Persian Music: Studies in Structure and Cultural Context*, 2nd ed. Champaign, Ill.: Elephant and Cat.

Nooshin, Laudan. 1996. "The Processes of Creation and Re-Creation in Persian Classical Music." Ph.D. dissertation, University of London.

———. 1998. "The Song of the Nightingale: Processes of Improvisation in *Dastgāh Segāh* (Iranian Classical Music)." *British Journal of Ethnomusicology* 7:69–116.

Tsuge, Gen'ichi. 1974. "*Āvāz*: A Study of the Rhythmic Aspects in Classical Iranian Music." Ph.D. dissertation, Wesleyan University.

Yarshater, Ehsan. 1974. "Affinities between Persian Poetry and Music." In *Studies in the Art and Literature of the Near East*, ed. Peter Chelkowski, 59–78. Salt Lake City and New York: University of Utah and New York University.

Youssefzadeh, Ameneh. 1997. "Les bardes bakhshi du Khorassan iranien." Thesis, Université de Paris-X.

———. 2000. "The Situation of Music in Iran since the Revolution: The Role of Official Organizations." *British Journal of Ethnomusicology* 9(2):35–61.

———, comp. 1998. *Iran: Bardes du Khorassan*. OCORA C 560136. Compact disk.

Snapshot: ʿAlī Āqā Almājoqī: The Life of a Khorasani *Bakhshi*

Ameneh Youssefzadeh

ʿAlī ʿAlīreżāʾī, known as ʿAlī Āqā Almājoqī, was born in Almājoq, a small village southeast of Qūchān in northern Khorasan. This province in northeastern Iran is inhabited by a variety of ethnic groups, especially in its northern, most populated part. After the Persians, the Turks are the oldest inhabitants (speaking a distinctive Turkic language), and there are also Turkmens as well as a substantial Kurdish community (which dates from the sixteenth century). This variety makes for a rich musical tradition, and one of the foremost representatives of that tradition is the bard, or *bakhshi*, a term that has also denoted, at different periods, shamans and Buddhist priests. Among the Kazakh, Kyrghyz, and Uighur peoples, it still refers to a shaman; among the Turkmens, Khorasani Turks, and Uzbeks, the *bakhshi* survives mainly as a singer and reciter of epics. Accompanying himself on the *dūtār*, a long-necked lute with two strings, he is the carrier of a centuries-old oral art—a trilingual repertoire that has Turkic, Kurdish, and Persian elements. ʿAlī Āqā Almājoqī (figure 1) perfectly exemplifies the *bakhshi*'s art and repertoire.

FIGURE 1 ʿAlī Āqā playing the *dūtār* at home. At his feet are *ketābche* containing poems and texts. Photo by Ameneh Youssefzadeh, 1996.

ʿAlī Āqā was born around 1932, the son of a Kurdish father and a Turkish mother. He studied for nine years at a Qurʾānic school (*maktab*), learning to read and write Persian and Kurdish and recite the Qurʾān. His was a family of farmers, and he says of his milieu: "There was no *sāz-zan* 'instrumentalist' (that is, no *dūtār* player) in our family. However, my father was *ahl-e ẕowq* 'a man of taste' and *ahl-e ʿeshq* 'a man of love'. He said his prayers regularly, yet there was no lack of singing and dancing at home."

From his earliest childhood ʿAlī Āqā was in close touch with local musical traditions. He sang with the *ʿāsheq-hā*—groups of musicians who provide entertainment at village festivities and dances; they play *sornā* and *dohol*, *qūshme* (double clarinet) and *dohol*, or *kamānche* and *dohol*. The bards, who are also present on these occasions, usually perform in the evening; a bard plays solo or is accompanied by a disciple or son, and the recital is aimed at the more attentive listeners.

When ʿAlī Āqā was fourteen, his expressive, powerful voice was noticed by the bard Avāz Bakhshī, who later introduced him to Moḥammad Ḥosein Yegāne (1918–1992). Yegāne, a famous *bakhshi* (and barber), became his *ostād* 'master', taught him to play the *dūtār*, and passed on to him a vast repertoire. "He treated me like his son, and I owe him everything. All the melodies (*āhang*) that were in his *sīne* 'chest', 'memory' he passed on to me, without ever wanting anything in return. He would take me to a *majles* (a gathering at a wedding, a circumcision, or the like) when he performed. He taught me how these gatherings were arranged, where I should sit, what kind of poems I should sing. From the day he saw that I could hold my own, he let me perform alone."

In the old days, *bakhshis* were attached to the court or to a potentate or prince; today, however, they cannot live by their art alone and must find other employment. Quite a few are barbers (*ārāyeshgar*); the connection between these two professions is ancient. They also often function as local doctors—a reminder of the bard's shamanic past. ʿAlī Almājoqī was a shepherd and afterward worked as a builder's laborer; he is now unemployed.

At one time in his life, ʿAlī Āqā (and his is not an isolated case) stopped practicing his art for fifteen years. Perhaps he stopped because his uncle, a preacher at a mosque, saw him at a wedding and told him: "You shouldn't play the *tār* (that is, the *dūtār*); with your voice, you had better turn your eyes toward the *manbar* 'pulpit'." ʿAlī Almājoqī himself explains his long silence by his interest in religious writings.

His prodigious memory and sonorous voice prompted him to participate, like other *bakhshis*, in religious ceremonies during Ramadan and the months of Moḥarram and Ṣafar (when the Shīʿa commemorate the martyrdom of Imām Ḥosein and his family). He performs as a *nowḥe-khān* 'singer of lamentations' or tells the tragic tale of Ḥosein. ʿAlī Āqā has often functioned as *shabih-khān* 'impersonator' at representations of the *taʿziye*, a Shīʿa religious drama. At mourning ceremonies (*majles-e ʿazā*), he recites verses of the Qur'ān.

Like that of most *bakhshis*, ʿAlī Āqā's repertoire consists essentially of two genres. The first genre includes poems by such authors as Jaʿfar Qolī (a nineteenth-century Kurdish poet of Khorasan who led an almost legendary life), and Makhtum Qolī (an eighteenth-century Turkmen poet); there are also popular Persian quatrains (*chārbeitī*), as well as Turkic and Kurdish poems describing the exploits of regional rebels in the early twentieth century. The second genre, which is specific to the *bakhshi* and has analogues in other Turkic traditions, is the narrative called *dāstān* 'story'. Each narrative uses a mixture of sung verse and spoken prose and may last for several hours. The prose, related in the third person, expounds the framework of the story. The verse passages convey the characters' direct speech, especially that of an emotional nature. The poems have a regular strophic structure with instrumental refrains and interludes. The versified passages are always accompanied by the *dūtār* and may be sung on their own, without a prose narration of the story.

Some of these narratives are common to other traditions of the Turkic-speaking world. They are based on three major themes: love (the thwarted adventures of the hero and his beloved, as, for example, in *Ṭāher and Zohre* or *Maʿṣūm and Afrūzparī*); mystical (*ʿerfānī*) and religious experience (*Ibrāhīm Adham*, *Bābā Rowshān*); and heroism (*Koroğlu*).

ʿAlī Āqā knows a large number of melody types and may use the same tune for poems of varied content. He explains that "the interpreter has hundreds of melodies (*āhang*) at his disposal. According to his audience's mood and the poems selected, he can choose happy (*shād*), moving (*sūznāk*), martial (*razmī*), or melancholy (*ḥoznāvar*) airs." The *bakhshi* can also adapt different Turkish, Kurdish, or Persian poems to the same melody types used for the *dāstān*.

Although a considerable part of the bards' repertoire is drawn from oral tradition, some of the stories and poems have been committed to writing in manuscripts or popular publications like chapbooks. Some of these come from Azerbaijan, Bukhara, or Khiva; others are of unknown origin. The bards exchange them and copy the contents into a personal *ketābche* 'copybook'. Most have one or more of these books, in which they jot down the texts of stories as well as certain poems. ʿAlī Āqā claims to have twenty *ketāb-e 'āsheqī* 'books with love stories', though they serve merely as reminders. A bard rarely uses such a book during a recital.

'Alī Almājoqī has himself written verses in both Persian and Kurdish, for example about the *Jebhe* (the front in the war with Iraq), the *22nd Bahman* (the day of the Islamic Revolution), *Ḥażrat-e Fāṭeme* (the Prophet's daughter), and *Ḥekāyat-e Ḥaẓrat-e Moḥammad* (the story of the Prophet Muhammad), inspired by a verse of the Qur'ān. He sings them to the same tunes that he uses for the versified parts of the *dāstān* or poems of other authors.

Although 'Alī Āqā married twice and has children—four sons and two daughters—none of them has followed his career. Nor has he any disciples as such, though young students sometimes stay with him to learn tunes and stories.

The *bakhshi* has always commanded respect in northern Khorasan. After a difficult period during the Islamic Revolution (when music was banned and instruments were destroyed), he is now considered the custodian of a cultural heritage (*mirāṣ-e farhangī*). 'Alī Almājoqī has performed, alone or accompanied by his master, Yegāne, at festivals organized by the Ministry of Culture and Islamic Guidance and by the Organization for Islamic Propaganda, which has issued two sets of cassettes on which his performances are represented. This official recognition has allowed music to recover the legitimacy it was long denied in Iran.

The *Aşıq* and His Music in Northwest Iran (Azerbaijan)

Charlotte F. Albright

The *Aşıq*
Performance Venues
The *Saz* and Other Instruments
The Music of the *Aşıq*
The Poetry of the *Aşıq*

Azerbaijan lies between modern-day Turkey and the southwest coast of the Caspian Sea. The northern portion belonged to the Soviet Union from 1920 to 1991 and is now an independent republic. The southern portion lies to the south of the Araxes River, in Iran. For most of the last five hundred years, all or part of Azerbaijan has been a part of Iran, intially under the Safavids, whose first shāh, Ismāʿīl, declared that Iran would henceforth be a Shīʿa Muslim (rather than Sunni Muslim) state; then under the Zands, the Qajars, and, in the twentieth century, the Pahlavis and the Islamic Republic. Although the Safavids controlled all of Azerbaijan and parts of Armenia and Georgia, subsequent dynasties lost much of this territory to the Russians.

In pre-Islamic times the inhabitants of Azerbaijan were first Zoroastrian, then Christian. Muslim Turks began to move into the area from the east as early as the ninth century C.E., many eventually moving on into Anatolia. Today the population of Iranian Azerbaijan includes enclaves of Nestorian Christians, Armenians, and Kurds, with Turks constituting a strong majority. They speak Azerbaijani, a Turkic language; Azerbaijani and the Turkish spoken in Turkey are to some extent mutually intelligible. The music of the region has its own character: a recognizably Turkic idiom influenced by proximity to the music of the Armenian and Georgian peoples. [See MUSICAL TRADITIONS OF AZERBAIJAN.]

This article examines the music of the *aşıq* (plural, *aşıqlar*), a professional minstrel who sings his own songs as well as love songs and epic poetry he has learned from other minstrels. I consider, in turn, the nature of the *aşıq*'s profession; the venues in which he performs; his main instrument, the *saz*, and other accompanying instruments; his music; and his poetry.

My descriptions of the music and performance settings are drawn from fieldwork in the two northwest provinces of Iran—East Azerbaijan and West Azerbaijan, which are separated along much of their north-south axis by a large and extremely salty lake, Lake Orumiye (formerly Lake Reża'iye). This lake has separated the people living on its eastern and western shores to such a degree that their local dialects are noticeably different, and their music, though recognizably Azerbaijani, has different characteristics. The music of *aşıqlar* in Iranian Azerbaijan is similar to that of their counterparts in the republic of Azerbaijan, just across Iran's northern border. Azerbaijani Turks also live in the eastern provinces of Turkey. Turks who celebrate the music and dance of

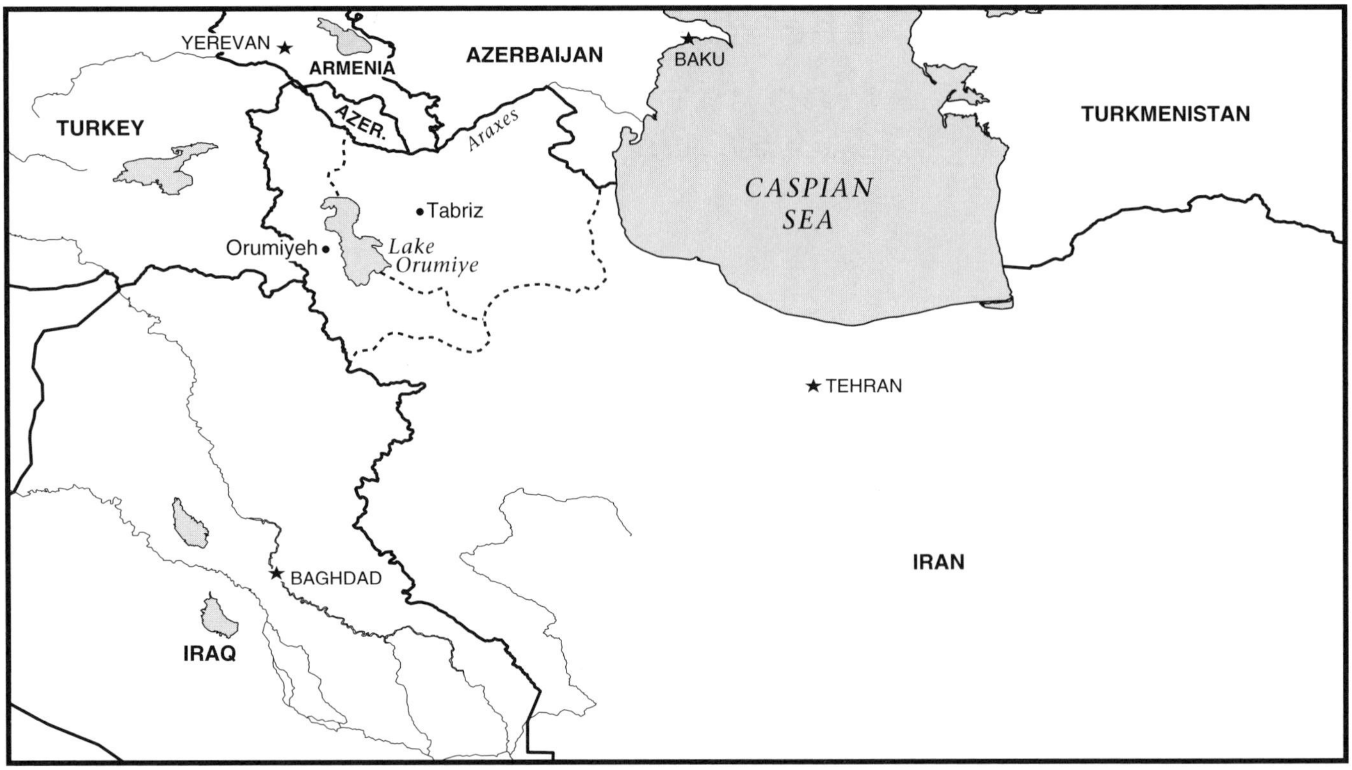

Northwestern Iran, eastern Turkey, and part of the (former) Soviet Union. Azerbaijani Turks live in this region today.

the various regions of Turkey in amateur and state-sponsored dance troupes often include Azerbaijani music in their repertoire.

THE *AŞIQ*

Professional minstrelsy is a long-standing tradition of most Turkic peoples across Central Asia and into Turkey. In Turkey the performer is called *âşık* (the same word in Turkish orthography), and his instrument is the *saz*, which comes in many shapes and sizes. Among the Turkmens, who live east of the Caspian Sea, minstrels are called *bagşy* (often spelled *bakhshī* when transliterated from Persian) and play a two-stringed, long-necked plucked lute known as the *dūtār*. In earlier times the *bagşy* combined the vocations of musician and shaman and was often a figure of considerable power. Other minstrels and shamans have accompanied their performances on a variety of fretted or fretless, plucked or bowed, long-necked and not-so-long-necked lutes. The Kyrgyz *akin* or *manaschi* (who specializes in the long epic *Manas*) may perform on the *komuz,* a plucked fretless lute, whereas his Kazakh counterpart may use the *qobuz,* a concave-fronted bowed lute. (For minstrel traditions of Central Asia, see Chadwick and Zhirmunsky 1969; Reichl 1992.)

The predecessors of today's *aşıq* came to Azerbaijan with the Turks. They were often part of a ruler's retinue, responsible for praising the ruler, his family, his horses, and his prowess in battle. Shah Ismāʿīl (r. 1501–1524) enjoyed the *aşıq*'s music so much that he learned to perform it himself and composed songs about Shīʿa Islam after he declared Iran to be a Shīʿa nation (Caferoğlu 1965:646). The word *aşıq* (Arabic for lover) appears in literature for the first time in the fifteenth century. Before then, similar minstrels were called *ozan* (Başgöz 1952:331). Several suggestions have been made as to why the name *aşıq* was given to these musicians. In the mid-nineteenth century, Alexander Chodzko gave one reasonable explanation:

> Aushek signifies properly "enamoured." In northern Persia, this word designates the professional singer, who singly, or in the company of jugglers, rope-dancers,

> and sometimes monkeys, perambulate[s] the towns, villages and encampments of the nomades, attend[s] the wedding ceremonies and festivals, amuse[s] the people with music, puns, songs, etc. (1842:12–13).

In northern Afghanistan, Slobin found the terms *'asheq* 'in love', *mast* 'drunk', and *majnūn* 'mad' used to describe musicians. He concluded that these terms indicated a belief that musicians must be inspired to write poetry and perform music well (Slobin 1976:24–25). Başgöz (1952:332) and Boratav (1965:34) noted similar attitudes toward Turkish *âşıklar*.

The *aşıqlar* I worked with in Tabriz and Orumiye did not offer explanations of the term but reported that they themselves, and others whom they knew, had been "called" in some special way to take up the profession. 'Aşıq Rasul, my chief informant in Tabriz, said he had a dream in which someone appeared, offered him a small *saz*, and asked if he could play it. Rasul picked up the instrument and immediately began playing. When he awoke, he was able to play the *saz* the first time he tried. 'Aşıq Dehqan of Orumiye began to study the *saz* and learn poems after he fell in love with a cousin; he and his cousin were too young to marry, so he turned to music for consolation. Other *aşıqlar* came to their profession by more ordinary paths. Aşıq Josef in Orumiye and Aşıq Qeşem in Kondrud followed in the footsteps of their musician fathers. Others apprenticed themselves to established *aşıqlar* because they regarded the profession as a good way to make money.

Regardless of how or why men become *aşıqlar*, most apprentice themselves to established musicians. This apprenticeship is similar to master-pupil relationships in other Asian cultures. Not only is the pupil expected to learn the master's music, but usually he also serves the master in other ways—for instance, by carrying the master's instrument. If the pupil earns money as he advances in musical skill, he gives his earnings to the master.

The concept of ranking, apparent in the master-apprentice hierarchy, carries over to ensembles. When an *aşıq* performs with a *balaban* player (the *balaban* is a double-reed aerophone with a cylindrical bore) and a *qaval* (tambourine) player, as he often does in East Azerbaijan, he is always the group leader (figure 1). The *balaban* player usually carries the *aşıq*'s *saz*, removes its cover before the performance, and replaces the cover afterward. All proceeds of the performance go to the *aşıq*, who then divides them.

Nowadays, of course, *aşıqlar* have access to less traditional means of learning the repertoire. Collections of *aşıq* poetry have been published in Baku, capital of the

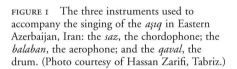

FIGURE 1 The three instruments used to accompany the singing of the *aşıq* in Eastern Azerbaijan, Iran: the *saz*, the chordophone; the *balaban*, the aerophone; and the *qaval*, the drum. (Photo courtesy of Hassan Zarifi, Tabriz.)

republic of Azerbaijan. These were available in bookstores in Tabriz in the 1970s. In Iran, at least before the revolution of 1979, anyone could buy a wide variety of tapes and phonograph recordings of *aşıq* music from both Iran and what was then the Azerbaijan S.S.R. People also taped performances broadcast on local and national radio and television. All these print and audio resources have been used by young men who want to learn the art of the *aşıq*.

PERFORMANCE VENUES

In West Azerbaijan the *aşıq* is a solo performer. In East Azerbaijan the *aşıq* performs by himself when he sings but is joined during the instrumental interludes by a *balaban* and sometimes a *qaval*.

Traditionally *aşıqlar* performed in coffeehouses and at weddings. In the larger cities, such as Tabriz and Orumiye, it is perhaps easier to find an *aşıq* in a coffeehouse (so called despite the fact that most patrons drink tea). In the 1970s, the coffeehouses in Tabriz where *aşıqlar* performed were located near the bus terminal and a large produce market. Village men who had come to town for the day could easily stop in at these coffeehouses and listen to an *aşıq*. Apparently there had once been other coffeehouses in Tabriz where *aşıqlar* performed, but the increasing popularity of the tape recorder and cassette recordings in Iran had driven all but the best *aşıqlar* out of the business.

The atmosphere of the coffeehouse is informal, though certain customs are observed by patrons and *aşıqlar* alike. The audience is exclusively male, even if women are not explicitly barred from entering. Members of the audience enter the coffeehouse, greet friends, and order a glass of tea. Some men order water pipes, whose bubbly sound blends with the music of the *aşıq* and the clinking of tea glasses.

Either the *aşıq* chooses his own songs or members of the audience request their favorites; the *aşıq* is given a tip for singing requests. Men who make no special requests still pay a nominal fee to hear the performance. As he performs, the *aşıq* walks up and down the aisles between the tables and chairs. He stops and sings before friends, honored guests, or people making special requests.

People judge an *aşıq* by his ability to remember poetry and the *dastanlar* 'stories', and by his interpretation of the songs and stories. A good performer should add appropriate emotions and feelings for the characters he describes. Perhaps as a result of this requirement, good *aşıqlar* are often impressive, charismatic figures. Virtuosity in playing the *saz* is also important, but less so than knowledge of the repertoire and vocal techniques.

Aşıqlar also appear at the festivities connected with weddings. Although performances at weddings are seasonal, they are much more lucrative than coffeehouse performances. In the Tabriz area the guests and family of the groom usually contribute money for the musicians. Sometimes the young men are allowed to dance with the unmarried girls, and they pay the performing musicians for this privilege. Wedding festivities may last from three days to a week.

In addition to their work in coffeehouses and at wedding celebrations, *aşıqlar* have also performed for radio or television broadcasts.

THE *SAZ* AND OTHER INSTRUMENTS

The Azerbaijani *saz* is a long-necked, fretted, plucked lute (figure 2). The origin of its name is unclear. In Persian, *sāz* is a generic term for any musical instrument, particularly a stringed instrument; it is also the present-tense stem of the verb *sākhtan* 'to build'. In Turkish, *saz* refers to a number of long-necked lutes, or to music in general. Most likely Turks borrowed the Persian word for the *aşıq*'s instrument.

The *saz* played in Iranian Azerbaijan has a length of about 105 centimeters, of which 41 centimeters is the length of the resonator. The resonating cavity is made of

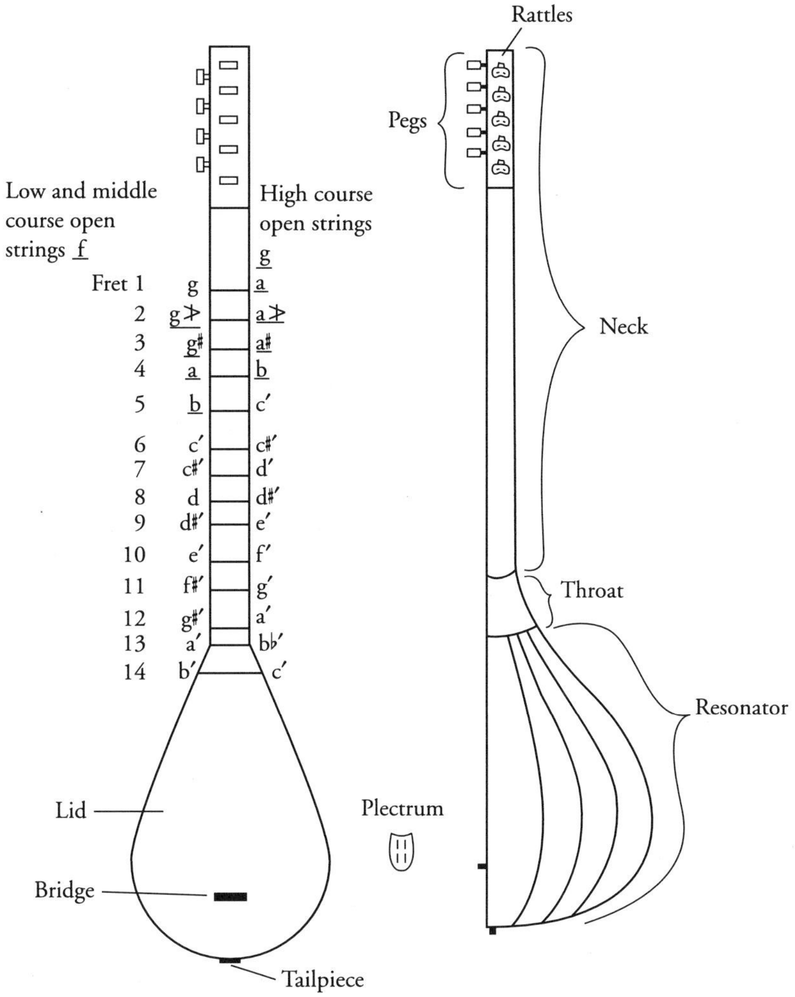

FIGURE 2 The Azerbaijani *saz*, front and side views. Underlined pitches are below middle C. The pitch produced at fret 2, G *sori*, lies between G-natural and G-sharp.

mulberry wood. The bowl is formed by gluing together nine or ten picket-shaped wooden ribs. This cavity is then completely covered with thin slats of wood. To allow sounds to escape the resonator, about twenty small holes are drilled through its cover. The neck of the *saz* is about 54 centimeters long and is made of walnut, which is harder and resists warping better than mulberry. The neck and resonator are joined by a "throat" about 10 centimeters long, also made of walnut. The resonator, throat, and neck of the instrument are often highly ornamented with gazelle horn, camel bone, and mother-of-pearl. Mother-of-pearl rattles are also attached to the neck on the side away from the performer.

The Azerbaijani *saz* has nine steel strings grouped in triple courses, which bear the Persian names for low, middle, and high pitches: *bəm*, *vəsət*, and *zil* (a variant of the Persian *zīr*). The strings are most often tuned close to the pitches *f*, *f*, and g (underlined pitches refer to the octave below middle C on the piano). The *zil* course is used for the melody, whereas the *vəsət* and *bəm* courses are the drone strings. Sometimes the player uses the *bəm* course to supply a melody pitch, by stopping the strings with his thumb. Performers in Orumiye may remove the two strings from the middle course closest to the *zil* course; this allows them to play just the *zil* course, with the drone strings silent. The *aşıq* strums the *saz* strings with an oblong, flexible plectrum made of cherry bark.

The fourteen frets (*pərdələr*) of the *saz* are made of wound sheep gut. Figure 2 shows the scale produced with these frets in the vicinity of Tabriz, the capital of East Azerbaijan. The scale on instruments played in West Azerbaijan may vary slightly.

There are only two nonchromatic intervals in the *saz* scale—those between the first and second frets, and between the second and third frets, are quarter tones. In practice, though, fret two is not used in most Azerbaijani melodies except as an ornamental pitch. Azerbaijani music is, thus, essentially chromatic. The Turkish *saz*—a close relative of the Azerbaijani *saz*—comes in several sizes, and its tunings vary considerably (see Picken 1975).

In the Iranian province of West Azerbaijan, the *aşıq* performs by himself, without backup musicians; this is also the practice of *aşıklar* in Turkey. In East Azerbaijan, however, the *aşıq* usually performs with a *balaban* and often a *qaval*. The *balaban*, as noted above, is a cylindrical-bore double-reed instrument; it is about 35 centimeters long and has seven finger holes and one thumbhole; the bore is about 1.5 centimeters in diameter. This instrument can be carved out of several kinds of wood, including mulberry. The double reed is made by flattening a piece of cane on one end and crimping the other end while it is still malleable so that it fits into the body of the instrument. The reeds are large: 2 centimeters wide where pressed flat. As with most reed aerophones, the reeds require special care and must be soaked in water to soften before they are played. Because the *balaban*'s sound is loud (it might remind symphony-goers of a loud English horn), it is played only when the *aşıq* is not singing. The *balaban* player (called *balabançü*) uses his cheeks as air reservoirs and uses circular breathing. The *balaban* or a similar instrument is also played in the republic of Azerbaijan, where it is often called *düdük*, and in Turkey, where it is called *mey* or *ney*. On a Radio Baku recording included in UNESCO's *Musical Anthology of the Orient*, two *düdükler* play together with a drum. One *düdük* plays only a drone part and is called the *dəmkeş* 'breath drawer' in Persian and Azerbaijani.

The *qaval* is the frame drum known as *dāīre* in Persian-speaking Iran. It is between 40 and 50 centimeters in diameter and has circular metal rattles attached all around the inside of the wooden frame over which the skin is stretched and glued. The drummer holds the *qaval* directly in front of himself with both hands. He can achieve a variety of low and high pitches depending on where and how he strikes the drumhead. The *qaval* is used to accompany both the music of the *aşıq* and music derived from the Persian court tradition. Unlike the *saz* and *balaban*, it is also played by women.

THE MUSIC OF THE *AŞIQ*

The *aşıqlar* in Iranian Azerbaijan are not much concerned with music theory. Musicians call any melody they use to accompany their songs a *hava* 'air' or 'tune' (from Persian; plural, *havalar*). The term is also used in Turkey, where *oyun havası*, for instance, is the generic term for a dance tune. In Iranian Azerbaijan each *hava* has a name (such as *Misrī* 'Egyptian'), and the *aşıq* customarily plays certain tunes with particular poems or epic tales. The *aşıqlar* do not try to connect their *havalar* to the systems used to classify modes in the art music of Iran, the Azerbaijan Republic, and Turkey.

When analyzed, the *havalar* exhibit a coherent tonal structure that has the following characteristics:

- A set of pitches, or scale
- Fairly discrete tessituras and a hierarchy of pitches in each tessitura
- A preferred tuning
- A drone pitch
- A cadential formula

Analysis of these characteristics reveals that the *havalar* of East and West Iranian Azerbaijan have different tonal qualities and thus need to be grouped separately. Nonetheless, some *havalar* in Iranian Azerbaijan share many tonal characteristics and can be grouped together (see Albright 1976a, b). To give an indication of the tonal, formal, and rhythmic components of an Azerbaijani *hava*, I will look at one from Tabriz (eastern style) and one from Orumiye (western style).

A typical, and popular, *hava* from East Azerbaijan is *Qürbati* (figure 3). The pitches used resemble an F major scale with a flat seventh (or the Gregorian Mixolydian mode). Tonally, the piece can be divided into two groups of pitches (or tessituras): the lowest pitches, marked (a) in figure 3, from F to c; then higher pitches, marked (b), up to c'. In the lower tessitura, the melodic figures start on c and use it as a kind of reciting tone which always resolves to B-flat. Each melodic segment ends with a cadential formula leading back to F. As the *aşıq* performs this piece on his *saz*, the lower-course strings, which are tuned to F, sound continuously to provide the drone. The performer who selects *hava Qürbati* to accompany his singing of a poem will use

FIGURE 3 The *hava Qürbati* as performed by Aşıq Rasul Qorbani, Tabriz, 1974. The symbol that consists of a circle with a descender (familiar to cellists) refers to a pitch played on the low strings with the thumb. Transcription by Charlotte Albright.

the melodic segments over and over, with many variations, in between the verses of poetry. In the recording on which this transcription is based, Aşıq Rasul Qurbani of Tabriz sings the poem *Sarı köynək* 'Yellow Shirt' by the late Alesker of Baku, a famous *aşıq*. Of the *havalar* I recorded in Tabriz, all but one used the same Mixolydian scale, and many also featured a C reciting tone falling back to F. But several used reciting tones other than c and final tones other than F.

The *saz* may be tuned in a number of different ways, depending on the melody and the performer's taste. The basic tuning all over Iranian Azerbaijan is that given above, in which the *bəm* and *vəsət* courses are tuned to the same pitch and the *zil* course is tuned one whole tone higher. This tuning can be used for any of the *havalar*. All other tunings (figure 4) are alternatives to the basic tuning and involve moving the *vəsət* course either up or down, to be in tune with, or an octave lower than, fret 1, 3, 5, or 10. This gives the tuning a definite tonal bias.

Aşıqlar in West Azerbaijan use a wider variety of pitches in their *havalar*. Perhaps this is because they are soloists and do not have to match their melodies to the fixed pitches of the *balaban* used in East Azerbaijan. The *hava Halabi* (figure 5)—a piece that perhaps originated in Aleppo, Halab in Arabic—is fairly typical of those in the western province. Here, as in numerous *havalar* from the Orumiye region, the melody begins on one of the pitches between c and g, develops a melodic figure in that tessitura, then drops to the pitches from c down to F for the cadential formula (the five-beat measure beginning the third line of the transcription). In this performance the only reference to the drone, F, occurs when the performer occasionally strums the open strings (as at the beginning of the second line). In comparison with those of East Azerbaijan, the *hava* melodies performed in West Azerbaijan are composed in a wider variety of scale types, and they often start high in the pitches above c and then move to the pitches below c (the opposite of the tendency in East Azerbaijan).

The rhythms and meters used in the *havalar* are not usually complex. Most are duple or triple. Very rarely, other metric patterns occur, as in *Halabi*, where triple and duple meter alternate briefly. As the *aşıq* performs a *hava* on his *saz*, there are not normally any gaps, rests, or long pauses, since the sound of the instrument dies away almost immediately. The melodies move along in continuous streams of eighth or sixteenth notes.

FIGURE 4 Tunings of the *saz* in Iranian Azerbaijan. The first may always be used but is not used if another tuning is chosen; the others are optional.

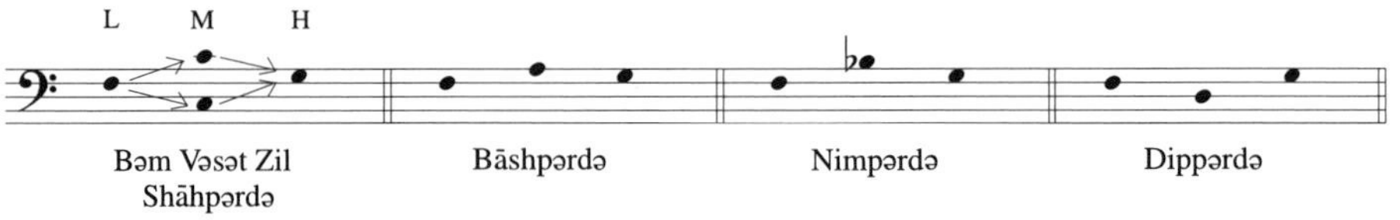

FIGURE 5 The *hava Halabi* as performed by Aşıq Dehqan, Orumiye, 1974. Transcription by Charlotte Albright.

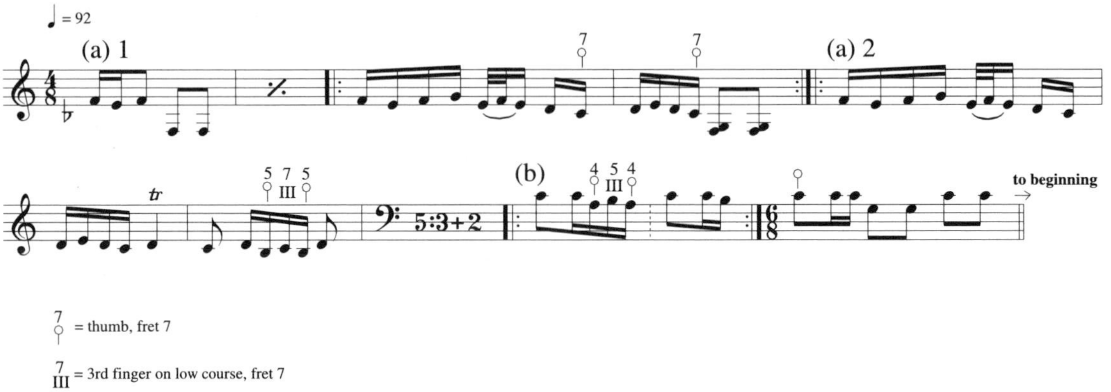

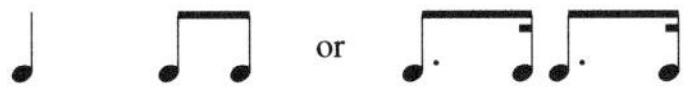

FIGURE 6 Rhythmic patterns.

Azerbaijani *saz* music often has a definite trochaic feeling, as does music for the Turkic long-necked lute in general. People like to ascribe this trochaic tendency to the nomadic origins of Turkic tribes. According to this theory, the trochaic rhythm recalls the sound of horses' hoofbeats. Whatever the source, rhythmic patterns such as those in figure 6 are common. Triplet figures are used, as in *Qürbati*, and free meter occurs as well, especially in the introductions to some *havalar*.

THE POETRY OF THE *AŞIQ*

Far more has been written about the *aşıq*'s poetry than about his music (Albright 1976a, b; Boratav 1965; Caferoğlu 1965). Collections of *aşıq* poetry have been published, particularly in Baku (Aleskerov 1972), so that an "official" written version can be compared with a performed version. Although many poetic forms have been recorded, particularly in the former Azerbaijan S.S.R., *aşıqlar* in Iranian Azerbaijan confine themselves largely to two forms: the lengthy epic poem called *dastan* (plural, *dastanlar*) in Azerbaijan and *hikâye* in Turkey; and the short lyric love poem called *aşıq havası* in Iran, *qoşma* in the republic of Azerbaijan, and *koşma* in Turkey.

The *dastanlar* are traditional epic poems, which form a major part of the literary heritage of Turkic peoples across Central Asia and into Turkey. An individual poem may be known among many Turkic groups and have many variations of plot and performance. Among the oldest is *Dede Qorqut*, which some scholars trace back to the thirteenth century (Lewis 1974). The main character in these tales, Dede Qorqut, was himself a legendary minstrel. Other *dastanlar* are heroic adventure stories, such as that about Koroğli, a warrior of superhuman strength. Others concern real historical personages, such as Shāh 'Abbās, the great Safavid Persian ruler. Many, such as *Kərəm və əsli*, tell the stories of ill-fated lovers.

Each epic takes several days, perhaps as many as fifteen, with the *aşıq* performing from ninety minutes to three hours each day. In a typical performance the *aşıq* does several things. After welcoming the audience members, he may ask them to recite a prayer, and he may sing one or two short lyrical poems. Once the audience is suitably "warmed up" and settled down, he begins to recite the *dastan* with a combination of spoken narration, including interpretation of any arcane bits of history, and sung poetry accompanied by the *saz* (or *saz*, *balaban*, and *qaval*). In the early 1970s, thirty *dastanlar* were still being performed in Iranian Azerbaijan.

The *aşıq havası,* unlike the lengthy *dastan,* is a relatively short poetic form. The poems are usually about unrequited love or the beauty of nature. Typically, a poem has three to five stanzas of four lines each. Each line has eleven syllables, divided as 6 + 5 or 4 + 4 + 3. The rhyme pattern in the first stanza is abcb (or abab) followed by dddb in the second stanza, eeeb in the third, and so forth. In the collected works of Aşıq Alesker (Aleskerov 1972), there are a number of different types of *qoşmə*, depending on the thematic content of the poem. A *güzellemə*, for instance, is a *qoşmə* dealing with love and nature (Başgöz 1952:33). Other forms include the *ustadnamə*, *şikayətnamə* (a poem of complaint), *təcnis*, and *bağlama*.

Here is an example of an *ashiq havası* (or *qoşmə*) composed by Sayyad and sung by Aşıq Rasul of Tabriz to the *hava Qürbati*. The rhyme syllable is *-ana* in the words *amana, imana, divana,* and *Kirmana.* The word *gəldim,* which follows the rhyme word, is a *redif* (from Persian *radīf* 'row'), a word repeated in every stanza but not considered part of the rhyme.

Fələyin əllinan çarxin qəhrimnan
Dunde ruzigarin amana gəldim.
Şükr Haqqa gördüm yar camalini
Elabir yetişdim imana gəldim

From the hand of fate, the wrath of fate,
I was helpless before the twists and turns of fate.
Thank God I saw my lover's beauty.
I heard so that I saw the truth of my belief.

əynina geyipdi yaşılı yali	She has put on a green vest.
Mənəm başqasina deməz xəyali	She has not told anyone but me her thoughts.
Öldürməyin qızlar Aşıq Ebdali	Don't kill Aşıq Abdali, girls!
ədalət eşitdim divana gəldim	I heard justice and came to court.
Sayyad diyar budir yarin soraqi	Sayyad says this is the place of the beloved.
əynina gəyipdir sudu boraqi	She has put on beautiful clothes.
Məhəlldən məhəll saddat soraqi	From place to place news was gathered.
Heyrətdən eşitdim Kirmana gəldim	I heard with surprise and came to Kirman.

To summarize, the *aşıq*, and his performance on the Azerbaijani *saz*, is one manifestation of the artistic culture brought to Iran and Turkey by Turkic tribes moving westward during the last millenium. Although the epic poetry, songs, and musical forms originally had a place in the tents of the khans, over time they have become the property of the lower classes in Iran. Most often, laborers, farmers, and villagers form the audience of today's *aşıq*. Just before the Islamic Revolution in 1979, the *aşıq* and his music became a symbol of Azerbaijani indigenous culture, and performances moved out of the coffeehouses and into local concert halls. It appears that this genre has remained popular in the years since the revolution.

REFERENCES

Albright, Charlotte F. 1976a. "The Music of Professional Musicians of Northwest Iran (Azerbaijan)." Ph.D. dissertation, University of Washington.

———. 1976b. "The Azerbaijani *'Ashiq* and His Performance of a *Dastan*." *Iranian Studies* 9:220–247.

———. 1988. "The Azerbaijani *'Ashiq*: A Musician's Adaptations to a Changing Society." *Edebiyat* (New Series) 2(1–2):205–217.

Aleskerov. 1972. *Aşıq Alesker*. 2 vols. Baku: Ilm.

Azerbaijan I: *A Musical Anthology of the Orient*, No. 24. n.d. Kassel: Bärenreiter-Musicaphon, BM 30 L 2024. (LP; notes by Habib H. Touma. Includes one excerpt of an *aşıq* and a duet of two *düdükler*.)

Başgöz, Ilhan. 1952. "Turkish Folk Stories about the Lives of Minstrels." *Journal of American Folklore* 65:331–339.

Boratav, Pertev Naili. 1965. "L'épopée et la 'hikāye.' " In *Philologiae Turcicae Fundamenta*, Vol. 2, 11–44. Wiesbaden: Franz Steiner.

Caferoğlu, Ahmet. 1965. "Die Aserbaidschanische Literatur." In *Philologiae Turcicae Fundamenta*, Vol. 2, 635–698. Wiesbaden: Franz Steiner.

Chadwick, Nora K., and Victor Zhirmunsky. 1969. *Oral Epics of Central Asia*. Cambridge: Cambridge University Press.

Chodzko, Alexander. 1842. *Specimens of the Popular Poetry of Persia*. London: Oriental Translation Fund.

During, Jean, 1989. *Azerbaidjan: Musique et chants des ashiqs—Ashiq Hasan, Emran Heydari, Alim Qasimov*. Geneva: Archives Internationales de Musique Populaire, AIMP XIX, VDE-Gallo CD-613. Compact disk.

During, Jean, and Eldar Mansurov. 1989. *Azerbayjan: Musique traditionnelle*. Paris: Le Chant du Monde LDX 274 901. Compact disk. (Music performed by *aşıqlar* from Baku, Azerbaijan.)

Lewis, Geoffrey. 1974. *The Book of Dede Korkut*. Harmondsworth, England: Penguin.

Picken, Laurence. 1975. *Folk Musical Instruments of Turkey*. London: Oxford University Press.

Reichl, Karl. 1992. *Turkic Oral Epic Poetry: Traditions, Forms, Poetic Structure*. New York: Garland.

Reinhard, Ursula, and Tiago de Oliveira Pinto. 1989. *Sänger und Poeten mit der Laute: Türkische Aşık und Ozan*. Veröffentlichungen des Museums für Völkerkunde Berlin, n.F. 47, Musikethnologische Abteilung 6. Berlin: Museum für Völkerkunde. (2 accompanying cassettes.)

Slobin, Mark. 1969. *Kirgiz Instrumental Music*. New York: Society for Asian Music.

———. 1976. *Music in the Culture of Northern Afghanistan*. Viking Fund Publications in Anthropology, no. 54. Tucson: University of Arizona Press.

Spector, Johanna. 1967. "Musical Tradition and Innovation." In *Central Asia: A Century of Russian Rule*, ed. Edward Allworth, 434–484. New York: Columbia University Press.

Tradition and History: The Case of Iran

Jean During

"Tradition" in Question
Emergence and Continuity of a Tradition

"TRADITION" IN QUESTION

It may seem obvious that art musics of the East are rightly called "traditional," particularly because many Eastern cultures themselves use that term: *aṣīl* or *sonnatī* in Persian and Arabic, *an'anevi* in Turkish. But "traditional" is an ill-defined concept, and the reality is not nearly so simple. While certain musical practices may well have developed somewhat more slowly or more regularly, others have undergone breaks in continuity and renewals that in some cases have been sharper and more frequent than those in Western music. It might actually make more sense to call the music that developed smoothly from Machaut to Debussy "traditional" than to use that label for Middle Eastern music, which, from an initial center in Baghdad in the eighth to tenth centuries, diverged into schools that are now quite different from one another.

In the specific case of Persian art music, one may argue against considering the forms developed in the nineteenth century "traditional," as they appear to have little in common with those described in ancient treatises and cultivated to this day in neighboring areas. The term *sonnatī* may have had an established meaning at the beginning of the twentieth century, but today it is not used with any consistency. If we consider art music, we can now identify the following categories:

"Traditional Iranian" (*sonnatī-ye īrānī*)
"Authentic" (*aṣīl*) Iranian
"New-style traditional" (*aṣīl-e novīn*)
Original "traditional Iranian" pieces

In addition, some people consider popular and regional (*maḥallī*, *maqāmī*) musics "traditional."

The understanding of *sonnatī* seems to have shifted in twentieth-century Iran. In view of the diversity of styles and genres, a more general category, *mellī* 'national' or "Iranian" music, was identified, and it is common to distinguish between *sonnatī* 'traditional' and *aṣīl* 'authentic'. These three categories can be though of as a pyramid, or as concentric circles:

Narrowest, top of pyramid or innermost circle: authentic music (*aṣīl*)
Traditional music (*sonnatī*)
Broadest, bottom of pyramid or outermost circle: Iranian or national music (*mellī*)

This first section of the article outlines the tradition as it obtains today in Iran, defining the relationships between authenticity, custom, territory, and nation. The second section evaluates the changes that have contributed to the development of a new form of tradition or to the advent of a certain form of modernity.

The heart of the tradition

As has been true for more than a century, the best-known traditional classical or scholarly Iranian music—simultaneously *mellī* 'national', *sonnatī* 'traditional', and *aṣīl* 'authentic'—has currently crystallized in the canonical repertoire known as the *radīf*, which was established and transmitted at the end of the nineteenth century, most notably by Mīrzā 'Abdollāh (c. 1843–1918). Certain compositions possibly dating back to the same period have been accepted as belonging to this repertoire.

Throughout the nineteenth century the best singers and instrumentalists, from different provinces of Iran, gradually gathered the components of a significant repertoire. It was organized in the form of a *radīf*, a model and a sequential order with variants that originated with different masters. The components are a modal introduction (*darāmad*), secondary modes (the "great" *gūshe-hā*; singular, *gūshe*) related to the basic mode, and independent melodies that may or may not be restricted to a single mode. In most components, rhythm and tempo are nonmeasured and quite flexible. Each fragment or piece was given a name. This profusion of standard melodies (*gūshe-hā*) was classified, on the basis of modal affinities, into twelve systems: seven
TRACK 4 *dastgāh-hā* (singular, *dastgāh*) and five derived *āvāz-hā* (singular, *āvāz*), each with about eight to sixty *gūshe-hā*.

The wider meaning of *radīf* can be distinguished from the restricted sense of one or another master's *radīf*. In its broadest sense the *radīf* is a repertoire of pieces meant
TRACK 28 to be played in a more or less prescribed order. It is also an exemplary model that enables one to learn (1) the repertoire of melodic types (*gūshe-hā*) and some virtually unchanging pieces; (2) the classification of modes and modulations, their structure, and their common traits; and (3) instrumental technique, the classical style, aesthetic principles, and implicit rules of composition and improvisation.

In its narrower sense, *radīf* has two meanings. First, it refers to the contents of a *dastgāh* or *āvāz* as defined by a master or a school, as when we say, "In so-and-so's version, the *radīf* of *shūr* has thirty *gūshe-hā*." Second, it refers to the special or fixed version of the body of *gūshe-hā* of the twelve modal systems taught by a master to his pupils, which corresponds to an original style or a specific musical instrument—as when we say, "The *darāmad* of *abū 'atā* is very different in X's *radīf* as compared with Y's" or "The *radīf* of Mīrzā 'Abdollāh suits the *setār* better."

As the *radīf* is not meant to be reproduced without change but can have variants and can give rise to new creations, we may ask which of its elements are fixed. Masters and the musical public accept changes only up to a point, beyond which the music is no longer "authentic" or "traditional" but only "Iranian" or "national." The pertinent criteria involve several factors:

1. Form and content: intervals, modes, melodic profile, ornaments, rhythm, timbre, ethos, and so on.
2. Process of transmission: orally or in musical notation; from master to disciple (by teaching) or by immersing oneself in the milieu; by self-teaching.
3. Means of production: instruments and type of ensemble (orchestral, vocal, amplified, and so on).
4. Performance and listening conditions: in a natural or constructed environment; with composition taking place in the mind or in writing; music recorded or performed in concert or broadcast by radio; length of the performance; and so on.
5. Social and cultural context: musician's social status; type of patronage; oral

or literate milieu; rural, tribal, or urban milieu; in ritual or traditional circumstances, or not; degree of familiarity with the audience; functionality of the music; spontaneity of the performance; relationship to nature; and so on.
6. Meaning and values: knowledge, symbolism, ethics, ethos, feelings, objectives, and so on.

To grasp the notion of tradition in each of these areas, I have recorded discussions I had in 1990 with Iranian musicians (identified in During 1994, acknowledgments) belonging to a variety of schools, all of whom shared a profound knowledge of the *radīf* as well as professional competence. Although these musicians rarely discussed areas 3, 4, and 5, they all insisted that the traditionality of music making is defined by certain forms—the *qāleb* 'master' or 'mold' forms, also known as *chahār-chūb* 'frame', *meḥvar-hā* 'axes', and *oṣūl* 'principles' (*oṣūl* is from the same root as *aṣīl* 'authentic'). These principles are exemplified particularly in the *radīf*.

Formal criteria and their symbolic dimension

According to the master Majīd Kīānī, "For the music to be considered traditional and in a line of continuity with ancient music, it must respect five axes: sonority and timbre, intervals [and, by extension, the modal system], rhythm, melodic movement, and ornamentation." Most of these axes relate to other arenas of culture or national life and define the "world" of the tradition. Thus, according to Kīānī, melodic movements—even descending movements—always include ascending elements, in a sawtooth pattern. This is deemed to convey an ancient philosophy of transcendence. Movements and ornaments that are solely descending are considered to be in poor taste, or vulgar, and to express decline and affliction. Rhythms are related to poetic meters and to the nursery rhymes that surround Iranians from early childhood.

Intervals and the *ḥāl*

All the musicians agreed on the importance of intervals, which they considered the heart of the tradition. Intervals are connected to the *ḥāl*, which has a dual meaning, signifying ethos or state of mind as well as inspiration. Intervals are also connected to the expression *ḥāl o ḥavā* 'ethos and atmosphere'. The relationship is circular: the singer's *ḥāl* produces the correct intervals (he or she requires a certain concentration, a good frame of mind); these intervals then produce the proper *ḥāl* (or carry the performer's *ḥāl*) and activate and sustain the performer's *ḥāl*. If the intervals are changed, the *ḥāl* is changed.

Objections arise not so much because one has left the traditional circle as because one has entered another circle, the culture and territory of others. We might say that scales and intervals exist in limited number and are in a sense like radio frequencies: as soon as we leave one frequency (the "bandwidth" of an interval) we pick up another station. Intervals are markers not only of ethos but of ethnicity and geocultural distinctiveness. To use another image, intervals function like the coloration and markings of birds, indicating ethnic "belonging" and delimiting territory. One way a tradition functions is by gathering a group or a people under a system of values, *sensus communis*. Some musicians say that sometime in the unknown past, Iranians abandoned the intervals that had also been played by the Arabs, to return to ancient, specifically Iranian intervals.

The determination of intervals is the condition for being able to play together and play truly. Intervals thus constitute the common language of any musical tradition. The ancient theorists (including al-Fārābī and Ṣafī al-Dīn) sought to bring the entire Islamic community together using the same scales. With the expansion of the empire, each community defined itself in terms of its own intervals and modes.

In function, intervals and intonations can be compared to accents in spoken language. When an Azerbaijani plays a Persian melody with his own intervals and timbres, he is said to have an "Azeri" accent. Such parallels between "mother tongue" and "maternal music" could be developed further, but the important point here is the connection between *ḥāl* and intervals. Intervals authenticate a musical form in the sense that they demonstrate the purity of its ethnic and national origins. Conversely, foreign intervals "corrupt" the music, for they do not correspond to the national *ḥāl o ḥavā*. In performance the musician's *ḥāl* proves the authenticity of his art. Music that is imitative (*taqlīdī*) has no *ḥāl* and is not authentic, even if it conforms perfectly to the appropriate norms.

Although they are connected, the *ḥāl* and intervals are unlike each other in nature. The *ḥāl* is by definition a personal aesthetic experience, unique, singular, incommunicable, subjective, sensed, escaping the intellect at every point. Intervals, on the other hand, exist in the domain of commonality and consensus. They can be objectified, measured, rationalized, and communicated. Intervals can be imagined as located at the intersection of two axes: a vertical axis for individual and transcendent communication (by means of the *ḥāl*) and a horizontal axis for communication limited by ethnic and geographic boundaries. According to the musicians, intervals define authenticity in two ways: by the purity of the form's ethnic origins (which encompass the whole Iranian nation-state) and by the intensity and nature of its aesthetic experience. In other words, authenticity is a "pure" product of national genius, unsullied by anything taken—borrowed or imitated—from beyond the border. But it is also the fruit of the individual aesthetic and emotional experience known as *ḥāl*, a kind of escape from oneself into grace and inspiration, without which the music remains banal and imitative.

The milieu: Nature and culture

Many musicians feel that instrumental timbre and intervals or elementary modal motifs reflect the nature of Iran:

> Kīānī: This music is made in a luminous land, inundated with sunlight, under a sky filled with brilliant stars. This must be reflected in the timbre of the instrument as well as in the sounds of the language, the voice, the song, and in painting, rugs, ceramics, and so on.

Traditional culture includes not only what is produced but also the relationship of the subject to his or her milieu. It is fundamentally synthetic and totalizing, integrating nature and culture—unlike modernity, which separates and opposes nature and culture. Each element refers to the whole: "In art," says Kīānī, "we find morality, religion, emotion, reason, reflection. Everything goes together."

One day Kīānī told the master Davāmī that he was afraid traditional music might disappear; but Davāmī began to laugh and answered, "No, this music is natural; as long as nature is there and God is there, this music will also be there." Nature is the space in which people live and sing. It is this whole that constitutes the traditional framework.

> The tradition encompasses all the melodies of Iran from all corners of the country. These are the melodies of natives, played with their blood, their emotions, their feeling, their labor. These are the melodies which unite them. This is what we call *sonnatī* and which in fact differs from Western music. . . . And if one wants to add anything at all, it will be within the scales, intervals, and melodies that reflect this ethos and ambience (*ḥāl o ḥavā*). (Zeydollah Ṭolū'ī)

Transmission

When the tradition is transmitted solely by the social milieu, it is more accurate to speak of immersion. When it occurs through the family, it is education (figures 1 and 2). Only when it is transmitted by one or several masters can we speak of tradition in the strong sense. Traditional teaching, which is fundamentally oral (*sīne be sīne* 'mem-

FIGURE 1 Mrs. Injegol and Ms. Bakht, Qaraqalpak bards, the daughter learning from the mother. Photo by Jean During.

ory to memory'), differs in several respects from "modern" teaching based on writing and verbalization. According to traditional musicians, the master teaches by example much more than by words. Silence, implicit assumptions, and allusions are important elements of traditional pedagogy.

> Kīānī: Why talk? We learn very well without it. . . . It is in Western music that everything is explained. . . . But in our era, and especially after the "renewal" that came about with Vazīrī (around 1930), we are obliged to discuss and argue, for example with students, so that they accept [what we are saying]. . . . In fact, the master says everything without ever speaking; it is with the other senses that one teaches.

Many musicians insist that traditional transmission must be oral. While it is true that Persian music does not allow itself to be imprisoned in notes, the reason for the importance of oral transmission is not merely technical:

> The notes are fine, but I learn a classical song with my eyes closed by repeating each phrase; this gives me another ambience than if I learn by looking at the notes. (Moḥammad Mūsavī)

Most masters today, especially singers, teach without notes, although they know the notes perfectly well. The older generation does not read notation or never uses it. In Persian music, notes are used only as a mnemonic device (During 1989b:198–199).

The ethics of balance

The effect sought by art music is a state of interior peace, harmony, and balance. In this view, Persian art "tries to establish a balance between all elements, especially between feelings and thoughts" (Kīānī), between personal and collective sentiment, and between technique and feeling (or expression). The modern attitude suffers from an excess of intellectualism in the modern West and an excess of sentimentality in the modern East. "My pain is not the pain of an individual; it is the pain of Everyman," said Ḥāfiẓ.

According to Dariūsh Ṣafvat, the valid or authentic *ḥāl* is that of a person whose conduct conforms to an ethic and who has developed such qualities as purity, rectitude, humility, and devotion (Safvat 1984:106–107). Kīānī also traces an ethical dividing line which returns once again to the concerns of the mystics. The essential point is effacement: "The master must be as though present before one. The traditional artist should always consider himself a student."

Authenticity

When we question musicians about the general direction of the tradition, the values and characteristics that usually emerge are the music's antiquity, its oral nature, its direct transmission from master to student, and the masters' authority—in particular, that of its founders. But the highest value attaches to authenticity (*eṣālat*), which is connected to quality, specific taste, and *keyfīyyat*—a term referring to an intimate, indescribable experience of the *ḥāl*. Two of these attributes, antiquity and authenticity, are conveyed by an image of roots (*rīshe*); this image simultaneously evokes the foundation of the music, its great age, its perennial nature, its depth, its interiority, the part that is hidden, and finally the land or territory, frequently cited in discussions of tradition.

> Roots are what grow under the surface. In a person, they also connote interiority, feelings, even spirituality. (Nāṣer Farhangfar)

> Traditional music must have . . . roots. It needs particular feelings in its substance or its interpretation, which cannot be described in words. (M. Shāpūr-Raḥīmī)

In the minds of Persian musicians and music lovers, the authenticity of the tradition is delimited by three concentric circles (an image that was used above for a different purpose). The outermost circle is race and language, that is, being Persian rather than Arab or Turkish. The second circle is geographic area: being from the center of Iran rather than from the periphery or from "greater Iran." The third circle, according to Kīānī, is education: within this culture one needs a good knowledge of poetry, calligraphy, and the other arts, and—beyond such knowledge—correct taste (*ẕowq*), sensibility (*eḥsās*), and more. These aspects of knowledge, crowned by one's moral qualities, constitute a good education (*adab*), without which one amounts to nothing. One progresses from the first circle to the second to the third until one reaches the center: this point is mysticism, understood in a general sense (During 1989a: 525–585; 1991a:167–75). What ensures the symbolic continuity and cohesion of Persian culture over the long term (that is, before and after Islam) is not so much language, which has evolved considerably; or geographic area, which has shrunk; or race, which has become mixed, but mysticism, and with it ethics and a certain spirit of dualism

FIGURE 2 Agā Hosein Qolī and his son and student, Alī Akbar Shahnāzī, two of the finest musicians of their time. Photo from Jean During.

and aesthetic sense. While many structural analogies can be drawn between religious and musical traditions, the musicians almost without exception used the analogy of the mystical domain and the *ḥāl* as a privileged means of access to that domain.

The center of the circle, the heart of the tradition (or, to adapt another image used above, the apex of the pyramid), is thus contact with the suprasensible, whether it be through prophetic revelation, mysticism more specifically construed, esotericism, philosophical intuition, or poetic or musical inspiration. Authentic knowledge is experiential in the sense that, in contrast to objective knowledge, it unifies subject and object in such a way that the subject finds himself or herself transformed. This is why Persian masters sometimes say, "It is not the person who makes the music, but the music which makes the person."

EMERGENCE AND CONTINUITY OF A TRADITION

The question of origins

When they are asked about the origins of their music, Iranian artists generally give two apparently contradictory responses. First, they say that the *radīf* goes back to ʿAlī Akbar Farāhānī, the father of Mīrzā ʿAbdollāh, who revived art music around 1845 to 1860; the names of the masters active between the seventeenth and early nineteenth centuries are unknown, and there is no evidence that they played the same music. Second, while recognizing the lack of evidence that the *radīf* is ancient, the vast majority of musicians are convinced that, under a broader definition, the kind of Persian music they play is directly traceable to an ancient past: through the Safavid era (sixteenth to seventeenth century), ʿAbdolqāder Marāghī (fourteenth to fifteenth century), Ṣafī al-Dīn Urmavī (thirteenth century), and Fārābī (tenth century) all the way to Bārbad (sixth century), the first great name of music that was wholly Iranian, preceding the Islamic era.

> Kīānī: Traditional music is defined this way: it follows in a continuous line with ancient music from its origins to our day, just as Western painting from its origins to our day is connected *without breaks*.

Some push this notion to its furthest limits; for example, one student maintained, "Our music goes back to the Achaemenians [fifth century B.C.E.]. There were changes, but the basis does not change: it is the same music but given a better interpretation. The *radīf* we have comes from Bārbad [sixth century]."

Thus, on the one hand the tradition was reinvented or transformed by ʿAlī Akbar, but on the other hand there were no breaks. If there was reinvention, we must ask ourselves what the word "tradition" means and in what way the new tradition is a continuation of the old. And if there was not, we must examine the meaning of this myth of renewal or mutation of the music attributed to a charismatic individual. Such questions—regarding music as well as other artifacts—can be asked of many other cultures.

Assessing change

In the past, one kind of music succeeded another, and in the absence of notation it was not possible to remember earlier music. Tradition was a page rewritten by each successive generation, which removed something and added something else. Today the pages have been preserved, and some people see no point in rewriting them. When there were no specific traces of change, one could believe in the continuity of tradition, but today one need only compare current music with records dating back to 1910 and notice the changes.

The obvious disparity between current musical forms and systems and those attested to by the great theorists may be minimized by the musicians' criteria. *No comparative method can determine the degree of subjectivity in assessing change*. The apparent

If an artist sometimes creates, or believes he is creating, new matrices, he may do so within the confines of superstructures or supermatrices that themselves remain immutable.

contradiction between stability and change comes from the fact that most musicians distinguish between several levels of abstraction in the traditional repertoire. The *radīf* is not only a repertoire but also a model (*olgū* 'matrix'), a collection of rules, an aesthetic framework (*chahār-chūb*). It is possible to affirm that change has affected the surface but not the ground, and that the invariance of the matrices has been preserved, however they have been used (use or custom being distinguished from "authenticity"). We should bear in mind that if an artist sometimes creates, or believes he is creating, new matrices, he may do so within the confines of superstructures or supermatrices that themselves remain immutable.

The cultural horizon

Although tradition (as a phenomenon, not as an object) transcends any single era and is thus beyond the present, it appears *in* time, by an initial manifestation. What anchors it is awareness of the meaning of an act; a mere fact cannot inaugurate a tradition. For the subject there is always a meaning floating over and above the form. Thus there is already a framework, a background of meaning against which the event is highlighted. The tradition concretizes what is already there. Hence it may be that musicians are telling the truth when they trace the tradition back to Bārbad or at least to Marāghī. For before 'Alī Akbar there was indeed something, even if only scattered elements, and there was an *expectation* of something new, the full meaning of which became apparent after 'Alī Akbar's arrival. It is worthwhile to sketch the cultural horizon that gave rise to or encouraged the development of a new tradition.

'Alī Akbar Farahānī was, incontestably, a genius, whose arrival at court in the mid-nineteenth century was an exceptional artistic event, hailed as such by the French ambassador, Count Gobineau. 'Alī Akbar eclipsed all other musicians, male and female, and became a legend in his own time. But if he was subsequently considered the founding father, he also came at an auspicious time, when the public's expectations had changed.

The second half of the nineteenth century, when this renaissance officially became a new tradition, was a period of upheaval in Iranian society and thought, and of a rise in nationalism. Shi'ism, which had been threatened with abolition in the eighteenth century, was now in the midst of a dynamic intellectual resurgence. In the mid-nineteenth century Iran's borders were established, and Iran regained its stability. Printing, photography, and newspapers appeared as the nation opened to the West. The shah (with his musicians) traveled to Europe on several occasions, and his emissaries there brought back military music and the concept of state religious drama (*ta'zīye*). New technologies were adopted, schools for the professional classes were created, and at the end of the century, soon after its introduction in Europe, the phonograph was used to record the court's great musicians. New political doctrines led to the adoption of a constitution in 1906. The *radīf* took firm shape toward the end of the nineteenth century (rather than in the middle). It is at this point that Iran began to enjoy a national musical language synthesized from the four corners of the country, just as literary Persian became the language of culture throughout the Islamic East.

The same conditions prevailed in Azerbaijan, which separated from Iran in 1828 and was even more open to foreign (especially Western) cultures. Here as well, toward 1880 a new tradition developed among music lovers and intellectuals. The result was a system identical to the *radīf* in organization and function and very close to it in content, but using a different code of intervals, mainly after the Soviet period.

Status and attitudes of artists

The artist's status evolved considerably as the new tradition took root. Before 'Alī Akbar, male and female court musicians played an entertainment repertoire, accompanied by dances. Under Naṣr al-Dīn Shāh (r. 1848–1896) two categories were established: "ordinary musicians" (*'āmme*) who played light music, and the "musicians of the elite" (*khāṣṣe*). This division, which may have been inspired by the protocols of the ancient Sasanian courts, led to an improvement in the status of musicians, or at least of stars. 'Alī Akbar was described as a "romantic" musician: "He also has all the defects that often come with such glory. He is extremely capricious, vain and anxious; his frequent indiscretions were the subject of anecdotes, and it is often a great and difficult affair to persuade him to let himself be heard" (Gobineau [1859] 1983:357).

An anecdote that has become legendary marks the turning point in relations between the musician and his public. Darvīsh Khān (1872–1926) was being pursued by his possessive patron, a Qājār prince, because he had performed at a private party without the prince's permission; in fact, the prince's executioner was ordered cut off Darvīsh's hands. Darvīsh, declaring that he was no slave, took refuge in the English embassy, where he received a warm welcome; he remained there until the ambassador was able to intervene with the prince and obtain his "enfranchisement." Thereafter, the artist was no longer in the prince's service but belonged to the entire nation. Art music spread to private circles, and musicians gained their autonomy and independence. Artists were freed from their social function, and scholarly music fell to talented amateurs and cultivated dilettantes, who reached the public through records, radio, and, later, concerts.

In the 1920s, Iranian music entered the modern era with an artist of an entirely new type, Colonel 'Alī Naqī Vazīrī. He was an agent of radical change and affirmed his individuality against tradition, though he knew the tradition well and derived his authority from it (this permitted him to introduce changes). Yet both in his behavior and in his style, he rejected custom, and he was in turn rejected by a large part of the public. He was, however, supported by the government, which was modern, lay, and constitutional. He became director of a conservatory on the Western model. More than half a century later, some people still say that he caused traditional music irreparable harm, although other people take a more balanced view, separating the positive from the negative.

Another revealing anecdote, from a few decades later, is the following. Ḥabīb Somā'ī (1905–1946), heir to a prestigious lineage of musicians, slapped the director of the national radio station to protest against the station's policy of directing its programming to a large public. Somā'ī's violent reaction symbolically marks the last phase of a process of democratization. Henceforth art music would be accessible to all, not only on records but on radio and cassettes, whose popularity grew much more quickly in the East than in the West. Now everyone could hear the finest artists and, even more often, artists who were not the finest. The experts' circle was broken, the music spread throughout consumer society, and everyone felt competent to evaluate it: ordinary people could decide which artists were talented, contradicting the opinion of the experts. The great masters retired from the scene, though they returned briefly during the 1970s, a period marked by a strong though short-lived return to traditional values (During 1994, ch. 9).

Toward the end of the nineteenth century, aristocrats had appropriated music, playing what they liked, when they liked, and in the way they liked, for themselves or circles of fans. With records and radio, art music came to the less cultivated bourgeois classes, losing its rigor and finesse; it became ingratiating and accessible. The masters, such as Darvīsh Khān and Abolhasan Ṣabā (1902–1957), had left the court and lived by giving lessons. To make their students happy, they had to lighten the *radīf*, removing the heavier parts and transmitting sweetened versions. The "sweetened" style (*shīrīn navāzī*) was a response to the demands of a new bourgeois society that had made its money quickly and had discovered luxury. Finally there was a return to classicism, which was quickly redirected anew by the pressure of events: the *radīf* was relegitimized as a technical point of reference and a source of inspiration, but the spirit of revolution sped the process of change.

Despite the fading of tradition as a concept, one aspect remains inviolate and transcendent: national feeling, that which is "Iranian." The artist is the one person who internalizes this world and reflects its image for the public. He is the nation's praise-singer, as he was the king's in the ancient monarchies. He sings for the people with or without the support of the government. His voice goes beyond the national borders for a few Western music-lovers, to sustain the diaspora or to represent the cultural force of the nation on the world stage.

The evolution of forms

The very order of the world seems to have been seriously questioned following contact with the West. After the fifteenth century, musical treatises were no longer regulated by the laws of mathematics. Three centuries later, the great tables analyzing the symbolic connection between music and the cosmic or natural order were no longer of concern to musicologists. In the nineteeth century, Iran produced few musical texts and left theory to scholars trained in Europe. When the Persian and Azerbaijani repertoires were reconstituted in the nineteenth century, the number twelve was maintained, but it had no connection with other orders of reality. At most, the twelve modes were distinguished by their expressive character, but even this is debatable, since here we enter the sphere of the relative and subjective.

The repertoire abandoned the solid structure of the suite or cycle (*nowbe*), which has a symbolic affinity with a natural and cosmic order. Henceforth the preferred musical form was the Persian equivalent of the *taqsīm*, free and improvised performance that uses the *radīf* framework and is essentially and by definition an art of discontinuity (*qsīm* means division). During the nineteenth century, this relatively "chaotic" form gained a central place in Iran. Music became an indeterminate individual means of expression using improvisation, which required managing the unforeseeable. The *taqsīm* form, even in its model version of the *radīf*, is undetermined in structure, content, and length. It must simply show some minimal unity and coherence in modal development and draw from a stock of tropes, clichés, figures, and groups of identifiable figures. This is, par excellence, an art for soloists and duets, in which an instrument may accompany singing. Small instrumental groups play only measured songs in unison as an introduction, intermezzo, or conclusion. Finally, the *radīf*, though it is also a vocal art (used in the *ghazal*), finds its power in instrumentation and gradually gains its autonomy from the word, with all that this implies about semantic, metric, and expressive constraints. The Arabs had already remarked, without understanding the attraction, that the Persians liked free instrumental musical forms. Yet it was in the modern era that musical forms developed separately from poetic and metric forms.

From the standpoint of rhythm as well—an aspect of the art that has an even stronger connection with the order of the cosmos—the nineteenth century witnessed an explosion, a fragmentation that transformed Persian music in its entirety. Time was fragmented both in the structure of performances (*nowbe* as against *taqsīm*) and in measured pieces that abandoned long cycles of 9, 12, 24, or 32 beats and long compositions. Only a few basic formulas were used, not exceeding 3/2 or 6/8 time (as in the *taṣnīf*, *reng*, and *pīsh-darāmad*). Within this narrow frame, individualized rhythmic structures emerged, and each tune had its specific accompaniment.

This principle has reached its height in our day, when percussion accompaniments are so odd and formulas are so detailed that the rhythm player must know the melody by heart and in extreme cases must follow sheet music. In the past, the rhythmic cycle and the melody were subject to a limited number of immutable principles. It was enough to know the formulas and to apply them passively to the corresponding tune. Together with the explosion of rhythmic cycles, the very framework of beats was seriously questioned, not only in unmeasured rhythms which are the basis of the *radīf* but, more subtly, in pieces that appear to be measured. For example, percussion that is regular must adapt to well-established time formulas which cannot be reduced to a formal measure or even a pulse. Between rubato and the subdivisions of pulse, some contemporary melodies defy classical musical analysis or at least make a radical break with classicism.

More recently, cassette recordings have led to new forms of performance that break completely with traditional performance conditions, which had already been modified by the demands of concert halls. Studio musicians see the music as a layering of sounds (using multiple tracks) and a montage of various discrete sequences. Thus they radically change all the techniques of musical notation and definitively break with the rules of orality, creating works "in vitro" (as it were) that are impossible to reproduce "in vivo."

Conclusion

Despite these signs of modernity, most Iranian musics remain attached to what musicians have defined as the immutable frames or axes of tradition. The slight changes in intervals foreseen by Vazīrī have been adopted only in theoretical treatises, modes have been preserved, and, even more curiously, no mode or modal type has been added for more than 150 years. The main instruments are still those of the nineteenth century, scarcely changed, despite the appearance of many new instruments, both Western (piano, violin, flute) and Eastern (*'ūd*, *qānūn*, and *rabāb*). Poetry and song still mobilize the public, and the sung *ghazal* remains the center of any musical performance, so much so that instrumentalists, breaking with the traditional separation of functions, have also begun to sing *taṣnif-hā*, solo or in a group, at the end of their concerts. Though some object to the ideology of the *ḥāl*, this objection is intended to purify it of its sensuality or elicit other kinds of emotion. The *ḥāl*, implicity opposed to technique or reason, remains the public's primary criterion. Beyond the formalism of classical tradition, the music refers to personal experience, insofar as the *ḥāl* alone guarantees authenticity. Perhaps this is why the progress of Iranian artists, although "modern," remains "traditional" insofar as the *ḥāl* is transpersonal, not individualized, permitting one to communicate by opening an intersubjective space while retaining one's own experience.

These observations do not allow us to conclude that the tradition will long retain the same system of values without being subjected to new conflicts. Perhaps the idea of tradition that I have described here, despite its historical and cultural universality, is susceptible to profound questioning. I sense that, in the East as elsewhere, music must learn to coexist with other visions of the world, which seek to go beyond the dichotomy between tradition and modernity. Perhaps all these currents simply announce the next redefinition of tradition.

TRANSLATED BY STEPHEN BLUM AND BETH RAPS.

REFERENCES

During, Jean. 1984. *La musique iranienne: Tradition et évolution*. Paris and Tehran: Institut Français d'Iranologie de Téhéran.

———. 1988. *Musique et extase: L'audition mystique dans la tradition soufie*. Paris: Albin Michel.

———. 1989a. *Musique et mystique dans les traditions de l'Iran*. Paris and Tehran: Institut Français de Recherches en Iran.

———. 1989b. "Les musiques d'Iran et du Moyen-Orient face à l'acculturation occidentale." In *Entre l'Iran et l'Occident: Adaptation et assimilation des idées et techniques occidentales en Iran*, ed. Yann Richard, 195–223. Paris: Éditions de la Maison des Sciences de l'Homme.

——— (with Zia Mirabdolbaghi and Dariush Safvat). 1991a. *The Art of Persian Music*. Washington D.C.,: Mage.

———. 1991b. *Le répertoire-modèle de la musique persane: Radif de târ et de setâr de Mirzâ 'Abdollâh*. Tehran: Sorūsh.

———. 1994. *Quelque chose se passe: Le sens de la tradition dans l'Orient musical*. Lagrasse: Verdier.

Gobineau, Joseph-Arthur, Comte de. [1859] 1983. *Trois ans en Asie (de 1855 à 1858)*, ed. Jean Gaulmier. In Gobineau, *Oeuvres*, 2:27–401. Paris: Gallimard (Bibliothèque de la Pléiade, 311).

Kīānī, Majīd. [1368] 1371. *Haft dastgāh-e mūsīqī-ye Īrān*. Tehran: Author and Mo'asese-ye Sāz-e Now Rūz.

Nettl, Bruno. [1987] 1992. *The Radif of Persian Music: Studies in Structure and Cultural Context*. Champaign, Ill.: Elephant and Cat.

Safvat, Dariush. 1984. "Musique et mystique," trans. Jean During. *Études Traditionnelles* 483:42–54, 484:94–109.

Varzi, Morteza. 1988. "Performer-Audience Relationships in the *Bazm*." In *Cultural Parameters of Iranian Musical Expression*, ed. Margaret Caton and Neil Siegel, 1–9. Redondo Beach, Calif.: Institute of Persian Performing Arts.

A New Approach to the Theory of Persian Art Music: The *Radīf* and the Modal System

Dariush Talai

The *Radīf*
Twentieth-Century Theories of Persian Music
The Modal System

The repertoire of Persian art music, together with its traditional order of classification, is called the *radīf*. To understand the concept of the *radīf* we must first understand that the *radīf* and the modal system are not identical. The *radīf* is a repertoire of melodies collected by different people at different times. Unlike Western art music, which is meant to be played exactly as written, the *radīf* is made up of traditional melodies, many of them derived from popular and folk sources, their origins obscured by the passage of time. I shall call them "flexible melodies" and discuss them at greater length below. The position of each melody in the *radīf* is determined by its modal characteristics. All the modes used in Persian art music can be found in the *radīf* but are not derived from it. Thus the discussion here presents the *radīf* as a repertoire organized by musicians to be used for both performance and instruction. The melodies of the *radīf* and the modal system are considered separately.

THE *RADĪF*

> The *radīf* is the principal emblem and the heart of Persian music. (Nūr 'Alī Borūmand)

The repertoire of Persian melodies was first organized into the *radīf* in the mid-nineteenth century. We do not know why Persian musicians formulated the idea of a *radīf* at this particular time. Even before then, they undoubtedly had their own store of memorized music, used for both teaching and performance; but perhaps the *radīf* aided them in their teaching, or perhaps the idea of a musical repertoire arose from their contact with Western music (Nettl 1992:4).

We do know that when the Qajars moved the capital to Tehran, and especially when Naṣr al-Dīn Shāh (r. 1848–1896) encouraged and protected artists, the best musicians migrated from other cities to Tehran, where they were patronized by the court of the shah and the princes or played at social gatherings. There was often an implicit but friendly rivalry among musicians who performed at these gatherings. Such occasions gave them an opportunity to exchange knowledge about music.

Mīrzā 'Abdollāh and Āqā Ḥosein Qolī

The oldest known *radīf-hā* come from two masters who were also brothers, Mīrzā 'Abdollāh (c.1843–1918) and Āqā Ḥosein Qolī (d. 1913). They spent a lifetime teaching their *radīf* with incredible conviction and rigor, and they educated the best musicians of the next generation. Their students were supposed to memorize the entire repertoire; therefore, it was important that the *radīf* be both complete and brief—as concise as possible. Since different people played the same melody in different ways, these two masters selected from among many versions of a melody to create their *radīf*.

Mīrzā 'Abdollāh's *radīf* contains about 250 pieces (*gūshe-hā*) organized into seven large complexes (*dastgāh-hā*) and five smaller, simpler ones (*āvāz-hā*). The same organization is found in all subsequent *radīf-hā*, but the number of *gūshe-hā* as well as their nomenclature and placement varies somewhat. The twentieth-century vocal master Mahmūd Karīmī left us a *radīf* with 145 *gūshe-hā*. The *radīf* of the *tār* and *setār*—plucked long-necked lutes—has more *gūshe-hā* because it includes all the vocal melodies as well as melodies just for instruments, such as *chahārmeżrāb-hā, reng-hā,* and the *gūshe-hā* of Baste Negār, Majles Afrūz, and others.

Since the idea of a *radīf* had originated with a family of musicians who played the *tār* and *setār,* the earliest *radīf-hā* are intimately linked to these instruments. Moreover, because the precise use of the *meżrāb* 'plectrum' or 'index fingernail' was very important for performance on the *tār* and *setār*, the melodies, often derived from vocal sources, necessarily became more regularized and structured. They also took on the performance style of the musicians, who—as artists and scholars of the tradition—transformed them into elaborate, cerebral art music.

The creation of a *radīf* to be used as a didactic tool and a basis for performance was a radical departure for the musicians of mid-nineteenth-century Persia. Most of the masters were reluctant to teach what they knew: they had gained their knowledge with difficulty, and each was distinguished by his individual mastery of his repertoire. For example, the father of Mīrzā 'Abdollāh and Āqā Ḥosein Qolī, Āqā 'Alī Akbar Farāhanī, who was a great *tār* player, died when his sons were children. Their uncle, Āqā Gholām Ḥosein, who was also a great *tār* player and became their stepfather, refused to teach them. To learn his repertoire, they were obliged, in their words, to "steal the pieces" by listening from outside the door when he practiced.

Sources of *gūshe-hā*

Each *gūshe* has a particular name and a distinct character. The origins of the *gūshe-hā* are diverse. Some, like those called *darāmad*, have a primarily modal role and are presumably derived from the principal *maqāmāt* 'modes' of ancient Persian music. Other kinds of *gūshe-hā* are recognized by their specific melodies. Their sources include folk and popular music; religious occasions (such as the *ta'ziye*); Sufi poetry and song; music associated with heroism, in particular descriptions of battle scenes when the *Shāh-nāme* (Iran's national epic) is performed in teahouses; and the traditional gymnasium *zūr-khāne*, where athletic exercises are accompanied by music.

Our information about the sources and formation of the *radīf* is not just hypothetical. The process of formation is ongoing: in the twentieth century, several new *gūshe-hā* were added to the repertoire. Abolḥasan Ṣabā (1902–1957)—a master of the *radīf*, a composer, and an influential teacher of Persian classical music—included melodies from the Caspian region in such *gūshe-hā* as *Deylamān* and *Amīrī*, and a melody from the dervish tradition called *Ṣadrī*. Maḥmūd Karīmī added *bayāt-e Shīrāz*, inspired by the music of the Azerbaijani *muğam* (the Azerbaijani pronunciation of *maqām*) of the same name, to the *āvāz* of *bayāt-e Eṣfahān*. As a part of his *radīf*, Ḥasan Kasā'ī, a famous master of the *ney*, played music such as the *gūshe hadāvandī*, which he attributed to his native city of Eṣfahān. 'Abdollāh Davāmī, the great master and transmitter of the *radīf*, who was inspired by the *radīf* of the *tār* and *setār*, created a vocal version of the *dastgāh* of *rāst panjgāh* for his *radīf*.

TRACK 28 The original nineteenth-century *radīf-hā* were created for players of the *tār* and *setār.* In the twentieth century, partial *radīf-hā* were created for other instruments, such as violin, *kamānche* 'spike fiddle', *santūr* 'hammered dulcimer', and *ney* 'end-blown flute'. Two complete vocal *radīf-hā* were recorded, one by 'Abdollāh Davāmī and the other by his pupil Maḥmūd Karīmī.

TRACK 8–4

Notation of the *radīf*

When Iranian musicians learned about Western music and musical notation, they began to notate the *radīf*, a valuable part of the heritage of Persian music that had previously been preserved by memorization. The first notators were Salar Mo'azzez (the student and successor of a French music instructor in Iran, Alfred Lemaire), Mehdī Qolī Hedāyat, and 'Alī Naqī Vazīrī. The first *radīf* to be published—by the ministry of culture and arts, in 1963—was the *tār radīf* of Mūsā Ma'rūfī. In the 1970s, the *radīf-hā* of several masters were recorded as well. As a result of efforts since the time of Mīrzā 'Abdollāh to preserve and make available the melodies of the *radīf*, we now have access to several versions, both recorded and notated.

Flexible melodies

As mentioned above, the melodic parts of the *radīf* are what I call "flexible melodies." Flexible melody is common in all kinds of music in Iran, especially in the very widespread unmeasured melodies, whose rhythm depends on the meter of the poetry. When Persian poetry is recited or sung, both long and short syllables are articulated in flexible units of time; nonetheless, short syllables are always sustained for a shorter time than long ones. Performances of flexible melodies vary because people have performed them many times under different circumstances. Such variations should be considered not as improvisation but as an aura infusing a melody; this aura is part of an ethnic or group collective memory of the melody—a memory that includes the melody itself, any poetry accompanying it, and its historical context.

TWENTIETH-CENTURY THEORIES OF PERSIAN MUSIC

The main intention of the creators of the *radīf* was to produce an organized repertoire for Persian music; they were not necessarily trying to impose an order on the modal system. Thus the relationship of the modes to this system was not clarified, and its pedagogy included no theoretical or explicative terms.

At the beginning of the twentieth century, Iranians tended to see the West as an ideal model. Western music had already been taught in Iran for more than three decades, and a number of Iranians had a thorough education in it. In fact, some of them questioned the value of Iranian music as a serious, dignified art and doubted that it should be taught in an institutional program of music study. Others, however, motivated in part by a spirit of nationalism, tried to revive Persian music and to create a theory relating it more closely to the perspective of Western classical music, which they regarded as more progressive.

The first person to develop a theory of Persian music was 'Alī Naqī Vazīrī, an exceptionally energetic leader. He had been a colonel in the army before he became a "soldier" of Iranian music, studying music in Europe and then returning to establish the first conservatory of Persian music in Tehran in 1923. Vazīrī was an accomplished *tār* player and knew the *radīf* well. In his study of Western music, he encountered the Western concept of modes. With this background he formulated a theory in which the *radīf* represented the Persian modal system. According to his system, each *dastgāh* consisted of a scale, for which he used the French word *gamme*, in turn consisting of two tetrachords separated by a whole step, as in a Western scale. In each scale, in which the signs for half-flat (*koron*) and half-sharp (*sorī*) are also used, the modal character of the *gūshe* was determined by the way each note of the melody functioned. For Vazīrī, three scale pitches were especially important: the most frequently repeated pitch (*shāhed*), the variable pitch (*motaghayyer*), and the pitch (*īst*) that ended most phases of the whole *gūshe.* Vazīrī's theory, in which individual *gūshe-hā* are modal genetic formulas, remains the basis of Persian modal concepts to this day.

However, the lack of a careful separation between the concept of modes and melodies immediately led to confusion among both musicians and scholars as to the nature of Persian music. Later, there was a split between musicians who remained faithful to the traditional melodies of the *radīf* and those who developed a more personal and quickly attainable form of musical expression based on modal elements: these two groups tended not to associate with one another, and they developed a mutual disregard. The *radīf* players used the term *moṭreb*—someone whose musical goal is solely entertainment—to describe the others, who for their part considered the music of the *radīf* players scholarly, *khoshk* 'dry', and lacking in artistic substance.

From the 1970s through the 1990s, both Iranian and Western musicologists were initiated into Persian music by scholars who believed that the *radīf* was its only worthwhile manifestation. As a result, musicologists studying Persian art music have often placed too much emphasis on the *radīf* as a modal system. For example, musicologists tried to define the term *gūshe* independently of the rest of the descriptive phrase of which it is usually a part. Its literal meaning is "corner," and it has no other sense than "piece" or "part." For Iranian musicians, what identifies a *gūshe* is its particular name—for example, *gūshe-ye gīlākī*.

Twentieth-century musicologists have also placed too much emphasis on analytically distinguishing different Iranian musical styles, such as folk, popular, religious, and classical or art music. But in reality there has always been tension and interplay between art music and the less formal genres. As Nayeb Asadollāh, the great *ney* master of the nineteenth century, said of himself, "I brought the *ney* from the sheep pen to the court of the shah." What made this interplay particularly vital in the Iranian context was the hostility of the religious establishment to music during various historical periods. At such times music could survive only as folk, religious, or dervish music, or as music accompanying storytelling—all of which were tolerated.

THE MODAL SYSTEM

I wish to propose a new way of understanding modes, combining the living repertoire of Persian modes both in their complex organization in the *radīf* and in their simpler and popular forms such as the *taṣnīf.* Interestingly, we see that although the melodies have vocal sources and may have a vocal character, their modal framework is closely related to the technical aspects of stringed instruments such as *'ūd*, *kamānche*, and *setār*. Therefore, in addition to the modes commonly used in folk, popular, and classical music, we will also consider the instruments used to perform them.

The fretting and tuning of stringed instruments was directly connected to the development of modes. We can deduce this from the fact that stringed instruments have been used to study intervals and tetrachords from antiquity, and from the fact that in the past, musicians were poet-singers first of all, accompanying their poetry and song with stringed instruments. The tuning of the strings and the frets guided the modal framework of the vocal phrasing. The purpose of this discussion is to show that Persian modes are based on a very solid intellectual construct. They can be better analyzed and understood on their own terms first, before we analyze melody.

Mode and interval

The modal system of Persian art music provides a set of frameworks. The system has much in common with the modal musics of this part of the world, such as those of the Turks, the Arabs, and to some extent the Indians. Two main dimensions, each characterized by intervals, are recognized: time and pitch. This conceptualization of time and pitch as two distinct phenomena is emphasized more in Persian music than in Western music.

The study of musical intervals is part of the study of harmonic laws; since antiquity, the octave, the fifth, and the fourth have been recognized as invariable, or fixed. The primary role of intervals and pitches in musical structures is confirmed by the perfect mathematical relationship between pitches when a string is divided in half, into thirds, or into quarters. In Persian music, the fourth is the most important interval and the smallest invariable interval. The usual tuning of the two melodic strings on the *tār* and *setār* is to a fourth. The third string, when it accompanies the first as a pedal tone, is tuned to the octave of the first string, which makes a fifth with the second string. The way these intervals work may be better understood as follows: when a fourth is inverted, it becomes a fifth, and the sum of the two intervals is an octave. For example, on the *setār* one would tune the highest string to C3 (middle C), the second to G2 (g below middle C), and the third to C2 (the octave below middle C).

Dāng **and interval**

For medieval scholars such as al-Kīndī (d. 874), al-Fārābī (d. 950), Ibn Sīnā (d. 1037), Ṣafī al-Dīn Urmavī (d. 1293), Qotb al-Dīn Shīrāzī (d. 1311), and ʿAbdolqāder Marāghī (d. 1435), the tetrachord, called *ẓolarbāʿ* in Arabic and *dāng* (plural, *dāng-hā*) in Persian, was the most important modal structural element. The tetrachord also corresponds to a physical area on the neck of instruments such as the *ʿūd*, *tār*, and *setār,* where the fingers can reach the notes without changing position. In medieval theories the open string (*moṭlaq*) and the names of the different fingers on the neck of the *ʿūd* designated the pitches used to make different sorts of tetrachords. The character of the tetrachord depends on the size of its two variable pitches (the intervals of the second and the third). Each tetrachord has its own unique genetic makeup.

Having studied the performance of Persian music and analyzed its intervals, I have concluded that all the Persian modes are based on four main kinds of *dāng-hā*, shown in figure 1 by the three intervals that separate the four notes of each *dāng*. These proposed intervals are in cents (based on a system whereby an octave is divided into 1,200 cents and each half tone is equal to 100 cents); each *dāng*, encompassing the interval of a fourth, is equal to 500 cents.

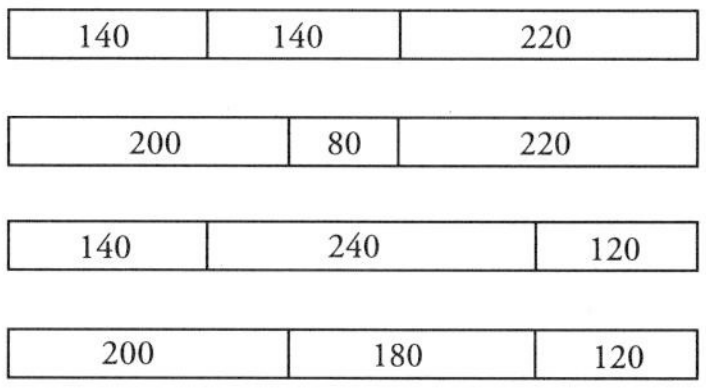

FIGURE 1 The four species of *dāng-hā*.

Figure 2 shows the names of the strings in the four kinds of *dāng-hā.* In the following discussion of modes, I name each of these *dāng-hā* by reference to its primary mode and identify each by the first letter of its name: C for *chahārgāh*, S for *shūr*, D for *dashtī*, and M for *māhūr*. I borrow the nomenclature used by medieval theorists and name the frets after the fingers that play them: *sabbāba*, *wusṭā*, *binṣir,* and *khinṣir*. *Zā'id* is an extra fret not named after a finger.

These *dāng-hā,* when played in the first position on a stringed instrument, are performed as shown in figure 2; but when they are transposed and interact, they must somehow be tempered because of the limitation imposed by the fixed intervals. The most common transposition occurs when the first pitch of the tetrachord begins on the *sabbāba* fret. For instance, on a two-stringed instrument whose strings are tuned to a fourth, the performer plays one *dāng* on the lower-pitched string beginning with the open string, and a second on the higher-pitched string. The performer begins to play the third *dāng* on the *sabbāba* fret of the higher string, which allows him to reach

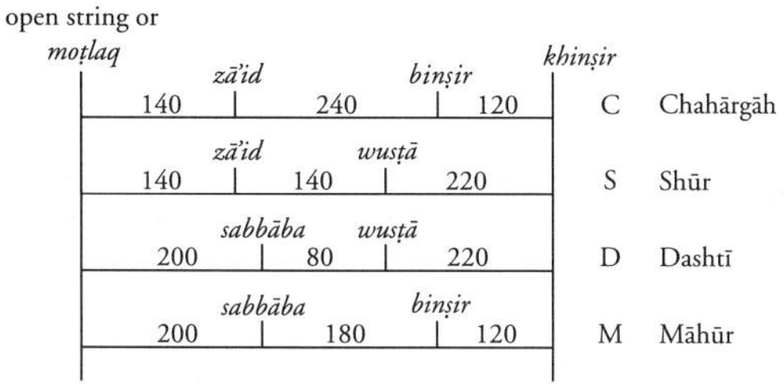

FIGURE 2 String names of the four kinds of *dāng-hā*.

the range of an octave. This transposition is an important modal shift that can be heard in both folk and popular music. The function of this process, called *owj* 'ascent', is obvious in simple musical forms whose range is about an octave.

In figure 3, the *dāng* beginning on the G string is G, AP, B♭, and C. The *dāng* on the C string is C, D, E♭, and F; and the third *dāng* starting from the *sabbāba* of the C string is D, EP, F, and G. The symbol P stands for *koron*, a pitch between, for instance, B♭ and B. In this figure, *dashtī*, one of the most common modes, is shown on a two-stringed instrument. To complete the octave, the *dāng* of *shūr* used for the *owj*, which is basically the same as the *shūr dāng* on the G string, is tempered—that is, the size of all three intervals is changed slightly to conform to the fixed frets.

To indicate all the frets used in one octave of a Persian stringed instrument, figure 4 shows the four main *dāng-hā* and their transpositions to the *sabbāba* and *khinṣir* frets. The main *dāng-hā*—*māhūr*, *chahārgāh*, *dashtī*, and *shūr*—begin with the open string. *Owj* and *shūshtarī* (the name of a *gūshe*) would begin on the *sabbāba* fret, and *zābol* (another *gūshe*) begins on the *khinṣir* fret and requires one additional fret not used in the other *dāng-hā*. Just as *owj* is the tempered version of the *shūr dāng*, *shūshtarī* may be seen as the tempered version of *chahārgāh*. *Zābol* is the same as *chahārgāh*.

Figure 5 shows the actual frets on the neck of the *tār* from which all the above *dāng-hā* will be derived. The frets on either side of the intervals of 60, 70, and 30 cents (DP and D, for instance) are never used in succession in Persian music. The interval relationships above G on the C string are the same as in the open string G in the octave below.

Tempered intervals

In practice, the intervals are never precise. They fluctuate between those we have called the four basic *dāng-hā* in figure 1 and their tempered forms in figure 6 (which shows the tempered form of the intervals in figure 4). The more complex the system and the greater the transposition and interaction of the *dāng-hā*, the more the intervals

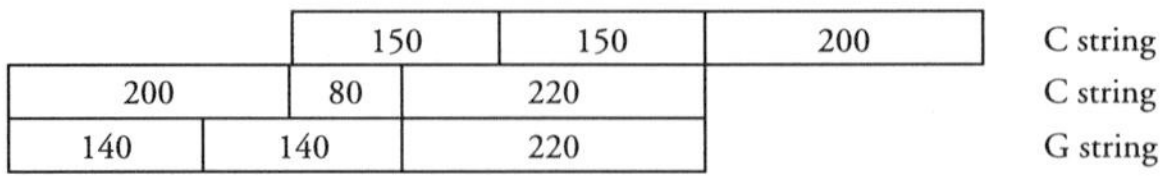

FIGURE 3 *Dashtī* mode on a two-stringed instrument.

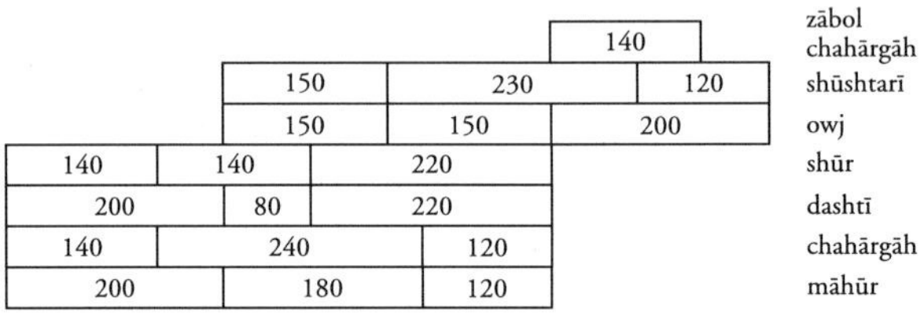

FIGURE 4 The four main *dāng-hā* and their transpositions to the *sabbāba* and *khinṣir* frets.

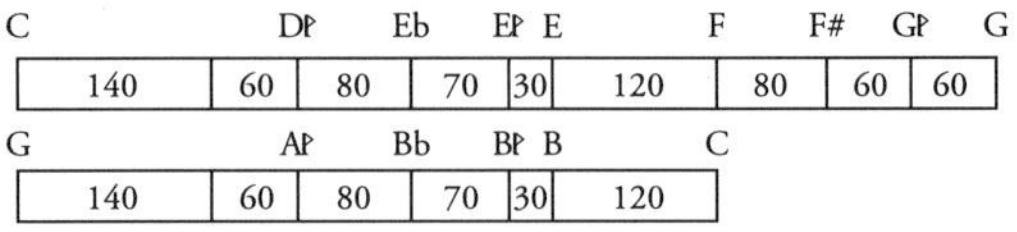

FIGURE 5 Actual frets on the *tār* from which the preceding *dāng-hā* are derived.

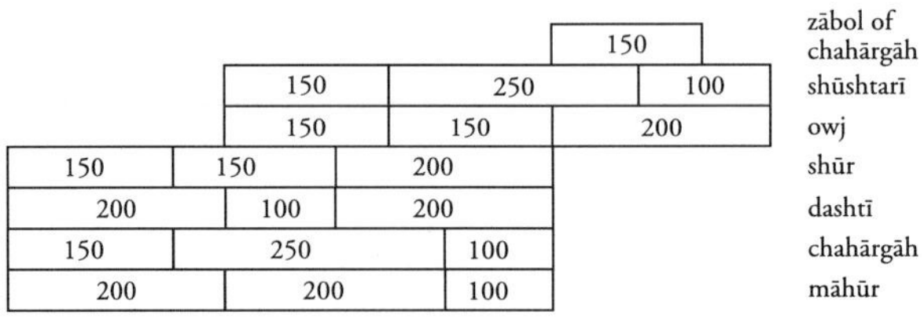

FIGURE 6 Tempered form of the intervals shown in figure 4.

need to be tempered on fretted stringed instruments. Since the intonation that results from tempering the intervals bothers the best musicians, the frets on the *tār* and *setār* have always remained movable, allowing the player to adjust them for each performance to achieve the most suitable tuning for each combination of modes. In the simple modes of folk and popular music, the intervals are closer to those of the basic *dāng-hā*. Moreover, the tempered intervals are better tolerated, for example, in the *dāng* of *māhūr* than in *chahārgāh*.

Māye

Here, I use *māye* (plural, *māye-ha*) in the sense of mode. However, there is no consensus among Persian theorists as to its exact meaning; it can also express such concepts as tonality and modal melody. The term *maqām* can also be used in this sense, interchangeably with *māye*. Actually, the term *māye* does not exist in the *radīf* system. When Persian musicians use this word among themselves, it refers to a unique mode in the context of Persian art music, whose organization and performance are multimodal. However, a Western musician, looking for a Persian equivalent of *mode*, would choose *māye*.

Each *māye* is made up of two *dāng-hā* in succession. Usually, the stress of the melodies in a given *māye* is on the note shared by the two *dāng-hā*. This pitch is most often the first note of the second *dāng*, but it can also be the second note or, more rarely, the third. Thus several *māye-hā* may share the same *dāng-hā* but be distinguished by their different stressed pitches. All together, I have identified eleven different ways of arranging the *dāng-hā* for the *māye-hā*. I have named them after the most important *gushe-hā* in which they appear in the *radīf* (figure 7).

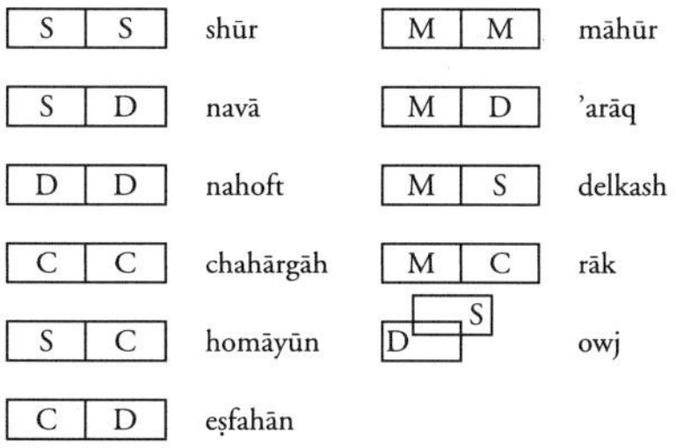

FIGURE 7 Arrangement of *dāng-hā* in the *māye-hā* of Persian art music.

All Persian modes are built on bitetrachordal systems, two conjunct tetrachords. However, other factors can also be involved in the distinction and realization of each mode. The main elements in this process are:

1. Type of bitetrachord
2. *Shāhed* 'witness'
3. *Īst* 'stop'
4. *Motaghayyer* 'variable'

Two secondary elements may be added. In certain situations, such as a free performance of modes, these elements may be considered confining and can be neglected:

5. Melodic curve
6. Melodic types peculiar to each *gūshe*

Dastgāh and āvāz

When Persian, Arabic, and Turkish music is performed, modes are combined. Mastering the art of combining them is one of the most important aspects of performance of these art musics. In Persian music, when two different *māye-hā* share a *dāng*, this *dāng* can be used as a bridge to modulate from one *māye* to the other. The modal structure of each *dastgāh* and *āvāz* is a combination of several *māye-hā* in a special range and order. Although these combinations are ordered in a traditional manner, they are defined and taught not by means of any modal terminology but by their specific melodies (*gūshe-hā*), which match each step in the modal progression.

Modal structures

Figures 8 to 20 are charts of the modal structures on which all the *dastgāh-hā* and *āvāz-hā* in the *radīf* rely. The *dastgāh-hā* are *shūr*, *navā*, *segāh*, *chahārgāh*, *homāyūn*, *māhūr*, and *rāst panjgāh*. The *āvāz-hā* are *abū 'atā*, *afshārī*, *bayāt-e tork*, *dashtī*, and *eṣfahān*. *Bayāt-e kord* is also played independently like an *āvāz*, but in the *radīf* it is

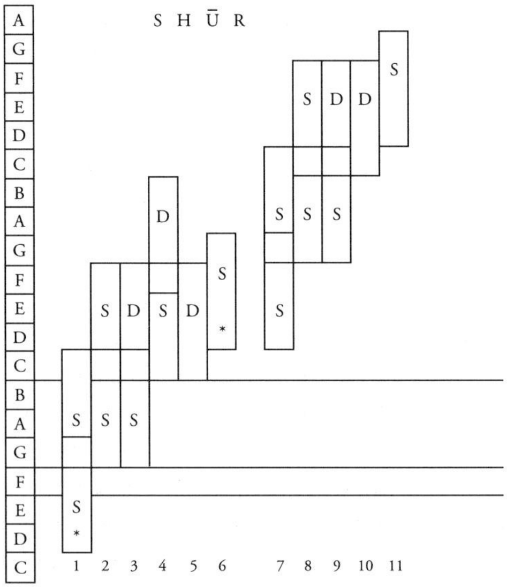

1. Darāmad of shūr
2. Owj
3. Salmak
4. Bozorg
5 and 6. ʿOzzal
7. Darāmad of shūr-e pa'in daste
8 and 9. Shahnāz, qarache, and razavī
10 and 11. Owj in shahrāshūb
(*Asterisks enclose an octave.)

FIGURE 8 Modal structure of *dastgāh shūr*.

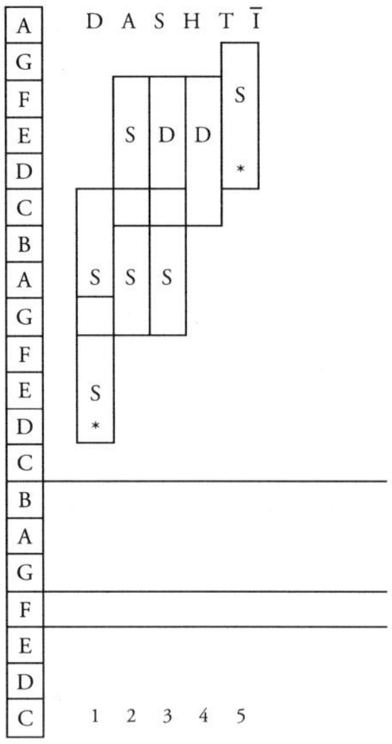

1, 2, and 3. Dashtī
5 and 6. Owj

FIGURE 9 Modal structure of *āvāz dashtī*.

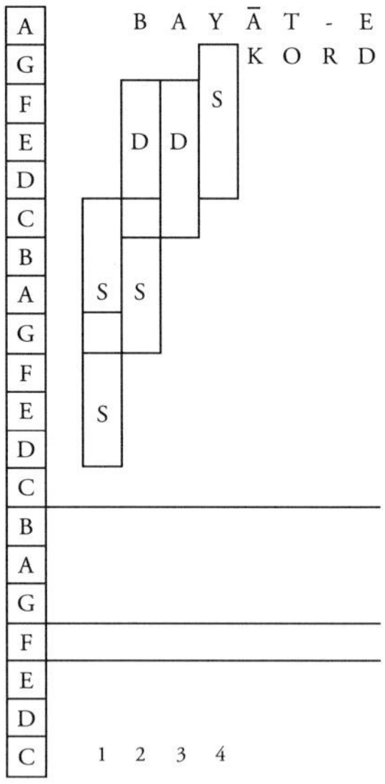

1 and 2. Bayāt-e kord
3 and 4. Owj

FIGURE 10 Modal structure of *bayāt-e kord*.

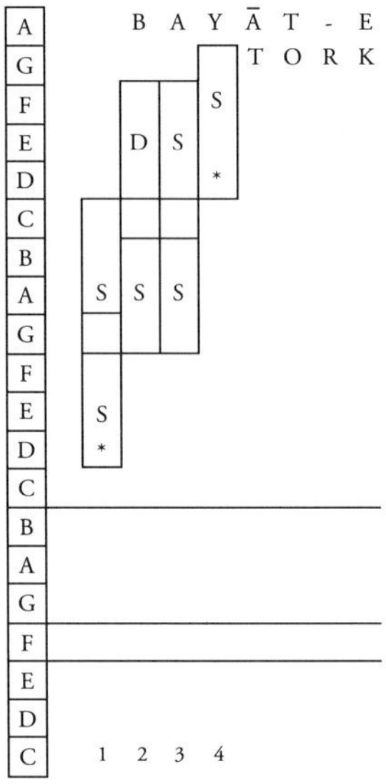

1 and 2. Bayāt-e tork
1. Ruḥ ol-arvāh
2. Mehrabānī
3 and 4. Shekaste

FIGURE 11 Modal structure of *āvāz bayāt-e tork*.

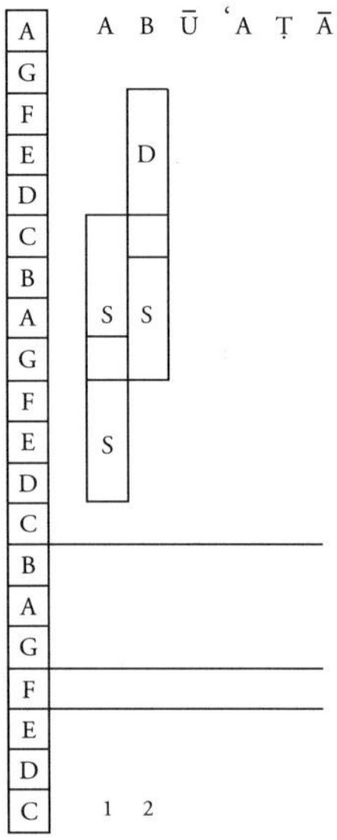

1. Abū ʿaṭā
2. Hejāz

FIGURE 12 Modal structure of *āvāz abū ʿaṭā*.

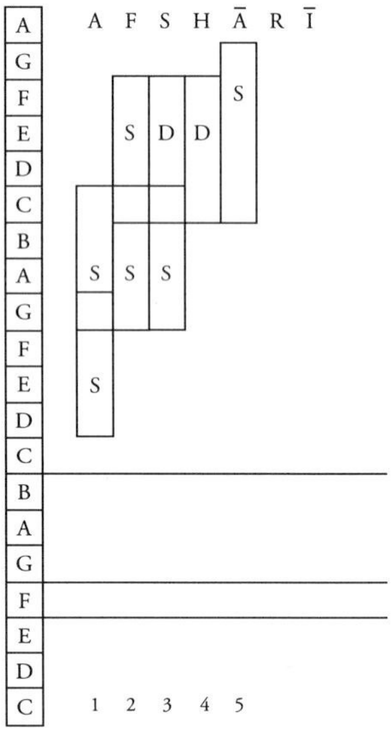

1, 2, and 3. Afshārī
4 and 5. ʿArāq

FIGURE 13 Modal structure of *āvāz afshārī*.

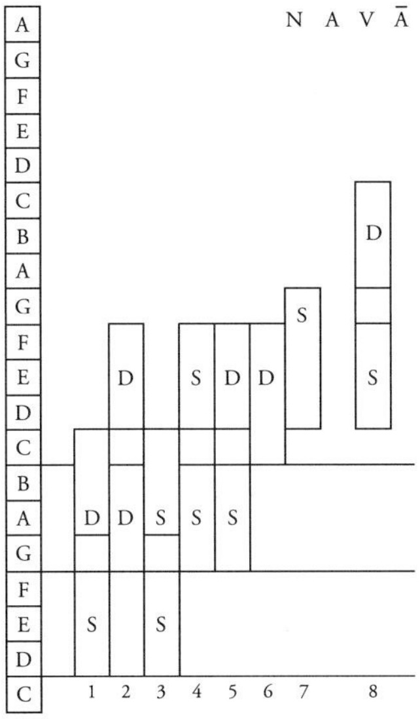

1. Darāmad of navā
1. Bayāt-e rāje (The stressed pitch is A.)
2. Nahoft
3. 'Ashīrān
4. Gavesht
5. Khojaste
5 and 7. Ḥosein
8. Būsalīk

FIGURE 14 Modal structure of *dastgāh navā*.

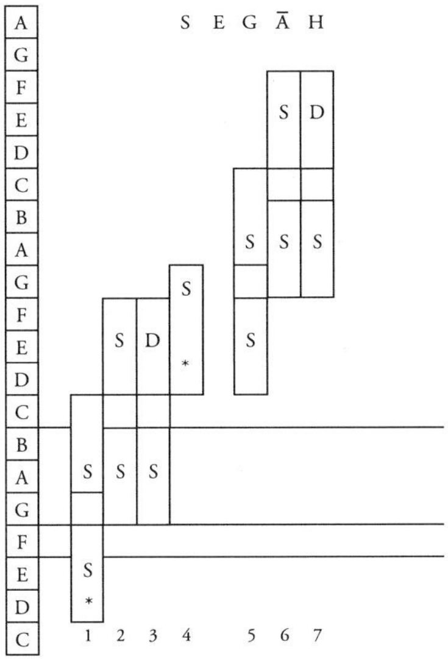

1 and 2. Darāmad of segāh
2. Zābol (Stressed pitch is C.)
2. Mūye (Stressed pitches are D♭ and Eb.)
3 and 4. Heṣār (C, D from number 3 and E♭, F, G from number 4. Stressed pitch is E♭.)
2 and 4. Mokhālef (C, D♭ from number 2 and E♭, F, G from number 4. The stressed pitch is F.)
5. Maqlūb
5 and 6. Rahāb and masīhī
5, 6, and 7. Shāh Khatā'ī
(* Asterisks enclose an octave.)

FIGURE 15 Modal structure of *dastgāh segāh*.

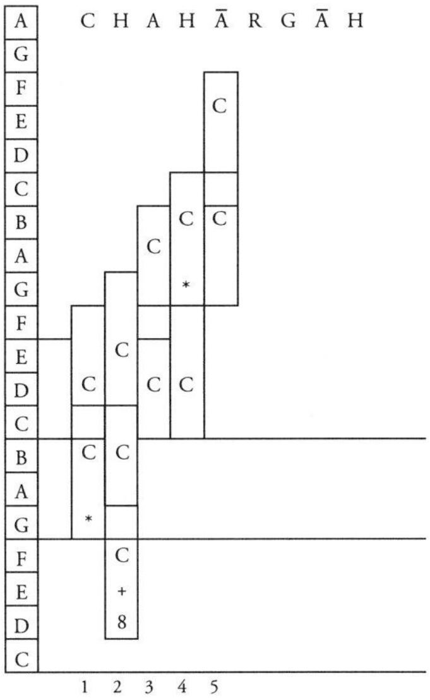

Lower C string serves primarily as a pedal tone (*vākhūn*), and the two other strings are the melody strings.

1. Darāmad of chahārgāh (Stressed pitch is C.)
1. Zābol (Stressed pitch is E.)
2. Heṣār is played one octave above (+ 8) and the G shown as stressed pitch is for this *gusheh*.
3. Mūye
4. Mokhālef and maghlūb
5. Manṣūrī
(* Asterisks enclose an octave.)

FIGURE 16 Modal structure of *dastgāh chahārgāh*.

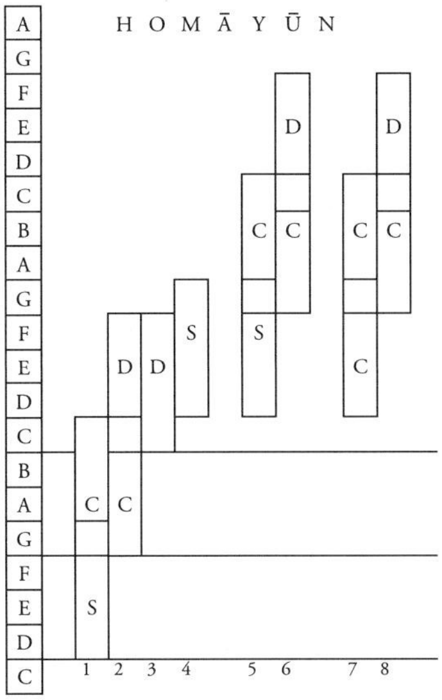

1. Darāmad of homāyūn
2. Chakāvak
2. Bīdād
3 and 4. Owj of bīdād
5 and 2. Nowrūz-e 'arab
6. Shūshtarī
7 and 8. Mavāliān

FIGURE 17 Modal structure of *dastgāh homāyūn*.

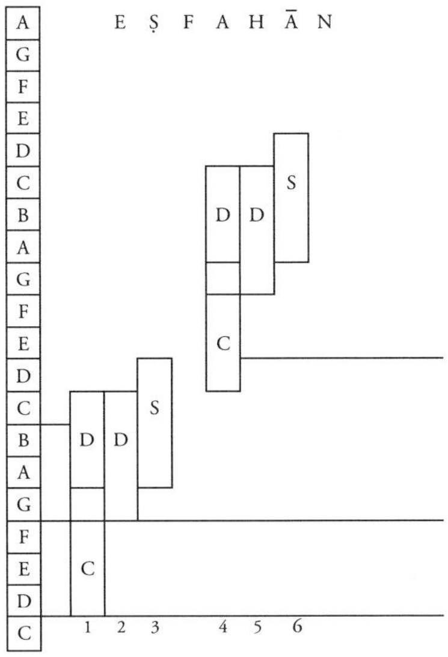

4. Eṣfahān
5 and 6. Owj
1, 2, and 3. Forūd (This part is the same as 4, 5, and 6 an octave lower, used for the descent of the *avaz*.)

FIGURE 18 Modal structure of *āvāz eṣfahān*.

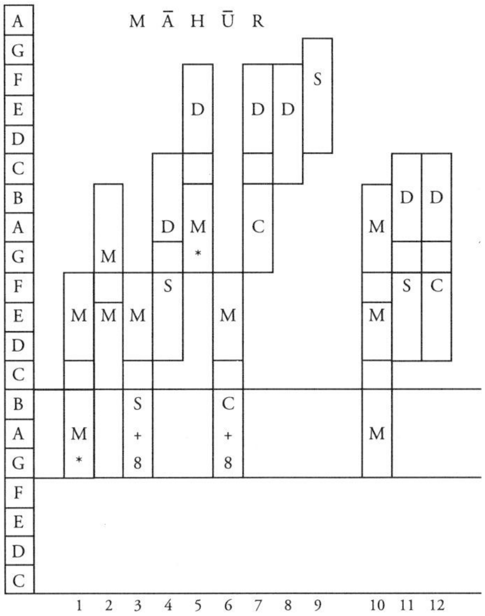

Lower C string serves primarily as a pedal tone (*vakhun*), and the two other strings are the melody strings.

1. Darāmad of māhūr
2. Heṣār māhūr (or pas māhūr)
3. Delkash
4. Shekaste
5. 'Arāq
6. Rāk
7. Rāk and Eṣfahānak
8 and 9. Ṣafīr-e rāk and ashūr
10. Sāqī nāme
11. Koshte
12. Ṣūfī nāme

FIGURE 19 Modal structure of *dastgāh māhūr*.

not counted as an independent *āvāz*; thus, the total number remains twelve: seven *dastgāh-hā* and five *āvāz-hā*. In figures 8 to 20:

1. The vertical keyboard at the left of each chart shows the widest range used for Persian music, six *dāng-hā*. These charts use the conventional pitches chosen for notation of the *radīf* of the *tār* and *setār*. In practice, the instruments can be tuned as much as a fourth lower (but not higher) than the conventional pitches.
2. The numbers along the bottom of the charts show the different components of the *dastgāh* structure. (The numbers are also used for reference in these comments.)
3. Because the position of the *māye-hā* and their relation to the open strings is important, the *dastgāh-hā* are presented with reference to the position used in the oldest *radīf*, that of Mīrzā 'Abdollāh. The horizontal lines designate the tuning of the open strings of the *tār* or *setār* for each *dastgāh*. Thus the tuning in *shūr*, for instance, is f, g, and c.
4. On the vertical keyboard, the thicker bottom line of a pitch shows that it is the stressed pitch in one of the sections of the *dastgāh*.
5. Two *dāng-hā* combined to form a *māye* have a pitch in common (except for the *māye-hā* of *delkash* and *rāk*). In the charts this pitch is designated as a square between the two *dāng-hā*. In Persian music, when an instrument does not have the high range of a melody, the pitches that are too high would ordinarily be transposed to the octave below. This means that the position of the two *dāng-hā* of the *māye* would be reversed (the higher would be played an octave lower). To better show the relationship of the *māye-hā* in the *dastgāh*, the *dāng-hā* for all the *māye-hā* are shown in the position in which they share a pitch. But *dāng-hā* designated + 8 are played an octave higher in the *dastgāh* of *māhūr* in numbers 3 and 6 and in the *dastgāh* of *chahārgāh* in number 2.
6. The *māye* of *owj* is shown throughout with the higher *dāng* only one tone higher than the *dāng* to its left, instead of stacked vertically. In *shūr*, for instance, *owj* appears in steps 6 and 11.
7. The names of the *gūshe-hā* listed below each chart are not all of the *gūshe-hā* in any given *māye* but the most important ones, which have a significant and distinctive modal character.

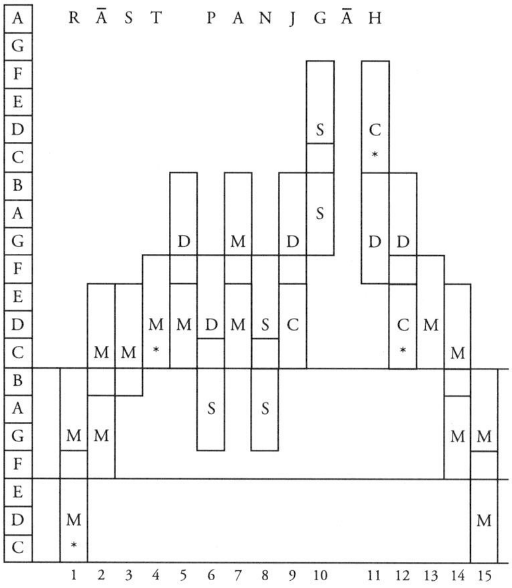

1 and 2. Rāst
3 and 4. 'Arāq (same function as owj)
5. 'Arāq and nahīb
6. Panjgāh and rūhafzā
6 and 4. 'Oshshāq
7. Sepehr
8. Bayāt-e 'ajam and qarache
9. Ṭarz and abolchap
10. Nowruz 'Arab and māvarā ol-nahr
11, 12, 13, 14, and 15. Farang (15 forūd)
(* Asterisks enclose an octave.)

FIGURE 20 Modal structure of *dastgāh rāst panjgāh*.

Note: This article is used with the permission of Mazda Publishers, Cosa Mesa, California.

REFERENCES

Barkeshlī, Mehdī. 1976. *Gām-hā va Dastgāh-hā-ye Mūsīqī-e Irān* (Scales and Dastgāhs of Iranian Music). Tehran: Ministry of Art and Culture.

Farhat, Hormoz. 1990. *The Dastgāh Concept in Persian Music*. Cambridge: Cambridge University Press.

Hannāneh, Morteză. 1988. *Gām-hā-ye Gomsbodeh* (The Lost Scales). Tehran: Soroush.

Khāleqī, Ruhollāh. 1954–1956. *Sargozasht-e mūsīqī-ye Īrān*. 2 vols. Tehran: Ebn-e Sina.

Kīānī, Majīd. 1992. *Haft Dastgāh-e Mūsīqī-e Irān* (Seven Dastgāhs of Iranian Music). Tehran: Iran Seda SITC-126. (Sound recording.)

———. 1998. *Mabānī-ye Nazarī-e Mūsīqī-e Irān* (The Basic Theory of Iranian Music). Tehran: Sarvsetah Cultural Institute.

Marāghī, 'Abd-al-Qādir. 1977. *Maqāsid al-Alhān*, ed. Taqī Bīnesh. Tehran: BTNK.

———. 1987. *Jāmi' al-Alhān*, ed. Taqī Bīnesh. Tehran: Institute for Studies in Art and Culture.

Ma'rūfī, Mūsā, ed. 1963. *Radīf-e mūsīqī-ye Īrān*. Tehran: Ministry of Culture and Art.

Mashhūn, Hassan. 1994. *Tārīkh-e Mūsīqī-e Irān* (History of Persian Music). Tehran: Sīmorgh and Fākhteh.

Mas'ūdiye [Massoudieh], Mohammad Teqī. [1978]. 1997. *Radīf-e āvāzī-ye musīqī-ye sonnatī-ye Īrān*. 2nd ed. Tehran: Iranian Music Association.

Nettl, Bruno. [1987]. 1992. *The Radif of Persian Music: Studies of Structure and Cultural Context*, rev. ed. Champaign, Ill.: Elephant and Cat.

Talai, Dariush. 1999. *Traditional Persian Art Music: The Radif of Mirza Abdollah*. Costa Mesa, Calif.: Mazda. (Includes five compact disks recorded in 1992.)

Vazīrī, Ali Naqī. 1934. *Mūsīqī-ye nazarī*. Tehran: Tolū'.

Zonis, Ella. 1973. *Classical Persian Music: An Introduction*. Cambridge, Mass.: Harvard University Press.

Dance in Iran

Anthony Shay

Dance in an Islamic Context
Regional Folk Dances
Solo Improvised Dance

As one of the world's oldest and most enduring cultural, linguistic, and political entities, Iran has for centuries provided settings for dance. Iconographic evidence of dance is seen on pottery dated as early as 5000 B.C.E. (Zokā'1978–1979). Choreographic activity has been documented mainly in observations by foreigners, from antiquity to our own time, and in artworks such as prehistoric pottery, silver work from the Sasanian period (224–650 C.E.), and miniatures from the twelfth century on. Since there is in general a paucity of documentation, it is impossible to reconstruct the dance of any historical period exactly. However, some observers have speculated about this (De Warren and Williams 1973, Rezvani 1962), and the historical evidence indicates cultural continuity in both group and solo dance forms.

Iran is, and most likely has always been, a region of immense ethnic and linguistic diversity, open to influences from many cultures, and its dance traditions reflect this diversity. In this article, the term *Iranian* encompasses the cultural and aesthetic expression of a wide region, which is also the area covered by literary and art histories of Iran: the Caucasus, Iran, Afghanistan, and Muslim areas in the former Soviet Union such as Uzbekistan and Tajikistan—in other words, an area much greater than the contemporary nation-state of Iran.

Two basic types of dance are performed in this Iranian cultural sphere, and in the Middle East generally. The first is regional folk dancing, most often (but not exclusively) performed in groups. The second is solo improvised dance (sometimes referred to as *majlesī* 'social' or 'party'). This second form often evokes a strongly negative reaction, reflected, now as in the past, in attempts to ban public performances of solo improvised dance and to marginalize professional performers. People in this area of the world sometimes seem to have what I call a "choreophobic" mentality; yet the same people who might condemn a solo performance in one context will happily perform a solo dance in another context—for example, at a wedding—and despite political bans in both Iran and Afghanistan, people will put themselves at risk of severe penalties to perform solo dances at weddings. Evidently, then, solo improvised dance is an ambiguous symbol in Iranian society, powerful but at the same time highly negative. It is nonetheless loved, performed, and frequently staged—at present in the United States and formerly throughout the Iranian cultural sphere.

Most Muslims view dance as the least of the arts, if indeed they consider it an art form at all.

DANCE IN AN ISLAMIC CONTEXT

Every researcher of dance or music in North Africa, the Middle East, or Central Asia soon confronts the fact that music and especially dance are often regarded with ambivalence and even hostility. Most Muslims view dance as the least of the arts, if indeed they consider it an art form at all. Many writers attribute this negative view of dance to Islam, but often without citing any supporting evidence. The historian Albert Hourani's thoughtful explanation (1991) of the care with which medieval Muslim scholars discussed the propriety of music and dance has not been sufficiently heeded by modern scholars, who tend to oversimplify this crucial issue. Thus we find claims such as Metin And's comment that "the austerity and rigidity of Islam did much to discourage music and dance and waged a relentless war against them" (1959:13) and the ethnomusicologist Hormoz Farhat's statement, "At the outset, Islamic religious leaders had assumed a hostile attitude towards music, and regarded it as a corrupting frivolity" (1990:4). One noted specialist in ethnic dance, La Meri, observed incorrectly that "Mohammed himself banned music and dance, and the arts withered" (adding, though, "But somehow they managed to keep alive"; 1961:44).

Although some members of the *'ulemā'*, including Ayatollāh Rūhollāh Khomeinī, have anathematized dance and attempted to ban public performances, Muslims' attitudes toward dance and music are more complex and diverse than And, Farhat, and La Meri would have us believe. If the Prophet Muhammad had indeed explicitly forbidden music and dance, or if there were a clear statement to that effect in the Qur'ān, the issue would have been resolved long ago, and these performing arts would not exist in the Islamic world.

Dancing and dance events in "choreophobic" societies such as many Islamic areas of North Africa, the Middle East, and Central Asia have received little scholarly attention, though this is changing. Some writers have extended the category of dance in an Islamic context to include spiritual practices and martial arts that incorporate patterned rhythmic movement. Iranians almost universally state that dance is found only on happy occasions; by contrast, spiritual or religious contexts are generally serious and often commemorate tragic events such as Ḥosein's martyrdom at Karbalā', calling forth deep grief among the participants. This raises the issue of which patterned movements actually constitute dance in an Islamic context and which do not. In my view, whether an activity should be characterized as dance can be determined by the intention of the participants and their audiences. In the words of Bousseloub, "When a Muslim performs ablutions and prepares himself to pray, he mentally announces his intention to pray and to address God. . . . Intention is everything, and must be followed by action. Clearly, their intent is to use turning to communicate with God, not to dance. The word dance cannot be used in religious or holy terms, except perhaps in quotation marks" (interview, 12 February 1993).

Such terms as *whirling dervishes* or *dancing dervishes* and *Sufi dancing* need to be reexamined; we should hesitate before subsuming group movements of a spiritual nature under the rubric *dance*. For many Shi'a men living in urban centers in the

Iranian cultural sphere, coordinated movements performed by groups (such as those found in *ʿazādārī*, the *zūr-khāne*, *zekr*, and other Sufi activities) largely replace dance. Because of the religious and spiritual fervor associated with these activities, they are often more popular than dance as forms of group expression.

REGIONAL FOLK DANCES

The northern and western regions of the Iranian cultural sphere, including Georgia, Armenia, Daghestan, Azerbaijan, Kurdistan, and Lorestan, are the eastern terminus of a choreographic "belt" which begins in Europe and in which patterned line, circle, and semicircle dances constitute the most common form of choreographic expression (for descriptions of dances, see Hasanov 1988; Lisitsian 1956–1972). In the folk dances of this Iranian region, the dancers are often linked by hand-holding of various sorts. The leader often executes special figures and gestures with his or her hand, in which a kerchief is held, to signal changes in foot patterns, in movements, or in the direction in which the group is moving.

By contrast, in the eastern and southern parts of the Iranian sphere—such as Khorasan, Fars, the Persian Gulf region, Baluchistan, Afghanistan, Turkmenistan, Uzbekistan, and Tajikistan—although regional dances are also performed in groups, the dancers do not touch one another. These dancers often carry scarves, sticks, or other objects with which to emphasize their movements. Here, some scope for improvisation is possible because of the relative freedom of each dancer's body; however, the dancers still conceive of themselves as part of a group, moving together (for descriptions of dances, see Hamada 1978; St. John 1993).

All these dances are usually associated with the countryside, though they may sometimes be seen in urban areas, particularly the line and circle dances. Because such a dance involves numerous participants, it is commonly performed outdoors. The dances are characterized by regional styles and—unlike solo improvised dance—by short patterned choreographic phrases that are repeated and embellished with variations.

Regional dances (such as the examples in figures 1 and 2), particularly those performed in lines and circles, may be seen at various events in southern California and other parts of the United States that have large communities of Azerbaijanis, Kurds, Assyrians, and Armenians who gather for communal celebrations.

FIGURE 1 Rice harvest dance from the village of Qāsemābad, Gilan Province. Avaz, Anthony Shay's International Dance Theatre; photo by Darren Young, 1995.

SOLO IMPROVISED DANCE

Whereas the specifically regional dance forms are usually performed in village and tribal areas, solo improvised dancing is frequently associated with urban life. In contrast to the regional dances, this dance form is performed in a highly individual and idiosyncratic style, though in a strikingly uniform manner with respect to performance and the underlying aesthetic and creative impulses. Such dancing can be seen from Tiflis in Georgia to western China, from Khiva in Uzbekistan to Shīrāz in southwestern Iran, and in the Iranian diaspora, especially in southern California. In this dance form, within the specific stylistic framework improvisational creativity is potentially limitless. The folk, classical, professional, and social dancing of the urban population is of this type. This dance tradition is both domestic and professional; it is a part of comic improvised theater (*rū-ḥowżī*, *sīyāh-bāzī*) and also of women's domestic theater (*bāzī-hā-ye nemāyeshī*; see Bezā'ī 1965; Shay 1995a).

Solo improvised dance draws from a large, rich reservoir of movement practices. During the course of such dances, highly experienced performers, both professional and amateur, use the shoulders, hips, torso, and head, and even nuanced movements of the lips and eyebrows; in fact, movements of the torso and the facial features offer the greatest aesthetic and "transgressive" potential. The use of eyebrows and other facial features is an unusual choreographic feature, which makes this dance form unique in the Middle East. Beautiful, intricate hand and arm movements are also highly prized in Iranian solo improvised dance, both domestic and professional. Unlike the *mudra* movements and gestures of classical Indian dance forms, the sometimes complex hand movements in Iranian solo improvised dance are abstract. Miming is a basic aspect of women's domestic theater, *bāzī-hā-ye nemāyeshī*, but it is idiosyncratic rather than codified (Shay 1995b).

Thus a skilled individual dancer has at his or her disposal an almost unlimited repertoire of movements and formulas for movement that can be composed and recombined in a dazzling array; a truly creative dancer is able to give unique, excitingly fresh performances. In both public and private performances, an enormous variety and many combinations of movements and moods—serious, playful, sensual, joyful, graceful, ethereal—may be experienced.

FIGURE 2 Gilberto Melendez of Avaz in *chūb-bāzī*, a stick dance from Khorasan Province, Iran. Avaz, Anthony Shay's International Dance Theatre; photo by Darren Young, 1995.

Both improvisation and geometry inform many genres of Iranian art (see Shay 1997), and the most important characteristics of this dance tradition are its connection with other performance practices through the use of improvisation and its connection with other visual forms through the use of geometric elements.

In performance, improvisation is a paramount feature of this dance form. Rarely do performers self-consciously consider their next movement, for dancing is as "natural" to the dancer as his or her native language; it is another form of culturally learned behavior. Also, a dancer rarely sustains the same movement for a prolonged period; rather, the movements flow from one to another with no perceptible boundary except, perhaps, for a brief, artful pose. Interestingly, this continous flow of movement, which exists in all the arts, is of special aesthetic value not only in dance and music but in visual arts such as calligraphy, rug-making, and ceramics. This intrinsic feature of "movement" is almost universally observed and remarked on by musicologists and art historians (see Farhat 1990; Hill and Grabar 1964; Pope 1964; Yūsofī 1994).

With regard to geometry, the movements in solo improvised dancing proceed from an aesthetic impulse intricately linked with and based on the geometric aesthetic that informs the visual arts in the Iranian-Islamic context and infuses the visual environment of this region. The geometric elements of the dance become most apparent in an accomplished performance in which the dancer's movements may be punctuated by effective pauses that create momentary poses—generally some interesting geometric form, such as turning to the side and curving both arms in an arc, with the hands placed near the head; or, alternatively, extending the arms and hands away from the body in a linear figure extending from the shoulders, with the torso and head leaning away from the extended arms, creating a long diagonal.

Dancers may use wood, stone, or metal clappers or finger cymbals to accent the rhythmic patterns of the music. This practice is rarer today than it once was, but it is still common in stage presentations. Although other rhythms are present, the most popular meters for dance throughout the Iranian cultural sphere are 6/8 and 7/8, in several variations. A musical composition specifically suited to dance performances is called *reng*.

Solo improvised dancing is occasionally performed by more than one person at the same time. This is not really a contradiction in terms, because although several people are dancing—at a large party, for instance, a sizable group may dance simultaneously—each person performs mostly without reference to the others, and the movements are highly individual. This genre forms the basis for public stage performances that are no longer improvised but are fashioned into routines or choreography set and performed in unison by the dancers.

REFERENCES

And, Metin. 1959. *Dances of Anatolian Turkey*. New York: Dance Perspectives.

Bezā'ī, Bahrām. 1965. *Nemāyesh dar Īrān* (Theater in Iran). Tehran: Keivān.

De Warren, Robert, and Peter Williams. 1973. "Discovery in Persia." *Dance and Dancers* 24 (January):28–32.

Farhat, Hormoz. 1990. *The Dastgāh Concept in Persian Music*. Cambridge: Cambridge University Press.

Hamada, Geoffrey Mark. 1978. "Dance and Islam: The Bojnurdi Kurds of Northeastern Iran." M.A. thesis, University of California, Los Angeles.

Hasanov, Kamal. 1988. *Azərbaycan qədim folklor rəqsləri* (Folk Dances of Old Azerbaijan). Baku: Işıg.

Hill, Derek, and Oleg Grabar. 1964. *Islamic Architecture and Its Decoration*. Chicago: University of Chicago Press.

Hourani, Albert. 1991. *History of the Arab Peoples*. Cambridge, Mass.: Harvard University Press.

La Meri [Russell Merriweather Hughes]. 1961. "Learning the Danse du Ventre." *Dance Perspectives* 10:43–47.

Lisitsian, Srbui. 1958–1972. *Starinnye pliaski i teatrl'nye presdtavleniia armanskogo naroda* (Ancient Dance and Theater Performance of the Armenian Nation). 2 vols. Yerevan: Armenian Academy of Sciences.

Pope, Arthur Upham, et al. 1964–1965. "Calligraphy: An Outline History." In *A Survey of Persian Art*, ed. Arthur Upham Pope et al., Vol. 4:1707–1742. Costa Mesa, Calif.: Mazda.

Rezvani, Medjid. 1962. *Le théâtre et la danse en Iran*. Paris: Maisonneuve et Larose.

Shay, Anthony. 1995a. "Dance and Non-Dance: Patterned Movement in Iran and Islam." *Iranian Studies* 28:61–78.

———. 1995b. "*Bazi-ha-ye namayeshi*: Iranian Women's Theatrical Plays." *Dance Research Journal* 27(2):16–24.

———. 1997. "Choreophobia: Iranian Solo Improvised Dance as Transgressive and Potentially 'Out-of-Control' Behavior in the Southern California Diaspora." Ph.D. dissertation, University of California, Riverside.

———. 1999. *Choreophobia: Solo Improvised Dance in the Iranian World*. Costa Mesa, Calif.: Mazda.

St. John, Katherine. 1988. "Afghan Atan." *Viltis* 47(1):23–24.

———. 1989. "Afghan Dance." *Folk Dance Scene* 24(2):8–18.

———. 1993. "Cultural and Historical Study of Selected Women's Dance from Herat, Afghanistan, 1970–1980." M.A. thesis, Brigham Young University, Provo, Utah.

Yūsofī, Gholam Hosein. 1994. "Calligraphy." *Encyclopaedia Iranica*, 680–718. London: Routledge and Kegan Paul.

Zokā', Yahyā. 1978–1979. "Tārīkh-e raqs dar Īrān" (A History of Dance in Iran). *Honar va Mardom* 16(188):2–12; 16(189):2–7; 16(191): 39–41; 16(192):22–28.

Music, Trance, and Therapy in Baluchistan

Jean During

The Relationship between Music, Trance, and Healing
The Power of Music

In Baluchi culture, every stage of human life from birth (when *shaptāgi* is sung for several days) to death (and *mōṭk* 'lament') is marked by music such as lullabies, circumcision songs (*sur*), and wedding songs (*nāzēnk, lāro, hālo*). Music expresses joy and sorrow (in *zahīrōk* 'deep memory,' and *līkū*) or brings about healing by driving away evil spirits, in the *gwātī* ceremony.

There are seven types of music in Iranian Baluchistan:

1. Traditional songs for weddings and celebrations, with a measured beat, including recent compositions that are sometimes inspired by Indo-Pakistani light music (*tarāne, sowt*, and so on).
2. Melismatic songs with an unmeasured beat (*līkū*) and their instrumental equivalent (*zahīrok*) played on the *sorūd*, a fiddle made of a single piece of wood with four melodic strings (including a drone string) and five to seven sympathetic strings.
3. Epic or courtly poems (*shēr*) with a measured, simple, repetitive refrain.
4. Songs of the bards (*sherwand* 'singers of poems', *pahlawān* 'champions' or *jangī* 'warriors') which combine recitative, instrumental ritornello, and melismatic sections. This genre is especially widespread in the south (Dashtyāri, Rāsk, Gwādar, and other places).
5. Religious songs of Sufi inspiration (in particular the repertoire of the Chestī order, accompanied by the *rabāb* 'plucked lute').
6. *Damāl, zekr*, and *verd* of the Qāderi or Refāi dervishes, accompanied only by the *doholak* 'cylindrical drum'.
7. *Gwātī, qalandarī*, or *gwātī-damāli* trance music, played on the *sorūd* 'fiddle' and the *donelī* 'double flute', with or without singing. The *gwātī* ritual or *lēb* is found only in the central and southern areas of Iranian Baluchistan: Irānshahr, Sarāvān, Rāsk, Qasr-e Qand, Dashtyārī, and Chāhbahār. In Pakistan it is found in the Makrān all the way to the city of Karachi, where hundreds of thousands of Baluchis live. This genre occupies a privileged position because of its complexity and richness of meaning.

The roots of the *gwātī* ritual go back to the archaic beginnings of Baluchi culture. The ritual itself represents a complex system of interaction between music, psychology,

The *gwātī* ritual represents a complex system of interaction between music, psychology, religion, and shamanism.

religion, and shamanism. Several aspects of that system are examined in this article, which draws on surveys made in Iran and Pakistan over a twenty-year period, and on discussions with officiants from Torbat in Pakistan.

THE RELATIONSHIP BETWEEN MUSIC, TRANCE, AND HEALING

If music can cure illness, its absence can make people ill. In the words of one officiant, "Those with pain are regenerated by music; their souls become fresh; they forget the pain. In the past there used to be festivals, dances, and music; people were not affected by pain and sorrow. Nowadays they hear music only once or twice a year, at weddings. Their sorrow is to have too much money or to have debts. Then, little by little, the sickness comes."

The *gwātī* ritual

Baluchis say that some people are possessed by an evil or ambivalent spirit, a *gwāt* or *parī*, sometimes called *jinn* or *bād*. *Gwāt* 'wind' means a spirit; *gwātī* is the adjective; *gwātī* alone means the patient who suffers from a *gwāt*. A *gwāt* manifests itself in various ways, rendering its victim weak, depressed, and anxious. Such patients, it is said, cannot be cured of the *gwāt*'s harmful effects by a doctor, a traditional physician, or a mullah performing Islamic incantations; they can find relief only through a treatment called *lēb* (from Arabic *la'ab* 'play'), which may be translated as "performance of the *gwātī* ritual." This healing process is set in motion by inducing and conducting a trance (*mastī* 'drunkenness') with the help of appropriate melodies, songs, or both. It is presided over by an officiant (*khalīfe*, *ostā*), assisted by professional musicians playing the *sorūd*. The *lēb* takes place in the house of the patient, who is surrounded by family members and friends. It must be repeated at least three nights in a row; some people say that it should be repeated for three, five, or seven consecutive nights.

A trance induced by music is assumed to be possession by the spirit, which is attracted by specific melodies and forced to manifest itself. This manifestation is usually accompanied by shivering and stirring—a kind of informal dance with jerks, cries, shouts, and tears—although some people move little and are content to nod gently. Sometimes the *gwātī* begins to sing; this is understood as a sign of the *gwāt*'s approval. Each patient uses a limited range of gestures, movements, and postures, but these are not stereotypical—they vary greatly from one patient to another. Three stages of trance may be distinguished. A state called *por shodan* 'being filled up' corresponds to the onset of shivering. It is followed by the kinetic trance, which ends with the collapse of the *gwātī*, once he or she has fed (*sīr shod*). The state of crisis (*mastī*) lasts from one to three hours, during which the musicians take only two or three short breaks. The patient is totally unaware of these states and will remember nothing afterward.

During a trance, the spirit may speak in what is heard as a foreign language (Arabic, Urdu, Hindi), or in Baluchi but with an odd voice which does not seem to be that of the possessed person. This usually happens during the last night of the cure, when the playing generally ends with a sacrifice and a ritual meal. The spirit will agree to leave the patient in peace for a year or several years, after which the playing, the sacrifice, the bargain, and the agreement must be renewed. The session establishes an acceptable *modus vivendi* between spirit and patient. In order to bind the spirit, the *ostā* or *khalīfe* who conducts the whole process must put himself or herself into a trance, generally from the beginning of the *lēb*.

Both men and women excel in this art; women, however, may treat only women, whereas a male *khalīfe* may treat women (though without touching them) as well as men. The officiants, who may also be performers or singers, are people who themselves were once possessed, were treated in the same way, and have progressively acquired a certain control over their trances.

This ritual relates to the healing of an individual and cannot be achieved without music, since the particular spirits involved can be conjured up only by specific music. Music is "offered" to them, generally in addition to perfume and the sacrifice of an animal or fowl. As for the relationship between music, trance, and healing, a musician in Torbat, Pakistan, distinguished three possibilities: (1) The patient may go into a trance, but the *jinn* does not listen to the music and does not go away. However, if the *jinn* reaches an agreement with the musician, he may leave on the first, second, or third day. (2) It may not be necessary for the patient to go into a trance in order to persuade the *jinn* to leave. (3) The patient may go into a trance and be cured; this third possibility is what usually happens.

Throughout the ritual the main element is music, played on the *sorūd* or the *donelī*, the former always accompanied by the rhythmic drone of the *tanbīre.* Other instruments (*doholak* or *bēnjo*) may join in, as may people who clap or sing. After an exorcism, the patient is expected to enter a trance whenever he or she hears the melody or melodies that precipitated the trance during the initial treatment.

The ritual is conducted with different degrees of intensity, according to the seriousness of the illness (Mas'ūdiye 1985 [1364]:20). In *sāz-e lēb* only the *sorūd is* used, possibly accompanying a woman's voice (*sāz* refers both to an instrument and to an instrumental piece). In *kopār-e lēb* the *doholak* is added; it can continue for one to four hours. *Valag-e lēb* is repeated several evenings in a row. *Khūn-e lēb* includes the sacrifice of a rooster, sheep, camel, or cow. In Karachi, *tobbuk-lēb* lasts an entire week and corresponds to an initiation into the functions of the *khalīfe*.

This ritual might appear to be a sort of shamanic session in which the patient's trance is central, but it is far from being that simple. A more careful examination finds considerable ambiguity and obscurity and raises numerous questions that reveal our lack of knowledge about phenomena of this type.

Psychological aspects

Baluchi ideas about the *gwātī* ritual fall into three general categories. One position treats the ritual as a matter of invisible occult powers or of the supernatural. A second position sees it as a matter of psychology and the therapeutic effect of music and dance; some people who take this view appeal to the concept of repression—but those who exclude any possibility of supernatural intervention are rare. For a third group, the ritual is an interplay of both the occult and psychology. A Cheshtī Sufi explained that all the afflictions endured by the *gwātī* originate in *'eshq* 'love' or 'desire' and *gham* 'melancholia' or 'frustration.' *Gwātī* handlers are well aware of the psychological dimension of the disease. In making a diagnosis, they ask patients about their dreams and speak with their families. Some also say that they can cure only patients who are married and have already, to a certain extent, satisfied their physical desires.

Psychoanalytic aspects, though important, are only a part of the healing process. Not all cases of possession by a *gwāt* have the same origin or the same intensity, as is suggested by the fact that the ritual has several levels (*sāz-e lēb*, *kopār-e lēb*, and so on). The ritual is also a means of social "reinsertion": the problem has been identified;

the patient has been recognized as a *gwātī*; the family has helped and indeed has spent much money. After the cure, a patient has been reborn (as is suggested by such details as the ritual meal and ablutions) and must not associate with bad people. Therapeutic effects of the trance may involve venting emotions and reducing stress. Although it is quite unpleasant to be bothered by a *gwāt,* the trance itself (or at least a trance of this type) may be very enjoyable, like drunkenness induced by wine. Some people observe wryly that in any Baluchi village many healthy people are eager to be "cured." Even within a relatively homogeneous society, we may find a wide range of trance or semitrance states.

For most people, the *gwātī* trance and Sufi ecstasy (and even the "intoxication" of snakes induced by snake charmers) are of the same nature and are designated by the same term, *mastī* 'intoxication'. The behavior of dervishes stirred by listening (*samā'*) or by the practice of *z̲ekr* (Arabic *dhikr* 'remembrance') is evidently not far removed from that of the *gwātī*. I have met some dervishes whose deep emotional and kinetic reactions were quite similar to, or even stronger than, those of a *gwātī*. Nonetheless, the *khalīfe* insists that one must not confound *gwātī* trance and Sufi intoxicated behavior. As a *gwātī* musician from Torbat explained, "There are two types of intoxication: those brought on by possession (*jinnī mastī*) and those brought on by [spiritual] love (*'eshqī mastī*). There is a great difference between the two. We can tell immediately if it is one or the other. The Sufi *faqīr* has only the intoxication of love. We know instinctively if it is the *jinn*. If it is the *jinn*, he says into the *faqīr*'s ear, 'This man is ill because I am within him.' "

The distinction between possession by a spirit and a mystical ecstatic trance may, at least in part, be linked to theological requirements. Theoretically, the difference between trance or ecstasy and possession is that possession is due to an external agent, generally a spirit displacing the personality of the subject, who remains unaware and is unable to control himself or herself. A strongly monotheistic doctrine like Sufism rules out any notion of possession by so-called gods or spirits; nor would divine possession be possible, given God's transcendence. However, Sufi assemblies for *z̲ekr* or *samā'* are generally called *ḥaḍra* 'presence', divine radiance falling on the meeting, attributed to the presence of the Prophet (or Imām 'Alī among the Shi'a, or possibly another spiritual entity such as Lā'l Shahbāz Qalandar for the *gwātī*).

Another level of trance might be called an "excitational trance," to paraphrase the Sufi term *tawājud* 'making an effort in order to achieve ecstasy'. It is easy and probably pleasant to dance, jerk, and shout in such a way that people think you are possessed. Women are more likely to do this, since in Baluchistan they have many reasons to feel oppressed by their society and culture. A man who denied belief in *gwātī* and *khalīfe*—except for his mother—told me that he had once seen several women in a trance at the same time, something that is quite uncommon. He concluded, however, that these women were merely simulating a trance when one of them asked a neighbor to "go and see if my baby is all right" and then resumed her trance. He also remembered concluding that several women were simulating the crisis stage when his mother (as dervishes do during the *z̲ekr*) suddenly went into ecstasy and shouted a powerful *huuu*!—whereupon the women, frightened, went to a corner and sat down quietly.

Another informant told me that he had overheard a *khalīfe* instructing a *gwātī* to put on a good "show" and had concluded from this that the *lēb* was mere simulation. Yet this *gwātī* had kept dancing and shouting and disturbing the musicians for an hour; this could be taken as evidence that the trickery lay only in a lack of ritualistic circumstances, since it is unlikely that a man could simulate such an intense trance state for so long. This may have been an instance of possession "for fun"—a kind of theatrical trance that was forced at the beginning but eventually became real.

I met a young man who claimed, half jokingly, to be a *gwātī* . He said that when he listened to music at festivals, he would fall into a strange state and would forget himself in the dance; of course he enjoyed this state, even though he was a bit afraid of it. In a *lēb*, where music is more appropriate and conditions encourage people to vent their emotions, he almost certainly would have behaved like a *gwātī*.

Music and social status

People have different relations with music according to their status and position in the sacred-secular continuum. At the apex we find the saints, the great Sufis. They are said to communicate with something beyond the natural world, partly by means of music (*ẕekr* and *qalandarī* tunes); their *dam* 'power of the breath' enables them to heal people and fulfill vows. In theory, they have nothing to do with the profane world. Their contact with the sacred dimension is enhanced by devotional practices in which music (*ẕekr*, *samāʿ*) has an important place as a means of reaching ecstasy. According to ancient Sufi sources, *samāʿ* also frees adepts from the pains of asceticism, refreshes their souls, and gives them energy and enthusiasm. This ideal model is followed by Sufis of lesser standing, called *faqīr* or *khalīfe*, or *faqīr dam* when they heal the sick with their prayers and breath.

The name *khalīfe* 'representative' suggests that the bearer is the delegate of a saint, living or deceased—that is, concretely connected to a Sufi order or devoted to a saint. "The *khalīfe*," one *gwātī* musician said, "receives permission to cure people from the great saints. . . . It is not necessary that the saint be living—the *khalīfe* has created a bond with him through devotion, attendance at his mausoleum, offerings, and so on." The terms *faqīr* and *khalīfe* are ambiguous, since they also refer to *gwātī* masters. The categories are assimilated by virtue of function or role: both are healers, but only the second uses music to this end. A *faqīr* who is particularly inclined toward ecstatic trance is called *malang*, and his practice (a kind of *samāʿ* or mystical concert) is called *damāl* (figure 1). The *malang*, like the *gwātī*, covers his head with a veil and dances to *qalandarī* music until he loses consciousness.

Noninitiates who are able to reach an altered state of consciousness (ecstasy, trance, agitation) while listening to music include (1) sensitive and religious people stirred by spiritual enthusiasm (*ʿeshq-e khodāʾī*) while hearing religious chants or tunes; (2) sick people under the influence of a malevolent spirit who are set free by falling into a trance; and (3) normal subjects who experience states similar to those of a *gwātī* while listening to secular music in a nonritualistic context, such as a festival.

Three kinds of people neglect or reject music: (1) Normal people who become sick owing to a lack of festivities and music. They often look down on those who make music (in this they are like people in category 3), though not on the music itself.

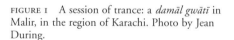

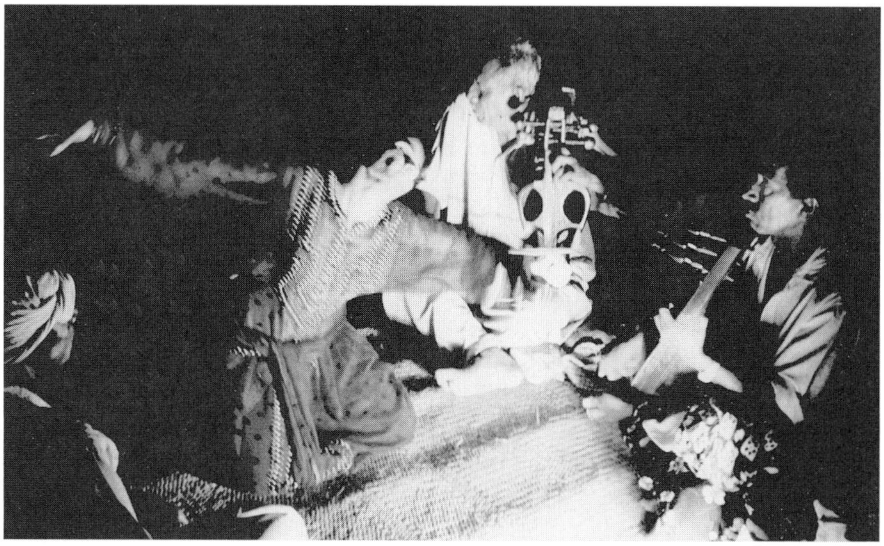

FIGURE 1 A session of trance: a *damāl gwātī* in Malir, in the region of Karachi. Photo by Jean During.

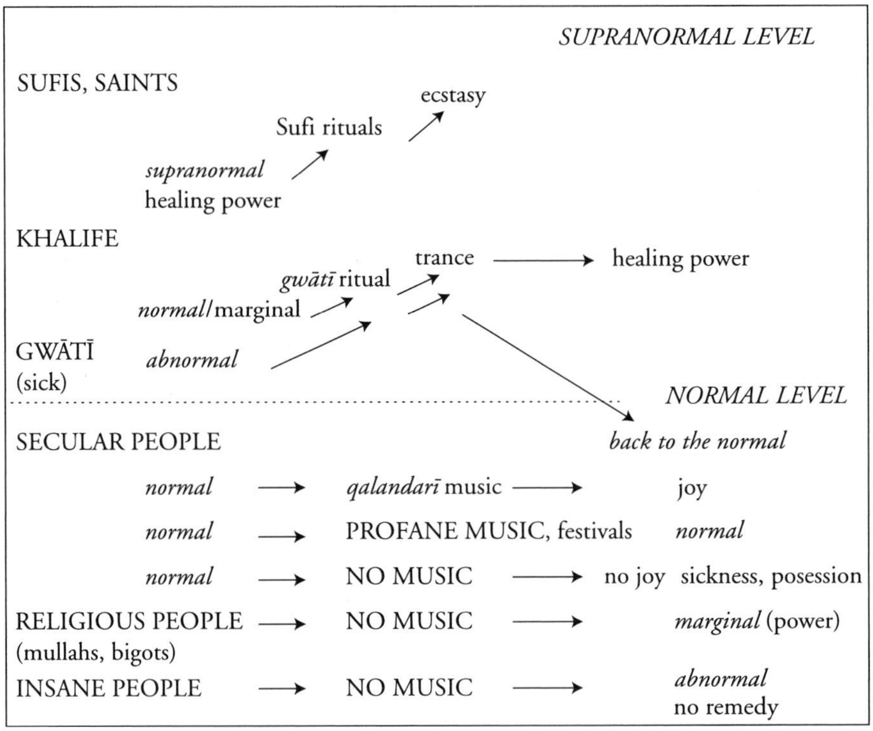

FIGURE 2 A model of the relationship between music, the sacred dimension, and Baluchi society.

(2) Insane people who are "allergic" to music and for whom nothing can be done. (3) Some bigots and mullahs who consider music illicit. They may indulge in religious chant, but they never consider this genre music. They are sometimes asked to perform minor exorcisms, not because of their personal power but because of their knowledge of Qur'ānic formulas on which talismans and incantations are based.

Any survey of the function of music in Baluchi society should take into account the role of spirits—*jinn*, *dīv*, *gwāt*, and the like. It is said that some of these spirits are pious while others are unbelievers, and that they react differently to music. Some (*dīv* and *zār*) are rather wild, others (*jinn* and *parī*) quite tame; they are even said to marry and have children with humans.

It would be unrealistic to look for a complete, coherent, logical structure in the relations between music, the sacred dimension, therapy, and Baluchi society. Apart from musicians and Sufis, common people do not have a clear concept of the subtle differences between possession, trance, ecstasy, excitation, spiritual emotion, and even the state of a snake charmed by music. Despite this reservation, a model of these complex relations is offered in figure 2.

THE POWER OF MUSIC

Music is such an essential element in ritual that nothing can be done without it. The *gwātī* cure is a kind of music therapy that induces trance states never attained in the course of secular festivities. There is no musical formula that automatically or magically elicits a trance state. When musicians are dealing with a first case, they must play the entire repertoire piece by piece until the *gwāt* clearly reacts to one piece—which must then be repeated continuously unless other tunes are found to produce the same effect on the *gwāt*. Although a *khalīfe* does not connect specific melodies with specific types of possession or illness, relationships of this kind would merit careful study. There does seem to be a secret affinity between the patient's temperament or symptoms and the tune that affects him or her, though we must not neglect the subjectivity of singers, the type of communication they establish with the *gwātī*, their own inner state (*ḥāl*), the manner in which they convey that state, and the order of the pieces, which may be fortuitous. Normally, subjects do not enter into a state of ecstasy on hearing the first piece; rather, they warm up gradually until they are susceptible to a tune whose particular virtue may lie only in being played at the right moment. Thereafter, this piece acts somewhat like the stimulus for a conditioned reflex; by hearing it again, the subjects can return to the state they experienced the first time they heard it. However, although a *gwātī* may need a specific tune to go into trance, he or she may be able to maintain that state with other tunes. This may be a matter of rhythm, tempo, and textual content (despite the fact that the tunes are often played without singing).

The character of *qalandarī* music

Gwātī or *qalandarī* music is an elaborate genre with subtle ornaments and rhythms that can be performed only by professionals. Technically, *gwātī* or *qalandarī* tunes share many characteristics with songs of celebration and epic poems, especially with respect to structure, rhythm, and style. Yet with a little experience one can immediately recognize *gwātī* music, despite its close relationship with other genres. Its ethos may be described as a certain harshness or aggressiveness in some tunes and a refinement of instrumental effects in others, capable at times of producing jubilation. In certain regions, the term *qalandarī* applies to music distinct from that played at an exorcism and includes religious songs that do not belong specifically to the *gwātī* repertoire. *Qalandarī* music is a genre highly esteemed by *sorūd* players, who regard it as a rich source of material and are free to add their own improvisation. It is in this genre that instrumental pieces reach the highest complexity and sophistication, due in part to the fact that, for some patients, the pieces are repeated throughout the night.

Distinctive traits of *qalandarī* music include these:

1. Freedom, creativity, versatility, and the possibility of improvisation and adaptation to different circumstances. Most pieces can be played to two or three different rhythms (with two, three, five, or six beats), even with a shifting of accents, and at different speeds. The words can also change.
2. Rhythmic ambiguity. The place of the first beat is often unclear or appears to shift according to subjective perceptions of the melody. This is achieved by syncopation or by an oscillation of rhythmic values between three and two beats. In some cases these techniques are combined (as a result of the rhythmic drone).
3. Two levels of perception, one evident and easy to grasp, the other internal, hidden, and subtle. The external level is a melody that anyone can reproduce by singing or playing it in a simple style. These melodies have a simple, symmetrical question-and-answer form—a brief, easy, attractive shape. However, their interpretation on the *sorūd* or *donelī* reaches a high level of sophistication due to short melismas, paraphrases and variants, and "pinpoint" ornamentation such as vibrato, glissandos, and trills.

Combining these technical elements makes it possible to repeat the same melodic form for a long time without producing boredom. The same music must be played in order to maintain the intensity of a trance and the unity of affect and mind. But this cannot be achieved by mere repetition, which might induce fatigue or a loss of attention. Microvariations within the same melody, along with an opening out of "perspective" due to the existence of several levels of perception, help to maintain attention.

A thorough analysis can cast light on these subtle or even hidden aspects, which may be sensed intuitively but demand considerable concentration and a great familiarity with the music of these regions if they are to be grasped and reproduced correctly. What appears at first hearing to be a simple four- or eight-bar melody may in fact consist of parallel rhythmic lines and may thus turn out to be a structure with different strata, some latent or implied. Just as two intersecting lines define a plane, and two

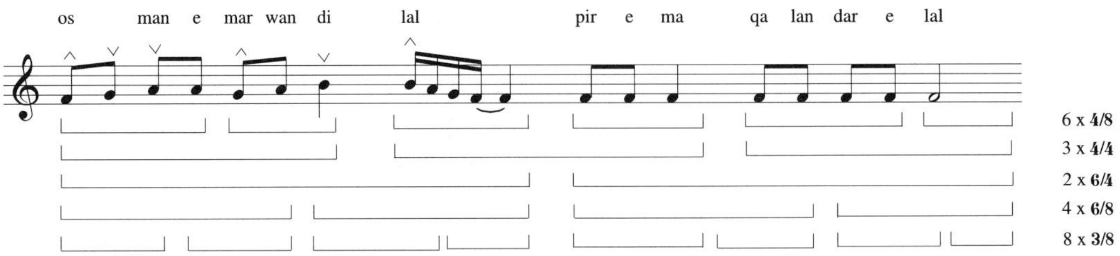

FIGURE 3 A melody whose structure can be seen in several ways.

intersecting planes define a volume, the crossing of two rhythmic lines or strata can be said to create a new spatial element that can justifiably be considered a volume. The concept of volume generates the concomitant idea of perspective and depth. This is an appealing analogy: the expressive depth of this music could derive from the depth of the spatiotemporal field.

Many types of music usually considered linear are in fact multidimensional. This is particularly true of all the 6/8 melodies that can be understood as 2 + 2 + 2 or 3 + 3 eighth notes. The structure of the melody in figure 3 can be seen in several ways, according to the position given to the strong beat—for example, six bars of 4/8, falling into two equal parts, each with a value of six quarter notes. The bowing is articulated in quarter-note values; this suggests 4/8 (2/4), and the ornamentation of the *sorūd* does not hint at anything else. The *tanbire*, however, plays a perfectly contrametric 3/8, whose strong beat coincides with the bow strokes only every 12 beats. Thus the overall phrasing is two groups of six quarter notes.

This allows different perspectives in the auditive image. The interplay of these parallel voices or strata creates a certain impression, whose underlying processes deserve further study. It would seem that on an elementary level the ear gives priority to one stratum, structuring the rhythm of the piece according to habit, culture, and sense of rhythm. This is why the changes that occur during a performance—breaks in rhythm, syncopation, accents, offbeats—can be confusing. But the musician hears all the levels at once and can direct his interpretation by emphasizing whichever level he chooses.

This music is designed above all to create an effect—to act on the psyche and induce a state of trance. The evidence suggests that the unfolding of the different strata, which is less evident in popular secular music, is intended precisely to induce such a state, in conjunction with other procedures. It can be suggested that the ambiguity inherent in some of these tunes, or the aspects hidden behind the smooth surface of a simple melody, will disorient many listeners and force them to abandon their intellectual and psychomotor references. This disorientation might well induce a state of mental confusion, helping to release rational or ordinary consciousness and prepare the way for the occurrence of a trance. According to this hypothesis, pieces in duple or quadruple time, which, unlike those in 6/8, are not rhythmically ambiguous, would act as a "restructuring" force.

To these elements one should add the emotional, expressive impact of the music performed by professionals, and sometimes also sung—with extraordinary communicative enthusiasm—by the participants. *Sorūd* players say that, for *gwātī* music, the highest tuning is the best.

The power of symbols

The dominant factor seems to be the symbolic and mystical dimension of the ritual, which is closely related to popular forms of Sufism. Without a ritualistic and mythical dimension, the *gwātī* cure would not work.

The *gwātī* ritual may be considered a kind of popular Sufi *samāʿ* 'mystic concert and dance' [see ISLAMIC HYMNODY IN EGYPT: *AL-INSHĀD AL-DĪNĪ*], on the basis of the following arguments:

1. The great majority of the songs in this repertoire are religious, most of them a kind of melodic *zekr*, sometimes called that. Most are devoted to La'l Shahbāz Qalandar (Sakhī Abu Bakr 'Osmān Marwandī, d. 1262), and musicians make pilgrimages to his tomb in order to acquire the supernatural powers that are said to enable them to master their difficult art. Other holy men invoked, in addition to the Prophet and 'Alī (the first Shi'a imām), are 'Abdolqāder Jilānī (d. 1166) and, less frequently, local saints (Shey Dāwud, Pir 'Omar) who are not known beyond Iranian Baluchistan.
2. Some of the tunes widespread in northern Makrān have been borrowed from the Sufi repertoire of the Cheshtī order settled near Sarāvān. Other features suggest connections with the Zikriyya, a marginal or heterodox Sufi movement of Baluchistan about which we know very little.
3. The music played in a *lēb* is called *qalandarī*, and after several years of therapy a *gwātī* may be called *malang* (a local term for dervish). A *qalandar* is a type of wandering dervish, familiar with ecstatic states, who has freed himself from outwardly religious and mundane laws. The word is repeated in almost all the choruses and might lead the *gwātī* to become possessed by the spirit or "image" of La'l Qalandar, or to identify himself or herself with an archetypal *qalandar*.
4. The term *khalīfe*, applied to the officiant, derives from the Sufi hierarchy.
5. In some regions one calls on the *khalīfe* and "offers" a seance so that his ecstatic trance will attract a blessing (*kheira*). Such sessions are called *damāl*, a term that has almost the same meaning for Sufis.
6. In the view of the common people (as opposed to that of connoisseurs), the ecstatic states of the Sufis and the *gwātī* trance are both considered a sort of intoxication (*mastī*).
7. We must also take into account the strong religious elements found in the ritual. The *khalīfe* must perform the ritual prayer before starting. It is also said that pious persons are immune to a *gwāt*.
8. When in a state of trance, a *khalīfe* may have clairvoyant powers comparable to those of a Sufi shaykh.

The *sīmorgh*

An important aspect of the *gwātī lēb* is the myth of the *sīmorgh*, a celestial bird endowed with a powerful mystical character. It is the archetypal perfect saint or Sufi shaykh, shaman, and medicine man in the form of a bird. In Sufi literature it symbolizes the human soul in search of the spiritual world. Every human being is a potential *sīmorgh*, and humans should unfold their wings in order to transcend the earthly condition. In Sufi imagery, the *sīmorgh* possesses the remedy for all diseases: one drop of its saliva will heal any wound, and a feather from its plumage will protect the possessor from harm. The *sīmorgh* is a cosmic singing bird, the origin of musical sound, both human and animal. The same meaning is found in the Greek myth of the kyknos phoenix (well known to Muslim philosophers) and appears as well in the Talmudic and Mandean traditions (During 1989:95–108; During 1990).

All these elements correspond perfectly to the position of this myth in *gwātī* music. We find the healing process; the role of the officiant (a kind of shaykh or shaman); the invocation of Shahbāz Qalandar, whose name (*shahbāz*) means "royal hawk" (a substitute for *sīmorgh*); and the attempts of sufferers to transcend their condition through ecstasy or trance. Furthermore, the most important *gwātī* piece is called *sīmorgh*. It has many variants and constitutes a genre in itself, which has generated many songs (just as, in myth, all music originates in the song of the *sīmorgh*). This sound is assimilated to the sound of a polyphonic aerophone, as in the Persian,

Mandean, and Greek forms of the myth: Baluchis say that the *sīmorgh* melody was originally destined for the *donelī* 'double flute'. The melody is very suggestive of the flight and song of a bird and has some polyphonic elements.

Opposed to this cosmic bird is the creeping snake, *mār*, represented in another important *gwātī* tune which is melodically related to that of the *sīmorgh*. Presumably the snake symbolizes the disease progressively dominated by the power of the music. The snake starts creeping but then rises and dances to the music, just as the patient lies on the floor at the beginning of the cure but then, after going into a trance, starts dancing. A further step in the imagery of the process of sublimation could be the intervention of the *sīmorgh* myth: the passage from earth to the air and sky through dance.

In view of all these elements, a schematic interpretation of the structure of the *gwātī* ritual and cure may be proposed. Negative aspects are transmuted into positive aspects as a *gwātī* gradually becomes a *malang* or perhaps a *khalīfe*, able to help another *gwātī* or even a non-*gwātī* who asks for intercession. Possession still obtains; but, in the imagery of the *gwātī*, the evil *gwāt* has been transformed into a helping spirit endowed with curative powers, like the *sīmorgh*.

This interpretation is my own, since healing is achieved without explicit verbal formulation, through the suggestive power of ritual and music and their symbolic meanings.

Translated by Beth Raps and Stephen Blum

REFERENCES

During, Jean. 1988a. *Musique et extase: L'audition mystique dans la tradition soufie*. Paris: Albin Michel.

———. 1988b. "Emotion and Trance: Musical Exorcism in Baluchestan." In *Cultural Parameters of Iranian Musical Expression*, ed. M. Caton and N. Siegel, 36–46. Redondo Beach, Calif.: Institute of Persian Performing Arts.

———. 1989. *Musique et mystique dans les traditions de l'Iran*. Paris: Institut Français de Recherches en Iran-Peeters.

———. 1990. "Der Mythos der Simorg." *Spektrum Iran* 3(3):3–19.

———. 1992a. "The Organization of Rhythm in Baluchi Trance Music." In *European Studies in Ethnomusicology: Historical Developments and Recent Trends*, ed. Max Peter Baumann, 282–302. Wilhelmshaven: Florian Noetzel.

———. 1992b. *Baloutchistan: Musique d'extase et de guérison*. Ocora, C580017-18. Compact disks. (Expanded edition of LP records issued under the same title in 1981.)

———. 1997a. "Devotion in Baluchistan." *Yearbook for Traditional Music* 29:39–56.

———. 1997b. *The Mystic Fiddle of the Proto-Gypsies, Masters of Trance Music*. Shanachie 65031. Compact disk.

———. 1997c. "Rhythmes ovoïdes et quadrature du cercle." *Cahiers de Musique Traditionelle* 10:17–36.

Lièvre, V., and J.-Y. Loude. 1990. *Le chamanisme des Kalash du Pakistan*. Paris: Éditions du C.N.R.S.

Massoudieh [Mas'ūdiye], Mohammad Taghi. 1973. "Hochzeitslieder aus Balūčestān." *Jahrbuch für Musikalische Volks- und Völkerkünde* 7:59–69. (With additional photographs, transcriptions, and LP disk.)

———. 1985 [1364]. *Mūsīqī-ye Balūchestān*. Tehran: Sorūsh.

———. 1988. *Musik in Balūčestān. Beiträge zur Ethnomusikologie*, Vol. 20. Hamburg: Karl Dieter Wagner.

Nāserī, A. 1979 [1358]. *Farhang-e mardom-e balūch*. Tehran.

Riāhī, A. 1978 [1356]. *Zār o bād o Balūch*. Tehran.

Section 8

Central Asia

Section 8
Central Asia

Central Asia comprises the core region of the famous Silk Road that linked East and West for centuries. Merchants and travelers of all sorts made their way from Europe, Africa, and western Asia to China using one of two main routes. Central Asian music manifests the intersections of the civilizations that traversed the region, settled in it, or governed it. In recent centuries, since the decline of the overland route, the music cultures of the region have become unfamiliar to those outside, but this region has a treasure trove of older musical practices with a strong resemblance to those of their Middle Eastern neighbors. One finds sung epic poetry, traditions of professional female musicians and dancers, and centuries-old classical and devotional expression. Minorities, notably the Jews of Bukhara, have served as bearers of broadly shared musical traditions. Historically, much musical performance has centered on life-cycle events.

The twentieth century witnessed successive attempts to preserve traditions through musical notation, audio and video recording, and institutionalized support of musicians. That century also saw the production of new and transformed music. Neoclassicists, such as Monâjât Yultichieva and Ilyas Malayev, have reframed the historic classical music of Uzbekistan. State ensembles and local practices have brought the repertoire into new settings. Pop artists such as Yulduz Usmanova seek fame on the "world beat." Local composers trained in European musical styles write symphonies.

"Central Asia" is fundamentally a European concept. The numerous ethnic and linguistic groups in the region have used more differentiated names to for local and regional identities. One cannot draw a firm boundary around Central Asia; here, as in most parts of the Middle East and Asia, cultural practices are shared across borders. In this context, musical performance serves as a medium for articulating varying and shifting local identities.

A Kyrgyz musician listens to a recording of himself. Photo by Theodore Levin, 1987.

Central Asia: Overview

Theodore Levin

Geographical and Cultural Boundaries
Islam in Central Asian Culture
Patterns of Settlement: The City and the Steppe
Music, Language, and National Identity
The Soviet Era
Central Asia in the Age of Globalization

The very name Central Asia suggests a region with imprecise borders. What constitutes the "central" portion of the huge Asian landmass? And from whose perspective is it "central"? Indeed, the notion of Central Asia as a coherent geocultural region is a European invention, and a relatively recent one at that. Indigenous peoples had their own mosaic of names for their territories, and the Russian, British, and Chinese imperial powers that jousted for control of the region in the nineteenth and twentieth centuries used still other names: Turkestan, Tartary, Transoxania, Xinjiang. No people goes by the ethnonym "Central Asian," and no linguists have posited a language group called "Central Asian." Rather, the peoples, languages, and territories of Central Asia represent identities whose domains may be larger or smaller than the region itself, however it is defined. One of the fascinations of Central Asia is the multitude of overlapping identities its inhabitants have developed for themselves—identities which have been in perpetual flux as a response to historical events and social change.

GEOGRAPHICAL AND CULTURAL BOUNDARIES

Central Asia as it is commonly understood at the beginning of the twenty-first century is a region defined by a mixture of geographical, political, and cultural boundaries. Most definitions would place the western extreme of the region at the shore of the Caspian Sea, a geographical demarcation. In the southwest, however, the conventional boundary is political: the border between Iran and Turkmenistan. And in the east, the distinct political border represented by the Chinese frontier is often disregarded in favor of an imagined cultural boundary farther to the east that encompasses the Uygurs of Chinese Xinjiang, a Muslim, Turkic-speaking people with strong cultural affinities to other Central Asian groups.

The northern and southern flanks of Central Asia are the most problematic. In the south, cultural coherence would argue for the inclusion of Afghanistan north of the Hindu Kush Mountains. However, the geographical boundary formed by the Amu Darya River, which also serves as a political frontier between Afghanistan and its northern neighbors Uzbekistan and Tajikistan, is frequently given priority, thus excluding Afghanistan altogether. In the north, the political border between Kazakhstan and Russia is commonly used as a demarcation; but from a demographic point of view, the north of Kazakhstan, with its large Slavic population, would be better con-

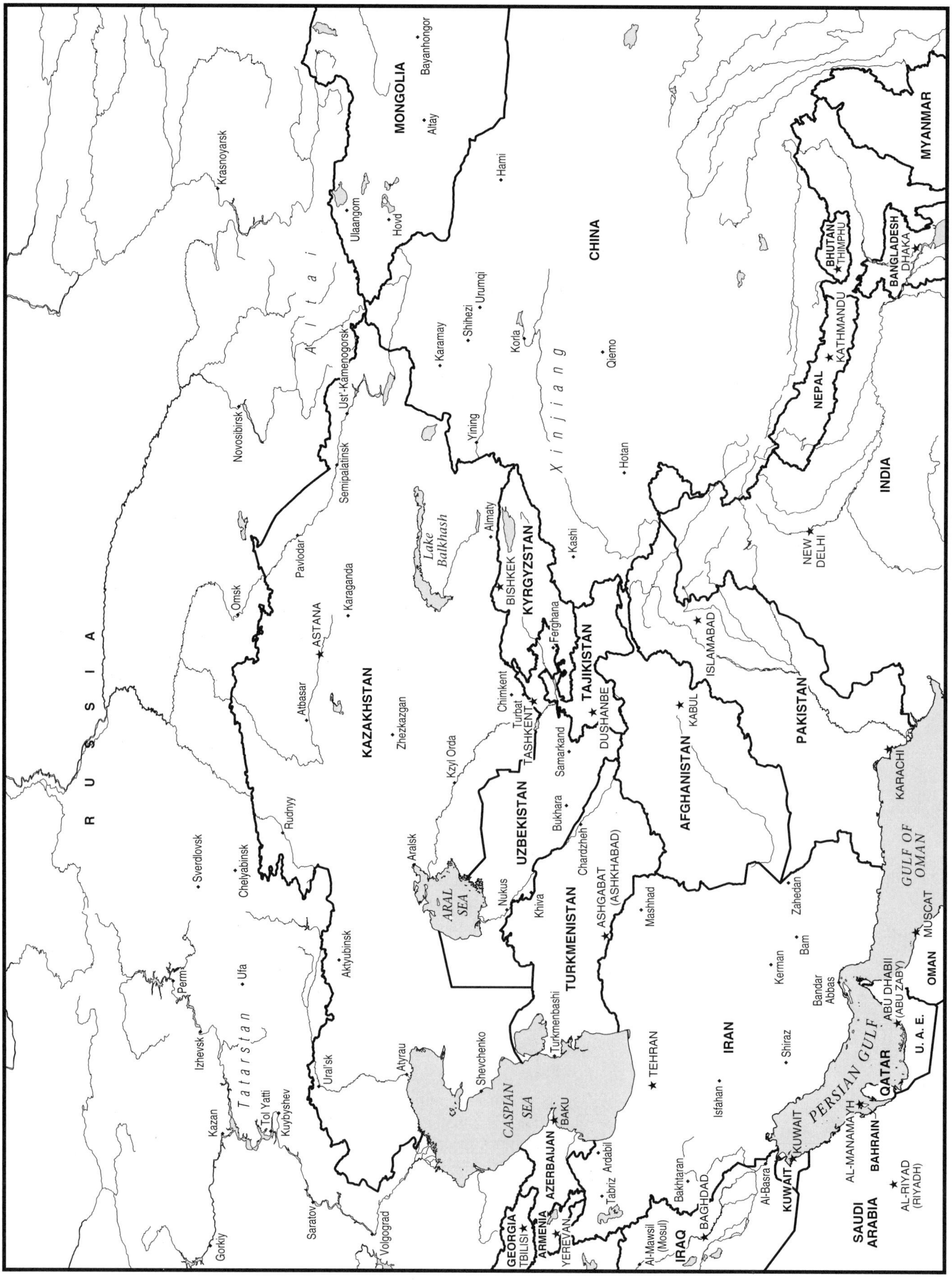

Central Asia.

sidered part of Russia. Conversely, the Altai region northeast of Kazakhstan, which includes Tuva, Khakasia, and Gorno-Altai and is considered part of Russian Siberia, has strong ethnolinguistic links to Central Asia. Finally, north of the Caspian Sea, Tatarstan—an autonomous republic within Russia that is the traditional territory of the Turkic-speaking Tatars—has never been included in geographic or political definitions of the region; but on the basis of ethnolinguistic and cultural ties, it probably ought to be.

Even if the conventional boundaries of Central Asia are of various types and their location is not entirely a matter of consensus, the region itself displays several kinds of broad coherence that represent defining features of society and culture. First, an overwhelming majority of the population identifies itself with Islam as an active religious practice, a cultural legacy, a worldview that informs everyday social life, or all of these.

Second, some 90 percent of the region's autochthonous population identify themselves with a Turkic ethnicity and speak a Turkic language as their native tongue. Most of the remaining 10 percent identify themselves with an Iranian ethnicity and speak an Iranian language, although many can also communicate in a Turkic language. Excluded from these figures are Russian-speaking Slavs—a group that began to populate Central Asia after the Czarist conquests in the latter half of the nineteenth century and during the Soviet era accounted for half or more of the population of the region's major cities. Since the end of the Soviet era, many Slavs have left Central Asia and resettled in Russia and Ukraine.

Third, over many centuries a close, even symbiotic, relationship has existed between sedentary peoples and nomads, making for recurring patterns of settlement and land use. Although pastoralism was sharply curtailed during the Soviet era, the special relationship between urban dwellers and pastoral herders is still part of the fabric of Central Asian life.

Fourth, in the nineteenth and twentieth centuries almost all of Central Asia came under the rule of Czarist Russia and subsequently the Soviet Union, which tried to bring about fundamental transformations in the organization, transmission, and expression of indigenous culture throughout its vast empire. Each of these social forces has contributed to shaping music and musical life in Central Asia.

ISLAM IN CENTRAL ASIAN CULTURE

Central Asia has been called a "double periphery"—that is, it forms the northeastern periphery of the Persianate Muslim realm, whose highest cultural aspirations arose from an urban sensibility; and simultaneously it forms the southwestern periphery of the Turco-Mongol nomadic realm, where expressive culture has traditionally been grounded in the life of the steppe.

City and steppe have produced quite different forms of music making, and it is not surprising that Islamic influences should be strongest in traditional urban repertoires and performance styles. Nonetheless, one cannot describe urban music in Central Asia simply as "Islamic." Rather, the influence of Islam must be situated in the context of particular times, places, and ruling dynasties, and examined with respect to specific social customs and practices. [See Sacred Music and Chant in Islamic Central Asia.]

The most common setting for live musical performance in the cities of Central Asia—particularly cities in the southern regions where Muslim influence has been strongest—is the festive celebration generically called *toi* in the region's local languages (figures 1 and 2). Virtually any event can provide an occasion for a *toi.* The most important events—a birth, a circumcision, or a marriage—can gather an enormous group of relatives and friends. Lesser occasions—a child's first day at school, a boy's first haircut, or in former times a girl's first veiling—are observed in smaller family gatherings.

FIGURE 1 Matrasul Matyakubov (center) plays the *surnai* with accompanists on *qairaq* 'clackers' and *dāyra* 'frame drum' in the center of old Khiva, 1994. Photographs in this article are by Theodore Levin.

FIGURE 2 Guests at a *toi*—a wedding fete—in Bukhara, 1993.

Whatever the size of a *toi,* two elements are obligatory: hospitality, called *dasturkhān* 'tablecloth', and live music to entertain the guests.

The gendering of performance

Before Russia colonized Central Asia and began to introduce European customs, Islamic tradition overwhelmingly dictated both the type of occasion appropriate for a *toi* and, to a large extent, the mode of celebration. One important influence on musical performance at these events has been the separate festivities for men and women—an abiding tradition that represents an extension of the separate male and female social worlds in Central Asia (although this separation tends to be less strict among nomadic groups accustomed to the close confines of encampments). Women's festivities have traditionally been served by female performers and men's festivities by male performers. In recent years, European-style celebrations that include both men and women have become increasingly common, yet in many cases they have supplemented rather than replaced the older gendered celebrations.

FIGURE 3 Shirin and Dilbar, wedding entertainers (*khalfa*) from Khiva, Uzbekistan, 1994.

Islamic traditions have dictated not only the gender of performers but the social background from which they tend to be drawn. For example, in the cities of Bukhara and Samarkand professional female entertainers called *sāzanda* lead dancing and singing among women. In the Khorezm region of northwest Uzbekistan, such wedding entertainers are known as *khalfa* (from Arabic *khalifa,* 'caliph', 'deputy', 'vicegerent', or 'assistant'; figure 3). Both types of performers have traditionally come from marginalized social groups: until recently, women who became *sāzandas* were overwhelmingly Bukharan Jews, while *khalfas* were typically from families of undistinguished lineage and were often crippled or blind (figure 4).

FIGURE 4 Muhammad Aminhon Nasriddinov, a blind singer of Bukhara, 1991.

The social marginalization of entertainers reflects the moral ambiguity that Islamic cultural tradition has ascribed to their profession. While marriage itself is imbued with a sense of sacred duty, the revelry associated with weddings has been morally suspect. In such a view, music and dance represent a powerful force that may lead humankind either upward toward prayer and contemplation of the divine or downward toward drunkenness and sensuality. As purveyors of dance music—even when they perform for men and women separately—wedding entertainers have been a lightning rod for fundamentalist pronouncements against celebration; and public celebration was prohibited under certain strict Muslim rulers such as Shah Murad (r. 1785–1800) and Emir Khadan (r. 1800–1825), particularly in Bukhara, known popularly as the "dome of Islam." Other rulers, however, permitted and even supported celebration; and the festivities associated with holidays such as *Nawruz* (the new year) and *Lola* (a tulip festival) as well as with weddings and other family celebrations offer evidence of an old tradition.

Music and dancing have also been a feature of men's celebration. At the end of the twentieth century, some performers could still remember seeing boy dancers called *bacha* who wore women's dresses and painted their lips and eyebrows. Under Soviet rule, the profession of *bacha* was made illegal, but although these dancers' number diminished, their tradition did not end. Other wedding entertainment was provided by a male singer-dancer called *mavrigikhān* (*mavrigi* 'from Merv'). Like socially marginalized female entertainers, the typical *mavrigikhān* has been descended from the Bukharan Irani or Farsi—members of Central Asia's Shi'ite minority who trace their ancestry to slaves captured in Iran by Turkmen tribesmen and brought via Merv to Bukhara.

FIGURE 5 Kyrgyz herder, 1977.

Musical structure and Islamic aesthetics

The musical repertoires performed at urban festive celebrations reflect Islamic influences no less than the social parameters of celebration itself. For example, song texts are typically drawn from Sufi-inspired poetry in which lyrical descriptions of earthly pleasure and beauty serve as an allegory for spiritual ascent toward the perfection of the divine. And at a more abstract level, musical structures, particularly in the most formally complex genres, also exemplify an aesthetic sensibility shaped by Muslim cultures. For a millennium, a continuous tradition of sophisticated urban art song evolved under the patronage of the Muslim nobility in Central Asia. Over time, this tradition assumed various local forms and names, but generically it is known as *maqām*. In Central Asia, *maqām* is itself one form of a more extensive tradition of what has been called court music, classical music, or elevated music, which extends through the core Muslim world and includes canonical repertoires and performance traditions in Turkey, Iran, Azerbaijan, and the Arab lands of the Middle East and North Africa.

In the Central Asian *maqām,* as well as in other local vocal genres to which it is related, a broad unifying principle is the gradual ascent of the melodic line through a series of discrete pitch areas to a melodic culmination called *awj* 'apogee'. The term *awj*, as its translation suggests, is borrowed from Islamic astronomy; it provides a cosmic and, by extension, metaphysical gloss to the moment of highest melodic ascent and greatest emotional tension. The symbolic significance of the "upward-looking" melodic style becomes even clearer when art song is contrasted with the "downward-looking" melodic style of the other great Central Asian musical tradition, oral epic, rooted in the pre-Islamic animist and shamanist beliefs of Turco-Mongol herders (figure 5). For animists and shamanists, the locus of spiritual power is the earthly world of nature, and it can hardly be a coincidence that the guttural, low-pitched recitative in which performers chant epic poetry orients the listener downward toward the earth, rather than upward toward the heavens.

Central Asian art song repertoires also illustrate the filigree embellishment and ornamentation of melody which is emblematic of Islamic aesthetics in music and sacred chant and whose fundamental model is the recitation of Islam's most sacred text, the Qur'ān. In contrast, for example, to the liquescent melodic lines of Indian *raga*, Central Asian art song is like a mosaic, clearly defining the tonal space of each melodic pitch. This mosaic quality is apparent in the sequencing not only of individual pitches but of entire blocks of melodic material. For example, certain instrumental pieces in the repertoire of Bukharan art song called *shash maqām* are formally structured according to a clearly audible "algebra" (a + ba + cba + dcba . . .) that is loosely analogous to the principle of repetition and variation in Bukharan decorative arts and, at a more abstract level, to the principle of arabesque that is a cornerstone of Islamic aesthetics.

Musical instruments typically used to accompany performers of art song—for example, the long-necked lutes called *tanbūr, tār,* and *dutār*—are designed not only to facilitate delicate melodic ornamentation like that of vocalists but also to reproduce the precise melodic intervals and scales that are the legacy of *'ilm-i mūsīqī*, the Islamic science of music. (The *tār* originated in the Caucasus but has been popular in Central Asia at least since the nineteenth century; the *dutār*, seen in figure 6, came into use in the 1920s and 1930s.) Intervals such as neutral thirds, which are halfway between a major and minor third, and scales with seventeen and nineteen tones to the octave, like those found on the *ṭār*, have a theoretical basis rationalized by the mathematical approach of Islamic musical science but are also preserved in actual performance practice.

At the opposite end of the musical spectrum from the refined melodies and veiled poetic symbolism of art song is the multimedia world of popular Islam, which has used song, chant, storytelling, theater, and dance as a means of propagating Islamic

FIGURE 6 Shuhrat Razzagov, a *dutār* virtuoso, 1994.

values and beliefs. Popular Islam engaged a broad cross-section of Central Asian urban society through the appeal of performers who were at once entertainers and preachers. These performers included the wandering dervishes, *qalandar*, who gathered street crowds to perform didactic spiritual songs for alms, and bards called *maddāh* who recited moralistic stories and chanted religious sayings and excerpts from the Qur'ān. Most of all, popular Islam engaged the followers of Sufism or Islamic mysticism, whose sacred rituals of *zikr* 'remembrance' included chanting, singing, and in some instances dancing.

PATTERNS OF SETTLEMENT: THE CITY AND THE STEPPE

Islamic influences on expressive culture that are historically strongest in the southern regions of Central Asia and are anchored in cities and towns have long intermingled with animist-shamanist influences that have flowed into Central Asia from the steppe regions in the northeast and have their source in the traditions of rural herding peoples. The confluence of these two cultural streams—one sedentary, Islamic, and Iranian; the other nomadic, animist, and Turko-Mongol—has contributed to the rich diversity of Central Asian expressive culture. After millennia of such intermingling, Turko-Mongol and Iranian cultural traditions have become so tightly interwoven that in many cases it is all but impossible—and perhaps pointless—to try to distinguish their ethnic origin. Yet in spite of myriad forms of cultural hybridization that have tended to merge the two currents of influence, broad distinctions remain between the cultural attributes of urban and rural Central Asia.

Rural stockbreeders have their own version of the urban *toi*, centered on the performance not of *bel canto* art song but of oral poetry, particularly epic poetry. [See KAZAKH MUSIC.] The consummate entertainer at such events is the bard, variously called *bakhshi, ashiq,* or *jrau.* The bardic repertoire consists of epic poems called *dāstān* and shorter poems called *terme,* both rendered in a guttural recitative to the accompaniment of two-stringed lutes such as the *dombra* and *dutār.* The *dāstān* is a repository of oral history, and the bard is the vessel through which this history is transmitted from one generation to the next. The social convention by which men maintain control over the bardic traditions assures them of the power of cultural memory and consequently of history itself. Yet the boundary between history and mythology is

FIGURE 7 *Dutār* maker in the Ferghana valley in Uzbekistan, 1987.

porous. The guttural, raspy vocal style of the bards presents an immediate contrast to the normal speaking and singing voice, creating an artistic and magical distance between everyday experience and the heroic world in which epic stories take place.

Epic poetry is overwhelmingly a male performance tradition—female epic singers, though not unknown, are rare—but women have their own vocal and instrumental genres. For example, in the towns and rural settlements of the Ferghana valley in Uzbekistan, groups of women commonly perform strophic dance songs known as *yalla* or *lapar* for their own entertainment, accompanying themselves on the frame drum (*dāyra*) and led by a singer-drummer known as *yallachi.* Women in the Ferghana region also play a form of two-stringed lute, the *dutār* (figure 7). Another instrument widely played by women in rural areas is the Jew's harp (*khomus*).

The same propensity for storytelling that shapes the musical style of the bards also infuses repertoires of instrumental music. Unlike pieces modeled on abstract formal motifs like the arabesque and performed on plucked long-necked lutes such as the *tanbūr* and *tār,* instrumental music that is part of a nomadic aesthetic typically narrates a story. The plot is generally known to listeners in advance and, just as with European program music, informed listeners are expected to be able to follow the story as it unfolds in a purely instrumental form—in this case, strummed on two-stringed lutes such as the *dombra* and *dutār.* These pieces, generically known as *kui,* often involve virtuoso strumming and fingering techniques, shifting rhythmic patterns, and flexible use of two-part polyphony. Other instruments, such as the *sybyzyk,* a short, single-reed pipe made from cane, and the *chang-kobuz,* a metal Jew's harp, are used to help the performer "imagine" a picture or a brief narrative program. Such music is more personal and intimate than communicative, and individual styles linked to the idiosyncratic techniques of one or another performer exist alongside canonical repertoires.

MUSIC, LANGUAGE, AND NATIONAL IDENTITY

While rural and urban populations throughout Central Asia gravitate toward different genres of music, other aspects of culture—in particular, language—strengthen the region's overall social cohesion. Just as the near ubiquity of Arabic bolsters social cohesion throughout the Middle East and North Africa, Turkic languages serve as a unifying force in Central Asia. However, unlike Arabic, which despite its many spoken dialects and local forms is identified at least nominally as a single language, the continuum of Turkic dialect in Central Asia has been fractured into nominally distinct though closely related languages. During the Soviet era, Soviet cultural policy was intended to break up ethnolinguistic and cultural continuities in Central Asia, with the goal of forging separate "national" identities centered on five Soviet republics: Kazakhstan, Khirgizia (now Kyrgyzstan), Tajikistan, Turkmenia (now Turkmenistan), and Uzbekistan. The cultural strategy for this region mirrored Soviet political strategy: *divisa et imperiam* 'divide and conquer'. Rather than reinforcing ethnolinguistic and cultural continuity throughout Central Asia, Soviet policy worked to undermine it.

Fearing an Islamist, pan-Turkic political alliance as a threat to Soviet power, Soviet cultural strategists stressed distinctions between one Central Asian people and another; and where these distinctions were not sufficiently marked, Soviet cultural policy manipulated language, literature, music, and other aspects of expressive culture to make them more apparent. Soviet publications on Central Asian music, such as the authoritative work of Victor Beliaev translated into English as *Central Asian Music* (Slobin and Slobin 1975), neatly correlated musical culture with Soviet political entities. Musical repertoires or genres that did not coincide with political boundaries were assigned in any event to a single republic. Soviet cultural policy had little tolerance for ambiguity. An example of the distortions perpetrated by such policies is the manipulation of the art song repertoire known as *shash maqām.*

Shash maqām, the court music tradition of the Bukharan emirs, has long been the joint cultural property of Uzbeks and Tajiks who lived side by side in the multi-
TRACK 30 ethnic cities of Bukhara and Samarkand. [See Classical Music of Uzbeks and Tajiks.] *Shash maqām* singers were typically bilingual in Uzbek (a Turkic language) and Tajik (an Iranian language), and their texts were drawn from classical poetry in
TRACK 31 both languages. These singers would switch almost unconsciously from one language to the other, and it is not uncommon to find Uzbek and Tajik couplets in the same song. But during the Soviet era, in order to bolster Soviet-created national identities ("Uzbek," "Tajik," and the like), the bilingual art song repertoire of Bukhara, Samarkand, and other cities was commonly divided into two separate entities: "Uzbek classical music" and "Tajik classical music," each with poetic texts exclusively in the "national" language of the appropriate republic. Commercial recordings, radio and television performances, musical pedagogy, and publications of musical notation all reflected this essentially political nomenclature. *Shash maqām,* for example, was split in two: a Tajik *shash maqām* was published in Dushanbe, Tajikistan, with Tajik texts; and an Uzbek *shash maqām* was published in Tashkent, with Uzbek texts.

By the early 1980s, this artificial division had become untenable, and the separate Tajik and Uzbek *māqām* repertoires were reterritorialized into what became known in Uzbekistan as the Uzbek-Tajik *shash maqām* and in Tajikistan as the Tajik-Uzbek *shash maqām.* In the intensely nationalistic atmosphere of post-Soviet Central Asia, particularly in Uzbekistan, *shash maqām* is again being used as a symbol of national identity and cultural tradition. Other republics seeking to bolster national cultural identity have also laid claim to particular repertoires or, in some cases, to particular works. For example, in Kyrgyzstan, the *Manas* epic, which in some versions consists of almost half a million lines of text (more than thirty times the length of Homer's *Odyssey*), has become the preeminent cultural symbol of nationhood. Indeed, Kyrgystan has developed a cult of the *Manas,* expressed through critical editions and recordings assembled by scholars, state-sponsored *Manas* festivals and competitions, and documentary films.

THE SOVIET ERA

The Russian conquest of Central Asia began in the middle of the nineteenth century and was formally completed in 1920, when the last of the region's feudal rulers—the emir of Bukhara and the khan of Khiva—were deposed. Through the 1920s, the erstwhile colonial territory of Russian Turkestan and the feudal city-states of Bukhara and Khiva were transformed, politically and culturally, into Soviet Central Asia. From the earliest years of Soviet rule, ideologically motivated cultural policies irrevocably changed local music and musical life.

Soviet cultural policy in Central Asia reflected broad Marxist-Leninist ideals concerning the role of art in socialist society: in all its forms, art should be accessible to the leading class of society—the proletariat—and should reaffirm the nation's political and social objectives. At an operational level, cultural strategists addressed the challenges of modernizing a region whose culture, like its politics, was officially viewed as backward and despotic. Following the Stalinist doctrine "nationalist in form, socialist in content," local music was adapted to conform to socialist themes. In song, for example, although the melodies remained unchanged, religious and spiritual lyrics were replaced by texts that proclaimed the glories of collective farms and five-year economic plans.

Even more disruptive to traditional music was the introduction of European cultural models for composition, performance, and pedagogy whose aim was to promote cultural enlightenment among indigenous Central Asian peoples. These models included musical notation, large ensembles such as orchestras and choirs, and an equally tempered tuning system like that of the piano, which made it possible to play instrumental music in a range of keys. The Soviet ministry of culture created a network of specialized music primary schools and high schools, and conservatories and institutes of musical research were opened in the capital cities of all the Central Asian republics. These institutions trained both performers and composers, whose craft revolved around using local folk music as a source for European-style compositions.

These models wreaked havoc on traditional forms of musical performance and pedagogy. The introduction and use of notation in music schools undermined orality, with its deep-rooted tradition of masters and disciples, as a method of transmission. Orchestras of reconstructed folk instruments transformed the subtle ornamentation and spare melodies of folksong into bloated cacophony. The neutral intervals and microtones that were the lifeblood of Central Asian urban music were associated with "feudalism" and were accordingly rejected and replaced by the whole tones and semitones of European major and minor scales.

In hindsight, the Soviet innovations in Central Asian musical life look paternalistic and Orientalist, but many artists and intellectuals—both Russians and representatives of indigenous peoples—became deeply committed to the project of building a cultural bridge between East and West. Even in the strongly nationalistic climate of post-Soviet Central Asia, official cultural policies have encouraged the continuation of Soviet-inspired hybrids such as orchestras of folk instruments and so-called *estrada* orchestras, which use a combination of European and indigenous instruments to transform local songs and tunes into vaudeville-like popular music. Conservatories and music institutes continue to turn out composers and performers of European-style concert music, and the nationalist aspirations of nineteenth-century Russian composers such as Tchaikovsky, Glinka, and Rimsky-Korsakov, who drew on native folk music, are still admired and are held up as a model for students. Noteworthy composers who have worked along these lines include Alexei Fedorovich Kozlovsky (1905–1977), Mutavaqqil Burxanov (b. 1916), and Mirsadyq Tajiyev (1944–1996).

CENTRAL ASIA IN THE AGE OF GLOBALIZATION

The beginning of the post-Soviet era in Central Asia has been characterized by strong cultural continuity but also by significant change. Each of the five Central Asian nations that declared independence after the breakup of the Soviet Union in 1991 has charted its own course in political and cultural affairs, yet all five have shared nativist tendencies which promote national heritage, history, and expressive culture. [Concerning contemporary Xinjiang, see WHEN UYGURS ENTERTAIN THEMSELVES

FIGURE 8 Young performers in Tashkent, Uzbekistan, 1999.

and MAQĀM IN THE TRADITION OF THE UYGURS.] For example, in Uzbekistan, many government-sponsored festivals and conferences have celebrated Uzbek heritage as expressed in architecture, literature, music, and dance (figure 8). The most venerated cities—Bukhara, Samarkand, and Khiva—have commemorated their antiquity with galas such as "Twenty-Five Hundred Years of Bukhara"; and traditional holidays such as *nawruz,* the Persian new year, which was suppressed during the Soviet era, have reemerged as a potent symbol of national identity. Music has had an important role in these events, not only as entertainment but as part of this symbolism.

While some state-sponsored festivals look backward, embracing heritage and tradition, others have emerged that showcase the place of Central Asia in global musical culture. For example, the festival "Voices of Asia" in Almaty, Kazakhstan, has featured fusion and crossover bands that might be viewed as descendants of the Soviet-era *estrada* orchestras, which performed ethnic pop music using a mixture of local and European instruments and musical languages. Young performers, such as Oleg Fesov from Tajikistan, Yulduz Usmanova from Uzbekistan, and the ensemble Ashkhabad from Turkmenistan, have made inroads into the global market for "world music," releasing recordings distributed by Western labels and touring a growing international network of world music festivals. Yulduz Usmanova, the self-styled "Madonna of Uzbekistan," has achieved enormous popularity in her own nation, yet her pop-star approach is tempered by respect for the traditional attitude of musicians who view music not as a commercial commodity but as a spiritual offering. Usmanova and her band still perform frequently at weddings in her native Tashkent, and they have been known to perform free when a family cannot afford to pay them.

Emigration spurred by the breakup of the Soviet Union has also changed the face of musical life in Central Asia. Fearing the consequences of nativism and nationalism, many Russians and other European-identified residents, including a sizable number of musicians, left the region. And beginning in the late 1970s, Bukharan Jews, who have lived in the cities of Central Asia for over a millennium and have made important contributions to urban performance traditions, emigrated *en masse* to Israel and the United States. At the turn of the twenty-first century, Bukharan Jewish communities in Tel Aviv and in Queens, New York, had a diverse, active musical life nourished by outstanding performers of classical *maqām,* lighter popular music, and Jewish liturgical and paraliturgical chant and song.

Central Asia's shifting political alignments and alliances, both among its own states and peoples and with the great powers that surround it, have resonated in music and musical life. Successive eras of conquest, devastation, détente, and renascence have produced a remarkable accretion of musical forms and influences. Some older traditions have disappeared, but more commonly older traditions have been reimagined in new forms. The intricacy and richness of the Central Asian musical landscape is not unlike a living arabesque that seamlessly merges repetition and variation into an unending pattern, at once familiar and endlessly provocative.

REFERENCES

Beliaev, Victor M., ed. 1950–1958. *Shashmaqām*, vols. 1–4. Moscow: Gosudarstvennoe Muzykalnoe Izdatelstvo.

During, Jean. 1998. *Musiques d'Asie centrale: L'esprit d'une tradition*. Paris: Cité de la Musique/ Actes Sud. Compact disk.

During, Jean, and Trjebinjac, Sabine. 1991. *Introduction à l'étude de la musique ouïgoure*. Bloomington: Indiana University Press.

Karomatov, Faizula M., ed. 1966–1975. *Shashmaqām*, vols. 1–6. Tashkent.

Levin, Theodore. 1996. *The Hundred Thousand Fools of God: Musical Travels in Central Asia (and Queens, New York)*. Bloomington: Indiana University Press. Compact disk.

Levin, Theodore. 2001b. "Making Marxist-Leninist Music in Uzbekistan." In *Drawing on Marx: Interdisciplinary Perspectives on Music*, ed. Regina Burckhardt Qureshi. New York: Garland.

Levin, Theodore, and Razia Sultanova. 2001a. "Uzbekistan." In *The New Grove Dictionary of Music and Musicians*, 2nd ed., ed. Stanley Sadie. London: Macmillan.

Rawski, Evelyn S. Forthcoming. "Cultural Interactions in East and Inner Asia." In *The Garland Encyclopedia of World Music*, Vol. 7, *East Asia: China, Japan, and Korea*, ed. Robert C. Provine, Yosihiko Tokumaru, and J. Lawrence Witzleben. New York: Routledge.

Slobin, Mark, and Greta Slobin, trans. and ed. 1975. *Central Asian Music*. Middletown, Conn.: Wesleyan University Press. (Adapted from Victor Beliaev. 1962. *Ocherki po istorii muzyki narodov SSSR*. Moscow.)

Sultanova, Razia. 1998. *Ritmika vokalnykh chastei shashmakoma*. Tashkent: Yani.

Yanov-Yanovskaya, Natalia Solomonovna. 1999. *Mutal' Burkhanov: Vremya, zhizn', tvorchestvo* (Mutal Burkhanov: His Times, Life, and Art). Tashkent: Media Land.

Zeranska-Kominek, Slawomira, with Arnold Lebeuf. 1997. *The Tale of Crazy Harman: The Musician and the Concept of Music in the Türkmen Epic Tale Harmna Däli*. Warsaw: Dialog.

Snapshot: Abdurahim Hamidov—An Eminent Contemporary Master

Jean During

Abdurahim Hamidov (figure 1) was born in 1952 into an old family of Tashkent. His ancestors were merchants and caravaners, and his father and grandfather were mullahs. He began learning music at the age of six by singing the entire repertoire of children's songs. A year later he began playing the *rabāb,* a long-necked lute; and at age nine he developed a passion for the *dutār*—another type of long-necked lute—and had his
TRACK 30 first lessons on it. His repertoire consisted of lively, modern virtuosic melodies like those on radio and television.

Hamidov studied in a music school (*bilimyurt*) typical of those found throughout the Soviet Union, but he was lucky in that at the age of sixteen he became part of the
TRACK 31 classical vocal ensemble of Salahudin Tokhtasinov. He soon became part of the musical life of Tashkent, which was very strong in the late 1960s. He was constantly invited to perform, and he became adept at learning melodies very quickly, even guessing their development after hearing just the first motifs.

FIGURE 1 Abdurahim Hamidov. Photo courtesy of Jean During.

In 1972, Hamidov entered the Tashkent Conservatory and met Fakhriddin Sādiqov (1914–1977), who completely overturned his concept of music. Sādiqov was the founder of the Uzbek school of instrumental music. At their first meeting, Hamidov played one of the virtuosic pieces in which he excelled. Sādiqov acted impressed and congratulated him. "Then," recounted Hamidov (in an interview with the author), "he took my *dutār,* loosened the strings by a fourth, and started to play so beautifully that I thought I'd pass out. His music was like honey or cream. I worked with him on the *dutār* for three years, which were for me like twenty years of study. Everything that I had learned before was false, and I thought that I'd never come to anything, but toward the end, I began to understand. After that, I worked an average of six hours a day; and after several years, I succeeded in finding myself as a musician." The difficulty consisted essentially in shaping the sound through the playing of the left hand so as to reproduce all the inflections of singing, creating moans and sighs on an instrument which in ordinary hands is used more for rhythm than melody.

Hamidov became the successor of Sādiqov and the most eminent representative of a prestigious line of dutārists, synthesizing the styles of Khwārezm and Ferghana that had evolved through several generations of performers: Fakhriddin Sādiqov, Kāmil-jān Jabbarov (d. 1974), Nur Muhammad Bāltayev, Qāzi Madrahimov, Muhiuddin Hāji Najmuddin, and finally Dārep Chola. Hamidov taught at the Tashkent Conservatory, and of his fifty students, five or six, including a young woman, have become masters in their own right.

Hamidov has been active not only as a performer but also as a recording artist. He recorded the complete canonic instrumental repertoire (*mushkilāt*) with a group he formed in the line of his teacher. He has composed half a dozen songs, though he does not think they are original enough to release. He performed on more than three hundred recordings before the local production and distribution of vinyl records declined precipitously following the breakup of the Soviet Union in 1991. He has made several concert tours in Europe and Asia as a soloist in the Bahār Ensemble and, since 1992, alone or with small ensembles which he directs in the purest form of classical tradition.

Hamidov frequently performs with well-known singers at traditional banquets where the most classical musical and poetic forms live on. For five years, he left the Tashkent Conservatory and made a living in the world of commerce. He returned to the conservatory in 1997 at the invitation of its new director, but without ceasing his business activities. He has several books and articles in press: on the genre *sawt,* on twentieth-century *dutār* players and their repertoire, and on the repertoire of Fatha Khān Mamadaliev (d. 1999). Listeners can get an idea of his art from several compact disks released in the West: *Ouzbekistan: L'art du dotār* (Paris, Ocora, 1997, recording and liner notes by Jean During) and *Asie centrale: Les maîtres du dotār* (Geneva, 1993, AIMP 26, recording and liner notes by Jean During). Hamidov is the coeditor of the compact disk *Ouzbekistan: Les grandes voix du passé, 1940–1965* (Uzbekistan: Great Voices of the Past, 1940–1965; Paris, Ocora, 1999, with a 24-page liner note, text in French and English).

TRANSLATED BY THEODORE LEVIN

The Classical Music of Uzbeks and Tajiks

Theodore Levin and Razia Sultanova

Three Traditions of Central Asian *Maqām*
The Relation of Music and Verse
***Maqām* in the Culture of Central Asian Islam**
The Soviet and Post-Soviet Performance Tradition
***Maqām* Ensembles**

The classical music of Central Asia is known as *maqām*, a name it shares with other repertoires of classical or court music in the core Muslim world. Like the Arabic, Turkish, and Iranian classical repertoires, local varieties of *maqām* in Central Asia—Bukharan, Khorezm, Ferghana-Tashkent, and Uyghur—constitute regional dialects of what is at root a common musical language. The Central Asian repertoires, however, are little known beyond the region, and the richness of their music and poetry is only beginning to become apparent to outsiders through recordings, international concert tours, and scholarly publications. Indeed, the Central Asian *maqām* represents a vast yet integrated artistic conception that encompasses music, metaphysics, ethics, and aesthetics.

TRACK 30

TRACK 31

THREE TRADITIONS OF CENTRAL ASIAN *MAQĀM*

Russian scholars who began studying indigenous music in Central Asia in the years following the Bolshevik Revolution were the first to use the term "classical music" to designate Central Asian *maqām.* Local scholars and musicians later adopted the terms "classical music" and "professional oral tradition music" to describe three distinct but related vocal and instrumental repertoires linked to the cities of Bukhara, Khiva, and Qoqand, all of which lie within the borders of present-day Uzbekistan. Bukhara is a multicultural city in which much of the population identifies itself as ethnically Tajik and is actively trilingual in Tajik, Uzbek, and Russian. The Bukharan *maqām* repertoire, known in Tajik as *shash* 'six' *maqām*, is performed with poetic texts in both Uzbek and Tajik, depending on the preference of performers and listeners, and has been elevated to a national cultural symbol in both Uzbekistan and Tajikistan. By contrast, the *maqām* repertoires associated with Khiva, known as the Khorezm *maqām*, and with Qoqand, known as the Ferghana-Tashkent *maqām*, are solidly within the present-day Uzbek cultural sphere: that is, they are largely performed by and for Uzbeks, although the Khorezm *maqām* has historically included both Persian and Uzbek texts.

Like other musical practices glossed as "classical" or "professional," the Central Asian *maqām* repertoires demand specially trained musicians and have evolved over at least a millennium in conjuction with erudite traditions of music theory and poetics. In the medieval Islamic world, as in medieval Christendom, music and music theory were linked with mathematics and the natural sciences, and the roots of the present

Uzbekistan and Tajikistan.

form and structure of Central Asian *maqām* are illuminated in a series of encyclopedic treatises produced between the tenth and seventeenth centuries by leading Islamic scholars such as al-Fārābī, Ibn Sīnā, Ṣayfī al-Dīn al-Urmawī, ʿAbd al-Qādir Marāghī, Kaukabi, and Darwīsh ʿAlī. [See Arabic Sources on Music: Eighth to Nineteenth Centuries.]

In Central Asia, classical music flourished during the reign of Timur (1337–1405) and the Timurid rulers who succeeded him. Timur made the city of Samarkand the capital of his empire, and to embellish it he gathered the finest architects, scholars, craftsmen, and musicians from his vast kingdom. The result was an opulent and diverse cultural life nourished by the intermingling of different artistic practices and aesthetic canons. By the end of the fifteenth century, the mighty Timurid Empire had begun to dissolve into smaller emirates and khanates ruled by local dynasties—the progenitors of the present-day Uzbeks—each with its own feudal court centered in a different city. These courts seem to have been a catalyst for the evolution of the Central Asian *maqām* tradition into distinct but related local styles and repertoires supported by the patronage of the feudal nobility and sometimes by Sufi sheikhs and their disciples. In addition to the Bukharan *shash maqām*, the Khorezm *maqām*, and the Ferghana-Tashkent *maqām*, these regional traditions include the so-called *on ikki* 'twelve' *maqām* of the Uygurs. The *on ikki maqām* comprises a related but somewhat more distant complex of styles and repertoires that may well have followed its own course of development over many centuries in the oasis cities of modern Chinese Xinjiang.

Bukharan *shash maqām*

The *shash maqām* is a monumental cycle of vocal and instrumental pieces that began to assume a canonical form toward the end of the eighteenth century and at present comprises a largely fixed repertoire. It consists of six constituent cycles, or suites, each of which is divided into an instrumental section (*mushqilāt*) and a vocal section (*nasr*). Each suite contains a series of pieces related by melodic resemblance but set in different metric-rhythmic genres.

In Central Asia, the term *maqām* has two meanings. As in other *maqām* traditions, it may refer to a melodic type or mode. More commonly, however, it designates a formal scheme—in particular, one of the lengthy suite cycles of the *shash maqām* or Khorezm *maqām* whose eponymous melodic type is prominently featured in the suite. For example, as a melodic type, *maqām buzruk* refers to an abstraction of melodic resemblance among all musical items called *buzruk.* The musicologist Harold Powers has described melodic types as occupying the tonal space between a "generalized tune" and a "particularized scale," with some kinds of melodic types tending toward the scale end of the continuum and others toward the tune end. In the Central Asian *maqām,* the concept of melodic type is strongly reified at the tune end. That is, musicians perform preexisting pieces drawn from one of the suites, rather than improvising melodies rooted in conventional melodic motifs and modal scales, as for example, in North Indian *rāga*.

The other meaning of *maqām*, that of a cycle or suite, is illustrated in figure 1. This table represents the formal scheme of the *shash maqām* as transcribed in an authoritative six-volume redaction published in Uzbekistan in the 1960s and 1970s by Karomatov and Rajabov. The division of vocal pieces into two groups is a relatively recent formalization of what appears to have been an older distinction between a fixed, canonical sequence of pieces and an open-ended sequence that followed it. The latter consisted of imitative pieces modeled on the melodic types and metric-rhythmic genres in the canonical section.

The first group of *shu'be* from the *rāst* suite is an example of how a single tune is metrically and rhythmically transformed to create different musical items related by melodic type. Here the melodic type is not *rāst* itself but *ushshāq*, a subsidiary melodic type within the *rāst* suite. Figure 2 shows the opening of the *ushshāq* tune in the three metric-rhythmic genres in which it occurs in the first group of *shu'be* in the *rāst* suite: *talqîn*, *nasr*, and *ufār.* Each genre is characterized by a repeating metric cycle called *usul* (the Arabic singular is *asl*). Note that the integrity of the common tune is overwhelmingly preserved in each item despite melodic and rhythmic variations.

The melodic development of each *shu'be* progresses through a series of structural divisions distinguished by tessitura: an introductory section, *darāmad*, set in a low tessitura leads to a section called *miyānkhāna* typically set at the interval of a fifth above the introduction. *Miyānkhāna* leads to *dunasr*, set an octave above the *darāmad*. *Awj* 'zenith', 'culmination' follows *dunasr*, after which the piece gradually descends to the original tessitura in a concluding section called *furāward.* The high-tessitura *awj* is both the musical and the dramatic climax and may assume various named canonical forms, such as *awj-i turk*, *muhayyar*, and *zebā pari*. *Awj* may also include melodic fragments drawn from another *shu'be*, called *namud,* which help create melodic unity in the *maqām* cycle as a whole.

Khorezm *maqām*

The Khorezm *maqām* is known colloquially as *alti-yarim* 'six-and-a-half' *makom* because one of its suites, *panjgāh*, contains only instrumental pieces and is thus counted as half a *maqām.* As a collection of suites consisting of an ordered sequence of musical items, the Khorezm *maqām* has clear parallels to the *shash maqām.* The items themselves, however, differ both in specific melodic content and in formal genre.

FIGURE 1 *Shash maqām*: contents and order. The names of the six *maqām* suites appear horizontally at the top; the left column lists the main genres of instrumental pieces and vocal songs in each suite, divided into their three formal units: instrumental section, first group of *shu'be*, second group of *shu'be*. (*Shu'be* 'branch' in Arabic here means a piece or musical item.)

Notes: Each intersection of a row and column represents an individual piece. The name of the piece is formed by linking the name of a metric-rhythmnic genre with the name of a melodic type, for example, *Tasnif-i Buzruk* (row 1, column 1).

An asterisk indicates that the name of the melodic type is the same as that of the *maqām* at the top of the column. Each *maqām* cycle, however, includes pieces that exemplify one or more subsidiary melodic types, and the names of these melodic types are entered in the table. For example, the metric-rhythmic genre *talqīn* is represented in the *buzruk* suite not by melodic type *buzruk* itself, but by *uzzāl*; thus, *Talqin-i Uzzal*.

Instrumental Section						
	Maqâm					
Genre	*Buzrak*	*Râst*	*Nawâ*	*Dugâh*	*Segâh*	*Irâq*
Tasnîf	*	*	*	*	*	*
Tarje	*		*	*	*	*
Gardûn	*	*	*	*		
Mukhammas	* Nasrullâ-î	* Panjgâh Ushshâq	* Bayât Huseynî	* Chârgâh Hâji Hâja Châr Sarkhâna	* Mirzâ Hakîm Ajâm	*
Saqîl	Sultan Islimî	Vazmin Râk-Râk	*	Ashkullâ	Bestenegâr	* (2) Kalân
Vocal Section: First Group of *Shu'be*						
Sarakhbâr	*	*	*	*	*	*
Tarâna	6	4	2	6	6	6
Talqîn	Uzzâl	Ushshâq	Bayât	Chârgâh	*	
Tarâna	*	*	*	*	*	
Mukhayar						*
Nasr	Uzzâl	Ushshâq	Bayât	Chârgâh		
Ufâr	Uzzâl	Ushshâq	Bayât	Chârgâh	*	*
Vocal Section: Second Group of *Shu'be*						
1st subsuite	Mûgûlcha-i Buzurk	Sowt-i Ushshâq	Sowt-i Nawâ	Sowt-i Chârgâh	Mûgulcha-i Segâh	(NONE)
Sowt		*	*	*	*	
Mûgulcha	*				*	
Talqîncha	*	*	*	*	*	
Chapandaz		*	*			
Qashqarcha	*	*	*	*	*	
Sâqînâma	*	*	*	*	*	
Ufâr	*	*	*	*	*	
2nd subsuite	Sowt-i Sarvinâz	Sowt-i Sabâ	Mûgulchâ-i Nawâ			
Mûgulcha	*	*	*			
Sowt	*	*				
Talqîncha	*	*	*	Qalindâr-i Dugâh		
Qashqarcha	*	*	*			
Sâqînâme	*	*	*			
Ufâr	*	*	*			
3rd subsuite	Irâq-i Bukhara	Sowt-i Kalân	Mustazâd-i Nawâ			
	Irâq					
Sowt		*				
Talqîncha	*	*	Mustazâd-i Nawâ Talqîncha-i Mustazâd-i Nawâ	Samandâr-i Dugâh		
Chapandâz	*	*				
Qashqarcha			*			
Sâqînâme	*	*	*			
Ufâr	*	*	*			
4th subsuite		Râk		Arâm-e-jân		

FIGURE 2 Opening of *ushshāq* tune in three metric-rhythmic genres in *maqām-i rāst*.

For example, the sequence of items in *maqām rāst* in the Khorezm *maqām* is as follows.

Instrumental section:	Vocal section:
tani maqām-i rāst	*tani maqam-i rāst*
tarji-i rāst	*tarāna*
peshrav- i gardūn	*talqīn*
muxammas i, ii, muxamas-i ushshāq	*farōd*
saqīl-i vazmin	*nasr-i sabā*
ufār	*suvāra*

Suvāra, a genre in the vocal section, is unique to Khorezm and is widely performed outside the *maqām* cycle as a freestanding art song. Certain pieces, such as *tarji-i rāst*, are performed in free rhythm, without the metrical delineation of *usul.* The Khorezm *maqām* contains only one *tarāna* in each suite, in contrast to the multiple *tarāna* pieces in the *shash maqām.*

Ferghana-Tashkent *maqām*

Of the three indigenous Central Asian *maqām* traditions, the Ferghana-Tashkent *maqām* is now most popular among local listeners. Also known as *chār* 'four' *maqām*, it consists of four independent suites: *bayāt*, *chargāh*, *dugāh-husayni*, and *gulyār-shahnāz*. Each contains an identical sequence of pieces distinguished by metric-rhythmic genre: *mugulcha*, *talqincha*, *qashqarcha*, *sāqināme*, and *ufār*. This is the sequence that twentieth-century performers of *shash maqām* appropriated and transformed into the second group of *shu'be* in each of the *shash maqām* suites except *irāq.* The Ferghana-Tashkent repertoire is lighter and faster than the *shash maqām* and Khorezm *maqām*, and local musicians call it *chapanlik* 'wild', 'daring', 'audacious' to suggest its eclectic fusion of urban court and rural nomadic styles.

THE RELATION OF MUSIC AND VERSE

At the center of the *maqām* tradition is vocal music. Singers have the greatest cachet among *maqām* performers, and the ability to reach a high tessitura pitch in the *awj*, or culmination, of a song and sustain it over an entire long breath is much admired by connoisseurs of classical music. Singing *maqām*, however, is far more than a display of virtuosity. The lyrical expressiveness of the *maqām* is also a means of conveying the beauty and symbolic power of the poetic texts. These texts belong to Islamic poets such as Hafez, Jamī, Nawā'i, Hilālī, Amirī, Bedil, Mashrab, and others who wrote in Persian and in a literary form of Turkic known as Chagatay. The texts, composed in classical forms such as *ghazal*, *mukhammas*, *mustazād*, and *rubaī*, are redolent with symbols drawn from Sufism, the mystical trend in Islam. The most salient of these symbols is love, which, while describing human feelings and activities, alludes metaphorically to love of the divine. Following are examples of poetic verse sung as lyrics in the *shash maqām.*

> She shot an arrow through my heart at point-blank range.
> The flames from me rose up, all intertwined.
> (Ghiyāsi)
>
> If you want to come to me, only come alone.
> For happiness and love, come alone.
> Your [half-open] lips are like a pistachio.
> Your tongue is like *halvah*.
> (Anonymous)
>
> O, my friend, if you ask for my soul, I'll give you my soul.
> Whatever is dearer than a soul, I'll also give you.
> (Anonymous)
>
> Like a nightingale in the garden, I sing for my roses.
> Like Majnun for his Leila, I sing.
> Like an owl, I live in a tumbledown place.
> Of the pain in my heart, I sing to that person who is like me.
> (Jazbi)
>
> Why did my beloved pass by me without paying me notice?
> Why didn't she see my tears and hear my wailing?
> Poor Hājji, how can you not cry from [the pain of] separation?
> I am like a reed in the steppe that grew so that whoever passed would cut me and take me along.
> (Hājji Huseyn-i Xangurti)

To convey the meaning of a text to listeners, singers must not only have a powerful voice with a broad range but also command the art of setting poetic texts properly to music. This art requires mastery of a prosodic system known as *aruz*, which has served as the basis of classical Arabic, Persian, and Turkic poetry from at least the ninth century virtually to the present.

The *aruz* system comprises a complex of quantitative meters, each with its own scansion formula analogous, for example, to the formulaic scansion of iambic pentameter or hexameter in English. Skilled performers understand how to accommodate the quantitative verse meter of a poetic text to the *usul* and melodic rhythm of a particular musical genre. Figure 3 shows the verse meters for poetry commonly set to music in the genres *nasr, talqīn*, and *ufār*. The meters are identified by their traditional Arabic nomenclature, with poetic feet spelled out in the Arabic *afa'īl*—rhythmic formulas serving as paradigms for recognized verse meters.

Talqīn and *ufār*, which share a verse meter but have different *usul* patterns and different melodic rhythms, demonstrate that the same verse meter can be set to different metric-rhythmic genres. But there must be a metric "common denominator"

FIGURE 3 Verse meters of *talqīn, ufār,* and *nasr*.

Ramal muṭamman maḥdūf (*talqīn' ufār*)

– ∪ – –   – ∪ – –   – ∪ – –   – ∪ –

fa:ʿila:tun fa:ʿila:tun fa:ʿila:tun fa:ʿilun

hazaj muṭamman sālim (*nasr*)

∪ – – –   ∪ – – –   ∪ – – –   ∪ – – –

mafa:ʿi:lun mafa:ʿi:lun mafa:ʿi:lun mafa:ʿi:lun

FIGURE 4 Initial two phrases of *talqīn-i ushshāq* and *ufār-i ushshāq* with scansion.

encompassing *usul* and verse meter that ensures metric-rhythmic accommodation between them. In *talqīn*, where verse meter is closely tied to melodic rhythm and *usul* to the shape of a phrase, such accommodation does not necessarily extend to the rhythmic details of each phrase but rather concerns a regularity of cyclic characteristics.

Figure 4 shows the initial two musical phrases of *talqīn-i ushshāq* and *ufār-i ushshāq*, corresponding to a couplet of poetic text. Scansion marks beneath the musical pitches show how a performer handles the relationship between verse meter and rhythmic values in the music, trying, wherever possible, to line up short rhythmic values in the music with syllables scanned as short in the text.

MAQĀM IN THE CULTURE OF CENTRAL ASIAN ISLAM

Until the 1920s, when the cultural policies of the newly founded Soviet Union began to transform musical life in the Soviet Central Asian republics, the social conventions surrounding music and other arts had been overwhelmingly shaped by Islamic beliefs and practices. As a canonical musical tradition rooted in urban culture, *maqām* was subject to strict social regulation that dictated where, when, and by whom it should be performed; how listeners should be affected by music and poetic texts; and through what mechanism knowledge should be transmitted to new generations of musicians.

The strictest social regulation was imposed on the *shash maqām*, the repertoire rooted in the feudal city of Bukhara, whose great tradition of Islamic learning and piety earned it the sobriquet "the dome of Islam." Music, viewed variously by Muslims

Music, viewed variously by Muslims as both a vessel of spirituality and a distraction from spirituality, had a morally ambiguous status in Bukhara.

as both a vessel of spirituality and a distraction from spirituality, had a morally ambiguous status in Bukhara. The Bukharan *shash maqām* was no exception. Notwithstanding its moralistic texts, the *shash maqām* was forbidden as a performance art under certain particularly strict emirs [see CENTRAL ASIA: OVERVIEW]. Other emirs, however, allowed public performances of the *shash maqām*, and the last emir, Alim Khan, who fled Bukhara in 1920 to escape the Bolsheviks, provided informal patronage to a retinue of court musicians. The most famous of these musicians was Levi Bābākhānov (1872–1926), popularly known as Leviche.

Like many other *shash maqām* singers, Leviche was Jewish—a descendent of Persian-speaking Jewish tradesmen and craftsmen who settled in Transoxania during the Timurid era or even before and became known as Bukharan Jews. From the late nineteenth century to the last quarter of the twentieth, several Jewish family lineages dominated the vocal performance of *shash maqām*. Mullaqand, Tālmas, and Bābākhān—Russified as Mullakandov, Tolmasov, and Bābākhānov—were household names among the musical connoisseurs of Bukhara, Samarkand, and Shahrisabz. (Tashkent's rise as the center of an academicized national culture came later.) Other well-known musicians, including Ata Jalāl, credited with being the "founder" of the *shash maqām*, were *chalas*—Jews who converted to Islam under duress and privately preserved elements of Jewish belief or practice. While the profession of musician was socially precarious for Sunni Muslims, who were the majority of Bukhara's population, it was both attractive and licit for Jews as well as other marginalized groups in this multiethnic city.

Although the emir of Bukhara invited musicians to entertain his family and his guests, Central Asian *maqām* seems never to have been confined to the social world of the feudal nobility or the mercantile elite. Rather, all three regional forms of *maqām* were popular with socially diverse listeners. Moreover, music served as a culturally unifying force; its poetic texts, infused with the moral values of Islam, were a hortatory device to guide and inspire listeners—many of whom were illiterate. Older performers alive at the end of the twentieth century could recall weddings at which vocalists belted out the Sufi-inspired lyrics of songs drawn from the *maqām* while a thousand guests sat in rapt attention. Often, as a performer reached the high-tessitura *awj*, the culmination, the listeners also cried aloud in ecstasy, participating in the rapture created by a powerful voice delivering words of deeply spiritual meaning. Individual songs were linked to form suites that, like the *maqām* cycles themselves, metaphorically spanned the entirety of human existence "from prayer to dance," as one performer described it. For example, the vocal section of the *shash maqām* begins with the lugubrious and introspective *sarakhbār* and progresses by the end of the first group of *shu'be* to the dancelike *ufār*.

By the beginning of the twenty-first century, the traditional social role of *maqām* performance as a central feature of festivities had been reduced to a single event in a typical wedding: *āsh*, the early-morning gathering of men for food and music. The *āsh* is a religious occasion, an extension of morning prayers that constitutes an offering to God and to ancestors. The fathers of the bride and groom pray for the continuation of their family lineage through their children's union. The music at an *āsh*—spiritual poetry set to slowly paced, drawn-out melodies—conveys the serious nature of the event.

Another casualty of the changing social context of *maqām* is the traditional artistic apprenticeship in which a disciple learns by imitating examples of a master's work. In classical Persian and Ottoman poetry, such mimetic or parallel creations are called *nazira,* and this term came to be used in music as well. The concept of *nazira* is based on in respect for elders and for tradition, a cornerstone of cultural values in Central Asia. To learn the art of performing *maqām,* a young student (*shagird*) typically apprenticed himself to a master musician (*ustaz*) for seven to ten years, during which time he memorized many pieces in precise detail. The end of this apprenticeship was marked by a ceremony, often following a type of examination, in which the master accepted the apprentice as a full-fledged professional qualified to create his own performance versions of pieces.

As long as the master-apprentice system remained rooted in oral transmission, it ensured the continuity of *maqām* as a canonical tradition while empowering talented performers to create new performance styles and compositions. But with the establishment of Soviet rule in Central Asia in the decade following the Bolshevik revolution of 1917, both the *shash maqām* and the Khorezm *maqām* began to attract the attention of musicologists and folklorists, first Russian and then Uzbek, who transcribed these repertoires into staff notation. As the use of notation became the norm in Soviet music schools and conservatories, the *maqām* traditions became not only canonical but also frozen in their published performance versions.

THE SOVIET AND POST-SOVIET PERFORMANCE TRADITION

The doyen of the Russian musicologists and folklorists in Central Asia was Victor Uspensky (1879–1949), born near Moscow but raised in the city of Osh on the border of Uzbekistan and Kyrgyzstan, where his father was in the government service. Uspensky graduated from the Saint Petersburg Conservatory in 1913, and in 1917 he managed to return to Central Asia as a member of an expedition launched from Saint Petersburg to study and gather examples of indigenous music. Uspensky's fieldwork led to his publication in 1924 of the first transcription of the *shash maqām* in staff notation, taken from the Bukharan musicians Ata Jalāl and Ata Ghiās. This publication, however, did not include song texts. Uspensky did not explain their absence in print, but in a letter to a fellow musicologist, Victor Beliaev, he made it clear that the texts had been excluded because of political sensitivities about language and nationality. The *shash maqām* texts that Uspensky transcribed from his Bukharan informants were mostly in Tajik Persian. Yet cultural leaders in Bukhara were eager to claim the *shash maqām* as an exemplar of an Uzbek "great tradition" in the arts. The most prominent of these leaders was Abdurauf Fitrat, the minister of enlightenment of the Bukharan People's Republic, an interregnum Muslim socialist state created from the remains of the Bukharan emirate before the establishment of the Soviet Republic of Uzbekistan. Fitrat's concern about the language of the *shash maqām* texts marked the introduction of the ideologically motivated "national question" into Central Asian cultural politics. Soviet policies regarding nationalities used art and culture to help articulate new national identities congruent with each of the Soviet Union's fifteen republics, such as Uzbek, Tajik, and Kazakh. In Central Asia, these identities were intended to replace those linked to the untidy amalgam of ethnolinguistic and regional groups in traditional Central Asian clan-based society—for instance, Qongrat, Qipchaq, and Sart.

Policies concerning nationalities affected the *shash maqām* in several ways. Most obviously, the repertoire was cloned into two variants, one associated with the republic of Uzbekistan and the other with the neighboring republic of Tajikistan. Most vocalists who performed the *shash maqām* were bilingual in Uzbek and Tajik and sang lyrics drawn from both languages. However, the government of Uzbekistan published a version of the *shash maqām* with exclusively Uzbek texts, while the "Tajik" *shash maqām* was published in Tajikistan in a version containing only Tajik texts. The *shash maqām* became a protean symbol of national identity, with scholars adjusting their discussion of the repertoire as political expediency demanded. In the edition of the *shash maqām* published in Uzbekistan in 1959, the musicologists Akbarov and Kon wrote: "We must suppose that the united effort of historians, Orientalists, and musicologists will lead in the near future to clarification of the problem of the origin and historical development of the *maqāmlar*, which are a remarkable monument to the centuries-old history of musical culture of the Uzbek people" (xxx). By contrast, in Victor Beliaev's edition of the *shash maqām* published in cooperation with the republic of Tajikistan in 1950, the following note appears in the introduction: "The classical music of the Tajik people, which is united under the general name *shash maqām*, together with other folk melodies and pieces, and with the musical culture of the great Russian people, is one of the fundamental sources of modern Soviet-Tajik musical culture and musical art" (11).

MAQĀM ENSEMBLES

The published transcriptions spurred the creation of large ensembles of musicians trained to read notation. Ensembles modeled on European orchestras and choirs began to appear in Central Asia in the 1920s as part of the Soviet Union's efforts to promote European cultural values among its many non-European peoples. Workers' choirs performed a mixture of arranged folk songs and newly composed revolutionary songs. After that came hybrid orchestras featuring a combination of European instruments and Uzbek instruments altered to facilitate a merging with European music. In 1927, a national folk music ensemble was organized at the fledgling Uzbek radio station in Samarkand, under the direction of Yunus Rajabī, who was an accomplished performer of *maqām* and a self-taught musicologist. In the late 1940s and early 1950s, however, *maqām* became an object of official scorn within the Uzbek cultural establishment. Echoing the infamous "struggle against formalism" launched by the Union of Composers in Moscow, the chairman of the Union of Composers of Uzbekistan, Sabir Babayev, issued a decree in 1951 entitled "About the Development of Monophonic Music," proclaiming that in monophonic music—which was to say *maqām*—no development was possible. Monophonic music, said Babayev, could not "properly reflect the new Soviet reality." *Maqām*, a highly visible symbol of feudal social traditions and

FIGURE 5 The ensemble Shash Maqām, founded and directed by Ari Bābākhānov (seated, second from left). Photo by Aleksandr Djumaev, Bukhara, 1998.

FIGURE 6 Ensemble of Uzbek traditional musicians. Photo by Razia Sultanova.

FIGURE 7 Fatakhān Mamadaliev. Photo by Razia Sultanova.

FIGURE 8 Monājāt Yulchieva, a well-known performer of classical song. Photo by Razia Sultanova.

Sufi-inspired spirituality, was a prime target for the "struggle against the past" by the Soviet ministry of culture. In 1952, all folk music ensembles at the Tashkent radio station were disbanded and replaced by recordings of European-style bands and orchestras whose musicians were reading notation. It was not until the cultural thaw of the Khrushchev era that *maqām* was politically rehabilitated (figures 5 and 6). In 1958, Yunus Rajabī was invited to create a *maqām* ensemble at the Tashkent radio station.

In pre-Soviet Bukhara, *maqām* would typically have been performed by a single singer, or sometimes by two or three singers who would trade vocal lines in a friendly competition, challenging one another to sing higher and higher, louder and louder. Singers provided their own spare instrumental accompaniment on the *tanbur* (a long-necked lute with three or four strings) and *dāyra* (a frame drum). By contrast, Rajabī's ensemble was like a chamber orchestra. In addition to *tanbur* and *dāyra*, it included *dutār* and Kashgar *rabāb* (long-necked lutes), *nay* (a transverse flute), *qoshnay* (an end-blown double pipe, each pipe with a single reed), *ghijak* (a spike fiddle), and *chang* (a struck zither similar to a hammer dulcimer). Vocal parts were performed not by one, two, or three singers but by a mixed chorus of male and female voices. Performances of the *shash maqām* took on the form of a grandiose cantata, with a conductor, antiphonal choirs, and orchestrated solo and tutti instrumental episodes.

While the bloated Soviet-era performance style epitomized by the Tashkent radio station's *maqām* ensemble remains a vestige of Soviet culture policy in post-Soviet Uzbekistan and Tajikistan, other performers and styles now have greater currency. The elegant, laconic instrumental pieces of Turgun Alimatov, a master performer on *tanbur*, *dutar*, and *sato* (a bowed *tanbur*), are newly composed miniatures modeled on the Ferghana-Tashkent *maqām*. Barno Iskhakova, a Bukharan Jewish singer revered by local connoisseurs of *maqām* for her luxuriant alto voice, legitimized the role of women in the *maqām* tradition. Jurabek Nabiyev, a virtuosic tenor from Khojand, Tajikistan, sings *shash maqām* with power and grace, accompanied by a small ensemble. Vocalists such as Mastane Yergashova, Fatakhān Mamadaliev (figure 7), Arifkhān Khatamov, and Monājāt Yulchieva (figure 8) not only earned renown as performers but had protégés to whom they transmitted their performance style and repertoire. Meanwhile, in the Bukharan Jewish diaspora communities of Tel Aviv, Israel, and Queens, New York, newly reconstituted ensembles perpetuate the tradition of Jewish *shash maqām* performers. For example, in Queens, the musician and poet Ilyas Malayev leads an eponymous group—the Ilyas Malayev Ensemble—whose performances of *shash maqām* are informed both by the traditions of pre-Soviet Bukhara and by the eclectic cultural life of Queens. Malayev sheds the ponderous textures of the Soviet-era *maqām* ensemble in favor of a lighter, faster style; yet in performances and recordings he re-creates the old sense of the *shash maqām* as a collection of suites—ordered sequences of pieces linked by a metric-rhythmic and melodic logic. On a recording of *maqām buzruk* made in 1998, Malayev shows the panoramic emotional range of the *shash maām*—from the somber meditative *sarakhbār* to the festive, dancelike *ufār.* Performed as a suite rather than, as became common in Soviet times, individual pieces taken out of context, the *shash maqām* is revealed as an extended metaphor of life itself: a musical and poetic journey through the emotional and spiritual worlds of human existence. That Malayev and his ensemble have been able to create from the *shash maqām* a music that is at once modern and traditional is evidence both of their great talent and of the eternal life of the *shash maqām.*

REFERENCES

Akbarov, I. A., and I. U. Kon. 1959. *Uzbekskaia narodnaia muzyka*, Vol. 5, *Bukharskie makomy*. Tashkent: Gos. Izdat. Khudozh. Lit.

Asie Centrale: Traditions classiques. 1993. Ocora/ Radio France C 560035–36. 2 compact disks.

At the Bazaar of Love: The Ilyas Malayev Ensemble. 1997. Shanachie Records 64081. Compact disk.

Beliaev, Victor M., ed. 1950–1958. *Shashmaqām*, Vols. 1–4. Moscow: Gosudarstvennoe Muzykalnoe-Izdatelstvo.

Djumaev, Alexander. 1993. "Power Structures, Culture Policy, and Traditional Music in Soviet Central Asia." *Yearbook for Traditional Music* 25:43–51.

During, Jean. 1998. *Musiques d'Asie centrale: L'esprit d'une tradition*. Paris: Cité de la Musique/ Actes Sud. Compact disk.

During, Jean, and Sabine Trebinjac. 1991. *Introduction à l'étude de la musique ouïgoure*. Bloomington: Indiana University Press.

Jung, Angelika. 1989. *Quellen der traditionellen Kunstmusik der Usbeken und Tadshiken Mittelasiens.* Hamburg: Karl Dieter Wagner.

Karomatov, Faizula M., ed. 1966–1975. *Shashmaqām*, Vols. 1–6. Tashkent.

Levin, Theodore. 1996. *The Hundred Thousand Fools of God: Musical Travels in Central Asia (and Queens, New York).* Bloomington: Indiana University Press. Compact disk.

Levin, Theodore. 2001. "Making Marxist-Leninist Music in Uzbekistan." In *Music and Marx: Ideas, Practice, Politics*, ed. Regina Burckhardt Qureshi. New York: Garland.

Levin, Theodore, and Razia Sultanova. 2001. "Uzbekistan." In *The New Grove Dictionary of Music and Musicians*, ed. Stanley Sadie. London: Macmillan.

Music of Khorezm. 1996. Auvidis/UNESCO D 8269. Compact disk.

Ouzbekistan: Monâjât Yultchieva (Maqam d'Asie centrale 1: Ferghana). 1994. Ocora/Radio France C 560060. Compact disk.

Ouzbekistan: Turgun Alimatov. 1995. Ocora/ Radio France C 560086. Compact disk.

Powers, Harold S. 1980. "[Mode:] Modal Entities in Western Asia and South Asia." In *The New Grove Dictionary of Music and Musicians*, Vol. 5(2, i):423–238. London: Macmillan. (See also 2nd ed.)

Slobin, Mark, and Greta Slobin, trans. and eds. 1975. *Central Asian Music*. Middletown, Conn.: Wesleyan University Press. Adapted from Viktor Beliaev. 1962. *Ocherki po istorii muzyki narodov S.S.S.R.* (Sketches of the Music History of the Peoples of the U.S.S.R.), Vol. 1. Moscow.

Sultanova, Razia. 1998. *Ritmika vokalnykh chastei shashmakoma*. Tashkent: Yani.

Yanov-Yanovskaya, Natalia Solomonovna. 1999. *Mutal' Burkhanov: Vremya, zhizn', tvorchestvo* (Mutal Burkhanov: His Times, Life, and Creativity). Tashkent: Media Land.

Zeranska-Kominek, Slawomira, with Arnold Lebeuf. 1997. *The Tale of Crazy Herman: The Musician and the Concept of Music in the Türkmen Epic Tale Harman Däli*. Warsaw: Dialog.

Music of Azerbaijan

Tamila Djani-Zade

Historical Overview
Musical Practice
Instruments
Modal Structure
The Art of *Muğam*
The *Aşıq*'s Art
Folk Song and Folk Dance

Since 1991 Azerbaijan has been an independent state in Transcaucasia, retaining the frontiers established in 1920 and 1936 for the Azerbaijan Soviet Socialist Republic. The national language is Azerbaijani or Azeri, which belongs to the southwestern or Oghuz group of Turkic languages and has been written in a modified Latin alphabet since 1992. (In this article, musical terms and most names are spelled according to this modified Latin alphabet, although more familiar spellings are used for authors known for their writings in Persian or Arabic, such as ʿAbdolqādir ibn Gheibī al-Marāghī, and for historical figures before the twentieth century.) The majority religion is Shiʿa Islam. The Araxes River is the southern boundary of the republic, and several million speakers of Azerbaijani live on the other side of the river, in northwest Iran. [See The *Aşıq* and His Music in Northwest Iran (Azerbaijan).]

The musical traditions of Azerbaijan are based on a mingling of two cultural strata—one formed from the influence of Turkic nomadic elements on the multiethnic civilization of Transcaucasia, the other from Iranian urban traditions that originated in the Sasanian era (224–651) and subsequently came under the influence of Arabic language, literature, and religion. In the period of Soviet hegemony, traditions of musical folklore common to the peoples of Transcaucasia were deliberately intensified, and the urban traditions oriented toward other civilizations (Muslim-Iranian in Azerbaijan, Monophysite Christian in Armenia, and Orthodox Christian in Georgia) were diminished.

Following a brief historical overview, this article looks at current musical practice, instruments, the structure of modes, the *muğam* as a cyclic genre, the art of the *aşıq*, and the principal genres of folk song and folk dance.

HISTORICAL OVERVIEW

Whereas the classical music of the Ottoman empire was formed under the influence of Arab (western Islamic) musical tradition, the court musical culture of Azerbaijan developed in the main channel of Iranian (eastern Islamic) musical tradition, despite the linguistic affinity with Ottoman Turkish. This was due, in part, to the important achievements of Persian literature in the classical poetic genres (*qasīde*, *ghazal*, *masnavī*, and so on), which preceded the formation of written literature in Azerbaijani and Ottoman Turkish.

FIGURE 1 The *məclis* of Oghuz-khan, 1528–1529 (Kerimov 1980).

Poets, scholars, and musicians from Azerbaijan were prominent at the courts of the Turkic rulers of the Seljuq and subsequent dynasties in Iran and Central Asia. For example, Munisa Mexseti Xanum of Ganja, a woman, was the favorite singer and poet of the Seljuq sultan Sanjar (r. 1118–1157), who was based in Khorasan. Poetry, treatises, and court music show so many commonalities throughout the Muslim world that it is difficult to single out features of Azerbaijani musical culture merely on the grounds of the language of a treatise or the birthplace of an author. Supraethnic civilizing factors were strengthened by intensive transfer of peoples, objects, and knowledge.

Court music was centered in Ganja, Nakhichevan, and Shemakha (from the tenth century the capital of the Shirvānshāhs in northeastern Azerbaijan, where the process of Turkization proceeded more slowly), along with Tabrīz, Marāghe, and later Baghdād. Music making at splendid feasts and gatherings (*məclislər*), during hunting and battles, and on urban streets is depicted in miniature paintings (figure 1) as well as in Persian verses (those of Qaṭrān Tabrīzī in the eleventh century, and Nezāmī of Ganja and Khāqānī of Shirvān in the twelfth), then in Turkic verses (those of ʻImādaddīn and Nesīmī in the fourteenth and fifteenth centuries, and Shāh Khatā'ī and the founder of Azerbaijani literature, Füzuli, in the sixteenth century).

The Azerbaijani musician and theorist ʻAbdolqādir ibn Gheibī al-Marāghī (d. 1435) mastered the theoretical canon of the systematist school of Safī al-Dīn ʻAbd al-Mumin al-Urmavī (d. 1294) and Quṭb al-Dīn al-Shīrāzī (d. 1311) at the court of Jalayirids in Tabrīz. After he was taken to Transoxiana and Khorasan by Tīmūr (r. 1370-1405), Marāghī played a central role in the dissemination and assimilation of the music theory and practice of the courts. He is the founding figure of Central Asian musical theory (treatises by ʻAbd al-Rahmān Jāmī, Zain al-ʻAbidin al-Huseini, and others adhere to his canon) and practice (the Tajik-Uzbek cycle *şaşmaqom* cycle preserves features of the genre *nuba* described in Marāghī 's treatises).

Iranian culture, further enriched by Shiʻa elements, continued to flourish in Azerbaijan under the Safavids (r. 1501–1722), an Azerbaijani dynasty whose capitals were successively Tabrīz, Qazvīn, and Esfahān. Northern Azerbaijan was incorporated into the Safavid state. The Shiʻa Safavids were continually at war with the Sunni Ottomans, who periodically conquered Transcaucasia. Russian political and economic interests added complications. Russia aspired to a sea outlet as well as to trade advantages; exports from Azerbaijan included oil, grains, cattle, silk from Shemakha, and rugs from Karabakh. After the reign of Nādir Qolīkhān Afshār (r. 1736–1747), several independent khanates were formed, including Kubin, Sheki, Karabakh, Shemakha, Baku, Ganja, and Nakhichevan. They were gradually annexed to Russia in the early nineteenth century. The outcome of the Russo-Iranian war (1828) fixed the border between the two states along the Araxes River. Northern Azerbaijan was incorporated into the Russian empire as the khanates were absorbed into the provinces of Bakinskaya and Elisavetopolskaya.

MUSICAL PRACTICE

The modern musical practices of Azerbaijan acquired their national features in the nineteenth and twentieth centuries. Folklore and the art of the *aşıq* were cultivated mainly in the countryside. The vocal and instrumental traditions that retained a close relation to Iranian culture flourished in the cities.

Urban musical life centered on performances in streets and squares; in the *zurxana* (gymnasium), caravansary, and *çayxana* 'teahouse'; and in the elite *məclislər* 'gatherings' of musicians, poets, and patrons of the arts in the homes of aristocrats (figure 2). There were *məclislər* in Nakhichevan, where Sattar, a famous *xanəndə* 'singer' from southern Azerbaijan, performed for the first time; and in Ganja, where Meşadi Camil

Amirov (1875–1928) worked. Many of the most outstanding musicians were born and raised in Shusha, where there were several *məclislər*.

The town of Shirvan in Shemakha was famous for the *məclis* of a musical activist, Mahmud Aqa, which was frequented by the great poet Seid Azim Şirvani. The musical traditions of Apsheron were formed at the *məclislər* in Baku (figure 3). The most popular were the evenings of Meşadi Melik Mansurov (1833–1909). The *muğam* experts of Baku gathered at his home, and outstanding musicians from Karabakh and other regions visited him. One of his sons, Mirza Mansur (1887–1967), became a famous *tar* player and the teacher of his nephew—Bahram Suleimanoğlı Mansurov (1911–1985), an outstanding *tar* player of the Soviet period.

The towns were the centers of Shi'a religious ceremonies, in which a great number of people assembled to stage the *təziye* religious dramas and *şaxsey-vaxsey* processions.

FIGURE 2 *The Dancers of Shamakh*, nineteenth century, by the Russian prince G. Gagarin (Shushinski 1985).

FIGURE 3 *A Musical Evening in Baku*, 1908 (Shushinski 1979).

FIGURE 4 The famous trio of Cabbar Kariağdı (1861–1944), *xanəndə*; Kurban Primov (1880–1965), *tar*; and Saşa Oğanezaşvili (1889–1932), *kəmançe* (Shushinski 1985).

During the mourning assemblies young singers performed the *dəstgahlar* in turn. The Shi'a *mərsiyə* 'lament' has retained its place in everyday musical life.

The European music heard in the new industrial center of Baku provided a model for the development of concerts featuring a *xanəndə-destesi* 'singer's ensemble'. The famous trio of Cabbar Kariağdı (1861–1944), *xanəndə*; Kurban Primov (1880–1965), *tar*; and Saşa Oğanezaşvili (1889–1932), *kəmançe* was one of these ensembles (figure 4). In the early twentieth century, theater and the possibility of opera were a subject of stormy debates in the press among members of the Azerbaijani intelligentsia. Uzeir Hacibekov (1885–1948), who studied in Moscow and Saint Petersburg, came to the fore at this time. As one who advocated the renovation of musical traditions, he created the *muğam* opera with *Leili və Mecnun* (1907) and other works, which were performed under his direction by singers and instrumentalists familiar with the traditional *muğam*.

In the Soviet period the staging of *muğam* operas helped to preserve the authentic *xanəndə* tradition, which was subjected to Soviet cultural propaganda from the 1930s onward. Under a simplistic division of culture into "proletarian" and "bourgeois," the Azerbaijani *aşıq* was regarded as a true representative of the national, peasant culture and the *xanəndə*, by contrast, as a servant of the urban bourgeoisie. The art of *muğam* was cultivated primarily in instrumental solos (in the short *muğam*) and in orchestras of folk instruments, with dance pieces predominating. The vocal-instrumental *dəstgah* was performed only occasionally from the 1930s to the 1950s; brief variants (*muğam-təsnifi*) replaced it. The text of any classical *qəzəl* sung to a *dəstgah* (often in Persian) by an old singer was subject to censorship.

Hacibekov, the *tar* player A. Bakixanov (1892–1973), and others incorporated performance on traditional instruments into the curriculum of educational institutions while struggling to preserve the seventeen-tone scale of the *tar* and the traditional *dəstgah*. A new generation of performers emerged, among them the *kəmançe* player Habil Aliev (b. 1927) and the *tar* players Haci Mammedov, Aliaqa Kuliev, Habib Bairamov, and Kamil Ahmadov. Instrumentalists performed the *muğam* with impressive virtuosity, but notated works (concertos, fantasies, and arrangements) constituted the greater part of the repertoire. The symphonic *muğam* was encouraged, and the underestimation of Azerbaijan's cultural and historical ties with Iran and, more broadly, with Islamic civilization, continued until the 1960s.

INSTRUMENTS

The contemporary musical culture of Azerbaijan does not preserve all the instruments mentioned in the poetry of Neẓāmī (more than thirty) and the treatises of Marāghī (more than forty). The most widely distributed instruments are a frame drum with metal rings (*dəf*); double-headed drums (*nağara*); paired clay kettledrums (*qoşa-nağara*); paired spoon-shaped wooden castanets (*şahşah*); two double-reed instruments, *zurna* and *balaban*, with a conical and cylindrical bore, respectively; the cylindrical whistle flute *tütek*; the spike fiddle *kəmançe*; and two long-necked plucked lutes, the *tar* and the *saz*. In addition the *'ud*, *tanbur*, and *qanun* are often used in orchestras of national instruments, and the rim-blown flute *nay* is often heard in the countryside. The small goblet-shaped Iranian drum, *zarb*, has been played since the 1950s.

The *dəf* or *qaval*, a medium-sized frame drum with numerous small metal rings, is often depicted in miniatures and mentioned in poetry; today it is included in many ensembles. In the *xanəndə-destesi*, where it is customarily played by the singer, it provides an obligatory accompaniment for several genres: *rəng*, *təsnif*, *dəraməd*, and *zərbi-muğam*.

Nağara is a general term for double-headed drums, which are classified as large (*kus*, *çilik*), medium (*əl, nağara*), and small (*cürə, bala*). They are played with sticks, with the palms of both hands, or with single or clustered fingers, depending on the type of ensemble. The *kus* and *çilik* are played with large curved beaters and accompany the *zurna*; the *cürə*, struck lightly with the hands, accompanies the *balaban*.

The *qoşa-nağara* is a pair of clay kettledrums of different sizes, tuned a fourth apart and played with two sticks on both the skin and the body. For the musicians known as *dumbulçu* 'drummer', the *qoşa-nağara* is a solo instrument. It is also used in various ensembles, most commonly with the *balaban*.

The *laçgutu*, found in the Lenkoran region and in the west, is a wooden rectangular bar with a slit, which is struck with a stick. It is played in ensembles with *balaban*, *zurna*, and accordion to accompany vocal groups and provide dance music.

The *zurna* has a loud, harsh sound. It is popular at festivals, performing dance melodies and marches in various ensembles. The tender sound of the *balaban* (*balaman*, *ney*, *yasty-balaban*) is heard in duets, where a master (*usta*) performs the melody and an assistant (*dəmkeş*) provides a drone; and in ensembles with *nağara* or *dəf*, or with *saz*. The cylindrical whistle flute *tütek* is widely used in rural areas for playing pastoral and dance tunes. The *tulum* or *tulup*, a diatonic bagpipe with double chanter and no separate drone pipe, is played mainly in the Nakhichevan and Lachin regions.

The spike fiddle *kəmançe* has a spherical body of wood and a rounded neck, without frets. In the early twentieth century Saşa Oğanezaşvili added a fourth string to the traditional three; the tuning is now e′–a–d–A.

The *saz* is widely distributed in rural areas among the *aşıqlar*, who use it to accompany their singing, and it is played in ensembles with *balaban* or *zurna* and drums. It has a deep oval body made of wood, a long neck with ten to fourteen frets, and eight to ten metal strings in three courses (d–G–c). Two courses are stopped and the third provides a drone. The player strikes all the strings simultaneously with a plectrum.

The *tar* has a wood body in the form of a figure eight. Its deep ovoid bowls are flattened at the bottom, and the upper side is entirely or partially covered by a membrane. The long neck has twenty-two movable frets and two fixed frets. In the second half of the nineteenth century, Mirza Sadıx Asadoğlı, an outstanding *tar* player known as Sadıxcan, improved the instrument by adding four to six sympathetic strings to the original five melody strings (tuned g–c′–C–G–c). He also straightened the back of the sound cavity, and this changed the manner of playing: the *tar* is now held against the chest rather than rested on the knee. The *tar* became the national Azerbaijani instrument, played in a great variety of ways. It is ubiquitous as a solo instrument, in ensembles with spike fiddle and frame drum, and in orchestras.

MODAL STRUCTURE

The tone system of Azerbaijani traditional music is most fully reflected in the fingerboard of the *tar*. The seventeen-tone scale, which differs from Arab and Persian scales, is produced on its main melodic string (figure 5*a*). Theoretical treatises discuss the division of the major Pythagorean tone (204 cents) into two minor semitones and a comma (90 + 90 + 24), as well as the possibility of forming a major semitone (114 = 90 + 24) or minor whole tone (180 = 90 + 90). An interval of 66 cents is produced on the *tar* by subtracting a comma from the minor semitone (90 – 24 = 66), shown in figure 5*a* by the *z*. The fact that frets for tones of 66 and 114 cents are fixed on the fingerboard indicates their special importance in musical practice.

This nontempered scale system is most fully realized in the art of the *muğam*. The Azerbaijani *muğam* of *segah* exists in several variants, which include thirds of different values. Use of the entire tonal range of the *tar* leads to the tempered system in which a semitone is lowered from 114 cents and raised from 90 cents; the difference of 10 cents is virtually indistinguishable to the ear (g to g-sharp = 90 cents; a to a-flat = 114 cents).

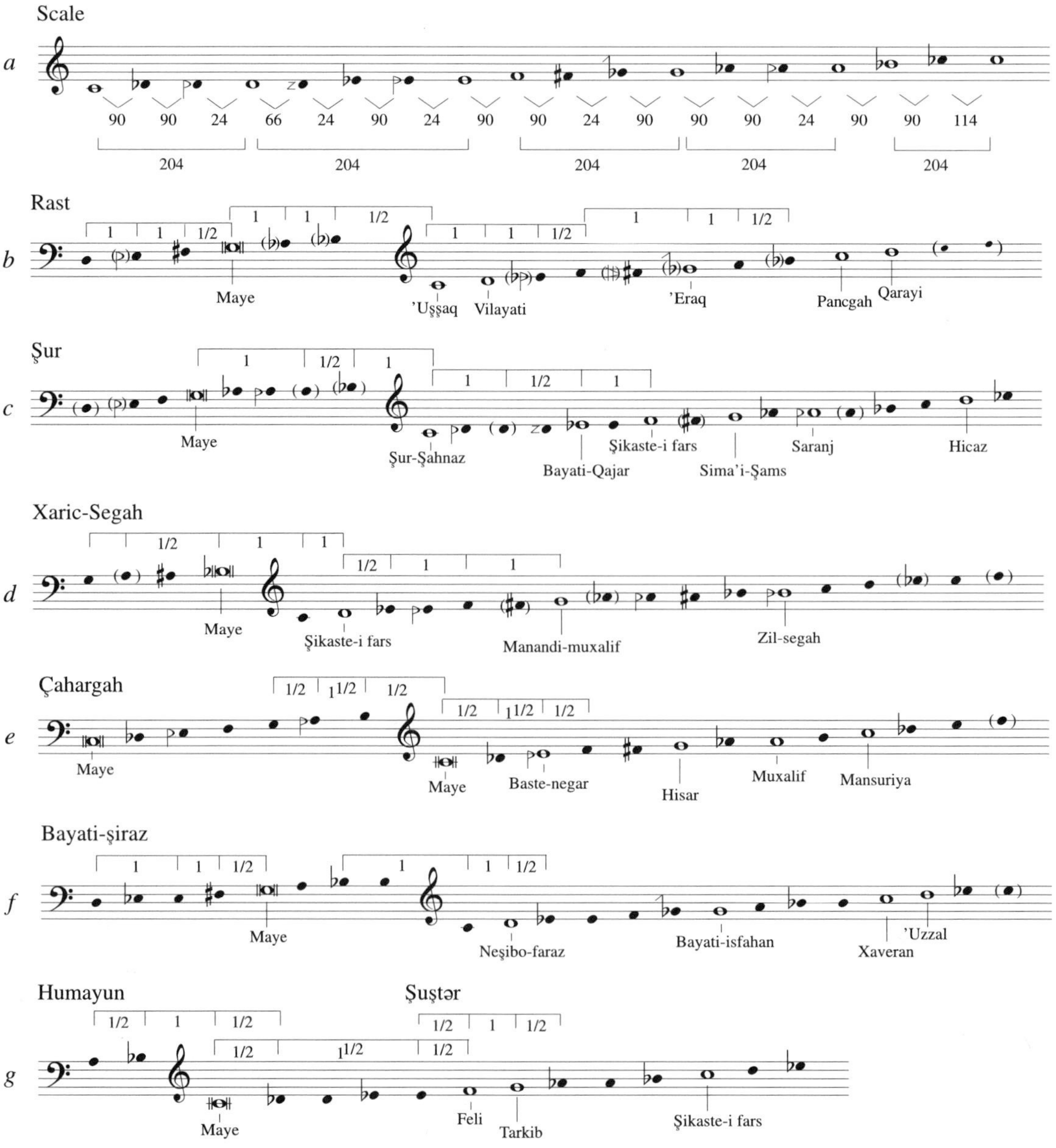

FIGURE 5 Scales of (a) the Azerbaijani *tar* and seven *muğam*, showing the locations of important branches (*şöbeler*): (b) *rast*, with five *şöbeler*; (c) *şur*, with six *şöbeler*; (d) *xaric-segah*, with three *şöbeler*; (e) *çahargah*, with four *şöbeler*; (f) *bayatı şiraz*, with four *şöbeler*; (g) *humayun* and *şüştər*, with three *şöbeler*

The rich scale system is a reflection of the diversity of the modes, called *maqāmāt* in treatises and now called *muğamlar* in Azerbaijan. The seven basic *muğamlar* are *rast, şur, segah, çahargah, bayatı şiraz, humayun,* and *şüştər*; as shown in figure 5*b–g*, the last two have similar scales. No less important than interval content in the system of mode formation are the position of the central tone—*mayə* 'basis'—and the characteristic melodic and cadential progressions. Many variants of the basic modes are used in practice. Some *muğamlar* have been formed by transposition, and some modes are branches (*şöbeler*) of the basic octave *muğamlar* (see the *şöbe* names indicated at appropriate points in figure 5*b–g*).

From the 1940s through the 1960s Uzeir Hacibekov and M. S. Ismailov worked out a diatonic system, based on heptatonic modes, that accounts for mode formation in Azerbaijani national music (folklore and music of the *aşıqlar*). Their system classifies modes according to the tetrachords with their different combinations of whole tones, half tones, and a one-and-a-half tone or augmented second. The seven basic *muğamlar* may define the mode of any genre of folk music: for example, a lullaby in *şur* or in *segah*. In figure 5*b–g* the diatonic systematization of Hacibekov and Ismailov is shown above every *muğam*.

THE ART OF *MUĞAM*

The highest achievement of Azerbaijani musical culture is the *muğam*, a polysemous term signifying a mode but also a genre, a form, and a specific manner of musical development. In Turkic usage, the term (derived from the Arabic word *maqām*) may have acquired new semantic content as early as the late nineteenth century, when the art of *muğam* began to be distinguished from other genres. In Azerbaijan this art is characterized above all by presentation of each *muğam* in solo performance, with no rhythmic cycle (*usul*) or rhythmic formulas. In their theoretical works (published in Russian and Azerbaijani), Hacibekov and Ismailov distinguished three classes of folk music according to the presence or absence of meter. The first class, *bəhrsiz* 'without meter', is the *muğam* that entails improvisation. The second, *bahrli* 'with meter', embraces folk song (*mahnı, təsnif*) and dance (*rəqs, rəng*). The third, *qarışıq bəhrli* 'mixed with meter', consists of rhythmic pieces (*zərbi-muğamlar*) in which nonmetrical declamation also has a place.

A *dəstgah* is the most complete *muğam*, a large cycle that includes virtually every urban traditional genre; the nonmetrical *şöbeler* and *guşeler* exist alongside the metrical (*dəraməd, rəng, təsnif,* and *diringi*). It is often called *muğam-dəstgah*. The current repertoire includes *rast, mahur, bayatı qajar, bayatı şiraz, çahargah*, several variants of *segah, şur,* and *humayun* (*şüştər*). The other independent small *muğamlar*—such as *rahab, şahnaz, bayatı kurd, qatar, daşti,* and *hicaz*—are *şöbeler* 'branches', tonal and melodic variants of the basic *muğamlar* (Zokhrabov 1991).

The names of *muğamlar* serve to distinguish their musical structures and are related to those in the treatises that describe *avaze, şöbe, guşe,* and *tərkib*. For example, the important *Vizūh al-arqām* 'Explanation of the Numbers' by Mir Möhsun Nəvvab of Shusha (written in 1884 and published in 1913) distinguishes six *dəstgahlar* (*rast, mahur, şahnaz, rahavi, çahargah, nava*); twelve *maqāmāt* (*rast, uşşaq, busalik, hüseyni, esfəhanək, zəngülə, rahavi, bozork, eraq, kuçek, nava, hicaz*); twenty-four *şöbeler* (among which are some of the currently popular *muğamlar*); twenty-four *guşeler*; and fifteen *āvāzāt* (most of which occur today).

Names may refer to frets on the necks of string instruments (*yegah, dügah, segah, çahargah, panjgah*); to characteristic melodic and rhythmic imagery (*balı kabutar* 'dove's wing', *neşib-o feraz* 'descent and ascent'); to personal names (*Şah Xəta'i, Mirza Hüseyn*); and in numerous cases to places or peoples (*esfəhan, kurd, ovshari, qajar, hicaz, azerbaijan*). The multiplicity of independent *muğam* compositions shows the absence of unification in this art. Versions of a *muğam* or *dəstgah* with the same name may vary according to regional tradition (of Karabakh, Baku, or Shemakha) or to the schools of different masters.

The artistic form of a *dəstgah* represents the *muğam* in process, according to a certain artistic scheme. The successive melodic patterns move around the central tone of each new *şöbe*, with continual returns to cadence patterns. In contemporary practice the first *şöbe*, which is often called *mayə*, can be preceded by the *bərdaşt* 'introduction', in which the basic melodic structure of the *mayə* sounds in the higher octave at the beginning and in the lower octave at the end, forming a characteristic cadence that concludes the *mayə* and the subsequent *guşeler*. In every *dəstgah* the tonal registers succeed one another in an individual manner, but always in the same direction—to the third, fourth, fifth, or octave above the central tone of the *mayə*.

In the scheme of succession of the *şöbeler* and *guşeler*, every Azerbaijani *dəstgah* constructs a specific musical form that, according to the Islamic artistic canon, represents a gradual ascent. The underlying model is the progress of a disciple (*murid*) along the mystic way (*təriq*) to perfection and his acquisition of new spiritual states or stations (*maqāmāt*) imbued with unexpected illuminations of the soul. The term *hal* is used for artistic evaluation of a *xanəndə*'s mastery, revealed in the culmination (*oc*) as the highest sense of beauty, toward which a master musician becomes a guide.

The poetry of the *qəzəl* is uniquely suitable to this musical form. Singers choose texts with images of love that are abstracted from the details of everyday life, sometimes with a characteristic mystic inspiration in the poet's conversation with the beloved. They use *qəzəllər* by such classic poets as Neẓāmī, Füzuli, Nesimi, Natavan, and Seyid Şirvani and by Soviet poets, notably Aqa Vahid. The high level of romantic expression is well represented by the first *beit* of Vahid's *qəzəl* that opens a recorded performance of the *dəstgah mahur-hindi*:

> Show me, beautiful one, your face, so that a flower would be ashamed,
> So that a butterfly, circling around, burned in the flame.
>
> It's enough that your intoxicating eyes create such treachery.
> Don't look at me so coquettishly; abandon your treachery.
>
> Your curly locks sleep peacefully on your bosom.
> Don't stir, don't awaken them, whatever you do.
>
> I can't explain to you what's in my soul
> The state doesn't exist that would allow you to understand me.
> (Melodiya C 30-17223-24, issued in 1980; translated by Theodore Levin)

The metric parts of a *dəstgah* cycle include the march-like introduction (*dəramad*), dance episodes (*rəng*), and short dance tunes (*diringa*), performed by the instrumental ensemble, as well as the vocal *təsnif*. These are inserted between the *şöbeler*, often at the end of the main parts. The dance character of the *təsnifler* and *rəngler* is based on either quantitative metrics—*əruz* (from Arabic *'arūz*) or syllabic metrics (*heca vəzni*). The contrast between the metrical insertions and the general lamenting character of the *muğam* declamation—like a contrast between spiritual and physical delight—is evident in the respective texts. In the *təsnif* the romantic feeling is addressed to a concrete terrestrial beloved, as in the folk genres *qoşma* and *bayatı*.

> O moonlike darling, you are yourself a moon.
> Descend for a while, become my beloved.
> Love for you possesses my heart.
> Come down to me, become my beloved.
> You are the only one, become my beloved.

The Azerbaijan *zərbi-muğam* is a unique genre in which metrically free vocal improvisation of a *xanəndə* is accompanied by a repeated rhythmic formula (*zərb*) in the instrumental ensemble. It is not lengthy and may have either its own name (*heyrati*, *arazbare*, *mani*, *ovşari*, *karami*) or the name of the culminating *şöbe* (such as *mansuriye* from *çahargah* or *sima'-i şams* from *şur*).

A separate group of *zərbi-muğamlar*, called *şekaste* 'broken' (which also designates a special type of calligraphy), fits plaintive lyrics to the tunes of the *zərbi-muğamlar*: *Karabakh-şekastesı*, *Şirvan-şekastesı*, *Kasma-* or *Baku-şekastesı*. Every *zərbi-muğam* is based on a principal *muğam* (*Karabakh-şekastesı* on *segah*, *heyrati* on *mahur-hindi*). This group mainly uses lyrical texts of the folk poetic genres (*bayatı* and *qoşma*) or portions of a *qəzəl*. A *xanəndə* skillfully presents the words, sometimes declaiming, sometimes pattering, sometimes with protracted and masterly vocalizing. The reiterated rhythmic pattern is based on either syllabic or quantitative (for instance, *ramal* and *hicaz*) meters. A good instrumentalist (*sazəndə*) must display a high level of skill in the performance of the extended dance introductions and *rəngler*.

THE *AŞIQ*'S ART

The art of the professional poets and singer-storytellers known as *aşıq* can be traced to the late sixteenth century, when the genres of epic and heroic-lyric *dastanlar* 'narratives'—such as *Koroğlu*, *Şah Ismail*, *Aşıq Qarib*, *Asli*, and *Kerim*—took shape and *aşıqlar* began to be distinguished by their names (Qurbani, *Aşıq* Abbas, Sary *Aşıq*, and so on). Samples of *aşıq* poetry begin to appear in seventeenth- and eighteenth-century manuscript collections.

People distinguish an *aşıq* according to his degree of mastery and creativity. An *aşıq ustad* 'master' is a skilled composer of verses and tunes he performs himself, and a wise teacher esteemed by everyone—for example, *Aşıq* Alesker (1821–1926) and *Aşıq* Molla-Cuma (nineteenth–twentieth century). An *el-şair* 'people's poet' creates verses but not tunes; he is often both a singer and a *saz* player. An *aşıq* may be simply a performer of the verses and tunes of others. In the past *haqq-aşıqlar* 'singers of the truth' performed a repertoire of verses with mystical content. A pejorative epithet, *yanşaq* 'windbag', is bestowed on some *aşıqlar*. A number of *aşıqlar* may reside in one village.

Three regions are distinguished according to different kinds of creativity. The *aşıqlar* of Karabakh, Nakhichevan, and Kel'badzhar (including Ağ *Aşıq*, *Aşıq* Alesker, and *Aşıq* Qurban) respect the classic traditions: solo singing accompanied by the *saz* and competitions (*dəyişmə*, figure 6) in which two singers try to maintain the meter

FIGURE 6 Competition (*dəyişmə*) between two *aşıqlar* in the 1950s (Abasova and Kasimov 1970).

FIGURE 7 The Congress of *Aşiqlar* of Azerbaijan (Bertlov et al., 1963).

and melody as they wittily respond to each other's riddles. The *aşıqlar* of Kirovabad, Shamkhor, Tauz, and Kazakh (including Hüseyn Şamkirli and Asad Rzaev) are also custodians of the tradition but have supplemented the *saz* accompaniment with a *balaban*. The *aşıqlar* of eastern Azerbaijan (Shemakha, Kyurdamir, and Sal'yany)—including Şakir Haiev and Panah Panaxov—have departed from tradition through their enthusiasm for dancing and their use of *muğam* and large ensembles with percussion and more than one *balaban*, which muffle the sound of the *saz*. These tendencies were strengthened during the Soviet period, as the repertoire came to include verses glorifying Lenin and Stalin as well as the labor and military exploits of the Soviet people, and as choruses, competitions, reviews, and congresses were organized (figure 7).

Nevertheless, in general the classic repertoire of the *aşıq* has been preserved. It consists of humorous, edifying, and lyric songs about love, beauty, nature, and everyday life. Musical meter and rhythm are defined by syllabic versification, *heca vəzni* (known among the *aşıq* as *barmaq hesabı* 'finger counting'). Quatrains with a certain type of rhyme predominate: *gerailı* with eight syllables divided as 4 + 4 or 5 + 3; *qoşma* with eleven syllables grouped as 6 + 5 or 4 + 4 + 3; *təcnis*, a type of *qoşma* in which the first and fourth lines are rhymed by homonyms; *müxəmməs*, a five-line stanza with fifteen or sixteen syllables grouped as 7 (8) + 8 (7) or 8 + 8; more rarely *qəzəl* and its varieties. In the *dastan* sung verses alternate with artistically spoken prose that tells of the epic hero's childhood, victories, and love. A favorite subject is the people's leader and defender of the poor, Koroğlu, who was a warrior and an *aşıq*. Several tunes associated with this *dastan* are also performed independently. The *aşıq*'s melodies use the diatonic modes, mainly the *muğam* of *şur*. The melodic range is based on an initial tetrachord, whose degrees are named like those of a *muğam*: *baş pərdə* 'initial fret', *orta pərdə* 'middle fret', and *ayaq pərdə* 'final fret'. After the *orta pərdə* the scale may be extended with other *pərdəler*. The chromatic tones added during the performance of one or another tune are often called by the name of a model melody, such as *təcnis pərdə* or *urfanı pərdə*. The *aşıq*'s art differs from the art of *muğam* not only by its repertoire and rural environment but also in singing style, which favors an open, laryngeal sound, as well as in the characteristic sound of the *saz* (chords based on thirds or droned fourths with an added second).

FOLK SONG AND FOLK DANCE

The musical folklore of Azerbaijan shows great variety and is thought to preserve ancient features. Work songs, which are correlated with the agricultural cycle (songs of plowing, weeding, harvesting, and so on), may include remnants of pagan sacrificial rites in appeals to animals and incantations of sun and rain. Round dances (*yallı*), which are also presumed to be ancient, have distinctive vocal and instrumental melodies, characterized by short, repetitive patterns (*oyun-yallı*, *raqs-yallı*, and so on).

Other vocal genres include lullabies, complaints about everyday life, and comic songs mocking human vices. Lyric songs (*mahnı*) are the most common, with texts (*bayatı* or *qoşma*) abounding in poetic metaphors and colorful descriptions of nature. Singers use many melismatic embellishments and repeated exclamations (such as *ay, aman* 'have mercy'; *can* 'soul'; and *balam* 'my child'). The melodic forms (binary; ternary with or without refrain) reflect the poetic structure: songs are divided into parts according to rhymed lines of text (two-, three-, and four-line). Nonrhyming single-line refrains appear between the verses, with additional words or exclamations.

Like singing, dancing (*rəqs*) is mainly solo. Graceful motions and fluent, richly ornamented melodies are typical of women's dances. Dance songs of the lyric genre *halay*, which are found throughout the southeastern region, are performed by two groups of women who sing antiphonally. Men's dances (*şalaho*, *pahlivanlar rəqsi* 'wrestlers' dance', and *kəndirbaz rəqsi* 'rope-walkers' dance') are fast and virtuosic, accompanied by *zurna* and percussion. The martial-heroic dance *cangi* 'warlike' is performed collectively. The rhythms of Azerbaijani dances, like those of the songs, are mostly duple with triple subdivision (6/8), sometimes changing to a marchlike duple (2/4). Until recently, a dance suite, *çaharzan*, was performed in many regions of Azerbaijan. It featured alternation of women's and men's dances, and of solo and group dances.

The song-dance repertoire is richly represented in the wedding ceremony, *toy*, which continues for ten to forty days, as well as in the new year's ceremony, *novruz*. The genre *mərsiyə*, derived from the Shi'a *təziye*, is a special type of lament for the martyred Shi'a imams—'Ali, his son Hüseyn, and their associates. *Mərsiyə* has a small melodic range (a third to a fifth) with a characteristic descending progression. It is distinguished from everyday laments by a clear melodic outline that avoids superfluous exclamations and cries. Here everything is subordinate to the verses of such poets as Füzuli, Şirvani, Qomri, and Sabir in the system of *əruz* versification, which are chanted according to the rules of *əruz* declamation and basic *muğam* intonations.

FIGURE 8 The instrument maker Farukh Abdul Rahimov playing the *tar*. Photo © Kevin Bubriski.

FIGURE 9 Musicians learning *muğam* at the Baku Conservatory. Photo © Kevin Bubriski.

The richness of Azerbaijan's musical traditions has only been suggested in this brief discussion of their history, practices, instruments (figure 8), and modes; the *muğam* (figure 9); the *aşıq*'s art; and folk genres.

REFERENCES

Abasova, El'mira, and Kubad Kasimov. 1970. *Ocherki muzyakl'nogo iskusstva Sovetskogo Azerbaidzhana 1920–1956*. Baku: Azerbaidzhanskoe Gosudarstvennoe Izdatel'stvo.

Babaev, Elxan. 1990. *Ritmika azerbaidzhanskogo destgyakha*. Baku: Işıq.

Badalbayli, Afarasiyab. 1969. *Izahlı monografik musiqi luqatı* (Monographic Explanatory Dictionary of Music). Baku: Elm.

Bagirova, Sanubar. 1992. "The Azerbaijanian Mugam: Artistic Idea and Structural Series." In *Regionale maqām-Traditionen in Geschichte und Gegenwart*, ed. Jürgen Elsner and Gisa Jähnichen, 28–50. Berlin: Maqam Study Group of the International Council for Traditional Music.

During, Jean. 1988. *La musique traditionnelle de l'Azerbayjan et la science des mugams*. Sammlung musikwissenschaftlicher Abhandlungen, 80. Baden-Baden: Koerner.

———. 1989. "The Modal System of Azarbâyjâni Art Music." In *Maqam—Raga—Zeilenmelodik: Konzeptionen und Prinzipien der Musikproduktion*, ed. Jürgen Elsner, 133–147. Berlin: Maqam Study Group of the International Council for Traditional Music.

Djani-Zade, Tamila. 1992. "Presentation of Maqâm in Dastgâh." In *Regionale maqām-Traditionen in Geschichte und Gegenwart*, ed. Jürgen Elsner and Gisa Jähnichen, 129–144. Berlin: Maqam Study Group of the International Council for Traditional Music.

———. 1997. "The Historical Destiny of Azerbaijanian Mugam in the Twentieth Century: Mugam between the Mugam Opera and Symphonic Mugams." In *The Structure and Idea of Maqām: Historical Approaches*, ed. Jürgen Elsner and Risto Pekka Pennanen, 193–195. Tampere: Department of Folk Tradition, University of Tampere.

Hacibekov, Uzeir. 1985 [1945]. *Principles of Azerbaijan Folk Music*, trans. G. Bairamov. Baku: YazıHı. (First published in Russian.)

Isazade, Ahmad, and Nariman Mammedov. 1984. *Azərbaycan xalq mahnıları va oyun havaları*. Baku: Elm.

Ismailov, M. S. 1984 [1960]. *Azərbaycan xalq musiqisinin janrları*. Baku: Işıq. (First published in Russian.)

———. 1992. "Azerbaijanian Magam and Mugam: Problems of Structure." In *Regionale maqâm-Traditionen in Geschichte und Gegenwart*, ed. Jürgen Elsner and Gisa Jähnichen, 524–539. Berlin: Maqam Study Group of the International Council for Traditional Music.

Kerimov, Kerim. 1980. *Azerbaydzahanskie minatury*. Baku: Işiq.

Mansurov, Eldar. 1984. *Azerbaidzhanskie daramady i rengi*. Baku: Işıq.

———. 1986. *Azerbaidzhanskie diringi i rengi*. Baku: Işıq.

———. 1990. *Azerbaidzhanskie starinnye narodnye napevy*. Baku: Işıq.

Rustamov, Said, et al. 1981. *Azərbaycan xalq mahnıları*. 2 vols. Baku: Işıq.

———. 1982. *Azərbaycan xalq rəngləri*. 2 vols. Baku: Işıq.

Shushinski, Firidun. 1979. *Narodnye pevtsy i muzykanty Azerbaidzhana*. Moscow: Sovetskii Kompozitor. (Azerbaijani version, 1985. *Azərbaycan xalq musiqiçiləri*. Baku: YazıHı.)

Vertkov, K., et al. 1963. *Atlas muzykal'nykh instrumentov narodov S.S.S.R.* Moskva.

Zokhrabov, Ramiz. 1983. *Azerbaidzhanskie tesnify*. Moscow: Sovetskii Kompozitor.

———. 1991. *Muğam*. Baku: Azarnaşr.

———. 1992. "The Problem of Melodics in Azerbaijanian Mugam-Dastgah." In *Regionale maqām-Traditionen in Geschichte und Gegenwart*, ed. Jürgen Elsner and Gisa Jähnichen, 570–593. Berlin: Maqam Study Group of the International Council for Traditional Music.

Audiovisual resources

During, Jean, comp. 1989a. *Azerbaidjan: Musique et chants des âshiq*. Geneva: Archives Internationales de Musique Populaire. AIMP 19, VDE CD-613. Compact disk.

———. 1989b. *Azerbayjan: Musique traditionnelle*. Paris: Le Chant du Monde. LDX 274 901. Compact disk.

Mansurov, Bahram. 1992 [1975]. *Azerbaijan Mugam*. Ivry-sur-Seine: Auvidis, D 8045. Compact disk.

Mugam d'Azerbaijan. Paris: Maison des Cultures du Monde. Eight compact disks. Inédit W260012 (1989), W260015 (1989), W260026 (1991), W260037 (1991), W260049 (1992), W260052 (1994), W260069 (1996), W260077 (1997). Vols. 1 and 2, Alem Kassimov; 3, Hâji Bâbâ Huseynov; 4, Trio Jabbâr Garyaghdu Oghlu; 5, Sakine Ismalov; 6. Trio Zulfi Azıgözelov, Agakhân Abdullaev; 7. Djanali Akberov (Trio Khân Shushinski); 8. Gandab Gulieva.

The Music of Azerbaijan. n.d. [c. 1970] A Musical Anthology of the Orient, 24. Kassel: Bärenreiter-Musicaphon BM 30 L 2024. LP record.

Sacred Music and Chant in Islamic Central Asia

Alexander Djumaev

Patterns of Culture in Central Asian Islam
The Development of Religious Music and Chant
Forms of Religious Music and Chant
The Role of Music in Central Asian Sufism
Religious Music in the Social World of Women

For a millennium, Central Asia has had a unified civilization linked by culture and economics, by a common political history, and, perhaps most crucially, by the cultural and religious preeminence of Islam. While adherents of other religions, particularly Orthodox Christianity and Judaism, have lived and continue to live in Central Asia, they have all in some measure adapted to the abiding influence of Islamic mores and institutions in the region. Yet Islam in Central Asia, although it is ubiquitous, is not monolithic. Rather, it has adapted to the particular patterns of culture in which it exists, ranging from Kazakh and Kyrgyz pastoralism to the sedentary agricultural and urban milieu that has been shaped primarily by Tajiks and Uzbeks.

PATTERNS OF CULTURE IN CENTRAL ASIAN ISLAM

The principal centers of Islamic culture in Central Asia are in the cities, and of these, Bukhara and Samarkand have played a particularly important role. The central institutions of Islam—mosque; *madrasah* 'religious college'; minaret; *khānaqā* 'Sufi dwelling'; and *mazār* 'tomb of a saint'—are concentrated in cities. The religious colleges of Bukhara trained Muslim clerics who served all over Central Asia and Kazakhstan as well as in the Volga-Ural region, the traditional territory of many of Russia's Muslim peoples. Among the inhabitants of oases and cities, the daily observance of religious customs and the practice of religious rituals were obligatory, and thus the influence of Islam on expressive culture was significant. City-dwelling Uzbeks and Tajiks attached particular importance to sacred music and chant, and to this day the core forms and genres of Islamic religious music in Central Asia are strongest in Uzbek and Tajik culture. By contrast, religious music has never been as important among peoples with a tradition of pastoralism—Kazakhs, Kyrgyz, and in particular the Turkmen, who were Islamized much later than the city dwellers. For example, the southern regions of Kazakhstan came under the influence of Islam only in the eleventh and twelfth centuries as a result of contact with the neighboring urban civilization of Tashkent and Bukhara; but in the central Kazakh steppe regions and in Kyrgyzstan, Islam did not begin to take root until the end of the eighteenth century. Muslims in Central Asia and Kazakhstan belong overwhelmingly to the Sunni branch of Islam. There is a Shi'i minority confined largely to the cities of Bukhara and Samarkand, and Ismaili Shi'is live in the Pamir Mountains of Tajikistan.

> The development of Islamic religious music and chant in Central Asia reflects the variety of ways in which Islam has been assimilated into the region—its diversity of local forms and its tendency to draw on a rich pre-Islamic musical legacy.

Broadly speaking, both in the cities and on the steppe, the practice of Islam diverged into two streams: on the one hand, an official canonical practice; on the other hand, various forms of popular Islam that represented a synthesis of Islamic and pre-Islamic cults and beliefs. Non-Islamic influences in popular Islam include Buddhism, shamanism, and cultic practices such as ancestor worship. To a large extent, these influences entered the world of Islam through Sufism, the mystical branch of Islam that flourished in Central Asia as early as the tenth century.

Sufism, which first arose in opposition to official Islam, eventually merged with it in the eighteenth and nineteenth centuries and subsequently began to replace it in practice. Sufi practices assumed a number of different forms, and Sufism created its own rituals connected with music, dance, and poetry. Popular Sufism relied on numerous holy places of pilgrimage and worship (*kadamjāi, ziyāratgāh*), whose locations can often be traced to pre-Islamic cultic practices at the same sites. Such sites can be found all across Central Asia and were distinguished according to a hierarchy of religious significance.

THE DEVELOPMENT OF RELIGIOUS MUSIC AND CHANT

When the first proselytizers of Islam reached Central Asia around the end of the seventh century, they found a panoply of religious practices both in cities and on the steppe. Ancestor cults, Buddhism, Christianity, Judaism, Zoroastrianism, Manichaeanism, and a variety of local animist-shamanist practices and beliefs all existed in Central Asia, and all used some form of poetry and music in their rituals. This poetry and music represented an intermingling of countless local traditions that had developed within Central Asia's historical geopolitical regions: Bactria, Sogd, Parthia, Tokharistan, Bukhara, Khwarezm, and others. Archaeological evidence suggests that in the pre-Islamic era religious music existed alongside secular court repertoires, military music, and music for festive ceremonial occasions. Sacred ceremonies, in particular those of the Buddhists, used a wide array of musical instruments. The development of this instrumental music was influenced by the civilizations of the ancient East, India, and Greece.

The development of Islamic religious music and chant in Central Asia reflects the variety of ways in which Islam has been assimilated into the region—its diversity of local forms and its tendency to draw on the region's rich pre-Islamic musical legacy. The Hanifite and Shafite schools of Islamic law which predominated in Transoxania (from Arabic *mā warā al-nah'* 'beyond the Oxus': the territory between the two great rivers, Amu Darya—the River Oxus of antiquity—and Syr Darya) were distinguished by a measured approach to music. From the very beginning of the Arab conquest of Khorasan and Transoxania, Islamic rulers displayed a great interest in local music and musicians. For example, the Umayyad caliphs ordered that lutenists and singers from Khorasan and Transoxania be brought to serve at their court in Baghdad. At the same time, however, Muslims struggled against the influence of expressive culture linked to other religions—Christianity, Judaism, and particularly "idol-worshiping" religions such as Buddhism, shamanism, and Zoroastrianism. Although early Islam had an essentially negative attitude toward music and entertainment, elements of pre-Islamic ritual chant and dance were incorporated into a variety of Islamic practices—above all, Sufism—and have been preserved to the present day.

From the tenth to the thirteenth centuries, Central Asia was overtaken by the Sufi movement. The appearance of communities of Sufis was followed in the twelfth century by the rise of organized brotherhoods: Hojagān, Yasawiyya, Kubrawiyya, and others. At their gatherings (*majlis*) Sufis practiced a special form of sacred music (*samā'*) and dance (*raks*), on the basis of which the ritual of *zikr* (Arabic *dhikr* 'remembrance') was born. The Sufi singer and reciter (*qawwāl*) became one of the main figures at these meetings. Sufi treatises of the tenth to eleventh centuries contain numerous debates as to whether or not music and dance were licit. One such manuscript, "Treatise on Listening," written at the beginning of the eleventh century, is preserved in the Beruni Oriental Institute of the Uzbekistan Academy of Sciences (inventory no. 3154/VI).

The Sufi *khānaqā* (figure 1) remained the repository of sacred musical traditions during the devastating Mongol invasions of the thirteenth century. These traditions flourished in the fourteenth and fifteenth centuries, when Central Asia entered a period of relatively stable cultural development under the rule of the Timurids. In Timurid Herat and Samarkand, the art of chanting the call to prayer (*azān*), reciting the Qur'ān, and delivering public sermons (*wa'iz*) reached a height. In the realm of popular Islam, wandering dervishes, *qalandar* (figure 2), and religious storytellers, *maddah* or *qissakhān*, propagated Islamic values through their songs and narratives.

The melding of official and popular forms of Islam, already evident in the fifteenth century, grew stronger between the sixteenth century and the first half of the nineteenth. Sufi *zikr* began to be conducted in mosques, thus combining the function of mosque and *khānaqā*. At the same time, the classical musical form *maqām* appeared in Sufi rituals, and the ritual practice of *zikr* by the Sufi brotherhoods assumed forms which were often divorced from the original practices of these brotherhoods.

Largely isolated from non-Islamic influences, the musical traditions of medieval Central Asia continued unbroken until the middle of the nineteenth century, when the region was annexed to the Russian Empire. Russia's conquest of Central Asia set the stage for an essentially new period of history in which Islamic culture came into direct contact with Russian and European civilization and began to absorb its influence. This contact ignited internal conflicts within Islam itself which were reflected

FIGURE 1 Sufi dwelling (*khānaqā*) of Hoja Ahmad Yassawi (d. 1166) in the city of Turkestan, Republic of Kazakhstan. Photo courtesy of Alexander Djumaev.

FIGURE 2 Central Asian wandering dervishes (*qalandar*) in the 1920s. Photo by Viktor Uspensky.

in the relationship of Islam to music and other arts. In the first two decades of the twentieth century this relationship was discussed in the local print media, and in books such as Hadi Keldibeki's *Music and Islam,* published in Ufa in 1909, which brought to Russian Turkestan new ideas about music education.

The historical period that began with the socialist revolution of 1917 and continued through the era of Soviet rule until the breakup of the Soviet Union in 1991 led to fundamental changes in the status of Islam in Central Asia. Communist-style modernization and Europeanization within an ideological framework of secularization and state atheism ruptured traditional culture and imposed strict limitations on the practice of religious life. In the 1920s, the government banned the practice of *zikr* in major religious centers; thereafter, *zikr* was transformed into a secret, illegal form of worship. Mosques and religious schools were closed, and spiritual leaders were defamed and persecuted. The performance or publication of songs with religious lyrics and connotations was discouraged or banned, and such songs, particularly when they were widely popular, were transformed by the substitution of secular, often overtly political, texts.

By contrast, the post-Soviet period has been characterized by a tendency toward a renaissance of spiritual religious values and traditions, including the practice of Islamic religious music and chant. This revival, however, has focused principally on the canonical practices of Islamic worship. Many old forms of music and ritual have been irrevocably lost and are now known now only through descriptions that predate the Bolshevik revolution.

FORMS OF RELIGIOUS MUSIC AND CHANT

Central Asian religious music and chant of the nineteenth and twentieth centuries can be divided into four distinct categories, ranging from relatively autonomous forms to forms strictly associated with specific liturgical functions and canonical performance traditions such as the call to prayer and the reading of the Qur'ān:

1. Chanting of canonical texts. The essential texts in this category are the call to prayer (*azān,* also locally called *bāng-i namaz* 'call to prayer') and recitation of the Qur'ān (Arabic *tajwīd*).

2. Ritual calendar songs. These songs are connected to the yearly cycle of Muslim holidays. One example is "*Yāh Ramazān*," sung during the month of Ramadan; another example is the mourning ceremony for the Shi'i martyrs 'Ali, Hasan, and Husayn performed during *ashura*—the first ten days of the month of Muharram.
3. Sufi ritual music and chant. This category includes various forms of *zikr* and spiritual concert (*samā'*) practiced by Central Asian Sufi orders and sects, as well as analogous forms used in funerals, healing, and other rituals and ceremonies.
4. Populist religious music and chant. This is a broad category that includes chant, declamation, and interpretation of spiritual poetry in Persian-Tajik and Turkic languages, conceived in a popular, accessible style. It also includes dance; theatricalized presentations on religious themes for popular consumption and entertainment (*tamāsha*) performed during Muslim festivals and religious events and at various male and female gatherings; and the propagation of Islamic values and beliefs in a popular form by professional singers and musicians, wandering dervishes (*qalandar*), and storytellers who narrate religious legends and history.

The call to prayer (*azān*)

The *azān* is traditionally chanted from the top of a minaret by a muezzin, a specially trained singer with a strong, expressive voice. In Bukhara at the end of the nineteenth century and the beginning of the twentieth, the muezzin of the emir began the *azān* that preceded each of the five daily prayers, thus signaling to other muezzins in the city that they should begin their own call to prayer. Ethnographic accounts report that the voice of the emir's muezzin was audible at a distance of nearly five miles.

The term *muezzin* was familiar to educated people, but in the popular world of Transoxania muezzins were usually called *azanchi* or *Sufi* (*Sopi*), terms still in use today. The personnel of a typical mosque included the imam (leader of a Muslim community) and *Sufi*, who also served as the mosque's custodian. A mosque usually served a neighborhood precinct (*mahalla* or *guzar*), a principal form of spatial and social organization in the late medieval Islamic city. While instructions for the canonical reading of sacred texts were to be found in Central Asian works on Islamic law (*fiqh*) and in other religious literature, the cities of Central Asia all had their own local traditions for performing the *azān*. Musical notation from the late nineteenth and early twentieth centuries confirms these distinct local traditions. In the twentieth century, the Bukharan style of chanting the *azān*, which is lyrical and melodic, has had wide popularity (*Bukhara: Musical Crossroads of Asia*, track 7).

Recitation of the Qur'ān

In prerevolutionary Central Asia, the Qur'ān occupied an exceptionally important place in the lives of Muslims, providing guidance for all spheres of human life from birth to death. Knowledge of the Qur'ān was highly valued, and every Muslim had memorized at least several key suras.

The profession of reciter (*qāri*, *hāfiz*) was considered pleasing to God and carried considerable social status. The word *qāri* usually became a part of a reciter's name (for example, "Mahmud Qāri"), indicating a special relationship to the sacred book. This profession was closely connected to music. Not infrequently, highly ranked professional singers began their path to the art with the study of the Qur'ān, as did the outstanding Uzbek singer of Soviet times, Muhiddin Qāri-Yakubov (1896–1957). Reciters studied in a school (*maktab*) affiliated with a mosque, a *madrasah,* a Sufi *khānaqā,* or a shrine, or in special institutions (*qarikhāna*) that educated and domiciled

Qur'ānic reciters and were supported by donations, bequests, and religious endowments (*waqf*). The boys chosen for such training were typically from poor families, orphans, or blind.

Like other forms of religious music and chant in Central Asia, recitation of the Qur'ān tended toward either of two contrasting performance styles: an official or "international" style, and an assortment of popular and more local styles. The official style, originating in Cairo and other religious centers of the Arab world, was the purview of professional reciters and the Islamic clergy and is characterized by formal strictness, lyricism, and rhythmic and melodic complexity. Professional reciters in this style typically used six or seven canonical melodic types, often borrowed directly from the Arabic tradition of the classical *maqām*. By contrast, local performance styles were practiced in daily life by Muslims who observed popular forms of Islam that arose along the byways and in the hinterlands of Central Asia. These local styles were characterized by melodic simplicity and accessibility and reflected local folk song: Kyrgyz folk melodies among the Kyrgyz, Kazakh melodies among the Kazakh, and so on.

In the twentieth century, the Bukharan style of Qur'ānic recitation, considered exemplary because of its refinement, was widely disseminated in Central Asia and in the steppe regions of Kazakhstan. To a large extent this dissemination resulted from the centralized training of mullahs, Qur'ānic reciters, and imams in Bukhara's religious colleges, in particular the famous late medieval *madrasah* Mir-i Arab. As the Soviet policy of state atheism lost its hold in Central Asia, recitation of the Qur'ān acquired new prestige. Recordings of Qur'ānic recitation were issued by the state-owned record company, Melodiya, and competitions for recitation of the Qur'ān were organized by religious authorities.

Music and chant for Muslim holidays

Ramadan

Music and other forms of entertainment were a central feature of Muslim festivities, particularly during the month of Ramadan. In Bukhara, the populace was notified that Ramadan had arrived by rhythmic drumming and music performed by the emir's military orchestra (*nakkarakhāna*), installed at the gates of his residence, called the *ark*. Following the daytime fast that is obligatory for observant Muslims during Ramadan, the emir's orchestra played after sunset. In Tashkent during the nights of Ramadan, a percussion orchestra consisting of kettledrums (*naghāra*) and other instruments performed from the roof of a house near the Shaykh Antahur Mosque. In other cities, special nighttime bazaars featured performances and pageantry by musicians, singers, and religious storytellers.

City-dwellers had favorite out-of-town religious sites, usually Sufi *khānaqā* and shrines set in picturesque gardens, where they gathered at the end of the daily fast. At night, they relaxed in these places, talking, eating, and watching various forms of popular entertainment. A site popular with the residents of Tashkent was the *khānaqā* and shrine of a follower of the Yassawiyya order, Shaykh Zengi-Ata, situated in a shady garden on the outskirts of the city. People from Bukhara and its surroundings—women and men on different days—visited the grave and *khānaqā* of the famous Sufi shaykh Bahauddin Naqshband, located in the suburbs, where well-known singers interpreted the works of Sufi-inspired poets such as Ḥāfiẓ, Mashrab, and Yassawi.

One of the genres performed during Ramadan was the *na'at*—a chanted song celebrating the life and deeds of the Prophet Muhammad. The *na'at* was characterized by a form of religious singing called *na'tkhāni* (Uzbek *na'tkhānlik*). The texts included compositions by professional poets as well as folk songs (*Bukhara: Musical Crossroads of Asia*, track 8).

Another genre sung during Ramadan consists of special greeting songs whose titles always include the word Ramadan (pronounced "Ramazan" in Central Asia): for instance, Uzbeks sang "*Iya Ramazan*"; Kazakhs, "*Jarapazan*"; Kyrgyz and Qaraqalpaqs, "*Zharamazan*"; and Turkmen, "*Yaremezan*." The singers were often children and teenagers strolling past the homes of neighbors. The texts wished the family happiness and well-being, the birth of a baby, and so on, and the singers received small gifts such as sweets or coins. Here is an Uzbek version of such a song:

Ramazān aytib keldik eshigingizga,	Serenading Ramazan, we came to your door.
Qochqordai oghil bersin beshigingizga.	Let it give to your cradle a son, strong as a ram.

The same words, with small changes, are sung by Kyrgyz as "*Zharamazan*" and by Kazakhs as "*Zharapazan*"—an illustration of the common poetic basis of the genre throughout Central Asia. The Kazakh version notated in figure 3 shows the limited melodic range and simple declamatory structure typical of the genre:

We are here to sing *zharapazan* in your home.
Please put an embroidered belt around our waist.
If you put an embroidered belt around our waist,
We'll go back to our home praising you.

In Uzbekistan, particularly in the eastern region of the Ferghana valley, women commonly performed songs called *rabbimmān* 'My Lord, God' during Ramadan. The following Uzbek example was recorded by the musical ethnographer Elena E. Romanovskaya in 1931 and illustrates a folk-inspired representation of Islam:

Rabbimmān, yāh rabbimmān, yāh ramazān,	Blessed is the month of Ramadan.
Khush mubārak, māhi ramazān.	In the air are various scents.
Havāda turli tumanning isi bār,	In the "four books" is the word of the Prophet.
Chār kitābda Mustafāning sozi bār	Blessed is the month of Ramadan.
Rabbimmān, yāh rabbimmān, yāh ramazān,	The month of Ramadan is for the community of Muhammad.
Muhammad ummatiga māhi ramazān	
Rabbimmān, yāh rabbimmān, yāh ramazān.	

The breaking of the fast at the end of Ramadan was observed as a major holiday (*ruza khayit* or *ruza bayram*). This holiday lasted three days, during which believers observed

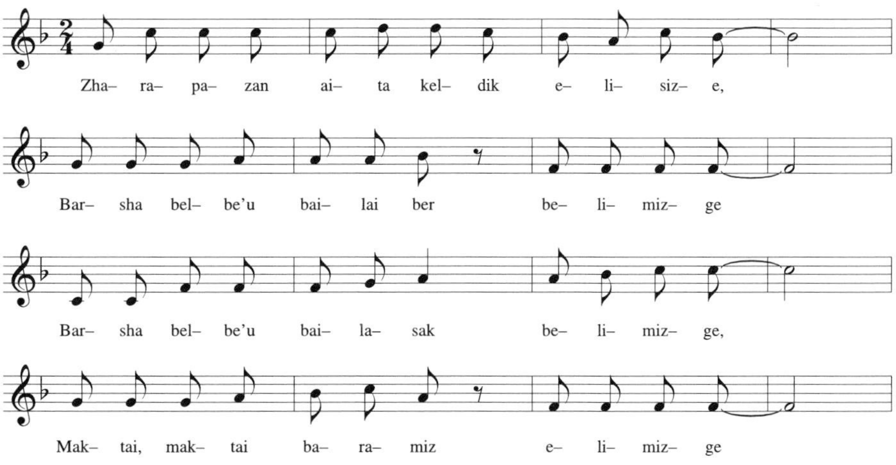

FIGURE 3 "*Zharapazan*," a Kazakh calendar-ritual song. (Transcription from Abdullaev 1994.)

the successful completion of the fast. Neighborhoods organized banquets and gave gifts to the mullahs. There were various forms of entertainment (*tamāsha*), including song, instrumental music, male dancers (*bacha*), clowns (*maskharabozi*), puppet theater, and acrobats. Representatives of various Sufi orders, itinerant dervishes, and religious storytellers sang and performed the ritual of *zikr*.

The most important holiday in Central Asia, the Feast of the Sacrifice (*kurban bairam* or *kurban khyit,* or simply *khyit*; Arabic *'īd al-aḍḥá*), was celebrated in an analogous way. It was held seventy days after the end of the Ramadan fast and lasted for three or four days, ending at the same time as the Pilgrimage. The Feast of the Sacrifice commemorates a test of faith, when Abraham—a prophet in Islam—prepared to sacrifice his son, Ismail, to Allah but at the last moment was instructed by Allah to replace Ismail with an animal. To mark this holiday, animals are sacrificed, large amounts of food are prepared and given away as an offering, friends visit one another, and people go to the graves of those who were close to them. Music and other performing arts are also an important part of of the Feast of the Sacrifice.

Mavlud

Another religious holiday, Mavlud (or *mavlūd al-nabī*), the birthday of the Prophet Muhammad, was also widely observed in Central Asia, on the twelfth day of the month of *rabi al-awwal*. Mavlud was an occasion for songs—also called *mavlud*—which, like the *na'at,* recounted the life and deeds of the Prophet. These *mavlud* songs typically had a short, simple refrain. During Mavlud, as during other holidays, people prepared food and listened to musical performances; and Sufi orders played an active role in the celebration. The person and deeds of the Prophet Muhammad were a central theme, expressed in sermons and stories as well as song.

Shiite ceremonies

Shiite ceremonies and rituals were widely observed in the cities of Central Asia and were seen as part of the common Islamic tradition. They included the period of mourning during the first ten days (*ashura*) of the month of Muharram that memorializes the Shiite martyrs Ali, Hasan, and Husayn. For *ashura,* Shiites had songs such as "*Shahādati imām Hasan, imām Husayn*" 'The Martyrs Imam Hasan and Imam Husayn', a special form of *zikr*, and sacred dance. In many parts of Bukhara inhabited by Iranians (who were known as Fārsi), there were Shiite prayer houses called *husayni-xāna* in the pre-Soviet period. The principal Shiite ceremonies, including laments for Imam Husayn and a special type of religious theater called *taziyah*, were conducted in these prayer houses. Women and men participated separately, and Sunni Bukharans also attended the annual mourning rituals of the Shiites.

THE ROLE OF MUSIC IN CENTRAL ASIAN SUFISM

Samā' and *zikr*

A number of major Sufi orders existed in Central Asia in the first third of the twentieth century, each with its own traditional territory. In the Khwarezm oasis was the Kubrawiyya; in the Bukhara-Samarkand region, the Naqshbandiyya; in Tashkent-Ferghana, there were the Yassawiyya and Qadiriyya. Almost everywhere were groups of wandering dervishes, *qalandar*. There were also small mystical groups, such as the Yazdakhum 'eleventh' in Bukhara. (Their name derives from the fact that they celebrated their *zikr* on the eleventh day of each month in memory of the famous medieval Sufi Abdulqadir Jilani, who died on the eleventh day of the month.)

All these orders performed the *zikr* as a ritual of sacred music, word, and dance. However, it took different forms, which ranged from the classical practice in the great *khānaqā* of Tajik-Uzbek urban society to various hybrid forms of prayer and healing rituals linked to shamanism (Kazakhstan), funerary rituals (in the mountainous regions of Tajikistan, Urā-Teppa, and Samarkand), and even dance intended as entertainment (among the Turkmen of western Turkmenistan). Among the Kyrgyz, the term *zikr* designated a broader set of activities practiced by itinerant dervishes known as *duwan*, from the Persian *diwana* 'mendicant', 'holy fool', 'possessed'.

There were two types of *zikr* in the ritual practice of the Central Asian orders: *zikr khafi* (or *khufi*), a silent, hidden *zikr*; and *zikr jakhri* (also *jari, jakhriyya*), loud *zikr*. In the silent *zikr* the name of Allah and the sacred formulas were pronounced silently; in the loud *zikr,* people sang, recited poetry aloud, and danced. Musical instruments were not used, except for the *dāyra* and, more rarely, the *safail*, a type of rattle. The loud *zikr* was traditionally practiced by the Kubrawiyya order in Khwarezm and the Yazdakhum sect in Bukhara, and in the nineteenth and early twentieth century it was adopted by many Sufi orders and groups throughout Central Asia. *Zikr* was conducted not only in the *khānaqā*, the special building constructed for this purpose, but also in shrines and mosques, at pilgrimage sites, and in the open air. Major centers for the performance of *zikr* included the Yassawi *khānaqā* in Turkestan, the shrine and *khānaqā* Zengi-Ata near Tashkent (where mass versions of *zikr* were conducted in the autumn), the *khānaqā* of Bahauddin Naqshband outside Bukhara, and the Shah-i Zinda complex in Samarkand. *Zikr* was held separately for men and women; women's *zikr* was usually led by an *ishan-bibi*, the wife of an *ishan*, a rural religious leader whose authority came not from a formal religious post but from a reputation for spiritual mastery among a circle of disciples.

The largest and most influential orders in Central Asia were the Naqshbandiyya and Yassawiyya. The Naqshbandiyya drew their membership primarily from the sedentary urban Tajik-speaking population of artisans, merchants, shopkeepers, and tradesmen. Its center was the *khānaqā* of Bahauddin Naqshband outside Bukhara, a site of mass pilgrimage (*ziyāratgāh*) where performers of spiritual songs and chant were always on hand to entertain visitors in return for alms. The Naqshbandiyya practiced silent and loud forms of *zikr* and used primarily Persian-Tajik mystical poetry.

The Yassawi order (sometimes known as the Jariyya, after the type of loud *zikr* they practiced) drew its membership primarily from the Turkic nomadic, seminomadic, and sedentary world. Its center was the *khānaqā* of Ahmad Yassawi (d. 1166) in the city of Turkestan (formerly Yassy) in present-day Kazakhstan. The form of loud *zikr* practiced there was known as *zikr arra* 'saw *zikr*', from a raspy, antiphonal chanting that sounded like sawing. The *zikr* was held once a week in the *khānaqā*, and during the season of mass pilgrimage (in the winter *chilla,* a forty-day period from the end of December to the beginning of February) it continued for three days in an underground room (*khilvat*).

FIGURE 4 Hoja Ahmad Yassawi's *Divan-i Hikmat*: the cover of a prerevolutionary lithograph published in Kagan, New Bukhara.

V. A. Uspenskii and Mahmud Akhmedov, two Soviet ethnographers who worked in the 1940s and 1950s, reported that the Yassawiyya "saw" *zikr* represented a multipart "composition" of between seven and fifteen vocal parts based primarily on the mystical poetry compiled in the *Hikmat* 'Wisdom' of Hoja Ahmad Yassawi (figure 4), with contributions from other Turkic-speaking poets including Alisher Nawāi, Fuzuli, Mashrab, Khuvaido, and Khalis. Persian-Tajik poetry was used much more rarely.

The *zikr* began with the recitation of the Qur'ān (*takbīr*) and then segued into a form of chanting called *chārzarb* 'four strokes', which constituted the basis of the *zikr*. From a musical perspective, *chārzarb* represented one of the names of God chanted in a metrical-rhythmic formula (*usūl*) consisting of four syllables within one breath. Usually the *chārzarb* reflected the four-beat rhythmic structure of the chanting of the Islamic creed called *tawḥīd*: *Lā illāha illa Allāh* 'There is no God but God', which is the nucleus of the loud *zikr* among the Yassawi and other orders. In chanting, the four rhythmically even accents are applied as follows (accented syllables are capitalized): *LA il-LA-ha IL -la Al-LAH.*

Analogous forms called *sezarb* (three syllables), *duzarb* (two syllables), and *yakzarb* (one syllable) together with the *chārzarb* formed a cycle of four metrical-rhythmic formulas. These and other syllable-based rhythmic formulas were designated by the word *zikr* in its narrow sense. Usually they were chanted by all the participants in the *zikr* at the beginning of the ceremony, between its parts, and as a repetitive ostinato during the whole event. Against this background, the soloist (*hāfiz*) sang devotional songs called *talqīn* which usually included one strophe of a poetic text from the *Hikmat*. Performance of the *talqīn* required a high level of artistry that was transmitted through lineages of musical specialists (*talqīnchi*). The Yassawi *zikr* also included a form of sacred dance which suggested the dance-incantation of shamans and in fact seems to have originated from it.

In the 1920s, after Soviet power was established in Central Asia, restrictions and prohibitions were placed on the practice of *zikr.* However, the practice was preserved through the entire Soviet era in remote settlements and, secretly, in cities such as Tashkent (figure 5), Namangan, Kokand, and Khojend.

Other forms of Sufi music

The classical *zikr* influenced many other forms and types of religious chant. One of these was known as *yakkakhāni* in Tajik and *yakkakhānlik* in Uzbek—the name means individual song. As a constituent part of the *zikr*, *yakkakhānlik* was usually performed during the breaks between the principal parts of the ritual or upon the conclusion of the entire cycle of the *zikr*, while the participants rested. In time, *yakkakhānlik* became an independent practice with its own style of singing.

Katta ashula 'great song' is another genre related to the chanting style of *zikr. Katta ashula* was widely performed in the Ferghana valley, particularly in the cities of Andijan, Ferghana, Kokand, Namangan, and Khojend, and in Tashkent and its environs. *Katta ashula* sets spiritual poetry in an unmetered, declamatory style sung loudly yet expressively, in a high tessitura. While it reflects the influence of the *zikr,* its poetic form also reflects the quantitative meters of the classical *aruz* system, whose origin was in Arabic and Persian poetry. Most *katta ashula* compositions are set to the poetic forms *ghazal*, *masnavi*, and *mukhammas*, and the musical material is through-composed: that is, rather than repeat a short musical structure through many couplets or quatrains of text, as in folk settings like those of the *Hikmat*, the melody of *katta ashula* develops to a point of culmination, called *awdj*, as is characteristic in Uzbek-Tajik songs from the classical *maqām* repertoire.

FIGURE 5 *Zikr* in Tashkent, Uzbekistan, in March 1958. Photo G. Rakushev (accompanying a recording made by Mahmud Akhmedov).

Another genre related to professional Sufi chanting was the *khānakāi* 'performed in the *khānaqā*'. This genre and its characteristic style are connected with the development of Sufi architecture, especially with the complex of buildings that contained the central domed hall where *zikr* was performed. As recently as the 1940s, the *khānakāi* was performed in Bukhara, and particular examples were notated by folklorists and musicians. Khwarezm had its own version of Sufi-inspired vocal music: a song cycle called *suvāra*, which, like *katta ashula* and *khānakāi*, set spiritual poetry to music. During the Soviet era, the religious texts of *katta ashula, suvāra,* and other vocal genres were largely replaced by secular words; but in post-Soviet Uzbekistan, singers have been restoring many of the old religious texts.

There were other religious organizations in Central Asia similar to the Sufi orders. The best known of these was the community of wandering dervishes (*qalandarlar*), which at times took the form of an independent order, the Qalandariyya. Many cities had a *qalandarkhāna* (*qalandar* house) where the wandering dervishes lived. These dervishes wandered through the neighborhoods and bazaars of the city, seeking alms and chanting prayers and spiritual songs, sometimes to the accompaniment of a noisy rattle (*safail*). They had their own traditions of vocal performance—based on an antiphonal alternation of chorus and soloist—and also practiced their own simplified form of *zikr*. The *duwan* of Kyrgyz popular culture was an itinerant figure similar to the *qalandar*.

Narrators of religious legends and history called *maddāh* were close in spirit to the *qalandar*, as well as to the Arab folk preacher of the first centuries of Islam, the *kassām* 'storyteller'. At the same time, they represented a folk version of the professional preachers (*wa'iz*) found throughout the Muslim world, including Central Asia. In the cities the *maddāhs* usually lived in a separate group or constituted an independent neighborhood called *maddāhkhān*. They were in close touch with musicians, wandering dervishes, and other like-minded denizens of the medieval city, and together with them created a kind of bohemian milieu. The principal repertoire of the *maddāh* consisted of *dastān*—narratives, stories, and legends with historical, religious, and homiletic content. They were well acquainted with music, knew a variety of spiritual songs and chants, and skillfully used theatrical methods of religious persuasion. Like the *qalandar*, the *maddāh* performed spiritual songs based on texts by Sufi poets, which used similar means of musical expression. The *maddāh* became noticeably more active during the major Muslim holidays.

Among Central Asian Sufis, wandering dervishes, and religious storytellers, the hermeneutic interpretation and singing of Sufi-inspired poetry by authors such as Yassawi, Mashrab, Bedil, and Ḥāfiẓ was very popular and constituted an independent type of spiritual art. Cities, towns, and even villages cultivated a tradition of spiritual gatherings devoted to the work of particular poets: a gathering devoted to the *Hikmat* of Yassawi was known as *Yassawikhānlik*; a gathering devoted to Ḥāfiẓ was a *Hāfizkhānlik*; a gathering devoted to Bedil was a *Bedilkhānlik*; and so on.

RELIGIOUS MUSIC IN THE SOCIAL WORLD OF WOMEN

In the social world of Central Asian women, religious and spiritual specialists typically had several different roles that all met women's spiritual and cultural needs. In Uzbekistan and Tajikistan, these figures included the *ātin āyi* 'teacher-mother' or *ātinbibi* 'teacher-grandmother', *khalfa* (a wedding entertainer in Khwarezm), *sāzanda* (a wedding entertainer in Bukhara), and *guyanda* (a professional mourner). Their major functions included reading the Qur'ān, saying prayers for women, lamenting and reciting poetry at funerals, singing spiritual songs and reading religious poetry at women's gatherings, and leading the *zikr* for women, sometimes for the specific purpose of healing. Folk forms of *zikr* also found an outlet in *sadr* or *samā'*, melodramatic or ecstatic funerary rituals performed by women. Chanting in the female *zikr* could

FIGURE 6 *Sezarb* from a women's *zikr*. Notated in 1940–1941 in Tashkent by Viktor Uspensky. (Here, there is a brief omission between staves 4 and 5; the text is: *Ashiqlari bekarar* . . .)

also follow a more classical form, as in the *sezarb* transcribed in figure 6, where a rhythmic formula containing one of the names of God follows every strophe:

Female singers (*zākir* and *ātin*) who had attained a high degree of vocal mastery performed the technique of "saw" *zikr*—imitation of the sound of a saw—which they learned through long years of practice. Women had their own forms of ritual associated with patrons of female professions and women's way of life, such as Bibi Fatima, Bibi Seshanba 'Mrs. Tuesday' (that being the day when women gathered to perform special songs, read prayers and poems, and share food), and Bibi Mushkul Kushād 'Mrs. Overcoming Difficulties'. These rituals included chants dedicated to mythical figures. In religious songs, women typically used the poems of Yassawi, Mashrab, Huvaidā, and other mystical poets.

Women's folk songs were usually sung at female social evenings, at weddings, and for festivals and rituals such as Lola (the tulip holiday) and Nawruz (the new year), particularly during the preparation of the ritual food *sumalak* (a type of porridge). The most popular musical instruments were the *dutār* and the *dāyra* and, in Khwarezm, the harmonium as well.

The declaration of independence by the new governments of Central Asia after the breakup of the Soviet Union in 1991 set off an intensive Islamic revival. In turn, this led to a revival of many forms of religious music that either had been forgotten or were being practiced illegally. For example, during Ramazan children have once again started visiting homes and even offices to ask for money or sweets. At the turn of the twenty-first century, religious music in Central Asia shows signs of reclaiming its former place as a central element in the spiritual culture of the region.

TRANSLATED BY THEODORE LEVIN

REFERENCES

Abdullaev, Rustam. 1994. *Obriadovaia Muzyka Tsentralnoi Azii.* Tashkent.

Bukhara: Musical Crossroads of Asia. 1991. Smithsonian Folkways 40050. Compact disk.

Kazakh Music

Alma Kunanbaeva

Cultural Aspects of Kazakh Nomadism
Musical Genres
The Oral Tradition
Instrumental Music: *Kyuiler*
Music and Musical Culture of the Soviet Period
Post-Soviet Kazakhstan

The Kazakhs are a Turkic-speaking people of Central Asia. Their nation, Kazakhstan, has an area about one-third that of the continental United States; it stretches almost 2,000 miles east to west, from the border of China to the Caspian Sea, and more than 1,200 miles north to south, from the southern Urals to the Tien Shan Mountains. At the end of the twentieth century, the population numbered some 16 million, of whom more than 1 million lived in the largest city, Almaty (Alma-Ata). Kazakhs make up about 50 percent of the population; the rest consists of Russians, Ukrainians, Germans, Koreans, Uyghurs, Uzbeks, Tartars, and nearly 100 other nationalities. Almost 3 million Kazakhs live outside Kazakhstan—most of them in Uzbekistan, Russia, China, and Mongolia.

CULTURAL ASPECTS OF KAZAKH NOMADISM

Since ancient times, the territory of present-day Kazakhstan has been inhabited by pastoral stockbreeders who raised sheep, cattle, horses, and camels. Animal husbandry was the only economic activity in the dry, harsh continental climate of the Kazakh steppe. The Kazakhs emerged from an amalgam of Turkic tribes in the mid-fifteenth century following the establishment of the Kazakh khanate in the Chu River Valley in southern Kazakhstan. Notwithstanding their large area of settlement, Kazakhs are unified by a common language and culture.

Kazakh society has traditionally been organized into three large *juze* 'kin groups' or (loosely) 'hordes': *Ouly* 'Senior', centered in the south and east of what is now Kazakhstan; *Orta* 'Middle', in the central region; and *Kishi* 'Younger', in the west. Each *juze* is divided into tribes and clans. Kinship is based on exogamy, and thus knowledge of genealogy is an essential component of traditional life which serves the practical function of preventing incest.

The ancient religion of the nomads is known as Tengrianism, after Tengri, the name of the sky deity, who represents the origin of maleness. Tengrianism is trinitarian, the other deities being Jer-Su, the female deity of earth and water; and Umai, the female protector of fertility and women in childbirth. By the end of the tenth century Islam had been established among the sedentary populations living in the south of present-day Kazakhstan, and by the sixteenth century Kazakhs had become Sunni

Among the Kazakhs, traditional culture is basically oral; in such a social context, it was natural for music to assume a role far greater than mere entertainment.

Muslims. Nowadays, many Kazakhs combine Islamic practices and beliefs with elements of Tengrianism.

Among the Kazakhs, as well as other Central Asian nomadic peoples, traditional culture is basically oral, and the specific features of orally preserved and transmitted knowledge provide a key to understanding this culture. Before the nineteenth century, literacy was confined to men educated in Islamic religious colleges; the vast majority of the Kazakh population absorbed whatever knowledge they had by listening and memorizing. In such a social context, it was natural for music to assume a role far greater than mere entertainment. Indeed, for the Kazakhs, music has been at the core of society, providing the mechanism through which social life is preserved and transmitted. For example, many kinds of music were incorporated into traditional hospitality rituals performed in the circular felt yurts that are home to the Kazakh nomads. Musical performances were typically accompanied by commentary, conversation, and interpretation. As a rule, each musical piece recounted the history of its own creation, and its performance included a story about its composer and about past performers. The listeners participated actively, influencing the choice of repertoire and encouraging the performers.

MUSICAL GENRES

Kazakh music includes both vocal and instrumental genres. Vocal music may be divided into folklore, consisting mainly of solo pieces sung by women which are closely linked to ritual and ceremonial functions; and professional music primarily performed by men who accompany themselves on an instrument, in social contexts not constrained by a ritual function. Distinctive features of professional oral music include formal teacher-student relationships, a high level of professionalism, and the distinguished social status of both vocalists and instrumentalists.

Kazakh vocal music exists within a framework of three social and artistic institutions: folk song (*änshilik*, from *än* 'melody'), improvised composition (*aqyndyq*, from *aqyn* 'poet-improviser'), and storytelling (*zhyraulyq*, from *zhyr* 'epic', 'epic poetry'). Each of these has particular performance genres. The genres have texts with common themes and rhetorical techniques such as contemplation, edification, exhortation, and a stringing together of historical events and personages; and they speak to a particular level of consciousness in performer and listener. For example, folk songs address the level of ordinary everyday consciousness; the *aqyn*—the poet-improviser—animates a kind of ritualized genealogical consciousness; and epics operate at an elevated level of aphoristic and symbolic consciousness. Ritual songs are to a certain extent embedded in the traditions of the poet-improviser and the epic (in the outline below, "calque" refers to this).

A schematic outline of the entire system of vocal genres in Kazakh traditional music might look like this (the discussion below, however, follows a somewhat different order):

I. Folk song tradition (*änshilik*)
   1. Ritual songs
   2. Lyrical songs
   3. Epic songs
II. Poet-improviser tradition (*aqyndyq*)
   1. *Aqyn* calque of ritual songs
   2. Professional lyric poetry
   3. *Aqyn* songs on epic subjects
   4. Genres of *aitys* (sung poetic competitions)
III. Epic tradition (*zhyraulyq*)
   1. Epic calque of ritual songs
   2. Epic tales in complete form (*zhyr*)
   3. Shorter narrative forms derived from epic: *tolghau*, *terme*, *osiet*, *naqyl söz*, *khat*, *soz*
   4. Epic poetry

The defining features of musical genres and traditions among the nomadic Kazakhs are rooted not in theory but in an entire complex of concrete melodic, textual, and stylistic characteristics and associations shaped by culture.

THE ORAL TRADITION

Folk songs

Folk song genres, performed mainly by women without instrumental accompaniment, are typically linked to ceremonial and ritual occasions such as weddings, funerals, and holidays.

Wedding songs include various types that accompany and comment on particular events: the bride's laments (*syngsu* and *tanysu*), opening the wedding (*toi bastar*), unveiling the bride's face (*betashar*), and saying farewell (*qoshtasu*). The most popular wedding song, "Zhar-Zhar," which is found in different versions throughout Central Asia, constitutes a genre of its own, defined by an antiphonal performance style in which two choirs—one male and one female—sing responsorially.

Funeral songs are another group of specific genres: herald songs announcing a death (*yestirtu*), songs of condolence (*kongil aitu*, *zhubatu*), and laments sung during the funeral ritual and at yearly memorials (*zhoqtau*, *zhylau*, *daus*).

Still another genre consists of songs or carols (*zharapazan*) for the Muslim fast of Ramadan [see SACRED MUSIC AND CHANT IN ISLAMIC CENTRAL ASIA]. Such ritual genres were not classified generically as "songs" (*än*, *öleng*) but were known by their specific functional designations: *synsu* (figure 1), *zhoqtau*, and so on.

In addition to songs connected to specific ceremonial and ritual events, women sing lyrical music called *qara öleng* 'simple song', which is also the name used to

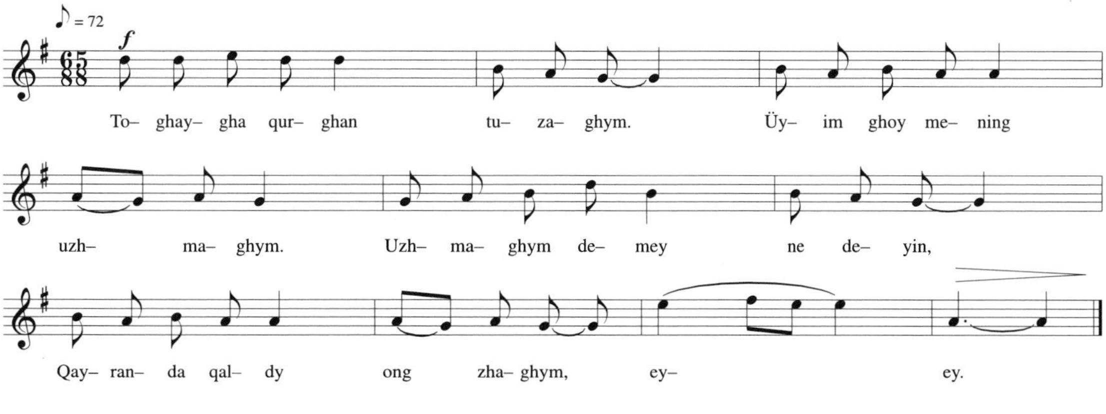

= 72
f
To– ghay– gha qur– ghan tu– za– ghym. Üy– im ghoy me– ning
uzh– ma– ghym. Uzh– ma– ghym de– mey ne de– yin,
Qay– ran– da qal– dy ong zha– ghym, ey– ey.

FIGURE 1 *Synsu* (Bekkhozina 1972, no. 40). Translation: "A trap is laid for me in the grove./My home is in paradise./What else do I have to call home/When my right side [my luck] is behind me?"

FIGURE 2 Almas Almatov (b. 1951), an epic singer from Kyzl-Orda, with one of his sons. Photo by Sergei Zhirkevich, 1990.

describe the verse form: eleven-syllable lines set in two quatrains. This music is typically performed at singing and oral poetry contests (*qaiym öleng*), at evening gatherings featuring vocal improvisations by the guests (*böket öleng*), and during exchanges of riddle songs (*zhumbaq öleng*).

The oral epic (*zhyraulyq*)

The epic tradition remains a living force in Kazakh culture. An oral epic is at once history, literature, and philosophy, and the carriers of this tradition—epic singers called *zhyrau*—have a special social role and occupy a special status (figure 2). The *zhyrau* were advisers to the khans and guardians of cultural history, linking older and younger generations and serving as models for the formation of ethnic identity by keeping historical memory alive. They were also successors to the shamans, whose authority was reduced by the arrival of Islam in the eighteenth century and by the power of the Soviet Union in the twentieth.

Central to the epic tradition are tales of heroes (*batyrlar zhyry*). In addition to the immensely long heroic tales known to the entire Turkic-speaking world, such as "Kör-ogly," "Alpamysh," and "Yedige," the Kazakh epic repertoire also includes tales disseminated only within the territory of a single clan (for example, "Oraq-Mamai," "Karasai-Qazi," and "Shora Batyr"). Such local tales abound in names and deeds of legendary personages and were often included in extensive genealogical cycles that carefully transmitted the history of a clan from one generation to the next. Another large group of epic tales consists of so-called lyric epics, whose central theme is true, strong love. Typically, a lyric epic is named after its heroine ("Qyz-Zhibek," "Sulu-shash," "Maqralqyz,") or her beloved ("Qozy Körpesh-Bayan Sulu").

The living epic tradition is not limited to heroic epics. Surrounding the epic tale (*zhyr*) is a large group of narrative songs and instrumental genres which at first glance seem unrelated to it. These include *terme* 'threading', *tolghau* 'contemplation', *ösiet* 'exhortation', *naqyl söz* 'homily', *arnau* 'dedication', *hat* 'letter', *maqtau* 'eulogy', and others that together make up the so-called small epic genres. These consist mainly of short songs without a narrative plot, philosophical homilies on life and death or on the place and purpose of human beings, missives, dedications, exhortations, and so on. These subgenres within the epic tradition include varieties of *terme* such as *bastau-än* 'introductory songs', which usually precede the performance of major tales and are used by the storyteller to invoke inspiration and to inform the audience which tales he knows; *tanysu*, in which the reciter introduces himself and gets to know the audience; and *tangdatu*, a kind of epic "menu" presented to the audience members so that they can choose what they want to hear.

As a whole, the world of the epic represents a traditional moral code that summarizes the values of a people. The preeminent role of epic is not narrative as such; rather, it is homiletic, making a case for underlying ethical values. Epic regulates social conduct, weaving individual lives into the fabric of history and concentrating past and future in a momentary present. Nomadic life demanded that younger generations know the history of their people in order to defend their interests and ensure their continuity. Such knowledge could come only from the epic tradition, which reflects the historical experience of the Kazakhs over many centuries and provides a flexible mechanism for transmitting it.

The epic world does not consist of separate pieces or poems; in particular, it does not consist of the subjects of these works. Rather, it consists of a process that makes the listener an active participant in the rhythm by which human life evolves or unfolds. Storytellers themselves understand their performance as the creation of a panorama of traditional life with which listeners can empathize, and this empathy becomes a way to measure the vitality of the human spirit. The time between moments of empathy is regarded as nothing more than a transitory bodily existence supported by the mem-

FIGURE 3 Shazynda Makhanbetov, master *dombra* maker in Kyzl-Orda. Photo courtesy of Mr. Makhanbetov, 16 June 1991.

ory of epic revelations. This concept of epic makes clear the importance of constantly renewing the dialogue between storyteller and audience, even when the text of an epic is well known to almost all the participants in that dialogue.

The survival of epic in its traditional social context depends on six elements of what might be called "epic culture":

1. An audience, which to some degree is like a censor, ensuring the continuity of traditions that it likes and finds meaningful.
2. Professional guilds of epic reciters, which organize oral transmission from teacher to student.
3. A sense of moral purpose among epic reciters, who view themselves not simply as singers but as responding to a higher calling. This sense of "calling" explains the widespread belief in the magical powers of the *zhyrau.*
4. Mastery of a specific epic performance style characterized by dramatically oratorical recitative which the performer delivers in a raspy, guttural voice, accompanying himself on a two-stringed *dombra* (figure 3). The accompaniment is interwoven with the text, and a performer cannot narrate a tale without it. The raspy vocal style is reminiscent of the sound of the *qobyz*, a two-stringed bowed lute played by Kazakh shamans.
5. Stability of regional traditions, with which epic exists in a complex symbiosis.
6. Mastery of the conventions of oral composition and performance. An epic unfolds within a specific formal structure: an introduction (*bastau*); a central section of recitative (*uzyn sonar* 'long hunt') based on a recurring rhythmic motive; and a conclusion (*qaiyrma* 'turn') in which the recitative slows down, breaking the vocal pulse of the story, and the text gives way to textless vocables performed in an ebullient style. Within this formal structure, the reciter composes the melodic recitative in the process of performance. Scholars have used the prosodic term *tirade* to describe the original and most ancient form of Kazakh epic composition: a verse form in which an indefinite number of lines are joined by a single rhyme pattern (figure 4). Epic *tirades* consisting of short verses are called *zhyr* (hence *zhyrau* 'singer of tales'). Using a *tirade* as the basic principle for creating a form allows the performer to make any number of varied repetitions of its components. A sequence of *tirade*s can be interrupted by spoken interludes, which do not disrupt the rapid pace of epic verse.

TRACK 29

For the epic tradition to survive, these six elements must function as a whole. The decay or elimination of even one of them will gradually lead to a transformation or even the disappearance of the tradition.

The poet-improviser tradition (*aqyndyq*)

A social function complementing that of the *zhyrau* was performed by the *aqyn* (plural, *aqyndar*)—a professional poet-improviser who took part in music and poetry contests called *aitys*, which were closely associated with shamanism. Like the *zhyrau*, the *aqyn* is said to acquire his gift in a miraculous way and has his own patrons, well-known *aqyndar* of the past who come to him and instruct him in dreams. The activities of the *aqyn* are comparable to those of the ancient Greek *aedes*, who represented their clans in song and poetry contests. The origins of the *aqyn* can be traced to priests who played a special role in initiation rites. *Aitys* 'to speak together' connotes verbal combat, usually a contest in the form of a dialogue between two or more poets or poet-singers. *Aitys* is a popular event among Kazakhs, often lasting an entire day and sometimes all night. Kazakh poetry contests took place on public holidays and during feasts in the presence of large gatherings. By custom, the defeated contestant was supposed to recite from memory the entire *aitys*, with all its dialogue and repartee. A

FIGURE 4 *Zhienbaygyng termesi*: example of the *tirade* form, transcribed from a performance by the epic singer Zhienbay Rustembekov (author's collection). Translation: "Let your bag of songs be seen/By the experts who pack themselves in./The robe that represents mastery/Has already been made for me."

classic example preserved in folkloric tradition is found in the epic "Birzhan-Sara," in which a defeated but scintillating young female *aqyn*, Sara Tastanbekqyzy (1878–1916), recounted her verbal duel with the great *aqyn* Birzhan-sal Qozhaghululy (1831–1897).

Aitys is not the only contest in Kazakh traditional culture. There are many traditional festivals and games: horseback riding contests (*bäige*), long-distance horse races (*alaman bäige*), trotting contests (*zhorgha zharys*), duels of horsemen armed with lances (*saiys*), horseback wrestling in which the aim is to pull an opponent from his saddle (*audaryspaq*), a goat chase (*kökpag tartu*), shooting with bows or rifles while riding a galloping horse (*jamby atu* or *altyn qabaq*), trick riding (*kümis alu*), wrestling (*qazaqsha küres*), contests between representatives of different guilds (which always include blacksmiths and comedians), rope-pulling contests, and "catch the girl" (*qyz quu*), in which the winner once had the right to marry the girl he caught. There are many variations on wedding games involving the bride and groom, their attendants, and relatives from both families. Like the *agones* of ancient Greece, these ritual games always involved a large number of participants and took place during events at which clans were represented—most frequently, weddings and memorials for the dead.

As the central domain of Kazakh poetic culture, *aitys* has many variations, including *aitys* between a young woman and a young man (*qyz ben jigit aitysy*), religious *aitys* (*din aitysy*), *aitys* in riddles (*jumbaq aitysy*), and *aitys* between poet-improvisers (*aqyndar aitysy*). These performers sometimes created an *aitys* on a specific subject—for example, an examination of knowledge of geography (*tau öleng, su öleng, jer öleng*)—and also engaged in mass contests of vocal improvisation during weddings (*qaim öleng*). Dialogue could be used to cast spells (*bädik*), and in children's songs, for example, a quarrel between a goat and a sheep. Contests between instrumentalists (*tartys*) were also popular.

In order to take part in a competition, contestants had to display professional mastery of their skill or subject matter and also had to meet three requirements:

1. Competition was forbidden between members of the same clan, and between clan members whose relation to the clan was through the father's lineage.
2. Every participant was obliged to praise his own clan and find fault with his opponent's clan.
3. During the competition, contestants were allowed to address their opponent in ways that violated normal etiquette. As a result, each *aitys* or *tartys* became an event of great social significance.

The lyric song tradition (*änshilik*)

Kazakh professional lyrical song reached its zenith in the second half of the nineteenth century and the beginning of the twentieth century. Performers of the various types of lyrical song—*änshi, sal, seri*—might be compared to the medieval troubadours who sang of chivalry, beauty, and harmony. Kazakh lyric singers, almost always men, were distinguished by their extravagant behavior and refined clothes and were much favored by the public. In contrast to the many genres of *aitys*, lyrical song was more unified.

The finest examples of professional lyric singing are from a region in central Kazakhstan known as the *Saryarqa* 'golden steppe'. The best-known singers of the Arqa school were Akhan-seri Qoramsinuly (1843–1913), Birzhan-sal Qozhagululy (1831–1894), Zhayau Musa Baizhanuly (1835–1929), Ibrai Sandybaiuly (1860–1932), Muhit Meraliuly (1841–1918), Mädi Bapiuly (1880–1921), Äset Naimanbaiuly (1867–1922), and Estai Berkenbaiuly (1874–1946). Ämre Qashaubaiuly (1888–1934) also became widely known beyond Kazakhstan; he performed with great success at two international exhibitions of decorative arts—in 1925 in Paris, where he received second prize, and in 1927 in Frankfurt. His voice was recorded on cylinders in the 1920s and transferred to LP recordings in the 1970s (Melodiya 31-37635). Twentieth-century singers who perpetuated the style of these great singer-composers include Manarbek Erzhanov (1901–1966), Zhusupbek Elebekov (1904–1977), and Zhanibek Karmenov (1949–1992). Their work has preserved Kazakh lyrical song in contemporary inventories of world song. However, the social turmoil of the Soviet era disrupted the tradition, and its most productive period is now past.

Lyrical songs are performed in a bel canto style that emphasizes intricate ornamentation, refined phrasing, and a melody resembling a cantilena. In lyrical song (unlike folk song), the melodies do not rely on formulas and thus have more freedom. Structurally, lyrical song is characterized by a strophic form that has an introduction and refrain, and verse lines of eleven syllables. Melodies are diatonic, with a range that often extends to two octaves. The introduction typically has a high tessitura and uses

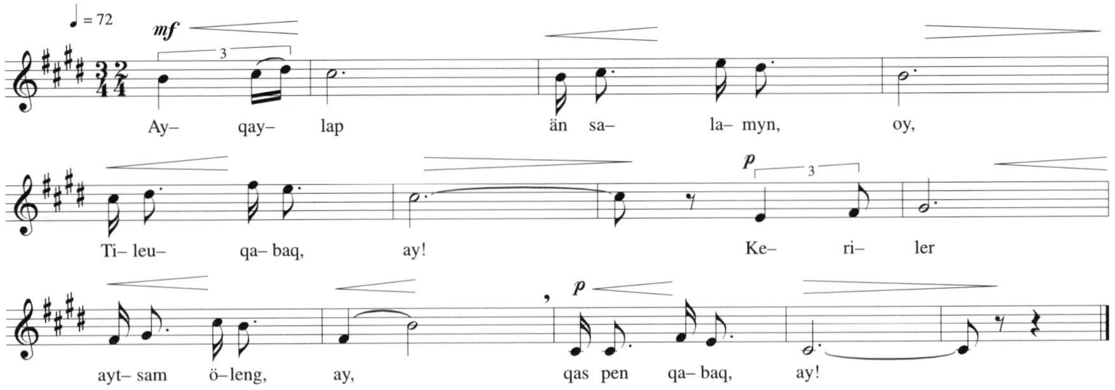

FIGURE 5 *Tileuqabaq* (Erzakovich 1994, no. 100; performed by Tamti Ibragimova, 1908–1982). Translation: "I sing the 'Tileuqabaq' very powerfully./When I'm singing, the [listeners'] foreheads and eyes are shining."

vocables rather than actual words. Refrains, also sung with vocables, are designed to show off the singer's vocal skills and the beauty of his voice. (The beginning of a lyrical song, "Tileuqabaq," is transcribed in figure 5.)

An essential characteristic of professional lyric singers was their insistence on preserving the attribution of a song to a particular singer-composer. This was accomplished in several ways: popular songs were always known by a specific title (in contrast to folk songs, which were typically nameless and were known simply by the first few words of the text); the composer's name was always included in the first couplet of the song; a canonical legend about the creation of the song or story typically preceded a performance; and reminicences about the composer became a part of the collective cultural memory.

The typical subject matter of lyrical songs may be divided into four categories:

1. Self-portraits in which the singer introduces himself in the first person; for example: "I belong to the clan of Argyn; they call me Äset the gifted," or "I am Shashubai, the son of Qoshkarbai."
2. Romance (the largest category).
3. The art of singing and the beauty of song.
4. Loss or parting—loss of youth, a loved one, a homeland, or life itself.

Professional lyric songs are always accompanied on the *dombra*—a plucked two-stringed lute. Unlike the *dombra* used by epic singers and by performers of the instrumental genre known as *kyui* (described below), the lyric *dombra* has a small resonator and a relatively short fingerboard with seven to eleven frets, and it is plucked rather than strummed (figure 6).

INSTRUMENTAL MUSIC: *KYUILER*

Of the large number of Kazakh musical instruments that existed in the past, only four survived at the beginning of the twentieth century: the *shang-qobyz*, *sybysghy*, *qyl-qobyz*, and *dombra*. The *shang-qobyz* is a Jew's harp mainly played by women; the *sybysghy* is an elongated open flute, approximately two feet long, made from the stem of umbelliferous plants or from wood, and played by shepherds.

The *qyl-qobyz*, a two-stringed bowed instrument, has a scoop-shaped body, chiseled from a whole piece of walnut or birchwood, and horsehair strings. The bow is held from beneath with the palm twisted to the side; the strings are tuned in the interval of a fourth or fifth and are played by lightly touching them to produce overtones (*flagolet*); the specific timbre comes from the absence of a fingerboard and the richness of the overtones. Music for *qobyz* is closely linked to the epic tradition, to mythology, and to shamanistic practices. The instrument is tuned differently for each kind of music: for epic recitation, the strings are set at the interval of a fourth; for music linked to shamanistic practices, they are set at the interval of a fifth. Per-

FIGURE 6 Bidas Rustembekov (b. 1951), a fourth-generation epic singer, performs for the author in Kyzl-Orda. Photo by Sergei Zhirkevich, 1990.

formers on the *qobyz* are called *qobyzshi*; one eminent player was Yqlas Dükenuly (1884–1916), whose instrumental pieces became the basis for the contemporary repertoire.

The *dombra*—a plucked long-necked lute—is the most popular instrument among contemporary Kazakhs. There are two types of *dombra.* The first, typical in western Kazakhstan, is pear-shaped and has a long, thin fingerboard with twelve, thirteen, or fourteen *perneler* 'frets' (singular, *perne*). The second type, common in southern, central, and eastern Kazakhstan, has a flat trapezoidal sound box (*shanaq*) and a shorter and broader fingerboard (*moiyn*) with seven, eight, or nine frets. Each fret has its own traditional name, which varies from region to region and from performer to performer. Often, a fret is associated with the name of a composition played on it (for example, *Turkimen Perne, Saryarqa Pernesi*). Strings (*shekter*) were once made of thin goat or sheep gut but later were manufactured from other readily available materials, such as fishing lines. Today, metal strings are also used. The *dombra* typically has two strings, although three-string and even four-string instruments existed in the past (for instance, in the Semipalatinsk region of Kazakhstan). The *dombra* has a range of two octaves, but the lower octave is the more important. The most colorful sound comes from the middle register (the fifth to tenth frets).

The *dombra* is used both to accompany songs and for independent instrumental solos known as *kyui* 'frame of mind', 'mood'. *Kyui* is a programmatic composition that resembles an instrumental poem. The title usually identifies the program, but traditionally the content of *kyui* is presented by the performer (*kyuishi*) before the piece is played. The content can be a legend or a simple story about the creation of the *kyui.* The legends represent a genre called *ängime*—an oral story.

Two types of *kyui* are distinguished by performance style: *tökpe* 'stream,' 'constant flow' is common in western Kazakhstan and consists of sweeping upward and downward movements of the right hand that produce a drone-like texture; *shertpe* 'plucking', 'flicking', 'fingering', found in all other parts of Kazakhstan, has no drone and is performed (as the name indicates) by plucking or flicking the strings with individual

FIGURE 7 *Sary-Arga* 'Golden Steppe', an example of *shertpe-kyui*.

fingers. The *kyui* of western Kazakhstan has two melodic lines whose interaction conceals the actual melody; by contrast, the *shertpe-kyui* is monophonic, and its melody is clearly audible (figure 7).

Prominent performers in the *tökpe* tradition include Qurmanghazy Saghyrbaiuly (1818–1879), Däületkerei Shyghaiuly (1820–1887), Qazanghap Tilepbergenuly (1854–1926), Espai Balustauly (1810–1901), Dina Nürpeisqyzy (1861–1955), and Seitek Orozalynuly (1861–1923). Well-known performers in the *shertpe* tradition include Tättimbet Qazanghapuly (1815–1862) and Sügir Äliuly (1890?–1961).

One genre performed on the *dombra* is the *tartys-kyui* 'contest piece' (also known as *aitys-quiler* in the Manghystau region of southwest Kazakhstan). Contest pieces are typically divided into three groups. From least to most demanding for the performer, these are:

1. Performing on the *dombra*.
2. Improvising an instrumental piece on a given theme.
3. Combining compositional mastery with the ability to memorize and reproduce a new *kyui* that a *dombra* player has heard only once.

MUSIC AND MUSICAL CULTURE OF THE SOVIET PERIOD

At the beginning of the Soviet period, Russian ethnographers and folklorists began the systematic collection and study of Kazakh music. The greatest of these early scholars was Alexander Zatayevich (1869–1936), who transcribed some 2,300 examples of Kazakh folk music, more than half of which appeared in two collections published in 1925 and 1931. A generation of scholars born in the first decades of the twentieth century continued Zateyevich's work and laid the foundation for modern Kazakh musicology and ethnomusicology.

In the 1920s and 1930s, Kazakh traditional culture was disrupted by a transition from nomadic to settled life imposed by Soviet ideology and power. This cultural revolution was dominated by European music, particularly the nineteenth-century Russian symphonic and operatic repertoire. An urbanization of culture, combined with other demographic shifts—Kazakhstan lost at least 25 percent of its native population while Russians were encouraged to migrate there—destroyed the professional status of oral culture, downgraded it to the level of folklore, and threatened the survival not only of oral tradition but of the musicians themselves.

The objective of Kazakhstan's cultural policy was to introduce European forms of art embellished with local ethnographic features. This policy in large part succeeded, leading to the creation of such hybrid musical institutions as the Kurmangazy State Orchestra of Folk Instruments, organized and directed by Ahmet Zhubanov. The Kazakh folk orchestra was inspired by Russian folk orchestras of the late nineteenth and early twentieth century, which themselves had been modeled on the European symphony orchestra. In the folk orchestra, traditional instruments were redesigned to produce the standard European scale, and consorts of Europeanized instruments, often playing in harmony, replaced solo performers. On the rare occasions when traditional masters were invited to perform in the new Soviet-style concerts, the most meaningful aspects of traditional performance—dialogue between performer and audience, storytelling, and legends that accompanied music making—were eliminated because they were considered incompatible with European concert music.

Formal instruction on reconstructed folk instruments began in 1934, when the Music College in the capital city of Alma-Ata created the first class in Kazakh folk instruments. In 1944, this college became the Alma-Ata State Conservatory (figure 8). Musical performance itself was institutionalized in the form of the Kazakh State Philharmonia, which was founded in 1935 and supervised the Kurmangazy Orchestra of Folk Instruments, the Kazakh Choir, a dance ensemble, and a large group of soloists including folk singers and instrumentalists.

In 1934, Evgeni Brusilovskii (1905–1981) of Saint Petersburg was commissioned to compose the first Kazakh opera. Brusilovskii's commission became *Qyz-Jibek* (the name of the heroine), which had a plot based on the theme of an epic tale and melodies drawn from lyrical songs. Other composers added to the nascent genre of Kazakh opera. For example, Muqan Tulebaev's *Birzhan and Sara* (1947) depicts a contest of poets and the affection shown toward the great poet-improvisers. Tulebaev did not simply quote folk tunes but contributed largely original music to the evolving national operatic style. Ahmet Zhubanov and Latif Khamidi's *Abai*, from a libretto by Mukhtar

FIGURE 8 Aitzhan Toqtaganov (b. 1946), a famous *dombra* player from Almaty and a professor at Almaty State Conservatory, named after Kurmangazy. Photo by Sergei Zhirkevich, 1990.

Auezov, illuminates the life of Abai Kunanbaev (1845–1904), a well-known Kazakh poet and thinker. Operatic composers strove to make their works broadly accessible by incorporating the perennially popular Kazakh bel canto lyrical song, and in time this genre, more than any other, came to epitomize Kazakh traditional music.

In the 1960s and 1970s Kazakh intellectuals began to turn away from the cultural politics of Russification and embrace a nativist interest in their own cultural history. The revival of Kazakh ethnicity was the catalyst for a comprehensive survey of oral tradition in Kazakhstan undertaken by Kazakh ethnomusicologists and folklorists. Another outcome was the creation in the 1980s of a traditional music ensemble, Otrar Sazy 'Tunes of Otrar', named after a city destroyed by Chinggis (Genghis) Khan. In contrast to the Europeanized folk orchestras, Otrar Sazy had authentic traditional instruments played in a traditional style.

POST-SOVIET KAZAKHSTAN

The 1990s brought to Kazakhstan long-awaited independence, which had a strong effect on perceptions of tradition and the role of traditional practices and beliefs. Ethnic self-identification and a renaissance of national culture, both material and spiritual, became burning issues and led to an explosion of interest in forms of literature and poetry that had previously been prohibited for political reasons. Russification and the artificial creation of "national" cultures gerrymandered to conform to the boundaries of the fifteen Soviet republics were replaced by a new concept of native ethnicity. Nativism both spurred interest in the archaic roots of Kazakh culture and encouraged reexamination of historical contacts between the Kazakhs and neighboring peoples in Central Asia, southern Siberia, and the Volga region.

The renaissance of tradition has been particularly striking in south and southwest Kazakhstan. For example, in the Kyzl-Orda region, where interest in the art of epic singing survived Soviet attempts to stifle it, a movement to restore social prestige to epic singers has resulted in the creation of a department of epic recitation (*zhyraulyk*) at Kyzl-Orda University that trains not only performers but also folklore collectors and researchers. Kyzl-Orda's initiative has led to the opening of centers to train traditional musicians in other regions of Kazakhstan.

Aitys has again become one of the most popular cultural events, drawing tens of thousands of audience members to each year's final round of competition in the Palace of the Republic in Almaty. The prestige of this competition is increased by the prizes awarded, which range from rare furs to foreign automobiles, all supplied by private sponsors.

The mass media have a significant role in disseminating traditional music. Weekly radio and television programs and an increasing number of articles in newspapers and magazines about the life and work of traditional musicians, both historical and contemporary, have brought fundamental changes in Kazakhstan's culture. Festivals, symposia, and conferences featuring folk performers from Kazakhstan and other nations settled by Turkic peoples also play an important role. During Soviet times, there was an emphasis on the cultural distinctiveness of the Central Asian nations; this has now given way to an awareness of cross-cultural similarities in musical genres, methods of sound production, and performance styles. The expanded horizons are most evident in the incorporation of new forms of sound production, such as the throat-singing of neighboring Tuva [see Music in Tuva].

At the same time that Kazakh musicians are seeking the archaic Turkic roots of their music, they are also striving to become part of contemporary global popular culture. Beginning in 1990, an annual international festival and performance competition in Almaty called *Aziya Dauysy* 'The Voice of Asia' has presented rising and world-class Asian popular musicians. During the first decade of this event, performers from more than sixty countries were represented, including well- known pop musicians

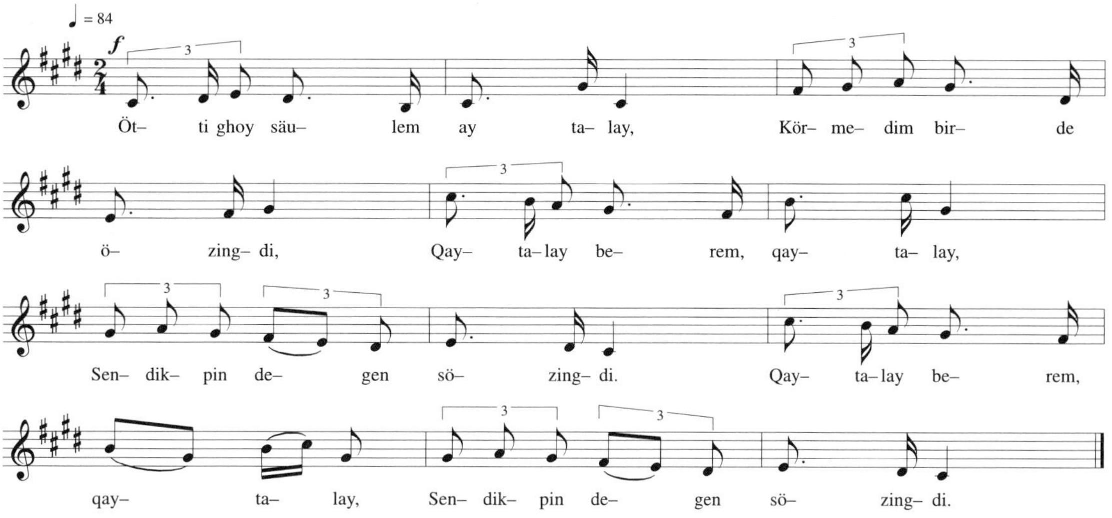

FIGURE 9 An example of Kazakh popular song (Bekkhozhina 1972, no. 195). Performer, Estileutov Zhengis (b. 1944); text by Tolegen Aybergenov, *aqyn* (1937–1967). Translation: "So many years have passed, my light./I did not see you even once./I'm just repeating again and again/Your saying 'I belong to you.'/ I'm just repeating again and again/Your saying 'I belong to you.'"

from Russia and the West. *Aziya Dauysy* has also resulted in the release of numerous compact disks.

The westernization of Kazakh popular culture is most evident in multinational cities and has been focused on urban teenagers. A parallel development might be called Kazakh traditional popular music (*estrada* in Russian)—a phenomenon that arose in the 1960s and 1970s under the strong influence of Soviet Russian popular song. From the beginning, this music, based on traditional melodies and focusing in particular on poetic texts, found its own voice, its own style, and, most important, its own audience. Venerable and enduring performers of traditional Kazakh popular music include Roza Baglanova (b. 1922), Bibigul Tulegenova (b. 1929), Yermeka Serkibaeva (b. 1926), Shamshi Kaldayakov (1930–c.1980); and Nurgis Tlendiev (1925–1996). Among city and town dwellers, the favorite songs of these singer-songwriters were often performed around a table. Later, a younger generation of singers added their own voices to indigenous popular music: Roza Rymbaeva (b. 1957), Nagima Eskalieva (b. 1954), and Alibek Dnishev (b. 1951). Popular song was mastered not only by professionals but also by amateur singer-songwriters who accompany themselves on the *dombra* and on the six-string and seven-string guitar. Frequently, these songs are based on the three-beat waltz rhythm beloved by Kazakhs, which is well suited to a musical "reading" of Kazakh syllabic poetry (figure 9).

As an emerging regional power with rich natural resources, Kazakhstan has the potential to create a well-funded cultural infrastructure to support a renaissance and a reenvisioning of indigenous performance traditions. Students of contemporary Central Asia have much to learn by observing how these ongoing cultural processes reflect deeper political and social currents in Kazakh society, and in the region at large.

TRANSLATED BY THEODORE LEVIN

REFERENCES

Abdibaev, Shaitursyn, comp. 1990. *An erkesi: Nartai turaly estelikter men maqalalar, zertteuler* (The Favorite of Song: Memoirs, Articles, and Studies of Nartai Bekezhanov). Almaty: Oner.

Abulkasimov, Babash. 1984. *Zhanr tolgau v kazakhskoi ustnoi poezii* (The Genre of the *Tolgau* in Kazakh Oral Poetry). Alma-Ata: Ghalym.

Akhmediarov, Q., comp. 1991. *Dina: Asem qongyr* (Dina [Nurpeisova]: The Beautiful Tune). Almaty: Oner.

Akhmetov, Zaki. 1964. *Kazakhskoe stikhoslozhenie* (Kazakh Versification). Alma-Ata: Nauka.

Akhmetova, Mariam. 1968. *Pesnia i sovremennost* (Song and Contemporaneity). Alma-Ata: Nauka.

———, comp. 1970. *Kazakhskie narodnye pesni* (Kazakh Folk Songs). Alma-Ata: Nauka.

———. 1984. *Traditsii kazakhskoi pesennoi kultury* (Traditions of Kazakh Song Culture). Alma-Ata: Nauka.

Akiner, Shirin. 1995. *The Formation of Kazakh Identity: From Tribe to Nation-state.* London:

Royal Institute of International Affairs, Russian and CIS Programme.

Amanova, Sayra. 1993. *Drevniaia instrumentalnaia muzyka kazakhov* (The Ancient Instrumental Music of the Kazakhs). Published summary of doctoral dissertation. Tashkent: Institut Iskusstvoznaniia.

Amirova, Dina. 1990. *Kazakhskaia professionalnaia lirika ustnoi traditsii (Pesenenoe iskusstvo Saryarki)* (Kazakh Professional Lyrics of the Oral Tradition [The Song Art of Saryarki]). Published summary of doctoral dissertation. Leningrad: Institut Teatra, Muzyki i Kinematografii.

Aravin, Petr. 1970. *Zhanry kazakhskoi instrumentalnoi muzyki* (Genres of Kazakh Instrumental Music). Alma-Ata.

———. 1978. *Stepnye sozvezdiia: Ocherki i etiudy o kazakhskoi muzyke* (The Constellation of the Steppe: Essays and Etudes on Kazakh Music). Alma-Ata: Zhalyn.

———. 1984. *Dauletkerei i kazakhskaia muzyka XIX veka.* (Dauletkerei and Kazakh Music of the Nineteenth Century). Moscow: Sovetskii Kompozitor.

Aravin, Petr, and Boris Erzakovich, comp. 1955. *Muzykalnaia kultura Kazakhstana: Sbornik statei i materialov* (Musical Culture of Kazakhstan: A Collection of Articles and Data). Alma-Ata: Nauka.

Asafev, Boris. 1987. *O narodnoi muzyke* (On Folk Music). Reconstructed and edited by Izaly Zemtsovsky and Alma Kunanbaeva. Leningrad: Muzyka.

Auezov, Mukhtar. 1975. *Abai.* Moscow: Progress. (Novel abridged and translated into English.)

Azerbaev, Kenen. 1977. *Boztorghai* (Skylark). Alma-Ata: Zhazushy.

Bacon, Elizabeth E. 1966, 1980, 1994. *Central Asians under Russian Rule: A Study in Culture Change.* Ithaca, N.Y.: Cornell University Press.

Baidildaev, Mardan. 1979. *Aqyn-zhyraular* (Folk Singers and Storytellers). Almaty: Ghylym.

Baigaskina, Asiya. 1973. "Evoliutsiia stikhotvornykh razmerov i logika razvitiia muzykalnoi formy kazakhskoi narodnoi pesni" (The Evolution of Poetic Meters and the Logic of Development of Form in Kazakh Folk Song). In *Problemy muzykalnogo folklora narodov SSSR*, ed. Izaly Zemtsovsky, 126–146. Moscow: Muzyka.

———. 1979. *O sootnoshenii slova i napeva v kazakhskoi pesne* (On the Correlation between Word and Tune in Kazakh Song). Published summary of doctoral dissertation. Alma-Ata.

———. 1991. *Ritmika kazakhskoi traditsionnoi pesni* (The Rhythmics of Kazakh Traditional Song). Alma-Ata: Qurmaghazy Conservatory.

Baikadamova, Baldyrgan. 1988. *Tematizm i forma kazakhskikh dombrovykh kyuev* (Musical Themes and Form of the Kazakh *Dombra Kyuis*). Published summary of doctoral dissertation. Tashkent: Institut Iskusstvoznaniia.

Baitenova, Gulsum. 1995. *Tsvety na pepelishche . . . Pesni-pisma, sozdannye vo vremia Velikoi Otechestvennoi voiny* (Flowers at the Site of Fire . . . Songs-Letters of the Period of the Great Patriotic War). Almaty: Daik-Press. (In Kazakh and Russian.)

Bekenov, Uali. 1981. *Kyui Tabighaty* (The Nature of *Kyui*). Almaty: Oner.

Bekkhozhina, Taliga. 1968. "Starinnyi svadebnyi tsikl kazakhsogo naroda" (The Ancient Wedding Cycle of the Kazakhs). *Muzykoznanie* 4.

———. 1972. *200 kazakhskikh pesen* (Two Hundred Kazakh Songs). Alma-Ata: Nauka.

———, ed. and comp. 1972. *Qazyna* (A Treasure). Almaty: Ghalym.

Beliaev, Viktor. 1975. *Central Asian Music: Essays in the History of the Music of the Peoples of the USSR*, ed. and annotator Mark Slobin; trans. (from Russian) Mark Slobin and Greta Slobin. Middletown, Conn.: Wesleyan University Press.

Bisenova, Gafura. 1995. *Pesennoe tvorchetsvo Abaia* (The Song Legacy of Abai). Almaty: Daik-Press.

Chadwick, Nora Kershaw, and Victor M. Zhirmunsky. 1969. *Oral Epics of Central Asia.* London: Cambridge University Press.

Chumbalova, Galiya. 1956, 1992. "Ocherk po istorii zapisi i izucheniia kazakhskoi muzyki dorevoliutsionnogo perioda" (An Essay on the History and Study of Kazakh Music in the Prerevolutionary Period). *Kazakhskaia muzyka*: 3–17.

Dernova, Varvara, ed. and comp. 1958. *Aleksandr Zataevich: Issledovaniia, Vospominaniia, Pis'ma, Dokumenty* (Aleksandr Zataevich: Studies, Memoirs, Letters, Papers). Alma-Ata: Oner.

———. 1966. *A. V. Zataevich i kazakhskaia narodnaia muzyka* (A. V. Zataevich and Kazakh Folk Music). Published summary of doctoral dissertation. Leningrad: Rimskii-Korsakov Conservatory.

———, ed. and comp. 1967. *Narodnaia muzyka v Kazakhstane* (Folk Music in Kazakhstan). Alma-Ata: Izd-vo "Kazakhstan."

———. 1986. "Tysiacha pesen" (One Thousand Songs). (On Aleksandr Zataevich). *Sovetskaia muzyka* 8:80–85.

Dzhanibekov, Uzbekali. 1990. *Ekho . . . Po sledam legendy o zolotoi dombre* (Echo . . . On the Trail of the Legend of the Golden *Dombra*). Alma-Ata: Oner.

Elemanova, Saida. 1984. *Professionalizm ustnoi traditsii v pesennoi kulture kazakhov* (Professionalism of the Oral Tradition in the Song Culture of Kazakhs). Published summary of doctoral dissertation. Leningrad: Rimskii-Korsakov Conservatory.

———. 1993. *Kazakhskaia muzykalnaia literatura: Uchebnik* (Kazakh Musical Literature: A Textbook). Alma-Ata: Oner.

Emsheimer, Ernest. 1956. "Singing Contests in Central Asia." *Journal of the International Folk Music Council* 8:26–29.

Erzakovich, Boris. 1954. *Kazakhskaia SSR* (The Kazakh SSR). Moskva: Gosudarstvennoe Muzykal'noe Izdatel'stvo.

———. 1955. *Qazaqstannyng khalyq anderi* (Folk Songs of Kazakhstan). Almaty: Ghylym.

———. 1956. *Narodnye pesni Kazakhstana: Etnograficheskii sbornik* (Folk Songs of Kazakhstan: An Ethnographic Collection). Alma-Ata: Nauka

———. 1961. *Kenen Azerbaev.* Moscow: Sovetskii kompozitor.

———. 1966. *Pesennaia kultura kazakhskogo naroda: muzykalno-istoricheskoe issledovanie* (The Song Culture of the Kazakhs: A Musical-Historical study). Alma-Ata: Nauka.

———. 1979. *Muzykalnoe nasledie kazakhskogo naroda* (Musical Legacy of the Kazakhs). Alma-Ata: Nauka.

———, ed. 1982. *Kazakhskii muzykalnyi folklor* (Kazakh Musical Folklore). Alma-Ata: "Ghylym" ("Nauka" Kazakhskoi SSR).

———. 1986. *Qazaq muzyka folklorynyng tarikhnamasy* (Historiography of Kazakh Musical Folklore). Almaty: Ghylym.

———. 1987. *U istokov kazakhskogo muzykoznaniia: po materialam russkikh uchenykh XIX v.* (At the Beginning of Kazakh Musicology: On the Data of Russian Scholars of the Nineteenth Century). Alma-Ata: Nauka.

———. 1994. *Qazaq khalqynyng ghashyqtyq anderi antologiiasy* (Anthology of the Kazakh Folk Love Songs). Almaty: Ghylym.

Esenuly, Aitzhan (Toqtaghanov). 1996. *Kyui—Tangirding kubiri* (*Kyui*—The Epistle of the Most High). Almaty: TOO "Daik-Press." (In Kazakh.) Also: 1997. *Kuyi—Poslanie Vsevyshenego*. Almaty: Kokil. (In Russian.)

Gaisin, Gennadii. 1986. *Garmonika i ee raznovidnosti v muzykalnoi kulture Kazakhstana* (The Accordion and Its Types in the Music Culture of Kazakhstan). Published summary of doctoral dissertation. Leningrad: Rimskii-Korsakov Conservatory.

Gizatov, Bisengali. 1976. *Ot kyuia do simfonii* (From *Kyui* to Symphony). Alma-Ata: Zhalyn.

———. 1989. *Sotsialno-estetichesie osnovy kazakhskoi narodnoi instrumentalnoi muzyki* (The Social-Aesthetic Basis of Kazakh Folk Instrumental Music). Alma-Ata: Nauka Kaz. SSR.

Grinkevich, Nikolai. 1984. *Kazakhskii gosudarstvennyj ordena Lenina akademicheskii teatr opery i baleta imeni Abaia* (The Kazakh State Lenin's Order Academic Theater of Opera and Ballet, Named after Abai). Alma-Ata: Oner.

Ibragimova, Tamti. 1985. *Pesnia, rozhedennaia v bitvakh: Ocherki o kazakhskikh kompozitorakh, pogibshikh v gody Velikoi Otechestvennoi voiny* (Song Born to Battles: Essays on Kazakh Composers Who Died in the Period of the Great Patriotic War). Alma-Ata: Oner. (Translated from Kazakh.)

Imanaliev, Zh., comp., and M. Aitkaliev, transcriptions. 1975. *Karatau Shertpeleri: Kyuiler zhinaghy* (Shertpe Karatau: A Collection of Kyuis). Almaty: Zhasushy.

Ismailov, Esmagambet. 1957. *Akyny: Monografiia o tvorchestve Zhambula i drugikh narodnykh akynov* (Aqyns: A Study of the Work of Dzhambul and Other Folk Singers). Alma-Ata: Nauka. Also: 1956. *Aqyndar*. Almaty. (1st ed., in Kazakh.)

Karakulov, Bulat. 1981. *Asyl mura: Nasledie. Muzykalno-etnographicheskii sbornik* (The Precious Heritage: A Musical-Ethnographic Collection). Alma-Ata: Ghalym.

Kazgulov, Bulat, and Nurila Shakhanova. 1989. "Traditsionnyi strunno-smychkovyi instrument kazakhov 'kylkobyz' (Po kollektsiiam MAE i polevym materialam)" (A Traditional String-Bow Instrument of the Kazakh '*Qylqobyz*' [Based on Collections of the Museum of Anthropology and Ethnography and Fieldwork]). In *Pamiatniki traditsionno-bytovoi kultury narodov Srednei Azii, Kazakhstana i Kavkaza*, 98–108. Leningrad: Nauka.

Ketegenova, Altyn, ed. 1979. *Makpal: 100 Songs.* (Velvet: One Hundred Songs.) Almaty: Zhalyn. (Songbook recorded by Mukan Tulebaev.)

Kidaish-Pokrovskaia, Nina, and Orazgul Nurmagambetova. 1975. *Qoblandy batyr: Kazakhskii geroicheskii epos (teksty i perevody)* (*Koblandy-batyr*: Kazakh Heroic Epic [texts and translations]). Moscow: Nauka. (Russian and Kazakh.)

Kirghizes et Kazakhs: Maîtres du komuz et du dombra. 1997. Paris: Ocora/Radio France, C 560121. (Compact disk.)

Kokumbaeva, Baglan. 1989. *Semeimo-obriadovye plachi kazakhov i liricheskie pesni na temy utraty* (The Family Ceremonial Laments of the Kazakhs and the Lyric Songs on Loss). Published summary of doctoral dissertation. Tashkent: Institut Iskusstvoznaniia.

Kopbaeva, Liazzat. 1991. *Kazakhskii kyui v riadu traditsionnykh zhanrov muzyki Srednei Azii* (The Kazakh *Kyui* among the Traditional Genres of Central Asian Music). Published summary of doctoral dissertation. Moscow: Chaikovsky Conservatory.

Kozhabekov, Ilias, ed. and comp. 1992. *Kazakhskaia muzyka: Traditsii i sovremennost'. Sbornik trudov* (Kazakh Music: Tradition and Contemporaneity. A Collection of Articles). Alma-Ata: Qurmanghazy Conservatory.

Kozhagululy, Birzhan-sal. 1983. *Lyailim-shrak* (My Dear Flame). Alma-Ata: Zhazushy. (Songbook.)

Kunanbaeva, Alma. 1982 "Spetsifika kazakhskogo epicheskogo intonirovaniia" (The Specificity of Kazakh Epic Intonation). *Soviet Music* 6:78–81.

———. 1984. *Problema kazakhskoi epicheskoi traditsii* (Music of the Kazakh Epic: The Problem of Kazakh Epic Tradition). Published summary of doctoral dissertation. Leningrad: Institut Teatra, Muzyki i Kinematografii.

———. 1985. "Fenomen muzykal'noi epicheskoi traditsii v kazakhskom folklore" (The Phenomenon of Musical Epic Tradition in Kazakh Folklore). *Artes Populares* 14:121–133. Also: 1992. *Kazakhskaia muzyka*: 34–43.

———. 1987. "Kazakhskii epos segodnia: Skazitel' i skazanie" (The Kazakh *Epos* Today: Story and Storyteller [or: Singer and Narrative]). *Soviet Ethnography* 4:101–110. (With English summary.)

———. 1989. "Zhanrovaia sistema kazakhskogo muzykalnogo eposa: Opyt obosnovaniia" (The System of Genres of the Kazakh *Epos*: Definition of the Problem). In *The Music of Epics*, ed. Izaly Zemtsovsky, 82–112. Yoshkar-Ola: Union of Composers.

———. 1990. "The Kazakh Epic: Modernization and Return." *Turkish Music Quarterly* 3(2, 3) (Spring-Summer):1–3.

———. 1995 "The Kazakh Zhyrau as the Singer of Tales." In *Ethnohistorische Wege und Lehrjahre eines Philosophen. Festschrift dedicated to Prof. Lawrence Krader*, ed. Dittmar Schorkowitz, 293–303. Frankfurt am Main: Peter Lang.

Levin, Theodore. 1996. *The Hundred Thousand Fools of God: Musical Travels in Central Asia (and Queens, New York)*. Bloomington: Indiana University Press.

Margulan, Alikei, 1959. "O nositeliakh drevnei poeticheskoi kultury kazakhskogo naroda" (On the Bearers of the Poetic Culture of the Kazakh People). In *Sbornik statei k 60-letiiu M.Auezova* (Collection of Articles for the Sixtieth Birthday of Mukhtar Auezov). Alma-Ata: Akademiia Nauk Kazakhskoi SSR.

Mergaliev, Tmat. 1972. *Dombyra sazy* (The *Dombra* Melody). Almaty: Ghylym.

———. 1980. *Zhanga dauir zhyrshysy* (The Singer of the New Epoch). Almaty: Ghylym.

Mongolia: Kazakh Songs and Epic Tradition of the West. C-580051. (Compact disk.)

Mongolie: Chants Kazakh et tradition epique de l'Ouest. 1993. Paris: Ocora 558 660. (Distribution: Harmonia Mundi. Compact disk.)

Morita, Minoru. 1992. *Music of Kazakhstan I: Songs Accompanied on* Dombra *and Solo* Kobyz. King Records (Tokyo, Japan), KICC 5166. World Music Library, 66. (Compact disk.)

———. 1995. *Music of Kazakhstan II:* Dombra *Music of Kazakhstan and Songs Accompanied on* Dombra. King Records (Tokyo, Japan), KICC 5199. World Music Library. (Compact disk.)

Mukhambetova, Asiya. 1976. *Narodnaia instrumentalnaia kultura kazakhov: Genezis i programmnost' v s vete evoliutsii form muzitsirovaniia* (The Instrumental Folk Music of the Kazakhs: Its Genesis and Its Programmatic Quality in Light of the Evolution of the Forms of Music Making). Published summary of doctoral dissertation. Leningrad: Institut Teatra, Muzyki i Kinematografii.

———, ed. and comp. 985. *Instrumentalnaia muzyka kazakhskogo naroda* (Instrumental Music of the Kazakhs). Alma-Ata: Oner.

———. 1989. "Kalendar' i zhanrovaia sistema traditsionnoi muzuki kazakhov" (The System of Calendar and Genre of the Traditional Music of the Kazakhs). In *Traditsii i perspektivy izucheniia muzykalnogo folklora narodov SSSR*, ed. E. E. Alekseev and L. I. Levin, 107–131. Moscow: Vsesoiuznyi Nauchno-Issledovatelskii Institut Iskusstvoznaniia.

———. 1990a. *Kazakhskii kyui kak sinkreticheskii zhanr* (The Kazakh *Kyui* as a Syncretic Genre). Alma-Ata: Qurmanghazy Conservatory.

———. 1990b. "Philosophical Problems of Being in the Art of the Kazakh Kuyshi." *Yearbook for Traditional Music* 22:36–41.

———, ed. 1990. *Pesennyi folklor narodov Kazakhstana* (The Sung Folklore of the Peoples of Kazakhstan). Alma-Ata: Qurmanghazy Conservatory.

———. 1995. "The Traditional Musical Culture of Kazakhs in the Social Context of the Twentieth Century." *World of Music* 37(3):66–83.

Nurmagambetova, Orazgul. 1988. *Kazakhskii geroicheskii epos Koblandy-batyr* (The Kazakh Heroic Epic *Qoblandy-batyr*). Alma-Ata: Ghylym.

Olcott, Martha Brill. 1995. *The Kazakhs*, 2nd ed. Stanford, Calif.: Hoover Institution Press, Stanford University Press.

Omarova, Gulzada. 1989. *Kazakhskaia kobyzovaia traditsiia* (The Kazakh *Kobyz* Tradition). Published summary of doctoral dissertation. Leningrad: Rimskii-Korsakov Conservatory.

Porter, James, ed. 1997. *Folklore and Traditional Music in the Former Soviet Union and Eastern Europe.* Los Angeles: University of California Los Angeles, Department of Ethnomusicology.

Qosbasarov, B., ed. 1988. *Kongyrzhai* (A Collection of *Kyuis* for *Kyl-Kobyz*). Almaty: Oner.

Qospakov, Zeinulla, comp. 1985. *Zhaiau Musa: Aq sisa.* (White Calico). Almaty: Oner. (Songs and *kyui* of Zhayau Musa Baizhanov.)

Raimbergenov, Abdulkhamit. 1984. *Qazanghap. Aqzhelen. Kyuiler* (The *Kyuis* of Qazanghap). Alma-Ata: Oner.

Raimbergenov, Abdulkhamit, and Saira Amanova. 1990. *Kyui qainary* (The Geyser of *Kyuis*). Almaty: Oner.

Reichl, Karl. 1992. *Turkic Oral Epic Poetry: Traditions, Forms. Poetic Structure.* New York: Garland.

Rustemov, Mukhamedzhan. 1983. *Nartai* (Aqyn Nartai). Almaty: Zhalyn.

Sandybaiuly, Ybyrai. 1995. *Gakku: A Songbook.* ed. Khairulla Zhuzbasov and Zinep Kospakov. Almaty: Oner (Art).

Sarybaev, Bolat. 1978a. *Kazakhskie muzykalnye instrumenty* (Kazakh Musical Instruments: A Study). Alma-Ata: Zhalyn.

———. 1978b. *Kazakhskie muzykalnye instrumenty* (Kazakh Musical Instruments). Alma-Ata: Zhalyn. (Illustrated album.)

Seidimbekov, Taraqty Aqseleu. 1992. *Kyui shezhire* (History of the *Kyui*). Almaty: Oner.

Shegebaev, Pernebek. 1986. "Applikaturno-intonatsionnaia osnova kazakhskoi dombrovoi muzyki" In *Problemy traditsionnoi instrumentalnoi muzyki narodov SSSR*, ed. Ihor Macijewski, 135–147. Leningrad: Institut Teatra, Muzyki i Kinematografii.

———. 1987. *Dombrovye kyui Zapadnogo Kazakhstana: Tradiitsionnaia forma i individualnyi stil'* (The *Dombra Kyuis* of Western Kazakhstan: The Traditional Form and Individual Style). Published summary of doctoral dissertation. Leningrad: Institut Teatra, Muzyki i Kinematografii.

Slobin, Mark. 1976. *Music in the Culture of Northern Afganistan.* Tucson: University of Arizona Press, published for Wenner-Gren Foundation for Anthropological Research.

Sydyqov, Qabibolla. 1974. *Aqyn-zhyraular* (The *Akyns* Improvisors). Almaty: Ghylym.

Tiftikidi, Nikolai. 1977. *Problema tempa i ritma v dombrovoi muzyke Zapadnogo Kazakhstana* (Tempo and Rhythm in the *Dombra* Music of Western Kazakhstan). Published summary of doctoral dissertation. Leningrad: Rimskii-Korsakov Conservatory.

Toqtaghanov, Aitzhan, ed. 1996. *Kyui Murata Uskenbaeva* (The *Kyuis* of Murat Uskenbaev). Almaty: Oner.

Tursynov, Edige. 1976. *Qazaq auyz adebietin zhasaushylardyn okilderi* (Types of Creators of Kazakh Oral Literature). Almaty: Ghylym. (In Kazakh.)

Usenov, Ermurat, ed. 1988. *Tattimbet Qazanghapuly: Sarzhailau. Kuyiler* (The Golden Steppe: *Kyui*). Almaty: Oner.

Utegalieva, Saule. 1987. *Funktsionalnyi kontekst muzykalnogo myshleniia kazakhskikh dombristov* (The Functional Context of Musical Thinking of the Kazakh *Dombra* Players). Published summary of doctoral dissertation. Leningrad: Institut Teatra, Muzyki i Kinematografii.

———. 1993. "The System of Images in the Dombra Tradition of Kazakhs." In *Proceedings of the First International Conference on Cognitive Musicology*, 270–282. Jyvaskyla: Jyvaskylan Yliopisto.

———, ed. and comp. 1996. *Traditsionnaia muzyka Azii: Issledovaniia i materialy* (Traditional Music of Asia: Study and Materials). Almaty: TOO "Daik-Press."

———. 1997. *Mangystauskaia dombrovaia traditsiia* (Mangystau *Dombra* Tradition). Almaty: Qurmanghazy Conservatory.

Vertkov, Konstantin, Georgiy Blagodatov, and Elsa Yazovitskaya. 1962, 1975. *Atlas muzikal'nikh instrumentov narodov SSSR.* (Atlas of Musical Instruments of the Peoples Inhabiting the U.S.S.R.). Moscow: Muzyka.

Vinogradov, Viktor. 1968. *Muzyka sovetskogo Vostoka: Ot unisona k polifonii* (Music of the Soviet Orient: From Unison to Polyphony). Moscow: Sovetskii Kompozitor.

Winner, Thomas Gustav. 1980. *The Oral Art and Literature of the Kazakhs of Russian Central Asia.* New York: Arno.

Zataevich, Aleksandr. 1925. *1000 pesen Kirgizskogo naroda (Napevy i melodii)* (One Thousand Songs of Kirghiz People: Tunes and Melodies). Orenburg: Kirgizskoe Gosudarstvennoe Izdatelstvo. Also: 1963. *1000 Songs of the Kazakh People*, 2nd ed. Moscow: Sovetskii Kompozitor; 1955. *Prodolzhenie "1000 pesen Kazakskogo naroda" togo zhe sobiratelia* (Continuation of *One Thousand Songs of the Kazakhs* by the Same Collector), 2nd ed. Moscow: Sovetskii.

———. 1931. *500 kazakhskikh pesen i kyuev Adaevskikh, Bukeevskikh, Semipalatinskikh i Uralskikh* (Five Hundred Songs and *Kyuis* of Aday, Bukey, Semipalatinsk, and the Ural Kazakhs). Alma-Ata: Narkompros Kazakskoi ASSR.

Zemtsovsky, Izaly, ed. and comp. 1991. *Narodnaia muzyka SSSR: Opyt diskografii* (Folk Music of the U.S.S.R.: An Attempt at a Discography), 41–49. Moscow: Ministry of Culture.

Zhanuzakova, Zaure, comp. 1964. *Kazakhskaia narodnaia instrumentalnaia muzyka: Kyui dlia dombry, kobyza i sybyzgi* (Kazakh Folk Instrumental Music: *Kyuis* for *Dombra*, *Kobyz*, and *Sybyzgy*). Alma-Ata: Galym.

Zharkinbekov, Musabek, ed. and transcription. 1987. *Korkyt. Elim-Ai: Kyuiler* (O, My Country: The *Kyuis* of Korkut). Almaty: Oner.

Zhirmunskii, Viktor. 1960. *On the Comparative Study of the Heroic Epic of the Peoples of Central Asia.* Moscow: Oriental Literature Publishing House.

Zhubanov, Akhmet. 1961. *Kyui Kurmanagazy.* Alma-Ata: Khudozhestvennaia Literatura.

———. 1967, 1975. *Zamana bylbyldary (Solov'i stoletii: Ocherki o zhizni i tvorchetve kazakhskikh narodnykh kompizitorov-pevtsov)* (The Nightingales of the Centuries: Essays on the Life and Work of Kazakh Folk Composers-Singers). Almaty: Zhazushy (Author). (1st ed. in Russian, 2nd ed. in Kazakh).

———. 1975. *Gasyrlar pernesi (Struny stoletii)* (The Strings of the Centuries). Almaty: Zhazushy (Author). (In Kazakh.) Also: 1956. Alma-Ata: Khudozhestvennaia Literatura. (1st ed., in Russian.)

———. 1976a. *An-Kui sapary* (The Journey of Song and *Kyui*). Almaty: Ghylym.

———. 1976b. "Kazakhskii narodnyii muzykalnyi nstrument—Dombra" (Kazakh Folk Music Instrument—*Dombra*). *Muzykoznanie* 8:9.

———. 1978. *Kurmangazy Sagyrbaev: Omiri men tvorchestvosy* (Kurmangazy Sagyrbaev: Life and Work). Almaty: Zhalyn. Also: 1936. Kzyylorda. (1st Kazakh ed.)

———. 1993. *Qurmanghazy kuileri qalai shyqqan?* (How Were the *Kyuis* of Qurmanghazy Composed?) Almaty: Zhalyn.

Zhubanov, Qudaibergen. 1936, 1990. "Qazaq muzykasynda kyui zhanrynyng paida boluy zhaily" (Toward the Formation of the *Kyui* Genre in Kazakh Music). In *Qudaibergen Zhubanov. Shygharmalar men esteliqter* (Articles and Memoirs), ed. Aqyrap Zhubanov. Almaty: Oner.

Zhusbasov, Khairulla. 1986. *Pesennyi folklor kazakhov Gornogo Altaia* (The Song Folklore of the Mountain Altai Kazakhs). Published summary of doctoral dissertation. Alma-Ata: Akademiia Nauk.

———. 1986. "Domb(y)ra—Starinnyi kazakhskii muzykalnyi instrument" (*Dombra*: The Ancient Musical Instrument of the Kazakhs). *Izvestiia Akademii Nauk KazSSR. Seriia filologicheskaia* 2:43–46.

———, comp. 1988. *Aqan seri: Mangmangger* [a horse's name]. Almaty: Oner.

———, comp. 1992. *Aset Naimanbaiuly: Inzhumarzhan* (A Coral: The Songs of Aset Naimanbaiuly). Almaty: Oner.

Music of Turkmenistan

Sławomira Żerańska-Kominek

The Turkmen People
The *Bagşy*
Elements of Theory
Performance Styles
Turkmen Musical Culture: Continuity and Change

The Turkmen people have a long history, and their music has been affected by numerous changes and numerous influences in the course of its development. The Turkmen music that has resulted is unique, and of great artistic value.

THE TURKMEN PEOPLE

The history of Turkmen ethnic identity is complex and protracted and still has many blank spots. When the Turkmen people first appeared under this name in the ninth century, they could certainly look back on a much older extraction. Farming tribes speaking Iranian languages (Bactrians, Sogdians, Ferganians, Margianians, Parthians, Khorezmians) had lands in the fertile oases of the Murgap and the Amu Darya (the Khorezmian oasis) in the latter half of the second millennium B.C.E. or early in the first century C.E. Nomadic tribes of the Massagetae (Sakas) inhabited deserts and steppes east of the Caspian Sea (the Kara Kum desert), the Ustyurt plateau, and the Kyzyl Kum desert in Transoxania (Mavarannahr). The Dahae were nomads in what is now southwestern Turkmenistan. Most ethnologists believe, on the strength of anthropological evidence and extant traits of material and spiritual culture, that today's Turkmens are descended from the nomadic tribes of Dahae-Massagetae and Iranian-speaking farming peoples.

About at the end of antiquity and the beginning of the modern era, nomadic tribes from the steppes of the Altai and Mongolia (Huns, Wu-Sun, Jüeh-chih) moved west toward the Aral Sea and into Transoxania, creating a great wave of movements of the native peoples there (Sakas, Massagetae, Tokharians). The migration of nomadic tribes came when Turkic-speaking groups were arriving in southern and western territories of Central Asia, especially in the sixth century, when the armies of the Turkish kaganate (551–744) conquered Transoxania. Another wave of Turkish invasions and population movements came from the tenth to twelfth centuries; this wave also involved Oghuz tribes, whom chroniclers in the early ninth century described as Turkmens.

In the ninth and tenth centuries the Oghuz inhabited a vast stretch between the Irtysh in the east and the mouth of the Volga in the west (territories to the south of Lake Balkhash, steppes around the Aral Sea, and the Ustyurt Plateau). But the largest Oghuz tribes lived along the Caspian Sea, in the lower Syr Darya, and on the Aral

The main actor on the Turkmen musical stage is the *bagşy,* who is simultaneously a narrator of epics, a poet, a singer, and a musician.

Sea. There were also Turkmen-Oghuz colonies in the south of today's Turkmenistan. The largest Oghuz groups at that time were the Salyr, along the lower Syr Darya; the Yazyr in Mangyshlak, western Ustyurt, and the Balkhan mountains; and the Gayï and Bayïndyr nomads, on the steppes of central Kazakhstan.

The Seljuk group of Turks split off from the strong tribal confederation of Oghuz in the ninth century. Following their defeat of the Ghaznavids, the Seljuks subjugated broad territories from Mavarannahr in the east to the banks of the Nile in the west. The Seljuk invasions pulled behind them massive shifts of Turkic-Oghuz tribes, many of which had left their previous territories by the end of the twelfth century to move eastward or toward China and India in the south and to the borders of Byzantium and Egypt in the west. Sporadic groups were scattered even further from the huge Oghuz-Turkic tide, into the Balkan peninsula, the Crimea, and the northern Caucasus. During the post-Seljuk period, the tribes that had stayed behind in Central Asia inhabited Mangyshlak and Ustyurt, the Kopet Dag mountains and the river valleys running through them, and the submontane southwestern territory of Paropamisus. The largest number of Turkmen-Oghuz tribes inhabited the Balkhan mountains, the Mangyshlak, steppes along the lower Etrek, and the territories of Saragt, Balkh, and Kerki (southeastern Turkmenistan). A number of Oghuz and Turkmens lived in the upper Syr Darya basin and in Iran.

In the thirteenth century the Turkmen tribes were pushed back from the territories swept by the Mongol invasion led by Genghis (Chingiz) Khan—that is, southeastern and southern Turkmenistan. Most Turkmens then moved west, settling in territories between the Balkhan mountains, the southwestern border of Khorezm on the Ustyurt, and the Mangyshlak, where they found the best pastures. At that point, the earlier Turkmen tribal structure changed. During the thirteenth century, a powerful tribal confederation called Ärsary developed in the Balkhan mountains; during the fourteenth century, Salyr Kazan established a Salyr confederation, including the tribes of Teke, Yomut, the Salyr "proper," the Saryk, and the Ärsary.

Factors such as weather and climate (as canals watering the Deryalyk were locked and water stopped flowing into the Sarygamysh), political events (assaults by the Nogays, Kalmuks, and Kazakhs), and demography (overpopulation of the Mangyshlak and northwestern Turkmenistan) led to large movements of Turkic tribes into agricultural territories, where they abandoned their nomadic lifestyle partly or altogether. That move began in the sixteenth century and lasted until the mid-nineteenth century. The migrant Turkmens first settled in the Etrek and Gorgan valleys, in the submontane territories of the Kopet Dag, and along both banks of the Amu Darya in its middle and upper parts. Later, in the eighteenth and nineteenth centuries, they took control of the Akhal, the Atek, the Tejen and Murgap oases, and a substantial part of the Khorezmian oasis. A small proportion of Turkmen tribes settled on the shores of the Caspian Sea.

Never in their history had Turkmens set up their own state: their territories were part of a succession of other states that rose and declined. Just before the Russian conquest of Central Asia, Turkmens lived in the Khiva khanate, as neighbors of the Bukhara emirate and Iran. When Russia finally took control of the Turkmen steppes in 1884, it set up a "Transcaspian region" east of the Caspian Sea. On the eve of the revolution of 1917, Turkmen tribes inhabited three administrative units: the Transcaspian region, the Khiva khanate, and the Bukhara emirate. In 1918, the Transcaspian region was incorporated into a newly created Turkistan republic. Two years later, a Bukhara republic and a Khorezm republic were created (from the former Bukhara emirate and Khiva khanate, respectively). A Turkmen republic—the Turkmen Soviet Socialist Republic—was created in 1924, embracing most of the Central Asian territories inhabited by Turkmens.

Today, ethnic Turkmens account for about 93 percent of Turkmenistan's population. Large groups live in southern Karakalpakstan, Tajikistan, the northern Caucasus (Stavropol region), and the Astrakhan region. Sizable Turkmen groups are also present in Afghanistan, Iran, Turkey, Iraq, and Syria.

THE *BAGŞY*

Turkmen culture is a complex synthesis of various indigenous traditions of western Central Asia and traditions of Turkic-speaking steppe peoples who came from the Altai or Mongolia. The Turkmens' resilient social structure helped their archaic traditions survive in a form that was only slightly affected by the new ideological influence of Islam. This feature of the Turkmens' culture has perhaps been best expressed in their music, which is rooted in shamanic beliefs and practices. One characteristic of the most ancient shamanic tradition of Turkic-speaking steppe peoples of Central Asia that has survived to this day—and has been a crucial element in the development of Turkmen musical culture in general—is the narrated heroic epic.

The main actor on the Turkmen musical stage is the *bagşy*, who is simultaneously a narrator of epics, a poet, a singer, and a musician. The etymology of the word *bagşy* is disputed: it may be linked to the Sanskrit word *bhikshum*, or it may be derived from the Chinese *po-shi* or *bag-si* 'teacher', 'wise'. The same word is used by Kazakhs, Kyrgyz, and Uygurs to describe a shaman, a soothsayer, a doctor who heals uttering charms, and a magician. In modern Turkmen, the closest translation of *bagşy* is 'inspired bard'—a singer of tales, poet, and musician. In the remote Turkmen past, the singing of tales was a job of shamans, and this link to shamanism still affects the *bagşy*'s self-perception and provides a key to many aspects of his tradition.

The image of the *bagşy*-shaman has survived in myths and legends, mainly in Turkmen tales known by the Persian name *dastan* or the Turkmen *dessan*. In a *dessan*, the *bagşy* is a man with magical power and wisdom, a healer, musician, and poet. His mythological model is Korkut, a character in a a famous Oghuz legend called *Görkut atanyng kitaby* 'The Book of Dede Korkut', a poetic account of this people's past. Korkut is a shaman, soothsayer, and sage, yet above all he is a singer and poet, an *ozan*. He plays a *qobuz* or a *dombra* (*tamdyr*) to accompany his songs lauding the deeds of tribal chiefs.

Some of Korkut's functions as *bagşy*-shaman have persisted to this day among Central Asian peoples. The Kazakh and Kyrgyz *baksy* are shamans and healers who play the *qobuz*. The Uyghur *baksy* are healers and musicians who play drums. The *bagşy* of Khorezm are *aşyk* (strolling folk poets) who perform the *dessan*.

Becoming a *bagşy*

As musician, poet, and narrator the Turkmen *bagşy* is distinguished above all by having a calling—a poetic gift that he has received while sleeping from a patron saint called Baba Ganbar (in southern and eastern Turkmenistan) or Aşyk Aÿdyñg (in northern Turkmenistan). The *bagşy* himself usually does not speak of this, however, since such a dream is a *bagşy*'s secret. A *bagşy* seeks an initiatory dream by going on pilgrimages and making sacrifices at the grave of a patron saint. Some believe that it is best to go on a pilgrimage on Wednesdays, several times in succession. In the evening, a pilgrim should "faithfully" sit down by the grave and play the *dutar* until dawn or until he has fallen asleep. In his dream, he might see the saint handing him wine or water to drink. "If you drink it all up, you will be a *bagşy*," the saying goes; "if you don't, you will wake up and will be only a musician."

Seeing a saint in a dream is a token that a musician has attained a a spiritual condition in which he can act as a *bagşy*. However, in general the right to use the title *bagşy* belongs only to a singer-narrator who has passed a course under the eyes of a *khalypa* 'master' (figure 1). Previously, candidates had to go through a broadly understood educational process at home and in the teacher's family, where they would remain for several years; the actual duration of this tutelage was not fixed but depended on the learner's progress. When a pupil had completed his education, the master would present the new *bagşy* to the community in a ritual of *pata* 'blessing'. Then, the young *bagşy* had to give a *toy* 'party' during which he would display his musical and narrative skill and would give his master a present. The master's *pata* authorized the new *bagşy* to practice the profession as a *khalal* 'legal' performer. Anyone who had not been granted a *pata* would be considered a *kharam* 'illegal' performer.

The *bagşy* in concert

The social backdrop

The *bagşy* (figure 2) performs mainly in connection with rites of passage. The event and the following party are called *toy*. Typically, the events that Turkmens celebrate most joyously are the birth of a son, a circumcision, the first haircut, weddings, and a man's sixty-second birthday (sixty-two being the age at which Muhammad died). But the *bagşy* also performs at purely social events. "These people," Arminius Vámbéry wrote in 1867, in his *Travels through Central Asia*, "take great delight in music and poetry. . . . Back home from looting raids (*alaman*) or after heroic deeds young warriors used to spend whole nights listening to recitals of songs and poetry. The desert holds few occasions for them to entertain themselves, but a *bagşy* can always be counted upon to be around."

FIGURE 1 *Khalypa* Mukhammet Rejebov-*Bagşy* and his pupil (Bäherden). Photo from Sławomira Żerańska-Kominek.

FIGURE 2 Ashyrmämmet Davudiv-*Bagşy*, Güych Nury Agdyev-Gyjakchy, and Aman Govshudov-Dutarchy. Photo from Sławomira Żerańska-Kominek.

Viktor A. Uspensky describes a *bagşy* concert in *Turkmen Music* (1979):

> At night . . . the whole village gathers in the home hosting the *bagşy*. The *bagşy* himself sits in the middle. By his side he has a teapot and a cup with green tea which he sips now and then to quell his thirst. Around him all people sit in total silence and rapture. Only rarely just before the performance you may hear someone cry "*bashlya-ver*" ['go on', 'start']. During the performance itself occasional voices are heard to say "*berkelya!*" ['excellent'], "*khay!*" [an exclamation of approval], "*chal!*" or "*chaly-ver!*" ['go on playing', 'pluck the strings'], "*sagbol!*" ['thank you'], "*ya Alla!*" ['O Allah'] and such. . . . The audience gets more and more excited; cries of praise for the *bagşy* are heard more and more often, as the carpet on which the *bagşy* sits is splattered with coins thrown by the delighted listeners to reward the *bagşy* for his efforts and to show their respect for him.

The repertoire

The *bagşy*'s repertoire includes the *dessan* and songs. A *dessan*, as noted above, is an epic tale; it is in prose and usually consists of monologues or dialogues. A *bagşy* who specializes in narrating tales is called a *dessançy-bagşy*. There is also the *tirmeç-bagşy*, who performs songs in verse based on a *dessan* or on poetry.

The Turkmen *dessan* falls into one of two categories. The first category includes material from the Oghuz epic cycle *Oghuz nama* 'The Tale of Oghuz': *Gorkut atanyng kitaby* 'The Book of Dede Korkut', *Körogly*, and a *dessan* called *Yusup ve Ahmet* attributed to Gurbanaly Magrupi, an eighteenth-century Turkmen poet. These *dessan*, known above all in northern Turkmenistan, are usually accompanied by a *dutar* (a two-stringed long-necked lute) and a *ghidjāk* (a spike fiddle).

The second category of *dessan* includes narratives that flourished especially in the sixteenth, seventeenth, and eighteenth centuries. They all fall between oral folk tales and classical written texts. A number of them (such as *Shasenem ve Garyp* and *Nejep Oglan*) are anonymous; others are the performers' own creation: tales, fables, and stories borrowed from folklore or from Persian or Turkish literature (examples include *Seypelmelek ve Metkhaljemal*, an eighteenth-century piece by Gurbanaly Magrupi; and

Yusup ve Züleykha by Nurmukhammet Anadalyp, 1710–1780). This second category of *dessan*, known mostly in southeastern Turkmenistan, especially in the Yolöten district, is accompanied by one or two *dutar*.

Tirmeçy-bagşy choose texts to their liking from different sources. During a concert, a *tirmeçy-bagşy* will perform poetic songs from various *dessan* and poems by various writers. The favorite choices seem to be texts by Magtymguly Pyragi (1733–1783), Nurmukhammet Andalyp (1710–1780), Abdylla Shabende (1720–1800), Seyitnazar Seyidi (1775–1836), Gurbandurdy Zelili (1795–1850), Kemine (1770–1840), and Mollanepes (1810–1862).

A *dessançy-bagşy* has in his repertoire at least one *dessan* and several songs to texts that are not taken from a *dessan*. Some narrators know by heart as many as five *dessan*. *Pälwan-bagşy* (1890–1939), for example, had a phenomenal memory and could recite twelve of the thirteen parts of the epic *Körgoly*, each of which is a huge self-contained *dessan*. A *tirmeçy-bagşy* should have in his repertoire at least a hundred songs, the minimum number sung during a *toy*. There are singers who know by heart five hundred, six hundred, or even a thousand pieces. In Turkmenistan, "pieces" means only the poetic texts. A tune by itself cannot be used to identify a piece, because many different poems may be recited to one tune—indeed, a *bagşy* is judged by his ability to adapt as many texts as possible to one tune. Some tunes are autonomous "pieces" with titles, but the title of such a tune is usually borrowed from a poem that is frequently performed to it. For instance, the title of the tune *Garybym* is taken from a poetic song from a *dessan*, *Şhasenem ve Garyp*. This tune can actually be used for no fewer than eleven different texts by different authors.

The pattern of a bagşy *concert*

The recital of a *dessan* is called *ýol* 'road' or 'journey'. The concept of transport is fundamental to a shaman's initiation, for it is believed to bring him into contact with the supernatural. Through the epic tales he recites, the *bagşy* is said to cross boundaries between worlds and to encounter supernatural beings. In shamanic cultures, narrating an epic tale was a journey in the same way as a shaman's ecstatic trance. Narrators were thought to be chosen by God, because—like shamans—they guided men's souls through worlds barred to common human understanding.

There is strong evidence that the epic narrative set the pattern of the *bagşy* concert, which is also called *ýol*, especially in northern Turkmenistan. A *bagşy*'s *ýol* has three phases: preliminary, middle, and concluding. The preliminary phase introduces the concert; how long this first part lasts depends on the expected duration of the performance. The longer the concert is likely to be, the longer this introductory phase will be. The middle phase is the longest part of the concert; during this part the *bagşy* "enters the right road," a phrase that refers to both his style and his emotionality. (It is at this point that the *bagşy*'s songs are actually called *ýol*.) The concluding phase is the culmination of the concert; this phase is relatively brief, consisting of just a few songs—no more than perhaps a dozen.

Each of the three stages is associated with a different atmosphere that the *bagşy* seeks to create. The first phase, emotionally neutral, focuses the audience's attention on the performance. The second phase is emotional; in this phase the emotion is steadily heightened. The peak of emotionality is reached in the ecstatic third phase. In any phase, the "being" is the *bagşy*'s own state of mind, which he communicates to his audience through music. The listeners' reactions, a very significant element in Turkmen tradition, stimulate the artist's mood. The audience's apprehension of the successive phases, then, is apparently a result of emotional communication between the performer and the listeners. There are never any fixed or clearly defined points of transition between the three phases, because in any specific musical situation each phase will depend on this emotional communication.

ELEMENTS OF THEORY

The three phases of a concert correspond, in Turkmen tradition, to three zones of tonal "space": low, middle, high. These zones are related to vocal registers, although concepts such as "zone" and "register" are of course relative; they depend on the skill and range of the individual singer. The low zone of tonal space (the lowest voice register) is used in the first phase. In the second and third phases, the music progresses to the middle and high zones (middle and high registers). This movement to higher registers is effected by altering the tuning of the *dutar*. As he begins his performance, a *bagşy* will tune his instrument as low as possible, adjusting it to the lowest register of his own voice. After some time, he raises the tuning by a quarter tone or a half tone—a change that the audience anticipates and enjoys, since the listeners expect the *bagşy* to be increasingly expressive and the emotional tension to rise. Consequently, frequent alteration of the tuning of the *dutar* is considered a sign of the *bagşy*'s artistry. Ideally, according to experienced performers, the pitch of the *dutar* should be changed seven times during a concert.

Despite these frequent alterations, Turkmen musicians identify three principal tunings of the *dutar*, corresponding to three zones of the tonal space. Here, as with vocal registers, there are no fixed boundary points, but the zones can perhaps be described as having approximately the ranges indicated:

1. Low—*pes çekim* 'the weakest stretch of the strings'; a–d^1 to c^1–f^1.
2. Middle—*orta çekim* 'middle stretch of the strings'; c^1-f^1 to e^1-a^1.
3. High—*beik çekim*, 'strongest stretch of the strings'; e^1-a^1 upward.

Particular songs are associated with each zone of tonal space, and thus with each phase of the concert. Accordingly, the entire vocal repertoire of the Turkmen *bagşy* falls into three classes: (1) songs for the low register (*yapbyldak aydymlar*), played during the first phase; (2) songs for the middle register (*orta aydymlar*), played in the second phase; (3) songs for the high register (*çekimli aydymlar*), played in third phase.

Theoretically, this classification of songs is based on the thirteen *perde* 'frets' of the *dutar*. The neck of the *dutar* has three parts: low, middle, and high. The upper border of the low part is at the fifth *perde* (or, according to some performers, the seventh). The upper end of the middle part is at the seventh *perde* (or the tenth). All other *perde* belong in the high part. Each class of songs, then, is associated with the appropriate part of the neck. In these terms, the Turkmen vocal repertoire can be classified as low songs (*yapbyldak*) of narrow range (a fourth or a fifth); middle songs (*orta aydymlar*) of medium range (an octave); and high songs (*çekimli aydymlar*) of wide range (more than an octave). *Yapbyldak* are regarded as easy pieces that present no major technical vocal problems; therefore, they are used for teaching a young *bagşy* during the first years of study. High songs are the most difficult of all, in terms of structure and vocal and expressive requirements.

In practice, this classification is relative and varies with the singer's vocal capacity, repertoire, and individual sense of register. Occasionally, at different concerts, one may hear the same songs performed in different phases. Nevertheless, within a single concert the classification is closely observed: high songs will not be performed in the low register, and low songs will not be performed in the high register. The sequence is shown in figure 3.

PERFORMANCE STYLES

The most characteristic feature of Turkmen *bagşy* music—and the feature that determines its expressive and aesthetic value—is the style of performance. This style fascinated the first observers and students of the tradition. Vámbéry wrote:

> In Etrek, one of those trouvères set up his yurt just by ours. The other day he came up to us with his *dutar*. Several young men promptly surrounded him and

FIGURE 3 Sequence of song classes in a *bagsy* concert.

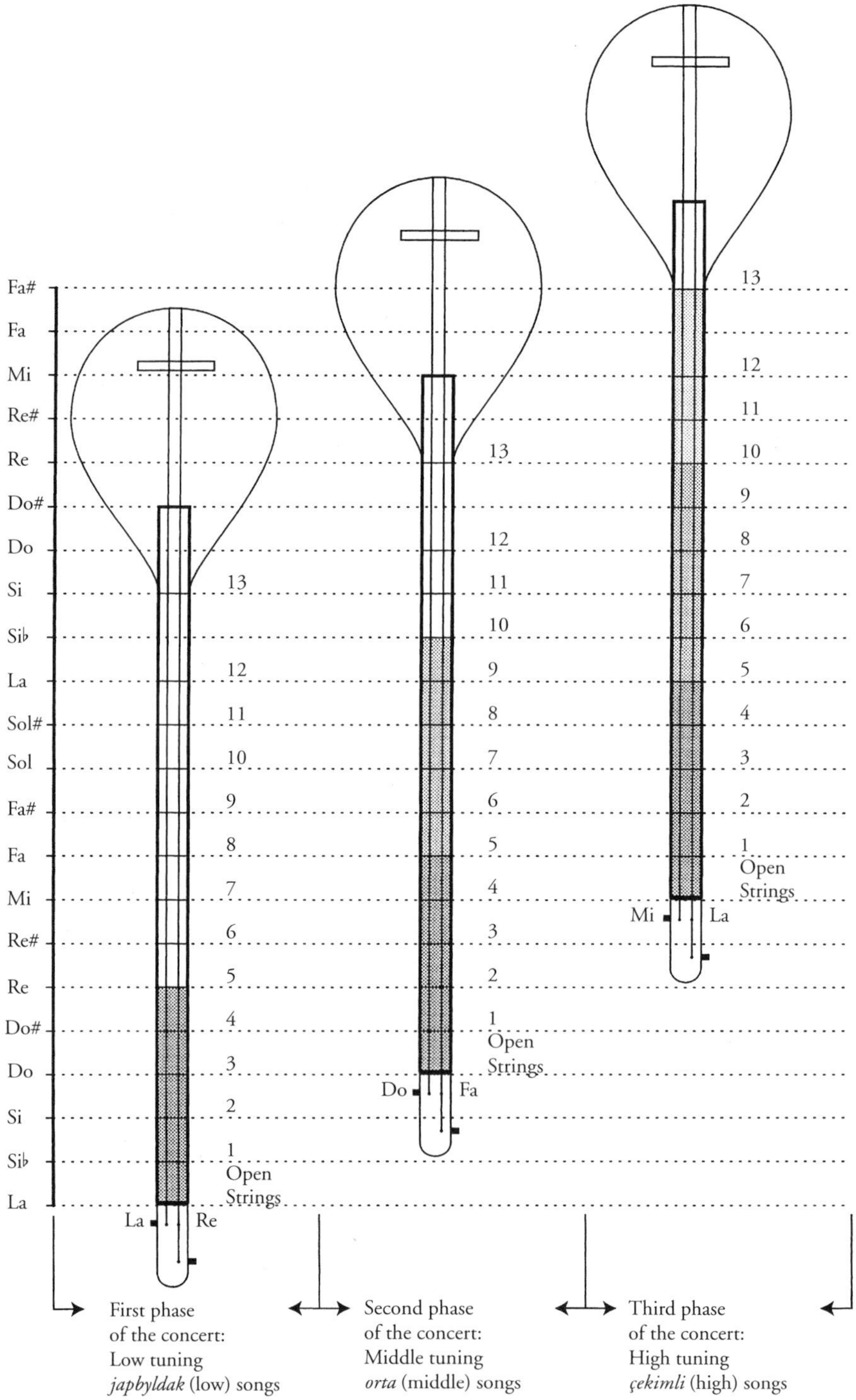

> he had to sing a heroic song. His singing consisted of a series of grating noises that sounded like snoring rather than singing. He plucked the strings of his *dutar*, at first slowly and very softly, but with time he got more excited, producing increasingly savage sounds.

Uspensky (1979) was likewise impressed by the unusual style of *bagsy* singing:

> The way the Yomut sing differs a lot from the music of other Turkmen tribes and sounds like a recitative interspersed with frequent exclamations, . . . spasmodic gulps, moans and protracted sounds much like vibrations of strings in the low register.

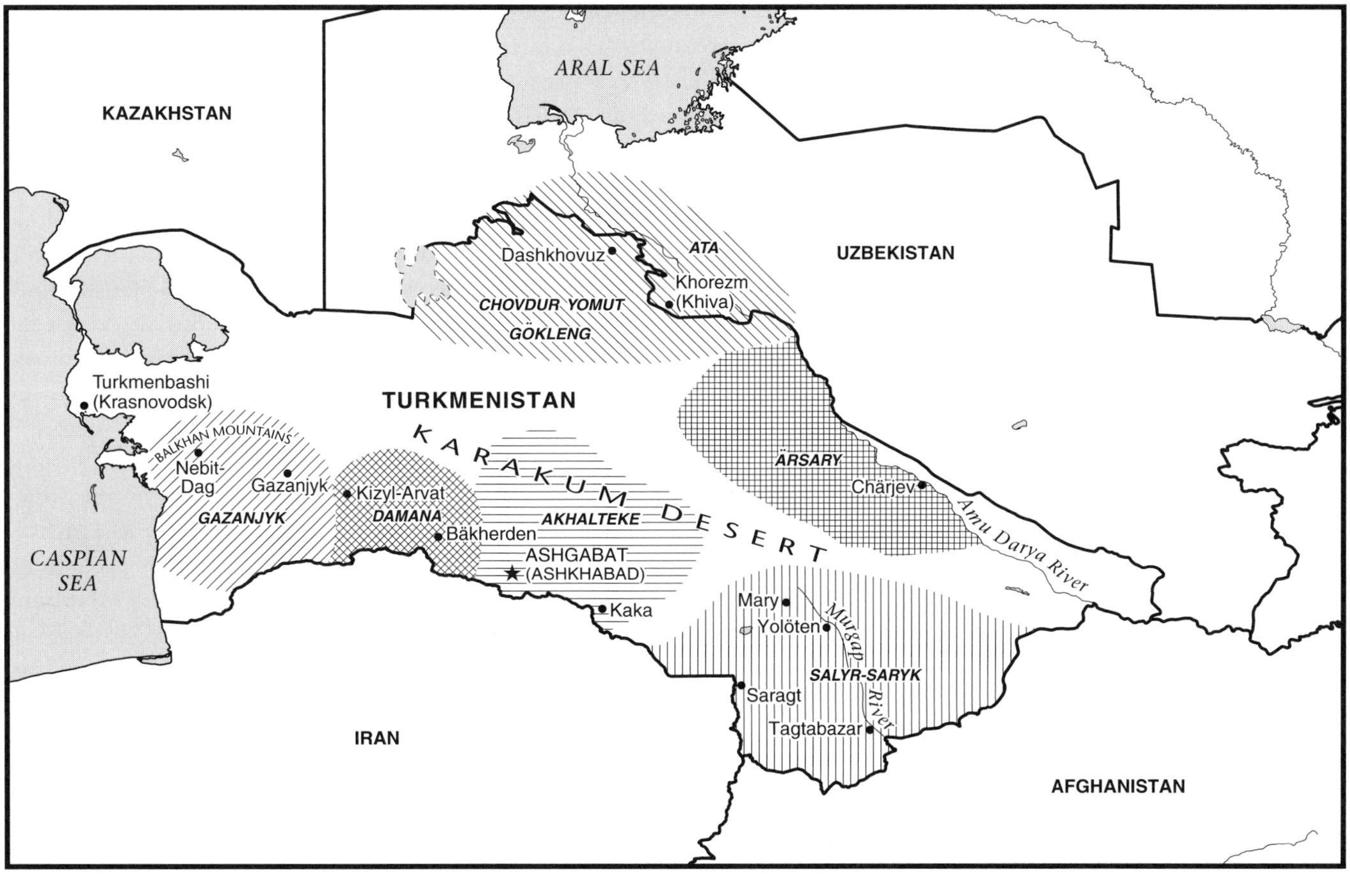

FIGURE 4 Distribution of performing styles, according to Turkmen *bagsy*.

The word *ÿol* is used to describe a performer's style as well as the recital of a *dessan*—it connotes the "direction" the *bagsy* has taken on his road or journey. A Turkmen *bagsy* has a very strong sense of stylistic identity, and performers distinguish at least eight styles (figure 4): Yomut-Gögleng, Çovdur, Ata, Ärsary, Saryk-Salyr, Akhal-Teke, *damana*, and Gazanjyk, which is also called the Yomut style in west Turkmenistan.

Except for *damana* 'foot of a hill' (a Persian term), these designations are all ethnonyms, suggesting a link between Turkmen tribes and musical styles. Actually, though, because of the vicissitudes of history—especially an apparently endless reshuffling of tribal structures—different traditions have merged, blurring their distinctive features. The performing styles in use today probably became established during the past two centuries, that is, when Turkmen tribes were no longer nomadic. Ethnocultural processes in Turkmenistan from the eighteenth to the early twentieth century eventually resulted in the emergence of two main, largely mutually opposed performing styles—northern (the Yomut-Gökleng, Çovdur, and Ata) and southern (Saryk-Salyr).

To the *bagsy*, style (*ÿol*) involves, equally, the repertoire, the purely musical properties of a performance, and the performer's body motions (gesticulation, mimicry, how he sits, how he holds the instrument, and so on). However, it is difficult to identify distinctive features in such general terms. More useful indicators of style may be the accompanying instrument or instruments, the way in which the instruments are handled, time, articulation, nonmusical effects, and vocal technique.

In southern or southeastern Turkmenistan, the *bagsy* is accompanied by one *dutar*—or occasionally two, and very rarely three, identically tuned. The *dutar*, an instrument that produces very soft sounds, repeats the melodic path of the tune and reinforces its rhythm; the *bagsy* touches the strings gently. In the north or northeast, the *dutar* is used as a rhythmic instrument in place of drums, which do not exist in Turkmen music. The *bagsy*'s playing is sharp, and the sound produced is quick and dry. The tune is played, always with slight precedence, by a *ghidjak* (an instrument that musicians in south Turkmenistan do not use for accompaniment). The high, shrill sound of the *ghidjak* makes the intonation and melody more precise and often dominates the performance.

The northern and southern styles also differ in tempo. In the south, tempi tend to be very slow, as a result of an increasing use of melisma, glissando-like "sobbing" combinations of notes, and prolonged pauses on vibrating sounds that disrupt the rhythm. In the north, tempi are quick or very quick. Because the text is performed syllabically, there are numerous interspersed ornaments and shouts, and rhythms are sharply pronounced.

One very distinctive feature of the *bagsy*'s art is a profusion of nonmusical acoustic effects, linked to shamanic magic spells. These effects depend largely on the *bagsy*'s personal preferences, although those preferences are influenced by general stylistic conventions. It would be impossible to list all the nonmusical effects that can be heard in a *bagsy* performance, but they can, roughly, be put into three categories: (1) rustling sounds (snoring, moaning, murmurs); (2) shouts or exclamations; (3) "barking" or "hiccups" called *djuk-djuk*. Categories 1 and 2 are more common in the northern style; in the southern style, which is much more restrained, such effects are often "musical"—that is, played at a definite pitch. In the north, there is a throaty murmur at an indefinite pitch; in the south, this becomes an effect called *hümlemek*, a murmur or slightly throaty singing on the syllable *hü* at a definite pitch in a low register. In the northern style, calls (*ey*, *ay*, *yarey*, *kha*, *akh*, and many more) as a rule have no pitch; in the south, they almost always have a definite pitch. The *djuk-djuk* (category 3) is a favorite ornament and is found in both northern and southern styles.

The difference between the northern and southern performing styles is largely determined by vocal techniques. In southeastern Turkmenistan, a *bagsy* usually sings in a broad, sonorous, slightly nasal voice. As he relaxes his vocal cords and takes advantage of the head as a resonator, he gets more breath, especially in a high register. Singing in a very high register is typical of the southern style. In the northern style, a throaty, flat, stifled, hoarse voice is typical. The northern style often involves recitatives in which there is little accuracy of intonation. The high tempo and the parlando articulation frequently blur the melodic line. In high registers, singing occasionally turns into screaming.

Differences in vocal techniques are particularly obvious in the articulation of nonmusical effects, especially in "hiccups" or "barking"—the *djuk-djuk*. In the southern style, the *djuk-djuk* is performed very narrowly (usually on the vowel *i* or *ü*) and very deeply, from the diaphragm. In the north, the *djuk-djuk* is shallow and guttural, performed on the vowels *e*, *a*, and *u*. In the south, a *bagsy* uses this effect sparingly, with great expression, as if in meditation; in the north it is performed spontaneously, casually.

The southern and northern styles are relatively stable patterns that can be replicated in different performances. Yet it is necessary to understand that the *bagsy*'s artistic and psychological personality is crucial to the final shape of the performance. Turkmen musicians value originality; indeed, it is one criterion of mastery. Thus performances by singers representing the same style may differ significantly. Master teachers (*khalypa*) are important in developing a singer's personal style, but an eminent master creates his own style, and this may be completely different from the styles that any of his disciples will develop.

A *bagsy* may give a performance that does not really follow any style. Such a performance is, in terms of the two main styles, a "compilation," but this does not make it any less valuable artistically or expressively. What all stylistically indeterminate performances have in common is that they freely use elements of either or both styles. *Bagsy* calling themselves Akhal-Teke, for example, combine the typically northern abundance of nonmusical effects with characteristic southern melodiousness. Akhal-Teke performances are very lively and quick. In the Gazanjyk style, the voice sounds a bit throaty, as in the northern style, but the repertoire of effects and the manner of articulation are closer to the southern style. In the *damana* style of southwestern Turkmenistan, very high registers are used and ornamental elements are quite restrained; but the *djuk-djuk* is performed as in the southern style. The most stylistically disparate performances seem to be those by *bagsy* describing themselves as Ärsary (in eastern Turkmenistan). An Ärsary *bagsy* will often sing alternately in the northern and southern styles during the same concert. Some Ärsary *bagsy* have a distinct voice—tense, thin, and nonthroaty—and perform a deep *djuk-djuk*. This voice, according to some commentators, imitates the sound of the *gargy tüydük*, the Turkmen flute.

TURKMEN MUSICAL CULTURE: CONTINUITY AND CHANGE

Russia's conquest of Central Asia was in many ways beneficial to the people there: it brought an end to tribal warfare and slavery, and it began a period of economic development, including railroads. On the other hand, Turkistan was for many years under a harsh, ruthless military regime that held the native population in disdain and crushed any show of discontent. A new era came after 1917, when Central Asia—along with other ethnic nations of the Russian empire—was subjected to a sweeping modernization and social engineering. Culture was important to the Bolshevik leaders, who wanted to create a new social consciousness, a "Soviet man" not bound by class or ethnicity; thus existing ethnic cultures had to give way to a uniform supranational Soviet culture. Ethnic traditions were not completely discarded, however; the overall policy was to modify their specific institutions, channels of transmission, substance, and functions.

The institutional foundations for a new culture began in Turkmenistan in the 1920s. Reading rooms, clubs, libraries, stands dispensing Communist propaganda, "red nooks," red *çaykhan* 'tearooms', and peasants' clubs were set up across the country. A national chain of educational institutions was managed by the Turkmen People's Education Division of the National Education Committee of the Turkistan Soviet Republic (Narkompros) until 1924, and after that by the Narkompros of the Turkmen Soviet Socialist Republic. In the mid-1930s state and regional Socialist Culture Houses were set up; these were renamed Folk Art Houses in 1935. A ministry of culture was established in 1953; it still controls the vast majority of cultural and educational institutions in Turkmenistan.

These institutions of the centralized cultural system were expected to carry out initiatives of the Communist Party, which included propaganda, a literacy program, the emancipation of women, and folk art. Articles in the press and party information were often read aloud in the reading rooms; and party declaimers replaced the professional traditional narrators (*kyssachy* or *kyssakhan*) who had recited *dessan* to illiterate Turkmens. To promote folk art, musical groups were founded and contests and festivals were organized. One format was the agitprop brigade or agitbrigade; these brigades were traveling groups consisting of a party agitator and several artists, usually *bagsy*. They went to farming cooperatives (*kolkhozes*) and to herders in the steppes.

The main purpose of the postrevolutionary recasting of Turkmen musical culture was "sovietization." In practice, this meant modernization (westernization) of local traditions on the one hand, and folklorization on the other. Uspensky, a student of folklore and a composer—the first to integrate Turkmen music into the Western idiom—is said to have played an important part in this effort. In the late 1920s, Western-type musical institutions were established in Turkmenistan. A Turkmen sec-

FIGURE 5 Concert commemorating the ninetieth anniversary of Puli Saryev-*bagsy*'s birth. Photo from Sławomira Żerańska-Kominek, 12 April 1991.

ondary art school was started in Ashkhabad in 1929; six years later, music schools for children and a branch of the Moscow Conservatory were established in Turkmenistan. The influential Union of Composers of Turkmenistan was set up in 1940 as a branch of the Union of Soviet Composers.

As noted above, the sovietization of Turkmen musical culture involved folklorization—the deliberate use of traditional cultural elements in forms that were alien to it, and in inauthentic contexts. Many eminent *bagsy* were actively involved in organizing arranged folk music, to be performed mainly by pop art groups. In 1929, the famous Sakhy Jepparov-*bagsy* took the initiative in forming an ensemble of folk instruments at the Aşgabat Dramatic Theater to accompany official shows and perform between acts; this group also worked as an agitbrigade. In 1930, a large ensemble was founded in Kizyl Arvat; in 1937, a representative folk instrument ensemble was formed at the state Folk Art House there. A folk group founded by Purli Saryev on Turkmen radio in 1928 was very popular, and in 1940 Mylly Tachmuradov formed a radio ensemble that performed as an official folk group for many years. Folk ensembles with the best singers and instrumentalists held important posts in music education institutions. Some *bagsy* learned their art in groups performing on Turkmen radio, and in orchestras, theaters, and Houses of Culture. One of the best-known *bagsy* in Turkmenistan today, Ödenyaz Nobat of Tagtabazar—the grandson of Kurban-*bagsy* and the son of Nobat Aman Sakhat-*bagsy*—received his education and made his entire career in such institutions.

The adaptation of traditional Turkmen culture to the rigors of the new sociopolitical system had far-reaching and irreversible consequences. Before the revolution, Turkmens had never had a national state, or anything like national self-awareness; but under Soviet rule, ironically, nationalism appeared as an unexpected side effect—Turkmens acquired a desire for self-determination and an ethnic cultural identity. This new awareness was derived from the original Turkmen cultural heritage, which now is a subject of increasing reflection and a widely shared value.

The changes under way in Turkmenistan are indicated by the initiative of a *kolkhoz* in Yolöten, the district of southeastern Turkmenistan where the grave of Baba Ganbar, the patron saint of the *bagsy*, is located. In 1990, the elders of the *kolkhoz* proclaimed a great festival to venerate the saint; in less than six months, a huge mausoleum had been built, and in April 1990 Baba Ganbar Day was celebrated for the first time. The event, organized by the community, was received enthusiastically as a demonstration—perhaps the first—of Turkmen national pride. There is also a rapidly spreading cult of famous *bagşy* of the past; commemorations have been organized for some of them, including Purli Saryev (figure 5). The birthdays of some living *bagşy* are also celebrated more and more frequently: the sixtieth birthday of Ödenyaz Nobat-*bagşy* of Tagtabazar and the seventieth birthday of Ilaman Annayev-*bagşy* of Dashkhovuz were acknowledged officially in Ashgabad in 1990.

As before, the *bagşy* who "tells the people what they do not know" is the main carrier of the Turkmen cultural heritage. His memory keeps alive the memory of his people, and he serves as a bridge between the past and the present.

REFERENCES

Gullyev, Shahym. 1985. *Iskusstvo turkmenskikh bakhshi*. Ylym: Ashgabad.

Slobin, Mark. 1976. *Music in the Culture of Northern Afganistan*. Tucson: University of Arizona Press.

Uspensky, Victor A., and Victor M. Belyaev. 1979. *Turkmenskaya muzika*. Ashkhabad: Turkmenistan

Żerańska-Kominek, Sławomira. 1990. "The Classification of Repertoire in Turkmen Traditional Music." *Journal of the Society for Asian Music* 31(2):90–109.

———. 1992a. "Mode: Process and/or Structure—Analytical Study of Turkmen Mukam Gökdepe." In *Studi e testi*. 1, *Secondo Convegno Europeo di Analisi Musicale*, ed. Rossana Dalmonte and Mario Baroni, 249–259. Trent: Università degli Studi di Trento.

———. 1992b. "The Turkmen Bakhshy: Shaman and/or Artist." In *European Studies in Ethnomusicology: Historical Developments and Recent Trends*, ed. M. P. Baumann, 303–317. Berlin: International Institute for Traditional Music.

———. 1992c. *Turkmenistan: Music of the Bakhshy*. Geneva: Archives Internationales de Musiques Populaires.VDE-GALLO. CD-651. (Compact disk.)

———. 1994. "Turkmen Epic Singing/Köroglu." In *Anthology of Traditional Music*. UNESCO Collection. Auvidis. Unesco D 8312.

———. 1995. "The Turkmen Musical Tradition and the Soviet Culture." In *Lux Oriente: Begegnugen der Kulturen in der Musikforschung. Festschrift Robert Günther zum 65 Geburstag*, ed. K. W. Niemöller, 419–427. Kassel: Gustav Bosse Verlag.

Music in Tuva

Theodore Levin

Tuva as a Cultural Area
Sound and Music as Mimesis
***Khöömei*: Throat-Singing**
Poetics of Tuvan Music
Musical Instruments
Tuvan Music as World Music

Westerners have mostly come into contact with the music of Tuva only since the early 1990s, as Tuvan "throat-singing" has become a presence on concert stages and in music festivals around the world. Adopted by rock stars, featured in movie soundtracks, and appropriated by mass-market ad campaigns, Tuvan music has truly entered global pop culture. But behind the currently popular forms of "fusion Tuvan," a long history of indigenous performance represents a fascinating tradition of sound art that challenges commonly held assumptions about the definition of music and its relationship to nature, culture, entertainment, and spirituality.

TUVA AS A CULTURAL AREA

Tuva (or Tyva, as it is called in the Tuvan language) is an autonomous republic within the Russian Federation that lies some 2,500 miles east of Moscow in the grasslands, forests, and mountainous plateaus of South Siberia. Tuva's southern border is international, dividing Russia from Mongolia. Its other borders mark political divisions within Russia: to the north, beyond the Sayan Mountains, is Khakasia; to the west, across the 13,000-foot peaks of the Altai range, is Gorno-Altai; to the east, at the headwaters of the Yenisei, one of Siberia's great rivers, is Buryatia. Each of these is an autonomous region or republic with its own language and culture.

Tuva is sparsely settled, with slightly more than 300,000 people occupying an area that extends roughly 500 miles east to west and 300 miles north to south. About a third of the population consists of Russians and other peoples who are not ethnically Tuvan. Most of the non-Tuvans live in Tuva's capital, Kyzyl (which means "red" in Turkic languages), a small city established during the time of the Bolshevik revolution.

The Tuvans are a Turkic people, and Tuvan—or Tuvinian, as it is sometimes called in English—is a Turkic language. This linguistic connection notwithstanding, Tuvans cannot easily speak with Turks from Turkey, for Tuvan is related to modern-day Turkish in much the same way as English is related to German. Turkic peoples have ancient roots in Inner Asia, and historians and archaeologists have generally agreed that the Altai-Sayan region, which includes Tuva, is one of the oldest wellsprings of Turkic civilization. Centuries of economically motivated migrations, military campaigns, and ethnic intermingling brought Turkic civilization southward to Central

Tuva.

Asia and westward to Anatolia, where it blossomed in urban forms under the Seljuks and later the Ottomans. As Islam spread from its birthplace in the Arabian Peninsula to become the state religion of vast portions of Central and West Asia, the Turkic inhabitants of these regions were Islamized, assimilating many of the cultural and linguistic conventions of the Islamic world. Islam, however, never came to Siberia. Siberian Turks—who include Tuvans (or Uriankhai, as they were called in the nineteenth-century ethnographic literature), Khakas, Yakuts, and many smaller groups—have preserved languages, religious customs, and expressive cultures with roots that predate the rise of Islam in the seventh century and betray no Islamic influence. Tuva's cultural autonomy, maintained despite centuries of political colonization by a succession of Mongol, Dzungar, Manchu, and Russian empires, has been bolstered both by the physical barriers of mountains, desert, and boggy forest that surround it and by the decentralized herding economy that has traditionally provided the livelihood of its inhabitants. This pastoral livelihood, closely linked with the natural world of the Tuvan grasslands, has supplied one of the vital resources of Tuvan music: landscapes and environmental sounds.

SOUND AND MUSIC AS MIMESIS

Animism and imitation

Tuvan herders have traditionally been animists. That is, they typically ascribe spiritual power to natural phenomena and pray to the spirits, literally "owners" or "hosts," of mountains, rivers, and caves, as well as to the spirits of wild animals such as bear, deer, and certain birds. The spirits of animals are themselves believed to animate and sanctify topographic features such as mountains, as is evident, for example, in the common word *xaïyrakan* 'bear', which also connotes a sacred mountain.

In Tuvan animism, the spiritual nature of mountains and rivers is manifested not only in their physical appearance (which in the case of mountains is typically anthropomorphized through analogies between topographic features and parts of the human body) but also in the sounds they produce—or can be made to produce through human agency. Thus, the echo that results from singing close to a cliff, and the interaction of a human voice with the gurgling water of a brook or the swishing air currents of a strong wind, may be imbued with spiritual power.

Living creatures, no less than inanimate places or landscapes, manifest spiritual power through sound. For humans, the key to animating and assimilating this spiritual power becomes, logically enough, the imitation of sounds. The fact that imitation, with its overtones of animist worship, is based on the sense of sound rather than, for example, sight—which would tend to lead to a mimesis of movement or physical expression, such as dance (as among some other Siberian peoples, including the Koriaks)—underscores the importance of sound as a physical stimulus, and the importance of listening in the traditional herding-hunting culture of the Tuvans.

FIGURE 1 From sound to song.

Iconic imitation of natural sounds	*Stylized imitation of natural sounds*	*Musical constructs*
ang-meng mal-magan öttü-neri (imitation of wild and domestic animals)	*khöömei* (throat-singing)	*uzun-yry* ('long song', lyrical song)
vocalizations and instruments such as *ediski* (single reed made to imitate female musk deer); *khirlee* (instrument used to imitate sounds of wind); *amyrga* (hunting horn used to imitate call of stag)	imitations on instruments such as *khomus* (Jew's harp), *igil* (two-stringed fiddle), *shoor* (flute)	autonomous instrumental pieces (*igilding ayalgalary*) *kyska* (short song)
shamanic vocalizations		intoned speech; prayers to the spirits of sacred places and animals

Sound or music?

Music has sometimes been broadly defined as "aestheticized sound." Whether highly structured or randomly produced, and whether considered by listeners to represent sublime harmony or an inharmonious affront to the ears, music strives to convey an aesthetic statement through sound. In the sound world of Tuva, however, the boundary between sound and music becomes vague. No Tuvan word covers the same semantic field as *music*. (*Khögzhüm,* a loan word from Mongolian, does broadly mean music, but it implies the use of musical instruments as opposed to voice alone.) Rather, the social functions, techniques of acoustical production, and formal styles of sound and music are described by a range of specialized terms. These functions, techniques, and styles might best be understood as points along a continuum—as shown in figure 1—ranging from *sound* to *song*, that is, from iconic imitation of natural sounds to stylized imitations of natural sounds to autonomous musical constructs.

Figure 1 represents distinctions of function and form in traditional Tuvan music that still play a role in the sound world of contemporary Tuva. These distinctions, however, are not absolute. For example, *khöömei* 'throat-singing', which is basically a form of stylized mimesis, is often used as a vocal technique in songs, particularly in *kozhamyk*. Likewise, instruments, including the *amyrga* and *ediski*, whose original function was iconic imitation are now included in arrangements of composed songs.

KHÖÖMEI: THROAT-SINGING

Throat singing, *khöömei*, is unquestionably Tuva's best-known musical artifact. The primary meaning of *khöömei,* a loan word from Mongolian, is throat or pharynx; throat-singing is the usual English translation. The noun *khöömei* is used for throat-singing in general, for a particular style of throat-singing, and also for something sung in the general *khöömei* style. Performers of *khöömei* are called *khöömeizhi*.

In *khöömei,* a single vocalist simultaneously produces two distinct tones: a low, sustained fundamental pitch, like the drone of a bagpipe, and a series of reinforced harmonics or overtones high above this drone. Using the throat as a precise type of band-pass filter that reinforces certain frequencies while attenuating others, singers are able to isolate and reinforce a single harmonic to such an extent that it sounds louder than the fundamental. By sequencing different reinforced harmonics in quick succession, vocalists produce the effect of "singing" a melody composed solely of harmonics.

Although the harmonic series of any fundamental pitch is potentially infinite, the portion of the series typically exploited in Tuvan *khöömei* extends from the sixth harmonic (two and a half octaves above the fundamental pitch) to the twelfth harmonic (three and a half octaves above the fundamental). This portion of the harmonic series includes seven harmonic pitches, of which two are scrupulously avoided by performers of *khöömei*: the seventh harmonic, whose pitch is a slightly flat dominant seventh relative to the fundamental; and the eleventh harmonic, a neutral pitch halfway between a perfect fourth and a tritone relative to the fundamental. The resulting harmonic scale expresses the strongly pentatonic character of many Tuvan melodies, demonstrating that for performers of *khöömei,* the harmonic series is not simply a naturalistic sonic resource but is musically shaped and stylized in ways that reflect ingrained cultural preferences. (The major second present in Tuvan pentatonic melodies is missing in the portion of the harmonic series exploited by singers, but this scale degree is implied by the melodic syntax.) Figure 2 shows the pitches typically used by Tuvan singers. The fact that an almost complete pentatonic scale is available within the very portion of the harmonic series in which individual harmonics can be most easily isolated and reinforced (the sixth through twefth harmonics) must surely contribute to the durability of *khöömei* as a cultural practice.

While the origins of *khöömei* are obscure, stories and legends underscore the notion that humankind learned to sing in such a way by imitating natural sounds whose timbres are rich in harmonics. These sounds include waterfalls, burbling brooks, bird songs, and strong wind exciting the strings of a zither, called *chatagan,* which Tuvan herders place on the roofs of their yurts to dry the instrument's gut strings.

Khöömeizhi, performers of *khöömei*, use harmonics to extemporize stylized imitations of sounds in the environment as well as to perform musical items—usually lasting not more than a minute or two—in which short segments of text sung in a raspy bass or baritone register are followed by textless codas consisting of reinforced harmonics. Performers describe these codas as expressions of exaltation at the beauty of nature or the power of love that no words can convey. Harmonics may also be used to perform the melodies of standardized songs. The melody of one such song, "*Artii-Sayir*" 'The Far Side of a Dry Riverbed', a favorite among *khöömeizhi*, is transcribed in figure 3.

Metrical songs with a rounded phrase structure such as "*Artii-Sayir*" represent a formal concept of *khöömei* quite different from extemporized imitations of natural sounds or harmonic codas to lyrical texts. For singers and acculturated listeners, the principal interest of these latter styles is not melody and meter but rather timbre and rhythm. The opening of one such *khöömei,* "Alash"—the name of a river—is transcribed in figure 4.

Subsequent iterations of the harmonic sequence are slightly varied, and pauses between one iteration and the next are of irregular length. These iterations should be understood not in the Western sense of a melody with many verses but as a series of discrete responses to images of beauty or feelings of ecstasy. The singer responds, then waits for further inspiration, then responds again. (On the Smithsonian Folkways compact disk that includes "Alash," recorded and edited by this author with a Russian and a Tuvan colleague, pauses between iterations were shortened and standardized in

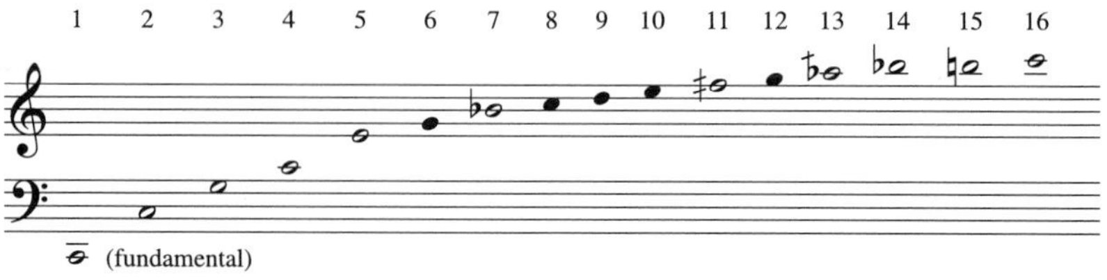

FIGURE 2 First sixteen pitches of the harmonic series. Pitches typically used by Tuvan singers are blackened.

FIGURE 3 *"Artii-Sayir."* The number above each note identifies the harmonic which produces that pitch. By convention, the first harmonic (1) is the fundamental pitch; thus the second harmonic (2) is that which sounds an octave higher, and successive harmonic multiples of 2 all produce successively higher octaves above the fundamental. Transcription by Theodore Levin.

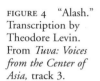

FIGURE 4 "Alash." Transcription by Theodore Levin. From *Tuva: Voices from the Center of Asia,* track 3.

an attempt to make the composition sound more "musical." Only later did we understand that the long and irregular pauses, far from reflecting a lack of musicianship on the part of the performer, were not intended to be perceived in metrical time.)

Still more melodically minimalist are *khöömei* that imitate sounds in the environment. Here, the entire exposition may revolve around a rhythmically pulsating ornamentation of just two or three harmonics. With melody all but nonexistent, the timbre and rhythm of the harmonics become the focus of interest (for example, see *Tuva: Voices from the Center of Asia*, "*Ezenggileer*," track 15). Among younger singers in Tuva, the type of purely mimetic *khöömei* represented by *ezenggileer* seems to be gradually giving way to a more melodic style of singing influenced by conventional song genres.

In Tuva, music scholars and performers alike divide *khöömei* into several canonical styles: *sygyt, kargyraa, borbangnadyr, ezenggileer,* and *khöömei* (which, as noted earlier, is the name of a particular style as well as the general term for throat-singing). Each style is characterized by a different type of vocal production. These core styles, however, are performed in highly individualized ways by different singers, and well-known throat-singers typically become identified not only with a manner of vocal production but with a specific tune that serves as a personal signature. For example, "Kombu *khöömei*" is a musical item identified by both vocal style and melody as belonging to the singer Kombu.

In the style known as *sygyt* 'whistle' (a Tuvan word), the fundamental drone pitch is typically in the baritone register and vocal production is highly tensed, yielding clear, piercing harmonics. *Khöömei* is sung in the same register as *sygyt,* but with less laryngeal tension and more nasal resonance. In *ezenggileer* (from *ezenggi* 'stirrup'), soft, shimmering harmonics produced by rapid vibration of the lips and tongue are sung over a low fundamental drone, imitating clinking stirrups on a horse in motion. *Borbangnadyr* (from an onomatopoeic word that suggests the sound of a round object rolling) designates a rhythmic treatment of harmonics that resembles the sound of rapid movement, typically of water, wind, or a horse. In *kargyraa* (from an onomatopoeic word for wheezing or speaking in a hoarse or husky voice), the fundamental pitch that is the source of harmonics is itself biphonic, consisting of both glottal and supraglottal oscillations at the interval of an octave. *Kargyraa* is the style of Tuvan throat-singing that most closely resembles the sound of Tibetan Buddhist chant, and it is possible that the Tibetan Buddhist practice represents a specialized application of the raspy double-source vocal timbre found in a variety of musical forms and genres among Inner Asian pastoralists.

POETICS OF TUVAN MUSIC

The aesthetic linking of humankind to the natural world expressed through *khöömei* is also present in other forms of Tuvan music. This link is particularly clear in songs known as *uzun yry* 'long song', so called because of their melismatic style—syllables of the text are melodically extended over long durations. In place of the sound mimesis exemplified by throat-singing, *uzun yry* uses poetic analogies to link the external world of landscapes and topographic features to the internal world of human feeling. The meaning of such an analogy may be unclear to listeners who are not intimately familiar with the particular landscape or topography described; thus knowledge of topography and toponymy plays an essential role in Tuvan poetics. Here is a quatrain from a Tuvan song. (*Shanchyg* is a description of a hill whose base is the shape of a bent forearm with the angle made by the elbow.)

Kara Shanchyg baarynga, Konggurgai	If you dig a well before the black Shanchyg, Konggurgai,
Kuduk kaskanza ünmes dep be, Konggurgai?	Why wouldn't [water] flow out, Konggurgai?
Kap-la kara uruglarny, Konggurgai	If you get engaged to a dark-skinned girl, Konggurgai
Kudalaza berbes dep be, Konggurgai?	Why wouldn't [her parents] give her away, Konggurgai?

Once one understands that Shanchyg is a dry place where water is unlikely to appear, the seemingly straightforward question in the first couplet becomes ironic. The second couplet offers what the poetic form makes clear is a parallel irony and reveals the meaning: the parents of the girl are no more likely to give her away then the well-digger is likely to find water.

Other examples of *uzun yry* place singer and listeners in a particular landscape by narrating a journey through it that is rich in toponymic references. In such songs, singers aim to induce nostalgia in listeners familiar with the landscapes they describe, and it is not uncommon for Tuvan men to weep upon hearing a poignantly sung description of a land where they have herded animals or ridden horseback. These toponymic songs also use poetic analogies between nature and culture. Following are three quatrains from the song "Bayan Dugai." In each quatrain, the first couplet describes a natural landscape and the second couplet draws a parallel with human life. (In the second quatrain, the term translated as *merry* is literally "joke black"; in the third quatrain, *hem* is a pun—the word also refers to foothills.)

Astyng-kishting turlaa bolgan	Argarlyg and Koshkarlyg
Argarlygny Koshkarlygny	Became places where the ermine and sable live.
Aldan-bezhen malchyn küzeesh	Bayan-Dugai is a place where forty or fifty herders
Kyshtaglai beer Bayan-Dugai	Camp during the autumn and winter.

Bayan-Dugai artyn kaastaan	The rear view of Bayan-Dugai is beautifully ornamented,
Bayan-Mandaam taanda charash	And my Bayan-Mandaa is just as beautiful.
Bashtanggyzy khadyp orar	The bridal head-ornament
Bashtak-kara Dugai kyzy	Worn by Dugai's merry daughter waves in the wind.
Ezimneri edektelgem	My Ezirlig and Byshkak [names of hills]
Ezirlimnyi Byshkaktymny	Whose forested slopes descend like a hem.
Edekteri estep-orar	Erge-Kara [a woman's name], that rascal
Erge-kara kulugurnu	Whose hem waves in the wind.

MUSICAL INSTRUMENTS

In Tuva, vocal and instrumental music intersect in a number of ways. The most evident intersection has to do with timbre, for example in the ubiquitous *khomus* 'Jew's harp': the player's buccal cavity is used to reinforce harmonics produced by the vibration of the instrument's tongue, a technique analogous to the reinforcement of vocally produced harmonics in *khöömei*. Upright fiddles such as the *igil* and *byzaanchy* are also played in a manner that accentuates the richness of their string harmonics, and in performance these harmonics become part of the instrument's narrative voice.

FIGURE 5 Andrei Chuldum-ool accompanies throat-singing on the *igil*, a two-stringed fiddle.

The notion that an instrument possesses a "voice" is not simply a metaphor in Tuva. Tuva's legacy of animism has imbued instruments with voices that are understood to be imitations of natural voices. The horsehead fiddle called *igil* is widely regarded as capable of telling stories; and in one traditional type of performance, the player of the *igil* explains the story he is going to "tell" and then plays it without any accompanying narration (figures 5 and 6). In one of the best-known of such stories, the *igil* narrates the legend of its own creation, and in so doing explains the cult of the horse exemplified by the horsehead atop its pegboard. In this legend, a man's beloved horse is driven over a cliff by a jealous landowner. As the horse's owner, a herder named Öskϋs-ool, vainly searches for him, the voice of the horse comes down from the heavens and instructs Öskϋs-ool where to find its body and how to use various parts of the body to construct an *igil*. (In fact, this instrument not only has a miniature horsehead on the pegboard but also incorporates horsehide, hair, and gut.) After building the *igil*, Öskϋs-ool begins to play it; the horse, hearing the sound,

FIGURE 6 The neck of the *igil*, here played by Kaigal-ool Khovalyg, is often topped by a horsehead, illustrating the cult of the horse in Tuvan music.

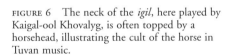

FIGURE 7 Anatoli Kuular, on an *amyrga*, imitates the mating call of a stag.

descends from the heavens, followed by a herd of stallions. This instrumentally performed legend represents an archaic type of program music: a listener who knows the story can indeed easily discern the flow of the narrative through the *igil*'s representation of various equine and human sounds.

Another example of a mimetic instrument is the Jew's harp, *khomus*. Jew's harps, like *khöömei*, serve a variety of musical functions ranging from sound mimesis to playing standard song melodies. A unique mimetic function of the *khomus* is the imitation of human speech. Many stories and legends tell of confidential messages encoded in the playing of the *khomus* and subsequently decoded by listeners sensitive to the instrument's phonetics. (A "talking *khomus*" is included on *Tuva, Among the Spirits*, track 17.)

In addition to the *khomus,* various aerophones are used to imitate natural sounds, although with a more limited range of mimetic subjects. Such instruments include the *ediski,* a single reed made to imitate the sounds of a female musk deer; the *khirlee,* a thin piece of wood that, when spun like a propeller on a tensed, twisted string, imitates the sound of wind; and the *amyrga* (figure 7), a hunting horn used to imitate the mating call of a stag.

TUVAN MUSIC AS WORLD MUSIC

Beginning in the early 1990s, Tuvan music began to reach an audience beyond Tuva itself through recordings and concert tours by self-managed ensembles that were descendants of the state-sponsored folk troupes of the Soviet era. The new ensembles capitalized on widespread interest in "world music" to present Tuvan music in forms ranging from respectfully authentic arrangements of throat-singing and balladlike long songs to fusion-inspired techno, jazz, and avant-garde appropriations. Among the diverse styles and genres of Tuvan music, throat-singing has had the greatest impact on the West. Tuvan throat-singers have participated in a wide range of collaborations with Western artists and have contributed to movie and television soundtracks, commercials, theater productions, and dance compositions. At the same time, the popularization of throat-singing has inspired acolytes around the world to try to learn how to produce reinforced harmonics, giving rise to novel styles, techniques, and theories about the aesthetics and metaphysics of harmonics—all independent of Tuva itself.

The enthusiastic reception of Tuvan music in the West coincided with—and very likely contributed to—a rise in the status of traditional music within Tuva (figure 8). During the Soviet era, throat-singing, along with other kinds of expressive culture

FIGURE 8 The folklorist Eduard Alekseyev records a herder as she chants a prayer and tosses fresh milk to nourish the spirits that protect her yurt.

officially viewed as undesirable vestiges of superstition, magic, and religion, was discouraged or banned. Today, by contrast, throat-singing occupies a place of honor in the pantheon of Tuvan artistic forms. A biannual *khöömei* festival and international competition and a *khöömei* research institute are sponsored by the Tuvan ministry of culture, and throat-singing has become a popular activity among young people. Girls and women, formerly discouraged from throat-singing because of a social taboo based on the belief that it could lead to infertility, are also learning to sing in Tuva.

As the popularity of throat-singing increases, however, stylistic diversity and individuality among performers in Tuva are giving way to increasing standardization, and other styles of music less dramatic or less commercially viable than throat-singing are gradually disappearing. The *limbi* and *shoor*, two types of flute, are all but extinct in Tuva, and outstanding performers on other instruments are in short supply. One can only hope that the revival of interest in *khöömei* will eventually have a similar affect on other aspects of Tuva's traditional musical life.

REFERENCES

Bloothooft, Gerrit, et al. 1992. "Acoustics and Perception of Overtone Singing." *Journal of the Acoustical Society of America* 92(4, part 1, October):1827–1836.

Levin, Theodore C., and Michael E. Edgerton. 1999. "The Throat Singers of Tuva." *Scientific American* 281(3):70–77.

Tuva: Among the Spirits. Smithsonian Folkways 40452. Compact disk.

Tuva: Voices from the Center of Asia. Smithsonian Folkways 40017. Compact disk.

When Uygurs Entertain Themselves

Sabine Trebinjac

The Twelve *Muqam*: *On Ikki Muqam*
The *Dolan Muqam* Repertoire

The autonomous region of Xinjiang (also known as Chinese Turkistan) is a vast land in Central Asia that covers one-sixth of the area of the People's Republic of China: 1.6 million square kilometers. Xinjiang is bordered by major mountain systems; its center is formed by two great basins and is mostly deserts (the Takla Makan, Lop Nur, and Dzongaria) dotted with oases. In this almost hostile environment live some 14 million Uygurs, according to the census of 1990. The Uygurs are primarily farmers but also shepherds. They are reputed to be clever musicians and light-footed dancers; in fact, this reputation has become something of a cliché.

The diversity of the Uygur musical repertoire is noteworthy, and fascinating. There are significant regional differences (for example, musical systems may go from predominantly heptatonic to pentatonic or even hexatonic), but in general Uygur music centers on two major forms: the *muqam* and "popular music," which is not related to *muqam*. We can summarize Uygur musical culture by saying that, except when there has been a death, anyone can play music at any time, with complete freedom to choose between *muqam* and popular songs. In both types, music, song, and dance are intimately linked. Another important aspect of the music is that in this Muslim society, men and women, young and old, enjoy it and play it together.

Let us look more closely at two examples of *muqam* performance. In the first case, we will be looking at *muqam* being played, or *muqam orunlimaq*. In the second case, we will be looking at *oynimaq* 'enjoyment, games and dance'.

THE TWELVE *MUQAM*: *ON IKKI MUQAM*

Among the diverse *muqam* traditions of Xinjiang, the "twelve *muqam*" repertoire enjoys the greatest prestige. Originating in the south—more precisely, in Kashgar—it has given birth to at least four derived forms: Ili, Khotan, Kucha, and Turfan.

We can broadly define a *muqam* as a modal, monodic suite, usually heptatonic, which has varying rhythmic cycles as well as unmeasured rhythms. Each suite lasts about two hours and is organized into three major sections: (1) the *bash muqam* or *muqäddimä* and *chong näghmä*, (2) the *dastan*, and (3) the *mäshräp*. Each section is made up of subsections, one leading into the next, alternating musical and sung pieces, and possibly danced pieces. The *mäshräp* section has two to seven subsections, also

FIGURE 1 A theatrical *muqam* performance. Photo courtesy of Xinjiang's People's Publishing.

known as *mäshräp*, characterized by a quick, continuously accelerating rhythm that pulls the listener in. This section has dance accompaniment from beginning to end.

One might hear a *muqam*, or more typically part of a *muqam*, during a religious holiday, at a wedding, or at a gathering of relatives or friends; but today, one usually goes to a theater to watch a *muqam* performance. It is important to note that this performance version—and the version of reference for the twelve *muqam*—comes from a recording made in the early 1960s of the Kashgar musician Turdi Akhon, which was transcribed by the Chinese musicologist Wan Tongshu. As a result, the spontaneity of informal performances is usually replaced in formal performances by considerable, or even very strict, rigidity. A very large number of instrumentalists, singers, and dancers appear, in flamboyant costumes; the women are covered in imitation jewelry that is not always clearly Uygur in origin; and a cardboard set or backdrop is intended to recall the splendor of the royal courts (figure 1). Thus, the twelve *muqam* are no longer traditional but are rather an example of state-sponsored traditionalism. They have been described by Levin (1996) as "frozen."

THE *DOLAN MUQAM* REPERTOIRE

The Dolan are an ethnic subgroup of the Uygurs, though they have been assimilated and therefore are not recognized officially as such. Unofficial estimates put their number at about 20,000. Their origin is uncertain and remains a subject of debate. Many Dolan claim that their group is of Mongolian origin and that their name comes from a Mongolian word, *duilän* or *turan* 'seven'; but if so, the name Dolan may have been given to them by the Mongols—in which case the Dolan themselves would not be Mongols. The Dolan live in the northern and western margins of the Takla Makan desert, and their economy is principally herding sheep. They have a strongly developed ethnic consciousness, and they always speak in terms of "the Uygurs" and "us." They have their own dialect, kinship terminology, myths, music, and musical instruments.

The Dolan say that twelve *muqam* exist, though they admit that today some have been forgotten. Thus, in the Mäkit region, only seven, eight, or nine are played; a few more are played in the north. The names of some Dolan suites are identical to Uygur names—*Rak*, *Özhal*, *Musaviräk*, *Bayat*, *Chargah*—whereas other names seem to be specifically Dolan: *Bom bayawan*, *Zil bayawan*, *Jula*, *Dogamät*, *Khodäk*, *Chöl bayawan*. In either case, though, the two repertoires have nothing in common. In fact, as though to mark the difference, the Uygurs have given the Dolan *muqam* a special category, *nakhsha usul muzikisi* 'music that is sung and danced'. The Dolan, for their part, call their music *millätlik muzikisi* 'ethnic music'.

A Dolan suite does not last more than six minutes, and it is danced from beginning to end. Each suite has five sections, one leading to the next: *muqam*, *chikitmä*, *sänäm*, *sänqäs*, and *sirilma*. Each suite has its own modal organization, predominantly hexatonic (except for two, *Dogamät* and *khodäk*, that are heptatonic). All the suites have the same rhythmic structure. All five sections can proceed only in this way: unmeasured *muqam*, 6/4 time, 2/4, 4/4, and finally 2/4—which can, as the tempo increases, become 5/8.

At least once a week, the Dolan participate in a *mäshräp* 'a place for rejoicing', 'assembly', 'party' (figure 2). A *mäshräp* is organized for a religious holiday, a marriage, a visit from distant relative, or the construction of a new house, or as reparation by a member of the village community. It is a party on a large scale, at which more than two hundred people may assemble outside or, during the winter, within the enclosure of a house. People who live in nearby oases come to join the *mäshräp*, and the festivities last for hours—until, it seems, the participants are exhausted. A *mäshräp* follows a fairly precise order and conforms to rigorous rules. Two men—the *bäg* and his subaltern, the *pässap*—are designated by the community to make sure that the rules are observed. The *bäg* has a title that is identical to the title formerly given to the person responsible for the community in general. He is chosen "*bäg* of the evening" for life, which means that he is the grand master of the *mäshräp*. The *pässap* watches over the dances to make sure they take place properly.

A *mäshräp* begins with an initial *muqam*. While a dozen peasants play the "head" of the *muqam*, which is unmeasured, the crowd gets ready to dance. During the next four parts, the different dance movements suggest a hunting scene. In the *chikitmä*, men and women, two by two, swinging their arms, dance a four-step figure tracing an oval: this represents hunters looking for animal tracks. Next, in the *sänäm*, the presence of the animal has been detected, and the men prepare their weapons while their wives light their way with a torch. Here, their steps trace a square and they hold their arms aloft. Then the *sänqäs* gathers all the dancers, one behind the other, in a large circle to walk around the "quarry" in the center. Finally, the joy of a successful hunt is expressed in the *sirilma*, in which each dancer spins as fast and as long as possible, and then leaves the dance (figure 3).

After three or four *muqam* interspersed with songs—during which, responding to fatigue, the musicians, dancers, and spectators exchange roles—different entertainments are organized, involving all the participants in the *mäshräp* again. Some of these

FIGURE 2 A Dolan *mäshräp*. Photo by Sabine Trebinjac, 1988.

FIGURE 3 Dolan dancers. Photo by Sabine Trebinjac, 1988.

entertainments are parodies; some are games involving role playing. They suggest the functions that structure Dolan social life, including, for example, a skit called "An Invitation to Tea" and one called "The Whip." In some games, sayings are used to relate the deterioration of a relationship. Such sayings may publicly expose a disagreement, using imitation but without overtly identifying the individuals concerned; this allows the audience to arbitrate the dispute and the two actors to be reconciled. When a young man extends two half-filled bowls to a young woman while improvising a few verses (as in "An Invitation to Tea"), he is publicly declaring his love and, in effect, submitting it for the approval or condemnation of the audience. When participants strike each other with a rolled-up scarf, they indicate the quality of their friendship: the harder they hit each other, the stronger their friendship is.

Muqam, songs, and nonmusical entertainment alternate in this way for hours—they may continue throughout the night. Each game has rules the participants cannot violate. Entering the dance at the wrong time, making the wrong movements, dumping the water out of the bowls, refusing a proffered scarf, contesting the audience's verdict, and not recognizing one's errors are infractions for which the *bäg* will impose the label *guna* 'sinner'. The sinner is pushed to the center of a circle formed by the crowd and must answer the question asked by the *bäg*: "Are you *namaqul* 'repentant', or are you *säwänliq* 'at fault'?" The sinner and the audience decide together what the answer is. A repentant sinner must expiate the sin by offering a sheep or money or organizing a new *mäshräp* the very next day. A sinner who pleads guilty must lie down and be hit by a stick, and then harassed by a man disguised as a woman; or he or she must perform various humiliating wagers.

The *mäshräp* are times of rejoicing and social cohesion and are important episodes for the Dolan, who like to say that they "need them to live." The very high proportion of Dolan who participate in *mäshräp*—an estimated 90 percent in the Mäkit region—attests to this. One peasant explained the fact that everyone knows how to sing and dance the *muqam* by saying that the Dolan must defend themselves from attacks by boar, unclean animals which, under Qur'ānic law, they may not touch:

> Starting in September or October, when the cold begins, the Yarkän River has no more water, and it runs into the sands of the Takla Makan. At this point, around the Mäkit, when the sun has barely risen, you see hordes of deer coming from the Takla Makan looking for a source of water. But in the evening, when the night falls, hordes of boar bolt from the Takla Makan, maybe two hundred

> or three hundred of them. Sometimes they come before the sorghum has been harvested, and trample and eat it. We have dogs and when they see the boar coming, they begin to bark. And that's our signal. The peasants of the village gather and sing the *muqam*. The whole village joins in. There may be over a hundred people singing and accompanying themselves on the *dap*, or a plate, or any other noisemaker. And the women begin to dance. We force the children to sing too, and we say that that is why everyone should know the *muqam*. Because of the many voices singing sharply and shouting, because of the blows on the *dap*, and the dances, the boar become frightened and flee. When a nearby village hears these songs, those villagers interpret the message quickly, and also begin to sing the *muqam* to keep the boar from coming down on them. We say that the *muqam* protects us from the boar—it's a much more effective weapon than guns!

In describing the necessity and utility of the *muqam,* the Dolan suggest the virtues they attribute to their music and their *mäshräp*.

During these festivities, music, song, dance, and entertainment alternate. As has been noted, the entertainments—sometimes parodies, sometimes role-playing games—are an important part of Dolan social life. Through these games, marriage can be proposed ("An Invitation to Tea"), friendship can be declared ("The Whip"), and disputes can be brought into the open and resolved (in imitative skits). The games involve not only the actors but also the spectators, who, as judges and arbiters, are just as important as the disputants.

The Kashgar *muqam* and the Dolan *muqam* represent a significant contrast. It is probably no accident that one belongs to the category of *kilassiki muzika* 'classical music' while the other belongs neither to classical music nor to *xälq nakhshisi* 'popular songs'. Whereas the first is, as we have seen, a form of state-sponsored traditionalism, the second is a form of ritual expression. The first is played, *orunlimaq*; the second is enjoyed, *oynimaq*.

TRANSLATED BY BETH RAPS

REFERENCES

Alibakieva, Tamara. 1986. *Uygurskie Istoritcheskie pesni*. Moscow: Sovietskiy Kompositor.

———. 1988. *On ikki muqam*. Alma Ata: Öner.

Dru, C. Gladney. 1991. "Sedentarization, Socioecology, and State Definition: The Ethnogenesis of the Uighur." In *Rulers from the Steppe: State Formation on the Eurasian Periphery*, ed. G. Seaman and D. Marks, 308–340. Los Angeles: University of Southern California, Ethnographics Press.

During, Jean. 1988. *La musique traditionnelle de l'Azerbayjan et la science des muqams*. Baden-Baden: Valentin Koener.

During, Jean, and Sabine Trebinjac. 1991. *Introduction au muqam ouïgour*. Papers on Inner Asia, no. 17. Bloomington: Indiana University, Research Institute for Inner Asian Studies.

Levin, Theodore. 1996. *The Hundred Thousand Fools of God: Musical Travels in Central Asia (and Queens, New York)*. Bloomington: Indiana University Press.

MacKerras, Colin. 1985a. "Traditional Uygur Performing Arts." *Asian Music* 16:29–58.

———. 1985b. "Uygur Performing Arts in Contemporary China." *China Quarterly* 101:58–77.

Trebinjac, Sabine. 1998. *Le pouvoir en chantant*, Vol. 1. Nanterre: Société d'Ethnologie.

Trebinjac, Sabine, and Jean During. 1990. *Turkestan chinois / Xinjiang, Musiques oïugoures*. Paris, Radio France OCORA C 559092-C 559093. (2 compact disks.)

Muqam in the Tradition of the Uygurs

Anna Czekanowska

The Concept of the Uygur *Muqam*
The Music of the *Muqam*
The *On Ikki* Repertoire
The Sequence of *Muqam*
Terminology
Instruments
Poetry
Sources for the *Muqam*

The Uygurs are among the oldest Turkic-speaking peoples. Uygur culture flourished along the tributaries of the rivers Tarim, Aksu, Yarkand, and Khotan; the most famous cities were Turfan, Kucha, Aksu, and Khotan. As a sedentary people who inhabited oases, the Uygurs were noticed, and their culture was appreciated, by the Chinese; Uygur culture contributed vitally to the development of music in Central Asia, and the Uygurs were active in the transitional trade known, famously, as the Silk Road. (The Silk Road was a caravan route linking China with the West; along this route were carried not only goods—such as silk being brought westward and silver being brought eastward—but also ideas. This ancient road became especially important at the time of Mongol supremacy in the fourteenth century C.E. Recently, it inspired a plan by the United Nations for a trans-Asian passage.)

The first record that may refer to the Uygurs is found on a stele dating from 460 C.E.: a name—*On Oghur* 'Ten Uygurs'—of a confederation of clans, then located in the north. Historians emphasize that the Uygurs are related to the Oghuz people, who in turn were related to the Huns from the Orghon River basin. They established a kingdom along the Orkhon River in the eighth century, but it was overrun by the Kyrgyz in 840. In consequence, the Uygurs migrated southwest, to the Tien Shan mountains. There they formed another independent kingdom in the Turfan region, which was overrun by Mongols in the thirteenth century. The Uygurs had an immense influence on Mongolian culture, and the Mongols adopted Uygur writing derived from Sogdian.

Historically, the Uygurs were shamanists or Buddhists. In the eighth century the upper Uygur classes accepted Manichaeism. In the tenth century the Kashgari Uygurs became Muslims, and Islam increasingly came to dominate the entire Uygur area. Today, the Uygurs are mainly Sunnite Muslims.

At present, there are more than 8 million Uygurs in China, most of them in the Xinjiang Autonomous Uygur Region in China's northwest. About 600,000 Uygurs live in the the post-Soviet republics. In recent history, the Uygurs were organized in small khanates like those of Kashgar, Khotan, and Yarkend. In 1955—six years after the establishment of the People's Republic—the Uygur Autonomous Region was created in China, but this did not imply an independent country. The Uygurs underwent a very difficult period during the Cultural Revolution in China, and their contem-

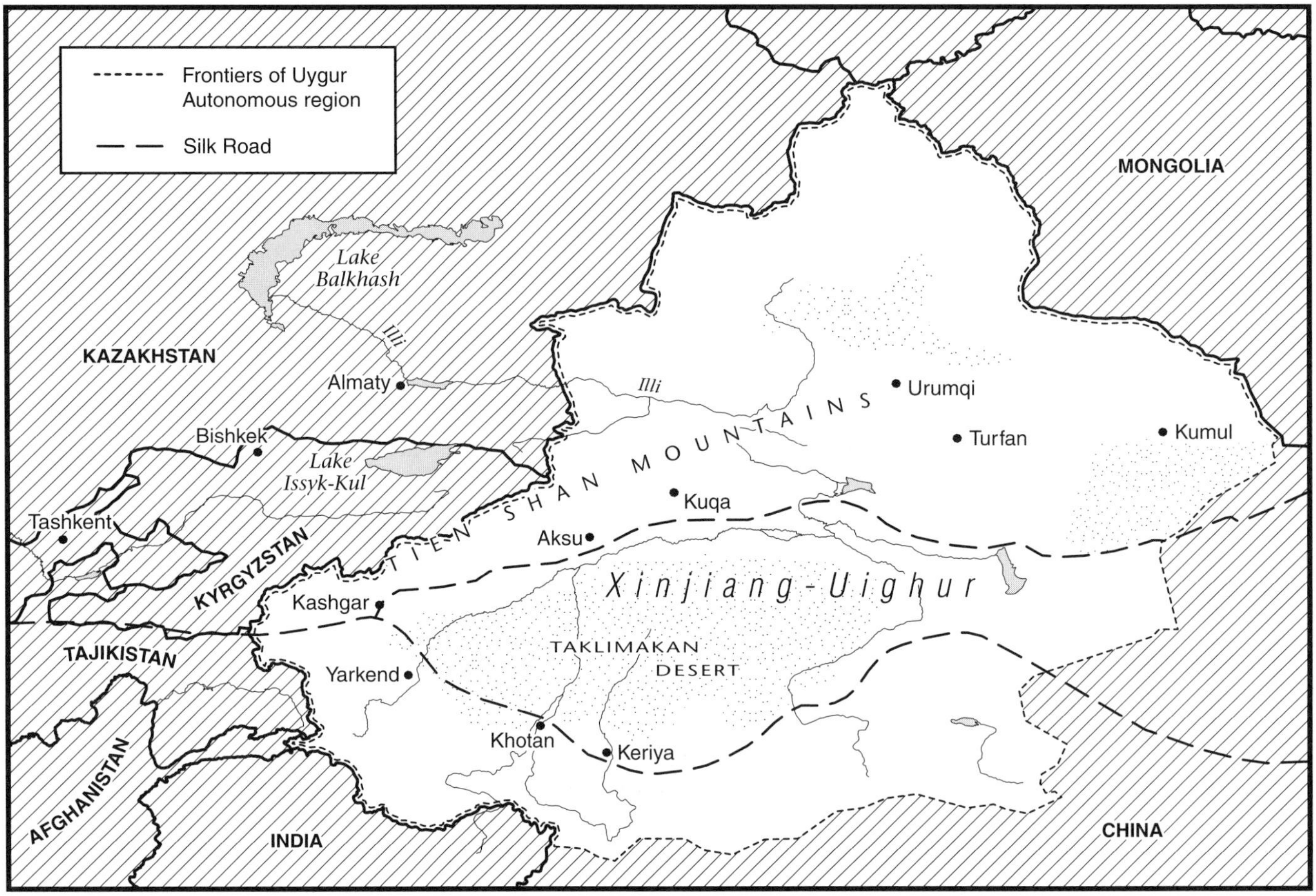

Xinjiang.

porary situation remains difficult. Remarkably, the political frontiers between China and Russia, and then between the Chinese People's Republic and the Soviet Union, did not divide the Uygur people, who have kept in contact with each other—in fact, intermarriages between Uygurs in the Chinese and post-Soviet regions are very popular. This continuing contact has been important for Uygur musical culture and the tradition of the Uygur *muqam*.

Both their history and their music are critical components of the Uygurs' identity. Traditions, whether historical or legendary, handed down from generation to generation form a background that many of them recognize and identify with. The concept of *muqam* called *on ikki* 'twelve' is crucial, helping the Uygurs to maintain a sense of their heritage despite the fact that they live today—as they have lived for hundreds of years—in a diaspora. In seeking to preserve their distinct identity and national awareness, Uygurs, wherever they live, hold fast to the tradition of *muqam*. The classical repertoire of *on ikki* reveals the complexity of Uygur culture, which has absorbed many contributions from other peoples—Persian, Chinese, Turkic, Arab, Indian, Mongol, and more. At the same time, Uygur culture has left its own unique mark on music and *muqam*.

THE CONCEPT OF THE UYGUR *MUQAM*

The term *muqam* as used by the Uygurs refers more to a sequence of pieces than to a mode or modal category. This sequence is comparable to a suite, although the Uygurs do not use that word to describe it.

Muqam may also refer to classical Uygur music and its repertoire in general. The term *on ikki*, which is widely used, indicates the number of *muqam* in the classical repertoire: twelve. The Kashgar Uygurs take pride in having preserved more *muqam* than other Central Asian peoples: the Dolan (who may be of Mongol descent and now speak a dialect of the Uygur language) preserve only nine *muqam*, and the Tadjiks and Uzbeks preserve only six. [See THE CLASSICAL MUSIC OF UZBEKS AND TAJIKS.] Uygur performers and listeners also find a link between the twelve *muqam* and the twelve signs of the zodiac, which is the organizational basis of the Central Asian calendar.

The concept of *muqam* is also applicable to the dramatic sequence within a particular *muqam*. This has to do not only with the order of the sections that make up a *muqam* but also with their character and how they are performed. Every *muqam* must have an introduction in a free rhythm, followed by a series of other sections subdivided into items that are quite diverse in nature and are differentiated by specific names. In Uygur theory, the hierarchy of sections and subsections is not expected to be recognized by performers or listeners; the names of particular items are more important. The complete sequence of *on ikki muqam* may contain as many as thirty items.

Although the number of sections of particular *muqam* varies from region to region, the basic principles of the sequence have much in common. The sections that follow the introduction must be clearly different from it; and the performance changes progressively, following the rhythmic dictates of the poetic text (this principle is called *aruz*) or the rhythm of an accompanying dance, or both. The last two sections should be danced, regardless of the rhythm of the poetic text and independently of the rhythm of certain set dances.

THE MUSIC OF THE *MUQAM*

The Uygur *muqam* differs from its counterparts developed by other Central Asian peoples. It has a more complicated rhythm and a well-developed melody of more than an octave, with many leaps. Perhaps the most original feature of the Uygur *muqam* is its tonal richness and fluidity. The melody continually moves between hepta-, hexa-, and pentatonics, and within each system there are numerous modulations. Another feature of the Uygur *muqam* is its clear construction—its transparent division into sections and subitems.

Differences can also be observed among Uygur traditions in various places: the People's Republic of China, the post-Soviet republics of Kazakhstan and Kyrgyzstan (mainly in Semirechye, a basin of seven rivers in the southeast, between lakes Balkhash and Issyk-Kul), and Uzbekistan. These differences are a result of regional traditions (Kashgar and Illi in the west, Khotan and Dolan in the south, Turfan and Qumul in the east); however, differences in performance usually result from different types of patronage. The tradition that developed in Soviet and post-Soviet Central Asia elaborates the whole cycle, which is usually arranged for large ensembles that were formerly supported by the state. Essentially, this tradition is part of a deliberate revival; nevertheless, it has surprising vitality. In the large ensembles of the post-Soviet regions, different groups of instrumentalists and singers—such as male, female, and mixed voices—are often contrasted, although singing in unison is also typical in large choirs. The Soviet tradition of ensemble performance is clearly influential here, as it also is in performances of *shash maqam* (Levin 1996). Such practices may call to mind modern Chinese performances, although performers and listeners would not say so; in fact, the Soviet and the modern Chinese practices both seem to be an invention of present-day conductors and instructors and have little to do with any early heritage. The tradition preserved by Uygurs living in China seems to be older. This *muqam* is often fragmented and appears today mainly in isolated pieces: in other words, traditional Uygurs in China do not perform developed cycles; their presentations are usually limited to sections of a *muqam* (Swets 1995; Trebinjac and During 1990). But the richness of their rhythm and melody is evidence of a much better preserved tradition.

In studying this music, it is often difficult to confirm information. Local listeners and performers sometimes simply repeat well-known stories about its history. Also, they may relate current musical instruments to instruments described in old sources simply because (as in the case of the lutes *dutar* and *rawap*) contemporary and ancient terms coincide; and it is true that some contemporary instruments are close to those revealed by iconography. All this makes it tempting to assume that the music has not changed, but in reality the sources and musical materials both require detailed examination.

Thus it is not easy to identify Uygur strata in theoretical concepts or terms. The Uygur theory of music is obviously related to the Persian-Arabic tradition. The concept of twelve *muqam* can be traced back to Ṣafī al-Dīn and to ʿAbd al-Qadīr ibn Ghaybī, sometimes also called al-Marāghī. From Central Asia, Abd al-Rahman Djami's treatise has been translated into Russian and is frequently consulted, especially in the former Soviet regions, but *muqam* names cannot be identified accurately from this source. Among the twelve *muqam* from various traditions, similar names do not refer to the same modes.

Still, certain musical principles can be discerned. The most characteristic modal formulas are small and are framed as tetra- or pentachords that are often repeated. These tonal structures often overlap and may be transposed to the fourth or fifth. Depending on the section, the rendition of the melody can be more or less flexible; the most flexible renditions are vocal parts that include chromatic pitches and microtones, *charaki*. (Some vocal sections of the *Chong näghmä*, for instance, require trained professional musicians.) Tonality can also vary by region; *muqam* from post-Soviet Central Asia, for example, have much greater tonal stability.

Rhythmic patterns (*usul*) are strongly affected by the poetic meters (*aruz*). Rhythmic formulas are also very short and are characterized by obvious shifts. The rhythm often involves unequal lengths of 2 and 3, resulting in different combinations such as $3 + 2 = 5$, $3 + 2 + 2 = 7$, and $3 + 2 + 2 + 2 = 9$. Typically, there are many repetitions of rhythmical motives, and a recurring pattern predominates. In rhythm as well as pitch, vocal sections are more variable than instrumental sections.

THE *ON IKKI* REPERTOIRE

The classical *on ikki* repertoire is organized into twelve *muqam* that are related to certain modes. Each mode is considered to have its own ethos; but neither this fact nor the relationship between *muqam* and modes means that a mode will be strictly preserved.

The *on ikki* repertoire is never performed as a whole—that would take too much time. Rather, in principle, performers concentrate on one *muqam*, and often only on chosen sections. Thus the longest performance does not last more than two hours. The contemporary *on ikki*, which is best preserved in the Kashgar version, has the twelve *muqam* listed in figure 1.

With regard to the ethos of *muqam*, there are some differences among performers and scholars. According to Alibakieva (1988), *muqam rak*, *nawa*, *adjam*, and *irak* are very serious and are dedicated to older people whereas *chap-bayat*, *mushavirak*, *pandjgah*, and *bayat* are joyful, optimistic, and dedicated to young people. However, Trebinjac considers *rak* joyful while Khashimov considers it reflective. Trebinjac also gives more precise indications not only about the age of people to whom *muqam* are dedicated but also about gender and status—for example, he describes *rak* as being for single women, *chap-bayat* for young married women, *pandjgah* for young single men, *mushavirak* for young married men, *(a)oshshak* and *chahargah* for orphans and people who are sad, *nawa* for lovers, and *segah* for hermits (1989; interview, 1978; Trebinjac and During 1990). The relationship between age, gender, and mood deserves detailed study.

FIGURE 1 Regional variations of the *muqam* repertoire.

	Kashgar muqam	*Qumul muqam*	*Dolan muqam*	
			Yarkend:	*Aksu:*
1.	*Rak*	*Dur*	*Rak*	*Bash mukam*
2.	*Chap-bayat*	*Udugdur*	*Bom bayavan*	*Bom bayavan*
3.	*Mushavirak*	*Mustazat*	*Zil bayavan*	*Mugal*
4.	*Chahargah*	*Khupti*	*Sim bayavan*	*Sim bayavan*
5.	*Pandjgah*	*Chap-bayat*	*Ozkhal*	*Samuk*
6.	*Ozkhal*	*Mushavirak*	*Djola*	*Djola*
7.	*Adjam*	*Uskhal*	*Mushavirak*	*Chol bayavan*
8.	*Oshshaq*	*Irak*	*Duhamiyat*	*Duhamiyat*
9.	*Bayat*	*Dolan mushavirak*	*Khudak*	*Bayavan*
10.	*Nawa*	*Rak*		
11.	*Segah*	*Chargah*		
12.	*Irak*	*Dugah*		

In addition to the famous *on ikki* known from the Kashgar *muqam*, there is the *on ikki* of the Qumul, which has different *muqam* and changes the classical order (Alibakieva 1988:27). There is also the repertoire of the Dolan, which has only nine *muqam* instead of twelve; this repertoire has two subregional variants: Yarkend and Aksu (figure 1).

THE SEQUENCE OF *MUQAM*

The classical *muqam* (Khashimov 1978) should start with an introduction that is initially in the lower register and in a slow tempo (figure 2). After a short instrumental prelude has been completed, the solo voice starts to present the main melody, which is accompanied by a stringed instrument.

This introduction should be followed by the first section, called *chong näghmä* 'great music'. The first section is the most essential one. It is to be understood as a presentation of many instruments, which are brought in successively. As the section progresses, the rhythm becomes more regular, but changes in the rhythmic pattern still occur.

The second section, *dastan*, is devoted to sung poetry and is often accompanied by dances. The essence of this section is contrast between vocal items (*dastan*) and instrumental elaborations (*märghul*) on the vocal parts. The most characteristic feature of this section is poetic additive rhythm (the *aruz* principle), presented in the vocal items and articulated by a *dap* (a single-headed frame drum). This rhythm contrasts clearly with the rhythm of the instrumental items (*märghul*), which is more standardized. In the *märghul* items the variety of instruments can be very rich (for instance, *nay*, *rawap*, *dutar*, *tämbür*, and *chang*); the melody, too, can be richly ornamented. Contrasts between solo and ensemble items are also very characteristic of this section.

The third and last section, *mäshräp* (or *mäsräp*; the name of a famous Uygur poet who lived from 1641 to 1711), is dominated by a kettledrum and is performed as a dance; it is loud and in a lively tempo. The *mäshräp* dances call for rhythmic sensitivity on the part of the musicians and dancers, although the metric pattern—which is often additive, 7/4—is more stable.

The *muqam* sequence has a definite profile, or dynamics. After the presentation of the melodic and rhythmic models and several repetitions and transformations of their motives, the performance becomes metrical and standardized, driven by a rhythmic pattern that becomes progressively more important. This leads the *muqam* to its *awdj* 'climax', which is reached in the higher register. After the *awdj*, the last melodic formulas appear, returning the *muqam* to its introductory melody. The sequence re-

FIGURE 2 *Muqam rak*, introduction.

turns to the lower register and to a slow tempo, usually performed as a vocal solo accompanied by the lute. The *muqam* has now reached its end.

There are regional differences in the *muqam* sequence. Such differences may depend on the number of climaxes, which in turn depends on performance traditions and on the context. The main question is whether the *chong näghmä* will satisfy the audience's expectations or whether the listeners will expect more—a climax in the *mäshräp* section.

Recent trends indicate that the *chong näghmä* is in decline, whereas the *dastan* and *mäshräp* are more popular. Performances at festivals are usually on a stage and involve mass dancing; such performances can be more or less traditional in character, in accordance with the occasion. In contrast, a more individual performance will concentrate on the substantial sections of the *muqam*. Individual accompanied song and the small ensemble including the *dap* seem to be most deeply rooted in tradition; in this kind of presentation the performer seems relatively independent and does not experience the pressures of a stereotyped group performance.

FIGURE 2 *(continued).*

Today, the classical *muqam* sequence is represented by the Kashgar version. The other regional variants of the sequence are fragmentary, are much shorter, and combine some sections and items differently. The northern *muqam* from the Illi river valley and the Qumul *muqam* are not as well documented historically, but the former seems to be influenced by Transoxania and the latter by the Chinese. The Dolan *muqam* (al-Shukur 1980) have five sections, are very short, and are dominated by dances and songs; the instrumental accompaniment has only a secondary role. The Dolan dances often symbolize hunting [see WHEN UYGURS ENTERTAIN THEMSELVES], ending with a fast round dance in which each dancer spins individually—as in the ritual dances of some Sufi brotherhoods.

TERMINOLOGY

The terminology of the *muqam* indicates how many functions it can have and how many associations it can evoke. This terminology includes simple technical indications such as "to put into order" (at the beginning), "to be on the main stress" (at the end), and starting with one or another fret, but it also suggests many other factors: moods, characteristics, a hierarchy of values (for instance, "doubly important"), geography ("a distant country"), and local concepts of "our own" versus "foreign." It can also reveal the participants' sensitivity, their artistic predispositions, their emotional involvement, and even their personal traits ("small but hard").

Such terminology points up the complexity of the Uygur legacy, and its many ethnic and regional components. A detailed analysis may find characteristics of particular traditions and predispositions to certain moods. Most interestingly, however, an analysis will find a general tendency for a sequence to lead from reflective sections to highly emotional sections and to end with what is expressed as "having enough." One finds this even in Dolan variants, which seem the furthest from the classical sequence of Kashgar *muqam*.

INSTRUMENTS

Contemporary practice features a variety of musical instruments, although some of them (such as the *balaman* and *qalun*) are old and in decline whereas others (such as the *chang*, a struck zither), are newer and appear often. Some instruments are played only in one region (for example, the Qomul *ghijäk*, a cross between the Chinese *erhu* and the Dolan *ghijäk*).

String instruments, and lutes in particular, are important in the *muqam* tradition, as is the *dap* (a one-sided frame drum 25 to 45 centimeters in diameter, with many iron rings played with the fingers). The *dap* is especially important in the *dastan* section, since it articulates the complex additive rhythm.

Lutes are of various kinds: for instance, some have numerous frets whereas the *rawap* is fretless. There may be drone strings (usually tuned down a fourth or fifth) as well as many sympathetic strings. The tuning of these lutes has many details in common, but the differences between instruments are crucial to local musical styles.

The most famous and most traditional lute is the *dutar* 'two strings.' The Uygur *dutar* (figure 3) is long and slender. The classical *dutar* should have silk strings tuned in fourths with frets scaled chromatically.

Another important instrument in the *muqam* tradition is the *tanbur*, which has three melodic strings of copper: the two outer strings are tuned in unison and the middle string is tuned a fourth below them. A skilled performer may produce as many as fourteen scales on this instrument.

The *rawap* appears in several varieties. These are well described by Rachel Harris, a British ethnomusicologist who has been working on music in Xinjiang since 1995.

> The Kashgar *rawap*, at around 90 cm, has a small bowl-shaped body covered with skin and five metal strings, and is decorated with ornamental horns (*möngüz*). The shorter herder's *rawap* (*qoychi rawap*), found in the Khotan region, measures around 70 cm and is strung with two paired or three sheep-gut strings. Both of these types are played by the narrative singers (*dastanchi* and *qoshaqchi*). The Dolan *rawap*, principal instrument in the Dolan muqam, with one melodic and several sympathetic strings and pear-shaped body, resembles the Afghan *rubab* more closely than the Kashgar *rawap*. The Qomul *rawap* is similar to the Dolan version, and is used in folksongs and in the Qumul muqam. The Kashgar *rawap* has more recently become a professional virtuoso solo and orchestral instrument (*täkämmul rawap*) with six metal strings tuned *do-do-sol-re-la-mi*. An equivalent bass *rawap* has also been added to professional orchestras. (Harris, forthcoming).

FIGURE 3 Uygur *dutur*. Photo from Theodore Levin.

The bowed *satar*, played in the introduction of the *muqam*, is a pear-shaped fiddle, quite long, with three strings, two of which are tuned in unison and one a fourth below. This instrument has twelve sympathetic strings. Its relative, the *ghijäk*, a spike fiddle with three metal or gut strings, is tuned in fourths.

A trapezoidal dulcimer called the *chang*, with metal strings that may reach three octaves, has replaced the older *qalon*.

Among the percussion instruments, the *dap* is the most traditional. The kettle-drum *naghra* is also played.

POETRY

Traditional *muqam* texts come from both classical and folk literature and from many Asian peoples. Elements from Persian literature are common in the oldest *muqam* texts, though often transformed or "folklorized." Among the important classic poets is the Persian Nizām al-Dīn Ibn Muḥammad Ilyās Ibn Yusuf (often called Nizami of Ganja). His poems are found throughout the Middle East, often "folklorized"—as in the famous stories *Layla and Majnun* and *Khosrov and Shirin*—and motives from his poetry appear in the Uygur texts.

Turkic poetry is more easily identified. Turkic texts derive from Chagatai and Azeri sources—for instance, the classic poetry of Ali Shir Nawai (b. 1441) and the poems of Seyid Imaddedin Nesimi (d. 1418) and Mehemed bin Suleyman Fuzuli (1495–1556). In folk transmissions, one can find the names of many other poets, such as Khirkati, Bilal Nazim, and Khuveyda.

The poems of the Uygur *muqam* usually have a syllabic structure with a clear concept of the verse. *Murabba*—a stanza consisting of four verses—is a very popular model. Often, a four-verse stanza will have a shorter or longer refrain. Certain rhyme schemes are widely used: for instance, aa, ba, ca; aaab, cccb, ddbb; and abab.

The most respected genre is the *ghazel*, a very short, very graceful love poem of ancient Arab-Persian heritage. In classical literature, it has five to twelve verses; but in Uygur literature it usually has only two. In this simplified Uygur form, the second verse often ends with the same word as the first, giving the effect of a refrain. In the example below (from Ali Shir Nawai, after Alibakieva 1988:89–94), *soran*, which corresponds to certain melodic and rhythmic motives, is used in this way:

Ferdlig zewkini sorman shewketu shah ehlidin
Ul sehbet lezzetin bekhanumanlardin soran.

Adjiz tupraghinda ishk ehlige elgen hekmi bar
Ketl hekmi eyleemekni kehrimanlardin soran.

The greatness of wisdom is unknown to the world of power.
You should turn to the poor people and ask them for help.

The weak people will not survive the experience of love.
Those who are sunk in lies will be lost. You should turn to the brave people.

The poems often use metaphors that make expressions of love and passion very dramatic. Some texts appeal directly to the *ghazel* tradition; an example is the direction "One needs to express *muqam rak* in a *ghazel* form" (Alibakieva 1988). Epic themes and stories of historical heroes are also present. In this poetry, moral judgments and warnings are emphasized; for instance, warnings against treachery, envy, and the limits of trust are very common.

Folk poetry from oral and printed sources is of great importance in *muqam*. One finds fragments of many well-known stories, such as *Farhad and Shirin*, *Yusuf and Ahmet*, *Gharip and Saman*, and *Tahir and Zukhra.* Usually, the name of a poem is that of the hero, or an adjective glorifying the hero: for instance, *Khuveyda* 'the magnificent' (a poet who died in 1780). Such "folklorized" poems are typical in the *dastan* and *mäshräp* sections of *muqam*. Today, more recent folk derivations have become more visible.

SOURCES FOR THE *MUQAM*

Iconography

Many archaeological records confirm a developed musical culture along the tributaries of the Khotan, Aksu, and Yarkend rivers much earlier than the Uygurs' activity can be identified. Beginning in the third century C.E., the culture of the Khotan oases was a base for the development of Uygur traditions, although it is not clear to what extent the Uygurs adopted this ancient culture or brought their own new one (Marco Polo 1954). A fascinating subject for Oriental Studies is the relation between Uygur culture and pre-Islamic cultures that flourished in ancient Iran and India (Sogd, Bactria, and Gandhara).

The iconography comes mainly from ancient sacred places. The oldest is that of the Khotan oases. Terra-cotta figurines indicate a wide range of instruments, especially flutes—there are many depictions of the syrinx, or panpipes (figure 4). A statue of a playing monkey (figure 5) is of special interest because it may be related to the dancing monkeys that became typical in later paintings (sixth to ninth centuries). Wall paintings from the caves of the monastery Ming-oy 'Thousand Caves' (from the year 500; figure 6) document a rich variety of instruments, some very sophisticated. The lutes are quite surprising: we find the *p'ipa-barbat*, *ghijäk*, *'oud*, *dutar*, and *rawap*. Flutes, drums, and dances are also depicted (Karomatov et al. 1987).

FIGURE 4 Panpipes: terra-cotta figurine from the oasis of Khotan, second to third century C.E. (Karomatov et al. 1987, number 174).

FIGURE 5 Monkey playing: figurine from the oasis of Khotan, second to third century C.E. (Karomatov et al.1987, number 183).

Narratives about music

Numerous legends referring directly to music and to *muqam* still exist and are well known to the Uygur people. One example is a story about "singing water" and music lessons:

> Khezr, a friend of God, . . . was the first to know how to sing. He taught what he knew to water, the indispensable source of all life, and water learned how to sing. When the first water-carrier heard the singing, he was charmed by those modulations born of waves, currents, and rapids, and after listening to the music accompanying his steps as he carried endless bucketfuls, he too learned how to sing. Then it was the turn of the mule-drivers to learn when they stopped at the water's edge for their animals to drink. And so, gradually, through water, everyone learned the singing of Khezr. (Trebinjac and During 1990)

Another example is a story about wandering through a labyrinth in order to disclose the secret of *muqam*. According to this legend, playing music and performing *muqam* are like going through a labyrinth of a thousand caves that hide treasures and a mystery (Czekanowska 1983). The present author found that local people relate this abstract legend to the system of caves of the real monastery Ming-oy. The "wanderer"—the participant in *muqam*—should try to discover the treasures of traditional Uygur wisdom, and the performance should help him in this quest. However, the quest is endless: the wanderer comes closer and closer to the truth but can never reach the end, which is complete understanding.

Some legends confirm historical events from the relatively recent past. One example is reminiscent of the story of the labyrinth—this is a popular story about a Russian archaeologist who was making excavations in the Ming-oy monastery and discovered a fresco so beautiful that he was overwhelmed and could work no longer. The next day, when he had recovered enough to return to the site, the lovely painting, except for one small fragment, had disappeared. The scienfic explanation is probably that the fresco was destroyed by its sudden exposure to air; but the local interpretation is that this is a warning against discovering the old sources of Uygur knowledge—a reminder that the search must be endless.

FIGURE 6 Wall painting of deities playing instruments, from the Kucha region, 500 C.E. (Karomatov et al. 1987, number 20).

Legends, and the concepts related to them, may be highly philosophical or very simple, even naive; the coexistence of abstract and simpler concepts suggests how complex and stratified the Uygur tradition is. References to the zodiac occur very frequently in Central Asia; and, as noted above, the twelve *muqam*—*on ikki*—are often linked to the twelve signs of the zodiac. *Muqam* is also sometimes compared to family relationships: "*Muqam* is our mother" or "*Muqam* is our parents" (Trebinjac and During 1990). Some concepts are particularly common—for instance, the idea of "stepping," that is, dancing and playing the *dap*. In this case, stepping may be a metaphor for eternal wandering; or, of course, it may refer to dance steps, to steps in playing the instrument, or to steps in mastering performance skills. Indeed, many legends involve acquiring and perfecting such skills, and this may explain why the *dap* is so highly regarded.

Written sources about *muqam*

Chinese records give the earliest written information about *muqam*. The oldest records (Alibakieva 1988:21) that can be connected to the *muqam* tradition date from the Sui dynasty (589–618) and concern a famous Uygur *p'ipa* player, singer, and theoretician named Sudjup. (It is not clear whether this name can be interpreted as signifying Turkic, or Seljuk, descent; the Seljuk, a Turkic-speaking people, were active in the Kashgar region beginning in the eleventh century, and perhaps earlier.) Chinese sources tell us that other musicians from Kucha were considered highly skilled, among them masters of the flute. There is no doubt that Uygur musicians were highly valued at the Chinese court, because during the reign of the emperor Wen (581–604) a special department (number 6) was created for the music of Kucha. Mantur is one famous musician mentioned in Chinese writings (Ehmet 1983:9).

Very important sources date from the Tang dynasty of 618–907 (al-Shukur 1980). They confirm that Uygur musicians and dancers were active at the Chinese court, and that much attention was paid to pantomime and to dances depicting lions and monkeys, which were called the "great performance" (a term that suggests the concept of "great music"). Some records concern a specific skill—playing an instrument with the fingers while dancing (Alibakieva 1988:22)—and some concern musical genres. According to some scholars, *chong näghmä* may have emerged as early as the eighth century (al Shukur 1980:43–46). There are also indications that during the Tang dynasty (684–712), graphic musical notation was already in use by the Uygur people (Ehmet 1983:9).

Musical instruments are often described in later writings, such as Marco Polo's; and some writings mention dances illustrating hunting, which suggest the Dolan *muqam*.

However, the Uygur *muqam* as such cannot be traced to very old sources, and scholars disagree about later sources, many of which seem to be secondary. Alibakieva (1988)—who is an expert in Russian, Armenian, and Uygur studies—has traced the beginning of the Uygur *muqam* to the tenth to twelfth centuries, if not earlier; but Trebinjac (1989) could not confirm the existence of *muqam* before the fifteenth century. The Persian-Arab history of *muqam* is the most abundant, but it applies to the music of Central Asia as a whole, and so the Uygur tradition is hard to identify. The Turkic version of *muqam* seems to be closer to that of Uygurs. Local sources (Ehmet 1983) confirm the existence of *muqam* in the sixteenth century—in particular, the activity of famous musicians from the Yarkend and Aksu regions and of Yusuf Kidirkhan Yarkendi, the creator of *muqam wisal* in the Dolan repertoire (Alibakieva 1988).

The history of the Uygur music and *muqam* in the nineteenth and twentieth centuries was well documented by historians of the time, especially Russian historians. These scholars focus on rhythmic factors and on the function of the *dap* in the mastery of "stepping."

Uygur scholars have made important contributions in recent years (Alibakieva 1988; Ehmet 1980; Khashimov 1978, 1981; Molla 1980; al-Shukur 1980), recounting in detail the activities of many musicians. They have noted, for instance, that many musicians took their names from their instruments—famous examples are Abd al Mulla Dombak at the turn of the nineteenth century and Rosi Tambir (1900–1957). Uygur authors also describe the emergence of new *muqam* in the present day: for example, in the 1940s, *muqam rukhshara* (composed by Zikri Alpitaev) and a new version of *yarkend* (composed by Nurmukh-Zammet). In interviewing musicians, one may sometimes receive the impression that they are unsure of the historical names of the *maqam* they play and thus come up with new names; however, the newly composed *muqam* are quite different from those in historical sources—and the creation of these new versions indicates the continuing vitality of the tradition.

Transcriptions and sound recordings

In performance as well, the *muqam* of today is different from the historical *maqām*, as can be seen by comparing contemporary recordings with recordings of only fifty years ago.

Transcriptions of *muqam* from folk traditions were first made in the 1950s. The classical Kashgar cycle was recorded by the ethnographer Van Tunshi in Urumchi, as performed by Rosi Tambir and the *satar* player Turdi Ak Hun al-Nagma (1881–1956). The Dolan *muqam* was recorded in 1956 by the Russian linguist Eduard Tenishev in the village of Tuvenki, with the help of a local informant, Mezmet Nyaz Memet.

The Kashgar *muqam* was published in Beijing in 1961 as *Uyghur Khelik Klassik Muzikisy: On Ikki Muqam*, in two volumes in Chinese and Uygur but without the poetic text. Two volumes of *on ikki* in the Uygur language were published in 1971 and 1987 in Alma-Aty. In the 1970s, the Soviet record company, Melodiya, started to record all twelve *on ikki muqam*. In 1988 Tamara Alibakieva published a volume on *muqam rak* and *muqam chap-bayat*, with commentary in Uygur and Russian and with musical transcriptions; this material corresponds to what was recorded by Melodiya and performed mainly in Soviet and post-Soviet Central Asia.

In 1990, Sabine Trebinjac and Jean During released two compact disks of Uygur music from China, with excellent commentary and samples of analysis (descriptions

Muqam is sometimes compared to family relationships: "*Muqam* is our mother" or "*Muqam* is our parents."

of scales and rhythmic patterns). In 1994 the whole *on ikki* was released in Urumchi on twenty-four cassettes. The musical notation and texts were published in twelve volumes in 1994. In 1995, Wouter Swets released a record of an Uygur ensemble, and another recording was released in 2001 by Globestyle.

Muqam as practiced by the Uygurs today has a dual purpose—individual and social. It is meant to support the Uygur identity and the political struggle for independence.

The contemporary changes in *muqam* necessitate changes in cultural policy. Cultural institutions of the recent past, exemplified by radio and festival ensembles, are being questioned and have a doubtful future. For instance, the famous ensemble Nawa (named for *muqam nawa*) of the Uygur Theater in Almaty no longer exists, nor does the Uygur Radio Ensemble in Tashkent. It is true that audiences are still interested in preserving this kind of staged performance. It is also true that during the Cultural Revolution in China, when Uygur music was banned, the Soviet Union continued to actively support this music, and its support was welcomed by Uygurs on both sides of the border. Today, however, the former patronage has been altered, and people are looking for new initiatives, often commercial. Examples include music ensembles that travel abroad to give concerts and release recordings (Swets 1995).

Pride in national music, and historical awareness of such music, can be a part of national consciousness. Thus the Uygurs are proud of preserving their rich *muqam* and of perfecting their musical skills. Globalization presents a constant danger of cultural dilution; but it is still virtually impossible to imagine an Uygur who does not recognize *muqam* as his or her own music.

Note: The author gratefully acknowledges the help and advice of Mrs. Ania Bylińska, Mr. Mir Younes Naderi, and Dr. Rachel Harris.

REFERENCES

Alibakieva, Tamara. 1988. *On ikki muqam* (The Twelve *Muqam*). Alma Ata: Oner.

Arshidinov, Batur, ed. 1987. *On ikki muqam.* Alma Ata: Zhazushy.

Czekanowska, Anna. 1983. "Aspects of the Classical Music of Uyghur People: Legend versus Reality." *Asian Music* 14(1):41–93.

During, Jean, and Sabine Trebinjac. 1991. *Introduction au muqam ouigour*. Papers on Inner Asia, no. 17, Central Asia. Bloomington: Indiana University, Research Institute for Inner Asian Studies.

Dvenadtsat uygurskikh mukamov (The Twelve Uygur *Muqam*). 1983–1986. Tashkent: Melodya Records, S-30. (LP disks.)

Ehmet, Hadji. 1983. *Deniz Unchirili*. Keshker.

Harris, Rachel. 1998. Music, identity and persuasion: Ethnic minority music in Xinjiang, China. Ph.D. diss., London University.

———. 2001. "Cassettes, Bazaars and Saving the Nation: The Uyghur Music Industry in Xinjiang, China." In Tim Craig and Richard King, eds., *Global Goes Local: Popular Culture in Asia.* Vancouver: University of British Columbia Press.

———. 2001. "Wang Luobin: 'Folksong King of the Northwest' or Song Thief? Copyright, Representation and Chinese 'Folksongs'." In Kevin Latham and Stuart Thompson, eds., *Consuming China: Approaches to Cultural Change in Contemporary China.* London: Curzon Press.

———. Forthcoming. "Music of the Uyghurs." In *Project Turk*. Istanbul: Yeni Turkiye.

Iunosov, Ravshan. 1992. *Makomy i mugamy: K tipologii zhanrov uzbekskoi i azerbaidzhanskoi professional'noi monodii*. Tashkent: Izd-vo "Fan" Akademii nauk Respubliki Uzbekistan.

Jami, Abd al-Rahman. 1960. *Traktat o Muzyke*, trans. V. M. Beliaeva. Tashkent: Izd-vo Akademii nauk Uzbekskoi S.S.R.

Kakuk, S. 1972. "Chants ouïghours de Chine." *Acta orientalia academiae scientiarum hungaricae* 25:415–429.

Karomatov, Faizulla, V. A. Meskeris, and Tamara Vyzgo. 1987. *Musikgeschichte in Bildern*, Band II, Lieferung 9. Leipzig: Deutscher Verlag für Musik.

Khashimov, Abd al-Aziz. 1978. "Structure du *muqam* ouïghour et les conditions de sa préservation." In *Mâqams, mugams, et composition contemporaine*, 130–138. Tashkent.

———. 1981. "Dvenadcat' Uygurskikh *Muqamov*." In *Professyonalnaya Muzyka Ustnoy Tradicy Blizhnego i Srednego Vostoka i Sovremennost*, ed. Faizulla Karomatov. Tashkent.

Levin, Theodore. 1996. *The Hundred Thousand Fools of God: Musical Travels in Central Asia (and Queens, New York)*. Bloomington: Indiana University Press.

Light, Nathan. 1998. Slippery paths: The performance and canonization of Turkic literature and Uyghur muqam song in Islam and modernity. Ph.D. diss., Indiana University.

Muhämmät, Imin Abduşukur. 1980. *Uyğur xälk kilassik muzikisi 'on ikki muqam' häqqidä* (The Twelve *Muqam*: Classical Music of the Uygur People). Urumqi: Millätlär Năshriyati.

Mackerras, Colin. 1985. "Traditional Uygur Performing Arts." *Asian Music* 16:29–58.

Molla, Majlesi Mulla binni. 1980. *Tavarikhi Musiyunn*. Urumqi.

Polo, Marco. 1954. *Opisanie Œwiata*, ed. A. L. Czerny. Warsaw.

———. 1986. *The Book of Ser Marco Polo*. New York: AMS.

Roberts, Sean. 1978. "Negotiating Locality, Islam, and National Culture in a Changing Borderlands: The Revival of the *Mäshräp* Ritual Among Young Uighur Men in the Ili Valley." *Central Asian Survey* 17(4):672–700.

al-Shukur, Muhammet Iamin Abd. 1980. *Shinzhannin Tan devridiki naksha-usul se'iti*. Urumqi.

Swets, Wouter. 1995. *Songs and Melodies of the Uygurs*. PAN Records 2027. (Compact disk with liner notes.)

Tongshu, Wan, ed. 1960. *On ikki muqam/Shi'er mukamu* (The Twelve *Muqam*). Beijing.

———. 1985. *Weiwuer zu yueqi* (Musical Instruments of the Uygurs). Urumqi.

Trebinjac, Sabine. 1989. "Musique ouïghoure de Chine: De l'authenticité à la folklorisation." In *Actes du Colloque ESCAS*. 3, *L'Asie Centrale et ses voisins: Paris, 1989*, 227–238. Paris: INALCO.

———. 1995. "Femme, seule et venue d'ailleurs: Trois atouts d'un ethnomusicologue au Turkestan chinois." *Cahier de Musiques Traditionnelles* 8:59–68.

Trebinjac, Sabine. 2000. *Le pouvoir en chantant: l'art de fabriquer une musique chinoise*. Nanterre: Société d'ethnologie.

Trebinjac, Sabine, and Jean During. 1990. *Turkestan Chinois/Xinjiang Musiques Ouigoures*. AIMP/OCORA Records, C 559092-3. (2 compact disks with liner notes.)

Uyğur kilasik muzikisi: Qumul muqamliri (Uygur Classical Music: The Qumul *Muqam*). 1994. Beijing. (Includes 10 cassette tapes.)

Uyğur on ikki muqam (The Uygur Twelve *Muqam*). 1994. Urumqi.

Uyghur Khelik Klassik Muzikisi—On ikki muqam. 1959, 1960. 2 vols. Beijing.

Section 9
Israel

Section 9
Israel

Constituted primarily by waves of immigrants beginning in the nineteenth century, Israeli society is an amalgam of peoples and cultures from Europe, Africa, North and South America, and Asia. Amateur and professional musicians came to Israel bringing musical instruments, skills, and ideas. There they variously created an Israeli musical culture and re-created the cultures of the lands from which they had come. Musical articulations of social identity range from symphony orchestras and chamber music groups begun by European Jews and sustained internationally by generations of Israeli virtuosos to new, westernized Israeli rock to the Mediterranean pop tunes of *mizraḥi* Jews from Arab lands. Israel is home to master musicians of the Iraqi *maqām*, the Bukharan *shashmaqam*, and the Persian classical *radīf*. Its musical religious practices include several systems for the cantillation of holy texts, impassioned Hasidic improvisations, and lively hymns (*piyutim*) often drawing from contrafacta melodies.

Within this rich mix of expression, the creation of new, native Israeli folk songs was encouraged by governmental agencies after the establishment of the state in 1948. Army entertainment troupes, local community organizations, and others produced a stream of song—printed, recorded, broadcast, and live. They created genres and styles indigenously Israeli.

The multiple musical styles that exist today in Israel reveal the complexity of the culture. Musical performance projects numerous, sometimes contested, identities that in turn form part of a broader discourse on the nature of Israeli society.

Tel Aviv, Israel.
Photo Researchers, Inc.
© Louis Goldman.

Israel: An Overview

Edwin Seroussi

Historical Background
Music in Israel
Traditional Music of Ethnic Communities
Israeli Folk Song
Popular Music
Music of Non-Jewish Communities

The complex web of Israeli society and culture and the cultural ideology of Zionism are reflected in the music of the country. Since the beginnings of the modern Jewish colonization of Palestine, attempts were made to forge a new identity through musical expression. In the early period of statehood, the support of musical performance, composition, dissemination, and education was in the hands of governmental agencies and thus was controlled by the political and cultural elite. This control by the establishment gradually weakened, particularly following the decentralization of the mass media in the early 1980s.

HISTORICAL BACKGROUND

The state of Israel is an outgrowth of complex political, social, and cultural processes among the Jewish people since the nineteenth century. Its roots are found in the latent religious longing for a return to Zion after two millennia of exile, in the influence of the Enlightenment on European Jews since the second half of the eighteenth century, and in the subsequent adoption by Jewish intellectuals in the nineteenth century of the concept of "nation" as a political entity with defined territorial boundaries as a solution to the particular Jewish existence in the diaspora. These developments offered a new option for solving the Jewish "problem": a secular national identity that would displace religious observance as the sole basis of Jewish identity. Specifically, secular Jewish intellectuals founded the Zionist movement, which held its first congress in Basel in 1897. This political movement aimed at establishing a Jewish state in Palestine (other places, such as Uganda and Argentina, were also considered). The success of the Zionist movement in achieving its goals cannot be detached from major historical events, such as the colonialist policies of the European powers in the Middle East (particularly Great Britain and France) after the dismemberment of the Ottoman Empire and, later, the Holocaust in Europe.

From the last two decades of the nineteenth century to 1948, the Jewish colonization of Palestine under Zionist ideology was characterized by waves of immigrants (*'aliyot* in Hebrew). The earliest *'aliyot* (c. 1900–1935) were Eastern European (Ashkenazi) Jews (mainly from Russia, Ukraine, Poland, Romania, and Hungary); later immigrants came from Germany. Small contingents of Sephardi and Oriental Jews

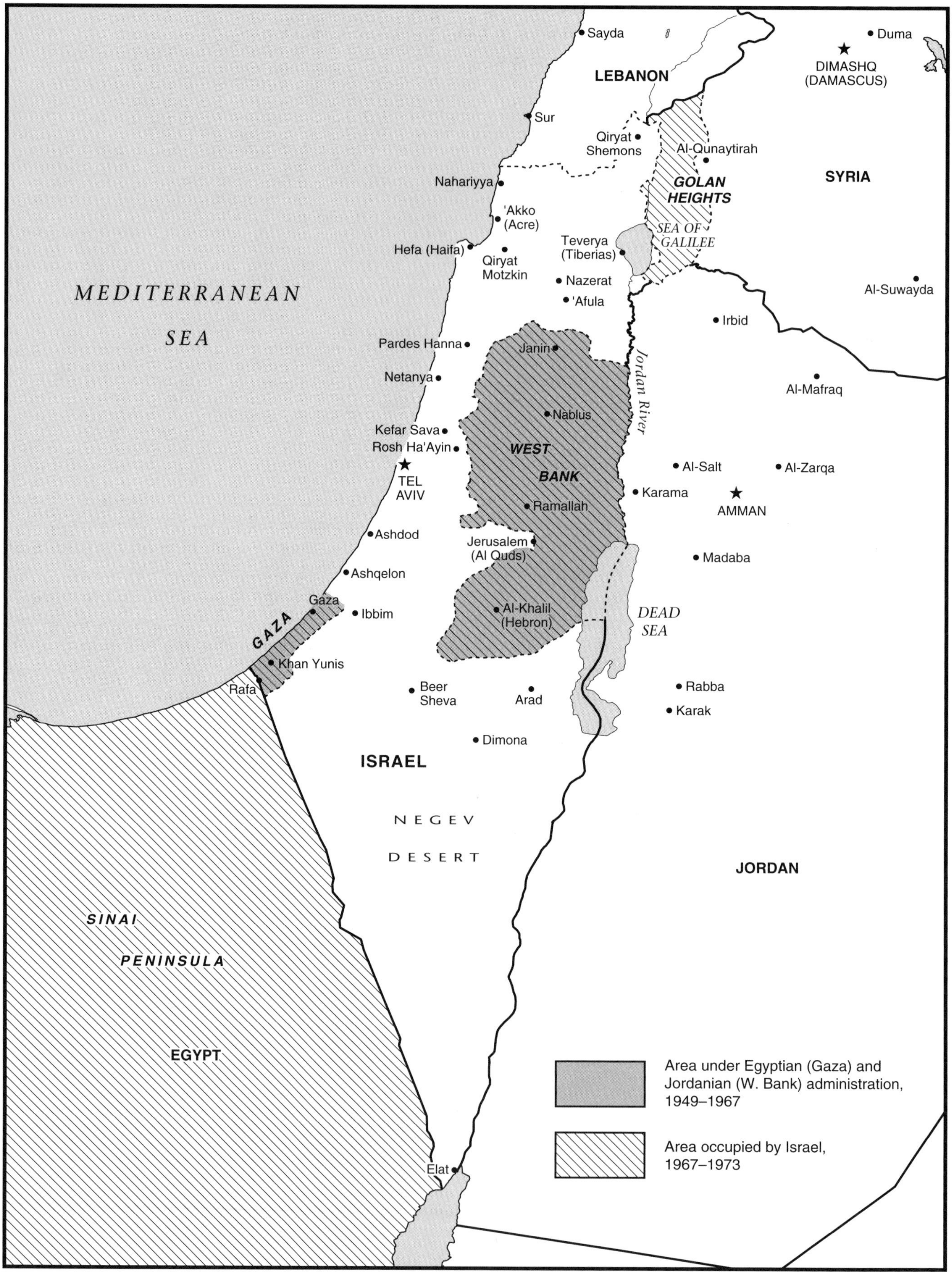

Sayda
Duma
DIMASHQ
(DAMASCUS)
LEBANON
Sur
Qiryat
Shemons
Al-Qunaytirah
SYRIA
Nahariyya
GOLAN
HEIGHTS
'Akko
(Acre)
Teverya
(Tiberias)
SEA OF
GALILEE
Hefa (Haifa)
Qiryat
Motzkin
MEDITERRANEAN
SEA
Nazerat
'Afula
Al-Suwayda
Irbid
Pardes Hanna
Janin
Netanya
Jordan River
Al-Mafraq
Nablus
Kefar Sava
Rosh Ha'Ayin
WEST
BANK
TEL
AVIV
Al-Salt
Al-Zarqa
Karama
AMMAN
Ramallah
Ashdod
Jerusalem
(Al Quds)
Madaba
Ashqelon
Gaza
Ibbim
Al-Khalil
(Hebron)
DEAD
SEA
GAZA
Khan Yunis
Rafa
Beer
Sheva
Arad
Rabba
Karak
Dimona
ISRAEL
NEGEV
DESERT
JORDAN
SINAI
PENINSULA
EGYPT
Area under Egyptian (Gaza) and Jordanian (W. Bank) administration, 1949–1967
Area occupied by Israel, 1967–1973
Elat

Israel.

from Islamic countries (Yemen, Persia, Bukhara, Morocco) and from Turkey, Greece, and Bulgaria arrived during the same period.

Zionism aroused the opposition of the Arab population of Palestine; after the 1920s, this opposition developed into a national conflict between Jews and Arabs. The decision of the United Nations on 29 November 1947 to partition Palestine into two states, one Jewish and one Arab, was not accepted by the Arab states (themselves emerging from the bonds of European colonialism). This rejection launched a war known in Israel as the War of Independence. The State of Israel was declared on 14 May 1948. Thereafter, major waves of immigration arrived from Islamic countries (Iraq, Iran, Syria, Yemen, North Africa) in the 1950s and from the Soviet Union, Eastern Europe, and Ethiopia from the 1960s until the present.

The Arab-Israeli conflict remained a permanent aspect of Israel's existence. Large Palestinian Arab (Muslim and Christian) and Druze minorities remained within the boundaries of Israel and became citizens of the state. In the aftermath of the Six-Day War (June 1967), Israel controlled a larger Palestinian population in the West Bank and the Gaza Strip. Following the Oslo accords of 1993, these territories were supposed to gradually disengage from Israel to become the Palestinian Authority.

The continuous stream of Jewish immigrants and the Arab-Israeli conflict are two keys to understanding present-day Israeli society and its culture. A native Jewish population, the Israelis, emerged out of the Eastern European Jews who laid down the basis for the state. The "Israeli" was conceived of as a "new" Jew, or *tsabar* (literally a type of cactus; this was a metaphor for native Israelis used by their own immigrant parents): secular, a speaker of modern Hebrew, and identified with Western values (particularly socialism).

The Zionist immigrants from Eastern Europe dominated the political, economic, and cultural infrastructure of the emerging state. They tried to "homogenize" the influx of immigrants from Islamic countries by introducing them, through the educational system, to the core values of secular Zionism. The chief concept used to describe this process was *mizug galuyot* 'ingathering of the exiles', the Israel version of the American "melting pot."

The cultural hegemony of the Zionist establishment has been challenged since the early 1970s, when issues such as ethnic diversity, socioeconomic disparities, and the role of religion in the state became contentious among different strata of Israeli society. Resistance to traditional "Israeliness" led to a more heterogeneous society. Today, Israelis define "belonging" in terms of ethnic or national origins (particularly among immigrants from the former Soviet Union in the 1990s), degree of allegiance to religious observance, and socioeconomic status rather than in terms of the traditional Zionist ethos and symbolism.

As noted above, the center of modern Israeli culture was the idea of a "new" Jew, exempted from the duties of religious observance, a worker on the simultaneously old and new land, and responsible for his or her own physical survival. A major factor in the formation of this culture is the renaissance of the Hebrew language as a means of creating a new reality symbolically linked to the biblical Jewish kingdom. The "new" Jew is, in sum, a cultural construct that is the antithesis of what Zionists perceived as the "diasporic" Jew.

Implied in the idea of the "new" Jew is the creation of a new culture, in two senses: the invention of a corpus of "cultural assets" (a new language, new songs, a new literature and theater, a new mythology, and so on) and the establishment of social networks and institutions to articulate, support, promote, and apply these assets. In spite of efforts to separate "Israeli" culture from past Jewish bonds, the relations between the new culture and the diasporic Jewish legacy and psyche remain complex even today.

The music of Israel involves controversy between different perceptions of "Israelness."

MUSIC IN ISRAEL

The variety of music in Israel is a result not only of the diverse Jewish ethnicities that gathered in the new state but also of the fact that the new society included different types of settlements, each with a distinctive musical life. Modern urban centers (particularly Tel Aviv), agricultural settlements (*moshav*), collective farms (*kibbutzim*), and peripheral "development towns" (*'ayyarot pituaḥ*) developed their own musical repertoires and activities, such as satirical cabaret, dance halls, and a network of educational and performing institutions of art music in the large cities; communal folk singing and small communal orchestras in the agricultural settlements; and traditional ethnic music in developmental towns consisting mostly of immigrants from Islamic countries.

The music of Israel, then, involves controversy between different perceptions of "Israeliness." The struggle for local identity is reflected in the different fields of musical creativity and activity. We can distinguish four such fields: the traditional music of ethnic communities (Jewish and non-Jewish), Israeli folk song, Israeli popular music, and Western art music.

TRADITIONAL MUSIC OF ETHNIC COMMUNITIES

Each Jewish community of the diaspora that immigrated to Israel brought its musical culture. A clear line must be drawn between the music of European (Ashkenazi) and non-European Jews. In the context of Israel, "ethnic" music means the music of the Jews from Islamic countries (and lately from Ethiopia as well). Since the founders of "Israeli" culture were Ashkenazi Jews, there is a commonsense identification of mainstream Israeli music with Western secular music (art and popular). "Ethnic" music connotes "otherness," usually, if not always, equated with the term *mizraḥi* 'Oriental'. This perception is now being contested, however. For example, in studies of the music of the synagogue, the concept of "ethnic" music is also applied to Ashkenazi communities.

A distinction should be made between urban and rural Jewish communities from Islamic countries. Jews from large cities (such as Teheran, Baghdad, Aleppo, Istanbul, Tunis, and Marrakech) were proficient in the styles of the "great" pan-Islamic art music traditions such as the Persian *dastgah*, the Azeri *mugham*, the Iraqi *maqām*, the Turkish *makam*, and the Andalusian *āla* from the Maghrib. Jews from small villages in the Atlas Mountains, the Eastern and Northern Caucasus, or Yemen brought with them more rural music traditions.

The fate of the different musical repertoires within each community varied. Undoubtedly, the main context for the continuity of Jewish ethnic music traditions in
TRACK 11 Israel is the synagogue (figure 1). The synagogue was the center of communal affairs in the diaspora until the middle of the nineteenth century in Europe, and until the emigration to Israel in the Islamic countries. In Israel it became exclusively a house of prayer with an identity derived from the ethnic origin of the majority of the congregation or from the musical style imposed by its leaders. This identity can be clear

FIGURE 1 Bar mitzvah in an Israeli synagogue. Photo from Edwin Seroussi.

or vague, depending on the location of the synagogue and on local demographics. There is, however, an ongoing process of homogenization in synagogue music, whereby dominant styles prevail over local traditions. The "Sephardi-Jerusalemite" style, based on the application of the Syrian-Egyptian *maqām* system to the Jewish liturgy, now dominates most synagogues of "Oriental" Jews in Israel. Still, some local styles can be heard in the synagogues of Yemenite and North African Jews. A similar process occurred in the synagogues of the Ashkenazi "national-religious" sector (Zionist orthodox Jews), which developed a style known as *nussaḥ eretz Yisrael* 'the tradition of the land of Israel'.

Songs associated with the life cycle—particularly with weddings—changed dramatically, although some traditional songs may have survived in new contexts alongside adopted repertoires. For instance, a small community of Jews from Haban, Yemen, was able to preserve substantial sections of its wedding repertoire while also adopting modern "Oriental" Israeli and "Hasidic" popular songs (Shay 1998). But this example is the exception rather than the rule. Larger ethnic communities, which were dispersed throughout Israel, were unable to maintain their traditional paraliturgical and secular repertoires. Entire repertoires, particularly women's songs in Jewish vernaculars—dialects such as Judeo-Spanish and Judeo-Arabic—disappeared or were utterly transformed into styles of popular music that appealed to large "nonethnic" audiences. This is true of songs in Judeo-Spanish (generically known as *romansot sefaradiyot*) that became popular in the 1960s (Seroussi 1996); it is also true of songs in Morrocan Judeo-Arabic revived by rock bands whose members were second- or third-generation immigrants from Morocco.

In most of their countries of origin, Jews from the Islamic world excelled in instrumental music. Some of their instrumental styles were pervasive in cafés and at private parties during the first years of immigration (the 1950s and 1960s). When Iraqi Jewish musicians, who had been outstanding performers in Iraq, came to Israel in the 1950s, they were engaged by the "Oriental music" orchestra of the Israel Broadcasting Authority. In more recent years, both the political and the cultural interests of Moroccan Jews (figure 2), the largest "ethnic" community in Israel, promoted the founding of an Israeli Andalusian orchestra. This organization presents traditional Moroccan art music in a new format—the symphony orchestra. Interestingly, it employs many Soviet Jewish immigrant musicians. In the 1990s, a large number of

FIGURE 2 Moroccan Jews singing and playing *'ud* and *tar* outside the tomb of Baba Sali during the remembrance of the anniversary of his death, Netivot, Israel. Photo from Edwin Seroussi.

professional Jewish musicians arrived from the eastern Caucasus and Central Asia; several ensembles playing instrumental music from these areas are now active in Israel. The instrumental music of Ashkenazi Jews, *klezmer* music, also continued in Israel, especially at national-religious and orthodox non-Zionist weddings. A local *klezmer* tradition developed that can be distinguished from its Eastern European and American counterpart (Mazor 2000). *Klezmer* music is seldom discussed in writings about Israeli music, because many European Jewish scholars are biased against perpetuating "diasporic" music in the modern state.

The continuance of ethnic musical traditions and the processes of change that these traditions underwent in the new context were related to complex, dynamic social and cultural variables (Shiloah and Cohen 1983). The interaction of different Jewish ethnic communities in Israel created an unprecedented situation in Jewish musical culture. Among its results, one may cite crossovers between Jewish ethnic styles, the standardization of ethnicity (such as the perception of a single "Yemenite" Jewish music, which obliterates distinctions between local Yemenite communities), and the transformation of traditional music into popular styles.

ISRAELI FOLK SONG

The main musical enterprise of the Zionist movement was to create a native Israeli folk song. Three terms—*shirei erets Yisrael* 'songs of the land of Israel'; *ha-zemer ha-'ivri* 'Hebrew song'; and *ha-shir ha-Ysraeli* 'Israeli song'—are used to describe "the folk song of the new Jewish society that came into being in the Land of Israel from the 1880s onwards" (Bayer 1980). Though frequently interchanged, these terms denote particular ways of perceiving this music. Only the first term, *shirei erets Yisrael*, is used today by the Israeli media and scholars of popular music. It defines a specific repertoire of songs in modern Hebrew that was canonized, particularly by being included in songbooks published by cultural institutions of the political establishment. Thus "folk" and "popular" music are intermingled to such an extent that it is difficult to distinguish between them. [See Popular Music in Israel.]

A unique characteristic of this "folk" song is its creation by composers. According to Shahar, "the song [is categorized] as having been created within the framework of the Zionist establishment, or at least with the intention of establishment acceptance" (1990:v–vi).

Shirei erets Yisrael is an amorphous repertoire of songs in different styles. It has its origins in Russian ballads and Eastern European songs brought by the founders of Israeli society in the first half of the twentieth century. Other songs germinated in the satirical theaters that entertained the young Jewish community between the late 1920s and the 1950s. The same composers who wrote for those theaters also wrote for the army entertainment troupes created during and after the War of Independence (Ne'eman 1980).

The lyrics of *shirei erets Yisrael* generally treat the landscape of Israel, the ethos of defending the state, and themes related to agriculture. The arrangements tend to be acoustic, accompanied by accordion or guitar. The repertoire is performed on ceremonial occasions or in *shirah betsibur* 'communal singing', a format (perhaps unique to Israel) in which the audience gathers in a club or recreation center to sing texts projected on a screen or distributed on paper (Eliram 1995).

Shirei erets Yisrael symbolizes patriotism and national consensus. Its social connotations are clear: this genre is a musical reflection of the ethos of Jewish society in Palestine, including elements from several historical eras and from both rural and urban experiences, and sublimating all the values venerated by the majority. However, it is difficult if not impossible to single out any structural, melodic, harmonic, or rhythmic characteristic common to all of *shirei erets Yisrael.*

One finds a complex relationship between written and oral transmission in this repertoire. What was created and accepted by the establishment of the Yishuv (and thereafter by musicologists) as "folk" has characteristics of what became known as state-sponsored "popular" music at the beginning of the twentieth century. This is particularly true of the composition, recording, and distribution in written form of songs by known composers. Although the printed songbooks could be considered a kind of sheet music, most of these composed folk songs were transmitted orally through communal singing. Real folk songs—by anonymous composers, transmitted orally with many variants, and based on several sources and styles—were written down and printed by the publishers of songbooks alongside composed songs.

Shirei erets Yisrael is thus a bridge between "composed" and "real" folk songs, and it came to constitute a specific category of popular music when a recording industry developed in Israel. The first collection of songs was recorded around 1933 by Avah, a pioneering but short-lived record company in Tel Aviv. Its title was *Mi-shirei Erets Israel* 'From the *Shirei Erets Yisrael.* As early as it is, this recorded collection reflects a complex musical scene. It includes composed folk songs, Hebrew versions of Yiddish folk songs, songs with religious content, and—significantly—cabaret songs. Stylistically, these songs draw on different sources, ranging from the dominant Russian style of the composed folk songs to the international styles of the 1930s adapted for Hebrew texts, such as Argentine tangos and foxtrots promoted by gramophones, radio, and motion pictures.

The new additions to the repertoire after the 1940s are songs related to the War of Independence (1948–1949), songs of the army entertainment groups of the 1950s, and songs in the international styles in vogue among the bourgeoisie. An early pamphlet dated 1951 consisting of texts of songs recorded by the popular singer Israel Itzhaki includes guarachas, boleros, slow-fox, tango, swing, beguine, waltz, samba, and a Romanian doina. In the mid-1950s songs by young Israeli-born composers such as Nahum Heiman and Naomi Shemer were added to the repertoire.

Shirei erets Yisrael is not a category of songs but an ongoing process through which music from different sources became a symbol of the collective historical consciousness and experience of Israeli society. This memory is rooted in the old Yishuv, was reinforced during the War of Independence, and took its present shape during statehood.

FIGURE 3 Selling music cassettes at an improvised stand, Netivot, Israel. Photo from Edwin Seroussi.

POPULAR MUSIC

The growth of large cities (Tel Aviv and Haifa) and the immigration of professional musicians from Poland and Germany led to the opening of musical theaters and cabarets where contemporary European songs were sung to Hebrew texts. The popular music industry was launched in the mid-1930s when a record company and a radio station opened in Palestine.

Until the 1970s, popular music was dominated by state-controlled cultural policies and mass media. The Israel Defense Forces were entertained by *lehakot tseva'iyot*, ensembles consisting of ten to fifteen young soldiers: singers and comedians coached by civilian artists who combined "native" elements with international popular styles such as swing jazz. The arrangements were based on group singing with short solos, accompanied by accordion and Arab tambourine. These entertainers' songs became widely popular through long-playing records and radio broadcasts. By the 1970s the distinction between military and civilian artists had been blurred, and artists of the Israeli Defense Forces became stars. This period also saw duos and trios, accompanied by acoustic instruments, who performed intimate songs called *pizmonim* or *shirei meshorerim* 'songs of the poets'. *Pizmonim* stressed individual urban experiences rather than collective agricultural themes. The performers expanded their repertoire to include Hebrew versions of French *chansons* and Greek pop songs. Despite the "mobilized" character of popular music at this time, international trends were apparent. Singers recorded and performed to the accompaniment of "jazz" ensembles in diverse styles, such as Latin American. The "light music" orchestra of Israel Radio contributed to this trend.

In response to foreign influences, the Israeli Song Festival was established by Israel Radio on Independence Day in 1960. The festival, modeled on European song festivals such as the San Remo Festival, included original solo songs accompanied by orchestral arrangements. Its goal was to encourage an "Israeli" style of popular music, but it faded away after 1970 when that goal became obsolete.

The 1960s saw the rise of Greek popular songs in Hebrew. These "Greek" songs were actually combined with ethnic Jewish and particularly Yemenite traditions, and they contained the seeds of a confrontation between popular music sanctioned by the establishment and non-Western styles. This music later became known as *muzika mizraḥit*. The democratization of the recording industry after the introduction of the cassette in 1972 had a revolutionary effect because it allowed the dissemination of the *mizraḥi* style on the fringes of the "official" music industry (figure 3). Socially, this style is identified with the working class. Despite its marginal status, *muzika mizraḥit* produced some performers who were major stars in terms of both their sales and the durability of their appeal to wide audiences (Horowitz 1994).

Since the 1970s, Israeli pop music has been characterized by rock aesthetics, internationalization, and stylistic diversification. Studios with state-of-the-art equipment have increased the quantity and and improved the quality of commercial recordings. These trends became even stronger when economic liberalization and a tilt toward Anglo-American culture were emphasized (Regev 1990).

Hebrew pop and rock comprise versions of all Western pop genres, such as rock, disco, rap, and middle-of-the-road. Hebrew pop uses the mechanisms of the Western music industry: stars, hit parades, top-twenty lists, early releases of singles, and concert tours. Many Hebrew pop songs are in Europop style. Israelis have won the Eurovision song contest three times. Other musicians have sought alternative avenues, such as Hebrew songs in bossa nova rhythms and Hebrew blues.

MUSIC OF NON-JEWISH COMMUNITIES

Non-Jewish communities in Israel include Christian and Muslim Arabs, bedouin tribes (in the Negev desert in the south), Druze (in Upper Galilee), and smaller groups such as the Cherkess, descendants of Caucasian immigrants. Israeli Arabs favor the same musical styles as their counterparts elsewhere in the Middle East. One finds local Palestinian folk traditions in Galilee that belong to the Syrian-Lebanese area (Bar-Yosef 1998), mainstream urban music from Egypt, local popular music (Regev 1993), and art music from the "great" pan-Islamic traditions. Of particular interest are the musical traditions of the Eastern churches of Jerusalem (Armenian, Coptic, Ethiopian, Greek Orthodox, Pravoslavic, and Syriac).

As a result of the economic boom of the 1990s, a large contingent of foreign workers arrived in Israel from Southeast Asia, Eastern Europe, Africa, and Latin America. Like all immigrant groups, each community developed venues where its own music could be heard. So far, there has been no serious study of the music of immigrant communities in Israel, but this is a subject that deserves attention.

The great diversity and vitality of musical activities in Israel clearly reflect the multicultural character of Israeli society. The quest for local "authenticity" is no different from that in other emerging nations consisting mostly of immigrants. In the early stages of statehood, it was believed that a constructed "Israeliness" could be widely accepted as a common denominator by immigrants, and state intervention in cultural policies was designed to promote this trend. Yet today, music is a major area of cultural controversy in Israel. For example, the current public debate over governmental support for "Oriental" culture may be symbolized as a conflict between the Israel Philharmonic Orchestra and the Israeli Andalusian Orchestra.

REFERENCES

Bar-Yosef, Amatzia. 1998. "Traditional Rural Style under a Process of Change: The Singing Style of the *Hadday*, Palestinian Folk Poet-Singers." *Asian Music* 29(2):57–82.

Bayer, Bathya. 1980. "Creation and Tradition in Israeli Folksongs: Some Specimens." *Aspects of Music in Israel*: 52–60. (Tel Aviv: Israeli Composers League.)

Bensky, Tova. 1989. "Ethnicity and the Shape of Musical State Patterns in an Israeli Urban Community." *Social Forces* 67(3):731–750.

Bohlman, Philip V. 1989. *The Land Where Two Streams Flow: Music in the German-Jewish Community in Israel*. Urbana: University of Illinois Press.

Bohlman, Philip V., and Mark Slobin, eds. 1986. *Music in the Ethnic Communities of Israel. Asian Music* 17(2, special issue).

Cohen, Eric, and Amnon Shiloah. 1985. "Major Trends of Change in Jewish Oriental Ethnic Music." *Popular Music* 5:199–223.

Eliram, Talila. 1995. "*Shirei Erets Israel*: The Formation and Meaning of a Popular Music

Repertoire at the End of the Twentieth Century." M.A. thesis, Bar-Ilan University. (In Hebrew.)

Hacohen, Eliyahu. 1985. *The Songs of Tel-Aviv 1909–1984*. Tel Aviv. (In Hebrew.)

Halper, Jeff, Pamela Squires-Kidron, and Edwin Seroussi. 1992. "Musica Mizraḥit and the Realignment of Israeli Society: The Case of Hayyim Moshe." In *1789–1989: Musique, histoire, démocratie*, ed. A. Hennion, Vol. 3:669–672. Paris: Éditions de la Maison des Sciences de l'Homme.

Halper, Jeff, Edwin Seroussi, and Pamela Squires-Kidron. 1989. "Musica Mizraḥit: Ethnicity and Class Culture in Israel." *Popular Music* 8:131–142.

Horowitz, Amy. 1994. "*Musika Yam Tikhonit Ysraelit* (Israeli Mediterranean Music): Cultural Boundaries and Disputed Territories." Ph.D. dissertation, University of Pennsylvania.

———. 1997. "Performance in Disputed Territory: Israeli Mediterranean Music." *Musical Performance* 1(3):43–53.

Mazor, Yacov. 2000. *The Klezmer Tradition in the Land of Israel*. Jerusalem: Jewish Music Research Center. (Yuval Music Series 6.)

Ne'eman, Amitay. 1980. "Light Music and Pop in Israel." *Aspects of Music in Israel*, 61–65. (Tel Aviv: Israeli Composers League.)

Regev, Motti. 1986. "The Musical Soundscape as a Contest Area: 'Oriental Music' and Israeli Popular Music." In *Media, Culture, and Society* 8:343–355. London: Sage.

———. 1989. "The Field of Popular Music in Israel. In *World Music, Politics, and Social Change*, ed. S. Firth, 145–155. Manchester: Manchester University Press.

———. 1990. "The Coming of Rock: Meaning, Content, and Structure in the Field of Popular Music in Israel." Ph.D. dissertation, Tel Aviv University. (In Hebrew.)

———. 1992. "Israeli Rock, or a Study in the Politics of Local Authenticity." *Popular Music* 11(1):1–14.

———. 1993. *Oud and Guitar: The Musical Culture of the Arabs in Israel*. Ra'nanah: Ha-Merkaz le-Ḥeḳer ha-Ḥevra be-Yisra'el. (In Hebrew.)

Seroussi, Edwin. 1996. *Popular Music in Israel: The First Fifty Years*. Cambridge, Mass.: Harvard College Library.

Shahar, Nathan. 1990. "The Eretz-Israeli Song 1920–1950: Sociomusical and Musical Aspects." Ph.D. dissertation, Hebrew University of Jerusalem. (In Hebrew.)

Shay, Yael. 1998. "Change and Continuity in the Wedding Music of the Jews of Habban." Ph.D. dissertation, Bar-Ilan University. (In Hebrew.)

Shiloah, Amnon, and Eric Cohen. 1983. "The Dynamics of Change in Jewish Oriental Ethnic Music in Israel." *Ethnomusicology* 27(2): 227–251.

Musical Life and Institutions in Israel: 1880–1990

Jehoash Hirshberg

Ottoman Rule: 1880–1914
The British Mandate: First Decade
From the Beginning of Central European Immigration to 1948
The State of Israel: 1948 to 1990

Israeli society has been shaped by one of the most intense migrations in modern history. The Jewish migration to Palestine has been repeatedly activated by religious longing for the Holy Land and by the modern political ideology of self-determination. Which countries of origin have been most prominent varied in response to changing conditions; in consequence, the Jewish community of Palestine before 1948—traditionally called the *yishuv* 'settlement'—and Israeli society since 1948 have fluctuated ethnically and culturally.

The principal agent of the intended fusion of disparate ethnic and cultural groups into a unified nation was modernized Hebrew. The ancient language of sacred texts and prayers had been dormant for centuries before it was revived in learned Jewish circles in Europe for literary and scholarly usage, and then systematically disseminated for daily use in the *yishuv*. After a period of heated controversy in the early twentieth century, the local pronunciation common among Sephardic Jews won out over the Ashkenazi pronunciation of Jews from Europe. Music was seen as catalyst in the dissemination of Hebrew, whether through group singing or through vocal performances in Hebrew.

The heterogeneous immigrant communities in Palestine were reluctant to give up their ethnic and cultural identity. Immigrants from the West modeled music on Western hierarchic institutions—formal concerts, performing ensembles, and professional music schools. Such models differed from the context-dependent and family-oriented musical activities of the self-contained ethnic communities of Jews from Yemen, Iraq, Morocco, Iran, and other Eastern cultures. These two models, though incompatible, could have coexisted; but the national ideology urged a gradual fusion, which created incessant tension. Music was required to contribute to a visionary national culture. Ironically, musicians, especially composers and critics, often found themselves working toward a goal whose nature—an unspecified orientation to the East—was not only vague but also disputed.

OTTOMAN RULE: 1880–1914

Musical life was limited by the small size of the *yishuv,* which had only 80,000 people in 1914, and by the suspicions of the Ottoman administration. However, certain events of that time turned out to be indicative of future developments. In 1895 the

> The principal agent of the intended fusion of disparate ethnic and cultural groups into a unified nation was modernized Hebrew; and music was seen as a catalyst in the dissemination of Hebrew, whether through group singing or through vocal performances.

founders of one of the first new agricultural settlements, Rishon Le-Tsiyon, formed a community orchestra that took part in all kinds of social and educational events and was well organized, with a salaried conductor and a strict constitution. In 1910, the German-born singer Shulamit Ruppin (1873–1912) founded the first conservatory in the Jewish community of the port town of Jaffa (8,000 Jews); it had a purely European curriculum—piano, violin, and theory. The musical community in the *yishuv* was not yet stratified. Amateurs and professionals performed together, and the same musicians were active in several fields. For example, the violinist Mosheh Hopenko, director of the music school after Shulamit Ruppin's death, earned a living as a violin teacher, a conductor, a piano and music dealer, and a concert manager.

The Jewish community in Jerusalem went through crucial social and economic changes at the turn of the century, signified by the opening of several modern educational institutions such as the Hebrew *gymnasium* and the Bezalel arts academy. In 1911 Shulamit Ruppin opened a branch in Jerusalem that soon became a small independent music school.

A bold attempt to bridge the gap between Western practice and Eastern traditions was made by the cantor and ethnomusicologist Abraham Z. Idelsohn (1882–1938), who conducted extensive fieldwork in Jerusalem from 1907 to 1921 among Jewish communities of ethnic Yemenite, Iraqi, and Persian origin. Idelsohn's prolific anthropological research revealed the wealth of Eastern Jewish traditions to musicians of Western training and attracted international attention to music in Palestine. His ambitious goal, to reconstruct the original heritage of the Hebrew temple, was unattainable, since the continuity of the ancient musical tradition had been irreparably ruptured. Still, his pioneering research, as recorded in his voluminous *Thesaurus*, not only made a lasting contribution to ethnomusicology but also became a source of musical material for many composers.

The *yishuv*, a new immigrant society, had no deep-rooted local folk song tradition. Nevertheless, the immigrant musicians recognized the unifying and communal power of songs, which were used in the context of daily work in the fields and on the roads, as well as on social occasions. The first group of folk songs was dominated by Hebrew translations and modifications of popular Russian songs, many of which were fully integrated into the local folk song corpus for years to come. Additional songs were derived from the Yiddish repertoire of Eastern Europe and from Hasidic songs.

The ravages of World War I generated a mass emigration of nearly a third of the Jewish population of Palestine and temporarily halted all musical activity in the country.

THE BRITISH MANDATE: FIRST DECADE

The wave of optimism that followed the establishment of a British administration over Palestine led to an immediate recovery of cultural activity and to two major waves of Jewish immigration. One wave, mostly from Russia, brought the *yishuv* up to 90,000 in 1923; the second, in 1924–1925, mostly from Poland, brought more than

50,000 additional immigrants. This second wave activated a rapid process of urbanization, which made Tel Aviv a vibrant cultural center called "the first Hebrew town"; Jerusalem acquired the character of a cosmopolitan city housing the British and Jewish administrations as well as Hebrew University (founded in 1925). The British mandate administration granted Jews full autonomy in education and in culture. No direct financial support was provided, but British officials regularly attended cultural events. The director of the Jerusalem Music School was the British pianist Sydney Seal, and the high commissioners frequently sponsored important musical events, especially in Jerusalem.

The renewed attraction of the *yishuv* as a promising Jewish cultural center induced the eminent critic, scholar, and composer Joel Engel (1868–1927) to move the activities of his Society for Jewish Folk Music (founded in Russia in 1908) to Palestine. Engel himself immigrated in 1924, along with several of his colleagues, notably Jacob Weinberg (1879–1958) and Solomon Rosowksy (1878–1962). After Engel's death, his project was continued by the pianist and pedagogue David Schorr (1867–1942), who merged a vision of Jewish national revival with a utopian socialist ideology as a point of departure for a large-scale educational project. Schorr's goal was a classless, well-educated Jewish society; the unifying power of music was to be applied to this end through lecture-recitals, mostly on Beethoven as a great humanitarian, and through the systematic establishment of a network of amateur choruses all over the country. Engel and Schorr also organized regular vocal recitals of music by Jewish composers, mostly former members of the Society for Jewish Folk Music. A vision of a return to the land of the Bible inspired the conductor Fordhaus Ben-Tsisi (1898–1979) to form the Bible Chorus in 1926. Combining religious fervor and a romantic belief in the power of religious masterpieces, Fordhaus presented large-scale biblical oratorios by Handel, Haydn, Mendelssohn, and others in Hebrew translations that frequently bordered on free paraphrase and ideological interpretation.

These musicians interpreted the concept of "Jewish music" in its broadest sense, as including not only music by Jewish composers but also great works on biblical and Jewish religious themes and texts. This interpretation was fiercely resisted by some critics, who rejected even the slightest trace of Western influence and wanted a national Jewish music to spring anew from purely Eastern sources of inspiration.

Both visionary utopianism and pragmatism led the Russian-born conductor Mark Golynkin (1875–1963) to launch the Palestine Opera in 1923. Golynkin considered opera a first step toward his hoped-for "Temple for the Arts" that would unite all performing institutions with a professional school for all the arts. Golynkin insisted on productions in Hebrew. For four seasons, the Palestine Opera produced seventeen operas (the standard Italian, French, and Russian repertoire, translated into Hebrew), playing to full houses; but a lack of funding and of a proper opera house led to the financial collapse of the venture in 1927.

With no financial base for a professional symphony orchestra, the relatively few instrumentalists in Palestine had to earn a living from silent films and coffeehouses. The conductor Max Lampel (1900–1985) put together ad hoc ensembles for symphonic concerts held outdoors or in makeshift auditoriums. These programs—which were well attended—included the standard eighteenth- and nineteenth-century repertoire. Several small chamber music societies sponsored high-quality concert series, mostly encouraged by the powerful personality of the British-born cellist Thelma Bentwich-Yellin (1895–1959), who immigrated in 1921 and was a student of Pablo Casals. Audiences in Palestine were so warm and enthusiastic that they attracted internationally acclaimed soloists for frequent concert tours, among them the violinists Henri Marteau, Jan Kubelik, and Jascha Heifetz and the pianists Leopold Godowsky and Arthur Rubinstein. Music was reviewed in the daily press by discriminating critics, such as David Rosolio (1898–1963) and Menashe Rabinowitz-Ravina (1899–1975), as well as by ideologically motivated and musically educated columnists, who helped avert a stale, provincial musical culture.

During the 1920s, numerous songs that would form a national folk repertoire were composed. The verses were frequently chosen from optimistic biblical passages, mostly in the Song of Songs and the Book of Psalms; but some verses were specially written, stressing idyllic scenes of village life and Orientalist scenes. Composers such as Yedidyha Admon-Gorochov (1894–1985), who immigrated in 1906, and Emanuel Amiran Pougatchov (b. 1909), who immigrated in 1924, renounced the predominant Russian folk idiom and searched for a new style that would incorporate Eastern motives and rhythms, as in Admon's "Camel's Song", in which alternating major and minor thirds suggest Arab intonation.

Hundreds of songs were printed and disseminated as inexpensive sheet music and even as postcards. They were taught by music teachers in elementary schools and kindergartens and performed by amateur choruses. On the other hand, only a few composers of art music were active in the 1920s; and the first national Hebrew opera, *The Pioneers* (1924) by Jacob Weinberg, was never performed in Palestine—there were no funds for a production of a new opera.

Severe economic depression and political unrest caused widespread unemployment and emigration which hampered the development of concert activity in the late 1920s. The only working ensemble at this time was the Concert Ensemble, a chamber orchestra that specialized in popular light classics and lasted for nearly three years.

FROM THE BEGINNING OF CENTRAL EUROPEAN IMMIGRATION TO 1948

After a period of economic depression and increased emigration, a large wave of Jewish immigrants came from Poland and Central Europe in response to the rise of Nazism in Germany. About 50,000 people arrived from Central Europe, most of whom were well-trained, well-educated academics and businessmen, who soon effected a major change in all facets of culture in the *yishuv*. They transplanted the tradition of *Hausmusik* to Palestine (Bohlman 1989) and constituted a discriminating, dedicated concert audience.

The most important musical event at this time was the inauguration of the Palestine Orchestra in December 1936. Its founder was the violinist Bronislaw Huberman (1882–1947), who had a grand vision of an international center for music and the arts in Palestine that would replace the declining West and would perform for a classless society. Faced with increasing persecution of Jews in central Europe, Huberman turned his project instead into an emergency operation that brought some seventy fine refugee musicians to Palestine. Huberman's ideology was music for the people; he eschewed what he considered European class snobbery, and for years to come his subscription series included special low-priced concerts for workers. The conductor of the first subscription series was the legendary Arturo Toscanini, who, as a demonstration against fascism, donated his performances. The Palestine Orchestra continued to perform under renowned international conductors, among them Molinari and Dobrowen, and thus set high professional standards from the outset. After the foundation of the state of Israel, the ensemble changed its name to the Israel Philharmonic Orchestra; from the start, it had a loyal corps of subscribers, some of whom held lifetime subscriptions.

With the establishment of the Palestine Orchestra, a process of specialization and stratification was completed. The orchestra organized itself as a cooperative run by an elected committee that determined its administrative, financial, and artistic policies. The success of the Palestine Orchestra contrasted with the failure of the operatic venture in Palestine; but some opera companies, though short-lived, continued to give low-budget productions of popular and chamber operas.

The musicians of the Palestine Orchestra made a significant contribution to chamber music; one example is the string quartet founded by the Hungarian-educated Lorand and Alice Fenyves, Oedoen Partos, and Laszlo Vince. They also established high standards of professional instrumental education in the country.

In March 1936 the British administration inaugurated a radio station, which broadcast on one channel in English, Arabic, and Hebrew. Music programs amounted to 25 percent of broadcast time in Hebrew, and they too had a significant influence on musical life; special emphasis was given to works by Jewish and local composers. Most concerts were broadcast live from the studio by a chamber ensemble, which soon became the nucleus of a radio orchestra, now the Jerusalem Symphony.

The migration included more than thirty well-trained composers, most from Central Europe, who settled in Palestine between 1931 and 1939. With a few exceptions—notably Stefan Wolpe (1902–1972), who immigrated to Palestine in 1935 but went on to the United States in 1939—these composers settled permanently in Palestine, where they launched creative and educational activities. They all acknowledged their obligation to participate in forming a national musical culture, though its precise nature could not be defined. Their music was subjected to severe criticism, based on their perceived contribution to an envisioned national style, but the reviewers frequently contradicted each other with regard to this contested concept.

Despite the hope of a national revival in the ancient homeland, no direct continuity could be established between the music of biblical times and modern music. Ancient traditions, such as the cantillations of the Bible, provided no more than elementary melodic figures, which lost all meaning when they were removed from their context. Moreover, even music that had acquired a "Jewish" connotation in Europe, such as Bloch's *Sacred Service* (*'Avodat ha-kodesh*), while highly respected by the *yishuv* audience, was still considered diaspora music inappropriate for the pioneers in Palestine.

With no existing model, local composers never formed a unified "national school"; they had come from different backgrounds and ideologies, and their creative activity remained individualized or even polarized. The German-born Erich Walter Sternberg (1891–1974), who immigated in 1931, advocated romantic individualism and believed that a genuine national style would gradually emerge as a natural outcome of high-quality professional creativity. His large-scale orchestral works *Twelve Tribes of Israel* (*Shnem 'Asar Shivtey Yisreel,* 1938) and *Joseph and His Brethren* (*Yosef ve-Eḥav*, 1942) are steeped in late-romantic German chromatic harmony, dense fugal polyphony, and excited melodic rhetoric. The German-born Paul Ben-Haim (Frankenburger, 1897–1984), who immigrated in 1933, developed an elaborate synthesis of traditional German polyphony, directional tonal organization, standard formats such as sonata form and ternary form, harmony influenced by Debussy and Ravel, and modal melody. Some of his melodic material was derived from local folk songs, as in *Variations on a Hebrew Tune* for piano trio (1937). Ben-Haim's First Symphony (1940) is a large-scale Mahlerian epic that symbolically relates the migrant experience, moving from an excited rhetorical quotation of the initial motive of Mahler's Second Symphony to a stylized arrangement of a motive from a traditional Persian song.

By contrast, Alexander U. Boskovitch (1907–1964), who migrated from Transylvania in 1938, based his compositional style on a well-articulated ideology—that composers should renounce romantic self-expression, considering themselves representatives of the collective spirit of the people and their work a national mission. Boskovitch expected composers in the *yishuv* to find an appropriate musical representation of the unique "static and dynamic landscape" of Palestine (an allusion to the dry desert climate and the scorching sun), by which he meant music with powerful, austere contrasts and the pathos and rhetoric of modern Sephardic-accented Hebrew and the Arabic spoken in Palestine. He refrained from quoting traditional tunes and folk songs directly, since he aspired to a fully internalized national style that would not be based on local ethnic models. In his *Semitic Suite* (*Suita Shemit*, 1945) Boskovitch discarded polyphony in favor of heterophonic textures, harmonies of superimposed fifths, small-range recurring dance figures, and imitation of microtones through cross-relations. Boskovitch coined the term "Mediterranean music," which was later taken up by the critic and composer Max Brod (1951). A similar ideology was adopted by the French-educated composer Menahem Avidom (Mahler-Kalkstein), who was born in 1908 and immigrated in 1925, in his lively *Mediterranean Sinfonietta* (Symphony No. 3, *Yam Tikhonit*).

Marc Lavry (1930–1967), who immigrated in 1935, advocated a popular, communicative folk style that would appeal to the masses. Lavry used a popular dance, the *hora*, which he extolled as an expression of the national spirit. This Palestinian dance (unrelated to the Romanian *hora lunga*) is characterized by short symmetrical phrases in square meter and by recurring syncopated rhythms. Lavry's song *Emek* (dedicated to the Jezre'el valley in northern of Palestine, a symbol of the heroism of Jewish agricultural settlements) combined a pastoral introduction with a *hora*. Later, he expanded *Emek* into a symphonic poem (1936). In Lavry's opera *Dan the Guard* (*Dan ha-Shomer*, 1945)—the first national opera produced in Palestine—an individual's emotional struggle in an isolated, besieged *kibbutz* is contrasted with the heroic endeavor of the collective of young and old settlers; the music is a semiotic contrast of different styles representing each character and each group.

Such a collective ideology deliberately blurs the distinction between concert music and folk music. Songs by Lavry were performed as both concert and folk pieces, and several songs by Boskovitch originally written as incidental music (for example, *Dudu*, *The Negev Song*) soon acquired the status of folk songs. Mordechai Seter (1916–1995) merged three strains in his *Sabbat Cantata* (*Kantatah le-Shabat*, 1940): the melodies quote traditional Yemenite tunes derived from Idelsohn's *Thesaurus*, which are worked out contrapuntally to resemble a motet and merge into diatonic dissonant harmony.

The immigrant composers' encounter with the East was partially accomplished through mediators, of whom the most important was the singer Bracha Zefira (1910–1990). [See Popular Music in Israel.] In 1939, Zefira began commissioning arrangements from most of the immigrant composers, and many of them later used the traditional melodies they had learned from her in their concert works. Ben-Haim, for instance, quoted and reworked more than thirty songs he had arranged for Zefira; the third movement of his Piano Concerto (1949) is one example. Classical Arab music was regularly performed in Palestine, especially on radio, by the composer and *'ūd* virtuoso 'Ezra Aharon (1903–1995), who was a royal musician at the court of the king of Iraq before immigrating in 1935. A Western-trained dancer, Yardenah Cohen, used live Arabic music in her performances of biblical scenes. Yet despite such mediators and their own increasing exposure to Arabic and Eastern ethnic traditions, the Western-trained composers never truly internalized Eastern music and did not sever their Western roots.

Along with the ideological interest in folk styles and collective nationalism, knowledge of new trends in Europe was constantly maintained through chamber concerts of works by composers such as Schoenberg and Hindemith; such concerts were organized by E. W. Sternberg, Peter E. Gradenwitz (1910–2001), and the cellist, composer, and scholar Joachim Stutschewsky (1891–1981), who immigrated in 1938.

The ethnomusicologists Robert Lachmann (1892–1939) and Edith Gerson-Kiwi (1908–1992), who both immigrated in 1935, established rigorous research at Hebrew University, where they founded the Phonogram Archives. During the 1940s, academies of music were opened in Tel Aviv and Jerusalem, closely modeled on Central European conservatories, notably those in Berlin and Budapest; the curriculum was based on competitive instrumental classes and courses in composition, theory, and history, although emphasis was given to courses in Jewish and non-European music.

Despite the centralization of the musical establishment in Tel Aviv and to a lesser extent in Jerusalem, local musical traditions and institutions developed in small towns and in the *kibbutz* movement, whose communal way of life called for specialized activities and ceremonies, especially on the traditional Jewish holidays. Although the *kibbutz* movement combined European socialism with a revolt against traditional Jewish religious orthodoxy, its members still felt a need to preserve the spirit of holidays; they developed new forms of celebrations, foremost of which was the seder (the celebration of Passover eve). At the *kibbutz* seder, original music by local musicians was performed alongside arranged classical excerpts, frequently by Bach and Handel, as well as folk songs.

An important aspect of the musical scene was the predominance and prestige of choral singing, which was considered a powerful means of education and unification. Local amateur choruses were formed on *kibbutzim*, among professionals such as physicians, and in schools; in fact, music teachers in schools were expected to be primarily choral directors.

In sum, when the *yishuv* gained political independence in 1948, an infrastructure of musical life had been firmly established and shaped.

THE STATE OF ISRAEL: 1948 TO 1990

Although World War II nearly isolated Palestine, musical activity continued; indeed, local initiatives were encouraged because musicians were unable to visit from abroad. The postwar years brought massive waves of refugee immigrants, greatly increasing the population and further diversifying it—Asian and African countries (Yemen, Egypt, Iraq, Morocco, Algeria, and India) were strongly represented. The official cultural policy during the 1950s and 1960s inclined toward the East; the preservation of Israel's non-European heritage was encouraged and supported. The Inbal Dance Theater, founded by the composer and choreographer Sara Levi-Tannay, took the rich tradition of the Yemenite community into a stylized, theatrical public context. Some immigrant groups used music to preserve their community; for example, the Tzadikov choir was a cohesive force among Bulgarian Jews who came to Israel during the 1950s.

International contact resumed immediately after the war; these contacts included the first tours of the Israel Philharmonic Orchestra in Europe and in the United States. New municipal orchestras were founded, such as the Israel Chamber Orchestra, the Haifa Orchestra, and the Be'er Sheba Sinfonietta. Several semiprofessional and professional choruses of various sizes have been formed since the 1950s; chief among them were the Philharmonic Choir founded by Eitan Lustig and the Rinat Chamber Choir founded by the conductor Gary Bertini. In 1977, an official directory listed fifty-nine professional performing groups, ranging from string quartets to choruses and orchestras.

In 1948 the American-born soprano Addis De Philip founded the Israeli Opera, which lasted for a generation, performing many operas, including the premiere of Menahem Avidom's *Aleksandrah*, and presenting leading international singers. However, it suffered from personal conflicts and a persistent shortage of funds; in general, opera remained secondary to symphonic and chamber music.

In 1949 the musicologist Peter E. Gradenwitz founded Israel Music Publications, (which later moved to Jerusalem under Stanley Simmonds). In 1961 it was complemented by the Israel Music Institute under the direction of William Elias (and later Paul Landau). These two houses have been responsible for most of the music publishing in Israel.

Israel's geographical and political isolation have increased the desire of musicians, officials, and audiences to maintain cultural contacts with the West, through visiting artists and national events. One important event is the annual Israel Festival, which began in 1961 and has sponsored ambitious productions by international artists. Stravinsky's *Abraham and Isaac* was commissioned for the Israel Festival, and the festival has given pioneer performances of early music such as *The Play of Daniel*, authentic performances of works such as the Saint Matthew Passion, and concerts of non-European music. The Jerusalem Music Center, initiated by the violinist Isaac Stern, has sponsored master classes by important performers and teachers. The Harp Contest and the Arthur Rubinstein Piano Competition have also helped make Israel an international venue for Western music.

Chamber music is a well-established and multifacted tradition in Israel, ranging from *Hausmusik* activity to professional concerts such as a series at the Tel Aviv Art Museum. Several chamber ensembles, notably the Tel Aviv Quartet (Ḥayim Taub, Yefim Boyko, Daniel Benyamini, and Uzi Wiesel), have existed for a generation.

Cultural exchange with the West has been of special importance to composers, who have responded vigorously to the challenge of the international avant-garde. From his earliest works on, Joseph Tal (Grünthal, b. 1910) was dedicated to new techniques, including traditional dodecaphonism (in his Symphony No. 2) and serialism. Tal was the founder of the first studio for electronic music in Israel, at Hebrew University. Other advanced studios were founded by Tsvi Avni and Yizhak Sadai at the academies of music in Jerusalem and Tel Aviv. During the 1950s, there was a second generation of Israeli composers, most of whom were born and educated in Israel. Controversy and pluralism notwithstanding, it appears that the initial repertoire did develop at least a vague image of what was expected from an "Israeli" composition (Hirshberg and Sagir 1978). Tsvi Avni (b. 1927) fused his own Eastern predilections with new influences such as Varèse and electronic music; an example is his orchestral work *Meditations on a Drama* (*Hirhurim al Drama*). The Hungarian-born Oedoen Partos (1907–1977), who immigrated in 1938, combined Yemenite and Arabic motives and rhythms with complex dodecaphonism—for example, in *Maqamat* (1959). Haim Alexander (b. 1915) used a folk idiom in *Five Dances* but later turned to strict serialism for his setting of the *Rubayiat of 'Umar Kahyyām* (1963). Boskovitch, in *Concerto da Camera* (1961) and *Ornaments* (*Ada'im*, 1964), boldly attempted to serialize rhythms of the Hebrew in the Bible and in ancient prayers.

Opera was revived with the opening of the New Israeli Opera in Tel Aviv in 1985. In Israel, operas have been produced mostly in the original languages with supertitles in Hebrew, and there has been a growing interest in the dramatic modern productions that have become prominent all over the world. The composer and conductor Noam Sheriff challenged the supremacy of the Israel Philharmonic by forming the ambitious Rishon le-Tsiyon orchestra, which also functions as the opera orchestra.

The "authentic performance" movement reached Israel in the early 1980s and soon gained momentum. Concerts of international and local artists included large-scale productions such as Monteverdi's *Vespers*. Workshops have been attended by many professional and amateur musicians who play early instruments.

With the rise of a third generation of Israeli-born composers, bolstered by immigrants, pluralism and diversification have further increased. Avant-garde music is somewhat less in vogue, and composers are again attempting to build bridges to the East. For instance, *Memory* (1982), by Mark Kopytman, who was born in Russia in 1929 and immigrated in 1972, opens with a traditional Yemenite song performed live by the folk artist Gilah Bashari; its melody is then worked out in complex orchestral heterophony. Ancient Jewish prayers have been featured in large-scale works by Ben-Zion Orgad (b. 1926) and André Hajdu (b. 1932). Other composers have retained the folklike clarity and simplicity of the Mediterranean school; an example is Yehezkiel Braun (b. 1922).

The 1970s saw immigration from the Soviet Union, the United States, and South America; since 1989, a much larger wave of immigration from the former Soviet Union has nearly doubled the number of active professional musicians in Israel. New orchestras have been founded, and local audiences have encountered different repertoires and performance styles. Ensembles of traditional music and dance of the Asian republics of the former Soviet Union have further diversified musical life in Israel. The full effect of the dramatic resettlement of Ethiopian Jewry is not yet realized, but successful ensembles of traditional Ethiopian music and dance have already been established.

The Israeli musical scene has been shaped and dominated by dialectical struggles between isolationism and cosmopolitanism. The concept of the melting pot has yielded to pressures to preserve immigrant cultures. Israeli musicians have always sought international recognition, and some have made their professional careers abroad, but many have kept their Israeli citizenship. The multiethnic society of Israel has formed a complex network of musical subcultures in which compartmentalized ethnic traditions (such as those of the Karaite Jews and the Samaritans) coexist with commercial panorientalism. As a rule, Western-oriented performing institutions attract enthusiastic audiences, and although the public taste is often said to be conservative and snobbish, new music has also attracted interested and discerning listeners.

REFERENCES

Adler, Israel, and Judith Cohen. 1976. *A. Z. Idelsohn Archives at the Jewish National and University Library: Catalogue*. Jerusalem: Magnes Press, Hebrew University.

Adler, I., B. Bayer, and E. Schleifer. 1986. *The Abraham Zvi Idelsohn Memorial Volume*. Jerusalem: Yuval Studies of the Jewish Music Research Center 5, Magnes Press.

Adler, Israel, ed. 1977. *A Directory of Music Institutions in Israel.* Jerusalem: Israel Section of the International Music Council.

Bahat, Avner. 1984. 'Eden Partosh: Hayav ve-yetsirato (Oedoen Partos: His Life and Works). Tel Aviv: Am Oved.

Bohlman, Philip. 1989. *The Land Where Two Streams Flow*. Urbana: University of Illinois Press.

Brod, Max. (1951) 1976. *Die Musik Israels: Revidierte Ausgabe mit einem zweiten Teil werden und Entwocklung der Music in Israel von H. W. Cohen*. Kassel: Bärenreiter.

Flam, Gila. 1986. "Bracha Zephira—A Case Study of Acculturation in Israeli Song." *Asian Music* 17:108–125.

Gerson-Kiwi, Edith. 1974. "Robert Lachmann: His Achievement and His Legacy." *Yuval* 3 (Jerusalem: Jewish Music Research Center):100–108.

Hirshberg, Jehoash. 1987. "Jerusalem Symphony Orchestra" and "Israel Philharmonic Orchestra." In *Symphony Orchestras of the World, Selected Profiles*, ed. Robert Craven, 200–207. New York: Greenwood.

———. 1990. *Paul Ben-Haim: His Life and Works.* Jerusalem: Israel Music Publications.

———. 1995–1996. *Music in the Jewish Community of Palestine, 1880–1948: A Social History.* Oxford: Oxford University Press.

Hirshberg, Jehoash, and David Sagiv. 1978. "The 'Israeli' in Israeli Music: The Audience Responds." *Israel Studies in Musicology* 1:159–173.

Ibbeken, Ida, and Tzvi Avni. 1969. *An Orchestra Is Born*. Tel Aviv: Israel Philharmonic Orchestra. (Compiled from the Huberman Archives.)

Idelsohn, Abraham Z. 1914–1932 *Thesaurus of Hebrew Oriental Melodies.* Leipzig: Breitkopf und Härtel.

Shahar, Nathan. 1989. "Ha-Shir ha-Erets Yisraeli: Hebetim musikaliyim ve-sotsiomusikaliyim ba-shanim 1920–1950 (The Erets Israeli Song 1920–1950: Sociomusical and Musical Aspects.)." Ph.D. dissertation, Hebrew University. (In Hebrew.)

Shiloah, Amnon. 1992. *Jewish Musical Traditions.* Detroit: Wayne State University Press.

Shiloah, Amnon, and Cohen, Eric. 1987. "The Dynamics of Change in Jewish Oriental Ethnic Music in Israel." *Ethnomusicology* 27:227–252.

Sikron, Moshe. 1957. *Immigration to Israel.* Jerusalem: Central Bureau of Statistics.

Tischler, Alice. 1989. *A Descriptive Bibliography of Art Music by Israeli Composers.* Warren, Mich.: Detroit Studies in Music Bibliography 62.

Snapshot: Mizraḥi Music in Israel—Zohar Argov and Zahava Ben Sing *Peraḥ be-Gani*

Amy Horowitz

The opening bars of the synthesizer's horn section prepare the ear for a Spanish bullfight. Brassy tones crest, then cool down, then pause as if expectantly. But no matador charges into the ring. Instead, a slender Yemenite man in a tight-fitting Western suit appears at stage left in the smoke-filled Club Ariana, in Jaffa. He walks to the microphone and fills the air with a single clear, piercing tone.

The sound shoots out from a deep well somewhere between his heart and head. It streams through every part of his throat and nose, lips, and cheeks, like unexpected rain winding down the crevices of a desert canyon. It is neither a cry nor a roar, though it evokes feelings that might be expressed by cries and roars. Overtones reverberate as he bends the note into a melismatic arch that conjures up Muslim and Jewish prayer.

Zohar Argov is performing the opening *muwwāl* of *Ha-Peraḥ be-Gani* 'The Flower in My Garden' in 1982. The *muwwāl* is an improvisation on a sound such as "ah" or "Ya lel" with which a singer opens a performance. By setting a meditative mood, the opening *muwwāl* focuses the attention of the singer and the audience.

In his performance of *Ha-Peraḥ be-Gani,* Argov's *muwwāl* answers the linear horn opening with carefully placed vocal spirals and twists of Eastern melisma (*silsulim*). His timbres soar like a bird. His vocal lines retrace the melody outlined by the horns, creating an interior path that bends the pitches and liberates the myriad microtones that live between the whole and half tones of Western scales.

The *muwwāl* lasts for 40 seconds and then gives way to Western drumbeats that underline the rhythmic drive of the song. In this well-known song, which the composer, Avihu Medina, classifies as "one of my Spanish works," the *muwwāl* marks a cultural nerve center. Between the Spanish Mediterranean horns and the Western beat, Argov's *muwwāl* assures the listener that the voice, with its Middle Eastern attitude and aesthetic, is the signature line. Argov's voice subverts expectation. He overtakes but does not obliterate the Spanish orchestra, with Hebrew lyrics that reclaim and celebrate its guttural sounds. He renders improvisational *silsulim* where Western notation calls for rest bars.

It is not only the intensity of his voice and its unlikely coalition with the musical accompaniment that shock the listeners into emotional attentiveness; it is the man himself. He has piercing black eyes and a hungry face (which, he has confessed, was deemed "too ugly for air time" by an apologetic television producer)—hungry not for

FIGURE 1 Zahava Ben. Photo by Amy Horowitz, 1992.

food but for approval. His movements are understated, yet the audience senses that the sound is flowing from a volcanic center. The listeners, a mixture of teenagers and middle-aged people, of Moroccans, Yemenites, Iraqis, Iranians, Georgians, and other Mizrahi communities, are on their feet, swaying to the music, clapping, singing, and dancing with arms raised above their heads. Some audience members climb onto the low stage. Argov offers them the microphone to sing a few bars. Others undulate and throw dollars and flowers toward the beloved singer.

Shoni Gavriel's Club Ariana in Jaffa was a leading Mizraḥi venue in the 1970s and 1980s. Zohar Argov, the leading Mizraḥi Israeli singer of the 1980s, considered it his home base. He and other Mizraḥi performers made a living by appearing at clubs, weddings, and neighborhood events. Their grueling performance schedules often included appearances at three different events in one night. Even so, few of them could survive on music alone. Their economic hardships were a result of their exclusion from mainstream European-centered Israeli music channels, and of the small size and thus the limited music market of the country.

A decade later, in 1992, a relatively new Mizraḥi woman singer, Zahava Ben (figure 1), took to an entirely different stage in a park in downtown Jerusalem, at an antidrug concert. She opened her performance in memory of Zohar Argov, with his signature song, *Ha-Peraḥ be-gani.* She was modestly dressed, but—like Argov—she captured the audience's emotional attention with her opening note.

By now, the audience had expanded beyond the limited Mizraḥi club network. In this park, European, Middle Eastern, and North African Israelis and Palestinians from Ramallah and Bethlehem rose to their feet and danced together to Ben's new version of the song that had brought Argov and Mizraḥi music into the mainstream Israeli canon and across the borders to Jordan, Lebanon, Syria, and Palestine.

Music of the Maghribi Jews in North Africa and Israel

Edwin Seroussi

Liturgical Music
Paraliturgial Music
Judeo-Arabic Folk Song
Judeo-Spanish Folk Song
Multilingual Songs
Instrumental Music
Magrhibi Jews in the General Musical Life of North Africa

North African Jewry (understood as Jews of the Maghribi, for example, Morocco, Algeria, Tunisia, and Libya, excluding Egypt) belongs geographically to Africa but culturally to the Islamic world (Shiloah 1972). Musically, North Africa is a crossroads of various traditions: Andulasian or Moorish in large urban centers on the coasts, Berber in remote internal areas such as the Atlas Mountains, and Middle Eastern (Turkish and Egyptian) because of the Ottoman conquest and the influence of Egyptian music on the contemporary music of the Arab countries. Sub-Saharan elements can be found in southern regions.

Jews established communities in North Africa as early as the second century C.E. Proselytizing by Jews in the Maghrib led to the existence of Judaized Berber tribes which, according to the historian Ibn Khaldun, inhabited the area before the Islamic conquest. In the following centuries Eastern Jews arrived in the Maghrib and Spain. From the ninth century on, Maghrib Jewry (except for the Berber tribes) may be considered together with Spanish Jewry, because of constant flow of leaders, intellectuals, and merchants from both sides of the Strait of Gibraltar. Expelled from Spain in 1492 and from Portugal in 1497, Peninsular Jews sought refuge in the Maghrib, where they joined the already established communities. The Judeo-Spanish or Sephardi influence in the culture of North Africa Jewry is noticeable in large cities of the northern shores, while in southern regions a more autochthonous type of Maghribi Jewish culture prevailed. Western European influence, which started in the late eighteenth century, intensified in the nineteenth century after the conquest of Maghribi territories by France (starting with Algeria) and Italy. However, enclaves of Berber Jews remained isolated from external influences until the twentieth century.

The historical and cultural distinction between the various segments of Maghribi Jewry is also reflected in its languages. Various Judeo-Arabic dialects, which also incorporate elements from Hebrew and European languages, predominate. Judeo-Spanish, once an important dialect, survived only in Spanish-dominated enclaves such as Tangier and Tetuan. Judeo-Berber dialects were spoken by the Jews in the Atlas Mountains. French and Italian become customary in the nineteenth century and later among the Europeanized, educated classes of large cities such as Casablanca and Tunis.

After the sixteenth century Sephardi Jews from North Africa moved to all corners of the Sephardi world: eastward to Palestine and Turkey and northward to Italy, the

Netherlands, and England. Thus traces of their synagogal music heritage can be also found in these countries. Waves of migration also occurred in the late nineteenth century, resulting in the establishment of Maghribi (mostly Moroccan or Algerian) communities in Palestine, France, and South America. In the twentieth century immigration increased, reaching its peak between 1948 and 1967, when the vast majority of North African Jews moved to Israel, France, and Canada, with smaller numbers immigrating to Latin America, Spain, and the United States. The bulk of the Maghribi Jews in Israel arrived from Morocco and Tunisia. They are the largest group within the non-European Jewish population of Israel.

Most research on the music of the Maghribi Jews was conducted outside the Maghrib. A. Z. Idelsohn, a pioneer in the study of this tradition, carried out his fieldwork in the Ma'aravi 'Maghribi' community (immigrants from Mogador, Fez, and Gibraltar) in Jerusalem around 1906 to 1920 (Idelsohn 1929). His findings should be taken with caution because his informants were a small contingent that had been detached from its sources for several decades. Liturgical recitatives predominate in this anthology. Music for paraliturgical events or folk songs in Jewish dialects are not included, except for Judeo-Spanish songs (only in the German edition) reproduced from Manuel M. Ortega's *Los hebreos en Marruecos* (published in Madrid in 1919).

Robert Lachmann (1892–1939) carried out a model study of Jewish music in the ancient Jewish community on the island of Djerba, off the coast of southern Tunisia (Lachmann 1940/1978). He studied all the musical genres, dividing them into categories on the basis of gender, social function, and structure: cantillation (mostly of biblical texts, in free rhythm) and sacred Hebrew poetry (liturgical and paraliturgical, mostly in measured rhythm), both sung by men; and women's songs in Judeo-Arabic, accompanied by percussion instruments. Being well acquainted with the Arab traditions of North Africa, Lachmann was able to trace the relations between the music of the Jews and their non-Jewish neighbors.

Edith Gerson-Kiwi, a student of Lachmann, continued the study of North African Jewish traditions, recording new immigrants as they arrived in Israel in the late 1940s. She focused on the communities of the Atlas Mountains (1967a, b). Gerson Kiwi points up the high degree of cultural contact between Jews and Berbers that is reflected in tonal organization of melodies and in musical-poetical genres: rhapsodic epic songs in which heroic episodes are sung using a modular melodic formula (figure 1), antiphonal dance songs (similar to the Berber *aḥwash*) performed at wedding and henna ceremonies, and songs related to pilgrimages to the tombs of saints. One characteristic of this tradition is its protopentatonic tonal organization (found in biblical cantillation and in the chanting of the Book of Zohar). According to Gerson-Kiwi, this feature indicates the ancient roots of Jewish-Berber music, which for ages remained unaffected by external influences.

Avigdor Herzog continued Lachmann's pioneering work on Djerba tradition, studying it in Israel and focusing on biblical cantillation (1963). Ruth Davis (1984–1985) returned to Djerba in the 1980s in Lachman's footsteps. [See MUSIC OF THE JEWS OF DJERBA, TUNISIA.]

Woman
♩ = 96
Am– ta– te– ne tit– la– ta chi– da– moi ich– laf– dim– na– ta iva– ra ler– ne tif– la– rat
Man
ich– la– ma te– me tit– la– ta chi– da– ra ich– laf ge– le– da drar ler– ne– tu la– rat.

FIGURE 1 Judeo-Arabic epic performed in alternation by a man and a woman (Gerson-Kiwi collection no. 4390 and 1967a:141). The text transcription is phonetic.

Despite such progress in the study of the history, literature, and folklore of the Maghribi Jews in Israel, studies of their music are still scant and are confined to specific topics. The ethnography of the Maghribi musical traditions was carried out by the Jewish Music Research Center and the National Sound Archive (Jewish National and University Library, Jerusalem). Most scholars focused on the Moroccan Jews, the largest Maghribi community in Israel (there have been no studies of traditions from Algeria, Tunisia, or Libya). The Moroccan *bakashot* (paraliturgical music) and its relation to the Andalusian Arabic tradition attracted wide attention (see Amzallag 1984, 1986, 1988, 1991; Chetrit 1991; Seroussi 1984, 1986, 1990; Shiloah 1980; Turel 1981). Judeo-Spanish folk song from north Morocco was intensively researched by Susana Weich-Shahak (1987, 1989, 1992). Liturgical melodies from the Maghrib are included in an anthology by Isaac Levy s(1964–1980). An important aspect of Maghribi synagogue music, the singing of psalms, was examined as part of a comprehensive study of this genre (Flender 1993).

Outside Israel, Judeo-Spanish folk song from North Morocco has also attracted wide attention. Pioneering work was carried out in the 1910s by the Spaniard scholar Manrique de Lara (Katz 1979). Following De Lara was another Spanish scholar, Larrea Palacin, whose publications (1952, 1954) encompass the entire Judeo-Spanish repertoire from Tetuán. More recently, Israel J. Katz, in cooperation with the literature scholars Samuel G. Armistead and Joseph H. Silverman, conducted a thorough study of the romance in North Africa (Armistead, Silverman, and Katz 1986). Judith Cohen (1988, 1989) studied Judeo-Spanish song in the Moroccan community in Montreal. In the same project, Dina Sabbah (1980) conducted studies of their liturgical music.

LITURGICAL MUSIC

The normative liturgy in Maghribi synagogues, as in every Jewish community, includes diverse musical structures. Biblical cantillation (according to Masoretic accents) and the recitation of prayers are in free rhythm, while other sections, particularly poetic ones (but also biblical verses and psalms) are sung to metric melodies. All these melodies are narrow in range, usually a perfect fifth (figure 2).

A characteristic of the musical performance of the liturgy is the active participation of the congregation. The absence of paid professional cantors is noticeable, and a service may be conducted by more than one individual. However, a professional *paytan* (a singer of *piyyutim*, religious poems) may perform whenever a special event, such as a wedding or bar mitzvah, takes place in the synagogue; he is paid by the host family. *Piyyutim* are added to the normative prayers during holidays too. These hymns are performed responsorially, between soloists and the congregation (figure 3).

Stylistic identity in the Maghribi liturgical tradition has not been addressed, but provisionally, several layers of musical influences can be discerned: autochthonous, Sephardi, and modern. The autochthonous layer includes elements that make the

FIGURE 2 *Hodu ladonay kir'u bishmo.* Initial verses from the sabbath morning prayer according to the Rabat-Casablanca tradition (from National Sound Archives, Jerusalem; transcribed by Edwin Seroussi).

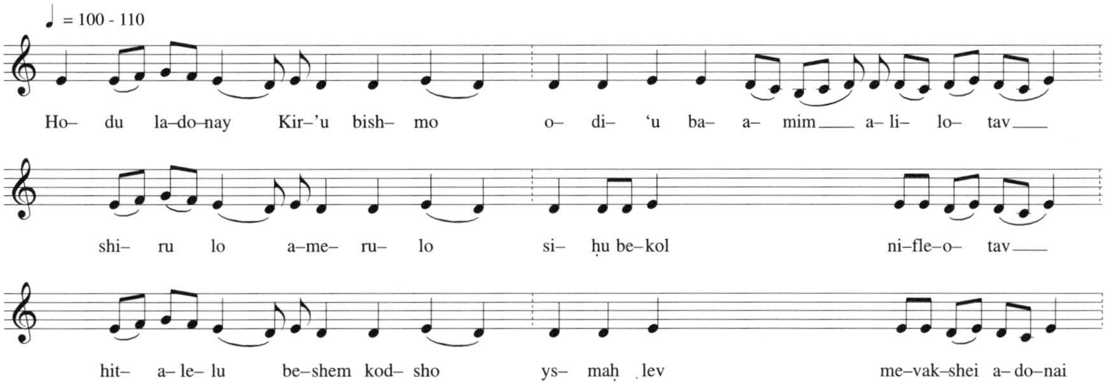

FIGURE 3 *Emunim arkhu shebaḥ la-el.* A *piyyut* (liturgical poem) for Passover according to the Djerba tradition (after Lachmann 1978:141).

Maghribi traditions unique relative to other Jewish traditions: a particular vocal quality, pentatonic tonal structures, compound meters, and syncopated rhythmic patterns. For example, a special manner of singing the psalms at the beginning of services with measured melodies is a hallmark of the Maghribi tradition, later spread by Moroccan and Tunisian cantors to Spanish-Portuguese communities in Amsterdam, Hamburg, London, and Livorno (Seroussi 1992).

The Sephardi connection reflects the interaction of Maghribi Jewry with Spanish and Portuguese immigrants immediately after the expulsion from the Iberian Peninsula, and in later periods. Examples from the oldest layers of Sephardi influence are found in the services for the high holy days, such as the *seliḥa* (a type of liturgical poem) for the new year *Atanu leḥallot panekha* (Avenary 1986). Later, Sephardi liturgical melodies were brought from Turkey and Palestine by *shadarim* 'emissaries' charged with raising funds for rabbinical academies and for the poor in the Holy Land.

The twentieth century brought an influx of modern music, especially through personnel associated with schools of the Alliance Israélite Universelle network. Liturgical music, particularly in the central synagogues of large cities, was not immune to ideas arriving from Parisian synagogues. For example, in the 1930s and 1940s there were attempts to establish choirs in some synagogues in Casablanca. A daily prayer book, *Sepher Tehiloth Israel* (1906), printed by Joseph Cohen in the "progressive" Portuguese community of Tunis, has an appendix of melodies by Beethoven, Mendelsohn, Meyerbeer, and Rossini set to Hebrew tests, amid transcriptions of traditional Maghribi tunes. Exposure to Western music may, however, have occurred earlier, in Gibraltar, where Jews had attended performances by British ensembles since the eighteenth century, as attested to by the famous poet Rabbi David ben Hassin from Morocco in his introduction to an anthology of his poems, *Tehillah le-David* (published in Amsterdam in 1807).

Finally, a major contemporary influence on Maghribi liturgical traditions is the "Jerusalemite" style predominant nowadays in Israel among Sephardi and Oriental

Jews. This style basically leans on Middle Eastern mainstream music, particularly that of Egyptian singers and composers such as Umm Kulthūm, Farīd al-Aṭrash, and Muhammed Abd al-Wahhāb (Eilam-Amzallag 1991). This style was already known in the 1920s in Tunis, through the services of the Jerusalemite Asher Mizraḥ, who was a cantor and a singer of nonreligious music there until the late 1950s.

There has been an ongoing quest for an "Andalusian" identity in Israeli liturgical music (Sharvit 1986). Despite the "Jerusalemite" influence on young Maghribi cantors, Maghribi styles can be still heard in synagogues of small development towns where the majority of the population is North African (for example, Dimonah, Yeroḥam, Netivot, and Ofakim in the Negev or Kiryat Shemonah, Hatsor ha-Gelilit, and Migdal ha-Emek in Galilee).

PARALITURGICAL MUSIC

TRACK 32

The paraliturgical tradition *bakashot* consists of singing Hebrew sacred poems during Saturday midnight vigils. Its rich musical content derives from the classic Andalusian tradition of Morocco. The involvement of Jews in this tradition is very old and can be traced to medieval Andalusia itself. Manuscript evidence exists from the late seventeenth century on. The tradition was also reported by early travelers (Host 1781) as well as by modern scholars such as Chottin (1939).

According to Chetrit (1991), the *bakashot* ceremony has three interrelated strands. First is a venerable tradition, found in Spain and Morocco before the expulsion of the Jews from the Peninsula in 1492, of singing sacred poems called *bakashot* 'supplications' before morning prayers. Second, there is an independent tradition of compound musical compositions called *treq* 'path' resembling the Andalusian *nawba*, which is performed at life-cycle and communal celebrations. Third, there is a tradition of creating Hebrew counterparts to the normative Arabic Andalusian repertoire of eleven *nawbāt* compiled by Muḥammad al-Ḥā'ik in Tetuan in the second half of the eighteenth century (figure 4). This tradition was first conceived by Rabbi Shelomo Choen of Marrakesh in the early nineteenth century.

Of the varied *bakashot* traditions that developed in Morocco, the one from Marrakesh-Mogador, whose texts appeared in *Shir yedidot* (first published in Marrakesh in 1921), eventually became predominant and has been perpetuated by most Moroccan Jews in Israel to this day. It was fostered especially after 1965, with the arrival in the country of R. David Buzaglo (d. 1975), who was considered its best exponent of his generation.

In this tradition, gatherings take place in synagogues early on Saturday morning for twenty weeks (twenty-four in leap years) from October to March, The event, which lasts for about three to four hours, includes prayers, *bakashot*, a cycle of *piyyutim* (based each Saturday on a different Andalusian-Arab mode), and a *qaṣīda* (a poem in an Arabic genre on the theme from the weekly portion of the Torah), all performed a capella. The evening is conducted by a professional performer (*paytan,* also called *muqaddam*) and a selected group of singers (*havura*). The congregation joins only in the refrains and responses. Parts of this same repertoire are performed with instrumental accompaniment on weekdays at family festivities and special concerts.

Traces of Andalusian musical modes and forms are found in Tunisia too. The earliest evidence of this tradition can be found in the *dīwān* of the seventeenth-century Tunisian Jewish poet Fradji Shawat, whose poems are divided according to Andalusian modes (manuscript in the private collection of M. Benayahu; see Hazan 1976). Later manuscripts of this kind are found in private collections (a facsimile of the title page of the collection *Sfina maaluf* was copied by Abraham Uzan in 1916 in Taieb). The book *Shirei zimra* (published in Tunis in 1905) contains the texts of the Hebrew Andalusian tradition that had been handed down until then as manuscripts. The study of the Tunisian Andalusian music tradition among the Jews remains a desideratum.

FIGURE 4 *Dai lamevin ki zehu ḥelko be-elohav*. Song from the *bakashot* repertoire in the Andalusian style: *ṭab'* 'mode' *al-ḥijāz al-kabīr*; *mīzān* 'rhythmic cycle' *al-qāyim wa-niṣf*.

Religious poetry is also sung during celebrations of the anniversary of a pious man's death. Such events include a pilgrimage to the tomb (*ziyāra*) or a reunion in a private house or a rented hall (*hilulah*). Today, the largest such celebration takes place at the tomb of Simeon Bar-Yoḥai in Meron, Upper Galilee, on the thirty-third day after Passover (*Lag ba-'omer*). *Piyyutim* and songs in Hebrew and Judeo-Arabic (*matruz*) are sung by men while women sing *qṣa'id*. Most songs are in praise of the saint, recounting his life and miracles, or the site of his tomb (Ben-Ami 1984). They are usually performed by invited professional *paytanim* with an accompanying ensemble (figure 5).

Another context for paraliturgical (as well as folk) music is the *Mimunah*, at the conclusion of Passover. This festivity, found only among Moroccan Jews, was originally celebrated with visits and exchanges of food between neighbors as well as picnics where music was performed. In Israel, the *Mimunah* has become almost a national celebration. On this day, traditional music can be heard on stages set up in state and city parks.

The paraliturgical repertoire is dynamic and has been continually renovated by melodies borrowed from religious and nonreligious works of singers and poets (for example, Arabic, Spanish, and French). This phenomenon, known in the scholarly literature as contrafactum, has drawn particular attention (for example, Armistead and Silverman 1973, 1981). One curious early instance is the use of *Mamrún se fué a la guerra,* the Spanish version of a popular ballad of French origin, whose melody is mentioned in a manuscript of 1824–1825 (J.N.U.L. Ms. Heb 80 3716, fol. 325r; see Armistead, Hassan, and Silverman 1974). Modern cases are equally interesting; the melody of the Scottish song "Auld Lang Syne" is widely used by Moroccan Jewish

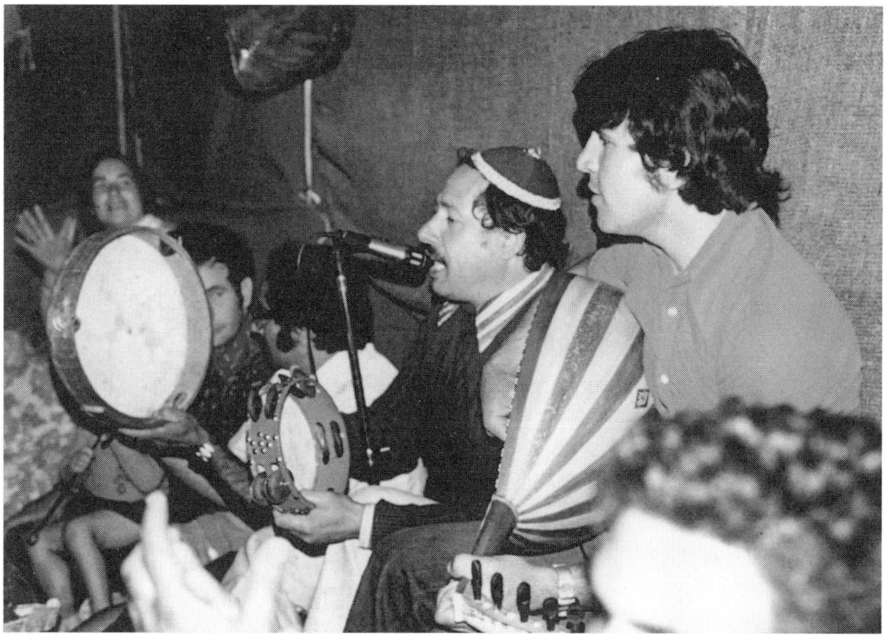

FIGURE 5 Moroccan Jews singing and playing *'ūd* and *tar* outside the tomb of Mimunah Baba Sali (Rabbi Yisrael Abuḥatsira) during his *hilulah*, Netivot, Israel. Photo by Varda Polak-Sahm.

singers for Hebrew *piyutim* such as *Yigdal elohim ḥay* and *Ki eshmera shabat*; this melody became known in Morocco through a French film. In Djerba, the local Jews set the Hebrew song *Dumiyah ve-libbi yilhav* 'In Silence My Heart Flames Up' to the tune of the French national anthem "La Marseillaise" when French officials visted the island.

Today, the *bakashot* of Moroccan Jews in Israel is one of the most vital Maghribi Jewish musical traditions. Widespread interest in Andalusian music in Hebrew led to the creation of schools of singers and an Andalusian orchestra supported by public funds. The interaction between Jewish and Arab musicians from Morocco was fostered in recent years by the peace process between Israel and its Arab neighbors. In Morocco and Israel, in public and private contexts, there were performances of Andalusian music in Arabic and Hebrew simultaneously.

JUDEO-ARABIC FOLK SONG

There has been hardly any musicological research on Judeo-Arabic folk songs in the Maghrib; one reason for this is the predominance of research on the music of Jews from major urban centers as opposed to more remote areas such as the Atlas or the south. However, since—as scholars of literature have pointed out (Chetrit 1994)—there is a close relationship between Jewish and Muslim folk poetry in cities such as Sefrou and Tefollalt, one can assume that there is also a close relationship in music.

Four genres of folk songs are found among Jews from Morocco: *milḥūn* and *qaṣīda* (sung by men), and *'arubī* and *mawwāl* (sung by women; Stillman 1978, 1980). *Milḥūn* borrowed its modes from Andalusian music, in a simplified form.

The most popular of these genres is the *'arubī*, which is performed at weddings, circumcisions, and other social gatherings, such as a visit by an important guest. It usually consists of five-line stanzas of ten syllables with fixed rhyme patterns (songs of as many as fifty stanzas have been collected). The melodies are taken from an existing repertoire that the singer adapts extemporaneously. The topics of *'arubī* are varied: love, the beauty of nature, the suffering and pain of loneliness, the cursing of enemies, and current events. In songs of this type composed during World War II, the figure of Adolf Hitler appeared. *'Arubī* in the form of a dialogue between a man and a woman usually include witty lines.

Chetrit (1981, 1994) groups Judeo-Arabic songs on the basis of function, distinguishing between "individual" and "social" songs. In "individual" songs the performer (usually a professional or semiprofessional woman) expresses personal feelings, in the first person and in a lyrical style. Besides the *'arubī* and *mawwāl,* these women sing birth and wedding songs and *nuwwāḥ* (mourning songs). "Social" songs treat, in the third person, topics of communal interest and thus are a source of information about customs, social and economical issues, ideological positions, and historical events. Many social songs are *qaṣīda*, such as the famous *L'qasida de-skhina*, which describes the preparation of a traditional meat stew (*skhina*) cooked on Friday and kept warm throughout the sabbath.

JUDEO-SPANISH FOLK SONG

In the cities of northern Morocco, around the Strait of Gibraltar, Jewish communities perpetuated Judeo-Spanish folk songs of three distinct genres: romances, *coplas*, and lyric songs. These are usually sung by women (solo or in groups); the lyric songs are accompanied by percussion instruments.

The *romance* is the most venerable genre in the Iberian legacy of the Jews. This is basically a solo ballad with epic and lyric elements; the music is structured as four phrases comprising two verses of sixteen syllables each. While similar in structure to its eastern Mediterranean counterparts, the Judeo-Spanish romance from northern Morocco has several stylistic features of its own: diatonic intonation, a tendency toward major-minor modes, and a preference for metric schemes combining duple and triple units (Etzion and Weich-Shahak 1988).

Coplas are strophic songs on Jewish topics such as holidays and historical events (Romero 1981). These are of more recent creation than the romances, are usually by known poets, and are set to different types of melodies whose structure depends on that of the text. A curious example *is El debate de las flores* 'Debate of the Flowers', a text from the Ottoman Sephardi tradition sung today only in Morocco. Its melody has a four-phrase structure and, like a romance tune, alternates duple and triple meter.

It is in the lyric songs that the influence of the local Judeo-Spanish dialect, *haketia*, and local folk customs appears. Most lyric songs are performed for events of the life cycle, particularly weddings (Weich-Shahak 1987, 1989). The melodies are more varied than those of the romances or *coplas*: in a lyric song, the melody usually consists of two to four phrases in different combinations and, in some cases, refrains sung by a group alternating with a soloist. A characteristic feature of these songs is the alteration of duple and triple meters such as 6/8 and 3/4 (figure 6). The Arab influence is noticeable in some of these songs; for example, one responsorial wedding song uses metaphors found in medieval Arabic poetry to describe the bride's body (Weich-Shahak 1989: no. 20). A very similar test is also found in the Judeo-Arabic repertoire (Ben-Ami 1971).

TRACK 33

Because northern Morocco is so close to the Iberian Peninsula geographically, its traditional romance and lyric folk songs have close musical and poetic ties to Spanish folk song. Thus, one finds not only texts of Iberian extraction but also some tunes common to both traditions. For example, the lullaby *Si este niño se durmiere*, recorded by Felipe Pedrell and Kurt Schindler at the turn of the twentieth century, has Jewish versions from Tetuán; and tunes used in Tetuán for the romance *Don Bueso y su hermana* are also widespread in Iberia. Undoubtedly, the Spanish influence increased after the conquest of Tetuán in 1860 and during the protectorate period (1912–1956), when Jews attended Spanish schools. One can find today in the Jewish repertoire traces of popular genres such as flamenco and zarzuela tunes and well-known Hispanic children's songs—for instance, *Arroz con leche* and *Don Gato*. The mass media have also widened the scope of the Judeo-Spanish repertoire in north Morocco, bringing popular Hispanic genres such as the Argentinean tango (Cohen 1989; Seroussi 1990).

FIGURE 6 *No me puso mi madre*. Judeo-Spanish wedding song from Alcazarquivir, northern Morocco (Weich-Shahak 1989:57).

MULTILINGUAL SONGS

Several Maghribi Jewish songs combine Hebrew with Judeo-Arabic or Judeo-Spanish. The first combination, known as *matruz*, treats religious and secular topics. Examples are a song in the praise of wine by the poet Shlomo Gozlan from the late eighteenth century and a song found in a manuscript from Taroudant about a poor teacher complaining that he lacks funds for Passover. The second combination is much rarer. One example still extant in the repertoire of singers is *Coplas de la Tora* 'Song of the Torah', which includes many Hebrew words in its strophes and has a refrain, *Hi torah lanu nitana*, that is entirely in Hebrew.

INSTRUMENTAL MUSIC

Banned from synagogue services by normative Jewish law, instrumental music is confined to two settings: within the community, at events related to the life cycle, particularly weddings and circumcisions; and outside the community, as entertainment for the gentile society. Jews were well-known instrumentalists, particularly in the Andalusian tradition (Ben Ami 1970). They performed in mixed ensembles with Muslims or in entirely Jewish bands. There is also evidence that instrumental music was performed by gentiles for Jews. Rabbi Avraham Ibn Musa (Tetuán c. 1680–Tunis 1733) noted: "I witnessed a scandal. . . . They [Jews from Tunis] bring to their houses in holidays, and sometimes on weekdays, gentiles that play *kinor* [the *kamanja*] and *nevel* [the *'ūd*] and *tof* [a drum, probably the *darbuka* or *ṭār*] and *ḥalil* [a wind instrument, perhaps a *ghayta* or *djouak*] . . . and men intermingle with women" (manuscript in the British Museum, 440, fol. 164v).

Traditional ensembles described in the eighteenth and nineteenth centuries by travelers such as the Italian Jew Samuel Romanelli or depicted by European artists such as Eugène Delacroix (Shiloah 1984) include an *'ūd* (short-necked lute), *kamanja* (bowed spike lute replaced in modern times by the European violin), *darbuka* (vessel drum), and *ṭār* (frame drum). Ensembles of this type are still popular among. Maghribi Jews in Israel, France, and Canada at both religious events and private parties.

MAGHRIBI JEWS IN THE GENERAL MUSICAL LIFE OF NORTH AFRICA

As mentioned above, Jews have been part of the general musical life of North African countries since time immemorial. In Libya, for example, Jewish men gained access to palace life "by virtue of their abilities as singers" (Goldberg 1990:26). But it was during the European protectorate in North Africa that the Jewish presence in musical life developed most significantly. The Jews had relatively more access to early means of modern musical transmission, such as publishing houses, radio stations, and the recording industry.

Algeria, where Jews were recognized as accomplished performers of the Andalusian *nawba*, is an exemple. The Jewish musician, publisher, and impresario Edmond-Nathan Yafil (1877–1928), founder of the musical society El-Moutribia in Alger, is considered a main figure in the renaissance of Algerian classic music in the twentieth century (Bouzar-Kasbadji 1988:39–86). Among the Jewish masters of the classic Algerian chant in the twentieth century is Saoud El Medioni, called Saoud l'Oranais. Jews were also performers of Algerian popular genres, such as *ḥawzī* from Tlemcen, *mahjūs* from Constantine (songs in the southern Algerian dialect accompanying dances), and the Algerian *sha'bī*. We may mention the blind singer and *'ūd* player Reinette Sultana Daoud, called Reinette l'Orainase, an expert in *ḥawzī*; Raymond Leyris of Constantine and his disciple Sylvain Ghrenassia, a violinist who was an expert in *ma'lūf*; Edmond Atlan, another disciple of Raymond's; and Enrico Macias, the son of Sylvain and son-in-law of Raymond (Teboul 1987). Macias popularized the music of Algeria in France.

Jews were also substantially represented in the creation and performance of general repertoires in Tunisia. Since the 1920s, the French- and Egyptian-influenced popular song of the city of Tunis was composed and performed by Jews such as Raoul Journo, Ḥabība Messika, Luezia Tunsia, Dhelomi 'Ami'el (born in Egypt), Bishi Slama (called Khaisa), and the cantor Asher Mizraḥi (Taieb 1989).

Moroccan folk poetry, which spread to Algeria, was popularized by Algerian *sha'bī* singers. The Algerian repertoire of the Moroccan *milḥūn* was adopted at the beginning of the twentieth century by the singers of Casablanca, who conceptualized it as a modernized version of their own traditional repertoire. These romantic-lyric songs—adapted and composed by Jewish poets and singers who were influenced by Muslim styles of Morocco and Algeria—is called *msalmani* or *djiri*. The *djiri* style, as performed by Jewish singers, became very popular and even permeated into the synagogue repertoires. Among the popular performers who specialized in this genre in Morocco are Zohara Elfassiya, Ibrahim Suiri, Elma'alma Nejma, and Sami Elmaghrebi, who was influenced by Salīm Halāī. In Israel, a chief representative of this genre is Sheikh Muizo (Moshe Attar). Leaning toward modern popular genres (typically disributed on commercial cassettes), this kind of song is widely appreciated by Maghribi Jews in Israel, France, and Canada.

REFERENCES

Abitbol-Mayost, Sam. 1992. *The Jewish Music of Fez.* Ottawa.

Alvarez-Pereyre, Frank, Tamar Alexander, Isaac Benabu, Iacob Ghelman, Ora Schwarzwald, and Susana Weich-Shahak. 1994. "Towards a Typology of the Judeo-Spanish Folksong: Gerineldo and the Romance Model." *Yuval* (*Studies of the Jewish Music Research Center*) 6:68–163.

Amzallag, Abraham. 1984. "The Qasida in 'Shir Yedidot': Sources, Texts, and Music." *Pe'amim* 19:88–112.

———. 1986. "Modal Aspects in the Singing of *Bakashot* by Moroccan Jews." Ph.D. dissertation, Hebrew University of Jerusalem.

———. 1988. "Shir Yedidot and the Poetry of the *Bakashot*." *Pe'amim* 32:94–116.

———. 1991. "Late Developments in the Music of the Jews from Morocco." *Miqqedem u-miyyam* 4:145–164.

Anahory-Librowicz, Oro, and Judith Cohen. 1986. "Modalidades expresivas de los cantos de boda judeo-españoles." *Revista de Dialectología y Tradiciones Populares* 41:189–209.

———. 1993. "Expressive Modes in the Judeo-Spanish Wedding Song"; "The Music of the Songs." In *New Horizons in Sephardic Studies*, ed. George Zucker and Yedida Stillman-Khalfon, 285–296, 297–304. Albany: State University of New York (SUNY) Press.

Armistead, Samuel G., and Joseph H. Silverman. 1973. "El cancionero judeo-español de Marruecos en el siglo XVIII (Incipits de los Ben Cur). *Nueva Revista de Filología Hispánica* 22(2):280–290.

——— and ———. 1977. *Romances judeo-españoles de Tanger recogidos por Zarita Nahón.* Madrid Catedra Seminario Menéndez Pidal.

——— and ———. 1981. "El antiguo cancionero sefardí: Citas de romances en himnarios hebreos (siglos XVI–XIX)." *Nueva Revista de Filología Hispánica* 30(2):453–512.

Armistead, Samuel G., Joseph H. Silverman, and Iacob M. Hassán. 1974. "Four Moroccan Judeo-Spanish Folksong Incipits (1824–1825)." *Hispanic Review* 42(1):83–87.

Armistead, Samuel G., Joseph H. Silverman, and Israel Katz. 1986. *Judeo-Spanish Ballads from Oral Tradition*. 1, *Epic Ballads.* Berkeley, Los Angeles, and London: University of California Press.

Avenary, Hanoch. 1986. "Persistence and Transformation of a Sephardi Penitential Hymn." *Yuval* (*Studies of the Jewish Music Research Center*) 5:181–232.

Ben-Ami, Issachar. 1970. "Jewish Musicians and Folk Bands in Morocco." *Tatslil* 10:54–58. (In Hebrew.)

———. 1971. "*Shabbat Hanadneda* (A Moroccan Jewish Wedding Song)." *Tatslil* 5:197–199.

———. 1975. "La *qsida* chez les juifs marocains." In *Le Judaisme marocain: Études ethno-culturelles*, ed. Issachar Ben-Ami, 105–119. Jerusalem: Rubin Mass.

———. 1984. "The Ziara and Hillula Songs." In *Saint Veneration among the Jews of Morocco,* ed. Issachar Ben-Ami, 99–146. Folklore Research Center Studies 8. Jerusalem: Magnes.

Bouzar-Kasbadji, Nadya. 1988. *L'émergence artistique algérienne au XXe siècle.* Alger.

Chetrit, Joseph. 1981. "The Personal and Social Song in Judeo-Arabic from Morocco." *Miqqedem u-miyyam* 1:185–230.

———. 1991. *Shirat ha-piyyutim ve-shirat bakashot shel yehudei marako* (The Singing of *Piyutim* and *Bakashot* of Moroccan Jews). Tel-Aviv: Moreshet Dorot.

———. 1994. *Ha-shirah ha-'Arvit-Yehudit shebikhetav bi-Tsefon Afrikah: 'Iyunim po'etiyim, leshoniyim ve-tarbutiyim.*

Chottin, Alexis. 1939. *Tableau de la musique marocaine*, 149–153. Paris: Geuthner.

Cohen, Judith. 1988. "Judeo-Spanish Songs in the Sephardic Communities of Montreal and Toronto: Survival, Function, and Change." Ph.D. dissertation, Université de Montréal.

———. 1989. "The Impact of Mass Media and Acculturation on the Judeo-Spanish Song Tradition in Montreal." In *World Music, Politics and Social Change,* ed. Simon Frith, 90–97. Manchester: Manchester University Press.

Davis, Ruth. 1984–1985. "Songs of the Jews on the Island of Djerba: A Comparison between Two Surveys—Hara Sghira (1929) and Hara Kebira (1978)." *Musica Judaica* 7 (1):23–33.

Eilam-Amzallag, Avraham. 1991. "Recent Changes in Moroccan Jewish Music," *Miqqedem u-miyyam* (Tradition and Change in the Culture of Moroccan and Oriental Jewry), ed. Joseph Chetrit, 4: 145–164. Haifa (In Hebrew.)

Etzion, Judith. 1989. "The Spanish and the Sephardi Romances: Musical Links." *Ethnomusicology* 32(2):1–37.

———, and Susana Weich-Shahak. 1988. "The Music of the Judeo-Spanish Romancero: Stylistic Features." *Anuario Musical* 43:221–250.

Fenton, Paul. 1975. "Les baqqaot d'orient et d'occident." *Revue des Études Juives* 134:101–121.

Flender, Reinhard. 1993. *Hebrew Psalmody*. Yuval Monograph Series 9. Jerusalem: Hebrew University.

Gerson-Kiwi, Edith. 1967a. "Migrating Patterns of Melody among the Berbers and Jews of the Atlas Mountains." *Journal of the IFMC* 19: 64–73.

———. 1967b. "The Jews of the Atlas Mountains: Their Folk Life and Folk Music." *Tatslil* 7:140–144. (In Hebrew.)

Goldberg, Harvey. 1990. *Jewish Life in Muslim Libya: Rivals and Relatives.* Chicago and London.

Hazan, Efraim. 1976. *The Poems of Fradji Shawat.* Jerusalem: Ben-Zvi Institute. (In Hebrew.)

Herzog, Avigdor. 1963. *The Intonation of the Pentateuch in the Heder of Tunis.* Tel Aviv: Israel Music Publications.

Host, George Hjersing. 1781. *Nachrichten von Morokos und Fes, im Lande selbst gesammelt in der Jahre 1760 bis 1768*, 258–263. Copenhagen.

Idelsohn, Abraham Z. 1929. *Hebräisch-orientalischer Melodienschatz,* Vol. 5: *Gesange der marokkanischen Juden*. Jerusalem-Berlin-Wien: Benjamin Harz Verlag.

Lachmann, Robert. 1978. *Gesänge der Juden auf der Insel Djerba*, ed. E. Gerson-Kiwi. Jerusalem: Hebrew University. (Abridged English edition, 1940, Jerusalem.)

Larrea Palacín, Arcadio. 1952. *Romances de Tetuán*. 2 vols. Madrid: Instituto de Estudios Africanos.

———. 1954. *Canciones rituales hispano-judias*. Madrid: Instituto de Estudios Africanos.

Levy, Isaac. 1964–1980. *Antología de la liturgia judeo-española*. 10 vols. Jerusalem: Author.

Katz, Israel. 1973. "The 'Myth' of the Sephardic Musical Legacy from Spain." In *Proceedings of the Fifth World Congress of Jewish Studies* 4: 237–243. Jerusalem: World Union of Jewish Studies.

———. 1979. "Manuel Manrique de Lara and the Tunes of the Moroccan Sephardic Ballad Tradition: Some Insights into a Much-Needed Critical Edition." In *El Romancero hoy: Nuevas fronteras,* ed. Antonio Sanchez Romeraldo, Diego Catalan, and Samuel G. Armistead, 75–87. Madrid: Seminario Menendez Pidal.

———. 1982. "On the Music of Three Romances from Tangier." *Estudios Sefardies* 1:129–131.

———. 1986. "'Contrafacta' and the Judeo-Spanish Romancero: A Musicological View." In *Hispanic Studies in Honor of Joseph Silverman,* ed. Joseph V. Recapito, 169–187. Newark, Del.: Juan de la Cuesta.

Ortega, Manuel L. 1919. *Los hebreos en Marruecos: Estudio histórico, político, y social.* Madrid: Editorial Hispano Africana.

Romero, Elena. 1981. "Las coplas sefardíes: Categorias y estado de la cuestión." In *Actas de las Jornadas de Estudios Sefaradíes,* 69–98. Caceres: Universidad de Extremadura.

Sabbah, Dina. 1980. "Le chant religieux chez les marocains d'Israel." M.A. thesis, Université de Montréal.

Seroussi, Edwin. 1984. "Change and Continuity in the Singing of *Bakkashot* among Moroccan Jews in Israel: Transformations in the Symbolic Meaning of a Traditional Music Custom." *Pe'amim* 19:113–129. (In Hebrew.)

———. 1986. "Politics, Ethnic Identity, and Music in Israel: The Case of the Moroccan *Bakkashot.*" *Asian Music* 17(2):32–45.

———. 1990. "La musica arábigo-andaluza en las *bakkashot* judeo-marroguíes: Estudio histórico y musical." *Anuario Musical* 45:297–315.

———. 1990. "The Growth of the Judeo-Spanish Folksong Repertory in the Twentieth Century." In *Proceedings of the Tenth World Congress of Jewish Studies,* division D, 2:173–180. Jerusalem: World Union of Jewish Studies.

———. 1992. "The Ancient Melodies: On the Antiquity of Music in the Sephardi Liturgy." *Pe'amim* 50:99–131. (In Hebrew.)

Seroussi, Edwin, and Susana Weich-Shahak. 1991. "Judeo-Spanish Contrafacts and Musical Adaptations: The Oral Tradition." *Orbis Musicae* 10:164–194.

Sharvit, Uri. 1986. "Diversity within Unity: Stylistic Change and Ethnic Continuity in Israeli Religious Music." *Asian Music* 17(2): 126–146.

Shiloah, Amnon. 1972. "Africa, North: Musical Traditions." *Encyclopedia Judaica* 16:1257–1260.

———. 1980. "La nuba et la célébration des *bakashot* en Maroc." In *Judaisme d'Afrique du Nord,* ed. Michel Abitbol, 108–113. Jerusalem: Ben-Zvi Institute.

———. 1984. "Impressions musicales des voyageurs européens en Afrique du Nord." In *Les relations intercommunautés juives en méditerranée occidentale XIIIe–XXe siècles,* ed. J. L. Miege, 275–280. Paris: Éditions du C.N.R.S.

Stillman, Yedida. 1978. "The Art of a Moroccan Folk Poetress." *Zeitschrift der Deutschen Morgenlandischen Gesellschaft* 128(1):65–89.

———. 1980. "The Art of Women Songs in Morocco." In *Judaisme d'Afrique du Nord,* ed. Michel Abitol, 161–171. Jerusalem: Ben-Zvi Institute. (In Hebrew.)

Taieb, Jacques. 1989. "Ya lil, ya lil . . ." In *Les juifs de Tunisie: Images et textes,* ed. Jacques Allali et al., 200–205. Paris: Éditions du Scribe.

Teboul, Annie. 1987. "Les musiciens." In *Les juifs d'Algérie: Images et textes,* 276–281. Paris: Éditions du Scribe.

Turel (Gilead), Tali. 1981. "Music in the Custom of the *Bakkashot* among Moroccan Jews in Israel." M.A. thesis, Tel Aviv University. (In Hebrew.)

Weich-Shahak, Susana. 1987. "Rites of Passage in the Judeo-Spanish Songs of Morocco." *Pe'amim* 30:105–124. (In Hebrew.)

———. 1989. *Judeo-Spanish Moroccan Songs for the Life Cycle.* Yuval Music Series 1. Jerusalem: Hebrew University.

———. 1992. *Música y tradiciones sefardíes.* Salamanca: Diputación de Salamanca.

Yurchenko, Henrietta. 1958. "The Music of the Jews in Morocco." *Year Book of the American Philosophical Society:* 518–520.

———. 1991. *Ne'im zemirot: 102 Selections of Sephardi Jewish Music.* Montreal.

Zafrani, Haim. 1977. *Poésie juive en Occident musulman,* 271–305. Paris: Geuthner.

Liturgical Music of the Yemenite Jews in Israel

Uri Sharvit

The Age of Yemenite Jewish Culture
Musical Motifs and Tropes
The Liturgical Text
Liturgical Tunes

The first organized immigration of a few hundred Yemenite families to what is now Israel and was then Palestine began in 1881–1882. There were two more waves of immigration in 1907 and 1918, but the largest wave—about 50,000 people—came in 1949–1950, immediately after the founding of the state of Israel. In Israel today, although acculturation is an ongoing process, the Yemenite Jews still tend to live together in homogeneous communities, where they attempt to maintain their traditional culture; they are proud of their tradition and often express their determination to keep it unchanged. This cultural persistence is reflected in their music, especially in their celebration of Jewish calendrical holidays and noncalendrical ceremonies.

THE AGE OF YEMENITE JEWISH CULTURE

When Jews first settled in Yemen is not known, but some historical evidence shows that there were Jews in Yemen in pre-Islamic days, as early as the fourth century C.E. Although the Yemenite Jews were always in contact with leaders of various Jewish centers around the world, they kept many aspects of their own culture different from that of these other Jews. The unique Yemenite Jewish culture seems to preserve very ancient features, and such features might support the traditional belief that the Jewish colony in Yemen originated in the commercial and naval enterprises of King Solomon with the queen of Sheba and with the countries of Offir and Tharshish in Africa around the tenth century B.C.E. Two phenomena in particular suggest that the Jewish Yemenite culture, as preserved today, is very old. The first of these is their unique pronunciation of Hebrew and Aramaic texts. The second has to do with the liturgical music of biblical recitations.

Older generations, especially people who were born in Yemen, still use a distinctive pronunciation, even in their everyday speech, and younger people as well use it in the synagogue, where it is obligatory for prayers. For example, the dotted gimel is a hard *g* in almost all other traditions, whereas the Yemenites pronounce it as a soft *g*, or *j*; and the undotted daleth, usually *d*, is pronouned like *th* in *this* by the Yemenites. There are also differences in their pronuciation of the vowels segol (which they pronounce like the first *a* in *attach*), patah (pronounced like the *a* in *bar*), qamats (pronounced like *o* in *god*), and holam (which sounds very close to the German *ö*).

No other Jewish group uses this delicate pronunciation: it differs clearly from the way most Hebrew consonants and vowels are spoken, and it has very meaningful implications for traditional Yemenite music.

The other feature that indicates the possible antiquity of the culture is connected directly with the liturgical music of biblical recitations. In other Jewish traditions, each of the twenty-eight symbols for cantillation, called tropes—as these appeared in printed Bibles—has its own fixed musical motif. The Yemenites, however, ignore most of the biblical tropes; they sing the biblical texts according to seven musical motifs, which are discussed below.

MUSICAL MOTIFS AND TROPES

Only one of the Yemenite motifs is attached to a special trope named *zirgå*; the other six have a specific terminology and are sung to seven syntactic disjunctives:

1. The cadential motif of a phrase is sung to the highest-degree disjunctive in a verse. It is indicated by the trope *silug* at the final word of the verse. The Yemenite term for this disjunctive, and for the next one, is *ma'amiḏ-ḥazaq* 'a strong standing'.
2. The same motif is also sung to the disjunctive of the next higher degree in a verse. It is indicated by the trope *aṭnåḥå* at the word that ends the middle part of the verse.
3. An interim motif, based on the opening part of the previous candential motif, is sung to the second-degree disjunctive. The Yemenite term for this disjunctive is *ma'amiḏ* 'standing'. It is indicated by eight tropes: *zågef ǧaḏö*, *zågef gåtån*, *sǎ̄gulåṭå*, *påzer*, *garne fårå*, *rabiya'*, *tabir*, and *tilšå yåmin*.
4. Another interim motif, based on the beginning of the opening part of the cadential motif, is sung to the third-degree disjunctive, *mafsig* 'pausing'. It too is indicated by eight tropes: *tifḥå*, *yǎṭiv mugdåm*, *påseg*, *fištå*, *šalšalaṭ*, *'azel wö-ate*, *ate*, and *tǎren tirsin*. However, the last three of these tropes are sung in this way only when they are followed by the trope *rabiya'*, which is one of the second-degree-disjunctive tropes. If any of these three is not followed by *rabiya'*, its function changes: that is, it becomes a second-degree disjunctive and is sung according to the *ma'amiḏ* motif above.
5. A motif that is based on the final part of the cadential motif, and is sung to the final *ma'amiḏ* (a second-degree disjunctive) of the verse, serves to herald the cadential motif. The Yemenite term for this function is *kissrah* 'breaking'. It can be indicated by any one of the eight tropes of the *ma'amiḏ* degree (the second-degree disjunctives in number 3 above).
6. The motif of the final *mafsig* (a third-degree disjunctive) of the whole verse is indicated by the trope *tifḥå* and might be described as the "essence" of the cadential motif.
7. The motif of the final *mafsig* of the first part of a verse is indicated by the same trope, *tifḥah*. Its musical structure, howeve, can be descrubed as the "essence" of the interim motif of the *ma'amiḏ* disjunctive (number 3 above).

Each these hierarchical motifs is sung on the stressed syllable of the final word of every syntactical clause. Therefore, the words receive their syntactic importance from the hierarchical motifs attached to them. This musical hierarchy is expressed structurally: all the motifs are parts of the cadential motif, which is the longest and the "richest." Such a phrase gives the singer, and the listener, a feeling of constant tension: a pull toward the musical goal—the final motif, which ends the phrase by presenting a musical culmination. (See figure 1.)

The Yemenites are aware that a tune may "become more revered," as they say, by "beautifying its performance." Usually, this is done by lengthening the duration of a

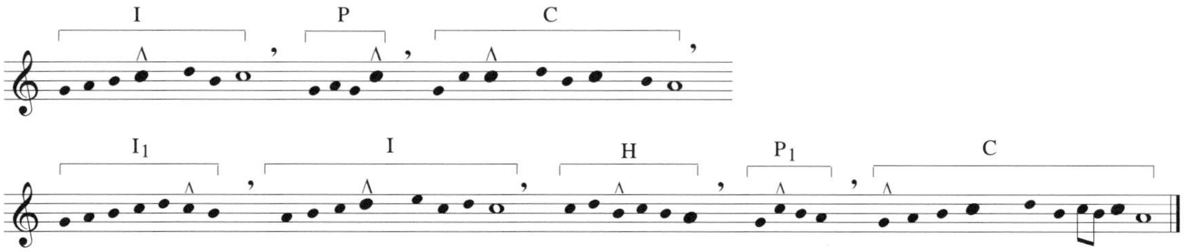

FIGURE 1 Motifs. (I) Interim motif of a *ma'amid*, a second-degree disjuctive. (I_1) Interim motif of a *mafsig*, a third-degree disjuctive. (P) Penultimate motif of the final *mafsig* of the first part of the verse. (P_1) Penultimate motif of the final *mafsig* of the whole verse. (C) Cadential motif. (H) Heralding motif. (^) Starting point of the melisma of the stressed syllable. The climactic point, C, is emphasized through motifs H and P_1, which are both based on the final part of the cadential motif, thus preparing for the closing sound.

motif: repeating some of the tones as well as adding a few others in order to heighten the ascending line of the opening part of the motif, thus widening its range. (See figure 2.)

These two musical features—a "drive" toward the end through hierarchical motifs of which the final one, the climax, is the most developed; and an elevation of a "simple" tune or motif to a more "revered" form by lengthening its duration and adding certain tones—are aesthetic principles that have an important sociocultural meaning in the life of the Yemenite Jews, particularly in their liturgy.

THE LITURGICAL TEXT

The liturgical text, which is common to all Jewish ethnic groups, is divided into many paragraphs, sung either as solo recitatives by the cantor or as a metrical rendering by the congregation. To mark the end of such a paragraph, its last verse is sung according to a more "revered" structure: a more developed rendering by the cantor or—in a congregational song—a switch from a measured meter to an unmeasured free rhythmic performance.

Another prevalent structural feature of the liturgical repertoire is heralding. Apart from the motif sung at the fixed syntactical place in scriptural recitations, we find various musical types and forms whose function is to prepare for the approaching end. These have in common, relative to the immediately preceding phrases, a certain element of surprise—a new motif, a new type of development, a sudden transposition, and so on. Also, they have a typical extramusical function.

A good example is found in the famous "priestly benediction." In the general Jewish liturgy in the synagogue, Jews who claim a family descent from Aaron the priest leave their seats at a certain point and gather in front of the Holy Ark. The text of the benediction consists of three verses (Numbers 6:24–26); each word is first sung by the cantor and then repeated by the priests. Following the final word of each verse, the congregation responds: "Amen." In the unique Yemenite practice, almost every word is sung using the same motif, whose final sound is the tonic (A in figure 3). The cantor sings a developed version, and the priests sing a "simple," more rhythmic version, in order to achieve unity. The first verse has three words and the second verse has five. The final words are sung in the same way but according to a different motif (H), whose ending sound is one tone below the tonic. Only the congregational amen is sung again according to the regular motif (A), which leads toward the "expected" finale on the tonic. Because every textual verse ends on the subtonic, the music also has a clear liturgical function, impelling the congregation to complete the musical

TRACK 34

FIGURE 2 A tune may be "beautified" by lengthening a motif. This kind of delicate structural development can also occur within a phrase. Here and in figure 1, motifs I and C are more developed in the second half of the phrase than in the first half.

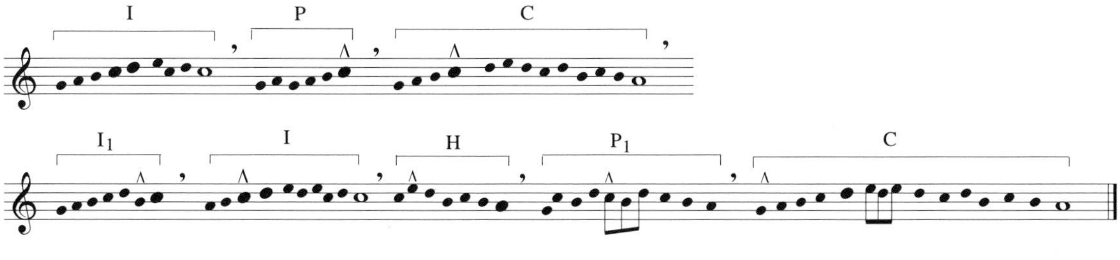

Verse 1:	A A H;	A (amen)
Verse 2:	A A A A H;	A (amen)

FIGURE 3 "Priestly benediction": scheme of the musical phrases. (A) motif ending on the tonic; (H) motif ending one tone below the tonic.

phrase by reaching the tonic. Since there are no more words to be used in such a verse, the only word that can be sung as the finale is the amen.

The music of the third verse closes the benediction. (See figure 4.) Another new motif is added on the penultimate word, whose final sound is a half tone higher than the tonic (P), enhancing the importance of the musical preparation. This verse has seven words; its musical scheme is:

Verse 3: A A A A A P H A (amen)

The tune we have been considering is just one of some twenty different tunes used for the yearly Jewish liturgy. A short description of the yearly liturgy may help to convey the general form and function of this repertoire in the Yemenite tradition. (See figure 5.)

The first part of the morning service for every weekday, *psuqei d'zimrah* 'verses of singing', consists of nine psalms, two chapters of Chronicles, and one chapter of Nehemiah. This line of biblical chapters ends with "The Song at the Sea" (Exodus 15). On sabbaths, festivals, and high holy days, nine more psalms are added. The whole first part is preceded and followed by two extensive blessings from postbiblical texts.

TRACK 35

The second part of the morning service consists of three paragraphs from the Pentateuch (Deuteronomy 6:5–9 and 11:13–21, and Numbers 15:37–41) whose title is *Shema' Yisra'el* 'Hear, O Israel'. Like the first part, this second part is preceded and followed by extensive blessings from postbiblical texts—in this case, by four such blessings, of which three open the part and one closes it. On sabbaths and festivals, there are minute changes in the text of the first opening blessing.

FIGURE 4 "Priestly benediction": typical performance of the five final motifs of the third verse.

	Weekday	*Monday and Thursday*	*Purim*	*Ninth of Ab*	*1st day of the month*	*Sabbath*	*Passover*	*Pentecost*	*Tabernacles*	*Tunes*	*High holidays*
1.	Psuqei d'zimrah	Psuqei d'zimrah	Psuqei d'zimrah	Psuqei d'zimrah	Psuqei d'zimrah	Psuqei d'zimrah (enlarged)	Psuqei d'zimrah (enlarged)	Psuqei d'zimrah (enlarged)	Psuqei d'zimrah (enlarged)	I, II, III, I	Psuqei d'zimrah (enlarged)
2.	Shema'	Shema'	Shema'	Shema'	Shema'	Shema' (minute change)	Shema' (minute change)	Shema' (minute change)	Shema' (minute change)	I, IV, I	Shema' (minute change)
3.	'Amidah	'Amidah	'Amidah	'Amidah	'Amidah	'Amidah	'Amidah	'Amidah	'Amidah	I	'Amidah
4.					Hallel	—	Hallel	Hallel	Hallel	V	—
5.									Hoshanot	VI	—
6.									Circuits Ecclesiastes (XI)	Songs 5–10 (as stated)	—
7.			Esther (IX)	Lamentations (X)			Song of Solomon (XI)	Ruth (XI)			
8.		Pentateuch	Pentateuch	Pentateuch	Pentateuch	Pentateuch + Prophets	Pentateuch + Prophets	Pentateuch + Prophets	Pentateuch + Prophets	VII VIII	Pentateuch + Prophets + Shofar
9.					Mussaf	Mussaf	Mussaf	Mussaf	Mussaf	I	Mussaf
10.	Final part	Final part	Final part	Final part	Final part (+ song 1)	Final part (+ song 2)	Final part (+ song 2)	Final part (+ song 2)	Final part (+ song 2)	I + songs as stated.	Final part

FIGURE 5 The yearly Jewish liturgy.

The third part, the *'amidah* 'standing' prayer, consists of three short opening blessings and three final blessings. On weekdays, thirteen more short blessings are inserted between these opening and final groups of blessings; but on sabbaths and festivals, just one extensive blessing is inserted.

The final part of the morning service is very short. It consists of one psalm (number 145), a group of several biblical verses, and three paragraphs from postbiblical texts.

On Mondays, Thursdays, the sabbath, festivals, high holidays—the two days of Rosh Hashanah (the new year) and Yom Kippur 'Day of Atonement'—and the first day of the (Jewish) month, the third part is followed by a special part: the public recitation of a certain portion of the Pentateuch. On the sabbaths, festivals, and high holidays, this Pentateuch portion is followed by a certain chapter of Prophets. Each first day of a month, each sabbath, each festival, and each of the three high holidays has its own fixed portion of the Pentateuch portion and its own chapter of Prophets. On Mondays and Thursday, however, the recitation consists of only a small part from the beginning of the material for the coming sabbath. The ceremony of taking the Pentateuch scroll from the Ark to the pulpit and returning it after the recitation consists of a slow procession accompanied by the singing of a few verses and psalms.

Another special part for sabbaths, festivals, the high holidays, and the first day of the month is the *mussaf*, the additional *'amidah* that is performed immediately after the public recitation. The main text of this *'amidah* is identical to that of the previous one: three opening blessings and three final belssings, along with the "sanctification" and the "priestly benediction" performed during the cantorial repetition. The only difference is the extensive blessing inserted between these opening and final groups of blessings.

On each of the three festivals—Passover, Pentecost, and Tabernacles—and also on the day of Purim and the ninth of Ab, the public recitation is preceded by reciting one of the "Five Scrolls":

Passover—Song of Solomon
Pentecost—Ruth
Ninth of Ab—Lamentations
Tabernacles—Ecclesiastes
Purim—Esther

Another inserted part is the *hallel*, that is, Psalms 113–118, surrounded by short opening and closing blessings. This part is performed on the three festivals as well as on the first day of the month, preceding the public recitation.

Three more special parts should be mentioned: the blowing of the *shofar* 'ram's horn' on the high holidays; the *hosha'not*, a procession around the pulpit on Tabernacles, in which the "Four Species" are carried; and the "circuit" of all the Pentateuch scrolls on the eighth day of Tabernacles, which includes singing and dancing.

LITURGICAL TUNES

Tunes for morning services

In Yemenite practice, the blessings that precede and follow the biblical chapters in parts 1, 2, and 3 are cantorial recitatives sung to the same tune (I), which was mentioned above as the tune of the "priestly benediction." The psalms in part 1 are sung by the congregation, to another tune (II). The "Song at the Sea" is also sung by the congregation, to a third tune (III) whose traditional name is *shirah* 'singing'. (See figure 6.) The three biblical chapters in part 2 are sung by the congregation to a fourth tune (IV).

Parts 1, 2, and 3, therefore, include cantorial singing to tune I and congregational singing to tunes II, III, and IV (see figure 5). The three congregational tunes are

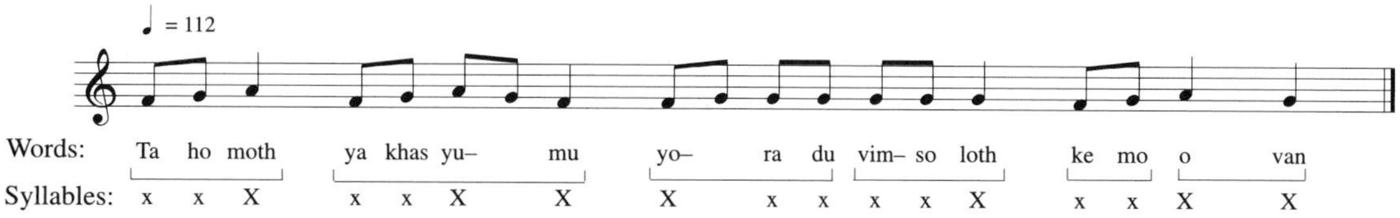
♩ = 112
Words: Ta ho moth ya khas yu– mu yo– ra du vim– so loth ke mo o van
Syllables: x x X x x X X X x x x x X x x X X

FIGURE 6 One phrase of *shirah* (tune III), from Exodus 15:5: (X) accented syllables; (x) unaccented syllables.

syllabic and measured and have only two rhythmic values: the shorter value is for unstressed syllables and the longer value is for stressed syllables.

The third part, the *'amidah*, is performed twice. First, the text is whispered by the congregation while standing (hence the title, "standing"). When everybody finishes and has been seated, the cantor repeats it to tune I. During this repetition, two "scenes" take place: the first, which precedes the third blessing, is called *kedushah* 'sanctification'; the second, which precedes the ultimate blessing, is the "priestly benediction" described above. The *kedushah* consists of three short responses between the cantor and the congregation, and the tune, like that of the priestly benediction, is performed in two ways: the cantor sings his verses in a developed version whereas the congregation sings its responses in a rhythmic, measured version.

These four tunes are the same for all morning services throughout the year. They are also sung on the sabbath, festivals, and high holidays, but in a more "revered" version. At the heart of both the cantorial and the congregational singing is the structural principle that the tunes are to serve the text. Indeed, these tunes are each constructed as a complete melodic unit covering a full verse; each such verse (or sentence) is sung using the same melodic unit. Therefore, one of the cantor's musical tasks is to deviate from the strictly repetitive nature of the music by elaborating the given motifs through trills, longer melismas, and so on.

The inner structure of any unit is similar to the structural principle of a biblical tune: the unit has at least two motifs, each covering a clause or a word. One motif is repeated (though with different nuances) several times, depending on how many words or clauses it covers; the final motif is the most important and therefore is fixed in every performance. Often there is also a third, penultimate motif ("heralding"), and one or two interim motifs. These structural principles also apply to the other eleven liturgical tunes, discussed below.

Tunes I, II, III, and IV are used for most parts of the liturgy as follows. The ninth part and most of the tenth are sung to tune I. Since the ninth part is another *'amidah*, similar to the *'amidah* of the third part, it is performed in exactly the same way as the third part. Most of the tenth part is also a cantorial recitative, but on sabbaths and festivals it ends with a certain poem sung by the congregation to a fixed measured, metric melody, song 1 (refer back to figure 5). The fourth part is sung to a special new tune (V), which is performed as a cantorial recitative in a "reverent" version, except for a few verses and the responsorial word "hallelujah," which is sung by the congregation in a measured rhythm. The same type of performance is used in the fifth part, which is part of the liturgy only on Tabernacles. It is sung to a special tune (VI), which is also used in the liturgy for the high holidays. The eighth day of Tabernacles is replete with songs and dances performed to about ten poems, each of which has its own metric tune, so that there are some ten different song tunes.

Finally, there are the tunes of the biblical recitations for parts 6 and 7 of the yearly liturgy. The Pentateuch recitation has its special tune (VII), and the following recitation from Prophets is done to another tune (VIII). Esther is sung to a special tune (IX); Lamentations is sung to yet another tune (X); and three books—Song of Solomon, Ruth, and Ecclesiastes—are sung to the same tune (XI). These five tunes (VII–XI) are all sung in accordance with the common cantillation system described above.

Tunes for evening services

In Jewish tradition, a day actually starts on the previous evening; thus the liturgical celebration of a festival or any other special day starts the evening before. The evening service has three parts. The first part consists of three chapters of the Pentateuch, as in the second part of the morning service. However, for the evening service there are two preceding blessings and two concluding blessings with postbiblical texts that differ from those of the morning service. The second part of the evening service is the *'amidah* prayer, which is performed now only by the congregants, who whisper it while standing. The third part is a short prayer with a postbiblical text. The evening service for the sabbath is unique in that its first part is preceded by a set of eight psalms, a special poem, and a chapter from a Talmudic tractate.

Yemenite traditional music follows this textual similarity to the morning services. The first part is sung exactly like the second part of the morning services with regard to the tunes (I and IV). The second part has no music. The third part is sung as a cantorial recitative to tune I. The sabbath eve service is exceptional, however: its opening section, which precedes the first part, consists of a congregational singing of the first six psalms to tune II, followed by a special metric tune (song 3), and ending with a measured new tune (XII) to which the congregation sings the remaining two psalms and the Talmudic chapter. The service ends with the singing of a certain poem to a metric melody (song 1).

Tunes for afternoon services

Another daily service, the afternoon service, is built on the following three sections: psalms 145, the *'amidah*, and a final part. On the sabbath, however, the first part is enlarged by an additional group of biblical verses (the same as in the final part of the morning service); and between the first two parts another part is inserted—the Pentateuch recitation. The first and the third parts are sung by the cantor to tune I, and the second part is done in exactly the same way as the third and the ninth parts of the morning services.

In all, Jewish Yemenite liturgical music consists of twenty-five tunes that can be divided into two main groups:

1. Cantorial solo recitatives. This group includes fifteen tunes, each of which is based on a fixed "kernel" of tones—mainly a fixed group of pitches each of which has its own structural function (such as opening tone, reciting tone, and final tone) and relative metric length within a context of unmeasured rhythmic values. Every "kernel" can be developed to some extent, but only in a fixed traditional way that maintains the general melodic contour and the "kernel" tones, including their function and metric interrelations.
2. Congregational singing of two types of tunes. The first type of congregational tunes includes some ten songs: fixed melodies constructed on the basis of measured rhythm and equal metric groupings. The second type includes the fifteen cantorial tunes to which a whole textual piece—usually a complete biblical chapter—is sung, or to which a few verses are sung during the appropriate cantorial piece, as a sort of response or antiphon. Such singing is based on an accepted set of variants of the motif "kernels" of a particular tune, sung syllabically in a measured rhythm, but—usually—not organized into equal metric groupings.

The cantorial recitations and the first type of congregational singing are the most meaningful tunes, because they express the congregants' sociocultural coherence by indicating a text or a festival and by "elevating" or "simplifying" the musical structure that signifies the textual form and affects the whole event.

REFERENCES

Bahat, Avner. 1995. "The 'Hallelot' in the Yemenite Diwan." *Yuval* 5:139–168.

Bahat, Noemi, and Avner Bahat. 1995. *Saperi Tamah*. Tel Aviv: E'eleh ba-tamar.

Brauer, Erich. 1933–1934. "Die Juden Jemens." *Kirat Sefer* 10:119, 236, 515.

———. 1934. *Ethnologie der jemenitischen Juden*. Heidelberg: C. Winter.

Gerson-Kiwi, Edith. 1965. "Women's Songs from the Yemen: Their Tonal Structure and Form." In *The Commonwealth of Music: In Honor of Curt Sachs*, 97. New York: Free Press.

———. 1968. "Vocal Folk Polyphonies of the Western Orient in Jewish Traditions." *Yuval* 1:169–193.

Goitein, S. D. F. 1937. *Von den Juden Jemens*. Berlin: Schocken.

———. 1955. "Portrait of a Yemenite Weavers' Village." *Jewish Social Studies* 27:3.

Idelsohn, A. Z. 1914–1932. *Hebraisch-oritentalischer Melodienschatz*. Leipzig and Berlin.

———. 1918. "The Jews of Yemen: Their Poetry and Music." *Reshumot* 1:3–66.

Kafaḥ, Yosef. 1961. *Halikhot Teman* (Customs of the Yemenites). Jerusalem: Mekhon Ben-Tsevi.

Ratsabi, Y. 1968. "Form and Melody in the Jewish Song of Yemen." *Tatslil* 8:15–22.

Ravina, M. 1938. "Manginot Yehudei Teman" (Jewish Yemenite Songs). In *Mi-Teman le-Tsiyon*, 194–216. Tel Aviv: n.p.

Sharvit, U. 1980. "The Role of Music in the Jewish Yemenite 'Heder.'" *Israel Studies in Musicology* 2:33–49.

———. 1981. "On the Role of Arts and Artistic Concepts in the Tradition of Yemenite Jewry." *Pe'amim* 10:119–130.

———. 1982. "The Musical Realization of Biblical Cantillation Symbols in the Jewish Yemenite Liturgy." *Yuval* 4:179–210.

———. 1986. "The Music and Its Function in the Traditional Singing of the Qasid: 'Abda birabi di halak.'" *Yuval* 5:192–234.

Sharvit, U., and Yehiel Adaqi. 1981. *A Treasury of Jewish Yemenite Chants*. Jerusalem: Israel Institute for Sacred Music.

Sharvit, U., and Simcha Arom. 1994. "Plurivocality in the Liturgical Music of the Jews of San'a (Yemen)." *Yuval* 6:34–67.

Sharvit, U., and E. Yaacov. 1984. "The 'Hallelot' of the Jews of Huggariyah and Those of Central Yemen." *Pe'amim* 19:130–162.

Shiloah, A. 1969. "The World of a Yemenite Folk Singer." *Tatslil* 9:144–149.

Spector, Johanna. 1952. "On the Trail of Oriental Jewish Music: Among the Yemenites." *Reconstructionist* 28:7–12.

Zefira, Bracha. 1978. *Kolot Rabim*. Tel Aviv: Masadah.

Music Scholarship in Israel

Amnon Shiloah

BEGINNINGS

The first attempts to explore the diversity of musical traditions in Israel go back to the pioneer generation of comparative musicologists who laid the foundations for all those who succeeded them. The initial step was taken by an exceptional scholar, Abraham Zvi Idelsohn, (1882–1938), who at first knew relatively little about some of the traditions he undertook to investigate. Idelsohn was born in a small Lithuanian town and received education and training as a cantor. Before the age of twenty, he left home for Germany, where he studied music theory and composition. He maintained contact with Jewish music by serving as a cantor, first in a synagogue in Regensburg (Germany) and then in Johannesburg (South Africa).

In 1906 Idelsohn moved to Palestine, settling in Jerusalem. It was there that he first encountered the multiplicity of Jewish and Arab traditions. Overwhelmed by the wealth of musical idioms surrounding him, Idelsohn decided to devote himself to gathering a living record from the lips of individuals still steeped in the traditions. His equipment for this tremendous project consisted of a phonograph—the cumbersome recording instrument newly invented by Edison—endless patience, and, of course, his own musical ability and background. The country at that time totally lacked any means of supporting his enterprise. However, he did receive some assistance from the Phonogrammarchiv in Vienna. Idelson's most important contribution is his monumental *Thesaurus of Hebrew Oriental Melodies* (1914–1932). The ten volumes, devoted to ten major musical traditions, include more than a thousand musical examples transcribed in Western notation, as well as extensive introductions covering history, language, dialect and accents, ethnography, and musical analysis.

Inspired by the concepts and approach of contemporary comparative musicologists, in subsequent studies Idelsohn sought to achieve a broad synthetical perspective, extending the scope of his research to Arab, Muslim, and Christian musical traditions, augmented with reflections on the roots of church music. Thus the body of knowledge he provided encompasses theoretical concepts about melodic archetypes that may have ancient roots; reading modes basically shared by all Jewish traditional reading, as well as the relation of those modes to folk songs that were unique to the Jewish people before its dispersion; the antiquity of the musical legacy of Oriental Jewish

Overwhelmed by the wealth of musical idioms surrounding him in Palestine, Idelsohn decided to devote himself to gathering a living record from individuals still steeped in the traditions.

communities; the relation between Jewish and church songs; the concept and principle of the Arab *maqām*; and the modal concept inherent in the East European Jewish *steiger*.

Idelsohn left Jerusalem and Palestine in 1921. After a year in Germany, where he made arrangements to publish his *Thesaurus*, he settled in the United States and was eventually invited to join the faculty of Hebrew Union College in Cincinnati. His major contributions during this period include *Jewish Music in Its Historical Development*, in which he summarized his basic ideas.

Just after Idelsohn's death in 1938, Eric Werner (1901–1989), a veteran scholar of Jewish music, emigrated to the United States and soon after his arrival was invited to become Idelson's successor at Hebrew Union College. Different in background, education, approach, and vision, Werner became profoundly interested in comparative liturgy and medieval Judaic musical sources. Thus the question of relations between church and synagogue in the realms of liturgy, words, and melody, as well as Jewish medieval sources related to music, became central to his research. Werner was among the organizers of the first international congress of Jewish music, held in Paris in 1957, with the eminent scholar Curt Sachs. The congress resolved to establish a *corpus musicae hebraicae*, publish an annual on Jewish music research, and develop phonogram archives; it also decided to found an international society of Jewish music, of which Sachs was elected honorary president.

For some fifteen years after Idelsohn's departure from Palestine in 1921, there was a vacuum in ethnic music research. Renewed activity came with Robert Lachmann (1892–1939). Under the Nazis, Lachmann was dismissed from his position as librarian in the Berlin State Library; in 1935, in response to an invitation from Judah L. Magnes, president of Hebrew University in Jerusalem, he came to Jerusalem to found a record archive. There, he renewed his acquaintance with the gifted musician and *'ūd* player 'Ezra Aharon, whom he had met in Cairo. Aharon was a member of the ensemble that represented Iraq at the first congress of Arabic music, where Lachmann was chosen to head the phonogram commission. Lachmann was well-versed in Arabic music, having done fieldwork and analytical studies while preparing his doctoral thesis on Tunisian music. He discovered the tradition of the Jewish community on the island of Djerba, near the Tunisian coast. The recordings Lachmann made there provided the source materials for his last work, *Study of Jewish Music in the Isle of Djerba*, published posthumously in 1940. When he moved to Jerusalem, he was able to bring 500 items of the Djerba recordings. During his last four years as head of the recording archives at Hebrew University, Lachmann recorded approximately 1,000 new items centered on Oriental liturgies including Jewish, Samaritan, Islamic, and Eastern Christian.

During the short time he was in Palestine before his death in 1939, Lachmann brought a new style to its ethnomusicological research and introduced norms based on his long experience as a comparative musicologist with extensive knowledge of Oriental music. Edith Gerson-Kiwi (1908–1992) later published a catalog of the

Lachmann documentary and record archives as well as a number of his posthumous texts (see below).

Edith Gerson-Kiwi and Herbert Lowenstein (1908–1994), better known by his Hebrew name, Hanoch Avenary, moved to Palestine at about the same time; they became the third link in the chain of development spanning the period between the eve of World War II and the creation of the state of Israel in 1948. They represent two different types of scholar with divergent backgrounds and approaches. Gerson-Kiwi was trained as a pianist and harpsichordist at the Berlin Stern Conservatory and the Leipzig Musikhochschule. She also studied performance practice and musicology with Wilibald Gurlitt in Freiburg, where she wrote her doctoral dissertation on the sixteenth-century Italian canzonette. When she moved to Palestine in 1935 to escape Nazi persecution, the environment was such that she could not utilize either her abilities as a performer or her expertise in musicology. But her brief collaboration with Lachmann was a catalyst: this exposure to the wealth of ethnic music traditions fascinated her, and her initial curiosity was soon transformed into a vital interest.

The massive immigration of Jewish communities in 1950, just two years after the creation of the state of Israel, offered Gerson-Kiwi an exceptional opportunity to revive the archive's recording project. She undertook to record the newcomers before they dispersed throughout the new country; and she and the dance specialist Gurit Kadman filmed documentaries of dances and songs of a number of groups. In 1953, Gerson-Kiwi's Ethnological Institute for Oriental Jewish Music (Makhon le-ḥeger ha-musiqa shel 'Adot Yisrael), with its thousands of recorded items, was taken over by Hebrew University; there, in 1955, she started to conduct study groups in ethnomusicology.

Gerson-Kiwi's writings, radio programs, and teaching were crucial in promoting Jewish, Arab, and Christian musical traditions in Israel and the rest of the world. She advanced a wide range of topics, from the music in the Bible to individual repertoires of Jewish and Arab women and men, touching on many aspects: folk, art, theoretical, social, and methodological. *The Persian Doctrine of Dastgah-Composition: A Phenomenological Study in the Musical Modes* (1963) and more particularly Gerson-Kiwi's collection of essays, *Migrations and Mutations of the Music in East and West* (1980), indicate her expansive research interests. She provides sections on instruments and instrumental forms, sacred chant in cults and religions, theory and treatises of the music of the Middle East, and music and society.

Avenary's professional life followed a different course. Unlike Gerson-Kiwi, whose studies combined performance and musicology from the outset, Avenary focused on musicology, contributing studies in literature and art history. In Germany, however, he was prevented from pursuing an academic career; he turned instead to publishing Jewish art in Berlin from 1932 until 1936, when he emigrated to Palestine. There he worked first as a publisher, then as a technical manager in industry; he later joined the Israeli Air Force Research Department. At the same time, however, he did musicological work privately; and after 1965 he embarked on an academic career, first as a research fellow at Hebrew University and later as a faculty member at Tel Aviv University.

Avenary dealt with many diverse aspects of the history of Jewish music from the Middle Ages to the nineteenth century, as well as with affinities between synagogue music and church music. His work encompasses biblical chants and accents, ancient and medieval sources, modality in Jewish and Christian traditions, and different versions of certain traditional melodies, with an emphasis on the laws of oral transmission. Among his major writings are *Studies in the Hebrew, Syrian, and Greek Liturgical Recitative* (1963), which investigates the ancient sources of recitative style; and *The Ashkenazi Tradition of the Biblical Chant between 1500 and 1900* (1978), in which sixteenth-century cantorial notations are compared with modern versions from Eastern and European nations. *Encounters of East and West in Music* (1979), a selection of his writings, was issued by Tel Aviv University on the occasion of his retirement. It includes articles in English and German dealing with musical instruments, modality in Jewish and Christian music, synagogue music, Jewish folklore as related to music, and problems in musicology from an Israeli perspective. His book *Kantor Salomon Sulzer und seine Zeit* (1985), which discusses a prominent and influential figure, Salomon Sulzer, provides a general picture of the nineteenth-century Viennese synagogue cantor.

Gerson-Kiwi and Avenary blazed a trail for a new generation of scholars, and for the diversification of ethnological activity.

A veteran composer, Me'ir Shim'on Geshuri, who came to Palestine in 1920, did research on Jewish music, particularly Hasidic songs. He wrote numerous articles, as well as a three-volume book in Hebrew on Hasidic music and dance, *Entsiklopediyah shel hāḥasidut* 'The Encyclopedia of Hasidism' (1956–1959). He was also one of the founders, in 1958, of the Israel Institute for Sacred Music.

In 1936 a German musicologist and publisher, Peter Gradenwitz, settled in Palestine. He founded Israeli Music Publications, which disseminated and promoted many works by Israeli composers; he also wrote a book in Hebrew to introduce Israeli music students and concertgoers to Western music—*Toldot ha-musiqa miyemot* 'The History of Music from Early Times until Today' (1939), the first comprehensive work on music that appeared in Israel. His book *Music and Musicians in Israel* (1952; revised ed. 1959) and two works in German issued outside Israel—*Wege zur Musik der Gegenwart* (1963, published in Stuttgart) and *Musik zwichen Orient und Okzident* (1977, published in Hamburg)—examined musical developments in Israel and their relation to the Orient. In this context one should mention another important book on music in Israel, written by Max Brod (a famous author who was Kafka's biographer) and annotated and edited by Yehuda Walter Cohen: *Die Musik Israels* (1976, published in Kassel).

In the early 1950s Leo Levy, an Italian-born scholar, gave a new impetus to ethnomusicological activity and broadened its scope. Levy had moved to Palestine in 1935, at age twenty-three. His main interests were Jewish and Oriental Christian liturgical music and the music of Italian and Mediterranean Jewish communities in Turkey, Greece, Bulgaria, Yugoslavia, and the island of Djerba in Tunisia. The material he collected in the course of his travels includes several rare documents; many of his Italian recordings are of particular importance, as they were obtained from the last surviving bearers of certain traditions. His important collection, essentially from the 1950s, supplements the material accumulated by Gerson-Kiwi during the period of mass immigration to Israel. Both collections are now in the National Archives at Hebrew University.

Finally, Johanna Spector, a Latvian-born ethnomusicologist who had lived in the United States since 1947, was a research fellow at Hebrew University between 1951 and 1953; she made an extensive collection of recordings in Israel, Morocco, and Turkey, including Samaritan and Yemenite music. A large part of her collection is also in the National Archives at Hebrew University. In 1954 she joined the Jewish Theological Seminary in New York, where she established the department of ethnomusicology in 1962.

THE ADVENT OF A GENERATION OF ISRAELI SCHOLARS

The 1960s were a turning point in the development and diversification of music research in Israel. Growth accelerated in several fields pertaining to music, as a result of several factors, the most important of which was an increasing institutionalization of research. The young school of Israeli musicology acquired momentum from official encouragement and support, which provided the essential means and tools. Of special importance is the establishment, in the course of five years, of musicology departments at Hebrew University in Jerusalem, Tel Aviv University, and Bar-Ilan University. This recognition of musicology as a university discipline was important in various ways: it offered numerous young Israelis who had had to take their doctorate in European and American universities, as well as newcomers interested in musicology who decided to make Israel their home, an opportunity to pursue an academic career in Israel. These young scholars represented different schools and backgrounds. Those who opted for ethnomusicological research or aspects of Jewish music found a fertile ground here. On the other hand, some Israeli musicologists who leaned toward Western historical musicology found themselves at a serious disadvantage: they felt isolated from Europe and the United States, where the vast majority of source material and research libraries are centered. Nevertheless, most if not all found ways to overcome these difficulties and to distinguish themselves internationally. Moreover, some of these musicologists took advantage of the abundant opportunities to study historical aspects of Jewish music available in Israel to anyone researching Jewish and non-Jewish minority groups. In the course of cultivating their areas of interest, they produced studies of great significance.

SALIENT FACTS AND EVENTS

In the early 1960s two Hebrew periodicals emerged, each associated with a newly founded musical institution. The first, *Dukhan*, was initiated by the Israel Institute for Sacred Music, established in 1958. Its first volume appeared in 1959 for the purpose of publishing the proceedings of the Institute's annual meetings, held during the festival of Hanukkah. It is exclusively devoted to subjects related to Jewish sacred music, for example, biblical cantillation and accents, prayer singing and cantorial art, and liturgical hymnody. Later on, the Israel Institute undertook additional publications—all in Hebrew—and made relevant recordings on similar subjects.

The second Hebrew periodical, *Tazlil* (also, *Tatslil*) is associated with the Haifa Music Museum and the AMLI library founded in 1957 by the music critic and writer Moshe Gorali. He did research on the music of ancient Israel, primarily attempting to reconstruct the instruments referred to in the Bible. The fruits of this project are displayed in the Haifa Museum. In 1960, Gorali published the first volume of *Tazlil*—a yearbook for musical studies and bibliography; it continued to appear regularly until 1980. The twenty volumes of *Tazlil* include contributions by almost all musicologists active in Israel; its articles are brief and treat a wide range of topics: general musicology, history of Jewish musicology, Jewish folk music and dance, ethnomusicology, Jewish music in Western art music, and so forth. English summaries of the major contributions are also provided.

In 1963, an important event helped put the young Israeli musicological school on the map, giving it an opening to and a perspective on the international scene. A congress held in Israel, "East and West in Music," was organized by the Israeli Council of Culture and Art in cooperation with the International Music Council of UNESCO and the International Folk Music Council. Leading scholars from all over the world were able to become acquainted with musical traditions in Israel and with the efforts being made by Israeli scholars to explore them. Indirectly, the congress was a mark of recognition for the achievements of the first generation of Israeli musicologists.

It is significant that in connection with this international congress, the newly created official publishing house, the Israel Music Institute, designed to promote Israeli art music, published seven monographs offering a cross section of studies concerned with Oriental and Jewish music. This panoramic series gave the guests from abroad an overview of musical scholarship in Israel.

The seven monographs include a first example of what later became known as archaeomusicology, Bathya Bayer's study *The Material Relics of Music in Ancient Palestine and Its Environs*, in which 250 archaeological finds from 3000 B.C.E. to the sixth century C.E. are listed and documented. Ancient sources of recitative are the theme of Avenary's *Studies in the Hebrew, Syrian, and Greek Liturgical Recitative*. The critic and composer Menashe Ravina investigates the old tradition of the Samaritans in *Organum and the Samaritans*. Avigdor Herzog, in *The Intonation of the Pentateuch in the Heder of Tunis*, analyzes Bible teaching and biblical cantillation as practiced by the religious schools of Tunis. The modern Israeli folk song, its characteristics, and its relation to ancient Hebrew music are treated by Michal Smoira-Roll in *Folk Song in Israel: An Analysis Attempted*. The two remaining monographs deal with Persian and Arabic art music. One, mentioned above, is Gerson-Kiwi's *The Persian Doctrine of Dastgah-Composition,* which analyzes one particular *dastgah* on the basis of the author's recordings of a young Jewish Iranian musician. The second, *Caractéristiques de l'art vocal arabe au Moyen Age* (1963), by Amnon Shiloah (the present author), deals with vocal art and techniques and discusses improvisation in reference to medieval Arab sources. This review of the monographs indicates the wide scope and diversity of scholarship already present in Israel at that early period.

NATIONAL SOUND ARCHIVES AND JEWISH MUSIC RESEARCH CENTER

In 1964, Israel Adler, upon returning to Israel after extended studies in Paris, took decisive steps toward complying with resolutions of the first International Congress of Jewish Music (Paris, 1957). He initiated the National Sound Archives (Phonotheka) at Hebrew University. With Herzog at its head, the Phonotheka quickly became an important central repository for existing collections and for those that were gradually being accumulated. More than 100,000 items of vastly variegated musical expressions testify to the wealth and diversity of Jewish and related musical traditions. This collection is also a trove of information for scholars who want to broaden their research perspectives.

The year 1964 also saw the foundation of the Jewish Music Research Center (Merkoz le-Musiḳah Yehudit) at Hebrew University. Its goal has been to establish a base for the two principal branches of research: ethnomusicological and historical. A team of research members was formed, consisting of Adler, director of the center; Avenary; Bayer; Gerson-Kiwi; Herzog; and Shiloah. They initiated the enormous project of preparing an inventory of Jewish music. This enterprise eventually led to the publication of two volumes by Adler: *Hebrew Writings Concerning Music in Manuscripts and Printed Books* (1975) and *Hebrew Notated Manuscripts* (1989), both part of the series Répertoire International des Sources Musicales.

In 1968, the first volume of *Yuval: Studies of the Jewish Music Research Center*, edited by Adler, Avenary, and Bayer, was published; the fourteen contributions included in the first issue reflected the diverse fields of research associated with Jewish music. Among the subjects treated were ancient Israeli and Samaritan music, stylistic aspects of various musical traditions, the relationship between synagogue and church music, critical edition of medieval sources, cantorial art, and the technique of musical analysis with the melograph. Five volumes of *Yuval,* along similar lines, have appeared so far; the Idelsohn Memorial Volume, published in 1986, was a tribute to the founder of the discipline that reflects his diverse interests. The name of the biblical inventor of music—Yuval—was also given to a series of longer monographs initiated by the research center in 1974; these include:

- I. Adler, *Musical Life and Tradition of the Portuguese Jewish Community of Amsterdam in the XVIII Century* (1974).
- R. Lachmann, *Posthumous Works,* Vol. 1, ed. E. Gerson-Kiwi (1974).
- I. Adler and J. Cohen, *Catalog of the Idelsohn Archives in the Jewish and University Library* (1976).
- A. Shiloah, *Music Subjects in the Zohar: Texts and Indices* (1977).

- D. Cohen and R. Katz, *The Israeli Folk Song: A Methodological Example of Computer Analysis of Monophonic Music* (1977).
- R. Lachmann, *Posthumous Works,* Vol. 2, ed. E. Gerson-Kiwi (1978).

DEPARTMENTS OF MUSICOLOGY AT ISRAELI UNIVERSITIES

With the opening of three departments of musicology between 1965 and 1969, ethnic and historical music research entered a new phase, paving the way for a new, locally trained generation of scholars, teachers, critics, and radio producers. It is interesting to note that in the beginning, eminent Jewish American musicologists were summoned by the three universities to establish and plan their respective departments. Thus in 1965 Alexander Ringer from the University of Illinois inaugurated Hebrew University's department in Jerusalem; a year later, Eric Werner, heir to Idelsohn's chair at Hebrew Union College in Cincinnati, opened the department at Tel Aviv University; and in 1970 Bar-Ilan University, a religious institution, called on Bathia Churgin from Vassar College to help establish its department. She is the daughter of the late Pinchas Churgin, a professor of Jewish history who was among the founders of Bar-Ilan University in 1955 and its first chancellor and president. Ringer and Werner served as visiting professors, but Bathia Churgin settled in Israel and was the chair of the musicology department at Bar-Ilan for many years. These three founders were instrumental in ensuring a strict disciplinary approach and high standards from the outset, although the subsequent efflorescence of each department has been essentially determined by the characteristics and major interests of its faculty.

Hebrew University's initial team included the well-known composer and theorist Josef Tal, who was also a founder and director of the Israel Center for Electronic Music at Hebrew University; Ruth Katz, whose interests embraced opera, sociology, and philosophy of music as well as ethnomusicology; Don Harrán, a renowned specialist in the Renaissance and humanism in music; and the present author, Amnon Shiloah, a specialist in Jewish and Arab musical traditions who combines a historical and an ethnomusicological approach. Dalia Cohen, a music theorist whose interests encompass Western and Eastern music, soon joined the faculty; she was the founder, in conjunction with Ruth Katz, of the Electronic Laboratory for the study of music, where they developed several models of the melograph (the most recent is designed to be used with a computer). The faculty also includes Jehoash Hirshberg, a specialist in fourteenth- and eighteenth-century musical styles who developed new areas of interest in Israeli music and ethnomusicology; Israel Adler, who continued to head the Jewish Music Research Center; Bathya Bayer, who is interested in the music of both ancient and modern Israel; the eminent Shenkarian expert and specialist in music appreciation Roger Kamien; and the renowned composer Mark Kopytman.

The music department of Tel Aviv University inaugurated its studies with a faculty that included the two pioneers Gerson-Kiwi and Avenary, in addition to Peter Gradenwitz and Herzl Shmueli, an eminent music educator whose main interests are Israeli song and art music as well as the early Romantics and music in England. Judith Cohen, who (like her colleague Shmueli) received a doctorate from the University of Zurich, specializes in late medieval and Renaissance music. Later, several others joined the department: David Bloch, an expert in performing practice of contemporary and avant-garde music; the composer Haim Alexander; Shay Burstyn, a specialist in late medieval and Renaissance music and the director of Cantilena, the Israeli ensemble of early music; and Judith Etzion, who concentrates on Spanish music and its relation to the Sephardi music—in which field she is doing research with Susana Weich-Shahak. For a limited period the faculty also included Joachim Braun, who later joined Bar-Ilan University; and Avner Bahat, who in 1978 founded the Jewish Music Center (Merkaz Ha'azanah le-Musikah Yehudit) at Bet ha-Tefutsot—the Jewish Diaspora Museum. Directed by Bahat, the center has a collection of recorded musical traditions

Following in the steps of Edith Gerson-Kiwi, a younger generation made extensive field recordings and published many studies of individual traditions.

and Israeli music, has published a series of music books in Hebrew, and has issued four records. The music critic Uri Eppstein, who took his doctorate in Japan and was awarded the Order of the Rising Sun (conferred by the emperor of Japan), gives courses on Japanese musical traditions at the University of Jerusalem and at Tel Aviv University.

In 1971, Tel Aviv University's department of musicology launched the first volume of *Orbis Musicae* to give scholars from Israel and other countries a forum for their work. Unlike *Yuval,* which was devoted exclusively to Jewish music, *Orbis* published articles on general musicology, with special emphasis on Mediterranean music. Nine volumes have been published so far.

In 1975, at Avenary's initiative, this department began a series called Documentation and Studies. Its principal purpose was to provide students with Hebrew versions of important musicological studies. The three monographs issued in Hebrew were published in 1978 in an annotated English translation (see below).

The Bar-Ilan faculty follows three main directions, reflecting its members' interests. One is connected with Bathia Churgin's major area. A second is inspired by the religious aspect of the institution. Churgin's interest centered on the early symphony and the classical period; consequently, precedence has been given to stylistic analysis and the process of composition, with emphasis on the classical and Romantic eras in Western music. This tendency found expression in a Beethoven research project that culminated in a conference held in 1987 and seven theses on Beethoven's works written under Churgin's guidance and supervision. The third direction—compatible with, and linking, these two fields of interest—is the ethnomusicological curriculum offered by B. Shamgar and the composer André Hajdu. The group whose interest centers on Jewish music includes Uri Sharvit, who combined research on ethnic musical traditions (emphasizing the Yemenites) with research on sociocultural aspects of change as they affect these traditions. With regard to the latter, Sharvit collaborated with Braun, who specialized in Baltic and Russian music and the Jewish musical traditions of that region. Others belonging to this group are Avigdor Herzog, who specializes in biblical chant and accents as well as Samaritan music; Ya'akov Mazor, whose main interest is Hasidic and *klezmer* music; and Edwin Seroussi, whose investigations have focused primarily on Sephardi music after the expulsion from Spain.

MUSICOLOGISTS AND THEIR AREAS OF INTEREST

Up to now, more than forty scholars in Israel have produced hundreds of articles and books in Hebrew as well as in major European languages. This output is notable for its contribution to a wide variety of spheres: Jewish music throughout history from biblical times to the present, the music of ancient Israel and other ancient civilizations, aspects of biblical and postbiblical chant, the relationship of synagogue and church music, study and critical editing of sources, research on living musical traditions of exiled Jewry and the imprint of local styles, the art and folk music of Middle Eastern cultures, newly born folk and art music in Israel, historical and systematic studies of

Western art music, and so on. Another interesting phenomenon is that Israeli scholars tend to specialize in more than one field and often shift from one area to another.

The music of ancient Israel and other ancient Middle Eastern civilizations is the field of Bathja Bayer, who is well-versed in archaeology and biblical studies. In addition to *Material Relics*, she published two authoritative contributions in *Yuval* 1 and 4, "The Biblical Nebel," which combined organology and musical theory of antiquity; and "The Titles of Psalms: A Renewed Investigation of an Old Problem." Among her important ongoing research projects is "The Mesopotamian Theory: A Reexamination of the Sources." Shlomo Hofman, whose interests include biblical and postbiblical scriptures, has published five manuals in Hebrew providing biblical, postbiblical, talmudic, and midrashic references to music.

The postbiblical domain—including history, transmission of synagogue music, relationships between synagogue and church music, Jewish medieval thought, and study and critical editing of sources—has received contributions from several scholars. Avenary has been discussed above. Israel Adler, in addition to the works described earlier, wrote *La pratique musicale savante dans quelques communautés juives en Europe aux 17 et 18e siècles* (1966). Both scholars, as well as the American Norman Golb, have also studied the notated fragments by Obadiah the proselyte (eleventh century). The present author, Amnon Shiloah, has given attention to the study and critical editing of Judeo-Arabic sources, emphasizing links between Jewish and Arab thought and theory; his research spans past and present and analyzes written sources and living traditions, the historical aspects being described in sociocultural contexts. His book *Jewish Musical Traditions* (1992), which is based on an earlier extensive Hebrew version, can be considered a link between ethnomusicological and historiomusicological studies.

The wealth of musical cultures from East and West in Israel has drawn the attention of many scholars and has shaped their investigations. Following in the steps of Gerson-Kiwi, a younger generation made extensive field recordings and published many studies of individual traditions. At least four scholars—Katz, Herzog, Hofman, and Ravina—have studied archaic Samaritan musical traditions. Hertzog was particularly interested in the biblical chant and accents of both Oriental and Ashkenazi traditions; his investigations encompassed, for example, the use of chironomy in reading the Torah and the emergence of a new style of chanting. The Jewish Yemenite musical tradition has been a major interest of Uri Sharvit, who, in addition to numerous articles, published the book *A Treasury of Jewish Yemenite Chants* (in Hebrew and English, issued in Jerusalem in 1981). He also studied sociocultural factors affecting traditional music in Israel. This subject has been treated in an extensive theoretical study by Shiloah and the sociologist Erik Cohen. The Qara'it tradition has also been an object of research for the historical musicologist Jehoash Hirshberg, who has published important material on the community. Joachim Braun has made valuable contributions to the study of Baltic and Russian music, emphasizing Jewish elements in Russian music and discussing Eastern Jewish musical folklore. In collaboration with his colleague Sharvit, he became involved in anthropological aspects of the traditional music of Israel.

Ashkenazi traditions have also been a focus of scholarship. Eli Schleifer, an expert in cantorial art, edited Chemjo Vinaver's magnificent collection and provided an enlightening bibliography raisonnée of Idelsohn's writings that was published in the memorial volume of *Yuval* (of which he is an editor). André Hajdu and Ya'akov Mazor jointly and separately contributed important studies on Hasidic and *klezmer* music; they also published *Otsar ha-Ḥasidut*, which contains transcriptions of 101 tunes. The useful documentary books of Cantor Yehoshuwa' Lev Ne'eman *ṭera be-ṭa'am* (1966) and *Nusaḥ la-ḥazan* (1968–1969) have to do with biblical chanting and traditional Ashkenazi prayer-tunes, respectively. The Sephardi musical heritage that survived in the Ottoman Empire, Morocco, and Europe after the expulsion from Spain in 1492 is the major area of research of Susana Weich-Shahak and Edwin Seroussi. Weich-Shahak, who served for years as a research member at the Jewish Music Research Center, published twenty-one articles on the Judeo-Spanish repertoire in the Balkans and Morocco. She also collaborated with Judith Etzion on important investigations of the relation between Spanish and Sephardi romances. Seroussi has studied liturgical and secular Sephardi music, Hebrew contrafacta (a subject also studied by Bahat), relations with neighboring indigenous musical traditions (Turkish music), and notable Jewish musicians. His book *Mi-zimrat kedem* is about the life and work of one musician: Isaac Algazi, from Turkey. Further contributions to the same general field were made by Avenary, Gerson-Kiwi, Isaac Levy, and Shiloah (the present author). Among Shiloah's ethnomusicological studies is *The Jewish Iraqi Musical Tradition* (1983), which emphasizes liturgy. Biblical cantillation and accents (*te'amim*) have always been a major concern for scholars; this topic has brought together a team of researchers—Dalia Cohen, Avigdor Herzog, Uri Sharvit, and Daniel Weil—to work on the elucidation of a theoretical model conceived by Weil. In collaboration with Cohen, Weil is pursuing a central objective: reconstruction of the biblical Masoretic cantillation and the establishment of a theoretical model of the original performance as a means of disclosing the principles of cantillation practice.

Some important research has centered on Arab folk and art music. Work done in this area by Idelsohn, Lachmann, and Gerson-Kiwi was described above. For some time now, this field has been a major interest of the present author, who has written more than fifty books and articles on history, sources, social and cultural life, and living musical traditions, including *La perfection des connaissances musicales* (1972), *The Epistle on Music of the Ikhwan al-Safa* (1978), and *The Theory of Music in Arabic Writings* (1979). Dalia Cohen, whose broad scope includes the liturgical music of Eastern churches, the modal concept in Arabic music, Arab folk music and acoustics, and the nature and meaning of musical parameters, has expounded her major ideas in an important book *Mizraḥ u-Ma'arav ba-Muzika* (published by East and West in Music in 1986). She examines prevalent tendencies, principles, and characteristics in musical and extramusical contexts in Western and nonwestern cultures. Collaborating with Ruth Katz, Cohen devoted many years to a huge research project, *Latent and Manifest Theory: A Maqam Tradition in Practice*; the work offers an extensive theoretical analysis of an oral tradition exemplified by Arabic folk song in Israel.

Israeli folk and art music is an area increasingly favored by musicologists. For a long time the return to the "land of Israel" that began at the end of the nineteenth century created acute problems for the Jewish population, stemming from the aspiration to create a national style that would synthesize Eastern and Western music. Hirshberg has concentrated on studies of a few composers who furthered Israeli folk and art music in the period preceding and immediately following statehood; one example is *Paul Ben-Haim: His Life and Works* (1981). Avner Bahat published a book on another composer, *Oedoen Partos: His Life and Works* (1984). Israeli folk song was the subject of an important contribution by Herzl Shmueli, *Ha-Zemer ha-Yisraeli* 'Israeli Song' (1971). Monographs by Michal Smoira-Roll, Dalia Cohen, and Ruth Katz have already been mentioned. Bathja Bayer, who also became involved in studying Israeli folk song, supervised Natan Shahar's Ph.D. thesis, "The Eretz-Israeli Song 1920–1950: Sociomusical and Musical Aspects."

Finally, there is Western art music. In view of Israel's distance from sources and documents, the achievments of researchers in this field have been remarkable. Don Harrán, who is considered a leading scholar of sixteenth- and seventeenth-century music, has produced major studies encompassing musical thought, theoretical writings, the relationship between word and tone, performance practice, and Jewish music as it relates to Western art music of specific periods. His critical editions include

"Maniera" il madrigale: Una raccolta di poesie musicali del Cinquecento (Biblioteca dell'Archium Romanicum I, 158, 1980); the third, fourth, and fifth volumes of *The Anthologies of Black-Note Madrigals* (1980–1981); and collected works of the Jewish composer Salomone Rossi, to be published in twelve volumes. His books include *Word-Tone Relations in Musical Thought: From Antiquity to the Seventeenth Century* (1986); *In Search of Harmony: Hebrew and Humanist Elements in the Sixteenth Century* (1988); and *In Defense of Music: The Case for Music as Argued by a Singer and Scholar of the Late Fifteenth Century* (1989). Ruth Katz, whose ethnomusicological work was mentioned above, is conducting research on opera as an institution—its proliferation and the way in which various styles have crystallized. She discusses these topics in depth in her book *Divining the Power of Music: Aesthetic Theory and the Origin of Opera* (1986); she has also collaborated with Carl Dalhaus on the four-volume work *Contemplating Music* (1987–1993). The research project she conducted with Dalia Cohen concerns the nature and meaning of musical parameters and the development of ways of calibration and of assessing changes in musicocultural contexts. Bathia Churgin, a specialist on Sammartini and the origin of the symphony, published the first critical edition of some of Sammartini's 177 trios in 1981; in 1984, she published a critical edition of ten symphonies with background and detailed analysis. She has also conducted two projects analyzing Beethoven's Fourth Symphony. Beth Shamgar is involved in research on the late classical and early Romantic eras. Judith Cohen is mainly concerned with the early works of Dufay and his time; she published a critical edition (from manuscript), *Six Anonymous l'Homme Armé Masses* (1968), and *Alfonso dalla Viola: Sechs Petrarca Madrigale zu vier Stimmen* (1989). In 1978, she edited *Eduard Birnbaum: Jewish Musicians at the Court of the Mantuan Dukes (1542–1628).* Among Hirshberg's topics are fourteenth-century musical style and theory, opera, and the origins of the concerto. In 1984 he published *Ten Italian Violin Concertos from Fonds Blancheton*. Shay Burstyn is involved in research on late medieval and early Renaissance music. Among his many studies is the article "The Arabian Influence Thesis Revisited"; he is preparing a scholarly edition of *Song of Songs Antiphons in Early Renaissance Musical Manuscripts*. Judith Etzion's research and publications, as already noted, deal with the sixteenth-century Spanish ballad and with Spanish polyphonic *cancioneros* of the sixteenth and seventeenth centuries. Roger Kamien, the great Schenkarian specialist, has contributed numerous studies to the analysis and performance of works by Mozart, Haydn, and Beethoven. A seventh edition of his *Music: An Appreciation* appeared in 2000; the fifth edition of his *Norton Scores: An Anthology for Listening* appeared in 1990.

This survey of musicological activities in Israel before and since its establishment as a state until the early 1990s indicates the impressive quality, quantity, and diversity of the young country's output in the field.

REFERENCES

Adler, Israel. 1966. *La pratique musicale savante dans quelques communautés juives en Europe aux XVIIe et XVIIIe siècles*. Paris: Mouton.

———. 1974. *Musical Life and Traditions of the Portuguese Jewish Community of Amsterdam in the XVIIIth century*. Jerusalem: Magnes Press, Hebrew University

———. 1975. *Hebrew Writings Concerning Music, in Manuscripts and Printed Books from Geonic Times up to 1800*. Munich: Henle Verlag.

———. 1989. *Hebrew Notated Manuscript Sources up to circa 1840: A Descriptive and Thematic Catalog with a Checklist of Printed Sources*. Munich: Henle Verlag.

Adler, Israel, Bathyah Bayer, and Eliyahu Schleifer. 1986. *Sefer Avraham Tsevi Idelson*. Jerusalem: Hotsa'at sefarim 'a.sh. Y.L. Magnes, ha-Universitah ha-Ivrit.

Adler, Israel, and Judith Cohen. 1976. *A. Z. Idelsohn Archives at the Jewish National and University Library: Catalog*. Jerusalem: Magnes Press, Hebrew University.

Avenary, Hanoch. 1963. *Studies in the Hebrew, Syrian, and Greek Liturgical Recitative*. Tel Aviv: Israel Music Institute

———. 1978. *The Ashkenazi Tradition of Biblical Chant between 1500 and 1900: Documentation and Musical Analysis*. Tel Aviv: Tel Aviv University; Council for Culture and Art, Ministry of Education and Culture.

———. 1979. *Encounters of East and West in Music: Selected Writings*. Tel Aviv: Faculty of Visual and Performing Arts, Department of Musicology, Tel Aviv University.

———, Walter Pass, and Nikolaus Vielmetti. 1985. *Kantor Salomon Sulzer und seine Zeit: Eine Dokumentation*. Sigmaringen: Jan Thorbecke Verlag.

Bahat, Avner. 1984. *'Eden Partosh ḥayav vi-yetsirato*. Tel Aviv: 'Am 'Oved.

Bayer, Bathyah. 1963. *The Material Relics of Music in Ancient Palestine and Its Environs: An Archeological Inventory*. Tel Aviv: Israel Music Institute.

———. 1968. "The Biblical Nebel." *Yuval* 1:89–131.

———. 1982. "The Titles of the Psalms." *Yuval* 4:29–123.

Birnbaum, Edward. 1978. *Jewish Musicians at the Court of the Mantuan Dukes (1542–1628)*, English ed. rev. and augmented by Judith Cohen. Tel Aviv: Tel Aviv University, Faculty of Fine Arts, School of Jewish Studies.

Brod, Max. 1976. *Die Musik Israels*. Rev. ed. Kassel: Bärenreiter.

Burstyn, Shai. 1990. "The Arabian Influence Revisited." *Current Musicology* 45–47:119–146.

Cohen, Dalia. 1986. *Mizraḥ u-ma'arav ba-muzika*. Jerusalem: Hotsa'at sefarim 'al shem Y. L. Magnes, ha-Universitah ha-'Ivrit.

Cohen, Dalia, and Ruth Katz. 1977. *The Israeli Folk Song: A Methodological Example of Computer Analysis of Monophonic Music*. Jerusalem: Magnes Press, Hebrew University.

Cohen, Judith. 1968. *The Six Anonymous L'Homme Armé Masses in Naples, Biblioteca Nazionale, MS VI E 40*. Dallas: American Institute of Musicology.

Dalla Viola, Alfonso. 1989. *Sechs Petrarca-Madrigale zu vier Stimmen*, ed. Judith Cohen. Wolfenbuttel: Moseler.

Etzion, Judith, ed. 1996. *El Cancionero de la Sablonara*. London: Tamesis.

Gerson-Kiwi, Edith. 1963. *The Persian Doctrine of Dastgah-Composition: A Phenomenological Study in the Musical Modes.* Tel Aviv: Israel Music Institute.

———. 1980. *Migrations and Mutations of the Music in East and West: Selected Writings*. Tel Aviv, Israel: Tel Aviv University, Faculty of Visual and Performing Arts, Department of Musicology.

Gradenwitz, Peter. 1956. *Toldot ha-muzika mi-yemot kedem 'ad yamenu eleh*, 4th ed. Jerusalem: R. Mas.

———. 1963. *Wege zur Musik der Gegenwart*. Stuttgart: W. Kohlhammer

———. 1977. *Musik zwischen Orient und Okzident*. Wilhelmshaven: Heinrichshofen.

———. 1978. *Music and Musicians in Israel: A Comprehensive Guide to Modern Israeli Music*, 3rd ed. Tel Aviv: Israeli Music Publications.

Hajdu, André, and Ya'kov Mazor. 1988. *Otsar ha-ḥasidut: 101 nigune riḳud Ḥasidiyim*, 2nd ed. Jerusalem: Renanot, ha-makhon le-muzika Yehudit.

Harrán Don, ed. 1978–81. *The Anthologies of Black-Note Madrigals*. 5 vol. Rome: American Institute of Musicology.

———. 1980. *"Maniera" e il madrigale : una raccolta di poesie musicali del Cinquecento*. Florence: Olschki.

———. 1986. *Word-Tone Relations in Musical Thought from Antiquity to the Seventeenth Century*. Neuhausen-Stuttgart: Hanssler-Verlag.

———. 1988. *In Search of Harmony: Hebrew and Humanist Elements in Sixteenth-Century Musical Thought*. Neuhausen-Stuttgart: Hanssler-Verlag for the American Institute of Musicology.

———. 1989. *In Defense of Music: The Case for Music as Argued by a Singer and Scholar of the Late Fifteenth Century*. Lincoln: University of Nebraska Press.

Herzog, Avigdor. 1963. *The Intonation of the Pentateuch in the Ḥeder of Tunis*. Tel Aviv: Israel Music Institute.

Hirshberg, Jehoash. 1984. *Ten Italian Violin Concertos from Fonds Blancheton*. Madison, Wis.: A-R Editions.

———. 1990. *Paul Ben-Haim: His Life and Works*. Jerusalem: Israeli Music Publications.

Hofman, Shlomo. 1974. *Mikra'e muzika: yalkut shel pesukim meha-Tanakh she-mahutam muzika be-'Ivrit, Anglit, Tsarfatit u-Sefaradit*. Tel Aviv: Makhon le-muzika Yisraelit.

———. 1989. *ha-Muzika ba-Talmud*. Tel Aviv: Makhon le-muzika Yisraelit.

Idelsohn, Abraham Zvi. 1914–1932. *Hebräisch-orientalischer Melodienschatz*. Leipzig: Breitkopf and Härtel.

———. 1992. *Jewish Music in Its Historical Development*. New York: Dover. (Reprint of 1929 ed.)

Kamien, Roger. 1990. *The Norton Scores: An Anthology for Listening*, 5th ed. New York: Norton.

———. 2000. *Music: An Appreciation*, 7th ed. Boston: McGraw-Hill.

Katz, Ruth. 1986. *Divining the Powers of Music: Aesthetic Theory and the Origins of Opera*. New York: Pendragon.

Katz, Ruth, and Carl Dahlhaus. 1987–1993. *Contemplating Music: Source Readings in the Aesthetics of Music*. 4 vols. New York: Pendragon.

Lachmann, Robert. 1940. *Jewish Cantillation and Song in the1sle of Djerba*. Jerusalem: Archives of Oriental Music, Hebrew University.

———. 1974, 1978. *Posthumous Works*, ed. Edith Gerson-Kiwi. 2 vols. Jerusalem: Magnes Press, Hebrew University.

Ne'eman, Yehoshu'a. 1966. *Ḳera bēta'am*. Jerusalem: ha-Makhon ha-Yisre'li le-musiḳah datit.

———. 1972. *Nusaḥ la-ḥazan: le-fi masoret ha-neginah ha-Liṭa'it Yerushalmit*. Jerusalem: ha-Makhon ha-Yisreli le-muzika datit.

Ravina, Menashe. 1963. *Organum and the Samaritans*, trans. Alan Marbe. Tel Aviv: Israel Music Institute.

Rossi, Salomono. 1995–. *Complete Works*, ed. Don Harrán. Rome: American Institute of Musicology.

Sammartini, Giovanni Battista. 1968. *The Symphonies of G. B. Sammartini*, ed. Bathia Churgin. Cambridge, Mass.: Harvard University Press.

———. 1981. *Sonate a tre stromenti: Six Notturnos for String Trio, Op. 7*, ed. Bathia Churgin. Chapel Hill: University of North Carolina Press.

Seroussi, Edwin. 1989. *Mi-zimrat kedem: ḥayav vi-yetsirato ha-musikalit shel ha-Rav Yitsḥak Algazi mi-Turkiyah*. Jerusalem: Renanot, Makhon le-muzika Yehudit.

Shahar, Natan. 1989. "Ha-Shir ha-Erets Yisraeli: hebetim musikaliyim ve-sotsiomusikaliyim ba-shanim 1920–1950." Ph.D. dissertation, Hebrew University, Jerusalem.

Shamgar, Beth. 1978. "The Retransition in the Piano Sonatas of Haydn, Mozart, and Beethoven." Ph. D. dissertation, New York University.

Sharvit, Uri. 1981. *A Treasury of Yemenite Jewish Chants: Yehiel Adaqi's Collection*. Jerusalem: Israel Institute for Sacred Music.

Shiloah, Amnon. 1963. *Caractéristiques de l'art vocal arabe au moyen-âge*. Tel Aviv: Israel Music Institute.

———. 1972. *La perfection des connaissances musicales: Al-Ḥasan ibn Aḥmad ibn 'Alī al-Kātib*. Paris: P. Geuthner.

———. 1977. *Music Subjects in the Zohar Texts and Indices*. Jerusalem: Magnes Press, Hebrew University.

———. 1978. *The Epistle on Music of the Ikhwān al-Ṣafā (Bagdad, Tenth Century)*. Tel Aviv: Tel Aviv University, Faculty of Fine Arts, School of Jewish Studies, Council for Culture and Art, Ministry of Education and Culture.

———. 1979. *The Theory of Music in Arabic Writings (c. 900–1900): Descriptive Catalog of Manuscripts in Libraries of Europe and the U.S.A.* Munich: G. Henle Verlag.

———. 1983. *The Musical Tradition of Iraqi Jews*. Or Yehuda: Iraqi Jew's Traditional Culture Center.

———. 1992. *Jewish Musical Traditions*. Detroit: Wayne State University Press.

Shiloah, Amnon, and Eric Cohen. 1983. "The Dynamics of Change in Jewish Oriental Ethnic Music in Israel." *Ethnomusicology* 27(2):227–252.

Shmueli, Herzl. 1971. *ha-Zemer ha-Yisre'eli*. Tel Aviv: ha-Merkaz le-tarbut ule-ḥinukh.

Smoira-Roll, Michal. 1963. *Folk Song in Israel: An Analysis Attempted*. Tel Aviv: Israel Music Institute.

Vinaver, Chemjo. 1985. *Anthology of Hassidic Music*, ed. Eliyahu Schleifer. Jerusalem: Jewish Music Research Center, Hebrew University of Jerusalem.

Weich-Shahak, Susana. 1989. *Judeo-Spanish Moroccan Songs for the Life Cycle*. Jerusalem: Jewish Music Research Center, Hebrew University of Jerusalem.

Weil, Daniel. 1994. *The Original Performance of the Tiberian Masoretic Accents: A Deductive Approach*. Jerusalem: ha-Universiṭah ha-'Ivrit.

Popular Music in Israel

Gila Flam

Popular Song before 1948
Popular Song since 1948

This article will introduce Israeli popular music—its history, content, style, creators, and meaning. In Israel, popular music consists mainly of songs. A popular song consists of a Hebrew text and a melody; such songs have been disseminated, from their beginning, both in written form (figure 1) and through oral tradition. Since the establishment of a recording industry in Israel in 1933, popular song has also been disseminated through recordings and radio; therefore, one can almost say that every Israeli song is a popular song, at least from the point of view of its origins and distribution.

Some of this music became "folk songs" performed by sing-along groups or as an accompaniment to "folk dances." Israeli institutions took part in creating a "folk song" tradition by training teachers, youth leaders, and musicians, and by producing musical materials for educational use. Thus the Israeli popular song was used—at least in the years before statehood and in the early years of the state—not only for entertainment but to create a national identity.

Although Israeli popular song was born as a Western music, it was always looking to the East, seeking to incorporate local elements such as Arab and Mediterranean material, in order to adapt to its new environment. From the late nineteenth century up to the present, song has looked eastward to ancient Zion, as reflected in the Israeli national hymn *Hatiḳvah* 'The Hope', published in 1886:

> As long as deep in the heart
> The soul of a Jew yearns,
> And toward the East
> An eye looks to Zion.
>
> Our hope is not yet lost
> The hope of two thousand years
> To be a free people in our land
> The land of Zion and Jerusalem.

The poem, written by Naphtali Herz-Imber (1856–1909) in Palestine when he was serving as a secretary and adviser on Jewish affairs to a Zionist leader, was set to a melody consciously based on a Moldavian-Romanian folk song by Samuel Cohen of

FIGURE 1 Sheet music of a song published for the tenth anniversary of settlements in the Negev (the desert area in the south), 1960. Lyrics and melody by Emanuel Zamir, published by the Workers' Union, Culture Department of the Settlements. (From Meir Noy Collection at the Jewish National and University Library, Music Department, Jerusalem.)

Rishon-le-Zion. This adaptation became a Hebrew folk song almost overnight, then the anthem of the Zionist movement, and then the national anthem of the state of Israel.

Hatiḳvah, like most Israeli songs, has a text that looks eastward but a melody based on European melodic types, mainly in a minor scale. The tension between East and West, between Ashkenazim (Jews from Europe) and Mizraḥim (Jews from Asia and Africa) living in Israel and between Israel and its neighboring Arab countries, is reflected in Israeli popular music. Israeli popular song mirrors the creation of Israeli culture and national identity.

A syncretic phenomenon, Israeli popular song adopts musical elements from a variety of sources, both Jewish and non-Jewish. It is an original creation, a form of composition that developed a complex aesthetic language and symbolism. Israeli song manifests a process of adopting elements from a variety of sources and forming new syntheses in order to express the individual and the group.

POPULAR SONG BEFORE 1948

Before the establishment of the state of Israel in 1948, Hebrew songs were disseminated as printed postcards, booklets, and other published materials. Hebrew songs were composed for the Zionist movement and were used to create a new symbolic and aesthetic vocabulary for the new nation. Early Hebrew popular songs were composed in Europe in the second half of the ninteenth century with the rise of the Zionist movement, which sought to bring the Jewish people back to their homeland—Zion or *erets Yisrael* 'the land of Israel'. (This was a biblical name for the land settled from 1880 until 1948 by Jews of the diaspora; it was used together with the term Palestine, the political designation for the British Mandate from 1918 to 1948). The Zionists also wanted to revive their ancient culture and their language, Hebrew. Therefore, the early Hebrew songs that described a longing for Zion came to *erets Yisrael* with the first settlers of the early *'aliyot* 'immigration' from Europe.

The lyrics created imaginary symbols of the past, the landscape of the Bible—the desert, the sun, camels—and the people of the Bible, shepherds and farmers. In these lyrics the composers searched for a new language, but they looked homeward, to Europe, for the music, adopting Russian and Eastern European Jewish melodies, in particular Yiddish songs and Hasidic tunes (most in a minor key and metrical rhythm), as well as German songs.

In addition to the folk songs of Eastern Europe, early composers found material in the liturgical and traditional music of "Oriental" Jews, especially those who had settled in Israel after 1880 from Yemen, Iraq, southeastern Europe, Ottoman Asia Minor, and Central Asia. These communities in Israel attracted the attention of the pioneering Jewish ethnomusicologist Abraham Zvi Idelsohn (1882–1938). Idelsohn immigrated to *erets Yisrael* in 1906 and did fieldwork among its Jewish communities, collecting their melodies. These were published as the *Thesaurus of Hebrew Oriental Melodies* (1914–1932) and were to have a significant influence on song composers. Idelsohn also composed his own songs and published them in numerous books; his books for schoolchildren are especially well-known.

Among the other early composers of Hebrew songs were Hanina Karzhevsky (1873–1926) and Joel Engel (1868–1927). Like Idelsohn, they had been musicologists and composers in Europe and immigrated to *erets Yisrael* as mature musicians. In spite of their ideological leanings, their melodies were closer to Yiddish song than to Arab or "Oriental" Jewish song.

In the years before statehoond, songwriters were very active and enormously productive. Natan Shaḥar found that at least 4,073 songs were printed during this period; he attributed the large production of song in *erets Yisrael* to the ideological potential it represented—its capacity to create "a culture which would be entirely new, but which would also be a renewal stemming from ancient foundations" (1989:vi–vii). The song repertoire not only mixed oral and written sources through the process of composition but also continued to rely on both oral and written transmission, forming a distinctive music history.

The recording of Hebrew songs began in Europe and the Americas at the end of the nineteenth century, on cylinders. The first Hebrew phonograph records were produced in the 1920s in Europe and the Americas; the first Israeli record company, Aḥva, was established in 1933 (Hakohen 1993:15–16). The Palestine Broadcasting Authority in Jerusalem began to program Jewish and Israeli song in 1936. After the establishment of the state in 1948, Kol-Yisrael, the national broadcasting authority, took over the British Mandate station and played an important role in disseminating Israeli popular song.

In 1929, the Yemini-born singer Bracha Zefira (1911–1984), an orphan who had been raised in Jerusalem by several "Oriental" Jewish families, introduced "Oriental" melodies to the new Hebrew composers. She began her career as a concert singer in Poland and Germany and introduced Yemeni-Jewish, Sephardic, and Arab tunes to Western musicians and audiences. (*Sephardic* originally referred to the Jews of Spain; later, the term was also used for Jews of the Balkans and other regions.) Zefira's encounter with Naḥum Nardi (1901–1974), a Russian Jewish pianist and composer, led to the first mixture of East and West in Hebrew song before statehood. Bracha Zefira sang the "Oriental" melodies and Nardi improvised a piano accompaniment in the Western tradition. Later, Nardi immigrated to Palestine and composed melodies with an Oriental flavor he had learned from Zefira, but the essence of the song remained Eastern European, with a predilection for minor scales and metrical rhythm.

Others who composed in an "Oriental" style were Sarah Levi-Tannay, Issac Levi, Nissan Cohen Melamed, Yedidya Admon (Gorokhov), Matityahu Shelem, Mordechai Zeira, David Zehavi, Yehuda Sharett, Daniel Samburski, Yitshak Edel, Yoel Valbeh,

Emanuel Amiran, and Nira Ḥen. European-born composers were trying to incorporate a new aesthetic language of the "imagined past" and "imagined East." It was not until many decades later, however, that a genuine fusion of East and West was achieved in Israeli popular music.

Before statehood, song lyrics articulated the Zionist ideology of social cooperation, returning to nature, returning to the land of the Bible and to biblical texts, and re-creating the rituals of biblical holidays in order to connect them with the agricultural cycle. The common theme of these songs was "work and homeland." The texts went along with the revival of the Hebrew language in its Sephardic pronunciation (rather than the Ashkenazi pronunciation used in Europe mainly for sacred texts) and the creation of new Hebrew literature and Israeli art. The musical instruments accompanying these songs were the accordion, which bridged Russian and Hebrew song; and the recorder, which suggested the image of the shepherd, an Arab or bedouin associated with the people of the Bible.

In the 1930s and 1940s the musical theaters of Tel Aviv supported popular (urban) hit songs, in which the chorus was the main attraction. These theaters created songs not only for the educational and functional Israeli holidays of the *kibbutz* but also for professional entertainers. Song texts of the 1940s were a reaction against the image created in the 1930s—a picture of shepherds and workers in the fields, all living in a magnificent landscape of hills and valleys, flowers, and wheat glowing in the rising sun. The lyrics of the 1940s expressed the individual's life and feelings and included satire on current events. This music was more in the style of the European and American "hit song," turning to the West rather than the East.

POPULAR SONG SINCE 1948

At the time of statehood and the War of Independence, a new phenomenon arose: the army entertainment band (*lehaka tsevai't*; figure 2). Initially, there were two bands, Chizbatron and Ḥishtron. Among the composers for these bands were Moshe Wilensky (1910–1997), Alexander Argov (1914–1996), Meir Noy (1922–1998), Shemuel Freshko (1914–1990), and David Zehavi (1910–1977). The band melodies were dominated by dance tunes such as the tango and foxtrot; in fact, such dance music was dominant generally in the 1950s.

While Moshe Wilensky and Alexander Argov introduced a rich melodic and harmonic language taken from their roots in Poland and Russia and adjusted structure

FIGURE 2 The army entertainment group Naḥal in performance. Photo from Government Press Office, Israel, 1970s.

and rhythm to the Hebrew text, other composers were looking for a local musical language. The search for a new tradition led some to of them to compose songs not in minor or major scales but in modes such as the Dorian. Among these composers are Gil Aldema (b. 1928), Imanuel Zamir (1925–1962), Dov Zelzer (b. 1932), Amitai Ne'eman (b. 1926), Joseph Hadar (b. 1926), and Yoḥanan Zarai (b. 1930). Emanuel Zamir (1925–1962) introduced the *debka* rhythm of the Arab folk dance into Hebrew song and Israeli dance. Some of the songs recalled the shepherds of the 1930s and were called "ho ho songs."

The song texts of the 1950s contributed to the mythic status of the War of Independence and the creation of the new Jewish state, telling of acts of heroism and commemorating fallen soldiers. These songs helped shape the new Israeli sabras (*tsabar*) and became part of a canon.

Naomi Shemer (b. 1930), the first Israeli-born songwriter, introduced songs in the 1960s that were a synthesis of the 1930s and 1940s. Shemer wrote both lyrics and melodies and was the first *tsabar* songwriter to introduce melodies in minor and major keys with the spice of a French *chanson*.

In the 1970s, along with Wilensky, Argov, and others of the early generation, a new generation of musicians, most of whom were Israeli-born, began to create songs. They included Nurit Hirsh (b. 1942), Yair Rosenblum (1944–1996), Yony Rechter, Shlomo Gronich, Mati Kaspi (b. 1949; figure 3), Shalom Ḥanokh (figure 4), and Miki Gavrielov. The generation of the 1970s was influenced, on the one hand, by early Israeli composers such as Wilensky and Argov and, on the other hand, by Western popular music and song, mainly British and American rock and roll. In the 1970s Israeli popular song discarded the accordion of the army entertainment groups in favor of electric guitars and drums; but the army groups were still active, performing new songs written for them by older and younger composers.

The 1970s also introduced the Israeli public to Hebrew rock. One of the founders of this style was Shmulik Kraus; along with other Israeli musicians, he established the first rock groups in Israel. During the 1970s, once again, an enormous number of songs in new styles were created. A new style called Hasidic pop represented Zionist religious groups in Israel and incorporated some Hasidic musical elements with texts taken from traditional Jewish sources such as the Bible.

The lyrics of the 1970s (like pop music in the West) expressed individual feelings more than collective nationalism. The music incorporated electric sounds

FIGURE 3 Mati Kaspi (or Matti Caspi) sings and accompanies himself at the piano. Photo from Government Press Office, Israel, 1980s.

FIGURE 4 Shalom Hanokh, a leader of Israeli rock, 1990s.

and introduced the modern "troubadour," the songwriter who was also the performer. The 1970s also introduced female troubadours, who had a major role in bringing new subjects and sounds to Israeli popular song. The female singers no longer performed only men's music but created songs with new feminine themes. Among these singers are Judith Ravitz, Nurit Galron, Corinne Alal, and to some extent Chava Alberstein.

In the late 1970s, and then even more in the 1980s, political and social changes and the decline of the myth of the *tsabar*—the ideology of gatherings of exiles—led to a new popular style called *muzika mizraḥit* 'Oriental music'. The young Mizraḥim, Israelis born to Jewish immigrants from Middle Eastern and other Muslim countries, created music that joined their old traditions and roots in Arab societies with new Israeli Western national song. This music also included a Greek sound, mediating between East and West and incorporating Middle Eastern instruments such as the *'ūd* and *buzuq*.

FIGURE 5 Zohar Argov in performance, 1980s.

Some of the leaders in this style are Avihu Medina, Zohar Argov (figure 5), and Margalit Tsan'ani, a Yemeni woman who performed songs in the Oriental style normally dominated by men. This music was a bridge between Israel and its neighbors and became very popular in Middle Eastern countries.

The 1990s were more pluralistic and accommodated different audiences with several styles of Israeli popular song: (1) Israeli popular song in a "folk" style, which continues the tradition of the 1930s; (2) Israeli rock, which began in the 1970s and became a vehicle for political protest; (3) Israeli Oriental music, which began essentially as Western music with an "Oriental" flavor and developed as *muzika mizraḥit* in the 1990s, attracting a large audience; (4) Hasidic pop, aimed at Zionist and Orthodox Jews in Israel, mainly Western in style but with some traditional Ashkenazi-Hasidic melodic elements. The 1990s also gave rise to "fusion" groups that combined traditional world music (mainly Jewish, but also non-Jewish) with jazz elements, classical European music, and rock. For the first time East and West were being presented as equals, albeit in Western-style concerts.

Thus Israeli popular music has moved from being a tool for the creation of national identity to an expression of ethnic identity, and it exists in various forms that reflect diversity and social change in the new nation.

REFERENCES

Bayer, Bathyah. 1971. "Ha-Tikvah." In *Encyclopaedia Judaica,* 7:1470–1472. Jerusalem: Encyclopaedia Judaica.

Bohlman, Philip V. 1994. "Shireh 'Am, Shireh Medinah (Folk Song, National Song)." In *Israeli Folk Music*, ed. Hans Nathan, 39–54. Madison, Wisc.: A-R Editions.

Cohen, Dalia, and Ruth Katz. 1977. *The Israeli Folk Song: A Methodological Example of Computer Analysis*. Jerusalem: Magnes Press of Hebrew University.

Hakohen, Eliyahu. 1993. "Ha-Takliṭ ha-'ivri, sibuvim rishonim: prakim badiskografiyah shel ha-zemer ha-'ivri" (The Hebrew Record, the First Rounds: Chapters in the Discography of Hebrew Song)." In *Ha-kol zahav*, ed. Yosi Mar-Ḥayim and Ya'ir Setavi, 9–20. Tel Aviv: Ma'ariv.

Idelsohn, A. Z. 1914–1932. *Hebraisch-orientalischer Melodienschatz*. 10 vols. Leipzig: Breitkopf and Härtel.

Shaḥar, Natan. 1989. "Ha-shir ha-Erets Yisraeli: hebetim musikaliyim ve-sotsiomusikaliyim ba-shanim 1920–1950 (Erets-Israeli Song, 1920–1950: Sociomusical and Musical Aspects)." Ph.D. dissertation, Hebrew University of Jerusalem.

Shiloah, Amnon, and Erik Cohen. 1983. "The Dynamics of Change in Jewish Oriental Ethnic Music in Israel." *Ethnomusicology* 27(2):227–252.

Glossary

Alexander J. Fisher

abyāt Vocal introduction to the *nūba* in Tunisian traditional music. (331, 451)

Acemaşiran Common Turkish *makam* resembling the Western major scale. (49)

ACCESS Arab Community Center for Economic and Social Services, an institution providing support for Arab music and musicians in Detroit, among other services. (286)

açiş Prelude in free rhythm to the Turkish instrumental *uzun hava*; also *ayak*. (81)

'açrī 'Contemporary', genre of Algerian popular music drawing on Western dance music. (270)

adhān Islamic call to prayer, performed five times per day by a solo vocalist from the mosque; also *azān*, *ezan*. (153, 165, 372, 475, 517, 525, 538, 673, 937)

adhān shar'ī Syllabic rendition of the *adhān*, or call to prayer, alternating between two notes a step apart. (155)

aghānī 'Songs', as in titles of early Arabic song collections, for example *Kitāb al-aghānī*; singular, *ughniya*. See also *ughniyya*. (367, 442, 551)

aghānī dīniyya 'Religious songs'. In Islamic hymnody in Egypt, songs combining the urban Arab music tradition with poetry containing Islamic themes. Popular singers may perform or record such songs for religious occasions. (165)

aghānī al-ghawṣ 'Diving songs', local term for pearl divers' songs in the Gulf region; also *nahma* 'animal sound' or 'voice of the whale'. (651)

aghānī shabābiyya 'Youth songs', popular musical tradition of the Mashriq characterized by brief songs with a Western-influenced, heavily synthesized accompaniment; also *aghānī al-jīl* 'new generation songs'. (555)

āghāz Initial tone of a *gūshe* in Iranian music. (65)

ağıt Turkish funeral dirge. (761)

ağız 'Dialect' (Turkish), referring to the specific regional character of Turkish folk melodies; in urban areas, also *tavır*. (82)

agwāl Small clay goblet-shaped drum used by the Moroccan Berbers; also *aqwāl*. (489)

āhang 'Tune' or 'melody type', Persian term adapted into Arabic as *hank* (plural, *hunūk*). (550, 839)

ahellil Song of praise by Moroccan Berbers for seasonal or life-cycle events; also *ahellel*. (484)

aḥidus Term used in the Tamazight region of Berber Morocco for a gathering of villagers, their participation in songs and dances, and the songs and dances themselves, accompanied by the beating or clapping of the feet or hands; also *ahidous*. (486)

aḥwash Moroccan collective dance accompanied by drums; in Berber Morocco, may also refer to the gathering of villagers, their participation in songs and dances, and the songs and dances themselves. (301, 480, 486, 1036)

aḥwash n'timgharin 'Women's *aḥwash*', women's version of the Moroccan Berber *aḥwash* involving poetic contests and dancing. (488)

aitys Kazakh music and poetry contest, usually taking the form of a competitive dialogue between two or more performers. (953)

aiyāi Ethical-meditative song genre of Algeria, performed by *gawwāl* 'singer-poets'. (466)

'ajam One of the primary Arab *maqāmāt*. (37, 49)

ajewwaq Traditional Berber flute; plural, *tajewwaqt*. (276)

akhal-teke Performance style of southern Turkmenistan. (973)

akhbār 'Accounts', in Arabic titles on the lives of musicians, such as *Akhbār al-mughannīn*; singular, *khabar*. (369)

akin Kyrgyz epic singer. (844)

aksak 'Limping', 'staggering', term for asymmetrical rhythmic patterns (*usūl*) in Turkish music. (759)

'al-hawá Type of Palestinian wedding song. (583)

āla (Musical) instrument; plural, *ālāt*. In Morocco, also refers to the classical Andalusian *nūba* repertoire. (401, 436, 449, 455, 1016)

āla mūsīqiyya 'Musical instrument'; plural, *ālāt mūsīqiyya*. Most widespread term for musical instrument in the Arab world. (401)

alafranga Turkish term for European aesthetic ideals, espoused in the *Tanzimat* period of the Ottoman Empire; cf. *alaturka*. (782)

'ālam-i mithāl World of analogies, between the world that can be sensed and the world of ideas; a way of musical understanding in the Islamic world. (187)

āla hawā'iyya 'Wind instrument', Arabic term for aerophones. (402, 413)

āla iqā'iyya 'Rhythmic instrument', Arabic term for membranophones and idiophones. (402)

āla jildiyya Specific Arabic term for membranophones; also *ālā dhāt al-jild*. (402)

āla watariyya 'Instrument with strings', Arabic term for chordophones. (402)

ālātī Instrumentalist; plural, *ālātiyya*. (313)

alaturka Turkish term referring to native Turkish aesthetic sensibilities, considered outmoded in the Ottoman *Tanzimat* period; cf. *alafranga*. (782)

Alevī 'Follower of Ali', Sufi-related Shi'ite religious group of Anatolia, encompassing Turks, Kurds, and Zazas, doctrinally related to the Bektaşī *tarikat*. (190, 755, 765, 793, 811)

'ālima 'Learned woman'; plural, *'awālīm*, professional female musician or dancer who performs for a female audience; also *'alma*. (305, 547, 615, 625)

aliyot Hebrew term for Jewish immigrants who settled in Palestine. (1013)

allun Large frame drum of the Atlas Mountains in Morocco; see *bandīr*. (486)

alti-yarim makom 'Six and a half *maqāmlar*', referring to the Khorezm (Khiva) *maqām* tradition of Uzbekistan. (911)

'amal 'Work', 'craft', the practical art (of music), in contrast to theory (*'ilm*); refers more specifically to the *ma'lūf* when performed in Sufi contexts. Also *'aml*. (369, 517)

'amal Song type within the Andalusian *nūba*. (12, 447)

amdyaz Male musicians of Morocco; plural, *imdyazn*. (489)

'amidah 'Standing'. In the Yemenite Jewish liturgy, prayer said while standing, consisting of a series of blessings. It forms the third part of the weekday morning service in the Yemenite Jewish liturgy. (1051)

amkhllf Sung poetry contest in the women's *aḥwash* of Berber Morocco. (488)

'āmme Ordinary musicians in Persia under Naṣr al-Dīn Shāh who performed light music. (861)

amssad Type of Berber *aḥidus* among the Ayt Yahya involving singing and dancing by young men; cf. *hayfa*. (487)

amyrga Tuvan hunting horn, used to imitate the mating call of a stag. (981)

än Kazakh term for melody. (950)

ana 'Mother', Turkish term for basic or fundamental meters. (85)

an'anevi 'Traditional' (Turkish). (853)

Andalusia (al-Andalus) Geographical term for the medieval Islamic civilization in Spain. (441, 455)

Andalusian North African branch of urban art music, thought to have originated in the Moorish Islamic courts of medieval Spain. (201, 433, 441, 464, 467, 495, 516, 1035)

'anqā' Medieval zither or dulcimer. (397)

änshi Kazakh lyric singer; also *sal*, *seri*. (955)

änshilik Term for Kazakh folk song. (950)

antuni Genre of peasant songs reflecting the life of homeless Armenians expelled from their land by foreign invaders. (724)

aqqayn Term for sung lyrics among Moroccan Berbers; also refers to seeds and certain nuts. (483)

aqyn Kazakh poet-improviser with shamanistic qualities who takes part in music and poetry contests. (950)

aqyndyq Kazakh term for improvised composition, derived from *aqyn* 'poet-improviser'. (950)

arabesk Syncretic urban popular genre, usually dated from 1969, and popular in Turkey throughout the 1970s and 1980s. (118, 231, 247, 255, 776)

arap tarzı 'Arab style' (Turkish), connoting an Arab, non-Turkish tradition in twentieth-century Turkish musical discourse. (784)

'arḍa Warrior song and dance of the bedouin of the Arabian Peninsula; also *'ardah*. (289, 546, 647, 665, 706)

'arḍa baḥriyya Dance performed by pearl fishers of the Gulf region when their ships are ready to return to shore. (708)

ardin Mauritanian ten- to twelve-stringed harp, traditionally played by women. (359)

arghūl Type of double clarinet used in the Mashriq and Maghrib, often with tubes of unequal length, one of which serves as a drone. (414, 545, 582)

argul Double clarinet of southern Turkey; cf. *arghūl*. (763)

'arruz Poetic meters that influence rhythmic patterns in Uygur music. (997)

ärsary Performance style of eastern Turkmenistan. (973)

'arūbī Improvisatory vocal genre originating in the rural area around Algiers, and stemming from Andalusian repertoires. Also, a common folksong genre among Moroccan Jews. (472, 1041)

'aruz Quantitative poetic meters in Turkish, classical Arabic, and Persian poetry. Also *'arūḍ*. (136, 782, 914, 944)

āsh Early-morning gathering of men for food and music at Central Asian weddings, a typical site for the performance of *maqām*. (916)

aṣḥāb al-ghinā' al-'arabī 'Advocates of Arab music', in ninth-century discussions with (*aṣḥāb al-mūsīqī*) 'advocates of Greek music theory'. (368)

aṣḥāb al-mūsīqī 'Advocates of Greek music theory'; cf. *aṣḥāb al-ghinā' al-'arabī*. (368)

'āsheq 'Lover', bard or minstrel who performs folk poetry and narrative song, found in many parts of Turkey and elsewhere. Also *ashiq*, *'ashiq*, *aşık*, *aşıq*. (345, 827, 839, 845, 901)

Ashkenazim Israeli Jews of European heritage. (199, 1065, 1072)

ashugh A professional musician of Armenia, replacing the traditional *gusan*. The *ashugh* has the same social role and professional character as the *gusan*, but the form and content of the music and some features of the performance differ. (724)

Ashura Shi'ite ceremony commemorating the martyrdom of the saints Hasan and Husayn in 680 C.E., observed in most Shi'ite communities. (544)

aşık See *'āsheq*. (114, 193, 250, 345, 762, 796, 801)

aṣīl Authentic, pure, unmixed, possessing roots (*rīshe*); a central term, for example, in Persian discourse on *sonnatī* 'traditional' music. (557, 853, 854)

aşıq See *'āsheq*. (843)

aşıq havası Short lyric love poem of Iranian Azerbaijan. (851)

assergig 'Trembling', a dance movement in the *aḥidus* of the Ayt Brahim (Moroccan Berbers). (487)

astara-n-igharïwn 'Shoulder walk', women's dance interpolated into the Moroccan Berber warrior dance *taskiwin*. (489)

'aṭābā Popular folk song genre of the Mashriq, similar to the *mawwāl*. In Palestinian wedding celebrations, it is a semi-improvisatory genre for sung poetic contests. (283, 545, 574, 582)

'aṭābā al-nashid Type of *'aṭābā* featuring song duels. (577)

ātin āyi 'Teacher-mother', female carrier of religious and spiritual traditions in Uzbekistan and Tajikistan; the term *ātin-bibi* 'teacher-grandmother' is also found. (945)

atışma Song duelling by Turkish minstrels. (82)

āvāz Melody, mode; singing governed by the quantitative poetic meters of classical Persian poetry; an instrumental solo based on appropriate sections of the Persian *radīf*; one of five or more secondary systems in Persian art music. (11, 17, 60, 131, 184, 751, 824, 854, 866)

'awālim 'Learned women'; singular, *'ālima*. Women's wedding party. (615, 618)

āwīhā Palestinian wedding song, sung by a woman and responded to with ululation by other guests. (582)

'awj 'Apogee', point of culmination in a musical phrase; also *awdj*, *'awdj*. Also refers to one of the major notes of the Arab fundamental scale. (34, 900, 913, 944)

awlād il-kār 'People of the trade', term used by the performers of Muḥammad 'Alī Street in Cairo to describe themselves. (619)

ayak Turkish term for mode; cf. *makam*. (81)

ayaq 'Foot, knee, leg' (Turkic): the cadence or return to the initial register of an Azerbaijani *muğam*; the lowest note in a tetrachord. (11)

'ayyāla Official tribal dance of the Emirates. (403)

āyīn The ritual of a *tarikat*, performed at set times and on set days, often accompanied by music; also *mukabbele*. The Mevlevī *āyīn* had the most elaborate musical compositions of all the Ottoman *tarikatlar*. (108, 114, 132, 191, 779)

ayīnhān Chanter of the Mevlevī *āyīn*. (189)

āyīn-i cem' 'Ritual of unity' of the Alevi and Bektaşi religious groups. (190)

'āzī Omani song of praise. (673)

'Azūziyya Tunisian Sufi brotherhood. (506)

bacha Traditional Central Asian boy dancer who dresses in women's garb, banned under Soviet rule. (899)

badḥan 'Jester' who entertains with rhymes and songs at Jewish weddings. (202)

bağlama Long-necked, fretted Turkish folk lute; see *saz*. (80, 244, 257, 763, 789, 795)

bagšy See *bakhshī*. (827)

bahr-e osul Term for rhythmic modes in Iranian classical music. (75)

baḳashot Night vigils held during the winter by Sephardi Jews; also refers to sacred poems sung before morning prayers by Moroccan and Spanish Jews prior to 1492. (202, 1037)

bakhshī In Iranian Khorasan and Turkmenistan, a bard who performs a traditional repertoire and, in some cases, original songs, accompanying himself or herself on the *dūtār*; spelled *bagšy* in Turkmen. (827, 839, 901)

bālābān Aerophone with a cylindrical bore and a large double reed, also called *düdük* and *mey*; it accompanies the *aşıq* in northwest Iran. (10, 845)

baladī 'Folk', 'of the folk'; common eight-beat rhythmic pattern in Arab folk music; also *maṣmūdī ṣaghīr*. Also refers to an Egyptian musical genre evocative of rural life. (89, 321)

bālah Yemeni dance involving poetic competition. (705)

bam 'Above' (Persian). On an *'ūd* or other lute, the string or course of strings that lies closest to the player's head and produces the lowest pitches. (8, 835)

bambūṭiyya From English *bumboat.* Dance of the Suez Canal Zone, possibly of Western origin, accompanied by the *simsimiyya, riqq,* and *darabukka.* (623)

bandīr Large circular Maghribi frame drum with snares; also *bendīr.* (276, 326, 418, 474, 498, 519, 633)

bar'a 'To surpass oneself', 'excellence', 'bravery'; men's warrior dance of the high plateaus of Yemen. Also *bara'.* (302, 706)

barbāṭ Greek term for lyre in the ancient world, an early precursor of the *'ūd*; plural, *barābit.* (12, 131, 358, 397, 1005)

bargham Cow horn used in Omani tribal traditions; also *barghum.* (416)

barwal One of the canonical rhythms of the *ma'lūf,* commonly used by the 'Īsāwiyya; also refers to a Maghribi vocal genre using this rhythm; plural, *brāwal, barāwīl.* (451, 517)

barwal nūba Shorter version of the Libyan *nūba.* (453)

bashraf 'Prelude', 'to go before' (from Persian *pīsh-row*); introductory instrumental form, of Turkish origin, found in various Arab suite forms and characterized by a long, complex rhythmic cycle. (451, 470, 550, 560)

basīṭ 'Simple', section of light music in the classical *nūba* repertoire. (447, 456, 460)

basta Traditional Iraqi strophic song, often used in Iraqi *maqām*; also *bista.* (551)

bastau Introductory section of a Kazakh epic tale. (952)

bāṭin Internal, hidden, esoteric. (186)

batyrlar zhyry Kazakh epic tales about heroes, the performance of which may be accompanied by narrative songs and instrumental genres. (952)

baxši Turkmen or Karakalpak epic singer; cf. *bakhshī.* (345)

bayt Line of poetry; in Kurdistan, sung narrative in rhymed verse; also *beyt* (135, 747)

bayt al-ḥikma 'House of Wisdom', scholarly institution founded by Caliph al-Ma'mun (r. 813–833) in Baghdad, which translated numerous Greek treatises into Arabic. (540)

bayyātī One of the primary Arab *maqāmāt*; *beyati* in Turkish. (33, 283)

bāz 'Falcon', small copper kettledrums used by Sufi and other religious orders in Iraq, Egypt, and Libya; also *ṭabl bāz* or *bāza.* (417, 626)

bāzī-hā-ye nemāyeshī Women's domestic theatre tradition in Iran. (878)

bazm Evening entertainments involving music in Iran. (140)

begenna Ethiopian lyre. (357)

Bektaşi Major Sufi *tarikat* of Turkey, doctrinally related to the Alevi group. (81, 114, 189, 793)

bəm From Persian *bam* 'above'. Triple course of strings on the Azerbaijani *saz* that is tuned to the lowest pitch and provides a drone. (847)

bemol Flat (Turkish). (82)

bendêr Term for a wooden circular frame drum in Kurdistan; cf. *bandīr.* (745)

bərdaşt 'Introduction' (Azerbaijani, from Persian), an introductory passage, moving from a higher to a lower register, in the *maye* of an Azerbaijani *muqam.* (928)

beste Major Turkish song genre using a wide variety of rhythmic cycles (*usūl*) and lengthy melodic lines, a primary constituent of the *fasıl.* (113, 773, 799)

Beth-Gazô 'Thesaurus', 'treasury'; in the Syrian Christian church, a collection of nonbiblical liturgical chants in the form of sung hymns and melodies, in which only the initial poetic meter is indicated. Also refers to a compendium of model strophes for Syriac poetry. (208, 228)

beyābānī 'Pertaining to the desert' (Persian), a vocal genre of southern Khorasan, sung in open, uninhabited spaces. (829)

beytbij Semiprofessional singer in Kurdistan. (748)

bilûlê asin End-blown flute made of iron pipe, common in Kurdish areas of western Iran; also *şimşal.* (746)

bimūl Flat (pitch). (34)

binşir Ring finger; the fret played by this finger. (869)

birleşik 'Compound', Turkish term for additive types of meters. (85)

bīyānū al-sharqī 'Oriental piano', term for the modified Western piano which was introduced into Egypt in the nineteenth century. (610)

blūr End-blown wooden flute in Kurdistan; also *bulūl, belwēr.* (745)

borbangnadyr Type of Tuvan *khöömei* involving a rhythmic treatment of harmonics suggesting rapid movement, for example of water, wind, or a horse. (983)

boru (Turkish) trumpet. (115, 767)

bozlak 'Song of anguish', form of Turkish *uzun hava* found throughout central-southern Anatolia and the Taurus Mountains. (761)

bozuk Long-necked Turkish lute; cf. *buzuq.* (115)

bṭāyḥī Vocal genre within the Maghribi *nūba*; also refers to a rhythmic cycle used in this genre. (450)

būga Metallic tubular drum used on national, social, and personal occasions in Yemen; also *mu'asti.* (420)

bughya Unmeasured instrumental prelude in the Maghribi *nūba.* (450)

būq Horn or trumpet. (444)

būq zamrī Horn. (444)

burmiyya From *barama* 'to twist'. Simple, quasi-stationary dance of the Siwa oasis of Egypt, involving a shuffling, hip-swinging action. (624)

būs Type of clarinet used in Saudi Arabia, played by shepherds and amateurs. (414)

buyūt 'Houses', a term used by al-Ḥaṣkafī in describing scalar degrees; singular, *bayt.* (366)

buzuq Long-necked lute of the eastern Arab world. (405, 554, 1074)

byzaanchy Type of upright Tuvan fiddle. (985)

čäčän Tatar epic singer. (345)

çağana Turkish military cymbals. (767)

çargâh A common melodic mode (*makam*) in Turkish folk music. (51, 84)

Celvetī Sufi *tarikat,* offshoot of the Halvetīye. (194)

cem Term for closed religious musical services by the Turkish Alevī sect; also *ayin, āyīn.* (794)

çeng Classical Turkish harp. (115, 774)

çengī Female professional dancers of Ottoman Turkey. (115)

cent One-hundredth of a Western tempered semitone, used in the measurement of intervals. (48; passim)

centonization Process which establishes the melody and poetic meter of hymns and melodies using set formulas. (210)

Cerrāhī Subdivision of the Halvetīye sect. (191)

çeyrek Quarter tone (Turkish). (82)

chāb rai '*Rai* of the young', form of Algerian *rai* which developed in the 1980s and featured Western electrophones such as the synthesizer and drum machine. (271)

chahār maqām 'Four *maqāmlar*', term for the Ferghana-Tashkent *maqām* tradition, consisting of the four independent suites *bayāt, chargāh, dugāh-husayni,* and *gulyār-shahnāz.* (913)

chahār meżrāb 'Four strokes' (Persian), a composition emphasizing instrumental virtuosity. (67, 132, 866)

Chalcedon, Council of Christian church council in 451 which condemned Monophysitism; the Maronite church evolved out of the Chalcedonian group, which believed in two natures of Christ within a single person. (207)

Chaldean Church Christian sect espousing the Eastern Syro-Antiochene rite, united with the Roman See from the seventeenth century. (208)

chālghī al-baghdādī 'Baghdadi ensemble', traditional ensemble for the performance of Iraqi *maqām,* consisting of two chordophones (*sanṭūr, jōza*) and two or three membranophones (*daff, dumbuk, naqqāra*). Also refers to a characteristically Iraqi compound form or suite. Also *jālghī al-baghdādī.* (8, 312, 410, 551)

chang In Xinjiang-Uygur, a trapezoidal dulcimer with metal strings which has replaced the older *kalun* or *kanun*; also refers to a Central Asian struck zither. (919, 999)

chang Medieval Persian harp; cf. *jank.* (138, 395)

chang-kobuz Metal Jew's harp of Central Asia. (902)

chap kuk In Iranian music, tuning for the female vocal range. (66)

charaki Chromatic pitches and microtones in Uygur music. (998)

chārbeitī 'Quatrain' (Persian), a genre of sung poetry consisting of couplets (that is, four half-lines) normally sung in succession, with or without instrumental accompaniment; also called *dobeitī* or *dobeytī* 'couplet'. (829, 840)

chārzarb 'Four strokes', form of rhythmic chanting in four beats of one of the names of God, forming the basis of Central Asian Sufi *zikr.* (943)

Chasidic pop Style of Israeli popular music appealing to Zionist religious groups in Israel, developed in the 1970s. (1074)

chatagan Tuvan zither. (982)

Chong nagma 'Great music', term for the first and most essential section of the Uygur *muqam,* in which various instruments enter successively; it follows a short instrumental prelude. (998)

Chronos protos Greek term meaning the shortest perceivable duration, used as the unit of measurement. It was the cornerstone of Arabic medieval rhythmic theories. (388)

chuyūkh / chaykāt 'Masters' or 'mistresses' of Algerian *rai*; also *shuyūkh, shaykāt.* (270)

çifte Turkish double clarinet with a box-shaped body. (765)

çifte-na're Small Turkish kettledrums. (115)

çöğür Long-necked plucked Turkish folk lute with movable frets. (795)

coplas Judeo-Spanish strophic songs on Jewish topics, sung by Moroccan Jews. (1042)

cümbüş Banjo-like Turkish lute. (764)

cura Small Turkish lute. (763)

dabka 'Stamping the feet', popular folk dance of the Mashriq; also *dabkah, dabkeh,* or *dabkih.* Also refers to a common folk-dance rhythm, adopted in Hebrew song and Israeli dance. (283, 545, 576, 1073)

daff In the Arab world, generic term for a frame drum or tambourine, sometimes containing snares; also *duff*; cf. *riqq.* (8, 91, 94, 180, 282, 295, 312, 359, 395, 418, 445)

daff zinjārī Iraqi tambourine with five pairs of small cymbals. (418)

dagg al-ḥabb Yemeni folk song accompanying the milling of grain. (698)

dā'ira Generic term for round frame drum; also *daire* (Turkish), *dāire.* Also refers to a short prelude in free rhythm in the Maghribi *nūba.* (8, 115, 451, 457, 828)

dāire-zangī Frame drum with attached metal rings. (828)

dal'ūna Folk song accompanying a line dance, or *dabkah,* among eastern Mediterranean rural communities; also *dal'ōna.* (545, 583)

dam Breath (spirit) that brings an effect. (885)

d'am In Armenian music, the tonic drone tone, usually provided by one of two *duduk* players. (731)

damana Performance style of southwestern Turkmenistan. (973)

d'amkash Musician who provides the drone pitch in Armenian music. (731)

dammām Polygonal frame drum used in Iraq. (419)

dān Omani women's ensemble. (674)

dāng (Persian): a tetrachord, in Persian music theory; equivalent to Arabic *zolarba'* or *dhū'l-arba'.* (869)

dap Single-headed frame drum of Xinkiang-Uygur. (999)

daqqa 'Beat', 'thrust', general term for rhythmic periods; plural, *daqqāt.* (98)

darabuka, darabukka See *darbūka.*

daraja Scale degree, pitch, note, or sound; plural, *darajāt.* (446)

darāmad 'Coming out' (Persian), one of the initial *gushe-hā* in a *dastgāh.* In the Central Asian *shash maqām,* also refers to an introductory section in a low tessitura in the melodic development of a *shu'be.* (60, 134, 836, 854, 866, 911)

ḍarb 'Beat', 'tap', 'pulse'; plural, *ḍurūb.* General term for rhythmic modes or periods. (98)

darbūka Goblet-shaped single-headed drum found throughout the Arab world; also *darbuka, darbeka, darabukka, darabuka, darbakkeh, darbukka.* (250, 266, 270, 407, 453, 468, 519)

***das'a,* greater** Rhythmic period in Yemenite music (*ḍarb, daqqa, īqā'*) with internal structure of 2 + 3 + 3 + 3. (93)

***das'a,* lesser** Rhythmic period in Yemenite music with internal structure of 3 + 2 + 2. (93, 687)

dasa' Traditional Yemeni dance for two performers. (709)

dāstān Sung poetic narrative of Turkey and Central Asia, performed by an *'āsheq* or *bakhshī.* Also *destan.* (81, 345, 762, 827, 840, 851, 901, 999)

daste In Iran, a group of men who meet to perform *nowḥe sīne-zanī* and *nowḥe zanjīr-zanī,* poetic laments for martyrs. (826)

dastgāh 'System', 'apparatus' (Persian; Azerbaijani *dəstgah*). One of the seven canonical systems (*shūr, segāh, chāhargāh, māhūr, homāyūn, navā, rāst panjgāh*) that constitute the *radīf,* or modal system, of Persian music. (11, 59, 129)

davul Large double-headed Turkish drum, generally appearing with the *zurna.* (764)

dawr Vocal composition, especially popular in nineteenth-century and early-twentieth-century Egyptian music, involving a degree of vocal improvisation; plural, *adwār.* It is performed by a vocal soloist accompanied by a chorus and *takht.* Also, *dōr.* (370, 547, 560, 569, 598)

dāyra See *dā'ira.* (902, 919, 943, 946)

ddikr Song of praise of God and the Prophet, sung by Moroccan Berbers (the Chleuh or Shleuh people) for seasonal or life-cycle events; plural, *ladkar.* (484)

ddrst 'Row', 'chain'; type of *aḥwash* dance of the Ida Ouzddout, referring to the arrangement of dancers into a long line. (488)

deblek Single-headed Turkish hourglass drum; cf. *darbuka.* (763)

dede Alevī holy man who supervises rituals and religious instruction. (794)

def Frame drum, with or without jingles; cf. *daff.* (745, 763, 825)

dəf Azerbaijani frame frum; cf. *def.* (8)

deff Square double-headed frame drum; cf. *daff.* (498)

dehol Double-headed cylindrical drum in Kurdistan, played by professional musicians, *mitirp*; cf. Turkish *davul,* Arabic *ṭabla.* (745)

deme Songs of mystical love, performed in Alevī ceremonies. (795)

dergāh Sufi lodge or *tekke,* especially one with an attached tomb. (191)

dervish A follower of a spiritual way in Islam. (107)

dessan From Persian *dāstān*; a long narrative epic of Turkmenistan. (967, 969, 970, 975)

dessanchy bagshy Singer of *dessan* in Turkmenistan. Also *dessançy bagşy.* (969)

devr-i kebīr Complex Turkish rhythmic cycle in 28/4, characterizing the *peşrev* genre. (91)

deyiş 'Poem' (Turkish); genre of mystical poetry. (81, 115, 790, 795)

dəyişmə 'Exchange' (Azerbaijani); a contest of sung poetry in which two *aşıqlar* exchange strophes. (929)

dhikr 'Remembrance'. In its general sense, this term refers to the remembrance of Allah by any means. More specifically, it refers to a portion of the Sufi liturgy: the regular chanting of a name of Allah, usually accompanied by regular body movements. Also *zikr.* (114, 147, 171, 180, 516, 543, 598, 625)

diez Sharp (Turkish). (82)

dīv Powerful demon in Iranian mythology. (886)

divān Musical genre of Turkish coffeehouses based on urbanized versions of Anatolian songs and urban *şarkı* and *türkü*; it typically begins a Turkish song duel. (80, 806)

dīwān Algerian ritual involving dance, music, poetry, and song; cf. *gnāwa, stambūlī.* (403)

diyār thaqāfa 'Houses of Culture' in modern Tunisia hosting a network of music clubs for the cultivation of *ma'lūf.* (330, 511)

diyāz Sharp (pitch). (35)

dobeitī See *chārbeitī.* (829)

dohol Cylindrical double-headed drum, usually played with a switch and a stick; cf. *dehol.* (828, 839)

doholak Double-headed cylindrical drum of Baluchistan, played with the hands; also called *dholak* and *drokkol*; cf. *dehol.* (881)

dombira Short-necked lute of Kyrgyzstan. (345)

dombra Plucked two-stringed long-necked lute of Central Asia. (901, 953)

donelī Baluchi double duct-flute, played with circular breathing. (10, 881)

dōtār Short-necked lute of Kyrgyzstan; cf. *dūtār.* (345)

Doxology Coptic hymn of praise for the Virgin Mary, saints, or angels. (221)

draj Lively vocal genre in the Maghribi *nūba;* plural, *adrāj.* (450)

dūbayt 'Two-line' (Persian); a form of Arab vocal music sung to paired lines of poetry. (370)

dudakdeğmez 'Lips don't touch'; form of Turkish song duelling in which the *aşık* must avoid the pronunciation of certain consonants, and is compelled to do so by placing a pin between the upper and lower palate. (808)

duduk Double-reed aerophone with a cylindrical bore, used mostly in ensembles. It has a warm and slightly nasal timbre and is very popular among folk and professional musicians; also *düdük, bālābān, mey.* (11, 729, 848)

dūkā One of the major notes of the Arab fundamental scale. (34)

dukhūl Short instrumental prelude in the Maghribi *nūba.* (451)

dūlāb Precomposed instrumental piece opens various Arab suite forms (*fāṣil, nūba, waṣla*). Also *dulab.* (563)

düm, tek Terms used for high and low drum pitches in Turkish musical metrics; see *dumm, tak.* (366, 772)

dumbuk Goblet-shaped single-headed drum; also *dumbak* or *dumbuq.* (8, 94, 312, 552, 682)

dumduma Small, deep kettledrum of the Tihāma made of clay or other appropriate materials, surrounded with straps and having a double skin; also called *ṭungura.* (7, 98)

dumm Low-pitched drum stroke; plural, *dumūm;* cf. *tak.* (7, 89, 549)

dunasr Third section in the melodic development of a *shu'be*, an octave above the opening *darāmad.* (911)

dūnāy Reed pipe with two tubes. (395)

durak Type of Turkish meter; also a musical genre associated with Sufi liturgy. (122, 769)

durbakkih Palestinian term for *darbūka*, or goblet-shaped drum. (587)

dūtār (dotār) 'Two strings' (Persian); long-necked plucked lute with two strings, called *bam* and *zīr.* (825, 839, 844, 900, 908, 919, 968, 999)

duwan From Persian *diwana*, 'mendicant', 'holy fool', 'possessed one'; term for itinerant dervishes in Kyrgyzstan. (943)

dûzele 'Of two reeds' (Kurdish), a double clarinet of Kurdistan; also *dödük, zimare.* (10, 746)

düzen Tuning (Turkish). (796)

ediski Tuvan single-reed aerophone, designed to imitate the sound of the female musk deer. (981)

ekphonetics Signs giving phonetic and rhythmic indications. (229)

elektrobağlama Electronically amplified Turkish *bağlama.* (257)

Ephesus, Council of Christian church council in 431 that condemned the Nestorian heresy, which proposed that Christ had two distinct natures and persons, one human and one divine. (207)

erebane Term for a circular wooden frame drum in Kurdistan; cf. *bendêr, def.* (745)

erets Yisrael 'Land of Israel'; Hebrew, biblical term for the land settled in Palestine between 1880 and 1948 by Jews of the diaspora. (1070)

eṣālat 'Authenticity' (Persian); in Iran, term of praise for music of quality and taste which invokes rapture, or *ḥāl*; see also *aṣīl* (858)

eshāre Ornament alluding to the next melodic tone in Persian music. (133)

estrada Russian term for regional, traditional popular music (as in Kazakhstan). (904)

ezan Call to prayer (Turkish); see *adhān.* (57, 768)

ezenggileer A strictly mimetic type of Tuvan *khöömei.* (983)

falsafat al-laḥn 'Philosophy of the melody', referring to stable forms out of which the Yemeni *'ūd* player develops variations. (687)

fann 'Art'; plural, *fūnun.* (671)

faqīr 'A poor person'; plural, *fuqārā.* Dervish, *malang*, or *qalandar.* (884)

far'awi Musical genre used in dancing at Palestinian wedding celebrations. (574, 584)

farīsa 'Hobby horse dance', women's dance of the Gulf region in which a performer wearing a cardboard horse costume dances in the midst of a circle of women playing tambourines. (709)

fartash 'Search'; Yemeni instrumental genre with variations on a short melodic motive. (687)

faryādī 'Crying out' (Persian); a vocal genre of southern Khorasan, sung in open, uninhabited spaces. (829)

fasıl Turkish suite form originating in the Ottoman court, beginning with a *peşrev* and containing *taksim*, a *saz semai*, and various song genres. (11, 57, 111, 113, 773, 779)

fāṣil Syrian suite form, similar to the *nūba* or *waṣla*, consisting of *muwashshaḥāt* in gradually livelier meters; cf. *fasıl.* (551, 563)

fasıl-i hanende Specifically vocal performance cycle in Ottoman Turkish music. (121)

fasıl-i sazende Specifically instrumental performance cycle in Ottoman Turkish music. (114)

faṣīla Families into which theorists group various *maqāmāt*; plural, *faṣā'il.* (43)

fawātiḥ Invocation of several individuals or groups, followed by the recitation of Sūrat al-Fātiḥa, the opening chapter of the Qur'ān), as a benediction. A sequence of call-response *fawātiḥ* usually opens and closes the Sufi *ḥaḍra.* (171)

felak 'Fate' (Persian, from Arabic); Afghan and Tajik equivalent of the Iranian genre *gharībī.* (830)

fijīrī 'Until dawn', popular song tradition of pearl fishermen in the Gulf region; also *fjirī, fijrī, fjīrī.* (404, 546, 651, 708)

firqa Group, troupe, ensemble; plural, *firaq.* Generally refers to a larger group than the chamber ensemble or *takht.* (8, 33, 98, 147, 317, 327, 454, 552, 642, 675)

firqat al-dān Term for women's ensemble in Oman, which may also include male drummers. (675)

firqat al-qurba Omani bagpipe ensemble. (675)

firqat al-razḥa Omani group practicing the arts of the sword, rituals involving sung poetry, dancing, and duels with swordplay; known generically as *al-razīf*; cf. *'arḍa.* (675)

Flexible melody Notion describing the melodic content of the Iranian *radīf*, in which a given melodic contour may be rhythmically elaborated in different ways according to meter of the poetry. (865)

forūd 'Descent' (Persian), a gradual return to and cadence in the initial low register, in a performance of Persian classical music. (134)

fulklūr 'Folklore', Lebanese urban repertoire embracing music, dance, and drama, dating from the 1950s. (553)

furāward Concluding section in the melodic development of a *shu'be.* (911)

fuṣūl Cycles in which individual *maqāmāt* may be ordered in the Iraqi *maqām*; singular, *fāṣil.* (11, 312)

gāh Ways of progressing through various *maqāmāt* (Persian). (131)

gargy tüydük Long end-blown Turkmen flute. (975)

Garip 'Strange'; Turkish romance about the minstrel Garip; also refers to a specific Turkish instrumental melody in free rhythm. (81)

garip ayağı Common melodic mode (*makam*) in Turkish folk music. (84)

gaṣba Term for the *nāy*, or flute, in North Africa; plural, *gaṣbāt.* Also *qaṣaba, shbēb*, or *shabbāba.* (413, 466)

gawwāl Singer-poet of Algeria; cf. *qawwāl.* (466)

gazanjyk Performance style of western Turkmenistan. (973)

gazel Major lyric form in Ottoman-Turkish poetry; free-rhythm improvised singing of such lyric texts, corresponding to the instrumental *taksīm.* (81, 116, 195, 782)

gazino Turkish nightclub music, dominated by Gypsy performers and styles; also *fasıl.* (57)

geçki Turkish term for modulation between two *makamlar.* (52)

geliri Term for Kurdish folk music. (752)

gezinti In Turkish *uzun hava*, instrumental preludes and interludes performed with vocal and instrumental melodies in strict meter. (81)

ghaita Term for a shawm or double-reed pipe in North Africa; also *ghayṭa*, *gaida*. (415, 498)

gharībī 'Condition of a stranger' (Persian); one type of Persian *chārbeitī*, with verses that refer to the singer's sense of isolation. (829)

gharnāṭī 'Granadan', regional term for Andalusian music in North Africa; also *ghurnāṭī* (269, 436, 449)

ghawāzī Local Egyptian dance entertainers. (545)

ghazal 'Flirtation', 'love'; the principal genre of classical poetry in Persian, Azerbaijani, and Turkish, dominating vocal performance of classical music in Iran and Azerbaijan; typically has five to seventeen lines; also *gazel* or *ghazel*. (60, 135, 301, 583, 685, 825, 833, 862, 914, 921, 944, 1004)

ghāziyya Female musician-dancer in Egypt; plural, *ghawāzī*. (305, 625)

ghijak Spike fiddle; also *ghichek*, *ghidjak*. (395, 919, 1004)

ghinā' 'Music', 'song'. (305, 361, 364, 538, 681)

ghinā' al-maqām 'Singing the *maqām*', since the 1930s, term for performance of the Iraqi *maqām*. (312)

ghinā' mulhī 'Entertaining music', term used by Ibn Ḥażm. (372)

ghinā' mutqan 'Perfect singing', term for art music in the medieval Middle East; also refers to modern, professional musical performances. (296, 591)

ghinā' al-Ṣan'ānī 'Song of Ṣan'ā'', term for the oldest urban tradition of classical vocal and instrumental music in Yemen. (685)

ghinnāwa Repertoire of Egyptian bedouin song. (306)

ghirbāl Early Arabic term, possibly referring to a round frame drum. (360, 696)

Ghrība 'Lonely one', 'stranger'; synagogue on the outskirts of Ḥāra Ṣghīra on the island of Djerba, a pilgrimage site for Jews and Muslims. (523)

gimbrī Long-necked lute of North Africa with two or three strings; also *gunbrī*, *ginbrī*, *gumbrī*, *jumbrī*, *hajiy*. (269, 403, 435)

gnāwa Moroccan ritual involving dance, music, poetry, and song; cf. *dīwān*, *stambūlī*. (403, 435, 487, 491)

govend Kurdish dance. (748)

goygoy Pejorative term for cetain "Arab" vocal practices in twentieth-century Turkish musical discourse. (784)

güçlü Dominant note in a Turkish *makam*. (772)

guffal Women's song of the Gulf region, sung to greet returning pearl fishers. (698)

gusan Professional Armenian musician, who is at once a storyteller, singer, instrumentalist, dancer, comedian, and tragic actor; also refers to an Armenian colloquial song genre. (723)

gūshe 'Corner' (Persian); one section of the *radīf* of Persian music, either a relatively fixed short composition or a melody type allowing for more or less elaborate realization in performance. (60, 132, 826, 854)

guyanda Female professional mourner in Central Asia. (945)

güzellemə A *qoşma* on themes of love and nature. (851)

gwāt 'Wind' (Baluchi); a spirit thought to be responsible for certain illnesses. The adjectival form, *gwātī*, may refer to the patient or to a musician involved in the healing ceremony. Also *parī*, *jinn*, or *bād*. (882)

gwātī Adjectival form of *gwāt* 'wind', referring to a Baluchi healing ritual in which trance is induced through music. (881)

ha-shir ha-Yisraeli 'Israeli song', denoting the canonical Israel folk song repertoire developed by the Zionist movement; also *ha-zemer ha-'ivri* 'Hebrew song'. (1018)

habrban One of the oldest genres of Armenian peasant song. (729)

hadharī* or *ḥaḍarī Urban popular music style of Algeria, especially of Oran; also *wahrāni* 'from Oran'. (269)

ḥadīth 'Sayings' of the Prophet Muḥammad, a source of Islamic law. (19, 294, 358, 371, 538)

ḥaḍra 'Presence'. The *ḥaḍra* is the primary corporate Sufi ritual, having as its goal a mystical experience of the divine presence; typically, it includes *fawātiḥ*, *ḥizb*, *dhikr*, and *inshād*. Religious sermons and Qur'ānic recitations may also be included; food, beverages, and perfumes are often presented to each participant. (147, 171, 185, 306, 474, 520, 521, 884)

ḥaḍrāt Women's musical ensemble of Tunisia. (437)

ḥāfiẓ 'Guardian', 'memorizer' (of the Qur'ān); also a general term for a musician who has committed a body of music to memory; also refers to a solo singer of devotional music in Central Asian Sufi *zikr* or a professional chanter of the Qur'ān in Turkey. (121, 939)

ḥafla Musical performance, concert. (265, 280, 637)

ḥaflat al-zaffāf Arab wedding party or procession; a Saudi women's wedding party. (691)

ḥāgir Large cylindrical drum of the Hadramawt, tensed by cords. (94)

hakāmma In the Darfur area of Sudan, a woman who sings to encourage warriors in battle. (359)

ḥajar Large double-headed cylindrical drum of the Arabian Peninsula. (404)

ḥāl Internal state, emotion, aesthetic or mystical rapture. (133, 149, 492, 886, 928)

ḥāl o ḥavā 'Condition', 'atmosphere', 'ambience'. In discourse about Persian music, refers to the situation of a musician or listener, or to an epoch. (856)

halakhah Jewish religious law. (199)

halay Turkish folk dance genre performed in central and eastern Anatolia. (814, 931)

halel In Syriac, acclamations of God based on the syllables that together make up God's name, *Elohim Aloho*, which is so sacred that speaking it is forbidden. (226)

halile Drum pair used in Mevlevī ceremonies. (769)

halk 'Folk music', 'people's' music; usually refers to rural Anatolian music. (83, 247)

Halk Eğitim Merkezleri 'People's Educational Centers', institutions that carried on the work of the *Halk Evleri* 'People's Houses' after 1960 in promoting Turkish folk music and culture. (77)

Halk Evleri 'People's Houses', from the 1930s to 1960, Turkish institutions that promoted the collection, preservation, teaching, and performance of folk music. (77, 797, 813)

halk hikayecileri 'Popular storytellers' of the Adana plain in Turkey. (82, 766)

hallel In Yemenite Jewish liturgy, the recitation of Psalms 113–118, preceded and followed by short blessings, for festivals and on the first day of each month. (1052)

ḥalqat al-lewa Omani ensemble consisting of twenty to forty male singers and dancers (descendants of slaves), who perform several types of circle dances. (675)

ḥalqat al-mālid Omani men's ensemble performing poetry, song, and dance in honor of the birth and life of the Prophet. (675, 682)

ḥalqat al-pākit Omani men's ensemble performing a type of musical theater at weddings. (675)

Halvetī Turkish Sufi *tarikat* that entered Anatolia from Azerbaijan in the fifteenth century and spread throughout the Ottoman Empire. (189, 768)

hāne Major subdivision of the seventeenth- and eighteenth-century *peşrev*. (91, 126, 773)

ḥarba 'Arrowhead', refrain in the performance of a *qaṣīda*, containing the poetic form, theme of the poem, and basic melody. (499)

ḥarīm Chorus. (677)

Ḥasidim Mystical sect of orthodox Ashkenazi Judaism. (200)

Hatikvah 'The Hope' (Hebrew), the Israeli national anthem. (1069, 1070)

Hausmusik 'Domestic music' (German-Yiddish); European domestic music tradition brought to Palestine by Central European Jews during the Nazi era. (1026)

havā 'Air' (Persian and Turkic, from Arabic *hawā*). Turkic term for a tune or melody type; refers to any melody used by an *aşıq*. (848)

ḥawfī Women's genre of Algerian urban folk music, related closely to *ḥawzī*. (269, 473)

ḥawzī Semipopular song style of Algeria, resembling the Andalusian *zajal* with respect to poetic form and generally having lyrics pertaining to love. (269, 407, 427, 472, 1044)

Haydar Alevī composition for voice and *bağlama*, using twentieth-century Bektaşī poetry, by the radio and recording artist Ali Ekber Çiçek. (797)

hayfa Berber *aḥidus* among the Ayt Yahya involving singing and dancing by mature men; also *taghzzaft*; cf. *amssad.* (487)

hazaj Light song style appropriate for love songs. (296, 447, 696)

ḥazanim Turkish term for Jewish cantors in major urban centers. (57)

ḥazanut Cantorial art of Eastern European Jews; also refers to composed religious music similar in social function to Western "art" music. (202)

hekayat Sung narrative in Kurdistan alternating spoken and sung prose; also *Đrokōstran.* (747)

ḥekāye Narrative alternating prose and verse, performed by an *'āsheq* or *bakhshī*; also *hikâye.* (803, 827, 851)

hey'at In Iran, a group of men who meet for religious exercises of various kinds. (826)

hicaz Common Turkish *makam*; cf. *ḥijāz.* (52, 84, 85)

ḥida' Folk song of the ancient Middle East, associated with camel-driving; in Palestine, a popular genre of improvised sung poetry. (537, 584, 665)

ḥijāz One of the primary Arab *maqāmāt*; also *hicaz* (Turkish). (36, 52, 154, 168, 312, 332, 555, 652)

hijikirini From *hij kirin* 'to make love', term for Kurdish love song, indistinguishable in form and structure from heroic songs. (748)

Hikmat 'Wisdom' of Hoja Ahmad Yassawi; mystical poetry often sung in the *zikr* of the Yassawi Sufi order of Uzbekistan-Kazakhstan. (943)

hilulah Jewish celebration on the anniversary of the death of a saintly person; plural, *hilulot.* (203, 1040)

hirmologion Byzantine compendium of model strophes within an eight-mode system. (209)

hirmos Byzantine model strophe. (208)

ḥizb Fixed group prayer, assembled by a Sufi *shaykh* from religious texts. A collection of *hizb* is associated with each Sufi order; one of these is typically recited during the *ḥaḍra.* (171, 517)

hjīnī Early form of bedouin sung poetry in the Arabian Peninsula. (665)

ḥomaynī Style of lyrical poetry, or *ghazal*, influenced by colloquial Yemeni Arabic. (495, 685)

homotony Measurment of the number syllables in a poetic line according to their accented stresses. (209)

horon Turkish folk dance genre performed in the Black Sea region, characterized by 7/16 meter. (87, 812)

horovel One of the most important genres of Armenian peasant work songs. The term derives from the exclamation *ho* and the word *arhavel* (meaning unploughed ground between two furrows) joined together. (728)

hora Popular Israeli dance, extolled by some Israeli composers (such as Mark Lavri) as a token of the national spirit. (1028)

hos Hymn of praise in the Coptic liturgy. (221)

hosha'not In Yemenite Jewish liturgy, procession around the pulpit during the festival of Tabernacles. (1052)

hubbān Line dance of Kuwait and the Emirates performed by Iranian immigrant communities, named after its signature instrument, the *hubbān* 'bagpipe'. (710)

ḥusaynī One of the notes of the Arab fundamental scale; also one of the *maqāmāt*; in Turkish, *hüseyni.* (34, 51, 83, 110, 118, 181, 769)

Husayni-xāna Shi'a prayer houses in pre-Soviet Bukhara, hosting laments for Imam Husayn as well as *taziyah*, religious theater. (942)

huzām One of the primary Arab *maqāmāt.* (37, 53, 84)

ibtihāl Supplications to God; these prayers are commonly performed as solo nonmetric *inshād*, especially before the dawn prayer and during Ramadan. (165)

'idda General Arabic term indicating specific groupings of musical instruments connected with specific musical arts. (401, 412, 656)

'iddat al-lewa 'Tools of *lewa*', term for an instrumental ensemble in the Gulf states, which accompanies the Afro-Arab *lewa* tradition of song and dance. (404)

igil Upright horsehead fiddle of Tuva, played so as to emphasize harmonic pitches. (981)

ilāhī Hymn or song of praise. (122, 191, 768, 780)

ilhamli ashik 'God-inspired poet', Turkish *aşık* thought to have received divine inspiration. (804)

illalah Poem or song in Alevī ceremonies, incorporating the *tahlīl* formula, meant to create an atmosphere of *zikr.* (795)

'ilm 'Science' (of music), in contrast to practical art, *'amal.* (369, 834)

'ilm al-tajwīd Art of Qur'ānic cantillation. (538)

'ilm-i mūsīqī 'Science of music', referring to the systematization of melodic intervals and scales. (540)

imazighen 'Free men', indigenous term by which Berber populations of Morocco and Algeria identify themselves; singular, *amazigh.* (274, 483)

imeddahen Professional Berber poets who travel from village to village, offering sung commentary on recent social and political affairs; also *imdyazen.* (274)

imzad Circular monochord fiddle of the Saharan regions of Algeria and Libya. (410)

inshād dīnī 'Islamic hymnody'. Melodic vocal recitation of poetry, performed as worship. Principal themes are supplications to and praise of Allah, and praise of the Prophet Muhammad. (19, 147, 165, 321, 568, 664)

inshād ṭab' al-naghma Vocal prelude in the Moroccan *nūba.* (450)

inṣirāf Vocal genre in the Maghribi *nūba*; also refers to a specific Maghribi rhythmic mode with a 5/8 or 10/8 cycle. (450, 457, 470, 473)

intifāḍa Palestinian revolt against Israeli rule, from 1987 on. (282, 635)

īqā' 'Falling', 'causing to fall', general Arabic term for rhythmic periods or modes; plural, *īqā'āt.* Also represented in the titles of early Arabic music theoretical works such as *Kitāb al-īqā'.* (89, 98, 103, 166, 329, 352, 364, 387, 506, 525, 538, 549, 559)

'iqd Tonal unit within each mode of a *nūba* defined by a characteristic succession of intervals; plural, *'uqūd.* (332)

'irāq Name of a melodic mode or *maqām*, first mentioned in the late fifth century A.H., eleventh century C.E. (37, 181, 365, 769)

irizi Drummed rhythm of the Moroccan Berbers, also referring to a type of dance tune in the Berber *aḥwash* of the Anti-Atlas Mountains. (483, 488)

ırlayış Popular Turkish musical form. (115)

'Īsāwiyya Tunisian Sufi brotherhood. (333, 403, 418, 506, 515)

iṣbahān Name of a mode, first mentioned by Ibn Sīnā. (365)

isqī al-'iṭāsh 'Give water to the thirsty!', an originally religious chant (*inshād*) sung in Aleppo during droughts and involving elaborate music and dance. (568)

iss Rest. (89, 549)

ist Tone that occurs at the end of a cadence in a Persian *gūshe.* (65, 134, 867)

istiftāḥ Maghribi instrumental or vocal prelude in free rhythm. (451)

istihlāl Medieval Arabic vocal prelude in free rhythm. (12, 388, 447, 652)

istikhbār Improvised prelude in the Algerian and Libyan *nūba.* (451, 470)

izli Light, amorous musical genre performed by the *imdyazn* (Moroccan Berber troupe); plural, *izlan.* (487)

izwirrign Moroccan wedding song. (479, 484)

jabd 'Captivation', term for the ecstatic state of a Sufi devotee. (519)

jadīd 'The new', term for newer, Western-influenced Egyptian repertoires from the 1930s and1940s. (558)

jafra Type of Palestinian wedding song. (583)

jahārka One of the major notes of the Arab fundamental scale; also *jahārkāh.* (34)

jahala Clay pot used as an idiophone by pearl fishermen of the Gulf region; also *jahla.* (404, 546, 651)

jalāla Rhythmic chanting of poetry of praise, accompanied by drums, in Omani wedding ceremonies and performed by a *ḥalqat al-mālid.* (678)

jalwih Palestinian song and dance for the bride's wedding eve celebration, usually conducted by an older woman from the village. (585)

jam' 'Collection', 'group'; Sufi assembly. Also refers to the joining of tetrachords to create different *maqāmāt.* (37, 180)

jangī 'Warrior'. In Baluchistan, a warrior or bard who sings epic tales. (881)

jank Andalusian harp. (444)

jank al-miṣrī 'Egyptian harp', described in the anonymous *Kashf al-humūm*; also *jank misrī.* (373)

jāriya General term for a slave girl who was a musical entertainer at early Arab courts; plural, *jawārī*; cf. *qayna.* (293)

javāb-e āvāz In Persian classical music, an immediate instrumental response to a phrase sung by the vocalist. (833)

jawq Small chamber ensemble that has traditionally performed *nūbāt* in Algeria. (454, 460, 470)

jawza Four-stringed spike fiddle used in Iraqi musical traditions, similar to the Persian *kamanche*; also *jawz, jōza, jōz'e.* (552)

Jazīrat al-Maghrib 'Island of the West', early Arab term for North Africa. (429)

jīm Conch trumpet. (678)

jinn Ambivalent spirit that may cause harm to humans. (180, 359, 456, 491, 537, 632, 674, 710, 882)

jins From Greek *genus*, referring to a tetrachord or pentachord from which a modal scale may be constructed; plural, *ajnās.* (16, 36, 369, 503, 701)

jirba Term for bagpipes in the Gulf states; also *gurba, habban.* (415)

jōqa Troupe of singer-poets, dancers, and musicians in the Arabian Peninsula. (668)

jōze Iraqi spike fiddle. (8, 312, 409)

jrāna Tunisian term for the violin; see *kamanja.* (421)

juljul Musical bell. (395)

juwwāk End-blown flute of North Africa; also *shabāba.* (407, 454, 489)

kabak kemane Turkish bowed spike lute. (763, 798)

kabbāde Heavy rattle with metal disks attached to the links of a chain; it is lifted and shaken by athletes in the Iranian *zūr-khāne.* (825)

kadamjāi Holy place of pilgrimage or worship; also *ziyarātgāx.* (936)

Kadīrī Major Sufi *tarikat* of the Muslim world, which entered the Ottoman Empire in the fifteenth century. (189, 811)

kaff Social dance of Upper Egypt in which one or more veiled women parade, pivot, advance, and retreat before a row of men. (624)

kaff al-'arab Common bedouin dance involving one or more female dancers interacting with a row of male singers. (624)

Kalenderi Common melodic mode in Turkish folk music; cf. *qalandar.* (80)

kamān Generic term for unfretted spike fiddle in the Arab world. It is also often used to describe the Western violin, which has come into widespread usage; also *kamānja, kamānche.* (8, 60, 133, 148, 269, 340, 410, 421, 453, etc.)

k'aman Long rectangular three- or four-stringed fiddle of Armenia. (734)

k'amanch'a Long Armenian spike fiddle with three or four strings and a round, skin-covered, and often beautifully decorated body. (733)

kamānja kabīra European viola, used in Algerian ensembles by the late nineteenth century. (470)

kankala Medieval one-stringed plucked instrument of Indian origin with a gourd-shaped box. (395)

k'anon Armenian trapezoidal zither with twenty-four courses and seventy-two total strings; see *qānūn.* (734)

kanun Plucked zither; see *qānūn.* (257, 774, 1003)

Kanz al-Tuḥaf 'Treasure of Rarities' (anonymous fourteenth-century Persian treatise). (835)

kār Major Turkish song genre, a primary constituent of the *fasıl.* (111, 119, 773)

karākīb Pair of medium-sized circular cymbals connected by a clasp, used in the Afro-Arab traditions of North Africa; in Morocco, *karkabūs*; in Libya, *shikshakāt.* (403)

Karakoyun 'Black sheep', name of a specific instrumental melody in the Turkish *uzun hava* in free rhythm. (81)

karar ses 'Resting tone' (Turkish), tonic note of a melody. (51, 82)

Karcığar Common melodic mode in Turkish music. (54, 84, 115)

kargyraa Type of Tuvan *khöömei* characterized by a low-pitched, raspy vocal production. (983)

karma 'Mixed', referring to meters in Turkish music. (85)

karnata Cylindrical shawm used by Turkmen populations in Iraq. (415)

karşılama Turkish folk dance genre performed mostly in Thrace, characterized by a 9/8 meter. (87, 814)

karşilaşma 'To encounter', 'to meet', Turkish term for song dueling. (801)

kasar Medium-sized double-headed drum played in Afro-Arab ceremonies in Iraq. (420)

kasīde Panegyric poem; any *ilāhī* poem sung in free rhythm during the *zikr*; see also *qaṣīda.* (192)

kaside Turkish term for vocal *taksīm* performed in Sufi rituals. (121, 192)

kaşık In Turkey, two spoons played like castanets, often accompanying dance. (763)

kasīr Small double-headed drum of Oman. (418, 676)

katta ashula 'Great song'; unmetered, declamatory setting of spiritual poetry in a high tessitura, widely performed in the Ferghana valley of Uzbekistan. (944)

kaval End-blown Turkish flute. (11, 81, 762, 799)

kawāla Reed flute resembling the *nāy*, but shorter and lacking the thumb hole. In Egypt, the *kawāla* is typically used to accompany Sufi *inshād* of the public *ḥaḍra.* Also *kawwala.* (170)

kelīme-i tevhīd 'There is no god but God'; formula of unity. (191)

keman Turkish fiddle; see *kamān.* (764)

kemane Turkish instrument resembling the Greek lyre. (763)

kemençe Turkish pear-shaped fiddle. (121, 758)

kemençe rûmî Small Turkish three-stringed fiddle. (774)

kəmənçe Azerbaijani spike fiddle; cf. *kamān.* (8, 924)

kemenche* Or *kemençe. Spike fiddle played by professional musicians, *mitirp*, in Kurdistan; also *riçek*; see *kamān.* (746)

Kerem Name of a minstrel; in the Turkish *uzun hava*, a specific instrumental melody in free rhythm; also refers to the fundamental mode, related to *hüseyni*, of Turkish folk music. (81)

kereshme Rhythmic realization of a *gūshe* in Persian music involving hemiola patterns. (67, 134)

khafīf Vocal genre within the Maghribi *nūba*; plural, *khfāyif.* (452, 457)

'khafīf Light, quick. (104)

khalīfa From Arabic *khalifa* 'caliph'; female wedding entertainer in Khorezm, Central Asia. (899, 945)

khalīfa Spiritual head of an Omani *ḥalqat al-mālid*, assisted by a *shawūsh.* (677)

khalīfe Officiant within a group of dervishes, perhaps the singer; the shaman or *ostā* in the *gwātī* ritual. (178, 191, 882)

khānaqāh Sufi dwelling; *khāneqāh* in Iran. (823, 935)

kharja Procession of a Sufi *ṭarīqa*, involving chanting and the playing of instruments. (520)

kharsha 'Decoration', improvised variation on sections of a basic melody in Yemeni tradition; plural, *kharashāt.* (687)

khashba 'Piece of wood', small single-headed Mesopotamian drum; also *khashaba*; cf. *ṭabla.* (416)

khāṣṣe 'Musicians of the elite' in Persia under Naṣr al-Dīn Shāh. (861)

khatim Concluding, lively vocal section within the Andalusian-Tunisian *nūba*; also *khatm*; plural, *akhtām.* (452, 457)

khawal Egyptian male dancer. (625)

khazer Armenian neumatic notation invented in the ninth century. (723)

khinṣir Little finger, or the fret played by this finger. (869)

khirkhsha Rattle usually intended for children, but used in selected musical traditions in Sudan (also *atetash*), Libya, and elsewhere; plural, *khirkhashāt.* (404)

khirlee In Tuva, a thin piece of wood that imitates the sound of wind when spun like a propeller on a tensed, twisted string. (981)

khitm Concluding section within Sufi performance of *ma'lūf*; cf. *khatim.* (519)

khögzhüm 'Music', Mongolian term for music, implying the use of musical instruments. (981)

khomus Jew's harp. (902, 981)

khöömei 'Throat', 'pharynx', Mongolian term for biphonic throat-singing in Tuva. (981)

khöömeizhi Performer of Tuvan *khöömei.* (981)

khumāsī Pentatonic *maqām* used in Nubian traditions. (644)

khushnī 'Nonentertainers', 'intruders', pejorative term for new musicians on Muḥammad 'Alī Street in Cairo; plural, *khashanā.* (619)

kibbutz Israeli communal settlement combining ideals of European socialism with a Jewish revolt against religious orthodoxy; plural, *kibbutzim.* (1016, 1028, 1072)

kilassiki muzika 'Classical music', referring to the *muqam* tradition of Uygur-Xinjiang. (993)

kinnāra Early Arabic term for a lyre; plural, *kinnārāt.* (358)

kirdān One of the major notes of the Arab fundamental scale. (34)

kırık hava 'Broken melody', category of Turkish folk music with melodies in strict meter. (79, 759)

kisr Type of lyre played by Nubians and Egyptian bedouin on the Red Sea coast. (412, 641)

Kitāb al-aghānī 'Book of Songs' by al-Iṣfahānī (d. 967), one of the most important medieval sources for Arab music. (12, 17, 291, 293, 349, 351, 370, 392, 396, 402, 541, 564, etc.)

klasik müziği 'Classical music' of Ottoman Turkey. (770)

klâsik Türk müziği 'Turkish classical music' performed by elite instrumentalists and singers and supported institutionally; also *klâsik Türk musikisi.* (47)

klezmer Traditional instrumental music of Ashkenazi Jews. (202, 1018, 1064)

köçek Dancing boys at Ottoman imperial festivals, or more recently at Turkish weddings; also *tavşan.* (115, 765, 779, 812)

koma sesler Microtonal pitches; Turkish. (82)

komuz Plucked fretless lute in Kyrgyzstan. (844)

kopuz Turkish folk lute. (80)

Koran See Qur'ān.

Köroğlu 'The Blind Man's Son', an epic of Central Asian origin. (81, 766, 952, 969)

koron Symbol for a half-flat in notation of Persian music. (60, 135, 867)

kös Large Turkish kettledrums. (115, 767)

koşma Common form of Turkish and Azerbaijani lyric verse with eleven- or eight-syllable lines, favored by minstrels; also *qoşma.* (81, 762, 851, 928)

krar Regional type of Ethiopian lyre. (358)

k'shots Armenian cult instrument made of silver plates with jingles. (736)

k'tsurt Form of Armenian sacred music. (737)

kūbah 'Drinking glass', early Arabic term for single-headed goblet drum. (360)

kudüm Small pair of drums used in Mevlevī ceremonies. (192, 769)

kurban bairam Feast of the Sacrifice, the most important religious holiday in Central Asia; also *kurban xayit, xayit;* Arabic, *id al-adkha, 'id al-aḍḥā.* (942)

kursī Short, quick instrumental introduction in the Andalusian-Algerian *nūba.* (451)

kwītra Short-necked lute of Morocco and Algeria. (405, 453, 470)

kyui 'Frame of mind', 'mood'; in Central Asia, an independent instrumental piece, played on lutes such as the *dombra* and *dutār*, that seeks to narrate a story; also *kui.* (902, 956)

kyuiler Term for Kazakh instrumental music. (956)

la'ba Yemeni dance performed by male couples, accompanied by the *mizmār.* (303)

Lag ba-'Omer Largest of the Jewish *hilulot*, festivals on the anniversary of the death of a saintly person, taking place on the thirty-third day after Passover; it is observed by Jews and Muslims alike on the island of Djerba. (203, 523, 1040)

***laḥn* (plural, *alḥān*)** 'Song', 'tune'; also refers to a model strophe in Arabic poetry. (208)

lahw 'Entertainment', 'idle pleasure', pejorative term for music in Islamic *samā'* literature; also *lahu.* (372, 538)

lāl al-'ūd 'Great shout', Omani dance consisting of antiphonal calls and slow, even-metered singing and dancing. (676)

lale devri 'Tulip time', cultural renaissance in eighteenth-century Turkey. (771)

l'amt Yearly gathering of drummers among the Shleuh group of Moroccan Berbers, in which playing and improvisation are learned. (487)

lapinka Marine shell horn of the Gulf region; also *yim* or *buk* in Oman. (416)

lavta Turkish lute. (758)

lawik Term in northern Iraq and western Iran for one genre of lyrical song. (748)

layālī 'Nights', section of vocal improvisation, analagous to instrumental *taqsīm*, and using the words *yā layl* 'O night!' or *yā 'aynī* 'O my eye!' (34, 121, 147, 388, 550, 567)

layla 'Night', Egyptian Sufi musical concert, performed at nighttime on religious and social occasions; plural, *layāli.* (147)

laylat al-ḥinna 'Henna night', a festivity preceding a wedding, during which the bride's and sometimes the groom's hands and feet are dyed with henna as a prophylactic against the evil eye; also *lailat al-hanna.* (627, 697)

lāzima Instrumental interlude; in Yemeni tradition, a short coda played at the end of a song which underlines the basic rhythm and characteristic pitches of the mode. (687)

le'b 'Play' in Arabic, also *lēb*; a Baluchi term for the *gwātī* ritual of possession or exorcism. (881)

lehakot tsva'iyot Troupes or ensembles for the entertainment of the Israeli Defense Forces; to the 1970s, their music combined "native" elements with international popular styles. (1020)

lewa Afro-Arab performance tradition in the Gulf states involving song and dance, accompanied by an instrumental ensemble featuring percussion instruments and the *ṣurnāy*, or oboe; also *līwa.* (403, 546, 678, 710)

līkū Baluchi form of melismatic singing. (881)

lmsaq Singing contest among Moroccan Berbers. (488)

lobsh 'Crowning hymn', Coptic nonbiblical text on a biblical theme, usually recited rather than chanted. (221)

longa 'Club', 'clubhouse', Turkish term for a Turko-Arab instrumental genre with a fixed rhythmic pattern, often appearing at the conclusion of a suite. (45, 91)

lōtār Circular, long-necked lute of the Moroccan Berbers. (405, 489)

lu'b 'Play', term sometimes applied to dance; see also *le'b.* (656, 704)

ma'allim Leader of the classical *nūba* ensemble in North Africa, who plays the *kwītra*; also *mu'allim, bāshā kyatrī.* (407)

ma'āni Spiritual meanings. (187)

madad 'Help', the assistance which God, through the saints, may provide to the sincere Muslim seeker. The Sufi *munshid* typically requests *madad* from various saints during his performance. (148, 171, 626)

madā'iḥ w-adhkār Sufi songs of praise or remembrance. (437)

madb Social performance of funeral laments, common in the eastern Mediterranean. (545)

maddāḥ Sufi religious storyteller; also *qissakhān.* (476, 901, 937, 945)

maddāḥa Algerian female musician. (305)

madīḥ 'Praise'. Any poem of praise, especially an encomium for the Prophet Muhammad. Such poems are frequently performed as *inshād*, especially in Sufi contexts. (148, 167, 414, 475, 568, 825)

madrūf Yemeni edge-blown open transverse flute with five fingerholes. (93)

maghna Turkish-influenced urban repertoire popular in Egypt from the mid-nineteenth to the early twentieth century; also *ṭarab.* Referred as *al-qadīm* 'the old' by conservative musicians. (557)

Maghrib Geographical term for the western, North African part of the Arab world, including Morocco, Algeria, and Tunisia. (201, 304, 364, 515, 535, 1035)

magrūna Double clarinet of the Maghrib; *majrūna.* In Tunisia appears with cow horn bells; cf. *tormāy, suggarat.* (306, 414, 624)

maḥallī 'Regional', with reference to rural or folkloric music in Iran. (853)

maḥall-i ẓuhūr Site of epiphany in a Sufi ceremony. (185)

maḥmūl 'Carried', early Arabic name for a mode, widely used in the East and in Muslim Spain before the seventh century A.H., thirteenth century C.E. (365)

mahrajān Outdoor weekend festival involving music, common in Arab-American communities. (280)

maḥṣūr Early Arabic mode name, cf. *maḥmūl.* (365)

Maimuna Festival originally among Moroccan Jews occurring on the last day of Passover; it is observed widely in modern Israel. (1040)

majles Term for a social gathering in Iran and Central Asia which may include performance of poetry and music; also *majlis.* (295, 626, 824, 840, 875, 937)

makab Large, low-pitched cylindrical drum tensed by cords in Bayt al-Faqīh/Tihāma. (99)

makam Turkish musical mode; plural, *makamlar;* see *maqām.* Can also refer to a song or tune. (31, 47, 79, 110, 114, 190, 256, 768, etc.)

makhdara Enclosed place or room in which the bride awaits the arrival of the groom. (102)

maktab In Central Asia, a school affiliated with a mosque, Sufi house, or shrine, in which Qur'ānic recitation is studied. (839, 939)

malang Term applied in eastern Iran and Pakistan to dervishes who are particularly inclined toward ecstatic trance; applied to a *gwātī* after several years of therapy. (885)

mahūn Colloquial North African language, used in popular genres like *'arūbī* and *ḥawzī;* also *milḥūn.* Also refers to a sung poetry tradition of Morocco. (416, 427, 472, 495)

mālid Omani ritual involving poetry, song, and body movements, in honor of the Prophet. (674)

ma'lūf Term for Andalusian (art) music of the Maghrib.Varieties include *ma'lūf al-hazl* 'frivolous' or 'profane', *ma'lūf al-jadd* 'serious' or 'sacred', and *ma'lūf al-khām* 'raw' or 'unrefined', a practice associated with Sufi brotherhoods characterized by unison singing accompanied by hand clapping or by percussion instruments. (325, 415, 433, 449, 455, 467, 501, 505, etc.)

Manas Kyrgyz heroic epic, a primary symbol of Kyrgyz nationhood. (345, 844, 903)

manascı Kyrgyz epic singer; also *semeteycı, manaschi.* (345, 844)

ma'nāwī Spiritual. (187)

mandala Geometrical sacred figure. (184)

mandole Combination of lute and mandolin, said to have been invented in Italy, which has been used in Algerian *sha'bī,* or popular, music since the 1930s. (421)

mani Common type of Turkish folk verse with seven- or eight-syllable lines, thought to have been the domain of women. (81, 762)

manjūr Jingle girdle made of animal hooves sewn on a piece of cloth, used in the Afro-Arab *nuban* ritual. (405, 546, 633)

maqām Generic term for melodic modes in the Arab world; plural, *maqāmāt.* In Central Asia, refers to a classical tradition of art song; see also *makam.* (11, 16, 31, 33, 46, 59, 113, 131, 148, 160, 166, 201, 209, 229, 283, 311, etc.)

al-maqām al-'irāqī Term evoking a primary urban vocal repertoire in Iraq involving a vocal soloist and a small instrumental ensemble. (8, 311, 403, 551, 1011, 1016)

maqāmāt al-aṣliyya Term designating the primary *maqāmāt.* (312)

maqsūm Common eight-beat rhythmic pattern. (89, 149)

marghul Instrumental elaborations of the *dastan* within the Uygur *mugam.* (999)

Maronite church Eastern Antiochene church that uses the Syriac language. (207, 229, 544)

marwaḥa See *mirwaḥa.* (215)

mashrap Derived from the name of the Uygur poet Mashrap (1641–1711), term for the final section of the Uygur *muqam,* involving dance and dominated by the kettledrum. (999)

Mashriq Eastern Arab world, usually including Egypt, Jordan, Lebanon, Iraq, Syria, and Palestine. (33, 317, 425, 533)

maṣmūdī ṣaghīr Common eight-beat rhythmic pattern; also *baladī.* (89, 691)

masnavī Classical Persian poetic form consisting of rhymed couplets. (70, 136, 831, 921, 944)

mäsräp Major section of the Uygur *muqam,* characterized by a quick, accelerating rhythm; also refers to a festive gathering among the Dolan people involving music. (989)

mastī 'Drunkenness', referring to the trance induced by the Baluchi *gwātī* ritual. (882)

matruz Song tradition of Maghribi Jews, treating religious and secular topics and combining Hebrew with Judeo-Arabic or Judeo-Spanish. (1043)

Mavlud Birthday of the Prophet Muhammad, widely observed in Central Asia; also *mavlud al-nabi.* Also refers to songs recounting the life and deeds of Muhammad, sung on the holiday of the same name. (942)

mavrigikhān Male singer-dancer of Central Asia, typically a descendant of Bukharan Irani or Farsi populations. (899)

mawwāl 'Causing to bend', 'repeatedly bending'. (1) Form of Arabic colloquial poetry, featuring clever wordplay. (2) Solo singing of Arabic poetry, nonmetric though sometimes with metric accompaniment, in the *maqām* modal system; often improvised. Also *muwal, muwwal.* (34, 167, 237, 313, 370, 388, 450, 544, 566, 628, 655, etc.)

mawwāl ḥalabī Aleppan version of *mawwāl.* (567)

maya Northeastern Turkish term for the *uzun hava* repertoire; also *varsağı* or *hoyrat.* (761)

māye In Persian music, two tetrachords that constitute the basis of a *dastgāh* or an important *gūshe,* along with characteristic melodic gestures; the "essence" of a mode. (59, 871, 927)

mazar Saint's tomb. (935)

mazhar See *mizhar.* (170, 418, 545, 626, 763)

mazmūm Early Arabic mode name, cf. *maḥmūl.* (365)

məclis 'Gathering', Azerbaijani spelling of Persian *majles,* from Arabic. (922)

Mediterranean music Term coined by the Israeli composer Alexander Boscovitch (1907–1964) to describe a style characterized by a rejection of European, Romantic tendencies in favor of expression of the collective will, geography, and culture of Palestine. (1028)

megiddo Traditional lyre of Palestine. (357)

mehter Turkish janissary band. (114, 190, 767)

mehter-i birūn 'Unofficial *mehter*', principal outdoor ensemble of Ottoman Turkey. (115)

mellī 'National', with reference to music of the Iranian nation; opposed to *mahallī* 'regional'. (853)

mersiye Laments for Imam Husayn, performed in Alevi ceremonies. (81, 122, 196, 768, 795, 924)

meşk 'Lesson', 'model' (Turkish), traditional pedagogical system for the training of vocalists in Turkey. (784)

mesnevī Narrative poem in couplets; usually the famous *mesnevī-i ma'nevī* of Cellālüddin Rūmī (1207–1273). (107, 196, 769)

meṣrā' Hemistich within a line of *ghazal.* (135)

Mevlevī Religious sect in Sufi Islam, known popularly as whirling dervishes. (107, 113, 132, 161, 184, 543, 755, 769, 779, 811)

mevlīd-i şerīf Birthday of the Prophet Muhammed; poem describing the birth of the Prophet; also *mevlit.* (193)

Mevlut Epic on the life of the Prophet in the Turkish *mesnevi* poetic style, composed by Süleyman Çelebi; also *Mevlit.* (57, 196, 769)

mey Turkish term for *bālābān* or *düdük,* a cylindrical double-reed aerophone; also *ney.* (10, 81, 764, 799, 848, 925)

meyan Third line of a four-line Turkish vocal composition, set apart by modulation or other means. (773)

meydan sazı Large Turkish lute. (763)

meẓrāb Stroke; plectrum or nail of index finger used in playing a string instrument; plucking technique. (866)

mḥorabih Palestinian improvisatory song for wedding processions. (585)

mihbash Bedouin mortar or pounder, pounded in particular rhythms and symbolizing social hospitality; also *mihba.* (404)

mijānā Popular genre of Mashriqī music. (283, 409)

mijwiz Single-reed double clarinet; also *mizwij.* (10, 283, 414, 545, 576)

milḥūn See *malḥūn.* (1041)

millî musiki 'National' style of music in the late Ottoman Empire, cultivated to appeal to Western tastes. (782)

Mimuna See Maimuna. (203, 265)

minjayra Lebanese end-blown flute. (545)

miraciye Turkish poem commemorating the Prophet's ascension to heaven; musical composition for such a poem, the most famous of which was composed by the Mevlevī Osman Dede (1652–1730). (57, 122, 195, 769)

miraçlama Song about Muhammad's ascension to heaven, performed in Alevi ceremonies. (795)

mīrāse farhangī 'Cultural heritage' (Persian, from Arabic *mīrāth*), a concept applied after the Iranian revolution of 1979 to certain musical repertoires, such as those of the *'āsheq* and the *bakhshī.* (823, 841)

mirfa' Shallow pot- or pan-shaped kettledrum, with head tensed by a turning ring, used particularly in the Yemeni highlands; plural, *marāfi'.* (7, 94, 417, 655)

mirwaḥa Idiophone with silver jingles attached to a circular silver disk, used in the Syrian, Maronite, Coptic, and Armenian Christian churches; the sound is thought to symbolize the murmuring of angels; also *marwaḥa.* (207, 401)

mirwās Small double-headed drum, used throughout southern Iraq and the Arabian Peninsula. (94, 404, 546, 652)

mishāliyya Instrumental prelude in free rhythm in the Moroccan *nūba.* (450)

mıskal Archaic Turkish pan flute, displaced by the *ney* in Ottoman Turkish ensembles. (108, 114, 774)

misket Common melodic mode (*makam*) in Turkish folk music. (83)

mistakhbār al-ṣan'a Term for an instrumental prelude in the *nūba* practice of Algiers; *mishāliyya* in Tlemcen. (451)

mitirp From Arabic *muṭrib*, professional musicians in Kurdistan, understood to be "Gypsies" or a minority. (745)

miyān 'Middle', middle section of a musical composition which usually modulates. (190)

miyānkhāna Second melodic section in the melodic development of a *shu'be.* (911)

mi'zaf Archaic term for lyre; plural, *ma'āzif.* Also *mi'zafa.* (295, 357, 395)

mīzān General term for rhythm or rhythmic periods, especially in North African music; plural, *mawāzīn.* (451, 457, 468, 518)

mizhar Skin-bellied lute of the medieval Middle East; also refers to an early type of frame drum. (295, 418)

mizmār General term for a double-reed aerophone in the Arab world; in Egypt, also *mizmār baladī, sibs-aba.* (93, 154, 303, 360, 395, 414, 545, 628, etc.)

mizmār al-jarāb Bagpipe. (395, 397)

mizmār wa-ṭābl baladī Egyptian ensemble of three *mizmār* players and two drummers. (415)

Mizraḥim 'Eastern' or 'Oriental' Jews of Asian and African heritage. (204, 261, 427, 1011, 1033)

mizwed North African bagpipe with a double clarinet attached to the bag; also *mizwid*; cf. *mizwij.* (415, 519)

mjarrad Five-beat rhythm associated with the 'Īsāwiyya of Tunis. (518)

Monophysitism Early Christian doctrine that Christ had a single nature, both human and divine; this doctrine was condemned by the Council of Chalcedon in 451. (207, 227)

morākab khāni Modulation between one *dastgāh* and another in Persian music; also *morākab navāzi.* (135)

morshed Spiritual guide, in a Sufi order; man whose singing and drumming directs the exercises in an Iranian *zūr-khāne*; also *murshid*, Arabic. (824)

motaqayyer 'Changing tone', tone within a Persian *gūshe* which changes depending on whether the melodic line ascends or descends; also *motaghayyer.* (62, 135, 867)

mōtk Baluchi lament for the dead. (881)

moṭlaq Open string; also *muṭlaq.* (869)

moṭreb In Iran, one member of a duo or small troupe that performs urban popular music; considered socially undesirable by religious leaders and others; cf. *muṭrib.* (139, 828, 868);

mṣaddar Introductory vocal genre with instrumental overture within the Maghribi *nūba*; plural, *mṣadrāt.* (327, 451, 470)

mṣaddar nūba Longer and more significant form of the Andalusian-Libyan *nūba.* (452)

msama' Traditional women's ensemble of Algeria; plural, *msama'āt.* (473)

mshāghlāt Vocal genre in the Andalusian-Tunisian *nūba* derived from popular songs. (452)

mshālya Instrumental introduction to the Algerian *nūba*; known in Algiers as *mustakhbar al-ṣan'a.* (470)

mu'adhdhin Performer of the *adhān*, or Islamic call to prayer; also *muezzin.* (153–155)

muezzin Performer of the *adhān*, or Islamic call to prayer; also *mu'adhdhin.* (153, 192, 568, 780, 939)

muğam Azerbaijani term for *maqām.* Also *mugam, mogam, mugham.* (8, 18, 23, 311, 552, 834, 921, 1016)

mughannī 'Singer', a singer or musician; more recent term for a soloist in the Iraqi *maqām.* (298, 313, 359, 686)

muḥarrak Type of song in the Andalusian *nūba*; plural, *muḥarrakāt.* (447, 456)

muḥarrikāt 'Moving', 'emotionally moved', section in the performance of the classical *nūba*; also *muḥarrakāt.* (456)

muḥāsaba Instrumental responses that enter into dialogue with the vocal part in the Iraqi *maqām.* (312)

muḥayyar *Maqām* similar to *maqām bayyātī.* (43, 51)

muhayyer Turkish melodic mode similar to *hüseyni.* (84)

mujarrad-i khiyāl Independent images in Islamic metaphysics. (187)

mujawwad 'Improved', 'beautified', melodically elaborate and intense style of Qur'ānic recitation; also *tartīl* or *tajwīd.* (160, 321)

mukabelle Mevlevī evening ceremony of *semā'*, sometimes applied to the *zikr* ceremony of other *tarikatlar.* (108, 191)

mukhammas Classical Arabic poetic form often used in Central Asian *maqām* traditions. (914)

mukhannath Male musician who dressed as a woman in medieval Medina and Mecca; plural, *mukhannathūn.* (296, 538)

mukhliṣ Final vocal piece within the Andalusian-Algerian *nūba.* (451)

mülāzime Major subdivision of the seventeenth- and eighteenth-century *peşrev.* (126)

mūlid Saint's day celebration; plural, *mawālid.* (147, 473, 617, 625)

munfaṣil 'Disjunct', type of tetrachordal joining. (37)

munshid General term for singer or vocalist, especially in a Sufi context; plural, *munshidīn.* (147, 165, 450, 543, 626)

mūnūlūj 'Monologue', through-composed song with great emotional intensity popular in twentieth-century Egypt. (548)

muqaddima Instrumental introduction; in the Iraqi *maqām*, either *muqaddima* or *taqsīm* (instrumental improvisation) is required in performance. (312)

muqam In Uygur music, term for a modal, monodic suite using varying rhythmic cycles as well as unmeasured rhythms. (184, 866, 989, 995)

murabba' Uygur poem with four-verse stanzas. Also a major Turkish vocal genre setting poetry in a nonmetered, improvisatory style. (120, 574, 628, 773, 1004)

murādā Women's dance of Qatar and Bahrain, in which the rhythm is created by foot stamping. (700, 710)

murāghī 'Recurring', 'repeating'; 'additional', 'supplementary', in Yemen. (99)

murakkaz Vocal genre within the Andalusian-Libyan *nūba.* (453)

murattal Unembellished style of Qur'ānic recitation; cf. *mujawwad*; also *tartīl* or *tajwīd*. (159)

musaf Special service in the Jewish liturgy for the sabbath, festivals, high holidays, and every first day of the Jewish month. (1052)

muṣawwitāt al-watariyya 'Chordophones', literal translation of the Greek term in a book title by al-Kindī. (373)

mushqilāt Instrumental section of a suite in the Bukharan tradition of *shash maqām*. (908)

mūsīqā 'Music', general term for music, usually implying the presence of melodic instruments. It can also refer to the theory of music, as opposed to practice (*ghinā*). (165, 182, 235, 367, 552, 557)

al-mūsīqā al-qadīma Term referring to traditional Egyptian classical music involving improvisation; cf. *al-turāth*. (161)

mustaftīḥ In the Sufi *dhikr*, the leader who regulates the tempo, movement, and chanting. (171)

mustazād Classical poetic form often used in Central Asian *maqām* traditions. (762, 914)

mutadākhil Overlapping type of tetrachordal joining. (37)

muṭawwal 'Stretched', Yemeni fixed composition with an unmeasured form. (689)

muṭawwala Slow, binary variant of the Yemeni *wasṭā* rhythm. (687)

muṭlaq Early Arabic mode name, cf. *maḥmūl*. (364)

muṭrib / muṭriba Performer of great talent who is thought to evoke *ṭarab*, or musical ecstasy; vocal soloist in a *takht* ensemble; lead songstress in a women's *firqa*. (167, 313, 551, 559, 682, 698, 745)

muttaṣil 'Joined', conjunct type of tetrachordal joining. (37)

muwashshaḥ A form of popular strophic Arab poetry that originated in Andalusian Spain as an alternative to the older *qaṣīda*. Also refers to a fixed vocal composition based on this poetic form. (24, 91, 167, 202, 237, 283, 370, 436, 443, etc.)

muzika mizraḥit 'Oriental music' or 'Mediterranean music', term for a genre of Israeli popular music that developed in the 1970s and 1980s, involving a mixture of traditional Arab idioms and instruments with Western-influenced Israeli song. (204, 261, 1020, 1033, 1074)

mzayyan Saudi dance involving poetic competition. (705)

mzayyin In Yemen, term for a professional musician of low social status, as a descendant of former slaves. (99, 303, 655)

na'ash Women's dance movement of the Arabian Peninsula, in which the dancer holds her right hand lightly on the upper chest while swinging her head and loose tresses; also *tanawush*, or *nuwwāsh* or *rishi*, in Yemen. (705)

na'at Muslim devotional song of praise, also *na't*. (122, 194, 940)

na'at-i şerîf Precomposed rubato form opening the Mevlevi *āyīn* ceremony. (110)

nabaṭī Cantillated bedouin poetry of the Arabian Peninsula. (652, 665)

naḍr Omani ceremony for the well-being of a newborn, involving poetry, hymns, and rhythmic body movements. (675)

nafīr North African metallic trumpet, played during Ramadan and for street processions during weddings. (415, 566)

nagarāt Pair of differently tuned drums used in North Africa; also *nagharāt, naqarāt*. (418, 453, 468)

nagham Mode or melody, interchangeable with *maqām*. 'Tones', a discipline of early Arabic music theory represented in book titles such as *Kitāb al-nagham*. (12, 33, 183, 364, 517, 564)

naghāra Kettledrums in Central Asia. (925, 940)

naghme 'Tune' in Iranian classical music, or subsidiary modal system derived from a *dastgāh*; similar to *āvāz*. (69)

nagla 'Passing', 'transition' between two melodies in a Yemeni suite, *qawma*. (689)

nağme Melody, Turkish. (80)

nahāwand One of the primary Arab *maqāmāt*. (36, 332, 555)

naḥḥām Professional singer of pearl divers' music of the Gulf. (546, 651)

naḥma 'Animal sound', 'voice of the whale', local term for pearl divers' songs in the Gulf region. (10, 651)

nakkaraxāna Term for an emir's military orchestra in traditional Bukhara. (940)

nakkare Kettledrums, Turkish; cf. *naqqāra*. (767)

naqqāl In Iran, a man who sings verses from Ferdowsī's epic *Shāh-nāme* in tea houses and other settings, perhaps adding prose narration of the stories. (827)

naqqālī Popular Persian tradition of prose storytelling and poetic recitation. (344, 827)

naqqāra Small kettledrum, usually played in pairs; plural, *naqqārāt*. (8, 312, 326, 395, 417, 498, 502, 566)

naqqāre Kettledrum, often played in pairs and found in various sizes; cf. *naqqāra*. (835)

naqrazān Small kettledrums, sometimes suspended from the player's neck. (631)

naqsh Vocal form in Arab music involving a prelude-like treatment of various *ghazal* tunes. (370, 827)

naqus Antiphonal singing of the Moroccan Atlas mountains, accompanied by idiophones made from found objects; also *nāqūs*. (303)

nāqūs General term describing metallic idiophones, including bells and cymbals. (219, 222, 403, 489)

narinik Term for lullabies in central Kurdistan; also may refer to certain wedding songs. (750)

nash'at kār Smaller Aleppan variant of the *'ūd*. (570)

nashīd Medieval Arabic vocal prelude in free rhythm; also a general term for song. (237, 388, 447, 456, 519, 664)

nashshād 'Singer of *nashīd*', singer of the Yemeni vocal suite or *tawshīḥ*. Also refers to Yemeni religious hymnody. (13, 307, 689)

nasr Vocal section within a suite in the Bukharan *shash maqām* tradition. (911)

na't Turkish poem praising the Prophet; musical genre stylistically related to the *durak*; cf. *na'at*. (769)

nawā One of the major notes of the Arab fundamental scale. (34, 312)

nawba Sung or instrumental suite in classical Arab music; see *nūba*. (184, 540, 1039)

nawḥ Lament. (538, 696)

nāy End-blown flute or reed pipe found throughout the Arab world, having six finger holes plus one thumbhole; plural, *nāyāt*. (8, 155, 186, 204, 282, 312, 327, 395, etc.)

nāzenk Baluchi wedding song genre. (881)

nazira Music created by a student in imitation of a master, a central idea in the transmission of Central Asian *maqām*. (917)

nefes Mystical hymn performed in Alevi ceremonies. (81, 114, 190, 768, 795)

nefîr Turkish trumpet; cf. *nafīr*. (115)

Nestorian heresy Belief, condemned by the Council of Ephesus in 431, that Christ had two distinct natures and persons. (207)

nevbet 'Striking the watch', music played by the janissary *mehter* ensemble in the early morning at the Ottoman court. (768)

ney End-blown rim flute, indigenous to Iran; cf. *nāy*. (137, 798, 828, 866)

ney Turkish flute; cf. *nāy*. (108, 755, 769, 774, 799, 848)

nigunei Meron 'Meron tunes' based on Arab, Turkish, Greek, and Druze tunes, performed in the *klezmer* repertoire for Jewish *hilulah* festivals. (203)

nigunim Vocal songs and improvisations performed during the Hasidic *tish*; singular, *nigun*. (202)

nihavent Common Turkish *makam* resembling the Western minor scale. (49)

nikriz Type of Turkish melodic mode, or *makam*. (84)

nimra Entertainment act; also used as a shorthand for entertainers; also *nimar*. (621)

nobān Possession ritual of the Gulf region. (180)

nowbe Suite or cycle of compositions in the system of Persian *radīf*; cf. *nūba*. (862)

nowḥe Poetic laments for the martyred Shi'a imams and members of their families; often performed responsorially with *sīne-zanī* or *zanjīr-zanī*. (826, 840)

Nowrūz Iranian new year, coinciding with the vernal equinox, widely celebrated by Persians, Kurds, Afghans, Tajiks and other Iranian peoples; also *nawruz*. (931, 946)

nozheh Medieval Persian dulcimer. (395)

nūba 'Suite' in Andalusian music, comprising a common stock of vocal and instrumental genres, each representing a different *īqā'* and performed in a given sequence; also *nawba*; plural, *nūbāt*. (11, 20, 327, 367, 407, 436, 441, 455, etc.)

nuban Afro-Arab possession and healing ritual involving sung poetry and dancing. (405, 412, 417, 546)

nūbat al-inqilābāt Folklike, simpler form of the Maghribi *nūba*. (470)

nūbat neqlāb *Nūba* of more recent origin and modest dimensions in the Algerian repertoire; seven of these join the twelve traditional *nūbat*. (450)

nūbat tūshiyya Originally instrumental overture within the Moroccan *nūba*, to which words were later adapted. (450)

nuqṭa Monetary tip. (617)

nusaḥ erets Yisrael 'Tradition of the land of Israel', musical style developed by the synagogues of the Ashkenazi national-religious sector. (1017)

nuwwaḥ Women's tradition of mourning songs among Moroccan Jews. (1042)

octo echos Byzantine system of melodic modes. Also *oktōēchos*. (11, 221)

oksh Belt rattle of goat hooves; also *mangour*. (633)

on ikki 'Twelve': term for classical *muqam*. (*maqām*) practice in Uygur (Xinkiang), referring more to a sequence of pieces in twelve *muqam* than to a modal category. (910, 989, 996)

ostā 'Master' (Baluchi), the officiant in the *gwātī* ritual; synonymous with *khalīfe*. (882)

ostād 'Master' (Persian), honorific term bestowed on those who have fully mastered musical and other arts. (59, 71, 134, 839)

oyun havalar Turkish dance tune; the term implies instrumental performance. (80)

oyun havası 'Dance tune' in Turkey, generic term. (848)

owj 'Climax', 'summit' (Persian), the highest register attained during a performance; cf. *'awj*; also the name of a *gūshe* in the *dastgāh* of *shūr* and the *āvāzāt* of *dashtī* and *bayāt-e esfahān*. (61, 134, 870)

ozan Archaic term for minstrel or poet in Iran, Turkey, and Azerbaijan; see *aşıq*. (80, 345, 765, 796, 844, 967)

özgün müziği 'Alternative' music with didactic, leftist tendencies, embraced by some Turkish Alevi. (251, 799)

pahlawān 'Champion', Baluchi performer of narrative songs that combine recitative, instrumental ritornello, and melismatic sections. (881)

p'andukht'i Genre of Armenian peasant songs reflecting the life of a *p'andukht*, one who is forced to live and work abroad. (724)

parda-dārī Solo performance genre in which a man recites and sings narratives in Persian while displaying a canvas painting of the story; also called *parda-gū'ī*. (827)

parde 'Curtain', 'membrane' (Persian); *pərdə* (Azerbaijani); one fret on a *dutār*, *sāz*, *tār*, or another chordophone; modal entity associated with a particular fret. (843)

parī Invisible creature; colorful, winged, rather feminine angel of ambivalent nature in Iranian mythology. (882)

parīkhān One who exorcises a *parī*. (881)

paşbend 'After the verse', Kurdish song in a relatively straightforward musical meter, performed after a vocal genre that avoids a recurring meter or rhythmic pattern. (11, 836)

pāye Rhythmic motive in Persian music. (137)

paytan Singer of Hebrew *piyyutim*, religious poems. (1037)

perde Fret on a Turkmen *dutar*. (971)

pərdələr Frets on an Azerbaijani *saz*. (847, 930)

peşrev Prelude in Turkish instrumental music with a fixed rhythmic pattern; *bashraf* in Arabic; also *peshrev*. (11, 80, 110, 114, 137, 194, 550, 767)

peste Rhythmic popular song that concludes the Iraqi *maqām* in secular contexts; cf. *bastah*, *tawshīḥ*. (312)

pīr Turkish spiritual elder; founder of a *tarikat*. (191)

pīsh darāmad Instrumental composition played by a melodic instrument and drum or by a small ensemble before the initial *gūshe-hā* of a Persian *dastgāh*. (137, 863)

pisheh Medieval Persian flute. (395)

piyuṭ Jewish festal song, setting Hebrew rhymed poetry; plural, *piyuṭim*. (202, 524, 1011, 1037)

pizmon Paraliturgical hymns; also popular Hebrew songs stressing urban, individualistic experiences instead of collective, agricultural topics, popular from the 1970s; plural, *pizmonim*. (1020)

psalis Psalms in the Coptic church; *madaya* in Arabic. (221)

psalmodiyya Choral service sung daily in the Coptic church. (221)

psuqei d'zimrah First part of the weekday morning service in the Yemenite Jewish liturgy. (1050)

qadd Strophic song in colloquial Arabic, associated with Aleppo; plural, *qudūd*. (551, 568)

qaḍīb Wand or stick. (297, 395)

qādriyya Women's musical genre of Algeria, setting multiple stanzas of love poetry; plural, *qādriyyāt*. (473)

qafl Rapid concluding song within a cycle of Andalusian-Moroccan *nūba*. (450, 458)

qafla Melodic or poetic cadence; plural, *qaflāt*. (11, 148, 446, 549)

qā'ida 'Basis', 'law', 'custom', 'pattern', referring the basic melodic and rhythmic structure of a song that must be reproduced in performance. (687)

qaiyrma 'Turn', conclusion of a Kazakh epic tale involving the performance of textless vocables. (953)

qalandar Dervish inclined to the state of ecstasy; the adjectival form, *qalandarī*, may refer to the music played in Baluchi *gwātī* rituals. (881, 901, 937)

qāleb In Persian music, a matrix, mold, model, or melodic structure that makes creative performance possible. (855)

qanbūṣ Yemeni short-necked lute; also *gabus*, *'ūd ṣan'ānī*, or *turbi*. (405, 654, 686)

qanṭara Relatively fast song within a cycle of the Andalusian-Moroccan *nūba*. (450, 457)

qānūn Trapezoidal plucked zither or psaltery found throughout the Arab world; plural, *qawānīn*. (8, 17, 39, 204, 263, 282, 312, 317, 322, 327, 395, 406, etc.)

qara öleng 'Simple song', lyrical songs sung by Kazakh women in various contexts. (951)

qarār Tonic pitch of a *maqām*; also *asās*. (34, 548)

qāri' Reciter of the Qur'ān; in Central Asia, also *hafiz*. Also refers to a solo male performer in the Iraqi *maqām*. (313, 551, 939)

qarrādī Genre of Palestinian improvised sung poetry. (587)

qaṣaba Open, edge-blown transverse flute with six fingerholes. (93)

qaṣīd Solo bedouin heroic vocal repertoire, accompanied by the *rabāba*; also *hudjeinī*, *hjīnī*. (409)

qaṣīda Poem in classical Arabic usually having a single rhyme scheme and meter throughout, following one of the sixteen poetic meters (*buḥūr*), or a musical composition setting such a poem; plural, *qaṣā'id*. (9, 148, 167, 203, 237, 313, 371, 447, 458, 470, etc.)

qaṣṣafiyya Lively Omani dance with weapons. (673)

qāvāl Azerbaijani frame drum (tambourine), 40–50 centimeters in diameter, with attached metal rings; accompanies performance of an *aşıq* in northwest Iran. (845, 925)

qawma Term for a suite of pieces in Yemeni tradition, related to the Andalusian *nūba*, containing three melodies of different rhythmic cycles and tempi. (689)

qawwāl Singer or reciter of the Qur'ān. Also refers more generally to a poet or singer. (545, 937)

qaycı Epic reciter in Altai culture. (345)

qāyim wa-nisf Vocal cycle within the Moroccan *nūba*. (450, 457)

qayna Singing-girl or songstress; possibly a slave in the home of a noble family; plural, *qaynāt* or *qiyān*. (291, 293, 358, 376, 537, 696)

qinīn Ancient Ethiopian lyre. (358)

qirā'a 'Reading', the correct reading of the Qur'ān. (372)

qirā'āt Scholarly discipline presenting and explaining authoritative interpretations of the Qur'ān. (158)

qirā'at al-maqām 'Reciting the *maqām*', traditional term for the singing of the Iraqi *maqām*. (312)

qiṣaṣ dīniyya 'Religious stories', religious or moralistic stories performed as a genre of *inshād*, by a solo *munshid* using a variety of literary and musical styles, with *takht* accompaniment. (167)

qiṭ'a General term for a musical piece. (45, 316)

qitāra Circular, five-stringed lyre found in upper Egypt and used in secular repertoires. (413)

qobız Horsehair fiddle. (345)

qobuz Concave, bowed lute of Central Asia; also *qobyz*, *qyl-qobyz*; cf. *qubūz*. (844, 953, 967)

qoshnay End-blown double-pipe aerophone of Central Asia with single reeds. (919)

qoş-nağara 'Pair of kettledrums', Azerbaijani. (925)

qrāqab Heavy Moroccan cymbals. (491)

quddām Rapid vocal movement within the Moroccan *nūba*. (450, 457)

Qur'ān Primary sacred text of Islam. (19, 132, 145, 148, 157, 179, 192, 295, 312, 321, 341, 353, 371, 388, etc.)

qūshme Possibly derived from Turkic *qoş-ney* 'pair of reeds'; double clarinet played in Iranian Khorasan, made of two equal lengths of bird bone. (836, 839)

rabāb Generic term for unfretted, bowed chordophones of various shapes and with varied numbers of strings; plural, *rabābāt*. Also *rabāba*, *rabābah*, *rababah*, *rbeb*, *rebab*, *ribāb*, *rribab*. (10, 269, 327, 340, 360, 395, 406, etc.)

rabāba Sudanese lyre. (357, 412)

rabbimman Women's genre of religious song, especially in the Ferghana valley of Uzbekistan. (941)

radīf 'Row' (Persian), the canonical repertoire of melody-types and modes, organized in the personal style of a great master Also, a word that follows the rhyming syllable or syllables in each line of a poem. (11, 18, 59, 129, 836, 851, 854, 865, 1011)

rāhber 'Leader' (Persian), a singer who assumes the leader's role in a ritual performance. (833)

raḥmānī Large double-headed drum of Oman. (420, 676)

rai 'Opinion', 'destiny', form of Algerian popular music that gained prominence in the 1980s, influenced by local Algerian and Western popular styles. (231, 269, 427, 438, 477)

ra'īs Leader of an ensemble. (676)

Ramadan Ninth month of the Islamic lunar calendar, during which the Qur'ān was first revealed to the Prophet Muhammad. During Ramadan, Muslims fast from dawn to sunset. *Inshād dīnī* is frequently performed during this month. (166, 191, 415, 473, 617, 668, 694, 840, 940, 951)

raqd Syriac lamentation dance. (361)

raqṣ Dance; also *raks*. (361, 704, 931, 937)

raqṣ bil-'aṣā 'Stick dance', sometimes accompanying the martial *taḥṭīb* dance of Egypt. (631)

raqṣ iskandarānī 'Alexandrian dance', acrobatic martial dance performed with various types of weapons in Lower Egypt. (627)

raqṣ al-khayl 'Horse dancing', Egyptian traditional dance in which a horse performs a variety of exercises to instrumental accompaniment; the rider may also dance standing on the horse's back. (628)

raqṣ al-sham'īdān Form of *raqṣ sharqī*, known in the West as a belly dance, in which the performer balances a weighty candelabrum on her head. (625)

raqṣ sharqī 'Oriental dance', characterized by articulated pelvic movements, common in Egypt; known in the West as belly dance. (624)

Rashīdiyya Institute Institute founded in Tunis in 1934 with the aim of preserving traditional Tunisian music. (326, 502, 505)

rāst Also *rast*. (1) Name of the principal mode of traditional Arab art and court music, first alluded to by Ibn Sīnā. (2) Name given to the open strings of the lute in Ibn Kurr's description of the tonal system. (3) One of the primary notes of the Arab fundamental scale. (34, 50, 154, 181, 312, 332, 365, 542, etc.)

rāst kūk In Iranian music, tuning for the male vocal range. (65)

rawap Ancient Uygur bowl-shaped lute; cf. *dūtār*. (999)

rāwī Bard or poet-singer. (667)

raysat Female singer-dancers of Morocco who perform in urban *rways* troupes. (490)

razḥa Omani men's warrior dance; cf. *'arḍa*. (647, 654, 680, 706)

reng Persian or Azerbaijani composition associated with dancing. Each *dastgāh* concludes with one or more *reng-hā*. (132, 834, 863, 866, 879, 925)

responsa 'Answers' to public queries by Jewish rabbis. (205)

riçak Term in Kurdistan for spike fiddle. (746)

ring In Oman, term for medium-sized cymbals that accompany the singing and dancing of professional groups; also *sehal*, *ṭāsa*. (403)

riqq Small frame drum or tambourine, usually with five small cymbals inserted into the frame, also called *duff* in Yemen. (8, 91, 148, 282, 317, 418, 547, 559, 616, 623)

rīshe 'Roots'; in Iran, term referring to the bases, age, depth, and origin of music. (858)

rīshqālā Model strophe in Syro-Maronite chant. (208)

robā'i Quatrain, classical Persian poetic form. (136)

romansot sfaradiyot Judeo-Spanish songs that became popular in Israel from the 1960s. (1017)

rongo Dance of Sudanese origin accompanied by the *ringu*, or xylophone. (630)

rowże-khān In Iran and elsewhere, a performer of narratives about the martyrdom of Imam Hosein, other Shī'a imams, or members of their families. (826)

rū-howżī Iranian comic improvised theater, involving solo dancing. (878)

rubāb Long-necked lute of medieval Persia and Central Asia. (395)

rubaī Classical poetic form often used in Central Asian *maqām* traditions. (914)

rūḥ Spirit. (182)

rways Sung poetry tradition among Moroccan Berbers of the Tashlhiyt region. (410, 489)

ṣabā One of the primary Arab *maqāmāt*. (37, 49, 85, 193, 312, 555)

saf Dance song performed by women of the Saharan Atlas for religious feasts. (474)

safail Type of rattle used in Central Asian *zikr* ceremonies. (943)

ṣaff Line of men acting as a chorus in Palestinian wedding celebrations. (573, 583)

ṣaffāqatān Archaic term for cymbals or castanets. (395)

safīna 'Vessel,' manuscript or printed collection of poetic texts; plural, *safā'in*. (506)

sagat tūra Large finger cymbals; also *ṣājāt*. (403, 626)

ṣaḥfa Shallow vessel drum of the north Tihāma, made of clay with an open bottom, two antipodal handles, and a turning ring for tightening the head. (94, 419)

ṣaḥn Gong-shaped flat dish made of thin metal, used as a percussion instrument. (94, 403, 687)

ṣaḥn nuḥāsī Flat circular copper tray used as a struck idiophone in Yemen. (403)

ṣa'īdī Common eight-beat rhythmic pattern, named after the Ṣa'īd region of Upper Egypt. (89)

ṣa'ir 'Poet', term for a singer of heroic songs in Kurdistan; also *lawjebij* 'sayer of songs'. (345, 747)

saj' Ancient rhymed prose; also refers to a quick, march-like Yemeni rhythmic pattern. (664, 687)

ṣājāt Small brass finger cymbals; also *sagāt*. (545)

salām 'Greeting', a musical salutation consisting of a popular song. (617)

salṭana Ecstatic state thought to arise from hearing or performing the *maqām*. (174, 549)

salyr-saryk Performance style of southeastern Turkmenistan. (973)

samā' 'Hearing', 'listening', especially in a Sufi context; also used as a synonym for music or a concert or recital. (19, 109, 118, 132, 158, 179, 371, etc.)

samāḥ Aleppan sacred dance, possibly related to the Turkish Alevi *sema* dance. (568)

samā'ī Common Arab instrumental overture, formally related to the Turkish *bashraf* or *peşrev.* (45, 91, 550, 563, 569)

sāmirī Poetic genre of the Arabian Peninsula performed with music and dance. (653, 709)

samrī Bedouin communal dance performed with antiphonal singing in the Mashriq; also refers to love songs of sedentary bedouin of the Arabian Peninsula. (409, 647, 665)

ṣan'a 'Art', term for the traditional Arab-Andalusian repertoire of the Maghrib. (407, 436, 449, 455, 467)

sanat 'Art' (German *Kunst*) music, usually referring to urban Turkish genres of the nineteenth and twentieth centuries. (247)

sanat musikisi 'Art music', term designating Turkish classical music. (47)

ṣanj Generic term for cymbals; also refers to a type of early harp, and possibly to a medieval Chinese gong. (360, 395, 566)

sankīn samā'ī Common 6/8 rhythmic pattern. (91)

santūr Trapezoidal zither struck with two mallets, today played largely in Iraq. (8, 64, 115, 137, 312, 398, 411, 421, 552, 774, etc.)

saqfa suwaysī 'Suez clapping', complex syncopated clapping performed during wedding celebrations in the Suez. (627)

sarakhbār Somber, meditative genre of Central Asian *maqām.* (916, 920)

sāri' Quicker variant of the Yemeni *wasṭā* rhythm. (687)

şarkı Urban form of the *türkü* folk song, first developed in the seventeenth century, and still current. (115, 190, 772)

sato Central Asian bowed lute; in Uygur Xinkiang, pear-shaped fiddle with three bowed strings and twelve sympathetic strings; related to *ghidjak.* (919, 1003)

sawākāt Vocal genre in the Andalusian-Tunisian *nūba* derived from popular songs. (452)

ṣawt 'Voice', 'sound', term for a classical Arab vocal repertoire; highly stylized song cycle of the Gulf region, often performed in prosperous homes; genre of popular music in the Gulf region. (101, 420, 456, 541, 552, 647, 651, 698, 709)

ṣawt al-tays Solo falsetto vocalist in a Tunisian ensemble. (502)

sayr 'Path', model for the unfolding of a *maqām* presented in theoretical or pedagogical contexts. (549)

sāz Long-necked, fretted, plucked Turkish and Azerbaijani folk lute; also a synonym of *sornā*; one tube of a double aerophone (as in Persian *dosāz* 'two tubes'); any musical instrument; harmony, concord. (10, 82, 248, 345, 405, 751, 763, 795, etc.)

s'az Armenian lute with a long pear-shaped body and long neck, usually with six to eight metal strings and ten to thirteen frets; cf. *sāz.* (734)

saz payı Instrumental interludes in Turkish vocal music. (773)

saz semai Primary composed instrumental form in Turkish music; also *saz semaisi.* (91, 121, 773, 779)

sāzanda Female wedding entertainer in Bukhara and Samarkand, Uzbekistan; cf. *khalfa.* (899, 945)

Şeb-i 'Arūs Mevlevī celebration on the anniversary of Jalûluddin Rûmî. (109)

Şehnaz Common Turkish *makam* featuring augmented-second intervals. (49)

selâm Section within the Mevlevi *āyīn* ceremony; also *selām.* (111, 114, 190)

şelpe Style of playing the Turkish *bağlama* with the fingertips, derived from Central Asian practice. (790, 796)

sema Ritual dance performed in Alevī ceremonies by couples. (568, 768, 795, 811)

semā' Medieval Sufi musical ritual, term inherited by Mevlevī sect, later also applied to the *zikr* of the Sunnī *tarikatlar* and to the *āyīn-i cem'* of the Alevī and Bektaşī sects. (114, 190, 811)

Sephardic Jews "Spanish Jews," today referring to non-Ashkenazi Jews in Israel. (58, 199, 427, 1035, 1063, 1064, 1071)

şer Kurdish heroic sung narrative; also *merxoş.* (747)

serraba Short introductory song in a quick meter, performed as part of *malḥūn.* (499)

şeşbendi Term for wedding songs in central Kurdistan, sung by close relatives of the bride and groom. (751)

setār 'Three strings' (Persian), a long-necked lute with four strings, plucked with the nail of the index finger. (10, 137, 866)

seyir Basic melody capturing the essentials of a Turkish *makam* for students. (48, 83, 121)

sez See *zorne.* (745)

sezarb Form of religious song in the Central Asian *zikr,* involving rhythmic refrains containing one of the names of God. (946)

shabbāba End-blown cane flute. (407, 545, 582)

sha'bī Urban popular style of North Africa, developed in the 1930s and influenced by Western jazz and popular music; also a generic term for "folk" music in the Mashriq. (275, 321, 421, 427, 475, 1044)

shabih See *ta'zīye.* (827, 840)

shadd Name for a mode in the school of al-Urmawī; plural, *shudūd.* (365)

Shādhiliyya One of the oldest and most prominent North African Sufi brotherhoods. (515)

shagird Apprentice or student to a master musician (*ustaz*) in Central Asia. (917)

shāhed 'Witness tone', tonal center of a *gūshe* in Persian music. (65, 134, 867)

shāh gūshe 'King *gūshe*', primary *gūshe* in Persian music, forming the basic modal sections of the *dastgāh* structure. (67, 134)

Shāh-nāme Epic poem in Persian composed by Ferdowsī in the tenth century C.E., fourth century A.H., formerly recited in tea houses by *naqqāl-hā*; also *Shāhnāma.* (340, 827, 866)

shāhrūd Type of medieval box zither. (395)

shā'ir Professional poet–epic singer; plural, *shu'arā'.* (340, 409, 545, 653, 664)

shambar Instrumental form in Algerian classical music, of Turkish origin. (470)

sham'idān 'Candelabra', dance with candelabra. (619)

shanbar Instrumental overture within the Andalusian-Tunisian *nūba.* (451)

shang-qobyz Kazakh term for a Jew's harp played mainly by women. (956)

shaptāgi Baluchi vocal genre, performed for six days following the birth of a child. (881)

sharakan Canonical hymns sung in the Armenian divine office. (737)

sharaknots Collection of *sharakan* hymns. (737)

sharḥ Popular couples dance of southern Yemen. (656, 709)

sharqī 'Eastern', term for Egyptian styles that became popular in twentieth-century Algeria along with jazz and European dance music. (269, 475)

shash maqām 'Six *maqāmāt*', repertoire of Uzbek and Tajik classical art song native to Bukhara and Samarkand; also *shashmakom, shashmaqom.* (11, 311, 900, 909, 922, 997, 1011)

shaykh Traditional honorary title bestowed on (1) an elder; (2) a tribal leader; (3) a religious scholar; (4) a Sufi spiritual leader; (5) a religious singer (*munshid*). (107, 147, 165, 186, 191, 327, etc.)

shēr Baluchi epic or courtly poem, sung with simple, measured refrains. (881)

shertpe 'Plucking', 'flicking', 'fingering'; type of Kazakh *kyui* (instrumental music) involving the plucking of strings by individual fingers. (957)

shibāba Shepherd's flute; see *shabbaba.* (636)

shikh Professional musicians of Berber Morocco; plural, *shikhāt.* (489)

shi'r Poetry. (342, 663)

shirah betsibur 'Communal singing', Israeli institution in which an audience gathers to sing songs whose texts are projected on a screen or distributed in paper. (1019)

shirei erets Yisrael 'Songs of the land of Israel'; specific repertoire of folk songs in modern Hebrew canonized by the political establishment. (262, 1018)

shīrīn navāzī 'Sweetened style' of the Persian *radīf* demanded by the new bourgeois society of twentieth-century Iran. (862)

sho'be Modal branch in Persian music. (11, 73, 131, 184)

shofar Ram's horn, blown on Jewish high holidays. (1052)

shūbāsh Precomposed congratulatory song performed at a Palestinian wedding for the entry of the groom after he has gotten dressed. (589)

shu'be 'Branch', referring to a subdivision of pieces within the Bukharan *shash maqām.* (17, 911, 916, 927)

shughl Vocal form in the Mashriq, similar to the *muwashshaḥ.* (370, 452, 568)

shūr The most fundamental and characteristic mode in the Iranian musical system. (59, 131, 826, 836, 854, 869, 926)

shūrī One of the primary Arab *maqāmāt.* (41)

sīkā One of the major notes of the Arab fundamental scale. (34, 57, 652, 687)

silsile Chain of initiates or genealogy reaching back to the Prophet. (194, 758)

sīmorgh Mythical bird in Iranian mythology, symbolizing the celestial soul, the spiritual guide and physician, the object of the quest; the most important piece of music in the Baluchi *gwātī* ceremony, with numerous variants. (179, 889)

simsimyya Small lyre with bowl-shaped body and five strings, used primarily in Egypt and Yemen. (93, 358, 412, 545, 623, 656)

sinād Genre of highly ornamented songs sung to classical Arabic poetry, typical of women's music of the medieval Arabian Peninsula. (696)

sīne be sīne 'Chest to chest' or, by extension, 'memory to memory' (Persian): oral transmission. (839, 856)

sīne-zanī 'Breast-beating' (Persian); responsorial singing of *nowḥe* by Shī'a men who strike their shoulders with small, light chains as they move in rhythm. (826)

sinkinī In the Gulf region, dance performed to mournful poetry while pearl divers' vessels were readied for sea. (708)

sipsi Small Turkish reed or bamboo clarinet. (763)

sīra Traditional genre of Arabic versified, heroic narratives; plural, *siyar.* (339, 628)

Sīrat Banī Hilāl Lengthy epic of the Banī Halāl bedouin tribe (Egypt), one of the last epics to survive in oral tradition. (340, 410)

sīyāh-bāzī Iranian comic improvised theater involving dance. (878)

snitra Algerian term (diminutive of *sanṭūr*) for the Western mandolin, introduced in the eighteenth century. (407, 421, 453)

sonnatī 'Traditional' (Persian, from Arabic), a term applied to numerous phenomena, including several types of music, following the Iranian revolution. (853)

sorī Symbol for a half-sharp in notation of Persian music. (867)

sornā Aerophone with conical bore, found in Iran. (828, 839)

sorūd Baluchi waisted fiddle with four strings and sympathetic strings, also called *soroz* and *qeychek.* (881)

sözlü ezgiler Turkish vocal melodies, such as the sung poetry of minstrels. (80)

sözlü oyun havalar Turkish dance songs. (80)

srnaj Term for a shawm in the Gulf region. (415)

stambūlī Tunisian ritual involving dance, music, poetry, and song; cf. *gnāwa, dīwān.* (403)

ṣuffarā Small Egyptian flute; also *suffāra, salamiyya.* (413, 545, 633)

Sufi Muslim participating in Sufism. (19, 107, 132, 145, 147, 161, 165, 177, 372, 403, 427, 431, etc.)

Sufism The mystical dimension of Islam, comprising social, doctrinal, and ritual aspects; considered by Sufis to constitute the essence of Islam. (129, 147, 170, 189, 515, 543, 625, 823, etc.)

suggarāt Double clarinet with cow horn bells used in Algeria; cf. *tormāy, magrūna.* (414)

suisin Small, three-stringed fretless lute with a skin-covered body, used in Morocco. (407, 499)

sulyāq Medieval term, probably denoting a lyre. (395)

ṣunūj Cymbals or castanets. (403)

ṣunūj al-aṣābi' Finger cymbals; Egypt, *sajāt*; Iraq, *chumparāt*; Morocco, *nuiqsāt*; Libya, *zel.* (403)

sur Baluchi circumcision song. (881)

ṣurnāy Type of oboe used in the Afro-Arab music of the Gulf region. Also an archaic term for flute or oboe. (395, 546, 705, 898, 1003)

suvāra Sufi-related song cycle of Khwarezm (Khorezm), Uzbekistan-Kazakhstan, setting spiritual poetry to music. (913, 945)

sybysghy Elongated open flute, played by Kazakh shepherds. (956)

sybyzyk Short, single-reed pipe made of cane, found in Central Asia. (902)

sygyt 'Whistle', type of Tuvan *khöömei* involving high, clear, piercing harmonics. (983)

Syriac Semitic language, derived from Aramaic, once spoken by the inhabitants of historical Syria. (208, 225)

Syro-Catholic church Christian church espousing the Western Syro-Antiochene rite, united with the Roman See since the eighteenth century. (208)

Syro-Orthodox church Christian church espousing the Western Syro-Antiochene rite. (208)

ṭab' Generic term for musical mode; plural, *ṭubū'.* Also refers to the nature, stamp, or character of a *nūba.* (12, 365, 381, 446, 452, 456, 470)

tabıl Large Turkish drum; also *davul.* (767)

ṭabl Generic term for various types of drums in the Arab world; plural, *ṭubūl.* (94, 115, 360, 395, 415, 444, 498, 566, 624, etc.)

ṭabl baladī Double-headed bass drum. (283, 545, 631)

ṭabl bōga Term used in Yemen for a large, low-pitched cylindrical drum tensed by cords. (99)

ṭabl al-lewa Tubular drum used in Yemeni possession ceremonies. (420)

ṭabl marad Term used in Zabīd/Tihāma, Yemen, for a large, low-pitched cylindrical drum tensed by cords (7, 99)

ṭabl mu'asṭā Term used in the Tihāma, Yemen, for a large, high-pitched cylindrical drum tensed by cords, played in ensembles accompanying dance. (7, 99)

ṭabl sāgh Term used in Bayt al-Faqīh–Tihāma for a large, high-pitched cylindrical drum tensed by cords; see *ṭabl mu'asṭā.* (99)

ṭabl al-ṣaghīr Small double-headed drum played by women on festive occasions in Yemen; also *ṭabl ṣaghīr.* (420)

***ṭabla* (plural, *ṭablāt*)** Generic term for drum; cf. *ṭabl.* Also may refer more specifically to a single-headed portable drum used throughout the Arab world; also *darbūka*; in Algeria, *gelal*; in Libya, *galal.* (31, 148, 170, 282, 416, 545, 559, 616, 642, 745)

t'agh In Armenian music, a sung poem, lyrical, dramatic, or solemnly laudatory. There are secular and religious *tagher.* (733)

Tahir Classical mode, or *makam,* found in Turkish folk music. (83)

taḥmīla Short, fixed instrumental composition involving call-and-response by various solo instruments, common in the Egyptian *takht* repertoire. (45, 550, 569)

taḥrīr Opening section of melismatic vocalization within the Iraqi *maqām*; also *badwa.* (135, 311, 551, 652)

taḥṭīb Egyptian martial dance in which the participants wield large bamboo or wooden staves. (628)

tajwīd Qur'ānic recitation, or the rules governing its proper performance; also may refer to the more melodically elaborate style of Qur'ānic recitation. (158, 165, 192, 321, 372, 517, 938)

tak High-pitched drum stroke; also *takk*; cf. *dumm.* (7, 89, 418, 549)

takbīr Qur'ānic recitation in Central Asian Sufi ceremonies. (943)

takhmīr 'Leavening', 'fermentation', term for the trance or ecstasy of a Sufi devotee. (517)

takht Small chamber ensemble of three to five or more musicians, common in the nineteenth-twentieth-century Mashriq; also *takht al-sharqī, takht sharqī.* (8, 33, 148, 170, 240, 312, 317, 406, 547, 559, etc.)

taksīm Solo instrumental improvisation (Turkish); see *taqsīm.* (11, 56, 108, 114, 196, 257, 758, 773)

ta'līf 'Composition', a discipline of early Arabic music theory, represented in book titles such as *Ta'līf al-alḥān.* (364)

tallunt Drum of the Moroccan Berbers. (488)

talqin Devotional songs in Sufi *zikr* or *dhikr*, transmitted through lineages of musical specialists, *talqinchi*. (911, 944)

talwīn Modulation from one mode, or *maqām*, to another. (446)

tal'wwatt Moroccan Berber flute. (489)

ṭambūra Lyre; also *ṭambra, ṭanbūra, ṭanbūrah*. (93, 405)

tamdyazt Moral or political type of song performed by the Moroccan Berber *imdyazn* troupe. (487)

tamssust Dance song of the Moroccan Berbers; also refers to the act of knocking down fruit from trees. (483)

tanaka Large jerrycan for oil or fat, used as an idiophone by Afro-Arab populations in the Gulf states in the *lewa* musical tradition; also *pato*. (403)

tanbīre Long-necked lute that provides a drone in Baluchi music (also *tanburag* and *setār*); a lyre of the Gulf region used in *nobān* ceremonies; cf. *ṭunbūr*. (825, 883)

ṭanbūra Song and dance tradition of the Gulf region, held as a weekly social event or on special occasions to treat maladies associated with spirit possession. The ritual is named for the lyre *tanbura*, which is commonly used in the ceremony; cf. *ṭambūra*. Also known as *nuban*, a term related to its Nubian roots. (546)

tanna Lowest-pitched of the three small cylindrical drums in the drum ensembles of Shiḥr (southern Hadramawt), generally known as *mirwās*. (96)

Tanzimat Period of reform in the nineteenth-century Ottoman empire, emphasizing the principle of westernization in society, culture, and aesthetics. (757, 781)

taqlīd 'Imitation' (Arabic); routine imitation, necessary in the early stages of musical apprenticeship but devalued in religious and artistic traditions. (856)

taqsīm Introductory instrumental section of music involving free improvisation; also *taqāsīm*. In performance of the Iraqi *maqām*, either *taqsīm* or *muqaddima* (instrumental introduction) is required; also *taksim*, Turkish. (34, 46, 121, 148, 170, 312, 388, 421, 499, 550, 559, 563, 567, 576, 593, 600, 692, 701, etc.)

ṭaqṭūqa Short strophic song, popular in early-twentieth-century Egypt. (548)

tār 'String' (Persian); a long-necked lute with three double courses of strings, found in Iran and Central Asia. (8, 130, 395, 828, 866, 900, 923)

ṭār Small round frame drum with small metal cymbals (tambourine), used in the Maghrib and Mashriq; also refers to a larger type of frame drum. (94, 270, 326, 407, 418, 453, 460, 499, 502, 519, 527, 545, 591, 628, 641, 653, 675, 692, 706, 734, 833, 1041)

t'ar Long-necked Armenian lute with a body in the shape of a figure-eight. It has a skin soundboard and five to nine, eleven, or fourteen strings; cf. *tār*. (725)

ṭarab Acute joy, enthusiasm, or grief; also, artistry. (149, 165, 187, 281, 305, 313, 354, 449, 517, 549, etc.)

ṭarab Traditional Yemeni lute covered in goatskin, also called *qanbūs*. (686)

tarāne Traditional Baluchi song for weddings and celebrations, derived from Indo-Pakistani light music. (881)

tarāwīd Light songs sung at henna parties preceding Palestinian weddings. (581)

ṭarda Egyptian combat game of presumed bedouin origin, involving the mutual pursuit of armed horsemen. (628)

tarfī' Medium-pitched drum of three small cylindrical drums in drum ensembles of Shiḥr (southern Hadramawt), generally known as *mirwās*. (96)

tarh Coptic hymn paraphrasing a biblical text. (221)

t'arija Small single-headed vase drum, typical in performance of Moroccan *malḥūn*. (416, 489, 499)

tarikat Turkish Sufi order; plural, *tarikatlar*; cf. *ṭarīqa*. (107, 119, 189)

ṭarīqa Sufi order; plural, *ṭuruq*. (171, 492, 516, 543, 625)

tarjama 'Translation', ornamented variation of a vocalist's melody by the instrumentalists of a *takht*. (149, 559)

tarjī' Technique in which text repetitions are sung to new, improvised melodies. (291)

tartīl (1) Qur'ānic recitation; (2) the less melodically elaborate style of Qur'ānic recitation; cf. *tajwīd*. (148, 159, 391)

tartys-kyui 'Contest piece' performed on the Kazakh *dombra*. (955)

ṭāsa Shallow dish-shaped kettledrum with head tensed by a turning ring, in modern practice using screws attached to the head assembly; widespread throughout Yemen, particulary in the highlands; also, a copper bowl struck with sticks, played in the 'Isāwa Sufi ritual of Morocco. (94, 403, 417, 655)

taṣdīra First, relatively slow song within a Andalusian-Moroccan *nūba* cycle. (450, 457)

tasfiq Hand clapping. (372, 692, 698)

taskiwin 'Powderhorns', warrior dances performed in the Moroccan Berber *aḥwash* by men in a circle. (489)

taslīm Concluding or refrain section, for example in the Iraqi *maqām*. (311)

taṣnīf Vocal composition with a poetic text in Persian or Azeri, included at specified points in performances of classical music and representing a simplification of the *radīf* system. (137, 834, 863, 868, 925, 928)

ta'thīr Effect, ethos. (177, 541)

tatyan Genre of eastern Turkish vocal music. (84)

tavājud Ecstasy; trance; forced ecstasy; psychic and unconscious conditioning in order to reach ecstasy. (884)

tavşan 'Rabbit', male dancer in Ottoman Turkish traditions; cf. *köçek*. (115)

tawāshī Internal musical segments embellishing the framework of an Andalusian *nūba*; plural, *tūshiya*. (450)

tawashīḥ dīniyya Genre of *inshād dīnī* performed by a solo *munshid* supported by a small chorus (*biṭāna*). (167)

tawḥīd Islamic creed, *Lā illāha illa Allāh* 'There is no God but God'. (678, 943)

tawshīḥ Rhythmic song; may conclude a performance of the Iraqi *maqām* in ritual contexts; cf. *peste*. (312, 452, 652)

tawshīḥ Type of vocal suite in Yemeni tradition, related to the *qawma*; also *tathlīth* 'tripling', referring to its threefold structure. (657, 689)

ta'zīye Dramatic representation of events surrounding the martyrdom of Imam Husayn or another Shī'a imam, in which imams and their supporters sing lines of verse while their opponents recite in an unmelodious manner; called *shabih* 'likeness' in Iranian Khorasan. (544, 827, 860, 866, 923, 931, 942)

tazrrart Responsorial song of Morocco; plural, *tizrrarin*. In some forms, men and women in separate rooms respond to one another. Also refers to a "limping" rhythm used in Moroccan Berber *ahwash*. (303, 481, 487)

tecvīt Qur'ānic recitation (Turkish); cf. *tajwīd*. (192, 768)

tekke Dervish lodge; place of meeting or residence for members of a *tarikat*. (81, 107, 117, 189, 780)

temcîd Night prayer sung in the mosque during the month of fasting (Turkish), associated with the Sufi liturgy. (195, 769)

Tengrianism Ancient trinitarian religion of Kazakh nomads, aspects of which many Kazakhs blend with Islamic beliefs. (949)

terkīb Subdivision of the *mülāzime* and *hāne* in the Turkish *peşrev*, consisting of two or more cycles (*devr*) of the *usūl*; used in a modular fashion in the early Ottoman *peşrev*. (126)

terme 'Threading', term for a variety of short narrative songs that surround the performance of the Kazakh epic tale. (901, 951)

tesbîh Morning prayer sung in the mosque during the month of fasting (Turkish). (195, 769)

teslim Refrain with a Turkish musical form; cf. *taslīm*. (773)

tevşīh Metrical hymn performed on the birthday of the Prophet or another holiday; cf. *tawshīh, tawashīḥ diniyya*. (122, 193, 769)

thaqīl 'Heavy', slow in tempo. (103, 389)

theotokia Hymns in honor of the Virgin Mary, sung in the Coptic church. (221)

thōb nashal Long traditional dancing dress on the Arabian peninsula. (692)

tidinit Long-necked lute, used in classical music by Arab tribes of Mauritania. (405)

tiqrqqawin Metal castanets used by Moroccan Berbers. (487)

tirade Borrowed Greek term referring to a verse form in which an indefinite number of lines are joined by a single rhyme pattern; it is used to describe an ancient form of Kazakh epic composition. (953)

tirmechy bagshy 'Collector', Turkmen singer of poems. Also *tirmeçy bagşy.* (969)

tırnak kemençe Fiddle played with the fingernails, native to nomads of southwestern Turkey. (763)

tish Hasidic traditional meal on the sabbath, involving singing (of *nigunim*) and dancing. (202)

tishbibt Metal flute, Egypt. (624)

toi Festive celebration involving hospitality and musical performance, common in Central Asia; see also *toy.* (897, 951)

tökpe 'Stream', 'flow', type of *kyui* (instrumental music) common in western Kazakhstan, consisting of sweeping movements of the right hand resulting in a drone-like texture. (957)

tombak Goblet drum named for the two basic sounds *dom* (struck in the center, lower in pitch, resonant) and *tak* (struck on the rim, brighter in timbre, dry); also called *ẓarb.* (137)

tormāy Egyptian double clarinet (*mizmār*) with cow horn bells; cf. *magrūna, suggarat.* (414)

toy 'Banquet' (Turkic); cf. *toi.* Festive celebration of a birth, circumcision, wedding, or the like; the major occasion for performances by an *'āsheq* or *bakhshī.* (827, 931, 968)

treq 'Path', Judeo-Spanish tradition of compound musical compositions resembling the Andalusian *nūba*, performed at life-cycle and communal celebrations. (1039)

trianto Metal triangle used in performance of Coptic chant. (222)

tuata Conical metal trumpet used in Iraqi Shi'ite centers during the ceremony of mourning for Husayn. (415)

tulum Turkish bagpipe. (763, 925)

ṭūmār Teacher's scroll outlining the narrative of a Persian epic, copied by the student. (344)

ṭumbara Yemeni lyre; cf. *ṭambūra.* (357, 412)

ṭunbūr Fretted, long-necked lute played with a plectrum; plural, *ṭanābīr.* Also *ṭanbūr, tanbur, tanbūr.* Also a rare early Arabic designation for lyre. (10, 82, 115, 130, 184, 357, 395, 405, etc.)

ṭungura Small, deep kettledrum of the Tihāma made of clay or other appropriate materials, surrounded with straps and having a double skin; also called *dumduma.* (7, 98)

ṭūra Medium-sized Egyptian cymbals, played in religious contexts. (170, 403)

turāth 'Heritage', generic term for classical Arab music. More specifically, may refer to an Egyptian style of classical music that emerged in the 1950s. (29, 235, 283, 317, 325, 511, 557, 564, 605)

Türk halk müziği 'Turkish folk music culture', promoted under the leadership of Mustafa Kemal Atatürk. (77)

türkü Turkish folk song. (80, 115, 195, 759)

tūshiyat al-kamāl Concluding instrumental piece within the Andalusian-Algerian *nūba.* (456)

tūshiya zīdān Classical instrumental overture of Algeria, found in varying forms in Tlemcen, Constantine, and Algiers. (467–468, 469)

'ūd Plucked Arab lute found throughout the Middle East; plural, *a'wād* or *'īdān.* (8, 16, 36, 45, 130, 148, 170, 204, 257, 263, 269, 279, 291, 295, 312, 317, 327, 352, 357, 364, 395, 402, etc.)

'ūd 'arbī Fretless short-necked Algerian lute with four pairs of strings; also *'ūd tūnisī* or *'ūd maghribī.* (327, 405, 453, 470, 502)

'ūd sharqī 'Eastern lute' of the Mashriq, with six pairs of strings. (327, 405, 407, 453, 527)

ufār Dancelike genre in Central Asian *maqām.* (911)

ughniyya 'Song', 'tune'; (plural, *ughniyyāt, aghānī*). Twentieth-century genre of long sectionalized colloquial song. Also *ughnīya.* (552, 558, 569)

uhzūja 'Swift song'; plural, *ahāzīj.* Piece concluding the performance of the classical *nūba*, synonymous with *ṭaqṭūqa*, a light, popular genre. (456)

urghanīn Byzantine organ. (395)

urjūza Poem in the *rajaz* metre, used for didactic purposes. (366)

urkestr 'Orchestra', English term adapted in the Mashriq. (552)

uşşak Common melodic mode (*makam*) in Turkish music. (54, 83, 110, 118, 772)

usṭā Chief of a group of performers; plural, *usṭāwāt.* (618)

ustādh Teacher. See also *ostād.* (313, 929)

ustaz Master musician in Central Asia. (917)

usul Rhythmic patterns in Uygur music; also refers to a repeating metric cycle in the Bukharan *shash maqām.* (911, 927, 943, 998)

usūl Turkish term for rhythmic cycles. (79, 85, 110, 113, 193, 767, 782)

uzun hava 'Long melody', category of Turkish folk music involving lengthy, quasi-improvisational melodies. (80, 759, 765)

uzun yry 'Long song', melismatic style of Tuvan *khöömei*, using poetic analogies to link the external world with human feelings. (981)

uzyn sonar 'Long hunt', central section of recitative in a Kazakh epic, based on a recurring rhythmic motive. (953)

varsağī Popular Turkish musical form. (115, 761)

velvele Subdivision of beats in the performance of Turkish rhythmic patterns, or *usûl.* (123, 773)

verd In Iran, a Sufi litany. (881)

vəsət 'Middle', the middle course of strings on the Azerbaijani *saz*, used as part of the drone. (847)

vipasan Armenian storyteller and poet of the Middle Ages. (723)

viyolonsel Cello, Turkish term. (758)

waḥda Common eight-beat rhythm in modern Arab vocal music. (92, 149, 631, 655)

wahhābiyya Omani dance with weapons, similar to the *qaṣṣafiyya.* (654, 676)

wa'iẓ Public sermon delivered by a Sufi. (937, 945)

wajd 'Ecstasy', mystical rapture that may result from proper performance of Sufi rituals, especially from *dhikr* and *inshād.* (166, 180, 519)

waṣla 'Stretch', 'connection', traditional vocal suite of the Mashriq, comparable to the Andalusian *nūba.* (11, 21, 148, 174, 370, 452, 551, 563, 567)

wasṭā Rhythmic period in Yemenite music with internal structure of 3 + 3 + 2. (93, 655, 687, 689)

wasṭā al-kawkabāniyya 'The Kawkabān *wasṭā*', triplet variant of the Yemeni *wasṭā* rhythm. (687)

wazn Rhythmic mode; plural, *awzān*; cf. *'īqā.* (90, 549)

wird Sufi religious litany. (185)

wusṭā Middle finger; the fret played by this finger. (869)

xälq naxsisi Term for popular songs in Uygur Xinjiang. (993)

xānakāi 'Performed in the *khānāqā*'; vocal genre related to Sufi chanting, especially in Uzbekistan. (945)

yakkaxāni 'Individual song', Tajik term; in Uzbek, *yakkaxānlik.* This is performed during breaks in the Central Asian Sufi *zikr.* (944)

yalla Women's repertoire of strophic dance songs in the Ferghana valley in Uzbekistan; also *lapar.* (902)

yanık 'Burned', 'consumed by love'; term for a Turkish solo repertoire for the *bağlama.* (80)

yarā'a Medieval flute. (395)

yarghūl Shepherd's flute of Palestine, similar to the *mijwiz* but with one melody and one drone pipe. See also *arghūl.* (545, 575, 636)

yaylı tanbur Long-necked bowed Turkish urban lute. (250, 758)

Yazdaxum 'Eleventh', Sufi group in Bukhara that celebrated *zikr* on the eleventh day of each month. (943)

yeniçeri Turkish janissary band. (21)

yeshivot Hebrew religious schools. (200, 526)

yishuv 'Settlement', term for the Jewish community of Palestine before 1948. (1023)

yol 'Road', 'wandering', 'direction'; Turkmen term referring to performance style, song, *dessan* or its narration, or a *bagshy* (*bagşy*) performance. (970)

yomut-gökleng Performance style of northern Turkmenistan. (973)

zaffa March or procession, often seen in weddings. (102, 616, 626, 643, 682)

zaffih Palestinian song for the shaving of the groom. (587)

zafina Early Arabic term for dance. (361)

zafn Type of dance that produces no sound and consists of moving the shoulders, eyebrows, head, and so on. (396)

zagharīt Cries of joy; ululation; singular, *zaghrūta*. (573, 582, 691, 699)

ẓāhir Apparent, manifest. (186–187)

żahīrok A Baluchi instrumental genre, equivalent to the vocal *līkū*. (881)

ẓā'id 'Extra' (Arabic), an additional fret, not named for a finger. Also *zā'id*. (869)

zajal A form of colloquial, popular Arabic poetry, first appearing in medieval Islamic Spain; plural, *azjāl*. Also refers to a musical setting of this poetry. (167, 229, 370, 436, 443, 458, 470, etc.)

zakir Musician who performs in Alevi ceremonies; also *güvende, sazende, aşık*. (191, 796)

zambra Moorish festival of song and dance. (449)

zammār Central figure in the Omani *ḥalqat al-lewa*, who plays a double-reed instrument or *mizmār*. (678)

zamr Early designation for a wind instrument; today refers to a Maghribi double clarinet; also *zammr*. (270, 306, 444)

zamzamāt Women's musical ensemble in Libya. (437)

zanj Cymbal; plural, *zunūj*. (476)

zanjīr-zanī 'Chain-striking' (Persian), responsorial singing of *nowḥe* by Shī'a men who strike their shoulders with small, light chains as they move in rhythm. (826, 833)

zār Evil spirit; by extension, a possession ritual of African origin widespread on the Red Sea and Gulf coasts. (180, 359, 412, 535, 632, 656, 674)

żarb Iranian goblet drum of walnut, clay, or plastic; also called *tombak*, with the exception of the large *żarb* played in the *zūr-khāne*. (8, 825, 925)

ẓarbī A particular rhythmic realization of a *gushe* in Persian music. (134)

ẓarīf al-ṭūl Palestinian wedding song. (583)

zāwiya Sufi lodge or shrine, typically built around the tomb of a saint; plural, *zāwāyā*. (327, 435, 493, 516)

zekr 'Remembrance' (of God); Persian, from Arabic *dhikr*; cf. *dhik, zikir*. Sufi method of verbal recall in the form of a litany. Also *ẕekr*. (833, 877, 881)

zeybek Turkish folk dance genre performed in the Aegean region. (812)

zhyr Kazakh term for epic or epic poetry. (950)

zhyrau Kazakh epic singer. (950)

zikir Invocation of God's name (Turkish); cf. *dhikr*. (769)

zikr See *dhikr*.

zikr jaxri 'Loud' *zikr*, Central Asian term; also *zikr jari* or *jaxriyya*. This involves singing, reciting poetry, and dancing. (943)

zikr khafi 'Silent' *zikr*, Central Asian term; also *zikr khufi*. The name of Allah and sacred formulas are pronounced silently; (943)

zil From Persian *zīr* 'below'. Triple course of strings on the Azerbaijani *saz*, tuned to the highest pitch and used for the melody. (847)

zil Cymbals, Turkish. (767)

zilli maşa 'Fire tongs with bells', type of Turkish idiophone. (765)

zīr 'Below' (Persian); on an *'ūd, dutār*, or *sāz*, the string or course of strings that lies farthest from the player's head and produces the highest pitches. (8, 835)

zıraw Epic reciter in Kazakhstan; also *aqın*. (345)

ẕolarbā' Arabic term for tetrachord. (869)

zorne From Turkish *zurna*, Arabic *mizmār*; double-reed aerophone used in Kurdistan; cf. *sez, zūrnā*. (745)

ẕowq 'Taste', 'passion', Persian. (858)

zūkra Double-reed aerophone of North Africa. (306, 415, 519)

zummār Oboes. (566)

zūr-khāne 'House of strength' (Persian); gymnasium in which men's athletic exercises are coordinated with the singing and drumming of a *morshed*. (824, 866, 877)

zurna Generic term for double-reed aerophone in the eastern Arab world; cf. *sornā*. (10, 115, 257, 263, 415, 566, 679, 764, 816, 925)

z'urna Armenian bell-mouth wind instrument made from wood or metal; cf. *zurna*. Because of its very strong sound, it is used as mostly an outdoor instrument. (729)

A Guide to Publications on Middle Eastern Music

Alexander J. Fisher

INTRODUCTION TO THE REGION

Abu Lughod, Lila. 1986. *Veiled Sentiments: Honor and Poetry in a Bedouin Society*. Berkeley and Los Angeles: University of California Press.

———. 1989. *Before European Hegemony: The World System* A.D. *1250–1350*. Oxford: Oxford University Press.

Adler, Israel. 1975. *Hebrew Writings Concerning Music, in Manusripts and Printed Books, from Geonic Times up to 1800*. Munich: G. Henle.

Angles, Higinio. 1943–1964. *La musica de las Cantigas de Santa Maria del rey Alfonso el Sabio*. Barcelona: Disputación Provincial de Barcelona, Biblioteca Central.

'Arafa, 'Abd al-Mun'im, and Ṣafar 'Alī. 1942. *Kitāb dirāsat al-'ūd*. Cairo: n.p.

Armbrust, Walter. 1996. *Mass Culture and Modernism in Egypt*. Cambridge: Cambridge University Press.

Barkechli, Mehdi. 1963. *La musique traditionnelle de l'Iran*. Tehran: Secrétariat d'État aux Beaux-Arts.

Bates, Daniel G., and Amal Rassam. 1983. *Peoples and Cultures of the Middle East*. Englewood Cliffs, N. J.: Prentice-Hall.

Bayer, Bathyah. 1963. *The Material Relics of Music in Ancient Palestine and Its Environs: An Archaeological Inventory*. Tel Aviv: Israel Music Institute.

Blench, Roger. 1984. "The Morphology and Distribution of Sub-Saharan Musical Instruments of North African, Middle Eastern, and Asian Origin." *Musica Asiatica* 4:155–191.

Blum, Stephen. 1972. "Musics in Contact: The Cultivations of Oral Repertoires in Meshed, Iran." Ph.D. dissertation, University of Illinois.

Bohlman, Philip. 1987. "The European Discovery of Music in the Islamic World and the 'Non-Western' in Nineteenth-Century Music History." *Journal of Musicology* 5(2):147–164.

Cachia, Pierre. 1973. "A Nineteenth-Century Arab's Observations on European Music." *Ethnomusicology* 17:41–51.

Campbell, Kay Hardy. 1999. "Days of Song and Dance." *Aramco World* 50(1):78–87.

Caton, Margaret. 1983. "The Classical Tasnif: A Genre of Persian Vocal Music." Ph.D. dissertation, University of California, Los Angeles.

Caton, Steven C. 1990. *"Peaks of Yemen I Summon": Poetry as Cultural Practice in a North Yemeni Tribe*. Berkeley: University of California Press.

———. 1999. *Lawrence of Arabia: A Film's Anthropology*. Berkeley: University of California Press.

Choudhury, Roy. 1957. "Music in Islam." *Journal of the Asiatic Society, Letters* 23(2):43–102.

Christianowitsch, Alexandre. 1863. *Esquisse historique de la musique arabe aux temps anciens, avec dessins d'instruments et quarante mélodies notées et harmonisées*. Cologne: M. Dumont-Schauberg.

Danielson, Virginia. 1997. *'The Voice of Egypt': Umm Kulthum, Arabic Song, and Egyptian Society in theTwentieth Century*. Chicago: University of Chicago Press.

Dauer, Alfons. 1985. *Tradition afrikanischer Blasorchester und Entstehung des Jazz*. Beiträge zur Jazzforschung, 7. Graz: Akademische Druck- und Verlagsanstalt.

D'Erlanger, Baron Rodolphe. 1930–1959. *La musique arabe*. Paris: Geuthner.

Description de l'Égypte. 1809–1822. Paris: Imprimerie Impériale.

Djumaev, Alexander. 1993. "Power Structures, Culture Policy, and Traditional Music in Soviet Central Asia." *Yearbook for Traditional Music* 25:43–50.

Doubleday, Veronica. 1999. "The Frame Drum in the Middle East: Women, Musical Instruments, and Power." *Ethnomusicology* 43(1):101–134.

During, Jean. 1984. *La musique iranienne: Tradition et évolution*. Paris: Recherche sur les Civilisations.

———. 1988a. *Musique et extase: L'audition spirituelle dans la tradition Soufie*. Paris: Albin Michel.

———. 1988b. *La musique traditionnelle de l'Azerbayjan et la science des muqams*. Baden-Baden: V. Koerner.

———. 1992. "L'oreille islamique: Dix années capitales de la vie musicale en Iran: 1980–1990." *Asian Music* 23(2):135–164.

———. 1994. *Quelque chose se passe: Le sens de la tradition dans l'Orient musical*. Lagrasse: Verdier.

During, Jean, Zia Mirabdolbaghi, and Dariush Safvat. 1991. *The Art of Persian Music*. Washington D.C.: Mage.

Eickelman, Dale F. [1981] 1998. *The Middle East and Central Asia: An Anthropological Approach*, 3rd ed. Upper Saddle River, N. J.: Prentice-Hall.

Elsner, Jürgen. 1997. "Listening to Arabic Music." *World of Music* 39(2):111–126.

Engel, Hans, 1987. *Die Stellung des Musikers im arabisch-islamischen Raum*. Bonn: Verlag für Systematische Musikwissenschaft.

Farhat, Hormoz. 1965. "The *Dastgah* Concept in Persian Music." Ph.D. dissertation, University of California, Los Angeles.

Farmer, Henry George. 1925. *The Arabian Influence on Musical Theory*. London: H. Reeves.

———. 1929. *History of Arabian Music to the Thirteenth Century*. London: Luzac.

———. 1933. *An Old Moorish Lute Tutor, Being Four Arabic Texts from Unique Manuscripts in the Biblioteca Nacional, Madrid (no. 334) and the Staatsbibliothek, Berlin (Lbg. 516)*. Glasgow: Civic.

———. [1939?] *The Structure of the Arabian and Persian Lute in the Middle Ages*. London: s.n.

———. 1943. *Sa'adyah Gaon on the Influence of Music*. London: A. Probsthain.

———. 1957. "Janitscharemusik." In *Die Musik in Geschichte und Gegenwart*. Kassel: Bärenreiter.

———. 1978. *Historical Facts for the Arabian Musical Influence*. New York: Arno.

———. 1997. *Studies in Oriental Music*. Frankfurt am Main: Institute for the History of Arabic-Islamic Science at Johann Wolfgang Goethe University.

al-Faruqi, Lois Ibsen. 1979. "The Status of Music in Muslim Nations: Evidence from the Arab World." *Asian Music* 12(1):56–85.

———. 1985a. "The Suite in Islamic History and Culture." *World of Music* 27(3): 46–64.

———. 1985b. "Music, Musicians and Muslim Law." *Asian Music* 17(1):3–36.

Feldman, Walter. 1996. *Music of the Ottoman Court: Makam Composition and the Early Ottoman Instrumental Repertoire*. Berlin: VWB (Verlag für Wissenschaft und Bildung).

Friedl, Erika. 1991. *Women of Deh Koh: Lives in an Iranian Village*. New York: Penguin.

Gavin, Carney. 1985. "The Earliest Arabian Recordings: Discoveries and Work Ahead." *Phonographic Bulletin* 43:38-45.

Gerson-Kiwi, Edith. 1980. *Migrations and Mutations of the Music in East and West: Selected Writings*. Tel Aviv: Tel Aviv University, Faculty of Visual and Performing Arts, Department of Musicology.

Goitein, S. D. 1967–1993. *A Mediterranean Society: The Jewish Communities of the Arab World as Portrayed in the Documents of the Cairo Geniza*. Berkeley: University of California Press.

Goldschmidt, Arthur. [1979] 1999. *A Concise History of the Middle East*, 6th ed. Boulder, Colo.: Westview.

Guignard, Michel. 1975. *Musique, honneur, et plaisir au Sahara*. Paris: Paul Geuthner. (Includes 45-rpm record.)

Hage, Louis. 1972–1991. *Musique maronite*. 4 vols. Kaslik, Lebanon: Bibliothèque de l'Université de Saint-Esprit.

Al-Ḥā'ik, Muḥammad ibn al-Ḥusayn. 1999. *Kunnāsh al-Ḥā'ik*. Rabat: Akadimiyat al-Mamlaka al-Maghribiyya.

Hassan, Scheherazade Qassim. 1980. *Les instruments de musique en Irak et leur rôle dans la société traditionnelle*. Paris: Mouton.

Hickmann, Hans. 1949. *Instruments de musique*. Cairo: Impr. de l'Institut Français d'Archéologie Orientale.

Hourani, Albert H. 1991. *A History of the Arab Peoples*. Cambridge, Mass.: Harvard University Press.

Husmann, Heinrich. 1970. "Die oktomodale Stichera und die Entwicklung des byzantinischen Oktoëchos." *Archiv für Musikwissenchaft* 27:304–325.

Ibn Khaldūn. 1967. *The Muqaddimah: An Introduction to History*, trans. Franz Rosenthal. 3 vols., 2nd ed. Princeton. N. J.: Princeton University Press.

al-Jabartī, 'Abd al-Raḥmān. 1993. *Napoleon in Egypt: Al-Jabartî's Chronicle of the French Occupation, 1798*, trans. Shmuel Moreh. Princeton and New York: Markus Wiener.

Al-Jāḥiz. 1980. *The Epistle on Singing-Girls of Jahiz*, ed. with trans. and commentary A. F. L. Beeston. Warminster, Wiltshire, England: Aris and Phillips.

Jeffery, Peter, 1994. "The Earliest Christian Chant Repertory Recovered: The Georgian Witnesses to Jerusalem Chant." *Journal of the American Musicological Society* 47:1–38.

Jung, Angelika. 1989. *Quellen der traditionellen Kunstmusik der Usbeken und Tadshiken Mittelasiens: Untersuchungen zur Entstehung und Entwicklung des šašmaqam*. Hamburg: Karl Dieter Wagner.

Kiesewetter, Raphael Georg. 1842. *Die Musik der Araber, nach Originalquellen dargestellt*. Leipzig: Breitkopf and Härtel.

Kitāb mu'tamar al-mūsīqā al-'arabiyya (Book of the Conference of Arab Music). 1933. Cairo: al-Maṭba'a al-Amīriyya.

Lachmann, Robert. 1929a. "Die Weise vom Löwen und der pythische Nomos." In *Musikwissenschaftliche Beiträge: Festschrift für Johannes Wolf*, 97–106. Berlin: M. Breslauer.

———. 1929b. *Musik des Orients*. Breslau: F. Hirt.

Lambert, Jean. 1997. *La médecine de l'âme: Le chant de Sanaa dans la société yéménite*. Nanterre: Société d'Ethnologie.

Lane, Edward William. [1836] 1978. *An Account of the Manners and Customs of the Modern Egyptians*. Reprint, The Hague: East-West Publications.

Lapidus, Ira M. 1988. *A History of Islamic Societies*. Cambridge: Cambridge University Press.

Lawergren, Bo. 1995–96. "The Spread of Harps between the Near and Far East during the First Millennium A.D.: Evidence of Buddhist Musical Cultures on the Silk Road." *Silk Road Art and Archaeology* 4:233–275.

———. 1997. "To Tune a String: Dichotomies and Diffusions between the Near and Far East." In *Ultra Terminum Vagari: Scritti in onore di Carl Nylander*, ed. B. Magnusson et al., 175–192. Rome: Quasar.

Levin, Theodore. 1984. "The Music and Tradition of the Bukharan Shashmaqam in Soviet Uzbekistan." Ph.D. dissertation, Princeton University.

———. 1993. "Western Central Asia and the Caucasus." In *Ethnomusicology: Historical and Regional Studies*, ed. Helen Myers. New York: Norton.

Marcus, Scott. 1989. "Arab Music Theory in the Modern Period." Ph.D. dissertation, University of California, Los Angeles.

Massoudieh, Muhammad. 1973. "Tradition und Wandel in der persischen Musik des 19. Jahrhunderts." In *Musikkulturen Asiens, Afrikas, und Ozeaniens im 19. Jahrhundert*, ed. Robert Günther, 73–96. Regensburg: Gustav Bosse.

———. 1995. *Radif-i avazi-i musiqi-i sunnati-i Iran*. Tehran: Instisharat-i Vizarat-i Farhang va Hunar, Anjuman Ishaah va Ala-i Musiqi.

———. 1996. *Manuscrits persans concernant la musique*. Munich: G. Henle.

Monroe, James T. 1970. *Islam and the Arabs in Spanish Scholarship (Sixteenth Century to the Present)*. Leiden: Brill.

———. 1986–1987. "A Sounding Brass and Tinkling Cymbal: Al-Halīl in Andalus (Two Notes on the Muwaššah)." *La Corónica* 15(2):252–258.

Mostyn, Trevor, and Albert H. Hourani, eds. 1983. *The Cambridge History of the Middle East and North Africa*. Cambridge: Cambridge University Press.

La musique arabe: Le congrès du Caire de 1932. 1992. Cairo: CEDEJ.

Nasr, Seyyed Hossein. 1987. *Islamic Art and Spirituality*. Albany: State University of New York Press.

Nelson, Kristina. 1985. *The Art of Reciting the Qur'ān*. Austin: University of Texas Press.

Nettl, Bruno. 1992. *The Radīf of Persian Music*. Champaign, Ill.: Elephant and Cat.

Neubauer, Eckhard. 1965. "Musiker am Hof der frühen Abbasiden." Inaug.-Diss., Frankfurt am Main, J. W. Goethe-Universität.

———. 1994. "Die acht 'Wege' der arabischen Musiklehre und der Oktoechos." *Zeitschrift für die Geschichte der arabisch-islamischen Wissenschaften* 9:373–414.

———. 1995–1996. "Al-Halīl ibn Ahmad und die Frühgeschichte der arabischen Lehre von den 'Tönen' und den musikalischen Metren." *Zeitschrift für die Geschichte der arabisch-islamischen Wissenschaften* 10:255–323.

———. 1997. "Zur Bedeutung der Begriffe Komponist und Komposition in der Musikgeschichte der islamischen Welt." *Zeitschrift für die Geschichte der arabisch-islamischen Wissenschaften* 11:307–363.

Newlandsmith, Ernest, 1931. *The Ancient Music of the Coptic Church*. London, 1931.

Petry, Carl F. 1991. *The Civilian Elite of Cairo in the Later Middle Ages*. Princeton, N. J.: Princeton University Press.

Picken, Laurence E. R., and Noël J. Nickson. 2000. *Some Ancient Connections Explored*. Vol. 7 of *Music from the Tang Court*. Cambridge: Cambridge University Press.

Poché, Christian, and Jean Lambert. 2000. *Musiques du monde arabe et musulman: Bibliographie et discographie*. Paris: Geuthner.

Racy, Ali Jihad. 1983a. "The Waslah: A Compound Form Principle in Egyptian Music." *Arab Studies Quarterly* 5:396–404.

———. 1983b. "Music in Nineteenth-Century Egypt: An Historical Sketch." *Selected Reports in Ethnomusicology* 4:157–179.

———. 1991. "Creativity and Ambience: An Ecstatic Feedback Model from Arab Music" *World of Music* 33(3):7–28.

Rahman, Fazlur. [1966] 1979. *Islam*, 2nd ed. Chicago: University of Chicago Press.

Ribera, Julian. 1912. *Discursos leídos ante la Real Academia Española*. Madrid: Iberica.

———. 1970. *Historia de la música árabe medieval y su influencia en la Española*. New York: AMS.

———. 1975. *Music in Ancient Arabia and Spain: Being La musica de las Cantigas*. New York: Da Capo.

Robson, James, and Henry George Farmer, eds. 1938. *Ancient Arabian Musical Instruments, as Described by al-Muffaddal ibn Salama (Ninth Century) in the Unique Istanbul Manuscript of the* Kitab al-malahi *in the Handwriting of Yaqut al-Mustasimi (d. 1298)*. Glasgow: Civic.

Robson, James. 1938. *Treatise on Listening to Music*. London: Royal Asiatic Society.

Said, Edward. 1978. *Orientalism*. New York: Pantheon.

Salvador-Daniel, Francisco. 1879. *La musique arabe: Ses rapports avec la musique grecque et le chant grégorien*. Algiers: A. Jourdan.

Sawa, George Dimitri. 1989. *Music Performance Practice in the Early Abbasid Era 132–320 A.H./*

750–A.D. 932. Toronto: Pontifical Institute of Mediaeval Studies.

Schlesinger, Kathryn. 1925. *Is European Musical Theory Indebted to the Arabs? Reply to "The Arabian Influence on Musical Theory" by H. G. Farmer*. London: H. Reeves.

Schuyler, Philip D. 1990. "Hearts and Minds: Three Attitudes toward Performance Practice and Music Theory in the Yemen Arab Republic." *Ethnomusicology* 34:1–18.

———. 1997. "*Qat*, Conversation, and Song: A Musical View of Yemeni Social Life." *Yearbook for Traditional Music* 29:57–73.

Shihāb al-Dīn Muḥammad ibn Ismā'īl. c. 1840. *Safīnat al-mulk wa-nafīsat al-fulk*. Cairo: Maṭba'at al-Jami'a.

Shiloah, Amnon. 1979. *The Theory of Music in Arabic Writings (c. 900–1900): A Descriptive Catalogue of Manuscripts in Libraries of Europe and the U.S.A.* Munich: G. Henle.

———. 1992. *Jewish Musical Traditions*. Detroit: Wayne State University Press.

———. 1995. *Music in the World of Islam: A Sociocultural Study*. Aldershot, Hants, England: Scolar.

Smith, J. A. 1994. "First-Century Christian Singing and Its Relationship to Contemporary Jewish Religious Song." *Music and Letters* 75:1–15.

Strunk, Oliver. 1942. "The Tonal System of Byzantine Music." *Musical Quarterly* 28:190–204.

———. 1950. *Source Readings in Music History*. New York: Norton.

Touma, Habib Hassan. 1973. "Die Musik der Araber im 19. Jahrhundert." In *Musikkulturen Asiens, Afrikas, und Ozeaniens im 19. Jahrhundert*, ed. Robert Günther, 49–72. Regensburg: Gustav Bosse.

———. 1996. *The Music of the Arabs*, trans. Laurie Schwartz. Portland, Ore.: Amadeus.

Van Nieuwkerk, Karin. 1995. *A Trade Like Any Other: Female Singers and Dancers in Egypt*. Austin: University of Texas Press.

Volney, Constantin-François Comte de. 1787. *Voyage en Syrie et en Égypte*. Paris: Desenne.

Werner, Eric. 1959–1984. *The Sacred Bridge: The Interdependence of Liturgy and Music in Synagogue and Church during the First Millennium*. 2 vols. London: Dobson; New York: Columbia University Press.

———. 1965. "Greek Ideas on Music in Judeo-Arabic Literature." In *The Commonwealth of Music*, ed. Gustav Reese and Rose Brandel. New York: Free Press.

West, M. L. 1994. "The Babylonian Musical Notation and the Hurrian Melodic Texts." *Music and Letters* 75:161–179.

Wright, Owen. 1992. *Words without Songs: A Musicological Study of an Early Ottoman Anthology and Its Precursors*. London: School of Oriental and African Studies, University of London.

———. 2000. *Demetrius Cantemir: The Collection of Notations*. London: School of Oriental and African Studies, University of London.

Yekta, Raouf. 1922. "La musique turque." In *Encyclopédie de la musique et dictionnaire du Conservatoire*, ed. A. Lavignac. Paris: Delagrave.

Zimmerman, Heidy. 2000. *Tora und Shira: Untersuchungen zur Musikauffassung des rabbinischen Judentums*. Bern: Peter Lang.

Zirbel, Katherine. 1999. "Musical Discursions: Spectacle, Experience, and Political Economy among Egyptian Performers in Globalizing Markets." Ph.D. dissertation, University of Michigan.

THEORY, COMPOSITION, AND PERFORMANCE

Adler, Israel. 1975. *Hebrew Writings Concerning Music in Manuscripts and Printed Books from Geonic Times up to 1800*. RISM, B IX². Munich: G. Henle.

And, Metin. 1976. *Turkish Dancing*. Ankara: Dost Yayınları.

———. 1987. *Culture, Performance, and Communication in Turkey*. Performance in Culture, 4. Tokyo: Institute for the Study of Languages and Cultures of Asia.

Andrews, Walter. 1976. *An Introduction to Ottoman Poetry*. Chicago: Bibliotheca Islamica.

Bakewell, Anderson. 1985. "Music." In *Studies on the Tihāmah*, ed. Francine Stone, 104–108. London: Longman.

Bartók, Béla. 1976. *Turkish Music from Asia Minor*, ed. Benjamin Suchoff with afterword by Kurt Reinhard. Princeton, N. J.: Princeton University Press.

Başgöz, Ilhan. 1972. "Folklore Studies and Nationalism in Turkey." *Journal of the Folklore Institute* 9:162–176.

Beken, Münir Nurettin, and Karl Signell. Forthcoming. "Confirming, Delaying, and Deceptive Elements in Turkish Improvisations." In *The Maqām Traditions of the Turkic Peoples: ICTM Study Group "Maqam," Proceedings of the 4th Meeting, Istanbul, 18–24 October 1998*, ed. Jürgen Elsner and Yalçin Tura. Istanbul: Istanbul Technical University.

Caron, Nelly, and Dariouche Safvate. 1966. *Les traditions musicales: Iran*. Buchet/Chastel: Institut International d'Études Comparatives de la Musique.

———. 1988. "Melodic Contour in Persian Music, and Its Connection to Poetic Form and Meaning." In *Cultural Parameters of Iranian Musical Expression*, ed. Margaret Caton and Neil Siegel, 18–26. Redondo Beach, Calif.: Institute of Persian Performing Arts.

Caton, Margaret. 1983. "The Classical Tasnif: A Genre of Persian Vocal Music." Ph.D. dissertation, University of California, Los Angeles.

———. 1984. "Bahá'í Influences on Mírzá 'Abdúlláh, Qájár Court Musician and Master of the *Radíf*." In *From Iran East and West*, ed. Juan Cole and Moojan Monen, 30–64, 187–190. Los Angeles: Kalimát.

Chabrier, Jean-Claude. 1985. "Élements d'une approche comparative des échelles théoriques arabo-irano-turques." *Revue de Musicologie* 71:39–77.

Connelly, Bridget. 1986. *Arab Folk Epic and Identity*. Berkeley: University of California Press.

Crow, Douglas Karim. 1984. "Samā': The Art of Listening in Islam." In *Maqām: Music of the Islamic World and Its Influences*, ed. Robert H. Browning, 30–33. New York: Alternative Museum.

Donald, Mary Ellen. 1985. *Arabic Tambourine: A Comprehensive Course in Techniques and Performances for the Tambourine, Tar, and Mazhar*. San Francisco: Mary Ellen Books.

During, Jean. 1975. "Éléments spirituel dans la musique traditionnelle iranienne contemporaine." *Sophia Perennis: Bulletin of the Imperial Iranian Academy of Philosophy* 1(2):129–154.

———. 1984. *La musique iranienne: Tradition et évolution*. Paris: Éditions Recherche sur les Civilisations.

———. 1987. "Acoustic Systems and Metaphysical Systems in Oriental Traditions." *World of Music* 29(2):19–28.

During, Jean, and Zia Mirabdolbaghi. 1991. *The Art of Persian Music*. Washington, D.C.: Mage.

Elsner, Jürgen. 1967. "Zu Prinzipien arabischer Musizierpraxis." *Jahrbuch für Musikalische Volks- und Völkerkunde* 3:90–95.

———. 1975. "Zum Problem des Maqām." *Acta Musicologica* 47:208–239.

———, ed. 1989a. *Maqam-Raga-Zeilenmelodik: Konzeptionen and Prinzipen der Musikproduktion. Materialien der 1. Arbeitstagung der Study Group "Maqām" beim International Council for Traditional Music vom 28. Juni bis 2. Juli 1988 in Berlin*. Berlin: National-Komitee.

———. 1989b. "Zum maqām-Prinzip. Tongruppenmelodik als Grundlage und Baustein musikalischer Produktion." In *Maqam-Raga-Zeilenmelodik*, ed. Jürgen Elsner, 7–39. Berlin: National-Komitee.

———. 1990. "Trommeln und Trommelensembles im Jemen." In *Beiträge zur traditionellen Musik*, ed. Andreas Michel and Jürgen Elsner, 18–37. Berlin: Humboldt Universität.

———. 1992. "Trommeln und Trommelspiel im Jemen." In *Von der Vielfalt der musikalischen Kultur, Festschrift für Josef Kuckertz*, ed. Rüdiger Schumacher, 183–205. Anif/Salzburg: Ursula Müller-Speiser.

Elsner, Jürgen, and Gisa Jänichen, eds. 1992. *Regionale maqām-Traditionen in Geschichte und Gegenwart. Materialien der 2. Arbeitstagung der Study Group "Maqām" des International Council for Traditional Music vom 23. bis 28. März in Gossen bei Berlin*. 2 vols. Berlin: s.n.

Elsner, Jürgen, and Risto Pekka Pennanen, eds. 1997. *The Structure and Idea of Maqām: Historical Approaches. Proceedings of the Third Meeting of the ICTM Maqām Study Group, Tampere—Virrat, 2–5 October 1995*. Tampere: University of Tampere.

D'Erlanger, Baron Rodolphe. 1930–1959. *La musique arabe*. 6 vols. Paris: Librairie Orientaliste Paul Geuthner.

Farhat, Hormoz. 1990. *The Dastgāh Concept in Persian Music*. Cambridge: Cambridge University Press.

Farmer, Henry George. 1936. "Musiki." In *Encyclopedia of Islam*, 749–755. Leiden: Brill.

———. 1973. *A History of Arabian Music to the Thirteenth Century*. London: Luzac.

al-Faruqi, Lois Ibsen. 1975. "The Muwashshah: A Vocal Form in Islamic Culture." *Ethnomusicology* 19:1–29.

———. 1978. "Ornamentation in Arabian Improvisational Music: A Study of Interrelatedness in the Arts." *World of Music* 20(1):17–32.

———. 1979. "The Status of Music in Muslim Nations: Evidence from the Arab World." *Asian Music* 12(1):56–85.

———. 1981. *An Annotated Glossary of Arabic Musical Terms*. Westport, Conn.: Greenwood.

———. 1985a. "Structural Segments in the Islamic Arts: The Musical 'Translation' of a Characteristic of the Literary and Visual Arts." *Asian Music* 16(1):59–81.

———. 1985b. "Music, Musicians, and Muslim Law." *Asian Music* 17(1):3–36.

Feldman, Walter. 1990. "Jewish Liturgical Music in Turkey." *Turkish Music Quarterly* 3(1):10–13.

———. 1996. *Music of the Ottoman Court: Makam, Composition, and the Early Ottoman Instrumental Repertoire*. Berlin: VWB (Verlag für Wissenschaft und Bildung).

Finnegan, Ruth. 1979. *Oral Poetry*. Cambridge: Cambridge University Press.

Gerson-Kiwi, Edith. 1963. *The Persian Doctrine of Dastga-Composition: A Phenomenological Study in the Musical Modes*. Tel-Aviv: Israel Music Institute.

Hassan, Scheherazade Qassim. 1980. *Les instruments de musique en Iraq et leur rôle dans la société traditionnelle*. Paris: École des Hautes Études en Sciences Sociales.

Karpat, Kemal. 1963. "The People's Houses in Turkey." *Middle East Journal* 17:55–67.

———. 1976. *The Gecekondu: Rural Migration and Urbanization*. Cambridge: Cambridge University Press.

Khatschi, Khatschi. 1962. *Der Dastgāh: Studien zur neuen persischen Musik*. Regensburg: Gustav Bosse Verlag.

Krüger-Wust, Wilhelm J. 1983. *Arabische Musik in europäischen Sprachen: Eine Bibliographie*. Wiesbaden: Otto Harrassowitz.

Laborde, Jean Benjamin de. 1780. *Essai sur la musique ancienne et moderne*, Vol. 1. Paris: Imprimerie de Ph.-D. Pierres.

Lambert, Jean. 1989. "Du 'chanteur' à 'l'artiste' vers un nouveau statut du musicien." *Yemen Sanaa, Peuples Méditerranéens* 46.

———. 1990. "La médecine de l'âme: Musique et musiciens dans la société citadine à Ṣan'ā'." Ph.D. dissertation, Paris.

Lewis, Bernard. 1968. *The Emergence of Modern Turkey*. London: Oxford University Press.

Lortat-Jacob, Bernard, ed. 1987. *L'improvisation dans les musiques de tradition orale*. Paris: SELAF.

Marcus, Scott. 1989a. "Arab Music Theory in the Modern Period," esp. 12–42. Ph.D. dissertation, University of California, Los Angeles.

———. 1989b "The Periodization of Modern Arab Music Theory: Continuity and Change in the Definition of the *Maqāmat*." *Pacific Review of Ethnomusicology* 5:35–49.

———. 1992. "Modulation in Arab Music: Documenting Oral Concepts, Performance Rules, and Strategies." *Ethnomusicology* 36(2):171–195.

———. 1993a. "Solo Instrumental Improvisation (Taqāsīm) in Arab Music." *Middle East Studies Association Bulletin* 27:108–111.

———. 1993b. "The Interface between Theory and Practice: The Case of Intonation in Arab Music." *Asian Music* 24(2):39–58.

Markoff, Irene Judyth. 1986a. "Musical Theory, Performance, and the Contemporary Bağlama Specialist in Turkey." Ph.D. dissertation, University of Washington, Seattle.

———. 1986b. "The Role of Expressive Culture in the Demystification of a Secret Sect of Islam." *World of Music* 28(3):42–56.

———. 1990/91. "The Ideology of Musical Practice and the Professional Turkish Folk Musician: Tempering the Creative Impulse." *Asian Music* 22(1):129–145.

Martin, Richard. 1982. *Islam: A Cultural Perspective*. Englewood Cliffs, N. J.: Prentice-Hall.

Ma'rufi, Musá, comp. 1963. *Les systèmes de la musique traditionnelle de l'Iran (Radif)*. Tehran: Ministry of Culture and Arts.

Massoudieh, Mohammad Taghi. 1968. *Āwāz-e Sur: Zur Melodiebildung in der persischen Kunstmusik*. Regensburg: Gustav Bosse Verlag.

———. 1996. *Manuscrits persans concernant la musique*. RISM B XII. Munich: G. Henle.

Modir, Hafez. 1986. "Model and Interpretation in Iranian Classical Music: The Performance Practice of Mahmoud Zoufonoun." Master's thesis, University of California, Los Angeles.

Nelson, Kristina. 1985. *The Art of Reciting the Qur'ān*. Austin: University of Texas Press.

Nettl, Bruno. 1987. *The Radif of Persian Music: Studies of Structure and Cultural Context*. Champaign, Ill.: Elephant and Cat.

Nieuwkerk, Karin van. 1995. *"A Trade Like Any Other": Female Singers and Dancers in Egypt*. Austin: University of Texas Press.

Ogger, Thomas. 1987. *Maqām Segāh/Sikāh. Vergleich der Kunstmusik des Iran und des Irak anhand eines maqām Modells*. Hamburg: Karl Dieter Wagner.

Pacholczyk, Josef. 1970. "Regulative Principles in the Koran Chant of Shaikh 'Abd'l Basit 'Abd's-Samad." Ph.D. dissertation, University of California, Los Angeles.

Picken, Laurence. 1975. *Folk Instruments of Turkey*. London: Oxford University Press.

Powers, Harold S. 1980. "Mode." In *The New Grove Dictionary of Music and Musicians*, ed. Stanley Sadie, 12:376–450. London: Macmillan.

———. 1988. "First Meeting of the ICTM Study Group on Maqām." *Yearbook for Traditional Music* 20:199–218.

———. 1989. "International *segāh*' and Its Nominal Equivalents in Central Asia and Kashmir." In *Maqam-Raga-Zeilenmelodik: Konzeptionen and Prinzipen der Musikproduktion. Materialien der 1. Arbeitstagung der Study Group "Maqām" beim International Council for Traditional Music vom 28. Juni bis 2. Juli 1988 in Berlin*, ed. Jürgen Elsner, 40–85. Berlin: National-Komitee.

Racy, Ali Jihad. 1976. "Record Industry and Egyptian Traditional Music: 1904–1932." *Ethnomusicology* 20(1):23–48.

———. 1977. "Musical Change and Commercial Recording in Egypt, 1904–1932." Ph.D. dissertation, University of Illinois, Champaign-Urbana.

———. 1991. "Creativity and Ambience: An Ecstatic Feedback Model from Arab Music" *World of Music* 33(3):7–28.

Reckord, Thomas. 1987. "Chant in Popular Iranian Shi'ism." Ph.D. dissertation, University of California, Los Angeles.

———. 1988. "The Role of Religious Chant in the Definition of the Iranian Aesthetic." In *Cultural Parameters of Iranian Musical Expression*, ed. Margaret Caton and Neil Siegel. Redondo Beach, Calif.: Institute of Persian Performing Arts.

Reichow, Jan. 1971. *Die Entfaltung eines Melodiemodells im Genus Sikāh*. Regensburg: Bosse.

Reinhard, Kurt, and Ursula Reinhard. 1984. *Musik der Türkei*. Wilhelmshaven: Heinrichshofen's Verlag.

Roychoudhury, M. L. 1957. "Music in Islam." *Journal of Asiatic Society, Letters* 23(2):43–102.

Sadeghi, Manoochehr. 1971. "Improvisation in Nonrhythmic Solo Instrumental Contemporary Persian Art Music." Master's thesis, California State University, Los Angeles.

Saygun, A. Adnan. 1976. *Béla Bartók's Folk Musical Research in Turkey*, ed. V. Laszlo. Budapest: Akademia Kiado.

Schneider, Marius. 1962. "Ragā-Maqām-Nomos." In *Die Musik in Geschichte und Gegenwart,* 10:1864–1868. Kassel: Bärenreiter.

Schuyler, Philip D. 1984. "Moroccan Andalusian Music." In *Maqām: Music of the Islamic World and Its Influences*, ed. Robert H. Browning, 14–17. New York: Alternative Museum.

Serjeant, Robert B. 1951. *Prose and Poetry from Hadramawt*. London: Taylor's Foreign Press.

Seroussi, Edwin. 1989a. *Mizimrat Qedem: The Life and Music of R. Isaac Algazi from Turkey*. Jerusalem: Renanot-Institute for Jewish Music.

———. 1989b. "The Turkish *Makam* in the Musical Culture of the Ottoman Jews: Sources and Examples." *Israeli Studies in Musicology* 5:55–68.

———. 1991. "The *Peşrev* as a Vocal Genre in Ottoman Hebrew Sources." *Turkish Music Quarterly* 4(3):1–9.

Shiloah, Amnon. 1974. "Le poète-musicien et la création poético-musicale en Moyen-Orient." *Yearbook of the International Folk Music Council* 6:52–63.

———. 1979. *The Theory of Music in Arabic Writings (c. 900–1900). Descriptive Catalogue of Manuscripts in Libraries of Europe and the U.S.A.* RISM B X. Munich: G. Henle.

———. 1981. "The Arabic Concept of Mode." *Journal of the American Musicological Society* 34(1):19–42.

———. 1992. *Jewish Musical Traditions*. Detroit: Wayne State University Press.

———. 1995. *Music in the World of Islam*. Detroit: Wayne State University Press.

Signell, Karl. 1977. *Makam: Modal Practice in Turkish Art Music*. Seattle: Asian Music.

———. 1986. *Makam: Modal Practice in Turkish Art Music*. New York: Da Capo. See also 1973. "Turkish Makam System in Contemporary Theory and Practice." Ph.D. dissertation. Ann Arbor, Mich.: UMI Research Press.

Simon, Artur, et al. 1997. "Modale Melodiekonzepte." In *Die Musik in Geschichte und Gegenwart*, 2nd ed., Sachteil 6:354–82. Kassel: Bärenreiter; Stuttgart: Metzler.

Stokes, Martin. 1992. *The Arabesk Debate*. Oxford: Clarendon.

Szabolcsi, Bence. 1965. "The Maqam Principle in Folk and Art-Music: The Type and Its Variants." In *A History of Melody*, 205–215. London: Barrie and Rockliff.

Touma, Habib Hassan. 1971. "The *Maqam* Phenomenon: An Improvisation Technique in the Music of the Middle East." *Ethnomusicology* 15:38–48.

———. 1975. "Die Koranrezitation: eine Form der religiösen Musik der Araber." *Beiträge zur Musik des vorderen Orients und seinen Einflussbereichen, Baessler-Archiv* 23(1):87–120.

———. 1976. *Der Maqam Bayati im arabischen Taqsim*. Hamburg: Karl Dieter Wagner.

———. 1996. *The Music of the Arabs*, trans. Laurie Schwartz. Portland, Ore.: Amadeus.

Tsuge, Gen'ichi. 1972. "A Note on the Iraqi Maqam." *Asian Music* 4(1):59–66.

———. 1974. "Āvāz: A Study of the Rhythmic Aspects in Classical Iranian Music." Ph.D. dissertation, Wesleyan University.

Varzi, Morteză. 1988. "Performance-Audience Relationships in the *Bazm*." In *Cultural Parameters of Iranian Musical Expression*, ed. Margaret Caton and Neil Siegel, 1–9. Redondo Beach, Calif.: Institute of Persian Performing Arts.

Vigreux, Philippe, ed. *Musique arabe: Le Congrès du Caire de 1932*. Cairo: CEDEJ.

Wright, Owen. 1978. *The Modal System of Arab and Persian Music, A.D. 1250–1300*. London Oriental Series, Vol. 28. Oxford: Oxford University Press.

———. 1988. "Aspects of Historical Change in the Turkish Classical Repertoire." *Musica Asiatica* 5:1–108.

———. 1992a. *Demetrius Cantemir: The Collection of Notations*. London: School of Oriental and African Studies, University of London.

———. 1992b. "Segah: An Historical Outline." In *Regionale maqām-Traditionen in Geschichte und Gegenwart. Materialien der 2. Arbeitstagung der Study Group "Maqām" des International Council for Traditional Music vom 23. bis 28. März in Gossen bei Berlin*, ed. Jürgen Elsner and Gisa Jähnichen, 480–509. Berlin: s.n.

Yammine, Habib. 1995. "Les hommes des tribus et leur musique (Hauts-plateaux yéménites, vallée d'al-Ahjur)." Ph.D. dissertation, Paris.

Yar-Shater, Ehsan. 1974. "Affinities between Persian Poetry and Music." In *Studies in Art and Literature of the Near East*, ed. Peter Chelkowski, 59–78. Salt Lake City: University of Utah.

Yekta, Rauf. 1921. "La musique turque." In *Encyclopédie de la musique et dictionnaire du Conservatoire*, ed. A. Lavignac, part 1, 5:2945–3064. Paris: C. Delagrave.

Zonis, Ella. 1973. *Classical Persian Music: An Introduction*. Cambridge, Mass.: Harvard University Press.

MUSIC IN RELIGIOUS EXPRESSION

Abdel-Malek, Kamal. 1995. *Muhammad in the Modern Egyptian Popular Ballad*. Leiden: Brill.

Abu Mrad, Nidaa. 1989. "Musicothérapie chez les Arabes au Moyen-Age." Thesis, Académie de Paris, Université René Descartes.

Ackerman, Phyllis. 1938–1939. "The Character of Persian Music." In *A Survey of Persian Art*, ed. Arthur Upham Pope, 2805–2817. London and New York: Oxford University Press.

Adler, Israel. 1975. *Hebrew Writings Concerning Music in Manuscripts and Printed Books from Geonic Times up to 1800*. München: G. Henle. RISM B IX².

———. 1982. "Problems in the Study of Jewish Music." In *Proceedings of the World Congress on Jewish Music, Jerusalem 1978*, ed. Judith Cohen, 15–26. Tel Aviv: Institute for the Translation of Hebrew Literature.

Aflākī, Shams al-Dīn Aḥmad. 1978. *Les saints des derviches tourneurs* (*Manāqib ul-'ārifīn*), trans. Clément Huart. 2 vols. Paris: Sindbad.

Ashqar, Paul. 1939. *Mélodies liturgiques syro-maronites*. Jounieh, Lebanon.

'Aṭṭār, Farīd al-Dīn. 1959. *The Tadhkiratu 'l-Awliya* (Memoirs of the Saints), ed. and trans. Reynold A. Nicholson. 2 vols. London and Leiden.

Bayer, Bathja. 1986. "The Announcement of the Institute of Jewish Music in Jerusalem by A. Z. Idelsohn and S. Z. Rivlin in 1910." *Yuval* 5:24–35.

Ben-Ami, Issachar. 1998. *Saint Veneration among the Jews in Morocco*. Detroit: Wayne State University Press.

Ben Rafael, E., and S. Sharot. 1991. *Ethnicity, Religion, and Class in Israeli Society*. Cambridge and New York: Cambridge University Press.

Birge, John Kingsley. 1937. *The Bektashi Order of Dervishes*. London: Luzac Oriental.

Borrel, Eugene. 1947. "Les poètes Kizil Bach et leur musique." *Revue des Études Islamiques* 15:157–190.

Borsai, Ilona. 1970–1971. "Charactéristiques générales du chant de la messe copte." *Studia Orientalia Christiana Aegyptica: Collectanea* 14:412–442.

———. 1974. "Y a-t'il un octoechos dans le système du chant copte?" *Studia Aegyptiaca* 1:39–53.

Bürgel, J. Christoph. 1988. *The Feather of Simurgh: The "Licit" Magic of the Arts in Medieval Islam*. New York: New York University Press.

Chottin, Alexis. 1938. *Tableau de la musique marocaine*. Paris: P. Geuthner.

Cody, Aelred. 1982. "The Early History of the Octoechos in Syria." In *East of Byzantium: Syria and Armenia in the Formative Period*. Washington, D.C.: Dumbarton Oaks.

Cohen, Boaz. 1935. "The Responsum of Maimonides Concerning Music." *Jewish Music Journal* 2, no. 2:1–7.

Corbin, Henry. 1960. *Terre céleste et corps de résurrection de l'Iran mazdéen à l'Iran shī'ite*. Paris: Buchet/Chastel. See also 1979. *Corps spirituel et Terre céleste: De l'Iran mazdéen à l'Iran shī'ite*. (2nd ed.)

———. 1993. *History of Islamic Philosophy*, trans. Liadain and Philip Sherrard. London and New York: Kegan Paul.

Dalmais, Irenee Henri. 1957. "L'apport des églises syriennes à l'hymnographie chrétienne." *L'Orient Syrien* 2(3):243–260.

Danielson, Virginia. 1997. *The Voice of Egypt: Umm Kulthum, Arabic Song, and Egyptian Society in the Twentieth Century*. Chicago: University of Chicago Press.

Denny, Frederick. 1980."The Adab of Qur'ān Recitation: Text and Context." In *International Congress for the Study of the Qur'ān*, ed. Anthony Johns, 143–160. Canberra: Australian National University.

———. 1986. "The Great Indonesian Qur'ān Chanting Tournament." *The World and I* 6:216–223.

———. 1988. "Qur'ān Recitation Training in Indonesia: A Survey of Contexts and Handbooks." In *Approaches to the History of Interpretation of the Qur'ān*, ed. Andrew Rippin, 288–306. Oxford: Clarendon.

———. 1989. "Qur'ān Recitation: A Tradition of Oral Performance and Transmission." *Oral Tradition* 4(1–2):5–26.

Deshen, Shlomo, and Moshe Shokeid. 1984. "Cultural Ethnicity in Israel: The Case of Middle Eastern Jews' Religiosity." *AJS Review* 9(2):247–271.

During, Jean. 1977. "The 'Imaginal' Dimension and Art of Iran." *World of Music* 19(3–4):24–34.

———. 1982. "Revelation and Spiritual Audition in Islam." *World of Music* 4:68–84.

———. 1987. "Le *samā'* de Ruzbehān Baqli Shirāzi." *Connaissance Religieuse* 2(4):191–197.

———. 1988. *Musique et extase: L'audition mystique dans la tradition soufie*. Paris: Albin Michel.

———. 1989. *Musique et mystique dans les traditions de l'Iran*. Paris: Institut Français de Recherche en Iran. Leuven: Diffusion, Éditions Peeters.

———. 1990a. "L'autre oreille: Le pouvoir mystique de la musique au Moyen-Orient." *Cahiers des Musiques Traditionnelles* 3:57–78.

———. 1990b. "Der Mythos der Simorg." *Spektrum Iran* 3(3):3–19.

———. 1992. "What is Sufi Music?" In *The Legacy of Persian Medieval Sufism*, ed. Leonard Lewisohn, 277–287. London: Khaniqahi Nimatullahi.

———. 2001. *L'âme des sons: La musique d'Ostad Elâhi (1895–1974)*. Paris: Éditions du Relié.

Eickelman, Dale. 1978. "The Art of Memory: Islamic Education and Its Social Reproduction." *Comparative Studies in Society and History* 20(4):485–516.

Erian, Nabila. 1986. "Coptic Music: An Egyptian Tradition." Ph.D. dissertation, University of Maryland, Park County.

D'Erlanger, Baron Rodolphe. 1930–1959. *La musique arabe*. 6 vols. Paris: P. Geuthner.

Farmer, Henry George. 1925–1926. "The Influence of Music from Arabic Sources." *Proceedings of the Musical Association* 52:89–124.

al-Farūqi, Lois Ibsen/Lamyā'. 1979. "Tartīl al-Qur'ān al-Karīm." In *Islamic Perspectives: Studies in Honor of Mawlāna Sayyid Abul 'A'lā Mawdūdi*, ed. Khurshid Ahmad and Zafar Ansari, 105–121. London: Islamic Foundation.

Feldman, Walter. 1992. "Musical Genres and Zikir of the Sunni Tarikats of Istanbul." In *The Dervish Lodge: Architecture, Art, and Sufism in Ottoman Turkey*, ed. Raymond Lifchez, 187–202. Berkeley: University of California Press.

———. 1993. "Mysticism, Didacticism, and Authority in the Liturgical Poetry of the Halvetī Dervishes of Istanbul." *Edebiyat* NS 4:243–65.

Frishkopf, Michael. 1996. "La voix du poète: *Ṭarab* et poésie dans le chant mystique soufi." *Egypte/Monde Arabe/CDEJ* 25:85–117.

Gastoué, Amédée. 1931. "La musique byzantine et le chant des églises d'Orient." In *Encyclopédie de la musique et dictionnaire du Conservatoire*, 1:541–556. Paris: Librairie Delagrave.

Gilsenan, Michael. 1973. *Saint and Sufi in Modern Egypt: An Essay in the Sociology of Religion*. Oxford: Clarendon.

Graham, William A. 1985. "The Qur'ān as Spoken Word: An Islamic Contribution to the Understanding of Scripture." In *Approaches to Islam in Religious Studies*, ed. Richard C. Martin, 23–40. Tucson: University of Arizona Pres.

———. 1987. *Beyond the Written Word: Oral Aspects of Scripture in the History of Religion*. Cambridge: Cambridge University Press.

Hage, Louis. 1963. "Réforme du chant maronite." *Cahiers de Philosophie et de Théologie* 2:7–27.

———. 1967. "Les mélodies-types dans le chant maronite." *Melto* 3:325–409.

———. 1969. "Le chant maronite." In *Encyclopédie des musiques sacrées,* 2:218–222. Paris: Éditions Labergerie. See also English translations: *Maronite Music*. 1978. London: Longman for the University of Essex; "Music of the Maronite Church." 1971. *Parole de l'Orient* 2(1):197–206.

———. 1972–. *Musique maronite*. Kaslik, Lebanon: Bibliothèque de l'Université de Saint-Esprit. Vol. 1: *Le chant syro-maronite* (1972). Vol. 2: *Le chant maronite* (1995). Vols. 3a and 3b: *Monuments du chant maronite* (1990–1991). Vols. 4a and 4b: *Analyse, classement, et références* (1990–1991).

———. 1980. "Lebanon." In *The New Grove Dictionary of Music and Musicians*, 10:573–576. London: Macmillan.

———. 1984a. "Siriaco, Canto." In *Dizionario enciclopedico universale della musica e dei musicisti, il lessico*, 4:308–309. Turin: UTET.

———. 1984b. "Les églises orientales non byzantines." In *Précis de musicologie*, ed. Jacques Chailley, 114–119. Paris: Presses Universitaires de France.

———. 1986. *Les strophes-types syriaques et leurs mètres poétiques du patriarche maronite Etienne Douayhi*. Kaslin, Lebanon: Bibliothèque de l'Université Saint-Esprit.

———. 1987. *The Syriac Model Strophes and Their Poetic Meters, by the Maronite Patriarch Stephen Douayhi*. Kaslik, Lebanon: University of the Holy Spirit.

———. 1997. *Précis de chant maronite*. Kaslik: Université Saint-Esprit de Kaslik.

———. 1997. Vol. 7: *Les strophes-types syriaques: Analyse, références, et classification*.

———. 1998. Vol. 8: *Écrits relatifs au chant syriaque et maronite*.

Hajdu, Andre. 1971. "Le niggun Meron." *Yuval: Studies of the Jewish Music Research Centre* 2:73–114.

Hajdu, Andre, and Yaacov Mazor. 1971. "Hasidim: The Musical Tradition of the Hasidism." In *Encyclopedia Judaica*, 7:1421–1432. Jerusalem: Encyclopedia Judaica; New York: Macmillan.

Halper, Jeff, Edwin Seroussi, and Pamela Squires-Kidron. 1989. "Musika Mizraḥit: Ethnicity and Class Culture in Israel." *Popular Music* 8:131–142.

Hannick, Théodose. 1969. "Syriens occidentaux et Syriens orientaux." In *Traditions chrétiennes des premiers siècles aux cultes révolutionnaires*. Vol. 2 of *Encylopédie des musiques sacrées*, ed. Jacques Porte, 214–217. Paris: Éditions Labergerie.

Hodgson, M. G. S. 1974. *The Venture of Islam*, Vol 1. Chicago: University of Chicago Press.

Hoffman, Valerie. 1995. *Sufism, Mystics, and Saints in Modern Egypt*. Columbia: University of South Carolina Press.

Horowitz, Amy. 1994. "Israeli Mediterranean Music: Cultural Boundaries and Disputed Territories." Ph.D. dissertation, University of Pennsylvania.

Hujvīrī, 'Alī ibn 'Uṣmān. 1976. *The "Kashf al-mahjub": The Oldest Persian Treatise on Sufism*, trans. Reynold A. Nicholson. Lahore: Islamic Book Foundation.

Husmann, Heinrich. 1967. *Die Melodien des chaldäischen Breviers Commune, nach den Traditionen Vorderasiens und der Malabarküste*. Rome: Pontificio Istituto per gli Studi Orientali.

———. 1969. "Die Tonarten der chaldäischen Breviergesänge." *Orientalia Christiana Periodica* 35:215–248.

———. 1969–1971. *Die Melodien der Jakobitischen Kirche*. Wien: Bohlau Kommissionsverlag.

———. 1970. "Arabische Maqamen in ostsyrischer Kirchenmusik." In *Musik als Gestalt und Erlebnis: Festschrift Walter Graf*, 102. Vienna: Böhlau.

———. 1971. "Hymnus und Troparion." In *Jahrbuch des Staatlichen Instituts für Musikforschung Preussischer Kulturbesitz Berlin*, 7–86. Berlin.

———. 1974. "Eine Konkordanztabelle syrischer Kirchentöne und arabischer Maqamen in einem syrischen Musiknotizbuch." In *Symposium Syriacum 1972*. Rome: Pont. Institutum Orientalium Studiorum.

———. 1976. "Madrase und Seblata—Repertoireuntersuchungen zu den Hymnen Ephraems des Syrers." *Acta Musicologica* 48:113–150.

Iamblichus (c. 250–c. 330). 1993. *Les mystères d'Egypte*, trans. Édouard des Places. Paris: Les Belles Lettres.

Ivánka, Endre von, et al., eds. 1971. *Handbuch der Ostkirchenkunde*. Düsseldorf: Patmos-Verlag.

Jargy, Simon. 1952. "La musique liturgique syrienne." In *Atti del Congresso Internazionale di Musica Sacra*, 166–169. Rome, Tournai, Paris: Desclée et Cie.

———. 1961. "Syrienne (musique)." In *Encyclopédie de la musique*, ed. François Michel, 3:992–993. Paris: Fasquelle.

———. 1971. *La musique arabe*. Paris: Presses Universitaires de France.

———. 1978. "The Folk Music of Syria and Lebanon." *World of Music* 1:79–89.

Jeannin, Jules, et al. 1924–1928. *Mélodies syriennes*. Paris: Leroux.

Kahn, Aharon. 1986–1989. "Music in Halakhic Perspective." *Journal of Jewish Music and Liturgy* 9:55–72, 10:32–49, 11:65–75.

Katz, Ruth. 1968. "The Singing of *Baqqashot* by Aleppo Jews." *Acta Musicologica* 40:65–85.

Kedem, Peri. 1991. "Dimensions of Jewish Religiosity." In *Tradition, Innovation, Conflict: Jewishness and Judaism in Contemporary Israel*, ed. Z. Sobel and B. Beit-Hallahmi, 251–272. Albany: State University of New York Press.

Khs-Burmester, O. H. E. 1967. *The Egyptian or Coptic Church: A Detailed Description of Her Liturgical Services and the Rites and Ceremonies Observed in the Administration of Her Sacraments*. Cairo: Publications de la Société d'Archéologie Copte.

Kuckertz, Josef. 1969. "Die Melodietypen der westsyrischen liturgischen Gesänge." *Kirchenmusikalisches Jahrbuch* 53:61–98.

Levi, Leo. 1957. "Les neumes, les notations bibliques, et le protochrétien." In *La musique sacrée au IIIème Congrès international de musique sacrée*, 147–155 [*La Revue musicale*, nos. 239–240]. Paris: Éditions Richard-Masse.

Lièvre, Viviane, and Jean-Yves Loude. 1990. *Le chamanisme des Kalash du Pakistan*. Paris: Éditions Recherche sur les Civilisations.

MacDonald, Duncan, ed. 1901–1902. "Emotional Religion in Islam as Affected by Music and Singing. Being a Translation of a Book of the *Ihyā 'Ulūm ad-Dīn* of al-Ghazzālī, with Analysis, Annotations, and Appendices." *Journal of the Royal Asiatic Society* (1901):195–252, 705–748; (1902):1–28, 195–252.

Martin, B. G. 1972. "A Short History of the Khalwati Order of Dervishes." In *Scholars, Saints, and Sufis*, ed. Nikki R. Keddie, 275–306. Berkeley: University of California Press.

Meinardus, Otto Friedrich August. 1989. *Monks and Monasteries of the Egyptian Deserts*, rev. ed. Cairo: American University in Cairo Press.

Ménard, Réné. 1952. "Notes sur les musiques arabes et coptes." *Les Cahiers Coptes* 2:48–54.

———. 1969. "Tradition copte." In *Traditions chrétiennes des premiers siècles aux cultes révolutionnaires*. Vol. 2 of *Encylopédie des musiques sacrées*, ed. Jacques Porte, 229–233. Paris: Éditions Labergerie.

Moftah, Ragheb. 1958. "The Coptic Music." *Bulletin de l'Institute des Études Coptes*.

Moftah, Ragheb, Margit Toth, and Martha Roy. 1998. *The Liturgy of St. Basil of the Coptic Orthodox Church*. Cairo: American University at Cairo Press.

Molé, Marijan. 1963. "La danse extatique en Islam." In *Les Danses Sacrées*, 145–280. Paris: Éditions du Seuil.

Nelson, Kristina. 1985. *The Art of Reciting the Qur'ān*. Austin: University of Texas Press.

Neubauer, Eckhard. 1990. "Arabische Anleitungen für Musiktherapie." *Zeitschrift für Geschichte der Arabisch-Islamischen Wissenschaften* 6:227–272.

Nieten, Ulrike. 1998. "Syrische Kirchenmusik." In *Die Musik in Geschichte und Gegenwart*, 9:185–200. Kassel: Bärenreiter.

Parisot, Dom Jean. 1899. *Rapport sur une mission scientifique en Turquie d'Asie*. Paris: E. Leroux.

———. 1901. "Les huit modes du chant syrien." *Tribune de Saint-Gervais* 7:258–262.

———. 1898. "Essai sur le chant litugique des églises orientales." *Revue de l'Orient Chrétien* 3:221–231.

Poché, Christian. 1978. "Zikr and Musicology." *World of Music* 20:59–73.

Qureshi, Regula. 1969. "Tarannum: The Chanting of Urdu Poetry." *Ethnomusicology* 13(3):425–468.

———. 1995. *Sufi Music of India and Pakistan*. Chicago: University of Chicago Press.

Rasmussen, Anne K. 2001. "The Qur'ān in Indonesian Daily Life: The Public Project of Musical Oratory." *Ethnomusicology* 45:30–57.

Robertson, Marian. 1984–1985. "The Reliability of the Oral Tradition in Preserving Coptic Music: A Comparison of Three Musical Transcriptions of an Extract from the Liturgy of St. Basil." *Bulletin of the Coptic Archaeology Society* 26 and 27.

———. 1986. "Vocal Music in the Early Coptic Church." *Coptologia* 6:23–28.

Robson, James, ed. 1938. *Tracts on Listening to Music, Being Ḏhamm al-malāhī, by Ibn abī'l-Dunyā, and Bawāriq al-ilmā', by Majd al-Dīn al-Tūsī al-Ghazālī*. London: Royal Asiatic Society.

Rouanet, J. 1922. "La musique arabe." In *Encyclopédie de la musique et dictionnaire du Conservatoire*, ed. A. Lavignac, 1(5):2676–2812. Paris: C. Delagrave.

Ṣafī al-Dīn. [1346] 1967. *Bihjat al-Rūḥ*, ed. Rabino de Borgomale. Tehran.

Sarrāj, Abū Naṣr 'Abd Allāh ibn 'Alī. 1914. *The Kitāb al-luma' fi 'l-Taṣawwuf of Abū Naṣr 'Abdallah b. 'Alī al-Sarrāj al-Ṭūsī*, ed. Reynold Alleyne Nicholson. Leiden: Brill; London: Luzac.

Schleifer, Eliyahu. 1995. "Current Trends of Liturgical Music in the Ashkenazi Liturgy." In *Jewish Musical Culture—Past and Present*. Vol. 37(1) of *World of Music*, ed. Uri Sharvit, 59–72. Basel, Kassel: Bärenreiter.

Schreiber, Baruch David. 1984–1985. "The Woman's Voice in the Synagogue." *Journal of Jewish Music and Liturgy* 7:27–32.

Sells, Michael. 1991. "Sound, Spirit, and Gender in *Sûrat al-Qadr*." *Journal of the American Oriental Society* 111(2):239–259.

———. 1993. "Sound and Meaning in *Surat al-Qari'a*." *Arabica* 40:403–430.

———, ed. 1999. *Approaching the Qur'ān—The Early Revelations*. Ashland, Ore.: White Cloud.

———. 2000. "A Literary Approach to the Hymnic Suras of the Qur'ān." In *Literary Structures of Religious Meaning in the Qur'ān*, ed. Issa Boullata, 3–25. London: Curzon.

Seroussi, Edwin. 1986. "Politics, Ethnic Identity, and Music in the Singing of *Bakkashot* among Moroccan Jews in Israel." *Asian Music* 17(2):32–45.

Sharvit, Uri. 1986. "Diversity within Unity: Stylistic Change and Ethnic Continuity in Israeli Religious Music." *Asian Music* 17(2):126–146.

El-Shawan, Salwa. 1975. "An Annotated Bibliography on Coptic Music." M.A. thesis, Columbia University.

Shiloah, Amnon. 1965, 1967. "L'épître sur la musique des Ikhwân al-Safâ." *Revue des Études Islamiques* 33:125–162; 37:159–193.

———, ed. 1972. *La perfection des connaissances musicales (al-Ḥasan ibn Aḥmad ibn 'Alī al-Kātib)*. Paris: P. Geuthner.

Slobin, Mark. 1989. *Chosen Voices: The Story of the American Cantorate*. Urbana and Chicago: University of Illinois Press.

Touma, Habib Hassan. 1975a. "Die Koranrezitation: Eine Form der religiösen Musik der Araber." *Bessler-Archiv*, Neue Folge, 23:87–133.

———. 1975b. *Die Musik der Araber*. Wilhelmshaven: Heinrichshofen's Verlag.

———. 1976. "Relations between Aesthetics and Improvisation in Arab Music." *World of Music* 18(2):33–36.

Tucci, Giuseppe. 1974. *Théorie et pratique du mandala*. Paris: Fayard.

Waugh, Earl H. 1989. *The Munshidiin of Egypt: Their World and Their Song*. Columbia: University of South Carolina Press.

Wegner, Ulrich. 1986. "Transmitting the Divine Revelation: Some Aspects of Textualism and Textual Variability in Qur'ānic Recitation." *World of Music* 27(3):57–78.

Weiss, Bernard, Morroe Berger, and M. A. Rauf, trans. 1975. *The Recited Koran: A History of the First Recorded Version by Labib as-Sa'id*. Princeton, N. J.: Darwin.

Wellesz, Egon. 1954a. "Early Christian Music." In *The New Oxford History of Music*, 2:1–13. London, New York, and Toronto: Oxford University Press.

———. 1954b. "Music of the Eastern Churches." In *The New Oxford History of Music*, 2:14–52. London, New York, and Toronto: Oxford University Press.

Werner, Eric. 1952. "The Common Ground in the Chant of Church and Synagogue.' In *Atti del Congresso Internazionale di Musica Sacra*, ed. Igino Angles, 134–148. Tournai: Desclée.

———. 1959. *The Sacred Bridge: The Interdependence of Liturgy and Music in Synagogue and Church during the First Millennium*. London: Dobson; New York: Columbia University Press.

Yalcin, Warda, and Esther Lamandier. 1997. *Chants de l'église d'Orient en araméen*. Paris: Aliénor.

POPULAR MUSIC AND THE MEDIA

Abraham, Sameer Y., and Nabeel Abraham. 1983. *Arabs in the New World: Studies on Arab-American Communities*. Detroit: Wayne State University Press, Urban Studies Center.

Alterman, Jon. 1998. *New Media, New Politics? From Satellite Television to the Internet in the Arab World*. Washington, D.C.: Washington Institute for Near East Policy.

Armbrust, Walter. 1996. *Mass Culture and Modernism in Egypt*. Cambridge: Cambridge University Press.

———. 1998. "When the Lights Go Down in Cairo: Cinema as Secular Ritual." *Visual Anthropology* 10(4):413–442.

———. 2000. "Farid Shauqi: Tough Guy, Family Man, Cinema Star." In *Imagined Masculinities: Male Identity and Culture in the Modern Middle East*, ed. Mai Ghoussoub and Emma Sinclair-Webb. London: Saqi.

Aswad, Barbara C., ed. 1974. *Arabic Speaking Communities in American Cities*. New York: Center for Migration Studies of New York.

Ayalon, Ami. 1995. *The Press in the Arab Middle East: A History*. Oxford: Oxford University Press.

Azzam, Nabil Salim. 1990. "Muhammad 'Abd al-Wahhab in Modern Egyptian Music." Ph.D. dissertation, University of California, Los Angeles.

Bourgeot, André. 1989. "Cultures, langues berbères, et folklorisation chez les Touaregs." In *Tradition et modernité dans les sociétés berbères*, ed. Tassadit Yacine, 33–52. Paris: Awal.

Brett, Michael, and Elizabeth Fentress. 1996. *The Berbers*. Oxford and Cambridge, Mass.: Blackwell.

Chaker, Salem. 1989a. *Berbères aujourd'hui*. Paris: L'Harmattan.

———. 1989b. "Une tradition de résistance et de lutte: La poésie berbère kabyle—un parcours poétique." *Revue du Monde Musulman et de la Méditerranée* 51(1):11–31.

Coon, Carleton Stevens. 1966. *Caravan: The Story of the Middle East*, rev. ed. New York: Holt.

Danielson, Virginia. 1988. "The Arab Middle East." In *Popular Musics of the Non-Western World*, ed. Peter Manuel, 141–160. New York: Oxford University Press.

———. 1996. "New Nightingales of the Nile: Popular Music in Egypt since the 1970s." *Popular Music* 15(3):299–312.

———. 1997. *The Voice of Egypt: Umm Kulthum, Arabic Song, and Egyptian Society in the Twentieth Century*. Chicago: University of Chicago Press.

Davis, Eric. 1983. *Challenging Colonialism: Bank Misr and Egyptian Industrialization, 1920–1941*. Princeton: Princeton, N.J.: University Press.

Djaad, Abdelkrim. 1979. "Idir, entre l'aède et le show." *Algérie Actualité* (August 2–8):22–23.

Djura. 1990. *Le voile du silence*. Paris: M. Lafon. See also 1992. *The Veil of Silence*, trans. Dorothy Blair. London: Quartet.

Ezzedine, Salah. 1966. "The Role of Music in Arabic Films." In *The Cinema in the Arab Countries*, ed. Georges Sadoul. Beirut: Interarab Center of Cinema and Television.

Gross, Joan E., and David A. McMurray. 1993. "Berber Origins and the Politics of Ethnicity in Colonial North African Discourse." *PoLAR: Political and Legal Anthropology Review* 16(2):39–57.

Gross, Joan E., D. McMurray, and Ted Swedenburg. 1996. "Arab Noise and Ramadan Nights: *Rai*, Rap, and Franco-Maghrebi Identities." In *Displacement, Diaspora, and Geographies of Identity*, ed. Smadar Lavie and Ted Swedenburg, 119–155. Durham, N.C.: Duke University Press.

Halper, Jeff, Edwin Seroussi, and Pamela Squires-Kidron. 1989. "Musica Mizrahit: Ethnicity and Class Culture in Israel." *Popular Music* 8:131–142.

Hirschkind, Charles. 2000. "Technologies of Islamic Piety: Cassette-Sermons and the Ethics of Listening." Ph.D. dissertation, Johns Hopkins University.

Hoogland, Eric, ed. 1987. *Crossing the Waters: Arabic-Speaking Immigrants to the United States before 1940*. Washington, D.C., and London: Smithsonian Institution Press.

Horowitz, Amy. 1994. "Israeli Mediterranean Music: Cultural Boundaries and Disputed Territories." Ph.D. dissertation, University of Pennsylvania.

Howell, Sally. 1998. "Picturing Women, Class, and Community in Arab Detroit: The Strange Case of Eva Habib." *Visual Anthropology* 10(2–4):209–226.

Kayal, Philip M., and Joseph M. Kayal. 1975. *The Syrian-Lebanese in America: A Study in Religion and Assimilation*. Boston: Twayne.

Lacoste-Du Jardin, Camille. 1978. "Chansons berbères, chansons pour vivre." *L'Histoire* 5:104–105.

Lefebure, Claude. 1984. "Ousman: La chanson berbère reverdie." *Annuaire de l'Afrique du Nord* 23:189–208.

Mandell, Joan. 1988. "Cultural Resilience through Change: Finding the Theme for *Tales from Arab Detroit*." *Visual Anthropology* 10(2–4):189–208.

Manuel, Peter. 1988. "The Non-Arab Middle East." In *Popular Musics of the Non-Western World*, ed. Peter Manuel, 161–170. New York: Oxford University Press.

———. 1993. *Cassette Culture: Popular Music and Technology in North India*. Chicago: University of Chicago Press.

Matoub, Lounes. 1995. *Rebelle*. Paris: Stock.

el-Mazzawi, Farid. 1966. "The U.A.R. Cinema and Its Relations with Television." In *The Cinema in the Arab Countries*, ed. Georges Sadoul. Beirut: Interarab Center of Cinema and Television.

McCarus, Ernest. 1984. *The Development of Arab-American Identity*. Ann Arbor: University of Michigan Press.

McDermott, Anthony. 1988. *Egypt from Nasser to Mubarak: A Flawed Revolution*. New York: Croom Helm.

Mehenni, Ferhat. 1983. "La chanson kabyle depuis dix ans." *Tafsut, Série Spéciale "Etudes et Débats"* 1:65–71.

Naaf, Alexa. 1985. *Becoming American: The Early Arab Immigrant Experience*. Carbondale: Southern Illinois University Press.

Racy, Ali Jihad. 1977. "Musical Change and Commercial Recording in Egypt, 1904–1932." Ph.D. dissertation, University of Illinois, Champagne-Urbana.

———. 1984. "Arab Music—An Overview." In *Maqam: Music of the Islamic World and Its Influences*, ed. Robert Browning, 9–13. New York: Alternative Museum.

———. 1991. "Creativity and Ambience: An Ecstatic Feedback Model from Arab Music." *World of Music* 33(3): 7–28.

Rasmussen, Anne. 1991. "Individuality and Musical Change in the Music of Arab Americans." Ph.D. dissertation, University of California, Los Angeles.

———. 1996. "Theory and Practice at the 'Arabic Orq': Digital Technology in Contemporary Arab Music Performance." *Popular Music* 15(3):345–365.

———. 1997. "The Music of Arab Detroit: A Musical Mecca in the Midwest." In *Musics of Multicultural America: A Study of Twelve Musical Communities*, ed. Kip Lornell and Anne K. Rasmussen, 73–100. New York: Schirmer.

———. Forthcoming. "The Sound of Culture, The Structure of Tradition: Musicians' Work in Arab America." In *Creating a New Arab World: Life on the Margins of Multicultural America*, ed. Andrew Shryock and Nabeel Abraham. Detroit: Wayne State University Press.

Regev, Moti. 1992. "Israeli Rock: Or a Study in the Politics of 'Local Authenticity.'" *Popular Music* 11:1–14.

Reynolds, Dwight F. 1998. "From the Delta to Detroit: Packaging a Folk Epic for a New Folk." *Visual Anthropology* 10(2–4):145–164.

Robins, Kevin, and David Morley. 1996. "Almanci, Yabanci." *Cultural Studies* 10(2):248–254.

Schuyler, Philip D. 1984. "Berber Professional Musicians in Performance." In *Performance Practice: Ethnomusicological Perspectives*, ed. Gérard Béhague, 91–148. London: Greenwood.

———. 1993. "A Folk Revival in Morocco." In *Everyday Life in the Muslim Middle East*, ed. Donna Lee Bowen and Evelyn A. Early, 287–293. Bloomington: Indiana University Press.

Seroussi, Edwin. 1996. *Popular Music in Israel: The First Fifty Years*. Cambridge, Mass.: Harvard College Library.

Shafik, Viola. 1998. *Arab Cinema: History and Cultural Continuity*. Cairo: American University in Cairo Press.

el-Shawan, Salwa Aziz. 1980. "Al-Musika al-Arabiyyah: A Category of Urban Music in Cairo, Egypt, 1927–1977." Ph.D. dissertation, Columbia University.

———. 1987. "Some Aspects of the Cassette Industry in Egypt." *World of Music* 29(2):32–45.

Shiloah, Amnon. 1992. "Eastern Sources in Israeli Music." *Ariel* 88:4–19.

Shiloah, Amnon, and Erik Cohen. 1983. "The Dynamics of Change in Jewish Oriental Music in Israel." *Ethnomusicology* 27(2):222–251.

——— and ———. 1985. "Major Trends of Change in Jewish Oriental Music in Israel." *Popular Music* 5:199–223.

Shryock, Andrew. 1998. "Mainstreaming Arabs: Filmmaking as Image Making in *Tales from Arab Detroit*." *Visual Anthropology* 10(2–4):165–188.

Stokes, Martin. 1992. *The Arabesk Debate: Music and Musicians in Modern Turkey*. Oxford: Clarendon.

Swedenburg, Ted. 1997. "Saida Sultan/Danna International: Transgender Pop and the Polysemiotics of Sex, Nation, and Ethnicity on the Israeli-Egyptian Border." *Musical Quarterly* 81:81–108.

Tekelioğlu, Orhan. 1996. "The Rise of a Spontaneous Synthesis: The Historical Background of Turkish Popular Music." *Middle Eastern Studies* 32(1):194–215.

Virolle-Souibès, Marie. 1995. *La chanson raï: De l'Algérie profonde à la scène*. Paris: Karthala.

Wallis, Roger, and Malm Krister. 1984. *Big Sounds from Small People: The Music Industry in Small Countries*. New York: Pendragon.

Waterbury, John. 1978. *Egypt: Burdens of the Past, Options for the Future*. Bloomington: Indiana University Press.

Yacine, Tassadit. 1989. *Ait Menguellat chante . . .* Paris: La Découverte/Awal.

Zogby, James, ed. 1984. *Taking Root, Bearing Fruit: The Arab-American Experience.* Washington, D.C.: American-Arab Anti-Discrimination Committee.

Zoulef, Boudjemaa, and Mohamed Dernouny. 1981. "L'identité culturelle au Maghreb à travers un corpus de chants contemporains." *Annuaire de l'Afrique du Nord* 20:1021–1051.

GENDER AND MUSIC

Abd ar-Rāziq, Aḥmad. 1973. *La femme au temps des Mamlouks en Égypte*. Cairo: Institut Français d'Archéologie Orientale du Caire.

Abu-Lughod, Lila. 1986. *Veiled Sentiments: Honor and Poetry in a Bedouin Society*. Berkeley: University of California Press.

———. 1990. "Shifting Politics in Bedouin Love Poetry." In *Language and the Politics of Emotion*, ed. Catherine A. Lutz and Lila Abu-Lughod, 24–45. Cambridge: Cambridge University Press, Éditions de la Maison des Sciences de l'Homme.

Basset, Henri. 1920. *Essai sur la littérature des Berbères*. Algiers: Jules Carbonel.

Brandily, Monique. 1986. "Qu'exprime-t-on par et dans la musique traditionnelle? Quelques exemples Libyens." *Maghreb Review* 2(2–4):53–57.

———. 1997. *Introduction aux musiques africaines*. Musiques du Monde. Cité de la Musique/Actes Sud. (Compact disk included.)

Caussin de Perceval, A. 1873. "Notices anecdotiques sur les principaux musiciens arabes des trois premiers siècles de l'islamisme." *Journal Asiatique*, 7th series, 2:397–592.

Danielson, Virginia. 1991. "Artists and Entrepreneurs: Female Singers in Cairo during the 1920s." In *Women in Middle Eastern History. Shifting Boundaries in Sex and Gender*, ed. Nikki R. Keddie and Beth Baron, 292–309. New Haven and London: Yale University Press.

———. 1997. *The Voice of Egypt: Umm Kulthūm, Arabic Song, and Egyptian Society in the Twentieth Century*. Chicago: University of Chicago Press.

Farmer, George Henry. [1929] 1994. *A History of Arabian Music to the Thirteenth Century*. London: Luzac Oriental.

Doubleday, Veronica. 1988. *Three Women of Herat*. London: Cape.

Ferchiou, Sophie. 1972. "Survivances mystiques et culte de possession dans le maraboutisme tunisien." *L'Homme* 12(3):47–69.

Hassan, Schéhérazade Qassim. 1980. *Les instruments de musique en Irak et leur rôle dans la société traditionnelle*. Paris: Mouton (Cahiers de l'Homme).

Herndon, Marcia, and Susanne Ziegler, eds. 1990. *Music, Gender, and Culture*. Wilhelmshaven: Florian Noetzel Verlag.

Huart, Clément. 1884. "Étude biographique sur trois musiciennes arabes." *Journal Asiatique*, 8th series, 3:141–187.

JaFran Jones, Lura. 1987. "A Sociohistorical Perspective on Tunisian Women as Professional Musicians." In *Women and Music in Cross-Cultural Perspective*, ed. Ellen Koskoff, 69–83. Urbana and Chicago: University of Illinois Press. (Originally published 1987. New York: Greenwood.)

al-Jahīz (d. 868). 1980. *The Epistle on Singing-Girls of Jahiz*, ed. and trans. A. F. L. Beeston. Warminster, Wiltshire: Aris and Phillips.

Jamous, Raymond. 1981. *Honneur et baraka: Les structures sociales traditionnelles dans le Rif.* Paris: Éditions de la Maison des Sciences de l'Homme.

Jansen, Willy. 1987. *Women without Men.* Leiden: Brill.

Jargy, Simon. 1971. *La musique arabe*. Paris: Presses Universitaires de France.

Koskoff, Ellen, ed. 1989. *Women and Music in Cross-Cultural Perspective*. Urbana and Chicago: University of Illinois Press. (Originally published 1987. New York: Greenwood.)

Kulthūm, Umm. 1976. "Umm Kulthūm." In *Middle Eastern Women Speak*, ed. Elizabeth Warnock and Basima Qattan Bezirgan. Austin: University of Texas Press.

Lambert, Jean. 1997. *La médecine de l'âme*. Hommes et Musiques. Nanterre: Société d'Ethnologie. (Compact disk included.)

Lortat-Jacob, Bernard. 1980. *Musique et fêtes au Haut-Atlas*. Paris: Mouton (Cahiers de l'Homme). (Compact disk included.)

———. 1994. *Musiques en fête*. Hommes et musiques. Nanterre: Société d'Ethnologie.

Mahfoufi, Mehenna. 1991. "Le répertoire musical d'un village berbère d'Algérie (Kabylie)." 2 vols. Ph.D. dissertation, Paris X-Nanterre University.

Meyers Sawa, Suzanne. 1987. "The Role of Women in Musical Life: The Medieval Arabo-Islamic Courts." *Canadian Woman Studies / Les Cahiers de la Femme* 8(2):93–95.

Nieuwkerk, Karin van. 1990. *Female Entertainment in Nineteenth- and Twentieth-Century Egypt*. Amsterdam: Middle East Research Associates.

———. 1995. *"A Trade Like Any Other": Female Singers and Dancers in Egypt*. Austin: University of Texas Press.

Rouget, Gilbert. 1980. *La musique et la transe: Esquisse d'une théorie générale des relations de la musique et de la possession.* Paris: Gallimard.

Rovsing-Olsen, Miriam. 1984. "Chants de mariage de l'Atlas marocain." 2 vols. Ph.D dissertation, Paris X-Nanterre University.

———. 1989. "Symbolique d'un rituel de mariage berbère: Une approche ethnomusicologique." *Anuario Musical* 44:259–291.

———. 1996. "Modalités d'organisation du chant berbère: Paroles et musique." *Journal of Mediterranean Studies: History, Culture, and Society in the Mediterranean World* 6(1):88–108.

———. 1997. *Chants et danses de l'Atlas (Maroc)*. Cité de la Musique/Actes Sud. (Compact disk included.)

Rowson, Everett K. 1991. "The Effeminates of Early Medina." *Journal of the American Oriental Society* 111(4):671–693.

Sakata, Hiromi Lorraine. 1983. *Music in the Mind: The Concepts of Music and Musician in Afghanistan*. Kent, Ohio: Kent State University Press.

———. 1989. "Hazara Women in Afghanistan: Innovators and Preservers of a Musical Tradition." In *Women and Music in Cross-Cultural Perspective*, ed. Ellen Koskoff, 85–95. Urbana and Chicago: University of Illinois Press. (Originally published 1987. New York: Greenwood.)

Sarkissian, Margaret. 1992. "Gender and Music." In *Ethnomusicology: An Introduction*, ed. Helen Myers, 337–348. The New Grove Handbooks in Music. London: Macmillan.

Sawa, George Dimitri. 1989. *Music Performance Practice in the Early 'Abbāsid Era 132–320* A.H. / A.D. *750–932*. Toronto: Pontifical Institute of Mediaeval Studies.

Schuyler, Philip D. 1984. "Berber Professional Musicians in Performance." In *Performance Practice: Ethnomusicological Perspectives*, ed. Gerard Béhague, 91–148. Westport, Conn.: Greenwood.

Shapiro, Anne Dhu. 1991. "A Critique of Current Research on Music and Gender." *World of Music* 33(2):5–13.

Siala, Mourad. 1994. "La hadra de Sfax: Rite soufi et musique de fête." 2 vols. Ph.D dissertation, Paris X-Nanterre University.

Stigelbauer, Michael. 1975. *Die Sängerinnen am Abbasidenhof um die Zeit des Kalifen al-Mutawakkil*. Vienna: Verband der Wissenschaftlichen Gesellschaften Österreichs.

Stokes, Martin. 1994. "Introduction: Ethnicity, Identity, and Music." In *Ethnicity, Identity, and Music: The Musical Constuction of Place*, ed. Martin Stokes, 1–27. Oxford and Providence, R.I.: Berg.

Villoteau, Guillaume André. 1812. *De l'état actuel de l'art musical en Egypte, ou relation historique et descriptive des recherches et observations faites sur la musique en ce pays*. Vol. 14 of *Description de l'Egypte ou recueil des observations et des recherches qui ont été faites en Egypte pendant l'expédition de l'armée française*. Paris: Imprimerie de C.L.F. Panckoucke.

Wright, Owen. 1983. "Music and Verse." In *Arabic Literature to the End of the Umayyad Period*, 433–489. Cambridge: Cambridge University Press.

Yammine, Habib. 1995. "Les hommes des tribus et leur musique (Haut-plateaux yéménites, vallée d'al-Ahjur)." 2 vols. Ph.D. dissertation, Paris, X-Nanterre University.

LEARNING AND TRANSMISSION

Başgöz, Ilhan. 1952. "Turkish Folk Stories about the Lives of Minstrels." *Journal of American Folklore* 65:331–339.

———. 1967. "Dream Motif in Turkish Folk Stories and Shamanistic Initiation." *Asian Folklore Studies* 26:1–18.

Blum, Stephen. 1972. "The Concept of the *'Asheq* in Northern Khorasan." *Asian Music* 4:27–47.

Chadwick, Nora K., and Victor Zhirmunsky. 1969. *Oral Epics of Central Asia*. Cambridge: Cambridge University Press.

Davis, Ruth. 1986a. "Modern Trends in the *Ma'lūf* of Tunisia: 1934–1984." Ph.D. dissertation, Princeton University.

———. 1986b. "Modern Trends in the Arab-Andalusian Music of Tunisia." *Maghreb Review* 11:58–63.

———. 1992. "The Effects of Notation in the Performance Practice of Tunisian Art Music." *World of Music* 34(1):35–114.

D'Erlanger, Rodolphe. 1917. "Au sujet de la musique arabe en Tunisie." *Revue Tunisienne* 24:91–95.

———. 1930–1959. *La musique arabe*. 6 vols. Paris: Librairie Orientaliste Paul Geuthner.

Hanaway, William L. "Formal Elements in the Persian Popular Romances." In *Iran: Continuity and Variety*, ed. Peter Chelkowski, 139–160. New York: Center for Near Eastern Studies, 1971.

———. 1978. "The Iranian Epics." In *Heroic Epic and Saga: An Introduction to the World's Great Epics*, ed. Felix J. Oinas, 76–98. Bloomington: Indiana University Press.

Hassan, Scheherazade. 1987. "Le makam irakien: Structures et réalisations." In *L'improvisation dans les musiques de tradition orale*, ed. Bernard Lortat-Jacob, 143–149. Paris: SELAF.

———. 1989. "Some Islamic Non-Arabic Elements of Influence on the Repertory of al Makam al 'Iraki." In *Maqam, Raga, Zeilenmelodik: Konzeptionen and Prinzipien der Musikproduktion. Materialen der 1. Arbeitstagung der Study Group "Maqām" beim International Council for Traditional Music vom 28. Juni bis 2. Juli 1988 in Berlin*, ed. Jürgen Elsner, 148–155. Berlin: [Nationalkomitee DDR des International Council for Traditional Music in Verbindung mit dem Sekretariat Internationale Nichtstaatliche Musikorganisationen].

———. 1992. "Choix de la musique et de la représentation irakienne au Congrès du Caire en 1932: Vers une étude de contexte." In *Musique Arabe: Le Congrès du Caire de 1932*, ed. Philippe Vigreux, 123–145. Cairo: CEDEJ.

———. 1992. "Survey of Written Sources on the Iraqi *Maqām*." In *Regionale Maqam-Traditionen in Geschichte und Gegenwart. Materialien der 2. Arbeitstagung der Study Group "maqam" des International Council for Traditional Music vom 23. bis 28. März in Gosen bei Berlin*, ed. Jürgen Elsner and Gisa Jähnichen, 252–275. Berlin: s.n.

Lane, Edward. 1895. *An Account of the Manners and Customs of the Modern Egyptians*. London: East-West.

Lord, Albert B. 1960. *The Singer of Tales*. Cambridge, Mass.: Harvard University Press.

Marcus, Scott. 1989. "Arab Music Theory in the Modern Period." Ph.D. dissertation, University of California, Los Angeles.

Moyle, Natalie K. 1990. *The Turkish Minstrel Tale Tradition*. Harvard Dissertations in Folklore and Oral Tradition. New York: Garland.

Page, Mary Ellen. 1977. "*Naqqāli* and Ferdowsi: Creativity in the Iranian National Tradition." Ph.D.dissertation, University of Pennsylvania.

Parry, Milman. 1987. *The Making of Homeric Verse*, ed. A. Parry. Oxford and New York: Oxford University Press.

Racy, Ali Jihad. 1977. "Musical Change and Commercial Recording in Egypt." Ph.D. dissertation, University of California, Los Angeles.

Reichl, Karl. 1985. "Oral Tradition and Performance of the Uzbek and Karakalpak Epic Singers." In *Fragen der mongolischen Heldendichtung*, ed. W. Heissig, 613–643. Wiesbaden: Otto Harrassowitz.

———. 1992. *Turkic Oral Epic Poetry: Traditions, Forms, Poetic Structure*. New York: Garland.

Reinhard, Ursula, and Tiago de Oliveira Pinto. 1989. *Sänger und Poeten mit der Laute: Türkische Aşik und Ozan*. Berlin: Dietrich Reimer Verlag.

Reynolds, Dwight F. 1995a. *Heroic Poets, Poetic Heroes: The Ethnography of Performance in an Arabic Oral Epic Tradition*. Ithaca, N.Y.: Cornell University Press.

———. 1995b. "Musical Dimensions of an Arabic Oral Epic Tradition." *Asian Music* 26(1):51–92.

———. 1996. "Crossing and Recrossing the Line." In *The World Observed: Reflections on the Fieldwork Process*, ed. Bruce Jackson and Edward Ives, 100–117. Chicago: University of Illinois Press.

el-Shawan, Salwa Aziz. 1980a. "*Al-Mūsīka al-Arabiyyah:* A Category of Urban Music in Cairo, Egypt, 1927–1977." Ph.D. dissertation, Columbia University.

———. 1980b. "The Sociopolitical Context of al-Musiqa al-'Arabiyyah in Cairo, Egypt: Politicies, Patronage, and Musical Change (1927–1977)." *Asian Music* 12(1):86–128.

———. 1982. "The Role of Mediators in the Transmission of al-Musika al-Arabiyyah in Twientieth-Century Cairo." *Yearbook for Traditional Music* 21:56–74.

———. 1984. "Traditional Arab Music Ensembles in Egypt since 1967: 'The Continuity of Tradition within a Contemporary Framework." *Ethnomusicology* 22(2):271–288.

Slyomovics, Susan E. 1987. *The Merchant of Art: An Egyptian Hilali Oral Epic Poet in Performance*. Berkeley and Los Angeles: University of California Press, 1987.

HISTORICAL ROOTS

Adler, Israel. 1975. *Hebrew Writings Concerning Music in Manuscripts and Printed Books from Geonic Times up to 1800*. RISM B IX[2]. Munich: G. Henle.

Anati, Emmanuel. 1968. *Rock-Art in Central Arabia*. Louvain: Institut Orientaliste.

Arberry, Arthur J., trans. [1935] 1977. *The Doctrine of the Ṣūfīs* (Kitāb al-Ta'arruf li-madhab ahl al-taṣawwuf). (From the Arabic of Abū Bakr al-Kalābādhī.) Cambridge: Cambridge University Press.

Baffioni, Carmela. 1984. "La scala pitagorica in al-Kindī." In *Studi in onore di Francesco Gabrieli nel suo ottantesimo compleanno*, ed. R. Traini. Rome: Università di Roma "La Sapienza," Dipartimento di Studi Orientali.

Barker, Andrew, ed. 1989. *Greek Musical Writings: II*. Cambridge and New York: Cambridge University Press.

Beeston, A. F. L., ed. and trans. 1980. *The Epistle on Singing-Girls of Jāḥiẓ*. Warminster: Aris and Phillips.

Beichert, Eugen. 1931. *Die Wissenschaft der Musik bei al-Fârâbî*. Regensburg: Pustet.

Berque, Jacques. 1995. *Musiques sur le fleuve: Les plus belles pages du Kitâb al-Aghânî*. Paris: Michel.

Berthier, Annie, and Amnon Shiloah. 1985. "À propos d'un 'Petit livre arabe de musique,' Oxford, Bodleian Library, Manuscrits Turcs XLII. Paris, Bibliothèque Nationale, Arabe 2480." *Revue de Musicologie* 71:164–177.

Bohlman, Philip V. 1987. "The European Discovery of Music in the Islamic World and the 'Non-Western' in Nineteenth-Century Music History." *Journal of Musicology* 5:147–163.

Braune, Gabriele. 1990. "Puls und Musik: Die Wirkung der griechischen Antike in arabischen medizinischen und musikalischen Traktaten." *Jahrbuch für Musikalische Volks- und Völkerkunde* 14:52–67.

Bürgel, Johann Christoph. 1979. "Musicotherapy in the Islamic Middle Ages as Reflected in Medical and Other Sources." In *History and Philosophy of Science*, ed. Hakim Mohammed Said. Islamabad: Hamdard Foundation Press.

Burnett, Charles. 1993. "European Knowledge of Arabic Texts Referring to Music: Some New Material." *Early Music History* 12:1–17.

Carlisle, Roxane Connick. 1973. "Women Singers in Darfur, Sudan Republic." *Anthropos* 68:758–800.

Carra de Vaux, Baron. 1891a. "Notice sur deux manuscrits arabes." *Journal Asiatique*, 8th series, 17:295–322.

———. 1891b. "Le traité des rapports musicaux ou l'Épître à Scharaf ed-Dîn, par Safi ed-Dîn 'Abd el-Mumin Albaghdâdî." *Journal Asiatique*, 8th series, 18:279–355.

Caussin de Perceval, A. 1873. "Notices anecdotiques sur les principaux musiciens arabes des trois premiers siècles de l'Islamisme." *Journal Asiatique*, 7th series, 2:397–592.

Centre des Musiques Arabes et Méditerranéennes, ed. 1992. *Les instruments de musique en Tunisie*. Tunis: Ministère de Culture.

Chabrier, Jean-Claude. 1985. "Éléments d'une approche comparative des échelles théoriques arabo-irano-turques." *Revue de Musicologie* 71:39–78.

———. 1996. "Musical Science." In *Encyclopedia of the History of Arabic Science*, ed. Roshdi Rashed. London and New York: Routledge.

Christianowitsch, Alexandre. 1863. *Esquisse historique de la musique arabe aux temps anciens*. Cologne: Dumont-Schauberg.

Clement of Alexandria. 1954. "Paedagogos (Christ the Educator)." In *Fathers of the Church*, Vol. 23. Washington: Catholic University of America Press.

Corriente, Federico, ed. and trans. 1988. *Poesía estrófica atribuida al místico granadino As-Sustarī (siglo XIII d.C.). (Preedición, traducción, estudio e índices)*. Madrid: Consejo Superior de Investigaciones Científicas. Instituto de Filologia. Departamento de Estudios Arabes.

Cortés García, Manuela. 1988. "Revisión de los manuscritos poético-musicales árabes, andalusíes, y magrebíes de la Biblioteca Nacional de Madrid." in *IV Congreso Internacional de Civilización Andalusí. Universidad de El Cairo*, 95–108. Cairo.

———. 1993. "Vigencia de la transmisión oral en el Kunnās al-Ḥā'ik (Cancionero de al-Ḥā'ik)," *Revista de musicología* 16:1942–1952.

———. 1995. "Nuevos datos para el estudio de la música en al-Andalus de dos autores granadinos: As-Sustarī e Ibn al-Jaṭīb." *Música Oral del Sur* 1:177–194.

———. 1996. "Sobre la música y sus efectos terapéuticos en la 'Epístola sobre las melodías' de Ibn Bāyya," *Revista de Musicología* 19:11–23.

Cowl, Carl, trans. 1966. "The Risāla fīhubr tā'līf al-alḥān of Ja'qūb ibn Isḥāq al-Kindī (790–874)." *Consort* 23:129–166.

Cruz Hernándes, Miguel. 1981. "La teoría musical de Ibn Sīnā en el Kitāb al-Sifā'." In *Milenario de Avicena*, ed. A. Badawi et al. Madrid: Instituto Hispano-Árabe de Cultura.

D'Erlanger, Baron Rodolphe. 1930–1959. *La musique arabe*. Paris: Librairie Orientaliste Paul Geuthner.

Dieterici, Friedrich. 1865. *Die Propaedeutik der Araber im zehnten Jahrhundert*. Berlin: Mittler. Reprints: 1969. Hildesheim: Olms; 1999. Frankfurt: Institute for the History of Arabic-Islamic Science.

Doughty, Charles. 1888. *Travels in Arabia Deserta*. Cambridge: University Press.

Ehrenkreutz, Stefan. 1980. "Medieval Arabic Music Theory and Contemporary Scholarship." *Arab Studies Quarterly* 2:249–265.

Elsner, Jürgen, and Paul Collaer. 1983. *Nordafrika*. Musikgeschichte in Bildern, Band I: Musikethnologie, Lieferung 8. Leipzig: Deutscher Verlag für Musik.

Elsner, Jürgen. 1969. "Remarks on the Big Argul." *Yearbook of the International Folk Music Council* 1:234–239.

al-Fārābī, Abū Naṣr (d. 950). 1967. *Kitāb al-Mūsīqī al-Kabīr*, ed. Ghaṭṭās 'Abd-al-Malik Khashaba. Revision and introduction by Maḥmūd Aḥmad al-Ḥifnī. Cairo: Dār al-Kātib al-'Arabī.

———. 1968–1969. "Die Theorie von Īqā'. I: Übersetzung des Kitāb al-Īqā'āt von Abū Naṣr al-Fārābī," trans. Eckhard Neubauer. *Oriens* 21–22:196–232.

———. 1994. "Die Theorie von Īqā'. II: Übersetzung des Kitāb Iḥṣā' al-Īqā'āt von Abū Naṣr al-Fārābī," trans. Eckhard Neubauer. *Oriens* 34:103–173.

Farmer, Henry George. [1929] 1973. *A History of Arabian Music to the Thirteenth Century*. London: Luzac.

———. 1929–30. "Greek Theorists of Music in Arabic Translation." *Isis* 13:325–333. Reprint: 1997. In H. G. Farmer, *Studies in Oriental Music*.

———. 1930. *Historical Facts for the Arabian Musical Influence*. London: Reeves.

———. 1931. *The Organ of the Ancients. From Eastern Sources (Hebrew, Syriac, and Arabic)*. London: Reeves. Reprint: 1997. In H. G. Farmer, *Studies in Oriental Music*.

———, ed. and trans. 1933. *An Old Moorish Lute Tutor: Being Four Arabic Texts from Unique Manuscripts in the Biblioteca Nacional, Madrid (No. 334) and the Staatsbibliothek, Berlin (Lbg. 516)*. Glasgow: Civic. Reprint: 1997. In H. G. Farmer, *Studies in Oriental Music*.

———, ed. and trans. 1934. *Al-Fārābī's Arabic-Latin Writings on Music in the* Iḥṣā' al-'ulūm *(Escorial Library, Madrid, No. 646),* De scientiis *(British Museum, Cott. MS. Vesp. B.X., and Bibl. Nat., Paris, No. 9335), and* De ortu scientiarum *(Bibl. Nat., Paris, No. 6298, and Bodleian Library, Oxford, No. 3623), etc.* Glasgow: Civic. Reprint: 1997. In H. G. Farmer, *Studies in Oriental Music*.

———. [1935] 1997. "A Maghribī Work on Musical Instruments." In *Studies in Oriental Music*, 2:151–165. Frankfurt am Main: Institute for the History of Arabic-Islamic Science.

———. [1937] 1997. "The Lute Scale of Avicenna." In *Studies in Oriental Music*, 2:175–187. Frankfurt am Main: Institute for the History of Arabic-Islamic Science.

———. 1941. "The Jewish Debt to Arabic Writers on Music." *Islamic Culture* 15:59–63. Reprint: 1997. In H. G. Farmer, *Studies in Oriental Music*.

———, trans. 1942. *Music: The Priceless Jewel. From the "Kitāb al-'iqd al-farīd" of Ibn 'Abd Rabbihi (d. 940)*. Bearsden: Author. Reprint: 1997. In H. G. Farmer, *Studies in Oriental Music*.

———. 1943. *Sa'adyah Gaon on the Influence of Music*. London: Arthur Probsthain. Reprint: 1997. In H. G. Farmer, *Studies in Oriental Music*.

———. 1945. *The Minstrelsy of "The Arabian Nights." A Study of Music and Musicians in the Arabic "Alf Laila wa Laila."* Bearsden: Author. Reprint: 1997. In H. G. Farmer, *Studies in Oriental Music.*

———. [1952] 1997. "The Religious Music of Islām." In *Studies in Oriental Music,* 1:123–128. Frankfurt am Main: Institute for the History of Arabic-Islamic Science.

———. 1955. "The Song Captions in the *Kitāb al-aghānī al-kabīr.*" *Transactions of the Glasgow University Oriental Society* 15:1–10. Reprint: 1997. In H. G. Farmer, *Studies in Oriental Music.*

———. 1957. "Al-Kindī on the 'Ēthos' of Rhythm, Colour, and Perfume." *Transactions of the Glasgow University Oriental Society* 16:29–38. Reprint: 1997. In H. G. Farmer, *Studies in Oriental Music.*

———, trans. 1959. "The Science of Music in the *Mafātīḥ al-'ulūm.*" *Transactions of the Glasgow University Oriental Society* 17:1–9. Reprint: 1997. In H. G. Farmer, *Studies in Oriental Music.*

———, trans. 1959–1961. "Tenth Century Arabic Books on Music: As Contained in 'Kitāb al-Fihrist' of Abu 'l-Faraj Muḥammad ibn al-Nadīm." *Annual of Leeds University Oriental Society* 2:37–47. Reprint: 1997. In H. G. Farmer, *Studies in Oriental Music.*

———. [1965a] 1997. "The Old Arabian Melodic Modes." In *Studies in Oriental Music,* 1:429–432. Frankfurt am Main: Institute for the History of Arabic-Islamic Science.

———. 1965b. *The Sources of Arabian Music: An Annotated Bibliography of Arabic Manuscripts Which Deal with the Theory, Practice, and History of Arabian Music from the Eighth to the Seventeenth Century.* Leiden: Brill.

———. 1966. *Islam: Musikgeschichte in Bildern.* ed. Heinrich Besseler and Max Schneider. Leipzig: VEB Deutscher Verlag für Musik.

———. [1986] 1997. *Studies in Oriental Music.* Vol. 1: *History and Theory.* (Reprint of writings published in 1925–1966.) Vol. 2: *Instruments and Military Music.* (Reprint of writings published in 1925–1969.) Frankfurt: Institute for the History of Arabic-Islamic Science. (First published 1986.)

al-Faruqi, Lois Ibsen. 1981. *An Annotated Glossary of Arabic Musical Terms.* Westport, Conn.: Greenwood.

———. 1982a. "Al Ghazālī on Samā'." In *Essays in Islamic and Comparative Studies. Papers Presented to the Islamic Studies Group of the American Academy of Religion,* ed. Isma'il Raji al Faruqi and Abdullah Omar Nasseef. Washington, D.C.: International Institute of Islamic Thought.

———. 1982b. "The Sharī'ah on Music and Musicians." In *Islamic Thought and Culture,* ed. Ismail R. al Faruqi. Herndon, Va.: International Institute of Islamic Thought.

———. 1985. "The Suite in Islamic History and Culture." *World of Music* 27(3):46–64.

Fischer, August. 1918. *Das Liederbuch eines marokkanischen Sängers. Nach einer in seinem Besitz befindlichen Handschrift herausgegeben, übersetzt und erläutert.* Leipzig: B.G. Teubner.

Frolova, Olga B. 1995. "Egyptian Folk Songs in the Unique Manuscripts of the St. Petersburg University Library." *Studia Orientalia* (Helsinki) 75:87–93.

García Gómez, Emilio. 1962. "Estudio del Dār al-ṭirāz, preceptiva egipcia de la muwaṣṣaḥa." *Al-Andalus* 27:21–104.

Gramlich, Richard, trans. 1978. *Die Gaben der Erkenntnisse des 'Umar as-Suhrawardī ('Awārif al-ma'ārif).* Wiesbaden: Steiner.

———, trans. 1989. *Das Sendschreiben al-Qušayrīs über das Sufitum.* Wiesbaden: Steiner.

———, trans. 1990. *Schlaglichter über das Sufitum. Abū Naṣr as-Sarrāǧs Kitāb al-luma'.* Stuttgart: Steiner.

———, trans. 1994. *Die Nahrung der Herzen. Abū Ṭālib al-Makkī's Qūt al-qulūb.* Stuttgart: Steiner.

Graziosi, P. 1964. "New Discoveries of Rock Painting in Ethiopia." *Antiquity* 150:96.

Gribetz, Arthur. 1991. "The *Samā'* Controversy: Sufi versus Legalist." *Studia Islamica* 74:43–62.

Guardiola, María Dolores. 1990. "Biografías de músicos en un manuscrito de al-Udfuwī." *Estudios Onomástico-Biográficos de al-Andalus* 3:335–350.

———. 1991. "La figure de la ḳayna dans les sources musicales." In *Le patrimoine andalou dans la culture arabe et espagnole.* Tunis. (Actes du VIIe Colloque Universitaire Tuniso-Espagnol. Tunis 3–10 février 1989.)

———. 1995. "Licitud de la venta de esclavas cantoras." In *Homenaje al Profesor José María Fárneas Besteiro,* 2:938–996. Granada: Universidad de Granada.

Guettat, Mahmoud. 1980. *La musique classique au Maghreb.* Paris: Sindbad.

Guignard, Michel. 1975. *Musique, honneur, et plaisir au Sahara.* Paris: Geuthner.

Gulisaschwili, Boris A. 1967. "Ibn Sina und die reine Stimmung." *Beiträge zur Musikwissenschaft* 9:272–283.

Haas, Max. 1989. "Antikenrezpetion in der arabischen Musiklehre: Al-Fārābī über musikalische Fantasie." In *Kontinuität und Transformation der Antike im Mittelalter,* ed. Willi Erzgräber, 261–269. Sigmaringen: Jan Thorbecke.

Hammerstein, Reinhold. 1986. *Macht und Klang: Tönende Automaten als Realität und Fiktion in der alten und mittelalterlichen Welt.* Bern: Francke.

Haq, Sirajul. 1944. "Samâ' and Raqṣ of the Darwishes." *Islamic Culture* 18:111–130.

al-Hassan, Ahmad Y., and Donald R. Hill. 1986. *Islamic Technology: An Illustrated History.* Cambridge: Cambridge University Press; Paris: UNESCO.

Hassan, Scheherazade Qassim. 1980. *Les instruments de musique en Irak et leur rôle dans la société traditionnelle.* New York and Paris: Cahiers de l'Homme; Mouton.

Hickmann, Hans. 1954. "Ägyptische Volksinstrumente." *Musica* 8:49–52, 97–100.

el-Hefny, Mahmoud, ed. and trans. 1931. *Ibn Sina's Musiklehre hauptsächlich an seinem "Naǧāt" erläutert.* Berlin: Hellwig.

al-Heitty, Abd al-Kareem. 1990. "The Contrasting Spheres of Free Women and Jawārī in the Literary Life of the Early 'Abbāsid Caliphate." *Al-Masāq* (Leeds) 3:31–51.

Hill, Donald R., ed. and trans. 1974. *Al-Gazarī: Kitāb fī ma'rifat al-ḥiyal al-handasiyya. The Book of Knowledge of Ingenious Mechanical Devices.* Dordrecht and Boston: Reidel.

Huart, Clément. 1884. "Étude biographique sur trois musiciennes arabes." *Journal Asiatique,* 8th series, 3:141–187.

Ibn Ghaybī, 'Abd al-Qādir (d. 1435). *Jāmi' al-Alḥān.* Oxford: Oxford University, Bodleian Library Marsh 282.

Ikhwān al-Ṣafā. 1976. *The Epistle on Music of the Ikhwān al-Ṣafā. Risāla fī al-Mūsīqī,* trans. Amnon Shiloah. Tel Aviv: Tel Aviv University.

al-Iṣbāhānī, Abū al-Faraj (d. 967). 1927–1974. *Kitāb al-aghānī.* 24 vols. Cairo: Dār al-Kutub.

Jahn, Alfred. 1902. *Die Mehri-Sprache in Südarabien.* Vienna: A. Hölder.

Jenkins, Jean, and Poul Røvsing-Olsen. 1976. *Music and Musical Instruments in the World of Islam.* London: Horniman Museum.

Kartomi, Margaret. 1990. "National Identity and Other Themes of Classification in the Arab World." In *On Concepts and Classifications of Musical Instruments,* 122–134. Chicago: University of Chicago Press.

Kazemi, Elke, ed. and trans. 1999. *Die bewegte Seele: Das spätantike Buch über das Wesen der Musik (Kitāb 'Unṣur al-mūsīqī) von Paulos/Būlos in arabischer Übersetzung vor dem Hintergrund der griechischen Ethoslehre.* Frankfurt: Institute for the History of Arabic-Islamic Science.

Kennedy, Philip F. 1998. *The Wine Song in Classical Arabic Poetry: Abū Nuwās and the Literary Tradition.* Oxford: Clarendon.

el-Kholy, Samha A. 1984. *The Function of Music in Islamic Culture in the Period up to 1100 C.E.* Cairo: General Egyptian Book Organization.

Kiesewetter, Raphael Georg. 1842. *Die Musik der Araber, nach Originalquellen dargestellt.* Leipzig: Breitkopf und Härtel.

Kilpatrick, Hilary. 1997. "Cosmic Correspondences: Songs as a Starting Point for an Encyclopaedic Portrayal of Culture." In *Pre-Modern Encyclopaedic Texts (Proceedings of the Second COMERS Congress, Groningen, 1–4 July 1996),* ed. P. Binkley. Leiden: Brill.

———. 1998. "The Transmission of Songs in Medieval Arabic Culture." In *Philosophy and Arts in the Islamic World (Proceedings of the Eighteenth Congress of the Union Européenne des Arabisants et Islamisants Held at the Katholieke Universiteit Leuven [September 3–September 9, 1996]),* ed. U. Vermeulen and D. de Smet. Leuven: Peeters.

———. 1999. "Princes, musiciens, et musicologues à la cour abbasside." In *Les intellectuels en*

Orient musulman: Statut et fonction, ed. F. Sanagustin. Cairo: Institut Français d'Archéologie Orientale.

Kosegarten, Johann Gottfried Ludwig. 1844. "Die moslemischen Schriftsteller über die Theorie der Musik." *Zeitschrift für die Kunde des Morgenlandes* (Bonn) 5:137–163.

Lachmann, Robert, and Mahmud el-Hefni, eds. 1931. *Ja'qūb Ibn Isḥāq al-Kindī: Risāla fī hubr tā'līf al-alḥān. Über die Komposition der Melodien*. Leipzig: Kistner and Siegel.

Land, Jan Pieter Nicolaas. 1885. "Recherches sur l'histoire de la gamme arabe." In *Actes du Sixième Congrès International des Orientalistes tenu en 1883 à Leide*. Deuxième partie, section 1, Sémitique:37–168. Leiden: Brill.

———. 1892. "Remarks on the Earliest Development of Arabic Music." In *Transactions of the Ninth International Congress of Orientalists. (Held in London, 5th to 12th September 1892.)*, 2:155–163. London.

———. 1922. "Tonschriftversuche und Melodieproben aus dem muhammedanischen Mittelalter." *Sammelbände für vergleichende Musikwissenschaft* 1:79–85.

Lane, Edward W. 1981. *Manners and Customs of the Modern Egyptians 1833–1835*. The Hague and London: East-West; Cairo: Livres de France.

Lerner, Ralph, and Muhsin Mahdi, ed. 1972. *Medieval Political Philosophy: A Source Book*. Ithaca, N. Y.: Cornell University Press.

Lyall, Sir Charles. 1913. *The Diwāns of 'Abīd ibn al-Abraṣ of Asad*. Leiden: Brill.

MacDonald, Duncan Black, trans. 1901–1902. "Emotional Religion in Islām as affected by Music and Singing: Being a Translation of a Book of the *Iḥyā' 'Ulūm ad-Dīn* of al-Ghazzālī." *Journal of the Royal Asiatic Society* (1901):195–252, 705–748; (1902):1–28.

al-Mallah, Issam. 1993. "The Increasing Role of Instrumental Music and Its Influence on Musical Life in Egypt." In *Actas del XV Congreso de la SIM. Revista de Musicología* 16:1246–1249.

———. 1997. *Arab Music and Musical Notation*. Tutzing: Hans Schneider.

Manik, Liberty. 1969. *Das arabische Tonsystem im Mittelalter*. Leiden: Brill.

———. 1979. "Zwei Fassungen einer von Ṣafī al-Dīn notierten Melodie." *Baessler-Archiv*, Neue Folge 23:145–151.

Marcus, Scott. 1989. "Arab Music Theory in the Modern Period." Ph.D. dissertation, University of California, Los Angeles.

Margoliouth, David Samuel, trans. 1935–1938, 1945–1948. "The Devil's Delusion [*Talbīs iblīs*] by Ibn Al-Jauzi." *Islamic Culture* 9–12, 19–22, passim.

Menander. 1862. *Scriptorum Graecorum Bibliotheca Aristophanis, Menandri, et Philemoni*. Paris: Firmin Didot.

Michot, Jean R. 1988. "L'Islam et le monde: al-Ghazâlî et Ibn Taymiyya à propos de la musique (*samâ'*)." In *Figures de la finitude: Études d'anthropologie philosophique*, ed. G. Florival et al. Louvain-la-Neuve: Éditions de l'Institut Supérieur de Philosophie, Librairie Peeters; Paris: Vrin.

———. 1991. *Musique et danse selon Ibn Taymiyya: Le Livre du* Samâ' *et de la Danse* (Kitāb al-Samā' wa l-Raqṣ) *compilé par le shaykh Muḥammad al-Manbijī*. Paris: Vrin.

Mokri, Mohammad. 1995. "La mélodie chez al-Fârâbî: Rôle, fondement, et définition." In *Persico-Kurdica: Contributions scientifiques aux études iraniennes*, ed. M. Mokri. Paris, Louvain: Peeters.

Monroe, James T. 1989. "Aḥmad al-Tīfāshī on Andalusian Music." *Modern Philology* 125:35–44.

Müller, Hans. 1980. *Die Kunst des Sklavenkaufs nach arabischen, persischen, und türkischen Ratgebern vom 10. bis zum 18. Jahrhundert*. Freiburg: Klaus Schwarz.

Neubauer, Eckhard. 1965. "Musiker am Hof der frühen 'Abbāsiden." Ph.D. dissertation, J. W. Goethe-Universität.

———. 1968–1969. "Die Theorie vom *īqā'*. I. Übersetzung des *Kitāb al-Īqā'āt* von Abū Naṣr al-Fārābī." *Oriens* 21–22:196–232. Reprint: 1998. In E. Neubauer, *Arabische Musiktheorie* (with facs. ed. of text).

———. 1987–1988. "Das Musikkapitel der *Gumal al-falsafa* von Muḥammad ibn 'Alī al-Hindī (1135 n.Chr.)." *Zeitschrift für Geschichte der arabisch-islamischen Wissenschaften* 4:51–59. Reprint: 1998. In E. Neubauer, *Arabische Musiktheorie* (with facs. ed. of text).

———. 1990. "Arabische Anleitungen zur Musiktherapie." *Zeitschrift für Geschichte der arabisch-islamischen Wissenschaften* 6:227–272.

———. 1993. "Der Bau der Laute und ihre Besaitung nach arabischen, persischen, und türkischen Quellen des 9. bis 15. Jahrhunderts." *Zeitschrift für Geschichte der arabisch-islamischen Wissenschaften* 8:279–378.

———. 1994. "Die Theorie vom *īqā'*. II. Übersetzung des *Kitāb Iḥṣā' al-īqā'āt* von Abū Naṣr al-Fārābī." *Oriens* 34:103–173. Reprint: 1998. In E. Neubauer, *Arabische Musiktheorie* (with facs. ed. of text).

———. 1995–1996. "Al-ɦalīl ibn Aḥmad und die Frühgeschichte der arabischen Lehre von den 'Tönen' und den musikalischen Metren. Mit einer Übersetzung des *Kitāb an-Naġam* von Yaḥyā ibn 'Alī al-Munaǧǧim." *Zeitschrift für Geschichte der arabisch-islamischen Wissenschaften* 10:255–323. Reprint: 1998. In E. Neubauer, *Arabische Musiktheorie* (with facs. ed. of text).

———. 1998. *Arabische Musiktheorie von den Anfängen bis zum 6./12. Jahrhundert. Studien, Übersetzungen und Texte in Faksimile*. Frankfurt: Institute for the History of Arabic-Islamic Science.

———. 2000. "Glimpses of Arab Music in Ottoman Times from Syrian and Egyptian Sources." *Zeitschrift für Geschichte der arabisch-islamischen Wissenschaften* 13:317–365.

Neubauer, Eckhard, and Elsbeth Neubauer. 1987–1988. "Henry George Farmer on Oriental Music: An Annotated Bibliography." *Zeitschrift für Geschichte der Arabisch-Islamischen Wissenschaften* 4:219–266.

Odeimi, Bechir. 1991. "Kitāb al-Imtā' wa-l-intifā': Un manuscrit sur la musique arabe de Ibn al-Darrāǧ." *Arabica* 38:40–56.

Pellat, Charles, trans. 1954. *Le livre de la couronne. Kitāb at-Tāǧ . . . attribué à Ǧāḥiẓ*. Paris: Les Belles Lettres.

———. 1955. *Le Kitāb at-Tarbī' wa-t-Tadwīr de Jāḥiz*. Damascus: Institut Français de Damas.

———, trans. 1963. "Les esclaves-chanteuses de Ǧāḥiẓ." *Arabica* 10:121–147.

Plumley, A. Gwendolen. 1976. *El Tanbur: The Sudanese Lyre or the Nubian Kissar*. Cambridge: Town and Gown.

Poché, Christian. 1984. "*'Arṭaba*," "*Duff*," "*Ghirbāl*," "*Kinnārāt*," "*Mi'zaf*," "*Mizmār*," "*Qinīn*," "*Rabāba*," "*Ṭunbūr*." In *The New Grove Dictionary of Musical Instruments*, ed. Stanley Sadie. London: Macmillan.

———. 1989. "Le partage des tâches: La femme dans la musique arabe." *Cahiers de l'Orient* 13:11–21.

Poché, Christian. 1993. "Un nouveau regard sur la musique d'al-Andalus: Le manuscrit d'al-Tīfāshī." *Revista de Musicología* 16(1):367–379.

Poché, Christian, and Jean Lambert. 2000. *Musiques du monde arabe et musulman: Bibliographie et discographie*. Paris: Geuthner.

Pollux, Julius. 1967. *Pollucis Onomasticon. Lexicographi Graeci*, Vol. 9, ed. Ericus Bethe. Stuttgart: Teubner.

Pourjavady, Nasrollah. 1990. "Zwei alte Werke über *samā'*." *Spektrum Iran* (Bonn) 3(2):37–59; 3(3):36–61.

Pouzet, Louis. 1983. "Prises de position autour du *samâ'* en Orient musulman au VIIe/XIIIe siècle." *Studia Islamica* 57:119–134.

Qureshi, Regula Burckhardt. 1991. "Sufi Music and the Historicity of Oral Tradition." In *Ethnomusicology and Modern Music History*, ed. Steven Blum, Philip V. Bohlman, and Daniel M. Neuman, 103–120. Urbana: University of Illinois Press.

Racy, Ali Jihad. 1988. *Tanbura Music of the Gulf*. Doha: Arab Gulf States Folklore Center.

———. 1991. "Historical Worldviews of Early Ethnomusicologists: An East-West Encounter in Cairo, 1932." In *Ethnomusicology and Modern Music History*, ed. Steven Blum, Philip V. Bohlman, and Daniel M. Neuman, 68–91. Urbana: University of Illinois Press.

———. 1994. "A Dialectical Perspective on Musical Instruments: The East Mediterranean Mijwiz." *Ethnomusicology* 38:37–57.

Randel, Don M. 1976. "Al-Fārābī and the Role of Arabic Music Theory in the Latin Middle Ages." *Journal of the American Musicological Society* 29:173–188.

Rashid, Subhi Anwar. 1984. *Mesopotamien*. Musikgeschichte in Bildern, Band II: Musik des Altertums, Lieferung 2. Leipzig: Deutscher Verlag für Musik.

Rasmussen, Anne. 1996. "Theory and Practice at the 'Arabic Orq': Digital Technology in Contemporary Arab Music Performance." *Popular Music* 15:345–365.

Rat, Gustave. 1899–1902. *Al-Mostaṭraf: Recueil des morceaux choisis ça et là dans toutes les branches de connaissances réputées attrayantes* par Šihâb-ad-dîn Aḥmad al-Abšîhî. *Ouvrage philologique, anecdotique, littéraire, et philosophique traduit pour la première fois*. 2 vols. Paris and Toulon.

Reinert, Benedikt. 1979. "Das Problem des pythagoräischen Kommas in der arabischen Musiktheorie." *Asiatische Studien* 33:199–217.

———. 1990. "Die arabische Musiktheorie zwischen autochthoner Tradition und griechischem Erbe." In *Die Blütezeit der arabischen Wissenschaft*, ed. Heinz Balmer and Beat Glaus. Zürich: Verlag der Fachvereine.

Reynolds, Dwight. 1995. *Heroic Poets, Poetic Heroes: The Ethnography of Performance in an Arabic Oral Epic Tradition*. Ithaca, N. Y.: Cornell University Press.

Ribera, Julián. 1929. *Music in Ancient Arabia and Spain: Being La música de las Cantigas*. London: Oxford University Press; Stanford, Calif.: Stanford University Press.

Rice, David Storm. 1958. "A Drawing of the Fatimid Period." *Bulletin of the School of Oriental and African Studies* 21:31–39.

Rimmer, Joan. 1969. *Ancient Musical Instruments of Western Asia in the British Museum*. London: Trustees of the British Museum.

Robson, James, ed. and trans. 1938. *Tracts on Listening to Music: Being* Dhamm al-malāhī *by Ibn abī 'l-Dunyā and* Bawāriq al-ilmā' *by Majd al-Dīn al-Ṭūsī al-Ghazālī*. London: Royal Asiatic Society.

———, trans. 1947–1953. "The Meaning of Ghinā'." *Journal of the Manchester University Egyptian and Oriental Society* 25:1–8.

———. 1952. "A Maghribi Ms. on Listening to Music." *Islamic Culture* 26:113–131.

———. 1957. "Muslim Controversy about the Lawfulness of Music." *Islamic Literature* 9:305–314.

———. 1958. "Some Arab Musical Instruments." *Islamic Culture* 32:171–185.

———. 1961. "Muslim Wedding Feasts." *Transactions of the Glasgow University Oriental Society* 18:1–14.

Robson, James, and Henry George Farmer. (Facs., trans.) 1938. *Ancient Arabian Musical Instruments: As Described by Al-Mufaḍḍal ibn Salama (Ninth Century) in the Unique Istanbul Manuscript of the* Kitāb al-malāhī *in the Handwriting of Yāqūt al-Musta'ṣimī (d. 1298)*. Glasgow: Civic.

Ronzevalle, Louis, ed. and trans. 1913. "Un traité de musique arabe moderne." *Mélanges de la Faculté Orientale, Université Saint-Joseph* 6:1–120.

Rosenthal, Franz, trans. 1958. *Ibn Khaldûn. The Muqaddimah. An Introduction to History*. New York: Pantheon.

———. 1966. "Two Graeco-Arabic Works on Music." *Proceedings of the American Philosophical Society* 110:261–268. Reprint: 1991. In F. Rosenthal, *Science and Medicine in Islam*. Aldershot: Variorum.

Rowson, Everett K. 1991. "The Effeminates of Early Medina." *Journal of the American Oriental Society* 111:671–693.

Ryckmans, Gonzague. 1934. *Les noms propres sud-sémitiques*. 3 vols. Louvain: Bureaux du Muséon.

Sachs, Curt. 1913. *Real-Lexikon der Musikinstrumente*. Berlin: J. Bard.

———. 1940. *The History of Musical Instruments*. New York: Norton.

Saint-Saëns, Camille. 1913. "Lyres et cythares." In *Encylopédie de la musique et dictionnaire du Conservatoire*, 1:538–540, ed. Albert Lavignac. Paris: C. Delagrave.

Salem, Elie A. 1977. *Hilāl al-Ṣābi'*. Rusūm Dār al-Khilāfah (*The Rules and Regulations of the 'Abbāsid Court*). Trans. from Arabic. Beirut: American University of Beirut.

Sawa, George Dimitri. 1981. "The Survival of Some Aspects of Performance Practice of Medieval Arabic Music." *Ethnomusicology* 25(1):73–86.

———. 1982. "Bridging One Millenium: Melodic Movement in al-Fārābī and Kolinski." In *Cross-Cultural Perspectives on Music*, ed. R. Falk and T. Rice. Toronto: University of Toronto Press.

———. 1983–1984. "Al-Fārābī's Theory of Īqā': An Empirically Derived Medieval Model of Rhythmic Analysis." *Progress Reports in Ethnomusicology* l(9):1–32.

———. 1984. "Musical Humour in the *Kitāb al-Aghānī* (Book of Songs)." In *Logos Islamikos: Studia Islamica in Honorem Georgii Michaelis Wickens*, ed. Roger M. Savory and Dionisius Agius, 35–50. Papers in Mediaeval Studies, 6. Toronto: Pontifical Institute of Mediaeval Studies.

———. 1985. "The Status and Role of the Secular Musician in *Kitāb al-Aghānī*." *Asian Music* 17(1):69–82.

———. 1989. *Music Performance Practice in the Early 'Abbāsid Era. 750–932 A.D.* Toronto: Pontifical Institute of Medieval Studies.

———. 1989. "The Differing World of the Music Historian and the Music Illuminator in Medieval Islamic Manuscripts." *Imago Musicae* 6:7–22.

———. 1989. "Oral Transmission in Arabic Music, Past and Present." *Oral Tradition* 4(1–2):254–265.

———. 1990. "Paradigms in al-Fārābī's Musical Writings." In *Paradigms in Medieval Thought: Applications in Medieval Disciplines*, ed. Nancy van Deusen and Alvin E. Ford, 81–92. Lewinston, N.Y.: Edwin Mellen.

———. 1997. "Editing and Translating Medieval Arabic Writings on Music." In *Music Discourse from Classical to Early Modern Times: Editing and Translating Texts*, ed. Maria Rika Maniates, 45–70. Toronto: University of Toronto Press.

Sezgin, Fuat. 1974. *Geschichte des arabischen Schrifttums*. Vol. 5, *Mathematik bis ca. 430 H.* Leiden: Brill.

Shehadeh, Kamal, Donald R. Hill, and Richard Lorch, eds. and trans. 1994. "Construction of a Fluting Machine by Apollonius the Carpenter." *Zeitschrift für Geschichte der arabisch-islamischen Wissenschaften* 9:326–356.

Shehadi, Fadlou. 1995. *Philosophies of Music in Medieval Islam*. Leiden: Brill.

Shawqi, Yusuf. 1994. *Dictionary of Traditional Music of Oman*. Rev. and expanded by Dieter Christensen. Intercultural Music Studies 6, International Institute for Traditional Music. Wilhelmshaven: Florian Noetzel Verlag.

Shiloah, Amnon. 1962. "Réflexions sur la danse artistique musulmane au Moyen-âge." *Cahiers de Civilisation Médiévale* 5:463–474.

———. 1963. *Caractéristiques de l'art vocale arabe au Moyen-âge*. Tel-Aviv: Israel Music Institute.

———, trans. 1964–1966. "L'épître sur la musique des Ikhwān alṢafā'." *Revue des Études Islamiques* 32:125–162; 34:159–193.

———, ed. and trans. 1968. "Deux textes arabes inédits sur la musique." *Yuval* l:22l–248. (Reprint: Shiloah 1993.)

———, ed. and trans. 1971a. "Un 'Problème Musical' inconnu de Thābit ibn Qurra." *Orbis Musicae* 1:25–38. (Reprint: Shiloah 1993.)

———. 1971b. "Les sept traités de musique dans le manuscrit 1705 de Manisa." *Israel Oriental Studies* 1:303–315.

———. 1972a. "The Simsimiyya: A String Instrument of the Red Sea." *Asian Music* 4:15–26.

———, trans. 1972b. *Al-Ḥasan ibn Aḥmad ibn 'Alī al-Kātib: La perfection des connaissances musicales*. Paris: Geuthner.

———. 1972c. "Ibn Hindū: Le médecin et la musique." *Israel Oriental Studies* 2:447–462. (Reprint: Shiloah 1993.)

———, trans. 1974. "Un ancien traité sur le *'ūd* d'Abū Yūsuf al-Kindī." *Israel Oriental Studies* 4:179–205.

———, trans. 1978a. *The Epistle on Music of the Ikhwān alṢafā'*. Tel Aviv: Tel Aviv University. (Reprint: Shiloah 1993.)

———. 1978b. "Reflets de la musique des divers peuples dans les écrits arabes sur la musique." In *Actes du Deuxième Congrès International d'Études des Cultures de la Méditerranée Occidentale*, ed. Micheline Galley, vol. 2. Algiers: Société Nationale d'Édition et de Diffusion.

———. 1979. *The Theory of Music in Arabic Writings (c. 900–1900): Descriptive Catalogue of Manuscripts in Libraries of Europe and the U.S.A.* Munich: Henle.

———. 1986. "Music in the Pre-Islamic Period as Reflected in Arabic Writings of the First Islamic Centuries." *Jerusalem Studies in Arabic and Islam* 7:109–120. (Reprint: Shiloah 1993.)

———. 1990. "Techniques of Scholarship in Medieval Arabic Musical Treatises." In *Music Theory and Its Sources: Antiquity and the Middle Ages*, ed. André Barbera. Notre Dame, Ind. (Reprint: Shiloah 1993.)

———. 1991. "Musical Modes and the Medical Dimension: The Arabic Sources (c. 900–c.1600)." In *Metaphor: A Musical Dimension*, ed. Jamie Croy Kassler. Sydney. (Reprint: Shiloah 1993.)

———. 1993. *The Dimension of Music in Islamic and Jewish Culture*. Aldershot: Variorum.

———. 1994. "Notions d'esthétique dans les traités arabes sur la musique." *Cahiers de Musiques Traditionnelles* 7:51–58.

———. 1997. "L'approche humaniste et métaphorique dans les premiers écrits arabes sur la musique." In *Festschrift Walter Wiora zum 90. Geburtstag*, ed. Christoph-Hellmut Mahling and Ruth Seiberts, 446–456. Tutzing: Hans Schneider.

———. 1997. "Music and Religion in Islam." *Acta Musicologica* 69:143–155.

Smith, Eli, trans. 1847. "A Treatise on Arab Music, Chiefly from a Work by Mikhâ'il Meshâkah, of Damascus." *Journal of the American Oriental Society* 1:171–217.

Sobh, Mahmud. 1995. "La poesía árabe, la música y el canto." *Anaquel de Estudios Árabes* 6:149–184.

Stigelbauer, Michael. 1975. *Die Sängerinnen am Abbasidenhof um die Zeit des Kalifen Al-Mutawakkil: Nach dem Kitāb al-Aġānī des Abu-l-Faraǧ al-Iṣbahānī und anderen Quellen dargestellt*. Vienna: VWGÖ.

el-Tawil, M. A. 1992. "Ibn Sina and Medieval Music (370–428 A.H/A.D. 980–1038): A New Edition of the Musical Section of Kitab al-Shifa and Kitab al-Najat plus a Comprehensive Study of His Life and Works on Music." Ph.D. dissertation, University of Exeter.

Terés, Elías, trans. 1971. "La epístola sobre el canto con música instrumental, de Ibn Ḥazm de Córdoba." *Al-Andalus* 36:203–214.

Vajda, Georges. 1980. "Un libelle contre la danse des soufis." *Studia Islamica* 51:163–177.

Valderrama, Fernando. 1986. "La música arábigo-andaluza." In *Actas del XII Congreso de la U.E.A.I. (Malaga, 1984)*. Madrid: Huertas.

van den Branden, Albert. 1966. *Histoire de Thamoud*. Beirut: Publications de l'Université Libanaise.

Vigreux, Philip. 1985. *La derbouka: Technique fondamentale et initiation aux rhythmes arabes*. Aix-en-Provence: Eddisud.

Villoteau, G. A. 1809–22. *De l'état actuel de l'art musical en Égypte*. Paris: Panckoucke.

———. 1813. "Description historique, technique, et littéraire des instruments de musique des orientaux." Vol. 14 of *Description de l'Egypte*. Paris: Pancoucke.

Weil, Jürgen W. 1975–1978. "Epigramme auf Musikerinnen [part 2 and 3: Künstlerinnen] in der Gedichtsammlung *Alf ǧāriya wa-ǧāriya*." *Rocznik orientalistyczny* 37 (1975):7–12; 39 (1977):137–141; 40 (1978):83–93.

Werner, Eric, and Isaiah Sonne. 1941–1943. "The Philosophy and Theory of Music in Judaeo-Arabic Literature." *Hebrew Union College Annual* 16 (1941):251–319; 17 (1942–43):511–573.

Werner, Eric. 1965. "Greek Ideas on Music in Judeo-Arabic Literature." In *The Commonwealth of Music: In Honor of Curt Sachs*, ed. Gustave Reese and Rose Brandel. New York: Free Press; London: Collier Macmillan.

Wiedemann, Eilhard. 1910. "Über die Herstellung von Glocken bei den Muslimen." *Mitteilungen zur Geschichte der Medizin und der Naturwissenschaften* 9:475–476. Reprint: 1984. In Wiedemann, *Gesammelte Schriften zur arabisch-islamischen Wissenschaftsgeschichte,* 1:475–476. Frankfurt.

———. 1910. "Über Musikautomaten bei den Arabern." In *Centenario della nascita di Michele Amari*, vol. 2. Palermo: Virzì. Reprint: 1984. In Wiedemann, *Gesammelte Schriften zur arabisch-islamischen Wissenschaftsgeschichte,* 1:451–472. Frankfurt.

———. 1914. "Über Musikautomaten." *Sitzungsberichte der Physikalisch-Medizinischen Societät in Erlangen* 46:17–26. Reprint: 1970. In Wiedemann, *Aufsätze zur arabischen Wissenschaftsgeschichte,* 2:47–56. Hildesheim and New York: Olms.

Wiedemann, Eilhard, and Fritz Hauser. 1918. "Byzantinische und arabische akustische Instrumente." *Archiv für die Geschichte der Naturwissenschaften und der Technik* 8:140–166. Reprint: 1984. In Wiedemann, *Gesammelte Schriften zur arabisch-islamischen Wissenschaftsgeschichte,* 3:1580–1606. Frankfurt.

———, and Wilhelm Müller. 1922–1923. "Zur Geschichte der Musik. l. Abschnitt über die Musik aus den Schlüsseln der Wissenschaft. 2. Angaben von al Akfânî über die Musik." *Sitzungsberichte der Physikalisch-Medizinischen Societät in Erlangen* 54–55:7–22. Reprint: 1970. In Wiedemann, *Aufsätze zur arabischen Wissenschaftsgeschichte,* 2:580–595. Hildesheim and New York: Olms.

Wright, Owen. 1966. "Ibn al-Munajjim and the Early Arabian Modes." *Galpin Society Journal* 19:27–48.

———. 1978. *The Modal System of Arab and Persian Music A.D. 1250–1300*. Oxford: Oxford University Press.

———. 1983. "Music and Verse." In *Arabic Literature to the End of the Umayyad Period*, ed. A. F. L. Beeston et al. Cambridge: Cambridge University Press.

———. 1995. "A Preliminary Version of the *Kitāb al-Adwār*." *Bulletin of the School of Oriental and African Studies* 58:455–478.

Yammine, Habib. 1999. "L'évolution de la notation rythmique dans la musique arabe du IXe à la fin du XXe siècle." *Cahiers de Musiques Traditionnelles* 12:95–121.

Zenkowsky, S. 1950. "*Zār* and *Tambūra* as Practised by the Women of Omdurman." *Sudan Notes and Records* 31:65–81.

Ziegler, Christiane. 1979. *Les instruments de musique égyptiens au musée du Louvre*. Paris: Éditions de la Réunion des Musées Nationaux.

NORTH AFRICA: THE MAGHRIB

Abassi, Hamadi, et al. 1991. *Tunis chante et danse: 1900–1950*. Les Éditions de la Méditerranée. Tunis: Alif.

'Abd al-Wahhāb, Ḥassan Ḥusnī. 1918. "Le développement de la musique arabe en Orient, Espagne, et Tunisie." *Revue Tunisienne* 25:106–117.

Abun-Nasr, Jamil M. 1975. *A History of the Maghrib*, 2nd ed. Cambridge: Cambridge University Press.

———. 1987. *A History of the Maghreb in the Islamic Period*. Cambridge: Cambridge University Press.

Arberry, A. J. 1965. *Arabic Poetry*. London: Cambridge University Press.

Aydoun, Ahmed. 1995. *Musiques du Maroc*. Casablanca: EDDIF.

Bourgeot, André. 1989. "Cultures, langues berbères, et folklorisation chez les Touaregs." In *Tradition et modernité dans les sociétés berbères*, ed. Yassadit Yacine, 33–52. Paris: Awal.

Bouzar-Kasbadji, Nadya. 1988. *L'émergence artistique algérienne au XXe siècle*. Algiers: Offices des Publications Universitaires.

Brandes, Edda. 1989. *Die Imẓad Musik der Kel-Ahaggar-Frauen in Süd-Algerien*. Göttingen: Edition Re.

Brett, Michael, and Elizabeth Fentress. 1996. *The Berbers*. Oxford and Cambridge, Mass.: Blackwell.

Brown, Kenneth L. 1985. "The Discrediting of a Sufi Movement in Tunisia." In *Islamic Dilemmas: Reformers, Nationalists, and Industrialization*, ed. Ernest Gellner, 146–168. The Southern Shore of the Mediterranean: Religion and Society, 25. Amsterdam, Berlin, and New York: Mouton.

Brunel, René. 1926. *Essai sur la confrérie religieuse des Aîssâoûa au Maroc*. Paris: Geuthner.

Centre des Musiques Arabes et Méditerranéennes. 1992. *Les instruments de musique en Tunisie*. Tunis: Centre des Musiques Arabes et Méditerranéennes.

Chaker, Salem. 1989a. *Berbères aujourd'hui*. Paris: L'Harmattan.

———. 1989b. "Une tradition de résistance et de lutte: La poésie berbère kabyle—Un parcours poétique." *Revue du Monde Musulman et de la Méditerranée* 51(1):11–31.

Chottin, Alexis. 1931–1933. *Corpus de musique marocaine*. Paris: Au Ménestrel Heugel.

———. 1938. *Tableau de la musique marocaine*. Paris: Librairie Orientaliste Paul Geuthner.

Collaer, Paul, and Jürgen Elsner. 1983. *Nordafrika: Musikgeschichte in Bildern*, 1(8), ed. Werner Bachman. Leipzig: Deutscher Verlag für Musik.

Compton, Linda Fish. 1976. *Andalusian Lyrical Poetry and Old Spanish Love Songs: The Muwashshah and Its Kharja*. New York: New York University Press.

Daoudi, Bouziane, and Hadj Miliani. 1996. *L'aventure du rai*. S.n.: Éditions du Seuil.

Davis, Ruth. 1985. "Songs of the Jews on the Island of Djerba: A Comparison between Two Surveys." *Musica Judaica* 7:23–33.

———. 1986a. "Modern Trends in the *Ma'lūf* of Tunisia: 1934–1984." Ph.D. dissertation, Princeton University.

———. 1986b. "Some Relations between Three Piyuṭim from Djerba and Three Arab Songs." *Maghreb Review* 11:134–44.

———. 1989. "Links between the Baron Rodolphe d'Erlanger and the Notation of Tunisian Art Music." In *Ethnomusicology and the Historical Dimension*, ed. Margot Lieth Philipp, 47–59. Ludwigsburg: Philipp Verlag.

———. 1992a. "The Tunisian Nūba as a Cyclic Genre: A Performance Analysis." In *Regionale maqām-Traditionen in Geschichte und Gegenwart. Materialien der 2. Arbeitstagung der Study Group "Maqām" des International Council for Traditional Music vom 23. bis 28. März in Gossen bei Berlin*, ed. Jürgen Elsner and Gisa Jähnichen, 83–114. Berlin: s.n.

———. 1992b. "The Effects of Notation on Performance Practice in Tunisian Art Music." *World of Music* 34(1):85–114.

———. 1993. "Tunisia and the Cairo Congress of Arab Music, 1932." *Maghreb Review* 18:83–102.

———. 1993. "Melodic and Rhythmic Genre in the Tunisian *nūba*." In *Ethnomusicologica II*, ed. F. Giannattasio and G. Giuriati, 71–87. Siena: Accademia Musicale Chigiana.

———. 1996. "The Art/Popular Music Paradigm and the Tunisian Ma'lūf." *Popular Music* 15:313–323.

———. 1997a. "Cultural Policy and the Tunisian Ma'lūf: Redefining a Tradition." *Ethnomusicology* 41:1–21.

———. 1997b. "Traditional Arab Music Ensembles in Tunis: Modernizing al-Turāth in the Shadow of Egypt." *Asian Music* 28(2):73–108.

———. In press. "*Piyuṭ* Melodies as Mirrors of Social Change in Djerba, Tunisia." *Musica Judaica* 14.

D'Erlanger, Rodolphe. 1917. "Au sujet de la musique arabe en Tunisie." *Revue Tunisienne* 24:91–95.

———. 1930–1959. *La musique arabe*. 6 vols. Paris: Libraire Orientaliste Paul Geuthner.

———. 1937. *Mélodies tunisiennes, hispano-arabes, arabo-berbères, juive, nègre*. Paris: Librairie Orientaliste Paul Geuthner.

Dermenghem, Emile, and Léo Barbès. 1951. "Essai sur la hadhra des Aïsaouia d'Algérie." *Revue Africaine* 84:289–314.

Djura. 1990. *Le voile du silence*. Paris: M. Lafon. See also 1992. *The Veil of Silence*, trans. Dorothy Blair. London: Quartet.

Elsner, Jürgen. (1985) 1990. "Der Rhythmus Inṣirāf: Zum Problem quantitativer Rhythmik." In *Schriftenreihe des Mecklenburgischen Folklorezentrums, Abteilung Tanz*, ed. Rosemarie Ehm-Schulz, 59–74. Neubrandenburg: Mecklenburgisches Folklore-Zentrum. Also in *Rhythmik und Metrik in traditionellen Musikkulturen*, ed. Oskár Elschek, 239–249. Bratislava: VEDA, Verlag der Slowakischen Akademie der Wissenschaften.

———. 1991a. "Formation of New Music Traditions in the Arab Countries of North Africa." In *Studies in Ethnomusicology*, Vol. 1, ed. Jürgen Elsner and Gisa Jähnichen, 33–45. Berlin: Humboldt-Universität.

———. 1991b. "The Forms of Classical Algerian Instrumental Music." In *Studies in Ethnomusicology*, Vol. 1, ed. Jürgen Elsner and Gisa Jähnichen, 20–32. Berlin: Humboldt-Universität.

———. 1992 (1993). "Présentation de la musique algérienne au Congrès du Caire." In *Musique arabe, Le Congrès du Caire de 1932*, ed. Sheherazade Qassim Hassan, 191–208. Cairo: CEDEJ. German version as "Zur Darstellung der algerischen Musik auf der ersten Konferenz für arabische Musik Kairo 1932." In *Studies in Ethnomusicology*, Vol. 3, ed. Jürgen Elsner and Gisa Jähnichen, 111–136. Berlin: Humboldt-Universität.

———. 1993. "Some Remarks on New Developments in the Music of Algerian Cities." *Revista de Musicología* 16(3):1240–1245.

———. 1997. "Bashraf und Cambar in Algerian Art Music." In *The Structure and Idea of maqām, Historical Approaches, Proceedings of the Third Meeting of the ICTM Maqām Study Group Tampere—Virrat, 2–5 October 1995*, ed. Jürgen Elsner and Risto Pekka Pennanen, 65–85. Tampere: Department of Folk Tradition, University of Tampere.

Farmer, Henry George. 1929. *A History of Arabian Music to the Thirteenth Century*. London: Luzac.

Gross, Joan E., and David A. McMurray. 1993. "Berber Origins and the Politics of Ethnicity in Colonial North African Discourse." *PoLAR: Political and Legal Anthropology Review* 16(2):39–57.

Guettat, Mahmoud. 1980. *La musique classique du Maghreb*. Paris: Sinbad.

———. 1986. *La tradition musicale arabe*. S.n.: Ministère de l'Education Nationale.

———. 1992. "La Tunisie dans les documents du Congrès du Caire de 1992." In *Musique arabe: Le Congrès du Caire de 1932*, ed. Philippe Vigreux, 69–86. Cairo: Editions CEDEJ.

Johnson, Pamela Ryden. 1979. "A Sufi Shrine in Modern Tunisia." Ph.D. dissertation, University of California, Berkeley.

Jones, Lura JaFran. 1977. "The 'Isawiyya of Tunisia and Their Music." Ph.D. dissertation, University of Washington.

———. 1982. "The Role of Sufi Brotherhoods in the Preservation of Tunisian Art Music." In *Essays in Islamic and Comparative Studies*, ed. Isma'il Raji al-Faruqi, 109–120. Herndon, Va.: International Institute of Islamic Thought.

———. 1987. "A Sociohistorical Perspective on Tunisian Women as Professional Musicians." In *Women and Music in Cross-Cultural Perspective*, 2nd ed., ed. Ellen Koskoff, 69–83. Champaign-Urbana: University of Illinois Prss.

———. 1991. "Women in Non-Western Music." In *Women and Music: A History*, ed. Karin Pendle, 314–330. Bloomington: Indiana University Press.

Jouad, Hassan. 1995. *Le calcul inconscient de l'improvisation: Poésie berbère, rythme, nombre, et sens*. Paris: Peeters.

Jouad, Hassan, and Bernard Lortat-Jacob. 1978. *La saison des fêtes dans une vallée du Haut-Atlas*. Paris: Seuil.

Julien, Charles-André. 1970. *History of North Africa from the Arab Conquest to 1830*. New York: Praeger.

Kacem, Abdelaziz. 1973. "La politique culturelle tunisienne." *Annuaire de l'Afrique du Nord* 12:29–44.

Kapchan, Deborah. 1999. "*Zajal* Poetry: A Preface." *Mediterraneans/Méditerranéennes* 11:45.

Kárpáti, J. 1961. "Mélodie, vers, et structure strophique dans la musique berbère (imazighen) du Maroc central." *Studia Musicologica* 1(3-4):451–473.

Keddie, Nikki R., ed. 1972. *Scholars, Saints, and Sufis: Muslim Religious Institutions since 1500*. Berkeley: University of California Press.

Laade, Wolfgang. 1962. *Tunisia*. Vol. 2, *Religious Songs and Cantillations from Tunisia*. Folkways FW 8862.

Lachmann, Robert. 1940. *Jewish Cantillation and Song in the Isle of Djerba*. Jerusalem: Azriel, Archives of Oriental Music, Hebrew University.

———. 1974. *Die Musik im Volksleben Nordafrikas und orientalische Musik und Antike*. Vol. 1 of *Posthumous Works*, ed. Edith Gerson-Kiwi. Jerusalem: Magnes.

Lachmann, Robert, and Edith Gerson-Kiwi, eds. 1978. *Gesänge der Juden auf der Insel Djerba*. Yuval Monograph Series 7. Jerusalem: Magnes Press, Hebrew University.

Lacoste-Du Jardin, Camille. 1978. "Chansons berbères, chansons pour vivre." *L'Histoire* 5:104–105.

Laoust, Emile. 1993. *Noces berbères: Les cérémonies du mariage au Maroc*. Aix-en-Provence: Edisud.

Lefébure, Claude. 1977. "La poésie féminine berbère comme mode de participation sociale." *Littérature Orale Arabo-Berbère* 8:109–142.

———. 1987. "Contrat mensonger, un chant d'*amdyaz* sur l'émigration." *Études et Documents Berbères* 3:28-46.

Liu, Benjamin M., and James T. Monroe. 1989. *Ten Hispano-Arabic Strophic Songs in the Modern Oral Tradition: Music and Texts*. Berkeley and Los Angeles: University of California Press.

Lortat-Jacob, Bernard. 1980. *Musique et fêtes au Haut-Atlas*. Paris: Mouton-EHESS.

———. 1994. *Musiques en fêtes*. Nanterre: Société d'Ethnologie.

Louati, Ali. 1995. *Le Baron d'Erlanger et son palais Ennajma Ezzahra à Sidi Bou Said.* Tunis: Editions Simpact.

el-Mahdi, Salah. 1972. *La musique arabe*. Paris: Alphonse Leduc.

Marcus, Scott. 1989. "Arab Music Theory in the Modern Period." Ph.D. dissertation, University of California, Los Angeles.

Marouf, Nadir, ed. 1995. *Le chant arabo-andalou: Essai sur le rurbain ou la topique de la norme et de la marge dans le patrimoine musical arabe. Colloque international, Lille 6–8 décembre 1991*. Paris: Éditions L'Harmattan.

Matoub, Lounes. 1995. *Rebelle*. Paris: Stock.

Mehenni, Ferhat. 1983. "La chanson kabyle depuis dix ans." *Tafsut, série spéciale "Etudes et débats"* 1:65–71.

Ministère de la Culture (Tunisia). 1995. *Centre des Musiques Arabes et Méditerranéennes.* Tunis: Simpact.

Monroe, James T. 1974. *Hispano-Arabic Poetry: A Student's Anthology*. Berkeley: University of California Press.

———. 1986–1987. "A Sounding Brass and Tinkling Cymbal: al-Halīl in Andalus (Two Notes on the Muwaššaha)." *Corónica* 15:252–258.

———. 1987. "The Tune or the Words? (Singing Hispano-Arabic Poetry)." *Al-Qantara* 8:265–317.

Moussali, Bernard. 1988. "Tunisia: Urban Music of Tunis." In *Congrès du Caire 1932*, 145–151. France: Édition Bibliothèque Nationale avec le concours de l'Institut du Monde Arabe.

Nykl, A. R. 1946. *Hispano-Arabic Poetry and Its Relations with the Old Provençal Troubadours*. Baltimore: Furst.

Pacholczyk, Josef. 1983. "The Relationship between the Nawba of Morocco and the Music of the Troubadours and Trouvères." *World of Music* 25(2):5–14.

Paris, André. 1921. "Haouach à Télouet." *Hespéris* 1:209-216.

Peyron, Michaël. 1991. *"Isaffen ghbanin (rivières profondes)": Poésies du Moyen-Atlas marocain traduites et annotées*. Casablanca: Wallada.

———. 1994. "Danse." *Encyclopédie Berbère* 14:2204–2213.

Plenckers, Leo J. 1989. *De muziek van de algerijnse muwashshaḥ*. Alkmaar: Rapporta B.V.

———. 1993. "Changes in the Algerian *san'a* Tradition and the Role of the Musicologist in the Process." *Revista de Musicología* 16(3):1255–1260.

Poché, Christian. 1995. *La musique arabo-andalouse*. S.n.: Cité de la Musique/Actes Sud.

Racy, Ali Jihad. 1991. "Historical Worldviews of Early Ethnomusicologists: An East-West Encounter in Cairo, 1932." In *Ethnomusicology and Modern Music History*, ed. Stephen Blum, Philip V. Bohlman, and Daniel M. Neuman, 68–91. Urbana and Chicago: University of Illinois Press.

Ribera, Julián. 1929. *Music in Ancient Arabia and Spain*. Stanford, Calif.: Stanford University Press.

Rouanet, Jules. 1913–1922. "La musique arabe" and "La musique arabe dans le Maghreb." In *Encyclopédie de Lavignac (Histoire de la musique)*, 5:2676–2812, 2813–2942. Paris: Delagrave.

Rovsing Olsen, Miriam. 1997. *Chants et danses de l'Atlas (Maroc)*. Pares: Cité de la Musique/Actes Sud.

Saadallah, Rabah. 1981. *Le chaâbi d'el-hadj M'hamed el-Anka*. Algiers: Dār al-kutub (La Maison des Livres).

Salvador-Daniel, Francisco. 1986. *Musique et instruments de musique du Maghreb*. Paris: La Boîte à Documents.

Schade-Poulsen, M. 1994. "Music and Men in Algeria. An Analysis of the Social Significance of Rai." Ph.D. dissertation, University of Copenhagen.

Schuyler, Philip D. 1978a. "*Rwais and Aḥwash*: Opposing Tendencies in Moroccan Berber Music and Society." *World of Music* 21(1):65–80.

———. 1978b. "Moroccan Andalusian Music." *World of Music* 21(1):33–46.

———. 1979a. "A Repertory of Ideas: The Music of the Rwais, Berber Professional Musicians from Southwestern Morocco." Ph.D. dissertation, University of Washington.

———. 1979b. "Music Education in Morocco: Three Models." *World of Music* 22(3):19-31.

———. 1984a. "Berber Professional Musicians in Performance." In *Performance Practice: Ethnomusicological Perspectives*, ed. Gérard Béhague, 91–148. London: Greenwood.

———. 1984b. "Moroccan Andalusian Music." In *Maqam: Music of the Islamic World and Its influences*, ed. Robert Browning. New York: Alternative Museum.

———. 1985. "The *Rwais* and the *Zawia*: Professional Musicians and the Rural Elite in Southwestern Morocco." *Asian Music* 17(1):114–131.

———. 1993a. "A Folk Revival in Morocco." In *Everyday Life in the Muslim Middle East*, ed. Donna Lee Bowen and Evelyn A. Early, 287–293. Bloomington: Indiana University Press.

———. 1993b. "Entertainment in the Marketplace." In *Everyday Life in the Muslim Middle East*, ed. Donna Lee Bowen and Evelyn Early, 276–280. Bloomington: Indiana University Press.

el-Shawan, Salwa Aziz. 1980. "Al-Mūsīka al-arabiyyah: A Category of Urban Music in Cairo, Egypt, 1927–1977." Ph.D. dissertation, Columbia University.

Speight, R. Marston. 1966. "Tunisia and Sufism." *Muslim World* 26:58–59.

Stern, Samuel M. 1964. "Andalusian Muwashshahs in the Musical Repertory of North Africa." In *Actas del Primer Congreso de Estudios Árabes e Islámicos, Córdoba, 1962*, 319–327. Madrid: Maestre.

———. 1974. *Hispano-Arabic Strophic Poetry*, ed. L. P. Harvey. Oxford: Clarendon.

Touma, Habib Hassan. 1998. *Die Nūbah Māyah: Zur Phänomenologie des Melos in der arabisch-andalusi Musik Marokkos*. Hildesheim: George Olms Verlag.

Trimingham, J. Spencer. 1971. *The Sufi Orders in Islam*. Oxford: Clarendon.

Udovitch, Abraham L., and Lucette Valensi. 1984. *The Last Arab Jews: The Communities of Jerba, Tunisia*. Chur, London, Paris, and New York: Harwood Academic.

Vocke, Sibylle. 1990. *Die markkanische Malhunpoesie.* Wiesbaden: Otto Harrassowitz.

Wansbrough, John. 1969. "Theme, Convention, and Prosody in the Vernacular Poetry of North Africa." *Bulletin of the School of Oriental and African Studies* 32:477–495.

Wulstan, David. 1982. "The Muwassah and Zağal Revisited." *Journal of the American Oriental Society* 102:247–264.

Yacine, Tassadit. 1989. *Ait Menguellat chante . . .* Paris: La Découverte/Awal.

Yafil, Edmond-Nathan. 1904–1924. *Répertoire de musique arabe et maure*. Nos. 1–29. Algiers.

Yelles-Chaouche, Mourad. 1986. *Le Ḥaufi: Poésie féminine et tradition orale au Maghreb*. Algiers: Office des Publications Universitaires.

Zoulef, Boudjemaa, and Mohamed Dernouny. 1981. "L'identité culturelle au Maghreb à travers un corpus de chants contemporains." *Annuaire de l'Afrique du Nord* 20:1021–1051.

THE EASTERN ARAB WORLD: THE MASHRIQ

Abdun, Salih, ed. 1971. *Genesi della "Aida": Con documentazione inedita*. Quaderni dell' Istituto di Studi Verdiani, Vol. 4. Parma: Tipografia "La Nazionale."

Abu-Haidar. 1988. "The Poetic Content of the Iraqi Maqam." *Journal of Arabic Literature* 19:128–141.

Alexandru, Tiberiu, and Emile A. Wahba. 1967. *The Folk Music of Egypt*. Cairo: Ministry of Culture.

Armbrust, Walter. 1996. *Mass Culture and Modernism in Egypt*. Cambridge: Cambridge University Press.

Azzam, Nabil. 1990. "Muḥammad 'Abd al-Wahhāb in Modern Egyptian Music." Ph.D. dissertation, University of California, Los Angeles.

Bailey, Clinton. 1974. "Bedouin Weddings in Sinai and the Negev." In *Studies in Marriage Customs*, ed. Issachar Ben-Ami and Dov Noy, 117–132. Jerusalem: Magnes.

al-Barghoti, 'A. 1963. "Arab Folk Songs from Jordan." Ph.D. dissertation, University of London.

Barker, John. 1876. *Syria and Egypt under the Last Five Sultans of Turkey*. London: Tinsley.

Berger, Morroe. 1961. "A Curious and Wonderful Gymnastic. . . ." *Dance Perspectives* 10:4–41.

Berner, Alfred. 1937. *Studien zur arabischen Musik auf Grund der gegenwärtigen Theorie und Praxis in Ägypten*. Leipzig: Kistner and Siegel.

Braune, Gabriele. 1987. *Die Qasida im Gesang von Umm Kultum: Die arabische Poesie im Repertoire der grössten ägyptischen Sängerin unserer Zeit*. Hamburg: Karl Dieter Wagner.

———. 1992. "Maqāmāt and Western Harmony in Egypt with Musical Examples of Sayyid Darwīs and Farīd al-'Atrās." In *Regionale maqām-Traditionen in Geschichte und Gegenwart. Materialien der 2. Arbeitstagung der Study Group "Maqām" des International Council for Traditional Music vom 23. bis 28. März in Gossen bei Berlin*, ed. Jürgen Elsner and Gisa Jähnichen, 75–82. Berlin: s.n.

Buonaventura, Wendy. 1989. *Serpent of the Nile: Women and Dance in the Arab World*. London: Saqi.

Clot-Bey, Antoine Barthelemy. 1840. *Aperçu général sur l'Egypte*. Paris: Fortin, Massin et Cie.

Dalman, G. 1901. *Palästinisher Diwan*. Leipzig.

Danielson, Virginia. 1989. "Cultural Authenticity in Egyptian Musical Expression." *Pacific Review of Ethnomusicology* 5:51–61.

———. 1991a. "Artists and Entrepreneurs: Female Singers in Cairo during the 1920s." In *Women in Middle Eastern History*, ed. Nikki R. Keddie and Beth Baron, 292–310. New Haven and London: Yale University Press.

———. 1991b. "Min al-Meshayikh: A View of Egyptian Musical Tradition." *Asian Music* 22(1):113–128.

———. 1997. *The Voice of Egypt: Umm Kulthūm, Arabic Song, and Egyptian Society in the Twentieth Century*. Chicago: University of Chicago Press.

D'Arvieux, Laurent. 1735. *Mémoires du Chevalier d'Arvieux*. 6 vols. Paris: Charles Jean-Baptiste Delespine.

De Laborde, Jean Benjamin. 1780. *Essai sur la musique ancienne et moderne*. 4 vols. Paris: Chez Eugène Onfroy.

D'Erlanger, Baron Rodolphe. 1930–1959. *La musique arabe*. Paris: Paul Geuthner.

Elsner, Jürgen. 1973. *Der Begriff des maqām in Ägypten in neuerer Zeit*. Leipzig: VEB Deutscher Verlag für Musik.

Collangettes, D. M. 1906. "La musique d'Alep." *Revue Musicale* 6:142.

Fahmy, Farida Melda. 1987. "The Creative Development of Mahmoud Reda, a Contemporary Egyptian Choreographer." M.A. thesis, University of California, Los Angeles.

Fakhri, Ahmed. 1973. *The Oases of Egypt*, Vol. 1. Cairo: American University in Cairo Press.

Farmer, Henry George. [1929] 1973. *A History of Arabian Music to the Thirteenth Century*. London: Luzac.

al-Faruqi, Lois Ibsen Lamya'. 1976–1977. "Dances of the Muslim Peoples." *Dance Scope* 11(1):43–51.

———. 1978. "Dance as an Expression of Islamic Culture." *Dance Research Journal* 10(2):6–13.

———. 1979. "The Status of Music in Muslim Nations: Evidence from the Arab World." *Asian Music* 12(1):56–85.

Fernea, Elizabeth, and Robert A. Fernea (with Aleya Rouchdy). 1991. *Nubian Ethnographies*. Prospect Heights, Ill.: Waveland.

Fernea, Robert A. 1966. "Initial Adaptations to Resettlement: A New Life for Egyptian Nubians." *Current Anthropology* 7(3):349–354.

———. 1973. *Nubians in Egypt: Peaceful People*. Austin: University of Texas Press.

Graham-Brown, Sarah. 1988. *Images of Women*. London: Quartet.

Granqvist, Hilma. 1931–35. *Marriage Conditions in a Palestinian Village*. Helsingfors: Akademische Buchhandlung.

Haddad, M. 1986. *Palestinian Folk Heritage Between Obliteration and Revival*. Taybih.

Hassan, Scheherazade Qassim. 1980. *Les instruments de musique en Irak et leur rôle dans la societé traditionnelle*. Paris: Mouton.

———. 1987. "Le makam irakien: Structures et réalisations." In *L'improvisation dans les musiques de tradition orale*, ed. Bernard Lortat-Jacob, 143–149. Paris: SELAF.

———. 1989. "Some Islamic Non-Arabic Elements of Influence on the Repertory on al-Maqām al-'Irāqī in Bagdad." In *Maqam-Raga-Zeilenmelodik: Konzeptionen and Prinzipen der Musikproduktion. Materialien der 1. Arbeitstagung der Study Group "Maqām" beim International Council for Traditional Music vom 28. Juni bis 2. Juli 1988 in Berlin*, ed. Jürgen Elsner, 148–155. Berlin: National-Komitee.

———. 1992. "Survey of Written Sources on the Iraqi Maqam." In *Regionale maqām-Traditionen in Geschichte und Gegenwart. Materialien der 2. Arbeitstagung der Study Group "Maqām" des International Council for Traditional Music vom 23. bis 28. März in Gossen bei Berlin*, ed. Jürgen Elsner and Gisa Jähnichen, 252–275. Berlin: s.n.

Haydar, 'Adnan. 1989. "The Development of Lebanese *Zajal*: Genre, Meter, and Verbal Duel." *Oral Tradition* 4(1–2) :189–212.

Jargy, Simon. 1970. *La poésie populaire traditionnelle chantée au Proche-Orient Arabe*. Paris: Mouton.

———. 1978. "Ḳasida." *Encyclopaedia of Islam* 4:713–714. Leiden: Brill.

Kennedy, John G. 1967. "Nubian Zar Ceremonies as Psychotherapy." *Human Organization* 26(4):185–194.

Al-Kholy, Samhah, and John Robison, eds. 1993. *Festschrift for Gamal Abd Al-Rahim*. Cairo: Binational Fulbright Commission in Egypt.

Koskoff, Ellen, ed. 1989. *Women and Music in Cross-Cultural Perspective*. Urbana and Chicago: University of Illinois Press.

Lagrange, Frédéric. 1996. *Musiques d'Egypte*. Paris: Cité de la Musique/Actes Sud.

Landau, Jacob M. 1958. *Studies in the Arab Theater and Cinema*. Philadelphia: University of Pennsylvania Press.

Lane, Edward W. 1936. *The Modern Egyptians*. London: Dent.

Linder, Sven. 1952. *Palästinische Volksgesänge*. Uppsala: Lundequistska Bokhandeln.

Marcus, Scott Lloyd. 1989. "Arab Music Theory in the Modern Period." Ph.D. dissertation, University of California, Los Angeles.

McPherson, J. W. 1941. *The Moulids of Egypt*. Cairo: Ptd. N. M. Press.

Molé, Marijan. 1963. "La danse extatique en Islam." In *Les danses sacrées*, ed. Jean Cazeneuve. Paris: Éditions du Seuil.

Murray, G. W. 1935. *Sons of Ishmael*. London: Routledge.

Nelson, Kristina. 1985. *The Art of Reciting the Qur'ān*. Austin: University of Texas Press.

Nettl, Bruno, and Ronald Riddle. 1973. "Taqsīm Nahawand: A Study of Sixteen Performances by Jihad Racy." *Yearbook of the International Folk Music Council* 5:11–50.

Neubauer, Eckhard. 1989. "Musique arabe en France 1630–1830." In *Le monde arabe dans la vie intellectuelle et culturelle en France*. Paris: Institut du Monde Arabe.

Nieuwkerk, Karin van. 1995. *"A Trade Like Any Other": Female Singers and Dancers in Egypt*. Austin: University of Texas Press.

Poché, Christian. 1995. *La musique arabo-andalouse*. Arles, Paris: Actes Sud et Cité de la Musique.

Racy, Ali Jihad. 1976. "Record Industry and Egyptian Traditional Music: 1904–1932." *Ethnomusicology* 20(1):23–48.

———. 1977. "Musical Change and Commercial Recording in Egypt, 1904–1932." Ph.D. dissertation, University of Illinois at Urbana-Champaign.

———. 1981. "Music in Contemporary Cairo: A Comparative Overview." *Asian Music* 13(1):4–26.

———. 1982. "Musical Aesthetics in Present-Day Cairo." *Ethnomusicology* 26:391–407.

———. 1983a. "Music in Nineteenth-Century Egypt: An Historical Sketch." *Selected Reports in Ethnomusicology* 4:157–79.

———. 1983b. "The Waṣlah: A Compound-Form Principle in Egyptian Music." *Arab Studies Quarterly* 5(4):396–403.

———. 1988. "Sound as Society: The Takht Music of Early Twentieth Century Cairo." *Selected Reports in Ethnomusicology* 7:139–70.

———. 1991a. "Creativity and Ambience: An Ecstatic Feedback Model from Arab Music." *World of Music* 33(3):7–28.

———. 1992. "Music." In *The Genius of Arab Civilization: Source of Renaissance*, 3rd ed., ed. John R. Hays, 151–171. New York: New York University Press.

———. 1996. "Heroes, Lovers, and Poet-Singers: The Bedouin Ethos in Music of the Arab Near-East." *Journal of American Folklore* 109 (434):404–424.

———. 1998. "Improvisation, Ecstasy, and Performance Dynamics in Arab Music." In *In the Course of Performance: Studies in the World of Musical Improvisation*, ed. Bruno Nettl and Melinda Russell, 95–112. Chicago and London: University of Chicago Press.

Russell, Alex[andre], and Pat[rick] Russell. 1794. *Natural History of Aleppo*. 2 vols. London: G. G. and J. Robinson.

Saarisalo, Aapeli. 1932. *Songs of the Druzes*. Helsinki.

Said, Edward. 1993. *Culture and Imperialism*. New York: Vintage.

Said, Mohamed Sayyid. 1999. "Cosmopolitanism and Cultural Autarky in Egypt." In *Cosmopolitanism, Identity, and Authenticity in the Middle East*, ed. Roel Meijer. Surrey: Curzon.

St. John, Bayle. 1973. *Village Life in Egypt*. New York: Arno.

Saleh, Magda. 1979. "A Documentation of the Ethnic Dance Traditions of the Arab Republic of Egypt." Ph.D. dissertation, New York University.

Saleh, Maher. 1965. "Horsemanship and the Horse Dance." *Al Funun al Shaabiya* (Folk Arts) 2:68–81.

Savary, [Claude Etienne]. 1785. *Lettres sur l'Egypte*. 3 vols. Paris: Chez Onfroy.

Sawa, George. 1989. *Music Performance Practice in the Early 'Abbasid Era, 132–320 A.H. / A.D. 750–932*. Toronto: Pontifical Institute of Mediaeval Studies.

Sbait, Dirgham. 1982. "Improvised Folk-Poetry of the Palestinians." Ph.D. dissertation, University of Washington.

———. 1986. "Poetic and Musical Structure in the Improvised-Sung Colloquial *Qasidah* of the Palestinian Poet-Singers." *Al-'Arabiyya* 19:75–108.

———. 1989. "Palestinian Improvised-Sung Poetry: The Genres of *Hida* and *Qarradi*—Performance and Transmission." *Oral Tradition* 4:213–235.

———. 1993. "Debate in the Improvised-Sung Poetry of the Palestinians." *Asian Folklore Studies* 52:93–117.

Schiff, Ze'ev and Ya'ari, Ehud. [1989] 1991. *Intifāḍa: The Palestinian Uprising—Israel's Third Front*, ed. and trans. Ina Friedman. New York: Simon and Schuster, Touchstone.

el-Shawan, Salwa. 1980a. "The Sociopolitical Context of *al-Musika al-'Arabiyyah* in Cairo, Egypt: Policies, Patronage, Institutions, and Musical Change (1927–1977)." *Asian Music* 12(1):86–129.

———. 1980b. "Al-Musika Al-'Arabiyah: A Category of Urban Music in Cairo, Egypt, 1927–1977." Ph.D. dissertation, University of Illinois, Urbana-Champaign.

———. 1982. "The Role of Mediators in the Transmission of Al-Musiqa Al-'Arabiyyah in Twentieth Century Cairo." *Yearbook for Traditional Music* 14:55–74.

———. 1984. "Traditional Arab Music Ensembles in Egypt since 1967: The Continuity of Tradition within a Contemporary Framework." *Ethnomusicology* 28(2):271–288.

———. 1985. "Western Music and Its Practitioners in Egypt (c. 1825–1985): The Integration of a New Musical Tradition in a Changing Environment." *Asian Music* 27(1):144–153.

Shelemay, Kay Kaufman. 1998. *Let Jasmine Rain Down: Song and Remembrance among Syrian Jews*. Chicago: University of Chicago Press.

Shiloah, Amnon. 1974. "A Group of Arabic Wedding Songs from the Village of Deyr al-Asad." In *Studies in Marriage Customs*, ed. Issachar Ben-Ami and Dov Noy, 267–296. Jerusalem: Magnes.

———. 1979. *The Theory of Music in Arabic Writings (c. 900–1900)*. Munich: G. Henle Verlag.

Simon, Artur. 1972. *Studien zur ägyptischen Volksmusik*. 2 vols. Hamburg: Karl Dieter Wagner.

Slyomovics, Susan. 1988. *The Merchant of Art: An Egyptian Hilali Oral Epic Poet in Performance*. Berkeley: University of California Press.

Sowayan, Saad A. 1989. "'Tonight My Gun Is Loaded': Poetic Dueling in Arabia." *Oral Tradition* 4(1–2):151–173.

Spector, Johanna. 1970. "Classical *'Ūd* Music in Egypt with Special Reference to Maqamat." *Ethnomusicology* 14:243–257.

Sulaiman, Khalid A. 1984. *Palestine and Modern Arab Poetry*. London: Zed.

Touma, Habib Hassan. 1996. *The Music of the Arabs*. Portland, Ore.: Amadeus.

Tsuge, Gen'ichi. 1972. "A Note on the Iraki Maqam." *Asian Music* 4(1):59–66.

Vatikiotis, P.J. 1985. *The History of Egypt from Muhammad Ali to Mubarak*, 3rd ed. Baltimore: Johns Hopkins University Press.

Villoteau, M. [Guillaume A.]. 1823. *Description historique, technique, et littéraire des instruments de musiques des Orientaux*. Vol. 13 of *Description de l'Egypte*. Paris: Panckoucke.

———. 1826. *De l'état actuel de l'art musical en Egypte*. Vol. 14 of *Description de l'Egypte*. Paris: Panckoucke.

Waugh, Earle H. 1989. *The Munshidin of Egypt: Their World and Their Song*. Columbia: University of South Carolina Press.

Wegner, Ulrich. 1982. *Abūdiya und mawwāl: Untersuchungen zur sprachlich-musikalischen Gestaltung im südirakischen Volksgesang*. 2 vols. Hamburg: Karl Dieter Wagner.

Wood, Leona. 1976. "Danse du ventre: A Fresh Appraisal." *Dance Research Journal* 8(2):18–30.

Zuhur, Sherifa, ed. 1998. *Images of Enchantment: Visual and Performing Arts of the Middle East*. Cairo: American University in Cairo Press.

MUSIC OF THE ARABIAN PENINSULA

Abbeele, Georges Van Den. 1992. *Travel as a Metaphor: From Montaigne to Rousseau*. Minneapolis: University of Minnesota Press.

Adler, Guido. 1903. "Sokotri-Musik." In *Die Mehri- und Soqotri-Sprache*. 2, *Südarabische Expedition der Akademie der Wissenschaften*, ed. David Heinrich Müller, 6:377–382. Vienna: A. Hölder.

Adra, Najwa. 1982. "Qabyala: The Tribal Concept in the Central Highlands Yemen Arab Republic." Ph.D. dissertation, Temple University.

———. 1993. "Tribal Dancing and Yemeni Nationalism: Steps to Unity." *Revue du Monde Musulman et de la Méditerranée* 67(l):161–168.

———. 1998. "Dance and Glance: Visualizing Tribal Identity in Highland Yemen." *Visual Anthropology* 11(1–2):55–101.

'Alī, Khalīl Ḥusayn. 1988. "*Al-'idda* Dance in Yemen." *Al Ma'thūrāt al-sha'biyya* 12:8–15.

Altorki, Soraya. 1986. *Women in Saudi Arabia*. New York: Columbia University Press.

Arom, Simha, and Uri Sharvit. 1994. "Plurivocality in the Liturgical Music of the Jews of San' (Yemen)." *Yuval* 6:34–67.

Bahat, Naomi, and Avner Bahat. 1980. "Traditional Scriptural-Reading Hand Movements as a Dance Source for Yemenite Jews." *Israel Dance* 5:22–23.

———. 1995. *Saperi Tama: The* Diwan *Songs of the Jews of Central Yemen, as Sung in the Manakha Community, Poetry-Music-Dance*. Tel Aviv: Beth Hatefutsoth.

Bahat-Ratzon, Naomi. 1975–1976. "Le saff-procession dansé dans les cérémonies du mariage druze." *Orbis Musicae* 5:45–65.

Bakewell, Anderson. 1985. "Music of the Tihamah." In *Studies on the Tihamah: The Report of the Tihama Expedition 1982,* ed. F. Stone, 104–108. London: Longman.

Barth, Fredrik. 1983. *Sohar, Culture, and Society in an Omani Town*. Baltimore: Johns Hopkins University Press.

Burckhardt, John Lewis. 1830. *Notes on the Bedouins and Wahabys*. 2 vols. London: Coburn and Bentley.

Campbell, Kay Hardy. 1979. "Arabian Wedding Nights." *Arab News* (August 1).

———. 1985. "Saudi Arabian Women's Music." *Habibi* 9(3).

———. 1977. "The Lives and Literary Patronage of 'Aishah Bint Talhah Ibn 'Ubayd Allah and Sukaynah Bint al-Husayn Ibn 'Ali in *Kitab al-Aghani*." Summa cum laude thesis, University of Minnesota.

———. 1980. "Why Sarah Uthman Wants to Expand beyond Wedding Party Audiences." *Arab News* (August 4).

Caton, Steven. 1991. *Peaks of Yemen I Summon: Poetry as Cultural Practice in a North Yemen Tribe*. Berkeley: University of California Press.

Christensen, Dieter. 1991. "Traditional Music, Nationalism, and Musicological Research." In *Music in the Dialogue of Cultures*, ed. Max Peter Baumann, 215–223. Wilmhelmshaven: Noetzel.

———. 1992. "Worlds of Music, Music of the World: The Case of Oman." In *World Music, Musics of the World*, ed. Max Peter Baumann, 107–122. Wilhelmshaven: Noetzel.

Deaver, Sherri. 1978. "Concealment versus Display: The Modern Saudi Woman." *Dance Research Journal* 10(2):14–18.

Dickson, Harold Richard Patrick. 1967. *The Arab of the Desert*, 4th ed. London: Allen and Unwin.

Elsner, Jürgen. 1990. "Trommeln und Trommelensembles im Jemen." In *Beiträge zur traditionellen Musik*, ed. A. Michel and Jürgen Elsner, 18–37. Berlin: Humboldt Universität.

Farmer, Henry G. 1929. "Meccan Musical Instruments." *Journal of the Royal Asiatic Society* 3:489–505. Reprint: 1997. In H. G. Farmer, *Studies in Oriental Music*, ed. Eckhard Neubauer, 2:79–100. Frankfurt am Main: Institute for the History of Arabic-Islamic Science at the Johann Wolfgang Goethe University.

———. [1929] 1967. *A History of Arabian Music to the Thirteenth Century*. London: Luzac.

Fox, Edward. 1990. "Arabian Delights." *Folk Roots* 86:21–23.

Galley, Micheline. 1996. "Creativity and Tradition: Mediterranean Folk Poetry in Sung Form." *Journal of Mediterranean Studies* 6(1).

Gavin, Carney E. S. 1985. "The Earliest Arabian Recordings: Discoveries and Work Ahead." *Phonographic Bulletin* (September):38–45.

Grandguillaume, Gilbert. 1982. "Valorisation et dévalorisation liées au contacts de cultures en Arabie Saoudite." In *Péninsule arabique aujourd'hui: Études par pays*, ed. P. Bonnenfant, 623–654. Paris: Éditions du CNRS.

al-Harbi, Salih. 1980. "Hommes et société des pêcheurs de perles au Koweit." Diplôme, l'École des Hautes Études, Paris.

Hassan, Scheherazade Qassim. 1976. "Musical Instruments among the Yezidi of Iraq." *Yearbook of the International Folk Music Council* 8:53–72.

Hofman, Shlomo. 1968. "The Density of a Yemenite Folk Tune." *Yearbook of the International Folk Music Council* 20:25–29.

Hood, Mantle. 1992. "Voiceprints of Traditional Omani Music." In *African Musicology: Current Trends*, 191–244. Los Angeles: University of California Press; Atlanta: Crossroads, African Studies Center.

Hurgronje, Snouck. [1888] 1931. *Mekka in the Latter Part of the Nineteenth Century*, trans. James Henry Monahan. Leiden: Brill.

Jargy, Simon. 1970. *La poésie populaire traditionnelle chantée au Proche-Orient arabe*. Paris: Mouton.

———. 1986. "Comments on the Concept and Characteristics of the Folk Music in the Gulf and Arabian Peninsula." *Al-Ma'ṯūrāt al-sha'biyya* (1 January).

———. 1987. "Aspects de la poésie chantée dans la tradition orale de la péninsule arabique." *Revue Musicale de la Suisse Romande* 40(1):2–12.

———. 1988. *La musique arabe*, 3rd ed. Paris: Presses Universitaires de France.

———. 1989. "Sung Poetry in the Oral Tradition of the Gulf Region and the Arabian Peninsula." *Oral Tradition* 4(1–2):174–188.

Jenkins, Jean, and Poul Røvsing-Olsen. 1976. *Music and Musical Instruments in the World of Islam*. London: World of Islam Festival Publishing.

Kanafani, Aida Sami. 1983. *Aesthetics and Ritual in the United Arab Emirates*. Beirut: American University in Beirut.

Kerbage, Toufic. 1983. *The Rhythms of Pearl Diver Music in Qatar*. Doha: Culture and Art Directorate, Ministry of Information.

———. 1986–87. "Tonernes univers." *Dansk Musik Tidsskrift* 61(4):162–168.

al-Kholaifi, Aisha. 1986. "Al-Muradah: The Female Dance in the Arabian Gulf." *Al-Ma'thūrāt al-sha'biyya* 3:104–129.

al-Khulayfi, Samia. 1995. *Le chant des femmes du Koweit*. Paris: DEA, Université de la Sorbonne-Paris IV.

al-Khusaibi, Said bin Nasser. 1985. *The Use of Traditional Music in the Development of Mass Media in Oman*. Beverly Hills, Calif.: University of Beverly Hills.

Lambert, Jean. 1993. "Identité nationale et régionalisme musical." In *Revue d'Études du Monde Musulman et Méditerranéen*, 67(1), *Le Yémen, passé et présent de l'unité*, 171–186. Aix-en-Provence.

———. 1995. "La musique dans la Maison-tour: Harmonies et Dissonances." In *Sanaa, architecture domestique et société*, ed. P. Bonnenfant, 165–173. Paris: CNRS-Éditions.

———. 1997. *La médecine de l'âme: Le chant de Ṣan'ā' dans la société yéménite*. Hommes et Musiques. Nanterre: Societé d'Ethnologie.

———. 2000. "Yemen." In *The New Grove Dictionary of Music and Musicians*, 2nd ed., 27:652–657. London: Macmillan.

Lonnet, Antoine, and Marie-Claude Simeone-Senelle. 1987. "Rābūt: Trance and Incantations in Mehri Folk Medicine." *Proceedings of the Seminar for Arabian Studies* 17:107–115.

el-Mahdi, Salah. 1976. "Les formes improvisées de la musique arabe." *World of Music* 18(3): 42–45.

el-Mallah, Issam. 1990. "Some Observations on the Naming of Musical Instruments and on Rhythm in Oman." *Yearbook of the International Folk Music Council* 22:123–126.

———. 1992. "Die Vorbereitung des Felles als Teil musikalischer Darbietungen in den arabischen Golfländern." In *Von der Vielfalt musikalischer Kultur: Festschrift für Josef Kuckertz—Zur Vollendung des 60. Lebensjahres*, 305–310. Anif/Salzburg: Müller-Speiser.

———. 1995. "Afrikanische Elemente in arabischen Musikkulturen." In *Altes im Neuen: Festschrift Theodor Göllner zum 65. Geburtstag*, 47–62. Tutzing: Hans Schneider.

———. 1996. *Arabische Musik und Notenschrift*. Münchner Veröffentlichungen zur Musikgeschichte, Vol. 53. Tutzing: Hans Schneider.

———. 1997. *Die Rolle der Frau im Musikleben Omans*. Tutzing: Hans Schneider.

Marks, Paul F. 1973. *Bibliography of Literature Concerning Yemenite-Jewish Music*. Detroit: Information Coordinators.

Morris, M. 1983. "Some Preliminary Remarks on a Collection of Poems and Songs of the Batahirah." *Journal of Oman Studies* 6(1):129–44.

Ogger, Thomas. 1987. *Maqam segah/sikah: Vergleich der Kunstmusik des Irak und des Iran anhand eines maqam-Modells*. Hamburg: Verlag der Musikalienhandlung K. D. Wagner.

Poché, Christian. 1978. "Zikr [Dhikr] and Musicology." *World of Music* 20(1):59–71.

———. 1981. "Rythme impair et danse boiteuse." *Cahiers Musique Culture Mémoire:* 97–101.

———. 1983. *Introduction à la musique de Djibouti*. Paris: Radio-France-Internationale, Centre de Documentation Africaine.

———. 1984. "Qanbūs." In *The New Grove Dictionary of Musical Instruments*, 3:168–169. London: Macmillan.

———. 1992. "Lyre of the Arab Gulf: Historical Roots, Geographical Link, and Social Context." *al-Ma'thurat al sh"biyyah* 27:7–17.

———. 1994a. "Pays du Golfe: De la frénésie sociale à l'accélération musicale." In *Adib*, ed. Y. Gonzales-Quijani and R. Boustani. Paris: IMA. (CD-ROM.)

———. 1994b. "De l'homme parfait . . . l'expressivité musicale: Courants esthétiques arabes au XXe siècle." *Cahiers de Musiques Traditionnelles* 7:59–74.

Pratt, Mary Louise. 1992. *Imperial Eyes: Travel Writing and Transculturation*. London: Routledge.

Ratzaby, Yehuda. 1986. "Yemenite *Qasid* Songs." *Yuval* 5:169–191.

al-Rifa'i, Hessa. 1985. "Sea Chanteys of Kuwait." *Arabian Studies* 7:88–95.

Rihani, Amin. 1930. "The Dance." In *Around the Coasts of Arabia*. Boston: Houghton Mifflin

Rossi, Ettore. 1939. *L'arabo parlato a Sanaa: Grammatica, testi, lessico*. Rome: Istituto per l'Oriente.

Røvsing-Olsen, Poul. 1964. "Enregistrements faits à Kuwait et à Bahrein." In *Les colloques de Wegimont, 4, 1958–1960, Ethnomusicologie III*, 137–170. Paris: Les Belles Lettres.

———. 1967. "La musique africaine dans le Golfe Persique." *Journal of the International Folk Music Council* 19:28–36.

———. 1974. "Six Versions de Taqsim en Maqam Rast." *Studia Instrumentorum Musicae Popularis* 3:197–202.

———. 1978. "The Vocal Bourdon in the Arab Gulf." *Anthropologiska Studier* 25–26:12–20.

———. 1980. "Arabian Gulf." In *The New Grove Dictionary of Music and Musicians*, 1:513–514. London: Macmillan.

al-Saud, Noura bint Muḥammad, al-Jawharah Muḥammad al-'Anqari, and Madeha Muḥammad al-'Atroush, eds. 1989. *Abha, Bilad Asir: Southwestern Region of the Kingdom of Saudi Arabia*. Riyadh: Published by the editors.

Schuyler, Philip. 1990. "Hearts and Minds: Three Attitudes towards Performance Practice and Music Theory in the Yemen Arab Republic." *Ethnomusicology* 34:1–18.

———. 1990–91. "Music and Tradition in Yemen." *Asian Music* 22(1):51–71.

Serjeant, Robert B. 1951. *South Arabian Poetry and Prose of Ḥaḍramawt*. London: Taylor's Foreign Press.

Sharvit, Uri. 1980. "The Role of Music in the Yemenite *Heder*." *Israel Studies in Musicology* 2:33–49.

Shawqi, Yusuf. 1994. *Dictionary of Traditional Music in Oman*. English ed., rev. and expanded by Dieter Christensen. Intercultural Music Studies, Vol. 6. Wilhelmshaven: F. Noetzel.

Shiloah, Amnon. 1972. "The *Simsimiyah*: A Stringed Instrument of the Red Sea Area." *Asian Music* 4(1):15.

———. 1980. "Arab Music: II. Folk Music." In *The New Grove Dictionary of Music and Musicians*, 1:526–539. London: Macmillan.

———. 1991. "The Jewish Yemenite Tradition: A Case Study of Two Women Poet-Musicians." In *Tradition and Its Future in Music*, 447–450. Osaka: Mita.

Sillamy, Jean-Claude. 1987. *La musique dans l'ancien Orient, ou, La théorie musicale suméro-babylonienne*. 2 vols. Ajaccio: Jean Claude Sillamy.

———. 1991. *Le principe de la modulation dans le fragment babylonien d'Ur: U.7/80 (XVIIIème siècle av. J.C.) (à partir d'un instrument de l'époque non identifié, le "gis za—mi")*. Ajaccio: Jean-Claude Sillamy.

Sowayan, Saad Abdullah. 1982. "The Prosodic Relationship of Nabati Poetry to Classical Arabic Poetry." *Journal of Arabic Linguistics* 8:72–79.

———. 1985. *Nabati Poetry: The Oral Poetry of Arabia*. Berkeley and Los Angeles: University of California Press.

———. 1989. "'Tonight My Gun Is Loaded': Poetic Dueling in Arabia." *Oral Tradition* 4(1–2):151–173.

Staub, Shalom. 1979. *A Review of the Literature and a Selective Bibliography of Yemenite Jewish Folklore and Ethnology with a Special Emphasis on Dance and Music, 1893–1978*. n.p.

Stone, Ruth. 1989. "Sound and Rhythm in Corporate Ritual in Saudi Arabia." In *Music and the Experience of God*, ed. Mary Collins et al. Edinburgh: Clark.

Tayash, Fahad. 1988. "Sameri Tradition and Zār Dance in Saudi Arabia." *Al-Ma'ṯūrāt al-Sha'biyya* 9:23–36.

Touma, Habib Hassan. 1975. *Die Musik der Araber*. Wilhelmshaven: Heinrichshofen.

———. 1977. "Le fidjri, forme de chant caractéristique des pêcheurs de perles de Bahrein." *World of Music* 19(3–4):128–132.

———. 1995. *The Music of the Arabs*. Portland, Ore.: Amadeus.

Wikan, Unni. 1982. *Behind the Veil: Women in Oman*. Baltimore: University of Chicago Press.

Wright, Owen. 1978. *The Modal System of Arab and Persian Music A.D. 1250–1300*. London: Oxford University Press.

———. 1992. "Segah: An Historical Outline." In *Regionale maqam-Traditionen in Geschichte und Gegenwart*, 480–509. Berlin: Humboldt-Universität, Institut für Musikwissenschaft und Musikerziehung.

———. 1995. "'Abd Al-Qadir Al-Maraghi and 'Ali B. Muhammad Bina'i: Two Fifteenth-Century Examples of Notation. Part 2: Commentary." *Bulletin, School of Oriental and African Studies* 58(1):17–39.

Yammine, Habib. 1991. "Correspondances entre la musique tribale et la musique citadine (Sana) dans la région des hauts plateaux yéménites." In *Le chant arabo-andalou: Colloque, Lille, 1991*, 119–128. Paris: Harmattan.

———. 1995. "Les hommes de tribu et leur musique (Hauts plateaux yéménites, vallée d'al-Ahjur)." Ph.D. dissertation, Université de Paris X-Nanterre.

ARMENIA

At'ayan, Robert A. 1999. *The Armenian Neume System of Notation*, trans. V. N. Nersessian. Richmond, Surrey, England: Curzon.

Chabrier, Jean-Claude. 1986–1987. "Remarques sur l'interprétation du système de Limončean par Komitas Vardapet." *Revue des Études Arméniennes* 20:507–20.

Dowsett, Charles, 1997. *Sayat'-Nova: An Eighteenth-Century Troubadour: A Literary and Biographical Study*. Leuven: Peeters.

Ertlbauer, A. 1985. *Geschichte und Theorie der einstimmigen armenischen Kirchenmusik: eine Kritik der bisherigen Forschung*. Vienna.

Kazandjian, Sirvart. 1984. *Les origines de la musique arménienne*. Paris: Éditions Astrid.

Kerovpyan, A. 1991. "Les *charakan* (*troparia*) et l'octoéchos arménien selon le *charaknots* (*tropologion* arménien) édité en 1875." In *Aspects de la musique liturgique au Moyen-Age*, ed. Christian Meyer, 93–123. Paris: Creaphis.

———. 1995. "Mündliche und schriftliche Überlieferung in der Musik der Armenier." In *Armenien: Wiederentdeckung einer alten Kulturlandschaft*, ed. K. Platt, 445–449. Bochum.

———. 1996. "Armenian Liturgical Chant: The System and Reflections on the Present Situation." *St. Nersess Theological Review* 1:25–42.

———. 1999. *Manuel de notation musicale arménienne moderne*. Vienna.

———. 1998. *Armenian Sacred and Folk Music*, trans. Edward Gulbekian. Richmond, Surrey: Curzon.

Komitas, Vardapet. 1986–1987. "La musique religieuse arménienne au XIXème siècle," trans. Léon Ketcheyan. *Revue des Études Arméniennes* 20:497–506.

Moses of Khoren. 1978. *History of the Armenians*, trans. Robert W. Thomson. Cambridge, Mass.: Harvard University Press.

Nersessian, Vrej, ed. 1978. *Essays on Armenian Music*. London: Kahn and Averill for the Institute of Armenian Music.

Sarafian, Krikor. 1959. *The Armenian Apostolic Church: Her Ceremonies, Sacraments, Main Feasts, and Prominent Saints*. Fresno, Calif.: Sunday School Council of the Armenian Diocese of California.

KURDISTAN

Allison, Christine. 1996. "Old and New Traditions in Badinan." In *Kurdish Culture and Identity*, ed. Philip G. Kreryenbroek and Christine Allison, 29–47. London and Atlantic Highlands, N. J.: Zed.

Blum, Stephen, and A. Hassanpour. 1996. "'The Morning of Freedom Rose Up.' Kurdish Popular Song and the Exigencies of Cultural Survival." *Popular Music* 15:325–43.

Bruinessen, Martin van. 1992. *Agha, Shaikh, and State: The Social and Political Structures of Kurdistan*. London: Zed.

Christensen, Dieter. 1961. "Kurdische Brautlieder aus dem Vilayet Hakkari. Süd-Ost Türkei." *Journal of the International Folk Music Council* 13:70–72.

———. 1963. "Tanzlieder der Hakkari-Kurden." *Jahrbuch für Musikalische Volks- und Völkerkunde* 1:11–47.

———. 1967a. "Die Musik der Kurden." *Mitteilungen der Berliner Gesellschaft für Anthropologie, Ethnologie, und Urgeschichte* 1:113–119.

———. 1967b. "Zur Mehrstimmigkeit in kurdischen Wechselgesängen." In *Festschrift für Walter Wiora zum 30. Dezember 1966*, ed. Ludwig Finscher and Christoph-Hellmut Mahling, 571–577. Kassel: Bärenreiter.

———. 1975. "Musical Style and Social Context in Kurdish Songs." *Asian Music* 6:1–6.

During, Jean. 1989. *Musique et mystique dans les traditions de l'Iran*. Paris: Institut Français de Recherche en Iran; Leuven: Peeters.

Kendal, Nezan. 1979. "Kurdish Music and Dance." *World of Music* 21(1):19–32.

Tatsumura, A. 1980. "Music and Culture of the Kurds." *Senri Ethnological Studies* 5:75–93.

TURKEY

Ahrens, Christian. 1970. *Instrumentale Musikstile an der osttürkische Schwarzmeerküste, eine vergleichende Untersuchung der Spielpraxis davul-zurna, kemençe und tulum*. Munich: Kommissionsverlag K. Renner.

———, et al. 1984. "Weine meine Laute . . ." In *Gedenkschrift Kurt Reinhard*, ed. Christian Ahrens, Rudolf Maria Brandl, and Felix Hoerburger, 37–56. Regensburg: Laaber-Verlag.

Akdemir, Hayrettin. 1992. *Die neue türkische Musik*. Berlin: Hitit-Verlag.

Aksoy, Bülent. 1989. "Is the Question of the Origin of Turkish Music Not Redundant?" *Turkish Musical Quarterly* 2(4):1–8.

And, Metin. 1959. "Dances of Anatolian Turkey." *Dance Perspectives* 3:3–77.

———. 1976. *A Pictorial History of Turkish Dancing: From Folk Dancing to Whirling Dervishes—Belly Dancing to Ballet*. Ankara: Dost Yayınları.

———. 1986a. "Opera and Ballet in Modern Turkey." In *The Transformation of Turkish Culture: The Atatürk Legacy*, ed. Günsel Renda and C. Max Kortepeter. Princeton, N. J.: Princeton University Press.

———. 1986b. "Les rituels et les danses extatiques mystiques de la Confrérie des Bektachis et des Alevis d'Anatolie." In *Transe, chamanisme, possession: De la fête à l'extase; Actes des deuxièmes rencontres internationales sur la fête et la communication, Nice Acropolis, 24–28 avril 1985*. Nice: Éditions Serre, Nice-Animation.

———. 1987. *Culture, Performance, and Communication in Turkey*. Performance in Culture, 4. Tokyo: Institute for the Study of Languages and Cultures of Asia.

Andrews, Walter. 1976. *An Introduction to Ottoman Poetry*. Chicago: Bibliotheca Islamica.

———. 1985. *Poetry's Voice, Society's Song: Ottoman Lyric Poetry*. Seattle: University of Washington Press.

Andrews, Walter, and Irene Markoff. 1987. "Poetry, the Arts, and Group Ethos in the Ideology of the Ottoman Empire." *Edebiyat* 1(1):28–70.

Bartók, Béla. 1976. *Turkish Folk Music from Asia Minor*, ed. Benjamin Suchoff. Princeton, N. J.: Princeton University Press.

Başgöz, Ilhan. 1952. "Turkish Folk Stories about the Lives of Minstrels." *Journal of American Folklore* 65:331–339.

———. 1967. "Dream Motif and Shamanistic Initiation." *Asian Folklore Studies* 1:1–18.

———. 1972. "Folklore Studies and Nationalism in Turkey." *Journal of the Folklore Institute* 9:162–176.

Beken, Münir Nurettin, and Karl Signell. In press. "Confirming, Delaying, and Deceptive Elements in Turkish Improvisations." *Proceedings of the ICTM Maqam Study Group*. Istanbul: Istanbul Technical University.

Bellah, Robert. 1958. "Religious Aspects of Modernization in Japan and Turkey." *American Journal of Sociology* 64:1–5.

Berkes, Niyazi, ed. 1981. *Turkish Nationalism and Western Civilization: Selected Essays of Ziya Gökalp*, trans. and ed. N. Berkes. Westport, Conn.: Greenwood.

Birge, John Kingsley. 1937. *The Bektashi Order of Dervishes*. London: Luzac.

Boratav, Pertev Naili. 1973. "La littérature populaire turque contemporaine." *Turcica* 5:47–67.

Brands, Horst Wilfrid. 1978. "Aytîş-Deyişme, Formen des Dichterwettstreits bei den Türkvölkern." In *Studies in Turkish Folklore*, ed. Ilhan Başgöz and Mark Glazer. Bloomington: [Indiana University].

Campbell, Richard G. 1968. *Zur Typologie der Schalenlanghalslaute*. Collection d'études musicologiques/Sammlung musikwissenschaftlicher Abhandlungen, 47. Strasbourg, Baden-Baden: Heitz.

Christensen, Dieter. 1963. "Tanzlieder der Hakkari-Kurden." *Jahrbuch für musikalische Volks- und Völkerkunde* 1:11–47.

Eberhard, Wolfram. 1955. *Minstrel Tales from Southeastern Turkey*. Berkeley and Los Angeles: University of California Press.

Eliade, Mircea. 1974. *Shamanism: Archaic Techniques of Ecstasy*. Princeton. N. J.: Princeton University Press.

Emsheimer, E. 1956. "Singing Contests in Central Asia." *International Folk Music Journal* 8:26–29.

Erdener, Yıdlıray. 1987. "Dueling Singers: Strategies and Interaction Processes among Turkish Minstrels." Ph.D. dissertation, Indiana University.

———. 1995. *The Song Contests of Turkish Minstrels: Improvised Poetry Sung to Traditional Music*. New York: Garland.

Erguner, Ahmed. 1990. "Alla Turca—Alla Franca: Les enjeux de la musique turque." *Cahiers de Musique Traditionnelles* 3:45–56.

Farmer, Henry G. 1937. *Turkish Instruments of Music in the Seventeenth Century*. Glasgow: Civic.

———. 1966. *Islam*. Musikgeschichte in Bildern, Vol. 3. Leipzig: Deutscher Verlag für Musik.

Feldman, Walter. 1990. "Jewish Liturgical Music in Turkey." *Turkish Music Quarterly* 3(1):10–13.

———. 1990–1991. "Cultural Authority and Authenticity in the Turkish Repertoire." *Asian Music* 22(1):73–111.

———. 1992. "Musical Genres and Zikir of the Sunni Tarikats of Istanbul." In *The Dervish Lodge: Architecture, Art, and Sufism in Ottoman Turkey*, ed. Raymond Lifchez, 187–202. Berkeley and Los Angeles: University of California Press.

———. 1993. "Ottoman Sources on the Development of the Taksîm." *Yearbook for Traditional Music* 25:1–28.

———. 1996. *Music of the Ottoman Court*. Intercultural Music Studies, 10. Berlin: International Institute for Traditional Music.

Finnegan, Ruth. 1979. *Oral Poetry*. Cambridge: Cambridge University Press.

Fisher, C. G., and A. W. Fisher. 1987. "Topkapı Sarayı in the Mid-Seventeenth Century: Bobovsk's Description." *Archivium Ottomanicum* 10:5–81.

Greve, Martin. 1995. *Die Europäisierung orientalischer Kunstmusik in der Türkei*. Frankfurt am Main: Peter Lang.

Hall, Leslie. 1989. "The Turlish *Fasıl*: Selected Repertoire." Ph.D. dissertation, University of Toronto.

Halman, Talât Sait, and Metin And. 1983. *Mevlana Celaleddin Rumi and the Whirling Dervishes.* Istanbul: Dost Yayınları.

Haq, Sirajul. 1944. "Samā' and Raqṣ of the Darwishes." *Islamic Culture* 18.2:111–130.

Inalcik, Halil. 1973. *The Ottoman Empire: The Classical Age 1300–1600.* New York: Praeger.

Jäger, Ralf Martin. 1996a. *Türkische Kunstmusik und ihre handschriftlichen Quellen aus dem 19. Jahrhundert.* Schriften zur Musikwissenschaft aus Münster, 7. Eisenach: K. D. Wagner.

———. 1996b. *Ktalog der hamparsum-notası-Manuskripte im Archiv des Konservatoriums der Universität Istanbul.* Schriften zur Musikwissenschaft aus Münster, 8. Eisenach: K. D. Wagner.

James, D. W. 1946. "Some Turkish Folk Dances." *Dancing Times* (October):14–15.

Karpat, Kemal. 1963. "The People's Houses in Turkey: Establishment and Growth." *Middle East Journal* 17:55–67.

———. 1976. *The Gecekondu: Rural Migration and Urbanization.* Cambridge: Cambridge University Press.

Kusić, Dane. 1996. "Discourse on Three Teravih Namazı-s in Istanbul." Ph.D. dissertation, University of Maryland.

Lewis, Bernard. 1968. *The Emergence of Modern Turkey.* London: Oxford University Press.

Mardin, Serif. 1984. "A Note on the Transformation of Religious Symbols." *Turcica* 16:119–120.

Markoff, Irene. 1986a. "Musical Theory, Performance and the Contemporary Bağlama Specialist in Turkey." Ph.D. dissertation, University of Washington, Seattle.

———. 1986. "The Role of Expressive Culture in the Demystification of a Secret Sect in Islam: The Case of the Alevis in Turkey." *World of Music* 28(3):42–45.

———. 1990–1991. "The Ideology of Musical Practice and the Professional Turkish Folk Musician: Tempering the Creative Impulse." *Asian Music* 22(1):129–145.

———. 1993. "Music, Saints, and Ritual: Samā' and the Alevis of Turkey." In *Manifestations of Sainthood in Islam*, ed. Grace Martin Smith and Carl. W. Ernst, 95–110. Istanbul: Isis.

———. 1995. "Introduction to Sufi Music and Ritual in Turkey." *MESA Bulletin* 29(2):157–160.

Mélikoff, Irène. 1974. "Le problème Kızılbaş." *Turcica* 6:49–67.

O'Connell, John M. 1996. "*Alaturka* Revisited: Style as History in Turkish Vocal Performance." Ph.D. dissertation, University of California Los Angeles.

Okyay, Erdoğan. 1976. *Melodische Gestaltelemente in den türkischen "Kırık hava."* Ankara: s.n.

Oransay, Gültekin. 1957. "Das Tonsystem der türkei-türkischen Kunstmusik." *Musikforschung* 10:250–264.

———. 1964. *Die traditionelle türkische Kunstmusik.* Ankara: Küğ-Veröffentlichung.

———. 1966. *Die melodische Linie und der Begriff Makam der traditionellen türkischen Kunstmusik vom 15. bis 19. Jahrhundert.* Ankara: Küğ-Veröffentlichung.

Öztürkmen, Arzu. 1993. "Folklore and Nationalism in Turkey." Ph.D. dissertation, University of Pennsylvania.

———. 1995. "The Alevi *Cem* Ritual and the Nationalization of *Semah* Dances." In *Dance and Ritual: Proceedings from the Eighteenth Symposium of the ICTM Study Group on Ethnochoreology.* Skierniewice.

———. 1994. "The Role of the People's Houses in the Making of National Culture in Turkey." *New Perspectives on Turkey* 11:159–181.

———. 1994. "Folk Dance and Nationalism in Turkey." In *Seventeenth Symposium of the Study Group on Ethnochoreology: 1992 Proceedings*, 83–86. Nafplion: Peloponnesian Folklore Foundation.

Picken, Laurence. 1975. *Folk Musical Instruments of Turkey.* London, New York, and Toronto: Oxford University Press.

Popescu-Judetz, Eugenia. 1981. *Studies in Oriental Arts: Dimitri Cantemir's Theory of Turkish Art Music.* Pittsburgh, Pa.: Institute of Folk Arts.

Radloff, V. 1885. *Proben der Volksliteratur der Türkischen Stamme*, Vol. 5. St. Petersburg: Akademie der Wissenschaft.

Reiche, Jens Peter. 1970. "Stilelemente südtürkischer Davul-Zurna-Stücke." *Jahrbuch für Musikalische Volks- und Völkerkunde* 5:9–54.

Reinhard, Kurt. 1956. "Zustand und Wandel der bäuerlichen Musik in der türkischen Provinz Adana." *Sociologus*, Neue Folge, 6:68–78.

———. 1956. "Types of Turkmenian Songs in Turkey." *Journal of the International Folk Music Council* 9:49–54.

———. 1960. "Ein türkischer Tanzliedtyp und seine außertürkischen Parallelen." *Baessler-Archiv*, Neue Folge, 8:131–169.

———. 1961. "Trommeltänze aus der Süd-Türkei." *Journal of the International Folk Music Council* 13:19–26.

———. 1961. "Zur Variantenbildung im türkischen Volkslied, dargestellt an einer Hirtenweise." In *Festschrift Heinrich Besseler zum 60. Geburtstag*, 21–34. Leipzig: Deutscher Verlag für Musik.

———. 1962. *Türkische Musik.* Berlin: Museum für Völkerkunde.

———. 1966. "Türkische Musik." In *Die Musik in Geschichte und Gegenwart* 13:954–968. Kassel: Bärenreiter.

———. 1966. "Musik am Schwarzen Meer: Erste Ergebnisse einer Forschungsreise in die Nordost-Türkei." *Jahrbuch für Musikalische Volks- und Völkerkunde* 2:9–58.

———. 1967. "Die Gegenwärtige Praxis des Epengesanges in der Türkei." In *Grazer und Münchener Balkanologische Studien: Beiträge zur Kenntnis Südosteuropas und des Nahen Orients*, 83–96. Munich: Trofenik.

———. 1967. "Die Quellensituation der türkischen Kunstmusik: Gedanken zur Frage mündlicher und schriftlicher Tradition und zum Problem Improvisation-Komposition." In *Festschrift Walter Wiora*, 578–582. Kassel: Bärenreiter.

———. 1969. "Cultivation and Encouragement of Traditional Music in Turkey: Creating a Wider Interest in Traditional Music." In *International Institute for Comparative Music Studies and Documentation, Berlin, 1969*, 160–169. Berlin.

———. 1970. "Strukturanalyse einer Hymne des türkischen Komponisten Itrî." In *Festschrift Walter Graf*, 158–177. Vienna: H. Böhlau.

———. 1972. "Grundlagen und Ergebnisse der Erforschung türkischer Musik." *Acta Musicologica* 44:266–280.

———. 1973a. "Vorderer Orient" and "Die Türkei im 19. Jahrhundert." In *Musikkulturen Asiens, Afrikas und Ozeaniens im 19. Jahrhundert*, ed. Robert Günther, 17–48. Regensburg: Gustave Bosse.

———. 1973b. "Musikalische Gestaltungsprinzipien der *âyın*, dargestellt an der anonymen Komposition im Makam pençgâh." In *Uluslararası Mevlâna Semineri*, 315–333. Ankara: Türkiye İş Bankası Kültür Yayınları.

———. 1974. "Die türkische Doppelklarinette çifte." *Baessler-Archiv*, Neue Folge, 22:139–163.

———. 1975. "Über die Beziehungen zwischen byzantinischer und türkischer Musik." In *Musica Antiqua. 4, Acta Scientifica*, 623–632. Bydgoszcz.

———. 1975. "Die Musikpflege türkischer Nomaden." *Zeitschrift für Ethnologie* 100:115–124.

———. 1976. "Über einige Beziehungen zwischen türkischer und griechischer Volksmusik." *Beiträge zue Ethnomusikologie* 4:9–18.

———. 1978. "Albert Bobovsky's Aufzeichnungen türkischer Musik als geschichtliche Quelle." In *Musica Antiqua* 5, *Acta Scientifica*, 373–382. Bydgoszcz.

———. 1979. "Spieltechnik und Musik der türkischen Kurzoboe mey." *Studia Instrumentorum Musicae Popularis* 6:111–119.

———. 1980a. "Turkey." In *The New Grove Dictionary of Music and Musicians,* 19:165–179. London: Macmillan.

———. 1980b. "Türkei." In *Außereuropäische Musik in Einzeldarstellungen*, 165–179. Munich: Deutscher Taschenbuchverlag; Kassel: Bärenreiter.

———. 1981a. "Mozarts Rezeption türkischer Musik." In *Bericht über den Internationalen Musikwissenschaftlichen Kongress, Berlin 1974*, 518–523. Kassel: Bärenreiter.

———. 1981b. "Turkish Miniatures as Sources of Music History." In *Music in East and West: Essays in Honor of Walter Kaufmann*, 143–166. New York.

———. 1984a. "Gestalten südtürkischer Totenklagen." In *"Weine, meine Laute . . ." Gedenkschrift für Kurt Reinhard*, ed. Christian Ahrens, Rudolf Maria Brandl, and Felix Hoerburger. Regensburg: Laaber-Verlag.

———. 1984b. "Das Na't des İtrî und seine Versionen." *Jahrbuch für Musikalische Volks- und Völkerkunde* 11:9–13.

Reinhard, Kurt, and Ursula Reinhard. 1968. *Auf der Fiedel mein . . . Volkslieder von der osttürkischen Schwarzmeerküste*. Veröffentlichungen des Museums für Völkerkunde Berlin, Neue Folge, Vol. 14. Berlin: Museum für Völkerkunde.

Reinhard, Kurt, and Ursula Reinhard.. 1969. *Turquie: Les traditions musicales*. Paris: Buchet-Chastel.

Reinhard, Kurt, and Ursula Reinhard. 1983. "Volksmusikelemente in der Türkischen Kunstmusik." In *II. Milletlerarası Türk Folklor Kongresi Bildiriler* 3:225–239. Ankara: Kültür ve Turizm Bakanlığı.

Reinhard, Kurt, and Ursula Reinhard. 1984. *Musik der Türkei*. 2 vols. Wilhelmshaven: Heinrichshofen.

Reinhard, Ursula. 1965. *Vor seinen Häusern eine Weide . . . Volksliedtexte aus der Süd-Türkei*. Veröffentlichungen des Museums für Völkerkunde Berlin, Neue Folge, Vol. 8. Berlin: Museum für Völkerkunde.

———. 1985. "Konstanz und Wandel im bağlama-Spiel und Gesang türkischer âşık und ihrer Lieder." *Studia Instrumentorum Musicae Popularis* 8:86–93.

———. 1985. "Das Musikleben in osmanischer Zeit." In *Türkische Kunst und Kultur aus osmanischer Zeit*, 1:159–163 and 213–222. Recklinghausen: A. Bongers.

———. 1987. "Westliche Einflüsse auf das türkische Musikleben einst und heute." In *Mozaik: Türkische Kultur in Berlin*, 37–44. Berlin: Arenhövel.

———. (1998, in press.) "Musik am türkischen Hof des 17. Jahrhunderts." Lecture, Akademie der Wissenschaften in Göttingen, June.

———. 1990. "The Veils Are Lifted." In *Music, Gender, and Culture*, ed. Marcia Herndon and Susanne Ziegler, 101–111. Wilhelmshaven: Florian Noetzel Verlag.

———. 1994a. "Epische Gesänge in der Türkei am Beispiel des Köroğlu-Epos." In *Historische Volksmusikforschung*, ed. Doris Stockmann and Annette Erler, 157–170. Göttingen: Edition Re.

———. 1994b. "Musik am türkischen Hof des 17. Jahrhunderts." In *Höfische Kultur in Südosteuropa: Abhandlungen der Akademie der Wissenschaften in Göttingen*, ed. Reinhard Lauer and Hans Georg Majer, 174–204. Göttingen: Vandenhoeck und Ruprecht.

———. 1997a. "Eine alte nomadische Singtechnik in der Türkei und auf dem Balkan und ihre instrumentale Wiederbelebung." In *Historical Studies on Folk and Traditional Music*, ed. Doris Stockmann and Jens Henrik Koudal, 167–176. Copenhagen: Danish Folklore Archives.

———. 1997b. "Dichtersänger im Nordosten der Türkei, in Armenien und Aserbaidschan; Ein Vergleich." *Jahrbuch für Musikalische Volks- und Völkerkunde* 16:71–92.

———. 2001. "Die Musik der Alewiten." In *Aleviler/Alewiten*, ed. Ismail Engin and Erhard Franz, 199–220. Hamburg: Deutsches Orient-Institut.

Reinhard, Ursula, and Tiago De Oliveria Pinto. 1989. *Sänger und Poeten mit der Laute, Türkische Âşık und Ozan*. Veröffentlichungen des Museums für Völkerkunde Berlin, Abteilung Musikethnologie Berlin (with 2 cassettes). Berlin: Museum für Völkerkunde, Dietrich Reimer Verlag.

Robins, Kevin, and David Morley. 1996. "Almanci, Yabanci." *Cultural Studies* 10(2):248–254.

Roemer, Hans R. 1990. "The Qizilbash Turcomans: Founders and Victims of the Safavid Theocracy." In *Intellectual Studies on Islam: Essays Written in Honor of Martin B. Dickson*, ed. Michel M. Mazzaoui and Vera B. Moreen, 27–39. Salt Lake City: University of Utah Press.

Saygun, Adnan. 1948. *Les divers aspects de la musique turque*. Ankara.

———. 1950. "Des danses d'Anatolie et de leur caractère rituel." *Journal of the International Folk Music Council* 2:10–14.

———. 1976. *Béla Bartók's Folk Music Research in Turkey*, ed. László Vikár. Budapest: Akadémiai Kiadó.

Seroussi, Edwin. 1989a. *Mizimrat Qedem: The Life and Music of R. Isaac Algazi from Turkey*. Jerusalem: Renanot-Institute for Jewish Music.

———. 1989b. "The Turkish *Makam* in the Musical Culture of the Ottoman Jews: Sources and Examples." *Israeli Studies in Musicology* 5:55–68.

———. 1991. "The *Peşrev* as a Vocal Genre in Ottoman Hebrew Sources." *Turkish Music Quarterly* 4(3):1–9.

Sezgin, Paméla J. Dorn. 1994. "*Hakhamim*, Dervishes, and Court Singers: The Relationship of Ottoman Jewish Music to Classical Turkish Music." In *The Jews of the Ottoman Empire*, ed. Avigdor Levy, 585–632. Princeton, N. J.: Darwin.

Shaw, Stanford. 1976–1977. *History of the Ottoman Empire and Modern Turkey*. 2 vols. Cambridge: Cambridge University Press.

Shiloah, Amnon. 1992. *Jewish Musical Traditions*. Detroit: Wayne State University Press.

Sieglin, Angelika. 1975. *Untersuchungen in den Peşrev des Tanburi Cemil Bey*. Hamburg: Karl Dieter Wagner.

———. 1984. *Instrumentalkompositionen der türkischen Kunstmusik in ihrer Beziehung zum Makam*. Hamburg: K. D. Wagner.

Signell, Karl L. 1977. *Makam: Modal Practice in Turkish Art Music*. Seattle: Asian Music.

———. 1988. "Mozart and the Mehter." *Turkish Music Quarterly* 1(1):34–36.

Stokes, Martin. 1992. *The Arabesk Debate: Music and Musicians in Modern Turkey*. Oxford: Oxford University Press.

Van Bruinessen, Martin. 1996. "Kurds, Turks, and the Alevi Revival in Turkey." *Middle East Report* 200:7–10

Wannig, Klaus-Detlev. 1980. *Der Dichter Karaca Oğlan. Studien zur türkischen Liebeslyrik*. Studien zur Sprache, Kultur und Geschichte der Türkvölker, 1. Freiburg: Schwarz.

Wright, Owen. 1988. "Aspects of Historical Change in the Turkish Classical Repertoire." *Musica Asiatica* 5:1–108.

———. 1990. "Çargah in Turkish Classical Music." *Bulletin of the School of Oriental and African Studies (University of London)* 53:224–244.

———. 1992a. *Demetrius Cantemir: The Collection of Notations*. Musicology Series, 1. London: School of Oriental and African Studies (University of London).

———. 1992b. *Words without Songs: A Musicological Study on an Early Ottoman Anthology and Its Precursors*. Musicology Series, 2. London: School of Oriental and African Studies (University of London).

Yalman, Nur. 1969. "Islamic Reform and the Mystic Tradition in Eastern Turkey." *European Journal of Sociology* 10(1):41–60.

Yekta Bey, Raouf. 1922. "La musique turque." In *Encyclopédie de la musique*, ed. Albert Lavignac, 1(5):2045–3064. Paris: C. Delagrave.

Zimmermann, Cornelia-Kalyoncu. 1985. *Deutsche Musiker in der Türkei im 20. Jahrhundert*. Frankfurt am Main, Bern, and New York: Peter Lang.

IRAN

Albright, Charlotte F. 1976. "The Music of Professional Musicians of Northwest Iran (Azerbaijan)." Ph.D. dissertation, University of Washington.

———. 1976. "The Azerbaijani *'Ashiq* and His Performance of a *Dastan*." *Iranian Studies* 9:220–247.

———. 1988. "The Azerbaijani 'Ashiq: A Musician's Adaptations to a Changing Society." *Edebiyat* n.s. 2(1–2):205–217.

Barkeshli, M. 1963. *La musique traditionnelle de l'Iran*. Tehran.

Başgöz, Ilhan. 1952. "Turkish Folk Stories about the Lives of Minstrels." *Journal of American Folklore* 65:331–39.

Blum, Stephen. 1972a. "Musics in Contact: The Cultivation of Oral Repertoires in Meshhed, Iran." Ph.D. dissertation, University of Illinois.

———. 1972b. "The Concept of the *'Asheq* in Northern Khorasan." *Asian Music* 4(1):27–47.

———. 1978. "Changing Roles of Performers in Meshhed and Bojnurd, Iran." In *Eight Urban Musical Cultures*, ed. Bruno Nettl, 19–95. Urbana: University of Illinois Press.

———. 1996. "Musical Questions and Answers in Iranian Xorāsān." *EM: Annuario degli Archivi di Etnomusicologia, Accademia Nazionale di Santa Cecilia* 4:145–63.

Boratav, Pertev Naili. 1965. "L'épopée et la 'hikâye.'" In *Philologiae Turcicae Fundamenta*, 2:11–44. Wiesbaden: Franz Steiner.

Borel, François. 1986. "La vièle, le tambour, et les génies du mal." In *Le mal et la douleur*, ed. J. Hainard and R. Kaehr, 199–205. Neuchâtel: Musée d'Ethnographie.

Caferoğlu, Ahmet. 1965. "Die Aserbaidschanische Literatur." In *Philologiae Turcicae Fundamenta*, 2:635–698. Wiesbaden: Franz Steiner.

Caron, Nelly. 1975. "The Ta'zieh: The Sacred Theatre of Iran." *World of Music* 17(4):3–10.

Caron, Nelly, and Dariouche Safvate. 1966. *Iran: Les traditions musicales*. Paris: Buchet/Chastel.

Chadwick, Nora K., and Victor Zhirmunsky. 1969. *Oral Epics of Central Asia*. Cambridge: Cambridge University Press.

Chelkowski, Peter J., ed. 1979. *Ta'ziye: Ritual and Drama in Iran*. New York: New York University Press.

———. 1991. "Popular Entertainment, Media, and Social Change in Twentieth-Century Iran." In *The Cambridge History of Iran*. Vol. 7, *From Nadir Shah to the Islamic Republic*, ed. Peter Avery, Gavin Hambly, and Charles Melville, 765–814. Cambridge: Cambridge University Press.

Chodzko, Alexander. 1842. *Specimens of the Popular Poetry of Persia*. London: Oriental Translation Fund.

De Warren, Robert, and Peter Williams. 1973. "Discovery in Persia." *Dance and Dancers* (January):28–32.

During, Jean. 1984. *La musique iranienne: Tradition et évolution*. Paris and Tehran: Institut Français d'Iranologie de Téhéran.

———. 1988a. *Musique et extase: L'audition mystique dans la tradition soufie*. Paris: Albin Michel.

———. 1988b. "Emotion and Trance: Musical Exorcism in Baluchestan." In *Cultural Parameters of Iranian Musical Expression*, ed. M. Caton and N. Siegel, 36–46. Redondo Beach, Calif.: Institute of Persian Performing Arts.

———. 1989a. *Musique et mystique dans les traditions de l'Iran*. Paris: Institut Français de Recherches en Iran-Peeters.

———. 1989b. "Les musiques d'Iran et du Moyen-Orient face à l'acculturation occidentale." In *Entre l'Iran et l'Occident: Adaptation et assimilation des idées et techniques occidentales en Iran*, ed. Yann Richard, 195–223. Paris: Éditions de la Maison des Sciences de l'Homme.

———. 1990. "Der Mythos der Simorg." *Spektrum Iran* 3(3):3–19.

———. 1991. *Le répertoire-modèle de la musique persane: Radif de târ et de setâr de Mirzâ 'Abdollâh*. Tehran: Sorūsh.

———. 1992a "The Organization of Rhythm in Baluchi Trance Music." In *European Studies in Ethnomusicology: Historical Developments and Recent Trends*, ed. Max Peter Baumann 282–302. Wilhelmshaven: Florian Noetzel.

———. 1992b "L'oreille islamique: Dix années capitales de la vie musicale en Iran: 1980–1990." *Asian Music* 23(2):135–164.

———. 1994. *Quelque chose se passe: Le sens de la tradition dans l'Orient musical*. Lagrasse: Verdier.

———. 1996. "La voix des esprits et la face cachée de la musique: Le parcours du maître Hâtam 'Asgari." In *Le voyage initiatique en terre d'Islam: Ascensions célestes et itinéraires spirituels*, ed. Mohammad Ali Amir-Moezzi, 335–373. Louvain and Paris: Peeters.

———. 1997a. "African Winds and Muslim Djinns: Trance, Healing, and Devotion in Baluchistan." *Yearbook for Traditional Music* 29:39–56.

———. 1997b. "Rhythmes ovôdes et quadrature du cycle." *Cahiers des Musiques Traditionnelles* 10:17–36.

During, Jean, with Zia Mirabdolbaghi and Dariush Safvat. 1991. *The Art of Persian Music*. Washington, D.C.: Mage.

Farhat, Hormoz. 1990. *The Dastgāh Concept in Persian Music*. Cambridge Studies in Ethnomusicology. Cambridge: Cambridge University Press.

Fatemi, Sasan. 1997. *La musique et la vie musicale du Mazanderan: Le problème du changement*. Thesis, Université de Paris-X.

Gobineau, Joseph-Arthur, Comte de. [1859] 1983. *Trois ans en Asie (de 1855 à 1858)*. Reprint: In *Oeuvres*, ed. Jean Gaulmier, 2:27–401. Paris: Gallimard.

Hamada, Geoffrey Mark. 1978. "Dance and Islam: The Bojnurdi Kurds of Northeastern Iran." M.A. thesis, University of California, Los Angeles.

Hassan, Schéhérazade Qassim. 1980. *Les instruments de musique en Irak et leur rôle dans la société traditionnelle*. Paris: Mouton.

Hill, Derek, and Oleg Grabar. 1964. *Islamic Architecture and Its Decoration*. Chicago: University of Chicago Press.

Hourani, Albert. 1991. *History of the Islamic Peoples*. Cambridge, Mass.: Harvard University Press.

Ivanov, Vladimir. 1926. "Notes on the Ethnology of Khurasan." *Geographical Journal* 67:143–158.

———. 1927. "Notes on Khorasani Kurdish." *Journal of the Asiatic Society of Bengal*, n.s. 23:166–235.

Jackson, Peter. 1989. "Bakši." In *Encyclopaedia Iranica*, ed. Ehsan Yarshater, 3:535–36. London: Routledge and Kegan Paul.

Kuckertz, Josef, and Mohammad Taghi Massoudieh. 1976. *Musik in Bušehr (Süd-Iran)*. 2 vols. Ngoma: Studien zur Volksmusik und aussereuropäischen Kunstmusik, 2. Munich and Salzburg: Katzbichler.

La Meri [Russell Merriweather Hughes]. 1961. "Learning the Danse du Ventre." *Dance Perspectives* 10:43–47.

Lewis, Geoffrey. 1974. *The Book of Dede Korkut*. Harmondsworth, England: Penguin.

Lièvre, Viviane, and Jean-Yves Loude. 1990. *Le chamanisme des Kalash du Pakistan*. Paris: Éditions Recherche sur les Civilisations.

Massoudieh, Mohammad Teqi. 1973. "Hochzeitslieder aus Balūčestān." *Jahrbuch für Musikalische Volks- und Völkerkünde* 7:59–69.

———. 1978. *Radif vocal de la musique traditionnelle de l'Iran*. Tehran.

———. 1988. *Musik in Balūčestān*. Beiträge zur Ethnomusikologie, 20. Hamburg: Karl Dieter Wagner.

———. 1992a. "Der Begriff des Maqām in der persischen Volksmusik." In *Von der Vielfalt musikalischer Kultur: Festschrift Josef Kuckertz zum 60. Geburtstag*, ed. Rüdiger Schumacher, 311–334. Anif/Salzburg: U. Müller-Speiser.

———. 1992b. "Die Begriffe Maqām und Dastgāh in der turkmenischen Musik des Iran." In *Regionale maqām-Traditionen in Geschichte und Gegenwart*, ed. Jürgen Elsner and Gisa Jähnichen, 377–397. Berlin: Study Group "Maqām" of the International Council for Traditional Music.

Nettl, Bruno. 1972. "Persian Popular Music in 1969." *Ethnomusicology* 16:218–239.

———. 1974. "Aspects of Form in the Instrumental Performance of the Persian *Āvāz*." *Ethnomusicology* 18:405–414.

———. 1978. "Persian Classical Music in Tehran: The Processes of Change." In *Eight Urban Musical Cultures*, ed. Bruno Nettl, 146–185. Urbana: University of Illinois Press.

———. 1992 [1987]. *The Radif of Persian Music: Studies of Structure and Cultural Context*, rev. ed. Champaign, Ill.: Elephant and Cat.

Nettl, Bruno, and Bela Foltin, Jr. 1974. *Daramad of Chahargah: A Study in the Performance Practice of Persian Music*. Detroit, Mich.: Information Coordinators.

Nooshin, Laudan. 1996. "The Processes of Creation and Re-Creation in Persian Classical Music." Ph.D. dissertation, University of London.

———. 1998. "The Song of the Nightingale: Processes of Improvisation in *Dastgāh Segāh* (Iranian Classical Music)." *British Journal of Ethnomusicology* 7:69–116.

Perry, John R. 1975. "Forced Migration in Iran during the Seventeenth and Eighteenth Centuries." *Iranian Studies* 8:199–215.

Picken, Laurence. 1975. *Folk Musical Instruments of Turkey*. London: Oxford University Press.

Reichl, Karl. 1992. *Turkic Oral Epic Poetry: Traditions, Forms, Poetic Structure*. New York: Garland.

Reinhard, Ursula, and Tiago de Oliveira Pinto. 1989. *Sänger und Poeten mit der Laute: Türkische Aşık und Ozan*. Veröffentlichungen des Museums für Völkerkunde Berlin, n.F. 47, Musikethnologische Abteilung 6. Berlin: Museum für Völkerkunde.

Rezvani, Medjid. 1962. *Le théâtre et la danse en Iran*. Paris: Maisonneuve et Larose.

Safvat, Dariush. 1984. "Musique et mystique," trans. Jean During. *Études Traditionnelles* 483:42–54, 484:94–109.

Shay, Anthony. 1995a. "Dance and Non-Dance: Patterned Movement in Iran and Islam." *Iranian Studies* 28:61–78.

———. 1995b. "*Bazi-ha-ye Namayeshi*: Iranian Women's Theatrical Plays." *Dance Research Journal* 27(2):16–24.

———. "Choreophobia: Iranian Solo Improvised Dance as Transgressive and Potentially 'Out-of-Control' Behavior in the Southern California Diaspora." Ph.D. dissertation, University of California, Riverside.

St. John, Katherine. 1988. "Afghan Atan." *Viltis* 47(1):23–4.

———. 1989. "Afghan Dance." *Folk Dance Scene* 24(2):8–18.

Slobin, Mark. 1969. *Kirgiz Instrumental Music*. New York: Society for Asian Music.

———. 1976. *Music in the Culture of Northern Afghanistan*. Viking Fund Publications in Anthropology, 54. Tucson: University of Arizona Press.

Spector, Johanna. 1967. "Musical Tradition and Innovation." In *Central Asia: A Century of Russian Rule*, ed. Edward Allworth, 434–484. New York: Columbia University Press.

Talai, Dariush. 1999. *Traditional Persian Art Music: The Radif of Mirza Abdollah*. Costa Mesa, Calif.: Mazda.

Tsuge, Gen'ichi. 1974. "*Āvāz*: A Study of the Rhythmic Aspects in Classical Iranian Music." Ph.D. dissertation, Wesleyan University.

Varzi, Morteza. 1988. "Performer-Audience Relationships in the *Bazm*." In *Cultural Parameters of Iranian Musical Expression*, ed. Margaret Caton and Neil Siegel, 1–9. Redondo Beach, Calif.: Institute of Persian Performing Arts.

Yarshater, Ehsan. 1974. "Affinities between Persian Poetry and Music." In *Studies in the Art and Literature of the Near East*, ed. Peter Chelkowski, 59–78. Salt Lake City and New York: University of Utah and New York University.

Youssefzadeh, Ameneh. 1996. "Les bardes *bakhshī* du Khorassan iranien." Dissertation, Université de Paris X-Nanterre.

Yūsofi, Gholam Hosein. 1994. "Calligraphy." *Encyclopaedia Iranica*, 680–718. London: Routledge and Kegan Paul.

Zonis, Ella. 1973. *Classical Persian Music: An Introduction*. Cambridge, Mass.: Harvard University Press.

CENTRAL ASIA

Akiner, Shirin. 1995. *The Formation of Kazakh Identity: From Tribe to Nation-State*. London: Royal Institute of International Affairs, Russian and CIS Programme.

Bacon, Elizabeth E. [1966] 1980. *Central Asians under Russian Rule: A Study in Culture Change*. Ithaca, N. Y.: Cornell University Press.

Beliaev, Victor, M., ed. 1950–1958. *Shashmaqâm*, Vols. 1–4. Moscow: Gosudarstvennoe Muzykalnoe Izdatelstvo.

———. 1975. *Central Asian Music: Essays in the History of the Music of the Peoples of the U.S.S.R.*, ed. and annotated Mark Slobin; trans. from Russian by Mark Slobin and Greta Slobin. Middletown, Conn.: Wesleyan University Press.

Chadwick, Nora Kershaw, and Victor M. Zhirmunsky. 1969. *Oral Epics of Central Asia*. London: Cambridge University Press.

Czekanowska, Anna. 1983. "Aspects of the Classical Music of Uyghur People: Legend versus Reality." *Asian Music* 14(1):41–93.

Djumaev, Alexander. 1993. "Power Structures, Culture Policy, and Traditional Music in Soviet Central Asia." *Yearbook for Traditional Music* 25:43–51.

Dru, C. Gladney. 1991. "Sedentarization, Socioecology, and State Definition: The Ethnogenesis of the Uighur." In *Rulers from the Steppe: State Formation on the Eurasian Periphery*, ed. G. Seaman and D. Marks, 308–340. Los Angeles: University of Southern California, Ethnographics Press.

During, Jean. 1988. *La musique traditionnelle de l'Azerbayjan et la science des muqams*. Baden-Baden: Valentin Koener.

During, Jean, and Sabine Trebinjac. 1991. *Introduction à l'étude de la musique ouïgoure*. Bloomington: Indiana University Press.

Emsheimer, Ernest. 1956. "Singing Contests in Central Asia." *Journal of the International Folk Music Council* 8:26–29.

Farmer, Henry George. 1937. *Turkish Instruments of Music in the Seventeenth Century as Described in the Siyahat Nama of Ewliya Chelebi*. Glasgow: Civic.

———. 1962. "Abdalqadir ibn Gaibi on Instruments of Music." *Oriens* 5:242–248.

———. 1965. *The Sources of Arabian Music: An Annotated Bibliography of Arabic Manuscripts Which Deal with the Theory, Practice, and History of Arabian Music from the Eighth to the Seventeenth Century*. Leiden: Brill.

Jung, Angelika. 1989. *Quellen der traditionellen Kunstmusik der Usbeken und Tadshiken Mittelasiens*. Hamburg: Karl Dieter Wagner.

Kakuk, S. 1972. "Chants ouïghours de Chine." *Acta Orientalia Academiae Scientiarum Hungaricae* 25:415–29.

Karomatov, Faizula M., ed. 1966–1975. *Shashmaqâm*, Vols. 1–6. Tashkent.

Karomatov, Faizula M., V. A. Meskeris, and Tamara Vyzgo. 1987. *Mittelasien*. Band II, Lieferung 9 of *Musikgeschichte in Bildern*. Leipzig: Deutscher Verlag für Musik.

Khashimov, Abd al-Aziz. 1978. "Structure du *muqam* ouïghour et les conditions de sa préservation." In *Mâqams, mugams, et composition contemporaine*, 130–138. Tashkent.

Kunanbaeva, Alma. 1990. "The Kazakh Epic: Modernization and Return." *Turkish Music Quarterly* 3(2–3):1–3.

———. 1995 "The Kazakh Zhyrau as the Singer of Tales." In *Ethnohistorische Wege und Lehrjahre eines Philosophen: Festschrift dedicated to Prof. Lawrence Krader*, ed. Dittmar Schorkowitz, 293–303. Frankfurt am Main: Peter Lang.

Levin, Theodore. 1996. *The Hundred Thousand Fools of God: Musical Travels in Central Asia (and Queens, New York)*. Bloomington: Indiana University Press.

———. 2001a. "Making Marxist-Leninist Music in Uzbekistan." In *Music and Marx: Ideas, Practice, Politics*, ed. Regula Burckhardt Qureshi. New York: Garland.

Levin, Theodore, and Razia Sultanova. 2001b. "Uzbekistan." In *The New Grove Dictionary of Music and Musicians*, 2nd ed., 26:180–189. London: Macmillan.

Mackerras, Colin. 1985a. "Traditional Uygur Performing Arts." *Asian Music* 16:29–58.

———. 1985b. "Uygur Performing Arts in Contemporary China." *China Quarterly* 101:58–77.

Mukhambetova, Asiya. 1990a. "Philosophical Problems of Being in the Art of the Kazakh Kuyshi." *Yearbook for Traditional Music* 22:36–41.

———. 1995. "The Traditional Musical Culture of Kazakhs in the Social Context of the 20th Century." *World of Music* 37(3):66–83.

Neubauer, Eckhard. 1969. "Musik zur Mongolenzeit in Iran und angrenzenden Ländern." *Islam* 54(3):233–260.

Olcott, Martha Brill. 1995. *The Kazakhs*, 2nd ed. Stanford, Calif.: Hoover Institution Press, Stanford University Press.

Porter, James, ed. 1997. *Folklore and Traditional Music in the Former Soviet Union and Eastern Europe*. Los Angeles: UCLA, Department of Ethnomusicology.

Powers, Harold S. 1980. "[Mode:] Modal Entities in Western Asia and South Asia." In *The New Grove Dictionary of Music and Musicians* 5(2, i):423–238. London: Macmillan.

Reichl, Karl. 1992. *Turkic Oral Epic Poetry: Traditions, Forms, Poetic Structure*. New York: Garland.

Slobin, Mark. 1976. *Music in the Culture of Northern Afganistan*. Tucson: University of Arizona Press, for Wenner-Gren Foundation for Anthropological Research.

Trebinjac, Sabine. 1989. "Musique ouïghoure de Chine: De l'authenticité à la folklorisation." In *Actes du colloque ESCAS III: L'Asie Centrale et ses voisins—Paris, 1989*, 227–238. Paris: INALCO.

———. 1995. "Femme, seule et venue d'ailleurs: Trois atouts d'un ethnomusicologue au Turkestan chinois." *Cahier de Musiques Traditionnelles* 8:59–68.

———. 1998. *Le pouvoir en chantant*, Vol. 1. Nanterre: Société d'Ethnologie.

Utegalieva, Saule. 1993. "The System of Images in the Dombra Tradition of Kazakhs." In *Proceedings of the First International Conference on Cognitive Musicology*, 270–282. Jyvaskyla: Jyvaskylan Yliopisto.

Winner, Thomas Gustav. 1980. *The Oral Art and Literature of the Kazakhs of Russian Central Asia.* New York: Arno.

Wright, Owen. 1978. *The Modal System of Arab and Persian Music, 1250–1300*. Oxford: Oxford University Press.

Zeranska-Kominek, Slawomira. 1990. "The Classification of Repertoire in Turkmen Traditional Music." *Journal of the Society for Asian Music* 31(2):90–109.

———. 1992a. "The Turkmen *Bakhshy*: Shaman and/or Artist." In *European Studies in Ethnomusicology: Historical Developments and Recent Trends*, ed. Max Peter Baumann, 303–317. Berlin: International Institute for Traditional Music.

———. 1992b. "Mode: Process and/or Structure—Analytical Study of Turkmen *Mukam Gökdepe*." In *Studi e testi 1. Secondo Convegno Europeo di Analisi Musicale*, ed. Rossana Dalmonte and Mario Baroni, 249–259. Trento: Universitá degli Studi di Trento.

———. 1995. "The Turkmen Musical Tradition and the Soviet Culture." In *Lux Oriente: Begegnungen der Kulturen in der Musikforschung—Festschrift Robert Günther zum 65. Geburtstag*, ed. K. W. Niemöller, 419–427. Kassel: Gustave Bosse Verlag.

Zeranska-Kominek, Slawomira, with Arnold Lebeuf. 1997. *The Tale of Crazy Harman: The Musician and the Concept of Music in the Türkmen Epic Tale "Harman Däli."* Warsaw: Dialog.

Zhirmunskii, Viktor. 1960. *On the Comparative Study of the Heroic Epic of the Peoples of Central Asia.* Moscow: Oriental Literature Publishing House.

ISRAEL

Adler, Israel. 1966. *La pratique musicale savante dans quelques communautés juives en Europe aux XVIIe et XVIIIe siècles*. Paris: Mouton.

———. 1974. *Musical life and traditions of the Portuguese Jewish community of Amsterdam in the XVIIIth century*. Jerusalem: Magnes Press, Hebrew University

———. 1975. *Hebrew Writings Concerning Music in Manuscripts and Printed Books from Geonic Times Up to 1800.* RISM B IX². München: G. Henle.

———, ed. 1977. *A Directory of Music Institutions in Israel*. Jerusalem: Israel Section of the International Music Council.

———. 1982. "Problems in the Study of Jewish Music." In *Proceedings of the World Congress on Jewish Music, Jerusalem 1978*, ed. Judith Cohen, 15–26. Tel Aviv: Institute for the Translation of Hebrew Literature.

———. 1989. *Hebrew Notated Manuscripts Sources Up to c. 1840: A Descriptive and Thematic Catalogue with a Checklist of Printed Sources*. Munich: Henle Verlag.

Adler, Israel, Bathyah Bayer, and E. Schleifer. 1986. *The Abraham Zvi Idelsohn Memorial Volume. Yuval* Studies of the Jewish Music Research Center, 5. Jerusalem: Magnes.

Adler, Israel, and Judith Cohen. 1976. *A. Z. Idelsohn Archives at the Jewish National and University Library: Catalogue*. Jerusalem: Magnes Press, Hebrew University.

Alvarez-Pereyre, F., T. Alexander, I. Benabu, I. Ghelman, O. Schwarzwald, and S. Weich-Shahak. 1991. "Towards a Typology of the Judeo-Spanish Folk Song: Gerineldo and the Romance Model." *Yuval* 6.

Armistead, Samuel G., and Joseph H. Silverman. 1973. "El cancionero judeo-español de arruecos en el siglo XVIII (Incipits de los Ben Cur)." *Nueva Revista de Filología Hispánica* 22(2):280–290.

Armistead, Samuel G., and Joseph H. Silverman. 1977. *Romances judeo-espanoles de Tanger recogidos por Zarita Nahon*. Madrid: Catedra Seminario Menedez Pidal.

Armistead, Samuel G., and Joseph H. Silverman. 1981. "El antiguo cancionero sefaradí: Citas de romances en himnarios hebreos (siglos XVI–XIX)." *Nueva Revista de Filología Hispánica* 30(2):453–512.

Armistead, Samuel G., Joseph H. Silverman, and Iacob M. Hassan. 1974. "Four Moroccan Judeo-Spanish Folksong Incipits (1824–1825)." *Hispanic Review* 42(1):83–87.

Armistead, Samuel G., Joseph H. Silverman, and and Israel J. Katz. 1986. *Judeo-Spanish Ballads from Oral Tradition*. 1, *Epic Ballads*. Berkeley: University of California Press.

Avenary, Hanoch. 1963. *Studies in the Hebrew, Syrian, and Greek Liturgical Recitative*. Tel Aviv: Israel Music Institute

———. 1972. "Music." In *Encyclopaedia Judaica*, 12:554–678. Jerusalem: Encyclopedia Judaica; New York: Macmillan.

———. 1978. *The Ashkenazi Tradition of Biblical Chant between 1500 and 1900: Documentation and Musical Analysis*. Tel Aviv: Tel Aviv University; Council for Culture and Art, Ministry of Education and Culture.

———. 1979. *Encounters of East and West in Music: Selected Writings*. Tel Aviv: Faculty of Visual and Performing Arts, Deptartment of Musicology, Tel Aviv University.

———. 1986. "Persistence and Transformation of a Sephardi Penitential Hymn." *Yuval* 5:181–232.

Avenary, Hanoch, Walter Pass, and Nikolaus Vielmetti. 1985. *Kantor Salomon Sulzer und seine Zeit: Eine Dokumentation*. Sigmaringen: Jan Thorbecke Verlag.

Bahat, Avner. 1986. "The 'Hallelot' in the Yemenite Diwan." *Yuval* 5:139–168.

Bar-Yosef, Amatzia. 1998. "Traditional Rural Style under a Process of Change: The Singing Style of the *Hadday*, Palestinian Folk Poet-Singers." *Asian Music* 29(2):57–82.

Bayer, Bathyah. 1963. *The Material Relics of Music in Ancient Palestine and Its Environs: An Archeological Inventory*. Tel Aviv, Israel Music Institute.

———. 1968. "The Biblical Nebel." *Yuval* 1:89-131.

———. 1980. "Creation and Tradition in Israeli Folksongs: Some Specimens." In *Aspects of Music in Israel*, 52–60. Tel Aviv.

———. 1982. "The Titles of the Psalms" *Yuval* 4:29-123.

———. 1986. "The Announcement of the Institute of Jewish Music in Jerusalem by A. Z. Idelsohn and S. Z. Rivlin in 1910." *Yuval* 5:24–35.

Ben-Ami, Issachar. 1975. "La qasida chez les juifs marocains." In *Le Judaisme Marocain: Études Ethno-Culturelles*, 105–119. Jerusalem: Rubin Mass.

———. 1984. "The Ziara and Hillula Songs." In *Saint Veneration among the Jews of Morocco*, 99–146. Jerusalem: Magnes.

Bensky, Tova. 1989. "Ethnicity and the Shape of Musical State Patterns in an Israeli Urban Community." *Social Forces* 67:731–750.

Bensky, Tova, Joachim Braun, and Uri Sharvit. 1986. "Towards a Study of Israeli Urban Musical Culture: The Case of Kiryat Ono." *Asian Music* 17(2):168–209.

Bohlman, Philip V. 1989. *The Land Where Two Streams Flow: Music in the German-Jewish Community in Israel*. Urbana: University of Illinois Press.

Bohlman, Philip V., and Mark Slobin, eds. 1986. *Music in the Ethnic Communities of Israel. Asian Music* 17(2, special issue).

Brauer, Erich. 1933–1934. "Die Juden Jemens." *Ḳiryat Sefer* 10:119, 236, 515.

———. 1934. *Ethnologie der jemenitischen Juden*. Heidelberg: C. Winter.

Brod, Max. [1951] 1976. *Die Musik Israels*, rev. ed. Kassel: Bärenreiter.

Burstyn, Shai. 1989–1990. "The 'Arabian Influence' Thesis Revisited." *Current Musicology* 45–47:119–146.

Chottin, Alexis. 1939. *Tableau de la musique marocaine*. Paris: Geuthner.

Cohen, Boaz. 1935. "The Responsum of Maimonides Concerning Music." *Jewish Music Journal* 2(2):1–7.

Cohen, Dalia, and Ruth Katz. 1978. *The Israeli Folk Song: A Methodological Example of Computer-analysis of Monophonic Music*. Jerusalem: Magnes Press, Hebrew University.

Cohen, Eric, and Amnon Shiloah. 1985. "Major Trends of Change in Jewish Oriental Ethnic Music." *Popular Music* 5:199–223.

Cohen, Judith. 1988. "Judeo-Spanish Songs in the Sephardic Communities of Montreal and Toronto: Survival, Function, and Change." Ph.D. dissertation, Université de Montréal.

———. 1989. "The Impact of Mass Media and Acculturation on the Judeo-Spanish Song Tradition in Montreal." In *World Music, Politics and Social Change*, ed. Simon Frith, 90–97. Manchester: Manchester University Press.

Cohen, Judith, and Oro Anahory-Librowicz. 1986. "Modalidades expresivas de los cantos de boda judeo-españoles." *Revista de Dialectología y Tradiciones Populares* 41:189–209.

Eliram, Talila. 1995. "*Shirei Eretz Israel*: The Formation and Meaning of a Popular Music Repertory at the End of the Twentieth Century." M.A. thesis, Bar-Ilan University.

Etzion, Judith. 1989. "The Spanish and the Sephardi Romances: Musical Links." *Ethnomusicology* 32(2): 1–37.

———, ed. 1996. *El cancionero de la Sablonara*. London: Tamesis.

Etzion, Judith, and Susana Weich-Shahak. 1988. "The Music of the Judeo-Spanish Romancero: Stylistic Features." *Anuario Musical* 43: 221–250.

Fenton, Paul. 1975. "Les baqqasot d'orient et d'occident." *Revue des Études Juives* 134:101–121.

Flam, Gila. 1986. "Bracha Zephira—A Case Study of Acculturation in Israeli Song." *Asian Music* 17:108–125.

Fleisher, Robert Jay. 1997. *Twenty Israeli Composers: Voices of a Culture*. Detroit: Wayne State University Press.

Flender, Reinhard. 1992. *Hebrew Psalmody*. Yuval Monograph Series, 9. Jerusalem: Hebrew University.

Gerson-Kiwi, Edith. 1963. *The Persian Doctrine of Dastgah-Composition: A Phenomenological Study in the Musical Modes.* Tel Aviv: Israel Music Institute.

———. 1965. "Women's Songs from the Yemen: Their Tonal Structure and Form." In *The Commonwealth of Music, in Honor of Curt Sachs*, 97. New York: Free Press.

———. 1967a. "Migrating Patterns of Melody among the Berbers and Jews of the Atlas Mountains." *Journal of the IFTM* 19:64–73.

———. 1968. "Vocal Folk Polyphonies of the Western Orient in Jewish Tradition." *Yuval* 1:169–193.

———. 1974. "Robert Lachmann: His Achievement and His Legacy." *Yuval* 3:100–108.

———. 1980. *Migrations and Mutations of the Music in East and West: Selected Writings*. Tel-Aviv, Israel: Tel Aviv University, Faculty of Visual and Performing Arts, Deptartment of Musicology.

Goitein, S. D. F. [1937] 1973. *From the Land of Sheba: Tales of the Jews of Yemen.* New York: Schocken.

———. 1955. "Portrait of a Yemenite Weavers' Village." *Jewish Social Studies* 17:3.

Gradenwitz, Peter. 1963. *Wege zur Musik der Gegenwart*. Stuttgart: W. Kohlhammer.

———. 1977. *Musik zwischen Orient und Okzident*. Wilhelmshaven: Heinrichshofen.

———. 1978. *Music and Musicians in Israel: A Comprehensive Guide to Modern Israeli Music*, 3rd ed. Tel Aviv: Israeli Music Publications.

Halper, Jeff, Edwin Seroussi, and Pamela Squires-Kidron. 1989. "Musica Mizrahit: Ethnicity and Class Culture in Israel." *Popular Music* 8:131–142.

———. 1992. "Musica Mizrahit and the Realignment of Israeli Society: The Case of Hayyim Moshe." In *1789–1989 Musique, Histoire, Démocratie*, ed. Antoine Hennion, 3:669–672. Paris: Éditions de la Maison des Sciences de l'Homme.

Hajdu, Andre, and Yaacov Mazor. 1971. "Hasidim: The Musical Tradition of the Hasidism." In *Encyclopedia Judaica*, 7:1421–1432. Jerusalem: Encyclopedia Judaica; New York: Macmillan.

Herzog, Avigdor. 1963. *The Intonation of the Pentateuch in the Heder of Tunis*. Tel-Aviv: Israel Music Institute.

Hirshberg, Jehoash. 1987. "Jerusalem Symphony Orchestra," "Israel Philharmonic Orchestra." In *Symphony Orchestras of the World: Selected Profiles*, ed. Robert Craven, 200–207. New York: Greenwood.

———. 1990. *Paul Ben-Haim: His Life and Works*. Jerusalem: Israeli Music Publications.

———. 1995. *Music in the Jewish Community of Palestine 1880–1948: A Social History*. Oxford: Clarendon; New York: Oxford University Press.

Hirshberg, Jehoash, and David Sagiv. 1978. "The 'Israeli' in Israeli Music: The Audience Responds." *Israel Studies in Musicology* 1:159–173.

Horowitz, Amy. 1994. "Israeli Mediterranean Music: Cultural Boundaries and Disputed Territories." Ph.D. dissertation, University of Pennsylvania.

———. 1997. "Performance in Disputed Territory: Israeli Mediterranean Music." *Musical Performance* 1(3):43–53.

Høst, Georg Hjersing. 1781. *Nachrichten von Morokos und Fes, im Lande selbst gesammelt in der Jahre 1760 bis 1768*. Copenhagen.

Ibbeken, Ida, and Tzvi Avni. 1969. *An Orchestra is Born*. Tel Aviv: Israel Philharmonic Orchestra.

Idelsohn, Abraham Zvi. 1914–1932. *Hebräisch-orientalischer Melodienschatz*. Leipzig: Breitkopf and Härtel.

———. 1918. "The Jews of Yemen: Their Poetry and Music." *Reshumot* 1:3–66.

———. [1929] 1992. *Jewish Music in Its Historical Development*. New York: Dover.

Kahn, Aharon. 1986–1989. "Music in Halakhic Perspective." *Journal of Jewish Music and Liturgy* 9:55–72, 10:32–49, 11:65–75.

Katz, Israel J. 1973. "The 'Myth' of the Sephardic Musical Legacy from Spain." *Proceedings of the Fifth World Congress of Jewish Studies* 4:237–243.

———. 1979. "Manuel Manrique de Lara and the Tunes of the Moroccan Sephardic Ballad Tradition: Some Insights into a Much-Needed Critical Edition." In *El Romancero hoy: Nuevas Fronteras*, ed. Antonio Sánchez Romeraldo, Diego Catalán, and Samuel G. Armistead, 75–87. Madrid: Catedra Seminario Menendez Pidal.

———. 1982. "On the Music of Three Romances from Tangíer." *Estudios Sefardies* 1:129–131.

———. 1986. "'Contrafacta' and the Judeo-Spanish Romancero: A Musicological View." In *Hispanic Studies in Honor of Joseph H. Silverman*, ed. Joseph V. Recapito, 169–187. Newark, Del.: Juan de la Cuesta.

Katz, Ruth. 1968. "The Singing of *Baqqashot* by Aleppo Jews." *Acta Musicologica* 40:65–85.

Keren, Zvi. 1980. *Contemporary Israeli Music: Its Sources and Stylistic Development*. Ramat-Gan, Israel: Bar-Ilan University Press.

Lachmann, Robert. 1940. *Jewish Cantillation and Song in the Isle of Djerba*. Jerusalem: Archives of Oriental Music, Hebrew University.

———. 1974, 1978. *Posthumous Works*, ed. Edith Gerson-Kiwi. 2 vols. Jerusalem: Magnes Press, Hebrew University.

———. 1978. *Gesänge der Juden auf der Insel Djerba*, ed. Edith Gerson-Kiwi. Jerusalem: Hebrew University.

Landman, Leo. 1972. *The Cantor: An Historical Perspective*. New York: Yeshiva University.

Larrea Palacín, Arcadio. 1952. *Romances de Tetuán*. 2 vols. Madrid: Instituto de Estudios Africanos.

———. 1954. *Canciones rituales hispano-judias*. Madrid: Instituto de Estudios Africanos.

Levy, Isaac. 1964–1980. *Antologia de la liturgia judeo-espanola*. 10 vols. Jerusalem: Author.

Lewis, Bernhard. 1984. *The Jews of Islam*. Princeton, N. J.: Princeton University Press.

Loeb, Laurence D. 1972. "The Jewish Musician and the Music of Fars." *Asian Music* 4(1):3–14.

Marks, Paul F. *Bibliography of Literature Concerning Yemenite-Jewish Music*. Detroit: Information Coordinators.

Mazor, Yacov. 2000. *The Klezmer Tradition in the Land of Israel*. Jerusalem: Jewish Music Research Center.

Nathan, Hans, ed. 1994. *Israeli Folk Music: Songs of the Early Pioneers*. Madison, Wisc.: A-R Editions.

Ne'eman, Amitay. 1980. "Light Music and Pop in Israel." In *Aspects of Music in Israel*, 61–65. Tel Aviv.

Ravina, Menashe. 1963. *Organum and the Samaritans*, trans. Alan Marbe. Tel Aviv: Israel Music Institute.

Regev, Moti. 1986. "The Musical Soundscape as a Contest Area: 'Oriental Music' and Israeli Popular Music." In *Media, Culture, and Society*, ed. Richard Collins et al., 8:343–355. London, Beverly Hills, and New Delhi: Sage.

———. 1989. "The Field of Popular Music in Israel." In *World Music, Politics and Social Change*, ed. Simon Frith, 145–155. Manchester: Manchester University Press.

———. 1992. "Israeli Rock, or a Study in the Politics of Local Authenticity." *Popular Music* 11(1):1–14.

Romero, Elena. 1981. "Las coplas sefardíes: Categorías y estado de la cuestión." In *Actas de las Jornadas de Estudios Sefaradíes*, 69–98. Cáceres: Universidad de Extremadura.

Sabbah, Dina. 1980. "Le chant religieux chez les marocains d'Israel." M.A. thesis, Université de Montréal.

Schleifer, Eliyahu. 1995. "Current Trends of Liturgical Music in the Ashkenazi Liturgy." In *Jewish Musical Culture—Past and Present*. Vol. 37(1) of *World of Music*, ed. Uri Sharvit, 59–72. Basel, Kassel: Bärenreiter.

Schreiber, Baruch David. 1984–1985. "The Woman's Voice in the Synagogue." *Journal of Jewish Music and Liturgy* 7:27–32.

Seroussi, Edwin. 1986. "Politics, Ethnic Identity, and Music in the Singing of *Bakkashot* among Moroccan Jews in Israel." *Asian Music* 17(2):32–45.

———. 1990a. "La musica arabigo-andaluza en las bakkashot judeo-marroquíes: Estudio histórico y musical." *Anuario Musical* 45:297–315.

———. 1990b. "The Growth of the Judeo-Spanish Folksong Repertory in the Twentieth Century." In *Proceedings of the Tenth World Congress of Jewish Studies*, 2:173–180. Jerusalem: World Union of Jewish Studies.

———. 1996. *Popular Music in Israel: The First Fifty Years*. Cambridge, Mass.: Harvard College Library.

Seroussi, Edwin, and Susana Weich-Shahak. 1991. "Judeo-Spanish Contrafacts and Musical Adaptations: The Oral Tradition." *Orbis Musicae* 10:164–194.

Sharvit, Uri. 1980. "The Role of Music in the Jewish Yemenite 'Heder.'" *Israel Studies in Musicology* 2:33–49.

———. 1981. "On the Role of Arts and Artistic Concepts in the Tradition of Yemenite Jewry." *Pe'amim* 10:119–130.

———. 1982. "The Musical Realization of Biblical Cantillation Symbols in the Jewish Yemenite Liturgy." *Yuval* 4:179–210.

———. 1986a. "Diversity within Unity: Stylistic Change and Ethnic Continuity in Israeli Religious Music." *Asian Music* 17(2):126–146.

———. 1986b. "The Music and Its Function in the Traditional Singing of the Qasid: 'Abda birabi di halak.'" *Yuval* 5:192–234.

———, ed. 1995. *Jewish Musical Culture—Past and Present*. Vol. 37(1) of *World of Music*. Basel, Kassel: Bärenreiter.

Sharvit, Uri, and Yehiel Adaqi. 1981. *A Treasury of Jewish Yemenite Chants*. Jerusalem: Israel Institute for Sacred Music.

Sharvit, Uri, and Simcha Arom. 1994. "Plurivocality in the Liturgical Music of the Jews of San'a (Yemen)." *Yuval* 6:34–67.

Sharvit, Uri, and E. Yaacov. 1984. "The 'Hallelot' of the Jews of Huggariyah and Those of Central Yemen." *Pe'amim* 19:130–162.

Shiloah, Amnon. 1969. "The World of a Yemenite Folk Singer." *Tatslil* 9:144–149.

———. 1972. "Africa, North: Musical Traditions." In *Encyclopaedia Judaica* 16:1257–1260. Jerusalem: Encyclopaedia Judaica.

———. 1977. *Music Subjects in the Zohar Texts and Indices*. Jerusalem: Magnes Press, Hebrew University.

———. 1980. "La muba et la célébration des bakashot en Maroc." In *Judaisme d'Afrique du Nord*, ed. Michel Abitbol, 108–113. Jerusalem: Ben-Zvi Institute.

———. 1983. *The Musical Tradition of Iraqi Jews*. Or Yehuda: Iraqi Jew's Traditional Culture Center.

———. 1984. "Impressions musicales des voyageurs européens en Afrique du Nord." In *Les relations intercommunautaires juives en Méditerranée occidentale*. Paris: Éditions du C.N.R.S.

———. 1992a. *Jewish Musical Traditions*. Detroit: Wayne University Press.

———. 1992b. "Eastern Sources in Israeli Music." *Ariel* 88:4–19.

Shiloah, Amnon, and Eric Cohen. 1983. "The Dynamics of Change in Jewish Oriental Ethnic Music in Israel." *Ethnomusicology* 27:227–251.

Sikron, Moshe. 1957. *Immigration to Israel*. Jerusalem: Central Bureau of Statistics.

Slobin, Mark. 1989. *Chosen Voices: The Story of the American Cantorate*. Urbana and Chicago: University of Illinois Press.

Smoira-Roll, Michal. 1963. *Folk Song in Israel: An Analysis Attempted*. Tel Aviv: Israel Music Institute.

Spector, Johanna. 1952. "On the Trail of Oriental Jewish Music: Among the Yemenites." *Reconstructionist* 18:7–12.

Tischler, Alice. 1989. *A Descriptive Bibliography of Art Music by Israeli Composers*. Warren, Mich.: Detroit Studies in Music Bibliography.

Vinaver, Chemjo. 1985. *Anthology of Hassidic Music*, ed. Eliyahu Schleifer. Jerusalem: Jewish Music Research Center, Hebrew University of Jerusalem.

Weich-Shahak, Susana. 1989. *Judeo-Spanish Moroccan Songs for the Life Cycle*. Jerusalem: Jewish Music Research Center, Hebrew University of Jerusalem.

Weil, Daniel. 1994. *The Original Performance of the Tiberian Masoretic Accents: A Deductive Approach*. Jerusalem: ha-Universiṭah ha-'Ivrit.

Werner, Eric. 1976. *A Voice Still Heard: The Sacred Songs of the Ashkenazi Jews*. University Park: Pennsylvania State University Press.

Yurchenko, Henrietta. 1958. "The Music of the Jews in Morocco." In *Year Book of the American Philosophical Society*, 518–520. Philadelphia: American Philosophical Society.

Zafrani, Haim. 1977. *Poésie juive en Occident musulman*. Paris: Geuthner.

A Guide to Recordings of Middle Eastern Music

Alexander J. Fisher

THE MAGHRIB

Aflak. 1994. *Marocain moderne / Aflak*. Paris: Les Artistes Arabes Associés, Club du Disque Arabe AAA102.

Ahouach, ahidous, et guedra. 1996. Les Artistes Arabes Associés, Club du Disque Arabe, AAA 131. Compact disk.

Alaoui, Amina. 1995. *Musique arabo-andalouse du Maroc*. Audivis B 6806. Compact disk.

Amārg al-Maghrib: Mukhtārāt min ghinā' wa-mūsīqa al-ruwāyis / Maroc: Anthologie des rwâyes. 1991. Paris: Maison des Cultures du Monde, W260023. 4 compact disks.

Antūlūjīyat al-alāh / Anthologie al-āla: Musique Andaluci-Marocaine. 1989–. Paris: Maison des Cultures du Monde and Rabat: Ministère de la Culture.

Vol. 1 (1989). Haj Abdelkrim al-Raïs and the Orchestre al-Brihi de Fès: *Nūbat gharībat al-ḥusayn*. W260010. 6 compact disks.

Vol. 2 (1990). Haj Mohamed Toud and the Orchestre Moulay Ahmed Loukili de Rabat: *Nūbat 'ushshāq*. W260014. 6 compact disks.

Vol. 3 (1992). Mohammed Larbi-Temsamani and the Orchestre du Conservatoire de Tètouan: *Nūbat iṣbahān*. W260024. 6 compact disks.

Vol. 4 (1992). Ahmed Zaytouni Sahraoui and the Orchetre de Tanger: *Nūbat raṣd*. W260027. 6 compact disks.

Vol. 5 (1992). Haj Abdelkrim al-Raïs and the Orchestre al-Brihi de Fès: *Nūbat istihlāl*. W260028. 7 compact disks.

Vol. 6 (1992). Haj Mohamed Toud and the Orchestre Moulay Ahmed Loukili de Rabat: *Nūbat raṣd al-dhil*. W260029. 6 compact disks.

Vol. 7 (1992). Ahmed Zaytouni Sahraoui and the Orchetre de Tanger: *Nūbat 'irāq 'ajam*. W260030. 7 compact disks.

Vol. 8 (1997). Haj Abdelkrim al-Raïs and the Orchestre al-Brihi de Fès: *Nūbat al-ḥijāz al-kabīr*. W260031. 7 compact disks.

Vol. 9 [c. 1990.] Mohammed Larbi-Temsamani and the Orchestre du Conservatoire de Tètouan: *Nūbat ramal al-māya*. W260032. 8 compact disks.

Vol. 10 (1992). Haj Abdelkrim al-Raïs and the Orchestre al-Brihi de Fès: *Nūbat al-ḥijāz al-mashriqī*. W260033. 5 compact disks.

Vol. 11. [c. 1990.] Ahmed Zaytouni Sahraoui and the Orchetre de Tanger: *Nūbat al-māya*. W260034. 7 compact disks.

Vol. 12 [c. 1990.] Mohammed Briouel and the Ensemble al-Āla du Ministère de la Culture du Maroc: *Mīzān quddām bawākir al-māya* and *Mīzān al-quddām al-jadīd*. W260035. 2 compact disks.

Arab Music. Music of the Near East. 1968. Lyrichord LLST 7186, 7198. LP disk.

Archives de la musique arabe. 1987–. Ocora C558678. Compact disk.

Augier, Pierre, comp. 1975. *Algeria (Sahara): Music of Gourara*. EMI Odeon 3C 064 18079. LP disk.

Aux sources du raï. Les cheikat: Chants de femme de l'ouest algérien. 1996. Les Artistes Arabes Associés, Club du Disque Arabe AAA 132. Compact disk.

Azem, Slimane. 1995. *Meltiyid matchfam*. Les Artistes Arabes Associés, Club du Disque Arabe AAA 135. Compact disk.

Ben Mahmoud, Abderrahman Sheikh. n.d. *La Sulâmiyya: Chants soufis de Tunis*. Institut du Monde Arabe 321025. Compact disk.

Ben Sari, Elarbi. 1995. *Gharnata: Congrès du Caire 1932*. Les Artistes Arabes Associés AAA 098. Compact disk.

Bent el Hocine, Fatna. 1999. *Barbès café: Trois cheikhates mythiques du Maroc*. Night and Day BAC 104. Compact disk.

Bin 'Ashūr, Daḥmān. 1990. *La Nouba*. Les Artistes Arabes Associés, Club du Disque Arabe AAA 022. Compact disk.

Bin Ḥasan, Muḥammad. 1994. *Malouf tunisien: Congrès du Caire 1932*. Les Artistes Arabes Associés, Club du Disque Arabe AAA 094. Compact disk.

Bilkhayyāt, 'Abd al-Hādī. 1990. *La chanson moderne au Maroc*. Paris: Artistes Arabes Associés, Club du Disque Arabe, AAA 012. Compact disk.

Bin 'Ashūr, Daḥmān. 1990. *Nouba*. Vol. 4. Les Artistes Arabes Associés, Club du Disque Arabe AAA 143. Compact disk.

Boniche, Lili. [c. 1997.] *Trésors de la chanson judéo-arabe*. Blue Silver 79 102 2 BS. Compact disk.

Bowles, Paul, comp. 1972. *Music of Morocco*. Washington, D.C.: Library of Congress Recording Laboratory, AFS L63–64. 2 LP disks.

Būshnāk, Luṭfī. 1993. *Mālūf Tūnisī*. Paris: Maison des Cultures du Monde W260053. Compact disk.

Chants de traverse: Récital de musiques judéo-marocaines. Paris: Atoll Music. 2 compact disks.

Chants sacrés du Sahara Algérien: Ahallîl de Gourara. 1994. Institut du Monde Arabe REF 50306–2. Compact disk.

Chaouli, Nacer Eddine. 1996. *Musique classique algérienne: Hawzi*. Les Artistes Arabes Associés AAA 149. Compact disk.

Chaouqi, Mohamed. 1995. *Les gnawa du Maroc: Ouled el 'abdi*. Audivis B 6805. Compact disk.

Chawqi, Ahmed. 1995. *Ahmed (oud)* and *Souad (qanoun) Chawki*. Paris: Les Artistes Arabes Associés, Club du Disque Arabe, AAA 133. 2 compact disks.

Cheikha, Cherifa and Hanifa. 1996. *Chants berbères: Cherifa* and *Hanifa*. 1996. Les Artistes Arabes Associés AAA 146. Compact disk.

Chekroun, Alain. 2000. *Chants des synagogues du Maghreb*. Magda MGD027. Compact disk.

Cherkauoi, Abdeslam. 1988. *The Arabic Tradition in Morrocan* [sic] *Music / Musique de tradition arabe*. Paris: Audivis, D 8002. Compact disk.

Congrès du Caire 1932: Musique arabe savante et populaire. 1988. Édition Bibliothèque Nationale—France/l'Institut du Monde Arabe, APN 88–9, 88–10. 2 compact disks.

Dali, Abdelkrim. 1998. *École de Tlemcen*. Vol. 2. *Abdelkrim Dali*. Les Artistes Arabes Associés AAA 147. Compact disk.

Dances and Trances: Moroccan Sufi Brotherhoods, Berber Street Musicians. 2000. World Arbiter 2002. Compact disk.

La daqqa: Tambours sacrés de Marrakech / Sacred drums from Marrakesh. 1999. Paris: Institut du Monde Arabe, 321028. Compact disk.

Le diwân de Biskra. 1996. Ocora/Radio France C 560088. Compact disk.

El Din, Hamza. 1964. *Music of Nubia*. Vanguard VSD-79164. LP disk.

Ezzahi, Ammar. 1996. *La chaâbi*. Les Artistes Arabes Associés, Club du Disque Arabe AAA 124. Compact disk.

Fergani, Hadj Mohamed Tahar. 1993. *La nuba maya*. Harmonia Mundi/Ocora C 560002. Compact disk.

Le folklore Kabyle: Musique et traditions. 1990. Les Artistes Arabes Associés AAA 033, Club du Disque Arabe CDA 401. Compact disk.

Gharnâti de Tlemçen. 1993. Ocora/Radio France C 560004. Compact disk.

Groupe Lemchaheb. 1989. *La chanson populaire marocaine*. Paris: Les Artistes Arabes Associés, AAA 008. Compact disk.

Haddarat. *Chants sacrés des femmes de Fez*. Al Sur CDAL 243. Compact disk.

Hādra des gnaoua d'Essaouira. 1993. Ocora/Radio France C560006. Compact disk.

Halali, Salim, 1990a. *Salim Halali en Algérie*. Les Artistes Arabes Associés AAA 023. Compact disk.

———. 1990b. *Salim Halali en Tunisie*. Les Artistes Arabes Associés AAA 036. Compact disk.

Hassan, Chalf. 1997. *Songs and Dances from Morocco*. EUCD 1393 ARC Music. Compact disk.

Le Hawzi: Sur des poèmes de Bentriki. 1994. Les Artistes Arabes Associés, Club du Disque Arabe AAA 081. Compact disk.

Hoggar: Musique des Touareg. 1994. Chant du Monde LDX 274974. Compact disk.

Kabyle chantée: Chants, rythmes, danses folkloriques de Kabylie. [n.d.] Les Artistes Arabes Associés AAA 160. Compact disk.

Khaznadji, Mohamed. 1993. *La nuba ghrib*. Harmonia Mundi/Ocora 560003. Compact disk.

Kheddam, Chérif. 1992. *Les maîtres de la chanson kabyle*. Vol. 4: *Chérif Kheddam*. Les Artistes Arabes Associés AAA060. Compact disk.

Krémer, Gérard. 1989. *Maroc: Documents recueillis au Maroc par Gérard Krémer*. Arion ARN 64079. Compact disk.

Kurd, Muḥammad. 1992. *La malouf Constantinois*. Vol. 1. Les Artistes Arabes Associés, Club du Disque Arabe AAA 051. Compact disk.

Laade, Wolfgang. 1962. *Tunisia*. Vol. 1: *The Classical Arab-Andalusian Music*. Vol. 2: *Religious Songs and Cantillations*. Vol. 3: *Folk Music*. Smithsonian Folkways FW 8861–8863. 3 LP disks.

Libye: Chants des oasis. n.d. Al-Sur CDAL 236-3. 3 compact disks.

Lortat-Jacob, Bernard. 1975. *Maroc: Musique berbère—Un mariage dans le Haut-Atlas oriental*. Vogue LDY 28.029. LP disk.

Lortat-Jacob, Bernard, and Gilbert Rouget. 1971. *Musique berbère du Haut-Atlas*. Collection Musée de l'Homme. Vogue LD 786. LP disk.

Lortat-Jacob, Bernard, and Hassan Jouad. 1979. *Berbères du Maroc "ahwash."* Collection CNRS/ Musée de l'Homme. Le Chant du Monde LDX 74705. LP disk.

Al-Maghrib: 'Ashr qaṣā'id min ṭarab al-milḥūn / Maroc: Anthologie d'al-melhûn. Traditions de Fes, Meknes, Salé, Marrakech. 1990. Morocco, Ministry of Culture, and Maison des Cultures du Monde, W260016. 3 compact disks.

Al-Maghrib: al-Ṭarab al-gharnāṭī: Nawbat al-ramal / Maroc: Musique gharnâtî. 1990. Paris: Maison des Cultures du Monde, W260017. Compact disk.

Mahieddine. 1996. *Musique classique arabo-andalouse*. Les Artistes Arabes Associés, Club du Disque Arabe AAA 138. Compact disk.

Le malouf tunisien Vol. 1. 1992. Les Artistes Arabes Associés AAA 054. Compact disk.

Le Malhûn de Meknès: Musique et chants du Maroc. 1994. Institut du Monde Arabe 50305-2. Compact disk.

Maroc. 1980. 1. *Musique Tachelhit: Raïs Lhaj Aomar Ouahrouch*. 2. *Moyen Atlas: Musique sacrée et profane*. Paris: Radio-France OCORA OCR 558587, 558560. 2 LP disks.

Maroc: À Marrakech, sur la Djemâa el-Fna. 1994. Chant du Monde LDX 274973. Compact disk.

Moroccan Street Music. [c. 1970.] Lyrichord LLST 7263. LP disk.

Moroccan Sufi Music. [c. 1970.] Lyrichord LLST 7238. LP disk.

Moyen-Atlas: Musique sacrée et profane. 1989. Ocora/Radio France C 559057. Compact disk.

Music of Islam and Sufism in Morocco. 1999. Rounder CD 5145. Compact disk.

Music of Morocco. 1966. Folkways Records FE 4339. LP disk.

Musique arabo-andalouse classique: Ensemble Masano Tazzi. 1995. Chant du Monde CMT 274 1007. Compact disk.

Musique classique andalou-maghrébine. 1988. Ocora C559016. Compact disk.

Musique classique: Maroc. n.d. Les Artistes Arabes Associés AAA006. Compact disk.

La musique Judéo-Arabe. 1992–1993. Les Artistes Arabes Associés 062-072. 2 compact disks.

Musique tunisienne. Enregistrements du Congrès du Caire. Gramophone HC 40–55 and HC 83–86. 20 compact disks.

Nass el Ghiwan. 1997. *Nass el Ghiwane*. Paris: Blue Silver 50620–2. Compact disk.

Nawbat al-aṣbahān. 1992. Paris: Maison des Cultures du Monde W260024. 6 compact disks.

Nawbat al-aṣbahān. 1993. Paris: Maison des Cultures du Monde W260046. Compact disk.

Nawbat al-dhīl. 1992. Paris: Maison des Cultures du Monde W260044. Compact disk.

Nawbat al-'irāq. 1993. Paris: Maison des Cultures du Monde W260047. Compact disk.

Nawbat al-ramal. 1992. Paris: Maison des Cultures du Monde W260045. Compact disk.

Nawbat al-sīkāh. 1994. Paris: Maison des Cultures du Monde W260059. Compact disk.

Nûba çika. Nûba zidane. Nûba des înklabat', mode moual. 1994. Ocora/Radio France C560044/45. 2 compact disks.

Olsen, Miriam, and Bernard Lortat-Jacob. 1994. *Maroc: Musique berbère du Haut-Atlas et de l'Anti-Atlas*. Le Chant du Monde LDX 274991. Compact disk.

Poèmes de Benshala. 1993. Les Artistes Arabes Associés, Club du Disque Arabe AAA 071. Compact disk.

Rayīs, 'Abd al-Karīm. 1993–1999. *Musique andalouse de Fès*. Paris: Institut du Monde Arabe, 321002–3. 2 compact disks.

Remitti, Cheikra. [c. 1990.] *Aux sources du raï*. Paris: Institut du Monde Arabe 503 09–2. Compact disk.

Rituel de transe: Les Assawa de Fès. 1999. Paris: Institut du Monde Arabe, 321011. Compact disk.

Sacred Music of the Moroccan Jews. 2000. Rounder CD 5087. 2 compact disks.

Sahara: Musiques du Gourara. 1991. Audivis D 8037. Compact disk.

Salah, Sadaoui. 1995. *Sadaoui Salah*. Vol. 1: *En Kabyle*. Les Artistes Arabes Associés AAA 106. Compact disk.

Saoudi, Nour-Eddine. 1998. *Nouba h'sine*. Les Artistes Arabes Associés AAA 167. Compact disk.

Saoula. 1993. *Hommage à* [Amraoui] *Missoum*. Les Artistes Arabes Associés AAA 086. Compact disk.

Schuyler, Philip D. 1978. *The Rwais: Moroccan Berber Musicians from the High Atlas*. Lyrichord LLST 7316. LP disk.

Tahar, Samir. 1996. *Oud*. Les Artistes Arabes Associés, Club du Disque Arabe AAA 136. Compact disk.

Tamar, Simone. 1993. *Malouf constantinois*. Vol. 3. Les Artistes Arabes Associés AAA 077. Compact disk.

Tazi, Massano. 1988. *Musique classique andalouse de Fès*. Ocora/Radio France C559035. Compact disk.

Tetma, Shaykhah. 1993. *École de Tlemcen: Cheikha Tetma*. Les Artistes Arabes Associés, Club du Disque Arabe AAA 067. Compact disk.

Tunisia. [c. 1970.] Musicaphon BM 30 L 2008. LP disk.

Zinelabidine, Mohamed. 1996. *Oud: De Carthage à Ifriqiya*. Les Artistes Arabes Associés, Club du Disque Arabe AAA 137. Compact disk.

THE MASHRIQ

'Abd al-Wahhāb, Muḥammad. [c. 1990.] *Fakkarūnī*. Ṣawt al-Qāhira, Sīdī 94 SDCD 01B16. Compact disk.

———. [c. 1990.] *Aghaddan alqāk*. Ṣawt al-Qāhira, Sīdī 94 SDCD 01B25. Compact disk.

———. 1990. *The Music of Mohamed Abdel Wahab*. Axiom 422-846 754-2. Compact disk.

———. 1996a. *Min ghayr layh*. EMI Arabia 310511-2. Compact disk.

———. 1996b. *Waṭaniyyāt*. EMI Arabia 310607-2, 310608-2. 2 compact disks.

———. 1997. *The HMV Recordings*. EMI Arabia 0946 310963-2. Compact disk.

L'âge d'or de la musique égyptienne. 1991. Les Artistes Arabes Associés, Club du Disque Arabe AAA 043. Compact disk.

Aḥmad, Zakarīyā. [c. 1990.] *Al-āhāt, kalimāt: al-Ustādh Bayram al-Tūnisī, laḥn al musīqār*. Ṣawt al-Qāhira, Sīdī 94 SDCD 01B30. Compact disk.

———. [c. 1990.] *Anā fī intiẓārak, kalimāt: Bayram al-Tūnisī, laḥn al-musīqār*. Ṣawt al-Qāhirah, Sīdī 94 SDCD 01B58. Compact disk.

———. [c. 1990.] *Al-awwilah fil-gharām*. Ṣawt al-Qāhira, Sīdī 94 SDCD 01B46. Compact disk.

———. [c. 1990.] *Ḥulm al-amal*. Ṣawt al-Qāhira, Sīdī 94 SDCD 01B29. Compact disk.

Arabian Music: Maqam. 1971. Philips 6586 006. LP disk.

Arabic and Druse Music. 1956. Folkways P 480. LP disk.

Arabic Love Songs and Dances of Lebanon. 1957. Folkways FW 8815. LP disk.

Arabic Songs of Lebanon and Egypt. 1956. Folkways FW 6925. LP disk.

Archives de la musique arabe. 1987–. Ocora C558678. Compact disks.

Asmahān. 1988. *Asmahan*. Les Artistes Arabes Associés, Club du Disque Arabe AAA 004. Compact disk.

———. 1992. *Asmahan: Archives des années 42/44*. Les Artistes Arabes Associés, Club du Disque Arabe AAA 049. Compact disk.

———. 1992. *Asmahan*. Vol. 3: *Archives des années 30*. Les Artistes Arabes Associés, Club du Disque Arabe AAA 059. Compact disk.

Aṭrash, Farīd. 1992. *Farid el Atrache: Les années 30*. Baidaphon/Club du Disque Arabe, AAA053. Compact disk.

Barrayn, Shaykh Ahmad. *Sufi Songs*. Long Distance 592323. Compact disk.

Bashīr, Munīr. [c. 1971.] *Iraq: Oud classique arabe par Munir Bashir*. Ocora OCR 63. LP disk.

———. 1988a. *Munir Bachir en concert*. Maison des Cultures du Monde W260006. Compact disk.

———. 1988b. *Récital: Solo de luth-oud*. Les Artistes Arabes Associés AAA 003, Club du Disque Arabe CDA 401. Compact disk.

———. 1998a. *L'art du 'ūd*. Ocora/Radio France C 580068. Compact disk.

———. 1993. *Maqamat*. Maison des Cultures du Monde W260050. Compact disk.

———. 1996. *Méditations*. Maison des Cultures du Monde W260071. Compact disk.

———. [c. 1990.] *Babylon Mood: Munir Bechir and His Quartet*. Voix de l'Orient, A. Cahine and Fils VDLCD 529. Compact disk.

Bashīr, Munīr, and Omar Bashīr. 1998b. *Duo de 'ūd*. Auvidis B 6874. Compact disk.

Beduin Music of Southern Sinai. 1978. Folkways FE 4204. LP disk.

Bulos, Afif Alvarez. 1961. *Songs of Lebanon, Syria, and Jordan*. Folkways FW 8816. LP disk.

Cafés chantants du Caire. 1995–1996. Les Artistes Arabes Associés AAA 099, AAA 115, Club du Disque Arabe CDA 401. 2 compact disks.

Chants de Baghdad par l'ensemble al-Tchâlghî al-baghdâdî. 1996. Institut du Monde Arabe IMA-CD 18. Compact disk.

Coptic Music. 1960. Folkways FR 8960. LP disk.

Dāyikh, Adīb. 1994. *L'art sublime du Ghazal*. Notes by Bernard Mousali. Nanterre: Al Sur, ALCD 143–144. 2 compact disks.

Église Syrienne Orthodoxe: Liturgie d'Antioche. 1992. Auvidis D 8039. Compact disk.

Egypte: Ordre Chazili 'al-Tariqa al-Hamidiyya al-Chaziliyya'. 1992. Arion ARN 64211. Compact disk.

Ensemble David. 1999. *Liturgies coptes*. Institut du Monde Arabe 321022. Compact disk.

Fakhrī, Ṣabāḥ. 1990. *Ṣabāḥ Fakhrī*. Dūnyāfūn LPD CD 501. Compact disk.

———. 1995. *Sabah Fakhri au palais des congrès*. Les Artistes Arabes Associés, Club du Disque Arabe AAA110. Compact disk.

Fayrūz. 1988a. *Fairuz*. Ṣawt al-Sharq, Voix de l'Orient VDLCD 502. Compact disk.

———. 1988b. *Fayrūz fī al-Ūlimbiyā / Le Liban à l'Olympia gala Fairuz à Paris*. Ṣawt al-Sharq, Voix de l'Orient VDLCD 503-4. 2 compact disks.

———. 1993. *Al-aghānī al-khālida*. Ṣawt al-Sharq, Voix de l'Orient VDLCD 560. Compact disk.

———. 1997. *Ma'akoum*. EMI Music Arabia 0946 310964-2 6. Compact disk.

Firqat al-Tanbûrah. 1999. *La simsimiyya de Port Saïd*. Institut du Monde Arabe 321026. Compact disk.

Ghazālī, Nāẓim. 1994a. *Nāẓim al-Ghazālī al-juz' al-awwal*. Bou Zaid Phone, Digital Press Hellas BUZCD 515. Compact disk.

———. 1994b. *Nāẓim al-Ghazālī al-juz' al-thānī*. Bou Zaid Phone, Digital Press Hellas BUZCD 516. Compact disk.

Ḥāfiẓ, 'Abd al-Ḥalīm. 1996. *Kariat al Fengan*. EMI Arabia 310502-2. Compact disk.

———. 1997. *Abdel Halim Hafez: Live at the Royal Albert Hall, London*. Virgin 310968–2. Compact disk.

Hage, Louis. 1971–1973. *Traditions musicales du Proche-Orient*. Beirut: Kaslik. 13 45-rpm disks.

———. 1979a. *Florilège de chants maronites*. Paris: SM. LP disk.

———. 1979b. *Chants syriaques de l'Église Maronite*. Paris: SM. LP disk.

———. 1982a. *Noëls maronites*. Paris: SM. LP disk.

———. 1982b. *Chants de la Passion et de Pâques*. Paris: SM. LP disk.

———. 1983. *Gesänge der maronitischen Kirche*. Christophorus. LP disk.

———. 1993. *Chants maronites traditionnels*. Paris: SM. Compact disk.

Ḥamdī, Balīgh. [c. 1990.] *Ba'īd 'annak*. Ṣawt al-Qāhira, Sīdī 94 SDCD 01B63. Compact disk.

———. [c. 1990.] *Bitfakkar fī mīn*. Ṣawt al-Qāhira, Sīdī 94 SDCD 01B62. Compact disk.

———. [c. 1990.] *Al-ḥubb kulluh*. Ṣawt al-Qāhira, Sīdī 94 SDCD 01B48. Compact disk.

Ḥarrāshī, Daḥmān. 1996. *Musique populaire algérienne: Dahmane Elharrachi*. Vol. 4: *Le chaâbi*. Les Artistes Arabes Associés AAA 142. Compact disk.

———. 1999. *Le chaâbi*. Vol. 5. Les Artistes Arabes Associés, Club du Disque Arabe AAA 183. Compact disk.

Ḥijāzī, Salāma. 1994. *Shaykh Salama Higazi*. Les Artistes Arabes Associés, Club du Disque Arabe AAA 085. Compact disk.

Ḥilmī, 'Abd al-Ḥayy. 1994. *Abd al-Hayy Hilmi*. Les Artistes Arabes Associés, Club du Disque Arabe AAA 075. Compact disk.

Iqa'at: Rythmes traditionnels. 1992. Auvidis D 8044. Compact disk.

Islamic Ritual Zikr in Aleppo / Rituel islamique zikr à Alep. 1989. Auvidis D 8013. Compact disk.

Jordanie: Chants bédouins, chants de mariage, chants des pêcheurs d'Aqaba. 1998. Maison des Cultures du Monde W260083. Compact disk.

Al-Kindī. 1998. *Le salon de musique d'Alep: L'art du chant classique Arabe*. Le Chant du Monde CML 5741108-9. 2 compact disks.

Laments of Lebanon. 1985. Folkways FE 4046. LP disk.

Mahmoud, Zein. 1997. *Chants sacrés de Haute-Egypte*. Paris: Institut du Monde Arabe IMA-CD 22. Compact disk.

Makkāwī, Sayyid. 1997. *Yā misahharnī*. Ṣawt al-Qāhira. Compact disk.

Manyalāwī, Yūsuf. 1993. *Shaykh Yûsuf Al-Manyalâwî (1847–1911)*. Les Artistes Arabes Associés AAA 065, Club du Disque Arabe CDA 401. Compact disk.

Mélodies judéo-arabes d'autrefois: Maghreb et Moyen Orient. 1997. Paris: Blue Silver Mélodie, 50556–2. Compact disk.

Mohamed, Matar. 1996. *Liban. Matar Muhammad (1939–1995): Hommage à un maître du buzuq*. Paris: Maison des Cultures du Monde W260068. Compact disk.

Moudallal, Sabri. 1994. *Chants sacrés et profanes de Syrie. Sabri Moudallal: Premier muezzin d'Alep*. Notes by Christian Poché. Paris: Institut du Monde Arabe, REF 303. Compact disk.

———. [c. 1990.] *Chants d'Alep*. Institut du Monde Arabe 321001. Compact disk.

Muezzins d'Alep. 1992. *Chants religieux de l'Islam*. Ocora 580038. Compact disk.

Muḥammad, Abū al-'Ilā. 1995. *Abu al-Ila Muhammad*. Les Artistes Arabes Associés AAA 114, Club du Disque Arabe CDA 401. Compact disk.

Music of the Nile Valley. [c. 1980.] Lyrichord LLST 7355. LP disk.

Musicians of the Nile. 1988. *Les musiciens du Nil*. Ocora C559006. Compact disk.

———. 1997. *Egypt: Music of the Nile from the Desert to the Sea*. Virgin 724384456924 LC 3098. 2 compact disks.

'Omar, Yusuf. [n.d.] *Iraq: Makamat par l'Ensemble al-Tchalghî al-Baghdâdî et Yusuf Omar*. Ocora OCR 79. LP disk.

———. 1995. *Le maqâm irakien*. Maison des Cultures du Monde W260063. 2 compact disks.

Qabbānjī, Muḥammad. 1994. *Le maqam en Irak: Congrès du Caire 1932*. Les Artistes Arabes Associés, Club du Disque Arabe AAA097. 2 compact disks.

Al-Qundarjī, Rashīd. 1996. *Musique savante d'Irak: Le fausset de Bagdad*. Nanterre: Al-Sur ALCD 183. Compact disk.

Racy, Ali Jihad. [c. 1978.] *Ancient Egypt: A Tribute*. Lyrichord LLST 7347. LP disk.

Redouane, Aïcha. 1993. *Egypte*. Ocora/Radio France C 560020. Compact disk.

Sabbāgh, Farḥān. 1992. *Récital de oud à Berlin*. Les Artistes Arabes Associés, Club du Disque Arabe AAA047. Compact disk.

Sāhir, Kāẓim. 1993. *al-'Azīz ghinā' wa-alḥān Kāẓim al-Sāhir*. Kuwait: Naẓā'ir NZR 08. Compact disk.

Sayyid Darwīsh. 1995. *Shaykh Sayyid Darwish*. Les Artistes Arabes Associés, Club du Disque Arabe AAA 096. Compact disk.

Shakkūr, Hamza. 1994. *Musique des derviches tourneurs de Damas*. Auvidis B 6813. Compact disk.

Shamma, Naseer. [c. 1995.] *Histoire d'amour orientale: Le luth de Baghdad*. Institut du Monde Arabe 50310-2. Compact disk.

Sunbāṭī, Riyāḍ. [c. 1990.] *Aghār min nasmat al-janūb*. Cairo: Ṣawt al-Qāhira, Sīdī 94 SDCD 01B31. Compact disk.

———. [c. 1990.] *Al-qalb ya'shaq kull jamīl*. Ṣawt al-Qāhira, Sīdī 94 SDCD 01B50. Compact disk.

———. [c. 1990.] *Aqbal al-layl*. Ṣawt al-Qāhira, Sīdī 94 SDCD 01B26. Compact disk.

———. [c. 1990.] *Aqūlak ayh*. Ṣawt al-Qāhira, Sīdī 94 SDCD 01B27. Compact disk.

———. [c. 1990.] *Arūḥ li-mīn*. Ṣawt al-Qāhira, Sīdī 94 SDCD 01B22. Compact disk.

———. [c. 1990.] *Dalīlī iḥtār*. Ṣawt al-Qāhira, Sīdī SDCD 01B19. Compact disk.

———. [c. 1990.] *Dhikriyāt*. Ṣawt al-Qāhira, Sīdī 94 SDCD 01B20. Compact disk.

———. [c. 1990.] *Ghanna al-rabī'*. Ṣawt al-Qāhira, Sīdī 94 SDCD 01B14. Compact disk.

———. [c. 1990.] *Ghulubt aṣāliḥ fī rūḥī*. Ṣawt al-Qāhira, Sīdī 94 SDCD 01B36. Compact disk.

———. [c. 1990.] *Hallit layālī al-qamar*. Ṣawt al-Qāhira, Sīdī 94 SDCD 01B77. Compact disk.

———. [c. 1990.] *Al-ḥubb kidah*. Ṣawt al-Qāhira, Sīdī 94 SDCD 01B47. Compact disk.

———. [c. 1990.] *Jaddidt ḥubbak layh*. Ṣawt al-Qāhira, Sīdī 94 SDCD 01B65. Compact disk.

———. [c. 1990.] *Lā yā ḥabībī*. Ṣawt al-Qāhira, Sīdī 94 SDCD 01B69. Compact disk.

———. [c. 1990.] *Lissah fākir*. Ṣawt al-Qāhira, Sīdī 94 SDCD 01B70. Compact disk.

———. [c. 1990.] *Udhkurīnī*. Ṣawt al-Qāhira, Sīdī 94 SDCD 01B21. Compact disk.

———. [c. 1990.] *Yā ṭūl 'adhābī*. Ṣawt al-Qāhira, Sīdī 94 SDCD 01B80. Compact disk.

———. [c. 1990.] *Yā ṭūlimnī*. Ṣawt al-Qāhira, Sīdī 94 SDCD 01B81. Compact disk.

Syria: Sunnite Islam. 1973. EMI Odeon 3C 064-17885. LP disk.

Syrie: Adīb Dāyikh et l'ensemble al-Kindī. 1995. Notes by Bernard Mousali. Paris: Institut du Monde Arabe REF 50314–2. Compact disk.

Touma, Habib Hassan. 1971. *The Music of the Syrian Orthodox Church*. UNESCO Collection, Musical Sources, Religious Psalmody, IV/2. LP disk.

———. 1996. *Église syriaque orthodoxe d'Antioche: Chants liturgiques du Carême et du Vendredi Saint*. Inedit W260072. Compact disk.

al-Tuḥāmī, Shaykh Yasīn. 1998. *The Magic of the Sufi Inshād: Sheikh Yasin al-Tuhami*. Long Distance 3039552 ARC 338. 2 compact disks.

Turāthīyāt: Munaqqa'āt 'Irāqīyah. [c. 1990.] Oak Park, Mich.: Spring Production 101. Compact disk.

Umm Kulthūm. 1989–. *Oum Kaltsoum*. 8 vols. Les Artistes Arabes Associés AAA005, 024–030, Club du Disque Arabe CDA 401. 8 compact disks.

———. [c. 1990.] *Aghānī waṭaniyyah. Juz' 1–2*. Cairo: Ṣawt al-Qāhira, Sīdī 94 SDCD 01B53–54. 2 compact disks.

———. [c. 1990.] *Anta al-ḥubb: Sayyidat al-ghinā' al-'arabī*. Sīdī 94 SDCD 01B59. Compact disk.

———. [c. 1990.] *Fīlm 'Āyidah*. Ṣawt al-Qāhira, Sīdī 94 SDCD 01B42. Compact disk.

———. [c. 1990.] *Fīlm Fāṭima*. Ṣawt al-Qāhira, Sīdī 94 SDCD 01B43. Compact disk.

———. [c. 1990.] *Fīlm Rābi'a al-'Adawiyyah*. Ṣawt al-Qāhira, Sīdī 94 SDCD 01B44. Compact disk.

———. [c. 1990.] *Qiṣṣat al-ams*. Ṣawt al-Qāhira, Sīdī 94 SDCD 01B17. Compact disk.

———. 1995–1997. *La diva*. 5 vols. EMI 352702, 310953-2, 310957-2, 310959-2, 310960-2. 5 compact disks.

———. 1998. *Sayyidat al-tarab*. EMI Arabia 310962-2. Compact disk.

Wasla d'Alep: Chants traditionnels de Syrie. 1988. Maison des Cultures du Monde MCM 260007. Compact disk.

Wenzel, Jochen, and Christian Poché. 1992. *Syrian Orthodox Church: Antioch Liturgy*. UNESCO/Audivis D 8039. Compact disk.

Yalcin, Warda, and Esther Lamandier. 1997. *Chants de l'Église d'Orient en araméen*. Alienor AL 1070. Compact disk.

THE ARABIAN PENINSULA

'Abduh, Muḥammad. 1991. *Sha'biyyāt*. Ṣawt al-Jazīra MACD 516-517. 2 compact disks.

Aman, Mohammed. 2001. *Arabie Saoudite. Mohammed Aman. Le majass, musique classique du Hijaz*. Ocora, Radio France. Compact disk.

Arabie Saoudite. Musique de 'Unayzah, ancienne cité du najd. 1999. Maison des Cultures du Monde W260087. Compact disk.

Archives de la musique arabe. 1987–. Ocora C558678. Compact disks.

Bahat, Noemi, and Avner Bahat. *The Yemenite Jews*. 1990. Auvidis D 8024. Compact disk.

Bakewell, Anderson. 1985. *The Afro-Arabian Crossroad: Music of the Tihama on the Red Sea, North Yemen*. Lyricord LLST 7384. LP disk.

Bhattacharya, Deben. n.d. (c. 1970). *Musique des bédouins*. Paris, Bam, Folklore et musiques de l'univers. LD 5783. LP disk.

Chant sacré du Yémen. 2000. Institut du Monde Arabe. Compact disk.

Chants du Hadramawt. 1998. Auvidis/UNESCO D 8273. Compact disk.

Christensen, Dieter. 1993. *Arts traditionels du Sultanat d'Oman*. Auvidis/UNESCO D 8211. Compact disk.

Congrès du Caire, 1932: Musique arabe, savante et populaire. 1988. Édition Bibliothèque Nationale, France APN 88-9, 88-10. 2 compact disks.

Fidjeri: Chants des pêcheurs de perles. 1992. Auvidis D 8046. Compact disk.

Hachlef, Ahmed. 1994. *La musique de Bahreïn: Anthologie de la musique arabe*. Club du Disque Arabe AAA 104. Compact disk.

Al-Hārithī, Muḥammad. 1997. *Le chant de Sanaa: Musique classique du Yémen*. Institut du Monde Arabe IMA-CD 26. Compact disk.

Hassan, Schéhérazade. 1998. *Yémen: Chants du Ḥadramawt*. Auvidis-UNESCO D 8273. Compact disk.

Ibn Faris, Muhammad, Dahi Ibn Walid, and Muhammad Zuwayid. 1994. *La musique de Bahreïn*. Les Artistes Arabes Associés, AAA 104. Compact disk.

Jargy, Simon. 1994a. *Les chants des femmes*. VDE CD 783. Compact disk.

———. 1994b. *Le sowt, musique des villes*. VDE CD 782. Compact disk.

Jargy, Simon, and Poul Røvsing Olsen. 1994. *Poésie chantée des bédouins*. VDE-Gallo VDE CD-780. Compact disk.

Jargy, Simon, and Ali Zakariyya al-Ansari. 1994. *A Musical Anthology of the Arabian Peninsula*. Vol. 1: *Sung Poetry of the Bedouins*. Vol. 2: *Music of the Pearl Divers*. Vol. 3: *Ṣawt, Music from the City*. Vol. 4: *Women's Songs*. Geneva: VDE-Gallo, CD 758-61. 4 compact disks.

Jenkins, Jean, and Poul Røvsing-Olsen. 1976. *Music in the World of Islam*. 1. *The Human Voice*; 2. *Lutes, Strings*; 4. *Flutes and Trumpets*; 5. *Reeds and Bagpipes*; 6. *Drums and Rhythms*. Tangent Records, TGS 131–136. LP disks.

Johnson, Ragnar. [1975] 1999. *Music from Yemen Arabia: Sanaani, Laheji, Adeni*. Rounder CD 5156. Compact disk.

———. 1975. *Music from Yemen Arabia: Samar*. Lyrichord LLST 7284. LP disk.

Krémer, Gérard. 1996. *Yémen: Musiques des hauts plateaux*. PlayaSound PS 65179. Compact disk.

Lambert, Jean. 1997. *Mohammed al-Hārithī: Chant et luth de Ṣan'ā'*. Institut du Monde Arabe, Media 7 IMA-CD 26. Compact disk.

Maddāh, Ṭalāl. 1986. *Sīdī Qum*. Sharikat Ṣawt al-Jazīrah al-'Arabīyah LP ALJAZ 1. LP disk.

El-Mallah, Issam. 1994. *Die Musik einer alten Hochkultur: Das Sultanat Oman*. Oman: Ministry of Information. Compact disk.

The Music of Islām. Vol. 11: *Yémen*. 1998. Celestial Harmonies, 13151-2. Compact disk.

Music of South Arabia. 1951. Folkways P 421. LP disk.

Musiques traditionnelles du Sultanat d'Oman. [c. 1990.] Paris: Buda Records 92703-2. Compact disk.

Poché, Christian. 1976. *Zaidi and Shafi'i: Islamic Religious Chanting from North Yemen*. UNESCO collection, Musical Sources, Philips 6586 040. LP disk.

Poché, Christian, and Jochen Wenzel. 1988. *Yémen du nord: Musique traditionnelle du nord*. Auvidis D 8004. Compact disk.

Racy, Ali Jihad. 1988. *Tanbura Music of the Gulf*, Vol. 2. Arab Gulf States Folklore Center. Cassette tape.

Røvsing Olsen, Poul. 1968. *Pêcheurs de perles et musiciens du Golfe Persique*. Ocora OCR 42. LP disk.

Saint-Hilaire, Alain, and Karen Saint-Hilaire. 1971. *Les Emirats du Golfe Arabique*. Alvarès, Paris. C 471. LP disk.

Shiloah, Amnon. 1978. *Bedouin Music of Southern Sinai*. Ethnic Folkways Records EE 4204. LP disk.

Al-Tawḥīd. 1994. Maison des Cultures du Monde, Auvidis W260001. Compact disk.

Touma, Habib Hassan. 1979. *Fidjeri Songs of the Bahrain Pearl Divers*. *Musical Sources*, Vol 23. UNESCO. Philips 064-18371. LP disk.

Yémen du nord: Musique traditionnelle du nord. 1988. Auvidis D 8004. Compact disk.

ARMENIA

Arménie: Chants liturgiques du moyen-âge. [c. 1970.] Ocora OCR 66. LP disk.

Arménie: Musique de tradition populaire. [c. 1970.] Ocora OCR 50. LP disk.

Arménie: Musique des Achough. [c. 1972.] Ocora OCR 59. LP disk.

Arménie: Musique instrumentale. [c. 1972.] Ocora OCR 67. LP disk.

Armianskaia dukhovnaia muzyka V–XIII vv (Armenian Sacred Music of the Fifth to Thirteenth Centuries). 1991. USSR: Melodiya 1000265. Compact disk.

Chants liturgiques arméniens: Chants liturgiques du Carême et des fêtes de Pâques (Armenian Liturgical Chant: Chant for Lent and Easter). 1989. Auvidis D 8015. Compact disk.

Chants liturgiques du moyen-âge et musique instrumentale. 1988. Ocora C559001. Compact disk.

Gasparian, Djivan. 1996. *Apricots from Eden*. Traditional Crossroads CD 4276. Compact disk.

———. 1999. *Armenia*. WDR/World Network 32.377. Compact disk.

———. 2000. *Armenian Fantasies*. Frankfurt am Main: Network Medien 34.801. Compact disk.

Hagopian, Richard. 1993. *Armenian Music through the Ages*. Smithsonian/Folkways SF 40414. Compact disk.

Kalaschjan. 1992. *Rural and Urban Traditional Music from Armenia*. Wergo 281505-2. Compact disk.

Komitas, Vardapet. 1970. *The Music of Komitas*. KCC 100 Komitas Centennial Committee. 2 LP disks.

———. 1989. *Arménia: Chants et danses populaires d'Arménie*. Empreinte digitale ED 13002. Compact disk.

———. 1990. *Yerketsoghutuink srbo pataraki / Divine Liturgy*. New Albion Records NA 033. Compact disk.

———. 1995. *The Voice of Komitas Vardapet*. Traditional Crossroads CD 4275. Compact disk.

Manukian, Yeghish. [c. 1995.]. *Arménie, sources*. Paris: Buda Records 92610-2. Compact disk.

Markarian, Varoujan. [1995.] *Armenian Chant*. Holyland 17. Compact disk.

Music of the Russian Middle East. 1951. Folkways P 416. LP disk.

Musique de tradition populaire et des Achough. 1993. Ocora/Radio France C 580005. Compact disk.

KURDISTAN

Christensen, Dieter. 1965. *Kurdish Folk Music from Western Iran*. New York: Ethnic Folkways Library FE 3103. LP disk.

Groupe Koma Zozan. 1990. *Chants et musiques du Kurdistan*. Arion ARN 64263. Compact disk.

Groupe Musical du Kurdistan. 1994. *Chants du Kurdistan*. Nanterre: Al-Sur ALCD 125. Compact disk.

Kurdish Folk Songs and Dances. 1955. Folkways FE 4469. LP disk.

Kurdistan. [1974] 1989. UNESCO Collection Audivis D8023. Compact disk.

Kurdistan: Zikr et chants soufis. 1994. Ocora/Radio France C 560071/72. 2 compact disks.

Music of Kurdistan. n.d. Koch 333362. Compact disk.

Musiques et chants du Kurdistan: Les espaces Kurdes. 1995. Les Artistes Arabes Associés AAA127. Compact disk.

Perwer, Şivan. 1989. *Chants du Kurdistan*. Audivis B6145. Compact disk.

Temo. 1995. *Chants et musique kurdes*. Auvidis B6815. Compact disk.

TURKEY

Archives de la musique turque. 1995. Ocora/Radio France C 560082. 2 compact disks.

Bacanos, Yorgo. 1998. *Udi Yorgo Bacanos, 1900–1977*. Traditional Crossroads CD 4287. Compact disk.

Bartók, Béla, comp. 1996. *Turkish Folk Music Collection*. Hungaroton HCD 18218-9. 2 compact disks.

Beken, Münir Nurettin. 1997. *The Art of the Turkish Ud*. Rounder CD 1135. Compact disk.

Cérémonie du djem alevi. 1998. Ocora/Radio France C 560125. Compact disk.

Chant des derviches de Turquie. 1988. Arion ARN 64061. Compact disk.

Çiçek, Ali Ekber. *Turkish Sufi Music: Folk Lute of Anatolia*. Lyrichord Stereo LLST 7392. Compact disk.

Les derviches de Turquie: Musique soufi. 1994. Playasound PS 65120. Compact disk.

Derviches tourneurs de Turquie: La cérémonie des Mevlevî. 1991. Arion ARN 64159. Compact disk.

Ensemble de Kudsi Erguner. 1990. *Fasl: Musique de l'empire ottoman*. Auvidis B 6737. Compact disk.

———. 1991. *Peshrev and Semai of Tanburi Djemil Bey*. CMP Records CMP CD 3013. Compact disk.

Erguner, Kudsi. 1979. *Meditation on the Ney*. Philips 6586 039. LP disk.

———. 1990. *Le ney turc*. Auvidis D 8204. Compact disk.

Firat, Ozan. 1992. *Musique des troubadours*. Auvidis B 6771. Compact disk.

Folk and Traditional Music of Turkey. 1956. Folkways FE 4404. LP disk.

Gençturk, Vedad. 1996. *L'art du 'ūd turc*. Arion ARN 60265. Compact disk.

Great Voices of Constantinople, 1927–33. 1997. Rounder CD 1113. Compact disk.

Les Janissaires: Musique martiale de l'Empire Ottoman. 1990. Auvidis B 6738. Compact disk.

Karaca, Kâni. 1998. *Cantillation coranique*. Ocora/Radio France C 560130. Compact disk.

Kartal, Göksel. 1994. *The Art of Taksim*. Traditional Crossroads CD TC4267. Compact disk.

Kenkulian, Hrant. 1994. *Udi Hrant*. Traditional Crossroads CD 4265, Compact disk.

———. 1995. *Udi Hrant: The Early Recordings*. Traditional Crossroads CD 4270-4271. 2 compact disks.

Makam. 1993. Musique classique ottomane. Al-Sur ALCD 114. Compact disk.

Masters of Turkish Music. 1990–1996. Rounder CD 1051, 1111. 2 compact disks.

Musique bektachi: Chants des Achik. 1996. Auvidis D 8069. Compact disk.

Musique de la cour Ottomane: Ensemble Ulvi Erguner. 1992. Al-Sur ALCD 108. Compact disk.

Musique classique turque: Hommage à Yunus Emre. 1991. Auvidis D 8303. Compact disk.

Musique populaire et classique de Turquie. 1991. Playasound PS 65069. Compact disk.

Musique savante ottomane. 1996. Les Artistes Arabes Associés AAA 130. Compact disk.

Musique traditionnelle turque. Pièces instrumentales. 1971. Ocora OCR 56. LP disk.

The Mystic Flutes of the Sufis. 1988. JVC VID-25005. Compact disk.

Necdet Yaşar Ensemble. 1992. *Music of Turkey*. Music of the World CDT-128. Compact disk.

Özkan, Talip. 1980. *Turquie: L'art vivant de Talip Özkan*. Ocora C 558561. LP disk.

———. 1992. *The Dark Fire*. Axiom 314-512 003-2. Compact disk.

———. 1993. *L'art vivant de Talip Özkan*. Ocora/Radio France C 580047. Compact disk.

———. 1994. *Turquie: L'art du tanbûr*. Ocora/Radio France C 560042. Compact disk.

Reinhard, Kurt, comp. 1971. *The Music of Turkey: The Music of the Whirling Dervishes (Mevlevi)*. Anthology AST 4003. LP disk.

The Road to Keşan: Turkish Rom and Regional Music of Thrace. 2000. Traditional Crossroads CD 6001. Compact disk.

The Sacred Koran: Recitations by Muezzins of Istanbul, the Ottoman Empire. 1988. JVC VID-25006. Compact disk.

Sağ, Arif. *Insan Olmaya Geldim*. Sembol Plak.

———, with Belkis Akkale. *Seher Yıldızı*. ASM Müzik Üretim.

Sağ, Tolga, Erdal Erzincan, and Ismail Özden. *Türküler Sevdamız*. ASM Müzik Üretim.

Şakır, Mehmet. 1998. *Le violon des yayla*. Ocora/Radio France C 560116. Compact disk.

Signell, Karl. 1970–1972. Turkish tape recordings. Signell collection, Archive of Folk Culture, Library of Congress, Washington, D.C. Recordings include concerts, interviews, mosque and Sufi musics, and many examples of *taksim*, *seyir*, and other genres. Index and copies available to qualified scholars.

Le sipsi des yayla / Sipsi of the Yayala. 1998. Ocora/Radio France C 560103. Compact disk.

Song Creators in Eastern Turkey. 1993. Smithsonian Folkways SF 40432. Compact disk.

Songs and Dances of Turkey. 1956. Folkways FW 8801. LP disk.

Sulukule: Rom Music of Istanbul. 1998. Traditional Crossroads CD 4289. Compact disk.

Tanbûrî Cemil Bey. 1994–1995. *Tanburi Cemil Bey*. Traditional Crossroads CD 4264, 4274. 3 compact disks.

Tanrıkorur, Cinuçen. 1986. *Turquie*. Ocora C558574. LP disk.

Tchinar, Feyzullah. 1995. *Chants sacrés d'Anatolie*. Ocora C 580057. Compact disk.

Tewari, Laxmi G. 1972. *Turkish Village Music*. Nonesuch H-72050. LP disk.

Turkey: A Musical Journey. 1975. Nonesuch H-72067. LP disk.

Turkey: An Esoteric Sufi Ceremony. n.d. JVC World Sounds. VICG-5345.

Turkey. 1: *The Music of the Mevlevi*. [c. 1960.] Bärenreiter-Musicaphon BM 30 L 2019. LP disk.

Turkey: Traditional Songs and Dances. [c. 1977.] Lyrichord LLST 7356. LP disk.

Turkish Folk Music. [c. 1976.] Lyrichord LLST 7289. LP disk.

Turkish Music. 2: *Classical and Religious Music*. [n d.]. Bärenreiter-Musicaphon BM 30 L 2020. LP disk.

Turquie, aşik: Chants d'amour et de sagesse d'Anatolie. 1991. Maison des Cultures du Monde W260025. Compact disk.

Turquie: Cérémonie des derviches Kadiri. 1990. VDE VDE CD-587. Compact disk.

Turquie: Chants sacrés d'Anatolie. 1973. Ocora OCR 65. LP disk.

Turquie: Concert de musique classique ottomane. 1995. Le Chant du Monde CMT 2741013. Compact disk.

Turquie: L'art du tanbûr ottoman. 1990. VDE VDE VD-586. Compact disk.

Turquie: Musique soufi. 1977. Ocora 558522. LP disk.

Turquie: Musique soufi, ilâhî, et nefes. 1991. Maison des Cultures du Monde W260021. Compact disk.

Turquie: Musique tzigane. 1984. Ocora 558649. LP disk.

Turquie: Musiques villageoises d'Anatolie. 1994. VDE VDE CD-797. Compact disk.

Turquie: Voyages d'Alain Gheebrant en Anatolie (1956–1957). 1985. Ocora 558634-558635. 2 LP disks.

Uzel, Nezih, and Kudsi Erguner. 1987. *Musique soufi*. Ocora C559017. Compact disk.

Women of Istanbul. 1998. Traditional Crossroads CD 4280. Compact disk.

The Works of Tatyos Efendi. 1996–. Traditional Crossroads TC4277-78. 2 compact disks.

IRAN

Akhbari, Djalal. 1996. *L'art du santūr persan*. Arion ARN 60351. Compact disk.

Alizādeh, Hossain. [c. 1995.] *Musique iranienne, improvisations*. Buda 92622-2 2 compact disks.

Alizādeh, Hossain, and Majdid Khaladj. 1998. *The Art of Improvisation*. Haus der Kulturen der Welt, Wergo 281530-2. Compact disk.

Anthology of Persian Music, 1930–1990. 1991. Washington, D.C.: Mage Publishers, Mage CD 22-1. Compact disk.

Bina, Sima. 1995. *Sima Bina: Persian Classical Music*. Nimbus NI 5391. Compact disk.

———. 1997. *Āvā-ye sahrā / Sounds from the Plain*. Canoga Park, Calif.: Caltex. Compact disk.

Chemirani, Djamchid. 1991. *Djamchid Chemirani, zarb*. Auvidis B 6752. Compact disk.

Dastgah nava. 1995. Traditional Crossroads CD 4273. Compact disk.

Digard, Jean-Pierre, comp. 1974. *Iran: Baxtyâri, nomades de la montagne*. SELAF-OROSTOM CETO 747. LP disk.

During, Jean, comp. 1979–1982. *Iran: Anthologie de la musique traditionnelle*. Ocora 558540, 558550, 558562, 558563. 4 LP disks.

———. [1981] 1992. *Baloutchistan: Musique d'extase et de guérison*. Ocora C580017-18. 2 compact disks.

———, comp. 1993. *Asie Centrale: Les maîtres du dotâr*. Geneva: Archives Internationales de Musique Populaire, AIMP 26. Compact disk.

———. 1997. *The Mystic Fiddle of the Proto-Gypsies, Masters of Trance Music*. Shanachie 65013. Compact disk.

Ensemble Moshtaq. [c. 1992.] *Musique savante persane*. Buda 92532-2. Compact disk.

Folk Music of Iran: The Luristan and Fars Provinces. [c. 1970.] Lyrichord LLST 7261. LP disk.

Googoosh. 2000. *Googoosh*. Pars Video, Caltex CLX 2046. 4 compact disks.

Ilāhī, Nūr ʿAli. 1996. *La musique céleste d'Ostâd Elâhi: Au luth sacré tanbûr*. Le Chant du Monde CMT 274 1026. Compact disk.

———. 1997. *Les chemins de l'amour divin / Paths of Divine Love. Ostad Elahi*. Le Chant du Monde CMT 2741083. Compact disk.

———. 1999. *Harmonies célestes*. Le Chant du Monde CMT 274 1122. Compact disk.

Iran. [c. 1970.] Bärenreiter Musicaphon BM 30 L 2004-5. 2 LP disks.

L'Iran: Le ney. 1973. CBS 65.414. LP disk.

Iran: Persian Classical Music. 1974. Elektra Nonesuch 72060. Compact disk.

Iranian Dastgah. 1971. Philips 6586 005. LP disk.

Izadi, Souroush. 1995. *La musique persane savante*. Auvidis B 6808. Compact disk.

Kalhor, Kayhan. 1997. *Ghazal: Lost Songs of the Silk Road. Persian and Indian Improvisations*. Shanachie 64096. Compact disk.

———. 1998. *Scattering Stars Like Dust*. Traditional Crossroads CD 4288. Compact disk.

The Kamkars. 1997. *Nightingale with a Broken Wing*. [London:] Womad WSCD 009. Compact disk.

Khaladj, Madjid. 1994. *Iran, l'art du tombak (zarb)*. Buda 92594-2. Compact disk.

———. [c. 1997.] *Le répertoire fondamental de Maître Tehrâni*. Buda 92672-2. Compact disk.

Kīanī, Majīd. 1991. *Majid Kiâni, santur*. Auvidis B 6756. Compact disk.

———. 1992. *Haft dastgāh-e mūsīqī-e Irān* (Seven *Dastgāh-hā* of Iranian Music). Tehran: Iran Seda SITC-126. Compact disk.

Kurdish Folk Music from Western Iran. 1966. Folkways FE 4103. LP disk.

Les maîtres de la musique traditionnelle. 1991–1992. Ocora/Radio France C 560024–560026. 3 compact disks.

Malek, Hossein. [n.d.] *Classical Music of Iran*. Lyrichord LLST 7403. LP disk.

Manahedji, Behnam. 1993. *Master of Persian Santoor*. Wergo SM 1508-2. Compact disk.

Marẓīyah. 1995. *Monadjat: Musique traditionnelle persane*. Auvidis B 6825. Compact disk.

Morādi, Shahmirza. 1994. *The Music of Lorestan, Iran: Shahmirza Morādi, Sornā*. Wyastone Leys, Monmouth, England: Nimbus NI 5397. Compact disk.

Musavi, Mohammad. [c. 1995.] *Iran: Le ney de Mohammad Musavi*. Buda 92645-2. Compact disk.

Music of Iran: The Tar. 1968–1970. Lyrichord LLST 7201, 7220. 2 LP disks.

Mūsīqī-ye navāḥī-ye Irān (Regional Music of Iran). 1998. Tehran: Anjoman-e Mūsīqī-ye Irān. 16 albums, each with six cassettes and a booklet.

Musique iranienne. 1992. Harmonia Mundi HMA 190391. Compact disk.

Musique persane. [1971] 1987. Ocora/Radio France C559008. Compact disk.

ʿOmoumi, Hossein. 1993. *Persian Classical Music: Hossein Omoumi, Ney*. Nimbus NI 5359. Compact disk.

———. 2000. *The Song of the Ney*. Nimbus NI 7061. 2 compact disks.

Pāyvar, Farāmarz. 1995. *Musique classique iranienne*. Al-Sur ALCD 164. Compact disk.

A Persian Heritage: Classical Music of Iran. 1974. Nonesuch H-72060. LP disk.

The Persian Santur: Music of Iran. 1970. Nonesuch H-72039. LP disk.

Persische Kunstmusik. 1972. Harmonia Mundi 1C 065-99 632. LP disk.

Rastigār-Nizhād, Nāṣir. 1964–1966. *Santūr Recital*. Lyrichord LL 7135, 7165, 7166. 3 LP disks.

Shadjariān, Mohammad Rezā. 1990. *Musique classique persane*. Ocora/Radio France C 559097. Compact disk.

Shadjariān, Mohammad Rezā, and Kayhan Kalhor. *Night Silence Desert*. Traditional Crossroads CD 80702-4299-2. Compact disk.

Shenāsā, Masʿoud. 1996. *Santour*. Les Artistes Arabes Associés AAA 140. Compact disk.

Shūshā. [c. 1972.] *Persian Love Songs and Mystic Chants*. Lyrichord LLST 7235. LP disk.

Sulaymānī, Qurbān. 1995. *Mūsīqī shamāl Khurāsān / Music of the Bards from Iran, Northern Khorasan*. Los Angeles: Kereshmeh Records, KCD-106. Compact disk.

The Tar: Music of Iran. n.d. Lyrichord LLST 7201. LP disk.

Tārif, Sadiq. 1995. *Chant et musique classiques persans*. Institut du Monde Arabe 50315-2. Compact disk.

Youssefzadeh, Ameneh, comp. *Bardes du Khorassan*. 1998. Ocora C 560136. Compact disk.

Zonis, Ella Mahler, and Ruhallah Khaleqi. 1991. *Classical Music of Iran: The Dastgah Systems*. Smithsonian Folkways CD SF 40039. Compact disk.

CENTRAL ASIA

Alimatov, Turgun. 1995. *Ouzbekistan: Turgun Alimatov*. Ocora/Radio France C 560086. Compact disk.

Asie Centrale: Traditions classiques. 1993. Ocora/Radio France C 560035–36. 2 compact disks.

At the Bazaar of Love: The Ilyas Malayev Ensemble. 1997. Shanachie Records 64081. Compact disk.

Azerbaijan 1. n.d. A Musical Anthology of the Orient, 24. Kassel: Bärenreiter-Musicaphon, BM 30 L 2024. LP disk.

Badakhshan: Pamir, chants et musiques du toit du monde. 2000. Buda 92744-2. Compact disk.

Bukhara: Musical Crossroads of Asia. Smithsonian Folkways 40050. Compact disk.

During, Jean. 1989. *Azerbaidjan: Musique et chants des ashiqs. Ashiq Hasan. Emran Heydari, Alim Qasimov*. Geneva: Archives Internationales de Musique Populaire, AIMP XIX, VDE-Gallo CD-613. Compact disk.

———. 1993. *Asie Centrale: Les maîtres du dotār*. 1993. Geneva, AIMP 26; VDE VDE CD-735. Compact disk.

———. 1998. *Musiques d'Asie Centrale: L'esprit d'une tradition*. Paris: Cité de la Musique/Actes Sud. Compact disk.

During, Jean, and Eldar Mansurov. 1989. *Azerbayjan: Musique traditionnelle*. Le Chant du Monde LDX 274 901. Compact disk.

Dvenadtsat uygurskikh mukamov (The Twelve Uighur *Muqam*). 1983–1986. Tashkent: Melodiya Records, S-30. LP disks.

Les grandes voix du passé (1940–1965) (Uzbekistan: Great Voices of the Past, 1940–1965.) 1999. Ocora/Radio France C 560142. Compact disk.

Hamidov, Abdorahim. 1997. *L'art du dotār*. Recording and notes by Jean During. Ocora/Radio France C 560111. Compact disk.

Huun-Huur-Tu. 1993. *Sixty Horses in My Herd: Old Songs and Tunes of Tuva*. Shanachie 64050. Compact disk.

———. 1994. *The Orphan's Lament*. Shanachie 64058. Compact disk.

Ilyas Malayev Ensemble. 1997. *At the Bazaar of Love: Timeless Central Asian Maqâm Music*. Shanachie 64081. Compact disk.

Kholov, Davlatmand. 1992. *Davlatmand: Musiques savantes et populaire du Tadjikistan*. Maison des Cultures du Monde/Auvidis W260038. Compact disk.

Kirghizes et Kazakhs: Mâitres du komuz et du dombra. 1997. Ocora/Radio France C 560121. Compact disk.

Levin, Theodore. 1999. *Tuva: Among the Spirits. Sound, Music, and Nature in Sakha and Tuva*. Smithsonian Folkways SFW 40452.

Maqâm Navâ. 1997. Ocora/Radio France C 560102. Compact disk.

Mongolie: Chants Kazakh et tradition épique de l'Ouest. 1993. Ocora/Radio France C 580051. Compact disk.

Morita, Minoru. 1992. *Music of Kazakhstan*. 1: *Songs Accompanied on Dombra and Solo Kobyz*. King Records (Tokyo, Japan), KICC 5166. Compact disk.

———. 1995. *Music of Kazakhstan*. II: *Dombra Music of Kazakhstan and Songs Accompanied on Dombra*. King Records (Tokyo, Japan), KICC 5199. Compact disk.

Music of Central Asia: Uzbekistan. 1991. Tokyo: World Music Library KICC 5108. Compact disk.

Music of Khorezm. 1996. Auvidis/UNESCO D 8269. Compact disk.

Music of the Russian Middle East. 1951. Folkways P 416. LP disk.

Musique sur les routes de la soie. 1992. Auvidis B 6776. Compact disk.

Musique tadjike du Badakhshan. 1993. Auvidis D 8212. Compact disk.

Musiques du Kirghizstan. [c. 1995.] Buda 92631-2. Compact disk.

Musiques traditionnelles d'Asie centrale: Chants harmoniqes touvas. 1995. Silex 225222. Compact disk.

Ouzbékistan: Musique classique instrumentale. 1998. VDE-Gallo VDE CD-974. Compact disk.

Songs and Dances of the S.S.R. Middle East. [1956.] Folkways FP 916. LP disk.

Songs and Melodies of the Uighurs. 1995. PAN Records 2027. Compact disk.

Tadjikistan: Chants des bardes. 1998. VDE-Gallo VDE CD-973. Compact disk.

Tadjikistan-Ouzbékistan: Tradition savante shash maqam. [c. 1995.] Buda 92639-2. Compact disk.

Trebinjac, Sabine, and Jean During. 1990. *Turkestan chinois / Xinjiang, Musiques ouïgoures*. Ocora/Radio France C 559092-3. 2 compact disks.

Turkmenistan: Chants des femmes bakhshi. 1995. Maison des Cultures du Monde W260064. Compact disk.

Tuva: Voices from the Center of Asia. Smithsonian Folkways 40017. Compact disk.

Uzlyau: Guttural Singing of the Peoples of the Sayan, Altai, and Ural Mountains. 1993. Pan Records PAN 2019CD. Compact disk.

Voyage en URSS: Anthologie de la musique instrumentale et vocal des peuples de l'URSS. [c. 1985.] Le Chant du Monde LDX 74001-74010. 10 LP disks.

Yultchieva, Monâjât. 1994. *Ouzbekistan: Monâjât Yultchieva* (*Maqam d'Asie Centrale*. 1: *Ferghana*). Ocora/Radio France C 560060. Compact disk.

Zerańska-Kominek, Slawomira. 1992. *Turkmenistan: Music of the Bakhshy*. VDE-Gallo CD-651. Compact disk.

———. 1994. *Turkmen Epic Singing: Köroglu*. Auvidis/UNESCO D 8213. Compact disk.

ISRAEL

Argov, Zohar. 1988. *Zohar Argov's Greatest Hits*. ACUM C.D.R. 990. Compact disk.

Ben, Zehava. 1999. *Best of Zehava Ben*. Paris: Atoll Music 521660-2. Compact disk.

Ben-Haim, Paul. 1962. *The Sweet Psalmist of Israel*. Columbia ML 5451. LP disk.

Bhattacharya, Deben. [c. 1960.] *In Israel Today: Songs of the Jews from Morocco*. New York: Westminster W-9806. LP disk.

———. [c. 1960.] *In Israel Today: Songs of the Jews from Yemen, the Atlas Mountains, Tunisia, and Spain*. New York: Westminster W-9810. LP disk.

———, comp. [1971.] *Music from Israel*. Argo ZFB 50. LP disk.

Boniche, Lili. [c. 1997.] *Trésors de la chanson Judéo-Arabe*. Blue Silver 79 102 2 BS. Compact disk.

Braun, Yehezkiel. 1996. *Yetsirot le-makhelah / Choral Works*. Tel Aviv: Bet ha-tefutsot BTR 9602. Compact disk.

Burning Bush. 1999. *Folksongs from Israel*. West Sussex: ARC Music EUCD1513. Compact disk.

Chants de traverse: Récital de musiques judéo-marocaines. Paris: Atoll Music. 2 compact disks.

Chants Hébreux d'Israël et d'Orient. 1995. Al Sur ALCD 139. Compact disk.

Chekroun, Alain. 2000. *Chants des synagogues du Maghreb*. Magda MGD027. Compact disk.

Damari, Shoshana. 1995. *Israeli, Yiddish, Yemenite, and Other Folk Songs*. Omega Vanguard Classics OVC 6025. Compact disk.

Danna International. 1998. *Diva*. Tel Aviv: Dancepool DANA1PCD. Compact disk.

Diaspora Yeshiva Band. 1998. *Land of Our Fathers / Erets avotenu*. Tel Aviv: RARE Productions. Compact disk.

Easter Ceremonies in Jerusalem. 1957. Folkways FR 8951. LP disk.

Einstein, Arik. [1969] 1995. *Puzy*. Tel Aviv: Phonokol 4070-2. Compact disk.

Ethnix. 1995. *Ha-Osef shel Etnix: Sefer disk*. Tel Aviv: Helicon HL8115. Compact disk.

Ha-Festival ha-Yisre'eli le-shire yeladim mispar. 14: *The Israeli Children's Song Festival Number 14*. 1983. Tel Aviv: Isradisc. LP disk.

Festival ha-zemer ha-Hasidi 1985 / Israeli Chassidic Festival 1985. Tel Aviv: Isra-Art Productions FEST-85. LP disk.

Fleischer, Tsippi. [c. 1999.] *Israel at Fifty*. Greenville: Opus One CD175. Compact disk.

Folk Music of Palestine. 1951. Folkways FE 4408. LP disk.

Gadalnu yahad: Osef ha-yovel shel Yisra'el, ha-musikah / Israel's 240 Greatest Songs in Celebration of Its Fiftieth Anniversary. 1998. Tel Aviv: Hed Arzi. 11 compact disks.

Ga'on, Yehoram. 1996. *Yehoram Ga'on*. Hed Arzi CD 15813. Compact disk.

———. 2000. *Osef ha-ladino ha-gadol / Ladino Masterpieces*. NMC Gold 20383-2, 20384-2, 20385-2. 6 compact disks.

Gavrielov, Miki. 1998. *Ha-Osef Miki Gavri'elov*. Phonokol 4138-2. Compact disk.

Gerson-Kiwi, Edith. [c. 1960.] *Oriental Music, Israel*. American Zionist Council E4 K1 5996. LP disk.

Great Artists Perform Israeli Music. 1975. Musical Heritage Society MHS 3241. LP disk.

Gronich, Shlomo. [c. 1994.] *Shelomoh Gronikh ve-makehlat*. Ramat Gan: Hed Arzi 15615. Compact disk.

Hadar, Joseph. 1997. *Erev shel shoshanim / Evening of Roses*. Tel Aviv: Phonokol 5125-2. Compact disk.

Ḥalonot ha-gevohim. 1967. *The High Windows*. Ramat Gan: Hed Arzi BAN 49-47. LP disk.

Hanokh, Shalom. 1993. *Shalom Hanokh be-hofa'ah ḥayah / Shalom Hanoch in Concert*. Tel Aviv: NMC NMC-82270-2. Compact disk.

Haran, Michael. 1988. *Israeli Music for Cello*. Israel Music Publications MII-CD-7. Compact disk.

Haza, Ofra. 2000. *Melody of the Heart*. Hed Arzi 64027. 3 compact disks.

Hirsh, Nurit. 1992. *Nurit Hirsh*. Ramat Gan: Hed Arzi CD 15508. Compact disk.

Hora. Songs and Dances of Israel. [1961.] Elektra EKL 186. LP disk.

Israel. Vol. 1: *Traditions liturgiques des communautés juives. Les jours du Kippour*. 1977. Ocora 558529. LP disk.

Israel. Vol. 2: *Les Juifs d'Ethiopie*. 1986. Ocora 558670. LP disk.

Jerusalem Great Synagogue Choir. 1994. *Jerusalem Great Synagogue Choir*. Studio Christal SCACD 11161. Compact disk.

Jewish and Israeli Folk Songs. 1959. Folkways FW 8740. LP disk.

Les juifs yéménites: Diwan judéo-yéménites. 1990. Auvidis D 8024. Compact disk.

Kaspi, Mati. 1992. *Mati Kaspi*. Tel Aviv: CBS Records 80779-2. Compact disk.

Kaveret. [1973] 1989. *Sipure Pugi / Poogy Tales*. Hed Arzi. Compact disk.

Kraus, Shmulik. 1992. *Galgal mistovev / Spinning Wheel*. Ramat Gan: Hed Arzi 14950. Compact disk.

Laḥaḳat ha-Naḥal. 1989. *Laḥaḳat ha-Naḥal: Ha-lehiṭim ha-gedolim, 1963–1972*. Hed Arzi 15408. Compact disk.

Leyris, Raymond. 1994. *Cheikh Raymond: Chant d'exil*. Tel Aviv: Magda Music MGD023. Compact disk.

Mazor, Y., ed. 1998. *The Klezmer Tradition in the Land of Israel*. Anthology of Music Traditions in Israel, AMTI CD 9802. Jerusalem: The Jewish Music Research Centre. Compact disk.

Melamed, Nissin Cohen. 1980. *Pirḳe ḥazanut u-fiyuṭim: Be-nusaḥ Yehude Sefarad ha-Yerushalmiyim*. IMI Records 2002/3. 2 LP disks.

Mi-shire tenu'ot ha-no'ar / Songs of Israel's Youth Movements. 1991. Hed Arzi 14469. Compact disk.

Morasha: Traditional Jewish Musical Heritage. 1978. Folkways FE 4203. LP disk.

La musique Judéo-Arabe. 1992–1993. Les Artistes Arabes Associés 062-072. 2 compact disks.

'Ofrah Ḥazah, Shoshanah Damri, Laḥaḳat ha-Naḥal, ha-Geva'ṭron, Shelishiyat Gesher ha-Yarḳon, Ariḳ Einstein ve-aḥerim: *Sharim et shirehem ha-mefursamim shel Mosheh Vilenski, Na'omi Shemer ve-Shayḳeh Paiḳov*. 1994. Hataḳlit C-3-071/73. 3 compact disks.

Osef festival shire yeladim. 1995–1996. Phonokol 4102-2, 4121-2. 4 compact disks.

Rinat Choir. 1993. *Rinat—Maḳhelah ḳamerit Yisre'elit: Haḳlaṭot meha-shanim 1972–1956 / Recordings from the Years 1956–1972*. Tel Aviv: NMC 1032-2. 3 compact disks.

Sacred Music of the Moroccan Jews. 2000. Rounder CD 5087. 2 compact disks.

Shalom ḥaver / Good-Bye, My Friend. 1996. Phonokol, Hed Arzi 20197-2. 2 compact disks.

Shemer, Naomi. 1991. *Artsi moladeti: Shireha ha-yafim shel No'omi Shemer / The Beautiful Songs of Naomi Shemer*. Haifa: Hataḳlit CD 201. Compact disk.

Un siècle de chansons judéo-arabes. 2000. Paris: NFB World NFB 160899. Compact disk.

Sulam. 1992. *Klezmer Music from Tel Aviv*. Wergo 281506-2. Compact disk.

Voice of the Turtle. 1997. *Full Circle: Music of the Spanish Jews of Jerusalem*. Titanic Ti-251. Compact disk.

Wilensky, Moshe. 1993. *Shalekhet ba-lev: Ha-shirim ha-ahuvim shel Mosheh Vilenski / The Favorite Songs of Moshe Wilensky*. Haifa: Hataḳlit CD 156. Compact disk.

World Music from Israel. 1998. Frémeaux FA079. 2 compact disks.

Yemenite Passover. [1957.] Folkways FW 8921. LP disk.

Yurchenco, Henrietta. 1994. *The Bride's Joys and Sorrows: Songs and Ballads of the Moroccan Jews as Sung by the Women of Tetuan, Morocco*. New York: Global Village CD 148. Compact disk.

Zahavi, David. 1980. *Yesh maḳom ba-'Eden shire David Zehavi li-yeladim / Children's Songs by David Zahavi*. Tel Aviv: CBS Records, 84316. LP disk.

A Guide to Films and Videos of Middle Eastern Music

Alexander J. Fisher

Ali, Aisha. *Dances of Egypt.* Los Angeles: Araf. Videocassette.

———. 1995. *Dances of North Africa.* Araf. Videocassette.

Basic Middle Eastern Drums and Rhythms, Vol. 1. 1992. Portland, Ore.: Brothers of the Baladi. Videocassette.

Belic, Roko. 2000. *Genghis Blues.* Medium/New Video. Videocassette.

Bhattacharya, Deven. 1992. *Ecstatic Circle.* Guilford, Conn.: Distributed by Audio-Forum. Videocassette.

Cultural Fest. 1988. Jerusalem: Israel Film Service. Videocassette.

Dumon, Dirk. 1996. *I Am a Sufi, I Am a Muslim.* Princeton, N.J.: Films for the Humanities and Sciences. Videocassette.

Elef peraḥim: Festival Dalyah 1968. 1987. Jerusalem: Israel Film Service. Videocassette.

Fayrūz. *Fayrūz fī 'l-Qāhira 67.* 1993. Santa Monica, Calif.: Sufian Video Company. Videocassette.

Genini, Izza. 1987. *Hymns of Praise: Les confréries religieuses au moussem Moulay Idriss Zerhoum.* First Run/Icarus Films. Videocassette.

———. 1989. *Malhoune: la parole chantée.* First Run/Icarus Films. Videocassette.

———. 1990. *Gnaouas.* New York: First Run/Icarus Films. Videocassette.

———. 1993. *Airs en terre berbère: Vibrations en Haut-Atlas.* New York: First Run/Icarus Films. 2 videocassettes.

———. [c. 1994.] *Lutes and Delights.* First Run/Icarus Films. Videocassette.

———. [1990s.] *Aita.* First Run/Icarus Films. Videocassette.

Going on Fifty: The Israel Philharmonic Orchestra with Zubin Mehta. 1986. West Long Branch, N.J.: Kultur International Films. Videocassette.

Goldman, Michal. 1996. *Umm Kulthūm: A Voice Like Egypt.* Waltham, Mass.: Documentary Educational Resources. Videocassette.

Goodman, Ruth. 1985. *Night on the Sea of Galilee: Israel Folk Dance Festival.* Long Branch, N.J.: Kultur. Videocassette.

Grabias, David. 1996. *Asiklar: Those Who Are in Love.* Watertown, Mass.: Documentary Educational Resources. Videocassette.

Great Cantors in Cinema. 1993. Waltham, Mass.: National Center for Jewish Film. Videocassette.

Green Voices: A Program of Songs with Artists from Israel's Kibbutsim. 1988. Jerusalem: Israel film Service. Videocassette.

Haza, Ofra. 1988. *Ofra Haza: From Sunset till Dawn.* Teaneck, N.J.: Ergo Media. Videocassette.

Israel: Sounds in Search of a Home. 1999. Teaneck, N.J.: Ergo Media. Videocassette.

The JVC Video of World Music and Dance. 1988. Tokyo: JVC. 30 videocassettes.

Landoff, Brita. 1995. *Shiwayyah li-qalbī washiwayyah li-rabbī / Lite för mitte hjarta och lite för min Gud.* New York: Filmmakers Library. Videocassette.

el-Mallah, Issam. 1997. *The Role of Women in Omani Musical Life.* Tutzing: Hans Schneider. Includes videocassette.

Mandell, Joan. 1995. *Tales from Arab Detroit.* Detroit and Los Angeles: ACCESS and Olive Branch Productions. Videocassette.

Montgomery, Steve. 1995. *Morocco: The Past and Present of Djemma el Fna.* New York: Filmmakers Library. Videocassette.

Racy, Ali Jihad. 1983. *The Master Musicians of Jahjouka.* Long Beach, Calif.: Mendizza and Associates. Videocassette.

Smith, Huston. 1998. *Islamic Mysticism: The Sufi Way.* Wellspring Media. Videocassette.

Tlalim, Asher. 1994. *Morocco: The Music of the Jews of Morocco.* Teaneck, N.J.: Ergo Media. Videocassette.

Toub, Martin D. 1998. Exploring the World of Music. South Burlington, Vt.: Annenberg/CPB Project. 12 videocassettes.

Umm Kulthūm. [1970] 1982. *Sahrah ma'a al-Sayyidah Umm Kulthūm: Inta 'umrī & Yā msahharnī / Oum Kalsoum Concert: It Omry, Yam Sahreney.* Anaheim, Calif.: Ṣawt wa-Ṣūrah, Arabian Video Entertainment. Videocassette.

Under African Skies. Vol. 3, *Algeria.* 1989. London: BBC Videos for Education and Training. Videocassette.

Wickett, Elizabeth. 1990. *For Those Who Sail to Heaven.* New York: First Run/Icarus Films. Videocassette.

Wilets, Bernard. [1968] [1995?]. Discovering the Music of the Middle East. Huntsville, Tex.: Educational Video. Videocassette.

Zehavah Ben: The Solitary Star. 1988. Teaneck, N.J.: Ergo Media. Videocassette.

Notes on the Audio Examples

1. Eastern Arab Art Music: *taqāsīm* (solo improvisation) in *maqām bayyātī* and *Samā'ī Bayyātī al-'Aryān* (excerpt) (3:51)

   Performed on the *'ūd* (fretless lute) by Ali Jihad Racy with *riqq* (tambourine) accompaniment by Souhail Kaspar. Racy's *taqāsīm*, divided into multiple sections by a combination of cadential phrases and pauses, shows many characteristic features of *maqām bayyātī* [see The Eastern Arab System of Melodic Modes in Theory and Practice: A Case Study of *Maqām Bayyātī*] and also illustrates the performer's artistic freedom to step beyond traditional modal boundaries, for example with the use of a G-sharp accidental. The *taqāsīm* is followed by the first two sections (the first *khāna* and *taslīm*) of *Samā'ī Bayyātī*, composed by the Egyptian *qānūn* player Ibrāhīm al-'Aryān (1898–1953). Each of these sections contains five measures of the 10/8 *samā'ī* rhythm [see Rhythmic Modes in Middle Eastern Music, figures 3 and 4].

   From *Mystical Legacies: Ali Jihad Racy Performs Music of the Middle East*, Lyrichord compact disk 7437, with permission. Recorded live at the J. Paul Getty Museum as part of the Los Angeles Festival, 1993. Copyright © Lyrichord Discs Inc.

2. Turkish Mevlevi *taksim* (solo improvisation) in *makam beyati* (excerpt) (2:47)

   Performed on the *ney* (reed flute) by the late Akagündüz Kutbay, in the context of a Mevlevi ("whirling dervishes") recording. The excerpt begins with the concluding phrases of the vocal *Naat* performed by Kani Karaca, followed by ritual strokes on the *kudüm* drums. Kutbay then begins a 10 1/2-minute *baş takşimi* (opening improvisation) introducing *beyati*, the *makam* of the *ayin* (ritual music composition of the Mevlevi order) to follow. Normally, the *baş takşimi* ignores the preceding *Naat* (in *makam rast*) and directly establishes the *makam* and pitch level of the composition to follow. Instead, Kutbay's first phrase echoes the closing tones of the *Naat*. His second phrase deftly reinterprets those tones: starting with the *Naat*'s finalis, now the third degree of *beyati*, Kutbay rises a whole step to establish *beyati*'s all-important fourth degree, and then continues to present a characteristic *beyati seyir* (including the "warmed"—lowered—second degree, signaling the new finalis) in the second phrase, finally falling to the new finalis at the end of the third phrase. In the fourth phrase, he emphasizes another important *beyati* tonal center, its sixth degree. At 2:30, in the closing moment of Kutbay's *beyati* exposition, he touches on an expected taste of *makam hicaz* on the fourth degree, or *makam karcığar* based on the same note as *beyati* [see Contemporary Turkish *Makam* Practice].

   Recorded in Atlantic Studios, New York City, 1978. Released in 1987 on LP as *Music of the Whirling Dervishes*; re-released on CD under same title, Atlantic 7 82493-2. Used with permission from Atlantic.

3. Turkish classical *taksim* (solo improvisation), in *makam beyati* (3:37)

   Performed on the *ud* (fretless lute) by Münir Nurettin Beken. Beken, a leading Turkish *ud* artist, performs a full *taksim* consisting of exposition–*meyan* (modulation section)–return. The first phrase of his exposition typically emphasizes the fourth scalar degree, the dominant of *beyati*; its lower neighbor, the flat third; and the secondary tonal center, the flat sixth. The expected taste of *makam hicaz* on the dominant, or *makam karcığar* from *beyati*'s finalis, comes at 0:26. Ending the exposition with a full cadence on *beyati*'s finalis, Beken begins the *meyan* at 1:06 with *makam eviç-ferahnak*, visits *makam hicaz* (2:05), and returns to *beyati* (2:45). He touches briefly on other *makamlar* throughout the *meyan* and return [see Contemporary Turkish *Makam* Practice].

   Recorded for this volume at Jack Straw Studios in Seattle, Washington, United States. Used with permission of the artist.

4. Classical Persian *dastgāh-e shūr* (3:48)

   An improvisation on *kamānche* (a four-stringed spiked fiddle) performed by Ostad Morteza Varzi to illustrate modal progression in the *dastgāh* of *shūr* [see The Concept of Mode in Iranian Music: *Shūr*], including the *gūshehā* of *darāmad* (starting at 0:00); *salmak* (1:07); *shahnāz* (1:48), which includes the *gūshehā* of *qarache* (2:19) and *razavi* (2:23); *ḥoseyni* (2:57); and *forud* (3:27). Although this music is primarily nonmetered, Varzi has included excerpts in *salmak*, *shahnāz*, and *ḥoseyni* in *kereshme* rhythm (a hemiola pattern).

   Recorded for this volume in Los Angeles on 9 July 2001.

5. Yemeni drumming from the Ḥaḍramawt: *Īqā' al-Rubūṭ*, performed by Nawba Na'īmāt of Shiḥr, Yemen 1:25

   In Shiḥr the old Arabic term *nawba* (*noba*, in dialect) has been retained as a designation for music ensembles. In this respect it refers to the regular obligation of the ensemble to perform for weddings and other festivities. The profession of musician, considered to be of low social status, is normally hereditary. In this example and track 7, members of the 'Abd al-Mu'īn family take leading roles. The main singer, who also plays the *mirwās*, is Farḥa 'Abd al-Mu'īn. Ghazāl 'Abd al-Mu'īn plays the cylindrical drum (*ḥāgir*) while Faṭūm Sa'id Bā Ṣāliḥ and Khadīja Sālimīn play the other shallow cylindrical drums [see Rhythmic Structure and Drum Improvisation in Yemen, figures 3, 4, 7, and 8].

   Tracks 5–8 recorded by Jürgen Elsner.

6. Yemeni highland drumming: *Ḍarbat Sayyārī*, performed by Aḥmad Muḥammad J'ūf (*ṭāsa*) and Ṣāliḥ Muḥammad Ṣāliḥ (*mirfa'*) of Ḍāli', Yemen (0:33)

Highland drumming, featuring the shallow kettledrums *ṭāsa* and *mirfa'*, may be among the oldest traditions of Yemen. Its sonic layering and differentiation make it distinct from the drumming of the Ḥaḍramawt or the Tihāma. The *ṭāsa* is characterized by its sharp, energetic presentation of the rhythm; this may at times influence the *mirfa'*, which is dedicated solely to the rhythmic foundation [see Rhythmic Structure and Drum Improvisation in Yemen, figure 16]. The name *Sayyārī* refers to a rhythm (*ḍarb*) as well as to a dance. In Ḍāli', *sayyārī* dancing is the province of women.

7. Yemeni drumming from the Ḥaḍramawt: *Īqā' al-Istimā'*, performed by Firqat al-Zirbādī of Shiḥr, Yemen (1:20)

Weddings, celebrated by men and women in separate spaces, feature a comprehensive repertoire of songs and dances with various functions. The ensembles, which accompany the men's public celebrations, differ from the women's *noba* in that they also include the flute. In the Firqat al-Zirbādī, whose name derives from *zirbādī*, a multipart, rhythmically varied men's dance, two members of the 'Abd al-Mu'īn musical family again play a central role. In the *īqā' al-Istimā'*, as in the *Rubūṭ*, a characteristic tendency toward ternary rhythmic structures may be observed; this is a basis of the fascinating musicianship attributed to Yemenite performers [see Rhythmic Structure and Drum Improvisation in Yemen, figures 17 and 18].

8. Yemeni drumming from the Tihāma: *Raqṣat al-Mansarī*, performed by Firqa Sha'biyya of Zabīd, Yemen (1:04)

The notation [see Rhythmic Structure and Drum Improvisation in Yemen, figure 19] follows the recording, which itself arose as a special recording for scholarly study. Thus no melody instrument is present; however, the individual layers of the drumming for dancing (*raqṣ*) can easily be followed. The *mansarī* rhythm, with its overlapping of binary- and ternary-structured voices, and indeed the binary and ternary elements of the *mirfa'*, can serve as a good example of the elaborate, through-composed rhythm of Yemenite music. Despite the leveling characteristic of the modern age, such intricate rhythms may still be commonly found in different layers of Yemen's rich musical culture.

9. Islamic vocal music: *Inshād* in the public *ḥaḍra* (2:39)

Performed by Shaykh Yāsīn al-Tuhāmī (*munshid*), with *takht* accompaniment, including *kamanjā*, *'ūd*, *duff*, *riqq*, and *ṭabla*.

A poignant moment in a public Ṣūfī *ḥaḍra* performance by Egypt's most famous Ṣūfī *munshid*, illustrating the improvisatory interactions among performers [see Snapshot: Shaykh Yāsīn al-Tuhāmī in the Public Ḥaḍra]. Shaykh Yāsīn begins the excerpt in *maqām nahāwand*, *ḍarb waḥda kabīra*. The poem, a classical *qaṣīda* by the famous nineteenth-century Aleppine Sufi, Shaykh Abū al-Huda al-Ṣayyādī (head of the Rifā'i order and religious adviser to the Ottoman sultan 'Abd al-Ḥamīd), is an ecstatic, esoteric meditation on mystical union using symbols and metaphors typical of Sufi poetry throughout the ages. In this excerpt, Shaykh Yāsīn sings the following two lines (hemistitches are separated by /, lines by //): *Taraktu li maḥwi l-ghayri fī ḥāni jam'ina / wa buḥtu bi ḥāli fī bisāṭ 'al-'aliyyati // tukhāṭibuni bi l-layli a'rif ramzaha / wa adrī ma'ānīha wa law bi l-'ishārati.* 'I left the others to obliteration in the tavern of our union / and revealed my state in the Holy Presence. // It addresses me by night—I know its signs / and understand its meanings, though by intimations'.

Recorded outdoors in the village of 'Izbat al-Mansi, Ṭanṭa, Egypt; around midnight, 17 January 1994.

10. Islamic vocal music: *Ibtihālāt* (1:09)

Performed by Shaykh 'Awaḍ Abū Laylā, *mubtahil*.

Performing inside the mosque without meter or accompaniment, the *munshid* begins with prose praises and supplications to God in *maqām rāst* and then turns to a religious *qaṣīda* (classical Arabic poem). This short excerpt captures that transition (marked sonically by a modulation to *maqām nahāwand*), beginning with a standard prose supplication. Text: *'Afwaka wa riḍāka wa ḥusna liqāka yā rabb.* 'Your forgiveness and satisfaction, and a good meeting with You, O Lord!' (The melodic formula used here to set *yā rabb* is a stereotype commonly used by the *mubtahilīn*.)

Following this supplication comes the first line of poetry: *Mīlādu 'aḥmada nūrun sāṭi'un ḍuḥa / 'amma l-bariyyata qāsīha wa dānīha.* 'Aḥmad's birthday is the brilliant light of forenoon, / which pervaded all creation, far and near'. The *qaṣīda* is a *madīḥ*, praising the Prophet Muhammad (Aḥmad) by describing his miraculous life. After presenting six more lines in a similar style, the *munshid* sings prose requests for blessings on the Prophet and then launches immediately into the dawn call to prayer (*adhān al-fajr*). The entire *ibtihālāt* performance lasts about 10 minutes [see Islamic Hymnody in Egypt: *Al-Inshād al-Dīnī*].

Recorded at Masjid al-Nūr, 'Abbāsiyya, Cairo, Egypt, before dawn on 15 July 1997.

11. Jewish cantillation: *Bereshit bara* 'In the beginning', Genesis 1:1–5 (1:01)

Biblical reading following the cantillation accents. A portion from the Pentateuch (the five books of Moses) is read by an expert reader at the synagogue during sabbath services. The reading of the entire Pentateuch is completed in a yearly cycle that starts with the festival of *Simhat Torah* 'Rejoicing of the Torah' in early October. The opening portion of the whole cycle, which is included in this recording, is read in a festive manner. Sung by Menashe Cohen from Khalkis, Greece [see Music in the Religious Experience of Israeli Jews].

Recorded by Amnon Shiloah in Greece, 9 August 1970. Courtesy of National Sound Archives, Jewish National and University Library, Jerusalem, Yc 277.

12. Eastern Christian chant (2:53)

A Syro-Maronite chant (line A) with two Syro-Maronite-Arabic chants (lines B and C) adapted by the "refashioning" procedure to two paraliturgical Arabic texts.

The three texts are sung during Holy Week. Chant B is taken from a studio recording with instruments that are not usually used inside a church. Chant C is usually sung in a responsorial manner (solo and congregation) [see Maronite Music, figure 3]. Performed by the Choir of the University of the Holy Spirit at Kaslik (Lebanon); female soloist: Majdala.

Translation: (A) "He is killed in Egypt, the real lamb; and knifed in Zion the Easter lamb." (B) "O my people and my companions, where is the reliable pact; where is the gratitude of the love, the amiability and the forgiveness?" (C) "I am the sad Mother, and nobody consoles me. That the death of your Son be a life for those that ask for it."

13. Berber women's wedding song from the Anti-Atlas (1:21)

Beginning of the initial song of the series, performed upon the arrival of the men of the honor guard (*imsalan*) at the bride's house. The women are singing antiphonally, and three ululations precede the song [see A Wedding in the Atlas Mountains].

Recorded by Miriam Rovsing Olsen, Ida Ouzddout, Anti-Atlas, Morocco, 1979. Copyright © Miriam Rovsing Olsen.

14. Berber wedding song, *aḥwash*, from the Anti-Atlas (2:27)

Beginning of *tamssust* in a women's *aḥwash* (*aḥwash n-timgharin*) [see Berber Musics in Morocco]. The example fades into a male soloist singing laudatory poetry while standing in the center of a circle of women. This is followed by the women's antiphonal response in sung poetry beginning with the last verse sung by the poet. The beginning of the dance is marked by a progressive introduction of the women's hand clapping, of drums (a two-headed drum, *ganga*; and several frame drums, *tilluna*), and of metal clappers (*tiqrqqawin*). The singing is punctuated by ululations from women in the audience.

Recorded by Miriam Rovsing Olsen, Ida Ouzddout, Anti-Atlas, Morocco, 1979. Copyright © Miriam Rovsing Olsen.

15. Berber warrior dance, *taskiwin*, from the High Atlas (1:36)

The part of the warrior dance *taskiwin* called *assus* 'shaking', performed by three *tal'wwatt* flute players and three players of the *tallunt* frame drum, who are standing in the center of twenty-one dancers moving in a circle each with a small goblet-shaped drum (*agwal*) [see Berber Musics in Morocco]. When the dancers shake their left shoulder, the small bells attached to their *taskiwin* 'powderhorns' (singular, *tiskt*) tinkle. This example comprises twice the rhythmic sequence called *'awd bu-lḥrb* 'the repetition of the exercise of war', on which the flute players are playing a drone. Ululations of women in the audience can be heard. This *taskiwin* is directed by Lahsen Wakrim, who plays the lead frame drum.

Recorded by Miriam Rovsing Olsen, Ida Oumahmoud, High Atlas, Morocco, 1975. Copyright © Miriam Rovsing Olsen.

16. Palestinian folk song, *dal'onā* (1:42)

[For tracks 16, 17, and 18, see Palestinian Wedding Songs.] The Palestinian repertoire called *dal'onā* 'song to the flirtatious girl' is commonly performed during weddings. Performances typically include a series of Palestinian folk songs and variations on well-known melodies, tunes, and topics, particularly *ghazal* 'love'. A group of dancers performs the *dabkih* dance in the style of northern Galilee while musicians play *dal'onā* tunes and male or female vocalists sing the lyrics. Traditional village weddings commonly feature the *mijwiz* (a double clarinet) or *urghul* (a wind instrument consisting of two pipes of unequal length). In this example the singer Walīd 'Ābid is accompanied by the professional musicians of his group playing *'ūd* (lute), violin, *durbakkih* (single-headed drum), *daff* (tambourine), and *nāy* (reed flute). This quatrain, sung in *maqām bayyātī*, is one of hundreds in the *dal'onā* repertoire.

Translation: "Mother, O Mother, where is my beloved? / They separated us with a mountain. / I will cross the sea and sit in his lap. / I will drink from the water of the olive tree spring."

Recorded live at a Palestinian wedding in Shafā 'Amr in Galilee, summer 1978. Ḍirghām Ḥ. Sbait Collection, 1982.

17. Palestinian line dance, *saḥjih* (0:50)

Saḥjih is the most popular event during the evening of the groom's party at traditional Palestinian weddings. A team of two professional poet-singers improvise various genres of folk poems. The *ḥidā*, a popular genre of the *saḥjih* repertoire, is sung in couplets, quatrains, or eight-line stanzas, followed by the dancers' refrains. As the poet-singers switch from one type of *ḥidā* to another, they accelerate the tempo. In this example the poet-singers Jihād Sbait and Ḥannā Sbait alternate quatrains (*ḥidā mrabb'*) in *maqām bayyātī* describing the mood of the dancers and the guests at the wedding.

Recorded live at a Palestinian wedding in Fassūṭah, Galilee, 1976. Ḍirghām Ḥ. Sbait Collection, 1982.

18. Palestinian shaving song, *zaffih* (0:42)

The groom's public shaving party in preparation for his marriage is a touching moment of pleasure mixed with sadness prompted by the groom's impending departure from his parents' home. The mother of the groom begins the singing of the *zaffih* repertoire. If she cannot sing, she invites a well-known female soloist to lead the singing. The soloist sings one couplet at a time, and the audience repeats it as a refrain. Songs are accompanied by folk dances, clapping, and traditional or modern instruments. In this example the female poet-singer soloist, Wardih Sbait, sings precomposed and impromptu verses. The lyrics include these lines (translated): "We shaved the groom; we wish to shave his best man next [that is, the singers wish him to be married soon]. / May the right hand of the groom's barber be safe. / We shaved the groom; congratulations to his mother."

Recorded live at a wedding in Haifa, 1978. Ḍirghām Ḥ. Sbait Collection, 1982.

19. *Qurba* 'bagpipe' dance at a wedding in Oman (2:18)

In 1987, a young military bagpiper and some young drummers came together at a youth club in Sahham to jam, setting off what would within a few years become a rage among young people in northern Oman. Drawing on older musical genres and incorporating male dancing, "Gulf songs" known through the media, and amplification, *qurba* quickly became a form of popular music and has since spread across the entire country. In addition to the Scottish bagpipe, the ensemble includes various drums of African and Near Eastern types, tambourines, singers, and dancers to animate the onlookers—who may enter the circle to dance themselves [see Musical Life in Sohar, Oman].

Recorded by Dieter Christensen in Mejis, Sohar, Oman, July 1990.

20. Yemeni vocal music with lute accompaniment (3:06)

Hasan al-'Ajamī (voice and four-course Yemeni lute, *qanbūs* or *ṭurbī*) presents a part of the compound form *qawma*, beginning with an instrumental introduction that includes a short prelude (*fertash*) and then the *das'a* (11/8) rhythmic cycle. The use of measured time distinguishes the introduction from the *taqāsīm* or *taksim* of other Middle Eastern traditions (see tracks 1, 2, and 3). Finally al-ʿAjamī begins to sing the poem *Qif bī ʿalā l-masʾa* (by Ahmad ʿAbd al-Rahmān al-Anisī, d. 1825) [see AL-GHINĀʾ AL-ṢANʿĀNĪ: POETRY AND MUSIC IN ṢANʿĀʾ, YEMEN].

Translation: "Stop half the slope, at the gate of the peace / And celebrate your feelings in the night. / Compose your verses in the mystic path / And cover the vice with a pudic veil."

Recorded in concert, Institut du Monde Arabe, Paris, by Rainer Engel, March 1998. From *Yémen—Le chant de Sanaa* (Sanaan Singing)*: H. al-Ajami et A. Ushaysh.* HM321029, distribution Harmonia Mundi. Courtesy of Institut du Monde Arabe, Paris.

21. Yemeni vocal music with copper-plate percussion (excerpt) (2:15)

Ahmad ʿUshaysh plays the *wastā* (4/4) rhythmic cycle on the copper plate and continues singing the poem *Al-nās ʿalayk aqlaqūnī* (anonymous). Translation: "People bothered me about you, O little one. / They mentioned your name and asked me questions. / I said : 'Whose name is this? Introduce me! / It's the name of someone I've never set eyes on.'"

Then he switches to the *sāriʿ* cycle (4/4, the same as *wastā*, but faster) and sings *ʿAzīm al-rajā* (anonymous). Translation: "Thou to whom all our desires do turn. / I beseech Thee, by Thy power, / By Thy fine names, by the sacred Table [upon which Allah writes the decrees of destiny], and by the pen."

These two pieces are the last parts of the compound *qawma* form [see AL-GHINĀʾ AL-ṢANʿĀNĪ: POETRY AND MUSIC IN ṢANʿĀʾ, YEMEN].

Recorded in concert, Institut du Monde Arabe, Paris, by Rainer Engel, March 1998. From *Yémen—Le chant de Sanaa* (Sanaan Singing)*: H. al-Ajami et A. Ushaysh.* HM321029, distribution Harmonia Mundi. Courtesy of Institut du Monde Arabe, Paris.

22. Saudi women's wedding song, *Bāʿūnī* (3:20)

The Saudi songstress ʿItāb and her all-women ensemble perform *Bāʿūnī* to entertain women guests at a wedding in Jeddah, Saudi Arabia, in the late 1970s. While the *ʿūd* states the melody line quietly in the introduction and refrains, the vocals and multilayered drumming dominate. ʿItāb's drummers sing and play *daff, darbukka,* and a full complement of frame drums, *ṭārāt* (singular, *ṭar*), producing a wide tonal range as well as a highly syncopated rhythmic texture. ʿItāb was very popular in the Saudi women's wedding party circuit at that time, and her popularity is reflected in the audience's enthusiastic clapping and whistling. The crowd also cheers intermittently during the song—most likely to applaud a dancer who has executed a difficult move, such as swinging her long hair in an arc overhead [see MUSIC IN PERFORMANCE: A SAUDI WOMEN'S WEDDING PARTY and WOMEN'S MUSIC OF THE SAUDI ARABIAN PENINSULA].

Recorded in Jeddah, Saudi Arabia, c. 1978.

23. Kurdish epic song, *Hasu* (1:52)

Ali Çetin (age fifty), a well-known poet-singer (*lawjebij*) of the Doski Kurds, entertains guests of a tribal leader with a narrative about the exploits of young Hasu (Hasan). As is the custom in central Kurdistan, he sings without instrumental accompaniment, alternating long-drawn-out melismas at the beginning and end of phrases with rapid recitation in between. The high, "fine" voice quality is characteristic of professional bards [see KURDISTAN for tracks 23 and 24].

Field recording 65/71 by Dieter Christensen in Gewar, Hakkari, Turkey, June 1965.

24. Kurdish dance songs: *Ax lê Nurê, Henokê gerowwêre, Xwastîme* (2:32)

Excerpt from an uninterrupted sequence of sixteen dance songs recorded during a wedding. The track starts with the last strophe of "O Nure," then changes to "Hannah in the Crowd" and continues with "I Am Engaged." Two groups of two or three men, all of the Acar family, alternate in singing the short strophes while dancing in a single line, their shoulders touching. The texts describe the beauty of the girls named in most song titles.

Field recording 65/174-6 by Dieter Christensen, in Zomayê Meydanê Zengîl, Hakkari, Turkey, July 1965.

25. Turkish Alevī song with *bağlama* accompaniment: *Haydar, Haydar* ("I wandered around for fourteen thousand years in the guise of a moth") (2:55)

The quest for spiritual intoxication invoked in the mystical verses of the Bektashi dervish and poet Sidkı (1863–1928) together with Alevī sacred melodies inspired *Haydar, Haydar,* created by the virtuoso Alevī artist Ali Ekber Çiçek in the mid-1960s. This unique composition is divided into three parts. First, there is a six-second introduction that reveals some of the lower degrees of the folk mode *yanık kerem,* which is similar to *nikriz makam* on the *bağlama* (folk lute). Second, there a technically demanding prelude that alternates meters of 9/8 (2223) and 10/8 (2323) in combination with complex plectrum configurations that create multidimensional rhythmic ostinati. Third, there is the verse proper (in 2323), set to music borrowed from the Alevī *aşık* or *dede* Süleyman Elver (from the Malatya region of eastern Turkey) and refashioned somewhat [see ALEVI IDENTITY AND EXPRESSIVE CULTURE and ASPECTS OF TURKISH FOLK MUSIC THEORY].

The 45-rpm disk was recorded in 1965 in Turkey (Columbia 45-RT 736; 7XT2 7902).

26. *Gharībī,* lyric song of Khorasan province, Iran (2:21)

Sung by Gholām Lūṭī (age thirty-five), a professional entertainer (*moṭreb*) who normally sang and danced with members of his troupe at weddings and other celebrations. He described this genre as "a kind of tune (*āhang*) belonging to someone who came from another region and misses his mother and father and sings several verses" [see IRAN: AN INTRODUCTION, figure 3].

Recorded by Stephen Blum in Mashhad, Iran, 27 April 1969.

27. Persian narrative song, *Sayyed Moḥammad Khān* (0:55)

Sung by an ironsmith (*ḥaddād*), Moḥammad Shāʿer Karemī (age sixty), as he paused while making knives to entertain a friend and two visitors [see IRAN: AN INTRODUCTION, figure 4*a*].

Recorded by Stephen Blum in Āb Kūh, a suburb of Mashhad, Iran, 30 April 1969.

28. Persian classical music: *Masnavi* in the *dastgāh* of *māhur* arranged and performed by Leyli Atashkar on the *setār*, a four-stringed long-necked lute (3:28)

Masnavi chanting is an independent genre of Sufi song and is part of the classical repertoire. The text is usually drawn from the famous *Masnavi* of Jalāloddin Rumi (thirteenth century). The most distinctive characteristic of *masnavi* chanting is its poetic meter, - *u* - - / - *u* - - / - *u*, which is often performed very flexibly.

This example is in *dastgāh māhur* and was transmitted by the singer 'Abdollāh Davāmi. It has characteristics of both Sufi and classical styles. It is a structural model that can be adapted to any *dastgāh* and any poem in this meter; it has a sense of rhythm, although it is unmetered; and it has more modulations than would usually be found in such a short example. This selection has a *darāmad* (introduction, a melodic theme in *māhur*), a passage in *shekaste*, and a final section in *delkash*, with intervening returns to the initial mode. The tuning (fa do sol do) is a special one, rarely used nowadays, that gives this version a flavor of olden times. Leyli Atashkar (b. 1960) has preserved a very classical style on the *setār*.

Recorded for this volume by Jean During in Tashkent, 2001.

29. Kazakh epic song, *zhyr* (2:04)

A traditional Kazakh epic singer (*zhyrau*), Shamshat Tolepova (b. 1938; Karmakchi region of Kzylorda province, Republic of Kazakhstan), performs with *dombra* (two-stringed long-neck lute) [see KAZAKH MUSIC]. Each line of text is separated from the next by a brief instrumental interlude.

Translation: "A friend's heart is a mirror—be careful, don't break it! / A friend's heart is a spring—be careful, don't spit on it! / A friend's heart is a *dombra*—be careful, don't break its pegs!"

Recorded in Saint Petersburg, Russia, by Alma Kunanbaeva, 1990.

30. Uzbek classical song, *Sarabaxi Ōrōm-i Jōn* 'Peace of the Soul' in *maqām dugāh* (or *dugōh*), *saraxbōr* (4/4) rhythm (3:55)

Performed by Nadira Pirmatova (vocal) and his master, Abdurahim Hamidov, on *dutār* (a two-stringed lute) with *dōyra* (frame drum) accompaniment [see THE CLASSICAL MUSIC OF UZBEKS AND TAJIKS].

The *dugāh maqām* contains two pieces of the genre *saraxbōr* 'introduction', of which the first is in *dugāh* and the second, *Ōrōm-i Jōn*, much less developed, follows the development phase of the *dugāh* itself. This example is one of the best-known melodies in the *shash maqām* repertoire; the version here has been condensed and is slightly "uzbekified" compared with Bukharan *shash maqām*. The poem, in the Chagatay language (an ancestor of modern Uzbek), is by Bābur, founder of the Moghul dynasty (c. 1500): *Jonimdin o'zga yori vafodor topmadim / Ko'nglumdin o'zga mahrami asror topmadin.* 'Other than my own soul, I have found no loyal friend. / Other than my own heart, I have found no one in whom to confide my secrets'.

Recorded for this volume by Jean During in Tashkent, 2001.

31. Uzbek classical instrumental dance piece, *Oynasin Dugah* (2:32)

Performed on *dutār*, *ṭanbur* (another long-necked lute), and violin, with *dōyra* accompaniment.

This is in the mode *dugōh* (*dugāh*) in a nonclassical,unnamed rhythm. It was composed about sixty years ago by the master musician Yunus Rajabi. This classical genre appeared during the 1930s, in part to suppress the *maqām* repertoire [see THE CLASSICAL MUSIC OF UZBEKS AND TAJIKS]. The artists heard on tracks 30 and 31 include Nōdira Pirmatova (b. 1976), accompanied by Abdruahim Hamidov on the *dutār* [see SNAPSHOT: ABDURAHIM HAMIDOV—AN EMINENT CONTEMPORARY MASTER]; Shuhrat Razzaqov (Hamidov's disciple) on the *tanbur*, Ahmadjōn Dōdōev on the violin, which he holds vertically; and Hōjimmurōd Safarov on the *dōyra*.

Recorded by Jean During, 1998.

32. Moroccan Jewish song, *Shokhant bassadeh* 'She That Dwelleth in the Field' (1:35)

A *piyyut* (religious poem) for the festival of *Shavuot* (Pentecost) inspired by the text of the biblical Song of Songs. Sung by Yeshu'a Azulay and Meir Shriki from Morocco in Hebrew and Arabic, accompanied by *'ūd*. This tune is in the classical Moroccan-Jewish Andalusian style [see MUSIC OF THE MAGHRIBI JEWS OF NORTH AFRICA AND ISRAEL].

Recorded by Dina Berdugo-Sabbah in Beit Shemesh, Israel, 1974. Courtesy of National Sound Archives, Jewish National and University Library, Jerusalem, Yc 709.

33. Moroccan Jewish wedding songs, *Y fuerame a bañar* 'I Went to Bathe' (1:59)

A string of very short wedding songs in the Judeo-Spanish dialect of North Morocco (*haketia*). Sung by Ginnette Benabou accompanied by Jackie Benabou (*darbukka*) and Menashe Elbaz (*sonaja*, a small frame drum with cymbals) [see MUSIC OF THE MAGHRIBI JEWS OF NORTH AFRICA AND ISRAEL].

Recorded by Susana Weich Shahak at National Sound Archives, 31 January 1984. Courtesy of National Sound Archives, Jewish National and University Library, Jerusalem, Yc 2261

34. Jewish-Yemenite priests' blessing (2:05)

At a certain point during the daily morning service, members of the congregation who are—according to their family tradition—descendants of the biblical Aaron the Priest gather in front of the Ark (where the Pentateuch scrolls are stored), and bless the rest of the congregation. The blessing consists of three biblical verses (Numbers 6:24–26) performed word by word. The cantor sings every word according to a repetitive tune in a very ornate way; the priests repeat the word with the same tune, but avoiding the embellishments so that the meter is more emphasized. This enables them to pay attention to the homophonic sound, resulting in a "parallel organum" of an interval of a fourth or a fifth. The last words of the three verses are sung in a different tune that ends on the subtonic, "preparing" the cadential tune that ends on the tonic, and sung by the congregation on the responsorial word "Amen" at the end of every verse. This "preparatory" tune of the last word of the third verse is preceded by an additional new tune sung on the penultimate word, intensifying the preparation of the cadential tune sung on the final "Amen" that closes the blessing. The example consists of the last two verses [see LITURGICAL MUSIC OF THE YEMENITE JEWS IN ISRAEL for tracks 34 and 35].

Recorded by Uri Sharvit, Jerusalem, 1978.

35. Jewish-Yemenite liturgical song, *The Song of the Sea* (1:35)

The biblical text (Exodus 14:30–31 and 15:1–36) is sung by the Jewish-Yemenite congregation during the morning service on every sabbath and holiday. The tune is built on one model phrase repeated with every verse of text. The example consists of nine verses (15:2–10). It illustrates a conventional phenomenon of creating "transpositions" through frequent initiatives by individuals, adults as well as boys, who, deciding to lower the pitch by one tone or to raise it by a fifth, gradually pull the whole congregation with them. This creates the sound of "pseudo-organum" until the rest of the congregation joins the individual's new pitch.

Recorded by Uri Sharvit, Jerusalem, 1978.

Note: An abridged version of these notes is provided as liner notes accompanying the compact disk.

Compiled by Scott Marcus

Index

Page numbers in *italic* indicate pages on which illustrations appear.